taff Services
Printing
Research
blic Relations
counting, etc.

Circulation
Director

Subscription
Sales Mgr.

Newsstand
Sales Mgr.

Fulfillment

Mgr.
ct Mail

Mgr.
Agents

Field
Salespeople

Current
Subscribers

Subscriber
Renewals

1984 WRITER'S MARKET®

WHERE TO SELL WHAT YOU WRITE

Edited by Bernadine Clark

Writer's
Digest
Books

Cincinnati, Ohio

Acknowledgments

The editor wishes to acknowledge P.J. Schemenaur (*Writer's Market* editor, 1981-83) for her contribution in setting the stage for this edition.

Distributed in Canada by Prentice-Hall of Canada Ltd., 1870 Birchmount Road, Scarborough, Ontario M1P 2J7, and in Australia and New Zealand by Bookwise (Aust.) Pty. Ltd., 101 Argus Street, Cheltenham, V1C 3192, Australia.

Library of Congress Catalog Number 31-20772
International Standard Serial Number 0084-2729
International Standard Book Number 0-89879-120-0

Contents

The Profession

The Markets

666 Trade, Technical, and Professional Journals

The Profession

Introduction

Old Sam Johnson said any man who wrote, and did not write for money, was a plain damn fool.

—Introduction
Writer's Market, 1943-44

Forty years later, it's still sage advice. And every new edition of *Writer's Market* is proof that words matter and quality writing can be sold.

Writers meet here annually to see what's brewing in the world of freelance writing. They come to discover new markets and acquaint themselves with editorial changes in old ones. They come to learn about the comings and goings of this writing business.

So whether you string your words together on a charcoal grey video screen or every other line of a blue-lined yellow tablet. . . welcome to the 1984 edition of *Writer's Market*.

If you're going after your first byline or your fifty-first, this fresh, new edition is your working guide to getting there.

We've contacted editors, publishers, producers and program directors on your behalf. We've asked them to give us pertinent information about their editorial needs and how these have changed since last year. In addition, we've contacted new publications or publishers not included in previous editions to see if they welcome freelance submissions.

The results of this year's update? Hundreds of changes in editorial contact persons, addresses, kinds of manuscripts wanted, payment rates and reporting times. Hundreds of new markets (indicated with a ‡ to the left of the listing). And a few hundred previously listed markets excluded from this edition. (See p. 4 for additional information on how editorial needs are secured and why some markets are not included.)

Headlines (big things to notice). The lineup that follows is an overview of new or expanded features in this edition of *Writer's Market*. Get a sense of the freelance industry by reading this headline information.

- Upfront articles discussing the advantages of being a specialist or generalist writer—and related comments from professional writers and editors.
- Section introductions that offer tips and industry trends. . . to be read before you test the waters.
- Book Publisher Subject Index (p. 195) of over 90 categories, designed to streamline your search for an appropriate publisher.

- Profiles of editors and writers who share a variety of reflections on writing, their jobs and each other.
- Software Publishers section offering freelance computer programmers outlets for their creative talents.
- Appendix of updated information concerning manuscript mechanics, submissions, copyright and payment rates for hundreds of writing jobs. A new section on query letters offers tips on how to write them and a sample letter that resulted in a manuscript sale.

Footnotes (little things that matter). These tips are included as reminders to read carefully the editorial listings. Pay close attention to what's said and what isn't. Seasoned freelancers always read footnotes.

- Editorial needs. Editors generally spell out what they want to see from you. If there's not a fiction subhead in the listing, don't send your short story; don't even bother querying. Notice article length, audience and editorial slant in tailoring your submissions.
- Tips. Read the entire market listing. Some of the most telling information comes at the end. Here's where editors give you practical advice for making headway at their magazine, publishing company, ad agency or production firm.
- Editors' preferences, likes and dislikes regarding computer printout and disk submissions. If the editor has not supplied this information in the listing, contact him before you assume he will read your dot-matrix manuscript.
- Money matters. Listings throughout *Writer's Market* are paying markets, with the exception of some entries in the following sections: Lifestyles and Poetry in the Consumer section, and Journalism in the Trade section.

There you have it—a rundown of this 55th edition of *Writer's Market*. The contents are yours to digest. Read *WM* for information and inspiration. Read it often; use it well. This is 1984, after all. There are Olympic medals to be won, writing careers to be launched, and money to be made. And because words matter, there are manuscripts to be sold. Let's get on with it.

—Bernadine Clark

Using Your Writer's Market

How to Read a Market Listing

A good writer is a careful reader, especially when consulting *WM* market listings. Each listing must be read carefully and *interpreted* before you jump to your typewriter. Remember these tips:

• Information regarding the emphasis and audience of a publication gives important clues to the slant and style your submissions should take.

• Figures listing the number of freelance manuscripts purchased are approximations, but they indicate a market's openness.

• Figures for manuscript lengths preferred by editors are limits to keep in mind when submitting material or suggesting manuscript length in a query letter. However, a story should be told in the space it requires—no more and no less.

• Look for markets that pay on acceptance, *not* "on publication." Payment here is immediate, and not dependent on when your story appears in print.

• Look, too, for markets that don't buy all rights, and don't make "work-for-hire" contract agreements (in which the market, and not the author, owns the article's copyright). Retain rights you might be able to resell. (Information regarding a publication's openness to previously published work is also listed.)

• Don't abuse openness to simultaneous submissions or phone queries. Use these routes only when your "hot" story will be chilled by usual submission procedures. Also, openness to photocopied submissions *does not* imply that simultaneous submissions are OK.

• Check a market's receptiveness to computer printout and disk submissions, as well as preference for letter-quality over dot-matrix type. If no mention is made of printout or disk submissions, check with the editor before mailing your computer-generated manuscript or query.

• Listed reporting times are approximate. Give editors about six extra weeks before following up politely on queries or submissions.

• Enclose a self-addressed, stamped envelope (SASE) in *any* correspondence with editors.

• If a listing instructs you to query, please query. If it instructs you to send a complete manuscript, send a complete manuscript. If either is OK, a query may save you time and labor on a manuscript.

• Address a cover letter or query to a specific editor by name. If the name is not easily recognizable as to gender, use the full name (without the titles—Mr., Mrs., or Ms.) on both the envelope and the letter (e.g., Dear Dale Smith:).

• Don't abuse the editor's willingness to distribute free sample copies. Purchase samples at newsstands if possible, but *always* get a sample copy before querying or making a submission. A good writer is a careful reader, and a sample of your target publication should be at the top of your reading list.

• If the editor advises in the listing that a sample copy is available for a price and a SASE—but does not specify the size of the SASE—look at the publication's description. If it is a tabloid, newspaper or magazine, you'll need to enclose a 9x12 SASE with three first class stamps affixed. If the publication is a newsletter, chances are it will weigh less than an ounce, so a business-size SASE with one first class stamp affixed should be sufficient. Generally speaking, if a sample copy is available for a price (without SASE), assume that postage is included in the price quoted. Most guidelines are available for a business-size envelope with one first class stamp (unless otherwise specified).

Important

- Listings are based on editorial questionnaires and interviews. They are *not* advertisements, *nor* are markets reported on here endorsed by *WM* editors.
- Information in listings is as current as possible, but editors come and go, companies and publications move, and editorial needs change between the publication date of *Writer's Market* and the day you buy it. Listings for new markets and changes in others can be found throughout the year in *Writer's Digest*, the monthly magazine for freelancers. If you know of a market not listed in this book, write us and give the market's name and address; we will solicit it for the next edition.
- When looking for a specific market, check the index. A market might not be listed for one of these reasons: 1) It doesn't solicit freelance material. 2) It has gone out of business. 3) It doesn't pay for material (we have, however, included nonpaying listings in the journalism, lifestyles, and poetry categories because publication in these magazines could be valuable to a writer). 4) It has failed to verify or update its listing for the 1984 edition. 5) It requests not to be listed. 6) Complaints have been received about it, and it hasn't answered *Writer's Market* inquiries satisfactorily. 7) It buys few manuscripts, thereby constituting a very small market for freelancers. 8) It was in the midst of being sold at press time, and rather than disclose premature details, we chose not to list it.
- *Writer's Market* reserves the right to exclude any listing.

In the interests of promoting good, clean sport *and* stimulating your own particular muse, the 1984 *Writer's Market* begins with a hearty debate. Should freelance writers develop a writing specialty or cultivate a generalist approach to their craft?

We've asked two freelancers (who practice what they preach) to present their sides of the issue. Their respective cases are followed by additional insights into the question offered by professional writers and editors.

The winner of the debate? You decide. And then decide which route seems "right" for you.

The Case for Specialists

BY SANDRA DARK

Would you purchase a life insurance policy from a washing machine salesman? Would you have a valuable painting appraised by an auto mechanic? Would you hire a radiologist to fill out your income tax return?

Of course not.

But, it could be that you've been asking editors to do just that.

Talent, skill, and determination aside, one of the freelance writer's most important tools is salesmanship. You (the writer) cannot hope to sell your product (the manuscript or idea) unless you can convince the consumer (the editor *and* the reader) that you know what you are writing about. In my experience, the simplest way to accomplish that is to develop a specialty.

What is a Specialist

Anyone can be a specialty writer. If you have a job, a hobby, or do volunteer work, you already have the foundation. Doctors who write for the *Journal of the American Medical Association* are specialists. So are amateur hobbyists who sell woodworking articles to *Handyman*, or trout fishing pieces to *Field and Stream*, or gardening articles to *The Mother Earth News*.

It isn't absolutely necessary that you be specially trained or formally educated in your specialty, although that certainly gives you a running start on your competition. The important thing is that you be able to write about a subject with some measure of authority. Personal experience frequently plays a more important role than schooling in specialty writing. A weekend hang-gliding enthusiast is likely to produce a far more interesting and exciting story on his sport than, say, an aeronautical engineer who has never had the somewhat dubious thrill of sailing off a cliff into thin air.

Basically, specializing is a matter of using your own personal or professional strong points. For instance, you never see a great weight lifter with skinny legs, or a track star who is built like a Sherman tank. Athletes know how to cash in on their individual strengths, and there is no reason why writers cannot do the same.

Being an imaginative lot by nature, many writers recoil at the thought of being boxed in by the word *specialist*. That's nonsense. Specialty articles can be slanted to hit almost any market, even the most general. A single recent issue of *Review*, Eastern Airline's in-flight publication, printed articles in such diverse specialties as health, art, travel, outdoors, real estate, food, economics, sports and language. I've

Sandra Dark is a freelancer who writes a column for Organic Gardening *from her home in Norman, Oklahoma. Her current writing specialty is novels, and she is presently working on a medical thriller for publication in 1984.*

sold gardening-related material to a wide range of publications, including a mail-order shopping magazine, women's magazines and gardening markets.

Isaac Asimov, the successful science-and-space writer, is a classic example of a specialist. He has the entire universe to play around with, and certainly no one could accuse him of being boxed in by his subject. Julia Child is another writer who has taken full advantage of her culinary interest/expertise, turning out a stream of very successful cookbooks and columns.

But you don't have to be a scientific whiz . . . or any kind of whiz, for that matter . . . to be a specialist. Believe me, my reputation as a garden writing specialist far outstrips my actual gardening abilities (which is not to say that I'm a plant-killer . . . I *can* garden, and well enough to have done field trials for seed companies for the past three years). The difference is that I have developed a considerable bank of information sources ranging from home gardeners (great for anecdotes!) to university professors. I have educated myself well beyond the level of the average gardener.

How much of an expert must you be to qualify as a specialty writer? Less than you might think. It all hinges on the strength of your files and Rolodex. After all, Esther Pauline Lederer never claims to be a trained psychologist. Better known as *Ann Landers*, Lederer regularly consults experts in the process of turning out her popular, long-running, syndicated advice column.

Specialist vs. Generalist

You may not yet have the confidence or the credits of an Ann Landers, but as a specialist you'll soon realize many benefits. I've found that breaking in as a specialist can provide a shortcut between writing-on-speculation and getting firm assignments with kill fees. Spec-writing often is a necessity for beginners trying to break in to the highly competitive marketplace. But, the word "specialist" has a way of perking the interest of wary editors.

The goals of the specialist are similar to those of the generalist writer: regular sales to more and higher-paying markets. The difference lies mostly in outlook and strategy. While the generalist takes the "shotgun" approach, wading into each new writing project through relatively uncharted waters, the specialist consolidates his efforts by honing a subject area that is familiar to him.

The specialist also has an advantage over the generalist in that nearly all his "excess" research for one article can be turned into grist for future stories. I once used research from a tree-planting article to add punch to a piece on mail ordering trees, in addition to juicing up my regular monthly column in *Organic Gardening*. Unlike the generalist, who skips from subject to subject, the specialist can draw from an always deepening well of readily available sources.

I know, because I've worked both sides of the street. I started out as a generalist. And after three years of hard work, I was *still* starting out.

Almost in desperation, and totally by accident, I turned an avid gardening hobby into a writing specialty that has since netted scores of sales in more than a dozen different publications. Within a year of pinpointing and focusing my specialty, editors were already beginning to call *me* with unsolicited assignments, including a monthly column in a nationally published gardening magazine. Which goes to show that editors *are* hungry for material, regardless of the rejection slips that might glut your mailbox.

But how do you convince an editor that you are a specialist? The same way you convince him that you are a writer, period. By firing off an intriguing, attention-getting query letter describing your proposal, including your special qualifications for writing it. If you're proposing a wildlife-related story and have worked for years as a zoo volunteer, then, by all means, say so. If your idea is on increasing your car's gasoline mileage and you are an experienced auto mechanic, the editor will want to know about it. And it goes without saying that if you already have published credits in your specialty—even one—they should be mentioned.

Once you have captured an editor's attention, it's time to turn to producing a well-researched, well-thought-out, specialty article.

Specialize in What

Often, writers are specialists without even realizing it; they fail to take full advantage of their standing. Larry Dale Brimmer, a San Diego-based freelancer, writes on fitness/exercise, travel and gardening. Only recently did he stop to analyze his overall sales, and conclude that gardening articles contributed most to his income. By focusing on his bread-and-butter "specialty," he now hopes to reduce rejection and increase future sales.

This does not mean that Brimmer must, or even should, entirely drop his secondary fitness/exercise and travel specialties. They will simply move a notch lower on his priorities list. As markets fluctuate (magazine markets are as fluid as the mercury in a thermometer), and Brimmer's own interests change over the years, he may even decide to rearrange those priorities. Or, shift to a completely new specialty. Knowing when to shift gears can be just as important and profitable as establishing a specialty in the first place.

How do you go about choosing a potentially profitable writing specialty? If you've ever bought groceries, you have the basic idea. First, prepare a shopping list of your areas of expertise and/or interest. Don't leave out anything. Firsthand knowledge of child rearing or house painting might be just as important as work on NASA's Apollo program. If you've restored a '57 Chevy, or have a talent for entertaining large crowds, throw that in as well.

Next, compare your list, item by item, with the related category divisions in your *Writer's Market* to determine potential marketability. Some items on your list might fit into more than one category. For instance, my gardening specialty has sales potential in *Home and Garden* publications, as well as *Women's*, *General Interest*, and *Regional*, among others. Keep in mind that the more markets that are available for your specialty, the greater your chances for future sales. Also, a broad market base reduces the main drawback of specialty writing: *market drought*. That occurs when an entire sector of specialty markets suddenly dries up. It happened to the CB market several years ago. It also happened to specialty fiction writers at about the same time, when the bottom fell out of the once-booming gothic market.

Before making the final decision on your specialty, decide which is your greater immediate motivation: glory or greed. Some markets (such as *Religious*) are wide open and eager for new writers, but pay slave wages. Higher-paying markets, on the other hand, are more selective and less easy to break in to.

How to Become a Specialist

Once you've settled on a specialty, begin building a foundation. I continually search magazines, newspapers, and book stores for material pertaining to my specialty, and file it away for future reference. My Rolodex contains the names, addresses, and phone numbers of every expert or source of information I've come across in the gardening or agricultural field, including more than 65 mail order nurseries. (Often, experts can refer you to other experts, expanding on your valuable source list.) I'm on the media mailing lists of various nurseries, as well as agricultural cooperative extension services in several states. I've joined gardening and garden writers' organizations, and find their newsletters and mailings provide inspiration for article ideas and information on the latest trends in the booming gardening industry. Since my local public library is weak on gardening reference books, I invested in a couple of gardening encyclopedias that have since paid for themselves many times over.

You cannot be a successful specialist *or* generalist writer without knowing where to find the best and latest information in your field. Off-the-top-of-the-head articles might net you a few sales in the beginning, but continued success in the highly competitive word marketplace is based on solid, informative articles that editors feel are worthy to pass along to their readers.

But, your main investment will be in *effort*, not dollars. Reading (and what writer doesn't like to read?), absorbing, and filing away every scrap of information available on your specialty should become a habit, if not a compulsion. I also visit public gardens, garden shops, farmers' markets, and any other place that might be a source of information, or trigger an idea. Not only will the process of continual osmosis broaden your knowledge of your specialty, it will also keep your imagination active and creative.

The deeper you probe into your specialty, the greater are your chances of coming up with fresh new slants on subjects. A different viewpoint can make even the most jaded editor rub his hands together. For instance, after a good dozen people had complained to me that they were the kiss of death to houseplants, I wrote "Houseplants for Purple Thumbs," which sold to *Lady's Circle*. In the March 1983 issue of *Organic Gardening*, Porter Shimer writes about how gardening can affect your sleep. There is bound to be a nutrition specialist out there somewhere who can tell us how to diet on fast foods.

Tools of the Trade

Books are part of building your specialty foundation. Home reference libraries for your specialty are nice and can be handy time-savers for basic research needs. But, they are an unnecessary expense for the beginning specialist if there is a large municipal or university library nearby. Even a small library can be a boon if it has interlibrary lending arrangements with a larger facility. I can use the extensive University of Oklahoma library for research but, because I'm not a student, I cannot check out books. Since I'm not keen on sitting on hard library chairs for days on end, poring over often tedious books, I simply jot down the titles and authors, and then order them through my local public library. When they arrive on loan from the university—a process that takes anywhere from a couple of days to a week, assuming that a student hasn't beaten me to them—I can borrow them from the public library for the standard two-week period and plow through them in the comfort of my easy chair.

One last word on home reference libraries: they can put a major crimp in your bank account. I shop book store sales and have gotten some terrific buys from mail order companies offering remaindered books (such as a fully-illustrated, 16-volume gardening encyclopedia for $35). Even so, I've always made it a practice to spend only a certain percentage of my specialty writing income on specialty reference materials. This doesn't shock my budget and it gives me added incentive to work toward more and larger sales.

People Resources

The heart and soul of a specialist writer's bag of tricks are his sources of expert information. After all, there are times when even the experts must consult other experts. Here is where it really helps to have a basic knowledge of your subject matter. You aren't so likely to ask questions that will turn off an expert and make him less receptive to providing vital information in the future. The importance of establishing a relationship of mutual respect with the occupants of your Rolodex (so you can turn to them again and again) cannot be overemphasized.

Beginners often get off to a rocky start on those relationships, and I'm as guilty of that as anyone. Some years ago, while preparing an article for an early issue of *The New Farm*, I managed to corral a USDA meat additives expert for a telephone interview. The move from *gardening* to *farming* was a giant leap to me, and the expert caught on right away that I was in slightly over my head (a not uncommon problem, it seems to me, for beginning *generalists* who hop from subject to subject). That perception hardly brought out his compassionate side. He stomped all over my ego like a Marine Corps Drill Instructor. I had what I considered to be a carefully prepared list of basic questions to ask him. But, as it turned out, they were *too* basic. He let me know in no uncertain terms (he got downright sarcastic!) that he thought I was wasting his time by asking questions that were beneath his level of expertise. It still rankles to admit it, but he was right. Although I did get the information I needed, I was wringing wet by the time I hung up. The gentleman's Rolodex card still bears the notation, "Good source . . . but *be prepared!*"

That experience taught me to interview the expert only *after* doing the basic background research. They have neither the time nor the inclination to do your homework for you. And if you ask only concise, knowledgeable questions, your expert sources are more likely to open up to you the next time you call on them.

Where do you begin a list of specialty sources? Public relations people are excellent sources of quotes and information, although you must keep in mind that their viewpoints tend to be sharply slanted. They are usually talkative and willing to spend seemingly limitless amounts of time with you. Your local librarian can help you track down names and addresses of major industries and organizations in your specialty field, most of which have PR departments.

If possible, however, bypass the PR rep's blizzard conditions and go straight to the hard source. If you're an outdoors specialist doing an article on fishing tackle, become familiar with manufacturers, and ask to talk with the fellow who actually designs and field tests the equipment. I interviewed a university field researcher for the article on tree planting, a government soil conservationist for a soil erosion piece, and a truck farmer for an article on an obscure squash plant.

Armed with an arsenal of experts, the specialist writer who is already well-grounded in the basics of his field usually has less homework to do than the generalist before getting down to the nitty-gritty of his article research and writing. You might even think you don't *need* an expert, and perhaps you're right in some cases. But there is nothing like a quote directly from the horse's mouth to add weight to an article, and grab an editor's attention. So, don't be tempted to hide your Rolodex under your typewriter cover.

Opportunities for Specialists

For the writer with large ambitions, specializing has one outstanding advantage that is tough to beat: specialty books are always in demand, and the specialty writer has the inside track. Although I've yet to write a nonfiction specialty book, I've had enthusiastic responses from editors on preliminary specialty book proposals, and have had several requests that I co-author books—all on the basis of my magazine specialty articles.

I've also found that the instincts developed by specializing work well with researching for fiction. I've recently completed an espionage thriller that required a great deal of research, including interviewing a U.S. Border Patrol agent working a lonely stretch of highway in South Texas. (I went there prepared with a tight list of questions, and bled him of enough information in fifteen minutes flat to write an entire chapter I hadn't even planned on.) My files are loaded with intelligence-related research material that never made it into that book . . . but that will be part of another project.

I'm currently collaborating with an M.D. on a medical thriller. When it comes to research, this bears a closer relationship to my nonfiction gardening specialty than you might think. Both physicians and doctors of horticulture (and related sciences) deal with living, breathing, hormone-stimulated organisms. They have a maddening fondness for fifty-cent words that require a great deal of translation to make them palatable to the average reader. (My esteemed partner emphasizes the flora-fauna correlation by referring to the *head* as a "gourd.")

For nonfiction writers hoping to make a transition into fiction, I highly recommend specializing. The better you know your subject (be it science, spies, cowboys, or high finance), the more realism you can add to your plots. For instance, millions of Robert Ludlum fans are convinced (wrongly) that he once worked for the CIA. As an espionage-thriller specialist, Ludlum takes details seriously, and probably knows the exact voltage in the electrically charged fence surrounding the CIA's Langley, Virginia headquarters. It's the cumulative effect of seemingly innocuous details that can make a story come alive.

A Specialist in the 80s

Writers in this decade are faced with a deluge of opportunities. Specializing is a good way to break in to the writing field (and add order to these opportunities) even if, at heart, you are a generalist. I've noticed that since I've established myself as a specialist, editors are far more receptive to offering me assignments outside my specialty area. This makes the transition from one specialty to another, when and if necessary, much easier.

Responding to pressure from increasingly sophisticated and demanding readers, publications are becoming more and more specialized each year. As the trend continues, it's only natural that a growing number of editors will turn to specialty writers to fill their specialty needs. Specialists can best provide the depth of writing that editors and readers expect. It's a simple matter of supply-and-demand. By developing a strong, marketable specialty, you can supply that demand . . . and shift your writing career into high gear.

The Case for Generalists

BY GARY TURBAK

The writing world is full of choices. Should you write for adults or for children? Fiction or nonfiction? How about humor? Should you write about your own experiences or someone else's?

Or, is it possible to do all of these? Should you—can you—be all things to all editors?

I believe you can . . . and should. I think you should hitch your writing wagon to the brightest star of all. I think you should become a generalist.

What is a Generalist

A generalist knows no bounds. He can research and write about anything that interests him . . . or an editor. He can go bear trapping with a biologist, climb on a rooftop with a chimney sweep, or jet across the country (at a magazine's expense) to hear firsthand the poignant story of a missing child that has been found. I know. As a generalist writer, I have done all these things.

A generalist is free to follow current trends or to relive the past. He may make readers laugh one day and cry the next. A generalist's writing is restricted only by his innate abilities and his imagination. He is the freest of all writers.

A successful generalist is any writer who will allow his mind to wander and who has confidence in his skills. It matters not where (or whether) you went to college or how you were brought up. You can be a successful generalist as easily in Wyoming as in Washington, D.C. I make my living as a generalist writer in Montana, about as far from a throbbing metropolis as you can get.

If you seem never to have time to read all the books and magazines you'd like, to visit all the places you want, or meet enough interesting people . . . you're probably primed to be a good generalist. If your interests range from macrame to Zen you can be a generalist. Keeping a ravenous curiosity well fed is a major personal goal and a common trait among many generalists. My own has led me to investigate ancient medical practices, wildlife poachers, funeral planning, filmmaking, barter clubs, classic hoaxes, and worm raising. I've written and sold articles about each of these subjects.

Story ideas are everywhere, and only a generalist can take advantage of all of them. He sees every person, place, thing in the context of a potential story idea. Has your neighbor devised a unique way to make furniture? Might a travel magazine be interested in that rustic lodge down the road? Does your local school have an effective program for combating teen drug use?

A generalist is constantly on the alert for article ideas; he learns to recognize salable topics and angles. He approaches a story idea in a way specialists cannot. I call it bleeding. I try to bleed every idea for as many sales as I can. After you have chosen a market for the central idea, try to determine who else might be interested. Many topics are loaded with spin-off potential.

I once wrote a straightforward article for *The Elks Magazine* about woodburning stoves. As an outgrowth of that original idea, I also sold pieces on woodburner safety (*Harrowsmith*), cleaning a woodburner chimney (*Family Handyman*), a profile of a professional chimney sweep (*Blair and Ketchum's Country Journal*), and a general look at other uses of wood energy (*The American Legion magazine*). It's not al-

Gary Turbak is a freelance writer from Missoula, Montana, who says, "I've always got a project going." His "projects" have appeared in a variety of publications, including Outdoor Life, Reader's Digest, National Wildlife, Kiwanis, Family Handyman, Connecticut Business Times *and* Harrowsmith.

ways possible to bleed this many sales out of a single topic, but you should try. You must refine the idea to fit a particular audience—and a discriminating editor.

Specialist vs. Generalist

Maybe you've heard the argument that editors prefer to work with specialists rather than generalists. Bullfeathers! Oh sure, a few technical areas (such as computer programming or brain surgery) may be out of bounds for most generalists, but I believe most editors couldn't care less (and often don't even know) if this is your first or 50th article on a given topic. When querying, tout your credentials by listing your most prestigious publications, regardless of the genre.

Most magazine editors are wise enough to realize that good articles come more often from good writers than from experts in any given field. A good freelancer can research and write about almost any topic, but experts aren't automatically publishable writers. If specialist writers are making sale after sale, it's because they are effective writers, not because they're experts in the field. You'll establish credibility with an editor only by producing good stories for him, not by proffering a reputation you may have acquired somewhere else.

Let's say the editor of a major popular magazine is looking for a general audience story on how a nuclear bomb works. Who is more likely to produce a good article—a nuclear physicist or a freelance writer? I'll bet on the writer every time. The physicist's article is likely to bulge with formulas, theories, and equations. And the specialist, I think, runs the risk of becoming too familiar with his topic. Because he knows his subject so thoroughly, he may lose track of what his readers already do or do not know. A good generalist writer, on the other hand, knows how to take that same information, assimilate it, and produce an informative story anyone can understand. Because each topic is fresh and new to a generalist, he brings to the research the same curiosity that readers would.

If editors know that writers produce better articles than experts, why should they care if you, as a writer, have already written one or 50 articles about nuclear bombs? The editor may even be seeking exactly the fresh approach only a newcomer can give.

And don't fret about being labeled a "shotgunner." Your accumulated sales to a variety of magazines in a variety of topics can only speak well of you. Having numerous publishing credits is always a plus, regardless of their origin. Remember, the writing "depth" editors are looking for comes *within* an article via thorough research, not by writing many stories about the same topic.

That crucial first sale (and most subsequent ones) will invariably come by way of a professional query . . . followed by an equally professional manuscript. The process of writing and selling is no different for generalists than for anyone else. It's just that generalists complete the process in a greater variety of publications than do specialists.

Why *You* Should be a Generalist

The most obvious benefit of being a generalist is increased sales. When you're free to write about virtually anything, potential markets are almost unlimited. Let's compare two writers—a car-care specialist and a broad-based generalist. How many magazines run articles about car care? There are a few major ones like *Popular Mechanics* and *Mechanics Illustrated*. The travel magazines occasionally use such features. So do homeowner publications. A woman's magazine will infrequently run a car-care story. Let's be generous and say there are 50 potential markets for this specialist. That's a darn small field to work with, considering the tremendous number of freelancers in business today.

I think a specialist severely restricts his selling potential. Sure, a few car care specialists may have more work than they can handle, but the average freelancer often gets lost in the shuffle. You don't see K-Mart or Sears selling their products only to a selected few customers, do you?

In contrast, the generalist has tremendous market potential. *Writer's Market* lists 4,000 places to sell what you write, and any good generalist is capable of tapping hundreds—maybe thousands—of those markets, *including* the 50 publications interested in car care stories.

A more personal benefit of being a generalist lies in the tremendous amount of diverse information you can tuck away in your mind. As a generalist, you can get paid for learning about Egyptian history, gold mining, leukemia, and hundreds of other topics.

And by freeing yourself of topic restraints, you'll also stand a better chance of avoiding writer burnout. I don't know about you, but I grow weary of a subject after even two weeks of intensive research and writing. When that happens, there's a chance my writing could get flat and boring. I'd suffer, and my readers would, too. But because I flit from woodburners to baseball, I am always fresh, always ready to give readers my best shot. They deserve nothing less.

I think it's important for a beginning writer to choose consciously to be a generalist. Many a beginner is plagued by timidity. He thinks he's limited to writing about whatever single topic got him interested in writing in the first place. He sees himself as a woodworker or teacher or athlete who also is a writer. He needs to reverse that perception—to see himself as a writer who also works with wood, teaches, or is an athlete. Say it out loud: "I'm a freelance writer, and I'm a generalist. I can and will write about anything that interests me."

Affirming this credo (or choosing not to affirm it) is an individual, personal decision. Not every writer should be a generalist, just as not everyone is cut out to be a parent or public speaker. To be an effective generalist, you must have an active imagination, an insatiable curiosity, and good research and writing skills.

Periodically, you may want to reevaluate your status as a generalist. If you have trouble coming up with article ideas in different subject areas, maybe generalism isn't for you. If you find yourself repeatedly returning to one topic for story ideas, your efforts elsewhere might be futile shots in the dark. If you find a niche where every idea sells and every story is worth $2,000, you'll likely want to stay with that topic. (And so will I. Call me and share the wealth.) But I'll bet you become addicted to the freedom and unlimited markets afforded the generalist writer.

How to Become a Generalist

One way to cultivate a generalist outlook and tap into those markets is by reading. Read magazines of all sorts, even the kind for which you have never written. Go to the library or newsstand and browse the magazines that are unfamiliar to you. Take notes if you like. Perhaps your goal may be to become familiar with one new magazine each week. *Cats Magazine* may not seem to hold much promise right now, but next month when your neighbor buys a pair of purebred Siamese and starts breeding them, you'll be glad you know about that new market.

Read at least one newspaper thoroughly each day. Clip and keep any article that even remotely suggests a story idea to you. My most lucrative article idea (the problem of missing children) came out of my morning newspaper. From that one tiny newspaper story I ended up writing two major articles which netted me about $5,500, including reprint fees.

Watch and listen to news broadcasts and other informational programs on television and radio. Which topics are hot? If "Sixty Minutes" is doing a piece on medical quacks today, you may land an assignment to write about them next week. Stay informed.

Listen to the people around you. If you hear, as I did, two retailers complaining about the number of bad checks they receive or buzzing about the advantages of barter clubs, you'll know, as I did, that you've just been handed a couple of article ideas.

Tools of the Trade

To launch those ideas into salable articles and research other writing projects, you need access to a generalist's equipment. *Writer's Market* is as close as we come to having a Bible. If you haven't done so already, spend a couple evenings *reading Writer's Market* the way you would a novel—page by page. There are markets out there of which you could not possibly have dreamed . . . and about which you'll never know unless you thoroughly examine this book. Via *Writer's Market* I have sold articles to *The Old Bottle Magazine, Ruralite, On Campus Report*, and many other publications I wouldn't have discovered any other way.

Other musts for your home library are an encyclopedia set, almanac, dictionary, thesaurus (used sparingly), and copy of *The Elements of Style*. Within arm's reach I also have *The Careful Writer*, and *Plain English Handbook. The Associated Press Stylebook and Libel Manual* (or one of the other comprehensive style guides) can help you be consistent with your abbreviations, punctuation and usage.

Become familiar with *Reader's Guide to Periodical Literature* and *The Encyclopedia of Associations*. The former provides a complete indexing of the topics, titles, and authors in scores of popular magazines. The latter puts you in touch with thousands of organizations capable of supplying you with information and experts on everything from rodeo cowboys to cerebral palsy. Your public library probably has both.

Make friends with your librarians and learn to take full advantage of the services your library provides. If yours offers an interlibrary loan service (whereby you can get virtually any book in the country) or computerized data search, learn how to use these tools. Become a thorough researcher.

If you live anywhere near a college or university, become familiar with the facilities and people there. Universities are storehouses of experts, books, theses, and research information.

Ask a lot of questions. Of everyone. If you meet someone who has an unusual occupation, is doing unique research, or is concerned about a little-known social problem, quiz him. If you read of individuals or institutions engaged in interesting work, write to them and ask for information. Make notes about every thing and everyone who may now or someday be part of a story. Write everything down. Trust nothing to your memory. Establish a card file of people and organizations who may be of help to you.

Keep everything practically forever—letters from sources, reports, studies, pamphlets, photographs, interview tapes and transcripts, photocopied information, names, addresses and phone numbers. If you can't afford filing cabinets, store the material in sturdy cardboard boxes. You never know when you may need the material again.

Opportunities for Generalists

The writing opportunities and the chances for dipping into those cardboard boxes are as varied as the subjects you write about. You may begin with a local market or query an editor of a regional publication. The difficulty of breaking into any market usually is directly proportional to the payment a publication makes. The higher the pay, the stiffer the competition. Many generalists choose to begin at the lower end of the pay scale, where it's relatively easy to break in and where hundreds of smaller magazines are looking for material.

As you refine your skills and get a few publishing credits, you can move up the payment ladder. There may be drawbacks to being a freelance generalist, but the availability of markets isn't one of them.

Your tremendous flexibility as a generalist may even allow you to expand your writing career into totally new areas. You're used to trying new things. Though about 90 percent of my writing is nonfiction magazine articles, my generalist approach gives me even greater latitude for sales.

A couple years ago, I did a bit of advertising and began writing employment resumes for job seekers in my community. After I had about 100 such documents to my credit, I wrote a book showing people how to prepare their own resumes. My second book (naturally on a completely different topic) is a travel guide to Montana. I've also written two brochures, one for a Midwest utility company explaining the pros and cons of heating with wood; the other, a promotional tool for an employment counseling service. When a nearby city needed a newcomer's guide, I got the job of writing and shooting pictures for it.

Recently, I happened to read a couple of supposedly humorous fiction pieces in outdoor magazines. They didn't seem *that* funny, and I thought I could do better. Though fiction—and especially humorous fiction—was foreign to me, trying new things was not. These haven't been published yet, but I'm confident they will be.

I didn't set out to discover any of these "different" markets. Rather, I remained open so they might find me. My skill lies not in amassing knowledge of any single topic or genre, but in having the confidence to adapt my craft to virtually any type of writing work. Maybe I'll write a screenplay next or some serious short stories. And there's that novel I've been thinking about . . .

Let diversity be a way of life for you. When the opportunity arises to venture into a completely different kind of writing, you will be prepared for the challenge.

A Generalist in the 80s

Perhaps the greatest test for a generalist writer lies in his ability to stay attuned to the ever-changing needs of hundreds of editors. In honing our ideas sharp to fit a particular publication. In keeping our writing crisp and fresh and free of jargon. In maintaining our composure and direction while dozens of new ideas fight for a place in our minds.

The generalist fits into the new technological age like Cinderella's foot in the slipper. This is the era of the generalist writer. Scores of new publications are born each year, all clamoring for effective freelancers. With computers and data banks becoming increasingly available to writers, more information than ever before is at our disposal. Word processors are setting us free from the drudgery of typing to use our time more effectively by exploring topics and markets we knew nothing about only yesterday.

Some say this decade will usher in a new age of information as important as the industrial revolution of the 18th century. And readers will need informed writers who can describe complex scientific experiments in layman's terms; interpret the spiritual mysteries of space; and look ahead to the time when today's science fiction becomes fact. As a flexible generalist, you can ride the crest of the information revolution because you're a pro at exploring and adapting to new fields and new markets.

What the Writers Say

If we could know exactly what the world will be like in the future, it would make perfect sense to become a specialist. The fact is, however, that we have very little idea of what sorts of writing will be considered of value a number of years from now. (Who in the world would have supposed a decade ago that anyone could publish a book on running? Not me, certainly.) So if we want to be purely pragmatic about the matter—if, that is, we want to *sell* above all else—it's probably safer, and smarter, to be a generalist. I suspect, however, that theory doesn't matter much here, and that what counts most is people's individual bent. In the end, we all wind up doing pretty much what our minds have best suited us to do. A good thing, too.

—James Fixx
Jim Fixx's Second Book of Running; Jackpot!

It depends on your particular bent. I started out to be a science fiction writer and nothing else—and I ended up writing on anything under the sun. I don't think it's the sort of thing you can plan.

—Isaac Asimov
Asimov on Science Fiction; Universe

First decide that what you want to say is worth saying, and then decide on how you are going to say it. For example, your content might be a serious issue, but your method might be humor. Whether you develop into a specialist or generalist is incidental to your subject matter and should not be something decided at the beginning of your career. Your subject matter may lead you into an area of special interest, but this cannot be predetermined.

—Laurence J. Peter
Peter's People; The Peter Plan: A Proposal for Survival

A writer benefits, I think, from attempting many things; he or she writes better prose for having attempted poetry, and better fiction for having done nonfiction. Write every sort of thing that amuses you, especially when young and beginning. On the other hand, aim at some sort of market if you intend to make a living at writing; this aim will doubtless involve some specializing.

—John Updike
Rabbit is Rich; Poorhouse Fair

It helps to be well versed in a specialty—that's how I got to where I am today. But to be a good writer of fact or fiction, you must have a well-rounded education and broad interests. Otherwise, your writing will be limited and dull.

—Jane Brody
Jane Brody's The New York Times Guide to Personal Health;
Jane Brody's Nutrition Book

There are two tips I would offer beginning writers: 1) Writing for fame or fortune is a fool's errand; 2) Write out of a passion, a caring, a need. The rest will follow.

—Sidney Sheldon
Master of the Game; Rage of Angels

I don't think a writer should limit himself or herself to a particular specialty, particularly in the beginning. To write as much as possible, about as big a variety of topics as possible—this is essential. Long before I wrote a novel (writing novels is, and has always been, my first and persistent love), I wrote short stories, nonfiction magazine articles, newspaper columns, profiles. All of this sharpened my talent; every byline convinced me I was a professional writer. And when the proper time came, I wrote that first novel, and have been writing them ever since. To me, specialty writing means confinement. And the ability to write is too various a talent to place limitations on it. Even now I write occasional articles (book reviews, columns, etc.) to keep myself fresh and sharp.

—Robert Cormier
I Am the Cheese; Take Me Where the Good Times Are

In the early stages I certainly think I would try to develop as a "generalist writer." . . . Actually it seems better to *me* if you don't *ever* become a "specialist." Life is less interesting for the writer if his expertise is only in coral reef fish or New England regional cooking. [But] if you are eventually going to become a specialist, it is still important to get published as much as you can in the early days, or nobody will ever pay attention to your specialty.

—Helen Gurley Brown
*Having It All; Cosmopolitan's Love Book:
A Guide to Ecstasy in Bed*

You must be the kind of writer you *want* to be. Writing is a creative art. Like all arts, it represents the expression of your unique perception of life. It is a statement of something that, because you are uniquely *you*, no one else can replicate. Therefore, if you do not make the statement, it will never be made. Certainly, you earn a living by grinding out what others see, or request that you see, but you will only become *important* when you share your special way of seeing. For it is that quality which is inherent in every art that lives.

—Leo Buscaglia
Love; Living, Loving, & Learning

What the Editors Say

We welcome the generalist writer. It normally takes a working pro a few queries to figure out what we're looking for and to deliver the particular military angle we want in almost every story. But after that breaking-in period, we can be a modest but steady market for the pro. We'd like to hear from more of them. They have only to be willing to get to know our special audience.

—Bruce Thorstad
Off Duty Magazine

We much prefer specialist writers because they are usually more into their subject—more complete and thorough.

—Robin M. Thompson
Rosicrucian Digest

Specialist, generalist—it doesn't matter as long as they can supply material of interest to our readers. Our readers are pet shop owners, pet suppliers, commercial breeders, distributors and manufacturers. They are concerned about pets—how to get them to market profitably and healthy, how to solve the industry problems, and how to stay in business. A specialist could do it well, but sometimes a good reporter, who has not seen the industry up close for such a long time, has more excitement. Accuracy of reporting is the key—plus, of course, good writing.

—Bob Behme
Pet Business

We're always looking for new ideas and writers! We'll also work with a person in whom we see talent, but isn't quite there yet. If your specialty is comedy, of course we're very interested. However, if it is comedy, chances are you've already tried writing for us . . .

—John Ficarra
MAD Magazine

Generalists are fine if they are enterprising enough to research the needs of our market. If they need too much help from us in finding leads, interviews, etc., I discourage them. Ours is a very specialized market, and my experience with generalists is that they are unwilling or unable to do the spadework necessary to adapt their work to our readers.

—Sheila Gibbons
Ladycom Magazine

The *Old Cars Price Guide* requires some degree of specialization, but nothing that a good generalist couldn't research in an afternoon or two. The specialist is probably better suited to my editorial needs, although specialists in the old car field tend to fear writing about value considerations.

—John Gunnell
Krause Publications

We find that even writers who specialize in housing and related fields can seldom supply enough integrated technical information couched in decent, idiomatic English. We prefer to deal directly with the people who do the work.

—Mark Alvarez
Fine Homebuilding

We do not require any particular credentials in our writers, but so many of our articles have a heavy medical slant that writers without some knowledge of medicine can feel quite shy about writing for us. It is easier for the writer if he or she has some experience writing on medical subjects for a lay audience.

—Joan Lippert
Health Magazine

Content is the key. Expertise often is contained in the writer's personal experience. Specialized writers are OK if they write in a popular style from the base of their expertise/authority.

—E. Lee Sizemore
Living with Teenagers

It's more important for a freelancer to be a good writer, rather than highly specialized. A good writer can learn to do research; it's harder to learn good writing.

—Susan Spann
Selling Direct

The Markets

Book Publishers

This time, like all times, is a very
good one if we but know what to do with it.

—Ralph W. Emerson

What writers should do with this time in book publishing is a good question. In updating our *Writer's Market* listings for 1984, we asked editors/publishers for their predictions for the short-term future of their particular sector of the industry. Those who answered generally responded in one of three ways: with cautious optimism for modest growth; with a "wait and see what the economy does" attitude; with the question, "Who can predict?" One especially succinct editor wrote simply, "Say your prayers."

These less-than-definitive answers from industry representatives were not given without thought. The truth is there are no clear-cut answers. Here's why. The industry is currently preoccupied with figuring out how electronic publishing will permanently affect operations. Some book publishers are running willy nilly to get in on a slice of the computer software pie; others are taking a guarded stance, hoping to learn from the mistakes of the first generation go-getters.

Apart from the computer flurry, publishers of all sizes and persuasions are working hard to defend themselves against further losses at the cash register (there haven't been many banner years in book publishing lately). Some commercial publishers are putting more promotional oomph into their backlist books—those titles that keep selling over a number of years. University presses are picking up commercially published books whose copyrights have expired; smaller college presses are even licensing books originally published by some of the bigger university publishers.

Amidst all of this are the book buyers who are just getting back on their feet as the economy creeps forward. Sales growth and just how people will put their discretionary income to use is anybody's guess. Both consumers and publishers are at a crossroads.

This is not to say that book publishing is at a standstill. Hardly.

There's plenty brewing in the industry. The number of newly published books in America is higher than ever—some 45,000 new titles made it to press in the last year. And, according to the Data Services Division at R.R. Bowker (publishers of *Books in Print*, *Publishers Weekly*, etc.), some 300 new book publishers enter the marketplace each month.

Small and independent presses, traditionally known to promote narrow-audience books and usually on a shoestring, appear to be opening up to manuscripts with greater commercial success potential. In a related comment, one small press editor writes that as he sees it, "the university and small independent presses are the last refuge of risk taking in the industry." Many of the smaller publishers are also taking on books they can market directly (through direct response and direct mail), rather than relying on major book and department store chains.

In a similar show of "looking out for us" are the regional publishers who continue to add variety and life to the country's bookshelves. (Notice the significant number of publishers in our book publisher index that indicate an interest in regional topics.) The networks of cooperation growing between regional booksellers and their publishing counterparts may reflect that New York and Los Angeles do not speak for the whole country. Regional publishers fill gaps for readers who look for strong identification in the books they buy.

Publishers are also looking for identification—with writers they add to their catalogs. They are looking for authors willing to make a commitment both to their subject matter and their publisher. One Midwestern company tells us the primary ingredient in its search for writers is that they have direct experience in what they are writing about. A West Coast publisher says he looks for new and veteran writers with whom he can nurture a long-term publishing relationship. With uncertainty in the industry, editors/publishers are quick to go with known quantities—writers they know they can work with and who have been successful in the past.

Other trends in the industry indicating the printed word lives include the following:

- the computer book explosion. From beginner books to texts for individual computer systems, to manuals for parents and real estate personnel, to tutorials for business and school, and on and on . . . the sales have surpassed any prophet's wildest projections.
- specialty books. Self-help, diet, exercise and health books continue to be strong sellers.
- how-to books. Anything on teaching you how to make money, manage your finances or live to be a hundred has an audience.
- romance. Fiction sales are led by tales of passion and emotion followed by mysteries, historicals and suspense. Consult *Fiction Writer's Market* (Writer's Digest Books) for a detailed look at fiction markets.
- nonfiction. Good technical writing in science, communications and technology has a solid niche. The audiences are well defined—but once established in the field, you could become a household word. Travel-related books continue to be popular.
- biography and autobiography. Rock stars, public figures and entertainers are top sellers.
- relevance. There is a heightened interest in contemporary concerns, both personal and global. Books on nuclear war, acid rain, and how to raise your child into the twenty-first century signal growing interest in quality-of-life topics.

So what does the confusing combination of flat sales, limited risk taking, increased publishing activity and buying trends mean for writers? It means knowing what to do with your book idea or manuscript is probably the single most important step on the road to getting published. *It means you must know the markets.*

Before you get to the actual tapping of those publishers, though, your homework includes getting to know your competition. Become very familiar with the *Subject Guide To Books In Print*. This three-volume reference book (its companions are *Books in Print—Authors* and *Books in Print—Titles*) is available in any library. It lists authors and titles of books according to topic/field/subject. Knowing what's already out there will help you tailor your book with a different slant or an unusual direction.

Get to know the comings and goings of the book industry. Read *Publishers*

Weekly where you can recognize industry trends and read sneak previews of new and not-yet-released titles. Study book publisher catalogs that tell you a lot more than just book prices. Careful scrutiny will suggest the style and image a particular publisher is aiming for. Most publishers will send a catalog free or for a nominal postage charge. Does your book idea complement the line they already have? Be critical and thorough in your pre-submission research.

When you know the marketplace, you might be ready to query a publisher—usually with your proposal (including a synopsis of the project, a description of your audience, your qualifications for writing, etc.). The query should run under two pages, unless the subject is complex. For a nonfiction book, add a proposed Table of Contents; for a fiction manuscript, add up to 50 pages of sample writing you've already done. Wait for a publisher to request anything more. If an editor is interested in nonfiction, he may ask for a few sample chapters; for fiction, the complete manuscript is often requested.

Use the book publisher index at the end of this section to streamline your search for a market. Learn about those publishers that indicate interest in your subject area. But don't just query all the companies under, for example, "business and economics." Reading the individual listings for the publishers under that heading will reveal that some are interested only in how-to operate a beauty salon—still others may want high school textbook material. They will not automatically be receptive to your interpretations of the Laffer curve. Save time for yourself and the editors who receive your submissions.

Because publishers frequently have their own submission requirements, be sure to read the *Writer's Market* entries carefully—and all the way through. The more than 800 publishers listed here have taken the time to tell you what they want. Follow their directions. If you have a word processor and plan to submit a computer print-out manuscript, be sure the publisher is receptive to such submissions. If the listing says send outline and two sample chapters, do just that.

Too many editors/publishers tell us they are drowning in misdirected manuscripts and outlines or queries that arrive without SASE. Some have even asked us not to include them in this year's edition, because they have neither the staff nor the patience to wade through unsolicited manuscripts or poorly prepared proposals.

The writer who knows where to direct his manuscript and proposals won't have to worry about their landing on some editor's slush pile. He recognizes that *this* time in book publishing is a very good one.

A & P FEATURE PUBLICATIONS, A division of The Atlantic & Pacific Commerce Co., Inc. Box 6639, Oakland CA 94603-9989. Chief Editor: Ernst H. Mikkelsen. Publishes hardcover and paperback originals. Averages 2-6 titles/year. Pays 4-16% royalty "depending upon marketing methods used. Advances paid before or on date of publication." Simultaneous and photocopied submissions OK. Reports in 1 month.
Nonfiction: For parents or married couples: Health, recreation, children, and subjects related to developing higher value systems within families. Submit outline/synopsis and sample chapters.

A & W PUBLISHERS, INC., 95 Madison Ave., New York NY 10016. (212)725-4970. Imprints include A&W Visual Library, Sphere Books and Gallahad Books. Executive Editor: Carolyn Trager. Publishes hardcover and paperback originals (80%) and hardcover and paperback reprints (20%). Published 70 titles in 1983. Pays standard royalty; offers variable advance. Simultaneous and photocopied submissions OK. SASE. Reports in 2 months. Free book catalog.
Nonfiction: Beauty, fitness, child care, humor, women's interest, financial advice and self-help. Needs include all areas of general nonfiction. Query first with outline/synopsis and sample chapters. "Do not send photos or artwork that are irreplaceable."
Recent Nonfiction Titles: *America Wants to Know*; *Image Impact for Men*; and *Face Care*.
Fiction: Mainstream. Needs trade books of general interest. Submit complete ms.
Recent Fiction Titles: *Arthur Dimmesdale*; *Bullion*.

---

*Asterisk preceding a listing indicates that individual subsidy publishing or co-publishing (where author pays part or all of publishing costs) is also available. Those firms that specialize in total subsidy publishing are listed at the end of the book publishers' section.

ABBEY PRESS, St. Meinrad IN 47577. (812)357-8011. Publisher: Keith McClellan, OSB. Publishes original paperbacks. Averages 8 titles/year. Pays definite royalty on net sales. Query with outline and sample chapter. Reports in 3 weeks. SASE.
Nonfiction: "Primarily books aimed at married and family life enrichment. The materials must be typed and readable and must show some promise for the author (good grammar, etc.)."
Recent Nonfiction Titles: *Walk On in Peace*, by Dorothy Edgerton; *Building Family: An Act of Faith*, by Paul Connolly; and *The Challenge of Fatherhood*, by Hugh Stanley.

‡ABBOTT, LANGER & ASSOCIATES, 548 1st St., Crete IL 60417. (312)672-4200. Managing Consultant: Dr. Steven Langer. Publishes trade paperback originals and loose-leaf books. Averages 12 titles/year. Pays 10-15% royalty; no advance. Photocopied submissions OK. Computer printouts and disk submissions OK. SASE. Reports in 2 weeks on queries; 1 month on mss.
Nonfiction: How-to, reference, technical on some phase of personnel administration or industrial relations. Especially needs "a very limited number (3-5) of books dealing with very specialized topics in the field of personnel management, wages and salary administration, training, recruitment, selection, labor relations, etc." Publishes for personnel directors, wage and salary administrators, training directors, etc. Query.
Recent Nonfiction Titles: *Compensation of Industrial Engineers (7th Ed.)*, by S. Langer (pay survey report); *Income in Sales/Marketing Management (3rd Ed.)*, by S. Langer (salary survey report); and *How to Develop & Conduct a Pay/Benefits Survey*, by Carl F. Lutz.

ABC-CLIO, INC., 2040 A.P.S., Santa Barbara CA 93103. (805)963-4221. Vice President, Publishing: Dr. Gail Schlachter. Clio Books Editor: Barbara H. Pope. Publishes hardcover originals (95%) and paperback reprints (5%). Averages 15-20 titles/year. Pays 10-12% royalty on net price; no advance. Photocopied submissions OK. Disk submissions "must be compatible with our equipment; check with us first." Reports in 2 months. SASE. Free book catalog.
Nonfiction: Bibliographic guides, reference books, dictionaries, directories in the field of history and political science (specifically in ethnic studies, war/peace issues, comparative and international politics, women's studies, environmental studies, library science-acquisition guides, collection guides for the reference librarian, or for the el-hi market). Mss on comparative politics should be forwarded directly to the series editor, Prof. Peter H. Merkl; bibliographies on war/peace issues may be forwarded to Prof. Richard D. Burns; reference guides may be forwarded to Dr. Gail Schlachter; dictionaries in political science may be forwarded to Jack C. Plano. Query or submit outline/synopsis and 2-3 sample chapters.
Recent Nonfiction Titles: *Guide to American Foreign Relations since 1700*, by Richard Dean Burns; *Peace and War: A Guide to Bibliographies*, by Berenice A. Carroll, Clinton F. Fink, and Jane E. Mohraz; *Empire on the Pacific: A Study in American Continental Expansion*, reprint edition, by Norman A. Graebner; *TAPS for a Jim Crow Army: Letters from Black Soldiers in World War II*, by Phillip McGuire; *Energy Information Guide: Volume I, General and Alternative Energy Sources, Volume II, Nuclear and Electric Power*, by R. David Weber; *Political and Social Science Journals: A Handbook for Writers and Reviewers*; *World War II from an American Perspective: An Annotated Bibliography*; *European Immigration and Ethnicity in the United States and Canada: A Historical Bibliography*, by David L. Brye.

ABINGDON PRESS, 201 8th Ave. S., Box 801, Nashville TN 37202. (615)749-6403. Editorial Director: Ronald P. Patterson. Managing Editor: Robert Hill Jr. Editor/Professional Books: R. Donald Hardy. Senior Editor/Reference Books: Carey J. Gifford. Editor of Lay Books: Mary Ruth Howes. Editor of Academic Books: Pierce S. Ellis Jr. Editor of Children Books: Ernestine Calhoun. Publishes paperback originals and reprints. Published 120 titles last year. Pays royalty. Query with outline and samples. Write for ms preparation guide. Reports in 6 weeks. SASE.
Nonfiction: Religious-lay and professional, children's books and academic texts. Length: 32-200 pages.
Recent Nonfiction Titles: *Introduction to Old Testament Study*, by J. Hayes; *Contagious Congregation*, by G. Hunter (evangelism); and *If I Were Starting My Family Again*, by J. Drescher.
Fiction: Juveniles only.
Recent Fiction Titles: *A Sweetheart for Valentine*, by L. Balian (baby adopted by entire village); and *The Devil's Workshop*, by K. Marcuse (historical fiction about Johann Gutenberg).
Tips: "A short, pithy book is ahead of the game. Long, rambling books are a luxury few can afford."

HARRY N. ABRAMS, INC., 110 E. 59th St., New York NY 10022. (212)758-8600. Subsidiary of Times Mirror Co. President, Publisher and Editor-in-Chief: Paul Gottlieb. Publishes hardcover and "a few" paperback originals. Averages 65 titles/year. "We are one of the few publishers who publish almost exclusively illustrated books. We consider ourselves the leading publishers of art books and high quality artwork in the US." Offers variable advance. Prefers no simultaneous submissions; photocopied submissions OK. SASE. Reports in 3 months. Free book catalog.
Nonfiction: Art, nature and science and outdoor recreation. Needs illustrated books for art and art history, museums. Submit outline/synopsis and sample chapters and illustrations.

Recent Nonfiction Titles: *Secrets of the Gnomes*, by Poortuliet; *The National Museum of Natural History*, by Kopper; and *The Vatican*.

ABT BOOKS, Subsidiary of Abt Associates, Inc., 55 Wheeler St., Cambridge MA 02138. (617)492-7100. Editor-in-Chief: Clark C. Abt. Publishes hardcover and trade paperback originals. Averages 30 titles/year. Pays 10-15% royalty on receipts; offers negotiable advance. Photocopied submissions OK. SASE. Reports on queries in 3 weeks; 1 month on mss. Free book catalog.
Nonfiction: Business and world economy, social science and social issues. Subjects include business and economics, crime, housing, health, politics, psychology, sociology and research methods. "Social policy studies based on extensive research; how-to books on research methods; and business strategy. Our readers are professional and business groups with the 'need to know'; e.g., how housing programs work, how to conduct survey research, how to meet the public-involvement requirements under state and federal law." No belles-lettres. Submit outline/synopsis and sample chapters.
Recent Nonfiction Titles: *Henderson on Corporate Strategy*, by Bruce Henderson; *The Winding Passage* , by Daniel Bell (social theory); and *The Politics of Welfare*, by Blanche Bernstein (city and state policy).

ACADEMIC PRESS, INC., 111 5th Ave., New York NY 10003. (212)741-6851. Editorial Vice President: E.V. Cohen. Pays variable royalty. Publishes over 400 titles/year. Reports in 1 month. SASE.
Nonfiction: Specializes in scientific, mathematical, technical and medical works. Textbooks and reference works only in natural, behavioral-social sciences at college and research levels. Submit outline, preface and sample chapter. Books for researchers only, not general public.
Recent Nonfiction Titles: *Nonlinear Laser Spectroscopy*; *Lipoprotein Kinetics and Modeling*.

ACADEMY CHICAGO, 425 N. Michigan Ave., Chicago IL 60611. (312)644-1723. Editorial Director/Senior Editor: Anita Miller. Publishes hardcover and paperback originals (35%) and reprints (65%). Averages 40 titles/year. Pays 7-10% royalty; no advance. Photocopied submissions OK. Reports in 2 months. SASE.
Nonfiction: Adult; travel, historical. No how-to, cookbooks, self-help, etc. Query or submit sample chapters. "Do *not* send whole books. We find synopses defeating. We look first of all for good writing style, professional organization; after subject matter, that's important. Sample chapters are most helpful."
Recent Nonfiction Titles: *The Fair Women* , by Jeanne M. Weimann; and *Henry VIII*, by Lacey Baldwin Smith.
Fiction: "We would consider mysteries with one detective for series." No "romantic" fiction, or religious or sexist material; nothing avant-garde. "We can no longer do children's books or young adults."
Recent Fiction Titles: *Six Sgt. Beef Mysteries*, by Leo Bruce; and *Murder at the Red October*, by Anthony Alcott.
Tips: "We are very interested in good nonfiction history and biography. We are also interested in quality fiction and will consider once-published books that deserve reprinting."

‡ACCELERATED DEVELOPMENT, INC., 3400 Kilgore Ave., Muncie IN 47304. (317)284-7511. Executive Vice President: Mrs. Lucile Hollis. Publishes textbooks/paperback originals. Averages 6-8 titles/year. Computer printout submissions OK; prefers letter quality to dot matrix. Disk submissions OK if compatible with CPT equipment. Pays 6-15% royalty on net price. SASE. Reports in 3 months. Free book catalog.
Nonfiction: Reference books and textbooks on psychology, counseling, guidance and counseling, teacher education and death education. Especially needs "psychologically-based textbook or reference materials, death education material, theories of counseling psychology, techniques of counseling, and gerontological counseling." Publishes for professors, counselors, teachers, college and secondary students, psychologists, death educators, psychological therapists, and other health service providers. "Write for the graduate level student." Submit outline/synopsis and 2 sample chapters.
Recent Nonfiction Titles: *Role Model Blacks*, by Carroll Miller; *Managing Anxiety and Stress*, by James Archer Jr.; and *Leadership and Administration in Student Affairs*, by Ted Miller, Roger Winston Jr.; and William Mendenhall.

ACCENT BOOKS, A Division of Accent Publications, 12100 W. 6th Ave., Box 15337, Denver CO 80215; (303)988-5300. Executive Editor: Jerry A. Wilke. Managing Editor: Edith A. Quinlan. Publishes evangelical Christian paperbacks, almost exclusively nonfiction (including teacher training books), though an occasional superior novel may be considered. Averages 24 titles/yr. Pays royalty on cover price. Query or submit 2 sample chapters and a brief synopsis of each chapter, together with contents page. No computer printout or disk submissions. Include SASE. Do not submit full manuscript unless requested. Reports in 3-8 weeks. Free author's information sheet on request.
Recent Nonfiction Titles: *Bible Country*; *The Remarkable Spaceship Earth*; *Guilt-Free Snacking*; *Something More Than Love . . . The X-Factor in a Good Marriage*.

ACE SCIENCE FICTION, The Berkley Publishing Group, 200 Madison Ave., New York NY 10016. (212)686-9820. Publishes paperback originals and reprints. Publishes 160 titles/year.
Fiction: Science fiction and fantasy. Query with outline and 3 sample chapters. Reports in 2 months. SASE.

ACROPOLIS BOOKS, LTD., Subsidiary of Colortone Press, 2400 17th St., NW, Washington DC 20009. (202)387-6805. Publisher: Alphons J. Hackl. Publishes hardcover and trade paperback originals. Averages 25 titles/year. Pays individually negotiated royalty. SASE. Reports in 2 months. Free book catalog.
Nonfiction: How-to, reference and self-help. Subjects include nutrition and cooking, health, nature, beauty/fashion, senior citizens and money management. "We will be looking for manuscripts dealing with fashion and beauty, and self development. We also will be continuing our teacher books for early childhood education. Our audience includes general adult consumers, professional elementary school teachers and children." Submit outline/synopsis and sample chapters.
Recent Nonfiction Titles: *Color Me Beautiful*, by Carole Jackson (fashion beauty); *The Retirement Money Book*, by Ferd Navheim; and *The Touchlings*, by Michael W. Fox (children's fantasy creatures).

BOB ADAMS, INC., 2045 Commonwealth Ave., Brighton MA 02135. (617)782-5707. Contact: Submissions Editor. Publishes hardcover and trade paperback originals. Averages 10 titles/yr. Pays variable royalty. Simultaneous and photocopied submissions OK. SASE. Reports in 1 month on queries; 2 months on manuscripts.
Nonfiction: How-to, reference, technical on business and economics (with special emphasis on careers and job-hunting). "We are interested in seeing proposals and summaries for career planning and job-hunting books of all types. We are also interested in seeing database-type books of all types, local and regional information books of all types. We will consider publishing books in all other nonfiction categories. We will consider books for both the general book market as well as the library market. Please submit query first and only send manuscript upon request. We can not be responsible for unsolicited manuscripts.
Recent Nonfiction Titles: *The Metropolitan Washington Job Bank*, Adams and Fiedler; *Career Connections*, by Boyd, Ramsauer & Senft (both career books).

ADDISON-WESLEY PUBLISHING CO., INC., General Books Division, Jacob Way, Reading MA 01867. Publisher: Ann Dilworth. Executive Editor: Dorothy Coover. Publishes hardcover and paperback originals. Publishes 50 titles/year. Pays royalty. Simultaneous and photocopied submissions OK. SASE. Reports in 3-4 weeks. Free book catalog.
Nonfiction: Biography, business/economics, health, how-to, nature, photography, politics, psychology, recreation, science, self-help, sociology and sports. "Also needs books on 'tools for living' related to finance, everyday law, health, education, and parenting by people well-known and respected in their field. No cookbooks or books on transactional analysis." Query, then submit outline/synopsis and 1 sample chapter.
Recent Nonfiction Titles: *More Joy of Photography*, by the editors at Eastman Kodak Company; *Theory Z*, by William Ouchi; and *The Fifth Generation*, by Edward Feigenbaum and Pamela McCorduck.
Tips: Queries/mss may be routed to other editors in the publishing group.

AERO PUBLISHERS, INC., 329 W. Aviation Rd., Fallbrook CA 92028. (714)728-8456. President: Ernest J. Gentle. Publishes hardcover and paperback originals. Pays 10% royalty. Simultaneous and photocopied submissions OK. Reports in 2 months. SASE. Free catalog.
Nonfiction: "Manuscripts submitted must be restricted to the fields of aviation and space and should be technical or semitechnical or historical in nature. Manuscripts should be 50,000-100,000 words in length and well illustrated." Accepts nonfiction translations from German and Spanish. No personal biographies. Submit outline/synopsis and 2 sample chapters.
Recent Nonfiction Titles: *Aviation and Space Dictionary, 6th Edition*, by Gentle and Reithmaier; *Space Shuttle: America's Wings to the Future*, by M. Kaplan; and *Seven Decades of Progress: The Story of General Electric Aircraft Engine Division*, by W. Schoneberger.

AGLOW PUBLICATIONS, Subsidiary of Women's Aglow Fellowship, Box I, Lynnwood WA 98036. (206)775-7282. Associate Editor: JoAnne Sekowsky. Publishes mass market paperback originals. Averages 2-3 books, 2-3 minibooks, 1-2 booklets/year. Pays up to 7½% maximum royalty on retail price "depending on amount of editorial work needed"; buys some mss outright. No advance. Photocopied submissions OK. Computer printout submissions OK. SASE. Reports in 1 month on queries; 1½ months on mss. Free book catalog.
Nonfiction: Cookbook, self-help and Bible studies. Subjects include religion (Christian only). Accepts nonfiction and fiction translations. "We are always on the lookout for good women's testimonies. We also publish Bible studies, booklets and mini-books. Please familiarize yourself with our materials before submitting. Our needs and formats are very specific." Query or submit outline/synopsis and first 3 sample chapters or complete ms.
Recent Nonfiction Titles: *Flair in the Kitchen* (cookbook); *Fran*, by Fran Lance/Pat King (autobiography); and *Reflections* (devotional).

Fiction: Religious. "We are a Christian women's publishing house. We do not publish secular material or material directed toward a men's audience." Query or submit outline/synopsis and sample chapters or complete ms.

Recent Fiction Title: *Love Is for Tomorrow*, by Hope Traver (gothic-Christian).

Tips: "Our books are largely bought by evangelical, charismatic Christian women—although many of our books, especially cookbooks have a much larger audience."

‡**AHSAHTA PRESS**, Boise State University, Dept. of English, 1910 University Dr., Boise ID 83725. (208)385-1246. Co-Editor: Tom Trusky. Publishes trade paperback originals. Averages 3 titles/year. Pays 25% royalty on retail price. "Royalty commences with 3rd printing." Simultaneous and photocopied submissions OK. Prefers letter quality to dot matrix printout submissions. SASE. Reports in 2 weeks on queries; 3 months on mss.

Poetry: Contemporary western American poetry collections. No "rhymed verse; 'songs of the sage'; 'buckaroo ballads'; purple mountain's majesty; coyote wisdom; Jesus-in-the-prairie; 'nice' verse." Accepts poetry translations from native American languages, Spanish and Basque. Submit 15 samples with SASE between February and April. "Write incredible, original poetry."

Recent Poetry Titles: *Hannah's Travel*, by Richard Speakes (western woman's diary); *Laws of the Land*, by David Baker (poems of Utah); and *Agua Negra*, by Leo Romero (Hispanics of New Mexico).

*****ALASKA NATURE PRESS**, Box 632, Eagle River AK 99577. Editor/Publisher: Ben Guild. Publishes hardcover and paperback originals. Plans to offer subsidy publishing "as needed—estimated 10%." Averages 2 titles/year. Pays 10% royalty on retail price; no advance. Simultaneous and photocopied submissions OK. No computer printout or disk submissions. SASE. Reports in 2 months.

Nonfiction: Alaska material only: animals, biography, history, how-to, juveniles, nature, photography, poetry, recreation, wildlife, nature and self-help. No hunting or fishing tales. Query or submit outline/synopsis and 2-3 sample chapters or complete ms. Accepts photos/artwork with ms. "As a specialty publishing house (we take *only* Alaskans material) the work *must* have an impact on Alaska or people interested in Alaska—for Alaska."

Fiction: Alaska material only: adventure, historical, romance and suspense. Query editor/publisher, Box 632, Eagle River AK 99577. "SASE, please." Reports in 2 months.

ALASKA NORTHWEST PUBLISHING CO., Box 4-EEE, Anchorage AK 99509. Editor and Publisher: Robert A. Henning. Publishes primarily paperback originals. Averages 12 titles/year. Most contracts call for straight 10% royalty. Free book catalog. "Rejections are made promptly, unless we have 3 or 4 possibilities in the same general field and it's a matter of which one gets the decision. That could take 3 months." SASE.

Nonfiction: "Alaska, northern British Columbia, Yukon, Northwest Territories and northwest United States are subject areas. Emphasis on life in the last frontier, history, biography, cookbooks, travel, field guides, juveniles and outdoor subjects. Writer must be familiar with area first-hand. We listen to any ideas." Query with outline, sample chapters, and any relevant photographs preferred.

ALBA HOUSE, 2187 Victory Blvd., Staten Island, New York NY 10314. (212)761-0047. Editor-in-Chief: Anthony L. Chenevey. Publishes hardcover and paperback originals (90%) and reprints (10%). Specializes in religious books. "We publish shorter editions than many publishers in our field." Pays 10% royalty on retail price. Averages 15 titles/year. Query. State availability of photos/illustrations. Simultaneous and photocopied submissions OK. Reports in 2-4 weeks. SASE. Free book catalog.

Nonfiction: Publishes philosophy, psychology, religious, sociology, textbooks and Biblical books. Accepts nonfiction translations from French, German or Spanish. Submit outline/synopsis and 1-2 sample chapters.

Recent Nonfiction Titles: *The Making of a Pastoral Person*, by Gerald Niklas; *Broken But Loved*, by George Maloney; and *Depression and the Integrated Life*, by Berg & McCartney.

Tips: "We look to new authors." Queries/mss may be routed to other editors in the publishing group.

ALFRED PUBLISHING CO., INC., 15335 Morrison St., Box 5964, Sherman Oaks CA 91413. (213)995-8811. Vice President: Steven Manus. Publishes trade paperback originals (Alfred Handy Guides). Averages 24 titles/year. Pays variable royalty; buys some mss outright for $1,500; offers negotiable advance. Simultaneous submissions OK. SASE. Reports in 2 months. Free book catalog.

Nonfiction: How-to. Subjects include computers and business. Length: 15,000 words. Submit outline/synopsis and 1 sample chapter.

Recent Nonfiction Titles: *How to Buy a Personal Computer*, by Shrum; *How to Use the IBM Personal Computer*, by Nolan.

‡**ALLEGHENY PRESS**, Box 220, Elgin PA 16413. Editor: Bonnie Henderson. Publishes hardcover originals and trade paperback originals and reprints. Averages 4 titles/year. Pays 10-20% royalty on wholesale price. Simultaneous and photocopied submissions OK. SASE. Reports in 2 weeks on queries; 1 month on mss.

Nonfiction: How-to, self-help, textbook on animals, cooking and foods, hobbies, nature, recreation, travel. Especially needs college lab manuals and texts and nature and outdoor books. Publishes for college students, outdoor enthusiasts, armchair geographers. Submit outline/synopsis and sample chapters.
Recent Nonfiction Titles: *Alaska Highway Journal*, by Tomikel (travelogue); *Mineral Identification*, by Kohland (science); and *Basic Meteorology*, by Moses (text).

ALLEN & UNWIN, INC., 9 Winchester Terrace, Winchester MA 01890. (617)729-0830. Executive Vice President: Mark Streatfeild. Publishes hardcover and paperback originals. Averages 150 titles/year. Simultaneous and photocopied submissions OK. SASE. Reports in 2-3 weeks. Book catalog for SASE.
Nonfiction: Business/economics; history; literature; literary criticism; philosophy; politics; reference; science; sociology; technical; textbooks. Especially needs advanced university material; must be of international interest. Submit outline/synopsis and sample chapters.

ALLEN PUBLISHING CO., 5711 Graves Ave., Encino CA 91316. Publisher: Michael Wiener. Publishes paperback originals. Averages 3 titles/year. Pays 10% royalty on net price; no advance. Simultaneous and photocopied submissions OK. "Author queries welcome from new or established writers. Do not send manuscript or sample chapter." Accepts photos/artwork. Reports in 2 weeks. SASE "essential." One-page author guidelines available for SASE.
Nonfiction: "Self-help material, 25,000-50,000 words, aimed at wealth-builders. We want to reach the vast audience of opportunity seekers who, for instance, purchased *Lazy Man's Way to Riches*, by Joe Karbo. Material must be original and authoritative, not rehashed from other sources. Most of what we market is sold via mail order in softcover book form. No home fix-it, hobby hints, health or 'cure' books, or 'faith' stories, poetry or fiction. We are a specialty publisher and will not consider any book not fitting the above description."
Recent Nonfiction Titles: *Making it Rich in the 1980's*; *101 Easy Businesses You Can Start Now—Even If You're Just About Flat Broke*; *How To Have It Made In 90 Days*.

ALLYN AND BACON, INC., 7 Wells Ave., Newton MA 02149. Editors: Gary Folven (college texts), Linda Vahey (el-hi texts), Jack Stone (professional books). Publishes hardcover and paperback originals. Publishes 200 titles/year. "Our contracts are competitive within the standard industry framework of royalties." Reports in 1-3 months. SASE.
Nonfiction: "We are primarily a textbook, technical and professional book publisher. Authoritative works of quality. No fiction or poetry." Will consider business, medicine, reference, scientific, self-help and how-to, sociology, sports, technical mss and other course-related texts. Letter should accompany ms with author information, ms prospectus, etc. Query or submit complete ms.

ALMAR PRESS, 4105 Marietta Dr., Binghamton NY 13903. (607)722-0265. Editor-in-Chief: A.N. Weiner. Managing Editor: M.F. Weiner. Publishes hardcover and paperback originals and reprints. Averages 6 titles/year. Pays 10% royalty; no advance. Prefers exclusive submissions; however, simultaneous (if so indicated) and photocopied submissions OK. Reports in 1 month. SASE must be included. Catalog for SASE.
Nonfiction: Publishes business, technical, and consumer books and reports. "These main subjects include general business, financial, travel, career, technology, personal help, hobbies, general medical, general legal, and how-to. *Almar Reports* are business and technology subjects published for management use and prepared in 8½x11 and book format. Publications are printed and bound in soft covers as required. Reprint publications represent a new aspect of our business." Submit outline/synopsis and sample chapters. Looks for information in the proposed book that makes it different or unusual enough to attract book buyers.
Recent Nonfiction Titles: *Solo Games: 12 Exciting New Board Games to Be Played by One Person*, by H. David Jackson; *How to Live with Your Children*, by D.H. Fontenelle; *How to Buy, Install and Maintain Your Own Telephone Equipment*, by La Carrubba and Zimmer.

ALPINE PUBLICATIONS, INC., 1901 S. Garfield St., Loveland CO 80537. Managing Editor: B.J. McKinney. Publishes hardcover and paperback originals. Averages 4 titles/year. Pays 7-15% royalty; "occasionally a small advance is offered." Simultaneous and photocopied submissions OK if so indicated. No computer printout or disk submissions. SASE. Reports in 6 weeks. Free catalog for SASE.
Nonfiction: "Alpine Publications is seeking book-length nonfiction mss with illustrations on the care, management, health, training or characteristics of various breeds of dogs, horses, and cats. We specialize in books for the serious owner/breeder, so they must be written by persons knowledgeable in these fields or be well-researched and documented. Our books provide in-depth coverage, present new techniques, and specific 'how-to' instruction. We are not interested in books about reptiles or exotic pets." Accepts artwork/photos. Query. Submit outline/synopsis and 3-5 sample chapters or submit complete ms.
Recent Nonfiction Titles: *Sheltie Talk*, by McKinney and Rieseberg (breed book on Shetland Sheepdogs); *Canine Hip Dysplasia*; *How to Raise a Puppy You Can Live With*, by Rutherford; *Collie Concept* (breed book on collies), by Roos.

ALYSON PUBLICATIONS, INC., Box 2783, Boston MA 02208. (617)542-5679. Publisher: Sasha Alyson. Publishes trade paperback originals and reprints. Averages 12 titles/year. Pays 8-15% royalty on net price; buys some mss outright for $200-1,000; offers average $600 advance. Computer printout submissions OK; prefers letter quality to dot matrix. SASE. Reports in 2 weeks on queries; 5 weeks on mss. Looks for "writing ability and content suitable for our house." Book catalog for business size SAE and 3 first class stamps.
Nonfiction: Subjects include gay/lesbian/feminist. "We are especially interested in nonfiction providing a positive approach to gay/lesbian and feminist issues." Accepts nonfiction translations. Submit one-page synopsis.
Recent Nonfiction Titles: *The Men With the Pink Triangle*, by Heinz Heger (history); *Reflections of a Rock Lobster*, by Aaron Fricke (autobiography).
Fiction: Gay novels. Accepts fiction translations. Submit 1-page synopsis.
Recent Fiction Title: *Between Friends*, by Gillian E. Hanscombe (lesbian fiction).
Tips: "We publish many books by new authors."

AMERICAN ASTRONAUTICAL SOCIETY, (Univelt, Inc., Publisher), Box 28130, San Diego CA 92128. (619)746-4005. Editorial Director: H. Jacobs. Publishes hardcover originals. Averages 8-10 titles/year. Pays 10% royalty on retail price; no advance. Simultaneous and photocopied submissions OK. Computer printout submissions OK; prefers letter quality to dot matrix. Reports in 4 weeks. SASE. Free book catalog.
Nonfiction: Proceedings or monographs in the field of astronautics, including applications of aerospace technology to Earth's problems. "Our books must be space-oriented or space related. They are meant for technical libraries, research establishments and the aerospace industry worldwide." Submit outline/synopsis and 1-2 sample chapters.
Recent Nonfiction Titles: *Soviet Lunar and Planetary Exploration*, by N.L. Johnson; and *Guidance and Control 1982*, by R.D. Culp.

‡*AMERICAN ATHEIST PRESS, Subsidiary of Society of Separationists, Inc., Box 2117, Austin TX 78768. (512)485-1244. Editor/Director: Jon G. Murray. Publishes trade paperback and mass market paperback originals (50%) and reprints. Averages 15 titles/year. Subsidy publishes 5% of books (100% cost of first printing). Pays 7% royalty on wholesale price. Simultaneous and photocopied submissions OK. SASE. Reports in 1 week on queries; 3 weeks on manuscripts. Free book catalog.
Nonfiction: Biography and Atheism. Publishes books based on solid research in Atheism for "anyone interested in finding out the truth about religion. Accepts nonfiction translations. Reprints of Atheist classics do well. We envision more of these, as well as up-to-date refinements on the position of Atheism in the world. Synthesize science and Atheism, including accurate, detailed biographies of the most significant people and descriptions of the most significant developments. No promotions of religious or superstitious beliefs." Submit the complete ms.
Recent Nonfiction Titles: *The Best of Dial-an-Atheist Vol. I, Chicago*, by the Illinois chapter of American Atheists (Atheist messages); *All the Questions You Ever Wanted to Ask American Atheists With All the Answers*, by Dr. Madalyn Murray O'Hair; and *sepher tolduth jeshu*, by ancient jews (Jewish life of Christ).

AMERICAN BABY BOOKS, Harlequin Enterprises, 11315 Watertown Plank Rd., Milwaukee WI 53226. (414)771-0226. Editorial offices: 575 Lexington Ave., New York NY 10022. President: Dan Wood. Publishes trade paperback originals and reprints. Averages 20 titles/year.
Nonfiction: How-to, reference and self-help. Subjects include parenting. Query "with concept" or submit outline/synopsis and 1 sample chapter or complete ms. Computer printout submissions OK; prefers letter quality to dot matrix.
Recent Nonfiction Titles: *What Shall I Name the Baby, Keepsake Record Book, The First Year of Life, New Mother's Cookbook*, and *American Baby Handbook*, by American Baby Editors.

AMERICAN CATHOLIC PRESS, 1223 Rossell Ave., Oak Park IL 60302. (312)386-1366. Editorial Director: Father Michael Gilligan. Publishes hardcover originals (90%) and hardcover and paperback reprints (10%). Published 4 titles in 1979, 2 in 1980. "Most of our sales are by direct mail, although we do work through retail outlets." Pays by outright purchase of $25-100; no advance. Simultaneous and photocopied submissions OK. Computer printouts OK; dot matrix printouts acceptable. Reports in 2 months. SASE. Free book catalog.
Nonfiction: "We publish books on the Roman Catholic Liturgy, for the most part books on religious music and educational books and pamphlets. We also publish religious songs for church use, including Psalms as well as choral and instrumental arrangements. We are very interested in new music, meant for use in church services. Books, or even pamphlets, on the Roman Catholic Mass are especially welcome. We have no interest in secular topics and are not interested in religious poetry of any kind." Query. Recently published *The Role of Music in the New Roman Liturgy*, by W. Herring (educational); *Noise in Our Solemn Assemblies*, by R. Keifer (educational); and *Song Leader's Handbook*, by W. Callahan (music).

‡**AMERICAN COUNCIL FOR THE ARTS**, 570 7th Ave., New York NY 10018. (212)354-6655. Manager of Publishing: Robert Porter. Publishes hardcover and trade paperback originals. Averages 5-8 titles/year. Pays 10-15% royalty on wholesale or retail price. Simultaneous and photocopied submissions OK. Computer printout submissions OK. SASE. Reports in 3 weeks on queries; 2 months on mss. Free book catalog.
Nonfiction: How-to, reference, technical, textbook and professional books on business and economics—nonprofit management, recreation, sociology, travel—all as they pertain to the arts. Books on the arts in areas of management, reference, public policy, and role in society (i.e., city life, travel, recreation, education, etc.). Especially needs books on nonprofit management skills, especially the arts (i.e., marketing, planning); public policy in the arts; resource directories for the arts; and practical discussions of ways the arts can be integrated into specific aspects of everyday life. Publishes for artists, professionals, and trustees of arts organizations and agencies; university faculty and students; professionals and trustees of nonprofit institutions. No mss on the aesthetics of specific arts disciplines or biographies. Query or submit outline/synopsis and 3-4 sample chapters. Accepts artwork and/or photos.
Recent Nonfiction Titles: *Live the Good Life!*, by Wolf Von Eckardt (reference-sociology-arts); *Out of the Red: Strategies for Effective Corporate Fundraising*, by W. Grant Brownrigg (how-to); and *Presenting Performances*, by Thomas Wolf (how-to).

AMERICAN PHILATELIC SOCIETY, Box 8000, State College PA 16801. (814)237-3803. Editor: Richard L. Sine. Publishes hardcover originals (85%), and hardcover reprints (15%). Averages 4 titles/year. Pays 5-10% royalty. Photocopied submissions OK. Computer printout submissions OK; prefers letter quality to dot matrix. SASE. Reports in 2 weeks on queries; 3+ months on mss. Free book catalog.
Nonfiction: How-to, reference and technical. Subjects include hobbies. Accepts nonfiction translations. "We're interested in anything showing solid research into various areas of stamp collecting." Query "if not a member of our society" or submit complete ms or at least 3 sample chapters. Accepts photos/artwork with ms.
Recent Nonfiction Titles: *The Admiral Issue of Canada*, by George C. Marler (reference); *100 Trivia Quizzes on Stamp Collecting*, by Bill Olcheski; *APS Stamp Identifier*, (reference).

‡**AMERICAN PRESS**, 520 Commonwealth Ave., #416, Boston MA 02215. (617)247-0022. Executive Editor: Malcolm Fox. Publishes paperback texts, study guides, lab manuals. Average 150 titles/year. Pays 5-15% royalty on wholesale price; offers average $200 advance "for typing and/or illustrations." Simultaneous and photocopied submissions OK. Computer printout and disk submissions OK. SASE. Reports in 6 weeks.
Nonfiction: Textbooks on Americana, animals, art, business and economics, health, history, philosophy, politics, psychology, religion, sports, biology, chemistry, physics, math. Accepts nonfiction translations from Spanish. "No foreign language texts at this time." Query or submit outline/synopsis and 1 sample chapter.
Recent Nonfiction Titles: *Meat Science*, by Smith (text and lab); *Intermediate Algebra*, by Scott (text); and *Geology*, by Long (text).

AMERICAN SOLAR ENERGY SOCIETY, US (American) Section of International Solar Energy Society, 110 W. 34th St., New York NY 10001. (212)736-8727. Book publisher and independent book producer/packager. Director of Publications: Albert Henderson. Publishes hardcover originals. Averages 12 titles/year. Publishes some books based on "marketability (i.e., serving useful and valuable purpose) for professional audience." Pays royalty and by arrangement "on the merits of the proposal." SASE. Reports in 1 month on queries; 3 weeks plus on mss.
Nonfiction: How-to, reference, technical, textbook on art (architectural design); business and economics; politics (public policy and law); engineering; applied physics; building and construction. Immediate needs include professional books on solar energy. No mss on other subjects. Query.
Recent Nonfiction Titles: *Passive Cooling*, by Bowen, et al. (survey); *Solar Energy Information*, by Ubico (survey); and *Satellites and Solar Radiation Forecasing*, by Bahm (survey).

AMPHOTO, 1515 Broadway, New York NY 10036. (212)764-7300. Senior Editor: Michael O'Connor. Publishes hardcover and paperback originals. Averages 20 titles/year. Pays royalty, or by outright purchase; offers variable advance. Simultaneous and photocopied submissions OK. Reports in 1 month. SASE. Free book catalog.
Nonfiction: "Photography instruction only. We cover all technical and how-to aspects. Few portfolios or picture books." Submit outline/synopsis, sample chapters and sample photos. Looks for "practical value to the readers, marketing info."
Recent Nonfiction Titles: *The Fashion Photographer*, by Robert Farber; *Advertising Photography*, by Allyn Solomon; and *Focus on Special Effects*, by Don and Marie Carroll.
Tips: "Consult the photo magazines for book ideas."

AND BOOKS, 702 S. Michigan, South Bend IN 46618. (219)232-3134. Editor: Janos Szebedinszky. Publishes trade paperback originals. Averages 15-25 titles/year. Pays standard royalty on retail price. Simultaneous and photocopied submissions OK. Disk submissions OK. SASE. Reports in 2 weeks on queries; 5 weeks on mss. Free book catalog.

Nonfiction: Subjects include: current affairs, computers, business, economics, music, philosophy, sociology, media, folklore, self-help, natural living, women's issues. "All material must be literate and salable." No college theses, found-out descriptions, diaries, autobiographies of civil servants, pet stories, hunting and fishing guides, technical journals, investment guides or family genealogies." Query (preferred) or submit 2-3 sample chapters/complete ms.

Recent Nonfiction Titles: *Play To Live*, by A. Watts (philosophy); *Black Book of Polish Censorship*, by A. Niczow (current affairs); *Breast Cancer Handbook*, by D. Dewar (women's and medical self-help); *Small Time Operator Computer Edition*, by E. Krause with B. Kamaroff (computers, technology).

Tips: Queries/mss may be routed to other editors in the publishing group.

ANDERSON PUBLISHING CO., Suite 501, 602 Main St., Cincinnati OH 45201. (513)421-4393. Editorial Director: Jean Martin. Publishes hardcover and paperback originals (98%) and reprints (2%). Publishes 14 titles/year. Pays 15-18% royalty; "advance in selected cases." Simultaneous and photocopied submissions OK. Reports in 2 months. SASE. Free book catalog.

Nonfiction: Law, and law-related books, and criminal justice criminology texts (justice administration legal series). Query or submit outline/chapters with vitae.

Recent Nonfiction Titles: *Justice As Fairness*, by D. Fogel/J. Hudson; *The Law Dictionary*, by W. Gilmer; and *Criminal Careers*, by Gwynne Nettler.

AND/OR PRESS, Box 2246, Berkeley CA 94702. Publisher: Carlene Schnabel. Paperback originals (90%); hardcover and paperback reprints (10%). Specializes in "nonfiction works with youth market interest. We function as an alternative information resource." Pays 5-10% royalty; offers average advance of 10% of first print run. Averages maximum of 8 titles/year. Computer printout and disk submissions OK. Reports in 2 weeks to 3 months. SASE. Prefers outline with 1-3 sample chapters.

Nonfiction: Publishes appropriate technology, human potential, the future, health and nutrition, travel and psycho-pharmacology books. Also alternative lifestyle books.

Recent Nonfiction Titles: *Network Revolution: Confessions of a Computer Scientist*, by Jacques Vallee; and *Right Where You Are Sitting Now: Further Tales of the Illuminati*, by Robert Anton Wilson.

ANDREWS AND McMEEL, INC., 4400 Johnson Dr., Fairway KS 66205. Editorial Director: Donna Martin. Publishes hardcover and paperback originals. Publishes 30 titles annually. Pays royalty on retail price. "Not currently reading unsolicited mss. Publishing program mainly related to features of Universal Press Syndicate, parent company of Andrews & McMeel."

‡**ANGEL PRESS/PUBLISHERS**, 561 Tyler, Monterey CA 93940. (408)372-1658. Associate Editors: Raye Allan and Marianne Bingham. Publishes hardcover originals and reprints and mass market paperback originals. Averages 2-4 titles/year. Pays negotiable royalty; cash return (actual). No advance. Simultaneous and photocopied submissions OK. SASE. Reports in 3 weeks on queries; "several" months on mss.

Nonfiction: Biography, how-to, humor, self-help, spiritual/metaphysical. Subjects include Americana, animals, health, history, hobbies, nature, philosophy, photography, politics, psychology, recreation, religion and sociology. Especially needs "well-written, well-conceived books in the areas of controversy, erotica, feminist, humor, satire; plus any book that is unusually well written and is potentially a good seller in its field." Query before submitting ms.

Recent Nonfiction Titles: *Living with Angels*, by Dorie D'Angelo (spiritual/inspirational); *Having Your Baby at Home*, by Kathy Fielding (women's); *The Lesbian Path*, by Margaret Cruikshank (women's—New Age).

Fiction: Adventure, confession, erotica, fantasy, humor, mainstream, religious, metaphysical, human potential. "Fiction is not our main thrust. No out-and-out pornography. Professionalism is the key word." Query before submitting ms.

Recent Fiction Titles: *Re'lize whut Ahm Talkin' 'Bout?*, by Steve Chennault (black English).

ANNA PUBLISHING, INC., Box 218, Ocoee FL 32761. Book publisher and independent book producer/packager. President: Darrell K. Wolfe. Publishes hardcover originals and trade paperback originals and reprints. Averages 20 titles/year. Subsidy publishes 2 books/year, based on subject matter. "We do not solicit subsidized books." Pays 10-20% royalty on wholesale or retail price; buys some mss outright for $250-1,500. No advance. Photocopied submissions OK. SASE. Reports in 2 weeks on queries; 1 month on mss. Book catalog for 6x9 SAE and 35¢ postage.

Nonfiction: Cookbook, how-to, illustrated book, reference (psychology), physical fitness. Subjects include cooking and foods, health, sports. Publishes for college instructors, professionals, and advanced or advancing physical fitness experts. Query or submit outline/synopsis and sample chapters.

Recent Nonfiction Titles: *With Wings as Eagles*, by Gresham; *The Child Management Program for Abusive Parents*, by Wolfe (psychology); and *Feeling People*, by Hannig.

APPALACHIAN MOUNTAIN CLUB BOOKS, 5 Joy St., Boston MA 02108. (617)523-0636. Director of Publications: Sally Carrel. Publishes hardcover and paperback originals (80%) and reprints (20%). Averages 8 titles/year. Offers 5-10% royalty on retail price; offers average advance: $1,000. Simultaneous and photocopied submissions OK. SASE. Reports in 2 months. Free book catalog.
Nonfiction: How-to; nature; recreation; and sports. "The Appalachian Mountain Club is a non-profit public service organization dedicated to outdoor recreation and conservation, primarily in the Northeast. Most of our books to date have been hiking and canoeing guidebooks to specific regions. We have also done 'how-to' books on trail building, canoeing, growth planning. Others include mountaineering, memoirs, historical reprint, mountain photography, environmental primer, ski touring. Any book we do must fall under the charter of the AMC." Does *not* want to see mechanized sports (e.g., snowmobiling); "no 'how to save the world' essays." Query first.
Recent Nonfiction Titles: *Wilderness Search and Rescue*, by Tim J. Setnicka; and *White Water Handbook*, by John Urban and T. Walley Williams.
Tips: "Most of our books are by new or unknown authors."

APPLE PRESS, 5536 SE Harlow, Milwaukie OR 97222. (503)659-2475. Senior Editor: Judith S. Majors. Publishes paperback originals. Averages 3-5 titles/year. Pays 7-10% royalty on retail price; offers average advance $200-500. Computer printout submissions OK "as long as they're legible." SASE. Reports in 4-6 weeks.
Nonfiction: Health and self-help. Query first. Accepts outline/synopsis and 2 sample chapters. Looks for "well done research and accuracy." SASE.
Recent Nonfiction Titles: *Sugar Free Kid's Cookery* (calculated youth cookbook); *Diet Out Oregon*; *Sugar Free Microwavery*; and *Sugar Free Sweets and Treats*.

APPLE-WOOD BOOKS, INC., Box 2870, Cambridge MA 02139. (617)923-9337. Editorial Director: Phil Zuckerman. Publishes hardcover and trade paperback originals. Averages 14 titles/year. Pays 10-15% royalty on wholesale price; offers $250-2,500 advance. Simultaneous and photocopied submissions OK. SASE. Reports in 3 weeks on queries; 3 months on mss. Book catalog for 8½x11 SAE and 2 first class stamps.
Nonfiction: Subjects include history, politics and sociology. "Books concerning social themes and New Englandia. We publish for a young, literary audience." No how-to or cookbooks. Query.
Recent Nonfiction Titles: *Cocktails at Somoza's*, by Richard Elman (political); and *Crossing Over*, by Richard Currey (political journal).
Fiction: "We don't consider fiction by category, but by quality. We publish the future great American writers." Query or submit outline/synopsis and sample chapters.
Recent Fiction Titles: *P-town Stories*, by R.D. Skillings; *Candace & Other Stories*, by Alan Cheuse; and *Death By Dreaming*, by Jon Manchip White.

THE AQUARIAN PRESS LTD., Denington Estate, Wellingborough, Northamptonshire NN8 2RQ England. Editor-in-Chief: Michael Cox. Hardcover and paperback originals. Pays 8-10% royalty. Photocopied submissions OK. Computer printout and disk submissions OK; prefers letter quality to dot matrix. SAE and International Reply Coupons. Reports in 2-4 weeks. Free book catalog.
Nonfiction: Publishes books on comparative religion, magic, metaphysics, mysticism, occultism, parapsychology and esoteric philosophy. Length: 30,000-100,000 words. Looks for "a clear indication that the author has thought about his market; a fundamental ability to *communicate* ideas—authority in combination with readability."

ARBOR HOUSE, Subsidiary of Hearst Corp., 235 E. 45th St., New York NY 10017. Publisher: Donald I. Fine. Publishes hardcover and trade paperback originals and reprints. Pays standard royalty; offers negotiable advance. SASE. Free book catalog.
Nonfiction: Autobiography, cookbook, how-to, and self-help. Subjects include Americana (possibly), art (possibly), business and economics, cooking and foods, health, history, politics, psychology, recreation, religion (possibly) and sports (on golf, tennis, or sailing). Query or submit outline/synopsis and sample chapters to "The Editors."
Recent Nonfiction Titles: *All About Jewelry*, by Rose Leiman Goldemberg; *The Berenstains' Baby Book*, by Stan and Jan Berenstain; *Tennessee Williams: An Intimate Biography*, by Dakin Williams.
Fiction: "Superior fiction—everything from romance to science fiction and adventure. Stay away from formula novels. No gothic novels unless they are truly exceptional." Query or submit outline/synopsis and sample chapters to "The Editors."
Recent Fiction Titles: *Murder in the Smithsonian*, by Margaret Truman; *Stick*, by Elmore Leonard; and *Pinocchio's Nose*, by Jerome Charyn.

ARCHER EDITIONS PRESS, 318 Fry Branch Rd., Lynnville TN 38472. Editorial Director: Wanda Hicks. Publishes hardcover and paperback originals (60%) and paperback reprints (40%). Pays 15% royalty on wholesale price; occasionally offers $250-750 advance. Averages 1-6 titles/year. Simultaneous and photocopied submissions OK. Reports in 2-3 months. SASE. Free book catalog.
Nonfiction: "We are interested in books that could go to the academic and public library market in the fields of history, literature and art. We would especially like biographies in this field." Query.
Recent Nonfiction Titles: *Thomas Francis Meagher*, by W.F. Lyons (Civil War reprint); and *Lost Sandstones and Lonely Skies*, by Jesse Stuart (essays).
Fiction: "We are doing a limited amount of fiction of a somewhat academic nature by established authors."
Recent Fiction Titles: *The Autobiography of Cassandra; Princess and Prophetess of Troy*, by Ursule Molinaro.

ARCHITECTURAL BOOK PUBLISHING CO., INC., 10 E. 40th St., New York NY 10016. (212)689-5400. Editor: Walter Frese. Averages 10 titles/year. Royalty is percentage of retail price. Prefers queries, outlines and 2 sample chapters with number of illustrations. Reports in 2 weeks. SASE.
Architecture and Industrial Arts: Publishes architecture, decoration, and reference books on city planning and industrial arts. Accepts nonfiction translations. Also interested in history, biography, and science of architecture and decoration.

ARCO PUBLISHING, INC., 219 Park Ave. S., New York NY 10003. Senior Editor, Consumer Books (trade): Madelyn Larsen. Pays advance against royalties. Simultaneous submissions OK; "inform us if so." Materials submitted without sufficient postage will not be returned.
Nonfiction: Publishes business; crafts and collecting; pet care and training; horses (all aspects); self-help (medical and financial); sports instruction (no spectator sports: baseball, football, etc.); how-to; militaria. "Our readers are people who want information, instruction and technical know-how from their books. They want to learn something tangible." No fiction, poetry, cookbooks, biographies, autobiographies, religion or personal "true" accounts of persons or pets. Prefers letter of inquiry with a contents page and 1 sample chapter. Educational Books, Linda Bernbach, Editor; Career guidance, test preparation and study guides, Ellen Lichtenstein, Editor; Medical Review Books, Don Simmons, Director of the Medical Division, medicine and psychiatry (technical and authoritative). Same requirements as for consumer books.

ARCsoft PUBLISHERS, Box 132, Woodsboro MD 21798. (301)845-8856. Publisher: Anthony R. Curtis. Publishes trade paperback originals. Averages 20 titles/year. Pays 10% royalty on net sales; offers variable advance. Simultaneous and photocopied submissions OK. Computer printout submissions OK; prefers letter quality to dot matrix. SASE. Reports in 1 month on queries; 10 weeks on mss. Free book catalog.
Nonfiction: How-to, reference, technical and textbook. "We publish books in personal computing and electronics, especially for beginners in each field. In computers, we need books of programs, buyers guides, how-to-use-them books, for as many different brand names of computers as are on the market. In electronics, books for newcomers to the hobby." Accepts nonfiction translations. Query or submit outline/synopsis and 1 sample chapter. Looks for "ability to cover (our desired) subject thoroughly, writing quality and interest."
Recent Nonfiction Titles: *The Color Computer Songbook*, by Ron Clark (music programs for TRS-80); *Murder in the Mansion and Other Computer Adventures*, by Jim Cole (programs for pocket computers); and *25 Electronics Projects for Beginners*, by Bob Greene.

ARIEL PRESS, 2557 Wickliffe Rd., Columbus OH 43221. (614)451-2030. The Publishing House of Light. Publisher: Carl Japikse. Publishes hardcover and trade paperback originals. Averages 12 titles/year. Pays average 10% royalty on retail price. No advance. Simultaneous submissions OK. No computer printout or disk submissions. SASE. Reports in 2 months. Book catalog for 6½x9½ size SAE and first class stamp.
Nonfiction: Personal growth, creativity, holistic health and psychic phenomena. No book reviews or reports on what is already known. Query.
Recent Nonfiction Titles: *Active Meditation: The Western Tradition*, by Robert R. Leichtman, MD and Carl Japikse; and *To Parent Or Not*, by C. Norman and Mary Charlotte Shealy.
Tips: "We have very high standards in terms of quality of content and writing. It is mandatory that the writer submitting to us be familiar with what we already publish."

‡*M. ARMAN PUBLISHING, INC., 175 W. Granada Blvd., Suite 200, Ormond Beach FL 32074. (904)673-5576. Mailing address: Box 785, Ormond Beach FL 32074. Contact: Mike Arman. Publishes trade paperback originals and reprints. Averages 6-8 titles/year. Subsidy publishes 10% of books. Pays 10% royalty on wholesale price. No advance. Photocopied submissions OK. Computer printout and disk submissions OK. SASE. Reports in 1 week on queries; 3 weeks on mss. Book catalog for business-sized SASE with 37¢ postage.
Nonfiction: How-to, reference, technical, textbook on hobbies, recreation, sports, travel. Accepts nonfiction translations. "Motorcycle and aircraft technical books only." Publishes for enthusiasts. Submit complete ms. Accepts photos/artwork with ms.

Recent Nonfiction Titles: *Special Tools for Harley Davidson*, by Arman and Heinrichs; (uses and availability of special tools for HD motorcycles); *A Guide to Autogyros*, by Crowe (construction, flight training, operation of autogyros); and *Motorcycle Electrics Without Pain*, by Arman (electrical troubleshooting guide for motorcyles).
Fiction: "Motorcycle or aircraft-related only." Accepts fiction translations. Immediate needs are "slim," but not non-existent. Submit complete ms.
Recent Fiction Title: *Motorcycle Summers*, by Gately (G-rated short stories about motorcycling).

ART DIRECTION BOOK COMPANY, 10 E. 39th St., New York NY 10016. (212)889-6500. Editorial Director: Don Barron. Senior Editor: Lawrence Oberwager. Publishes hardcover and paperback originals. Publishes 15-20 titles/year. Pays 10% royalty on retail price; offers average advance: $1,000. Photocopied submissions OK. SASE. Reports in 3 months. Free book catalog.
Nonfiction: Commercial art; ad art how-to; and textbooks. Accepts photos/artwork. Query first with outline/synopsis and 1 sample chapter. "We are interested in books for the professional advertising art field—that is, books for art directors, designers, et. al; also entry level books for commercial and advertising art students in such fields as typography, photography, paste-up, illustration, clip-art, design, layout and graphic arts."
Recent Nonfiction Titles: *An Insider's Guide to Advertising Music*, by Walt Woodward; *Creative Visual Thinking*, by Morton Garchik; *Encyclopedia of the Air Brush*, by Steven Rubelmann; *Treasury of German Trade Marks 1850-1925*; and *Encyclopedia of Calligraphy Styles*.

ARTECH HOUSE, INC., 610 Washington St., Dedham MA 02026. (617)326-8220. Editor: Dennis Ricci. Publishes hardcover originals. Averages 15-18 titles/year. Offers 10-15% royalty on net price. No advance. Simultaneous and photocopied submissions OK. SASE. Reports in 1½ months. No book catalog.
Nonfiction: Technical. "High quality treatments of the state-of-the-art in electronic technologies, including radar, microwave, telecommunications, and medical subjects. We do *not* want anything non-scientific or technical in any area not cited above." Submit outline/synopsis and sample chapters or complete ms.
Recent Nonfiction Titles: *Intro to Synthetic Array and Imaging Radar*, by S.A. Hovanessian, Ph.D. (radar); and *GaAs Fet Principles and Technology*, by J.V. DiLorenzo, Ph.D. (circuit design).

‡**ARTISTS & WRITERS PUBLICATIONS**, Drawer 668, San Rafael CA 94915. (415)456-1213. Book publisher and independent book producer/packager. Publisher: Owen S. Haddock. Publishes trade paperback originals. Averages 5 titles/year. Pays 5% royalty. Simultaneous submissions OK. SASE. Reports in 3 weeks on queries; 2 weeks on mss.
Nonfiction: Cookbook, how-to, self-help on business and economics, cooking and foods, hobbies, politics, education. "Interested in: How to use special cooking utensils; how to write and communicate in general; how to explain new political movements such as Libertarian ideas." Publishes for any audience captivated by a unique-practical cooking utensil or highly involved in new educational or political philosophy. No mss without a specific market. "Writer should state own perceptions about the available market in query." Query "only."
Recent Nonfiction Titles: *The New T-Fal French Cookbook*, by Marguerite Thomas (how to use non-stick cookware); *The Lifetime Cookbook*, by Evelyn Radcliffe (how to use waterless cookware); and *School District Spelling Manual*, by Margaret Elliot (spelling for teachers).

ASI PUBLISHERS, INC., 127 Madison Ave., New York NY 10016. Director of Publishing: Laurie Sue Brochway. Publishes hardcover and paperback originals and reprints. Pays 7½% royalty based on retail and wholesale price; no advance. Averages 8-10 titles/year. Book catalog for SASE. Will consider photocopied submissions. Computer printout submissions OK. Query. Submit outline and sample chapters or complete ms. Mss should be typed, double-spaced. SASE. Reports in 3 weeks.
Nonfiction: "We specialize in guides to balancing inner space, e.g., natural healing, astrology, new age consciousness, etc. Our editors are themselves specialists in the areas published. We will accept technical material with limited sales potential."
Recent Nonfiction Titles: *Tales from a Unicorn* (Mario James), ed. by Laurie Sue Brochway.

ASSOCIATED BOOK PUBLISHERS, INC., Box 5657, Scottsdale AZ 85261-5657. (602)998-5223. Editor: Ivan Kapetanovic. Publishes hardcover and paperback originals. "Offer outright payment or standard minimum book contract. We have not made a practice of giving advances." Averages 3-4 titles/year. Will consider photocopied submissions. Computer printout submissions OK. Submit outline and 1 sample chapter, or submit complete ms. Reports in 3 weeks. "We are not responsible for unsolicited materials unless return postage is enclosed."
Nonfiction: "We would especially consider publication of books suitable for elementary, junior high and high school students, in the field of guidance, including occupational information, college entrance and orientation, personal and social problems and how to pass tests of all kinds. In addition to the categories listed below, we are interested in bibliographies in all subject areas and in textbooks for elementary through high school grades. Books published in following categories: economics, linguistics, dictionaries, education, children's books,

cooking and nutrition, gardening, history, hobby and crafts, self-help and how-to, sociology and guidance. Accepts nonfiction translations. No strict length requirements.''
Recent Nonfiction Title: *Croatian Cuisine*, by Kapetanovic.

*ASSOCIATED BOOKSELLERS, 147 McKinley Ave., Bridgeport CT 06606. (203)366-5494. Editor-in-Chief: Alex M. Yudkin. Hardcover and paperback originals. Averages 8 titles/year. Pays 10% royalty on wholesale or retail price; advance averages $500. Subsidy publishes 10% of books. Subsidy publishing is offered ''if the marketing potential is limited.'' Query. Simultaneous and photocopied submissions OK. Reports in 2-4 weeks. SASE. Book catalog for SASE.
Nonfiction: Publishes how-to, hobbies, recreation, self-help, and sports books.
Recent Titles: *Key to Judo*; *Ketsugo*, by Ishi Black; and *Kashi-No-Bo*, by Claude St. Denise.

‡ASTRO COMPUTING SERVICES, Box 16430, San Diego CA 92116. (619)297-9203. Editorial Director: Maritha Pottenger. Publishes hardcover and trade paperback originals (95%) and trade paperback reprints. Averages 12 titles/year. Pays 15% royalty and ''monies received by publisher.'' Offers ''highly variable'' advance. Simultaneous and photocopied submissions OK. Computer printout and disk submissions OK; prefers letter quality to dot matrix. SASE. Reports in 2 weeks on queries; 3 months on mss. Free book catalog.
Nonfiction: Biography, humor, reference, self-help, technical, textbook on astrology, holistic health, psychology—usually astrologically-inclined. Occasionally accepts nonfiction translations from German and French. ''We're interested primarily in high quality astrological manuscripts, particularly (but not exclusively) with an academic and psychological slant. We're also quickly expanding our line of books in related fields, including holistic health and exploration of 'inner realities' and self-realization. We reach a strong representation both of the general public and students and professionals in the field of which we publish.'' Query or submit outline/synopsis and 1 sample chapter.
Recent Nonfiction Titles: *The Only Way to . . . Learn Astrology*, by March and McEvers (astrology text series); *Healing with the Horoscope, A Guide to Counseling*, by Pottenger; and *The American Book of Nutrition & Medical Astrology*, by Nauman.

ATHENEUM PUBLISHERS, 597 5th Ave., New York NY 10017. Editor-in-Chief: Thomas A. Stewart. Published 170 titles in 1979. Simultaneous and photocopied submissions OK. Reports in 6 weeks. SASE.
Nonfiction: General trade material dealing with politics, psychology, popular health, cookbooks, sports, biographies and general interest. Length: 40,000 words minimum. Query or submit outline/synopsis and a sample chapter.
Recent Nonfiction Titles: *Short Circuit*, by Michael Mewshaw; and *Voices: A Life of Frank O'Connor*, by James Matthews.
Fiction: ''We are not interested in unsolicited fiction.''

ATHENEUM PUBLISHERS, INC., Juvenile Department, 597 5th Ave., New York NY 10017. Editor: Jean Karl. Publishes hardcover originals and paperback reprints. Averages 55 titles/year. Reports in 6 weeks. Computer printout submissions OK. SASE.
Nonfiction: Juvenile books for ages 3-16. Picture books for ages 3-8. ''We have no special needs; we publish whatever comes in that interests us.'' Accepts artwork/photos ''of professional quality.''
Tips: ''Most submissions are poorly conceived, poorly written. Think deeper and learn to put words on paper in a way that conveys that depth to readers, without being didactic.''

ATHLETIC PRESS, Box 50314, Pasadena CA 91108. (213)283-3446. Editor-in-Chief: Donald Duke. Publishes paperback originals. Specializes in sports conditioning books. Pays 10% royalty; no advance. Averages 3 titles/year. Query or submit complete ms. ''Illustrations will be requested when we believe ms is publishable.'' Simultaneous and photocopied submissions OK. Reports in 2-4 weeks. SASE. Free book catalog.
Nonfiction: Publishes sports books.

ATLANTIC MONTHLY PRESS, 8 Arlington St., Boston MA 02116. (617)536-9500. Director: Upton Birnie Brady. Associate Director, Children's Books: Melanie Kroupa. Managing Editor: Natalie Greenberg. Averages 36 titles/year. ''Advance and royalties depend on the nature of the book, the stature of the author, and the subject matter.'' SASE.
Nonfiction: Publishes, in association with Little, Brown and Company, general nonfiction, biography, autobiography, science, philosophy, the arts, belles lettres, history and world affairs. Looks for ''intelligence, coherence, organization, good writing (which comes first), neatness of presentation—and a covering letter.'' Length: 70,000-200,000 words.
Recent Nonfiction Titles: *Blue Highways*, by William Least Heat Moon; *Distant Water*, by William W. Warner.

Fiction: Publishes, in association with Little, Brown and Company, general fiction, juveniles and poetry. Length: 70,000-200,000 words.
Recent Fiction Title: *Rogue Justice*, by Geoffrey Household.

AUGSBURG PUBLISHING HOUSE, 426 S. 5th St., Box 1209, Minneapolis MN 55440. (612)330-3432. Director, Book Department: Roland Seboldt. Publishes hardcover and paperback originals (95%) and paperback reprints (5%). Publishes 45 titles/year. Pays 10-15% royalty on retail price; offers variable advance. Simultaneous and photocopied submissions OK. Reports in 6 weeks. SASE.
Nonfiction: Health, psychology, religion, self-help and textbooks. "We are looking for manuscripts that apply scientific knowledge and Christian faith to the needs of people as individuals, in groups and in society." Query or submit outline/synopsis and a sample chapter or submit complete ms.
Recent Nonfiction Titles: *The Friendship Factor*, by Alan Loy McGinnis; *Adventure Inward*, by Morton T. Kelsey (Christian growth through personal journal writing); and *Stress/Unstress*, by Keith W. Sehnert, MD.
Tips: "We are looking for good contemporary stories with a Christian theme for the young readers in age categories 8-11, 12-14, and 15 and up." Submit complete ms.

*AUTO BOOK PRESS, 1511 Grand Ave., San Marcos CA 92069. (714)744-2567. Editorial Director: William Carroll. Publishes hardcover and paperback originals. Publishes 3 titles/year. Subsidy publishes 25% of books based on "author's exposure in the field." Pays 15% royalty; offers variable advance. Simultaneous and photocopied submissions OK. Computer printout submissions OK. Reports in 2 weeks. SASE. Free book catalog.
Nonfiction: Automotive material only: technical or definitive how-to. Query. Accepts outline/synopsis and 3 sample chapters. Recently published *Brief History of San Marcos*, by Carroll (area history); *Honda Civic Guide*, by Carroll; and *How to Sell*, by Woodward (sales hints).

AVALON BOOKS, Thomas Bouregy & Co., Inc., 22 E. 60th St., New York NY 10022. Editor: Rita Brenig. "We like the writers to focus on the plot, drama, and characters, not the background." Publishes hardcover originals. Publishes 60 titles/year. Pays $400 advance which is applied against sales of the first 3,500 copies of the book. SASE. Reports in 12 weeks. Free book list for SASE.
Fiction: "We want well-plotted, fast-moving light romances, romance-mysteries, gothics, westerns, and nurse-romance books of about 50,000 words." Submit one-page synopsis or submit complete ms. No sample chapters or long outlines. SASE.
Recent Fiction Titles: *Mists of Revilla*, by Juanita Tyree Osborne; *Nurse Sarah's Confusion*, by Mary Curtis Bowers.

AVANT BOOKS, 3719 6th Ave., San Diego CA 92103. Publisher: Michael Gosney. Publishes trade paperback originals. Averages 8 titles/year. Pays 9-20% royalty on wholesale price. Simultaneous (if so advised) and photocopied submissions OK. SASE. Reports in 2 months on queries, 3 months on mss. Book catalog $1.50.
Nonfiction: Subjects include art, health, nature, philosophy, psychology and social commentary. "Books dealing with contemporary thought, global culture, consciousness, vital ecological issues, social movements, 'new renaissance' art and writing. Also some 'how-to' and 'self-help' titles." No overly esoteric; political; single-group or viewpoint orientation (as opposed to more universal, holistic, planetary). Submit outline/synopsis and sample chapters or complete ms. of "quality, relevance, originality."
Recent Nonfiction Titles: *Deep Ecology*, ed. by Michael Tobias; *Return to Meaningfulness*, by Robert Powell (philosophy); and *The Personal Fitness Workbook*, by Tom Murphy.
Fiction: "Experimental, contemporary plays, and progressive fiction melding science fiction and 'consciousness' genres. Titles which represent the creative leading edge; East/West synthesis; ecological awareness; consciousness; 'new renaissance' mythologies. No '60s throwbacks; overly narcissistic works; overly specialized subjects or scenarios." Submit outline/synopsis and sample chapters only.
Recent Fiction Titles: *Buddha*, by Nikos Kazantzakis (drama) and *Vital Signs*, by Michael Weiner (contemporary novel).

‡AVE MARIA PRESS, Notre Dame IN 46556. (219)287-2831. Editor: Frank J. Cunningham. Publishes trade paperback originals. Averages 16-20 titles/year. Pays 7-8% royalty on retail price. Offers average $600 advance. Photocopied submissions OK. SASE. Reports in 1 week on queries; 6 weeks on mss. Free book catalog.
Nonfiction: Religion and textbooks. "Our books are for 'a basically Catholic audience,' though we have a broad interfaith appeal." Submit outline synopsis and sample chapters.
Recent Nonfiction Titles: *Walking with Loneliness*, by Paula Ripple (self-help); *Words to Love By . . .*, by Mother Teresa (inspirational); and *Blessings for God's People*, by Thomas Simons (practical resource).

*AVI PUBLISHING CO., 250 Post Rd. E., Box 831, Westport CT 06881. (203)226-0738. Managing Editor: James R. Ice, PhD. Hardcover and paperback originals. Specializes in publication of books in the fields of food science and technology, food service, nutrition, hospitality, health, agriculture and aquaculture. Pays 10% royalty, based on list price on the first 3,000 copies sold; $500 average advance (paid only on typing and art bills). "Subsidy publishes symposia; subject matter within the areas of food, nutrition, agriculture and health, endorsed by appropriate professional organizations in the area of our specialty." Publishes 30 titles/year. Reports in 1 month. SASE. Free book catalog.

Nonfiction: Publishes books on foods, agriculture, nutrition and health, scientific, technical, textbooks and reference works. Accepts nonfiction translations. Query or "submit a 500-word summary, a preface, a table of contents, estimated number of pages in manuscript, 1-2 sample chapters, when to be completed and a biographical sketch." Accepts artwork and/or photos.

Recent Nonfiction Titles: *World Fish Farming, 2nd ed.*, by Brown; *Foodservice Standards Series*, by L.J. Minor; *The Practice of Hospitality Management*, by Pizam, Lewis and Manning; *Landscape Plants in Design*, by Martin.

AVIATION BOOK CO., 1640 Victory Blvd., Glendale CA 91201. (213)240-1771. Editor: Walter P. Winner. Publishes hardcover and paperback originals and reprints. Averages 5 titles/year. Pays royalty on retail price. No advance. Free book catalog. Query with outline. Reports in 2 months. SASE.

Nonfiction: Aviation books, primarily of a technical nature and pertaining to pilot training. Young adult level and up. Also aeronautical history. Asks of ms, "Does it fill a void in available books on subject?" or, "Is it better than available material?" Recently published *Airmen's Information Manual*, by Winner (pilot training); *Their Eyes on the Skies*, by Martin Cole (aeronautics history); *Wings of Man: Biography of Capt. Dick Merrell*, by King.

AVON BOOKS, 959 8th Ave., New York NY 10019. President/Publisher: Walter Meade. Editorial Director: Page Cuddy. Publishes paperback originals (48%) and paperback reprints (52%). Averages 300 titles/year. Pay and advance are negotiable. Simultaneous and photocopied submissions OK. Computer printout submissions OK. SASE. Reports in 8 weeks. Buys 10-20 unsolicited mss/year. Free book catalog for SASE.

Nonfiction: Animals, biography, business/economics, cookbooks/cooking, health, history, hobbies, how-to, humor, juveniles, music, nature, philosophy, photography, poetry, politics, psychology, recreation, reference, religion, science, self-help, sociology, and sports. No textbooks. Submit outline/synopsis and sample chapters.

Recent Nonfiction Titles: *Your Own Money*, by Sylvia Porter; *When Bad Things Happen to Good People*, by Rabbi Kushner.

Fiction: Adventure, fantasy, gothic, historical, mainstream, mystery, religious, romance, science fiction, suspense, and western. Submit outline/synopsis, sample chapters and SASE.

Recent Fiction Title: *A Rose in Winter*, by Kathleen Woodiwess.

AZTEX CORP., 1126 N. 6th Ave., Box 50046, Tucson AZ 85703. (608)882-4656. Publishes hardcover and paperback originals. Averages 15 titles/year. Pays 10% royalty. Computer printout letter quality submissions OK; inquire about compatibility for disk submissions. SASE. Reports in 3 months. Free catalog. *Author-Publisher Handbook* $3.95.

Nonfiction: "We specialize in transportation subjects (how-to and history) and early childhood education." Accepts nonfiction translations. Submit outline/synopsis and 2 sample chapters or complete ms. Accepts artwork/photos. Looks for "accuracy, thoroughness, and interesting presentation."

Recent Nonfiction Titles: *MGA—A History and Restoration Guide* , by Robert Vitrikas; *Teach Me—Baby Wants to Learn*, by Larry A. Morris, Ph.D.; *Driving To Win*, by Bob Holbert, et. al.

B.W.M.T., INC., 279 Collingwood, San Francisco CA 94114. (415)431-0458. Editor: Michael J. Smith. Publishes trade paperback originals. Averages 2-3 titles/year. Pays a share in percentage of net profits. Simultaneous and photocopied submissions OK. Computer printout submissions OK. SASE. Reports in 1 week on queries; 1 month on mss.

Nonfiction: Biography, reference, self-help, historical/interviews on politics, psychology, sociology. "We are interested in all materials, fiction and nonfiction, which add to the knowledge and understanding of black and other Third World gay/lesbian people and their friends." No mss unrelated to the above statement. Accepts nonfiction translations. Query or submit outline/synopsis and 5 sample chapters or complete ms.

Recent Nonfiction Title: *Colorful People and Places*, by Michael J. Smith (guide to interracial, Third World gay and lesbian groups and social places).

Fiction: Ethnic, historical. Accepts fiction translations. See requirements for nonfiction. Query or submit outline/synopsis and 5 sample chapters or complete ms.

BAHAMAS INTERNATIONAL PUBLISHING CO., LTD., Box 1914, Nassau, The Bahamas. (809)322-1149. Editorial Director: Michael A. Symonette. Publishes paperback originals. Averages 18-24 titles/year. Buys mss outright for $250-1,000; offers average $250 advance. Simultaneous and photocopied submissions OK. SASE. Reports in 6 weeks. Book catalog $3. Sample copies of books $6.95 postpaid.

Imprints: *The Island Press, Ltd.* and *The Herald, Ltd.*
Nonfiction: Biography. Subjects include history. Query. "Unsolicited mss are not accepted."
Recent Nonfiction Titles: *Discovery of a Nation* (illustrated history of The Bahamas); *The New Bahamians*; *The Tax Haven Story.*
Fiction: Mainstream. "We will consider only mainstream fiction of the highest literary quality, suitable for European as well as North American readers. We are not really interested in fiction built around the standard commercial formula of today. We are concerned with substantial themes and the development of ideas. There should be strong characterization and a meaningful story line. Ours is a limited but highly literate international market. *Absolutely no* romances, gothics, science fiction, confessions, occult, fantasy, or variations on these themes in any form." Query. "Unsolicited mss are not accepted."
Recent Fiction Titles: *The Best of the Herald (Anthology); The Stone Kings; The Sunlit Wheel; Something a Little Like Love; Refugees;* and *A Winter Passage.*
Poetry: "We are considering poetry." Serious full-length dramatic works. Queries only.

*BAKER BOOK HOUSE COMPANY, Box 6287, Grand Rapids MI 49506. (616)676-9185. Editorial Director: Dan Van't Kerkhoff. Publishes hardcover and paperback originals (40%) and paperback reprints (60%). Averages 100 titles/year. Subsidy publishes 1% of books. Subsidy contract is offered "if title is in harmony with our line" and author has religious writing experience. Pays 5-10% royalty. Also buys booklet-length mss by outright purchase: $250-500. No advance. Simultaneous and photocopied submissions OK. Computer printout submissions OK "if legible"; prefers letter quality to dot matrix. SASE. Reports in 4 weeks. Book catalog for SASE.
Nonfiction: Humor; juvenile; philosophy; psychology; religion; self-help; and textbook. "All must be of religious nature." Submit outline/synopsis and 2-3 sample chapters (more, if chapters are brief) or submit complete ms.
Recent Nonfiction Titles: *Taming Tension*, by P. Keller (self-help); *Happiness is a Choice*, by P. Meier and F. Minirth (psychology); and *Dating: Guidelines from the Bible*, by Scott Kirby; and *The Wounded Parent* by Guy Greenfield.
Fiction: "Juvenile adventure with religious flavor." Submit complete ms.
Recent Fiction Titles: *Naya Nuke: Girl Who Ran*, by Kenneth Thomasma; *Cross-Country To Danger*, by John C. Hall.

BALE BOOKS, Box 2727, New Orleans LA 70176. Editor-in-Chief: Don Bale Jr. Publishes hardcover and paperback originals and reprints. Offers standard 10-12½-15% royalty contract on wholesale or retail price; no advance. Sometimes purchases mss outright for $500. Averages 10 titles/year. "Most books are sold through publicity and ads in the coin newspapers." Book catalog for SASE. Will consider photocopied submissions. Computer printout and disk submissions OK; prefers letter quality to dot matrix printouts. "Send ms by registered or certified mail. Be sure copy of ms is retained." Reports usually within several months. SASE.
Nonfiction: "Our specialty is coin and stock market investment books; especially coin investment books and coin price guides. We are open to any new ideas in the area of numismatics. The writer should write for a teenage through adult level. Lead the reader by the hand like a teacher, building chapter by chapter. Our books sometimes have a light, humorous treatment, but not necessarily." Looks for "good English, construction and content, and sales potential." Submit outline/synopsis and 3 sample chapters.
Recent Nonfiction Titles: *How to Find Valuable, Old Scarce Coins*; and *A Gold Mine in Gold*, by Bale.

BALLANTINE BOOKS, Division of Random House, 201 E. 50th St., New York NY 10022. "Science fiction and fantasy should be sent to Judy Lynn, Del Rey editor-in-chief, Del Rey Books. Proposals for trade books, poster books, calendars, etc., should be directed to Joelle Delbourgo, editor of trade books. Proposals including sample chapters for contemporary and historical fiction and romances should be sent to Pamela Strickler, senior editor of Ballantine or Michaela Hamilton, senior editor of Fawcett." Publishes trade and mass market paperback originals and reprints. Royalty contract varies. Published 350 titles last year; about 25% were originals.
General: General fiction and nonfiction, science fiction and fantasy. "Not interested in poetry or books exclusively for children; books under 50,000 words are too short for consideration. Since we are a mass market house, books which have a heavy regional flavor would be inappropriate for our list."
Recent Titles: *Living, Loving and Learning*, by Leo Buscaglia; *Chameleon*, by William Diehl; *The One Tree*, by Stephen R. Donaldson; *Twice Shy*, by Dick Francis.

BALLINGER PUBLISHING CO., 54 Church St., Harvard Square, Cambridge MA 02138. (617)492-0670. Editor: Carol Franco. Publishes hardcover originals. Averages 70 titles/year. Pays royalty by arrangement. Simultaneous and photocopied submissions OK. SASE. Reports in 1 month. Free book catalog.
Nonfiction: Professional and reference books in social and behavioral sciences, energy, economics, business, finance, high technology, and international relations. Submit outline/synopsis and sample chapters or submit complete ms.

Recent Nonfiction Titles: *Global Stakes: The Future of High Technology in America*, by James Botkin, Dan Dimancescu and Ray Stata; and *Robotics: Applications and Social Implications*, by Robert U. Ayres and Steven M. Miller.

BANKERS PUBLISHING CO., 210 South St., Boston MA 02111. (617)426-4495. Executive Editor: Robert I. Roen. Publishes hardcover originals. Averages 7 titles/year. Pays 10-15% royalty on both wholesale and retail price; buys some mss outright for negotiable fee. SASE. Computer printout submissions OK. Reports in 2 months. Book catalog for 5½x8½ SAE and 1 first class stamp.
Nonfiction: How-to reference texts on banking only for banking professionals. "Because of their nature, our books remain useful for many years (it is not unusual for a title to remain in print for 5-10 years). However, some of our technical titles are revised and updated frequently." Looks for "the ability of the author to communicate practical, how-to technical knowledge to the reader in an understanding way." Submit outline/synopsis and 2 sample chapters.
Recent Nonfiction Titles: *Accounts Receivable & Inventory Lending*, 2nd ed., by David A. Robinson; *Commercial Problem Loans*, 2nd ed., by Bob Behrens; and *Bank Audits and Examination*, by John Savage.
Tips: "As long as a book contains technical, necessary information about doing a particular banking job, it does well. We try to provide bankers with information and guidance not available anywhere else. Most of our writers are experienced bankers, but we are willing to consider a professional researcher/writer for some projects. We seek to work with new authors."

BANTAM BOOKS, INC., 666 5th Ave., New York NY 10103. Imprints include Skylark, For Young Readers, Sweet Dreams, Peacock Press, New Age Books, Windstone, Bantam Classics. (212)765-6500. President/CEO: Lou Wolfe. Executive Vice President/COO: Alberto Vitale. Vice President and Publisher: Jack Romanos. Vice President and Associate Editorial Director: Allan Barnard. Editorial Director/Vice President, Adult Fiction and Nonfiction Books: Linda Grey. Publishes mass market, trade paperback, and hardcover books for adults, young adults (ages 12-17), and young readers (ages 8-12), fiction and nonfiction reprints and originals. Pays variable royalty and advance. Queries must be accompanied by outline and sample chapters, but publisher does not accept unsolicited manuscripts. Queries will be considered for joint hardcover/paperback imprint. SASE.
Nonfiction: Material will be returned unread unless sent at Bantam's request. Please query as appropriate. Grace Bechtold, Vice President and Executive Editor, Religious and Inspirational Books; Brad Miner, Senior Editor, Religious and Inspirational Books; Toni Burbank, Executive Editor (women's studies, school and college); Fred Klein, Vice President and Executive Editor/Media (Guiness Book of World Records); Senior Editors: Linda Price (cookbooks, health); Linda Cunningham (business, finance); LuAnn Walther (school and college, classics); Tobi Saunders (science); Nessa Rapoport (Bantam Jewish Bookshelf).
Fiction: Fred Klein, Vice-President and Executive Editor/Media (TV and Movie tie-ins); Irwyn Applebaum, Publishing Manager (westerns); Senior Editors: Linda Price (mysteries); Peter Guzzardi (sports and general fiction); Carolyn Nichols (Loveswept); Brad Miner (war series); Tobi Sanders (general), Lou Aronica, Editor, Science Fiction and Fantasy; Elizabeth Barrett, Associate Editor, Loveswept. Young Adult titles: Ron Buehl, Vice President/Editorial Director; Judy Gitenstein, books for young readers.
Tips: Looks for queries with a "style that is not too formal or wordy; an approach that is refreshing and different; a look at the subject that is innovative and creative; a topic that is marketable and salable; and a product that is packageable."

*BANYAN BOOKS, INC., Box 431160, Miami FL 33243. (305)665-6011. Director: Ellen Edelen. Publishes hardcover and paperback originals (90%) and reprints (10%). Averages 6 titles/year. Specializes in Florida regional and natural history books. Pays 10% royalty on retail price; no advance. Subsidy publishes 10% of books; "worthwhile books that fill a gap in the market, but whose sales potential is limited." Send prints if illustrations are to be used with ms. Photocopied submissions OK. Reports in 1 month. SASE. Free book catalog.
Nonfiction: Publishes regional hist y and books on nature and horticulture. Submission of outline/synopsis, sample chapters preferred, but will ccept queries.
Recent Nonfiction Title: *Seashore ife of Florida and the Caribbean*, by Gilbert Voss.
Tips: "Look for gaps in material avail ble in bookstores and libraries; ask booksellers and librarians what they are asked for that is not readily availaole. Be aware of trends and what is being accepted for publication."

A.S. BARNES AND CO., INC., 9601 Aero Dr., San Diego CA 92123. (714)457-3200. President: Gifford T. Foley. Editorial Director: Modeste Williams. Publishes hardcover and paperback originals and reprints. Contract negotiable. Pays 10-15% royalty. Advance varies, depending on author's previous works and nature of book. Averages 10-25 titles/year. Will send a catalog. Query or submit outline, synopsis and sample chapters, plus SASE. Reports in 6-8 weeks.
Nonfiction: Adult nonfiction on general interest subjects with special emphasis on cinema and performing arts, contemporary issues, US history (particularly Civil War and WW II), sports, collecting and crafts. Looks

for "market identification, synopsis with rationale for book, unique features, sample chapters to demonstrate writing style and subject development, commentary on strengths and weaknesses of competing titles."
Recent Nonfiction Titles: *McQueen*; *The Day Richmond Died*; and *It's Alive*.

BARNES & NOBLE, Division of Harper & Row, 10 E. 53rd St., New York NY 10022. (212)593-7000. Editor: Jeanne Flagg. Editorial Director: Irving Levey. Publishes paperback originals (50%) and paperback reprints (50%). Averages 40 titles/year. Pays standard paperback royalties for reprints; offers variable advance. Simultaneous and photocopied submissions OK. SASE. Reports in 1 month.
Nonfiction: Education paperbacks including "College Outline Series" (summaries of college subjects) and Everyday Handbooks (self-teaching books on academic subjects, and skills and hobbies). Query or submit outline/synopsis and sample chapters. Looks for "an indication that the author knows the subject he is writing about and that he can present it clearly and logically."
Recent Nonfiction Titles: *Introduction to Computer Science*; Coloring Concepts books: *Botany Coloring Book* and *Human Evolution Coloring Book*.

BARRON'S EDUCATIONAL SERIES, INC., 113 Crossways Park Dr., Woodbury NY 11797. Publishes hardcover and paperback originals. Publishes 170 titles/year. Pays royalty, based on both wholesale and retail price. Simultaneous and photocopied submissions OK. Computer printout and disk submissions OK. Reports in 3 months. SASE. Free book catalog.
Nonfiction: Adult education, art, cookbooks, foreign language, review books, guidance, juvenile, sports, test preparation materials and textbooks. Accepts artwork/photos. Query or submit outline/synopsis and 2-3 sample chapters. Accepts nonfiction translations.
Recent Nonfiction Titles: *How to Prepare for the Regents Competency Examination in Reading*, by Dr. Robert Fredericks and Dr. Barbara Erdman Lipner (test preparation); *Judith Olney's Entertainments*, by Judith Olney (cookbook); and *How to Beat Test Anxiety*, by James Divine and David W. Kylen (guidance).

BASIC BOOKS, INC., 10 E. 53rd St., New York NY 10022. (212)593-7057. Editorial Director: Martin Kessler. Publishes hardcover originals (80%) and paperback reprints "of own hardcovers" (20%). Publishes 60 titles/year. Pays standard royalty; negotiates advance depending on projects. SASE. Reports in 6 weeks.
Nonfiction: Political, social, behavorial and economics for universities and trade. Prefers submission of complete ms; outline/synopsis and sample chapters acceptable.
Recent Nonfiction Titles: *Godel-Escher-Bach*, by D. Hofstadter (thinking computers and their relation to culture); *Zero-Sum Society*, by L. Thurow; and *Freud—Biologist of the Mind*, by F. Sulloway (intellectual biography of Freud).

BEACON PRESS, 25 Beacon St., Boston MA 02108. (617)742-2110. Contact: Director, Wendy J. Strothman. Publishes hardcover originals (50%) and paperback reprints (50%). Averages 30 titles/year. "Our audience is composed of liberal/religious and other book readers interested in a wide variety of subjects pertaining to the social and political issues facing contemporary society." Pays 7½% royalty on retail price (paperback); 10% on hardbound; advance averages $3,000. Photocopied submissions OK. Reports in 2 months. SASE. Free book catalog.
Nonfiction: General nonfiction, religion, world affairs, sociology, psychology, women's studies, political science, art, literature, philosophy and self-help. Query.
Recent Nonfiction Titles: *Strange Gods: The Great American Cult Scare*, by David Bromley and Anson Shupe; *The 50/50 Marriage*, by Gayle Kimball; *Media Monopoly*, by Ben Bagdikian.
Tips: "Our books address the critical issues of our time and provide guidance and inspiration so that people may lead more effective, caring, and responsible lives."

BEAU LAC PUBLISHERS, Box 248, Chuluota FL 32766. Publishes hardcover and paperback originals. SASE.
Nonfiction: "Military subjects. Specialist in the social side of service life." Query. Recently published *The Officer's Family Social Guide*; *Military Weddings and the Military Ball*; *Military Memories*, all by M.P. Gross.

BEAUFORT BOOKS, INC., 9 E. 40th St., New York NY 10016. (212)685-8588. Editorial Director: Susan Suffes. Publishes hardcover and trade paperback originals (100%). Averages 40-50 titles/year. Pays 7½-15% royalty on retail price; offers variable advance. Simultaneous and photocopied submissions OK. No computer printout or disk submissions. SASE. Reports in 2 weeks on queries; 1 month on mss. Book catalog for 6x9 SAE and 2 first class stamps.
Nonfiction: Biography, cookbook, how-to, illustrated book, self-help and young adult. Subjects include cooking and foods, health, business, sports, humor, history, hobbies, psychology and recreation. Query, or submit outline/synopsis and 3 sample chapters or complete ms.
Recent Nonfiction Titles: *Home Before Morning: The Story of an Army Nurse in Vietnam* (autobiography); *Kempei Tai: The History of the Japanese Secret Service*; and *The Special Guest Cookbook*.

Fiction: Adventure, and literary novels. "No first novels, no science fiction." Accepts fiction translations from French. Query or submit complete ms.
Recent Fiction Titles: *Impressionist* (adult novel, based on the life of the artist Mary Cassett), by Joan King; *Dracula's Diary* (literary "who sucks"), by Michael Geane and Michael Corby.

THE BENJAMIN COMPANY, INC., One Westchester Plaza, Elmsford NY 10523. (914)592-8088. President: Ted Benjamin. Publishes hardcover and paperback originals. Averages 10-12 titles/year. Buys mss by outright purchase. Offers advance. Simultaneous and photocopied submissions OK. Reports in 2 months.
Nonfiction: Business/economics, cookbooks, cooking and foods, health, hobbies, how-to, self-help, sports and consumerism. "Ours is a very specialized kind of publishing—for clients (industrial and association) to use in promotional, PR, or educational programs. If an author has an idea for a book, and close connections with a company that might be interested in using that book, we will be very interested in working together with the author to 'sell' the program and the idea of a special book for that company. Once published, our books do get trade distribution, through a distributing publisher, so the author generally sees the book in regular book outlets as well as in the special programs undertaken by the sponsoring company. Normally we do not encourage submission of mss. We usually commission an author to write for us. The most helpful thing an author can do is to let us know what he or she has written, or what subjects he or she feels competent to write about. We will contact the author when our needs indicate that the author might be the right person to produce a needed ms." Query. Submit outline/synopsis and 1 sample chapter. Looks for "possibility of tie-in with sponsoring company or association."
Recent Nonfiction Titles: *Complete Dessert Cookbook* (C&H Sugar); *Getting More for Your Money*, for the Council of Better Business Bureaus; *Kenmore Microwave Cooking*, for Sears, Roebuck.

BENNETT PUBLISHING CO., 809 W. Detweiller Dr., Peoria IL 61615. (309)691-4454. Editorial Director: Michael Kenny. Publishes hardcover and paperback originals. Specializes in textbooks and related materials. Pays 10% royalty for textbooks "based on cash received, less for supplements"; no advance. Averages 30 titles/year. Query "with 1-2 sample chapters that represent much of the book; not a general introduction if the ms is mostly specific 'how-to' instructions." Photocopied submissions OK. Reports in 2-4 weeks. SASE. Free book catalog.
Nonfiction: Publishes textbooks and related items for home economics, industrial education, and art programs in schools, junior high and above. Wants "content with good coverage of subject matter in a course in one of our fields; intelligent organization; and clear expression." Prefers author to submit art and/or prints with text matter.
Recent Nonfiction Titles: *Living Today*, by Dr. Irene Oppenheim (home economics textbook); *Introduction to Photo-Offset Lithography* , by Dr. Kenneth Hird (industrial arts textbook); and *Residential Electrical Wiring*, by Dr. Rex Miller (industrial education textbook).

THE BERKLEY PUBLISHING GROUP, (publishers of Berkley/Jove/Charter/SECOND CHANCE AT LOVE/Tempo young adult fiction/Ace Science Fiction), 200 Madison Ave., New York NY 10016. (212)686-9820. Vice President/Editorial Director: Roger Cooper. Editor-in-Chief: Nancy Coffey. Executive editor: Beverly Lewis. Publishes paperback originals (60%) and reprints (40%). Publishes approx. 700 titles/yr. Pays 6-10% royalty on retail price; offers advance. SASE. Reports in 6 months.
Nonfiction: How-to, inspirational, family life, philosophy, and nutrition.
Recent Nonfiction Titles: *Nam*, by Mark Baker; *Human Options*, by Norman Cousins; *Mister Rogers Talks with Parents*, by Fred Rogers and Barry Head; *From Peak to Peek Principle*, by Robert H. Schuller.
Fiction: Adventure, historical, mainstream men's adventure, young adult, suspense, western, occult, and romance, science fiction. Submit outline & first 3 chapters.
Recent Fiction Titles: *Dinner at the Homesick Restaurant*, by Anne Tyler; *The Case of Lucy Bending*, by Lawrence Sanders; *An Accidental Woman*, by Richard Neely; *White Plague*, by Frank Herbert; *Death Beam*, by Robert Moss; *This Promised Land*, by Gloria Goldreich; *Reap the Savage Wind*, by Ellen Tanner Marsh.
Young Adult Fiction Titles: *Before Love*, by Gloria Mikowitz; *Swak*, by Judith Enderle; *Three's a Crowd*, by Nola Carlson.

BETHANY HOUSE PUBLISHERS, 6820 Auto Club Rd., Minneapolis MN 55438. (612)944-2121. Managing Editor: Carol Johnson. Publishes hardcover and paperback originals (85%) and paperback reprints (15%). "Contracts negotiable." Averages 50 titles/year. Simultaneous and photocopied submissions OK. Computer printout submissions OK; prefers letter quality to dot matrix. Reports in 1-2 months. Free book catalog on request.
Nonfiction: Publishes reference (lay-oriented), devotional (evangelical, charismatic) and self-help books. Accepts nonfiction translations. "No poetry, please." Query. Looks for "interesting subject, quality writing style, authoritative presentation, unique approach, sound Christian truth."
Recent Nonfiction Titles: *Today's Dictionary of the Bible*(reference); *If God Loves Me, Why Can't I Get My*

Locker Open?, by Lorraine Peterson; and *Telling Yourself the Truth*, by Marie Chapian/William Backus (self-help).

Fiction: Well-written stories with a Christian message. Submit outline and 2-3 sample chapters.

Recent Fiction Titles: *Kara*, by Carole Gift Page (young adult romance); *Love Comes Softly*, by Janette Oke (prairie romance); and *The Fisherman's Lady*, by George MacDonald (gothic).

BETTER HOMES AND GARDENS BOOKS, 1716 Locust St., Des Moines IA 50336. Editor: Gerald Knox. Publishes hardcover originals and reprints. Publishes 20 titles/year. "Ordinarily we pay an outright fee for work (amount depending on the scope of the assignment). If the book is the work of one author, we sometimes offer royalties in addition to the fee." Prefers outlines and 1 sample chapter, but will accept complete ms. Will consider photocopied submissions. No computer printout or disk submissions. Reports in 6 weeks. SASE.

Nonfiction: "We publish nonfiction in many family and home service categories, including gardening, decorating and remodeling, sewing and crafts, money management, entertaining, handyman's topics, cooking and nutrition, and other subjects of home service value. Emphasis is on how-to and on stimulating people to action. We require concise, factual writing. Audience is primarily husbands and wives with home and family as their main center of interest. Style should be informative and lively with a straightforward approach. Stress the positive. Emphasis is entirely on reader service. We approach the general audience with a confident air, instilling in them a desire and the motivation to accomplish things. Food book areas that we have already dealt with in detail are currently overworked by writers submitting to us. We rely heavily on a staff of home economist editors for food books. We are interested in non-food books that can serve mail order and book club requirements (to sell at least for $9.95 and up) as well as trade. Rarely is our first printing of a book less than 100,000 copies. Publisher recommends careful study of specific *Better Homes and Gardens* book titles before submitting material."

Tips: Queries/mss may be routed to other editors in the publishing group.

‡**BETTERWAY PUBLICATIONS, INC.**, General Delivery, White Hall VA 22987. (804)823-5661. Senior Editor: Robert F. Hostage. Publishes hardcover and trade paperback originals. Averages 10-12 titles/year. Pays 10-15% royalty on wholesale price. Advance averages $500. Simultaneous and photocopied submissions OK. SASE. Reports in 3 weeks on queries; 1 month on mss. Free book catalog.

Nonfiction: Cookbook, how-to, illustrated book, juvenile, reference, self-help, nutrition and diet. Subjects include business and economics, cooking and foods, health, gardening and homemaking. Especially wants "useful how-to and reference books for homemakers; practical and inspirational books for women who want personal/business fulfillments and a strong home and family life; how-to books for juveniles and adolescents; cookbooks; books on health and nutrition; books on contemporary issues affecting personal and family lives." Submit outline/synopsis and sample chapters.

Recent Nonfiction Titles: *Unpuzzling Your Past—A Basic Guide to Genealogy*, by Emily A. Croom; *Teen is a Four-Letter Word—A Survival Kit for Parents*, by Joan W. Anderson; *Am I Still Visible—A Woman's Triumph Over Anorexia Nervosa*, by Sandra H. Heater.

BILINGUAL EDUCATIONAL SERVICES, INC., 1607 Hope St., South Pasadena CA 91030. (213)682-3456. General Manager: Joann N. Baker. Publishes hardcover and paperback originals. Averages 2 titles/year. Negotiates royalty; offers no advance. Simultaneous and photocopied submissions OK. SASE. Reports in 3 months. Book catalog for 9x12 SASE.

Nonfiction: Publishes adult and juvenile nonfiction. Interested in "anything which will appeal to Spanish-speaking people, especially Chicano and Southwest US topics—high-interest low-vocabulary—easy to translate into Spanish." Also interested in English as a second language materials. Submit outline/synopsis and sample chapters. Submit complete ms if intended for translation.

Recent Nonfiction Titles: *Knowledge Aid Picture Dictionary*; *450 Years of Chicano History*; and *US Government in Action* (Spanish translation of English textbook).

Fiction: Publishes adult and juvenile fiction. Same subject requirements as nonfiction.

*BINFORD & MORT, PUBLISHERS, 2536 SE 11th Ave., Box 42368, Portland OR 97242. (503)238-9666. Publisher: Mrs. Janet E. Binford. Editor-in-Chief: L.K. Phillips. Publishes hardcover and paperback originals (80%) and reprints (20%). Pays 10% royalty on retail price; offers variable advance (to established authors). Occasionally does some subsidy publishing, "when ms merits it, but it does not fit into our type of publishing." Publishes about 24 titles annually. Reports in 2-4 months. SASE. Free book catalog.

Nonfiction: Publishes books about the Pacific Northwest, mainly in the historical field. Also Americana, biography, cookbooks, cooking and foods, history, nature, photography, recreation, reference, sports, and travel. Query.

Recent Nonfiction Titles: *Blood on the Half Shell*, by Al Qualman; *Heave To! You'll Drown Yourselves!*, by Stan Allyn; *Shaninko People*, by Helen G. Rees.

Fiction: Publishes historical and western books. Must be strongly laced with historical background.

BIOMEDICAL PUBLICATIONS, Box 495, Davis CA 95617. (916)756-8453. General Manager: L. Mak. Averages 3-5 titles/year. Pays 10-20% royalty on wholesale or retail price; offers negotiable advance. Simultaneous and photocopied submissions OK. Computer printout and disk submissions OK. SASE. Reports in 1 week on queries; 3 weeks on mss. Free book catalog.

Nonfiction: Reference, technical and textbook. Subjects include health and biomedical sciences. Accepts nonfiction translations from German, French and Spanish. "Manuscripts on industrial toxicology, environmental contamination, drug and chemical toxicology, pharmacology and pharmacokinetics, clinical chemistry, forensic science. Our readers include toxicologists, pharmacologists, clinical pharmacists, pathologists, forensic scientists and attorneys." Query or submit outline/synopsis and 1-2 sample chapters.

Recent Nonfiction Titles: *Forensic Toxicology*, by Cravey (textbook); *Review Questions in Analytical Toxicology*, by Wallace (study guide); and *Industrial Chemical Exposure*, by Lauwerys (reference).

*BIWORLD PUBLISHERS, INC., 671 N. State, Orem UT 84057. (801)224-5803. Vice President: Al Lisonbee. Publishes hardcover and trade paperback originals. Averages 12-20 titles/year. Subsidy publishes 10% of books, based on each individual case. Pays 8-12% royalty on retail price; no advance. Simultaneous and photocopied submissions OK. SASE. Reports in 2 weeks on queries; 1 month on mss. Free book catalog.

Nonfiction: Cookbook, how-to, reference, self-help and textbook. Subjects include cooking and foods, health and nature. "We're looking for reputable, professionally-done, well-researched manuscripts dealing in health, natural medicine, etc." Submit outline/synopsis and sample chapters or complete ms.

Recent Nonfiction Titles: *Today's Herbal Health*, by Louise Tenney; *Healing Energies*, by Stephen Shepard; and *Health in the Space Age*, by Ladean Griffin.

Tips: "The health field is just now dawning. Health-related books of quality research are in demand."

‡BKMK PRESS, College of A&S, UMKC, 5100 Rockhill Rd., Kansas City MO 64110. (816)276-1305. Editor: Dan Jaffe. Averages 6 titles/year. Pays by individual agreement. Photocopied submissions OK. SASE. Reports in 1 month on queries; 6 months on mss. Free book catalog.

Fiction: Ethnic, experimental, mainstream. "We are new to publishing fiction and plan only one book in each of the next few years. We are interested in fiction of high literary merit but which may not have enough commercial appeal to be accepted elsewhere. We plan either a collection of short stories by a single author or an anthology of short stories. We are not interested in commercial fare." Query.

Poetry: "We publish about half a dozen poetry books a year. We specialize in, but are not limited to poets of the Midwest." Accepts poetry translations. No sentimental poetry. Query.

Recent Poetry Titles: *Honeymoon*, by William Kloefkorn; *No Dancing, No Acts of Dancing*, by Phyllis Janik; and *Fields, Archas, Pitches, Turfs*, Richard Kostelanetz (avant garde).

Tips: "We are interested in working with new talent as well as with more established poets. We recommend publishing in several magazines before querying us about a book-length manuscript. The same applies for fiction writers. We envision our readers as sensitive to and knowledgeable about literature."

THE BLACKSBURG GROUP, INC., Box 242, Blacksburg VA 24060. (703)951-9030. President: Jonathan A. Titus, Ph.D. Editorial Director: Christopher A. Titus, Ph.D. Senior Editor: J.R. Smallwood. "Our group writes and edits books from outside authors. Our books are published by technical publishers. We offer competitive royalties, advances for technical works, and we offer our writers many advantages not found with most technical publishers. We are not agents and do not take any portion of the author's royalties for our publishing efforts." Publishes paperback originals. Averages 12 titles/year. Pays 7½-13% royalty; offers advance. Photocopied submissions OK. Computer printout and disk submissions OK; "authors should call first to see if formats for disk submissions are the same." Prefers letter quality to dot matrix printouts. SASE. Reports in 1 month. Free book catalog.

Nonfiction: Computers and electronics; how-to (electronic projects); reference, technical and textbooks (computers, electronics, and computer programming). Especially interested in "microcomputer applications (hardware and software), VIC-20, Commodore-64, TI99/4 and other computer applications and programs, digital and analog electronics, fiber optics, books with experiments/projects/hands-on learning, robotics, and home satellite TV." Query, submit outline/synopsis introduction and sample chapter or complete ms. Looks for "complete coverage of the material at a level suitable for the reader to whom the book is directed. Careful organization and attention to detail, and technically correct and timely (up-to-date) material. At least three people look at our incoming book proposals."

Recent Nonfiction Titles: *Introduction to Electronic Speech Synthesis*, by Neil Sclater; *STD Bus Interfacing*, by C.A. Titus, et al.; *FORTH Programming*, by Leo Scanlon (all computer-electronic).

JOHN F. BLAIR, PUBLISHER, 1406 Plaza Dr., Winston-Salem NC 27103. (919)768-1374. Editor-in-Chief: John F. Blair. Publishes hardcover originals, trade paperbacks and reprints. Royalty to be negotiated. Free book catalog. Submit synopsis/outline and first 3 chapters or complete ms. Computer printout submissions OK; prefers letter quality to dot matrix. Reports in 3 months. SASE.

Nonfiction: Especially interested in well-researched adult biography and history. Preference given to books dealing with Southeastern United States. Also interested in environment, politics, recreation, humor, education and Americana. Looks for utility and significance.

Recent Nonfiction Titles: *Landscaping with Native Plants*, by Cordelia Penn; *W.W. Holden: A Political Biography*, by Edgar E. Folk and Bynum Shaw.

Fiction: "We are most interested in serious novels of substance and imagination with contemporary settings. No category fiction. Juveniles should be for ages 9-14; no picture books. We are not accepting poetry mss at this time."

Recent Fiction Titles: *Tales of the South Carolina Low Country*, by Nancy Rhyne; *Banners Over Terre d'Or*, by Gay Weeks Neale.

THE BOBBS-MERRILL CO., INC., 630 3rd Ave., New York NY 10017. Executive Editor: Margaret B. Parkinson. Publishes hardcover originals and some trade paper originals and reprints. Pays 10-15% royalty on retail price and variable advances depending on author's reputation and nature of book. Publishes 22 titles/year. Simultaneous and photocopied submissions OK. Reports in 1 month on queries; 2 months on mss. SASE.

Nonfiction: Biography, cookbook, how-to, self-help, psychology, medicine. Subjects include parenting, cooking and foods, health, diet, and sports. Query through agent only. All unsolicited mss are returned unopened.

Recent Nonfiction Titles: *To Love a Child*, by Nancy Reagan; *Understanding Pregnancy and Childbirth*, by Sheldon H. Cherry, M.D.; *Plumbing for Dummies*, by Don Fredriksson.

BOOKCRAFT, INC., 1848 W. 2300 South, Salt Lake City UT 84119. (802)972-6180. Senior Editor: H. George Bickerstaff. Publishes (mainly hardcover) originals and reprints. Pays standard 10-12½-15% royalty on retail price; "we rarely make an advance on a new author." Averages 25 titles/year. Will send information for authors to a writer on request. Query. Will consider photocopied submissions. Computer printout submissions OK; prefers letter quality to dot matrix. "Include contents page with ms." Reports in about 2 months. SASE.

Nonfiction: "We publish for members of The Church of Jesus Christ of Latter-Day Saints (Mormons) and do not distribute to the national market. All our books are closely oriented to the faith and practices of the LDS church. We will be glad to review such mss, but mss which have merely a general religious appeal are not acceptable. Ideal book lengths range from about 64 pages to 160 or so, depending on subject, presentation, and age level. We look for a fresh approach—rehashes of well-known concepts or doctrines not acceptable. Mss should be anecdotal unless truly scholarly or on a specialized subject. Outlook must be positive. We do not publish anti-Mormon works. We don't publish poetry, plays, personal philosophizings, family histories, or personal histories. We also publish short and moderate length books for Mormon youth, about ages 14 to 19, mostly nonfiction. These reflect LDS principles without being 'preachy'; must be motivational. 20,000-30,000 words is about the length, though we would accept good longer mss. This is a tough area to write in, and the mortality rate for such mss is high. We only publish 1 or 2 new juvenile titles annually."

Recent Nonfiction Titles: *The Divine Center*, by Stephen R. Covey; *To Him That Believeth*, by Frederick Babbel; and *I'm Somebody Special*, by Pat Allen (juvenile).

Fiction: Must be closely oriented to LDS faith and practices.

Recent Fiction Titles: *Corker*, by Anya Bateman (contemporary novel); and *The Bishop's Horse Race*, by Blaine and Brenton Yorgason (humorous adventure).

BOOKS FOR BUSINESS, INC., 1100 17th St. NW, Washington, D.C. 20036. (202)466-2372. Publishes hardcover and paperback originals (80%) and reprints. Specializes in high-priced books on business or international trade and legal reference works for lawyers and law libraries. Accepts nonfiction translations in international law. Averages 6 titles/year. "Looking for a unique content area geared to business and/or the entrepreneur. New and different concepts are welcomed. Usually royalties start at 10%; sometimes 5% for anthologies, but this is not a fixed rule." No advance. Simultaneous and photocopied submissions OK. "SASE is a must." Computer printout submissions OK. Reports in 1-2 months. Book catalog for SASE.

Recent Nonfiction Titles: *Legal Barriers to Solar Heating and Cooling of Buildings*; *How to Develop & Manage a Successful Condominium*; and *Panamanian Business Laws*.

Tips: "Reference and how-to books should not date themselves. Their main purpose should be years of survival. We are only interested in law, professional, and reference books. We no longer sell to the book trade and thus cannot handle books on business intended for a general audience." Queries/mss may be routed to other editors in the publishing group.

BOREALIS PRESS, LTD., 9 Ashburn Dr., Nepean, Ontario, Canada K2E 6N4. Editorial Director: Frank Tierney. Senior Editor: Glenn Clever. Publishes hardcover and paperback originals. Averages 20 titles/year. Pays 10% royalty on retail price; no advance. Reports in 12 weeks. SAE and International Reply Coupons. Book catalog $1.

Nonfiction: "Only material Canadian in content." Query. Looks for "style in use and language; reader interest; and maturity of outlook."

Recent Nonfiction Titles: *The Canadian Parliamentary Handbook*, edited by John Bejermi; *The Quebec Problem*, by William O'Grady (an analysis of Quebec separatism); and *Wry and Ginger*, by Jack Howard (humor).
Fiction: "Only material Canadian in content." Query.
Recent Fiction Titles: *Tale Spinners in a Spruce Tipi*, by Evalyn Gantreau (collection of Cree Indian tales in English); *Strike at Eldorado*, by Carl Hortic (novel of labor problems and love in Ontario); and *The Secret of Ivy Lea*, by Janice Cavan (teenage novel set in the Thousand Islands of the St. Lawrence).

THE BORGO PRESS, Box 2845, San Bernardino CA 92406. (714)884-5813. Publishers: R. Reginald and Mary A. Burgess. Publishes hardcover and paperback originals. Averages 35 titles/year. Pays royalty on retail price: "10% of gross, with a 12% escalator." No advance. "Most of our sales are to the library market." Computer printout submissions OK; "will accept diskettes compatible with IBM PC or disk cartridge for Tallgrass Cartridge Tape/Hardfile System." Reports in 2 months. SASE. Free book catalog for SASE.
Nonfiction: Publishes literary critiques, historical research, film critiques, interview volumes, biographies, social studies, political science, and reference works for library and academic markets. Query with letter or outline/synopsis and 1 sample chapter. Accepts nonfiction translations. "We appreciate people who've looked at our books before submitting proposals; all of the books in our Milford series, for example, are based around a certain format that we prefer using."
Recent Nonfiction Titles: *Anti-Sartre, With an Essay on Camus*, by Colin Wilson; *Candle for Poland: 469 Days of Solidarity*, by Dr. Leszek Szymanski; and *The Jewish Holocaust: An Annotated Guide to Books in English*, by Marty Bloomberg. Established monographic series include: The Milford Series: Popular Writers of Today; I. O. Evans Studies in the Philosophy & Criticism of Literature; Stokvis Studies in Historical Chronology & Thought; Great Issues of the Day; The Borgo Reference Library; Borgo Bioviews; The Woodstock Series: Popular Music of Today; Malcolm Hulke Studies in Cinema and Theatre.

‡*DON BOSCO PUBLICATIONS, 475 N. Ave., Box T, New Rochelle NY 10802. (914)576-0122. Subsidiaries include Salesiana Publishers. Editorial Director: James Hurley. Publishes hardcover and trade paperback originals. Averages 8 titles/year. Subsidy publishes 12% of books. "We judge the content of the manuscript and quality to be sure it fits the description of our house." Pays 6-10% royalty on retail price; offers average $100 advance. Computer printout submissions OK; prefers letter quality to dot matrix. SASE. Reports in 1 week on queries; 2 months on mss. Free book catalog.
Nonfiction: Biography, juvenile, textbook on Roman Catholic religion and sports. "Biographies of outstanding Christian men and women of today. Sports for youngsters and young adults. We are a new publisher with wide experience in school marketing, especially in religious education field." Accepts nonfiction translations from Italian and Spanish. Query or submit outline/synopsis and 2 sample chapters.
Recent Nonfiction Titles: *Gospel According to Barabbas*, by Salvatore Grillo; and *Don Bosco and the Salesians*, by Moran Wirth; and *General Mickey*, by Peter Lappin.
Fiction: "We will consider only religious fiction this year." Query.
Tips: Queries/mss may be routed to other editors in the publishing group.

THOMAS BOUREGY AND CO., INC., 22 E. 60th St., New York NY 10022. Editor: Rita Brenig. Offers advance on publication date. Averages 60 titles/year. Reports in 3 months. SASE.
Imprints: *Avalon Books* (fiction).
Fiction: Romances, nurse/romances, westerns and gothic novels. Avoid sensationalist elements. Send one-page query with SASE. No sample chapters. Length: about 50,000 words.
Recent Fiction Titles: *Mists of Revilla*, by Juanita Tyree Osborne; *Nurse Sarah's Confusion*, by Mary Curtis Bowers.

R.R. BOWKER CO., 1180 Avenue of the Americas, New York NY 10036. (212)764-5100. Editor-in-Chief, Book Division: Paul Doebler. Pays negotiable royalty. Reports in 2 months. SASE.
Nonfiction: Publishes books for the book trade and library field, professional books, reference books and bibliographies. Query; "send in a very thoroughly developed proposal with a table of contents, representative chapters, and analysis of the competition with your idea."

BRADBURY PRESS, INC., 2 Overhill Rd., Scarsdale NY 10583. (914)472-5100. Editor-in-Chief: Richard Jackson. Publishes hardcover originals for children and young adults. Averages 15 titles/year. An affiliate of Macmillan, Inc. Pays 10% royalty or 5% on retail price to author, 5% to artist; advance averages $2,000. Reports in 3 months. SASE. Book catalog for 37¢
Fiction: Contemporary fiction; adventure and humor. Also "stories about real kids; special interest in realistic dialogue." No adult manuscripts. No fantasy or religious material. Submit complete ms.
Recent Fiction Titles: *Tiger Eyes*, by Judy Blume; *Tunnel Vision*, by Fran Arrick; and *Star Boy*, by Paul Goble.
Tips: "Blockbusters make it *possible* to take risks; we still do first novels."

‡*BRADSON PRESS, INC., 120 Longfellow St., Thousand Oaks CA 91360. (805)496-8212. President: Donn Delson. Publishes trade paperback originals and reprints. Averages 3 titles/year. Subsidy publishes 50% of books "depending on quality of work and market potential." Pays 5-12% royalty. Simultaneous and photocopied submissions OK. SASE. Reports in 6 weeks. Free book catalog.
Nonfiction: Humor, juvenile, reference, self-help and technical covering health, hobbies, psychology, sociology, sports, entertainment and communications. "Self-help and how-to books are our primary focus—also interested in unique humorous concepts for mass market." No history, politics, religion. Submit outline/synopsis and sample chapters.
Recent Nonfiction Title: *Motion Picture Distribution: An Accountant's Perspective*, by D. Leedy.
Fiction: Humor. No religious or western material. Submit outline/synopsis and sample chapters.

CHARLES T. BRANFORD CO., Box 41, Newton Centre MA 02159. (617)964-2441. Editor-in-Chief: I.F. Jacobs. Hardcover and paperback originals (80%) and reprints (20%). Offers 10% royalty on retail price. No advance. Publishes about 4 titles annually. Photocopied submissions OK. Computer printout and disk submissions OK. Reports in 2 weeks. SASE. Free book catalog.
Nonfiction: Hobbies; how-to; recreation; and self-help. Accepts nonfiction translations. Query first. Accepts artwork/photos.
Recent Nonfiction Titles: *Embroidery in Religion & Ceremonial*, by Beryl Dean; *20th Century Embroidery in Great Britain, Vol. I*, by C. Howard; *Birds of Prey*, by E. Ford; *Falconry in Mews & Field*, by E. Ford; *Creative Design in Bobbin Lace*, by A. Collier; *Technique of Metal Thread Embroidery*, by B. Dawson.

GEORGE BRAZILLER, INC., 1 Park Ave., New York NY 10016. Offers standard 10-12½-15% royalty contract; Offers variable advance depending on author's reputation and nature of book. Computer printout submissions OK; prefers letter quality to dot matrix. No unsolicited mss. Reports in 6 weeks. SASE.
General Fiction and Nonfiction: Publishes fiction and nonfiction; literature, art, philosophy, history. Accepts nonfiction, fiction and poetry translations "provided clearance from foreign publisher is obtained." Query. Accepts outline/synopsis and 2 sample chapters.

BREVET PRESS, INC., Box 1404, Sioux Falls SD 57101. Editor-in-Chief: Donald P. Mackintosh. Managing Editor: Peter E. Reid. Publishes hardcover and paperback originals (67%) and reprints (33%). Specializes in business management, history, place names, historical marker series. Pays 5% royalty; advance averages $1,000. Query; "after query, detailed instructions will follow if we are interested." Send copies if photos/illustrations are to accompany ms. Simultaneous and photocopied submissions OK. Reports in 1-2 months. SASE. Free book catalog.
Nonfiction: Publishes Americana (A. Melton, editor); business (D.P. Mackintosh, editor); history (B. Mackintosh, editor); and technical books (Peter Reid, editor). Recently published *Illinois Historical Markers and Sites* (nonfiction historical series); and *Challenge*, by R. Karolevitz (history).

BRIARCLIFF PRESS PUBLISHERS, 11 Wimbledon Ct., Jericho NY 11753. Editorial Director: Trudy Settel. Senior Editor: J. Frieman. Publishes hardcover and paperback originals. Averages 5-7 titles/year. Pays $4,000-5,000 by outright purchase; average advance of $1,000. "We do not use unsolicited manuscripts. Ours are custom books prepared for businesses and assignments are initiated by us."
Nonfiction: How-to, cookbooks, sports, travel, fitness/health, business and finance, diet, gardening, and crafts. "We want our books to be designed to meet the needs of specific business." Query. Accepts outline and 2 sample chapters. Computer printout submissions OK; prefers letter quality to dot matrix. Accepts nonfiction translations from French, German, Italian.
Recent Nonfiction Title: *Amana Microwave Oven Cookbook*, by C. Adams.

BRICK HOUSE PUBLISHING CO., 34 Essex St., Andover MA 01810 (617)475-9568. Publisher: Jack D. Howell. Publishes hardcover and paperback originals. Averages 12 titles/year. Pays 7-10% royalty on paperback and 10-15% on hardcover. Photocopied submissions OK. Reports in 4 weeks. SASE. Free book catalog.
Nonfiction: Trade paperbacks generally in the $6-12 range. Alternative sources of energy and environmental material; "and would like to diversify into other how-to and alternative lifestyle books. We will consider any quality nonfiction trade material."
Recent Nonfiction Titles: *Passive Solar Energy*, by Bruce Anderson and Malcolm Wells; and *Solar Retrofit*, by Dan Reif; *Seeds of Promise: The First Real Hearings on The Nuclear Arms Freeze*, by the Federation of American Scientists.
Tips: "Include complete prospectus telling why and for whom you are writing, listing all aspects, graphs, photos, line drawings, length, etc."

*BRIGHAM YOUNG UNIVERSITY PRESS, University Press Bldg., Provo UT 84602. Managing Editor: Howard A. Christy. Publishes hardcover and paperback originals (85%) and reprints (15%). Averages 8 titles/year. "We subsidy publish 15% of our books. If a book has scholarly merit but little potential for repaying the

cost of publication, we encourage the author to seek a subsidy from an institution or foundation." Pays royalties based on estimated market potential, ranging 0-15% of wholesale price; offers very small advances. Reports in 3-6 weeks. SASE. Free book catalog.
Nonfiction: Scholarly nonfiction, textbooks, and high-level popularizations. "We are interested in high-quality work from any discipline, but we focus mainly on Western regional studies, law, the social sciences, preschool education and outdoor recreation, and especially anthropological studies dealing with the American Indian. No length preferences. We do not publish fiction or children's literature." Query. Accepts with outline/synopsis and 2 sample chapters.
Recent Nonfiction Titles: *Indeh: An Apache Odyssey*, by Eve Ball; and *On Being a Christian and a Lawyer*, by Thomas Shaffer.

BROADMAN PRESS, 127 9th Ave. N, Nashville TN 37234. Editorial Director: Thomas L. Clark. Publishes hardcover and paperback originals (85%) and reprints (15%). Averages 100 titles/year. Pays 10% royalty on retail price; no advance. Photocopied submissions OK "only if they're sharp and clear." SASE. Reports in 2 months.
Nonfiction: Religion. "We are open to freelance submissions in the children's and inspirational area. Materials in both areas must be suited for a conservative Protestant readership. No poetry, biography, sermons, or anything outside the area of the Protestant tradition." Query, submit outline/synopsis and sample chapters, or submit complete ms.
Fiction: Religious. "We publish almost no fiction—less than five titles per year. For our occasional publication we want not only a very good story, but also one that sets forth Christian values. Nothing that lacks a positive Christian emphasis; nothing that fails to sustain reader interest." Submit complete ms.
Tips: "Bible study is very good for us, but our publishing is largely restricted in this area to works that we enlist on the basis of specific author qualifications."

WILLIAM C. BROWN CO., PUBLISHERS, 2460 Kerper Blvd., Dubuque IA 52001. President, College and Professional Division: Lawrence E. Cremer. Publishes 110 titles/year. Pays variable royalty on net price. SASE. Query. Accepts outline/synopsis and 2 sample chapters. Computer printout and disk submissions OK.
Nonfiction: College textbooks. Accepts photos/artwork with ms. "Be aware of the reading level for the intended audience."
Recent Nonfiction Titles: *Visicalc for Apple II*; *Advanced Visicalc for IBM PC*, by Desautels; *Introduction to Graphics for IBM PC*, *Data File Management for IBM PC*, *User's Guide with Applications for IBM PC* by Grillo/Robertson; *Karate* by Kim/Leland; *Self-Defense for Women* by Monkerud/Heiny; *Weight Training* by Rasch; *Swimming* by Vickers/Vincent; *Learning to Use Pocket Computers*, *Programs for the Pocket Computer* by Zimmerman/Conrad.
Tips: Queries/mss may be routed to other editors in the publishing group.

‡*BRUNSWICK PUBLISHING CO., Box 555, Lawrenceville VA 23868. (804)848-3865. Publisher: Marianne S. Raymond. Publishes hardcover originals, trade and mass market paperback originals. Averages 5-6 titles/year. Subsidy publishes 80% of books based on "author-publisher dialogue." Payment is based on "individual contracts according to work." Photocopied submissions OK. SAE. Reports in 2 weeks on queries; 3 weeks on mss. Book catalog for business size SAE.
Nonfiction: Biography, coffee table book, cookbook, how-to, humor, illustrated book, juvenile, reference, self-help, technical and textbook. Subjects include Americana, animals, business and economics, cooking and foods, health, history, hobbies, music, nature, philosophy, politics, psychology, religion, sociology, travel, biography, black experience and ethnic experience. "Not limited to any particular subject, but interested in Third World authors and subjects to continue Third World Monograph series." Query or submit outline/synopsis and sample chapters. Looks for "quality, originality, utility."
Recent Nonfiction Titles: *Dictionary of Politics*, by Walter J. Raymond, S.J.D., Ph.D. (reference); *Philosophy of Education and Third World Perspective*, by Festus C. Okafor, Ph.D. (textbook); and *The Nkrumah Regime*, by Charles Jarmon, Ph.D. (monograph).
Fiction: "Will consider fiction mainly on subsidy basis—not limited to special topics." Adventure, erotica, ethnic, historical, humor, mainstream and romance. Query or submit outline/synopsis and sample chapters.
Poetry: "Poetry published only on subsidy basis as of now—not limited to any particular subject."
Recent Poetry Titles: *The Footprints of Jesus*, by Isabel H. Lancaster (religious).
Tips: "Try to be very original in material or presentation. Offer your readers excellent advice (how-to, self-help). Don't take one person's opinion of what constitutes a 'good' or 'bad' manuscript as final."

BUCKNELL UNIVERSITY PRESS, Lewisburg PA 17837. (717)524-3674. Subsidiary of Associated University Presses. Director: Mills F. Edgerton, Jr. Publishes hardcover originals. Averages 18-20 titles/year. Pays royalty. Photocopied submissions OK. Reports in 2-4 weeks on queries; 3-6 months on mss. Book catalog free on request.
Nonfiction: Scholarly art, history, music, philosophy, politics, psychology, religion, sociology. "In all fields,

our criterion is scholarly presentation; mss must be addressed toward the scholarly community." Query.
Recent Nonfiction Titles: *New Americans: The Westerner and the Modern Experience in the American Novel*,
by Glen A. Love; *Milton and the Middle Ages*, ed. by John Mulryan; *Laud's Laboratory: The Diocese of Bath
and Wells in the Early Seventeenth Century*, by Margaret Stieg.

BYLS PRESS, Department of Bet Yoatz Library Services, 6247 N. Francisco Ave., Chicago IL 60659.
(312)262-8959. President: Daniel D. Stuhlman. Publishes trade paperback originals. Averages 3 titles/year.
Pays 7½-15% on wholesale price; no advance. Photocopied submissions OK. Computer printout submissions
OK; diskettes must be North Star 5¼" SD. SASE. Reports in 1 week on queries; reporting time on mss "depends on material." Free book catalog.
Nonfiction: How-to (for teachers); and juvenile. Subjects include baking and religion ("stories aimed at children for Jewish holidays"). "We're looking for children's books for Jewish holidays that can be made into
computer personalized books. In particular we need books for Sukkot, Shabbat, and Purim. We also need titles
for our teacher education series." Query; "no agents, authors only. Do not submit ideas without examining our
books and ask yourself if a book idea fits what we are looking for."
Recent Nonfiction Titles: *Library of Congress Subject Headings for Judaica*; *My Own Hanukah Story*, by D.
Stuhlman (children's); and *My Own Pesah Story*, by D. Stuhlman (children's).
Fiction: Religious (stories for Jewish children). No expository fiction. "All unsolicited mss are returned unopened."

CALIFORNIA INSTITUTE OF PUBLIC AFFAIRS, Box 10, Claremont CA 91711. (714)624-5212. President/Director: T.C. Trzyna. Assistant: Lizanne Fleming. Publishes paperback originals. Averages 6-8 titles/
year. Negotiates royalties and outright purchases; also for some types of mss authors are not paid. Rarely offers
advance. Simultaneous and photocopied submissions OK. SASE. Reports in 3 weeks. Free book catalog.
Nonfiction: "The California Institute of Public Affairs is a research foundation affiliated with The Claremont
Colleges. Most of our books are written by our staff; however, we are open to publishing material by other writers that fits into our program and several titles have come to us 'over the transom.' Our list is very specialized.
We do not want to see mss that do not fit exactly into our very specialized fields of interest and format. We publish in two fairly narrow fields and all submissions must fit into one of them: (1) California reference books,
that is, either directories or bibliographies relating to California; and (2) reference books on global environmental and natural resource problems. Several titles have been co-published with such houses as Marquis
Who's Who, Inc. and the Sierra Club. A prospective author should request and examine our list before submitting an idea or outline." Query or submit outline/synopsis and sample chapters (biographic information useful).
Recent Nonfiction Titles: *The United States and the Global Environment: A Guide to American Organizations*, by staff (information guide); *California Museum Directory*, by Kimberly Mueller (guidebook); *World
Directory of Environmental Organizations*, by Trzyna et al. (information guide).

CAMARO PUBLISHING CO., Box 90430, Los Angeles CA 90009. (213)837-7500. Editor-in-Chief: Garth
W. Bishop. Publishes hardcover and paperback originals. Pays royalty on wholesale price. "Every contract is
different. Many books are bought outright." Published 14 titles last year. Query. SASE.
Nonfiction: Books on travel, food, wine, health and success.
Recent Nonfiction Title: *Old California Almanac of Fairs & Festivals*.

CAMBRIDGE BOOK COMPANY, 888 7th Ave., New York NY 10106. (212)957-5300. Vice President Editorial: Brian Schenk. Publishes paperback originals in adult education. Averages 25 titles/year. Pays usually
flat fee only; occasionally pays 6% royalty on institutional net price; offers small advance. Photocopied submissions OK. Computer printout submissions OK. SASE. Reports in 1 month. Free book catalog.
Nonfiction: Basic skills—adult education only—emphasizing alternative programs. Vocational, pre-GED,
ESL. Submit prospectus and sample lesson only. No phone calls. Looks for "marketability (how broad and
how stable the market is for the program); understanding of adult students (learning styles and needs); thoroughness of design of program (will it require substantial editing? How does the design relate to current educational practice); and cost factors, possible production problems."
Recent Nonfiction Titles: Best known for GED preparation material. Recently published *English Spoken
Here* (ESL program); and *Living in the Reader's World* (ABE reading program).

CAMBRIDGE UNIVERSITY PRESS, 32 E. 57th St., New York NY 10022. Editorial Director: Colin Day.
Publishes hardcover and paperback originals. Publishes 500 titles/year. Pays 10% royalty on retail price; 6% on
paperbacks; no advance. Query. Computer printout and disk submissions OK. Reports in 2 weeks to 6 months.
SASE.
Nonfiction and Textbooks: Anthropology, archeology, economics, life sciences, mathematics, psychology,
upper-level textbooks, academic trade, scholarly monographs, biography, history, music. Looking for academic excellence in all work submitted. Department Editors: Elizabeth Maguire (humanities), Susan Milmoe

(psychology), Frank Smith (history, political science), David Tranah (mathematics, physical sciences), Richard Ziemacki (history of science, life sciences), Susan Allen-Mills (social anthropology, sociology), Ellen Shaw (English as second language).
Recent Nonfiction Title: *Children's Early Thought*.

CAMELOT BOOKS, Children's Book Imprint of Avon Books, a division of the Hearst Corp., 959 8th Ave., New York NY 10019. (212)262-7454. Editorial Director: Jean Feiwel. Publishes paperback or inals (25%) and reprints (75%). Averages 48 titles/year. Pays 6-10% royalty on retail price; minimum ad' ice $1,500. Query or submit outline/synopsis and 6 sample chapters. Simultaneous and photocopied sut ssions OK. Computer printout submissions OK. SASE. Reports in 8 weeks. Free book catalog.
Nonfiction: Animals, health, history, how-to, humor, and self-help.
Recent Nonfiction Titles: *Basic Fun: Computer Games, Puzzles & Problems Children Can W* , by Susan Lipscomb, Margaret Ann Zuanich; *PUNCH!* by R.R. Knudson.
Fiction: Adventure, fantasy, humor, mainstream, mystery, science fiction, picture books an uspense.
Recent Fiction Titles: *Don't Make Me Smile*, by Barbara Park; *The Westing Game*, by Ellen iskin; *Good Work, Amelia Bedelia*, by Peggy Parish; and *Bunnicula*, by James and Deborah Howe.
Tips: Queries/mss may be routed to other editors in the publishing group.

CAPRA PRESS, Box 2068, Santa Barbara CA 93120. (805)966-4590. Editor-in-Chief loel Young. Publishes hardcover and paperback originals. Specializes in documentary lifestyle books, and t raphies (no fiction). Pays 8% royalty on wholesale price; advance averages $1,000. Averages 14 titles/y State availability of photos and/or illustrations to accompany ms. Simultaneous submissions OK "if we told where else it has been sent." Reports in 1 month. Looks for "coherent and original ideas, good writin with California origination, yet having national appeal." SASE. Book catalog for SASE.
Nonfiction: Publishes western contemporary nonfiction (30,000 words); biography (30,000 v ls); how-to; and nature books "for the more serious reader with an exploring mind." Submit outline/synor and sample chapters.
Recent Nonfiction Titles: *Hot Springs of the Southwest*, by Jason Loam; *Black Sun*, by Edw Abbey; *Los Angeles: The Enormous Village*, by John Weaver (popular history); *The Great Notorious Salo* *of San Francisco*, by Jane Chamberlin.

*ARISTIDE D. CARATZAS, PUBLISHER, Box 210, 481 Main St., New Rochelle NY 1 . (914)632-8487. Managing Director: Marybeth Sollins. Publishes 80% hardcover and paperback original d 20% d-cover and paperback reprints. Averages 20 titles/year. Subsidy publishes 5% of books sed on ms "commercially marginal, though of importance to a particular field." Pays 10% royalty. Phot pied submissions OK. Computer printout submissions OK; disk submissions OK "if compatible with equipment." SASE. Reports in 3 months. Free book catalog on request.
Nonfiction: Subjects include art, history, philosophy, photography, politics, religion and tra . Query first, or submit outline/synopsis and 2-3 sample chapters. Accepts artwork/photos. All unsolicited s are returned unopened; "we cannot be responsible for lost unsolicited mss." Looks for "suitability with publications program; credentials of the author; and quality and economic justification of the work." Ac ts nonfiction translations from German, French, Italian and modern Greek.
Recent Nonfiction Title: *The Rediscovery of Greece*, by F. M. Tsigakou.

CAREER PUBLISHING, INC., 931 N. Main St., Box 5486, Orange CA 92667. (714)99 8471. Contact: Senior Editor. Publishes paperback originals. Averages 6-23 titles/year. Pays 10% royalty on holesale price; no advance. Simultaneous (if so informed with names of others to whom submissions have be n sent) and photocopied submissions OK. Reports in 2 months. SASE. Book catalog 25¢.
Nonfiction: Guidance material, home economics, word processing, allied health, diction ies, etc. "Textbooks should provide core upon which class curriculum can be based: textbook, workbook c kit with 'hands-on' activities and exercises, and teacher's guide. Should incorporate modern and ef ective teaching techniques. Should lead to a job objective. We also publish support materials for existing cou es, and are open to unique, marketable ideas with schools in mind. Reading level should be controlled appro riately—usually 8th-9th grade equivalent for vocational school and community college level courses. Any sign of sexism or racism will disqualify the work. No career awareness masquerading as career training." Submit outline/synopsis and 2 sample chapters and table of contents or complete ms.
Recent Nonfiction Titles: *Trucking: A Truck Driver's Training Handbook Course*, by Ken Gilliland and J. Millard; *Dictation With Foreign Accents*, by L. Rowe; *Medical Office Management*, by G.E. Bonito; *Microcomputer Courseware* with Educational Software, by Peter Braun Ph.D.
Tips: "Authors should be aware of vocational/career areas with inadequate or no training textbooks, submit ideas and samples to fill the gap."

CAROLINA BIOLOGICAL SUPPLY CO., 2700 York Rd., Burlington NC 27215. (919)584-0381. Head, Scientific Publications: Dr. Phillip L. Owens. Publishes paperback originals. Averages 15 titles/year. Pays 10% royalty on sales. Simultaneous and photocopied submissions OK. No computer printout or disk submissions. SASE. Reports in 2 weeks on queries.
Nonfiction: Self-help, technical, textbook on animals, health, nature, biology, science. "Will consider short (10,000 words) mss of general interest to high school and college students on health, computers, biology, physics, astronomy, microscopes, etc. Longer mss less favored but will be considered." Query first. Accepts photos/artwork with ms.
Recent Nonfiction Titles: *Test-tube Babies*, by R.G. Edwards (monograph); *Electron Microscopy*, by Friedrich Kopp (monograph); *Dinosaurs*, by J.H. Ostrom (monograph); *What About Alcohol*, by Alex and Jane Comfort.

CAROLRHODA BOOKS, INC., 241 1st Ave. N., Minneapolis MN 55401. (612)332-3345. Editor: Susan Pearson. Publishes hardcover originals. Averages 30-40 titles/year. Pays negotiable royalty; buys new authors' mss outright. Simultaneous and photocopied submissions OK. SASE. Reports in 3 months. Book catalog for 9x12 SAE and 88¢ postage.
Nonfiction: Juvenile (easy to read, grades 1-2) on early American history. Accepts translations. Submit complete ms.
Recent Nonfiction Titles: *Cornstalks & Cannonballs*, by Barbara Mitchell (history for young readers).
Fiction: Humor, mystery, science fiction. "Light fiction for 7-11 year olds." Submit outline/synopsis and 2 sample chapters.
Recent Fiction Titles: *A Matter of Pride*, by Emily Crofford; *Harriet's Recital*, by Nancy Carlson; and *Calamity Kate*, by Terry Deary.

CARSTENS PUBLICATIONS, INC., Hobby Book Division, Box 700, Newton NJ 07860. (201)383-3355. Publisher: Harold H. Carstens. Publishes paperback originals. Averages 5 titles/year. Pays 10% royalty on retail price; offers average advance. SASE. Book catalog for SASE.
Nonfiction: Model railroading, toy trains, model aviation, railroads and model hobbies. "We have scheduled or planned titles on several railroads as well as model railroad and model airplane books. Authors must know their field intimately since our readers are active modelers. Our railroad books presently are primarily photographic essays on specific railroads. Writers cannot write about somebody else's hobby with authority. If they do, we can't use them." Query.
Recent Nonfiction Titles: *The Central Vermont Railway*, by Beaudette; *Colorado Memories of the NG Circle*, by Krause and Grenard; and *Design Handbook for Model RR*, by Paul Mallery.

CATHOLIC TRUTH SOCIETY, 38/40 Eccleston Square, London, England SW1V 1PD. (01)834-4392. Editorial Director: David Murphy. Publishes hardcover and paperback originals (70%) and reprints (30%). Averages 80 titles/year. Pays in outright purchase of $50-400; no advance. Simultaneous and photocopied submissions OK. Computer printout submissions OK. Reports in 4 weeks. SASE. Free book catalog.
Nonfiction: Books dealing with how to solve problems in personal relationships, parenthood, teen-age, widowhood, sickness and death, especially drawing on Christian and Catholic tradition for inspiration; simple accounts of points of interest in Catholic faith, for non-Catholic readership; and books of prayer and devotion. Accepts artwork/photos. Query, submit outline/synopsis and sample chapter, or submit complete ms.
Recent Nonfiction Titles: *Disabled from Birth—What Parents Should Know*, by Prof. R.B. Zachary; *Brandt: the Christian Connection*, by Rev. Patrick O'Mahony; *Study Guide to "The Final Report" of the Anglican/Roman Catholic International Commission*, by the English Anglican/Roman Catholic Committee.

CATHOLIC UNIVERSITY OF AMERICA PRESS, 620 Michigan Ave. NE, Washington DC 20064. (202)635-5052. Director: Dr. David J. McGonagle. Manager: Miss Marian E. Goode. Averages 5-10 titles/year. Pays 10% royalty on wholesale or retail price. Query with sample chapter plus outline of entire work, along with curriculum vita and list of previous publications. Reports in 2 months. SASE.
Nonfiction: Publishes history, biography, languages and literature, philosophy, religion, church-state relations, social studies. No doctoral dissertations. Length: 200,000-500,000 words.
Recent Nonfiction Titles: *The Three-Personed God: The Trinity as a Mystery of Salvation*, by William J. Hill; *Ethica Thomistica*, by Ralph McInerny; *Origen: Homilies on Genesis and Exodus*, translated by Ronald Heine; and *The Presence of Stoicism in Medieval Thought*, by Gerard Verbeke.

‡THE CAXTON PRINTERS, LTD., 312 Main St., Box 700, Caldwell ID 83605. (208)459-7421. Vice President: Gordon Gipson. Publishes hardcover and trade paperback originals. Publishes 6-12 titles/year. Audience includes Westerners, students, historians and researchers. Pays royalty; average advance $500-8,000. Simultaneous and photocopied submissions OK. SASE. Reports in 2 weeks on queries; 8 weeks on mss. Free book catalog.

Nonfiction: "Coffee table," Americana and Western Americana. "We need good Western Americana, preferably copiously illustrated with unpublished photos." Query.

Recent Nonfiction Titles: *Grand Teton National Park—A Guide and Reference Book*, by Cliff McAdams; *Railroads Through the Coeur D' Alenes*, by John V. Wood; *The John Muir Trail*, by Don and Roberta Lowe.

CBI PUBLISHING CO., INC., 51 Sleeper St., Boston MA 02210. (617)426-2224. President: Mike A. Tucker. Senior Editor, Foodservice: Phil Mason. Senior Editor, Business: George Abbott. Publishes hardcover and paperback originals. Averages 45-50 titles/year. Pays 10-15% royalty on net sale. Simultaneous and photocopied submissions OK. SASE. Reports in 2 weeks. Free book catalog.
Nonfiction: Business professional, cookbooks/cooking, healthcare, small business, reference, computer science, textbooks, and travel. "We would like to see more professional and reference in foodservice, small business management, management training, consumer cookbooks, health care planning and management, textbooks in hospitality, and business computer service." Submit outline/synopsis and sample chapters.
Recent Nonfiction Titles: *The Book of Great Hors D' Oeuvre*, by Terence Janericco; *Microprocessors for Managers* (a decision makers guide), by Ron Krutz; and *Survival Guide to Computer Systems*, by Bill Perry (general management).

‡CEDARSHOUSE PRESS, 406 W. 28th St., Bryan TX 77801. (713)822-5615. Editor: Paul Christensen. Publishes hardcover originals and trade paperback reprints. Averages 4-8 titles/year. Pays 5-8% royalty on retail price. Photocopied submissions OK. No computer printout or disk submissions. SASE. Reports in 6 weeks on queries; 4 months on mss.
Nonfiction: Biography, reference, belles lettres on Americana, history, philosophy, politics, travel. "Studie of neglected American authors, fiction, poetry, nonfiction; controversial historical subjects—race relatic , leftist political systems in US, generation studies of Americans in 20th century, commentary on contempor y society, etc." Publishes for Southwestern readers interested in the lore and mythology of the region; reade of innovative and experimental fiction and verse; historical and critical writing appealing to writers, soc observers, general interest audiences." No pop studies, slick prose, magazine writing, superficial s eys, trendy concepts, coffee table book writing, photo books, private journals and survival memoirs, etc. Q ry or submit outline/synopsis and 3 sample chapters.
Recent Nonfiction Titles: *A Bibliography of Texas Poets 1945-1982*, by S. Turner; *Essays in Postm ernism*, edited by P. Christensen (criticism); and *Profile: J.H. Griffin*, by R. Bonazzi (biography).
Fiction: "Very low priority; no particular needs at this time except for distinguished mss of e rimental prose." No conventional fiction of any type. Query.
Poetry: "Long poems of an experimental attitude; regional poetry stressing unique perception of nd and people; Southwestern topics; books tightly ordered and innovative." Accepts poetry translations fr French and Spanish. No conventional lyrics, collections of verse, theme books, confessional writing, m oirs, travelogues, scenic poems, anthologies. Submit 6-10 samples.
Recent Poetry Titles: *Old and Lost Rivers* and *The Vectory*, by Christensen (lyric poetry); d *Osiris at the Roller Derby*, by J. Simmons (lyric sequence).
Tips: Queries/mss may be routed to other editors in the publishing group.

CELESTIAL ARTS, Box 7327, Berkeley CA 94707. (415)524-1801. Editorial Di r: George Young. Publishes paperback originals, adult and children's books. Publishes 20 titles/year. S taneous and photocopied submissions OK. Computer printout submissions OK; prefers letter quality t t matrix. SASE. Reports in 3 months. Book catalog for $1.
Nonfiction: Celestial Arts publishes biography, cookbooks/cooking, health, hum psychology, recreation and self-help. No poetry. "Submit 2-3 sample chapters and outline; no original c y. If return requested, include postage."
Recent Nonfiction Titles: *Love Is Letting Go of Fear*, by Jerry Jampolsky; *The ly Diet There Is*, by Sondra Ray; and *Remember the Secret*, by Elisabeth Kubler-Ross.

CENTER FOR NONPROFIT ORGANIZATIONS, INC., 203 W. 25th St., 3rd Fl., New York NY 10001. (212)989-9026. Vice President: Robert Hess. SASE. Reports in 2 weeks "with SASE." Book catalog for SAE and 1 first class stamp. Send samples of published articles and/or research relating to associations and organizations such as community groups, co-ops, arts, youth, health, social service and education. Writers should also send an outline of new article ideas in these areas. The Center will respond detailing needs for future publications and make arrangements for assignments.
Nonfiction: How-to, reference and self-help. Subjects include business and economics, hobbies, nonprofit organizations, tax exemption, management and fundraising. "We seek articles for periodicals relating to hobby-into-career, fundraising, nonprofit organizations, community development, arts management, volunteers, board development, etc." Interested in books on single people. Submit outline/synopsis and sample chapters.
Recent Nonfiction Title: *Contacts*, by H. Fischer (individual management).

*CHAMPION ATHLETE PUBLISHING COMPANY, Box 2936, Richmond VA 23235. Editor: Dr. George B. Dintiman. Publishes hardcover and paperback originals. Averages 3 titles/year. Pays 15% royalty on wholesale or retail price. Simultaneous and photocopied submissions OK. SASE. Reports in 4 weeks. Brochure for $1.

Nonfiction: Health, sports and textbooks (physical education/athletics). Exercise texts for the college class market and other texts targeted for a specific course. Accepts nonfiction translations from Spanish. Books are published for the participant and not the coach. "We are only interested in health and sports areas or texts designed for physical education service or major classes." Submit outline/synopsis and 1 sample chapter or submit complete ms.

Recent Nonfiction Titles: *Doctor Tennis*, by J. Myers (tennis conditioning and injury prevention guide); *How to Run Faster*, by G. Dintiman; and *P.E. Activities Manual*, by Barrow, et al.

CHARTER BOOKS, The Berkley Publishing Group, 200 Madison Ave., New York NY 10016. (212)686-9820. Publishes paperback originals and reprints (50%). Publishes over 100 titles/year.

Nonfiction: General nonfiction, business. No unsolicited mss accepted.

Fiction: General fiction, suspense, adventure, espionage, epic/saga, westerns, gothics, mysteries, romances. No short stories or novellas. No unsolicited mss accepted.

Recent Fiction Titles: *The Hollow Men*, by Sean Flannery; and *The Patriarch*, by Chaim Bermant.

THE CHATHAM PRESS, a subsidiary of Devin-Adair Publishers, 143 Sound Beach Ave., Old Greenwich CT 06870. Publishes hardcover and paperback originals, reprints, and anthologies. "Standard book contract does not always apply if the book is heavily illustrated. Average advance is low." Averages 14 titles/year. Free book catalog. Query with outline and 3 sample chapters. Computer printout and disk submissions OK. Reports in 2 weeks. SASE.

Nonfiction: Publishes mostly "regional history and natural history, involving mainly Northeast Seaboard and the Carolinas, mostly illustrated, with emphasis on conservation and outdoor recreation." Accepts artwork/photos. Accepts nonfiction translations from French and German.

Recent Nonfiction Titles: *Striped Bass and Other Cape Cod Fish* (updated); *A Beachcomber's Guidebook*; *Strangers at the Door: Ellis Island and Castle Gardens* (reprint); *A Guide to the Outer Banks*; *The Connecticut Yankee Almanac*.

CHELSEA HOUSE, 133 Christopher St., New York NY 10014. (212)924-6414. Subsidiaries include Belvedere (reprints). Senior Editor: Joy Johannessen. Publishes originals (50%) and trade paperback reprints (50%). Averages 10-12 titles/year. Pays 6% minimum royalty. SASE. Reports in 6 weeks. Book catalog for business size SAE and 1 first class stamp.

Nonfiction: Biography, cookbook, illustrated book, reference and self-help. Subjects include Americana ("a biggie"), animals, art, business and economics, cooking and foods, health, history, philosophy, politics, psychology, recreation, religion, sociology, sports. Submit outline/synopsis and sample chapters.

Recent Nonfiction Titles: *The Rage to Convince*, by Marcel Bleustein-Blanchet; *The Trouble With Advertising*, by John O'Toole; and *Mae West Autobiography*.

Fiction: "Open to any new ideas." Submit outline/synopsis and sample chapters.

Recent Fiction Title: *Roomshot*, by Ted Perry.

Tips: "We would like to reprint books of enduring interest with updated introductions by current experts."

CHICAGO REVIEW PRESS, 213 W. Institute Place, Chicago IL 60610. (312)337-0747. Editor: Linda Matthews. Publishes hardcover and trade paperback originals. Averages 12 titles/year. Pays 7-15% royalty on retail price; offers average $2,000 advance. Simultaneous and photocopied submissions OK. Letter-quality computer printout submissions OK. Interested in disk submissions, "but want to discuss format with author." SASE. Reports in 3 weeks on queries; 2 months on mss. Free book catalog.

Nonfiction: Cookbook, how-to, reference, self-help and guidebooks. Subjects include cooking and foods, health, hobbies, recreation, sports and travel. "We especially need Chicago guidebooks, national-interest, popular how-to or self-help books, career guides, books on writing, and trendy nonfiction with strong subrights possibilities." Query or submit outline/synopsis and 2-3 sample chapters. Looks for "clear thinking, lively writing, salable idea."

Recent Nonfiction Titles: *Whatever Happened to the Quiz Kids?*, by Ruth Duskin Feldman (popular sociology); *Test for Success*, by Dr. Harry E. Gunn (popular psychology); *Crime Movie Quiz Book*, by Jay Robert Nash (quizzes and love for movie buffs).

The double dagger (‡) before a listing indicates that the listing is new in this edition. New markets are often the most receptive to freelance contributions.

CHILDRENS PRESS, 1224 W. Van Buren St., Chicago IL 60607. (312)666-4200. Editorial Director: Fran Dyra. Pays in outright purchase or offers small advance against royalty. Averages 80 titles/year. Reports in 12 weeks. SASE. Simultaneous submissions OK. Computer printout submissions OK.

Juveniles: For supplementary use in elementary and secondary schools; picture books for early childhood and beginning readers; high-interest, easy reading material. Specific categories include social studies and science. Length: 50-10,000 words. For picture books, needs are very broad. They should be geared from preschool to grade 3. "We have a strong tendency to publish books in series. Odds are against a single book that couldn't, if sales warrant, develop into a series." Length: 50-1,000 words. Send outline with 1 sample chapter; complete ms for picture books. Accepts translations. Accepts artwork and photos, "but best to submit ms first." Do not send finished artwork with ms.

Recent Nonfiction Titles: *World of Racing Series* (7 titles); *True Book Series* (80 titles); *World at War* (10 titles); and *Enchantment of the World Series* (8 titles).

Fiction: For supplementary use in elementary and secondary schools. Length: 50-10,000 words. Picture books from preschool to grade 3. Length: 50-1,000 words. Send outline with sample chapters; complete ms for picture books. Do not send finished artwork with ms.

Tips: Submissions often "lack originality. Too often authors talk 'down' to young readers. First it must be a good story, then it can have an educational or moral point. We're looking for writers in the science and technology areas."

CHILTON BOOK CO., Chilton Way, Radnor PA 19089. Editorial Director: Alan F. Turner. Publishes hardcover and trade paperback originals. Publishes 90 titles/year. Pays royalty; average advance. Simultaneous and photocopied submissions OK. Computer printouts OK. SASE. Reports in 3 weeks.

Nonfiction: Business/economics, computers, crafts, how-to and technical. "We only want to see any manuscripts with informational value." Query or submit outline/synopsis and 2-3 sample chapters.

Recent Nonfiction Titles: *The Small Business Computer Handbook*; *How To Work In Stained Glass*, 2nd ed.; *Irma's Gardening Hints*; *The Book of Sampler Quilts*.

CHINA BOOKS, 2929 24th St., San Francisco CA 94110. (415)282-2994. Editorial Director: Foster Stockwall. Publishes trade paperback originals. Averages 6 titles/year. Pays average 8% royalty; offers negotiable advance. Simultaneous and photocopied submissions OK. SASE. Reports in 2 weeks. Book catalog $1.

Nonfiction: Biography, cookbook, illustrated book, reference on Chinese history, travel, and things related to the People's Republic of China. Accepts artwork/photos. "Books about China or things Chinese that are new or unusual." Query. Accepts Chinese translations.

Recent Nonfiction Titles: *Chinese Paper Cuts*, by Florence Temko; *Bridge to China*, by Donald Gledhill (travel); and *Milton & Matilda*, by Nancy Besst (juvenile).

Tips: Queries/mss may be routed to other editors in the publishing group.

CHOSEN BOOKS, Lincoln VA 22078. (703)338-4131. Associate Publisher: Leonard E. LeSourd. Hardcover and paperback originals. Averages 12 titles/year. Computer printouts in Courier 72, 10 pitch OK; prefers letter quality to dot matrix. Free book catalog for SASE.

Religion: Seeks out teaching and personal experience books of Christian content with high quality. Length: 40,000-60,000 words. Query. Submit 1-2 page synopsis.

Recent Nonfiction Titles: *Story Bible*, by Catherine Marshall; *Facets of the Faith*, by Everett L. Fullam; *The Last Word on the Middle East*, by Derek Prince.

Tips: "Write a book that grips the reader in the first pages and then holds him through all chapters. Give the reader a 'you are there feeling.' "

CHRISTIAN CLASSICS, Box 30, Westminster MD 21157. (301)848-3065. Director: John J. McHale. Publishes hardcover originals (5%), and hardcover reprints (95%). Averages 10 titles/year. Pays 10% royalty; buys some mss outright for $500-2,000. Photocopied submissions OK. SASE. Reports in 2 months. Free book catalog.

Nonfiction: Subjects include psychology and religion. "We're looking for general books of religious interest." Query.

Recent Nonfiction Titles: *Summa Theologica*, by St. Thomas Aquinas (complete English edition in 5 volumes); *Lives of the Saints*, by Alban Butler (religious); and *The Angels and Their Mission*, by Jean Danielou, S.J. (religious).

Tips: "Think about mass market paperback possibilities."

CHRONICLE BOOKS, 870 Market St., San Francisco CA 94102. Editorial Director: Larry L. Smith. Publishes hardcover and paperback originals. Publishes 25 titles annually. Pays 6-10% royalty on retail price; negotiates advance. Simultaneous and photocopied submissions OK. Computer printout submissions OK. SASE. Reports in 1 month.

Nonfiction: West Coast regional and recreational guidebooks; West Coast regional histories; art and architec-

ture; and natural history. No fiction, science fiction, drama or poetry. "Our readers are literate, sophisticated and interested in the world around them. Writers should, for this audience, shun tired topics and stay somewhat future-oriented." Query or submit outline/synopsis and 2 sample chapters. Accepts photos/artwork.
Recent Nonfiction Titles: *50 West Coast Artists*; *Ancient Cities of the Southwest*; and *Mark Twain in California*.

CITADEL PRESS, 120 Enterprise Ave., Secaucus NJ 07094. (212)736-0007. Editorial Director: Allan J. Wilson. Publishes hardcover originals and paperback reprints. Pays 10% royalty on hardcover, 5-7% on paperback; offers average $2,000 advance. Simultaneous and photocopied submissions OK. No computer printout or disk submissions. Reports in 2 months. SASE.
Nonfiction: Biography, film, psychology, humor and history. Also seeks "off-beat material," but no "poetry, religion, politics." Accepts nonfiction and fiction translations. Query. Accepts outline/synopsis and 3 sample chapters.
Recent Nonfiction Titles: *Moe Howard and the Three Stooges*, by M. Howard (filmography); *The Great American Amusement Parks*, by G. Kyriazi (Americana); and *Documentary History of the Negro People in the U.S.* , by H. Aptheker (history).

CLARION BOOKS, Ticknor & Fields: a Houghton Mifflin Company. 52 Vanderbilt Ave., New York NY 10017. Editor and Publisher: James C. Giblin. Senior Editor for Nonfiction: Ann Troy. Publishes hardcover originals. Averages 25-28 titles/year. Pays 5-10% royalty on retail price; $1,000-2,000 advance, depending on whether project is a picture book or a longer work for older children. Photocopied submissions OK. Computer printout submissions OK; prefers letter quality to dot matrix. No multiple submissions. SASE. Reports in 6-8 weeks. Free book catalog.
Nonfiction: Americana, biography, hi-los, holiday, humor, nature,photo essays and word play. Prefers books for younger children. Accepts artwork/photos. Query.
Recent Nonfiction Titles: *Junk Food, Fast Food, Health Food*, by Lila Perl (nutrition); *Make Noise, Make Merry*, by Miriam Chaikin (Purim); *What Has Ten Legs and Eats Corn Flakes?*, by Ron Roy (pet care).
Fiction: Adventure, fantasy, humor, mystery, science fiction and suspense. "We would like to see more humorous contemporary stories that young people of 8-12 or 10-14 can identify with readily." Accepts fiction translations. Query on ms of more than 50 pages. Looks for "freshness, enthusiasm—in short, life" (fiction and nonfiction).
Recent Fiction Titles: *I'll Always Remember You . . . Maybe*, by Stella Pevsner (teenage story); *The Time of the Witch*, by Mary Downing Hahn (contemporary drama); and *The Tempering*, by Gloria Skurzynski (historical novel).

*ARTHUR H. CLARK CO., Box 230, Glendale CA 92109. (213)245-9119. Editorial Director: Robert A. Clark. Publishes hardcover originals. Averages 8 titles/year. Subsidy publishes 10% of books based on whether they are "high-risk sales." Pays 10% minimum royalty on wholesale prices. Photocopied submissions OK. Computer printout submissions OK; prefers letter quality to dot matrix. SASE. Reports in 1 week on queries; 2 months on mss. Free book catalog.
Nonfiction: Biography, reference and historical nonfiction. Subjects include Americana and history. "We're looking for documentary source material in western American history." Query or submit outline/synopsis and 3 sample chapters. Looks for "content, form, style."
Recent Nonfiction Titles: *Covered Wagon Women* (10 vol. series), edited by Kenneth L. Holmes; *The Betrayal of Liliuokalani*, by Helena G. Allen; and *The Custer Trail*, by John Carroll.

T&T CLARK LTD., 36 George St., Edinburgh Scotland EH2 2LQ. (031)225-4703. Editorial Director: Geoffrey Green. Publishes hardcover and paperback originals (25%) and reprints (75%). Averages 50 titles/year. Pays 5-10% royalty based on wholesale or retail price. May offer 250 pounds advance. Simultaneous and photocopied submissions OK. Computer printout and disk submissions OK. SASE. Reports in 4 weeks. Free book catalog.
Nonfiction: Religion; philosophy; and history. Accepts translations. Top level academic. Query first.
Recent Nonfiction Titles: *A History of Christian Doctrine*, by H. Cunliffe-Jones (religion/theology/history student textbook); *Great Themes of the New Testament*, by W. Barclay (popular commentary); and *Ethics*, by Karl Barth (theology).

CLARKE, IRWIN & CO., LTD., 791 St. Clair Ave., W., Toronto, Ontario, Canada M6C 1B8. Publishes hardcover and paperback originals (90%) and reprints (10%). Specializes in Canadian subjects. Pays variable royalty, minimum of 10%. Publishes about 25 titles a year. Submit outline/synopsis and sample chapters or complete ms. Must be typed double-spaced. "Don't send only copy." Send samples of prints for illustration. Photocopied submissions OK. Reports in 2 months. SASE.
Nonfiction: Publishes juveniles and books on Canadiana, art, arts and sciences, biography, history, how-to, nature, politics, recreation, sports, textbooks, travel.

Recent Nonfiction Titles: *Discovering Your Scottish Roots*, by Alwyn James; *Mad About Muffins*, by Angela Clubb.
Fiction: Publishes juveniles, adventure, historical, humorous, and mainstream books.
Recent Fiction Titles: *Murder on Location*, by Howard Engel; *Disneyland Hostage*, by Eric Wilson.

‡*CLCB PRESS, Subsidiary of CLCBI International, 5901 Plainfield Dr., Charlotte NC 28215. (704)536-2662. President: Mr. Rozier Sinclair. Publishes hardcover, trade paperback and mass market paperback originals and hardcover, trade paperback, and mass market paperback reprints. Averages 8-12 titles/year. Subsidy publishes 50% of books. Pays variable royalty or makes outright purchase of 10-25¢/word. Reports in 3 days on queries; 1 month on mss. Imprints include Rainbow-Unicorn Press.
Nonfiction: Biography, "coffee table" book, cookbook, how-to, humor, illustrated book, juvenile, reference, self-help, technical and textbook. Subjects include Americana, animals, art, business and economics, cooking and foods, health, history, hobbies, music, nature, philosophy, photography, politics, psychology, recreation, religion, sociology, sports and travel. Particularly interested in travel and photography works. Query with outline/synopsis and sample chapters.
Fiction: Adventure, confession, ethnic, experimental, fantasy, gothic, historical, humor, mainstream, mystery, religious, romance and science fiction. Submit outline/synopsis and sample chapters.
Poetry: Submit 12 samples.

CLIFFS NOTES, INC., Box 80728, Lincoln NE 68501. (402)477-6971. Editor: Michele Spence. Publishes trade paperback originals. Averages 10 titles/year. Pays royalty on wholesale price. Buys some mss outright; "full payment on acceptance of ms." SASE. Reports in 1 month. Free book catalog.
Nonfiction: Self-help, textbook. "We publish self-help study aids directed to junior high through graduate school audience. Publications include *Cliffs Notes*, *Cliffs Test Preparation Guides*, *Cliffs Speed and Hearing Series*, and other study guides. Most authors are experienced teachers, usually with advanced degrees. Some books also appeal to a general lay audience." Query.

COBBLESMITH, Box 191, RFD 1, Freeport ME 04032. Editor-in-Chief: Gene H. Byington. Publishes hardcover and paperback originals (90%); hardcover and paperback reprints (10%). Averages 3 titles/year. Pays 10% royalty on list price; no advance. Simultaneous and photocopied submissions OK. Computer printout and disk submissions OK. SASE. Query first. *"Unsolicited mss often are treated as though only a little better than unsolicited third class mail."* Reports in 4 months minimum. Free book-catalog.
Nonfiction: Americana and art topics (especially New England and antiques); law (popular, self-help); cookbooks, cooking and foods; gardening; psychology (applied—not theory); how-to (home and homestead crafts); philosophy (educational and new developments); sociology (applied, not theory); material on alternative lifestyles; nature, travel (offbeat guide books); and self-help. Accepts nonfiction, fiction and poetry translations.
Recent Nonfiction Titles: *Across the Running Tide* (environment); *Our Classroom Is Wild America*, by Michael Cohen; and *The Day the White Whales Came to Bangor*, by Gerald Hausman (children/environment).

COLES PUBLISHING CO., LTD., 90 Ronson Dr., Rexdale, Ontario, Canada M9W 1C1. (416)249-9121. Vice President of Publishing and New Product Development/Editorial Director: Jeffrey Cole. Publishes hardcover and paperback originals (40%) and reprints (60%). Averages 25 titles/year. "We are a subsidiary company of 'Coles, the Book People,' a chain of 235 bookstores throughout Canada and America." Pays by outright purchase of $500-$2,500; advance averages $500. Simultaneous and photocopied submissions OK. Reports in 3 weeks. SAE and International Reply Coupons.
Nonfiction: "We publish in the following areas: education, language, science, math, pet care, gardening, cookbooks, medicine and health, occult, business, reference, technical and do-it-yourself, crafts and hobbies, antiques, games, and sports." No philosophy, religion, history or biography. Submit outline/synopsis and sample chapters.
Recent Nonfiction Titles: *Food Processor Magic*; *Enjoying Cruising Under Sail*.

COLLECTOR BOOKS, Box 3009, Paducah KY 42001. Editor: Steve Quertermous. Publishes hardcover and paperback originals. Pays 5% royalty on retail; no advance. Publishes 25-30 titles/year. Send prints or transparencies if illustrations are to accompany ms. Disk submissions OK if arranged prior to submission; "material must be compatible with our system." SASE. Reports in 2-4 weeks. Free book catalog.
Nonfiction: "We only publish books on antiques and collectibles. We require our authors to be very knowledgeable in their respective fields and have access to a large representative sampling of the particular subject concerned." Query. Accepts outline/synopsis and 2-3 sample chapters. Recently published *Collector's Encyclopedia of Depression Glass*, by G. Florence; *Madame Alexander Collector Dolls*, by P. Smith; and *Primitives and Folk Art, Our Handmade Heritage*, by Catherine Thuro.

COLLEGE-HILL PRESS, 4284 41st St., San Diego CA 92105. (619)563-8899. Promotions Manager: Karen Jackson. Publishes hardcover and trade paperback originals. Averages 15 titles/year. Pays average 10%

royalty on retail price. Reports in 1 week. SASE. Free book catalog.
Nonfiction: Reference, textbook, medical. Subjects include speech, hearing, language, special education, medicine. Query and request "editorial and marketing questionnaire."
Recent Nonfiction Titles: *Educating and Understanding Autistic Children,* edited by Koegel, PhD, Rincover, PhD and Egel, PhD; and *Communication Programming for the Severely Handicapped,* by Musselwhite and St. Louis.

‡**COLLIER MACMILLAN CANADA, LTD.**, 1125 B Leslie St., Don Mills, Ontario, Canada. Publishes both originals and reprints in hardcover and paperback. Advance varies, depending on author's reputation and nature of book. Published 35 titles last year. Reports in 6 weeks. SAE and International Reply Coupons.
General Nonfiction: "Topical subjects of special interest to Canadians." Query.
Textbooks: Mathematics, language arts, and reading: mainly texts conforming to Canadian curriculum requirements. Also resource books, either paperback or pamphlet for senior elementary and high schools. Length: open.

COLORADO ASSOCIATED UNIVERSITY PRESS, Box 480, 1338 Grandview Ave., University of Colorado, Boulder CO 80309. (303)492-7191. Editor: Frederick Rinehart. Publishes hardcover and paperback originals. Averages 10 titles/year. Pays 10-12½-15% royalty contract on wholesale or retail price; "no advances." Free book catalog. Will consider photocopied submissions "if not sent simultaneously to another publisher." Computer printout submissions OK. Query first with table of contents, preface or opening chapter. Reports in 3 months. SASE.
Nonfiction: "Scholarly and regional." Length: 250-500 ms pages.
Recent Nonfiction Titles: *Chemicals and Cancer,* by Matthew S. Meselson (biology); *The Virginius Affair,* by Richard H. Bradford (history); and *Imperial Science and National Survival,* by David Montgomery (general science; politics).

***COLUMBIA PUBLISHING CO., INC.**, Frenchtown NJ 08825. (201)996-2141. Editorial Director: Bernard Rabb. Publishes hardcover originals. Pays 10% royalty; offers average advance. "Subsidy publishing is rarely offered and then only if we feel the book to be worthy to have our name on it." Simultaneous and photocopied submissions OK. Computer printout submissions OK; prefers letter quality to dot matrix. Reports in 6 months or longer. SASE.
Nonfiction: Biography, theater, film, dance, classical music, political science, business, recreation, and nature/ecology. Accepts nonfiction and fiction translations from French and German. "We do not want spy novels, westerns, romances, science fiction, mysteries, fad books, religious titles, sex guides, photography books, or academic books not applicable to a lay audience." Submit complete ms. Accepts artwork/photos.
Recent Nonfiction Titles: *The Deathday of Socrates,* by Eckstein; *Wayside Simples and Grateful Herbs,* by Abraitys; and *Conductors on Conducting,* by Jacobson (classical music).
Fiction: Literary novels—serious fiction only. Submit complete ms.
Recent Fiction Title: *Cousin Drewey and the Holy Twister,* by Sinclair.

COLUMBIA UNIVERSITY PRESS, 562 W. 113th St., New York NY 10025. (212)678-6777. Director and Editor-in-Chief: John D. Moore. Publishes hardcover and paperback originals. Pays negotiable royalty. Query. SASE.
Nonfiction: "General interest nonfiction of scholarly value." *Scholarly:* Books in the fields of literature, philosophy, fine arts, Oriental studies, history, social sciences, science, law.

‡**COMMONERS' PUBLISHING**, 432 Rideau St., Ottawa, Ontario, Canada K1N 5Z1. (613)233-4997. Editorial Director: Glenn Cheriton. Senior Editors: Lucille Shaw, Maridee Winters. Publishes hardcover and paperback originals. Royalties paid yearly based on 10% of sales, list. Photocopied submissions OK. "We do not like simultaneous submissions." Computer printout submissions OK. Reports in 4 months. SAE and International Reply Coupons. Book catalog for SAE and International Reply Coupons.
Nonfiction: Self-help, alternative lifestyles and crafts books. Accepts artwork/photos. Submit complete ms. Accepts translations from French.
Recent Nonfiction Title: *Kidding Around Ottawa,* by Gold and McDuff.
Fiction: Canadian short stories, plays and fiction; also full-length novels with Canadian themes, locations, and authors; and Canadian poetry. Submit complete ms.
Recent Fiction Titles: *Secret of Happiness,* by Smith (poetry); *Still Close to the Island,* by Dabydeen (short stories); and *All for Margarita,* by Darrel Wansley (stories).
Tips: Queries/mss may be routed to other editors in the publishing group.

COMMUNICATION SKILL BUILDERS, INC., Box 42050, Tucson AZ 85733. (602)323-7500. Acquisitions/Editorial Manager: Ellen B. North. Publishes paperback originals, kits, games, software, audio cassettes, and micro records. 60 titles for 1983. Pays negotiable royalty on wholesale or retail price. No

simultaneous submissions; photocopied submissions OK. SASE. Reports in 4 months. Free book catalogs—
Special Education and Gifted.
Special Education Material: Articulation therapy, language remediation and development; hearing impaired; adult communicative disorders; physically handicapped/developmentally delayed; learning disabled.
Gifted Material: All areas K-12. Query. Looks for "theoretical soundness, practically, usefulness."
Recent Nonfiction Titles: Special Education: *The Microphonograph Program for Aphasia*; *Let's Articulate*. Gifted: *Capture Creativity*.

COMMUNICATIONS PRESS, INC., 1346 Connecticut Ave., NW Washington DC 20036. (202)785-0865. President: Mary Louise Hollowell. Publishes hardcover, trade paperback, and professional/text paperback originals. Averages 1-4 titles/year. Pays royalty or honorarium; offers "nominal, if any" advance. Computer printout proposals OK. SASE. Reports in 1 month. Free book catalog.
Nonfiction: Reference, technical and textbook. Subjects include business and economics (communications); journalism and communications; performing arts; and politics and sociology (science/technology, public affairs and communications). Accepts outline/synopsis and 2 sample chapters.
Recent Nonfiction Titles: *How to Act & Eat at the Same Time: The Business of Landing a Professional Acting Job*, by Tom Logan; *The Cable/Broadband Communications Book, Volume 3, 1982-1983*, edited by Mary Louise Hollowell; *Creating Original Programming for Cable TV*, edited by Wm. Drew Shaffer and Richard Wheelwright; and *Cable TV Renewals & Refranchising*, edited by Jean Rice.

COMPACT PUBLICATIONS, INC., 3014 Willow Lane, Hollywood FL 33021. (305)983-6464. Editor: Virginia Aronson. Publishes trade paperback originals. Averages 6 titles/year. Buys mss outright for $3,000 minimum (average 10¢/word). No advance. Simultaneous submissions OK. SASE. Reports in 1 month. Free book catalog.
Nonfiction: Cookbook, how-to, and diet and health guides. Subjects include cooking and foods, health, others with mass market appeal. Books marketed in supermarkets and convenience stores to 70% female audience. Query.
Recent Nonfiction Titles: *Doctor's Cholesterol and Low Salt Diet Guide*, by Dr. Sylvan Lewis, MD.; *Joy o Being Thin*, by Dr. Neal Edison, MD; and *Cook Your Weight Off*, by Virginia Aronson, RD.

COMPCARE PUBLICATIONS, 2415 Annapolis Lane, Minneapolis MN 55441. Publisher: Arnold un- ing. Publishes hardcover and trade paperback originals and reprints. Averages 10-15 titles/year. Pays gotia- ble royalty; offers negotiable advance. Simultaneous and photocopied submissions OK. SASE. Re ts in 2 months. Free book catalog.
Nonfiction: Personal growth books on alcoholism/chemical dependency, weight control, per al relation- ships, stress management, parenting. "Prefer to hear from writers with credentials in the field y are writing about. Very little chance of publication for divorce experiences or personal recovery from a olism or drug addiction." Query.
Recent Nonfiction Titles: *The Sexual Addiction*, by Patrick J. Carnes, PhD; *Hug Thera* , by Kathleen Keat- ing; *Do I Have to Give Up Me to be Loved by You?*, by Jordan Paul.

COMPUTER SCIENCE PRESS, INC., 11 Taft Ct., Rockville MD 20850. (30 51-9050. President: Bar- bara B. Friedman. Publishes hardcover and paperback originals. Averages 20 es/year. Pays royalty on wholesale price; no advance. Simultaneous and photocopied submissions OK Computer printout and disk submissions OK. Reports ASAP. SASE. Free book catalog.
Nonfiction: "Technical books in all aspects of computer science, computer engineering, computer chess, electrical engineering and telecommunications. Both text and reference books. Will also consider public ap- peal 'trade' books in computer science, mss. and diskettes for computer education at all levels: elementary, secondary and college." Also publishes bibliographies in computer science areas and the quarterly *Journal of VLSI Systems & Computations* and *Journal of Telecommunication Networks*. Query or submit complete ms. "We prefer 3 copies of manuscripts." Looks for "technical accuracy of the material and reason this approach is being taken. We would also like a covering letter stating what the author sees as the competition for this work and why this work is superior."
Recent Nonfiction Titles: *Algorithms for Graphics and Image Processing*, by Theo Pavlidis; *Understanding Computer Systems*, by Harold Lawson; and *Bits 'n Bytes About Computing: A Computer Literacy Primer*, by R. Heller and C. D. Martin.

‡**COMPUTER SKILL BUILDERS**, Box 42050, Tucson AZ 85733. (602)323-7500. Managing Editor: Wil- liam G. Crider. Publishes trade and mass market paperback originals. Averages 20-30 titles/year. Pays negotia- ble royalty on wholesale price. No advance. Photocopied submissions OK. Computer printout and disk submissions OK. SASE. Reports in 2 weeks on queries; 2 months on mss. Book catalog for 9x12 SAE and 2 first class stamps.
Nonfiction: How-to, reference, self-help, technical and textbook on computers in education. Interested in

"anything to do with computers in education." Query or submit outline/synopsis and sample chapters.
Recent Nonfiction Titles: *Math Skill Builders*; *Greeting Cards*.

CONCORDIA PUBLISHING HOUSE, 3558 S. Jefferson Ave., St. Louis MO 63118. Pays royalty on retail price; outright purchase in some cases. Averages 62 titles/year. Submit outline and sample chapter for nonfiction; complete ms for fiction. Reports in 3 months. SASE. Free book catalog.
Nonfiction: Publishes Protestant, general religious, theological books and periodicals, music works and juveniles. "As a religious publisher, we look for mss that deal with ways that readers can apply Christian beliefs and principles to daily living. Any ms that deals specifically with theology and/or doctrine should conform to the tenets of the Lutheran Church-Missouri Synod. We suggest that, if authors have any doubt about their submissions in light of what kind of mss we want, they should first correspond with us."
Fiction: Publishes adult fiction, juvenile picture and beginner books. "We look for mss that deal with Bible stories, Bible history and Christian missions."

‡**CONGDON & WEED, INC.**, 298 5th Ave., New York NY 10001. (212)736-4883. Assistant Editor: Georgina Schiller. Publishes hardcover and trade paperback originals and trade paperback reprints. Averages 30-35 titles/year. Pays royalty on retail price. Simultaneous and photocopied submissions OK. SASE. Reports in 3 months. Book catalog for 7x10 SAE and 54¢ postage.
Nonfiction: Biography, coffee table book, cookbook, humor, illustrated book, and guide book. Subjects include Americana, art, business and economics, cooking and foods, health, history, music, philosophy, politics, psychology and travel. No inspirational books. Submit outlines/synopsis and sample chapters.
Recent Nonfiction Titles: *Growing Up*, by Russell Baker (autobiography); *The Web That has No Weaver: Understanding Chinese Medicine*, by Ted Kaptchuk (medical); and *The Big Time*, by Glenn Kaplan (career guide).
Fiction: No genre books of any description. Submit complete ms.
Recent Fiction Titles: *Bluebird Canyon*, by Dan McCall (literary fiction); and *Natural Causes*, by Jonathan Valin (mystery/detective).

CONGRESSIONAL QUARTERLY PRESS, 1414 22nd St. NW, Washington DC 20037. (202)887-8642. Director: Joanne Daniels. Publishes hardcover and paperback originals. Pays standard college royalty on wholesale price; offers college text advance. Simultaneous and photocopied submissions OK. SASE. Reports in 6 months. Free book catalog on request.
Nonfiction: "We are probably the most distinguished publisher in the area of Congress and US government." College texts American politics. Submit outline and prospectus. "Virtually all our books are written by experienced scholars."
Recent Nonfiction Titles: *Congress Reconsidered*, 2nd Edition, by Dodd and Oppenheimer; *Goodbye to Goodtime Charlie: The American Governorship Transformed*, 2nd ed., by Larry Sabato; *Interest Group Politics*, by Cigler and Loomis; *Public Policy and the Aging*, by William W. Lammers.

CONSUMER REPORTS BOOKS, Subsidiary of Consumers Union. Subsidiaries include *Consumer Reports* magazine and *Penny Power*, (magazine for children 8-14). 256 Washington St., Mt. Vernon NY 10550. (914)667-9400. Director, Consumer Reports Books: Jonathan Leff. Publishes trade paperback originals (50%), and trade paperback reprints (50%). Averages 5-10 titles/year. Pays variable royalty on retail price; buys some mss outright. Simultaneous and photocopied submissions OK. Reports in 1 month on queries; 2 months on mss. Free book listing.
Nonfiction: Cookbook, how-to, reference, self-help and technical; how-to books for children. Subjects include business and economics, cooking and foods, health, music and consumer guidance. Submit outline/synopsis and 1-2 sample chapters.
Recent Nonfiction Titles: *Guide to Used Cars*, *Top Tips from Consumer Reports*; *The Consumers Union Report on Life Insurance* (buying guidance); and *The Medicine Show* ("practical guide to health problems and products"), all by Editors of Consumer Reports Books.

CONTEMPORARY BOOKS, 180 N. Michigan Ave., Chicago IL 60601. (312)782-9181. Publisher: Harvey Plotnick. Executive Editor: Nancy Crossman. Adult Education Director: Wendy Harris. Publishes hardcover and trade paperbacks. Averages 110 titles/year. Pays sliding scale of royalties for cloth; most frequently 7½% for paperback. Offers small advance. Simultaneous submissions OK, if so advised. Reports in 3 weeks, longer on complete ms.
Nonfiction: Sports instructional, fitness and health, how-to, self improvement, leisure activities, hobbies, practical business, women's interest, and cookbooks. Also publishes GED and adult basic education materials. Prefers query first with outline/synopsis and sample chapter. "We look at everything; and we do, in fact, publish occasional titles that come in over the transom." Looks for "clarity, insight, high regard for the reader."
Recent Nonfiction Titles: *Male Practice*, by Dr. Robert Mendelsohn; *Winning Body Building*, by Franco Columbu; *How We Made a Million Dollars Recycling Great Old Houses*, by Sam and Mary Weir; and *The Art of*

Cooking for the Diabetic, by Katharine Middleton and Mary Abbott Hess.
Fiction: An occasional unusual title. Seldom more than one fiction book per list.

THE CONTINUUM PUBLISHING CORPORATION, 575 Lexington Ave., New York NY 10022. (212)421-4800. Contact: The Editors. Publishes hardcover and paperback originals (95%) and paperback reprints (5%). Publishes 30 titles/year. Pays average 10-12½-15% royalty on hardcover; 7½% on retail paperback; offers an advance. Photocopied submissions OK. SASE. Reports in 2 months. Free book catalog.
Nonfiction: Current affairs, social and educational concerns, psychology, philosophy, sociology, literary criticism, history, biography and self help. Query.
Recent Nonfiction Titles: *Starving for Attention*, by Cherry Boone O'Neill; and *Whole-Life Parenting*, by James and Mary Kenny (counseling and self-help).

DAVID C. COOK PUBLISHING CO., Adult (General) Division, 850 N. Grove, Elgin IL 60120. (312)741-2400. General Titles Managing Editor: Mrs. Janet Hoover Thoma. Publishes hardcover and paperback originals (98%) and paperback and hardcover reprints (2%). Averages 20 titles/year. Pays 8-15% royalty on retail price; offers variable advance. Simultaneous and photocopied submissions OK (only if so indicated in a letter). Computer printout submissions OK. SASE. Reports in 4 months.
Nonfiction: Religious. "Our primary emphasis is in the nonfiction area. We are interested in inspirational books which help people grow in their Christian faith and which minister to people's needs when they hurt, i.e., loss of a loved one; depression; etc. The spiritual element must be evident and Bible-based, but it doesn't necessarily need to dominate the story. Be careful not to get too preachy. We are interested in biographies of famous or unusual people who have a faith which can challenge the reader. Also, books on current topics from a Christian viewpoint are given serious consideration, e.g., personal finances; marriage; etc." Submit outline/synopsis and first two chapters. In your cover letter, include the theme of your proposed book and its uniqueness, who you think will buy the book, and something about your spiritual, literary, educational, and professional background. Accepts artwork and photos; nonfiction and fiction translations. Query first.
Recent Nonfiction Titles: *The Graham Kerr Step-By-Step Cookbook*; and *The Second American Revolution*, by John Whitehead.
Fiction: Religious; "We are considering good manuscripts that deal in a creative way with Church history, the current religious scene, or science fiction/fantasy from a Christian viewpoint."
Recent Fiction Titles: *Master of MacKenzie Station*, by Kathleen Yapp; and *Olympia*, by Dr. Elgin Groseclose.
Tips: Queries/mss may be routed to other editors in the publishing group. "Write in a popular style that makes people want to read what you have written."

DAVID C. COOK PUBLISHING CO., Chariot Books, 850 N. Grove, Elgin IL 60120. (312)741-2400. Managing Editor: Janet Hoover Thoma. Associate Editor: Susan Zitzman. Publishes hardcover and paperback originals and paperback reprints for children and teens. Averages 30-35 titles/year. Pays 4-8% royalty on retail price. SASE required. Reports in 3 months. Writer's guidelines for 9x12 SASE.
Nonfiction: "We're particularly interested in books that teach the child about the Bible in fun and interesting ways—not just Bible story rehashes. Also books that help children understand their feelings and problems; books about animals, sports, science, or true stories of young people whose Christian faith is a vital part of an interesting life." Query. "We prefer a 2- to 4-page synopsis and first 2 chapters." No unsolicited mss.
Recent Nonfiction Titles: *Sometimes I Get Lonely* (Psalm 42 for Children), by Elspeth Campbell Murphy; *The Christian Kids' Almanac*, by Bob Flood.
Fiction: "We want books with a spiritual dimension that is an integral inevitable part of the story. The plot should involve spiritual as well as external conflict, and the characters should resolve these conflicts through faith in God. Yet the stories should be entertaining and compelling. We are always looking for books that are humorous and books that can be part of a series. For the Pennypincher series we need sports fiction for the 10- to 14-year-old boy, and romances for 10- to 14-year-old girls. Also need more titles for the Making Choices series, in which reader is main character, and story has many possible endings.
Recent Fiction Titles: *The Droodles Storybook of Proverbs*, by Ray and Sally Cioni; *The Cereal Box Adventures* (A Making Choices Book), by Barbara Bartholomew; and *Lost in the Shenandoahs*, by Ron Wilson.
Tips: "The author should sell us his manuscript, not only providing a sampling of the book, but also explaining the book's uniqueness, why the book will sell, and why the author is qualified to write it."

‡**COPLEY BOOKS**, Subsidiary of The Copley Press, Inc., (Copley Newspapers), Box 957, La Jolla CA 92038. (619)454-1842, 454-0411. Manager: Jean I. Bradford. Publishes hardcover originals. Averages 1-2 titles/year. Pays royalty; "individual agreement with author for each publication." Simultaneous and photocopied submissions OK. SASE. Reports in "a few weeks." Free book catalog.
Nonfiction: Biography, "coffee table" book, illustrated book on Americana, art or Western history. Needs mss on "the history of California (including Baja) and the West; aspects of western contemporary and earlier history, not widely covered previously; diaries, letters of western pioneers; ecology; water needs in the West,

and solutions; Indian lore; Hispanic history and contemporary status." Query or submit outline/synopsis and sample chapters.

Recent Nonfiction Titles: *Last of the Californios*, by Harry Crosby (nonfiction about people living as their ancestors did 200 years ago); *Window on the Sea*, by Herbert L. Minshall (changes in the California coastline); *The California to Remember*, by Richard F. Pourade (nostalgic view of old places and old scenes).

CORDOVAN PRESS, Division of Cordovan Corp., Publishers, 5314 Bingle Rd., Houston TX 77092. (713)688-8811. Director: Delton Simmons. Publishes hardcover and paperback originals and reprints. Pays negotiable royalty. Averages 5 titles/year.
Nonfiction: Professional business and finance; business self-help. General interest and regional trade, on Texana, western and southwestern history, Texas and southwestern travel and guidebooks. Query.

‡**THE CORINTHIAN PRESS**, Subsidiary of EDR Corp., 3592 Lee Rd., Shaker Heights OH 44120. (216)751-7300. Editor: Dave Cockley. Publishes hardcover and trade paperback originals. Averages 3-4 titles/year. Pays 10-15% royalty on wholesale price. Simultaneous and photocopied submissions OK; prefers originals. SASE. Reports in 1 month on queries; 2 months on mss. Free book catalog.
Nonfiction: How-to, juvenile, self-help, technical, and books of regional interest. Subjects include business and economics, health and travel. "We are primarily interested in business books targeted to highly specialized audiences and books of regional interest. Submit outline/synopsis and sample chapters.
Recent Nonfiction Titles: *Your Skin & How to Live In It*, by Dr. Jerome Z. Litt (self-help); *A Manager's Guide to Industrial Robots*, by Ken Susnjara (business); and *Benjamin and the Big Game*, by Dave Cockley (juvenile).

CORNELL MARITIME PRESS, INC., Box 456, Centreville MD 21617. Managing Editor: Willard A. Lockwood. Publishes original hardcover and quality paperbacks. Averages 10 titles/year. Payment is negotiable but royalties do not exceed 10% for first 5,000 copies, 12½% for second 5,000 copies, 15% on all additional. Revised editions revert to original royalty schedule. Free book catalog. Send queries first, accompanied by writing samples and outlines of book ideas. Reports in 2-4 weeks. SASE.
Nonfiction: Marine subjects, highly technical; manuals; how-to books on maritime subjects. Tidewater Publishers imprint publishes books on regional history, folklore and wildlife of the Chesapeake Bay and the Delmarva Peninsula.
Recent Nonfiction Titles: *Nautical Rules of the Road* (2nd ed.); *Stability and Trim for the Ship's Officer* (3rd ed.); *Navigator's Pocket Calculator Handbook*; *Shipwrecks on the Chesapeake*.

R.D. CORTINA CO., INC., 17 Riverside Ave., Westport CT 06880. (203)227-8471. General Editor: MacDonald Brown. Pays on a fee or a royalty basis. Published 27 titles last year. "Do not send unsolicited mss; send outline and sample chapter." Reports in 2 months or less.
Textbooks: Publishes foreign language and ESL teaching textbooks for self-study and school; also publishes language teaching phonograph records and tapes. Materials of special ESL interest. Word length varies.

COUGAR BOOKS, Box 22246, Sacramento CA 95822. Editorial Director: Alan Pritchard. Publishes paperback originals. Averages 5 titles/year. Pays 7-10% royalty on wholesale or retail price; outright purchases negotiable. Simultaneous and photocopied submissions OK. Computer printout and disk submissions OK; "query first to be sure disk is compatible or use modem." SASE. Reports in 2 months. Book catalog sent for #10 SASE.
Nonfiction: Trends in nutrition, health, child care, parenting. Accepts artwork/photos. "We're picking up subject areas in which California is pioneering." Query first or submit outline/synopsis and 2 sample chapters.
Recent Nonfiction Titles: *Mommy, I'm Hungry-How to Feed Your Child Nutritiously*, by P. McIntyre; *Alternative Birth*, by K. Anderson; *Midwife Murder Case*, by J. Bowers and Rosalie Tarpening; *Mommy & Me Exercises*, by Christie Costanzo.

COWARD, McCANN & GEOGHEGAN, Books for Boys and Girls, 200 Madison Ave., New York NY 10016. (212)576-8900. Editor-in-Chief, Books for Boys and Girls: Refna Wilkin. Averages 24 children's titles/year. Pays royalties on juvenile. Advances are competitive. Query. SASE.
Nonfiction: "Our publishing program is small and selective but we will consider nonfiction for ages 4 and up. The outline should indicate the aspects of the subject to be covered and the age level, and samples should indicate writing style, type of treatment, etc."
Fiction: Fiction for ages 4 and up. "An outline should give a synopsis of the plot with some ideas of the characters, and should indicate age level; chapters should include samples of narrative and dialogue."

COWARD McCANN, INC., 200 Madison Ave., New York NY 10016. (212)576-8900. President: Peter Israel. Editor-in-Chief: Phyllis Grann. Publishes hardcover originals. "We publish about 60 adult titles a year." Pays 10-15% royalty on retail prices. No unsolicited mss. No response without SASE.

Nonfiction: Animals, biography, health, history, how-to, juveniles, nature, politics, psychology, recreation, science, self-help, sociology and sports. "We are looking for nonfiction books on topics of current and/or lasting popular interest, for general, not specialized audiences. Our scope is broad; our needs are for quality manuscripts marketable in the hardcover arena. We do not want manuscripts in specialized or technical fields that require extensive design and art work that lead to high cover prices." Query with SASE only.
Recent Nonfiction Titles: *Lyle Official Antiques Review*; *The Rise of Theodore Roosevelt*, by Edmund Morris; and *Great Expectations*, by Landon Jones.
Fiction: Adventure, mainstream, mystery, romance and suspense. "We also want espionage thrillers and mysteries, although the market for these is not as strong as it once was. We do not want science fiction, fantasy or experimental novels." Query with SASE only.
Recent Fiction Titles: *The Defector*, by Evelyn Anthony; *Prizzi's Honor*, by Richard Condon; *For Special Services*, by John Gardner; and *Shadowland*, by Peter Straub.

CRAFTSMAN BOOK CO. OF AMERICA, 6058 Corte Del Cedro, Box 6500, Carlsbad CA 92008. (714)438-7828. Editor-in-Chief: Gary Moselle. Publishes paperback originals. Pays royalty of 12½% of gross revenues, regardless of quantity sold. Averages 10 titles/year. "More than 60% of our sales are directly to the consumer, and since royalties are based on gross revenues the author's share is maximized." Will send free catalog and author's submission guide on request. Will consider photocopied submissions. Computer printout submissions OK; disk submissions OK "if compatible with our computers." Submit query or outline. Reports in 2 weeks. SASE.
Nonfiction: "We publish practical references for professional builders and are aggressively seeking manuscripts related to construction, the building trades, civil engineering, construction cost estimating and construction management. Ours are not how-to books for homeowners. Emphasis is on step-by-step instructions, illustrations, charts, reference data, checklists, forms, samples, cost estimates, estimating data, rules of thumb, and procedures that solve actual problems in the field or in the builder's office. Each book covers a limited subject fully, becomes the owner's primary reference on that subject, has a high utility to cost ratio, and helps the owner make a better living in his profession. We like to see ideas and queries for books in their early stages; we work with first-time authors, prefer an outline or query, and look for completeness in the coverage of the topic, and clear, simple writing."
Recent Nonfiction Titles: *Contractor's Guide to the Building Code*, by Jack Hageman; *Estimating Electrical Construction*, by Ed Tyler; and *Construction Superintending*, by Leslie Cole.

CRAIN BOOKS, 740 Rush St., Chicago IL 60611. Director: Jack Graham. Publishes hardcover and paperback originals. Averages 12-18 titles/year. Pays royalty on net revenues, makes an advance only under exceptional circumstances. Send contact sheet if photos/illustrations are to accompany ms. Reports in 2 months. SASE. Free book catalog.
Nonfiction: Publishes business books exclusively both for the professional and academic market. Subject areas: advertising and marketing; insurance; finance and investment; business management, international business. Basically interested in "practical, nuts-and-bolts, how-to approach by experts in the field." Wants to see "outline, table of contents (down to B heads), and 2-3 sample chapters."
Recent Nonfiction Titles: *Public Money Manager's Handbook*, edited by Nathaniel Guild; *Response Television*, by John Witek; and *An Executive Guide to Commercial Property and Casualty Insurance*, by Edward W. Siver; *Cable: An Advertiser's Guide to the New Electronic Library*, by Ronald B. Kaatz.

CREATIVE ARTS BOOK COMPANY, Modern Authors Monograph Series; Black Lizard Books; CA Communications Books. 833 Bancroft Way, Berkeley CA 94710. (415)848-4777. Publisher: Donald S. Ellis. Senior Editor: Barry Gifford. Sales Director: Richard Flood. Publishes hardcover and paperback originals (50%) and paperback reprints (50%). Averages 12 titles/year. Pays 5-10% royalty on retail price or buys some mss outright for $500-$10,000. Offers minimum $500 advance. Simultaneous and photocopied submissions OK. SASE. Reports in 3 weeks. Free book catalog.
Nonfiction: Alternative health and foods, cookbooks, how-to, but open to anything *brilliant* (except poetry).
Recent Nonfiction Titles: *The Art of Seeing*, by Aldous Huxley (eye improvement); *The Not Strictly Vegetarian Cookbook*, by Lois Fishkin and Susan DiMarco; *Tempeh Primer*, by Joel Andersen and Robin Clute.
Fiction: "Looking for serious literary fiction of broad appeal."
Recent Fiction Titles: *View of Dawn in the Tropics*, by G. Cabrera-Infante; *Blood on the Dining-Room Floor*, by Gertrude Stein; and *A Totally Free Man: An Unauthorized Autobiography of Fidel Castro*, by John Krich.

CREATIVE BOOK CO., 8210 Varna Ave., Van Nuys CA 91402. (213)988-2334. Editor-in-Chief: Sol H. Marshall. Publishes paperback originals. Full schedule for 1983. Do not submit until 1984. Pays $50-200 in outright purchase. Simultaneous and photocopied submissions OK. SASE. Reports in 2 weeks. Book catalog for SASE.
Nonfiction: Cookbooks/cooking; fund raising and public relations for education and community services. Query or submit outline/synopsis and 2-3 sample chapters or submit complete ms for shorter material.

Recent Nonfiction Titles: *Ten Reasons Editors Hate Publicists, And Ten Reasons They Like 'Em*, by Sol H. Marshall; *Selling Out: A Guide for Promoting Community Theatre*, by Steven F. Marshall; *Recipes My Milwaukee Mother Taught Me*, by Dolly Medress; *Recipes in Rhyme*, by Marion G. Marshall.

CREATIVE PUBLISHING, Box 9292, College Station TX 77840. (713)696-7907. Editor: Theresa Earle. Publishes hardcover originals and trade paperback reprints. Averages 2-3 titles/year. Pays negotiable royalty. Simultaneous submissions OK. Computer printout submissions OK; prefers letter quality to dot matrix. Reports in 1 week. Book catalog for business size SAE and 1 first class stamp.
Nonfiction: Biography, reference on western history. Query.
Recent Nonfiction Titles: *The O.K. Corral Inquest*, by Alford E. Turner; *Henry Brown, Outlaw Marshall*, by Bill O'Neal; *El Paso Lawman*, by Fred Egloff; *The Train Robbing Bunch*, by Rick Miller.

CRESCENDO PUBLISHING, 132 W. 22nd, New York NY 10011. Publishes hardcover and paperback originals and reprints. Offers standard 10-12½-15% royalty contract; "advances are rare; sometimes made when we seek out an author." Published 20 titles last year. Will look at queries or completed mss. SASE. Address submissions to Gerald Krimm. Reports in 6 weeks.
Music: Tradebooks in music. Length: open.

CRESTWOOD HOUSE, INC., Box 3427, Mankato MN 56001. (507)388-1616. Contact: Editorial Director. Publishes hardcover originals. Averages 25 titles/year. "All fees are negotiated based upon subject matter, length of publication, and additional work furnished." Occasionally offers advance. Simultaneous and photocopied submissions OK. No computer printout or disk submissions. SASE.
Nonfiction: "Crestwood House publishes high-interest, low-vocabulary books for children with a reading level of grades 3-5. Our books are always published in series which have related subject matter (probably 5-10 titles per series). We do sports, recreation, and other current topics of high interest to children and young adults. Books are generally between 48-64 pages; no mss accepted under 5,000 or over 10,000 words. All books include a generous number of photographs." Submit complete ms.
Recent Nonfiction Titles: *The Whitetail*, by Ahlstrom (wildlife series); *Trucks*, by Sheffer.
Fiction: Same basic requirements as nonfiction. Science fiction; adventure; and sports. No pre-school through 1st grade material.
Recent Fiction Title: *Save the Dam*, by Siroff.

‡**CRICKET PUBLICATIONS**, Box 8771, Toledo OH 43623. Editor: Amy Danforth. Publishes hardcover and mass market paperback originals. Averages 2-3 titles/year. Pays 10-20% royalty on wholesale price or makes outright purchase of $1 per line for poetry. No advance. Simultaneous and photocopied submissions OK. SASE. Reports in 6 weeks.
Nonfiction: Juvenile and poetry.
Fiction: Juvenile adventure, fantasy, mystery and humor. "No religious or goody-goody stories." Query or submit complete ms. "Stories must be well written and interesting."
Poetry: Short, humorous, rhyming poems; short nature poems for children; and story poems for children. For short poems 4-10 lines, submit in batches of 5-10 poems.
Recent Poetry Title: *Animal Fair*, by Amy Danforth (humorous).

THE CROSSING PRESS, Box 640, Trumansburg NY 14886. Co-Publishers: Elaine Gill or John Gill. Publishes hardcover and trade paperback originals. Averages 10-12 titles/year. Pays royalty. Simultaneous and photocopied submissions OK. Reports in 2 weeks on queries; 1 month on mss. Free book catalog.
Nonfiction: Cookbook, how-to, literary and feminist. Subjects include cooking; health; gays and feminism. Accepts nonfiction, fiction and poetry translations. Submit outline and sample chapter.
Recent Nonfiction Title: *The Whole Birth Catalog*.
Fiction: Feminism (good literary material). Submit outline and sample chapter.
Recent Fiction Titles: *Folly*; *Gay Touch*.

CROSSWAY BOOKS, 9825 W. Roosevelt Rd., Westchester IL 60153. Subsidiary of Good News Publishers. Editor-in-Chief: Jan P. Dennis. Publishes hardcover and trade paperback originals. Averages 25 titles/year. Pays negotiable royalty; offers negotiable advance. Simultaneous and photocopied submissions OK. SASE. Reports in 6-8 weeks. Book catalog for 9x12 SAE and 2 first class stamps.
Nonfiction: Subjects include issues on Christianity in contemporary culture; Christian doctrine; church history. Accepts translations from European languages. "All books must be written out of Christian perspective or world view." Query by phone or letter with 3-5 sample chapters or submit complete ms. Accepts artwork/photos.
Recent Nonfiction Title: *A Christian Manifesto*, by Frances Schaeffer.
Fiction: Mainstream; science fiction; fantasy (genuinely creative in the tradition of C.S. Lewis, J.R.R. Tolkien and Madeleine L'Engle); and juvenile age 6 and up to young adult. No formula romance. Submit com-

plete ms. "All fiction must be written from a genuine Christian perspective."
Recent Fiction Titles: *Alpha Centauri*, by Robert Siegel; *In the Hall of the Dragon King*, by Stephen R. Lawhead; *Poppa John*, by Larry Woiwode; *The Holy Fool*, by Harold Fickett.

CROWELL/LIPPINCOTT JUNIOR BOOKS, see Harper & Row Junior Books Group.

CROWN PUBLISHERS, INC., 1 Park Ave., New York NY 10016. (212)532-9200. Imprints include Clarkson N. Potter/Arlington House, Barre, Harmony and Julian Press. Editor-in-Chief: Betty A. Prashker. Publishes hardcover and paperback originals. Publishes 250 titles/year. Simultaneous and photocopied submissions OK. SASE. Reports in 6 weeks.
Nonfiction: Americana, animals, art, biography, cookbooks/cooking, health, history, hobbies, how-to, humor, juveniles, music, nature, philosophy, photography, politics, psychology, recreation, reference, science, self-help, and sports. Query or submit outline/synopsis and sample chapters.
Recent Titles: *Mistral's Daughter*, by Judith Krantz; *The Valley of Horses*, by Jean M. Auel; *Like the Universe and Everything*, by Douglas Adams.

THE CUMBERLAND PRESS, INC., Box 296, Freeport ME 04032. (207)865-6045. Editor: Mary Louise Bridge. Pays 10% royalty on retail price. No advance. Averages 4-6 titles/year. Query. SASE.
Nonfiction: "We are interested in nonfiction books for national market (especially how-to, calligraphy, philosophy, economics) and regional manuscripts, particularly New England and Rocky Mountain States." Looks for marketability, quality, organization.
Recent Nonfiction Titles: *These I Do Remember: Fragments From the Holocaust*, by Gerda Haas; and *Pen Dance*, by Bonnie Spiegel.

CURTIN & LONDON, INC., 6 Vernon St., Somerville MA 02145. (617)625-1200. Contact: Katie Carlone. Publishes hardcover and paperback originals. Publishes 12 titles/year. Pays 5-15% royalty on wholesale price; offers minimum $500 advance. Simultaneous and photocopied submissions OK. Computer printout submissions OK; disk submissions OK if IBM DOS, Osborne or Apple II Plus. SASE. Reports in 1-2 weeks. Free book catalog.
Nonfiction: How-to and technical in photography and personal computing at all levels. Accepts artwork/photos. Especially needs "books with a strong visual approach using line art, photographs and captions to explain how-to subjects." Does not want picture books. Query first.
Recent Nonfiction Titles: *An Apple Business Users Guide: Planning and Budgeting*; *An IBM PC Business Users Guide: Controlling Financial Performance*; *The Book of 35mm Photography*.

ROBERT F. DAME, INC., 511 Research Rd., Richmond VA 23236. (804)794-9442. President: Robert F. Dame. Publishes hardcover and paperback originals. Publishes 30 titles/year. Pays 15% royalty on list price. Simultaneous and photocopied submissions OK. SASE. Reports in 4 weeks.
Nonfiction: Business/economics, reference and textbooks (banking, finance and accounting) and executive development. Submit outline/synopsis and sample chapters.
Recent Nonfiction Titles: *Asset Liability Management: A Model for Commercial Banks*, by Olson, Sollenberger and O'Connell (executive development); *A Guide to Supply-Side Economics*, by Thomas J. Hailstone; and *Interest Rate Futures: Concepts and Issues*, by Robert W. Kolb and Gerald Gay.

DANCE HORIZONS, 1801 E. 26th St., Brooklyn NY 11229. (212)627-0477. Editorial Director: A.J. Pischl. Publishes hardcover and paperback originals (40%) and paperback reprints (60%). Averages 9 titles/year. Pays 10% royalty on retail price; offers average $500 advance. Simultaneous and photocopied submissions OK. SASE. Reports in 1 month. Free book catalog.
Nonfiction: "Anything dealing with dance." Query first.
Recent Nonfiction Titles: *Philosophical Essays on Dance*, edited by Gordon Fancher and Gerald Myers; *Letters on Dancing and Ballets*, by Jean Georges Noverre; and *Letters From a Ballet Master: The Correspondence of Arthur Saint-Leon*, edited by Ivor Guest.

DANTE UNIVERSITY OF AMERICA PRESS, INC., Box 635, Weston MA 02193. Contact: Manuscripts Editor. Publishes hardcover originals and reprints, and trade paperback originals and reprints. Averages 3-5 titles/year. Pays royalty; offers negotiable advance. Simultaneous and photocopied submissions OK. Computer printouts and disk submissions OK; prefers letter quality printouts. SASE. Reports in 6 weeks on queries; 2 months on mss. Book catalog for business size SAE and 1 first class stamp.
Nonfiction: Biography, reference, reprints and nonfiction and fiction translations from Italian and Latin. Subjects include general scholarly nonfiction, Renaissance thought and letter, Italian language and linguistics, Italian-American history and culture and bilingual education. Query first. Accepts outline/synopsis and 4 sample chapters.
Recent Nonfiction Titles: *An Ode to America's Independence: A Bilingual Edition*, by Alfieri; *Italian Panel*

Paintings of the 14th and 15th Centuries, by Boskovits; *Dante Studies Volume I: Dante in the 20th Century*; *Italian Conversation*, by Gorjanc.
Poetry: "There is a chance that we would use Renaissance poetry translations."

DARTNELL CORP., 4660 N. Ravenswood Ave., Chicago IL 60640. (312)561-4000. Senior Vice-President: Norman F. Guess. Publishes manuals, reports, hardcovers. Royalties: sliding scale based "usually on retail price. Published 7 titles last year." Send outline and sample chapter. Reports in 4 weeks. SASE.
Business: Interested in new material on business skills and techniques in management, supervision, administration, advertising sales, etc.
Recent Nonfiction Titles: *Quality Circles*, by Ron Kreposki and Beverly Scott; and *Desk-Top Computers*, by Rosa and Miller.

DARWIN PUBLICATIONS, 850 N. Hollywood Way, Burbank CA 91505. (213)848-0944. Executive Editor: Victoria Darwin. Publishes hardcover and trade paperback originals and reprints. Averages 3-4 titles/year. Pays 10% royalty on retail price. Simultaneous and photocopied submissions OK. Computer printout submissions OK (printout paper should be separated and collated with sprocket holes detached); "only letter quality is acceptable." SASE. Reports in 2 weeks on queries; 1 month on mss. Free book catalog.
Nonfiction: "Coffee table" book, how-to, illustrated book, reference and technical. Subjects include Americana, history, hobbies, nature, railroading, recreation and travel. "Manuscripts on adventurous topics, with interesting photos, (mostly b&w). In-depth research with casual writing style. Although railroad topics provide the mainstay of our line, we are broadening our scope." Query. Accepts outline/synopsis and 1-2 sample chapters. "We look at overall scope and treatment of the topic, the author's writing style, how photos and illustrations complement the text, and how much editing it will require in light of its salability (its editorial cost-effectiveness)."
Recent Nonfiction Titles: *The Movie Railroads*, by Larry Jensen ("coffee table" book); *Sunset Blvd: America's Dream Street*, by Kennelley and Hankey (pictorial history); and *The Brown Book*, by R.A. Brown (brass locomotive models).

DATA AND RESEARCH TECHNOLOGY CORP., D.A.R.T. Corp., 1102 McNeilly Ave., Pittsburgh PA 15216. Editor: Frank X. McNulty. Pays 10% royalty; buys some mss outright. Computer printout submissions OK. SASE. Reports in 3 weeks.
Nonfiction: Publishes the "Answers:" (series of select bibliographies). Current and original bibliographies as reference sources for specific audiences like telecommunications managers, condominium owners, or people interested in computer applications, etc. "To be accepted for publication, the quality must meet the approval of any serious researcher or librarian. The references must include a brief abstract, title, publisher, pages, price. The bibliography should include not only books, but periodicals, tapes, any audiovisuals, videotapes and discs, trade associations, etc." Also looks at any authoritative, specific manuscripts in the field of bibliography. Query with SASE. Accepts outline/synopsis and 1 sample chapter.

MAY DAVENPORT, PUBLISHERS, 26313 Purissima Rd., Los Altos Hills CA 94022. (415)948-6499. Editor/Publisher: May Davenport. Hardcover and trade paperback originals. Averages 3-4 titles/year. Pays 15% royalty on retail price; no advance. Photocopied submissions OK. Computer printout submissions OK. SASE. Reports in 3 weeks. Paperback book with listings of title $2.50.
Imprints: md Books (nonfiction and fiction), May Davenport, editor.
Nonfiction: Humor, juvenile and textbook. Accepts artwork/photos. Subjects include Americana, animals, art, music and nature. Accepts nonfiction translations from Spanish. Our readers are students in elementary and secondary public school districts, as well as correctional institutes of learning, etc." No "hack writing." Query. SASE. Accepts outline/synopsis and 1 sample chapter.
Recent Nonfiction Titles: *John Hawk—White Man, Black Man, Indian Chief*, by Beatrice S. Levin; *The ABC of Ecology*, by Frances Wosmek; and *Unusual Animals A to Z*, by Darlene Bakko.
Fiction: Adventure, ethnic, fantasy, humor, mystery and suspense. "We're overstocked with picture books and first readers; prefer stories for the tv-oriented teenagers (30,000-45,000 words.) Entertain while informing." No sex or violence. Query with SASE.
Recent Fiction Titles: *Eagle Trap*, by Ronald G. Bliss; *The Manuscript*, by Stephenie Slahor; and *Dudley Smithwright*, by Marcus Steinour.
Tips: "Make people laugh. Humor has a place, too."

DAVIS PUBLICATIONS, INC., 50 Portland St., Worcester MA 01608. (617)754-7201. Acquisitions Editor: Wyatt Wade. Averages 5-10 titles/year. Pays 10-15% royalty. Computer printout submissions OK. Write for copy of guidelines for authors. Submit outline, sample chapters and illustrations. Enclose return postage.
Art and Reference: Publishes art, design and craft books. Accepts nonfiction translations. "Keep in mind the intended audience. Our readers are *viewers*, as well. All illustrations should be collated separately from the text, but keyed to the text. Photos should be good quality original prints. Well-selected illustrations can ex-

plain, amplify, and enhance the text. We average 2-4 photos/page. We like to see technique photos as well as illustrations of finished artwork. Recent books have been on papermaking, airbrush painting, jewelry, design, puppets, programs for the artistically gifted, quilting, and water color painting.''

‡**STEVE DAVIS PUBLISHING**, Box 190831, Dallas TX 75219. Publisher: Steve Davis. Publishes hardcover and trade paperback originals. Averages 6-10 titles/year. Pays 10-20% royalty on net price. "Royalties, terms and advance are negotiable." Photocopied submissions OK. SASE. Reports in 2 weeks on queries; 1 month on mss. Free book catalog.
Nonfiction: How-to, reference, self-help, technical, textbook on personal computers, modern technology and communications arts. "We want to see unique, timely, helpful information for personal computer users." No religion, medicine or psychology. Query or submit outline/synopsis and sample chapters.
Recent Nonfiction Title: *Programs for the TI Home Computer*, by Steve Davis.
Fiction: Experimental, fantasy, humor and science fiction. "We do not expect to publish primarily fiction. However, would consider something fresh and unique." No mass market westerns, romance, religious, etc. Query or submit outline/synopsis and sample chapters.

DAW BOOKS, INC., 1633 Broadway, New York NY 10019. Editor: Donald A. Wollheim. Publishes science fiction paperback originals (80%) and reprints (20%). Publishes 62 titles/year. Pays 6% royalty; $2,500 advance and up. Simultaneous submissions "returned at once unread." SASE. Reports in 6 weeks. Free book catalog.
Fiction: "We are interested in science fiction and fantasy novels only. We do not publish any other category of fiction. We are not seeking collections of short stories or ideas for anthologies. We do not want any nonfiction manuscripts." Submit complete ms.
Recent Fiction Titles: *Thendara House*, by Marion Zimmer Bradley; *The Pride of Chanur*, by C.J. Cherryh; *An Oath to Mida*, by Sharon Green.

DBI BOOKS, INC., 1 Northfield Plaza, Northfield IL 60093. Subsidiary of Dun & Bradstreet, Technical Publishing Co. (312)441-7010. Vice President, Publisher: Sheldon L. Factor. Publishes trade paperback originals. Averages 15-20 titles/year. Pays negotiable royalty on retail price; buys some mss outright. Reports in 2 weeks on queries; 3 weeks on mss. SASE. Free book catalog.
Nonfiction: Subjects include recreation and sports. Specifically needs how-to books on guns, hunting, fishing, camping and various participant sports. No spectator sports. Query or submit outline/synopsis and sample chapters.
Recent Nonfiction Titles: *Gun Digest*, edited by Ken Warner (technical gun book); *Gambler's Digest*, by Clement McQuaid; and *Bowhunter's Digest*, by Cheri Elliot.

JOHN DE GRAFF, INC., Distributed by International Marine Publishing Co., Camden ME 04843. Editorial: Clinton Corners NY 12514. (914)266-5800. President: John G. DeGraff. Publishes hardcover originals. Averages 2-3 titles/year. Pays 10% royalty on retail price. Simultaneous and photocopied submissions OK. SASE. Reports in 2 weeks on queries; 1 month on mss. Free book catalog.
Nonfiction: Nautical (pleasure boating). "Our books are for yachtsmen, boat builders and naval architects. We're interested in the how-to aspects, rather than boating experiences." Submit complete ms.
Recent Nonfiction Titles: *Yachtsmen's Legal Guide to Co-ownership*, by Odin; *Sailing Years, a Memoir*, by Coles; and *Marine Survey Manual for Fiberglass Boats*, by Edmunds.

DELACORTE PRESS, 245 E. 47th St., New York NY 10017. (212)605-3000. Editor-in-Chief: Jackie Farber. Publishes hardcover originals. Publishes 30 titles/year. Pays 10-12½-15% royalty; average advance. Simultaneous and photocopied submissions OK. SASE. Reports in 2 months.
Fiction and General Nonfiction: Query or outline or brief proposal, or complete ms accepted only through an agent; otherwise returned unopened. No mss for children's or young adult books accepted in this division.
Recent Nonfiction Titles: *Holy Blood, Holy Grail*, by Henry Lincoln, Michael Baigent and Richard Leigh; *Victim*, by Gary Kinder; *The Cox Report*, by Allan Cox; *Buying the Night Flight* by George Anne Geyer.
Recent Fiction Titles: *Noble House*, by James Clavell; *Eden Burning*, by Belva Plain; *Life Sentences*, by Elizabeth Forsythe Hailey; *Crossings*, by Danielle Steele; *Deadeye Dick*, by Kurt Vonnegut.

DELAIR PUBLISHING COMPANY, INC., 420 Lexington Ave., New York NY 10170. (212)867-2255. Editor: Louise L. Apfelbaum. Executive Editor: Edward T. Finnegan. Publishes hardcover and paperback originals (80%) and reprints (20%). Averages 45 titles/year. Pays royalty; offers advance; other arrangements, depending on work. SASE. Simultaneous and photocopied submissions OK. Computer printout submissions OK.
Imprints: *Culinary Arts Institute* (cookbooks).
Nonfiction: Cookbooks; women's interest; consumerism; how-to; juvenile (to age 9); reference and self-help books about cooking, entertaining and foods; crafts; home maintenance, decorating and improvement; health;

medicine; travel. Accepts nonfiction translations. Query or submit outline/synopsis and 2 sample chapters. Accepts artwork/photos.

Recent Nonfiction Titles: *German and Viennese Cooking*; *The Salad Book*; *Coping with Your Headaches*, by Seymour Diamond, M.D.; *The ABC Dinosaur Book*, by Jill Kingdon; *Be a Home Videogame Superstar*, by E. Zavisca, Ph.D., and G. Beltowski.

Tips: "We are actively looking for manuscripts with very broad mass appeal (primarily to homemakers). Heavily illustrated books OK; cookbooks should contain a minimum of 200 recipes, though can be much longer."

DELL PUBLISHING CO., INC., 1 Dag Hammarskjold Plaza, New York NY 10017. Imprints include Dell, Delacorte Press, Delta Books, Dell Trade Paperbacks, Laurel, Delacorte Press Books for Young Readers, Candlelight Books, Yearling and Laurel Leaf. Publishes hardcover and paperback originals and reprints. Publishes 500 titles/year. Pays royalty on retail price. "General guidelines for unagented submissions. Please adhere strictly to the following procedure: 1) Do not send manuscript, sample chapters or art work; 2) Do not register, certify or insure your letter; 3) Send only a 3-page synopsis or outline with a cover letter stating previous work published or relevant experience." Simultaneous and photocopied submissions OK. Reports in 3 months. SASE.

Nonfiction: "Because Dell is comprised of several imprints, each with its own editorial department, we ask you to carefully review the following information and direct your submission to the appropriate department. Your envelope must be marked, Attention: (blank) Editorial Department—Proposal. Fill in the blank with one of the following: Delacorte: Publishes in hardcover. Looks for popular nonfiction (*My Mother, Myself*; *Holy Blood, Holy Grail*). Delta and Dell Trade: Publishes in trade paperback; rarely publishes original fiction; looks for useful, substantial guides (*Feed Your Kids Right*); entertaining, amusing nonfiction (*Cult Movies*); serious work in the area of modern society (*Killing Our Own*). Yearling and Laurel Leaf: Publishes in paperback and hardcover for children and young adults, grades 7-12. Purse: Publishes miniature paperbacks about 60 pages in length on topics of current consumer interest, e.g., diet, exercise, coin prices, etc."

Fiction: Refer to the above guidelines. Delacorte: Publishes top-notch commercial fiction in hardcover (e.g., *Bread Upon the Waters*; *Remembrance*). Dell: Publishes mass-market paperbacks; rarely publishes original nonfiction; looks for family sagas, historical romances, sexy modern romance, adventure and suspense, thrillers, occult/horror and war novels. Especially interested in submissions for our Candlelight Ecstasy Line. Not currently publishing original mysteries, westerns or science fiction.

DELMAR PUBLISHERS, INC., 2 Computer Dr., W., Box 15-015, Albany NY 12212. (518)459-1150. Director of Publishing: G.C. Spatz. Publishes hardcover and paperback textbooks. Averages 50 titles/year. Pays royalty on wholesale price. SASE. Reports in 2 weeks on queries; 2 months on submissions. Free book catalog.

Nonfiction: Subjects include business and data processing; allied health/nursing; childcare; mathematics; agriculture/horticulture texts; and textbooks for most vocational and technical subjects. Accepts artwork/photos. Books are used in secondary and postsecondary schools. Query and submit outline/synopsis and 2-3 sample chapters.

Recent Nonfiction Titles: *Vocational Technical Mathematics*, by Robert D. Smith; *Understanding Child Development*, by Rosalind Charlesworth; *Pediatric Nursing*, by Patricia A. Lesner; *Advertising Practices*, by Francis S. King; *Landscaping*, by Jack E. Ingels; and *Understanding Construction Drawings*, by Mark Huth.

Tips: Queries/mss may be routed to other editors in the publishing group.

DELTA BOOKS, Division of Dell Publishing Co., 1 Dag Hammarskjold Plaza, New York NY 10017. (212)605-3000. Editor-in-Chief: Jackie Farber. Publishes trade paperback reprints and originals. Averages 30 titles/year. Pays 6-7½% royalty; average advance. Simultaneous and photocopied submissions OK. SASE. Reports in 2 months. Book catalog for 8½x11 SASE.

Nonfiction: Consciousness, cookbooks/cooking, health, how-to, humor, music, New Age, photography, politics, recreation, reference, science, self-help and sports. "We would like to see books on popular music, social history, social criticism and analysis, and child care. We do not want to see biography, philosophy, academic books, textbooks, juveniles, or poetry books." Query or submit outline/synopsis and sample chapters. Prefers submissions through agents.

Recent Nonfiction Titles: *Parent's Magazine Mother's Encyclopedia*; *Death of the Sun*, by John Gribbin; and *Holistic Medicine*, by Kenneth Pelletier.

Fiction: "We are looking for original, innovative and contemporary novels." Submit through an agent.

Recent Fiction Titles: *Going After Cacciato*, by Tim O'Brien; *Black Tickets*, by Jayne Anne Phillips (collection of powerful short stories); *Legends of the Fall*, by Jim Harison; and *A Dove of the East*, by Mark Helprin.

RED DEMBNER ENTERPRISES CORP., 1841 Broadway, New York NY 10023. (212)265-1250. Editorial Director: S. Arthur Dembner. Senior Editor: Anna Dembner. Imprints include Dembner Books. Publishes hardcover and trade paperback originals. Averages 10 titles/year. Offers royalty on retail price. "Advances are negotiable—from bare bones on up." Simultaneous and photocopied submissions OK. SASE. Reports in 2-3 weeks.

Nonfiction: Biography, business/economics; health; history; hobbies; how-to; nature; philosophy; politics; psychology; recreation; reference; science; and self-help. "We're interested in upbeat, intelligent, informative mss. No cult, fad, or sex books. We prefer books that are worth reading, and even keeping." Submit outline/synopsis and sample chapters with SASE.

Recent Nonfiction Titles: *Isaac Asimov Presents Super Quiz*, by I. Asimov (compilation); and *One Word Leads to Another*, by M. Paisner (etymology).

Fiction: Adventure; historical; mainstream; mystery; and suspense. "We are prepared to publish a limited number of well-written, non-sensational works of fiction." Submit outline/synopsis and sample chapters with SASE.

Recent Fiction Titles: *Like Father*, by D. Black; *Search in Gomorrah*, by Daniel Panger; and *Deliverance in Shanghai*, by G. Agel and Eugene Boe.

*DENEAU PUBLISHERS & CO. LTD., 281 Lisgar St., Ottawa, Ontario, Canada K2P 0E1. (613)233-4075. Editorial Director: Barbara Stevenson. Publishes 93% hardcover and paperback originals and 7% paperback reprints. Averages 12 titles/year. Negotiates royalty and advance. Simultaneous and photocopied submissions OK. Computer printout submissions OK; prefers letter quality to dot matrix. SASE. Reports in 2 months. Free book catalog.

Nonfiction: Business/economics, social issues, politics, recreation, and travel. Submit outline/synopsis and 1-2 sample chapters.

Recent Nonfiction Titles: *Working People*, by Desmond Morton; *The Eighth Night of Creation*, by Jerome Deshusses (philosophy); and *An Eclectic Eel*, by Dalton Camp (politics).

Fiction: Literary. Submit outline and 1-2 sample chapters.

Recent Fiction Titles: *From a Seaside Town*, by Norman Levine (short stories); *Cock-Eyed Optimists*, by Dorothy O'Connell (short stories); and *By Grand Central Station I Sat Down and Wept* by Elizabeth Smart (novel).

T.S. DENISON & CO., INC., 9601 Newton Ave., S. Minneapolis MN 55431. Editor-in-Chief: W.E. Rosenfelt. Publishes teacher aid materials. Royalty varies, usually $80-100 per 1,000 sold, 8-10% on occasion; no advance. Send prints if photos are to accompany ms. Photocopied submissions OK. No computer printout or disk submissions. Reports in 2-4 weeks. SASE. Book catalog for SASE.

Nonfiction: Specializes in bulletin board books, early childhood books. Submit complete ms.

‡DENLINGER'S PUBLISHERS, LTD., Box 76, Fairfax VA 22030. (703)631-1500. Publisher: William W. Denlinger. Publishes hardcover and trade paperback originals, mass market paperback originals and hardcover and trade paperback reprints. Averages 12 titles/year. Pays variable royalty. No advance. Simultaneous and photocopied submissions OK. SASE. Reports in 1 week on queries; 6 weeks on mss.

Nonfiction: Biography, "coffee table" book, how-to and technical books on Americana and animals. Query.

Recent Nonfiction Titles: Series of Dog Breed Books—*Dogs on the Frontier*, by John E. Bauer.

Fiction: Historical and animal (dog). Query.

Recent Fiction Title: *Mandingo*.

*DETSELIG ENTERPRISES LTD., Box G399, Calgary, Alberta, Canada T3A 2G3. President: T.E. Giles. Publishes hardcover and trade paperback originals. Averages 6-8 titles/year. Subsidy publishes 15% of books. "The quality of the material and writing must be of a very high standard." Pays 8-13% royalty on wholesale price. No advance. Simultaneous and photocopied submissions OK. Computer printout submissions OK; prefers letter quality to dot matrix. SASE. Reports in 1 month on queries; 4 months on mss. Free book catalog.

Nonfiction: Biography, "coffee table" book, cookbook, reference, technical and textbook. Subjects include business and economics, cooking and foods, health, history, hobbies, psychology and sociology. "Most of our books will emphasize the Canadian scene." Immediate needs are university and college textbooks. No radical politics and religion. Query.

Recent Nonfiction Titles: *The Canadian Coal Industry*, by F. Anton; *Laird of the West*, by J. Chalmers; *Models of Classroom Management*, by J. Martin; *Strangled Roots*, by I. Quiring; *Personal Development*, by J. and W. Martin; *Roxene*, by W. Stephenson.

DEVELOPMENT SYSTEMS CORP., 500 N. Dearborn, Chicago IL 60610. (312)836-4400. Acquisitions Coordinator, Real Estate/Business/Professional Books: Alice Tell. Acquisitions Coordinator, Real Estate Textbooks: Bobbye Middendorf. Acquisitions Editor, Financial Services Textbooks: Ivy Lester. Publishes hardcover and paperback originals. Averages 50 titles/year. Pays 5-15% royalty. No advance. Simultaneous and photocopied submissions OK. Computer printout submissions OK. SASE. Reports in 2 months. Free book catalog.

Imprints: Real Estate Education Co., Educational Methods, Inc., Longman Financial Services Publications.

Nonfiction: "Development Systems Corporation publishes books for real estate professionals and other financial services professionals (banking, insurance, securities). Any topics appropriate for this market are of interest." Submit outline and 1-3 sample chapters (but not the first chapter) or complete ms.

Recent Nonfiction Titles: *Real Estate Law*, by Frank Gibson, Elliot Klayman, and James Karp (basic introduction law textbook); *Power Real Estate Selling*, by William Pivar (helps real estate salespeople increase their selling skills); *Taxation of Real Estate in the United States*, by Thomas A. Bodden (professional reference book that explains how real estate is taxed).

THE DEVIN-ADAIR CO., INC., Subsidiary: The Chatham Press, 143 Sound Beach Ave., Old Greenwich CT 06870. (203)637-4531. Editor: Jane Andrassi. Publishes hardcover and paperback originals (90%) and reprints (10%). Royalty on sliding scale, 5-25%; "average advance is low." Averages 38 titles/year. Send prints to illustrate ms. No simultaneous submissions. Computer printout submissions OK; disk submissions must be compatible with present equipment. SASE. Free book catalog.
Nonfiction: Publishes Americana, business, how-to, politics, history, medicine, nature, economics, sports and travel books. New lines: personal computer books and homeopathic books. Accepts translations. Query or submit outline/synopsis and sample chapters. Looks for "early interest, uniqueness, economy of expression, good style, and new information."
Recent Nonfiction Titles: *The IRS vs. the Middle Class*, by Martin A. Larson; *Is Public Education Necessary?*, by Samuel L. Blumenfeld (history); *Light, Radiation, and You*, by John N. Ott (health); *How to Select a Personal Computer*, by Ursula Connor; *The Original 1887 White House Cookbook*, by Hugo Ziemann; *Games in Applesoft Basic*, by Peter Gabriele; *The Homosexual Network*, by Enrique Rueda; *DMSO: New Healing Power*, by Dr. Morton Walker.
Tips: "We purposely seek to publish books of high quality manufacture. We spend 8% more on production than necessary to insure a better-quality book."

*DHARMA PUBLISHING, 2425 Hillside Ave., Berkeley CA 94704. (415)548-5407. Editor: Betty Cook. Publishes hardcover and paperback originals (90%) and paperback reprints (10%). Publishes 10 titles/year. Pays 5-7% royalty on retail price; no advance. Subsidy publishes 5% of books. SASE. Reports in 1-2 months. Free book catalog.
Nonfiction: Art (Tibetan and other Buddhist); biography (Buddhist); history (Asia and Buddhism); philosophy (Buddhist); photography (Buddhist); psychology (Buddhist); religion (Buddhism); and self-help. "We want translations of Buddhist texts from Tibetan or Sanskrit. Please—no original discussions of Buddhist topics." Query. Recently published *Life and Liberation of Padmasambhava*, by Yeshe Tsogyal (biography); *Time, Space, and Knowledge*, by Tarthang Tulkv (philosophy/religion); *Tibet in Pictures*, by LiGotami Govinda (photography); and *Buddha's Lions*, by Abhayadatta (biography).

THE DIAL PRESS, Doubleday, Inc., 245 Park Ave., New York NY 10167. (212)953-4561. Publishes hardcover and paperback originals. Averages 60 titles/year. Pays royalty on retail price. Simultaneous and photocopied submissions OK. Reports in 6 weeks. SASE.
Nonfiction: "All general trade nonfiction is of interest." Submit outline/synopsis and sample chapters.
Recent Nonfiction Titles: *In War's Dark Shadow*, by Bruce Lincoln; and *Kathleen Kennedy*, by Lynne McTaggert.
Fiction: All general adult categories. Submit outline/synopsis and sample chapters.
Recent Fiction Titles: *The Birth of the People's Republic of Antarctica*, by John Calvin Batchelor; *The Chester A. Arthur Conspiracy*, by William Wiegand; *Fatal Obsession*, by Stephen Greenleaf.

DILITHIUM PRESS, Suite E, 11000 SW 11th St., Beaverton OR 97005. (503)646-2713. Editorial Director: Merl Miller. Publishes paperback originals and software. Averages 25-30 titles/year. Pays 5-25% royalty on wholesale or retail price; average advance. Photocopied submissions OK. Computer printout and disk submissions OK. SASE. Reports in 2 months. Free book catalog.
Nonfiction: Textbooks and books about microcomputers. "We are looking for manuscripts in the field of microcomputers. Topics should be geared to general information, hardware and software." Accepts outline/synopsis and 4-5 sample chapters. Query.
Recent Nonfiction Titles: *Computers for Everybody*, by Jerry Willis and Merl Miller; *Bits, Bytes and Buzzwords*, by Mark Garetz; *How to Use Super Calc*, by Deborrah Smithy-Willis.

DILLON PRESS, INC., 500 S. 3rd St., Minneapolis MN 55415. (612)333-2691. Editorial Director: (Ms.) Uva Dillon. Senior Editor: Tom Schneider. Juvenile Fiction Editor: (Mr.) Terry Hopkins. Publishes hardcover originals. Averages 25-30 titles/year. Pays royalty and by outright purchase. Submit complete ms or outline and 1 sample chapter. Computer printout submissions OK. No disk submissions. Reports in 6 weeks. SASE.
Nonfiction: "We are actively seeking manuscripts for the juvenile educational market." Areas of interest: science, wildlife, environment, biography, heritage, crafts and outdoor activities, and contemporary issues. Accepts artwork/photos. Recently published: *China: From Emperors to Communes*, by Chris and Janie Filstrap

(juvenile); *Bill Cosby*, by Harold and Geraldine Woods (juvenile); and *The Dangers of Strangers*, by Carole G. Vogel and Kathryn A. Goldner (juvenile).

Fiction: We are looking for engaging stories that will appeal to K-6 readers. Areas of interest: animal/nature tales, mysteries, science fiction, and stories that focus on the lifestyles, problems, and experiences of today's young people.

Tips: "Writers can best tailor their material to our needs by making themselves aware of the subjects and people who appeal to today's youngsters."

DIMENSION BOOKS, INC., Box 811, Denville NJ 07834-0811. (201)627-4334. Contact: Thomas P. Coffey. Publishes 35 titles/year. Pays "regular royalty schedule" based on retail price; advance is negotiable. No computer printout or disk submissions. Book catalog for SASE. Reports in 1 week on receipt of mss. SASE.

General Nonfiction: Publishes general nonfiction including religion, principally Roman Catholic. Also psychology. Accepts nonfiction translations. Query. Accepts outline/synopsis and 3 sample chapters. Length: 40,000 words minimum. Recently published *Looking for Jesus*, by A. van Kaam; *Called By Name*, by P. van Breemen; and *Certain as the Dawn*, by Peter van Breemen.

DOANE-WESTERN, INC., 8900 Manchester Road, St. Louis MO 63144. (314)968-1000. Editor, Books and Special Projects: Tom Corey. Publishes hardcover and paperback originals. Averages 3 titles/year. Pays 8% of the gross sales. Submit outline/synopsis and sample chapter. Reports in 1-2 months. SASE.

Nonfiction: "Publishes books written for farmers and ranchers and others involved in agribusiness. Most titles are guides, handbooks, references or how-to books. Books that sell to this audience offer specific advice and assistance, not overviews or general interest."

Recent Nonfiction Titles: *Buying & Selling Farmland*, by Jundt; and *Farm Buildings: From Planning to Completion*, by Phillips.

DODD, MEAD & CO., 79 Madison Ave., New York NY 10016. (212)685-6464. Includes Everest House imprint. Senior Editors: Jerry Gross, Allen T. Klots, Evan Marshall, Margaret Norton. Royalty basis: 10-15%. Advances vary, depending on the sales potential of the book. A contract for nonfiction books is offered on the basis of a query, a suggested outline and a sample chapter. Write for permission before sending mss. Averages 150 titles annually. Adult fiction, history, philosophy, the arts, and religion should be addressed to Editorial Department. Reports in 1 month. SASE.

General Fiction and Nonfiction: Publishes book-length mss. Length: 70,000-100,000 words. Fiction and nonfiction of high quality, mysteries and romantic novels of suspense, biography, popular science, travel, yachting and other sports, music and other arts. Very rarely buys photographs or poetry.

Juveniles: Length: 1,500-75,000 words. Children's Books Editor: Mrs. Joe Ann Daly.

‡DOLL READER, Subsidiary of Hobby House Press, Inc., 900 Frederick St., Cumberland MD 21502. (301)759-3770. Subsidiaries include *Doll Reader* and *The Teddy Bear and Friends Magazine*. Publisher: Gary R. Ruddell. Publishes hardcover originals. Averages 10 + titles/year. Pays a royalty. Simultaneous and photocopied submissions OK. SASE. Reports in 2 weeks. Free book catalog.

Nonfiction: Doll-related books. "We publish books pertaining to dolls and teddy bears as a collector's hobby; we also publish pattern books. The *Doll Reader* is published 8 times a year dealing with the hobby of doll collecting. We appeal to those people who are doll collectors, miniature collectors, as well as people who sew for dolls. Our magazine has a worldwide circulation of close to 40,000." Query or submit outline/synopsis. *The Teddy Bear and Friends Magazine* is published quarterly.

Recent Nonfiction Titles: *5th Blue Book of Dolls and Values*, by Jan Foulke (price guide for dolls); *The 3rd Doll Catalog*, edited by Donna Felger (guide to the doll world); *Best of the Doll Reader*, edited by Virginia Heyerdahl (compendium of articles from *Doll Reader*); and *Kestner, King of Dollmakers*, by Jan Foulke (reference on Kestner dolls).

THE DONNING COMPANY/PUBLISHERS, INC., 5659 Virginia Beach Blvd., Norfolk VA 23502. Editorial Director: Robert S. Friedman. Publishes hardcover and paperback originals. Averages 30-35 titles/year. Pays 10-12½-15% royalty on retail price, up to 50% discount (hardcover titles); 8-10-12% royalty on paperback; advance "negotiable." Simultaneous (if so informed) and photocopied submissions OK. Computer printout and disk submissions OK. Reports in 12 weeks. SASE. Book catalog for SASE.

Nonfiction: Wants material for 3 series: 1) Portraits of American Cities Series (pictorial histories of American cities with 300 illustrations, primarily photographs, with fully descriptive captions and historical overview text of approximately 10,000 words. "The intent is to capture the character of a community in transition, from earliest known settlers to the present. Author need not be a professional historian, but must have close ties to the community and cooperation of local historians and private and public photo archives); 2) Regional Specialty Books (specialty, regional cookbooks, popular history and art collections); and 3) Unilaw Library imprint (Editor: Richard Horwege. Religious, inspirational, metaphysical subjects and themes). Accepts nonfiction translations. "Prefer complete manuscript, if not a thorough outline and 3 sample chapters. We look for professionally presented material, with helpful marketing and promotion suggestions if author has any." Accepts artwork/photos.

Recent Nonfiction Titles: *Portland (OR): A Pictorial History*, by Harry Stein, Kathleen Ryan and Mark Beach; and *Elvis: His Spiritual Journey*, by Jess Stearn.

Fiction: Starblaze Editions imprint. Editor: Hank Stine.

Recent Fiction Titles: *Myth Conceptions*, by Robert Asprin (science fiction); *Web of Darkness*, by Marion Zimmer Bradley (science fiction); and *Voices? Voices!*, by Stefan Grunwald (metaphysical fiction).

Tips: "Beginning writers are finding it harder to get published because of the increasing number of copies needed to break even. Regional appeal books are easier to place, and authors should consider doing more of them to break into print." Queries/mss may be routed to other editors in the publishing group.

DOUBLEDAY & CO., INC., 245 Park Ave., New York NY 10167. (212)953-4561. Managing Editor: Karen Van Westering. Publishes hardcover and paperback originals; publishes paperback reprints under Anchor, Dolphin and Image imprints. Offers standard 10-12½-15% royalty on retail price; offers variable advance. Reports in 2½ months. Publishes over 500 titles/year. Special submission requirements outlined below. Query with outline and sample chapters for both fiction and nonfiction. "Your letter of inquiry should be addressed to the Editorial Department. The letter may be as short as one page, but no longer than six pages (double-spaced). Use a separate letter for each submission. The first sentence should tell us whether your book is a novel, a biography, a mystery, or whatever. The first paragraph should give us an idea of what your book is about. This description should be clear and straightforward. If your book is a novel, please give us an engaging summary of the plot and background, and a quick sketch of the major characters. If you have already been published, give us details at the end of your letter. You should also tell us of any credentials or experience that particularly qualify you to write your book. For a nonfiction book, it will be helpful to you to consult the *Subject Guide to Books in Print* (available in most libraries) so that you are aware of other books on the same or similar subjects as your own, and can tell us how your book differs from them. Finally, letters of inquiry should be inviting and typed with a good ribbon. If we ask to see your ms, it should be submitted double-spaced on white paper. You should retain a carbon copy, since we cannot assume responsibility for loss or damage to mss. Sufficient postage, in the form of loose stamps, should accompany your submission if your ms is to be returned in the event it is not accepted for publication."

Nonfiction and Fiction: "Doubleday has a policy concerning the handling of manuscripts. We return unopened and unread all complete manuscripts, accompanied by a form telling how we would like submissions made. However, in 2 areas, we will accept complete manuscripts: mysteries and science fiction. These mss should be addressed to the appropriate editor (for example, Science Fiction Editor) and not just to Doubleday. We presently have a moratorium on books for young readers, and poetry publishing and are not accepting mss."

DOUBLEDAY CANADA, LTD., 105 Bond St., Toronto, Ontario, Canada M5B 1Y3. (416)977-7891. Senior Editor: Janet Turnbull. Publishes hardcover originals. Publishes 15-20 titles/year. Pays royalty on retail price; advance "varies." Simultaneous and photocopied submissions OK. Reports in 3 months. Free book catalog.

Nonfiction: General interest. "We do not specialize, but the major part of our list consists of biography, popular history, and subjects of contemporary interest. Our main concern is to publish books of particular interest to the Canadian market, although our books are published in the US as well. We will consider any nonfiction proposal." Query or submit outline/synopsis and 3 or 4 sample chapters.

Recent Nonfiction Titles: *The Other Mrs. Diefenbaker*, by Simma Holt, *The Presidents and the Prime Ministers: Washington and Ottawa Face to Face: The Myth of Bilateral Bliss*, by Lawrence Martin; *For Services Rendered: Leslie James Bennett and the RCMP Security Service*, by John Sawatsky; *Signing On: The Birth of Radio in Canada*, by Bill McNeil and Morris Wolfe; *The Silence of Jesus: The Authentic Voice of the Historical Man*, by James Breech; *Five Hundred Years of New Words*, by William Sherk; *Disappearances: Tales of Canadians Who Vanished*, by Derrick Murdoch; *The Company Store: James Bryson McLachlan and the Cape Breton Coal Miners*, by John Mellor.

Fiction: "No particular preferences as to style or genre. We publish both 'literary' and 'commercial' books. Once again, we are most interested in adult fiction with a Canadian angle (author, setting, subject). Of course, we hope they have North American potential as well." Query or submit outline/synopsis and opening chapters.

Recent Fiction Titles: *The Other Woman*, by Joy Fielding; *Home Game*, by Paul Quarrington; *Smith and Other Events* by Paul St. Pierre; *Lusts*, by Clark Blaise.

Tips: Looks for "identification of genre of work; straightforward description of what book is about; indication of whether work is completed or in progress; covering letter detailing writer's publishing history, any credentials or experience that particularly qualifies him/her to do the proposed book." In fiction, studies plot summary and brief sketch of major characters. Queries/mss may be routed to other editors in the publishing group.

DOW JONES-IRWIN, (Business and Finance) 1818 Ridge Rd., Homewood IL 60430. (312)798-6000. Executive Editor: Ralph Rieves. Publishes originals only. Royalty schedule and advance negotiable. Publishes 60 titles annually. Reports in 2 weeks. SASE.
Nonfiction: Business and financial subjects. Query with outline. Queries/mss may be routed to other editors in the publishing group.
Recent Nonfiction Titles: *Money Market: Myth, Reality and Practice*, by Marcia Stigum; *Modern Portfolio Theory*, by Robert Hagen (investing); and *Tax Shelters*, by Robert E. and Barbara M. Swanson.

DOW JONES-IRWIN, (Psychology and Sociology) 1818 Ridge Rd., Homewood IL 60430. (312)798-6000. Senior Editor: Michael Jeffers. Subsidiary of Richard D. Irwin. Subsidiaries include Dorsey Professional Series. Publishes hardcover originals. Averages 70 titles/year. Pays 10-15% royalty on retail price; offers average $1,500-2,000 advance. Simultaneous and photocopied submissions OK. SASE. Reports in 3 weeks on queries; 1 month on mss. Free book catalog.
Nonfiction: How-to and technical on psychology, sociology and social work. Immediate needs include clinical psychology, genetic research, psychopharmacology. No self-help or child care mss. Submit outline/synopsis and sample chapters.
Recent Nonfiction Titles: *The Clinical Measurement Package: A Field Manual*, by Walter W. Hudson; *Psychotherapy and Patient Relationships*, by Michael J. Lambert; *A Guide to Family Financial Counseling: Credit, Debt, and Money Management*, by Mary G. Van Arsdale; *Clinical Psychology Handbook*, 2 volumes, by Eugene Walker.

‡**DOWN EAST BOOKS**, Subsidiary of Down East Enterprise, Inc., Box 679, Camden ME 04843. (207)594-9544. Assistant to Publisher: Karin Womer. Publishes hardcover and trade paperback originals and hardcover and trade paperback reprints. Averages 10-20 titles/year. Pays 10-15% on wholesale price. Offers average $200 advance. Simultaneous and photocopied submissions OK. SASE. Reports in 2 weeks on queries; 3 months on mss. Free book catalog.
Nonfiction: Biography, "coffee table" book, cookbook, humor, illustrated book, juvenile, reference and textbook. Subjects include Americana, art, cooking and foods, history, nature, photography and recreation. "Our books are for New Englanders and others with a fondness for New England and the New England way of life and people with an interest in a coastal and forest environment." Query.
Recent Nonfiction Titles: *Lost Bar Harbor*, by G.W. Helfrich (history); *A Foraging Vacation*, by Raquel Boehmer (nature guide); and *Maine's Historic Places*, by Frank Beard and Betty Smith (history).
Fiction: Humor, mystery and juvenile. Query.
Recent Fiction Titles: *Zachary Goes Ground-Fishing*, by Alice Larkin (juvenile); *Storm Treasure*, by Robert Packie (juvenile mystery); and *The Littlest Lighthouse*, by Ruth Sargent (juvenile).

‡***DRAGON'S TEETH PRESS**, El Dorado National Forest, Georgetown CA 95634. (916)333-4224. Editor: Cornel Lengyel. Publishes trade paperback originals. Averages 6 titles/year. Subsidy publishes 25% of books; applies "if book has high literary merit, but very limited market." Pays 10% royalty on retail price, or in copies. Simultaneous and photocopied submissions OK. SASE. Reports in 2 weeks on queries; 1 month on mss. Book catalog for SASE with 63¢ postage.
Nonfiction: Music and philosophy. Publishes for 500 poets, or potential poets. Query or submit outline/synopsis and sample chapters.
Poetry: "Highly original works of potential literary genius. No trite, trivial or trendy ego-exhibitions." Submit 10 samples or the complete ms.
Recent Poetry Titles: *The Liam Poems*, by Thomas Heffernan (lyric poetry); *The Devil Comes to Wittenberg*, by George Hitchcock; and *Dispatches From the Fields*, by R. Henri (lyric poetry).

THE DRAGONSBREATH PRESS, Rt. 1, Sister Bay WI 54234. Editor: Fred Johnson. Publishes hardcover and trade paperback originals. Averages 1 title/year. Payment conditions "to be arranged"; no advance. Simultaneous and photocopied submissions OK. Computer printout submissions OK "if readable." SASE. Reports in 1 month on queries; 2 months on mss.
Nonfiction: Biography, humor, illustrated book. Subjects include Americana, art, history and photography. "We're interested in anything suited to handmade book production—short biography, history, original artwork, photography. The Dragonsbreath Press is a small press producing handmade limited edition books including original artwork meant for collectors of fine art and books who appreciate letterpress printing. This audience accepts a handmade book as a work of art." Query first; do not submit ms.
Fiction: Adventure, erotica, experimental, fantasy, horror, humor, mystery, science fiction. "We are looking for short, well-written stories which lend themselves to illustration and deserve to be made into fine, handmade books." *No long, novel-length* manuscripts or *children's books*. Query first; do not submit ms.
Recent Fiction Title: *How I Became Popular Overnight*, by F.W. Johnson (mystery/humor).
Poetry: "We're looking for good readable poetry relating emotions, feelings, experiences. No religious,

sweet-Hallmark style or divorce poems." Submit 3 samples with query; submit complete ms "when requested."

Tips: "Because of many delays on projects, we are not looking for manuscripts to read until 1984. Please do not submit mss unless they have been requested."

DRAMA BOOK PUBLISHERS, 821 Broadway, New York NY 10003. (212)228-3400. Contact: Ralph Pine or Judith C. Rudnicki. Publishes hardcover and paperback originals and reprints. Royalty varies; advance varies; negotiable. Computer printout submissions OK; "but query first." Averages 15 titles/year. Reports in 4 to 8 weeks. SASE.
Nonfiction: Books for and about performing arts theory and practice: acting, directing; voice, speech, movement, dance; makeup; costume, set, lighting design; technical theatre, stagecraft; stage management; producing; arts management, business and legal; film and video; theory, criticism, reference; playwriting; theatre history. Accepts nonfiction and drama translations. Query; accepts 1-3 sample chapters; no complete mss.
Fiction: Plays and musicals.

‡DREADNAUGHT, 46 Harbord St., Toronto, Ontario, Canada M5S 1G2. (416)979-2752. Publishes hardcover and trade and mass market paperback originals. Averages 6 titles/year. Pays 5-7% royalty on retail price. SASE. No computer printout or disk submissions. Reports in 6 weeks on queries; 3 months on mss. Book catalog for a business-sized SASE with 32¢ Canadian postage.
Nonfiction: Coffee table book, cookbook, illustrated book, juvenile, reference, datebooks on art, cooking and foods, history, hobbies, travel, Canadiana. Accepts translations of nonfiction, fiction and poetry. "We are developing lists in the areas of Canadiana, cooking, datebooks and diaries." Publishes for a large, varied, educated, urbane audience. No philosophy, religion, sociology. Query. Accepts photos/artwork. "Unsolicited mss are received with horror and disgust."
Recent Nonfiction Titles: *Canada Illustrated: 19th Century Engraving*, by Albert Moritz (art book); *1983 Canadian Engagement Diary*, by Theresa Moritz/Ann Jansen (datebook); and *Food 101: Student's Guide to Quick & Easy Cooking*, by Cathy Smith.

DREAM GARDEN PRESS, 1199 Iola Ave., Salt Lake City UT 84104. (801)355-2154. Editor: Marc Brown. Publishes hardcover and trade paperback originals (50%) and reprints (50%). Averages 8 titles/year. Pays 10-17½% royalty on retail price. No advance. Photocopied submissions OK. SASE. Reports in 2 weeks on queries; 2 months on mss. Free book catalog.
Imprints: *Western Wilderness Calendars*, *Ned Ludd Books* (nonfiction books on the environment, deep ecology, etc.) Ken Sanders, owner; Marc Brown, editor.
Nonfiction: How-to and environmental. Subjects include Americana, art, history, nature and photography. Looks for mss "with some sort of regional slant; either the author writing about the West in some manner or being a western author. No mss that are too academic or technical/professional." Query or submit outline/synopsis and sample chapters.
Recent Nonfiction Titles: *The Fiddleback: Lore of the Line Camp*, by Owen Ulph (essays); *Footprints in the Wilderness: A History of the Lost Rhoades Mines*, by Gale Rhoades (regional western Americana); and *Treasure Mountain Home: Park City Revisited*, by George Thompson (regional western Americana).
Fiction: Adventure, experimental, fantasy, historical, horror, mystery, science fiction, western and environmental fiction. "Well written insightful regional books about the West, defined in its broadest sense. Good genre fiction." Query or submit outline/synopsis and sample chapters.
Recent Fiction Title: *The Leather Throne*, by Owen Ulph (western fiction).
Tips: "Please don't send us any submissions if all you're interested in are royalty checks and movie rights, rather than the quality of what you've written and how it's produced."

DRYAD PRESS, 15 Sherman Ave., Takoma Park MD 20912. Also: 2943 Broderick St., San Francisco CA 94123. Editor/Publisher: Merrrill Leffler. Editor/Publisher: Neil Lehrman. Publishes hardcover and trade paperback originals. Averages 3 titles/year. Pays 8-10% royalty on retail price. No advance. Simultaneous and photocopied submissions OK. SASE. Reports in 2 weeks; 2 months on mss. Free book catalog.
Nonfiction: "We rarely publish nonfiction, though we are considering literary manuscripts." Publishes for a literary, not necessarily university, audience. Submit outline/synopsis and sample chapters.
Fiction: Submit outline/synopsis and sample chapters.
Recent Fiction Titles: *Perdut*, by Neil Lehrman (novel); and *The Secret Seed*, by Sidney Sulkin (7 stories and 20 poems).
Poetry: Submit 10 samples.
Recent Poetry Titles: *The Feel of the Rock: Poems of the Three Decades*, by Reed Whittemore; *From the Backyard of the Diaspora*, by Myra Sklarew; and *With Wanda: Town & Country Poems*, by Paul Zimmer.

‡*DUCK DOWN PRESS, Box 1047, Fallon NV 89406. (702)423-6643. Editor/Publisher: Kirk Robertson. Publishes trade paperback originals. Averages 3-5 titles/year. Subsidy (combination of NEA and private funds)

publishes 50% of books. Pays in copies and royalties on "amount above expenses." No photocopied submissions. SASE. Reports in 1 week on queries; 3 weeks on mss. Book catalog for 6x9 SAE and 2 first class stamps.
Imprints: Windriver Series (fiction and poetry).
Nonfiction: Art and photography.
Fiction: Quality post-modern literature. Query with outline/synopsis and sample.
Recent Fiction Titles: *The Chase*, by Gerald Locklin (novel); and *The Wages of Sin*, by Gerald Haslam (collection of short fiction).
Poetry: Publishes 2-4 titles/year. No juvenile, rhymed or metrical. Submit 5-10 poems.
Recent Poetry Titles: *The Broken Face of Sommer*, by Michael Hogan; *Cruisin at the Limit: Selected Poems 1968-78*, by Dr. Wagner; and *Reasons and Methods*, by Kirk Robertson.

‡**DUFOUR EDITIONS, INC.**, Box 449, Chester Springs PA 19425. (215)458-5005. Associate Editor: Kristin Dufour. Publishes hardcover and trade paperback originals and reprints. Averages 10 titles/year. Pays "as negotiated." Simultaneous and photocopied submissions OK. SASE. Reports in 1 month on queries; 6 months on mss. Free book catalog.
Nonfiction: Biography, cookbook, juvenile, textbook, humanities on Americana, art, cooking and foods, history, music, philosophy, politics, psychology, religion. Accepts nonfiction, fiction and poetry translations. Publishes for public and university libraries. Query or submit outline/synopsis and 2 sample chapters.
Recent Nonfiction Titles: *Five Religions in the 20th Century*, by W. Owen Cole (religious textbook); *These Were the Greeks*, by H.D. Amos and A.G.P. Lang (classics textbook); and *Dynamics of European Nuclear Disarmament*, by Alva Myrdal and others (political).
Fiction: Confession, ethnic, experimental, fantasy, historical, humor, mainstream, romance, feminist. Query or submit outline/synopsis and 2 sample chapters.
Recent Fiction Title: *The Knife*, by Peadar O'Donnell (historical).
Poetry: Submit 6 samples.

DUQUESNE UNIVERSITY PRESS, 600 Forbes Ave., Pittsburgh PA 15282. (412)434-6610. Averages 9 titles/year. Pays 10% royalty on net sales; no advance. Query. Reports in 3 months. Enclose return postage.
Nonfiction: Scholarly books in the humanities, social sciences for academics, libraries, college bookstores and educated laypersons. Length: open. Looks for scholarship.
Recent Nonfiction Titles: *Hart Crane's Holy Vision: White Buildings*, by Alfred Hanley; *Foundations of a Critical Psychology*, by Theo de Boer (psychology); and *Philosophy and Archaic Experience*, edited by John Sallis (philosophy).

‡**DURST PUBLICATIONS**, 29-28 41st Ave., Long Island City NY 11101. (212)706-0303. Owner: Sanford Durst. Publishes hardcover and trade paperback originals (30%) and reprints. Averages 20+ titles/year. Pays variable royalty. SASE. Reports in 1 month. Book catalog for business size SAE and 75¢ postage.
Nonfiction: How-to and reference on Americana, art, business and economics, cooking and foods, hobbies—primarily coin collecting, stamp collecting, antiques, legal. Especially needs reference books and how-to on coins, medals, tokens, paper money, art, antiques—illustrated with valuations or rarities, if possible. Publishes for dealers, libraries, collectors, attorneys. Submit outline/synopsis and sample chapters.
Recent Nonfiction Titles: *Buying & Selling Country Land*, by D. Reisman (practical/legal); *The Golden Key*, by E. Levine (investment in gold); and *Copyright Practice & Procedure*, by S. Durst (practical/legal).
Tips: "Write in simple English. Do not repeat yourself. Present matter in logical, orderly form. Try to illustrate."

DUSTBOOKS, Box 100, Paradise CA 95969. (916)877-6110. Publisher: Len Fulton. Publishes hardcover and paperback originals. Averages 7 titles/year. Offers 15% royalty. Offers average $500 advance. Simultaneous and photocopied submissions OK if so informed. SASE. Reports in 1-2 months. Free book catalog.
Nonfiction: Technical. "DustBooks would like to see manuscripts dealing with microcomputers (software, hardware) and water (any aspect). Must be technically sound and well-written. We have at present no titles in these areas. These represent an expansion of our interests." Submit outline/synopsis and sample chapters.

E.P. DUTTON, 2 Park Ave., New York NY 10016. (212)725-1818. Publisher, Children's Books: Ann Durell. Senior Editor: Julie Amper. Averages 50 titles/year. Pays royalty on list price; offers variable advance. Considers unsolicited mss. "Please send query letter first on all except picture book mss."
Juvenile: Picture books; Smart Cats (beginning readers); stories for ages 8-12; Skinny Books (Hi-lo for 12 and up). Accepts artwork/photos. Emphasis on books that will be current and popular as well as well written.
Recent Juvenile Fiction Titles: *When I was Young in the Mountains*, by Cynthia Rylant and Diane Goode (picture book); *The Kestrel*, by Lloyd Alexander; *That Game from Outer Space*, by Stephen Manes.
Tips: Queries/mss may be routed to other editors in the publishing group.

EAKIN PUBLICATIONS, INC., Box 23066, Austin TX 78735. (512)288-1771. Imprints include Nortex. Editorial Director: Edwin M. Eakin. Publishes hardcover and paperback originals (95%); and reprints (5%). Averages 25-30 titles/year. Pays 10-12-15% in royalty. Simultaneous and photocopied submissions OK. SASE. Reports in 3 months. Free book catalog sent on request.
Nonfiction: History, juvenile history and folklore. Specifically needs biographies of well-known Texas people, current Texas politics and history for the grades 3-9. Query first or submit outline/synopsis and sample chapters.
Recent Nonfiction Titles: *Memoirs of a Texas Pioneer Grandmother* (translation), by Goeth and Guenther; *Fifty Years of Texas Politics*, by Richard Morehead; *The Unsinkable Titanic Thompson*, by C. Stowers.
Fiction: Historical fiction for school market. Specifically need juveniles that relate to Texas. Query or submit outline/synopsis and sample chapters.
Recent Fiction Titles: *Jim Bowie*, *Stephen F. Austin* and *William B. Travis*, all by Jean Flynn (juvenile); *Texas Yesterday and Today*, by Hancock and Venable (juvenile).

THE EAST WOODS PRESS, (Trade name of Fast & McMillan Publishers, Inc.), 429 E. Blvd., Charlotte NC 28203. Editorial Director: Sally Hill McMillan. Publishes hardcover and paperback originals for "travelers and seekers of alternative lifestyles." Publishes 10 titles/year. Pays 8-10% royalty on retail price; 5% on wholesale price. Reports in 2-4 weeks. SASE. Book catalog for SASE.
Nonfiction: "We are mainly interested in travel and the outdoors. Regional guidebooks are our specialty, but anything on travel and outdoors will be considered." Submit outline/synopsis and 2-3 sample chapters. "A list of competitive books should be submitted, along with specific reasons why this manuscript should be published. Also, maps and art should be supplied by the author."
Recent Nonfiction Titles: *The Best Bed & Breakfast in the World*, by Sigourney Welles; *Free Campgrounds, USA*, by Mary VanMeer; *Carpentry: Tips & Tricks from an Old-Style Carpenter*, by Bob Syvanen.

‡EASTVIEW EDITIONS, INC., Box 783, Westfield NJ 07091. (201)233-0474. Subsidiary includes Glenn Associates. Manager: Mr. N. Glenn. Publishes hardcover and trade paperback originals (90%) and reprints. Averages 12 titles/year. Pays standard royalty contract; offers negotiable advance. Simultaneous and photocopied submissions OK. Computer printout submissions OK. SASE. Reports in 6 weeks. Free book catalog.
Nonfiction: Illustrated books on the arts, history, hobbies, music, nature, photography, design, dance, antiques. Also does limited editions of nature and art books. Considers all material for domestic and international publication. Submit outline and 2-3 sample chapters, table of contents; "description of the book, what the author envisions." Accepts artwork/photos. Will distribute to book trade and libraries; (national and international) books privately printed.
Recent Nonfiction Titles: *Logic and Design*, by Krome Barrett; *The Rise of Architectural History*, by B. Watkins; *The Wedgwood Circle, 1730-1897*, by Barbara Wedgwood (history); and *Textiles by William Morris & Co.*, by Oliver Fairclough and Emmeline Leary.

THE ECCO PRESS, Subsidiaries include *Antaeus*, 18 W. 30th St., New York NY 10001. (212)685-8240. Editor: Daniel Halpern. Associate and Managing Editor: Megan Ratner. Publishes hardcover and trade paperback originals and reprints. Averages 12 titles/year. Pays 5-15% royalty on retail price; offers average $300 advance. Photocopied submissions OK. SASE. Reports in 1 week on queries; 2 months on mss. Free book catalog.
Nonfiction: Cookbook and literary criticism. "Can do only 1 or 2 books." No scientific, historical or sociological mss. Query.
Recent Nonfiction Titles: *Eating in America*, by Waverley Root (food history); *Babel to Byzantium*, by James Dickey (literary criticism); and *The Structure of Verse*, by Harvey Gross (prosody).
Fiction: Experimental, mainstream, and serious or 'literary' fiction. "Can do 1 or possibly 2 novels or short story collections." Query.
Recent Fiction Titles: *Zara*, by Meredith Steinbach (novel); *In the Garden of the North American Martyrs*, by Tobias Wolff (short stories); and *The Ghostly Lover*, by Elizabeth Hardwick (reprint novel).
Poetry: One or two new collections. No religious, inspirational, etc. Submit 4-6 samples.
Recent Poetry Titles: *Descending Figure*, by Louise Gluck; *Praise*, by Robert Hass; and *Rwen Doggeries*, by James Tabe.

EDITS PUBLISHERS, Box 7234, San Diego CA 92107. (619)488-1666. Editorial Director: Robert R. Knapp. Publishes hardcover and paperback originals. Averages 4 titles/year. Pays variable royalty on retail price; no advance. Photocopied submissions OK. Reports in 1-2 months. SASE. Book catalog for SASE.
Nonfiction: "Edits publishes scientific and text books in social sciences, particularly counseling and guidance, psychology, statistics and education." Query or submit sample chapters. Recently published *Actualizing Therapy*, by E. Shostrom (therapy text); *Naked Therapist*, by S. Kopp; and *Handbook in Research and Evaluation*, by S. Isaac.

*EDUCATION ASSOCIATES, Box 8021, Athens GA 30603. (404)542-4244. Editor, Text Division: D. Keith Osborn. Publishes hardcover and trade paperback originals. Averages 2-6 titles/year. Subsidy publishes 50% of books. "We may publish a textbook which has a very limited audience . . . but we still believe that the book will make a contribution to the educational field." Buys mss "on individual basis." Photocopied submissions OK. SASE. Reports in 3 weeks on queries; 6 weeks on mss.
Nonfiction: How-to and textbook. Subjects include psychology and education. "Books in the fields of early childhood education and middle school education. Do not wish basic textbooks. Rather, are interested in more specific areas of interest in above fields. We are more interested in small runs on topics of more limited nature than general texts." Query with outline/synopsis and sample chapters. "Prefer query. If interested, will request total manuscript."
Recent Nonfiction Titles: *Discipline & Classroom Management*, by D.K. Osborn (college text); *Source Book for the Middle School*, by M. Compton (reference text for middle school students); and *Cognitive Tasks*, by J. Dyson (college text).

EDUCATIONAL DEVELOPMENT CORP., Usborne/Hayes, 8141 E. 44th St., Tulsa OK 74145. (800)331-4418. General Manager: Rich Howard. Publishes hardcover and trade and mass market paperback originals and reprints. Averages 50 titles/year. Pays average 5% royalty on wholesale price; buys some mss outright; offers negotiable advance. Simultaneous submissions OK. SASE. Reports in 1 month. Free book catalog.
Nonfiction: Juvenile (preschool—age 12). Subjects include animals, hobbies, nature, sports, computers, travel, world of the future, young engineers, wizards, princes, King Arthur, Robinson Crusoe. "Highly colorful quality books." Query or submit outline/synopsis.

WILLIAM B. EERDMANS PUBLISHING CO., Christian University Press, 255 Jefferson Ave. SE, Grand Rapids MI 49503. (616)459-4591. Editor-in-Chief: Jon Pott. Publishes hardcover and paperback originals (80%) and reprints (20%). Averages 55 titles/year. Pays 7½-10% royalty on retail price; usually no advance. Simultaneous and photocopied submissions OK. Computer printout submissions OK; prefers letter quality to dot matrix. SASE. Reports in 3 weeks for queries and 4 months for mss. Looks for "quality and relevance." Free book catalog.
Nonfiction: History, philosophy, psychology, reference, religion, sociology and textbooks. "Approximately 80% of our publications are religious—specifically Protestant and largely of the more academic or theological (as opposed to devotional, inspirational or celebrity-conversion type of book) variety. Our history and 'social studies' titles aim, similarly at an academic audience; some of them are 'documentary' histories. We prefer writers take the time to notice if we have published anything at all in the same category as their manuscript before sending it to us." Accepts nonfiction translations. Query. Accepts outline/synopsis and 2-3 sample chapters.
Recent Nonfiction Titles: *Documentary History of Religion in America*, ed. by Edwin S. Gaustad (history); *Spirituality and Human Emotion*, by Robert Roberts (theology); and *John Cheever: The Hobgoblin Company of Love*, by George Hunt (literary criticism).

*EFFECTIVE LEARNING, INC., 7 N. MacQuesten Pkwy., Box 2212, Mt. Vernon NY 10551. (914)664-7944. Editor: William Brandon. Publishes hardcover and paperback originals (95%) and reprints (5%). Averages 6-10 titles/year. Subsidy publishes 2% of books. Simultaneous submissions OK. Query. SASE. Reports in 1-2 months. Free book catalog.
Nonfiction: Americana, biography, business, cookbooks, cooking and food, economics, history, hobbies, how-to, multimedia material, nature, philosophy, politics, reference, religious, scientific, self-help, sociology, technical, textbooks and travel. "All manuscripts should be sent to the editorial review committee." Recently published *The Middle East: Imperatives & Choices*, by Alon Ben-Meir (politics).

ENSLOW PUBLISHERS, Bloy St. and Ramsey Ave., Box 777, Hillside NJ 07205. (201)964-4116. Editor: Ridley Enslow. Publishes hardcover and paperback originals. Averages 30 titles/year. Pays 10-15% royalty on retail price or net price; offers $500-5,000 advance. Query. Photocopied submissions OK. Computer printout and disk submissions OK. SASE. Reports in 2 weeks. Free book catalog.
Nonfiction: Biography, business/economics, health, hobbies, how-to, juveniles, philosophy, psychology, recreation, reference, science, self-help, sociology, sports and technical. Accepts artwork/photos and nonfiction translations. Accepts outline/synopsis and 2 sample chapters.
Recent Nonfiction Titles: *Comets: A Descriptive Catalog*, by Kronk (science); *Solar Cells: What You Always Wanted to Know*, by Laws (how-to); *Justice Sandra Day O'Connor*, by Fox (juvenile biography).

ENTELEK, Ward-Whidden House/The Hill, Box 1303, Portsmouth NH 03801. Editor-in-Chief: Albert E. Hickey. Publishes paperback originals. Offers royalty on retail price of 5% trade; 10% textbook. No advance. Averages 4-5 titles/year. Free catalog. Photocopied and simultaneous submissions OK. Submit outline and sample chapters or submit complete ms. Reports in 1 week. SASE.

Nonfiction: Publishes computer books and software of special interest to educators. Length: 3,000 words minimum.
Recent Nonfiction Titles: *Genetics With the Computer*; *Physics with the Computer*; *3-D Computer Graphics*, and *Navigation with a Microcomputer*.

ENTERPRISE PUBLISHING CO., INC., 725 Market St., Wilmington DE 19801. (302)654-0110. Editor and Publisher: T.N. Peterson. Publishes hardcover and paperback originals, "with an increasing interest in newsletters and periodicals." Averages 4 titles/year. Pays royalty on wholesale or retail price. Advance averages $1,000. Simultaneous and photocopied submissions OK, but "let us know." Reports in 1 month. SASE. Catalog and writers' guidelines for SASE.
Nonfiction: "Subjects of interest to small business owners/entrepreneurs. They are highly independent and self-sufficient, and of an apolitical to conservative political leaning. They need practical information, as opposed to theoretical: self-help topics on business, including starting and managing a small enterprise, advertising, marketing, raising capital, public relations, tax avoidance and personal finance." Business/economics, legal self-help, and business how-to. Query; all unsolicited mss are returned unopened.
Recent Nonfiction Titles: *Big Tax Savings for Small Business*, by Joseph R. Oliver; *Basic Book of Business Agreements* and *How to Save Your Business*, by Arnold S. Goldstein; and *Make Money by Moonlighting*, by Jack Lander.

ENVIRONMENTAL DESIGN & RESEARCH CENTER, 261 Port Royal Ave., Foster City CA 94404. Contact: Dr. Kaiman Lee. Publishes hardcover originals. Averages 5 titles/year. Pays 15-18% royalty. SASE. Reports in 2 weeks on queries; 3 weeks on submissions. Free book catalog.
Nonfiction: Reference, technical, textbook and encyclopedic. Subjects include business and economics (personal finance); architecture; energy; and environment. "We're looking for mss on personal financial and survival planning. Our books are highly technical but of current material." Submit complete ms.
Recent Nonfiction Titles: *Encyclopedia of Financial and Personal Survival: 650 Coping Strategies*, by K. Lee and R. Yang; *Kaiman's Encyclopedia of Energy Topics*, by K. Lee; and *Environmental Court Cases Related to Buildings*, by K. Lee.

*PAUL S. ERIKSSON, PUBLISHER, Battell Bldg., Middlebury VT 05753. (802)388-7303. President: Paul S. Eriksson. Publishes hardcover and paperback trade originals (99%) and paperback trade reprints (1%). Averages 5-10 titles/year. Pays 10-15% royalty on retail price; advance offered if necessary. Subsidy publishes 5% of books. "We have to like the book and probably the author." Photocopied submissions OK. SASE. Reports in 3 weeks. Free book catalog.
Nonfiction: Americana, birds (ornithology), art, biography, business/economics, cookbooks/cooking/foods, health, history, hobbies, how-to, humor, music, nature, philosophy, photography, politics, psychology, recreation, self-help, sociology, sports and travel. Submit outline/synopsis and sample chapters. Looks for "intelligence, excitement, salability."
Recent Nonfiction Titles: *Steinbeck and Covici*, by Thomas Fensch; *It's A Pig World Out There*, by Phyllis Demong; and *Flight of the Storm Petrel*, by Ronald M. Lockley.
Fiction: Mainstream. Submit outline/synopsis and sample chapters.
Recent Fiction Title: *The Deadly Dream*, by Theodore S. Drachman, M.D.

EROS PUBLISHING CO., INC., Box 604, Reseda CA 91335. "Not in the market for freelance material."

ESSCO, Akron Airport, Akron OH 44306. (216)733-6241. President/Editorial Director: Ernest Stadvec. Publishes paperback originals. Averages 14 titles/year. Pays 10% royalty on retail price for the first 1,000 and 15% thereafter; no advance. Simultaneous and photocopied submissions OK. SASE. Reports in 2 weeks. Free book catalog.
Nonfiction: Biography, history, hobbies, how-to, technical and textbooks, all on aviation. Specifically needs aviation-related subjects, aircraft guide books, training manuals, aircraft picture books, historical books and military aviation. Query.
Recent Nonfiction Titles: *The Eternal Twin Beech*, by E. Stadvec (historical); and *The Aircraft Value Guide*, by E. Stadvec.

*ETC PUBLICATIONS, Drawer ETC, Palm Springs CA 92263. (619)325-5352. Editorial Director: LeeOna S. Hostrop. Senior Editor: Dr. Richard W. Hostrop. Publishes hardcover and paperback originals. Subsidy publishes 5-10% of books. Averages 12 titles/year. Offers 5-15% royalty, based on wholesale and retail price. No advance. Simultaneous and photocopied submissions OK. Computer printout submissions OK; prefers letter quality to dot matrix. SASE. Reports in 3 weeks. Book catalog $2.
Nonfiction: Biography; business/economics; how-to; psychology; recreation; reference; self-help; sociology; sports; technical; and textbooks. Accepts artwork/photos. Accepts nonfiction translations. Submit complete ms.

Recent Nonfiction Titles: *The Fans Vote! 100 Baseball Superstars*, by R. Bartlett (sports); *Vampires Are*, by S. Kaplan (occult); *The Creative Writer's Phrase-Finder*, by Edward Prestwood (how-to).
Tips: "*ETC* is particularly interested in textbook titles for use in college courses in professional education—also reference titles in all areas."

EVANS AND CO., INC., 216 E. 49 St., New York NY 10017. Editor-in-Chief: Herbert M. Katz. Publishes hardcover originals. Royalty schedule to be negotiated. Averages 30 titles annually. Will consider photocopied submissions. Computer printout and disk submissions OK. "No mss should be sent unsolicited. A letter of inquiry is essential." Reports in 6-8 weeks. SASE.
General Fiction and Nonfiction: "We publish a general trade list of adult fiction and nonfiction, cookbooks and semi-reference works. The emphasis is on selectivity since we publish only 30 titles a year. Our fiction list represents an attempt to combine quality with commercial potential. Our most successful nonfiction titles have been related to the behavioral sciences. No limitation on subject. A writer should clearly indicate what his book is all about, frequently the task the writer performs least well. His credentials, although important, mean less than his ability to convince this company that he understands his subject and that he has the ability to communicate a message worth hearing."
Tips: "Writers should review our catalog (available for 9x12 envelope with 2 stamps) or the *Publishers Trade List Annual* before making submissions."

EXANIMO PRESS, 23520 Hwy 12, Segundo CO 81070. Editor: Dean Miller. Publishes hardcover and trade paperback originals. Averages 6-10 titles/year. Pays 10% minimum royalty on retail price; buys some mss outright for $500-1,500; no advance. Photocopied submissions OK. No computer printout or disk submissions. SASE. Reports in 1 month on queries; 2 weeks on mss. Book catalog for SAE and 1 first class stamp.
Nonfiction: How-to and technical. Subjects include prospecting; small mining; treasure hunting; self-employment; dowsing (water witching); and self- or family-improvement from an economical point of view. Accepts nonfiction translations from German or French (on dowsing and mining only). "We would like to publish one book per month in our particular field which is mining, prospecting, and treasure hunting. Our style and format is approximately 8x10" pages with books running from 40 to 104 pages. We prefer a profusely illustrated book and our artist will make finished sketches from rough drawings. Accepts artwork/photos. Our books are aimed at the adventuresome person or family and people who want to get out of the rat race and into a profitable activity that relieves them of audits, inspections and red tape. No copy-artistry, please, and no read-and-rewrites; we want hard-core mining material from people with at least 10 full years of experience." Query. Accepts outline/synopsis, 1 sample chapter and intended table of contents.
Recent Nonfiction Titles: *Midas Manual—How to Earn Money as Your Own Boss*; *Miser's Manual—How to Save Part of What You Earn and Grow Rich*; and *Encyclopedia of Dowsing*.
Tips: "Investigate the market and find a publisher whose specialty is in accord with your proposed book or books. Most try to create a good working relationship and pave the way for future books which will obviously pave the way for a higher financial return for you. The secret is to get a first book published in order to give leverage for future books. Specialize in 1 field and develop a reputation for technically accurate books and get 2 or 3 titles into print and then look forward to an ascending career in writing."

FACTS ON FILE, INC., 460 Park Ave. S., New York NY 10016. (212)683-2244. Editorial Director: Eleanora Schoenebaum. Publishes hardcover originals (75%) and reprints (25%). Averages 120 titles/year. Offers "usually 15% royalty of net proceeds, sometimes 10% of list price." Also buys some mss by outright purchase: $2,000-50,000. Advance averages $7,000. Simultaneous and photocopied submissions OK. SASE. Reports in 4 weeks. Book catalog for SASE.
Nonfiction: Reference for libraries and trade in art; biography; business/economics; history; music; nature; energy; politics; psychology; science; self-help; sociology; and travel. "All books must be essentially reference or information-oriented, but given that, the subject matter can be almost anything." Does *not* want "juvenile books, textbooks, Ph.D. theses, opinionated books." Submit outline/synopsis and sample chapters. Looks for "organization, comprehensiveness, clarity."
Recent Nonfiction Titles: *World Paychecks: Who Makes What, Where, and Why*, by David Harrop (reference); *Safe Delivery: Protecting Your Baby During High Risk Pregnancy*, by Dr. Roger Freeman and Susan Pescar (health reference); and *World Press Encyclopedia*, edited by George Kurian (reference).

FAIRCHILD BOOKS & VISUALS, Book Division, 7 E. 12th St., New York NY 10003. Manager: E.B. Gold. Publishes hardcover and paperback originals. Offers standard minimum book contract; no advance. Pays 10% of net sales distributed twice annually. Published 12 titles last year. Photocopied submissions OK. No computer printout or disk submissions. Free book catalog. Query, giving subject matter, brief outline and at least 1 sample chapter. Enclose return postage.
Business and Textbooks: Publishes business books and textbooks relating to fashion, electronics, marketing, retailing, career education, advertising, home economics, and management. Length: open. Recently

published *Fairchild's Designer's/Stylist's Handbook*, by Gioello; and *Fashion Advertising and Promotion*, by Winters/Goodman.

FAIRMONT PRESS INC., Box 14227, Atlanta GA 30324. (404)447-5314. Director of Operations: V. Oviatt. Publishes hardcover originals. Averages 4-8 titles/year. Pays 5-12% royalty. SASE. Reports in 6 weeks. Free book catalog.
Nonfiction: How-to, reference, science, self-help, technical, energy, plant engineering, environment, safety. Submit outline/synopsis and sample chapters.
Recent Nonfiction Title: *Handbook on Selling to the US Military*, by Richard K. Miller, C.E.M.

‡*FALCON PRESS PUBLISHING CO., INC., 324 Fuller, Box 731, Helena MT 59624. (406)442-6597. Publisher: Bill Schneider. Publishes hardcover and trade paperback originals. Averages 5-8 titles/year. Subsidy publishes 10% of books. Pays 8-15% royalty on net price. Simultaneous and photocopied submissions OK. SASE. Reports in 3 weeks on queries; 6 weeks on mss. Free book catalog.
Nonfiction: "Coffee table" book, cookbook, how-to and self-help. Subjects include Americana, cooking and foods, health, history, hobbies, nature, photography, recreation, sports and travel. "We're primarily interested in recreational guidebooks." No fiction or poetry. Query only. Do not send ms.
Recent Nonfiction Titles: *The Hiker's Guide to Utah*, by Dave Hall; *The Traveler's Guide to Montana*, by Gary Turbak; *The Dakota Image*, by Bill Schneider.

FALKYNOR BOOKS, 4950 SW 70th Ave., Davie FL 33314. (305)791-1562. Executive Director: Michael Blate. Publishes hardcover and trade paperback originals. Averages 3-4 titles/year. Buys mss outright. Simultaneous submissions OK. SASE. Reports in 2 weeks. Book catalog for business size SAE and 1 first class stamp.
Nonfiction: Self-help (natural and self-health) techniques. Subjects include health. Submit outline and sample chapters "after querying first."
Recent Nonfiction Titles: *The Natural Healers Acupressure Handbook*, by Michael Blate (self-health); *The Natural Healers Acupressure Handbook Book II*, by Michael Blate; *First Aid Using Simple Remedies*, by Michael Blate.

THE FAMILY ALBUM, Rt. 1, Box 42, Glen Rock PA 17327. (717)235-2134. Contact: Ron Lieberman. Publishes hardcover originals and reprints. Averages 4 titles/year. Pays royalty on wholesale price. Simultaneous and photocopied submissions OK. Computer printout and disk submissions OK. SASE. Reports in 2 months.
Nonfiction: "Significant works in the field of (nonfiction) bibliography. Worthy submission in the field of Pennsylvania-history, biography, folk art and lore. We are also seeking materials relating to books, literacy, and national development. Special emphasis on Third World countries, and the role of printing in international development." No religious material. Submit outline/synopsis and sample chapters.

FARM JOURNAL BOOKS, W. Washington Sq., Philadelphia PA 19105. (215)574-1342. Subsidiary of *Farm Journal*. Managing Editor: Nancy Steele. Publishes hardcover and trade paperback originals. Averages 4-12 titles/year. Pays 5-8% royalty on retail price; offers average $3,000 advance. SASE. Computer printout and disk submissions OK. Reports in 2 weeks on queries; 1 month on mss. Queries/mss may be routed to other editors in the publishing group.
Nonfiction: Cookbook, how-to. Immediate needs include original craft books, especially books for people who sew. No rural nostalgia. Query. Accepts outline/synopsis and 2 sample chapters.
Recent Nonfiction Titles: *More Scap Saver's Stitchery*, by Sandra Lounsbury Foose (how-to); *Let's Make a Patchwork Quilt*, by MacDonald and Shafer (how-to); *Farm Journal's Complete Cake Decorating Book*, by food editors of *FJ* (cooking).

FARNSWORTH PUBLISHING CO., INC., 78 Randall Ave., Rockville Centre NY 11570. (516)536-8400. President: Lee Rosler. Publishes hardcover and paperback originals. "Standard royalty applies, but 5% is payable on mail order sales." Publishes 20 titles/year. Computer printout submissions accepted "for consideration"; prefers letter quality. Reports in 2 months. SASE.
General Nonfiction, Business and Professional: "Our books generally fall into 2 categories: books that appeal to executives, lawyers, accountants and life underwriters and other salespeople (subject matter may cover selling techniques, estate planning, taxation, money management, etc.); and books that appeal to the general population—generally in the financial and self-improvement areas—and are marketable by direct mail and mail order, in addition to bookstore sales." Submit outline/synopsis and 3 sample chapters.
Recent Nonfiction Titles: *Executive Wealthbuilding Plans*, by Paul Bullock and William Kautter; *Making It In Management The Japanese Way*, by Raymond Dreyfack; *A Treasury of Business Opportunities for the '80s*, by David D. Seltz; and *Living Together—The Complete Guide To Personal Relationships*, by Mort Katz, MSSW.

FARRAR, STRAUS AND GIROUX, INC., 19 Union Square West, New York NY 10003. Children's Editor: Stephen Roxburgh. Publishes hardcover originals. Pays royalty; advance. Photocopied submissions OK. SASE. Reports in 3 months. Catalog for SASE.

Nonfiction: History, humor, juveniles, philosophy, psychology, science and sociology. "We are primarily interested in nonfiction for the junior high and up age group." Submit outline/synopsis and sample chapters.

Recent Nonfiction Titles: *South Africa: Coming of Age Under Apartheid*, by Jason and Ettegale Laure; and *Upon the Head of the Goat*, by Aranka Siegal; *Pack, Band and Colony: The World of Social Animals*, by Judith and Herbert Kohl.

Fiction: Adventure, fantasy, historical, humor, mainstream, mystery, romance, science fiction, suspense and western. "We particularly want to see contemporary fiction for 7-10 and 10-and-up age group." Submit outline/synopsis and sample chapters.

Recent Fiction Titles: *Hi My Name is Henley*, by Colby Rodowsky; *Annie On My Mind*, by Nancy Garden; and *Chester Cricket's Pigeon Ride*, by George Selden, illustrated by Garth Williams.

FAWCETT BOOKS, 201 E. 50th St., New York NY 10022. See Random House, Inc.

FREDERICK FELL PUBLISHERS, INC., 386 Park Ave., S., New York NY 10016. (212)685-9017. Editor: Ms. Mercer Warriner. Publishes hardcover and paperback originals (95%) and reprints (5%). Pays 10% royalty, based on wholesale or retail price. Publishes 25 titles/year. Send sample prints or contact sheet if photos/illustrations are to accompany ms. Photocopied submissions OK. Reports in 2 months. SASE. Free book catalog.

Nonfiction: Diet, business, hobbies, how-to, medicine and psychiatry, pets, psychology, recreation, reference, inspiration, self-help and sports books. Query with outline and 3 sample chapters.

Recent Nonfiction Titles: *No Bull Selling*, by Hank Triszer; *Complete Wedding Planner*, by Edith Gilbert.

THE FEMINIST PRESS, Box 334, Old Westbury NY 11568. (516)997-7660. Publishes paperback and hardcover originals and historical reprints. Averages 12-15 titles/year. Pays 10% royalty on net sales; no advance. Simultaneous and photocopied submissions OK. Reports in 3 months. Query or submit outline/synopsis and sample chapters.

Adult Books: Jo Baird, Editor. Feminist books for a general trade and women's studies audience. "We publish biographies, reprints of lost feminist literature, women's history, bibliographies and educational materials. No material without a feminist viewpoint. No contemporary adult fiction, drama, or poetry." Looks for "feminist perspective, interesting subject, potential use in women's studies classroom, sensitivity to issues of race and class, clear writing style, general grasp of subject."

Recent Nonfiction Titles: *Lesbian Studies*, edited by Cruikshank (anthology); *How to Get Money for Research*, by Rubin (text, how-to); and *The Silent Partner*, by Phelps (fiction reprint).

Children's Books: "We publish juvenile fiction and biographies. No picture books." Recently published *Tatterhood and Other Tales*, by E. Phelps (folklore); *The Lilith Summer*, by H. Irwin; and *The Boy Who Wanted a Baby*, by W. Lichtman.

Tips: "Submit a proposal for an important feminist work that is sophisticated in its analysis, yet popular in its writing style. Both historical and contemporary subjects will be considered. We are especially interested in works that appeal to both a trade audience and a women's studies classroom market."

‡**FIESTA CITY PUBLISHERS**, 740 Sky View Dr., Box 5861, Santa Barbara CA 93108. (805)969-2891. President: Frank E. Cooke. Publishes hardcover and mass market paperback originals. Averages 3 titles/year. Pays 5-15% royalty on retail price. No advance. Simultaneous and photocopied submissions OK. SASE. Reports in 2 weeks on queries; 1 month on mss. Book catalog for 4x9½ SAE.

Nonfiction: Cookbook, self-help and musical subjects. "How-to books on playing instruments, writing music, marketing songs; any music-related material (including bios or autobios of famous music world personalities. Nothing personalized or dull." Query or submit complete ms.

Recent Nonfiction Titles: *Write That Song!*, by Frank E. Cooke (self-help); *Cooking with Music*, by Ann and Frank Cooke (recipes from famous people and music); and *Kids Can Write Songs, Too*, by Frank E. Cooke (self-help).

‡**FIL-AM-BEL PUBLICATIONS, INC.**, Box 87450, Chicago IL 60680-0450. Editor/Publisher: Tomas P. Rizal, Jr. Publishes hardcover and mass market paperback originals. Averages 5 titles/year. Pays 4-8% royalty on retail price; buys some mss outright $200-400. "Additional 5% royalty after sales of 2,000 or more of our 60-page pamphlets." Offers $50 advance on acceptance. Photocopied submissions OK. SASE. Reports in 6 weeks on queries; 3 months on mss. Writer's guidelines available.

Nonfiction: Pamphlets and books related to the Philippines or Philippine-American relationships. "We get too many full-length book manuscripts; we need more pamphlet length (60 pages plus or minus); we need more on geographical areas in the Philippines and on 'great men' biographies not only of Filipinos, but of Americans pertinent to the Philippines. "No political propaganda or anything not related to Philippines or Filipinos or Fil-Am relations." Query.

Recent Nonfiction Titles: *Empires in the Filipino Ethnic Travel Market*, by "Lolo Bob" Johnston (analysis of travel industry in US); *Quezon*, by "Lolo Bob" Johnston (biography).

Fiction: "We have not published fiction as yet—but would consider it. At least some characters, however, must be either Filipinos or Filipino-Americans." Query.

Poetry: Poetry must involve Filipinos, Filipino-Americans, or subjects of interest to them. Submit 3 poems.

Recent Poetry Title: *Poems from the Ilonggo*, by Nathaniel C. Sanchez (lyric).

*THE FILTER PRESS, Box 5, Palmer Lake CO 80133. (303)481-2523. Editorial Director: Gilbert L. Campbell. Senior Editor: Lollie W. Campbell. Publishes hardcover and paperback originals (50%) and reprints (50%). Publishes 8 titles/year. Subsidy publishes about 20% of titles/year. "These are usually family histories in short runs, although subjects have ranged from preaching, ranching, history debunking, to a study of UFOs. If we feel we can market a book profitably for us and the author, and it is a good book and the author feels he needs it published, we will consider it." Pays 10% royalty on net price; no advance. Simultaneous and photo-copied submissions OK. Reports in 2-3 weeks. "Must have SASE." Book catalog for SASE.

Nonfiction: "Cookbooks must appeal to Westerners, campers, and tourists. Accepts nonfiction translations. We have one cookbook on game cookery, one on pancakes, one on camp cooking, one on Southwestern Indian recipes, two on Mexican cooking for the Anglo bride. Also Western legends, Indians, ghost towns, and other Western Americana, as we are quite regional. We must stay at or near our 64-page limit, as most booklets are sold softbound, saddle stitched. We have done some verse of Western interest. Our morgue of antique wood engravings is used extensively, so books with a Western Victorian feel fit in best. Western Americana on our list includes Indians, explorations, lawmen, and bandits. We have Butch Cassidy and Pat Garrett. Family histories and very local history have not done well for us. Writers must remember we are small, publish few books, and they must be things that a tourist will buy to take home, although we are in many Eastern book-stores." Query; "it is much cheaper and safer to send a query and SASE than to send the manuscript to us cold." Accepts artwork/photos.

Recent Nonfiction Titles: *Violet Soup*, by Daniel Beshoar; *People of the Crimson Evening*, by Ruth Underhill; *Mexican Recipe Shortcuts*, by Helen Duran.

FJORD PRESS, Box 615, Corte Madera CA 94925. (415)924-9566. Editors: Steven T. Murray and Susan Doran. Publishes trade paperback originals and reprints. Averages 3-6 titles/year. Pays 1-7.5% royalty on retail price (to translators only); sometimes offers advance. Simultaneous (if so advised) and photocopied submissions OK. Computer printout submissions OK; prefers letter quality to dot matrix. SASE. Reports in 6 weeks on queries. Book catalog for business size envelope and 1 first class stamp.

Nonfiction: Subjects include cooking and foods (European); history (European); nature (European ecology, animals, natural history); travel (literary only); and women (European). "Acquired through European publishers, but open to suggestions from translators." No original American mss. Query first with resume and submit outline/synopsis and sample chapters. Looks "first for an interesting style. Second, a good story. Third, the magic ingredient that makes the book worth translating and publishing here."

Recent Nonfiction Title: *Evening Light*, by Stephan Hermlin (memoirs—East German).

Fiction: Adventure; fantasy; historical (particularly Scandinavian and German); mainstream (modern European literature and 19th century classics); science fiction; suspense (spy and international thrillers); and women's mainstream from any language. "Translations of modern or contemporary European novels that have not been done in English before; or of modern classics that should be reprinted." Interested in ethnic American fiction. Query first with resume, and submit outline/synopsis and sample chapters.

Recent Fiction Titles: *Fitzcarraldo*, by Werner Herzog; *The Witches' Circles*, by Kerstin Ekman (Swedish novel); and *Stolen Spring*, by Hans Scherfig (Danish satire).

Poetry: "Limited to one book per year, modern classics only (European)." No American mss. Submit 5 to 10 samples.

Recent Poetry Title: *Love & Solitude*, by Edith Sodergran (Finnish-Swedish classic).

Tips: Accepts translations; "our specialty is Germanic, but we are looking for others (mainly European and Latin American)."

FLARE BOOKS, Young Adult Imprint of Avon Books, a division of the Hearst Corp., 959 8th Ave., New York NY 10019. (212)262-7454. Editorial Director: Jean Feiwel. Publishes mass market paperback originals (50%) and reprints (50%). "We have published young adult books under the *Avon* imprint. Those books are now under the *Avon-Flare* imprint." Pays 6-10% royalty; offers average $1,500 advance. Simultaneous and photocopied submissions OK. Computer printouts OK. SASE. Reports in 6 weeks.

Nonfiction: Self-help. Subjects include health and psychology. Query or submit outline/synopsis and 6 sample chapters.

Recent Nonfiction Title: *Am I Normal?*, by Jeanne Betancourt.

Fiction: Adventure, ethnic, experimental, fantasy, humor, mainstream, mystery, romance, science fiction,

suspense and contemporary. Mss appropriate to age 12-20. Submit outline/synopsis and 6 sample chapters.
Recent Fiction Titles: *Waiting Games*, by Bruce and Carole Hart; *I Love You, Stupid!*, by Harry Mazer; *The Grounding of Group 6*, by Julian Thompson.
Tips: Queries/mss may be routed to other editors in the publishing group.

FLEET PRESS CORP., 160 5th Ave., New York NY 10010. (212)243-6100. Editor: Susan Nueckel. Publishes hardcover and paperback originals and reprints. Royalty schedule and advance "varies." Published 11 titles in 1980. Free book catalog. Reports in 6 weeks. Enclose return postage with ms.
General Nonfiction: "History, biography, arts, religion, general nonfiction, sports." Length: 45,000 words. Query with outline; no unsolicited mss.
Juveniles: Nonfiction only. Stress on social studies and minority subjects; for ages 8-15. Length: 25,000 words. Query with outline; no unsolicited mss.

FOCAL PRESS, Division of Butterworth Publishers, 10 Tower Office Park, Woburn MA 01801. (617)933-8260. General Manager and Editor: Arlyn S. Powell. Publishes hardcover and paperback originals. Publishes 35 titles/year. Offers royalty; rate negotiable. Advances paid. Simultaneous and photocopied submissions OK. SASE. Reports in usually 6 weeks. Free book catalog.
Nonfiction: "We publish only in the fields of photography, cinematography, audiovisual and broadcasting—how-to books for beginning amateur to advanced level research monographs." Does *not* want to see books of pictures or portfolios. Submit outline/synopsis and sample chapters or complete ms. "We look for a logical format, strong writing, and an *organized*, well-planned presentation."
Recent Nonfiction Titles: *Nikon/Nikkormat Way*, by Keppler; *Monochrome Darkroom Practice*, by Coote; *The Use of Microphones*, by Nisbett.

FODOR'S TRAVEL GUIDES, 2 Park Ave., New York NY 10016. (212)340-9800. President and Publisher: James Louttit. Executive Vice President/Editorial: Alan Tucker. Publishes hardcover and paperback originals. Averages 70 titles/year.
Nonfiction: "We are the publishers of dated travel guides—regions, countries, cities, and special tourist attractions. We do not solicit manuscripts on a royalty basis, but we are interested in travel writers and/or experts who will and can cover an area of the globe for Fodor's for a fee." Submit credentials and samples of work.
Recent Nonfiction Titles: *Fodor's Scotland; Fodor's New York City; Fodor's Texas; Fodor's Korea.*

FOLCRAFT LIBRARY EDITIONS/NORWOOD EDITIONS, 842 Main St., Darby PA 19023. (215)583-4550. President: Hassie Weiman. Publishes hardcover originals (library bound). Publishes 300 titles/year. Pays standard royalty rates; offers variable advance. Simultaneous and photocopied submissions OK. SASE. Reports in 3 months.
Nonfiction: Scholarly materials in the humanities by scholars and active researchers associated with universities. Submit complete ms.
Recent Nonfiction Titles: *Native American Music*, by M. Herndon; *The Kibbutz, A Bibliography*, by Schor, et al.; and *Democracy and Change: The Kibbutz and Social Theory*, by Rosner.

FORDHAM UNIVERSITY PRESS, University Box L, Bronx NY 10458. (212)579-2320. Director: H.G. Fletcher. Averages 8 titles/year. Pays royalty on sales income. Send written queries only; do not send unsolicited manuscripts. SASE. Reports in 1 week. Free book catalog.
Nonfiction: Humanities. "We would like the writer to use the *MLA Style Sheet*, latest edition. We do not want dissertations or fiction material."
Recent Nonfiction Titles: *The Value of Justice*, edited by Charles A. Kelbley; *The Metaphysics of Experience*, by Elizabeth M. Kraus; *Conservative-Millenarians*, by Paul Gottfried; *Evil and a Good God*, by Bruce Reichenbach.

FORMAN PUBLISHING, Suite 206, 11661 San Vicente Blvd., Los Angeles CA 90049. (213)820-8672. President: Len Forman. Publishes hardcover and mass market paperback originals. Averages 6 titles/year. Pays standard royalty. Photocopied submissions OK. SASE. Reports in 1 month.
Nonfiction: Cookbook, how-to, self-help. Accepts nonfiction translations. Submit outline/synopsis and 3 sample chapters.
Recent Nonfiction Titles: *How to Save a Fortune on Life Insurance*, by Barry Kaye.
Fiction: Mainstream. Submit outline/synopsis and 3 sample chapters.
Recent Fiction Titles: *Talisman*, by James Nugent (occult); and *Circles*, by Doris Mortman.

FORTRESS PRESS, 2900 Queen Lane, Philadelphia PA 19129. (215)848-6800. Editorial Director: Norman A. Hjelm. Publishes hardcover and paperback originals. Specializes in general religion for laity and clergy; academic texts and monographs in theology (all areas). Pays 7½% royalty on paperbacks; 10% on hardcover; modest advance. Mss must follow *Chicago Manual of Style* (13th edition). Photocopied submissions OK.

Computer printout submissions OK. Reports in 90 days. SASE. Free book catalog.
Nonfiction: Publishes theology, religious and self-help books. Accepts nonfiction translations. Query. Accepts outline/synopsis and 2 sample chapters. No religious poetry or fiction.
Recent Nonfiction Titles: *Thank God, It's Monday*, by William Diehl; *Christian Maturity and Christian Success*, by Daniel Jenkins; *A Chance to Change: Women and Men in the Church*, by Betty Thompson; and *Introduction to the New Testament* (two vols.), by Helmut Koester.

FRANCISCAN HERALD PRESS, 1434 W. 51st St., Chicago IL 60609. (312)254-4462. Editor: The Rev. Mark Hegener, O.F.M. Senior Editor: Marion A. Habig. Imprints include *Synthesis Booklets* and *Herald Biblical Booklets*. Publishes hardcover and paperback originals (90%) and reprints (10%). Averages 40 titles/year. Pays 8-12% royalty on both wholesale and retail price; offers $200-1,000 advance. Photocopied submissions OK. Computer printout submissions OK; disk submissions "only after acceptance of the work." SASE. Reports in 2 weeks. Free book catalog.
Nonfiction: "We are publishers of Franciscan literature for the various branches of the Franciscan Order: history, philosophy, theology, Franciscan spirituality and biographies of Franciscan saints and blessed." Accepts nonfiction translations from German, French, Italian, Spanish. Query or submit outline/synopsis and 1 sample chapter. Accepts artwork/photos. Recently published *The Franciscan Book of Saints*, by M. Habig; *The Credo of Pope Paul VI: Theological Commentary*, by C. Pozo, S.J.; and *The Principles of Catholic Moral Life*, edited by William E. May.

THE FREE PRESS, Division of the Macmillan Publishing Co., Inc., 866 3rd Ave., New York NY 10022. President: Allan Wittman. Publisher: Kenneth J. Bowman. Averages 150 titles/year. Royalty schedule varies. Send 1-3 sample chapters, outline, and query letter before submitting mss. "Prefers camera-ready copy to machine-readable media." Reports in 3 weeks. SASE.
Nonfiction: Professional books and textbooks. Publishes college texts, adult nonfiction, and professional books in the social sciences, humanities and business. Accepts artwork/photos. Looks for "identifiable target audience, evidence of writing ability." Accepts nonfiction translations.

‡**FROMM INTERNATIONAL PUBLISHING CORP.**, 560 Lexington Ave., New York NY 10022. (212)308-4010. Marketing Director/Managing Editor: Anne O'Malley. Publishes hardcover and trade paperback originals and trade paperback reprints. Averages 10 titles/year. Pays negotiable royalty. Offers negotiable advance. Photocopied submissions OK. SASE. Reports in 3 weeks. Free book catalog.
Nonfiction: Biography, history, politics and sociology. No cookbooks, diet books, sports books. Send complete ms.
Recent Nonfiction Title: *A Crack in the Wall*, by Horst Kruger (memoir).
Fiction: Historical, humor, mainstream and suspense. No romance, westerns, horror, gothic. Submit outline/synopsis and sample chapters.
Recent Fiction Titles: *A People Betrayed: November 1918, A German Revolution*, by Alfred Doblin (historical fiction); *The Sydney Circle*, by Alice Ekert-Rotholz (suspense/romance); and *Gillyflower Kid*, by Christine Bruckner (historical fiction).

C.J. FROMPOVICH PUBLICATIONS, RD 1, Chestnut Rd., Coopersburg PA 18036. (215)346-8461. Contact: Publisher. Publishes trade and mass market paperback originals. Averages 3 titles/year. Pays 10% royalty on wholesale price. No advance. Reports in 1 month. Book catalog for business size SAE and 1 first class stamp.
Nonfiction: Self-help, technical on natural nutrition. Submit outline/synopsis and sample chapters.
Recent Nonfiction Titles: *Understanding Body Chemistry and Hair, Mineral Analysis*, by Catherine Frompovich; *A Very Important Person's Workbook*, by Virginia Braxton; and *The Fox in Shangri-la*, by Zayren Hoffman and Catherine Frompovich.

‡**FRONT ROW EXPERIENCE**, 540 Discovery Bay Blvd., Byron CA 94514. (415)634-5710. Editor: Frank Alexander. Publishes trade paperback originals. Averages 3 titles/year. Pays 5-10% royalty on net sales. Simultaneous and photocopied submissions OK. Computer printout submissions OK; prefers letter quality to dot matrix. "We return submissions but not without a SASE." Reports in 1 week on queries; 1 month on mss. Free book catalog.
Nonfiction: How-to, reference, curriculum guides for movement education, perceptual-motor development. Especially needs innovative curriculum guides. Publishes for elementary physical education directors, elementary and preschool teachers, YMCA activity directors, occupational therapists, physical therapists, Head Start teachers. Accepts nonfiction translations from Spanish and French. No mss outside of movement education, special education, perceptual-motor development. Accepts artwork/photos. Query. Accepts outline/synopsis and 3 sample chapters.
Recent Nonfiction Titles: *Step by Step*, by Sheila Kogan; *Successful Movement Challenges*, by Jack Capon; and *Classroom-Made Movement Materials*, by Tom Hall.

‡**GALAXY PUBLICATIONS**, Subsidiary of Ideal Opportunities, Corp., 4550 N. Bay Rd., Miami Beach FL 33140. (305)672-4000 or 672-0666. President: Walter B. Lebowitz. Publishes hardcover and trade paperback originals. Averages 3 titles/year. Payment is determined on an individual basis. Simultaneous and photocopied submissions OK. SASE. Reports in 1 month on queries; 2 months on mss.
Nonfiction: Biography, coffee table book, how-to, humor, illustrated book, self-help, textbook. Subjects include business and economics, health, hobbies, music, politics, psychology, recreation, sociology, travel. Primarily interested in taxes, tax shelters, finance, investments and business-related topics for investors, business readers and professionals. Submit outline/synopsis and sample chapters or complete ms.
Recent Nonfiction Titles: *Year End Tax Planning*; *Tax Shelter Guide*; *Expressions*, by Jessica Jordan (poetry); and *The Best Little Bachelor Book in Florida*, by Jessica Jordan.
Fiction: Adventure, fantasy, horror, humor, mainstream, mystery, romance. Submit outline/synopsis and sample chapters or send complete ms.

GAMBLER'S BOOK CLUB, GBC Press, Box 4115, Las Vegas NV 89127. (702)382-7555. Editorial Director: John Luckman. Publishes paperback originals (67%) and reprints (33%). Averages 10 titles/year. Pays 10% royalty on sales income; advance averages $300. Photocopied submissions OK. Computer printout submissions OK. Reports in 1 month. SASE. Twenty-page book catalog free.
Nonfiction: 20,000-word minimum mss pertaining to gambling or to games on which people wager money. Accepts nonfiction translations. Submit complete ms (preferred) or at least 4 chapters. Recently published *Theory of Blackjack*, by Peter A. Griffin; *Class in Thoroughbred Racing*, by Chuck Badone; *Betting the Bases*, by Mike Lee (baseball betting); *Craps—A Smart Shooter's Guide*, by Thomas Midgley (shooting craps to win); and *The Tote Board is Alive and Well*, by Milt Gaines (gambling, pari-mutuel betting); *Handicapper's Condition Book* and *Literature of Thoroughbred Handicapping*, 1965-82 both by James Quinn; *Gamblers of Yesteryear* (History of European gambling spas), by Russell Barnhart.
Tips: "Especially interested in books on regional games; sports betting; on ethnic games and games on which no books have been written."

GAMBLING TIMES, 1018 N. Cole, Hollywood CA 90038. (213)466-5261. Associate Publisher, Book Division: Arnold Abrams. Publishes hardcover and softcover. Averages 35 titles/year. Pays 9-11% royalty on retail price for hardcover; 4-6% on softcover. Simultaneous and photocopied submissions OK. SASE. Reports in 1 month.
Nonfiction: How-to. "Straight gambling material related to gambling systems, betting methods, etc. Also interested in political, economic and legal issues surrounding gambling inside and outside the US." Submit sample chapters. Gambling-related books only.

GUY GANNETT BOOKS, Subsidiary of Guy Gannett Publishing Co., 390 Congress St., Portland ME 04101. (207)775-5811. Editorial Director: Allan A. Swenson. Publishes hardcover originals and trade paperback originals and reprints. Averages 10 titles/year. Pays 6-14% royalty on retail price; offers average $1,500 advance. Simultaneous and photocopied submissions OK. Computer printout and disk submissions OK; prefers letter quality to dot matrix. SASE. Reports in 1 month on queries; 6 weeks on mss. Free book catalog.
Nonfiction: Biography, cookbook, how-to, humor, juvenile and self-help. Subjects include Americana, animals, cooking and foods, history, nature and travel. "We're looking for books of wide appeal based on Maine and New England themes and topics. We publish the 'Best of Maine' books—expanding to be the 'Best of New England.' Our audience is a broad base of readers interested in New England history, traditions, folklore, heritage and outdoors." Accepts artwork/photos. Submit outline/synopsis and 3-4 sample chapters.
Recent Nonfiction Titles: *Islands of Maine, Where America Really Began*, by Bill Caldwell (history); *The Psychic Search*, by Shirley Harrison and Lynn Franklin; and *Faces of Maine*, by Bob Niss (history).
Tips: Queries/mss may be routed to other editors in the publishing group.

GARBER COMMUNICATIONS, INC., (affiliates: Steinerbooks, Spiritual Science Library, Rudolf Steiner Publications, Freedeeds Books, Biograf Publications), 5 Garber Hill Rd., Blauvelt NY 10913. (914)359-9292. Editor: Paul M. Allen. Publishes hardcover and paperback originals and reprints. Averages 15 titles/year. Pays 5-7% royalty on retail price; advance averages $500. Free book catalog. Query with outline and first, middle and last chapters for nonfiction. Will consider photocopied submissions. No computer printout or disk submissions. Reports in 2 months. SASE.
Nonfiction: Spiritual sciences, occult, philosophical, metaphysical, ESP. These are for our Steiner Books division only. Serious nonfiction. Philosophy and Spiritual Sciences: Bernard J. Garber.
Recent Nonfiction Titles: *Citizens of the Cosmos*, by Beredene Jocelyn (astrology and life after death); *Graphology: The Science of Handwriting*, by Henry Frith; and *Spiritual Research*, by Rudolf Steiner.
Fiction: Bernard J. Garber, editor. The new genre called Spiritual Fiction ® Publications. "We are now looking for original manuscripts or rewrites of classics in modern terms."
Recent Fiction Titles: *Zanoni*, by Sir Edward Bulwer-Lytton; *Romance of Two Worlds*, by Marie Corelli; and *Seraphita*, by Honore de Balzac.

GARDEN WAY PUBLISHING, Charlotte VT 05445. (802)425-2171. Editor: Roger Griffith. Publishes hardcover and paperback originals. Publishes 12 titles/year. Offers a flat fee arrangement varying with book's scope, or royalty, which usually pays author 6% of book's retail price. Advances are negotiable, but usually range from $1,500 to $3,000. "We stress continued promotion of titles and sales over many years." Emphasizes direct mail sales, plus sales to bookstores through salesmen. Photocopied submissions OK. Computer printout and disk submissions OK; prefers letter quality to dot matrix printouts. Enclose return postage.
Nonfiction: Books on gardening, cooking, animal husbandry, homesteading and energy conservation. Accepts artwork/photos. Emphasis should be on how-to. Length requirements are flexible. "The writer should remember the reader will buy his book to learn to do something, so that all information to accomplish this must be given. We are publishing specifically for the person who is concerned about natural resources and a deteriorating life style and wants to do something about it." Would like to see energy books with emphasis on what the individual can do. Query with outline and 2-3 sample chapters.
Recent Nonfiction Title: *Joy of Gardening*, by Dick Raymond.

GARLAND PUBLISHING, INC., 136 Madison Ave., New York NY 10016. (212)686-7492. Editor-in-Chief: Art Stickney. Publishes hardcover originals. Averages 100 titles/year. Pays 10-15% royalty on wholesale price. "Depending on marketability, some copies may be royalty-exempt, or author may prepare camera-ready copy." Simultaneous and photocopied submissions OK. Computer printout submissions OK; prefers letter quality to dot matrix. Reports in 2 weeks on queries; 1 month on mss. Free book catalog.
Nonfiction: Reference books for libraries. Humanities and social sciences. Accepts nonfiction translations. "We're interested in reference books—bibliographies, sourcebooks, indexes, etc.—in all fields." Submit outline/synopsis and 1-2 sample chapters.
Recent Nonfiction Titles: *A Directory of Religious Bodies in the US*, by Melton (directory); *Folk Song Index*, by Brunnings (index to 1,000 books); and *America's White Working-Class Women: A Historical Bibliography*, by Kennedy.

GARLINGHOUSE COMPANY, 320 SW 33rd St., Box 299, Topeka KS 66601. (913)267-2490. President: Whitney Garlinghouse. Publishes trade paperback originals. Averages 2-5 titles/year. Usually pays 6% royalty on retail price; sometimes offers advances of up to $1,500; buys some mss outright. Simultaneous and photocopied submissions OK. Computer printout submissions OK; prefers letter quality to dot matrix. SASE. Reports in 1 month.
Nonfiction: How-to relating to the home. Suitable subject areas include home building and design; underground homes and other innovative building techniques; home remodeling and repairs; solar energy; energy conservation in the home; home projects; furniture making and restoration; and home workshop aids. Principally interested in books that deal specifically with saving (or making) money. Accepts nonfiction translations. Submit outline/synopsis and 3 sample chapters. "Please list credentials with submissions."
Recent Nonfiction Titles: *Traditional Home Plans* and *Small Home Plans*, both by Garlinghouse.

GASLIGHT PUBLICATIONS, 112 E. 2nd St., Bloomington IN 47401. (812)332-5169. Publisher: Jack Tracy. Publishes hardcover originals (50%) and hardcover reprints (50%). Averages 6-8 titles/year. Pays 10% minimum royalty on retail price; no advance. Simultaneous and photocopied submissions OK. SASE. Reports in 1 month.
Nonfiction: "Studies in A. Conan Doyle, Sherlock Holmes and related Victoriana. Serious, well-researched, not necessarily for the specialist. 12,000 words minimum. Our publications are usually heavily illustrated, and a generous number of appropriate illustrations will materially enhance a book's chances for acceptance." No ephemera, parodies, pastiches or "untold tales." Query or submit outline/synopsis, sample chapters or complete ms.
Recent Nonfiction Titles: *Origins of Sherlock Holmes*, by Walter Klinefelter (literary history); *The Game Is Afoot: A Travel Guide to the England of Sherlock Holmes*, by David L. Hammer (travel); *A Study in Surmise: The Making of Sherlock Holmes*, by Michael Harrison (literary analysis).

‡**GAY SUNSHINE PRESS**, Box 40397, San Francisco CA 94140. (415)824-3184. Editor: Winston Leyland. Publishes hardcover and trade paperback originals and trade paperback reprints. Averages 7 titles/year. Pays royalty or makes outright purchase. Photocopied submissions OK. SASE. Reports in 3 weeks on queries; 1 month on mss. Book catalog $1.
Nonfiction: How-to and gay lifestyle topics. "We're interested in innovative literary nonfiction which deals with gay lifestyles." No long personal accounts (e.g. "how I came out"), academic or overly formal titles. No books that are too specialized (e.g., homosexuality in the ancient world). Query. "After query is returned by us, submit outline/synopsis and sample chapters. All unsolicited mss are returned unopened."
Recent Nonfiction Titles: *Gay Sunshine Interviews*, Volume 2, edited by W. Leyland (gay literary/political interviews); *Look Back in Joy*, by Malcolm Boyd (short personal autobiographical pieces); and *Sex: True Homosexual Experiences*, Volume 3, (true sexual accounts by various people).
Fiction: Erotica, ethnic, experimental, historical, mystery, science fiction and gay fiction in translation. "In-

Close-up

Peter McWilliams, Writer

His credits read like a patchwork quilt. Nine volumes of love poetry, a book on TM, one on surviving the loss of a love, two books on computers/word processing—with two more coming out this year, a computer column appearing in forty newspapers nationwide. And Peter McWilliams didn't consciously plan to do any of it.

The poetry started in high school when a teacher let him write poems on society instead of turning in five sociology book reports. "I was writing the poems and falling in love at the same time," says McWilliams, "and pretty soon I realized they were love poems. And people started wanting copies." At age 17, he self-published his first volume.

"Now I write because it's my job," he says. "And the books that tend to be the most successful have been those written out of my desire to communicate my interests."

McWilliams admits, however, that he's been in the right place at the right time with his book ideas. "I happened to be ready with a product when it got interesting. I had not thought that I would write a book about computers, though. I just wanted a computer for myself because I'm a terrible speller and I hate rewriting. I'm not a great fan of computers for everybody, but for writers I think they're the most important invention since the writing down of things. They have changed my life as a writer, and I thought other writers might want to know about them."

Though he writes about computers in a light-and-lively style (one *New York Times* reviewer described him as "writing with a continuous giggle"), he's committed to them—both as an enhancer of the creative process (no more crossing out!) and a vehicle for selling writing. Crisp-looking computer printout manuscripts and query letters are his tools. The key to getting published, he says, is to keep that submission process going. "It doesn't happen overnight, but slowly you start to gain acceptance.

"Any writer who doesn't think of himself as a business person is kidding himself. Too often writers have this fantasy that some publisher is supposed to come through their town and convince them over a three-hour lunch that they should be kind enough to submit their manuscript. It just doesn't happen that way. You've got to sell yourself."

McWilliams recognizes, however, that in addition to writing fulltime and marketing your work, you have to eat, too. And he offers this formula for survival. "When you start in a fulltime profession, especially one connected with creativity, plan on at least two years of paying your dues. That means you've got to support yourself in some way other than your writing. Be a waiter or a short-order cook during the day so you can write fulltime at night." (McWilliams worked in a restaurant and an auto factory, and sold encyclopedias to support himself in the early days.)

For all his successes, McWilliams is quick to reiterate that writing is plain hard work. "And staring at a video screen is just like staring at a sheet of paper. Everyone thinks they can be a writer. Most people don't understand what's involved. The real writers persevere. The ones that don't, either don't have enough fortitude and they probably wouldn't succeed anyway, or they fall in love with the glamour of writing as opposed to the writing of writing."

terested in well-written novels on gay themes; also short story collections. We have a high literary standard for fiction." Query. "After query is returned by us, submit outline/synopsis and sample chapters. All unsolicited mss are returned unopened."

Recent Fiction Titles: *The Boy from Beirut*, by Robin Maugham; *A Thirsty Evil*, by Gore Vidal (short fiction); and *Adonis Garcia*, by Luis Zapata (novel in translation from Spanish).

*GENEALOGICAL PUBLISHING CO., INC., 111 Water St., Baltimore MD 21202. (301)837-8271. Editor-in-Chief: Michael H. Tepper, Ph.D. Publishes hardcover originals and reprints. Offers straight 10% royalty on retail price. Does about 10% subsidy publishing. Averages 80 titles/year. Will consider photocopied submissions. Prefers query first, but will look at outline and sample chapter or complete ms. Reports "immediately." Enclose SAE and return postage.

Reference, genealogy, and immigration records: "Our requirements are unusual, so we usually treat each author and his subject in a way particularly appropriate to his special skills and subject matter. Guidelines are flexible, though it is expected that an author will consult with us in depth. Most, though not all, of our original publications are offset from camera-ready typescript. Since most genealogical reference works are compilations of vital records and similar data, tabular formats are common. We hope to receive more ms material covering vital records and ships' passenger lists. We want family history compendia, basic methodology in genealogy, local history (for example, county histories, particularly those containing genealogy), heraldry, and immigration records. Recently published *Index to the 1820 Census of Virginia*, by J. Felldin; *Heraldic Design*, by H. Child; *Genealogies of Virginia Families*, 5 volumes; and *Passenger Arrivals at the Port of Baltimore, 1820-1834*.

GENERAL HALL, INC., 23-45 Corporal Kennedy St., Bayside NY 11360. (212)423-9397. Publisher: Ravi Mehra. Publishes hardcover and trade paperback originals. Averages 5-6 titles/year. Pays 10-15% royalty. Simultaneous and photocopied submissions OK. Computer printout and disk submissions OK. SASE. Reports in 6 weeks.

Nonfiction: Reference and textbook. Subjects include Americana, blacks, business and economics, politics, psychology and sociology. Submit complete ms.

Recent Nonfiction Titles: *A New Look At Black Families*, 2nd ed., by Charles V. Willie; *Mainstreaming Outsiders—The Production of Black Professionals*, by James E. Blackwell; *Democracy in Education—Boyd H. Bode*, by Robert V. Bullough Jr.; and *Crime, Justice and Society*, by Calvin J. Larson.

‡THE J. PAUL GETTY MUSEUM, Subsidiary of The J. Paul Getty Museum Trust, Box 2112, Santa Monica CA 90406. (213)459-2306. Editor: Sandra Knudsen Morgan. Publishes hardcover and trade paperback originals (80%) and reprints. Averages 10 titles/year. Pays 6-12% royalty on retail price; buys some mss outright; offers average $500 advance. Photocopied submissions OK. SASE. Reports in 1 month. Free book catalog.

Nonfiction: Reference and scholarly on art and history. "Scholarly titles and well-researched general and children's titles on topics related to the museum's three collections: Greek and Roman art and architectures (especially the Villa dei Papiri), Old Master paintings of the Renaissance and Baroque, and French decorative arts of the Regence through Napoleonic periods." No non-European art. Query.

Recent Nonfiction Titles: *Greek and Roman Sculpture in America*, by C.C. Vermeule (picture catalog); *Ancient Herbs in the JPGM Gardens*, by J. D'Andrea (herb introduction); and *Skopas in Malibu*, by A. Stewart (monograph).

THE K.S. GINIGER CO., INC., 235 Park Ave., S., New York NY 10003. (212)533-5080. President: Kenneth Seeman Giniger. Book publisher and independent book producer/packager. Publishes hardcover, trade, and paperback originals. Averages 8 titles/year. Pays royalty on wholesale or retail price. SASE. No computer printout or disk submissions. Reports in 2 weeks.

Nonfiction: Biography, cookbook, how-to, juvenile, reference and self-help. Accepts artwork/photos. Subjects include Americana, art, cooking and foods, health, history, hobbies, religion, sports and travel. Query with SASE. Accepts outline/synopsis; 1 sample chapter. All unsolicited mss are returned unread "if postage is enclosed." Looks for "good idea and power of expressing it with clarity and interest."

Recent Nonfiction Titles: *Churchill and the Generals*, by Barrie Pitt (history); *The Complete Gymnastics Book*, by Frank Bare (sports); *The Duchess of Windsor*, by Diana Mosley (biography); and *European Detours*, by Nino Lo Bello (travel).

GINN AND CO., 191 Spring St., Lexington MA 02173. (617)861-1670. Elementary Editor: Ralph Hayashida. Secondary Editor: Robert Feaster. Royalty schedule: from 10% of net on a secondary book to 4% on elementary materials. "We are doing a significant number of books on a work-for-hire or fee basis." Averages 200 titles/year. Sample chapters, complete or partially complete mss will be considered. Computer printout and disk submissions OK. Reports in 2 to 6 weeks. Enclose return postage.

Textbooks: Publishers of textbooks and instructional materials for elementary and secondary schools.

Recent Nonfiction Titles: *A History of the United States*, by Dan Boorstin and Brooks Kelly (American history); and *Ginn Reading Program*.
Tips: Queries/mss may be routed to other editors in the publishing group.

GLOBE MINI MAGS, 2112 S. Congress Ave., West Palm Beach FL 33406. (305)433-1551. Associate Editor: Toby Donahue. Averages 120 titles/year. Buys some mss outright; "negotiated individually." No advance. SASE. Reports in 1 month. Queries/mss may be routed to other editors in the publishing group.
Nonfiction: "We publish 64-page mini mag handbooks sold at variety stores, supermarkets, and gift shops." Subjects include nutrition and foods, health, diets and exercises. Accepts artwork/photos. "We prefer a query letter with the writer's credentials and a *brief* description of the proposed mini mag."
Recent Nonfiction Titles: *Aerobic Dancing* (exercise); and *Herbal Diets* (weight loss).

THE GLOBE PEQUOT PRESS, INC., Old Chester Rd., Box Q, Chester CT 06412. (203)526-9571. Vice President/Publications Director: Linda Kennedy. Publishes hardcover and paperback originals (95%) and paperback reprints (5%). Averages 15 titles/year. Offers 7½-10% royalty on retail price; advances offered "for specific expenses only." Simultaneous and photocopied submissions OK. SASE. Reports in 3 weeks. Book catalog for SASE.
Nonfiction: New England: Americana; recreation (outdoor books); and travel (guide books). Some regional history and cookbooks. "Guide books are especially promising today; with a guide book people can plan travel itineraries in advance, save time and money. Books with a New England-wide focus will be considered most seriously." No doctoral theses, genealogies or textbooks. Submit outline/synopsis and sample chapters.
Recent Nonfiction Titles: *Guide to the Recommended Country Inns of New England*, by E. Squier (New England guide/travel book); *The Boston Globe's Historic Walks in Old Boston*, by John Harris; and *In and Out of Boston With (or Without) Children*, by Bernice Chesler.

GMG PUBLISHING, 25 W. 43rd St., New York NY 10036. (212)354-8840. President: Gerald Galison. Publishes hardcover and trade paperback originals (90%) and reprints (10%), illustrated and text only. Averages 10 titles/year. Pays negotiable royalty; offers negotiable advance. Simultaneous submissions OK. Computer printout and disk submissions OK; prefers letter quality to dot matrix printouts. SASE. Reports in 2 weeks.
Nonfiction: Soft science, natural history, the arts. Accepts nonfiction translations. "Open to quality projects in topics of current interest." Query. Accepts outline/synopsis and 1 sample chapter.
Recent Nonfiction Titles: *What's for Lunch?*, and *Animal Breeding at the Zoo*, by Sally Tongren; and *First Lady's Cookbook*, by Margaret Klapthor (reprint and update).

GOLDEN BOOKS, Western Publishing Co., Inc., 850 3rd Ave., New York NY 10022. Publisher: Walter Retan. Editorial Director, Adult Books: Jonathan P. Latimer. Editorial Director, Juvenile Books: Janet B. Campbell. Averages 200 titles/year. Pays royalty; buys some mss outright.
Nonfiction: Adult nonfiction, especially family-oriented how-to subjects. Children's books, including picturebooks, concept books, novelty books, information books. Query before submitting ms. Looks for "completeness, an indication that the author knows his subject and audience."
Fiction: Children's picturebooks and young fiction. Query before submitting ms.

‡*THE GOLDEN QUILL PRESS, Avery Rd., Francestown NH 03043. (603)547-6622. Owner: Edward T. Dell Jr. Publishes hardcover originals. Averages 25 titles/year. Subsidy publishes 90% of books "depending on past sales records." Pays 10% maximum royalty on retail price. Photocopied submissions OK. SASE. Reports in 2 weeks on queries; 1 month on mss. Free book catalog.
Nonfiction: Biography. Query or submit complete ms.
Poetry: All types. Submit complete ms.

GOLDEN WEST BOOKS, Box 80250, San Marino CA 91108. (213)283-3446. Editor-in-Chief: Donald Duke. Managing Editor: Jeff Dunning. Publishes hardcover and paperback originals. Pays 10% royalty contract; no advance. Simultaneous and photocopied submissions OK. Reports in 2-4 weeks. SASE. Free book catalog.
Nonfiction: Publishes selected western Americana and transportation Americana. Query or submit complete ms. "Illustrations and photographs will be examined if we like ms."
Recent Nonfiction Title: *California Redwood Industry*, by Lynwood Carranco.

‡GOLDEN WEST PUBLISHERS, 4113 N. Longview, Phoenix AZ 85014. (602)265-4392. Editor: Hal Mitchell. Publishes trade paperback originals. Averages 4 titles/year. Pays 6-10% royalty on retail price or makes outright purchase of $500-2,500. No advances. Simultaneous and photocopied submissions OK; prefer query letter first. SASE. Reports in 2 weeks on queries; 1 month on mss. Book catalog for business-size SAE and 1 first class stamp.

Nonfiction: Cookbooks, how-to, humor, guide books and self-help books. Subjects include Americana, animals, cooking and foods, health, history, photography, the outdoors, travel and the West or Southwest. No religion or poetry. Query or submit outline/synopsis and sample chapters.
Recent Titles: *Arizona Adventure*, by Marshall Trimble (history); *Arizona—Off the Beaten Path*, by Thelma Heatwole (travel guide); *Mexican Family Favorites Cook Book*, by M.T. Bermudez; and *Fools' Gold*, by Robert Sikorsky (history, travel).

GRAPHIC ARTS CENTER PUBLISHING CO., 3019 NW Yeon Ave., Box 10306, Portland OR 97210. (503)226-2402. President: Betty A. Sechser. Assistant Publisher and Editor: Douglas Pfeiffer. Publishes hardcover originals. Averages 6-10 titles/year. Pays outright purchase averaging $3,000 (less for paperbacks); small advance. Simultaneous and photocopied submissions OK. No computer printout or disk submissions. Reports in 3 weeks. SASE. Free book catalog.
Nonfiction: "All titles are pictorials with text. Text usually runs separately from the pictorial treatment. State and regional book series are published under the imprint name (D.B.A.) Belding. Several of the new series of pictorial books have also been begun and length and style are more flexible." Query.

‡***GRAPHIC IMAGE PUBLICATIONS**, Box 1740, La Jolla CA 92038. (619)457-0344. President: Hurb Crow. Publishes trade and mass market paperback originals. Averages 5 titles/year. Subsidy publishes 10% of books based on "length of experience and success of prior works." Pays 5-15% royalty on wholesale price; advance negotiable. Query with outline/synopsis and 2 sample chapters, attn: Managing Editor: Judy Delp. Must have SASE for response. Reports in 2 months. Simultaneous and photocopied submissions OK.
Nonfiction: How-to, cookbooks, photography, young adult, textbook and travel. "We publish for students and others with a desire to learn on their own; and for people who love to travel and to know about the areas they visit." Accepts artwork/photos.
Recent Nonfiction Titles: *Photojournalism*, by C.R. Learn (text); and *Baja California Sur*, by S.R. Hoffmaster (travel).
Fiction: Erotica, fantasy, children's stories and definitely romance.
Fiction Title: *Night Vision*, by Erin Hahn (suspense).
Poetry: We need poetry that is short, humorous or scenic for calendars and greeting cards. Be creative. Submit 10 samples.
Tips: "Be professional in your query, and let us know a little about yourself, be positive." Queries/mss may be routed to other editors in the publishing group.

GRAY'S PUBLISHING, LTD., Box 2160, Sidney, BC, Canada V8L 3S6. (604)656-4454. Editor: Maralyn Horsdal. Publishes hardcover and paperback originals and reprints. Offers standard royalty contract on retail price. Averages 4 titles/year. Query with outline and 3-4 sample chapters. Reports in 6-10 weeks. SAE and International Reply Coupons.
Nonfiction: Wants "nonfiction, Canadiana," especially Pacific Northwest. Biography, natural history, history, nautical. Looks for "good writing and worthwhile marketable topic." Accepts artwork/photos. Length: 60,000-120,000 words.
Recent Nonfiction Titles: *The Columbia Is Coming!*, by Doris Andersen (history); *Skeena, River of Destiny*, by R. G. Large (updated history reprint); and *The Gulf Islands Explorer*, by Bruce Obee (guide).

GREAT OCEAN PUBLISHERS, 1823 N. Lincoln St., Arlington VA 22207. (703)525-0909. President: Mark Esterman. Publishes hardcover and trade paperback originals (90%) and hardcover reprints (10%). Averages 3 titles/year. Pays 8-10% hardcover royalty; 6-8% paperback on retail price; occasionally offers advance. Simultaneous (if so indicated) and photocopied submissions OK. Reports in 3 weeks.
Nonfiction: Biography, how-to, illustrated book, reference, self-help, technical. Subjects include art, business and economics, child care/development, health, history, music, philosophy, politics, religion. "Any subject is fine as long as it meets our standards of quality." Submit outline/synopsis and sample chapters. Accepts artwork/photos. "SASE *must* be included with all material to be returned." Looks for "1) good writing; 2) clear evidence that ms is intended as a *book*, not a long collection of weakly organized small pieces; 3) good organization. Not to mention a worthwhile, interesting subject." Accepts nonfiction translations—query first.
Recent Nonfiction Titles: *Essays on Marriage*, by Seikan Hasegawa; *The Eye Book*, by Ben Esterman, MD (eye care); and *Beethoven Remembered*, by Wegeler and Ries.
Fiction: Serious fiction. "Quality of writer and writing more important than genre." Query before sending unsolicited fiction mss.

GREAT OUTDOORS PUBLISHING CO., 4747 28th St. N., St. Petersburg FL 33714. (813)522-3453. Editor-in-Chief: Charles Allyn. Publishes paperback originals. Offers royalty of 5% on retail price. No advance. Published 8 titles last year. Will consider photocopied submissions and simultaneous submissions. Query for nonfiction. Reports in 1 month. Enclose return postage. Will send title listings on request with SASE.
Nonfiction: Books of regional interest. Fishing, gardening, shelling in Florida. Also publishes some cook-

books of Southern emphasis. Should be straightforward, how-to style with consideration for the hobbyist or sportsman who needs the basic facts without flowery phrasing. "No other publisher is geared to the tourist market in Florida. Our books are low-cost and especially suited to their market." Would like to see more shell books with illustrations. No personal narratives or pet books. Department editors: Joyce Allyn, cooking, nature, recreation; Charles Allyn, self-help and how-to. Length: cooking, 9,000-17,000 words; nature, 52,000-90,000 words; self-help, how-to, sports, hobbies and recreation, 9,000-17,000 words.

GREEN BARON BOOK & FILM CO., 7130 Chippewa Rd., Colorado Springs CO 80915. Managing Editor: Charles Rutter. Publishes hardcover and trade and mass market paperback originals (90%); and mass market reprints (10%). Averages 14 titles/year. Pays 10-20% on retail price. No advance. Simultaneous and photocopied submissions OK. SASE. Reports in 1 month on queries; 4 months on mss.
Nonfiction: Cookbook, how-to, humor, illustrated book, juvenile, textbook and children's coloring books. Subjects include business and economics, cooking and foods, nature and religion. Immediate needs are computer language (textbook and programs) and business textbooks. No memoirs, Ma and Pa, biography. Query.
Recent Nonfiction Titles: *The Complete Guide to Wholesale*, by Weichsecher (instructional); *How to Stop Smoking Now*, by Weichsecher; and *Computers and Your Church*, by Rutter (textbook).
Fiction: Adventure (children's and teenagers'); fantasy (with gospel message); gothic; historical; humor (down home); mainstream; mystery; religious (open door); romance (with values of chastity, love of God); science fiction; suspense; western (stressing honesty, cowboy in white hat); and children's. "We are a fiction-oriented company. We prefer books of the above types stressing Christian values, love of people, love of God, honesty, good triumphing over evil, etc." No mss with profanity, excessive violence, or sex just to liven the book. Query first on all mss.
Recent Fiction Titles: *Church of the Side Door Pullmam*, by Charlotte Trejos (adventure); and *The Last Trip Home*, by Charles Rutter (mystery).
Tips: "We are being deluged by mss without SASE or with personal checks for return postage. SASE, please. Agents included."

GREEN HILL PUBLISHERS, 722 Columbus St., Ottawa IL 61350. (815)434-7905. (Distributed by Caroline House, Aurora IL). Publisher and Editorial Director: Jameson Campaigne Jr. Senior Editor: Richard S. Wheeler. Publishes hardcover and paperback originals (85%) and reprints (15%) and distributes for other publishers. Publishes 12 titles/year. Pays 6-15% royalty; outright purchase averages $2,500. Advance averages $2,000. Simultaneous and photocopied submissions OK. Computer printout submissions OK; prefers letter quality to dot matrix. Reports in 3 months. SASE. Book catalog for SASE.
Nonfiction: Racquet sports, how-to, guides and biographies (of major subjects). Some fiction. Query; all unsolicited mss are returned unopened.
Recent Titles: *The Reagan Wit*, by Bill Adler; *Here's Erma: The Bombecking of America*, by Norman King; and *The Connoisseur's Guide to Beer*, by James Robertson.
Fiction: *Carry the Wind*, by Terry Johnston; *Sword of the North*, by Richard White.

*WARREN H. GREEN, INC., 8356 Olive Blvd., St. Louis MO 63132. Editor: Warren H. Green. Publishes hardcover originals. Offers "10-20% sliding scale of royalties based on quantity distributed. All books are short run, highly specialized, with no advance." About 5% of books are subsidy published. Averages 90 titles/year. "37% of total marketing is overseas." Will send a catalog to a writer on request. Will consider photocopied submissions. Submit outline and sample chapters. "Publisher requires 300- to 500-word statement of scope, plan, and purpose of book, together with curriculum vitae of author." Reports in 60-90 days.
Medical and Scientific: "Specialty monographs for practicing physicians and medical researchers. Books of 160 pages upward. Illustrated as required by subject. Medical books are non-textbook type, usually specialties within specialties, and no general books for a given specialty. For example, separate books on each facet of radiology, and not one complete book on radiology. Authors must be authorities in their chosen fields and accepted as such by their peers. Books should be designed for all doctors in English-speaking world engaged in full or part-time activity discussed in book. We would like to increase publications in the fields of radiology, anesthesiology, pathology, psychiatry, surgery and orthopedic surgery, obstetrics and gynecology, and speech and hearing."
Recent Nonfiction Titles: *Basic Neuroradiology*, by Sarwar; *Atlas of Neuroanatomy with Radiologic Correlation and Pathologic Illustration*, by Dublin; *Abdominal C.T.*, by Sorgen; *Physical Basis of Computed Tomography*, by Marshall.

GREEN TIGER PRESS, 1061 India St., San Diego CA 92101. (619)238-1001. Editor: Harold Darling. Publishes hardcover and trade paperback originals and reprints. Averages 15 titles/year. Pays 10% minimum royalty on retail price; offers average $350 advance. Simultaneous and photocopied submissions OK. SASE. Reports in 2 weeks on queries; 2 months on mss. Free book catalog.
Imprints: *Star & Elephant* (nonfiction and fiction).
Nonfiction: Illustrated book and juvenile. Subjects include art and poetry.

Recent Nonfiction Title: *The World of Carl Larsson* (commentary on life and work of illustrator includes over 400 illustrations).
Fiction: Juvenile, fantasy, myth, art.
Recent Fiction Titles: *The Animals' Ball*, by Helene Tersac; *Nimby*, by Jasper Tomkins; *A Phenomenal Alphabet Book*, by Cooper Edens.
Poetry: Submit 3 samples.
Recent Poetry Titles: *With Secret Friends*, by Cooper Edens; and *Lost Wine*, by John Theobald (7 centuries of French/English lyric poetry).
Tips: "We look for manuscripts containing a romantic, visionary or imaginative quality, often with a mythic feeling where fantasy and reality co-exist. Since we are a visually-oriented house, we look for manuscripts whose texts readily conjure up visual imagery."

THE STEPHEN GREENE PRESS/LEWIS PUBLISHING, Box 1000, Brattleboro VT 05301. (802)257-7757. Editorial Director: Thomas Begner. Publishes hardcover and paperback originals (99%); hardcover and paperback reprints (1%). Averages 30 titles/year. Royalty "variable; advances are small." Send contact sheet or prints to illustrate ms. Photocopied submissions OK. Reports in 6 weeks. SASE. Book catalog for SASE.
Nonfiction: Americana; cookbooks, cooking and foods; history; how-to (self-reliance); nature and environment; recreation; self-help; sports (outdoor and horse); popular technology; popular psychology and social science; and regional (New England). "We see our audience as mainly college-educated men and women, 30 and over. They are regular book buyers and readers. They probably have pronounced interests, hobby or professional, in subjects that our books treat. Authors can assess their needs by looking critically at what we have published."
Recent Nonfiction Titles: *What Psychology Knows*, by Dan Goleman and Jonathan Freedman; *Successful Cold Climate Gardening*, by Hill; and *The Kids' Book of Divorce*, by Eric Rolfes et al.

GREENLEAF CLASSICS, INC., Box 20194, San Diego CA 92120. Acquisitions Editor: Ralph Vaughan. Publishes paperback originals. Specializes in adult erotic fiction. Publishes 360 titles/year. Pays by outright purchase about 2½ months after acceptance. Photocopied submissions OK. No computer printout or disk submissions. Reports in 2-4 weeks. "NO mss will be returned unless accompanied by return postage." Writer's guidelines for SASE.
Fiction: Erotic novels. "All stories must have a sexual theme. They must be contemporary novels dealing with the serious problems of everyday people. All plots are structured so that characters must get involved in erotic situations. Write from the female viewpoint. *Request our guidelines before beginning any project for us.*" Preferred length: 35,000 words. Complete ms preferred; or at least 3 sample chapters.

GREENWOOD PRESS, Box 5007, Westport CT 06881. (203)226-3571. Vice President, Editorial: James Sabin. Averages 180 titles/year. Pays negotiable royalty; offers negotiable advance. Simultaneous and photocopied submissions OK. "We encourage our authors to submit manuscripts on disk or mag tape." SASE. Reports in 6 weeks. Free book catalog.
Nonfiction: Reference (dictionaries and handbooks); professional books for lawyers and public officials; and scholarly monographs. Accepts nonfiction translations from French, German, Italian and Spanish. Query or submit prospectus, 1 sample chapter and vita.
Recent Nonfiction Titles: *Dictionary of Mexican-American History*, by Matt Meier and Feliciano Rivera; *International Handbook of Contemporary Architecture*, by 50-75 contributors; and *International Handbook of Contemporary Librarianship*, by 50-75 contributors.

GREGG DIVISION, McGraw-Hill Book Co., 1221 Avenue of the Americas, New York NY 10020. Vice President: Robert C. Bowen. Publishes hardcover and softcover instructional material for secondary and post-secondary education market. "Contracts negotiable; no advances." Query. "We accept very few unsolicited mss." Reports in 1-2 months. Enclose return postage with query. Publishes books on typewriting, office education, shorthand, accounting and data processing, distribution and marketing, trade and industrial education, health and consumer education and word processing.
Recent Nonfiction Titles: *Accounting Systems and Procedures*, by Weaver et al.; *Word Processing and Information Systems*, by M. Popyc; *Digital Computer Electronics*, by A.P. Malvino.

GROUPWORK TODAY, INC., Box 258, South Plainfield NJ 07080. Editor-in-Chief: Harry E. Moore Jr. Publishes hardcover and paperback originals. Averages 4-6 titles/year. Offers $100 advance against royalties on receipt of contract and completion of ms ready for publication; 10% of gross receipts from sale of book. Books are marketed by direct mail to Groupwork Agency executives and professionals (YMCA, YWCA, Scouts, Salvation Army, colleges, directors of organized camps, and libraries). Will send catalog to a writer for SASE with 37¢ in stamps. "Also will answer specific questions from an author considering us as a publisher." Will not consider simultaneous submissions. No computer printout or disk submissions. Submit outline and 3 sample chapters for nonfiction. Reports in 6-8 weeks. Enclose return postage.

Nonfiction: "We are publishers of books and materials for professionals and volunteers who work with people in groups. Titles are also used by colleges for texts and resources. Some of our materials are also suited to the needs of professionals who work with individuals. Groupwork agency management, finance, program development and personnel development are among the subjects of interest to us. Writers must be thoroughly familiar with 'people work' and have fresh insights to offer. New writers are most welcome here. Lengths are open but usually run 40,000-60,000 words." Readers are mainly social agency administrators and professional staff members. Groupwork materials are also read by volunteers serving in the social agencies. Mss are judged by experienced professionals in social agencies. The company is advised on policy direction by a council of advisors from national agencies and colleges across the nation. "We also are publishing our 'monogram' series to deal with the most important problems with which social work agencies must deal today."

Recent Nonfiction Titles: *Helping Women: Counseling Girls and Women in a Decade of Change*, by Gloria Sklansky and Linda Algazi; *Guide to Creative Giving*, by Bernard P. Taylor; and *Meaning Well is Not Enough: Perspectives on Volunteering*, by Jane M. Park.

Tips: "If a writer will send material only on which he or she has done as much work as possible to make a good outline, a sample chapter or two to indicate writing ability, and the idea is a contribution to our field, we will spend all kinds of time guiding the author to completion of the work."

GROVE PRESS, 196 W. Houston St., New York NY 10014. Editorial Director: Barney Rosset. Imprints include Evergreen and Black Cat books. Publishes hardcover and paperback originals (50%) and paperback reprints (50%). Averages 40 titles/year. Simultaneous and photocopied submissions OK. Computer printout and disk submissions OK; prefers letter quality to dot matrix. SASE. "We accept no phone calls concerning mss, requests for catalogs and other information." Free book catalog.

Nonfiction: Biography, health, history, how-to, philosophy, politics, psychology, self-help, and sports. Accepts nonfiction translations. Accepts outline/synopsis and 3 sample chapters.

Recent Nonfiction Titles: *The Cancer Syndrome*, by Ralph Moss (medicine, current affairs, investigative report on the cancer industry); *Nutrition and Vitamin Therapy*, by Michael Lesser, MD (health, nutrition); and *The Story of Motown*, by Peter Benjaminson.

Fiction: Novels.

Recent Fiction Title: *The Harder They Come*, by Michael Thelwell.

GRYPHON HOUSE, INC., 3706 Otis St., Box 275, Mt. Rainier MD 20712. (301)779-6200. President Editor: Larry Rood. Publishes trade paperback originals. Averages 3 titles/year. Pays 10-12½% royalty on retail price; offers average $300 advance. Photocopied submissions OK. Computer printout submissions OK. SASE. Reports in 2 weeks. Book catalog for 9x12 SAE and 2 first class stamps. Writer's guidelines for SASE.

Nonfiction: How-to and creative educational activities for parents and teachers to do with preschool children, ages 1-5. "We are specialty publishers and do not consider anything at present out of the above category. Our audience includes parents and teachers in preschools, nursery schools, day care centers and kindergartens." Query or submit outline/synopsis and 1 sample chapter. Looks for "brevity, clarity and an explanation of how this book is unique."

Recent Nonfiction Titles: *A Parent's Guide to Day Care; Bubbles, Rainbows and Worms: Science Experiments for Pre-School Children*, by Brown; *Easy Woodstuff for Kids*, by Thompson; and *Hug a Tree and Other Things to do Outdoors with Young Children*, by Rockwell, et.al.

‡*GUERNICA EDITIONS, Box 633, Station N.D.G., Montreal, Quebec, Canada H4A 3R1. (514)481-5569. President/Editor: Antonio D'Alfonso. Publishes hardcover and trade paperback originals and hardcover and trade paperback reprints. Averages 10 titles/year. Subsidy publishes 50% of titles. "Subsidy in Canada is received only when the author is established, Canadian-born, active in the country's cultural world. The others we subsidize ourselves." Pays 3-10% royalty on retail price. Makes outright purchase of $200-5,000. Offers 7¢/word advance for translators. Photocopied submissions OK. IRC required. "American stamps are of no use to us in Canada." Reports in 1 month on queries; 6 weeks on mss. Free book catalog.

Nonfiction: Biography, humor, juvenile, reference and textbook. Subjects include art, history, music, nature, philosophy, photography, politics, psychology, recreation, religion and Canadiana. "We are looking for essays on history, philosophy, religion, politics, film, and other topics which can be used as discussion books." Query.

Fiction: Erotica, ethnic, historical, mystery, science fiction and suspense. "We wish to open up into the fiction world. No country is a country without its fiction writers. Canada is growing some fine fiction writers. We'd like to read you. No first novels." Query.

Poetry: "We wish to have writers in translation. Any writer who has translated Italian poetry is welcomed. Full books only. Not single poems by different authors, unless modern, and used as an anthology. First books will have no place in the next couple of years." Submit samples.

Recent Poetry Titles: *Concrete City (Selected Poems 1972-1982)*, by Claude Beausoleil (translated by Ray Chamberlain); *Alchemy of the Body*, by Juan Garcia (translated by Marc Plourde); *Black Tongue*, by Antonio D'Alfonso.

GUIDANCE CENTRE, Faculty of Education, University of Toronto, 252 Bloor St. W., Toronto, Ontario, Canada M5S 2Y3. (416)978-3210. Editorial Director: S.J. Totton. Coordinating Editor: Hazel Ross. Publishes hardcover and paperback originals. Averages 15 titles/year. Pays in royalties. Reports in 1 month. Submissions returned "only if Canadian postage is sent." Free book catalog.
Nonfiction: "The Guidance Centre is interested in publications related to career planning and guidance and in measurement and evaluation. Also general education. No manuscripts which have confined their references and illustrations to United States material." Submit complete ms. Consult Chicago *Manual of Style*.
Recent Nonfiction Titles: *Career Information: A Bibliography of Publications About Careers in Canada*, by Sybil Huffman and James Huffman; *What Can I do This Summer?* 1983 edition, by C.L. Bedal.

***GULF PUBLISHING CO.**, Box 2608, Houston TX 77001. (713)529-4301. Vice President: C.A. Umbach Jr. Editor-in-Chief: B.J. Lowe. Imprint: Lone Star Books (regional Texas books). Publishes hardcover and large format paperback originals. Pays 10% royalty on net income; advance averages $300-2,000. Averages 40-50 titles/year. Subsidy publishes 1-2 titles a year. Simultaneous and photocopied submissions OK. Computer printout and disk submissions OK; prefers letter quality to dot matrix printouts. Reports in 1-2 months. SASE. Free book catalog.
Nonfiction: Business, reference, regional trade, regional gardening, scientific and self-help. "We are the world's largest specialized publisher to the energy industries." Submit outline/synopsis and 1-2 sample chapters.
Recent Nonfiction Titles: *Historic Texas Inns and Hotels*, by Ed Syers; and *Creative Worklife*, by Don Scobel (management).

H.P. BOOKS, Box 5367, Tucson AZ 85703. Executive Editor: Rick Bailey. Publishes hardcover and paperback originals. Specializes in how-to books in several fields, all photo-illustrated. Pays royalty on wholesale price; advance negotiable. Averages 40-45 titles/year. Simultaneous and photocopied submissions OK. "We delight in disk submissions—as long as they're compatible with out Wang VS 100 system. *No printouts*." Reports in 2-4 weeks. SASE. Free book catalog.
Nonfiction: Cookbooks; cooking and foods; gardening; hobbies; how-to; leisure activities; photography; automotive; health; recreation; self-help; art techniques; and technical books. Most books are 160 pages minimum; "word count varies with the format." Query and state number and type of illustrations available. Accepts introdution and 1 sample chapter. "We *require* author to supply photos and illustrations to our specifications."
Recent Nonfiction Titles: *Microwave Cookbook: The Complete Guide*, by Pat Josler; *Vegetable Cookery*, by Lou Pappas; *Spas & Hot Tubs*, by Cort Sinnes; *Pruning: How-To Guide for Gardeners*, by Stebbins & McCaskey; *Doll Collecting for Fun & Profit*, by Mildred & Colleen Seeley.

H.W.H. CREATIVE PRODUCTIONS, INC., 87-53 167th St., Jamaica NY 11432. (212)297-2208. President: Willis Hogans Jr. Publishes hardcover and trade paperback originals. Averages 5 titles/year. Pays 10-15% royalty on wholesale price; offers average $200 advance. Photocopied submissions OK. SASE. Reports in 1 month on queries; 2 months on mss.
Imprints: *Phase One Graphic* (nonfiction and fiction), Mrs. Maxine Bayliss, editorial contact person.
Nonfiction: Biography, cookbook, humor, illustrated book and self-help. Subjects include Americana, animals, art, cooking and foods, health, hobbies, nature, photography (as a creative art form), recreation, travel and energy. Particularly interested in cookbooks, personalities, self portraits, new forms of energy, high technology. Submit outline/synopsis and sample chapters.
Recent Nonfiction Titles: *Euphrates Black Pages*, Euphrates Inc. (classified book) and *New Distributor Orientation Manual*, T&M Assoc. (instructional manual).
Fiction: Confession, ethnic, experimental, fantasy, humor, mainstream, romance, science fiction, suspense and plays. "Mindblowing science fiction, clean romance, experimental writing on any subject, children's stories." Submit outline/synopsis and sample chapters.
Recent Fiction Titles: *The Land of the Blue and Purple Clouds*, by Willis Hogans Jr. (science fiction); *That Time Again* (fantasy); and *The Last Tree in the World* (fantasy).

HAMMOND, INC., 515 Valley St., Maplewood NJ 07040. (201)763-6000. General Trade Editor: Warren Cox. Hardcover and paperback originals. "Books are negotiated from flat fee for outright purchase to advances against standard royalties, depending on subject." Published 5 titles in 1981. Submit outline/synopsis and sample chapters. State availability of photos/illustrations. Simultanous submissions OK. Reports in 2-4 weeks. SASE. Book catalog for SASE.
Nonfiction: Publishes Americana, art, business, cookbooks, history, hobbies, how-to, humor, nature, recreation, reference, sports and travel books.
Recent Nonfiction Titles: *What's What*, by David Fisher and Reginald Bragonier Jr.; *The Times Atlas of World History*; *The Hammond Almanac*; *The Book of Why*, by Robert L. Shook; *Famous Brands Cookbook*; *Cordial Cookery*, by Marjorie White.

HANCOCK HOUSE PUBLISHERS LTD., 1431 Harrison Ave., Blaine WA 98230. Editor-in-Chief: David Hancock. Hardcover and paperback originals (85%) and reprints (15%). Pays 10% royalty on list price; $500 minimum advance. Publishes 40 titles/year. State availability of photos and/or illustrations to accompany ms. Computer printout submissions OK; prefers letter quality to dot matrix. Reports in 1-2 months. SASE. Free book catalog.
Nonfiction: Publishes (in order of preference): craft, anthropology, sport, nature, history, biography, reference, Americana and Canadian, cookbooks, cooking and foods, hobbies, how-to, photography, recreation, self-help, and travel books. Needs 25 new titles on northwestern history and nature; 25 titles on small farm crops and animals. Query or send complete ms including photos. Looks for "a very complete outline and table of contents."
Recent Nonfiction Titles: *My Spirit Soars*, by Chief Dan George; *David Ingram's Investment Guide*; and *Roadside Wildflowers of the Northeast* and *Roadside Wildflowers of the Northwest.*

*HARBOR PUBLISHING, INC., 1668 Lombard St., San Francisco CA 94123. (415)775-4740. Publisher: Jack E. Jennings. Publishes hardcover and paperback originals. Averages 16 titles/year. Subsidy publishes 15% of books. Pays 5-15% royalty on wholesale price. Photocopied submissions OK. SASE. Reports in 2 weeks on queries; 2 months on mss. Book catalog for business size SAE and 2 first class stamps.
Nonfiction: How-to, self-help. Subjects include animals, business and economics, cooking and foods, health, psychology; and investment/tax. Accepts artwork/photos. "How-to in regard to finance, investments; self-help in psychology, health for the adult professional and layman." Accepts outline/synopsis and 3 sample chapters.
Recent Nonfiction Titles: *101 Loopholes in Reagan Tax Package*, by Bill Greene (tax avoidance strategy); *Grants Game; How To Get Free Money*, by Lawrence Lee; and *Kathy Cooks . . . Naturally*, by Kathy Hoshijo.

HARCOURT BRACE JOVANOVICH, 1250 6th Ave., San Diego CA 92101. Director of Trade Books Department: Peter Jovanovich. Publishes hardcover and paperback originals and reprints. SASE.

‡HARCOURT BRACE JOVANOVICH LEGAL & PROFESSIONAL PUBLICATIONS, INC., Subsidiary of Harcourt Brace Jovanovich, Inc., 14415 S. Main St., Gardena CA 90248. (213)321-3275. Subsidiaries include Law Distributors, Gilbert Printing, Gilbert Law & Legalines, Bar/Bri Law Reviews. President: Meyer Fisher. Publishes trade paperback originals and trade paperback reprints. Averages 6 titles/year. Pays 7-10% royalty on wholesale price. Offers $1,000-6,000 advance. Simultaneous submissions OK. Computer printout submissions OK. SASE. Reports in 3 weeks on queries; 2 months on mss. Queries/mss may be routed to other editors in the publishing group. Free book catalog.
Nonfiction: How-to, reference law books for minors, self-help, technical, textbook, law outlines and study aids. Subjects include business and economics, psychology, professional law, C.P.A., criminal justice. Especially needs books on "juvenile laws, psychology for law people, law for law people. Does not want biography, cookbooks, health, humor, politics, religious books. Submit outline/synopsis and 6 sample chapters.
Recent Nonfiction Titles: *California Laws Relating to Minors*, by Dale Ely (juvenile justice); *Counselors' Dictionary*, by Dale Ely (psychology dictionary); and *Administrative Law*, by Asimov.

HARIAN CREATIVE PRESS—BOOKS, Box 189, Clifton Park NY 12065. (518)885-7397, 885-6699. Publisher & Executive Editor: Dr. Harry Barba. Publishes hardcover and trade and mass market paperback originals and reprints. Averages 3-6 titles/year. Pays 15% royalty; offers advance "for an exceptional submission." Simultaneous and photocopied submissions OK. No computer printout or disk submissions. SASE. Reports in 1 month on queries; 2-3 months on mss. Book catalog for business size SASE.
Imprints: Barba-Cue Specials and Harian Creative Awards, (nonfiction and fiction). Dr. Harry Barba, publisher. What's Cooking In—?, ed. by Harry Barba and Marian Barba.
Nonfiction: Biography, "coffee table" book, cookbook, how-to, humor, illustrated book, juvenile, reference, self-help, technical and textbook. Accepts translations. Subjects include Americana, animals, art, business and economics, cooking and foods, health, history, hobbies, music, nature, philosophy, photography, politics, psychology, recreation, sociology, travel and belles lettres. Accepts artwork/photos. "Our readers are both the quality reader and the general reader; the reader with a conscience and a wish to be entertained while being put in connection with life, himself (or herself), and fellow humankind. We prefer full manuscript submissions."
Fiction: "We prefer full manuscript submissions."
Recent Fiction Titles: *The Day the World Went Sane*, by Harry Barba (novelette); *Saratoga* and *Girl On the Beach*, by Karen Watson; *Clown, Feeling Beautiful*, by Margaret Kingery; and *The Gospel Accoridng to Everyman*, by Harry Barba.
Poetry: "Socially functional poetry. No obscenity, pornography for its own sake, etc."
Recent Poetry Titles: "Poems," by Harold Bond (new psyche); *Verses Vice Verses*, by Richard Loughlin (all genres); and *The Magellan Heart*, by Donald A. Sears (all genres).

Tips: "The writer would do well to consult our print-out on social/functional writing and art before submitting manuscripts to us. Also, familiarize yourself with what we have already published." Queries/mss may be routed to other editors in the publishing group.

HARLEQUIN BOOKS, (formerly Harlequin Enterprises, Ltd.), 225 Duncan Mill Rd., Don Mills, Ontario, Canada M3B 3K9. (416)445-5860. Imprints include Harlequin Romance, Harlequin Presents, Superromances, and Harlequin American Romance. Publishes paperback originals. Pays royalty on retail price; offers advance. Photocopied submissions OK. No computer printout or disk submissions. SAE and International Reply Coupons. Reports in 3-5 months.
Fiction: For Harlequin Romance and Harlequin Presents submit to Jennifer Campbell, Senior Editor. Outline/synopsis and sample chapters OK. For Superromance submit to Star Helmer, Editorial Director. Outline/synopsis and sample chapters OK. For Harlequin American Romance submit to Vivian Stephens, Editorial Director, Harlequin Books, 919 3rd Ave., 15th Floor, New York NY 10022. Complete mss only.
Tips: "This is a tough market. The odds against you are high, but the rewards are great if you hit."

HARMONY BOOKS, 1 Park Ave., New York NY 10016. (212)532-9200. Division of Crown Publishers. Executive Editor: Esther Mitgang. Assistant Editor: Douglas Abrams. Publishes hardcover and paperback originals (95%) and reprints (5%). Publishes 40 titles/year. Royalties vary with project; advance varies.
Nonfiction: Art, cookbooks, cooking and foods, music and photography. Needs popular topics for adults. Submit outline/synopsis and sample chapters. Unsolicited mss will not be accepted.
Recent Nonfiction Titles: *New American Cuisine*, by the *Metropolitan Home* (cooking); *Doveen*, by S. N. Behrman (biography); and *Hangover Handbook*, by David Outerbridge (humor).
Fiction: Mainstream. Unsolicited mss will not be accepted.
Recent Fiction Titles: *Captain Blood*, by Michael Blodgett; and *Restaurant at the End of the Universe*, by Douglas Adams.

‡HARPER & ROW JUNIOR BOOKS GROUP, 10 E. 53rd St., New York NY 10022. (212)593-7044. Imprints include: Harper & Row Junior Books, including Charlotte Zolotow Books; T.Y. Crowell and Lippincott Junior Books. Publisher: Elizabeth Gordon. Editors: Charlotte Zolotow, Marilyn Kriney, Barbara Fenton, Lucille Schultz, Laura Geringer, Robert Warren. Publishes hardcover originals and paperback reprints—picture books, easy-to-read, middle-grade, teenage, and young adult novels. Published 64 titles in 1983 (Harper, cloth); 29 titles (Harper, paperback); 34 titles (Crowell); 20 titles (Lippincott). Query; submit complete ms; submit outline/synopsis and sample chapters through agent. SASE for query and ms. Photocopied submissions OK. "Please identify simultaneous submissions." Reports in 3 months. Pays average royalty of 10%. Royalties on picture books shared with illustrators. Offers advance. Book catalog for SAE.
Nonfiction: Science, history, social studies, sports.
Fiction: Fantasy, animal, spy/adventure, science fiction, problem novels, contemporary.
Recent Titles: (Harper) *The Philharmonic Gets Dressed*, by Karla Kuskin, pictures by Marc Simont (ages 4-8); *The Book of Pigericks*, by Arnold Lobel (ages 5-8); *The Wish Giver*, by Bill Brittain (ages 8-12); *The Magical Adventures of Pretty Pearl*, by Virginia Hamilton (ages 11 and up). (Crowell) *A Medieval Feast*, by Aliki (all ages); *Cars and How They Go*, by Joanna Cole, pictures by Gail Gibbons (ages 7-11); *Rain and Hail*, by Franklyn M. Branley (ages 5-8). (Lippincott) *Crocker*, by Kin Platt (ages 12 and up); *Gobs of Goo*, by Vicki Cobb (ages 6-8).
Tips: "Write from your own experience and the child you once were. Read widely in the field of adult and children's literature. Realize that writing for children is a difficult challenge."

HARPER & ROW PUBLISHERS, INC., 10 E. 53rd St., New York NY 10022. (212)593-7000. Imprints include Barnes & Noble; and Harper & Row-San Francisco (religious books only); Perennial; Colophon; and Torchbooks. Contact: Managing Editor. Publishes hardcover and paperback originals, and paperback reprints. Publishes 300 titles/year. Pays standard royalties; advances negotiable. No unsolicited queries or mss. SASE. Reports on queries in 6 weeks.
Nonfiction: Americana, animals, art, biography, business/economics, cookbooks, health, history, how-to, humor, music, nature, philosophy, photography, poetry, politics, psychology, reference, religion, science, self-help, sociology, sports and travel. "No technical books."
Fiction: Adventure, fantasy, gothic, historical, mainstream, mystery, romance, science fiction, suspense, western and literary. "We look for a strong story line and exceptional literary talent."

THE HARVARD COMMON PRESS, 535 Albany St., Boston MA 02118. (617)423-5803. Editorial Director: Kathleen Cushman. Publishes hardcover and trade paperback originals and reprints. Averages 8 titles/year. Pays royalty; offers average $1,000 advance. Simultaneous and photocopied submissions OK. Computer printout and disk submissions OK; prefers letter quality to dot matrix printouts. SASE. Reports in 1 month. Catalog for 9x11½ SAE and 2 first class stamps.
Nonfiction: Biography, cookbook, how-to, humor, reference and self-help. Subjects include Americana,

business and economics, cooking and foods, health, history, hobbies, music, nature, politics, psychology, recreation, sociology, sports and travel. "We want strong, practical books with an idealistic bias—books that help people gain control over a particular area of their lives, whether it's family matters, business or financial matters, health, travel, or careers. We're open to any good nonfiction proposal that shows evidence of strong organization and writing. First-time authors are welcome." Accepts nonfiction translations. Submit outline/synopsis and 1-3 sample chapters.

Recent Nonfiction Titles: *A Young Person's Guide to Military Service*, by Jeff Bradley (practical guide); *Starting a Small Restaurant*, by Daniel Miller (small enterprise); and *Helping Children Cope with Separation and Loss*, by Claudia Jewett (family matters).

HARVARD UNIVERSITY PRESS, 79 Garden St., Cambridge MA 02138. (617)495-2601. Director: Arthur J. Rosenthal. Editor-in-Chief: Maud Wilcox. Publishes hardcover and paperback originals and reprints. Publishes 120 titles/year. Free book catalog.
Nonfiction: "We publish only scholarly nonfiction." No fiction.

HARVEST HOUSE, 1075 Arrowsmith, Eugene OR 97402. Editor: Eileen L. Mason. Pays 8% royalty on the retail price to first-time authors; 10% on the retail price to previously published authors. SASE. Reports in 3 weeks.
Nonfiction: Evangelical books that help the hurts of people. How-to books which proclaim the gospel, sometimes in a limited way; Bible-related study books which are topical and promote the cuase of evangelical literature; and books in the health field with a biblical connection. Not fundamentalist in approach, but rather, progressive evangelical. No biographies, autobiographies, science, history fiction, children's books, bookletsized works or poetry. Submit contents page, three chapters, and synopsis.

HARVEY HOUSE PUBLISHERS, 20 Waterside Plaza, New York NY 10010. Publisher: L.F. Reeves. Publishes hardcover originals. Averages 22-25 titles/year. Pays 5% minimum royalty based on wholesale or retail price; advance "depends on the manuscript." Simultaneous (if so informed) and photocopied submissions OK. No computer printout or disk submissions. Reports in 3 weeks. "Manuscripts and queries without SASE will be destroyed."
Nonfiction: Juvenile leisure-time activity books. "We have successful books on skateboards, minicycles, hang gliding, etc. Our biography series 'Star People' covers athletes; we have books on Dorothy Hamill, Tracy Austin, Janet Guthrie, Reggie Jackson and people in the news. Also occasional science books." No religious, self-help, strictly adult, textbooks or travel books. Query.
Recent Nonfiction Title: *Kitty O'Neil*, by Ireland (biography).
Fiction: "We publish only a couple of novels a year. No science fiction, romances, fantasy, talking animal stories or rehashed fairy tales." Query.
Recent Fiction Title: *Hot Wire*, by William Butterworth (teenage employment problems).

HASTINGS HOUSE PUBLISHERS, INC., 10 E. 40th St., New York NY 10016. (212)689-5400. Editor: Walter Frese. Hardcover and paperback originals (80%) and reprints (20%). Averages 60 titles/year. 10% minimum royalty. Reports in 1-2 weeks. No computer printout or disk submissions. SASE. Free book catalog.
Nonfiction: Publishes Americana, graphic arts, biography, cookbooks, cooking and foods, history, juveniles, photography, recreation, sports and travel. Accepts nonfiction translations. Query or submit outline/synopsis and 2 sample chapters. Accepts artwork/photos. Recently published *Food Processor Magic*, by Hemingway/DeLima (cooking); *Inside ABC-American Broadcasting Company's Rise to Power*, by Sterling/Quinlan; *Philadelphia in Color*, by Hayes/Noll/Tavs.

*HAWKES PUBLISHING, INC., 3775 S. 5th W., Salt Lake City UT 84115. (801)262-5555. President: John Hawkes. Publishes hardcover and trade paperback originals. Averages 24 titles/year. Subsidy publishes 25% of books/year based on "how promising they are." Pays varying royalty of 10% on retail price to 10% on wholesale; no advance. Photocopied submissions OK. SASE. Reports in 1 month on queries; 3 months on mss. Free book catalog.
Nonfiction: Cookbook, how-to and self-help. Subjects include cooking and foods, health, history, hobbies and psychology. Query or submit outline/synopsis and sample chapters.
Recent Nonfiction Titles: *Lord, Why Me? Understanding Adversity*, by Larry Davis; *Your Wedding—Saving Hundreds of Dollars*, by Betty Peterson; *Hurry Home Dad, Today I'm Going to Die*, by Jeannie Davis.

HAYDEN BOOK CO., INC., 50 Essex St., Rochelle Park NJ 07662. (201)843-0550. Editorial Director: Michael Violano. Publishes hardcover and paperback originals. Publishes 70 titles/year. Pays 12-15% royalty; offers "minimal" advance. Simultaneous (if so identified) and photocopied submissions OK. Reports in 6 weeks. SASE. Free book catalog.
Technical: Publishes technician-level and engineering texts and references on microcomputers, digital elec-

tronics, electricity and robotics; computer science; text and references for food service and restaurant management; texts and references for senior high schools, in English and composition.

‡**HAZELDEN FOUNDATION**, Dept. of Educational Materials, Box 176, Center City MN 55012. (612)257-4010. Managing Editor: Linda Peterson. Publishes hardcover and trade paperback originals. Averages 40 titles/year. Pays 7-9% royalty on retail price; buys some mss outright; offers $150-300+ advance. Simultaneous and photocopied submissions OK. Computer printout submissions OK. SASE. "We immediately acknowledge receipt. A decision is usually made within 2 months."
Nonfiction: Reference, self-help, technical on philosophy, psychology, sociology, addictions. "We are seeking mss of pamphlet or booklet length. The subject matter, ideally, will center around alcoholism, drug abuse or other addictions. The focus would be on the prevention, recovery from, or understanding of an addiction." Publishes for people recovering from an addiction and those close to them; people seeking information about alcoholism/drug abuse; professionals who help such people. No personal stories or poetry. Submit outline/synopsis, introduction and 2 sample chapters.
Recent Nonfiction Titles: *It Happens to Doctors, Too*, by Abraham Twerski, MD; *Do's & Don'ts*, by Hazelden Family Center (workbook); and *Inside the Adolescent Alcoholic*, by Ann Marie Krupski (booklet).

HEALTH PROFESSION PUBLISHING, McGraw-Hill Book Co., 1221 Avenue of the Americas, New York NY 10020. Editorial Director: Robert P. McGraw. Publishes 60 titles/year. Pays on royalty basis. SASE.
Textbooks: Publishes textbooks, major reference books and continuing education materials in the field of medicine.
Recent Nonfiction Titles: *Cranial Computed Tomography*, by Lee and Rao; *Principles of Surgery*, by Schwartz, et. al.

‡***HEART OF THE LAKES PUBLISHING**, 2989 Lodi Rd., Interlaken NY 14847-0299. (607)532-4997. Contact: Walter Steesy. Publishes hardcover and trade paperback originals and hardcover and trade paperback reprints. Averages 10-15 titles/year. Subsidy publishes 50% of books/year, "depending on type of material and potential sales." Payment is "worked out individually." Simultaneous and photocopied submissions OK. SASE. Reports in 1 week on queries; 2 weeks on mss. Current books flyer for busness size SAE and 1 first class stamp; full catalog $2.
Nonfiction: New York state and New England history and genealogy. Query.
Recent Nonfiction Titles: *Their Own Voices: Oral History Recorded in 1840 in Washington County, New York*, by Asa Fitch, c 1840 (edited by Wiston Adler); *The Man Who Owned the Pistols*, by Helene Phelen (local history/biography); and *St. Lawrence County (New York) History*, by Durant & Peirce (reprint of 1878 edition).
Fiction: "Not looking for any, but will review any that deal with New York state historical subjects."

D.C. HEATH & CO., 125 Spring St., Lexington MA 02173. (617)862-6650. College Division Editorial Director: Barbara Piercecchi. Division Editor-in-Chief: Robert Marshall. Lexington Books General Manager: Michael McCarroll. Collamore Press General Manager: Geoff Gunn. Publishes hardcover and paperback textbooks and professional scholarly and medical books. Averages 300 titles/year. Offers standard royalty rates. Query. Computer printout and disk submissions OK. "Final revised mss accepted are published within 1 year." SASE.
Textbooks: "Texts at the college level in psychology, history, political science, chemistry, math, biology, physics, economics, modern languages, English, business, and computer science. Also publishes professional reference books: "Advanced-level research studies in the social sciences, library science, and in technical fields (Lexington Books) and medical books (The Collamore Press)." Length varies.
Tips: Queries/mss may be routed to other editors in the publishing group.

‡**HEATH CO.**, Subsidiary of Zenith Radio Corp., Hilltop Rd., St. Joseph MI 49085. (616)982-3200. Senior Educational Product Developer: Richard Krajewski. Publishes educational courses in three-ring binders and in paperback. Averages 10 titles/year. Pays royalty on wholesale price. Computer printout and disk submissions OK. SASE. Reports in 1 month. Free book catalog.
Nonfiction: Technical and textbook on computers and electronics. Publishes for technicians and professionals. Accepts artwork/photos. "Prospective authors should write to us for our current needs. They should also include their resumes when they write." No material outside the area of technology and science. Query.
Recent Nonfiction Titles: *Voice Synthesis*; *Microcomputer Interfacing*, by Andrew Staugarrd; and *Advanced Amateur Radio Course*.

HEINLE & HEINLE PUBLISHERS, INC., Subsidiary of Science Books International, Inc., 286 Congress St., Boston MA 02210. (617)451-1940. President: Charles H. Heinle. Editor: Stanley Galek. Averages 15 titles/year. Pays 6-15% royalty on net price; no advance. SASE. Reports in 3 weeks on queries; 3 months on mss. Free book catalog.

Nonfiction: Textbook. "Foreign language and English as a second or foreign language and English as a second or foreign language text and non-text materials. Before writing the book, submit complete prospectus along with sample chapters, and specify market and competitive position of proposed text."

Recent Nonfiction Titles: *Toward a Philosophy of Second Language Learning and Teaching*, by Kenneth D. Chastain (teaching methods); *How to Learn a Foreign Language*, by Paul Pimsleur (foreign language learning); and *Vida y voces del mundo hispanico*, by P. Smith, H. Babbitt, H. Frey and A. Tejeda (Spanish textbook).

Fiction: "Education materials in foreign language." Query.

*HERALD PRESS, Mennonite Publishing House, 616 Walnut Ave., Scottdale PA 15683. (412)887-8500. Book Editor: Paul M. Schrock. Publishes hardcover and paperback originals and reprints. Averages 35 titles/year. Several titles a year are subsidized by church organizations. "Subsidy is accepted only for books sponsored by an official board or committee of the Mennonite Church to meet discriminating needs when a book is not otherwise economically feasible." Pays 10-15% royalty on retail price; no advance. Photocopied submissions OK. Computer printout and disk submissions OK; prefers letter quality to dot matrix printouts. SASE. Catalog 50¢. Reports in 3 weeks.

Nonfiction: Biography (religious); cookbooks; history (church); how-to; juveniles; devotional/inspirational; psychology (religion); reference (Mennonite); religion; missions and evangelism; self-help (Christian); sociology (of religion); peace and social issues; and textbooks (Christian). Query. Accepts outline/synopsis and 1 sample chapter. Looks for "a fresh perspective; competence of the writer in the subject treated (professional credentials if applicable); crisp use of language; neatness of manuscript; ability of author/manuscript to immediately capture attention and sustain interest."

Recent Nonfiction Titles: *Faith in a Nuclear Age*, by Dave Beachey; *Caring Enough to Hear and Be Heard*, by David Augsburger; *The Church and Persons with Handicaps*, by H. Oliver Ohsberg; and *A New Way to Live*, by Neta Jackson.

Fiction: Adventure (juvenile); historical and religious. Query.

Recent Fiction Titles: *Danger in the Pines*, by Ruth Nulton Moore; *For Conscience Sake*, by Solomon Stucky.

‡HERE'S LIFE PUBLISHERS, INC., Subsidiary of Campus Crusade for Christ, Box 1576, San Bernardino CA 92404. (714)886-7981. Editorial Director: Les Stobbe. Publishes hardcover and trade paperback originals and mass market paperback originals. Averages 40 titles/year. Pays 15% royalty on wholesale price. Offers $1,000-2,000 advance. Simultaneous and photocopied submissions OK. SASE. Reports in 1 month on queries; 3 months on mss. Book catalog for 8½x11 SAE and $2 postage. Writer's guidelines available.

Nonfiction: Biography, how-to, illustrated book, reference and self-help. Subjects include religion and sports (religious). Needs "books in the areas of evangelism, Christian growth and family life; must reflect basic understanding of ministry and mission of Campus Crusade for Christ. No metaphysical or missionary biography." Query or submit outline/synopsis and sample chapters.

Recent Nonfiction Titles: *Love Unlocks Every Door*, by Arlis Priest with Al Jansen (biographical); *Live, Grow and Be Free*, by Dennis Gibson (how-to); and *Starting Point*, by Ken Green (teen Bible study).

*HERITAGE BOOKS, INC., 3602 Maureen, Bowie MD 20715. (301)464-1159. Editorial Director: Laird C. Towle. Publishes hardcover and paperback originals (20%) and reprints (80%). Averages 4 titles/year. "Quality of the book is of prime importance; next is its relevance to our fields of interest." Pays 10% royalty on retail price; occasional advance. Simultaneous and photocopied submissions OK. Computer printout submissions OK; prefers letter quality to dot matrix. Reports in 1 month. SASE. Free book catalog.

Nonfiction: "We particularly desire nonfiction titles dealing with history and genealogy including how-to and reference works, as well as conventional histories and genealogies. The titles should be either of national interest or restricted to New England. Other subject matter will be considered provided that it is of either national or New England interest. We prefer writers to query, submit an outline/synopsis, or submit a complete ms, in that order, depending on the stage the writer has reached in the preparation of his work."

Recent Nonfiction Titles: *New Hampshire Genealogical Research Guide*, by Towle and Brown; *Genealogical Periodical Annual Index, Vol. 18*, by Mayhew and Towle; *1790-1840 Federal Censuses, Provincetown, Mass.*, by Ferguson; and *History of Framingham, Mass.*, by Barry.

HERMAN PUBLISHING, 45 Newbury St., Boston MA 02116. (617)536-5810. Editor: Sanford M. Herman. Publishes hardcover and paperback originals. Averages 20 titles/year. "Standard 10% royalty (7% on paperbacks) up to break-even point; higher beyond." Advance varies, depending on author's reputation and nature of book. Will send copy of current catalog on request. Send query, outline and sample chapter to C.A. Herman. Reports in 2 months, "longer if jammed up." SASE.

Nonfiction: Business, technical reference, the arts, health, self-improvement, careers, electronics, architecture, communications arts, engineering, commerce, finance, technology, food service and home economics, health care, management, manufacturing, marketing and selling. "It might be worth noting that we also perform a unique service. We will market books in the areas mentioned above that may have been privately published by the author or by a small publisher. Naturally, we must first see a sample copy and be satisfied that we can market it." Writing must be factual and authoritative. No length limits.

Recent Nonfiction Titles: *Professional Engineer's License Guide*, by Joseph D. Eckard; *The Manufacturer's Representative*, by Frank LeBell (marketing and selling); and *Trade Shows in the Marketing Mix*, by Hanlon.

HIGH/COO PRESS, Route #1, Battle Ground IN 47920. (317)567-2596. Editors: Randy and Shirley Brooks. Publishes originals. Averages 5 titles/year. Pays 15% minimum royalty on retail price saddle-stitched after production expenses. SASE. Reports in 2 weeks on queries; 2 months on mss. Book catalog for 5x7 SAE and 2 first class stamps. Sample chapbook $3.50 postpaid.

Nonfiction: Reference. Subjects include haiku books. "Every two years we publish a directory of haiku in English called *Haiku Review*. We list and review haiku books in print along with other haiku bibliography information. We have an international audience of poets and haiku enthusiasts. We do not seek or desire any mass market, but rather an informed, astute readership." Query.

Recent Nonfiction Title: *Haiku Review '82*, edited by Randy and Shirley Brooks (haiku directory).

Poetry: "We publish a chapbook of short poetry every 6 months. Each chapbook is 24-48 pages. We also publish 3-4 mini-chapbooks every year. Each mini is 12-24 pages. No poems with more than thirteen lines." Submit complete ms. "Sample our publications before submitting."

Recent Poetry Titles: *Sun Faced Haiku/Moon Faced Haiku*, by Alan Gettis (2 volumes); *Wind in the Keys*, by LeRoy Gorman; *Barbwire Holds Its Ground*, by Randy Brooks (Kansas haiku); and *A Cappella*, by Margherita Faulkner.

HOLIDAY HOUSE, 18 E. 53rd St., New York NY 10022. (212)688-0085. Editorial Director: Margery Cuyler. Publishes hardcover originals. Averages 25-30 titles/year. Pays in royalties based on retail price; offers variable advance. Photocopied submissions OK. Computer printouts and disk submissions OK. Reports in 2 months. SASE. Free book catalog.

Nonfiction and Fiction: General fiction and nonfiction for young readers—pre-school through high school. "It's better to submit the ms without art." Submit outline/synopsis and 3 sample chapters or complete ms. "No certified, insured or registered mail accepted."

Recent Titles: *Banana Blitz*, by Florence Parry Heide; *Germs!*, by Dorothy Hinshaw Patent.

HOLLOWAY HOUSE PUBLISHING CO., 8060 Melrose Ave., Los Angeles CA 90046. (213)653-8060. Editorial Director: Robert Leighton. Publishes paperback originals (95%) and reprints (5%). Averages 30 titles/year. Pays royalty based on retail price. Photocopied submissions OK. Prefer outline and 3 sample chapters. No computer printout or disk submissions. SASE. Reports in 6 weeks. Free book catalog for SASE.

Nonfiction and Fiction: "Holloway House is the largest publisher of Black Experience literature. We are in the market for hard-hitting contemporary stories with easily identifiable characters and locations. Dialogue must be realistic, with authentic slang and current 'street' language. A strain of sex is acceptable but not essential. Action, people and places must be thoroughly depicted and graphically presented." Black romance line newly launched—Holloway House Heartline Romances, designed to appeal to middle class black women paralleling other romance lines designed for white readers. Gambling and Game Books-from time to time publishes gambling books along the line of *How to Win*, *World's Greatest Winning Systems*, *Backgammon*, *How to Play and Win at Gin Rummy*, etc. Send query letter and/or outline with one sample chapter. SASE. Length: 60,000 words.

Recent Nonfiction Title: *How to Win*, by Mike Goodman.

Recent Fiction Titles: *Treat Them Like Animals*, by Rae Stewart (black women in prison); and *Love's Velvet Song*, by Geraldine Greene (black romance).

HOLMES & MEIER PUBLISHERS, INC., 30 Irving Place, New York NY 10003. (212)254-4100. Publisher: Max J. Holmes. Publishes hardcover and paperback originals (50%) and reprints (50%). Publishes 120 titles/year. Pays variable royalty. Computer printout and disk submissions OK. SASE. Reports in 3 months. Free book catalog.

Nonfiction: Americana, art, biography, business/economics, history, music, nature, politics, psychology, reference, sociology and textbooks. Accepts nonfiction translations. "We are noted as a scholarly publishing house and are pleased with our reputation of excellence in the field. However, while we will continue to publish books for academic and professional audiences, we are expanding our list to reach the broader non-academic intellectual community. We will continue to build on our strengths in the social sciences, humanities and natural sciences. We do not want how-to and self-help material." Accepts artwork/photos. Query first and submit outline/synopsis, sample chapters and curriculum vitae and idea of intended market/audience.

Recent Nonfiction Titles: *Gender and Literary Voice*, edited by Janet Todd (women's studies); *Central*

America: Anatomy of a Crisis, by Richard E. Feinberg; *Hitler's Death Camps*, by Konnilyn Feig; and *Léon Blum*, by Jean Lacouture.

HOLT, RINEHART & WINSTON OF CANADA, LTD., 55 Horner Ave., Toronto, Ontario Canada M8Z 4X6. (416)255-4491. School Editor-in-Chief: William Park. College Editor-in-Chief: Ron Munro. Publishes hardcover and paperback text originals for the El-Hi, community college and university markets. Royalty varies according to type of book; pays $200-500 for anthologies. No advance. Simultaneous and photocopied submissions OK. Reports in 1-3 months. SAE and International Reply Coupons. Free book catalog.
Nonfiction: Education texts. Query.
Recent Nonfiction Titles: *Music Canada*, general editor, Penny Louise Brooks; *Elementary School Music Programme*; *Personnel Management*, by Stone & Meltz (college personnel text).

HORIZON PRESS, 156 5th Ave., New York NY 10010. Pays royalty based on both wholesale and retail price. Royalty schedule standard scale from 10% to 15%. Averages 24 titles/year. Free book catalog. Reports in 3 months. No computer printout or disk submissions. Accepts nonfiction and fiction translations. SASE. "Insurance cost for guaranteed return."
Nonfiction: History, literature, science, biography, the arts, general. Length: 40,000 words and up. Accepts photos/artwork. Query with full description.
Recent Nonfiction Titles: *"Friend and Lover": The Life of Louise Bryant*, by Virginia Gardner; *Innovative Furniture in America*, by David Hanks; *My Thirty Years' War*, *The Fiery Fountains* and *The Strange Necessity*, all by Margaret Anderson; *Yesto Life*, by Corliss Lamont.
Fiction: Query with full description. Recently published *Sun Dogs*, by Robert Olen Butler; *The Refusers*, by Stanley Burnshaw. "We rarely publish fiction."

HOUGHTON MIFFLIN CO., 2 Park St., Boston MA 02108. (617)725-5000. Editor-in-Chief: Austin G. Olney. Managing Editor: Linda L. Glick. Hardcover and paperback originals (90%) and paperback reprints (10%). Royalty of 6% on retail price for paperbacks; 10-15% on sliding scale for standard fiction and nonfiction; advance varies widely. Publishes 125 titles/year. Simultaneous submissions and photocopied submissions OK. No computer printout or disk submissions. Reports in 6-8 weeks. SASE.
Nonfiction: Americana, natural history, animals, biography, cookbooks/cooking/food, health, history, how-to, juveniles, poetry, politics, psychology and self-help. Query.
Recent Nonfiction Titles: *Recalled by Life*, by Anthony J. Sattilaro, M.D.; *Escape From Sobibor*, by Richard Rashke.
Fiction: Historical, mainstream, mystery, science fiction and suspense. Query.
Recent Fiction Titles: *Fairland, Fairland*, by A.B. Guthrie; *The Mosquito Coast*, by Paul Theroux; and *Triptych*, by Dora Landey and Elinor Klein.
Tips: Quries/mss may be routed to other editors in the publishing group.

HOUGHTON MIFFLIN CO., Children's Trade Books, 2 Park St., Boston MA 02108. (617)725-5953. Contact: Editor. Publishes hardcover originals and trade paperback reprints (some simultaneous hard/soft). Averages 45-50 titles/year. Pays standard royalty; offers advance. SASE. Reports in 1 month on queries; 2 months on mss. Free book catalog.
Nonfiction: General juvenile nonfiction. "We'll consider most ideas." Submit outline/synopsis and sample chapters.
Fiction: "We publish fiction for a children's audience of all ages." Submit complete ms.

‡HOUNSLOW PRESS, Subsidiary of Anthony R. Hawke Ltd., 124 Parkview Ave., Willowdale, Ontario, Canada M2N 3Y5. (416)225-9176. President: Anthony Hawke. Publishes hardcover and trade paperback originals and reprints. Averages 6 titles/year. Pays 5-15% royalty on retail price; offers average $500 advance. Simultaneous and photocopied submissions OK. No computer printout or disk submissions. Reports in 1 week on queries; 2 weeks on mss. Free book catalog.
Nonfiction: Biography, coffee table book, cookbook, how-to, humor, illustrated book, juvenile, reference, self-help on animals, art, business and economics, cooking and foods, health, history, hobbies, nature, philosophy, photography, politics, psychology, recreation, religion, travel. Publishes for a general audience. "We do well with cookbooks and photography books about Canadian themes." Query. Accepts outline/synopsis and 4 sample chapters.
Recent Nonfiction Titles: *A Canadian Country Diary & Recipe Book*, by Ruth Mason (cookbook); *The Colour of New Brunswick*, by Stuart Trueman (photography); and *The Great Canadian Alphabet Book*, by Philip Johnson (children's book).
Fiction: Adventure, humor, mainstream. Query.
Poetry: Submit 20 samples.
Recent Poetry Titles: *Into a Blue Morning*, by C.H. Gervais; *Symmetries*, by Marin Sorescu; and *Beyond Lables*, by Robert Zend.

HOUSE OF COLLECTIBLES, INC., 1900 Premier Row, Orlando FL 32809. Publishes hardcover and trade paperback originals. Royalty is based on the stature of the author, the subject and the ms. Average advance is $1,000. Published 50 titles last year. Exclusive publisher of official price guides. Complete distribution and marketing range in all fields with heavy coverage on the collectible markets. Will consider photocopied submissions. Mss must be typed, double spaced with sample illustrations, when necessary. Reports in 2 months. Enclose return postage. Will send catalog to writer on request.
Nonfiction: "On the subject of collectibles (antiques, numismatics, philatelics) and how-to-do books, we prefer an author who knows his or her subject thoroughly. Any special treatment of emphasis is a matter of decision for the author." Submit outline and sample chapters.

HOWARD UNIVERSITY PRESS, 2900 Van Ness St. NW, Washington DC 20008. (202)686-6696. Managing Editor: Renee Mayfield. Publishes hardcover and paperback originals (90%), and hardcover reprints (10%). Averages 14 titles/year. Pays 5-15% royalty; offers average $500 advance. Simultaneous and photocopied submissions OK. SASE. Reports in 2 months. Free book catalog.
Nonfiction: Biography and reference. Subjects include Americana, art, business and economics, health, history, music, philosophy, photography, politics, psychology, religion, sociology, sports, science and literary criticism. "We would be pleased to receive inquiries concerning projects of an original, scholarly, conceptual nature on the above subjects as they pertain to minorities in the US or to people in the Third World. In Black studies, works that relate Black Americans to the Diaspora and, continually, works that serve to integrate Black history from slavery to WWII." No textbooks or personal revelations having no foundation in scholarly or journalistic methods.
Recent Nonfiction Titles: *Global Dimensions of the African Diaspora*, ed. by Joseph E. Harris (history); *Imperialism and Dependency*, by Daniel Offiong (economics, politics); *Pan-Africanism: The Idea and Movement, 1776-1963*, by P. Olisanwuche Esedebe (history); *Transformation and Resillency in Africa*, ed. by Pearl T. Robinson and Elliott P. Skinner (history); *Reluctant Reformers*, revised edition, by Robert Allen (history); *Singers of Daybreak*, revised edition, by Houston A. Baker, Jr. (literary criticism).
Fiction: Experimental and mainstream. "Our needs in this area are minimal. We will probably be aware of and seek out any projects we would do in this area." Query.
Tips: "Visit bookstores and college campuses, and tune in to what is being bought, read, researched and argued."

HOWELL-NORTH BOOKS, 9601 Aero Dr., San Diego CA 92123. (619)560-5163. President: Gifford T. Foley. Editorial Director: Modeste Williams. Publishes hardcover originals (95%) and some softcover (5%). Averages 10-15 titles/year. Pays 10-15% royalty. Generally no advance. Reports in 2 months. SASE.
Nonfiction: Railroad books. Also, to lesser degree, western Americana, marine and outdoor adventure. No autobiography, few biographies. Query. Provide statement of purpose for work, market identification, author vita.
Recent Nonfiction Titles: *MoPac Power*, by Joe Collias; *The Thousand-Mile Summer*, by Colin Fletcher; and *Rail City: Chicago, U.S.A.*, by George Douglas.

HUDSON HILLS PRESS, INC., Suite 301, 220 5th Ave., New York NY 10001. (212)889-3090. President/Editorial Director: Paul Anbinder. Publishes hardcover and paperback originals. Averages 6-8 titles/year. Offers royalties of 5-8% on retail price. Average advance: $5,000. Simultaneous and photocopied submissions OK. SASE. Reports in 4 weeks. Free book catalog.
Nonfiction: Art and photography. "We are only interested in publishing books about art and photography, or collections of photographs (photo essays or monographs)." Query first, then submit outline/synopsis and sample chapters including illustrations.
Recent Nonfiction Titles: *Hearst Castle, San Simeon*, by Thomas R. Aidala and Curtis Bruce; *The Prints of Frank Stella*, by Richard H. Axsom; and *Picasso's Concrete Sculptures*, by Sally Fairweather.

HUMANICS LIMITED, 1182 W. Peachtree St. NE, Atlanta GA 30309. (404)874-2176. President: Gary B. Wilson. Publishes softcover, educational and trade paperback originals. Averages 10 titles/year. Pays average 10% royalty on net sales; buys some mss outright. No computer printout or disk submissions. Reports in 8 weeks. Free book catalog.
Nonfiction: Juvenile, self-help, textbook and teacher resource books. Subjects include cooking and foods, health, psychology, sociology, education and parenting. Submit outline/synopsis and at least 3 sample chapters. Accepts artwork and photos.
Recent Nonfiction Titles: *Love Notes*, by Angie Rose (parenting); *Real Talk*, by George M. Gazda and William C. Childers, PhD (friendship and helping skills); *Energy*, by Carolyn S. Diener; *Kids Who Hate School*, by Lawrence J. Greene (parenting); *The Best Chance Diet*, by Joe D. Goldstrich, M.D., F.A.C.C. (health & nutrition); *Exploring Feelings*, by Susan B. Newman, Ph.D. and Renée Panoff (children's activity book).

CARL HUNGNESS PUBLISHING, Box 24308, Speedway IN 46224. (317)244-4792. Editorial Director: Carl Hungness. Publishes hardcover and paperback originals. Pays "negotiable" outright purchase. Reports in 3 weeks. SASE. Free book catalog.

Nonfiction: Stories relating to professional automobile racing. No sports car racing or drag racing material. Query. Recently published *Indianapolis 500 Yearbook*, by C. Hungness and others (historical); and *The Mighty Midgets*, by J.C. Fox (historical).

*HUNTER HOUSE, INC., Subsidiary of Servire, B.V. the Netherlands, Box 1302, Claremont CA 91711. (714)624-2277. General Manager: Kiran S. Rana. Publishes hardcover and trade paperback originals. Averages 4 titles/year. Subsidy publishes 10-25% of books based on "commercial non-viability yet sound content and editorial familiarity." Pays 7½% average royalty on retail price; offers average $250 advance. Simultaneous submissions OK. Computer printout submissions OK. SASE. Reports in 2 weeks on queries; 3 months on mss.

Nonfiction: How-to. Subjects include family and health topics, psychology and sociology. "Psychology and psychotherapy written for professionals/academics." Accepts nonfiction and poetry translations from German, French and Spanish. Query or submit outline/synopsis and 3-5 sample chapters. Looks for familiarity with subject, objectivity, writing style and creative thought." Interested in developing original illustrated books for co-publication.

Recent Nonfiction Titles: *LSD Psychotherapy*, by Dr. Stan Grof (text and general); *Once a Month*, by Dr. Katharine Dalton; and *Questioning Techniques*, by Dr. Artur Kaiser.

Tips: Queries/mss may be routed to other editors in the publishing group.

HURTIG PUBLISHERS LTD., 10560 105th St., Edmonton, Alberta, Canada T5H 2W7. (403)426-2359. Editorial Manager: José Druker. Hardcover and paperback originals (80%) and reprints (20%). Averages 12 titles/year. Typically pays 10% royalty on first 7,000 copies; 12% on next 7,000; 15% thereafter. Advance averages $500-1,000. State availability of photos and/or illustrations to accompany ms. Photocopied submissions OK. Computer printouts OK; "will read anything legible—must be hard copy printout. Prefers letter of inquiry first. Reports in 2-3 months. SASE. Free book catalog.

Nonfiction: Publishes biographies of well-known Canadians; Canadian history; humor; nature; topical Canadian politics and economics; reference (Canadian); and material about native Canadians "aimed at the nationalistic Canadian interested in politics, the North and energy policy." No poetry or original fiction. Query or submit outline/synopsis and 1-2 sample chapters; or submit complete ms. Very few unsolicited manuscripts published. Looks for "suitability of topic to general publishing program; market interest in topic; qualifications of writer to treat that topic well; quality of writing."

Recent Nonfiction Titles: *The Art of Canadian Nature Photography*, by J.A. Kraulis (nature); *Canadian Newspapers/The Inside Story*, edited by Walter Stewart (socio-economic, current events); and *Pitseolak: A Canadian Tragedy*, by David F. Raine.

ICARUS PRESS, INC., Box 1225, South Bend IN 46624. (219)233-6020. Editorial Director: Bruce M. Fingerhut. Publishes hardcover and paperback originals. Averages 15 titles/year. Offers 10-15% royalty based on wholesale price. Average advance: $2,000. Simultaneous and photocopied submissions OK (if so indicated). No computer printout or disk submissions. SASE. Reports in 1 month. Free book catalog.

Nonfiction: Americana; biography; history; recreation; sports; and travel (regional). Accepts nonfiction translations. "Our interests in sports, whether of the self-help, coaching, or history genre, remain high. As to history, biography, current affairs, etc., such manuscripts as we publish must be real trade titles—with national appeal. We do *not* want to see poetry, photography, art, hobbies (other than those immediately connected with sports), or cookbooks." Accepts artwork/photos. Query first, then submit outline/synopsis and 2-4 sample chapters. Looks for "originality, flair of style, writing competence."

Recent Nonfiction Titles: *Beating the Bushes*, by Frank Dolson (sports); *The Dodgers*, by Jean Pitrone and Joan Elwart (biography), *Long Time Gone*, by Curt Smith (history/politics).

Fiction: Mainstream. "We shall probably not be publishing any fiction for the next year or two, although our intention is to publish fiction as soon as possible." Does *not* want to see confession, romance, science fiction, or western. Query first, then submit outline/synopsis and sample chapters.

‡*IDEAL WORLD PUBLISHING CO., Box 1237-EG, Melbourne FL 32936-1237. New Idea Publishing Co. is a division of Ideal World Publishing Co. Publisher: Harold Pallatz. Publishes hardcover and paperback originals and reprints. Averages 3 titles/year. Offers subsidy publication of "difficult-to-place" manuscripts. "If your book has marketing potential which major publishers have failed to recognize due to their own business strategy, we can help you get published. We offer you a special subsidy plan which includes typing, printing, binding and distribution. Fee starts at $50 for short runs, depending upon number of pages, copies, etc. 75% of titles subsidy published. Photocopied submissions OK. Computer printout submissions OK. "Query, first, please." Reports in 2-4 weeks. *"No material will be returned unless SASE is attached."*

Health: "Natural approaches to good health through nutrition, herbs, vegetarianism, vitamins, unusual medical approaches for specific ailments, particularly from authorities in the field. Any style is acceptable, but it must hold the reader's attention and make for fairly smooth nonintensive (no brain taxation) requirements. Ideas should be in a simple, easygoing pace.'' Also publishes energy-related books: alternative energy themes, particularly do-it-yourself hybrid vehicles. "The scope of our publishing is confined to health and energy nonfiction; we do not accept fiction or poetry.''

Recent Nonfiction Title: *Hybrid Manual*, by Harold Pallatz (electric cars).

IDEALS PUBLISHING CORP., 11315 Watertown Plank Rd., Milwaukee WI 53226. Vice President, Publishing:James A. Kuse. Imprints include *Good Friends* (juvenile) and *Successful* (how-to books for the homeowner). Publishes hardcover and paperback originals, and greeting booklets. Published 75 titles in 1979, 80 in 1980. Pays variable royalty; offers advance only on assigned projects. Photocopied submissions OK. SASE. Reports in 4-6 weeks.

Nonfiction: Cookbooks. Length: 300 recipes. *Successful* imprint includes books of approximately 60,000 words on do-it-yourself home projects. Often buys manuscripts with illustrating photographs.

Recent Nonfiction Titles: *Chinese Cookbook*; and *Kitchen Planning and Remodeling*.

Fiction: Juveniles under the *Good Friends* imprint. "Stories which are fun to read, entertaining yet instructive without being overly didactic.'' Often buys illustrated children's manuscripts. Query. Length varies.

‡ILLUMINATI, Suite 204, 8812 W. Pico Blvd., Los Angeles CA 90035. (213)271-1460. Editor: P. Schneidre. Publishes hardcover and trade paperback originals. Averages 10 titles/year. Pays 10-15% royalty on retail price. Offers average $150 advance. Photocopied submissions OK. SASE. Reports in 2 weeks on queries; 3 weeks on mss. Book catalog for 9x12 SAE and 37¢ postage.

Imprint: tadbooks (fiction).

Nonfiction: "Coffee table'' book; literature and art. Submit outline/synopsis and sample chapters.

Poetry: "We will be needing several 'tadbooks'—i.e., small book mss comprised, probably, of a single long poem, an illustrated poem or a sequence of poems.'' No light verse or haiku. Submit complete ms.

Recent Poetry Titles: *A Horse of a Different Color*, by Greg Kuzma; *Naked Charm*, by Lyn Lifshin; and *Americruiser*, by F.A. Nettelbeck.

INDIANA UNIVERSITY PRESS, 10th & Morton Sts., Bloomington IN 47405. (812)337-4203. Director: John Gallman. Publishes hardcover and paperback originals (75%) and paperback reprints (25%). Averages 75-80 titles/year. Pays maximum 10% royalty on retail price; offers occasional advance. Photocopied submissions OK. Reports in 2 months. SASE. Free book catalog.

Nonfiction: Scholarly books on humanities, history, philosophy, translations, semiotics, public policy, film, music, linguistics, social sciences, regional materials, African studies, women's studies, and serious nonfiction for the general reader. Query or submit outline/synopsis and sample chapters. "Queries should include as much descriptive material as is necessary to convey scope and market appeal to us.''

Recent Nonfiction Titles: *Eisenhower's Lieutenants: The Campaign of France and Germany, 1944-1945*, by Russell F. Weigley; *Handbook of American Folklore*, edited by Richard M. Dorson; *The Stardust Road*, by Hoagy Carmichael.

Fiction: Query or submit outline/synopsis.

INSTITUTE FOR BUSINESS PLANNING, Division of Prentice-Hall, Sylvan Ave., Englewood Cliffs NJ 07632. (201)592-3080. Managing Editor: Anthony Vlamis. Publishes hardcover originals and paperback reprints. Averages 15 titles/year. Pays 5% maximum royalty (direct mail) and 15% royalty (trade retail). Average advance: $1,500-2,000. No simultaneous submissions; photocopied submissions OK. SASE. Reports in 4-6 weeks. Free book catalog.

Nonfiction: Business/economics; how-to ("high level professional audience; not how to make money in mail order or other pedestrian books''); and reference. "We seek practical professional reference books in the following areas: accounting, business management, estate planning and administration, real estate, law, especially trial related subjects, taxation and finance. Areas open for future considerations are: banking, insurance, and financial planning.'' Does *not* want inspirational and selling mss. Query first or submit outline/synopsis and sample chapters. Looks for "a unique salable central idea or unusual presentation of familiar material that makes it easily understandable and applicable.''

Recent Nonfiction Titles: *Desk Book for Setting Up a Closely-Held Corporation*, by R. Hess (law); *Professional's Guide to the Estate Tax Audit*, by J. C. Berger and M. D. Brody (tax); *Taking Cash Out of the Closely Held Corporation*, by L. Silton (business management).

*INSTITUTE FOR THE STUDY OF HUMAN ISSUES, (ISHI Publications), Suite 252, 3401 Market St., Philadelphia PA 19104. (215)387-9002. Director of Publications: Betty Crapivinsky-Jutkowitz. Managing Editor: Brad Fisher. Publishes hardcover and paperback originals (85%) and hardcover reprints (15%). Averages 18 titles/year. Subsidy publishes 10% of books. Pays 10-12½% royalty on wholesale price; no advance. Photocopied submissions OK. Reports in 3 months. SASE. Free book catalog.

Nonfiction: Books on political science, history, anthropology, folklore, sociology, economics and macro-economics, suitable for students and scholars in these fields. Accepts nonfiction translations. Submit outline/synopsis and 2 or more sample chapters. Recently published *Hitler Over Germany*, by Otis Mitchell (political history); *The US and the Philippines*, by Stephen Rosskamm Shalom (political science/foreign affairs); and *The German Legends of the Brothers Grimm*, translated by Donald Ward (folklore).

INTERCULTURAL PRESS, INC., 70 W. Hubbard St., Chicago IL 60610. (312)321-0075. Contact: David S. Hoopes, Editor-in-Chief, 130 North Rd., Vershire VT 05079. (802)685-4448. Publishes hardcover and trade paperback originals. Averages 5-15 titles/year. Pays royalty; occasionally offers small advance. Simultaneous and photocopied submissions OK. Computer printout submissions OK; prefers letter quality to dot matrix. SASE. Reports in "several weeks" on queries; 2 months on mss. Free book catalog.
Nonfiction: How-to, reference, self-help, textbook and theory. Subjects include business and economics, philosophy, politics, psychology, sociology, travel, or "any book with an international or domestic intercultural, multicultural or cross-cultural focus, i.e., a focus on the cultural factors in personal, social, political or economic relations. We want books with an international or domestic intercultural or multicultural focus, especially those on business operations (how to be effective in intercultural business activities) and education (textbooks for teaching intercultural subjects, for instance). Our books are published for educators in the intercultural field, business people who are engaged in international business, and anyone else who works in an international occupation or has had intercultural experience. No mss that don't have an intercultural focus." Accepts nonfiction translations. Query "if there is any question of suitability (we can tell quickly from a good query)," or submit outline/synopsis. Do not submit mss unless invited.
Recent Nonfiction Titles: *Survival Kit for Overseas Living*, by Robert Kohls (how-to); *Multicultural Education: The Cross-Cultural Training Approach*, edited by Peggy Pusch (text); and *American Cultural Patterns: A Cross-Cultural Perspective*, by Edward Stewart (theory/text).

INTERGALACTIC PUBLISHING CO., Box 188, Clementon NJ 08021. (609)783-0910. Contact: Samuel W. Valenza, Jr. Publishes trade paperback originals. Averages 3 titles/year. "We have a unique setup for teachers: 50% royalty paid on 1st edition after costs; 60-40 split on subsequent editions after costs." Pays royalty on both wholesale and retail price; offers average $100 advance. Simultaneous and photocopied submissions OK. SASE. Reports in 1 month on queries; 2 months on mss. Free book catalog.
Nonfiction: Technical and textbook. Subjects include "educational methods and motivational materials in the areas of math and science. Materials, texts and how-to vehicles that accent mathematics and sciences at the K-12 level in an 'applied' sense, particularly mss developed in classrooms by teachers of mathematics. We also produce games, and AV materials related to these areas. Our readers include academia on a secondary and junior college level; also high school and junior libraries, and media centers." Submit complete ms. Accepts artwork/photos.
Recent Nonfiction Titles: *The Mathematics of the Energy Crisis*, by R. Gagliardi; *The Mathematics Laboratory in the Elementary School, How? What? and Who?*, by F. Swetz; and *Geometrical Theorems in Slides*, by V. Madan (21 slides plus 16-page booklet).
Fiction: "Math and science if related to teachable concepts. A title is applicable only if it is uniquely suited to our list; e.g., 'Professor Googol's Math Primer.' " Submit complete ms.
Tips: "Our market is limited, but books accenting the *application of learned material* on the secondary level are doing best, since our market as a whole is concerned with *motivation* in education."

INTERNATIONAL MARINE PUBLISHING CO., 21 Elm St., Camden ME 04843. President: Roger C. Taylor. Managing Editor: Kathleen M. Brandes. Publishes hardcover and paperback originals. Averages 15 titles/year. "Standard royalties, based on retail price, with advances." Free mail-order catalog. "Material in all stages welcome. We prefer queries first with 2-3 sample chapters. We like unsolicited manuscripts as long as the authors are patient. Computer printout submission is fine. We are not yet geared up to receive submissions on disk"; prefers letter quality to dot matrix. Reports in 6 weeks. Return postage necessary.
Marine Nonfiction: "Marine nonfiction only—but a wide range of subjects within that category: boatbuilding, boat design, yachting, seamanship, boat maintenance, maritime history, etc." All books are illustrated black and white only. Accepts artwork/photos. Accepts nonfiction translations from French, German and Italian. Recently published *Practical Yacht Joinery*, by Fred P. Bingham; *The Racing-Cruiser*, second edition, by Richard Henderson; *Cruising Rigs and Rigging*, by Ross Norgrove.

Market conditions are constantly changing! If this is 1985 or later, buy the newest edition of *Writer's Market* at your favorite bookstore or order directly from Writer's Digest Books.

‡**INTERNATIONAL PUBLISHERS CO., INC.**, #1301, 381 Park Ave. S., New York NY 10016. (212)685-2864. President: Betty Smith. Publishes hardcover and trade paperback originals and trade paperback reprints. Averages 10-20 titles/year. Pays 5% royalty on paperback retail price; maximum 10% royalty on cloth retail price. No advance. Simultaneous and photocopied submissions OK. SASE. Reports in 1 month on queries; 6 months on mss. Free book catalog.

Nonfiction: Biography, reference and textbook. Subjects include Americana, art, business and economics, history, music, philosophy, politics, psychology, sociology and Marxist-Leninist classics. "Books on labor, black studies and women's studies have high priority." Query or submit outline/synopsis and sample chapters.

Recent Nonfiction Titles: *My Shaping-Up Years*, by Art Shields (autobiography); *History of US Labor Movement*, Volume 6, by Philip Foner (history); and *Encounters in Democracy*, by Margrit Pittman (politics).

Fiction: "We publish very little fiction. We are considering an anthology of original short stories and a novel on working class life; perhaps a series of young adult titles." Query or submit outline/synopsis and sample chapters.

Recent Fiction Title: *Salute to Spring*, by Meridel LeSueur (short stories).

Poetry: "We rarely publish individual poets, usually anthologies."

Recent Poetry Titles: *Leaving the Bough*, ed. by Roger Gaess (anthology of newer poets); and *Voices from Wah'kon-tah*, ed. by Dodge and McCullough (anthology of US Indian poetry).

INTERNATIONAL SELF-COUNSEL PRESS, LTD., 306 W. 25th St., North Vancouver, British Columbia, Canada V7N 2G1. (604)986-3366. President: Diana R. Douglas. Editor-in-Chief: Lois Richardson. Publishes trade paperback originals. Publishes 50 titles/year. Pays 10% royalty on wholesale price; no advance. Simultaneous and photocopied submissions OK. Computer printout submissions OK; prefers letter quality to dot matrix. Reports in 4-6 weeks. SASE. Free book catalog.

Nonfiction: "Books only on law and business for the layperson (how-to)." Submit outline/synopsis and sample chapters. Follow Chicago *Manual of Style*. Recently published *Financial Control for the Small Business*, by Michael Coltman; *Media Law Handbook*, by Stuart Robertson; *Assertiveness for Managers*, by Diana Cawood.

‡*THE INTERNATIONAL UNIVERSITY PRESS**, Subsidiary of The International University Foundation, 1301 S. Noland Rd., Independence MO 64055. (816)461-3633. Editor: Dr. John Wayne Johnston. Publishes hardcover originals and trade and mass market paperback originals. Averages 100 titles/year. Subsidy publishes 50% of books. "Such decisions are made by a committee based on internal criteria." Pays "percentage, based on size of first run." Simultaneous and photocopied submissions OK. Computer printout submissions OK; prefers letter quality to dot matrix. SASE. Reports in 1 month on queries; 4 months on mss.

Nonfiction: Biography, reference, technical, textbook on art, business and economics, health, history, music, philosophy, politics, psychology, religion, sociology, sports. Especially needs "any manuscript that exhibits coherence, originality, adequate command of the language, and few, if any, mechanical errors. Must have serious intent and some market appeal." Publishes for a "small, select group of readers of quality work." No poorly written work on any topic. Submit complete ms. Accepts poetry translations from Spanish.

Recent Nonfiction Titles: *Playwriting Principles*, by Philip P. Shaps; *Supervision of Student Teachers*, by Vanda S. Steele; and *Application of Psychoanalytic Psychology*, by Maurice Apprey.

Fiction: Fantasy, gothic, historical, horror, humor, mainstream, mystery, romance, science fiction, suspense, western. "This is a new area for our press and we hope to review a large number of fiction mss with an eye to publishing a growing volume of such works. No erotica or any work of questionable general interest to a sober, serious reading audience." Submit complete ms.

Poetry: "We will consider poetry mss of 50 pages or more either in form of long, epic poems or a collection of shorter works." Submit complete ms. Accepts poetry translations from Spanish.

INTERNATIONAL WEALTH SUCCESS, Box 186, Merrick NY 11566. (516)766-5850. Editor: Tyler G. Hicks. Averages 10 titles/year. Pays 10% royalty on wholesale or retail price. Usual advance is $1,000, but this varies, depending on author's reputation and nature of book. Will consider photocopied submissions. Query. Reports in 4 weeks. Enclose return postage.

Self-Help and How-to: "Techniques, methods, sources for building wealth. Highly personal, how-to-do-it with plenty of case histories. Books are aimed at the wealth builder and are highly sympathetic to his and her problems." Financing, business success, venture capital, etc. Length 60,000-70,000 words.

Recent Nonfiction Title: *How to Grow Rich in Real Estate*, by Nielsen.

Tips: "Concentrate on practical, hands-on books showing people how to build wealth today, starting with very little cash. Most of the manuscripts we get today assume that everyone has money to invest in gold, rare coins, stocks, etc. This is not so! There are millions who haven't made it yet. This is *our* audience, an audience that can build great wealth for a writer who tells these people what to do, where to do it and how to do it. Forget theories; concentrate on the day-to-day business of making money from one's own business and you've got it made!"

THE INTERSTATE PRINTERS & PUBLISHERS, INC., 19-27 N. Jackson St., Box 594, Danville IL 61832-0594. (217)446-0500-0594. Acquisitions: Russell L. Guin. Managing Editor: Ronald L. McDaniel. Hardcover and paperback originals. Usual royalty is 10% of wholesale price; no advance. Publishes about 50 titles/year. Markets books by mail and exhibits. Computer printout submissions OK; prefers letter quality to dot matrix. Reports in 1-2 months. SASE. Free book catalog.

Nonfiction: Publishes high school and college textbooks; agriculture; special education; trade and industrial; home economics; athletics; career education; outdoor education; school law; marriage counseling; and learning disabilities books. "We favor, but do not limit ourselves to, works which are designed for class—quantity rather than single-copy sale." Accepts artwork/photos. Query or submit outline/synopsis and 2-3 sample chapters.

Recent Nonfiction Titles: *Rabbit Production*, 5th ed., by Peter R. Cheeke, et al.; and *Assessment of Fluency in School-Age Children*, by Julia Thompson.

INTERVARSITY PRESS, Box F, Downers Grove IL 60515. (312)964-5700. Editorial Director: James W. Sire. Publishes hardcover and paperback originals. Averages 40 titles/year. Pays 10% royalty on retail price; advance averages $500. "Indicate simultaneous submissions." Photocopied submissions OK. Computer printout submissions OK "if they're clear"; prefers letter quality to dot matrix. Reports in 16 weeks. SASE. Free book catalog.

Nonfiction: "InterVarsity Press publishes books geared to the presentation of Biblical Christianity in its various relations to personal life, art, literature, sociology, psychology, philosophy, history and so forth. Though we are primarily publishers of trade books, we are cognizant of the textbook market at the college, university and seminary level within the general religious field. The audience for which the books are published is composed primarily of university students and graduates; stylistic treatment varies from topic to topic and from fairly simple popularizations for college freshmen to extremely scholarly works primarily designed to be read by scholars." Accepts nonfiction translations. Query or submit outline/synopsis and 2 sample chapters. Recently published *Out of the Saltshaker: Evangelism as a Way of Life*, by Rebecca Manley Pippert; *Liberating the Church*, by Howard Synder (practical theology); and *Between Heaven and Hell*, by Peter Kreeft.

*IOWA STATE UNIVERSITY PRESS, 2121 S. State Ave., Ames IA 50010. (515)294-5280. Director: Merritt Bailey. Managing Editor: Judith Gildner. Hardcover and paperback originals. Pays 10-12½-15% royalty on wholesale price; no advance. Subsidy publishes 10-50% of titles, based on sales potential of book and contribution to scholarship. Averages 35 titles/year. Send contrasting b&w glossy prints to illustrate ms. Simultaneous submissions OK, if advised; photocopied,submissions OK if accompanied by an explanation. Reports in 2-4 months. SASE. Free book catalog.

Nonfiction: Publishes biography, history, scientific/technical textbooks, the arts and sciences, statistics and mathematics, and medical and veterinary sciences. Accepts nonfiction translations. Submit outline/synopsis and several sample chapters, preferably not in sequence; must be double-speaced throughout. Looks for "unique approach to subject; clear, concise narrative; and effective integration of scholarly apparatus."

Recent Nonfiction Titles: *American Farmer and the New Deal*, by Theodore Saloutos; *Multivariate Statistical Methods*, by Marvin J. Karson; and *Private Pilot*, by Sarah Rambo.

ISI PRESS, Subsidiary of Institute for Scientific Information, 3501 Market St., Philadelphia PA 19104. (215)386-0100. Director: Robert A. Day. Publishes hardcover originals. Averages 6 titles/year. Pays 10% royalty on retail price; offers average $500 advance. No computer printout or disk submissions. SASE. Reports in 1 week on queries; 6 weeks on mss.

Nonfiction: How-to and technical on communications. "We are developing a strong professional writing series. In general, we publish scholarly and professional books concerned with communications: writing, editing, publishing, etc." Query or submit outline/synopsis and 1 sample chapter.

Recent Nonfiction Titles: *How to Write and Publish a Scientific Paper*, by R.A. Day (professional); *Essays of an Information Scientist*, by E. Garfield (professional); and *Faces of Science*, by V.V. Nalimov (scholarly).

ISLAND PRESS, Star Route 1, Box 38, Covelo CA 95428. Executive Director: Barbara Dean. Publishes paperback originals. Publishes 4 titles/year. Pays 10-15% royalty on retail price; offers $500 average advance. Simultaneous and photocopied submissions OK. Computer printout submissions OK. SASE. Reports in 3 months. Free book catalog for 8½x11 SASE.

Nonfiction: "We specialize in books on the environment and on human experience. We would welcome well-researched, technically accurate material on particular aspects of nature, conservation, animal life; also on true, personal experience in nature or personal growth. Emphasis on protection of wilderness, living with nature and human experience as means of spiritual growth. No poetry, science fiction, historical romance, children's books or textbooks. Also we are not interested in new age fads or trendy material." Query or submit outline/synopsis and 2 sample chapters.

Recent Nonfiction Titles: *Tree Talk: The People and Politics of Timber*, by Ray Raphael (voices from industry and environmentalists); *The Trail North: A Solo Journey on the Pacific Crest*, by Hawk Greenway (a young man's journey by horseback); and *Building an Ark*, by Phillip M. Hoose (strategies for natural diversity through land protection).

Fiction: "We are interested only in the unusual fiction that would merge with our primarily nonfiction list; fiction dealing with environmental consciousness or with human experience leading to personal/spiritual growth." No gothic, science fiction, romance, confession, etc. Query or submit outline/synopsis and 2 sample chapters.

Recent Fiction Titles: *The Search For Goodbye-To-Rains*, by P. McHugh (young man's odyssey across America to find himself); and *No Substitute for Madness*, by Ron Jones (six stories from a teacher and his unusual kids).

JALMAR PRESS, INC., B.L. Winch & Associates, 45 Hitching Post Dr., Bldg. 2, Rolling Hills Estates CA 90274. (213)547-1240. Editor: Suzanne Mikesell. Publishes trade paperback originals. Averages 6 titles/year. Pays 5-15% on net sales. Simultaneous and photocopied submissions OK. Computer printout and disk submissions OK. SASE. Reports in 1 month on queries; 3 months on mss. Free book catalog on request.

Nonfiction: How-to, illustrated book, self-help and educational. Subjects include health and psychology. Easy-to-read, helpful, purposeful books for schools, families, adults and children, that assist positive mental health, self-esteem development. No technical, academic-oriented manuscripts. Must be practical—reach a wide audience. Accepts artwork/photos. Query or submit outline synopsis and 2 sample chapters or complete ms.

Recent Nonfiction Titles: *Unicorns Are Real: A Right-Brained Approach to Learning*, by Barbara Vitale; *"He Hit Me Back First!" Creative Visualization Activities for Parenting and Teaching*, by Eva Fugitt; and *Charles The Clown's Guide to Children's Parties*, by Charles and Linda Kraus.

JAMESTOWN PUBLISHERS, INC., Box 6743, Providence RI 02940. (401)351-1915. Senior Editor: Ted Knight. Publishes paperback supplementary reading text/workbooks. Averages 25-30 titles/year. Pays 10% royalty on retail price; buys some mss outright; offers variable advance. SASE. Reports in 1 month. Free book catalog.

Nonfiction: Textbook. "Materials for improving reading and study skills for K-12, college, or adult education." Submit outline/synopsis and sample chapters.

Recent Nonfiction Titles: *Learning to Study*, by Charles T. Mangrum II, Ed. D. (elementary study skills series); *Skill Drills*, ed. by Edward Spargo (comprehension work sheets, grades 4-6); *Six-Way Paragraphs, Middle and Advanced Levels*, by Walter Pauk, Ph.D.

Fiction: "We occasionally use original fiction as the basis for comprehension exercises and drills." Submit outline/synopsis and sample chapters.

JANUS BOOK PUBLISHERS, 2501 Industrial Pkwy., W., Hayward CA 94545. (415)785-9625. Vice President: Charles Kahn. Averages 10-12 titles/year. Pays 4-10% royalty on retail price or buys some mss by outright purchase; average advance. Query or submit outline/synopsis and 2-3 sample chapters. Computer printout submissions OK. SASE. Reports in 3 weeks. Free book catalog.

Nonfiction: "We publish work texts written at a 2.5 reading level for young adults with limited reading ability."

Recent Titles: *It's Our Government*, by William Lefkowitz and Richard Uhlich; *Keeping Fit*, by Anita Schwartz and Deborah Guth; *The Five Senses*, by Nancy Lobb.

JH PRESS, Box 294, Village Station, New York NY 10014. (212)255-4713. Publisher: Terry Helbing. Publishes trade paperback originals. Averages 3 titles/year. Pays 6-10% royalty on retail price; offers average $100 advance. Simultaneous and photocopied submissions OK. SASE. Reports in 2 weeks. Free book catalog.

Nonfiction: Subjects include drama and theater. "Studies of gay theater or gay plays." Query.

Recent Nonfiction Title: *Gay Theatre Alliance Directory of Gay Plays*, by Terry Helbing.

Fiction: Drama and theater. "Gay plays that have been produced but not previously published." Query.

Recent Fiction Titles: *Forever After*, by Doric Wilson (play); *News Boy*, by Arch Brown (play); *Last Summer At Bluefish Cove*, by Jane Chambers (play); *Pines '79*, by Terry Miller (play); *Street Theater*, by Doric Wilson (play); *The Dinosaur Plays*, by C.D. Arnold (play).

JOHNS HOPKINS UNIVERSITY PRESS, Baltimore MD 21218. Editorial Director: Anders Richter. Publishes mostly clothbound originals and paperback reprints; some paperback originals. Publishes 100 titles/year. Payment varies; contract negotiated with author. Reports in 2 months. SASE.

Nonfiction: Publishes scholarly books and journals, biomedical sciences, history, literary theory and criticism, wildlife biology and management, psychology, political science, regional material, and economics. Accepts nonfiction translations. Query. Accepts outline/synopsis and 2-3 sample chapters. Length: 50,000 words minimum.

Recent Nonfiction Title: *Women Scientists In America*, by Margaret G. Rossiter.

Fiction: Occasional fiction by invitation only.

JOHNSON BOOKS, 1880 S. 57th Ct., Boulder CO 80301. (303)443-1576. Editorial Director: Michael McNierney. Publishes hardcover and paperback originals and reprints. Publishes 8-10 titles/year. Royalties vary. Computer printout submissions OK "if clear and easy to read with proper line-spacing, wide margins, etc." Prefers letter quality to dot matrix. SASE. Reports in 1-2 months. Free book catalog.

Nonfiction: General nonfiction, cookbooks, how-to, western regional history, environmental subjects, science, geology, nature, outdoor recreation and sports. Accepts nonfiction translations. "We are primarily interested in books for the informed popular market, though we will consider vividly written scholarly works. As a small publisher, we are able to give every submission close personal attention." Query first or call. Accepts outline/synopsis and 3 sample chapters. Looks for "good writing, thorough research, professional presentation and appropriate style. Marketing suggestions from writers are helpful."

Recent Nonfiction Titles: *Skiing Right*, by Horst Abraham; *Colorado Front Range: A Landscape Divided*, by Gleaves Whitney; *Colorado Scenic Guide*, by Lee Gregory.

JONATHAN DAVID PUBLISHERS, 68-22 Eliot Ave., Middle Village NY 11379. (212)456-8611. Editor-in-Chief: Alfred J. Kolatch. Publishes hardcover and paperback originals. Averages 25-30 titles/year. Pays standard royalty. Reports in 3 weeks. SASE.

Nonfiction: Adult nonfiction books for a general audience. Americana, cookbooks, cooking and foods, how-to, recreation, reference, self-help and sports. "We specialize in Judaica." Query.

Recent Nonfiction Titles: *Cooking Kosher: The Natural Way*, by Jane Kinderlehrer; *The Jewish Book of Why*, by A. J. Kolatch; *Golda*, by Robert Slater; *Great Jews in Sports*, by Robert Slater; *The Baseball Catalogue*, by Dan Schlossberg; and *Football Made Easy*, by Sam DeLuca.

JOSSEY-BASS, INC., PUBLISHERS, 433 California St., San Francisco CA 94104. (415)433-1740. Editorial Director: Allen Jossey-Bass. Publishes hardcover and paperback originals. Averages 100 titles/year. Pays 10-15% royalty on net receipts; no advance. Simultaneous (if so informed) and photocopied submissions OK. Computer printout submissions OK; prefers letter quality to dot matrix. Reports in 4 weeks. SASE. Free book catalog.

Nonfiction: Professional, scholarly books for senior administrators, faculty, researchers, graduate students, and professionals in private practice. Research-based books developed for practical application. "We do not want undergraduate texts or collections of previously published materials." Submit outline/synopsis and 3-4 sample chapters.

Recent Nonfiction Titles: *The Tactics of Change*, by Richard Fisch, John Weakland and Lynn Segal; and *The State of the Nation and the Agenda for Higher Education*, by Howard R. Bowen.

JUDSON PRESS, Valley Forge PA 19481. (215)768-2116. General Manager: Harold L. Twiss. Publishes hardcover and paperback originals. Generally 10% royalty on retail price. "Payment of an advance depends on author's reputation and nature of book." Publishes 40 titles/year. Free book catalog. Query with outline and 2-3 sample chapters. Computer printout submissions OK; letter quality only. Reports in 3 months. Enclose return postage.

Religion: Adult religious nonfiction of 30,000-80,000 words. "Our audience is mostly church members who seek to have a more fulfilling personal spiritual life and want to do a better job as Christians in their church and other relationships."

Recent Nonfiction Titles: *Prayer—the Vital Link*, by William J. Krutza; *Reaching Out to the Unchurched*, by Douglas W. Johnson; *Open to Glory*, by Carol Doran and Thomas H. Troeger.

KALMBACH PUBLISHING CO., 1027 N. 7th St., Milwaukee WI 53233. (414)272-2060. Editorial Director: David P. Morgan. Books Editor: Bob Hayden. Publishes hardcover and paperback originals (80%) and paperback reprints (20%). Averages 10 titles/year. Offers 5-8% royalty on retail price. Average advance: $1,000. No simultaneous or photocopied submissions. Computer printout and disk submissions OK. SASE. Reports in 8 weeks. Free book catalog.

Nonfiction: Hobbies; how-to; and recreation. "Our book publishing effort is in railroading and hobby how-to-do-it titles *only*." Query first. "I welcome telephone inquiries. They save me a lot of time, and they can save an author a lot of misconceptions and wasted work." In written query, want to see "a detailed outline of two or three pages and a complete sample chapter with photos, drawings, and how-to text."

Recent Nonfiction Titles: *Scale Reference Data: World War Two Jet Fighters*, by Don Berliner (data for aircraft modelers); *How to Build Miniature Furniture & Room Settings*, by Judy Beals (miniatures); and *34 New Electronic Projects for Model Railroaders*, by Peter J. Thorne (model railroading).

Tips: "Our books are about half text and and half illustrations. Any author who wants to publish with us must be able to furnish good photographs and rough drawings before we'll consider contracting for his book."

WILLIAM KAUFMANN, INC., 95 1st St., Los Altos CA 94022. Editor-in-Chief: William Kaufmann. Hardcover and paperback originals (90%) and reprints (10%). "Generally offers standard minimum book contract of 10-12½-15% but special requirements of book may call for lower royalties"; no advance. Averages 15

titles/year. State availability of photos and/or illustrations to accompany ms. Simultaneous and photocopied submissions OK. Computer printout submissions OK. Reports in 1-2 months. SASE. Free book catalog.
Nonfiction: "We specialize in not being specialized; we look primarily for originality and quality." Publishes Americana; art; biography; business; computer science; economics; history; how-to; humor; medicine and psychiatry; nature; psychology; recreation; scientific; sports; and textbooks. Does not want to see cookbooks, novels, poetry, inspirational/religious or erotica. Query.
Recent Nonfiction Titles: *Copyediting—A Practical Guide*, by Karen Judd.

‡**KAV BOOKS, INC.**, Box 1134, New York NY 10159. (212)505-6076. President: Dr. T.M. Kemnitz. Publishes hardcover and trade paperback originals. Averages 53 titles/year. Pays 5-10% royalty on wholesale price. Photocopied submissions OK. SASE. Reports in 3 weeks. Free book catalog.
Nonfiction: Cookbook, how-to, juvenile, self-help on Americana particularly crafts/how-to; cooking and foods—canning, preservation, growing; games, puzzles, brain teasers. Especially needs a major series on energy—solar, wind, etc.; food—canning; house—building, design. "Our present audience is almost entirely school teachers: our marketing, via direct mail. In 1983 we will be expanding into the how-to areas and be looking for an audience of homeowners, handymen, people interested in crafts, etc." Query or submit outline/synopsis and sample chapters or complete ms.
Recent Nonfiction Titles: *Stories to Stretch Minds*, by Levy (brain teasers); *Geography for the Quick*, by Stanley (brain teasers); and *Creative Encounters*, by Mize (classroom).
Fiction: Mainstream, mystery. "We will do a small number of novels aimed specifically at a teacher audience." Submit outline/synopsis and sample chapters or complete ms.

KEATS PUBLISHING, INC., 27 Pine St., Box 876, New Canaan CT 06840. (203)966-8721. Editor: Ms. An Keats. Publishes hardcover and paperback originals and reprints, and one magazine on health and nutrition. Offers standard royalty contract. Advance varies. Free book catalog. Query with outline and sample chapter. Reports in 3 months. Enclose return postage.
Nonfiction: "Natural health, special interest. Also, mss with promotion and premium potential. In natural health, anything having to do with the current interest in ecology, natural health cookbooks, diet books, organic gardening, etc." Length: open.
Religion: "Largely in the conservative Protestant field."

KENT STATE UNIVERSITY PRESS, Kent State University, Kent OH 44242. (216)672-7913. Director: Paul H. Rohmann. Publishes hardcover and paperback originals and some reprints. Standard minimum book contract on net sales; rarely offers advance. Averages 10-12 titles/year. Free book catalog. "Always write a letter of inquiry before submitting mss. We can publish only a limited number of titles each year and can frequently tell in advance whether or not we would be interested in a particular ms. This practice saves both our time and that of the author, not to mention postage costs. If interested we will ask for complete ms. Decisions based on in-house readings and 2 by outside scholars in the field of the study." Computer printout submissions OK; prefers letter quality to dot matrix. Reports in 10 weeks. Enclose return postage.
Nonfiction: Especially interested in "scholarly works in history of high quality, particularly any titles of regional interest for Ohio. Also will consider scholarly biographies, literary studies, archeological research, the arts, and general nonfiction."
Recent Nonfiction Titles: *A Fearful Innocence*, by Frances Davis (memoir); *The Righteous Remnant: The House of David*, by Robert S. Fogarty (history); and *Medieval Woman's Guide to Health*, by Beryl Rowland (medieval studies).

KERN PUBLICATIONS, Subsidiary of Data Dynamics, Inc., 190 Duck Hill Rd., Box 1029, Duxbury MA 02332. (617)934-0445. Senior Editor: Pam Korites. Publishes trade paperback originals and microcomupter software. Averages 6 titles/year. Pays 15-25% royalty on wholesale price. Simultaneous and photocopied submissions OK. SASE. Reports in 2 weeks. Free book catalog.
Nonfiction: How-to, technical, textbook and computer software in book form. Subjects include business and economics, and computer software marketing and development. "We publish two lines of books: 1) How to Sell Computer Software, and 2) How to Write Computer Software. We also publish Packaged Software for Microcomputers. Our needs in the first category include anything that relates to the marketing of computer software. Examples are case studies of successful software entrepreneurs, legal tips for software marketers, descriptions of specific markets for computer software, etc. In the second category, we are interested in books that include computer program listings. Of special interest are how-to books in this area. We are also interested in nontechnical books and programs, such as business applications, as long as they relate to microcomputers. Of special interest are computer-aided design and manufacturing, robotics, computer graphics, and computer-aided instruction. Also, our publications must be of immediate interest to the computer and educational communities and must be highly professional in technical content. No mss of merely academic interest." Query or submit outline/synopsis and sample chapters.

Recent Nonfiction Titles: *How To Sell Your Micro Software*; *The 1983 Software Writer's Market*; *Graphic Software For Micros*; *IBMpc Graphics*; *Structural Analysis and Micros*; *Data Plotting Software for Micros*.

KIRKLEY PRESS, INC., 7677 Canton Center Dr., Baltimore MD 21224. Editor: Jay Weitzel. Publishes paperback 16-page booklets and paycheck stuffer folders. "We buy mss outright and pay upon acceptance. Payment (total) varies between $200 and $300, depending on subject and strength with which written. Sample of our material sent on request." No computer printout or disk submissions. Send complete ms. "We try to answer in 2 weeks." Enclose return postage.
Business: "We publish small booklets which are sold to businesses for distribution to employees and newsletters which are mailed monthly to business executives. They attempt to stimulate or motivate employees to improve work habits. Basically they are pep talks for employees. We need writers who are so close to the problems of present-day employee attitudes that they can take one of those problems and write about it in a warm, human, understanding, personal style and language that will appeal to the employee and which the employer will find to his advantage to distribute to the employees." Length: 2,400-2,600 words.
Recent Nonfiction Titles: *Action People*, by H.K. Dugdale; *Engery Saving Ideas*; and *If You Were the Boss*, by D. Shiel.
Tips: Newsletter articles accepted on business letter techniques; in-house and external newsletters; direct mail techniques; electronic and subliminal communications; effective public speaking and graphic techniques. Length: 100-250 words. Pays 10¢/word. Send complete ms. SASE.

B. KLEIN PUBLICATIONS, Box 8503, Coral Springs FL 33065. (305)752-1708. Editor-in-Chief: Bernard Klein. Hardcover and paperback originals. Specializes in directories, annuals, who's who type of books; bibliography, business opportunity, reference books. Averages 15-20 titles/year. Pays 10% royalty on wholesale price, "but we're negotiable." Advance "depends on many factors." Markets books by direct mail and mail order. Simultaneous and photocopied submissions OK. Reports in 1-2 weeks. SASE. Catalog for SASE.
Nonfiction: Business, hobbies, how-to, reference, self-help, directories and bibliographies. Query or submit outline/synopsis and sample chapters or complete ms.
Recent Nonfiction Titles: *Reference Encyclopedia of the American Indian*; *Your Business, Your Son and You*, by J. McQuaig (nonfiction); *Guide to American Directories*; and *Mail Order Business Directory*.

ALFRED A. KNOPF, INC., 201 E. 50th St., New York NY 10022. (212)751-2600. Senior Editor: Ashbel Green. Children's Book Editor: Ms. Frances Foster. Publishes hardcover and paperback originals (90%) and paperback reprints (10%). Published 163 titles in 1981. Royalties and advance "vary." Simultaneous (if so informed) and photocopied submissions OK. Reports in 2-4 weeks. Book catalog for SASE.
Nonfiction: Book-length nonfiction, including books of scholarly merit. Preferred length: 40,000-150,000 words. "A good nonfiction writer should be able to follow the latest scholarship in any field of human knowledge, and fill in the abstractions of scholarship for the benefit of the general reader by means of good, concrete, sensory reporting." Query.
Recent Nonfiction Titles: *Californians*, by J. Houston (contemporary affairs); *The Sporty Game*, by J. Newhouse (business); and *Mussolini*, by P. Smith (biography).
Fiction: Publishes book-length fiction of literary merit by known or unknown writers. Length: 30,000-150,000 words. Submit complete ms.
Recent Fiction Titles: *The Patriot Game*, by G.V. Higgins and *Cry to Heaven*, by Anne Rice.

KNOWLEDGE INDUSTRY PUBLICATIONS, INC., 701 Westchester Ave., White Plains, NY 10604. (914)328-9157. Editor-in-Chief: Efrem Sigel. Publishes hardcover and paperback originals. Averages 40 titles/year. Offers 5%-10% royalty on wholesale price; also buys mss by outright purchase for minimum $500. Offers negotiable advance. No simultaneous submissions; photocopied submissions OK. SASE. Reports in 2 weeks. Free book catalog.
Nonfiction: Business/economics. Especially needs "communication and information technologies, TV and video, library and information science, office automation and office productivity." Query first, then submit outline/synopsis and sample chapters.
Recent Nonfiction Titles: *Who Owns the Media*, by Conpaine; *Video Discs*, by Sigel; *Library Information Manager's Guide to Online Services*, by Hoover; and *The Teleconferencing Handbook*, by Ellen Lazer, et. al.

JOHN KNOX PRESS, 341 Ponce de Leon Ave. NE, Atlanta GA 30308. (404)873-1549. Editor: Walter C. Sutton. Publishes hardcover and paperback originals and paperback reprints. Publishes 24 titles/year. Pays royalty on income received; no advance. Photocopied submissions OK. Computer printout submissions OK; prefers letter quality to dot matrix. SASE. Free book catalog.
Nonfiction: "We publish books dealing with Biblical studies, Christian faith and life, family relationships, Christian education, and the relationship of faith to history and culture." Accepts nonfiction translations; query first. Query or submit outline/synopsis and 1-2 sample chapters.

KARL KRAMER VERLAG GMBH & CO., Rotebuhlstrasse 40, D-7000, Stuttgart, Germany. 49-711-62-08-93. President/Editorial Director: Karl H. Kramer. Publishes hardcover and paperback originals. Averages 15 titles/year. Pays 10% minimum royalty; offers $500-$1,000 average advance. SASE. Reports in 2 months. Free book catalog.

Nonfiction: Architecture. Submit outline/synopsis and sample chapters or complete ms.

Recent Nonfiction Titles: *Multi-use Architecture*, by E. Zeidler; *Structuralisme*by A. Luchinger; and *Architektur der Zukunft-Zukunft der Architektur*, by J. Joedicke et al.

‡**THE KRANTZ COMPANY PUBLISHERS**, 2210 N. Burling, Chicago IL 60614. (312)472-4900. Publisher: L. Krantz. Publishes hardcover and trade paperback originals. Averages 4-5 titles/year. Pays royalty or makes outright purchase. Simultaneous submissions OK. SASE. Reports in 4 weeks. Free book catalog.

Nonfiction: Coffee table book, how-to, reference, self-help and general nonfiction in the areas of art and photography—some science. Query. No unsolicited mss accepted.

Recent Titles: *New York Art Review*, ed. by Les Krantz (art reference); *Antiques—Best of the Best*, by Marjorie Glass and Igor Alexander (general nonfiction).

‡*****KUMARIAN PRESS**, 29 Bishop Rd., West Hartford CT 06119. (203)232-4360. Publisher: Krishna Sondhi. Editorial Director: Ian Mayo-Smith. Publishes hardcover and trade paperback originals (80%) and reprints. Averages 4-6 titles/year. Subsidy publishes 5% of books. Pays 0-12% royalty on wholesale or retail price "depending on market. We are moving to net sales price." Simultaneous and photocopied submissions OK. Computer printout and disk submissions OK. Reports in 3 weeks on queries; 3 months on mss. Free book catalog.

Nonfiction: How-to, reference, textbook on business and economics, philosophy, politics, psychology, religion, sociology. "We specialize in books dealing with the development needs of developing countries and the transfer of administrative and management technologies." Especially needs academic, scholarly, social science philosophy, business, reference books, workbooks, monographs, and how-to books in the area of development. Publishes for professionals and students in the area of development in universities, training institutes, consulting firms in the US and overseas and international and US aid agencies and institutions; also for libraries and the well-informed public. Query (preferred) or submit outline/synopsis and 3 sample chapters "and use University of Chicago *Manual of Style*."

Recent Nonfiction Titles: *Managing Development: The Political Dimension*, by Lindenberg and Crosby (textbook); *Managing Rural Development: Peasant Participation in Rural Development*, by Bryant and White (monograph); and *Planning a Performance Improvement Project: A Practical Guide*, by Mayo-Smith (workbook).

LAKE VIEW PRESS, Box 25421, Chicago IL 60625. (312)935-2694. Director: Paul Elitzik. Publishes hardcover and paperback originals (100%). Averages 6 titles/year. Pays 10-15% royalty on retail price. No advance. Simultaneous and photocopied submissions OK. Computer printout submissions OK; prefers letter quality to dot matrix. SASE. Reports in 2 months. Free catalog.

Nonfiction: Films, Middle East, Afro-American, labor, women, Asia. Accepts artwork/photos; accepts nonfiction translations. "Our audience interest is current affairs, politics and the contemporary cultural scene." Submit outline, 2 sample chapters and author biography.

Recent Nonfiction Titles: *The Mossadegh Era: Roost of the Iranian Revolution*, by Sepehr Zabih; *Through Another Lens: The Cineaste Interviews*, edited by Dan Georgakas and Leonard Rubenstein; and *Latin American Film and Politics*, edited by Dennis West.

LAKEWOOD BOOKS, 4 Park Ave., New York NY 10016. Editorial Director: Donald Wigal, PhD. Publishes 64-page paperback originals. Publishes 38 titles/year. Pays on a work-for-hire basis. "Few exceptions." Simultaneous and photocopied submissions OK. Computer printout (letter quality) submissions OK. Reports in 2 months. SASE.

Nonfiction: "Our books are apparently bought by women who have families, or are attracted to a rather middle-of-the-road life style. Our titles are mainly self-help (exercise, diet) and informational (finances, how-to). We avoid controversial topics. Nonfiction which ties in with specific products welcomed by query. (e.g., '100 Tips on Using Brand X in the Garden')." No fiction, poetry, astrology, puzzle, cookbook or sport titles needed at present (1983-4). Query. Author should have "an awareness of our format (limitations and potential), and sensitivity to the mass market. Concise overview best." Accepts artwork/photos.

Recent Nonfiction Titles: *Shape Up Hips and Thighs*; *Kellogg's Pinch-an-Inch Shape-Up Planner*.

Tips: "Consider the competition and see what seems to be working. Find a slightly new approach and blend the tried-and-true with the innovative. An entertaining, yet informative book with a single concept sells the best, e.g., *The Flat Tummy Book*." Queries/mss may be routed to other editors in the publishing group.

‡**LAME JOHNNY PRESS**, Rt. 3, Box 9A, Hermosa SD 57744. (605)255-4466. Publisher: Linda M. Hasselstrom. Publishes hardcover and trade paperback originals (98%), and hardcover reprints (2%). Averages 2-5 ti-

tles/year. Pays 30-50% royalty on wholesale price. Photocopied submissions OK. Computer printout submissions OK; prefers letter quality to dot matrix. SASE. Reports in 6 weeks. Book catalog for business size SAE and 2 first class stamps.
Nonfiction: How-to and self-help. Subjects include Americana and history. Accepts nonfiction translations. "We do not search for nonfiction titles; accept only occasional rare ones that originate in the Great Plains." Looks for "enough of a sample of the writing to determine quality of the work—sample chapters should accompany synopsis or outline. Simply—good writing without bombast, or obtuseness; clear characters in whom the reader can develop an interest." Accepts artwork/photos. Submit complete ms.
Recent Nonfiction Titles: *The Book Book: A Publishing Handbook (for Beginners & Others)*, by L.M. Hasselstrom (how-to); and *Next-Year Country: One Woman's View*, by Alma Phillip (informal history).
Fiction: Historical (on the Great Plains only). "We consider only works by/about Great Plains, loosely defined or works with a geographically western subject matter, but not shoot-em-ups, love-my-gun, love-my-horse books. Quality determines acceptance." Submit complete ms or extensive plot outline.
Recent Fiction Titles: *Buffalo Gap: A French Ranch in Dakota*, 1887 Baron E. de Grancey (historical); and *A Country for Old Men and Other Stories*, by Zietlow (Great Plains short stories).
Poetry: "Quality determines acceptance; must be by/about the Great Plains." Submit complete ms.
Recent Poetry Titles: *Mato Come Heal Me*, by Craig Volk (based on history; Indian youth, 1880's); *Delivery*, by Carolyn Bell (on woman's awakening); and *Where Is Dancer's Hill?*, by Robert Schuler (short poems, influenced by Indian history and myth).
Tips: "Our readers in the Great Plains seek cultural pride. Readers outside the plains seek information, entertainment, and high-quality writing. Our authors participate in the publishing of their books; sometimes by helping finance the book (but we're *not* a subsidy publisher); sometimes in other ways. The entire process remains personal, with the writer involved in every step if he/she wishes to be."

LANCASTER, MILLER & SCHNOBRICH PUBLISHERS, 3165 Adeline St., Berkeley CA 94703. (415)845-3782. Editor and Publisher: Thomas Miller. Publishes trade hardcover and paperback originals. Averages 6-7 titles/year. Pays 6-8% royalty on paperbacks; 10-12% on hardcover; offers $3,000-30,000 advance. Simultaneous and photocopied submissions OK. Computer printout submissions OK. SASE. Reports in 2 weeks. Free book catalog.
Imprint: *Asian Humanities Press* (scholarly books, art and thought).
Nonfiction: Computer books, picture books, art books for trade and special markets. "Full color, black and white when appropriate." Art, photography, graphic design, architecture, industrial design for worldwide market. (Also picture books for western region.) Accepts artwork/photos.
Recent Nonfiction Titles: *Jukebox: The Golden Age*, text by Lynch and Henkin, photos by Tsuruta; *Chinatown: San Francisco*, text by R. Reinhardt, photos by Peter Perkins; and *Goddesses*, by Mayumi Oda.

‡*****LANCELOT PRESS LTD.**, Box 425, Hantsport, Nova Scotia, Canada B0P 1P0. (902)684-9129. Editor: William Pope. Publishes trade paperback originals. Averages 18 titles/year. Subsidy publishes 20% of books, based on whether or not books will sell 1,000 copies. Pays 10-12% royalty on retail price. Photocopied submissions OK. SASE. Reports in 3 weeks on queries; 1 month on mss. Free book catalog.
Nonfiction: Biography, coffee table book, cookbook, humor, illustrated book, juvenile, regional on art, cooking and foods, health, history, hobbies, nature, politics, recreation, religion, sports, travel. "We consider any good book of its kind, but more success has been achieved with books of regional interest. We do well with books pertaining to the sea." No technical, specialized subjects. Query or submit outline/synopsis and sample chapters.
Recent Nonfiction Titles: *The Monctonians, Volume 2*, by J.E. Belliueau (regional history); *Laugh and Grow Fit*, by Lester Sellick (humour and health); and *Rubbing Shoulders*, by Ernest Rhuda (autobiography).

LANDMARK BOOKS, 2200 66th St. W., Minneapolis MN 55423. CEO: Patrick Fleming. Editor-in-Chief: Joyce Hovelsrud. Publishes hardcover and paperback originals. Pays standard royalty. Averages 6-10 titles/year. Photocopied and simultaneous submissions OK if so indicated. No computer printout or disk submissions. SASE. Reports in 6 weeks. Free book catalog and writer's guidelines.
Nonfiction: "We're a religious market looking for manuscripts on subjects of current issues and interest, which are appropriate for both religious and general markets. Material must be scripturally sound. We do not publish watered down religion and are interested in material with impact." Query or submit complete ms. Looks for "subjects that are timely and timeless." Want to see "the thrust of the subject in synopsis; the comment the author is making; where he is going with a subject and how he's going to develop it in his outline." In the completed ms wants "something of impact, order, relevance, *good* writing, and a recognizable style." Accepts translations.
Recent Nonfiction Titles: *So Help Me God*, by John McCollister (the faith of America's presidents); *The Madam Celeste*, by Celeste Horvath with Maria Castellano; and *I Talked About You Today—To God*, by Ruth Grant.

LANE AND ASSOCIATES, INC., Box 3063, La Jolla CA 92038. (619)275-3030. President: Gloria J. Lane. Publishes hardcover and paperback originals. Averages 5 titles/year. Pays 10-15% royalty on wholesale or retail price; offers average $200 advance. Buys some mss outright for $200-$500. Simultaneous and photocopied submissions OK. Computer printout and disk submissions OK. SASE. Reports in 6 weeks. Free book catalog for SASE.
Nonfiction: Business/economics, reference, science, self-help, technical and textbooks. Looking for women-oriented business-management books. Also, interested in unique self-help mss. No religion, fiction, politics or poetry. Submit outline/synopsis and 3 sample chapters.
Recent Nonfiction Titles: *Who's Who Among San Diego Women: The Power Source* (1982-83 Edition), edited by G. Lane (reference); *The Women's Basic Training Manual*, edited by G. Lane (anthology); *Take Back the Power (A Guide to Self-Actualization and Success)*, by G. Lane (self-help); *Positive Concepts for Success*, by G. Lane (self help); and *Who's Who Among San Diego Women: The Power Source* (1984-85 edition), ed. by G. Lane (reference).

‡**LARANMARK PRESS**, Box 253, Neshkoro WI 54960. (414)293-8216. President/Editor-in-Chief: Larry D. Names. Contact: Karen Cassiani or Susan Jacobson. Publishes hardcover and paperback originals. Averages 6-12 titles/year. Pays 8% royalty on the first 50,000 copies; 10% on the next 50,000; 12% thereafter; 15% on hardcover; sometimes offers $150-1,000 advance. Computer printout and disk submissions OK; prefers letter quality to dot matrix printouts.
Nonfiction: Adult books for hardcover line on sports, cooking, Americana, history, how-tos. Accepts artwork/photos; accepts nonfiction translations. Query with outline/synopsis and 3 sample chapters, or submit through agent.
Recent Nonfiction Title: *The Packer Legend: An Inside Look*, by John B. Torinus.
Fiction: Adventure, humor, historical, horror, mystery, science fiction, mainstream, western for paperback line. Accepts fiction translations. Query or submit through agent.
Recent Fiction Titles: *The PK Factor*, by C.H. Martin; and *Hunter's Orange*, by Richard Lundeen.

LARKSDALE, 133 S. Heights Blvd., Houston TX 77007. (713)869-9092. Publisher: James Goodman. Editor-in-Chief: Nancy Buquoi Adleman. Managing Editor: Brad Sagstetter. Publishes hardcover and paperback originals. Averages 20 titles/year. Pays standard royalty contract; no advance. Simultaneous (if so indicated) and photocopied submissions OK. Computer printout submissions OK. "SASE, means stamped container for return, not a check for postage." Reports in 3 months.
Imprints: *The Linolean Press* (religious). *The Lindahl Press* (general). *Harle House* (mass market paperback).
Nonfiction: Religion (Christian doctrine). General trade publisher. No off-color work accepted. Submit *complete* ms to publisher. Accepts artwork/photos. Looks for "an uplifting moral purpose, quality writing, salability in mss."
Recent Nonfiction Titles: *Search for Truth*, by Natasha Rawson; and *The Official Redneck Handbook*, by Jack S. Moore.
Recent Fiction Titles: *Officer in Trouble*, by Jim Viner; *The Last Grey Wolf*, by Tom Townsend; *Rose*, by Gleonda Kachelmeier; *Wake of a Lawyer*, by Aubrey Holmes; and *The Clone Machine*, by Allen Hahn.

LARKSPUR PUBLICATIONS, Box 211, Bowmansville NY 14026. (716)337-2578. Vice President: Judith E. Donaldson. Vice President: George H. Brown. Publishes mass market paperback originals. Averages 4-6 titles/year. Pays 5-10% royalty on wholesale price. Photocopied submissions OK. SASE. Reports in 1 month on queries; 2 months on mss.
Nonfiction: Illustrated book and juvenile. Subjects include animals, recreation, religion, sports, travel and game books. Query or submit outline/synopsis and sample chapters.
Recent Nonfiction Titles: *Travel Game* books (series of 3), by Judith E. Donaldson; *Doodles Diddles Puzzles Quizzies & Fun Stuff*, by George H. Brown; *Doodles Diddles Puzzles Quizzies & Fun Stuff*, Vol. 2, by Judith E. Donaldson.

LAW-ARTS PUBLISHERS, Suite 500, 2001 Wilshire Blvd., Santa Monica CA 90403. Editorial Director: Joseph Taubman. Publishes hardcover and paperback originals (90%) and paperback reprints (10%). Pays 10% royalty; no advance. Simultaneous and photocopied submissions OK. Reports in 1 month. SASE.
Nonfiction: Legal-related, in-depth textbooks; books on creative work, audiovisual techniques, management, publicity, etc. No photography books. Submit outline/synopsis and sample chapters. Recently published *Performing Arts Management and Law*, by J. Taubman; *Professional Sports and the Law*, by L. Sobel; and *Video for Lawyers*, by Ellen Miller.

‡**LE BEACON PRESSE**, Dept. WM 84, Suite 7, 2921 E. Madison St., Seattle WA 98112. (206)322-1431. Coordinator: Keith S. Gormezand. Publishes trade and mass market paperback originals and reprints. Aver-

ages 5-10 titles/year. Pays 20-25% royalty; buys some mss outright for $100-1,000. Simultaneous and photo-copied submissions OK. SASE.

Nonfiction: Humor, reference and technical. Subjects include Americana, art, business and economics, cooking and foods, photography, politics, recreation and travel. Accepts translations. "In the near future we will need 5 reference books, 3 with political themes and 1 autobiographical novel." All unsolicited mss are returned unopened. Query first.

Recent Nonfiction Titles: *Who's Who Among Hispanic-Americans*; *Who's Who in Iowa*; and *Name Identification*, by Keith S. Gormezand (political).

Fiction: Adventure, erotica, ethnic, experimental, historical, horror, humor, mystery, science fiction and suspense. Query. All unsolicited mss are returned unopened.

Poetry: "Will publish 3, 36-page poetry books." Submit maximum 3 poems with cover letter.

Recent Poetry Titles: *36 Flavors*, by Gormezand (ethnic); and *Mongrel Harmony*, by Davis.

‡**LEARNING ENDEAVORS**, 13262 Europa Court, Apple Valley MN 55124. (612)432-0710. Editor: Elizabeth Swiderski. Publishes hardcover and trade paperback originals and mass market paperback originals. Averages 1-3 titles/year. Pays 10% maximum royalty on wholesale price. Photocopied submissions OK. SASE. Reports in 3 weeks on queries; 2 months on mss.

Nonfiction: Education and special education textbooks. "We use material which is used by the teacher of students with learning difficulties. Books should be usable in the classroom and pointed toward a single or multiple grades." Query.

Recent Nonfiction Title: *Study Skills: Learning Made Easier*, by Swiderski/Zettel (study guide).

LEARNING PUBLICATIONS, INC., Box 1326, Holmes Beach FL 33509. (616)372-1045. Associate Editor: Lois Carl. Publishes hardcover and trade paperback originals. Averages 10 titles/year. Pays 5-15% royalty on wholesale price. No advance. Photocopied submissions OK. SASE. Reports in 3 weeks on queries; 3 months on mss. Free book catalog.

Nonfiction: How-to, reference, self-help, technical, textbook on art, psychology, sociology, reference books for counselors, teachers, and school administrators. Books to help parents of children with reading problems and special needs (impaired, gifted, etc.); or art activity books for teachers. Query or submit outline synopsis and sample chapters.

Recent Nonfiction Titles: *All Children Create: An Elementary Art Curriculum*, by Sefkow and Berger (art activities for the classroom); *Sex Discrimination in Educational Employment*, by Stoddard; *Children of Alcoholics*, by Ackerman; *Microcomputers in Education*, by Joiner, et. al; and *Creating Effective Schools*, by Brookover, et. al.

LEATHER STOCKING BOOKS, Box 19746, West Allis WI 53219. (414)778-1120. Editor: Carlton Sitz. Publishes hardcover and original paperbacks. Average 3-5 titles/year. Pays 10% royalty on wholesale price; no advance. Simultaneous and photocopied submissions OK. SASE. Reports in 2 months.

Nonfiction: Frontier history, guns, outdoor (how-to), military. Query.

Recent Nonfiction Titles: *Famous Guns & Gunners*, by Virines; and *Rube Burrow/King of the Train Robbers*, by Breihan.

LEBHAR-FRIEDMAN, 425 Park Ave., New York NY 10022. (212)371-9400. Chief Editor: Barbara Miller. Publishes hardcover and paperback originals (100%). Averages 17-20 titles/year. Pays royalty on wholesale price; no advance. Photocopied submissions OK. No computer printout or disk submissions. Reports in 4-8 weeks. SASE. Book catalog for SASE.

Nonfiction: "Most of our books published are for the retail business field (food service and supermarket). Our market is directed at both the retailer, administrator, and the college and junior college student wishing to enter the field and needing a good hard look at the facts and how-to's of the business. We are not interested in the generalist approach but with specifics that will be of importance to the business person." Submit outline/synopsis and 1-3 sample chapters.

Recent Nonfiction Titles: *More Than They Bargained For: The Rise and Fall of Korvette's*, by Isadore Beamesh; *Great Restaurant Innovators*, Charles Bernstein; and *General Merchandise in Food Stores*, by Levis and Converse.

‡**LEE'S BOOKS FOR YOUNG READERS**, Box 111, 813 West Ave., O'Neil Professional Bldg., Wellington TX 79095. (806)447-5445. Independent book producer/packager. Publisher: Lee Templeton. Publishes hardcover originals. Averages 8 titles/year. Pays 10% minimum royalty on wholesale price. No advance. No computer printout or disk submissions. Free book catalog.

Nonfiction: Biography. "Our books are nonfiction history of young heroes. All our books are written for 'reluctant' readers in junior high school market (10-14 age group), to be sold to junior (middle) school libraries. We will consider queries about young American heroes, male or female, that historians overlooked." All unsolicited mss are returned unopened.

Recent Nonfiction Titles: *Cannon Boy of the Alamo*, *The Death of Jimmy Littlewolf*, and *Columbus' Cabin Boy*, all by Lee Templeton.

LESTER AND ORPEN DENNYS, LTD., PUBLISHERS, 78 Sullivan St., Toronto, Ontario M5T 1C1, Canada. (416)593-9602. President: Malcolm Lester. Vice President: Louise Dennys. Publishes hardcover and trade paperback originals. Offers standard minimum book contract of 10-12½-15% on retail price. Averages 20 titles/year. Free book catalog. Will consider photocopied submissions. Query with outline and one sample chapter showing style and treatment. Submit complete ms only for fiction, or if writer has been published before. Reports in 2 months. SAE and International Reply Coupons; no return unless necessary postage included.
General Fiction and Nonfiction: "Our basic philosophy of publishing only carefully selected books is stronger than ever; each and every title reflects a uniqueness in concept, careful and imaginative editing and design, and powerful and creative promotion." Publishes adult trade fiction, mystery, thriller, biography, sociology, economics and philosophy.
Recent Titles: *Images: Contemporary Canadian Realism*, by Marci and Louise Lipman; *Monseigneur Quixote*, by Graham Greene; and *Samaritan*, by Philippe van Rjndt (fiction).

THE LEWIS PUBLISHING CO., 15 Muzzey St., Lexington MA 02173. (617)861-0170. Publisher: Thomas Begner. Publishes hardcover and trade paperback originals. Averages 10 titles/year. Pays negotiable royalty; offers variable advance. No computer printout or disk submissions. Reports in 1 month. Book catalog 50¢.
Nonfiction: Popular social science. Submit outline/synopsis and 3 sample chapters.
Recent Nonfiction Titles: *The Kids Book of Divorce*, by The Unit at the Fairweather School; and *What Psychology Knows That Everyone Should*, by Daniel Goleman.

LIBERTY PUBLISHING COMPANY, INC., 50 Scott Adam Rd., Cockeysville MD 21030. (301)667-6680. Publisher: Jeffrey B. Little. Publishes hardcover and mostly trade paperback originals. Averages 10-12 titles/year. Pays 8-12% royalty on wholesale or retail price; buys some mss outright for $500-1,500; offers average $500 advance. Photocopied submissions OK. Computer printout submissions OK. Reports in 2 weeks on queries; 2 months on mss. "Exclusive distribution arrangements with self-publishers possible."
Imprints: Liberty Personal Counsel Library, J. Little, publisher.
Nonfiction: Biography, cookbook, how-to, illustrated book, self-help. Subjects include Americana; business and economics; cooking and foods; history; hobbies; photography (b&w only); recreation; sports; travel; educational; parent guides. Accepts nonfiction translations. "How-to or self-help books dealing with concrete advice written by people qualified to address the subject. Extensive graphic possibilities preferred. No self improvement books dealing with psychology and mind improvement. No poetry, please." Query with author biography or submit outline/synopsis and 3 sample chapters.
Recent Nonfiction Titles: *Understanding Wall Street*, by J. Little (business guide for the layman investor); *The #1 Home Business Book*, by G. Delany (self-help book for the new entrepreneur); and *The Essential Book of Shellfish*, by Robert Robinson (fully illustrated guide to preparing and dismantling shellfish).

*LIBRA PUBLISHERS, INC., 391 Willets Rd., Roslyn Heights NY 11577. (516)484-4950. Publishes hardcover and paperback originals. Specializes in the behavioral sciences. Averages 15 titles/year. 10-15% royalty on retail price; no advance. Subsidy publishes a small percentage of books (those which have obvious marketing problems or are too specialized). Simultaneous and photocopied submissions OK. Computer printout and disk submissions OK; prefers letter quality to dot matrix. Reports in 1-2 weeks. SASE. Free book catalog.
Nonfiction: Mss in all subject areas will be given consideration, but main interest is in the behavioral sciences. Submit outline/synopsis and 3 sample chapters. Recently published *The Glimpe*, by Joyce MacIver; *The Rhythm Factor in Human Behavior*, by Salvatore J. Garzino; *Please Stand By—Your Mother's Missing*, by Shirley Bennett Tallman and Nancy Pahl Gilsenan; *Consciousness: Natural and Artificial*, by James T. Culbertson.

LIBRARIES UNLIMITED, Box 263, Littleton CO 80160. (303)770-1220. Editor-in-Chief: Bohdan S. Wynar. Publishes hardcover and paperback originals (95%) and hardcover reprints (5%). Averages 30-40 titles/year. Specializes in library science and reference books, 10% royalty on net sales; advance averages $500. Marketed by direct mail to 40,000 libraries and schools in this country and abroad. Query or submit outline/synopsis and sample chapters. All prospective authors are required to fill out an author questionnaire. Query if photos/illustrations are to accompany ms. Reports in 2 months. SASE. Free book catalog.
Nonfiction: Publishes reference and library science text books. Looks for professional experience.
Recent Nonfiction Titles: *Introduction to Cataloging and Classification*, by Bohdan S. Wynar; *Genreflecting: A Guide to Reading Interests in Genre Fiction*, by Betty Rosenberg; *Educational Software Directory: A Subject Guide to Microcomputer Software*, compiled by Marilyn J. Chartrand and Constance D. Williams for Corporate Monitor, Inc.

‡**PHILIP LIEF AND ASSOCIATES**, Cagney Hill Road, Southfield MA 01259. (413)229-2686. Editor: Marsha Fink. Produces trade paperback originals. Averages 12 titles/year. Shares royalty; buys some mss outright. Simultaneous and photocopied submissions OK. SASE. Reports in 1 month on queries; 2 months on mss. Free book catalog.
Nonfiction: Coffee table book, reference, illustrated book. Query.
Fiction: All types of humor.
Recent Fiction Titles: *The Burbank Diet*, by Lola Peters; *I Hate Cats, Cubes, Pac-Man and You, Too!*, by L. Beltz; and *The Cat's Book of Etiquette* by Hodge. Query.

LIFE ENRICHMENT PUBLISHER, 1308 Harrison Ave., Canton OH 44706. (216)454-1598. Publisher: Dennis Bartow. Publishes trade paperback originals. Averages 5 titles/year. Pays 10-15% royalty on wholesale price; offers negotiable advance. Simultaneous submissions OK. No computer printout or disk submissions. Reports in 4 weeks.
Nonfiction: Reference. "Instructional and inspirational religious material, spiritual healing, church administration and program tools." Query.

LIGHTBOOKS, Box 1268, Twain Harte CA 95383. (209)533-4222. Publisher: Paul Castle. Publishes hardcover and paperback originals. Averages 4-6 titles/year. Pays 10-15% royalty on wholesale or retail price; no advance. Simultaneous and photocopied submissions OK. SASE. Reports in 4 weeks.
Nonfiction: Photography. "We are always interested in good mss on technique and/or business of photography. We especially want mss on *marketing* one's photography. We don't want mss on art criticism of photography, collections of art photos, basic photo teaching books, or anything other than books on the technique and/or business of photography. Query, if the idea is good, we'll ask for outline/synopsis and sample chapters." Recently published *How to Produce and Mass Market Your Creative Photography*, by Kenneth Townend; and *Outdoor Photography How to Shoot it, How to Sell it*, by Robert McQuilkin.
Tips: "We need more anecdotes and illustrations (word) to amplify the writer's points. We particularly look for skilled photographers who are doing something very well and can communicate their expertise to others. We are willing to work with such individuals on extensive re-write and editing, if what they have to say is valuable."

LIGUORI PUBLICATIONS, Book and Pamphlet Dept., 1 Liguori Dr., Liguori MO 63057. (314)464-2500. Editor-in-Chief: Rev. Christopher Farrell, C.SS.R. Managing Editor: Roger Marchand. Publishes paperback originals. Specializes in Catholic-Christian religious materials. Averages 30 titles/year. Pays 8% royalty on books; flat fee on pamphlets and teacher's guides; no advance. Query or submit outline/synopsis and 1 sample chapter; "never submit total book." State availability of photos and/or illustrations. Photocopied submissions OK. Computer printouts (letter quality) OK; disk submissions from TRS-80 Model III in a 1.3 system/1.0 version OK "if sent with computer printout." Reports in 3-5 weeks. SASE. Free book catalog.
Nonfiction: Publishes doctrinal, inspirational, Biblical, self-help and educational materials. Looks for "thought and language that speak to the basic practical and religious concerns of contemporary Catholic Christians."
Recent Nonfiction Titles: *Jesus Loves You: A Catholic Catechism for the Primary Grades*; *Following Christ: A Handbook of Catholic Moral Teaching*; *Biblical Guidelines for Discovering God's Kingdom*; and *Dealing with Depression: A Whole-Person Approach*.
Tips: "People seek light on real-life concerns. Writers lead and educate in light of Good News shared in faith-community."

LIPPINCOTT JUNIOR BOOKS, see Harper & Row Junior Books Group.

LITTLE, BROWN AND CO., INC., 34 Beacon St., Boston MA 02106. Contact: Editorial Department, Trade Division. Publishes hardcover and paperback originals and paperback reprints. Publishes 100 titles/year. "Royalty and advance agreements vary from book to book and are discussed with the author at the time an offer is made." Submissions only from authors who have had a book published or have been published in professional or literary journals, newspapers or magazines." Reports in 6-8 weeks for queries/proposals. SASE. Free book catalog.
Nonfiction: "Some how-to books, select and distinctive cookbooks, biographies, history, science and sports." Submissions only from authors who have had a book published or have been published in professional or literary journals, newspapers or magazines. Query or submit outline/synopsis and sample chapters.
Recent Nonfiction Titles: *Crockett's Flower Garden*;, by James Underwood Crockett; *Years of Upheaval*, by Henry Kissinger; and *The Last Lion*, by William Manchester.
Fiction: Contemporary popular fiction as well as fiction of literary distinction. "Our poetry list is extremely limited; those collections of poems that we do publish are usually the work of poets who have gained recogni-

tion through publication in literary reviews and various periodicals." Query or submit outline/synopsis and sample chapters.

Recent Fiction Titles: *War and Remembrance*, by Herman Wouk; and *Ancient Evenings*, by Norman Mailer.

*LLEWELLYN PUBLICATIONS, Box 43383, St. Paul MN 55164-0383. (612)291-1970. President: Carl L. Weschcke. Publishes hardcover and trade paperback originals. Averages 6-12 titles/year. Subsidy publishes 5% of books "if it appears to be a viable proposition with too limited a market for our economics to justify, and if the author has the resources." Pays 10% maximum royalty on both wholesale and retail price. Simultaneous and photocopied submissions OK. Computer printout submissions OK; prefers letter quality to dot matrix. SASE. Reports in 2 weeks on queries; 2 months on mss. Book catalog 50¢.

Nonfiction: Coffee table book, how-to, reference, self-help and textbook. Subjects include nature, philosophy, psychology and religion. Accepts nonfiction translations. "We specialize in astrology and the occult, broadly defined. We cater to sincere students and professionals in astrology, students and intelligent lay-people interested in the reality of astrology and occultism, the self-help and the farming and gardening market (for lunar and organic planting). We only want astrology or occult—but not 'pop' stuff! No 'celebrity' stuff! No satanist or devil possession, etc." Submit outline/synopsis and 2 sample chapters or complete ms, along with the writer's concept of the value of the book to the intended audience and his evaluation of the potential he believes the book to have.

Recent Nonfiction Titles: *The Llewellyn Practical Guide to Astral Projection*, by Melita Denning and Osborne Phillips (occult; parasychology: out-of-body-experience); *Brujeria*, by Mary Virginia Devine (Mexican-Amercan folk magic); *The Llewellyn Practical Guide to the Magic of the Tarot*, by Denning and Phillips (how to read, and shape, the future through tarot images in ritual, meditation, dance and drama); *Magical Herbalism*, by Scott Cunningham (the magical lore and technology of herbs).

Fiction: Erotica (with a Tantric theme); mystery (with an occult theme); science fiction (with an occult theme); and suspense (with an occult theme). "We're booked up pretty solid, but will consider exceptional works. No 'satanist,' 'devil-worship,' 'demon possession,' 'saved from witchcraft,' or material from writers not actually—and really—knowledgeable about the occult or parapsychological theme or data included in fiction, or nonfiction." Query.

Recent Fiction Title: *The Secrets of Dr. Taverner*, by Dion Fortune (short stories of ceremonial magic and psychotherapy with the aid of supersensible knowledge).

LODESTAR BOOKS, Division of E. P. Dutton, 2 Park Ave., New York NY 10016. (212)725-1818. Editorial Director: Virginia Buckley. Hardcover originals. Publishes juveniles, young adults, fiction and nonfiction; no picture books. Averages 25 titles/year. Pays royalty on list price; advance offered. State availability of photos and/or illustrations. Photocopied submissions OK. Computer printout submissions OK. Reports in 2-4 months. SASE.

Nonfiction: Query or submit outline/synopsis and 2-3 sample chapters including "theme, chapter-by-chapter outline, and 1 or 2 completed chapters."

Fiction: Publishes only for young adults and juveniles: adventure, fantasy, humorous, contemporary, mystery, science fiction, suspense and western books. Submit complete ms.

Tips: Queries/mss may be routed to other editors in the publishing group.

LOIRY PUBLISHING HOUSE, Suite 6, 635 S. Orange Ave., Sarasota FL 33577. (813)365-1959. Executive Editor: William S. Loiry. Publishes hardcover and trade paperback originals. Pays negotiable royalty. No advance. Simultaneous and photocopied submissions OK. SASE. Reports in 1 month.

Nonfiction: How-to, juvenile, reference, self-help, textbook. Human Relations: effective living, sexuality, male/female relations, parenting, race relations; children and youth: conditions of youth, youth policy, youth programs, youth activism; politics: what's really going on in politics and government and why. Query.

Recent Nonfiction Titles: *A Time to Live*, by David A. Loiry, PhD and Carol J. Loiry, MA (human relations); *Winning with Science*, by William S. Loiry (children and youth); and *The Impact of Youth Part 1: The Past*, by William S. Loiry (children and youth).

*LONE STAR PUBLISHERS, INC., Box 9774, Austin TX 78766. (512)255-2333. Editorial Director: A.J. Lerager. Publishes hardcover and paperback originals. Averages 3 titles/year. Subsidy publishes approximately 1 title/year based on "the subject matter, the author's reputation, the potential market, the capital investment, etc." Pays 12½-15% royalty on wholesale or retail price; no advance. Simultaneous and photocopied submissions OK. Reports in 3 weeks. SASE. Free book catalog.

Nonfiction: College textbooks; how-to; cookbooks; self-help and sports. No poetry. Query. Recently published *The Texas Press Women's Cookbook*, by D. Hunt, K. Pill and B. Field (cookbook); *Poverty, Manpower, & Social Security*, by P. Brinker and J. Klos (college text); *Retail Management*, by Roger A. Dickinson; and *Economics for the Voter*, by M.L. Greenhut and Charles Stewart.

LONGMAN, INC., 19 W. 44th St., New York NY 10036. (212)764-3950. Head of Services Division: Diana Scholefield. Director, College and Professional Book Division: Lane Akers. Director, Schools/ELT Divisions: Robert Cornford. Publishes hardcover and paperback originals. Publishes 60 titles/year. Pays variable royalty; offers average $1,000 advance. Photocopied submissions OK. SASE. Reports in 6 weeks.
Nonfiction: Textbooks only (college and professional). History, music, politics, psychology, reference, sociology, and English as a second language. No trade, art or juvenile, El-hi texts. Query.

‡*LOST ROADS PUBLISHERS**, Box 310, Eureka Springs AR 72632. Editors: C.D. Wright, Forrest Gander. Publishes hardcover and trade paperback originals. Averages 3 titles/year. Subsidy publishes 75% of books based on "whether or not we have received a grant which covers the work." Pays 5-10% royalty on retail price; pays in copies/$200 cash payment. Simultaneous and photocopied submissions OK. Computer printout submissions OK; prefers letter quality to dot matrix. SASE. Reports in 1 month on queries; 2 months on mss. Free book catalog.
Fiction: Erotica, ethnic, experimental, mainstream, documentary prose, b&w visual art. Especially needs experimental, political and mainstream. Accepts fiction translations. Query. Accepts outline/synopsis and 2 sample chapters.
Recent Fiction Titles: *Trouble in Paradise*, by Zuleyka Benitez (narrative drawings); and forthcoming, an undisclosed work of documentary prose by Carolyn Forehé.
Poetry: "All contemporary poetry, works in translation and long poems." Submit 8 samples.
Recent Poetry Titles: *The Battlefield Where the Moon Says I Love You*, by Frank Stanford (one 23,000-line poem); *Very Rich Hours*, by Frances Mayes (prose poems); and *No Seige Is Absolute*, translation of René Char by Franz Wright.

LOTHROP, LEE & SHEPARD BOOKS, Division of William Morrow Company, 105 Madison Ave., New York NY 10016. (212)889-3050. Editor-in-Chief: Dorothy Briley. Hardcover original children's books only. Royalty and advance vary according to type of book. Averages 55 titles/year. State availability of photos to accompany ms. Photocopied submissions OK, but originals preferred. Computer printout submissions OK; no disk submissions. Reports in 4-6 weeks. SASE. Free book catalog.
Juveniles: Publishes picture books, general nonfiction, and novels. Submit outline/synopsis and sample chapters for nonfiction. Juvenile fiction emphasis on contemporary novels, but also includes adventure, fantasy, historical, humorous, mystery, science fiction and suspense. Submit complete ms for fiction. Looks for "organization, clarity, creativity, literary style." Accepts artwork/photos.
Recent Titles: *The Kissimmee Kid*, by Vera and Bill Cleaver; *You Can't Be Timid With a Trumpet*, by Betty Lou English (photoessay on orchestra); and *Sunshine*, by Jan Ormerod.

LOUISIANA STATE UNIVERSITY PRESS, Baton Rouge LA 70803. (504)388-6618. Assistant Director and Executive Editor: Beverly Jarrett. Director: L.E. Phillabaum. Averages 60 titles/year. Pays royalty on wholesale price; no advance. Photocopied submissions OK. SASE. Reports in 1 month (queries); 1-6 months (mss). Free book catalog.
Nonfiction: "We would like to have mss on humanities and social sciences, with special emphasis on Southern history and literature; Southern studies; French studies; political philosophy; music, especially jazz." Query.
Recent Nonfiction Titles: *The Selected Essays of T. Harry Williams* (biography); *Winston Churchill's World View: Statesmanship and Power*, by Kenneth Thompson.

‡*THE LOWELL PRESS, INC.**, 115 E. 31st St., Box 1877, Kansas City MO 64141. (816)753-4545. Editor: Barbara Funk. Publishes hardcover and trade paperback originals (50%) and reprints. Averages 5-10 titles/year. Subsidy publishes 33% of books. Simultaneous submissions OK. SASE. Reports in 1 month. Free book catalog.
Nonfiction: Coffee table book, humor, illustrated book on Americana, animals, art, nature, photography, travel only. Query.
Recent Nonfiction Titles: *A Day Late and A Dollar Short*, by Spike Van Cleve (Americana, humor); *Missouri*, by Bill Nunn (nature, travel); and *No More Buffalo*, by Bob Scriver (art).

‡LYNX HOUSE PRESS**, Box 800, Amherst MA 01004. (503)777-3102. Fiction Editor: Domenic Stansberry. Poetry Editor: Chris Howell. Publishes hardcover and trade paperback originals. Averages 5 titles/year. Pays in copies plus percentage on 2nd printing. Simultaneous and photocopied submissions OK. No computer printout or disk submissions. SASE. Reports in 1 month on queries; 2 months on mss. Book catalog $1.
Fiction: Literary. Accepts fiction and poetry translations. "We are not actively seeking manuscripts but will consider poetry and fiction of high literary quality by writers with substantial publication in literary presses who have not yet had their work collected in book form. We are *not* interested in genre or mass market literature." Sumbit outline/synopsis and sample chapters to D. Stansberry, Box 800, Amherst MA 01004.
Recent Fiction Titles: *Becoming Coyote*, by Wayne Ude (novel); *35¢ Thrills*, by Joyce Thompson (stories); and *Blount's Anvil*, by Don Hendrie (novel).

Poetry: Literary. Submit 8-10 samples to Chris Howell, 6116 S.E. Mitchell, Portland OR 97206.
Recent Poetry Titles: *Lost in the Bonewheel Factory*, by Yusef Kumanyaaka; *The Dog That Was Barking Yesterday*, by Patricia Goedicke; and *Homefront*, by Bill Tremslay.

‡**McCLELLAND AND STEWART, LTD.**, 25 Hollinger Rd., Toronto, Ontario, Canada M4B 3G2. Publisher: L.E. McKnight. Publishes hardcover and paperback originals. Offers sliding scale of royalty on copies sold. Advance varies. Free book catalog. Submit outline and 3 sample chapters for nonfiction and fiction. No computer printout or disk submissions. Reports in 6 weeks, average. SAE and International Reply Coupons.
Nonfiction, Poetry and Fiction: Publishes "Canadian fiction and poetry. Nonfiction in the humanities and social sciences, with emphasis on Canadian concerns. Coffee table books on art, architecture, sculpture and Canadian history." Accepts artwork/photos. Will also consider general adult trade fiction, biography, history, nature, photography, politics, sociology, textbooks. Accepts nonfiction and fiction translations.

MARGARET K. McELDERRY BOOKS, Atheneum Publishers, Inc., 597 5th Ave., New York NY 10017. Editor: Margaret K. McElderry. Publishes hardcover originals. Publishes 30-35 titles/year. Pays royalty on retail price. Reports in 6 weeks. SASE.
Nonfiction and Fiction: Quality material for preschoolers to 16-year-olds. Looks for "originality of ideas, clarity and felicity of expression, well-organized plot (fiction) or exposition (nonfiction) quality."
Recent Titles: *A Jar of Dreams*, by Yoshiko Uchida; and *Circle of Fire*, by William Hooks.

McFARLAND & COMPANY, INC., PUBLISHERS, Box 611, Jefferson NC 28640. (919)246-4460. President: Robert Franklin. Publishes hardcover and "quality" paperback originals; a non-"trade" publisher. Averages 28 titles/year. Pays 10-12½% royalty on gross sales income; no advance. Simultaneous and photocopied submissions OK "if announced." Reports in 2 weeks.
Nonfiction: Scholarly monographs, reference, technical and professional. Subjects include Americana, art, business and economics, chess, drama/theatre, health, cinema/radio/TV (very strong here), history, literature, librarianship (very strong here), music, parapsychology, religion, sociology, sports/recreation, women's studies, world affairs. "We will consider *any* scholarly book—with authorial maturity and competent grasp of subject. Reference books are particularly wanted—fresh material (i.e., not in head-to-head competition with an established title). We don't like mss of fewer than 200 double-spaced typed pages. Our market consists of libraries, mainly. Also professional schools' textbook users, and some individuals such as college professors. Our film books are the only ones going to bookstores." No memoirs, poetry, children's books, personal essays. Query or submit outline/synopsis and sample chapters.
Recent Nonfiction Titles: *Lust for Fame: The Stage Career of John Wilkes Booth*, by Gordon Samples (biography/reference/criticism); *Famous Phrases from History*, by Charles F. Hemphill, Jr. (reference); and *Musicians' Autobiographies*, by John L. Adams (bibliography).
Tips: "Don't worry about 'writing skills'—we have editors. What we want is real *knowledge* of an area in which there is not good information coverage at present. Plus reliability (so we don't feel we have to check absolutely everything)."

McGRAW-HILL BOOK CO., College Textbooks Division, 1221 Avenue of the Americas, New York NY 10020. (212)997-2271. Editorial Director: William Willey. Editor-in-Chief, Engineering: B.J. Clark. Editor-in-Chief, Arts and Sciences: Philip Butcher. Publisher, Health Professions Division: J. Dereck Jeffers. Publishes hardcover and paperback originals, reprints, translations and anthologies. Pays 10-12½-15% royalty on hardcover and 7½% royalty on retail price of paperback. Reports in 3 weeks. SASE.
Nonfiction: The College Division publishes textbooks. The writer must know the college curriculum and course structure. Also publishes scientific texts and reference books in business, economics, computers, engineering, social sciences, physical sciences, and mathematics. Material should be scientifically and factually accurate. Most, but not all, books should be designed for existing courses offered in various disciplines of study. Books should have superior presentations and be more up-to-date than existing textbooks.

McGRAW-HILL BOOK CO., General Division, 1221 Avenue of the Americas, New York NY 10020. General Manager: Thomas J. Dembofsky. Publishes hardcover and trade paperback (40%) and trade paperback reprints (60%). Averages 100 titles/year. Prefers mss submitted through agents. No response to authors without SASE.
Nonfiction: How-to, self-help and books from academics on business and economics, health, psychology, recreation, sociology. Submit outline/synopsis and sample chapters.
Fiction: Mainstream. No short stories or poetry. Mss submitted through agents only.

McGRAW-HILL BOOK CO., Professional and Reference Division, 1221 Avenue of the Americas, New York NY 10020. General Manager: Peter Nalle; Multi/volume Encyclopedia Editor-in-Chief: Sybil Parker; Business Editor-in-Chief: William Sabin; Handbooks and Technical Books Editor-in-Chief: Harold B. Crawford; Computing and Software Editor-in-Chief: Tyler G. Hicks. Hardcover and paperback originals, reprints, translations and anthologies. Pays 10-12½-15% royalty on net price on hardcover and 7½% royalty on retail price on paperback. Reports in 3 weeks. SASE.

Nonfiction: Publishes books for engineers, architects, scientists and business people who need information on the professional level. Some of these books also find use in college and technical institute courses. This division also publishes multi-volume encyclopedias (which are usually staff-prepared using work from outside contributors who are specialists in their fields) and one-volume encyclopedias prepared by experts in a given field. The professional books are usually written by graduate engineers, architects, scientists or business people (such as accountants, lawyers, stockbrokers, etc.). Authors of the professional books are expected to be highly qualified in their fields. Such qualifications are the result of education and experience in the field; these qualifications are prerequisite for authorship. The multi-volume encyclopedias rarely accept contributions from freelancers because the above education and experience qualifications are also necessary. Single-volume encyclopedias are usually prepared by subject specialists; again freelancers are seldom used unless they have the necessary experience and educational background.

DAVID McKAY CO., INC., 2 Park Ave., New York NY 10016. Editor: James Louttit. Publishes hardcover and paperback originals. Averages 20 titles/year. "No unsolicited manuscripts or proposals considered or acknowledged."

‡MACLAY & ASSOCIATES, INC., Box 16253, Baltimore MD 21210. (301)235-7985. President: John Maclay. Publishes hardcover and trade paperback originals and hardcover and trade paperback reprints. Averages 12 titles/year. Pays 10% royalty. Simultaneous and photocopied submissions OK. SASE. Reports in 1 month. Free book catalog.
Fiction: Mainstream. Looking for 12,500-15,000-word short novels—10/year. No juvenile fiction. Send complete ms.
Recent Fiction Titles: *Hour*, by J.N. Williamson; *Silent Strides*, by A. Ross Metzger; and *Black & White*, by J.L Bruce.

MACMILLAN OF CANADA, 146 Front St., W., Suite 685, Toronto, Ontario, Canada M5J 1G2. Publisher: Douglas M. Gibson. Editor-in-Chief: Anne Holloway. Publishes hardcover originals and paperback reprints. Averages 25 titles/year. 10% royalty on retail price. Sample chapters and outlines only acceptable form of submission. Computer printout submissions OK "if clear and legible." Reports in 10 weeks. SAE and International Reply Coupons. Book catalog for SAE and International Reply Coupons.
Nonfiction: "We publish Canadian authors on all sorts of subjects and books of all sorts that are about Canada. Biography; history; art; current affairs; how-to; and juveniles. Particularly looking for good topical nonfiction." Accepts artwork/photos. Accepts translations. Accepts outline/synopsis and 3, 4 or 5 sample chapters "depending on length of total manuscript."
Recent Nonfiction Titles: *Louisbourg Portraits*, by Christopher Moore (popular Canadian history); *Grits*, by Christina McCall-Newman (politics); *Start with $1,000*, by J.J. Brown & Jerry Ackerman (financial advice).
Fiction: Query.
Recent Fiction Titles: *The Moons of Jupiter*, by Alice Munro; *Stargate*, by Pauline Gedge; *The Teacher's Daughter*, by Richard D. Wright.

MACMILLAN PUBLISHING CO., INC., 866 3rd Ave., New York NY 10022. Publishes hardcover and paperback originals and reprints. Averages 130 titles/year. Will consider juvenile submissions only. Address mss to Children's Book Department. Enclose return postage.
Juveniles: Children's books.

MCPHERSON & COMPANY, Box 638, New Paltz NY 12561. Editor: Bruce McPherson. Imprints: Treacle Press, Documentext. Publishes hardcover and paperback originals, paperback reprints. Averages 5 titles/year. Pays royalty. No unsolicited manuscripts—query first with SASE. Reports in 3 weeks to 2 months.
Fiction and Nonfiction: "We issue novels, anthologies, books of literary criticism, anthropology, film studies, etc., and plan to expand into the areas of alternative lifestyle and contemporary politics." Accepts fiction translations. Recently published *Brakhage Scrapbook: Collected Writings 1964-1980*, by Stan Brakhage; *Something Else Press: An Annotated Bibliography*, by Peter Frank; *Positions with White Roses*, by Ursule Molinaro.

MADRONA PUBLISHERS, INC., Box 22667, Seattle WA 98122. (206)325-3973. President: Daniel J. Levant. Editorial Director: Sara Levant. Publishes hardcover and paperback originals (90%) and paperback reprints (10%). Averages 6 titles/year. Pays 7½-15% royalty on wholesale or retail price; offers $1,000 average advance. Simultaneous and photocopied submissions OK. Computer printout submissions OK. SASE. Reports in 6 weeks. Free book catalog.
Nonfiction: Americana, biography, cookbooks, cooking and foods, health, history, hobbies, how-to, humor, photography, politics, psychology, recreation, self-help and travel. Query, submit outline/synopsis and at least

2 sample chapters or complete ms. Accepts nonfiction and fiction translations.
Recent Nonfiction Titles: *Under the Influence*, by Dr. James Milam and Katherine Ketcham; and *The Last Great Race*, by Tim Jones.

*MANYLAND BOOKS, INC., 84-39 90th St., Woodhaven NY 11421. (212)441-6768. Editor-in-Chief: Stepas Zobarskas. Publishes hardcover and paperback originals. Pays 5-10-12½-15% royalty on wholesale price; no advance. About 25% of books are subsidy published. Averages 20 titles/year. Photocopied submissions OK. Submit complete ms. Reports in 8-10 weeks. Enclose return postage with ms.
Fiction, Nonfiction, Poetry, and Juveniles: "Manyland is concerned primarily with the literature of the lesser known countries. It has already published a score of novels, collections of short stories, folk tales, juvenile books, works of poetry, essays, and historical studies. Most of the publications have more than local interest. Their content and value transcend natural boundaries. They have universal appeal. We are interested in both new and established writers. We will consider any subject as long as it is well-written. No length requirements. We are especially interested in memoirs, biographies, anthologies." Accepts translations.
Recent Nonfiction Titles: *Anna Marinkovitch*, by Edward Iskovic; *A Look at Modern Ghana*, by Katheren Obeng; *The Exitingest Things*, by Peter Thorpe; *Escape to China*, by Anna Lincoln.
Tips: Queries/mss may be routed to other editors in the publishing group.

‡MARATHON INTERNATIONAL PUBLISHING COMPANY, INC., Dept. WM, Box 33008, Louisville KY 40232. (502)245-1566. President: Jim Wortham. Publishes hardcover originals, trade paperback originals, trade paperback reprints. Averages 10 titles/year. Pays 10% royalty on wholesale. Simultaneous and photocopied submissions OK. No computer printout or disk submissions. SASE. Reports in 1 week on queries; 2 weeks on mss. Book catalog for 6x9 SAE and 4 first class stamps.
Nonfiction: Cookbooks, how-to, self-help on business and economics, and offbeat humor. Especially needs how-to make extra money-type manuscripts; self-improvement; how a person can be happier and more prosperous. Does not want biography or textbooks. Query. Will consider poetry manuscripts for subsidy publication only.
Recent Nonfiction Titles: *How to Make Money in Penny Stocks*, by Jim Scott (financial); *Convert Your Car to Alcohol*, by Keat Drane (alternative energy); *Run Your Car on Sunshine*, by James Blake (alternative energy); and *So You Want to Write a Cookbook*, by Judy Rehmel.

‡*MARINER PUBLISHING COMPANY, INC., 10927 N. Dale Mabry, Tampa FL 33618. (813)962-8136. Editor: Jack Sandler. Publishes hardcover trade paperback and mass market paperback originals. Averages 15-20 titles/year. Subsidy publishes about 50% of books depending on "market and author evaluation." Pays 8-18% royalty on retail price, or pays negotiable rates. Simultaneous and photocopied submissions OK. SASE. Reports in "weeks" on queries and mss. Free book catalog.
Nonfiction: Biography, cookbook, how-to, humor, illustrated book, juvenile, reference, self-help, technical and textbook. Subjects include cooking and foods, health, history, philosophy, psychology, recreation, religion, sociology and sports. Query, submit outline/synopsis and sample chapters or submit complete ms.
Recent Nonfiction Titles: *The Complete Guide to Women's Health*, by Shephard & Shephard (self-help health); *Human Sexuality: Current Perspectives*, by Sandler, Myerson & Kinder (health textbook); *Univalent Functions*, by Dr. A.W. Goodman (textbook); and *Elementary Applied Calculus*, by J.S. Ratti (textbook).
Fiction: All types. Query or submit complete ms.

MEADOWBROOK PRESS, 18318 Minnetonka Blvd., Deephaven MN 55391. (612)473-5400. Senior Editor: Kathe Grooms. Publishes trade paperback originals (with small print-runs of hardcover copies). Averages 8-12 titles/year. Pays variable royalty; buys some mss outright or by assigning them as works-for-hire. Simultaneous and photocopied submissions OK. SASE. Book catalog for SASE.
Nonfiction: How-to, juvenile, self-help and consumer reference. Subjects include cooking and foods; health (on dieting, nutrition); travel; parenting; consumer interest (on money-saving); children's activities. No standard cookbooks; technical books; biographies or memoirs. "We prefer a query first; then we will request an outline and/or sample material."
Recent Nonfiction Titles: *The Parent's Guide to Baby & Child Medical Care*, ed. by Terril H. Hart, M.D.; *Free Stuff for Kids*, by The Free Stuff Editors; and *Economy Motel Guide*, by The Meadowbrook Reference Group.
Tips: "Note that the majority of our books are produced in-house, *not* by authors. In addition, most of our concepts are developed by the staff."

MEDICAL ECONOMICS BOOKS, Division of Medical Economics Co., 680 Kinderkamack, Oradell NJ 07649. Company also publishes magazines and references for doctors, nurses, pharmacists, laboratorians. Acquisitions Director: Elizabeth A. Stueck. Editor: Reuben Barr. Publishes hardcover, paperback, and spiral bound originals. Averages 36 titles/year. Pays by individual arrangement. Simultaneous and photocopied submissions OK. Computer printout submissions OK. SASE. Reports in 6 weeks. Free book catalog. Tests freelancers for rewriting and editing assignments.

Nonfiction: Clinical and practice-financial management references, handbooks, manuals. Medical—primary care—all fields; obstetrics and gynecology, pathology and laboratory medicine. Nursing for the practicing nurse. Submit table of contents and prospectus. Accepts artwork/photos.

Recent Nonfiction Titles: *Management of High-Risk Pregnancy*, by John Queenan, MD; *Tax Strategy for Physicians*, by Larry L. Farber; and *Managing the Critically Ill Effectively*, by Margaret Van Meter, RN.

Tips: "Our mission is to provide the practicing health care professional with high quality, clearly-written, practical, useful books." Queries/mss may be routed to other editors in the publishing group.

MEDICAL EXAMINATION PUBLISHING CO., INC., 3003 New Hyde Park Rd., New Hyde Park NY 11042. Editors: Janice Resniek and Esther Gumpert. Royalty schedule is negotiable. Free catalog. Submit outline. Reports in 1 month.

Medical: Medical texts and medical review books; monographs and training material for the medical, nursing and allied health professions.

MED-PSYCH PUBLICATIONS, Box 19746, West Allis, WI 53219. (414)778-1120. Editorial Director: Timothy E. Knier. Publishes hardcover and paperback originals. Averages 6-8 titles/year. Pays 10% royalty on wholesale price; no advance. Simultaneous and photocopied submissions OK. SASE. Reports in 2 months. Book catalog $1.

Nonfiction: Health, how-to psychology, and self-help. "We would like to see more para-psychology, folk medicine and counseling material. We do not want any text books." Query.

Recent Nonfiction Titles: *Second Chance*, by Sydney Banks; and *Sanity, Insanity and Common Sense*, by Suarez and Mills.

*MEMPHIS STATE UNIVERSITY PRESS, Memphis State University, Memphis TN 38152. (901)454-2752. Editor-in-Chief: J. Ralph Randolph. Publishes hardcover and paperback originals. Averages 5 titles/year. Each contract is subject to negotiation. Does about 10% subsidy publishing. Free book catalog and writer's guidelines. Will consider photocopied submissions. No computer printout or disk submissions. Query. Accepts outline/synopsis and 2 sample chapters. Reports in 3-6 months. SASE.

General Nonfiction: Regional emphasis. "We publish scholarly and trade nonfiction, books in the humanities, social sciences, and regional material. Interested in nonfiction material within the lower Mississippi River Valley. Tennessee history, and regional folklore."

Recent Nonfiction Titles: *A Guide to Wildflowers of the Mid-South*, by Arlo I. Smith (natural history); *Memphis Memoirs*, by Paul Coppock (history); and *Home Place*, by Robert Drake (growing up in west Tennessee).

Tips: Considering new material on a very limited basis until 1984.

MERCER UNIVERSITY PRESS, Macon GA 31207. (912)744-2880. Editor-in-Chief: Edd Rowell. Publishes hardcover originals. Averages 40 titles/year. Pays royalty. Simultaneous submissions OK. Computer printout and disk submissions OK. SASE. Reports in 2 weeks. Free book catalog.

Nonfiction: Reference, textbook. Subjects include history (of the American South); philosophy (Kant studies); religion, theology and biblical studies. Accepts nonfiction translations (German theology). Query. Accepts outline/synopsis and 2 sample chapters.

Recent Nonfiction Titles: *History and Criticism of the Marcan Hypothesis*, by Hans-Herbert Stoldt, and *The American Quest for the City of God*, by Leland D. Baldwin.

ARTHUR MERIWETHER, INC., 1529 Brook Dr., Downers Grove IL 60515. Editor-in-Chief: Arthur L. Zapel Jr. Publishes paperback originals on how-to subjects relating to youth activities or communication arts. Averages 10 book titles and 35 plays (1-act and 3-act)/year. Payment by royalty arrangement, based on wholesale and retail price. Marketed by direct mail. Book catalog $1. Editorial guidelines also available. Query, or a "brief synopsis or outline together with a brief page or 2 of writing style. Do not send ms until after response from us." Reports in 1 month. Enclose return postage.

Education: Mss for educational use in schools and churches. Subjects include speech, drama and English. Religious, self-help, how-to, sociology, Bible-study books are also published. Accepts artwork/photos and translations.

Recent Nonfiction Titles: *Playwriting for Amateurs*, by Thomas J. Hatton; *Who is the Man Called Jesus*, by Janet and Philip Meili; and *The Tangerine-Flavored Peanut Butter Gang*, by James Weekley.

Drama: Plays, satire and comedy. "We publish 25-35 yearly."

CHARLES E. MERRILL PUBLISHING CO., a Bell & Howell Co., 1300 Alum Creek Dr., Columbus OH 43216. Publishes hardcover and paperback originals. "Royalties and contract terms vary with the nature of the material. They are very competitive within each market area. Some projects are handled on an outright purchase basis." Publishes approximately 200 titles/year. Submit outline/synopsis and 3 sample chapters. Reports in 4-12 weeks. Will accept simultaneous submissions if notified. SASE.

Education Division: Editor: Ann Turpie. Publishes texts, workbooks, instructional tapes, overhead projection transparencies and programmed materials for elementary, junior high and high schools in all subject areas, primarily language arts and literature, mathematics, science and social studies (no juvenile stories or novels). **College Division:** Editor-in-Chief, Education, Special Education and Humanities, Business, Mathematics, Science and Technology: Alan B. Borne. Publishes college texts and multimedia programs.

JULIAN MESSNER,(Simon & Schuster Division of Gulf & Western Corp.), 1230 Avenue of the Americas, New York NY 10020. Editor-in-Chief: Iris Rosoff. Senior editor for elementary grades: Madelyn Klein Anderson. Senior Editor for junior and senior high school: Jane Steltenpohl. Hardcover originals. Averages 70 titles/year. Royalty varies. Advance averages $2,000. State availability of photos and/or illustrations to accompany ms. "Propose book ideas to start with. If the editor is interested, we will ask for detailed outline and sample chapters." Reports in 2-3 months. SASE. Free book catalog.
Juveniles: Nonfiction books only for young people.
Recent Nonfiction Titles: *Allergies and You*, by Sheila Burns; *Girls Can Be Anything They Want*, by Patricia Foot; *Solar Energy in Tomorrow's World*, by Reed Millard; and *The Stop Smoking Book for Teens*, by Curtis W. Casewit.

‡METAMORPHOUS PRESS, Subsidiary of Metamorphosis Enterprises, Inc., Box 1712, Lake Oswego OR 97034. (503)635-6709. Editor: Paul Roberge. Publishes hardcover, trade paperback and mass market paperback originals and hardcover and trade paperback reprints. Averages 6-8 titles/year. Pays 5-10% royalty on wholesale prices. No advance. Simultaneous and photocopied submissions OK. SASE. Reports in 1 week on queries; 1 month on mss. Free book catalog.
Nonfiction: Biography, how-to, illustrated book, reference, self-help, technical and textbook—all related to behavioral science only. Subjects include business and economics, health, psychology, sociology and new ideas in behavioral science. "We are interested in any well-proven new idea or philosophy in the behavioral science areas." Submit complete ms.
Recent Nonfiction Titles: *Magic Demystified*, by Lewis/Puchelik (psychology/communication); *Basic Techniques in NLP*, by Mell (subject overview workbook with cassette); and *Unfair Advantage*, by Moine (business communication).

‡MICROTREND, INC., 18141 Lawson Valley Rd., Jamul CA 92035. (619)445-8590. Publisher: Leslie S. Smith. Publishes trade paperback originals. Averages 12 titles/year. Pays 10-15% royalty on wholesale price. Offers variable advance. Simultaneous and photocopied submissions OK. SASE. Reports in 2 weeks on queries; 1 month on mss. Write for book catalog.
Nonfiction: How-to, self-help, and technical—only microcomputer subjects. Query.
Recent Titles: *IBM Graphics*, by Van Buren (how-to); *Encyclopedia of Operating Systems*, by Microtrend Staff (reference); and *Overcoming Computer Anxiety*, by Fry (self-help). Release date for these titles is February 1984.

‡MILLCREEK PRESS, Subsidiary of M.W.H. Limited, Box 10, 525 Main St., Bath, Ontario, Canada K0H 1G0. (613)352-7730. President: Michael Whitford. Publishes trade paperback originals. Averages 10 titles/year. Pays 10-12% royalty on retail price. "No advances to date." Photocopied submissions OK. Computer printout submissions OK; prefers letter quality to dot matrix. SAE and IRCs outside US. Reports in 2 weeks on queries; 6 weeks on mss.
Nonfiction: How-to, reference, self-help, technical, textbooks on hobbies, crafts, "post-retirement activities." No energy, ecology, keeping fit, religion. Accepts artwork/photos. Submit outline/synopsis and 3 sample chapters or complete ms. Accepts nonfiction translations from German and French.
Recent Nonfiction Titles: *Making It—A Guide to Successful Craft Retailing*, by various authors (how-to); *Human Factors in Furniture Design*, by M. Whitford.

MILLER BOOKS, 2908 W. Valley Blvd., Alhambra CA 91803. (213)284-7607. Subsidiaries include *San Gabriel Valley Magazine*, Miller Press and Miller Electric. Publisher: Joseph Miller. Publishes hardcover and trade paperback originals, and hardcover reprints. Averages 4 titles/year. Pays 10-15% royalty on retail price; buys some mss outright. Simultaneous and photocopied submissions OK. SASE ("no returns on erotic material"). Reports in 2 weeks on queries; 2 months on mss. Free book catalog.
Nonfiction: Cookbook, how-to, self-help, textbook and remedial textbooks. Subjects include Americana, animals, cooking and foods, history, philosophy and politics. "Remedial manuscripts are needed in most fields." No erotica. Submit complete ms. "Please don't send letters. Let us see your work."
Recent Nonfiction Title: *Republican Chaos*, by J. Miller (political textbook).
Fiction: Adventure, historical, humor, mystery and western. No erotica. Submit complete ms.
Recent Fiction Titles: *The Magic Story*, by F.V.R. Dey (positive thinking); *Headless Horseman*, by H. Boye (mystery and adventure); *Every Feeling Is Desire*, by James J. Smith.
Tips: "Write something good about people, places and our country. Avoid the negative—it doesn't sell."

*MIMIR PUBLISHERS, INC., Box 5011, Madison WI 53705. Editor-in-Chief: Henry H. Bakken. Hardcover and paperback originals. Specializes in books in the social sciences at college level. Averages 3-10 titles/year. 15% royalty on list price, "but nearly all titles are determined on a special contract." No advance. Subsidy publishes 50% of books. Subsidy publishing is offered "if the author wishes to proceed on our 50/50 type contract and share in the proceeds. Under this contract the author gets all the proceeds until he recovers his venture capital." Query or submit complete ms. Simultaneous ("if indicated") and photocopied submissions OK. Computer printout submissions OK. Reports in 2-4 months. SASE. Free book catalog.
Nonfiction: Publishes Americana; biography (limited); business; economics; history; law; philosophy; politics; sociology; and textbooks. Accepts artwork/photos.
Recent Nonfiction Titles: *The Hills of Home*, by Bakken; and *Wisconsin Income Tax Guide for Individuals*, by J.B. Bower.

MIT PRESS, 28 Carleton St., Cambridge MA 02142. (617)253-1693. Contact: Acquisition Department. Averages 100 titles/year. Pays 8-10% royalty on wholesale or retail price; $500-1,000 advance. SASE. Reports in 4-6 weeks. Free book catalog.
Nonfiction: Computer science/artificial intelligence, civil engineering/transportation, neuroscience, linguistics/psychology/philosophy, architecture, design, visual communication, economics, management, business, physics, math, history of science and technology. "Our books must reflect a certain level of technological sophistication. We do not want fiction, poetry, literary criticism, education, pure philosophy, European history before 1920, belles-lettres, drama, personal philosophies, or children's books." Submit outline/synopsis and sample chapters.
Recent Nonfiction Titles: *Architecture, Poetry, and Number in the Royal Palace at Caserta*, by George L. Hersey; *Folded, Spindled, and Mutilated—Economic Analysis and U.S. v. IBM*, by Fisher, et al.; *A Generative Theory of Tonal Music*, by Fred Lerdahl and Ray Jackendoff.

MODERN CURRICULUM PRESS, (formerly Follett's Children's Books), Children's Books, 13900 Prospect Road, Cleveland OH 44136. Contact: Mr. Lynn Keller. Publishes hardcover originals and some paperback reprints. Pays negotiable royalty and advance. Photocopied manuscripts are OK. Computer printout submissions OK. Reports in 4-6 weeks. SASE. Book catalog for SASE.
Tips: "We will be reviewing fiction and nonfiction mss for books of first and second grade reading level. Vocabulary should be limited to words that lowest grade reader can read and recognize themselves. It is not necessary to provide illustrations as those are handled by the publisher."

MONITOR BOOK CO., INC., 195 S. Beverly Dr., Beverly Hills CA 90212. (213)271-5558. Editor-in-Chief: Alan F. Pater. Hardcover originals. Pays 10% minimum royalty or by outright purchase, depending on circumstances; no advance. Send prints if photos and/or illustrations are to accompany ms. Reports in 2-4 months. No computer printout or disk submissions. SASE. Book catalog for SASE.
Nonfiction: Americana, biographies (only of well-known personalities); law and reference books. Recently published *What They Said in 1982: The Yearbook of World Opinion* (current quotations); *Anthology of Magazine Verse for 1981*; *United States Battleships: A History of America's Greatest Fighting Fleet*; *Galli-Curci's Life of Song* (a biography of the renowned opera coloratura); and *Children in Court*.

*MOREHOUSE-BARLOW CO., INC., 78 Danbury Rd., Wilton CT 06897. Editorial Director: Theodore A. McConnell. Publishes hardcover and paperback originals. Averages 20 titles/year. Pay 10% royalty on retail price. Simultaneous and photocopied submissions OK. No computer printout or disk submissions. SASE.
Nonfiction: Specializes in Anglican religious publishing. Theology, ethics, church history, pastoral counseling, liturgy and religious education. Accepts outline/synopsis and 3-5 sample chapters. No fiction, poetry or drama.
Recent Nonfiction Titles: *The Spirit of Anglicanism*, by William J. Wolf; *A Faithful Church*, by O.C. Edwards and John Westerhoff; and *The Episcopal Church Annual*.

WILLIAM MORROW AND CO., 105 Madison Ave., New York NY 10016. Publisher: Sherry W. Arden. Payment is on standard royalty basis. Query letter on all books. No unsolicited mss or proposals. Mss and proposals should be submitted through a literary agent.
Imprints: *Greenwillow Books* (juveniles), Susan Hirschman, editor. *Lothrop, Lee and Shephard* (juveniles), Dorothy Briley, editor. *Morrow Junior Books* (juveniles), David Reuther, editor. *Quill* (trade paperback), James D. Landis, publisher.
Affiliates: *Hearst Books* (trade). Editorial Director: Joan Nagy. *Hearst Marine Books* (nautical). Publisher: Paul Larsen.
General Trade: Publishes adult fiction, nonfiction, history, biography, arts, religion, poetry, how-to books and cookbooks. Length: 50,000-100,000 words.
Recent Titles: *The Man from St. Petersburg*, by Ken Follett; *Indecent Exposure*, by David McClintick; *The*

One Minute Manager, by Kenneth Blanchard Ph.D. and Spencer Johnson M.D.; and *Master of the Game*, by Sidney Sheldon.

MORROW JUNIOR BOOKS, 105 Madison Ave., New York NY 10016. (212)889-3050. Editor-in-Chief: David L. Reuther. Senior Editor: Pamela Pollock. Publishes hardcover originals. Publishes 50 titles/year. All contracts negotiated separately; advance varies. No simultaneous or photocopied submissions. SASE. Reports in 6 weeks. Free book catalog.
Nonfiction: Juveniles (trade books). No textbooks. Query.
Fiction: Juveniles (trade books).

MOSAIC PRESS, 358 Oliver Rd., Cincinnati OH 45215. (513)761-5977. Publisher: Miriam Irwin. Publishes hardcover originals. Averages 11 titles/year. Buys mss outright for $50. Simultaneous and photocopied submissions OK. Computer printout submissions OK. SASE. Reports in 2 weeks; "but our production, if ms is accepted, often takes 2 or 3 years." Book catalog $3.
Nonfiction: Biography, cookbook, humor, illustrated book and satire. Subjects include Americana, animals, art, business and economics, cooking and foods, health, history, hobbies, music, nature, sports and travel. Accepts artwork/photos. Interested in "beautifully written, delightful text. If factual, it must be extremely correct and authoritative. Our books are intended to delight, both in their miniature size, beautiful bindings and excellent writing." No occult, pornography, science fiction, fantasy or how-to. Query or submit outline/synopsis and sample chapters or complete ms.
Recent Nonfiction Titles: *Chess*, by Dr. R.R. McCready; *Lichens*, by Marj Westhafer (nature); and *The Lamp*, by Virginia Douglas Dawson (biography of Lloyd C. Douglas).

MOTORBOOKS INTERNATIONAL PUBLISHERS & WHOLESALERS, INC., Box 2, Osceola WI 54020. Director of Publications: William F. Kosfeld. Senior Editor: Barbara K. Harold. Hardcover and paperback originals. Offers 7-15% royalty on wholesale or retail price. Average advance: $1,500. Averages 10-12 titles/year. Simultaneous and photocopied submissions OK. Computer printout submissions OK. Reports in 2-3 months. SASE. Free book catalog.
Nonfiction: Publishes biography; history; how-to; photography; and motor sports as they relate to cars, trucks, motorcycles, motor sports and aviation (domestic and foreign). Submit outline/synopsis, 1-2 sample chapters and sample of illustrations. Accepts nonfiction translations from German/Italian. "State qualifications for doing book." Prefers not to see repair manuals.
Recent Nonfiction Titles: *Illustrated Ferrari Buyer's Guide*, by Dean Batchelor; *Automotive Fuel Injection Systems*, by Jan Norbye; and *Muscle Car Mania*, by Mitch Frumkin.

MOTT MEDIA, INC., PUBLISHERS, 1000 E. Huron, Milford MI 48042. Editor: Leonard George Goss. Associated with Evangelical Book Club. Hardcover and paperback originals (75%) and paperback reprints (25%). Averages 20-25 titles/year. Specializes in religious books, including trade and Christian school textbooks. Pays variable royalty on retail, depending on type of book. Query or submit outline/synopsis and sample chapters. Photocopied submissions OK. Reports in 1 month. SASE. Free book catalog.
Nonfiction: Publishes Americana (religious slant); biography (for juveniles on famous Christians, adventure-filled; for adults on Christian people, scholarly, new slant for marketing); how-to (for pastors, Christian laymen); juvenile (biographies, 30,000-40,000 words); politics (conservative, Christian approach); religious (conservative Christian); self-help (religious); and textbooks (all levels from a Christian perspective, all subject fields). No preschool materials. Main emphasis of all mss must be religious. Wants to know "vocation, present position and education of author; brief description of the contents of the book; basic readership for which the mss. was written; brief explanation of why the ms differs from other books on the same subject; the author's interpretation of the significance of this ms."
Recent Nonfiction Titles: *Social Justice and the Christian Church*, by Ronald Nash; *The Wisdom of God*, by David Jeremiah; *The Christian Legal Advisor*, by John Eidsmoe.
Fiction: "We're beginning to consider a limited amount of fiction for the Christian consumer. No overt moral or crisis decision necessary, but fiction must demonstrate a Christian perspective."

*MOUNTAIN PRESS PUBLISHING CO., 1600 North Ave. W, Missoula MT 59806. Publisher: David P. Flaccus. Hardcover and paperback originals (90%) and reprints (10%). Royalty of 12% of net amount received; no advance. Subsidy publishes less than 5% of books. "Top-quality work in very limited market only." Averages 12 titles/year. State availability of photos and/or illustrations to accompany ms. Simultaneous submissions OK. Computer printout and disk submissions OK. Reports in 2-4 weeks. SASE. Free book catalog.
Nonfiction: Publishes history (western Americana); hobbies, how-to (angling, hunting); nature (geology, habitat and conservation); outdoor recreation (backpacking, fishing, etc.); technical (wood design and technology); and textbooks. Looks for "target audience, organization, quality of writing and style compatibility with current list and goals." Accepts nonfiction translations.

Recent Nonfiction Titles: *Death, Too, for the-Heavy-Runner*, by Ben Bennett; *We Seized Our Rifles*, by Lee Silliman; and *American Frontier Tales*, by Helen Addison Howard.

MOUNTAIN STATE PRESS, University of Charleston, Charleston WV 25304. Publishes hardcover and paperback originals. Pays royalty. No advance. SASE with queries or submissions. Effort is made to report within in a reasonable time, "but we ask for patience."
Nonfiction, Fiction: Especially interested in books about West Virginia or by West Virginians, but without stereotyped characters or shallow viewpoint.
Nonfiction Titles: *As I Remember It*; *Peaceful Patriot*.
Fiction Titles: *Life at an Early Age*; *Six Miles Out*.
Poetry Titles: *Of Bitter Choice*; *Anse on Island Creek*.
Tips: Positive approach preferred. Obvious insertions of place names or sensational scenes not appreciated.

THE MOUNTAINEERS BOOKS, 715 Pike St., Seattle WA 98101. (206)682-4636. Manager: Donna DeShazo. Publishes hardcover and paperback originals (85%) and reprints (15%). Averages 10-15 titles/year. Offers 10-15% royalty based on wholesale or retail price. Offers advance on occasion. Photocopied submissions OK. SASE. Reports in 6-8 weeks. Free book catalog.
Nonfiction: Recreation; sports; and outdoor "how-to" books. Accepts artwork/photos. "We specialize only in books dealing with mountaineering, hiking, backpacking, skiing, snowshoeing, canoeing, bicycling, etc. These can be either how-to-do-it, where-to-do-it (guidebooks), or accounts of mountain-related experiences." Does *not* want to see "anything dealing with hunting; fishing or motorized travel." Submit outline/synopsis and minimum of 2 sample chapters. Accepts nonfiction translations. Looks for "expert knowledge, good organization."
Recent Nonfiction Titles: *Trekking in Nepal*, by Stephen Bezruchka (guidebook); *The Last Step*, by Rick Ridgeway (expedition account); and *Snowshoeing*, by Gene Prater (how-to).
Fiction: Adventure and humor. Accepts fiction translations. "We might consider an exceptionally well-done book-length manuscript on mountaineering. It could be humorous and/or could be aimed at the juvenile audience." Does *not* want poetry or mystery. Query first.

JOHN MUIR PUBLICATIONS, Box 613, Santa Fe NM 87501. (505)982-4078. Project Co-ordinator: Lisa Cron. Publishes trade paperback originals. Averages 6 titles/year. Pays 8-12% royalty; offers variable advance. Simultaneous and photocopied submissions OK. Computer printout submissions OK. SASE. Reports in 1 month on queries; 2 months on mss. Free book catalog.
Nonfiction: How-to, illustrated book and self-help. Accepts artwork/photos. Subjects include automobile repair manuals, health, music, and travel. "We are interested in manuscripts written with warmth, wit, humor and accuracy and which help promote self-sufficiency. The topic of such a submission is open; we'll look at almost anything. However, we don't publish theory books or political treatises or books like 'The History of Tennis Memorabilia'; in other words, we want manuscripts that offer practical applications." Submit outline/synopsis and at least 3 sample chapters.
Recent Nonfiction Titles: *A Guide to Midwifery*, by Elizabeth Davis; *The People's Guide to Camping in Mexico*, by Carl Franz; and *How to Keep Your VW Rabbit Alive*, by Richard Sealey.
Tips: Readers include "counterculture people and those in the mainstream who have become dissatisfied with the status quo. *Please* take a look at our books before submitting a manuscript. We continue to get textbook-type submissions—dryly written, and with no practical application. It is their friendliness and humor that set our books apart. Also we often get queries for 'the children's book editor' or 'the poetry editor' when a bit of research would reveal we publish neither children's nor poetry books."

MUSEUM OF NEW MEXICO PRESS, Box 2087, Santa Fe NM 87503. (505)827-2352. Editor-in-Chief: Sarah Nestor. Director: James Mafchir. Hardcover and paperback originals (90%) and reprints (10%). Averages 4-6 titles/year. Royalty of 10% of list after first 1,000 copies; no advance. Prints preferred for illustrations; transparencies best for color. Sources of photos or illustrations should be indicated for each. Simultaneous and photocopied submissions OK. Submit complete mss, addressed to James Mafchir, Publisher. Mss should be typed double-spaced, follow Chicago *Manual of Style*, and be accompanied by information about the author's credentials and professional background. Reports in 1-2 months. SASE. Free book catalog.
Nonfiction: "We publish both popular and scholarly books on regional anthropology, history, fine and folk arts; geography, natural history, the Americas and the Southwest; regional cookbooks. Art, biography (regional and Southwest); music, nature, reference, scientific and technical. Accepts nonfiction translations.

‡**MUSEUM OF NORTHERN ARIZONA PRESS**, Box 720, Rt. 4, Flagstaff AZ 86001. (602)774-5211. Managing Editor: Diana Lubick. Publishes hardcover and trade paperback originals. Averages 6-8 titles/year. Pays one-time fee on acceptance of ms and at subsequent reprints. No advance. Simultaneous and photocopied submissions OK. No computer printout or disk submissions. SASE. Reports in 1 month on queries; 2 months on mss. Free book catalog.

Nonfiction: Coffee table book, reference, technical on Southwest, art, nature, science. Especially needs ms "relating directly to the culture and history of the Colorado Plateau for people interested in the Southwest—science, the arts and culture." Query or submit outline/synopsis and 3-4 sample chapters. Accepts artwork/photos.

Recent Nonfiction Titles: *Basket Weavers* (Indian arts and crafts); *Water on the Plateau* (science), *Aspects of Vertebrate* (pabeotology), by multiple authors; *Navajo Painting* (Navajo easel art); *Dinosaurs of the Colorado Plateau* (dinosaurs).

Fiction, Poetry: Accepts fiction and poetry translations from Hopi and Navajo.

MUSIC SALES CORP., 799 Broadway, New York NY 10003. (212)254-2100. Imprints include *Acorn, Amsco, Anfor, Ariel, Award, Consolidated, Embassy, Oak, Yorktown, Music Sales Ltd.*, London, *Wise Pub., Ashdown Ltd.*, and *Music Sales*, Australia. Editor-in-Chief: Eugene Weintraub. Contact: Barry Edward, President (NY office). Publishes paperback originals (95%) and reprints (5%). Publishes 75 titles/year. Standard publishing contracts. Simultaneous and photocopied submissions OK.

Nonfiction: Instructional music books on blues, bluegrass, classical, folk and jazz; also technical, theory, reference and pop music personalities. Music Sales Corporation publishes and distributes a complete line of quality music instruction books for every musician from beginner to professional.

Recent Nonfiction Titles: *Jazz Violin*, by Stephane Grappelli and Matt Glaser (history, technique, transcriptions); *Fingerpicking Gershwin*, by John Miller (guitar arrangements); *Studio Recording*, by Fred Miller; *Teaching Piano*, by Denis Agay; *About a Bunch of Roses Folksongs*, (England, Scotland, et al); *Masters of Old Time Fiddling*, by Miles Krassen.

THE NAIAD PRESS, INC., Box 10543, Tallahassee FL 32302. (904)539-9322. Editorial Director: Barbara Grier. Publishes paperback originals. Averages 12 titles/year. Pays 20% royalty on wholesale or retail price; no advance. Reports in 6 weeks. SASE. Book catalog for SASE.

Fiction: "We publish lesbian fiction, preferably lesbian/feminist fiction. We are not impressed with the 'oh woe' school and prefer realistic (i.e., happy) novels." Query. "We emphasize fiction, and are reading manuscripts in that area heavily now."

Recent Fiction and Nonfiction Titles: *Faultline*, by Sheila Ortiz Taylor; *To the Cleveland Station*, by Carol Anne Douglas; and *Mrs. Porter's Letter*, by Vicki P. McConnell.

*NATIONAL ASSOCIATION OF COLLEGE AND UNIVERSITY BUSINESS OFFICERS, One Dupont Circle, Suite 510, Washington DC 20036. (202)861-2500. Director, Communications: Mr. Abbott Wainright. Publishes hardcover and trade paperback originals. Averages 5 titles/year. Subsidy publishes 40% of books based on "relevance to publisher's subject needs." Buys mss outright for $500-2,000. Simultaneous and photocopied submissions OK. SASE. Reports in 1 week on queries; 3 weeks on mss. Free book catalog.

Imprints: *NACUBO*, (nonfiction), Mr. Abbott Wainright, Director, Communications.

Nonfiction: Technical and textbook. Subjects include business and economics. "We're looking for mss on the effects of demographic changes in the traditional college-age population on colleges and universities; also, mss on college and university planning, management, accounting, costing, investments, real estate, financial reporting, and personnel administration. We publish books that provide immediate help with real problems, as opposed to conceptual studies. Our audience is made up of college and university senior administrators." Query or submit outline/synopsis and sample chapters or complete ms which demonstrates "applicability to business and financial administration in higher education. We have a narrow audience, so recommend queries if there is any doubt."

Recent Nonfiction Titles: *College & University Business Administration*, 4th ed., edited by Welzenbach; *A Cost Accounting Handbook for College & University*, by James A. Hyatt; *Contracting for Services*, by Claudia Madsen; *Financial Conditions of Colleges and Universities*, by Nathan Dickmeyer.

NATIONAL BOOK COMPANY, 333 S.W. Park Ave., Portland OR 97205. (503)228-6345. Imprints include Halcyon House. Editorial Director: Carl W. Salser. Senior Editor: John R. Kimmel. Manager of Copyrights: Lucille Fry. Publishes hardcover and paperback originals (95%) and paperback reprints (2%). Averages 28 titles/year. Pays 5-15% royalty on wholesale or retail price; no advance. Simultaneous and photocopied submissions OK. Computer printout submissions OK. SASE. Reports in 2 months. Free catalog for SASE.

Nonfiction: Art, business/economics, health, history, music, politics, psychology, reference, science, technical and textbooks (materials suitable for educational uses in all categories). "The vast majority of titles are individualized instruction programs for educational consumers. Prospective authors should be aware of this and be prepared for this type of format, although content, style and appropriateness of subject matter are the major criteria by which submissions are judged. We are most interested in materials in the areas of the language arts, social studies and the sciences." Query, submit outline/synopsis and 2-5 sample chapters or complete ms.

Recent Nonfiction Titles: *Introductory Chemistry*, by E. Bushman; *Statistics*, by N. Crowhurst; *Personal Shorthand, Cardinal Series* Books 1, 2 and 3, by Barrett, Salser and Yerian.

THE NATIONAL GALLERY OF CANADA, Publications Division, Ottawa, Ontario, Canada K1A 0M8. (613)995-6526. Head: Peter L. Smith. Publishes hardcover and paperback originals. Averages 15 titles/year. Pays in outright purchase of $1,500-2,500; advance averages $700. Photocopied submissions OK. Reports in 3 months. SASE. Free sales catalog.

Nonfiction: "In general, we publish only *solicited* manuscripts on art, particularly Canadian art, and must, publish them in English and French. Exhibition catalogs are commissioned, but we are open (upon approval by Curatorial general editors) to mss for the various series, monographic and otherwise, that we publish. All mss should be directed to our Editorial Coordinator, who doubles as manuscript editor. Since we publish translations into French, authors have access to French Canada and the rest of Francophonie. Because our titles are distributed by University of Chicago Press, authors have the attention of European as well as American markets."

Recent Nonfiction Titles: *Modernism in Quebec Art 1916-1946*, by Jean-René Ostiguy; *Richard Long*, by Richard Long; *Fantin-Latour*, by Douglas Druick and Michel Hoog.

NATIONAL PUBLISHERS OF THE BLACK HILLS, INC., Fair Chase Publications, Box 302, Rapid City SD 57709. (605)394-4993. Senior Editor: Jean Babrick. Publishes hardcover and trade and mass market paperback originals and trade paperback reprints. Averages 10 titles/year. Pays negotiable royalty; offers negotiable advance. Simultaneous and photocopied submissions OK. Computer printout and disk submissions OK; prefers letter quality to dot matrix printouts. SASE. Reports in 3 weeks on queries; 5 weeks on mss.

Imprints: *Fair Chase* (outdoor topics from adventure to how-to; nature-oriented "coffee table" books), John Hauer, publisher, (605)394-4995.

Nonfiction: "Coffee table" book, technical, textbook on animals (wild); business and economics texts; medical administrative assisting; computer science texts; native; travel; English texts. Immediate needs include basic electronics texts, basic geophysical surveying texts, technical writing texts (for post high-school education market). Outdoor books of many types, but preferably with a "Fair Chase" theme. Nature themes will also receive consideration. Query or submit outline/synopsis and 3 sample chapters or complete ms.

Recent Nonfiction Titles: *Tourism*, by Jan van Harssel (travel textbook); *Business Mathematics*, by Marie Ritten (math textbook); and *Fundamentals of English*, by Torrey, Sloat and Kinyon (English textbook); NATARS (computer reservations textbook); *Orthopedics* (medical assisting textbook).

NATIONAL TEXTBOOK CO., 4255 W. Touhy Ave., Lincolnwood IL 60646-1975. (312)679-4210. Editorial Director: Leonard I. Fiddle. Mss purchased on either royalty or buy-out basis. Averages 9 titles/year. Free book catalog and writer's guidelines. Send sample chapter and outline or contents. Reports in 4 months. Enclose return postage.

Textbooks: Major emphasis being given to language arts area, especially secondary level material. Gay E. Menges, Language Arts Editor.

Recent Nonfiction Titles: *Reading by Doing*, by Simmons & Palmer (critical reading); *Play Production Today*, by Beck et al. (theater); and *Writing by Doing*, by Sohn and Enger (composition).

NATUREGRAPH PUBLISHERS, INC., Box 1075, Happy Camp CA 96039. (916)493-5353. Editor: Barbara Brown. Quality trade books. Averages 5 titles/year. "We offer 10% of wholesale; 12½% after 10,000 copies are sold. To speed things up, queries should include: 1)summary, 2)detailed outline, 3)comparison to related books, 4)2 sample chapters, 5)availability and samples of any photos or illustrations, 6)author background. Send ms only on request." Photocopied submissions OK. No computer printout or disk submissions. Reports in 1-2 months. SASE. Free book catalog.

Nonfiction: Primarily publishes nonfiction for the layman in 7 general areas: natural history (biology, geology, ecology, astronomy); American Indian (historical and contemporary); outdoor living (backpacking, wild edibles, etc.); land and gardening (modern homesteading); crafts and how-to; holistic health (natural foods and healing arts); PRISM Editions (Baha'i and other new age approaches to harmonious living). All material must be well-grounded; author must be professional, and in command of effective style. Our natural history and American Indian lines can be geared for educational markets."

Recent Nonfiction Titles: *All the World Is Kin*, by Bernice Espy Hicks; *Circle Without End*, By Frances G. and Gerald S. Lombardi (sourcebook of American Indian ethics); *The Northwoods Wildlife Region*, by Jay and Constance Conrader; and *Oaks of North America*, by Howard Miller and Samuel Lamb.

THE NAUTICAL & AVIATION PUBLISHING CO. OF AMERICA, INC., 8 Randall St., Annapolis MD 21401. (301)267-8522. President: Mr. Jan Snouck-Hurgronje. Publishes hardcover originals (33%) and reprints (33%) and imported books (33%). Pays 14-18% royalty on net selling price; sometimes offers advance. Simultaneous and photocopied submissions OK. No computer printout or disk submissions. Reports in 2 weeks.

Nonfiction: History, biography, reference. Accepts nonfiction translations from Russian, German, and Japanese. Especially needs mss on military topics, history, reference. Looking for books on individual aircraft and

Marine Corps history. Submit outline/synopsis, 2-3 sample chapters and table of contents. Accepts artwork/photos.
Recent Nonfiction Titles: *Naval Air War Series* and *American Submarine*, 2nd ed., by Norman Polmar.
Fiction: Military. "Would consider reprinting of original novels." Submit complete ms.

NAVAL INSTITUTE PRESS, Annapolis MD 21402. Acquisitions Editors: Richard R. Hobbs, Deborah Guberti. Press Director: Thomas F. Epley. Averages 30 titles/year. Pays 14-18-21% royalty based on net sales; modest advance. Simultaneous and photocopied submissions OK. SASE. Reports in 2 weeks (queries); 6 weeks (others). Free book catalog.
Nonfiction: "We are interested in naval and maritime subjects: navigation, naval history, biographies of naval leaders and naval aviation."
Fiction: Limited, very high quality fiction on naval and maritime themes.
Recent Titles: *U.S. Aircraft Carriers: An Illustrated Design History*, by Norman Friedman; *Empires in the Balance: Japanese and Allied Pacific Strategies to April 1942*, by H.P. Willmott; and *Battleship Sailor*, by Theodore C. Mason.

NAZARENE PUBLISHING HOUSE, Box 527, Kansas City MO 64141. Trade name: Beacon Hill Press of Kansas City. Betty Fuhrman. Publishes hardcover and paperback originals and reprints. Offers "standard contract (sometimes flat rate purchase). Advance on royalty is paid on first 1,000 copies at publication date. Pays 10% on first 10,000 copies and 12% on subsequent copies at the end of each calendar year." Averages 60-65 titles/year, 5-10 of them freelance. Follow *Chicago Manual of Style*. Address all mss to Book Editor. Queries/mss may be routed to other editors in the publishing group. Reports in 2-5 months. "Book Committee meets quarterly to select, from the mss which they have been reading in the interim, those which will be published." Query. SASE.
Nonfiction: "Basically religious, (inspirational, devotional, Bible study, beliefs). Doctrinally must conform to the evangelical, Wesleyan tradition. Conservative view of Bible. Personal religious experience. We want the accent on victorious life, definitely upbeat. Social action themes must have spiritual base and motivation. Popular style books should be under 128 pages." Interested in business and professional books on church administration, Sunday school, etc. Textbooks are "almost exclusively done on assignment." Query. Accepts outline/synopsis and sample chapters. Length: 10,000-30,000 words.
Recent Nonfiction Titles: *Justin, Heaven's Baby*, by Sharon Marshall; *Where On Earth Is God?*, by Richard Howard; *Building a Caring-Sharing Community of Believers*, by Elvin M. Powers; *Enjoy!*, by Virginia Kirley Leih.
Fiction: "Currently a moratorium on fiction."

NC PRESS, 31 Portland St., Toronto, Ontario, Canada M5V 2V9. (416)593-6284. Editorial Director: Caroline Walker. Publishes hardcover and paperback originals and reprints and a full line of children's books. Averages 10-15 titles/year. Pays royalty on list under 50% discount. Simultaneous and photocopied submissions OK. Computer printout and Wordstar CP/M 8" diskettes preferred. SASE. Free book catalog.
Nonfiction: "We generally publish books of social/political relevance either on contemporary topics of concern (current events, ecology, etc.), or historical studies. We publish primarily Canadiana. US authors must have US co-publisher—i.e., we're only interested in Canadian rights and cannot publish US authors without US co-publisher." Accepts nonfiction translations from French. Submit outline/synopsis and 1-2 sample chapters.
Recent Nonfiction Titles: *This Thing of Darkness*, by Norman Elder (travel/anthropology); *Beginnings*, edited by John Moss (literary criticism); and *Columbo's Book of Marvels and Names and Nicknames*, by John Robert Colombo (trivia).

NELLEN PUBLISHING CO., INC., Box 18, Newton NJ 07860. (201)948-3141. Editorial Director: Nancy W. Dunn. Senior Editor: M.F. Valentine. Publishes hardcover and paperback originals. Publishes 10 titles/year. Pays 10-12½-15% royalty on wholesale price; no advance. Photocopied submissions OK. Reports in 2-4 weeks. SASE. Free book catalog.
Nonfiction: "We are seeking titles of interest to both trade and scholarly markets. Our emphasis is on the trade. If a book is addressed to the scholarly or technical market we may ask the author to rewrite with the larger market in mind. Our subject areas are wide: history, politics, economics, health, crime, self-help, management, the arts, etc. We are especially interested in Americana books on names (like our Smith book) and genealogy." Submit outline/synopsis and sample chapters. "With a clear synopsis of the book we appreciate knowing something about the author. We prefer authors with published works to their credit. If not books, at least magazine or journal articles."
Recent Nonfiction Titles: *The Book of Smith*, by Edson C. Smith (fact book); *Managing Change*, by John Flaherty (management); and *Roots of Crime*, by Thomas Marsh.

THOMAS NELSON PUBLISHERS, Nelson Place at Elm Hill Pike, Nashville TN 37214. (615)889-9000. Editor: Lawrence M. Stone. Publishes hardcover and paperback originals (95%) and reprints (5%). Averages 65 titles/year. Pays royalty or by outright purchase; sometimes an advance. Photocopied submissions OK. Computer printout submissions OK. SASE. Reports in 6-8 weeks. Book catalog for SASE.
Nonfiction: Reference, and religious (must be orthodox Christian in theology). Accepts outline/synopsis and 3 sample chapters. Looks for "orthodoxy, honesty, quality, validity."
Recent Nonfiction Titles: *Guideposts Family Topical Concordance to the Bible* (reference); *Guest of the Revolution*, by Kathryn Koob (biography); and *The Secret Kingdom*, by Pat Robertson with Bob Slosser (religious).
Recent Fiction Titles: *The Wisest Fools*, by Michael Ross; and *Chase the Wind*, by Deborah Lawrence and Aggie Villanueva.

NELSON-HALL PUBLISHERS, 111 N. Canal St., Chicago IL 60606. (312)922-0856. Editorial Director: Harold Wise, Ph.D. Publishes hardcover and paperback originals. Averages 105 titles/year. Pays 15% maximum royalty on retail price; average advance. Photocopied submissions OK. SASE. Reports in 1 month. Free book catalog.
Nonfiction: Textbooks and general scholarly books in the social sciences. Query.
Recent Nonfiction Titles: *Criminal Evidence*, by Waltz; *Contemporary American Social Problems*, by Bagby; *Guide to Confident Public Speaking*, by Sayer; *Introductory Philosophy*, by McLaren.

NEW AMERICAN LIBRARY, 1633 Broadway, New York NY 10019. (212)397-8000. Imprints include Signet, Mentor, Classic, Plume and Meridian. Publisher: Elaine Koster. Editor-in-Chief/Paperback: William Grose. Editor-in-Chief/Hardcover: John Dodds. Publishes hardcover and paperback originals and hardcover reprints. Publishes 350 titles/year. Royalty is "variable;" offers "substantial" advance. Simultaneous and photocopied submissions OK. Computer printout submissions OK. Reports in 2 months. SASE. Free book catalog.
Tips: Queries/mss may be routed to other editors in the publishing group.

‡NEW CENTURY PUBLISHERS, INC., Recent corporate acquisitions: Follett trade books, Butterick, Association Press, Winchester Press. General Books Editorial Offices: 245 E. 72nd St., New York NY 10021. (212)628-2733. Editor: Robin Little. Publishes hardcover originals, trade paperback originals, hardcover and trade paperback reprints. Averages 50 titles/year. Pays 10-15% royalty on retail price; buys some mss outright for $1,500-7,500. Offers average $5,000 advance. Simultaneous and photocopied submissions OK. No computer printout or disk submissions. SASE. Reports in 3 weeks on queries; 1 month on mss. Free book catalog.
Nonfiction: Biography, coffee table book, cookbook, how-to, humor, illustrated book, juvenile, reference, self-help and technical books on Americana, animals, art, business and economics, cooking and foods, health, history, hobbies, music, nature, philosophy, photography, politics, psychology, recreation, religion, sociology, sports and travel. Accepts artwork/photos. "Since our books are very broad based, we do not limit the kinds of nonfiction we publish except submissions that are in bad taste. We are looking for well-written, popular and original books." Accepts nonfiction translations from French, German, Spanish. Submit complete ms.
Recent Nonfiction Titles: *In Search of Gandhi*, by Sir Richard Attenborough (autobiography); *The IRA Handbook*, by Michael Pancheri and David Flynn (financial); and *Executive Style*, by Diana Jewell and Mary Fiedorek (fashion).

NEW LEAF PRESS, INC., Box 1045, Harrison AR 72061. Editor-in-Chief: Bertha Sprenger. Hardcover and paperback originals. Publishes 10 titles/year. Specializes in charismatic books. Pays 10% royalty on first 10,000 copies, paid once a year; no advance. Send photos and illustrations to accompany ms. Simultaneous and photocopied submissions OK. Computer printout and disk submissions OK. SASE. Reports in 3 months. Free book catalog.
Nonfiction: Biography; self-help. Charismatic books; life stories; how-to live the Christian life. Length: 100-400 pages. Submit complete ms.
Recent Titles: *Run to the Roar*, by Tammy Bakker with Cliff Dudley (fear); *Released to Reign*, by Charles Trombley (the Christian's place); and *Supreme Commander*, by Col. Henry C. Godman with Cliff Dudley (testimony and history).

NEW READERS PRESS, Publishing division of Laubach Literacy International, Box 131, Syracuse NY 13210. Assistant Editorial Director: Kay Koschnick. Publishes paperback originals. Averages 15 titles/year. "Most of our sales are to public education systems, including adult basic education programs, with some sales to volunteer literacy programs, private human-services agencies, prisons, and libraries with outreach programs for poor readers." Pays royalty on retail price, or by outright purchase. "Rate varies according to type of publication and length of ms." Advance is "different in each case, but does not exceed projected royalty for first year." Photocopied submissions OK. Computer printout and disk submissions OK; prefers letter quality to dot matrix printouts. Reports in 2 months. SASE. Free book catalog.

Nonfiction: "Our audience is adults and older teenagers with limited reading skills (6th grade level and below). We publish basic education materials in reading and writing, math, social studies, health, science, and English-as-a-second-language for double illiterates. We are particularly interested in materials that fulfill curriculum requirements in these areas. Mss must be not only easy to read (3rd-6th grade level) but mature in tone and concepts. We would consider submissions in the curriculum areas of reading skills development, composition, grammar, practical math, social studies (economics and U.S. history), science, self-awareness and human relations, and adapting to U.S. culture (for functionally illiterate English-as-a-second language students). We would also consider materials for specialized audiences of nonreaders, such as the learning disabled or speakers of nonstandard dialects. We are not interested in biography, poetry, or anything at all written for children." Accepts outline/synopsis and 1-3 sample chapters depending on how representative of the total they are." Recently published: *Breakthrough to Math Series*, by Glassboro State College Adult Education Resource Center; *Crime and the Law*, by Maxine Phillips; and *Focus on Phonics-3*, by Gail Rice (student workbook and teacher's edition).

Fiction: "We're looking for original, realistic fiction written for adults, but written at a 3rd-grade reading level. We want well-developed believable characters in realistic situations. We want mss of approximately 12,000 to 15,000 words that can be published as short novels. We are not interested in formula fiction but would consider adventure, mystery, or romance of interest to the adult or teenager. We do not want simplified versions of already published works." Query. Looks for "plots of interest to our audience without too many characters or too much complication."

Recent Fiction Titles: *A New Life* by Roy Sorrels; *Just Once*, by Mary Blount Christian.

NEW YORK UNIVERSITY PRESS, Washington Square, New York NY 10003. (212)598-2886. Contact: Editor. Publishes hardcover and scholarly paperback originals. Averages 50 titles/year. Pays negotiable royalty. No advance. Reports in 3 weeks. Free book catalog.

Nonfiction: Scholarly works in the areas of art history; history; New York City regional history; philosophy; politics; literary criticism; medieval studies. Submit precis and vita.

Recent Nonfiction Titles: *Watergate Games*, by Douglas Muzzio (game theory by a political scientist); *Medieval Experience*, by Jill Claster; and *The Victorian Imagination*, by William E. Buckler (literary criticism).

‡NEW YORK ZOETROPE, INC., 80 E. 11th St., New York NY 10003. (212)254-8235. Contact: James Monaco. Publishes hardcover and trade paperback originals and hardcover and trade paperback reprints. Averages 25 titles/year. Pays 10-20% royalty on wholesale prices or makes outright purchase of $500-1,000. Offers average $200 advance. Simultaneous and photocopied submissions OK. SASE. Reports in 2 weeks on queries; 2 months on mss.

Nonfiction: Coffee table book, juvenile, reference, technical and textbook. Subjects include business and economics, travel and media. Interested especially in computer subjects. No fiction. Query.

Recent Nonfiction Titles: *The Running Game*, by John O'Leary (journal); *Encyclopedia of Television*, by Les Brown (reference); and *Hollywood: The First 100 Years*, by Torrence (art).

NEWCASTLE PUBLISHING CO., INC., 13419 Saticoy, North Hollywood CA 91605. (213)873-3191. Editor-in-Chief: Alfred Saunders. Publishes trade paperback originals and trade paperback reprints. Averages 8 titles/year. Pays 5-10% royalty on retail price; no advance. Simultaneous and photocopied submissions OK. SASE. Reports in 3 weeks on queries; 6 weeks on mss. Free book catalog.

Nonfiction: How-to, self-help, metaphysical, new age. Subjects include health (physical fitness, diet and nutrition); psychology; and religion. "Our audience is made up of college students and college-age non-students; also, adults aged 25 and up." No biography or travel. Query or submit outline/synopsis and sample chapters. Looks for "something to grab the reader so that he/she will readily remember that passage."

Recent Nonfiction Titles: *Handwriting Analysis: The Complete Basic Book*, by Amend & Ruiz (occult/psychology); *Numerology: The Complete Guide*, by Matthew Goodwin (occult); *Past Lives/Future Lives*, by Dr. Bruce Goldberg (occult/psychology); and *Energy Ecstasy and Your Vital Chakras*, by Bernard Gunther.

NICHOLS PUBLISHING CO., Box 96, New York NY 10024. Editorial Director: Linda Kahn. Publishes hardcover originals. Averages 25-30 titles/year. Simultaneous and photocopied submissions OK. Computer printout submissions OK. Reports in 6 weeks. SASE. Book catalog for SASE.

Nonfiction: Professional/academic materials in architecture, business, education, engineering, international affairs, investment, and energy topics. Accepts artwork/photos. Query with outline, table of contents, 2 sample chapters.

Recent Nonfiction Titles: *The Financing and Financial Control of Small Enterprise Development*, by Ray and Hutchison; *Microcomputers in Building Appraisal*, by Brandon and Moore; *Dictionary of New Information Technology*, by Meadows; *World Yearbook of Education: Computers and Education*.

‡NIMBUS PUBLISHING LIMITED, Subsidiary of H.H. Marshall Ltd., Box 9301, Station A, Halifax, Nova Scotia, Canada B3K 5N5. (902)454-8381. Contact: Elizabeth Eve. Publishes hardcover and trade paperback originals (90%) and trade paperback reprints. Averages 5 titles/year. Pays 4-10% royalty on retail price. Photocopied submissions OK. Computer printout and disk submissions OK. SASE. Reports in 2 months on queries; 4 months on mss. Free book catalog.

Imprints: Petheric Press (nonfiction and fiction), contact: Elizabeth Eve.

Nonfiction: Biography, coffee table books, cookbooks, how-to, humor, illustrated books, juvenile, books of regional interest on art, cooking and foods, history, nature, travel, regional. Accepts artwork/photos. "We do some specialized publishing; otherwise, our audience is the tourist and trade market in Nova Scotia." Query or submit outline/synopsis and a minimum of 1 sample chapter.

Recent Nonfiction Titles: *Common Sense Book of Canoeing*, by Keating (guide to canoeing); *Halifax*, by Hines (96-page book of colored pictures of the city); *Canada's Flowers*; *History of the Corvettes 1939-45*, by Lynch.

‡**NORTH LIGHT**, Imprint of Writer's Digest Books, 32 Berwick Court, Fairfield CT 06430. (203)336-4225. Editor/Design Director: Fritz Henning. Publishes hardcover originals and trade paperback originals. Averages 8-10 titles/year. Pays 10% royalty on net receipts. Offers $1,000-3,000 advance. Simultaneous submissions and photographs of artwork OK. SASE. Reports in 2 weeks on queries; 2 months on mss. Free book catalog.

Nonfiction: How-to and reference art books. Subjects include instructional art. Especially needs books on acrylic painting; framing paintings/making frames; drawing basics; pen and ink drawing. Does not want "prestige-type art books not focusing on how-to art instruction." Query or submit outline/synopsis and examples of artwork.

Recent Nonfiction Titles: *Watercolor Energies*, by Frank Webb (art instruction—intermediate level); *Painter's Guide to Lithography*, by John Muench (instruction—advanced); and *Graphics Handbook*, by Howard Munce (instruction—beginners).

NORTHEASTERN UNIVERSITY PRESS, 17 Cushing Hall, Northeastern University, 360 Huntingon Ave., Boston MA 02115. (617)437-2783. Editors: Robilee Smith and Deborah Kops. Publishes hardcover originals and paperback reprints. Averages 10 titles/year. Pays 7-10% royalty on wholesale price. Simultaneous and photocopied submissions OK. "Both computer printout and disk submissions are welcome for production purposes, but submissions must be printed on paper for our review process." SASE. Reports in 1 month on queries; 3 months on mss.

Nonfiction: Biography, reference and scholarly. Subjects include history, music, politics, French literature, criminal justice, literary criticism, women's studies, New England regional and scholarly material. "We are looking for scholarly works of high quality, particularly in the fields of American history, criminal justice, literary criticism, French literature, music and women's studies. Our books are read by scholars, students, and a limited trade audience." Submit outline/synopsis and 2-3 sample chapters.

Recent Nonfiction Titles: *The Divine Politician: Samuel Cooper and the American Revolution in Boston*, by Charles Akers (American history); *Judge, Lawyer, Victim, Thief: Women, Gender Roles and Criminal Justice*, edited by Nicole Rafter and Elizabeth Stanko; and *Letters of H. L. Mencken*, edited by Guy L. Forgue (literature reprint).

Poetry: "We will consider translations, particularly of French poetry." Submit complete ms.

Recent Poetry Title: *Roof Slates and Other Poems of Pierre Reverdy*, by Mary Ann Caws and Patricia Terry (verse and prose translations of the French).

NORTHERN ILLINOIS UNIVERSITY PRESS, DeKalb IL 60115. (815)753-1826. Director: M.L. Livingston. Pays 10-15% royalty on wholesale price. SASE. Free catalog.

Nonfiction: "The NIU Press publishes mainly history, literary criticism and regional studies. It does not consider collections of previously published articles, essays, etc., nor do we consider unsolicited poetry." Accepts nonfiction translations. Query with outline/synopsis and 1-3 sample chapters.

NORTHLAND PRESS, Box N, Flagstaff AZ 86002. (602)774-5251. Hardcover and paperback originals (80%) and reprints (20%). Advance varies. Averages 10 titles/year. Pays royalty on wholesale or retail price. Transparencies and contact sheet required for photos and/or illustrations to accompany ms. Simultaneous and photocopied submissions OK. Reports in 6-8 weeks. SASE. Free book catalog.

Nonfiction: Publishes Western Americana, Indian arts and culture, Southwestern natural history and fine photography with a western orientation. Query. "Submit a proposal including an outline of the book, a sample chapter, the introduction or preface and sample illustrations. Include an inventory of items sent." Looks for "clearly developed treatment of subject; tightly constructed presentation; an outline of author's background; pertinent research reference. Author should include assessment of intended audience (potential buyers and market) and other books published on same subject matter."

Recent Nonfiction Titles: *Pletka*; *CO Bar: Bill Owen Depicts the Historic Babbitt Ranch*, by Marshall Tiemble; and *Designs from the Ancient Mimbrenos with a Hope Interpretation*, by Fred Kabatie.

W.W. NORTON CO., INC., 500 5th Ave., New York NY 10110. (212)354-5500. Managing Editor: Sterling Lawrence. Royalty varies on retail price; advance varies. Publishes 213 titles/year. Photocopied and simultaneous submissions OK. Computer printout submissions OK. Submit outline and/or 2-3 sample chapters for fiction and nonfiction. Return of material not guaranteed without SASE. Reports in 4 weeks.

Nonfiction and Fiction: "General, adult fiction and nonfiction of all kinds on nearly all subjects and of the highest quality possible within the limits of each particular book." Last year there were 56 book club rights sales; 30 mass paperback reprint sales; "innumerable serializations, second serial, syndication, translations, etc." Looks for "clear, intelligent, creative writing on original subjects or with original characters."

Recent Titles: *Enjoying Old Age*, by B.F. Skinner; *After Long Silence*, by Michael Straight; *The Healing Heart*, by Norman Cousins; *Oswald's Game* by Jean Davison.

Tips: "Long novels are too expensive—keep them under 350 pages (manuscript pages)."

NOYES DATA CORP., (including Noyes Press and Noyes Publications), Noyes Bldg., Park Ridge NJ 07656. Publishes hardcover originals. Averages 60 titles/year. Pays 10%-12% royalty on retail price; advance varies, depending on author's reputation and nature of book. Free book catalog. Query Editorial Department. Reports in 1-2 weeks. Enclose return postage.

Nonfiction: (Noyes Press) "Art, classical studies, archeology, history. Material directed to the intelligent adult and the academic market."

Technical: (Noyes Publications) Publishes practical industrial processing science; technical, economic books pertaining to chemistry, chemical engineering, food, textile, energy, pollution control, primarily those of interest to the business executive. Length: 50,000-250,000 words.

NURSECO, INC., Box 145, Pacific Palisades CA 90272. (213)454-6597. Publisher: Margo Neal. Publishes hardcover and trade paperback originals and textbooks. Averages 15 titles/year. Pays 6% minimum royalty; offers negotiable advance. Simultaneous and photocopied submissions OK. SASE. Reports in 1 month. Free book catalog.

Nonfiction: Reference on nursing. Resources for working nurses. No medical mss. Submit outline/synopsis.

Recent Nonfiction Titles: *Nursing Care Planning Guide 1-5*, by Margo Neal; *Nurses Business*; *AJN 1983 Nursig Boards Review*, by American Journal of Nursing Company.

OAK TREE PUBLICATIONS, INC., 9601 Aero Dr., San Diego CA 92123. Editorial Assistant: Modeste Williams. Publishes hardcover and paperback originals. Averages 15-25 titles/year. Offers variable advance. SASE. Reports in 2 months.

Nonfiction: Adult books on current social, adult, and parenting concerns; juvenile nonfiction (7-11): books that inform in entertaining format. Unique craft, activity, science, and aid-in-development (i.e., parent participation) books.

Recent Nonfiction Titles: *What You Think of Me Is None of My Business*, by Rev. T. Cole-Whittaker; *I Wish I Had A Computer That Makes Waffles*, by Dr. Fitzhugh Dodson; *Kids Encyclopedia of Things to Make and Do*, *Facing Alcoholism*, by Robert McCormick; and *Getting Off to College*, by Melody Martin.

Fiction: Educational and informational children's books.

Recent Fiction Titles: *Carnival Kidnap Caper*, by Dr. F. Dodson and P. Reuben; and *Where the Deer and the Cantaloupe Play*, by T. Ernesto Bethancourt.

OCCUPATIONAL AWARENESS, Box 948, Los Alamitos CA 90720. Editor-in-Chief: Ms. Edith Ericksen. Publishes originals. Averages 10 titles/year. Offers standard contract. Average advance $1,500. Photocopied submissions/computer printouts OK. Submit outline and 3 sample chapters for professional books and textbooks. Accepts artwork/photos. SASE.

Nonfiction: Materials on behavior/adjustment (no TA), textbooks, workbooks, kits, career guidance, relating careers to curricula, special education, tests.

‡OCTAMERON ASSOCIATES, 820 Fontaine St., Alexandria VA 22302. (703)836-1019. Editorial Director: Karen Stokstad. Publishes trade paperback originals. Averages 10 titles/year. Pays 10-15% royalty on wholesale price. Simultaneous submissions OK. SASE. Reports in 1 week. Free book catalog.

Nonfiction: Reference and self-help, post-secondary education subjects. Especially interested in "paying-for-college and college admission guides." Does not want books unrelated to postsecondary education. Query. Accepts outline/synopsis and 2 sample chapters.

Recent Nonfiction Titles: *How We Do It*, by Ed Wall; (self-help); *Earn & Learn*, by Joseph Re (self-help); and *Don't Miss Out*, by Bob Leider (self-help).

OCTOBER PRESS, INC., 200 Park Ave. S., Suite 1320, New York NY 10003. (212)477-1251. Director: Mark Iocolano. Book producer; co-publishing programs. "Currently, October Press is developing several business and technical books for photographers, designers, and other users of photography." Pays variable

rate, depending upon project. "We cannot handle unsolicited proposals." Reports in 3 weeks.
Nonfiction: How-to, illustrated book, juvenile, technical on hobbies, photography, professional handbooks.

ODDO PUBLISHING, INC., Box 68, Beauregard Blvd., Fayetteville GA 30214. (404)461-7627. Managing Editor: Genevieve Oddo. Publishes hardcover and paperback originals. Scripts are usually purchased outright. "We judge all scripts independently." Royalty considered for special scripts only. Book catalog 50¢. Send complete ms, typed clearly. No computer printout or disk submissions. Reports in 3-4 months. "Ms will not be returned without SASE."
Juveniles: Publishes language arts, workbooks in math, writing (English), photophonics, science (space and oceanography), and social studies for schools, libraries, and trade. Interested in children's supplementary readers in the areas of language arts, math, science, social studies, etc. "Texts run from 1,500 to 3,500 words. Ecology, space, oceanography, and pollution are subjects of interest. Books on patriotism. Ms must be easy to read, general, and not set to outdated themes. It must lend itself to full color illustration. No stories of grandmother long ago. No love angle, permissive language, or immoral words or statements."
Recent Titles: *Bobby Bear Meets Cousin Boo*; *Timmy Tiger and the Masked Bandit*; *Let's Walk Safely*; *Bobby Bear and the Blizzard*; *Bobby Bear Goes to the Beach.*

OHARA PUBLICATIONS, INC., 1813 Victory Place, Box 7728, Burbank CA 91510-7728. Editor: Gregory Lee. Publishes trade paperback originals. Averages 12 titles/year. Pays royalty. Photocopied submissions OK. SASE. Reports in 3 weeks on queries; 6 weeks on mss. Free book catalog.
Nonfiction: Martial arts. "We decide to do a book on a specific martial art, then seek out the most qualified material artist to do a 'how to' book on that art for us." No mss that do *not* pertain to martial arts systems (their histories, techniques, philosophy, etc.) Query first, then submit outline/synopsis and sample chapters.
Recent Nonfiction Titles: *Ideals of the Samurai*, translated by William S. Wilson; *Kicks for Competition*, by Chong Lee; *Modern Amis*, by Romy Presas.

OHIO STATE UNIVERSITY PRESS, 2070 Neil Ave., Columbus OH 43210. (614)422-6930. Director: Weldon A. Kefauver. Pays royalty on wholesale or retail price. Averages 20 titles/year. Query letter preferred with outline and sample chapters. Reports in 2 months. Ms held longer with author's permission. Enclose return postage.
Nonfiction: Publishes history, biography, science, philosophy, the arts, political science, law, literature, economics, education, sociology, anthropology, geography, and general scholarly nonfiction. No length limitations.

*OHIO UNIVERSITY PRESS, Scott Quad, Ohio University, Athens OH 45701. (614)594-5505. Imprints include *Ohio University Press* and *Swallow Press*. Director: Patricia Elisar. Associate Director: Holly Panich. Publishes hardcover and paperback originals (97%) and reprints (3%). Averages 40-45 titles/year. Subsidy publishes 6% of titles, based on projected market. Pays in royalties starting at 1,500 copies based on wholesale or retail price. No advance. Photocopied submissions OK. Reports in 3-5 months. SASE. Free book catalog.
Nonfiction: "General scholarly nonfiction with particular emphasis on 19th century literary criticism. Also history, social sciences, philosophy, business, western regional works and miscellaneous categories." Query.
Recent Nonfiction Titles: *Little Sparrow: A Portrait of Sophia Kovalevsky*, by Don Kennedy; *The First Pictorial History of the American Oil and Gas Industry*, by Ruth Sheldon Knowles.

THE OLD ARMY PRESS, Box 2243, Ft. Collins CO 80522. (303)226-2788. Editor-in-Chief: Michael J. Koury. Hardcover and paperback originals (90%) and reprints (10%). Averages 5-10 titles year. Specializes in western Americana. Pays 10% royalty; no advance. State availability of photos and/or illustrations to accompany ms. Simultaneous and photocopied submissions OK. SASE. Free book catalog.
Nonfiction: Publishes Americana (60,000 words or less); and history (60,000 words or less). Query. Looks for "material that falls within our historical field of subject matter."
Recent Nonfiction Titles: *Dust to Dust*, by J. Gaddy; *Tour Guide to Old Western Forts*, by Herbert M. Hart; *Centennial Campaign*, by John S. Gray; and *Roll on the Little Big Horn*, new edition, by Carroll and Price.

ONCE UPON A PLANET, INC., Box 220, Bayside NY 11361. (212)961-9240. President: Charles Faraone. Publishes trade paperback originals. Averages 10 titles/year. Pays 5-10% royalty on wholesale price; buys some mss outright for $1,000-up; offers average $500-2,000 advance. Simultaneous and photocopied submissions OK. Computer printout submissions OK. SASE. Reports in 1 month on queries; 5 weeks on mss. Book catalog for SASE.
Nonfiction: How-to (satirical), humor, illustrated book and self-help (satirical). Subjects include philosophy, psychology and "anything funny. Our books are small (4x5½; 32 pp.), making it possible to try many topics and titles. We are currently entering the full sized trade paperback market with expanded versions of our bestsellers. We are attempting to publish a large selection of humorous books on both humorous and serious subjects. Nothing controversial (unless it's very well done)." Query or submit outline/synopsis and 2-3 sample

chapters. Accepts artwork/photos.

Recent Nonfiction Titles: *Why I Hate Men*, by various authors (humor); *How to Drive Like a Selfish Bastard*, by Charles Faraone (humor); and *A Man's Guide to Housework*, by Bruce Pollack (humor).

Fiction: "We are not interested in any fiction at this time."

101 PRODUCTIONS, 834 Mission St., San Francisco CA 94103. (415)495-6040. Editor-in-Chief: Jacqueline Killeen. Publishes paperback originals. Offers standard minimum book contract on retail prices. Averages 12 titles/year. Free book catalog. Will consider photocopied submissions. Computer printout and disk submissions OK; "we are equipped to edit and typeset from disks, providing the software is compatible." Query. No unsolicited mss will be read. SASE.

Nonfiction: All nonfiction, mostly how-to: cookbooks, the home, gardening, outdoors, travel. Heavy emphasis on graphics and illustrations. Accepts artwork/photos. Most books are 192 pages.

Recent Nonfiction Titles: *Fifteen Minute Meals*, by Emalee Chapman; *Front Row Center*, by Jack Books; and *Restaurants Los Angeles*, Colman Andrews.

OPEN COURT PUBLISHING CO., Box 599, LaSalle IL 61301. Publisher: M. Blouke Carus. General Manager: Howard R. Webber. Marketing Manager: Alwin B. Carus. Averages 5-10 titles/year. Royalty contracts negotiable for each book. Computer printout submissions OK; prefers letter quality to dot matrix. Query. Accepts outline/synopsis and 2-3 sample chapters. Reports in 6-8 weeks. Enclose return postage.

Nonfiction: Philosophy, psychology, mathematics, comparative religion, education, chemistry, orientalia and related scholarly topics. Accepts nonfiction translations from German and French. "This is a publishing house run as an intellectual enterprise, to reflect the concerns of its staff and as a service to the world of learning."

Recent Nonfiction Titles: *Tomorrow, Capitalism: The Economics of Economic Freedom*, by Henri Lepage (economics); *Jungian Analysis*, edited by M. Stein (psychology); *The Philosophy of Jean-Paul Sartre*, edited by P.J. Schillp (philosophy)

OPTIMUM PUBLISHING INTERNATIONAL INC., 511 Place D'Armes. Montreal, Quebec, Canada H2Y 2W7. (514)844-8468. Managing Director and Editor-in-Chief: Michael S. Baxendale. Hardcover and paperback originals and reprints. 10% royalty on retail price. Averages 21 titles/year. Publishes in both official Canadian languages (English and French). Query or submit outline/synopsis and sample chapters. Photocopied submissions OK. Reports in 2-4 weeks. SAE and International Reply Coupons.

Nonfiction: Biography; cookbooks, cooking and foods; gardening; history; natural history; how-to; health; nature; crafts; photography; art; self-help; crime; sports; and travel books.

Recent Nonfiction Titles: *Inmate*, by George D. Scott, MD with Bill Trent; *Ski Alpine; Les Consequences*, by Margaret Trudeau; *Creative Parenting*, by William Sears, MD; and *The Illustrated Encyclopedia of Houseplants*, by Jud Arnold.

ORBIS BOOKS, Maryknoll NY 10545. (914)941-7590. Editor: Philip Scharper. Publishes paperback originals. Publishes 30 titles/year. 7-8½-10% royalty on retail prices; advance averages $1,000. Query with outline, 2 sample chapters, and prospectus. Computer printout and disk submissions OK. Reports in 4 to 6 weeks. Enclose return postage.

Nonfiction: "Religious developments in Asia, Africa, and Latin America. Christian missions. Justice and peace. Christianity and world religions."

Recent Nonfiction Titles: *Religion and Social Conflict*, by Otto Nadura; *The Power of the Poor in History*, by Gustavo Gutierrey; *Parenting for Peace and Justice*, by James and Kathy McInniss.

OREGON STATE UNIVERSITY PRESS, 101 Waldo Hall, Corvallis OR 97331. (503)754-3166. Hardcover and paperback originals. Averages 5-10 titles/year. Pays royalty on wholesale price. No advance. Submit contact sheet of photos and/or illustrations to accompany ms. Reports in 4 months. SASE. Free book catalog for SASE.

Nonfiction: Publishes Americana; biography; economics; history; nature; philosophy; energy and recreation; reference; scientific (biological sciences only); technical (energy); and American literary criticism books. Emphasis on Pacific or Northwestern topics. Submit outline/synopsis and sample chapters.

Recent Nonfiction Titles: *Contemporary Northwest Writing*, by R. Carlson (anthology); and *Salmonid Ecosystems of the North Pacific*, by W. McNeil and D. Himsworth (marine biology).

ORYX PRESS, 2214 N. Central Ave., Phoenix AZ 85004. (602)254-6156. President/Editorial Director: Phyllis B. Steckler. Publishes hardcover and paperback originals. Averages 35 titles/year. Pays 10-15% royalty on net receipts; no advance. Simultaneous and photocopied submissions OK. Computer printout submissions OK; disk submissions "depend upon computer protocol." SASE. Reports in 8 weeks. Queries/mss may be routed to other editors in the publishing group. Free book catalog.

Nonfiction: Bibliographies; directories; education; general reference; library and information science; and agriculture monographs. Publishes nonfiction for public, college and university, junior college and special libraries; education faculty members; agriculture specialists. Accepts artwork/photos. Query or submit outline/synopsis and 1 sample chapter, or complete ms.

Recent Nonfiction Titles: *Evolution vs Creationism: The Public Education Controversy*, ed. by Zetterberg (resource for teachers and librarians); *Diffusing Censorship*, by Jones (library information science monograph); *Directory of Nursing Home Facilities*, ed. by Mongeau (reference).

OTTENHEIMER PUBLISHERS, INC., 300 Reisterstown Rd., Baltimore MD 21208. (301)484-2100. President: Allen Hirsh Jr. Publishes hardcover and paperback originals. Publishes 250 titles/year. Negotiates royalty and advance. Photocopied submissions OK. Reports in 1 month.
Nonfiction: Cookbooks, reference, gardening, home repair and decorating, automotive and medical for the layperson. Submit outline/synopsis and sample chapters or complete ms.

OUR SUNDAY VISITOR, INC., 200 Noll Plaza, Huntington IN 46750. (219)356-8400. Managing Editor: Robert Lockwood. Publishes paperback and hardcover originals and reprints. Pays variable royalty on net receipts; offers average $500 advance. Averages 20-30 titles a year. Reports in 1 month on most queries and submissions. SASE. Free author's guide and catalog.
Nonfiction: Catholic viewpoints on current issues; reference and guidance; Bibles and devotional books; Catholic heritage books. Prefers to see well-developed proposals as first submission with "annotated outline, three sample chapters, definition of intended market."
Recent Nonfiction Titles: *Strange Gods: Contemporary Religious Cults in America*, by William Whalen; and *Forever Family: Our Adventures in Adopting Older Children*, by Ruth Piepenbrink.

‡**OUTBOOKS INC.**, 217 Kimball Ave., Golden CO 80401. Contact: Wiliam R. Jones. Publishes trade paperback originals and reprints. Averages 10 titles/year. Pays 5% royalty on retail price. Simultaneous and photocopied submissions OK. No computer printout or disk submissions. SASE. Reports in 1 month on queries; 2 months on mss. Free book catalog "as available."
Nonfiction: Cookbook, how-to, regional books on Americana, animals, cooking and foods, history, hobbies, nature, photography, recreation, sports, travel. Accepts artwork/photos. Publishes for "lay enthusiasts in American history, outdoors, and natural history, ecology, conservation." Query. Accepts outline/synopsis and 1 sample chapter.
Recent Nonfiction Titles: *Evidence and the Custer Enigma*, by Jerome A. Greene; *Rock Art and the American Indian*, by Campbell Grant; and *Ten Trail Trips in Yosemite National Park*, by William R. Jones (trade paperbacks).

***OUTDOOR EMPIRE PUBLISHING, INC.**, Box C-19000, Seattle WA 98109. Associate Publisher: Fay Ainsworth. Publishes trade paperback originals (25%) and reprints (75%). Averages 25 titles/year. Subsidy publishes 50% of books based on market potential of subject. Buys some mss outright for $500, or by special contract depending upon project. Simultaneous and photocopied submissions OK. Computer printout and disk submissions OK; prefers letter quality to dot matrix submissions. SASE. Reports in 1 month. Book catalog for business size SAE and 1 first class stamp.
Nonfiction: How-to, self-help, textbook, workbook-texts on recreation and sports for ages 10 through adult. "Contemporary how-to treatment of various subjects in the areas of outdoor recreation: Boating, fishing, hunting, camping, bicycling, mopeds, 4-wheel drives, survival, emergency preparedness." No mss on professional team sports, or outdoor travel journals. Accepts artwork/photos. Query or submit outline/synopsis and sample chapters or complete ms.
Recent Nonfiction Titles: *Better Boating—A Guide to Safety Afloat*, *Set Your Sights*, and *The Bicyclist's Guide*, all by various contributors.

OUTDOOR LIFE BOOKS, Book Division, Times Mirror Magazines (subsidiary of Times Mirror Co.), 380 Madison Ave., New York NY 10017. Editor: John Sill. Publishes books for Outdoor Life Book Club that are also distributed by major trade publishers. Pays royalty and advance relative to book list price. SASE.
Nonfiction: Guides on hunting, fishing, firearms, outdoor lore, wildlife—all of broad appeal to national sportsman audience. Submit author resume, outline, sample chapters, and sample illustrations for heavily illustrated small books to 35,000 words and large books to 150,000 words. Looks for "either a description of each chapter's contents or a subject-by-subject breakout. Sample rough drawings and photographs: either color transparencies, any size or 8x10 b&w glossies."

OWLSWOOD PRODUCTIONS, INC., 287 Harbor Way, S., San Francisco CA 94080. (415)583-8050. Editor: Susan H. Herbert. Publishes trade paperback originals. Averages 2 titles/year. Buys some mss outright; offers advance. Simultaneous and photocopied submissions OK. SASE. Reports in 1 week.
Nonfiction: Cookbook. Subjects include cooking and foods. "Our books are for anyone interested in good, wholesome foods." Query or submit outline/synopsis and sample chapters.

Recent Nonfiction Titles: *Chicken Favorites*, by MK Hollander (cookbook); and *Ground Beef Favorites*, by B. Brauer (cookbook).

OXFORD UNIVERSITY PRESS, INC., 200 Madison Ave., New York NY 10016. (212)679-7300. Editor-in-Chief: Sheldon Meyer. Publishes hardcover originals and paperback reprints. Publishes over 100 titles/year. Pays standard royalty; offers variable advance. Photocopied submissions OK. SASE. Free book catalog.
Nonfiction: American history, music, political science, reference books. Submit outline/synopsis and sample chapters.
Recent Nonfiction Titles: *Franklin D. Roosevelt and American Foreign Policy* (political history); *Jerome Kern* (biography); *American Musical Theatre* (popular history); *The Majority Finds Its Past* (women's history); *Descent from Glory* (history).

OXMOOR HOUSE, (Division of The Southern Progress Corp.), Box 2262, Birmingham AL 35202. Director: Don Logan. Editor: John Logue. Publishes hardcover and paperback originals. Pays on royalty basis or fee. Averages 13 titles/year. Submit outline and sample chapter. Reports in 1 month. SASE.
Nonfiction: "Publishes books of general interest to Southern readers—cookbooks, garden books; books on crafts, sewing, photography, art, outdoors, antiques and how-to topics.
Recent Nonfiction Titles: *The Timeless River, Quilted Clothing*; *Country Antiques and Collectibles*; and *Cookbook for Two*.

P. A. R., INC., Abbott Park Place, Providence RI 02903. (401)331-0130. President: Barry M. Smith. Hardcover and paperback originals. Specializes in textbooks for business schools, junior or community colleges, and adult continuing education programs. Pays 10% royalty. Markets through fall and winter workshops throughout the country with special seminars that are periodically held by authors and sales staff. State availability of photos or illustrations to furnish at a later date. Simultaneous submissions OK. Computer printout submissions OK. Reports in 2-4 months. SASE. Free book catalog.
Nonfiction: Michael K. Groleau, managing director. Business, economics, law, politics, psychology, sociology, technical, textbooks. Accepts outline/synopsis and 2 sample chapters.
Recent Titles: *The Person You Are* (personal development); *Concepts of Business* (management); *Powereading* (reading).

PACIFIC BOOKS, PUBLISHERS, Box 558, Palo Alto CA 94302. (415)856-0550. Editor: Henry Ponleithner. Royalty schedule varies with book. No advance. Averages 8 titles/year. Will send catalog on request. Send complete ms. Computer printout submissions OK "if clean, typewriter-quality." Reports "promptly." SASE.
Nonfiction: General interest, professional, technical and scholarly nonfiction trade books. Specialties include western Americana and Hawaiiana. Looks for "well-written, documented material of interest to a significant audience." Accepts artwork/photos and translations.
Recent Nonfiction Titles: *What Comes After You Say, "I Love You?"*, by James R. Hine (marriage); and *Mountain Climber: George B. Bayley, 1840-1894*, by Evelyn Hyman Chase (biography).
Textbooks and Reference: Text and reference books; high school and college.

PADRE PRODUCTIONS, Box 1275, San Luis Obispo CA 93406. Editor-in-Chief: Lachlan P. MacDonald. Publishes hardcover and paperback originals (90%) and reprints (10%). Pays 6% minimum royalty; advance ranges from $200-1,000. Averages 4-8 titles/year. State availability of photos and/or illustrations or include contact sheet or stat. Simultaneous submissions OK. Reports in 2-6 months. Mss and queries without SASE are not answered. Book catalog for SASE.
Nonfiction: Publishes Americana (antiques); art; business opportunities; collectibles; cookbooks; history (local California); hobbies; how-to; investments for the layman; nature (with illustrations); photography; poetry; publishing; recreation; reference; self-help; and travel books. Query or submit outline and 2-3 sample chapters. "Ample packaging; type all material; don't send slides unless asked." Looks for "literacy, flair, intelligence."
Recent Nonfiction Titles: *Pioneer California*, by Margaret Roberts (history); *Electrical Collectibles*, by Don Fredgant (antiques); *The Guide to Whale Watching*, by L.P. MacDonald; and *Handwriting Analysis*, by David Battan.
Fiction: Publishes (in order of preference): fantasy, contemporary, juvenile. Juveniles for 10-14 year readers, (about 160 pages with strong illustrative possibilities). Submit complete manuscript.

THE PAGURIAN CORPORATION LIMITED, 13 Hazelton Ave., Toronto, Ontario, Canada M5R 2E1. (416)968-0255. Editor-in-Chief: Christopher Ondaatje. Publishes paperback and hardcover originals and reprints. Offers negotiable royalty contract. Advance negotiable. Averages 5 titles/year. Photocopied submissions OK. Computer printout submissions OK; prefers letter quality to dot matrix. Submit 2-page outline, synopsis or chapter headings and contents. Reports "immediately." SAE and International Reply Coupons.

Nonfiction: Publishes general interest trade and art books. Accepts artwork/photos. Will consider fine arts, outdoor and cookbooks. Length: 40,000-70,000 words.

PALADIN PRESS, Box 1307, Boulder CO 80306. (303)443-7250. President/Publisher: Peder C. Lund. General Manager: Timothy J. Leifield. Editorial Director: Virginia Thomas. Publishes hardcover and paperback originals (80%) and paperback reprints (20%). Averages 22 titles/year. Pays 10-12-15% royalty on net sales. Simultaneous and photocopied submissions OK. Reports in 1 month. SASE. Free book catalog.
Nonfiction: "Paladin Press primarily publishes original manuscripts on military science, weaponry, self-defense, the martial arts, survival, police science, guerrilla warfare and fieldcraft, and within the last two years, humor. Survival and how-to manuscripts, as well as pictorial histories, are given priority. Manuals on building weapons, when technically accurate and cleanly presented, are encouraged. If applicable, send sample photographs and line drawings with outline and sample chapters." Query or submit outline/synopsis and sample chapters.
Recent Nonfiction Titles: *Up Yours*, by George Hayduke (humor); *Life or Death: Emergency Medical Techniques*, by Sharon Carter (outdoors); *Ninja Death Touch*, by Ashida Kim (martial arts); and *The Complete Book of Taekwon Do Forms*, by Keith Yates (martial arts).

PANTHEON BOOKS, Division of Random House, Inc., 201 E. 50th St., New York NY 10022. Managing Editor: Betsy Amster. Published more than 60 titles last year. Pays royalty on retail price. Address queries to Don Guttenplan, Adult Editorial Department (15th Floor). Computer printout submissions OK. Enclose return postage.
Nonfiction: Emphasis on Asia, international politics, radical social theory, history, medicine, women's studies, and law. Recreational guides and practical how-to books as well. Query letters only. No manuscripts accepted.
Recent Nonfiction Titles: *Secrets*, by Sissela Bok; *Gender*, by Ivan Illich; *The Nuclear Delusion*, by George Kennan.
Juveniles: Publishes some juveniles. Address queries to Juvenile Editorial Department (6th floor).
Fiction: Publishes fewer than 5 novels each year, primarily mysteries. Queries on fiction not accepted.
Tips: Queries/mss may be routed to other editors in the publishing group.

PARA RESEARCH, Whistlestop Mall, Rockport MA 01966. (617)546-3413. Editor: Shaun Levesque. Publishes trade paperback originals (90%) and reprints (10%). Averages 8-10 titles/year. Pays 5-10% royalty on publisher's net; buys some mss outright for negotiable fee; offer average $1,000 advance. Simultaneous and photocopied submissions OK. SASE. Reports in 2 weeks on queries; 2 months on mss.
Nonfiction: How-to, self-help, and metaphysical on health, psychology, and astrology/occult. No biography or autobiography. Submit outline/synopsis and sample chapters.
Recent Nonfiction Titles: *Get a Job in 60 Seconds*, by Steve Kravette (self-help); *Horoscope Symbols*, by Robert Hand (astrology); *Astral Projection*, by Brad Steiger (occult); *Quit Smoking*, by Curtis Casewit (health).

PARADOX PUBLISHING CO., 2476 Buttonwood Court, Florissant MO 63031. (314)838-0241. Subsidiary of Paradox Enterprises, Inc. Senior Editor: Curt Scarborough. Publishes hardcover and trade paperback originals. Averages 12 titles/year. No advance. Simultaneous and photocopied submissions OK. SASE. Reports in 2 weeks on queries; 1 month on mss.
Nonfiction: How-to and self-help on health, philosophy, psychology, religion, sociology. "We specialize in Christian how-to books—self-help, ethics, psychology, etc. Looking for promising how-to books for paperback line: 64-page books; approximately 20,000 words. Also interested in original ideas for full-length hardback books." Query.
Recent Nonfiction Title: *Choice Sermons From Missouri Pulpits*, by Gerald Young (compilation of sermons).

PARENTS MAGAZINE PRESS, A division of Parents' Magazine Enterprises, Inc., 685 3rd Ave., New York NY 10017. (212)878-8612. Editorial Director: Stephanie Calmenson. Publishes hardcover originals. Averages 14 titles/year. Pays flat fee for Parents' book club edition; royalty for trade and library editions which are distributed by Elsevier-Dutton. Computer printout and disk submissions OK. SASE. Reports in 6-8 weeks.
Nonfiction: "We are not doing any nonfiction at this time."
Fiction: "We publish only easy-to-read, full color picture books for children 2-7. Average text/art pages about 38, in a 48-page self-ended book. Approximately 400-600 words. Emphasis is on humor, action, and child appeal. No message stories." Submit complete ms.
Recent Titles: *Detective Bob and the Great Ape Escape*, by David Harrison, pictures by Ned Delaney; *Get Well, Clown-Arounds*, by Joanna Cole, pictures by Jerry Smith; *Sandcake*, by Frank Asch.

PARENTS PRODUCTIONS, Box 16352, San Francisco CA 94116. (415)753-1313. Editor: Gregory Frazier. Publishes trade paperback originals. Averages 3-6 titles/year. Pays 5-15% royalty on wholesale price. Buys some mss outright for $500-5,000. No advance. Simultaneous and photocopied submissions OK. SASE.

Reports in 3 weeks on queries; 1 month on mss.
Nonfiction: Cookbook, how-to, humor, illustrated book, reference, self-help (as they relate to childcare/parenting). Subjects include art, cooking and foods, health, hobbies, music, parenting, photography, psychology, recreation and travel. "We want *popular* treatments of crafts, how-to, and gift-type books directed to parents of infants and toddlers and young children. We will also consider non-book material such as record books, stationery and other paper products." No children's books and storybooks or any highly technical or clinical material. Query or submit outline/synopsis and sample chapters or complete ms.
Recent Nonfiction Title: *Your Child's Astrological Birthday Book*, by Dennis Redmond (record book).

PARKER PUBLISHING CO., West Nyack NY 10994. Publishes hardcover originals and paperback reprints. Pays 10% royalty; 5% mail order and book clubs. Publishes 85 titles/year. Will send catalog on request. Reports in 3-5 weeks.
Nonfiction: Publishes practical, self-help, how-to books. Subject areas include popular health, letterwriting, electronics, education, secretarial, selling, personal and business self-improvement. Length: 65,000 words.
Recent Nonfiction Titles: *Power Selling by Telephone*, by Masser and Leeds; *Secretary's Modern Guide to English Usage*, by Vermes; and *Doctor Morrison's Amazing Healing Foods*, by Morrison.

‡PATH PRESS, INC., Suite 625, 53 W. Jackson Blvd., Chicago IL 60604. (312)663-0167. Editorial Director: Herman C. Gilbert. Publishes hardcover and trade paperback originals and hardcover and trade paperback reprints. Averages 10 titles/year. Distributed by Chicago Review Press. Pays 10-15% royalty on retail price. Simultaneous and photocopied submissions OK. SASE. Reports in 3 weeks on queries; 1 month on mss.
Nonfiction: Biography, how-to and reference. Subjects include art, history, philosophy, politics, religion, sociology and sports (all with a black slant). Interested in books dealing with black demands in the fields of politics and economics; also black autobiography and biography "Ours is a general audience with emphasis on black and Third World." Query or submit outline/synopsis and sample chapters.
Recent Nonfiction Title: *American Diary: Personal History of the Black Press*, by Enoch P. Waters (autobiography).
Fiction: Adventure, confession, ethnic, historical, humor, mystery and romance. "We publish stories treating black life." Query or submit outline/synopsis and sample chapters.
Recent Fiction Title: *The Negotiations*, by Herman Cromwell Gilbert (political suspense).
Recent Poetry Title: *The Best of the Best* (anthology—black poets).

PAULIST PRESS, 545 Island Road, Ramsey, NJ 07446. (201)825-7300. Publisher: Rev. Kevin A. Lynch. Managing Editor: Donald Brophy. Publishes hardcover and paperback originals (90%) and paperback reprints (10%). Averages 100 titles/year. Pays royalty on retail price; sometimes an advance. Photocopied submissions OK. SASE. Reports in 4 weeks.
Nonfiction: Philosophy, religion, self-help, and textbooks (religious subject). Accepts nonfiction translations from German, French and Spanish. "We would like to see theology (Catholic and ecumenical Christian), popular spirituality, liturgy, and religious education texts." Submit outline/synopsis and 2 sample chapters.
Recent Nonfiction Titles: *Healing Life's Hurts*, by Dennis and Matthew Linn (spirituality); *Fundamental Theology*, by Gerald O'Collins (theology); *Antioch and Rome*, by R. Brown and J. Meier (New Testament studies); and *Invisible Partners*, by John Sanford (psychology).

PELICAN PUBLISHING CO., INC., 1101 Monroe St., Box 189, Gretna LA 70053. (504)368-1175. Imprints include *Pelican Publishing House*, *Paddlewheel Publications*, *Dixie Press*, *Hope Publications*, *Friends of the Cabildo*, *Sam Mims*, *Jackson Square Press*, and *Mississippi Library Association*. Editor-in-Chief: James Calhoun. Editor: Frumie Selchen. Publishes hardcover and paperback originals (90%) and reprints (10%). Publishes 50-75 titles/year. Pays 10-15% royalty on wholesale price; sometimes offers advance. "Please send us a photocopy and retain the original. Exclusive submissions preferred. SASE if ms to be returned; otherwise it will be discarded if not accepted. Reports in 3 months. While we will use care, we accept no responsibility for unsolicited manuscripts."
Nonfiction: Art; cookbooks/cooking; self-help (especially motivational); inspirational and travel (guidebooks). Accepts nonfiction translations. Submit outline/synopsis and sample chapters. "We look for clarity and conciseness of expression and presentation in a synopsis/outline, and we ask to see those that will most likely yield proposals that will fit our list and that we feel we can market successfully. We look for completed manuscripts that are well written and will require little editing, that contain subject matter that is in line with our publishing program." Accepts artwork/photos.
Recent Nonfiction Titles: *Best Editorial Cartoons of the Year* (annual series); *Maverick guides* (annual series); *Whistling in the Dark*, by Fred Lowery, the blind whistler; *South to Louisiana, The Music of the Cajun Bayous*, by John Broven; *Traditional Irish Recipes*, by George Thomson.
Fiction: Novels. "We are actively seeking well-written fiction."
Recent Fiction Title: *Henry Hamilton, Graduate Ghost*, by Marilyn Redmond (juvenile/adult fiction).

PENGUIN BOOKS, 625 Madison Ave., New York NY 10022. Editorial Director: Kathryn Court. Publishes paperback originals (5-10%) and reprints (90-95%). Publishes 200 titles/year. Pays standard royalty on retail price; offers variable advance. Photocopied submissions OK. SASE. Reports in 6 weeks. Free book catalog. **Nonfiction:** Educational handbooks on health and humor. "We publish very little original fiction or poetry." Accepts nonfiction, fiction and poetry translations. Submit outline/synopsis and at least 3 sample chapters. **Recent Nonfiction Titles:** *At Dawn We Slept*, by Gordon Prange; *Getting To Yes*, by Roger Fisher and William Ury; *The Read-Aloud Handbook*, by Jim Trelease.

THE PENNSYLVANIA STATE UNIVERSITY PRESS, 215 Wagner Bldg., University Park PA 16802. (814)865-1327. Editor-in-Chief: Jack Pickering. Hardcover and paperback originals. Specializes in books of scholarly value, and/or regional interest. Averages 40 titles/year. Pays 10% royalty on wholesale price; no advance. Maintains own distribution company in England which serves the British Empire, Europe, etc. Submit outline/synopsis and 2 sample chapters plus endorsement by a scholar at a university or research institution. Simultaneous and photocopied submissions OK. Reports in 2-4 months. SASE. Free book catalog. **Nonfiction:** Publishes scholarly books on agriculture, art, business, economics, history, medicine and psychiatry, music, nature, philosophy, politics, psychology, religions, science, sociology, technology, women's studies, black studies, and *Keystone Books* (a paperback series concentrating on topics of special interest to those living in the mid-Atlantic states.) Accepts nonfiction translations. Looks for "content and form acceptable to scholars (as attested by a recognized scholar)." **Recent Nonfiction Titles:** *Rivers of Pennsylvania*, by T. Palmer (nature, conservation, history); *Clouds and Storms*, by F. H. Ludlam (meteorology); and *The Development of Plato's Metaphysics*, by Henry Teloh (philosophy).

‡PENNWELL BOOKS, Box 1260, Tulsa OK 74132. (918)663-4220. Acquisitions Editor: Gerald L. Farrar. Publishes hardcover originals on petroleum/energy. Averages 30 titles/year. Pays 10-15% royalty on retail price. No advance. SASE. Reports in 1 week on queries; 2 weeks on mss. Free book catalog. **Nonfiction:** Technical books on petroleum engineering. No "novel, alternative energy (solar, hydrogen) or fiction with an oilfield topic." Submit outline/synopsis and sample chapters. **Recent Nonfiction Titles:** *Fundamentals of Oil & Gas Accounting*, by Gallun/Stevenson (petro accounting, suitable for college market); *Drilling and Producing Offshore*, by Hall (offshore D&P techniques—reference); *HP-41 Reservoir Engineering Manual*, by Meehan/Vogel (calculator programs for engineers).

PEREGRINE SMITH, BOOKS, Box 667, Layton UT 84041. (801)544-9800. Editorial Director: Buckley C. Jeppson. Publishes hardcover and paperback originals (80%) and reprints (20%). Pays 10% royalty on wholesale price; no advance. Photocopied submissions OK. Computer printout submissions OK; letter quality only. Reports in 3 months. SASE. Book catalog 37¢. **Nonfiction:** "Western American history, natural history, American architecture, art history and fine arts. We consider biographical, historical, descriptive and analytical studies in all of the above. Much emphasis is also placed on pictorial content. Many of our books are used as university texts." Query or submit outline/synopsis and 2 sample chapters. Accepts artwork/photos. Accepts nonfiction translations from French. Consult *Chicago Manual of Style*. Recently published *Spectacular Vernacular*, by J. Bourgeois; *Edward Weston on Photography*, by P. Bunnell; *California People*, by C. Dunlap; *A Toulouse-Lautrec Album*, by G. Beaute. **Fiction:** "We mainly publish reprints or anthologies of American writers." Query or submit outline/synopsis and 2 sample chapters. "No unsolicited manuscripts accepted. Query first." Looks for "style, readable, intelligent, careful writing. Must be geared to a competitive commercial market." Accepts fiction translations from French. **Tips:** "Write seriously. If fiction, no potboilers, bestseller movie tie-in type hype books and no science fiction. We like Pynchon and Gaddis. If nonfiction, only serious, well-researched critical, historical or craft-related topics. No self-help books."

THE PERFECTION FORM CO., Suite 15, 8350 Hickman Rd., Des Moines IA 50322. (515)278-0133. Editor: M. Kathleen Myers. Publishes paperback originals for sale in secondary schools. Publishes 10 titles/year. Pays royalty; offers small advance on publication. Simultaneous and photocopied submissions OK. SASE. Reports in 8 weeks. Free book catalog. **Fiction:** Original mss of approximately 20,000-30,000 words written for young adult audiences ages 12-18. Wholesome, high interest books. Adventure stories, humor, school problems, personal conflict and choice, sports, family, courage and endurance. Submit chapter and outline or complete ms.

*PERIVALE PRESS, 13830 Erwin St., Van Nuys CA 91401. (213)785-4671. Publisher: Lawrence P. Spingarn. Publishes trade paperback originals and trade paperback reprints. Averages 2-3 titles/year. Subsidy publishes 25% of books. "If the book's appeal is limited, we ask a subsidy to cover printing that is returnable from proceeds after one year." Pays 10-15% royalty or through grants. Simultaneous and photocopied submissions OK. SASE. Reports in 1 week on queries; 2 months on mss. Book catalog for business size SAE and 1 first class stamp.

Nonfiction: Humor and criticism. Subjects include criticism. Accepts translations from French, German, Italian, Portuguese and Spanish. "We are open to any new ideas that come along, particularly cook books, herbals and humor." Query. Accepts outline/synopsis and 2 sample chapters.

Recent Nonfiction Title: *Not-so-Simple Neil Simon*, by Edythe McGovern (criticism of dramatic work of Neil Simon).

Fiction: Experimental and mainstream; "open." No novels over 120 pages. Query. Looks for "a good story line with believable characters (fiction); a modern tone with competent translations (poetry anthologies of foreign literature). The first few sample chapters should be gripping."

Recent Fiction Titles: *Rice Powder*, by Sergio Galindo (novella; translation); *Mountainhouse*, by Patt McDermitt (novella; regional fiction, California); *The Blue Door*, by Lawrence Spingarn (stories); and *Fire & Water* by Elisabeth Stevens (stories).

Poetry: No poetry by individuals is now considered. Watch for next poetry chapbook competition.

Recent Poetry Titles: *Open to the Sun*, edited by Nora Wieser (anthology of Latin-American women poets by women); *Birds of Prey*, by Joyce Mansour (surrealist French poetry in translation); and *The Dark Playground*, by Lawrence Spingarn (satirical and polemical poetry).

Tips: "Study the trends in one particular field. Length is a factor. In all cases we hope for either grants from foundations or a returnable author subsidy written into the contract."

PERSEA BOOKS, 225 LaFayette St., New York City NY 10012. (212)431-5270. Editorial Director: Karen Braziller. Publisher: Michael Braziller. Publishes hardcover and paperback originals and reprints. Averages 10 titles/year. Pays 6-15% royalty. Offers average $500 advance. Simultaneous and photocopied submissions OK. SASE. Reports in 2 months.

Nonfiction: Poetry, critical essays and literary criticism. "Authors must send query letters first. If no query letter is sent unsolicited manuscripts will not be considered."

Recent Nonfiction Title: *The Book of the City of Ladies*, by Christine de Pizan.

Fiction: Experimental; historical; mainstream; and autobiographical fiction. Query.

Recent Fiction Titles: *A Meditation*, by Juan Benet; and *The Rock Pool*, by Cyril Connolly.

PERSEPHONE PRESS, Box 7222, Watertown MA 02172. (617)924-0336. Executives: Pat McGloin and Gloria Z. Greenfield. Publishes trade paperback originals. Averages 4 titles/year. Simultaneous and photocopied submissions OK. No computer printout or disk submissions. SASE. Reports in 1 month on queries; 3 months on mss. Free book catalog.

Nonfiction: Lesbian/women's books. Subjects include history, philosophy, politics, psychology, religion, sociology and lesbian/women's issues. "Persephone Press is interested in publishing innovative and provocative books by women with a strong lesbian sensibility. Our audience is general, but mainly consists of women, both lesbians and straights. We do not publish manuscripts by men." Query. Presently not accepting unsolicited mss. All unsolicited mss are returned unopened.

Recent Nonfiction Titles: *This Bridge Called My Back: Writings by Radical Women of Color*, edited by Moraga and Anzaldua; and *Nice Jewish Girls: A Lesbian Anthology*, edited by Evelyn Torton Beck.

Fiction: Adventure, confession, erotica, ethnic, experimental, fantasy, historical, humor, mystery, romance, science fiction and women's/lesbian. "Innovative and provocative fiction by women with a strong lesbian sensibility. No fiction by men." Query. All unsolicited mss are returned unopened.

Recent Fiction Titles: *Choices*, by Nancy Toder (novel about lesbian love); *The Wanderground: Stories of the Hill Women*, by Sally Gearhart (Utopian novel); *Zami: A New Spelling of My Name*, by Audre Lorde (biomythography).

Poetry: "Innovative and provocative poetry by women with a strong lesbian sensibility. We do not publish poetry by individual authors, nor do we publish works by men." Query.

Recent Poetry Titles: *Claiming an Identity They Taught Me to Despise*, by Michelle Cliff (prose-poetry); *Lesbian Poetry: An Anthology*, by Elly Bulkin/Joan Larkin Eds. (lesbian poetry); and *Keeper of Accounts*, by Irena Klepfisz.

PETERSEN PUBLISHING COMPANY, 6725 Sunset Blvd., Los Angeles CA 90028. (213)657-5100. Sales Promotion Manager: Mike Clifford. Publisher and Editorial Director, Specialty Publications: Lee Kelley. Publishes hardcover and paperback originals. Averages 11 titles/year. Pays royalty. Photocopied submissions OK. SASE. Reports in 4 weeks. Free book catalog for SASE.

Nonfiction: How-to and nonfiction works relating to automotive, Americana, art, sports and hobbies. Size and format variable. Particulary interested in titles in any field written by an acknowledged expert in that area. Query or submit outline/synopsis and sample chapters.

Recent Nonfiction Titles: *Toyota Tune-Up*, (in-house on auto repair); *Labrador Retriever*, by Richard Wolters; and *Maneaters*, by Peter Chastick.

PETERSON'S GUIDES, INC., Box 2123, Princeton NJ 08540. (609)924-5338. Publisher/President: Peter W. Hegener. Editorial Director: Karen C. Hegener. Publishes paperback originals. Averages 25 titles/year. Pays 8-12% royalty on "net price after discount;" buys some mss outright; offers advance. Photocopied submissions OK. SASE. Reports in 2 months. Free book catalog for SASE.
Nonfiction: Educational and career reference works. Submit complete ms or outline. Looks for "appropriateness of contents to our market, accuracy of information and use of reliable information sources, and writing style suitable for audience."
Recent Nonfiction Title: *Jobs for English Majors and Other Smart People*, by John Munschauer.

PETROCELLI BOOKS, INC., 1101 State Road, Princeton NJ 08540. (609)924-5851. Editorial Director: O.R. Petrocelli. Senior Editor: Roy Grisham. Publishes hardcover and paperback originals. Publishes 18 titles/year. Offers 12½-18% royalties. No advance. Simultaneous and photocopied submissions OK. Computer printout submissions OK; prefers letter quality to dot matrix. SASE. Reports in 4 weeks. Free book catalog.
Nonfiction: Business/economics; reference; technical; and textbooks. Submit outline/synopsis and 1-2 sample chapters.
Recent Nonfiction Titles: *Management Fraud*, by Elliot and Willingham (business); *Computer Optimization Techniques*, by W. Conley (computer/mathematics); and *Sexual Harassment*, by Mary C. Meyer.

PHILOMEL BOOKS, Division of The Putnam Publishing Group, 51 Madison Ave., New York NY 10010. (212)869-9200. Editor-in-Chief: Ann Beneduce. Editors: Linda Falken, Joan Knight. Publishes quality hardcover originals. Publishes 15-30 titles/year. Pays standard royalty. Advance negotiable. Photocopied submissions OK. No multiple submissions, please. SASE. Reports in 2 months. Free book catalog on request.
Nonfiction: Young adult and children's picture books. Does not want to see alphabet books or workbooks. Query first. Looks for "interesting theme; writing quality; suitability to our market."
Recent Nonfiction Title: *Sight and Seeing: A World of Light and Color*, by Hilda Simon.
Fiction: Young adult and children's book on any topic. Query to Patricia Rogers. Unsolicited manuscripts will be returned unopened. "We regret this change in procedure, but simply haven't the staff to cope with manuscripts unless we have authorized their submission in response to a previously submitted query letter."

PICKWICK PUBLICATIONS, 4137 Timberlane Dr., Allison Park PA 15101. Editorial Director: Dikran Y. Hadidian. Publishes paperback originals and reprints. Averages 3-6 titles/year. Pays 8-10% royalty on wholesale or retail price; no advance. Photocopied submissions OK. Computer printout and disk submissions OK. Reports in 2 months. SASE. Free book catalog.
Nonfiction: Religious and scholarly mss in Biblical archeology, Biblical studies, church history and theology. Also reprints of outstanding out-of-print titles and original texts and translations. Accepts nonfiction translations from French or German. No popular religious material. Query. Accepts outline/synopsis and 2 sample chapters. Consult *MLA Style Sheet* or Turabian's *A Manual for Writers*.
Recent Nonfiction Titles: *Reformed Roots* . . . , by Irena Bachus (historical-Biblical); and *Orientation by Disorientation*, by Spencer (literary and Biblical literary criticism).

PILOT BOOKS, 103 Cooper St., Babylon NY 11702. (516)422-2225. Publishes paperback originals. Offers standard royalty contract based on wholesale or retail price. Usual advance is $250, but this varies, depending on author's reputation and nature of book. Averages 20-30 titles/year. Send outline. Reports in 4 weeks. Enclose return postage.
General Nonfiction, Reference, and Business: "Publishes financial, business, travel, career, personal guides and training manuals. Our training manuals are utilized by America's giant corporations, as well as the government." Directories and books on moneymaking opportunities. Wants "clear, concise treatment of subject matter." Length: 8,000-30,000 words.
Recent Nonfiction Titles: *Starting and Operating a Word Processing Service*, by Jean Murray; and *The Senior Citizen's Guide to Budget Travel in the US and Canada*, by Paige Palmer.

PINE MOUNTAIN PRESS, INC., Box 19746, West Allis WI 53219. (414)778-1120. President: Robert W. Pradt. Publishes hardcover and quality paperback originals. Averages 8 titles/year. Pays 10-12% royalty on wholesale price. No advance. Simultaneous and photocopied submissions OK. Computer printout and disk submissions OK. SASE. Reports in 3 months. Book catalog for business size SAE and 1 first class stamp.
Imprints: *Leatherstocking* (frontier history, firearms, outdoor how-to's); *Med-Psych Publications* (psychology and folk medicine text books to popular markets).
Nonfiction: Humor, inspirational. Query or submit outline/synopsis and 2 sample chapters.
Recent Nonfiction Titles: *Sanity, Insanity and Common Sense*, by Enrique Suarez and Roger Mills; *How Sensuous Are You*, by Christy Lynn (professional); and *Rube Burrow, King of the Train Robbers*, by Carl Breihan (history).
Tips: "Once we start working with a writer we look for ideas only, not complete manuscripts." Queries/mss may be routed to other editors in the publishing group.

PINNACLE BOOKS, 1430 Broadway, New York NY 10018. Editor-in-Chief: Sondra Ordover. Publishes paperback originals and reprints. "Contracts and terms are standard and primarily competitive." Publishes 160 titles/year. Pays royalty on retail price. Catalog and requirements memo for SASE. "Will no longer accept unsolicited mss. Most books are assigned to known writers or developed through established agents. However, an intelligent, literate and descriptive letter of query will often be given serious consideration." SASE.
General: "Books range from general nonfiction to commercial trade fiction in most popular categories. Pinnacle's list is aimed for wide popular appeal, with fast-moving, highly compelling escape reading, adventure, espionage, historical intrigue and romance, science fiction, western, popular sociological issues, topical nonfiction. Seems to be a better acceptance of nonfiction and good commercial contemporary romance—both in the Helen Van Slyke and Jacqueline Susann style."
Tips: "Become familiar with our list of published books, and follow our instructions. It is a difficult market—paperbacks—with publishers competing for rack space. Watch what sells best and follow the trends as closely as possible. Study the original books that work, as well as the reprints. Good, persuasive query letters are the best and fastest tools you have to get an editor's attention. The idea, or angle is vital . . . then we trust the author has or can complete the manuscript."

PITMAN LEARNING, 6 Davis Dr., Belmont CA 94002. Publisher, Book Publishing Group: Mel Cebulash. Averages 50-70 titles/year. Pays royalty on wholesale price or fee outright. Photocopied submissions OK. SASE. Query or submit outline/synopsis and sample chapters. Reports in 1 month. Free book catalog.
Nonfiction: "We don't want to see material for the general trade market—our basic-skills and life-skills books are sold to elementary, secondary and adult basic education schools. Query.
Recent Nonfiction Title: *That's Life*, by Reiff/Clews (remedial/basic skills in a life-skills context).
Fiction: "We are looking for easy-to-read fiction written to a vocabulary scale we provide and suitable for the junior high school through adult basic education market. We are not looking for juvenile fiction, but prefer the major characters to be adults in adult situations. Sex role stereotyping is taboo."
Recent Fiction Titles: *Doomsday Journal* (6 young adult science disaster novels, incuding teacher's guide); and *Life School* (40 modules of life skills instruction for the high school or adult student reading at the 1st to 4th grade level).

‡**PLANET BOOKS, A Trade Paperback Division of Once Upon A Planet, Inc.**, Box 220, Bayside NY 11361. (212)961-9240. Editor: Philip Faraone. Publishes trade paperback originals and reprints. Averages 3 titles/year. Pays 5-10% royalty on wholesale price or makes outright purchase of $1,000 minimum. Offers average advance of $500-2,000. Simultaneous and photocopied submissions OK. SASE. Reports in 4 weeks on queries; 5 weeks on mss. Book catalog for business-size SAE and 1 first class stamp.
Nonfiction: How-to (satirical); humor; illustrated book; self-help (satirical); cartoons. Subjects include philosophy, psychology, sociology—anything funny. "We seek original potential high-volume sellers and are not interested in knock-offs of current best-sellers, e.g., *Real Writers Don't Steal Ideas*, or *The Official Knock-off Handbook*, etc. No fiction. We are not interested in erotic material." Query or submit outline/synopsis and sample chapters.
Recent Titles: *Why I Hate Men*, ed. by Claudia Charles; *Let's Hug!*, ed. by Josleen Wilson; and *How to Drive Like a Selfish Bastard*, ed. by Josleen Wilson (all humor).
Tips: "We try to address ourselves to large targeted groups (women, huggers, drivers) for maximum sales from a limited number of titles."

PLATT & MUNK PUBLISHERS, Division of Grosset & Dunlap, 51 Madison Ave., New York NY 10010. Senior Editor: Teresa A. Kennedy. Publishes hardcover and paperback originals. Averages 40-50 titles/year. Pays $1,000-3,500 in outright purchase; advance negotiable. Simultaneous and photocopied submissions OK. SASE. Reports in 6 weeks.
Nonfiction Juvenile: "We are particularly interested in series proposals rather than individual manuscripts, though everything submitted will be read. Nature, science, and light technology type books are all of interest. Submit proposal or query first, please." Looks for "new ways of looking at the world of children; no cutesy stuff."
Recent Nonfiction Titles: *Mysterious Seas*, by Mary Elting; *Birds of the World*, by Polly Greenberg; *Computer Programming 1, 2, 3*, by Dwight and Patricia Harris.
Fiction: Juvenile—all types, picture books for 3-7 age group and some higher. Also interested in anthology-type works and collections with a fresh approach.
Recent Fiction Titles: *The Illustrated Treasury of Fairy Tales*, edited by T. Kennedy; and *The Platt & Munk Treasury of Stories for Children*; and *Ghosts & Goblins*, by Tim Kirk.
Tips: "We want something new—a proposal for a new series for the ordinary picture book. You have a better chance, if you have new ideas."

PLENUM PUBLISHING CORP., 233 Spring St., New York NY 10013. Imprints include Da Capo Press, Consultants Bureau, IFI/Plenum Data Corporation, Plenum Press, Plenum Medical Book Company, Plenum

Scientific. President: Martin Tash. Executive Vice President: Mark Shaw. Publishes hardcover and paperback reprints. Publishes 300 titles/year.

Nonfiction: Scientific, medical and technical books including the social and behavioral sciences, physics, engineering and mathematics. Da Capo division publishes art, music, photography, dance and film.

‡PLURIBUS PRESS, INC., Division of Teach'em, Inc., 160 E. Illinois St., Chicago IL 60611. Assistant Editor: Ellen Slezak. Publishes hardcover and trade paperback originals. Averages 8-12 titles/year. Pays royalty. Simultaneous and photocopied submissions (if so advised) OK. Will consider computer printout submissions. SASE. Reports in 1 month.

Nonfiction: How-to, self-help, technical, textbooks on business and economics, health, psychology, sports, management "for adult professionals interested in improving the quality of their work and home life. In particular we want material that shows how to or is in self-help, technical, or textbook form with emphasis on health and education administration. Will consider proposals in the following areas: business/management, psychology, and sports. We will consider humorous treatment. No fiction, poetry, art, nature, history, juvenile, politics, religion, travel, biography or autobiography considered." Query or submit outline/synopsis and 3 sample chapters.

Recent Nonfiction Titles: *The Healing Mission and the Business Ethic*, by Robert M. Cunningham, Jr. (health care); *How to Make Decisions That Payoff*, by J. Daniel Mathein and Morris B. Squire (general management); and *Making Success a Habit*, by Steve Musseau (self-help/management).

POCKET BOOKS, 1230 Avenue of the Americas, New York NY 10020. Paperback originals and reprints. Published 300 titles last year. Pays royalty on retail price. Query only; include SASE. No unsolicited mss, except for imprints which follow: *Timescape, Tapestry, Archway.*

Imprints: *Washington Square Press* (high-quality mass market). *Timescape* (science fiction and fantasy). *Archway* (children and young adults). *Poseidon Press* (hardcover fiction and nonfiction). *Tapestry* (historical romance).

General: History, biography, general nonfiction and adult fiction (mysteries, science fiction, romance, westerns). Reference books.

Recent Nonfiction Titles: *What About the Russians—and Nuclear War*, by Ground Zero; and *The Invisible Bankers*, by Andrew Tobias.

Recent Fiction Titles: *This Calder Range*, by Janet Dailey (contemporary romance); *Lace*, by Shirley Conran; and *The Prodigal Daughter*, by Jeffrey Archer.

POET GALLERY PRESS, 224 W. 29th St., New York NY 10001. Editor: E.J. Pavlos. Publishes paperback originals. Pays standard 10-12½-15% royalty contract. Averages 5 titles/year. Submit complete ms only. Enclose return postage with ms.

Nonfiction: "We are a small specialty house, and we place our emphasis on publishing the works of young Americans currently living in Europe. We are interested in creative writing rather than commercial writing. We publish for writers who live overseas, who write and live, who produce writings from the self. Our books might turn out to be commercial, but that is a secondary consideration. We expect to emphasize poetry; however, our list will be concerned with all aspects of literature: the novel, plays, and cinema, as well as criticism. We urge that authors recognize our imposed restrictions; we cannot, and do not wish at this time to compete with major publishing companies." Recently published *Sarah*, by Gamela; *Iris Elegy*, by Hakim; and *Balancing Act: A Congruence of Symbols*.

Tips: "The major problem with submissions is that while the works submitted are works of 'love,' the writers have not learned their craft! Read, write, study." Looks for "quality: 1) a mastery of craft; 2) an expression worth the craft; and 3) craft worth the expression."

POLARIS PRESS, 16540 Camellia Terrace, Los Gatos CA 95030. (408)356-7795. Editor: Edward W. Ludwig. Paperback originals; considers reprints, depending upon reputation of author. Specializes in science fiction and college-level books with appeal to general public. Averages 3 titles/year. Pays 6% royalty on retail price; advance averages $100-300. Send contact sheets or prints if photos and/or illustrations are to accompany ms. Simultaneous and photocopied submissions OK. Reports in 1-2 weeks. SASE. Free book catalog with 50¢ postage.

Fiction: Fantasy and science fiction 60,000-90,000 words. "Please, *no* mss which require extensive (and expensive) use of color in inner pages." No juvenile or general fiction. Query.

Recent Fiction Titles: *The Seven Shapes of Solomon*; *Bean & Eleven Others*, by Ludwig (anthology of previously published science and science fantasy stories); and *Gumshan: The Chinese American Saga*, by Loo.

Tips: "Query to determine immediate needs, which are usually specialized. List briefly main interests and qualifications. Will accept 2 sample chapters plus synopsis. There is little chance that a nonsolicited manuscript will be accepted spontaneously."

POPULAR SCIENCE BOOKS, Book Division, Times Mirror Magazines, Inc., (subsidiary of Times Mirror Co.), 380 Madison Ave., New York NY 10017. Editor: John Sill. Publishes books for Popular Science Book Club that are also distributed by major trade publishers. Pays royalty and advance relative to book list price. SASE.
Nonfiction: Do-it-yourself guides on home and shop how-to, wood-working, cabinet making, housebuilding, home repairs, energy savings, car care. Submit author resume, outline, sample chapters, and sample illustrations for heavily illustrated small books to 35,000 words and large books to 150,000 words. Looks for "either a description of each chapter's contents or a subject-by-subject breakout. Sample rough drawings and photographs: either color tranparencies, any size, or 8x10 b&w glossies."

PORTER SARGENT PUBLISHERS, INC., 11 Beacon St., Boston MA 02108. (617)523-1670. Publishes hardcover and paperback originals, reprints, translations and anthologies. Averages 4 titles/year. Pays royalty on retail price. "Each contract is dealt with on an individual basis with the author." Free book catalog. Send query with brief description, table of contents, sample chapter and information regarding author's background. Computer printout and disk submissions OK. Enclose return postage. Looks for "originality and clear and concise treatment and availability of subject."
Reference, Special Education, and Academic Nonfiction: "Handbook Series and Special Education Series offer standard, definitive reference works in private education and writings and texts in special education. The Extending Horizons Series is an outspoken, unconventional series which presents topics of importance in contemporary affairs and the social sciences." This series is particularly directed to the college adoption market. Nonfiction only. Accepts nonfiction translations from French and Spanish. Contact Christopher Leonesio.
Recent Nonfiction Titles: *Social Power and Political Freedom*, by G. Sharp (political science); and *Workplace Democracy and Social Change*, by F. Lindenfeld and J. Rothschild-Whitt (sociology).

POTENTIALS DEVELOPMENT FOR HEALTH & AGING SERVICES, Suite 321, 775 Main St., Buffalo NY 14203. (716)842-2658. Editor: Mary V. Kirchhofer. Publishes paperback originals. Averages 6 titles/year. Pays 5-10% royalty on retail price. Simultaneous submissions OK. SASE. Reports in 6 weeks. Free book catalog for SASE.
Nonfiction: Human development mss with emphasis on mental, physical and emotional health for older adults. "We seek material of interest to those working with elderly people in the community and in institutional settings. We need textbooks for practical gerontological education." Query or submit outline/synopsis and 3 sample chapters. Looks for "suitable subject matter, writing style and organization."
Recent Nonfiction Title: *What Shall I Do with a Hundred Years? Creative Writing I and II*, by Pat Quigley.

CLARKSON N. POTTER, INC., 1 Park Ave., New York NY 10016. (212)532-9200. Editorial Director: Carol Southern. Director of Operations: Michael Fragnito. Publishes hardcover and trade paperbacks. Pays 10% royalty on hardcover; 5-7½% on paperback, varying escalations; advance depends on type of book and reputation or experience of author. Averages 35 titles/year. Samples of prints may be included with outline. Photocopied submissions OK. No computer printout or disk submissions. Reports in 2-4 weeks. SASE. Free book catalog.
Nonfiction: Publishes Americana, art, autobiography, biography, cooking and foods, decorating, history, how-to, humor, juvenile, nature, photography, self-help style and annotated literature. "Mss must be cleanly typed on 8½x11 non-erasable bond; double-spaced. Chicago *Manual of Style* is preferred." Accepts artwork and photos. Query or submit outline/synopsis and sample chapters. Accepts nonfiction translations.
Recent Nonfiction Titles: *How to Make Love to a Woman*, by Michael Morgenstern; *Entertaining*, by Martha Stewart; *French Style*, by Susie Slegin.
Fiction: Quality.
Recent Fiction Titles: *Arcadio*, by William Goyen; *Colombian Gold*, by Jaime Maurifue.

PRECEDENT PUBLISHING, INC., 520 N. Michigan Ave., Chicago IL 60611. (312)828-0420. Editorial Director: Louis A. Knafla. Publishes hardcover and paperback originals. Pays 10% royalty. Reports in 1 month on queries; 2 months on mss. No computer printout or disk submissions. SASE. Free book catalog: SASE.
Nonfiction: Scholarly books: history, Afro-American life, philosophy, war and peace. No fiction or poetry. Query, including outline of chapters, synopsis of book, author's resume, maximum number of words projected and tentative date of ms. Accepts nonfiction translations. Recently published *Envelopes of Sound*, by Grele (oral history); *Perception, Theory, Commitment*, by Brown (philosophy/science); *US Diplomatic Codes*, by Weber (history); *Heidegger, Man and Thinker*, edited by Sheehan; *Forgotten Victim: History of the Civilian*, by Hartigan (military, political science/law).

PRENTICE-HALL, Children's Book Division, Englewood Cliffs NJ 07632. Manuscripts Editor: Rose Lopez. Publishes hardcover and paperback originals and paperback reprints. Publishes "roughly 30 hardcovers, and about 15 paperbacks/year. Pays royalty; average advance. No computer printout or disk submissions.

SASE. Reports in 6 weeks. Book catalog for SASE.

Nonfiction: All subjects, all age groups but special interest in topical science and technology, art, social sciences, "star" biography (7-10 of outlaws, magicians and other characters), current events (7-10 and 9-12), health (teenage problems by MDs only), history (any unusual approaches), humor (no jokes or riddles but funny fiction), music (keen interest in basic approaches, no biographies), sociology (8-12), and sports (6-9), puzzle and participation (6-8). Query. Accepts outline/synopsis and 5-6 sample chapters from published writers; entire ms from unpublished writers.

Recent Nonfiction Titles: *Future Life: The Biotechnology Revolution*, by Dr. Alvin and Virginia B. Silverstein; *The Lippizaners and the Spanish Riding School of Vienna*, by Philippe Dumas; and *Life on a Barge: A Sketchbook*, by Huck Scarry.

Fiction: Gothic, humor, mainstream and mystery. Submit outline/synopsis and sample chapters.

Recent Fiction Titles: *The Voyage of the Lucky Dragon*, by Jack Bennett (family adventure, ages 10 and up); *Go Ask Alice* (documentary); *Stairway to Doom: A Miss Mallard Mystery*, by Robert Quackenbush (detective mystery, ages 6-9).

Picture Books: Accent on humor.

Recent Picture Books: *Happy Birthday, Moon*, written and illustrated by Frank Asch; *Hugo and the Space Dog*, written and illustrated by Lee Lorenz; *To Bed, to Bed*, by Mischa Richter (wordless); and *Silly Goose*, by Jack Kent.

PRENTICE-HALL, INC., General Publishing Division, Englewood Cliffs NJ 07632. Editorial Director: Lynne A. Lumsden. Publishes hardcover and simultaneous trade paperback originals. Will consider unsolicited photocopied submissions on nonfiction topics, but not responsible for returning unsolicited manuscripts. Computer printout and disk submissions OK; prefers letter quality to dot matrix. SASE must be included in order to receive a response in 6-8 weeks. "No responses will be sent nor materials returned on proposals for fiction, poetry, romances, westerns, personal life stories, or for other subjects we do not publish."

Nonfiction: Educational, professional, or how-to subjects like computers (books and software), business, health, music and other performing arts, psychology, science, art, travel, nature, religion, sports, self-help, vocational-technical subjects, hobbies, recreation, and reference. Length 60,000 words. Accepts nonfiction translations.

Tips: "The writer should submit his/her work profesionally prepared and typewritten." Submit outline and 2-3 sample chapters. Queries/mss may be routed to other editors in the publishing group.

THE PRESERVATION PRESS, National Trust for Historic Preservation, 1785 Massachusetts Ave. NW, Washington DC 20036. Publishes nonfiction books and periodicals on historic preservation (saving and reusing the "built environment"). Averages 4-6 titles/year. Books are often commissioned by the publisher. Subject matter encompasses architecture and architectural history, neighborhood preservation, regional planning, preservation law, building restoration and rural area conservation. No local history. Query. Looks for "relevance to national preservation-oriented audience; educational or instructional value; depth; uniqueness; need in field."

Recent Nonfiction Titles: *New Energy From Old Buildings*; *Respectable Rehabilitation: Answers to Your Questions About Old Buildings*.

PRESIDIO PRESS, 31 Pamaron Way, Novato CA 94947. (415)883-1373. Editor-in-Chief: Adele Horwitz. Senior Editor: Joan Griffin. Publishes hardcover and paperback originals. Pays 15% on net price royalty; offers nominal advance. Photocopied submissions OK. Computer printout submissions OK; disk submissions "depending on equipment used." SASE. Reports in 3 months. Free book catalog.

Nonfiction: California, regional, contemporary military history. No scholarly mss or fiction. Accepts nonfiction translations. Query or submit outline/synopsis and 3 sample chapters.

Recent Nonfiction Titles: *San Francisco: Story of a City*, by J. McGloin (history); *Strategy for Defeat*, by U.S. Sharp (popular military affairs); and *We Led the Way: Darby's Rangers*, by W. Baumer (popular WW II history).

PRESS PACIFICA, Box 47, Kailua HI 96734. Publisher: Jane Wilkins Pultz. Publishes hardcover and paperback originals (50%) and reprints (50%). Averages 4 titles/year. Pays 10% royalty "with escalations" on retail price; advance averages $100. Simultaneous and photocopied ("if on good white paper and very readable") submissions OK. No computer printout or disk submissions. Reports in 1-3 months. SASE. Book catalog for 50¢.

Nonfiction: Publishes Hawaii authors only. History (especially women and Hawaii); Hawaiiana; women (history, biography, anthologies, feminist theory); self-help; and how-to. Accepts nonfiction translations from French, Portuguese, Oriental and Polynesian. "We are open to new authors who have expertise in their field." Children's books with Hawaii theme. No technical or supernatural material. Accepts artwork/photos. Submit outline/synopsis and 2-3 sample chapters. "Subject matter, expertise, writing and exposition must be impeccable."

Recent Nonfiction Titles: *Botanist Visit to Hawaii in 1831*; *Easy Cooking—The Island Way*; and *Japanese Bon Dance in Hawaii*.

PRESSWORKS, INC., Suite 225, 2800 Routh St., Dallas TX 75201. (214)749-1044. President: Anne Dickson. Publishes hardcover originals. Averages 17 titles/year. Pays variable royalty on retail price; offers variable advance. Simultaneous and photocopied submissions OK. Computer printout submissions OK; prefers letter quality to dot matrix. SASE. Reports in 1 month on queries; reporting time varies on mss. Free book catalog.
Nonfiction: Reference. Subjects include Americana, art, business and economics, history, and other branches of the humanities. Accepts artwork/photos. Consumers are libraries and scholars, trade bookstores, rare book dealers. Submit outline/synopsis and 3 sample chapters or complete ms. Looks for "good, clean style and timely subject." Accepts nonfiction translations.
Recent Nonfiction Titles: *First Printings of Texas Authors*, by Cameron Northouse (reference); and *The Fifty Best Books on Texas*, by A. C. Greene.
Fiction: Humor and/or intense feeling with well-developed dialogue. Accepts fiction translations.

PRICE/STERN/SLOAN INC., PUBLISHERS, 410 N. La Cienega Blvd., Los Angeles CA 90048. Imprints include *Cliff House Books*, *Serendipity Books*, *Troubador Press* and *Laughter Library*. Executive Editor: L.L. Sloan. Editorial Director: Lawrence S. Dietz. Publishes trade paperback originals. Averages 100-120 titles/year. Pays royalty on wholesale price, or by outright purchase; small or no advance. Simultaneous and photocopied submissions OK. SASE. Reports in 6-8 weeks. Book catalog for SASE.
Nonfiction: Humor; self-help; and satire (limited). Submit outline/synopsis and sample chapters. "Most titles are unique in concept as well as execution and are geared for the so-called gift market."

PRINCETON BOOK CO., PUBLISHERS, Box 109, Princeton NJ 08540. (201)297-8370. Editorial Director: Charles Woodford. Publishes hardcover and paperback originals (70%) and reprints (30%). Averages 5-7 titles/year. Pays 10% royalty; no advance. Simultaneous and photocopied submissions OK. Reports in 6 weeks. SASE. Free book catalog.
Nonfiction: Professional books and college textbooks on education, physical education, dance, sociology and recreation. No "books that have a strictly trade market." Submit outline/synopsis and sample chapters with vita. Looks for "originality of ideas and/or scholarship; writing style; marketing potential; author's credentials."
Recent Nonfiction Titles: *Making It Till Friday: A Guide to Successful Classroom Management*, by Long/Frye (college textbook); *Recreational Leadership*, by Shivers (professional book); and *The Acquisition of Motor Skill*, by Kleinman (professional book).

*PRINCETON UNIVERSITY PRESS, 41 William St., Princeton NJ 08540. (609)542-4900. Associate Director and Editor: R. Miriam Brokaw. Publishes hardcover and trade paperback ("very few") originals and reprints. Averages 130 titles/year. Subsidy assists 50% of books, "when we don't break even on the first printing." Pays 15% maximum royalty on retail price; offers minimum $1,000 advance ("but rarely"). Simultaneous (rarely) and photocopied submissions OK. SASE. Reports in 1 week on queries; 1 month on mss "if unsuitable" or 4 months "if suitable."
Nonfiction: Biography, reference and technical. Subjects include art, literature, history, music, politics, religion, sociology and poetry. "We're looking for any scholarly book with an importance of subject, clear writing." Query.
Recent Nonfiction Titles: *Bertolt Brecht in America*, by James K. Lyon (literature); *Japan Over Two Centuries*, by Marius B. Jansen (Asian history); and *Medical Thinking*, by Lester B. King (medicine).
Poetry: "Poetry submissions (original and in translation) are judged in competition. Write Mrs. Marjorie Sherwood." Submit complete ms.

‡PRINTEMPS BOOKS, INC., Box 746, Wilmette IL 60091. (312)251-5418. Secretary-Treasurer: Beatrice Penovich. Publishes trade paperbacks. Averages 3 titles/year. Pays royalty or buys some mss outright, "to be agreed upon." No advance. SASE. Reports in 1 month on mss.
Fiction: Adventure, ethnic, fantasy, humor, mystery, suspense, children's stories (short). "Our aim is to both entertain and educate students who have less than average reading skills. We envision publication of a collection of stories suitable for high school students who have a very limited vocabulary." Publishes for school systems and over-the-counter purchases. Submit complete ms.

PROMETHEUS BOOKS, INC., 700 E. Amherst St., Buffalo NY 14215. (716)837-2475. Editor-in-Chief: Paul Kurtz. Director of Advertising and Promotion: Victor Gulotta. Publishes hardcover and trade paperback originals. Averages 24 titles/year. Pays 5-10% royalty on wholesale price; offers negotiable advance. Computer printout submissions OK. SASE. Reports in 1 month. Free book catalog.
Nonfiction and Fiction: Textbook and trade. Subjects include philosophy, science, psychology, religion, sociology, medical ethics, biography, literature and criticism. "Prometheus is an independent publishing house

with a commitment to maximizing the availability of books of high scholarly merit and popular intrigue. We welcome manuscript proposals suitable to our publishing program, which focuses on the humanities and social and natural sciences. One area of specialization in which we have experienced tremendous growth is scientific criticism of 'paranormal phenomena.' We also are interested in examining proposals for competitive college texts, both primary and supplementary.'' Accepts nonfiction translations. Submission of popular trade nonfiction is also encouraged. Submit outline/synopsis and ''at least the first few'' chapters. Accepts artwork/photos.
Recent Titles: *The Roving Mind*, by Isaac Asimov (science); *Sam Holman*, by James T. Farrell (fiction); *Flim-Flam!*, by James Randi (science and psychology); *Mark Twain: Selected Writings of an American Skeptic*, edited by Victor Doyno (biography).

PRUETT PUBLISHING CO., 2928 Pearl, Boulder CO 80302. Managing Editor: Gerald Keenan. Averages 25-30 titles/year. Royalty contract on wholesale price. No advance. ''Most books that we publish are aimed at special interest groups. As a small publisher, we feel most comfortable in dealing with a segment of the market that is very clearly identifiable, and one we know we can reach with our resources.'' Free catalog on request. Mss must conform to the Chicago *Manual of Style*. Legible photocopies acceptable. Any disk submissions would have to interface with present typesetting system. Query. Reports in 2-4 weeks. SASE.
General Adult Nonfiction and Textbooks: Pictorial railroad histories; outdoor activities related to the Intermountain West; some Western Americana. Accepts artwork/photos. Textbooks with a regional (Intermountain) aspect for pre-school through college level. Does not want to see anything with the personal reminiscence angle or biographical studies of little-known personalities. ''Like most small publishers, we try to emphasize quality from start to finish, because, for the most part, our titles are going to a specialized market that is very quality conscious. We also feel that one of our strong points is the personal involvement ('touch') so often absent in a much larger organization.'' Accepts outline/synopsis and 3 sample chapters. Recently published *N&W: Giant of Steam*, by Jeffries (railroadiana); *Montana: Our Land and People*, by Lang and Myers; and *Evening Before the Diesel*, by Foss.

‡**THE PUBLISHING WARD, INC.**, Box 9077, Fort Collins CO 80525. Editor: Dan S. Ward. Publishes hardcover and trade paperback originals. Averages 4-6 titles/year. Pays 10-15% royalty on wholesale price. No advance. Simultaneous and photocopied submissions (if good copies) OK. Computer printout submissions OK, if letter quality on 8½x11 paper; disk submissions OK, if query first. SASE. Reports in 3 weeks on queries; 6 weeks on mss.
Nonfiction: Humor, ancient history, crossword puzzles for a ''general, well-read audience.'' Especially needs ''unique, innovative approaches to standard subjects.'' Query.
Recent Nonfiction Title: *Crosswords for People Who are Bored with Crosswords*, by D.S. Ward (crossword puzzles).
Fiction: Historical, humor, science fiction for a ''general, well-read audience.'' Especially needs ''well researched historical novels; science fiction and futuristic novels with realistic characters. We insist on good narrative presentation and quality plots. Length: 60,000-150,000 words.'' No fantasy. Submit complete ms.
Recent Fiction Title: *Dawn, The Chosen*, by D.S. Ward (science fiction love story).

PURDUE UNIVERSITY PRESS, South Campus Courts, D., West Lafayette IN 47907. (317)494-2035. Director: William J. Whalen. Managing Editor: Verna Emery. Publishes hardcover and paperback originals. Specializes in scholarly books from all areas of academic endeavor. Pays 10% royalty on list price; no advance. Publishes 6 titles/year. Photocopied submissions OK ''if author will verify that it does not mean simultaneous submission elsewhere.'' No computer printout or disk submissions. Reports in 2-4 months. SASE. Free book catalog.
Nonfiction: Publishes agriculture, Americana, art (but no color plates), biography, communication, economics, engineering, history, horticulture, literature, nature, philosophy, political science, psychology, scientific, sociology, and literary criticism. ''Works of scholarship only.'' Submit complete ms only.
Recent Nonfiction Titles: *The Falcon and the Eagle: Montenegro and Austria-Hungary, 1908-1914*, by John D. Treadway; *Plain Talk*, edited by Carol Burke; *Ultimately Fiction: Design in Modern American Literary Biography*, by Dennis W. Petrie; and *Black-White Contact in Schools: Its Social and Academic Effects*, by Martin Patchen.

Q.E.D. INFORMATION SCIENCES, INC., 170 Linden St., Box 181, Wellesley MA 02181. (617)237-5656. Editor: Edwin F. Kerr. Publishes trade paperback originals. Averages 10 titles/year. Pays 10-15% royalty on retail price. Photocopied submissions OK. Computer printout and disk submissions OK. SASE. Reports in 1 week on queries; 3 weeks on mss. Free book catalog.
Nonfiction: Technical. Subjects include computers and database technology. ''Our books are read by data processing managers and technicians.'' Submit outline/synopsis and 2 sample chapters.
Recent Nonfiction Titles: *Managing Systems Maintenance*, by W. Perry (technical); *Design Guide for CODASYL DBMS*, by R. Perron (technical); and *Managing for Productivity in Data Processing*, by J. Johnson (technical).

‡**QUALITY PUBLICATIONS, INC.**, Box 2633, Lakewood OH 44107. Executive Editor: Gary S. Skeens. Associate Editor: Robin S. Moser. Publishes trade paperback originals. Averages 7 titles/year. Pays 10-20% royalty on retail price. No advance. Simultaneous and photocopied submissions OK. Computer printout and disk submissions OK. SAE. Reports in 1 week on queries; 2 months on mss. Book catalog for 6x9 SAE and 3 first class stamps.

Fiction: Adventure, erotica, mainstream, western. Accepts fiction and poetry translations from French, Spanish and Russian. Publishes for an "open audience: wide range of backgrounds, experiences, education; those who feel to the very marrow of their bone. No weak plot or character development, dishonesty with writers' work or themselves, pornography." Query. "We will not be actively seeking manuscripts between 1983 and 1985, though we will look at any strong queries that might be sent in."

Recent Fiction Titles: *As Any Mount of Its Snows*, by Joseph Davey and *Black Badges Are Bad Business and Other Stories*, by 3 authors (story collections).

Poetry: No "pornography, weak style, development lapses, poor image usage." Submit 10-15 samples.

Recent Poetry Titles: *Playground Poems*, by Yvonne L. Rusiniak (serious); *Offering*, by Skip Johnson (inspirational); *The Dancer*, by Gary S. Skeens (serious/street); *Sing Loud & Long of Leafy Trees*, by Laverne Rison (serious); and *Poems, and Roses . . . A Lady*, by Gary S. Skeens (love/searching).

‡**QUE CORP.**, 7960 Castleway Dr., Indianapolis IN 46250. (317)842-7162. Managing Editor: Paul Mangin. Publishes trade paperback originals. Averages 18-22 titles/year. Pays 7-10% royalty on wholesale price; variable royalty on retail price; buys some mss outright. Simultaneous (if so advised) and photocopied submissions OK. Computer printout submissions OK; disk submissions compatible with IBM 3740 55/50 8" or IBM PC 5¼" or Osborne 5¼". SASE. Reports in 2 weeks on queries; 1 month on mss. Book catalog for business-sized SAE and 1 first class stamp.

Nonfiction: How-to, reference books, technical, textbooks on business (related to microcomputers and word processing), hobbies (microcomputers), and microcomputer systems and evaluations. Especially needs manuscripts on microcomputers, word processing and home or educational use of microcomputers. Query or submit outline/synopsis and 2-4 sample chapters or complete ms.

Recent Nonfiction Titles: *IBM's Personal Computer*, by DeVoney and Summe (computer systems analysis); *CP/M Word Processing*, by DeVoney (software evaluations); and *VisiCalc Models for Business*, by Cobb (planning tool use); *Timex/Sinclair 1000 User's Guide (Vols. 1&2)* (programming guide); *Super Calc Super Models for Business*; *The Osborne Portable Computer*.

‡**QUICKSILVER PRODUCTIONS**, Box 340, Ashland OR 97520. (503)482-5343. Manager: Nancy Hozer. Publishes mass market paperback originals. Averages 4 titles/year. Pays 7½-8% royalty. Free book catalog. Computer printout submissions OK; "we prefer disk submissions."

Nonfiction: Cookbooks, and calendars on astrology.

Recent Nonfiction Titles: *Celestial Influences 83*, by Jim Maynard (wall calendar); *Pocket Astrologer 83*, by Jim Maynard (calendar); *Putting It Up With Honey*, by Susann Geiskopf (cookbook); *Celestial Guide 83*, by Jim Maynard (engagement calendar); *The Vegetarian Treasure Chest*, by Winifred Graham (cookbook).

QUINTESSENCE PUBLISHING CO., INC., 8 S. Michigan Ave., Chicago IL 60603. (312)782-3221. Publisher: H.W. Haase. Vice President, Editorial: Tomoko Tsuchiya. Publishes hardcover and trade paperback originals. Averages 22 titles/year. Pays average 10% royalty. Computer printout and disk submissions OK. SASE. Reports in 2 weeks.

Nonfiction: Technical (on all aspects of dentistry). Accepts artwork/photos. Submit outline/synopsis and 2-4 sample chapters.

R & E RESEARCH ASSOC., Box 2008, Saratoga CA 95070. (415)494-1112. Publisher: R. Reed. Publishes trade paperback originals. Averages 60 titles/year. Pays 10-15% royalty on retail price; no advance. Photocopied submissions OK. SASE. Reports in 1 month. Free book catalog.

Nonfiction: How-to, reference, self-help, textbook and scholarly. Subjects include Americana, business and economics, health, history, politics, psychology, sociology and education. "We would like how-to books, manuals for educators, self-help books, and reference materials." Query or submit outline/synopsis and sample chapters.

Recent Nonfiction Titles: *Tips on Having a Successful Sale*; *Teacher Survival Handbook*.

R & R NEWKIRK, ITT Publishing, Box 1727, Indianapolis IN 46206. (317)297-4360. Editor: Anne Shropshire. Publishes trade paperback originals. Averages 12 titles/year. Pays 10-15% royalty on retail price. Simultaneous and photocopied submissions OK. No computer printout or disk submissions. SASE. Reports in 2 weeks on queries; 1 month on mss. Free book catalog.

Nonfiction: Self-help/motivational, technical, and sales techniques/methods. Subjects include how-to for life insurance selling. "Our books are written for life insurance agents, managers and trainers. We publish 1 softcover book per month—have scheduled prospective mss through April, 1984, but this is not an inflexible

schedule and we can alter it in consideration of a publishable ms. Material must pertain to sales." Submit outline/synopsis and 3 sample chapters or complete ms. Looks for "clear, crisp writing; a fully developed theme."
Recent Nonfiction Titles: *Time Management*, by Dennis Hensley (motivation/how-to); *Inflation-Proof Your Retirement*, by Lawrence Bell; and *Section 303 Stock Redemption*, by Leo Hodges (technical training).
Tips: "Research thoroughly your intended audience and direct your work to their needs. Subject should be appropriate to the life insurance (particularly sales) market, and the more defined the subject matter, the better."

RAND McNALLY & CO. PUBLISHING GROUP, Box 7600, Chicago IL 60680. Variable royalty and advance schedule. Some outright purchases. Photocopied submissions OK. SASE.
Nonfiction: Focus on geographically-related subjects. Travel and other reference works. Query first.
Recent Nonfiction Titles: *Places Rated Retirement Guide*; *Colorado: Rocky Mountain Country*; *Bill Kurtis on Assignment*.
Juvenile: Picture books, young information books. Query first.

RANDOM HOUSE, INC., 201 E. 50th St., New York NY 10022. Also publishes Vintage Books. Publishes hardcover and paperback originals and reprints. Payment as per standard minimum book contracts. Query. SASE.
Fiction and Nonfiction: Publishes fiction and nonfiction of the "highest standards."
Poetry: Some poetry volumes.

RANDOM HOUSE, INC., School Division, 201 E. 50th St., New York NY 10022. (212)751-2600. Managing Editor: Gerry Gabianelli. Publishes textbooks, paperbacks, and worktexts for school market. Averages 40 titles/year. Pays royalty or buys ms outright; "depending on the nature of the project." Reports in 2 months.
Nonfiction: Textbooks and workbooks in reading, language arts and math—K-8, English and social studies for secondary level. Submit outline/synopsis and 2-3 sample chapters.

*RANGER ASSOCIATES, INC., Box 1357, Manassas VA 22110. (703)369-5336. Publications Director: Sharon M. Lane. Publishes hardcover and trade paperback originals and reprints. Averages 5 titles/year. Subsidy publishes 25% of books based on "the literary quality of the manuscript and a board decision as to the profitability of the book for the client. We will not print a book which we feel will not sell." Pays 5-12% royalty on wholesale price; on retail price for those sold at retail. Simultaneous and photocopied submissions OK. Computer printout submissions OK. Disk submissions should be compatible with Tandy Corp. TRS-80 Model I. SASE. Reports in 3 weeks on queries; 6 weeks on mss. Free book catalog "when available."
Imprints: *Ranger Press* (fiction and nonfiction); Ranger Book Club (military nonfiction). Sharon M. Lane, director, publications.
Nonfiction: Biography, how-to, humor, illustrated book, juvenile and self-help; "will consider all types." Subjects include business and economics, history, hobbies, recreation, sports and travel; "will consider others. We are particularly interested in manuscripts about elite military units and leaders, e.g., rangers, paratroopers, commandos and irregular forces. We would like to receive original works on the Ranger Battalions of WWII, the Ranger Companies of the Korean War, and Ranger/Special Forces Advisors in Vietnam. Our audience is the mass of American readers searching for well researched, well written books on elite military units and leaders. We address our advertising to soldiers, veterans and their families." Query or submit outline/synopsis and 3 sample chapters. Accepts artwork/photos. Looks for "organization, creativity, intelligence." Accepts nonfiction translations from French, German and Spanish.
Recent Nonfiction Titles: *Lead the Way, Rangers!*, by Henry S. Glassman (history); *Pillars of the Pentagon*, by Nita Scoggan (religious); *An Infantryman's Journal*, by John F. Hummer (autobiography); *Job Sharing*, by Penny Jensen and Shelley Kuenning (how-to).
Fiction: "Our preference is for nonfiction during the coming year; however, we will consider exceptional work in some areas of fiction." No erotica. Query or submit outline/synopsis and sample chapters.
Recent Fiction Titles: *Goodness Gracious*, by Harry P. Levitt (juvenile); *The Pestilence Plot*, by Betty Ann Patterson (adult novel).

REALTORS NATIONAL MARKETING INSTITUTE, Affiliate of National Association of Realtors, 430 N. Michigan Ave., Chicago IL 60611. (312)670-3780. Director of Publishing: Barbara Gamez-Craig. Publishes hardcover and trade paperback originals. Averages 12 titles/year. Pays 10% maximum on retail price; offers advance: "50% of estimated royalties from sales of first printing." Simultaneous and photocopied submissions OK. SASE. Reports in 2 months. Free book catalog.
Nonfiction: How-to, reference, self-help and technical. Subjects include business and economics (realty-oriented) and professional real estate. "We're interested in real estate-oriented mss on commercial-investment (basic how-to); residential-creative; and management strategies and motivation for real estate professionals." Submit outline/synopsis and sample chapter.
Recent Nonfiction Titles: *Real Estate Data—Your Market & Your Firm*, by George D. Herman; *Home Buying—The Complete Illustrated Guide*, by Henry Harrison; *The Condominium Home—A Special Marketing*

Challenge, by Janet Scavo; *Role Playing*, by Alice McIntyre; *Success Strategies for Investment Real Estate*, by Jerry D. Anderson.

A.H. & A.W. REED LTD., Box 14-029, Wellington, 3, New Zealand. Tel. 873-045. Subsidiaries include Reed Books Ltd; Tangent Publications Ltd. Publishes hardcover and trade and mass market paperback originals and reprints. Averages 50 titles/year. Pays 10% royalty on retail price; buys some mss outright for $2,000-15,000; offers average $250 advance, "dependent on author's needs. SASE. Reports in 2 weeks on queries; 1 month on mss. Free book catalog.
Nonfiction: Biography, "coffee table" book, cookbook, how-to, illustrated book, reference, self-help on New Zealand, animals, art, business, cooking and foods, health, history, hobbies, nature, photography, politics, recreation, sociology, sports, travel, photo essays of New Zealand. No mss that are too "overseas" in content for New Zealand publication or adaptation. Submit outline/synopsis and sample chapters.
Recent Nonfiction Titles: *I Passed This Way*, by Sylvia Ashton-Warner (autobiography); *Native Trees of NZ*, by Prof. John Salmon (natural history); and *Craft New Zealand*, by Doreen Blumhardt and Brian Brake (art/craft).

REGAL BOOKS, Division of Gospel Light Publications, 2300 Knoll Dr., Ventura CA 93003. Senior Editor: Donald E. Pugh. Publishes hardcover and paperback originals. Averages 35 titles/year. Pays 10% royalty on paperback titles, 10% net for curriculum books; 10% net for children's books. Photocopied submissions OK. Computer printouts OK. Reports in 2 months. SASE.
Nonfiction: Missions; Bible studies (Old and New Testament); Christian living; counseling (self-help); contemporary concerns; evangelism (church growth); marriage and family; youth; communication resources; teaching enrichment resources; Bible commentary for Laymen Series; and fiction (no romance). Query or submit detailed outline/synopsis and 2-3 sample chapters.
Recent Nonfiction Titles: *The Friendless American Mule*, by David W. Smith (Christian life); *The Church Unleashed*, by Frank Tillapaugh (church growth); *Caring Enough to Hear*, by David Augsburger.
Recent Children's Titles: *The Boy Who Made God Smile*, by Don Goodman; and *Night of Fire, Days of Rain*, by Robert Zoller.
Tips: Queries/mss may be routed to other editors in the publishing group.

REGENTS PUBLISHING CO., INC., 2 Park Ave., New York NY 10016. Averages 50 titles/year. ESL Acquisitions Editor: John Chapman. Spanish Language Editor: Lolita Koch. Computerized Instruction Editor: David Tillyer. Publishes English as a Second Language and Spanish language textbooks, as well as computer-assisted instruction programs for the same market. Prefers complete proposals, including description of target market, comparison with similar materials already on the market, description of age/grade/difficulty level, as well as table of contents and at least 3 sample units.
Textbooks: Publishes ESL/EFL and Spanish language textbooks for all ages. Produces ESP materials for business, science, etc.
Software: Produces ESL practice materials for use with microcomputers in home and school settings.
Recent Text Titles: *Spectrum* (an adult notional/functional ESL series); *Regents Readers* (36-book ESL reading series); *Grammarwork* (a 4-book ESL grammar practice series).

REGNERY/GATEWAY, INC., 360 W. Superior St., Chicago IL 60610. Publisher: Douglas Hofmeister. President: Henry Regnery. Vice President: Clyde P. Peters. Senior Managing Editor: Robert F. Scott, Box 131, Croton-on-Hudson NY 10520. Publishes hardcover and paperback originals (50%) and paperback reprints (50%). Averages 12-15 titles/year. Pays royalty. Simultaneous and photocopied submissions OK. Computer printout submissions OK. SASE. Reports in 1 month. Free book catalog.
Nonfiction: Biography, business/economics, history, philosophy, politics, psychology, religion, science, sociology, travel and education (teaching). Accepts nonfiction translations. "We are looking for books on current affairs—of either political, legal, social, environmental, educational or historical interest. Books heavy on sex and obscene brutality should not be submitted. Please, no fiction, verse, or children's literature." Inquiries preferred, or submit outline/synopsis and 1 sample chapter. Looks for "a novel approach to the subject, expertise of the author, clean, respectable writing, salability of the proposed work."
Recent Nonfiction Titles: *Fat City: How Washington Wastes Your Taxes*, by D. Lambro (investigative report on federal government); *Abuse of Trust: A Report on the Nader Network*, by Dan M. Burt; and *From Under the Rubble*, by Alexandr Solzhenitsyn (essays from six dissidents).

RESOURCE PUBLICATIONS, INC., Box 444, Saratoga CA 95070. Editorial Director: William Burns. Publishes paperback originals. Publishes 8 titles/year. "If the author can present and defend a personal publicity effort, or otherwise demonstrate demand, and the work is in our field, we will consider it." Pays 8% royalty; no advance. Photocopied submissions (with written assurance that work is not being submitted simultaneously) OK. "We prefer disk submissions, plus printout (CP/M). Reports in 2 months. SASE.
Nonfiction: "We look for creative source books for the religious education, worship, religious art, architec-

ture fields. How-to books, especially for contemporary religious art forms, are of particular interest (dance, mime, drama, choral reading, singing, music, musicianship, bannermaking, statuary, or any visual art form). No heavy theoretical, philosophical, or theological tomes. Nothing utterly unrelated or unrelatable to the religious market as described above. "We're starting a new line of how-to books for personal computer applications, and science applications." Query or submit outline/synopsis and sample chapters. Accepts artwork/photos and translations.
Recent Nonfiction Titles: *Banners and Such,* by Ortegel (how-to); *Blessings: A Reappraisal,* by Tom Simons (history/theology); and *Through the Eye of a Rose Window,* by Richard S. Vosko (design).
Fiction: "Light works providing examples of good expression through the religious art forms. Any collected short works in the areas of drama, dance, song, stories, anecdotes or good visual art. Long poems or illustrated light novels which entertain while teaching a life value which could be useful in religious education or to the religious market at large." Query or submit outline/synopsis and sample chapters.
Recent Fiction Titles: *Psalms of the Still Country,* by Ed Ingebretsen, SJ (poetry); *In Season and Out,* by Bruce Clanton, SDS (stories); and *Parables for Little People,* by Larry Castaghola (stories).
Tips: "Prepare a clear outline of the work and an ambitious schedule of public appearances to help make it known and present both as a proposal to the publisher. With our company a work that can be serialized or systematically excerpted in our periodicals is always given special attention."

RESTON PUBLISHING CO.,Subsidiary of Prentice-Hall, 11480 Sunset Hills Rd., Reston VA 22090. President: David M. Ungerer. Publishes hardcover originals. Offers standard minimum book contract of 10-12-15% on net sales; advance varies. Averages 200 titles/year. Free catalog on request. Will consider photocopied submissions. Computer printout and disk submissions OK. Submit outline and a minimum of 2 sample chapters. Looks for "rationale for writing book, writing style, market." Reports immediately. Enclose return postage.
Textbooks: "We look for titles in agriculture; business and real estate; engineering; computer science; paramedical field; nursing. Primarily for the junior college and vocational/technical school market. Professionally oriented books for in-service practitioners and professionals. All material should be written to appeal to these markets in style and subject. We are able to attract the best experts in all phases of academic and professional life to write our books. But we are always seeking new material in all areas of publishing, any area that is represented by courses at any post-secondary level." Accepts artwork/photos.
Recent Nonfiction Title: *Power of Money Dynamics,* by Van Caspal.

FLEMING H. REVELL CO., Central Ave., Old Tappan NJ 07675. Imprints include Power Books and Spire. Editorial Director: Dr. Victor L. Oliver. Managing Editor: Norma F. Chimento. Publishes hardcover and paperback originals and reprints. Publishes 80 titles/year. Wants no poetry. Pays royalty on retail price; sometimes an advance. Simultaneous and photocopied submissions OK. SASE. Reports in 2 months. Book catalog for SASE.
Nonfiction: Religion and inspirational. "All books must appeal to Protestant-evangelical readers." Query.
Recent Nonfiction Titles: *Changepoints,* by Joyce Landorf; *The Battle for the Mind,* by Tim LaHaye; *The Complete Book of Baby and Child Care for Christian Parents,* by Herbert Ketterman, MD and Grace Ketterman, MD; *Griffiti: Devotion for Guys, Devotion for Girls,* by J. David Schmidt; *Gennie, The Huguenot Women,* by Bette M. Ross; *Be A New Christian All Your Life,* by Raymond C. Artland.
Fiction: Protestant-evangelical religion and inspiration. Query or submit 3-6 sample chapters or complete ms.
Recent Fiction Title: *Song of Deborah,* by Bette M. Ross.

REVIEW AND HERALD PUBLISHING ASSOCIATION, 55 West Oak Ridge Dr., Hagerstown MD 21740. Editor-in-Chief: Richard W. Coffen. Publishes hardcover and paperback originals. Specializes in religiously oriented books. Averages 30-40 titles/year. Pays 5-10% royalty on retail price; advance averages $100. Simultaneous and photocopied submissions OK. Computer printout submissions OK. SASE. Reports in 2-4 months. Free brochure.
Nonfiction: Juveniles (religiously oriented only; 20,000-60,000 words; 128 pages average); nature (128 pages average); and religious (20,000-60,000 words; 128 pages average). Query or submit outline/synopsis and 2-3 sample chapters. Looks for "literary style, constructive tone, factual accuracy, compatibility with Adventist theology and life style, and length of manuscript."
Recent Nonfiction Titles: *High Rider,* by O. Tom Allen; *Food for Your Health and Efficiency,* by Marion Vollmer; and *On My Back, Looking Up,* by Evelyn Orser.
Tips: "Familiarize yourself with Adventist theology because Review and Herald Publishing Association is owned and operated by the Seventh-day Adventist Church. We are accepting fewer, but better-written manuscripts."

REYMONT ASSOCIATES, 6556 SW Maple Lane, Boca Raton FL 33433. Editor-in-Chief: D.J. Scherer. Managing Editor: Felicia Scherer. Paperback originals. Pays 10-12-15% royalty on wholesale price; no advance. Submit outline/synopsis and 2 sample chapters. Simultaneous and photocopied submissions OK. Com-

puter printout submissions OK. Reports in 2 weeks. SASE. Book catalog for SASE.
Nonfiction: Publishes business reports; how-to; unique directories; bibliographies. " 'Net' writing; no rhetoric. Aim for 7,500-10,000 words."
Recent Nonfiction Titles: *Improving EDP Software Production*; *Preventing Misuse of EDP Systems*; *How to Make Money With Pen & Ink Drawings*; *Consumers Guide to Mobile Home Living*.

RICHBORO PRESS, Box 1, Richboro PA 18954. (215)364-2212. Editor: George Moore. Publishes hardcover and trade paperback originals. Averages 6 titles/year. Pays 10% royalty on retail price. SASE. Reports in 6 weeks on queries; 3 months on mss. Free book catalog.
Nonfiction: Cookbook, how-to, gardening. Subjects include cooking and foods. Query.
Recent Nonfiction Titles: *Italian Herb Cooking*, by Daneo; *Handbook of Medieval Herbs*, by Moore; and *Breads*, by Bird.

‡*THE RIVERDALE COMPANY, INC., PUBLISHERS**, 5506 Kenilworth Ave., Riverdale MD 20737. (301)864-2029. President: John Adams. Publishes hardcover originals. Averages 6-8 titles/year. Pays 15% maximum royalty on wholesale price. Photocopied submissions OK. Computer printout submissions OK. SASE. Reports in 1 week on queries; 1 month on mss. Free book catalog.
Nonfiction: "We publish technical and social science textbooks for scholars, students, policy makers; tour, restaurant and recreational guides for the mass market." Subjects include economics, history, politics, psychology, sociology, and travel. Especially needs "social science manuscripts on South Asia or South Asia-Africa. Will consider college text proposals in economics and South Asian Studies; travel guides for Washington DC and immediate area." Query. Accepts outline/synopsis and 2-3 sample chapters.

ROSEBRIER PUBLISHING CO., Box 1725, Blowing Rock NC 28605. (704)295-7614. Publishes hardcover originals. Averages 3 titles/year. Pays standard royalty contract. Simultaneous and photocopied submissions OK. No computer printout or disk submissions. Reports in 3-4 weeks. Book catalog for business size SAE and 1 first class stamp.
Nonfiction: Juvenile. Submit outline/synopsis and sample chapters. Accepts artwork/photos.
Recent Nonfiction Titles: *Miss Lucy*, *Rabbit Family*, and *Montgomery Mole*, by Beverly Rose.
Fiction: Fantasy (juvenile, illustrated). Stories with a moral for preschool to 5th graders to be bound in a leather-look with gold title.

THE ROSEN PUBLISHING GROUP, 29 E. 21st St., New York NY 10010. (212)777-3017. President: Roger Rosen. Imprints include Pelion Press (music titles). Publishes hardcover originals. Entire firm averages 46 titles/year; young adult division averages 6 titles/year. Pays royalty or makes outright purchase. Simultaneous and photocopied submissions OK. No computer printout or disk submissions. SASE. Reports in 3-4 weeks. Free book catalog.
Nonfiction: Juvenile, reference, self-help and textbook. Subjects include art, health, coping, and music. "Our books are geared to the young adult audience whom we reach via school and public libraries. Most of the books we publish are related to guidance-career and personal adjustment. We also publish material on the theater, music and art, as well as journalism for schools. Interested in supplementary material for enrichment of school curriculum. Manuscripts in the young-adult nonfiction areas of vocational guidance, personal and social adjustment, journalism, theater. For Pelion Press, mss on classical music, emphasis on opera and singing." Query or submit outline/synopsis and sample chapters.
Recent Nonfiction Titles: *Coping with Academic Anxiety*, by Ottens; *Exploring Careers in the Computer Field*, by Weintraub; and *Speech and Drama Club Activities*, by Ratliff.

ROSS BOOKS, Box 4340, Berkeley CA 94704. President: Franz Ross. Publishes hardcover and paperback originals (85%) and paperback reprints (15%). Averages 7-10 titles/year. Offers 8-12% royalties on net price. Average advance: 10% of the first print run. Simultaneous and photocopied submissions OK. Computer printout and disk submissions for TRS-80 OK. SASE. Reports in 1 month. Free book catalog.
Nonfiction: General career finding, bicycle books, popular how-to science, garden books, music, general how-to, some natural foods and eastern religion. Especially wants general career finding, popular how-to science and how-to's. No political, fiction, poetry or children's books. Accepts artwork/photos. Submit outline/synopsis and 2 sample chapters with SASE. Accepts nonfiction translations.
Recent Nonfiction Titles: *Living on Two Wheels*; *Holography Handbook*; *Rock, Water & Marsh Gardens*; *Roadside Guide to Bike Repairs*.

‡**ROSSEL BOOKS**, 44 Dunbow Dr., Chappaqua NY 10514. (914)238-8954. President: Seymour Rossel. Publishes hardcover originals (90%) and trade paperback originals and reprints (10%). Averages 6-8 titles/year. "We subsidy publish only books which have been sponsored by foundations, organizations, etc." Pays royalty on wholesale or retail price. Negotiates advance. Photocopied submissions OK. SASE. Reports in 2 weeks on queries; 1 month on mss. Book catalog for business-size SAE and 37¢ postage.

Nonfiction: Cookbook, how-to, illustrated book, juvenile, reference, textbook, and Judaica in all fields—art, cooking and foods, history, philosophy, photography, politics, psychology, religion, sociology, and travel. "We currently seek juvenile nonfiction manuscripts on Jewish subjects; adult manuscripts on being Jewish in America, Jews on the frontier, interesting anecdotal histories with Jewish content, and collections of American Jewish photos. We do not publish adult Jewish fiction. However, we do wish to see juvenile fiction in the Judaica field." Submit outline/synopsis and sample chapters.

Recent Nonfiction Titles: *Promise of a New Spring: The Holocaust & Renewal*, by Gerda W. Klein (a child's primer on the Holocaust and its meaning); *The River of Light*, by L. Kushner (modern Jewish mysticism); *The Bar Kokhba Syndrome*, by Y. Harkabi (military history of the war fought 132-135 B.C.E.).

Fiction: Juvenile Jewish adventure, ethnic, historical, mystery, religious, romance and science fiction. Submit outline synopsis and sample chapters.

Tips: "Within the next year, Rossel Books will be initiating a new publishing imprint, LONGHORN BOOKS. Longhorn will seek to do Texas-oriented material for the Texas regional marketplace. We would be glad to see submissions for this new imprint as well."

ROSS-ERIKSON, INC., PUBLISHERS, 629 State St., Santa Barbara CA 93101. (805)962-1175. Editor: Roy (Buzz) Erikson. Managing Editor: George Erikson. Publishes hardcover and trade paperback originals, and hardcover and trade paperback reprints. Averages 6 titles/year. Pays 7-10% royalty; offers average $500 advance. Simultaneous and photocopied submissions OK. Computer printout and disk submissions OK. SASE. Reports in 2 months on queries; 6 months on mss. Free book catalog.

Nonfiction: How-to, self-help, anthropology, philosophy, and comparative religion. Accepts nonfiction translations from German and Spanish. Subjects include art; health; philosophy; psychology; religion (comparative). Query or submit outline/synopsis and 1-2 sample chapters. Looks for "strength of style, accuracy in nonfiction works, talent." Accepts artwork/photos.

Recent Nonfiction Titles: *The Don Juan Papers*, by Richard deMille (anthropology, philosophy and science); *Maria Sabina: Her Life and Chants*, by Alvaro Estrada (oral autobiography of Mazatec Indian Shaman); and *Unstress Yourself!*, by Stuart Litvak (self-help).

Fiction: No fiction or poetry being considered this year.

‡**ROSSI PUBLICATIONS**, Box 2001, Beverly Hills CA 90213. Editor: B. Simon. Publishes trade paperback originals. Averages 5-10 titles/year. Pays negotiable royalty. Photocopied submissions OK. SASE. Reports in 1 month on mss.

Nonfiction: Cookbooks, how-to, self-help on cooking and foods and health. Especially needs how-to mss. Submit complete mss.

Recent Nonfiction Titles: *Kosher Konnection*, by Bennet Simon (dining guide); *California Directory of Healing Art Practioners*, by R. Wener (directory); and *Buying Real Estate for Pennies*, by Sam Cambell (how-to).

ROUTLEDGE & KEGAN PAUL, LTD., 9 Park St., Boston MA 02108. Director: Bob Paul. Editor: Carol Baker. Publishes hardcover and paperback originals and reprints. Pays standard 10-12½-15% wholesale royalty contract "on clothbound editions, if the books are not part of a series"; usual advance is $1,000-3,000. Averages 200 titles/year. Query with outline and sample chapters. Submit complete ms "only after going through outline and sample chapters step." Reports in 2-3 months. Enclose check for return postage.

Nonfiction: "Academic, reference, and scholarly levels: social sciences, philosophy and logic, psychology, parapsychology, oriental religions, history, political science and education. Our books generally form a reputable series under the general editorship of distinguished academics in their fields. The approach should be similar to the styles adopted by Cambridge University Press, Harvard University Press and others." Interested in material for the International Library of Sociology, International Library of Philosophy, International Library of Psychology and US Policy and Welfare. Length: 50,000-150,000 words.

*****ROWE PUBLISHING CORP.**, 3906 N. 69th St., Milwaukee WI 53216. (414)438-0685. Subsidiaries include: The Diver's Bookstore and Aquatronics. Administrative Editor: Sheila Shane. Publishes trade paperback originals. Averages 8-10 titles/year. Subsidy publishes 10% of books. "If the book appears to have a limited scope or is totally regional in nature, we might arrange a limited run edition to test the market. In such a case, author contributes." Pays 10% royalty. Photocopied submissions OK. Computer printout submissions OK. SASE. Reports in 1 month. Book catalog $1.

Nonfiction: How-to, reference, technical on Americana, history, recreation, sports, travel. Accepts artwork/photos. "All subjects should relate to dive/marine themes. At present we are a specialty house. We invite submissions. Looking for material concerning the diver (scuba). We review submissions from around the world. We are interested in seeing manuscripts dealing with how-to, informational, marine history, regional guides, and dive adventure." Accepts nonfiction translations from German and French. Query or submit outline/synopsis and 2-3 sample chapters.

Recent Nonfiction Titles: *Make Money in Diving*, by Jon-Paul Giguere; *Shipwrecks of New England*, by Ja-

mes F. Jenney (history); and *Bottle Diving*, by James Frederick.
Tips: Queries/mss may be routed to other editors in the publishing group.

ROWMAN & ALLENHELD, PUBLISHERS, Division of Littlefield Adams & Co., 81 Adams Dr., Totowa NJ 07512. Vice President/Publisher: Matthew Held. Publishes hardcover and paperback originals (95%) and hardcover and paperback reprints (5%). Pays 5-12½% royalty on net sales; offers no advance. Simultaneous submissions OK. SASE. Reports in 2 months. Free book catalog.
Nonfiction: Art, business/economics, health, photography, politics, psychology, reference, science, sociology, technical and textbooks. "We publish scholarly studies in these fields with special emphasis on international studies (development, 3rd World, trade, finance, agricultural), labor economics and agricultural science. Our authors are typically academics writing for other professionals, for government bodies and other organizations which utilize primary research." Submit outline/synopsis and sample chapters.
Recent Nonfiction Title: *Banks and the Balance of Payments*, by Benjamin J. Cohen in collaboration with Fabio Basagni (private lending in the international adjustment process).

ROYAL PUBLISHING CO., Subsidiary of ROMC (Recipes of the Month Club), Box 5027, Beverly Hills CA 90210. (213)277-7220. President: Mrs. Harold Klein. Publishes hardcover, trade, and mass market paperback originals (100%). Averages 4 titles/year. Pays 8-12% royalty on retail price; buys some mss outright. No simultaneous submissions. Photocopied submissions OK. SASE. Free book catalog.
Nonfiction: Cookbook. "We especially need cookbooks, diet, food history and specialty cookbooks." Submit complete ms with SASE.
Recent Nonfiction Titles: *Joy of Eating*, *Joy of Entertaining* and *Great Beginnings and Happy Endings*, all by Darling (cookbooks).

‡RPM PRESS, INC., Box 157, Verndale MN 54681. (218)631-4707. Publisher: David Hietala. Publishes 90% trade paperback originals and 10% trade paperback reprints. Averages 10-12 titles/year. Pays 6-10% royalty on retail price or makes outright purchase of $500-2,000. Average advance is $500. Simultaneous and photocopied submissions OK. SASE. Reports in 4 weeks on queries; 6 weeks on mss. Book catalog for 9x12 SAE and $1.50 postage.
Nonfiction: How-to, reference and technical books on business and economics, agriculture and engineering. "We are looking for how-to-do-it books specifically related to describing how to set up successful small business operations or manage certain aspects of such operations. For example, a how-to-do-it book on how to set up a successful home-based microcomputer mail order software business would definitely catch our attention. People who buy our books are entrepreneurs or would-be entrepreneurs, so we like to hear from people who have developed successful small businesses of any kind and are willing to tell others how to do it. We are interested in working with new or established authors. The primary ingredient is that they have direct experience in the business they are covering, or at least be willing to research it to the extent that they actually gain the know-how. We are entirely receptive to hearing all ideas and are interested in working with authors who—once they establish themselves with us—are willing to work with us on a long-term basis on assignment. We are not interested in anything outside of the how-to-do-it arena. We focus on information you can put to work." Query.
Recent Titles: *The Work Measurement Handbook*, by D. Hietala (engineering); *Vocational Diagnosis of the Mentally Handicapped*, (government human relations reprint); *Selling to Industry and Government*, by P. McCray (marketing for nonprofit agencies).

RUSSICA PUBLISHERS, INC., 799 Broadway, New York NY 10003. (212)473-7480. Contact: Valery Kuharets. Publishes trade paperback originals (50%) and reprints (50%). Averages 15 titles/year. Pays 10-15% royalty on retail price. Photocopied submissions OK. SASE. Reports in 2 weeks. Free book catalog.
Nonfiction: Biography and humor. Subjects include history. "We're looking for biographies of prominent Russians or Slavs and histories of Russian art and culture. Manuscripts in Russian are always wanted." Submit complete ms.
Recent Nonfiction Titles: *Uncensored Russian Limericks*, by V. Kozlovsky (folklore); and *The Fate of Traitor*, by Nikolaevsky (history).
Fiction: Adventure, erotica, ethnic, horror, humor, mystery and suspense. "Russian language manuscripts only." Submit complete ms.
Recent Fiction Titles: *Poetry*, by Marina Tsvetaeva; *Prose* (2 volumes), by M. Tsvetaeva; and *The Hand (Ruka)*, by Iuz Aleshkovsky.
Poetry: Modern Russian poetry. Submit complete ms.

The double dagger (‡) before a listing indicates that the listing is new in this edition. New markets are often the most receptive to freelance contributions.

Recent Poetry Titles: *The Nets (Seti)*, by M. Kuzmin; *Anthology of Russian Lyrics*, compiled by Sviatopolk—Mirsky; and *Collection of Poems*, by V. Khodasevich.

RUTGERS UNIVERSITY PRESS, 30 College Ave., New Brunswick NJ 08903. Averages 35 titles/year. Pays royalty on retail price. Free book catalog. Final decision depends on time required to secure competent professional reading reports. Enclose return postage.
Nonfiction: Scholarly books in history, literary criticism, anthropology, sociology, women's studies and criminal justice. Regional nonfiction must deal with mid-Atlantic region with emphasis on New Jersey. Query. Length: 60,000 words minimum.
Recent Nonfiction Titles: *Ancient Maya Civilization*, by Norman Hammond; *The Logic and Limits of Trust*, by Bernard Barber; *Defoe and the Uses of Narrative*, by Michael M. Boardman.

S. C. E.-EDITIONS L'ETINCELLE, 3449 Rue St-Denis, Montreal, Quebec, Canada H2X 3L1. (514)843-7663. President: Robert Davies. Publishes trade paperback originals. Averages 12 titles/year. Pays 8-12% royalty on retail price; offers average $1,000. Simultaneous and photocopied submissions OK. SASE. Reports in 8 weeks on queries; 3 months on mss. Free book catalog.
Imprints: *L'Etincelle* (nonfiction and fiction), Robert Davies, President.
Nonfiction: Biography, cookbook, how-to, humor, reference and self-help. Subjects include animals, business and economics, cooking and foods, health, history, hobbies, nature, philosophy, politics, psychology, recreation, sociology, sports and travel. Accepts nonfiction translations. "We are looking for about 5 translatable works of nonfiction, in any popular field. Our audience includes French-speaking readers in all major markets in the world." No "topics of interest only to Americans." Query or submit outline/synopsis and 3 sample chapters.
Recent Nonfiction Titles: *Sports Massage*; *Growing Your Own Mushrooms*; *Bioclimatic Housing*; and *Vitamin C and Cancer*.

SAIL BOOKS, Division of Sail Publishers, Inc., 34 Commercial Wharf, Boston MA 02110. Editor: Stanley Grayson. Publishes hardcover originals. Averages 8 titles/year. Pays 10-15% royalty on retail price; 5% on price received by mail order; offers average $3,500 advance. Simultaneous and photocopied submissions OK ("must be clear"). SASE. Reports in 1 month on queries; 6 months on mss.
Nonfiction: How-to and adventure. Subjects include sports (sailing only). "We're interested in instructional texts with illustrations—some real adventure." Query.
Recent Nonfiction Titles: *Blown Away*, by Payson (how-to/adventure); *Blue Water*, by Griffith (how-to/adventure); *Cooking On the Go*, by Groeme (shipboard cooking); *The Sunfish Book*, by Will White (racing/how to/tuning history); *Yarns*, (adventure/exploration); *Sailing Craft*, by Frank Rosenow (yacht development, design and anecdotes).

ST. ANTHONY MESSENGER PRESS, 1615 Republic St., Cincinnati OH 45210. Editor-in-Chief: The Rev. Norman Perry, O.F.M. Publishes paperback originals. Averages 12 titles/year. Pays 6-8% royalty on retail price; offers $500 average advance. Books are sold in bulk to groups (study clubs, high school or college classes) and in bookstores. Will send free catalog to writer on request. Will consider photocopied submissions if they are not simultaneous submissions to other publishers. Query or submit outline and 2 sample chapters. Enclose return postage.
Religion: "We try to reach the Catholic market with topics near the heart of the ordinary Catholic's belief. We want to offer insight and inspiration and thus give people support in living a Christian life in a pluralistic society. We are not interested in an academic or abstract approach. Our emphasis is on popular writing with examples, specifics, color and anecdotes." Length: 25,000-40,000 words.
Recent Nonfiction Titles: *Six Ways to Pray from Six Great Saints*, by Gloria Hutchinson; *The Healing Mysteries: A Rosary for the Sick*, by Joanne Turpin; and *Marriage: Sacrament of Hope and Challenge*, by Wm. P. Roberts.

ST. LUKE'S PRESS, Mid-Memphis Tower, 1407 Union, Memphis TN 38104. (901)357-5441. Subsidiaries include Raccoon Books, Inc. (literary non-profit); American Blake Foundation (scholarly non-profit). Managing Editor: Roger Easson, Ph.D. Averages 5-6 titles/year. Pays 10% minimum royalty on retail price; offers average $100-200. Simultaneous and photocopied submissions OK. Computer printout preferred for initial contact; disk submissions if compatible with Apple II equipment on TRS-80. SASE. Reports in 3 months. Book catalog $1.
Nonfiction: Biography. "The author or content must have some logical connection with the Mid-South region." Submit story line and 3 sample chapters. Accepts translations.
Recent Nonfiction Titles: *Laughing Stock*, by T.S. Stribling (autobiography); and *Abiding Appalachia: Where Mountain and Atom Meet*, by Marilou Bonham Thompson.
Fiction: Regional—Mid-South. Submit story line and 3 sample chapters.

Recent Fiction Title: *Gayoso Bayou*, by Edward Hatcher.
Poetry: *Poetry Is You*, by Douglas Hinkle.

ST. MARTIN'S PRESS, 175 5th Ave., New York NY 10010. Averages 550 titles/year. SASE. Reports "promptly."
General: Publishes general fiction and nonfiction; major interest in adult fiction and nonfiction, history, self-help, political science, popular science, biography, scholarly, popular reference, etc. "No children's books." Query. "It takes very persuasive credentials to prompt us to commission a book or outline."
Recent Titles: *Trade Wind*, by M.M. Kaye (romantic historical); *The Lord God Made Them All*, by James Herriot; and *Mary Ellen's Help Yourself Diet*, by Mary Ellen Pinkham.
Textbooks: College textbooks. Query.

HOWARD W. SAMS & CO., INC., 4300 W. 62nd St., Indianapolis IN 46268. Manager of Acquisitions: C.P. Oliphant. Payment depends on quantity, quality, salability. Offers both royalty arrangements or outright purchase. Prefers queries, outlines, and sample chapters. Usually reports within 30 days. SASE.
Nonfiction: Technical and engineering books on computers, electronics, security, robots, video and telecommunications.

SCARECROW PRESS, INC., 52 Liberty St., Metuchen NJ 08840. Senior Editor: Bill Eshelman. Editor: Barbara Lee. Publishes hardcover originals. Averages 110 titles/year. Pays 10% royalty on list price of first 1,500 copies; 15% on list price thereafter. No advance. Photocopied submissions OK. SASE. Reports in 2 weeks. Free book catalog.
Nonfiction: Music. Needs reference books, bibliographies, women's studies and movies. Query.

SCHENKMAN PUBLISHING CO., INC., 3 Mt. Auburn Place, Cambridge MA 02138. (617)492-4952. Editor-in-Chief: Alfred S. Schenkman. Publishes hardcover and paperback originals. Specializes in textbooks and professional and technical books. Averages 60 titles/year. Royalty varies on net sales, but averages 10%. "In some cases, no royalties are paid on first 2,000 copies sold." No advance. State availability of photos and/or illustrations. Simultaneous and photocopied submissions OK. Reports in 1-2 months. SASE. Free book catalog.
Nonfiction: Publishes economics, history, psychology, sociology, textbooks and professional and technical books. Query.
Recent Nonfiction Titles: *Black in White America*, by Sidney Willhelm; *Women and the Law: A Social Historical Perspective*, edited by D. Kelly Weisberg; and *Public Relations for Public Schools*, by Doyle Bantner.

SCHIFFER PUBLISHERS, LTD., Box E, Exton PA 19341. (215)696-1001. Editorial Director: Peter Schiffer. Publishes hardcover and paperback originals (80%) and reprints. (20%). Averages 20 titles/year. Offers 10-15% royalty on wholesale price. No advance. No simultaneous or photocopied submissions. SASE. Reports in 4 weeks. Book catalog for SASE.
Nonfiction: Americana; art; cookbooks, cooking and food; history; and gardening. Especially needs books on antiques, art, cooking and collectibles. Submit outline/synopsis and sample chapters.

SCHIRMER BOOKS, Macmillan Publishing Co., Inc., 866 3rd Ave., New York NY 10022. Senior Editor: Mary Beth Payne. Publishes hardcover and paperback originals (90%) and paperback reprints (10%). Pays royalty on wholesale or retail price; small advance. Publishes 20 books/year. Submit photos and/or illustrations "if central to the book, not if decorative or tangential." Photocopied and simultaneous submissions OK. Reports in 6 weeks. SASE. Book catalog for SASE.
Nonfiction: Publishes books on the performing arts specializing in music, dance and theater; college texts; coffee table books; biographies; reference; and how-to. Submit outline/synopsis and sample chapters.
Recent Nonfiction Titles: *Pavlova*, by John and Roberta Lazzarini (coffee table); *Recorded Classical Music, A Critical Guide to Compositions and Performances*, by Arthur Cohn; *Teaching Woodwinds*, by Gene Saucier; and *Schirmer History of Music*, by Rosensteil.

SCHOCKEN BOOKS, INC., 200 Madison Ave., New York NY 10016. (212)685-6500. Editorial Director: Emile Capouya. Publishes hardcover and paperback originals and paperback reprints and simultaneous. Publishes 56 titles/year. Pays standard royalty; offers variable advance. Photocopied submissions OK. SASE. Reports in 6 weeks. Free book catalog.
Nonfiction: Needs books of Jewish interest, academic sociology, and children's (mythology and folktales). Submit outline/synopsis and sample chapters.
Recent Nonfiction Titles: *Brain Games*, by Richard B. Fisher; *The Art of Starvation*, by Sheila MacLeod; and *Women's Diaries of the Westward Journey*, by Lillian Schlissel.

SCHOLARLY RESOURCES, INC., 104 Greenhill Ave., Wilmington DE 19805. (302)654-7713. Managing Editor: Philip G. Johnson. Publishes hardcover and trade paperback originals (60%). Averages 15 hardcover titles/year. Pays 5-15% royalty on retail price. Simultaneous and photocopied submissions OK. SASE. Reports in 2 weeks on queries; 2 months on mss. Free book catalog.
Nonfiction: Reference. Subjects include history, sociology and political science. "We are interested in bibliography and other reference material as well as historical research and interpretative works on modern America, modern China, and diplomatic history. Our audience includes university and public libraries; some course adoption." Query or submit outline/synopsis and sample chapters.
Recent Nonfiction Titles: *The People's Republic of China: A Documentary Survey* (5 vols.), by Harold C. Hinton (reference); *The Warsaw Pact: Political Purpose and Military Means*, edited by Robert W. Clawson and Lawrence S. Kaplan; *Yamashita Precedent: War Crimes Command Responsibility*, by Richard L. Lall.

SCHOLASTIC, INC., 730 Broadway, New York NY 10003. (212)505-3000. Editor: Ann Reit. Lines include Wildfire and Windswept. Publishes trade paperback originals. Averages 24 titles/year. Pays 6% royalty on retail price. No computer printout or disk submissions. Reports in 3 months. Tip sheet for business-sized SASE with 20¢ postage.
Fiction: Gothic (Windswept line); romance (Wildlife line). "All books should be 40,000-45,000 words for 12 to 15 year old girls who are average to good readers." Query. Request tip sheet and follow guidelines carefully before submitting outline and three sample chapters.
Tips: Queries/mss may be routed to other editors in the publishing group.

SCHOLASTIC, INC., Pretzel Books, 730 Broadway, New York NY 10036. (212)505-3000. Editor: Molly Harrington. Publishes trade paperback and book club originals. Averages 6-8 titles/year. Pays 6% royalty on retail price; buys some mss outright for $3,000-4,000; $2,500 advance. Photocopied submissions OK. SASE. Reports in 1 month. Free book catalog.
Nonfiction: Juvenile, puzzle books. "Puzzle manuscripts containing one kind of puzzle (crosswords, word finds mazes, etc.) or manuscripts containing all different kinds of puzzles. Manuscripts written with a specific theme in mind (joke-puzzles, space, video, etc.) will also be considered. The puzzles should be geared for children ages 9-12. I'm looking for a fun, humorous, snappy approach, as well as good puzzle-making." No mss where the puzzles are fashioned around a licensed character (Superman, Peanuts, etc.) or a particular movie (*Star Wars*, *Raiders of the Lost Ark*, etc.). Submit puzzle and samples or complete ms.
Recent Nonfiction Titles: *Super Puzzlemix*, by Karen Markoe and Louis Phillips; *Monster Mazes*, by Tom Eaton; and *Puzzle Panic*, by Donna Pape and Jeanette Grote.

SCHOLASTIC-TAB PUBLICATIONS, 123 Newkirk Rd., Richmond Hill, Ontario, Canada L4C 3G5. (416)883-5300. Subsidiary of Scholastic, Inc. Acquisitions Editor: Sandra Bogart. Publishes hardcover, trade paperback and mass market paperback originals (80%), and paperback reprints (20%). Averages 35 titles/year in English and French. Pays royalty on list price; advance "depends on probable print run." Simultaneous (if so advised) and photocopied submissions OK. SASE. Reports in 3 weeks on queries; 3 months on mss. Book catalog for SAE.
Imprints: *North Winds Press* (nonfiction and fiction), Sandra Bogart, acquisitions editor.
Nonfiction: How-to, humor and juvenile. Subjects include animals, hobbies, crafts, puzzle books, mystery and adventure stories; from Canadian authors only. Submit outline/synopsis and sample chapters with basic storyline; sample of author's style of "an engaging story with a compelling and imaginative storyline, strong and convincing characters, and an immediate, lively writing style" or complete ms.
Recent Nonfiction Titles: *Seeds & Weeds, A Book of Country Crafts*, by Mary Alice Downie and Jillian Gilliland; *Police Story*, by Michael Barnes (informational); and *Puzzlemania*, by Lillian Marcus.
Fiction: Adventure, fantasy, humor, mainstream, mystery, romance, science fiction and suspense, suitable for ages 6-18, from Canadian authors only. No historical or occult fiction. Submit outline/synopsis and sample chapters or complete ms.
Recent Fiction Titles: *The Toothpaste Genie*, by Frances Duncan (fantasy); *Don't Call Me Sugarbaby*, by Dorothy Joan Harris; *The Vandarian Incident*, by Martyn Godfrey.

SCHOLIUM INTERNATIONAL, INC., 265 Great Neck Rd., Great Neck NY 11021. Editor-in-Chief: Arthur L. Candido. Publishes hardcover and paperback originals. Averages 19 titles/year. Standard minimum book contract of 10%. Free book catalog. Will consider photocopied submissions. No computer printout or disk submissions. Query. Reports in 2 weeks. SASE.
Science and Technology: Subjects include cryogenics, electronics, aviation, medicine, physics, etc. "We also publish books in other areas whenever it is felt the manuscript has good sales and reception potential. Contact us prior to sending ms, outlining subject, number of pages and other pertinent information which would enable us to make a decision as to whether we would want to review the manuscript. If interested, we will contact author; if no response, we are not interested in reviewing complete manuscript."

*ABNER SCHRAM LTD., 36 Park St., Montclair NJ 07042. (201)256-8600. Executive Editor: Spencer Carr. Publishes hardcover and paperback originals. Averages 33 titles/year. Subsidy publishes 3-4% books. Offers 7½-10% royalty; very limited advance. Simultaneous and photocopied submissions OK. SASE. Reports in 2 months. Book catalog for 8x10½ SASE.
Nonfiction: "Our main thrust is art and art history." Also interested in the slight outer periphery of art history and wants some idea of photos that could illustrate the book. Query first.
Recent Nonfiction Titles: *Chines Brush Work*, by Arthur Kwo; *Arshile Gorky*, by Harry Rand; and *Religious Paintings of Jan Steen*, by B. Kirschenbaum (art history).

CHARLES SCRIBNER'S SONS, 597 5th Ave., New York NY 10017. Director of Trade Publishing: Jacek K. Galazka. Publishes hardcover originals and hardcover and paperback reprints. Averages 300 titles/year. "Our contract terms, royalties and advances vary, depending on the nature of the project." Reports in 1-2 months. Enclose return postage.
General: Publishes adult fiction and nonfiction, practical books, science for the layman, health and business books. Queries only.
Recent Titles: *Innocent Blood*, by P.D. James (mystery); *The Male*, by Dr. Sherman Silber (health); and *Earthly Pleasures*, by Roger Swain (science).

CHARLES SCRIBNER'S SONS, Children's Books Department, 597 5th Ave., New York NY 10017. (212)486-4035. Editorial Director, Children's Books: Clare Costello. Publishes hardcover originals and paperback reprints of own titles. Averages 40 titles/year. Pays royalty on retail price; offers advance. Photocopied submissions OK. SASE. Free book catalog.
Nonfiction: Animals, art, biography, health, hobbies, humor, nature, photography, recreation, science and sports. Query.
Recent Nonfiction Title: *So You're Adopted*, by Fred Towledge.
Fiction: Adventure, fantasy, historical, humor, mainstream, mystery, science fiction and suspense. Submit outline/synopsis and sample chapters.
Recent Fiction Title: *Stone Pony*, by Patricia Calvert.

THE SEABURY PRESS, 815 2nd Ave., New York NY 10017. (212)557-0500. Publishes hardcover and paperback originals (85%) and paperback (adult only) reprints (15%). Publishes 50 titles/year. Pays 7-10% royalty; offers variable advance. Photocopied submissions OK. Computer printout and disk submissions OK; prefers letter quality to dot matrix. SASE. Reports in 6-8 weeks. Free book catalog.
Nonfiction: Theology, inspiration, liturgy, religious education. Accepts nonfiction translations. Query. Accepts outline/synopsis and 2 sample chapters.
Recent Nonfiction Titles: *The Way of the Heart*, by H. Nouwen; *Jesus and the Hunger for Things Unknown*, by Pierre Talec; and *Living Simply*, by David Crean.
Tips: Queries/mss may be routed to other editors in the publishing group.

SECOND CHANCE AT LOVE, 200 Madison Ave., New York NY 10016. (212)686-9820. Subsidiary of Berkley Publishing Group. Senior Editor: Ellen Edwards. Publishes mass market paperback originals. Averages 72 titles/year. Pays 2-6% royalty; averages $5,000 advance. Photocopied submissions OK. Computer printout and disk submissions OK; prefers letter quality to dot matrix printouts. Reports in 6 weeks.
Fiction: Contemporary romance. Accepts 3 sample chapters and detailed chapter-by-chapter outline. Query and request writer's guidelines.
Recent Fiction Titles: *Relentless Desire*, by Sandra Brown (contemporary romance); *Taken by Storm*, by Kay Robbins (contemporary romance); *A Lasting Treasure*, by Cally Hughes (contemporary romance).
Tips: "We're launching a new romance line under the Second Chance at Love umbrella. It will be called To Have and to Hold and will deal with married love. Guidelines are available. Will publish 36 titles/year; advances and royalties are the same as for Second Chance at Love."

‡SELF-COUNSEL PRESS, INC., Subsidiary of International Self-Counsel Press, Ltd., 1303 N. Northgate Way, Seattle WA 98133. (206)522-8383. Editor-in-Chief: Lois Richardson. Publishes trade paperback originals. Averages 15 new titles/year. Pays 10% royalty on wholesale price. Simultaneous and photocopied submissions OK. SASE. Reports in 6 weeks on queries; 2 months on mss. Free book catalog.
Nonfiction: How-to and reference on law, business and economics. Books on starting and running specific businesses applicable to both Canada and the US. Do-it-yourself and self-help law books for laypeople. No general "how to start a business" books. Query or submit outline/synopsis and sample chapters.
Recent Nonfiction Titles: *Collection Techniques for the Small Business*, by Tim Paulsen; *Media Law Handbook*, by Stuart Robertson; and *Start and Run a Successful Beauty Salon*, by Paul Pogue.

SERVANT PUBLICATIONS, 840 Airport Blvd., Box 8617, Ann Arbor MI 48107. (313)761-8505. Managing Editor: James W. Manney. Publishes hardcover, trade and mass market paperback originals (80%), and trade paperback reprints (20%). Averages 25 titles/year. Pays 10% royalty on retail price. Reports in 1 month. Free book catalog.

Nonfiction: Subjects include religion. "We're looking for practical Christian teaching, Scripture, current problems facing the Christian Church, and inspiration." No heterodox or non-Christian approaches. Query or submit brief outline/synopsis and 1 sample chapter. All unsolicited mss are returned unopened.

Recent Nonfiction Titles: *What Is Secular Humanism*, by James Hitchcock; *The Savage My Kinsman*, by Elisabeth Elliot; and *A Crisis of Truth*, by Ralph Martin.

‡*SEVEN LOCKS PRESS, INC.**, Subsidiary of Calvin Kytle Associates, Box 72, Cabin John MD 20818. (202)638-1598. Contact: Managing Editor. Publishes hardcover and trade paperback originals (60%) and reprints (40%). Averages 4 titles/year. Subsidy publishes 35% of books. "Thus far, we have not published any books subsidized by the author, and are unlikely to change this policy in the future. All our subsidy publishing has been in connection with professional associations and foundations. If an author's work greatly interests us but has insufficient sales potential, we will try to find a partial subsidy from an organization likely to have a particular interest in the book." Pays 10-15% royalty on retail price. No advance. Simultaneous (if so advised) and photocopied submissions OK. SASE. Reports in 2 weeks on queries; 2 months on mss. Book catalog for business size envelope and 1 first class stamp. "Original and intelligent nonfiction on important subjects: public policy formation, politics, liberal economics, journalism, and health. Also looking for subjects of particular interest to those living in the Washington, D.C./MD/VA area. Should be suitable for an interested and well-educated lay audience (policy makers, journalists, economists, literate issue- or problem-oriented readers) as well as for supplemental reading in college courses; libraries. No textbooks, no short-lived, trendy topics. The author should be very well informed about his subject, have a distinct and engaging style, and have something to say. We particularly value the original thinker, who has command of the facts and a writing style to bring it all home." Query first.

Recent Nonfiction Titles: *Beyond Despair*, by Robert Theobald; *Parkinson's: A Patient's View*, by Sidney Dorros; *Polls Apart*, by John P. Robinson, Robert Meadow and *Home on the Canal*, by Elizabeth Kytle.

‡**SEVEN SEAS PRESS**, Subsidiary of Davis Publications, 524 Thames St., Newport RI 02840. (401)847-1683. Editor: James Gilbert. Publishes hardcover originals. Averages 12 titles/year. Pays 8-12½% on gross receipts. Offers average $1,500 advance. Simultaneous and photocopied submissions OK. SASE. Reports in 1 month. Free book catalog.

Nonfiction: "Coffee table" book, cookbook, how-to, humor, illustrated book, reference and technical. "All our titles are in the nautical/marine field. We specialize in informative books that help cruising sailors, in particular, enjoy their sport. We also publish a line of high-adventure paperbacks that deal with the sea or sea-related topics." Maximum 2/year. Not interested in any nonfiction that is not of use or benefit to the cruising sailor. Query or submit outline/synopsis and sample chapters.

Recent Nonfiction Titles: *The Complete Live-Aboard Book*, by Katy Burke (how to live aboard a boat); *Boatcook II*, by Donna Marxer (boat cookbook); and *Sailor's Sketchbook*, by Bruce Bingham (drawings to help boatowners upgrade their boats).

Fiction: Adventure, horror, mystery, romance, suspense—must be sea-related. Query or submit outline/synopsis and sample chapters.

‡**SHAMBHALA PUBLICATIONS, INC.**, 1920 13th St., Boulder CO 80302. (303)449-6111. Subsidiaries include Great Eastern Book Co. Managing Editor: Larry Mermelstein. Publishes hardcover originals and trade paperback originals and reprints. Averages 25-30 titles/year. Pays royalty on retail price. Simultaneous and photocopied submissions OK. SASE. Reports in 5 weeks on queries; 6 weeks on mss. Free book catalog.

Imprints: Prajna Press; Great Eastern; Hermes House; Shambhala.

Nonfiction: Cookbook, self-help and trade paperbacks. Subjects include art, business and economics, cooking and foods, health, history, music, nature, philosophy, psychology, religion, Oriental studies, literature, astrology and science. Submit outline/synopsis and sample chapters. "We do not return mss received unless they are accompanied by SASE."

Recent Nonfiction Title: *Space, Time and Medicine*, by Larry Dossey.

HAROLD SHAW PUBLISHERS, 388 Gundersen Dr., Box 567, Wheaton IL 60189. (312)665-6700. Managing Editor: Megs Singer. Publishes hardcover and paperback originals (80%) and paperback reprints (20%). Averages 20 titles/year. Offers 5-10% royalty on retail price. Average advance (only with established authors): $300-1,000. Simultaneous and photocopied submissions OK. Computer printout submissions OK. SASE. Reports in 1 month. Free book catalog.

Nonfiction: How-to; juveniles; poetry; literary; religion; and self-help. Especially needs "manuscripts dealing with the needs of Christians in today's changing world. We are specially looking for mss on guilt, forgiveness, marriage (if it is handled in an original and creative way), pain and suffering. Also any well-done books on doctrine or Biblical exposition. If it is not for the Christian market, we don't want to see it. We do not want to see poetry unless the poet is already established and has a reading audience. Mss must be high in quality and

creativity.'' Query first, then submit outline/synopsis and 3-4 sample chapters.
Recent Nonfiction Titles: *Called & Committed*, by D. Watson (Biblical exposition and practical application); *Walking on Water*, by Madeleine L' Engle (Christian perspective on art); *Small Groups*, by Bob and Win Couchman (church renewal, how-to); and *Luke: Following Jesus*, by Sharrel Keyes (inductive Bible study guide).

SHERIDAN HOUSE, INC., 175 Orawaupum St., White Plains NY 10606. (914)948-1806. President: Lothar Simon. Publishes trade and text originals and reprints. Averages 10 titles/year. Pays 10% royalty on wholesale price. SASE. Reports in 6 weeks on queries; 3 months on mss. Free book catalog.
Nonfiction: How-to, reference, technical, textbook. Subjects include boating, seamanship, marine engineering, naval architecture, international law, patents, licensing, research and development, criminology. No general topics. Query or submit outline/synopsis and sample chapters.
Recent Nonfiction Titles: *In the Wake of the Spray*, by K. Slack (boating reprint); *Templeman on Marine Insurance*, revised by R.J. Lambeth; and *Israel Studies in Criminology*, by S. Shoham (monograph).

THE SHOE STRING PRESS, (Archon Books, Linnet Books, Library Professional Publications), 995 Sherman Ave., Hamden CT 06514. (203)248-6307. Distributor for the Connecticut Academy of Arts and Sciences. President: James Thorpe III. Publishes 60 titles/year. Royalty on net; no advance. Computer printout submissions OK. Reports in 4-6 weeks. SASE.
Nonfiction: Publishes scholarly books: history, biography, literary criticism, reference, geography, bibliography, military history, information science, library science, education and general adult nonfiction. Accepts nonfiction translations. Preferred length: 40,000-130,000 words, though there is no set limit. Query with table of contents and 2-3 sample chapters. Accepts artwork/photos.
Recent Nonfiction Titles: *Harold Nicholson· A Biography*, by James Lees-Milne; *Third World Conflict and International Security*, by Christopher Bertram; and *Creative Uses of Children's Literature*, by Mary Ann Paulin.
Tips: Queries/mss may be routed to other editors in the publishing group.

SIERRA CLUB BOOKS, 2034 Fillmore St., San Francisco CA 94115. (415)931-7950. Editor-in-Chief: Daniel Moses. Publishes hardcover and paperback originals (95%) and reprints (5%). Averages 14 titles/year. Offers 8-12½% royalty on retail price. Average advance: $7,000. Simultaneous and photocopied submissions OK. SASE. Reports in 2 months. Free book catalog.
Nonfiction: Animals; health; history (natural); how-to (outdoors); juveniles; nature; philosophy; photography; recreation (outdoors, nonmechanical); science; sports (outdoors); and travel (by foot or bicycle). ''The Sierra Club was founded to help people to explore, enjoy and preserve the nation's forests, waters, wildlife and wilderness. The books program looks to publish quality trade books about the outdoors and the protection of natural resources. Specifically, we are interested in undeveloped land (not philosophical but informational), nuclear power, self-sufficiency, natural history, politics and the environment, and juvenile books with an ecological theme.'' Does *not* want ''personal, lyrical, philosophical books on the great outdoors; proposals for large color photographic books without substantial text; how-to books on building things outdoors; books on motorized travel; or any but the most professional studies of animals.'' Query first, submit outline/synopsis and sample chapters, or submit complete ms.
Recent Nonfiction Titles: *Nukespeak*, by Stephen Hilgartner, Richard Bell and Rory O'Connor (an exploration of the language and history of the nuclear power industry); *The Mountains of North America*, by Fred Beckey (pictorial); *Hiking the North Cascades*, by Fred T. Darvill, Jr. (one of a series of guides to the terrain, flora and fauna of a specific geographical area).
Fiction: Adventure; historical; mainstream; and science fiction. ''We do very little fiction, but will consider a fiction manuscript if its theme fits our philosophical aims: the enjoyment and protection of the environment.'' Does *not* want ''any ms with animals or plants that talk; apocalyptic plots.'' Query first, submit outline/synopsis and sample chapters, or submit complete ms.
Recent Fiction Title: *The River Why*, by David James Duncan.

SIGNPOST BOOKS, 8912 192nd SW, Edmonds WA 98020. Editor-in-Chief: Cliff Cameron. Publishes paperback originals. Averages 3-4 titles/year. Offers standard minimum book contract of 6% on retail price. Free book catalog. Computer printout submissions OK. Query. Accepts outline/synopsis and 2-3 sample chapters. Reports in 3 weeks. SASE.
Nonfiction: ''Books on outdoor subjects emphasizing self-propelled activity such as hiking, canoeing, bicycling, camping and related interests. Books should have strong environmental material for a general audience, where applicable.''
Recent Nonfiction Titles: *Stehekin: The Enchanted Valley*, by Fred Darvill Jr. (hiking and nature guide); and *Trails of Western Idaho*, by Margaret Fuller (hiking guide).
Tips: Queries/mss may be routed to other editors in the publishing group.

SILHOUETTE BOOKS, Subsidiary of Simon & Schuster/Pocket Books, 1230 Avenue of the Americas, New York NY 10020. (212)586-6151. Editor-in-Chief: Karen Solem. Publishes mass market paperback originals. Averages 312 titles/year. Pays royalty; buys some mss outright. Photocopied submissions OK. Computer printout submissions OK; prefers letter quality to dot matrix. SASE. Reports in 5 weeks on queries; 3 months on mss. "Tip-sheets are available upon request."

Imprints: *Silhouette Romances* (contemporary adult romances); 50,000-55,000 words. *Silhouette Special Editions* (contemporary adult romances); 75,000-80,000 words. *Silhouette Desires* (contemporary adult romances); 55,000-65,000 words. *Silhouette First Loves* (contemporary young adult romances); 50,000-55,000 words. *Silhouette Intimate Moments* (contemporary adult romances); 75,000-85,000 words.

Fiction: Romance (contemporary romance for adults and young adults). "We are particularly interested in seeing mss for the Special Edition, Desire and Intimate Moments lines, though we will consider submissions for all 5 lines. No mss other than contemporary romances of the type outlined above. No medical." Submit complete ms. Ms should "follow our general format, yet have an individuality and life of its own that will make it stand out in the readers' minds."

Recent Fiction Titles: *Dreams of Evening*, by Kristin James; *After the Rain*, by Linda Shaw; *To Tame the Hunter*, by Stephanie James.

SILVER BURDETT, Subsidiary of SFN Companies, Inc., 250 James St., Morristown NJ 07960. Editor-in-Chief: Charlotte Gemmel. Publishes hardcover and paperback originals. Publishes 180 titles/year. "Textbook rates only, el-hi range." Computer printout and disk submissions OK. Query. SASE.

Education: Produces educational materials for preschoolers, elementary and high school students. Among materials produced: textbooks, teachers' materials, other print and nonprint classroom materials including educational courseware, manipulatives and audiovisual aids (silent and sound 16mm films and filmstrips, records, multimedia kits, overhead transparencies, tapes, etc.). Assigns projects to qualified writers on occasion. Writer must have understanding of school market and school learning materials.

Tips: Queries/mss may be routed to other editors in the publishing group.

SIMON & SCHUSTER, Trade Books Division, 1230 Avenue of the Americas, New York NY 10020. Administrative Editor: Daniel Johnson. "If we accept a book for publication, business arrangements are worked out with the author or his agent and a contract is drawn up. The specific terms vary according to the type of book and other considerations. Royalty rates are more or less standard among publishers. Special arrangements are made for anthologies, translations and projects involving editorial research services." "All unsolicited mss will be returned unread. Only mss submitted by agents or recommended to us by friends or actively solicited by us will be considered. In such cases, our requirements are as follows: All mss submitted for consideration should be marked to the attention of a specific editor. It usually takes at least three weeks for the author to be notified of a decision—often longer. Sufficient postage for return by first-class registered mail, or instructions for return by express collect, in case of rejection, should be included. Mss must be typewritten, double-spaced, on one side of the sheet only. We suggest margins of about one inch all around and the standard 8"x11" typewriter paper." Prefers complete mss. Computer printout submissions OK; prefers letter quality to dot matrix.

General: "Simon and Schuster publishes books of adult fiction, history, biography, science, philosophy, the arts and popular culture, running 50,000 words or more. Our program does not, however, include school textbooks, extremely technical or highly specialized works, or, as a general rule, poetry or plays. Exceptions have been made, of course, for extraordinary mss of great distinction or significance."

Tips: Queries/mss may be routed to other editors in the publishing group.

*SLAVICA PUBLISHERS, INC., Box 14388, Columbus OH 43214. (614)268-4002. President/Editor: Charles E. Gribble. Publishes hardcover and paperback originals (90%) and reprints (10%). Averages 20 titles/year. Subsidy publishes 1/3-1/2 of books. "All manuscripts are read for quality; if they pass that test, then we talk about money. We *never* accept full subsidies on a book, and we *never* publish anything that has not passed the scrutiny of expert readers. Most subsidies are very small (usually in the range of $200-800)." Offers 10-15% royalty on retail price; "for some books, royalties do not begin until specified number has been sold." No advance. "Only in exceptional circumstances will we consider simultaneous submissions, and only if we are informed of it. We strongly prefer good photocopied submissions rather than the original." No computer printout or disk submissions. Query first. SASE. Reports in 1 week to 4 months (more in some cases). Free book catalog.

Nonfiction: Biography; history; reference; textbooks; travel; language study; literature; folklore; and literary criticism. "We publish books dealing with almost any aspect of the peoples, languages, literatures, history, cultures of Eastern Europe and the Soviet Union, as well as general linguistics and Balkan studies. We do not publish original fiction and in general do not publish books dealing with areas of the world other than Eastern Europe, the USSR and the Balkans (except for linguistics, which may deal with any area)." Accepts nonfiction translations from Eastern European languages. Query first. Looks for authors of scholarly and textbooks who know their fields and write clearly.

Recent Nonfiction Titles: *Brain and Language*, by Roman Jakobson (linguistics); *Guide to the Slavonic Lan-*

guages (Third Edition), by R.G.A. de Bray (language study and linguistics); and *Sologub's Literary Children: Keys to a Symbolist's Prose*, by Stanley J. Rabinowitz.

Tips: "A large percentage of our authors are academics, but we would be happy to hear from other authors as well. Very few of our books sell well enough to make the author much money, since the field in which we work is so small. The few that do make money are normally textbooks."

SLEEPY HOLLOW PRESS, 150 White Plains Rd., Tarrytown NY 10591. (914)631-8200. Editor-in-Chief: Saverio Procario. Managing Editor: James R. Gullickson. Publishing hardcover originals (85%) and hardcover reprints (15%). Pays 5-10% (net) royalty; advance negotiable. Averages 4-5 titles/year. State availability of photos and/or illustrations to accompany ms. Simultaneous and photocopied submissions OK. Reports in 1-2 months. SASE. Free book catalog.

Nonfiction: Publishes Americana; art (American decorative arts); cooking and foods (historical); history (especially American, New York state and colonial through modern times); technical (17th- to 19th-Century technology); travel (regional and New York state); American literature and literary criticism (especially 19th-Century). Query the Managing Editor. Looks for "clear statement of theme, neatness, grammar and style."

Recent Nonfiction Titles: *Material Culture of the Wooden Age*, edited by Brooke Hindle; *American Industrialization, Economic Expansion, and the Law*, edited by Joseph R. Frese, SJ and Jacob Judd; *Officers and Gentlemen: Historic West Point in Photographs*, by Jeffrey Simpson.

THE SMITH, 5 Beekman St., New York NY 10038. Publishes hardcover and paperback originals. The Smith is owned by the Generalist Association, Inc., a nonprofit organization, which gives to writers awards averaging $500 for book projects. Averages 5 titles/year. Free book catalog. Send query first for nonfiction; sample chapter preferred for fiction. Reports in 2 months. SASE.

Nonfiction and Fiction: "Original fiction—no specific schools or categories; for nonfiction, the more controversial, the better." Accepts artwork/photos. Managing Editor: Tom Tolnay.

Recent Titles: *Two Friends*, by Menke Katz and Henry Smith (poet friends speak in verse); *The Word and Beyond*, by Donald Phelps, Dick Higgins and Richard Morris (literary criticism); and *No Goodbye*, by Stephen Philbaick (poetry).

‡THE ALLEN SMITH CO., 1435 N. Meridian St., Indianapolis IN 46202. (317)634-4098. President: Robert C. Lewis. Publishes hardcover and trade paperback originals. Averages 10 titles/year. Pays standard royalty; variable advance. Photocopied submissions OK. SASE. Reports in 3 weeks on queries; 1 month on mss. Free book catalog.

Nonfiction: How-to, reference, technical and textbook. Subjects include business and economics, law and law-related, medicolegal and consumer-related for professionals, executives and lay persons. Query.

Recent Nonfiction Titles: *Farm Income Tax Manual*, by O'Byrne and Davenport; *Liability of Corporate Officers & Directors*, by Knepper; *Unmarried Couples and the Law*, by Douthwaite; *Lawyers' Medical Cyclopedia*, by Frankel and Zimmerly; and *Medical Malpractice*, by Harney.

SOCIAL SCIENCE EDUCATION CONSORTIUM, INC., (SSEC), 855 Broadway, Boulder CO 80302. (303)492-8154. Publications Manager: Laurel R. Singleton. Publishes trade paperback originals. Averages 8-10 titles/year. Pays up to $600 honorarium. Photocopied submissions OK. Computer printout submissions OK. SASE. "At the end of each calendar year we establish a forthcoming list for the whole year. Before that time, we can only respond tentatively to prospective authors. Definite 'nos' receive responses within 30 days." Free book catalog.

Nonfiction: Reference and professional books for educators. Subjects include economics, history, politics, psychology, sociology and education. "We are always looking for useful, original resources that social studies educators can use in the classroom and in planning curriculum and staff-development programs. We also publish some scholarly research in social science education." No material "that would not be of direct interest to social studies educators, administrators, teacher educators, and preservice teachers." Query or submit outline/synopsis and 2 sample chapters. Looks for "content of direct interest to social studies, educators, administrators, teacher educators, and preservice teachers. Also, tight organization, up-to-date information and references, reasonable length (200-400 ms. pages)."

Recent Nonfiction Titles: *Teachers Have Rights, Too: What Educators Should Know About School Law*, by Leigh Stelzer and Joanna Banthin (review of educators' legal rights, status); *Data Book of Social Studies Materials and Resources*, vol. 6 (annual), edited by Laurel Singleton (analyses and descriptions of new social studies materials); and *Global Issues: Activities and Resources for the High School Teacher*, by Kenneth A. Switzer and Paul T. Mulloy (lessons and student materials).

Tips: "The SSEC is a not-for-profit educational service organization. One of our ongoing activities is a small, short-run publications program. All of our publications are designed for professionals in some aspect and at some level of education, particularly social studies/social science education. In fact, without exception, all of our publications are written and edited by people who fit that description. Our books are sold exclusively by direct mail. Thus, a freelance writer whose main motivation is to make money by selling manuscripts probably would not find us to be an attractive market. We pay only a modest honorarium, although some royalty arrangements will also be forthcoming; most of our authors are motivated by desire for professional growth, prestige, and service.''

‡SOS PUBLICATIONS, Subsidiary of Bradley Products, 4223-25 W. Jefferson Blvd., Los Angeles CA 90016. (213)730-1815. Publisher: Paul Bradley. Publishes trade paperback originals. Averages 4 titles/year. Pays royalty on wholesale price. Photocopied submissions OK. SASE. Reports in 6-8 weeks. Free book catalog.
Fiction: Contact Fiction Editor. Mystery, romance and suspense. Send complete ms for publisher's review.
Tips: ''We are enlarging our scope of publishing to the novel form with special attention to mysteries, thrillers, romance stories and new traditional fiction.''

SOUTH END PRESS, 302 Columbus Ave., Boston MA 02116. (617)266-0629. Publishes trade paperback and hardcover originals (70%) and trade paperback reprints. Averages 22 nonfiction titles/yr. Pays 8% royalty on retail price. Simultaneous submissions OK. ''Letter quality computer printout submissions are fine.'' Reports in 6-8 weeks. Free book catalog.
Nonfiction: Subjects include politics, economics, feminism, social change, radical cultural criticism, explorations of race, class, and sex oppression and liberation. No conservative political themes. Submit outline/synopsis and 1-2 sample chapter(s).
Fiction: Not accepting unsolicited fiction manuscripts or queries.

SOUTHERN ILLINOIS UNIVERSITY PRESS, Box 3697, Carbondale IL 62901. (618)453-2281. Director: Kenney Withers. Averages 50 titles/year. Pays 10-12.5% royalty on net price. Simultaneous and photocopied submissions OK. SASE. Reports in 6 weeks. Free book catalog.
Nonfiction: ''We are interested in humanities, social sciences and contemporary affairs material. No dissertations or collections of previously published articles.'' Accepts nonfiction translations from French, German, Scandinavian and Hebrew. Query.
Recent Nonfiction Title: *Thomas Pynchon*, by Cowart (literary criticism).

SOUTHERN METHODIST UNIVERSITY PRESS, Dallas TX 75275. (214)692-2263. Director *ad interim* and Editor: Charlotte T. Whaley. Averages 10 titles/year. Payment is on royalty basis: 10% of list up to 2,500 copies; 12% for 2,500-5,000 copies; 15% thereafter; no advance. Free book catalog. Computer printout submissions OK ''as long as copy is clear and double-spaced.'' Appreciates query letters, outlines and 1-2 sample chapters. Reports ''tend to be slow for promising mss requiring outside reading by authorities.'' Enclose return postage.
Nonfiction: Regional and scholarly nonfiction. History, economics, biography, folklore literature, anthropology, geology, international and constitutional law, American studies. Length: open.
Recent Nonfiction Titles: *Mexican Folktales from the Borderland*, by Riley Aiken; *Unconventional Methods in Exploration for Petroleum and Natural Gas: II*, edited by B.M. Gottlieb; *From Token to Triumph: The Texas Republicans Since 1920*, by Roger M. Olien; *Protestantism and the American University: An Intellectual Biography of William Warren Sweet*, by James L. Ash, Jr.; *The War-Making Powers of the President: Constitutional and International Law Aspects*, by An Van Wynen Thomas and A.J. Thomas, Jr.; revised and enlarged edition of *Tall Tales from Texas Cow Camps*, by Mody C. Boatright.

‡SOVEREIGN PRESS, 326 Harris Rd., Rochester WA 98579. Senior Editor: Marguerite Pedersen. Publishes hardcover and trade paperback originals. Averages 5 titles/year. Pays by individual agreements. ''Payments before publishing are bonus rather than advance.'' Simultaneous and photocopied submissions OK. Computer printout submissions OK. SASE. Reports in 1 month on queries and mss. Book catalog $1. ''We have a unique dedication to the culture of individual sovereignty and put out a special catalog that gives full details of our publishing policy. We want no inquiries and no submissions from anyone not acquainted with our unique orientation.''
Nonfiction: Social orientation books on history, philosophy, politics, religion (individual sovereignty only). Publishes for ''those seeking a way to integrate personal ideals with universal realities.'' Especially needs ''works effectively promoting the *culture* of individual sovereignty.'' Submit complete ms.
Recent Nonfiction Titles: *World Controlled Humans*, by John Harland (history) and *American Christian Bible*, by Thomas Jefferson and Erik Holden (Christianity for individual sovereigns).
Fiction: ''Historical novels and fictional projections that promote individual sovereignty.'' Especially needs ''perceptively conceived historical novels of Northern European life before individual sovereignty was corrupted by theocracy; fictional projections for a *practical* society of sovereign individuals.'' Submit complete ms.

Recent Fiction Titles: *The Curse of the Ring* and *The Ring Cycle*, by Melvin Gorham (projection of Richard Wagner's Ring operas into 21st century).

SPECIAL LIBRARIES ASSN., 235 Park Ave. S., New York NY 10003. (212)477-9250. Director, Information Services: Nancy M. Viggiano. Publishes hardcover originals. Averages 10 titles/year. Pays 15% royalty on income over expenses. No advance. Computer printout and disk submissions OK; prefers letter quality to dot matrix. SASE. Reports in 1 month on queries; 3 months on mss. Free book catalog.
Nonfiction: Reference, technical, textbooks, professional development for librarians and information managers. Query or submit outline/synopsis and 3 sample chapters.
Recent Nonfiction Titles: *Closing the Corporate Library*, by J.M. Matarazzo; *Special Libraries: A Guide for Management, 2nd ed.*, by J.L. Ahrensfeld, et al; *Picture Sources 4*, comp. by Ernest Robl; and *Issues and Involvement: Alberta Brown Lectures in Special Librarianship* 1978-1980, comp. by Pamela Jobin and Marcy Murphy.

SPRING PUBLICATIONS, INC., 2719 Routh St., Dallas TX 75201. (214)698-0933. Editor-in-Chief: Randolph Severson. Publishes trade paperback originals. Averages 5 titles/year. Pays 8% royalty on wholesale price; offers negotiable advance. Simultaneous submissions OK. SASE. Reports in 3 months. Free book catalog.
Nonfiction: Reference on depth psychology, mythology. "Alternative therapies, lifestyles and thought." Query.
Recent Nonfiction Titles: *The New Polytheism*, by David R. Miller (psychologists' study of religion); and *Soul and Money*, (essays by psychotherapists).

SRS ENTERPRISES, INC./SCIENTIFIC RESEARCH SERVICES, Division of Gambling Times, Inc., 1018 N. Cole Ave., Hollywood CA 90038. (213)461-3366. Book Department: Arnold L. Abrams. Publishes hardcover and trade and mass market paperback originals. Averages 6 titles/year. Pays 10% royalty on retail price; no advance. Simultaneous and photocopied submissions OK. SASE. Reports in 6 weeks on queries; 3 months on mss.
Nonfiction: How-to. Subjects cover only gambling. "We're looking for books on all types of gambling and gambling-related activities." Submit outline/synopsis and sample chapters.
Recent Nonfiction Titles: *Million Dollar Blackjack*, by Ken Uston (how to play and win at 21); *Winning Blackjack*, by Stanley Roberts; *Gaming Around the World*; *Psyching Out Vegas*, Marvin Karlins; *Gambling Times Guide to Crads*, by N.B. Winkiess, Jr.
Fiction: Query.

STACKPOLE BOOKS, Box 1831, Harrisburg PA 17105. (717)234-5091. Editors: Ruth Dennison-TeDesco and Judith Schnell. Publishes hardcover and quality paperback originals. Publishes approximately 50 titles/year. "Proposals should include a 2- to 4-page outline and 2 or 3 sample chapters, plus a summary of the book's contents and appeal and author's credentials." Simultaneous and photocopied submissions OK. Computer printout submissions OK. SASE. Free author's guidelines describing publishing program and submissions procedure.
Nonfiction: Outdoor-related subject areas—firearms, fishing, hunting, military, wildlife, outdoor skills, space exploration, crafts, and cookbooks. Accepts artwork/photos.

STANDARD PUBLISHING, 8121 Hamilton Ave., Cincinnati OH 45231. (513)931-4050. Publisher and Vice President: Ralph M. Small. Publishes hardcover and paperback originals (85%) and reprints (15%). Specializes in religious books. Averages 60 titles/year. Pays 10% usual royalty on wholesale price. Advance averages $200-1,500. Query or submit outline/synopsis and 2-3 sample chapters. Reports in 1-2 months. SASE.
Nonfiction: Publishes how-to; crafts (to be used in Christian education); juveniles; reference; Christian education; quiz; puzzle and religious; and college textbooks (religious). All mss must pertain to religion.
Recent Nonfiction Titles: *Frankly Feminine*, by Gloria Hope Hawley (God's idea of womanhood); *Adventures in Being a Parent*, by Shirley Pollack; and *Fun Ideas for Family Devotions*, by Ginger Jurries and Karen Mulder.
Fiction: Publishes religious, devotional books.
Recent Fiction Title: *6 Thorne Twin Adventure Books*, by Dayle Courtney (teen adventure).

STANFORD UNIVERSITY PRESS, Stanford CA 94305. (415)497-9434. Editor: J.G. Bell. Averages 32 titles/year. Pays 10-15% royalty; "rarely" offers advance. Photocopied submissions OK. SASE. Reports in 3 weeks. Free book catalog.
Nonfiction: Books on European history, the history of China and Japan, anthropology, psychology, taxonomy, literature and Latin American studies. Query.
Recent Nonfiction Titles: *MITI and the Japanese Miracle: The Growth of Industrial Policy, 1925-1975*, by Chalmers Johnson; and *Bernard Shaw, The Darker Side*, by Arnold Silver.

‡**STAR PUBLISHING CO.**, Subsidiary of Star Business Group, Inc., Box 68, Belmont CA 94002. (415)591-3505. Subsidiaries include University Software, Belmont Books. Editor: Stuart Hoffman. Publishes hardcover and trade paperback originals. Averages 20 titles/year. Pays royalty on wholesale price. No advance. Photocopied submissions OK. SASE. Reports in 1 month on queries; 2 months on mss.
Nonfiction: Primarily textbooks—art, business and economics, photography, mathematics, biology, education. Query.

***STATE HISTORICAL SOCIETY OF WISCONSIN**, 816 State St., Madison WI 53706. (608)262-9604. Editorial Director: Paul H. Hass. Senior Editor: William C. Marten. Publishes hardcover and paperback originals (90%) and hardcover reprints (10%). Publishes 2 titles/year. Subsidy publishes 66% of titles based on "an educated guess on the availability of a subsidy from some source and the strength of the market for the title." Pays 10% royalty; no advance. Photocopied submissions OK. Reports in 8 weeks. SASE. Free book catalog.
Nonfiction: "Research and interpretation in history of the American Middle West—broadly construed as the Mississippi Valley. Must be thoroughly documented but on topics of sufficient interest to attract the layman as well as the scholar. 150,000-200,000 words of text, exclusive of footnotes and other back matter. No extremely narrowly focused monographs on non-Wisconsin subjects."
Recent Nonfiction Titles: *The Documentary History of the Ratification of the Constitution: Volume XIV,* , edited by John Kaminski; *Swedes in Wisconsin,* by Frederick Hale; *The Welsh in Wisconsin,* by Phillips G. Danies; and *The Flavor of Wisconsin: An Informal History of Food and Eating in the Badger State,* by Harva Hachten.

STEIN AND DAY PUBLISHERS, Scarborough House, Briarcliff Manor NY 10510. Averages 100 titles/ year. Offers standard royalty contract. No unsolicited mss without querying first. Nonfiction, send outline or summary and sample chapter. *Must* furnish SASE with all fiction and nonfiction queries.
General: Publishes general adult fiction and nonfiction books; no juveniles or college. All types of nonfiction except technical. Quality fiction. Minimum length: 65,000 words. Recently published *Guadalcanal,* by Edwin P. Hoyt; *Politicians, Socialism and Historians,* by A.J.P. Taylor; and *Dillinger,* by Harry Patterson.

STERLING PUBLISHING, 2 Park Ave., New York NY 10016. (212)532-7160. Acquisitions Manager: Sheila Anne Barry. Publishes hardcover and paperback originals (75%) and reprints (25%). Averages 80 titles/ year. Pays royalty; offers advance. Simultaneous and photocopied submissions OK. Reports in 4-6 weeks. SASE. Book catalog for SASE.
Nonfiction: Alternative lifestyle, fiber arts, games, health, Americana, business, foods, economics, hobbies, how-to, humor, medicine, music, occult, pets, photography, psychology, recreation, reference, self-help, sports, theater (how-to), technical, wine and woodworking. Query or submit complete chapter list, detailed outline/synopsis and 2 sample chapters with photos if necessary. Recently published *Underground Houses,* by R. Roy (how-to); *Complete Diabetic Cookbook,* by M. Finsand (health); and *Biggest Riddle Book in the World.*

‡***STIPES PUBLISHING CO.**, 10-12 Chester St., Champaign IL 61820. (217)356-8391. Contact: Robert Watts. Publishes hardcover originals. Averages 25 titles/year. Subsidy publishes 4% of books, "determined by scholarly contribution of the book." Pays 15% maximum royalty on retail price. Photocopied submissions OK. Computer printout submissions OK; no disks without prior request. SASE. Reports in 2 weeks on queries; 2 months on mss.
Nonfiction: Technical (some areas), textbooks on business and economics, music, agriculture/horticulture and recreation. "All of our books in the trade area are books that also have a college text market." No "books unrelated to educational fields taught at the college level." Submit outline/synopsis and 1 sample chapter.
Recent Nonfiction Titles: *Manual of Woody Landscape Plants,* by Michael Dirr (college text and general reference); *Keyboard Musicianship, Group Piano for Adults,* by James Lyke (college text and general use for private teachers); and *An Introduction to Cinematography,* by John Mercer (college text and general use).

STONE WALL PRESS, INC., 1241 30th St., NW, Washington DC 20007. President/Publisher: Henry Wheelwright. Publishes hardcover and trade paperback originals. Averages 2-5 titles/year. Pays standard royalty; offers minimal advance. Simultaneous and photocopied submissions OK. Computer printouts OK. SASE. Reports in 2 weeks. Book catalog for business size SAE and 1 first class stamp.
Nonfiction: How-to and environmental/outdoor. "Unique, practical, illustrated how-to outdoor books (camping, fishing, hiking, hunting, etc.) and environmental books for the general public." Query. Looks for "concise, sharp writing style with humorous touches; a rough table of contents for an idea of the direction of the book, a new approach or topic which hasn't been done recently." Accepts outline/synopsis and 5 sample chapters.
Recent Nonfiction Titles: *These Are the Endangered,* by Cadieux (environmental); *The Natural World Cookbook,* by Freitus (wild edibles); *Backpacking for Trout,* by Cairns; and *Plant Extinction: A Global Crisis,* by Koopowitz and Kaye.

‡**STONEYDALE PRESS PUBLISHING CO.**, 295 Kootenai Creek Rd., Stevensville MT 59870. (406)777-5269. Publisher: Dale A. Burk. Publishes hardcover and trade paperback originals. Averages 6-8 titles/year. Pays 10-12% on wholesale price or makes outright purchase. Offers average $500 advance. SASE. Reports in 1 month. Book catalog for SAE and 1 first class stamp.
Nonfiction: Biography, "coffee table" book and how-to on Americana, art, history, nature, recreation, travel and Montana topics. "We're looking for good outdoor recreation book ideas for our area (Northern Rocky Mountains, Pacific Northwest); historical ideas from the same region not overly done in the past. Also open to 'coffee table' format books, if we can be convinced a market exists for a specific idea." Query.
Recent Nonfiction Titles: *Families That Take in Friends*, by Joel H. Bernstein (history/western Americana); *Bugling for Elk*, by Dwight Schuh (hunting how-to); *Elmer Sprunger: Wildlife Artist*, by Dale A. Burk (biography of artist); and *Young People's Guide to Yellowstone Park*, by Ruth Burk (recreation-travel guide).

STRAWBERRY HILL PRESS, 2594 15th Ave., San Francisco CA 94127. President: Jean-Louis Brindamour, Ph.D. Senior Editors: Donna L. Osgood, Renee Renouf, Jane Cormack. Publishes paperback originals. Publishes 12 titles/year. "We are a small house, proud of what we do, and intending to stay relatively small (that does not mean that we will do a less-than-professional job in marketing our books, however). The author-publisher relationship is vital, from the moment the contract is signed until there are no more books to sell, and we operate on that premise. We do no hardcovers, and, for the moment at least, our format is limited strictly to 6x9 quality paperbacks, prices between $4.95-10.95. We never print fewer than 5,000 copies in a first printing, with reprintings also never falling below that same figure." Pays 10-20% royalty on wholesale price; no advance. Photocopied submissions OK. Computer printout submissions OK; "disk must be compatible with our TRS 80 system." Reports in 2 months. SASE. Book catalog for SASE.
Nonfiction: Self-help; inspiration (not religion); cookbooks; health and nutrition; aging; diet; popular philosophy; metaphysics; alternative life styles; Third World; minority histories; oral history and popular medicine. Accepts nonfiction and fiction translations. No religion, sports, craft books, photography or fine art material. Submit outline/synopsis and 1 sample chapter.
Recent Nonfiction Titles: *Kimiko's World*, by Kimiko Sugano; and *Uncle Sam Must be Losing the War*, by Bill Downey.
Recent Fiction Title: *Five Rivers to Death*, by Melvin A. Casberg, M.D.

STRUCTURES PUBLISHING CO., Ideals Publishing Corp., Box 1101, Milwaukee WI 53201. Editor: David Schansberg. Publishes paperback originals. Averages 11 titles/year. Offers standard 10-12% royalty contract on selling price. Advance varies, depending on author's reputation and nature of book. Will send a catalog to a writer on request. Submit outline and sample chapters. Photocopied submissions OK. Reports in 4-6 weeks. Enclose return postage.
Technical and How-To: Books related to home remodeling, repair and building. Successful Series published for do-it-yourself homeowners. Will consider structure, construction, building, remodeling, home improvement, and decorating-related topics. "Manuscripts are commissioned, usually. Book illustration and photography expertise of interest."
Recent Nonfiction Titles: *Successful Homeowners Tools*, by James Ritchie; *Putting It All Together*, by Robert Scharff (fastening materials together); and *Successful Home Electrical Wiring*, by Larry Mueller.
Tips: "Manuscripts must be comprehensive, well researched and written and reflect the most current trends of the home improvement and construction markets."

LYLE STUART, INC., 120 Enterprise Ave., Secaucus NJ 07094. (201)866-0490, (212)736-1141. Subsidiaries include Citadel Press and University Books. President: Lyle Stuart. Publishes hardcover and trade paperback originals, and trade paperback reprints. Averages 70 titles/year. Pays 10-12% royalty on retail price; offers "low advance." SASE.
Nonfiction: Biography, "coffee table" book, how-to, humor, illustrated book and self-help. Subjects include Americana, art, business and economics, health, history, music and politics. "The percentage of acceptable over-the-transom mss has been so low during the years that we are no longer reading unsolicited material."
Recent Nonfiction Titles: *Jackie Mason's America*, by Jackie Mason; *The Day the Bunny Died*, by Victor Lownes; *Vegetarian Child*, by Joy Gross.

SHERWOOD SUGDEN & COMPANY, PUBLISHERS, 1117 8th St., La Salle IL 61301. (815)223-1231. Publisher: Sherwood Sugden. Publishes hardcover and trade paperback originals and reprints. Averages 8 titles/year. Pays 4-12% royalty. Simultaneous and photocopied submissions OK. Computer printout submissions OK. SASE. Reports in 3 weeks on queries; 3 months on mss. Book catalog for business size SAE.
Nonfiction: Subjects include history; philosophy; politics; religion (Christian, especially Roman Catholic); and literary criticism. "We're looking for lucid presentations and defenses of orthodox Roman Catholic doctrine, Church history and lives of the Saints aimed at the average intelligent reader. (Possibly one or two scholarly works of the same sort as well.) Works of criticism of British or American authors: perhaps a biography or two; also a work in elementary syllogistic logic. The audience for our books ranges from the bright high school

student with a curiosity about ideas through the mature general reader. Certain of our titles (perhaps 30% of our annual output) will appeal chiefly to the advanced student or scholar in the relevant disciplines." Submit outline/synopsis and 1 sample chapter.

Recent Nonfiction Titles: *Why Poe Drank Liquor: Vol. II of The Prophetic Poet and the Spirit of the Age*, by Marion Montgomery; *Angels, Apes, and Men*, by Stanley Jaki; *Generations of the Faithful Heart: On the Literature of the South*, by M.E. Bradford; *Escape from Scepticism: Liberal Education as if Truth Mattered*, by Christopher Derrick.

SUMMIT BOOKS, Division of Simon & Schuster, 1230 Avenue of the Americas, New York NY 10020. (212)246-2471. President and Editor-in-Chief: Jim Silberman. Publishes hardcover originals. Averages 30 titles/year. Pays standard royalty; offers variable advance. Simultaneous and photocopied submissions OK. SASE. Reports in 2 months.

Nonfiction: General trade list; no poetry. Query or submit outline/synopsis and sample chapters.

Fiction: General trade list; no short stories, no category books and no poetry.

*SUN PUBLISHING CO., Box 4383, Albuquerque NM 87196. (505)255-6550. Editor-in-Chief: Skip Whitson. Publishes hardcover and paperback originals (20%) and reprints (80%). Averages 30 titles/year. Pays 8% royalty; no advance. Will subsidy publish "if we think the book is good enough and if we have the money to do it, we'll publish it on our own; otherwise, the author will have to put up the money." Query or submit outline/synopsis, 2 sample chapters and table of contents. "Do not send complete ms unless requested to do so." Send photocopies if photos/illustrations are to accompany ms. Simultaneous and photocopied submissions OK. Computer printout submissions OK; prefers letter quality to dot matrix. Reports in 2-4 months. SASE. Book list for SASE.

Nonfiction: Publishes Americana, art, biography, cookbooks, history, how-to, politics, scientific, self-help, metaphysical, Oriental and new age books. "40-200-page lengths are preferred." Looks for brevity and clarity.

Recent Fiction Titles: *Rolling Thunder: The Coming Earth Changes*, by J.R. Jochmans; *Oracles of Nostradamus*, by Charles Ward; and *Principles of Occult Healing*, by Mary Weeks Burnett, MD.

Fiction: Publishes some science fiction books.

Tips: "We are looking for manuscripts on the Coming Earth Changes, for outright purchase."

THE SUNSTONE PRESS, Box 2321, Santa Fe NM 87501. (505)988-4418. Editor-in-Chief: James C. Smith Jr. Publishes paperback originals; "sometimes hardcover originals." Averages 16 titles/year. Pays royalty on wholesale price. Free book catalog. Query. Looks for "strong regional appeal (southwestern). Computer printout submissions OK. Reports in 2 months. Enclose return postage.

Nonfiction: How-to series craft books. Books on the history of the Southwest; poetry. Length: open.

Recent Nonfiction Titles: *Done In The Sun*, by Anne Hillerman (juvenile science); *How to Paint and Sell Your Art*, by Marcia Muth (how-to); *Wild Horses*, by Eva Pendleton Henderson (autobiography).

Fiction: Publishes "for readers who use the subject matter to elevate their impressions of our world, our immediate society, families and friends."

Recent Fiction Titles: *Curandero*, by Jose Ortiz y Pino (Southwest fiction); *Walks Two Worlds*, by Robert Fox (Navajo theme); *Mother Ditch*, by Oliver LaFarge (Southwest fiction).

Poetry: *Stone Run: Tidings*, by Cynthia Grenfell.

SUSANN PUBLICATIONS, INC., 3110 N. Fitzhugh, Dallas TX 75204. (214)528-8940. Publisher: Susan Goldstein. Publishes paperback originals. Averages 3 titles/year. Offers 10-15% royalty on retail price. No advance. Simultaneous and photocopied submissions OK. SASE. Reports in 4 weeks.

Nonfiction: Cookbooks, cooking and foods; health; how-to; humor; and self-help. "We are interested in how-to books which specifically help us toward self improvement. We are a female-owned company. We do not want to see sexist, chauvinistic or anti-woman material." Query first "always!"

Recent Nonfiction Titles: *The Underground Shopper Series: Dallas/Fort Worth, New York City, Houston, Austin/San Antonio*, staff-written (shopping guides); and *Greatest Little Bachelor Book in Texas*, staff-written (guide to bachelors).

Tips: "Take some time with your query letter. Mistakes are very unappealing. Include biographical information (limit to one paragraph) with an eye to what is promotable about yourself."

‡SWIFTWATER BOOKS, Box 22026, Tampa FL 33622. Contact: Editorial Department. Book packager publishing hardcover and trade paperback originals. Averages 12 titles/year. Pays royalty occasionally; mostly makes outright purchase. Advances are "extremely rare." Simultaneous and photocopied submissions OK. Does not return submissions unless accompanied by SASE. Reports in 6 weeks on queries; 4 months on mss.

Nonfiction: "Coffee table" book, cookbook, how-to, reference, technical, textbook. Subjects include business and economics, cooking and foods, photography and law. "We package books with both US and foreign publishers, and needs are often unpredictable. We will keep qualification letters of authors on file. Our strongest areas are business, law and cookbooks. We are also looking for several books for the gay male market, and a non-pornographic book of male nude photographs. We may also be interested in books on Hawaii and Puerto Rico. We have a strong need for material of Irish interest. There are no completely banned subjects, but if yours is outside our listed specialties, please send a query instead of a complete manuscript.'' Query with reference to a completed ms or send complete ms.

Recent Nonfiction Titles: *Tax Havens for the Multinational Corporation*, by Center for Business Information (tax law); *Tax Havens and Their Uses*, by US Treasury Department (tax law); *Handbook of Lubricants*, by NASA (reference).

Fiction: Erotic (gay male only) and science fiction. Fiction needs are limited. Query with reference to completed ms or send complete ms.

Tips: ''Most of our books are published for an international audience, although some business titles are suited only for a domestic audience. We have developed several specialized niches, and produce books in these narrow specialties for publishers not equipped to serve these markets.''

SYBEX, INC., 2344 6th St., Berkeley CA 94710. (415)848-8233. Editor-in-Chief: Dr. Rudolph S. Langer. Acquisitions Editor: Michael McGrath. Publishes hardcover and paperback originals. Averages 40 titles/year. Royalty rates vary. Average $2,500 advance. Simultaneous and photocopied submissions OK. ''We prefer hard copy for proposal evaluations and encourage our authors to submit Wordstar diskettes upon completion of their manuscripts. Wordstar word processor diskettes preferred. Reports in 2 months. Free book catalog.

Nonfiction: Computer and electronics. ''Manuscripts most publishable in the field of microprocessors, microcomputers, hardware, LSI, programming, programming languages, applications, automation, telecommunications.'' Submit outline/synopsis and 2-3 sample chapters. Accepts nonfiction translations from French or German. Looks for ''clear writing; technical accuracy; logical presentation of material; and good selection of material, such that the most important aspects of the subject matter are thoroughly covered; well-focused subject matter; and well-thought-out organization that helps the reader understand the material. And marketability.''

Recent Nonfiction Titles: *The CP/M Handbook*; *BASIC for Business*; *Introduction to WordStar*; *Doing Business with Visicak*; and *The Apple Connection*.

Tips: Queries/mss may be routed to other editors in the publishing group.

SYLVAN PRESS, Box 15125, Richmond VA 23227. Editor-in-Chief: Sylvia Manolatos. Art Director: Lelia C. Koplin. Senior Editor: Frederica D. Garcia. Editorial Director: Peter Katz. Publishes paperback originals. Averages 5 titles/year. Pays 10% royalty; no advance. Photocopied submissions OK. No computer printout or disk submissions. Reports in 3 months. ''All submissions *must* be accompanied by SASE. Not responsible for mss submitted without return postage enclosed.''

Nonfiction: Poetry. ''We want to see collections of serious poetry for possible publication as paperback chapbooks not to exceed 30 pages. Also, we are interested in individual poems for consideration in our anthologies, *Sylvan Sequence* and *Sylvan Song*. We do not want to see trite verse of any kind and prefer shorter poems. We use very little religious poetry, 'everyday' type verse, or poems about children.'' Accepts b&w artwork; and poetry translations from Spanish, German, French or Russian.

Recent Nonfiction Titles: *Thoughts on Monsters*, by Lawrence Vershel; *Woven Tapestries*, by Rupert Conrad.

Tips: ''Sylvan Press is trying to create a market for serious poets who want to see their works in print. We are a small specialty publisher. Our emphasis is on literary quality. At present, we are in the process of publishing 2 anthologies of poetry as well as 2 individual collections of verse. We also publish a quarterly poetry magazine *Serenade*.''

*SYMMES SYSTEMS, Box 8101, Atlanta GA 30306. Editor-in-Chief: E. C. Symmes. Publishes hardcover and paperback originals. Pays 10% royalty on wholesale price. ''Contracts are usually written for the individual title and may have different terms.'' No advance. Does 40% subsidy publishing. Will consider photocopied and simultaneous submissions. Computer printout submissions OK; prefers letter quality to dot matrix. Acknowledges receipt in 10 days; evaluation within 1 month. Query. SASE.

Nonfiction and Nature: ''Our books have mostly been in the art of bonsai (miniature trees). We are publishing quality information for laypersons (hobbyists). Most of the titles introduce information that is totally new for the hobbyist.'' Clear and concise writing style. Accepts artwork/photos. Text must be topical, showing state-of-the-art. All books so far have been illustrated with photos and/or drawings. Would like to see more material on bonsai and other horticultural subjects; also photography and collecting photographica. Length: open.

Recent Nonfiction Title: *Physician's Guide to Nutritional Therapy*, by Anderson.

SYRACUSE UNIVERSITY PRESS, 1600 Jamesville Ave., Syracuse NY 13210. (315)423-2596. Director/Editor: Arpena Mesrobian. Averages 25 titles/year. Pays royalty on net sales. Simultaneous and photocopied submissions OK ''only if we are informed.'' Computer printout submissions OK. SASE. Reports in 2 weeks on queries; ''longer on submissions.'' Free book catalog.

Nonfiction: ''The best opportunities for freelance writers are in our nonfiction program of books on New York

state. We have published regional books by people with limited formal education, but they were thoroughly acquainted with their subjects, and they wrote simply and directly about them. No vague descriptions or assumptions that a reference to a name (in the case of a biography) or place is sufficient information. The author must make a case for the importance of his subject." Query. Accepts outline/synopsis and at least 2 sample chapters.
Recent Nonfiction Titles: *Three Eyes on the Past: Exploring New York Folk Life*, by Janis C. Jones; *A Lasting Spring: Jessie Catherine Kinsley Daughter of the Oneida Community*, ed. by Jane Kinsley; *Gustav Stickley, The Craftsman*, by Mary Ann Smith.

‡**T.F.H. PUBLICATIONS, INC.**, 211 W. Sylvania Ave., Neptune City NJ 07727. (201)988-8400. Managing Editor: Neal Pronek. Publishes hardcover and trade paperback originals. Averages 30 titles/year. Pays 7½-12½% royalty on wholesale or retail price; buys most mss outright. Simultaneous and photocopied submissions OK. No computer printout or disk submissions. SASE. Reports in 1 week on queries; 2 weeks on mss. Book catalog for 9x12 SAE with $1.90 postage.
Nonfiction: How-to on animals (especially pets) and nature; technical (fish taxonomy) for owners of pet animals; tropical fish hobbyists. Especially needs "books that tell people how to care for and (where applicable) breed animals kept as pets. Manuscript/photo packages have better chance of acceptance than manuscript alone." Query or submit outline/synopsis and 1 sample chapter.
Recent Nonfiction Titles: *The Book of the Cocker Spaniel*, by Joan Brearley; *Handbook of Macaws*, by Dr. A.E. Decoteau; and *Beginning with Snakes*, by Richard Stratton.

TAB BOOKS, INC., Blue Ridge Summit PA 17214. (717)794-2191. Vice President: Ray Collins. Publishes hardcover and paperback originals and reprints. Publishes 200 titles per year. Pays variable royalty and advance. Buys some mss outright for a negotiable fee. Photocopied submissions OK (except for art). Computer printout submissions OK; prefers letter quality to dot matrix. Reports in 6 weeks. SASE. Free book catalog and manuscript preparation guide.
Nonfiction: TAB publishes titles in such fields as computer hardware; computer software; solar and alternate energy; marine line; aviation; automotive; music technology; consumer medicine; electronics; electrical and electronics repair; amateur radio; shortwave listening; model railroading; toys; hobbies; drawing; animals and animal power; practical skills with projects; building furniture; basic how-to for the house; building large structures; calculators; robotics; telephones; model radio control; TV servicing; audio, recording, hi-fi and stereo; electronic music; electric motors; electrical wiring; electronic test equipment; video programming; CATV, MATV and CCTV; broadcasting; photography and film; appliance servicing and repair; advertising; antiques and restoration; bicycles; crafts; farmsteading; hobby electronics; home construction; license study guides; mathematics; metalworking; reference books; schematics and manuals; small gasoline engines; two-way radio and CB; and woodworking. Accepts nonfiction translations.

TANDEM PRESS PUBLISHERS, Box 237, Tannersville PA 18372. (717)629-2250. Editor-in-Chief: Judith Keith. Hardcover originals. Averages 4 titles/year. 10-12½-15% royalty on retail price. Sometimes offers an advance. "This is handled with each author individually." Photocopied submissions OK. SASE. Reports in 2-4 weeks. Book catalog for SASE. Does not accept multiple submissions. Computer printout submissions OK. Also handles sales of original paperback to major houses.
Nonfiction: Cookbooks, cooking and foods; how-to; multimedia material; nature; pets; psychology; recreation; self-help; and sports books. Query. Accepts outline/synopsis and 3 sample chapters. Looks for "salability . . . which means an interesting story told with talent."
Recent Nonfiction Title: *I Haven't a Thing to Wear*, by J. Keith (how-to on clothes and accessories).
Fiction: Adventure; confession; fantasy; historical; mainstream; mystery; religious; romance; and suspense. Submit outline/synopsis and 3 sample chapters to Elisa Fitzgerald.
Recent Fiction Title: *Desires of Thy Hearts*, by Joan Cruz (historical romance).

TAPLINGER PUBLISHING, CO., INC., 132 W. 22nd, New York NY 10011. (212)741-0801. Imprints include Crescendo (music), Pentalic (calligraphy). Editors: Ms. Bobs Pinkerton and Roy E. Thomas. Publishes hardcover originals. Publishes 75 titles/year. Pays standard royalty; offers variable advance. Simultaneous and photocopied submissions OK. No computer printout or disk submissions. SASE. Reports in 10 weeks.
Nonfiction: Art, biography, history, current affairs, theatre, general trade and belles-lettres. No juveniles. Query.
Fiction: Serious contemporary quality fiction. Accepts fiction translations. No juveniles.

J.P. TARCHER, INC., 9110 Sunset Blvd., Los Angeles CA 90069. (213)273-3274. President and Editor-in-Chief: Jeremy P. Tarcher. Publishes hardcover and trade paperback originals. Pays 10-12½-15% royalty on hardcover list price; offers advance "competitive in the industry." Averages 35 titles/year. State availability of photos and/or illustrations to accompany ms. Simultaneous and photocopied submissions OK. Reports in 3-5 weeks. SASE. Free book catalog.
Fiction and Nonfiction: Publishes popular psychology, sociology, health and fitness, alternative medicine,

consciousness, gardening, cooking, and humor. Submit outline/synopsis and sample chapters. Recently published *Drawing on the Right Side of the Brain*, by B. Edwards, Ph.D.; *The Aquarian Conspiracy*, by M. Feruson; and *Joy's Way*, by B. Joy, M.D.

Recent Nonfiction Titles: *Psychology of Romantic Love*, by Nathaniel Branden; *Make It Easy in Your Kitchen*, by L.B. Grad; *Marva Collins Way*, by Marva Collins; *Writing the Natural*, by G. Rico.

‡**ALISTER TAYLOR PUBLISHERS**, The Old Post Office, Martinborough, New Zealand. (553)69847. Subsidiaries include Glenberrie Press, Student Publications Ltd. Managing Director: Alister Taylor. Publishes hardcover and trade paperback originals. Averages 15-20 titles/year. Pays 7½-15% royalty on retail price; buys some mss outright for $5,000-75,000. Advance "depends on the project." Photocopied submissions OK. SAE and IRCs. Reports in 2 weeks on queries; 3 months on mss. Free book catalog.
Nonfiction: Biography, "coffee table" books, illustrated books, juvenile, reference books, self-help on art, history, photography, politics, sports. Publishes for "literate audience interested in definitive quality books." Especially needs "illustrated catalogues raisonne of major painters; major books on the thoroughbred and Arab horse." Query or submit outline/synopsis and sample chapters.
Recent Nonfiction Titles: *Notable English and Irish Thoroughbreds*, (definitive racing book); *Eugene von Everard: German Romantic in the Antipodes* (biography and catalogue raisonne); and *Legend of the Kiwi*, (children's 4-8).
Fiction: New Zealand-Australian fiction only. Query or submit outline/synopsis and sample chapters.
Recent Fiction Titles: *Pet Shop*, by Ian Middleton and *For Mine Is the Kingdom*, by John A. Lee (novels).
Poetry: New Zealand poetry only. Submit complete ms.
Recent Poetry Title: *Collected Poems 1947-81*, by Alistar Campbell.

‡**TAYLOR PUBLISHING CO.**, Subsidiary of Insilco, Box 597, Dallas 1X 75221. (214)637-2800. Senior Editor: Pierce Watters. Editorial Director: J. Nelson Black. Publishes hardcover and trade paperback originals and hardcover and trade paperback reprints. Averages 10-20 titles/year. Pays 10% minimum royalty on wholesale price or makes outright purchase of $2,500 minimum. Simultaneous and photocopied submissions OK. SASE. Reports in 6 weeks on queries; 4 months on mss. Free book catalog.
Nonfiction: Send queries to Pierce Watters. Biography, "coffee table" book, cookbook, how-to, humor, illustrated book, reference, self-help, technical and textbook. Subjects include Americana, art, business and economics, cooking and foods, health, history, nature, photography, recreation, sports, travel and Texana. Interested in gardening, sports and business (sales and management) books—nonfiction with a regional slant and a national appeal. Query or submit outline/synopsis and sample chapters.
Recent Nonfiction Titles: *Journey to Triumph*, by Carlton Stowers (sports); *Neil Sperry's Complete Guide to Texas Gardening*, by Neil Sperry; and *Texas Sports Almanac*, edited by Bob O'Brien.

TEACHER UPDATE, INC., Box 205, Saddle River NJ 07458. (201)327-8486. Editorial Director: Donna Papalia. Senior Editor: Nick Roes. Editorial Assistant: Nancy Roes. Publishes hardcover and paperback originals. Averages 6 titles/year. Pays royalty; buys some mss outright by arrangement; offers variable advance. Photocopied submissions OK. SASE. Reports in 1 month. Free book catalog for SASE.
Nonfiction: Education, consumer and general interest. Query, submit outline/synopsis and sample chapters or complete ms.
Recent Nonfiction Titles: *Helping Children Watch TV*, by N. Roes (handbook); *America's Lowest Cost Colleges*, by N. Roes (directory); *Poems For Young Children*, by editors of *Teacher Update* (poetry); and *The Do Nothing Way to Beauty And Health*, by Mimi (beauty and health).

TEACHERS COLLEGE PRESS, 1234 Amsterdam Ave., New York NY 10027. (212)678-3929. Director: Thomas M. Rotell. Publishes hardcover and paperback originals (90%) and reprints (1%). Royalty varies; offers advance. Averages 75 titles/year. Reports in 3-6 months. SASE. Free book catalog.
Nonfiction: "This university press concentrates on books in the field of education in the broadest sense from early childhood to higher education: good classroom practices, teacher training, special education, innovative trends and issues, administration and supervision, film, continuing and adult education, all areas of the curriculum, comparative education, dental, guidance and counseling and the politics, economics, nursing, philosophy, sociology and history of education. The press also issues classroom materials for students at all levels, with a strong emphasis on reading and writing." Submit outline/synopsis and sample chapters.
Recent Nonfiction Title: *Parent's Handbook on School Testing*, by Boehm White.

TEMPLE UNIVERSITY PRESS, Broad and Oxford Sts., Philadelphia PA 19122. (215)787-8787. Editor-in-Chief: Michael Ames. Publishes 35 titles/year. Pays royalty on wholesale price. Photocopied submissions OK. SASE. Reports in 3 months. Free book catalog.
Nonfiction: American history, public policy and regional (Philadelphia area). "All books should be scholarly. Authors are generally connected with a university. No memoirs, fiction or poetry." Uses University of Chicago *Manual of Style*. Query.

Recent Nonfiction Titles: *Charlotte Perkins Gilman*, by Mary A. Hill; and *Policy and Politics in Britain*, by Douglas Ashford.

TEMPO BOOKS, A division of The Berkley Publishing Group, 200 Madison Ave., New York NY 10016. (212)686-9820. Publishes hardcover reprints and paperback originals. Nonfiction and fiction titles for young adults. Buys manuscripts on royalty basis. Submit 3 chapters and synopsis. SASE. Reports in 5-8 weeks. **Fiction:** Contemporary romances and problem novels for ages 11 to 18. "We are looking for contemporary young adult fiction dealing in all subjects." Submit outline/synopsis and sample chapters. **Recent Fiction Titles:** *The Leaving*, by Lynn Hall; *Kid Brother*, by Kevin Mulligan; *S.W.A.K. Sealed With a Kiss*, by Judith Enderle (a Caprice Romance); and *A Love Song For Becky*, by Francess Lin Lantz (a Caprice Romance).

TEN SPEED PRESS, Box 7123, Berkeley CA 94707. Editor: P. Wood. Publishes hardcover and paperback originals and reprints. Offers royalty of 8% of list price; 12½% after 100,000 copies are sold. Offers average $3,000 advance. Averages 15 titles/year. Will send catalog to writer on request for SASE. Submit outline and sample chapters for nonfiction. Computer printout and disk submissions OK. Reports in 1 month. Enclose return postage.
Nonfiction: Americana, gardening, cookbooks, cooking and foods, history, humor, law, nature, self-help, how-to, sports, hobbies, recreation and pets and travel. Publishes mostly trade paperbacks. Subjects range from bicycle books to William Blake's illustrations. "We will consider any first-rate nonfiction material that we feel will have a long shelf life and be a credit to our list." No set requirements. Some recipe books and career development books.
Recent Nonfiction Titles: *How To Get The Degree You Want*, by John Bear; *The Enchanted Broccoli Forest*, by Mollie Katzen (vegetarian cooking).

TEXAS A&M UNIVERSITY PRESS, Drawer C, College Station TX 77843. (409)845-1436. Director: Lloyd G. Lyman. Publishes 30 titles/year. Pays in royalties. Photocopied submissions OK. Computer printout submissions OK "if clean and legible"; prefers letter quality to dot matrix. SASE. Reports in 1 week (queries); 1 month (submissions). Free book catalog.
Nonfiction: History, natural history, environmental history, economics, agriculture and regional studies. Accepts nonfiction translations. "We do not want fiction and poetry." Query. Accepts outline/synopsis and 2-3 sample chapters.
Recent Nonfiction Titles: *The Sharks of North American Waters*, by José I. Castro (natural history); *Ashbel Smith of Texas: Pioneer, Patriot, Statesman, 1805-1886*, by Elizabeth Silverthorne (biography); and *Lumberjacks and Legislators: Political Economy of the US Lumber Industry, 1890-1941*, by William G. Robbins (environmental history).

TEXAS CHRISTIAN UNIVERSITY PRESS, Box 30783, TCU, Fort Worth TX 76129. (817)921-7822. Associate Director: Keith Gregory. Editor: Judy Alter. Publishes hardcover originals, some reprints. Averages 10 titles/year. Pays royalty. Simultaneous and photocopied submissions OK. Computer printout submissions OK. No disk submissions. Reports "as soon as possible."
Nonfiction: American studies, Texana, literature and criticism. "We are looking for good scholarly monographs, other serious scholarly work and regional titles of significance." Accepts artwork/photos. Query. **Recent Nonfiction Titles:** *Kiowa Voices*, by Boyd; *The Complete Short Stories of Anthony Trollope*; *Lone Star and Double Eagle*, by Goyne.

‡**TEXAS INSTRUMENTS LEARNING CENTER**, Subsidiary of Texas Instruments Inc., Box 225012, M/S 54, Dallas TX 75265. (214)995-5516. Manager, Product Development: Gerald Luecke. Publishes hardcover and trade paperback originals. Averages 3-6 titles/year. Pays fixed fee per printed page for each book. Photocopied submissions OK. Computer printout submissions OK; prefers letter quality to dot matrix. SASE. Reports in 2 weeks on queries; 1 month on mss. Free book catalog.
Nonfiction: Reference books, self-help, technical, textbooks on semiconductor technology, electronics, computers and their application. Publishes for hobbyists, technicians, continuing education, vocational schools, community colleges, industrial learning and training centers. "We publish books that enhance the understanding and use of the technologies that Texas Instruments uses for its products and for the extended use of the products that result from those technologies." No non-technical or unrelated themes. Submit outline/synopsis and 1 sample chapter. Accepts artwork/photos. "We normally work from outline agreed on for contract before writing begins. We would accept submissions but disclosure form needs to be signed to protect both parties."
Recent Nonfiction Titles: *Understanding Computer Science*, by R.G. Walker; *Understanding Microprocessors*, by D. Cannon and G. Luecke; *Understanding Automotive Electronics*, by W. Ribbens and N. Mansour; *Understanding Solid-State Electronics*, by Staff of Texas Instruments; and *Understanding Telephone Electronics*, by J.L. Fike and G.E. Friend.

Close-up

Philip Wood, Editor & Publisher
Ten Speed Press

You don't have to talk with Philip Wood for very long to sense his commitment to quality writing. It's a dedication that stems from more than 20 years in the book business.

"I had ten years in the field before I started Ten Speed Press in 1971," says Wood. "I started it basically because Penguin wouldn't publish a couple of books I thought were good."

Ten Speed was launched with a book called *Anybody's Bike Book* (hence the company's name) "that sold a thousand copies a day for a couple of years." But then Wood began branching out into other subject areas. "The best position for a publisher is to be in many different fields at one time," he says. Reflecting the same philosophy, Ten Speed has recently purchased Celestial Arts—publishers of self-help, humor, health and recreation titles.

"We don't discriminate between specialist and generalist writers or subjects. We look for fine writing that ranks well in its field," says Wood. "I don't care what the subject is—physics or mushrooms, bicycles or woodworking. If we can determine that a book is excellently written, that's sufficient reason to publish it."

Wood receives between 100 and 200 manuscripts and outlines each month. All submissions are logged in and get a preliminary reading. If the first reader likes the look of a manuscript, it is sent to Wood and two other editors who make the final decision. "We each read it, consider it, put it on a pile; we sleep on it and talk about it on and off for 30 days or so. Sometimes it takes longer, especially if we get something that's not complete."

The kinds of manuscripts Wood publishes are those that give continuity to Ten Speed's list. "We want books that help sell each other. We want a certain level of quality; we want something

that's not like other books on the subject. And I like to think that since we're small, we can wait for the unusual book to come along. I look for excellence—and excellence can be cleverness; it can be great, good humor; it can be something scholarly."

Wood thinks he gets a fair amount of quality submissions for two reasons. "I think people tend to send book manuscripts to a publisher based on what they have seen that publisher produce—and that's gratifying. The other thing is many of our authors recommend writers to us, people they would like to see on our list with their books."

A beginning writer has a good chance to be noticed at Ten Speed. "In fact, many of our authors were beginning writers who self-published their first books. Both of our bestsellers, *The Moosewood Cookbook* and *What Color Is Your Parachute?* were originally self-published.

"I think it's always good for an author to explain what his relationship to his subject is, and whether it's going to be an ongoing interest. If he just wants to get into print, make some money, and go on to something else, that is one kind of book. But if his life's been devoted to learning a subject thoroughly, and this book is just one part of the larger process, I want to know that. I respect that kind of commitment on the part of a writer. That can have a lot of influence on how carefully we look at a book or an idea."

TEXAS MONTHLY PRESS, INC., Subsidiary of Mediatex Communications Corp., Box 1569, Austin TX 78767. (512)476-7085. Senior Editor: Barbara Rodriguez. Publishes hardcover and trade paperback originals (80%), and trade paperback reprints (20%). Averages 16 titles/year. Pays royalty on retail price; offers average $2,500 advance. Simultaneous and photocopied submissions OK. Computer printout submissions OK; prefers letter quality to dot matrix. SASE. Reports in 2 weeks on queries; 2 months on mss. Free book catalog. Imprints: *Texas Monthly Press* (fiction and nonfiction) Barbara Rodriguez, editor.
Nonfiction: Biography, "coffee table" book, cookbook, humor, guidebook, illustrated book and reference. Subjects include Texana, art, business and economics, cooking and foods, history, nature, photography, politics, recreation, sports and travel. Texas and California-related subjects only. "Especially interested in biographies of distinguished Texans in all fields." Query or submit outline/synopsis and 3 sample chapters. Accepts artwork/photos.
Recent Nonfiction Titles: *The Only Texas Cookbook*, by Linda Eckhardt; *Out of the Forties*, by Nicholas Lemann (history); *The Snakes of Texas*, by Alan Tennant (zoology); *Mexico: The Texas Monthly Guidebook*, by Hilary Hylton.
Fiction: Adventure, ethnic, historical, mainstream, mystery, suspense and western. "All stories must be set in Texas." No experimental, erotica, confession, gothic, romance or poetry. Query or submit outline/synopsis and 3 sample chapters. No unsolicited mss.
Recent Fiction Titles: *The Gay Place*, by William Brammer (political); *A Family Likeness*, by Janis Stout (generational saga); and *The Power Exchange*, by Alan Erwin (suspense).

TEXAS WESTERN PRESS, The University of Texas at El Paso, El Paso TX 79968. (915)747-5688. Director/Editor: Hugh W. Treadwell. Publishes hardcover and paperback originals. Publishes 9-10 titles/year. "We are a university press, not a commercial house; therefore, payment is in books and prestige more than money. We sell to libraries and serious readers of serious nonfiction." Will send a catalog to a writer on request. Query. Will consider photocopied submissions. Follow *MLA Style Sheet*. Reports in 1 to 3 months.
Nonfiction: "Scholarly books. Historic and cultural accounts of the Southwest (west Texas, southern New Mexico, and northern Mexico). Some literary works, occasional scientific titles. Our *Southwestern Studies* use mss of 20,000 words. Our hardback books range from 30,000 words up. The writer should use good exposition in his work. Most of our work requires documentation. We favor a scholarly, but not overly pedantic, style. We specialize in superior book design."
Recent Nonfiction Titles: *The Urban Southwest*, by Bradford Luckingham; and *Pass of the North II*, by C.L. Sonnichsen.

*THE THEOSOPHICAL PUBLISHING HOUSE, Subsidiary of The Theosophical Society in America, 306 W. Geneva Rd., Wheaton IL 60189. (312)665-0123. Senior Editor: Shirley Nicholson. Publishes trade paperback originals. Averages 12 titles/year. Subsidy publishes 40% of books based on "author need and quality and theme of manuscript." Pays 10-12% royalty on retail price; offers average $1,500 advance. Simultaneous and photocopied submissions OK. Computer printout submissions OK; prefers letter quality to dot matrix. SASE. Reports in 1 week on queries, 2 months on mss. Free book catalog.
Imprints: *Quest* (nonfiction), Shirley Nicholson, senior editor.
Nonfiction: Self-help. Subjects include health, philosophy, psychology (trans-personal), religion and occultism. "TPH seeks works on philosophy, psychology, comparative religion, etc., which are compatible with the theosophical philosophy. Our audience includes the 'new age' consciousness community plus all religious groups, professors, general public." No "material which does not fit the description of needs outlined above." Accepts nonfiction translations. Query or submit outline/synopsis and sample chapters.
Recent Nonfiction Titles: *The Shaman and the Medicine Wheel*, by Evelyn Eaton; *The Opening of the Wisdom Eye*, by The Dalai Lama; and *The Gospels as a Mandala of Wisdom*, by Geddes MacGregor.

THE THORNDIKE PRESS, One Mile Rd., Box 157, Thorndike ME 04986. (207)948-2962. Senior Editor: Timothy A. Loeb. Publishes hardcover and paperback originals (25%) and reprints (75%). Averages 98 titles/year. No subsidy publishing. Offers 10-15% of wholesale receipts; also buys mss by outright purchase: $500-2,000. Average advance: $1,000. Simultaneous and photocopied submissions OK. Computer printout submissions OK. SASE. Reports in 2 months. Free book catalog.
Nonfiction: Americana (especially Maine and the Northeast); animals; humor; nature; and all subjects of regional interest. Especially needs "manuscripts relating to the wilderness and oudoor recreation (hunting, fishing, etc.) in the Northeast US." No poetry, young adult or children's books. Submit outline/synopsis and 2-3 sample chapters. Accepts artwork/photos.
Recent Nonfiction Titles: Fly Fishing in Maine, by A. Raychard (guide); *Second Sunrise, Nuclear War: The Untold Story*, by Michael Pogodzinski; *Trout and Salmon Fishing in Northern New England*, by Al Raychard; *Eastern Birds of Prey*, by Neal Clark.
Fiction: Mystery; humor (New England); nostalgia; and regional interests (Maine and New England). "We will always consider exceptional manuscripts, but currently have enough for general plans. Prefer short works." No young adult or children's books; no poetry. Submit outline/synopsis and 2-3 sample chapters.

Recent Fiction Titles: *Adventure in a Model T*, by Arthur Macdougall (Dud Dean stories); *Neighborly Relations*, by Edwin Merry (growing up in the 1920s); *Stories Told in the Kitchen*, by Morse; *Champagne and a Gardener*; *A Little Maine Murder*, by B.J. Morison; *What Use are Moose?*, by Peter Farrow (humor).
Tips: "We are moving away from Maine-only-type books and looking for a wider audience. The majority of our publishing consists of large print editions of current best sellers for the visually impaired (88 titles a year). For original books, we seek outdoors/nature guides, New England humor, nostalgia, mystery and general fiction of a high degree of literary merit. We are *not* publishing poetry, children's or young adult adventure/suspense, cookbooks, science fiction, erotica, or mass-market fiction or romances."

THORSONS PUBLISHERS, LTD, Denington Estate, Wellingborough, Northamptonshire NN8 2RQ England. Editor-in-Chief: J.R. Hardaker. Publishes hardcover and paperback originals and reprints. Pays 8-10% royalty. Photocopied submissions OK. Computer printout submissions OK; prefers letter quality to dot matrix. SAE and International Reply Coupons. Reports in 2-4 weeks. Free book catalog.
Nonfiction: Natural health and healing, natural food and vegetarian cookery, alternative medicine, hypnotism and hypnotherapy, practical psychology, inspiration, mind training, personal improvement, self-help themes, books for women, special diets, animal rights, public speaking topics, yoga and related disciplines. Submit outline/synopsis and 3 sample chapters.
Tips: Queries/mss may be routed to other editors in the publishing group.

THREE CONTINENTS PRESS, 1346 Connecticut Ave. NW, Washington DC 20036. Publisher/Editor-in-Chief: Donald E. Herdeck. Publishes hardcover and paperback originals (90%) and reprints (10%). Pays 10% royalty; advance "only on delivery of complete ms which is found acceptable; usually $300." Prefers photocopied submissions. State availability of photos/illustrations. Simultaneous submissions OK. No computer printout or disk submissions. Reports in 6 months. SASE. Free book catalog.
Nonfiction and Fiction: Specializes in African, Caribbean and Middle Eastern (Arabic and Persian) literature and criticism and translation, third world literature and history. Scholarly, well-prepared mss; creative writing. Fiction, poetry, criticism, history and translations of creative writing. "We search for books which will make clear the complexity and value of African literature and culture, including bilingual texts (African language/English translations) of previously unpublished authors from less well-known areas of Africa. We are always interested in genuine contributions to understanding African and Caribbean culture." Length: 50,000-125,000 words. Query. "Please do not submit ms unless we ask for it." Recently published *Fire: Six Writers from Angola, Mozambique, and Cape Verde*, by D. Burness; *Black Shack Alley* (from Joseph Zobel's Martiniquian novel, La rue Cases-Nègres); *African Language Literatures*, by Albert S. Gerard; *Holy Violence: The Revolutionary Thought of Frantz Fanon*, by B. Marie Perinbam; and *Heremakhonon*, by Maryse Condé (a Guadeloupian novel translated from the French).

‡**THUNDER'S MOUTH PRESS**, Box 780, New York NY 10025. (212)866-4329. Publisher: Neil Ortenberg. Publishes hardcover and trade paperback originals and reprints. Averages 6 titles/year. Pays 5-10% royalty on retail price; offers average $200 advance. Photocopied submissions OK. Reports in 3 weeks on queries; 2 months on mss. Book catalog for SAE with 20¢ postage.
Nonfiction: Biography, cookbook, how-to, self-help on cooking and foods, history, philosophy, politics, sociology. Publishes for "college students, academics, politically left of center, ethnic, social activists, women, etc. We basically do poetry and fiction now, but intend to start doing nonfiction over the next few years. How-to books, or biographies, history books, cookbooks would be fine." No cat books. Query or submit outline/synopsis and sample chapters.
Fiction: Erotica, ethnic, experimental, historical, humor, science fiction, political. "We are interested in doing anywhere from 3-5 novels per year, particularly highly literary or socially relevant novels." No romance novels. Query or submit outline/synopsis and sample chapters.
Recent Fiction Titles: *America Made Me*, by Hans Koning and *Dos Indios*, by Harold Jaffe (novels).
Poetry: "We intend to publish 3-5 books of poetry per year." No elitist poetry, rhymes poetry, religious poetry." Submit complete ms.
Recent Poetry Titles: *From Sand Creek*, by Simon Ortiz (native American); *Mojo Hands Call/I Must Go*, by Sterling Plumpp (jazz poetry); and *She Had Some Horses*, by Joy Harjo (native American).

TIMBER PRESS, Box 1631, Beaverton OR 97075. (503)292-2606. Editor: Richard Abel. Publishes hardcover and paperback originals. Publishes 10 titles/year. Pays 10-20% royalty; "sometimes" offers advance. Photocopied submissions OK. Computer printout submissions OK. SASE. Reports in 2 months. Free book catalog.
Nonfiction: Arts and crafts, natural history, Northwest regional material, forestry and horticulture. Accepts nonfiction translations from German. Query or submit outline/synopsis and 3-4 sample chapters. Accepts artwork/photos. Recently published *Complete Book of Roses*, by Krussmann (horticulture); *Native Clays and Glazes for North American Potters*, by Ralph Mason (arts and crafts).

TIME-LIFE BOOKS INC., 777 Duke St., Alexandria VA 22314. (703)960-5000. Editor: George Constable. Publishes hardcover originals. Publishes 40 titles/year. "We have no minimum or maximum fee because our needs vary tremendously. Advance, as such, is not offered. Author is paid as he completes part of contracted work." Books are almost entirely staff-generated and staff-produced, and distribution is primarily through mail order sale. Query to the Director of Corporate Development. SASE.
Nonfiction: "General interest books. Most books tend to be heavily illustrated (by staff), with text written by assigned authors. We very rarely accept mss or book ideas submitted from outside our staff." Length: open.
Recent Nonfiction Titles: *The Healthy Heart* (Health Series); *The First Aviators* (Epic of Flight Series); and *Japan at War* (WWII Series).

TIMES BOOKS, The New York Times Book Co., Inc., 3 Park Ave., New York NY 10016. (212)725-2050. Vice President, Editor-in-Chief: Jonathan B. Segal. Senior Editor: Kathleen Moloney. Senior Editor: Elisabeth Scharlatt. Assistant Editor: William J. Zirinsky. Publishes hardcover and paperback originals (75%) and reprints (25%). Publishes 35 titles/year. Pays royalty; average advance.
Nonfiction: Business/economics, cookbooks, current affairs, cooking, self-help and sports. Accepts only solicited manuscripts.
Recent Nonfiction Titles: *The Last Hero: Wild Bill Donovan*, by Anthony Cave Brown; *Princess*, by Robert Lacey; *Jane Brody's The New York Times Guide to Personal Health*, by Jane E. Brody; *What's The Good Word?*, by William Safire.

TL ENTERPRISES, INC., Book Division, 29901 Agoura Rd., Agoura CA 91301. (213)991-4980. Editor-in-Chief: Alice M. Dauro. Publishes hardcover and trade and mass market paperback originals. Averages 2 titles/year. Pays 5-10% royalty on retail price; offers average $6,000 advance. No computer printout or disk submissions. Reports in 1 month.
Nonfiction: Cookbook, how-to, reference, technical and travel/touring. Subjects include cooking and foods, hobbies, nature, recreation and travel. Accepts artwork/photos. "We have 9 mss in our publishing pipeline at present, so our immediate needs are satisfied. But we *do* read all queries, we will direct mail-test titles of promise, and we will give test winners an immediate home. At present, our book market consists of RV owners and motorcycle touring enthusiasts—so we want to see nothing that does not have a specific interest to one group or the other. For now, our book audience is our magazine audience—the million or more people who read *Trailer Life*, *Motor Home*, *Rider*, et al.—together with the 407,000 families who belong to our Good Sam (RV owners') Club." Query with outline/synopsis and 3 sample chapters ("3 chapters only"). All unsolicited mss are returned unopened.
Recent Nonfiction Titles: *Rider's Complete Guide to Motorcycle Touring*, by Dick Blom; *Guide to Full-Time RVing*, by Don Wright; *TL'S Secrets of Successful RVing*, by John Thompson (RVing how-to); and *RX For RV Performance and Mileage*, by Bill Estes and John Geraghty.

TOMPSON & RUTTER INC., Box 297, Grantham NH 03753. (603)863-4392. President: Frances T. Rutter. Publishes trade paperback originals. Averages 4 titles/year. Pays average 10% royalty on wholesale price. No advance. Simultaneous submissions OK. Reports in 1 month. Included in Shoe String Press catalog.
Nonfiction: Local history and New England folklore. Query with 1 page sample of published writing.
Recent Nonfiction Titles: *It Happened in New Hampshire*, by Fairfax Downey; *A Question of Age*, by Kathryn Martin; and *Winnowings from the Granite State*, by Henry Fitts.

TOR BOOKS, 8-10 W. 36th St., New York NY 10018. (212)564-0150. Managing Editor: Katya Pendill. Publishes mass market and trade paperback originals (75% "and growing") and reprints (25%). Averages 72 books/year. Pays 6-8% royalty; offers negotiable advance. Simultaneous and photocopied submissions OK. Computer printout and disk submissions OK. SASE. Reports in 1 month.
Fiction: Horror, science fiction, occult, and some fantasy. In the near future: thrillers. Submit outline/synopsis and 4-5 sample chapters.
Recent Fiction Titles: *Targets*, by Donald E. McQuinn; *The Descent of Anansi*, by Larry Niven and Steven Barnes; *The First Book of Swords*, by Fred Saberhagen; *The Playground*, by T.M. Wright.
Tips: "We're pretty broad in the occult, horror and fantasy but more straightforward in science fiction and thrillers, tending to stay with certain authors and certain types of work."

THE TOUCHSTONE PRESS, Box 81, Beaverton OR 97075. (503)646-8081. Editor-in-Chief: Thomas K. Worcester. Publishes paperback originals. Specializes in field guide books. Royalty of 10% of retail price; seldom offers an advance. Averages 3 titles/year. Photocopied submissions OK, "but don't expect response without SASE." Reports in 1-2 months. SASE. Free book catalog. No fiction or poetry.
Nonfiction: Cookbooks, cooking and foods; history, hobbies, how-to, recreation, sports and travel books. "Must be within the range of our outdoor styles." Query with "synopsis: the idea; and sample chapters. Query should demonstrate the skill to accomplish what the idea suggests."

Recent Nonfiction Titles: *35 Hiking Trails, Columbia River Gorge*, by Don and Roberta Lowe; and *Leftovers: Better the Second Time Around*, by Virginia Wright Kupiec.

TRADO-MEDIC BOOKS, (Division of *Conch Magazine*, Ltd., Publishers), 102 Normal Ave. (Symphony Circle), Buffalo NY 14213. (716)885-3686. Editorial Director: Dr. S.O. Anozie. Senior Editor: Dr. Philip Singer. Publishes hardcover and paperback originals. Averages 4-6 titles/year. "Terms vary from book to book, though they often do involve a royalty on the retail price. No simultaneous submissions; photocopied submissions OK. Reports in 1-2 months. Book catalog for SASE.
Nonfiction: Health; psychology; reference; and sociology. "Trado-Medic Books serves the informational needs and interests of an international academic community in the fields of medical anthropology, medical sociology, social psychiatry, ethnopsychiatry, community health, health-care delivery and the libraries and institutions that serve it." Query first. Looks for "competence and readability." All unsolicited mss are returned unopened.
Recent Nonfiction Titles: *Traditional Healing: New Science or New Colonialism?*, edited with an introduction by Professor Philip Singer; *Resources for Third World Health Planners: A Selected Subject Bibliography*, edited by Philip Singer and Elizabeth Titus; and *Hair Techniques & Alternatives to Baldness*, by John Mayhew.

TRANSACTION BOOKS, Rutgers University, New Brunswick NJ 08903. (201)932-2280. Book Division Director: Dalia Buzin. Publishes hardcover and paperback originals (65%) and reprints (35%). Specializes in scholarly social science books. Averages 50 titles/year. Royalty "depends almost entirely on individual contract; we've gone anywhere from 2-15%." No advance. No photocopied submissions. Send original ribbon copy. Reports in 1-4 months. SASE. Free book catalog.
Nonfiction: Americana, art, biography, economics, history, law, medicine and psychiatry, music, philosophy, politics, psychology, reference, scientific, sociology, technical and textbooks. "All must be scholarly social science or related." Query or submit outline/synopsis. Do not submit sample chapters. We evaluate complete manuscripts only. Accepts nonfiction translations. Use Chicago *Manual of Style*." Looks for "scholarly content, presentation, methodology, and target audience." State availability of photos/illustrations and send one photocopied example.
Recent Nonfiction Titles: *The Vietnam Trauma*, by Paul Kattenburg (political science); *The Artist and Political Vision*, edited by Benjamin Barber and Michael J. Gargas McGrath (communication and culture/political science); and *Cuban Communism*, 4th ed., edited by Irving Louis Horowitz (Third World Studies).

‡**TREE BY THE RIVER PUBLISHING**, 4375 Highland Place, Riverside CA 92506. (714)682-8942. Editor: Bill Dalton. Publishes hardcover and trade paperback originals. Averages 5 titles/year. Pays 3-5% royalty on retail price or makes outright purchase of $300-2,000. No advance. Simultaneous and photocopied submissions OK. SASE. Reports in 1 month. Free book catalog.
Imprint: Music Business Books.
Nonfiction: How-to, western Americana, history, music and the music business and travel. "Writers should first query. When the writer receives permission to mail his manuscript, he need only include the first and second chapter with a brief outline of remaining chapters. We also invite writers to send us their ideas for a new book on a subject we cover. All unsolicited mss are returned unopened."
Recent Nonfiction Titles: *Rosa May: The Search for a Mining Camp Legend*; *The Guide to Bodie*; and *The Songwriter's Demo Manual* (all by George Williams III).

TREND HOUSE, Box 611, St. Petersburg FL 33731. (813)893-8111. Chairman: Eugene C. Patterson. President: John B. Lake. General Manager: Andrew P. Corty. Publishes hardcover and paperback originals and reprints. Specializes in books on Florida—all categories. Pays royalty; no advance. Books are marketed through *Florida Trend* magazine. Photocopied submissions OK. Reports in 2-4 weeks. SASE.
Nonfiction: Business, economics, history, law, politics, reference, textbooks and travel. "All books pertain to Florida." Query. State availability of photos and/or illustrations.
Recent Nonfiction Titles: *Directory of Florida Industries*, by Chambers of Commerce; and *The Florida Statistical Abstract*, by University of Florida Press.

*****TRIUMPH PUBLISHING CO.**, Box 292, Altadena CA 91001. (213)797-0075. Editor-in-Chief: William Dankenbring. Hardcover and paperback originals. Pays 5-10% royalty; no advance. Subsidy publishes occasionally "depending upon the merits of the book." Averages 3 titles/year. State availability of photos and/or artwork to accompany ms. Simultaneous and photocopied submissions OK. Reports in 1-2 months. SASE. Free book catalog.
Nonfiction: History, science, theological, Biblical, family and health.
Recent Nonfiction Titles: *Stories for Young People*, by Henderson; *Armageddon! How Much Longer?*, by Dankenbring; and *Millennial Agriculture-The New Eden*, by Syltie.

TROUBADOR PRESS, Suite 205, 1 Sutter St., San Francisco CA 94104. (415)397-3716. Editorial Director: Malcolm K. Whyte. Publishes hardcover and paperback originals. Averages 6-8 titles/year. Pays royalty. Advance averages $500-1,000. Simultaneous and photocopied submissions OK. Computer printout submissions OK; prefers letter quality to dot matrix. Reports in 1 month. SASE. Book catalog for SASE.

Nonfiction: "Troubador Press publishes project, activity, entertainment, art, game, nature, craft and cookbooks. All titles feature original art and exceptional graphics. Primarily nonfiction. Current series include creative cut-outs; mazes and other puzzle books; color and story books; how-to-draw and other art and entertainment books. Interested in expanding on themes of 80 current titles. We like books which have the potential to develop into series." Query or submit outline/synopsis and 2-3 sample chapters with conciseness and clarity of a good idea. Accepts artwork/photos.

Recent Nonfiction Titles: *Bear Coloring Album*; *How to Draw Spaceships and Robots*, by Larry Evans; and *Gorey Cats Paper Dolls*, by Edward Gorey.

Tips: "We have always, and will continue to publish new, unpublished authors along with established writers/ artists and licensed properties. We feel the mix is good and healthy." Queries/mss may be routed to other editors in the publishing group.

TURNSTONE BOOKS, Denington Estate, Wellingborough, Northamptonshire, England NN8 2RQ. Editors: John Hardaker and Michael Cox. Hardcover and paperback originals and reprints. 7½% royalty on paperbacks; 10% on hardcovers. Photocopied submissions OK. Computer printout submissions OK; prefers letter quality to dot matrix. SASE. Reports in 1-2 months. Free book catalog.

Nonfiction: Pre-history, archaeology (alternative), earth mysteries, psychology, personal development, health and healing, ecology, lifestyle, new age topics, social issues. Submit outline/synopsis and 3 sample chapters.

Tips: Queries/mss may be routed to other editors in the publishing group.

CHARLES E. TUTTLE CO., INC., Publishers & Booksellers, Suido 1-chome, 2-6, Bunkyo-ku, Tokyo, Japan. Publishes originals and reprints, "handles all matters of editing, production and administration including royalties, rights and permissions." Pays $500 against 10% royalty on retail price; advance varies. Averages 30 titles/year. Book catalog $1. Send complete mss or queries accompanied by outlines or sample chapters and biographical data. US and Canada distributors: Publishers and Booksellers, Drawer F, 26-30 Main St., Rutland VT 05701. Reports in 4-6 weeks. SASE.

Nonfiction: Specializes in publishing books about Oriental art, culture, language and sociology as well as history, literature, cookery, sport and children's books which relate to Asia, the Hawaiian Islands, Australia and the Pacific areas. Also interested in Americana, especially antique collecting, architecture, genealogy and Canadiana. No poetry and fiction except that of Oriental themes. Accepts translations. Normal book length only. Looks for "subject matter related to Asia, particularly Japan; authority of the author; balance and logical order in the structure of the ms; presentation—minimum of spelling/grammatical errors, double-spaced typing."

Recent Nonfiction Titles: *The Ninja and Their Secret Fighting Art*, by Stephen K. Hayes; *Judo Formal Techniques*, by Tadao Otaki and Donn F. Draeger; *Stories from a Tearoom Window*, by Shigenori Chikamatsu; *Guide to the Tale of Genji*, by William J. Puette; *Changing Japanese Attitudes Toward Modernization*, edited by Marius B. Jansen; *A Glimpse at the Art of Japan*, by James Jackson Jarves; *Impressions of Japanese Architecture and the Allied Arts*, by Ralph Adams Cram; *Japanese Words and Their Uses*, by Akira Miura.

TWAYNE PUBLISHERS, A division of G.K. Hall & Co., 70 Lincoln St., Boston MA 02111. (617)423-3990. Editor: Caroline L. Birdsall. Payment is on royalty basis. Computer printout submissions OK; prefers letter quality to dot matrix. Publishes 120 titles/year. Query. Reports in 5 weeks. Enclose return postage.

Nonfiction: Publishes scholarly books and volumes for the general reader in series. Literary criticism, biography, history of immigration, film studies, musical criticism, women's studies, social studies, scholarly annuals and critical editions.

Recent Titles: *Joseph Conrad*, by Adam Gillon; *Critical Essays on Richard Wright*; and *Howard Hawks*, by Leland Poague.

Tips: Queries/mss may be routed to other editors in the publishing group.

TWENTY-THIRD PUBLICATIONS, INC., 185 Willow St., Box 180, Mystic CT 06355. (203)536-2611. Acquisitions: William Holub. Publishes trade paperback originals. Averages 8 titles/year. Pays average 10% royalty on wholesale price. No simultaneous submissions. SASE. Reports in 3 weeks. Book catalog for 9x12 SAE and 2 first class stamps.

Nonfiction: Religious education, adult education (Roman Catholic). "Our audience is teachers, mainstream and educators." Query.

Recent Nonfiction Titles: *Concise Catholic Dictionary for Parents and Religion Teachers*, by Reynolds and Rosemary Ekstrom; and *Little Things Mean a Lot*, by Marie McIntyre.

TYNDALE HOUSE PUBLISHERS, INC., 336 Gundersen Dr., Wheaton IL 60187. (312)668-8300. Editor-in-Chief and Acquisitions: Wendell Hawley. Publishes hardcover and trade paperback originals (90%) and hardcover and mass paperback reprints (10%). Publishes 100 titles/year. Pays 10% royalty; negotiable advance. Simultaneous queries OK; prefers original submissions. Reports in 6 weeks. SASE. Free book catalog.
Nonfiction: Religious books only: personal experience, family living, marriage, Bible reference works and commentaries, Christian living, devotional, inspirational, church and social issues, Bible prophecy, theology and doctrine, counseling and Christian psychology, Christian apologetics and church history. Submit table of contents, chapter summary, preface, first two chapters and one later chapter.
Fiction: Bible and contemporary novels. Christian romances, westerns, adventure. Junior high fiction. Submit outline/synopsis and sample chapters.

U.S. GAMES SYSTEMS, INC., 38 E. 32nd St., New York NY 10016. (212)685-4300. President: Stuart Kaplan. Publishes hardcover and trade paperback originals. Averages 10 titles/year. Pays royalty. Simultaneous and photocopied submissions OK. SASE. Reports in 1 month. Book catalog $1.
Nonfiction: Reference on tarot cards, history of playing cards. "Must be something new, different, and worthwhile limited to those subjects." Submit outline/synopsis and sample chapters.
Recent Nonfiction Titles: *The Encyclopedia of Tarot*, by Stuart Kaplan; *Crowley's Book of Thoth*; and *Waite's Pictorial Key to the Tarot*.
Tips: Prefers publishing books when accompanied by artwork for new tarot cards.

‡**ULTRALIGHT PUBLICATIONS, INC.**, Box 234, Hammelstown PA 17036. (717)566-0468. Editor: Michael A. Markowski. Publishes hardcover and trade paperback originals. Averages 6 titles/year. Pays 10-15% royalty on wholesale price; buys some mss outright; offers average $1,000 advance. Simultaneous and photocopied submissions OK. SASE. Reports in 3 weeks on queries; 2 months on mss. Free book catalog.
Nonfiction: How to, technical on hobbies (model airplanes), aviation. Publishes for "aviation buffs, dreamers and enthusiasts. We are looking for titles in the homebuilt, ultralight, sport and general aviation fields. We are interested in how-to, technical and reference books of short to medium length that will serve recognized and emerging aviation needs." We are also interested in automotive historical, reference and how-to titles. Query or submit outline/synopsis and 3 sample chapters.
Recent Nonfiction Titles: *Ultralight Airmanship*, by Lamie (how-to); *Ultralight Flight*, by Markowski (reference and how-to); *Ultralight Propulsion*, by Brinks (how-to); and *Ultralight Aircraft*, by Markowski (reference and how-to).

‡**UNDERWOOD/MILLER**, 239 N. 4th St., Columbia PA 17512. (717)684-2925. Contact: Chuck Miller. Publishes hardcover and trade paperback originals and hardcover reprints. Averages 12 titles/year. Pays 10% royalty on retail price; offers average $1,000-2,000 advance. Simultaneous and photocopied submissions OK. SASE. Reports in 1 month on queries and mss. Free book catalog.
Nonfiction: Reference; critical studies of science fiction, horror and fantasy authors. Publishes for "hard-core science fiction and fantasy collectors and institutional libraries. Our books are full cloth, smyth-sewn and made with acid-free paper. We are looking for specific studies of science fiction and fantasy authors. We also publish illustrated bibliographies of SF authors." Query.
Recent Nonfiction Titles: *FEAR ITSELF: The Horror Fiction of Stephen King*, edited by Tim Underwood and Chuck Miller (critical study of King); *PKD: A Philip K. Dick Bibliography* and *DeCamp: An L. Sprague de Camp Bibliography*, by Daniel JH Levack (illustrated bibliographies).
Fiction: Fantasy, horror, science fiction. "We publish limited edition SF and Fantasy novels and collections for the collectors and library markets." Query.
Recent Fiction Titles: *Gilden-Fire*, by Stephen R. Donaldson (fantasy); *Lost Moons*, by Jack Vance (short story collection); and *Eye of Cat*, by Roger Zelazny (science fiction novel).

UNIVELT, INC., Box 28130, San Diego CA 92128. (619)746-4005. Editorial Director: H. Jacobs. Publishes hardcover originals. Averages 8 titles/year. Pays 10% royalty on actual sales; no advance. Simultaneous and photocopied submissions OK. Computer printout submissions OK; prefers letter quality to dot matrix. Reports in 4 weeks. SASE. Free book catalog.
Nonfiction: Publishes in the field of aerospace, especially astronautics, and technical communications, but including application of aerospace technology to Earth's problems. Submit outline/synopsis and 1-2 sample chapters.
Recent Nonfiction Titles: *Handbook of Soviet Manned Space Flight*; *Science Fiction and Space Futures*; *Between Sputnik and the Shuttle*.
Tips: Queries/mss may be routed to other editors in the publishing group.

*****UNIVERSE BOOKS**, 381 Park Ave. S., New York NY 10016. (212)685-7400. Editorial Director: Louis Barron. Publishes hardcover and paperback originals (95%) and reprints (5%). Averages 45 titles/year. Offers 10-15% royalty on retail price (hardbound books). "On a few extra-illustrated art books and on special studies with a limited market we may pay a smaller royalty." Average advance: $1,000-4,000. Subsidy publishes 5% of books; "if a book makes a genuine contribution to knowledge but is a commercial risk, we might perhaps accept a subsidy from a foundation or other organization, but not directly from the author." Simultaneous and photocopied submissions OK. Computer printout submissions OK; prefers letter quality to dot matrix. "Will not return material without postage-paid SAE." Reports in 2 weeks. Book catalog if 35¢ in stamps (not SASE) is enclosed.

Nonfiction: Animals, art, economics, history, nature, performing arts, politics, reference and science. Universe also pays secondary attention to biography, health and how-to. Also uses "discussions of specific animal, bird or plant species; social histories of specific types of artifacts or social institutions; art histories of specific types of artifacts or symbols. We publish books in the following categories: antiques, crafts and collectibles, art, architecture and design, history, life, physical and agricultural sciences, ballet, music, contemporary problems, social sciences (especially books on survival, appropriate technology, and the limits to growth). We do not publish fiction, poetry, cookbooks, criticism or belles lettres." Accepts artwork/photos. Submit outline/synopsis and 2-3 sample chapters. Accepts nonfiction French and German translations.

Recent Nonfiction Titles: *The Ballerina* and *Pas de Deux*, by S. Montague; *Goya*, by Fred Licht (art history); *Enterprise Zones*, by Stuart M. Butler; *Field Guide to North American Orchids*, by Williams and Williams.

UNIVERSITY ASSOCIATES, INC., 8517 Production Ave., Box 26240, San Diego CA 92126. (619)578-5900. President: J. William Pfeiffer. Publishes paperback originals (65%) and reprints (35%). Specializes in practical materials for human relations trainers, consultants, etc. Pays average 10% royalty; no advance. Markets books by direct mail. Simultaneous submissions OK. No computer printout or disk submissions. SASE. Reports in 2-4 months. Free book catalog.

Nonfiction: Marion Mettler, Vice-President, publications. Publishes (in order of preference) human resource development and group-oriented material; management education and community relations and personal growth; business. No materials for grammar school or high school classroom teachers. Use *American Psychological Association Style Manual*. Query. Send prints or completed art or rough sketches to accompany ms.

Recent Nonfiction Titles: *The 1983 Annual Handbook for Facilitators, Trainers, and Consultants*, by J.W. Pfeiffer and L.D. Goodstein; *Making Meetings Work*, by Leland Bradford; and *The Schutz Measures*, by Will Schutz.

UNIVERSITY OF ALABAMA PRESS, Box 2877, University AL 35486. Director: Malcolm MacDonald. Publishes hardcover originals. Published 31 titles last year. "Maximum royalty (on wholesale price) is 10%; no advances made." Photocopied submissions OK. Enclose return postage. Free book catalog.

Nonfiction: Biography, business, economics, history, music, philosophy, politics, religion and sociology. Considers upon merit almost any subject of scholarly interest, but specializes in linguistics and philology, political science and public administration, literary criticism and biography, philosophy, and history. Accepts nonfiction translations.

Recent Nonfiction Titles: *A History of Metals in Colonial America* (US history); and *Judge Frank Johnson*, by Yarbrough (biography).

UNIVERSITY OF ARIZONA PRESS, 1615 E. Speedway, Tucson AZ 85719. (602)621-1441. Director: Stephen Cox. Publishes hardcover and paperback originals and reprints. "Contracts are individually negotiated, but as a 'scholarly publishing house' operating primarily on informational works, does not pay any advances. Also, royalty starting point may be after sale of first 1,000 copies, by virtue of the nature of the publishing program." Averages 25-30 titles/year. Free catalog and editorial guidelines. Will consider photocopied submissions if ms is not undergoing consideration at another publishing house. "Must have this assurance." Query and submit outline and sample chapters. Reports on material within 90 days. SASE.

Nonfiction: "Significant works of a regional nature about Arizona, the Southwest and Mexico; and books of merit in subject matter fields strongly identified with the universities in Arizona; i.e., anthropology, arid lands studies, space sciences, Asian studies, Southwest Indians, Mexico, etc. No "personal diary types of Western Americana, mainly directed only toward family interest, rather than broad general interest."

Recent Nonfiction Titles: *I-Mary: A Biography of Mary Austin*, by Augusta Fink; *Once a River: Birdlife and Habitat Changes on the Middle Gila*, by Amadeo Rea; *Hopi Photographers/Hopi Images*, compiled by Victor Masayesva and Erin Younger.

‡THE UNIVERSITY OF ARKANSAS PRESS, 201 Ozark St., Fayetteville AR 72701. (501)575-3246. Director: Miller Williams. Publishes hardcover and trade paperback originals and reprints. Averages 6-10 titles/year. Pays 10% royalty on wholesale price. No advance. Simultaneous submissions OK "if cleared in advance." Photocopied submissions OK "for screening only; if accepted, original plus photocopy is required." Computer printout submissions OK "for screening." SASE. Reports in 2 weeks on queries; 3 months on mss. Free book catalog.

Nonfiction: Biography, literary criticism, regional studies. Publishes for "educated humanist, generalist." Especially needs "critical works on modern American writers; Southern, British and intellectual history; general Southern regional studies." Accepts translations. No non-books, how-to, juvenile, self-help, technical or textbooks. Submit outline/synopsis and 3-5 sample chapters.

Recent Nonfiction Titles: *The Hound of Conscience: WWI Draft Resistance in England*, by Thomas Kennedy (history); *We Are Called Human: The Poetry of Richard Hugo*, by Michael Allen (literary criticism); and *Critical Discourse in the Old South*, by Michael O'Brien (intellectual history).

Fiction: Mainstream. "We are primarily interested in high-energy short stories." No confession, erotica, religious, romance, western. Submit outline/synopsis and sample chapters.

Recent Fiction Titles: *In The Land of Dreamy Dreams*, by Ellen Gilchrist (short stories); *A Record As Long As Your Arm*, by George Garrett (short stories); and *Simpkinsville And Vicinity*, by Ruth McEnery Stuart (short stories).

Poetry: "We are eclectic in our view of poetry and are willing to read most any submission, but are more often convinced by the short lyric, formal or free, original or in translation." No "rant or cant." Submit complete ms.

Recent Poetry Titles: *Life On the Edge Of the Continent*, by Ronald Koertge (lyric; free verse); *Story Hour*, by Sara Henderson Hay (sonnets); and *Cuckolds, Clerics and Countrymen*, translated by John DuVal, notes by Raymond Eichmann (French Fabliaux in translation).

UNIVERSITY OF CALIFORNIA PRESS, 2223 Fulton St., Berkeley CA 94720. Director: James H. Clark. Assistant Director: Stanley Holwitz. New York Office, Room 513, 50 E. 42 St., New York NY 10017. London Office CCJ, Ltd., Ely House, 37 Dover St., London W1X 4HQ, England. Publishes hardcover and paperback originals and reprints. "On books likely to do more than return their costs, a standard royalty contract beginning at 10% is paid; on paperbacks it is less." Published 201 titles last year. Queries are always advisable, accompanied by outlines or sample material. Accepts nonfiction translations. Send to Berkeley address. Reports vary, depending on the subject. Enclose return postage.

Nonfiction: "It should be clear that most of our publications are hardcover nonfiction written by scholars." Publishes scholarly books including art, literary studies, social sciences, natural sciences and some high-level popularizations. No length preferences.

Fiction and Poetry: Publishes fiction and poetry only in translation, usually in bilingual editions.

*UNIVERSITY OF IOWA PRESS, Graphic Services Bldg., Iowa City IA 52242. (319)353-3181. Editor: Art Pflughaupt. Publishes hardcover and paperback originals. Averages 7 titles/year. Pays 10% royalty on retail price. Subsidy publishes 5% of books. Subsidy publishing is offered "if a scholarly institution will advance a subsidy to support publication of a worthwhile book. We market mostly by direct mailing of fliers to groups with special interests in our titles." Query or submit outline/synopsis and 3 sample chapters. Use University of *Chicago Manual of Style*. State availability of photos/illustrations. Photocopied submissions OK. Computer printout submissions OK; prefers letter quality to dot matrix. Reports in 2-4 months. SASE. Free book catalog.

Nonfiction: Publishes art; economics; history; music; philosophy; reference; and scientific books. Accepts nonfiction, fiction and poetry translations. "We do not publish children's books, or any poetry or short fiction except the Iowa Translation Series and the Iowa School of Letters Award for short fiction." Looks for "evidence of original research; reliable sources; clarity of organization, complete development of theme with documentation and supportive footnotes and/or bibliography; and a substantive contribution to knowledge in the field treated."

Recent Nonfiction Titles: *A Bibliographical Guide to Midwestern Literature*, edited by Gerald C. Nemanic; *Crisis and Conflict: World News Reporting Between Two Wars*, by Robert W. Desmond; *Interpreting Kant*, ed. by Moltke S. Gram; and *A Bibliography of Computer Music*, by Sandra L. Tjepkema.

*UNIVERSITY OF MASSACHUSETTS PRESS, Box 429, Amherst MA 01004. (413)545-2217. Editorial Director: Bruce Wilcox. Acquisitions Editor: Richard Martin. Publishes hardcover and paperback originals (95%) reprints and imports (5%). Averages 25-30 titles/year. "Royalties depend on character of book; if offered, generally at 10% of list price. Advance rarely offered." Subsidy publishes 10% of books; "Press specifies subsidy requirement on basis of estimated edition loss." No author subsidies accepted. Simultaneous (if advised) and photocopied submissions OK. Computer printout submissions OK; prefers letter quality to dot matrix. No disk submissions. Preliminary report in 6 weeks. SASE. Free book catalog.

Nonfiction: Publishes Afro-American studies, art, biography, criticism, history, natural history, philosophy, poetry, politics, psychology, and sociology in original and reprint editions. Accepts artwork/photos. Submit outline/synopsis and 1-2 sample chapters. Accepts nonfiction translations.

Recent Nonfiction Titles: *Ever-Expanding Horizons: The Dual Informational Sources of Human Evolution*, by Carl P. Swanson (natural science); *Jerome Liebling Photographs*, by Jerome Liebling (arts); *Lydia Maria Child: Selected Letters, 1817-1880*, Milton Meltzer and Patricia G. Holland, eds., Francine Krasno, associate ed. (women's studies).

Tips: "As members of AAUP, we sometimes route (queries/mss) to other university presses."

UNIVERSITY OF MICHIGAN PRESS, 839 Greene St., Ann Arbor MI 48106. (313)764-4394. Editorial Director: Walter E. Sears. Senior Editor: Mary C. Erwin. Publishes hardcover and paperback originals (95%) and reprints (5%). Averages 35-40 titles/year. Pays 10% royalty on retail price but primarily on net; offers advance. Simultaneous and photocopied submissions OK. SASE. Reports in 2 weeks. Free book catalog.
Nonfiction: Americana; animals; art; biography; business/economics; health; history; music; nature; philosophy; photography; psychology; recreation; reference; religion; science; sociology; technical; textbooks; and travel. No dissertations. Query first.
Recent Nonfiction Titles: *Nuclear Power: Technology on Trial*, by J. Duderstadt and C. Kikuchi; *Wind Power and Other Energy Options*, by D.R. Inglis; and *Code of the Quipu*, by Marcia and Robert Ascher (mathematics and culture).

UNIVERSITY OF MISSOURI PRESS, 200 Lewis Hall, Columbia MO 65211. (314)882-7641. Director: Edward D. King. Associate Director: Susan E. McGregor. Publishes hardcover and paperback originals and paperback reprints. Averages 30 titles/year. Pays 10% royalty on net receipts; no advance. Photocopied submissions OK. Reports in 6 months. SASE. Free book catalog.
Nonfiction: "Scholarly publisher interested in history, literary criticism, political science, social science, music, art, art history, and original poetry." Also regional books about Missouri and the Midwest. "We do not publish mathematics or hard sciences." Query or submit outline/synopsis and sample chapters. Consult Chicago *Manual of Style*.
Recent Nonfiction Titles: *Painters of the Humble Truth: Masterpieces of American Still Life 1901-1939*, by William H. Gerdts; *Mark Twain's Escape from Time: A Study of Patterns and Images*, by Susan K. Harris (literary criticism); and *The Forgotten Frontier: Urban Planning in the American West*, by John W. Reps.
Fiction: "Will be reading fiction manuscripts again in February, 1984. We publish original short fiction in Breakthrough Series, not to exceed 35,000 words. May be short story collection or novella. We also publish poetry and drama in the same series. No limitations on subject matter." Query. Recently published *Winter Weeds*, by Harry Humes; *Delta Q*, by Alvin Greenberg; *Daffodils or the Death of Love*, by Corinne Demas Bliss.

UNIVERSITY OF NEBRASKA PRESS, 901 N. 17th St., Lincoln NE 68588. Humanities Editor: Bill Regier. Publishes hardcover and paperback originals (60%) and hardcover and paperback reprints (40%). Specializes in scholarly nonfiction; some regional books; reprints of Western Americana; natural history. Royalty is usually graduated from 10% on wholesale price for original books; no advance. Averages 40 new titles, 30 paperback reprints (*Bison Books*)/year. Computer printout submissions OK. SASE. Reports in 2-4 months. Free book catalog.
Nonfiction: Publishes Americana, biography, history, nature, photography, psychology, sports, literature, agriculture and American Indian themes. Accepts nonfiction and fiction translations. Query. Accepts outline/synopsis, 2 sample chapters and introduction. Looks for "an indication that the author knows his subject thoroughly and interprets it intelligently."
Recent Nonfiction Titles: *The City and the Saloon: Denver 1858-1916*, by Thomas J. Noel (Western history); and *Yuwipi: Vision and Experience in Oglala Ritual*, by William K. Powers (American anthropology).

UNIVERSITY OF NEVADA PRESS, Reno NV 89557. (702)784-6573. Director: Robert Laxalt. Editor: Nicholas M. Cady. Publishes hardcover and paperback originals (90%) and reprints (10%). Averages 6 titles/year. Pays 10-15% royalty on retail price; advance depends on title. Simultaneous (if so indicated) and photocopied submissions OK. Computer printout submissions OK; prefers letter quality to dot matrix. Preliminary reports in 2 months. Free book catalog.
Nonfiction: Specifically needs regional history and natural history, anthropology, biographies and Basque studies. "We are the first university press to sustain a sound series on Basque studies—New World and Old World." No juvenile books or cookbooks. Submit outline/synopsis and 1-2 sample chapters.
Recent Nonfiction Titles: *The Piñon Pine: A Natural and Cultural History*, by Ronald M. Lanner; *Nevada Printing History: A Bibliography*, by Robert D. Armstrong; *Navarra: The Durable Kingdom*, by Rachel Bard.

‡*UNIVERSITY OF NEW MEXICO PRESS**, Journalism 220, Albuquerque NM 87131. (505)277-2346. Senior Editor: Elizabeth C. Hadas. Publishes hardcover and trade paperback originals and hardcover and trade paperback reprints. Averages 60 titles/year. Subsidy publishes 10% of books "depending upon nature of ms." Pays maximum 10% royalty on wholesale price. Photocopied submissions OK. SASE. Reports in 2 weeks on queries; 6 months on mss. Free book catalog.
Nonfiction: Scholarly and regional books covering Americana, art, history, nature and photography. Query.
Recent Nonfiction Titles: *Textiles of the Prehistoric Southwest*, by Kate Kent (illustrated monograph); *America's Ancient Treasures*, by Franklin and Mary Folsom (guide book); *Tribalism in Crisis*, by Larry W. Burt (scholarly history).
Fiction: "No original fiction. Any fiction mss will be returned unread if accompanied by SASE. Otherwise, they will be discarded."

THE UNIVERSITY OF NORTH CAROLINA PRESS, Box 2288, Chapel Hill NC 27514. (919)966-3561. Editor-in-Chief: Iris Tillman Hill. Publishes hardcover and paperback originals. Specializes in scholarly books and regional trade books. Royalty schedule "varies." No advance. Averages 50 titles/year. "As a university press, we do not have the resources for mass marketing books." Send prints to illustrate ms only if they are a major part of the book. Photocopied submissions OK. Reports in 2-5 months. SASE. Free book catalog.
Nonfiction: "Our major fields are American and European history." Also scholarly books on Americana, classics, oral history, political science, urban studies, religious studies, psychology and sociology. History books on law and music. Books on nature, particularly on the Southeast; literary studies. Submit outline/synopsis and sample chapters. Must follow University of Chicago *Manual of Style*. Looks for "intellectual excellence and clear writing."
Recent Nonfiction Titles: *A Revolutionary People at War*, by C. Royster; *Women of the Republic*, by Linda Kerber (early American history and women's studies); and *Down and Out in the Great Depression*, by Robert S. McElvaine.

UNIVERSITY OF NOTRE DAME PRESS, Notre Dame IN 46556. Editor: Ann Rice. Publishes hardcover and paperback originals and paperback reprints. Pays 10-12½-15% royalty; no advance. Publishes 30-35 titles/year. Free book catalog. Will consider photocopied submissions. Query. Reports in 2 months. SASE.
Nonfiction: "Scholarly books, serious nonfiction of general interest; book-length only. Especially in the areas of philosophy; theology; history; sociology; English literature (Middle English period, and modern literature criticism in the area of relation of literature and theology); government; international relations; and Mexican-American studies.
Recent Nonfiction Titles: *Five Biblical Portraits*, by Elie Wiesel; *Race and Class in the Southwest*, by M. Barrera; and *After Virtue*, by Alasdair MacIntyre.

*****UNIVERSITY OF OKLAHOMA PRESS**, 1005 Asp Ave., Norman OK 73019. (405)325-5111. Editor-in-Chief: John Drayton. Publishes hardcover and paperback originals (85%); and reprints (15%). Averages 50 titles/year. Royalty ranges from 0-15% on wholesale price, "depending on market potential"; no advance. Submit sample photos. Photocopied submissions OK. Computer printout submissions OK; prefers letter quality to dot matrix. Reports in 2-4 months. SASE. Book catalog for SASE.
Nonfiction: Publishes North American Indian studies; Western history; Americana and art (Indian and Western); Mesoamerican studies; Western Oklahoma; classical studies; literary criticism; philosophy. Poetry and fiction not invited. Query, including outline, 1-2 sample chapters and author résumé. Accepts nonfiction translations from Spanish, German and French.
Recent Nonfiction Titles: *The Rocky Mountains: A Vision for Artists in the Nineteenth Century*, by Patricia Trenton and Peter Hassrick (Western history); *Barbarians and Romans: The Birth Struggle of Europe, A.D. 400-700*, by Justine Davis Randers-Pehrson (classical studies); *Sarah Winnemucca of the Northern Paiutes*, by Gae Whitney Canfield (Indian studies); *American Autographs*, by Charles Hamilton (Americana).

*****UNIVERSITY OF PENNSYLVANIA PRESS**, 3933 Walnut St., Philadelphia PA 19104. (215)243-6261. Director: Maurice English. Hardcover and paperback originals (90%) and reprints (10%). Pays 10% royalty on wholesale price for first 5,000 copies sold; 12½% for next 5,000 copies sold; 15% thereafter; no advance. Averages 45 titles/year. Subsidy publishes 10% of books. Subsidy publishing is determined by: evaluation obtained by the press from outside specialists; work approved by Press Editorial Committee; subsidy approved by funding organization. State availability of photos and/or illustrations to accompany ms, with copies of illustrations. Photocopied submissions OK. Computer printout and disk submissions OK; "only letter quality printouts are acceptable." Reports in 1-3 months. SASE. Free book catalog.
Nonfiction: Publishes Americana; biography; business (especially management); economics; history and psychiatry; philosophy; politics; psychology; reference; scientific; sociological; technical; folklore and folk life books. "Serious books that serve the scholar and the professional." Follow the University of Chicago *Manual of Style*. Query with outline and 1-4 sample chapters addressed to the editor.
Recent Nonfiction Titles: *Passing the Time in Ballymenone*, by Henry Glassie; *Autobiographical Occasions and Original Acts*, by Albert Stone; *The Papers of William Penn*, edited by Richard S. Dunn and Mary Maples Dunn; *Blacks in the Law*, by Geraldine R. Segal.
Tips: Queries/mss may be routed to other editors in the publishing group.

UNIVERSITY OF PITTSBURGH PRESS, 127 N. Bellefield Ave., Pittsburgh PA 15260. (412)624-4110. Director: Frederick A. Hetzel. Managing Editor: Catherine Marshall. Publishes hardcover and paperback originals. Publishes 30 titles/year. Pays 12½% royalty on hardcover, 8% on paperback; no advance. Photocopied submissions OK. Computer printout submissions OK; prefers letter quality to dot matrix. Reports in 1-4 months. SASE. Free book catalog.
Nonfiction: Scholarly nonfiction. No textbooks or general nonfiction of an unscholarly nature. Submit outline/synopsis and 1 sample chapter. Recently published *Cuba Between Empires, 1878-1902*, by Louis A.

Pérez, Jr.; *The Politics of Public Utility Regulation*, by William T. Gormley, Jr.; and *The Intimate Act of Choreography*, by Lynne Anne Blom and Tarin Chaplin.

THE UNIVERSITY OF TENNESSEE PRESS, 293 Communications Bldg., Knoxville TN 37916. Contact: Acquisitions Editor. Averages 25 titles/year. Pays negotiable royalty on retail price. Photocopied submissions OK. "We can only review hard copy. Printouts tend not to be legible. Word-processed material printed with a good printer is, of course, fine. We do not find it cost-effective to try to copyedit and typeset from disk (yet)." Prefers letter quality to dot matrix printouts. SASE. Reports in 1 week on queries; "in 1 month on submissions we have encouraged." Free catalog and writer's guidelines.

Nonfiction: American history, political science, film studies, sports studies, literary criticism, anthropology, folklore and regional studies. Prefers "scholarly treatment and a readable style. Authors usually have PhDs. No fiction, poetry or plays." Submit outline/synopsis, author vita, and 2 sample chapters.

Recent Nonfiction Titles: *Victims: A True Story of the Civil War*, by Phillip Paludan (history); and *The Wild and the Tame: Nature and Culture in the American Rodeo*, by Elizabeth Atwood Lawrence (anthropology).

Tips: "Our market is in several groups: scholars; educated readers with special interests in given scholarly subjects; and the general educated public interested in Tennessee, Appalachia and the South. Not all our books appeal to all these groups, of course. But any given book must appeal to at least one of them."

UNIVERSITY OF TEXAS PRESS, Box 7819, Austin TX 78712. Managing Editor: Barbara Spielman. Averages 60 titles/year. Pays royalty usually based on net income; occasionally offers advance. Photocopied submissions OK. SASE. Reports in 8 weeks. Free catalog and writer's guidelines.

Nonfiction: General scholarly subjects: human social science, economics, anthropology, archeology, chemistry, physics, math, sciences, political science, psychology, linguistics, photography and comparative literature. Also uses specialty titles related to the Southwest, national trade titles, regional trade titles and studies in the sciences and humanities. "No popular psychology or popular books." Accepts artwork/photos. Query or submit outline/synopsis and 2 sample chapters. Accepts nonfiction and fiction translations.

Recent Nonfiction Titles: *The Greeks*, by Ken Dover; *Petroleum Politics*; and *The Texas Railroad Commission*, by David F. Prindle.

Tips: "It's difficult to make a ms over 400 double spaced pages into a feasible book. Authors should take special care to edit out extraneous material." Looks for sharply focused, in-depth treatments of important topics.

UNIVERSITY OF UTAH PRESS, University of Utah, 101 University Services Bldg., Salt Lake City UT 84112. (801)581-6771. Director: Stephen H. Hess. Publishes hardcover and paperback originals and reprints. Pays 10% royalty on net income on first 2,000 copies sold; 12% on 2,001 to 4,000 copies sold; 15% thereafter. Royalty schedule varies on paperback editions. No advance. Averages 12 titles/year. Free book catalog. Query with outline and 3 sample chapters. Author should specify page length in query. Reports in 6-8 months. SASE.

Nonfiction: Scholarly books on Western history, philosophy, anthropology, Mesoamerican studies, folklore, Middle Eastern studies. Accepts nonfiction translations.

Recent Nonfiction Titles: *Codex en Cruz*, by Charles E. Dibble; *Plato's Poetics*, by Morriss Henry Partee; *Buried Unsung: Louis Tikas and the Ludlow Massacre*, by Zeese Papanikolas; *Religion, Reason, and Truth: Historical Essays in the Philosophy of Religion*, by Sterling M. McMurrin; and *Quarry*, by Carole Oles.

UNIVERSITY OF WISCONSIN PRESS, 114 N. Murray St., Madison WI 53715. (608)262-4928 (telex: 265452). Director: Allen N. Fitchen. Acquisitions Editor: Peter J. Givler. Publishes hardcover and paperback originals, reprints and translations. Pays standard royalties on retail price; no advance. Averages 40-50 titles/year. Send complete ms. Follow *Chicago Manual of Style*. Reports in 3 months. Enclose return postage with ms.

Nonfiction: Publishes general nonfiction based on scholarly research. "Among university publishers, geographical orientation and environmental emphasis distinguishes this university press." Looks for "originality, significance, quality of the research represented, literary quality, and breadth of interest to the educated community at large." Accepts nonfiction translations.

Recent Nonfiction Titles: *Fishes of Wisconsin*, by George C. Becker; *Chemical Demonstrations: A Handbook for Teachers of Chemistry*, by Bassam Z. Shakhashiri, Glen E. Dirreen, and collaborators; *Ancient Greek Art and Iconography*, ed. by Warren G. Moon.

UNIVERSITY PRESS OF AMERICA, 4720 Boston Way, Lanham MD 20706. (301)459-3366. Editorial Director: James E. Lyons. Publishes hardcover and paperback originals (95%) and reprints (5%). Averages 450 titles/year. Pays 5-15% royalty on wholesale price; no advance. Simultaneous and photocopied submissions OK. Reports in 6 weeks. SASE. Free book catalog.

Nonfiction: Scholarly monographs, college, and graduate level textbooks in history, economics, business, psychology, political science, African studies, black studies, philosophy, religion, sociology, music, art, literature, drama, and education. No juvenile or el-hi material. Submit outline.

Recent Nonfiction Titles: *African Society, Culture, and Politics*, edited by C. Mojekwu; *The Weimar in Crisis: Cuno's Germany*, by A. Cornebise; and *Thirteen Thinkers: An Introduction to Philosophy*, by G. Kreyche.

UNIVERSITY PRESS OF KANSAS, (formerly Regents Press of Kansas), 303 Carruth, Lawrence KS 66045. (913)864-4154. Editor: Fred Woodward. Hardcover and paperback originals. Averages 15 titles/year. Royalties negotiable. No advance. Markets books by advertising and direct mail, chiefly to libraries and scholars. "State availability of illustrations if they add significantly to the ms." Photocopied submissions OK. Reports in 2-4 months. SASE. Free book catalog.
Nonfiction: Publishes biography, history, psychology, philosophy, politics, regional subjects, and scholarly nonfiction books. Query.
Recent Nonfiction Titles: *The Spanish-American War and President McKinley* (history); *Economic Issues and National Security* (politics); and *Kansas in Color* (regional).

UNIVERSITY PRESS OF KENTUCKY, 102 Lafferty Hall, Lexington KY 40506. (606)257-2951. Director: Kenneth Cherry. Editor-in-Chief: Jerome Crouch. Managing Editor: Evalin F. Douglas. Hardcover originals (95%); paperback reprints (5%). Pays 10% royalty after first 1,000 copies; no advance. State availability of photos and/or artwork to accompany ms. "Author is ultimately responsible for submitting all artwork in camera-ready form." Computer printout submissions OK; prefers letter quality to dot matrix. Reports in 2-4 months. SASE. Free book catalog.
Nonfiction: Publishes (in order of preference): history, political science, literary criticism and history, politics, anthropology, law, philosophy; medical history and nature. "All mss must receive an endorsement (secured by the press) from a scholar in the appropriate area of learning and must be approved by an editorial board before final acceptance." No original fiction, poetry, drama or textbooks. Query or submit outline/synopsis with 1 sample chapter. Accepts artwork/photos. Recently published *The Republican Right since 1945*, by David W. Reinhard; *The Classic Racehorse*, by Peter Willett; and *Travel Literature and the Evolution of the Novel*, by Percy G. Adams.
Tips: Queries/mss may be routed to other editors in the publishing group.

*UNIVERSITY PRESS OF MISSISSIPPI, 3825 Ridgewood Rd., Jackson MS 39211. (601)982-6205. Director: Barney McKee. Publishes hardcover and paperback originals (90%) and reprints (10%). Averages 18 titles/year. Subsidy publishes 60% of books. Pays 10% net royalty on first printing and 12% net on additional printings. No advance. Photocopied submissions OK. SASE. Reports in 1 month. Free book catalog.
Nonfiction: Americana; art; biography; business/economics; history; philosophy; photography; politics; psychology; sociology; literary criticism; and folklore. Especially needs regional studies (Mississippi architecture, art, historical figures), and literary studies, particularly mss on William Faulkner and Eudora Welty. Submit outline/synopsis and sample chapters.
Recent Nonfiction Titles: *The South and Film*, edited by Warren French; *Black Folk Art in America*, by Jane Livingston and John Beardsley; and *Marilee*, by Elizabeth Spencer.

*UNIVERSITY PRESS OF NEW ENGLAND, 3 Lebanon St., Hanover NH 03755. (603)646-3349. "University Press of New England is a consortium of university presses. Some books—those published for one of the consortium members—carry the joint imprint of New England and the member: Dartmouth, Brandeis, Brown, Tufts, Clark, Universities of New Hampshire, Vermont and Rhode Island." Director and Editor: Thomas L. McFarland. Publishes hardcover and trade paperback originals (90%) and trade paperback reprints (10%). Averages 30 titles/year. Subsidy publishes 80% of books. Pays standard royalty; occasionally offers advance. Photocopied submissions OK. Computer printout and disk submissions OK; prefers letter quality to dot matrix printouts. SASE. Reports in 1 month. Free book catalog.
Nonfiction: Americana (regional—New England), art, biography, business/economics, history, music, nature, philosophy, politics, psychology, reference, science, sociology, technical, textbooks and regional (New England). No festschriften, memoirs or unrevised doctoral dissertations. Only a few symposium collections accepted. Accepts nonfiction translations. Submit outline/synopsis and 1-2 sample chapters.
Recent Nonfiction Titles: *The Work of Augustus Saint Gaudens*, by John H. Dryfhout (art); *The Life of a Simple Man*, by Emile Guillaumin (history); *The Bells of the Kremlin*, by Arvo Tuominen (politics); *French and Germans, Germans and French*, by Richard Cobb (history).

UNIVERSITY PRESS OF THE PACIFIC, INC., Box 66129, Seattle WA 98166. Publishes hardcover and paperback originals (50%) and reprints (50%). Averages 10 titles/year. Pays 5-10% royalty; buys some mss outright; no advance. Simultaneous and photocopied submissions OK. SASE. Reports in 2-4 months.
Nonfiction: Business/economics, history, politics, reference, science, technical and textbooks. We are looking for scholarly and reference books which are unique in content. Our advertising media concentrates on the library marketplace, yet we do sell some to the trade. We are not interested in popular trade books." Query.
Recent Nonfiction Titles: *World Within Worlds*, by I. Asimov (historical account of science); *Business in 1990*, by A. Starchild (anthology on business); *Powerhouse of the Atom*, by K. Gladkov (science); and *Science*

Fiction of Konstantin Tsiolkovsky, by K. Tsiolkovsky.
Tips: "We will also consider text for specialized courses where a professor can identify a specific market at his own or at other institutions; however, we will be buying very little in 1984. We are in the process of changing our method of operation to specialize in producing on-demand and very short-run reference publications for the academic community."

*UNIVERSITY PRESS OF VIRGINIA, Box 3608, University Station, Charlottesville VA 22903. (804)924-3468. Editor-in-Chief: Walker Cowen. Publishes hardcover and paperback originals (95%) and reprints (5%). Averages 45 titles/year. Royalty on retail depends on the market for the book; sometimes none is made. "We subsidy publish 40% of our books, based on cost vs. probable market." Photocopied submissions OK. Computer printout submissions OK; accepts only letter quality printouts. Returns rejected material within a week. Reports on acceptances in 1-2 months. SASE. Free catalog.
Nonfiction: Publishes Americana, business, history, law, medicine and psychiatry, politics, reference, scientific, bibliography, and decorative arts books. "Write a letter to the director, describing content of the manuscript, plus length. Also specify if maps, tables, illustrations, etc., are included. Please, no educational or sociological or psychological manuscripts." Accepts nonfiction translations from French.
Recent Nonfiction Titles: *Waterpower: A History of Industrial Power in the United States, 1780-1930*, by Lewis C. Hunter; *Against the Grain: Southern Radicals and Prophets, 1929-1959*, by Anthony P. Dunbar; *1789: The Emblems of Reason*, by Jean Starobinski.

‡UTAH STATE UNIVERSITY PRESS, Utah State University, Logan UT 84322. (801)750-1362. Director: Linda Speth. Publishes hardcover and trade paperback originals and hardcover and trade paperback reprints. Averages 6 titles/year. Pays 10-15% royalty on retail price. No advance. Simultaneous submissions OK. SASE. Reports in 2 weeks on queries; 2 months on mss. Free book catalog.
Nonfiction: Biography, reference and textbook on Americana, history, politics and science. "Particularly interested in book-length scholarly manuscripts dealing with western history, western literature (western Americana). All manuscript submission must have a scholarly focus." Submit complete ms.
Recent Nonfiction Titles: *Diary of Charles Lowell Walker*, by Karl and Katherine Larsen (diary); *Blazing Crosses in Zion: The KKK in Utah*, by Larry R. Gerlach (history); and *Jack London on the Road*, by Richard Etulain (literary criticism and diary).
Poetry: "At the present time, we have accepted several poetry mss and will not be reading poetry submissions for one year."
Recent Poetry Titles: *Stone Roses: Poems from Transylvania*, by Keith Wilson; *To Remember What Is Lost*, by Kenneth Brewer; *Selected Poems of Francis Jammes*, by Barry Gifford and Bettina Dickie (translation); and *While Dancing Feet Shatter the Earth*, by Keith Wilson.

‡VANCE BIBLIOGRAPHIES, 112 N. Charter, Box 229, Monticello IL 61856. (217)762-3831. Editor: Mary Vance. Publishes trade paperback originals. Averages 480 titles/year, 240/imprints. Pays $100 honorarium, 10-20 author's copies. Photocopied submissions OK. Computer printout submissions OK. SASE. Reports in 1 week on queries; 2 weeks on mss. Free book catalog.
Imprints: *Architecture Series: Bibliography* and *Public Administration Series: Bibliography*, Mary Vance, editor.
Nonfiction: Reference bibliographies on public administration and/or architecture and related subject areas. Publishes for "graduate students and professionals in the field; primary customers are libraries." Query or submit complete ms.
Recent Nonfiction Titles: *Pedestrian Facilities Design in Architecture*, by R.B. Harmon; *City Neighborhood: An Architectural Guide to Preservation* (bibliography, Architecture Series); *National Health Care Systems*, by B. Rylko-Bauer/K. Bletzer; and *Legal Aspects of Residential Solar Access*, by D. Brown (bibliography, PA series).

VANGUARD PRESS, INC., 424 Madison Ave., New York NY 10017. Editor-in-Chief: Mrs. Bernice S. Woll. Publishes hardcover originals and reprints. Publishes 20 titles/year. Offers 7½-15% royalty on retail price; also buys mss outright; pays variable advance. Simultaneous and photocopied submissions OK. SASE. Reports in 8 weeks.
Nonfiction: Animals; art; biography (especially of musicians, artists and political figures); business (management, making money, how-to); cookbooks (gourmet and diet books); cooking and foods; history (scholarly, but written with flair); hobbies (crafts, especially sewing); how-to; humor; juveniles (folk stories, nature and art topics); music (no scores, but anything pertaining to the field—also, jazz); nature (ecology and nature adventure); philosophy; poetry; politics (current issues); psychology; religion in literature and society (no tracts); current sociology studies; sports; travel; juvenile science; and literary criticism. "No textbooks, reference books or technical material." Query or submit outline/synopsis and sample chapters.
Recent Nonfiction Titles: *Cellulite*, by Beverly Cox; and *Chosin: Heroic Ordeal of the Korean War*, by Eric Hammel.

Fiction: Believable adventure, experimental, humor, mystery, modern suspense and "good literature." No confessions, erotica or gothics. Query or submit outline/synopsis and sample chapters.
Recent Fiction Titles: *To Keep Our Honor Clean*, by E. McDowell (military training); *The Fence*, by B. McGinnis; and *Green Island*, by Michael Schmidt.

*VESTA PUBLICATIONS, LTD., Box 1641, Cornwall, Ontario, Canada K6H 5V6. (613)932-2135. Editor-in-Chief: Stephen Gill. Paperback and hardcover originals. 10% minimum royalty on wholesale price. Subsidy publishes 5% of books. "We ask a writer to subsidize a part of the cost of printing; normally, it is 50%. We do so when we find that the book does not have a wide market, as in the case of university theses and the author's first collection of poems. The writer gets 50 free copies and 10% royalty on paperback editions." No advance. Publishes 16 titles/year. State availability of photos and/or illustrations to accompany ms. Simultaneous submissions OK if so informed. Photocopied submissions OK. Reports in 1 week on queries; 1 month on mss. SAE and International Reply Coupons. Free book catalog.
Nonfiction: Publishes Americana, art, biography, cookbooks, cooking and foods, history, philosophy, poetry, politics, reference, religious. Accepts nonfiction translations. Query or submit complete ms. Looks for knowledge of the language and subject. "Query letters and mss should be accompanied by synopsis of the book and biographical notes."
Recent Nonfiction Titles: *A Crack in the Mosaic: Canada's Race Relations in Crisis*, by David Lazarus; *Famine*, by Edward Pike; and *The Money Tree*, by Herbert Hart Hutner.

VGM CAREER HORIZONS, (Division of National Textbook Co.), 4255 W. Touhy Ave., Lincolnwood IL 60646-1975. (312)679-4210. Editorial Director: Leonard Fiddle. Senior Editor: Barbara Wood Donner. Publishes hardcover and paperback originals. Averages 20-30 titles/year. Mss purchased on either royalty or buy-out basis. No simultaneous submissions; photocopied submissions OK. SASE. Reports in 6 weeks. Book catalog for large SASE.
Career Guidance Books: "We are interested in all professional and vocational areas. Our titles are marketed to a senior high school, college and trade audience, so readability and reading level (10-12) of books in the series is especially important. VGM books are used by students and others considering careers in specific areas, and contain basic information of the history and development of the field; its educational requirements; specialties and working conditions; how to write a resume, interview, and get started in the field; and salaries and benefits. Additionally, we expect to be producing more general career guidance and women's career development materials in the next year or two. We are open to all suggestions in this area, although all proposals should be of relevance to young adults, as well as to older career changers. Since our titles are largely formatted, potential writers should always query first, requesting information on already-published titles and format and structure." Looks for "a comprehensive, orderly synthesis of the material, and an interesting presentation that is clear and accurate."
Recent Nonfiction Titles: *Opportunities in Film*, by Jan Bone; *Opportunities in Fire Protection Services*, by Ronny J. Coleman; *Opportunities in Health and Medical Careers*, by I. Donald Snook, Jr.; *Opportunities in Transportation*, by Adrian Paradis.
Tips: "On most projects, we prefer writers who have considerable knowledge of their subjects, although freelance writers who research well are also considered. Although the content of most titles is similar, the ability to present fairly cut-and-dried information in an upbeat, interesting manner is heavily in an author's favor."

VICTOR BOOKS, Box 1825, Wheaton IL 60187. (312)668-6000. Executive Editor: James R. Adair. Trade paperbacks, mass market paperbacks and hardcover originals. Averages 50 titles/year. Pays "competitive royalties on retail price with advances." Prefers outline/synopsis and sample chapters, but queries are acceptable. Reports in 1-2 months. SASE. Free book catalog and author's brochure.
Nonfiction: Only religious themes. "Writers must know the evangelical market well and their material should have substance. Many of our books are by ministers, Bible teachers, seminar speakers, counselors and subject experts. Freelancers can team with nonwriting experts to ghost or co-author books to fit our line. We prefer to see a brief outline to show where the book is going, accompanied by at least 2 sample chapters to give an indication of writing and content. Writing must have a popular touch, clearly communicate, and be biblically based." Also publishes reference books with religious themes for children and adults.
Recent Nonfiction Titles: *Bold Commitment*, by Colleen and Louis Evans, Jr.; *The Power Delusion*, by Anthony Campolo Jr.; and *The Power of a Positive Self-Image*, by Clifford Baird.
Fiction: "Fiction queries are being considered, both children and adults."

THE VIKING PENGUIN, INC., 40 W. 23rd St., New York NY 10010. Published over 300 titles last year. Pays royalty. Query letter only. Manuscripts considered only when sent through agent or intermediary to specific editor. SASE. Reports in 6 weeks.
Imprints: *Studio Books* (art, photography, etc.). *Viking Junior Books. The Viking Press* (adult fiction and nonfiction).

VISION HOUSE PUBLISHERS, INC., 2300 Knoll Dr., Ventura CA 93003. (805)644-9721. Senior Editor: Donald Pugh. Publishes hardcover and trade and mass market paperback originals. Averages 6-10 titles/year. Pays 5-10% on retail price. Photocopied submissions OK. Computer printout submissions OK. SASE. Reports in 3 months. SASE. Book catalog for 9x12 SAE and 4 first class stamps.
Nonfiction: Biography, how-to, humor, reference, self-help. Subjects include family, psychology, religion (Christian) and comparative religion. "The thrust of Vision House over the next year will be nonfiction, with a heavy emphasis on books that lend themselves to total media packages (i.e., books that are adaptable to audio and video cassettes or film)." Query or submit outline/synopsis and 2-3 sample chapters.
Recent Nonfiction Titles: *Too Proud To Die*, by Roger Helle (personal story); *Before the Crisis*, by John M. Montgomery (leadership); *Calm Down*, by Gary Collins (psychological).

*VOLCANO PRESS, INC., 330 Ellis St., San Francisco CA 94102. (415)664-5600. President: Ruth Gottstein. Publishes trade paperback originals. Averages 4 titles/year. Publishes some mss by author participation (co-venture). Pays royalty; buys some mss outright. Simultaneous and photocopied submissions OK. Computer printout submissions OK; prefers letter quality to dot matrix. SASE. Reports in 3 months. Book catalog for business size SAE and 1 first class stamp.
Nonfiction: Women and social change. Subjects include business and economics, health, history, philosophy, politics, psychology, sociology and travel. "I would be very interested in a manuscript on the Carnegie Libraries—I'd like to do a critique of them in history—together with some photos." Query or submit outline/synopsis (½page description) and sample chapters. "No telephone solicitations."
Recent Nonfiction Titles: *Battered Wives*, by Del Martin (sociology); *Period*, by Gardner-Louland, et al. (for girls on menstruation); *Conspiracy of Silence: The Trauma of Incest*, by Sandra Butler; *Learning to Live Without Violence: A Handbook for Men*, by David Jay Sonkin and Michael Durphy (anger control/redirection for batterers).

J. WESTON WALCH, PUBLISHER, Box 658, Portland ME 04104. (207)772-2846. Managing Editor: Richard S. Kimball. Senior Editor: Jane Carter. Publishes paperback originals. Averages 120 titles/year. Offers 10-15% royalty on gross receipts. Buys some titles by outright purchase; offers $100-1,000. No advance. No simultaneous submissions; photocopied submissions OK. Computer printout and disk submissions OK; prefers letter quality to dot matrix. SASE. Reports in 3 weeks. Free book catalog.
Nonfiction: Art; business; economics; English; foreign language; government; health; history; music; psychology; recreation; science; social science; sociology; and sports. "We publish only supplementary educational material for sale to secondary schools throughout the United States and Canada. Formats include books, posters, ditto master sets, visual master sets (masters for making transparencies), cassettes, filmstrips, microcomputer courseware, and mixed packages. Most titles are assigned by us, though we occasionally accept an author's unsolicited submission. We have a great need for author-artist teams and for authors who can write at third- to tenth-grade levels. We do *not* want basic texts, anthologies or industrial arts titles. Most of our authors—but not all—have secondary teaching experience. I cannot stress too much the advantages that an author-artist team would have in approaching us and probably other publishers." Query first. Looks for "sense of organization, writing ability, knowledge of subject, skill of communicating with intended audience." Accepts artwork/photos.
Recent Nonfiction Titles: *My Problem Is . . .* , by Margaret Dewey (teenagers' problems); *BASICally Speaking: A Beginner's Workbook*, by Thomas J. Speelhoffer (high school business and math courses); and *Survival Listening Skills Activity Pack*, by Thomas A. Smith (English).

WALKER AND CO., 720 5th Ave., New York NY 10019. Editor-in-Chief: Richard Winslow. Senior Editor: Ruth Cavin. Hardcover and paperback originals (90%) and reprints (10%). Averages 92 titles/year. Pays 10-12-15% royalty on retail price or by outright purchase; advance averages $1,000-2,500 "but could be higher or lower." Publishes 80 titles annually. Query or submit outline/synopsis and sample chapters. Submit samples of photos/illustrations to accompany ms. Photocopied submissions OK. SASE. Free book catalog.
Nonfiction: Publishes Americana; art; biography; business; cookbooks, cooking and foods; histories; hobbies; how-to; juveniles; medicine and psychiatry; multimedia material; music; nature; pets; psychology; recreation; reference; popular science; self-help; sports; travel; and gardening books. Recently published *The New York Philharmonic Guide to the Symphony*, by E. Downs (music nonfiction); *How to Make Your Child a Winner*, by Dr. Victor B. Cline (parenting); and *The Collapsing Universe*, by Isaac Asimov (nonfiction).
Fiction: Mystery; science fiction; suspense; gothics; regency books; historical romance and westerns.
Recent Fiction Title: *The Twelve Deaths of Christmas*, by Marian Babson (mystery).

WALLACE—HOMESTEAD BOOK CO., 1912 Grand Ave., Des Moines IA 50309. (515)243-6181. Editorial Director: Jim Leimkuhler. Publishes hardcover and paperback originals. Averages 20 titles/year. Offers 10% royalty on net price. No advance. Simultaneous and photocopied submissions OK. SASE. Reports in 6 weeks. Free book catalog.
Nonfiction: Antiques, collectibles and needlecraft. Query first, submit outline/synopsis and sample chapters

or submit complete ms.

Recent Nonfiction Titles: *Super Quilter II*, by Hassel; *Patchwork Plus*, by Lamphier; and *American Oak Furniture*, by Robert and Harriett Swedberg.

WANDERER BOOKS, Division of Simon & Schuster, 1230 Avenue of the Americas, New York NY 10020. (212)245-6400. Editor-in-Chief: Wendy Barish. Publishes hardcover, trade and mass market paperback originals. Averages 60 titles/year. Pays 2-6% royalty on retail price; buys some mss outright. Simultaneous submissions OK. SASE. Reports in 2 weeks on queries; 2 months on mss. Book catalog for SAE.
Nonfiction: Juvenile. Subjects include art, health, hobbies and recreation. "We are looking for solid backlist nonfiction for the next year or so, for ages 8-14. No science, nature, history, or other school- and library-oriented nonfiction. We are a trade and mass market publishing imprint for children."
Recent Nonfiction Titles: *The Complete Babysitter's Handbook*, by Barkin and James; *I Can Draw Horses*; *Simon & Schuster Question and Answer Book*.
Fiction: Adventure, humor, mystery and science fiction. "We are looking for novels for young people ages 8-14, in light, humorous style, or mystery/adventure style." No heavy, topical, social issue-oriented teenage fiction. Query or submit outline/synopsis and sample chapters or complete ms.
Recent Fiction Titles: *Clue in the Ancient Disguise*; *Crater of Mystery*.

FREDERICK WARNE & CO., INC., 2 Park Ave., New York NY 10016. Editor, Books for Young People: Jonathan Lanman. Publishes juvenile hardcover originals. Offers 10% royalty contract. Averages 15-20 titles/year. Minimum advance is $1,000. Submit outline and 3-4 sample chapters for nonfiction and fiction. Letter-quality computer printout submissions OK. "Ms will not be considered unless requested." Reports in 10 weeks.
Juveniles: Hardcover trade books for children and young adults. Accepts artwork/photos. Picture books (ages 4-7), fiction and nonfiction for the middle reader (ages 7-12) and young adults (ages 11 and up). Mss must combine a high-interest level with fine writing. Prefers to see fewer picture books and more submissions for 8- to 12-year-olds.
Recent Titles: *Where the Buffaloes Begin*, by Olaf Baker, illustrated by Stephen Gammell; *My Mom Travels a Lot*, by Caroline Feller Bauer, illustrated by Nancy Winslow Parker; and *The Night Journey*, by Kathryn Lasky, drawings by Trina Schart Hyman.

WATSON-GUPTILL PUBLICATIONS, 1515 Broadway, New York NY 10036. Imprints include Watson-Guptill, Amphoto, Whitney Library of Design, Billboard Books, Art & Antiques. Publishes originals. Pays 10-12½-15% royalty; usual advance is $1,000, but average varies depending on author's reputation and nature of book. Averages 60 titles/year. Address queries (followed by outlines and 1-3 sample chapters) to David E. Lewis, Executive Editor. Computer printout and disk submissions OK; prefers letter quality to dot matrix. Reports on queries within 1 month. Enclose return postage.
Art: Publishes art instruction, photography and architecture books. Interested only in how-to books in any field of painting, graphic design, and photography and professional books in architecture and interior design. Looks for "a strong concept or theme that is carried out in a thoughtful, well-organized manner." Length: open.
Tips: Queries/mss may be routed to other editors in the publishing group.

WAYNE STATE UNIVERSITY PRESS, 5959 Woodward Ave., Detroit MI 48202. (313)577-4606. Director: B.M. Goldman. Editor: J. Owen. Publishes hardcover and paperback originals. "Standard royalty schedule" on wholesale price; no advance. Publishes 30 titles/year. Reports in 1-6 months. SASE. Free book catalog.
Nonfiction: Publishes Americana, biography, economics, history, law, medicine and psychiatry, music, philosophy, politics, psychology, religious, and sociology books. Query or submit outline/synopsis and sample chapters. "Do not send photos unless requested, or send photocopies."
Recent Nonfiction Titles: *The Third Globe*, edited by Walter Hodges, Schoenbaum and Lenard Leone (theater); and *Long Night's Journey Into Day*, by Eckardt and Eckardt.

WEBSTER DIVISION, McGraw-Hill Book Co., 1221 Avenue of the Americas, New York NY 10020. General Manager: Jack L. Farnsworth. Royalties vary. "Our royalty and advance schedules are competitive with the industry." Photocopied submissions OK. Reports in 2-4 weeks. SASE.
Textbooks: Publishes software and instructional materials for elementary and secondary schools. Subject areas served include social studies, science, reading and language arts, home economics, health, foreign languages, computer literary and mathematics. "Material is generally part of a series, system, or program done in connection with other writers, teachers, testing experts, et al. Material must be matched to the psychological age level, with reading achievement and other educational prerequisites in mind."

WESLEYAN UNIVERSITY PRESS, 110 Mt. Vernon, Middletown CT 06457. Director: Jeannette Hopkins. Publishes 25-30 titles/year. Photocopied submissions OK. No computer printout or disk submissions. SASE. Reports in approximately 4 months.
Nonfiction: Concentration on American history and American studies, public affairs, poetry and theater. Accepts poetry translations. Query.

WESTERN ISLANDS, 395 Concord Ave., Belmont MA 02178. Editor: C.O. Mann. Publishes hardcover and paperback originals (75%) and reprints (25%). Averages 4 titles/year. Pays 10% of list price royalty on hardcover, 5% on paperback; no advance. Simultaneous and photocopied submissions OK. Reports in 2 months. SASE. Book catalog for SASE.
Nonfiction: "We are interested in conservative books on current events: economics, politics, contemporary history, etc. We are not interested in biographies, autobiographies (unless by a famous conservative), fiction, poetry, etc. Anti-communist books, if not overly autobiographical, are welcome." Query or submit complete ms. Recently published *To Covet Honor,* by H. Alexander; *The Siecus Circle,* by C. Chambers; *Nicaragua Betrayed,* by A. Somoza/J. Cox; *The UN Conspiracy,* by Robert L. Lee.

‡**WESTERN PRODUCER PRAIRIE BOOKS,** Box 2500, Saskatoon, Saskatchewan, Canada S7K 2C4. Manager: Rob Sanders. Publishes hardcover and paperback originals (95%) and reprints (5%). Specializes in nonfiction historical and natural history works set in Western Canada. Pays negotiable royalty on list price. Averages 15 titles/year. Submit contact sheets or prints if illustrations are to accompany ms. Simultaneous submissions OK. Computer printout and disk submissions OK. Reports in 2-4 months. SAE and International Reply Coupons. Free book catalog.
Nonfiction: Publishes history, nature, photography, biography, reference, agriculture, economics, politics and cookbooks. Accepts artwork/photos. Submit outline, synopsis and 2-3 sample chapters. Accepts nonfiction and fiction translations. Recently published *Wild Mammals of Western Canada,* by Savage (natural history); *Bacchanalia Revisited,* by G. Gray; and *Butter Down the Well,* by R. Collins.

WESTERN TANAGER PRESS, 1111 Pacific Ave., Santa Cruz CA 95060. (408)425-1111. Publishes hardcover and trade paperback originals (50%), and hardcover and trade paperback reprints (50%). Averages 3 titles/year.
Nonfiction: Biography and history. "We are looking for works of local and regional history dealing with California. This includes biography, natural history, art and politics. Also interested in travel." Query. Looks for "a well-written, well-thought-out project with a specific audience in mind."

WESTERNLORE PRESS, Box 35305, Tucson AZ 85740. Editor: Lynn R. Bailey. Publishes 6-12 titles/ year. Pays standard royalties on retail price "except in special cases." Query. Reports in 60 days. Enclose return postage with query.
Americana: Publishes Western Americana of a scholarly and semi-scholarly nature: anthropology, history, biography, historic sites, restoration, and ethnohistory pertaining to the greater American West. Republication of rare and out-of-print books. Length: 25,000-100,000 words.

‡**WESTIN COMMUNICATIONS,** Suite 31, 5760 Owensmouth Ave., Woodland Hills CA 91367. (313)340-6515. Acquisitions Editor: Carla M. Klein. Publishes trade paperback originals. Averages 15 titles/ year. Pays royalty; buys some mss outright. Simultaneous and photocopied submissions OK. Computer printout submissions OK; prefers letter quality to dot matrix. SASE. Reports in 1 week on queries; 1 month on mss. Book catalog for business size SAE and 1 first class stamp.
Nonfiction: How-to, reference books, technical, textbooks, test preparations on business and economics, computer science. Especially needs "college-level study review books in science, business and economics, mathematics, computers as part of Westin Study Review Series; career evaluation and test preparation books for college students; dictionaries in selected technical fields. No topic which cannot successfully be marketed to college students through college stores or to professionals by direct mail." Query or submit outline/synopsis and 1 sample chapter.
Recent Nonfiction Titles: *Cost Accounting* and *Business Law*, by G. Klein (study review books); and *Statistics for Business and Economics*, by C. Cagan (trade book for professionals).

THE WESTMINSTER PRESS, Department CBE, 925 Chestnut St., Philadelphia PA 19107. (215)928-2700. Children's Book Editor: Barbara S. Bates. Publishes hardcover originals. Publishes 12 juveniles. Royalty on retail price and advance "vary with author's experience and credentials, and the amount of illustration needed." Photocopied submissions OK if not simultaneous. Computer printout submissions OK; prefers letter quality to dot matrix. Reports in 3 months. SASE. Book catalog for SASE.
Nonfiction: Juvenile only, for readers 8-14. Consumer education; self-help; self-awareness; social studies; recreation and how-to; and sports and hobbies. Query or submit outline/synopsis and 2-3 sample chapters. Accepts photos. Looks for "originality, relevance, author reputation, quality."

Recent Nonfiction Titles: *My Diary—My World*, by Elizabeth Yates (social studies/career); and *Feeling Good About Myself* (self-awareness).
Fiction: Juvenile only, for ages 8-13. Adventure; humor; mystery; family; science fiction; and suspense. No picture books or stories in verse. Submit outline/synopsis and sample chapters.
Recent Fiction Titles: *The Pig at 37 Pinecrest Drive*, by Susan Fleming (family humor); *Summer of the Green Star*, by Robert C. Lee (science fiction).
Tips: "An agent does not get more attention here than direct submission."

*WESTVIEW PRESS, 5500 Central Ave., Boulder CO 80301. (303)444-3541. Publisher/President: F.A. Praeger. Associate Publisher/Vice President: Lynne Rienner. Hardcover and paperback originals (90%), lecture notes, reference books, and paperback texts (10%). Specializes in scholarly monographs or conference reports with strong emphasis on applied science, both social and natural. Zero to 12% royalty on net price, depending on market. Accepts subsidies for a small number of books, "but only in the case of first class scholarly material for a limited market when books need to be priced low, or when the manuscripts have unusual difficulties such as Chinese or Sanskrit characters; the usual quality standards of a top-flight university press apply, and subsidies must be furnished by institutions, not by individuals." Averages 200 titles/year. Markets books mainly by direct mail. State availability of photos and/or illustrations to accompany manuscript. No computer printout or disk submissions. Reports in 1-4 months. SASE. Free book catalog.
Nonfiction: Agricultural/food, public policy, energy, natural resources, international economics and business, international relations, area studies, geography, science and technology policy, sociology, anthropology, reference, military affairs, health. Looks for "scholarly excellence and scientific relevance." Query and submit 2 sample chapters. Use University of Chicago *Manual of Style*. "Unsolicited manuscripts receive low priority; inquire before submitting projects."
Recent Nonfiction Titles: *Animal Agriculture*, edited by Wilson G. Pond; and *Renewable Resources*, edited by Dennis Little.

‡WETHERALL PUBLISHING CO., 510 1st Ave. N., Minneapolis MN 55403. (612)339-3363. Director of Acquisitions: Judy Galbraith. Publishes trade paperback originals. Averages 6 titles/year. Pays 6-12% royalty on retail price or makes outright purchase of $1,000 minimum. Average advance $1,000. SASE. Reports in 2 weeks on queries; 3 weeks on mss. Book catalog for 6½x9½ SAE and 1 first class stamp.
Nonfiction: How-to, humor, juvenile and self-help. Subjects include business and economics, health, education, books for gifted children and parents. "We expect to be publishing more titles for small business and considerably more for gifted children and parents. These in addition to some humor, health and diet, and other general subject areas." Query or submit outline/synopsis and sample chapters.
Recent Nonfiction Titles: *Quit*, by Charles F. Wetherall (psychology, how to stop smoking); *Complete Book of Fearless Flying*, by Penny Angel-Levy (psychology, overcoming fear of flying); and *How to Tell If He's Cheating*, by Mary Poulos Wilde (humor); *The Gifted Kids Survival Guide*, by Judy Galbraith.

WHITAKER HOUSE, Pittsburgh and Colfax Sts., Springdale PA 15144. (412)274-4440. Editor: Victoria L. Mlinar. Paperback originals (40%) and reprints (60%). "We publish only Christian books." Royalty negotiated based on the cover price of the book. Advance only under certain circumstances. Publishes about 20-25 titles annually. "We market books in Christian book stores and in rack-jobbing locations such as supermarkets and drug stores." Looking for teaching books with personal experiences used throughout, typed, double-spaced, about 200 pages in length. Simultaneous and photocopied submissions OK. Reports in about 6 weeks. SASE.
Nonfiction: Publishes only very select biography or autobiography (testimony of spirit-filled Christians; 60,000 words); publishes mostly how-to books ("how to move on in your Christian walk"; 60,000 words); religious ("don't want heavy theology"; 60,000 words). Accepts outline/synopsis and 2-3 sample chapters. "Please note that we want teaching books that give the author's life experiences as well as solid Christian teaching." Looks for "well-written informative work that *follows our specifications*."
Recent Nonfiction Titles: *Victory Over Depression*, (teaching-how-to); *How To Conquer Fear* (teaching-how-to); and *With Christ in the School of Prayer*, by Andrew Murray (reprint).

THE WHITSTON PUBLISHING CO., Box 958, Troy NY 12181. (518)283-4363. Editorial Director: Jean Goode. Publishes hardcover originals. Averages 20 titles/year. Pays 10-12-15% royalty on wholesale price; no advance. Simultaneous and photocopied submissions OK. Computer printout submissions OK; "if good quality." Reports in 1 year. SASE. Book catalog $1.
Nonfiction: "We publish scholarly and critical books in the arts, humanities and some of the social sciences. We also publish reference books, bibliographies, indexes and checklists. We do not want author bibliographies in general unless they are unusual and unusually scholarly. We are, however, much interested in catalogs and inventories of library collections of individuals, such as the catalog of the Evelyn Waugh Collection at the Humanities Research Center, the University of Texas at Austin; and collections of interest to the specific scholarly community, such as surveys of early black newspapers in libraries in the US, etc." Query or submit complete

ms. Accepts poetry translations from French and Spanish.

Recent Nonfiction Titles: *Marcel Duchamp: Eros C'est la Vie*, by A. Marquis (biography); *The Letters of Randolph Bourne*, by E. Sandeen; *A Proust Dictionary*, by M. Vogely; *Women Poets of Pre-Revolutionary America, 1650-1775*, by P. Cowell; and *W.B. Yeats and the Emergence of the Irish Free State*, by R. Krimm.

WILDERNESS PRESS, 2440 Bancroft Way, Berkeley CA 94704. (415)843-8080. Editorial Director: Thomas Winnett. Publishes paperback originals. Averages 4 titles/year. Pays 8-10% royalty on retail price; advance averages $200. Simultaneous and photocopied submissions OK. Reports in 2 weeks. SASE. Book catalog for SASE.

Nonfiction: "We publish books about the outdoors. Most of our books are trail guides for hikers and backpackers, but we also publish how-to books about the outdoors and perhaps will publish personal adventures. The manuscript must be accurate. The author must research an area thoroughly in person. If he is writing a trail guide, he must walk all the trails in the area his book is about. The outlook must be strongly conservationist. The style must be appropriate for a highly literate audience." Query, submit outline/synopsis and sample chapters, or submit complete ms demonstrating "accuracy, literacy, and popularity of subject area."

Recent Nonfiction Titles: *Point Reyes*, by Dorothy Whitnah; and *Peninsula Trails*, by Jean Rusmore and Frances Spangle.

JOHN WILEY & SONS, INC., 605 3rd Ave., New York NY 10158. (212)850-6000. Publishes hardcover and paperback originals. Publishes 1000 titles/year. Pays variable royalties on wholesale price. Follow *MLA Style Sheet*. Simultaneous and photocopied submissions OK. Disk submissions OK. "We are actively seeking software authors." Reports in 6 months. SASE. Free book catalog.

Nonfiction: Publishes college textbooks, professional reference titles, trade books, journals and computer software in engineering, social sciences, computer science, business, life sciences, politics, law and medicine. Query or submit outline/synopsis and 2 sample chapters.

Recent Nonfiction Titles: *"Do It My Way Or You're Fired!*, by Ewing; *Golden Delicious Games for the Apple Computer*, by Franklin, Koltnow and Finkel; and *The Negro Almanac, 4th edition*, ed. by Ploski, Williams.

Tips: Queries/mss may be routed to other editors in the publishing group.

WILSHIRE BOOK CO., 12015 Sherman Rd., North Hollywood CA 91605. (213)875-1711. Editorial Director: Melvin Powers. Publishes paperback originals (50%) and reprints (50%). Publishes 50 titles/year. Pays 5% minimum royalty; "advance varies with nature of the book." Simultaneous and photocopied submissions OK. SASE. Reports in 2 weeks. Catalog for SASE.

Nonfiction: Calligraphy, health, hobbies, how-to, psychology, recreation, self-help and sports. "We are always looking for self-help and psychological books, such as *Psycho-Cybernetics* and *Guide to Rational Living*. We need manuscripts teaching mail order and advertising. We publish 70 horse books. "All that I need is the concept of the book to determine if the project is viable. I welcome phone calls to discuss manuscripts with authors."

Recent Nonfiction Titles: *How to Write a Good Advertisement*, by V. Schwab; *United States Mail Order Shopper's Guide*, by Susan Spitzer; and *Calligraphy Made Easy*, Tina Serafini.

WIMMER BROTHERS BOOKS, 4210 B.F. Goodrich Blvd., Box 18408, Memphis TN 38118. (901)362-8900. Editorial Director: Richard Anderson. Senior Editor: Janine Buford Earney. Publishes hardcover and paperback originals. Averages 4-5 titles/year. Offers 10-15% royalty on wholesale price. No advance. SASE. Reports in 2 months. Book catalog for SASE.

Nonfiction: Cookbooks, cooking and foods; and how-to. Especially needs specialized cookbooks and how-to books dealing with home entertainment. Submit complete ms. Looks for "interesting angle, well-edited recipes in the book and good grammar."

Recent Nonfiction Titles: *The Pastors' Wives Cookbook*, by S. DuBose (cookbook); *Forgotten Recipes*, by Jaine Rodack (cookbook); and *Wining and Dining with John Grisanti* (cookbook).

B.L. WINCH & ASSOCIATES, 45 Hitching Post Dr., Bldg. 2, Rolling Hills Estates CA 90274. (213)539-6434. Editorial Director: B.L. Winch. Production Editor: J. Lovelady. Senior Editor: Susan Mikesell. Publishes paperback originals and reprints. Averages 4-8 titles/year. Offers 5-15% royalty on wholesale or retail price. Simultaneous and photocopied submissions OK. SASE. Reports in 3 months. Free book catalog.

Nonfiction: Parent-oriented self-help materials (infant to teen), material for the gifted, affective curriculum, guidebooks and strategies, classroom management, guidebooks, infant development materials. "Prefer completed ms."

Recent Nonfiction Titles: *Unicorns Are Real*, by Barbara Vitale; *He Hit Me Back First!*, by Eva Fugitt; *Charles the Clown's Guide to Children's Parties*, by Charles and Linda Kraus.

WINCHESTER PRESS, Imprint of New Century Publishers, Inc., 220 Old New Brunswick Rd., Piscataway NJ 08854. Editor-in-Chief: Robert Elman. Publishes hardcover and paperback originals. Pays 10-12½-15%

royalty on retail price; offers $2,500 average advance. Averages 15-20 titles/year. "Submit sample photos and some idea of total number projected for final book." Simultaneous and photocopied submissions OK. Reports in 3 months. Looks for "good organization, defined audience potential, original and accurate information and good photographs." SASE. Free book catalog.

Nonfiction: Main interest is in leisure activities, outdoor sports, crafts and related subjects. Publishes cookbooks related to fish and game; how-to (sports and sporting equipment); pets (hunting dogs); recreation (outdoor); sports (hunting, fishing, etc.); and technical (firearms, boats and motors, fishing tackle, etc.). Submit outline/synopsis and sample chapters.

Recent Nonfiction Titles: *The Muzzleloading Hunter*, by Rick Hacker; *Women's Guide to Outdoor Sports*, by Sheila Link; and *Angler's Guide to Jigs and Jigging*, by Kenn Oberrecht.

Tips: "The writing of leisure-activities books—particularly how-to books—has vastly improved in recent years. Mss must now be better written and must reflect new ideas and new information if they are to be considered for publication by Winchester Press. Recreational equipment and opportunities have expanded, and writers must also be up-to-date journalists."

WINDSOR PUBLICATIONS, 21220 Erwin St., Woodland Hills CA 91365. Editorial/Photographic Director: Glenn R. Kopp. Senior Publications Editor: Rita Johnson. "We publish pictorial civic publications, business directories, and relocation guides for chambers of commerce, boards of realtors, etc. Our audience is anyone considering relocating or visiting another part of the country, and our publications document in pictures and words every aspect of a city or area. Writers, photographers and photo/journalists work on assignment only, after having demonstrated ability through samples. Publications are annual or biennial, vary in size and are titled with the name of a city. Circulation is controlled. Writers and writer/photographers with strong interview, reporting and travel writing experience are especially sought." Queries, stating writing and/or photography experience including tearsheets, are welcome. Computer printout (letter quality) submissions OK; disks must be compatible with WANG VS80, IBM PC or Radio Shack II with CPM. Reports in 2 weeks. SASE. Sample copy, writer's and photographer's guidelines sent on request.

Nonfiction: "All mss assigned. Unsolicited manuscripts and/or photos not wanted." Buys 150-200/year. Length: 3,000-10,000 words. Pays $500-2,400 on acceptance for all rights.

Photos: Photography for each publication usually assigned to photographer or photo/journalist on per-day rate plus expenses. Also purchase stock, speculative and existing photos on one-time use basis if they pertain to future publications. 35mm and larger color transparencies, b&w contact sheets and negatives or b&w prints (5x7 to 8x10) are acceptable; no color prints. Complete captions required. Photo guidelines, sample copy and upcoming photo needs will be sent in response to all queries. SASE.

‡WINGBOW PRESS, Subsidiary of Bookpeople, 2940 Seventh St., Berkeley CA 94710. (415)549-3030. Editor: Randy Fingland. Publishes hardcover and trade paperback originals and trade paperback reprints. Averages 3-4 titles/year. Pays 7-10% royalty on retail price; offers average $500 advance. Photocopied submissions OK. Computer printout submissions OK. SASE. Reports in 3 weeks on queries; 9 weeks on mss. Free book catalog.

Nonfiction: Coffee table books, how-to, illustrated books, juvenile, reference books, self-help on business and economics, hobbies, psychology, sociology. Especially needs regional guides to San Francisco Bay area. Accepts artwork/photos. No psychology, cooking, gardening or textbooks. Query or submit outline/synopsis and 1-5 sample chapters. Accepts nonfiction, fiction and poetry translations.

Recent Nonfiction Title: *Bargain Hunting in Bay Area*, by Sally Socolich (consumer reference).

Fiction: Adventure, confession, erotica, fantasy, historical, mainstream, mystery, science fiction, suspense. Especially needs "very strongly written mss as indicated by Recent Fiction Titles." No romance. Query or submit outline/synopsis and 1-5 sample chapters.

Recent Fiction Titles: *Coyotes Journal*, edited by James Koller (anthology); *Philosophers Stone*, and *God of Labyrinth*, by Colin Wilson (novels); and *High Desire*, by Leslie Simon (feminist/erotica).

Poetry: "Strongly written, usually not rhyming, modern verse. No philosophical or political diatribes." Submit complete ms.

Recent Poetry Titles: *Hello La Jolla*, by Edward Dorn (free verse); *Loba*, by Diane di Prima (free verse); and *Collected Works of Billy the Kid*, by Michael Ondaatje (free verse).

Tips: Queries/mss may be routed to other editors in the publishing group.

WINSTON PRESS, INC., CBS Educational Publishing, 430 Oak Grove, Minneapolis MN 55403. (612)871-7000. Trade Books Editorial Director: Wayne Paulson. Curriculum Editorial Director: Dee Ready. Publishes hardcover and paperback originals (90%) and reprints (10%). Publishes 40 trade titles/year. Pays royalty on net; advance varies. Photocopied submissions OK. Computer printout submissions OK. SASE. Reports in 2 months. Book catalog for SASE.

Nonfiction: "Religion and human development. Curriculum materials for preschool through adult education. Specialized and general trade books, gift and photography books." Query or submit outline/synopsis and 2 sample chapters. Looks for "a clear, popular writing style, responsible scholarship (but not a scholarly style), and fresh ideas." Accepts artwork/photos. Accepts nonfiction translations.

Recent Nonfiction Titles: *Women's Reality*, by Anne Wilson Schaef; *Catholicism*, by Richard P. McBrien; *Gene McCarthy's Minnesota*, by Eugene McCarthy; and *Traits of a Healthy Family*, by Dolores Curran.

WINSTON-DEREK PUBLISHERS, Pennywell Dr., Box 90883, Nashville TN 37209. (615)329-1319. President: James W. Peebles. Publishes hardcover, trade and mass market paperback originals (5%). Averages 15-20 titles/year. Pays 10-15% royalty on retail price; advance varies. Simultaneous and photocopied submissions OK. SASE. Reports in 1 month on queries; 6 weeks on mss.
Nonfiction: Biography, juvenile and poetry. Subjects include Americana; philosophy (contemporary format); cookbooks; religion (noncultism); travel; poetry and inspirational. Length: 50,000 words or less. Submit outline/first 2 or 4 consecutive chapters. No political or technical material.
Recent Nonfiction Titles: *Gays Under Grace*, by Maury Johnston (a gay Christian's response to the moral majority); *A Survey of African and Black Theology*, by Jamamogi Watumbi (theology); *Thirty Days of April*, by Catherine Huff (the abused child talks).
Fiction: Ethnic (non-defamatory); religious (theologically sound); suspense (highly plotted); and Americana (minorities and whites in positive relationships). Length: 50,000 words or less. "We can use fiction with a semi-historical plot; must be based or centered around actual facts and events—Americana, religion, gothic, and science fiction. Submit outline/synopsis and first 2 or 4 consecutive chapters. Unsolicited manuscripts will be returned unopened.
Recent Fiction Titles: *The Golden Circle*, by David Collins and Evelyn Witter (Americana); *The Black Friar*, by Arthur L. McLaughlin; *Night Wood*, by Darlene Goodenow (an Althea Bantree mystery selection).
Children's Books: "We are looking for books on relevant aspects of growing up and understanding life's situations. No funny animals talking."
Recent Children's Book Titles: *The Hey God Series: What is Christmas?; What is America?; Where Are You? Hurry!* and *Hey, God! Listen!* by Roxie Cawood Gibson.
Poetry: "Should be inspirational and divine—poetry that is suitable for meditation. We will also accept poetry about nature and life. No simple plainsong, etc." Submit complete ms for all poetry.
Recent Poetry Titles: *Some Gentle Moving Thing*, by James C. Floyd; *Ranson From a Poet*, by Jerry W. Elkins; and *Feathers on the Wind*, by Walter Nelms.
Tips: "The American audience is looking for less violent material. Outstanding biographies are quite successful, as are books dealing with the simplicity of man and his relationship with his environs. Our new imprint is *Scythe Books*, the children's division of Winston-Derek Publishers. We need material for adolescents within the 9-13 age group. These manuscripts should help young people with motivation for learning and succeeding, goal setting and character building. Biographies of famous women and men are always welcome. Stories must have a new twist."

ALAN WOFSY FINE ARTS, Box 2210, San Francisco CA 94126. Publishes hardcover and paperback originals (50%) and hardcover reprints (50%). Specializes in art reference books, specifically catalogs of graphic artists; bibliographies related to fine presses and the art of the book. Pays negotiable fee on retail price; offers advance. Publishes 5 titles annually. SASE. Reports in 2-4 weeks. Free book catalog.
Nonfiction: Publishes reference books on art. Query.

WOLF HOUSE BOOKS, Box 6657, Grand Rapids MI 49506. (616)245-8812. Editorial Director: Richard Weiderman. Publishes hardcover and paperback originals (50%) and reprints (50%). Published 5 titles in 1979. Offers 10% royalty. No advance. Simultaneous and photocopied submissions OK. Computer printout and disk submissions OK. Reports in 4 weeks. SASE. Book catalog for SASE.
Nonfiction: Literary criticism and biography and other studies (e.g. bibliography, etc.) on Jack London. Query.
Recent Nonfiction Titles: *Alien Worlds of Jack London*, by D.L. Walker; *White Logic: Jack London's Short Stories*, by J.I. McClintock; *Jack London at Yale*, by A. Irvine; *Jack London and the Amateur Press*, by Robert H. Woodward.

WOODBRIDGE PRESS PUBLISHING CO., Box 6189, Santa Barbara CA 93111. Editor-in-Chief: Howard B. Weeks. Publishes hardcover and paperback originals. Standard royalty contract. Rarely gives an advance. Will consider photocopied submissions. Computer printout submissions OK. Query. Returns rejected material and reports on material accepted for publication as soon as possible. Accepts no responsibility for such material other than as may be stated in a written publishing agreement. Enclose return postage with query.
General Nonfiction: "How-to books on personal health and well-being. Should offer the reader valuable new information or insights on anything from recreation to diet to mental health that will enable him to achieve greater personal fulfillment, with emphasis on that goal. Should minimize broad philosophy and maximize specific, useful information." Length: Books range from 96 to 300 pages. Also publishes cookbooks and gardening books and humor.

Recent Nonfiction Titles: *Discovering Natural Foods*, by Bruder; *I May Not Be Totally Perfect, But Parts of Me Are Excellent*, by Brilliant; and *Anyone for Insomnia?*, by Armour.

*WOODSONG GRAPHICS, Stoney Hill Rd., Box 231, New Hope PA 18938. (215)794-8321. Editor: Ellen P. Bordner. Publishes hardcover and trade paperback originals. Averages 3 titles/year. Subsidy publishes 35% of books based on "quality of material, motivation of author in distributing his work, and cost factors (which depend on the type of material involved), plus our own feelings on its marketability." Pays royalty on retail price; offers average $100 advance. Simultaneous submissions OK. No computer printout or disk submissions. SASE. Reports in two weeks on queries; reports on full manuscripts *can* take several months, depending on the amount of material already in the house. "We do everything possible to facilitate replies, but we have a small staff and want to give every manuscript a thoughtful reading."
Nonfiction: Biography, cookbook, how-to, humor, illustrated book, juvenile, reference, self-help. Subjects include cooking and foods, hobbies, philosophy, psychology. "We're happy to look at anything of good quality, but we're not equipped to handle lavish color spreads at this time. Needs are very open, and we're interested in seeing any subject, provided it's handled with competence and style. Good writing from unknowns is also welcome." No heavily pornographic mss; only minimal interest in technical manuals of any kind. Query or submit outline/synopsis and. at least 2 sample chapters. Accepts artwork/photos.
Fiction: Adventure, experimental, fantasy, gothic, historical, humor, mainstream, mystery, romance, science fiction, suspense, western. "In fiction, we simply are looking for writing that carries the reader off into new experiences. I find it difficult to define what they should be, but look forward to recognizing such material when it comes." No pornography or "sick" material. Submit outline/synopsis and sample chapters.
Poetry: "Again, serious pornography is about the only taboo here." Submit 6 samples or complete ms.

WORLD ALMANAC PUBLICATIONS, 200 Park Ave., New York NY 10166. (212)557-9652. Editorial Director: Hana Umlauf Lane. Publisher of *The World Almanac*. Publishes hardcover and trade paperback originals. Averages 8 titles/year. Pays 5-15% on retail price. No simultaneous or photocopied submissions. Computer printout submissions OK. SASE. Reports in 3 weeks. Free book catalog.
Nonfiction: Reference. "We look for reference books, like *The World Almanac*, but popular and entertaining. We expect at least a synopsis/outline and sample chapters, and would like to see completed manuscript." Accepts artwork/photos.
Recent Nonfiction Titles: *The World Almanac Book of World War II*; *The Where to Sell Anything and Everything Book*; and *The Last Time When: The World Almanac Dictionary of Dates*.

WORLD NATURAL HISTORY PUBLICATIONS, Division of Plexus Publishing, Inc., 143 Old Marlton Pike, Medford NJ 08055. (609)654-6500. Editorial Director: Thomas Hogan. Publishes hardcover and paperback originals. Averages 4 titles/year. Pays 10-20% royalty on wholesale price, buys some booklets outright for $250-1,000; offers average $500-1,000 advance. Simultaneous and photocopied submissions OK. SASE. Reports in 2 months. Book catalog for SASE.
Nonfiction: Animals, biography of naturalists, nature and reference. "We are looking for mss of about 300-400 pages for our series *Introduction to* ... some group of plants or animals designed for high school and undergraduate college use and for amateur naturalists. We will consider any book on a nature/biology subject, particularly those of a reference (permanent) nature. No philosophy or psychology; no gardening; generally not interested in travel, but will consider travel that gives sound ecological information." Also interested in mss of about 20 to 40 pages in length for feature articles in *Biology Digest* (guidelines for these available with SASE). Always query.
Recent Nonfiction Titles: *The Naturalist's Directory and Almanac*, (reference); *Exploring the Sea*, by John Fine; and *Taxonomists' Glossary of Mosquito Anatomy*, by R. Harbach and K. Knight.
Tips: "Write a book that is absolutely accurate and that has been reviewed by specialists to eliminate misstatement of fact."

JOHN WRIGHT/PSG INC., 545 Great Rd., Littleton MA 01460. (617)486-8971. President/Publisher: Frank Paparello. Hardcover and paperback originals. Pays royalty on net revenues. Specializes in publishing medical and dental books, newsletters, and journals for the professional and student markets. Pays 10-15% royalty; no advance. Send prints of photos to accompany ms. Simultaneous submissions OK. No computer printout or disk submissions. Reports in 2-4 weeks. SASE. Free book catalog.
Nonfiction: Medical, dental books, newsletters, and journals. Accepts artwork/photos. Request proposal form. Query or submit complete ms.
Recent Nonfiction Titles: *Drug Therapy in Psychiatry*, by Bernstein; *Child Abuse and Neglect*, by Eheling; *Essential Surgical Practice*, by Cushieri.
Tips: Queries/mss may be routed to other editors in the publishing group.

WRITER'S DIGEST BOOKS, 9933 Alliance Rd., Cincinnati OH 45242. (513)984-0717. Editor-in-Chief: Carol Cartaino. Publishes hardcover and paperback originals (nonfiction only) about writing, photography, songwriting, art, and other creative pursuits; selected trade titles. Pays variable royalty depending upon type of book; offers $3,000 average advance. Published 23 titles in 1983. Simultaneous (if so advised) and photocopied submissions OK. "Disk submission OK for final revised ms if compatible with our system. Printouts fine, especially if on double-wide paper so we have a huge righthand margin." Prefers letter quality to dot matrix. Reports in 3 months. Enclose return postage. Book catalog for SASE.

Nonfiction: "We're seeking up-to-date, instructional treatments by authors who can write from successful experience—how-to, reference, and other books about writing, photography, and other categories as described. Should be well-researched, yet lively and anecdotal. Also interested in seeing self-published books in the above areas. No fiction or poetry! Send sample, sales record, and reviews." Query or submit outline/synopsis and 3 sample chapters. Accepts artwork/photos. "Be prepared to explain how the proposed book differs from existing books on the subject."

Recent Nonfiction Titles: *Writing for the Joy of It*, by Leonard Knott; *The Complete Guide to Writing Nonfiction*, by the American Society of Journalists and Authors; *How to Write a Play*, by Raymond Hull; *Getting the Words Right*, by Theodore A. Rees Cheney; *Starting—and Succeeding—in Your Own Photography Business*, by Jeanne Thwaites; *Developing the Creative Edge in Photography*, by Bert Eifer; *Partnering*, by Lois Rosenthal.

THE WRITING WORKS DIVISION, Box 24947, Seattle WA 98124. (206)323-4300. Subsidiary of Cone-Heiden, Inc. President: Merle E. Dowd. Publishes hardcover and trade paperback originals. Averages 4-6 titles/year. Pays 5-10% on retail price; offers average $500-1,000 advance. SASE. Reports in 2 weeks on queries; 1 month on mss. Free book catalog.

Imprints: *Writing Works* (nonfiction), Merle Dowd, president. *Morse Press* (nonfiction, religious), Rohn Pelley, editorial director.

Nonfiction: "Coffee table" book, regional guide, religious. Subjects include health (natural foods), history, nature, recreation, religion and travel. Needs "regional travel and guides; special religious (Lutheran) programs, dramas and education." No nostalgia or poetry. Query or submit outline/synopsis and 2 sample chapters. "Also needed is a statement of where the market is, the constituency for the book and promotion ideas."

Recent Nonfiction Titles: *Barr on Backgammon*, by Ted Barr (game instruction); and *Seattle's Super Shopper*, 4th ed., by Priscilla Johnston and Dinah Stotler.

YALE UNIVERSITY PRESS, 92A Yale Station, New Haven CT 06520. Editor-in-Chief: Edward Tripp. Publishes hardcover and paperback originals (96%) and reprints (4%). Averages 120 titles/year. Pays 5-10% royalty on retail price. Photocopied submissions OK. Reports in 2-3 months. SASE. Book catalog for SASE.

Nonfiction: Works of original scholarship in the humanities, social sciences and hard sciences. No fiction, cookbooks or popular nonfiction. Query or submit outline/synopsis and sample chapters.

Recent Nonfiction Titles: *Hannah Rendt; for Love of the World,* by Elizabeth Young-Bruehl; *Nary Chestnut's Civil War*, by C. Van Woodward.

YANKEE BOOKS, Main St., Dublin NH 03444. (603)563-8111. Subsidiary of Yankee Publishing Inc. Editorial Director: Sharon M. Smith. Publishes trade paperback originals. Averages 8-10 titles/year. Pays royalty; buys some mss outright ("details depend on individual contract"); offers $500-1,000 advance. Simultaneous and photocopied (if clear) submissions OK. Computer printout submissions OK "if legible." SASE. Reports in 2 weeks on queries; 3 weeks on mss. Free book catalog.

Nonfiction: Coffee table book, cookbook, how-to, illustrated book, reference, self-help, New England-related subjects, antiques. Subjects include Americana (particularly New England); antiques; cooking; gardening; history (folklore and popular history, not scholarly); crafts; New England-related themes; photography; travel (solely New England). No scholarly history; any even slightly off-color humor; highly technical works, and biographies of worthy but not strikingly interesting persons. Query or submit outline/synopsis and sample chapters or complete ms.

Recent Nonfiction Titles: *Great New England Recipes* (cookbook); *Trips with Children in New England* (New England travel); *The Clock Watcher's Cookbook*.

‡**ZEBRA BOOKS**, Subsidiary of Norfolk Publishing Co., 475 Park Ave. S., New York NY 10016. (212)889-2299. Executive Editor: Leslie Gelbman. Publishes mass market paperback originals and reprints. Averages 150 titles/year. Pays royalty on retail price or makes outright purchase. Simultaneous and photocopied submissions OK. SASE. Reports in 2 months on queries; 3 months on mss. Book catalog for business-size SAE and 37¢ postage.

Nonfiction: Biography, how-to, humor and self-help. Subjects include health, history and psychology. "We are open to many areas, especially self-help, stress, money management, child-rearing, health, war (WWII, Vietnam), celebrity biographies." No nature, art, music, photography, religion or philosophy. Query or submit outline/synopsis and sample chapters.

Recent Nonfiction Titles: *Dustin Hoffman*, by Jeff Lenburg; *Self-Esteem: The Key to Your Child's Well-Being*, by Clemes and Bean; and *Escape from Laos*, by Dieter Dengler.

Fiction: Adventure, confession, erotica, gothic, historical, horror, humor, mainstream, romance and suspense. Tip sheet on historical romances, gothics, family sagas, adult romances and women's contemporary fiction is available. No poetry or short story collections. Query with synopsis and several sample chapters. SASE is a must.

Recent Fiction Titles: *Brazen Ecstasy*, by Janelle Taylor (historical romance); *Heritage*, by Lewis Orde (saga); and *The Warlord*, by Jason Frost (men's adventure).

CHARLOTTE ZOLOTOW BOOKS, see Harper & Row Junior Books group.

THE ZONDERVAN CORP., 1415 Lake Drive, SE, Grand Rapids MI 49506. (616)698-6900. Manuscript Review Editor: Julie Ackerman Link. Publishes hardcover and trade and mass market paperback originals (60%), and trade and mass market paperback reprints (40%). Averages 100 titles/year. Pays royalty of 14% of the net amount received on sales of cloth and softcover trade editions and 12% of net amount received on sales of mass market paperbacks; offers variable advance. Simultaneous (if so indicated) and photocopied submissions OK. "Computer printout submissions are acceptable, but the author should separate the perforated pages." SASE. Reports in 6 weeks on queries. Catalog for 9x12 SAE and $1.22 postage.

Nonfiction: Biography, coffee table book, how-to, humor, illustrated book, reference, devotional and gift, self-help, textbook on philosophy, psychology, religion, sociology. "All from religious perspective (evangelical, protestant)." Immediate needs include "books that take a fresh approach to issues and problems in protestant, evangelical community; books that offer new insights into solving personal and interpersonal problems; books that encourage readers to mature spiritually." No mss written from a mystical or occult point of view. Query or submit outline/synopsis and 2 sample chapters.

Recent Nonfiction Titles: *Forgive and Be Free*, by Richard P. Walters (personal development); *The Religion of Power*, by Cheryl Forbes (contemporary issues); and *A Feast of Families*, by Virginia Stem Owens (family).

Fiction: "Books that deal realistically and creatively with relevant social and religious issues." No mss for new children's books. Query or submit outline/synopsis and 2 sample chapters.

Recent Fiction Titles: *MacIntosh Mountain*, by Vic Kelly (contemporary/family issues); *Love's Sweet Promise*, by Susan C. Feldhake (adult/contemporary romance); and *Splendini*, by Scott Pinzon (juvenile/adventure).

Subsidy Book Publishers

The following listings are for book publishing companies who are totally subsidy publishers, meaning they do no standard trade publishing, and will publish a work only if the author is willing to underwrite the entire amount of the venture. This can be costly, and may run into thousands of dollars, usually returning less than 25% of the initial investment.

Read any literature or contracts carefully and thoroughly, being sure that all conditions of the venture (binding, editing, promotion, number of copies to be printed, number of copies to be bound, etc.) are spelled out specifically.

De Young Press, Rt. 2 (Perkins), Box 14, Hull IA 51239.

Dorrance & Company, 828 Lancaster Ave., Bryn Mawr PA 19010.

Exposition Press, 325 Rabro Dr., Smithtown NY 11787.

Mojave Books, 7040 Darby Ave., Reseda CA 91335.

Peter Randall, Publisher, Box 4726, Portsmouth NH 03801.

Vantage Press, 516 W. 34th St., New York NY 10001.

Book Publishers Subject Index

Nonfiction

Use this subject index to locate book publishers interested in your writing topic. Notice parenthetical phrases (following publishers' names) which offer additional information to help you identify those publishers that might be most receptive to your work. For example, Oryx Press is listed in the Agriculture/Horticulture subject area—but they want only reference-type submissions.

When you find a publisher that seems "right" for your book idea or manuscript, read carefully the corresponding market listing. A publisher may be categorized as publishing ethnic nonfiction. But unless you read through the entire *Writer's Market* entry, you will not know that only Greek-related manuscripts or materials on the history of southwestern American Indians are welcome.

Agriculture/Horticulture. Allen & Unwin, Inc.; Avi Pubg Co. (textbook); Banyan Books, Inc.; Brigham Young Univ. Press; Delmar Pubrs, Inc. (textbook); Doane-Western, Inc.; Hancock House Pubrs, Ltd.; The Interstate Printers & Pubrs, Inc. (textbook); Oryx Press (reference); The Pennsylvania State Univ. Press (scholarly); Purdue Univ. Press (scholarly); Reston Pubg Co. (textbook); Rowman & Allenheld, Pubrs (scholarly); Stipes Pubg Co. (textbook); Texas A&M Univ. Press (scholarly); Universe Books; Univ. of Nebraska Press (scholarly); Univ. Press of America (scholarly); Western Producer Prairie Books; Westview Press (scholarly).

Alternative Lifestyles. And Books; And/Or Press; Avant Books; Brick House Pubg Co.; Cobblesmith; Commoners' Pubg; Creative Arts Book Co.; Ideal World Pubg Co.; McPherson & Co.; Naturegraph Pubrs, Inc.; South End Press; Spring Pubns, Inc.; Sterling Pubg; Strawberry Hill Press; Thorsons Pubrs, Ltd.; Turnstone Books.

Americana. Allegheny Press (textbook); Amer. Press (textbook); Angel Press/Pubrs; Binford & Mort, Pubrs; John F. Blair, Pubr; Brevet Press, Inc.; Brunswick Pubg Co.; The Caxton Printers, Ltd.; Cedarshouse Press; Chelsea House; Clarion Books (how-to); Arthur H. Clark Co.; CLCB Press; Cobblesmith; Coles Pubg, Co., Ltd.; Congdon & Weed, Inc.; Copley Books; Coward McCann, Inc.; Crown Pubrs Inc.; Darwin Pubns (reference); May Davenport, Pubrs; Denlinger's Pubrs, Ltd.; The Devin-Adair Co., Inc.; Down East Books; The Dragonsbreath Press; Dream Garden Press; Dufour Editions, Inc.; Durst Pubns (reference); Paul S. Eriksson, Pubr; Falcon Press Pubg Co., Inc.; The Filter Press; Guy Gannett Books; General Hall, Inc. (reference); The K.S. Giniger Co., Inc.; The Globe Pequot Press, Inc.; Golden West Books; Green Tiger Press (juvenile); The Stephen Greene Press/Lewis Pubg; H.W.H. Creative Productions, Inc.; Hammond, Inc.; Hancock House Pubrs, Ltd.; Harian Creative Press Books; Harper & Row Pubrs, Inc.; The Harvard Common Press; Hastings House Pubrs, Inc.; Holmes & Meier Pubrs, Inc.; Houghton Mifflin Co.; Hounslow Press; Howard Univ. Press (scholarly); Icarus Press, Inc.; International Pubrs Co., Inc.; Jonathan David Pubrs; Wm. Kaufman, Inc.; Lame Johnny Press; Laranmark Press; Le Beacon Presse; Liberty Pubg Co., Inc.; The Lowell Press, Inc.; McFarland & Co., Inc., Pubrs (reference); Madrona Pubrs, Inc.; Miller Books; Mimir Pubrs, Inc.; Monitor Book Co., Inc.; Mosaic Press; Mott Media, Inc., Pubrs; New Century Pubrs, Inc.; Northland Press; The Old Army Press; Oregon State Univ. Press; Outbooks, Inc.; Pacific Books, Pubrs (scholarly); Padre Productions; Petersen Pubg Co.; Clarkson N. Potter, Inc.; Pressworks, Inc. (reference); Purdue Univ. Press (scholarly); R&E Research Assoc.; Rowe Pubg Corp.; Schiffer Pubrs, Ltd.; Sleepy Hollow Press; Sterling Pubg; Stoneydale Press Pubg,

Co.; Lyle Stuart, Inc.; Sun Pubg Co.; Taylor Pubg Co.; Ten Speed Press; The Thorndike Press; Transaction Books (scholarly); Tree By The River Pubg; Charles E. Tuttle Co., Inc.; Univ. of Michigan Press (scholarly); Univ. of Nebraska Press (scholarly); Univ. of New Mexico Press (scholarly); The Univ. of N. Carolina Press (scholarly); Univ. of Pennsylvania Press (scholarly); Univ. Press of Mississippi; Univ. Press of New England (scholarly); Univ. Press of Virginia (scholarly); Utah State Univ. Press (scholarly); Vance Bibliographies (bibliographies); Vesta Pubns, Ltd.; Walker & Co.; Wayne State Univ. Press (scholarly); Westernlore Press (scholarly); Yankee Books (reference).

Animals. Alaska Nature Press; Alpine Pubns Inc.; American Press (textbook); Angel Press/Pubrs; Arco Pubg Inc. (how-to); Avon Books; Brunswick Pubg Co.; Camelot Books; Carolina Biological Supply Co. (textbook); Chelsea House; CLCB Press; Collier MacMillan Canada, Ltd.; David C. Cook Pubg Co. (juvenile); Crown Pubrs, Inc.; May Davenport, Pubrs; Dillon Press, Inc. (juvenile); Educational Development Corp. (juvenile); Paul S. Eriksson, Pubrs; Frederich Fell Pubrs, Inc.; Fjord Press; Guy Gannett Books; Garden Way Pubg; H.W.H. Creative Productions, Inc.; Hancock House Pubrs Ltd.; Harbor Pubg, Inc.; Harian Creative Press Books; Harper & Row Pubrs, Inc.; Houghton Mifflin Co.; Iowa State Univ. Press (textbook); Island Press; The Lowell Press, Inc.; Miller Books; Mosaic Press; National Pubrs of the Black Hills, Inc. (textbook); New Century Pubrs, Inc.; S.C.E.-Editions L'Etincelle; Scholastic-Tab Pubns.; Charles Scribner's Sons (juvenile); Sierra Club Books; Sterling Pubg; T.F.H. Pubns, Inc. (how-to & technical); Tab Books; Tandem Press Pubrs; Ten Speed Press; The Thorndike Press; Thorsons Pubrs, Ltd.; Universe Books; Univ. of Michigan Press (scholarly); Vanguard Press, Inc.; Walker & Co.; World Natural History Pubns (reference).

Anthropology/Archaeology. Brigham Young Univ. Press; Cambridge Univ. Press (textbook); Hancock House Pubrs Ltd.; Inst. for the Study of Human Issues; McPherson & Co.; Museum of New Mexico Press (scholarly); Noyes Data Corp. (scholarly); Ohio State Univ. Press (scholarly); Pickwick Pubns (scholarly); Ross-Erikson, Inc., Pubrs; Rutgers Univ. Press (scholarly); Southern Methodist Univ. Press (scholarly); Stanford Univ. Press; Trado-Medic Books (reference); Turnstone Books; Univ. of Arizona Press (scholarly); Univ. of Nevada Press (scholarly); The Univ. of Tennessee Press (scholarly); Univ. of Texas Press (scholarly); Univ. of Utah Press (scholarly); Univ. Press of Kentucky (scholarly); Westernlore Press (scholarly); Westview Press (scholarly).

Art and Architecture. Harry N. Abrams, Inc.; American Press (textbook); Amer. Solar Energy Society (reference); Archer Editions Press; Architectural Book Pub. Co.; Art Direction Book Co. (how-to & textbook); Avant Books; Barron's Educational Series, Inc.; Beacon Press; Bennett Pubg Co. (textbook); George Braziller, Inc.; Bucknell Univ. Press (scholarly); Aristide D. Caratzas, Pubr; Chelsea House; Chronicle Books; Clarke, Irwin & Co., Ltd.; CLCB Press; Cobblesmith; Columbia Univ. Press (scholarly); Congdon & Weed, Inc.; Copley Books; Crown Pubrs, Inc.; May Davenport, Pubrs; Davis Pubns, Inc. (reference); Denlinger's Pubrs, Ltd.; The Donning Co./Pubrs, Inc.; Down East Books; The Dragonsbreath Press; Dream Garden Press; Duck Down Press; Dufour Editions, Inc.; Durst Pubns (how-to); Eastview Editions, Inc.; Effective Learning, Inc.; Environmental Design & Research Center (reference); Facts on File, Inc. (reference); The J. Paul Getty Museum (reference & scholarly); The K.S. Giniger Co., Inc.; Great Ocean Pubrs; Green Tiger Press (juvenile); Guernica Editions; H.P. Books; Hammond, Inc.; Harian Creative Press Books; Harmony Books; Harper & Row Pubrs, Inc.; Hastings House Pubrs, Inc.; Herman Pubg; Holmes & Meier Pubrs, Inc.; Hounslow Press; Howard Univ. Press (scholarly); Hudson Hills Press, Inc.; Illuminati; International Pubrs Co., Inc.; The International Univ. Press (textbook); Wm. Kaufman, Inc.; Karl Kramer Verlag GMBH & Co.; Krantz Co. Pubns (reference); Lancaster, Miller & Schnobrich Pubrs (scholarly); Lancelot Press Ltd.; Learning Pubns, Inc. (how-to & textbook); Le Beacon Presse; The Lowell Press, Inc.; McClelland & Stewart, Ltd.; McFarland & Co., Inc., Pubrs (reference); McGraw-Hill Book Co., Professional & Reference Div. (reference); Macmillan of Canada; MIT Press (scholarly); Wm. Morrow & Co.; Mosaic Press; Museum of Northern Arizona Press (reference); National Book Company (textbook); The National Gallery of Canada; New Century Pubrs, Inc.; New York Univ. Press (scholarly); Nichols Pubg Co. (scholarly); North Light (how-to & reference); Noyes Data Corp.

(scholarly); Ohio State Univ. Press (scholarly); Optimum Pubg International Inc.; Oxmoor House; Padre Productions; The Pagurian Corp. Ltd.; Parents Productions; Path Press, Inc. (reference); Pelican Pubg, Co., Inc.; The Pennsylvania State Univ. Press (scholarly); Peregrine Smith Books; Petersen Pubg Co.; Clarkson N. Potter, Inc.; Prentice-Hall (juvenile); Prentice-Hall, Inc.; The Preservation Press; Pressworks, Inc. (reference); Princeton Univ. Press (scholarly); Purdue Univ. Press (scholarly); A.H. & A.W. Reed Ltd.; Resource Pubns, Inc.; Rosen Publishing Group (reference); Rossel Books; Ross-Erikson, Inc., Pubrs; Rowman & Allenheld, Pubrs (scholarly); Schiffer Pubrs Ltd.; Abner Schram Ltd.; Charles Scribner's Sons (juvenile); Shambhala Pubns, Inc.; Sheridan House, Inc. (reference); Simon & Schuster; Sleepy Hollow Press; Star Pubg Co. (textbook); Sterling Pubg; Stoneydale Press Pubg Co.; Structures Pubg Co. (how-to); Lyle Stuart, Inc.; Sun Pubg Co.; Teplinger Pubg Co., Inc.; Taylor Pubg Co.; Transaction Books (scholarly); Troubador Press; Charles E. Tuttle Co., Inc.; Universe Books; Univ. of California Press (scholarly); Univ. of Iowa Press (scholarly); Univ. of Massachusetts Press (scholarly); Univ. of Michigan Press (scholarly); Univ. of Missouri Press (scholarly); Univ. of New Mexico Press (scholarly); Univ. Press of Mississippi; Univ. Press of New England (scholarly); Vanguard Press, Inc. (juvenile); Vesta Pubns, Inc.; The Viking Penguin, Inc.; J. Weston Walch, Pubr (textbook); Walker & Co.; Wanderer Books (juvenile); Watson-Guptill Pubns (how-to); Western Tanager Press; The Whitston Pubg Co. (scholarly); Winston-Derek Pubrs; Alan Wofsy Fine Arts (reference & bibliographies).

Astrology/Psychic Phenomena. The Aquarian Press Ltd.; Ariel Press; Asi Pubrs, Inc.; Astro Computing Services (textbook & reference); Coles Pubg Co., Ltd.; Garber Communications, Inc.; Intercultural Press, Inc.; Llewellyn Pubns (reference & how-to); Newcastle Pubg Co., Inc.; Para Research; Pitman Learning; Porter Sargent Pubrs, Inc.; Regal Books; Shambhala Pubns Inc.; Sterling Pubg; Strawberry Hill Press; Sun Pubg Co.; The Theosophical Pubg House; Turnstone Books; U.S. Games Systems, Inc.

Bibliography. ABC-Clio, Inc.; Associated Book Pubrs, Inc.; R.R. Bowker Co.; Data & Research Technology Corp.; The Family Album; The Feminist Press; Garland Pubg Inc.; B. Klein Pubns; Oryx Press; Reymont Assoc.; Scarecrow Press, Inc.; The Shoe String Press (scholarly); Univ. Press of Virginia (scholarly); The Whitston Pubg Co. (scholarly).

Biography. Academy Chicago; Addison-Wesley Pubg Co., Inc.; Alaska Nature Press; Alaska Northwest Pubg Co.; Amer. Atheist Press; Archer Editions Press; Architectural Book Pubg Co.; Astro Computing Services; Atheneum Pubrs; Atlantic Monthly Press (and autobiography); Avon Books; B.W.M.T., Inc.; Bahamas International Pubg Co., Ltd.; Beaufort Books, Inc.; Binford & Mort, Pubrs; John F. Blair, Pubr; The Bobbs-Merrill Co., Inc.; The Borgo Press; Don Bosco Pubns; Brunswick Pubg Co.; Cambridge Univ. Press; Capra Press; Catholic Univ. of America Press (scholarly); Cedarshouse Press; Celestial Arts; China Books; Citadel Press; Clarion Books (how-to); Arthur H. Clark Co.; Clarke, Irwin & Co., Ltd.; CLCB Press; Columbia Pubg Co., Inc.; Congdon & Weed, Inc.; The Continuum Pubg Corp.; David C. Cook Pubg Co.; Copley Books; Coward McCann, Inc.; Creative Pubg; Crown Pubrs, Inc.; Dante Univ. of America Press, Inc.; Red Dembner Enterprises Corp.; Detselig Enterprises Ltd.; Dillon Press, Inc. (juvenile); Dodd, Mead & Co.; Doubleday Canada, Ltd.; Down East Books; The Dragonsbreath Press; Dufour Editions, Inc.; Effective Learning, Inc.; Enslow Pubrs; Paul S. Eriksson, Pubr; Essco; ETC Pubrs; Facts on File, Inc.; The Family Album; The Feminist Press (juvenile); Fiesta City Pubrs; Fil-Am-Bel Pubns, Inc.; Fleet Press Corp.; Franciscan Herald Press; Fromm International Pubg Co.; Guy Gannett Books; The K.S. Giniger Co., Inc.; The Golden Quill Press; Gray's Pubg, Ltd.; Great Ocean Pubrs; Green Hill Pubrs; Green Tiger Press (juvenile); Grove Press; Guernica Editions; H.W.H. Creative Productions, Inc.; Hancock House Pubrs Ltd.; Harian Creative Press Books; Harper & Row Pubrs, Inc.; The Harvard Common Press; Harvey House Pubrs (juvenile); Hastings House Pubrs, Inc.; Holmes & Meier Pubrs, Inc.; Horizon Press; Houghton Mifflin Co.; Hounslow Press; Howard Univ. Press (scholarly); Hurtig Pubrs Ltd.; Icarus Press, Inc.; International Pubrs Co., Inc.; The International Univ. Press (scholarly); Iowa State Univ. Press; Wm. Kaufman, Inc.; Lancelot Press Ltd.; Lee's Books for Young Readers (juvenile); Lester & Orpen Dennys, Ltd., Pubrs; Liberty Pubg Co., Inc.; Little, Brown & Co., Inc.; McClelland & Stewart, Ltd.; Macmillan of Canada; Madrona Pubrs, Inc.;

Manyland Books, Inc.; Mariner Pubg Co., Inc.; Metamorphous Press; Mimir Pubrs, Inc.; Monitor Book Co., Inc.; Wm. Morrow & Co.; Mosaic Press; Motorbooks International Pubrs & Wholesalers, Inc.; Mott Media, Inc., Pubrs (juvenile); The Nautical & Aviation Pubg Co. of America, Inc.; Naval Inst. Press; New Century Pubrs, Inc.; Nimbus Pubg Ltd.; Northeastern Univ. Press; Ohio State Univ. Press (scholarly); Optimum Pubg International Inc.; Oregon State Univ. Press; Path Press, Inc.; Pocket Books; Clarkson N. Potter, Inc. (and autobiography); Prentice-Hall (juvenile); Princeton Univ. Press; Prometheus Books, Inc.; Purdue Univ. Press (scholarly); Ranger Assoc., Inc.; A.H. & A.W. Reed Ltd.; Regnery/Gateway, Inc.; Russica Pubrs, Inc.; S.C.E.-Editions L'Etincelle; St. Luke's Press; St. Martin's Press; Schirmer Books; Charles Scribner's Sons (juvenile); The Shoe String Press (scholarly); Simon & Schuster; Slavica Pubrs, Inc.; Southern Methodist Univ. Press (scholarly); Stoneydale Press Pubg Co.; Lyle Stuart, Inc.; Sun Pubg Co.; Taplinger Pubg Co., Inc.; Texas Monthly Press, Inc.; Thunder's Mouth Press; Transaction Books (scholarly); Twayne Pubrs; Universe Books; Univ. of Alabama Press; The Univ. of Arkansas Press; Univ. of Massachusetts Press (scholarly); Univ. of Michigan Press (scholarly); Univ. of Nebraska Press (scholarly); Univ. of Nevada Press (scholarly); Univ. of Pennsylvania Press (scholarly); Univ. Press of Kansas (scholarly); Univ. Press of Mississippi; Univ. Press of New England (scholarly); Vanguard Press, Inc.; Vesta Pubns, Ltd.; Vision House Pubrs, Inc.; Walker & Co.; Wayne State Univ. Press (scholarly); Western Producer Prairie Books; Western Tanager Press; Westernlore Press (scholarly); Winston-Derek Pubrs; Wolf House Books; Woodsong Graphics; World Natural History Pubns; The Zondervan Corp.

Business and Economics. ABT Books; Bob Adams, Inc. (reference); Addison-Wesley Pubg Co., Inc.; Alfred Pubg Co., Inc.; (how-to); Allen & Unwin, Inc.; Allen Pubg Co., (how-to); Allyn & Bacon, Inc. (textbook); Almar Press; Amer. Council for the Arts (reference); American Press (textbook); Amer. Solar Energy Society (reference); And Books; Arbor House; Arco Pubg, Inc. (how-to); Artists & Writers Pubns (how-to); Associated Book Pubrs, Inc.; Avon Books; Ballinger Pubg Co. (reference); Bankers Pubg Co. (reference); Bantam Books, Inc.; Basic Books, Inc.; The Benjamin Co., Inc.; Betterway Pubns, Inc.; Books For Business, Inc. (reference); Brevet Press, Inc.; Briarcliff Press Pubrs; Brunswick Pubg Co.; Cambridge Univ. Press (textbook); Center For Nonprofit Organizations, Inc. (how-to); Charter Books; Chelsea House; Chilton Book Co.; CLCB Press; Coles Pubg Co., Ltd.; Columbia Pubg Co., Inc.; Communications Press, Inc. (reference); Congdon & Weed, Inc.; Consumer Reports Books (reference); Cordovan Press; The Corinthian Press; Crain Books (textbook); The Cumberland Press, Inc.; Robert F. Dame, Inc. (textbook & reference); Dartnell Corp.; Delmar Pubrs, Inc. (textbook); Red Dembner Enterprises Corp.; Deneau Pubrs & Co. Ltd.; Development Systems Corp. (real estate); The Devin-Adair Co., Inc.; Dow Jones-Irwin (business and finance); Durst Pubns (reference); Effective Learning, Inc.; Enslow Pubrs; Enterprise Pubg Co., Inc.; Environmental Design & Research Center (reference); Paul S. Eriksson, Pubr; ETC Pubns; Exanimo Press; Facts on File, Inc. (reference); Fairchild Books & Visuals (textbook); Farnsworth Pubg Co., Inc.; Frederick Fell Pubrs, Inc.; The Free Press (textbook & reference); Galaxy Pubns (textbook); General Hall, Inc. (textbook); Great Ocean Pubrs; Green Baron Book & Film Co. (textbook); Gregg Division (textbook); Gulf Pubg Co.; Hammond, Inc.; Harbor Pubg, Inc.; Harcourt Brace Jovanovich Legal & Professional Pubns, Inc. (reference); Harian Creative Press Books; Harper & Row Pbrs, Inc.; The Harvard Common Press; D.C. Heath & Co. (textbook); Herman Pubg; Holmes & Meier Pubrs, Inc.; Hounslow Press; Howard Univ. Press (scholarly); Inst. for Business Planning (how-to & reference); Inst. for the Study of Human Issues; Intercultural Press, Inc. (how-to); International Pubrs Co., Inc.; International Self-Counsel Press, Ltd. (how-to); The International Univ. Press (textbook); Johns Hopkins Univ. Press (scholarly); Wm. Kaufman, Inc.; Kirkley Press, Inc.; B. Klein Pubns; Knowledge Industry Pubns, Inc.; Kumarian Press (textbook & scholarly); Lane & Assoc., Inc.; Lebhar-Friedman; Le Beacon Presse; Lester & Orpen Dennys, Ltd., Pubrs; Liberty Pubg Co., Inc.; McFarland & Co., Inc., Pubrs (reference); McGraw-Hill Book Co., College Texts (reference); McGraw-Hill Book Co., General Div.; McGraw-Hill Book Co., Professional & Reference Div. (reference); Marathon International Pubg Co., Inc. (self-help); Charles E. Merrill Pubg Co. (textbook); Metamorphous Press; Mimir Pubrs Inc.; MIT Press (scholarly); Mosaic Press; National Assoc. of College & University Business Officers (textbook & technical); National Book Company (textbook); National Pubrs of the Black Hills, Inc. (textbook); Nellen

Pubg; New Century Pubrs, Inc.; New York Zoetrope, Inc. (textbook & reference); Nichols Pubg Co. (scholarly); Noyes Data Corp. (technical); Ohio Univ. Press (scholarly); Oregon State Univ. Press; P.A.R., Inc.; Padre Productions; Parker Pubg Co. (how-to); The Pennsylvania State Univ. Press (scholarly); Petrocelli Books, Inc.; Pilot Books (reference); Pluribus Press, Inc. (how-to); Prentice-Hall, Inc.; Pressworks, Inc. (reference); Purdue Univ. Press (scholarly); Que Corp. (textbook); R&E Research Assoc.; R&R Newkirk (technical); Ranger Assoc. Inc.; Realtors National Marketing Institute (how-to & reference); Regnery/Gateway, Inc.; Reston Pubg Co. (textbook); Reymont Assoc.; The Riverdale Co., Inc. Pubrs (textbook); Rowman & Allenheld, Pubrs (scholarly); RPM Press (how-to); S.C.E.-Editions L'Etincelle; Schenkman Pubg Co., Inc. (textbook); Charles Scribner's Sons; Self-Counsel Press, Inc. (how-to & reference); Seven Locks Press, Inc.; Shambhala Pubns, Inc.; The Allen Smith Co. (reference); Social Science Education Consortium, Inc. (reference); South End Press (gov't & politics); Southern Methodist Univ. Press (scholarly); Star Pubg Co. (textbook); Sterling Pubg; Stipes Pubg Co. (textbook); Lyle Stuart, Inc.; Swiftwater Books (reference); Taylor Pubg Co.; Teachers College Press; Texas A&M Univ. Press (scholarly); Times Books; Transaction Books (scholarly); Trend House; Universe Books; University Assoc., Inc.; Univ. of Alabama Press (scholarly); Univ. of Iowa Press (scholarly); Univ. of Michigan Press (scholarly); Univ. of Pennsylvania Press (scholarly); Univ. of Texas Press (scholarly); Univ. Press of America (scholarly); Univ. Press of Mississippi; Univ. Press of New England (scholarly); Univ. Press of the Pacific, Inc. (scholarly); Univ. Press of Virginia (scholarly); Vanguard Press, Inc. (how-to); J. Weston Walch, Pubrs (textbook); Walker & Co.; Wayne State Univ. Press (scholarly); Western Islands; Western Producer Prairie Books; Westin Communications (textbook & reference); Wetherall Pubg Co. (how-to); John Wiley & Sons, Inc. (reference); Wingbow Press (self-help).

Career Guidance. Bob Adams, Inc. (reference); Almar Press; Arco Pub., Inc.; Associated Book Pubrs, Inc.; Barron's Educational Series, Inc.; Career Pubg, Inc.; The Chatham Press; Chicago Review Press; Fairchild Books & Visuals; Guidance Centre; Herman Pubg; The Interstate Printers & Pubrs, Inc. (textbook); Petersen's Guides, Inc. (reference); Pilot Books (reference); The Rosen Pubg Group (young adult); Ross Books; Teachers College Press; VGM Career Horizons; Westin Communications.

Communications. And Books; Avant Books; Bradson Press, Inc.; Career Pubg Inc.; Chicago Review Press; College-Hill Press (reference); Communication Skill Builders, Inc.; Communications Press, Inc. (reference); Drama Book Pubrs (reference); Focal Press (how-to); Herman Pubg; ISI Press (how-to); Kirkley Press, Inc.; Knowledge Industry Pubns, Inc.; Law-Arts Pubrs (textbook); Arthur Merriwether, Inc. (textbook & juvenile); National Pubrs of the Black Hills, Inc. (textbook); New York Zoetrope, Inc. (reference); Oryx Press (reference); Padre Productions; Purdue Univ. Press (scholarly); Random House, Inc. (textbook); Regal Books; The Rosen Pubg Group (young adult); Seven Locks Press, Inc.; The Shoe String Press (scholarly); Special Libraries Assn. (textbook & references); Univelt, Inc. (technical); University Assoc., Inc.; Writer's Digest Books (how-to & reference).

Community/Public Affairs. A.S. Barnes & Co., Inc.; Center for Nonprofit Organizations, Inc. (reference); Communications Press, Inc.; The Continuum Pubg Corp.; Creative Book Co.; Deneau Pubrs & Co. Ltd.; Groupwork Today, Inc.; Indiana Univ. Press; Loiry Pubg House (reference); Macmillan of Canada; NC Press; Seven Locks Press, Inc.; Temple Univ. Press (scholarly); Trado-Medic Books (health & medicine); University Assoc., Inc.; Vance Bibliographies (bibliographies); Wesleyan Univ. Press (scholarly); Westview Press (scholarly).

Computers and Electronics. Alfred Pubg Co., Inc. (how-to); And Books; ARCsoft Pubrs (how-to, reference & textbook); Artech House, Inc.; The Blacksburg Group, Inc. (textbook & reference); Carolina Biological Supply Co.; Chilton Book Co.; Computer Science Press (bibliographies, reference, textbook & general nonfiction); Computer Skill Builders; Curtin & London, Inc. (how-to); Steve Davis Pubg (reference, how-to & technical); Delmar Pubrs, Inc. (textbook); dilithium Press (textbook); Dustbooks; Educational Development Corp. (juvenile); Entelek; Fairchild Books & Visuals (textbook); Green Baron Book & Film Co. (textbook); Hayden Book Co., Inc. (reference); D.C. Heath & Co. (textbook); Heath Co. (technical &

textbook); Herman Pubg; Intervarsity Press (textbook); Wm. Kaufman, Inc.; Kern Pubns (how-to, textbook & technical); Lancaster, Miller & Schnobrich Pubrs; McGraw-Hill Book Co., College Text Div. (reference); Microtrend, Inc.; MIT Press (scholarly); National Pubrs of the Black Hills, Inc. (textbook); New York Zoetrope, Inc. (reference & technical); Path Press, Inc. (reference); Prentice-Hall, Inc.; Q.E.D. Information Sciences, Inc. (technical); Que Corp. (how-to, reference & technical); Regents Pubg Co. Inc. (text book); Resource Pubns Inc. (how-to); Reston Pubg Co. (textbook); Howard W. Sams & Co., Inc. (technical); Sybex, Inc.; Tab Books, Inc.; Texas Instruments Learning Center (reference & technical); Univ. Press of Virginia (scholarly); Webster Division (how-to); Westin Communications (textbook & reference); John Wiley & Sons, Inc.

Consumer Affairs. Almar Press; Consumer Reports Books (reference); Delair Pubg Co., Inc.; Dell Pubg Co., Inc.; Gregg Division (textbook); Meadowbrook Press; The Allen Smith Co. (reference); Teacher Update, Inc.; The Westminster Press (juvenile).

Cooking/Foods/Nutrition. Acropolis Books, Ltd. (how-to & reference); Aglow Pubns; Alaska Northwest Pubg Co.; Allegheny Press (how-to); Angel Press/Pubrs; Anna Publishing, Inc.; Apple Press; Arbor House; Artists & Writers Pubns; Associated Book Pubrs, Inc.; Atheneum Pubrs; Avi Pubg Co. (textbook); Avon Books; Bantam Books, Inc.; Barron's Educational Series, Inc.; Beaufort Books, Inc.; The Benjamin Co., Inc.; The Berkley Pubg Group; Better Homes & Gardens Books; Betterway Pubns, Inc.; Binford & Mort, Pubrs; Biworld Pubrs, Inc.; The Bobbs-Merrill Co., Inc. (how-to); Briarcliff Press Pubrs; Brunswick Pubg Co.; Byls Press; Camaro Pubg Co.; Celestial Arts; Chelsea House; Chicago Review Press; China Books; CLCB Press; Cobblesmith; Coles Pubg Co., Ltd.; Compact Pubns, Inc.; Congdon & Weed, Inc.; Consumer Reports Books (how-to); Contemporary Books; Cougar Books; Creative Arts Book Co.; Creative Book Co.; The Crossing Press; Crown Pubrs Inc.; Delair Pubg Co., Inc.; Delta Books; Detselig Enterprises Ltd.; Down East Books; Dreadnaught; Dufour Editions, Inc.; Durst Pubns (how-to); The Ecco Press; Effective Learning, Inc.; Paul S. Eriksson, Pubr; Evans & Co.; Falcon Press Pubg Co., Inc.; Farm Journal Books; Frederick Fell Pubrs, Inc.; The Filter Press; Fjord Press; Forman Pubg; C.J. Frompovich Pubns (technical); Guy Gannett Books; Garden Way Pubg; The K.S. Giniger Co., Inc.; Globe Mini Mags; The Globe Pequot Press, Inc.; Graphic Image Pubns; Great Outdoors Pubg Co.; Green Baron Book & Film Co.; The Stephen Greene Press/Lewis Pubg; H.P. Books; H.W.H. Creative Productions, Inc.; Hammond, Inc.; Hancock House Pubrs Ltd.; Harbor Pubg, Inc.; Harian Creative Press Books; Harmony Books; Harper & Row Pubrs, Inc.; The Harvard Common Press; Hastings House Pubrs, Inc.; Hawkes Pubg, Inc. (how-to); Hayden Book Co., Inc. (textbook); Herald Press; Houghton Mifflin Co.; Hounslow Press; Humanics Ltd.; Ideals Pubg Corp.; Johnson Books; Jonathan David Pubrs; Kav Books, Inc. (how-to); Keats Pubg, Inc.; Lancelot Press Ltd.; Laranmark Press; Le Beacon Presse; Liberty Pubg Co., Inc.; Little, Brown & Co., Inc.; Lone Star Pubrs; Madrona Pubrs, Inc.; Marathon International Pubg Co., Inc.; Mariner Pubg Co., Inc.; Meadowbrook Press; Miller Books (how-to); Wm. Morrow & Co.; Mosaic Press; New Century Pubrs, Inc.; Nimbus Pubg Ltd.; 101 Productions (how-to); Optimum Pubg International, Inc.; Ottenheimer Pubrs, Inc.; Outbooks Inc.; Owlswood Productions, Inc.; Oxmoor House; Padre Productions; The Pagurian Corp. Ltd.; Parents Productions; Pelican Pubg Co., Inc.; Perivale Press; Clarkson N. Potter, Inc.; A.H. & A.W. Reed Ltd.; Richboro Press; Ross Books; Rossel Books; Royal Pubg Co.; S.C.E.-Editions L'Etincelle; Schiffer Pubrs, Ltd.; Seven Seas Press; Shambhala Pubns, Inc.; Sleepy Hollow Press; Stackpole Books; Sterling Pubg; Strawberry Hill Press; Sun Pubg Co.; Susann Pubns, Inc.; Swiftwater Books (how-to); Tandem Press Pubrs; J.P. Tarcher, Inc.; Taylor Pubg Co.; Ten Speed Press; Texas Monthly Press, Inc.; Thorsons Pubrs, Ltd.; Thunder's Mouth Press; Times Books; TL Enterprises, Inc. (how-to); The Touchstone Press; Troubador Press; Univ. Press of Virginia (scholarly); Vanguard Press, Inc.; Vesta Pubns, Ltd.; Walker & Co.; Western Producer Prairie Books; Wimmer Bros. Books; Winchester Press; Woodbridge Press Pubg Co.; Woodsong Graphics; Yankee Books (how-to).

Counseling. Accelerated Development, Inc. (textbook & reference); Barron's Educational Series; Consumer Reports Books (how-to); Edits Pubrs (reference); Groupwork Today, Inc.; The Interstate Printers & Pubrs, Inc. (textbook); Learning Pubns, Inc. (reference); Med-Psych

Pubns; Morehouse-Barlow Co., Inc.; Mott Media, Inc., Pubrs; New Leaf Press, Inc.; Occupational Awareness; Rosen Publishing Group (young adult); Teachers College Press; Tyndale House Pubrs, Inc.

Crafts. Arco Pub., Inc. (how-to); Associated Book Pubrs, Inc.; A.S. Barnes & Co., Inc.; Better Homes & Gardens Books; Charles T. Branford Co. (how-to); Briarcliff Pubrs; Chilton Book Co.; Collector Books; Commoners' Pubg; Davis Pubns, Inc. (reference); Delair Pubg Co., Inc. (how-to); Dillon Press, Inc. (juvenile); Doll Reader; Farm Journal Books; Hancock House Pubrs Ltd.; House of Collectibles (how-to); Kav Books, Inc. (how-to); Millcreek Press (how-to & reference); Naturegraph Pubrs, Inc.; Oak Tree Publications, Inc. (how-to); Optimum Pubg International Inc.; Oxmoor House; Parents Productions; Popular Science Books (how-to); Scholastic-Tab Pubns; Stackpole Books; Standard Pubg (how-to); The Sunstone Press (how-to); Tab Books, Inc.; Timber Press; Troubador Press; Universe Books; Vanguard Press, Inc.; Wallace Homestead Book Co.; Winchester Press (how-to); Yankee Books.

Datebooks and Calendars. Dreadnaught; Quicksilver Productions. Also see the Greeting Card Publishers section of *Writer's Market*.

Education(al). Accelerated Development, Inc. (textbook & reference); Acropolis Books, Ltd.; Addison-Wesley Pubg Co., Inc.; Amer. Catholic Press; Anderson Pubg Co.; Arco Pubg Co., Inc.; Artists & Writers Pubns (how-to); Associated Book Pubrs, Inc.; Aztex Corp.; Bantam Books, Inc.; Barnes & Noble; Barron's Educational Series, Inc.; Bilingual Educational Series, Inc. (juvenile); John F. Blair, Pubr; Brigham Young Univ. Press; Byls Press; Cambridge Book Co.; Cliffs Notes, Inc.; Coles Pubg Co. Ltd.; Communication Skill Builders, Inc.; Computer Skill Builders; The Continuum Pubg Corp.; R.D. Cortina Co., Inc.; Dante Univ. of America Press, Inc.; T.S. Denison & Co., Inc.; Edits Pubrs (reference); Education Associates (textbook); Entelek; The Feminist Press; Front Row Experience; Gregg Division; Gryphon House, Inc.; Guidance Centre; Holt, Rinehart & Winston of Canada, Ltd. (textbook); Humanics Ltd.; Intergalactic Pubg Co.; The Interstate Printers & Pubrs, Inc. (textbook); Jamestown Pubrs Inc.; Janus Book Pubrs; Learning Endeavors; Learning Pubns, Inc. (reference); Liberty Pubg Co., Inc.; Liguori Pubns; Arthur Merriwether, Inc. (juvenile); Charles E. Merrill Pubg Co. (textbook); Morehouse-Barlow Co., Inc.; National Book Co.; New Readers Press; Nichols Pubg Co. (scholarly); Occupational Awareness; Octameron Assoc.; Ohio State Univ. Press (scholarly); Open Court Pubg Co.; Oryx Press; Parker Pubg Co. (how-to); Princeton Book Co., Pubrs (textbook); R&E Research Assoc.; Regents Pubg Co., Inc.; Regnery/Gateway, Inc.; Resource Pubns, Inc.; Routledge & Kegan Paul, Ltd. (scholarly); The Seabury Press; The Shoe String Press (scholarly); Silver Burdett; Social Science Education Consortium, Inc. (reference); Teacher Update, Inc.; Teachers College Press; Twenty-Third Pubns, Inc.; Univ. Press of America (scholarly); Webster Division (how-to); Wetherall Pubg Co.; B.L. Winch & Assoc.; Winston Press.

Ethnic. ABC-Clio, Inc. (reference); And Books; B.W.M.T., Inc.; Bilingual Educational Services, Inc. (juvenile); Borealis Press, Ltd.; Brunswick Pubg Co.; Byls Press; China Books; Columbia Univ. Press (scholarly); Dante Univ. of America Press, Inc.; Fil-Am-Bel Pubns Inc.; Fleet Press Corp. (juvenile); Genealogical Pubg Co., Inc.; General Hall, Inc. (reference); Guernica Editions; Heart of the Lakes Pubg; Heritage Books, Inc.; Holloway House Pubg Co.; Inst. for the Study of Human Issues; International Pubrs Co., Inc.; Manyland Books, Inc.; Museum of New Mexico Press (scholarly); Museum of Northern Arizona Press (reference); Naturegraph Pubrs Inc.; Nellen Pubg; Northland Press; Path Press, Inc.; The Pennsylvania State Univ. Press (scholarly); Precedent Pubg, Inc. (scholarly); A.H. & A.W. Reed Ltd.; Schocken Books; Shambhala Pubns, Inc.; Slavica Pubrs, Inc.; State Historical Society of Wisconsin; Strawberry Hill Press; Sun Pubg Co.; Texas Western Press (scholarly); Three Continents Press; Charles E. Tuttle Co., Inc.; Univ. of Arizona Press (scholarly); Univ. of Massachusetts Press (scholarly); Univ. of Nebraska Press (scholarly); Univ. of Nevada Press (scholarly); Univ. of Oklahoma Press (scholarly); Univ. of Pennsylvania Press (scholarly); Univ. of Utah Press (scholarly); Univ. Press of America (scholarly); Westernlore Press (scholarly); Yankee Books.

Fashion/Beauty. A&W Pub., Inc.; Acropolis Books, Ltd. (how-to & reference); Fairchild Books & Visuals (textbook).

Games and Entertainment. Coles Pubg Co., Ltd.; Contemporary Books; Dell Pubg Co., Inc.; Gambler's Book Club; Gambling Times; H.P. Books; Holloway House Pubg Co.; Kav Books, Inc.; Knowledge Industry Pubns, Inc.; McFarland & Co., Inc., Pubrs (reference); Prentice-Hall (juvenile); The Publishing Ward, Inc.; Scholastic, Inc. (puzzles for juveniles); Scholastic-Tab Pubns; SRS Enterprises, Inc./Scientific Research Services; Sterling Pubg; Tab Books, Inc.; Troubador Press; U.S. Games Systems, Inc.; Winchester Press.

Gardening and Plants. Associated Book Pubrs, Inc.; Banyan Books, Inc.; Better Homes & Gardens Books; Betterway Pubns, Inc. (how-to); Briarcliff Press Pubrs; Cobblesmith; Coles Pubg Co., Ltd.; Delmar Pubrs, Inc. (textbook); Garden Way Pubg; Great Outdoors Pubg Co.; Gulf Pubg Co.; H.P. Books; Keats Pubg, Inc.; Naturegraph Pubrs, Inc.; 101 Productions (how-to); Optimum Pubg International Inc.; Ottenheimer Pubrs, Inc.; Perivale Press; Richboro Press; Ross Books; Schiffer Pubrs, Ltd.; Symmes Systems; J.P. Tarcher, Inc.; Taylor Pubg Co.; Ten Speed Press; Timber Press; Universe Books; Walker & Co.; Woodbridge Press Pubg Co.; Yankee Books.

Gay and Lesbian. Alyson Pubns, Inc.; The Crossing Press; Gay Sunshine Press; JH Press; Persephone Press; Swiftwater Books; Thorsons Pubrs, Ltd. (how-to).

General Nonfiction. Academy Chicago; Atheneum Pubrs; Ballantine Books; A.S. Barnes & Co., Inc.; Beacon Press; Charter Books; Delacorte Press; Dell Pubg Co., Inc.; The Dial Press; Doubleday Canada Ltd.; Evans & Co.; Wm. Morrow & Co.; New Amer. Library; W.W. Norton Co., Inc.; Pacific Books, Pubrs; Pinnacle Books; Pocket Books; Pruett Pubg Co.; Random House, Inc.; St. Martin's Press; Charles Scribner's Sons; The Shoe String Press; The Smith; Stein & Day Pubrs; Summit Books; Taplinger Pubg, Co., Inc.; Teacher Update, Inc.; Time-Life Books, Inc.; The Viking Penguin, Inc.

Government and Politics. ABC-Clio, Inc. (reference); ABT Books; Addison-Wesley Pubg Co., Inc.; Allen & Unwin, Inc.; American Press (textbook); Amer. Solar Energy Society (reference); Angel Press/Pubrs; Apple-Wood Books, Inc.; Arbor House; Atheneum Pubrs; Avon Books; Basic Books, Inc.; Beacon Press; John F. Blair, Pubr; The Borgo Press; Brunswick Pubg Co.; Bucknell Univ. Press (scholarly); Aristide D. Caratzas, Pubr; Cedarshouse Press; Chelsea House; Clarke, Irwin & Co., Inc.; CLCB Press; Columbia Pubg Co., Inc.; Communications Press, Inc.; Congdon & Weed, Inc.; Coward McCann, Inc.; Crown Pubrs, Inc.; Delta Books; Red Dembner Enterprises Corp.; Deneau Pubrs & Co. Ltd.; The Devin-Adair Co., Inc.; Dufour Editions, Inc.; Effective Learning, Inc.; Paul S. Eriksson, Pubr; Facts on File, Inc. (reference); Fromm International Pubg Co.; General Hall, Inc. (textbook); Great Ocean Pubrs; Grove Press; Guernica Editions; Harian Creative Press Books; Harper & Row Pubrs, Inc.; The Harvard Common Press; D.C. Heath & Co. (textbook); Holmes & Meier Pubrs, Inc.; Houghton Mifflin Co.; Hounslow Press; Howard Univ. Press (scholarly); Hurtig Pubrs Ltd.; Inst. for the Study of Human Issues; Intercultural Press, Inc. (reference); International Pubrs Co., Inc.; The International Univ. Press (textbook); Johns Hopkins Univ. Press (scholarly); Kumarian Press (textbook); Le Beacon Presse; Loiry Pubg House (reference); Longman, Inc. (textbook); McClelland & Stewart, Ltd.; McPherson & Co.; Madrona Pubrs, Inc.; Miller Books; Mimir Pubrs, Inc.; Mott Media Inc., Pubrs; National Book Co. (textbook); NC Press; Nellen Pubg; New Century Pubrs, Inc.; New York Univ. Press (scholarly); Northeastern Univ. Press (reference); Ohio State Univ. Press (scholarly); Oxford Univ. Press, Inc. (scholarly); P.A.R., Inc.; Pantheon Books; Path Press, Inc. (reference); The Pennsylvania State Univ. Press (scholarly); Persephone Press; Princeton Univ. Press (scholarly); R&E Research Assoc.; A.H. & A.W. Reed Ltd.; Regnery/Gateway, Inc.; The Riverdale Co., Inc., Pubrs (textbook); Rossel Books; Routledge & Kegan Paul, Ltd. (scholarly); Rowman & Allenheld Pubrs (scholarly); S.C.E.-Editions L'Etincelle; St. Martin's Press; Scholarly Resources, Inc. (scholarly); Seven Locks Press; Social Science Education Consortium, Inc. (reference); Sovereign Press; Lyle

Stuart, Inc.; Sherwood Sugden & Co., Pubrs; Sun Pubg Co.; Teachers College Press; Texas Monthly Press, Inc.; Thunder's Mouth Press; Transaction Books (scholarly); Trend House; Universe Books; Univ. of Alabama Press (scholarly); Univ. of Massachusetts Press (scholarly); Univ. of N. Carolina Press (scholarly); Univ. of Notre Dame Press (scholarly); Univ. of Pennsylvania Press (scholarly); Univ. of Tennessee Press (scholarly); Univ. of Texas Press (scholarly); Univ. Press of America (scholarly); Univ. Press of Kansas (scholarly); Univ. Press of Kentucky (scholarly); Univ. Press of Mississippi; Univ. Press of New England (scholarly); Univ. Press of the Pacific, Inc. (scholarly); Univ. Press of Virginia (scholarly); Utah State Univ. Press (scholarly); Vanguard Press, Inc.; Vesta Pubns, Ltd.; J. Weston Walch, Pubr (textbook); Wayne State Univ. Press (scholarly); Western Islands; Western Tanager Books; John Wiley & Sons, Inc. (reference).

Health and Medicine. ABT Books; Academic Press, Inc. (scholarly); Acropolis Books, Ltd. (how-to & reference); Addison-Wesley Pubg Co., Inc.; Allyn & Bacon, Inc. (textbook); Almar Press; American Press (textbook); And/Or Press; Angel Press/Pubrs; Anna Pubg (reference); Apple Press; Arbor House; Arco Pub., Inc. (reference); Ariel Press; Artech House, Inc. (technical); Asi Pubrs, Inc.; Astro Computing Services (textbook & reference); Atheneum Pubrs; Augsburg Pubg House; Avant Books; Avi Pubg Co. (textbook); Avon Books; Bantam Books, Inc.; Beaufort Books, Inc.; The Benjamin Co., Inc.; Betterway Pubns, Inc.; Biomedical Pubns (reference & textbook); Biworld Pubrs, Inc. (reference); The Bobbs-Merrill Co., Inc.; Bradson Press, Inc.; Briarcliff Press Pubrs; Brunswick Pubg Co.; Camaro Pubg Co.; Cambridge Univ. Press (textbook); Camelot Books; Career Pubg Inc.; Carolina Biological Supply Co. (textbook); Celestial Arts; Champion Athlete Pubg Co.; Chelsea House; CLCB Press; Coles Pubg Co., Ltd.; College-Hill Press (textbook & reference); Compact Publications, Inc.; Compcare Pubns (self-help); Congdon & Weed, Inc.; Consumer Reports Books (reference); Contemporary Books; Copley Books; The Corinthian Press; Cougar Books; Coward McCann, Inc.; Creative Arts Book Co.; The Crossing Press; Crown Pubrs, Inc.; Delair Pubg Co., Inc. (how-to); Delmar Pubrs, Inc. (textbook); Delta Books; Red Dembner Enterprises Corp.; Detselig Enterprises Ltd.; The Devin-Adair Co., In.; Dow Jones-Irwin (technical); Enslow Pubrs; Paul S. Eriksson, Pubr; Falcon Press Pubg Co., Inc.; Falkynor Books (self-help); Frederick Fell Pubrs, Inc.; Flare Books (young adult); The K.S. Giniger Co., Inc.; Globe Mini Mags; Great Ocean Pubrs; Warren H. Green, Inc. (scholarly); Gregg Division (textbook); Grove Press; H.P. Books; H.W.H. Creative Productions, Inc.; Harbor Pubg Inc.; Harian Creative Press Books; Harper & Row Pubrs, Inc.; The Harvard Common Press; Hawkes Pubg Inc. (how-to); Hazelden Foundation; Health Profession Pubg (textbook & reference); D.C. Heath & Co. (reference); Herman Pubg; Houghton Mifflin Co.; Hounslow Press; Howard Univ. Press (scholarly); Humanics Ltd.; Hunter House, Inc.; Ideal World Pubg Co.; The International Univ. Press (textbook); Iowa State Univ. Press (textbook); Jalmar Press, Inc. (how-to); Johns Hopkins Univ. Press (scholarly); Wm. Kaufman, Inc.; Keats Pubg Inc.; McFarland & Co., Inc., Pubrs (reference); McGraw-Hill Book Co., General Div.; Madrona Pubrs, Inc.; Mariner Pubg Co., Inc.; Meadowbrook Press; Medical Economics Books (reference); Medical Examination Pubg Co., Inc. (textbook); Med-Psych Pubns; Metamorphous Press; Mosaic Press; John Muir Pubns (how-to); National Book Co. (textbook); Naturegraph Pubrs, Inc.; Nellen Pubg; New Century Pubrs, Inc.; Newcastle Pubg Co., Inc.; Nurseco, Inc. (reference); Optimum Pubg International Inc.; Ottenheimer Pubrs, Inc.; Pantheon Books; Para Research; Parents Productions; Parker Pubg Co. (how-to); Penguin Books; The Pennsylvania State Univ. Press (scholarly); Plenum Pubg Corp.; Pluribus Press, Inc. (reference); Potentials Development for Health & Aging Services; Prentice-Hall (juvenile); Quintessence Pubg Co., Inc. (technical); R&E Research Assoc.; A.H. & A.W. Reed Ltd.; Reston Pubg Co. (textbook); The Rosen Pubg Group (reference); Ross-Erikson, Inc., Pubrs; Rowman & Allenheld, Pubrs (scholarly); S.C.E.-Editions L'Etincelle; Scholium International Inc.; Charles Scribner's Sons; Charles Scribner's Sons (juvenile); Seven Locks Press, Inc.; Shambhala Pubns, Inc.; Sierra Club Books; Sterling Pubg; Strawberry Hill Press; Lyle Stuart, Inc.; Susann Pubns, Inc.; J.P. Tarcher, Inc.; Teachers College Press; The Theosophical Pubg House; Thorsons Pubrs, Ltd.; Trado-Medic Books (reference); Transaction Books (scholarly); Triumph Pubg Co.; Turnstone Books; Universe Books; J. Weston Walch, Pubr (textbook); Walker & Co.; Wanderer Books (juvenile); Wayne State Univ. Press (scholarly);

Westview Press (scholarly); Wetherall Pubg Co. (self-help); John Wiley & Sons, Inc. (reference); Wilshire Book Co.; Woodbridge Press Pubg Co. (how-to); John Wright/PSG Inc. (reference); The Writing Works Division; Zebra Books.

History. ABC-Clio, Inc. (reference); Academy Chicago; Alaska Northwest Pubg Co.; Allen & Unwin, Inc.; American Press (textbook); Angel Press/Pubrs; Apple-Wood Books, Inc.; Arbor House; Archer Editions Press; Associated Book Pubrs, Inc.; Atlantic Monthly Press; Avon Books; Bahamas International Pubg Co., Ltd.; Banyan Books, Inc.; A.S. Barnes & Co., Inc.; Beaufort Books, Inc.; Binford & Mort, Pubrs; John F. Blair, Pubr; The Borgo Press; George Braziller, Inc.; Brevet Press, Inc.; Brunswick Pubg Co.; Bucknell Univ. Press (scholarly); Cambridge Univ. Press; Camelot Books; Aristide D. Caratzas, Pubr; Carolrhoda Books, Inc. (juvenile); Catholic Univ. of America Press (scholarly); Cedarshouse Press; Chelsea House; China Books; Citadel Press; Arthur H. Clark Co.; T&T Clark Ltd.; Clarke, Irwin & Co., Ltd.; CLCB Press; Columbia Univ. Press (scholarly); Congdon & Weed, Inc.; The Continuum Pubg Corp.; Cordovan Press; Coward McCann, Inc.; Creative Pubg (reference); Crossway Books; Crown Pubrs Inc.; Darwin Pubns (reference); Red Dembner Enterprises Corp.; Detselig Enterprises Ltd.; The Devin-Adair Co., Inc.; Dillon Press, Inc. (juvenile); The Donning Co./Pubrs, Inc.; Doubleday Canada, Ltd.; Down East Books; The Dragonsbreath Press; Dream Garden Press; Dufour Editions, Inc.; Eakin Press (juvenile); Eastview Editions, Inc.; Educational Development Corp. (juvenile); Wm. B. Eerdmans Pubg Co.; Effective Learning, Inc.; Paul S. Eriksson, Pubr; Essco; Facts on File, Inc.; Falcon Press Pubg Co., Inc.; Farrar, Straus & Giroux, Inc. (young adult); Fjord Press; Fleet Press Corp.; Franciscan Herald Press; Fromm International Pubg Co.; Guy Gannett Books; Gaslight Pubns; Genealogical Pubg Co., Inc.; The J. Paul Getty Museum (reference & scholarly); The K.S. Giniger Co., Inc.; The Globe Pequot Press, Inc.; GMG Pubg; Gray's Pubg, Ltd.; Great Ocean Pubrs; The Stephen Greene Press/Lewis Pubg; Grove Press; Guernica Editions; Hammond Inc.; Hancock House Pubrs Ltd.; Harian Creative Press Books; Harper & Row Junior Books Group (juvenile); Harper & Row Pubrs, Inc.; The Harvard Common Press; Hastings House Pubrs, Inc.; Hawkes Pubg, Co.; Heart of the Lakes Pubg; D.C. Heath & Co. (textbook); Herald Press; Heritage Books, Inc.; Holmes & Meier Pubrs, Inc.; Horizon Press; Houghton Mifflin Co.; Hounslow Press; Howard Univ. Press (scholarly); Hurtig Pubrs Ltd.; Icarus Press, Inc.; Indiana Univ. Press; Inst. for the Study of Human Issues; International Marine Pubg Co.; International Pubrs Co., Inc.; The International Univ. Press (textbook); Iowa State Univ. Press; Johns Hopkins Univ. Press (scholarly); Johnson Books; Wm. Kaufman, Inc.; Kent State Univ. Press (scholarly); Lame Johnny Press; Lancelot Press Ltd.; Laranmark Press; Leather Stocking Books; Liberty Pubg Co., Inc.; Little, Brown & Co., Inc.; Longman, Inc. (textbook); McClelland & Stewart, Ltd.; McFarland & Co., Inc., Pubrs (reference); Macmillan of Canada; Madrona Pubrs, Inc.; Mariner Pubg Co., Inc.; Mercer Univ. Press (reference); Miller Books; Mimir Pubrs, Inc.; Wm. Morrow & Co.; Mosaic Press; Motorbooks International Pubrs & Wholesalers, Inc.; Mountain Press Pubg Co.; Museum of New Mexico Press (scholarly); Museum of Northern Arizona Press (reference); National Book Co. (textbook); Naturegraph Pubrs, Inc.; The Nautical & Aviation Pubg Co. of America, Inc.; NC Press; Nellen Pubg; New Century Pubrs, Inc.; New Readers Press; New York Univ. Press (scholarly); Nimbus Pubg Ltd.; Northeastern Univ. Press (reference); Northern Illinois Univ. Press (scholarly); Noyes Data Corp. (scholarly); Ohio State Univ. Press (scholarly); Ohio Univ. Press (scholarly); The Old Army Press; Optimum Pubg International Inc.; Oregon State Univ. Press; Outbooks Inc.; Oxford Univ. Press, Inc. (scholarly); Padre Productions; Paladin Press; Pantheon Books; Path Press, Inc. (reference); The Pennsylvania State Univ. Press (scholarly); Peregrine Smith Books; Persephone Press, Pickwick Pubns; Pine Mountain Press, Inc.; Pocket Books; Clarkson N. Potter, Inc.; Precedent Pubg, Inc. (scholarly); Prentice-Hall (juvenile); The Preservation Press; Presidio Press; Press Pacifica; Pressworks, Inc. (reference); Princeton Univ. Press (scholarly); Purdue Univ. Press (scholarly); R&E Research Assoc.; Ranger Assoc., Inc.; A.H. & A.W. Reed Ltd.; Regnery/Gateway Inc.; The Riverdale Co., Inc., Pubrs (textbook); Rossel Books; Routledge & Kegan Paul, Ltd. (scholarly); Rowe Pubg Corp.; Russica Pubrs, Inc.; Rutgers Univ. Press (scholarly); S.C.E.-Editions L'Etincelle; St. Martin's Press; Schenkman Pubg Co., Inc. (textbook); Schiffer Pubrs, Ltd.; Scholarly Resources, Inc. (scholarly & bibliographies); Shambhala Pubns, Inc.; The Shoe String Press (scholarly); Simon & Schuster; Slavica Pubrs,

Inc.; Sleepy Hollow Press (technical); Social Science Education Consortium, Inc. (reference); Sovereign Press; Southern Methodist Univ. Press (scholarly); Stanford Univ. Press; State Historical Society of Wisconsin; Stoneydale Press Pubg Co.; Strawberry Hill Press; Lyle Stuart, Inc.; Sherwood Sugden & Co., Pubrs; Sun Pubg Co.; The Sunstone Press; Taplinger Pubg Co., Inc.; Temple Univ. Press (scholarly); Ten Speed Press; Texas A&M Univ. Press (scholarly); Texas Monthly Press, Inc.; Texas Western Press (scholarly); Three Continents Press; Thunder's Mouth Press; Tompson & Rutter Inc.; The Touchstone Press; Transaction Books (scholarly); Tree by the River Pubg; Trend House; Triumph Pubg Co.; Turnstone Books; Charles E. Tuttle Co., Inc.; Universe Books; Univ. of Alabama Press (scholarly); Univ. of Arkansas Press (scholarly); Univ. of Iowa Press (scholarly); Univ. of Massachusetts Press (scholarly); Univ. of Missouri Press (scholarly); Univ. of Nebraska Press (scholarly); Univ. of Nevada Press (scholarly); Univ. of New Mexico Press (scholarly); Univ. of N. Carolina Press (scholarly); Univ. of Notre Dame Press (scholarly); Univ. of Oklahoma Press (scholarly); Univ. of Pennsylvania Press (scholarly); Univ. of Tennessee Press (scholarly); Univ. of Utah Press (scholarly); Univ. Press of America (scholarly); Univ. Press of Kansas (scholarly); Univ. Press of Kentucky (scholarly & health & medicine); Univ. Press of Mississippi; Univ. Press of New England (scholarly); Univ. Press of the Pacific, Inc. (scholarly); Univ. Press of Virginia (scholarly); Utah State Univ. Press (scholarly); Vanguard Press, Inc.; Vesta Pubns, Ltd.; J. Weston Walch, Pubr, (textbook); Walker & Co.; Wayne State Univ. Press (scholarly); Wesleyan Univ. Press (scholarly); Western Islands; Western Producer Prairie Books; Western Tanager Books; Westernlore Press (scholarly); The Writing Works Division; Yankee Books; Zebra Books.

Hobby. Allegheny Press (how-to); Almar Press; Amer. Philatelic Society (how-to & reference); Angel Press/Pubrs; Arco Pubg, Inc. (how-to); M. Arman Pubg Inc. (how-to, textbook & reference); Artists & Writers Pubns (how-to); Associated Booksellers (how-to); Associated Book Pubrs, Inc.; Avon Books; Bale Books; Barnes & Noble (how-to); Beaufort Books, Inc.; The Benjamin Co., Inc.; Bradson Press, Inc.; Charles T. Branford Co. (how-to); Brunswick Pubg Co.; Carstens Pubns, Inc.; Chicago Review Press (reference); CLCB Press; Coles Pubg Co., Ltd.; Collector Books; Contemporary Books (how-to); Crown Pubrs Inc.; Darwin Pubns (how-to); Red Dembner Enterprises Corp.; Detselig Enterprises Ltd.; Doll Reader; Durst Pubns (how-to); Eastview Editions, Inc.; Educational Development Corp. (juvenile); Effective Learning, Inc.; Enslow Pubrs; Paul S. Eriksson, Pubr; Essco; Falcon Press Pubg Co., Inc.; Frederick Fell Pubrs, Inc.; The K.S. Giniger Co., Inc.; H.P. Books; H.W.H. Creative Productions, Inc.; Hammond, Inc.; Hancock House Pubrs Ltd.; Harian Creative Press Books; The Harvard Common Press; Hawkes Pubg Inc. (how-to); Hounslow Press; House of Collectibles (how-to); Kalmbach Pubg Co. (how-to); B. Klein Pubns; Liberty Pubg Co., Inc.; Madrona Pubrs, Inc.; Millcreek Press (how-to & reference); Mosaic Press; Mountain Press Pubg Co., New Century Pubrs, Inc.; October Press, Inc. (technical); Outbooks Inc.; Oxmoor House; Padre Productions; Parents Productions; Petersen Pubg Co. (how-to); Popular Science Books (how-to); Prentice-Hall, Inc.; Ranger Assoc., Inc.; A.H. & A.W. Reed Ltd.; S.C.E.-Editions L'Etincelle; Schiffer Pubrs Ltd.; Scholastic-Tab Pubns; Charles Scribner's Sons (juvenile); Sterling Pubg; Tab Books, Inc.; Ten Speed Press; TL Enterprises, Inc. (how-to); The Touchstone Press; Ultralight Pubns, Inc. (technical); Walker & Co.; Wallace Homestead Book Co.; Wanderer Books (juvenile); Wilshire Book Co.; Wingbow Press (how-to); Woodsong Graphics.

Home and Family Life. A&P Feature Pubns; A&W Pubg, Inc.; Abbey Press; Addison-Wesley Pubg Co., Inc.; Amer. Baby Books; Aztex Corp.; Bennett Pubg Co. (textbook); The Berkley Pubg Group; Better Homes & Gardens Books; Betterway Pubns, Inc. (how-to & reference); The Bobbs-Merrill Co., Inc. (how-to); Career Pubg; Catholic Truth Society (how-to); Cobblesmith (how-to); Compcare Pubns (how-to); David C. Cook Pubg Co.; Cougar Books; Delair Pubg Co., Inc. (how-to); Delmar Pubrs, Inc. (textbook); Delta Books; Fairchild Books & Visuals (textbook); Garlinghouse Co. (how-to); Golden Books; Great Ocean Pubrs; Gryphon House (how-to); Here's Life Pubrs Inc.; Herman Pubg; Humanics Ltd.; Hunter House, Inc.; Ideals Pubg Corp.; The Interstate Printers & Pubrs, Inc. (textbook); John Knox Press; Lakewood Books (self-help); Loiry Pubg House (reference); Meadowbrook Press; Oak Tree Pubns, Inc.; 101 Productions (how-to); Ottenheimer Pubrs, Inc.; Parents Productions (self-help); Popular Science Books (how-to); Regal Books; Harold Shaw Pubrs; Sterling Pubg; Structures Pubg Co. (how-to); Tab Books, Inc. (how-to); Triumph Pubg Co.; Tyndale House Pubrs, Inc.; Vision House Pubrs, Inc.; Wimmer Bros. Books (how-to); B.L. Winch & Assoc. (self-help).

How-to. Addison-Wesley Pubg Co., Inc.; Angel Press/Pubrs; Anna Pubg, Inc.; Barnes & Noble; The Berkley Pubg Group; Biworld Pubrs; Briarcliff Press Pubrs; Camelot Books; Capra Press; Chicago Review Press; Chilton Book Co.; Clarke, Irwin & Co., Ltd.; Computer Skill Builders; The Corinthian Press; Coward McCann, Inc.; Creative Arts Book Co.; Crown Pubrs, Inc.; Dell Pubg Co., Inc.; Delta Books; Red Dembner Enterprises Corp.; The Devin-Adair Co., Inc.; Dream Garden Press; Effective Learning, Inc.; Enslow Pubrs; Paul S. Eriksson, Pubr; Essco; ETC Pubns; Exanimo Press; Fairmont Press Inc.; Falcon Press Pubg Co., Inc.; Farm Journal Books; Frderick Fell Pubrs, Inc.; Forman Pubg; Front Row Experience; Gambling Times; Gay Sunshine Press; The K.S. Giniger Co., Inc.; Golden Books; Graphic Image Pubns; Green Baron Book & Film Co.; Green Hill Pubrs; Grove Press; H.P. Books; Hammond, Inc.; Harcourt Brace Jovanovich Legal & Professional Pubns, Inc.; Harper & Row Pubrs, Inc.; The Harvard Common Press; Herald Press; Here's Life Pubrs, Inc.; Ideals Pubg Corp.; Johnson Books; Jonathan David Pubrs; Wm. Kaufman, Inc.; B. Klein Pubns; Lame Johnny Press; Laranmark Press; Liberty Pubg Co., Inc.; Little, Brown & Co., Inc.; Loiry Pubg House; Lone Star Pubrs; Macmillan of Canada; Madrona Pubrs, Inc.; Mariner Pubg Co., Inc.; Meadowbrook Press; Arthur Merriwether, Inc. (juvenile); Metamorphous Press; Wm. Morrow & Co.; Motorbooks International Pubrs & Wholesalers, Inc.; Naturegraph Pubrs, Inc.; New Century Pubrs, Inc.; Newcastle Pubg Co., Inc.; Nimbus Pubg Ltd.; Once Upon a Planet, Inc.; Optimum Pubg International Inc.; Outbooks Inc.; Outdoor Empire Pubg, Inc.; Oxmoor House; Padre Productions; Pantheon Books; Para Research; Parents Productions; Pluribus Press, Inc.; Clarkson N. Potter, Inc.; Prentice-Hall, Inc.; Press Pacifica; R&E Research Assoc.; Ranger Assoc., Inc.; Reymont Assoc.; Richboro Press; Rossel Books; Scholastic-Tab Pubns; Harold Shaw Pubrs; Sierra Club Books; Stoneydale Press Pubg Co.; Sun Pubg Co.; Tandem Press Pubrs; Taylor Pubg Co.; Ten Speed Press; Thunder's Mouth Press; The Touchstone Press; Ultralight Pubrs, Inc.; Vision House Pubrs, Inc.; The Westminster Press (juvenile); Wilshire Book Co.; Woodsong Graphics; Zebra Books; The Zondervan Corp. Also see specific subject categories.

Humanities. Amer. Council for the Arts (reference); Duquesne Univ. Press (scholarly); Folcraft Library Editions/Norwood Editions (scholarly); Fordham Univ. Press (scholarly); The Free Press (textbook & reference); Garland Pubg Inc. (reference); Holmes & Meier Pubrs, Inc.; Indiana Univ. Press; McClelland & Stewart, Ltd.; Pressworks, Inc. (reference); Prometheus Books, Inc.; Southern Illinois Univ. Press; Univ. of Texas Press (scholarly); The Whitston Pubg Co. (scholarly); Yale University Press (scholarly).

Humor. Angel Press/Pubrs; Avon Books; Baker Book House Co.; John F. Blair, Pubr; Bradson Press, Inc.; Camelot Books; Celestial Arts; Citadel Press; Clarion Books (how-to); Congdon & Weed, Inc.; Crown Pubrs, Inc.; May Davenport, Pubrs; Delta Books; The Dragonsbreath Press; Paul S. Eriksson, Pubr; Farrar, Straus & Giroux, Inc. (young adult); Green Baron Book & Film Co.; Guernica Editions; H.W.H. Creative Productions, Inc.; Hammond, Inc.; Harian Creative Press Books; Harper & Row Pubrs, Inc.; The Harvard Common Press; Hounslow Press; Hurtig Pubrs Ltd.; Wm. Kaufman, Inc.; Lancelot Press Ltd.; Le Beacon Presse; The Lowell Press, Inc.; Madrona Pubrs, Inc.; Marathon International Pubg Co., Inc.; Mosaic Press; New Century Pubrs Inc.; Nimbus Pubg Ltd.; Once Upon a Planet, Inc.; Paladin Press; Parents Productions; Penguin Books; Perivale Press; Pine Mountain Press; Planet Books (how-to); Clarkson N. Potter, Inc.; Prentice-Hall (juvenile); Price/Stern/Sloan, Inc., Pubrs; Princeton Univ. Press; The Pubg Ward, Inc.; Ranger Assoc., Inc.; Russica Pubrs, Inc.; S.C.E.-Editions L'Etincelle; Scholastic, Inc. (juvenile); Scholastic-Tab Pubns; Charles Scribner's Sons (juvenile); Sterling Pubg; Lyle Stuart, Inc.; Susann Pubns, Inc.; Ten Speed Press; Texas Monthly Press, Inc.; The Thorndike Press; Vanguard Press, Inc.; Vision House Pubrs, Inc.; Wetherall Pubg Co. (home & family life); Woodbridge Press Pubg Co.; Woodsong Graphics; Zebra Books; The Zondervan Corp.

Juvenile. Abingdon Press; Alaska Nature Press; Alaska Northwest Pubg Co.; Angel Press/Pubrs; Apple Press; Associated Book Pubrs, Inc.; Atheneum Pubrs, Inc.; Augsburg Pubg House; Avon Books; Baker Book House Co.; Bantam Books, Inc.; Betterway Pubns, Inc. (how-to); Don Bosco Pubns; Bradson Press, Inc.; Broadman Press; Brunswick Pubg Co.; Clarke, Irwin & Co., Ltd.; CLCB Press; Concordia Pubg House; Consumer Reports Books; The Corinthian Press; Coward McCann, Inc.; Coward, McCann & Geoghegan; Cricket Pubns; Crown Pubrs, Inc.; May Davenport, Pubrs; Delair Pubg Co., Inc.; Dell Pubg Co., Inc.; T.S. Denison & Co., Inc.; Down East Books; Dreadnaught; Dufour Editions, Inc.; E.P. Dutton; Enslow Pubrs; Farrar, Straus & Giroux, Inc.; Guy Gannett Books; The K.S. Giniger Co., Inc.; Golden Books; Green Baron Book & Film Co.; Gryphon House (how-to); Guernica Editions; Harvey House Pubrs; Hastings House Pubrs, Inc.; Herald Press; Holiday House; Houghton Mifflin Co.; Hounslow Press; Kav Books, Inc.; Lancelot Press Ltd.; Loiry Pubg House; Lothrop, Lee & Shepard Books; Margaret K. McElderry Books; Macmillan of Canada; Macmillan Pubg Co., Inc.; Mariner Pubg Co., Inc.; Meadowbrook Press; Julian Messner; Modern Curriculum Press; Morrow Junior Books; New Century Pubrs, Inc.; Nimbus Pubg Ltd.; Oak Tree Pubns; October Press, Inc.; Pantheon Books; Philomel Books; Clarkson N. Potter, Inc.; Press Pacific; Rand McNally (reference); Rosebrier Pubg Co.; Rossel Books; Schocken Books; Scholastic, Inc.; Scholastic-Tab Pubns; Harold Shaw Pubrs; Sierra Club Books; Standard Pubg; The Viking Penguin, Inc.; Walker & Co.; Fredrick Warne & Co., Inc.; Wetherall Pubg Co.; Wingbow Press; Winston-Derek Pubrs; Woodsong Graphics. Also see specific subject categories.

Labor and Management. Abbott, Langer & Assoc. (reference); Center for Nonprofit Organizations, Inc.; Crain Books (textbook); Robert F. Dame, Inc. (reference); Dartnell Corp.; Groupwork Today, Inc.; Herman Pubg; International Pubrs Co., Inc.; Kirkley Press, Inc.; Lake View Press; MIT Press (scholarly); National Assoc. of College & University Business Officers; Nellen Pubg; Realtors National Marketing Institute (reference); Rowman & Allenheld, Pubrs (scholarly); University Assoc., Inc..

Language and Literature. Allen & Unwin, Inc.; Archer Editions Press; Associated Book Pubrs, Inc.; Bantam Books, Inc.; Barron's Educational Series, Inc.; Beacon Press; George Braziller, Inc.; Cambridge Book Co.; Catholic Univ. of America Press (scholarly); Cedarshouse Press (reference); Coles Pubg Co., Ltd.; College-Hill Press (reference); Collier MacMillan Canada, Ltd. (textbook); Columbia Univ. Press (scholarly); Communication Skill Builders, Inc.; The Continuum Pubg Corp.; R.D. Cortina Co., Inc. (textbook); The Crossing Press; Dante Univ. of America Press, Inc.; Dryad Press; Gaslight Pubns; Hayden Book Co., Inc. (textbook); D.C. Heath & Co. (textbook); Heinle & Heinle Pubrs, Inc. (textbook); High/Coo Press (reference); Horizon Press; Illuminati; Indiana Univ. Press; Jamestown Pubrs, Inc. (textbook); Johns Hopkins Univ. Press (scholarly); Longman, Inc. (textbook); McFarland & Co., Inc., Pubrs (reference); Charles E. Merrill Pubg Co. (textbook); MIT Press (scholarly); National Book Co. (textbook); National Pubrs of the Black Hills, Inc. (textbook); National Textbook Co. (textbook); New Readers Press; New York Univ. Press; Northeastern Univ. Press (scholarly); Oddo Pubg Inc. (juvenile); Ohio State Univ. Press (scholarly); Oregon State Univ. Press; Poet Gallery Press; Princeton Univ. Press (scholarly); Prometheus Books, Inc.; Purdue Univ. Press (scholarly); Random House, Inc. (textbook); Regents Pubg Co., Inc.; Shambhala Pubns, Inc.; Slavica Pubrs, Inc.; Sleepy Hollow Press; Southern Methodist Univ. Press (scholarly); Spring Pubns, Inc.; Stanford Univ. Press; Taplinger Pubg Co., Inc.; Texas Christian Univ. Press; Three Continents Press; Charles E. Tuttle Co., Inc.; Underwood/Miller (reference); Univ. of Alabama Press (scholarly); Univ. of Arkansas Press (scholarly); Univ. of California Press (scholarly); Univ. of Nebraska Press (scholarly); Univ. of Notre Dame Press (scholarly); Univ. of Texas Press (scholarly); Univ. Press of America (scholarly); Univ. Press of Mississippi; Utah State Univ. Press (scholarly); J. Weston Walch, Pubr (textbook); Webster Division (textbook).

Law/Criminal Justice. Addison-Wesley Pubg Co., Inc.; Amer. Solar Energy Society (reference); Anderson Pubg Co. (textbook & reference); Books For Business, Inc. (reference); Brigham Young Univ. Press; Cobblesmith; Farnsworth Pubg Co., Inc.; Greenwood Press; Harcourt Brace Jovanovich Legal & Professional Pubns, Inc. (textbook, technical & reference);

Inst. for Business Planning (reference); International Self-Counsel Press, Ltd. (how-to); Law-Arts Pubrs (textbook); McGraw-Hill Book Co., Professional & Reference Div. (reference); Mimir Pubrs, Inc.; Monitor Book Co.; Nellen Pubg; Northeastern Univ. Press (reference); Optimum Pubg International Inc.; P.A.R., Inc.; Pantheon Books; Rutgers Univ. Press, (scholarly); Self-Counsel Press, Inc. (how-to & reference); Sheridan House, Inc. (reference); The Allen Smith Co., (reference); Southern Methodist Univ. Press (scholarly); Ten Speed Press; Transaction Books (scholarly); Trend House; The Univ. of N. Carolina Press (scholarly); Univ. Press of Kentucky (scholarly); Univ. Press of Virginia (scholarly); Wayne State Univ. Press (scholarly); John Wiley & Sons, Inc. (reference).

Literary Criticism. Allen & Unwin, Inc.; The Borgo Press; The Ecco Press; Howard Univ. Press; McPherson & Co.; Northern Illinois Univ. Press; Perivale Press; Persea Books; Poet Gallery Press; Prometheus Books, Inc.; Rutgers Univ. Press; The Shoe String Press; Slavica Pubrs Inc.; Sleepy Hollow Press; Sherwood Sugden & Co., Pubrs; Texas Christian Univ. Press; Three Continents Press; Twayne Pubrs; Underwood/Miller; Univ. of Alabama Press; Univ. of Arkansas Press; Univ. of Massachusetts Press; Univ. of Missouri Press; Univ. of N. Carolina Press; Univ. of Notre Dame Press; Univ. of Oklahoma Press; Univ. of Tennessee Press; Univ. Press of Kentucky; Vanguard Press, Inc.; Wolf House Books.

Marine Subjects. Cornell Maritime Press, Inc. (technical & how-to); Gray's Pubg Ltd.; Howell-North Books; International Marine Pubg Co.; Lancelot Press Ltd.; Naval Institute Press (history); Rowe Pubg Corp.; Sail Books; Seven Seas Press (reference); Sheridan House, Inc. (reference).

Military. Arco Pubg, Inc.; Beau Lac Pubrs; Essco; Leather Stocking Books; The Nautical & Aviation Pubg Co. of America, Inc. (reference); Paladin Press; Precedent Pubg, Inc. (scholarly); Presidio Press; Ranger Assoc., Inc.; The Shoe String Press (scholarly); Stackpole Books; Westview Press (scholarly).

Money and Finances. A&W Pubg, Inc.; Acropolis Books, Ltd. (reference & how-to); Addison-Wesley Pubg Co., Inc.; Almar Press; Bale Books; Bankers Pubg Co. (reference); Bantam Books, Inc.; The Benjamin Co., Inc.; Better Homes & Gardens Books; Center for Nonprofit Organizations, Inc. (how-to); Contemporary Books (how-to); David C. Cook Pubg Co.; Cordovan Press; Robert F. Dame, Inc. (textbook & reference); Development Systems Corp.; Dow Jones-Irwin (business and finance); Enterprise Pubg Co., Inc.; Environmental Design & Research Center (reference); Farnsworth Pubg Co., Inc.; Galaxy Pubns (textbook); Harbor Pubg, Inc. (how-to); Herman Pubg; Inst. for Business Planning (reference); International Self-Counsel Press, Ltd. (how-to); Lakewood Books (self-help); Marathon International Pubg Co., Inc. (self-help); Medical Economics Books (reference); National Assoc. of College & Univ. Business Officers (textbook); Nichols Pubg Co. (scholarly); Padre Productions; Pilot Books (reference); R&R Newkirk; Realtors National Marketing Institute (self-help); Vanguard Press, Inc. (how-to).

Music and Dance. Amer. Catholic Press; And Books; Atlantic Monthly Press; Bucknell Univ. Press (scholarly); Cambridge Univ. Press; Columbia Pubg Co., Inc.; Columbia Univ. Press (scholarly); Communications Press, Inc.; Concordia Pubg House; Congdon & Weed, Inc.; Consumer Reports Books (reference); Crescendo Pubg; Crown Pubrs Inc.; Dance Horizons; May Davenport, Pubrs; Dodd-Mead & Co.; Dragon's Teeth Press; Drama Book Pubrs (reference); Dufour Editions, Inc.; Eastview Editions, Inc.; Paul S. Eriksson, Pubr; Facts on File, Inc. (reference); Fiesta City Pubrs (how-to & self-help); Front Row Experience; Great Ocean Pubrs; Guernica Editions; Harmony Books; The Harvard Common Press; Holmes & Meier Pubrs, Inc.; Howard Univ. Press (scholarly); International Pubrs Co., Inc.; The International Univ. Press (textbook); McFarland & Co., Inc., Pubrs (reference); Wm. Morrow & Co.; Mosaic Press; John Muir Pubns; Music Sales Corp. (how-to); National Book Co. (textbook); New Century Pubrs, Inc.; Northeastern Univ. Press (reference); Ohio State Univ. Press (scholarly); Oxford Univ. Press, Inc.; The Pagurian Corp. Ltd.; Parents Productions; Pennsylvania State

Univ. Press (scholarly); Prentice-Hall (juvenile); Prentice-Hall, Inc.; Princeton Book Co., Pubrs (textbook); Princeton Univ. Press (scholarly); Resource Pubns, Inc.; The Rosen Pubg Group (reference); Ross Books; Scarecrow Press, Inc.; Schirmer Books (textbook & reference); Shambhala Pubns, Inc.; Simon & Schuster; Sterling Pubg; Stipes Pubg Co. (textbook); Lyle Stuart, Inc.; Tree by the River Pubg (how-to); Twayne Pubrs (scholarly); Universe Books; Univ. of Alabama Press (scholarly); Univ. of Iowa Press (scholarly); Univ. of Missouri Press (scholarly); Univ. of N. Carolina Press (scholarly); Univ. Press of America (scholarly); Univ. Press of New England (scholarly); J. Weston Walch, Pubr (textbook); Walker & Co.; Wayne State Univ. Press (scholarly); The Whitston Pubg Co. (scholarly).

Nature and Environment. ABC-Clio, Inc. (reference); Harry N. Abrams, Inc.; Acropolis Books, Ltd. (how-to & reference); Addison-Wesley Pubg Co., Inc.; Alaska Nature Press; Alaska Northwest Pubg Co.; Allegheny Press (textbook); Amer. Solar Energy Society (reference); Angel Press/Pubrs; Appalachian Mountain Club Books; Avant Books; Avon Books; Banyan Books, Inc.; Binford & Mort, Pubrs; Biomedical Pubns (reference); Biworld Pubrs, Inc. (reference); John F. Blair, Pubr; Brick House Pubg Co.; Brunswick Pubg Co.; Calif. Inst. of Public Affairs (reference); Capra Press; Carolina Biological Supply Co. (textbook); The Chatham Press; Chronicle Books; Clarion Books (how-to); Clarke, Irwin & Co., Ltd.; CLCB Press; Cobblesmith; Collier MacMillan Canada Ltd.; Columbia Pubg Co., Inc.; Coward McCann, Inc.; Crown Pubrs Inc.; Darwin Pubns (reference); May Davenport, Pubrs; Red Dembner Enterprises Corp.; The Devin-Adair Co., Inc.; Dillon Press, Inc. (juvenile); Down East Books; Dream Garden Press; Dustbooks; The East Woods Press; Eastview Editions, Inc.; Educational Development Corp. (juvenile); Effective Learning, Inc.; Environmental Design & Research Center (reference); Paul S. Eriksson, Pubr; Facts on File, Inc. (reference); Fairmont Press Inc.; Falcon Press Pubg Co., Inc.; Fjord Press; Guy Gannett Books; Garden Way Pubg; Garlinghouse Co. (how-to); GMG Pubg; Gray's Pubg, Ltd.; Green Baron Book & Film Co.; The Stephen Greene Press/Lewis Pubg; Guernica Editions; H.W.H. Creative Productions, Inc.; Hammond, Inc.; Hancock House Pubrs Ltd.; Harper & Row Pubrs, Inc.; The Harvard Common Press; Holmes & Meier Pubrs, Inc.; Houghton Mifflin Co.; Hounslow Press; Hurtig Pubrs Ltd.; Ideal World Pubg Co.; Island Press; Johns Hopkins Univ. Press (scholarly); Johnson Books; Wm. Kaufman, Inc.; Keats Pubg Inc.; Lancelot Press, Ltd.; Llewellyn Pubns (reference); The Lowell Press, Inc.; McClelland & Stewart, Ltd.; Mosaic Press; Mountain Press Pubg Co.; Museum of New Mexico Press (scholarly); Museum of Northern Arizona Press (reference); National Pubrs of the Black Hills, Inc.; Naturegraph Pubrs Inc.; NC Press; New Century Pubrs, Inc.; Nichols Pubg Co. (scholarly); Nimbus Pubg Ltd.; Northland Press; Noyes Data Corp. (technical); Oddo Pubg Co. (juvenile); Optimum Pubg International, Inc.; Oregon State Univ. Press; Outbooks Inc.; Outdoor Life Books; Padre Productions; The Pagurian Corp. Ltd.; The Pennsylvania State Univ. Press (scholarly); Pennwell Books (reference & technical); Peregrine Smith, Books; Platt & Munk Pubrs (juvenile); Clarkson N. Potter, Inc.; Prentice-Hall, Inc.; Purdue Univ. Press (scholarly); A.H. & A.W. Reed Ltd.; Regnery/Gateway, Inc.; Review & Herald Pubg Assoc. (juvenile); S.C.E.-Editions L'Etincelle; Charles Scribner's Sons (juvenile); Shambhala Pubns, Inc.; Signpost Books; Stackpole Books; Stipes Pubg Co. (textbook); Stone Wall Press, Inc. (how-to); Stoneydale Press Pubg Co.; Symmes Systems; T.F.H. Pubns, Inc. (how-to); Tandem Press Pubrs; Ten Speed Press; Texas A&M Univ. Press (scholarly); Texas Monthly Press, Inc.; The Thorndike Press; Timber Press; TL Enterprises, Inc.; Troubador Press; Turnstone Books; Universe Books; Univ. of Massachusetts Press (scholarly); Univ. of Michigan Press (scholarly); Univ. of Nebraska Press (scholarly); Univ. of Nevada Press (scholarly); Univ. of New Mexico Press (scholarly); Univ. of N. Carolina Press (scholarly); Univ. of Wisconsin Press (scholarly); Univ. Press of Kentucky (scholarly); Univ. Press of New England (scholarly); Vanguard Press, Inc. (juvenile); Walker & Co.; Western Producer Prairie Books; Western Tanager Press; Westview Press (scholarly); Wilderness Press; World Natural History Pubns (reference); The Writing Works Division.

Philosophy. Alba House; Allen & Unwin, Inc.; American Atheist Press; American Press (textbook); And Books; And/Or Press; Angel Press/Pubrs; The Aquarian Press Ltd.; Ariel Press; Atlantic Monthly Press; Avant Books; Avon Books; Baker Book House Co.; Beacon Press; The

Berkley Pubg Group; George Braziller, Inc.; Brunswick Pubg Co.; Bucknell Univ. Press (scholarly); Aristide D. Caratzas, Pubr; Catholic Univ. of America Press (scholarly); Cedarshouse Press; Chelsea House; T&T Clark Ltd.; CLCB Press; Cobblesmith; Columbia Univ. Press (scholarly); Congdon & Weed, Inc.; The Continuum Pubg Corp.; Crown Pubrs Inc.; The Cumberland Press, Inc.; Dante Univ. of America Press, Inc.; Red Dembner Enterprises Corp.; Dragon's Teeth Press; Dufour Editions, Inc.; Wm. B. Eerdmans Pubg Co.; Effective Learning, Inc.; Enslow Pubrs; Paul S. Eriksson, Pubr; Farrar, Straus & Giroux, Inc.; Franciscan Herald Press; Garber Communications, Inc.; Great Ocean Pubrs; Green Tiger Press (juvenile); Grove Press; Guernica Editions; Harian Creative Press Books; Harper & Row Pubrs, Inc.; Hazelden Foundation (technical); Hounslow Press; Howard Univ. Press (scholarly); Indiana Univ. Press; Intercultural Press, Inc. (reference); International Pubrs Co., Inc.; The International Univ. Press (textbook); Kumarian Press (textbook); Lester V. Orpen Dennys, Ltd., Pubrs; Llewellyn Pubns (reference); Mariner Pubg Co., Inc.; Mercer Univ. Press (textbook & reference); Miller Books; Mimir Pubrs, Inc.; New Century Pubrs, Inc.; New York Univ. Press (scholarly); Ohara Pubns, Inc.; Ohio State Univ. Press (scholarly); Ohio Univ. Press (scholarly); Once Upon a Planet, Inc.; Open Court Pubg Co.; Oregon State Univ. Press; Paradox Pubg Co. (self-help); Path Press, Inc. (reference); Paulist Press; The Pennsylvania State Univ. Press (scholarly); Persephone Press; Precedent Pubg, Inc. (scholarly); Prometheus Books, Inc.; Purdue Univ. Press (scholarly); Rossel Books; Ross-Erikson, Inc., Pubrs; Routledge & Kegan Paul, Ltd. (scholarly); S.C.E.-Editions L'Etincelle; Shambhala Pubns, Inc.; Sierra Club Books; Simon & Schuster; Sovereign Press; South End Press; Strawberry Hill Press; Sherwood Sugden & Co., Pubrs; Teachers College Press; The Theosophical Pubg House; Thunder's Mouth Press; Transaction Books (scholarly); Univ. of Alabama Press (scholarly); Univ. of Iowa Press (scholarly); Univ. of Massachusetts Press (scholarly); Univ. of Michigan Press (scholarly); Univ. of Notre Dame Press (scholarly); Univ. of Oklahoma Press (scholarly); Univ. of Pennsylvania Press (scholarly); Univ. of Utah Press (scholarly); Univ. Press of America (scholarly); Univ. Press of Kansas (scholarly); Univ. Press of Kentucky (scholarly); Univ. Press of Mississippi; Univ. Press of New England (scholarly); Vanguard Press, Inc.; Vesta Pubns, Ltd.; Volcano Press, Inc.; Wayne State Univ. Press (scholarly); Western Islands; Winston-Derek, Pubrs; Woodsong Graphics; The Zondervan Corp. (textbook).

Photography. Addison-Wesley Pubg Co., Inc.; Alaska Nature Press; Amphoto (technical & how-to); Angel Press/Pubrs; Art Direction Book Co. (how-to); Avon Books; Binford & Mort, Pubrs; Aristide D. Caratzas, Pubr; CLCB Press; Crown Pubrs, Inc.; Curtin & London, Inc. (how-to & technical); Delta Books; Dodd, Mead & Co.; Down East Books; The Dragonsbreath Press; Dream Garden Press; Duck Down Press; Eastview Editions, Inc.; Paul S. Eriksson, Pubr; Falcon Press Pubg Co., Inc.; Focal Press (how-to); Graphic Image Pubns; Guernica Editions; H.P. Books; H.W.H. Creative Productions, Inc.; Hancock House Pubrs Ltd.; Harian Creative Press Books; Harmony Books; Harper & Row Pubrs, Inc.; Hastings House Pubrs, Inc.; Hounslow Press; Howard Univ. Press (scholarly); Hudson Hills Press, Inc.; Krantz Co. Pubns (reference); Lancaster, Miller & Schnobrich Pubrs; Le Beacon Presse; Liberty Pubg Co., Inc.; Lightbooks (how-to); The Lowell Press, Inc.; McClelland & Stewart, Ltd.; Madrona Pubrs, Inc.; Motorbooks International Pubrs & Wholesalers, Inc.; New Century Pubrs, Inc.; Northland Press; October Press, Inc. (technical); Optimum Pubg International Inc.; Outbooks Inc. (how-to); Oxmoor House; Padre Productions; Parents Productions; Clarkson N. Potter, Inc.; A.H. & A.W. Reed Ltd.; Rossel Books; Rowman & Allenheld, Pubrs (scholarly); Charles Scribner's Sons (juvenile); Sierra Club Books; Star Pubg Co. (textbook); Sterling Pubg; Swiftwater Books; Tab Books, Inc.; Taylor Pubg Co.; Texas Monthly Press, Inc.; Univ. of Michigan Press (scholarly); Univ. of Nebraska Press (scholarly); Univ. of New Mexico Press (scholarly); Univ. of Texas Press (scholarly); Univ. Press of Mississippi; The Viking Penguin, Inc.; Watson-Guptill Pubns (how-to); Western Producer Prairie Books; Winston Books; Writer's Digest Books (how-to & reference); Yankee Books.

Picture Books. Camelot Books; Children's Press; Concordia Pubg House; E.P. Dutton; Golden Books; Harper & Row-Junior Books; Parents Magazine Press; Platt & Munk Pubrs; Prentice-Hall; Rand McNally; Frederick Warne & Co., Inc.

Plays. Avant Books; Commoners' Pubg; H.W.H. Creative Productions, Inc.; Drama Book Publishers; JH Press. Also see the Scriptwriting/Playwriting section of *Writer's Market*.

Poetry. Ahsahta Press; Avon Books; BKMK Press; Brunswick Pubg Co.; Cedarshouse Press; CLCB Press; Commoners' Pubg; Cricket Pubns; Dragon's Teeth Press; The Dragonsbreath Press; Dryad Press; Duck Down Press; Dufour Editions, Inc.; The Ecco Press; The Golden Quill Press; Graphic Image Pubns; Green Tiger Press (juvenile); Guernica Editions; Harian Creative Press Books; High/Coo Press; Houghton Mifflin Co.; Illuminati; The International Univ. Press; Lame Johnny Press; Le Beacon Presse; Lost Roads Pubrs; McClelland & Stewart, Ltd.; Marathon International Pubg Co., Inc.; Wm. Morrow Co.; Mountain State Press; Northeastern Univ. Press; Padre Productions; Persea Books; Persephone Press; Poet Gallery Press; Princeton Univ. Press; Quality Pubns, Inc.; Random House, Inc.; Resource Pubns, Inc.; St. Luke's Press; The Sunstone Press; Sylvan Press; Three Continents Press; Univ. of Arkansas Press; Univ. of Massachusetts Press (scholarly); Univ. of Missouri Press; Vanguard Press, Inc.; Vesta Pubns, Inc.; Wesleyan Univ. Press; Wingbow Press; Winston-Derek Pubrs; Woodsong Graphics.

Psychology. ABT Books; Accelerated Development, Inc. (textbook & reference); Addison-Wesley Pubg Co., Inc.; Alba House; American Press (textbook); Angel Press/Pubrs; Anna Publishing, Inc. (reference); The Aquarian Press Ltd.; Arbor House; Astro Computing Services (textbook & reference); Atheneum Pubrs; Augsburg Pubg House; Avant Books; Avon Books; B.W.M.T., Inc.; Baker Book House Co.; Basic Books, Inc.; Beacon Press; Beaufort Books, Inc.; The Bobbs-Merrill Co., Inc.; Bradson Press, Inc.; Brunswick Pubg Co.; Bucknell Univ. Press (scholarly); Cambridge Univ. Press (textbook); Celestial Arts; Chelsea House; Christian Classics; Citadel Press; CLCB Press; Cobblesmith; Congdon & Weed, Inc.; The Continuum Pubg Corp.; Coward McCann, Inc.; Crown Pubrs Inc.; Red Dembner Enterprises Corp.; Detselig Enterprises Ltd.; Dimension Books, Inc.; Dow Jones-Irwin (psychology and sociology); Dufour Editions, Inc.; Edits Pubrs (reference); Education Associates (textbook); Wm. B. Eerdmans Pubg Co.; Enslow Pubrs; Paul S. Eriksson, Pubr; ETC Pubns; Facts on File, Inc. (reference); Farrar, Straus & Giroux, Inc.; Frederick Fell Pubrs, Inc.; Flare Books (young adults); General Hall, Inc. (textbook); The Stephen Greene Press/Lewis Pubg (how-to); Grove Press; Guernica Editions; Harbor Pubg, Inc. (self-help); Harcourt Brace Jovanovich Legal & Professional Pubns, Inc. (reference); Harian Creative Press Books; Harper & Row Pubrs, Inc.; The Harvard Common Press; Hawkes Pubg Inc. (self-help); Hazelden Foundation (technical); D.C. Heath & Co. (textbook); Herald Press; Holmes & Meier Pubrs, Inc.; Houghton Mifflin Co.; Hounslow Press; Howard Univ. Press (scholarly); Humanics Ltd.; Hunter House, Inc.; Intercultural Press, Inc. (reference); International Pubrs Co., Inc.; The International Univ. Press (textbook); Jalmar Press, Inc.; Johns Hopkins Univ. Press (scholarly); Wm. Kaufman, Inc.; Kumarian Press (textbook); Learning Pubns, Inc. (reference); Libra Pubrs, Inc.; Llewellyn Pubns (reference); Longman, Inc. (textbook); McFarland & Co., Inc., Pubrs (reference); McGraw-Hill Book Co., General Div.; Madrona Pubrs, Inc.; Mariner Pubg Co., Inc.; Med-Psych Pubns (how-to); Metamorphous Press; MIT Press (scholarly); National Book Co. (textbook); New Century Pubrs, Inc.; Newcastle Pubg Co., Inc.; Once Upon a Planet, Inc.; Open Court Pubg Co.; P.A.R., Inc.; Para Research; Paradox Pubg Co. (self-help); Parents Productions; Persephone Press; Pine Mountain Press, Inc.; Pluribus Press, Inc. (how-to); Prentice-Hall, Inc.; Prometheus Books, Inc.; Purdue Univ. Press (scholarly); R&E Research Assoc.; Regnery/Gateway, Inc.; The Riverdale Co., Inc., Pubrs (textbook); Rossel Books; Ross-Erikson, Inc., Pubrs; Routledge & Kegan Paul, Ltd. (scholarly); Rowman & Allenheld, Pubrs (scholarly); S.C.E.-Editions L'Etincelle; Schenkman Pubg Co., Inc. (textbook); Shambhala Pubns, Inc.; Social Science Education Consortium, Inc. (reference); Spring Pubns, Inc. (reference); Stanford Univ. Press; Sterling Pubg; Tandem Press Pubrs; J.P. Tarcher, Inc.; The Theosophical Pubg House; Transaction Books (scholarly); Turnstone Books; Univ. of Massachusetts Press (scholarly); Univ. of Michigan Press (scholarly); Univ. of Nebraska Press (scholarly); Univ. of N. Carolina Press (scholarly); Univ. of Pennsylvania Press (scholarly); Univ. of Texas Press (scholarly); Univ. Press of America (scholarly); Univ. Press of Kansas (scholarly); Univ. Press of Mississippi; Vision House Pubrs, Inc.; Volcano Press, Inc.; J. Weston Walch Pubr (textbook);

Walker & Co.; Wayne State Univ. Press (scholarly); Wilshire Book Co.; Woodsong Graphics; Zebra Books; The Zondervan Corp. (textbook).

Recreation. Harry N. Abrams, Inc.; Addison-Wesley Pubg Co., Inc.; Alaska Nature Press; Allegheny Press (textbook); Amer. Council for the Arts (reference); Angel Press/Pubrs; Appalachian Mountain Club Books; Arbor House; M. Arman Pubg Inc. (how-to, textbook & reference); Associated Booksellers (how-to); Avon Books; Beaufort Books, Inc.; Binford & Mort Pubrs; John F. Blair, Pubr; Charles T. Branford Co.; Brigham Young Univ. Press; Celestial Arts; Chelsea House; Chicago Review Press (reference); Chronicle Books; Clarke, Irwin & Co., Ltd.; CLCB Press; Columbia Pubg Co., Inc.; Coward McCann, Inc.; Crestwood House, Inc. (juvenile); Crown Pubrs Inc.; Darwin Pubns (reference); DBI Books, Inc.; John De Graff, Inc. (how-to); Delta Books; Red Dembner Enterprises Corp.; Deneau Pubrs & Co. Ltd.; Dillon Press, Inc. (juvenile); Down East Books; The East Woods Press; Enslow Pubrs; Paul S. Eriksson, Pubr; ETC Pubns; Falcon Press Pubg Co., Inc.; Frederick Fell Pubrs, Inc.; Front Row Experience; Guy Gannett Books; The Globe Pequot Press, Inc.; Great Outdoors Pubg Co.; The Stephen Greene Press/Lewis Pubg; Guernica Editions; H.P. Books; H.W.H. Creative Productions, Inc.; Hammond, Inc.; Hancock House Pubrs Ltd.; Harian Creative Press Books; The Harvard Common Press; Harvey House Pubrs (juvenile); Hastings House Pubrs, Inc.; Hounslow Press; Icarus Press, Inc.; International Marine Pubg Co.; Johnson Books; Jonathan David Pubrs; Wm. Kaufman, Inc.; Leather Stocking Books; Le Beacon Presse; Liberty Pubg Co., Inc.; McFarland & Co., Inc., Pubrs (reference); McGraw-Hill Book Co., General Div.; Madrona Pubrs, Inc.; Mariner Pubg Co., Inc.; Mountain Press Pubg Co.; The Mountaineers Books (how-to); New Century Pubrs, Inc.; Occupational Awareness; Oregon State Univ. Press; Outbooks Inc.; Outdoor Empire Pubg Inc. (textbook); Padre Productions; Pantheon Books (reference); Parents Productions; Prentice-Hall, Inc.; Princeton Book Co., Pubrs (textbook); Ranger Assoc., Inc.; A.H. & A.W. Reed Ltd.; The Riverdale Co., Inc., Pubrs; Ross Books; Rowe Pubg Corp.; S.C.E.-Editions L'Etincelle; Charles Scribner's Sons (juvenile); Sierra Club Books; Signpost Books; Stackpole Books; Sterling Pubg; Stipes Pubg Co. (textbook); Stone Wall Press, Inc. (how-to); Stoneydale Press Pubg Co.; Tandem Press Pubrs; Taylor Pubg Co.; Ten Speed Press; Texas Monthly Press, Inc.; The Thorndike Press; TL Enterprises, Inc.; The Touchstone Press; Univ. of Michigan Press (scholarly); J. Weston Walch, Pubr (textbook); Walker & Co.; Wanderer Books (juvenile); The Westminster Press (juvenile); Wilderness Press; Wilshire Book Co.; Winchester Press (how-to); Woodbridge Press Pubg Co. (how-to); The Writing Works Division.

Reference. Allen & Unwin, Inc.; Allyn & Bacon, Inc.; B.W.M.T., Inc.; Bethany House Pubrs; Binford & Mort, Pubrs; The Borgo Press; R.R. Bowker Co.; Bradson Press, Inc.; Brunswick Pubg Co.; Arthur H. Clark Co.; Coles Pubg Co., Ltd.; Computer Skill Builders; Craftsman Book Co. of Amer.; Crown Pubrs, Inc.; Dante Univ. of America Press, Inc.; Delair Pubg Co., Inc.; Delta Books; Red Dembner Enterprises Corp.; Detselig Enterprises Ltd.; Dreadnaught; Wm. B. Eerdmans Pubg Co.; Effective Learning, Inc.; Enslow Pubrs; ETC Pubns; Fairmont Press Inc.; Frederick Fell Pubrs, Inc.; Front Row Experience; Genealogical Pubg Co., Inc.; The K.S. Giniger Co., Inc.; Great Ocean Pubrs; Greenwood Press; Guernica Editions; Gulf Pubg Co.; Hammond, Inc.; Hancock House Pubrs Ltd.; Harper & Row Pubrs, Inc.; The Harvard Common Press; Hazelden Foundation; Holmes & Meier Pubrs Inc.; Howard Univ. Press (scholarly); Hurtig Pubrs Ltd.; International Pubrs Co., Inc.; The International Univ. Press; Jonathan David Pubrs; B. Klein Pubns; Lane & Assoc., Inc.; Le Beacon Presse; Libraries Unlimited; Philip Lief & Assoc.; Loiry Pubg House; Mariner Pubg Co., Inc.; Metamorphous Press; Monitor Book Co., Inc.; National Book Co.; Thomas Nelson Pubrs; New Century Pubrs, Inc.; Octameron Assoc.; Oregon State Univ. Press; Ottenheimer Pubrs, Inc.; Oxford Univ. Press, Inc. (scholarly); Pacific Books Pubrs; Padre Productions; Parents Productions; Petrocelli Books, Inc.; Pocket Books; Prentice-Hall, Inc.; Princeton Univ. Press; R&E Research Assoc.; A.H. & A.W. Reed Ltd.; The Rosen Pubg Group (young adult); Rossel Books; S.C.E.-Editions L'Etincelle; St. Martin's Press; Scarecrow Press, Inc.; The Shoe String Press (scholarly); Slavica Pubrs, Inc.; Social Science Education Consortium, Inc.; Standard Pubg; Sterling Pubg; Taylor Pubg Co.; Texas Monthly Press, Inc.; Transaction Books (scholarly); Trend House; Universe Books; Univ. Press of New England (scholarly); Univ. Press of the Pacific, Inc. (scholarly); Vesta Pubns, Ltd.; Vision House Pubrs, Inc.; Western Producer Prairie Books; Windsor Pubns; Woodsong Graphics; World Almanac Pubns. Also see specific subject categories.

Regional. Alaska Northwest Pubg Co.; Appalachian Mountain Club Books; Apple-Wood Books, Inc.; Banyan Books, Inc.; Binford & Mort, Pubrs; Borealis Press, Ltd.; Brigham Young Univ. Press; Calif. Inst. of Public Affairs (reference); Capra Press; The Caxton Printers, Ltd.; The Chatham Press; Chronicle Books; Colorado Associated Univ. Press; Copley Books; Cordovan Press; The Corinthian Press; The Cumberland Press; The Donning Co./Pubrs, Inc.; Doubleday Canada, Ltd.; Down East Books; Dreadnaught; Dream Garden Press; The East Woods Press; The Family Album; The Filter Press; Guy Gannett Books; The Globe Pequot Press, Inc.; Golden West Books; Graphic Arts Center Pubg Co.; Gray's Pubg Ltd.; Great Outdoors Pubg Co.; The Stephen Greene Press/Lewis Pubg; Guernica Editions; Gulf Pubg Co.; Hancock House Pubrs Ltd.; Heart of the Lakes Pubg; Heritage Books, Inc.; Howell-North Books; Hurtig Pubrs.Ltd.; Indiana Univ. Press; Johns Hopkins Univ. Press (scholarly); Johnson Books; Kent State Univ. Press; Lancelot Press Ltd.; McClelland & Stewart, Ltd.; Macmillan of Canada; Memphis State Univ. Press; Mountain Press Pubg Co.; Mountain State Press; Museum of New Mexico Press (scholarly); Museum of Northern Arizona Press (reference); NC Press; New York Univ. Press (scholarly); Nimbus Pubg Ltd.; Northeastern Univ. Press; Northern Illinois Univ. Press (scholarly); Northland Press; Ohio Univ. Press; Outbooks Inc.; Oxmoor House; Pacific Books Pubrs (scholarly); The Pennsylvania State Univ. Press; Peregrine Smith, Books; The Preservation Press; Presidio Press; Press Pacifica; Pruett Pubg Co.; Rand McNally (reference); A.H. & A.W. Reed Ltd.; St. Luke's Press; Southern Methodist Univ. Press; State Historical Society of Wisconsin; Stoneydale Press Pubg Co.; The Sunstone Press; Syracuse Univ. Press; Taylor Pubg Co.; Temple Univ. Press (scholarly); Texas A&M Univ. Press (scholarly); Texas Christian Univ. Press; Texas Monthly Press, Inc.; Texas Western Press (scholarly); The Thorndike Press; Timber Press; Tompson & Rutter Inc.; Trend House; Charles E. Tuttle Co., Inc.; Univ. of Arizona Press (scholarly); Univ. of Arkansas Press; Univ. of Nevada Press; Univ. of New Mexico Press; Univ. of Tennessee Press (scholarly); Univ. of Texas Press (scholarly); Univ. of Wisconsin Press (scholarly); Univ. Press of Kansas; Univ. Press of Mississippi; Univ. Press of New England (scholarly); Utah State Univ. Press (scholarly); Westernlore Press (scholarly); Wingbow Press; The Writing Works Division; Yankee Books.

Religion. Abingdon Press; Accent Books; Aglow Pubns; Alba House; Amer. Atheist Press; Amer. Catholic Press; American Press (textbook); Angel Press/Pubrs; The Aquarian Press Ltd.; Augsburg Pubg House; Ave Maria Press; Avon Books; Baker Book House Co. (textbook); Bantam Books, Inc.; Beacon Press; Bethany House Pubrs; Don Bosco Pubns (textbook); Broadman Press; Brunswick Pubg Co.; Bucknell Univ. Press (scholarly); Byls Press; Aristide D. Caratzas, Pubr; Catholic Truth Society; Catholic Univ. of America Press (scholarly); Chelsea House; Chosen Books; Christian Classics; T&T Clark Ltd.; CLCB Press; Concordia Pubg House; David C. Cook Pubg Co.; David C. Cook Pubg Co. (juvenile); Crossway Books; Dimension Books, Inc.; The Donning Co./Pubrs, Inc.; Dufour Editions, Inc.; Wm. B. Eerdmans Pubg Co.; Effective Learning, Inc.; Fleet Press Corp.; Fortress Press; Franciscan Herald Press; The K.S. Giniger Co., Inc.; Great Ocean Pubrs; Green Baron Book & Film Co.; Green Tiger Press (juvenile); Guernica Editions; Harvest House; Here's Life Pubrs, Inc.; Hounslow Press; Howard Univ. Press (scholarly); The International Univ. Press (textbook); Judson Press; Keats Pubg, Inc.; John Knox Press; Kumarian Press (textbook); Lancelot Press Ltd.; Landmark Books; Larksdale; Life Enrichment Pubr (reference); Liguori Pubns; Llewellyn Pubns (reference); McFarland & Co., Inc., Pubrs (reference); Mariner Pubg Co., Inc.; Mercer Univ. Press (reference); Arthur Merriwether, Inc. (juvenile); Morehouse-Barlow Co., Inc.; Wm. Morrow & Co.; Mott Media, Inc., Pubrs; Nazarene Pubg House; Thomas Nelson Pubrs; New Century Pubrs, Inc.; New Leaf Press, Inc.; Newcastle Pubg Co., Inc.; Open Court Pubg Co.; Orbis Books; Our Sunday Visitor, Inc.; Paradox Pubg Co. (how-to & self-help); Paulist Press (textbook); The Pennsylvania State Univ. Press (scholarly); Persephone Press; Pickwick Pubns (scholarly); Prentice-Hall, Inc.; Princeton Univ. Press (scholarly); Prometheus Books, Inc.; Regal Books; Regnery/Gateway, Inc.; Resource Pubns, Inc.; Fleming H. Revell Co.; Review &

Herald Pubg Assoc. (juvenile); Ross Books; Rossel Books; Ross-Erikson, Inc., Pubrs; Routledge & Kegan Paul Ltd. (reference); St. Anthony Messenger Press; The Seabury Press; Servant Pubns; Shambhala Pubns, Inc.; Harold Shaw Pubrs; Sovereign Press; Standard Pubg (textbook); Sherwood Sugden & Co., Pubrs; The Theosophical Pubg House; Triumph Pubg Co.; Twenty-Third Pubns, Inc.; Tyndale House Pubrs, Inc.; Univ. of Alabama Press (scholarly); Univ. of Michigan Press (scholarly); Univ. of N. Carolina Press (scholarly); Univ. of Notre Dame Press (scholarly); Univ. Press of America (scholarly); Univ. Press of New England (scholarly); Vesta Pubns, Ltd.; Victor Books; Vision House Pubrs, Inc.; Wayne State Univ. Press (scholarly); Whitaker House (biography); Winston Press; Winston-Derek Pubrs; The Writing Works Division; The Zondervan Corp. (textbook and reference).

Scholarly. Brigham Young Univ. Press; Cambridge Univ. Press; Colorado Associated Univ. Press; Columbia Univ. Press; Dante Univ. of America Press, Inc.; Greenwood Press; Harvard Univ. Press; Indiana Univ. Press; Intervarsity Press; ISI Press; Jossey-Bass, Inc., Pubrs; Alfred A. Knopf, Inc.; McFarland & Co., Inc., Pubrs; Memphis State Univ. Press; Open Court Pubg Co.; R&E Research Assoc.; St. Martin's Press; Social Science Education Consortium, Inc.; Texas Christian Univ. Press; Twayne Pubrs; Univ. of Pittsburgh Press; Western Tanager Press. Also see specific subject categories.

Science and Technology. Harry N. Abrams; Academic Press, Inc. (scholarly); Addison-Wesley Pubg Co., Inc.; Aero Publishers, Inc.; Allen & Unwin, Inc.; Allyn & Bacon, Inc. (reference); Almar Press; Amer. Astronautical Society; American Press (textbook); Amer. Solar Energy Society (technical); And/Or Press; Artech House, Inc.; Atlantic Monthly Press; Avon Books; Ballinger Pubg Co. (reference); Bantam Books, Inc.; Biomedical Pubns (textbook & technical); The Blacksburg Group, Inc.; Cambridge Univ. Press (textbook); Carolina Biological Supply Co. (textbook); Childrens Press (juvenile); Coles Pubg Co., Ltd.; Collier MacMillan Canada, Ltd. (textbook); Columbia Univ. Press (scholarly); Computer Science Press, Inc. (general nonfiction); David C. Cook Pubg Co. (juvenile); Coward McCann, Inc.; Crown Pubrs Inc.; Steve Davis Pubg; Delmar Pubrs, Inc. (textbook); Delta Books; Red Dembner Enterprises Corp.; Dillon Press, Inc. (juvenile); Dodd, Mead & Co.; Educational Development Corp. (juvenile); Effective Learning, Inc.; Enslow Pubrs; Facts on File, Inc. (reference); Fairmont Press Inc.; Farrar, Straus & Giroux, Inc.; Warren H. Green Inc. (scholarly); Gulf Pubg Co.; H.W.H. Creative Productions, Inc.; Harper & Row Junior Books Group (juvenile); Harper & Row Pubrs, Inc.; Harvey House Pubrs (juvenile); Hayden Book Co., Inc. (reference); D.C. Heath & Co. (textbook); Heath Co. (technical & textbook); Herman Pubg; Holmes & Meier Pubrs, Inc.; Horizon Press; Howard Univ. Press (scholarly); Intergalactic Pubg Co. (how-to & textbook); Iowa State Univ. Press (textbook); Johnson Books; Wm. Kaufman Inc.; Knowledge Industry Pubns, Inc.; Krantz Co. Pubns (reference); Lane & Assoc., Inc.; Little, Brown & Co., Inc.; McGraw-Hill Book Co., General Div. (reference); McGraw-Hill Book Co., Professional & Reference Div. (reference); Charles E. Merrill Pubg Co. (textbook); MIT Press (scholarly); Museum of Northern Arizona Press (reference); National Book Co. (textbook); New Readers Press; Nichols Pubg Co. (scholarly); Noyes Data Corp. (technical); Oddo Pubg (juvenile); Ohio State Univ. Press (scholarly); Open Court Pubg Co.; Oregon State Univ. Press; Parker Pubg Co. (how-to); The Pennsylvania State Univ. Press (scholarly); Platt & Munk Pubrs (juvenile); Plenum Pubg Corp.; Prentice-Hall (juvenile); Prentice-Hall Inc.; Prometheus Books, Inc.; Purdue Univ. Press (scholarly); Regnery/Gateway, Inc.; Resource Pubns, Inc. (how-to); Reston Pubg Co. (textbook); Ross Books (how-to); Rowman & Allenheld, Pubrs (scholarly); St. Martin's Press; Howard H. Sams & Co., Inc. (technical); Scholium International, Inc.; Charles Scribner's Sons; Charles Scribner's Sons (juvenile); Shambhala Pubns, Inc.; Sheridan House, Inc. (reference); Sierra Club Books; Simon & Schuster; Sun Pubg Co.; Tab Books, Inc.; Texas Instruments Learning Center (textbook); Transaction Books (scholarly); Triumph Pubg Co.; Univelt, Inc.; Universe Books; Univ. of Arizona Press (scholarly); Univ. of California Press (scholarly); Univ. of Iowa Press (scholarly); Univ. of Michigan Press (scholarly); Univ. of Pennsylvania Press (scholarly); Univ. of Texas Press (scholarly); Univ. Press of New England (scholarly); Univ. Press of the Pacific, Inc. (scholarly); Utah State Univ. Press (scholarly); J. Weston Walch, Pubr (textbook); Walker & Co.; Webster Division (textbook); John Wiley & Sons, Inc. (reference); Yale University Press (scholarly).

Self-Help. A&W Pubg, Inc.; Addison-Wesley Pubg Co., Inc.; Aglow Pubns; Alaska Nature Press; Allen Pubg Co.; Allyn & Bacon, Inc. (reference); Amer. Baby Books; And Books; Angel Press/Pubrs; Apple Press; Arco Pubg, Inc.; Ariel Press; Asi Pubrs, Inc.; Associated Booksellers; Associated Book Pubrs, Inc.; Astro Computing Services; Augsburg Pubg House; Ave Maria Press; Avon Books; B.W.M.T., Inc.; Baker Book House Co.; Beacon Press; Beaufort Books, Inc.; The Benjamin Co., Inc.; Bethany House Pubrs; Betterway Pubns, Inc.; Biworld Pubrs, Inc. (health & medicine); The Bobbs-Merrill Co., Inc.; Bradson Press, Inc.; Charles T. Branford Co.; Brunswick Pubg Co.; Camelot Books; Carolina Biological Supply Co.; Celestial Arts; Chicago Review Press; Cliffs Notes, Inc. (textbook); Cobblesmith; Commoner's Pubg; Consumer Reports Books; Contemporary Books; The Continuum Pubg Corp.; The Corinthian Press; Coward McCann, Inc.; Crown Pubrs Inc.; Delair Pubg Co., Inc.; Delta Books; Red Dembner Enterprise Corp.; Effective Learning, Inc.; Enslow Pubrs; Paul S. Eriksson, Pubr; ETC Pubns; Exanimo Press; Facts on File, Inc. (reference); Fairmont Press Inc.; Frederick Fell Pubrs, Inc.; Flare Books (young adult); Forman Pubg; Fortress Press; C.J. Frompovich Pubns; Guy Gannett Books; The K.S. Giniger Co., Inc.; Great Ocean Pubrs; The Stephen Greene Press/Lewis Pubg (how-to); Grove Press; Gulf Pubg Co.; H.P. Books; Hancock House Pubrs Ltd.; Harcourt Brace Jovanovich Legal & Professional Pubrs, Inc.; Harper & Row Pubrs, Inc.; The Harvard Common Press; Hazelden Foundation; Here's Life Pubrs, Inc.; Herman Pubg; Houghton Mifflin Co.; Jalmar Press; Jonathan David Pubrs; Kav Books, Inc.; B. Klein Pubrs; Lane & Assoc., Inc.; Learning Pubns, Inc.; Liguori Pubns; Loiry Pubg House; Lone Star Pubrs; McGraw-Hill Book Co., General Div. (how-to); Madrona Pubrs, Inc.; Mariner Pubg Co., Inc.; Meadowbrook Press; Med-Psych Pubns; Metamorphous Press; Millcreek Press; John Muir Pubns; Nellen Pubg; New Leaf Press, Inc.; Newcastle Pubg Co., Inc.; Octameron Assoc.; Ohara Pubns, Inc.; Once Upon a Planet, Inc.; Optimum Pubg International Inc.; Outdoor Empire Pubg Inc.; Padre Productions; Paladin Press; Para Research; Parker Pubg Co.; Paulist Press; Pelican Pubg Co., Inc.; Planet Books (humor); Pluribus Press, Inc.; Clarkson N. Potter, Inc.; Precedent Pubg, Inc. (scholarly); Prentice-Hall, Inc.; Press Pacifica; Price/Stern/Sloan, Inc., Pubrs; R&E Research Assoc.; The Rosen Pubg Group (young adult); St. Martin's Press; Shambhala Pubns, Inc.; Harold Shaw Pubrs; Sterling Pubg; Strawberry Hill Press; Sun Pubg Co.; Tandem Press Pubrs; Taylor Pubg Co.; Ten Speed Press; Texas Instruments Learning Center; Thorsons Pubrs, Ltd.; Times Books; Vision House Pubrs, Inc.; Walker & Co.; The Westminster Press (juvenile); Wetherall Pubg Co.; Whitaker House (religion); Wilshire Book Co.; Woodsong Graphics; Yankee Books; Zebra Books; The Zondervan Corp.

Social Sciences. ABT Books; Academic Press, Inc. (scholarly); Apple-Wood Books, Inc.; Avant Books; Ballinger Pubg Co. (reference); Catholic Univ. of America Press (scholarly); Columbia Univ. Press (scholarly); The Continuum Pubg Corp.; Delta Books; Duquesne Univ. Press (scholarly); Edits Pubrs (reference); Evans & Co.; The Free Press (textbook & reference); Garland Pubg Inc. (reference); GMG Pubg; The Stephen Greene Press/Lewis Pubg; Groupwork Today, Inc.; Harper & Row Junior Books Group (juvenile); D.C. Heath & Co. (reference); Holmes & Meier Pubrs, Inc.; Indiana Univ. Press; Iowa State Univ. Press (textbook); Kumarian Press (scholarly); The Lewis Pubg Co.; McClelland & Stewart, Ltd.; McGraw-Hill Book Co., College Text Div. (reference); Memphis State Univ. Press; Nelson-Hall Pubrs (textbook & scholarly); Oak Tree Pubns, Inc.; Oddo Pubg Inc. (how-to); Ohio Univ. Press (scholarly); Plenum Pubg Corp.; Porter Sargent Pubrs Inc.; Pretice-Hall (juvenile); Random House, Inc. (textbook); The Riverdale Co., Inc., Pubrs (textbook); Routledge & Kegan Paul, Ltd. (scholarly); Southern Illinois Univ. Press; Transaction Books (scholarly); Turnstone Books; Twayne Pubrs; Univ. of California Press (scholarly); Univ. of Missouri Press (scholarly); Univ. of Texas Press (scholarly); Volcano Press, Inc.; J. Weston Walch, Pubr (textbook); Webster Division (textbook); The Westernlore Press (juvenile); Westview Press (scholarly); The Whitston Pubg Co. (scholarly); John Wiley & Sons, Inc. (reference); Yale University Press (scholarly).

Sociology. ABT Books; Addison-Wesley Pubg Co., Inc.; Alba House; Allyn & Bacon, Inc. (reference); Amer. Council for the Arts (reference); And Books; Angel Press/Pubrs; Apple-Wood Books, Inc.; Associated Book Pubrs Inc.; Avon Books; Basic Books, Inc.; Beacon

Press; Bradson Press, Inc.; Brunswick Pubg Co.; Bucknell Univ. Press (scholarly); Chelsea House; CLCB Press; Cobblesmith; Communications Press, Inc.; The Continuum Pubg Corp.; Coward McCann, Inc.; Detselig Enterprises Ltd.; Dow Jones-Irwin (psychology and sociology); Wm. B. Eerdmans Pubg Co.; Effective Learning, Inc.; Enslow Pubrs; Paul S. Eriksson, Pubr; ETC Pubns; Facts on File, Inc. (reference); Farrar, Straus & Giroux, Inc.; Fromm International Pubg Co.; General Hall, Inc. (textbook); Harian Creative Press Books; Harper & Row Pubrs, Inc.; The Harvard Common Press; Hazelden Foundation (technical); Herald Press; Holmes & Meier Pubrs, Inc.; Howard Univ. Press (scholarly); Humanics Ltd.; Hunter House Inc.; Inst. for the Study of Human Issues; Intercultural Press, Inc. (reference); International Pubrs Co., Inc.; The International Univ. Press (textbook); Kumarian Press (textbook); Learning Pubns, Inc. (reference); Lester & Orpen Dennys, Ltd., Pubrs; Longman, Inc. (textbook); McClelland & Stewart, Ltd.; McFarland & Co., Inc., Pubrs (reference); McGraw-Hill Book Co., General Div.; Mariner Pubg Co., Inc.; Arthur Merriwether, Inc. (juvenile); Metamorphous Press; Mimir Pubrs Inc.; New Century Pubrs, Inc.; Ohio State Univ. Press (scholarly); P.A.R., Inc.; Paradox Pubg Co. (self-help); Path Press, Inc. (reference); The Pennsylvania State Univ. Press (scholarly); Persephone Press; Prentice-Hall (juvenile); Princeton Book Co., Pubrs (textbook); Princeton Univ. Press (scholarly); Prometheus Books, Inc.; Purdue Univ. Press (scholarly); R&E Research Assoc.; A.H. & A.W. Reed Ltd.; Regnery/Gateway, Inc.; The Riverdale Co., Inc., Pubrs (textbook); Rossel Books; Rowman & Allenheld, Pubrs (scholarly); RPM Press (how-to); Rutgers Univ. Press (scholarly); S.C.E.-Editions L'Etincelle; Schenkman Pubg Co., Inc. (textbook); Schocken Books (scholarly); Scholarly Resources, Inc. (scholarly); Social Science Education Consortium, Inc. (reference); J.P. Tarcher, Inc.; Teachers College Press; Thunder's Mouth Press; Transaction Books (scholarly); Charles E. Tuttle Co., Inc.; Univ. of Massachusetts Press (scholarly); Univ. of Michigan Press (scholarly); Univ. of N. Carolina Press (scholarly); Univ. of Notre Dame Press (scholarly); Univ. Press of Mississippi; Univ. Press of New England (scholarly); Volcano Press, Inc.; J. Weston Walch, Pubr (textbook); Wayne State Univ. Press (scholarly); Wingbow Press (reference); The Zondervan Corp. (textbook).

Sports. Addison-Wesley Pubg Co., Inc.; Allyn & Bacon, Inc. (reference); Almar Press; American Press (textbook); Anderson Pubg Co. (textbook); Anna Pubg, Inc. (reference); Appalachian Mountain Club Books; Arbor House; Arco Pubg, Inc. (how-to); M. Arman Pubg, Inc. (how-to, textbook & reference); Associated Booksellers; Atheneum Pubrs; Athletic Press; Avon Books; A.S. Barnes & Co., Inc.; Barron's Educational Series, Inc.; The Benjamin Co., Inc.; Binford & Mort, Pubrs; The Bobbs-Merrill Co., Inc.; Don Bosco Pubns; Bradson Press, Inc.; Briarcliff Press Pubrs; Champion Athlete Pubg Co. (textbook); Chelsea House; Clarke, Irwin & Co., Ltd.; CLCB Press; Coles Pubg Co., Ltd.; Columbia Univ. Press (scholarly); Contemporary Books (how-to); David C. Cook Pubg Co. (juvenile); Coward McCann, Inc.; Crestwood House, Inc. (juvenile); Crown Pubrs Inc.; DBI Books, Inc.; Delta Books; The Devin-Adair Co.; Inc.; Dodd-Mead & Co.; Educational Development Corp. (juvenile); Enslow Pubrs; Paul S. Eriksson, Pubr; ETC Pubns; Falcon Press Pubg Co., Inc.; Frederick Fell Pubrs, Inc.; Fleet Press Corp.; The K.S. Giniger Co., Inc.; Green Hill Pubrs; The Stephen Greene Press/Lewis Pubg; Grove Press; Hammond, Inc.; Hancock House Pubrs Ltd.; Harper & Row Junior Books Group (juvenile); Harper & Row Pubrs, Inc.; The Harvard Common Press; Hastings House Pubrs, Inc.; Howard Univ. Press (scholarly); Carl Hungness Pubg; Icarus Press, Inc.; The International Univ. Press (textbook); The Interstate Printers & Pubrs, Inc. (textbook); Johnson Books; Jonathan David Pubrs; Wm. Kaufman, Inc.; Lancelot Press Ltd.; Laranmark Press; Liberty Pubg Co., Inc.; Little, Brown & Co., Inc.; Lone Star Pubrs; McFarland & Co., Inc., Pubrs (reference); Mariner Pubg Co., Inc.; Mosaic Press; Motorbooks International Pubrs & Wholesalers, Inc.; Mountain Press Pubg Co. (how-to); The Mountaineers Books (how-to); New Century Pubrs, Inc.; Ohio State Univ. Press (scholarly); Optimum Pubg International Inc.; Outbooks Inc.; Outdoor Pubg Inc. (textbook); Outdoor Life Books; Path Press, Inc. (reference); Petersen Pubg Co. (how-to); Pluribus Press, Inc.; Prentice-Hall (juvenile); Prentice-Hall, Inc.; Ranger Assoc., Inc.; A.H. & A.W. Reed Ltd.; Rowe Pubg Corp.; S.C.E.-Editions L'Etincelle; Sail Books (how-to); Charles Scribner's Sons (juvenile); Sierra Club Books; Sterling Pubg; Stone Wall Press, Inc. (how-to); Swiftwater Books (reference); Tandem Press Pubrs; J.P. Tarcher, Inc.; Taylor Pubg Co.; Ten Speed Press; Texas Monthly Press, Inc.; Times Books; The Touchstone Press; Ultralight Pubns,

Inc.; Univ. of Nebraska Press (scholarly); The Univ. of Tennessee Press (scholarly); J. Weston Walch, Pubr (textbook); Walker & Co.; Wilshire Book Co.; Winchester Press.

Stage and Film. Atlantic Monthly Press; A.S. Barnes & Co., Inc.; The Borgo Press; Bradson Press, Inc.; Citadel Press; Columbia Pubg Co., Inc.; Communications Press, Inc.; Drama Book Pubrs (reference); Indiana Univ. Press; JH Press; Lake View Press; Law-Arts Pubrs (textbook); McFarland & Co., Inc., Pubrs (reference); McPherson & Co.; Poet Gallery Press; Rosen Publishing Group (reference); Scarecrow Press, Inc.; Schirmer Books; Sterling Pubg; Tab Books, Inc.; Taplinger Pubg, Co., Inc.; Twayne Pubrs; Univ. of Tennessee Press (scholarly); Wesleyan Univ. Press (scholarly).

Technical. Allen & Unwin, Inc.; Allyn & Bacon, Inc.; Almar Press; Bradson Press, Inc.; Brevet Press, Inc.; Brunswick Pubg Co.; Carolina Biological Supply Co.; Chilton Book Co.; Computer Skill Builders; The Corinthian Press; Craftsman Book Co. of America; Effective Learning, Inc.; Enslow Pubrs; Environmental Design & Research Center; Essco; ETC Pubns; Fairmont Press, Inc.; Great Ocean Pubrs; H.P. Books; D.C. Heath & Co. (reference); Intergalactic Pubg Co.; The International Univ. Press; Iowa State Univ. Press (textbook); Lane & Assoc. Inc.; Le Beacon Presse; Mariner Pubg Co., Inc.; Metamorphous Press; Mountain Press Pubg Co.; Oregon State Univ. Press; P.A.R., Inc.; Petrocelli Books, Inc.; Plenum Pubg Corp.; R&R Newkirk; The Riverdale Co., Inc., Pubrs; Rowman & Allenheld, Pubrs (scholarly); RPM Press (how-to); Schenkman Pubg Co., Inc.; Taylor Pubg Co.; Texas Instruments Learning Center; TL Enterprises, Inc.; Univ. of Michigan Press (scholarly); Univ. Press of New England (scholarly); Univ. Press of the Pacific, Inc. (scholarly); Westin Communications.

Textbook. Abingdon Press; Alba House; Allen & Unwin, Inc.; Augsburg Pubg House; Ave Maria Press; Barron's Educational Series, Inc.; William C. Brown Co., Pubrs; Brunswick Pubg Co.; Career Pubg Inc.; Computer Skill Builders; May Davenport Pubrs; Detselig Enterprises Ltd.; Dufour Editions, Inc.; Wm. B. Eerdmans Pubg Co.; Effective Learning, Inc.; Essco; ETC Pubns; Ginn & Co.; Graphic Image Pubns; Gregg Division; Guernica Editions; Holmes & Meier Pubrs Inc.; International Pubrs Co., Inc.; Wm. Kaufman, Inc.; Lane & Assoc., Inc.; Learning Endeavors; Libraries Unlimited; Loiry Pubg House; Lone Star Pubrs, Inc.; McClelland & Stewart, Ltd.; McGraw-Hill Book Co., College Text Book Div.; Mariner Pubg Co., Inc.; Charles E. Merrill Pubg Co.; Metamorphous Press; Mimir Pubrs, Inc.; Mott Media, Inc., Pubrs; Mountain Press Pubg Co.; National Book Co.; Occupational Awareness; P.A.R., Inc.; Pacific Books, Pubrs; Petrocelli Books, Inc.; Potentials Development for Health & Aging Services; Prometheus Books, Inc.; Pruett Pubg Co.; R&E Research, Assoc.; Regents Pubg Co., Inc.; The Rosen Pubg Group (young adult); Rowman & Allenheld, Pubrs (scholarly); Silver Burdett; Slavica Pubrs, Inc.; Taylor Pubg Co.; Trend House; Univ. of Michigan Press (scholarly); Univ. Press of New England (scholarly); Univ. Press of the Pacific, Inc. (scholarly); John Wiley & Sons, Inc. Also see specific subject categories.

Transportation. Aero Pubrs, Inc.; Amer. Astronautical Society; Auto Book Press (technical); Aviation Book Co. (technical); Aztex Corp. (how-to & history); Darwin Pubns (reference); John De Graff, Inc. (how-to); Golden West Books; H.P. Books; Howell-North Books; International Marine Pubg Co.; Kalmbach Pubg Co. (reference); MIT Press (scholarly); Motorbooks International Pubrs & Wholesalers, Inc.; John Muir Pubns (how-to); The Nautical & Aviation Pubg Co. of America, Inc.; Outdoor Empire Pubg Inc.; Petersen Pubg Co. (how-to); Pruett Pubg Co.; Ross Books; Scholium International, Inc.; Tab Books, Inc.; Ultralight Pubns, Inc.

Travel. Academy Chicago; Alaska Northwest Pubg Co.; Allegheny Press (reference); Almar Press; Amer. Council for the Arts (reference); And/Or Press; M. Arman Pubg, Inc. (how-to, textbook & reference); Binford & Mort, Pubrs; Briarcliff Press Pubrs; Brunswick Pubg Co.; Camaro Pubg Co.; Aristide D. Caratzas, Pubr; Cedarshouse Press; China Books; Clarke, Irwin & Co., Ltd.; CLCB Press; Cobblesmith; Congdon & Weed, Inc.; The Corinthian Press; Darwin Pubns (reference); Delair Pubg Co., Inc.; Deneau Pubrs & Co. Ltd.; The Devin-Adair Co., Inc.;

Dodd-Mead & Co.; The East Woods Press; Educational Development Corp. (juvenile); Effective Learning, Inc.; Paul S. Eriksson, Pubr; Facts on File, Inc. (reference); Falcon Press Pubg Co., Inc.; Fjord Press; Fodor's Travel Guides; Guy Gannett Books; The K.S. Giniger Co., Inc.; The Globe Pequot Press, Inc.; Graphic Image Pubns; H.W.H. Creative Productions, Inc.; Hammond, Inc.; Hancock House Pubrs Ltd.; Harian Creative Press Books; Harper & Row Pubrs, Inc.; The Harvard Common Press; Hastings House Pubrs, Inc.; Hounslow Press; Icarus Press, Inc.; Intercultural Press, Inc. (reference); Lancelot Press Ltd.; Le Beacon Presse; Liberty Pubg Co., Inc.; The Lowell Press, Inc.; Madrona Pubrs, Inc.; Meadowbrook Press; Mosaic Press; John Muir Pubrs; National Pubrs of the Black Hills, Inc.; New Century Pubrs, Inc.; New York Zoetrope, Inc.; Nimbus Pubg Ltd.; 101 Productions; Optimum Pubg International Inc.; Outbooks Inc.; Padre Productions; Parents Productions; Pelican Pubg Co., Inc.; Pilot Books (reference); Prentice-Hall, Inc.; Rand McNally (reference); Ranger Assoc., Inc.; A.H. & A.W. Reed Ltd.; Regnery/Gateway, Inc.; The Riverdale Co., Inc., Pubrs; Rossel Books; Rowe Pubg Corp.; S.C.E.-Editions L'Etincelle; Sierra Club Books; Slavica Pubrs, Inc.; Sleepy Hollow Press; Stoneydale Press Pubg Co.; Ten Speed Press; Texas Monthly Press, Inc.; TL Enterprises, Inc.; The Touchstone Press; Tree by the River Pubg; Trend House; Univ. of Michigan Press; Walker & Co.; Winston-Derek Pubrs; The Writing Works Division; Yankee Books.

Women's Studies/Feminism. A&W Pubg, Inc.; ABC-Clio, Inc. (reference); Alyson Pubns, Inc.; And Books; Bantam Books, Inc.; Beacon Press; Contemporary Books; Delair Pubg Co., Inc.; The Feminist Press; Indiana Univ. Press; International Pubrs Co., Inc.; Lake View Press; Lane & Assoc., Inc.; Northeastern Univ. Press (reference); Pantheon Books; The Pennsylvania State Univ. Press (scholarly); Persephone Press; Press Pacifica; Rutgers Univ. Press (scholarly); Scarecrow Press, Inc.; South End Press; Susann Pubns Inc. (self-help); Thorsons Pubrs Ltd.; Thunder's Mouth Press; Twayne Pubrs (scholarly); Volcano Press, Inc.·

World Affairs. ABC-Clio, Inc. (reference); ABT Books; And Books; Atlantic Monthly Press; Avant Books; B.W.M.T., Inc.; Ballinger Pubg Co. (reference); Beacon Press; Calif. Inst. of Public Affairs (reference); China Books; The Family Album; Intercultural Press, Inc. (how-to); Kumarian Press (reference); Lake View Press; Manyland Books, Inc.; NC Press; Nichols Pubg Co. (scholarly); Open Court Pubg Co.; Orbis Books; Pantheon Books; Regnery/Gateway, Inc.; Routledge & Kegan Paul, Ltd. (scholarly); Rowman & Allenheld, Pubrs (scholarly); Southern Illinois Univ. Press; Stanford Univ. Press; Strawberry Hill Press; Univ. of Notre Dame Press (scholarly); Univ. of Utah Press (scholarly); Westview Press (scholarly).

Young Adult. Dell Pubg Co., Inc.; Graphic Image Pubns; Harper & Row Junior Books; Holiday House; Lodestar Books; Rosen Pubg Group (textbooks); Tempo Books; Frederick Warne & Co., Inc. Also see specific subject categories.

Fiction

Use this subject index to identify book publishers either devoted completely to fiction or publishing fiction in addition to their nonfiction lines. Notice parenthetical phrases (following publishers' names) that offer more information about the kind of fiction manuscripts (juvenile, young adult, etc.) accepted.

As with the nonfiction markets, be sure to read the complete editorial listing. In addition to telling you exactly what they like to see in fiction manuscripts, editors often include tips and advice for writers interested in submitting material to them. For a comprehensive list of fiction publishers, consult *Fiction Writer's Market* (Writer's Digest Books).

Adventure. Alaska Nature Press; Angel Press/Pubrs; Arbor House; M. Arman Pubg, Inc.; Avon Books; Baker Book House Co. (juvenile); Beaufort Books; The Berkley Pubg Group;

Bradbury Press, Inc. (young adult); Brunswick Pubg Co.; Camelot Books; Charter Books; Clarion Books (juvenile); Clarke, Irwin & Co., Ltd.; CLCB Press; Coward McCann, Inc.; Crestwood House, Inc. (juvenile); Cricket Pubns (juvenile); May Davenport, Pubrs; Dell Pubg Co., Inc.; Red Dembner Enterprises Corp.; The Dragonsbreath Press; Dream Garden Press; Farrar, Straus & Giroux, Inc. (juvenile and young adult); Fjord Press; Flare Books (young adult); Green Baron Book & Film Co. (young adult); Green Tiger Press; Harper & Row Junior Books (juvenile); Harper & Row Pubrs, Inc. (juvenile); Herald Press (juvenile); Hounslow Press; Laranmark Press; Le Beacon Presse; Lodestar Books (juvenile); Lothrop, Lee & Shepard Books (juvenile); Miller Books; The Mountaineers Books; New Readers Press; Path Press, Inc.; The Perfection Form Co. (young adult); Persephone Press; Pinnacle Books; Printemps Books, Inc. (young adult); Quality Pubns, Inc.; Rossel Books (juvenile); Russica Pubrs, Inc.; Scholastic-Tab Pubns (juvenile); Charles Scribner's Sons (juvenile); Seven Seas Press; Sierra Club Books; Tandem Press Pubrs; Texas Monthly Press, Inc.; Vanguard Press, Inc.; Wanderer Books; The Westminster Press (juvenile); Wingbow Press; Woodsong Graphics; Zebra Books.

Confession. Angel Press/Pubrs; CLCB Press; Dufour Editions, Inc.; H.W.H. Creative Productions, Inc.; Path Press, Inc.; Persephone Press; Tandem Press Pubrs; Wingbow Press; Zebra Books.

Erotica. Angel Press/Pubrs; Brunswick Pubg Co.; The Dragonsbreath Press; Gay Sunshine Press; Graphic Image Pubns; Greenleaf Classics, Inc.; Guernica Editions; Le Beacon Presse; Llewellyn Pubns; Lost Roads Pubrs; Persephone Press; Quality Pubns, Inc.; Russica Pubrs, Inc.; Swiftwater Books; Thunder's Mouth Press; Wingbow Press; Zebra Books.

Ethnic. BKMK Press; B.W.M.T., Inc.; Bilingual Educational Services, Inc. (juvenile); Borealis Press, Ltd.; Brunswick Pubg Co.; CLCB Press; May Davenport, Pubrs; Dufour Editions, Inc.; Fil-Am-Bel Pubrs, Inc.; Flare Books (young adult); Gay Sunshine Press; Guernica Editions; H.W.H. Creative Productions, Inc.; Le Beacon Presse; Lost Roads Pubrs; McClelland & Stewart, Ltd.; Path Press, Inc.; Persephone Press; Printemps Books, Inc. (young adult); Rossel Books (juvenile); Russica Pubrs, Inc.; Texas Monthly Press, Inc.; Thunder's Mouth Press; Winston-Derek Pubrs.

Experimental. Avant Books; BKMK Press; CLCB Press; The Dragonsbreath Press; Dream Garden Press; Dufour Editions, Inc.; The Ecco Press; Flare Books (young adult); Gay Sunshine Press; Green Tiger Press (juvenile); H.W.H. Creative Productions; Howard University Press; Le Beacon Presse; Lost Roads Pubrs; Perivale Press; Persea Books; Persephone Press; Thunder's Mouth Press; Vanguard Press, Inc.; Woodsong Graphics.

Fantasy. Ace Science Fiction; Angel Press/Pubrs; Avon Books; Ballantine Books; Bantam Books Inc.; Camelot Books; Clarion Books (juvenile); CLCB Press; Cricket Pubns (juvenile); Crossway Books; May Davenport, Pubrs; Daw Books, Inc.; The Dragonsbreath Press; Dream Garden Press; Dufour Editions, Inc.; Farrar, Straus & Giroux, Inc. (juvenile); Fjord Press; Flare Books (young adult); Graphic Image Pubns; Green Baron Book & Film Co.; Green Tiger Press (juvenile); H.W.H. Creative Productions, Inc.; Harper & Row Junior Books (juvenile); Harper & Row Pubrs, Inc.; The International Univ. Press; Lodestar Books (juvenile); Lothrop, Lee & Shepard Books (juvenile); Padre Productions; Persephone Press; Polaris Press; Printemps Books, Inc. (young adult); Rosebrier Pubg Co. (juvenile); Scholastic-Tab Pubns (juvenile); Charles Scribner's Sons (juvenile); Tandem Press Pubrs; Tor Books; Wingbow Press; Woodsong Graphics.

Feminist. The Crossing Press; Dufour Editions, Inc.

Gay/Lesbian. Alyson Pubns, Inc.; Gay Sunshine Press; JH Press; The Naiad Press, Inc.; Persephone Press.

Gothic. Avalon Books; Avon Books; Bethany House Pubrs; Thomas Bouregy & Co., Inc.; Charter Books; CLCB Press; Green Baron Book & Film Co.; Harper & Row Pubrs, Inc.; The

International Univ. Press; Prentice-Hall (juvenile); Scholastic, Inc. (young adult); Woodsong Graphics; Zebra Books.

Historical. Alaska Nature Press; Avon Books; B.W.M.T., Inc.; Ballantine Books; The Berkley Pubg Group; Brunswick Pubg Co.; Clarke, Irwin & Co., Ltd.; CLCB Press; David C. Cook Pubg Co.; Dell Pubg Co., Inc.; Red Dembner Enterprises Corp.; Denlinger's Pubrs Ltd.; Dream Garden Press; Dufour Editions, Inc.; Eakin Press (juvenile and young adult); Farrar, Straus & Giroux, Inc. (juvenile); Fjord Press; Fromm International Pubg Co.; Gay Sunshine Press; Green Baron Book & Film Co.; Guernica Editions; Harper & Row Pubrs, Inc.; Herald Press; Houghton Mifflin Co.; The International Univ. Press; Lame Johnny Press; Laranmark Press; Le Beacon Presse; Lothrop, Lee & Shepard Books (juvenile); Miller Books; Path Press, Inc.; Persea Books; Persephone Press; Pinnacle Books; The Publishing Ward, Inc.; Rossel Books (juvenile); Charles Scribner's Sons (juvenile); Sierra Club Books; Sovereign Press; Tandem Press Pubrs; Texas Monthly Press, Inc.; Thunder's Mouth Press; Wingbow Press; Woodsong Graphics; Zebra Books.

Horror. The Dragonsbreath Press; Dream Garden Press; The International Univ. Press; Laranmark Press; Le Beacon Presse; Lodestar Books (young adult); Russica Pubrs, Inc.; Seven Seas Press; Tor Books; Zebra Books.

Humor. Angel Press/Pubrs; Bradbury Press, Inc. (young adult); Bradson Press, Inc.; Brunswick Pubg Co.; Camelot Books; Carolrhoda Books, Inc. (juvenile); Clarion Books (juvenile); Clarke, Irwin & Co., Ltd.; CLCB Press; David C. Cook Pubg, Co. (juvenile); Cricket Pubns (juvenile); May Davenport, Pubrs; Down East Books; The Dragonsbreath Press; Dufour Editions, Inc.; Farrar, Straus & Giroux, Inc. (juvenile); Flare Books (young adult); Fromm International Pubg, Co.; Green Baron Book & Film Co.; H.W.H. Creative Productions, Inc.; Hounslow Press; The International Univ. Press; Laranmark Press; Le Beacon Presse; Philip Lief & Assoc.; Lothrop, Lee & Shepard Books (juvenile); Miller Books; The Mountaineers Books; Parents Magazine Press (juvenile); Path Press, Inc.; The Perfection Form Co. (young adult); Persephone Press; Prentice-Hall (juvenile); Pressworks, Inc.; Printemps Books, Inc. (young adult); The Publishing Ward, Inc.; Russica Pubrs, Inc.; Scholastic-Tab Pubns (juvenile); Charles Scribner's Sons (juvenile); The Thorndike Press; Thunder's Mouth Press; Vanguard Press, Inc.; Wanderer Books; The Westminster Press (juvenile); Zebra Books.

Juvenile. Abingdon Press; Bantam Books, Inc.; John F. Blair, Pubr; Bradbury Press, Inc.; Clarke, Irwin & Co., Ltd.; Coward, McCann & Geoghegan; Crossway Books; Down East Books; E.P. Dutton; The Feminist Press; Graphic Image Pubns; Green Baron Book & Film Co.; H.W.H. Creative Productions, Inc.; Holiday House; Houghton Mifflin Co.; Ideals Pubg, Corp.; Margaret K. McElderry Books; Macmillan Pubg Co., Inc.; Modern Curriculum Press; Morrow Junior Books; Oak Tree Pubns, Inc.; Padre Productions; Philomel Books; Platt & Munk Pubrs; Printemps Books, Inc.; Victor Books; Frederick Warne & Co., Inc.

Literary. Beaufort Books, Inc.; Columbia Pubg Co., Inc.; Creative Arts Book Co.; Deneau Pubrs & Co. Ltd.; Doubleday Canada, Ltd.; The Ecco Press; Great Ocean Pubrs; Harper & Row Pubrs, Inc.; Alfred A. Knopf, Inc.; Little, Brown & Co., Inc.; Lynx House Press; Taplinger Pubg Co., Inc.; Thunder's Mouth Press.

Mainstream/Contemporary. A&W Pub., Inc.; Angel Press/Pubrs; Avon Books; BKMK Press; Bahamas International Pubg Co., Ltd.; The Berkley Pubg Group; John F. Blair, Pubr; George Braziller, Inc.; Brunswick Pubg Co.; Camelot Books; Charter Books; Clarke, Irwin & Co., Ltd.; CLCB Press; Coward McCann, Inc.; Crossway Books; Dell Pubg Co., Inc.; Delta Books; Red Dembner Enterprises Corp.; The Dial Press; Dillon Press, Inc. (juvenile); Doubleday Canada, Ltd.; Duck Down Press (post-modern); Dufour Editions, Inc.; The Ecco Press; Evans & Co.; Farrar, Straus & Giroux, Inc. (juvenile); Fjord Press; Flare Books (young adult); Forman Pubg; Fromm International Pubg Co.; Grove Press; H.W.H. Creative Productions Inc.; Harian Creative Press Books; Harmony Books; Harper & Row Junior Books (juvenile); Harper & Row Pubrs, Inc.; Houghton Mifflin Co.; Hounslow Press; Howard Univ. Press; Icarus Press; The International Univ. Press; Kav Books, Inc.; Laranmark Press; Lester & Orpen Dennys, Ltd., Pubrs; Little, Brown & Co., Inc.; Lost Roads Pubrs; McClelland & Stewart, Ltd.; McGraw-Hill Book Co.; Maclay & Assoc., Inc.; Wm. Morrow & Co.; W.W. Norton Co., Inc.; Padre Productions; Pelican Pubg Co., Inc.; Perivale Press; Persea Books; Prentice-Hall (juvenile); Quality Pubns, Inc.; Random House, Inc.; Scholastic-Tab Pubns (juvenile); Charles Scribner's Sons; Charles Scribner's Sons (juvenile); Sierra Club Books; Simon & Schuster; The Smith; Stein & Day Pubrs; Summit Books; Tandem Press Pubrs; Texas Monthly Press, Inc.; Thorndike Press (nostalgia); The Univ. of Arkansas Press; The Viking Penguin, Inc.; Wingbow Press; Woodsong Graphics; Zebra Books.

Military. Bantam Books, Inc.; Dell Pubg Co., Inc.; The Nautical & Aviation Pubg Co. of America, Inc.

Mystery. Academy Chicago; Avalon Books; Avon Books; Bantam Books, Inc.; Camelot Books; Carolrhoda Books, Inc. (juvenile); Charter Books; Clarion Books (juvenile); CLCB Press; Coward McCann, Inc.; May Davenport, Pubrs; Red Dembner Enterprises Corp.; Dillon Press, Inc. (juvenile); Dodd-Mead & Co.; Doubleday & Co., Inc.; Down East Books; The Dragonsbreath Press; Dream Garden Press; Farrar, Straus & Giroux, Inc. (young adult); Flare Books (young adult); Gay Sunshine Press; Green Baron Book & Film Co.; Guernica Editions; Harper & Row Pubrs, Inc.; Houghton Mifflin Co.; The International Univ. Press; Kav Books, Inc.; Laranmark Press; Le Beacon Presse; Lester & Orpen Dennys, Ltd., Pubrs; Llewellyn Pubns; Lodestar Books (young adult); Lothrop, Lee & Shepard Books (juvenile); Miller Books; New Readers Press; Pantheon Books; Path Press, Inc.; Persephone Press; Pocket Books; Prentice-Hall (juvenile); Printemps Books, Inc. (young adult); Russica Pubrs, Inc.; Scholastic-Tab Pubns (juvenile); Charles Scribner's Sons (juvenile); Seven Seas Press; SOS Pubns; Tandem Press Pubrs; Texas Monthly Press, Inc.; The Thorndike Press; Vanguard Press, Inc.; Wanderer Books; The Westminster Press (juvenile); Wingbow Press; Woodsong Graphics.

Occult. The Berkley Pubg Group; Dell Pubg Co., Inc.; Llewellyn Pubns; Tor Books.

Regional. Mountain State Press; St. Luke's Press; The Thorndike Press.

Religious. Aglow Pubns; Angel Press/Pubrs; Avon Books; Baker Book House Co. (juvenile); Don Bosco Pubns; Broadman Press; Byls Press (juvenile); CLCB Press; Concordia Pubg House; David C. Cook Pubg Co.; David C. Cook Pubg Co. (juvenile); Green Baron Book & Film Co.; Herald Press; Mott Media, Inc., Pubrs; Resource Pubns, Inc.; Fleming H. Revell Co.; Standard Pubg; Tandem Press Pubrs; Tyndale House Pubrs, Inc.; Victor Books; Winston-Derek Pubrs; The Zondervan Corp.

Romance. Alaska Nature Press; Arbor House; Avalon Books; Avon Books; Ballantine Books; The Berkley Pubg Group; Bethany House Pubrs (young adult); Thomas Bouregy & Co., Inc.; Brunswick Pubg Co.; Charter Books; CLCB Press; David C. Cook Pubg Co. (young adult); Coward McCann, Inc.; Dell Pubg Co., Inc.; Dodd-Mead & Co.; Dufour Editions, Inc.; Farrar, Straus & Giroux, Inc. (young adult); Flare Books (young adult); Graphic Image Pubrs; Green Baron Book & Film Co.; H.W.H. Creative Productions, Inc.; Harlequin Books; Harper & Row Pubrs, Inc.; Holloway House Pubg Co.; The International Univ. Press; New Readers Press; Persephone Press; Pinnacle Books; Pocket Books; Scholastic, Inc. (young adult); Scholastic-Tab Pubns (young adult); Second Chance At Love; Seven Seas Press; Silhouette Books (young adult); SOS Publications; Tandem Press Pubrs; Woodsong Graphics; Zebra Books.

Science Fiction. Ace Science Fiction; Arbor House; Avon Books; Ballantine Books; Bantam Books, Inc.; The Berkley Pubg Group; Camelot Books; Carolrhoda Books, Inc. (juvenile); Charter Books; Clarion Books (juvenile); CLCB Press; David C. Cook Pubg Co.; Crestwood House, Inc. (juvenile); Crossway Books; Daw Books, Inc.; Dillon Press, Inc.

(juvenile); The Donning Co./Pubrs, Inc.; Doubleday & Co., Inc.; The Dragonsbreath Press; Dream Garden Press; Farrar, Straus & Giroux, Inc. (young adult); Fjord Press; Flare Books (young adult); Gay Sunshine Press; Green Baron Book & Film Co.; Guernica Editions; H.W.H. Creative Productions, Inc.; Harper & Row Junior Books (juvenile); Harper & Row Pubrs, Inc.; Houghton Mifflin Co.; The International Univ. Press; Laranmark Press; Le Beacon Presse; Llewellyn Pubns; Lodestar Books (young adult); Lothrop, Lee & Shepard Books (juvenile); Persephone Press; Pinnacle Books; Pocket Books; Polaris Press; The Publishing Ward, Inc.; Scholastic-Tab Pubns (juvenile); Charles Scribner's Sons (juvenile); Sierra Club Books; Swiftwater Books; Thunder's Mouth Press; Tor Books; Wanderer Books; The Westminster Press (juvenile); Wingbow Press; Woodsong Graphics.

Spiritual. Commoners' Pubg; Doubleday Canada, Ltd.; Dream Garden Press; Garber Communications, Inc.; Island Press; The Sunstone Press.

Sports. Bantam Books, Inc.; David C. Cook Pubg Co. (juvenile); Crestwood House, Inc. (juvenile); The Perfection Form Co. (young adult).

Suspense. Alaska Nature Press; Avon Books; The Berkley Pubg Group; Camelot Books; Charter Books; Clarion Books (juvenile); Coward, McCann, Inc.; May Davenport, Pubrs; Dell Pubg Co., Inc.; Red Dembner Enterprises Corp.; Farrar, Straus & Giroux, Inc. (young adult); Fjord Press; Flare Books (young adult); Fromm International Pubg Co.; Green Baron Book & Film Co.; Guernica Editions; H.W.H. Creative Productions, Inc.; Harper & Row Pubrs, Inc.; Houghton Mifflin Co.; The International Univ. Press; Le Beacon Presse; Lester & Orpen Dennys, Ltd., Pubrs; Llewellyn Pubns; Lodestar Books (young adult); Lothrop, Lee & Shepard Books (juvenile); Printemps Books, Inc. (young adult); Russica Pubrs, Inc.; Scholastic-Tab Pubns (juvenile); Charles Scribner's Sons (juvenile); Seven Seas Press; SOS Pubns; Tandem Press Pubrs; Texas Monthly Press, Inc.; Vanguard Press, Inc.; The Westminster Press (juvenile); Wingbow Press; Winston-Derek Pubrs; Woodsong Graphics; Zebra Books.

Western. Avalon Books; Avon Books; Bantam Books, Inc.; The Berkley Pubg Group; Thomas Bouregy & Co., Inc.; Charter Books; Dream Garden Press; Farrar, Straus & Giroux, Inc. (young adult); Green Baron Book & Film Co.; Harper & Row Pubrs, Inc.; The International Univ. Press; Laranmark Press; Lodestar Books (young adult); Miller Books; Pinnacle Books; Pocket Books; Quality Pubns, Inc.; Texas Monthly Press, Inc.; Woodsong Graphics.

Young Adult. Bantam Books, Inc.; The Berkley Pubg Group; Crossway Books; Harper & Row Junior Books Group; Holiday House; Margaret K. McElderry Books; Philomel Books; Pitman Learning; Tempo Books; Frederick Warne & Co., Inc.

Company Publications

One of the ways employers promote cohesion within the ranks of their staff is through a company newsletter, magazine or bulletin. A company publication is a fringe benefit. But as a nicety and not a necessity, it is often vulnerable to budget cuts and belt tightening. Quite a few company publications listed in the 1983 *Writer's Market* are not included in this edition. Twenty-five percent of last year's entries were "killed" for any of these reasons: they are no longer being published; they have become one-person operations and cannot handle any freelance material; they have temporarily ceased publication but plan to return with a new format when their funding returns; they have reduced page count or frequency to the point where they have a backlog of unused freelance material.

Even though the freelance opportunities in house organs have changed, the rules for getting published in them remain the same. Reading the market listings is essential because the direction, depth and thrust of each publication are unique. Some are very specific and are read in-house by employees—they keep workers abreast of company policies and events. Others broaden their audience to include stockholders in search of pertinent financial information. Still others are promotional tools written and edited for customers. Some resemble trade journals because of their technical style and approach. Finally, company publications may be directed at sales reps who want selling techniques, or dealers who are interested in hearing from the manufacturers of the products they sell.

Whatever the particular slant of the company publication, manuscripts must have a strong company tie-in. They must pivot on the products or services the firm offers. Editors of these magazines are looking for new twists and angles for presenting material to their well-defined audiences. Another important point to remember about submitting material to these markets is that photos are generally a plus.

For a name and address list of over 3,000 company magazines and other house organs consult Volume 5 of *Working Press of the Nation* (Automated Marketing Systems, National Research Bureau, 310 S. Michigan Ave., Chicago IL 60604) available in most large public libraries.

ADVANCES FOR MEDICINE, Hewlett-Packard Medical Products Group, 100 5th Ave., Waltham MA 02254. (617)890-6300. Editor: Carol Lasky. Magazine published 5 times/year for medical professionals—physicians, nurses, biotechnicians, hospital administrators covering Hewlett-Packard's wide range of products and services, with an international emphasis. Circ. 120,000. Pays on acceptance. Buys one-time rights or makes work-for-hire assignments. Simultaneous queries, and simultaneous, photocopied, and previously published submissions OK. SASE. Reports in 5 weeks. Free sample copy.
Nonfiction: Book excerpts; expose; interview/profile; new product releases; personal experience (of medical professionals); technical (application stories must feature Hewlett-Packard instrumentation). Buys 7 mss/year. Query with clips of published work or send complete ms. Length: 300-2,500 words. Pays $100 minimum.
Photos: Steve Cahill, photo editor. State availability of photos or send photos with ms. Reviews contact sheets. Captions, model release, and identification of subjects required.
Tips: "Submit articles with a human tone on how a specific procedure/HP product has changed (made more efficient, accurate) medical care—stress *unique* applications. Start with a case study of a patient problem, introduce the potential solution, spice with quotations by physicians, show how the problem is solved and an advancement has been realized—include technological information."

BAROID NEWS BULLETIN, Box 1675, Houston TX 77251. Editor-in-Chief: Jennifer Daigle. 50% freelance written. Emphasizes the petroleum industry for a cross-section of ages, education and interests, although most readers are employed by the energy industries. Quarterly magazine; 36 pages. Circ. 20,000. Pays on acceptance. Buys first North American serial rights. Byline given. Submit seasonal/holiday material 1 year in advance. Computer printout and disk submissions OK; prefers letter quality to dot matrix printouts. SASE. Reports in 5 weeks. Free sample copy and writer's guidelines.
Nonfiction: General interest and historical. No travel articles or poetry. Buys 12 mss/year. Complete ms preferred. Length: 1,000-3,000 words. Pays 8-10¢/word.

Photos: "Photos may be used in the publication, or as reference for illustration art." Submit b&w prints. No additional payment for photos accepted with ms. Captions preferred. Buys first North American serial rights.
Tips: Manuscripts accompanied by good quality photos or illustrations stand a much better chance of acceptance.

BARTER COMMUNIQUE, Full Circle Marketing Corp., Box 2527, Sarasota FL 33578. (813)349-3300. Editor-in-Chief: Robert J. Murely. Emphasizes bartering for radio and TV station owners, cable TV, newspaper and magazine publishers and select travel and advertising agency presidents. Semiannual tabloid; 48 pages. Circ. 50,000. Pays on publication. Rights purchased vary with author and material. Phone queries OK. Simultaneous, photocopied and previously published submissions OK. Computer printout and disk submissions OK. SASE. Reports in 4 weeks. Free sample copy and writer's guidelines.
Nonfiction: Articles on "barter" (trading products, goods and services, primarily travel and advertising). Length: 1,000 words. "Would like to see travel mss on southeast US and the Bahamas, and unique articles on media of all kinds. Include photos where applicable. No mss on barter for products, goods and services—primarily travel and media—but also excess inventory of business to business." Pays $30-50.
Tips: "Computer installation will improve our ability to communicate."

BRISTOL-MYERS NEW YORK, 345 Park Ave., New York NY 10154. (212)546-4000. Editor: Arlene Elzweig. Emphasizes consumer and pharmaceutical products for employees. Monthly magazine. Circ. 2,000. Pays on publication. Buys first rights. Simultaneous and photocopied submissions OK. SASE. Reports in 3 weeks. Free sample copy.
Nonfiction: Company news, employee news, job safety, new products, photo features and profiles. "Company tie-in essential. We emphasize stories that help employees understand the company and its operations better." Buys less than 1 ms/issue. Query. Length: 350-750 words. Pays $100-300.

‡**CALLIGRANEWS, The Calligrafree Company's Newsletter**, Box 96, Brookville OH 45309. (513)833-5677. Editor: A. Lincoln. Bimonthly newsletter covering calligraphy for teachers and professionals. "We introduce new books and tools and announce important events. We also use the 4-page insert to deal with one specific 'how to' theme in calligraphy. The insert is '. . . Talk', i.e., 'Brushtalk,' 'Pentalk,' 'Papertalk,' etc. The series is planned for 26 individual issues (or inserts), but will be expanded." Circ. 5,000+. Pays on acceptance. Byline given. Buys all rights. Submit seasonal/holiday material 3 months in advance. Simultaneous queries and photocopied submissions OK. Computer printout submissions and floppy disk for Apple computers OK. SASE. Reports in 1 month. Sample copy for SAE and 1 first class stamp; free writer's guidelines.
Nonfiction: How-to, inspirational, interview/profile, new product, opinion, personal experience, photo feature—all related to calligraphy. Also needs b&w catalog cover ideas. "No personal write-ups slanted toward free advertising for author." Query with clips. Length: 500-2,500 words. Pays $50-150.
Photos: Send photos with ms. Pays $5-25/5x7 b&w prints. Captions, model release and identification of subjects required. Buys all rights.
Tips: "Study the subject thoroughly—research in library titles helps. The readers are teachers and professionals and know their trade. Best area for freelancers is in coverage of the numerous exhibits and shows each year in most cities. Also, reports on successful teachers of calligraphy. How To Do It is needed, especially in high tech areas—as in computer calligraphy. Will probably expand size and scope to include handwriting in elementary schools."

CATERPILLAR WORLD, Caterpillar Tractor Co., 100 NE Adams AB1D, Peoria IL 61629. (309)675-4724. Editor: Tod Watts. 10% freelance written. Emphasizes "anything of interest about Caterpillar people, plants, or products. The magazine is distributed to 100,000 Caterpillar people and friends worldwide. It's printed in French and English. Readers' ages, interests and education vary all over the map." Quarterly magazine; 24-32 pages. Pays on acceptance. Byline given. Computer printout and disk submissions OK. First submission is always on speculation. Free sample copy.
Nonfiction: "Everything should have a Caterpillar tie. It doesn't have to be strong, but it has to be there. How-to (buy one piece of equipment and become a millionaire, etc.); general interest (anything that may be of interest to Cat people worldwide); humor (it's hard to find something humorous yet interesting to an international audience; we'd like to see it, however); interview (with any appropriate person: contractor, operator, legislator, etc.); new product (large projects using Cat equipment; must have human interest); personal experience (would be interesting to hear from an equipment operator/writer); photo feature (on anything of interest to Cat people; should feature people as well as product); and profile (of Cat equipment users, etc.). Prints occasional lifestyle and health articles (but must apply to international audience). Written approval by the subjects of the article is a must." Query. Length: "Whatever the story is worth."
Photos: "The only articles we accept without photos are those obviously illustrated by artwork." State availability of photos in query. Captions and model release required.
Tips: "Best way to get story ideas is to stop in at local Cat dealers and ask about big sales, events, etc."

‡**COMPASS**, Marine Office of America Corporation (MOAC), 180 Maiden Lane, New York NY 10038. (212)440-7718. Editor: Ms. Patricia Phillips. Semiannual magazine of the Marine Office of America Corporation covering insurance. Magazine is distributed world wide to persons in marine (agents, brokers, risk managers) insurance and the media. Circ. 25,000. Pays half on acceptance, half on publication. Byline given. Offers $250 kill fee. Not copyrighted. Buys all rights and makes work-for-hire assignments. Simultaneous queries, and simultaneous, photocopied, and previously published submissions OK. Reports in 2 weeks on queries; 4 weeks on mss. Free sample copy and writer's guidelines.
Nonfiction: Arthur Domingo, articles editor. (212)564-4065. General interest, historical/nostalgic, technical. "Historical/nostalgia should relate to ships, trains, airplanes, balloons, bridges, sea and land expeditions, seaports, and transportation of all types. General interest includes marine and transportation subjects; fishing industry; and environmental events—improvements relating to inland waterways, space travel, satellites. Articles must have human interest. Technical articles may cover energy exploration and development—offshore oil and gas drilling, developing new sources of electric power and solar energy; usages of coal, water, wind to generate electric power; special cargo handling such as containerization on land and sea. Articles must not be overly technical and should have reader interest." No book excerpts, exposes, how-to, humor or opinion. Buys 14 mss/year. Query with or without published clips. Length: 1,500-2,000 words. Pays $1,000 maximum.
Photos: Robert A. Cooney, photo editor. (212)838-6200. State availability of photos. Reviews b&w and color transparencies and prints. Captions and identification of subjects required. Buys one-time rights.
Tips: "Send a brief outline of the story idea to articles editor mentioning also the availability of photographs in b&w and color. All articles must be thoroughly researched and original. Articles should have human interest through the device of interviews."

THE COMPASS, Mobil Sales and Supply Corp., 150 E. 42nd St., New York NY 10017. Editor-in-Chief: R. Gordon MacKenzie. 60% freelance written. Emphasizes marine or maritime activities for the major international deep sea shipowners and ship operators who are Mobil's marine customers. 40 pages. Circ. 20,000. Pays on acceptance. Buys one-time rights. Byline given. Simultaneous, photocopied and previously published submissions OK. SASE. Reports in 2 weeks. Free sample copy.
Nonfiction: Marine material only. General interest, historical, nostalgia, new product, personal experience and technical. No travelogues. Query or submit complete ms. Length: 2,000-4,000 words. Pays $125-250.
Photos: Purchased with accompanying ms. Submit 5x7 or larger b&w prints or 35mm color transparencies. Offers no additional payment for photos accepted with ms. Captions preferred. Buys one-time rights. Model release required.

CORRESPONDENT, Aid Association for Lutherans, Appleton WI 54919. (414)734-5721. Editor: Linda J. Peterson. Emphasizes fraternal insurance for Lutherans and their families. Quarterly magazine. Circ. 800,000. Pays on publication. Buys one-time rights. Simultaneous and photocopied submissions OK. SASE. Reports in 1 month. Free sample copy.
Nonfiction: Profiles of Lutherans doing unusual jobs. Company tie-in essential. Buys 2-3 mss/year. Rarely uses submitted mss. Query. Length: 500-1,500 words. Pays 10¢/word.
Photos: Pays $5 for b&w glossy prints; $10 for color prints or slides.

CORVETTE NEWS, c/o GM Photographic, 3001 Van Dyke, Warren MI 48090. Managing Editor: Becky Bodnar. For Corvette owners worldwide. Quarterly magazine. Circ. 75,000. Buys all rights. Pays on acceptance. Free sample copy and editorial guidelines. Query. Computer printout submissions OK; prefers letter quality to dot matrix. SASE.
Nonfiction: "Articles must be of interest to this audience. Subjects considered include: (1) Technical articles dealing with restorations, engines, paint, body work, suspension, parts searches, etc. (2) Competition, 'Vettes vs. 'Vettes, or 'Vettes vs. others. (3) Profiles of Corvette owners/drivers. (4) General interest articles, such as the unusual history of a particular early model Corvette, and perhaps its restoration; one owner's do-it-yourself engine repair procedures, maintenance procedures; Corvettes in unusual service; hobbies involving Corvettes; sports involving Corvettes. (5) Celebrity owner profiles. (6) Special Corvette events such as races, drags, rallies, concourse, gymkhanas, slaloms. (7) Travel, in USA or abroad, via Corvette. (8) Corvette club activities. We're willing to consider articles on Corvette owner lifestyles. This could include pieces not only about the mechanically-minded (who own Corvettes) but also about the fashion-conscious and people seeking the active good life. No articles negative to cars in general and Corvette in particular or articles not connected, in some way, to Corvette. Send an approximately 100-word prospectus on the proposed article and add a statement about how you are prepared to supplement it with drawings or photographs." Length: 1,200-3,600 words. Pays $150 minimum.
Photos: Color transparencies required. Offers no additional payment for photos accepted with ms.
Tips: "We are always looking for new ideas, new writing approaches. However, unless the writer has a solid knowledge about the car—either owns one, has driven one, or comes in contact with people who do own the car—the input is of little value."

CREDITHRIFTALK, CREDITHRIFT Financial, Box 59, Evansville IN 47701. (812)464-6638. Editor-in-Chief: Gregory E. Thomas. Emphasizes consumer finance. All readers are employees of CREDITHRIFT Financial or one of its financial or insurance subsidiaries, age range 18-65, with most in the 25-45 bracket. Most are high school graduates with one year of college, interested in company advancement. Monthly magazine; 12-16 pages. Circ. 3,000. Pays on acceptance. Not copyrighted. Pays 100% kill fee. Byline given only if requested. Submit seasonal/holiday material 5 months in advance of issue date. Simultaneous, photocopied and previously published submissions OK. Reports in 2 weeks. Free sample copy for SASE.
Nonfiction: Interview (must be with company employee; subject need not be limited to consumer finance and could center on employee's personal experience, hobby, volunteer work, etc.); personal opinion; photo feature (employee engaged in a unique activity); profile (employee); and finance industry trends. Query. Length: 800-3,000 words. Pays $50 minimum.
Photos: State availability of photos. Pays $15 minimum/b&w photo; submit contact sheet. Captions preferred. Buys one-time rights. Model release required "in some cases where a non-employee is included in the photo."

THE ENERGY PEOPLE, PSE&G, 80 Park Plaza, 4A, Newark NJ 07101. (201)430-5989. Editor: Eugene Murphy. For employees. Quarterly magazine. Circ. 19,000. Pays on acceptance. Not copyrighted. Simultaneous, photocopied and previously published submissions OK. SASE. Reports in 3 weeks. Free sample copy.
Nonfiction: Company news, employee news and humor (industry-related). Company tie-in preferred. Buys 3 mss/year. Query with clips of published work. Pays $75-200.

THE FLYING A, Aeroquip Corp., 300 S. East Ave., Jackson MI 49203. (517)787-8121. Editor-in-Chief: Wayne D. Thomas. 10% freelance written. Emphasizes Aeroquip customers and products. Quarterly magazine; 24 pages. Circ. 30,000. Pays on acceptance. Buys first rights. Simultaneous submissions OK. No computer printouts or disk submissions. Reports in 1 month.
Nonfiction: General interest (feature stories with emphasis on free enterprise, business-related or historical articles with broad appeal, human interest.) "An Aeroquip tie-in in a human interest story is helpful." No jokes, no sample copies; no cartoons, no short fillers. Buys 3-4 mss/issue. Query with biographic sketch and clips of published work. Length: not to exceed five typewritten pages. Pays $50 minimum.
Photos: "Photos are by specific story assignment only."
Fillers: Human interest nonfiction. Pays $50 minimum for a two-page article. No personal anecdotes, recipes or fiction. "Suggest the writer contact editor by letter with proposed story outline."
Tips: "We publish a marketing-oriented magazine as opposed to an employee publication. Despite our title, we are *not* an aviation magazine."

FRIENDLY EXCHANGE, Webb Company, 1999 Shepard Rd., St. Paul MN 55116. (612)690-7383. Editor: Adele Malott. Quarterly magazine "designed to encourage the sharing or exchange of ideas, information and fun among its readers, for young, traditional families between the ages of 19 and 39 who live in the western half of the United States." Estab. 1981. Circ. 4.5 million. Pays on acceptance. Offers 25% kill fee. Buys first North American serial rights and non-exclusive reprint rights for use in other Webb publications. Submit seasonal/holiday material 9 months in advance. Simultaneous queries and photocopied submissions OK. SASE. Reports in 8 weeks. Sample copy free for 9x12 SASE and 98¢ postage; writer's guidelines free for business-size SAE and 1 first class stamp.
Nonfiction: General interest (family activities, sports and outdoors, consumer topics, personal finance); historical/nostalgic (heritage and culture); how-to (decorate and garden); travel (domestic); and lifestyle. "Whenever possible, a story should be told through the experiences of actual people or families in such a way that our readers will want to share experiences they have had with similar activities or interests. No product publicity material." Buys 10 unsolicited mss/year. Query. Length: 1,000-2,500 words. Pays $300-700/article.
Photos: Contact: *Friendly Exchange* Art Director, Webb Company. Send photos with ms. Pays $150-400 for 35mm color transparencies; and $75 for 8x10 b&w prints. Pays on publication.
Columns/Departments: All columns and departments rely on reader-generated ideas, recipes, household hints, etc. Study articles from November 1981 and August 1982 "The Storytellers" and "Candy Lightner's Campaign" as models.

FRIENDS MAGAZINE, Ceco Publishing Co., 30400 Van Dyke Blvd., Warren MI 48093. (313)575-9400. Editor: Bill Gray. 75% freelance written. "The only common bond our audience shares is they own Chevrolets." Monthly magazine; 32 pages. Circ. 2,000,000. Pays on acceptance. Rights vary. Submit seasonal/holi-

---

day material 6 months in advance. Simultaneous and photocopied submissions OK. SASE. Reports in 4 weeks. Free sample copy and writer's guidelines.

Nonfiction: General interest (lifestyle); historical (when story has contemporary parallel); humor (any subject, but rarely accept first person); travel (only with a strong hook); and photo feature (strong photo essays that say something about American lifestyle). "We're looking for freelancers who can spot lifestyle trends with national impact. We're looking for fresh ideas. We'd like to break national feature stories."

Photos: State availability of photos. Pays $50 for b&w contact sheets and $75 for 35mm color transparencies. Captions and model releases required.

GEMCO COURIER, A Publication for Members of America's Finest Membership Department Stores, Lucky Stores, Inc., 6565 Knott Ave., Box 5001, Buena Park CA 90622. Articles Editor: Robyn McGee. Monthly advertising supplement used to promote Gemco merchandise. Circ. 5.5 million. Pays on acceptance. Buys first North America serial rights. Photocopied submissions OK. Computer printout and disk submissions OK. SASE. Reports in 6 weeks. Sample copy for 9x12 SASE; writer's guidelines for business-size SASE.

Nonfiction: General interest, how-to, interviews/profiles. "In addition, each month we run a number of features that emphasize ways our members can improve their homes and skills, and lower their cost of living. Articles receiving the best response in the past have been self-help, family-oriented, and general interest features. Many of our articles feature items carried in our stores. The best way a freelancer can begin writing for us is to familiarize himself/herself with our merchandise, either by 'shopping' our stores or through back issues of the *Courier*." No biography, humor, historical, personal experiences, anecdotes, trivia, poetry, fiction, first-person narratives, or articles of a religious/political/controversial nature. Length: 225-1,000 words. Query. Pays $75-400.

‡GO GREYHOUND, The Greyhound Corp., Greyhound Tower - 1810, Phoenix AZ 85077. (602)248-5714. Editor: Donald L. Behnke. Quarterly in-house publication for Greyhound shareholders, employees and other interested individuals. Circ. 200,000. Pays on acceptance. No byline given. Buys one-time rights. Submit seasonal/holiday material 9 months in advance. Simultaneous queries and simultaneous and photocopied submissions OK. Reports in 3 months. Free sample copy and writer's guidelines.

Nonfiction: Mary Jo Orkild, publications assistant. Travel (to places reached by Greyhound bus). "We review features about historic, scenic or entertainment attractions that can be reached by Greyhound bus." No personal experience stories. Buys 4 mss/year. Query or send complete ms. Length: 500-800 words. Pays $350 maximum with color pictures.

Photos: Mary Jo Orkild, publications assistant. "Articles must be accompanied by a minimum of 12 good quality color transparencies from which we may choose to illustrate the story." Payment included with purchase of ms. Reviews 35mm and larger color transparencies and 5x7 color prints.

Tips: "Follow our writer's guidelines. We must see accompanying transparencies and we require excellent color pictures to accompany travel stories. Will only review stories with pictures—professional quality. Articles submitted without required transparencies will not be considered. Do not send personal experience travel on bus."

INLAND, The Magazine of the Middle West, Inland Steel Co., 30 W. Monroe St., Chicago IL 60603. (312)346-0300. Managing Editor: Sheldon A. Mix. Emphasizes steel products, services and company personnel. Quarterly magazine; 24 pages. Circ. 12,000. Pays on acceptance. Buys one-time rights. Kill fee: "We have always paid the full fee on articles that have been killed." Byline given. Submit seasonal/holiday material at least a year in advance. Simultaneous submissions OK. Computer printout and disk submissions OK; prefers letter quality to dot matrix printouts. SASE. Reports in 6-8 weeks. Free sample copy.

Nonfiction: Articles, essays, humorous commentaries and pictorial essays. "We encourage individuality. Half of each issue deals with staff-written steel subjects; half with widely ranging nonsteel matter. Articles and essays related somehow to the Midwest (Illinois, Wisconsin, Minnesota, Michigan, Missouri, Iowa, Nebraska, Kansas, North Dakota, South Dakota, Indiana and Ohio) in such subject areas as history, folklore, sports, humor, the seasons, current scene generally; nostalgia and reminiscence if well done and appeal are broad enough. But subject is less important than treatment. We like perceptive, thoughtful writing, and fresh ideas and approaches. Please don't send slight, rehashed historical pieces or any articles of purely local interest." Personal experience, profile, humor, historical, think articles, personal opinion and photo essays. No "nostalgia that is merely sentimental and superficial and that doesn't move the reader, or rehashes of historical personalities and highlights." Buys 10-15 unsolicited mss/year. Length: 1,200-5,000 words. Payment depends on individual assignment or unsolicited submission.

Photos: Purchased with or without mss. Captions required. "Payment for pictorial essay same as for text feature."

Tips: "Our publication particularly needs humor that is neither threadbare nor in questionable taste, and shorter pieces (800-1,500 words) in which word-choice and wit are especially important. A writer who knows our needs and believes in himself should keep trying." Recent published material: "The Emancipation of Mary

Todd Lincoln'' (history, No. 1, 1983) and ''The City of Big Shoulders Is Sweet on Modern Sculpture'' (Chicago sculpture, Special Issue combining Nos. 3-4, 1982).

THE LEADING EDGE, of exploration, Society of Exploration Geophysicists, Box 3098, Tulsa OK 74101. Editor: Theodore Barrington. Assistant Editor: Robert Dean Clark. Monthly magazine covering the ''successes, failures, aspirations, frustrations of earth scientists plus general interest—as broad as *Harper's*, *Atlantic Monthly*, et al.'' Estab. 1982. Circ. 50,000. Pays on publication. Byline given. Offers $100 kill fee. Submit seasonal/holiday material 2 months in advance. Simultaneous queries OK. SASE. Reports in 2 weeks on queries; 6 weeks on mss.
Nonfiction: General interest, historical/nostalgic, satire, opinion. No whimsy, pornography, how-to. Buys 10-15 mss/year. Send complete ms. Length: 500-5,000 words. Pays $50-1,500.
Fiction: Fantasy, mainstream. Buys 10 mss/year. Send complete ms. Length: 1,000-5,000 words. Pays $50-1,500.
Poetry: Serious and light verse, traditional and free. ''Only criterion is excellence of writing.'' Buys 10-15 poems/year. Submit maximum 6 poems. Length: 4-50 lines. Pays $10-500.
Fillers: Jokes, anecdotes, short humor. Buys 100-200/year. Length: 25-250 lines. Pays $5-50.

MARATHON WORLD, Marathon Oil Co., 539 S. Main St., Findlay OH 45840. (419)422-2121. Editor-in-Chief: Norman V. Richards. 20% freelance written. Emphasizes petroleum/energy for educators, legislators, government officials, libraries, community leaders, students and employees. Quarterly magazine; 24 pages. Circ. 45,000. Pays on acceptance. Buys first North American serial rights. Pays 20% kill fee. Byline given on contents page, not with article. Photocopied submissions OK. SASE. Reports in 3 weeks. Free sample copy and writer's guidelines.
Nonfiction: Informational features. Especially needs ''articles on subjects to help readers live better, handle problems (economic, social, personal, medical) more effectively, and generally get more out of life. We like articles on self-awareness, science, cultural events, outdoor sports and activities, and Americana in areas where Marathon operates (primarily Midwest). No articles promoting travel by car. No local sights or festivals; subjects should have broader geographic base. Freelancers should not attempt to sell articles on Marathon or oil industry operations; these are staff written.'' Buys 1-2 mss/issue. Query. Length: 800-1,500 words. Pays $800-1,200.
Photos: Photos generally not purchased with accompanying ms. Art director makes assignments to professional photographers. Pay negotiable.
Tips: ''Because of the special nature of the *World* as a corporate external publication and the special limits imposed on content, the best approach is through initial query. Include as many details as possible in a 1-2 page letter.''

MORE BUSINESS, 11 Wimbledon Court, Jerico NY 11753. Editor: Trudy Settel. ''We sell publications material to business for consumer use (incentives, communication, public relations)—look for book ideas and manuscripts.'' Monthly magazine. Circ. 10,000. Pays on acceptance. Buys all rights. SASE. Reports in 1 month.
Nonfiction: General interest, how-to, vocational techniques, nostalgia, photo feature, profile and travel. Buys 10-20 mss/year. Word length varies with article. Payment negotiable. Query. Pays $4,000-7,000 for book mss.

THE PRESS, The Greater Buffalo Press, Inc., 302 Grote St., Buffalo NY 14207. Managing Editor: Mary Lou Vogt. Quarterly tabloid for advertising executives at Sunday newspapers, ad agencies, retail chains and cartoonists who create the Sunday funnies. Circ. 4,000. Pays on acceptance. Buys all rights. Photocopied submissions and previously published submissions OK. No computer printout or disk submissions. SASE. Reports in 4 weeks. Sample copy 50¢; free writer's guidelines.
Nonfiction: Short biographies of people in advertising, retailing, business, or unusual occupations. No travel/leisure or personal experience articles. Back issues sent upon written request. Buys 4-6 mss/issue. Query. Length: 800-1,500 words. Pays $100-125.
Photos: State availability of photos (with ms only). Uses 35mm transparencies or larger (color preferred). Offers no additional payment for photos accepted with ms. Captions optional. Photos are usually returned after publication. ''We do not accept photographs or artwork unless they accompany a ms.''

RAYTHEON MAGAZINE, Raytheon Company, 141 Spring St., Lexington MA 02173. (617)862-6600, ext. 2415. Editor-in-Chief: Robert P. Suarez. Quarterly magazine for Raytheon stockholders, employees, customers, suppliers, plant city officials, libraries, interested persons. ''Ours is a company publication that strives to avoid sounding like a company publication. All stories must involve some aspect of Raytheon or its products.'' Estab. 1981. Circ. 200,000. Pays on acceptance. Byline given. Free sample copy.
Nonfiction: General interest, humor, interview/profile, new product, nostalgia, photo feature, technical and travel. ''This is a corporate publication designed to illustrate the breadth of Raytheon Company in a low-key manner through six general-interest articles per issue. Photos are used liberally, top quality and exclusively col-

or. Stories are by assignment only." Buys 5 mss/issue. Query with clips of published work, stating specialties, credentials and other publication credits. Length: 800-1,000 words. Pays $750-1,000/article.
Tips: "Submit resume and magazine-style writing samples. We are looking for established writers who are capable of crisp, interesting magazine journalism. We are not looking to promote Raytheon, but rather to inform our audience about the company, very subtly. Heavy marketing-style or house organ writing is of no interest to us."

ROSEBURG WOODSMAN, Roseburg Lumber Co., c/o Hugh Dwight Advertising, Suite 101, 4908 SW Griffith Dr., Beaverton OR 97005. Editor: Shirley P. Rogers. Monthly magazine for wholesale and retail lumber dealers and other buyers of forest products, such as furniture manufacturers. Emphasis on wood products, including company products. Publishes a special Christmas issue. Circ. 8,000. Buys all rights. No byline given. Buys approximately 15-20 mss/year. Pays on publication. Free sample copy and writer's guidelines. No photocopied or simultaneous submissions; no computer printout or disk submissions. Submit seasonal material 6 months in advance. Reports in 1 week.
Nonfiction: Features on the "residential, commercial and industrial applications of wood products, such as lumber plywood, prefinished wall paneling, and particleboard, particularly Roseburg Lumber Co. products. We look for unique or unusual uses of wood and stories on hobbyists and craftsmen. No 'clever,' 'wise' or witty contributions unless they tell a fascinating story and are well-illustrated. No fillers, isolated photos or inadequately illustrated articles." Query or submit complete ms. Length: 250-500 words. Pays $50-$100.
Photos: "Photos are essential. Good pictures will sell us on a story. B&w photos immediately relegate a story to secondary position." Prefers 120 color transparencies but 35mm is acceptable. Pays $25-$50/color transparency or color-corrected print; more for cover photo. Pays $10-$15/b&w glossy print purchased with ms.
Tips: "I sometimes hire a freelancer 'on assignment' at a higher rate. Send letter specifying experience, publications, types of stories and geographic area covered. We have an absolute need for good, striking, interesting photos."

RURALITE, Box 557, Forest Grove OR 97116. (503)357-2105. Editor: Ken Dollinger. Monthly magazine primarily slanted toward small town and rural families, served by consumer-owned electric utilities in Washington, Oregon, Idaho, Nevada and Alaska. "Ours is an old-fashioned down-home publication, with something for all members of the family." Circ. 203,000. Buys first North American rights. Byline given. Pays on acceptance. Submit seasonal material at least 3 months in advance. Computer printout submissions OK. Query. SASE. Sample copies $1; guidelines for SASE.
Nonfiction: Walter J. Wentz, nonfiction editor. Primarily human-interest stories about rural or small-town folk, preferably living in areas (Northwest states and Alaska) served by Rural Electric Cooperatives. Articles emphasize self-reliance, overcoming of obstacles, cooperative effort, hard or interesting work, unusual or interesting avocations, odd or unusual hobbies or histories, public spirit or service, humor. Will also consider how-to, advice for rural folk, little-known and interesting Northwest history, people or events. "Looking specifically for energy (sources, use, conservation) slant and items relating to rural electric cooperatives." No "sentimental nostalgia or subjects outside the Pacific Northwest; nothing racy." Buys 15-20 mss/year. Length: 500-1,500 words. Pays $30-100, depending upon length, quality, appropriateness and interest, number and quality of photos.
Photos: Reviews b&w negatives with contact sheets. Offers no additional payment for photos accepted with ms.

SEVENTY SIX MAGAZINE, Box 7600, Los Angeles CA 90051. Editor: Sergio Ortiz. Bimonthly publication of the Union Oil Company for employees, retirees, elected officials and community leaders. Not copyrighted. Buys 5-6 mss/year. Pays on acceptance. Free sample copy. Reports "as soon as possible." SASE.
Nonfiction: Buys informational, profile, historical articles about the petroleum industry, Union Oil Company, or Union Oil's employees or retirees. No articles about service stations or dealers. No travel features. "Please query first." Pays 20¢/word minimum.
Photos: Only 2¼x2¼ color transparencies purchased with mss for extra payment. Captions required.

SMALL WORLD, Volkswagen of America, 888 W. Big Beaver Rd. Box 3951, Troy MI 48099. Editor: Ed Rabinowitz. Magazine published 5 times/year for Volkswagen owners in the United States. Circ. 300,000. Buys all rights. Byline given. Buys 10-12 mss/year. Pays on acceptance. Free writer's guidelines. Computer printout and disk submissions OK. Reports in 6 weeks. SASE.
Nonfiction: "Interesting stories on people using Volkswagens; useful owner modifications of the vehicle; travel pieces with the emphasis on people, not places; Volkswagenmania stories, personality pieces, inspirational and true adventure articles. VW arts and crafts, etc. The style should be light. All stories must have a VW tie-in, preferably with a new generation VW model, i.e., Rabbit, Pickup, Scirocco, Jetta, Vanagon or Quantum. Our approach is subtle, however, and we try to avoid obvious product puffery, since *Small World* is not an advertising medium. We prefer a first-person, people-oriented handling. No basic travelogues; articles on older VWs; stay away from Beetle stories. With all story ideas, please query first. All unsolicited manuscripts will

be returned unopened. Though queries should be no longer than 2 pages, they ought to include a working title, a short, general summary of the article, and an outline of the specific points to be covered. We strongly advise writers to read at least 2 past issues before working on a story." Length: 1,500 words maximum; shorter pieces, some as short as 450 words, often receive closer attention." Pays $100 per printed page for photographs and text; otherwise, a portion of that amount, depending on the space allotted. Most stories go 2 pages; some run 3 or 4.

Photos: Submit photo samples with query. Photos purchased with ms; captions required. "We prefer color transparencies, 35mm or larger. All photos should carry the photographer's name and address. If the photographer is not the author, both names should appear on the first page of the text. Where possible, we would like a selection of at least 40 transparencies. It is recommended that at least one show the principal character or author; another, all or a recognizable portion of a VW in the locale of the story. Quality photography can often sell a story that might be otherwise rejected. Every picture should be identified or explained." Model releases required. Pays $250 maximum for front cover photo.

Fillers: "Short, humorous anecdotes about Volkswagens." Pays $15.

Tips: "Style of the publication and its content are being structured toward more upscale, affluent buyer. VW drivers are not the same as those who used to drive the Beetle."

SUNSHINE SERVICE NEWS, Florida Power & Light Co., Box 529100, Miami FL 33152. (305)552-4895 or 3523. Editor: Derek Davis. Monthly employee newspaper for the electrical utility industry. Circ. 13,500. Pays on publication. Not copyrighted. Reports in 2 weeks. Free sample copy.

Nonfiction: Company news, employee news, general interest, historical, how-to, humor and job safety. Company tie-in preferred. Query. Pays $25-100.

TIME BREAK, AMF Geo Space Corp., Box 36374, Houston TX 77036. (713)666-1611. Editor: Lee C. Dominey. Quarterly (March, June, September, December). "The purpose of *Time Break* is to inform 'friends and customers' about new products and applications plus trends and items of interest in the geophysical exploration field. It includes technical and semitechnical articles." Circ. 4,000. Pays on acceptance. Buys all rights. Byline given. Submit seasonal/holiday material 3 months in advance of issue date. Simultaneous and previously published submissions OK. SASE. Reports in 1 month. Free sample copy.

Nonfiction: "All articles need to be related to seismic exploration." General interest (to people engaged in seismic exploration); historical; interview; and nostalgia. Query. Length: 500-5,000 words. Pays $50-250.

Photos: "Hopefully, *all* articles in the magazine have photos." State availability of photos. Pays $10-50 for b&w photos. Captions preferred. Buys all rights. Model release required.

Tips: "Some knowledge of the seismic exploration industry is a *must*. Magazine is now published quarterly, but is smaller in size than previously."

WDS FORUM, Writer's Digest School, 9933 Alliance Rd., Cincinnati OH 45242. (513)984-0717. Editor: Kirk Polking. Bimonthly magazine covering writing techniques and marketing for students of courses in fiction and nonfiction writing offered by Writer's Digest School. Circ. 5,000. Pays on acceptance. Buys one-time rights. Pays 25% kill fee. Byline given. Phone queries OK. Submit seasonal/holiday material 3 months in advance of issue date. Simultaneous, photocopied and previously published submissions OK. SASE. Reports in 3 weeks. Free sample copy.

Nonfiction: How-to (write or market short stories, articles, novels, poetry, etc.); and interviews (with well-known authors of short stories, novels and books). Buys 10 mss/year. Query. Length: 500-1,500 words. Pays $10-30.

Photos: Pays $5 for 8x10 b&w prints of well-known writers to accompany mss. Captions required. Buys one-time rights.

Consumer Publications

To have ideas is paradise, to work them out
is hell.
—Maurice Maeterlinck

The working out of ideas often results in sheer delight on both sides of a manuscript. "There's nothing more exhilarating," says a senior editor at a national general interest magazine, "than getting a good manuscript—one that really works and is right for you."

Consider that statement an open invitation for quality manuscripts from the editorial community listed in the consumer magazine section of *Writer's Market*. Quality is the watchword; because with more people than ever taking pencil to paper or fingers to word processor keys, the competition is stiff. Even among lesser-known and heretofore "little" magazines, the road to a byline is not often paved.

Publication in any size magazine has always been important to furthering a writing career. Especially for fiction writers, whose genre is often the first to be cut back when book publishers go for a commercial blockbuster, being published in magazines is a valuable achievement. Legendary authors including Gertrude Stein and Sherwood Anderson had their early exposure in magazines.

Whether you plan to use magazine writing as a stepping stone or a plateau, you should know the business is big. The more you know about what editors and readers want, the more prepared you will be to give it to them. We've compiled the following industry trends from information supplied us by the editors whose magazines are listed in *Writer's Market*.

● shorter articles. Many magazines are experimenting with format and design (usually in hopes of increasing sales and cutting costs). They are changing column size, layout, use of art/photography. The consensus is that shorter articles stand a better chance of being used—and being read. Editors are looking for tight writing.

● documentation. Editors are aware of the sophistication of their readers and the accuracy they demand. With some editorial staffs being trimmed, editors don't always have the people power to double and triple check facts. Therefore, an increasing number of them are requesting freelancers to include references and documentation with their articles. Though the actual references will probably not be used on the printed page, editors will know the resources used. One magazine editor reminds freelancers of the "need for accurate reporting."

● computer magazines. Paralleling the proliferation of computer books and software, magazines are offering computer users/owners ongoing, hands-on advice and answers. Some industry observers believe computer publications will dominate the magazine marketplace during the next few years. Writing for these publications is straightforward and often technical—articles are frequently written by users for users. There's no room here for writers only mildly interested in the computer revolution. Writers for these magazines are in-the-know, and they can translate their expertise into language that computer novices can understand. Editors recognize their worth and are willing and able to respond with high payments.

● specialty magazines. Computer publications aren't the only items on the magazine menu. Though magazine start-ups aren't breaking any records, those that are new are geared to a well-defined audience or subject. These specialty publications are being distributed through nontraditional outlets to reach directly their target audience. For example, some men's magazines have been distributed at auto parts stores; computer magazines at computer retailers; sewing and needlepoint publications near cash registers of fabric stores. Special interests continue to be pursued. Diet and health magazines are still strong. Romance publications reflect the country's current fascination with emotion. Lifestyle magazines—be they for singles, widowers, swingers or homosexuals—are also big. One editor wrote us that the public is "demanding to be informed on a thought-provoking level that stimulates them into introspection and improves their self-esteem at their particular level of social consciousness." That thought seems on target as magazines such as *Nuclear Times* and *The American Bystander* make their presence felt.

● editor-writer relations. We've heard complaints many times from both sides, and one editor-writer of a Texas-based publication aptly puts it this way: "Here's my vote for editorial etiquette. Writers and editors should treat each other with more respect and consideration. As someone who works on both sides of the coin, I've noticed a sad lack of professionalism in this business many of us claim to take seriously."

Part of being a professional writer means knowing your industry. Study magazine racks, library periodical divisions and the publications that appear at the barber shop or physician's office. Don't just read titles. Don't assume something titled *The Cutting Edge* is a magazine for knife collectors. It could be a trade publication for knife manufacturers or a hobby magazine for stained glass cutters. The topic, editorial slant and audience must all be considered before you submit a query or manuscript to an editor. Be sure to get copies of those magazines you intend to write for. Avoid a rejection slip that says, "Interesting idea, but not right for us."

Other aspects of professionalism include the following:

● query letter. Make it telling, crisp and honest. This is your first step to that editorial invitation for quality manuscripts. Refer to the Appendix for more details on how to write effective queries.

● research. Syndicated columnist Ellen Goodman has said that you won't last long in the writing business if you don't do the research. That means ferreting out facts, tracking down primary sources and double checking information. Researching fiction is equally important. You'll frustrate a lot of editors and lose a lot of readers if you don't know the history for your Spanish-American War story.

● organization and rewriting. Don't wait for an editor to tell you that the manuscript needs to be tightened, reworked or developed further. There's little time for coaching in the magazine business. And editors will be less likely to use you again if they remember the major surgery they had to do on your earlier submission.

● computer printout submissions. Most of the editors who responded to our question about printout submissions said they prefer letter-quality to dot matrix type. Some, however, do not want to receive printout submissions. This information is included in the listing. Fewer editors are receptive to disk submissions because of the problems with incompatible systems. In any case, if an editor has not specified in the listing his preference for these newer kinds of submissions, check before you send yours.

● word count. This is a frequent editorial lament. If the *Writer's Market* guidelines say 1,000-2,000 words, no 5,000-word article, no matter how brilliant, is going to thrill an editor. (Most editors report that the length problem is usually "too long" and rarely "too short.")

● slant. If you have queried a number of editors and have no takers, consider changing the focus of your article. You can repackage the research you've done to fit a different market. An article on water beetles may not interest *National Wildlife* right now, but what about telling children who read *Ranger Rick* about the mysteries of the flitting creatures? Perhaps fishermen who read *Field and Stream* would be intrigued to know more about the darting insects they watch while waiting for a tug on their lines.

● Keep in touch with editorial changes and magazines' freelance needs by reading *Writer's Digest* magazine. The monthly publication capsules new and updated information on various freelance markets. Consult the following columns: The Markets, New York Market Letter, The West Market Report, Poetry Notes and Market Update.

In addition to the professional tips described above, we remind writers of the basics of submitting queries and manuscripts. Include SASE; heed deadlines; proofread your writing. Attending to the basics will ensure proper treatment of your quality manuscript. And chances are good that editors will continue to extend their invitation.

Animal

These publications deal with pets, racing and show horses, other pleasure animals and wildlife. Magazines about animals bred and raised for the market are classified in the Farm category. Publications about horse racing will be found in the Sports section.

ANIMAL KINGDOM, New York Zoological Park, Bronx NY 10460. (212)220-5121. Editor: Eugene J. Walter Jr. Bimonthly magazine for members of zoological societies, individuals interested in wildlife, zoos and aquariums. Buys all rights. Usually pays 25% kill fee but it varies according to length, amount of work involved, etc. Byline given. No computer printout or disk submissions. Pays on acceptance. Reports in 8 months. SASE.
Nonfiction: Wildlife articles dealing with wildlife, natural history, conservation or behavior. Articles must be scientifically well-grounded, but written for a general audience, not scientific journal readers. Recent article example: "Zhen-Zhen, Rare Treasure of Sichuan" (December 1982-January 1983). No pets, domestic animals, or botany. Length: 1,500-3,000 words. Pays $250-750 (average is $500). State availability of photos. Payment for photos purchased with mss is negotiable.
Tips: "It helps to be a working scientist dealing directly with animals in the wild, or a scientist working in a zoo such as a staff member here at the New York Zoological Society. I cannot be too encouraging to anyone who lacks field experience. Many authors who send us unsolicited mss are nonscientists who are doing their research in libraries. They're simply working from scientific literature and writing it up for popular consumption. There are a fair number of others who are backyard naturalists, so to speak, and while their observations may be personal, they are not well grounded scientifically. It has nothing to do with whether or not they are good or bad writers. In fact, some of our authors are not especially good writers, but they are able to provide us with fresh, original material and new insights into animal behavior and biology. That sort of thing is impossible from someone who is working from books."

‡**ANIMAL REVIEW,** Stonehedge Co., Box 985, Pocasset MA 02559. (617)563-5704. Editor: Charray Bryant. Bimonthly magazine covering animals and animal issues for the New England animal lover. Provides educational information and news about animals. Estab. 1982. Circ. 5,000. Pays on publication. Byline given. Buys one-time rights. Submit seasonal/holiday material 6 months in advance. Simultaneous queries, and simultaneous, photocopied and previously published submissions OK. SASE. Reports in 2 weeks on queries; 6 weeks on mss. Sample copy $2; writer's guidelines for business size SAE and 1 first class stamp.
Nonfiction: Expose (agencies or individuals severely abusing animals or "ripping off" animal lovers); general interest (of or pertaining to New England animal lovers); how-to (animal care/training, build-it-yourself projects); humor (whenever possible); inspirational (acts and ideas of courage); interview/profile (with animal experts in their respective fields); opinion (guest editorial column on any topic of animal interest); personal experience (if educational); photo feature (with animal as main character); animal profiles—writing technique secondary to knowledge of the subject. "We do not publish articles about breeding animals or 'how to make money with animals.' " Buys 18-24 mss/year. Query with published clips. Length: open. Pays in copies or to maximum 30¢/published line—about 6¢/word.
Photos: Animals as main character in photos. State availability of photos. Pays $15 maximum for 5x7 and 8x10 b&w and color prints.
Poetry: Traditional. Buys 6-8 poems/year. Submit maximum 3 poems. Length: 8 lines minimum. Pays in copies or to maximum 20¢/published line.

Fillers: Clippings, anecdotes, short humor, newsbreaks. Length: open. Pays in copies or maximum 10-15¢/ published line.
Tips: *"Animal Review* is an ideal publication for anyone who is an aspiring animal journalist—length is secondary to topic. Because *AR* is a not-for-profit magazine, we prefer to pay in advertising/subscription credits whenever possible. We depend heavily upon outside contributions."

ANIMALS, MSPCA, 350 S. Huntington Ave., Boston MA 02130. Editor: Susan Burns. Bimonthly magazine for members of the MSPCA. 40 pages. Circ. 15,000. Pays on publication. Buys one-time rights. Photocopied and previously published submissions OK. Computer printout submissions OK; prefers letter quality to dot matrix. OK. Reports in 2 weeks. Sample copy $1.25 with 8½x11 SASE; writer's guidelines for SASE.
Nonfiction: Uses practical articles on animal care; humane/animal protection issues; animal profiles; true pet stories (*not mawkish*) and research essays on animal protection. Nonsentimental approach. Length: 300-3,000 words. Pays 2¢/word.
Photos: Pays $10 for 5x7 or larger b&w prints; $30 for color transparencies with accompanying ms or on assignment. Uses photo essays and original photos of artistic distinction for "Gallery" department.

APPALOOSA NEWS, Box 8403, Moscow ID 83843. (208)882-5578. Monthly magazine covering Appaloosa horses for Appaloosa owners and breeders, and people interested in horses. 200 pages. Circ. 24,000. Buys all rights. Byline given. Phone queries OK. Seasonal/holiday material should be submitted 3 months in advance. No computer printouts or disk submissions. SASE. Reports in 1 month. Free sample copy to serious writers only.
Nonfiction: How-to (horse-related articles); historical (history of Appaloosas); informational; interview (horse-related persons—trainer, owner, racer, etc.); photo feature; profile (must be authentic); and technical. "We are only interested in articles about Appaloosa horses; no western artist features or general horsemanship articles." Submit complete ms. Buys 15-20 unsolicited mss/year. Pays $35-300.
Photos: Reviews 8x10 or 5x7 b&w glossy prints or color transparencies for cover. Offers no additional payment for photos accepted with accompanying ms. Captions required. Pays $75 for cover use.
Columns/Departments: Regional reports for Appaloosa Horse Club, horse shows, sales, races, etc. Send complete ms.
Tips: "Feature stories about top youth, trainers and breeders involved in Appaloosas are especially liked by our readers—especially those with tips on how they got to where they are today. Mss with photos are more likely to be used; we will pay up to $300 if manuscript is very good and accompanied by photos. Although we use a few first- and second-person articles, third-person, professionally presented articles are definitely preferred." Recent article examples: "Broodmare Power at Sheldak Ranch," (March 1983); and "Myrtle Brown, An Appaloosa Pioneer" (April 1983).

CALIFORNIA HORSE REVIEW, The Largest All-Breeds Horse Magazine in the Nation, Related Industries Corp., Box 646, North Highlands CA 95660. (916)485-4301. Editor: Dan Kemp. Monthly magazine covering all equines, for "professional trainers, breeders and amateurs whose main interest is in caring for, showing and riding their horses. Articles provide entertainment and factual information to these readers. Emphasis is on equines in the West and most particularly in California." Circ. 7,500. Pays on acceptance. Byline given. Pays $50 kill fee. Buys first North American serial rights. Submit seasonal/holiday material 3 months in advance. Photocopied submissions OK. SASE. Reports in 3 weeks. Sample copy $1; writer's guidelines for business size SAE and 1 first class stamp.
Nonfiction: Historical/nostalgic, how-to, humor, inspirational, interview/profile, personal experience, photo feature, technical and travel. "Thirty to forty percent of the magazine is freelance written. We want material for major articles concerning health, training, equipment and interviews with wellknown personalities in the equine field. No general-interest articles or articles not aimed at Western horse owners, trainers or breeders." Recent article examples: "Old Beck—The Fertile Mule" (December 1981); and "Equine Embryo Transfer" (January 1982). Buys 120 mss/year. Query. Length: 1,200-3,000 words. Pays $35-125.
Photos: "Photos are purchased as a part of the editorial package; however, we do buy cover photos for $75."
Fiction: Adventure, historical, humorous, mainstream, novel excerpts and western. No general interest fiction; must be horse-oriented. Buys 12 mss/year. Length: 1,200-2,500 words. Pays $45-125.
Tips: "We are more apt to purchase material from horsemen who have some writing skill than from writers who have little horse knowledge. Interviews of trainers, breeders or others well known in the horse world are always sought. Readers want factual information written in clear, understandable fashion. Photos are necessary to illustrate many nonfiction articles. A writer in this field should also be a photographer and should continually work to sharpen writing skills."

THE CANADIAN HORSE, 7240 Woodbine Ave., Suite 210, Markham, Ontario, Canada L3R 1A4. (416)495-7722. Publisher: Evelyn Spragg. For thoroughbred horsemen. Monthly magazine. Circ. 5,500. Buys all rights. Pays on publication. Query first, "with a letter that demonstrates your knowledge of and fa-

miliarity with our magazine." Enclose SAE and International Reply Coupons.
Nonfiction: Material on thoroughbred racing and breeding. Pays approximately $100/article.

‡**CANINE CHRONICLE,** Routledge Publications, Inc., Box 115, Montpelier IN 47359. (317)728-2464. Editor: Ric Routledge. Weekly tabloid covering purebred dogs for people who breed and show them. Circ. 7,000. Pays on acceptance. Byline given. Buys all rights. Submit seasonal/holiday material 3 months in advance. Simultaneous queries and photocopied and previously published submissions OK. SASE. Reports in 3 weeks on queries and mss. Free sample copy.
Nonfiction: How-to (on grooming, feeding, handling, breeding, kennels); history; interviews and features about the people behind the dogs. Buys 25 mss/year. Query or send complete ms. Pays average of $100 for 1,500 words, "though we are not a stickler on length if the subject is covered."
Photos: State availability of photos. Reviews 5x7 b&w prints. Captions and identification of subjects required. Buys all rights.
Columns/Departments: Query or send complete ms.
Fiction: "We use a limited amount of fiction. Stay away from 'Boy meets dog.' " Buys 5 mss/year. Send complete ms.

CAT FANCY, Fancy Publications, Inc., Box 4030, San Clemente CA 92672. (714)498-1600. Editor: Linda Lewis. Monthly magazine for men and women of all ages interested in all phases of cat ownership. 64 pages. Circ. 100,000. Pays after publication. Buys first American serial rights. Byline given. Submit seasonal/holiday material 4 months in advance. SASE. Reports in 6 weeks. Sample copy $2.50; free writer's guidelines with SASE.
Nonfiction: Historical; medical; how-to; humor; informational; personal experience; photo feature and technical. Buys 5 mss/issue. Send complete ms. Length: 500-3,000 words. Pays 3-5¢/word.
Photos: Photos purchased with or without accompanying ms. Pays $10 minimum for 8x10 b&w glossy prints; $50-100 for 35mm or 2¼x2¼ color transparencies. Send prints and transparencies. Model release required.
Fiction: Adventure; fantasy; historical and humorous; nothing written with cats speaking. Buys 1 ms/issue. Send complete ms. Length: 500-3,000 words. Pays 3¢/word.
Poetry: Avant-garde, free verse, haiku, light verse and traditional. Buys 5 poems/issue. Length: 5-50 lines. Pays $10.
Fillers: News worthy or unusual; items with photo and cartoons. Buys 10 fillers/year. Length: 100-500 words. Pays $20-35.

CATS MAGAZINE, Box 4106, Pittsburgh PA 15202. Executive Editor: Jean Amelia Laux. (412)766-1662. Co-Editor: Linda J. Walton, Box 37, Port Orange FL 32019. Monthly magazine for men and women of all ages; cat enthusiasts, vets and geneticists. Circ. 75,000. Buys first North American serial rights and Japanese first rights. Byline given. Buys 50 mss/year. Pays on publication. Free sample copy. Submit seasonal/Christmas material 6 months in advance. Reports in 6-8 weeks. SASE.
Nonfiction: "Cat health, cat breed articles, articles on the cat in art, literature, history, human culture, cats in the news. Cat pets of popular personalities. In general how cats and cat people are contributing to our society. We're more serious, more scientific, but we do like an occasional light or humorous article portraying cats and humans, however, as they really are. No talking cats! Would like to see something on psychological benefits of cat ownership; how do cat-owning families differ from others?" Length: 800-2,500 words. Pays $15-75. Photos purchased with or without accompanying ms. Captions optional. Pays $10 minimum for 4x5 or larger b&w photos; $150 minimum for color (cover). Prefers 2x2 minimum, but can use 35mm (transparencies only). "We use color for cover only. Prefer cats as part of scenes rather than stiff portraits." Send transparencies to Box 37, Port Orange FL 32019. Please mark each transparency with name and address.
Fiction and Poetry: Science fiction, fantasy and humorous fiction; cat themes only. Length: 800-2,500 words. Pays $15-$100. Poetry in traditional forms, blank or free verse, avant-garde forms and some light verse; cat themes only. Length: 4-64 lines. Pays 30¢/line.
Tips: "We sometimes hold articles due to a backlog. Please advise if you have a time limit."

CONTINENTAL HORSEMAN, Box 479, Weatherford TX 76086. (817)594-0257. Editor: Sandy Crawford. Monthly magazine covering the quarter horse industry only. Circ. 14,000. Pays on publication. Byline given. Buys first rights. Submit seasonal/holiday material 2 months in advance. SASE. Reports in 2 weeks on queries. Sample copy $2.
Nonfiction: General interest, inspirational, new product, personal experience, travel—all related to quarter horses; how-to (train horses, break horses and colts). Length: open. Pays $5-100.
Photos: Reviews b&w prints. Captions, identification of subjects required. Buys one-time rights.
Columns/Departments: Send complete ms.

DOG FANCY, Fancy Publications, Inc., Box 4030, San Clemente CA 92672. (714)498-1600. Editor: Linda Lewis. Monthly magazine for men and women of all ages interested in all phases of dog ownership. Circ.

80,000. Pays after publication. Buys first American serial rights. Byline given. Submit seasonal/holiday material 4 months in advance. Sample copy $2.50; free writer's guidelines. SASE.

Nonfiction: Historical, medical, how-to, humor, informational, interview, personal experience, photo feature, profile and technical. Buys 5 mss/issue. Length: 500-3,000 words. Pays 3¢/word.

Photos: Photos purchased with or without accompanying ms. Pays $10 minimum for 8x10 b&w glossy prints; $50-100 for 35mm or 2¼x2¼ color transparencies. Send prints and transparencies. Model release required.

Fiction: Adventure, fantasy, historical and humorous. Buys 5 mss/year. Send complete ms. Length: 500-3,000 words. Pays 3¢/word.

Fillers: "Need short, punchy photo fillers and cartoons." Buys 10 fillers/year. Pays $20-35.

FAMILY PET, Box 22964, Tampa FL 33622. Editor-in-Chief: M. Linda Sabella. Quarterly magazine about pets and primarily for pet owners in Florida. "Our readers are all ages; many show pets, most have more than one pet, and most are in Florida." Averages 16 pages. Circ. 2,500. Pays on publication. Buys one-time rights. SASE. Reports in 6-8 weeks. Sample copy and writer's guidelines for SASE.

Nonfiction: Historical (especially breed histories); how-to (training and grooming hints); humor (or living with pets); informational; personal experience; photo feature; and travel (with pets). Buys 1-2 mss/issue. Send complete ms. Length: 500-1,000 words. Pays $5-20. Maximum $20 for article/photo package.

Photos: Purchased with or without accompanying ms. Captions required. Pays $3-5 for 5x7 b&w glossy prints used inside. Send prints. Pays $10 for photos used on cover.

Columns/Departments: New Books (reviews of recent issues in pet field). Send complete ms. Length: 200-400 words. Pays $3-5. Open to suggestions for new columns/departments.

Poetry: Light verse, prefers rhyme. Buys 1/issue. Length: 12-16 lines preferred. Pays $3-5.

Fillers: Jokes, gags, anecdotes, puzzles and short humor. Buys 4-5 fillers/year. Length: 100-350 words. Pays $2-5.

‡**THE GREYHOUND REVIEW, Official Publication of the National Greyhound Association**, National Greyhound Association, Box 543, Abilene KS 67410. (913)263-4660. Editor: Gary Guccione. Monthly magazine covering greyhound breeding and racing for greyhound owners. Circ. 4,200. Pays on publication. Byline given. Not copyrighted. Buys one-time rights. Submit seasonal/holiday material 3 months in advance. Simultaneous queries and photocopied and previously published submissions OK. SASE. Reports in 4 weeks. Free sample copy and writer's guidelines.

Nonfiction: Janie Allen, articles editor. Book excerpts; general interest; historical/nostalgic; how-to (train greyhounds, better care for greyhounds, etc.); humor; interview/profile; opinion; personal experience; photo feature; technical. Not interested in articles of general interest that greyhound owners will find too fundamental. Buys 60 mss/year. Send complete ms. Length: 1,000-10,000 words. Pays $40-100.

Photos: Send photos with ms. Pays $10-50 for 5x7 b&w and color prints. Identification of subjects required.

Columns/Departments: Janie Allen, column/department editor. "Our Readers Write"—consideration of all mss relevant to all pertinent greyhound issues. Buys 10 mss/year. Send complete ms. Length: 1,000-5,000 words. Pays $40-100.

Tips: "Get acquainted with the greyhound scene in your local area (track, etc.) and submit feature on a particular owner or greyhound currently making news. A couple b&w pics accompanying the article will enhance its chances of being used. Because our readership receives the magazine about one month after deadline, the time element needs to be considered. Articles should still be pertinent by the time they reach readership."

HORSE AND HORSEMAN, Box HH, Capistrano Beach CA 92624. Editor: Mark Thiffault. 75% freelance written. For owners of pleasure horses; predominantly female with main interest in show/pleasure riding. Monthly magazine; 74 pages. Circ. 96,000. Buys all rights. Byline given. Buys 40-50 mss/year. Pays on acceptance. Sample copy $1.50 and writer's guidelines free with SASE. Submit special material (horse and tack care; veterinary medicine pieces in winter and spring issues) 3 months in advance. Reports in 1 month. Query or submit complete ms. SASE.

Nonfiction and Photos: Training tips, do-it-yourself pieces, grooming and feeding, stable management, tack maintenance, sports, personalities, rodeo and general horse-related features. Emphasis must be on informing, rather than merely entertaining. Aimed primarily at the beginner, but with information for experienced horsemen. Subject matter must have thorough, in-depth appraisal. Interested in more English (hunter/jumper) riding/training copy, plus pieces on driving horses and special horse areas like Tennessee Walkers and other gaited breeds. More factual breed histories. Uses informational, how-to, personal experience, interview, profile, humor, historical, nostalgia, successful business operations, technical articles. Length: 2,500 words average. Pays $75-200. B&w photos (4x5 and larger) purchased with or without mss. Pays $4-10 when purchased without ms. Uses original color transparencies (35mm and larger). No duplicates. Pays $100 for cover use. Payment for inside editorial color is negotiated.

‡**HORSE ILLUSTRATED**, Fancy Publications, Inc., Box 4030, San Clemente CA 92672. (714)498-1600. Editor: Linda Lewis. Monthly magazine for men and women of all ages interested in all phases of horse owner-

ship. Circ. 40,000. Pays after publication. Buys first North American serial rights. Submit seasonal/holiday material 4 months in advance. Sample copy $2.50; free writer's guidelines. SASE.
Nonfiction: Medical, how-to, humor, informational, interview, photo feature, profile, technical and sport. Buys 5 mss/issue. Length: 500-2,500 words. Pays 3-5¢/word.
Photos: Photos purchased with or without accompanying ms. Pays $10 minimum for 8x10 b&w glossy prints; $50-100 for 35mm 2¼x2¼ color transparencies. Send prints and transparencies. Model release required.
Fiction: Adventure and humor. Buys 5 mss/year. Send complete ms. Length: 500-2,000 words. Pays 3¢/word.
Fillers: Newsworthy or unusual items with photo and cartoons. Buys 10/year. Pays $20-35.

HORSE WOMEN, Rich Publishing, Inc., 41919 Moreno Rd., Temecula CA 92390. Editor: Ray Rich. Annual magazine covering western and English riding for those interested in taking better care of their horse and improving their riding. Magazine is tailored for working women and family women who are interested in riding or caring for equines. Circ. 80,000. Pays on publication. Buys all rights. Offers 100% kill fee. Byline given. Phone queries OK. Submit seasonal/holiday material 3 months in advance. SASE. Reports in 1 month. Sample copy $3; free writer's guidelines.
Nonfiction: How-to (anything relating to western and English riding, jumping, barrel racing, etc.); humor; interview (with well-known professional trainers); new product (want new product releases, description of the product and b&w photo, featuring the latest in western and English tack and clothing) and photo feature (preferably foaling). Buys 10-15 mss/issue. Query or send complete ms. Length: 1,000-2,500 words. Pays $40-50/printed page depending on quality and number of photos.
Photos: Send photos with ms. Offers no additional payment for 5x7 or 8x10 b&w glossy prints. Pays extra for color photos. Captions preferred.

HORSEMAN MAGAZINE, 5314 Bingle Rd., Houston TX 77092. (713)688-8811. Editor: David Gaines. Monthly magazine for people who own and ride horses for pleasure and competition. Majority own western stock horses and compete in western type horse shows as a hobby or business. Many have owned horses for many years. Circ. 175,474. Rights purchased vary with author and material. Buys first North American serial rights. Byline given. Pays on publication. Free sample copy and writer's guidelines. Submit seasonal material 4 months in advance. Reports in 3 weeks. Query. SASE.
Nonfiction and Photos: "How-to articles on horsemanship, training, grooming, exhibiting, horsekeeping, and history dealing with horses. We really like articles from professional trainers, or articles about their methods written by freelancers. The approach is to educate and inform readers as to how they can ride, train, keep and enjoy their horses more." Length: 1,000-2,500 words. Pays up to 7-10¢/word. Photos purchased with accompanying ms or on assignment. Captions required. Pays $10 minimum for 5x7 or 8x10 b&w prints; 35mm or 120 negatives. Pays $25 for inside color. Prefers transparencies. Buys all rights.
Tips: "Send article ideas with very narrow focus. Indicate depth. Use know-how from top experts or send us good, concise articles about specific training problems with detailed explanation of correction. Otherwise, stick to fringe articles: humor, photo essay, Horseman Travelog. The articles need to be packed with information, but we don't always mean step-by-step how to. Make them readable."

HORSEMEN'S YANKEE PEDLAR NEWSPAPER, Box H, Auburn MA 01501. (617)832-9638. Publisher: Nancy L. Khoury. Editor: Jane K. Sullivan. "All-breed monthly newspaper for horse enthusiasts of all ages and incomes, from one-horse owners to large commercial stables. Covers region from New Jersey to Massachusetts." Circ. 12,000. Pays on publication. Buys all rights for one year. Submit seasonal/holiday material 3 months in advance of issue date. SASE. Reports in 1 month. Sample copy $1.25.
Nonfiction: Humor, educational and interview about horses and the people involved with them. Pays $2/published inch. Buys 50 mss/year. Submit complete ms or outline. Length: 1,500 words maximum.
Photos: Purchased with ms. Captions and photo credit required. Buys 1 cover photo/month; pays $10. Submit b&w prints. Pays $5.
Columns/Departments: Area news column. Buys 85-95/year. Length: 1,200-1,400 words. Pays 75¢/column inch. Query.
Tips: "Query with outline of angle of story, approximate length and date when story will be submitted. Stories should be people oriented and horse focused. Send newsworthy, timely pieces, such as stories that are applicable to the season, for example: foaling in the spring or how to keep a horse healthy through the winter. We like to see how-to's, features about special horse people and anything that has to do with the preservation of horses and their rights as creatures deserving a chance to survive."

HORSEPLAY, Box 545, Gaithersburg MD 20877. (301)840-1866. Editor: Cordelia Doucet. Monthly (except combined issue January and February) magazine covering horses and horse sports for a readership interested in horses, especially people who show, event and hunt. 60-80 pages. Circ. 46,000. Pays within 30 days after publication. Copyrighted. All rights reserved. Pays negotiable kill fee. Byline given. Phone queries OK. No computer printouts or disk submissions. Submit all material 2 months in advance. SASE. Reports in 6 weeks. Sample copy $2.50; free writer's guidelines.

Nonfiction: How-to (various aspects of horsemanship, course designing, stable management, putting on horse shows, etc.); humor; interview; photo feature; profile and technical. Buys 50 mss/year. Length: 1,000-3,000 words. Pays $30-130.

Photos: Cathy Mitchell, art director. Purchased on assignment. Captions required. Query or send contact sheet, prints or transparencies. Pays $10 for 8x10 b&w glossy prints; $125 maximum for color transparencies (cover only).

Tips: "Write requesting our writer's guidelines and a sample copy. Study both. No fiction, western riding, or racing articles." Model article study is "November Hill" (March 1982).

HORSES ALL, Rocky Top Holdings, Ltd., Box 550, Nanton, Alberta, Canada T0L 1R0. (403)646-2144. Editor: Jacki French. Monthly tabloid for horse owners, 75% rural, 25% urban. Circ. 15,200. Pays on publication. Buys one-time rights. Phone queries OK. Submit seasonal material 3 months in advance. Simultaneous, photocopied (if clear), and previously published submissions OK. Reports on queries in 5 weeks; on mss in 6 weeks. Sample copy $1.

Nonfiction: Interview, humor and personal experience. Query. Pays $20-100.

Photos: State availability of photos. Captions required.

Columns/Departments: Length: 1-2 columns. Query. Open to suggestions for new columns/departments. Query Doug French.

Fiction: Historical and western. Query. Pays $20-100.

THE MORGAN HORSE, American Morgan Horse Association, Box 1, Westmoreland NY 13490. (315)735-7522. Acting Editor: Wayne G. Hipsley. Monthly breed journal covering the training, showing, and vet care of Morgan horses. Circ. 9,000. Pays on publication. Byline given. Buys all rights. Submit seasonal/holiday material 3 months in advance. Simultaneous queries and simultaneous, photocopied, and previously published submissions OK (subject to editor's discretion). SASE. Reports in 3 months. Sample copy $2 (price may vary with issue); writer's guidelines for business size SAE and 1 first class stamp.

Nonfiction: How-to (trailering, driving, training, etc.); human interest (if highly unusual); interview/profile (of respected Morgan personalities); veterinary articles. January-Morgan Grand National; February-Stallions; March-Versatility; April-Driving; May-Mare; June-Youth; August-Historical; September-Gelding; October-Foal; November-International; December-Horse Buying. "No articles with less-than-national interest or material dealing with half-bred Morgans." Buys 10-15 mss/year. Query with clips of published work. Length: 500-3,000 words. Pays 5¢/word.

Photos: Send photos with ms. Pays $5 minimum for 8x10 b&w prints. Captions, model release, and identification of subjects required.

Tips: "We like to see completed manuscripts from new writers and welcome articles on veterinary breakthroughs and training."

NORTHEAST HORSEMAN, Henley Sales, Ltd., Box 131, Hampden ME 04444. (207)862-3808. Editor: Stephen Kinney. Monthly magazine covering all breeds of horses and disciplines of horsemanship. For professional trainers, show people and amateur riders in New York, New England and Maritime Canada. Pays on publication. Unsolicited mss not returned.

Nonfiction: Each issue features a type of riding or a particular breed. Covers events and personalities regionally; uses occasional opinion pieces; question-and-answer interviews. Send resume and clippings (not returned); mss on assignment only.

Tips: "We prefer phone queries from local freelancers."

PAINT HORSE JOURNAL, American Paint Horse Association, Box 18519, Fort Worth TX 76118. (817)439-3400. Managing Editor: Phil Livingston. For people who raise, breed and show paint horses. Monthly magazine. Circ. 14,000. Pays on acceptance. Normally buys all rights. Pays negotiable kill fee. Byline given. Phone queries OK. Submit seasonal/holiday material 3 months in advance. Photocopied and previously published submissions OK. SASE. Reports in 1 month. Free sample copy and writer's guidelines.

Nonfiction: General interest (personality pieces on well-known owners of paints); historical (paint horses in the past—particular horses and the breed in general); how-to (train and show horses); and photo feature (paint horses). Buys 4-5 mss/issue. Send complete ms. Pays $50-250.

Photos: Send photos with ms. Offers no additional payment for photos accepted with accompanying ms. Uses 3x5 or larger b&w glossy prints; 3x5 color transparencies. Captions preferred. Normally buys all rights.

Tips: "*PHJ* needs breeder-trainer articles from areas far-distant from our office. Photos with copy are almost always essential. Well-written first person articles welcome. Humor, too. Submit well-written items that show a definite understanding of the horse business. Use proper equine terminology and proper grounding in ability to communicate thoughts."

‡PERFORMANCE HORSEMAN, Gum Tree Store Press, Inc. Gum Tree Corner, Unionville PA 19375. (215)692-6220. Editor-in-Chief: Pamela Goold. Managing Editor: Carol Clark. Monthly magazine covering

Western horsemanship and horse care. Circ. 35,000. Pays on acceptance. Byline given. Offers negotiable kill fee. Buys all rights. Computer printout submissions OK; prefers letter quality to dot matrix. SASE. Reports in 2 months on queries and mss. Sample copy for 9x12 SAE; free writer's guidelines.

Nonfiction: Miranda Lorraine, articles editor. How-to (on riding, training, horse care, horse health); interviews (with top western riders and trainers, and researchers or veterinarians on breakthroughs, new developments/methods); photo feature (must be how-to of a specific stable skill). "Be familiar with our format and content. Query with name and credentials of a trainer or top horseman, along with slant for the story. Personal experience stories must contain how-to information. We are not interested in writer's own opinion or method; interview must be with proven trainer. No puff pieces on a horseman, yarns, tales of the Old West—must be how-to material." Buys 25 mss/year. Query.

Photos: State availability of photos. Identification of subjects required.

Tips: "First person training articles are most open to freelancers. Keep stories in first person with subject of story 'I'; accompany with colorful biography."

‡**PET HOSPITAL NEWS,** Impressions Writing Service, 5804 E. New York, Indianapolis IN 46219. (317)357-2760. Editor: Tim Altom. Bimonthly newsletter on domestic and wild animals syndicated to veterinarians nationwide to be mailed to their clients' homes. Estab. 1982. Circ. 75,000. Pays on acceptance. No byline given. Buys all rights. Submit seasonal/holiday material 6 months in advance. Simultaneous and photocopied submissions OK. SASE. Reports in 2 weeks. Free sample copy and writer's guidelines.

Nonfiction: General interest, historical/nostalgic, humor. "We use stories of unusual pets or pet-related subjects, except technical matters. No 'weird' pets, but stories about animals not normally thought of as pets will be considered. No advice pieces. We need a definite journalistic style." Also looks for pet or animal historicals; how pets or other animals have fit into man's world; humorous articles about wild or domestic animals. "Nothing downbeat; nothing critical of veterinarians or animal care industry; nothing technical concerning veterinary medicine." Buys 6-10 mss/year. Query. Length: 500-750 words. Pays $50-75.

Photos: State availability of photos. Pays $10-25 for 8x10 b&w prints. Model release required.

Tips: "You can be bouncy and fun while being informative and enlightening. First page only is open to freelancers. We get serious *inside* the newsletter."

PRACTICAL HORSEMAN, Gum Tree Store Press Inc., Gum Tree Corner, Unionville PA 19375. Editor-in-Chief: Pamela Goold. Articles Editor: Miranda Lorraine. Monthly magazine for knowledgeable horsemen interested in breeding, raising and training thoroughbred and thoroughbred-type horses for show, eventing, dressage, racing or hunting, and pleasure riding. Circ. 55,000. Pays on publication. Buys all rights. Simultaneous and photocopied submissions OK, but will not use any submission unless withdrawn from other publishers. SASE. Reports in 2 months. Free sample copy and writer's guidelines.

Nonfiction: How-to interviews with top professional horsemen in hunter/jumper; dressage; veterinary and stable management articles; photo features; and step-by-step ideas for barn building, grooming, trimming, and feeding and management tips. Buys 3-4 mss/issue. Query with sample of writing or complete ms. Length: open. Pays $200 and up.

Photos: Purchased on assignment. Captions required. Query. Pays $7.50 minimum for b&w glossy prints (5x7 minimum size); $100 maximum for 35mm or 2¼x2¼ color transparencies for covers.

‡**PURE-BRED DOGS AMERICAN KENNEL GAZETTE,** American Kennel Club, Inc., 51 Madison Ave., New York NY 10010. (212)696-8330, ext. 8331 or 8332. Editor: Ms. Pat Beresford. Managing Editor: Ms. Jan Saeger. Monthly magazine covering dogs. "Reaches pure-bred dog breeders, owners. All articles published must be related to the pure-bred dog fancy—dog showing, judging, breeding, health and medicine, grooming, training, the dog in art or literature as well as some personal experience pieces." Circ. 48,000. Pays on publication. Byline given. Buys all rights. Submit seasonal/holiday material 6 months in advance. Simultaneous queries and photocopied and previously published submissions OK "on rare occasions". Reports in 1 month. Free sample copy and writer's guidelines.

Nonfiction: General interest, historical/nostalgic, how-to, humor, interview/profile, personal experience, photo feature, technical, medical. No personal experience or opinion that is not of interest to the pure-bred dog fancier. Buys about 50 mss/year. Send complete ms. Length: 750-3,000 words. Pays $50-150 and up "depending on article."

Photos: Send photos with accompanying query or ms. Reviews 8x10 b&w and color prints or slides. Pay depends on entire article. Model release and identification of subjects required.

Fiction: Adventure, humorous stories related to dogs. Buys about 2 mss/year. Send complete ms. Length: 750-3,000 words. Pays $50-250, depending on ms.

Poetry: Light verse, traditional. Buys about 5/year. Length: open. Pays $50-150.

Fillers: Anecdotes, short humor, newsbreaks. Length: 750 words maximum. Pays $50 maximum.

Tips: "We simply like to have completed manuscripts and any ideas submitted. If we like the work or see potential, we will contact the writer. Most of the editorial features section is open to freelancers. We like to see in-depth coverage with good photo illustrations."

THE QUARTER HORSE JOURNAL, Box 9105, Amarillo TX 79105. (806)376-4811. Editor-in-Chief: Audie Rackley. Official publication of the American Quarter Horse Association. Monthly magazine; 650 pages. Circ. 89,000. Pays on acceptance. Buys all rights or first rights. Submit seasonal/holiday material 2 months in advance. SASE. Reports in 2 weeks. Free sample copy and writer's guidelines.
Nonfiction: Historical ("those that retain our western heritage"); how-to (fitting, grooming, showing, or anything that relates to owning, showing, or breeding); informational (educational clinics, current news); interview (feature-type stories—must be about established people who have made a contribution to the business); new product; personal opinion; and technical (medical updates, new surgery procedures, etc.). Buys 30 mss/year. Length: 800-2,500 words. Pays $50-200.
Photos: Purchased with accompanying ms. Captions required. Send prints or transparencies. Uses 5x7 or 8x10 b&w glossy prints; 2¼x2¼ or 4x5 color transparencies. Offers no additional payment for photos accepted with accompanying ms.

THE WESTERN HORSEMAN, Box 7980, Colorado Springs CO 80933. Editor: Chan Bergen. Monthly magazine covering western horsemanship. Circ. 177,532. Pays on acceptance. Buys first-time rights. Byline given. Submit seasonal/holiday material 3 months in advance. SASE. Reports in 3 weeks. Sample copy $1.50.
Nonfiction: How-to (horse training, care of horses, tips, etc.); and informational (on rodeos, ranch life, historical articles of the West emphasizing horses). Length: 1,500 words. Pays $85-135; "sometimes higher by special arrangement." Since a good part of the magazine is staff written, suggest query first.
Photos: Send photos with ms. Offers no additional payment for photos. Uses 5x7 or 8x10 b&w glossy prints and 35mm transparencies. Captions required.
Tips: "Submit clean copy with professional quality photos. Stay away from generalities. Writing style should show a deep interest in horses coupled with a wide knowledge of the subject."

Art

Art publications included here are magazines of and about art, art history, and specific art forms written both for art patrons and artists. Publications addressing the business and management concerns of the art industry are listed in the Art, Design, and Collectibles category of the Trade Journals section.

THE AMERICAN ART JOURNAL, Kennedy Galleries, Inc., 40 W. 57th St., 5th Floor, New York NY 10019. (212)541-9600. Editor-in-Chief: Jane Van N. Turano. Scholarly magazine of American art history of the 17th, 18th, 19th and 20th centuries, including painting, sculpture, architecture, decorative arts, etc., for people with a serious interest in American art, and who are already knowledgeable about the subject. Readers are scholars, curators, collectors, students of American art, or persons who have a strong interest in Americana. Quarterly magazine; 96 pages. Circ. 2,000. Pays on acceptance. Buys all rights. Byline given. Photocopied submissions OK. SASE. Reports in 2 months. Sample copy $7.
Nonfiction: "All articles are historical in the sense that they are all about some phase or aspect of American art history." No how-to articles or reviews of exhibitions. No book reviews or opinion pieces. No human interest approaches to artists' lives. No articles written in a casual or "folksy" style. *Writing style must be formal and serious.* Buys 25-30 mss/year. Submit complete ms "with good cover letter." Length: 2,500-8,000 words. Pays $300-400.
Photos: Purchased with accompanying ms. Captions required. Uses b&w only. Offers no additional payment for photos accepted with accompanying ms.
Tips: "Actually, our range of interest is quite broad. Any topic within our time frame is acceptable if it is well researched, well written, and illustrated. Whenever possible, all mss must be accompanied by b&w photographs which have been integrated into the text by the use of numbers."

‡**AMERICAN INDIAN ART MAGAZINE**, American Indian Art, Inc., 7314 E. Osborn Dr., Scottsdale AZ 85251. (602)994-5445. Managing Editor: Roanne P. Goldfein. Quarterly magazine covering Native American art, historic and contemporary, including new research on any aspect of Native American art. Circ. 15,000. Pays on publication. Byline given. Buys one-time and first rights. Submit seasonal/holiday material 6 months in advance. Simultaneous queries OK. Reports in 2 weeks on queries; 2 months on mss. Free sample copy and writer's guidelines.
Nonfiction: New research on any aspect of Native American art. No previously published work or personal interviews with artists. Buys 12-18 mss/year. Query. Length: 1,000-2,500 words. Pays $75-300.
Tips: "We are devoted to the great variety of textiles, ceramics, jewelry and artifacts of Native American artists—in articles (with bibliographies) appealing to laymen and professionals."

‡**ART & ARTISTS,** Oil Pastel Association, 304 Highmount Terrace, Upper-Nyack-on-Hudson NY 10960. Editor: Sheila Elliot. Quarterly magazine covering art and artists. "Our artists are either working in or interested in oil pastel; we will always be interested in articles with a slant toward this medium. We are, however, open to and interested in all well-researched articles with any art subject matter." Estab. 1983. Circ. under 1,000. Pays on publication. Byline given. Buys first North American serial rights, first rights and second serial (reprint) rights. Submit seasonal/holiday material 6 months in advance. Simultaneous queries, and simultaneous, photocopied and previously published (specify where published) submissions OK. SASE. Will return mss only if adequate postage and envelope is provided. Reports in 1 month on queries; 2 months on mss. Sample copy for $3, 9x12 SAE and 4 first class stamps; writer's guidelines for 5x9 SAE and 2 first class stamps.
Nonfiction: Historical/nostalgic (interviews of persons close to historic art scene or who knew prominent artists); how-to (art or art-related, such as marketing your art, legal, etc.); humor (art-related, short); interview/profile (artists or fine arts figures such as influential museum directors, art consultants, etc.); new product (art materials); opinion (art issues); personal experience; photo feature; technical; travel (good art locations and inexpensive hotels, hostels, etc.). Buys 50 mss/year. Query. Length: 500-7,500 words. Pays $10 "for 500 words and up."
Photos: State availability of photos. Pays $1 for b&w contact sheets and 5x7 or 8x10 prints; $2 for 35mm color transparencies and 5x7 or 8x10 color prints. Captions, model release and identification of subjects required. Buys one-time rights.
Columns/Departments: Review of Reviews (reviews of art exhibit reviews especially outside New York City area). Book reviews are staff written. Interested in teacher feature contributions. Buys 50 mss/year. Send complete ms. Length: 25-800 words. Pays $1 "for 25 words and up."
Fiction: "We would consider fiction that dealt with inner struggles of artists, such as 'why am I painting' or 'can I have children and do art, too?' Serious probing nature. We would also consider art-related humor. Although we do not plan to use fiction regularly, if you have something you are really excited about, consider submitting to us." Will consider high-quality shorts and short shorts. Send complete ms. Pays $25 for short stories.
Poetry: Free verse, haiku, light verse, traditional. "Nothing overly long." Buys 15 poems/year. Submit maximum 10 poems. Length: 2-24 lines. Pays $1.
Fillers: Clippings, anecdotes, short humor, newsbreaks. Buys 50/year. Length: 25-500 words. Pays $1.
Tips: "We are a fledgling magazine that needs all kinds of material. Study the art magazines that are currently on the market, especially *American Artist* for practicing artist articles, and *Art in America* and other expensive glossies for 'think' pieces and reviews. We are inclined to be indulgent of relatively weak writing techniques, provided the writer has something to say and is willing to work with us and accept extensive editing. Hence, we are an excellent submission ground for new, as yet, 'un-polished' writers. Whenever possible, we will request revisions of the writer, or submit our own revisions to author for approval. We especially need and will continue to need art exhibition reviews, especially in USA outside New York City area, Canada and foreign art capitals. Reviews should be informed and scholarly, and show clearly the theoretical context from which the reviewer analyzes. A brief credentials page should accompany queries and reviews."

‡**ART NEW ENGLAND, A Resource for the Visual Arts,** 353 Washington St., Brighton MA 02135. (617)782-3008. Editors: Carla Munsat, Stephanie Adelman. Visual arts tabloid published ten times/year. Provides "a comprehensive index for regional exhibitions, lectures and films. Articles focus on different aspects of painting, sculpture, graphics, crafts, photography, and architecture; features include interviews and profiles on new or established artists, curators and other leaders in the art community. Articles on the business of art and collecting are also included." Circ. 15,000. Pays on publication. Byline given. Submit seasonal/holiday material 2 months in advance. SASE. Sample copy $1.75; free writer's guidelines.
Nonfiction: Book excerpts and book reviews (fine arts, photography, crafts, architecture); interview/profile (on new and established artists, curators and other members of the art community); opinion (on artists' rights, etc.); personal experience (from artist's or curator's point of view); photo feature (art). No articles or reviews *not* related to the visual arts. "We are only interested in art-related subjects." Buys 30 mss/year. Query with resume and clips. Length: 900-1,500 words (features only). Pays $50 maximum features only; reviews less.
Tips: "Features and reviews are most open to freelancers."

‡**ART WEST MAGAZINE, The Foremost Western Art Journal,** Art West, Inc., 303 E. Main St., Box 1799, Bozeman MT 59715. (406)586-5411. Editor: Helori M. Graff. Bimonthly publication covering Western and wildlife art. "In addition to keeping our readers informed of trends in the Western and wildlife art scenes, our major form of presentation is profiles of the individual artists—covering everything—technique, philosophies, lifestyle, etc." Circ. 38,500. Pays on acceptance. Byline given. Offers 50% kill fee. Buys first North American serial rights. Submit seasonal/holiday material 8 months in advance. SASE. Reports in 2 months. Sample copy for 9x12 SAE and $2.50 postage; writer's guidelines for business-size SAE and 1 first class stamp.
Nonfiction: Expose (art market, re: Western and wildlife art); historical (Western artists); interview/profile (artists/gallery owners); opinion (forum for opinions on art-related topics); photo feature (artists, techniques,

museum and gallery openings); technical (methods artists employ); travel (towns considered havens for artists). "Don't complete a profile on an artist before Editorial Board makes the decision to publish feature on that artist (send query with photographs of artist's work first)." Buys 50 mss/year. Query with published clips. Length: 1,200-3,000 words. "Writers are paid for the article as a whole; this is not calculated on the basis of the number of words."

Columns/Departments: Art Tomes (reviews of Western, wildlife, or general art, art publications); In Review (reviews of art shows); Art Events (events, trends in Western, wildlife art). Buys 20-30 mss/year. Query with published clips. Length: 200-1,500 words.

Tips: "*Art West* profiles are typically written in clear, lively and unaffected prose which entertains as well as informs readers of the artist's background, personality, interests, artistic methods, style, philosophies, hopes for the future. Readers have indicated a desire to know about each artist's techniques. Please enclose clips. Relate why writer is interested, qualified for this type of subject. Come to us with a story idea—not entire manuscript. If writer is proposing a particular artist as topic of article, please query first and enclose varied sampling of that artist's work (photographs, transparencies, brochure, etc.)."

‡**THE ARTIST'S MAGAZINE**, F&W Publishing Co., 9933 Alliance Rd., Cincinnati OH 45242. Editor: William Fletcher. Monthly (9 times/year) magazine covering art instruction. "Ours is a highly visual approach to teaching the serious amateur artist techniques that will help him improve his skills and market his work. The style should be crisp and immediately engaging." Estab. 1984. Circ. 60,000. Pays on acceptance. Byline given. Offers 20% kill fee. Buys first North American serial rights and second serial (reprint) rights. Submit seasonal/holiday material 6 months in advance. Simultaneous queries, and photocopied and previously published submissions OK "as long as noted as such." SASE. Reports in 3 weeks. Sample copy for 9x12 SAE plus postage; free writer's guidelines.

Nonfiction: Book excerpts; historical/nostalgic; how-to (every aspect of technique for painting, drawing and the business of art); inspirational (how an artist may have succeeded through hard work, determination, etc.); opinion; interview/profile; new product. "Every article type must instruct the reader in some way." Special issues include: educational issue (the virtues of training, workshops, etc.) and artists' tools issue (perhaps an historical view). No unillustrated articles. Buys 50 mss/year. Query. Length: 500-2,500 words. Pays $50-350.

Photos: "Photos are purchased with every sort of article, but are essential in any instructional piece." Pays $5-35 for b&w contact sheet; $25-100 for 35mm color transparencies. Captions required. Buys one-time rights.

Columns/Departments: Book reviews; Art Life (brief items about art and artists); The Market (*unique* galleries, markets for artists). Buys 300 mss/year. Send complete ms. Length: 25-250 words. Pays $5-50.

Tips: "Look at several issues carefully and read the author's guidelines carefully. We are especially happy to get excellent visuals which illustrate the article and the 4-color separations for such visuals."

ARTS MAGAZINE, 23 E. 26th St., New York NY 10010. (212)685-8500. Editor: Richard Martin. A journal of contemporary art, art criticism, analysis and history, particularly for artists, scholars, museum officials, art teachers and students, and collectors. Monthly, except July and August. Circ. 28,500. Buys all rights. Pays on publication. Query. SASE.

Nonfiction and Photos: Art criticism, analysis and history. Topical reference to museum or gallery exhibition preferred. Length: 1,500-2,500 words. Pays $100, with opportunity for negotiation. B&w glossies or color transparencies customarily supplied by related museums or galleries.

‡**ARTVIEWS**, Visual Arts Ontario, 417 Queen's Quay West, Toronto, Ontario, Canada M5V 1A2. (416)366-1607. Editor: Gail J. Habs. Assistant Editor: Rachel Rafelman. Quarterly magazine "exploring the current visual arts scene—issues, events, major exhibitions—particularly as they pertain to Ontario's art community." Circ. 4,500. Pays on acceptance. Byline given. Offers 25% kill fee. Buys one-time rights. Simultaneous queries and previously published submissions OK. SASE. Reports in 2 weeks on queries; 5 weeks on mss. Free sample copy and writer's guidelines.

Nonfiction: Interview/profile, opinion, photo feature, art issues. No exhibition reviews. Buys 8 mss/year. Query with published clips if available. Length: 500-1,500 words. Pays $50-150.

Photos: State availability of photos. Pays $10-25 for 8x10 b&w prints. Captions and identification of subjects required.

Fillers: Newsbreaks, art, cartoons. Buys variable number of mss/year. Length: 200-500 words. Pays $5-25.

CRAFT RANGE, The Mountain Plains Crafts Journal, 6800 W. Oregon Dr., Denver CO 80226. (303)986-4891. Editor: Waynelle Wilder. Bimonthly tabloid covering criticism, review, artists, shows, galleries, institutions and issues related to contemporary crafts and arts in areas west of the Mississippi River, excluding the West Coast states. Circ. 1,000. Pays on publication. Byline given. Buys one-time rights. Simultaneous queries, simultaneous, photocopied and previously published submissions OK. Computer printout submissions OK; prefers letter quality to dot matrix. SASE. Reports on queries and mss in 1 month. Sample copy free; writer's guidelines free for business size SASE and 1 first class stamp.

Nonfiction: General interest (craft related); interview/profile (artists); personal experience; photo feature; and

book reviews. No how-to-do crafts, or business/marketing. Query. Length: 250-1,500 words. Pays $30-50/article.
Photos: State availability of photos. Reviews 5x7 or larger b&w glossy prints. Cost of photos are reimbursed. Model release and identification of subjects required. "Try to get public relations photos from the gallery or artist."

DESIGN FOR ARTS IN EDUCATION MAGAZINE, Heldref Publications, 4000 Albemarle St. NW, Washington DC 20016. (202)362-6445. Publisher: Cornelius W. Vahle. Managing Editor: Jane Scully. "For teachers, art specialists, administrators, and parents who work with children in education." Bimonthly magazine. Byline given. Accompanying photographs encouraged. SASE. Reports in 8-10 weeks. Sample copy $3. Editorial guidelines for SASE.
Nonfiction: *Design* deals with architecture, dance, the environmental arts, folk arts, literature, media, museums, music, opera, theatre and the visual arts, as well as their relationships with each other. The articles are aimed at teachers, administrators, parents and professionals both within and outside of the arts fields. Articles will range from theory to practice, from exemplary programs to learning theory in and among the arts disciplines and other curricular areas. Emphasis will be on information about the arts and their place, focus, and impact on education and the educational process. Submit complete ms. Length: 1,000-2,000 words.

FORMAT: ART & THE WORLD, Seven Oaks Press, 405 S. 7th St., St. Charles IL 60174. (312)584-0187. Editor: Ms. C.L. Morrison. Quarterly magazine covering art and society. "Our audience consists of three groups: artists wanting to know more about survival and the effectiveness in the current art system (visual and other arts); women exploring their role, opportunities, and situation in the art world; and writer/editors involved in the small-press literary community. We are practical, straight-talking and non-sexist—not a glossy coffee-table art magazine, but instead a budget-conscious vehicle by which creative people can communicate ideas, experiences and proposals for change. Subscribers are 30% Midwest, 20% West Coast, 20% East Coast, with the rest scattered in the US and a tiny segment of Europe." Circ. 700. Pays on publication. Byline given. "We copyright for the author; some assignments are on a work-for-hire basis." Photocopied submissions OK. SASE. Reports in 1 month. Sample copy $3.
Nonfiction: Opinion, personal experience, and some historical subjects involving a new interpretation. "Subjects we are particularly interested in now include: artists as workers (self-employment and being an employee); artist's social role; proposals for education of artists; how do artists make their work known; using art-knowledge in everyday life; how artists can affect the direction of industry and consumer preference; opinions about government funding; how current society affects current art; how past society and living conditions affected past art; and artists' personal experiences with one thing or another—i.e., real life episodes. No articles that say, 'I don't understand modern art—it's all a bunch of ridiculous stuff,' or murder mysteries in which the hard working cop is uplifted by the artist-victim's work." Send complete ms. Length: 300-3,000 words. Pays $5-15 plus up to 1 pound of contributor's copies.
Fiction: "Art-related, or 'odd' subjects." Buys 10 mss/year. Length: 250-1,000 words. Pays $5-15 and/or 1 pound of contributor's copies.
Poetry: Avant-garde, free verse and traditional. Poetry should be subject-oriented. Subjects are social critique, art and sex-role identity. No "romantic, organic sense-impressions, word-pictures, pure language, and so forth." Buys 25 mss/year. Submit maximum 10 poems. Length: 8-40 lines. Pays 1 pound of contributor's copies.
Tips: "A writer can break in with us by being straightforward, outspoken, original, well informed, individualistic, concerned. Our general tone, however, is not angry. We are often quite light and humorous. Try to avoid 'complaining' and feature concrete observation, evaluation and proposals. We would like to receive more articles and interviews—well written and not repeats of information published 1,000 times before. If the writer has no real-life experience, i.e., is all textbooks and academia, forget it. Material should be knowledgeable, but not so remote as to lack everyday application."

‡**FOUR WINDS, The International Forum for Native American Art, Literature and History,** Hundred Arrows Press, Box 156, Austin TX 78767. (512)472-7701. Editor: Charles J. Lohrmann. Assistant Editor: Christy Walker. Quarterly magazine covering Native American and western art, literature and history. "Emphasis is on collecting Native American art." Circ. 10,000. Pays on publication. Byline given. Buys one-time rights. SASE. Reports in 1 month. Sample copy $5.50.
Nonfiction: Articles dealing with Native American art, literature and history. Publishes 12-16 mss/year. "Please send an outline of article with writing sample and personal background. We rarely accept unsolicited submissions." Query. Length: 750-2,500 words. Pays $100-300.
Photos: State availability of photos. Reviews contact sheets. "All photograph submissions should be approved prior to submission." Captions, model release and identification of subjects required. Buys one-time rights. "Agreements regarding size, format, and payment are made prior to submission."
Columns/Departments: Book reviews, Museum reviews, Gallery reviews, News/Notes, Calendar of Events. Buys 8-12 mss/year. Query with clips of published work. Length: 750-1,000 words. Pays $50-150.

Fiction: Writing by Native American authors or fiction concerning Native American art, literature, or history. Also considers material on American West. Buys 4-6 mss/year. Query by letter with clips of published work or telephone. Length: 1,000-2,500 words. Pays $150-300.

Poetry: Avant-garde, free verse, traditional. No "over-romanticized or mystical poetic images of American Indians." Buys 6-8/year. Length: open. Pays $30-75.

Fillers: Rarely purchases fillers.

Tips: "Writers should have academic background or personal experience with Native American or Western art and history. While most of our articles and photographs are from freelance contributors, all are experienced in the field."

FUNNYWORLD, THE MAGAZINE OF ANIMATION & COMIC ART, Box 1633, New York NY 10001. For animation and comic art collectors and others in the field. Quarterly magazine; 56 pages. Circ. 7,000. Pays on publication. Buys all rights. Photocopied and previously published work OK. Computer print-out submission OK. SASE. Reports in 1 month. Sample copy $3.50.

Nonfiction: Historical (history of animation and its creators; history of comic books, characters and creators); interview (with creators of comics and animated cartoons); and reviews (of materials in this field). Buys 6 unsolicited mss/year. Query. Pays $50 minimum.

Photos: "Photos of creators, film stills, comic strips and art used extensively." State availability of photos. Pay varies for 8x10 b&w and color glossy prints. Offers no additional payment for photos accepted with ms. Captions preferred.

GLASS, Box 23383, Portland OR 97223. Editor: Maureen R. Michelson. A fine arts quarterly publication that showcases all aspects of glass art as well as artists, collectors, museum exhibits, etc. Appeals to artists, hobbyists, museums, galleries, collectors and anyone else interested in looking at glass art. Circ. 30,000. Pays 1 month after publication.

Nonfiction: "This magazine showcases glass as a fine art, showing only the best. We are looking for artists' profiles, exhibit reviews, special features. Writing for this publication requires considerable knowledge about the medium." Pays $400 maximum.

GLASS STUDIO, Box 23383, Portland OR 97223. Editor: Maureen R. Michelson. For artists, craftspeople, and hobbyists working in blown glass, stained glass, conceptual glass, as well as collectors, museum curators, gallery and shop owners, students in the arts, and anyone else interested in glass art. Monthly. Circ. 30,000. Computer printout submissions OK; prefers letter quality to dot matrix. Pays 1 month after publication.

Nonfiction: "We are looking for technical articles, how-to articles from people who know what they're talking about. Also, features on artists, glass companies, and unusual stories related to glass art. Remember, you are writing for a specific audience that either works with glass or collects it." Pays $200 maximum.

Photos: No additional payment for photos used with mss.

METALSMITH, Society of North American Goldsmiths, 2489 St. Ann Dr., Green Bay WI 54301. Editor: Sarah Bodine. Editorial address: 1 Penn Lyle Rd., Princeton Jct. NJ 08550. Quarterly magazine covering craft metalwork and metal arts for people who work in metal and those interested in the field, including museum curators, collectors and teachers. The magazine covers all aspects of the craft including historical and technical articles, business and marketing advice and exhibition reviews. Circ. 2,300. Pays on publication. Byline given. Buys first North American serial rights. Submit seasonal/holiday material 6 months in advance. Photocopied and previously published submissions (foreign) OK. Computer printout submission OK; prefers letter quality to dot matrix. SASE. Reports in 1 month on queries; 6 weeks on mss.

Nonfiction: Expose (metals, markets, theft); historical/nostalgic; how-to (advanced-level metalsmithing techniques); humor; inspirational; interview/profile; opinion (regular column); personal experience; photo feature; technical (research); travel (Metalsmith's Guides to Cities). Special issues include: Annual Summer Program Listing and Suppliers Listing. Buys 15 mss/year. Recent article example: "The Toolmaker's Art" (Winter 1982-83). Query with clips of published work and indicate "experience in the field or related fields." Length: 1,000-3,500 words. Pays $25-100/article.

Columns/Departments: Exhibition reviews; Issues: Galleries, Marketing and Business Advice, Metalsmith's Guides to Cities and Regions, and Book Reviews. Buys 20 mss/year. Query with clips of published work. Length: 250-3,000 words. Pays $10-50/article.

Tips: "The discovery of new talent is a priority—queries about innovative work which has not received much publicity are welcome. Almost all our writing is done by freelancers. Those knowledgeable in the field and who have previous experience in writing analysis and criticism are most sought after. *Metalsmith* is looking to build a stable of crafts writers and so far have found these few and far between. Those who both have a feeling for metalwork of all kinds and a sharp pencil are sought. Articles must have some substance. We do not go for two-page spreads, so an idea submitted must have thematic unity and depth. We are not looking for pretty pictures of metalwork, but analysis, presentation of new or undiscovered talent and historical documentation. A few lines of explanation of a story idea are therefore helpful."

THE ORIGINAL ART REPORT, Box 1641, Chicago IL 60690. Editor and Publisher: Frank Salantrie. Emphasizes "visual art conditions from the visual artists', and general public's perspective." Monthly newsletter; 6 pages. No computer printouts or disk submissions. Pays on publication. SASE. Reports in 2 weeks. Sample copy $1.25.

Nonfiction: Expose (art galleries, government agencies ripping off artists, or ignoring them), historical (perspective pieces relating to now), humor (whenever possible), informational (material that is unavailable in other art publications), inspirational (acts and ideas of courage), interview (with artists, other experts; serious material), personal opinion, technical (brief items to recall traditional methods of producing art), travel (places in the world where artists are welcome and honored), philosophical, economic, aesthetic, and artistic. "No vanity profiles of artists, arts organizations, and arts promoters' operations." Buys 4-5 mss/year. Query or submit complete ms. Length: 1,000 words maximum. Pays 1¢/word.

Columns/Departments: New column: In Back of the Individual Artist. "Artists express their views about non-art topics. After all, artists are in this world, too!;" WOW (Worth One Wow), Worth Repeating, and Worth Repeating Again. "Basically, these are reprint items with introduction to give context and source, including complete name and address of publication. Looking for insightful, succinct commentary." Submit complete ms. Length: 500 words maximum. Pays ½¢/word.

Tips: "I get excited when ideas are proposed which address substantive problems of individual artist in the art condition and as they affect the general population. Send original material that is direct and to the point, opinionated and knowledgeable. Write in a factual style with clarity. No straight educational or historical stuff, please." Recent article example: "Money, Museums, and History" (Vol. 6, No. 8).

‡PLATE WORLD, The Magazine of Collector's Plates, Plate World Ltd., 6054 W. Touhy, Chicago IL 60648. (312)763-7773. Editor: Sam Bauman. Associate Editor: Alyson Wycoff. Bimonthly magazine. "We write exclusively about limited edition collector's plates/artists/makers. Our audience is involved in plates as collectors or retailers, makers or producers." Circ. 75,000. Pays on publication. Byline given. Offers 50% kill fee. Makes work-for-hire assignments. Submit seasonal/holiday material 5 months in advance. Computer printout submissions OK. Reports in 2 weeks on queries; 1 week on mss. Sample copy $3.50; free writer's guidelines.

Nonfiction: Interview/profile (how artists create, biography of artist); photo feature (about artist or plate manufacturer). No critical attacks on industry. Buys 10 mss/year. Query. Pays $100-400.

Photos: Mike Reagan, art director. Human interest, technical. State availability of photos. Reviews transparencies. Pays negotiable rate. Identification of subjects required. Buys all rights.

Tips: Profiles of artists working in plates is the area most open to freelancers.

SOUTHWEST ART, Box 13037, Houston TX 77219. (713)850-0990. Editor: Susan Hallsten McGarry. Emphasizes art—painting and sculpture. Monthly. Pays on 10th of the month of publication. Buys first rights. Photocopied submissions OK. SASE. Reports in 3 months. Sample copy $6.

Nonfiction: Informational, interview, personal opinion, and profile. "We publish articles about artists and art trends, concentrating on a geographical area west of the Mississippi. Articles should explore the artist's personality, philosophy, media and techniques, and means by which they convey ideas." Buys approximately 100 mss/year. Must submit 20 color prints/transparencies along with a full biography of the artist. If artist is accepted, article length is 2,000 words minimum. Pays $200 base.

Tips: "Submit both published and unpublished samples of your writing. An indication of how quickly you work and your availability on short notice is helpful."

WESTART, Box 1396, Auburn CA 95603. (916)885-0969. Editor-in-Chief: Martha Garcia. Emphasizes art for practicing artists and artist/craftsmen; students of art and art patrons. Semimonthly tabloid; 20 pages. Circ. 7,500. Pays on publication. Buys all rights. Byline given. Phone queries OK. Photocopied submissions OK. Sample copy 50¢; free writer's guidelines.

Nonfiction: Informational; photo feature and profile. No hobbies. Buys 6-8 mss/year. Query or submit complete ms. Length: 700-800 words. Pays 30¢/column inch.

Photos: Purchased with or without accompanying ms. Send b&w prints. Pays 30¢/column inch.

Tips: "We publish information which is current—that is, we will use a review of an exhibition only if exhibition is still open on date of publication. Therefore, reviewer must be familiar with our printing deadlines and news deadlines."

Association, Club, and Fraternal

These publications keep members, friends and institutions informed of the ideals, objectives, projects, and activities of the sponsoring club or organization. Club-financed magazines that carry material not directly related to the group's activities (for example, *The American Legion Magazine* in the General Interest section) are classified by their subject matter in the Consumer and Trade Journals sections of this book.

CALIFORNIA HIGHWAY PATROLMAN, California Association of Highway Patrolmen, 2030 V St., Sacramento CA 95818. (916)452-6751. Editor: Richard York. Monthly magazine; 100 plus pages. Circ. 18,000. Pays on publication. Buys all rights. SASE. Reports in 2 months. Free sample copy.
Nonfiction: Publishes articles on transportation safety and driver education. "Topics can include autos, boats, bicycles, motorcycles, snowmobiles, recreational vehicles and pedestrian safety. We are also in the market for travel pieces and articles on early California. We are *not* a technical journal for teachers and traffic safety experts, but rather a general interest publication geared toward the layman." Pays 2½¢/word.
Photos: "Illustrated articles always receive preference." Pays $2.50/b&w photo. Captions and model releases required.

D.A.C. NEWS, Detroit Athletic Club, 241 Madison Ave., Detroit MI 48226. Editor: John H. Worthington. For business and professional men. Much of the magazine is devoted to member activities, including social events and athletic activities at the club. Magazine published 9 times/year. Pays after publication. Buys first rights. Byline given. SASE. Reports in 1 month. Sample copy for 9x12 SASE.
Nonfiction: General interest articles, usually male-oriented, about sports (pro football, baseball, squash, golf, skiing and tennis); travel (to exclusive resorts and offbeat places); drama; personalities; health (jogging, tennis elbow, coronary caution); and some humor, if extremely well-done. Some nostalgia (football greats, big band era are best examples). "We would like to see articles on eccentric millionaires, sunken treasure, the world's biggest yacht, old English pubs, the economy, football's greatest games, offbeat resorts and gourmet foods." Buys 5-6 unsolicited mss/year. Send complete ms. Length: 750-3,000 words. Pays $50-250.
Photos: Send photos with ms. Offers no additional payment for photos accepted with mss.
Tips: "Tell us your story idea and where you have been published previously. Give us a brief synopsis of one idea. Express a cheerful willingness to rewrite along our lines." Recent article example: "Detroit Lions' '57 Championship Team" (October, 1982).

THE ELKS MAGAZINE, 425 W. Diversey, Chicago IL 60614. Managing Editor: Donald Stahl. Emphasizes general interest with family appeal. Magazine published 10 times/year. 56 pages. Circ. 1,600,000. Pays on acceptance. Buys first North American serial rights. SASE. Reports in 6 weeks. Free sample copy and writer's guidelines.
Nonfiction: Articles of information, business, contemporary life problems and situations, or just interesting topics, ranging from medicine, science, and history, to sports. "The articles should not just be a rehash of existing material. They must be fresh, provocative, thought provoking, well researched and documented. No fiction, travel or political articles, fillers or verse. Buys 2-3 mss/issue. Written query a must. No phone queries. Length 2,000-3,500 words. Pays $150-500.
Photos: Purchased with or without accompanying manuscript (for cover). Captions required. Query with b&w photos or send transparencies. Uses 8x10 or 5x7 b&w glossies and 35mm or 2¼x2¼ color transparencies (for cover). Pays $250 minimum for color (cover). Offers no additional payment for photos accepted with mss.
Tips: "Since we continue to offer sample copies and guidelines for the asking there is no excuse for being unfamiliar with *The Elks Magazine*. A submission, following a query letter go-ahead would do best to include several b&w prints, if the piece lends itself to illustration."

THE KIWANIS MAGAZINE, 3636 Woodview Trace, Indianapolis IN 46268. Executive Editor: Scott Pemberton. Magazine published 10 times/year for business and professional men and their families. Circ. 300,000. Buys first North American serial rights. Pays 20-40% kill fee. Byline given. Pays on acceptance. Free sample copy. Computer printout submissions OK "If clear and paper is of good quality. Prefer writers separate sheets before submission." Reports in 1 month. SASE.
Nonfiction and Photos: Articles about social and civic betterment, business, education, religion, family, sports, health, recreation, etc. Emphasis on objectivity, intelligent analysis and thorough research of contemporary problems. Concise, lively writing, absence of cliches, and impartial presentation of controversy required. Especially needs "articles on business and professional topics that will directly assist the readers in their own businesses (generally independent retailers and companies of less than 25 employees) or careers. We

have an increasing need for articles of international interest and those that will enlighten our readers about the problems of underprivileged children and the handicapped." Length: 1,500-3,000 words. Pays $300-600. "No fiction, personal essays, fillers or verse of any kind. A light or humorous approach welcomed where subject is appropriate and all other requirements are observed. Detailed queries can save work and submission time. We often accept photos submitted with mss, but we do not pay extra for them; they are considered part of the price of the ms. Our rate for a ms with good photos is higher than for one without." Query.

LEADER, The Order of United Commercial Travelers of America, 632 N. Park St., Box 159019, Columbus OH 43215. (614)228-3276. Editor-in-Chief: James R. Eggert. Emphasizes fraternalism for its officers and active membership. Magazine published 6 times/year; 32 pages. Circ. 20,000. Pays on publication. Buys all rights. Byline given. Submit seasonal/holiday material 3 months in advance. SASE. Reports in 1 week. Free sample copy and writer's guidelines.
Nonfiction: Fraternal/volunteer articles; no anecdotes, jokes, or material written from the first-person point of view. Submit complete ms. Length: 500-1,000 words. Pays 1½¢/word.
Photos: State availability of photos with ms. Pays $5 for b&w glossy prints. Captions preferred. Buys all rights. Model release required.
Tips: "The *Leader* is primarily a fraternal publication. We are looking for articles dealing with fraternal topics, as well as volunteer opportunities, for our four chief civic causes: Aid to Retarded Citizens; Cancer Education/ Prevention; Safety; and Youth."

THE LION, 300 22nd St., Oak Brook IL 60570. (312)986-1700. Editor-in-Chief: Roy Schaetzel. Senior Editor: Robert Kleinfelder. Covers service club organization for Lions Club members and their families. Monthly magazine; 36 pages. Circ. 670,000. Pays on acceptance. Buys all rights. Byline given. Phone queries OK. Photocopied submissions OK. No computer printouts or disk submissions. SASE. Reports in 2 weeks. Free sample copy and writer's guidelines.
Nonfiction: Informational (stories of interest to civic-minded men) and photo feature (must be of a Lions Club service project). No travel, biography, or personal experiences. No sensationalism. Prefers anecdotes in articles. Buys 4 mss/issue. Query. Length: 500-2,200. Pays $50-400.
Photos: Purchased with or without accompanying ms or on assignment. Captions required. Query for photos. B&w and color glossies at least 5x7 or 35mm color slides. Total purchase price for ms includes payment for photos, accepted with ms. "Be sure photos are clear and as candid as possible."
Tips: "The Lions Club project proposed for assignment should be large enough in scope to warrant feature-length treatment. Ascertain first the amount of money raised or the number of people who benefit as a result of the project."

NATIONAL 4-H NEWS, 7100 Connecticut Ave., Chevy Chase MD 20815. (301)656-9000, ext. 219. Editor: Suzanne C. Harting. For "volunteers of a wide range of ages who lead 4-H clubs; most with high school, many with college education, whose primary reason for reading us is their interest in working with kids in informal youth education projects, ranging from aerospace to sewing, and almost anything in between." Monthly. Circ. 90,000. Buys first serial or one-time rights. Computer printout and disk submissions OK. Buys about 1-2 unsolicited mss/year. Pays on acceptance. Free sample copy and writer's guidelines. Query with outline. "We are very specialized, and unless a writer has been published in our magazine before, he more than likely doesn't have a clue to what we can use. When query comes about a specific topic, we often can suggest angles that make it usable." Submit seasonal material 1 year in advance. Reports in 1 month. SASE.
Nonfiction: "Education and child psychology from authorities, written in light, easy-to-read fashion with specific suggestions how the layman can apply principles in volunteer work with youth; how-to-do-it pieces about genuinely new and interesting crafts of any kind. Craft articles must be fresh in style and ideas, and tell how to make something worthwhile . . . almost anything that tells about kids having fun and learning outside the classroom, including how they became interested, most effective programs, etc., always with enough detail and examples, so reader can repeat project or program with his or her group, merely by reading the article. Speak directly to our reader (you) without preaching. Tell him in a conversational manner how he might work better with kids to help them have fun and learn at the same time. Use lots of genuine examples (although names and dates are not important) to illustrate points. Use contractions when applicable. Write in a concise, interesting way. Our readers have other jobs and not a lot of time to spend with us. Will not print personal reminiscences, stories on 'How this 4-H club made good' or about state or county fair winners." Length: 3-8 pages, typewritten, doublespaced. Payment up to $200, depending on quality and accompanying photos or illustrations.
Photos: State availability of photos. "Photos must be genuinely candid, of excellent technical quality and preferably shot 'available light' or in that style; must show young people or adults and young people having fun learning something. How-to photos or drawings must supplement instructional texts. Photos do not necessarily have to include people. Photos are usually purchased with accompanying ms, with no additional payment. Captions required. If we use an excellent single photo, we generally pay $25 and up."
Tips: There will be "more emphasis on interpersonal skills, techniques for working with kids, more focus on

Close-up

Robert Kleinfelder
Senior Editor, *The Lion*

Some association, club and fraternal magazines can send writers' words around the world. And writers don't need a passport or membership card to take the trip.

What they do need, according to Robert Kleinfelder, senior editor of the Lions Clubs International's monthly magazine, is an understanding of the market they are writing for.

The Lion, with a circulation exceeding 1.25 million, has 25 separate editions in 18 languages. Kleinfelder works to keep the US and Canadian edition as international as possible, while reporting state and local service projects.

Unlike some fraternal publications, *The Lion* does not cover ceremonies or social functions. Kleinfelder buys articles on Lions service projects that he hopes other clubs will follow and general-interest stories for civic-minded men.

And in fact, articles on American or Canadian service projects sometimes prompt overseas clubs to start similar programs. A Lions Club in Japan, for example, started a camp for children with diabetes—after an article about the Texas Lions clubs' camp appeared in *The Lion*. This is one of the rewards of Kleinfelder's job—and of the writers whose words are published in *The Lion* and read around the world.

Kleinfelder, a 15-year veteran of *The Lion*, gets about 25 to 30 queries, manuscripts and cartoons each week. Submissions vie to be among the five to eight bylined articles in each edition. About 90 percent of these bylined pieces are written by non-Lion members.

What concerns Kleinfelder is the five or six submissions that might arrive in a day's mail—totally unrelated to the magazine's format and audience. Despite the fact that the magazine is clearly geared for the 670,000 Lions members and their families, he occasionally gets material suited for men's magazines. "It's up to writers," says Kleinfelder, "to take the responsibility to tailor their submissions to our readership."

To ensure that a subject is "right" for *The Lion*, Kleinfelder encourages writers to contact him by phone with article ideas, especially if they will be visiting an area where a major Lion project is planned.

But a phone query does not mean that the writer won't have to organize ideas before writing the story. If the idea fits the magazine's content, Kleinfelder then asks for a detailed letter with facts and an outline for the proposed article. He also reminds potential *Lion* writers never to overlook the importance of anecdotes, details, and pictures with a story. "Writers who aren't really interested in details have no place in the business," he says.

The advice is grounded in experience, as Kleinfelder, himself, is a sometimes freelancer. He tells writers, "Don't get discouraged if you don't sell an article on the first try." For a writer seeking a byline in a high-circulation club magazine, like *The Lion*, heeding that advice and knowing the publication's audience are good ways to increase your chances of being read around the world.

—Paula Deimling

the family. Familiarity with the 4-H program and philosophy is most helpful. Write for sample copy. I judge a writer's technical skills by the grammar and syntax of query letter; seldom ask for a ms I think will require extensive reorganization or heavy editing." Recent article example: "We the People" June-July 1982.

THE OPTIMIST MAGAZINE, Optimist International, 4494 Lindell Blvd., St. Louis MO 63108. (314)371-6000. Editor: Dennis R. Osterwisch. Monthly magazine about the work of Optimist clubs and members for the 140,000 members of the Optimist clubs in the United States and Canada. Circ. 140,000. Pays on acceptance. Buys first North American serial rights. Submit seasonal material 3 months in advance. Photocopied and previously published submissions OK. Computer printout and disk submissions OK; prefers letter quality to dot matrix printouts. SASE. Reports in 1 week. Free sample copy.
Nonfiction: General interest (people, places and things that would interest men dedicated to community service through volunteer work); interview (members who have in some way distinguished themselves). No articles of a negative nature. "A well-written article on some unusual Optimist-related activity with good action photos will probably be purchased, as well as, upbeat general interest articles that point out the good side of life, anything that promotes fellowship, international understanding, respect for the law, and anything that highlights what's good about the youth of today." Buys 2-3 mss/issue. Query. "Submit a letter that conveys your ability to turn out a well-written article and tells exactly what the scope of the article will be and whether photos are available." Length: 1,000-1,500 words. Pays $75-125.
Photos: State availability of photos. Payment negotiated. Captions preferred. Buys all rights. "No mug shots or people lined up against the wall shaking hands. We're always looking for good color photos relating to Optimist activities that could be used on our front cover. Colors must be sharp and the composition must be suitable to fit an 8½x11 cover."
Tips: "We are mainly interested in seeing general-interest articles from freelancers because most club activities are better covered by club members. We're open to almost any idea; that's why all queries will be carefully considered. We don't want stories about a writer's Uncle Clem who 'had a rough life but always kept a smile on his face.' If you don't know about Optimist International, ask for our free sample magazine." Recently published article: "Volunteer Burnout" (the problem of letting one or two volunteers "do everything").

PERSPECTIVE, Pioneer Clubs, Division of Pioneer Ministries, Inc., Box 788, Wheaton IL 60189. (312)293-1600. Editor: Julie Smith. "All subscribers are volunteer leaders of clubs for girls and boys in grades 1-12. Clubs are sponsored by evangelical, conservative churches throughout North America." Quarterly magazine; 32 pages. Circ. 24,000. Pays on acceptance. Buys first North American serial rights. Submit seasonal/holiday material 9 months in advance. Simultaneous submissions OK. No computer printouts or disk submissions. SASE. Reports in 6 weeks. Sample copy $1; writer's guidelines for SASE.
Nonfiction: How-to (projects for clubs, crafts, cooking, service), informational (relationships, human development, mission education, outdoor activities), inspirational (Bible studies, adult leading youths), interview (Christian education leaders), personal experience (of club leaders). Buys 4-10 mss/year; 3 unsolicited/year. Byline given. Query. Length: 200-1,500 words. Pays $10-60.
Columns/Departments: Storehouse (craft, game, activity, outdoor activity suggestions—all related to club projects for any age between grades 1-12). Buys 8-10 mss/year. Submit complete ms. Length: 150-250 words. Pays $8-10.
Tips: "Submit articles directly related to club work, practical in nature, i.e., ideas for leader training in communication, Bible knowledge, teaching skills. They must have practical application. We want substance—not ephemeral ideas. In addition to a summary of the article idea and evidence that the writer has knowledge of the subject, we want evidence that the author understands our purpose and philosophy. We're doing more and more inhouse writing—less purchasing of any freelance." Recent article example: "One Week at a Time" (spring 1982).

PORTS O' CALL, Box 530, Santa Rosa CA 95402. (707)542-0898. Editor: William A. Breniman. Newsbook of the Society of Wireless Pioneers. Society members are mostly early-day wireless "brass-pounders" who sent code signals from ships or manned shore stations handling wireless or radio traffic. Biannually. Not copyrighted. Pays on acceptance. No computer printout or disk submissions. Reports on submissions "within 30 days (depending on workload)." SASE.
Nonfiction: Articles about early-day wireless as used in ship-shore and high power operation; radar, electronic aids, SOS calls, etc. Early-day ships, records, etc. "Writers should remember that our members have gone to sea for years and would be critical of material that is not authentic. We are not interested in any aspect of amateur radio. We are interested in authentic articles dealing with ships (since about 1910)." Oddities about the sea and weather as it affects shipping. Buys 45 unsolicited mss/year. Query. Length: 500-2,000 words. Pays 1-5¢/word.
Photos: Fred B. Rosebury, department editor. Purchased with mss. Unusual shots of sea or ships. Wireless pioneers. Prefers b&w, "4x5 would be the most preferable size but it really doesn't make too much difference as long as the photos are sharp and the subject interests us." Fine if veloxed, but not necessary. Pays $2.50-10;

"according to our appraisal of our interest." Ship photos of various nations, including postcard size, if clear, 25¢-$1 each.

Poetry: Ships, marine slant (not military), shipping, weather, wireless. No restrictions. Pays $1-$2.50 each.

Tips: "Material will also be considered for our *Ports O' Call* biannual and *Sparks Journal*, a quarterly tabloid newsletter. *Sparks* (published yearly) takes most of the contents used in *Port O' Call*, published now every 2 years in encyclopedic format and content. *The Sparks Journal*, published quarterly in tabloid form carries much of the early days, first hand history of wireless (episodes and experiences). Also, *Wireless Almanac* contains much nautical data relating to radio and wireless used at sea."

THE ROTARIAN, 1600 Ridge Ave., Evanston IL 60201. (312)328-0100. Editor: Willmon L. White. 50% freelance written. For Rotarian business and professional men and their families; for schools, libraries, hospitals, etc. Monthly. Circ. 490,300. Usually buys all rights. Pays on acceptance. Free sample copy and editorial fact sheet. Query preferred. Reports in 1 month. SASE.

Nonfiction: "The field for freelance articles is in the general interest category. These run the gamut from inspirational guidelines for daily living to such weighty concerns as world hunger, peace, and preservation of environment. Recent articles have dealt with international illiteracy, salary, energy, dehumanization of the elderly, and worldwide drug abuse and prevention. Articles should appeal to an international audience and should in some way help Rotarians help other people. An article may increase a reader's understanding of world affairs, thereby making him a better world citizen. It may educate him in civic matters, thus helping him improve his town. It may help him to become a better employer, or a better human being. We are interested in articles on unusual Rotary club projects or really unusual Rotarians. We carry debates and symposiums, but we are careful to show more than one point of view. We present arguments for effective politics and business ethics, but avoid expose and muckraking. Controversy is welcome if it gets our readers to think but does not offend ethnic or religious groups. In short, the rationale of the organization is one of hope and encouragement and belief in the power of individuals talking and working together." Length: 2,000 words maximum. Payment varies.

Photos: Purchased with mss or with captions only. Prefers 2¼x2¼ or larger color transparencies, but also uses 35mm. B&w prints and photo essays. Vertical shots preferred to horizontal. Scenes of international interest. Color cover.

Poetry and Fillers: "Currently overstocked on serious poetry, but will look at short, light verse." Pays $2 a line. Pays $10 for brief poems. "We occasionally buy short humor pieces."

‡**THE SAMPLE CASE**, The Order of United Commercial Travelers of America, 632 N. Park St., Box 159019, Columbus OH 43215. (614)228-3276. Acting Editor: Elizabeth M. Kowalski. Quarterly magazine covering travel/leisure topics and news for members of the United Commercial Travelers. Circ. 186,000. Pays on publication. Byline given. Buys one-time rights. Submit seasonal/holiday material 3 months in advance. Simultaneous queries and submissions OK. SASE. Reports in 3 months. Free sample copy and writer's guidelines.

Nonfiction: Expose (insurance, business, finance, legal, health, recreational topics); travel (cities/regions in the US and Canada); food/cuisine; health/fitness/safety; hobbies/entertainment; fraternal/civic activities. No fiction or personal experience written from first person point of view. Query. Length: 500-2,000 words. Pays 10¢/word.

Photos: Jeffrey T. Haycock, art director. State availability of photos. Pays minimum $20 for 5x7 b&w or larger prints; $30 for 35mm or larger color transparencies used inside. Captions required.

Columns/Departments: Traveline (a regular column featuring information on certain travel topics—packing, train excursions, golf packages, etc.). Query with published clips. Length: 500-2,000 words. Pays 10¢/word.

THE SERTOMAN, Sertoma International, 1912 E. Meyer Blvd., Kansas City MO 64132. (816)333-8300. Editor: Patrick W. Burke. Quarterly magazine with "service to mankind" as its motto edited for business and professional men. Circ 35,000. Pays on acceptance. Byline given. Buys one-time rights. Submit seasonal material 3 months in advance. Simultaneous, photocopied and previously published submissions OK. SASE. Reports in 2 weeks. Free sample copy.

Nonfiction: General interest (social civic issues, energy, finance, retirement, alcohol, drug abuse); and humor (in daily living). "We're especially interested in articles on speech and hearing, Sertoma's international sponsorship." Buys 2 mss/issue. Query with clips of previously published work. Length: 500-2,000 words. Pays $25-100.

Photos: Pays $5 minimum/5x7 b&w glossy prints. Captions and model release required. Buys one-time rights.

THE TOASTMASTER, Box 10400, Santa Ana CA 92711. (714)542-6793. Editor-in-Chief: Debbie Horn. Covers communication and leadership techniques; self-development for members of Toastmasters International, Inc. Monthly magazine; 32 pages. Circ. 95,000. Pays on acceptance. Buys all rights. Byline given. Photocopied submissions and previously published work OK. No computer printout or disk submissions. SASE. Reports in 3 weeks. Free sample copy and writer's guidelines.

Nonfiction: How-to (improve speaking, listening, thinking skills; on leadership or management techniques, etc., with realistic examples), humor (on leadership, communications or management techniques), interviews (with communications or management experts offering advice that members can directly apply to their self-development efforts; should contain "how to" information). No articles on fear of speaking, time management, meeting planning or basic speaking techniques. Buys 20-30 mss/year. Query. Length: 1,800-3,000 words. Pays $25-150.

Photos: Purchased with or without ms. Query. Pays $10-50 for 5x7 or 8x10 b&w glossy prints; $35-75 for color transparencies. Offers no additional payment for photos accepted with ms.

Tips: "Study our magazine and send us (after a query) material that is related. Since we get a number of articles from our members on 'how to build a speech,' freelancers should concentrate on more specific subjects such as body language, etc. We're a nonprofit organization, so if they're looking to get rich on one article, they can probably forget it. But we do offer inexperienced freelancers an opportunity to get published in a magazine that will give their work international exposure. Offer ideas on subjects that haven't been covered in the past two years (membership turnover period), interviews with celebrities discussing their speaking techniques and success secrets. We prefer a lively writing style with lots of quotes and anecdotes rather than an academic approach."

WOODMEN OF THE WORLD MAGAZINE, 1700 Farnam St., Omaha NE 68102. (402)342-1890, ext. 302. Editor: Leland A. Larson. 20% freelance written. Published by Woodmen of the World Life Insurance Society for "people of all ages in all walks of life. We have both adult and children readers from all types of American families." Monthly. Circ. 467,000. Not copyrighted. Buys 20 mss/year. Byline given. Pays on acceptance. Will send a sample copy to a writer on request. Will consider photocopied and simultaneous submissions. Prefers letter quality to dot matrix computer printout submissions. Submit complete ms. Submit seasonal material 3 months in advance. Reports in 5 weeks. SASE.

Nonfiction: "General interest articles which appeal to the American family—travel, history, art, new products, how-to, sports, hobbies, food, home decorating, family expenses, etc. Because we are a fraternal benefit society operating under a lodge system, we often carry stories on how a number of people can enjoy social or recreational activities as a group. No special approach required. We want more 'consumer type' articles, humor, historical articles, think pieces, nostalgia, photo articles." Recent article example: "Botanical Columbus" (January 1982). Buys 15-24 unsolicited mss/year. Length: 1,500 words or less. Pays $10 minimum, 5¢/word depending on count.

Photos: Purchased with or without mss; captions optional "but suggested." Uses 8x10 glossy prints, 4x5 transparencies ("and possibly down to 35mm"). Payment "depends on use." For b&w photos, pays $25 for cover, $10 for inside. Color prices vary according to use and quality with $100 maximum. Minimum of $25 for inside use; up to $100 for covers.

Fiction: Humorous and historical short stories. Length: 1,500 words or less. Pays "$10 minimum or 5¢/word, depending on count."

Astrology and Psychic

The following publications regard astrology, psychic phenomena, ESP experiences, and related subjects as sciences or as objects of serious scientific research.

AMERICAN ASTROLOGY, Clancy Publications, Inc., 2505 N. Alvernon Way, Tucson AZ 85712. (602)327-3476. Editor: Joanne S. Clancy. 50% freelance written. For all ages, all walks of life. Monthly magazine; 112 pages. Circ. 265,000. Buys all rights. Buys 50-75 mss/year. No computer printout or disk submissions. Pays on publication. Free writer's guidelines. Reports in 1 month. Submit complete ms. SASE.

Nonfiction: Astrological material, often combined with astronomy. More interested in presenting results of research material and data based on time of birth, instead of special Sun-sign readings. Source of birth data must be included. No occult. Length: 3,500 words. "Payment is made according to the astrological knowledge and expertise of the writer."

Tips: Clancy Publications also publishes a 158-page yearbook, *American Astrology Digest.* Articles of about 3,500 words based on astrology that concern environment, sports, vocation, health, etc., will be given prompt consideration for the yearbook.

DOORWAYS TO THE MIND, Aries Productions, Inc., 652 Emerson Ct., Creve Coeur MO 63141. (314)872-9127. Editor: Beverly C. Jaegers. Managing Editor: G. Weingart. Quarterly magazine covering mind development, PSI, practical ESP, stocks and Wall Street, and criminal detection with ESP, predictions. For a general audience interested in mental development and self-help ESP using Russian/USA methods. Pays on publication. Byline given. Not copyrighted. Buys one-time rights. Submit seasonal/holiday material 4 months in advance. Simultaneous queries, and simultaneous, photocopied, and previously published submissions OK. No computer printout or disk submissions. SASE. Reports in 6 weeks. Sample copy for $1, 9x12 SAE, and 3 first class stamps; writer's guidelines for business size SAE and 2 first class stamps.

Nonfiction: Michael Christopher, articles editor. Book excerpts, general interest, inspirational, interview/profile, opinion. Not interested in articles on witchcraft, the occult, UFOs, space creatures or space vehicles, etc. Buys 4-10 mss/year. Send complete ms. Length: 1,000-10,000 words. Pays $10 minimum.

Columns/Departments: Michael Christopher, column/department editor. News & Notes, Book Reviews. Buys 10-12 mss/year. Send complete ms. Length: 200-350 words. Pays $5 minimum.

Poetry: Light verse, traditional. Buys 3-4/year. Submit maximum 5 poems. Pays $5 minimum.

Fillers: Clippings, newsbreaks. Buys variable number/year. Length: 200-550 words. Pays $5 minimum.

Tips: "Write realistically. Include helpful data on ESP development, mind control and special studies such as grapho analysis, astrology, archeology, and crime detection with ESP."

FATE, Clark Publishing Co., 500 Hyacinth Place, Highland Park IL 60035. Editor: Mary Margaret Fuller. 70% freelance written. Monthly. Buys all rights; occasionally North American serial rights only. Byline given. Pays on publication. Query. Reports in 2 months. SASE.

Nonfiction and Fillers: Personal psychic experiences, 300-500 words. Pays $10. New frontiers of science, and ancient civilizations, 2,000-3,000 words; also parapsychology, occultism, witchcraft, magic, spiritual healing miracles, flying saucers, etc. Must include complete authenticating details. Prefers interesting accounts of single events rather than roundups. "We very frequently accept manuscripts from new writers; the majority are individuals' first-person accounts of their own psychic experience. We do need to have all details, where, when, why, who and what, included for complete documentation." Pays minimum of 5¢/word. Fillers should be fully authenticated. Length: 100-300 words.

Photos: Buys good glossy prints with mss. Pays $5-10.

HOROSCOPE, The World's Leading Astrological Magazine, Dell Publishing Co., Inc., 1 Dag Hammarskjold Plaza, 245 E. 47th St., New York NY 10017. (212)605-3439. Editor: Julia A. Wagner. Monthly magazine covering "mundane astrology, self-help, problem analysis. Audience is middle class in the age group 15-80." Circ. 240,000. Pays on acceptance. Byline given. Buys all rights. Submit seasonal/holiday material 6 months in advance. Simultaneous queries OK, but not submissions. SASE. Reports in 2 weeks on queries; 3 months on mss. Free sample copy and writer's guidelines.

Nonfiction: General interest, how-to, technical. Articles must be based on the tropical, not the sidereal, zodiac. No series, planets in the signs, planets in the houses. Buys 75 mss/year. Query. Length: 1,000-2,000 words. Pays 7¢/word.

Fillers: Anecdotes. Buys 240/year. Length: 30-100 words. Pays 7¢/word.

Tips: "You must be skilled as an astrologer and a writer. How-to and self-help articles are most open to freelancers."

HOROSCOPE GUIDE, Box 70, West Springfield MA 01090. Contact: Editor. For persons interested in astrology as it touches their daily lives; all ages. Monthly. Circ. 60,000. Buys all rights. Byline given. Buys 40 mss/year. Pays on acceptance. Sample copy for $1.50. Photocopied submissions OK. Submit seasonal material 5 months in advance. Submit complete ms. SASE.

Nonfiction, Poetry and Fillers: Wants anything of good interest to the average astrology buff, preferably not so technical as to require more than basic knowledge of birth sign by reader. Mss should be light, readable, entertaining and sometimes humorous. Not as detailed and technical as other astrology magazines, "with the astro-writer doing the interpreting without long-winded reference to his methods at every juncture. We are less reverent of astrological red tape." Wants mss about man-woman relationships, preferably in entertaining and occasionally humorous fashion. No textbook-type material. Does not want to see a teacher's type of approach to the subject. Length: 900-4,000 words. Pays 2-3¢/word. Buys traditional forms of poetry. Length: 4-16 lines. Pays $2-$8.

Tips: "Best way to break in with us is with some lively Sun-sign type piece involving some area of man-woman relationships—love, sex, marriage, divorce, differing views on money, religion, child-raising, in-laws, vacations, politics, lifestyles, or whatever."

NEW REALITIES, Suite 408, 680 Beach St., San Francisco CA 94109. (415)776-2600. Editor: James Bolen. 20% freelance written. For general public interested in total wellness, personal growth and in holistic approach to living. Straightforward, entertaining material on new environments, the healing arts, new spirituality, consciousness research, and the frontiers of human potential and the mind. Bimonthly. Buys all rights. Pays on publication. Reports in 6 weeks. Query. SASE.

Nonfiction and Photos: "Documented articles on mental, physical and spiritual holistic dimensions of humankind. Balanced reporting, no editorializing. No personal experiences as such. Accept profiles of leaders in the field. Must have documented evidence about holistic leaders, healers, researchers. Short bibliography for further reading." Length: 1,500-3,500 words. Pays $75-250.

Automotive and Motorcycle

Publications listed in this section detail the maintenance, operation, performance, racing and judging of automobiles, and recreational vehicles. Publications that treat vehicles as a means of transportation or shelter instead of as a hobby or sport are classified in the Travel, Camping, and Trailer category. Journals for teamsters, service station operators, and auto dealers will be found in the Auto and Truck classification of the Trade Journals section.

AMERICAN MOTORCYCLIST, American Motorcyclist Association, Box 141, Westerville OH 43081. (614)891-2425. Managing Editor: Bill Amick. For "enthusiastic motorcyclists, investing considerable time and money in the sport. Unlike most motorcycle magazines, we never publish road tests or product evaluations unless they are related to safety or anti-theft. We emphasize the motorcyclist, not the vehicle." Monthly magazine. Circ. 126,000. Pays on publication. Rights purchased vary with author and material. Pays 25-50% kill fee. Byline given. Query. No computer printouts or disk submissions. Submit seasonal/holiday material 4 months in advance. SASE. Reports in 1 month. Sample copy $1.25.
Nonfiction: How-to (different and/or unusual ways to use a motorcycle or have fun on one); historical (the heritage of motorcycling, particularly as it relates to the AMA); interviews (with interesting personalities in the world of motorcycling); photo feature (quality work on any aspect of motorcycling); and technical (well-researched articles on safe riding techniques). No product evaluations or stories on motorcycling events not sanctioned by the AMA. Buys 10-15 mss/year. Query. Length: 500 words minimum. Pays minimum $2/published column inch.
Photos: Greg Harrison, associate editor. Purchased with or without accompanying ms, or on assignment. Captions required. Query. Pays $15 minimum per photo published.
Tips: "Accuracy and reliability are prime factors in our work with freelancers. We emphasize the rider, not the motorcycle itself. It's always best to query us first and the further in advance the better to allow for scheduling."

‡**AUTOBUFF MAGAZINE, The Magazine for the Adult Automotive Enthusiast**, Carnaby Communications Corp., Box 88690, Atlanta GA 30356-8690. (404)394-0010. Editor: D.B. Naef. Managing Editor: F. Fittanto. Bimonthly magazine covering high-performance automobiles for 18-34-year-old males with high discretionary incomes and an interest in beautiful women. Estab. 1982. Circ. 200,000. Pays ½ on acceptance, ½ on publication. Byline given. Buys one-time rights. Simultaneous and photocopied submissions OK. SASE. Reports in 3 weeks. Sample copy for 9x12 SAE and $1.22 postage; writer's guidelines for SAE and 1 first class stamp.
Nonfiction: How-to (high performance automotive); humor (auto related); technical (high performance automotive). No women's lib, gay material. "Each issue features the finest 'street machines' the country has to offer along with the most attractive female models to be found anywhere." Buys 12 mss/year. Send complete ms. Length: 1,500-2,500 words. Pays $150-250.
Photos: Send photos with ms. Review 2¼ or 35mm color transparencies and 8x10 b&w prints. Captions and model release required. Buys all rights.
Fiction: Adventure, erotica, humorous. Buys 15 mss/year. Send complete ms. Length: 2,000-3,000 words. Pays $150-250.

AUTOMOBILE QUARTERLY, 221 Nassau St., Princeton NJ 08540. (609)924-7555. Editor-in-Chief: L. Scott Bailey. Emphasizes automobiles and automobile history. Quarterly hardbound magazine; 112 pages. Circ. 40,000. Pays on acceptance. Buys all rights. Pays expenses as kill fee. Byline given. SASE. Reports in 3 weeks. Sample copy $12.95.
Nonfiction: Authoritative articles relating to the automobile and automobile history. Historical, interview and nostalgia. Buys 5 mss/issue. Query. Length: 2,000-20,000 words. Pays $200-800.
Photos: Purchased on assignment. Captions required. Query. Uses 8x10 b&w glossy prints and 4x5 color transparencies. "Payment varies with assignment and is negotiated prior to assignment."
Tips: "Familiarity with the magazine a *must*."

AUTOWEEK, Crain Consumer Group, Inc., 965 E. Jefferson, Detroit MI 48207. (313)567-9520. Managing Editor: John Mulhere. Emphasizes automobile racing and the auto industry, domestic and international. Weekly tabloid. Circ. 150,000. Pays on publication. Byline "generally given." Buys first North American serial rights or by agreement with author. Submit seasonal material 2 months in advance. SASE. Reports in 2-4 weeks. Free sample copy and writer's guidelines.
Nonfiction: Wide variety of articles from nostalgia to news reports, driving impressions to technical analyses,

personality profiles to 'sneak' previews of future products. "We maintain a fulltime staff in Detroit, with a group of regular correspondents around the country and overseas. We do, however, solicit manuscripts from literate, knowledgeable writers." Recent article example: Dutch Mandel's "In Search of the Van Culture" in the April 11, 1983 issue. Buys 24 mss/year. Length: 1,000-2,500 words. Query. Pays negotiable rates.
Photos: Pays $15/b&w; $35/color transparency.

BMX ACTION, Wizard Publications, 3162 Kashiwa, Torrance CA 90505. (213)539-9213. Editor: Steve Giberson. Publisher/Managing Editor: Bob Osborn. Monthly magazine covering bicycle motocross for "all young people (average reader: 14.5-year-old male) . . . whether they're actively racing or not." Circ. 150,000. Pays on publication. Byline given. Offers negotiable kill fee. Buys all rights. Submit seasonal/holiday material 6 months in advance. Photocopied submissions OK. SASE. Reports in 1 month on queries; 5 weeks on mss. Sample copy $2; writer's guidelines for business size SASE and 20¢ postage.
Nonfiction: General interest (impact of BMX, growth, etc.), how-to (BMX racing, bike repair, riding techniques, race preparation, nutrition, bike maintenance), humor ("doesn't hurt in any of our pieces"), interview/profile (with established BMX stars, etc.), personal experience (only if tied to 'how-to'), photo feature ("will consider, but our photos are tops"), technical (product review and evaluation—query first), travel (BMX should be central theme . . . and how it's growing in other countries). No race coverage ("we do that ourselves!") and local track stories not of national interest. Query with clips of published work if available. Length: 1,500-2,500 words. Pays $25-250.
Photos: Bob Osborn, photo editor. Needs "good action shots." Pays $10-30 for 35mm color transparencies (more for cover shots). Pays $5-25 for 8x10 b&w prints. Captions and identification of subjects required.

BMX PLUS MAGAZINE, Daisy/Hi-Torque Publishing Co., Inc., 10600 Sepulveda Blvd., Mission Hills CA 91345. (714)545-6012. Editor: John Ker. Managing Editor: Dean Bradley. Monthly magazine covering the sport of bicycle motocross for a youthful readership (95% male, aged 8-25). Circ. 89,000. Pays on publication. Byline given. Buys one-time rights. Submit seasonal/holiday material 3 months in advance. Simultaneous queries and submissions OK. SASE. Reports in 2 months. Sample copy $2; writer's guidelines for business size SAE and 1 first class stamp.
Nonfiction: Historical/nostaglic, how-to, humor, interview/profile, new product, photo feature, technical, travel. "No articles for a general audience; our readers are BMX fanatics." Buys 20 mss/year. Send complete ms. Length: 500-1,500 words. Pays $30-250.
Photos: "Photography is the key to our magazine. Send us some exciting and/or unusual photos of hot riders in action." Send photos with ms. Pays $25 for color photo published; $10 for b&w photos. Reviews 35mm color transparencies and b&w negatives and 8x10 prints. Captions and identification of subjects required.
Tips: "The sport of BMX is very young. The opportunities for talented writers and photographers in this field are wide open. Send us a good interview or race story with photos. Race coverage is the area that's easiest to break into. It must be a *big* race, preferably international in scope. Submit story within one week of completion of race."

CANADIAN MOTORCYCLE RIDER, Hodgson Publishing Co., 1948 Queen St. E., Toronto, Ontario, Canada M4L 1H6. (416)690-0566. Editor: Dave Dutton. Bimonthly magazine for motorcycle enthusiasts. Circ. 55,000. Pays on acceptance. Byline given. Buys one-time rights and second serial (reprint) rights. Submit seasonal/holiday material 4 months in advance. Simultaneous queries, and photocopied and previously published submissions OK. SASE. Reports in 1 week on queries; 2 weeks on mss. Sample copy $1.75.
Nonfiction: Book excerpts, general interest, historical/nostalgic, how-to, humor, interview/profile, new product, opinion, personal experience, photo feature, technical, travel. "We look kindly on stories that are a little more skeptical, a little funnier, a tad more literate and a shade less technical than the norm." No "under-researched first person recitations of last summer's vacation trip; pompous, under-researched technobabble." Buys 30 mss/year. Query with clips of published work. Length: 500-3,000 words. Pays $25-150.
Columns/Departments: 'First Kicks'—opening section of 500-1,250 word short articles on wide variety of topics: opinion and news. Buys variable number mss/year.
Tips: "Simply provide a concise, entertaining 100-word outline of what you have in mind. Many of our writers have never previously been published."

CAR AND DRIVER, 2002 Hogback Rd., Ann Arbor MI 48104. (313)994-0055. Editor/Publisher: David E. Davis Jr. For auto enthusiasts; college-educated, professional, median 24-30 years of age. Monthly magazine; 120 pages. Circ. 740,000. Rights purchased vary with author and material. Buys all rights or first North American serial rights. Buys 10-12 unsolicited mss/year. Pays on acceptance. Submit seasonal material 4 months in advance. Query with clips of previously published work. Reports in 2 months. SASE.
Nonfiction and Photos: Non-anecdotal articles about the more sophisticated treatment of autos and motor racing. Exciting, interesting cars. Automotive road tests, informational articles on cars and equipment; some satire and humor. Personalities, past and present, in the automotive industry and automotive sports. "Treat readers as intellectual equals. Emphasis on people as well as hardware." Informational, how-to, humor, histor-

ical, think articles, and nostalgia. Length: 750-2,000 words. Pays $200-1,500. B&w photos purchased with accompanying mss with no additional payment. Also buys mini-features for FYI department. Length: about 500 words. Pays $100-500.

Tips: "It is best to start off with an interesting query and to stay away from nuts-and-bolts stuff since that will be handled in-house or by an acknowledged expert. Our goal is to be absolutely without flaw in our presentation of automotive facts, but we strive to be every bit as entertaining as we are informative."

CAR COLLECTOR/CAR CLASSICS, Classic Publishing, Inc., Suite 144, 8601 Dunwoody Pl., Atlanta GA 30338. Editor: Donald R. Peterson. For people interested in all facets of classic, milestone, antique, special interest and sports cars; also mascots, models, restoration, license plates and memorabilia. Monthly magazine; 76 pages. Circ. 55,000. Pays on publication. Submit seasonal/holiday material 4 months in advance. Photocopied submissions OK. SASE. Reports in 2 months. Sample copy: $2 and free writer's guidelines.
Nonfiction: General interest, historical, how-to, humor, inspirational, interview, nostalgia, personal opinion, profile, photo feature, technical and travel. Buys 75-100 mss/year. Query with clips of published work. Buys 24-36 unsolicited mss/year. Length: 300-2,500 words. Pays 5¢/word minimum.
Photos: State availability of photos with ms. Offers additional payment for photos with accompanying mss. Uses b&w glossy prints; color transparencies. Pays a minimum of $75 for cover and centerfold color; $10 for inside color; $5 for inside b&w. Buys one-time rights. Captions and model release required.
Columns/Departments: "Rarely add a new columnist but we are open to suggestions." Buys 36/year. Query with clips of published work. Length: 2,000 maximum; prefer 1,000-2,000 words. Pays 5¢/word.
Tips: Recent article example: "The Two Roads Home" (April 1982).

CAR CRAFT, Petersen Publishing Co., 8490 Sunset Blvd., Los Angeles CA 90069. (213)657-5100, ext. 345. Editor: Jon Asher. For men and women, 18-34, "enthusiastic owners of 1949 and newer muscle cars." Monthly magazine; 132 pages. Circ. 400,000. Study past issues before making submissions or story suggestions. Buys all rights. Buys 2-10 mss/year. Computer printout submissions OK. Pays generally on publication, on acceptance under special circumstances. Query. SASE.
Nonfiction and Photos: How-to articles ranging from the basics to fairly sophisticated automotive modifications. Drag racing feature stories and some general car features on modified late model automobiles. Especially interested in do-it-yourself automotive tips, suspension modifications, mileage improvers and even shop tips and homemade tools. Stories about drag racing personalities are generally of more interest than stories about racing machinery. Length: open. Pays $100-200/page. Art director: J.R. Martinez. Photos purchased with or without accompanying text. Captions suggested, but optional. Reviews 8x10 b&w glossy prints; 35mm or 2¼x2¼ color negotiable. Pays $30 for b&w, color negotiable. "Pay rate higher for complete story, i.e. photos, captions, headline, subtitle: the works, ready to go."

CAR EXCHANGE MAGAZINE, Krause Publications, 700 E. State St., Iola WI 54990. Editor: Richard Johnson. Monthly magazine devoted to postwar automotive hobby (cars between 1946 and 1972) for 18-40 year old automobile collectors and enthusiasts with average to above average education. Circ. 137,000. Pays on acceptance. Computer printouts and disk submissions OK; prefers letter quality to dot matrix printouts. Submit seasonal material 4 months in advance. SASE. Reports in 1 month on queries. Free sample copy; free writer's guidelines with SASE.
Nonfiction: Historical; how-to (restore, buy, sell, store, transport); humor; interview (past designers who worked on cars); new product (products for collectors, calendars, tools, polishing); photo feature (car collector, meets, shows); technical (repairs). "No 'local club does this or that, local man restores car,' or 'a story about my car.' " Buys 80-120 mss/year. Query. Length: 300-2,000 words. Pays 5¢/word.
Photos: "We do not accept manuscripts without accompanying art." Send photos with ms. Pays $5/5x7 b&w glossy prints. Pays $50 minimum/2¼x2¼ or 4x5 color transparencies.
Columns/Departments: Book reviews, short subjects. Buys 24 mss/year. Send complete ms with dust jacket. Length: 100-500 words.
Fiction: Adventure, experimental, historical and mainstream. "Must have emphasis on postwar collectible cars." Length: 500-2,000 words. Pays 4¢/word.
Tips: "The best way to break in is to know the subject and consider the audience carefully. Write short, lively prose. We're expanding—more market for writers."

CARMAG, Canadian Automobile Repair & Maintenance, CARM Publishing, Inc., 41 Mutual St., Toronto, Ontario, Canada M5B 2A7. (416)363-3013. Editor: Ed Belitsky. Bimonthly do-it-yourself automotive magazine for the practical motorist. Circ. 72,000. Pays on publication. Byline given. Offers $50-100 kill fee. Buys first rights. No computer printouts or disk submissions. Submit seasonal/holiday material 2 months in advance. SASE. Reports in 1 month. Free sample copy.
Nonfiction: How-to, interview/profile, photo feature, technical. Buys 30 mss/year. Query or send complete ms. Length: 600-1,200 words. Pays $100-250.
Photos: Send photos with ms. Reviews 35mm color transparencies; 5x7 or 4x5 color prints. Captions, model

release, and identification of sujects required. "We do not buy manuscripts without photos if applicable."
Tips: "We emphasize quality of content, not quality of graphics. Our writers must research their subjects well. A brief note with an idea outline is probably the best way to begin. The editor may then offer a preferred angle of approach to the subject."

CARS MAGAZINE, Arden Communications, Inc., Box 567, Mt. Kisco NY 10549. Editor:Tom Segnit. Covers automotive high performance: factory muscle cars, hot street machines, drag race cars, and racing. For enthusiasts from early teens through 30s, some older, who have fairly technical knowledge of cars. Bimonthly magazine. Circ. 110,000. Pays on publication. Buys one-time or all rights. Byline given. Phone queries OK. SASE. Reports in 3 months. Sample copy $1.75.
Nonfiction: How-to (budget hop-ups, speed tricks, suspension modification, customizing, repair, body work, or race car building); informational and new product offerings; high-performance or automotive humor; interviews and profiles (of prominent people in drag racing or automotive field); historical and nostalgia (looking back on hot rods, muscle cars of the '50s and '60s); technical (drivetrain and suspension subjects). "We're currently looking for new (auto) products performance reports, substantiated with reputable facts and figures, and photos." Buys 12 mss/issue. Submit complete ms. Length: 500-3,000 words. Pays $100-500.
Photos: Pays $25 for b&w 8x10 glossy prints and $50 for 35mm or larger transparencies without accompanying mss. Offers no additional payment for photos accompanying mss. Model release required.
Tips: "Having a background in the automotive field and knowing how to package a story with photos and captions are pluses."

CORVETTE FEVER, Prospect Publishing Co., Inc., Box 55532, Ft. Washington MD 20744. (301)839-2221. Publisher: Patricia E. Stivers. Bimonthly magazine; 64-84 pages. Circ. 35,000. Pays on publication. Buys first and reprint rights. Byline given. Phone queries OK. Submit seasonal/holiday material 4 months in advance. Photocopied submissions OK. Computer printout submissions OK if double spaced. SASE. Reports in 4 weeks. Sample copy and writer's guidelines $2.
Nonfiction: General interest (event coverage, personal experience); historical (special or unusual Corvette historical topics); how-to (technical and mechanical articles, photos are a must); humor (Corvette-related humor); interview (with important Corvette persons, race drivers, technical persons, club officials, etc.); nostalgia (relating to early Corvette car and development); personal experiences (related to Corvette car use and experiences); profile (prominent and well-known Corvette personalities wanted for interviews and articles); photo feature (centerspread in color of Corvette and Vette owner; photo essays on renovation, customizing and show cars); technical (any aspect of Corvette improvement or custom articles); and travel (relating to Corvette use and adventure). Buys 4-6 mss/issue. Query or send complete ms. Length: 500-2,500 words. Pays $40-300.
Photos: Send photos with ms. Pays $5 for 5x7 b&w glossy prints; $10 for color contact sheets and transparencies. Captions preferred; model release required.
Columns/Departments: Innovative Ideas, In Print, Model Shop, Pit Stop, Schlick Shift and Tech Vette. Buys 5 mss/issue. Send complete ms. Length: 300-800 words. Pays $24-200.
Fiction: "Any type of story as long as it is related to the Corvette." Buys 1-2 mss/issue. Send complete ms. Length: 500-2,500 words. Pays $40-200.
Fillers: Clippings, jokes, gags, anecdotes, short humor and newsbreaks. Buys 2-3/issue. Length: 25-150 words. Pays $2-15.

‡**CUSTOM BIKE/CHOPPER**, Touring Bike Publishing, Inc., 4247 E. La Palma Ave., Anaheim CA 92807. (714)996-5111. Managing Editor: Rose Warren. Monthly magazine for the street custom motorcycle rider and performance motorcycle enthusiast. Circ. 98,992. Pays on publication. Byline given. Buys all rights. Submit seasonal/holiday material 6 months in advance. Simultaneous queries and previously published submissions OK. Computer printout and disk submissions OK. SASE. Reports in 1 month. Sample copy $3; writer's guidelines for SASE.
Nonfiction: Rosemarie Warren, articles editor. Historical/nostalgic, how-to, humor, interview/profile, personal experience, photo feature, technical. Buys 35 mss/year. Length: open. Pays variable fee depending on material.
Photos: Reviews color transparencies. Pays variable rate depending on quality. Captions, model release and identification of subjects required. Buys all rights.
Tips: Reader's Bike section is most open to freelancers. "Must have a nice-looking custom motorcycle. We need words and photos about bikes. Also could use historical articles dealing with motorcycles."

CYCLE, Ziff-Davis Publishing, Co., 780-A Lakefield Rd., Westlake Village CA 91361. (213)889-4360. Editor: Phil Schilling. Executive Editor: Don Phillipson. Monthly magazine covering motorcycles for motorcycle owners (mostly men). Circ. 450,000. Pays on publication. Byline given. Buys first North American serial rights. Submit seasonal/holiday queries 4 months in advance. Simultaneous queries and photocopied submissions OK. Computer printout and disk submissions OK; prefers letter quality to dot matrix printouts. SASE. Reports in 1 month. Free sample copy.

Nonfiction: Investigative, historical, interview/profile (of racing personalities or others in the industry); photo feature; technical (theory or practice); travel (long-distance trips anywhere in the world); reports on racing; and investigative articles. Query "with references." Length: 2,000-4,000 words. Pays $400-700.

Photos: Pays $20-100 for b&w prints; $50-200 for 35mm color transparencies. Model release and identification of subjects required. Buys one-time rights.

CYCLE CANADA, Brave Beaver Pressworks Ltd., 290 Jarvis St., Toronto, Ontario, Canada M5B 2C5. (416)977-6318. Editor: John Cooper. Managing Editor: Bruce Reeve. Monthly magazine covering motorcycling. Circ. 50,000. Pays on publication. Byline given. Buys first North American serial rights. No computer printouts or disk submissions. Submit seasonal/holiday material 3 months in advance. SASE. Reports in 3 weeks. Sample copy $2.50.

Nonfiction: Road tests of new motorcycles, product and accessories testing, reports of Canadian races and world-class events, technical articles, touring stories, and motorcycling news from around the world. No poetry or crash stories. Buys 15 mss/year. Send complete ms. Length: 50-2,500 words. Pays $10-250.

Photos: Send photos with ms. Pays $10-25 for 8x10 b&w prints. Identification of subjects required. Buys one-time rights.

Fiction: Humorous. No racing stories or crash stories. Buys 2-3 mss/year. Send complete ms. Length: 500-1,000 words. Pays $50-100.

CYCLE NEWS, WEST, 2201 Cherry Ave., Box 498, Long Beach CA 90801. (213)427-7433. Senior Editor: Dale Brown. Publisher: Sharon Clayton. Emphasizes motorcycle recreation for motorcycle racers and recreationists west of Mississippi River. Weekly tabloid; 48 pages. Circ. 50,000. Pays on 15th of month for work published in issues cover-dated the previous month. Buys all rights. SASE. Reports in 1 month. Free writer's guidelines.

Nonfiction: Expose; how-to; historical; humor; informational; interview (racers); personal experience (racing, nonracing with a point); personal opinion (land use, emission control, etc.); photo feature; profile (personality profiles); technical; and travel (off-road trips, "bikepacking"). Buys 1,000 mss/year. Submit complete ms. Pays $2/column inch.

Photos: Purchased with or without accompanying manuscript. Captions required. Submit contact sheet, prints, negatives or transparencies. Pays $5 minimum for 5x7 or 8x10 glossy prints; $10 minimum for 35mm slides or 2¼x2¼ color transparencies. Model release required. No additional payment for photos accepted with accompanying ms.

CYCLE WORLD, 1499 Monrovia Ave., Newport Beach CA 92663. Editor: Allan Girdler. For active motorcyclists, "young, affluent, educated, very perceptive." Subject matter includes "road tests (staff-written), features on special bikes, customs, racers, racing events; technical and how-to features involving mechanical modifications." Monthly. Circ. 350,000. Buys all rights. Buys 200-300 mss/year from freelancers. Pays on publication. Sample copy $1; free writer's guidelines. Submit seasonal material 2½ months in advance. Reports in 6 weeks. Query. SASE.

Nonfiction: Buys informative, well-researched, technical, theory and how-to articles; interviews; profiles; humor; and historical pieces. Taboos include articles about "wives learning to ride; 'my first motorcycle.' " Length: 800-5,000 words. Pays $75-100/published page. Columns include Competition, which contains short, local racing stories with photos. Column length: 300-400 words. Pays $75-100/published page.

Photos: Purchased with or without ms, or on assignment. "We need funny photos with a motorcycle theme." Captions optional. Pays $50 for 1-page; $25-35 for half page. 8x10 b&w glossy prints, 35mm color transparencies.

Fiction: Humorous stories. No racing fiction or "rhapsodic poetry." Length: 1,500-3,000 words. Pays $75 minimum/published page.

DUNE BUGGIES & HOT VWS, Wright Publishing Co., Inc., Box 2260, Costa Mesa CA 92626. Editor: Lane Evans. Monthly magazine. Circ. 85,000. Pays on publication. Buys one-time rights. Submit seasonal or holiday material 3 months in advance. Computer printout submissions OK; prefers letter quality to dot matrix printouts. SASE. Free sample copy.

Nonfiction: Technical how-to and informational articles. No first person articles. Buys 6-8 mss/issue. Submit complete ms. Length: 500-2,000 words. Pays $60/published page.

Photos: Purchased with ms. Captions required. Send contact sheet. Pays $12.50 maximum for 8x10 b&w glossy prints; $15 minimum for color negs or slides.

EASYRIDERS MAGAZINE, Entertainment for Adult Bikers, Box 52, Malibu CA 90265. (213)889-8701. Lou Kimzey. For "adult men—men who own, or desire to own, expensive custom motorcycles. The individualist—a rugged guy who enjoys riding a chopper and all the good times derived from it." Monthly. Circ. 488,000. Buys all rights. Buys 36-48 mss/year. Pays on acceptance. Sample copy $1. Reports in 2-3 weeks. SASE.

Nonfiction, Fiction, and Fillers: Department Editor: Louis Bosque. "Masculine, candid material of interest to men. Must be bike-oriented, but can be anything of interest to any rugged man. It is suggested that everyone read a copy before submitting—it's not *Boy's Life*. Light, easy, conversational writing style wanted, like men would speak to each other without women being around. Gut level, friendly, man-to-man. Should be bike-oriented or of interest to a man who rides a motorcycle. *Easyriders* is entirely different from all other motorcycle magazines in that it stresses the lifestyle and good times surrounding the owning of a motorcycle—it's aimed at the rider and is nontechnical, while the others are nuts and bolts. Not interested in overly technical motorcycle articles. We carry no articles that preach or talk down to the reader, or attempt to tell him what he should or shouldn't do." Buys personal experience, interviews, especially humor, expose (of Big Brother, big government, red, white and blue, motorcycle-oriented) articles. Length: 1,000-3,000 words. Pays 10¢/word minimum, depending on length and use in magazine. "It's the subject matter and how well it's done—not length, that determines amount paid." Risque jokes, fillers, short humor. Length: open. Pays on acceptance.

Photos: Department Editor: Pete Chiodo. B&w glossy prints, 35mm color, 2¼x2¼ color transparencies purchased with mss. "We are only interested in *exclusive* photos of exclusive bikes that have never been published in, or photographed by, a national motorcycle or chopper publication. Bikes should be approved by editorial board before going to expense of shooting. Submit sample photos—Polaroids will do. Send enough samples for editorial board to get good idea of the bike's quality, originality, workmanship, interesting features, coloring." Payment is $50-$250 for cover, $100-350 for centerspread, $20 for b&w and $35 for color for "In the Wind," $25 up for arty, unusual shots, and $100-225 for a complete feature.

Fiction: "Gut level language okay. Any sex scenes, not to be too graphic in detail. Dope may be implied, but not graphically detailed. Must be biker male-oriented, but doesn't have to dwell on that fact. Only interested in hard-hitting, rugged fiction." Length: 2,000-3,500 words. Pays 10¢/word minimum, depending on quality, length and use in magazine.

Tips: "There is no mystery about breaking into our publication as long as the material is aimed directly at our macho, intelligent, male audience."

THE EJAG NEWS MAGAZINE, EJAG Publications, Box J, Carlisle MA 01741. (617)369-5531. Editor: Lori R. Toepel. Monthly magazine covering "everything about Jaguar and Daimler autos for readers ranging from corporate presidents to local car-fixers; Sunday mechanics—all Jaguar-Daimler fans." Circ. 24,000. Pays on acceptance. Byline given. Offers $10-25 kill fee. Buys all rights unless otherwise negotiated. Submit seasonal/holiday material 3 months in advance. Computer printout submissions OK; prefers letter quality to dot matrix "if easily readable." SASE. Reports in 1 month. Free sample copy and writer's guidelines.

Nonfiction: General interest (on auto field in general); historical/nostalgic (on Jaguars of previous eras, in USA and abroad); how-to (do it yourself pieces in depth for maintenance, repair, restoration); interview/profile (of Jag owners, racers, factory people, collectors); new product (anything applicable to Jaguars); personal experience ("A Funny Thing Happened on the Way . . . " in a Jag—regular feature with reader participation); photo feature (on beautiful Jaguars, technical procedures, restorations); technical (do-it-yourself or general tech background); and travel (long distance driving techs. How to manage a Jag in the city; where to park, what to see). "No club news or club meets (we have direct lines to these). No technical articles that sound like manuals." Buys 25 or more unsolicited mss/year. Query. Length: 1,200-5,000 words. "Longer article accepted—for splitting into several months installments." Pays 3-10¢/word.

Photos: State availability of photos. Pays $5 maximum for 35mm, 3x3 color transparencies and 3x5 and 5x7 prints. Caption, model release and identification of subjects (if possible) required. Buys one-time rights.

Tips: "We welcome unpublished writers *but* you must know the subject. No non-Jaguar auto material."

FOUR WHEELER MAGAZINE, 21216 Vanowen St., Canoga Park CA 91303. (213)992-4777. President/Publisher: Jon Pelzer. Executive Editor: Dianne Jacob. Emphasizes four-wheel-drive vehicles competition, off-road adventure. Monthly magazine; 108 pages. Circ. 170,000. Pays on publication. Buys first rights. Written queries only. Submit seasonal/holiday material at least 4 months in advance. SASE. Reports in 1 month. Sample copy $2 plus postage. Writer's guidelines for SASE.

Nonfiction: 4WD competition and adventure articles, technical ideas, how-to's, and vehicle features about a unique 4WD vehicle. "We like adventure: mud-running through treacherous timber trails, old desert ghost town four-wheeling trips, coverage of ice-racing jeeps; and unusual 4WD vehicles such as customized trucks, 4WD conversions. See features by Willie Worthy, Rich Johnson and Russ Leadabrand." Query or send complete ms. Length: 2,500 words maximum; average 2-4 pages when published. Pays variable rate.

Photos: Requires excellent quality photos, e.g. 10 b&w glossy 8x10s, 6 color transparencies. Captions required.

Tips: "Technical material is difficult to come by. A new writer has a better chance of success with us if he can offer new technical articles, maintenance and performance tips. Also, we like unique custom vehicle features."

HOT ROD, Petersen Publishing Co., 8490 Sunset Blvd., Los Angeles CA 90069. (213)657-5100. Editor: Leonard Emanuelson. For readers 10 to 60 years old with automotive high performance, street rod, truck, drag racing and street machine interest. Monthly magazine; 120 pages. Circ. 900,000. Buys all rights. Byline given. Pays on acceptance. Free editorial guidelines. Submit seasonal material 4 months in advance. Reports on accepted and rejected material "as soon as possible." SASE.

Nonfiction and Photos: Wants how-to, interview, profile, photo, new product and technical pieces. Length: 2-12 ms pages. Pays $100-225/printed page. "Freelance quantity at *Hot Rod* will undoubtedly decline; staff will originate most material. Foresee more need for photo essays, less for the written word. We accept very little unsolicited (written) freelance or nontechnical material." Photos purchased with or without accompanying ms and on assignment. Sometimes offers no additional payment for photos accepted with ms. Captions required. Pays $25 for b&w prints and $25 minimum for color.

Tips: "Freelance approach should be tailored for specific type and subject matter writer is dealing with. If it is of a basic automotive technical nature, then story slant and info should be aimed at the backyard enthusiasts. What we do is attempt to entertain while educating and offering exceptional dollar value."

KEEPIN' TRACK OF VETTES, Box 48, Spring Valley NY 10977. (914)425-2649. Editor: Shelli Finkel. For Corvette owners and enthusiasts. Monthly magazine; 68-84 pages. Circ. 38,000. Pays on publication. Buys all rights. Byline given. Submit seasonal/holiday material 2-3 months in advance. SASE. Reports in 3-4 weeks. Free sample copy and writer's guidelines.

Nonfiction: Expose (telling of Corvette problems with parts, etc.); historical (any and all aspects of Corvette developments); how-to (restorations, engine work, suspension, race, swapmeets); humor; informational; interview (query); nostalgia; personal experience; personal opinion; photo feature; profile (query); technical; and travel. Buys 8-10 mss/issue. Query or submit complete ms. Pays $50-200.

Photos: Send photo with ms. Pays $10-35 for b&w contact sheets or negatives; $10-50 for 35mm color transparencies; offers no additional payment for photos with accompanying ms.

‡KIT CAR QUARTERLY, Box 9527, San Jose CA 95157. (408)295-2222. Editor: Philip B. Hood. Managing Editor: William R. Mazer. Quarterly magazine on full-size, driveable automobiles in kit form for assembly at home. "*Kit Car Quarterly* aims to reach automotive do-it-yourselfers and anyone with a love for beautiful automobiles. We emphasize in-depth profiles of individual Kit Cars, good color photography, and how-to features." Estab. 1981. Circ. 75,000. Pays on publication. Byline given. Offers $25 kill fee. Buys one-time or all rights. Submit seasonal/holiday material 5 months in advance. Simultaneous queries and simultaneous, photocopied and previously published submissions OK. SASE. Reports in 1 month; sample copy $1; free writer's guidelines.

Nonfiction: How-to (build up articles on Kit Cars, hints for Kit Car assembly); interview/profile (designers/manufacturers with photos of cars and designs); new product (any products related to Kit Cars); personal experience (owner profiles of customized kits); photo feature (of unusual custom, hand-built autos). No articles knocking the entire industry. Buys 25 mss/year. Query or submit complete ms. Length: 500-2,500 words. Pays $35-250 (with photos).

Photos: Send photos with ms. Pays $5-25 for 35mm or larger color transparencies; $2-10 for 5x7 b&w prints. Model release and identification of subjects required.

Fiction: Would be interested in seeing automotive fiction. Do not currently buy any.

Tips: "Find a company with a photoworthy kit. Get all the facts, i.e., price of kit, contents, time to assemble, unique features, advantages and disadvantages of the particular car. Give the reader a 'hands on' feel for the car."

MOTOCROSS ACTION MAGAZINE, 10600 Sepulveda Blvd., Mission Hills CA 91345. (213)981-2317. Editor: Jody Weisel. For "primarily young and male, average age 12 to 30, though an increasing number of females is noticed. Education varies considerably. They are interested in off-road racing motorcycles, as either a profession or a hobby." Monthly magazine. Circ. 100,000. Buys all rights. Buys 20-25 mss/year. Pays on publication. Sample copy $1.50. Will consider photocopied but no simultaneous submissions. Reports in 1-6 months. Query. SASE.

Nonfiction and Photos: Wants "articles on important national and international motocross events, interviews with top professionals, technical pieces, and in-depth investigative reporting. Short stories and/or poetry will be greeted with a heartfelt yawn. It's best to obtain a copy of the magazine and read recent stories. Stories should be brief and to the point, though flair is appreciated. Top photography is a must. No blatant hero worship. For the coming year, we want to see articles on the evolution of Motocross from a backyard to a big-time, multi-million dollar sport and business." Takes informational, how-to, profile, humor and photo pieces. Length: 500-2,000 words. Pays $25-200. Photos purchased with accompanying ms with extra payment and on assignment. Captions optional. Pays $8-10 for 8x10 b&w glossy prints; $25-50 for 35mm or 2¼x2¼ color slides.

MOTOR TREND, Petersen Publishing Co., 8490 Sunset Blvd., Los Angeles CA 90069. (213)657-5100. Editor: Tony Swan. For automotive enthusiasts and general interest consumers. Monthly. Circ. 750,000. Buys all rights. "Fact-filled query suggested for all freelancers." Reports in 30 days. SASE.

Nonfiction: Automotive and related subjects that have national appeal. Emphasis on domestic and imported cars, roadtests, driving impressions, auto classics, money-saving ideas for the motorist, and high-performance features for the enthusiast's news tips on new products, pickups, long-term automotive projects. Packed with facts.

Photos: Buys photos, particularly of prototype cars and assorted automotive matter. Pays $25-250 for b&w glossy prints or 2¼x2¼ color transparencies.

Fillers: Automotive newsbreaks. Any length.

MOTORCYCLIST MAGAZINE, Petersen Publishing, 8490 Sunset Blvd., Los Angeles CA 90069. (213)657-5100. Editor-in-Chief: Art Friedman. Managing Editor: Tracey Hurst. Emphasizes motorcycles or motorcycle enthusiasts. Monthly magazine; 100 pages. Circ. 250,000. Pays on publication. Buys all rights. Byline given. Written queries preferred. SASE. Reports in 3 months. Free writer's guidelines.

Nonfiction: How-to, humor, informational, interview, new product, photo feature, profile and technical. Buys 12-25 mss/year. Length: 500-2,000 words. Pays $25-1,000.

Photos: Paul Gordon, photo editor. Reviews contact sheets and negatives. Pays $25-100 for 8x10 b&w prints; $75-200 for 35mm color transparencies. Captions, model release and identification of subjects required.

Columns/Departments: Hotline (short news items); Hotcap (short competition news); Last Page (humorous, bizarre, tip-type items); Sport (features on competitions, racers—timeliness is important). Buys 10/year. Send complete ms. Length: 50 words minimum.

Fiction: Adventure, fantasy, humorous. Buys 1-2 mss/year. Send complete ms.

Fillers: Short humor and newsbreaks. Buys 20/year. Length: 50-250 words. Pays $25-50.

OFF-ROAD MAG, Argus Publishing, Suite 316, 12301 Wilshire Blvd., Los Angeles CA 90025. (213)820-3601. Editor: Mike Parris. Monthly magazine covering off-pavement vehicles, particularly 4-wheel drive, utility, and pickup trucks; and off-road racing and rallying vehicles. Readers are owners and people who aspire to own off-road vehicles, as well as those who intend to modify engines and other components for off-road use. Circ. 120,000. Pays on publication. Byline given. Buys all rights, "but may reassign rights upon request. Submit seasonal/holiday material 4 months in advance. SASE. Reports in 1 month. Writer's guidelines for business size SAE and 1 first class stamp.

Nonfiction: Technical (modification); travel (and adventure in the continental US); off-road groups; and land-closures. "The key to writing for us is technical expertise. You must be knowledgeable on the subject." Buys 50 mss/year. Send complete ms and photos or diagrams. Length: 2,000-3,000 words. Pays $125-400.

Photos: Send photos with ms. Reviews 35mm color transparenices and 8x10 b&w glossy prints.

Fillers: Fix it, How-to. Buys 25/year. Length: 750-1,000 words. Pays $50-100.

‡ON TRACK MAGAZINE, The Auto Racing Newsmagazine, Paul Oxman Publishing, Unit M, 17165 Newhope St., Fountain Valley CA 92708. (714)966-1131. Editor: John Zimmermann. Managing Editor: Cheryl Cooper. Bimonthly tabloid covering auto racing. Estab. 1981. Circ. 25,000. Pays on publication. Byline given. Not copyrighted. Buys first North American serial rights. Simultaneous queries and simultanous submissions and photocopied submissions OK. SASE. Reports in 6 weeks.

Nonfiction: General interest, how-to, interview/profile, opinion, personal experience, photo feature, technical—all related to auto racing. Query. Length: 250-3,000 words. Pays $3/column inch; some rates negotiable.

Photos: Anne Peyton, photo editor. State availability of photos. Pays $50 for 35mm color transparency, $7.50 for 5x7 b&w print. Buys one-time rights.

PETERSEN'S 4-WHEEL & OFF-ROAD, Petersen Publishing Company, 8490 Sunset Blvd., Los Angeles CA 90069. (213)657-5100. Editor: Craig Caldwell. Managing Editor: Catherine Selfridge. Monthly magazine covering automotive four-wheel drive vehicles. "We appeal to the off-road enthusiast who plays hard and likes to have fun with his or her 4x4. Our approach is slanted toward showing how to do-it-yourself when it comes to maintaining or modifying an off-road vehicle." Pays on acceptance. Byline given. Pays 50% kill fee. Buys all rights. Submit seasonal/holiday material 6 months in advance. Computer printout and disk submissions OK; prefers letter quality to dot matrix. SASE. Reports in 3 weeks.

Nonfiction: How-to (modify a vehicle); interview/profile (of racers, engineers); photo feature (modified vehicles); and technical (modification of a vehicle). No first-person accounts of anything; no travel features. Buys 6-10 mss/year. Query or send complete ms. Length: 300-1,500 words. Pays $50-500.

Photos: Barry Wiggins, photo editor. Pays $10-75 for color transparencies; $5-25 for 8x10 b&w prints. Captions, model release, and identification of subjects required. Buys all rights.

Columns/Departments: Tailgate (miscellaneous automotive news). Buys 6 mss/year. Send complete ms. Length: 20-100 words. Pays $10-25.

Tips: "The best way to break in is with a well-photographed, action feature on a modified vehicle. Study our magazine for style and content. We do not deviate much from established editorial concept. Keep copy short, information accurate, and photos in focus."

PICKUP, VAN & 4WD MAGAZINE, Petersen Publishing Co., 8490 Sunset Blvd., Los Angeles CA 90069. (213)657-5100. Editor: John J. Jelinek. Managing Editor: Michael Tighe. Covers street pickups and vans. Monthly magazine. Circ. 235,000. Pays on publication. Buys all rights. Pays kill fee "depending on assignment." Byline given. Submit seasonal/holiday material 3-4 months in advance. Photocopied submissions OK "with guarantee of exclusivity." Query and request writer's guidelines, "Contributor's Memo." SASE. Reports 1-2 months. Free writer's guidelines.
Nonfiction: How-to (modifications to light duty trucks, such as extra seats, tool storage, body and mechanical repairs, modifications, etc.), historical/nostalgic (restored trucks), technical and travel (2-wheel drive travel only, must show vehicle being used). Buys 2-3 mss/per issue. Submit complete ms. Length: 1,000-3,000 words. Pays $75/published page.
Photos: Purchased with accompanying manuscript or on assignment. Captions required. Query for photos. Pays $10-75 for 8x10 b&w glossy prints; $25-75 for 35mm or 2¼x2¼ color transparencies; offers no additional payment for photos accepted with ms. Model release required.

RIDER, 29901 Agoura Rd., Agoura CA 91301. Editor: Tash Matsuoka. For owners and prospective buyers of motorcycles to be used for touring, sport riding, and commuting. Monthly magazine; 100-160 pages. Buys all rights. Pays on publication. Sample copy $1. Free writer's guidelines. Query first. Submit seasonal material 3 months in advance. Photocopied submissions OK. Computer printouts and disk submissions OK; prefers letter quality to dot matrix printouts. Reports in 1 month. SASE.
Nonfiction and Photos: Articles directly related to motorcycle touring, camping, commuting and sport riding including travel, human interest, safety, novelty, do-it-yourself and technical. "Articles which portray the unique thrill of motorcycling." Should be written in clean, contemporary style aimed at a sharp, knowledgeable reader. Buys informational how-to, personal experience, profile, historical, nostalgia, personal opinion, travel and technical. Length is flexible. Pays $50 for Favorite Ride feature and $150-450 for major articles. Offers no additional payment for photos purchased with ms. Captions required. "Quality photographs are critical. Graphics are emphasized in *Rider*, and we must have photos with good visual impact."

ROAD & TRACK, 1499 Monrovia Avenue, Newport Beach CA 92663. Editor: John Dinkel. For knowledgeable car enthusiasts. Monthly magazine. Buys all rights. Query. Computer printouts and disk submissions OK; prefers letter quality to dot matrix printouts. Reports in 6 weeks. SASE.
Nonfiction: "The editor welcomes freelance material, but if the writer is not thoroughly familiar with the kind of material used in the magazine, he is wasting both his time and the magazine's time. *Road & Track* material is highly specialized and that old car story in the files has no chance of being accepted. More serious, comprehensive and in-depth treatment of particular areas of automotive interest." Recent article example: "The Crasher" (February 1982). Pays 12-25¢/word minimum depending upon subject covered and qualifications and experience of author.
Tips: "Freelancer must have intimate knowledge of the magazine. Unless he can quote chapter and verse for the last 20 years of publication he's probably wasting his time and mine."

ROAD KING MAGAZINE, 23060 S. Cicero Ave., Richton Park IL 60471. Editor-in-Chief: George Friend. 10% freelance written. Truck driver leisure reading publication. Quarterly: 48 pages. Circ. 226,515. Pays on acceptance. Buys all rights. Byline given "always on fiction—if requested on nonfiction—copyright mentioned only if requested." Submit seasonal/holiday material 3 months in advance. Simultaneous and photocopied submissions OK. Sample copy for 7x10 SASE with 54¢ postage or get free sample copy at any Union 76 truck stop.
Nonfiction: Trucker slant or general interest, humor, and photo feature. No articles on violence or sex. Name and quote release required. Submit complete ms. Length: 500-2,500 words. Pays $50-150.
Photos: Submit photos with accompanying ms. No additional payment for b&w contact sheets or 2¼x2¼ color transparencies. Captions preferred. Buys first rights. Model release required.
Fiction: Adventure, historical, humorous, mystery, suspense rescue-type and western. Especially about truckers. No stories on sex and violence. "We're looking for quality writing." Buys 4 mss/year. Submit complete ms. Length: Approximately 1,200 words. Pays $400.
Fillers: Jokes, gags, anecdotes and short humor. Buys 20-25/year. Length: 50-500 words. Pays $5-100.
Tips: No collect phone calls or postcard requests. "We don't appreciate letters we have to answer." No certified, insured or registered mail. No queries. "Do not submit mss or art or photos using registered mail, certified mail or insured mail. Publisher will not accept such materials from the post office. Publisher will not discuss refusal with writer. Nothing personal, just legal. Do not write and ask if we would like such and such article or outline. We buy only from original and complete mss submitted on speculation. Do not ask for writer's guidelines. See above and/or get copy of magazine and be familiar with our format before submitting anything. Never phone for free copy as we will not have such phone calls."

ROAD RIDER, Box 678, South Laguna CA 92677. Editor: Roger Hull. Covers touring and camping on motorcycles for a family-oriented audience. Monthly magazine; 96 pages. Circ. 70,000. Pays on acceptance.

Buys all rights. Submit seasonal/holiday material 6 months in advance. No computer printouts or disk submissions. SASE. Reports in 1 month. Sample copy $3; free writer's guidelines with SASE.

Nonfiction: "We will consider any articles providing they are of sound base so far as motorcycling knowledge is concerned. Must be cycle-oriented. How-to's usually are of technical nature and require experience. We would love to see more humorous cycle experience type of material. Cycling personalities are also big here. We try to do three or four historical pieces per year. All evaluation/testing pieces are done in house. Travel pieces need good photos; same thing is true on historical or nostalgia material." No beginner articles. Buys 48 mss/year. Query or send complete ms. Length: 300-1,500 words. Pays $100-200.

Photos: Send photos with ms. Offers no additional payment for photos accepted with accompanying ms. Prefers 5x7 b&w glossy prints or 35mm color transparencies. Captions and model release required.

Fiction: "We are open for good, motorcycling fiction which is slanted toward a family-type audience. No erotica." Buys 2-3 mss/year. Send complete ms. Length: 300-2,000 words. Pays $100-150.

Tips: "We are an enthusiast publication—as such, it is virtually impossible to sell here unless the writer is also an enthusiast and actively involved in the sport. A good, well-written, brief item dealing with a motorcycle trip, accompanied by top quality b&w and color photos receives prime time editorial attention. We are always on the lookout for good material from eastern seaboard or Midwest. Best way to hit this market is to buy and study a sample issue prior to submitting. Most of our contributors are Road Rider People. If you are unsure as to what Road Rider People refers, you will probably not be able to sell to this magazine. We continue to be overstocked on following: beginner articles (all ages, sexes, etc.), journal-format travel articles (not welcome) and travel articles from Southwestern US."

STOCK CAR RACING MAGAZINE, Box 715, Ipswich MA 01938. Editor: Dick Berggren. For stock car racing fans and competitors. Monthly magazine; 100 pages. Circ. 120,000. Pays on publication. Buys all rights. Byline given. No computer printout or disk submissions. SASE. Reports in 6 weeks.

Nonfiction: "Uses nonfiction on stock car drivers, cars, and races. We are interested in the story behind the story in stock car and sprint car racing. We want interesting profiles and colorful, nationally interesting features." Query. Buys 50-60 mss/year. Length: 100-6,000 words. Pays $10-350.

Photos: State availability of photos. Pays $20 for 8x10 b&w photos; $50-250 for 35mm or larger color transparencies. Captions required.

Tips: "We get more queries than stories. We just don't get as much material as we want to buy. We have more room for stories than ever before. We are an excellent market with 18 issues per year."

STREET RODDER MAGAZINE, TRM Publications, Inc., 2145 W. LaPalma, Anaheim CA 92801. Editorial Director: Jerry Dexter. For the automotive enthusiast with an interest in street-driven, modified old cars built prior to 1949. Monthly magazine. Circ. 105,000. Buys all rights. Pays on publication. Sample copy $2; free writer's guidelines. No photocopied or simultaneous submissions; no computer printout or disk submissions. Reports in 1 month. Query or submit complete ms. SASE.

Nonfiction and Photos: "We need coverage of events and cars that we can't get to. Street rod event (rod runs); how-to technical articles; features on individual street rods. We don't need features on local (Southern California) street rods, events or shops. We stress a straightforward style; accurate and complete details; easy to understand (though not 'simple') technical material. Need good, clear, complete and well-photographed technical and how-to articles on pertinent street rod modifications or conversions. We very seldom accept a story without photos." Buys 10-12 unsolicited mss/year. Length: 250-1,500 words. Pays $50-70/page. Average payment for 2-page feature using 5x7 or 8x10 b&w photos is $100. "We demand good close-ups of details and 10-20 views, so that we can pick 5 or 6 for the photo layout."

Tips: "We regularly encourage new freelancers to submit material to us. They must have a knowledge of the street rod itself and how it is built. Our readers build and own pre-1949 cars that are modernized with late model engines, etc. We would like to see more photo features on non-Ford rods."

SUPER CHEVY, Argus Publishing, Suite 316, 12301 Wilshire Blvd., Los Angeles CA 90025. (213)820-3601. Editor: Doug Marion. Feature Editor: Jeff Tann. Monthly magazine covering Chevrolet automobiles for anyone associated with Chevys—owners, mechanics, car builders and racing drivers. Circ. 160,000. Pays on acceptance. Byline given. Buys all rights. Submit seasonal/holiday material 4 months in advance. Simultaneous queries OK. Reports in 2 weeks on queries; 1 week on mss. Free sample copy.

Nonfiction: Historical (classic Chevy); interview; race coverage (drag, stock and sprint car). Buys 25 mss/year. Query by phone or letter. Length: 300-1,500 words. Pays $75-100/printed page.

Photos: State availability of photos. Pays $25-60/35mm color transparency; $10 minimum/5x7 or 8x10 b&w glossy print. Captions and model release required.

SUPER STOCK AND DRAG ILLUSTRATED, Lopez Publications, 602 Montgomery St., Alexandria VA 22314. Editor: Steve Collison. Monthly magazine for "mostly blue-collar males between 18-40 years old; high performance, drag racing oriented." Circ. 85,000. Pays on publication. Buys all rights. Byline given. Simultaneous and photocopied submissions OK. SASE. Reports in 6 weeks. Sample copy $2.

Nonfiction: Interview (with prominent drag racers); profile (on local or national drag cars); photo features (on drag racing cars or racing events); and technical. Buys 120 mss/year. Query or submit complete ms to 135 Walnut Ave., Atco NJ 08004. Length: 500-2,000 words maximum. Pays $50-250.
Photos: Purchased with accompanying ms. Captions required. Submit prints or transparencies. Pays $10 for 8x10 b&w glossy prints; $50-300 for 35mm color transparencies.
Fiction: Adventure, humorous. Must be drag racing oriented. Submit complete ms. Length: 500-2,000 words. Pays $75-300.

‡**TOURING BIKE**, Touring Bike Publishing Co., Inc., 4247 E. La Palma Ave., Anaheim CA 92807. (714)996-5111. Editor: John Warren. Managing Editor: Rosemarie Warren. Monthly magazine for the touring street and performance motorcycle rider. Circ. 73,180. Pays on publication. Byline given. Buys all rights. Submit seasonal/holiday material 6 months in advance. Simultaneous queries OK. Computer printout and disk submissions OK. SASE. Reports in 1 month. Sample copy $3; free writer's guidelines with SASE.
Nonfiction: Historical/nostalgic, how-to (dealing with maintenance, riding technique, product selection, installation and use); humor, interview/profile, personal experience, technical, travel. Buys 35 mss/year. Send complete ms. Length: open. Pays variable rate depending on material.
Photos: Send photos with ms. Reviews color transparencies. Payment "depends on quality of photos." Captions, model release and identification of subjects required. Buys all rights.
Tips: "Feature department is the area most open to freelancers. We are looking for well-written travel articles relating to touring by motorcycle."

VW & PORSCHE, Argus Publishers, Suite 316, 12301 Wilshire Blvd., Los Angeles CA 90025. (213)820-3601. Editor: Greg Brown. Bimonthly magazine covering VW and Porsche and Audi cars for owners of VWs and Porsches. Circ. 65,000. Pays one month before publication. Byline given. Kill fee varies. Buys one-time rights. Submit seasonal/holiday material 4 months in advance. SASE. Reports in 2 weeks on queries. Free sample copy.
Nonfiction: How-to (restore, maintain or tune-up); Special, modified or restored VWs and Porsches. Buys 30-35 mss/year. Query. Length: 1,000-2,500 words. Pays $60-75/printed page. "More if color pictures are used."
Photos: State availability of photos. Reviews 8x10 glossy prints. Identification of subjects required. "Photo payment included in page price."
Tips: "Whoever writes for a 'nut' book should research their material extremely well. Our readers want straight, honest, new information. Errors are caught at once."

Aviation

Publications in this section aim at professional and private pilots, and at aviation enthusiasts in general. Magazines intended for passengers of commercial airlines are grouped in a separate In-Flight category. Technical aviation and space journals, and publications for airport operators, aircraft dealers and others in aviation businesses are listed under Aviation and Space in the Trade Journals section.

‡**AERO**, Macro/Comm Corp., Box 4030, San Clemente CA 92572. (714)498-1600. Editor: Dennis Shattuck. 50% freelance written. For owners of private aircraft. "We take a unique, but limited view within our field." Circ. 75,000. Buys first North American serial rights. Buys about 20-30 mss/year. Pays after publication. Sample copy $3; writer's guidelines for SASE. Will consider photocopied submissions if guaranteed original. No simultaneous submissions. Reports in 2 months. Query. SASE.
Nonfiction: Material on aircraft products, developments in aviation, specific airplane test reports, travel by aircraft, development and use of airports. All must be related to general aviation field. Length: 1,000-4,000 words. Pays $75-250.
Photos: Pays $15 for 8x10 b&w glossy prints purchased with mss or on assignment. Pays $150 for color transparencies used on cover.
Columns/Departments: Weather flying, instrument flight refresher, new products.
Tips: "Freelancer must know the subject about which he is writing; use good grammar; know the publication for which he's writing; remember that we try to relate to the middle segment of the business/pleasure flying public. We see too many 'first flight' type of articles. Our market is more sophisticated than that. Most writers do not do enough research on their subject. Would like to see more material on business-related flying, more on people involved in flying."

AIR LINE PILOT, 1625 Massachussetts Ave. NW, Washington DC 20036. (202)797-4176. Editor-in-Chief: C.V. Glines. Managing Editor: Anne Kelleher. Covers commercial aviation issues for members of Air Line Pilots Association (ALPA). Monthly magazine; 48-64 pages. Circ. 45,000. Pays on acceptance. Buys all rights. Computer printouts and disk submissions OK; printout must be letter quality. Submit seasonal material 4 months in advance. SASE. Reports in 1 month. Free sample copy and writer's guidelines with correctly sized SASE only.
Nonfiction: Historical (aviation/personal or equipment, aviation firsts); informational (aviation safety, related equipment or aircraft aids); interview (aviation personality); nostalgia (aviation history); photo feature; profile (airline pilots; must be ALPA members); and technical. No book reviews or advice on piloting techniques. Buys 15 mss/year. Query. Length: 1,000-2,500 words. Pays $100-500.
Photos: State availability of photos with query. Purchased with or without accompanying ms. Captions required. Pays $10-25 for 8x10 b&w glossy prints; $20-250 for 35mm or 2¼x2¼ color transparencies. Covers: Pays $250.
Tips: "Unless a writer is experienced in the technical aspects of aviation, he is more likely to score with a pilot profile or aviation historical piece."

AOPA PILOT, 421 Aviation Way, Frederick MD 21701. (301)695-2350. Editor: Edward G. Tripp. For aircraft owners, pilots, and the complete spectrum of the general aviation industry. Official magazine of the Aircraft Owners and Pilots Association. Monthly. Circ. 260,000. Pays on acceptance. Reports in 2 months. Queries preferred. No computer disk submissions. SASE. Sample copy $2.
Nonfiction: Factual articles up to 2,500 words that will inform, educate and entertain pilots and aircraft owners ranging from the student to the seasoned professional. These pieces should be generously illustrated with good quality photos, diagrams or sketches. Quality and accuracy essential. Topics covered include maintenance, operating technique, reports on new and used aircraft, avionics and other aviation equipment, places to fly (travel), governmental policies (local, state and federal) relating to general aviation. Additional features on weather in relation to flying, legal aspects of aviation, flight education, pilot fitness, and aviation history are used occasionally. No commonplace first-solo or fly-in/local-event stories. Pays $400 maximum.
Photos: Pays $25 minimum for each photo or sketch used. Original b&w negatives or color slides should be made available.

‡**FLIGHT REPORTS**, Peter Katz Productions, Inc., 1280 Saw Mill River Rd., Yonkers NY 10710. (914)423-6000. Editor: Mary Hunt. Managing Editor: Peter J. Katz. Monthly travel magazine for pilots and aircraft owners. Pays on publication. Byline given. Buys all rights. Submit seasonal/holiday material 2 months in advance. SASE. Reports in 2 weeks. Sample copy $1.
Nonfiction: Destination reports include what to do, where to stay, and airport facilities for domestic travel and Canada only. No foreign travel. Buys variable number of mss/year. Query. Length: 750-1,500 words. Pays $25-50.
Photos: State availability of photos. Pays $5 for 3½x5½ b&w and color prints. Captions required.
Tips: "Pilot's license and cross country flying experience is helpful. Some aviation background is required."

FLYING, Ziff-Davis Publishing Co., 1 Park Ave., New York NY 10016. (212)725-3500. Editor-in-Chief: Richard L. Collins. Editorial Coordinator: Yamile Martin. 5% freelance written. For private and commercial pilots involved with, or interested in, the use of general-aviation aircraft (not airline or military) for business and pleasure. Monthly magazine; 116 pages. Circ. 370,000. Pay on acceptance. Buys one-time rights. Submit seasonal/holiday material 4 months in advance of issue date. SASE. Reports in 3 weeks.
Nonfiction: How-to (piloting and other aviation techniques); and technical (aviation-related). No articles on "My Trip" travel accounts, or historical features. Buys about 12 mss/year. Submit complete ms. Length: 750-3,500 words. Pays $50-1,000.
Columns/Departments: "I Learned About Flying From That" personal experience. Pays $100 minimum.
Tips: "New ideas and approaches are a must. Tone must be correct for knowledgeable pilots rather than the non-flying public. Facts must be absolutely accurate."

‡**FREQUENT FLYER**, Dun & Bradstreet, 888 7th Ave., New York NY 10106. Editor: Coleman A. Lollar. Monthly magazine covering business travel (airlines/airports/aviation) for mostly male high-level business executive readership. Circ. 300,000. Pays on acceptance. Byline given. Offers $75 kill fee. Buys all rights. Submit seasonal/holiday material 6 months in advance. SASE. Reports in 2 months on queries; 1 month on mss. Free sample copy and writer's guidelines.
Nonfiction: Book excerpts, expose, new product, technical, travel, news reporting, in particular on airports/aircraft/airlines/hotel/credit card/car rental. Not interested in queries on stress or anything written in the first person; no profiles, humor or interviews. "*FF* reports on travel as part of an executive's job. We do not assume that he enjoys travel, and neither should the freelancer." Buys 100 mss/year. Query with published clips. Length: 800-3,000 words. Pays $100-500.

Photos: Eve Cohen, photo editor. "We accept both b&w and color contact sheets, transparencies and prints; rates negotiable." Buys one-time rights.

Tips: "We publish very little destination material, preferring articles about how deregulation, airport developments, etc., have affected air services to a destination, rather than descriptive articles. We avoid all travel articles that sound promotional. We publish general business/economic features when they directly relate to the reader as a *mobile* businessman (portable computers, foreign banking, credit card/traveler's check development, etc.). We do not report on other business topics. We like service articles, but not in the usual 'how-to' format: our readers travel too much (average of almost 50 roundtrips a year) to be told how to pack a bag, or how to stay in touch with the office. In service articles, we prefer a review of how frequent travelers handle certain situations rather than how they *should* handle them. Unrequested mss will probably not be read. Give us a good, solid story idea. If accepted, expect a fairly detailed assignment from us. We rewrite heavily. Overly sensitive authors may want to avoid us."

GENERAL AVIATION NEWS, Drawer 1416, Snyder TX 79549. (915)573-6318, 1-800-351-1372 (Texas 1-800-592-4484). Editor-in-Chief: Norval Kennedy. 20% freelance written. For pilots, aircraft owners, mechanics, aircraft dealers and related business people. Weekly tabloid; 28 pages. Circ. 30,000. Pays on acceptance. Buys all rights. Byline given "only on features and short features, not on straight news stories." Phone queries OK. Submit seasonal/holiday material 1 month in advance. Photocopied submissions OK. Computer printout and disk submissions OK. SASE. "*GAN* will verify manuscript arrival immediately. Proposal or rejection in 6 weeks." Sample copy $1; writer's guidelines for SASE.

Nonfiction: General aviation articles that would be of interest to nationwide audience; articles and features of interest to corporate aviation (businesses and people that own and operate one or more business aircraft). No articles on commercial or military airplanes, UFOs or accidents. Buys up to 50 mss/year. Submit complete ms. Buys 10-20 unsolicited mss/year. Length: 2,000 words maximum. Pays $25/1,000 words.

Photos: Send photo material with accompanying ms. Pays $3-5 for 4x5 b&w or color prints. Captions required. Buys all rights.

Tips: "Knowing about business aviation is helpful, but the freelancer who can put together a good story about any aspect of it could also have a good chance of selling. I would be happy to discuss specifics on phone. Follow the advice in the front of *Writer's Market!*"

HOMEBUILT AIRCRAFT MAGAZINE, Werner & Werner Corp., Suite 201, 16200 Ventura Blvd., Encino CA 91436. (213)986-8400. Editorial Director: Steve Werner. Monthly magazine covering all aspects of homebuilding aircraft. Circ. 35,000. Pays on publication. Buys all rights. SASE. Reports in 1 month. Sample copy $2.50.

Nonfiction: How-to articles (construction methods from kits and scratch); informational (building techniques, materials); personal experiences (with building/flying; vintage homebuilts; homebuilt ultralights). Buys 75 mss/year. Query. Length: 1,000-3,000 words. Pays $100-300.

Photos: State availability of photos. Offers no additional payment for photos accepted with ms. Prefers 8x10, 2¼x2¼ or 35mm slides.

PLANE & PILOT MAGAZINE, Werner & Werner Corp., Suite 201, 16200 Ventura Blvd., Encino CA 91436. (213)986-8400. Editorial Director: Steve Werner. 75% freelance written. Emphasizes all aspects of general aviation—personal and business. Monthly magazine. Circ. 70,000. Pays on publication. Buys all rights. Query. Submit seasonal/holiday material 6 months in advance. SASE. Reports in 1 month. Sample copy $2.50.

Nonfiction: How-to articles (emergency procedures; weather); informational (proficiency; aircraft reports; jobs and schools; avionics); personal experience (regular features on "Flight I'll Never Forget;" travel). Buys 100 mss/year. Length: 1,000-3,000 words. Pays $100-300.

Photos: State availability of photos in query. Offers no additional payment for photos accepted with ms. Prefers 8x10 b&w prints and 2¼x2¼ or 35mm slides.

PRIVATE PILOT, Macro/Comm Corp., Box 4030, San Clemente CA 92672. (714)498-1600. Editor: Dennis Shattuck. 60% freelance written. For owner/pilots of private aircraft, for student pilots and others aspiring to attain additional ratings and experience. "We take a unique, but limited view within our field." Circ. 85,000. Buys first North American serial rights. Buys about 30-60 mss/year. Pays after publication. Sample copy $2; writer's guidelines for SASE. Will consider photocopied submissions if guaranteed original. No simultaneous submissions. Computer printout submissions OK "if double spaced and have upper and lower case letters." Reports in 2 months. Query. SASE.

Nonfiction: Material on techniques of flying, developments in aviation, product and specific airplane test reports, travel by aircraft, development and use of airports. All must be related to general aviation field. Recent article examples: "NASA's Electronic Airplane" (March 1982). No personal experience articles. Length: 1,000-4,000 words. Pays $75-250.

Photos: Pays $15 for 8x10 b&w glossy prints purchased with mss or on assignment. Pays $150 for color transparencies used on cover.

Columns/Departments: Business flying, homebuilt/experimental aircraft, pilot's logbook. Length: 1,000 words. Pays $50-125.

Tips: "Freelancer must know the subject about which he is writing; use good grammar; know the publication for which he's writing; remember that we try to relate to the middle segment of the business/pleasure flying public. We see too many 'first flight' type of articles. Our market is more sophisticated than that. Most writers do not do enough research on their subject. Would like to see more material on business-related flying, more on people involved in flying."

ULTRALIGHT AIRCRAFT MAGAZINE, Werner & Werner Corp., Suite 201, 16200 Ventura Blvd., Encino CA 91436. (213)986-8400. Editorial Director: Steve Werner. Bimonthly magazine covering all aspects of ultralight aviation. Circ. 60,000. Pays on publication. Buys all rights. SASE. Reports in 1 month. Sample copy $2.50.

Nonfiction: How-to articles (building from kits and scratch); informational (building/flying techniques, aircraft reports, regulations, safety); personal experience (with building/flying, prototypes, new models). Buys 75 mss/year. Query. Length: 1,000-3,000 words. Pays $100-300.

Photos: State availability of photos. Offers no additional payment for photos accepted with ms. Prefers 8x10, 2¼x2¼ or 35mm slides.

ULTRALIGHT FLYER, Ultralight Flyer, Inc., Box 98786, Tacoma WA 98499. (206)588-1743. Managing Editor: Dave Sclair. Monthly tabloid covering ultralight aviation nationwide. Provides upbeat coverage of ultralight news activities, and politics. Circ. 20,000. Pays on publication. Byline given. Buys one-time rights. Submit seasonal/holiday material 1 month in advance. Simultaneous queries, and photocopied and previously published submissions (from non competitive publications) OK. Computer printout and disk submissions OK. SASE. Reports in 1 week on queries; 2 weeks on mss. Sample copy $2; writer's guidelines for business size SAE.

Nonfiction: General interest; historical/nostalgic; how-to (safety practices, maintenance); humor; inspirational; interview/profile; new product; opinion (letters to editor); personal experience; photo feature; technical; travel. "No 'gee whiz' type articles aimed at non-pilot audiences." Buys 100-200 mss/year. Query or send complete ms. Length: 250-1,500 words. Pays $20-150.

Photos: "Good pics a must." Send photos with ms. Pays negotiable rates for color transparencies; $10-20 for b&w contact sheet, negatives and 5x7 or larger prints. Identification of subjects required.

Tips: "We will have more special subject editions."

‡ULTRALIGHT PILOT, 421 Aviation Way, Frederick MD 21701. (301)695-2350. Editor: Thomas A. Horne. For ultralight owners, pilots and aviation industry. Official magazine of the Ultralight Division of the Aircraft Owners and Pilots Association. Bimonthly. Circ. 6,000. Pays on acceptance. Reports in 2 months. SASE. Queries preferred. Sample copy $3.

Nonfiction: Factual articles up to 2,500 words that will inform, educate and entertain ultralight pilots and owners. Pieces should be illustrated with good quality photos, diagrams or sketches. Quality and accuracy essential. Topics covered include maintenance, operating techniques, reports on aircraft and equipment, governmental policies (local, state and federal) relating to ultralight pilots and operations. Features on weather in relation to flying, legal aspects of aviation, flight education, aircraft and parts construction, pilot fitness and aviation history also are used occasionally. Pays $100 maximum.

Photos: Pays $25 minimum for each photo or sketch used. Original b&w negatives or color slides should be made available.

WESTERN FLYER, N.W. Flyer, Inc., Box 98786, Tacoma WA 98499. (206)588-1743. Managing Editor: Dave Sclair. Biweekly tabloid covering general aviation. Provides "upbeat coverage of aviation news, activities, and politics of general and sport aviation." Circ. 20,000. Pays on publication. Byline given. Buys one-time rights. Submit seasonal/holiday material 1 month in advance. Simultaneous queries and photocopied and previously published submissions (from noncompetitive publications) OK. SASE. Reports in 1 week on queries; 2 weeks on mss. Sample copy $2; writer's guidelines for business size SAE.

Nonfiction: General interest; historical/nostalgic; how-to (safety practices, maintenance); humor; inspirational; interview/profile; new product; opinion (letters to editor); personal experience; photo feature; technical; travel. "Every other issue is a special issue. Send for list. No 'gee-whiz' type articles aimed at non-pilot audiences." Buys 100 mss/year. Query or send complete ms. Length: 250-1,500 words. Pays $15-100.

Photos: "Good pics a must." Send photos with ms. Pays $10-20 for b&w contact sheet, negatives, and 5x7 or larger prints. Identification of subjects required.

WINGS MAGAZINE, Division of Corvus Publishing Group, Ltd., Suite 158, 1224 53rd Ave., NE, Calgary, Alberta, Canada T2E 7E2. (403)275-9457. Publisher: Paul Skinner. Covers private, commercial and military aviation. Readers are age 15-70 and are predominantly people employed in aviation or with a hobbyist's interest in the field. Bimonthly magazine. Circ. 10,500. Pays on publication. Buys first rights. Phone queries OK. SAE and IRCs. Sample copy $2.50.

Nonfiction: Historical (mainly Canadian history); how-to (technical); informational (technical aviation); interview (Canadian personalities in aviation circles); new product, photo feature; profile (Canadian individuals); technical; travel (flying-related); aircraft handling tests and technical evaluation of new products. Recent example: Canadian Armed Forces Search and Rescue article (Vol. 23, No. 2). No poetry or cartoons. Query; include phone number (with area code). Length: 500-2,000 words. Pays $50-200.

Photos: State availability of photos in query. Purchased with or without accompanying ms. Captions required. Offers no additional payment for photos accepted with ms. Pays $5-20 for 5x7 b&w glossy prints; $25-50 for 35mm color transparencies.

Tips: The writer must have a technical grounding in aviation, be employed in aviation, be a knowledgeable buff or a licensed pilot. Be sure story idea is unique and would be of interest to a Canadian audience. The audience has a high level of technical insight and needs reading material that is newsworthy and informative to the industry executive, aviation expert and worker.

Business and Finance

National and regional publications of general interest to business executives form below. Those in the National grouping cover business trends nationwide, and include some material on the general theory and practice of business and financial management for consumers and members of the business community. Those in the Regional grouping report on the business climates of specific regions.

Magazines that use material on national business trends and the general theory and practice of business and financial management, but which have a technical slant, are classified in the Trade Journals section, under the Business Management, Finance, Industrial Operation and Management, or Management and Supervision categories.

National

BARRON'S NATIONAL BUSINESS AND FINANCIAL WEEKLY, 22 Cortlandt St., New York NY 10007. (212)285-5243. Editorial Director and Publisher: Robert M. Bleiberg. Editor: Alan Abelson. For business and investment people. Weekly. Free sample copy. Buys all rights. Pays on publication. SASE.

Nonfiction: Articles about various industries with investment point of view; shorter articles on particular companies, their past performance and future prospects. "Must be suitable for our specialized readership." Length: 2,000 minimum. Pays $500-1,000 for articles. Articles considered on speculation only.

Columns/Departments: News and Views. Pays $200-400.

Tips: "News and Views might be a good way to break in, but the key thing to remember here is these pieces must be fully researched and thoroughly documented."

‡**BETTER BUSINESS, National Minority Business Council, Inc.,** 235 E. 42nd St., New York NY 10017. (214)573-2385. Editor: John F. Robinson. Quarterly magazine covering small/minority business. Estab. 1981. Circ. 9,200. Pays on publication. Byline given. Buys first North American serial rights and all rights. Submit material 1 month in advance. Computer printout and disk submissions OK; prefers letter quality to dot matrix printouts. SASE. Sample copy for $2 and 9x12 SAE with $1.20 postage; free writer's guidelines.

Nonfiction: Interview/profile, technical. Buys 10 mss/year. Query with clips. Length: 3,000-5,000 words. Pays $300-350.

Photos: State availability of photos. Reviews b&w prints. Captions required. Buys all rights.

BUSINESS WEEK, 1221 Avenue of the Americas, New York NY 10020. Does not solicit freelance material.

COMMODITY JOURNAL, American Association of Commodity Traders, 10 Park St., Concord NH 03301. Editor: Arthur N. Economou. For investors interested in commodity trading based on cash, forward and option markets, alternative energy sources and foreign currencies. Bimonthly tabloid. Circ. 150,000. Pays on publication. Buys all rights. Byline given. Written queries OK. Photocopied and previously published submissions

OK. No computer printouts or disk submissions. SASE. Reports in 1 month. Free sample copy and writer's guidelines.

Nonfiction: Technical (alternative energy sources; commodity and foreign currency, trading, investing and hedging; commodity markets and foreign currency trends; written intelligibly for general public). "We are not interested in articles concerning the conventional futures market, except insofar as the spot or cash-based markets provide a better alternative." Buys 4 mss/issue. Query. Length: 1,000-2,500 words. Pays 10¢/word.

D&B REPORTS, Dun & Bradstreet, 99 Church St., New York NY 10007. (212)285-7683. Editor: Patricia W. Hamilton. Bimonthly magazine for owners and top managers of small businesses (average sales of $9 million annually.) Circ. 71,630. Pays on acceptance. Byline given. Buys all rights. Simultaneous queries OK. SASE. Reports in 2 weeks. Free sample copy and writer's guidelines.

Nonfiction: How-to (small business management; cash management; finance); interview/profile (of innovative managers); new product (how developed and marketed). "Articles provide concrete, hands-on information on how to manage more effectively. Articles on scientific developments or social change with implications for business are also of interest." Buys 8-12 mss/year. Query with clips of published work. Length: 2,000-3,000 words. Pays $500 minimum.

DOLLARS & SENSE, National Taxpayers Union, 325 Pennsylvania Ave. SE, Washington DC 20003. Editor-in-Chief: M. Fiddes. 10% freelance written. Emphasizes taxes and government spending for a diverse readership. Monthly newspaper; 8-12 pages. Circ. 120,000. Pays on publication. Buys all rights. Submit seasonal/holiday material 1 month in advance. Previously published submissions OK. SASE. Free sample copy and writer's guidelines.

Nonfiction: Exposé dealing with wasteful government spending and excessive regulation of the economy. Buys 7 mss/year. Query. Length: 500-1,500 words. Pays $25-100. "We look for original material on subjects overlooked by the national press and other political magazines. Probably the best approach is to take a little-known area of government mismanagement and examine it closely. The articles we like most are those that examine a federal program that is not only poorly managed and wasteful, but also self-defeating, hurting the very people it is designed to help. We are also interested in the long-term harm done by different kinds of taxation. Articles on IRS harassment and abuses are always needed and welcome. We have no use for financial or investment advice or broad philosophical pieces."

‡**DONOGHUE'S MONEY FUND REPORT®** , The Donoghue Organization, Inc., 360 Woodland St., Box 540, Holliston MA 01746. (617)429-5930. Senior Editor: Jeffrey L. Seglin. Weekly newsletter covering the money market mutual fund industry. Pays "upon completion of assigned article." No byline given. Makes work-for-hire assignments. Simultaneous queries, and simultaneous and photocopied submissions OK. SASE. Reports in 8 weeks. Free sample copy and writer's guidelines.

Nonfiction: How-to, new product, technical; coverage of industry conferences and regulatory board meetings. "We use news updates in the money market mutual fund industry and news stories with focus on how news will affect participants in the money market." No fiction. Buys variable number of mss/year. Query with published clips. Length: 100-500 words. Pays $75-100 for 400-500 words; "depends on article content."

Tips: Also publishes *Donoghue's Moneyletter* (for consumers interested in investment advice) and *The Cash Manager* (for cash management professionals).

DUN'S BUSINESS MONTH, Dun & Bradstreet Publications Corp., 875 3rd Ave., New York NY 10022. (212)489-2200. Editor: Clem Morgello. Emphasizes business, management and finances for a readership "concentrated among senior executives of those companies that have a net worth of $1 million or more." Monthly magazine. Circ. 284,000. Pays on acceptance. Buys all rights. Submit seasonal/holiday material 3 months in advance. Photocopied submissions OK. Reports in 1 month. Sample copy $2.50.

Nonfiction: Business and government, historical (business; i.e., law or case history), management (new trends, composition), finance and accounting, informational, interview, personal opinion and company profile. Buys 12 mss/year. Query first. Length: 1,200-2,500 words. Pays $200 minimum.

Photos: Art Director. Purchased with accompanying ms. Query first. Pays $75 for b&w photos; $150 for color.

Tips: "Make query short and clearly to the point. Also important—what distinguishes proposed story from others of its type."

THE EXECUTIVE FEMALE, NAFE, Suite 1440, 120 E. 56th St., New York NY 10022. (212)371-0740. Executive Editor: Karin Abarbanel. Managing Editor: Susan Strecker. Emphasizes "upbeat and useful career and financial information for the upwardly mobile female." Bimonthly magazine; 60 pages. Circ. 60,000. Byline given. Pays on publication. Submit seasonal/holiday material 6 months in advance. Simultaneous and photocopied submissions OK. SASE. Reports in 3 months. Sample copy $1.50; free writer's guidelines.

Nonfiction: Profile (of successful working women and the story of their careers), and technical (stories of women entrepreneurs, and career advancement and financial planning for women). "Articles on any aspect of career advancement and financial planning for women are welcomed." Sample topics: investment, coping with inflation, money-saving ideas, financial planning, business communication, time and stress management, and career goal setting and advancement. No negative or radical "women's lib" material. Queries preferred. Buys 3 unsolicited mss/year. Length: 800-1,500 words. Pays $50 minimum.

Columns/Departments: Profiles (interviews with successful women in a wide range of fields, preferably nontraditional areas for women); Entrepreneur's Corner (successful female business owners with unique ideas); Horizons (career planning, personal and professional goal-setting); and $$$ and You (specific financial issues, social security, tax planning). Buys 1-2/issue. Queries preferred. Length: 800-1,200 words. Pays $50 minimum.

Tips: "Write with more depth. I have the feeling that most are just writing off the tops of their heads to have articles 'out there.' "

‡**FACT, The Money Management Magazine**, 711 3rd Ave., New York NY 10017. (212)687-3965. Editor-in-Chief: Daniel M. Kehrer. Monthly personal money management and investment magazine for sophisticated readers. Estab. 1982. Circ. 150,000. Pays on acceptance. Byline given. Offers 25% kill fee. Buys first rights and non-exclusive (reprint) rights. Simultaneous queries OK. SASE. Reports in 6 weeks. Free sample copy.
Nonfiction: General interest (specific money management topics); how-to (invest in specific areas); new product. No business articles; no "how-to-balance your checkbook" articles. Writers must be knowledgeable and use lots of sidebars and tables. Buys 100 mss/year. Query with published clips. Length: 1,000-2,500 words. Pays $250-700.
Photos: Contact: Art Director. State availability of photos. Pays $25-120 for color transparencies. Captions, model release and identification of subjects required. Buys one-time rights.
Columns/Departments: Stocks, mutual funds, precious metals, bonds, real estate, collectibles, taxes, insurance, cash management, banking. Buys 50-60 mss/year. Query with published clips. Length: 1,500-1,800 words. Pays $250-600.
Tips: "Show writing credentials and expertise on a subject. Try something fresh, with photo possibilities. Read the magazine. Our readers are sophisticated about investments and money management."

FORBES, 60 5th Ave., New York NY 10011. "We occasionally buy freelance material. When a writer of some standing (or whose work is at least known to us) is going abroad or into an area where we don't have regular staff or bureau coverage, we have given assignments or sometimes helped on travel expenses." Pays negotiable kill fee. Byline usually given.

FORTUNE, 1271 Avenue of the Americas, New York NY 10020. Staff-written, but does buy a few freelance articles and pays well for them. Query first. SASE.

MONEY, Time-Life Bldg., Rockefeller Center, New York NY 10020. Managing Editor: Marshall Loeb. For the middle- to upper-income, sophisticated, well-educated reader. Major subjects: personal investing, financial planning, spending, saving and borrowing, careers, travel. Some freelance material.

‡**PERSONAL AND PROFESSIONAL, The Independent Magazine For Digital Personal Computer Users**, Personal Press, Inc., Box 114, Springhouse PA 19477. (215)542-7008. Managing Editor: James L. Trichon. Triannual (monthly in 1984) magazine of personal computers for business people who are personal computer users. Estab. 1983. Circ. 30,000. Pays on publication. Byline given. Offers 100% kill fee. Simultaneous queries and photocopied and previously published submissions OK. Reports in 1 month on queries; 2 weeks on mss. Free sample copy and writer's guidelines.
Nonfiction: Book reviews; general interest; how-to (use a computer, software, etc.); interview/profile (of computer leaders); personal experience (user articles); technical (all aspects of hardware and software); all types of articles dealing with PC market. No opinion pieces. Buys 200-250 mss/year. Query. Length: 1,500-5,000 words. Pays $100-500 "depending on the piece."

‡**REFERENCE MAGAZINE, The Business Journal for IBM Personal Computing**, Constant Communications, Inc., Box 1200, Amherst NH 03031. (603)673-9544. Editor: John DiCocco. Bimonthly (monthly in 1984) business magazine covering uses and users of the IBM personal computer. "Readers include middle managers, executive vice presidents, mom-'n'-pop entrepreneurs. Neither the data processing manager nor the software writer are part of our audience. We are a business publication first, computer magazine second, addressing the needs and interests of IBM Personal Computer users. We are totally independent; that is, not affiliated with IBM." Estab. 1982. Circ. 40,000. Pays on acceptance. Byline given. Buys first rights. Submit seasonal/holiday material 3 months in advance. No simultaneous, photocopied or previously published submissions. Reports in 1 month on queries; 3 weeks on mss. Sampl copy $3; free writer's guidelines.
Nonfiction: General interest (business computer); interview/profile (people finding success and/or new applications for personal computers); opinion (software or hardware reviews); "expertise" (an area of personal computing in which you have expertise, presented to readers in a nontechnical way). Special issues include

Taxes and the PC; Integrated Software Packages; Working at Home; Creativity and the PC: The Business of Microcomputers. No fiction, jokes, lines and lines of computer programs, or overly simple writing. Buys 4-8 mss/issue. Query with clips of published work. Length: 1,500-5,000 words. Pays approximately 15¢/word.
Tips: "We think of the PC as a business tool, liberator, and creativity enhancer. Our plain English editorial style is directed at the business reader who is a newcomer to the computer age, with little or no knowledge (*or interest!*) in the technical slide. Thus our articles are concerned with those activities of personal computers and computerists that add to office productivity. Like most business publications, we also run corporate profiles, case histories, and interviews as long as they relate to this field. The people who get published by *Reference* are those who can put a semi-technical subject into the kind of language that time-conscious business readers can understand and appreciate. We don't want 'too cute' or 'condescending tekkie.' Write *Wall Street Journal* style. A different theme every issue calls for changing expertise in personal computing areas. However, we are always looking for new applications of personal computers, and the p.c. business itself. We'll be a monthly beginning January 1984."

‡**THE STOCK MARKET MAGAZINE, Voice of the Small Investor**, Wall Street Publishing Institute, Inc., 16 School St., Yonkers NY 10701. (914)423-4566. Editor: Angelo R. Martinelli. Managing Editor: Bernard D. Brown. Monthly magazine covering the financial world with emphasis on companies in an uptrend (must be publicly owned). Circ. 50,000. Pays on publication. Bylines used occasionally. Buys all rights and second serial (reprint) rights. No computer printouts or disk submissions. Submit seasonal material 6 weeks in advance. Reports in 3 weeks.
Nonfiction: "No publicity puffs wanted." Query. Length: 800-2,400 words. Pays $50 minimum/assignment.

‡**SYLVIA PORTER'S PERSONAL FINANCE MAGAZINE**, Davis Publications, Inc., 380 Lexington Ave., New York NY 10017. (212)557-9100. Editor: Patricia Estess. Managing Editor: Elana Lore. Bimonthly magazine covering personal finance and consumer economics. Estab. 1983. Pays on acceptance. Byline given. Offers 20% kill fee. Buys all rights. Submit seasonal/holiday material 4 months in advance. No simultaneous queries. No simultaneous, photocopied or previously published submissions. SASE. Reports in 2 months. Free sample copy; writer's guidelines are available.
Nonfiction: General interest (financial). Only articles dealing with personal finance; no financially technical articles. Query with published clips. Length: 1,000-1,500 words. Pays negotiable rates.
Columns/Departments: Funny Money (send mss to editor, Funny Money). "Funny Money is looking for personal stories of humorous observation or experience in the fields of saving, spending, borrowing, investing." Buys 50 mss/year. Send complete ms. Length: about 150 words. Pays $25.
Tips: "The magazine is grounded on the personal relationship between reader and writer. Writers and editors have the responsibility of giving the reader the impression that an article was written 'for me'—and, indeed, it will have been. Send a cover letter with original ideas or slants about personal finance articles you'd like to do for us, accompanied by clippings of your previously published work. The features section is most open to freelancers. We will be covering topics such as budgeting, saving, investing, real estate, taxes, in each issue. Features must be accurate, personal in tone, and must sparkle."

‡**TECHNICAL ANALYSIS OF STOCKS AND COMMODITIES, The Traders Magazine**, Box 46518, Seattle WA 98146. (206)938-0570. Editor: Jack K. Hutson. Bimonthly magazine covering trading stocks and commodities. Estab. 1982. Circ. 1,000. Pays on acceptance. Byline given. Offers 50% kill fee. Buys first rights and second serial (reprint) rights. Photocopied and previously published submissions OK. SASE. Reports in 3 weeks on queries; 4 weeks on mss. Sample copy $5; detailed writer's guidelines for business-size SAE and 2 first class stamps.
Nonfiction: Reviews (new software or hardware on the market that can make a trader's life easier; comparative reviews of books, articles, etc.); how-to (make a trade); technical (trading and software aids to trading); utilities (charting or computer programs, surveys, statistics, or information to help the trader study or interpret market movements); humor (unusual incidents of market occurrences, cartoons). No newsletter-type, buy-sell recommendations. Program listings longer than 15-20 lines should be accompanied by diskette or cassette tapes. Buys 60 mss/year. Query with published clips if available or send complete ms. Length: 1,500-4,000 words. Pays $100-500. (Applies base rate and premium rate—write for information).
Photos: Kevin O. Donohoe, photo editor. State availability of photos. Pays $15-50 for 8½x11 b&w glossy prints. Captions, model release and identification of subjects required. Buys one-time rights.
Columns/Departments: Buys 10 mss/year. Query. Length: 800-1,600 words. Pays $50-200.
Fillers: Kevin O. Donohoe, fillers editor. Jokes. Buys 20/year. Length: 10-500 words. Pays $10-50.
Tips: "Describe how to use chart work and other technical analysis in day-to-day trading of stocks or commodities. A blow-by-blow account of how a trade was made, including the trader's thought processes, is, to our subscribers, the very best received story. One of our prime considerations is to instruct in a manner that the lay person can comprehend. We are not hyper-critical of writing style. The completeness and accuracy of submitted material is of the utmost consideration. Write for detailed writer's guidelines."

TRAVEL SMART FOR BUSINESS, Communications House, 40 Beechdale Rd., Dobbs Ferry NY 10522. (914)693-8300. Editor/Publisher: H.J. Teison. Managing Editor: Mary Hunt. Monthly newsletter covering travel and information on keeping travel costs down for business travelers and business travel managers. Circ. 2,000. Pays on publication. No byline given. "Writers are listed as contributors." Offers 25% kill fee. Buys first North American serial rights. SASE. Reports in 6 weeks. Sample copy for $2, business size SAE, and 2 first class stamps; writer's guidelines free for business size SAE and 1 first class stamp.

Nonfiction: Expose (of "inside" travel facts and companies dealing in travel); how-to (pick a meeting site, save money on travel); reviews of facilities and restaurants); analysis of specific trends in travel affecting business travelers. No general travel information, backgrounders, or non-business-oriented articles. "We're looking for value-oriented, concise, factual articles." Buys 20 mss/year. Query with clips of published work. Length: 250-1,500 words. Pays $20-150.

Columns/Departments: Deal Alert (latest offers for business travelers from commuter airlines, hotels, and car rental companies in specific parts of the country. Send complete ms. Length: 25-500 words. Pays $5-25.

Tips: "We are primarily staff written, with a few regular writers. Contributions to 'Deal Alert' are welcome and can take the form of clips, etc. Know the travel business or have business travel experience. People with a specific area of experience or expertise have the inside track."

‡**WASHINGTON REPORT**, US Chamber of Commerce, 1615 H St. NW, Washington DC 20062. (202)463-5663. Editor: Michael Lewis. Managing Editor: Al Holzinger. Weekly tabloid on government actions affecting business. Circ. 100,000. Pays on publication. Byline given. Buys all rights. Simultaneous queries OK. SASE. Reports in 3 weeks. Sample copy 60¢.

Nonfiction: Expose (government); opinion (relating to federal government). "News coverage is without bias. Opinion pieces reflect a pro-business, conservative philosophy." Buys 60 mss/year. Query with published clips if available. Length: 250-500 words. Pays $100-500.

Columns/Departments: Pieces on government issues related to business or areas of business directly related to government. Buys 20 mss/year. Length: 600-700 words. Pays $100 minimum.

Tips: "Freelancers should submit a specific story idea and give background information about themselves, including writing samples."

WEEKDAY, Enterprise Publications, Suite 3417, 20 N. Wacker Dr., Chicago IL 60606. For the average employee in business and industry. Circ. 30,000. Buys all rights. Byline given. Pays on acceptance. SASE.

Nonfiction and Photos: Uses articles slanted toward the average man, with the purpose of increasing his understanding of the business world and helping him be more successful in it. Also uses articles on "How to Get Along With Other People," and informative articles on meeting everyday problems—consumer buying, legal problems, community affairs, real estate, education, human relations, etc. Length: approximately 1,000 words maximum. Pays $15-40. Uses b&w human interest photos.

Regional

AUSTIN MAGAZINE, Austin Chamber of Commerce, Box 1967, Austin TX 78767. (512)478-9383. Editor: Hal Susskind. A business and community magazine dedicated to telling the story of Austin and its people to Chamber of Commerce members and the community. Magazine published monthly by the Chamber; 72-128 pages. Circ. 9,500. Copyrighted. Pays kill fee. Byline given "except if the story has to be completely rewritten; the author would be given credit for his input but he may not be given a byline." Sample copy for $1.75. Will consider original mss only. Computer printout and disk submissions OK; prefer letter quality to dot matrix printouts. Reports within 3 months. SASE.

Nonfiction and Photos: Articles should deal with interesting businesses or organizations, events, people, or phenomena relating to the Austin community and in particular Chamber of Commerce members. Articles are also accepted on Austin's entertainment scene and the arts. Length: 1,000 to 2,000 words. Pays $30-200. B&w photos are purchased with mss.

BUSINESS LIFE MAGAZINE, Canada's Business Magazine, Suite 705, 6299 Airport Rd., Mississauga, Ontario, Canada L4U 1N3. Editor: Jurgen Lindhorst. Managing Editor: Susan Marshall. Monthly magazine covering general business; politics/business; socio-economic trends as they apply to business. "We are acutely aware of the interplay between business and government and many of our articles reflect this interplay. Prime interest is in Canadian writers." Circ. 92,879. Pays 30 days after acceptance. Byline given. Offers 100% kill fee if story specifically assigned by the editors and then not published through internal decision; 10% if specifically assigned by editors and then found to be qualitatively unacceptable. Buys all rights. Simultaneous queries, photocopied and previously published submissions OK, "providing exclusive rights are offered." SASE. Reports in 1 month on queries; 2 months on mss. Free sample copy.

Nonfiction: How-to, interview/profile, general business. Buys 30-40 mss/year. Query with clips of published

work. Length: 1,750-3,500 words. Pays $300-1,000 (Canadian funds).
Photos: State availability of photos. Pays $25 maximum for color transparencies in 120 format. Captions required.

BUSINESS NEWS, Business News, 7908 Convoy Court, San Diego CA 92111. (619)565-2636. Editor: Hal Betancourt. Tabloid published every other Monday for "company executives and middle-management personnel." Estab. 1981. Circ. 10,000. Pays in 30 days of invoice. Byline given. Offers 100% kill fee. Buys one-time rights. Submit seasonal/holiday material 2 months in advance. Simultaneous queries and photocopied and previously published submissions OK. Computer printout submissions OK; letter quality only. SASE. Reports in 1 week. Sample copy for $1 and 9x12 SAE with 52¢ postage.
Nonfiction: How-to (be more successful), interview/profile, personal experience, technical, "all material must be business oriented." Buys 12 mss/year. Query with clips of published work. Length: 750-1,000 words. Pays $27-48.
Columns/Departments: Buys 3 mss/year. Query with clips of published work. Length: 500-750 words. Pays $25.
Tips: How-to (be better at work, successful, etc.) section most open to freelancers. Business computer systems information that is easy to understand will be needed.

THE BUSINESS TIMES, The Connecticut Business Times, Inc., 544 Tolland St., East Hartford CT 06108. (203)289-9341. Managing Editor: Deborah Hallberg. Monthly tabloid covering business and financial news within Connecticut for "the top executive or business owner in Connecticut." Circ. 25,000. Pays on publication. Byline given. Buys exclusive rights within Connecticut. Phone queries OK. Submit seasonal/holiday material 1 month in advance. Simultaneous queries and previously published submissions OK. No computer printout or disk submissions. SASE. Reports in 1 month. Sample copy $1.
Nonfiction: Interview/profile (of a Connecticut business person with a unique story); new product (pertaining to Connecticut only). "Features include legislative updates, state-of-the-economy analysis, industry profiles, etc. We use very little national news. It helps if out-of-state freelancers specialize in one area, e.g., real estate. Articles should be written with the business *owner*—not the office manager or secretary—in mind." Special monthly supplements include: computers, office design, word processing, copiers, real estate, tax shelters, transportation service, telecommunications, banking & finance, energy. "We have a need for material for our monthly advertising supplements. These are usually nuts & bolts kind of articles—state-of-the-art, etc." No articles on improving sales techniques, time management, stress management, cash flow management or how to choose a computer. Buys 4-5 mss/year. Query with clips of published works. Length: 800-1,500 words. Pays $1/column inch.
Photos: State availability of photos. Reviews 8x10 b&w prints. Pays $15/first photo, $10 each additional photo. Captions required. Buys exclusive rights within Connecticut.

‡**BUSINESS TO BUSINESS**, Tallahassee's Business Magazine, Business to Business, Inc., Box 6085, Tallahassee FL 32314. (904)222-7072. Editor: Howard Libin. Monthly tabloid covering business in the North Florida-South Georgia Big Bend region. Estab. 1982. Circ. 16,000. Pays on acceptance. Byline given "generally." Offers 30% kill fee. Buys one-time rights. Submit seasonal/holiday material 4 months in advance. Photocopied and previously published submissions OK. SASE. Reports in 2 weeks on queries; 3 weeks on mss. Sample copy for 9x12 SAE and 4 first class stamps; writer's guidelines for SAE and 1 first class stamp.
Nonfiction: Book excerpts (reviews of business related books—Megatrends, Positioning); In search of excellence (topics of interest to business-minded people); historical/nostalgic (only pertaining to the Big Bend); how-to (select the right typewriter, adding machine, secretary, phone system, insurance plan); new products; technical (articles on finance marketing, investment, advertising and real estate as it applies to small business). Special "inserts" planned: advertising, office of the future, consulting, taxes. "No really basic material. Writers must assume that readers have some idea of business vocabulary. No new business profiles, or material without local handle." Buys 30-50 mss/year. Query with published clips if available. Length: 600-2,000 words. Pays $40-200.
Photos: Peter Denes, Bob O'Lary, photo editors. State availability of photos. Pays $5-20 for b&w contact sheet and b&w prints. Identification of subjects required.
Columns/Departments: "Shorts accepted on all aspects of doing business. Each story should tackle one topic and guide reader from question to conclusion. General appeal for all trades and industries." Buys 50-70 mss/year. Query with published clips if available. Length: 600-1,000 words. Pays $40-75.
Tips: "Send a query with past writing sample included. If it seems that a writer is capable of putting together an interesting 500-800 word piece dealing with small business operation, we're willing to give them a try. Meeting deadlines determines writer's future with us. We're open to short department pieces on management, finance, marketing, investments, real estate. Must be tightly written—direct and to the point; yet keep it casual."

CALIFORNIA BUSINESS, Suite 711, 6420 Wilshire Blvd., Los Angeles CA 90048. (213)653-9340. Editor: Mike Harris. Emphasizes Western business for business executives, businessmen, market analysts, etc. Monthly magazine. Pays on publication. Buys first rights. Pays negotiable kill fee. Byline usually given. Simultaneous submissions OK. SASE. Reports in 6 weeks. Sample copy $1; SASE for writer's guidelines.
Nonfiction: General business pieces, most with California focus (coverage of other Western states is less than 2%). "We also do trends for industries, company features and an occasional piece on business men and women who've done something unique or have something to say relating to their field of expertise." Buys 3-4 mss/issue. Query. Length: 1,000-2,000 words. Pays $200-450.
Photos: State availability of photos. Pay negotiable for b&w prints and color transparencies. Captions and model release required.
Tips: Query should be 2-3 paragraphs with samples of writing.

CARIBBEAN BUSINESS NEWS, Suite 332, 111 Queen St. E., Toronto, Ontario, Canada M5C 1S2. (416)368-6451. Managing Editor: Colin Rickards. 3% freelance written. Emphasizes business and financial news affecting the entire Caribbean area for upper- and middle-echelon business/management people worldwide. Bimonthly magazine, 32-40 pages. Circ. 7,000. Pays on publication. Buys all rights. Byline given "but there might be a circumstance, at our discretion, where a byline would not be given." Phone queries OK. Photocopied and previously published submissions OK. SAE and IRC. Reports in 2 weeks. Free sample copy.
Nonfiction: General interest, interview and business/financial articles on Caribbean topics. Recent article example: "US Virgin Islands Broaden Industrial Base." No travel material. Buys 8 mss/year. Query. Length: 500-1,000 words. Pays $100-250.
Photos: Pays $40 minimum for 5x7 or 8x10 b&w prints. Captions required.
Tips: "We are looking for the offbeat in business. Recent articles include the business side of treasure diving in Dominica and the business side of being a beauty queen. Emphasis must be on business/finance."

COLORADO BUSINESS MAGAZINE, Titsch and Associates, Box 5400 T.A., Denver CO 80217. (303)295-0900. Executive Editor: Ann Feeney. Editor: Sharon Almirall. Monthly magazine covering business. Circ. 20,634. Pays on publication. Byline given. Offers negotiable kill fee. Buys first North American serial rights. Submit seasonal/holiday material 4 months in advance. Simultaneous queries, and photocopied and previously published submissions (on occasion). Computer printout submissions OK; prefers letter quality to dot matrix printouts. Disk submissions OK "if hard copy is attached." SASE. Reports in 2 weeks.
Nonfiction: Business-oriented articles only with Colorado "hook"; must be oriented to manager or executive. Buys 12 mss/year. Query. Length: 1,500-2,000 words. Pays $150-200.

COMMERCE MAGAZINE, 130 S. Michigan Ave., Chicago IL 60603. (312)786-0111. Editor: Carol Johnson. For top businessmen and industrial leaders in greater Chicago area. Also sent to chairmen and presidents of *Fortune* 1,000 firms throughout the United States. Monthly magazine; varies from 100 to 300 pages (8½x11½). Circ. 15,000. Buys all rights. Buys 30-40 mss/year. Pays on acceptance. Query. SASE.
Nonfiction: Business articles and pieces of general interest to top business executives. "We select our freelancers and assign topics. Many of our writers are from local newspapers. Considerable freelance material is used but almost exclusively on assignment from Chicago—area specialists within a particular business sector."

CORPORATE MONTHLY, 105 Chestnut St., Philadelphia PA 19106. Editor: Tom Bubeck. Emphasizes general business-oriented local material. Local writers preferred. Articles usually require some human interest angles, for anyone in business in the Delaware Valley. Monthly magazine. Pays on publication. Buys first North American serial rights. SASE.
Nonfiction: "New trends in business; exclusive reports on subjects relating to the business of the Delaware Valley; health and quality of life articles; technical articles of general interest—like 'How to Sell Your Business'; a fresh look or unique perspective on area problems." Mostly staff written. Query. Length: 800-2,000 words. Payment negotiated if query is accepted.
Tips: "We are buying virtually nothing from writers we don't already know. We get more good queries than we can handle from local writers. We are not a good market for freelancers at this time."

CRAIN'S CLEVELAND BUSINESS, 140 Public Square, Cleveland OH 44114. (216)522-1383. Editor: Jacques Neher. Weekly tabloid about business in the 7 county area surrounding Cleveland and Akron for upper income executives, professionals and entrepreneurs. Circ. 25,000. Average issue includes 2-3 freelance news or feature articles. Pays on publication. Byline given. Buys first North American serial rights. Phone queries OK. Reports in 3 weeks. Free writer's guidelines.
Nonfiction: "We are interested in business and political events and their impact on the Cleveland area business community. We also want local news developments and trends of significance to business life in the Cleveland-Akron-Lorain area." Buys 2-3 mss/issue. Query. Length: 500-1,200 words. Pays $5 column inch for news stories; $3/column inch for special section features.

Photos: State availability of photos. Reviews 5x7 b&w glossy prints. Pays $10/photo used. Captions required. Buys one-time rights.

EXECUTIVE, Airmedia, 2973 Weston Rd., Weston, Ontario, Canada M9N 3R3. (416)741-1112. Publisher: Donald Coote. Assistant Editor: Mary Louise Burke. Monthly business magazine covering financial, political, company profiles for presidents and senior management. Circ. 53,000. Pays on publication. Byline given. Buys first rights. Simultaneous queries OK. SASE. Reports in 1 month. Free sample copy.
Nonfiction: Executives in the news. Query with clips of published work.
Photos: Reviews photos. Identification of subjects required. Buys one-time rights.

EXECUTIVE REPORT, Riverview Publications, 213 S. Craig St., Pittsburgh PA 15213. (412)687-4803. Editor: Charles W. Shane. Monthly magazine concentrating on the business, industry and finance of western Pennsylvania. Estab. 1981. Circ. 16,000. Pays within 20 days of publication. Byline given. Submit seasonal/holiday material 3 months in advance. Simultaneous queries, and photocopied, simultaneous, and previously published submissions OK. No computer printout or disk submissions. SASE. Sample copy $2; free writer's guidelines.
Nonfiction: Deborah J. Ord, articles editor. Expose, interview/profile, new product, opinion, personal experience, travel. Buys 10-14 mss/year. Query with clips of published work. Length: 1,000-3,000 words. Pays $100-500.

THE FINANCIAL POST, Maclean Hunter, Ltd., 777 Bay St., Toronto, Ontario, Canada M5W 1A7. Editor-in-Chief: Neville J. Nankivell. Executive Editor: Dalton S. Robertson. Copy & Design Editor: Christopher Watson. 10% freelance written. Emphasizes Canadian business, investment/finance and public affairs. Weekly newspaper. Circ. 200,000. Pays on publication. Buys one-time rights. Pays 50% kill fee. Byline given. Reports in 2-3 weeks. Sample copy $1.
Nonfiction: Useful news and information for executives, managers and investors in Canada. Buys 3 mss/issue. Query. Length: 700-800 words. Pays 15-20¢/word.
Photos: State availability of photos with query. Pays $25-50 for 8x10 b&w glossy prints. Captions required. Buys one-time rights.

FINANCIAL POST MAGAZINE, Maclean Hunter, Ltd., 481 University Ave., Toronto, Ontario, Canada M5W 1A7. (416)596-5658. Editor: Paul A. Rush. Monthly magazine covering Canadian business. Circ. 225,000. Pays on acceptance. Byline given. Offers 50% kill fee. Buys first North American serial rights. Submit seasonal/holiday material 3 months in advance. Simultaneous queries OK. SASE. Reports in 1 month. Free sample copy.
Nonfiction: Book excerpts, general interest, interview/profile, new product. No articles on women in management, stress, travel, U.S. politics and money, or fashion. Canadian angle required.

HOUSTON BUSINESS JOURNAL, Cordovan Corp., an E.W. Scripps subsidiary, 5314 Bingle Rd., Houston TX 77092. (713)688-8811. Emphasizes Houston business. Weekly tabloid. Circ. 20,000. Pays on publication. Buys all rights. Byline given. Phone queries OK ("but prefer mail"). Submit seasonal/holiday material 2 months in advance. SASE. Reports in 1 month. Sample copy $1.
Nonfiction: Local emphasis exposé (business, if documented), how-to (finance, business, management, lifestyle), informational (money-making), interview (local business topics), nostalgia (possible, if business), profile (local business executives), personal experience and photo feature. Length: 500-2,000 words. Pays $3/column inch.
Photos: State availability of photos or send photos with ms. Pays $10 for b&w prints. Buys all rights. Captions required.

‡**ILLINOIS BUSINESS,** Crain Communications, Inc., 740 N. Rush, Chicago IL 60611. (312)280-3163. Editor: Joe Cappo. Managing Editor: Alan Rosenthal. Quarterly business publication for company presidents, owners, board chairmen, state officials. Estab. 1982. Circ. 25,000. Pays on acceptance. (All articles are on a work-for-hire basis.) Simultaneous queries OK "if so advised." Reports in 1 month.
Nonfiction: "Anything to do with Illinois business and economics." Buys 64 mss/year. (All articles are commissioned.) Query with published clips. Length: 2,500 words maximum. Pays $300 and up; average feature-length article pays $1,000.
Photos: "Illinois photographers only should contact the magazine about possible assignments." Buys first rights.
Tips: "Read our publication before submitting a query. All material must be about Illinois business. The magazine is seeking Illinois writers and photographers who can cover Illinois business subjects."

INDIANA BUSINESS, Suite 248, 9302 N. Meridian, Indianapolis IN 46260. (317)844-8627. Editor: Joan S. Marie. Monthly magazine. Pays on publication. Rights negotiable. Computer printout submissions OK. SASE. Free sample copy.

Nonfiction: "All articles must relate to Indiana business and must be of interest to a broad range of business and professional people." Especially interested in articles on agri-business, international affairs as they affect Indiana business, executive health issues, new science and technology projects happening in Indiana. "We don't want plain 'ole' success stories. We would like to hear about successes but only as they pertain to current issues, trends, (i.e., a real estate company that has made it big because they got in on the Economic Development Bonds and invested in renovation property)." Buys 15-20 mss/year. Query or send complete ms. Pay negotiable.

Photos: State availability of photos. Pay negotiable for b&w or color photos. Captions and model release required.

Tips: "A query letter must show that the author is familiar with our publication. It should also be concise but catchy. Be willing to submit samples and/or articles on speculation. We are very interested in articles that flow well—business-like but not dry. Also, the more timely, the better. Be specific about a person, product, company, new program, etc. Stay away from generalizations. The magazine now has 3 new sections: Agri-Business, International Affairs, New Technologies."

‡**JEFFERSON BUSINESS**, 3033 N. Causeway Blvd., Metairie LA 70002. (504)362-4310. Editor: Lan Sluder. Metro/regional business newsweekly tabloid covering business and professional news in the metro New Orleans area. Edited for upscale business executives, professionals and business owners. Pays on acceptance. Byline given. Buys available rights; at least exclusive in Louisiana. Submit seasonal/holiday material 1 month in advance. Simultaneous queries and simultaneous, photocopied and previously published submissions OK. Computer printout and disk submissions OK; prefers letter quality to dot matrix printouts. SASE. Reports in 2 weeks. Sample copy for 9x12 SAE and 8 first class stamps. Writer's guidelines for business size SAE and 1 first class stamp.

Nonfiction: Book excerpts (from quality business books); expose (none about politics); general interest (about power, money, and winning and losing); how-to (well written for savvy business person); humor (only with a business slant); interview/profile (with people in New Orleans area or with a direct tie); new product (only in Louisiana); personal experience (in business); photo feature, technical (on energy, taxes, real estate, etc.). "We have special issues on real estate, finance, executive toys and dozens of other subjects of interest to executives." No "how-to's that are boring rehashes of common sense business practices." Buys 100+ mss/year. Send complete ms. Length: 500-1,800 words. Pays $35-200.

Photos: Send photos with ms. Pays $5-40 for 5x7 b&w prints. Captions, model release and identification of subjects required. Buys one-time rights.

Columns/Departments: "We occasionally buy mss to run in our rotating 'Leisure' column on executive lifestyles. Also, money management columns, of interest to top executives and professionals." Buys 50/year. Send complete ms. Length: 800-2,000 words. Pays $50-75.

Tips: "Write good, dense copy that makes business sound exciting. We look seriously at anything with a solid local connection—mainly Jefferson and Orleans Parishes—but we don't ignore other Louisiana business developments."

KANSAS BUSINESS NEWS, Kansas Business Publishing Co., Inc., Suite 124, 3601 S.W. 29th, Topeka KS 66614. (913)293-3010. Editor: Dan Bearth. Monthly magazine about Kansas business for the businessmen, executives and professionals who want to how what is going on in the state that will affect the way they do business, their profits, labor requirements, etc. All submissions must relate to local business conditions. Circ. 15,000. Pays on publication. Buys all rights. Phone queries OK. Submit seasonal material 3 months in advance. Simultaneous and previously published submissions OK. SASE. Free sample copy.

Nonfiction: How-to, humor, interview, profile, and technical. Query only. Pays $25-100.

Photos: Editor: Marsh Galloway. State availability of photos or send photos with ms. Reviews b&w contact sheets and negatives. Offers no additional payment for photos accepted with ms. Captions preferred; model release required. Buys all rights.

Columns/Departments: Management, Finance, Government, Personnel Management, Taxes, Computers and Technology, Insurance, Labor Relations and Investment. Query only. Pays $25 minimum.

KENTUCKY BUSINESS LEDGER, Box 3508, Louisville KY 40201. (502)589-5464. Editor: Dot Ridings. Emphasizes Kentucky business and finance. Monthly tabloid. Circ. 13,000. Pays on publication. Buys all rights. Byline given at editor's option. Phone queries OK. Submit seasonal/holiday material 1 month in advance of issue date. Simultaneous, photocopied and previously published submissions OK. Prefers letter quality to dot matrix computer printout submissions. SASE. Reports in 2 weeks. Sample copy $1.50; free writer's guidelines.

Nonfiction: How-to (tips for businesses on exporting, dealing with government, cutting costs, increasing profits—must have specific Kentucky angle); interview (government officials on issues important to Kentucky businesspersons); new product (new uses for coal;—"We are not interested in every company's new flange or gasket"); profile (of Kentucky businesspersons); and articles on the meanings of government laws and regulations to Kentucky businesses. "We get too many industry-wide trend stories, which we use hardly at all. We must have a strong Kentucky link to any story." No humor, book reviews or personal advice. Buys 25-30 mss/ year. Query. Length: 2,000 words maximum. "We went from a 16" page to 13½"—so are running shorter articles." Pays $1.50/inch.

Photos: State availability of photos with query. Pays $10 up for b&w glossy prints.

Tips: "On technical subjects from unknown freelancers, we need a statement of expertise and/or previous work within the subject area."

LOS ANGELES BUSINESS JOURNAL, Cordovan Corp., Suite 506, 3727 W. 6th St., Los Angeles CA 90020. Editor: Charles M. Heschmeyer. Weekly tabloid covering business developments within the Los Angeles area for business executives, managers and entrepreneurs. The publication is designed to help the decision-making process for businessmen in the areas of new trends and ideas important to commerce and industry. Circ. 15,000 guaranteed. Pays on publication. Buys all rights. Computer printout and disk submissions OK.

Nonfiction: "We are interested in Los Angeles area industry or business trend stories, as well as executive or company profiles. Illustrate trends with specific figures. Length: 800-3,000 words. No column material; hard news of business features only. Buys 24 mss/year. Query. Pays $3/column inch, $25/b&w picture used with story.

Tips: "Submit a story line query of two-three-or four sentences. List the specific points expected to be covered in the article."

‡MIAMI VALLEY BUSINESS JOURNAL, Gramarye Communications, Inc., Suite 600, 4 S. Main St., Dayton OH 45402. (513)461-9700. Editor: Kathleen Turner. Weekly tabloid covering business developments, trends, expansions and new product and/or service opportunities for managers, investors and business professionals. Estab. 1982. Circ. 5000+ Pays on publication. Byline given occasionally. Buys first rights. Simultaneous queries and photocopied submissions OK. SASE. Reports in 1 week on queries; 2 weeks on mss. Sample copy 75¢; writer's guidelines for 9x12 SAE and 3 first class stamps.

.Nonfiction: Humor (business oriented); interview/profile, new product, opinion, technical (on business R&D). Query with clips if available. Length: 250-2,500 words. Pays 40¢/published line for feature; 20¢/ published line for commentary.

MID-SOUTH BUSINESS, Mid-South Communications, Inc., Suite 232, 4515 Poplar St., Memphis TN 38117. (901)685-2411. Editor: Barney DuBois. Weekley tabloid covering industry, trade, agribusiness and finance in west Tennessee, north Mississippi, east Arkansas, and the Missouri Bootheel. "Articles should be timely and relevant to business in our region." Circ. 9,000. Pays on acceptance. Byline given. Pays $50 kill fee. Buys one-time rights, second serial (reprint) rights, and makes work-for-hire assignments. Submit seasonal/holiday material 2 months in advance. Simultaneous queries and submissions OK. Computer printout and disk submissions OK. SASE. Reports in 2 weeks. Free sample copy.

Nonfiction: Expose; historical/nostalgic; interview/profile; business features and trends. "All must relate to business in our area." Buys 130 mss/year. Query with or without clips of published work or send complete ms. Length: 750-2,000 words. Pays $80-200.

Photos: State availability of photos or send photos with ms. Pays $25-50 for 5x7 b&w prints. Identification of subjects required. Buys one-time rights.

Tips: "We welcome freelancers who can do features and articles on business in the smaller cities of our region. We are now a weekly, so our stories need to be more timely."

NEW JERSEY BUSINESS, Hotel Robert Treat, 50 Park Place, Newark NJ 07102. (201)623-8359. Executive Editor: James Prior. Emphasizes business in the state of New Jersey. Monthly magazine. Pays on acceptance. Buys all rights. Simultaneous and previously published work OK. SASE. Reports in 3 weeks. Sample copy $1.

Nonfiction: "All freelance articles are upon assignment, and they deal with business and industry either directly or more infrequently, indirectly pertaining to New Jersey." Buys 6 mss/year. Query or send clips of published work. Pays $150-200.

Photos: Send photos with ms. Captions preferred.

The double dagger (‡) before a listing indicates that the listing is new in this edition. New markets are often the most receptive to freelance contributions.

NEW MEXICO BUSINESS JOURNAL, New Mexico's Magazine of Management, Southwest Publications, Inc., Box 1788, Albuquerque NM 87103. (505)243-5581. Editor: Paul Young. Monthly magazine covering industry and management news. Circ. 14,000. Pays on publication. Byline given. Buys one-time rights. Submit seasonal/holiday material 3 months in advance. Simultaneous queries and simultaneous, photocopied and previously published submissions OK. No computer printout or disk submissions. SASE. Reports as soon as possible. Sample copy $2; free writer's guidelines.
Nonfiction: How-to (manage, invest); business interest; technical (accounting procedures, etc.). No consumer, travel, personal history or human interest articles. Query with clips of published work. Length: 500-1,500 words. Pays 5¢/word.
Photos: Send photos with query. Pays $5 for 5x7 b&w prints. Captions and identification of subjects required.

NORTHWEST INVESTMENT REVIEW, #400, 534 SW 3rd Ave., Portland OR 97204. (503)224-6004. Editor-in-Chief: Shannon P. Pratt. For investors, advisors and corporate leaders who pay $195 a year to read about the 400 Northwestern/Intermountain/Hawaiian publicly held corporations covered by this and a companion publication. "Newsletter published at least 50 times/year (weekly)." Pays on publication. Query. Reports in 1 month.
Nonfiction: "We need top quality highly regional articles, covering public companies headquartered or having major operations in Hawaii, Alaska, Oregon, Washington, Idaho, Montana, Colorado, Wyoming, Utah and the two western provinces of Canada. Must appeal to investors. Length: 500-2500 words. Pay negotiable. Many are done for a fee; no set minimum."
Tips: "All work must be well researched. Ideally, freelancers should be from business page writing or finance/security backgrounds."

‡**OHIO BUSINESS**, (formerly *Northern Ohio Business Journal*), Business Journal Publishing Co., 425 Hanna Bldg., Cleveland OH 44115. (216)621-1644. Editor: Jim Lorincz. Managing Editor: Lys Ann Shore. Monthly magazine covering business-related subjects with an Ohio slant. "Our readers are corporate executives and small business owners around the state." Circ. 35,000. Pays on acceptance. Byline given. Submit seasonal/holiday material 2 months in advance. No previously published or simultaneous submissions. SASE. Reports in 1 month. Sample copy $2.
Nonfiction: Business and finance. "Writers can request our editorial calendar, compiled each year for the coming year. Generally one special topic per issue." Buys 6 or fewer mss/year. Query with or without published clips. Length: 1,000-2,000 words. Pays 20¢/word maximum.
Photos: State availability of photos. Pays negotiable rates for b&w and color transparencies and prints. Buys one-time rights.
Tips: "Target stories to our subject (business) and our region (Ohio). Best bets are composite stories that combine information from a variety of sources, preferably from around the state. Ask for our editorial calendar as a help in your planning."

‡**OKLAHOMA ECONOMIC DEVELOPMENT NEWS**, Oklahoma Economic Development Department, Box 53424, Oklahoma City OK 73152. (405)521-2181. Editor: Carol Miller. Bimonthly "magapaper" covering news about new and expanding industries in Oklahoma for Oklahoma manufacturers. Estab. 1983. Circ. 17,000. Pays on acceptance. No byline given. Not copyrighted. Buys one-time rights. Submit seasonal/holiday material 2 months in advance. Simultaneous queries, and simultaneous, photocopied, and previously published submissions OK. SASE. Reports in 2 weeks. Free sample copy and writer's guidelines.
Nonfiction: General interest, interview/profile, and new product. No articles about retail, farm or service operations, or anything not about Oklahoma business. Buys variable number mss/year. Query with clips of published work. Length: 1,300 words maximum. Pays negotiable rates.
Photos: Send photos with ms. Reviews b&w contact sheet and prints.
Tips: "It's important that the subject of the story is vital and appropriate to our publication."

OREGON BUSINESS, MIF Publications, Suite 875, 1515 SW 5th Ave., Portland OR 97201. (503)288-1332. Editor: Robert Hill. Monthly magazine covering business in Oregon. Estab. 1981. Circ. 20,000. Pays on publication. Byline given. Buys second serial (reprint) rights. Submit seasonal/holiday material 3 months in advance. Photocopied and previously published submissions OK. SASE. Reports in 1 month. Sample copy for business size SAE and $1.05 postage.
Nonfiction: General interest (real estate, business, investing, small business); interview/profile (business leaders); new products. Special issues include tourism, world trade, finance. "We need articles on real estate or small businss in Oregon, outside the Portland area." Buys 24 mss/year. Query with clips of published work. Length: 900-2,000 words. Pays 10¢/word minimum; $200 maximum.

PAREX BUSNESS JOURNALS, (*Charlotte Business Journal, Cincinnati Business Journal, Columbus Business Journal, Ohio Tavern News*), Box 222, Worthington OH 43085. (614)888-6005. Publisher: Paul Parshall. Editor: Elliot Blair Smith. Emphasizes business for an upper and middle class management audience.

Publication covers anything with a balance sheet. Monthly combined circ. 50,000 (unaudited). Phone queries OK. For editorial calendar, send SASE. Reports in 2 weeks on queries. Free sample copy with 8^{FRA}/1/2x11 SASE. Buys 10-12 freelance articles/issue. Byline given. (Sometimes an idea presented will be purchased.)
Nonfiction: Interviews with top executives of successful companies telling how company started, where it is now, and where it is heading; profile—past and future of given company; new product—how it affects a company; and technical breakthroughs which affect business. Length: 650-800 words. Pays $25.
Photos: State availability of photos. Pays $5 for 5x7 b&w glossy print. Captions required. Buys one-time rights. (Generally does not pay for photos.)
Columns/Departments: "We occasionally run guest columns—obtain an editorial calendar."

PHOENIX BUSINESS JOURNAL, Cordovan Corp., 1817 N. 3rd St., Phoenix AZ 85004. (602)271-4712. Editor: Tom Kuhn. Weekly tabloid covering business economics for CEOs and top corporate managers. Circ. 6,100. Pays on publication. Byline given. Buys all rights. Submit seasonal/holiday material 1 month in advance. Simultaneous queries ("if so indicated") and previously published submissions OK. SASE. Reports in 1 week. Sample copy free.
Nonfiction: How-to (solve management problems); interview/profile (of entrepreneurs); and "news affecting all types of Phoenix area corporations, large and small. Our audience is all local." Buys 250 mss/year. Query by phone. Length: open. Pays average $2.75/column inch.

REGARDIES: THE MAGAZINE OF WASHINGTON BUSINESS, 1010 Wisconsin Ave., NW, Washington DC 20007. (202)342-0410. Editor: Henry Fortunato. Bimonthly magazine covering business in the Washington DC metropolitan area for Washington business executives. Circ. 30,000. Pays within 30 days after publication. Byline given. Pays variable kill fee. Buys all rights. Computer printout and disk submissions OK; prefers letter quality to dot matrix. Submit seasonal/holiday material 3 months in advance. Reports in 3 weeks. Sample copy free.
Nonfiction: Profiles (of business leaders), investigative reporting, real estate, advertising, politics, lifestyle, media, retailing, communications, labor issues, and financial issues—all on the Washington business scene. "If it isn't the kind of story that could just as easily run in a city magazine or a national magazine like *Harper's*, *Atlantic*, *Esquire*, etc., I don't want to see it." Buys 90 mss/year. Length: 4,000 words average. Buys 5-6/issue. Pays "generally 20¢/word."
Columns/Departments: Length: 1,500 words average. Buys 8-12/issue. Pays 20¢/word.

SEATTLE BUSINESS MAGAZINE, Seattle Chamber of Commerce, 1200-1 Union Square, Seattle WA 98101. (206)447-7214. Editor-in-Chief: Ed Sullivan. Emphasizes regional socio-economic affairs. For business and government leaders, civic leaders, regional businessmen, educators, opinion makers, and the general public. Monthly magazine; 56 pages. Circ. 7,100. Pays on publication. Buys all rights. Submit seasonal/holiday material 2 months in advance. Previously published submissions OK. SASE. Reports in 1 month. Free sample copy.
Nonfiction: Informational (socio-economic affairs) and technical. Buys 1-2 mss/issue. Query. Length: 500-2,500 words. Pays $50-300.
Photos: Purchased with accompanying ms or on assignment. Captions required. Pays $50-100 for b&w photos. Total purchase price for ms includes payment for photos. Model release required.
Tips: "The freelancer must be able to write—and have a basic awareness of and sympathy for—the interests and problems of the business community as these relate to the community at large."

TIDEWATER VIRGINIAN, Suite A, 711 W. 21st, Norfolk VA 23517. Executive Editor: Marilyn Goldman. 90% freelance written. Published by six Tidewater area chambers of commerce. Monthly magazine for business management people. Circ. 7,300. Byline given. Buys 60 mss/year. Pays on publication. Sample copy $1.50. Photocopied and simultaneous submissions OK. Reports in 3 weeks. Query or submit complete ms. SASE.
Nonfiction: Articles dealing with business and industry in Virginia primarily; the surrounding area of southeastern Virginia (Tidewater area). Profiles, successful business operations, new product, merchandising techniques and business articles. Length: 500-2,500 words. Pays $25-150.
Tips: Recently published article: "Ole! A New Style in Dining" (trends in local and national restaurants).

‡**WASHINGTON BUSINESS JOURNAL**, Cordovan Corp., An E.W. Scripps subsidiary, Suite 430, 6862 Elm St., McLean VA 22101. (703)442-4900. Editor: Jack Mayne. Weekly tabloid covering business, in the District of Columbia, suburban Maryland and Northern Virginia areas for business persons in middle management as well as chief executive officers. Estab. 1982. Circ. 10,800. Pays on publication. Byline given. Not copyrighted. Buys all rights. SASE. Reports in 4 weeks on queries; 3 weeks on mss. Sample copy $1.
Nonfiction: Interview/profile (of a local figure—public or small entrepreneur); new product (inventions or patents from area people); business. Special issues are published frequently. Editorial calendar available on request. No generic or *national* business topics. Query with published clips or submit complete ms. Length: 600-

1,800 words. Pays $3-6/column inch.

Photos: State availability or send photos with ms. Pays negotiable rates for 8x10 b&w prints. Identification of subjects required.

Tips: "Queries should have decent writing samples attached. Manuscripts should be well researched, well written and thorough. Neatness and quality of presentation is a plus, as is accurate spelling and grammar. *WBJ* is interested in all business topics including: technology, real estate, accounting, associations, law, science, education, government, etc. Information sources should be high level and subject should be timely. Accompanying sidebars, photographs and graphs are also well received."

WESTERN INVESTOR, (formerly *Northwest Stock Guide*), Northwest/Intermountain/Hawaii Investment Information, Willamette Management Associates, 534 SW 3rd Ave., Portland OR 97204. (503)224-6004. Editor: S.P. Pratt. Quarterly magazine for the investment community of the Pacific Northwest, the Intermountain States and Hawaii. For stock brokers, corporate officers, financial analysts, trust officers, CPAs, investors, etc. Circ. 15,000. Pays on publication. Byline given. Buys one time and second serial (reprint) rights and makes work-for-hire assignments. Simultaneous queries and simultaneous, photocopied and previously published submissions OK. SASE. Reports in 6 weeks. Sample copy for $1.50 and SASE; writer's guidelines for SAE.

Nonfiction: General business interest ("trends, people, companies within our region"); new products. "Each issue carries a particular industry theme." Buys 8-12 mss/year. Query. Length: 200-5,000 words. Pays $50 minimum.

Photos: State availability of photos. Pays $10 minimum for 5x7 (or larger) b&w prints. Buys one-time rights.

Tips: "Send us a one-page introduction including your financial writing background, story ideas, availability for assignment work, credits, etc. What we want at this point is a good working file of authors to draw from; let us know your special areas of interest and expertise. Newspaper business page writers would be good candidates. If you live and work in the Northwest, so much the better."

WESTERN NEW YORK MAGAZINE, Buffalo Area Chamber of Commerce, 107 Delaware Ave., Buffalo NY 14202. (716)849-6689. Editor: J. Patrick Donlon. Monthly magazine of the Buffalo-Niagara Falls area. "Tells the story of Buffalo and western New York, with special emphasis on business and industry annd secondary emphasis on quality of life subjects." Circ. 8,000. Pays on acceptance. Byline given. Offers $150 kill fee. Not copyrighted. Buys all rights. Submit seasonal/holiday material 3 months in advance. Simultaneous queries OK. No computer printouts or disk submissions. SASE. Reports in 1 month. Sample copy for $2, 9x12 SAE and 3 first class stamps; writer's guidelines for business size SAE and 1 first class stamp.

Nonfiction: General interest (business, finance, commerce); historical/nostalgic (Buffalo, Niagara Falls); how-to (business management); interview/profile (community leader); western New York industry, quality of life. "Broad-based items preferred over single firm or organization. Submit articles that provide insight into business operations, marketing, finance, promotion, and nuts-and-bolts approach to small business management. No nationwide or even New York statewide articles or pieces on specific companies, products, services." Buys 30 mss/year. Query with clips of published work. Length: 1,000-2,500 words. Pays $150-300.

Photos: Amy R. Pope, art director. State availability of photos. Pays $10-25 for 5x7 b&w prints; reviews contact sheet.

Child Care and Parental Guidance

The publications below highlight child care and parental guidance. Other categories that include markets that buy items about child care for special columns and features are: Religious, and Women's in Consumer Publications; Education in Trade Journals.

AMERICAN BABY MAGAZINE, 575 Lexington Ave., New York NY 10022. (212)752-0775. Editor-in-Chief: Judith Nolte. 30% freelance written. Emphasizes how-to and medical information for expectant and new parents. Monthly magazine. Circ. 1,000,000. Pays on acceptance. Buys one-time rights. Byline given. Submit seasonal/holiday material 5 months in advance. Simultaneous, photocopied and previously published submissions OK. Computer printout and disk submissions OK; prefers letter quality to dot matrix printouts. SASE. Reports in 1 month. Writer's guidelines and sample copy with SASE only.

Nonfiction: How-to (on pregnancy and child-related subjects); interview (with medical authority on some subject of interest to expectant and new parents); personal experience; personal opinion; and profile (well-known figure in child care). No humor. Buys 7-10 mss/issue. Submit complete ms. Length: 1,000-2,000 words. Pays $200-350.

Tips: Send very brief biography with submissions.

BABY TALK, 185 Madison Ave., New York NY 10016. Editor: Patricia Irons. For new and expectant parents. Monthly. Circ. 900,000. Buys one-time rights. Pays on acceptance. Submit complete ms. SASE.

Nonfiction and Photos: Articles on all phases of baby care. Also true, unpublished accounts of pregnancy, life with baby or young children. B&w and color photos are sometimes purchased with or without ms. Buys 50-60 unsolicited mss/year. Payment varies.

‡**BE BETTER FAMILIES**, Be Center, Inc., Box 280, Fairview NC 28730. (704)628-3179. Editor: Russell A. Rachels. Bimonthly magazine on "family life, improving family relationships and helping parents and their kids understand each other." Estab. 1983. Circ. 3,000. Pays on acceptance. Byline given. Buys variable rights. Submit seasonal/holiday material 3 months in advance. Simultaneous queries, and simultaneous, photocopied and previously published submissions OK. SASE. Reports in 2 weeks on queries; 3 weeks on mss. Sample copy for 9x12 SAE and 2 first class stamps; writer's guidelines for business size SAE and 1 first class stamp.

Nonfiction: Expose (on the Department of Social Services); general interest; how-to (solve family problems); interview/profile (with professionals in the field of family/teen relations); opinion (drugs, sex, alcohol, school, law); personal experience (how you faced a family crisis and solved it); review of books by professionals in a related field. "We don't want to see any articles that do not have a family relationships tie-in." Buys 50 mss/year. Query or send complete ms. Length: 1,000-5,000 words. Ideal length is 1,500-2,500 words. Pays 3-5¢/word.

Poetry: Virginia K. Sheffer, poetry editor. Free verse, light verse, traditional. Must have family relationships tie-in. Buys 20 poems/year. Submit maximum 4 poems. Length: 8-40 lines. Pays $5-20.

Fillers: Clippings, short humor, newsbreaks. Buys "many" fillers/year. Length: 300-600 words. Pays 3-5¢/word.

Tips: "We are looking for articles that are helpful, informative and deal with the problems faced by parents and the youth of today. Most open to book reviews and personal experiences."

EXPECTING, 685 3rd Ave., New York NY 10017. (212)878-8700. Editor: Evelyn A. Podsiadlo. Assistant Editor: Grace Lang. Issued quarterly for expectant mothers. Circ. 1,000,000. Buys all rights. Pays 100% kill fee. Byline given. Pays on acceptance. Reports in 2-4 weeks. Free writer's guidelines. SASE.

Nonfiction: Prenatal development, layette and nursery planning, budgeting, health, fashion, husband-wife relationships, naming the baby, minor discomforts, childbirth, expectant fathers, working while pregnant, etc. Length: 800-1,600 words. Pays $100-200 for feature articles, somewhat more for specialists.

Fillers: Short humor and interesting or unusual happenings during pregnancy or at the hospital; maximum 100 words, $10 on publication; submissions to "Happenings" are not returned.

Poetry: Occasionally buys subject-related poetry; all forms. Length: 12-64 lines. Pays $10-30.

FAMILY JOURNAL, 1205 University Ave., Columbia MO 65201. (314)875-3003. Editor: Debra McAlear Gluck. Associate Editor: Kathleen Horrigan. Bimonthly magazine covering families with children up to about 8 years of age, for "the educated parent, aged 25-45, who desires sensible, useful information and advice. The reading audience is assumed to be sophisticated. Fathers are also readers of *Family Journal*, and are active in all decisions affecting the welfare of the child." Pays on publication. Byline given. Buys all rights. Submit seasonal/holiday material 6 months in advance. Simultaneous queries, and simultaneous, photocopied, and previously published submissions OK. Computer printout and disk submissions OK; must be double spaced with wide margins. SASE. Reports in 6-8 weeks. Writer's guidelines for SASE.

Nonfiction: General interest, how-to, humor, interview/profile, personal experience, pregnancy, childbirth, and childrearing through preadolescence. "We look for articles that deal with the above subject areas in a lucid style. The magazine is pro-family, and it addresses such topics as single parents, parents who adopt, infertility, and the many cultural influences on families. The magazine does not take a political or religious stand." Buys 25 mss/year. Send complete ms. Length: 1,000-2,500 words. Pays $50.

Photos: Pays $25 for the first photo of an assignment, $10 each for subsequent photos on the same assignment. Model release required. Buys one-time rights.

Columns/Departments: Computer Software, Books for Parents, Adoption, Food, Books for Children. Buys 25 mss/year. Send complete ms. Length: 1,000-1,500 words. Pays $20-150.

Fillers: Practical information. Buys 10/year. Length: 700-1,000 words. Pays $20-50.

Tips: "Writing ability and the magazine's editorial needs are taken into consideration in deciding payment. One's professional background is of less importance than the actual writing. *Family Journal* looks for writers who can articulate an experiential viewpoint as a parent." No telephone queries accepted.

GIFTED CHILDREN NEWSLETTER, For the Parents of Children with Great Promise, Box 115, Sewell NJ 08080. (609)582-0277. Editor: Dr. James Alvino. Assistant Editor: Agnes Gibbons. Monthly newsletter covering parenting and education of gifted children for parents. Circ. 40,000. Pays on acceptance. Byline given. Buys all rights and first rights. Submit seasonal/holiday material four months in advance. Simultaneous queries, and simultaneous, photocopied, and previously published submissions OK. No computer printout or disk submissions. SASE. Reports in 1 month on queries; 2 months on mss. Sample copy and writer's guidelines for 9x12 SASE.

Nonfiction: Book excerpts; historical/nostalgic; how-to (on parenting of gifted kids); humor; inspirational; interview/profile; new product; opinion; and personal experience. "Our Special Reports section is most accessible to freelancers." Query with clips of published work or send complete ms. Buys 36 unsolicited mss/year. Length: 1,000-2,500 words. Pays $25-200.

Tips: "It is helpful if freelancers provide copies of research papers to back up the article."

HOME LIFE, Sunday School Board, 127 9th Ave., N., Nashville TN 37234. (615)251-2271. Editor-in-Chief: Reuben Herring. Emphasizes Christian family life. For married adults of all ages, but especially newlyweds and middle-aged marrieds. Monthly magazine; 64 pages. Circ. 800,000. Pays on acceptance. Buys all rights. Byline given. Phone queries OK, but written queries preferred. Submit seasonal/holiday material 12 months in advance. Computer printout submissions OK; prefers letter quality to dot matrix. SASE. Reports in 6 weeks. Free sample copy and writer's guidelines.

Nonfiction: How-to (good articles on marriage and child care); informational (about some current family-related issue of national significance such as "Television and the Christian Family" or "Whatever Happened to Good Nutrition?"); personal experience (informed articles by people who have solved family problems in healthy, constructive ways). "No column material. We are not interested in material that will not in some way enrich Christian marriage or family life." Buys 150-200 mss/year. Submit complete ms. Length: 1,200-2,400 words. Pays 4¢/word.

Fiction: "Our fiction should be family-related and should show a strong moral about how families face and solve problems constructively." Buys 12-18 mss/year. Submit complete ms. Length: 1,600-2,400 words. Pays 4¢/word.

Tips: "Study the magazine to see our unique slant on Christian family life. We prefer a life-centered case study approach, rather than theoretical essays on family life. Our top priority is marriage enrichment material."

L.A. PARENT/PONY RIDE MAGAZINE, The Magazine for Parents in Southern California, (formerly *Pony Ride Magazine*), Pony Publications, Box 65795, Los Angeles CA 90065. (213)240-PONY. Editor: Jack Bierman. Managing Editor: Greg Doyle. Monthly tabloid covering parenting. Circ. 60,000. Pays on publication. Byline given. Buys all rights. Submit seasonal/holiday material 3 months in advance. Simultaneous queries and previously published submissions OK. SASE. Reports in 1 month. Sample copy $1; free writer's guidelines.

Nonfiction: Steve Linder, articles editor. General interest, how-to. "We focus on southern California activities for families, and do round-up pieces, i.e., a guide to private schools, fishing spots." Buys 10-15mss/year. Query with clips of published work. Length: 700-1,200 words. Pays $50-75.

MOTHERS TODAY, (formerly *Mothers' Manual*), 441 Lexington Ave., New York NY 10017. Editor-in-Chief: Janet Spencer King. Emphasizes pregnancy and parenting of young children. Bimonthly magazine; 60-72 pages. Circ. 900,000. Pays on publication. Buys all rights. Pays 20% kill fee. No computer printout or disk submissions. SASE required. Reports in 6 weeks. Sample copy $1.25.

Nonfiction: Well-researched, and well-documented how-to, humor, informational, inspirational, personal experience and opinion stories. Read the magazine before submitting complete ms. Length: 500-2,000 words. Pays $50-650.

Poetry: Lyn Roessler, poetry editor. Free verse, light verse and traditional. "We are looking for good humor; short, crisp poetry, upbeat, amusing poetry as well as narrative." Pays $10-30.

Tips: "Send a short finished piece written in the first person. Follow with a query for a second piece on a different subject. We like to cultivate good writers."

NETWORK, The Paper for Parents, National Committee for Citizens in Education, 410 Wilde Lake Village Green, Columbia MD 21044. (301)997-9300. Editor: Chrissie Bamber. Tabloid published 8 times during the school year covering parent/citizen involvement in public schools. Circ. 6,000. Pays on publication. Byline given. Buys one-time rights, all rights and makes work-for-hire assignments. Submit seasonal/holiday material 3 months in advance. Simultaneous queries and photocopied submissions OK. Computer printout submissions OK; prefers letter quality to dot matrix. SASE. Reports in 2 weeks. Free sample copy; writer's guidelines for #10 SAE and 20¢ postage.

Nonfiction: Book excerpts (elementary and secondary public education); expose (of school systems which attempt to reduce public access); how-to (improve schools through parent/citizen participation); humor (related to public school issues); opinion (school-related issues); personal experience (school-related issues). "It is our intention to provide balanced coverage of current developments and continuing issues and to place the facts about schools in a perspective useful to parents. No highly technical or scholarly articles about education; no child rearing articles or personal opinion not backed by research or concrete examples.'' Buys 4-6 mss/year. Query with clips of published work or send complete ms. Length: 1,000-1,500 words. Pays $25-100.

Tips: "Readers want articles of substance with information they can use and act on, not headlines which promise much but deliver only the most shallow analysis of the subject. Information first, style second. A high personal commitment to public schools and preferably first-hand experience is the greatest asset. A clear and simple writing style, easily understood by a wide range of lay readers is a must.''

PARENT'S CHOICE, Parents' Choice Foundation, Box 185, Waban MA 02168. (617)332-1298. Editor: Diana Huss Green. Emphasizes reviews of children's media, designed to alert parents to trends and events in books, TV, records, films, toys, educational issues, and computer software. Pays on publication. Buys all rights. Phone queries OK. SASE. Reports in 2 months. Sample copy $2; writer's guidelines $1.

Nonfiction: General interest (to parents interested in uses of the media); how-to (use books, films, TV, toys, games and records); humor; essays (on social and political issues related to media); interview (with writers of fiction for young adults and children, and directors, producers of films and TV); personal experience; photo feature (of parents and children, grandparents and children) and profile. Buys 10 mss/issue. Query. Pays $25 minimum.

Photos: State availability of photos. Offers no additional payment for photos accompanying ms. Uses b&w prints. Captions preferred.

Columns/Departments: A Parent's Essay and Choice Books; computer software reviews. Send complete ms. Length: 1,500-1,700 words.

PARENTS MAGAZINE, 685 3rd Ave., New York NY 10017. Editor: Elizabeth Crow. 25% freelance written. Monthly. Circ. 1,640,000. Usually buys first North American serial rights; sometimes buys all rights. Pays $100-350 kill fee. Byline given "except for 'Parents Report' or short items for which we pay only $20-75 and purchase all rights." Pays on acceptance. Reports in approximately 3 weeks. Query. SASE.

Nonfiction: "We are interested in well-documented articles on the development and behavior of preschool, school-age, and adolescent children and their parents; good, practical guides to the routines of baby care; articles which offer professional insights into family and marriage relationships; reports of new trends and significant research findings in education and in mental and physical health; articles encouraging informed citizen action on matters of social concern. Especially need articles on women's issues, pregnancy, birth, baby care and early childhood. We prefer a warm, colloquial style of writing, one which avoids the extremes of either slang or technical jargon. Anecdotes and examples should be used to illustrate points which can then be summed up by straight exposition." Length: 2,500 words maximum. Payment varies; pays $300 minimum.

Fillers: Anecdotes for "Parents Exchange," illustrative of parental problem-solving with children and teenagers. Pays $20 on publication.

‡**PEDIATRICS FOR PARENTS, The Newsletter for Caring Parents**, Pediatrics for Parents, Inc., 181 Broadway, Bangor ME 04401. (207)947-0221. Editor: Richard J. Sagall, M.D. Managing Editor: Judith Frost. Monthly newsletter covering medical aspects of raising children and educating parents about children's health. Estab. 1981. Circ. 2,800. Pays on publication. Byline given. Buys first North American serial and second serial (reprint) rights. Rights always include right to publish article in our books on "Best of . . ." series. Submit seasonal/holiday material 6 months in advance. Simultaneous queries, and simultaneous, photocopied and previously published submissions OK. SASE. Reports in 1 month on queries; 6 weeks on mss. Sample copy $1, 9x12 SAE and 2 first class stamps; writer's guidelines for business size SAE and 1 first class stamp.

Nonfiction: Book reviews; how-to (feed healthy kids, exercise, practice wellness, etc.); new product; technical (explaining medical concepts in shirtsleeve language). No general parenting articles. Buys 24 mss/year. Query with published clips or submit complete ms. Length: 25-1,000 words. Pays 2-5¢/edited word.

Columns/Departments: Book reviews; Please Send Me (material available to parents for free or at nominal cost); Pedia-Tricks (medically-oriented parenting tips that work). Buys 12 mss/year. Send complete ms. Pays $15-250. Pays 2¢/edited word.

Poetry: Light verse. No poetry extolling parenting and/or children. Pays $5-10.

Fillers: Clippings, anecdotes, short humor. Buys more than 10/year. Length: 25-150 words. Pays 2¢/edited word.

Tips: "We are dedicated to taking the mystery out of medicine for young parents. Therefore, we write in clear and understandable language (but not simplistic language) to help people understand and deal intelligently with complex disease processes, treatments, prevention, wellness, etc. Our articles must be well researched and documented. Detailed references must always be attached to any article for documentation, but not for publication. We strongly urge freelancers to read one or two issues before writing.''

Close-up

Elizabeth Crow
Editor-in-Chief, *Parents*

Nearly five years ago, Elizabeth Crow was hired to oversee the re-launch of *Parents* magazine. Today, the monthly women's service publication has nearly 1.7 million readers and a niche all its own, because "we treat our readers as grownups and not simply baby-rearing machines. We're geared exclusively to parents—and especially young mothers, many of whom first subscribe when they are pregnant," says Crow.

As editor-in-chief, Crow's role is a broad one. "I administer; I read, hire and fire; I write heads and bring in new writers. My children say my job consists of typing and talking." And communication is certainly a big part of the job. "I think of my role as not just an expeditor—not just somebody who separates the good ideas from the bad ones. I try to work with writers, and cultivate those I like. I like to figure out with them what their specialty or strengths could be. I try to have a sensitivity to their likes and dislikes."

Though currently over inventoried, Crow says "good writers are always welcome at *Parents*." She prefers to be contacted by query.

"I like to see a well-focused story idea that has a point of view general enough to be of interest to most of the women in our audience who range from pregnant women to mothers of young teenagers. At the same time, the information has to be specific enough to be news.

"I'm also interested in articles about the mother's quality of life as a woman. Articles about friendships, coping with family life in a positive way, marital relations—pieces about having a happy life as a person as well as a mother. Right now we're kind of up to our gills in articles on child behavior and development," she says.

Qualified writers don't need a page of credits to consider submitting a query

to *Parents*. "I have nothing against beginning writers," says Crow, "as long as they don't write like beginners. In fact, some of our most successful writers have rarely been published except in a local newspaper. These are writers who happen to have a touch that's right for us, and they are interested in our subject matter."

Whether they are generalists or specialists, there are ideal writers with whom Crow especially enjoys working. "They're hard workers. That's the most important thing. Nothing burns me up more than getting an article that reads fine at first glance, and then I realize that I've read half the quotes in other magazines and that it's just a cut-and-paste job. I want writers who will call the researcher and get new quotes, who will bother to understand the material well enough to bring a fresh approach to it."

Beyond that, Crow reminds writers that the basics—heeding deadlines, knowing the magazine, appreciating it for itself—are all traits of an ideal writer.

Crow says that the secret to getting published is not to get discouraged. "If I reject 12 story ideas in a row," she says, "it doesn't mean I won't *love* the 13th—and it may be the beginning of a long and profitable relationship with a freelancer. For most writers, it takes awhile to get the knack. But once a freelancer's got it—he's got it forever."

College, Career, and Alumni

There are two kinds of publications in this category: the first is a university publication written for students, alumni and friends of a particular institution; the second speaks to college students in general about college life, careers and job hunting.

ALCALDE, Box 7278, Austin TX 78712. (512)476-6271. Editor: Ernestine Wheelock. Editorial Assistant: Leigh Sander. Bimonthly magazine. Circ. 39,000. Pays on publication. Buys all rights. Submit seasonal/holiday material 5 months in advance. SASE. Reports in 2 weeks.
Nonfiction: General interest; historical (University of Texas, research, and faculty profile); humor (humorous University of Texas incidents or profiles that include background data); interviews (University of Texas subjects); nostalgia (University of Texas traditions); profile (students, faculty or alumni); and technical (University of Texas research on a subject or product). Recent article example: "UT: Bigger, Better, Richer" (November-December 1981). "It's about the University of Texas; it is well written and crowds a lot of material into relatively few words; it's a serious subject written in a readable style; it appeals to our readers, the alumni of the University of Texas." No subjects lacking taste or quality, or not connected with the University of Texas. Buys 30 mss/year. Query. Length: 1,000-1,800 words. Pays according to importance of article.

THE BLACK COLLEGIAN, 1240 South Broad St., New Orleans LA 70125. (504)821-5694. Editor: Kalamu ya Salaam. 40% freelance written. For black college students and recent graduates with an interest in black cultural awareness, sports, news, personalities, history, trends, current events and job opportunities. Published bimonthly during school year; 160 pages. Circ. 179,000. Rights purchased usually first North American serial rights. Byline given. Buys 6 unsolicited mss/year. Pays on publication. Will send sample copy to writer for $2. Write for copy of guidelines for writers. Will consider photocopied and simultaneous submissions. Computer printout or disk submissions OK. Submit special material 3 months in advance of issue date (Careers in Sciences, August; Computers/Grad School, November; Engineering and Travel/Summer Programs, January; Finance and Jobs, March; Medicine, May). Returns rejected material in 1½ months. Query. SASE.
Nonfiction and Photos: Material on careers, sports, black history, news analysis. Articles on problems and opportunities confronting black college students and recent graduates. Informational, personal experience, profile, inspirational, humor, think pieces, travel. Recent article example: "Negating Affirmative Action: The Reagan Initiative" (February/March 1982). Length: 500-4,500 words. Pays $25-350. B&w photos or color transparencies purchased with or without mss. 5x7 *and* 8x10 preferred. Pays $35/b&w; $50/color.

‡BYU TODAY, Brigham Young University, C-341 ASB, Provo UT 84602. (801)378-7321. Editor: Ken Shelton. University/alumni tabloid published 8 times/year. "It represents America's largest church-related institution of higher learning, Brigham Young University (26,000 enrollment). Readers are generally well educated and heavily involved in family, church, career and community activities." Circ. 180,000. Pays on acceptance. Byline given. Offers $50 kill fee. Buys first rights. Submit seasonal/holiday material 3 months in advance. Computer printout and disk submissions OK. Reports in 4 weeks. Free sample copy and writer's guidelines.
Nonfiction: General interest, historical/nostalgic, how-to (especially topics in career-family management); humor, inspirational (not sentimental); interview/profile, opinion, photo feature, sports. "All articles should relate to the interests of the University and its alumni. We also publish a few freelance book reviews and short alumni profiles." Buys 10-16 mss/year. Query with clips if available or send complete ms. Length: 1,500-2,500 words. Pays $100-250.
Tips: "Choose to write about an interesting individual who studied or taught at BYU or about a current issue or event that would be of general interest to BYU alumni. Produce a lively, quote-filled article or an insightful essay."

‡CARNEGIE-MELLON MAGAZINE, Carnegie-Mellon University, Pittsburgh PA 15213. (412)578-2900. Editor: Ann Curran. Alumni publication issued fall, winter, spring covering university activities, alumni profiles, etc. Estab. 1982. Circ. 41,000. Pays on acceptance. Byline given. Not copyrighted. Submit seasonal/holiday material 4 months in advance. Simultaneous queries OK. SASE. Reports in 1 month.
Nonfiction: Book excerpts (faculty alumni); general interest; humor; interview/profile; photo feature. "We use general interest stories linked to CMU activities and research." No unsolicited mss. Buys 5 features and 5-10 alumni profiles/year. Query with published clips. Length: 2,500-6,000 words. Pays $250 or negotiable rate.
Poetry: Avant-garde, free verse. No previously published poetry. No payment.
Tips: "Consideration is given to professional writers among alumni."

COLLEGIATE CAREER WOMAN, Equal Opportunity Publications, Inc., 44 Broadway, Greenlawn NY 11740. (516)261-8899. Editor: James Schneider. Magazine published 3 times/year ("fall, winter, spring; geared to college year") covering career guidance for college women. Strives "to aid women in developing career abilities to the fullest potential; improve job hunting skills; present career opportunities; provide personal resources; help cope with discrimination." Audience is 92% college juniors and seniors; 8% working graduates. Circ. 10,500. "Controlled circulation, distributed through college guidance and placement offices." Pays on publication. Byline given. Buys first North American serial rights; one-time rights; all rights; simultaneous rights; first rights; second serial (reprint) rights; as required. "Deadline dates: fall, July 15; winter, October 15; spring, January 10. Simultaneous queries, and simultaneous, photocopied and previously published submissions OK. Computer printout and disk submissions OK; prefers typed mss. SASE. Free sample copy and writer's guidelines.

Nonfiction: Book excerpts (on self-improvement, role models, success stories, employment helps); general interest (on special concerns of women); historical/nostalgic (on women's achievements, progress, and hopes for the future); how-to (on self-evaluation, job-finding skills, adjustment, coping with the real world); humor (student or career related); inspirational (encouragement and guidance); interview/profile (of successful career women, outstanding students); new product (new career opportunities); opinion (on women's progress, male attitudes, discrimination); personal experience (student and career experiences); technical (on career fields offering opportunities for women); travel (on overseas job opportunities); and contributions to the development of the whole person. Prefers not to see general stories about women's issues, but those specifically related to careers. Wants more profiles of successful career women. Special issues include career opportunities for liberal arts graduates. Buys 15-21 mss/year. Query with or without clips of published work or send complete ms. Length: 1,250-3,000 words.

Photos: James Schneider, photo editor. Captions, model release and identification of subjects required, "if necessary." Buys one-time rights, all rights, and other rights "as needed and available." More pictures needed.

EQUAL OPPORTUNITY, The Nation's Only Multi-Ethnic Recruitment Magazine for Black, Hispanic, Native American & Asian College Grads, Equal Opportunity Publications, Inc., 44 Broadway, Greenlawn NY 11740. (516)261-8899. Editor: James Schneider. Magazine published 3 times/year ("fall, winter, spring; geared to college academic year") covering career guidance for minorities of ethnic origin. "Our audience is 90% college juniors and seniors, 10% working graduates. An understanding of educational and career problems of minorities is essential." Circ. 15,000. "Controlled circulation, distributed through college guidance and placement offices." Pays on publication. Byline given. Buys first North American serial rights; one-time rights; all rights; simultaneous rights; first rights; second serial (reprint) rights; others as available. "Deadline dates: fall, July 11; winter, October 10; spring, January 20. Simultaneous queries, and simultaneous, photocopied and previously published submissions OK. Computer printout and disk submissions OK; prefers typed mss. SASE. Free sample copy and writer's guidelines.

Nonfiction: Book excerpts and articles (on self-improvement, role models); general interest (on specific minority concerns); historical/nostalgic; how-to (on job-hunting skills, personal finance, better living, adjustment, coping with discrimination); humor (student or career related); inspirational (on thought, leader encouragement and guidance); interview/profile (minority role models); new product (new career opportunities); opinion (problems of ethnic minorities); personal experience (professional and student study and career experiences); technical (on career fields offering opportunities for ethnic minorities); travel (on overseas job opportunities); and coverage of black, Hispanic, American Indian and Asian interests. Special issues include career opportunities for liberal arts graduates. "Prefers not to see political or socially-sensitive subjects." Buys 10-15 mss/year. Query with or without clips of published work. Length: 1,250-3,000 words.

Photos: Captions, model release and identification of subjects required, "if necessary." Buys one-time rights, all rights, and other rights "as available."

Tips: "More role-model profiles and more use of graphics and art will affect writers in the year ahead."

HIS, 5206 Main St., Downers Grove IL 60515. (312)964-5700. Editor: Linda Doll. Issued monthly from October-June for collegiate students, faculty, administrators and graduate students interested in the evangelical Christian persuasion. "It is an interdenominational, Biblical presentation, combining insights on Scripture and everyday life on campus. We need sophisticated humor, outstanding fiction with a Christian base, articles of interest to non-Christian readers." Buys first rights. Pays on acceptance. Reports in 3 months. SASE.

Nonfiction and Fiction: "Articles dealing with practical aspects of Christian living on campus, relating contemporary issues to Biblical principles. Should show relationship between Christianity and various fields of study, Christian doctrine, or missions." Submit complete ms. Buys 55 unsolicited mss/year. Recent article example "Beyond Celibacy" (May 1982). Length: 2,000 words maximum. Pays $35-70.

Poetry: Pays $10-20.

Tips: "Direct your principles and illustrations at the college milieu. Avoid preachiness and attacks on various Christian ministries or groups; share your insights on a peer basis."

MAKING IT!, Careers Newsmagazine, 2109 Broadway, Rm. 4155, New York NY 10023. (212)575-9018. Editor: Karen Rubin. Magazine published 4 times/year covering career opportunities for professionals and managers; specifically entry-level opportunities for college and graduate school students and strategic moves for employed professionals. "We are a newsmagazine with a news-feature format; we discourage generalized 'how-to' articles in favor of in-depth profiles of companies, agencies and industries. We will be looking for writers who have specialty in a particular area or interest and can become regular contributors." Estab. 1982. Circ. 30,000. Pays on publication (in most cases). Byline given. Offers 20% kill fee. Copyrighted. Makes work-for-hire assignments. Submit seasonal/holiday material 2 months in advance. Simultaneous queries OK. SASE. Reports in 2 months. Sample copy $1.50; writer's guidelines for business size SAE and 2 first class stamps.
Nonfiction: How-to ("we accept only a few, but these should relate to resume, interview, strategies for getting jobs); interview/profile (success stories and profiles about people who have "made it"); personal experience (strategies for getting the job you want). No superficial or general articles about careers or getting jobs. Buys variable number mss/year. Query with or without clips of published work. Length: 1,000-2,000 words. Pays $50-250.
Photos: "Photos that show young people in the work environment." State availability of photos. Pays $5-50 for contact sheets and 8x10 b&w prints. Captions and identification of subjects required. Buys one-time rights.

MISSISSIPPI STATE UNIVERSITY ALUMNUS, Mississippi State University, Alumni Association, Editorial Office, Box 5328, Mississippi State MS 39762. (601)325-3442. Editor-in-Chief: Linsey H. Wright. Emphasizes articles about Mississippi State graduates and former students. For well-educated and affluent audience. Quarterly magazine; 36 pages. Circ. 16,443. Pays on publication. Buys one-time rights. Pays 25% kill fee. Byline given. Phone queries OK. Submit seasonal/holiday material 3 months in advance. Simultaneous, photocopied and previously published submissions OK. SASE. Reports in 1 month. Free sample copy
Nonfiction: Historical, humor (with strong MSU flavor; nothing risque), informational, inspirational, interview (with MSU grads), nostalgia (early days at MSU), personal experience, profile and travel (by MSU grads, but must be of wide interest to other grads). Computer printout and disk submissions OK. Recent article example: "The River's Not Too Wide for Morrison." "The story dealt with an MSU graduate in nuclear engineering who is now a country-western song writer in Nashville." Buys 2-3 mss/year ("but welcome more submissions.") Send complete ms. Length: 500-2,500 words. Pays $50-150 (including photos, if used).
Photos: Offers no additional payment for photos purchased with accompanying ms. Captions required. Uses 5x7 and 8x10 b&w photos and color transparencies of any size.
Columns/Departments: Statesmen, "a section of the *Alumnus* that features briefs about alumni achievements and professional or business advancement. We do not use engagements, marriages or births. There is no payment for Statesmen briefs."
Tips: "We welcome articles about MSU grads in interesting occupations and have used stories on off-shore drillers, miners, horse trainers, etc. We also want profiles on prominent MSU alumni and have carried pieces on Senator John C. Stennis, comedian Jerry Clower, professional football players and coaches, and Eugene Butler, editor-in-chief of *Progressive Farmer* magazine. We feature three alumni in each issue, alumni who have risen to prominence in their fields or who are engaged in unusual occupations or who are involved in unusual hobbies."

NATIONAL FORUM: THE PHI KAPPA PHI JOURNAL, The Honor Society of Phi Kappa Phi, East Tennessee State University, Box 19420A, Johnson City TN 37614. (615)929-5347. Editor: Stephen W. White. Managing Editor: Elaine M. Smoot. Quarterly interdisciplinary, scholarly journal. "We are an interdisciplinary journal that publishes crisp, nontechnical analyses of issues of social and scientific concern as well as scholarly treatments of different aspects of culture." Circ. 90,000. Pays on publication. Byline given. Buys all rights. Submit seasonal/holiday material 6 months in advance. Computer printout submissions OK; can accept 5¼" diskettes compatible with Lanier No-Problem Word Processor. Telecommunications capabilities if author has compatible equipment/software. SASE. Reports in 6 weeks on queries; 2 months on mss. Sample copy 65¢; free writer's guidelines.
Nonfiction: General interest, interview/profile and opinion. No how-to or biographical articles. Each issue is devoted to the exploration of a particular theme. Upcoming theme issues: Conflict Resolution and Peacemaking, Health and Nutrition, Trends Analysis. Recent article examples: "The Next Industrial Revolution" and "Work and American Expectations." Query with clips of published work. Buys 15 unsolicited mss/year. Length: 1,500-2,000 words. Pays $50-200.
Photos: State availability of photos. Identification of subjects required. Buys one-time rights.
Columns/Departments: Educational Dilemmas in the 80s and Book Review Section. Buys 8 mss/year for Educational Dilemmas, 40 book reviews. Length: Book reviews—400-800 words. Educational Dilemmas—1,500-1,800 words. Pays $15-25 for book reviews; $50/printed page, Educational Dilemmas.
Fiction: Humorous and short stories. Buys 2-4 mss/year. Length: 1,500-1,800 words. Pays $50/printed page.
Poetry: Poetry Editors: Professor Van K. Brock, Professor Daniel Fogel. Avant garde, free verse, haiku, light verse, traditional. No love poetry. Buys 20 mss/year. Submit 5 poems maximum. Prefers shorter poems.

NOTRE DAME MAGAZINE, University of Notre Dame, Box M, Notre Dame IN 46556. (219)239-5335. Editor: Walton R. Collins. Managing Editor: James Winters. Magazine published 5 times/year (February, May, July, October, December) covering news of Notre Dame and education and issues affecting the Roman Catholic Church. "We are interested in the moral, ethical and spiritual issues of the day and how Christians live in today's world. We are universal in scope and Catholic in viewpoint and serve Notre Dame students, alumni, friends an constituencies." Circ. 87,000. Pays on acceptance. Byline given. Offers $250 kill fee. Buys first rights. Simultaneous queries OK. SASE. Reports in 3 weeks. Free sample copy.
Nonfiction: Opinion, personal experience, religion. "All articles must be of interest to Christian/Catholic readers who are well educated and active in their communities." Buys 35 mss/year. Query with clips of published work. Length: 600-2,000 words. Pays $500-1,500.
Photos: State availability of photos. Reviews b&w contact sheets, color transparencies, and 8x10 prints. Model release and identification of subjects required. Buys one-time rights.

‡ON CAMPUS, The Magazine for College Freshmen, Inter-Collegiate Press, Inc., 6015 Travis Lane, Box 10, Shawnee Mission KS 66201. (913)432-8100. Editor: Ellen Parker. Annual magazine covering topics of interest to first-semester college freshmen. Estab. 1982. Circ. 300,000. Pays on acceptance. Byline given. Buys all rights. Submit seasonal/holiday material 3 months in advance. Simultaneous queries OK. Reports in 1 month on queries. Free sample copy and writer's guidelines.
Nonfiction: Book excerpts, general interest, historical/nostalgic, how-to, humor, inspirational, interview/profile, opinion, personal experience, photo feature, travel, book reviews. "We use such editorial topics as career guidance and information, course selection guidance, study hints and methods, health and fitness, fashion, campus lifestyles, housing options, humorous essays on life as a college freshman, newsy shorts on campus life, reviews of self-help books, and interviews with students, college personnel or people who are successful in their careers." No "articles written in a 'preachy' tone; articles that assume freshmen are totally unsophisticated; articles casually mentioning sex, drugs or alcohol." Buys 6 mss/year. Query with clips of published work. Length: 1,000-3,500 words. Pays $100-400.
Photos: College-related shots, either b&w or 4-color. State availability of photos. Pays $50-300 for color transparencies; $25-100 for 8x10 b&w prints. Captions and identification of subjects required.
Columns/Departments: Quick tips (survival tips—finances, health, study aids, etc.); Campus Crier (news briefs of interest to college students). Buys 4 mss/year. Query with clips of published work. Length: 200-1,000 words. Pays $30-150.
Fillers: Newsbreaks. Buys 2/year. Length: 100-400 words. Pays $30-100.
Tips: "It's easy to be published by us—just write a lively, entertaining informative article of interest to our readers. Send us any good ideas you have, along with some clips, and we'll give serious consideration. The style is breezy, entertaining and easy-to-read, yet informative. Many stories take a 'how-to' approach. First person accepted in essays, but second and third person is preferred in features and shorts."

OSU OUTREACH, Room 313A, Public Information Bldg., Oklahoma State University, Stillwater OK 74078. (405)624-6009. Editor: Doug Dollar. Quarterly magazine for OSU alumni. Circ. 11,500. Pays on acceptance. Byline given. Buys one-time rights. Submit seasonal/holiday material 3 months in advance. Simultaneous, photocopied and previously published submissions OK. SASE. Reports in 2 weeks. Free sample copy for 9x12 SASE.
Nonfiction: General interest; humor (with strong OSU tie); interview (with OSU grads); historical/nostalgic (OSU traditions, early days events, people, the campus); interview/profile (OSU subjects); personal experience; and photo feature. "Subjects must have strong connection to OSU, and must be of interest to alumni." Buys 5 mss/year. Query with clips of published work or send complete ms. Length: 500-2,000 words. Pays $15-25 (including photos, if used).
Photos: State availability of photos. Pays $5-15 for 5x7 b&w prints; reviews b&w contact sheets. Captions required. Buys one-time rights.
Columns/Departments: Campus, sports, alumni. Buys 30 mss/year. Send complete ms. Length: 100-300 words. Pays $5-10.
Tips: "Items on alumni personalities are of great value if they have strong human-interest appeal. We prefer a tight style."

PRINCETON ALUMNI WEEKLY, Princeton University Press, 41 William St., Princeton NJ 08540. (609)452-4885. Editor: Charles L. Creesy. Managing Editor: Margaret M. Keenan. Biweekly (during the academic year) magazine covering Princeton University and higher education for Princeton alumni, students, faculty, staff and friends. "We assume familiarity with and interest in the university." Circ. 48,000. Pays on publication. Byline given. Offers $100 kill fee. Buys one-time rights. Submit seasonal/holiday material 2 months in advance. Simultaneous queries or photocopied submissions OK. Computer printout and disk submissions OK; prefers letter quality to dot matrix printouts. Reports "ASAP." Sample copy for 9x12 SAE and 71¢ postage.
Nonfiction: Book excerpts, general interest, historical/nostalgic, interview/profile, opinion, personal experi-

ence, photo feature. "Connection to Princeton essential. Remember, it's for an upscale educated audience." Special issue on education and economics (February). Buys 20 mss/year. Query with clips of published work. Length: 1,000-6,000 words. Pays $75-450.

Photos: State availability of photos. Pays $25-50 for 8x10 b&w prints; $50-100 for color transparencies. Reviews (for ordering purposes) b&w contact sheet. Captions and identification of subjects required.

Columns/Departments: "Columnists must have a Princeton connection (alumnus, student, etc.)." Buys 50 mss/year. Query with clips of published work. Length: 750-1,500 words. Pays $50-150.

THE PURDUE ALUMNUS, Purdue Alumni Association, Purdue Memorial Union, West Lafayette IN 47907. (317)494-5184. Editor: Gay L. Totte. Magazine published 9 times/year (except February, June, August) covering subjects of interest to Purdue University alumni. Circ. 55,000. Pays on publication. Byline given. Buys first rights and makes work-for-hire assignments. Submit seasonal/holiday material 2 months in advance. Simultaneous queries, and simultaneous, photocopied, and previously published submissions OK. SASE. Reports in 1 week on queries; 2 weeks on mss. Free sample copy.

Nonfiction: Book excerpts, general interest, historical/nostalgic, humor, interview/profile, personal experience. Focus is on campus news, issues, opinions of interest to 50,000 members of the Alumni Association. Feature style, primarily university-oriented. Issues relevant to education. Buys 12 mss/year. Length: 3,000 words maximum. Pays $15 minimum.

Photos: State availability of photos. Reviews b&w contact sheet or 5x7 prints.

Tips: "We're always anxious for new material, and depend rather heavily on freelancers. We don't pay much, but we do credit and have a well-educated, worldwide audience."

THE STUDENT, 127 9th Ave. N., Nashville TN 37234. Editor: W. Howard Bramlette. Publication of National Student Ministries of the Southern Baptist Convention. For college students; focusing on freshman and sophomore levels. Published 12 times during the school year. Circ. 25,000. Buys all rights. Payment on acceptance. Mss should be double spaced on white paper with 50-space line, 25 lines/page. Prefers complete ms rather than query. Reports usually in 6 weeks. SASE. Free sample copy.

Nonfiction: Contemporary questions, problems, and issues facing college students viewed from a Christian perspective to develop high moral and ethical values. The struggle for integrity in self-concept and the need to cultivate interpersonal relationships directed by Christian love. Length: 800-1,000 words. Length: 1,000 words maximum. Pays 3½¢/word after editing with reserved right to edit accepted material.

Fiction: Satire and parody on college life, humorous episodes; emphasize clean fun and the ability to grow and be uplifted through humor. Contemporary fiction involving student life, on campus as well as off. Length: 1,000-1,500 words. Pays 3½¢/word.

UNM ALUMNUS, University of New Mexico Alumni Association Magazine, Alumni Association, University of New Mexico, Suite 200, Student Union Bldg., Albuquerque NM 87131. (505)277-5813. Editor: Donald Burge. Tabloid published 9 times/year (except for February, July and November) for alumni and friends of the University of New Mexico. Circ. 50,000. Pays on publication. Byline given. Offers 25% kill fee. Not copyrighted. Buys one-time rights; makes work-for-hire assignments. Submit seasonal/holiday material 4 months in advance. Simultaneous queries, and simultaneous, photocopied, and previously published submissions OK. Computer printout and disk submissions OK. SASE. Reports in 1 month. Free sample copy.

Nonfiction: General interest; historical/nostalgic; humor; inspirational; interview/profile (of alumni who have achieved success in their fields or hold unusual jobs and/or hobbies); personal experience; photo feature. "If it isn't about the University of New Mexico or a UNM alumnus we can't use it. We particulary need more personality profiles/interviews of alumni who live far away from the UNM area. Our definition of 'alumnus' is quite broad and includes all students who ever attended UNM as well as former faculty or staff." Buys 9-15 mss/year. Query or send complete ms. Length: 350-1,200 words. Pays $25-100.

Photos: "Photos are essential, but I prefer to use 1 large good quality photo to several smaller photos." State availability of photos. Pays $5 for 5x7 b&w prints. Model release and identification of subjects required.

Tips: "Our features section is most open to freelancers. It profiles individual alumni or University programs. Keep the writing tight because we can't usually give you more than 1 page, and only very rarely will we go beyond 2 pages."

Consumer Service and Business Opportunity

These publications tell readers how to get the most for their money—either in goods purchased or in earnings from investment in a small business of their own. Publications for business executives and the informed public are listed under Business and Finance. Those on how to run specific businesses are classified in Trade, Technical and Professional Journals.

BEST BUYS, the Magazine for Smart Shoppers, 150 5th Ave., New York NY 10011. (212)675-4777. Editor: Carol J. Richards. Publisher: Jon J. Bloomberg. Monthly magazine covering various products/goods for consumers. Circ. 100,000. Pays on publication. Byline given for original stories. Buys all rights. Submit consumer-oriented material 4 months in advance on speculation. Photocopied submissions OK. Does not return manuscripts. Notification upon acceptance. Writer's guidelines free for business size SAE and 1 first class stamp. No computer printout or disk submissions.
Nonfiction: General interest (educational articles for consumers); and how-to (bargain, find good buys). Buys 10-20 mss/year. Query with brief biography plus b&w photos. Length: 850-1,200 words. Pays $50 per 850-word printed page. No fiction or humor.
Photos: State availability of photos. Reviews 5x7 b&w glossy prints. Captions, model releases, and identification of subjects required.
Tips: "We look for research-oriented people who can write with an unbiased slant, correctly and with meticulous care to accuracy of copy."

CONSUMER LIFE, 840 S. Broadway, Hicksville NY 11590. Editorial Director: Cathy Grieger. Quarterly magazine for perceptive members of Unity Buying Service who are primarily "working men and women with a family who want to be educated consumers." Circ. 1,000,000. Pays on acceptance. Byline given. Offers 25% kill fee. Buys all rights. Reports in 8 weeks on queries; in 1 month on mss.
Nonfiction: General interest (any story of value to a consumer: health organizations; home maintenance; tax and legal angles of starting a business; shopping for garden supplies and equipment by mail; travel (luggage; brochures; travel agents); how-to (do your own repairs; and shop for materials); products (criteria in shopping for a product—no brand names); and technical (purchasing-oriented articles, such as shopping for stereo equipment). Buys 5-7 mss/issue. Query with clips of published work. Length: 1,800 words. Pays $300.
Columns/Departments: Readers' Tips (household hints and shopping ideas). Buys 15 mss/issue. Send complete ms. Length: 50 words minimum. Pays $5 minimum.

CONSUMER REPORTS, 256 Washington St., Mt. Vernon NY 10550. Editor: Irwin Landau. Staff-written.

CONSUMERS DIGEST MAGAZINE, Consumers Digest, Inc., 5705 N. Lincoln Ave., Chicago IL 60659. (312)275-3590. Editor: Michael J. Connelly. Emphasizes anything of consumer interest. Bimonthly magazine. Circ. 900,000. Pays on publication. Buys all rights. SASE. Reports in 1 month. Free guidelines to published writers only.
Nonfiction: Exposé; general interest (on advice to consumers and consumer buying products, service, health, business, investments, insurance and money management); new products and travel. Buys 10 mss/issue. Query. Length: 1,500-3,000 words. Pays 20¢/word.
Tips: "Send short query with samples of published work."

CONSUMERS' RESEARCH MAGAZINE, Box 168, Washington NJ 07882. Technical Editor: F.J. Schlink. Monthly. Byline given "except when the article as written requires extensive editing, improvement, amplification, which may occur when a nontechnical person writes in a field where engineering, physical science, chemical, toxicological, economic or nutritional knowledge is essential." Limited amount of freelance material used. Query. SASE.
Nonfiction: Articles of practical interest to consumers concerned with tests and expert judgment of goods and services they buy. Must be accurate and well-supported by chemical, engineering, general science, medical, economic, or other expert or professional knowledge of subject matter of articles on consumer economic problems, investments and finance. Recent article examples: "Trials of the Sweeteners" (November 1979); "Quartz-Controlled Alarm Clocks," (February 1982); and "The ABCs of Shopping for Tires," (February 1982). Pays approximately $100/page.
Photos: Buys limited number b&w glossy prints with mss only. Pays $5 minimum. "Photos are accepted only if they are clearly relevant to the article being published or essential to understanding of points made or discussed."

‡**DIRECT, For People Who Love To Shop At Home**, Direct Magazine Partners, Suite 1825, 60 E. 42nd St., New York NY 10165. (212)883-1995. Editor: Susan Crandell. Bimonthly magazine covering products and subjects of interest to mail-order shoppers. Estab. 1981. Circ. 150,000. Pays on publication. Byline given. Payment negotiated individually. Buys first North American serial rights. Submit seasonal/holiday material 6 months in advance. Rarely accepts previously published submissions. SASE. Reports in 1 month. Sample copy $2.
Nonfiction: Articles on products and subjects of interest to mail-order shoppers. Buys 6-9 mss/year. Length: 1,000-2,000 words. Query. Pays $500-750.

ECONOMIC FACTS, The National Research Bureau, Inc., 424 N. 3rd St., Burlington IA 52601. Editor-in-Chief: Doris Ruschill. Magazine for industrial workers of all ages. Published 4 times/year. Circ. 30,000. Pays on publication. Buys all rights. Byline given. Submit seasonal/holiday material 3-4 months in advance of issue date. Previously published submissions OK. SASE. Reports in 1 week. Free sample copy and writer's guidelines.
Nonfiction: Rhonda Wilson, articles editor. General interest (private enterprise, government data, graphs, taxes and health care). Buys 3-5 mss/year. Query with outline of article. Length: 400-600 words.

ENTREPRENEUR MAGAZINE, 2311 Pontius, Los Angeles CA 90064. (213)473-0838. Publisher: Chase Revel. Editor: Ron Smith. For a readership looking for highly profitable opportunities in small businesses, as owners, investors or franchisees. Monthly magazine. Circ. 200,000. Pays on acceptance. Buys all rights. Byline given. Submit seasonal/holiday material 2 months in advance of issue date. Photocopied submissions OK. SASE. Reports in 1 month. Sample copy $3; free writer's guidelines.
Nonfiction: How-to (in-depth start-up details on 'hot' business opportunities like tanning parlors or computer stores). Buys 50 mss/year. Query with clips of published work. Length: 1,200-2,000 words. Pays $200-500 for features; $100 for featurettes.
Photos: "We need good b&w glossy prints to illustrate articles." Offers additional payment for photos accepted with ms. Uses 8x10 b&w glossy prints or standard transparencies. Captions preferred. Buys all rights. Model release required.
Columns/Departments: New Products; New Ideas; Promo Gimmicks; and Frauds. Query. Length: 200-500 words. Pays $25-50.

FDA CONSUMER, 5600 Fishers Lane, Rockville MD 20857. (301)443-3220. Editor: Roger W. Miller. For "all consumers of products regulated by the Food and Drug Administration." A federal government publication. Monthly magazine. December/January and July/August issues combined. Circ. 16,000. Not copyrighted. Pays 50% kill fee. Byline given. "All purchases automatically become part of public domain." Buys 4-5 freelance mss a year. Pays after acceptance. Query. "We cannot be responsible for any work by writer not agreed upon by prior contract." Computer printout submissions OK. SASE.
Nonfiction: "Articles of an educational nature concerning purchase and use of FDA regulated products and specific FDA programs and actions to protect the consumer's health and pocketbook. Authoritative and official agency viewpoints emanating from agency policy and actions in administrating the Food, Drug and Cosmetic Act and a number of other statutes. All articles subject to clearance by the appropriate FDA experts as well as acceptance by the editor. The magazine speaks for the federal government only. Articles based on facts and FDA policy only. We cannot consider any unsolicited material. All articles based on prior arrangement by contract. The nature and subject matter and clearances required are so exacting that it is difficult for a writer working outside the Washington DC metropolitan area to produce an acceptable article." Length: average, 2,000 words. Pays $1,000.
Photos: B&w photos are purchased on assignment only.

INCOME OPPORTUNITIES, 380 Lexington Ave., New York NY 10017. Editor: Joseph V. Daffron. Managing Editor: Ruth E. Messinger. For all who are seeking business opportunities, full- or part-time. Monthly magazine. Buys all rights. Buys 50-60 mss/year. No photocopied or simultaneous submissions; no computer printout or disk submissions. Two special directory issues contain articles on selling techniques, mail order, import/export, franchising and business ideas. Reports in 2 weeks. Query with outline of article development. SASE.
Nonfiction and Photos: Regularly covered are such subjects as mail order, direct selling, franchising, party plans, selling techniques and the marketing of handcrafted or homecrafted products. Wanted are ideas for the aspiring entrepreneur (no material that is purely inspirational); examples of successful business methods that might be duplicated. No material that is purely inspirational. Length: 800 words for a short; 2,000-3,000 words for a major article. "Payment rates vary according to length and quality of the submission."
Tips: "Study recent issues of the magazine. Best bets for newcomers: Interview-based report on a successful small business venture."

‡**INDEPENDENCE, A Digest for the Self-Employed**, Agora Publishing, 2201 St. Paul St., Baltimore MD 21218. (301)235-7961. Editor-in-Chief: Elizabeth W. Philip. Monthly newsletter covering time-saving, money-saving information for the self-employed person who believes in being independent—philosophically, financially and personally. Estab. 1982. Circ. 5,000. Pays on acceptance. Byline given. Buys first North American and second serial rights. Simultaneous queries and photocopied and previously published submissions OK. SASE. Reports in 1 month on queries; 6 weeks on mss. Sample copy $2; writer's guidelines for business size SASE.
Columns/Departments: Legal; Investment Notes; New Business Opportunities; Personal Motivation. Length: 1,000-2,000 words; prefers 1,000 words. Pays $5-100.

LOTTERY PLAYER'S MAGAZINE, National Lottery List, Intergalactic Publishing Company, Box 188, Clementon NJ 08021. (609)783-0910. Editor: Samuel W. Valenza Jr. Monthly tabloid covering lottery players in 17 states, lottery games, gaming, travel, recreation associated with the lottery. Estab. 1981. Circ. 45,000. Pays on publication. Byline given. Offers 10% kill fee. Buys simultaneous, first, and second serial (reprint) rights; also makes work-for-hire assignments. Submit seasonal/holiday material 2-3 months in advance. Simultaneous queries, and simultaneous, photocopied, and previously published submissions OK. Computer printout and disk submissions OK; prefers letter quality to dot matrix printouts. SASE. Reports in 1 month on queries; 2 months on mss. Free sample copy.
Nonfiction: Book excerpts, expose, general interest, historical/nostalgic, how-to, humor, interview/profile, new product, opinion, personal experience, travel. All mss must pertain to lotteries, games of chance, lottery operations and their directors, popular gaming places (Las Vegas, Atlantic City, Monte Carlo, etc.), and lottery winners and losers. Special issues include Lottery List Annual, a list of winning numbers and relevant analysis for previous year. Buys 6-10 mss/year. Query with clips of published work or send complete ms. Length: 200-1,500 words. Pays $60-250.
Photos: Send photos with ms. Pays $10-25 for b&w prints; reviews contact sheet. Captions, model release and identification of subjects required. Buys one-time rights.
Columns/Departments: Numerology column (discussing relationship of numbers to everyday life—lucky numbers, etc.); reviews of books on gaming, games of chance." Buys variable number mss/year. Query with clips of published work or send complete ms. Length: 200-400 words. Pays $60-100.
Fiction: T.K. Fos, fiction editor. Adventure, fantasy, historical, humorous, romance—associated with lottery. Buys 1-2 mss/year. Query with clips of published work. Length: 1,000-2,500 words. Pays $200-500.
Fillers: Clippings, jokes, gags, anecdotes. Buys 20-40 fillers/year. Length: 25-100 lines. Pays $20-50.
Tips: "We would like to establish contact with photojournalists in the states with lotteries for the express purpose of covering millionaire and other big chance drawings on a regular basis. We will pay regular rates and agreed upon expenses. States are: New Hampshire, New York, Nevada, Connecticut, Pennsylvania, Massachusetts, Michigan, Maryland, Rhode Island, Maine, Illinois, Ohio, Delaware, Vermont, Colorado, Arizona."

MONEY MAKER, Your Guide to Financial Security & Wealth, Consumers Digest, Inc., 5705 Lincoln Ave., Chicago IL 60659. (312)275-3590. Editor: John Manos. Bimonthly magazine covering investment markets for unsophisticated investors. "Instructions for neophyte investors to increase their capital." Circ. 450,000. Pays on publication. Byline given. Offers 25% kill fee. Buys all rights. Simultaneous queries and photocopied submissions OK. Reports in 3-6 weeks on queries; 3 months on mss. Free sample copy and writer's guidelines.
Nonfiction: How-to (on investment areas); analysis of specific markets. "Indicate your areas of financial expertise." Buys 60 mss/year. Query with clips of published work if available. Length: 1,000-3,000 words. Pays $200-600 + .

THE NATIONAL SUPERMARKET SHOPPER, (formerly *Supermarket Shopper*), American Coupon Club, Inc., 500 Franklin Square, New York NY 11010. President: Martin Sloane. Editor-in-Chief: Ruth Brooks. Emphasizes smart supermarket shopping and the use of cents-off coupons and refund offers for "a wide audience of supermarket shoppers who want to save money. The editorial slant is definitely consumer-oriented." Monthly; 52 pages. Circ. 100,000. Pays on publication. Buys all rights. Byline given. Simultaneous, photocopied and previously published submissions OK. SASE. Reports in 10 weeks. Free sample copy; writer's guidelines for SASE.
Nonfiction: Lee Shore, managing editor. General interest; exposé (of supermarket operations, management, coupon misredemption); how-to (save money at the supermarket, tips, dollar stretchers; etc.); humor; interview (of top management, food manufacturers or supermarkets); new product (food, household products); and personal experience (couponing and refunding). Buys 2-3 mss/issue. Send complete ms. Length: 750-2,500 words. Pays 5¢/published word.
Fiction: "We use fiction occasionally if the events are in context of supermarket shopping." Query. Length: 750-2,500 words. Pays 5¢/published word.
Fillers: Jokes, short humor and newsbreaks. Buys 1-2/issue. Length: 50-200 words. Pays $5-10.

Tips: "The best way to break in is to read a copy of our magazine and get an idea of the type of material we publish. The consumer viewpoint is utmost in our minds."

PRIVILEGE, Associated BankCard Holders, #2 Executive Campus, Cherry Hill NJ 08002. (609)665-3332. Editor: Kenneth N. Bauso. Publication Director: Monique Whitaker. Bimonthly magazine covering consumer finance, consumer services and consumer interests for bank credit card holders. Circ. 200,000. Pays on publication. Byline given. Buys one-time rights. Submit seasonal/holiday material 3 months in advance. Simultaneous queries and simultaneous, photocopied and previously published submissions OK. SASE. Reports in 2 weeks on queries; 1 month on mss. Sample copy for 9x12 SASE (with 6 first class stamps); free writer's guidelines.
Nonfiction: General interest (product background, e.g., how chocolate is made, packaged); how-to (buy any consumer product or service); humor (as it applies to consumers); interview/profile (of business people); new product (background, availability); travel. No "political, cause-oriented, sexual or product-biased material." Buys 35 mss/year. Query with clips. Length: 400-3,000 words. Pays $100-1,000.
Columns/Departments: Insurance; Legal; Leisuretime; Wardrobe Corner (any consumer information on clothing); Quest for the Best (buying the best consumer product of any kind); You Won't Believe It (humor with a consumer slant); Dollars and Sense (financial advice on investment). Buys 60 mss/year. Query with clips. Length: 500-1,000 words. Pays $100-200.
Tips: "We do read all submitted material, but it will save the author time and effort if he submits specifically requested material. We answer promptly. Feature and subfeature material should be current and mainstream."

PUBLIC CITIZEN, Public Citizen, Inc., Box 19404, Washington DC 20036. Editor: David Bollier. Quarterly magazine covering consumer issues for "contributors to Public Citizen, a consortium of five consumer groups established by Ralph Nader in the public interest: Congress Watch, the Health Research Group, the Critical Mass Energy Project, the Litigation Group, and the Tax Reform Group. Our readers have joined Public Citizen because they believe the consumer should have a voice in the products he or she buys, the quality of our environment, good government, and citizen rights in our democracy." Circ. 45,000. Pays on publication. Byline given. Buys first rights. Submit seasonal/holiday material 4 months in advance. Photocopied submissions OK. SASE. Reports in 1 month on queries; 2 months on mss. Sample copy available.
Nonfiction: Exposé (of government waste and inaction and corporate wrongdoing); general interest (features on how consumer groups are helping themselves); how-to (start consumer groups such as co-ops, etc.); interview/profile (of business or consumer leaders, or of government officials in positions that affect consumers); and photo feature (dealing with consumer power). "We are looking for stories that go to the heart of an issue and explain how it affects individuals. Articles must be in-depth investigations that expose poor business practices or bad government or that call attention to positive accomplishments. Send us stories that consumers will feel they learned something important from or that they can gain inspiration from to continue the fight for consumer rights. All facts are double checked by our fact-checkers." No "fillers, jokes or puzzles." Query or send complete ms. Length: 500-2,500 words. Pays $125 maximum/article.
Photos: State availability of photos. Reviews 5x7 b&w prints. "Photos are paid for with payment for ms." Captions required. Buys one-time rights.
Columns/Departments: Politics As Usual (short features on consumer issues); Focus on Books ("book reviews"). Query or send complete ms—"no clips please." Length: 500-1,000 words. Pays $125 maximum/article.
Tips: No first-person articles, political rhetoric, or "mood" pieces; *Public Citizen* is a highly factual advocacy magazine. Knowledge of the public interest movement, consumer issues, and Washington politics is a plus.

TOWERS CLUB, USA NEWSLETTER, The Original Information-By-Mail, Direct-Marketing Newsletter, Towers Club Press, Box 2038, Vancouver WA 98668. (206)699-4428. Editor: Jerry Buchanan. Newsletter published 10 times/year (not published in August or December) covering entrepreneurism (especially selling useful information by mail). Circ. 5,000. Pays on publication. Byline given. Buys one-time rights. Submit seasonal/holiday material 10 weeks in advance. Simultaneous, photocopied, and previously published submissions OK. Computer printout submissions or 7" diskettes with Scriptsit software OK. SASE. Reports in 2 weeks. Sample copy for $3 and 38¢ postage.
Nonfiction: Exposé (of mail order fraud); how-to (personal experience in self-publishing and marketing). "Welcomes well-written articles of successful self publishing/marketing ventures. Must be current, and preferably written by the person who actually did the work and reaped the rewards. There's very little we will not consider, *IF* it pertains to unique money-making enterprises that can be operated from the home." Buys 10 mss/year. Send complete ms. Length: 500-1,000 words. Pays $10-35.

VENTURE, The Magazine for Entrepreneurs, Venture Magazine, Inc., 35 W. 45th St., New York NY 10036. Editor: Carl Burgen. Monthly magazine about entrepreneurs for people owning their own businesses, starting new businesses or wanting to do so. Pays on acceptance. Buys first-time rights. SASE. Free sample copy.

Nonfiction: "We are looking for stories on new startups of companies and current news on venture capital and entrepreneurs." Buys 20-25 mss/issue. Query with clips of previously published work. Length: 800-3,000 words. Pays $300-1,000.

WINNING, National Reporter Publications, Inc., 15115 S. 76th E. Ave., Bixby OK 74008. (918)366-4441. Editor: Ruth Rosauer. Monthly tabloid covering "winning in all its aspects to help you cash in on the best things in life." Circ. 200,000. Pays on publication. Byline given. Buys all rights or first North American serial rights. Submit seasonal/holiday material 3 months in advance. Simultaneous queries and submissions OK. Computer printout and disk submissions OK; prefers letter quality to dot matrix printouts. SASE. Reports in 1 month. Free sample copy.
Nonfiction: How-to (succeed/win); inspirational; money making/saving ideas for the homemaker; and articles on winning/winners. Buys 48-60 mss/year. Length: 300-1,200 words. Pays 5¢/word.
Photos: State availability of photos. Pays $25 maximum for 5x7 b&w prints.

Detective and Crime

These publications are markets for nonfiction accounts from the world of espionage and crime. Markets for criminal fiction (mysteries) are listed in Mystery publications.

DETECTIVE CASES, Detective Files Group, 1440 St. Catherine St. W., Montreal, Quebec, Canada H3G 1S2. Editor-in-Chief: Dominick A. Merle. Art Director: Art Ball. Bimonthly magazine. See *Detective Files*.

DETECTIVE DRAGNET, Detective Files Group, 1440 St. Catherine St. W., Montreal, Quebec, Canada H3G 1S2. Editor-in-Chief: Dominick A. Merle. Art Director: Art Ball. Bimonthly magazine; 72 pages. See *Detective Files*.

DETECTIVE FILES, Detective Files Group, 1440 St. Catherine St. W., Montreal, Quebec, Canada H3G 1S2. Editor-in-Chief: Dominick A. Merle. Art Director: Art Ball. Bimonthly magazine; 72 pages. Pays on acceptance. Buys all rights. Photocopied submissions OK. SASE. Reports in 4 weeks. Free sample copy and writer's guidelines.
Nonfiction: True crime stories. "Do a thorough job; don't double-sell (sell an article to more than one market); and deliver, and you can have a steady market. Neatness, clarity and pace will help you make the sale." Query. Length: 3,500-6,000 words. Pays $175-300.
Photos: Purchased with accompanying ms; no additional payment.

THE DOSSIER, English Department, SUNY, Oneonta NY 13820. (607)431-3514. Editor: Richard L. Knudson. Quarterly magazine covering the world of espionage—real and fictional spies. Estab. 1981. Circ. 800. Payment method negotiable. Byline given. Buys negotiable rights. Simultaneous queries, and photocopied and previously published submissions OK. Computer printout and disk submissions OK. SASE. Reports in 2 weeks. Sample copy $3.
Nonfiction: Historical, how-to, interview/profile, new product, personal experience, photo feature, technical. No "fanzine" articles. Buys 20-30 mss/year. Query. Length: 500-2,000 words. Pays $30 minimum.
Photos: Send photos with ms. Pays $5 minimum for b&w prints. Captions, model release and identification of subjects required. Buys one-time rights.
Columns/Departments: "Book and film reviews should run about 500 words and aim at a sophisticated spy enthusiast." Buys 20-30 mss/year. Query. Length: 400-700 words. Pays $30 minimum.
Tips: "A writer should know his subject thoroughly; articles must be well-researched and documented (in the text). We're just getting started and are looking for writers willing to give us a break dollar-wise to become regulars later on when we can afford higher fees. No fiction or poetry."

FRONT PAGE DETECTIVE, INSIDE DETECTIVE, Official Detective Group, R.G.H. Publishing Corp., 460 W. 34th St., 20th Floor, New York NY 10001. (212)947-6500. Editor-in-Chief: Art Crockett. Editor of Front Page and Inside: Rose Mandelsberg.
Nonfiction: The focus of these two publications is similar to the others in the Official Detective Group, but concentrates more on pre-trial stories. Byline given. For further details, see *Official Detective*.

HEADQUARTERS DETECTIVE, Detective Files Group, 1440 St. Catherine St. W., Montreal, Quebec, Canada H3G 1S2. Editor-in-Chief: Dominick A. Merle. Art Director: Art Ball. Bimonthly magazine; 72 pages. See *Detective Files*.

MASTER DETECTIVE, Official Detective Group, R.G.H. Publishing Corp., 460 W. 34th St., New York NY 10001. Editor-in-Chief: Art Crockett. Managing Editor: Christos K. Ziros. Monthly. Circ. 350,000. Buys 9-10 mss/issue. See *Official Detective*.

OFFICIAL DETECTIVE, Official Detective Group, R.G.H. Publishing Corp., 460 W. 34th St., New York NY 10001. Editor-in-Chief: Art Crockett. Managing Editor: Christos Mirtsopoulos. "For detective story or police buffs whose tastes run to *true*, rather than fictional crime/mysteries." Monthly magazine. Circ. 500,000. Pays on acceptance. Buys all rights. Byline given. Phone queries OK. SASE. Reports in 2 weeks.
Nonfiction: "Only *fact* detective stories. We are actively trying to develop new writers, and we'll work closely with those who show promise and can take the discipline required by our material. It's not difficult to write, but it demands meticulous attention to facts, truth, clarity, detail. Queries are essential with us, but I'd say the quickest rejection goes to the writer who sends in a story on a case that should never have been written for us because it lacks the most important ingredient, namely solid, superlative detective work. We also dislike pieces with multiple defendants, unless all have been convicted." Buys 150 mss/year. Query. Length: 5,000-6,000 words. Pays $250.
Photos: Purchased with accompanying mss. Captions required. Send prints for inside use; transparencies for covers. Pays $12.50 minimum for b&w glossy prints, 4x5 minimum. Pays $200 minimum for 2¼x2¼ or 35mm transparencies. Model release required for color photos used on cover.
Tips: Send a detailed query on the case to be submitted. Include: locale; victim's name; type of crime; suspect's name; status of the case (indictment, trial concluded, disposition, etc.); amount and quality of detective work; dates; and availability and number of pictures. "We're always impressed by details of the writer's credentials."

STARTLING DETECTIVE, Detective Files Group, 1440 St. Catherine St. W., Montreal, Quebec, Canada H3G 1S2. Editor-in-Chief: Dominick A. Merle. Art Director: Art Ball. Bimonthly magazine; 72 pages. See *Detective Files*.

TRUE DETECTIVE, Official Detective Group, R.G.H. Publishing Corp., 460 W. 34th St., New York NY 10001. Editor-in-Chief: Art Crockett. Managing Editor: Christos Mirtsopoulos. Monthly. Circ. 500,000. Buys 11-12 mss/issue. Byline given. See *Official Detective*.

TRUE POLICE CASES, Detective Files Group, 1440 St. Catherine St. W., Montreal, Quebec, Canada H3G 1S2. Editor-in-Chief: Dominick A. Merle. Art Director: Art Ball. Bimonthly magazine; 72 pages. See *Detective Files*.

Ethnic/Minority

The interests and concerns of diverse nationalities and religions are represented by publications in this category. General interest lifestyle magazines for these groups are also included. Additional markets for writing with an ethnic orientation are located in the following sections: Book Publishers; College, Career, and Alumni; Juvenile; Men's; and Women's.

‡**ABOUT. . .TIME MAGAZINE**, 30 Genesee St., Rochester NY 14611. (716)235-7150. Editor: Carolyne S. Blount. Monthly magazine for blacks and minorities. Circ. 18,400. Pays on publication. Byline given. Offers 20% kill fee. Buys negotiable rights. Submit seasonal/holiday material 3 months in advance. Simultaneous queries and previously published submissions OK. SASE. Reports in 2 weeks on queries; 6 weeks on mss. Sample copy for $1 and 9x12 SAE.
Nonfiction: General interest; how-to (save money, repair and make things, improve health); humor; interview/profile; opinion; photo feature; travel; health; sports. Special issues include black/hispanic women, business, health, education, entertainment. No erotica. Buys 60 mss/year. Query. Length: 500-5,000 words. Pays $30-100.
Photos: Send photos with query. Pays $3-7 for 3x5 b&w prints. Captions, model release and identification of subjects required. Buys all rights.
Columns/Departments: Fiction, Book/Film/Record/Theatrical Reviews, Hobnobbing (PSAs, etc.), Reci-

pes, How-to, Poetry, Health. Buys 80 mss/year. Query. Length: 75-5,000 words. Pays $20-50.
Fiction: Ethnic (black/hispanic). No erotica, etc. Buys 10 mss/year. Send complete ms. Length: 500-2,500 words. Pays $20-50.
Poetry: Free verse, haiku, light verse, traditional. No avant-garde, erotica. Submit maximum 12 poems. Length: 60-150 lines. No payment for poetry.
Fillers: Short humor. Buys 15/year. Length: open. Pays $10-30.
Tips: "Information should be presented in a factual, positive and uplifting manner. *About . . .Time* documents the struggle by individuals, groups and organizations to keep a positive momentum going in the black communities. It deals with philosophy as well as strategy and presents numerous real-to-life examples of what is being done. Even local stories should reflect a national theme. Examine a copy of our publication. We feature one major topic (business, entertainment, women, etc.) in a single issue. Our cover story is usually an interview with a leader or influencing force in the subject area we cover."

AMERICAN DANE MAGAZINE, Danish Brotherhood in America, Box 31748, Omaha NE 68131. (402)341-5049. Administrative Editor: Howard Christensen. Submit only material with Danish ethnic flavor. Monthly magazine. Circ. 11,000. Pays on publication. Buys all rights. Submit seasonal/holiday material 12 months in advance (particularly Christmas). Photocopied or previously published submissions OK. SASE. Byline given. Reports in 2 months. Sample copy $1. Free writer's guidelines.
Nonfiction: Historical; humor (satirical, dry wit notoriously Danish); informational (Danish items, Denmark or Danish-American involvements); inspirational (honest inter-relationships); interview; nostalgia; personal experience; photo feature and travel. Buys 10-15 unsolicited mss/year. Length: 1,500 words maximum. Pays $25-50.
Photos: Purchased on assignment. Pays $10-25 for b&w. Total purchase price for ms includes payment for photos. Model release required.
Fiction: Danish adventure, historical, humorous, mystery, romance and suspense. Must have Danish appeal. Buys 12 mss/year. Query. Length: 500-1,500 words. Pays $25-50.
Fillers: Puzzles (crossword, anagrams, etc.) and short humor. Query. Length: 50-300 words.

‡**AN GAEL, Irish Traditional Culture Alive in America Today,** The Irish Arts Center, 553 W. 51st St., New York NY 10019. (212)757-3318. Editor: Kathleen Murphy. Quarterly magazine covering the heritage of the Irish people with emphasis on the Irish-American experience. Material in the Irish language, as well as English is welcome. Written for all those who want to maintain or actively pursue Irish arts, history and language. Estab. 1982. Circ. 2,500. Pays on acceptance. Byline given. Submit seasonal/holiday material 6 months in advance. Photocopied submissions OK. "We cannot return submissions." Reports in 1 month. Free sample copy.
Nonfiction: Humor, photo feature. Articles include periodic features on Irish language; traditional music, dance and visual arts; Irish-American community profiles; fiction and poetry in both English and Irish; interviews with and profiles of cultural figures; and reviews of cultural activities, drama, books, films and records. Buys 30 mss/year. Send complete ms. Length: 1,000 words maximum. Pays $10.
Photos: Descriptive of traditional Irish subject matter. Reviews 8x10 b&w glossy prints. Identification of subject required. Buys one-time rights.

ARARAT, The Armenian General Benevolent Union, 585 Saddle River Rd., Saddle Brook NJ 07662. Editor-in-Chief: Leo Hamalian. Emphasizes Armenian life and culture for Americans of Armenian descent and Armenian immigrants. "Most are well-educated; some are Old World." Quarterly magazine. Circ. 2,400. Pays on publication. Buys first North American serial rights. Submit seasonal/holiday material at least 3 months in advance. Photocopied and previously published submissions OK. SASE. Reports in 6 weeks. Sample copy $2.50.
Nonfiction: Historical (history of Armenian people, of leaders, etc.); interviews (with prominent or interesting Armenians in any field, but articles are preferred); profile (on subjects relating to Armenian life and culture); personal experience (revealing aspects of typical Armenian life); travel (in Armenia and Armenian communities throughout the world and the US). Buys 3 mss/issue. Query. Length: 1,000-6,000 words. Pays $25-100.
Columns/Departments: Reviews of books by Armenians or relating to Armenians. Buys 6/issue. Query. Pays $25. Open to suggestions for new columns/departments.
Fiction: Any stories dealing with Armenian life in America or in the old country. Buys 4 mss/year. Query. Length: 2,000-5,000 words. Pays $35-75.
Poetry: Any verse that is Armenian in theme. Buys 6/issue. Pays $10.
Tips: "Read the magazine, and write about the kind of subjects we are obviously interested in, e.g., Kirlian photography, Aram Avakian's films, etc. Remember that we have become almost totally ethnic in subject matter, but we want articles that present the Armenian to the rest of the world in an interesting way."

ATTENZIONE, Adam Publications, Inc., 152 Madison Ave., New York NY 10016. Editor: Lois Spritzer. Executive Editor: Maria Terrone. Monthly magazine emphasizing Italian-Americans for people who have an interest "in Italy and Italian-Americans, in their political, social and economic endeavors. We are a general interest magazine for a special interest group." Circ. 165,000. Pays 30 days after publication. Buys first North American serial rights. Submit seasonal material 5 months in advance. SASE. Reports in 2 months on queries.
Nonfiction: Expose; general interest; historical (relating to something of current interest); humor; interview; profile; and travel (1 issue/year devoted extensively to travel in Italy). Buys 6 mss/issue. Query. Length: 1,500-2,500 words. Pays $350-600.

BALTIMORE JEWISH TIMES, 2104 N. Charles St., Baltimore MD 21218. (301)752-3504. Editor: Gary Rosenblatt. Weekly magazine covering subjects of interest to Jewish readers. "*Baltimore Jewish Times* reaches 20,000 Baltimore-area Jewish homes, as well as several thousand elsewhere in the US and Canada; almost anything of interest to that audience is of interest to us. This includes reportage, general interest articles, personal opinion, and personal experience pieces about every kind of Jewish subject from narrowly religious issues to popular sociology; from the Mideast, to the streets of Brooklyn, to the suburbs of Baltimore. We run articles of special interest to purely secular Jews as well as to highly observant ones. We are Orthodox, Conservative, and Reform all at once. We are spiritual and mundane. We are establishment and we are alternative culture." Circ. 20,000. Pays on publication. Byline given. Buys one-time rights, first rights, or second serial (reprint) rights. Submit seasonal/holiday material 2 months in advance. Simultaneous queries, and photocopied and previously published submissions OK. "We will not return submissions without SASE." Reports in 6 weeks. Sample copy $2.
Nonfiction: Barbara Pash, editorial assistant. Book excerpts, expose, general interest, historical/nostalgic, humor, interview/profile, opinion, personal experience and photo feature. "We are inundated with Israel personal experience and Holocaust-related articles, so submissions on these subjects must be of particularly highquality." Buys 100 mss/year. "Established writers query; others send complete ms." Length: 1,200-6,000 words. Pays $25-250.
Photos: Kim Muller-Thym, graphics editor. Send photos with ms. Pays $10-35 for 8x10 b&w prints.
Fiction: Barbara Pash, editorial assistant. "We'll occasionally run a high-quality short story with a Jewish theme." Buys 6 mss/year. Send complete ms. Length: 1,200-6,000 words. Pays $25-250.

BLACK ENTERPRISE MAGAZINE, For Black Men and Women Who Want to Get Ahead, Earl G. Graves Publishing Co., 295 Madison Ave., New York NY 10017. (212)889-8220. Editor: Earl G. Graves. Managing Editor: Elliott Lee. Monthly magazine covering black economic development and business for a highly-educated, affluent, black, middle-class audience interested in business, politics, careers and international issues. Circ. 260,000. Pays on acceptance. Byline given. Offers 25% kill fee. Buys all rights. Submit seasonal/holiday material 4 months in advance. Simultaneous queries OK. Reports in 2 weeks on queries; 1 month on mss. Sample copy and writer's guidelines free.
Nonfiction: Expose, general interest, how-to, interview/profile, technical, travel and short, hard-news items of black interest. "We emphasize the how-to aspect." Special issues include: Careers, February; Black Business, June; and Money Management, October. "No fiction or poetry; no 'rags-to-riches,' ordinary-guy stories, please." Buys 30-40 mss/year. Query with clips of published work. Send "a short, succinct letter that lets us know the point of the piece, the elements involved, and *why* our readers would want to read it." Length: 600-3,000 words. Pays $100-800/article.
Columns/Departments: Sheryl Hilliard, senior editor. In the News (short, hard-news pieces on issues of black interest); and Personal Finance (aimed at middle-income readers). Buys 50-60 mss/year. Query with clips of published work. Length: 300-1,000 words. Pays $75-300/article.
Tips: "We have stayed away from trivia and first-person pieces on the belief that our readers want hard-nosed reporting and innovative analysis of issues that concern them. *Black Enterprise* has a mission of informing, educating and entertaining an upscale, affluent audience that wants issues addressed from its unique perspective. We are most open to 'In the News,' an expression of a sensitivity to issues/events/trends that have an impact on black people."

BLACK FUTURE, Williams Communication, Inc., Box 1849, Orangeburg SC 29115. (803)531-1662. Editor and Publisher: Cecil J. Williams. Quarterly magazine covering trends, with emphasis on people achieving. "*Black Future* also publishes a state edition (South Carolina) which utilizes some material contained in the national edition." Circ. 60,000. Pays on publication. Byline given. Buys all rights "but we will consider buying other rights." Submit seasonal/holiday material 3 months in advance. Simultaneous queries, and simultaneous, photocopied, and previously published submissions OK. SASE. Reports in 1 month. Sample copy $3 via 1st class.
Nonfiction: How-to (home repair, decorating, saving money); humor; inspirational; interview/profile; new product; opinion; personal experience; photo feature; and travel. Buys 4-6 mss/year. Query with outline or send complete ms. Length: 3,000 words maximum. Pays $25-350.
Photos: Send photos with ms. Reviews b&w or color 35 mm transparencies and 8x10 b&w prints. Captions

and model release required. Buys one-time rights. Pays negotiable fee.
Columns/Departments: Spectrum (news bits and short pieces); People Shaping the Future; and Modern Living (food, travel, habitat). Buys 15-20 mss/year. Send complete ms. Length: 500-1,000 words. Pays $25.
Fiction: "We're looking for stories of a sociological nature." Buys 2-4 mss/year. Send complete ms. Length: 1,000 words minimum. Pays $100.
Tips: "A writer should get our magazine and become familiar with it before submitting anything."

‡**CLUBDATE MAGAZINE, Magazine of the Good Life in Cleveland, U.S.A.**, MBC, Inc., 13726 Kinsman Ave., Cleveland OH 44120. (216)752-8410. Editor: Madelyne Blunt. Managing Editor: Carol Evyans. Bimonthly general interest magazine for the middle and upper income urban black family. Covers travel, food, book review, advice, etc., as well as cultural features on issues related to life in the urban center—housing, etc. Circ. 25,000. Pays on publication. Byline given. Buys first North American serial rights, first rights and makes work-for-hire assignments. Submit seasonal/holiday material 3 months in advance. Simultaneous queries and photocopied submissions OK. Prefers letter quality to dot matrix printout submissions. SASE. Reports in 2 weeks on queries; 1 month on mss. Sample copy $1.75; writer's guidelines for 9x12 SAE and 60¢ postage.
Nonfiction: Book excerpts (especially interested in these); expose (on shoplifting, etc.); general interest; how-to; humor; inspirational (success stories, unique jobs); interview/profile (of local people or people who once lived in Cleveland); new product (special interest with photo); opinion (editorial comment); personal experiences (as they relate to local folks); photo feature (of black people only); travel (with photos); fashion (with photos, black models or no models; accessories for men and women). Special issues include Christmas; Fashion (fall); and Travel. Query with clips, if available. Length: 1,000-3,500 words. Pays $150 minimum.
Photos: State availability with query letter or manuscript. Send photos with accompanying query or manuscript. Good quality and variety. Reviews contact sheets. Captions, model release and identification of subjects required. Buys one-time rights.
Columns/Departments: Advice to lovelorn, sex problems, Your Health, how-to (fashion tips, beauty). Buys 18/year. Query with clips of published work. Length: 500-1,000 words. Pays variable rate.
Tips: "We are expanding number of pages."

‡**COLORADO BLACK LIFESTYLE**, Downing Publishing, Inc., 2250 Downing, Denver CO 80205. (303)830-2101. Editor: John W. Hoffman. Managing Editor: Tom Murray. Monthly magazine for blacks in Colorado. Estab. 1982. Circ. 20,000. Pays on publication. Byline given. Buys all rights. No computer printout or disk submissions. Submit seasonal/holiday material 3 months in advance. SASE. Reports in 2 weeks on queries; 1 month on mss. Sample copy $2.
Nonfiction: Expose (all types); general interest, historical/nostalgic, humor, inspirational, interview/profile, personal experience; photo feature. No essays. Buys 24 mss/year. Length: 3,000 words maximum. Pays $50-150.
Photos: Send photos with ms. Pays $10-30 for color transparencies and 8x10 b&w prints. Captions, model release (if needed) and identification of subjects required. Buys one-time rights.
Fiction: Adventure, erotica, ethnic, historical, humorous, mystery, romance, science fiction, western. "Fiction needs to have black slant." Buys 12 mss/year. Send complete ms. Length: 4,000 words maximum. Pays $75-150.
Poetry: Buys 75/year. Submit maximum 10 poems. Pays $5-25.

CONGRESS MONTHLY, American Jewish Congress, 15 E. 84th St., New York NY 10028. (212)879-4500. Managing Editor: Nancy Miller. Magazine published 8 times/year covering topics of concern to the American Jewish community representing a wide range of views. Distributed mainly to the members of the American Jewish Congress; readers are intellectual, Jewish, involved. Circ. 35,000. Pays on publication. Byline given. Not copyrighted. Buys one-time rights. Submit seasonal/holiday material 2 months in advance. No photocopied and previously published submissions. No computer printout or disk submissions. Reports in 2 months.
Nonfiction: General interest ("current topical issues geared toward our audience"). No technical material. Buys 6 unsolicited mss/year. Recent article example: "Behind the Scenes With the Press in Lebanon" (February/March 1983). Send complete ms. Length: 2,500 words maximum. Pays $50-75/article.
Photos: State availability of photos. Reviews b&w prints. "Photos are paid for with payment for ms."
Columns/Departments: Book, film, art and music reviews. Buys 12 mss/year. Send complete ms. Length: 1,200 words maximum. Pays $50-75/article.
Fiction: Mainstream ("must have some kind of a 'hook' for a Jewish magazine"). Buys 6 mss/year. Send complete ms. Length: 3,000 words maximum. Pays $50-75/article.
Poetry: Traditional. Buys 6/year. Pays $10.
Tips: Read the magazine before submitting material.

EBONY MAGAZINE, 820 S. Michigan Ave., Chicago IL 60605. Editor: John H. Johnson. Managing Editor: Charles L. Sanders. For black readers of the US, Africa, and the Caribbean. Monthly. Circ. 1,500,000.

Buys all rights. Buys about 10 mss/year. "We are now fully staffed, buying few mss." Pays on publication. Submit seasonal material 2 months in advance. Query. Reports in 1 month. SASE.

Nonfiction: Achievement and human interest stories about, or of concern to, black readers. Interviews, profiles and humor pieces are bought. Length: 1,500 words maximum. "Study magazine and needs carefully. Perhaps one out of 50 submissions interests us. Most are totally irrelevant to our needs and are simply returned." Pays $150 minimum.

Photos: Purchased with mss, and with captions only. Buys 8x10 glossy prints, color transparencies, 35mm color. Submit negatives and contact sheets when possible. Offers no additional payment for photos accepted with mss.

ESSENCE, 1500 Broadway, New York NY 10036. (212)730-4260. Editor-in-Chief: Susan L. Taylor. Executive Editor: Audrey Edwards. Managing Editor: John Stoltenberg. Senior Editors: Alice C. Jones-Miller, Cheryl Everette. Emphasizes black women. Monthly magazine; 150 pages. Circ. 700,000. Pays on acceptance. Makes assignments on work-for-hire basis. 3 month lead time. Pays 25% kill fee. Byline given. Submit seasonal/holiday material 6 months in advance. Computer printout submissions OK. SASE. Reports in 2 months. Sample copy $1.25; free writer's guidelines.

Features: "We're looking for articles that inspire and inform black women. Our readers are interested and aware; the topics we include in each issue are provocative. Every article should move the *Essence* woman emotionally and intellectually. We welcome queries from good writers on a wide range of topics: general interest, historical, how-to, humor, self-help, relationships, work, personality interview, personal experience, political issues, personal opinion." Buys 200 mss/year. Query. Length: 1,500-2,000 words. Pays $300-1,000.

Photos: Ron Albrecht, art director. State availability of photos with query. Pays $75-200 for b&w prints; $100-300 for color transparencies. Captions and model release required.

Columns/Departments: Query department editors: Contemporary Living (home, food, lifestyle, consumer information): Stephanie Stokes Oliver. Travel & Entertainment: Stephanie Renfrow Hamilton; Health & Fitness: Wista J. Johnson; Careers: Elaine C. Ray. Query. Length: About 1,000 words. Pays $100 minimum. No unsolicited poetry.

Tips: "We're using much less fiction; more self-improvement pieces, 'relationship' articles and career information."

GREEK ACCENT, Greek Accent Publishing Corp., 41-17 Crescent St., Long Island City NY 11101. (212)784-2960. Editor: George Kalogerakis. Magazine published 11 times/year (combined July-August issue). "We are a publication for and about Greek-Americans and philhellenes." Circ. 20,000. Pays on publication. Byline given. Offers 20% kill fee. Buys first North American serial rights. Submit seasonal/holiday material 1 year in advance. Photocopied submissions OK. Computer printout and disk submissions OK; prefers letter quality to dot matrix printouts. SASE. Reports in 1 month on queries; 3 months on mss. Sample copy $2.50 for 9x12 SAE and 83¢ postage.

Nonfiction: Amalia Melis, articles editor. Book excerpts; expose; historical/nostalgic (historical more than nostalgic); how-to (only with a Greek slant, about Greece or Greeks); humor; interview/profile; new product (made or manufactured by Greeks or Greek-Americans); travel. No " 'My Trip to Samothraki,' articles or 'Greece Through the Eyes of a Non-Greek.' We publish articles on Greeks and Greece, on Greek-Americans who have succeeded at their work in some important way or who are doing unusual things, and on general interest subjects that might specifically interest our audience, such as the role of Greek Orthodox priests' wives, the crisis in Greek-US political relations, the Cyprus problem, Greek school education in the US, and large Greek-American communities like Astoria, New York." Query with clips of published work. "We buy almost no unsolicited articles—we work exclusively from queries." Length: 3,500-6,000 words. Pays variable rates.

Photos: John Thomsen, art director. State availability of photos. Pays $10 for 8x10 prints or contact sheets; $15 for color transparencies. Model release and identification of subjects required. Buys one-time rights.

Fiction: Ethnic, fantasy, historical, humorous, mainstream, mystery. No novels, Greek or Greek-American stereotyping. All fiction must in some way have a Greek theme. Send complete ms. Length: 1,500-3,000 words. Pays $100-200.

Tips: "Try to deal with problems and concerns peculiar to or of specific interest to Greek-Americans, rather than concentrating solely on Greece. With regard to Greece, heritage-historical-genealogical articles are of interest. We'd rather have investigative, informative articles than paeans to the glory that was Greece. Also, we do a semi-regular feature called 'Profile of a Parish,' spotlighting different parishes throughout the country. We'd especially like to see 'Profiles' of parishes outside the New York, New Jersey, Connecticut area. We'd like pieces on neighborhoods or communities outside this area, too. Probably the easiest way to get published here is to do a good, in-depth piece on a large, active Greek-American community in the Midwest, West, or South, and back it up with pictures. The more we get from outside the tri-state area, the happier we'll be."

THE HIGHLANDER, Angus J. Ray Associates, Inc., Box 397, Barrington IL 60010. (312)382-1035. Editor: Angus J. Ray. Managing Editor: Ethyl Kennedy Ray. Bimonthly magazine covering Scottish history, clans, genealogy, travel/history, and Scottish/American activities. Circ. 28,000. Pays on acceptance. Byline

Close-up

Cheryl Everette
Senior Editor, *Essence*

With a public relations and editorial background ("I learned it all on the job") in newspapers, book publishing and magazines, Cheryl Everette landed her first job at *Essence* magazine in 1979. "I'd always dreamed about working at *Essence*," says Everette, whose first position at the magazine was travel editor; today she is a senior editor.

"We talk directly to black American women who want to get ahead in their careers and their personal lives; they may want to grow psychologically or spiritually. That's the thread that runs through the magazine."

The real challenge, according to Everette, is that since there is not just *one* kind of black American woman, "we have a lot of ground to cover. There are black women on welfare, black women who are vice presidents of corporations, and everything in between. But whoever the black American woman is, if she's trying to move her life ahead, she can relate to *Essence*."

Everette says the magazine is like other women's publications in that it is service oriented. But *Essence* is different from other women's magazines "because we tend to talk to our readers like they are our sisters. Our tone is different from *Redbook*. When we say 'we', we mean black women."

Everette is dedicated to her readership and reflects that commitment in carrying out her editorial duties. In addition to receiving queries and manuscripts, she refines department material; attends editorial planning meetings; and supervises the newly created Grapevine section of the magazine which reports on new trends and looks at people and events in the news.

"I read through department material and manuscripts as if I were the reader out there. I look for things that aren't clear, seem wrong, or are handled insensitively. Every word, every photo is important to our readers and they have certain expectations about the magazine. I think writers need to remember that, too."

The ideal *Essence* writer, says Everette, is tuned in to the magazine's readers. Writers may be black, white, male or female. They may be excellent reporters or essayists. "We have some writers (but not enough!) who are good at humor. And we're always looking for good writers. They have a chance to break in if they just read us."

Reading the magazine ensures writers they will be in touch with the sensitivities of black American women. "I get annoyed with writers who want to do a piece that black women have no interest in. Someone once called me and wanted to do a profile of a male celebrity who is notorious for not even liking black women. The fact is—black women don't care what that person has to say. That's the sensitivity I'm talking about."

Along with knowing *Essence* readers, writers should know what the magazine has done. "It's a waste of time to get a query about a piece we published two months ago."

As for queries themselves, "I like to have a sense of what the article is going to do; what slant it's going to take; who the writer is going to talk to. I don't like vague query letters because they usually indicate that the writing's going to be pretty vague."

given. Buys first North American serial rights or second serial (reprint) rights. Submit seasonal/holiday material 6 months in advance. Photocopied and previously published submissions OK. SASE. Reports in 1 month. Sample copy and writer's guidelines free.

Nonfiction: Historical/nostalgic. "No fiction; no articles unrelated to Scotland." Buys 20 mss/year. Query. Length: 750-2,000 words. Pays $50-100.

Photos: State availability of photos. Pays $5-10 for 8x10 b&w prints. Reviews b&w contact sheets. Identification of subjects required. Buys one-time rights.

Tips: "Submit something that has appeared elsewhere."

INSIDE, The Jewish Exponent Magazine, Federation of Jewish Agencies of Greater Philadelphia, 226 S. 16th St., Philadelphia PA 19102. (215)895-5700. Editor: Jane Biberman. Managing Editor: Robin Fogel. Quarterly Jewish community magazine—for a 25 years and older, general interest Jewish readership. Circ. 75,000. Pays on acceptance. Byline given. Offers 20% kill fee. Buys one-time rights. Submit seasonal/holiday material 3 months in advance. Simultaneous queries OK. SASE. Reports in 3 weeks on queries; 1 month on mss. Sample copy $1.50; free writer's guidelines.

Nonfiction: Book excerpts; general interest; historical/nostalgic; humor; interview/profile; travel. Philadelphia angle desirable. No personal religious experiences or trips to Israel. Buys 50 mss/year. Query. Length: 1,000-3,000 words. Pays $100-400.

Photos: State availability of photos. Reviews color and b&w transparencies. Identification of subjects required.

Tips: "Personalities—very well known—and humor with a Jewish slant are needed."

JADE, The Asian American Magazine, 842 S. Citrus, Los Angeles CA 90036. (213)937-8659. Editor/Publisher: Gerald Jann. Managing Editor: Edward T. Foster. Quarterly magazine covering Asian-American people and events for Asian-Americans. Circ. 30,000. Pays on publication. Byline given. Offers 25% kill fee. Buys first North American serial rights. Submit seasonal/holiday material 6 months in advance. Simultaneous queries and photocopied submissions OK. Computer printout submissions OK; prefers letter quality to dot matrix. SASE. Reports in 3 weeks. Sample copy $1; writer's guidelines for business size SAE and 1 first class stamp.

Nonfiction: Interview/profile (Asian-Americans in unusual situations or occupations especially successful people active in communities). Buys 15 unsolicited mss/year. Send complete ms. Length: 4,000 words maximum. Pays $25-200.

Photos: Photos are a *must* with all stories. Send photos with ms. Reviews 35mm color transparencies and 5x7 color and b&w glossy prints. Model release and identification of subjects required. Buys one-time rights.

Columns/Departments: Open to new suggestions for columns/departments.

Fillers: Newsbreaks. Pays $10-25.

Tips: "We're especially interested in hearing from writers who are not on the West Coast."

JET, 820 S. Michigan Ave., Chicago IL 60605. Executive Editor and Associate Publisher: Robert E. Johnson. For black readers interested in current news and trends. Weekly. Circ. 800,000. Pays 100% kill fee. No byline. Study magazine before submitting. SASE.

Nonfiction: Articles on topics of current, timely interest to black readers. News items and features: religion, education, African affairs, civil rights, politics and entertainment. Buys informational articles, interviews, profiles, spot news and personal experience articles. Length: varies. Payment negotiated.

Photos: Photo essays. Payment negotiable.

THE JEWISH MONTHLY, 1640 Rhode Island NW, Washington DC 20036. (202)857-6645. Editor: Marc Silver. Published by B'nai B'rith. Monthly magazine. Buys North American serial rights. Pays on publication. SASE.

Nonfiction: Articles of interest to the Jewish community: economic, demographic, political, social, biographical, cultural, travel. No immigrant reminiscences. Queries (with clips of published work) should be direct, well-organized and map out the story. Buys 5-10 unsolicited mss/year. Length: 4,000 words maximum. Pays up to 10¢/word.

JEWISH POST AND OPINION, National Jewish Post, Inc., 2120 N. Meridian St., Indianapolis IN 46202. (317)927-7800. Editor: Gabriel Cohen. Weekly tabloid covering only news of Jewish interest. Circ. 112,000. Pays on publication. Byline given.

Nonfiction: "Straight reporting of hard news and human interest feature stories involving Jews." Length: 500-750 words for features. Pays 4¢/word. "No articles now, please, but we use stringers (correspondents) all throughout North America at 4¢ a word for news published." Information to involve Jewish person or incident.

‡**METROPOLITAN MAGAZINE, Washington DC Issue,** 13116 Country Ridge Dr., Germantown MD 20874. Managing Editor: Barbara Cummings. Monthly magazine featuring articles and investigative pieces

with a DC background for black, highly mobile, middle class audience. Estab. 1982. Pays on acceptance. Photocopied submissions OK. SASE. Reports "promptly." Sample copy and writer's guidelines $2.
Nonfiction: Feature articles on black lifestyles, history; investigative pieces with DC background; interview/profile (of black business, government, education, sports, media, and arts figures); consumer education and information. Query with 2 writing samples. Length: 750-4,500 words. Pays $85-300.
Columns/Departments: Subjects of interest to the black community. Query with 2 writing samples. Length: 750-4,500 words. Pays $85-300.

MIDSTREAM, A Monthly Jewish Review, 515 Park Ave., New York NY 10022. Editor: Joel Carmichael. Monthly. Circ. 14,000. Buys first rights. Byline given. Pays after publication. Reports in 2 months. SASE.
Nonfiction: "Articles offering a critical interpretation of the past, searching examination of the present, and affording a medium for independent opinion and creative cultural expression. Articles on the political and social scene in Israel, on Jews in Russia and the US; generally it helps to have a Zionist orientation. If you're going abroad, we would like to see what you might have to report on a Jewish community abroad." Buys historical and think pieces, primarily of Jewish and related content. Pays 5¢/word.
Fiction: Primarily of Jewish and related content. Pays 5¢/word.
Tips: "A book review would be the best way to start. Send us a sample review or a clip, let us know your area of interest, suggest books you would like to review. The author should briefly outline the subject and theme of his article and give a brief account of his background or credentials in this field. Since we are a monthly, we look for critical analysis rather than a 'journalistic' approach."

MOMENT MAGAZINE, 462 Boylston St., Boston MA 02116. (617)536-6252. Editor: Leonard Fein. Emphasizes Jewish affairs. Monthly magazine. Circ. 25,000. Pays on publication. Buys all rights. Pays 25% kill fee on commissioned articles. Byline given. Phone queries OK. Computer printout submissions OK. Submit seasonal/holiday material 6 months in advance. Reports in 6 weeks. Sample copy $2.50.
Nonfiction: Expose, how-to, informational, historical, political, humor, nostalgia, cultural, social action, profile and personal experience. Must have Jewish content. "We have a heavy backlog of poetry. A very high percentage of the material we receive deals with the Holocaust; we also get a large number of articles and stories focusing on grandparents. It's not that we don't want to see them, but we accept very few." Top literary quality only. Buys 100 mss/year. Query or submit complete ms. Length: 1,000-5,000 words. Pays $50 minimum.
Fiction: "We use only the highest quality fiction. Stories should have high Jewish content." Buys 6 mss/year. Submit complete ms. Length: 1,000-5,000 words. Pays $100-400.
Tips: "Read the magazine. Submit relevant material. Send a comprehensive letter that will outline elements to be covered as well as overall thrust of the article. It is helpful to include sources that will be used, and a brief summary of your experience (other publications, relevant credentials)."

‡**PHOENIX JEWISH NEWS**, Phoenix Jewish News, Inc., 1536 W. Thomas Rd., Phoenix AZ 85015. (602)264-0536. Executive Editor: Flo Eckstein. Managing Editor: Leni Reiss. Biweekly tabloid covering subjects of interest to Jewish readers. Circ. 5,000. Pays on publication. Byline given. Not copyrighted. Submit seasonal/holiday material 3 months in advance. Simultaneous queries, and simultaneous, photocopied, and previously published submissions OK. SASE. Reports in 4 weeks. Sample copy for SAE and $1 postage.
Nonfiction: General interest, historical/nostalgic, interview/profile, opinion, personal experience, photo feature, travel. Special issues incude Back to School; Summer Camps; Party Planning; Bridal; Jewish Holidays. Buys 25 mss/year. Query with published clips or send complete ms. Length: 1,000-2,500 words. Pays $25-100.
Photos: Send photos with query or ms. Pays $10 for 8x10 b&w prints. Captions required.
Tips: "Our newspaper reaches across the religious, political, social and economic spectrum of Jewish residents in this burgeoning southwestern metropolitan area."

PRESENT TENSE: The Magazine of World Jewish Affairs, 165 E. 56th St., New York NY 10022. (212)751-4000. Editor: Murray Polner. For college-educated, Jewish-oriented audience interested in Jewish life throughout the world. Quarterly magazine. Circ. 50,000. No computer printout or disk submissions. Buys all rights. Byline given. Buys 60 mss/year. Pays on publication. Sample copy $3. Reports in 6-8 weeks. Query. SASE.
Nonfiction: Quality reportage of contemporary events (a la *Harper's*, *New Yorker*, etc.). Personal experience, profiles and photo essays. Length: 3,000 words maximum. Pays $100-250.

‡**PROINI GREEK-AMERICAN NEWSPAPER, Proini Weekly**, Petallides Publishing Co. Inc., 9-11 E. 37th St., New York NY 10016. (212)578-4480. Editor: Dody Tsiantar. Weekly tabloid newspaper covering national and world news, Greek and Greek-American issues, problems, people. "We cover Greek-American communities, success stories, celebrities, leaders in the arts, business, and academia, human-interest stories relating to Greeks, travel to Greece and Cyprus, seasonal articles relating to Greek religious or national holi-

days or events (e.g., Christmas, Easter, March 25, October 28, the Turkish invasion of Cyprus)." Circ. 25,000. Pays on publication. Byline given. Offers 10% kill fee. Buys first North American serial rights. Submit seasonal/holiday material 2 months in advance. Simultaneous queries OK. SASE. Reports in 4 weeks on queries; 4 weeks on mss. Sample copy $1.

Nonfiction: Expose, historical/nostalgic, interview/profile, new product, photo feature, travel, art, culture, business. All must be Greek or Greek-American related. No pseudo-philosophical ramblings. Buys 25 mss/year. Query with clips. Length: 1,000-1,500 words. Pays $50-250.

Photos: John Haronides, photo editor. "We look for first-rate b&w glossy prints." Send photos with query or ms. Pays $5-15 for b&w prints, bought with ms, singly, or as series. Uses 5-10 photos for picture stories; pays $50-80 for double spread without ms. Captions, model release, and identification of subjects required. Buys one-time rights.

Columns/Departments: Book and film reviews (on Greek subjects or by Greek writers, directors, composers); Community (about Greek-American organizations, parishes, enclaves). Send complete ms. Length: 500-1,000 words. Pays $25-50.

Fiction: Ethnic-Greek. "Avoid Greek stereotyping, excessive violence, graphic sex, obscene language. The paper is read by the entire family. We are interested in young writers of merit." Send complete ms. Length: 500-1,500 words. Pays $50-75.

Fillers: Newsbreaks about Greeks and Greek-Americans. Length: 100-200 words. Pays $10-15 with b&w photos.

Tips: "We want original, informative, lively pieces that illuminate an aspect of Greek culture or life in America. Travel articles on Greece must be well researched, factual, sophisticated. Investigative pieces and personality profiles are more apt to be published than historical/nostalgic. Follow *Writer's Market* guidelines on submissions."

SCANDINAVIAN REVIEW, American-Scandinavian Foundation, 127 E. 73rd St., New York NY 10021. (212)879-9779. Editor: Judith Walker. "The majority of our readership is over 30, well educated, and in the middle income bracket. Most similar to readers of *Smithsonian* and *Saturday Review*. Have interest in Scandinavia by birth or education." Quarterly magazine. Circ. 6,000. Pays on publication. Buys all rights. Byline given. Previously published material (if published abroad) OK. SASE. Reports in 2 months. Sample copy $4.

Nonfiction: Historical, informational, interview, photo feature and travel. "Modern life and culture in Scandinavia." No literary criticism, American-Scandinavian memoirs, sociology, or academic writing in general. Buys 10 unsolicited mss/year. Recent article example: "Arctic Policies—What the Greenlanders Want" (June 1983). Send complete ms. Length: maximum 3,500 words. Pays $50-200.

Photos: Purchased with accompanying ms. Captions required. Submit prints or transparencies. Prefers sharp, high contrast b&w enlargements. Total purchase price for ms includes payment for photos.

Fiction: Literature. Only work translated from the Scandinavian. Buys 4-10 mss/year. Send complete ms. Length: 3,000 words maximum. Pays $75-125.

Poetry: Translations of contemporary Scandinavian poetry. Buys 5-20 poems/year. Pays $10.

Tips: "We will be using more Scandinavian authors and American translators; and commissioning more articles, so that we are even less open to freelancers."

‡**SEPIA, "Information With Style,"** Sepia Magazine, Inc., 8701 Wilshire Blvd., Beverly Hills CA 90211. (213)659-2152. Associate Editor: Susan M. Reed. Executive Editor: Clint C. Wilson. Monthly magazine covering informative, general interest, lifestyle subjects for primarily a black audience. "The new *Sepia* has a general interest-lifestyle format which is primarily targeted toward a black audience, but we also see it as a 'crossover' magazine." Circ. 135,000. Pays on publication. Byline given. Offers $50 kill fee. "We reserve all rights." Submit seasonal/holiday material 4 months in advance. Simultaneous queries, and simultaneous, photocopied, and previously published submissions OK. SASE. Reports in 1 month. Sample copy for 9x12 SAE and 3 first class stamps; writer's guidelines for business size SAE and 1 first class stamp.

Nonfiction: Book excerpts; general interest; historical/nostalgic; how-to (relating to time-saving projects, money-saving projects, investment tips, etc.); humor; inspirational; interview/profile; technical; travel. Special upcoming issues include Olympics sports features; features on women with special contributions (business, political, charitable, etc.). "No hand-written submissions; no racist, 'black-power', or downtrodden blacks subject matter; no hard sex." Query with published clips or send complete ms. Length: 650-3,000 words. Pays $75-200.

Photos: State availability of photos. Pays $15 for 2x3 color transparencies and 8x10 b&w prints. "Photos are judged on an individual basis by the art director to determine payment." Model release and identification of subjects required.

Columns/Departments: Homefront; Personal Finance; Career Horizons; First Person Singular (grooming, health, medicine, etc.). Query with published clips or send complete ms. Length: 650-800 words. Pays $75 maximum.

Fiction: Adventure, condensed novels, ethnic, fantasy, historical, humorous, mystery, novel excerpts, romance, science fiction, serialized novels, suspense. No hard sex. Query with published clips or send complete

ms. Length: 2,500-3,000 words. Pays $75-200.
Poetry: Avant-garde, free verse, light verse, traditional. No cliched or stereotypical subject matter. Submit maximum 4 poems. Length: 650-3,000 lines. Pays $75-200.
Fillers: Cartoons. Pays $15-30.
Tips: "Study the format and style of the magazine so that you can fully understand the magazine's intent, thereby being able to successfully write for that audience. Freelancers have best chance in Homefront, Career Horizons, First Person Singular, Personal Finance departments. Writing should be informative yet in an interesting, conversational style."

SOUTHERN JEWISH WEEKLY, Box 3297, Jacksonville FL 32206. (904)355-3459. Editor: Isadore Moscovitz. For a Jewish audience. General subject matter is human interest and short stories. Weekly. Circ. 28,500. Pays on acceptance. Not copyrighted. Buys all rights. Submit seasonal/holiday material 1 month in advance. SASE. Reports in 1 week. Free sample copy and writer's guidelines.
Nonfiction: "Any type of article as long as it is of Southern Jewish interest." Buys 15 mss/year. Length: 250-500 words. Pays $10-100.
Photos: State availability of photos. Pays $5-15 for b&w prints.

Food and Drink

Magazines appealing to readers' appreciation of fine wines and fine foods are classified here. Journals aimed at food processing, manufacturing, and retailing will be found in Trade Journals. Magazines covering nutrition for the general public are listed in the Health and Fitness category.

BON APPETIT, Knapp Communications, 5900 Wilshire Blvd., Los Angeles CA 90036. Editor-in-Chief: Paige Rense. Editor: Marilou Vaughan. Emphasizes food, cooking and wine "for affluent young, active men and women, interested in the good things of life." Monthly magazine. Circ. 1.3 million. Pays on acceptance for first rights. Submit seasonal/holiday material 6 months in advance. Reports in 6 weeks.
Nonfiction: William J. Garry, managing editor. How-to cook, and food articles with recipes. No historical food pieces. "We use only highly skilled food and wine writers." Query. Length: 2,000 words. Pay varies.

CUISINE, 1515 Broadway, New York NY 10036. (212)719-6201. Editor-in-Chief: Patricia Brown. "The magazine of fine foods and creative living." Monthly. Study several issues of the publication and query first. SASE. Unsolicited mss not accepted.

FINE DINING, Connell Publications, Inc., 1897 N.E. 164 St., N. Miami FL 33162. Editor/Publisher: Sean O'Connell. Articles Editor: Joanne Taylor. Emphasizes restaurant dining and gourmet cuisine. Bimonthly magazine; one edition: New York, Florida, Philadelphia, and Washington. Circ. 65,000. Pays on publication. Buys all rights. Byline given. Submit seasonal/holiday material 3 months in advance. Prefer original manuscripts over photocopies. No computer printout or disk submissions. SASE. Reports in 2 months. Sample copy $2.75 (includes postage and handling).
Nonfiction: Restaurant reviews, famous restaurant stories with recipes; famous hotel stories with fine dining rooms; country inns; interviews with chefs; travel/food articles with emphasis on cuisine and recipes; celebrity interviews with recipes. No humor about food or food puzzles. Buys 6 mss/year. Query with clips of published work. Length: 1,000-1,500 words.
Photos: Send photos with ms. Color close-up slides of food and/or 8x10 b&w glossy prints of exterior shots of inn, restaurant, and indoor dining rooms. Captions required.
Columns/Departments: Wines of Our Times (domestic and imported); Taking Off (short travel getaway with recipes); Celebrity Cook (favorite recipe of celebrity); Cookbook Comments (book reviews and excerpted recipes).

FOOD & WINE, Int. Review of Food & Wine Associates, an affiliate of American Express Publishing Corp., 1120 Avenue of the Americas, New York NY 10036. (212)386-5600. Editor: William Rice. Managing Editor: Warren Picower. Monthly magazine covering food and wine for "an upscale audience who cook, entertain, dine out and travel stylishly." Circ. 400,000. Pays on acceptance. Byline or "signer" at the end is given. Pays 25% kill fee. Buys one-time world rights. Submit seasonal/holiday material 6 months in advance. Computer printout submissions OK, "if completely legible"; prefers letter quality to dot matrix. SASE. Reports in 1 month; "letters of agreement are issued on every assignment."
Nonfiction: Contact: Catherine Bigwood, senior editor. How-to entertain, prepare, or equip or remodel a

kitchen; interview/profile (of chefs, restaurateurs, or persons who entertain well and are especially knowledgeable in food and wine); and "very specialized articles on food and wine worldwide." Contact John and Elin Walker on all beverage queries. Buys 75 mss/year. Query, "detailing an idea with a special slant for our magazine." Length: 1,000-2,200 words; "2,200-word maximum with or without recipes." Pays $800-1,800, "depending on length, amount of work involved, and quality."

Columns/Departments: Contact: Restaurants: Stephanie Curtis; Wine & Beverages: John and Elin Walker. Query. Length: 200-500 words. Pays $200. What's New: Warren Picower. Query. Length 100-200 words. Pays $100.

Tips: "A number of pieces are bought cold from writers we are not familiar with."

GOURMET, 560 Lexington Ave., New York NY 10022. (212)371-1330. Managing Editor: Miss Gail Zweigenthal. For moneyed, educated, traveled, food-wise men and women. Monthly. Purchases copyright, but grants book reprint rights with credit. Pays on acceptance. Suggests a study of several issues to understand type of material required. Reports in 2 months. Query. "If you haven't written for us before, you should enclose some samples of previous work. Articles from writers who have not previously been published in *Gourmet* are always on speculation." SASE.

Nonfiction: Uses articles on subjects related to food and wine—travel, adventure, reminiscence, fishing and hunting experiences. Prefers personal experiences to researched material. Recipes included as necessary. Not interested in nutrition, dieting, penny-saving or bizarre foods, or in interviews with chefs or food experts, or in reports of food contests, festivals or wine tastings. Buys recipes only as part of an article with interesting material to introduce them and make them appealing. "Gourmet Holidays" written by staff contributors only. The same is true for material including specific hotel or restaurant recommendations. Sophisticated, light, nontechnical. Length: 2,500-3,000 words. Current needs include American regional pieces (no restaurants). Pays $650 minimum.

Tips: "Personal reminiscences are the easiest way to break in, since we always use staff writers when recommending hotels or restaurants. Our biggest problem with freelancers is that they are not familiar with our style or that they fail to treat their material with enough sophistication or depth. We don't want pieces which sound like press releases or which simply describe what's there. We like to really cover a subject and literary value is important. We'd very much like to see more regional American material. It seems to be much easier to get people traipsing around Europe."

GREAT RECIPES OF THE WORLD, Great Recipes Publishing Associates, 333 Sylvan Ave., Englewood Cliffs NJ 07632. (201)569-2424. Editor: John Golden. Monthly magazine covering food for Middle America. Estab. 1981. Circ. 850,000. Byline given. Buys first North American serial rights. Submit seasonal/holiday material 6 months in advance. Simultaneous queries, and simultaneous and photocopied submissions OK. SASE. Reports in 4 weeks on queries. Sample copy 50¢.

Nonfiction: "This is a working magazine for people who shop in supermarkets. Category articles include recipes that are simple but interesting. Our magazine is meant to be taken into the kitchen, not left on the coffee table." Buys about 30 mss/year. Query with clips of published work. Length: 500-4,000 words. Pays $100 minimum.

Tips: "We're interested in recipe, travel and entertaining-at-home articles. Only published writers need apply."

THE WINE SPECTATOR, M. Shanken Communications, Inc., Opera Plaza Suite 2040, 601 Van Ness Ave., San Francisco CA 94102. (415)673-2040. Editor and Publisher: Marvin R. Shanken. Twice monthly newspaper covering wine. Circ. 32,000. Byline given. Buys first rights. Query seasonal/holiday material 3 months in advance. Simultaneous queries and photocopied submissions OK. Computer printout submissions OK "as long as they are properly formatted." SASE. Reports in 3 weeks. Sample copy $1; free writer's guideline.

Nonfiction: General interest (about wine or wine events); historical (on wine); how-to (build a wine cellar, taste wine, decant, etc.); humor; interview/profile (of wine; vintners, wineries); opinion; and photo feature. No "winery promotional pieces or articles by writers who lack sufficient knowledge to write below just surface data." Query with clips of published work. Length: 800-900 words average. Pays $100/base.

Photos: Send photos with ms. Pays $25 minimum for b&w contact sheets and 5x7 prints. Identification of subjects required. Buys one-time rights.

Tips: "A solid knowledge of wine is a must. Query letters help, detailing the story idea. New, refreshing ideas which have not been covered before stand a good chance of acceptance. *The Wine Spectator* is a consumer-oriented *newspaper* but we are interested in some trade stories; brevity is essential."

WINE TIDINGS, Kylix International, Ltd., 5165 Sherbrooke St. W., 414, Montreal, Quebec, Canada H4A 1T6. (514)481-5892. Managing Editor: Mrs. Judy Rochester. Magazine published 8 times/year primarily for men with incomes of over $30,000. "Covers anything happening on the wine scene in Canada." Circ. 14,600. Pays on publication. Byline given. Buys all rights. Submit seasonal/holiday material 3 months in advance. Pre-

fers letter quality to dot matrix printout submissions. Reports in 1 month.
Nonfiction: J. Rochester, articles editor. General interest; historical; humor; interview/profile; new product (and developments in the Canadian and US wine industries); opinion; personal experience; photo feature; travel (to wine-producing countries). "All must pertain to wine or wine-related topics and should reflect author's basic knowledge of and interest in wine." Buys 20-30 mss/year. Query with clips of published work or send complete ms. Length: 500-2,000 words. Pays $25-150.
Photos: State availability of photos. Pays $10-100 for color prints; $10 for b&w prints. Identification of subjects required. Buys one-time rights.

WINE WORLD MAGAZINE, Suite 115, 6308 Woodman Ave., Van Nuys CA 91401. (213)785-6050. Editor-Publisher: Dee Sindt. For the wine-loving public (adults of all ages) who wish to learn more about wine. Bimonthly magazine; 48 pages. Buys first North American serial rights. Buys about 50 mss/year. Pays on publication. Send $1 for sample copy and writer's guidelines. No photocopied submissions. Simultaneous submissions OK, "if spelled out." Reports in 30 days. Query. SASE.
Nonfiction: "Wine-oriented material written with an in-depth knowledge of the subject, designed to meet the needs of the novice and connoisseur alike. Wine technology advancements, wine history, profiles of vintners the world over. Educational articles only. No first-person accounts. Must be objective, informative reporting on economic trends, new technological developments in vinification, vine hybridizing, and vineyard care. New wineries and new marketing trends. We restrict our editorial content to wine, and wine-oriented material. Will accept restaurant articles—good wine lists. No more basic wine information. No articles from instant wine experts. Authors must be qualified in this highly technical field." Length: 750-2,000 words. Pays $50-100.

WOMEN'S CIRCLE HOME COOKING, Box 1952, Brooksville FL 33512. Editor: Barbara Hall Pedersen. For women (and some men) of all ages who really enjoy cooking. "Our readers collect and exchange recipes. They are neither food faddists nor gourmets, but practical women and men trying to serve attractive and nutritious meals. Many work fulltime, and most are on limited budgets." Monthly magazine; 72 pages. Circ. 225,000. Pays on acceptance. Buys all rights. Submit seasonal/holiday material 6 months in advance. No computer printout or disk submissions. SASE. Reports in 2-8 weeks. Sample copy for large SASE.
Nonfiction: Expose, historical, how-to, informational, inspirational, nostalgia, photo feature and travel. "We like a little humor with our food, for the sake of the digestion. Keep articles light. Stress economy and efficiency. Remember that at least half our readers must cook after working a fulltime job. Draw on personal experience to write an informative article on some aspect of cooking. We're a reader participation magazine. We don't go in for fad diets, or strange combinations of food which claim to cure anything." No medical advice or sick or gross humor. Buys 24 mss/year. Query. Length: 50-1,000 words. Pays 2-5¢/word.
Photos: State availability of photos. Pays $5 for 4x5 b&w or color sharp glossy prints; $35 minimum for 35 mm, 2¼x2¼ and 4x5 transparencies used on cover.
Fiction: Humorous fiction, related to cooking and foods. Length: 1,200 words maximum. Pays 2-5¢/word.
Poetry: Light verse related to cooking and foods. Length: 30 lines. Pays $5/verse.
Fillers: Short humorous fillers. Length: 100 words. Pays 2-5¢/word.
Tips: "We will buy slightly fewer mss in the year ahead due to an oversupply."

Games and Puzzles

Man's fascination with game playing and problem solving is verified by the existence of publications devoted to puzzles and games. These publications are written by and for game enthusiasts—people interested both in traditional games and word puzzles and newer role-playing adventure games. Other puzzle markets may be found in the Juvenile section.

CHESS LIFE, United States Chess Federation, 186 Route 9W, New Windsor NY 12550. (914)562-8350. Editor: Frank Elley. Monthly magazine covering the chess world. Circ. 60,000. Pays variable fee. Byline given. Offers kill fee. Buys all or negotiable rights. Submit seasonal/holiday material 8 months in advance. Simultaneous queries, and simultaneous, photocopied and previously published submissions OK. Computer printout submissions OK; prefers letter quality to dot matrix. SASE. Reports in 1 month. Free sample copy and writer's guidelines.
Nonfiction: General interest, historical/nostalgic, interview/profile, technical—all must have some relation to chess. No "stories about personal experiences with chess. Example: 'My First Chess Tournament.' " Buys 30-40 mss/year. Query with samples "if new to publication." Length: 3,000 words maximum.

Photos: Reviews b&w contact sheet and prints, and color prints and slides. Captions, model release and identification of subjects required. Buys all or negotiable rights.

Fiction: "Chess-related, high quality." Buys 1-2 mss/year. Pays variable fee.

Tips: "Articles must be written from an informed point of view—not from view of the curious amateur. Most of our writers are specialized in that they have sound credentials as chessplayers. Freelancers in major population areas (except New York and Los Angeles, which we already have covered) who are interested in short personality profiles and perhaps news reporting have the best opportunities. We're looking for more personality pieces on chessplayers around the country. Not just the stars, but local masters, talented youths, dedicated volunteers. Freelancers interested in such pieces might let us know of their interest and their range. Could be we know of an interesting story that needs covering in their territory."

‡**DRAGON® MAGAZINE, Monthly Adventure Role-Playing Aid**, TSR Hobbies, Inc., Box 110, Lake Geneva WI 53147. (414)248-3625. Editor: Kim Mohan. Monthly magazine of role-playing and adventure games and new trends in the gaming industry for adolescents and up. Circ. 120,000. Pays on publication. Byline given. Buys first North American serial rights for fiction; all rights for most articles. Submit seasonal/holiday material 6 months in advance. Simultaneous queries and photocopied submissions OK. SASE. Reports in 2 weeks on queries; 5 weeks on submissions. Sample copy $3; writer's guidelines for business size SAE and 2 first class stamps.

Nonfiction: Articles on the hobby of gaming and fantasy role-playing. No general articles on gaming hobby; "our article needs are *very* specialized. Writers should be experienced in gaming hobby and role-playing." Buys 100 mss/year. Query. Length: 1,000-10,000 words. Pays 3½-5¢/word.

Fiction: Patrick Price, fiction editor. Adventure, fantasy, science fiction, pieces which deal with gaming hobby. No fiction based on a religious, metaphysical or philosophical theme; no rehashes of other authors' work or ideas. Buys 10 mss/year. Query. Length: 3,000-10,000 words. Pays 4-6¢/word.

Tips: "*Dragon Magazine* and the related publications of Dragon Publishing are *not* periodicals that the 'average reader' appreciates or understands. A writer must *be* a reader, and must share the serious interest in gaming our readers possess."

GAMES, Playboy Enterprises, Inc., 515 Madison Ave., New York NY 10022. Editor: Ronnie Shushan. Monthly magazine featuring games, puzzles, mazes and brainteasers for people 18-49 interested in paper and pencil games. Circ. 650,000. Average issue includes 5-7 feature articles, paper and pencil games and fillers, bylined columns and 1-3 contests. Pays on publication. Byline given. Offers 25% kill fee. Buys all rights. Submit seasonal material 6 months in advance. Book reprints considered. Reports in 6 weeks. Free writer's guidelines with SASE.

Nonfiction: "We are looking for visual puzzles, rebuses, brainteasers and logic puzzles. We also want newsbreaks, new games, inventions, and news items of interest to game players." Buys 4-6 mss/issue. Query. Length: 500-2,000 words. Usually pays $110/published page.

Columns/Departments: Wild Cards (25-200 words, short brainteasers, 25-100 words plays, number games, anecdotes and quotes on games). Buys 6-10 mss/issue. Send complete ms. Length: 25-200 words. Pays $10-100.

Fillers: Editor: Will Shortz. Crosswords, cryptograms and word games. Pays $25-100.

‡**THE JOURNAL OF 20TH CENTURY WARGAMING**, 1002 Warrington Dr., Austin TX 78753. (512)475-6719. Editor: Nick Schuessler. Hobby gaming magazine published 4-6 times/year covering twentieth century wargaming and military history aimed for a mature, adult wargaming audience. Circ. 800. Pays on publication. Byline given. Simultaneous queries and simultaneous, photocopied and previously published submissions OK. SASE. Reports in 1 month. Sample copy $2.50; free writer's guidelines.

Nonfiction: Historical, new product, opinion. "All articles about games must deal with both the game itself, and also with the history that directs the game. Straight game review pieces, with simple descriptions of components and mechanics, are not accepted. Reviews or feature articles must compare the title under consideration to other titles previously published, as well as discuss both the history behind the game and how that history is (or is not) incorporated into the game design. Book reviews must provide a tie-in with either a game already published or a possible game topic." Query. Length: open. Pays negotiable rates "on a case by case" basis.

OFFICIAL CROSSWORD PUZZLES, DELL CROSSWORD PUZZLES, POCKET CROSSWORD PUZZLES, DELL WORD SEARCH PUZZLES, OFFICIAL WORD SEARCH PUZZLES, DELL PENCIL PUZZLES AND WORD GAMES, OFFICIAL PENCIL PUZZLES & WORD GAMES, DELL CROSSWORD SPECIALS, DELL CROSSWORDS AND VARIETY PUZZLES, DELL CROSSWORD PUZZLES PAPERBACK BOOK SERIES, Dell Puzzle Publications, 245 E. 47th St., New York NY 10017. Editor: Rosalind Moore. For "all ages from 8 to 80—people whose interests are puzzles, both crosswords and variety features." Buys all rights. SASE.

Puzzles: "We publish puzzles of all kinds, but the market here is limited to those who are able to construct quality pieces that can compete with the real professionals. See our magazines; they are the best guide to our needs. We publish quality puzzles, which are well-conceived and well-edited, with appeal to solvers of all ages and in about every walk of life. We are the world's leading publishers of puzzle publications and are distributed in many countries around the world in addition to the continental US. However, no foreign language puzzles, please! Our market for crosswords and Anacrostics is very small, since long-time contributors supply most of the needs in those areas. However, we are always willing to see material of unusual quality, or with a new or original approach. Since most of our publications feature variety puzzles in addition to the usual features, we are especially interested in seeing quizzes, picture features, and new and unusual puzzle features of all kinds. Please do not send us remakes of features we are now using. We are interested only in new ideas. Kriss Krosses and Word Searches are an active market here. However, constructors who wish to enter this field must query us first before submitting any material whatever. Prices vary with the feature, but ours are comparable with the highest in the general puzzle field."

ORIGINAL CROSSWORD PUZZLES, EASY-TIMED CROSSWORD PUZZLES, 387 Park Ave. S, New York NY 10016. (212)576-9246. Editorial Director: Arthur Goodman. Bimonthly. Buys all rights. Pays on acceptance. Refer to current issue available on newsstand as guide to type of material wanted. Submissions must be accompanied by SASE for return.
Puzzles: Original adult crossword puzzles; sizes 15x15 and 13x13; easy, medium and hard. Pays $10 minimum.

STRATEGY & TACTICS, Simulation Publications, Inc., 257 Park Ave. S., New York NY 10010. (212)673-4103. Managing Editor: Michael E. Moore. Bimonthly magazine covering military history for "professionally-oriented people in the hobby of adventure gaming." Circ. 35,000. Pays on publication. Byline given. Buys all rights. Reports in 1 month. Sample copy $6; writer's guidelines for SASE.
Nonfiction: Historical/political ("There are two major articles solicited from our stable of freelancers in each issue, each concentrating on a major battle, military campaign, historical period.) No general history and historical narrative-type articles not dealing with specific battles or campaigns." Buys 12 mss/year. Query. Length: 10,000-12,000 words. Pays 5¢/word.
Photos: State availability of photos. Reviews 8x10 b&w glossy prints.
Columns/Departments: Book reviews, adventure game reviews, historical trivia. Buys 50-200 mss/year. Send complete ms. "Historical trivia for 'For Your Information' column, book reviews and military/historical simulation game reviews are mostly unsolicited." Length: 500-1,000 words. Pays 3¢/word.
Tips: "The best way to break in is to thoroughly read a sample copy and play the game. It is awfully hard to understand the kind of information my readers want (and I need in an article) unless you have at least tried a game and seen a typical issue. Any writer who exhibits some knowledge of what a simulation game is, has a good military historical knowledge and background, and can write in English has a good chance of being commissioned by us. We are specifically looking for military (not general) historians and writers, and those who have no interest in or knowledge of military history and terminology would probably be wasting our time and theirs by submitting material."

‡THIEVES' GUILD, Gamelords, Ltd., 18616 Grosbeak Terrace, Gaithersburg MD 20879. (301)258-0775. Editor: Richard Meyer. Fantasy/science fiction, role-playing, adventure game scenarios published 3 times/ year for primarily male readers, ages 18 and up. "Role-playing adventures designed for thieves or other criminal types in fantasy/medieval world." Circ. 3,000-5,000. Pays royalty quarterly or on publication. Byline given. Buys variable rights ("please query") and makes work-for-hire assignments. Simultaneous queries, and simultaneous and photocopied submissions OK. SASE. Reports in 1 month on queries; 2 months on mss. Free sample copy and writer's guidelines.
Fiction: Fantasy and science fiction. "We publish role-playing game material *only*—no short stories, or other non-game material." Buys less than 10 mss/year. Query with published clips if available. Length: 5,000-20,000 words. "Payment is usually a royalty of varying percentages, depending on length and amount of editing necessary by editorial staff to meet game requirements. Please query."
Tips: "Some familiarity with how a role-playing game is played is essential, since a game scenario is not the same as a short story. Some background in fantasy or science fiction literature is helpful. We would be happy to provide further guidance to serious queries. Our biggest need is for fantasy role-playing scenarios (or science fiction). We have other publications besides *Thieves' Guild* and might be interested in other game ideas, particularly adventure or historical."

General Interest

Publications classified here are edited for national, general audiences and carry articles on a variety of subjects appealing to a broad spectrum of people. Other markets for general interest material will be found in these Consumer categories: Ethnic/Minority, In-Flight, Lifestyles, Men's, Regional, and Women's. Some company publications also cover general-interest topics.

‡**THE AMERICAN BYSTANDER, A Journal of Humor and Ideas,** 444 Park Ave. S, New York NY 10016. (212)362-9260. Editor: M.B. Kaye. Managing Editor: H. Berlin. Bimonthly tabloid covering the "original views of artists ad writers commenting humorously on all aspects of life. We're sort of an American *Punch*; *The American Bystander* is positioned to serve the audience that has outgrown *National Lampoon*, finds *The New Yorker* too conservative, and *Rolling Stone* topically restricted." Estab. 1982. Pays on acceptance. Byline given. Offers 20% kill fee. Buys first rights and second serial (reprint) rights. Submit seasonal/holiday material 4 months in advance. Simultaneous queries, and simultaneous and photocopied submissions OK. Computer printout submissions OK; prefers letter quality to dot matrix. SASE. Reports in 3 weeks. Sample copy for $2, 12x16 SAE and $1 postage; writer's guidelines for business size SAE and 1 first class stamp.
Nonfiction: Book excerpts, expose, general interest, historical/nostalgic, humor, opinion, personal experiences, photo feature. No self-help, how-tos. Buys 30 mss/year. Send complete ms. Length: 600-5,000 words. Pays $500-3,000.
Photos: Send photos with ms. Pays $50-500 for b&w and color prints. Buys 3-time rights: 1 for issue; 1 for reprint anthology; 1 for foreign.
Columns/Departments: Advertising; Wall Street/Finance; Show Business; General Observe columns. Buys 60 mss/year. Send complete ms. Length: 500-1,500 words. Pays $100-500.
Fiction: "All types as long as writing is honest, original, intelligent." Will be using more regional fiction. Buys 40 mss/year. Send complete ms. Length: 6,000 words maximum. Pays $500-2,000.
Poetry: Avant-garde, free verse, haiku, light verse, traditional. Buys 12/year. Length: open. Pays $50-500.
Fillers: Clippings, jokes, anecdotes, short humor, newsbreaks. Length: open.

THE AMERICAN LEGION MAGAZINE, Box 1055, Indianapolis IN 46206. (317)635-8411. Editor: Daniel S. Wheeler. Monthly. Circ. 2,500,000. Computer printout and disk submissions OK; prefers letter quality to dot matrix printouts. Reports on submissions "promptly." Buys first North American serial rights. Byline given. Pays on acceptance. SASE.
Nonfiction: Query first, but will consider unsolicited mss. "Prefer an outline query. Relate your article's thesis or purpose, tell why you are qualified to write it, the approach you will take and any authorities you intend to interview. War remembrance pieces of a personal nature (vs. historic in perspective) should be in ms form." Uses current world affairs, topics of contemporary interest, little-known happenings in American history and 20th century war-remembrance pieces. No personality profiles, travel or regional topics. Buys 60 mss/year. Length: 2,500 words maximum. Pays $100-1000.
Photos: Chiefly on assignment.
Poetry: Short, humorous verse. Pays $4.50/line, minimum $10.
Fillers: Short, tasteful jokes, humorous anecdotes and epigrams. Pays $10-20.
Tips: Query should include author's qualifications for writing a technical or complex article. Also include: thesis, length, outline and conclusion. "Send a thorough query into which some thought has obviously gone. Submit material that is suitable for us, showing that you have read several issues. Attach a few clips of previously published material. *The American Legion Magazine* is a general-interest publication which puts a premium on good taste and well-written articles about subjects of wide interest."

THE ATLANTIC MONTHLY, 8 Arlington St., Boston MA 02116. (617)536-9500. Editor-in-Chief: William Whitworth. For a professional, academic audience interested in politics, science, arts and general culture. Monthly magazine. Circ. 400,000. Pays soon after acceptance. Buys first North American serial rights. Pays negotiable kill fee "though chiefly to established writers." Byline given. Phone queries OK though written queries preferred. Submit seasonal/holiday material 3-5 months in advance. Simultaneous and photocopied submissions OK, if so indicated. SASE. Reports in 2-6 weeks. Sample copy $2.
Nonfiction: General interest, historical, humor, interview, nostalgia, personal experience, personal opinion, profile and travel. Query with clips of published work or send complete ms. Length: 1,000-6,000 words. Pays $1,500 and up/article.
Fiction: Mainstream. Buys 2 mss/issue. Send complete ms. Length: 2,000-6,000 words. Pays $2,000 and up/story.
Poetry: Avant-garde, free verse, light verse and traditional. "No concrete or haiku poetry." Buys 2-3 poems/issue. Submit in batches of 8 or less. Length: 100 lines maximum. Pays $3 and up/line.

A BETTER LIFE FOR YOU, The National Research Bureau, Inc., 424 N. 3rd St., Burlington IA 52601. (319)752-5415. Editor: Rhonda Wilson. Editorial Supervisor: Doris J. Ruschill. For industrial workers of all ages. Quarterly magazine. Pays on publication. Buys all rights. Previously published submissions OK. No computer printout or disk submissions. SASE. Reports in 3 weeks. Free writer's guidelines.
Nonfiction: General interest (steps to better health, on-the-job attitudes); how-to (perform better on the job, do home repair jobs, and keep up maintenance on a car). Buys 10-12 mss/year. Query or send outline. Length: 400-600 words. Pays 4¢/word.

CAPPER'S WEEKLY, Stauffer Communications, Inc., 616 Jefferson St., Topeka KS 66607. (913)295-1108. Editor: Dorothy Harvey. Emphasizes home and family for readers who live in small towns and on farms. Biweekly tabloid. Circ. 416,000. Pays for poetry on acceptance; articles on publication. Buys first North American serial rights: Submit seasonal/holiday material 2 months in advance. SASE. Reports in 3 weeks, 2 months for serialized novels. Sample copy 50¢.
Nonfiction: Historical (local museums, etc.), inspirational, nostalgia, travel (local slants) and people stories (accomplishments, collections, etc.). Buys 25 mss/year. Submit complete ms. Length: 700 words maximum. Pays $1/inch.
Photos: Purchased with accompanying ms. Submit prints. Pays $5 for 8x10 b&w glossy prints. Total purchase price for ms includes payment for photos. Limited market for color photos (35mm color slides, please).
Columns/Departments: Heart of the Home (homemakers' letters, recipes, hints), Hometown Heartbeat (descriptive). Submit complete ms. Length: 300 words maximum. Pays $2-10.
Fiction: Novel-length mystery and romance mss. No explicit sex, violence or profanity. Buys 2-3 mss/year. Query. Pays $150-200.
Poetry: Free verse, haiku, light verse, traditional. Buys 4-5/issue. Limit submissions to batches of 5-6. Length: 4-16 lines. Pays $3-5.
Tips: "Study a few issues of publication. Most rejections are for material that is 1) too long; 2) unsuitable (as short stories which we never use); or 3) out of character for our paper (too sexy, too much profanity, etc.). On occasion we must cut material to fit column space."

CHANGING TIMES, The Kiplinger Magazine, 1729 H St. NW, Washington DC 20006. Editor: Marjorie White. For general, adult audience interested in consumer information. Monthly. Circ. 1,500,000. Buys all rights. Reports in 1 month. SASE. Pays on acceptance. Thorough documentation required.
Nonfiction: "Most material is staff-written but we accept some freelance." Query with clips of published work. Bylines only on lighthearted personal essays, 500 words.

THE CHRISTIAN SCIENCE MONITOR, 1 Norway St., Boston MA 02115. (617)262-2300, ext. 2303. Editor: Earl W. Foell. International newspaper issued daily except Saturdays, Sundays and holidays in North America; weekly international edition. Special issues: travel, winter vacation and international travel, summer vacation, autumn vacation, and others. February and September: fashion. Circ. 184,000. Buys all newspaper rights for 3 months following publication. Buys limited number of mss, "top quality only." Pays on acceptance or publication, "depending on department." Submit seasonal material 2 months in advance. Reports in 4 weeks. Submit only complete original ms. SASE.
Nonfiction: Feature Editor, Robert P. Hey. In-depth features and essays. "Style should be bright but not cute, concise but thoroughly researched. Try to humanize news or feature writing so reader identifies with it. Avoid sensationalism, crime and disaster. Accent constructive, solution-oriented treatment of subjects. Home Forum page buys essays of 400-800 words. Pays $50-100. Buys poetry of high quality in a wide variety (traditional, blank and free verse). Pays $20 average. Education, arts, real estate, travel, living, garden, furnishings, and science pages will consider articles not usually more than 800 words appropriate to respective subjects." Pays $50-100.

COMMENTARY, 165 E. 56th St., New York NY 10022. (212)751-4000. Editor: Norman Podhoretz. Monthly magazine. Circ. 50,000. Buys all rights. Byline given. "All of our material is done freelance, though much of it is commissioned." Pays on publication. Query, or submit complete ms. Reports in 1 month. SASE.
Nonfiction: Editor: Brenda Brown. Thoughtful essays on political, social and cultural themes; general, as well as with special Jewish content. Length: 3,000 to 7,000 words. Pays approximately $100/printed page.
Fiction: Editor: Marion Magid. Uses some mainstream fiction. Length: varies.

THE DEAF CANADIAN MAGAZINE, Box 1291, Edmonton, Alberta, Canada T5J 2M8. Editor: David Burnett. For "general consumers who are deaf, parents of deaf children/adults, professionals on deafness, teachers, ministers, and government officials." Monthly magazine. Circ. 160,000. Pays on publication. "Although the publication is copyrighted, we do not purchase any rights which are reserved to the individual contributor." Byline given. Submit seasonal/holiday material 2 months in advance. Simultaneous, photocopied and previously published submissions OK. *Contributions cannot be acknowledged or returned.* Sample copy $3.

Nonfiction: Expose (education), how-to (skills, jobs, etc.), historical, humor, informational (deafness difficulties), inspirational, interview, new product, personal experience, personal opinion, photo feature (with captions), profile, technical and travel. "Mss must relate to deafness or the deaf world." Buys 1-10 mss/issue. Submit complete ms. Length: 3,000 words maximum. Pays $20-100. "Articles should be illustrated with at least 4 good b&w photos."

Photos: Purchased with accompanying ms or on assignment. Captions required (not less than 15 words). Query. Pays $20 for 2½x3 (preferably) and 5x7 b&w glossy prints; $100 for color transparencies used as cover. Total purchase price for ms includes payment for photos.

Columns/Departments: Here and There, Sports and Recreation, Foreign, Cultural Events and Books. Submit complete ms. Length: 1 page maximum. Pays $30-100. Open to suggestions for new columns/departments.

Fiction: Adventure, experimental, historical, humorous, mystery, mainstream, religious, romance, science fiction, suspense, condensed novels and serialized novels. Buys 1-10 mss/issue. Length: 3,000 words maximum. Pays $50-100.

Fillers: Clippings, jokes, gags, anecdotes, newsbreaks, puzzles and short humor. Must be related to deafness or the deaf world. Buys 1-20 mss/issue. Submit complete ms. Length: 1 page maximum. Pays $1-50.

‡**DIALOGUE, The Magazine for the Visually Impaired**, Dialogue Publications, Inc., 3100 Oak Park Ave., Berwyn IL 60402. (312)749-1908. Editor: Louise Kimbrough. Quarterly magazine of issues, topics and opportunities related to the visually impaired. Pays on acceptance. Byline given. Buys all rights "with generous reprint rights." Submit seasonal/holiday material 6 months in advance. Photocopied submissions OK. SASE. Reports in 2 weeks on queries; 1 month on mss. Free sample copy to visually-impaired writers; writer's guidelines for business-size SAE and 1 first class stamp.

Nonfiction: "Writers should indicate nature and severity of visual handicap." How-to (cope with various aspects of blindness); humor; interview/profile; new product (of interest to visually impaired); opinion; personal experience; technical (adaptations for use without sight); travel (personal experiences of visually-impaired travelers); and first person articles about careers in which individual blind persons have succeeded. No "Aren't blind people wonderful" articles; articles that are slanted towards sighted general audience. Buys 60 mss/year. Query with published clips or submit complete ms. Length: 3,000 words maximum. Prefers shorter lengths but will use longer articles if subject warrants. Pays $10-50.

Photos: Paula Oto, photo editor. Photographs of paintings, sculpture and pottery by visually-handicapped artists; and photos taken by visually-impaired persons. State availability or send photos with ms. Pays $10-20 for 3½x4¾ b&w prints. Identification of subjects required. Buys one-time rights.

Columns/Departments: ABAPITA ("Ain't Blindness a Pain in the Anatomy")—short anecdotes relating to blindness; Recipe Round-UP; Around the House (household hints); Vox Pop (see magazine); Puzzle Box (see magazine and guidelines); book reviews of books written by visually-impaired authors; Beyond the Armchair (travel personal experience); Backscratcher (a column of questions, answers, hints). Buys 80 mss/year. Send complete ms. Payment varies.

Fiction: "Writers should state nature and severity of visual handicap." Annette Victorin, fiction editor. Adventure, fantasy, historical, humorous, mainstream, mystery, science fiction, suspense, western. No plotless fiction or stories with unbelievable characters; no horror; no explicit sex and no vulgar language. Buys 12 mss/year. Send complete ms. Length: 3,000 words maximum; shorter lengths preferred. Pays $10-50.

Poetry: "Writers should indicate nature and severity of visual impairment." Annette Victorin, poetry editor. Free verse, haiku, light verse, traditional. No religious poetry or any poetry with more than 20 lines. Buys 30 poems/year. Submit maximum 3 poems. Length: 20 lines maximum. Pays $5-20.

Fillers: Jokes, anecdotes, short humor. Buys few mss/year. Length: 100 words maximum. Payment varies.

Tips: "*Dialogue* cannot consider manuscripts from authors with 20/20 vision or those who can read regular print with ordinary glasses. Any person unable to read ordinary print who has helpful information to share with others in this category will find a ready market. We believe that blind people are capable, competent, responsible citizens and the material we publish reflects this view. This is not to say we never sound a negative note but criticism should be constructive."

EASY LIVING MAGAZINE, The Webb Co., 1999 Shepard Rd., St. Paul MN 55116. (612)690-7228. Editor: Paula Kringle. Associate Editor: Gayle Bonneville. Emphasizes financial topics, personal improvement, lifestyle, family activities, consumer, travel and food articles for a high-income audience 30-60 years of age. Distributed by Creative Marketing Enterprises, Inc. Quarterly magazine. Circ. 250,000. Pays on acceptance. Buys one-time rights and nonexclusive reprint rights. Submit seasonal/holiday material 1 year in advance. Photocopied submissions OK. SASE. Reports on queries and mss in 3-6 weeks. Free sample copy and writer's guidelines. Nonfiction only. Query. Length: 1,000-2,000 words. Pays $200-500.

Photos: Contact Rudy Schnasse at (612)690-7396 for current rates.

‡**EQUINOX: THE MAGAZINE OF CANADIAN DISCOVERY**, Equinox Publishing, 7 Queen Victoria Dr., Camden East, Ontario, Canada K0K 1J0. (613)378-6651. Editor: James Lawrence. Executive Editor: Frank B. Edwards. Managing Editor: Barry Estabrook. Bimonthly magazine. "We publish in-depth profiles

of people, places and animals to show readers the real stories behind subjects of general interest in the fields of science and geography.'' Circ. 150,000. Pays on acceptance. Byline given. Offers 50% kill fee. Buys first North American serial rights. Submit seasonal/holiday material 1 year in advance. SAE and IRCs. Computer printout submissions OK; prefers letter quality to dot matrix. Reports in 6 weeks. Sample copy $5; free writer's guidelines.

Nonfiction: Book excerpts (occasionally); geography; science; art. No travel articles. Buys 40 mss/year. Query. ''Our biggest need is for science stories. We do not touch unsolicited feature manuscripts.'' Length: 5,000-10,000 words. Pays $1,000-negotiated.

Photos: Send photos with ms. Reviews color transparencies—must be of professional quality; no prints or negatives. Captions and identification of subjects required. Buys one-time rights.

Columns/Departments: Kathryn MacDonald, editor. Nexus, current science that isn't covered by daily media. ''Our most urgent need.'' Buys 80/year. Query with clips of published work. Length: 500-1,000 words. Pays $100-300.

Tips: Submit 'Nexus' ideas to us—the 'only' route to a feature is through the 'Nexus' department if writers are untried.''

FAMILY WEEKLY, 1515 Broadway, New York NY 10036. Editor: Arthur Cooper. Managing Editor: Tim Mulligan. No longer accepting unsolicited mss, but will consider queries. SASE.

FORD TIMES, Ford Motor Co., Box 1899, The American Rd., Rm. 765, Dearborn MI 48121. Managing Editor: Arnold S. Hirsch. ''General-interest magazine designed to attract all ages.'' Monthly magazine. Circ. 1,000,000. Buys first serial rights. Pays kill fee. Byline given. Buys about 100 mss/year. Pays on acceptance. Free sample copy and writer's guidelines. Submit seasonal material 6 months in advance. Computer printout submissions OK. Reports in 2 months. SASE.

Nonfiction: ''Almost anything relating to contemporary American life that leans toward the upbeat. Topics include vacation ideas, personality profiles, insights into big cities and small towns, the arts, the outdoors, and sports. We strive to be colorful, lively and, above all, interesting. We try to avoid subjects that have appeared in other publications or in our own.'' Length: 1,500-2,000 words maximum. Query required unless previous contributor. Pays $400 minimum for full-length articles.

Photos: ''Speculative submission of high-quality color transparencies and b&w photos with mss is welcomed. We need bright, geographically strong photos showing people. We need releases for people whose identity is readily apparent in photos.''

FUTURIFIC MAGAZINE, 280 Madison Ave., New York NY 10016. (212)684-4913. Editor: Balint Szent-Miklosy. Monthly. The name derives from future and terrific. ''We report on what is coming in all areas of life from international affairs to the arts and sciences. Mostly read by high income, well-educated government and corporate people.'' Circ. 6,000. Pays on publication. Byline given. Buys one-time rights. Simultaneous, photocopied and previously published submissions OK. Computer printout submissions OK. SASE. Reports in 1 week. Sample copy for 9x12 SAE and 37¢ postage.

Nonfiction: Book excerpts, expose, general interest, how to forecast the future—seriously; humor, interview/profile, new product, photo feature, technical. No historical, opinion or gloom and doom. Send complete ms. Length: 5,000 words maximum. Pay is open. ''The writer tells us how much. If the material and price are right, we are in business.''

Photos: Send photos with ms. Reviews b&w prints. ''The photographer lets us know how much he/she wants.'' Identification of subjects required.

Columns/Departments: Medical breakthroughs, new products, inventions, etc. ''Anything that is new or about to be new.'' Send complete ms. Length: 5,000 words maximum. ''The writer tells us the price. We either accept or reject.''

Poetry: Avant-garde, free verse, haiku, light verse, traditional. ''Must deal with the future.'' No gloom and doom or sad poetry. Buys 12/year. Submit unlimited number of poems. Length: open. Pay is ''up to the poet.''

Fillers: Clippings, jokes, gags, anecdotes, short humor, newsbreaks. ''Must deal with the future.'' Length: open. Pay is ''up to the person submitting.''

Tips: ''We seek to maintain a light-hearted, professional look at forecasting. Be upbeat and show a loving expectation for the marvels of the future.''

GEO, Knapp Communications Corp., 600 Madison Ave., New York NY 10022. (212)223-0001. Contact: David Maxey. Monthly magazine giving ''a new view of our world in terms of science, environment, places and issues for sophisticated people with wide ranging international interests.'' Circ. 250,000. Pays on acceptance. Buys first North American serial rights. Submit seasonal material 4 months in advance. Simultaneous and photocopied submissions OK. SASE. Reports in 2 months. Sample copy $5.

Nonfiction: Historical (natural history); interview (of authorities in fields of *Geo*'s interest); opinion (essays); personal experience; photo feature (of recent topics, such as the tops of New York skyscrapers or machine parts as art); technical (frontiers of technology, science and medicine); and new scientific thinking, top level scientific research, such as studying the squid to learn about the human nervous system. "No pure travel pieces." Buys 8-10 mss/issue. "It is relatively rare that we use an unsolicited manuscript, and we do not encourage their submission. We prefer concise, clearly stated queries, explaining the story idea, the proposed approach and the photographic possibilities. Short clips from other publications are helpful. *Geo* stories often require a hefty investment, so it is unusual that we send an inexperienced writer on assignment." Query with clips of published work. Length: 3,000 words maximum. Pays $2,500 average. "The writer does not need to be an authority but must get to the top people in science, the environment and current issues."

Photos: Elizabeth Biondi, editor. State availability of photos. Reviews all sizes color prints and transparencies. Gives guarantee upon acceptance against $250/page upon publication. Captions and model release required. Buys one-time rights.

Tips: "All story ideas must have a very strong photo tie-in. You need not take photos. *Geo* will provide the photographer."

GLOBE, Cedar Square, 2112 S. Congress Ave., West Palm Beach FL 33406. Assistant Editor: Bill Dick. "For everyone in the family over 18. *Globe* readers are the same people you meet on the street, and in supermarket lines, average hard-working Americans who prefer easily digested tabloid news." Weekly national tabloid newspaper. Circ. 2,000,000. Byline given. SASE.

Nonfiction, Photos and Fillers: Photo Editor: Alistair Duncan. We want features on well-known personalities, offbeat people, places, events and activities. No personal essays. Current issue is best guide. Stories are best that don't grow stale quickly. No padding. Remember—we are serving a family audience. All material must be in good taste. If it's been written up in a major newspaper or magazine, we already know about it." Buys informational, how-to, interview, profile, inspirational, humor, historical, exposé, photo, spot news. Length: 1,000 words maximum; average 500-800 words. Pays $250 maximum (special rates for "blockbuster" material). Photos are purchased with or without ms, and on assignment. Captions are required. Pays $50 minimum for 8x10 b&w glossy prints. "Competitive payment on exclusives."

Tips: "*Globe* is constantly looking for human interest subject material from throughout the United States and much of the best comes from America's smaller cities and villages, not necessarily from the larger urban areas. Therefore, we are likely to be more responsive to an article from a new writer than many other publications. This, of course, is equally true of photographs. A major mistake of new writers is that they have failed to determine the type and style of our content and in the ever-changing tabloid field, this is a most important consideration. It is also wise to keep in mind that what is of interest to you or to the people in your area may not be of equal interest to a national readership. Determine the limits of interest first. And, importantly, the material you send us must be such that it won't be 'stale' by the time it reaches the readers."

GOOD READING, Henry F. Henrichs Publications, Litchfield IL 62056. (217)324-2322. Monthly magazine. Circ. 12,000. Buys 10-15 unsolicited mss/year. Computer printout and disk submissions OK; prefers letter quality to dot matrix printouts. Buys first North American serial rights. Pays on acceptance. SASE.

Nonfiction: Accurate articles on current or factual subjects, adventure or important places. Material based on incidents related to business or personal experiences that reveal the elements of success in human relationships. Humorous material welcome. Uses one quiz a month. All published material is wholesome and noncontroversial. "We particularly enjoy historical travel articles or foreign travel articles with clear, b&w glossy photos, and we avoid material that emphasizes the financial aspects of traveling." No "over emphasized or common topics; no how-to articles or expositions." Length: 500-900 words. Pays $20-100.

Photos: Good quality b&w glossy prints illustrating an article are desirable and should be submitted with the article.

Fillers: 200-500 words. Pays $10-20.

Poetry: Does not pay for poetry, but publishes 4-5/month. Prefers pleasantly rhythmic humorous or uplifting material of 4-16 lines.

Tips: "We have raised the rate of payment slightly, especially for manuscripts accompanied by b/w glossy photographs."

GRIT, Stauffer Communications, Inc., 208 W. 3rd St., Williamsport PA 17701. (717)326-1771. Editor: Naomi L. Woolever. For a general readership of all ages in small-town and rural America. Tabloid newspaper. Weekly. Circ. 900,000. Buys first serial rights and second serial (reprint) rights. Byline given. Buys 1,000-1,500 mss/year. Pays on acceptance for freelance material; on publication for reader participation feature material. Sample copy $1; free writer's guideline. Reports in 2-4 weeks. Query or submit complete ms. No computer printouts or disk submissions. SASE.

Nonfiction and Photos: Assignment Editor: Joanne Decker. "Want mss about six basic areas of interest: people, religion, jobs (how individuals feel about their work), recreation, spirit of community (tradition or nostalgia that binds residents of a town together), necessities (stories about people and how they cope—food, shelter, etc.) Also want sociological pieces about rural transportation and health problems or how a town deals effectively with vandalism or crime. Also first person articles of 300 words or less about a person's narrowest escape, funniest moment, a turning point in life or recollections of something from the past, i.e. a flood, a fire, or some other dramatic happening that the person experienced." Wants good Easter, Christmas and holiday material. Mss should show some person or group involved in an unusual and/or uplifting way. "We lean heavily toward human interest, whatever the subject. Writing should be simple and down-to-earth." No "articles promoting alcoholic beverages, immoral behavior, narcotics, unpatriotic acts." Length: 500 words maximum. Pays 12¢/word for first or exclusive rights; 6¢/word for second or reprint rights. Photos purchased with or without ms. Captions required. Size: prefers 8x10 for b&w, but will consider 5x7. Transparencies only for color. Pays $25 for b&w photos accompanying ms; $100 for front cover color.

Poetry: Joanne Decker. Buys traditional forms of poetry and light verse. Length: preferably 20 lines maximum. Pays $6 for 4 lines and under, plus 50¢/line for each additional line.

Tips: "The freelancer would do well to write for a copy of our Guidelines for Freelancers. Everything is spelled out there about how-to's, submission methods, etc. All manuscripts should include in upper right-hand corner of first page the number of words and whether it's first or second rights."

HARPER'S MAGAZINE, 2 Park Ave., Room 1809, New York NY 10016. (212)481-5220. Editor: Michael Kinsley. 90% freelance written. For well-educated, socially concerned, widely read men and women and college students who are active in community and political affairs. Monthly. Circ. 140,000. Rights purchased vary with author and material. Buys approximately 6 non-agented, non-commissioned, non-book-excerpted mss/year. Pays negotiable kill fee. Byline given. Pays on acceptance. Sample copy $2.50. Will look only at material submitted through agents or that which is the result of a query. Computer printout submissions OK "if easily readable; prefers letter quality to dot matrix. Reports in 5 weeks. SASE.

Nonfiction: "For writers working with agents or who will query first only, our requirements are: public affairs, literary, international and local reporting, humor." No interviews. Also buys exposés and essays. Complete mss and queries must include SASEs. No unsolicited fiction or poems will be accepted. Length: 1,500-6,000 words. Pays $250-1,500.

Photos: Jan Drews, art director. Occasionally purchased with mss; others by assignment. Pays $35-400.

Columns/Departments: Publishes pieces between 1,000 and 2,000 words as columns in both the front and back of the magazine. "These should be construed as topical essays on all manner of subjects (politics, the arts, crime, business, etc.) to which the author can bring the force of passionately informed statements."

‡THE HUMAN, A Magazine of Life Issues, The Uncertified Human Publishing Co., Ltd., 1295 Gerrard St., E., Toronto, Ontario, Canada M4L 1Y8. (416)535-6487. Editor: Jessica M. Pegis. Managing Editor: Denyse Handler. Monthly magazine covering life and death issues and social concerns in a technological society for college-educated readers whose concern is "the enhancement of human life before and after birth. They like analysis—no lectures or movement rhetoric." Circ. 10,000. Pays on publication. Byline given. Not copyrighted. Buys first North American serial rights and second serial (reprint) rights. Submit seasonal/holiday material 6 months in advance. Simultaneous queries, and simultaneous, photocopied and previously published submissions "OK as long as identified as such." SASE. Reports in 6 weeks. Sample copy $1; writer's guidelines $1. "Please send International Postage Coupons for manuscripts. US stamps end up in our 'Stamps Around the World Album.'"

Nonfiction: Exposé (on medical racketeering); general interest ("we're happy to look at medium length articles on death and dying, suicide, child abuse, adoption, food and population concerns in developing countries. Will consider articles on TV violence, capital punishment or the psychology of war"); humor (coping with a handicap, growing old); interview/profile (of people active in field of human rights); new product (for the retarded or physically handicapped); opinion (500 words on any subject relative to our concerns); technical (prenatal surgery, fetal alcohol syndrome and drug addiction; premature baby survival; biological aspects of aging; enhancing the potential of the mentally retarded through special education; new family planning methods, excluding abortion). "No religious tracts, unresearched opinions, term essays, anything that would offend any reasonable minority or oppose the legal right to life of any group including children before birth. No population doomsday or anti-people rhetoric." Buys 10-12 mss/year. Query with published clips. Length: 1,000-2,800 words. Pays 3¢/word (Canadian funds).

Columns/Departments: Opinion; Quiz (question/answer column, approx. 200 words, presenting factual and statistical information in a succinct, readable way, e.g., "What is the percentage of retarded children in Ontario currently enrolled in a school program?"). "We're looking for cliché busters in this column." Buys 2-3 mss/year. Send complete ms. Length: 100-300 words. Pays 3¢/word (Canadian funds).

Poetry: Free verse, light verse, limericks. "No anti-abortion poems or social justice discourses." Buys 2-3 poems/year. Submit maximum 3 poems. Length: 2-12 lines. Pays 25¢/line (Canadian funds).

Tips: "Keep writing fresh, pungent and jargon free. We welcome new writers and are happy to see them develop, but our standards are high. A sample of your work, published or not, is essential. We are interested in reviews of books, plays and movies pertaining to science or medicine and human rights."

IDEALS MAGAZINE, 11315 Watertown Plank Rd., Milwaukee WI 53226. Vice-President, Publishing: James A. Kuse. Editor: Ralph Luedtke. Family-oriented magazine of general interest published 8 times/year with seasonal themes: Valentine's Day, Easter, Mother's Day, Father's Day, friendship, Americana, Thanksgiving

Day and Christmas. Pays on publication. Byline given. Buys one-time rights. Submit seasonal material 6 months in advance. Photocopied and previously published submissions OK. Reports on mss in 6 weeks. Sample copy for $1 postage and handling; writer's guidelines for SASE.

Nonfiction: General interest (holidays, seasons, family, nature, crafts); nostalgia (family oriented); profile (notable people); and travel. Buys 8-10 mss/issue. Length: 800 words minimum. Query or send complete ms. Pays $100-300.

Photos: State availability of photos with ms. Buys one-time rights.

Fiction: Limited use. Length: 800 words minimum.

Poetry: Short to medium length. Pays variable rate.

KNOWLEDGE, Official Publication of the World Olympiads of Knowledge, RSC Publishers, 568 Trail Lake Dr., Drawer 16489, Ft. Worth TX 76133. (817)292-4272. Editor: Dr. O.A. Battista. Managing Editor: N.L. Matous. For lay and professional audiences of all occupations. Quarterly magazine; 60 pages. Circ. 1,000. Pays on publication. Buys all rights. Byline given. Submit seasonal/holiday material 6 months in advance. No computer printouts or disk submissions. SASE. Reports in 2 weeks. Sample copy $4.

Nonfiction: Informational—original new knowledge that will prove mentally or physically beneficial to all lay readers. Buys 30 unsolicited mss/year. Query. Length: 1,500 words maximum. Pays $50 minimum.

Columns/Departments: Journal section uses maverick and speculative ideas that other magazines will not publish and reference.

L'ACTUALITE, Maclean Hunter, 625 President Kennedy, Montreal, Quebec, Canada H3A 1K5. (514)845-5141. Editor: Mr. Jean Pare. Monthly French language magazine featuring international and lifestyles reporting. Circ. 250,000. Pays on acceptance. Byline given. Buys first North American serial or one-time rights. Submit seasonal/holiday material 4 months in advance. Simultaneous queries and photocopied submissions OK. SASE. Reports in 2 weeks. Free sample copy.

Nonfiction: General interest, interview/profile. Special issues include skiing. Buys 70 mss/year. Query. Length: 1,500-2,700 words. Pays $500-1,000.

LIFE, Time & Life Bldg., Rockefeller Center, New York NY 10020. (212)841-3871. Managing Editor: Richard B. Stolley. Monthly general interest picture magazine for people of all ages, backgrounds and interests. Circ. 1.3 million. Average issue includes one feature. Pays on acceptance. Byline given. Offers $500 kill fee. Buys first North American serial rights. Submit seasonal material 2-3 months in advance. Simultaneous and photocopied submissions OK. Computer printout submissions OK, prefers letter quality to dot matrix. SASE. Reports in 6 weeks on queries; immediately on mss.

Nonfiction: "We've done articles on anything in the world of interest to the general reader and on people of importance. It's extremely difficult to break in since we buy so few articles. Most of the magazine is pictures. We're looking for very high quality writing. We select writers who we think match the subject they are writing about." Buys 1-2 mss/issue. Query with clips of previously published work. Length: 2,000-5,000 words. Pays $3,000 minimum.

Columns/Departments: Portrait (1,200-word essay on a well-known person). "We like to do these on people in the news." Buys 1 ms/issue. Query with clips of previously published work. Length: 1,200 words. Pays $2,000.

MACLEAN'S, Maclean Hunter Bldg., 777 Bay St., 7th, Toronto, Canada M5W 1A7. (416)596-5386. Contact: Section Editors (listed in masthead). For news-oriented audience. Weekly newsmagazine; 90 pages. Circ. 650,000. Frequently buys first North American serial rights. Pays on acceptance. "Query with 200- or 300-word outline before sending material." Reports in 2 weeks. Computer printout and disk submissions (MO-PASS) OK. SAE and International Reply Coupons.

Nonfiction: "We have the conventional newsmagazine departments (Canada, world, business, people, plus science, medicine, law, art, music, etc.) with roughly the same treatment as other newsmagazines. We specialize in subjects that are primarily of Canadian interest and there is now more emphasis on international—particularly U.S.—news. Most material is now written by staffers or retainer freelancers, but we are open to suggestions from abroad, especially in world, business and departments (like medicine, lifestyles, etc.). Freelancers should write for a free copy of the magazine and study the approach." Length: 400-3,500 words. Pays $300-1,500.

NATIONAL ENQUIRER, Lantana FL 33464. Editor: Iain Calder. Weekly tabloid. Circ. 5,250,000. Pays on acceptance at executive level, or negotiable kill fee. Query. "Story idea must be accepted first. We're no longer accepting unsolicited mss and all spec material will be returned unread." SASE.

Nonfiction and Photos: Any subject appealing to a mass audience. Requires fresh slant on topical news stories, waste of taxpayers' money by government, the entire field of the occult, how-to articles, rags to riches success stories, medical firsts, scientific breakthroughs, human drama, adventure and personality profiles. "The best way to understand our requirements is to study the paper." Pays $375-600 for most completed features, plus separate lead fees; more with photos. "Payments in excess of $2,000 are not unusual; we will pay more for really top, circulation-boosting blockbusters." Uses single or series b&w and color photos that must be attention-grabbing. Wide range; anything from animal photos to great action photos. "We'll bid against any other magazine for once-in-lifetime pictures."

NATIONAL GEOGRAPHIC MAGAZINE, 17th and M Sts. NW, Washington DC 20036. Editor: Wilbur E. Garrett. Address queries to Senior Assistant Editor. For members of the National Geographic Society. Monthly. Circ. 10,700,000. 50% freelance written. Buys first publication rights for magazine, with warranty to use the material in other National Geographic Society copyrighted publications for additional compensation. Pays 50% kill fee. Byline given. Buys 40-50 mss/year. Pays on acceptance. Reports in 2-4 weeks. Query by letter. Writers should study several recent issues of *National Geographic* and send for leaflets "Writing for *National Geographic*" and "*National Geographic* Photo Requirements." SASE. Sample copy $1.70.
Nonfiction and Photos: "First-person narratives, making it easy for the reader to share the author's experience and observations. Writing should include plenty of human-interest incident, authentic direct quotation, and a bit of humor where appropriate. Accuracy is fundamental. Contemporary problems such as those of pollution and ecology are treated on a factual basis. The magazine is especially seeking short American place pieces with a strong regional 'people' flavor. The use of many clear, sharp color photographs in all articles makes lengthy word descriptions unnecessary. Potential writers need not be concerned about submitting photos. These are handled by professional photographers. Historical background, in most cases, should be kept to the minimum needed for understanding the present." Length: 8,000 words maximum for major articles. Shorts of 2,000-4,000 words "are always needed." Pays $3,000-8,000 (and, in some cases, more) for acceptable articles. "A paragraph on an article idea should be submitted to the senior assistant editor. Please do not phone. If the idea is appealing, he will ask for a two-page outline for further consideration." Photographers are advised to submit a generous selection of photographs with brief, descriptive captions to Bruce A. McElfresh, Assistant Editor.
Tips: "Send 4 or 5 one-paragraph ideas. If any are promising, author will be asked for an outline. Read the latest issues to see what we want."

THE NEW YORK ANTIQUE ALMANAC, The New York Eye Publishing Co., Inc., Box 335, Lawrence NY 11559. (516)371-3300. Editor-in-Chief: Carol Nadel. Emphasizes antiques, art, investments and nostalgia. Tabloid published 10 times/year. Circ. 42,000. Pays on publication. Buys all rights. Byline given. Phone queries OK. Submit seasonal/holiday material "whenever available." Previously published submissions OK but must advise. SASE. Reports in 6 weeks. Free sample copy.
Nonfiction: Expose (fraudulent practices); historical (museums, exhibitions, folklore, background of events); how-to (clean, restore, travel, shop, invest); humor (jokes, cartoons, satire); informational; inspirational (essays); interviews (authors, shopkeepers, show managers, appraisers); nostalgia ("The Good Old Days" remembered various ways); personal experience (anything dealing with antiques, art, investments, nostalgia); opinion; photo feature (antique shows, art shows, fairs, crafts markets, restorations); profile; technical (repairing, purchasing, restoring); travel (shopping guides and tips) and investment; economics, and financial reviews. Also purchases puzzles and quizzes related to antiques or nostalgia. Pays $25. Buys 9 mss/issue. Query or submit complete ms. Length: 3,000 words maximum. Pays $15-70. "Expenses for accompanying photos will be reimbursed."
Photos: "Occasionally, we have photo essays (auctions, shows, street fairs, human interest) and pay $5/photo with caption."
Fillers: Personal experiences, commentaries, anecdotes. "Limited only by author's imagination." Buys 45 mss/year. Pays $5-15.
Tips: "Articles on shows or antique coverage accompanied by photos are definitely preferred."

THE NEW YORKER, 25 W. 43rd St., New York NY 10036. Editor: William Shawn. Weekly. Circ. 500,000. Reports in 2 months. Pays on acceptance. SASE.
Nonfiction, Fiction and Fillers: Single factual pieces run from 3,000-10,000 words. Long fact pieces are usually staff-written. So is "Talk of the Town," although ideas for this department are bought. Pays good rates. Uses fiction, both serious and light, from 1,000-6,000 words. About 90% of the fillers come from contributors with or without taglines (extra pay if the tagline is used).

THE OLD FARMER'S ALMANAC, Yankee Publishing, Inc., Dublin, NH 03444. (603)563-8111. Editor: Judson D. Hale, Sr. Annual magazine; "a traditional collection of astronomical information, weather forecasts, and feature articles related to country living, for a general audience." Circ. 3.5 million. Pays on acceptance. Byline given. Rights purchased are negotiable. Submit material for the next year's issue by February. Photocopied submissions OK. Computer printout submissions OK. SASE. Reports in 1 month.
Nonfiction: Historical, humor, biography, gardening, science and philosophy. "We want fresh and unusual material. This is a national magazine with a nationwide readership." Buys 5-10 mss/year. Query with clips of published work. Length: 1,500 words average. Pays $300 minimum.

Columns/Departments: Anecdotes and Pleasantries (short, self-contained items); and Rainy Day Amusements (puzzles, word games, quizzes). Buys 10 mss/year. Send complete ms. Length: 250-500 words. Pays $50 and up.
Fillers: Anecdotes. Length: 300 words minimum.

ON MAGAZINE, The Positive News of People and Events, Scott/Shannon Inc., Box 4822, Springfield MO 65808. (417)864-8820. Publisher: Doug Wead. Editor: Mary Achor. Quarterly magazine. Circ. 200,000. Pays on publication. Byline given. Buys first rights. Submit seasonal/holiday material 4 months in advance. Simultaneous queries, and simultaneous, photocopied, and previously published submissions OK. Computer printout and disk submissions OK. SASE. Reports in 1 month on queries; 6 weeks on mss. Sample copy for 50¢ and 10x13 SAE with $1 postage. Free writer's guidelines for business-sized SAE and 20¢ postage.
Nonfiction: Mary Achor, articles editor. Expose, general interest, historical, how-to, inspirational, interview/profile, photo feature, travel. Covers a broad range of departments: news, entertainment, sports, business, health, adventure, travel, etc. "All stories must have a positive slant, although investigative materials are welcomed." No personal experience, localized or regionalized stories, negative (uncorrective) articles. Buys 20 mss/year. Query with clips of published work. Length: 1,000-2,000 words. Pays $75-250.
Columns/Departments: Letters to Editor, short paragraphs of special interest (unusual people or events), news-oriented clips, book reviews. Buys 50 mss/year. Send complete ms. Length: 25-250 words. Pays $5-30.

‡**OPENERS, America's Library Newspaper**, American Library Association, 50 E. Huron St., Chicago IL 60611. (312)944-6780. Editor: Ann M. Cunniff. Managing Editor: Marcia Kuszman. Quarterly tabloid covering books, fitness and sports, art, music, TV and radio, movies, health, etc., as they relate/tie into the library. Distributed free to library patrons. *Openers* is designed to be used outside the library to encourage library use and inside as a bonus to library patrons to help broaden their reading interests. Estab. 1981. Circ. 170,000. Pays on publication. Byline given. Buys all rights. Submit seasonal/holiday material 3 months in advance. Simultaneous queries, and simultaneous and photocopied submissions OK. SASE. Reports in 2 months. Sample copy for 9x12 SAE.
Nonfiction: General interest, how-to and humor as they tie-in to reading or books. "Send us an outline first." Buys 25+ mss/year. Query with published clips. Length: 600-2,000 words. Pays $50-100.

PARADE, Parade Publications, Inc., 750 3rd Ave., New York NY 10017. (212)573-7000. Editor: Walter Anderson. Weekly magazine for a general interest audience. Circ. 23 million. Pays on acceptance. Kill fee varies in amount. Buys first North American serial rights. Submit seasonal/holiday material 3 months in advance. SASE. Reports in 2 weeks on queries. Writer's guidelines free for 4x9 SAE and 1 first class stamp.
Nonfiction: General interest (on science, business or anything of interest to a broad general audience); interview/profile (of news figures, celebrities and people of national significance); and "provocative topical pieces of news value." No fashion, travel, poetry, quizzes, or fillers. Buys 25 unsolicited mss/year. Address queries to articles editor. Length: 800-1,500 words. Pays $1,000 minimum.
Photos: Send photos with ms.
Tips: "Send a well-researched, well-written query targeted to our market. Please, no phone queries. We're interested in well-written exclusive manuscripts on topics of news interest."

PEOPLE IN ACTION, (formerly *People on Parade*), Meridian Publishing Co., 1720 Washington Blvd., Box 2315, Ogden UT 84404. (801)394-9446. Editor: Dick Harris. Associate Editor: Peggie Bingham. For employees, stockholders, customers and clients of 2,000 business and industrial firms. 90% freelance written. Monthly magazine; 28 pages. Circ. 450,000. Pays on acceptance. Buys first North American rights. Byline given. Submit seasonal/holiday material 6 months in advance. Computer printout and disk submissions OK; prefers letter quality to dot matrix printouts. SASE. Reports in 3-4 weeks. Sample copy 50¢; free writer's guidelines with SASE.
Nonfiction: "*PIA* focuses on people—active, interesting, exciting, busy people; personality profiles on people succeeding, achieving, doing things." Humorous, informational, inspirational. "We want material from all regions of the country and about all types of people. Big-name writers are fine, but we know there is a lot of talent among the little knowns, and we encourage them to submit their ideas. We read everything that comes in, but writers will save their time and ours by writing a good, tantalizing query. *PIA* has a strong family-community orientation. Without being maudlin or pious, we cherish the work ethic, personal courage and dedication to the American dream. So we look for material that reflects positively on the man/woman who succeeds through diligence, resourcefulness and imagination, or finds fulfillment through service to community or country. Tell us about people whose lives and accomplishments inspire and encourage others. We are still looking for personality profiles on successful people. We also have a Celebrity Chef page—we like featuring a well-known person with his favorite recipes. We like humor and nostalgia. We want tight writing, with lively quotes and anecdotes. We're overstocked with stories on handicapped people (blind TV repairmen, etc.) and senior citizens with new hobbies. No "lifestyle" stories or social issues. Pictures should be fresh, sharp, unposed, showing action, involvement." Buys 8-10 mss/issue. Length: 400-1,000 words. Pays 15¢/word.

Photos: State availability of photos. Purchased with or without mss or on assignment. Captions required. Pays $20 for 8x10 b&w glossy print; $35 for 35mm, $2\frac{1}{4}$x$2\frac{1}{4}$ or 4x5 color used inside; up to $300 for cover color. Model release required.

Columns/Departments: Wit Stop (humor pieces). Length: 600-800 words.

Fillers: "We welcome fillers and shorts with a humorous touch, featuring interesting, successful, busy people." Buys 1-2/issue. Length: 200-300 words. Pays 15¢/word.

Tips: "*People in Action* has started a celebrity cooking section. We feature a celebrity each month with his/her favorite foods or recipes, meal planning, dieting tips, etc. Length should be 500-600 words, and we need at least one color transparency of the celebrity in the kitchen, dining, etc. Pays 15¢/word, $35 for a color photo. We pay on acceptance. Everything comes to us on spec. Send for a sample copy or guidelines so you know what we're looking for—our word limits, photo requirements etc. Don't send snap shots or manuscripts that are over our word limit. *Always include SASE.* No phone queries, please. We're always looking for humor pieces for our 'Wit Stop' feature. Subtle humor—not forced."

PEOPLE WEEKLY, Time, Inc., Time & Life Bldg., Rockefeller Center, New York NY 10020. Editor: Patricia Ryan. For a general audience. Weekly. Circ. 2.6 million. Rights purchased vary with author and material. Usually buys first North American serial rights with right to syndicate, splitting net proceeds with author 50/50. Pays on acceptance. Query. SASE.

Nonfiction and Photos: "Nearly all material is staff-produced, but we do consider specific story suggestions (not manuscripts) from freelancers. Every story must have a strong personality focus. Payment varies from $200 for Lookouts to $1,000 for Bios. Photo payment is $300/page for b&w, minimum $100. Prefer minimum size of 8x10 from original negatives."

READER'S DIGEST, Pleasantville NY 10570. Monthly. Circ. 18 million. Includes general interest features for the broadest possible spectrum of readership. "Items intended for a particular feature should be directed to the editor in charge of that feature, although the contribution may later be referred to another section of the magazine as seeming more suitable. Original contributions (which become the property of *Reader's Digest* upon acceptance and payment by *Reader's Digest*) should be typewritten if possible. No computer printout or disk submissions. When material is from a published source, please give the name and date of publication and the page number. Contributions cannot be acknowledged or returned.

Columns/Departments: "Life in These United States contributions must be true, unpublished stories from one's own experience, revelatory of adult human nature, and providing appealing or humorous sidelights on the American scene. Maximum length: 300 words. Address Life in U.S. Editor. Payment rate on publication: $300. True and unpublished stories are also solicited for Humor in Uniform, Campus Comedy and All in a Day's Work. Maximum length: 300 words. Payment rate on publication: $300. Address Humor in Uniform, Campus Comedy or All in a Day's Work Editor. Toward More Picturesque Speech: The first contributor of each item used in this department is paid $35. Contributions should be dated, and the sources must be given. Address: Picturesque Speech Editor. For items used in Laughter, the Best Medicine, Personal Glimpses, Quotable Quotes, and elsewhere in the magazine, payment is made at the following rates: to the *first* contributor of each item from a published source, $35. For original material, $15 per *Digest* two-column line, with a minimum payment of $35. Address: Excerpts Editor."

Tips: "Send a good nonfiction general interest article, preferably in print and on a subject not recently discussed in *Reader's Digest*. We are also willing to consider a well-developed written query."

READERS NUTSHELL, Allied Publications, Drawer 189, Palm Beach FL 33480. Editor: Constance Dorval-Bernal. Bimonthly magazine for customers of insurance agents. 50% insurance-related material; 50% general interest. Circ. 69,000. Pays on acceptance. Buys one-time rights. Phone queries OK. Submit seasonal material 6 months in advance. Simultaneous, photocopied and previously published submissions OK. SASE. Reports in 2 weeks on queries; in 1 month on mss. Sample copy $1; free writer's guidelines.

Nonfiction: Insurance-related; general interest (non-controversial home, family, and safety articles); humor; interview (of famous people). Buys 2 mss/issue. Send complete ms. Length: 400-800 words. Pays 5¢/published word. "Freelancers should limit submissions to 600 words, with good black and white photos."

Photos: Send photos with ms. Pays $5 for 8x10 b&w glossy prints. Captions preferred; model release required.

Fillers: Puzzles. Pays $10.

READERS REVIEW, The National Research Bureau, Inc., 424 N. 3rd St., Burlington IA 52601. Editor: Rhonda Wilson. Editorial Supervisor: Doris J. Ruschill. "For industrial workers of all ages." Quarterly magazine. Pays on publication. Buys all rights. Previously published submissions OK. No computer printout or disk submissions. SASE. Reports in 3 weeks. Free writer's guidelines.

Nonfiction: General interest (steps to better health, attitudes on the job); how-to (perform better on the job, do home repairs, car maintenance); and travel. No articles on car repair, stress and tension. Buys 10-12 mss/year. Query with outline. Length: 400-600 words. Pays 4¢/word.

THE SATURDAY EVENING POST, The Saturday Evening Post Society, 1100 Waterway Blvd., Indianapolis, IN 46202. (317)634-1100. Editor-in-Chief: Cory Ser Vaas M.D. Executive Editor: Ted Kreiter. For general readership. Magazine published 9 times/year; 144 pages. Circ. 535,000. Pays on publication. Buys all rights. Simultaneous and photocopied submissions OK. SASE. Reports in 1 month. Free writer's guidelines for SASE.

Nonfiction: Lori Davis, nonfiction editor. How-to (health, general living); humor; informational; people (celebrities and ordinary but interesting personalities); inspirational (for religious columns); interview; personal experience (especially travel, yachting, etc.); personal opinion; photo feature; profile; travel and small magazine "pick-ups." Buys 5 mss/issue. Query. Length: 1,500-3,000 words. Pays $100-1,000.

Photos: Photo Editor: Patrick Perry. Photos purchased with or without accompanying ms. Pays $25 minimum for b&w photos; $50 minimum for color photos. Offers no additional payment for photos accepted with mss. Model release required.

Columns/Departments: Editorials ($100 each); Food ($150-450); Medical Mailbox ($50-250); Religion Column ($100-250) and Travel ($150-450).

Fiction: Fiction editor: Jack Gramling. Adventure; fantasy; humorous; mainstream; mystery; romance; science fiction; suspense; western; and condensed novels. Buys 5 mss/issue. Query. Length: 1,500-3,000 words. Pays $150-750.

Fillers: Fillers Editor: Bob Ehrgot. Jokes, gags, anecdotes, cartoons, postscripts and short humor. Buys 1 filler/issue. Length: 500-1,000 words. Pays $10-100.

Tips: "Interested in topics related to science, government, the arts, personalities with inspirational careers and humor. We read unsolicited material."

‡**SATURDAY REVIEW**, Saturday Review Publishing Co., 1205 University, Columbia MO 65201 (314)875-3003. Managing Editor: Bruce Van Wyngarden. Bimonthly magazine covering literature and the arts for a highly literate audience. Circ. 250,000. Pays on publication. Byline given. Buys first North American serial rights. Submit seasonal/holiday material 6 months in advance. SASE. Reports in 2 weeks. Sample copy for $2.50, 9x12 SAE and 2 first class stamps.

Nonfiction: Book excerpts; interview/profile (with artists and writers); coverage of a cultural or an artistic event. Buys 30 mss/year. Send complete ms. Length: 800-2,500 words. Pays $500-1,500.

Photos: Regina Setser, photo editor. Send photos with ms. Pays $50-500 for color transparencies; $35-100 for 5x7 b&w prints. Model release and identification of subjects required. Buys one-time rights.

Fiction: Buys 1 or fewer mss/year. Send complete ms. Length: 2,500 words maximum.

Fillers: Clarence Brown, cartoon editor. Send cartoons to Box 704, Kingston NJ 08528.

Tips: "Features should involve a profile of an important artist or writer—preferably one who has just produced or is about to produce an important work. Avoid the obvious and the overdone; we don't want to do the same people everyone else is doing."

SELECTED READING, The National Research Bureau, Inc., 424 N. 3rd St., Burlington IA 52601. Editor: Rhonda Wilson. Editorial Supervisor: Doris J. Ruschill. For industrial workers of all ages. Quarterly magazine. Pays on publication. Buys all rights. Previously published submissions OK. No computer printout or disk submissions. SASE. Reports in 3 weeks. Free writer's guidelines.

Nonfiction: General interest (economics, health, safety, working relationships); how-to; and travel (out-of-the way places). No material on car repair. Buys 10-12 mss/year. Query. A short outline or synopsis is best. Lists of titles are no help. Length: 400-600 words. Pays 4¢/word.

SIGNATURE—The Diner's Club Magazine from Citicorp, 880 3rd Ave., New York NY 10016. Editor: Horace Sutton. Basically for Diner's Club members (but subscriptions open to all)—"businesspersons, urban, affluent and traveled." Monthly. Circ. 690,000. Pays on acceptance. Buys first rights. Buys 75 mss/year. Submit seasonal material at least 3 months in advance. Computer printout submissions OK "if easily readable." Returns rejected material in 3 weeks. Query. SASE. Free writer's guidelines.

Nonfiction: Buys virtually all nonfiction from freelance writers. Front-of-the-book pieces deal with photography, sport, fitness, acquisitions. Length: Generally 1,200-1,500 words. Pays $700-900. "While travel and travel-related pieces are the major portion of the so-called 'well' or central part of the book, we will entertain any feature-length piece that relates to the art of living well or at least living interestingly. That could include such pieces as 'In Search of the Ultimate Deli' to 'Traveling in the State Department plane with the Secretary of State.' Writing is of high quality and while celebrated bylines are sought and used, the market is open to any writer of talent and style. Writers who join the 'stable' are used with frequency." Feature length: 2,000-3,000 words. Pays $1,200 and up.

Photos: "Photographers are assigned to major pieces and often accompany the writer. In almost no cases are writers expected to take their own photographs. Quality standard in pictures is high and highly selective. Photography rates on request to the art director."

Tips: "While we are heavy on travel in all its phases, that is far out Ladakh and Yemen and near at hand, e.g., Hemingway's Venice, we do try to embrace the many facets that make up the art of living well. So we are involved with good food, cuisine trends, sport in all forms, the arts, the stage and films and such concomitant subjects to be added this year as fitness and finance.''

SMITHSONIAN MAGAZINE, 900 Jefferson Drive, Washington DC 20560. Articles Editor: Marlane A. Liddell. For ''associate members of the Smithsonian Institution; 85% with college education.'' Monthly. Circ. 2 million. Payment for each article to be negotiated depending on our needs and the article's length and excellence. Pays on acceptance. Submit seasonal material 3 months in advance. Reports in 6 weeks. Query. Computer printout and disk submissions OK. SASE.
Nonfiction: ''Our mandate from the Smithsonian Institution says we are to be interested in the same things which now interest or should interest the Institution: cultural and fine arts, history, natural sciences, hard sciences, etc.'' Length: 750-4,500 words; pay negotiable. No fiction or poetry.
Photos: Purchased with or without ms and on assignment. Captions required. Pays $350/full color page.

THE STAR, 730 3rd Ave., New York NY 10017. (212)557-9200. Editor/Publisher: Ian G. Rae. Executive Editor: Phil Bunton. 25-40% freelance written. ''For every family; all the family—kids, teenagers, young parents and grandparents.'' Weekly tabloid; 48 pages. Circ. 3.5 million. Buys all rights, second serial (reprint) rights, and first North American serial rights. Pays negotiable kill fee. Byline given. Submit seasonal/holiday material 2-3 months in advance of issue date. No computer printout or disk submissions. SASE. Free sample copy and writer's guidelines.
Nonfiction: Malcolm Abrams, managing editor. Exposé (government waste, consumer, education, anything affecting family); general interest (human interest, consumerism, informational, family and women's interest); how-to (psychological, practical on all subjects affecting readers); interview (celebrity or human interest); new product; photo feature; profile (celebrity or national figure); travel (how-to cheaply); health; medical; and diet. No first-person articles. Buys 50 mss/issue. Query or submit complete ms. Length: 500-800 words. Pays $50-1,500.
Photos: State availability of photos with query or ms. Pays $25-100 for 8x10 b&w glossy prints, contact sheets or negatives; $125-1,000 for 35mm color transparencies. Captions required. Buys one-time, or all rights.
Fillers: Statistical-informational. Length: 50-400 words. Pays $15-100.

‡**STYLING MAGAZINE**, 2425 Sothern Ave., Shreveport LA 71104. (318)227-2342. Editor: Anthony Garner. Managing Editor: Christopher W. Smith. Monthly magazine covering fashion, architecture, food, people and art. ''Our goal is to deliver an educated, intellectual, cosmopolitan publication to an audience of complex diversity.'' Estab. 1983. Circ. 600,000. Pays on publication. Byline given. Offers 50% kill fee. Buys one-time rights. Submit seasonal/holiday material 3 months in advance. Simultaneous queries and simultaneous submissions OK. SASE. Reports in 6 weeks. Sample copy $2.50; writer's guidelines for 9x12 SAE and $1 postage.
Nonfiction: Interview/profile. ''Each month, *Styling's* Conversation interview will concentrate on people in the areas of fashion, architecture, art, theater, design, food, books, music and similar 'trendy and current' issues. All interviews will be published in a question-answer format with a brief introduction by the author. No articles on politics or religion, please.'' Buys 12-18 mss/year. Query with published clips and brief outline. Length: 1,000-1,500 words. Pays $500-750.
Columns/Departments: Paula K. Hester, column/department editor. ''Fashion section is produced monthly by our staff. However, we welcome for review any queries, with a brief outline, concerning men's and women's fashion. We will also be accepting film, book, music, and theater reviews on an approval basis. Reviews should be limited to a more sophisticated subject matter. We would also be interested in obtaining a regular columnist for reviews.'' Buys 12-18 mss/year. Query with published clips. Length: 600-1,000 words. Payment varies with type of article.
Fiction: Humorous. ''We would enjoy submissions from writers with an intellectual flair for satire and dry wit. Avoid any highly-controversial or sensitive areas.'' Buys variable number of mss/year. Send complete ms. Length: 500-1,200 words. Payment starts at $200, depends on length and quality.
Tips: ''We are looking for fresh writers who are in tune with an everchanging world and can relate what is happening today to our readers in an intellectual fashion. We will rely 100% upon freelance writers to supply our monthly interview, Conversations. While there are certain known personalities who would be excellent subjects, we are interested in people whose creativity and innovation in their work are influencing the way we live. Designers, architects, artists, musicians and similar people are wonderful candidates.''

SUNSHINE MAGAZINE, Henry F. Henrichs Publications, Litchfield IL 62056. (217)324-2322. 75% freelance written. For general audience of all ages. Monthly magazine. Circ. 90,000. Buys 120-140 unsolicited mss/year. Buys first North American serial rights. Pays on acceptance. Sample copy 50¢; free writer's guidelines. Complimentary copy sent to included authors on publication. Submit seasonal material 7 months in advance. Computer printout and disk submissions OK; prefers letter quality to dot matrix printouts. Reports in 1-2 months. Submit complete ms. SASE.
Nonfiction: ''We accept some short articles, but they must be especially interesting or inspirational. *Sunshine Magazine* is not a religious publication, and purely religious material is rarely used. We desire carefully written

Close-up

James Cerruti
Senior Assistant Editor
National Geographic

Being published in *National Geographic* is a little like singing in Carnegie Hall. The magazine is an institution. With 11 million readers and a keepsake quality (nobody throws *NG* away!) that both teaches and entertains, the magazine is a masterpiece of professional writing.

Ask Jim Cerruti. He's been on the editorial staff for the past 21 years, working with professional writers to produce a product of permanence.

"I work with contract writers," says Cerruti, "those who make their living by writing. About 50 percent of *Geographic* is staff written; the other half is made up of about 30 percent professional writers and 20 percent academics—those who aren't writers, but who have a topic we think they could do a good story on."

As might be expected of a prestigious publication, the procedure for breaking into *Geographic*'s pages is quite elaborate. "A writer should not send an outline and certainly not a manuscript," advises Cerruti, "but just two or three lines on three or four subjects or ideas he wants to write about. If there's one good idea among the four, I'll write and tell him to develop it into a two-page outline. When the outline comes in, and if I think it's good, I'll send it to an area specialist who (if he agrees with me) puts it through to the planning council—made up of senior assistant editors. We all have a copy and vote on all the proposed submissions. Later we meet again with the editor to bat around our ideas about these subjects. And then the editor decides. The result is we come up with five or ten ideas every six weeks."

The originators of those ideas get detailed assignment letters. Cerruti tells writers what *Geographic* expects: in-depth articles told in terms of people—human geography. "Authors appreciate being told specifically what needs to be done with a piece," Cerruti says.

And he is qualified to know what makes a story right. During his editorial career—15 years at *Holiday* magazine before coming to *NG*—Cerruti has worked with such writers as John Steinbeck, Ernest Hemingway, Joyce Cary, Jacques Barzun, Charles McCarry and Tom Wolfe. "If there's anything to be said about working with people like that, it's that they are easy to work with. The more famous the writer you are working with, the greater likelihood you're going to get a trouble-free story."

An editor's biggest frustration, he says, is the problem writers have with word count. "Even the most experienced writer will turn in a story long. It makes extra work all around.

"To receive a very good manuscript is always a thrill—and that's not every manuscript. I'd say 80 percent of them need some revision."

Though Cerruti isn't revising or reading *NG*'s manuscripts any more (he retired in the summer of 1983) he continues to have a good feeling about the magazine and the printed word. "Magazines will survive because people want something they can take at their own pace. Video gets away from you. But with a magazine like *Geographic*, you can sit down and study it whenever you want—think about all the other things you know related to a particular picture, for example. People will always want permanence and variety. Magazines like *Geographic* give them that."

features about persons or events that have real human interest—that give a 'lift.' " Recent article example: "Bus Stop" (January 1982). Length: 100-300 words. Pays $10-50.

Columns/Departments: My Most Extraordinary Experience—Yes, It Happened to Me. Must be in first person, deal with a very unusual or surprising situation and have a positive approach. Length: 350-600 words. Payment: $25. Favorite Meditation and Gem of the Month, inspirational essays not exceeding 200 words. Payment: $20.

Fiction: "Stories must be wholesome, well-written, with clearly defined plots. There should be a purpose for each story, but any moral or lesson should be well-concealed in the plot development. Humorous stories are welcome. Avoid trite plots. A surprising climax is most desirable. Material should be uplifting, and noncontroversial." Length: 400-1,200 words. Youth story: 400-700 words. Pays $20-100.

Poetry: Buys one poem for special feature each month. Payment: $15. Uses several other poems each month but does not purchase these. Prefers pleasantly rhythmic, humorous or uplifting material. Length: 4-16 lines.

Fillers: 100-200 words. Payment: $10.

Tips: "We prefer not to receive queries. Enclose a SASE, be neat, accurate and surprising, but wholesome. Do not send anything dealing with alcohol, violence, divorce, death or depression."

TOWN AND COUNTRY, 1700 Broadway, New York NY 10019. Managing Editor: Jean Barkhorn. For upper-income Americans. Monthly. Not a large market for freelancers. Always query first. SASE.

Nonfiction: Department Editor: Frank Zachary. "We're always trying to find ideas that can be developed into good articles that will make appealing cover lines." Wants provocative and controversial pieces. Length: 1,500-2,000 words. Pays $750. Also buys shorter pieces for which pay varies.

Us, Peters Publishing, 215 Lexington Ave., New York NY 10016. (212)340-7577. Editor-in-Chief: Richard Kaplan. Biweekly magazine featuring personalities for readers from 18-34. Circ. 1.1 million. Computer printout and disk submissions OK. Pays on publication. Buys all rights. Reports in 2 weeks.

Nonfiction: Richard Sanders, senior articles editor. General interest (human interest pieces with political, sports and religious tie-ins, fashion, entertainment, science, medicine); interview (of Hollywood figures); profiles (of trend and style setters, political personalities, sports figures) and photo feature (personalities, not necessarily celebrities). No humor or essays. "We are looking for the odd story, the unusual story, featuring colorful and unusual people." Buys 5 mss/issue. Query with clips of previously published work. Length: 750-800 words. Pays $350-400.

Photos: State availability of photos. Reviews b&w prints. "Color is OK, but we will convert to black and white. We've got to have stories with pictures."

Tips: "We do what we call anticipatory journalism. That means you should peg the story to a specific date. For example, a story about an unusual track star would work best if published close to the date of the star's most important race. The editors work 5-6 weeks ahead on stories. Query with a one-paragraph description of the proposed subject."

WHAT MAKES PEOPLE SUCCESSFUL, The National Research Bureau, Inc., 424 N. 3rd St., Burlington IA 52601. Editor: Rhonda Wilson. Editorial Supervisor: Doris J. Ruschill. For industrial workers of all ages. Published quarterly. Pays on publication. Buys all rights. Previously published submissions OK. No computer printout or disk submissions. SASE. Reports in 3 weeks. Free writer's guidelines.

Nonfiction: How-to (be successful); general interest (personality, employee morale, guides to successful living, biographies of successful persons, etc.); experience; opinion. No material on health. Buys 3-4 mss/issue. Query with outline. Length: 400-600 words. Pays 4¢/word.

Health and Fitness

Nearly every general interest publication is a potential market for an appropriate health article. Those listed here specialize in covering health and fitness-related topics for a popular audience. Bodybuilding and running magazines list in the Sports/Miscellaneous section.

ACCENT ON LIVING, Box 700, Bloomington IL 61701. (309)378-2961. Editor: Raymond C. Cheever. For physically disabled persons and rehabilitation professionals. Quarterly magazine; 128 pages. Circ. 19,000. Buys one-time rights unless otherwise specified. Byline usually given. Buys 50-60 unsolicited mss/year. Pays on publication. Sample copy $1.50; free writer's guidelines. Photocopied submissions OK. Computer printout and disk submissions OK. Reports in 2 weeks. SASE.
Nonfiction: Betty Garee, assistant editor. Articles about new devices that would make a disabled person with limited physical mobility more independent; should include description, availability, and photos. Medical breakthroughs for disabled people. Intelligent discussion articles on acceptance of physically disabled persons in normal living situations; topics may be architectural barriers, housing, transportation, educational or job opportunities, organizations, or other areas. How-to articles concerning everyday living giving specific, helpful information so the reader can carry out the idea himself. News articles about active disabled persons or groups. Good strong interviews. Vacations, accessible places to go, sports, organizations, humorous incidents, self improvement, and sexual or personal adjustment—all related to physically handicapped persons. No religious-type articles. Length: 250-1,000 words. Pays 10¢/word for article as it appears in magazine (after editing and/or condensing by staff). Query.
Photos: Pays $5 minimum for b&w photos purchased with accompanying captions. Amount will depend on quality of photos and subject matter.
Tips: "We read all manuscripts so one writer won't get preferred treatment over another. Make sure that you are writing to disabled people, not a general audience. We are looking for upbeat material. Hint to writers: Ask a friend who is disabled to read your article before sending it to *Accent*. Make sure that he understands your major points, and the sequence or procedure."

ALCOHOLISM, The National Magazine, Alcom, Inc., Box C19051, Queen Anne Station, Seattle WA 98109. (206)362-8162. Associate Editor: Gale Robinette. Managing Editor: Anthony White. Bimonthly magazine covering alcoholism, treatment, recovery. Circ. 30,000. Pays on publication. Byline given. Offers 20-50% kill fee. Buys first rights. Submit seasonal/holiday material 6 months in advance. Simultaneous queries, and simultaneous and photocopied submissions OK. SASE. Reports in 1 month. Sample copy $5; writer's guidelines for business-size SAE and 1 first class stamp.
Nonfiction: How-to, humor, interview/profile, opinion, "popularizations of research." New interest in business success through recovery. Special issues include Research Focus and Intervention Focus. No "this is how bad I was"; "this is how bad my parents (brother, etc.) were." Stress "the adventure of recovery" instead of the agony of the disease. No fiction. Especially interested in humor. Buys 20 major features/year. Query with clips of published work or send complete ms. Length: 300-2,000 words. Pays 10¢/word; $100/published page.
Photos: State availability of photos. Captions, model release, and identification of subjects required. Buys one-time rights.
Columns/Departments: "Clinician's Perspective"; Soapbox (on issues); "Road to Recovery": tips on ways of enhancing recovery. Buys 12-24 items/year. Send complete ms. Length: 500-750 words. Pays 10¢/word; $100/published page.
Poetry: Free verse, light verse, traditional (lucid). Wants recovery-oriented material only. No "surrealism; alcoholics are rotten; ain't it terrible on skid row. No grim poetry, please." Buys 1-2/ issue. Submit maximum 5 poems. Length: 2-20 lines. Pays $5-25.
Fillers: Short humor, newsbreaks. Pays $5 minimum; 10¢/word "on longer items."
Tips: "We need writers who know something about alcoholism—something more than personal experience and superficial acquaintance—writers who make tough material readable and palatable for a popular and professional audience. We are always on the lookout for well-researched popularizations of research. We try to run one personal experience per issue dealing with recovery—how the alcoholic finds ways to make sobriety worth being sober for." Editors also interested in working with writers outside the US.

AMERICAN HEALTH MAGAZINE, Fitness of Body and Mind, American Health Partners, 80 Fifth Ave., New York NY 10011. (212)242-2460. Editor-in-Chief: T George Harris. Editor: Joel Gurin. Executive Editor: Hara Marano. Bimonthly general interest magazine that covers both scientific and "lifestyle" aspects of health, including laboratory research, clinical advances, fitness, holistic healing and nutrition. Estab. 1982. Circ. 550,000. Pays on acceptance. Byline given. Offers 25% kill fee. Buys all rights; "negotiable, in some cases." Submit seasonal/holiday material 6 months in advance. Computer printout submissions OK. SASE. Reports in 6 weeks. Sample copy for $2 and $1.75 first class postage and handling; writer's guidelines for 4x9 SAE and 1 first class stamp.

Nonfiction: Mail to Editorial/Features. Book excerpts; how-to; humor (if anyone can be funny, yes); interview/profile (health or fitness related); new product (health or fitness related); photo feature (any solid feature or news item relating to health); technical. No first-person narratives, mechanical research reports, weight loss plans or recipes. "Stories should be written clearly, without jargon. Information should be new, authoritative and helpful to the readers. No first-person narrative about illness or recovery from an illness or accident." Buys 50 mss/year. Query with 2 clips of published work. "Absolutely *no* complete mss." Length: 750-3,000 words. Pays $500-2,000.

Photos: Mail to Editorial/Photo. Send photos with query. Pays $75-400 for 35mm transparencies and 8x10 prints "depending on use." Captions and identification of subjects required. Buys one-time rights.

Columns/Departments: Mail to Editorial/News. Technology Update, Consumer Alert, Medical News, Fitness Report, Health Styles, Nutrition Report, Tooth Report, Footwork, Body/Mind, and Skin, Scent and Hair. Buys 400 mss/year. Query with clips of published work. Length: 250-750 words. Pays $125-375.

Fillers: Mail to Editorial/Fillers. Anecdotes, newsbreaks. Buys 30/year. Length: 20-50 words. Pays $10-25.

Tips: "Queries should be short (no longer than a page), snappy and to the point. Think short; think news. Give us a good angle and a paragraph of background. Queries only. We do not take responsibility for materials not accompanied by SASE."

BESTWAYS MAGAZINE, Box 2028, Carson City NV 89702. Editor/Publisher: Barbara Bassett. Emphasizes health, diet and nutrition. Monthly magazine; 120 pages. Circ. 200,000. Pays on publication. Buys all rights. Byline given. Submit seasonal/holiday material 6 months in advance. SASE. Reports in 6 weeks. Sample copy and writer's guidelines for SASE.

Nonfiction: General interest (nutrition, physical fitness, preventive medicine, vitamins and minerals); how-to (natural cosmetics, diet and exercise); and technical (vitamins, minerals, weight control and nutrition). "No direct or implied endorsements of refined flours, grains or sugar, tobacco, alcohol, caffeine, drugs or patent medicines." Buys 4 mss/issue. Query. Length: 2,000 words. Pays $150.

Photos: State availability of photos with query. Pays $5 for 4x5 b&w glossy prints; $15 for 2¼x2¼ color transparencies. Captions preferred. Buys all rights. Model release required.

‡CELEBRATE HEALTH DIGEST, Bergan Mercy, Inc., 7500 Mercy Rd., Omaha NB 68124. (402)398-6303. Editor: David DeButts. Quarterly consumer-oriented magazine focusing on positive, upbeat news and features in the health/medical field. Estab. 1981. Circ. 25,000. Pays on acceptance. Byline given. Offers 25% kill fee. Buys variable rights "depending on author and material." Submit seasonal/holiday material 6 months in advance. Simultaneous queries, and simultaneous and photocopied submissions OK. SASE. Reports in 4 weeks. Sample copy $1; writer's guidelines for business-size SAE and 1 first class stamp.

Nonfiction: Health book reviews; general interest (family health); historical/nostalgic (medical); how-to (exercise, diet, keep fit); interview/profile (of doctors, health experts); new product (exercise equipment, sports clothing). "Nothing on pro-abortion, sterilization or artificial birth control." Buys 6-12 mss/year. Query with published clips or send complete ms. Length: 500-2,500 words. Pays $50-500.

Photos: Send photos with query or ms. Pays $25-50 for b&w contact sheets and negatives; $50-100 for 2¼ or 4x5 color transparencies used inside; $100 for color covers. "35mm is OK for color, too, but must be Kodachrome." Captions, model release and identification of subjects required. Buys variable rights.

Columns/Departments: Medical; Living; World of Work; Childhood; Nutrition; Prime Time (elderly). Buys 10 mss/year. Query with published clips or send complete ms. Length: 500-2,500 words. Pays $50-500.

Tips: "Columns are most open to freelancers. Writing should be crisp, snappy. The publication is edited according to the Associated Press stylebook. Interested in latest developments in health care facilities; all aspects of physical, mental and emotional health. Use authoritative sources. No medical jargon."

‡D.I.N. NEWSERVICE, D.I.N. Publications, Suite 7, 2050 E. University Dr., Phoenix AZ 85034. (602)257-0764. Editor: Jim Parker. Bimonthly magazine covering behavior and health; published by the Do It Now Foundation. Estab. 1983. Circ. 10,000. Pays on publication. Byline given. Offers 30% kill fee. Buys first North American serial rights. Simultaneous queries and photocopied submissions OK. SASE. Reports in 1 month. Sample copy $2.

Nonfiction: "News and features exploring current developments in human health and behavior, and the constellation of issues and events impacting health and behavior." Buys features, profiles, interviews, and opinions. Buys 5 mss/issue. Length: 500-3,500 words. Pays $50-400. Also buys news shorts. Length: 50-300 words. Pays $5-25.

Photos: Pays $10-50 for each b&w or color photo purchased with ms. More for assigned photos.

Columns/Departments: Newsfronts (shorts on current developments in health, behavior, substance abuse, consciousness, media, technology, etc.); Informat (specialized information on various behavioral health topics); Backwords (unusual or off-beat shorts and mini-features); Guestcolumn (guest opinion and commentary);

Postscripts (personal commentary on current news and events).

Tips: "Be authoritative but readable. Don't be afraid to be provocative if you have something to say. Study a sample copy for our viewpoint and style. If a topic interests you, chances are that it will interest us, too—unless it's already been run into the ground by major media. Query first. We'll turn down an interview with God if we ran an interview with God in our last issue."

FRUITFUL YIELD NEWSLETTER, The Fruitful Yield, Inc., 721 N. Yale, Villa Park IL 60181. (312)833-8288. Editor: Doug Murguia. Quarterly national newsletter covering natural foods, vitamins and herbs. Features subjects ranging from prenatal care to health and nutrition for all age groups. Circ. 15,000. Pays on publication. Buys first rights. Phone queries OK. Submit seasonal material 2 months in advance. Photocopied submissions OK. Reports in 3 months. Free sample copy and writer's guidelines for SASE.

Nonfiction: "We are interested in three main types of articles: 1) detailed, documented articles written for the layman telling of the latest research findings in the field of nutrition; 2) personal experience articles telling how natural foods, vitamins or herbs help you or a friend overcome or relieve an ailment (should be detailed and describe your program); 3) recipes using natural foods and/or giving cooking hints." Length: 250-500 words. Send complete ms. Buys 60 mss/yr. Pays $10-20. "We also buy short book reviews on related subjects." Length: 100-200 words. Buys 6 mss/yr. Pays $10.

Tips: "Be familiar with our content. We're looking for specific detailed, documented articles that make no assumptions. Use direct quotes from authorities."

FRUITION, The Plan, Box 872-WM, Santa Cruz CA 95061. (408)429-3020. Biannual newsletter covering healthful living/creation of public food tree nurseries and relative social and horticultural matters. Circ. 300. Payment method negotiable. Byline given. Offers negotiable kill fee. Buys first rights. Simultaneous queries, and simultaneous and photocopied, previously published submissions OK. Computer printout and disk submissions OK; prefers letter quality to dot matrix. SASE. Reports in 2-4 weeks. Sample copy $2; writer's guidelines for SASE.

Nonfiction: General interest, historical/nostalgic, how-to, inspirational, interview/profile, personal experience, photo feature—all must relate to public access—food trees, foraging fruit and nuts, and related social and horticultural matters. No articles "involving gardening with chemicals, or cloning plants. No articles on health with references to using therapies or medicines." Buys 4-6 mss/year. Length: 750-5,000 words. Pays negotiable fee.

Photos: Sunshine Nelson, photo editor. State availability of photos. Pays negotiable fee for b&w contact sheet and 3x3 or larger prints. Identification of subjects required. Buys one-time rights.

Poetry: E. Eagle, poetry editor. Avant-garde, free verse, haiku, light verse, traditional. Buys 4-6/year. Submit maximum 6 poems. Length: 2 lines-750 words. Pays negotiable fee.

Fillers: Clippings, short humor, newsbreaks. Buys 6-10/year. Length: 125-400 words. Pays negotiable fee.

GOODSTAY, Hart, Inc., 22 Throckmorton St., Freehold NJ 07728. (201)780-4278. Executive Editor: Arthur S. Schreiber. Features human interest for patients in hospitals (adults only). "We want to help them 'escape' their present environment. Tell them how to buffer the time between discharge and return to normal routine." Monthly magazine. Circ. 50,000. Byline given. Pays on acceptance. Submit seasonal/holiday material 3 months in advance. Simultaneous, photocopied and previously published submissions OK. SASE. Reports in 2 months. Writer's guidelines available—send SASE.

Nonfiction: General interest (hobbies, second careers, interesting careers, educational opportunities); how-to (understand everyday activity: weather forecasting, hobbies); travel; and photo feature. "No overseas travel, how to care for indoor plants, nostalgia. No discussion of diseases or disorders." Buys 6 mss/issue. Send complete ms. Length: 250-1,500 words. Pays $50-150.

Photos: State availability of photos or send photos with ms. High quality color and/or b&w. Offers no additional payment for photos accepted with ms. Captions preferred; model release required. Buys one-time rights.

Columns/Departments: Away (travel for one week or less), and Living Plants (how to care for seasonal plants, flowers in patient's room). Buys 2 mss/issue. Query. Length: 250-1,500 words. Pays $50-150.

Tips: Articles should be "upbeat diversion for adult patients, mostly in suburban communities. They can be on most any subject, except disease or disorders and religion, and we most appreciate those that are written very well, showing intelligence and a good sense of humor. A refreshing new glance at a familiar subject is what we are looking for. Try to imagine patient reading the article. If article is tedious or offensive in any way, or suggests hobbies that are too expensive or too strenuous for a convalescing person, it should not be submitted."

HEALTH, 149 5th Ave., New York NY 10010. Editor: Hank Herman. For health-minded men and women. Magazine; 66 pages. Monthly. Circ. 850,000. Rights purchased vary with author and material. Pays 20% kill fee. Byline given. Pays within 8 weeks of acceptance. Sample copy $2. Reports in 6 weeks. Query with fresh, new approaches; strongly angled. Submit complete ms for first-person articles. Computer printout and disk submissions OK. SASE.

Nonfiction: Articles on all aspects of health: physical; sexual; mental; emotional advocacy articles; and medical breakthroughs. No "all about" articles (for example, "All About Mental Health"). Informational (nutrition, fitness, diet and beauty), how-to, personal experience, interview, profile, think articles, expose. Length: 500-2,500 words. Pays $350-1,000. Also needed are brief (200-600 word) items on medical advances for the "Breakthrough" section (query optional).

Tips: For major articles, query with one-page sample of style intended for the whole story, and include an outline and author's background. "We don't often buy an unsolicited story or idea, but we often get back to a freelancer who has queried us when we get an idea that he or she might be qualified to write."

‡HEALTH & LONGEVITY REPORT, Agora Publishing, 2201 St. Paul St., Baltimore MD 21218. Editor-in-Chief: Elizabeth W. Philip. Monthly newsletter covering new research into aging and life extension. Estab. 1982. Circ. 5,000. Pays on acceptance. Byline given. Buys first North American and second serial rights. Simultaneous queries, and photocopied and previously published submissions OK. SASE. Reports in 1 month on queries; 6 weeks on mss. Sample copy $2; writer's guidelines for business-size SASE.
Nonfiction: "Articles must be okayed with editor first—and must be thoroughly documented." Length: 1,000-2,000 words; prefers 1,000 words. Pays $5-100.

‡LET'S LIVE MAGAZINE, Oxford Industries, Inc., 4444 N. Larchmont Blvd., Box 74908, Los Angeles CA 90004. (213)469-3901. Managing Editor: Keith Stepro. Associate Publisher: Peggy MacDonald. Emphasizes nutrition. Monthly magazine; 160 pages. Circ. 140,000. Pays on publication. Buys all rights. Byline given unless: "it is a pen name and author fails to furnish legal name; vast amount of editing is required (byline is then shared with the editors of *Let's Live*); it is an interview by assignment in which 'questioner' is *LL* (*Let's Live*)." Submit seasonal/holiday material 4 months in advance. SASE. Reports in 3 weeks for queries; 6 weeks for mss. Sample copy $2; free writer's guidelines.
Nonfiction: Exposé (of misleading claims for benefits of drug products or food in treatment of physical disorders); general interest (effects of vitamins, minerals and nutrients in improvement of health or afflictions); historical (documentation of experiments or treatment establishing value of nutrients as boon to health); how-to (acquire strength and vitality, improve health of children and prepare tasty health-food meals); inspirational (first-person accounts of triumph over disease through substitution of natural foods and nutritional supplements for drugs and surgery); interview (benefits of research and/or case studies in establishing prevention as key to good health); advertised new product (120-180 words plus 5x7 or glossy of product); personal experience ("my story" feature in conquering poor health); personal opinion (views of orthonolecular doctors or their patients on value of health foods toward maintainin good health); profile (background and/or medical history of preventive medicine, MDs or PhDs, in advancement of nutrition); and health food recipes ($5 on publication). "We do not want kookie first-person accounts of experiences with drugs or junk foods, faddist healers or unorthodox treatments." Buys 10-15 mss/issue. Query with clips of published work. Length: 750-2,000 words. Pays $50-250.
Photos: State availability of photos with ms. Pays $17.50-35 for 8x10 b&w glossy prinst; $35-60 for 8x10 color or prints and 35mm color transparencies. $150 for good cover shot. Captions and model releases required.
Columns/Departments: My Story and Interviews. Buys 1-2/issue. Query. Length: 750-1,200 words. Pays $50-250.
Tips: "We want writers with heavy experience in researching non-surgical medical subjects, interviewing authoritative MDs and hospital administrators, with the ability to simplify technical and clinical information for the layman. A captivating lead and structural flow are essential."

LISTEN MAGAZINE, 6830 Laurel St. NW, Washington DC 20012. (202)722-6726. Editor: Francis A. Soper. 50% freelance written. Specializes in drug prevention, presenting positive alternatives to various drug dependencies. "*Listen* is used in many high school classes, in addition to use by professionals: medical personnel, counselors, law enforcement officers, educators, youth workers, etc." Monthly magazine, 32 pages. Circ. 150,000. Buys all rights unless otherwise arranged with the author. Byline given. Buys 100-200 mss/year. Pays on acceptance. Sample copy $1; free writer's guidelines. Reports in 4 weeks. Query. SASE.
Nonfiction: Seeks articles that deal with causes of drug use such as poor self-concept, family relations, social skills or peer pressure. Especially interested in youth-slanted articles or personality interviews encouraging nonalcoholic and nondrug ways of life. Teenage point of view is essential. Popularized medical, legal and educational articles. Also seeks narratives which portray teens dealing with youth conflicts, especially those related to the use of or temptation to use harmful substances. Growth of the main character should be shown. "We don't want typical alcoholic story/skid-row bum, AA stories. We are also being inundated with drunk-driving accident stories. Unless yours is unique, consider another topic." Buys 75-100 unsolicited mss/year. Length:

The double dagger (‡) before a listing indicates that the listing is new in this edition. New markets are often the most receptive to freelance contributions.

500-1,500 words. Pays 4-7¢/word.

Photos: Purchased with accompanying ms. Captions required. Pays $5-15 per b&w print (5x7, but 8x10 preferred). Color preferred, but b&w acceptable.

Poetry: Blank verse and free verse only. Seeks image-invoking, easily illustrated poems of 5-15 lines to combine with photo or illustration to make a poster. Pays $15 maximum.

Fillers: Word square/general puzzles are also considered. Pays $15.

Tips: "True stories are good, especially if they have a unique angle. Other authoritative articles need a fresh approach. In query, briefly summarize article idea and logic of why you feel it's good." Recent article examples: "Inhalants—High Way to a Big Fall" (April 1983) and "How to Face a Crisis" (February 1983).

‡**MUSCLE & FITNESS**, Weider Health & Fitness, 21100 Erwin St., Woodland Hills CA 91367. (213)884-6800. Editor: Bill Reynolds. Managing Editor: Zbigniew Kindela. Monthly magazine covering bodybuilding/physical fitness for fitness-minded men/women ages 15-40. Circ. 300,000+. Pays 30 days after acceptance. Byline given. Buys all rights. Photocopied and occasionally previously published submissions (such as excerpts) OK. Computer printout and disk submissions OK. SASE. Reports in 6 weeks.

Nonfiction: Book excerpts (occasionally, if within our philosophy); how-to (only within our philosophy); inspirational; interview/profile. No article on unknown bodybuilders; unauthoritative pieces. No humor, astrology or erotica. Buys 100+ mss/year. Query with clips or send complete ms. Length: open. Pays $50/short column; $300-400/major feature.

Photos: Joe Weider, photo editor. Send proof sheets or transparencies. Pays negotiable rate for contact sheets, 60mm and 35mm transparencies, 8x10 prints. Captions, model release and identification of subjects required. Buys all rights. "We are using more and more color every issue. Photos are worthless if not of a top bodybuilder or well-known athlete."

Columns/Departments: See an issue of the magazine. Buys 100+/year. Query with clips of published work or send complete ms. Length: 500-700 words. Pays $50-75.

Tips: "We are probably most receptive in area of columns (always regular feature of magazine, but published with variety of authors and authoritative nutrition pieces). Also profiles of famous bodybuilders (only if writer has access to athlete, plus approval from us)."

‡**NUTRITION ACTION**, Center for Science in the Public Interest, 1755 S. St., NW, Washington DC 20009. (202)332-9110. Editor: Greg Moyer. Monthly magazine covering food-related consumer issues for membership of consumer group. Circ. 30,000. Pays on acceptance. Byline given. Offers about 20% kill fee. Buys one-time rights and makes work-for-hire and variety of other arrangements. Submit seasonal/holiday material 4 months in advance. Simultaneous queries OK. Computer printout submissions. SASE. Reports in 2 months.

Nonfiction: Expose (on government or industry); how-to (limited use of food preparation features); interview/profile (on local food activists). "Articles must endorse the tie between good nutrition and good health as described by USDA-HHS Dietary Guidelines for Americans." Buys 4 mss/year. Query with clips. Length: 750-2,000 words. Pays $75-200.

Tips: "Have working knowledge of food/nutrition controversies derived from study or personal experience. Catch us with a crisp query that demonstrates ability to write a great lead. How-tos and interview/profiles are most open to freelancers."

‡**PATIENT MAGAZINE**, American Health Publications, 500 3rd St., Wausau WI 54401. (715)845-2112. Editor: Judith C. Patterson. Annual magazine for hospitalized patients covering equipment, care, treatment and facilities. Estab. 1982. Circ. 500,000. Pays on acceptance. No byline given. Submit seasonal/holiday material 6 months in advance. Simultaneous queries OK. SASE. Reports in 3 months. Free sample copy.

Nonfiction: "Besides informing, educating and entertaining the patient/consumer, we are also a marketing tool for hospitals." No controversial issues or general consumer pieces. Buys 20-40 mss/year. Query with clips of published work. Length: 500-700 words. Pays negotiable rates.

Photos: Reviews 8x10 prints.

SAN DIEGO COUNTY'S HEALTH AND RESOURCE GUIDE, Community Resource Group, Box 81702, San Diego CA 92138. (714)299-3718. Editor: Patricia F. Doering. Annual book published each August covering health for an audience consisting of anyone interested in health and community resources, and health professionals who purchase a specially bound version of the same guide. Circ. 5,000. Pays on publication. Submit all material 3 months in advance. Previously published submissions preferred due to deadlines. SASE required. Reports in 3 weeks on queries; in 3 months on mss. If available, sample copy $5.

Nonfiction: General interest (cancer, heart disease, exercise); how-to (related to health, how-to enter a nursing home, prepare for old age, avoid catastrophic illness and related costs, etc.); interview; profile; new product; and photo features (b/w only—drugs, alcohol, mental health and aging). "Nothing offbeat. No first-person stories. We are particularly in need of current statistical data which keeps the public informed of current trends and advances within both traditional medicine and holistic medicine. We are not a 'borderline' or 'off-beat' medical publication, but one wishing to keep the public informed of all areas in health." Query with clips of previously published work. "We will *not* return manuscripts without SASE." Buys 3-4 unsolicited mss/year. Length: 300-1,500 words. Pays $25-500.

Tips: "We are most open to freelancers in the areas of mental health, aging, child diseases, cancer, hospital stories, drugs and alcoholism. However, successful treatment stories must be documented. Best time to submit January-June, annually. Best *way* to submit—1-2 pages of ms to give us idea of story and style with cover letter. Our publication date moves annually according to funding. We need to retain ms longer than usual as a result. We prefer writers to simultaneously submit elsewhere if possible to allow the writer a sale—rather than our exclusively holding onto materials."

SHAPE, Merging Mind and Body Fitness, Weider Enterprises, 21100 Erwin St., Woodland Hills CA 91367. (213)884-6800. Editor: Christine MacIntyre. Managing Editor: Betty Granoff. Monthly magazine covering women's health and fitness. Estab. 1981. Circ 550,000. Pays on acceptance. Offers 1/3 kill fee. Buys all rights and reprint rights. Submit seasonal/holiday material 8 months in advance. "Query first on previously published submissions." Reports in 1 month on queries; 3 weeks on mss.

Nonfiction: Judie Lewellen, articles editor. Book excerpts; expose (health, fitness related); how-to (get fit); interview/profile (of fit women); travel (spas). "We use health and fitness articles written by professionals in their specific fields. No articles which haven't been queried first." Query with or without clips of published work. Length: 500-2,000 words. Pays negotiable fee.

SLIMMER, Health and Beauty for the Total Woman, Playgirl Magazine, 3420 Ocean Park Blvd., Santa Monica CA 90405. (213)450-0900. Editor: Angela Hynes. Bimonthly magazine covering health and beauty for "college-educated single or married women, ages 18-34, interested in physical fitness and weight loss." Circ. 250,000. Pays 30 days after acceptance. Byline given. Buys all rights. Submit seasonal/holiday queries 6 months in advance. SASE. Reports in 1 month.

Nonfiction: Fitness and nutrition. "We look for well-researched material—the newer the better—by expert writers." No fad diets, celebrity interviews/round-ups, fashion or first-person articles. Buys 7-9 unsolicited mss/year. Query with clips of published work. Length: 2,500-3,000 words. Pays $300.

Photos: State availability of photos.

TOTAL FITNESS, National Reporter Publications, Inc., 15115 S. 76th E. Ave., Bixby OK 74008. (918)366-4441. Editor: Ruth Belanger Rosauer. Magazine covers fitness and health topics of interest to men and women between the ages of 25-55 who are serious about their physical well-being. Magazine published 12 times per year. Circ. 100,000. Pays on publication. Byline given. Rights negotiable. "Dislikes computer printout or disk submissions but evaluates the ms on its merit." SASE. Reports in 2 months or less. Free sample copy and writer's guidelines.

Nonfiction: General interest health topics (adult onset epilepsy, how to avoid back pain); nutrition, diets and recipes (low-sodium, carob, vegetarian); interview/profile (of "average" people who have managed to fit fitness into their lives—an IBM executive who finds time to train for the Iron Man Triathlon, a school teacher who took up long-distance running after a heart attack); personal experiences (almost anything can be written from the personal angle, but it must be well written). No fluff pieces or unsubstantiated health articles. "Articles are meant to inspire and/or instruct readers in the area of fitness." Buys 150 mss/year. Two or three paragraph query with clips of published work preferred. Length: 1,500-3,000 words. Pays $75-300.

TOTAL HEALTH, Trio Publications, 1800 N. Highland Ave., Los Angeles CA 90028. (213)464-4626. Editor: Robert L. Smith. Bimonthly magazine devoted to holistic health for a family-oriented readership. Circ. 60,000. Pays on publication. Buys first rights. Submit seasonal material 2½ months in advance. Photocopied submissions OK. SASE. Reports on queries in 3 weeks; on mss in 1 month. Sample copy $1.

Nonfiction: Expose; general interest (family health, nutrition and mental health); how-to (exercise, diet, meditate, prepare natural food); inspirational (meditation); new product (exercise equipment, sports clothing, solar energy, natural foods); and personal experience. No articles on Eastern religions. Buys 25 unsolicited mss/year. Length: 1,800-2,600 words. Pays $50-75.

Photos: Pays $15 maximum/5x7 and 8x10 b&w glossy print. Pays $25 maximum/5x7 and 8x10 color print. Offers no additional payment for photos accepted with ms. Captions and model release required. Buys one-time rights.

Columns/Departments: Buys 18 mss/year. Send complete ms. Length: 1,000-1,500 words. Pays $50-75.

WEIGHT WATCHERS MAGAZINE, 575 Lexington Ave., New York NY 10022. (212)888-9166. Editor-in-Chief: Linda Konner. Managing Editor: Fred Levine. Monthly publication for those interested in weight loss and weight maintenance through sensible eating and health/nutrition guidance. Circ. 700,000. Buys 18-30 unsolicited mss/year. Pays on acceptance. Reports in 4 weeks. Sample copy and writer's guidelines $1.25.

Nonfiction: Subject matter should be related to food, health or weight loss, but not specific diets. Would like to see researched articles related to the psychological aspects of weight loss and control and suggestions for making the battle easier. Inspirational success stories of weight loss following the Weight Watchers Program also accepted. "Before-and-after weight loss story ideas dealing either with celebrities or 'real people' should be sent to Trisha Thompson, associate editor." Length: 1,500 words maximum. Pays $200-600.

THE YOGA JOURNAL, California Yoga Teachers Association, 2054 University Ave., Berkeley CA 94704. (415)841-9200. Editor: Maia Madden. Bimonthly magazine covering yoga, holistic health, conscious living, spiritual practices, nutrition. "We reach a middle-class, educated audience interested in self-improvement and higher consciousness." Circ. 25,000. Pays on publication. Byline given. Offers $35 kill fee. Buys first North American serial rights. Submit seasonal/holiday material 4 months in advance. Simultaneous queries and photocopied submissions OK. SASE. Reports in 6 weeks on queries; 2 months on mss. Sample copy $2.50; free writer's guidelines.
Nonfiction: Book excerpts; how-to (exercise, yoga, massage, etc.); inspirational (yoga or related); interview/profile; opinion; personal experience; photo feature; travel (if about yoga). "Yoga is our main concern, and we especially like stories about people teaching or practicing Yoga in unusual ways. Nothing too far-out and mystical. Prefer stories about Americans incorporating yoga, meditation, etc., into their normal lives." Buys 40 mss/year. Query. Length: 750-3,500 words. Pays $35-100.
Photos: Terry Duffy, art editor. Send photos with ms. Pays $100-150 for color transparencies; $10-15 for 8x10 b&w prints. Model release (for cover only) and identification of subjects required. Buys one-time rights.
Columns/Departments: Forum; Food (vegetarian, text and recipes); Music (reviews of New Age music); Book Reviews. Buys 12-15 mss/year. Pays $10-25.
Tips: "We always read submissions. We are very open to freelance material and want to encourage writers to submit to our magazine. We're looking for out-of-state contributors."

YOUR LIFE AND HEALTH, 55 W. Oak Ridge Dr., Hagerstown MD 21740. Contact: Editor. Monthly. Circ. 50,000. Buys all rights. Byline given. Buys 90-135 unsolicited mss/year. Pays on acceptance. Sample copy $1.25. Free writer's guidelines. Submit seasonal health articles 6 months in advance. No computer printout or disk submissions. Reports on material within 1-3 months. SASE.
Nonfiction: General subject matter consists of "short, concise articles that simply and clearly present a concept in the field of health. Emphasis on prevention; faddism avoided." Approach should be a "simple, interesting style for laymen. Readability important. Medical jargon avoided. Material should be reliable and include latest findings. We are perhaps more conservative than other magazines in our field. Not seeking sensationalism." Buys informational, interview, some humor. "Greatest single problem is returning articles for proper and thorough documentation. References to other lay journals not acceptable." Recent article example: "Dressing for the Weather" (March 1982). Length: 2,000 words maximum. Pays $50-150.
Photos: Sometimes buys 5x7 or larger b&w glossy prints with mss. Color photos usually by staff ("but not always; we'll look at quality color slides from authors").
Poetry: Buys limited amount of health-related light verse. Pays $10.
Tips: "Information should be accurate, up-to-date, footnoted (when applicable); from reliable sources, but written in lay person's language. Interesting style. Neat copy. Originals not photocopies. Prefer seeing finished manuscript rather than query."

History

This section covers magazines emphasizing the history of an era or region; as well as those written for historical collectors, genealogy enthusiasts, and historic preservationists. Antique and other history markets are listed in the Hobby and Craft category.

AMERICAN HERITAGE, 10 Rockefeller Plaza, New York NY 10020. Editor: Byron Dobell. Bimonthly. Circ. 125,000. Usually buys all rights. Byline given. Buys 20 uncommissioned mss/year. Pays on acceptance. Before submitting, "check our five- and ten-year and annual indexes to see whether we have already treated the subject." Submit seasonal material 12 months in advance. Computer printout and disk submissions OK; prefers letter quality to dot matrix printouts. Reports in 1 month. Query. SASE.
Nonfiction: Wants "historical articles intended for intelligent lay readers rather than professional historians." Emphasis is on authenticity, accuracy and verve. "Interesting documents, photographs and drawings are always welcome." Style should stress "readability and accuracy." Length: 1,500-5,000 words.
Tips: "We have over the years published quite a few firsts from young writers whose historical knowledge, research methods and writing skills met our standards. Everything depends on the quality of the material. We don't really care whether the author is 20 and unknown, or 80 and famous."

AMERICAN HISTORY ILLUSTRATED, Box 8200, Harrisburg PA 17105. (717)657-9555. Editor: Patricia L. Faust. Aimed at general public with an interest in sound, well-researched history. Monthly except July and August. Buys all rights. Byline given. Pays on acceptance. Sample copy $2; free writer's guidelines. "Do not bind the manuscript or put it in a folder or such. Simply paperclip it. We prefer a ribbon copy, not a carbon or photocopy. No computer printout or disk submissions. No multiple submissions, please. It is best to consult several back issues before submitting any material, in order to see what we have already covered and to get an idea of our editorial preferences. Please include annotations and a reading list of materials used in preparing the article." Reports in 1 month on queries; 3 months on mss. Query and include suggestions for illustrations. "Prefer concise one-page summaries emphasizing article's unique properties." SASE.

Nonfiction: US history from 1492 to the Korean War. Topics include biographic, military, social, cultural and political. Need "more human interest material." Also covers the US in relation to the rest of the world, as in World Wars I and II. Style should be readable and entertaining, but not glib or casual. Slant generally up to the author. No shallow research or extensive quotation; no personal accounts/memoirs or travel articles. Buys 20 unsolicited mss/year. Length: 2,500-3,500 words. Short features 1,500-2,000 words considered. Pays $50-350.

Photos: Occasionally buys 8x10 glossy prints with mss; welcomes suggestions for illustrations.

Tips: "Query first and be willing to submit on speculation. Be willing to revise if necessary."

THE AMERICAN WEST, 3033 N. Campbell Ave., Tucson AZ 85719. Managing Editor: Mae Reid-Bills. Editor: Thomas W. Pew, Jr. Published by the Buffalo Bill Memorial Association, Cody WY. Sponsored by the Western History Association. Emphasizes Western American history, the old and the living West. Bimonthly magazine; 80 pages. Circ. 140,000. Pays within 2-4 weeks of acceptance. Buys first North American periodical rights, plus anthology rights. Byline given. Submit seasonal/holiday material 6 months in advance. Photocopied submissions OK. SASE. Reports in 6-8 weeks. Query first.

Nonfiction: Historical (lively, nonacademic, but carefully researched and accurate articles of interest to the intelligent general reader, having some direct relationship to Western American history); and pictorial feature (presenting the life and works of an outstanding Old Western painter or photographer). Length: approx. 3,000 words. Shorter regular features range from 850-1,000 words (best bets for unsolicited mss): "Gourmet & Grub" (historical background of a western recipe); "Shelters & Households" (history behind a Western architectural form); "Hidden Inns and Lost Trails" (history behind Western landmarks and places to stay—no commercial promotion). Pays $200-800.

Photos: Captions required. Also "Western Snapshots" ("submissions from readers of interesting old photos 'that tell a story of a bygone day'"). Payment on acceptance.

Tips: "We strive to connect what the West was with what it is today and what it is likely to become. We seek dynamic, absorbing articles that reflect good research and thoughtful organization of historical details around a strong central story line. We define 'the West' as the United States west of the Mississippi River, and, in proper context, Canada and Mexico."

BRITISH HERITAGE, Incorporating British History Illustrated, Historical Times, Inc., 2245 Kohn Rd., Box 8200, Harrisburg PA 17105. (717)657-9555. Executive Editor: Gail Huganie. Bimonthly magazine covering British history and travel in the British Isles and Commonwealth countries. "*British Heritage* aims to present aspects of Britain's history and culture in an entertaining and informative manner." Circ. 60,000. Pays on acceptance. Byline given. Makes work-for-hire assignments. Simultaneous queries and simultaneous submissions OK. No computer printout or disk submissions. SASE. Reports in 2 weeks on queries; 12 weeks on mss. Sample copy $4; free writer's guidelines for SAE and 1 first class stamp.

Nonfiction: Historical (British history). "Though we insist on sound research for both historical and general interest articles, the sources need not be exclusively primary ones, especially where the field has been thoroughly covered by reliable scholars. We prefer a popular to a scholarly style, but no fictionalisation. All thoughts and conversations must be borne out by memoirs or other sound evidence. We advocate simplicity and clarity of style, but not at the cost of over-simplification. Because of the great range of subject matter in Britain's 2,000 year history, we prefer to cover significant rather than trivial aspects of people, issues, events and places. We have, however, no bias against the little-known or controversial subject *per se* as long as it is interesting." No fiction, personal experience articles or poetry. Buys 30 unsolicited mss/year. Query with clips of published work. Length: 1,000-4,000 words. Pays $65/1,000 words; $400 maximum.

Photos: State availability of photos or send photocopies. "We use our own photographers, but like to consider work associated with British culture and history." Pays $20 maximum for color transparencies; $10 maximum for b&w prints. Captions and identification of subjects required. Buys one-time rights.

Tips: "No footnotes needed but sources are required. English style and spelling only. Please read the magazine for hints on style and subject matter. Grab the readers' attention as early as possible, and don't be afraid to use humor. We look for accurate research written in a flowing, interesting style with excellent opportunities for illustration. Provide a list of further reading. There will be greater emphasis in the year ahead on historical sites both in the British Isles and in Commonwealth countries such as West Indies, Australia, Africa and other; increased emphasis on shops, stately homes, museums and other areas of tourist interest."

CAMPAIGN, Lowry Enterprises, Box 896, Fallbrook CA 92028. Editor: Don Lowry. Emphasizes wargaming and military history. Quarterly magazine. Circ. 1,800. Pays on publication. Buys all rights. Byline given. Photocopied and previously published submissions OK but must be identified as such. Only letter-quality computer submissions OK. SASE. Reports in 3 weeks on queries; in 2 months on mss. Sample copy $2.75; free writer's guidelines.
Nonfiction: Historical (military); how-to (create a game, play well, design game); interview (with game designer, publisher); new products (reviews); personal experiences (description of game played to illustrate strategy); personal opinion (on game reviews); and photo feature (new games, conventions). No fiction. Buys 8-10 mss/year. Query or send complete ms. Pays $6/printed page.
Photos: State availability of photos or send photos with ms. Pays $6/printed page for b&w glossy prints; and color will be printed as b&w. Captions preferred.
Tips: "A conversational style is best, like a letter to a friend. Prefer to see entire manuscripts."

CHICAGO HISTORY, Chicago Historical Society, Clark St. at North Ave., Chicago IL 60614. (312)642-4600. Editor: Timothy Jacobson. Emphasizes history for history scholars, buffs and academics. Quarterly magazine. Circ. 6,500. Pays on acceptance. Buys all rights, second serial (reprint) rights and one-time rights. Byline given. Ribbon copy preferred. SASE. Reports in 2 months. Sample copy $1; free writer's guidelines.
Nonfiction: Historical (of Chicago and the Old Northwest). "Articles should be well researched, based on original primary source material, analytical, informative, and directed at a popular audience, but one with a special interest in history." No articles on Frontier Chicago, Fort Dearborn or Chicago authors. Buys 12-16 unsolicited mss/year. Recent article example: "Big Red in Bronzeville" (Summer 1981). Query. Length: 4,000 words maximum. Pays $75-250. Query should include a clear sketch, outline of the proposed article, with as many major points suggested as possible."
Tips: "The manuscripts we like best were usually done for a college or graduate school class."

CIVIL WAR TIMES ILLUSTRATED, 2245 Kohn Rd., Box 8200, Harrisburg PA 17105. (717)657-9555. Editor: John E. Stanchak. Magazine published monthly except July and August. Circ. 120,000. Pays on acceptance. Buys all rights, first rights or one-time rights, or makes work-for-hire assignments. Submit seasonal/holiday material 1 year in advance. SASE. Reports in 2 weeks on queries; 3 months on mss. Sample copy $2; free writer's guidelines.
Nonfiction: Profile, photo feature, and Civil War historical material. "Positively no fiction or poetry." Buys 20 mss/year. Recent article example: "The 20th Maine: Fighting for Little Round Top" (February 1983). Length: 2,500-5,000 words. Query. Pays $50-350.
Photos: Jeanne Collins, art director. State availability. Pays $5-25 for 8x10 b&w glossy prints or 4x5 color transparencies.
Tips: "We're very open to new submissions. Querying us after reading several back issues, then submitting illustration and art possibilities along with the query letter is the best 'in.' Never base the narrative solely on family stories or accounts. Submissions must be written in a popular style, but based on solid academic research. Manuscripts are required to have marginal source annotations."

EL PALACIO, MAGAZINE OF THE MUSEUM OF NEW MEXICO, (formerly *El Palacio, Quarterly Journal of the Museum of New Mexico*), Museum of New Mexico Press, Box 2087, Santa Fe NM 87503. (505)827-6454. Editor-in-Chief: Jane Shattuck Rosenfelt. Emphasizes anthropology, ethnology, history, folk and fine arts, Southwestern culture, natural history, and geography as these topics pertain to the Museum of New Mexico and the Southwest. Quarterly magazine; 48 pages. Circ. 2,500. Pays on publication. We hope "to attract more professional writers who can translate new and complex information into material that will fascinate and inform a general educated readership." Acquires all rights that can be reassigned to the writer. Byline given. Phone queries OK. Submit seasonal/holiday queries 1 year in advance. Photocopied and computer printout submissions OK. SASE. Reports in 4-6 weeks. Sample copy $3; free writer's guidelines.
Nonfiction: Historical (on Southwest; substantive but readable—not too technical); how-to (folk art and craft on the authentic); archeology (Southwest); informational (more in the fields of geography and natural history); photo essay; anthropology. Buys 5-6 unsolicited mss/year. Recent article documented Hispanic arts and crafts: such art contained in the museum; vanishing Hispanic art; Hispanic chests (photo essay). "Other articles that have been very successful are a photo-essay on Chaco Canyon and other archeological spots of interest in the state and an article on Indian baskets and their function in Indian life." Prefer query and writer's credentials. Length: 1,750-4,000 words. Pays $50 honorarium minimum.
Photos: Photos often purchased with accompanying ms, some on assignment. Prefers b&w prints. Informative captions required. Pays "on contract" for 5x7 (or larger) b&w photos and 5x7 or 8½x11 prints or 35mm color transparencies. Send prints and transparencies. Total purchase price for ms includes payment for photos.
Columns/Departments: The Museum's World, Photo Essay, Books (reviews of interest to *El Palacio* readers), Of Special Note (highlights a museum exhibit or event).
Tips: "*El Palacio* magazine offers a unique opportunity for writers with technical ability to have their work published and seen by influential professionals as well as avidly interested lay readers. The magazine is highly

regarded in its field. The writer should have strong writing skills, an understanding of the Southwest and of the field written about. Be able to communicate technical concepts to the educated reader. We like to have a bibliography, list of sources, or suggested reading list with nearly every submission.''

GORHAM GENEALOGY AND HISTORY, 1365 Edgecliff Dr., Los Angeles CA 90026. (213)633-1888. Publisher/Editor: Daniel J. Gorham. Quarterly magazine covering all branches of history and genealogy of Gorham family. Estab. 1981. Circ. 2,983. Pays on acceptance. Byline given. Offers 50% kill fee. Buys all rights. Submit seasonal/holiday material 8 months in advance. Previously published work OK. SASE. Reports in 3 weeks on queries; 2 months on mss. Sample copy $2.
Nonfiction: Book excerpts; expose; general interest; historical/nostaglic, humor; interview/profile; new product (about innovations in capturing, storing and retrieving data; personal experience; photo feature; travel. Query or send complete ms. Length: 500-3,000 words. Pays $75-300; or 2¢/word.
Photos: Send photos with ms. Pays $10-50 for 5x7 or larger b&w prints. Buys one-time rights.
Tips: ''Need historical articles: places named after the Gorhams; Gorham pioneers, soldiers, horse thiefs; present day Gorhams, various Gorham family trees; how to trace your family tree; interviews of persons involved in genealogy.''

HISTORIC PRESERVATION, National Trust for Historic Preservation, 1785 Massachusetts Ave. NW, Washington DC 20036. Editor: Thomas J. Colin. A benefit of membership in the National Trust for Historic Preservation. Read by professional planners and preservationists but more importantly, by well-educated people with a strong interest in preserving America's architectural and cultural heritage. Bimonthly magazine. Circ. 140,000. Pays on acceptance. May buy all, second serial (reprint), or one-time rights. SASE. Reports in 2-4 weeks. Free writer's guidelines.
Nonfiction: ''Willing to review queries from professional writers on subjects directly and indirectly related to historic preservation, including efforts to save buildings, structures and rural and urban neighborhoods of historical, architectural and cultural significance. No local history; must relate to sites, objects, buildings, people involved in preservation, and neighborhoods specifically. Also interested in maritime and archeological subjects relating to heritage preservation. Indirectly related subjects OK, such as old-style regional foods, cultural traditions. Interesting, well-written feature stories with a preservation angle are sought. Most material prepared on a commissioned basis. Writer must be very familiar with our subject matter, which deals with a specialized field, in order to present a unique publication idea.'' Length: 1,000-2,500 words. Pays $600 maximum.
Photos: Query or send contact sheet. Pays $10-50 for 8x10 b&w glossy prints purchased without mss or on assignment; $40-70 for color.

‡**MILITARY COLLECTOR'S JOURNAL, The Magazine for the Military Collector/Historian**, Box 523, Trexlertown PA 18087. (215)395-7374. Editor: Dr. David Valuska. Bimonthly magazine covering history and collecting for collectors of militaria who are ''extremely sophisticated in military history.'' Circ. 2,000. Pays on publication. Byline given. Buys first North American serial rights, one-time rights and negotiable rights. Submit seasonal/holiday material 3 months in advance. Simultaneous queries and photocopied submissions OK. SASE. Reports in 3 weeks. Sample copy $3.
Nonfiction: Military history, Civil War to present; militaria collecting. Buys 30 mss/year. Query or send complete ms. Length: 2,000 words maximum. Pays $20-50.
Photos: B&w, tintypes, etchings, other b&w illustrations. State availability or send photos with ms. Captions required. No additional payment for photos; ''chances for use of article are greatly increased with accompanying photos.''
Tips: ''Articles must be thoroughly and accurately researched. We are looking avidly for regular contributors who can produce what our readers are looking for—regardless of previous credits.''

‡**THE MUZZLELOADING ARTILLERYMAN**, Century Publications, Inc., 3 Church St., Winchester MA 01890. (617)729-8100. Editor: C. Peter Jorgensen. Quarterly magazine covering antique artillery, fortifications, and crew-served weapons up to 1900 for competition shooters, collectors and living history reenactors using muzzleloading artillery; ''emphasis on Revolutionary War and Civil War but includes everyone interested in pre-1900 artillery and fortifications, preservation, construction of replicas, etc.'' Circ. 3,100. Pays on publication. Byline given. Not copyrighted. Buys one-time rights. Simultaneous queries, and simultaneous, photocopied and previously published submissions OK. SASE. Reports in 3 weeks. Free sample copy and writer's guidelines.
Nonfiction: Historical/nostalgic; how-to (reproduce ordnance equipment/sights/implements tools/accessories, etc.); interview/profile; new product; opinion (must be accompanied by detailed background of writer and include references); personal experience; photo feature; technical (must have footnotes); travel (where to find interesting antique cannon). Buys 24-30 mss/year. Send complete ms. Length: 300 words minimum. Pays $20-60.

Photos: Send photos with ms. Pays $5 for 5x7 and larger b&w prints. Captions and identification of subjects required.

Tips: "We regularly use freelance contributions for Places-to-Visit, Cannon Safety, The Workshop and Unit Profiles departments. Also need pieces on unusual cannon or cannon with a known and unique history."

NORTH CAROLINA HISTORICAL REVIEW, Historical Publications Section, Archives and History, 109 E. Jones St., Raleigh NC 27611. (919)733-7442. Editor: Marie D. Moore. Emphasizes scholarly historical subjects for historians and others interested in history, with emphasis on the history of North Carolina. Quarterly magazine; 100 pages. Circ. 2,000. Buys all rights. Phone queries OK. Computer printout submissions OK; prefers letter quality to dot matrix. SASE. Reports in 3 months. Free writer's guidelines.

Nonfiction: Articles relating to North Carolina history in particular, Southern history in general. Topics about which relatively little is known or are new interpretations of familiar subjects. All articles must be based on primary sources and footnoted. Buys 6 unsolicited mss/year. Recent article example: "North Carolina Slave Courts, 1715-1785" (January, 1983). Length: 15-25 typed pages. Pays $10/article.

NORTH SOUTH TRADER, 8020 New Hampshire Ave., Langley Park MD 20783. (301)434-4080. Editor: Wm. S. Mussenden. Covers all aspects of American Civil War history with special attention to artifacts of the period for Civil War historians, collectors, relic hunters, libraries and museums. Bimonthly magazine; 52 to 68 (8½x11) pages. Circ. 10,000. Rights purchased vary with author and material. Usually buys all rights. Buys 60 mss/year. Pays on publication. Sample copy and writer's guidelines $1. Photocopied and simultaneous submissions OK. Reports in 3 weeks. Query first or submit complete ms. SASE.

Nonfiction and Photos: General subject matter deals with famous, and/or unusual people/events of the Civil War, military artifacts (weapons, accoutrements, uniforms, etc.), battlefield preservation, relic restoration, and historical information on battles, politics, and commerce. Prefers a factual or documentary approach to subject matter. Also concerned with current events such as battle reenactments, living history, and relic show coverage. Emphasis on current findings (archaeology) and research related to these artifacts. Not interested in treasure magazine type articles. Length: 500-3,000 words. Pays 2¢/word plus b&w photos are purchased with or without ms. Captions required. Pays $2.

OLD WEST, Western Publications, Iola WI. (715)445-2214. Editor: Jim Dullenty. Byline given. See *True West*.

PERSIMMON HILL, 1700 NE 63rd St., Oklahoma City OK 73111. Editor: Dean Krakel. Senior Editor: Sara Dobberteen. For an audience interested in Western art, Western history, ranching and rodeo; historians, artists, ranchers, art galleries, schools, libraries. Publication of the National Cowboy Hall of Fame and Western Heritage Center. Quarterly. Circ. 25,000. Buys all rights. Byline given. Buys 12-14 mss/year. Pays on publication. Sample copy $3. Reporting time on mss accepted for publication varies. Returns rejected material immediately. Query. SASE.

Nonfiction: Historical and contemporary articles on famous Western figures connected with pioneering the American West; Western art; rodeo; cowboys; etc. (or biographies of such people); stories of Western flora and animal life; environmental subjects. Only thoroughly researched and historically authentic material is considered. May have a humorous approach to subject. Not interested in articles that reappraise, or in any way put the West and its personalities in an unfavorable light. No "broad, sweeping, superficial pieces; i.e., the California Gold Rush or rehashed pieces on Billy the Kid, etc." Length: 2,000-3,000 words. Pays $200 minimum.

Photos: B&w glossy prints or color transparencies purchased with or without ms, or on assignment. Pays according to quality and importance for b&w and color. Suggested captions appreciated.

TRUE WEST, Western Publications, Iola WI 54990. Editor: Jim Dullenty. Monthly magazine. Circ. 90,000. Pays on acceptance. Buys first North American serial rights. Byline given. "Magazine is distributed nationally, but if not on the newsstands in a particular location will send sample copy for $1. Queries should give proposed length of article, what rights are offered, whether pix are available, and enough information for us to check our file for material covered or on hand. Example: an ageless query, "Would you like an article on a mountain man?" Without his name, we simply can't say." No computer printout or disk submissions. SASE.

Nonfiction: "Factual accounts regarding people, places and events of the frontier West (1830-1910). Sources are required. Fast-paced action, adventure, gun fights, Indian raids, and those things which contribute to an exciting story. We want stories about outlaws, lawmen and the major personalities of the Old West. If based on family papers, records, memoirs, etc., reminiscences must be accurate as to dates and events. Unless the author is telling of his/her own experiences, please use third person whenever possible; that is, give the people names: 'James Brown,' instead of Grandfather, etc. Family relationship can be stated at end. We also receive considerable material which is good local history, but would have limited appeal for a national readership." Length: 500-3,000 words; "Rarely will anything longer be accepted." Pay 5¢/word and up.

Photos: "All mss must be accompanied by usable b&w photos. We want at least two photos per 1,000 words. Photos are returned after publication." Pays $15/photo for all rights; $10/photo for one-time use.

VIRGINIA CAVALCADE, Virginia State Library, Richmond VA 23219. Primarily for readers with an interest in Virginia history. Quarterly magazine; 48 pages. Circ. 12,000. Buys all rights. Byline given. Buys 12-15 mss/year. Pays on acceptance. Sample copy $2; free writer's guidelines. Rarely considers simultaneous submissions. No computer printout or disk submissions. Submit seasonal material 15-18 months in advance. Reports in 4 weeks to 1 year. Query. SASE.
Nonfiction: "We welcome readable and factually accurate articles that are relevant to some phase of Virginia history. Art, architecture, literature, education, business, technology and transportation are all acceptable subjects, as well as political and military affairs. Articles must be based on thorough, scholarly research. We require footnotes but do not publish them. Any period from the age of exploration to the mid-20th century, and any geographical section or area of the state may be represented. Must deal with subjects that will appeal to a broad readership, rather than to a very restricted group or locality. Articles must be suitable for illustration, although it is not necessary that the author provide the pictures. If the author does have pertinent illustrations or knows their location, the editor appreciates information concerning them." Length: approximately 3,500 words. Pays $100.
Photos: Uses 8x10 b&w glossy prints; color transparencies should be at least 4x5.

Hobby and Craft

Collectors, do-it-yourselfers, and craftsmen are the readers of these magazines. Publications covering antiques and miniatures are listed here. Publications for electronics and radio hobbyists are included in the Science classification.

AMERICAN BOOK COLLECTOR, 274 Madison Ave., New York NY 10016. (212)685-2250. Consulting Editor: Anthony Fair. Bimonthly magazine on book collecting from the 15th century to the present for individuals, rare book dealers, librarians, and others interested in books and bibliomania. Circ. 3,500. Pays on publication. Submit seasonal material 3 months in advance. Photocopied and previously published submissions OK. Computer printout and disk submissions (IBM PC) OK, "others by special arrangement"; prefers letter quality to dot matrix printouts. SASE. Reports in 2 weeks. Sample copy and writer's guidelines for $3.50.
Nonfiction: General interest (some facet of book collecting: category of books; taste and technique; artist; printer; binder); interview (prominent book collectors; producers of contemporary fine and limited editions; scholars; librarians); and reviews of exhibitions. Buys 5-10 unsolicited mss/year. "We absolutely require queries with clips of previously published work." Length: 1,500-3,500 words. Pays 5¢/word.
Photos: State availability of photos. Prefers b&w glossy prints of any size. Offers no additional payment for photos accompanying ms. Captions and model release required. Buys one-time rights.
Columns/Departments: Contact editor. Book reviews of books on book collecting, gallery exhibitions.
Tips: "Query should include precise description of proposed article accompanied by description of author's background plus indication of extent of illustrations."

‡**AMERICAN CLAY EXCHANGE**, Page One Publications, Box 2674, La Mesa CA 92041. (619)697-5922. Editor: Susan N. Cox. Monthly newsletter on any subjects relating to American made pottery—old or new—with an emphasis on antiques and collectibles for collectors, buyers and sellers of American made pottery, earthenware, china, etc. Pays on publication. "We sometimes pay on acceptance if we want the manuscript badly. If article has not been printed within 3 months, we will pay for it anyway." Byline given. Buys all rights or first rights "if stated when manuscript submitted." Submit seasonal/holiday material 4 months in advance. No computer printout or disk submissions. SASE. Reports in 1 month on queries; 2 months on mss. Sample copy $1.50; free writer's guidelines.
Nonfiction: Book reviews (on books pertaining to American made pottery, china, earthenware); historical/nostalgic (on museums and historical societies in the U.S. if they handle pottery, etc.); how-to (identify pieces, clean, find them); interview/profile (if artist is up-and-coming). No "I found a piece of pottery for 10¢ at a flea market" types. Buys 30 mss/year. Query or send complete ms. Length: 1,000 words maximum. Pays $5-100+.
Photos: Janet Culver, photo editor. Send photos with ms. Pays $5 for b&w prints. Captions required. Buys all rights; "will consider one-time rights."
Tips: "Know the subject they are writing about including marks and values of pieces found. Telling a reader what 'marks' are on pieces is most essential. Their best bet is to write a short (200-300 word) article with a few photos and marks. We are a small company willing to work with writers who have good, salable ideas and know our product. Any article that deals effectively with a little known company or artist during the 1900-1950 era is most sought after. We will be adding a section devoted to dinnerware, mostly from the 1900-1950 era—same guidelines."

AMERICAN COLLECTOR, Drawer C, 100 E. San Antonio, Kermit TX 79745. Editor: Randy Ormsby. 80% freelance written. Emphasizes collecting for antique buffs, collectors of all kinds, dealers, and investors. Monthly tabloid; 48 pages. Circ. 100,000. Pays on publication. Buys all rights. Byline given. Submit seasonal/holiday material 3 months in advance of issue date. Legible computer printouts OK. SASE. Reports in 1 month. Sample copy $1; free writer's guidelines.

Nonfiction: Expose (fake collectibles and fake antiques); how-to (evaluate, protect an item, tips on finding or buying, and prices); interview; unusual collections and/or collectors; personal experience (related to collecting); and photo feature (related to collecting). No nostalgia pieces. "No poetry; no general looks at established collecting (dolls, toys, stamps, coins, books, furniture) that contain no new or relevant information." Buys 50-75 unsolicited mss/year. Recent article example: "Dial T for Telephones" (March 1982). Submit complete ms. Length: 500-1,200 words. Pays $1/inch.

Photos: Submit photo material with accompanying ms. Pays $5 for 8x10 b&w glossy prints and $10-25 for 35mm or 2¼x2¼ color transparencies. Captions required. Buys all rights.

Tips: "When submitting, freelancers should include a complete package consisting of ms in final form, any illustrative material and proper captions for any photos. Always include a phone number for the editor's convenience. Before submitting, secure a copy of our Writer's Guide and study it carefully."

AMERICAN CRAFT, American Craft Council Publishers, 401 Park Ave., S., New York NY 10016. Editor: Lois Moran. Senior Editor: Patricia Dandignac. Bimonthly. Circ. 39,000. Published by American Craft Council for professional and avocational craftsmen, artists, teachers, architects, designers, decorators, collectors, connoisseurs and the consumer public. Pays on publication. Free sample copy. Reports "as soon as possible." Query. Computer printout and disk submissions OK. SASE.

Nonfiction: Articles on the subject of creative work in clay, fiber, glass, metal, wood, etc. Discussions of the technology and the ideas of artists working in the above media. Not interested in amateur crafts. Length: 2,000 words. Pays $250-300.

Photos: Pays $35-150 for stock photos; $50-350 for commissioned photos.

AMERICAN INDIAN BASKETRY MAGAZINE, Box 66124, Portland OR 97266. (503)771-8540. Editor: John M. Gogol. Quarterly magazine about American Indian basketry for collectors, native Americans, anthropologists, craftspeople and the general public. Circ. 5,000. Pays on publication. Buys all rights. Phone queries OK. Simultaneous, photocopied and previously published submissions OK. SASE. Reports in 3 weeks. Sample copy $6.95.

Nonfiction: Historical (of American Indian basketry); how-to (step by step articles on how traditional baskets are made); interview (with basketmakers); profile (of basketmakers); photo feature (of collections and basketmakers); and technical. Buys 8 mss/year. Send complete ms. Pays $10-100.

Photos: Send photos with ms. Reviews 8x10 b&w glossy prints. Offers no additional payment for photos accepted with ms but will purchase individual photos also. Captions and model release preferred. Rights vary.

Tips: "To break in, be knowledgeable about the subject. Write interestingly about the life and craft of the basketmaker."

AMERICANA, 29 W. 38th St., New York NY 10018. (212)398-1550. Editor: Michael Durham. Bimonthly magazine featuring contemporary uses of the American past for "people who like to adapt historical ways to modern living." Circ. 300,000. Pays on acceptance. Byline given. Buys all rights. Submit seasonal material 6 months in advance. SASE. Reports in 6 weeks. Sample copy $1.95; SASE *required* for writer's guidelines.

Nonfiction: General interest (crafts, architecture, cooking, gardening, restorations, antiques, preservation, decorating, collecting, people who are active in these fields and museums); and travel (to historic sites, restored villages, hotels, inns, and events celebrating the past). "Familiarize yourself with the magazine. You must write from first-hand knowledge, not just historical research. Send a well-thought idea. Send a few snapshots of a home restoration or whatever you are writing about." Especially needs material for Christmas and Thanksgiving issues. Buys 10 mss/issue. Query with clips of previously published work. Length: 2,000 words minimum. Pays $350 minimum.

Columns/Departments: On Exhibit (short piece on an upcoming exhibit, $75-350); How-to (usually restoration or preservation of an historical object, 2,000 words, $350); Sampler (newsy items to fit the whole magazine, 500 words, $75); In the Marketplace (market analysis of a category of historical objects, 2,000 words, $350); Book Reviews ($50-75); In the Days Ahead (text and calendar of events such as antique shows or craft shows, 1,000 words, $350).

THE ANTIQUARIAN, Box 798, Huntington NY 11743. (516)271-8990. Editor-in-Chief: Marguerite Cantine. Managing Editor: Elizabeth Kilpatrick. Emphasizes antiques and 19th-century or earlier art. Monthly tabloid. Circ. 15,000. Pays on publication. Buys all rights. Pays 10% kill fee. Byline given. Submit seasonal/holiday material 3 months in advance. SASE with proper postage. Reports in 6 weeks. Sample copy for 12x15½ SASE with $1.25 postage attached.

Nonfiction: How-to (refinish furniture, repair glass, restore old houses, paintings, rebind books, resilver glass, etc.); general interest (relations of buyers and dealers at antique shows/sales, auction reports); historical (data, personal and otherwise, on famous people in the arts and antiques field); interview; photo feature (auctions, must have caption on item including selling price); profile (wants articles around movie stars and actors who collect antiques; query); and travel (historical sites of interest in New York, New Jersey, Connecticut, Pennsylvania and Delaware). Wants concise articles, accurate research; no material on art deco, collectibles, anything made after 1900, cutesy things to 'remake' from antiques, or flea markets and crafts shows. Buys 6 mss/year. Submit complete ms. Length: 200-2,000 words. Pays 3¢/word.
Photos: Pays 50¢-$1 for 3½x5 glossy b&w prints. Captions required. Buys all rights. Model release required.
Tips: "Don't write an article unless you *love* this field. Antiques belong to a neurotic group. Collecting is a sickness as expensive as gambling, and twice as hard to break, because we are all content in our insanity. Don't write like a textbook. Write as though you were carrying on a nice conversation with your mother. No pretensions. No superiority. Simple, warm, one-to-one, natural, day-to-day, neighbor-over-coffee writing. If you don't follow the instructions regarding the SASE, don't expect a reply. Don't telephone us for jobs or instruction. Submit all material through proper presentation."

‡**ANTIQUE MARKET TABLOID**, 10305 Calumet Dr., Silver Spring MD 20901. (301)681-9090. Editor: Jim Hrivnak. Managing Editor: Marc Montefusco. Monthly tabloid covering antiques. Estab. 1981. Circ. 15,000. Pays on acceptance. Byline given. Buys all rights. Submit seasonal/holiday material 3 months in advance. Simultaneous queries and submissions OK. Computer printout submissions OK; prefers letter quality to dot matrix. SASE. Reports in 2 months. Sample copy for 9x12 SAE and $1 postage.
Nonfiction: General interest, historical/nostalgic, how-to, humor, opinion, photo feature, technical. "Only antique-related material; no personal profiles." Buys 40-50 mss/year. Send complete ms. Length: 600-2,500 words. Pays $25-100.
Photos: Send photos with ms. Reviews 5x7 b&w prints. Captions and identification of subjects required. Buys all rights.
Columns/Departments: Send complete ms. Length: 600-2,500 words.

ANTIQUE MONTHLY, Boone, Inc., Drawer 2, Tuscaloosa AL 35402. (205)345-0272. Editor/Publisher: Gray D. Boone. Managing Editor: Anita G. Mason. Monthly tabloid covering art, antiques, and major museum shows. "More than half are college graduates; over 27% have post-graduate degrees. Fifty-nine percent are in $35,000 and over income bracket. Average number of years readers have been collecting art/antiques is 20.5/years." Circ. 65,100. Pays on publication. Buys all rights. Submit seasonal/holiday material 2 months in advance. Photocopied submissions OK. SASE. Reports in 1 month on queries and mss. Free sample copy.
Nonfiction: Historical (pertaining to art, furniture, glass, etc. styles); travel (historic sites, restorations); museum exhibitions; and book reviews. Recent article examples: Any "market articles—what Chinese rugs are selling for now (April 1982); prices for Paul Storr silver (April 1982) and stylistic discussions such as Rose Porcelains (March 1982). No personal material. Buys 6-10 unsolicited mss/year. Length: 1,000-1,500 words. Pays $125 minimum/article.
Photos: "Black and whites stand a better chance of being used than color." State availability of photos. Reviews color transparencies and 5x7 b&w prints. "We rarely pay for photos; usually we pay only for costs incurred by the writer, and this must be on prior agreement." Captions required.
Tips: "Freelancers are important because they offer the ability to cover stories that regular staff and correspondents cannot cover."

THE ANTIQUE TRADER WEEKLY, Box 1050, Dubuque IA 52001. (319)588-2073. Editor: Kyle D. Husfloen. 50% freelance written. For collectors and dealers in antiques and collectibles. Weekly newspaper; 90-120 pages. Circ. 90,000. Buys all rights. Buys about 60 mss/year. Payment at beginning of month following publication. Sample copy 50¢; free writer's guidelines. Photocopied and simultaneous submissions OK. Submit seasonal material (holidays) 4 months in advance. Query or submit complete ms. No computer printout or disk submissions. SASE.
Nonfiction: "We invite authoritative and well-researched articles on all types of antiques and collectors' items and in-depth stories on specific types of antiques and collectibles. No human interest stories. We do not pay for brief information on new shops opening or other material printed as service to the antiques hobby." Pays $5-50 for feature articles; $50-150 for feature cover stories.
Photos: Submit a liberal number of good b&w photos to accompany article. Uses 35mm or larger color transparencies for cover. Offers no additional payment for photos accompanying mss.
Tips: "Send concise, polite letter stating the topic to be covered in the story and the writer's qualifications. No 'cute' letters rambling on about some 'imaginative' story idea. Writers who have a concise yet readable style and know their topic are always appreciated. I am most interested in those who have personal collecting experience or can put together a knowledgeable and informative feature after interviewing a serious collector/authority."

BANK NOTE REPORTER, Krause Publications, 700 E. State St., Iola WI 54990. (715)445-2214. Editor: Bob Lemke. Monthly tabloid for advanced collectors of US and world paper money. Circ. 4,250. Pays on acceptance. Byline given. Buys first North American serial rights. Photocopied submissions OK. Computer printout submissions OK; prefers letter quality to dot matrix. SASE. Reports in 2 weeks. Free sample copy.
Nonfiction: "We review articles covering any phase of paper money collecting including investing, display, storage, history, art, story behind a particular piece of paper money and the business of paper money." No news items. "Our staff covers the hard news." Buys 4 mss/issue. Send complete ms. Length: 500-3,000 words. Pays 3¢/word to first-time contributors; negotiates fee for later articles.
Photos: Pays $5 minimum for 5x7 b&w glossy prints. Captions and model release required.

THE BLADE MAGAZINE, Stonewall Bldg., Suite 104, 112 Lee Parkway Dr., Chattanooga TN 37421. Editor: J. Bruce Voyles. For knife enthusiasts who want to know as much as possible about quality knives and edged weapons. Bimonthly magazine. Pays on publication. Buys all rights. Submit seasonal/holiday material 6 months in advance. Previously published submissions OK. SASE. Reports in 6 weeks. Sample copy $2.25.
Nonfiction: Historical (on knives and weapons); how-to; interview (knifemakers); new product; nostalgia; personal experience; photo feature; profile and technical. No poetry. Buys 75 unsolicited mss/year. Query with "short letter describing subject to be covered. We will respond as to our interest in the subject. We do not contract on the basis of a letter. We evaluate manuscripts and make our decision on that basis." Length: 1,000-2,000 words. Pays 5¢/word minimum.
Photos: Send photos with ms. Pays $5 for 8x10 b&w glossy prints; $25-75 for 35mm color transparencies. Captions required.
Tips: "The ideal article for us concerns a knife maker or a historical article on an old factory—full of well-researched long lost facts with entertaining anecdotes."

THE BOOK-MART, Box 72, Lake Wales FL 33853. Editor: Robert Pohle. Publisher: Mae Pohle McKinley. 60% freelance written. Emphasizes book collecting and the used book trade. Monthly half-tabloid; 36 pages. Circ. 2,000. Pays on publication. Buys one-time rights. Submit seasonal/holiday material 6 weeks in advance. Simultaneous, photocopied and previously published submissions OK. SASE. Reports in 6 weeks. Sample copy for 40¢ in postage.
Nonfiction: "Especially need articles of interest to book dealers and collectors containing bibliographical and pricing data." Expose (literary forgeries); general interest (articles about regional authors, especially those highly collected); historical (about books, authors, publishers, printers, booksellers); how-to (book conservation and restoration techniques, no amateur binding); interview (if in field of interest); nostalgia (articles about paper collectibles, especially those with pricing information); personal experience; and travel (literary landmarks). "No rambling accounts with no specific focus or articles about an unknown poet who has published his/her first book." Buys 48 unsolicited mss/year. Query. Length: 1,000-2,500 words. Pays 50¢/column inch.
Photos: State availability of photos with query. Pays $5 minimum for 5x7 or larger b&w glossy or matte finish prints. Buys one-time rights.
Columns/Departments: Profiles of Dealers, Collectors; "I Collect." Query "unless of a timely nature." Pays 50¢/column inch.

COINS, Krause Publications, 700 E. State St., Iola WI 54990. (715)445-2214. Assistant to the Publisher: Bob Lemke. Monthly magazine about United States and foreign coins for all levels of collectors, investors and dealers. Circ. 130,000. Average issue includes 8 features.
Nonfiction: "We'd like to see articles on any phase of the coin hobby; collection, investing, displaying, history, art, the story behind the coin, unusual collections, profiles on dealers and the business of coins." No news items. "Our staff covers the hard news." Buys 8 mss/issue. Send complete ms. Computer printout submissions OK; prefers letter quality to dot matrix. Length: 500-5,000 words. Pays 3¢/word to first-time contributors; fee negotiated for later articles.
Photos: Pays $5 minimum for b&w prints. Pays $25 minimum for 35mm color transparencies used. Captions and model release required. Buys first rights.

‡**COLLECTIBLES ILLUSTRATED**, Yankee Publishing Inc., Main St., Dublin NH 03444. (603)563-8111. Editor: Charles J. Jordan. Bimonthly magazine for people interested in collectibles. "Our editorial emphasis is on the new fields of collecting which are sweeping the country, items which have largely gained collecting status over the past quarter of a century and often date back no further than 100 years (although we are flexible on this)." Estab. 1982. Circ. 85,000. Pays on acceptance. Byline given. Offers variable kill fee. Buys all rights preferably, but will negotiate. Submit seasonal/holiday material 4-5 months in advance. SASE. Reports in 2 weeks on queries; 3 weeks on mss. Free sample copy and writer's guidelines.
Nonfiction: General interest, historical/nostalgic (with collectibles slant); how-to (preserve, restore and display collectibles); interview/profile (on celebrity collectors and collectors-profiles); travel (trips collectors can take to see public collectors/museums). "We are always in special need of celebrity collectors and 'Collector's

Trip' features." No "canned" material, stories on antiques or non-American collectibles. Buys 50 mss/year. Query with clips. Length: 500-2,500 words. Pays $300-400 average.

Photos: State availability of photos. Pays $50 average for b&w contact sheets and 35mm color transparencies. Identification of subjects required. Buys all rights preferably, but will negotiate.

Columns/Departments: Display Case (newsy wrap-up of latest events of the collecting world—new exhibits, auctions, etc.). Buys 6-10/year. Query with clips of published work. Length: 200-700 words. Pays $25-100.

Tips: "We welcome writers and are interested in developing new first time writers with promise. Areas most open to freelancers are: Collector profiles ('lively stories about collectors with plenty of good quotes'); Features (no writing 'off the top of your head.' Quote experts, facts, information.)."

COLLECTOR EDITIONS QUARTERLY, 170 5th Ave., New York NY 10010. Editor: R. C. Rowe. For collectors, mostly 30 to 65 in any rural or suburban, affluent area; reasonably well-educated. Quarterly. Circ. 80,000. Rights purchased vary with author and material. Buys all rights; first North American serial rights; first serial rights; second serial (reprint) rights; simultaneous rights. Buys 15-30 mss/year. "First assignments are always done on a speculative basis." Pays on publication. Will send sample copy to writer for $1. Photocopied submissions OK. Query with outline. Reports in 6-8 weeks. SASE.

Nonfiction: "Short features about collecting, written in tight, newsy style. We specialize in contemporary (postwar) collectibles. Particularly interested in items affected by scarcity; focus on glass and ceramics." Informational, how-to, interview, profile, expose, nostalgia. Length: 500-2,500 words. Pays $50-150. Columns cover stamps, porcelains, glass, western art and graphics. Length: 750 words. Pays $75.

Photos: B&w and color photos purchased with accompanying ms with no additional payment. Also purchased without ms and on assignment. Captions are required. "Wants clear, distinct, full-frame image that says something." Pays $10-50.

COLLECTORS MART, (formerly *Antique & Collectors Mart*), 15100 W. Kellogg, Wichita KS 67235. (316)772-9750. Marketplace for art, antiques, and limited editions. Publisher: William Bales, Jr. Pays on publication. Buys first rights. Photocopied submissions OK. No computer printout or disk submissions. SASE. Reports in 1 month. Sample copy $1.

Nonfiction: Antique, art, and limited editions investment topics but must be educational and authenticated. No first-party stories. Prefers active current events, market trends, historical sites and items, etc. Buys 22-24 unsolicited mss/year. Recent article example: "The First Fan Magazines" (January 1983). Query. Length: 500-1,000 words. Pays $1/column inch but special articles negotiable.

Photos: State availability of photos. Pays $5 for 5x7 or 8x10 b&w glossy prints; $10 for 35mm color transparencies.

Columns/Departments: Market trends, book reviews, quality antique items, profile studies, historical places and up-to-date investment guides. Query. Open to suggestions for new columns/departments.

Fillers: Anecdotes, newsbreaks, auction reports, show reports and price reports. Length: 50-200 words. Pays $1/column inch.

Tips: "Publication will lean more heavily toward antiques. Each issue will focus a special section on one facet of collecting. Query for subject schedule."

COLLECTORS NEWS, 606 8th St., Box 156, Grundy Center IA 50638. (319)824-5456. Editor: Linda Kruger. For dealers in, and collectors of, antiques. Monthly tabloid newspaper; 60-84 pages. Circ. 30,000. Buys 100 mss/year. Byline given. Pays on publication. Free sample copy. Submit seasonal material (holidays) 2 months in advance. Reports in 4 weeks. Query or submit complete ms. SASE.

Nonfiction: Only factual articles pertaining to some phase of collecting or interesting collections. Informational; profile; nostalgia. Length: 1,200 words minimum; 1,600 words average. Pays 75¢/column inch.

Photos: Offers no additional payment for b&w photos used with mss. Captions required.

Tips: "A freelancer can best contribute by writing for our writer's guidelines and a sample copy of our paper to see the length of articles, our style, type of article needed, or where he could fill a gap. He might also ask what subject matter we are in need of at the time and should tell us what subjects he could cover in the collecting field."

CRAFTS 'N THINGS, 14 Main St., Park Ridge IL 60068. (312)825-2161. Editor: Nancy Tosh. Assistant Editor: Jackie Thielen. Bimonthly magazine covering crafts for "mostly women, around age 40." Circ. 250,000. Pays on publication. Byline, photo and brief bio given. Buys one-time rights. Submit seasonal/holiday material 6 months in advance. Simultaneous queries, and photocopied and previously published submissions OK ("if so indicated"). SASE. Reports in 1 month. Free sample copy.

Nonfiction: How-to (do a craft project). Buys 7-14 mss/issue. "Send in a photo of the item and complete directions. We will consider it, and return if not accepted. Length: 1-4 magazine pages. Pays $50-200, "depending on how much staff work is required."

Photos: "Generally, we will ask that you send the item so we can photograph it ourselves."

Tips: "We're looking harder for people who can craft than people who can write."

CRAFTSWOMAN, Daedalus Publications, Inc., 1153 Oxford Rd., Deerfield IL 60015. (312)945-1769. Editor: Anne Patterson Dee. Bimonthly magazine covering craftswomen and their work. Estab. 1981. Pays on publication. Byline given. Buys one-time rights. Submit seasonal/holiday material 2 months in advance. Photocopied, simultaneous and previously published submissions OK. Computer printout and 5¼" disk submissions OK. SASE. Reports in 3 weeks. Sample copy $2.50.

Nonfiction: General interest (on craftswomen and their work); historical/nostalgic (quilting, stained glass, pottery, weaving, wood, etc.); how-to (run a shop; sell wholesale; do a trade show; promote shows; work with a sales rep, etc.); interview/profile (with successful craftswomen, shop owners, etc.); personal experience ("how I make money selling my designs," etc.); travel (collective pieces on shops in San Francisco, e.g., or selling at shows in Florida in the winter). No "how-to-make-it articles." Buys 30 mss/year. Query or send complete ms if reprint. Length: 500-1,500 words. Pays $10-35.

Photos: "Especially need cover photos." Send photos with ms. Reviews 5x6 or 8x10 b&w glossy prints. Buys one-time rights.

Tips: "We need concise, well-written articles with lots of specifics, quotes and accompanying b&w photos. We are very receptive to freelancers and want to hear from you."

‡**CREATIVE CRAFTS AND MINIATURES**, (incorporating *Creative Crafts* and *The Miniature Magazine*), Carstens Publications, Inc., Box 700, Newtown NJ 07860. Editor: Wendie R. Blanchard. Bimonthly magazine covering crafts and miniatures for the serious adult hobbyist. "Quality how-to articles, biographical profiles, book and product reviews, events, question and answer columns, product testing and articles requested by readers of both magazines." Estab. 1982. Circ. 150,000 + . Pays on publication. Buys all rights. Byline given. Submit seasonal/holiday material 7 months in advance. SASE. Reports in one month. Sample copy and writer's guidelines $1.50.

Nonfiction: How-to (step-by-step of specific projects or general techniques; instructions must be clearly written and accompanied by b&w procedural photos and/or drawings); articles dealing with the crafting and collecting aspects of craft projects and miniatures (dollhouses, etc.). Query. Length: 1,200 words average. Pays $50/magazine page.

Photos: Purchased with accompanying ms.

Columns/Departments: Going Places (places to visit: fairs, museums, craft shows). Query. Length: 1,200 words average. Pays $50/magazine page.

Tips: "We desire articles written by craftsmen (or collectors) knowledgeable about hobbies/miniatures. Our need is for quality crafts that offer some challenge to the hobbyist. When photographing miniatures, be sure to include some photos that have a scale relationship, i.e., a coin or a hand next to the miniature to give an idea of proportion. Request a sample copy of our new magazine and the updated writers' guidelines, and grow with us."

‡**DOLLS, The Collector's Magazine**, Acquire Publishing Co., Inc., 170 5th Ave., New York NY 10010. (212)989-8700. Editor: Robert Campbell Rowe. Managing Editor: Krystyna Poray Goddu. Quarterly magazine covering doll collecting "for collectors of antique, contemporary and reproduction dolls. We publish well-researched, professionally written articles that are illustrated with photographs of high quality, color or black-and-white." Estab. 1982. Circ. 20,000. Pays on publication. Byline given. "Almost all first mss are on speculation. We rarely kill assigned stories, but fee would be about 33% of article fee." Buys first North American serial rights ("almost always"). Submit seasonal/holiday material 6 months in advance. Photocopied submissions considered (not preferred); previously published submissions OK. Reports in 2 months. Sample copy $2; free writer's guidelines.

Nonfiction: Krystyna Poray Goddu, managing editor. Book excerpts; historical (with collecting angle); how-to (make doll clothes with clear instructions, diagrams, etc.); interview/profile (on doll artists or collectors with outstanding collections); new product (just photos and captions; "we do not pay for these, but regard them as publicity"); opinion ("A Personal Definition of Dolls"); technical (doll restoration advice by experts only); travel (museums, collections and artists around the world). "No sentimental, uninformed 'my doll collection' or 'my grandma's doll collection' stories or trade magazine-type stories on shops, etc. Our readers are knowledgeable collectors." Query with clips. Length: 500-2,500 words. Pays $100-350.

Photos: Managing Editor. Send photos with accompanying query or ms. Review 4x5 color transparencies; 4x5 or 8x10 b&w prints. "We do not buy photographs submitted without mss or unless we have assigned them; we pay for the manuscript/photos package in one fee." Captions required. Buys one-time rights.

Columns/Departments: Managing editor. Dolls Views—a miscellany of news and views of the doll world includes reports on upcoming or recently held events; possibly reviews of new books. "*Not* the place for new dolls, auction prices or dates; we have regular contributors or staff assigned to those columns." Query with clips if available or send complete ms. Length: 200-500 words. Pays $25-75. Doll View items are unbylined.

Fillers: "We don't really use fillers, but would consider if we got something very good. Hints on restoring, for example, or a nice illustration." Length: 500 words maximum. Pays $25-75.

Tips: "We need experts in the field who are also good writers. Freelancers who are not experts should know their particular story thoroughly and do background research to get the facts correct. Well-written queries from writers outside NYC area especially welcome. Non-experts should stay away from technical or specific subjects (restoration, price trends). Short profiles of doll artists or a story of a local museum collection, with good photos, might catch our interest. Editors want to know they are getting something from a writer they cannot get from anyone else. Good writing should be a given, a starting point. After that, it's what you know.''

EARLY AMERICAN LIFE, Historical Times, Inc., Box 8200, Harrisburg PA 17105. Editor: Frances Carnahan. 70% freelance written. For "people who are interested in capturing the warmth and beauty of the 1600 to 1900 period and using it in their homes and lives today. They are interested in arts, crafts, travel, restoration, collecting.'' Bimonthly magazine; 100 pages. Circ. 350,000. Buys all rights. Buys 50 mss/year. Pays on acceptance. Free sample copy and writer's guidelines. Photocopied submissions OK. Reports in 1 month. Query or submit complete ms. SASE.
Nonfiction: "Social history (the story of the people, not epic heroes and battles); crafts such as woodworking and needlepoint; travel to historic sites; country inns; antiques and reproductions; refinishing and restoration; architecture and decorating. We try to entertain as we inform, but always attempt to give the reader something he can do. While we're always on the lookout for good pieces on any of our subjects, the 'travel to historic sites' theme is most frequently submitted. Would like to see more how-to-do-it (well-illustrated) on how real people did something great to their homes.'' Length: 750-3,000 words. Pays $50-400.
Photos: Pays $10 for 5x7 (and up) b&w photos used with mss; minimum of $25 for color. Prefers 2¼x2¼ and up, but can work from 35mm.
Tips: "Get a feeling for today's early Americans, the folks who are visiting flea markets, auctions, junkyards, the antique shops. They are our readers and they hunger for ideas on how to bring the warmth and beauty of early America into their lives. Then, conceive a new approach to satisfying their related interests in arts, crafts, travel to historic sites, and the story of the people of the 1600-1900 period. Write to entertain and inform at the same time, and be prepared to help us with illustrations, or sources for them.''

‡**EDGES, The Official Publication of the American Blade Collectors**, American Blade, Inc., Stonewall Bldg., Suite 104, 212 Lee Parkway Dr., Chattanooga TN 37421. Editor: J. Bruce Voyles. Bimonthly tabloid covering the knife business. Estab. 1982. Circ. 20,000. Pays on publication. Byline given. Buys all rights. Submit seasonal/holiday material 6 months in advance. Simultaneous queries, and photocopied and previously published submissions OK "as long as they are exclusive to our market." SASE. Reports in 5 months. Acknowledges receipt of queries and ms in 6 weeks. Sample copy $1.
Nonfiction: Book excerpts; expose; general interest; historical (well-researched); how-to; humor; new product; opinion; personal experience; photo feature; technical. "We look for articles on all aspects of the knife business, including technological advances, profiles, knife shows, and well-researched history. Ours is not a hard market to break into if the writer is willing to do a little research. To have a copy is almost a requirement.'' Buys 150 mss/year. Send complete ms. Length: 50-3,000 words "or more if material warrants additional length." Pays 5¢/word.
Photos: Pays $5 for 5x7 b&w prints. Captions and model release required (if persons are identifiable).
Fillers: Clippings, jokes, gags, anecdotes, short humor, newsbreaks.
Tips: "If writers haven't studied the publication, don't bother to submit an article. If they have studied it, we're an easy market to sell to.'' Buys 80% of the article geared to "the knife business.''

FIBERARTS, The Magazine of Textiles, 50 College St., Asheville NC 28801. (704)253-0467. Editor: Rob Pulleyn. Bimonthly magazine covering textiles as art and craft (weaving, quilting, surface design, stitchery, knitting, crochet, etc.) for textile artists, craftspeople, hobbyists, teachers, museum and gallery staffs, collectors and enthusiasts. Circ. 26,000. Pays on publication. Byline given. Rights purchased are negotiable. Submit seasonal/holiday material 8 months in advance. Editorial guidelines and style sheet available. SASE. Reporting time varies. Sample copy $3.
Nonfiction: Book excerpts; historical/nostalgic; how-to; humor; interview/profile; opinion; personal experience; photo feature; technical; travel (for the textile enthusiast, e.g., collecting rugs in Turkey); and education, trends, exhibition reviews and textile news. Buys 25-50 mss/year. Recent example: Article on how to buy a knitting machine (March/April 1982). Query. "Please be very specific about your proposal. Also an important consideration in accepting an article is the kind of photos—35mm slides and/or b&w glossies—that you can provide as illustration. We like to see photos in advance.'' Length: 250-1,200 words. Pays $25-150/article.
Tips: "Our writers are very familiar with the textile field and this is what we look for in a new writer. The writer should also be familiar with *Fiberarts*, the magazine. We outline our upcoming issue in a column called '50 College St.' far enough in advance for a prospective writer to be aware of our future needs in proposing an article.''

‡**FINESCALE MODELER**, Kalmbach Publishing Co., 1027 N. 7th St., Milwaukee WI 53233. (414)272-2060. Editor: Bob Hayden. Quarterly magazine "devoted to how-to-do-it modeling information for scale modelbuilders who build non-operating aircraft, tanks, boats, automobiles, figures, dioramas, and science fiction and fantasy models.'' Estab. 1982. Circ. 25,000. Computer printout and disk submissions OK. Pays on ac-

ceptance. Byline given. Buys all rights. SASE. Reports in 1 month on queries; 6 weeks on mss. Sample copy for 9x12 SAE and 3 first class stamps; free writer's guidelines.

Nonfiction: How-to (build scale models); technical (research information for building models). Query or send complete ms. Length: 750-3,000 words. Pays $30/published page minimum.

Photos: Send photos with ms. Pays $7.50 minimum for color transparencies and 5x7 b&w prints. Captions and identification of subjects required. Buys one-time rights.

Columns/Departments: FSM Showcase (photos plus description of model); FSM Tips and Techniques (modelbuilding hints and tips). Buys 25-50/year. Query or send complete ms. Length: 100-1,000 words. Pays $10-75.

Tips: "A freelancer can best break in first, through hints and tips, then through feature articles. Most people who write for FSM are modelers first, writers second. This is a specialty magazine for a special, quite expert audience. Essentially, 99% of our writers will come from that audience."

THE FRANKLIN MINT ALMANAC, Franklin Center PA 19091. (215)459-7016. Editor: Samuel H. Young. Associate Editor: Rosemary Rennicke. Bimonthly magazine covering collecting, emphasizing numismatics, philatelics, porcelain, crystal, books, records and graphics for members of Franklin Mint Collectors Society who are regular customers and others who request. Circ. 1,200,000. Pays on acceptance. Byline given. Pays negotiable kill fee. Buys one-time rights. Submit seasonal/holiday material 9 months in advance. Simultaneous queries, and simultaneous, photocopied, and previously published submissions OK. Reports in 1 week on queries.

Nonfiction: General interest (topics related to products offered by the Franklin Mint); interview/profile (with well-known people who collect or Franklin Mint collectors); and types of collections. Buys 8 mss/year. Query. Length: 1,500-2,000 words. Pays $500 average/article.

Photos: State availability of photos.

Fillers: Newsbreaks related to collecting. Pays negotiable fee.

Tips: Expanding audiences in Europe and Asia. "Solid writing credentials and a knowledge of collecting are a plus."

GEMS AND MINERALS, Box 687, Mentone CA 92359. (714)794-1173. Editor: Jack R. Cox. Monthly for the professional and amateur gem cutter, jewelry maker, mineral collector and rockhound. Buys first North American serial rights. Byline given. Pays on publication. Free sample copy and writer's guidelines. Query. Reports in 4 weeks. SASE.

Nonfiction: Material must have how-to slant. No personality stories. Field trips to mineral or gem collecting localities used; must be accurate and give details so they can be found. Instructions on how to cut gems; design and creation of jewelry. Four to eight typed pages plus illustrations preferred, but do not limit if subject is important. Frequently good articles are serialized if too long for one issue. Buys 75-120 unsolicited mss/year. Recent article example: "An Introduction to Meet Point Faceting" (March 1982). Pays 50¢/inch for text.

Photos: Pays for b&w prints as part of text. Pays $1 inch for color photos as published.

Tips: "Because we are a specialty magazine, it is difficult for a writer to prepare a suitable story for us unless he is familiar with the subject matter: jewelry making, gem cutting, mineral collecting and display, and fossil collecting. Our readers want accurate instructions on how to do it and where they can collect gemstones and minerals in the field. The majority of our articles are purchased from freelance writers, most of whom are hobbyists (rockhounds) or have technical knowledge of one of the subjects. Infrequently, a freelancer with no knowledge of the subject interviews an expert (gem cutter, jewelry maker, etc.) and gets what this expert tells him down on paper for a good how-to article. However, the problem here is that if the expert neglects to mention all the steps in his process, the writer does not realize it. Then, there is a delay while we check it out. My best advice to a freelance writer is to send for a sample copy of our magazine and author's specification sheet which will tell him what we need. We are interested in helping new writers and try to answer them personally, giving any pointers that we think will be of value to them. Let us emphasize that our readers want how-to and where-to stories. They are not at all interested in personality sketches about one of their fellow hobbyists."

‡THE GOODFELLOW REVIEW OF CRAFTS, Goodfellow Catalog Press, Box 4520, Berkeley CA 94704. (415)428-0142. Editor: Christopher Weills. Bimonthly newspaper for craftspeople about their work and lifestyle and general public. Circ. 20,000. Pays on publication. Byline given. Offers negotiable kill fee. Buys one-time rights. Submit seasonal/holiday material 4 months in advance. Simultaneous queries and simultaneous, photocopied and previously published submissions OK. Computer printout submissions OK. SASE. Reports in 3 weeks. Sample copy $1.50; free writer's guidelines.

Nonfiction: General interest (related to crafts but not necessarily limited to people with knowledge of crafts); historical/nostalgic; how-to (for craftspeople, i.e., legal advice, marketing strategy, resources); interview/profile (of craftspeople); new product (new or unusual craft); personal experience (by craftsperson); technical (for craftspeople, i.e., woodworking technique, etc.). Buys 18-24 mss/year. Query with clips. Length: 1,000-3,500 words. Pays $25-45.

Photos: Alison M. White, photo editor. Send photos with ms. Pays $5-10 for 5x7 b&w prints. Captions and identification of subjects required. Buys one-time rights.

Columns/Departments: Portfolio (short introduction to new craftspeople); Book Reviews. Buys 10/year. Query. Length: 500-1,000 words. Pays $20-45.

Tips: "We appreciate a professional style and want to introduce readers to new, very talented artisans. We also like how-to articles that entice readers to try new methods. There will be stronger emphasis on national crafts news. We are interested in general trends and in hearing about craftspeople from all over the U.S. and Canada. Articles are most open area for freelancers."

‡**HANDMADE**, Lark Communications, 50 College St., Asheville NC 28801. (704)253-0468. Editor: Rob Pulleyn. Bimonthly how-to crafts magazine featuring projects in all crafts (needlework, knitting, sewing, crafts, etc.). Circ. 10,000. Pays on publication. Byline given. Offers negotiable kill fee. We make work-for-hire assignments. Submit seasonal/holiday material 6 months in advance. Photocopied submissions OK. Computer printout submissions OK; prefers letter quality to dot matrix. SASE. Reports in 3 weeks. Sample copy $2; writer's guidelines for business size SAE and 20¢ postage.

Nonfiction: Historical/nostalgic (crafts-related—traditional crafts, foreign crafts, etc.); how-to (crafts, all kinds with specific information); humor (crafts, "how to buy" sewing machine, etc.); interview/profile (of craftspeople); photo feature (craft show; can be of a person at work, photos of crafts inspiration, such as shots of Africans wearing batik clothing, etc.); technical; travel (visit to foreign places, crafts related). Buys 200-300 mss/year. Query with clips. Length: 250-2,000 words. Pays $50-400.

Photos: Send photos with ms (if possible). Reviews 35mm or 4x5 transparencies. Payment included in total fee. Captions and identification of subjects required. Buys all rights.

HANDS ON!, Shopsmith Inc., 750 Center Drive, Vandalia OH 45377. (513)898-6070. Contact: Editor. Bimonthly magazine for woodworkers and do-it-yourselfers. Circ. 1,000,000. Pays on acceptance. Byline given. Buys rights by agreement. Query. SASE. Reports in 3 weeks. Free sample copy and guidelines.

Nonfiction: Craftspersons' profiles must focus on creative use of Shopsmith tools; specific projects; and how to duplicate the project at home. "How-to research is crucial—methods and techniques tied to specific projects. Rough sketches OK; we supply professional drafting." General woodworking articles must focus on well-slanted information: wood joinery, turning, choosing and using material, working efficiently, alternative techniques with power tools, safety, finishing, the therapy of woodworking, joys and economy of doing it yourself. How-to projects: large or small, must feature use of Shopsmith tools. "Our nonprofessional woodworkers are looking to be 'heroes' to their loved ones, respected by their friends and affirmed in their choice of an avocation. We offer an authoritative variety of original project plans and tips in each issue, as well as freshly-slanted woodworking information with the aim to enable them to become better woodworkers." Query. Length: 1500 words maximum. Pays $250-500 published page.

Photos: Send with ms. Pays $10-25 for 8x10 b&w glossy prints and color transparencies. Buys one-time rights or as agreed.

Columns/Departments: Money Makers (projects that can be sold for quick cash); Almanac (short features on wide variety of woodworking themes); Workshop Safety (short reminders). Pays $25-50.

Tips: "Aim to make the joys of woodworking clearly, with authority, and in a non-intimidating manner. Present information clearly, with authority, and in a non-intimidating manner. Find a 'you can do it' slant. Get to know our tools. There is very little 'new' information in woodworking, but plenty of information that needs fresh presentation. Find a woodworker who has something to say about planning, constructing, finishing."

HANDWOVEN, From Interweave Press, 306 N. Washington, Loveland CO 80537. (303)669-7672. Editor: Linda C. Ligon. Bimonthly magazine (except July) covering handweaving, spinning and dyeing. Audience includes "practicing textile craftsmen. Article should show considerable depth of knowledge of subject, though tone should be informal and accessible." Circ. 25,000. Pays on publication. Byline given. Pays 50% kill fee. Buys first North American serial rights. Simultaneous queries and photocopied submissions OK. Computer printout submissions OK; prefers letter quality to dot matrix. SASE. Sample copy for $3.50 and 8½x11 SAE; free writer's guidelines.

Nonfiction: Historical and how-to (on weaving and other craft techniques; specific items with instructions); interview/profile (of successful and/or interesting textile craftsmen); and technical (on handweaving, spinning and dyeing technology). "All articles must contain a high level of in-depth information. Our readers are very knowledgeable about these subjects." Query. Length: 2,000 words. Pays $35-100.

Photos: State availability of photos. Identification of subjects required.

Tips: "We're particularly interested in articles about new weaving and spinning techniques as well as applying these techniques to finished products."

‡**THE HOME SHOP MACHINIST**, The Home Shop Machinist, Inc., 2779 Aero Park Dr., Box 1810, Traverse City MI 49685. (616)946-3712. Editor: Joe D. Rice. Bimonthly magazine covering machining and metalworking for the hobbyist. Estab. 1982. Circ. 17,200. Pays on publication. Byline given. Buys first North

American serial rights. Simultaneous submissions OK. SASE. Reports in 3 weeks. Free sample copy and writer's guidelines.

Nonfiction: How-to (projects designed to upgrade present shop equipment or hobby model projects that require machining); technical (should pertain to metalworking, machining, drafting, layout, welding or foundry work for the hobbyist). No fiction. Buys 50 mss/year. Query or send complete ms. Length: open; "whatever it takes to do a thorough job." Pays $20/published page, plus $6/published photo; $40/page for camera-ready art; and $40 for b&w cover photo.

Photos: Send photos with ms. Pays $6-40 for 5x7 b&w prints. Captions and identification of subjects required.

Columns/Departments: Welding; Sheetmetal; Book Reviews; New Product Reviews. "Writer should become familiar with our magazine before submitting. Query first." Buys 8 mss/year. Length: 600-1,500 words. Pays $20-50.

Fillers: Machining tips/shortcuts. Buys 12-15/year. Length: 100-300 words. Pays $15-32.

Tips: "The writer should be experienced in the area of metalworking and machining; should be extremely thorough in explanations of methods, processes—always with an eye to safety; should provide good quality b&w photos and/or clear drawings to aid in description. Visuals are of increasing importance to our readers. Carefully planned photos, drawings and charts will carry a submission to our magazine much farther along the path to publication."

LAPIDARY JOURNAL, Box 80937, San Diego CA 92138. Editor: Pansy D. Kraus. For "all ages interested in the lapidary hobby." Monthly. Rights purchased vary with author and material. Buys all rights or first serial rights. Byline given. Pays on publication. Free sample copy and writer's guidelines. Photocopied submissions OK. Query. SASE.

Nonfiction: Publishes "articles pertaining to gem cutting, gem collecting and jewelry making for the hobbyist." Buys informational, how-to, personal experience, historical, travel and technical articles. Pays 1¢/word.

Photos: Buys good contrast b&w photos. Contact editor for color. Payment varies according to size.

‡**LIVE STEAM**, Live Steam, Inc., 2779 Aero Park Dr., Box 629, Traverse City MI 49685. (616)941-7160. Editor: Joe D. Rice. Monthly magazine covering steam-powered models and full-size engines (i.e., locomotives, traction, cars, boats, stationary, etc.) "Our readers are hobbyists, many of whom are building their engines from scratch. We are interested in anything that has to do with the world of live steam-powered machinery." Circ. 12,800. Pays on publication. Byline given. Buys first North American serial rights. Simultaneous submissions OK. SASE. Reports in 3 weeks. Free sample copy and writer's guidelines.

Nonfiction: Historical/nostalgic; how-to (build projects powered by steam); new product; personal experience; photo feature; technical (must be within the context of steam-powered machinery or on machining techniques). No fiction. Buys 50 mss/year. Query or send complete ms. Length: 500-3,000 words. Pays $20/published page—$500 maximum.

Photos: Send photos with ms. Pays $40/page of finished art. Pays $6-40 for 5x7 b&w prints. Captions and identification of subjects required.

Columns/Departments: Steam traction engines; steamboats; stationary steam; steam autos. Buys 6-8 mss/year. Query. Length: 1,000-3,000 words. Pays $20-50.

Tips: "At least half of all our material is from the freelancer. Requesting a sample copy and author's guide will be a good place to start. The writer must be well-versed in the nature of live steam equipment and the hobby of scale modeling such equipment. Technical and historical accuracy is an absolute must."

LONG ISLAND HERITAGE, A Journal of and Guide to the History, Art, Architecture and Antiques of Long Island, Community Newspapers, Inc., 29 Continental Pl., Glen Cove NY 11542. (516)676-1200. Editor: Tim O'Brien. Monthly tabloid covering history, art, antiques, architecture with emphasis on Long Island and New York state "written for the 'old' loving lifestyle." Estab. 1981. Circ. 18,000. Byline given. Offers 10% kill fee. Buys one-time and simultaneous rights and makes work-for-hire assignments. Submit seasonal/holiday material 4 months in advance. Simultaneous queries, and simultaneous, photocopied and previously published submissions OK. Computer printout submissions OK "only if printout is readable, workable size and in upper and lower case"; prefers letter quality to dot matrix. SASE. Reports in 1 week on queries; 3 weeks on mss. Sample copy for 9x12 SAE and $1.05 postage; writer's guidelines for business size SAE and 1 first class stamp.

Nonfiction: General interest (antiques: explain one particular area of collecting); historical/nostalgic (Long Island histories, collecting old things, etc.); how-to (start a collection, find specific antiques, insure your collection, see your collection, etc.); humor ("we'd love to have some antique humor"); personal experience (how you started a successful collection); photo feature (on antiques, Long Island historical events, etc). Special issues include Americana, Colonial Christmas, Dolls & Toys. Buys 36-50 mss/year. Query with clips of published work or send complete ms. Length: 400-1,200 words. Pays $15-25.

Photos: State availability of photos. Pays $5-7.50 for 5x7 and 8x10 b&w prints. Captions and identification of subjects required.

Columns/Departments: Buys 15 mss/year. Query with clips of published work or send complete ms. Length: 200-400 words. Pays $5-15.

Tips: "Whenever possible we look for a Long Island connection in any article. General stories on furniture, antiques, etc. could be done by someone anywhere; we can add the local angle in a side bar. Most history-related stories are strictly Long Island. About 60% of our publication is freelance written; 40% of that is from first-time writers. We are constantly searching for new writers."

LOOSE CHANGE, Mead Publishing Corp., 21176 Alameda St., Long Beach CA 90810. (213)549-0730. Publisher: Daniel R. Mead. Monthly magazine covering collecting and investing in antique coin-operated machines. "Our audience is mainly male. Readers are all collectors or enthusiasts of antique coin-operated machines, particularly antique slot machines. Subscribers are, in general, not heavy readers." Circ. 3,000. Pays on acceptance. Byline given. Prefers to buy all rights, but also buys first and reprint rights. "We may allow author to reprint upon request in non-competitive publications." Photocopied submissions OK. Previously published submissions must be accompanied by complete list of previous sales, including sale dates. SASE. Reports in 1 month on queries; 6 weeks on mss. Sample copy $1; free writer's guidelines.

Nonfiction: Historical/nostalgic, how-to, interview/profile, opinion, personal experience, photo feature and technical. "Articles illustrated with clear, black and white photos are always considered much more favorably than articles without photos (we have a picture-oriented audience). The writer must be knowledgeable about his subject because our readers are knowledgeable and will spot inaccuracies." Buys up to 50 mss/year. Recent article example: "Jack in the Slots" (February 1982). Length: 900-6,000 words; 3,500-12,000, cover stories. Pays $150 maximum, inside stories; $250 maximum, cover stories.

Photos: "Captions should tell a complete story without reference to the body text." Send photos with ms. Reviews 8x10 b&w glossy prints. Captions required. "Purchase price for articles includes payment for photos."

Fiction: "All fiction must have a gambling/coin-operated-machine angle. Very low emphasis is placed on fiction. Stories must be exceptional to be acceptable for our readers." Buys maximum 6 mss/year. Send complete ms. Length: 800-2,500 words. Pays $60 maximum.

LOST TREASURE, 15115 S. 76th E. Ave., Bixby OK 74008. Editor: Michael Rieke. 95% freelance written. For treasure hunting hobbyists, bottle and relic collectors, amateur prospectors and miners. Monthly magazine; 72 pages. Circ. 55,000. Buys all rights. Byline given. Buys 100 mss/year. Pays on publication. Free sample copy and writer's guidelines. Will consider photocopied submissions. No simultaneous submissions. Reports in 6-8 weeks. Submit complete ms. SASE.

Nonfiction: How-to articles about treasure hunting, coinshooting, personal, profiles, stories about actual hunts. *Avoid* writing about the more famous treasures and lost mines. Length: 100-1,500 words. Pays 3¢/word.

Photos: Pays $5-10 for b&w glossy prints purchased with mss. Captions required. Pays $150 for color transparencies used on cover; 35mm minimum size.

McCALL'S NEEDLEWORK & CRAFTS MAGAZINE, 825 7th Ave. (7th fl.), New York NY 10019. Editor: Margaret Gilman. Bimonthly. All rights bought for original needlework and handicraft designs. SASE.

Nonfiction: Submit preliminary color photos for editorial consideration. Accepted made-up items must be accompanied by directions, diagrams and charts. Payment ranges from a few dollars to a few hundred dollars.

THE MAGAZINE ANTIQUES, Straight Enterprises, 551 5th Ave., New York NY 10176. (212)922-1818. Editor/Publisher: Wendell Garrett. Managing Editor: Alfred Mayor. Monthly magazine covering art, antiques and architecture for collectors, dealers, scholars and institutions. Circ. 57,985. Pays on publication. Byline given. Buys all rights. Submit seasonal/holiday material 6 months in advance. SASE. Reports in 6 months on mss.

Nonfiction: "Articles generally present new research results that pertain to art, architecture, fine arts, artists or towns, and that either correct or add to the existing record. We lean toward American art, but include some European art with an American connection." Special issues include: May, *American Furniture* and November, *American Painting*. Buys 48 mss/year. Send complete ms "and photos to give an idea." Length: 1,500-2,000 words. Pays 10¢/published word.

Photos: Reviews 4x5 transparencies and 8x10 glossy prints. "Generally we assign photos to freelancers who work with us regularly." Pay "varies widely."

Columns/Departments: Collector's Notes, Karen M. Jones (updates on the record); Current and Coming, Sarah B. Sherrill (exhibitions, forums, symposiums); Clues & Footnotes, Eleanor H. Gustafson (footnote-worthy quotations on the arts, crafts and architecture of an earlier era, from historical sources printed on manuscript); Museum Accessions, Eleanor H. Gustafson; Letters from London. "Contributors to Clues & Footnotes are paid $10 lawful money on publication." Book reviews and queries, Allison M. Eckardt.

MAKE IT WITH LEATHER, Box 1386, Fort Worth TX 76101. (817)335-4161. Editor: Earl F. Warren. Buys all rights. Byline given except for news releases or if ghosted or written on assignment with predetermined no byline. Bimonthly. Circ. 60,000. Buys 60 or more mss/year. Pays on publication. Free sample copy and writer's guidelines. Reports in 6-8 weeks. SASE.

Nonfiction: "How-to-do-it leathercraft stories illustrated with cutting patterns, carving patterns. First-person approach even though article may be ghosted. Story can be for professional or novice. Strong on details; logical progression in steps; easy to follow how-to-do-it." Length: 2,000 words or less suggested. Payment normally starts at $50 plus $10 per illustration. "All articles judged on merit and may range to '$250 plus' per ms. Depends on project and work involved by author."

Photos: 5x7, or larger, b&w photos of reproduction quality purchased with mss. Captions required. Color of professional quality is used on cover at $50/accepted photo. Ektachrome transparencies or sheet film stock. Negatives needed with all print film stock. All photos are used to illustrate project on step-by-step basis and finished item. "We can do photos in our studio if product sample is sent. No charge, but no payment for photos to writer. Letting us 'do it our way' does help on some marginal story ideas and mss since we can add such things as artists' sketches or drawings to improve the presentation."

Fillers: "Tips and Hints." Short practical hints for doing leathercraft or protecting tools, new ways of doing things, etc. Length: 100 words maximum. Pays $10 minimum.

Tips: "There are plenty of leathercraftsmen around who don't feel qualified to write up a project or who don't have the time to do it. Put their ideas and projects down on paper for them and share the payment. We need plenty of small, quick, easy-to-do ideas; things that we can do in one page are in short supply."

MINIATURE COLLECTOR, Acquire Publishing Co., Inc., 170 5th Ave., New York NY 10010. (212)989-8700. Editor: Peter Dwyer. Managing Editor: Krystyna Poray Goddu. Bimonthly magazine; 72 pages. Circ. 60,000. Byline given. Pays on publication. Submit seasonal/holiday material 4 months in advance. Photocopied and previously published submissions OK. SASE. Reports in 6-8 weeks. Sample copy $1.

Nonfiction: How-to (detailed furniture and accessories projects in l/12th scale with accurate patterns and illustrations); interview (with miniaturists, well-established collectors, museum curators with pictures); new product (very short-caption type pieces—no payment); photo feature (show reports, heavily photographic, with captions stressing pieces and availability of new and unusual pieces); and profile (of collectors with photos). Buys 3-6 mss/issue. Query. Length: 600-1,200 words. Pays $100-200. First manuscripts usually on speculation.

Photos: Send photos with ms; usually buys photo/manuscript package. Buys one-time rights. Captions required.

MODEL RAILROADER, 1027 N. 7th St., Milwaukee WI 53233. Editor: Russell G. Larson. For hobbyists interested in scale model railroading. Monthly. Buys exclusive rights. Study publication before submitting material. Reports on submissions within 4 weeks. Query. SASE.

Nonfiction: Wants construction articles on specific model railroad projects (structures, cars, locomotives, scenery, benchwork, etc.). Also photo stories showing model railroads. First-hand knowledge of subject almost always necessary for acceptable slant. Pays base rate of $54/page.

Photos: Buys photos with detailed descriptive captions only. Pays $7.50 and up, depending on size and use. Color: double b&w rate. Full color cover: $210.

THE NATIONAL KNIFE COLLECTOR, The Official Magazine of the National Knife Collectors Association, Box 21070, Chattanooga TN 37421. (615)892-5007 or 899-9456. Editor/Publisher: James V. Allday. Monthly magazine covering knife collection, manufacturing, hand crafting, selling, buying, trading; stresses "integrity in all dealings involving knives and bladed tools/weapons." Circ. 15,000. Pays on publication. Byline given. Buys all rights. Submit seasonal/holiday material 2 months in advance. Simultaneous queries OK. Computer printout and TRS-80 Mod III Scripsit disk submissions OK. SASE. Reports in 1 week on queries; 2 weeks on mss. Sample copy for $1, 9x12 SAE and 6 first class stamps; writer's guidelines for business size SAE and 2 first class stamps.

Nonfiction: Analytical pieces, book reviews, general interest, historical, how-to, interview/profile, new product, personal experience, photo feature, technical, travel. "We need freelance material for our special knifemaker issue in July of each year." Buys 1-2 mss/year. Query with clips of published work. Length: 900-2,500 words. Pays 10¢/word.

Photos: State availability of photos. Pays $7 for 5x7 b&w prints. Captions, model release, identification of subjects required.

Columns/Departments: Analytical reviews of knife, cutlery books. Buys 6 mss/year. Send complete ms. Length: 100-300 words. Pays 5-7¢/word.

Fiction: Adventure, historical, humorous, mainstream. No "non knife-related stuff." Buys 1 ms/year. Send complete item. Length: 300-700 words. Pays 5-7¢/word.

Poetry: Avant-garde, free verse, haiku, light verse, traditional, songs. Buys 6/year. "Unlimited number of poems can be submitted at one time." Length: 10-100 lines. Pays 10¢/word.

Fillers: Clippings, jokes, gags, anecdotes, short humor, newsbreaks. Buys 10/year. Length: 10-50 words. Pays $10-15.

Tips: "Get acquainted with the knife world and knife specialists by attending a knife show or the National

Knife Museum in Chattanooga. We're a feature magazine aimed at knife collectors/investors.''

‡**NATIONAL PROSPECTOR'S GAZETTE**, Gazette Publishing, Main St., Ames NB 68621. (402)727-9833. Editor: Dean Miller. Managing Editor: Paul Tainter. Bimonthly hobby tabloid for small prospectors, coin hunters, dowsers and those interested in buried treasure. Circ. 10,000. Pays on publication. Byline given. Not copyrighted. Buys all rights. Simultaneous queries and photocopied submissions OK. SASE. Reports in 1 month on queries; 6 weeks on mss. Sample copy 50¢; free writer's guidelines.

Nonfiction: General interest (rockhounding); historical/nostalgic (old west/lost treasure, Civil War battles); how-to (save money, operate mining equipment and metal detectors, dowsing techniques); personal experience (related to the field—nothing phony). Particularly looking for good, factual articles on east and south treasure hunting or prospecting. No phony, fictional stories which contain dialogue that is intentionally or obviously fictional. Buys variable number of mss. Send complete ms. Length: 1,500-3,000 words. Pays $30-50.

Photos: Send photos with ms. Reviews b&w negatives and 3x5 b&w prints. Pays $3 for large feature photo used to illustrate articles. Captions required.

NEEDLE & THREAD, Happy Hands Publishing, 4949 Byers, Ft. Worth TX 76107. (817)732-7494. Editor: Margaret Dittman. Bimonthly how-to magazine covering home sewing of all types for people interested in sewing fashions, home decorations and gifts. Estab. 1981. Circ. 750,000. Pays on acceptance. Byline given. Buys negotiable rights. Simultaneous queries and simultaneous and previously published submissions OK (if indicated where else they were submitted). Computer printout and disk submissions OK "so long as quality is not compromised." Reports in 6 weeks. Sample copy $3.

Nonfiction: How-to (with completed sewing projects); and interview/profile (of outstanding seamstresses and designers). Buys 120 mss/year. Query with snapshots of projects or clips of published work. Pays negotiable fee depending on the project.

Tips: "All projects must be original designs. On garments a manufactured pattern may be used with original decorative techniques."

NEEDLECRAFT FOR TODAY, Happy Hands Publishing, 4949 Byers, Ft. Worth TX 76107. (817)732-7494. Editor: Kay Holmquist. Bimonthly magazine for needlecraft enthusiasts. Circ. 1,100,000. Pays on acceptance "of total project." Designer credit given. Buys negotiable rights. Submit seasonal/holiday material 1 year in advance. Computer printout submissions OK "so long as it's black and clear enough for a typesetter to read"; prefers letter quality to dot matrix. SASE. Reports in 1 week. Sample copy $3; free writer's guidelines with SASE.

Nonfiction: "Crochet, needlepoint, quilting, counted cross-stitch, knitting and dollmaking, are used basically every issue. Any fiber project is of interest to us including fashions, wall hangings, home decorative items and toys—but of the highest quality and workmanship. How-to must be originally designed project. Provide a finished sample, chart, pattern, list of material and instructions." Buys 240 mss/year. Length: average 1,500 words. Pays "by arrangement, depending on the project."

Photos: "We photograph most finished projects ourselves." Send color photos with query.

Columns/Departments: Forum, guest speaker on any subject of interest to needlecrafters. Needlecraft Principles explains a craft to a beginner. Send complete ms. Pays $100-200.

Tips: "Writer must be able to write very clear step-by-step instructions for original projects submitted. We seek small bazaar items to advanced projects made from commercially available materials. Be an experienced needlecrafter."

NOSTALGIAWORLD, for Collectors and Fans, Box 231, North Haven CT 06473. (203)239-4891. Editor: Bonnie Roth. Managing Editor: Stanley N. Lozowski. Bimonthly tabloid covering entertainment collectibles. "Our readership is interested in articles on all eras—everything from early Hollywood, the big bands, country-western, rock n' roll to jazz, pop, and rhythm and blues. Many of our readers belong to fan clubs." Circ. 5,000-10,000. Pays on publication. Byline given. Buys all rights. Submit seasonal/holiday material 6 months in advance. Simultaneous queries, and simultaneous, photocopied, and previously published submissions OK. Computer printout and disk submissions OK; prefers letter quality to dot matrix printouts. SASE. Reports in 4 weeks on queries; 6 weeks on mss. Sample copy $2; writer's guidelines for legal size SAE and 1 first class stamp.

Nonfiction: Historical/nostalgic; how-to (get started in collecting); and interview/profile (of movie, recording, or sport stars). "Articles must be aimed toward the collector and provide insight into a specific area of collecting. *Nostalgiaworld* readers collect records, gum cards, toys, sheet music, movie magazines, posters and memorabilia, personality items, comics, baseball, sports memorabilia. We do *not* cater to antiques, glass, or other non-entertainment collectibles. Buys 20-30 unsolicited mss/year. All submissions must be double-spaced and typewritten."

Photos: Send photos with ms. Pays $10-25 for 5x7 b&w prints; reviews b&w contact sheets. Captions and identification of subjects required. Buys all rights.

Columns/Departments: Video Memories (early TV); and 78 RPM-For Collectors Only (advice and tips for the collector of 78 RPM recordings; prices, values, outstanding rarities). Buys varying number of mss/year. Query or send complete ms. Length: 500-1,500 words. Pays $10-25.

Tips: "Most readers are curious to find out what their collectibles are worth. With inflation running at such a high rate, people are investing in nostalgia items more than ever. *Nostalgiaworld* provides a place to buy and sell and also lists conventions and collectors' meets across the country. Our publication is interested in the entertainment field as it evolved in the twentieth century. Our readers collect anything and everything related to this field."

NUMISMATIC NEWS, Krause Publications, 700 E. State St., Iola WI 54990. (715)445-2214. Editor: Bob Lemke. Weekly magazine about United States coins, medals, tokens, and collecting for beginning and advanced collectors. Circ. 55,000. Pays on acceptance. Byline given. Buys first North American serial rights. Photocopied submissions OK. Computer printout submissions OK; prefers letter quality to dot matrix. SASE. Reports in 2 weeks. Free sample copy.

Nonfiction: "We're seeking features on any phase of coin collecting and investing." No news items. "Our staff covers the hard news." Buys 3-4 mss/issue. Send complete ms. Length: 500-3,000 words. Pays first time contributors 3¢/word; negotiates fees for others.

Photos: Send photos with ms. Pays $5 minimum for 5x7 b&w glossy prints. Captions and model release required.

NUTSHELL NEWS, Boynton and Associates, Clifton House, Clifton VA 22024. (703)830-1000. Editor: Ann Ruble. Monthly magazine about miniatures for miniatures enthusiasts, collectors, craftspeople and hobbyists. "*Nutshell News* is the only magazine in the miniatures field which offers readers comprehensive coverage of all facets of miniature collecting and crafting." Circ. 35,000. Pays on publication. Buys all rights in the field. Phone queries OK, "but would prefer letters and photos." Submit seasonal material 4 months in advance. Previously published submissions OK ("if they did not appear in a competing magazine"). Reports in 2 months. Sample copy $2.75; free writer's guidelines for SASE.

Nonfiction: Interview/profile of craftspeople specializing in miniatures. Research articles on design periods and styles. Articles on private and museum collections of miniatures. How-to articles on decorating, building miniature furniture, dollhouses, rooms, accessories. Show reports, book reviews, new product information. "We need stringers nationwide to work on an assignment basis, preferably freelancers with knowledge in the miniatures field to cover interviews with craftspeople and report on miniature shows." Buys 10 mss/issue. Query with "photos of the work to be written about. We're looking for craftspeople doing fine quality work, or collectors with top notch collections. Photos give us an idea of this quality." Length: 1,200-1,500 words. Pays 10¢/published word.

Photos: Pays $7.50 minimum for 5x7 b&w glossy prints. Pays $10 maximum for 35mm or larger color transparencies. Captions required.

OHIO ANTIQUE REVIEW, Box 538, Worthington OH 43085. Managing Editor: Charles Muller. (614)885-9757. 60% freelance written. For an antique-oriented readership, "generally well-educated, interested in folk art and other early American items." Monthly tabloid. Circ. 10,000. Pays on publication date assigned at time of purchase. Buys first North American serial rights and one-time rights. Byline given. Phone queries OK. Submit seasonal/holiday material 3 months in advance. Simultaneous, photocopied and previously published submissions OK. Computer printout submissions OK; prefers letter quality to dot matrix. SASE. Reports in 1 month. Free sample copy and writer's guidelines.

Nonfiction: "The articles we desire concern history and production of furniture, pottery, china, and other antiques of the period prior to the 1880s. In some cases, contemporary folk art items are acceptable. We are also interested in reporting on antique shows and auctions with statements on conditions and prices. We do not want articles on contemporary collectibles." Buys 5-8 mss/issue. Query with clips of published work. Query should show "author's familiarity with antiques and the kinds of antiques, and an interest in the historical development of artifacts relating to early America." Length: 200-2,000 words. Pays $75-100.

Photos: State availability of photos with query. Payment included in ms price. Uses 5x7 or larger glossy b&w prints. Captions required. Articles with photographs receive preference.

Tips: "Give us a call and let us know of specific interests. We are more concerned with the background in antiques than in writing abilities. The writing can be edited, but the knowledge imparted is of primary interest."

THE OLD BOTTLE MAGAZINE, Box 243, Bend OR 97701. (503)382-6978. Editor: Shirley Asher. For collectors of old bottles, insulators, relics. Monthly. Circ. 3,500. Buys all rights. Byline given. Buys 35 mss/year. Pays on acceptance. Will send a sample copy to a writer on request. No query required. Reports in 1 month. SASE.

Nonfiction, Photos and Fillers: "We are soliciting factual accounts on specific old bottles, canning jars, insulators and relics." Stories of a general nature on these subjects not wanted. "Interviews of collectors are usually not suitable when written by noncollectors. A knowledge of the subject is imperative. Would highly recommend potential contributors study an issue before making submissions. Articles that tie certain old bottles to a historical background are desired." Length: 250-2,500 words. Pays $10/published page. B&w glossy prints and clippings purchased separately. Pays $5.

OLD CARS NEWSPAPER, Krause Publications, 700 E. State St., Iola WI 54990. (715)445-2214. Editor: Tony Hossain. 40% freelance written. "Our readers collect, drive and restore everything from 1899 locomobiles to '76 Cadillac convertibles. They cover all age and income groups." Weekly tabloid; 60 pages. Circ. 95,000. Pays on acceptance. Buys all rights. Phone queries OK. Byline given. SASE. Reports in 2 months. Sample copy 50¢.
Nonfiction: Historical (sites related to auto history, interesting oldsters from the automobile past, etc.); how-to (good restoration articles); interview (with important national-level personages in the car hobby); nostalgia (auto-related, and only occasionally); and photo feature (by knowing hobby reporters, definite query). Buys 4 mss/issue. Query. Pays 3¢/word.
Photos: State availability of photos with query. Pays $5 for 5x7 b&w glossy prints. Captions required. Buys all rights.
Columns/Departments: Book reviews (new releases for hobbyists). Buys 1 ms/issue. Query. Pays 3¢/word.
Fillers: Newsbreaks. Buys 50/year. Pays 3¢/word.
Tips: "Must know automotive hobby well. One writer caught the editor's eye by submitting excellent drawings with his manuscript."

‡OLD CARS PRICE GUIDE, Krause Publications, 700 E. State St., Iola WI 54990. (715)445-2214. Editor: John A. Gunnell. Quarterly magazine of old car prices for old car hobbyists and investors. Circ. 85,000. Pays on acceptance. Byline given. Buys first North American serial rights. Submit seasonal/holiday material 3 months in advance. Computer printout and disk submissions OK. Reports in 1 week. Sample copy $2.25 and 8x10 SASE.
Nonfiction: How-to (buy, sell, collector cars); opinion (on car values market); technical (how to fix a car to increase value); investment angles. "All articles should be car-value related and include information or actual price lists on recent sales (of more than one car). Articles about brands or types of cars *not* covered in regular price lists are preferred. Plenty of research and knowledge of the old car marketplace is usually essential. Photos required with all articles. No historic or nostalgic pieces." Buys 8-12 mss/year. Send complete ms. Length: 600-1,000 words. Pays $75-150.
Photos: Send photos with ms. Pays $50 minimum for 4x4 color transparencies used on cover; $5 for b&w prints; "undetermined for color." Captions and identification of subjects required. Buys one-time rights.
Columns/Departments: Book Review (books on car values or investments). Buys 4 mss/year. Send complete ms. Length: 100-300 words. Pays 3¢/word; $5/photo.
Fillers: Jokes, gags, anecdotes, short humor, newsbreaks (related to old car values). Pays 3¢/word.

PACIFIC WOODWORKER, Box 4881, Santa Rosa CA 95402. (707)525-8494. Editor: Jean Davis. Bimonthly magazine covering woodworking, wood carving, cabinetmaking for the small cabinet shop owner, wood craftsperson, advanced hobbyist or wood carver. Estab. 1981. Circ. 5,000. Pays on publication. Byline given. Buys first North American serial rights. Simultaneous queries and photocopied submissions OK if identified as such. "Would consider computer printout or disk submissions from someone whose published or unpublished work I had already seen." SASE. Reports in 1 month on mss. Sample copy $1; writer's guidelines for SAE and 1 first class stamp.
Nonfiction: Historical (on woodworking techniques); how-to skills of interest to small business craftsmen; interview/profile (of successful small wood crafters); new product (of interest to woodworkers); personal experience (related to running a small shop/selling/designing woodcraft products); technical (woodcraft related). "Specific topics we would like to see include: finishing techniques, workshop organization, workshop efficiency and shortcut hints, workshop safety, characteristics of specific woods, successful marketing techniques for the small shop owner, how to start a woodworking business, interviews with prominent woodworkers (especially if accompanied by quality photos of them and their work), new products and their use. No beginner level/hobby shop woodworking projects. No material on people/events outside our region (Western US)." Buys 30 mss/year. Query or send complete ms. Length: 350-1,500 words maximum. Pays $75 maximum.
Photos: Chod Harris, photo editor. "We especially like articles accompanied by top quality, black and white glossy photos. Also need cover photos." State availability of photos in query, or send with ms. B&w 8x10 glossy prints preferred. Pays $5-25. Captions required. Buys all photo rights. Photos returned if requested.
Columns/Departments: Marketing Techniques, New Ideas and Products, Show Reviews, Shortcuts That Work, Restoration and Architectural Woodworking. Buys 20 mss/year. Query or send complete ms. Length: 250-500 words. Pays $50 maximum.
Tips: "Knowledge of the subject matter through personal experience is most essential for our writers. Good ideas and solid know-how are more important than authors' previous publications. We will work with less experienced writers to develop and express workable ideas."

QUILTER'S NEWSLETTER MAGAZINE, Box 394, Wheatridge CO 80033. Editor: Bonnie Leman. Monthly. Circ. 130,000. Buys first or second North American serial rights. Buys 15 mss/year. Pays on acceptance. Free sample copy. Reports in 3-4 weeks. Submit complete ms. SASE.

Nonfiction: "We are interested in articles on the subject of quilts and quiltmakers *only*. We are not interested in anything relating to 'Grandma's Scrap Quilts,' but could use material about contemporary quilting." Pays 3¢/ word minimum.

Photos: Additional payment for photos depends on quality.

Fillers: Related to quilts and quiltmakers only.

Tips: "Be specific, brief, and professional in tone. Study our magazine to learn the kind of thing we like. Send us material which fits into our format, but which is different enough to be interesting. Realize that we think we're the best quilt magazine on the market and that we're aspiring to be even better, then send us the cream off the top of your quilt material."

RAILROAD MODEL CRAFTSMAN, Box 700, Newton NJ 07860. (201)383-3355. Managing Editor: William C. Schaumburg. 75% freelance written. For "model railroad hobbyists, in all scales and gauges." Monthly. Circ. 97,000. Buys all rights. Buys 50-100 mss/year. Pays on publication. Sample copy $1.75. Submit seasonal material 6 months in advance. SASE requested for writer's and photographer's information.

Nonfiction: "How-to and descriptive model railroad features written by persons who did the work are preferred. Almost all our features and articles are written by active model railroaders familiar with the hobby. It is difficult for non-modelers to know how to approach writing for this field." Minimum payment: $1.75/column inch of copy ($50/page).

Photos: Purchased with or without mss. Buys sharp 8x10 glossy prints and 35mm or larger color transparencies. Minimum payments: $10 for photos or $2/diagonal inch of published b&w photos, $3 for color transparencies and $100 for covers which must tie in with article in that issue. Caption information required.

‡ROCKY MOUNTAIN MINIATURE JOURNAL, Box 3315, Littleton CO 80122. (303)779-6154. Editor: Norm Nielsen. Bimonthly magazine covering dollhouses and miniatures for collectors and crafters in the miniature hobby. Estab. 1981. Circ. 1,200. Pays on publication. Byline given. Buys one-time rights. Submit seasonal/holiday material 2 months in advance. SASE. Sample copy $2.25; writer's guidelines for SAE.

Nonfiction: Only how-to articles on dollhouses and related miniatures topics. Query first. Pays 2¢/word.

Photos: Send photos with ms. Reviews 5x7 or 8x10 b&w glossies. Identification of subjects required.

Tips: "We use how-to pieces on subjects such as making furniture and modeling clay flowers—crafts that can be adapted to dollhouses or miniatures."

JOEL SATER'S ANTIQUES & AUCTION NEWS, 225 W. Market St., Marietta PA 17547. (717)426-1956. Managing Editor: Joel Sater. Editor: Denise Murphy. For dealers and buyers of antiques, nostalgics and collectibles; and those who follow antique shows and shops. Biweekly tabloid; 24-28 pages. Circ. 80,000. Pays on publication. Buys all rights. Phone queries OK. Submit seasonal/holiday material 3 months in advance. Simultaneous (if so notified), photocopied and previously published submissions OK. SASE. Reports in 6 weeks. Free sample copy (must identify *Writer's Market*).

Nonfiction: Historical (related to American artifacts or material culture); how-to (restoring and preserving antiques and collectibles); informational (research on antiques or collectibles; "news about activities in our field"); interview; nostalgia; personal experience; photo feature; profile; and travel. Buys 100-150 mss/year. Query or submit complete ms. Length: 500-2,500 words. Pays $5-25.

Photos: Purchased with or without accompanying ms. Captions required. Send prints. Pays $2-10 for b&w photos. Offers no additional payment for photos purchased with mss.

SCOTT STAMP MONTHLY, (formerly *Scott's Monthly Stamp Journal*), 3 E. 57th St., New York NY 10022. (212)371-5700. Editor: Ira S. Zweifach. For stamp collectors, from the beginner to the sophisticated philatelist. Monthly magazine; 132 pages. Circ. 30,000. Rights purchased vary with author and material. Byline given. Usually buys all rights. Buys 8-9 unsolicited mss/year. Pays within 1 month after acceptance. Submit seasonal or holiday material 3 months in advance. Reports in 4 weeks. SASE.

Nonfiction: "We want articles of a serious philatelic nature, ranging in length from 1,500-2,500 words. We are also in the market for articles, written in an engaging fashion, concerning the remote byways and often-overlooked aspects of the hobby. Writing should be clear and concise, and subjects should be well-researched and documented. Illustrative material should also accompany articles whenever possible." Query. Pays $200-250.

Photos: State availability of photos. Offers no additional payment for b&w photos used with mss.

Tips: "*Scott Stamp Monthly* is undergoing a complete change. Although most material deals with stamps, new writers are invited to seek assignments. It is not necessary to be a stamp collector or a published professional. You must be a good writer, and be willing to do careful research on strong material. Because our emphasis is on lively, interesting articles about stamps, including historical perspectives and human interest slants, we are open to writers who can produce the same. Of course, if you are an experienced philatelist, so much the better."

We do not want stories about the picture on a stamp taken from a history book or an encyclopedia and dressed up to look like research. We want articles written from a philatelic standpoint. If idea is good and not a basic re-hash, we are interested.''

‡SEW NEWS, The Newspaper for People who Sew, Sew News, Inc., 208 S. Main, Seattle WA 98104. (206)624-4665. Bimonthly newspaper covering sewing—fashion and crafts for a mostly female audience, age 30-60, ranging from beginning home-sewers to professional dressmakers. "Our readers sew for creative satisfaction and to save money." Circ. 50,000. Pays on publication. Byline given. Offers $15 minimum kill fee. Buys first North American serial rights. Submit seasonal/holiday material 4 months in advance. Simultaneous queries OK. SASE. Reports in 1 month. Sample copy $1.50 postpaid; writer's guidelines for letter size SAE and 1 first class stamp.
Nonfiction: Laura Rehrmann and Jane Meyer, articles editors. How-to, interview/profile, opinion, photo feature. "All articles must be related to sewing. We look for articles on specific sewing techniques and tips, sewing for fashion, craft how-to's, gift ideas, textile and product information, sewing for sports, and feature articles on people in the sewing industry. No cutesy articles or windy testimonials; no kitsch-y crafts. We want straightforward articles with neither a folksy nor an old-school textbook style." Buys 150 mss/year. Query with published clips. Length: 200-2,000 words. Pays $35-150.
Photos: Send photos with query or ms. Pays $10 for 8x10 b&w prints. Buys one-time rights.
Tips: "Every article should be upbeat and express the fun, creativity and excitement of sewing. Every article should teach a specific technique, inspire the reader to try a new project, or tell of an interesting person, company, historical vignette, etc., related to sewing. Writing must be lively and to-the-point; instructions must be clear, concise and free of jargon.''

THE SPINNING WHEEL, 1981 Moreland Pkwy., Annapolis MD 21401. (301)267-7655. Publisher: Richard Sherry. For antique collectors and dealers. 6 times a year. Computer printout submissions OK; prefers letter quality to dot matrix. Pays on publication. Buys exclusive rights unless author wishes some reservations. Byline given. SASE.
Nonfiction: Authentic, well-researched material on antiques in any and all collecting areas; home decorating ideas with antiques. Prefers combined scholar-student-amateur appeal. No first-person or family history. Prefers draft or outline first. Requires bibliography with each ms. Quality illustrations, color if available. Length: 500-1,500 words. Pays minimum $1/published inch, including pictures.
Photos: Photos and professional line drawings accepted. Photos should be top quality b&w, no smaller than 5x7. If of individual items shown in groups, each should be separated for mechanical expediency. Avoid fancy groupings. 4-color transparencies for illustrations must also be top quality (35mm or 4x5).
Tips: "Find out what young collectors are buying at modest prices and write about it.''

‡SPIN-OFF, Interweave Press, 306 N. Washington, Loveland CO 80537. (303)669-7672. Editors: Lee Raven, Anne Bliss. Quarterly magazine covering handspinning, dyeing, techniques and projects for using hand-spun fibers. Audience includes "practicing textile/fiber craftsmen. Article should show considerable depth of knowledge of subject, though the tone should be informal and accessible." Circ. 6,000. Pays on publication. Byline given. Pays 50% kill fee. Buys first North American serial rights. Simultaneous queries and photocopied submissions OK. SASE. Sample copy $2.50 and 8½x11 SAE; free writer's guidelines.
Nonfiction: Historical and how-to (on spinning; knitted, crocheted, woven projects from handspun fibers with instructions); interview/profile (of successful and/or interesting fiber craftsmen); and technical (on spinning, dyeing or fiber technology, use, properties). "All articles must contain a high level of in-depth information. Our readers are very knowledgeable about these subjects." Query. Length: 2,000 words. Pays $25-100.
Photos: State availability of photos. Identification of subjects required.

‡SPORTS COLLECTORS DIGEST, Krause Publications, 700 E. State St., Iola WI 54990. (715)445-2214. Editor: Steve Ellingboe. Sports memorabilia magazine published 26 times/year. "We serve collectors of sports memorabilia—baseball cards, yearbooks, programs, autographs, jerseys, bats, balls, books, magazines, ticket stubs, etc." Circ. 14,000. Pays on acceptance. Byline given. Buys first North American serial rights. Submit seasonal/holiday material 3 months in advance. Simultaneous queries and photocopied submissions OK. SASE. Reports in 5 weeks on queries; 2 months on mss. Free sample copy and writer's guidelines.
Nonfiction: General interest (new card issues; research on older sets); historical/nostalgic (old stadiums, old collectibles, etc.); how-to (buy cards, sell cards and other collectibles; display collectibles, ways to get autographs, jerseys, and other memorabilia); interview/profile (or well-known collectors, ball players—but must focus on collectibles); new product (new card sets); personal experience ("what I collect and why"-type stories). No sports stories. "We are not competing with *The Sporting News*, *Sports Illustrated* or your daily paper. Sports collectibles only!" Buys 40-60 mss/year. Query. Length: 300-3,000 words; prefers 1,000 words. Pays $10-50.
Photos: Unusual collectibles. State availability of photos. Pays $5-15 for b&w prints. Identification of subjects required. Buys all rights.

Columns/Departments: "We have all the columnists we need, but welcome ideas for new columns." Buys 100-150 mss/year. Query. Length: 600-3,000 words. Pays $15-60.

Tips: "If you are a collector, you know what collectors are interested in. Write about it. No shallow, puff pieces. Our readers are too smart for that. Only well-researched articles about sports memorabilia and collecting. Some sports nostalgia pieces are OK. Open to 'what I collect and why'-type features. Write only about the areas you know about. Many of our writers do not receive payment; they submit articles for the satisfaction and prestige and to help their fellow hobbyists. It's that kind of hobby and that kind of magazine."

‡**STAMP WORLD, Fun & Profit Through Stamps,** Amos Press Inc., 911 Vandemark Rd., Sidney OH 45367. (513)498-2111, ext. 264. Editor: Fred Boughner. Monthly magazine covering stamp and postal history collecting for beginning to average stamp collectors and those with just a mild interest. Estab. 1981. Circ. 35,000+. Pays on acceptance. Byline given. Offers 40% kill fee. Buys first North American serial rights. Submit seasonal/holiday material 4 months in advance. Simultaneous queries and previously published submissions OK. SASE. Reports in 3 weeks on queries; 1 month on mss. Writer's guidelines for SAE with 20¢ postage.

Nonfiction: Historical/nostalgic; how-to (on rudiments of stamp buying, collecting); humor (stamp-related); interview/profile (of famous collectors and famous people who collect). No technical articles on stamps, printing, etc. or articles that "put down" collecting in general. Buys 120 mss/year. Query with clips if available. Length: 1,800-3,500 words. Pays $85-200.

Photos: Ed Heys, photo editor. State availability of photos or send photos with ms. Pays variable rate for contact sheets, negatives, 4x5 color transparencies and 8x10 b&w prints. Identification of subjects required.

Fiction: Adventure, fantasy, historical, horror, humorous, mystery, science fiction. "All fiction *must* be stamp or postally related." Buys 10 mss/year. Query. Length: 2,000-3,000 words. Pays $150-250.

Fillers: Anecdotes, short humor. Buys 15-20/year. Length: 50-150 words. Pays $20-35.

Tips: "Writer need not be a collector. We look for lively, easy-to-read pieces on stamp history, personalities and humor. Ability to write is more important than philatelic knowledge."

‡**STANDARD CATALOG OF AMERICAN CARS 1899-1942,** Krause Publications, 700 E. State St., Iola WI 54990. (715)445-2214. Editor: John A. Gunnell. Annual catalog of antique, classic and special-interest automobile prices, technical data and historical facts. Pays on acceptance. Byline given. Buys all rights.

Nonfiction: Needs are primarily for technical data on pre-war American automobiles. "This includes engine and chassis specifications; production totals; code numbers and interpretations; optional equipment and standard equipment information and estimates of current prices for specific models. Each contributor to the *Catalog* will be assigned the task of collecting data on a certain, specific brand of car. Factual correctness of data is essential. Data sheets for compiling the data to a standard format can be provided." Pays negotiable rates. Query first for assignments.

TREASURE, Jess Publishing, 16146 Covello St., Van Nuys CA 91406. (213)988-6910. Editor-in-Chief: David Weeks. Managing Editor: Jim Williams. Emphasizes treasure hunting and metal detecting. Monthly magazine. Circ. 100,000. Pays on publication. Buys all rights. Byline given. Phone queries OK. Submit seasonal/holiday material 4 months in advance. Previously published submissions OK. SASE. Reports in 2 months. Free writer's guidelines.

Nonfiction: Jim Williams, articles editor. How-to (coinshooting and treasure hunting tips); informational and historical (location of lost treasures with emphasis on the lesser-known); interviews (with treasure hunters); profiles (successful treasure hunters and metal detector hobbyists); personal experience (treasure hunting); technical (advice on use of metal detectors and metal detector designs). Buys 6-8 mss/issue. Send complete ms. Length: 300-3,000 words. Pays $30-200. "Our rate of payment varies considerably depending upon the proficiency of the author, the quality of the photographs, the importance of the subject matter, and the amount of useful information given."

Photos: Offers no additional payment for 5x7 or 8x10 b&w glossy prints used with mss. Pays $50 minimum for color transparencies (120 or 2¼x2¼). Color for cover only. Model release required.

Tips: "Clear photos and other illustrations are a must."

TRI-STATE TRADER, Mayhill Publishing, Box 90, Knightstown IN 46148. Editor: Robert M. Reed. Weekly newspaper covering antiques, auctions, collectibles, genealogy for collectors nationwide interested in history and past lifestyles. Circ. 38,000. Pays on publication. Byline given. Buys one-time rights. Submit seasonal/holiday material 3 months in advance. Simultaneous queries and photocopied and previously published submissions OK. SASE. Reports in 3 weeks on queries; 1 month on mss. Sample copy for SAE and 60¢ postage; free writer's guidelines.

Nonfiction: Historical/nostalgic (of interest to collectors). "We're always interested in brief articles of historical places, events and persons, past lifestyles and how today's antiques are used." Buys 175 mss/year. Query. Length: 300-1,100 words. Pays variable rates.

Fillers: History, places, dates, etc. Length: 30-150 words.

Tips: "We're interested in general news relating to collectibles and history. Read the *TST* and know this market. We are open to most any writer, but our readers are most knowledgeable on our topics and expect the same from writers."

WESTERN & EASTERN TREASURES, People's Publishing, Inc., Box Z, Arcata CA 95521. Editor: Rosemary Anderson. Emphasizes treasure hunting for all ages, entire range in education, coast-to-coast readership. Monthly magazine. Circ. 70,000. Computer printout and disk submissions OK; prefers letter quality to dot matrix. Pays on publication. Buys all rights. SASE. Reports in 4 weeks. Sample copy and writer's guidelines for 50¢.
Nonfiction: How-to (use of equipment, how to look for rocks, gems, prospect for gold, where to look for treasures, rocks, etc., "first-person" experiences). "No purely historical manuscripts or manuscripts that require two-part segments, or more." Buys 200 unsolicited mss/year. Submit complete ms. Length: maximum 1,500 words. Pays 2¢/word maximum.
Photos: Purchased with accompanying ms. Captions required. Submit prints or transparencies. Pays $5 maximum for 3x5 and up b&w glossy prints; $10 maximum for 35mm and up color transparencies. Model release required.
Columns/Departments: Detector Clinic, Tip of the Month. Buys 50/year. Send complete ms. Length: 800-1,500 words. Pays 2¢/word maximum. Open to suggestions for new columns or departments; address Rosemary Anderson.

THE WOODWORKER'S JOURNAL, Madrigal Publishing Co., Inc., 25 Town View Dr., Box 1629, New Milford CT 06776. (203)355-2697. Editor: James J. McQuillan. Managing Editor: Thomas G. Begnal. Bimonthly magazine covering woodworking for woodworking hobbyists of all levels of skill. Circ. 75,000. Pays on acceptance. Byline given. Buys all rights. Submit seasonal/holiday material 3 months in advance. SASE. Reports in 5 weeks. Free sample copy and writer's guidelines.
Nonfiction: "In each issue, we try to offer a variety of plans—some selected with the novice in mind, others for the more experienced cabinetmaker. We also like to offer a variety of furniture styles, i.e., contemporary, colonial, Spanish, etc. We are always in the market for original plans for all types of furniture, wood accessories, jigs, and other shop equipment. We are also interested in seeing carving and marquetry projects." Buys 20-30 mss/year. Send complete ms. Length "varies with project." Pays $80-120/page. "Payment rate is for a complete project submission, consisting of dimensioned sketches, a write-up explaining how the project was built, and at least one high-quality b&w photo."
Photos: Send photos with ms. Reviews 5x7 b&w prints. "Photo payment is included in our basic payment rate of $80-120/page for a complete project submission." Captions required. Buys all rights.

THE WORKBASKET, 4251 Pennsylvania Ave., Kansas City MO 64111. Editor: Roma Jean Rice. Issued monthly except bimonthly June-July and November-December. Buys first rights. Pays on acceptance. Query. Reports in 6 weeks. SASE.
Nonfiction: Interested in articles of 400-500 words of step-by-step directions for craft projects and gardening articles of 200-500 words. Pays 7¢/word.
Photos: Pays $7-10 for 8x10 glossies with ms.
Columns/Departments: "Readers' Recipes" (original recipes from readers); "Making Cents" (short how-to section featuring ideas for pin money from readers).

WORKBENCH, 4251 Pennsylvania Ave., Kansas City MO 64111. (816)531-5730. Editor: Jay W. Hedden. 90% freelance written. For woodworkers. Circ. 800,000. Pays on acceptance. Buys all rights. Byline given if requested. Reports in 2-4 weeks. Query. SASE. Free sample copy and writer's guidelines.
Nonfiction: "In the last couple of years, we have increased our emphasis on home improvement and home maintenance, and now we are getting into alternate energy projects. Ours is a nuts-and-bolts approach, rather than telling how someone has done it. Because most of our readers own their own homes, we stress 'retrofitting' of energy-saving devices, rather than saying they should rush out and buy or build a solar home. Energy conservation is another subject we cover thoroughly; insulation, weatherstripping, making your own storm windows. We still are very strong in woodworking, cabinetmaking and furniture construction. Projects range from simple toys to complicated reproductions of furniture now in museums." Pays: $125/published page, up or down depending on quality of submission.
Columns/Departments: Shop tips bring $20 maximum with drawing and/or photo.
Tips: "If you can consistently provide good material, including photos, your rates will go up, and you will get assignments. The field is wide open, but only if you produce quality material and clear, sharp b&w photos. If we pay less than the rate, it's because we have to supply photos, information, drawings or details the contributor has overlooked. Contributors should look over the published story to see what they should include next time. Our editors are skilled woodworkers, do-it-yourselfers and photographers. We have a complete woodworking shop at the office and we use it often to check out construction details of projects submitted to us."

WORLD COIN NEWS, Krause Publications, 700 E. State, Iola WI 54990. (715)445-2214. Editor-in-Chief: Russ Rulau. Weekly newspaper about non-United States coin collecting for novices and advanced collectors of foreign coins, medals, and paper money. Circ. 15,000. Pays on acceptance. Byline given. Buys first North American serial rights; first reprint rights. Submit seasonal material 1 month in advance. Simultaneous and photocopied submissions OK. Reports in 2 weeks. Free sample copy.
Nonfiction: "Send us timely news stories related to collecting foreign coins and current information on coin values and markets." Send complete ms. Buys 30 mss/year. Length: 500-2,000 words. Pays 3¢/word to first-time contributors; fees negotiated for later articles.
Photos: Send photos with ms. Pays $5 minimum for b&w prints. Captions and model release required. Buys first rights and first reprint rights.

YESTERYEAR, Yesteryear Publications, Box 2, Princeton WI 54968. (414)295-3969. Editor: Michael Jacobi. For antique dealers and collectors, people interested in collecting just about anything, and nostalgia buffs. Monthly tabloid. Circ. 6,000. Pays on publication. Buys one-time rights. Byline given. Submit seasonal/holiday material 3 months in advance. Simultaneous, photocopied and previously published submissions OK. No computer printout or disk submissions. SASE. Reports in 1 month for queries; 1 month for mss. Sample copy $1.
Nonfiction: General interest (basically, anything pertaining to antiques, collectible items or nostalgia in general); historical (again, pertaining to the above categories); how-to (refinishing antiques, how to collect). The more specific and detailed, the better. "We do not want personal experience or opinion articles." Buys 36 mss/year. Send complete ms. Pays $5-25.
Photos: Send photos with ms. Pays $5 for 5x7 b&w glossy or matte prints; $5 for 5x7 color prints. Captions preferred.
Columns/Departments: "We will consider new column concepts as long as they fit into the general areas of antiques, collectibles, nostalgia." Buys 3/issue. Send complete ms. Pays $5-25.

Home and Garden

AUSTIN HOMES & GARDENS, Diversified Productions, Inc., 1800 Rio Grande, Austin TX 78701. (512)474-7666. Managing Editor: Marsia Hart Reese. Monthly magazine emphasizing Austin, Texas homes, people, events, and gardens for current, former, and prospective residents. Circ. 11,000. Average issue includes 15 articles. Pays on publication. Byline given. Buys first North American serial rights. Local phone queries OK. Photocopied submissions OK. Computer printout submissions OK "as long as there are margins on the paper without holes in them"; prefers letter quality to dot matrix. SASE. Reports in 1 month. Sample copy $1.
Nonfiction: General interest (interior design; trends in home furnishings and landscaping; arts and crafts); historical (local); how-to (on home or garden); new product (for home or gardening); and fashion feature. Buys 7 mss/issue. Query. Length: 700-1,500 words. Pays $75 minimum.
Columns/Departments: Departments include The Errant Epicure (outstanding local restaurants); Breakaway (travel in or near Austin); and Profile (interesting Austin people). Query. Length: 500-1,000 words. Pays $100 minimum.
Tips: "Always looking for good freelances, but can only work with writers who live in our area and are familiar with our publication."

BETTER HOMES AND GARDENS, 1716 Locust St., Des Moines IA 50336. (515)284-3000. Editor: Gordon G. Greer. For "middle-and-up income, homeowning and community-concerned families." Monthly. Circ. 8,000,000. Buys all rights. Pays on acceptance. Query preferred. Submit seasonal material 1 year in advance. Mss should be directed to the department where the story line is strongest. SASE.
Nonfiction: "Freelance material is used in areas of travel, health, cars, money management, and home entertainment. Reading the magazine will give the writer the best idea of our style. We do not deal with political subjects or areas not connected with the home, community and family." Length: 500-2,000 words. Pays top rates based on estimated length of published article; $100-2,000.
Photos: Shot under the direction of the editors. Purchased with mss.
Tips: "Follow and study the magazine, to see what we do and how we do it. There are no secrets, after all; it's all there on the printed page. Having studied several issues, the writer should come up with one or several ideas that interest him, and, hopefully, us. The next step is to write a good query letter. It needn't be more than a page in length (for each idea), and should include a good stab at a title, a specific angle, and a couple of paragraphs devoted to the main points of the article. This method is not guaranteed to produce a sale, of course; there is no magic formula. But it's still the best way I know to have an idea considered."

CANADIAN DO IT YOURSELF MAGAZINE, Centre Publications Ltd., Suite 1, 2000 Ellesmere Rd., Scarborough, Ontario, Canada M1H 2W4. (416)438-1153. Editor: Jo Ann Stevenson. Publications Director: G.S. Werlick. Magazine published 8 times/year for home do-it-yourselfers. Circ. 65,000. Pays on publication. Byline given. Buys all rights. Submit seasonal/holiday material 6 months in advance. SASE. Reports in 1 month on queries. Free sample copy.
Nonfiction: How-to (home improvement, woodworking, crafts, etc.). Buys variable number mss/year. Length: 500-3,000 words. Pays $200-600.
Photos: Send photos with ms.

CANADIAN WORKSHOP, The Magazine for All Home Do-It-Yourselfers, Nordais Publications, Unit 6, 3781 Victoria Park Ave., Scarborough, Ontario, Canada M1W 3K5. (416)492-7330. Editor: Bob Pennycook. Monthly magazine covering the "do-it-yourself market including projects, renovation and restoration, gardening, maintenance and decoration. Canadian writers only, please." Circ. 55,000. Pays on publication. Byline given. Offers 75% kill fee. Buys all rights. Submit seasonal/holiday material 6 months in advance. Simultaneous queries OK. SASE. Reports in 3 weeks. Sample copy $2; free writer's guidelines.
Nonfiction: How-to (gardening, home and home machinery maintenance, renovation projects, woodworking projects). Buys 20-40 mss/year. Query with clips of published work. Length: 1,500-4,000 words. Pays $150-400.
Photos: Send photos with ms. Pays $20-150 for 2¼x2¼ color transparencies; covers higher; $10-50 for b&w contact sheets. Captions, model release, and identification of subjects required.
Tips: "Freelancers must be aware of our magazine format. Product-types used in how-to articles must be readily available across Canada. Deadlines for articles are 5 months in advance of cover date. How-to's should be detailed enough for the amateur but appealing to the experienced."

COLORADO HOMES & LIFESTYLES, Suite 154, 2550 31st St., Denver CO 80216. (303)433-6533. Editor: Mary McCall. Bimonthly magazine covering Colorado homes and lifestyles for designers and upper-middle-class and high income households. Circ. 33,000. Pays on publication. Byline given. Buys all rights. Submit seasonal/holiday material 6 months in advance. Simultaneous queries and photocopied submissions OK. Computer printout submissions OK: prefers letter quality to dot matrix. SASE. Reports in 1 month.
Nonfiction: Fine furnishings in the home, gardening and plants, decorating and design, and fine food and entertaining. Buys 24 mss/year. Send complete ms. Length: 800-1,500 words. "For celebrity features (Colorado celebrity and home) pay is $300-1500. For unique, well-researched pieces on Colorado people, places, etc., pay is 15-50¢/word. For regular articles, 10-20¢/word. The more specialized and Colorado-oriented your article is, the more generous we are."
Photos: Send photos with ms. Reviews 35mm color transparencies and b&w glossy prints. Identification of subjects required.

ECM NEWSLETTERS, INC., Suite F57, 8520 Sweetwater, Houston TX 77037. (713)591-6015. Editor: Jo Konen. Five monthly newsletters covering real estate and housing interests. Purchased by real estate sales associates to be given at no charge to consumers. Circ. 500,000. Pays on acceptance. Buys all rights. Submit seasonal material 6 months in advance. Photocopied submissions OK. SASE. Reports in 1 month on queries. Sample copy and writer's guidelines for business size SASE.
Nonfiction: "In general, we are looking for light subject matter. We are interested in general interest articles, household hints, health, statistics, vacation and travel, seasonal/holiday, how-to, short anecdotes, quotes from well-known persons, and good real estate articles. Unusual recipes are welcome if accompanied by high-quality color photos. No controversial subject matter, no opinionated articles on current issues, and no brand names. No regional-interest subjects (subjects should be applicable throughout the U.S.)" Material should be informative without being overly sales-oriented. Buys 315 unsolicited mss/year. Recent article example: "It Pays to Learn the Language" (March 1983). Query. Length: 20-200 words. Pays 10¢/word minimum, $25 for recipe/photo combination.
Photos: State availability of color photos. "We no longer accept b&w photos." Pays $20 for color slides/prints. Captions preferred. Buys all rights.
Tips: "We now publish 5 4-color newsletters per month and are in need of quality material, both manuscripts and photos, particularly in the non-technical real estate field. We can now pay up to 20¢/word for real estate material with good photo illustration, plus payment for the photo."

FAMILY HANDYMAN, Webb Co., 1999 Shepard Rd., St. Paul MN 55116. Editor: Joseph R. Provey. Emphasizes do-it-yourself home maintenance, repair and improvement. Publishes 10 issues yearly. Magazine; 100 plus pages. Circ. 1,100,000. Pays on acceptance. Submit seasonal material 6 months in advance. Computer printout submissions OK. SASE. Reports in 4-6 weeks. Free sample copy and writer's guidelines.
Nonfiction: How to do home, lawn and garden maintenance; repairs; remodeling; and shop projects. Recent article example: "TFH Designs and Builds a Potting Bench" (March 1982). Buys 10 unsolicited mss/issue. Query or send complete ms. Length: 700-1,200 words. Pays $50-1,500 depending on length, whether color or

b&w photos used, and quality of entire piece.

Photos: Send photos with ms. Uses 5x7 or 8x10 b&w glossy or 35mm or larger color transparencies. Offers additional payment for photos purchased with mss. Captions and model releases required.

Tips: Especially needs small-scale home remodeling, maintenance and repair projects and material on improving mobile homes.

FLOWER AND GARDEN MAGAZINE, 4251 Pennsylvania, Kansas City MO 64111. Editor-in-Chief: Rachel Snyder. For home gardeners. Bimonthly. Picture magazine. Circ. 600,000. Buys first rights. Byline given. Pays on acceptance. Free writer's guidelines. Query. Reports in 6 weeks. SASE.

Nonfiction: Interested in illustrated articles on how to do certain types of gardening, descriptive articles about individual plants. Flower arranging, landscape design, house plants, patio gardening are other aspects covered. "The approach we stress is practical (how-to-do-it, what-to-do-it-with). We try to stress plain talk, clarity, economy of words. An article should be tailored for a national audience." Buys 20-30 mss/year. Length: 500-1,500 words. Pays 7¢/word or more, depending on quality and kind of material.

Photos: Pays up to $12.50/5x7 or 8x10 b&w prints, depending on quality, suitability. Also buys color transparencies, 35mm and larger. "We are using more 4 color illustrations." Pays $30-125 for these, depending on size and use.

Tips: "Prospective author needs good grounding in gardening practice and literature. Then offer well-researched and well-written material appropriate to the experience level of our audience. Use botanical names as well as common. Illustrations help sell the story. Describe special qualifications for writing the particular proposed subject." Recent published article: "Flowering Holiday Cacti."

‡GARDEN DESIGN, The Fine Art of Residential Landscape Architecture, Publication Board of the American Society of Landscape Architects, 1190 E. Broadway, Louisville KY 40204. (502)589-1167. Editor: Norman Kent Johnson. Managing Editor: Susan Rademacher Frey. Quarterly magazine covering garden making, garden history, garden design emphasizing the *design* aspects of gardening, rather than horticulture. "Design elements and considerations are presented in clear, simple language for both laymen and professionals." Estab. 1982. Circ. 19,000. Pays on publication. Byline given. Offers negotiable kill fee. Buys one-time rights and makes work-for-hire assignments. Submit seasonal/holiday material 1 year in advance. Previously published submissions OK. SASE. Reports in 2 weeks on queries; 5 weeks on mss. Sample copy $4.

Nonfiction: Historical/nostalgic, interview/profile, opinion, personal experience, photo feature, travel. Photographic and editorial content addresses specific seasons—spring, summer, autumn, winter. No detailed horticultural or tecnical articles. Buys 20-30 mss/year. Query with published clips. Length: 500-3,000 words. Pays $50-250.

Photos: Send photos with query or ms. Pays $50-100 for 35mm color transparencies and 8x10 b&w prints. Captions, model release and identification of subjects required.

Columns/Departments: The Garden Life (personality profiles); Plant Page (design applications of plants); Seasonal Specifics; The Garden Traveler (public gardens outside U.S.); Focal Point (personal perspectives); Bookshelf (book reviews); Eclectic (items/events of interest). Buys 10-15 mss/year. Query with published clips. Length: 100-1,500 words. Pays $50-250.

Tips: "We emphasize the experience of gardening over technique. Our editorial core covers an array of subjects—historical, contemporary, large and small gardens. Departments follow specific subjects—travel, plants, people, etc. Samples of previously published work are welcomed. Outlines or brief article descriptions of specific subjects are helpful. We are willing to work with authors in tailoring specific subjects and style with them."

GARDEN MAGAZINE, The Garden Society, A Division of the New York Botanical Garden, Bronx Park, Bronx NY 10458. Editor: Ann Botshon. Emphasizes horticulture, environment and botany for a diverse readership, largely college graduates and professionals united by a common interest in plants and the environment. Many are members of botanical gardens and arboreta. Bimonthly magazine. Circ. 28,000. Buys all rights. Submit seasonal/holiday material 4 months in advance. Photocopied submissions OK. SASE. Reports in 2 months. Sample copy $2.

Nonfiction: Ann Botshon, editor. "All articles must be of high quality, meticulously researched and botanically accurate." Expose (environmental subjects); how-to (horticultural techniques, must be unusual and verifiable); general interest (plants of interest, botanical information, ecology); humor (pertaining to botany and horticulture); photo feature (pertaining to plants and the environment); and travel (great gardens of the world). Buys 15-20 unsolicited mss/year. Recent article example: "The Real and True Shamrock" (March/April 1982). Query with clips of published work. Length: 500-2,500 words. Pays $50-300.

Photos: Tim Metevier, designer. Pays $35-50/5x7 b&w glossy print; $40-150/4x5 or 35mm color transparency. Captions preferred. Buys one-time rights.

Tips: "We appreciate some evidence that the freelancer has studied our magazine and understands our special requirements."

GARDENS FOR ALL NEWS, Newsmagazine of the National Association for Gardening, Gardens for All, 180 Flynn Ave., Burlington VT 05401. (802)863-1308; 863-1321. Editor: Ruth W. Page. Monthly tabloid covering food gardening and food trees. "We publish not only how-to-garden techniques, but also news that affects gardeners and items on gardens for special purposes like therapy, education, feed the hungry, etc." No general information on gardening. "Our material is for more experienced gardeners." Circ. 150,000. Pays on acceptance. Byline given. Buys one-time rights. Submit seasonal/holiday material 4 months in advance. Photocopied and previously published submissions OK. Computer printout submissions OK. SASE. Reports in 2 weeks on queries; 1 month on mss. Sample copy and writer's guidelines for $1.
Nonfiction: How-to, humor, inspirational, interview/profile, new product, personal experience, photo feature, and technical. "All articles must be connected with food-gardening." Buys 80-100 mss/year. Query. Length: 300-3,500 words. Pays $15-200/article.
Photos: Kit Anderson, photo editor. Send photos with ms. Pays $5-15 for b&w photos; $15-35 for color photos. Captions, model releases and identification of subjects required.

GURNEY'S GARDENING NEWS, A Family Newspaper for Gurney Gardeners, Gurney Seed and Nursery Co., 2nd and Capitol, Yankton SD 57079. (605)665-4451. Editor: Janet Henderson. Bimonthly tabloid covering gardening, horticulture and related subjects for home gardeners. Circ. 30,000. Pays on acceptance. Byline given. Buys first North American serial rights, but will consider second serial (reprint) rights. Submit seasonal/holiday material 6 months in advance. Computer printout submissions OK. SASE. Reports in 1 month on queries; 2 months on mss. Sample copy for 9x12 SAE; writer's guidelines for business size SAE.
Nonfiction: "We are interested in well-researched, well-written and illustrated articles on all aspects of home gardening. We prefer articles that stress the practical approach to gardening and are easy to understand. We don't want articles which sound like a rehash of material from a horticultural encyclopedia or how-to-garden guide. We rarely buy articles without accompanying photos or illustrations. We look for a unique slant, a fresh approach, new gardening techniques that work and interesting anecdotes. Especially need short (300-500 words) articles on practical gardening tips, hints, methods. We are interested in: how-to (raise vegetables, flowers, bulbs, trees); interview/profile (of gardeners); photo feature (of garden activities); and technical (horticultural-related)." Buys 70 unsolicited mss/year. Query. Length: 700-2,500 words. Pays $50-375. Also buys articles on gardening projects and activities for children. Length: 500-1,000 words. Pays $30-100.
Photos: Purchases photos with ms. Also buys photo features, essays. Pays $10-85 for 5x7 or 8x10 b&w prints or contact sheets. Caption, model release and identification of subjects required. Buys one-time rights.
Tips: "Please time articles to coincide with the proper season. A word of caution: Our readers know gardening. If you don't, don't write for us."

HERB QUARTERLY, Box 275. New Fane VT 05345. (802)257-7045. Editor: Sallie Ballantine. Quarterly magazine about herbs for enthusiasts interested in herbal aspects of gardening or cooking, history and folklore. Circ. 18,000. Pays on publication. Buys first North American serial rights. Phone queries OK. Computer printout and disk submissions OK; prefers letter quality to dot matrix. SASE. Reports in 1 month. Sample copy $3.50.
Nonfiction: General interest (plant sciences, landscaping); historical (concerning the use and folklore of herbs); how-to (related to crafts, cooking and cultivation); humor; interview (of a famous person involved with herbs); profile; travel (looking for herbs); personal experience; and photo feature. No fiction. Send complete ms. Length: 1,500-3,000 words. Pays $25 minimum.
Photos: "Cover quality." Pays $25/layout minimum for 8x10 b&w prints.

HOME BUYERS GUIDE, Bryan Publications, Inc., 3355 Via Lido, Newport Beach CA 92663. Editor: Janie Murphy. Emphasizes new homes available for homebuyers and homebuilders. Monthly tabloid. Circ. 115,000. Pays on publication. Buys first North American serial rights. Photocopied submissions OK. Previously published work OK, but state where and when it appeared. SASE. Reports in 2 months.
Nonfiction: General interest (taxes, insurance, home safety, mortgages); how-to (beat high prices, select wallpaper, set up a tool bench, panel a wall); and opinion (by experts in a field, e.g., a CPA on taxes). "Gear all material to the California homeowner and consumer. Write in an informative yet entertaining style. Give examples the reader can identify with." Buys 2 mss/issue. Send complete ms. Length: 500-1,500 words. Pays $75-200.
Photos: Send photos with ms. Uses b&w 8x10 glossy prints and 4x5 color transparencies. Offers no additional payment for photos accepted with ms. Captions preferred, model release required. Buys one-time rights.
Columns/Departments: Energy, Taxes, Finance, Community Planning, Home Safety, Architecture and Design, New Products; and Personalizing Your Home (how homeowners have customized development homes). Buys 2 mss/issue. Send complete ms. Length: 500-1,200 words. Pays $75-200.

HOME MAGAZINE, Home Magazine, Ltd., 690 Kinderkamack Rd., Oradell NJ 07649. (201)967-7520. Editor: Olivia Buehl. Executive Editor: Louise I. Driben. Monthly magazine covering home remodeling, home improving and home building. "*Home* tells homeowners how to remodel, improve, or redecorate an existing home, build a new home, and deal effectively with architects, designers, contractors, and building supply dealers.'' Circ. 500,000. Pays on acceptance. Byline given. Pays negotiable kill fee. Buys all rights and makes work-for-hire assignments. Submit seasonal material 6 months in advance. SASE. Reports in 3 weeks on queries; 6 weeks on mss. Sample copy $2.

Nonfiction: How-to (homeowner-oriented, do-it-yourself projects); and financial subjects of interest to homeowners, e.g., taxes, insurance, etc. Buys 50-60 mss/year. Query with clips of published work. Length: 200-2,500 words. Pays $150-1,500.

THE HOMEOWNER, THE HOW TO MAGAZINE, (formerly *Homeowners How To Handbook* and *Homeowners How To*), 3 Park Ave., New York NY 10016. Editor: Jim Liston. A publication of Family Media, Inc. Bimonthly. Circ. 500,000. Buys first rights. Pays 50% kill fee. Byline given. Pays on acceptance. Sample copy $1.50; address request to Circulation Department. Submit seasonal material 7 months in advance. No computer printout or disk submissions. Reports in 3 weeks. SASE.

Nonfiction: Wants how-to information based on facts and experience—not theory. No material on gardening or decorating. ''Design ideas should be original and uncomplicated. They should be directed at young homeowners working with simple tools, and if possible, the kind of project that can be completed on a weekend. Likes articles on good before-and-after remodelings. All articles should contain a list of necessary materials and tools.'' Length: 1,800 words maximum. Pays $150/published page maximum.

Photos: Offers no additional payment for b&w photos used with mss. ''Photos are as important as words. B&w preferred. 4x5's are OK, but 8x10's are better.''

Fillers: Problem Solvers, a regular filler feature, pays $25 per captioned photo that contains a work-saving hint or solves a problem.

Tips: ''Send snapshots or even pencil sketches or plans of remodeling projects with query. To break in a writer should show a willingness to submit the proposed article on speculation. (Once a writer has proved himself to us, this is not required).''

HORTICULTURE, The Magazine of American Gardening, 300 Massachusetts Ave., Boston MA 02115. Editor: Thomas C. Cooper. Published by the Horticulture Associates. Monthly. ''We buy only first North American serial rights to mss; one-time use rights for photos.'' Byline given. Pays on acceptance. Query. Reports in 6 weeks. SASE.

Nonfiction and Photos: Uses articles from 2,000-5,000 words on all aspects of gardening. ''We cover indoors and outdoors, edibles and ornamentals, noteworthy gardens and gardeners.'' Study publication. Photos: color transparencies and top quality b&w prints, preferably 8x10 only; ''accurately identified.''

HOUSE & GARDEN, The Conde Nast Bldg; 350 Madison Ave., New York NY 10017. Editor-in-Chief: Louis Oliver Gropp. Editors: Denise Otis and Martin Filler. For cultured, sophisticated upper-income brackets. Monthly. Circ. 600,000. Buys all rights. Pays on acceptance. ''Study magazine before querying.'' Reports immediately. Query with clips of published work. SASE.

Nonfiction: Anything to do with architecture, decorating, gardens and the fine arts. Length: about 1,500 words. Payment varies. Shelley Wanger, is articles editor.

Photos: Photos purchased with mss only.

Tips: ''This is a very tough market to break into. We very seldom assign from queries and do not read unsolicited material. Read the magazine closely for style and avoid service or how-to material. However if you understand our needs and provide something that's really good, there's always a chance. It's best to send a query first and a sample of previous writing.''

HOUSE BEAUTIFUL, The Hearst Corp., 1700 Broadway, New York NY 10019. (212)903-5000. Editor: JoAnn Barwick. Executive Editor: Margaret Kennedy. Senior Editor/Copy: Carol Cooper Garey. Emphasizes design, architecture and building. Monthly magazine; 200 pages. Circ. 840,000. Pays on acceptance. Byline given. Submit seasonal/holiday material 4 months in advance of issue date. SASE. Reports in 5 weeks.

Nonfiction: Historical (landmark buildings and restorations); how-to (kitchen, bath remodeling service); humor; interview; new product; profile. Submit query with detailed outline or complete ms. Length: 300-1,000 words. Pays varying rates.

Photos: State availability of photos with ms.

LOG HOME GUIDE FOR BUILDERS & BUYERS, Muir Publishing Company Ltd., 1 Pacific Ave., Gardenvale, Quebec, Canada H9X 1B0. (514)457-2045. Editor: Doris Muir. (705)754-2201. Quarterly magazine covering the buying and building of log homes. ''We publish for persons who want to buy or build their own log home. The writer should always keep in mind that this is a special type of person—usually a back-to-the-land, back-to-tradition type of individual who is looking for practical information on how to buy or build a log home.'' Circ. ''50,000 and rising.'' Pays on publication. Byline given. Buys one-time rights. Submit seasonal/holiday material 4 months in advance. Simultaneous queries, and simultaneous (''writer should explain''), photocopied, and previously published submissions OK. No computer printout or disk submissions. Reports in

2 weeks. Sample copy $2.75 (postage included).

Nonfiction: Fred G. Dafoe, assistant editor. General interest; historical/nostalgic (log home historic sites; restoration of old log structures); how-to (anything to do with building log homes); inspirational (" 'Sweat equity—encouraging people that they can build their own home for less cost"); interview/profile (with persons who have built their own log homes); new product ("or new company manufacturing log homes—check with us first"); personal experience ("authors own experience with building his own log home, with photos is ideal); photo feature (on author or on anyone else building his own log home); technical (for "Techno-log" section; specific construction details, i.e. truss sections); also, "would like photo/interview/profile stories on famous persons and their log homes—how they did it, where they got their logs, etc." Interested in log commercial structures. "Please no exaggeration—this is a truthful, back-to-basics type of magazine trying to help the person interested in log homes." Buys 25 mss/year. Recent article example: "Not Your Run-of-the Mill Log Cabin" (spring 1982). Query with clips of published work or send complete ms. "Prefer queries first with photo of subject house" Length: open. Pays $50 minimum.

Photos: State availability of photos. Send photos with query "if possible. It would help us to get a real idea of what's involved." Pays $5-25 for b&w or color prints. "All payments are arranged with individual authors/submitters." Captions and identification of subjects required. Buys one-time rights.

Columns/Departments: Pro-Log (short news pieces of interest to the log-building world); Techno-Log (technical articles, i.e. solar energy systems; any illustrations welcome); and Book-Log (book reviews only, on books related to log building and alternate energy; "check with us first"). Buys "possible 50-75 mss/year. Query with clips of published work or send complete ms. Length: 100-1,000 words or more. All payments are arranged with individual authors/submitters." No need to enclose SASE.

‡**LOG HOUSE MAGAZINE**, Box 1205, Prince George, British Columbia, Canada V2L 4V3. Contact: Editor-in-Chief. "For a middle- to upper-income audience; well-educated, men and women of all ages. Everyone needs a home, but these are the people who have the energy, the drive, the intelligence to want to create a superior home with their own hands." Annual magazine; 96 pages. Circ. 20,000. Pays on publication day. Buys one-time rights. Byline given. No computer printout or disk submissions. Reports in 1 week.

Nonfiction: Historical (on excellent log construction methods), how-to (do any part/portion of a good solid timber house), informational, humor, inspirational, interview (with a practicing, professional builder, or a factual one on an individual who built a good house), new product (if relevant), personal experience (house building), photo feature (on good log buildings of a permanent residential nature; absolutely no cabins or rotting hulks), and technical (preservatives, tools). Query. Length: open. Pays $50 minimum.

Photos: Mary Mackie, photo editor. Purchased with accompanying ms. Captions required. Send contact sheet. Pays $3 minimum/5x7 b&w glossy print (negatives appreciated); $10 minimum for 2¼x2¼ transparencies.

METROPOLITAN HOME, 750 3rd Ave., New York NY 10017. Editor-in-Chief: Dorothy Kalins. For city dwellers. Monthly magazine; 110 pages. Circ. 750,000. Buys all rights. Buys 60-100 mss/year. Pays on acceptance. Submit seasonal material 6 months in advance. Computer printout and disk submissions OK "as long as they are readable." Reports in 2 months. Query. SASE.

Nonfiction: Joanna Kratz, article editor. "Service material specifically for people who live in cities on interior designs, collectibles, equity, wines, liquor and real estate. Thorough, factual, informative articles." Buys 60-100 mss/year. Query. Length: 300-1,000 words. Pays $600-800.

Photos: B&w photos and color are purchased only on assignment.

Columns/Departments: Wanderlusting, High Spirits (wine and liquor), Equity and Real Estate. Length: 300-1,000 words. Pays $600-800.

‡**N.Y. HABITAT MAGAZINE, For Co-op, Condominium and Loft Living**, The Carol Group, Ltd., 241 W. 23rd St., New York NY 10011. (212)741-0114. Editor: Carol J. Ott. Managing Editor: Tom Soter. Bimonthly magazine covering co-op, condo and loft living in metropolitan New York for "sophisticated, affluent and educated readers interested in maintaining the value of their homes and buying new homes." Estab. 1982. Circ. 10,000. Pays on publication. Byline given. Offers negotiable kill fee. Buys first North American serial rights. Submit seasonal/holiday material 3 months in advance. SASE. Reports in 3 weeks. Sample copy for $3, 9x12 SAE and 5 first class stamps; writer's guidelines for business size SAE and 1 first class stamp.

Nonfiction: Only material relating to co-op and condominium living in New York metropolitan area. Buys 20 mss/year. Query with published clips. Length: 750-1,500 words. Pays $25-250.

NEW SHELTER, Rodale Press, 33 E. Minor St., Emmaus PA 18049. Executive Editor: Laurence R. Stains. Articles Editor: Marguerite Smolen. Magazine published 9 times/year about energy-efficient homes. Circ. 650,000. Pays on acceptance. Buys all rights. Submit seasonal material at least 6 months in advance. Computer printout submissions OK; prefers letter quality to dot matrix. SASE. Reports in 6 weeks.

Nonfiction: "We are the magazine of innovative home designs and projects of use to our audience of advanced do-it-yourselfers. We are looking for the work of innovators who are at the cutting edge of affordable housing, alternate energy, water and resource conservation, etc. Our subtitle is, "Innovative Answers For Today's Homeowners," and that really says it all. We don't want run-of-the-mill, wooden how-to prose. We want lively writing about what real people have done with their homes, telling how and why our readers should do the same." Query with clips of previously published work. Length: 1,000-5,000 words. Rate of payment depends on quality of ms.

Photos: Art director: John Johanek. State availability of photos. Pays $15-25 for b&w contact sheets with negatives and 8x10 glossy prints with ms. Pays $25 minimum for 2x2 or 35mm color transparencies. Captions and model release required.

Tips: No hobby/craft or overly general, simplistic articles.

1001 HOME IDEAS, Family Media, 3 Park Ave., New York NY 10016. Editor-in-Chief: Anne Anderson. Managing Editor: Ellen Emory. "We're primarily an interior design magazine for mainstream America." Monthly. Circ. 1.4 million. SASE. Sample copy and writer's guidelines for $2 and SASE. Query first. Buys variable rights. Pays on acceptance.

Nonfiction: Interior design material and home service articles on food, gardening, money-saving tips. Length: 2,000 words maximum.

Photos: "Freelance photographs rarely accepted." Interior design queries should include snapshots of room and clear descriptions of the room and its contents. Professional photographers may contact Robert Thornton, art director, about possible assignments. Send SASE with sufficient postage.

Tips: "Our readers are looking for easy, attractive, and cost-effective ideas in a step-by-step format. Persons who want to suggest a room for possible inclusion in the magazine may do so by sending a query with detailed descriptions of the room and snapshots. Don't hire a professional photographer just to show us what the room looks like."

ORGANIC GARDENING, Rodale Press Publications, 33 E. Minor St., Emmaus PA 18049. (215)967-5171. Managing Editor: Jack Ruttle. For a readership "interested in health and conservation, in growing plants, vegetables and fruits without chemicals, and in protecting the environment." Monthly magazine; 160-240 pages. Circ. 1,200,000. Buys all rights and the right to reuse in other Rodale Press Publications with agreed additional payment. Pays 25% kill fee, "if we agree to one." Byline given. Buys 400-500 mss/year. Pays on acceptance. Free sample copy and writer's guidelines. Reports in 4-6 weeks. Query or submit complete ms. "Query with full details, no hype." SASE.

Nonfiction: "Factual and informative articles or fillers, especially on food gardening and family self-sufficiency, stressing organic methods. Interested in all crops, soil topics, indoor gardening, greenhouses; natural foods preparation, storage, etc.; biological pest control; variety breeding, nutrition, recycling, energy conservation; community and club gardening. Strong on specific details, step-by-step how-to, thorough research. We do not want to see generalized garden success stories: We print detailed stories on growing food. We would like to see material on garden techniques, raising fruit organically, grains, new and old vegetables; effective composting, soil building, waste recycling, food preparation, and insect control. Emphasis is on interesting, practical information, presented accurately." Length: 1,000-2,000 words for features. Pays $200-600.

Photos: B&w and color purchased with mss or on assignment. Enlarged b&w glossy print and/or negative preferred. Pays $15-25. 2¼x2¼ (or larger) color transparencies.

Fillers: Fillers on above topics are also used. Length: 150-500 words. Pays $50-100.

Tips: "Read the magazine regularly, like a hawk."

PHOENIX HOME/GARDEN, Arizona Home Garden, Inc., Suite 601, 1001 North Central, Phoenix AZ 85004. (602)258-9766. Editor: Manya Winsted. Associate Editors: Nora Burba and Joe Kullman. Monthly magazine covering homes, entertainment and gardening for Phoenix area residents interested in better living. Estab. 1980. Circ. 31,000. Pays on publication. Byline given. Buys all rights. Submit seasonal/holiday material 6 months in advance. Simultaneous queries OK. SASE. Reports in 6 weeks on queries. Sample copy $1.95.

Nonfiction: Book excerpts; general interest (on gardening, entertainment, food); historical (on furnishings related to homes); how-to (on home improvement or decorating); new product (for the home or garden); photo feature; and travel (of interest to Phoenix residents). Buys 100 or more mss/year. Query with clips of published work. Length: 2,000 words maximum. Pays $75-300/article.

Columns/Departments: Book Reviews (800-1,000 words); Crafts; and Homeworks (decorative how-to projects). Buys 125 mss/year. Query.

Fillers: Newsbreaks ("Sampler" describes "neat new products for the home in local stores"; "All's Fare" describes "food-related items of local interest, such as products or eateries"). Pays $20-25 (item and photo).

Tips: "It's not a closed shop. I want the brightest, freshest, most accurate material available."

SAN DIEGO HOME/GARDEN, Westward Press, Box 1471, San Diego CA 92101. (714)233-4567. Editor: Peter Jensen. Copy Editor: Kathryn Benson. Monthly magazine covering homes and gardens and nearby travel for 30 to 40 year old residents of San Diego city and county. Circ. 30,000. Pays on publication. Byline given. Submit seasonal material 3 months in advance. Photocopied submissions OK. Computer printout or disk sub-

missions OK; prefers letter quality to dot matrix. Reports in 1 month. Free writer's guidelines for SASE.
Nonfiction: General interest (service articles with plenty of factual information, prices and "where to buy" on home needs); how-to (save energy, garden, cook); new product (for the house); photo feature (on houses and gardens) and architecture; home improvement; remodeling and real estate. Articles must have local slant. Buys 10-15 unsolicited mss/year. Recent article example: "Proteas" (February 1982). Query with clips of previously published work. Length: 500-2,000 words. Pays $50-200.
Tips: "No out-of-town, out-of-state material."

SELECT HOMES MAGAZINE, (formerly *Select Home Designs*), 382 W. Broadway, Vancouver, British Columbia, Canada V5Y 1R2. (604)879-4144. Published 5 times/year: January, March, May, July, September. Circ. 100,000. Editor: Ralph Westbrook. Emphasizes building, renovations, additions, decorating, furnishing, single-family residential and recreational homes. Life-style articles associated with home and cottage activities, i.e., skiing, boating, water sports, regattae. Pays half on acceptance, half on publication. Byline and photo credits given. Submit 45-60 days in advance of issue publication. Buys first Canadian serial rights. Simultaneous, photocopied and previously published submissions OK. No computer printout or disk submissions. Reports in 2 weeks. Sample copy $1; free writer's guidelines.
Nonfiction: Preferred length: 250-2,000 words, depends on topic. Pays 10¢/word. Prefers cut-lines be included with submitted photographic prints.
Photos: "We are a 4-color consumer publication, prefer photographer to use negative film and submit contact sheets for our consideration from which we can request either negatives or finished, sized prints." Pays $5 minimum for b&w print, $10 for color negative, print or transparency. Pictures should not be sent unless intended for cover use; other cases, should be part of illustration for a story. Full bleed cover, vertical format; prefer 2¼x2¼ or larger format. 35mm for article illustrations only. Pays $200 for cover photos. Model release required. Prefer captions with photos.
Columns/Departments: "We have no existing columns or departments but are open to their establishment on a regular basis." Query. Pays 10¢/word.

SOUTHERN ACCENTS, W.R.C. Smith Publishing Co., 1760 Peachtree Rd. NW, Atlanta GA 30357. (404)874-4462. Editor: Lisa B. Newsom. Managing Editor: Diane Burrell. Emphasizes interior design and gardens of Southern homes for upper middle class and above. Most, but not all, readers live in the South. Read by interior designers and landscape architects "but most are simply people with varied vocations who are interested in interiors, collections, gardens and in the Southern cultural heritage and places of beauty." Quarterly magazine; 165 pages, mostly photographs. Circ. 130,000. Pays on publication. Buys all rights. Phone queries OK. Submit seasonal/holiday material 3 months in advance. SASE. Reports in 2-3 weeks. Sample copy $3.95; free writer's guidelines.
Nonfiction: Historical ("each issue carries at least one story on the renovation of a Southern home or historical garden; we're also interested in histories of certain decorative art, forms—Chinese export porcelains and American coin silver are two we have covered in the past. These articles depend less on illustration and can run considerably longer than 600 words"); "the didactic articles should help our readers learn to be more sophisticated collectors, e.g: 'A Primer for the Buyer of English Antique Furniture' "; interview and photo feature ("the majority of our articles describe the architecture and interior design of a house and simply tell how it got to look that way; text should tell the story and explicit captions should spell out names of manufacturers of fabrics, furniture, etc., origins of decorative articles. We use mostly color photos."). Buys 2-3 mss/issue. Query with clips of published work. Length: 1,000 words.
Photos: "We need to see photos in order to be able to judge whether or not we would be interested in the story." Never uses b&w photos. Payment varies for 4x5 or 2¼x2¼ color transparencies. Captions required.
Tips: Writers should have some expertise and credentials in the area in which they are writing, such as knowledge of period furniture and interior design.

‡THE SPROUTLETTER, Sprouting Publications, Box 62, Ashland OR 97520. (503)482-5627. Editor: Jeff Breakey. Bimonthly newsletter covering sprouting, live foods and indoor food gardening. "We emphasize growing foods (especially sprouts) indoors for health, economy, nutrition and food self-sufficiency. We also cover topics related to sprouting, live foods and holistic health." Circ. 1,400. Pays on publication. Byline given. Offers 50% kill fee. Buys first North American serial rights. Submit seasonal/holiday material 2 months in advance. Previously published submissions OK. SASE. Reports in 2 weeks on queries; 3 weeks on mss. Sample copy $1.50; writer's guidelines for business size SAE and 1 first class stamp.
Nonfiction: General interest (raw foods, sprouting, holistic health); how-to (grow sprouts, all kinds of foods indoors; build devices for sprouting or indoor gardening); personal experience (in sprouting or related areas); technical (experiments with growing sprouts). No common health food/vitamin articles or growing ornamental plants indoors (as opposed to food producing plants). Buys 3-5 mss/year. Query. Length: 500-2,400 words. Pays $10-40. "We give twice as much if payment is accepted in the form of subscriptions or advertising in *The Sproutletter* or in books or merchandise which we sell."

Columns/Departments: Book Reviews (books oriented toward sprouts or holistic health). Reviews are short and informative. News Items (interesting news items relating to sprouts or live foods); Recipes (mostly raw foods). Buys 4-8 mss/year. Query. Length: 120-400 words. Pays $1-6.
Poetry: Buys 1-2 poems/year. Submit maximum 3 poems. Length: 15-70 lines. Payment for poems is a half-year subscription.
Fillers: Short humor, newsbreaks. Buys 2-4/year. Length: 50-150 words. Pays $1-5.
Tips: "Writers should have a sincere interest in holistic health and in natural whole foods. We like writing which is optimistic, interesting and very informative. Articles should cover any given subject in-depth in an enjoyable and inspiring manner."

TEXAS GARDENER, The Magazine for Texas Gardeners, by Texas Gardners, Suntex Communications, Inc., Box 9005, Waco TX 76710. (817)772-1270. Editor: Chris S. Corby. Managing Editor: Ken Atkins. Bimonthly magazine covering vegetable and fruit production, ornamentals and home landscape information for home gardeners in Texas. Estab. 1981. Circ. 30,000. Pays on publication. Byline given. Buys all rights. Submit seasonal/holiday material 6 months in advance. SASE. Reports in 6 weeks. Sample copy $2.75; writer's guidelines for business size SAE and 1 first class stamp.
Nonfiction: How-to, humor, interview/profile, new product, photo feature. "We use feature articles that relate to Texas gardeners. We also like personality profiles on hobby gardeners and professional horticulturists who are doing something unique." Buys 50-100 mss/year. Query with clips of published work. Length: 800-2,400 words. Pays $50-200.
Photos: "We prefer superb color and b&w photos; 90% of photos used are color." State availability of photos. Pays negotiable rates for 2¼ color transparencies and 8x10 b&w prints and contact sheets. Model release and identification of subjects required.
Tips: "First, be a Texan. Then come up with a good idea of interest to home gardeners in this state. Be specific. Stick to feature topics like "How Alley Gardening Became a Texas Tradition." Leave topics like "How to Control Fire Blight" to the experts. High quality photos could make the difference. We would like to add several writers to our group of regular contributors and would make assignments on a regular basis."

WHITCHAPPEL'S HERBAL, 12 Old Street Rd., Box 272, Peterborough NH 03458. (603)924-3758. Editor: Lee Whitfield. Quarterly magazine covering growing and using herbs for flavor, fragrance, for color and for good health. Circ. 12,000. Pays on publication. Byline given. Assigned articles paid if used or not. Buys one-time rights or makes work-for-hire assignments. Submit seasonal/holiday material 4 months in advance. Simultaneous queries, and simultaneous, photocopied and previously published submissions OK. SASE. Reports in 3 weeks. Sample copy $3; writer's guidelines for SAE and 1 first class stamp.
Nonfiction: How-to (grow and use herbs, do herbal crafts); interview/profile (of herb growers, dealers); new product (in gardening, cooking); photo feature (see interview); travel (herbal cooking in foreign countries). Special issues include: Fall 1982—herbal crafts. "Must be original material—no rehash of old herbals." Buys 20-25 mss/year. Query with clips of published work or send complete ms. Length: 300-3,000 words. Pays 10¢/word.
Photos: State availability of photos with ms. Pays $10-50 for color transparencies and b&w prints. Model release and identification of subjects required. Buys one-time rights.
Columns/Departments: Eating Out (US or foreign restaurants with herb recipes); The Herb Shop (profile of shops, owners). Buys 8 mss/year. Length: 300-1,000 words. Pays 10¢/word.
Fiction: "Herblore only." Buys 1 ms/year. Query.
Tips: "Our contributors are all experienced gardeners and cooks who have studied and used herbs."

YOUR HOME, Meridian Publishing, Box 2315, Ogden UT 84404. Editor: Peggie Bingham. Monthly magazine; 12 pages. Circ. 650,000. Distributed to businesses, with their inserts, as house organs. A pictorial magazine with emphasis on home and garden decorating and improvement. We prefer manuscripts with photos, color and/or b&w. 400-1,000 words. Pays 15¢/word. $20 for b&w, $25 for color transparencies or slides. Computer printout and disk submissions OK; prefers letter quality to dot matrix printouts. Buys first-time rights. Credit line given. Payment on acceptance. 6 months lead time. Send SASE for guidelines. 50¢ for sample copy.
Tips: "To break in a lot depends on the 'quality' photos which accompany the submissions."

Home Computing

This section lists publications for users and owners of personal computers. Business applications for home computers are covered in the Consumer Business and Finance section. Publications for data processing personnel are listed in that section of Trade Journals. Software publishers interested in freelance computer programs are listed in a separate section (see the Table of Contents) of *Writer's Market*. Writer's Digest Books also publishes the *1984 Programmer's Market*, a new title directed to the writing and marketing of freelance computer programs.

‡**A.N.A.L.O.G. COMPUTING, The Magazine for ATARI Computer Owners**, A.N.A.L.O.G. Magazine Corp., Box 23, Worcester MA 01603. (617)892-9230. Editors: Michael DesChenes/Lee H. Pappas. Managing Editor: Jon A. Bell. Bimonthly magazine covering the Atari home computer. Estab. 1981. Pays on publication. Byline given. Buys all rights. Submit seasonal/holiday material 2 months in advance. Photocopied submissions OK. Computer printout or disk submissions OK "as long as the disk submission is prepared with one of the more common Atari word processing programs." Reports in 2 weeks. Sample copy $3; writer's guidelines for business-size SASE.
Nonfiction: How-to and technical. "We publish beginner's articles, educational programs, utilities, multi-function tutorials, do-it-yourself hardware articles (such as how-to build your own 400 keyboard), and games (preferably arcade-style in BASIC and/or ASSEMBLY language). We also publish reviews of Atari software and hardware." Buys 150 mss/year. Send complete ms. Length: open. Pays $60/typeset magazine page.
Photos: Send photos with ms. Reviews 5x7 b&w prints. Captions required; "clipped to the photo or taped to the back." Buys all rights.
Columns/Departments: Atari software and hardware reviews. Buys 30 mss/year. Send complete ms. Length: open.
Tips: "Almost all submissions are from people who read the magazine regularly and use the Atari home computers. We have published many first-time authors. We have published programs written in BASIC, ASSEMBLY, PILOT, FORTH, LISP, and some information on PASCAL. When submitting any program over 30 lines, authors must send a copy of the program on magnetic media, either cassette or disk. We strive to publish personable, down-to-earth articles as long as the style does not impair the technical aspects of the article. Authors should avoid sterile, lifeless prose. Occasional humor (detailing how the author uses his or her computer or tackles a programming problem) is welcome. No fiction. We will be going monthly in the not-too-distant future."

‡**ANTIC MAGAZINE, The Atari Resource**, Antic Publishing Co., 600 18th St., San Francisco CA 94107. (415)864-3858. Editor: James Capparell. Managing Editor: Robert DeWitt. Monthly magazine for Atari 400/800 computer users and owners of Atari game machines, compatible equipment and software. Estab. 1982. Circ. 70,000. Pays partial on acceptance; balance on publication. Byline given. Offers $60 kill fee. Buys all rights. Submit seasonal/holiday material 3 months in advance. Simultaneous queries and photocopied submissions OK. SASE. Reports in 2 weeks on queries; 4 weeks on mss. Sample copy $2.50; free writer's guidelines.
Nonfiction: How-to, interview/profile, new product, photo feature, technical. Special issues include Education (Sept.) and Buyer's Guide (Dec.). No generalized, non-technical articles. Buys 250 mss/year. Query or send complete ms. Length: 500-2,500 words. Pays $20-180.
Photos: State availability of photos or send photos with ms. Reviews color transparencies and b&w prints; b&w should accompany article. Identification of subjects required.
Columns/Departments: Starting Line (beginner's column); Assembly Language (for advanced programmers); Profiles (personalities in the business); Product Reviews (software/hardware products). Buys 36 mss/year. Query or send complete ms. Length: 1,500-2,500 words. Pays $120-180.
Tips: "Write for the Product Reviews section. Contact Editor: Deborah Burns. 500-1,000 words on a new software or hardware product for the Atari 400/800 computers. Give a clear description; personal experience with product; comparison with other available products."

BYTE MAGAZINE, 70 Main St., Peterborough NH 03458. (603)924-9281. Editor: Lawrence J. Curran. Monthly magazine covering personal computers for college-educated, professional users of computers. Circ. 360,000. Pays on publication. Buys all rights. Photocopied submissions OK. Double-spaced computer printout and disk submissions OK; prefers letter quality to dot matrix printouts. SASE. Reports on rejections in 3 months; in 6 months if accepted. Sample copy $2.95; writer's guidelines for SASE.
Nonfiction: How-to (technical information about computers) and technical. Buys 160 mss/year. Query. Length: 20,000 words maximum. Pays $50/typeset magazine page maximum.
Tips: "Many *Byte* authors are regular readers of the magazine, and most readers use a computer either at home

or at work. Back issues of the magazine give prospective authors an idea of the type of article published in *Byte*. Articles can take one of several forms: tutorial articles on a given subject, how-to articles detailing a specific implementation of a hardware or software project done on a small computer, survey articles on the future of microcomputers, and sometimes theoretical articles describing work in computer science (if written in an informal, 'friendly' style). Authors with less technical orientation should consider writing for our sister publication, *Popular Computing Magazine*. Author's guides are available for both publications."

‡**THE COLOR COMPUTER MAGAZINE for TRS-80 Color Computer and TDP-100 Users**, New England Publications, Highland Mill, Camden ME 04843. (207)236-9621. Editor: Kerry Leichtman. Monthly magazine covering "new ways for readers to use their TRS-80 Color Computers and TDP-100s. Articles are aimed at the novice and expert and speak with enthusiasm and authority." Estab. 1983. Circ. 30,000 (initially). Pays on acceptance. Byline given. Buys all rights. Submit seasonal/holiday material 5 months in advance. Simultaneous queries OK. Computer printout or disk submissions OK. SASE. Reports in 3 weeks on queries; 6 weeks on mss. Sample copy for $2.95 and 9x12 SASE; free writer's guidelines.

Nonfiction: How-to ("main editorial focus is describing how to use your computer"); interview/profile; new product; technical; reviews. No "I am a computer widow" articles. No "good golly, I own my very own computer" material. Buys 120 mss/year. Query with tape of program. Pays $50/published page (average article pays $100-250).

Photos: State availability of photos with query letter or manuscript or send photos with accompanying query or manuscript if possible. Pays $5 for 35mm b&w or color transparencies; $5 for 8x10 b&w or color prints. Captions required.

Fiction: Adventure, humorous, science fiction. Number of mss bought each year "will depend on quality of submissions." Send complete ms. Length: 1,000-3,000 words. Pays $65-250.

Fillers: Quick Tips. Number of items/year "open." Length: 25-250 words. Pays $5-25.

Tips: "Read the magazine. If an article doesn't give readers another program to use, or deeper insight into their Color Computer we don't want it. Otherwise breaking in is as easy as a trip to the post office. Writers should replace their typewriters with microcomputers. Not only will word processing capabilities help them, but articles about computer's uses are in heavy demand. People who write well are badly needed. You don't have to be a 'technical whiz' to break into this field—just curious and creative."

‡**COMMODORE, The Microcomputer Magazine**, Commodore Business Machines, 1200 Wilson Dr., West Chester PA 19380. (215)436-4211. Editor: Diane Lebold. Publisher: Neil Harris. Bimonthly magazine for owners of Commodore computers, using them for business, programming, education, communications, art, etc. Estab. 1981. Circ. 70,000. Pays on publication. Byline given. Buys first North American serial rights, all rights, second serial rights, and makes work-for-hire assignments. Submit seasonal/holiday material 5 months in advance. Simultaneous queries and previously published submissions OK. SASE. Reports in 1 month on queries; 2 months on mss. Free sample copy; writer's guidelines for legal size SAE and 1 first class stamp.

Nonfiction: Book reviews; how-to (write programs, use software); humor; new product (reviews); personal experience; photo feature; technical. "Write for guidelines." No articles mentioning other brands of computers. Buys 50 mss/year. Query or send complete ms. Length: 1,000-10,000 words. Pays $25-50/page.

Photos: Send photos with ms. Reviews 5x7 b&w and color prints. Captions required. Buys all rights.

Tips: "Write or phone the editor. Talk about several specific ideas. Use Commodore computers. We're open to programming techniques and product reviews."

‡**COMPUTE! The Leading Magazine of Home, Educational, and Recreational Computing**, Small System Service, 505 Edwardia Dr., Greensboro NC 27409. (919)275-9809. Editor: Robert Lock. Managing Editor: Kathleen Martinek. Monthly magazine covering consumer and personal computing. Circ. 315,000. Pays on acceptance. Byline given. Buys all rights. Submit seasonal/holiday material 6 months in advance. Simultaneous queries OK. SASE. Reports in 2 weeks on queries; 3 weeks on mss. Sample copy $2.50; free writer's guidelines.

Nonfiction: How-to (compute); personal experience (with programming/computers); technical (programs, games, utility programs for computers). No reviews. Send complete ms. Length: 500 words minimum. Pays $75-600.

Photos: Reviews 5x7 b&w glossy prints.

Tips: "We stress clarity and a tutorial approach and publish computer programs for many popular computers. Write for guidelines."

‡**COMPUTE!'s GAZETTE**, Small System Services, 505 Edwardia Dr., Greensboro NC 27409. (919)275-9809. Editor: Robert Lock. Managing Editor: Kathleen Martinek. Monthly magazine of consumer and personal computing for owners/users of VIC and Commodore 64 computer systems. "Our audience is mostly beginning and novice computer users." Estab. 1983. Circ. 80,000. Pays on acceptance. Byline given. Buys all rights. Submit seasonal/holiday material 6 months in advance. Simultaneous queries OK. SASE. Reports in 2

weeks on queries; 3 weeks on mss. Sample copy $2.50; free writer's guidelines.

Nonfiction: How-to (compute); personal experience (with programming/computers); technical (programs, games, utility programs for computers). No reviews. "We stress clarity, and a tutorial approach, and publish quality computer programs for VIC and Commodore 64 computers. Follow the suggestions in our author's guide. Send complete ms. Length: 500 words minimum. Pays $70 minimum.

‡**COMPUTING NOW!**, Unit 6, 25 Overlea Blvd., Toronto, Ontario, Canada M4H 1B1. (416)423-3262. Editor: Steve Rimmer. 60% freelance written. Editorial coverage is for first-time microcomputer buyers and those still discovering the potential of their computer system. Covers small business and home use. Monthly magazine. 96 pages. Circulation 25,000. Pays on publication. Buys all rights. Byline given. Phone queries OK. Photocopied submissions OK. Reports in 4 weeks maximum. Sample copy $3. Free writer's guidelines and list of articles sought.

Nonfiction: Technical articles written for a beginner's market; applications. Buys 50 mss/year. Recent article example: "What really is CP/M?" (April 1983). Query. Length: 800-4,000 words. Pays $75-100/page ($80 per 1,000 words).

Photos: Should be supplied if possible. Captions required. Buys all rights.

CREATIVE COMPUTING, 39 E. Hanover Ave., Morris Plains NJ 07950. Editor: Elizabeth Staples. Managing Editor: Peter J. Fee. Monthly magazine covering the use of computers in homes, businesses and schools for students, faculty, hobbyists—everyone interested in the effects of computers on society and the use of computers in school, at home or at work. Circ. 225,000. Pays on acceptance. "Buys first rights and usually first reprint rights so as to publish in 'Best of' volumes; then rights automatically revert to author." Byline given. Submit all material at least 4 months in advance. Computer printout and disk submissions OK; letter quality or dot matrix printout acceptable but dot matrix print should have descenders. SASE. Reports in 2 weeks. Sample copy $2.95.

Nonfiction: Reviews of new hardware and software; how-to (building a computer at home, personal computer applications and software); informational (computer careers; simulations on computers; problem-solving techniques; use in a particular institution or discipline such as medicine, education, music, animation, space exploration, business or home use); historical articles (history of computers, or of a certain discipline, like computers and animation); interviews (with personalities in the hobbyist field, old-timers in the computer industry or someone doing innovative work); personal experience (first-person accounts of using hardware or software); and technical (programs, games and simulations with printouts). Buys 200 mss/year. Length: 500-3,000 words. Pays $50-100/printed page.

Photos: Usually purchased with mss, with no additional payment, but sometimes pays $3-50 for b&w glossy prints or $10-150 for any size color.

‡**DESKTOP COMPUTING**, Wayne Green Inc., 80 Pine St., Peterborough NH 03458. (603)924-9471. Managing Editor: Daniel Sullivan. Monthly magazine covering microcomputers. "Nontechnical articles on microcomputer purchase and use by business people with little or no technical knowledge about computers." Estab. 1981. Circ. 50,000. Pays on publication. Byline given. Buys all rights. Simultaneous queries and simultaneous and photocopied submissions OK. Reports in 3 weeks on queries; 6 weeks on mss. Free sample copy; writer's guidelines for business size SAE and 1 first class stamp.

Nonfiction: Michael Thompson, articles editor. General interest (microcomputer industry); how-to (select systems and features for particular business applications); new product (microcomputer systems and software). No " 'war stories' of individual trials and tribulations of having bought a particular microcomputer system." Buys 100-125 mss/year. Length: 1,200-2,400 words. Pays $75-400.

Photos: Send photos with ms. Reviews b&w and color prints. No standard pay rate. Model release and identification of subjects required.

Columns/Departments: Ken Sheldon, column/department editor. Book reviews, systems reviews, software reviews on microcomputers. Buys 24/year. Query. Length: 800-1,600 words. Pays $50-175.

80 MICROCOMPUTING, 80 Magazine St., Peterborough NH 03458. (603)924-9471. Publisher: Wayne Green. Editor: Eric Maloney. Monthly magazine about microcomputing for "owners and users of TRS-80 by Radio Shack." Circ. 140,000. Pays 25% on acceptance, remainder on publication or in 9 months, whichever comes first. Buys all rights. Written queries preferred. Photocopied submissions OK. "Require hard copy of articles and disk or tape of programs. Computer printouts of articles OK." SASE. Reports in 2 months. Sample copy $2.50; writer's guidelines for SAE.

Nonfiction: Applications programs for business, education, science, home and hobby; utilities; programming techniques; tutorials. "We're looking for articles that will help the beginning, intermediate, and advanced TRS-80 microcomputer user become a better programmer. We also publish hardware construction projects. We buy about 40 manuscripts per issue. Query first; we are glutted!" Length: 1,000 words average. Pays $50/printed page.

Reviews: Writers interested in reviewing current available software are asked to query the review editor, stating areas of interest and equipment owned. Buys 8-15 reviews per issue.

Photos: Offers no additional payment for photos accepted with ms. Captions and model release required. Buys all rights.

INFOWORLD, The Newsweekly for Microcomputer Users, Popular Computing, Inc., Suite 303, 530 Lytton Ave., Palo Alto CA 94301. (415)328-4602. Editor-in-Chief: Maggie Canon. Editor: John C. Dvorak. Weekly magazine "dedicated to the small-computer user in the home, business, and classroom. We put special emphasis on telling the audience of microcomputer users what is good and bad about the products on the market today. We also relay information about technological breakthroughs and trends." Estab. 1980. Circ. 45,000. Pays on publication. Byline given. Offers negotiable kill fee. Buys first North American serial rights. Submit seasonal/holiday material 1 month in advance. SASE. Sample copy for 14x17 SAE; free writer's guidelines.

Nonfiction: General interest, historical/nostalgic, humor, interview/proile, new product, opinion, personal experience, photo feature, technical. Special issues include show coverage. No program listings, short stories, personal vendettas. Buys 100 mss/year. Query with clips of published work. "Articles must be submitted with line lengths of 37 characters and must not exceed 8 pages of double-spaced type. Pays $1.80-3/column inch including photos used in publication.

Photos: State availability of photos or send photos with ms. Reviews 8½x11 prints. Captions, model releases, and identification of subjects required. Buys one-time rights.

Columns/Departments: "Columns are written by writers who have committed to producing a column a month—these columns are limited in number." Buys 75 mss/year. Query with clips of published work. Length: requirements "same as article." Pays negotiable fee.

MICRO, The 6502/6809 Journal, MICRO INK, Inc., 10 Northern Blvd., Northwood Executive Park, Amherst NH 03031. Editor: Marjorie Morse. Monthly magazine covering applications, programming techniques, aids or enhancements, resources for the intermediate to advanced microcomputer user. Circ. 40,000. Pays on publication. Byline given. Buys all rights. Simultaneous queries not accepted. Photocopied submissions OK. SASE. Reports in 3 weeks on queries; 1 month on mss. Sample copy $2.50; free writer's guidelines.

Nonfiction: How-to (use a microcomputer); new product (reviews of software/hardware microcomputer products); technical (programming techniques, aids, applications for microcomputers). Need freelance material covering books on microcomputer use. Buys 200 mss/year. Send complete ms. Length: 250-3,000 words. Pays $50-100/page.

Columns/Departments: System specific columns on Atari, 6809, TRS-80 Color, etc. Buys 36 mss/year. Query or send complete ms. Length: 1,500 words maximum. Pays negotiable fee.

Fillers: Jokes, anecdotes, short humor, newsbreaks (about microcomputers). Buys 100/year. Length: 500 words maximum. Pays negotiable fee.

Tips: "It is very easy to break in if you submit useful information on the in-depth use of 6502 or 6809 microcomputer systems. Send neat, professional-looking submissions with programs on magnetic media to Marjorie Morse, editor."

MICRO DISCOVERY, The Non-Technical Magazine of Personal Computing, Micro Digest, Inc., Suite 206, 5242 Katella Ave., Los Alamitos CA 90720. (213)493-4441. Editor: Alan Mertan. Monthly magazine covering home computers. "*Micro Discovery* magazine will be aimed at the person who does not already own a personal computer, someone who has recently purchased one, or a person who may be considering a purchase but would like a bit of guidance and background information." Estab. 1982. Pays on acceptance. Buys all rights. Submit seasonal/holiday material 4 months in advance. Simultaneous queries, photocopied, simultaneous (if indicated) and previously published submissions OK. SASE. Reports in 1 month on queries; 2 months on mss. Free sample copy and writer's guidelines with SASE.

Nonfiction: General interest (application of micros, topics of general interest to those recently initiated into home/personal computing—or those with no previous knowledge of subject); how-to (get started, install); humor (mishaps); interview/profile (of industry personalities); new product (anything new in industry of merit and interest for the non-technical person); personal experience (problems encountered, resolutions); photo feature. No technical data or, "How to Re-Solder Your Computer!" Length: 2,000-4,000 words; "longer negotiable." Pays $250-750.

Photos: State availability of photos with ms. Pays negotiable rate for photos. Captions, model release and identification of subjects required. Buys all rights.

Columns/Departments: "Primarily staff written. Will consider reviews of software." Length: 600-1,000 words. Pays $50 minimum.

Fillers: Clippings, jokes, gags, anecdotes, short humor, newsbreaks. "All deal with personal computers or computers in general." Length: open.

Tips: Best way to break in is with "general articles that may help break down the fear that people have about computers. Freelancers should not attempt to be too technical. Look for new and interesting applications of home computers."

‡**MICRO MOONLIGHTER NEWSLETTER**, 4121 Buckthorn Ct., Lewisville TX 75028. (214)221-5169. Editor: J. Norman Goode. Managing Editor: Mary K. Goode. Monthly newsletter covering personal computing. "Hard hitting techniques for establishing, building and maintaining a home-based business using a personal computer." Estab. 1981. Pays on acceptance. Byline given. Buys all rights. Computer printout or disk submissions OK. "We can accept any ASCII format on 5¼" diskettes under CP/M or TRSDOS formats." SASE. Reports in 1 month. Sample copy $1.

Nonfiction: Book excerpts, expose, general interest, how-to, interview/profile, new product, opinion, personal experience, technical, business case studies. Buys 24 mss/year. Query or send complete ms. Length: 500-6,000 words. Pays 3-5¢/word.

Columns/Departments: Business Case Studies. Buys 12/year. Query or send complete ms. Length: 500-6,000 words. Pays 3-5¢/word.

Tips: "Writers should submit articles of interest to personal computer owners, those who are interested in starting a home business using the personal computer, and/or articles on products associated with personal computers." Especially open to material on "cottage industry and entrepreneurship." Business Case Studies is most open to freelancers.

MICROCOMPUTING, 73 Magazine St., Peterborough NH 03458. (603)924-9471. Publisher: Wayne Green. Assistant Publisher: Jeff Detray. Managing Editor: Dennis Brisson. Monthly magazine about microcomputing for microcomputer users, businessmen interested in computer systems and students who want to learn about computers. Circ. 100,000. Pays on acceptance. Buys all rights. Phone queries OK. Submit seasonal/holiday material 4 months in advance. Photocopied submissions OK. SASE. Reports in 3 weeks. Sample copy $2.95; writer's guidelines for SASE.

Nonfiction: General interest (the how and why of design, programs, algorithms, program modules, and experimental work in advanced fields); how-to (use for a hobby, in educational programs, business, etc.); humor; new product (evaluations); and technical (all related to microcomputers, with diagrams included on a separate sheet). Buys 25-35 mss/issue. Query. Length: 3,000 words minimum. Pays $35-50/page.

Photos: Reviews 5x7 and 8x10 b&w glossy prints. Pays $150 minimum for 8x10 color glossy prints and transparencies. Especially needs microcomputer with a person in the picture (vertical). Offers no additional payment for photos accepted with ms. Captions and model release required.

Fiction: Query.

Tips: "Use as few buzzwords as possible. Remember that *Microcomputing* is trying to interest newcomers in this field, not scare them away. Use the first person and subheadings."

‡**NIBBLE, The Reference for Apple Computing**, Micro-SPARC Inc., 10 Lewis St., Lincoln MA 01773. (617)259-9710. Editor: Mike Harvey. Magazine published 8 times/year covering personal computing for Apple computers for middle/upper middle income professionals who own Apple or Apple-compatible computers. Circ. 55,000. Pays on acceptance. Byline given. Buys all rights. Submit seasonal/holiday material 4 months in advance. Simultaneous queries and submissions OK. SASE. Reports in 1 week on queries; 3 weeks on mss. Sample copy $3.50; free writer's guidelines.

Nonfiction: D. Szetela, articles editor. How-to (on programming); new product; personal experience (home/small business personal computer applications and programs). Buys 400 mss/year. Send complete ms. Length: 300-15,000 words. Pays $50-500.

Columns/Departments: D. Szetela, column/department editor. Beginning Basic Programming, VisiCalc, Graphics, Assy Language Programming, Legal. Buys 100 mss/year. Send complete ms. Length: 300-2,000 words. Pays $100-200.

Tips: "Submit original personal computer programs for Apple computers—explain what they do, how to use them, how they work, and how the techniques can be used in the reader's own programs."

‡**PC, The Independent Guide to IBM Personal Computers**, Ziff-Davis Publishing Co., 1 Park Ave., New York NY 10016. (212)725-4694. Editor: Jonathan Lazarus. Executive Editor: Corey Sandler. Monthly magazine for users/owners of IBM Personal Computers and compatible systems. Estab. 1981. Pays on acceptance. Byline given. Buys all rights. Submit seasonal/holiday material 5 months in advance to executive editor. Photocopied submissions OK. SASE. Reports in 4 weeks. Sample copy $5.

Nonfiction: How-to (software and hardware); interview/profile; technical; product evaluations; programs. Query first for fiction. Buys 300 mss/year. Send complete ms. Length: 1,000-8,000 words.

‡**PC WORLD, The Personal Computer Magazine for IBM PCs and Compatibles**, PC World Communications, Inc., 555 De Haro St., San Francisco CA 94107. (415)861-3861. Monthly magazine covering IBM Personal Computers and compatibles. Estab. 1982. Circ. 300,000. Pays on acceptance. Byline given. Buys first world serial rights and second serial (reprint) rights. Submit seasonal/holiday material at least 3 months in advance. Simultaneous queries and previously published submissions OK. SASE. Reports in 6 weeks on queries; 4 weeks on mss. Sample copy $5; writer's guidelines for 9x12 SAE and 2 first class stamps.

Nonfiction: How-to, interview/profile, new product and technical. "*PC World* is composed of 4 sections:

State of the Art, Review, Hands On, and Community. In State of the Art, articles cover developing technologies.in the computer industry. In Review, new hardware and software are critically and objectively analyzed by experienced users. Hands On offers 'how-to' articles, giving readers instructions on patching Wordstar, setting up VisiCalc worksheets, inserting memory boards, developing programming skills and other related topics. Community covers a wide range of subjects, focusing on how society is being shaped by the influx of microcomputers in work places, schools and homes.'' No articles not related to the IBM PC or compatibles. 80% freelance written. Query with or without published clips or send complete ms. Length: 1,000-8,000 words. Pays $200-1,000.

Columns/Departments: REMark (personal opinions abou microcomputer-related issues); User Group Dispatch (IBM PC User Group topics). Buys 24 mss/year. Query with or without published clips or send complete ms. Length: 500-3,000 words. Pays $150-250.

Fillers: Anecdotes, newsbreaks. Buys 150/year. Length: 50-400 words. Pays $50 maximum. Send submissions to PC World View.

Tips: ''Familiarity with the IBM PC or technical knowledge about its operations often determines whether we accept a query. Send all queries to the attention of Proposals—Editorial Department. The Hands On section is especially open to freelancers with practical applications to offer.''

‡**PERSONAL COMPUTER AGE, The Definitive Journal for the IBM Personal Computer User**, Personal Computer Age, 10057 Commerce Ave., Tujunga CA 91042. (213)352-7811. Editor: Jack Crone. Managing Editor: Bob Embry. Monthly magazine covering the IBM Personal Computer. ''Practical how-to guidance and technical education for the IBM PC user.'' Estab. 1981. Circ. 50,000. Pays on publication. Byline given. Offers negotiable kill fee. Buys first rights and yearly anthology rights. Submit holiday/seasonal material 3 months in advance. Simultaneous queries, and photocopied and previously published submissions OK. Reports in 3 weeks. Sample copy $3.50.

Nonfiction: How-to (use IBM PC, etc.); humor (occasional); technical (IBM PC only); tutorials on computer technology oriented to the IBM PC. No ''history or industry overviews.'' Buys 250 mss/year. Query with clips. Length: 6,000 words maximum. Pays 6¢/word.

Photos: State availability of photos with query letter or manuscript ''only if pro-quality photographer.'' Buys one-time rights.

Fillers: Clippings, jokes, gags, anecdotes, short humor, newsbreaks. Buys 100/year. Pays negotiable rate.

Tips: ''Orient your thinking and writing to what the IBM PC user really needs to know to get the most out of his computer. Open with a concise tutorial, then go to specifics. Almost all articles are freelance-written. Don't assume the reader has your technical background—spell it out for him. Clear, sequential story organization is important. Don't ramble and philosophize—get to the point and stick to it. We need less traditional, dry technical writing and more stylish popular stuff, but with the same technical competence.''

‡**PERSONAL COMPUTER NEWS**, (formerly *Computer Trader*), Box 848, Pt. Reyes CA 94956. (415)669-7554. Editor: Kim Huegel. Monthly tabloid covering home and personal computer hardware, peripherals, software and video games. ''Interest and expertise, on the beginner to advanced level, in home and personal computers in layman's terms.'' Estab. 1982. Circ. 20,000. Pays on publication. Byline given. Offers 40% kill fee. Buys first North American serial rights, second serial (reprint) rights and makes work-for-hire assignments. Submit seasonal/holiday material 4 months in advance. Simultaneous queries, and simultaneous, photocopied, and previously published submissions OK. Computer printout submissions OK; prefers letter quality to dot matrix. SASE. Reports in 3 weeks on queries; 2 weeks on mss. Sample copy $3; writer's guidelines free with SASE.

Nonfiction: Book excerpts (new computer book releases); general interest (hardware, peripherals, software); historical/nostalgic; how-to (programming, hands-on day-to-day exposure, games); inspirational (getting over the hurdles of getting started); new product (hardware, peripherals, software, trends); opinion (trends); personal experience (hands-on learning and successful experience with home and p.c.'s); photo feature (new equipment); technical (hardware, peripherals, software); kids and computers; computer uses; the latest happenings. ''Inaccurate, amateurish, poorly researched articles will be met with a shrug. Good quality, clearly-explained articles are what to aim for.'' Buys 100+ mss/year. Send complete ms. Length: 200-3,500 words. Pays $20-350.

Photos: Send photos with ms. Pays $5-15 for b&w negatives, prints. Captions, model release and identificaton of subjects required. Buys one-time rights.

Columns/Departments: Book reviews, hardware reviews, software reviews, peripheral reviews, games, interviews, State of the Art, Letters, Hardware Index, Hardware/Software of the Month, Software Index, Computer Literacy, Computer Beginners and Pros. Buys 100+ items/year. Query or send complete ms. Length: 200-1,500 words. Pays $20-150.

Poetry: Avant-garde, free verse, haiku, light verse, traditional. Does not want ''anything not relating to information, computers and life.'' Buys 12-15/year. Submit maximum 3 poems. Length: 4-16 lines. Pays $5-25.

Fillers: Clippings, short humor, newsbreaks. Buys 50/year. Length: 50-250 words. Pays $5-25.

Tips: ''The freelancer should have an interest and expertise, a fascination, with home and personal computers.

Accuracy of information is vital and timeliness in this rapidly changing business is imperative. We welcome freelancers to contribute to all departments. If you are terrific in a hands-on sense with home and personal computers, but you're a bit worried about your writing skills . . . not to worry. We will polish up your prose a bit if necessary. Good material welcome.''

PERSONAL COMPUTING, Hayden Publishing Company, Inc., 50 Essex St., Rochelle Park NJ 07662. (201)843-0550, ext. 220. Managing Editor: Ernie Baxter. Monthly magazine covering small business, office, home and school computing. Monthly magazine. Circ. 35,000. Pays on publication. Buys all rights. Byline given. Submit seasonal/holiday material 4 months in advance. Photocopied submissions OK, but state if material is not multiple submission. SASE. Sample copy $3; free writer's guidelines.
Nonfiction: Business applications articles, issues concerning computer users and the experience of computing; general interest (related to microcomputers); how-to use computers; humor (fiction relating to computers and personal stories concerning computers); interview (with prominent figures in the field); new product (review, but not puff piece, must be objective); nostalgia (only if related to computing); computer chess and computer bridge; personal experience (someone who has worked with a specific system and has learned something readers can benefit from); opinion (editorials, or opinion of someone in field); photo feature (only if accompanied by article); profile (of prominent person in field); and technical (program writing, debugging; especially good are applications for business, education, or home use). No articles on product hype, personal experiences that don't pass anything on to the reader, games that have been published in similar form already, and puzzles. Buys 10 mss/issue. Query with outline preferred. Buys 12 unsolicited mss/year. Length: 1,000 words minimum. Pay varies.
Photos: State availability of photos with query or ms. Offers no additional payment for b&w or color pictures. Captions preferred. Buys all rights.
Columns/Departments: Editorials (on any topic in the field); Future Computing (a detailed look at one or more aspects of what's going on in the field and what's projected); *PC* Interview (of prominent figures in the field); Outlook (unusual applications, goings on, or stories about computers); Computer Chess (and other games) and Products (product reviews, comments on, criticism of, and comparison). Does not accept unsolicited reviews.

POPULAR COMPUTING MAGAZINE, 70 Main St., Peterborough, NH 03458. (603)924-9281. Managing Editor: Richard L. Friedman. McGraw-Hill monthly magazine covering personal computers directed particularly at beginners and professional people such as educators, attorneys, doctors and so on. Circ. 300,000. Pays on acceptance. Buys first North American serial rights. Photocopied submissions OK. SASE. Reports in 2 months. Sample copy $2.75.
Nonfiction: ''Articles should contain information about buying personal computers plus reviews of computers and other material related to personal computers.'' Buys 200 mss/year. Send detailed query letter to managing editor.
Tips: ''Visit personal computer stores or read any of the books on the market pertaining to personal computers. The ideal *Popular Computing Magazine* article popularizes personal computer concepts without talking down to the reader. Articles should be free of computer jargon as much as possible. Send query letter before submitting manuscript.''

‡**PORTABLE COMPUTER**, Miller Freeman Publications, 500 Howard St., San Francisco CA 94105. (415)397-1881. Editor: Steve Schneiderman. Managing Editor: Leonard Grzanka. Bimonthly magazine covering portable computer technology and applications for the non-technical portable computer user. Estab. 1983. Circ. 40,000. Pays on acceptance. Byline given. Offers kill fee. Buys first rights. Submit seasonal/holiday material 3 months in advance. Simultaneous queries and photocopied submissions OK. SASE. Reports in 1 month. Free writer's guidelines.
Nonfiction: General interest, how-to, humor, interview/profile, new product, personal experience. Query with published clips if available. Length: 1,000-5,000 words. Pays $100-1,000.
Photos: State availability of photos. Reviews b&w prints. Identification of subjects required. Buys one-time rights.
Tips: ''Send resume with 2 published samples.''

‡**POWER/PLAY, Home Computing**, Commodore Business Machines, 1200 Wilson Dr., West Chester PA 19380. (215)436-4211. Editor: Diane Lebold. Publisher: Neil Harris. Quarterly magazine covering games and home computing for new computer owners interested in recreational computing. ''Many readers are children.'' Estab. 1982. Circ. 70,000. Pays on publication. Byline given. Buys first North American serial rights, all rights, second serial (reprint) rights, and makes work-for-hire assignments. Submit seasonal/holiday material 6 months in advance. Simultaneous queries and previously published submissions OK. SASE. Reports in 1 month on queries; 2 months on mss. Free sample copy; writer's guidelines for legal size SAE and 1 first class stamp.
Nonfiction: Book reviews; how-to (beat games); humor; new product (reviews); personal experience (learning

from computers); photo feature; computers for kids. "No highly technical material. Send that to *Commodore Magazine* instead." Buys 30 mss/year. Query or send complete ms. Length: 1,000-8,000 words. Pays $25-50/page.

Photos: Send photos with ms. Reviews 5x7 b&w and color prints. Captions and identification of subjects required. Buys all rights.

Tips: "We're open to game reviews and advice and game programs. Find an interesting slant on computing at home!"

‡**SOFTALK FOR THE IBM PERSONAL COMPUTER**, Softalk Publishing Inc., 11160 McCormick St., North Hollywood CA 91601. (213)980-5074. Editor: Craig Stinson. Managing Editor: Mike Tighe. Monthly consumer and trade publication for novice to expert readers involved with the IBM Personal Computer. Estab. 1982. Pays on publication; on acceptance for material received by deadline. Byline given. Buys all rights. Simultaneous queries OK "if presented as such"; photocopied submissions OK "if neat and legible." SASE. Reports in 2 weeks on queries; 1 month on mss. Sample copy $3.

Nonfiction: How-to; humor; interview/profile (query); new product (query); personal experience; photo feature; technical. All must be personal computer related. "Writers should emphasize news and personal interest, but avoid the words 'I' and 'me.' " Query. Pays 10-12¢/word.

Photos: Kurt A. Wahlner, photo editor. State availability of photos. Reviews b&w contact sheet, 6x6, 6x7 or 35mm color transparencies and 8x10 b&w prints. Captions and identification of subjects required. Buys one-time rights.

‡**SOFTSIDE MAGAZINE**, Softside Publications, Inc., 6 South St., Milford NH 03055. (603)673-0585. Editor: Randal L. Kottwitz. Managing Editor: Carolyn Nolan. Monthly magazine of home and hobby microcomputing for the home user of Apple, Atari, IBM-PC and TRS-80 microcomputers. Circ. 50,000. Pays on publication. Byline given. Offers 20% kill fee. Buys mostly one-time rights; also all rights, seond serial (reprint) rights, and makes work-for-hire assignments "depending on the article." Submit seasonal/holiday material 4 months in advance. Simultaneous queries, and photocopied and previously published submissions OK. "We encourage submissions on disk and pay a premium for them." SASE. Reports in 2 weeks on queries; 1 month on mss. Sample copy for 9x12 SAE and 9 first class stamps; writer's guidelines for business-size SAE and 2 first class stamps.

Nonfiction: Book excerpts, how-to (hardware and software tutorials), humor, interview/profile, new product, photo feature and technical. Special issues include Microcomputer Graphics, Microcomputer Music, Computers in Education, Computer Telecommunications, Personal Finance and the Computer. "Social comment articles should deal with some aspect of computers' effects on society." No articles on business computing. Buys 150 mss/year. Query with clips if available or send complete ms. Length: 1,000-8,000 words. Pays $65-500.

Photos: Send photos with ms. Pays $10-50 for 35mm color transparencies; $5-40 for 5x7 b&w prints. Captions, model release and identification of subjects required. Buys one-time rights.

Columns/Departments: Microcomputer software reviews, related book reviews, hardware reviews. "Reviews should be complete with recommendations for improvement in product and use reports." Buys 50 mss/year. Query with clips or send complete ms. Length: 1,000-3,000 words. Pays $75-200.

Fiction: Experimental, fantasy, humorous and science fiction. Buys 10 mss/year. Send complete ms. Length: 500-2,000 words. Pays $40-125.

Fillers: Short humor, newsbreaks. Buys 15-20/year. Length: 200-1,000 words. Pays $10-50.

Tips: "Extra consideration is given to text submitted on computer diskette for TRS-80, Apple, Atari or IBM-PC computers. Call for details."

‡**SYNC, The Magazine for Sinclair and Timex/Sinclair Users**, Ahl Computing, 39 E. Hanover Ave., Morris Plains NJ 07950. (201)540-0445. Editor-in-Chief: David Ahl. Managing Editor: Paul Grosjean. Bimonthly magazine covering computer tutorials and applications. Estab. 1981. Circ. 30,000. Pays on acceptance. Byline given. Buys first rights, second serial (reprint) rights and book reprint rights. Submit seasonal/holiday material 6 months in advance. Photocopied submissions OK. SASE. Reports in 1 month on queries; 4 months on mss. Writer's guidelines for business-size SAE and 1 first class stamp.

Nonfiction: How-to (use the Sinclair and Timex/Sinclair computer series); new products (for this computer series); technical (how the series works and how to make hardware items for it). "Provide solid, concise, clear tutorial articles with illustrative programs where appropriate that will help Sinclair and Timex/Sinclair computer users get more out of their computers." No fiction or articles not relevant to the computer series served. Buys 120 mss/year. Query or send complete ms. Length: 1,000-2,000 words. Pays $25/published page.

Photos: State availability of photos. Reviews 3½x5 and larger b&w and color prints. Photos are paid for with payment for ms. Captions and model release required. Buys first serial and reprint rights.

SYNTAX, Syntax ZX80, Inc., Rd. 2 Box 457, Bolton Rd., Harvard MA 01451. (617)456-3661. Editor: Ann L. Zevnik. Monthly newsletter covering Timex Sinclair and ZX81 microcomputers for owners of all levels of expertise. Circ. 10,000. Pays on acceptance; 7¢ every 6 characters including punctuation. Token fee for programs. Byline given. Buys all rights; "nonexclusive." Submit seasonal/holiday material 2 months in advance. Photocopied submissions OK. SASE.

Nonfiction: How-to (hardware projects, software tutorials); new product (Timex Sinclair-related peripherals); technical (programs: business, educational, home, utility, math or game programs written in BASIC or Z80 machine language. Explanations of machine technical workings). "We need clearly written stories and reviews to both interest experts and educate beginners. An extremely tight style is especially important to our newsletter format. No long, chatty stories. We are a newsletter whose main purpose is to give readers as much information as possible in a minimum space. Set them to thinking rather than drowning them in explanation." Buys 48 mss/year. Length: 100-900 words.

Columns/Departments: "We need reviews of Timex Sinclair-related books on hardware and programming and reviews of software and hardware. Again, the piece must be user-oriented, but objective. Please include company or manufacturer's name, address and telephone number." Query. Length: 100-900 words.

Fillers: Newsbreaks (short-short information, such as 1-2 line commands to access computer memory). "Mostly staff-written but would buy 30/year if available." Length: 15-100 words.

Tips: "Demonstrate knowledge of Timex Sinclair computer, electronics, or programming and be able to express technical concepts clearly and simply. We have no strict submission requirements but prefer typed copy double-spaced and programs on cassette. For hardware projects and software stories make sure instructions are specific and clear, and writing should be super-tight. Of course, all project and programs must work."

Humor

Publications herein specialize in cartoon panel humor, gaglines or prose humor. Other publications that use humor can be found in nearly every category in this book. Some of these have special needs for major humor pieces; some use humor as fillers; many others are simply interested in material that meets their ordinary fiction or nonfiction requirements but has a humorous slant. For a closer look at writing humor, consult *How to Write and Sell (Your Sense of) Humor*, by Gene Perret (Writer's Digest Books).

‡**LONE STAR: A Magazine of Humor**, Lone Star Publications of Humor, Suite 103, Box 29000, San Antonio TX 78229. Editor: Lauren I. Barnett Scharf. Bimonthly humor magazine for "the general public and 'comedy connoisseur' as well as the professional humorist." Estab. 1982. Circ. 1,000. Pays on publication; "but we try to pay before that." Buys first North American serial rights, first rights and occasionally second serial (reprint) rights. Submit seasonal/holiday material 2 months in advance. Photocopied submissions and "sometimes" previously published work OK. SASE. Reports in 2 weeks on queries; 5 weeks on mss. Sample copy $1.95; writer's guidelines for business-size SAE and 1 first class stamp.

Nonfiction: Humor (on anything topical/timeless); interview/profile (of anyone professionally involved in humor); opinion (reviews of stand-up comedians, comedy plays, humorous books, *anything* concerned with comedy). "Inquire about possible theme issues." Buys 6 mss/year. Query with clips of published work if available. Length: 500-1,000 words; average is 700-800 words. Pays $5-20 and contributor's copy.

Fiction: Humorous. Buys variable mss/year. Query with clips if available or send complete ms. Length: 500-1,000 words. Pays $5-20 and contributor's copy.

Poetry: Free verse, light verse, traditional, clerihews, limericks. "Nothing too 'artsy' to be funny." Buys 10-20/year. Submit maximum 5 poems. Length: 4-16 lines. Pays $2-10.

Fillers: Clippings, jokes, gags, anecdotes, short humor, newsbreaks—"must be humorous or humor-related." Buys 20-30 mss/year. Length: 450 words maximum. Pays $1-5.

Tips: "We *do* like to know a writer's professional background. However, telling us that you've sold material to Phyllis Diller or that you're a personal friend of Isaac Asimov will not convince us to buy anything we don't find funny. Conversely, those with no background sales in humor should feel free to submit their material. The only real criteria are that it be original and *funny!* We recommend that those who are unfamiliar with *Lone Star* purchase a sample issue before submitting their work. However, this is *not* a requirement."

MAD MAGAZINE, 485 Madison Ave., New York NY 10022. Editor: Al Feldstein. Buys all rights. Byline given.

Humor & Satire: "You know you're almost a *Mad* writer when: You include a self-addressed, stamped envelope with each submission. You realize we are a visual magazine and we don't print prose, text or first/second/third-person narratives. You don't send us stuff like the above saying, 'I'm sure one of your great artists can do wonders with this!' You first submit a 'premise' for an article, and show us how you're going to treat it with three or four examples, describing the visuals (sketches not necessary). You don't send in 'timely' material, knowing it takes about 6 months between typewriter and on-the-stands. You don't send poems, song parodies, fold-ins, movie and/or TV show satires, Lighter Sides or other standard features. You understand that individual criticism of art or script is impossible due to the enormous amount of submissions we receive. You don't ask for assignments or staff jobs since *Mad* is strictly a freelance operation. You concentrate on new ideas and concepts other than things we've done (and over-done), like 'You Know You're a . . . When. . . .' " Buys 200-300 unsolicited mss/year.

ORBEN'S CURRENT COMEDY, 1200 N. Nash St., #1122, Arlington VA 22209. (703)522-3666. Editor: Robert Orben. For "speakers, toastmasters, businessmen, public relations people, communications professionals." Biweekly. Buys all rights. Pays at the end of the month for material used in issues published that month. "Material should be typed and submitted on standard size paper. Please leave 3 spaces between each item. Computer printout and disk submissions OK; prefers letter quality to dot matrix printouts. Unused material will be returned to the writer within a few days if SASE is enclosed. We do not send rejection slips. If SASE is not enclosed, all material will be destroyed after being considered except for items purchased."
Fillers: "We are looking for funny, performable one-liners, short jokes and stories that are related to happenings in the news, fads, trends and topical subjects. The accent is on laugh-out-loud comedy. Ask yourself, 'Will this line get a laugh if performed in public?' Material should be written in a conversational style and, if the joke permits it, the inclusion of dialogue is a plus. We are particularly interested in material that can be used by speakers and toastmasters: lines for beginning a speech, ending a speech, acknowledging an introduction, specific occasions, anything that would be of use to a person making a speech. We can use lines to be used at roasts, sales meetings, presentations, conventions, seminars and conferences. Short, sharp comment on business trends, fads and events is also desirable. Please do not send us material that's primarily written to be read rather than spoken. We have little use for definitions, epigrams, puns, etc. The submissions must be original. If material is sent to us that we find to be copied or rewritten from some other source, we will no longer consider material from the contributor." Pays $5.
Tips: "Follow the instructions in our guidelines. Although they are quite specific, we have received everything from epic poems to serious novels."

In-Flight

With the addition of a rail passenger magazine listing in this section, perhaps it should be titled Enroute. But for the most part, this category lists publications read by commercial airline passengers. Editors of in-flight magazines use a variety of general-interest material, as well as travel and popular aviation articles.

‡**ABOARD**, Aeroperú/Air Panamá/Air Paraguay/Lloyd Aéreo Boliviano/Lan-Chile/TACA/VIASA, North-South Net, Inc., 135 Madeira Ave., Coral Gables FL 33134. (305)442-0752/2667/2989. Editor: Amaury Cruz. Quarterly magazine covering destinations for the Peruvian, Panamanian, Paraguayan, Bolivian, Chilean, Salvadoran and Venezuelan national airlines. Entertaining, upbeat stories for the passengers. Circ. 100,000 average. Pays on publication. Byline given. Buys simultaneous and second serial (reprint) rights. Simultaneous queries, and simultaneous, photocopied and previously published submissions OK. Computer printout submissions OK. SASE. Reports in 2 weeks on queries; 6 weeks on mss. Sample copy for 9x12 SAE and $1.90 postage; writer's guidelines for 4x9½ SAE and 1 first class stamp.
Nonfiction: General interest, new product, photo feature, technical, travel, sports, business, science, technology or topical pieces. Nothing "political, downbeat or in any way offensive to Latin American sensibilities." Buys 20-25 mss/year. Query with clips if available or send complete ms. No resumés or letters from writers explaining their qualifications. Length: 250-1,500 words. Pays $50-150 (with photos).
Photos: State availability of photos or send photos with ms. Pays $10-50 for 35mm color transparencies; $5-20 for 5x7 b&w prints. Captions, model releases and identification of subjects required. Buys "non-exclusive use one-time and the right to re-use color separation after return of the original."
Tips: "Study *Aboard* and other inflights, write exciting, succinct stories with an upbeat slant and enclose photos with captions. Break in with destination pieces for the individual airline or those shared by all seven. Writers must be accurate. Photos are almost always indispensable. Manuscripts are accepted either in English or Spanish. Translation rights must be granted. All manuscripts are subject to editing and condensation."

ALASKAFEST, Seattle Northwest Publishing Co., Suite 503, 1932 1st Ave., Seattle WA 98101. (206)682-5871. Editor: Ed Reading. For travelers on Alaska Airlines. Monthly magazine; 64-80 pages. Circ. 25,000-

35,000 (depending on season). Pays within 2 weeks of publication. Buys first rights. Byline given. Submit seasonal/holiday material 4 months in advance. Computer printout or disk submissions OK; letter quality or dot matrix printouts acceptable "as long as the letters have ascenders and descenders. No OCR." SASE. Query with clips of published work. "A smart query begins with the lead of the story and is written in the style of the story. We don't get many like that." Free sample copy and writer's guidelines.

Nonfiction: The audience is predominantly male, business travelers. We cover not only Alaska, but the whole West Coast. Editorial content includes general-interest, adventure travel, business, life-style, and think pieces. We continue to look for humor and fiction. Buys 40 unsolicited mss/year. Length: 800-2,500 words. Pays $75-400.

Photos: State availability of photos with mss or send photos with ms. Pays $25-100 for b&w prints; $40-200 for color transparencies. Captions required.

Tips: "Read a copy of the magazine. Then send something I would publish. Show, don't tell. Do not send anything that could appear in a newspaper Sunday supplement or Sunday travel section."

AMERICAN WAY, Mail Drop 3D08, Box 61616, Dallas-Fort Worth Airport TX 75261. (817)355-1583. Editor: Walter A. Damtoft. The inflight magazine for American Airlines. Monthly magazine. Pays on acceptance. Buys various rights depending on author and material. Sometimes pays kill fee. Byline given. Submit seasonal/holiday material 7 months in advance. Letter quality computer printouts and Olivetti WP disk submissions OK. Reports in 4 months. SASE. Free sample copy.

Nonfiction: Broadly oriented rather than travel-oriented. "Seek timely articles that deal with almost any subject. Avoid controversial subjects or advocacy articles." Query (phone queries discouraged). "We would like writing samples that show a writer's abilities and scope. These will not be returned. We have no patience with writers who haven't familiarized themselves with the magazine." Submit Attn: Articles Editor. Nearly all articles written by a well-established group of freelancers. Length: 1,500-1,750 words for think pieces, interviews, profiles, humor, nostalgia, travel pieces, sports articles and how-to. Pays $300 minimum.

Tips: "Write interestingly and populate articles with real people who have something to say. Show a special concern for spelling of proper names. Send a query letter that is inherently interesting. It can almost be like a letter telling a friend about something interesting. Don't tell me *why* I should be interested."

‡AMTRAK EXPRESS, East/West Network, Inc., 34 E. 51st St., New York NY 10022. (212)888-5900. Editor: James A. Frank. Monthly magazine for Amtrak riders who are upscale and discriminating. Estab. 1981. Circ. 160,000. Pays on acceptance. Byline given. Offers ¼ kill fee. Buys first North American serial rights. Submit seasonal/holiday material 6 months in advance. Simultaneous queries OK. SASE. Reports in 3 weeks on queries; 2 weeks on mss. Sample copy for $2, 9x12 SAE and 3 first class stamps. Writer's guidelines for business size SAE and 1 first class stamp.

Nonfiction: General interest; humor; interview/profile; photo feature; travel (only within Amtrak territory); business; science/technology. No poetry, personal experiences, train trip experiences. "We have moved away from mostly business articles to cover lifestyle, 'the good life,' personalities, consumer items and travel (limited amounts)." Buys 75 mss/year. Query with published clips. Length: 1,800-2,200 words. Pays $500-750.

Photos: State availability of photos. Pays $75-175 for 5x7 or 8x10 b&w prints; $125-400 for 35mm color transparencies. Identification of subjects required. Buys one-time rights.

Columns/Departments: Health; Books; Sports; Business; Money ("should be a specific topic, well explained, informational and useful to readers"). Buys 35 mss/year. Query with published clips. Length: 1,200-1,800 words. Pays $350-500.

Tips: "Send a good idea, well explained with a detailed query that also tells something about you and your credits. We like to use new people, but we need some proof of competence."

‡CONTINENTAL MAGAZINE, The Magazine to Broaden Business Horizons, East/West Network, Suite 800, 5900 Wilshire Blvd., Los Angeles CA 90036. (213)937-5810. Editor: Ellen Alperstein. Associate Editor: Joan Yee. Monthly magazine covering business (and some travel and leisure activities) for upscale readers. Pays on acceptance. Byline given. Offers ⅓ to ¼ kill fee. Buys first North American serial rights. Submit seasonal/holiday material 4 months in advance. Simultaneous queries OK "provided writer informs us that it's submitted simultaneously." Reports in 3 weeks on queries. SASE a must. Sample copy $2 (requests to Dottie Hogan); writer's guidelines for SAE and 1 first class stamp.

Nonfiction: Fast Track (a substantial profile of a business person with a demonstrable record of success); Closeup (solid pieces of business reporting on subjects with implications in the business world at large); f-Stops (photo essay relating to industry with "an aesthetic graphic appeal"); Top of the Line (a color spread on "a person, place, product or service that is, without a doubt, the best"); The Savvy Shopper (service feature to advise the traveling executive in the consumer marketplace); humor (as long as it has a business angle); any subject (sports, science, fashion, leisure, architecture and design) as long as it has a business angle; Going Places (a major travel story with color photos offering "substantial service information to the Continental traveler"). Buys 130 features and department material/year. Length: 800-2,500 words. Pays $250-650 "plus some expenses." Query.

Columns/Departments: Creative Thinking (profiles of inventive people); On the Job With (first person accounts of people at work); Second Time Around (profiles of successful career changers); Grapevine (tips from readers only on restaurants, hotels, business services geared to the business traveler—a reader's forum); At Ease (leisure activities for maximizing nonworking hours); Last Laugh (monthly anecdote detailing in first person a resounding failure of an otherwise notable, successful person). Buys 75 mss/year. Length 800-2,000 words. Pays $250-350. Query.

DELTA SKY, Halsey Publishing, 12955 Biscayne Blvd., N. Miami FL 33181. (305)893-1520. Editor: Donna Dupuy. Audience is Delta Air Lines passengers. Monthly magazine. Circ. over 3 million monthly. "Unsolicited materials are rarely used, and only text/photo packages are considered." Details and guidelines for SASE.

EAST/WEST NETWORK, INC., 34 E. 51st St., New York NY 10022. Publisher: Fred R. Smith. Publishes monthly inflight publications: *Continental* (Continental Airlines), *Republic Scene* (Republic Airlines), *Ozark Magazine* (Ozark Airlines), *United* (United Airlines), *PSA Magazine* (Pacific Southwest Airlines), *ReView* (Eastern Airlines), *Texas Flyer,* (Texas International), *USAir* (US Air), *PanAm Clipper* (Pan-Am), *Western* (Western Airlines) and *Express* (Amtrak). Combined circ. 1.5 million. Pays within 60 days of acceptance. Buys one only East/West Network Publication: author retains other rights. Pays 50% kill fee. Byline given. SASE. No telephone queries. Reports in 1 month.
Nonfiction: "Magazines publish articles of interest to consumer magazine audience that are timely and have national significance." No first person stories, airline stories, politics or downbeat material. Queries with published work for *United, PanAm, USAir, Express* and *ReView* should be sent to New York office. Queries for all other publications should be sent to the West Coast office to Editor and name of publication at 5900 Wilshire Blvd., Los Angeles CA 90036. Length: 1,000-2,500 words. Pays $300-800. See individual listings for more information.
Photos: Wants no photos sent by writers.

INFLIGHT, Meridian Publishing Co., Box 2315, Ogden UT 84404. (801)394-9446. Editor: Dick Harris. Associate Editor: Peggie Bingham. Bimonthly magazine covering general-interest topics. Readers are "business-oriented, predominantly male, age 30-50, middle-to-high income, well-educated, who travel extensively in connection with business and personal affairs, like sports, and are moving up professionally. Our magazine aims at providing short, brightly-written articles that inform and entertain." Pays on acceptance. Byline given. Buys first North American serial rights and second serial (reprint) rights. Submit seasonal/holiday material 6 months in advance. Computer printout and disk submissions OK; prefers letter quality to dot matrix printouts. SASE. Reports in 2 weeks on queries and mss. Sample copy 50¢ with 9x12 SAE and 40¢ postage; writer's guideline free for #10 SAE and 20¢ postage.
Nonfiction: General interest, historical/nostalgic, how-to, humor, inspirational, interview/profile, photo feature and travel. No "exposes, think pieces, social issues, 'lifestyle' pieces, off-color humor or politics." Buys 50 mss/year. Query. Length: 400-1,200 words. Pays up to 15¢/word.
Photos: State availability of photos. Pays $35-50 for 35mm or 4x5 color transparencies; $20 for 8x10 b&w prints. Captions and identification of subjects required. Buys one-time rights.
Fillers: Short humor. "This is the most accessible section to freelancers. We're looking for short, humorous pieces of 300-400 words or 1-page humor features of about 800 words." Buys 20-30/year.

NORTHWEST ORIENT MAGAZINE, (formerly *Northwest Passages*), The Webb Co., 1999 Shepard Rd., St. Paul MN 55116. Editor-in-Chief: Jean Marie Hamilton. Columns Editor: Paul Froiland. 80% freelance written. For Northwest Orient Airlines passengers. Monthly magazine. Pays on acceptance. Buys first magazine rights and nonexclusive reprint rights. Reports in 1 month. Query with clips of published work. SASE. Sample copy $2; free writer's guidelines.
Nonfiction: How-to (on business, health, etc.,—no crafts); informational (sports, business trends, lifestyle, current issues); interviews and profiles (on interesting people who are saying things of significance); entertainment (television, movies, the arts); science; politics; travel (no what-to-see, where-to-stay pieces); and business management. Buys 4 unsolicited mss/year. Recent article example: "A Matter of Style: Senators Nancy Kassebaum and Paula Hawkins." Length: 2,000-3,000 words. Pays $300-1,000.
Photos: Purchased with mss and on assignment. Query. Pays $25-75/b&w; $50-100/color; $200/cover shots. For photos purchased with mss, "the package price is negotiated ahead of time." Model release required.
Columns/Departments: Sports and Health, The Arts, Pop psychology quizzes, Science, Travel and Finances. Buys 20 unsolicited mss/year. Recent column example: "The Superbrokers" (January 1982). Length 800-1,200 words. Pays $100-250.

‡OZARK MAGAZINE, East/West Network, 5900 Wilshire Blvd., Los Angeles CA 90036. Editor: Laura Doss. Monthly general interest inflight magazine slanted for a Midwest audience. Pays on acceptance. Byline given. Offers 10% kill fee. Buys first North American serial rights. Submit seasonal/holiday material 6 months

Close-up

Richard Busch, Editor
USAir Magazine

Photo by Olwen Woodier

Giving form and continuity to a publication that reaches an-"educated, affluent, mixed bag of people" is no small task; and Richard Busch is involved at every step. He reads queries, edits manuscripts, assigns articles, reviews photos and layouts, and checks galleys and page proofs, in addition to the administrative duties of his job as editor of *USAir* Magazine. "And I snatch moments to read mail," he adds.

Busch came to *USAir* at its inception in 1979. With him he brought editorial experience from *Life* and *Popular Photography*, and insight from having freelanced as a writer/photographer for three years.

Busch sees his job as one of bridging the gap between ideas and their fruition. "I'm the orchestrator who has to put it all together so it comes out with a style, a clarity and a readability. It's my duty to correct or eliminate confusion and contradiction. I have to be a champion both of the writer and the audience. My relationship with writers is a positive one when both of us go into it with a common purpose—communication. That's what we're about."

But with only one other editor and an art department the equivalent of 1½ fulltime people, time for communication is at a premium. "We don't have a lot of time to talk to writers," he says. "Telephone queries just don't work. But I don't mind getting a manuscript because I can tell pretty quickly whether it's for us." And for beginning writers (those without published clips), a complete manuscript is probably the best route to take. "It's always great to get a good manuscript out of the blue—it's a totally known quantity.

"With queries, I look to see what the person has in mind, and I look at what they've done before. A good query is short and concise and thought out in terms of *USAir*. It may have at least a working title expressing in a few short words the essence of the piece. Writing a headline is a good device because it forces you to focus the piece. If you can't do it in a few words, you haven't honed it. If I have to say 'what's this guy talking about; what does he want to do?'— lights flash, and I know there's a problem."

Another problem Busch sees in manuscripts that cross his desk is an unfamiliarity with *USAir Magazine*. "I know it's difficult because you can't buy us on the newsstand, but our *Writer's Market* listing will tell you how to get a sample copy. A lot of freelancers waste their time and postage with queries that have no chance in our market. We're a domestic airline; yet I get queries every month wanting to do a story on 'traveling down the Rhine.' "

What kinds of subjects does Busch want to see from freelancers? "We're general interest and visually oriented. Each month we run a six-to-eight-page portfolio and usually use a destination piece, something on sports, and a piece on business. Beyond that, we run the gamut—nature, science, health, food. And because we're based in the Northeast, we use some regional things, too.'

In addition to following these editorial formulas for *USAir*, Busch is very receptive to article ideas. "One of the great things about the fact there are freelancers out there," he says, "is that they're always hitting us with ideas nobody here has thought of before."

in advance. Simultaneous queries OK. SASE. Reports in 3 weeks on queries; 2 weeks on mss. Sample copy $2.

Nonfiction: General interest, historical/nostalgic, humor, interview/profile, personal experience, photo feature, travel, food, fashion, sports. All articles must somehow relate to the Midwest. Buys 150-175 mss/year. Query with published clips or send complete ms. Length: 1,700-2,500 words. Pays $250-600.

Photos: State availability of photos, or send photos with ms. Reviews 35mm transparencies. Identification of subjects required. Buys one-time rights.

Columns/Departments: Hometown; Sports; Business; Lifestyle; The Right Stuff; Media; Outdoors. Buys 35-45 mss/year. Query with published clips or send cmplete ms. Length: 1,700 words maximum. Pays $250-300.

‡**PACE MAGAZINE, Piedmont Airlines Inflight Publication**, Fisher-Harrison Publications, 338 N. Elm St., Greensboro NC 27401. (919)378-9651. Publisher: Bonnie McElveen Hunter. Managing Editor: Leslie P. Daisy. Bimonthly magazine covering travel, business, sports, collections. Circ. 2 million in a bimonthly period. Pays on publication. Byline given. Buys first North American serial rights. Submit holiday/seasonal material 6 months in advance. SASE. Reports in 1 month. Sample copy for SAE; free writer's guidelines.

Nonfiction: General interest, historical/nostalgic, humor, interview/profile, travel. No personal or religious pieces. Buys 60 mss/year. Send complete ms. Length: 1,000-2,000 words. Pays $75-200.

Photos: Send photos with accompanying ms. Reviews transparencies. Captions required. Buys one-time rights.

Fiction: Not at this time.

Tips: Send "good letter and clean manuscript. Write often—something may hit home." Especially open to travel, domestic, history, nostalgia, business management articles.

‡**PACIFIC EXPRESS MAGAZINE/SKIES WEST**, Skies West Publishing Co., 0612 SW Idaho, Portland OR 97201. (503)244-2299. Editor: James R. Rullo. Managing Editor: Diane Hayes. Monthly inflight publication for regional airline passengers—affluent, well-educated business people in the western US. Circ. 52,500/month. Pays on publication. Byline given. Buys first North American serial rights. Submit seasonal/holiday material 6 months in advance. Simultaneous queries and photocopied submissions OK. SASE. Reports in 3 weeks. Sample copy for $3, 8x10 SAE and 71¢ postage; writer's guidelines for business-size SAE and 1 first class stamp.

Nonfiction: Interview/profile, travel, business and investment. Buys 50 mss/year. Query. Length: 500-1,500 words. Pays $50-250.

Photos: Send photos with query or ms. Reviews color transparencies and b&w prints. Captions and identification of subjects required. Buys one-time rights.

Columns/Departments: Business Insight, Computer Technology, Office Automation, Investment. Buys 35 mss/year. Query. Length: 200-1,000 words. Pays $20-100.

Tips: "Don't focus on one specific, local business, but rather on an industry."

PAN-AM CLIPPER, East/West Network, 34 E. 51st St., New York NY 10022. (212)888-5900. Editor: Gayle Welling. Associate Editor: Trish Leader. Monthly magazine for passengers of Pan Am Airways (50% US, 50% foreign persons travelling on business or pleasure). Circ. 300,000. Pays on acceptance. Buys first world serial rights. Submit seasonal material 4 months in advance. Photocopied submissions OK. SASE. Reports in 1 month.

Nonfiction: General interest; interview (internationally important); profile; travel (destination pieces on unusual people and events of interest); humor (of worldwide appeal); technical (science and technology); other (great stories of sports of international interest). Length: 1,500 words maximum. Query with clips of previously published work.

Photos: Photo Editor: G. Woodford Pratt. State availability of photos. Reviews 8x10 b&w glossy prints and 35mm color transparencies. Pays ASMP rates. Captions and model release required. Buys one-time rights.

PSA MAGAZINE, East/West Network, Inc., Suite 800, 5900 Wilshire Blvd., Los Angeles CA 90036. (213)937-5810. Editor: Al Austin. 90% freelance written. Monthly magazine; 160 pages. Pays within 60 days after acceptance. Buys first rights. Pays 25% kill fee. Byline given. Submit seasonal/holiday material 4 months in advance of issue date. Simultaneous and photocopied submissions OK. SASE. Sample copy $2.

Nonfiction: Prefers California/West Coast slant. General interest; interview (top-level government, entertainment, sports figures); new product (trends, survey field); profile; and business (with California and West Coast

orientation). Buys 10 mss/issue. Query. Length: 500-2,000 words. Pays $150-700.
Photos: State availability of photos with query. Pays ASMP rates for b&w contact sheets or negatives and 35mm or 2¼x2¼ color transparencies. Captions required. Buys one-time rights. Model release required.
Columns/Departments: Business Trends. Buys 1 ms/issue. Query. Length: 700-1,500 words. Pays $100-400.

REPUBLIC SCENE, East/West Network, Inc., 5900 Wilshire Blvd., Los Angeles CA 90036. (213)937-5810. Editor: Jerry Lazar. Monthly in-flight magazine of Republic Airlines covering general nonfiction for predominantly male business travelers. Circ. 170,000 copies. Pays on acceptance. Byline given. Pays ⅓ kill fee. Buys first North American serial rights. Submit seasonal/holiday material at least 3 months in advance. SASE. Reports in 2 weeks on queries; 1 month on mss. Sample copy and writer's guidelines for $2.
Nonfiction: General interest, humor, interview/profile, photo feature and travel. "Material must be non-controversial." No reviews. Buys 96 mss/year. Query with clips of published work. Length: 2,000-3,000 words. Pays $250-600.
Photos: Sandy Silbert, art director. State availability of photos. Pays $75 minimum for color transparenices; $25 minimum for 8x10 b&w glossy prints. Captions preferred. Model releases required "where applicable." Buys one-time rights.
Columns/Departments: "Columns cover wine, personal finance, science, health, law, sports and fitness. No reviews, but subjects vary widely. We mostly use writers whose work we know." Buys 24 mss/year. Length: 750-1,500 words. Pays $200-400.

SKYLITE, Halsey Publishing Co., 12955 Biscayne Blvd., North Miami FL 33181. (305)893-1520. Editor: Julio C. Zangroniz. Monthly magazine aimed "to serve the corporate executive who flies in the private aircraft serviced by Butler Aviation in the US, and all editorial content is tailored to this audience's needs and interests." Estab. 1981. Circ. 20,000. Pays on publication. Byline given. Offers 50% kill fee. Buys first rights. Submit seasonal/holiday material in advance. Simultaneous queries OK. Computer printout and disk submissions OK. SASE a must! Reports in 3 months. Sample copy for $3 and 4x9 SAE with 20¢ postage; writer's guidelines for 4x9 SAE with 20¢ postage.
Nonfiction: General interest; historical/nostalgic; interview/profile (of corporate executives); travel (domestic and overseas); sports; science; consumer. No stories dealing with politics, sex, drugs or violent crime. Buys 85-95 mss/year. Query with clips of published work, if available. Length: 1,200-2,000 words. Pays $300-500.
Photos: "*Skylite* buys text-photo packages: no separate fee for photos." State availability of photos with ms. Prefers 2x2 transparencies or larger. Captions required. Buys one-time rights.
Tips: "Try to think the way corporate executives do—and orient your queries accordingly. Be patient, be persistent—don't let a rejection, or two or three discourage you."

USAIR MAGAZINE, East/West Network, 34 E. 51st St., New York NY 10022. Editor: Richard Busch. Senior Editor: John Atwood. A monthly general interest magazine published for airline passengers, many of whom are business travelers, male, with a high income and college education. Circ. 150,000. Pays on acceptance. Buys first rights. Submit seasonal material 6 months in advance. Photocopied submissions OK. Computer printout and disk submissions OK. SASE. Reports in 2 weeks. Sample copy $2; free writer's guidelines with SASE.
Nonfiction: Travel, business, sports, health, food, personal finance, nature, the arts, science, photography. "No downbeat stories or controversial articles." Buys 100 mss/year. Query with clips of previously published work. Length: 1,000-1,300 words. Pays $400-1,000.
Photos: Send photos with ms. Pays $75-150/b&w print, depending on size; color from $100-250/print or slide. Captions preferred; model release required. Buys one-time rights.
Columns/Departments: Sports, food, money, health, business, living, science, and photography. Buys 3-4 mss/issue. Query. Length: 1,200-1,800 words.
Tips: "Send irresistible ideas and proof that you can write."

Juvenile

This section of *Writer's Market* includes publications for children aged 2-12. Magazines for young people 12-18 appear in a separate Teen and Young Adult category. *Writing for Children and Teenagers*, by Lee Wyndham (revised by Arnold Madison, Writer's Digest Books) offers information and advice on writing for both of these age groups.

Most of the following publications are produced by religious groups, and wherever possible, the specific denomination is given. For the writer with a story or article slanted to a specific age group, the sub-index which follows is a quick reference to markets for his story in that age group.

Those editors who are willing to receive simultaneous submissions are indicated. (This is the technique of mailing the same story at the same time to a number of low-paying religious markets of nonoverlapping circulation. In each case, the writer, when making a simultaneous submission, should so advise the editor. In fact, some editors advise a query over a complete manuscript when you're considering making a simultaneous submission.) The few mass circulation, nondenominational publications included in this section that have good pay rates are not interested in simultaneous submissions and should not be approached with this technique. Magazines that pay good rates expect, and deserve, the exclusive use of material.

Writers will also note in some of the listings that editors will buy "second rights" to stories. This refers to a story which has been previously published in a magazine and to which the writer has already sold "first rights." Payment is usually less for the re-use of a story than for first-time publication.

Juvenile Publications Classified by Age

Two- to Five-Year-Olds: *Chickadee, Children's Playmate, The Friend, Highlights for Children, Humpty Dumpty, Odyssey, Our Little Friend, Primary Treasure, Ranger Rick, Story Friends, Turtle Magazine for Preschool Kids, Wee Wisdom.*

Six- to Eight-Year-Olds: *Bible-in-Life Friends, Chickadee, Children's Playmate, Dash, Ebony Jr!, The Friend, Highlights for Children, Humpty Dumpty, Jack and Jill, My Devotions, Odyssey, Our Little Friend, Pockets, Primary Treasure, R-A-D-A-R, Ranger Rick, Story Friends, Touch, Trails, Wee Wisdom, Wonder Time, The Young Crusader, Young Judaean.*

Nine- to Twelve-Year-Olds: *Action, Ahoy, Bible-in-Life Pix, Child's Life, Clubhouse, Cobblestone, Crusader Magazine, Dash, Discoveries, Ebony Jr!, The Friend, Health Explorer, Highlights for Children, Jack and Jill, Jr. Medical Detective, Junior Trails, My Devotions, On the Line, Pockets, R-A-D-A-R, Ranger Rick, Story Friends, 3-2-1 Contact, Touch, Trails, Wee Wisdom, The Young Crusader, Young Judaean.*

ACTION, Dept. of Christian Education, Free Methodist Headquarters, 901 College Ave., Winona Lake IN 46590. (219)267-7656. Editor: Vera Bethel. For "57% girls, 43% boys, age 9-11; 48% city, 23% small towns." Weekly magazine. Circ. 25,000. Pays on publication. Rights purchased vary; may buy simultaneous rights, second serial rights or first North American serial rights. Submit seasonal/holiday material 3 months in advance. Simultaneous and previously published submissions OK. Reports in 1 month. Free sample copy and writer's guidelines.
Nonfiction: How-to (make gifts and craft articles); informational (nature articles with pix); historical (short biographies except Lincoln and Washington); and personal experience (my favorite vacation, my pet, my hobby, etc.). Buys 50 mss/year. Submit complete ms with photos. Length: 200-500 words. Pays $15. SASE must be enclosed; no return without it.
Fiction: Adventure, humorous, mystery and religious. Buys 50 mss/year. Submit complete ms. Length: 1,000 words. Pays $25. SASE must be enclosed; no return without it.
Poetry: Free verse, haiku, light verse, traditional, devotional and nature. Buys 20/year. Limit submissions to batches of 5-6. Length: 4-16 lines. Pays $5.
Tips: "Send interview articles with children about their pets, their hobbies, a recent or special vacation—all with pix if possible. Kids like to read about other kids."

AHOY, A Children's Magazine, Suite 209B, 2021 Brunswick St., Halifax, Nova Scotia, Canada B3K 2Y5. (902)422-8230. Editor: Holly Book. Managing Editor: Jane Cowie. Quarterly magazine designed to "encourage children to read, enjoy learning and have fun—all at the same time." Circ. 5,000. Pays on publication. By-line given. Buys first North American serial rights. Submit seasonal/holiday material 6 months in advance. Simultaneous queries and photocopied submissions OK. Computer printout submissions OK; prefers letter quality to dot matrix. SASE. Reports in 3 weeks on queries; 2 months on mss. Sample copy $1.75 (Canadian funds) and 8x11 SAE and 2 first class stamps (Canadian postage); writer's guidelines for SAE and 1 first class stamp (Canadian postage).
Nonfiction: Holly Book, editor. General interest (to children); how-to; interview/profile ("meet the . . . "

feature, i.e., policeman, fireman, etc.; also of children with particular interest, i.e., skater, actor). Buys 4-6 mss/year. Send complete ms. Length: 300-1,000 words. Pays $15-30.

Photos: "We will accept b&w photos with a manuscript, but we do not buy photos."

Columns/Departments: "Museum Corner"—articles relating to a subject that might be dealt with in a museum, i.e, fossils, diaries, astrology. Send complete ms. Length: 500-1,000 words. Pays $15-30.

Fiction: Holly Book, editor. Adventure, fantasy, historical, humorous, mystery. "We're always looking for good fiction—particularly adventure." No patronizing or sexist stories; no fiction aimed at children aged 8 and under. Buys 4-6 mss/year. Send complete ms. Length: 500-1,200 words. Pays $15-30.

Poetry: Holly Book, editor. Light verse. Buys 4-6/year. Length: 10 lines minimum. Pays $15-30.

Fillers: "Jokes—usually from children."

Tips: "We are very open to contributions. The most successful stories are those which an adult might enjoy also. Too often the material we receive is quite condescending to children." Recent article examples: "Creating Cartoon Magic," "The Thinking Kid's Guide to Holiday Shopping," (Winter 1982).

‡**BIBLE-IN-LIFE FRIENDS, A David C. Cook Class and Family Paper for Primaries**, (formerly *Bible-in-Life Reader*), D.C. Cook Publishing Co., 850 N. Grove Ave., Elgin IL 60120. (312)741-2400. Editor: Ramona Warren. Administrative Editor: Rita West. Weekly newspaper sold on a quarterly basis covering Bible stories and other stories/columns that teach biblical truths. "A take-home paper for first and second graders designed to support the Sunday School lessons taught in the *Bible-in-Life* curriculum." Estab. 1982 (revised format). Pays on acceptance. Byline given. Offers variable kill fee. Buys all rights and makes work-for-hire assignments. Submit seasonal/holiday material 9 months in advance. SASE. Reports in 6 weeks. Free sample copy and writer's guidelines.

Nonfiction: Book excerpts (chilren's books teaching spiritual truths); historical (about famous Christians); how-to (make projects; live the Christian life); interview/profile (with families of primary children); personal experience (of children who applied biblical principles to their lives); photo feature (of children involved in Sunday School projects; other items of interest to young children); Bible stories. "We publish 4 parents' editions per year." Buys 20 work-for-hire mss/year. "Since we make work-for-hire assignments, we very rarely buy unsolicited manuscripts. However, a writer may send samples of writing when requesting to write for us. Writers must complete a trial test assignment before becoming a regular writer for *Friends*." Pays $25-75.

Columns/Departments: "In each issue we publish a Parents' Corner column, designed to help parents carry the Truths taught in Sunday School into the home. These columns suggest activities for the parents to complete with their children at home. We're looking for fresh creative ideas." Buys 52/year. Pays $35 maximum.

Fiction: Fantasy, humorous, religious. "All stories should teach a biblical concept, be action-packed and appealing to young readers." No overly didactic, "preachy" stories. Buys 52 mss/year. Pays $30-40.

Poetry: Free verse, light verse, traditional. Nothing symbolic or "preachy"; no play-on-words. Buys 15/year (work-for-hire). Length: 5-20 lines. Pays $5-30.

Fillers: Puzzles for 1st-2nd grade children. Buys 52/year. Pays $15.

Tips: "A freelancer may write to the editor, requesting Guidelines and a Writer Information Sheet. After the writer completes and returns this sheet to us, we will send him a trial assignment. If the assignment is acceptable, we will periodically send him work-for-hire assignments. We are a highly specialized publication, with very specific needs."

‡**BIBLE-IN-LIFE PIX**, David C. Cook Publishing Co., 850 N. Grove Ave., Elgin IL 60120. (312)741-2400. Editor: Robert Klausmeier. Weekly magazine covering Christian-oriented material for children aged 8-11. "Non-denominational Sunday School publication for grades 3-6. Features articles with curricular emphasis which help to apply the Christian faith to lives of children." Pays on acceptance. Byline given. Buys all rights and makes work-for-hire assignments. Submit seasonal/holiday material 1-1½ years in advance. SASE. Reports in 6 weeks. Sample copy for 8½x11 SAE and 2 first class stamps; free writer's guidelines.

Nonfiction: Historical/nostalgic, how-to, humor, inspirational, interview/profile, personal experience, photo feature. Query with clips. Length: 600 words. Pays $70.

Fiction: Adventure, historical, humorous, religious. Query with clips of published work. Length: 1,000 words. Pays $110.

Tips: "We rarely buy unsolicited manuscripts. Most assignments are made to meet specific curricular needs."

CHICKADEE MAGAZINE, The Magazine for Young Children, The Young Naturalist Foundation, 59 Front Street East, Toronto, Ontario, Canada M5E 1B3. (416)364-3333. Editor: Janis Nostbakken. Magazine published 10 times/year (except July and August) for 4-8 year-olds. "Aim: to interest children under eight in the world around them in a lively and entertaining way." Circ. 84,000. Pays on publication. Byline given. Buys all rights. Submit seasonal/holiday material up to 12 months in advance. Reports in 2½ months. Sample copy for $1.25 and IRCs; writer's guidelines for IRC.

Nonfiction: How-to (arts and crafts for children); personal experience (real children in real situations); photo feature (wildlife features). No articles for older children; no religious or moralistic features.

Photos: Send photos with ms. Reviews 35mm transparencies. Identification of subjects required.

Fiction: Adventure (relating to the 4-8 year old). No science fiction, fantasy, talking animal stories, religious articles. Send complete ms. Pays $100-300.

CHILD LIFE, Benjamin Franklin Literary & Medical Society, Inc., 1100 Waterway Blvd., Box 567, Indianapolis IN 46206. Editor: William Wagner. For youngsters 7-9. Monthly (except bimonthly issues in February/March, April/May, June/July and August/September) magazine. Pays on publication. Buys all rights. Byline given. Submit seasonal/holiday material 8 months in advance. Photocopied submissions OK. SASE. Reports in 10 weeks. Sample copy 75¢; writer's guidelines for SASE.
Nonfiction: Specifically need articles dealing with health, safety, nutrition, and exercise (including group sports). "We prefer not to sound encyclopedic in our presentation and therefore are always on the lookout for innovative ways to present our material. Articles on sports and sports figures are welcome, but they should try to influence youngsters to participate and learn the benefits of participation, both from a social and a physical point of view." In addition to health, seasonal articles are needed. Buys about 6 mss/issue. Submit complete ms; query not necessary. Length: 1,200 words maximum. Give word count on ms. Pays approximately 4¢/word.
Photos: Purchased only with accompanying ms. Captions and model release required. B&w glossies. Pays $5/photo used in publication. Buys one-time rights on most photos.
Fiction: Should emphasize some aspect of health, but not necessarily as a main theme. Seasonal stories also accepted. Buys about 2 mss/issue. Submit complete ms; query not necessary. Length: 500-1,500 words. Give word count on ms. Pays approximately 4¢/word.
Tips: "We would prefer *not* to see religious materials (as this is not our thrust, and we would rather leave this subject to those publications that specialize in that area); talking inanimate objects; or recipes that contain sugar, salt, or fatty meat products."

CHILDREN'S DIGEST, Benjamin Franklin Society, Box 567, Indianapolis IN 46206. (317)636-8881. Editor: Christine French Clark. Magazine published 8 times/year covering children's health for children ages 8-10. Pays on publication. Byline given. Buys all rights. Submit seasonal/holiday material 8 months in advance. Submit *only* complete manuscripts. "No queries, please." Photocopied submissions OK (if clear). SASE. Reports in 2 months. Sample copy 75¢; writer's guidelines for business size SAE and 1 first class stamp.
Nonfiction: Historical; interview/profile (biographical); craft ideas; health; nutrition; hygiene; exercise and safety. "We're especially interested in factual features that teach readers about the human body or encourage them to develop better health habits. We are *not* interested in material that is simply rewritten from encyclopedias. We try to present our health material in a way that instructs *and* entertains the reader." Buys 15-20 mss/year. Send complete ms. Length: 500-1,200 words. Pays 4¢/word.
Photos: State availability of photos. Pays $5-10 for 5x7 b&w glossy prints. Model release and identification of subjects required. Buys one-time rights.
Fiction: Adventure, humorous, mainstream and mystery. Stories should appeal to both boys and girls. "We need some stories that incorporate a health theme. However, we don't want stories that preach, preferring instead stories with implied morals. We like a light or humorous approach." Buys 15-20 mss/year. Length: 500-1,800 words. Pays 4¢/word.
Poetry: Pays $5 minimum.

CHILDREN'S PLAYMATE, 1100 Waterway Blvd., Box 567, Indianapolis IN 46206. (317)636-8881, ext. 247. Editor: Kathleen B. Mosher. "We are looking for articles, stories, and activities with a health, safety, exercise, or nutritionally oriented theme. Primarily we are concerned with preventative medicine. We try to present our material in a positive—not a negative—light, and we try to incorporate humor and a light approach wherever possible without minimizing the seriousness of what we are saying." Write for guidelines. For children, ages 5-7. Magazine published 8 times/year. Buys all rights. Byline given. Pays on publication. Sample copy 75¢; free writer's guidelines with SASE. No query. "We do not consider outlines. Reading the whole ms is the only way to give fair consideration. The editors cannot criticize, offer suggestions, or review unsolicited material that is not accepted." Submit seasonal material 8 months in advance. Reports in 2 months. Sometimes may hold mss for up to 1 year, with author's permission. "Material will not be returned unless accompanied by a self-addressed envelope and sufficient postage."
Nonfiction: Beginning science, 600 words maximum. Monthly "All about . . ." feature, 300-500 words, may be an interesting presentation on animals, people, events, objects or places, especially about good health, exercise, proper nutrition and safety. "Include number of words in articles." Buys 30 mss/year. Pays about 4¢/word.
Fiction: Short stories, not over 700 words for beginning readers. No inanimate, talking objects. Humorous stories, unusual plots. Vocabulary suitable for ages 5-7. Pays about 4¢/word. "Include number of words in stories."
Fillers: Puzzles, dot-to-dots, color-ins, hidden pictures and mazes. Buys 30 fillers/year. Payment varies.
Tips: Especially interested in stories, poems and articles about special holidays, customs and events. Recently published: "Jeremy Giraffe's Sore Throat" (humorous and health-oriented).

‡**CLUBHOUSE, Your Story Hour**, Box 15, Berrien Springs MI 49107. (616)471-3701. Editor: Elaine Meseraull. Magazine published 10 times/year covering many subjects with Christian approach. "Stories and features for fun for 9- to 13-year-olds. Main objectives: Let kids know that God loves them and provide a psychologically 'up' magazine that lets kids know that they are acceptable, 'neat' people." Circ. 10,000. Pays on acceptance. Byline given. Buys first North American serial rights, simultaneous and second serial (reprint) rights. Simultaneous queries, and simultaneous, photocopied and previously published submissions OK. SASE. Reports in 3 weeks. Sample copy for business or larger size SAE and 3 first class stamps; writer's guidelines for business size SAE and 1 first class stamp.

Nonfiction: How-to (crafts); personal experience; recipes (without sugar or artificial flavors and colors). "No stories in which kids start out 'bad' and by peer or adult pressure or circumstances are humiliated into becoming 'good.' " Send complete ms. Length: 750-800 words ($30); 1,000-1,200 words ($35).

Photos: Send photos with ms. Pays up to $20 for b&w prints. Buys one-time rights.

Columns/Departments: Body Shop (short stories or "ad" type material that is anti-smoking, drugs and alcohol and pro-good nutrition, etc.); Jr. Detective (secret codes, deduction problems, hidden pictures, etc.). Buys 10/year. Send complete ms. Length: 400 words maximum. Pays $10-30.

Fiction: Adventure, historical, humorous, mainstream. "Stories should depict bravery, kindness, etc., without overt or preachy Christian attitude." No science fiction, romance, confession, mystery. Buys 25-30 mss/year. Send complete ms. Length: 750-800 words ($30); 1,000-1,200 words ($35).

Poetry: Free verse, light verse, traditional. Buys 2-4/year. Submit 5 poems maximum. Length: 4-24 lines. Pays $5-20.

Fillers: Jokes, short humor, cartoons. Buys 10-20/year. Pay $10 maximum.

Tips: "All material for any given year is accepted April-May the year previous. Think from a kid's point of view and ask 'Would this story make me glad to be a kid?' Keep the stories moving, exciting, bright and tense. Stay within length guidelines."

COBBLESTONE, Cobblestone Publishing, Inc., 28 Main St., Peterborough NH 03458. (603)924-7209. Editor: Mark Corsey. Monthly magazine covering American history for children 8-13 years old. "Each issue presents a particular theme, approaching it from different angles, making it exciting as well as informative." Circ. 38,000. Pays on publication. Byline given. Buys all rights. Makes some assignments on a work-for-hire basis. All material must relate to monthly theme. Simultaneous and previously published submissions OK. Computer printout submissions OK. SASE. Sample copy $2.75; writer's guidelines for SASE.

Nonfiction: Historical/nostalgic, how-to, interview and personal experience. "Request a copy of the writer's guidelines to find out specific issue themes in upcoming months." Include SASE. No Revolutionary War memorabilia, particularly hometown guides to monuments. No material that editorializes rather than reports. Buys 5-8 mss/issue. Length: 500-1,200 words. Query with clips of previously published work. Pays up to 15¢/word.

Fiction: Adventure, historical, biographical fiction. Buys 1-2 mss/issue. Length: 800-1,500 words. Request free editorial guidelines sheet that explains upcoming issue themes and gives query deadlines. "Message" must be smoothly integrated with the story. Pays up to 15¢/word.

Poetry: Free verse, light verse and traditional. Buys 6 mss/year. Submit maximum 2 poems. Length: 5-100 lines. Pays $1.50/line.

Fillers: Word puzzles and mazes. Buys 1/issue. Pays $75 maximum.

Tips: "All material is considered on the basis of merit and appropriateness to theme. Query should state idea for material simply, with rationale for why material is applicable to theme. Request writers' guidelines (includes themes and query deadlines) before submitting a query. Include SASE."

CRUSADER MAGAZINE, Box 7244, Grand Rapids MI 49510. Editor: David Koetje. "*Crusader Magazine* shows boys (9-14) how God is at work in their lives and in the world around them." Magazine published 7 times/year. Circ. 13,000. Rights purchased vary with author and material. Byline given. Buys 15-20 mss/year. Pays on acceptance. Free sample copy and writer's guidelines. Photocopied and simultaneous submissions OK. Submit seasonal material (Christmas, Easter) at least 5 months in advance. Reports in 1 month. Query or submit complete ms. SASE.

Nonfiction: Articles about young boys' interests: sports, outdoor activities, bike riding, science, crafts, etc., and problems. Emphasis is on a Christian multi-racial perspective, but no simplistic moralisms. Informational, how-to, personal experience, interview, profile, inspirational, humor. Length: 500-1,500 words. Pays 2-5¢/word.

Photos: Pays $4-25 for b&w photos purchased with mss.

Fiction: "Considerable fiction is used. Fast-moving stories that appeal to a boy's sense of adventure or sense of humor are welcome. Avoid 'preachiness.' Avoid simplistic answers to complicated problems. Avoid long dialogue and little action." Length: 500-1,500 words. Pays 3¢/word minimum.

Fillers: Uses short humor and any type of puzzles as fillers.

DASH, Box 150, Wheaton IL 60187. Editor: Michael Chiapperino. For boys 8-11 years of age. Most subscribers are in a Christian Service Brigade program. Monthly magazine except for combined issues in April-May, July-August, October-November, January-February. Circ. 32,000. Rights purchased vary with author and material. Buys 8-10 mss/year. Pays on publication. Submit seasonal material 6 months in advance. Reports in 3 weeks. Query. SASE. Sample copy $1.

Nonfiction: "Our emphasis is on boys and how their belief in Jesus Christ affects their everyday lives." Uses short articles about boys of this age, problems they encounter. Interview, profile. Length: 1,000-1,500 words. Pays $30-70.

Photos: Pays $25 for 8x10 b&w photos for inside use.

Fiction: Avoid trite, condescending tone. Needs adventure, mystery action. A Christian truth should be worked into the storyline (not tacked on as a "moral of the story"). Length: 1,000-1,500 words. Pays $60-90.

Tips: "Queries must be succinct, well-written, and exciting to draw my interest. Send for sample copies, get a feel for our publication, then write something tailored specifically for us."

DISCOVERIES, 6401 The Paseo, Kansas City MO 64131. Editor: Mark York. For boys and girls 9-12 in the Church of the Nazarene. Weekly. Buys first rights and second rights. "We process only letter quality manuscripts; word processing with letter quality printers acceptable. Minimal comments on pre-printed form are made on rejected material." SASE.

Photos: Sometimes buys photos submitted with mss with captions only if subject has appeal. Send quality 8x10 photos.

Fiction: Stories with Christian emphasis on high ideals, wholesome social relationships and activities, right choices, Sabbath observance, church loyalty, and missions. Informal style. Submit complete ms. Length: 800-1,000 words. Pays 3¢/word for first rights and 2¢/word for second rights.

Tips: "The freelancer needs an understanding of the doctrine of the Church of the Nazarene and the Sunday School material for 3rd-6th graders."

EBONY JR!, Johnson Publishing Co., 820 S. Michigan Ave., Chicago IL 60605. (312)322-9272. Managing Editor: Marcia V. Roebuck-Hoard. For all children, but geared toward black children, ages 6-12. Monthly magazine (except bimonthly issues in June/July and August/September). Circ. 100,000. Pays on acceptance. Buys all rights, second serial (reprint) rights or first North American serial rights. Byline given. Submit seasonal/holiday material 4 months in advance. Previously published work OK. SASE. Acknowledges receipt of material in 3 weeks. Sample copy $1; free writer's guidelines.

Nonfiction: How-to (make things, gifts and crafts; cooking articles); informational (science experiments or articles explaining how things are made or where things come from); historical (events or people in black history); inspirational (career articles showing children they can become whatever they want); interviews; personal experience (taken from child's point of view); profiles (of black Americans who have done great things—especially need articles on those who have not been recognized). Buys 25 unsolicited mss/year. Query or submit complete ms. Length: 500-1,000 words. Pays $75-200.

Photos: Purchased with or without mss. Must be clear photos; no Instamatic prints. Pays $10-15/b&w; $25 maximum/color. Send prints and transparencies. Model release required.

Columns/Departments: *Ebony Jr!* News uses news of outstanding black children, reviews of books, movies, TV shows, of interest to children. Pays $25-400.

Fiction: Must be believable and include experiences black children can relate to. Adventure, fantasy, historical (stories on black musicians, singers, actors, astronomers, scientists, inventors, writers, politicians, leaders; any historical figures who can give black children positive images). No violence. Buys 2 mss/issue. Query or submit complete ms. Length: 300-1,500 words. Pays $75-200.

Poetry: Free verse, haiku, light verse, traditional forms of poetry. Buys 2/issue. No specific limit on number of submissions, but usually purchase no more than two at a time. Length: 5-50 lines; longer for stories in poetry form. Pays $15-100.

Fillers: Jokes, gags, anecdotes, newsbreaks and current events written at a child's level. Brain teasers, word games, crossword puzzles, guessing games, dot-to-dot games; games that are fun, yet educational. Pays $15-85.

Tips: "Those freelancers who have submitted material featuring an event or person who is/was relatively unknown to the general public, yet is the type of material that would have great relevance and interest to children in their everyday lives, are usually the successful writers."

THE FRIEND, 50 East North Temple, Salt Lake City UT 84150. Managing Editor: Vivian Paulsen. 75% freelance written. Appeals to children ages 4-12. Publication of The Church of Jesus Christ of Latter-day Saints. Issues feature different countries of the world, their cultures and children. Special issues: Christmas and Easter. Monthly. Circ. 200,000. Pays on acceptance. "Submit only complete ms—no queries, please." Submit seasonal material 6 months in advance. SASE. Free sample copy and guidelines for writers.

Nonfiction: Subjects of current interest, science, nature, pets, sports, foreign countries, and things to make and do. Length: 1,000 words maximum. Pays 7¢/word minimum.

Fiction: Seasonal and holiday stories; stories about other countries and their children. Wholesome and optimistic; high motive, plot, and action. Also simple, but suspense-filled mysteries. Character-building stories preferred. Length: 1,200 words maximum. Stories for younger children should not exceed 700 words. Pays 7¢/word minimum.

Poetry: Serious, humorous and holiday. Any form with child appeal. Pays $15.

Tips: "Do you remember how it feels to be a child? Can you write stories that appeal to children ages 4-12 in today's world? We're interested in stories with an international flavor and those that focus on present-day problems. Send material of high literary quality slanted to our editorial requirements. Let the child solve the problem—not some helpful, all-wise adult. No overt moralizing. Nonfiction should be creatively presented—not an array of facts strung together. Beware of being cutesy."

HEALTH EXPLORER, Children's Better Health Institute, Box 567, Indianapolis IN 46206. (317)636-8881. Editor: Ray A. Randolph. Quarterly health-oriented magazine for 5th grade readers. Estab. 1981. Pays on publication. Byline given. Buys variable rights. Submit seasonal/holiday material 8 months in advance. SASE. Reports in 10 weeks. Sample copy 75¢; writer's guidelines for business size SAE and 1 first class stamp.

Nonfiction: Health (diet, nutrition, exercise, environment, health fads). "No dogmatic or 'preachy' articles." Will consider historical articles and stories. Buys variable number mss/year. Send complete ms. Length: 500-1,000 words. Pays approximately 4¢/word.

Photos: Larry Simmons, photo editor. Send photos with ms. Pays $5 minimum for 8x10 b&w prints. Model release and identification of subjects required. Buys one-time rights.

Fiction: Health (nutrition, diet, exercise, environment, health fads). "No 'far out' stories. Setting and characters may be fictional but keep them factual." Buys variable number mss/year. Send complete ms. Length: 500-1,000 words. Pays approximately 4¢/word.

Tips: "Take a close look at the area of preventive health for children 9-11. Write something (nonfiction, fiction) that readers can use to increase their knowledge in the area of health and safety, and to improve and maintain health. Include list of sources or references used in manuscript."

HIGHLIGHTS FOR CHILDREN, 803 Church St., Honesdale PA 18431. Editor: Kent L. Brown Jr. For children 2-12. Magazine published 11 times/year. Circ. 1,500,000. Buys all rights. Pays on acceptance. Free writer's guidelines. Reports in about 2 months. Computer printout submissions OK. SASE.

Nonfiction: "We prefer factual features, including history and science, written by persons with rich background and mastery in their respective fields. Contributions always welcomed from new writers, especially engineers, scientists, historians, etc., who can interpret to children useful, interesting and authentic facts, but not of the bizarre type; also writers who have lived abroad and can interpret the ways of life, especially of children, in other countries, and who don't leave the impression that US ways are always the best. Sports material, biographies, articles of interest to children. Direct, simple style, interesting content, without word embellishment; not rewritten from encyclopedias. State background and qualifications for writing factual articles submitted. Include references or sources of information. Recent article example: "Crocodiles" (March 1982). Length: 900 words maximum. Pays $65 minimum. Also buys original party plans for children 7-12, clearly described in 400-700 words, including drawings or sample of items to be illustrated. Also, novel but tested ideas in crafts, with clear directions and made-up models. Projects must require only free or inexpensive, easy-to-obtain materials. Especially desirable if easy enough for early primary grades. Also, fingerplays with lots of action, easy for very young children to grasp and parents to dramatize. Avoid wordiness. Pays minimum $30 for party plans; $15 for crafts ideas; $25 for fingerplays.

Fiction: Unusual, wholesome stories appealing to both girls and boys. Vivid, full of action. "Engaging plot, strong characterization, lively language." Seeks stories that the child 8-12 will eagerly read, and the child 2-6 will like to hear when read aloud. "We print no stories just to be read aloud. We encourage authors not to hold themselves to controlled word lists. Avoid suggestion of material reward for upward striving. The main character should preferably overcome difficulties and frustrations through her or his own efforts. The story should leave a good moral and emotional residue. We especially need stories in the suspense-adventure-mystery category, and short (200 words and under) stories for the beginning reader, with an interesting plot and a number of picturable words. Also need rebuses, stories with urban settings, stories for beginning readers (500 words), humorous stories, and horse stories. We also need more material of one-page length (300-500 words), both fiction and factual. We need creative-thinking puzzles that can be illustrated, optical illusions, body teasers, and other 'fun' activities. War, crime and violence are taboo. Some fanciful stories wanted." Length: 400-900 words. Pays $65/minimum.

Tips: "We are pleased that many authors of children's literature report that their first published work was in the pages of *Highlights*. It is not our policy to consider fiction on the strength of the reputation of the author. We judge each submission on its own merits. With factual material, however, we do prefer either authorities in their fields or people with first-hand experience. In this manner we can avoid the encyclopedic article that merely restates information readily available elsewhere. Query with simple letter to establish whether the nonfiction *subject* is likely to be of interest. A beginning writer should first become familiar with the type of material which *Highlights* publishes. We are most eager for easy stories for very young readers, but realize that this is probably the most difficult kind of writing. Include special qualifications, if any, of author. Write for the child, not the editor.''

HUMPTY DUMPTY'S MAGAZINE, 1100 Waterway Blvd., Box 567, Indianapolis IN 46206. Editor: Christine French Clark. Magazine published 8 times/year stressing health, nutrition, hygiene, exercise, and safety for children ages 4 to 6. Combined issues: February/March, April/May, June/July, and August/September. Pays on publication. Buys all rights. Submit seasonal material 8 months in advance. Sample copy 75¢; writer's guidelines for SASE.
Nonfiction: ''Material with a health theme—nutrition, safety, exercise, hygiene—that encourages readers to develop better health habits without preaching. Very simple factual articles that creatively teach readers about their bodies. Simple crafts, some with emphasis on health.'' Submit complete ms. ''Include number of words in manuscript and Social Security number.'' Length: 600 words maximum. Pays 4¢/word.
Fiction: ''We're primarily interested in stories in rhyme and easy-to-read stories for the beginning reader. We use realistic stories and fantasy, some employing a health theme. We try to present our health material in a positive light, incorporating humor and a light approach wherever possible, without minimizing the seriousness of our message.'' Submit complete ms. ''Include number of words in manuscript and Social Security number.'' Length: 600 words maximum. Pays 4¢/word.
Poetry: Short, simple poems. Pays $5 minimum.

JACK AND JILL, 1100 Waterway Blvd., Box 567, Indianapolis IN 46206. (317)636-8881. Editor: William Wagner. For children 6-8. Magazine published 8 times/year. Buys all rights. Byline given. Pays on publication. Sample copy 75¢; writer's guidelines for SASE. Submit seasonal material 8 months in advance. Reports in about 2 months. May hold material seriously being considered for up to 6 months. ''Material will not be returned unless accompanied by self-addressed envelope with sufficient postage.''
Nonfiction: ''*Jack and Jill*'s primary purpose is to encourage children to read for pleasure. The editors are actively interested in material that will inform and instruct the young reader and challenge his intelligence, but it must first of all be enjoyable reading. Submissions should appeal to both boys and girls.'' Current needs are for articles, stories, and activities with a health, safety, exercise, or nutritionally oriented theme. ''We try to present our material in a positive—not a negative—light, and we try to incorporate humor and a light approach wherever possible without minimizing the seriousness of what we are saying. Fiction stories that deal with a health theme need not have health as the primary subject but should include it in some way in the course of events. Activities should be enjoyable to youngsters and encourage them to practice better health habits or teach them scientific facts about the body or nutrition. Articles should try not to be 'preachy,' but should be informative and appealing to young readers.'' Buys 95 mss/year. Length 500-1,200 words. Pays approximately 4¢/word.
Photos: When appropriate, should accompany mss. Sharp, contrasting b&w glossy prints. Pays $5 for each b&w photo.
Fiction: ''May include, but is not limited to, realistic stories, fantasy, adventure—set in the past, present, or future. All stories need plot structure, action and incident. Humor is highly desirable.'' Length: 500-1,200 words, short stories; 1,200 words/installment, serials of 2 parts. Pays approximately 4¢/word.
Fillers: ''Short plays, puzzles (including varied kinds of word and crossword puzzles), poems, games, science projects and creative construction projects. Instructions for activities should be clearly and simply written and accompanied by models or diagram sketches. Payment varies for fillers. Pays approximately 4¢/word for drama.
Tips: ''We have been accused of using the same authors over and over again, not keeping an open mind when it comes to giving new authors a chance. To some extent, perhaps we do lean a little heavier toward veteran authors. But there is a good reason for this. Authors who have been published in *Jack and Jill* over and over again have shown us that they can write the kind of material we are looking for. They obtain *current* issues of the magazine and *study* them to find out our present needs, and they write in a style that is compatible with our current editorial policies. We would reject a story by the world's best known author if it didn't fit our needs. After all, our young readers are more interested in reading a good story than they are in reading a good byline. We are constantly looking for new writers who have told a good story with an interesting slant—a story that is not full of outdated and time-worn expressions. If an author's material meets these requirements, then he stands as good a chance of getting published as anyone.''

JR. MEDICAL DETECTIVE, Children's Better Health Institute, Box 567, Indianapolis IN 46206. (317)636-8881. Editor: Ray A. Randolph. Quarterly medical ''mystery'' magazine for 6th grade readers. Estab. 1981. Pays on publication. Byline given. Buys variable rights. Submit seasonal/holiday material 8 months in advance. SASE. Reports in 10 weeks. Sample copy 75¢; writer's guidelines for business size SAE and 1 first class stamp.
Nonfiction: Medical ''mysteries''. Problems and solutions in area of diseases and illnesses. Buys variable number mss/year. Will consider historical material. Send complete ms. Length: 500-1,000 words. Pays approximately 4¢/word.

Photos: Send photos with ms. Pays $5 minimum for 8x10 b&w prints. Model release and identification of subjects required. Buys one-time rights.

Fiction: Medical "mysteries." Stories in fictional setting which present factual problems or medical conditions and factual solutions. No hardboiled detectives or trite solutions to 'unreal' problems." Buys variable number mss/year. Send complete ms. Length: 500-1,000 words. Pays approximately 4¢/word.

Tips: "Look around and find a medical health problem resulting from a condition or a disease. Lead the reader through the problem (investigation), and provide separate answer or include resolution in story. Include list of sources or references used in manuscript."

JUNIOR TRAILS, Gospel Publishing House, 1445 Boonville Ave., Springfield MO 65802. (417)862-2781. Editor: John Maempa. Weekly tabloid covering religious fiction; and biographical, historical, and scientific articles with a spiritual emphasis for boys and girls, ages 10 and 11. Circ. 95,000. Pays on acceptance. Byline given. Not copyrighted. Buys simultaneous rights, first rights, or second serial (reprint) rights. Submit seasonal/holiday material 1 year in advance. Simultaneous and previously published submissions OK. SASE. Reports in 6 weeks on queries; 2 months on mss. Sample copy for 9x12 SAE and 2 first class stamps; writer's guidelines for 9x12 SAE and 2 first class stamps.

Nonfiction: Biographical, historical, scientific (with spiritual lesson or emphasis). Buys 30-40 mss/year. Send complete ms. Length: 500-1,000 words. Pays 2-3¢/word.

Fiction: Adventure (with spiritual lesson or application); and religious. "We're looking for fiction that presents believable characters working out their problems according to Biblical principles. No fictionalized accounts of Bible stories or events." Buys 50-70 mss/year. Send complete ms. Length: 1,000-1,500 words. Pays 2-3¢/word.

Poetry: Free verse and light verse. Buys 6-8 mss/year. Pays 2¢/line.

Fillers: Anecdotes (with spiritual emphasis). Buys 15-20/year. Length: 200 words maximum. Pays 2-3¢/word.

Tips: "Junior-age children need to be alerted to the dangers of drugs, alcohol, smoking, etc. They need positive guidelines and believable examples relating to living a Christian life in an ever-changing world."

MY DEVOTIONS, Concordia Publishing House, 3558 S. Jefferson Ave., St. Louis MO 63118. Editor: Don Hoeferkamp. For young Christians, 8-13. Buys little freelance material. Guidelines for #10 SASE. Material is rejected here because of poor writing, lack of logic, and lack of Lutheran theology. Byline given. Pays $15/printed devotion.

ODYSSEY, AstroMedia Corp., 625 E. St. Paul Ave., Milwaukee WI 53202. (414)276-2689. Editor: Nancy Mack. Emphasizes astronomy and outer space for children of ages 8-12. Monthly magazine. Circ. 100,000. Pays on publication. Buys all or first North American serial rights. Submit seasonal/holiday material 3-4 months in advance. Photocopied and published submissions OK. Letter quality computer printout submissions OK. SASE. Reports in 6-8 weeks. Free sample copy,

Nonfiction: General interest (astronomy, outer space, spacecraft, planets, stars, etc.); how-to (astronomy projects, experiments, etc.); and photo feature (spacecraft, planets, stars, etc.). "No general overview articles; for example, a general article on the Space Shuttle, or a general article on stars. We do not want science fiction articles." Buys about 12 mss/year. Query with clips of previously published work. Length: 750-2,000 words. Pays $100.

Photos: State availability of photos. Pays $10 for all photos. Buys one-time rights. Captions preferred; model release required.

Tips: "Since I am overstocked and have a stable of regular writers, a query is very important. I often get several mss on the same subject and must reject them. Write a very specific proposal and indicate why it will interest kids. If the subject is very technical, indicate your qualifications to write about it."

ON THE LINE, Mennonite Publishing House, 616 Walnut Ave., Scottdale PA 15683. (412)887-8500. Editor: Helen Alderfer. For children 10-14. Weekly magazine. Circ. 17,650. Pays on acceptance. Buys one-time rights. Byline given. Submit seasonal/holiday material 6 months in advance. Simultaneous, photocopied and previously published submissions OK. SASE. Reports in 2 weeks.

Nonfiction: How-to (things to make with easy-to-get materials); and informational (500-word articles on wonders of nature, people who have made outstanding contributions). Buys 95 unsolicited mss/year. Recent article example: "The Important Things" (Apr. 4, 1982). Length: 500-1,200 words. Pays $10-24.

Photos: Photos purchased with or without accompanying ms. Pays $10-25 for 8x10 b&w photos. Total purchase price for ms includes payment for photos.

Columns/Departments: Fiction, adventure, humorous and religious. Buys 52 mss/year. Send complete ms. Length: 800-1,200 words. Pays $15-24.

Poetry: Light verse and religious. Length: 3-12 lines. Pays $5-15.

Tips: "Study the publication first. State theme and length of material in query."

OUR LITTLE FRIEND, PRIMARY TREASURE, Pacific Press Publishing Association, 1350 Villa St., Mountain View CA 94042. (415)961-2323, ext. 335. Editor: Louis Schutter. Published weekly for youngsters of the Seventh-day Adventist church. *Our Little Friend* is for children ages 2-6; *Primary Treasure*, 7-9. Buys first serial rights (international); or second serial (reprint) rights (international). Byline given. "The payment we make is for one magazine right. In most cases, it is for the first one. But we make payment for second and third rights also." Simultaneous submissions OK. No computer printout or disk submissions. "We do not purchase material during June, July and August." SASE.
Nonfiction: All stories must be based on fact, written in story form. True to life, character-building stories; written from viewpoint of child and giving emphasis to lessons of life needed for Christian living. True to life is emphasized here more than plot. Nature or science articles, but no fantasy; science must be very simple. All material should be educational or informative and stress moral attitude and religious principle. Buys 300 unsolicited mss/year.
Photos: 8x10 glossy prints for cover. "Photo payment: sliding scale according to quality."
Fiction: Should emphasize honesty, truthfulness, courtesy, health, and temperance, along with stories of heroism, adventure, nature and safety. 700-1,000 words for *Our Little Friend*, 600 or 1,200 words for *Primary Treasure*. Fictionalized Bible stories are not used. Recent story example: "Nothing Special Happens to Eric" *Primary Treasure* (November 6, 1981). Pays 1¢/word.
Poetry: Juvenile poetry. Up to 12 lines.
Fillers: Uses puzzles as fillers.
Tips: "We are in need of 1,200 word mss for the cover of *Primary Treasure*—an adventure story that has a premise or lesson embroidered into the plot. The cover story must have a scene that our illustrator can put his teeth into."

OWL MAGAZINE, The Discovery Magazine for Children, The Young Naturalist Foundation, 59 Front St. E., Toronto, Ontario, Canada M5E 1B3. (416)364-3333. Editor: Sylvia S. Funston. Magazine published 10 times/year (no July or August issues) covering natural science. Aims to interest children in their environment through accurate, factual information about the world around them presented in an easy, lively style. Circ. 125,000. Pays on publication. Byline given. Buys all rights and makes work-for-hire assignments. Submit seasonal/holiday material 1 year in advance. SASE. Reports in 10 weeks. Sample copy $1.25 and IRC; free writer's guidelines.
Nonfiction: How-to (activities, crafts); personal experience (real life children in real situations); photo feature (natural science, international wildlife, and outdoor features). "Write for editorial guidelines first; know your topic. Our magazine never talks down to children." No folk tales, problem stories with drugs, sex or moralistic views, fantasy, talking animal stories, sports or science fiction. Query with clips of published work.
Photos: State availability of photos. Reviews 35mm transparencies. Identification of subjects required.

‡**POCKETS, Devotional Magazine for Children**, The Upper Room, 1908 Grand Ave., Box 189, Nashville TN 37202. (615)327-2700. Editor: Judith E. Smith. Monthly magazine (except for January) for children 6-12, with articles specifically geared for ages 8-11. "The magazine offers stories, activities, prayers, poems—all geared to giving children a better understanding of themselves as children of God. Some of the material is not overtly religious but deals with situations, special seasons and holidays, ecological concerns from a Christian perspective. The overall goal is to build into a child's daily life a need for a devotional aspect." Estab. 1981. Circ. 70,000. Pays on acceptance. Byline given. Offers negotiable kill fee, when applicable. "We will attempt to publish every ms we formally accept." Buys newspaper and periodical rights. Submit seasonal/holiday material 1 year in advance. Previously published submissions OK. Prefers typed ms, but would read computer printout. SASE. Reports in 3 weeks on queries; 3 months on mss. Sample copy for 7x9 SAE and 3 first class stamps; writer's guidelines for business size SAE and 1 first class stamp.
Nonfiction: Historical/nostalgic, how-to, inspirational, interview/profile, opinion, personal experience, photo feature, retelling of Scripture. All articles on children's level. Special issues with Easter, Lenten, Thanksgiving, Christmas, All Saints themes. No "stories or articles dwelling on violence, containing sexual or racial stereotyping, relying on heavy moralizing to get a point across." Buys approximately 30 mss/year. Send complete ms. Length: 750-1,600 words. Pays 5¢/word and up. Honorarium for especially well-written articles.
Photos: State availability of photos with query letter or ms. Pays $50 minimum for color transparencies; $15-25 for b&w prints. Buys one-time rights.
Columns/Departments: Loaves and Fishes, deals with ecology, world hunger, nutrition, alternative celebrations, more responsible life styles; Pocketsful of Prayer, prayer activities; The Refrigerator Door, meaningful posters, sayings, poems, etc., to be torn out and hung on refrigerator door to share with the family; Pocketsful of Love, activities to share with the family, for example, a family activity around the dinner table; Role Model Story, true-life story based on well-known person or a significant person in the author's own life. Buys 11-25/year. Send complete ms. Length: 700-1,200 words, Role Model; others, 250 words. Pays 5¢/word and up. "All material must be documented through standard footnote material for verification. Writer should obtain permissions for use of previously copyrighted material which is quoted."
Fiction: Ethnic, fantasy, historical, mainstream, religious. All stories on children's level. No "violence, hor-

ror, sexual or racial stereotyping, or heavy moralizing." Buys 25 mss/year. Send complete ms. Length: 450-1,300 words. Pays 5¢/word and up.

Poetry: Cinquain, free verse, haiku, traditional. Nothing lengthy. Buys "perhaps 10"/year. Submit maximum 5 poems. Pays 50¢/line, $5-20 maximum.

Fillers: "Fillers should be in the form of children's games and activities—hidden word games, hidden picture games, crossword puzzles, maze, rebus and cartoons." Buys 24/year. Pays $5-25/activity.

Tips: "Send a well-written manuscript that does not 'write down' to children." All areas are open. "We are going to use more re-told Scripture stories and are seeking good writers."

PRIMARY TREASURE, Pacific Press Publishing Association, 1350 Villa St., Mountain View CA 94042. See *Our Little Friend.*

R-A-D-A-R, 8121 Hamilton Ave., Cincinnati OH 45231. (513)931-4050. Editor: Margaret Williams. 75% freelance written. For children 8-11 in Christian Sunday schools. Weekly. Rights purchased vary with author and material. Buys first serial rights or second serial (reprint) rights. Occasionally overstocked. Pays on acceptance. Submit seasonal material 12 months in advance. Reports in 4-6 weeks. SASE. Free sample copy.

Nonfiction: Articles on hobbies and handicrafts, nature, famous people, seasonal subjects, etc., written from a Christian viewpoint. No articles about historical figures with an absence of religious implication. Length: 500-1,000 words. Pays 2¢/word maximum.

Fiction: Short stories of heroism, adventure, travel, mystery, animals and biography. True or possible plots stressing clean, wholesome, Christian character-building ideas, but not preachy. Make prayer, church attendance, Christian living a natural part of the story. "We correlate our fiction and other features with a definite Bible lesson. Writers who want to meet our needs should send for a theme list." No talking animal stories, science fiction, Halloween stories or first-person stories from an adult's viewpoint. Length: 900-1,100 words; 2,000 words complete length for 2-part stories. Pays 2¢/word maximum.

RANGER RICK, National Wildlife Federation, 1412 16th St. NW, Washington DC 20036. (703)790-4270. Editorial Director: Trudy D. Farrand. For "children from ages 6-12, with the greatest concentration in the 7-10 age bracket." Monthly. Buys all world rights. Byline given "but occasionally, for very brief pieces, we will identify author by name at the end. Contributions to regular departments usually are not bylined." Pays on acceptance from $10-350, depending on length and content. "Anything written with a specific month in mind should be in our hands at least 10 months before that issue date." Query. No computer printout or disk submissions. SASE.

Nonfiction: "Articles may be written on any phase of nature, conservation, environmental problems, or natural science." Buys 20-25 unsolicited mss/year.

Fiction: "Same categories as nonfiction, but do not humanize wildlife. We limit the attributing of human qualities to animals in our regular feature, 'The Adventures of Ranger Rick.' The publisher, The National Wildlife Federation, discourages wildlife pets." Length: 900 words maximum.

Photos: "Photographs, when used, are paid for separately. It is not necessary that illustrations accompany material."

Tips: "Include in query details of what manuscript will cover; sample lead; evidence that you can write playfully or with great enthusiasm, purpose and excitement (formal, serious, dull queries indicate otherwise). Think of an exciting subject we haven't done recently, sell it effectively with query, produce manuscript of highest quality. Read past issues to learn successful styles and unique approaches to subjects. If your submission is commonplace in any way we won't want it."

STORY FRIENDS, Mennonite Publishing House, 616 Walnut Ave., Scottdale PA 15683. (412)887-8500. Editor: Marjorie Waybill. For children 4-9 years of age. Published monthly in weekly parts. Not copyrighted. Byline given. Pays on acceptance. Submit seasonal/holiday material 6 months in advance. SASE. Free sample copy.

Nonfiction: "The over-arching purpose of this publication is to portray Jesus as a friend and helper—a friend who cares about each happy and sad experience in the child's life. Persons who know Jesus have values which affect every area of their lives."

Fiction: "Stories of everyday experiences at home, at church, in school or at play can provide models of these values. Of special importance are relationships, patterns of forgiveness, respect, honesty, trust and caring. Prefer short stories that offer a wide variety of settings, acquaint children with a wide range of friends, and mirror the joys, fears, temptations and successes of the readers. *Story Friends* needs stories that speak to the needs and interests of children of a variety of ethnic backgrounds. Stories should provide patterns of forgiveness, respect, integrity, understanding, caring, sharing; increase the children's sense of self-worth through growing confidence in God's love for them as they are; help answer the children's questions about God, Jesus, the Bible, prayer, death, heaven; develop awe and reverence for God the Creator and for all of His creation; avoid preachiness, but have well-defined spiritual values as an integral part of each story; be plausible in plot; introduce chil-

dren to followers of Jesus Christ; and develop appreciation for our Mennonite heritage." Length: 300-800 words. Pays 2½-3¢/word.
Poetry: Traditional and free verse. Length: 3-12 lines. Pays $5.

3-2-1 CONTACT, Children's Television Workshop, One Lincoln Plaza, New York NY 10023. (212)595-3456. Editor: Andrew Gutelle. Associate Editor: Joanna Foley. Magazine published 10 times/year covering science for children 8-12. Circ. 300,000. Pays on acceptance. Submit seasonal material 6 months in advance. Simultaneous, photocopied and previously published submissions OK if so indicated. Reports in 1 month. Buys all rights "with some exceptions." Free writer's guidelines. SASE. Sample copy $1.25.
Nonfiction: General interest (space exploration, the human body, animals, current issues); profile (of interesting scientists or children in age group); photo feature (centered around a science theme); and role models of women scientists. No articles on travel not related to science. Buys 5 unsolicited mss/year. Query with clips of previously published work. Length: 700-1,000 words. Pays $150-300.
Photos: Reviews 8x10 b&w prints and 35mm color transparencies. Model release preferred.
Tips: "I prefer a short query, without manuscript, that makes it clear that an article is interesting. When sending an article, include your telephone number. Don't call us, we'll call you! Many submissions we receive are more like college research papers than feature stories. We like articles in which writers have interviewed kids or scientists, or discovered exciting events with a scientific angle. Library research is necessary; but if that's all you're doing, you aren't giving us anything we can't get ourselves. If your story needs a bibliography, chances are it's not right for us."

TOUCH, Box 7244, Grand Rapids MI 49510. Editor: Joanne Ilbrink. 50-60% freelance written. Purpose of publication is to show girls ages 8-15 how God is at work in their lives and in the world around them. Monthly magazine. Circ. 14,000. Pays on acceptance. Buys simultaneous, second serial and first North American serial rights. Byline given. Submit seasonal/holiday material 3-5 months in advance. Simultaneous, photocopied or previously published submissions OK. SASE. Reports in 3 weeks. Free sample copy and writer's guidelines.
Nonfiction: How-to (crafts girls can make easily and inexpensively); informational (write for issue themes); humor (needs much more); inspirational (seasonal and holiday); interview; travel; personal experience (avoid the testimony approach); and photo feature (query first). "Because our magazine is published around a monthly theme, requesting the letter we send out twice a year to our established freelancers would be most helpful. We do not want easy solutions or quick character changes from bad to good. No pietistic characters. Constant mention of God is not necessary, if the moral tone of the story is positive. We do not want stories that always have a good ending." Buys 36-45 unsolicited mss/year. Recent article example: "The Night I Prayed for Stephanie" (March 1982). Submit complete ms. Length: 100-1,000 words. Pays 2¢/word, depending on the amount of editing.
Photos: Purchased with or without ms. Submit 3x5 clear glossy prints. B&w only. Pays $5-25.
Fiction: Adventure (that girls could experience in their hometowns or places they might realistically visit), humorous, mystery (believable only), romance (stories that deal with awakening awareness of boys are appreciated), suspense (can be serialized) and religious (nothing preachy). Buys 20 mss/year. Submit complete ms. Length: 300-1,500 words. Pays 2¢/word.
Poetry: Free verse, haiku, light verse and traditional. Buys 10/year. Length: 50 lines maximum. Pays $5 minimum.
Fillers: Puzzles, short humor and cartoons. Buys 6/issue. Pays $2.50-7.
Tips: "Prefers not to see anything on the adult level, secular material, or violence."

TRAILS, Pioneer Ministries, Inc., Box 788, Wheaton IL 60189. Editor: LoraBeth Norton. Asscociate Editor: Lorraine Mulligan. Emphasizes the development of a Christian lifestyle for girls and boys, 6-12, most of whom are enrolled in the Pioneer Clubs program. It is kept general in content so it will appeal to a wider audience. Magazine published 5 times/year. Circ. 50,000. Pays on acceptance. Buys first, second, or simultaneous rights. Byline given. Submit seasonal/holiday material 6 months in advance. SASE. Reports in 4-8 weeks. Sample copy and writer's guidelines $1.50.
Nonfiction: How-to (crafts and puzzles); humor; informational; inspirational; and biography. Submit complete ms. Length: 800-1,500 words. Pays $25-50.
Fiction: Adventure, fantasy, historical, humorous, mainstream, mystery and religious. Buys 6 mss/issue. Submit complete ms. Length: 800-1,500 words. Pays $25-40.
Fillers: Puzzles. Pays $5-15.

‡**TURTLE MAGAZINE FOR PRESCHOOL KIDS,** Children's Better Health Institute, Benjamin Franklin Literary & Medical Society, Inc., 1100 Waterway Blvd., Box 567, Indianapolis IN 46206. (317)636-8881. Editor: Beth Wood Thomas. Monthly magazine (bimonthly February/March, April/May, June/July, August/September) for preschoolers—emphasizing health, safety, exercise, good nutrition. Circ. 250,000. Pays on publication. Byline given. Buys all rights. Submit seasonal/holiday material 8 months in advance. SASE. Reports in 10 weeks. Sample copy 75¢; writer's guidelines for business size SAE.

Fiction: Fantasy, humorous, health-related stories. No controversial material. Buys 30 mss/year. Submit complete ms. Length: 700 words maximum. Pays 4¢/word.

Poetry: "We use many stories in rhyme—vocabularly should be geared to a 3- to 5-year-old. Anthropomorphic stories and rhymes are especially effective for this age group to emphasize a moral or lesson without 'lecturing.' " Pays variable rates.

Tips: "We are primarily concerned with preventive medicine. This can encompass good hygiene, proper exercise and care of the body, good nutrition as well as awareness of those things that are bad for a growing child or an adult. We try to present our material in a positive—not a negative—light and to incorporate humor and a light approach wherever possible without minimizing the seriousness of what we are saying. Fiction stories that deal with a health theme need not have health as the primary subject but should include it in some way in the course of events. Study the magazine to learn the type of material being published. We like new ideas that will entertain as well as teach preschoolers."

WEE WISDOM, Unity Village MO 64065. Editor: Colleen Zuck. Magazine published 10 times/year. A Christian magazine for boys and girls aged 13 and under dedicated to the truths: that each person is a child of God and that as a child of God each person has an inner source of wisdom, power, love and health from his or her Father that can be applied in a practical manner to everyday life." Free sample copy, editorial policy on request. Buys first North American serial rights. Byline given. Pays on acceptance. SASE.

Nonfiction: Entertaining nature articles or projects, activities to encourage appreciation of all life. Pays 3¢/word minimum.

Fiction: "Character-building stories that encourage a positive self-image. Although entertaining enough to hold the interest of the older child, they should be readable by the third grader. Characters should be appealing but realistic; plots should be plausible, and all stories should be told in a forthright manner but without preaching. Life itself combines fun and humor with its more serious lessons, and our most interesting and helpful stories do the same thing. Language should be universal, avoiding the Sunday school image." Length: 500-800 words. Pay 3¢/word minimum.

Poetry: Very limited. Pays 50¢/line. Prefers short, seasonal or humorous poems. Also buys rhymed prose for "read alouds" and pays $15 minimum.

Fillers: Pays $3 minimum for puzzles and games.

WONDER TIME, 6401 The Paseo, Kansas City MO 64131. (816)333-7000. Editor: Evelyn Beals. Published weekly by Church of the Nazarene for children ages 6-8. Free sample copy. Buys first rights. Byline given. Pays on acceptance. SASE.

Fiction: Buys stories portraying Christian attitudes without being preachy. Uses stories for special days—stories teaching honesty, truthfulness, kindness, helpfulness or other important spiritual truths, and avoiding symbolism. "God should be spoken of as our Father who loves and cares for us; Jesus, as our Lord and Savior." Buys 150/mss year. Length: 400-600 words. Pays 3¢/word on acceptance.

Poetry: Uses verse which has seasonal or Christian emphasis. Length: 4-12 lines. Pays 25¢/line minimum-$2.50.

Tips: "Any stories that allude to church doctrine must be in keeping with Nazarene beliefs. Any type of fantasy must be in good taste and easily recognizable. Overstocked now with poetry and stories with general theme. Brochure with specific needs available with free sample." Recently published "a story of a little boy whose grandfather dies, showing how his faith in God and belief in heaven helps his grief"; and "a story about a boy talking to his dad about income taxes; relating it to the biblical command to give to God and to Caesar."

THE YOUNG CRUSADER, 1730 Chicago Ave., Evanston IL 60201. (312)864-1396. Managing Editor: Michael Vitucci. For children ages 6-12. Monthly. Not copyrighted. Pays on publication. Submit seasonal material 6 months in advance. Computer printout and disk submissions OK. SASE. Free sample copy.

Nonfiction: Uses articles on total abstinence, character-building and love of animals. Also science stories. Length: 600 words. Pays ½¢/word.

Fiction: Should emphasize Christian principles and world friendship. Also science stories. Length: 600 words. Pays ½¢/word.

Poetry: "Limit submissions to batches of 3." Pays 10¢/line.

YOUNG JUDAEAN, 50 W. 58th St., New York NY 10019. (212)355-7900, ext. 464, 465. Editor: Mordecai Newman. For Jewish children aged 8-13, and members of Young Judaea. Publication of Hadassah Zionist Youth Commission. All material must be on some Jewish theme. Special issues for Jewish/Israeli holidays, or particular Jewish themes which vary from year to year; for example, Hassidim, Holocaust, etc. Monthly (November through June). Circ. 8,000. Buys all rights, first North American serial rights or first serial rights. Byline given. Buys 3-6 mss/year. Payment in contributor's copies or small token payment. Sample copy and annual list of themes for 50¢. Prefers complete ms. Will consider photocopied and simultaneous submissions. No computer printout or disk submissions. Submit seasonal material 4 months in advance. Reports in 3 months. SASE.

Nonfiction: "Articles about Jewish-American life, Jewish historical and international interest. Israel and Zionist-oriented material. Try to awaken kids' Jewish consciousness by creative approach to Jewish history and religion, ethics and culture, politics and current events. Style can be didactic, but not patronizing." Informational (300-1,000 words), how-to (300-500 words), personal experience, interview, humor, historical, think articles, photo, travel, and reviews (books, theater and movies). Length: 500-1,200 words. Pays $20-40. "Token payments only, due to minuscule budget."

Photos: Photos purchased with accompanying mss. Captions required. 5x7 maximum. B&w preferred. Payment included with fee for article. Illustrations also accepted.

Fiction: Experimental, mainstream, mystery, suspense, adventure, science fiction, fantasy, humorous, religious and historical fiction. Length: 500-1,000 words. Pays $5-25. Must be of specific Jewish interest.

Poetry and Fillers: Traditional forms, blank verse, free verse, avant-garde forms and light verse. Poetry themes must relate to subject matter of magazine. Length: 25-100 lines. Pays $5-15. Newsbreaks, jokes and short humor purchased for $5.

Tips: "Think of an aspect of Jewish history/religion/culture which can be handled in a fresh, imaginative way, fictionally or factually. Don't preach; inform and entertain." Prefers not to get material with no Jewish relevance or material that deals with Jewish subject matter but from a Christian perspective.

Lifestyles

Publications listed here cover a wide range of special interests and philosophies. They offer writers a forum for unconventional views or serve as a voice for a particular audience or cause. Here are magazines for single and widowed people, vegetarians, homosexuals, atheists, survivalists, back-to-the-land advocates, and others interested in alternative outlooks and lifestyles. Also included are "free press" publications that do not pay except in copies.

THE ADVOCATE, Liberation Publications, Inc., Suite 225, Box 5847, 1730 S. Amphlett, San Mateo CA 94402. Editor-in-Chief: Robert I. McQueen. For gay men and women, aged 21-40; middle-class, college-educated, urban. Biweekly tabloid. Circ. 72,000. Pays on publication. Rights purchased vary with author and material. Byline given. SASE. Reports in 6 weeks.

Nonfiction: "Basically, the emphasis is on the dignity and joy of the gay lifestyle." News articles, interviews, lifestyle features. "Major interest in interviews or profiles of gay people whose names can be used." Informational, personal experience, humor, historical, photo feature, spot news. Query with "concrete description and writing sample." Length: open.

Photos: "Payment for b&w photos purchased without ms or on assignment depends on size of the reproduction."

‡**AMERICAN ATHEIST**, Gustav Broukal Press, Box 2117, Austin TX 78768. (512)458-1244. Editor: Dr. Madalyn Murray O'Hair. Managing Editor: Jon Garth Murray. Monthly magazine covering atheism and topics related to it and separation of state and church. Circ. 5,000. Pays in free subscription or 15 copies. Byline given. Buys one-time and all rights. Submit seasonal/holiday material 2 months in advance. Simultaneous queries and simultaneous, photocopied and previously published submissions OK. SASE. Reports in 1 week on queries; 3 months on mss. Free sample copy and writer's guidelines.

Nonfiction: Richard M. Smith, articles editor. Book excerpts, expose, general interest, historical, how-to, humor, interview/profile, opinion, personal experience and photo feature. No "religious or off-the-cuff, incoherent pieces which don't make a point." Buys 2 mss/year. Send complete ms. Length: 400-10,000 words. Pays $50 maximum.

Photos: Gerald Tholen, photo editor. Send photos with ms. Pays $15 maximum for 2x3 or 4x5 b&w prints. Identification of subjects required.

Columns/Departments: Richard M. Smith, column/department editor. Atheism. Send complete ms. Length: 400-10,000 words. Pays $25 maximum.

Poetry: Robin Eileen Murray O'Hair, poetry editor. Avant-garde, free verse, haiku, light verse, traditional. No religious poetry. Submit unlimited poems. Length: open.

Fillers: Richard M. Smith, fillers editor. Clippings, jokes, short humor, newsbreaks. Length: 300 words maximum.

ASCENSION FROM THE ASHES, The Alternative Magazine, AFTA Press, Suite #2, 153 George St., New Brunswick NJ 08901. (201)828-5467. Editor: Bill-Dale Marcinko. Quarterly magazine covering popular culture (TV, film, books and music) political and sexual issues for young adults (18-30) who are interested in rock music, films, literature and political and sexual issues. Circ. 25,000. Pays in copies. Acquires one-time rights. Phone queries OK. Submit seasonal material 1 month in advance. Simultaneous, photocopied and previously published submissions OK. SASE. Reports in 2 weeks. Sample copy $3.50.

Nonfiction: Humor (satires on popular books, TV, films, records and social issues); interview (of authors, TV/ film writers or directors, rock musicians and political movement leaders); opinion (reviews and reactions); profile; personal experience; and photo feature (on the making of a movie or TV program, coverage of a rock concert or political demonstration). *AFTA* also buys investigative articles on political, consumer, and religious fraud. Buys 75 unsolicited mss/year. Query with clips of previously published work. Pays in copies.

Photos: State availability of photos. Reviews b&w prints. Pays in copies.

Columns/Departments: Books, Etc. (book reviews, fiction and nonfiction of interest to a young counterculture audience); Demons in Dustjackets (horror and science fiction book reviews); and Medium Banal (TV reviews); Sprockets (film reviews); and Slipped Discs (record reviews). "We use short (3-4 paragraphs) reviews of comic books, underground comix, alternative magazines, recent books, television programs, films and rock albums, especially on gay, lesbian, and politically controversial small press magazines and books. Buys 50 mss/year. Query with clips of previously published work. Length: 100-1,000 words. Pays in copies.

Fiction: Short stories only. Experimental, erotic, humorous, science fiction, suspense and mainstream. Buys 10 mss/year. Query with clips of previously published work. Length: 3,000 words maximum. Pays in copies.

Fillers: "We print folk/rock songs on social issues with music. Buys 8 mss/year. Pays in copies. We also have a section in which readers describe their first-time sexual experiences (gay or straight)."

Tips: "Sending for a sample copy is probably the best way to familiarize yourself with the kind of writing in *AFTA*. Write with humor, simplicity, and intensity, first person if possible. Avoid being formal or academic in criticism. Write for a young adult audience. The short stories accepted generally have a style similar to the works of Vonnegut or Tom Robbins, very loose, playful and humorous. *AFTA* doesn't censor language in any submissions, and is known for printing material other magazines consider sexually and politically controversial."

THE BOSTON PHOENIX, 100 Massachusetts Ave., Boston MA 02115. (617)536-5390. Editor: Richard M. Gaines. 40% freelance written. For 18-40 age group, educated middle-class and post-counterculture. Weekly alternative newspaper; 124 pages. Circ. 135,000. Buys all rights. Pays at least 50% kill fee. Byline given. Pays on publication. Sample copy $1.50. Photocopied submissions OK. Computer printout submissions OK; letter quality only. No disks or cassettes. Reports in 6 weeks. Query letter preferable to ms. SASE.

Nonfiction: Sections are: News (local coverage, investigative, issues, some international affairs, features, think pieces and profiles); Lifestyle (features, service pieces, consumer-oriented tips, medical, food, some humor if topical, etc.); Arts (reviews, essays, interviews); Supplements (coverage of special-interest areas, e.g., stereo, skiing, automotive, computers, pro sound, education, apartments with local angle). Query Section Editor. "Liveliness, accuracy, and great literacy are absolutely required." No fiction or poetry. Pays 4¢/word and up.

CANADIAN CONNECTION, The Get Together Magazine, Box 237, Station K, Toronto, Ontario, Canada M4P 2G5. (416)487-7183. Editor: Dawn Evans. Managing Editor: C. Curl. Magazine published every 6 weeks for swingers. "We are interested in articles and stories directed at the new sexual openness that has come about with swingers and group sex." Estab. 1982. Circ. 50,000. Pays on acceptance. Byline given. Offers negotiated kill fee. Buys one-time rights or second serial (reprint) rights. Submit seasonal/holiday material 4 months in advance. Simultaneous queries and simultaneous, photocopied, and previously published submissions OK. SASE, IRCs outside Canada. Reports in 3 weeks. Sample copy for $5 and 9x12 SAE with 90¢ postage; IRCs outside Canada.

Nonfiction: How-to (on anything relating to sex); humor (of a sexual nature); new product (anything relating to sex); personal experience (of a sexual nature); travel (anything for swingers); swinging. Buys 14 mss/year. Query with clips of published work or send complete ms. Length: 1,000-3,000 words. Pays $75-200.

Photos: Send photos with ms. Pays $25-50 for color or b&w sheets, 35mm transparencies or prints. Model releases and identification of subjects required. Buys one-time rights.

Fiction: Adventure, confession, erotica, experimental, fantasy, humorous, swinging. Buys 14 mss/year. Query with clips of published work or send complete ms. Length: 1,000-3,000 words. Pays $75-200.

Fillers: Jokes, gags, anecdotes, short humor, newsbreaks. Buys 30/year. Length: open. Pays $10-50.

‡**THE CELIBATE WOMAN, A Journal for Women Who Are Celibate or Considering This Liberating Way of Relating to Others**, 3306 Ross Place NW, Washington DC 20008. (202)966-7783. Editor: Martha Allen. Biannual special interest magazine on celibacy and women. Estab. 1982. Byline given. Not copyrighted. SASE. Reports in weeks. Sample copy $4.

Nonfiction: Reflections on celibacy and sexuality. "The journal is a forum for presenting another view of sexuality—an opening up of alternatives in a sex-oriented society." Articles, artwork, letters, experiences, ideas and theory are welcome.

COSMOPOLITAN CONTACT, Pantheon Press, Box 1566, Fontana CA 92335. Editor-in-Chief: Romulus Rexner. Managing Editor: Nina Norvid. Assistant Editor: Irene Anders. Magazine irregularly published 2 or 3 times a year. "It is the publication's object to have as universal appeal as possible to students, graduates and others interested in international affairs, cooperation, contacts, travel, friendships, trade, exchanges, self-improvement and widening of mental horizons through multicultural interaction. This polyglot publication has worldwide distribution and participation, including the Communist countries. Writers participate in its distribution, editing and publishing." Circ. 1,500. Pays on publication in copies. Byline given. Simultaneous, photocopied and previously published submissions OK. SASE. Reports in 6 weeks. Sample copy $2.
Nonfiction: Expose (should concentrate on government; education; etc.); how-to; informational; inspiration; personal experience; personal opinion and travel. Submit complete ms. Buys 15-30 mss/year. Maximum 500 words. "Material designed to promote across all frontiers bonds of spiritual unity, intellectual understanding and sincere friendship among people by means of correspondence, meetings, publishing activities, tapes, records, exchange of hospitality, books, periodicals in various languages, hobbies and other contacts."
Poetry: Traditional. Length: Maximum 40 lines.
Tips: "Most of the material is not written by experts to enlighten or to amuse the readers, but it is written by the readers who also are freelance writers. The material is didactic, provocative, pragmatic—not art-for-art's sake—and tries to answer the reader's question, 'What can I do about it?' The addresses of all contributors are published in order to facilitate global contacts among our contributors, editors and readers/members. Instead of writing, e.g. about Lincoln or history, it is better to be an emancipator and to make history by promoting high ideals of mankind. Consequently, the material submitted to us should not be only descriptive, but it should be analytical, creative, action-and future-oriented. We are not interested in any contribution containing vulgar language, extreme, intolerant, pro-Soviet or anti-American opinions." Recent article example: "Mastery of Life" (Vol. XX, No. 34).

‡**DAY TONIGHT/NIGHT TODAY**, Box 353, Hull MA 02045. (617)925-0046. Editor: S.R. Jade. Magazine published 9 times a year for women writers. "We publish women only; non-sexist, non-racist; we try to provide a place for experimental and vivid writing by and for women." Estab. 1981. Circ. 1,250+. Pays in copies. Byline given. Rights revert to author. Simultaneous queries and simultaneous, photocopied and previously published submissions OK. Computer printout submissions OK. SASE. Reports in 1 month. Sample copy $2.50 and 9x12 SAE and 4 first class stamps; writer's guidelines for SAE and 1 first class stamp.
Nonfiction: Book excerpts, historical/nostaglic about specific women's lives or lifestyles; interview/profile. No travel, religious, fillers. Send complete ms. Length: 3,000 words maximum. Pays in copies.
Fiction: Condensed and serialized novels, ethnic, experimental, fantasy, suspense. Acquires about 15 mss/year. Length: 3,000 words maximum. Pays in copies.
Poetry: Avant-garde, free verse, haiku, light verse, traditional. No "gooey, sentimental, useless types of poetry." Acquires about 200/year. Submit maximum 6 poems. Pays in copies.
Tips: Poetry section is most open to freelancers. "We are especially interested in publishing works by women of color."

EARTH'S DAUGHTERS MAGAZINE, Box 41, Central Park Station, Buffalo NY 14215. Collective editorship. For people interested in literature and feminism. Publication schedule varies from 2-4 times a year. Circ. 1,000. Acquires first North American serial rights; copyright reverts to author after publication. Byline given. Pays in contributor's copies. Sample copy $3. Clear photocopied submissions and clear carbons OK. Prefers letter quality to dot matrix printout submissions. Reports "very slowly. Please be patient." Submit 3 or 4 poems maximum at a time; one short story/submission. "If part of larger work, please mention this." SASE.
Fiction: Feminist fiction of any and all modes. "Our subject is the experience and creative expression of women. We require a high level of technical skill and artistic intensity, and we are concerned with creative expression rather than propaganda. On occasion we publish feminist work by men." No anti-feminist material; no "hard-line, but shoddy, feminist work." Length: 1,500 words maximum. Pays in copies only.
Poetry: All modern, contemporary, avant-garde forms. Length: 40 lines maximum preferred with occasional exceptions.
Tips: "We're doing smaller issues, one of which will be by invitation only to past contributors."

‡**EARTHTONE, For People Tuned to the Earth**, Publication Development, Inc., Box 23383, Portland OR 97223. (503)620-3917. Editor: Mary Bisceglia. Associate Editor: Gordon J. Growden. Bimonthly "alternative" magazine covering self-sufficiency, back-to-the-land movement in the western US. Circ. 50,000. Pays on publication. Byline given. Buys first North American serial rights. Submit seasonal/holiday material 6 months in advance. Simultaneous queries and simultaneous and photocopied submissions OK. SASE. Reports in 1 month. Free sample copy; writer's guidelines for SAE and 1 first class stamp.
Nonfiction: General interest (on country living, food, folk art); historical/nostalgic; how-to (crafts, home projects, small scale low-cost building); humor; interview/profile (on people living this sort of lifestyle); new product (only if very unusual or revolutionary); personal experience (only if informative on various aspects of homesteading or country living and self-sufficient lifestyle); animal husbandry; health; energy; organic gar-

dening and recreation. How-to articles should be accompanied by photos or illustrations. All articles should have a western US angle. Buys 6-10 mss/issue. Query with published clips if available. Length: 500-3,000 words. Pays $50-300.

Tips: "Break in with a clearly written how-to on crafts, gardening, small scale low-cost building. Also, interesting personality sketches."

EAST WEST JOURNAL, East West Journal, Inc., 17 Station St., Box 1200, Brookline Village MA 02147. (617)232-1000. Editor: Steve Minkin. Emphasizes natural living for "people of all ages seeking balance in a world of change." Monthly magazine. Circ. 70,000. Pays on publication. Buys one-time rights. Byline given. Submit seasonal/holiday material 5 months in advance. Simultaneous, photocopied and previously published submissions OK. SASE. Reports in 1 month.

Nonfiction: Mark Mayell, nonfiction editor. Expose (of agribusiness, modern medicine, the oil and nuclear industries); interviews and features (on solar and alternative energies, vegetarianism, natural foods and organic farming and gardening, ecological and energy-efficient modes of transportation, natural healing, human-potential movement, whole food and technology); and near-death experiences. No negative, politically-oriented, or new-age material. "We're looking for original, first-person articles without jargon or opinions of any particular teachings; articles should reflect an intuitive approach." Recent article example: "In Search of Findhorn's Magic" (January 1983). Buys 15-20 mss/year. Query. Length: 1,500-2,500 words. Pays 5-10¢/word.

Photos: Send photos with ms. Pays $15-40 for b&w prints; $15-175 for 35mm color transparencies (cover only). Captions preferred; model release required.

Columns/Departments: Body, Food, Healing, Gardening, Alternative Energy and Spirit. Buys 15 mss/year. Submit complete ms. Length: 1,500-2,000 words. Pays 5-10¢/word.

FARMSTEAD MAGAZINE, Box 111, Freedom ME 04941. (207)382-6200. Editor-in-Chief: George Frangoulis. Magazine published 8 times/year covering gardening, small farming, homesteading, energy and home construction, and self-sufficiency. "We combine a practical, how-to approach with an appeal to aesthetic sense and taste." Circ. 150,000. Pays on publication. Buys first serial and reprint rights. Phone queries OK. Submit seasonal/holiday material 3 months in advance. SASE. Reports in 3 months. Free sample copy and writer's guidelines.

Nonfiction: General interest (related to rural living, gardening and farm life); how-to (gardening, farming, construction, conservation, wildlife, livestock, crafts, and rural living); interview (with interesting and/or inspirational people involved with agriculture, farm life or self-sufficiency); new product (reviews of new books); nostalgia (of rural living; farm life self-sufficiency); and occasionally travel (agriculture in other lands). No sentimentality or nostalgia. Buys 60 mss/year. Submit complete ms. Length: 1,000-5,000 words maximum. Pays $50-250.

Photos: State availability of photos with ms. Pay starts at $10 for each 5x7 b&w print used; starts at $25 for color; $50-100 for each color transparency used on cover.

Tips: "Contribute a thorough well-researched or first-hand-experience type article. B&w photos of good quality or careful diagrams or sketches are a boon. We look for an unusual but practical how-to article. An article sent in a folder is helpful. Presentation is important. We appreciate material from those who have lived and done what they are writing about. We like the how-to, hands-on approach; no theorizing." Send short factual pieces with good photos.

‡FIRST HAND, Experiences For Loving Men, Firsthand, Ltd., 310 Cedar Lane, Teaneck NJ 07666. (201)836-9177. Editor: Brandon Judell. Managing Editor: Jackie Lewis. Monthly magazine of homosexual erotica. Circ. 60,000. Pays 1 month after acceptance. Byline given. Buys first North American serial rights. Submit seasonal/holiday material 6 months in advance. Simultaneous queries and photocopied submissions OK. SASE. Reports in 3 weeks. Sample copy $3; free writer's guidelines.

Nonfiction: Book excerpts (should be erotic or offer advice); historical/nostalgic (gay life in the past); how-to (advice for homosexuals coming out); interview/profile (gay figure heads); personal experience ("this is our premise"); travel (where gays go); erotica. No violent or negative articles about gay life. No bestiality or child abuse. Buys 96 mss/year. Query with or without published clips or send complete ms. Length: 1,500-3,000 words. Pays $10-100.

Columns/Departments: Survival Kit (short nonfiction pieces about all aspects of gay life). Buys 48 mss/year. Query with or without published clips or send complete ms. Length: 400-800 words. Pays $25-50.

Fiction: Novel excerpts.

Poetry: Free verse, light verse. Buys 12/year. Submit maximum 5 poems. Length: 10-30 lines. Pays $15.

Fillers: Jokes, gags, anecdotes. Buys 30 mss/year. Length: 24-400 words. Pays $15-25.

Tips: "Half of each issue is written by our readers. In their letters, they share their lusts, hopes, loves and fears stemming from their homosexuality. The main articles which are bought from freelancers should display the same candor and honesty. *First Hand* is more than a magazine to get off on. It offers a support system to many homosexuals who feel isolated in the heterosexual community. Many of our readers are married. A few have never had gay sex. Most are very loyal and save every issue."

FLORIDA SINGLES MAGAZINE AND DATE BOOK, Box 83, Palm Beach FL 33480. Editor: Harold Alan. Bimonthly magazine covering "singles' problems with life, dating, children, etc., for single, divorced, widowed and separated persons who compose over 50% of the adult population over 18." Circ. 12,000. Pays on publication. Buys second serial rights and one-time rights. Simultaneous, photocopied and previously published submissions OK. SASE. Reports in 4 months.

Nonfiction: "We want any article that is general in nature dealing with any aspect of single life, dating, problems, etc." Buys 1-3 mss/issue. Send complete ms. Length: 800-1,400 words. Pays $10-30. "We are associated with 3 other singles magazines: the East Coast, Louisville KY, and Atlanta *Singles Magazine*. We pay up to $30 for the first time use of an article in the first publication and $15 each for each time reprinted in the other magazines."

Photos: Offers no additional payment for photos accepted with ms. Model release required.

Fiction: "We will look at any ms that is general in nature dealing with any aspect of single life, dating, problems, etc."

FOCUS: A JOURNAL FOR LESBIANS, Daughters of Bilitis, 1151 Massachusetts Ave., Cambridge MA 02138. A literary journal for lesbians of all ages and interests. Bimonthly magazine. "This is a magazine by lesbians for lesbians. We do not publish work by men, nor will we consider work that is male-centered. We are interested in writing that is relevant to our audience and which is also of high artistic quality." Circ. 400. Pays in contributor's copies. Obtains first rights. Byline given. Submit seasonal/holiday material 3 months in advance. Photocopied submissions OK. Computer printout OK; prefers letter quality to dot matrix. SASE. Reports in 3 months. Sample copy $1.35 and 35¢ postage.

Nonfiction: Historical; humor; informational; interview; personal experience; personal opinion; profile and book reviews. Send complete ms. Buys 30 unsolicited mss/year. Length: 3,000 words maximum.

Fiction: Relating to magazine theme. Confession; erotica; fantasy; historical; humorous; romance; and science fiction. Send complete ms. Length: 3,000 words maximum.

Poetry: Avant-garde; free verse; haiku; light verse; and traditional. Length: 200 words maximum.

Fillers: Short humor. Length: 200 words maximum.

Tips: "Be professional. Type your work, include a SASE, proofread, etc. We are very open to new writers; but sloppy, careless work is a real turn-off. Also, check out the magazine before submitting. Although we do accept nonfiction pieces, we prefer fiction. The tone of the journal is definitely literary. We are looking for quality writing rather than political correctness. Our primary concern is to bring together material that reflects all aspects of lesbian life and experience." Recent published articles: "Swinging" (March/April 1982); "Love at Forty-five" (January/February 1981).

‡THE FUTURIST, A Journal of Forecasts, Trends, and Ideas about the Future, World Future Society, 4916 St. Elmo Ave., Bethesda MD 20814. (301)656-8274. Editor: Edward S. Cornish. Bimonthly magazine on all aspects of the future for a general audience. *The Futurist* focuses on trends and developments that are likely to have a major impact on the way we live in the years ahead. It explores how changes in all areas—lifestyles, values, technology, government, economics, environmental affairs, etc.—will affect individuals and society in the next five to 50 years. We cover a very broad spectrum of topics—from assessing how a new technology like computers will affect the way people work to how the institution of marriage may change." Circ. 30,000. Byline given. Acquires variable rights "according to the article." Submit seasonal/holiday material 6 months in advance. Simultaneous queries and simultaneous (if so advised), photocopied and previously published submissions OK. SASE. Reports in 6 weeks on queries; 7 weeks on mss. Free sample copy and writer's guidelines.

Nonfiction: Eric Seaborg, assistant editor. Book excerpts, general interest, how-to, interview/profile, new product, opinion. "We are especially looking for articles on the social areas of the future of human values, relationships, lifestyles, etc. These 'soft' subjects seem to be much more difficult for informed speculation and projection than the "hard" area of technology and its effects." No "vague articles that say, 'Wouldn't it be nice if the future were like this, or if that happened in the future?' or articles lacking a future-orientation." Acquires 45-50 mss/year. Query with clips or send complete ms. Length: 500-5,000 words. Pays in copies.

Tips: "Feature articles in *The Futurist* are almost entirely freelance written. The 'Tomorrow in Brief' page and the 'World Trends and Forecasts' section are primarily staff written."

GAY NEWS, Masco Communications, 1108 Spruce, Philadelphia PA 19107. (215)625-8501. Senior Editor: Rick Grzesiak. Managing Editor/Owner: Mark Segal. Weekly tabloid covering news and features of interest to the lesbian and gay community. Circ. 15,000. Pays on publication. Byline given. Offers ⅓ kill fee. Buys one-time rights. Submit seasonal/holiday material 2 months in advance. Photocopied and previously published submissions OK. Computer printout submissions OK. SASE. Reports in 2 weeks on queries; 2 weeks on mss. Sample copy $1.

Nonfiction: Rich Grzesiak, senior editor. Book excerpts (with lesbian/gay themes or characters); expose (of enemies to lesbian/gay community); historical/nostalgic (gay history, 'herstory'); humor (satire welcome); interview/profile (of entertainment or activist personalities); opinion (about direction of gay movement and how

to achieve gay rights); travel (resorts that welcome gay tourists, i.e., Key West, San Francisco). "Reflect a constructive attitude toward gay issues. Politics has its place, but we present a balance of news, entertainment, opinion, investigative reporting and personality profiles that anyone (even your mother) can enjoy." Feature articles include gay press, gay health problems, S&M. No personal sexual experiences. Buys 40-50 mss/year. Query with clips of published work. Length: 750-2,500 words. Pays $20-75.
Photos: "Illustrations of the person, place or subject." State availability of photos. Pays $5 maximum for 5x7 b&w prints. Identification of subjects required. Buys one-time rights.
Columns/Departments: Book reviews of books with lesbian/gay themes or characters. Buys 20 mss/year. Query. Length: 750-1,000 words maximum. Pays $20 maximum.

HARROWSMITH MAGAZINE, Camden House Publishing, Ltd., Camden East, Ontario, Canada K0K 1J0. (613)378-6661. Editor/Publisher: James M. Lawrence. Published 6 times/year "for those interested in country life, nonchemical gardening, energy, self-sufficiency, folk arts, small-stock husbandry, owner-builder architecture and alternative styles of life." Circ. 150,000. Pays on acceptance. Buys first North American serial rights. Byline given. Submit seasonal/holiday material 6 months in advance. SAE and IRCs. Reports in 6 weeks. Sample copy $5; free writer's guidelines.
Nonfiction: Expose; how-to; general interest; humor; interview; photo feature; and profile. "We are always in need of quality gardening articles geared to northern conditions. No articles whose style feigns 'folksiness.' No how-to articles written by people who are not totally familiar with their subject. We feel that in this field simple research does not compensate for lack of long-time personal experience." Buys 10 mss/issue. Query. Length: 500-4,000 words. Pays $75-750 but will consider higher rates for major stories.
Photos: State availability of photos with query. Pays $50-250 for 8x10 b&w glossy prints and 35mm or larger color transparencies. Captions required. Buys one-time rights. "We regularly run photo essays for which we pay $250-750."
Tips: "We have standards of excellence as high as any publication in the country. However, we are by no means a closed market. Much of our material comes from unknown writers. We welcome and give thorough consideration to all freelance submissions. Magazine is read by Canadians who live in rural areas or who hope to make the urban to rural transition. They want to know as much about the realities of country life as the dreams. They expect quality writing, not folksy cliches."

HIGH TIMES, Trans-High Corp., 17 W. 60th St., New York NY 10023. (212)974-1990. Editor: Larry Sloman. Monthly magazine for persons under 35 interested in lifestyle changes, cultural trends, personal freedom, sex and drugs. "Our readers are independent, adventurous free-thinkers who want to control their own consciousness." Circ. 250,000. Pays on publication. Buys all rights or second serial (reprint) rights or first North American serial rights. Submit seasonal/holiday material 5 months in advance. SASE. Reports in 3 months. Sample copy $2.95.
Nonfiction: Expose (on political, government or biographical behind the scenes); general interest (political or cultural activities); historical (cultural, literary, dope history, political movements); how-to (that aids the enhancement of one's lifestyle); interview (of writers, scientists, musicians, entertainers and public figures); new product (on dope-related or lifestyle enhancing); nostalgia (cultural or dope-related); opinion (only from public figures); photo feature (on dope- or travel-related topics); profile, technical (explorations of technological breakthroughs related to personal lifestyle); travel (guides to places of interest to a young hip audience). "We want no material on 'my drug bust.' " Buys 5 mss/issue. Query with clips of published work. Length: 2,000-4,000 words. Pays $300-750.
Photos: Send photos with ms. Pays $25-150 for 8x10 glossy print per page; and $50-250 for 35mm color transparencies per page. Captions preferred; model releases required. Buys one-time rights.
Tips: "Think of article ideas that are too outrageous, visionary, radical or adventurous for any other magazine, e.g., 'Escape from Guadalajara' (October 1981)."

INTERNATIONAL LIVING, Agora Publishing, 2201 St. Paul St., Baltimore MD 21218. (301)235-7961. Editor: Elizabeth Philip. Monthly newsletter covering international lifestyles, travel and investment for Americans. Aimed at affluent and not-so-affluent dreamers to whom the romance of living overseas has a strong appeal, especially when it involves money-saving angles. Estab 1981. Circ. 28,000. Pays on acceptance. Byline given. Offers 50% kill fee, "but we prefer to have article rewritten." Buys first North American and second serial rights. Submit seasonal/holiday material 2 months in advance. Simultaneous queries, and photocopied and previously published work OK. SASE. Reports in 1 month on queries; 6 weeks on mss. Sample copy $2.50; writer's guidelines for business size SAE and 1 first class stamp.
Nonfiction: Book excerpts (overseas, travel, retirement investment, save money overseas); historical/nostalgic (travel, lifestyle abroad); how-to (save money, find a job overseas); interview/profile (famous people and other Americans living abroad); personal experience; travel (unusual, imaginative destinations, give how-to's and costs); other (financial aspects of overseas investment). "We want pithy, fact-packed articles. No vague, long-winded travel articles of well-trodden destinations or cute anecdotes." Buys 12 mss/year. Query with clips of published work or send complete ms. Length: 200-2,000 words. Pays $5 minimum.

Tips: "We are looking for writers who can combine original valuable information with a style that suggests the romance of life abroad. Break in with highly-specific, well-researched material combining subjective impressions of living in a foreign country or city with information on taxes, cost of living, residency requirements, employment and entertainment possibilities."

‡**INTRO MAGAZINE, The Single Source for Single People**, Intro International, Inc., Douglas Publishing, Inc., 3518 Cahuenga Blvd. W., Los Angeles CA 90068. (213)876-7221. Editor-in-Chief: Suzanne Douglas. Editor: Lori Kimball. Monthly magazine covering lifestyle/service exclusively for single people. Circ. 30,000. Pays on acceptance. Byline given. Offers 15% kill fee. Buys first North American serial rights, one-time and all rights. Makes work-for-hire assignments. Submit seasonal/holiday material 4 months in advance. Simultaneous queries and simultaneous, photocopied and previously published submissions OK. SASE. Reports in 2 months on queries; 1 month on mss. Sample copy $2; writer's guidelines for business-size SAE and 1 first class stamp.

Nonfiction: Book excerpts, general interest, humor, interview/profile, personal experience, photo feature. "No 'cope' pieces, erotic material, anything downbeat, anything family-oriented—our readers are 100% single, divorced or widowed." Buys variable number of mss/year. Query with clips if available. Length: 1,000-4,000 words. Pays $50-300.

Photos: Lynda Homler, art director. State availability of photos. Pays $50-300 for 35mm and 4x5 b&w and color transparencies; $50-200 for 8x10 b&w prints. Model release and identification of subjects required. Buys one-time and all rights.

Fiction: Adventure, humorous. No gothic romances or erotic fiction. Send complete ms. Length: 1,000-4,000 words. Pays $100-300.

Fillers: Short humor, newsbreaks, crosswords. Buys variable number of mss/year. Length: 50-200 words. Pays $10-30.

Tips: "We're most open to upbeat interviews and features of special interest to single people."

‡**JOINT ENDEAVOR, Endeavor News**, Inmate Welfare Club, Texas Department of Corrections, Box 32, Huntsville TX 77340. (713)295-6371. Editor/Publisher: William D. Walker, Jr. Managing Editor: James Hill. Associate Editor: Lonnie R. Griggs. Assistant Editor: Perry J. Green. Bimonthly magazine covering criminal justice, offender news, prison legislation and court actions. "Our readers are professionals, inmates, scholars and anyone with an interest in criminal justice. Subject matter deals with crime and corrections." Circ. 5,000, national and international. Pays in copies on publication. Byline given. "Rights approved upon credit." Submit seasonal/holiday material 2 months in advance. Simultaneous and photocopied submissions OK. Reports in 2 weeks on queries. Free sample copy and writer's guidelines.

Nonfiction: Book excerpts; general interest in correction or law; historical/nostalgic; how-to (any that relates to format); prison humor; interview/profile (relating to crime and corrections); opinion on crime and corrections (must be authentic); personal experience; biography; technical. Wants material on terrorism, crime, prisons, probation, youth offenders, criminal psychology, rape crisis, re-entry programs. Special issues include "Trends in the US Supreme Court"; "Prisons, The Crisis and Alternatives"; "Rape, The Laws and/or The Effects" and "Black Muslims In Prison." Send complete ms. Length: open. Pays in copies.

Photos: R.C. Castille, photo editor. Send photos with ms. Reviews 5x7 b&w prints. Identification of subjects required. All rights reserved.

Columns/Departments: Cause of Crime, Prison Rehabilitation, Viet Nam Veterans (those in prison) and Women In Prison. Accepts 200 mss/year. Send complete ms. Pays in copies.

Fiction: Carl A. Robins, fiction editor. Horror; humorous; mainstream (criminal justice related); mystery; romance (prison-related); serialized novels (very much needed, any type); suspense (criminal). No ethnic humor. Send complete ms. Length: open. Pays in copies.

Tips: Now accepting free-verse poetry and articles on sex in prison.

‡**LIVING SINGLE MAGAZINE**, The Dispatch Printing Co., 40 S. 3rd St., Columbus OH 43215. (614)461-5575. Editor: Jim O'Connor. Managing Editor: Esther Fisher. Monthly magazine on all aspects of single life. Circ. 7,000. Pays on publication. Byline given. Buys one-time rights. Submit seasonal/holiday material 4 months in advance. Simultaneous queries, and photocopied and previously published submissions OK. Computer printout submissions OK; prefers letter quality to dot matrix. SASE. Reports in 1 month. Sample copy $2; writer's guidelines for SAE and 1 first class stamp.

Nonfiction: General interest (all aspects of single life); how-to (home repair/decorating); interview/profile (single celebrity profiles); travel (single travel). "No fiction, poetry, personal experience or non-researched articles." Buys 70 mss/year. Query with clips or send complete ms. Length: 2,000 words minimum. Pays $100 minimum.

‡**MANIFEST**, Alternate Publishing, 15 Harriet St., San Francisco CA 94103. (415)864-3456. Editor: John W. Rowberry. Monthly tabloid covering gay men's lifestyle. "*Manifest* appeals to the leisure activities of contemporary gay men." Circ. 30,000. Pays on publication. Byline given. Offers 50% kill fee. Buys first North

American serial rights, one-time rights, and second serial (reprint) rights. Submit seasonal/holiday material 2 months in advance. Simultaneous queries and photocopied and previously published submissions (from non-USA sources) OK. Computer printout submission OK; prefers letter quality to dot matrix printouts. SASE. Reports in 1 week on queries; 3 weeks on mss. Sample copy $2; free writer's guidelines.

Nonfiction: Historical/nostalgic (gay historic figures); humor; interview/profile; photo feature; travel (gay traveler emphasis). No book, film and theatre reviews. "Fiction should be top caliber (brief is better)." No coming-out stories, non-gay related material. Buys 24-48 mss/year. Query or send complete ms; interview/profile and photo features, query first only. Length: 3,000 words minimum. Pays $50-125.

Photos: Send photos with ms. Pays $50-100 for 35mm color transparencies; $15-25 for 8x10 prints. Captions, model release and identification of subjects required. Buys one-time rights.

Fiction: Erotica, historical, humorous, mystery, novel excerpts, science fiction, suspense, western. No routine sex stories, experimental fiction, coming out stories. Buys 12 mss/year. Send complete ms. Length: 1,000 words minimum. Pays $50 minimum. No poetry.

Tips: "Know the magazine. Be creative. *Manifest* publishes *specific* material, so general articles that can be found elsewhere won't be found here; write about what you *know*. Be authoritative. *Manifest* is a great place for unknowns and near-unknowns. Editor will work with you to develop good material if inherent writing skills are present. Magazine is constantly expanding."

THE MOTHER EARTH NEWS, Box 70, Hendersonville NC 28791. (704)693-0211. Editor: Bruce Woods. Emphasizes "back-to-the-land self-sufficiency for the growing number of individuals who seek a more rational self-directed way of life." Bimonthly magazine. Circ. 1,000,000. Pays on acceptance. "We buy any rights we might ever need, while leaving the author free to resell the same material as often as he or she pleases." Byline given. Submit seasonal/holiday material 5 months in advance. Simultaneous, photocopied and previously published submissions OK if so indicated. SASE. Reports in 3 months. Sample copy $3; free writer's guidelines.

Nonfiction: Roselyn Edwards, submissions editor. How-to, home business, alternative energy systems, low cost—$100 and up—housing, energy-efficient structures, seasonal cooking, gardening and crafts. Buys 300-350 mss/year. Query or send complete ms. "A short, to-the-point paragraph is often enough. If it's a subject we don't need at all, we can answer immediately. If it tickles our imagination, we'll ask to take a look at the whole piece. No phone queries, please." Length: 300-3,000 words. Pays $100/minimum/published page.

Photos: Purchased with accompanying ms. Captions and credits required. Send prints or transparencies. Uses 8x10 b&w glossies; any size color transparencies. Include type of film, speed and lighting used. Total purchase price for ms includes payment for photos.

Columns/Departments: "Contributions to *Mother's* Down-Home Country Lore and Successful Swaps are rewarded by a one-year subscription; Bootstrap Business pays a two-year subscription; Profiles pays $25-50."

Fillers: Short how-to's on any subject normally covered by the magazine. Query. Length: 150-300 words. Pays $7.50-25.

Tips: "Probably the best way to break in is to send a tightly written, short (1,000 words), illustrated (with color transparencies) piece on a slightly offbeat facet of gardening, alternative energy, or country living. It's important that the writer get all the pertinent facts together, organize them logically, and present them in a fun-to-read fashion. Study our magazine, digest our writer's guidelines, and send us a concise article illustrated with color transparencies that we can't resist. We want articles that tell what real people are doing to take charge of their own lives. Articles should be well-documented and not just another repeat of something we've just done."

NEW AGE MAGAZINE, New Age Communications, 244 Brighton Ave., Box 1200, Allston MA 02134. (617)254-5400. Editor: Peggy Taylor. Monthly magazine covering alternative ideas and focusing on "what individuals can do to help solve the problems of the modern world." Circ. 55,000. Pays on publication. Byline given. Offers 50% kill fee. Buys one-time rights, first rights and second serial (reprint) rights, and makes work-for-hire assignments. Submit seasonal/holiday material 3 months in advance. Photocopied and previously published submissions OK. Computer printout submission OK; prefers letter quality to dot matrix. SASE. Reports in 6 weeks. Sample copy $2; writer's guidelines for business size SAE and 1 first class stamp.

Nonfiction: Sandy MacDonald, articles editor. Book excerpts (alternative ideas in all fields); expose (of spiritual groups, government, corporations); general interest; how-to; humor (personal growth); inspirational; interview/profile (of people doing positive things in the world); opinion; personal experience; photo feature; travel (inexpensive ways to travel). No recycled ideas. Special issues include biannual book supplements and quarterly seasonal guides. Buys 60 mss/year. Query with clips of published work or send complete ms. Length: 500-7,000 words. Pays $25-350.

Photos: Kathleen Gates, photo editor. Send photos with ms. Pays $25-75 for 8x10 b&w prints and contact sheets; $75-200 for 35mm color transparencies. Captions and identification of subjects required.

Columns/Departments: Sandy MacDonald, column/department editor. Book and film reviews (100-500 words), energy, politics, spirituality, family, humor, profiles, opinion, personal experience. Buys 60 mss/year. Query with clips of published work or send complete ms. Length: 500-1,500 words. Pays $25-75.

Fiction: Sandy MacDonald, fiction editor. Experimental, fantasy, humorous, novel excerpts, "new age" slant. Buys 6 mss/year. Send complete ms. Length: 1,200-4,000 words. Pays $60-200.

Poetry: Sandy MacDonald, poetry editor. Avant-garde, free verse, haiku. Buys 12/year. Submit maximum 4 poems. Length: 6-15 lines. Pays $15-30.

PILLOW TALK, 215 Lexington Ave., New York NY 10016. Editor: I. Catherine Duff. "For people interested in all areas of human relationships—meetings, dating, arguing, making up, sex (in all aspects). We're a light, fun, but helpful and reliable publication—a counselor, a friend, a shoulder to lean on, and an entertainment." Monthly magazine. Pays on publication. Buys all rights. Byline given unless author requests otherwise. No simultaneous or photocopied submissions. SASE. Reports in 1 month. Sample copy $1.75; writer's guidelines for SASE.

Nonfiction: How-to (romantic and sexual techniques, meeting new people, handling relationships, overcoming emotional hurdles); humor (sexual, romantic); interview (maybe in rare cases); personal experience (sexual/romantic scenarios if they illustrate a specific topic); and medical/technical (lightly done on sex-related health topics). "No out-and-out pornography unless incorporated in our sexual fantasy department. Should be top-class." Buys 11 mss/issue. Query. Length: 1,000-3,000 words. Pays $150-250.

Photos: State availability of photos with query. Pays $25-50 for b&w; $250 for color covers. Buys all rights. Model release required.

Columns/Departments: Front Entry, unusual and interesting news items. Healthworks, health related topics; Rear Entry, sexual fantasy. Regular columns on alternate lifestyles: The Gay Life, The Swinging Life and The Kinky Life. Query with clips of published work. Length: 1,250 words. Pays $150. Open to suggestions for new columns/departments.

Fiction: "Only sexual fantasy for our new Rear Entry department." Length: 2,000 words. Pays $100-150.

Fillers: Clippings and newsbreaks (funny, unusual items relating to the broad area of sex). Buys 6 clippings/issue. Pays $5.

Tips: A query letter to *Pillow Talk* should convince the editor that "the writer can write without pleading poverty, humor or the issue. Query anything—especially researched pieces—giving a one-paragraph outline of the intended angle."

‡**THE PYRAMID, The National Newsletter for the National Association for Widowed People, Inc.**, Box 3564, Springfield IL 62708. (217)522-4300. Editor: Dorothy Lee Doering. Managing Editor: Rosemarie T. Giles. Quarterly membership newsletter for widowed persons, professional corporations and persons that serve the widowed person, as well as interested community groups or organizations. Estab. 1982. Circ. 27,000. Pays on acceptance. Byline given. Buys second serial (reprint) rights. Submit seasonal/holiday material 2 months in advance. Photocopied and previously published submissions OK. SASE. Reports in 1 month. Free sample copy and writer's guidelines.

Columns/Departments: Health; Insurance; Investments; Social Security; Veterans Administration; Personal Glimpse; Cooking; Inspiration; Psychic. Buys 4 mss/year. Send complete ms. Length: 1,500-3,000 words. Pays $50-200.

Poetry: "Nothing of twos or married persons; we are dealing with widowed people." Buys 4 poems/year. Submit maximum 2 poems. Length: 100 lines maximum. Pays $5-25.

Fillers: Anecdotes, short humor, newsbreaks. Buys 4 mss/year. Length: 50-1,000 words. Pays $15-50.

Tips: "Research up-to-date information that affects the widowed person."

‡**QUARTERLY**, B.W.M.T., Inc., 279 Collingwood, San Francisco CA 94114. (415)431-0458. Editor: Michael J. Smith. Quarterly magazine of "interracial and Third World interest for gay/lesbian people. We are most interested in documenting the history of the various interracial and Third World gay/lesbian groups and their participants, particularly their anti-racist activist concerns." Circ. 2,500. Pays on acceptance. Byline given. Offers a 25% kill fee. Buys one-time rights. Simultaneous queries and simultaneous, photocopied and previously published submissions OK. Computer printout submission OK. SASE. Reports in 1 week on queries; 2 weeks on mss. Sample copy $5.

Nonfiction: Historical/nostalgic, interview/profile, opinion, personal experience. No pornography. Buys 6 mss/year. Query or send complete ms. Length: open. Pays $10-50.

Fiction: Ethnic, historical, novel excerpts. No pornography. Buys 2-3 mss/year. Query or send complete ms. Length: open. Pays $10-50.

Tips: "Writers must note the focus of our publication carefully. We particularly welcome black and other Third World contributors." Interviews/historical areas are most open to freelancers.

‡**RADICAL AMERICA**, Alternative Education Project, Inc., #14, 38 Union Square, Somerville MA 02143. (617)628-6585. Editor: John P. Demeter. Managing Editor: Donna Penn. Bimonthly political journal of radical history, socialism, feminism, and community and workplace organizing; cultural analysis and commentary. "*RA* is a popularly written, non-academic journal aimed at feminists, political activists and left academics written from socialist (independent) and feminist perspectives." Circ. 5,000. Pays in copies. Byline given. Buys all rights. Submit seasonal/holiday material 3 months in advance. Simultaneous queries and si-

multaneous, photocopied and previously published submissions OK. SASE. Reports in 2 weeks on queries; 1 month on mss. Sample copy $2; free writer's guidelines.

Nonfiction: James Stark, articles editor. Political opinion and history. No strictly journalistic accounts without analysis or commentary. Query with published clips. Length: 2,000-7,000 words. Pays in copies.

Photos: Phyllis Ewen, photo editor. State availability of photos. Pays $5-10 for b&w contact sheet. Captions and identification of subjects required. Buys one-time rights.

Poetry: J.S. Smutt, poetry editor. Avant-garde, free verse. No poetry without political or social theme. Length: 10-50 lines.

‡**REINCARNATION REPORT**, Sutphen Corp., Box 2010, Malibu CA 90265. (213)456-3934. Editor: Alan Vaughan. Associate Editor: Sharon Boyd. Monthly magazine dealing with reincarnation, and life-after-death studies. Estab. 1982. Circ. 25,000. Pays on publication. Byline given. Buys first North American serial rights. Simultaneous queries and photocopied submissions OK. Computer printout submissions OK. SASE. Reports in 4 weeks on queries and mss. Sample copy for 8½x11 SAE and 5 first class stamps; writer's guidelines for SASE.

Nonfiction: Book excerpts (on reincarnation and life after death); personal experience (verifiable experiences of reincarnation). "We are looking for personal experiences that change your viewpoint or have a karmic lesson. Keep the story simple. If some facts are boring, leave them out. Give the evidence that what you say is true. Don't be literary—be direct. Either charm the readers with your warm, personal and fast-paced story or shock them. Give them something to think about. If your story changed you, communicate that emotional experience so that readers can join in the excitement. We draw material from personal experiences, scientific experiments, hypnotic regression research, or anything that convinces us that you have a good point and can back it up." No esoteric, technical, theoretical material: "Tell us your stories, not your theories." No material on other psychic subjects. Buys 48 mss/year. Query. Length: 1,000-3,000 words. Pays $75-150.

Photos: State availability of photos. Pays $5-25 for 5x7 b&w prints. Captions and identification of subjects required. Buys one-time rights; all rights if assigned.

Columns/Departments: Why I Believe. "We want personal accounts of experiences that led a person to believe in reincarnation or other after-life states." Buys 24 mss/year. Send complete ms. Length: 500-800 words. Writers receive a T-shirt or tape.

Tips: "Start with your personal story of reincarnation, or someone you know. We're looking for facts, controversy, and scientific authority. Try a story on a past-life researcher in your town. Don't tell us why you think you were Joan of Arc. We're eager to print new writers with good stories and facts to back them. But there *must* be a tie-in with reincarnation or survival."

ROOM OF ONE'S OWN, A Feminist Journal of Literature & Criticism, Growing Room Collective, Box 46160, Station G, Vancouver, British Columbia, Canada V6R 4G5. Editors: Gayla Reid, Joanna Dean, Victoria Freeman, Eleanor Wachtel. Quarterly magazine of original fiction, poetry, literary criticism, and reviews of feminist concern. Circ 1,000. Pays on publication. Byline given. Buys one-time rights. Photocopied submissions OK. Computer printout submissions Ok "if readable and not in all caps"; prefers leter quality to dot matrix. SASE. Reports in 2 months. Sample copy $2.75.

Nonfiction: Interview/profile (of authors); literary criticism. Buys 8 mss/year. Send complete ms. Length: 1,500-6,000 words. Pays $10-25.

Fiction: "Quality short stories by women with a feminist outlook. Not interested in fiction written by men." Buys 12 mss/year. Send complete ms. Length: 1,500-6,000 words. Pays $25.

Poetry: Avant-garde, eclectic free verse, haiku. "Not interested in poetry from men." Buys 32/year. Submit maximum 10 poems. Length: open. Pays $10-25.

SAN FRANCISCO BAY GUARDIAN, 2700 19th St., San Francisco CA 94110. (415)824-7660. Editor/Publisher: Bruce Brugmann. Department Editors: Louis Dunn (photos); Alan Kay (articles). An alternative news weekly specializing in investigative, consumer and lifestyle reporting for a sophisticated, urban audience. Circ. 40,000. Buys first rights. Byline given. Buys 200 mss/year. Pays 2 months after publication. Photocopied submissions OK. SASE.

Nonfiction: Publishes "incisive local news stories, investigative reports, features, analysis and interpretation, how-to, consumer and entertainment reviews. All stories must have a Bay Area angle." Freelance material should have a "public interest advocacy journalism approach."

Photos: Purchased with or without mss.

Tips: "Work with our volunteer and intern projects in investigative, political and consumer reporting. We teach the techniques and send interns out to do investigative research. We like to talk to writers in our office before they begin doing a story."

‡**SINGLELIFE (MILWAUKEE) MAGAZINE**, SingleLife Enterprises, Inc., 3846 W. Wisconsin Ave., Milwaukee WI 53208. (414)933-9700. Editor: Gail Rose. Bimonthly magazine covering singles lifestyles. Estab. 1982. Circ. 15,000. Pays on publication. Byline given. Buys all rights. Submit seasonal/holiday material

3 months in advance. Simultaneous queries, and photocopied and previously published submissions OK. SASE. Reports in 3 months. Sample copy $2; writer's guidelines for business-size SAE and 1 first class stamp.

Nonfiction: Anne Lehmann, articles editor. Book excerpts, general interest, how-to, humor, opinion, personal experience, photo feature, travel. Buys 25 mss/year. Query with published clips or send complete ms. Length: 800-5,000 words. Pays $25-200.

Photos: Todd Treleven, photo editor. Send photos with query or ms. Pays $10-100 for b&w contact sheet, 2¼" transparencies and 8x10 prints; pays $20-200 for 2¼" color transparencies and 8x10 prints. Captions, model release and identification of subjects required.

Columns/Departments: Anne Lehmann, column/department editor. Film and record reviews; Book reviews; Humor (situational with singles emphasis); Single parenting column; Quips & Quotes (news briefs); Legal; Health. Buys 30 mss/year. Send complete ms. Length: 800-2,000 words. Pays $25-100.

Fiction: Will consider adventure, confession, humorous, mainstream, romance. Send complete ms. Length: open. Pays $50-150.

Poetry: Anne Lehmann, poetry editor. Avant-garde, free verse, haiku, light verse, traditional. Buys 10/year. Submit any number of poems. Length: open. Pays $10-100.

Fillers: Clippings, cartoons. Buys 20/year. Length: 100 words minimum. Pays $10.

Tips: Currently looking for someone to write a single parents column.

SINGLES SCENE MAGAZINE, Singles Scene, Inc., Suite T, 5600 McLeod NE, Albuquerque NM 87109. (505)881-5171. Editor: Linda Blocki. "The Singles Scene © National Network System consists of many monthly tabloid-type magazines published in various cities throughout the country. Each Singles Scene magazine is locally owned, but published under the Singles Scene tradename using the Singles Scene National Network System's general layout and format design plus a required number of articles that are furnished by the national office. Our magazines are aimed at the entire single adult marketplace of each city. Readers are generally of above-average intelligence, income and education. We request a creative but clean, thoughtful, straightforward writing style, making use of research/statistics whenever possible." Circulation varies from city to city; usually 20,000-45,000. Pays 2-3 weeks following publication. Byline and photo credits given. Buys first rights. Submit seasonal/holiday material 3 months in advance. Simultaneous queries and previously published submissions OK. Computer printout submissions OK "if done in upper and lower case (*not* all caps) and in dark print"; prefers letter quality to dot matrix. Query or send complete manuscript with SASE. Reports in 1 month. Writer's guidelines available with business-size SASE; sample copy of magazine with large, clasp SASE ($1 postage).

Nonfiction: "We're looking for articles that deal with every aspect of single living. All articles must be of national approach. We are NOT a 'swingers' magazine and will not accept articles of that nature. Subject matter may include interpersonal relationships, coping (with divorce, widowhood, a broken affair, jealousy, etc.), self-improvement, real estate, financial matters, health and fitness, single parenting, romance, human sexuality, entertaining, cooking, home improvements and decorating, spotlights on interesting (emphasis on *interesting* and *different*) singles, nutrition, sports, travel, senior singles, New Age topics, etc. We use some articles written from a strictly personal point of view, but in general we prefer material that combines personal experience/observation with quotes/anecdotes from knowledgeable sources/experts and facts/research." Length: ½ page (650-850 words); ¾ page (1,000-1,200), full page (1,500-1,800); special 1½-page feature (1,800-2,600). Note size/word length of story in upper right-hand corner of first page when submitting manuscript. Pays 4¢/word if published in just one magazine; 5¢/word if published in more than one.

Photos: State availability of photos. Photos purchased with or without ms. "Generic photos that might fit with any general articles are welcome." Cover shots must be color transparencies. " We want expressive-looking, not posed, innovative shots." Pays $5 minimum for 5x7 or 8x10 b&w prints and contact sheet; $100-125 for cover photo. Model release and identification of subjects required.

Tips: "We're rapidly expanding our network system to publish *Singles Scene* in cities all over the country. Thus we will need articles of a local nature to use in individual cities as well as those with a national approach. Right now we need far more 'national' stories that could be used in any of the *Singles Scene* magazines."

‡**SINGLES WORLD, A Magazine of and for Singles**, Box 5168, Phoenix AZ 85010. (602)954-5605. Editor: Reg A. Forder. Monthly magazine of the single life. Estab. 1982. Circ. 5,000. Pays on publication. Byline given. Buys first rights. Submit seasonal/holiday material 2 months in advance. Simultaneous queries and simultaneous, photocopied and previously published submissions OK. SASE. Reports in 2 weeks on queries; 1 month on mss. Sample copy for SAE and 2 first class stamps; free writer's guidelines.

Nonfiction: Expose, general interest, how-to, humor, inspirational, interview/profile, personal experience— must be of interest to singles. "Not interested in articles that dwell on negative aspects of single life." Buys 50 mss/year. Query with published clips if available or send complete ms. Length: 100-1,500 words. Pays $5-45.

Photos: State availability of photos. "Photos accepted without payment." Reviews b&w prints. Buys one-time rights.

Fiction: Humorous "with a singles slant." Buys variable number of mss/year. Query with clips if available or send complete ms. Length: 100-800 words. Pays $5-25.

Poetry: "We will consider all types of poetry if it has a singles slant; nothing negative." No payment. Buys variable number of poems/year. Submit maximum 3 poems. Length: 4-20 lines.

Fillers: Clippings, jokes, gags, anecdotes, short humor, newsbreaks—anything of interest to singles. Buys variable number/year. Length: 100 words maximum. Pays $5.

‡**SURVIVAL GUIDE**, McMullen Publishing, Inc., 2145 W. La Palma Ave., Anaheim CA 92801. (714)635-9040. Editor: Dave Epperson. Associate Editor: Katherine V. Row. Monthly magazine covering "self-reliance, defense, meeting day-to-day threats—survivalism for survivalists." Estab. 1981. Circ. 85,000. Pays on publication. Byline given. Offers 50% kill fee. Not copyrighted. Buys first North American serial rights. Submit seasonal/holiday material 5 months in advance. Computer printout submissions OK; prefers letter quality to dot matrix. SASE. Reports in 3 weeks. Sample copy $2.50; writer's guidelines for SAE.

Nonfiction: Expose (political); how-to; interview/profile; personal experience (how I survived); photo feature (equipment and techniques related to survival in all possible situations); emergency medical; food preservation; water purification; stealth tactics; self-defense; nutrition, tools, shelter, etc. "No general articles about how to survive. We want specifics and single subjects." Buys 60-100 mss/year. Query or send complete ms. Length: 1,500-4,000 words. Pays $125-400.

Photos: Send photos with ms. Pays $5-75 for b&w contact sheet or negatives; $20-100 for 35mm color transparencies or 8x10 b&w prints. Captions, model release and identification of subjects required. Buys all rights.

Tips: "We will be dealing more with weaponry and tactics than with food preservation, food storage, water purification and like matters. Know and appreciate the survivalist movement. Prepare material of relevant value to individuals who wish to sustain human life no matter what the circumstance. This magazine is a text and reference."

SURVIVE, Survive Publications, Inc., 5735 Arapahoe Ave., Boulder CO 80303. (303)449-2064. Editor: Robert K. Brown. Managing Editor: Kevin E. Steele. Monthly magazine presenting material that is essential to survivalists in a down-to-earth, non-hysterical manner. Estab. 1981. Circ. 80,000. Pays on publication. Byline given. Offers 25% of word count kill fee. Buys first North American serial rights or makes work-for-hire assignments. Submit seasonal/holiday material 5 months in advance. No computer printout or disk submissions. SASE. Reports in 2 months. Sample copy $2.50; writer's guidelines for business-sized SAE and 20¢ postage.

Nonfiction: How-to (self-reliance, survival); new product; technical. Special issues include nuclear survival, survival weapons, survival foods. "No knife fighting, offensive rather than defensive material, how to kill, etc." Buys 50 or more mss/year. Query. Length: 2,000-2,500 words. Pays $175-1,000.

Photos: State availability of photos. Captions, model release and identification of subjects required. Buys one-time rights.

Tips: "Feature articles should have highly technical data, charts, graphs boxed as sidebars; author's box should be 50 words." A trend toward general survival and away from the nuclear holocaust orientation—will affect writers in the year ahead.

‡**THE SURVIVORS MAGAZINE, Magazine for the Widowed**, Le'Dor, Inc., Box 3665, Springfield IL 62708. (217)522-1700, 522-4528. Editor: Dorothy Lee Doering. Managing Editor: Rosemarie T. Giles. Quarterly information magazine for widowed persons and the professionals who serve them. Circ. 27,000. Pays on acceptance within 60 days. Byline given. Buys first North American serial rights, one-time rights, all rights, simultaneous rights, first rights, second serial (reprint) rights and makes work-for-hire assignments. Submit seasonal/holiday material 2 months in advance. Simultaneous queries and simultaneous, photocopied and previously published submissions OK. SASE. Reports in 2 months. Sample copy $2; free writer's guidelines.

Nonfiction: Book excerpts (widowed); general interest; historical/nostalgic; how-to (repair, cook, quilt); humor; inspirational; interview/profile; opinion; personal experience; photo feature; travel; pets. Not interested in automobiles or anything that includes a wife and a husband. Send complete ms. Length: 500-5,000 words. Pays $40-700.

Photos: Seasonal, people—all types. Send photos with ms. Pays $30-100 for 3x3 color transparencies; $10-80 for b&w transparencies and 8x10 color prints. Identification of subjects required. Buys one-time and all rights.

Columns/Departments: Editorial Guest; History; Health; Profiles; Humor; Financial/Investments; Cooking; Travel; Book Review (of interest to widowed person); Human Interest. Buys 4 mss/year. Send complete ms. Length: 1,000-5,000 words. Pays $50-200.

Poetry: Free verse, light verse, traditional. No love poems where two persons are involved. Buys 2 poems/year. Submit maximum 4 poems. Length: open. Pays $14-40.

Fillers: Short humor, newsbreaks. Buys 7 mss/year. Length: 15-300 words. Pays $5-25.

Tips: "We like our articles geared toward the widowed—inspirational, first-hand experiences and accurate facts and research. We give the reading audience more depth and understanding about being widowed and how to go on living."

‡**TELEWOMAN, A Women's Newsletter**, Telewoman, Inc., Box 2306, Pleasant Hill CA 94523. Editor: Anne J. D'Arcy. Monthly networking newsletter covering women's networking resources, literary/art/photog-

raphy resources and connections for a lesbian and "woman-identified" readership. Circ. 400. Pays in copies. Byline given "on request." Not copyrighted. Simultaneous queries and simultaneous, photocopied and previously published submissions OK. SASE. Reports in 2 weeks on queries; 1 month on mss. Sample copy for $1, business-size SAE and 2 first class stamps.

Nonfiction: Book excerpts, interview/profile, personal experience, photo feature. No erotic material, political material, separatist slant. Send complete ms. Length: open.

Photos: Send photos of women with ms. Review b&w prints.

Fiction: Novel excerpts; religious (women's spirituality); romance; serialized novels. No erotic material.

Poetry: Avant-garde, free verse, haiku, light verse, traditional. No separatist, political, erotic content. Buys 60 poems/year. Submit unlimited poems with SASE. Length: 25 words maximum. Pays in contributor's copies.

Tips: Most open to poetry, book reviews and music reviews. "We provide books for book reviews."

‡**TRENDSETTERS MAGAZINE**, Trendsetter Publications, Inc., 650 Royal Palm Beach Blvd., Box 191, W. Palm Beach FL 33411. (305)793-6352. Editor: Cordell Tucker. Monthly magazine for unmarried adults with emphasis on entertainment, how-to, personal profiles, etc. Estab. 1982. Circ. 12,000. Pays on acceptance. Byline given. Offers negotiable kill fee. Buys one-time rights. Submit seasonal/holiday material 3 months in advance. Simultaneous queries and simultaneous submissions OK. SASE. Reports in 3 weeks on queries; 1 month on mss. Sample copy $2.50; writer's guidelines for SAE.

Nonfiction: General interest, how-to, interview/profile, photo feature, travel. "We look for a positive, upbeat approach to all single lifestyles. All submissions must be for and about unmarried adults." Buys 15-20 mss/year. Send complete ms. Length: 500-3,000 words. Pays $50-1,500.

Photos: "Preference always given to well-illustrated stories." Send photos with ms. Pays $20-100 for 35mm color transparencies; $10-300 for 8x10 b&w prints; reviews b&w contact sheet. Captions, model release and identification of subjects required.

Columns/Departments: Single Parent Family; Single Finances; Entertainment—Dining Out; Single Traveler; Older Singles; Cooking. Buys 15 mss/year. Query or send complete ms. Length: 500-1,500 words. Pays $250-1,500.

Fiction: Confession, historical, humorous, mainstream, romance. "Must apply to unmarried adults." Buys 10-12 mss/year. Query or send complete ms. Length: 500-2,000 words. Pays $150-2,000.

Fillers: Jokes, anecdotes, newsbreaks. Buys 3-5/year.

VEGETARIAN TIMES, Box 570, Oak Park IL 60303. (312)848-8120. Editor: Paul Barrett Obis Jr. Monthly magazine. Circ. 150,000. Rights purchased vary with author and material. Will buy first serial or simultaneous rights ("always includes right to use article in our books or 'Best of' series"). May pay 20% kill fee. Byline given unless extensive revisions are required or material is incorporated into a larger article. Buys 120 mss/year. Pays on publication. Sample copy $2. Photocopied and simultaneous submissions OK. Computer printout submissions OK. Submit seasonal material 6 months in advance. Reports in 1 month. Query. SASE.

Nonfiction: Features concise articles related to vegetarian cooking, health foods, and articles about vegetarians. "All material should be well-documented and researched. It would probably be best to see a sample copy." Informational, how-to, experience, interview, profile, historical, successful health food business operations and restaurant reviews. Length: average 1,500 words. Pays 5¢/word minimum. Will also use 500- to 1,000-word items for regular columns.

Photos: Pays $15 for b&w photos; $50 for color; b&w ferrotype preferred.

Tips: Write query with "brevity and clarity."

THE WASHINGTON BLADE, Washington Blade, Inc., Suite 315, 930 F St. NW, Washington DC 20004. (202)347-2038. Managing Editor: Steve Martz. Weekly tabloid covering the gay community for "gay men and women of all ages, oriented to living within the mainstream of society. Articles (subjects) should be written from or directed to a gay perspective." Circ. 20,000. Pays in 30 days. Byline given. Pays $15 kill fee. Buys first North American serial rights. Submit seasonal/holiday material 1 month in advance. Photocopied and previously published submissions OK. SASE. Reports in 1 month. Free sample copy and writer's guidelines.

Nonfiction: Expose (of government, private agency, church, etc., handling of gay-related issues); historical/nostalgic; interview/profile (of gay community/political leaders; persons, gay or non-gay, in positions to affect gay issues; outstanding achievers who happen to be gay; those who incorporate the gay lifestyle into their professions); photo feature (on a nationally or internationally historic gay event); and travel (on locales that welcome or cater to the gay traveler). *The Washington Blade* basically covers two areas: news and lifestyle. News coverage of DC area gay community, local and federal government actions relating to gays, some national news of interest to gays. Section also includes features on current events. Greatest opportunity for freelancers resides in current events, features, interviews, book reviews. Special issues include: Annual gay pride issue (early June). No sexually explicit material. Buys 30 mss/year, average. Query with clips of published work. Length: 500-1,500 words. Pays 3-5¢/word.

Photos: "A photo or graphic with feature/lifestyle articles is particularly important. Photo(s) with news stories are appreciated." State availability of photos. Reviews b&w contact sheets. Pays $15 minimum for 8x10 b&w glossy prints or 5x7 color glossy prints. Captions preferred. Model releases required. On assignment, photographer paid hourly rate plus film, expenses reimbursement. Publication retains all rights.

WOMEN'S RIGHTS LAW REPORTER, 15 Washington St., Newark NJ 07102. (201)648-5320. Legal journal emphasizing law and feminism for lawyers, students and feminists. Quarterly magazine. Circ. 1,300. No payment. Acquires all rights. SASE. Sample copy $5 individuals; $9 institutions.
Nonfiction: Historical and legal articles. Query or submit complete ms with published clips and education data. Length: 20-100 pages plus footnotes.

WOODSMOKE, Highland Publishing Co., Box 474, Centerville UT 84014. Editor: Richard Jamison. Quarterly magazine covering survival, aboriginal lifestyles, and primitive living for people of all ages with an outdoor interest. Circ. 1,500. Pays on publication. Buys one-time rights. Byline given. Submit seasonal/holiday material 2 months in advance. Photocopied and previously published submissions OK. Computer printout submission OK; prefers letter quality to dot matrix. SASE. Reports in 2 months. Sample copy $1.
Nonfiction: Historical (on pioneer and Indian historical trips and hardships); how-to (on self-sufficiency theme, primitive skills, etc.); and personal experience (how-to and interesting experiences in the outdoors, true survival experiences). "We do not want any *researched* articles on edible plants or herbal medicines. Actual experiences OK. No cute stories on animals, cooking dandelions or stupid jokes." Buys 10-14 unsolicited mss/year. "We are taking a new direction toward family outdoor experiences. We would like to see some projects that the family could enjoy together in the outdoors, preferably projects that emphasize skills." Send complete ms or query with SASE. Length: 500-2,000 words. Pays 2¢/word.
Photos: State availability of photos with ms. Offers no additional payment for photos accepted with ms. Uses only b&w prints. Captions preferred.
Columns/Departments: Wild and Free (wild edible plants and herbs); Recipe Box (natural and outdoor recipes); Survival Journal (true life survival experiences); and Who's Who (people with expertise in survival education or outdoor experience). Buys 6 columns/year. Send complete ms. Length: 500-1,000 words. Pays 2¢/word.
Poetry: Light verse and traditional. "We are open to verse that will fit our outdoor, homestead format." Submit in batches of 3. Pays $3 each.
Fillers: Appropriate jokes, gags, anecdotes, short humor and outdoor recipes. Buys 2/issue. Length: 50-100 words.
Tips: "Send a brief but thorough outline of the subject matter. We need qualifications—a biography or references. Please send for a sample before submitting. We get a lot of mss that just don't fit our format."

Literary and "Little"

Many talented American writers found first publication in magazines like these. Writers are reminded that many "littles" remain at one address for a limited time; others are sometimes unbusinesslike in their reporting on or returning of submissions. University-affiliated reviews are conscientious about manuscripts but some of these are also slow in replying to queries or returning submissions.

Magazines that specialize in publishing poetry or poetry criticism are found in the Poetry category. Several of the poetry markets also buy short stories and nonfiction related to the poetic arts.

For more information about fiction technique—and some specialized markets—see *Fiction Writer's Market*, published by Writer's Digest Books.

THE AMERICAN SCHOLAR, 1811 Q St. NW, Washington DC 20009. (202)265-3808. Editor: Joseph Epstein. "For college-educated, mid-20s and older, rather intellectual in orientation and interests." Quarterly magazine. Circ. 32,000. Buys right to publish; rights stay in author's possession. Byline given. Buys 20-30 mss/year. Pays on acceptance for publication. Sample copy $4; free writer's guidelines. No simultaneous submissions. Reports in 1 month. Query, with samples, if possible. SASE.
Nonfiction: "The aim of *The Scholar* is to fill the gap between the learned journals and the good magazines for a popular audience. We are interested not so much in the definitive analysis as in the lucid and creative exploration of what is going on in the fields of science, art, religion, politics, and national and foreign affairs. Advances in science particularly interest us." Informational, interview, profile, historical, think articles, and book reviews. Length: 3,500-4,000 words. Pays $350/article and $100 for reviews.

Poetry: Pays $50 for poetry on any theme. Approximately 5 poems published per issue. "We would like to see poetry that develops an image or a thought or event, without the use of a single cliche or contrived archaism. The most hackneyed subject matter is self-conscious love; the most tired verse is iambic pentameter with rhyming endings. The usual length of our poems is 30 lines. From 1-4 poems may be submitted at one time; *no more* for a careful reading. We urge prospective contributors to familiarize themselves with the type of poetry we have published by looking at the magazine."

Tips: "See our magazine in your public library before submitting material to us. Know what we publish and the quality of our articles."

ANTIOCH REVIEW, Box 148, Yellow Springs OH 45387. Editor: Robert S. Fogarty. For general, literary and academic audience. Quarterly. Computer printout submissions OK; prefers letter quality to dot matrix. Buys all rights. Byline given. Pays on publication. Reports in 4-6 weeks. SASE.

Nonfiction: "Contemporary articles in the humanities and social sciences, politics, economics, literature and all areas of broad intellectual concern. Somewhat scholarly, but never pedantic in style, eschewing all professional jargon. Lively, distinctive prose insisted upon." Length: 2,000-8,000 words. Pays $10/published page.

Fiction: Prefers a strong narrative line with strong, fresh insights into the human condition. No science fiction, fantasy, confessions. Pays $10/published page.

Poetry: Concrete visual imagery. No light or inspirational verse. Contributors should be familiar with the magazine before submitting.

THE ARK RIVER REVIEW, c/o A. Sobin, English Department, Wichita State University, Wichita KS 67208. Editors-in-Chief: Jonathan Katz, A.G. Sobin. 100% freelance written. For "the well-educated, college age and above; poets, writers, and the readers of contemporary poetry and fiction." Published biannually. Magazine; 85-150 pages. Circ. 1,000. Pays on publication. Buys all rights. Byline given. Photocopied submissions OK. "No dot matrix printouts." Reports in 1 month; finalists may take considerably longer. Sample copy, appropriate to your genre $2.50.

Fiction: "We print one fiction issue/year featuring chapbook-sized collections of the work of 3 writers. We will read manuscripts of 75-125 pages (short fiction or novella or novel excerpt), up to ⅓ of which may have been previously published in magazine form. We will consider only writers who have yet to publish a full-length book. Conventional fiction stands little chance. We are interested only in highly innovative and sophisticated material. Type and subject matter are far less important to us than the way in which the story is written. We are looking for freshness in approach, style and language. We suggest strongly that you read back issues before submitting." Buys 3 mss/issue. Send complete ms (no novels). Pays $250/manuscript and contributor's copies.

Poetry: "Poetry should be substantial, intelligent and serious (this doesn't mean it can't be funny). Any form is OK, though we almost never print rhyming poems or haiku. As in fiction, we print one poetry issue/year, which contains chapbook-sized collections of the work of 3 poets. We will read manuscripts of 15-30 pages, up to ⅓ of which may have been previously published in magazine form." Pays $250. Buys 3/issue.

Tips: "Your work should demonstrate to us that you know what has gone on in literature in the last 50 years, and that you're working toward something better. The best way to find out what we're after is to read back issues. Send complete ms and $2.50 handling fee, receive a free copy of the next issue appropriate to your genre. (No reading fee required of subscribers)." Queries and ms must be accompanied by SASE.

THE ATHENIAN, (formerly *New Arts Review*), Box 887, Athens GA 30603. Executive Editor: Roy Schwartzman. Editor-in-Chief: Jill Kirkpatrick. Monthly general-interest, literary magazine. Circ. 5,000 + . Pays on publication. Byline given. Buys all rights. Simultaneous, photocopied, and previously published submissions OK for fiction and poetry only. SASE. Reports in 2 weeks on queries; 1 month on mss. Sample copy $1.50.

Nonfiction: Interviews/profiles; book reviews; exposes; satire. "Anything that would interest a diverse readership." Buys 24 mss/year. Query or send complete ms. Length: 500-6,000 words.

Photos: Only with accompanying ms. Captions and identification of subjects required.

Fiction: No erotica or pornography. "We are very selective in fiction, but there is always room for new, original talent." Buys 24 mss/year. Length: 1,000-5,000 words.

Poetry: Any type. "Our poetry standards are extremely high, with less than 10% mss accepted. We look for vivid, powerful language in any form." Buys 60 mss/year. Submit maximum 5 poems. Length: 100 lines maximum.

Fillers: Cartoon, jokes, anecdotes. "We particularly need cartoons." Buys 36/year. Length: 100 words maximum.

Tips: "Address submissions to the appropriate department. *Writer's Digest* has rated us as one of the top 100 fiction markets, and we want to improve our standing as a showcase of new literary talent and well-written articles." Recent and upcoming articles and stories: expose on cable TV monopolies; interview with author Joseph Heller.

BLOOMSBURY REVIEW, Box 8928, Denver CO 80201. (303)455-0593. Editor: Tom Auer. Bimonthly magazine covering book reviews, stories and essays of interest to residents of the western states. Circ. 8,000. Pays 2 months after publication. Byline and one-line biography given. Buys one-time rights. Simultaneous queries OK. SASE. Reports in 3 months on queries and mss. Sample copy $2; free writer's guidelines with SASE.
Nonfiction: Historical/nostalgic (related to books and publishing); interview/profile (of prominent people in the book business such as authors and publishers); essays; and book reviews. "Submitting a book review is the best way to break into *Bloomsbury Review*." Query with clips of published work. Length: average 750 words. Pays $10 minimum."
Fiction: Adventure, ethnic, experimental, fantasy, historical, horror, humorous, mainstream, mystery, science fiction, suspense, and western.
Poetry: Avant-garde, free verse, haiku, light verse, traditional and all others. Buys 24/year. Pays $5 average.

BOOK FORUM, Hudson River Press, 38 E. 76th St., New York NY 10021. (212)861-8328. Editor: Marshall Hayes. Editorial Director: Marilyn Wood. Emphasizes contemporary literature, the arts, and foreign affairs for "intellectually sophisticated and knowledgeable professionals: university-level academics, writers, people in government, and the professions." Quarterly magazine; 192 pages. Circ. 5,200. Pays on publication. Buys all rights. Pays 33⅓% kill fee. Byline given. Phone queries OK. Photocopied submissions OK. SASE. Reports in 2 weeks. Sample copy $3.
Nonfiction: "We seek highly literate essays that would appeal to the same readership as, say, the *London Times Literary Supplement* or *Encounter*. Our readers are interested in professionally written, highly literate and informative essays, profiles and reviews in literature, the arts, behavior, and foreign and public affairs. We cannot use material designed for a mass readership, nor for the counterculture. Think of us as an Eastern establishment, somewhat snobbish literary and public affairs journal and you will have it right." General interest, interview (with select contemporary writers), profiles, and essays about contemporary writers. Buys 15-20 unsolicited mss/year. Query. Length: 1,400-3,000 words. Pays $25-100.
Tips: "To break in send with the query letter a sample of writing in an area relevant to our interests. If the writer wants to contribute book reviews, send a book review sample, published or not, of the kind of title we are likely to review—literary, social, biographical, art."

BOSTON REVIEW, (formerly *New Boston Review*), 10B Mt. Auburn St., Cambridge MA 02138. (617)492-5478. Editor: Nicholas Bromell. Managing Editor: Ann Parson. Bimonthly magazine of the arts, politics and culture. Circ. 10,000. Acquires all rights, unless author requests otherwise. Byline given. Photocopied and simultaneous submissions OK. No computer printout or disk submissions. SASE. Reports in 2 months. Sample copy $3.
Nonfiction: Critical essays and reviews; natural & social sciences, literature, music, painting, film, photography, dance, theatre. Buys 20 unsolicited mss/year. Length: 1,000-3,000 words.
Fiction: Length: 2,000-4,000 words. Pays according to length and author.
Poetry: Pays according to length and author.
Tips: Recent article examples: "Economics of the Arms Race"; "Beyond Literature as an Institution"; and "Women and Happiness."

THE CALIFORNIA QUARTERLY, 100 Sproul, University of California, Davis CA 95616. Editor: Elliot Gilbert. 95% freelance written. "Addressed to an audience of educated, literary, and general readers, interested in good writing on a variety of subjects, but emphasis is on poetry and fiction." Quarterly. Usually buys first North American serial rights. Reports in 2 months but the editorial office is closed from June 1 to September 30. SASE.
Nonfiction: Original, critical articles, interviews and book reviews. Length: 8,000 words maximum. Pays $2/published page.
Fiction: Department Editor: Diane Johnson. "Short fiction of quality with emphasis on stylistic distinction; contemporary themes, any subject." Experimental, mainstream. Buys 12 unsolicited mss/year. Length: 8,000 words maximum. Pays $2/published page.
Poetry: Department editor: Sandra M. Gilbert. "Original, all types; any subject appropriate for genuine poetic expression; any length suitable to subject." Buys 150 unsolicited poems/year. Pays $3/published page.

CANADIAN FICTION MAGAZINE, Box 946, Station F, Toronto, Ontario, Canada M4Y 2N9. Editor: Geoffrey Hancock. Emphasizes Canadian fiction, short stories and novel excerpts. Quarterly magazine; 148 pages. Circ. 1,800. Pays on publication. Buys first North American serial rights. Byline given. SASE (Canadian stamps). Reports in 4-6 weeks. Back issue $4.00 (in Canadian funds). Current issue $5.50 (in Canadian funds).
Nonfiction: Interview (must have a definite purpose, both as biography and as a critical tool focusing on problems and techniques) and book reviews (Canadian fiction only). Buys 35 mss/year. Query. Length: 1,000-3,000 words. Pays $10/printed page plus one-year subscription.

Photos: Purchased on assignment. Send prints. Pays $5 for 5x7 b&w glossy prints; $20 for cover. Model release required.

Fiction: "No restrictions on subject matter or theme. We are open to experimental and speculative fiction as well as traditional forms. Style content and form are the author's prerogative. We also publish self-contained sections of novel-in-progress and French-Canadian fiction in translation, as well as an annual special issue on a single author such as Mavis Gallant, Leon Rooke, Robert Harlow or Jane Rule. Please note that *CFM* is an anthology devoted exclusively to Canadian fiction. We publish only the works of writers and artists residing in Canada and Canadians living abroad."

Tips: "Prospective contributors must study several recent issues carefully. *CFM* is a serious professional literary magazine whose contributors include the finest writers in Canada."

CANADIAN LITERATURE; University of British Columbia, Vancouver, British Columbia, Canada V6T 1W5. Editor: W.H. New. Quarterly. Circ. 2,000. Not copyrighted. Pays on publication. Query "with a clear description of the project." SAE and International Reply Coupons.

Nonfiction: Articles of high quality on Canadian books and writers only. Articles should be scholarly and readable. No fiction or fillers. Length: 2,000-5,500 words. Pays $5/printed page.

CAROLINA QUARTERLY, University of North Carolina, Greenlaw Hall 066A, Chapel Hill NC 27514. (919)933-0244. Editor: Marc Manganaro. Managing Editor: Gregg Rugolo. Literary journal published 3 times/year. Circ. 1,000. Pays on publication. Byline given. Buys first North American serial rights. Photocopied submissions OK. SASE. Reports in 4 months. Sample copy $4 (includes postage); writer's guidelines for SAE and 1 first class stamp.

Nonfiction: Book excerpts and photo feature. "Nonfiction articles are not commissioned; used at editor's discretion." Buy 1-2 mss/year. Send complete ms. Length: 6,000 words.

Fiction: "We are interested in maturity: control over language; command of structure and technique; understanding of the possibilities and demands of prose narrative, with respect to stylistics, characterization, and point of view. What we want is precisely to discourage that which merely *pretends*. We publish a good many unsolicited stories; and *CQ* is a market for newcomer and professional alike." No pornography. Buys 12-18 mss/year. Send complete ms. Length: 7,000 words maximum. Pays $3/printed page.

Poetry: "*CQ* places no specific restrictions on the length, form or substance of poems considered for publication, though limited space makes inclusion of works of more than 300 lines impracticable." Submit 2-6 poems. Buys 60 mss/year. Pays $5/printed poem.

Tips: "*One* fiction ms at a time; no cover letter is necessary. Address to appropriate editor, not to general editor. Look at the magazine, a recent number if possible."

‡THE CHARITON REVIEW, Northeast Missouri State University, Kirksville MO 63501. (816)785-4499. Editor: Jim Barnes. Semi-annual (fall and spring) magazine covering contemporary fiction, poetry, translation, book reviews. Circ. 600. Pays on publication. Byline given. Buys first North American serial rights. No computer printout or disk submissions. SASE. Reports in 1 week on queries; 2 weeks on mss. Sample copy for $2 and 7x10 SAE and 63¢ postage.

Nonfiction: Book reviews. Buys 2-5 mss/year. Query or send complete ms. Length: 1,000-5,000. Pays $15.

Fiction: Adventure, ethnic, experimental, fantasy, horror, humorous, mainstream, mystery, novel excerpts, science fiction, western, traditional. "We are not interested in slick material." Buys 6-8 mss/year. Send complete ms. Length: 1,000-5,000 words. Pays $5/page.

Poetry: Avant-garde, free verse, traditional. Buys 50-55 poems/year. Submit maximum 10 poems. Length: open. Pays $5/page.

Tips: "Read *Chariton* and similar magazines. Know the difference between good literature and bad. Know what magazine might be interested in your work. We are not a trendy magazine. We publish only the best." All sections are open to freelancers, all material is freelance. "Know your market, or you are wasting your time—and mine."

CHICAGO SUN-TIMES SHOW/BOOK WEEK, *Chicago Sun-Times*, 401 N. Wabash Ave., Chicago IL 60611. (312)321-2131. Editor: Steven S. Duke. Emphasizes entertainment, arts and books. Weekly newspaper section. Circ. 750,000. Pays on publication. Buys all rights. Pays negotiable kill fee, except on speculative articles. Submit seasonal/holiday material at least 2 months in advance. Photocopied and previously published work OK. Computer printout submissions OK "if readable"; prefers letter quality to dot matrix. SASE. Reports in 3 weeks.

Nonfiction: "Articles and essays dealing with all the serious and lively arts—movies, theater (pro, semipro, amateur, foreign), filmmakers, painting, sculpture, music (all fields, from classical to rock—we have regular columnists in these fields). Our Book Week columns have from 6-8 reviews, mostly assigned. Material has to be very good because we have our own regular staffers who write almost every week. Writing must be tight. No warmed-over stuff of fan magazine type. No high-schoolish literary themes." Query. Length: 800-1,000 words. Pays $75-100.

CONFRONTATION, Long Island University, 1 University Plaza, Brooklyn NY 11201. (212)834-6170. Editor: Martin Tucker. 90% freelance written. Emphasizes creative writing for a "literate, educated, college-graduate audience." Semiannual magazine; 190 pages. Circ. 2,000. Pays on publication. Buys all rights. Pays 50% kill fee. Byline given. Phone queries OK. Simultaneous and photocopied submissions OK. Computer printout and disk submissions OK; prefers letter quality to dot matrix printouts. SASE. Reports in 2 months. Sample copy $1.50.

Nonfiction: "Articles are, basically, commissioned essays on a specific subject." Memoirs wanted. Buys 6 mss/year. Query. Length: 1,000-3,000 words. Pays $10-50.

Fiction: Ken Bernard, fiction editor. Experimental, humorous, mainstream. Buys 20 mss/year. Submit complete ms. Length: "completely open." Pays $15-75.

Poetry: W. Palmer, poetry editor. Avant-garde, free verse, haiku, light verse, traditional. Buys 40/year. Limit submissions to batches of 10. No length requirement. Pays $5-40.

Tips: "At this time we discourage fantasy and light verse. We do, however, read all mss."

CROSSCURRENTS, 2200 Glastonbury Rd., Westlake Village CA 91361. Editor: Linda Brown Michelson. Quarterly magazine featuring fiction and poetry for an educated audience. Estab. 1980. Circ. 2,100. Average issue includes 6-10 pieces of short fiction, 10-15 pieces of poetry and 1-2 pieces of nonfiction. Pays on acceptance. Byline given. Offers 50% kill fee. Buys first North American serial rights. Submit seasonal material 6 months in advance. Photocopied submissions OK. Computer printout submissions OK. SASE. Reports in 2 weeks on queries; in 6 weeks on mss. Sample copy $4; free writer's guidelines for SASE. No simultaneous submissions.

Nonfiction: Historical, interview, profile, memoirs and film. "Our only concern is well-crafted work, of the highest professional standard." Buys 4-7 mss/year. Query. Pays $35 minimum.

Photos: Photo editor: Michael Hughes. State availability of photos. Pays $10 minimum for b&w negative plus prints. Model release required. Buys one-time rights.

Fiction: "We try to remain open to all types of fiction." Buys 30-40 mss/year. Send complete ms. Length: 8,000 words maximum. Pays $35 minimum. Also pays in copies.

Poetry: Poetry editor: Pamela Camille. "We try to remain open to all types of poetry." Buys 50 mss/year. Submit maximum 5 poems. Pays $10 minimum. Also pays in copies.

Tips: "Study a sample issue of our publication, then send us something terrifically appropriate. We receive quite a bit of material that is well-done, but just not quite right for us."

THE DENVER QUARTERLY, University of Denver, Denver CO 80208. (303)753-2869. Editor: Eric Gould. For an intellectual/university readership. Quarterly magazine. Circ. 500. Pays on publication. Buys first North American serial rights. Phone queries OK. Photocopied (if explained as not simultaneous) submissions OK. SASE. Reports in 10 weeks. Sample copy $2. "Each issue may focus on a topic of contemporary, literary, and cultural concern. For example, Winter, 1980: Native American literature; future issues: Chicano literature, American translators, and contemporary Arabic poetry. Submissions need not coincide with these topics."

Nonfiction: Modern culture, literary analysis, theory and translations of same. Buys 10-12 mss/year. Send complete ms. Pays $5/printed page.

Fiction: Experimental, historical, traditional and translations of same. Buys 8-10 mss/year. Send complete ms. Pays $5/printed page.

Poetry: Avant-garde, free verse, traditional and translations of same. Buys 30 poems/year. Send poems. Pays $10/printed page.

Tips: "We decide on the basis of quality only. Prior publication is irrelevant. Promising material, even though rejected, will receive some personal comment from the editor; some material can be revised to meet our standards through such criticism. I receive more good stuff than *DQ* can accept, so there is some subjectivity and a good deal of luck involved in any final acceptance."

‡ENCOUNTER, Encounter, Ltd., 59 St. Martin's Lane, London WC2N 4JS, England. Editors: Melvin J. Lasky and Anthony Thwaite. Monthly magazine (except August and September) covering current affairs and the arts. Circ. 16,000. Pays on publication. Buys one-time rights. SASE or IRC. Reports in 2 weeks on queries; 6 weeks on mss. Sample copy $3 including surface mail cost.

Nonfiction: Mainly articles on current affairs. Length: 1,500-5,000 words. Pays variable fee, but "averages £20/1,000 words."

Fiction: "Just good up-market stories." Length: 1,500-5,000 words. Pays variable fee, averages £20/1,000 words.

Poetry: "Just good up-market poetry." Submit maximum 6 poems. Length: 12-100 lines. Pays variable fee.

Tips: "Study the magazine first. A straight submission will be carefully considered." Stories and poems most open to freelancers.

‡**EROTIC FICTION QUARTERLY**, EFQ Publications, Box 4958, San Francisco CA 94101. Editor: Richard Hiller. Quarterly creative fiction magazine covering sexual themes (roles, attitudes, behaviors) free of cliche or pretension. Estab. 1983. Pays on acceptance. Byline given. Buys all rights. Photocopied submissions OK. SASE. Writer's guidelines for SASE.
Fiction: Erotica (feminist); ethnic (new wave, etc.); experimental; fantasy; humorous; romance; science fiction; any story with sexual theme (not slant). No standard pornography; no "men's stories"; no contrived plots. Send complete ms. Length: 500-5,000 words, average 1,500 words. Pays $35 minimum.
Tips: "I specifically encourage beginners who have something to say regarding sexual attitudes, emotions, roles, etc. Story ideas should come from real life, not media; characters should be real people. There are essentially no restrictions on content, style, explicitness, etc.; *originality, clarity,* and *integrity* are most important."

EVENT, c/o Kwantlen College, Box 9030, Surrey, B.C., Canada, V3T 5H8. Managing Editor: Vye Flindall. For "those interested in literature and writing." Biannual magazine. Circ. 1,000. Uses 80-100 mss/year. Small payment and contributor's copies. Byline given. Photocopied and simultaneous submissions OK. Computer printout and disk submissions OK; prefers letter quality to dot matrix printouts. Reports in 4 months. Submit complete ms. SAE and International Reply Coupons.
Nonfiction: "High-quality work." Reviews of Canadian books and essays.
Fiction: Short stories and drama.
Poetry: Submit complete ms. "We are looking for high quality modern poetry."

FICTION INTERNATIONAL, St. Lawrence University, Canton NY 13617. Editor: Joe David Bellamy. For "readers interested in the best writing by talented writers working in new forms or working in old forms in especially fruitful new ways; readers interested in contemporary literary developments and possibilities." Published annually in mid-winter. Pays on publication. Copyrighted; rights revert to author. Reports in 1-3 months. SASE. Mss considered only from September through December of each year.
Fiction: Study publication. Previous contributors include: Asa Baber, Russell Banks, Jonathan Baumbach, T. Coraghessan Boyle, Rosellen Brown, Jerry Bumpus, David Madden, Joyce Carol Oates, Ronald Sukenick, Gordon Weaver and Robley Wilson Jr. Highly selective. Not an easy market for unsophisticated writers. No length limitations but "rarely use short-shorts or mss over 30 pages." Portions of novels acceptable if self-contained enough for independent publication.
Interviews: Seeking interviews with well-known or innovative fiction writers "able to discuss their ideas and aesthetic predilections intelligently."
Reviews: Review Editor: G. E. Murray. By assignment only. No payment. *Fiction International* also sponsors the annual $1,000 St. Lawrence Award for Fiction for an outstanding first collection of short fiction published in North America.

THE FIDDLEHEAD, University of New Brunswick, The Observatory, Box 4400, Fredericton, New Brunswick, Canada E3B 5A3. (506)454-3591. Editor: Peter Thomas. Quarterly magazine covering poetry, short fiction, photographs and book reviews. Circ. 1,045. Pays on publication. Not copyrighted. Buys first North American serial rights. Submit seasonal/holiday material 6 months in advance. Simultaneous queries, and photocopied submissions (if legible) OK. SAE and International Reply Coupons. Reports in 3 weeks on queries; 2 months on mss. Sample copy $4, Canada; $4.25, US.
Fiction: Michael Taylor and Bill Bauer. "Stories may be on any subject—acceptance is based on quality alone. Because the journal is heavily subsidized by the Canadian government, strong preference is given to Canadian writers." Buys 20 mss/year. Pays $20/page; $100/article.
Poetry: Robert.Gibbs. "Poetry may be on any subject—acceptance is based on quality alone. Because the journal is heavily subsidized by the Canadian government, strong preference is given to Canadian writers." Buys average of 60/year. Submit maximum 10 poems. Pays $20/page; $100 maximum.
Tips: "Quality alone is the criterion for publication. Return postage (Canadian, or International Reply Coupons) should accompany all mss."

‡**THE GENEVA REVIEW**, 19 rue Centrale, 1580 Avenches, Switzerland. Editor-in-Chief: Jed Curtis. Executive Editor: Collin Gonze. Literary magazine "serving much the same function that *The Paris Review* did before it relocated to the US." For intelligent English-speakers in Europe. 70% freelance written. Pays on acceptance. Simultaneous queries, and simultaneous and previously published submissions OK "if other submissions are made outside Europe."
Nonfiction: Contact Michael O'Regan. "Though mss of any genre are considered, there are two requirements: excellence in writing; and a European slant." Science developments, writer's life, essays, how-to-get-by-in-Europe (especially Switzerland), historical, the arts, politics, profiles and interviews (especially prominent English-language literary figures living in Europe), and 'the undefinable'. Query with published clips. Reports in 2-3 months. Length: open; but under 2,500 words preferred. Pays variable rates.
Fiction: Contact: S.F. Stromberg. Mainstream, historical, humorous, adventure, some experimental. One science fiction story/issue. "This is typically set somewhere in continental Europe, with at least one native Eng-

lish-speaker among the protagonists. For science fiction, 'European slant' might only mean the absence of an exclusively American viewpoint." Length: 2,000 words or less. Pays variable rates.
Poetry: Contact: Dorothy Oliveau. Any style OK. Submit maximum 5 poems. Length: 5-50 lines. Use of non-English words or sentences acceptable in giving flavor of some European nation.
Fillers: Jokes, anecdotes "always needed." Length: 250 words maximum.
Tips: "*TGR* draws primarily on the talents of English-language writers living anywhere in continental Europe (in conjunction with EWE, the English-Language Writers in Europe)."

GREAT RIVER REVIEW, 211 W. 7th, Winona MN 55987. Editors: Orval Lund, Fiction; Paul Wadden, Poetry; Susan Williams, Reviews. Published 2 times/year. Magazine; 145 pages. Pays on publication. Photocopied submissions OK. SASE. Reports in 3 months. Sample copy (back issues) $3; current issue $3.50.
Nonfiction: Essays on the region and articles on Midwestern writers. Query first on articles.
Fiction: Experimental and mainstream, but not mass circulation style. Buys 6-7 prose mss/issue, up to 30 poems. Length: 2,000-9,000 words.
Tips: Recent story examples: "The Round" (Vol. 3, No. 2) and "Going Home" (Vol. 4, No. 1).

‡**GREEN FEATHER MAGAZINE**, Quality Publications, Inc., Box 2633, Lakewood OH 44107. Editor: Gary S. Skeens. Assistant Editor: Robin S. Moser. Annual magazine covering poetry and fiction. Circ. 150. Pays on publication. Byline given. Buys first North American serial rights. Submit seasonal/holiday material 6 months in advance. Simultaneous queries, and simultaneous, photocopied and previously published submissions OK. Computer printout or disk submissions OK; prefers letter quality to dot matrix printouts. SASE. Reports in 1 week on queries; 1 month on mss. Sample copy $1; writer's guidelines for business size SAE and 1 first class stamp.
Photos: "Photos are used primarily for the magazine's cover. Open subject matter or query as to our needs at a particular time." Send photos with ms. Reviews 8x10 b&w prints. Model release and identification of subjects required. Buys one-time rights.
Fiction: Adventure, erotica, experimental, mainstream, and mystery. "No pornography or anything lacking strong sense of plot and character development." Buys 3 mss/year. Query. Length: 750-2,000 words. Pays $5-25.
Poetry: Free verse, light verse. Buys 25/year. Submit maximum 10 poems. Length: 5-30 lines. Pays $1-10.
Tips: "Prefers not to see anything of a pornographic, low-quality nature; poor plotting, dialogue, character development." Material must "grab the gut. Dishonesty will definitely be tossed back in the mail."

THE HUDSON REVIEW, 684 Park Ave., New York NY 10021. Managing Editor: Richard Smith. Quarterly. Pays on publication. Reports in 6-8 weeks. SASE for return of submissions.
Nonfiction: Articles, translations and reviews. Length: 8,000 words maximum.
Fiction: Uses "quality fiction". Length: 10,000 words maximum. Pays 2½¢/word.
Poetry: 50¢/line for poetry.
Tips: Unsolicited mss are not read during the months of June, July, August and September.

IMAGE MAGAZINE, A Magazine of the Arts, Cornerstone Press, Box 28048, St. Louis MO 63119. (314)752-3704. Managing Editor: Anthony J. Summers. Triannual literary journal "for the educated, open-minded, thinking person." Circ. 600. Pays on publication. Byline given. Offers negotiable kill fee. Buys one-time and negotiable rights. Simultaneous queries OK. SASE. Reports in 3 weeks on queries; 6 weeks on mss. Sample copy for $2 and 73¢ postage; free writer's guidelines.
Nonfiction: James J. Finnegan, articles editor. Expose, humor, interview/profile, opinion. "We're looking for a lot of material for Special Tenth Anniversary issue. Buys variable number mss/year. Length: open. Pays $1-100.
Fiction: Erotica, ethnic, experimental, fantasy, horror, humorous, novel excerpts, science fiction. No "cutesy, self-congratulating material." Buys variable number mss/year. Query or send complete ms. Length: open. Pays $1-100.
Poetry: Avant-garde, free verse, haiku, light verse, traditional. No "overly religious, Elvis poetry, 'The World is Neat and Happy' type, etc." Buys 20-100/year. Submit maximum 10 poems. Length: open. Pays $1-100.
Tips: "We receive very few reviews, interviews, interesting articles on the literary world, as well as plays, radio plays and experimental material. Try these for a better shot."

THE INTERCOLLEGIATE REVIEW, Intercollegiate Studies Institute, 14 S. Bryn Mawr Ave., Bryn Mawr PA 19010. (215)525-7501. Editor: Dr. Donald Roy. Emphasizes intellectual conservatism on cultural, economic, political, literary and philosophical issues. Biannual magazine; 64 pages. Circ. 25,000. Pays on publication. Buys all rights. Byline given. Phone queries OK. SASE. Reports in 6 months. Free sample copy.
Nonfiction: Political; historical; informational; and personal. Buys 8 unsolicited mss/issue. Query. Length: 1,000-5,000 words. Pays $50-150.

THE IOWA REVIEW, 308 EPB, The University of Iowa, Iowa City IA 52242. (319)353-6048. Editor: David Hamilton, with the help of colleagues, graduate assistants, and occasional guest editors. Quarterly magazine. Buys first rights. Photocopied submissions OK. SASE. Reports in 3 months.
Nonfiction: "We publish essays, stories and poems and would like for our essays not always to be works of academic criticism." Buys 65-85 unsolicited mss/year. Submit complete ms. Pays $1/line for verse; $10/page for prose.

JAM TO-DAY, Box 249, Northfield VT 05663. Editors: Judith Stanford and Don Stanford. Annual literary magazine featuring high-quality poetry, fiction and reviews. Especially interested in unknown or little-known authors. Circ. 300. Pays on publication. Byline given. Buys first rights. Photocopied submissions OK. SASE. Reports in 6 weeks. Sample copy $2.50.
Fiction: "We will consider quality fiction of almost any style or genre. However, we prefer not to receive material that is highly allegorical, abstruse, or heavily dependent on word play for its effect." Buys 1-2 mss/year. Send complete ms. Length: 1,500-7,500 words. Pays $5/page.
Poetry: Avant-garde, free verse, haiku, traditional. No light verse. Buys 30-50/year. Submit 5 poems maximum. Length: open. Pays $5/page.
Tips: "We expect a somewhat larger than usual issue, to mark our tenth anniversary of publication."

‡**JAPANOPHILE**, Box 223, Okemos MI 48864. Editor: Earl Snodgrass. For literate people who are interested in Japanese culture anywhere in the world. Quarterly magazine. Pays on publication. Buys first North American serial rights. Previously published submissions OK. SASE. Reports in 4 weeks. Sample copy $3.
Nonfiction: "We want material on Japanese culture in *North America or anywhere in the world*, even Japan. We want articles, preferably with pictures, about persons engaged in arts of Japanese origin: a Michigan naturalist who is a haiku poet, a potter who learned raku in Japan, a vivid 'I was there' account of a Go tournament in California. We use some travel articles if exceptionally well-written, but we are *not* a regional magazine about Japan. We are a little magazine, a literary magazine. Our particular slant is a certain kind of culture wherever it is in the world: Canada, the US, Europe, Japan. The culture includes flower arranging, haiku, religion, art, photography, fiction. It is important to study the magazine." Buys 8 mss/issue. Query or send complete ms. Length: 800-2,000 words. Pays $8-15.
Photos: State availability of photos. Pays $5 for 8x10 b&w glossy prints.
Fiction: Short stories to 5,000 words with a setting in Japan. Pays $20 and sometimes more. Best to see a sample copy.
Columns/Departments: "We are looking for columnists to write about cultural activities in Chicago, New York, Los Angeles, San Francisco, Tokyo and Honolulu. That is, one columnist for each city." Query. Length: 600-1,200 words. Pays $7-15.
Tips: Prefers to see more articles about Japanese culture in the US, Canada and Europe.

THE JOURNAL OF MEXICAN AMERICAN HISTORY, Box 13861-UCSB, Santa Barbara CA 93107. (805)968-5915. Editor-in-Chief: Joseph Peter Navarro. Emphasizes history for specialists in Mexican-American history, including professors, graduate and undergraduate students. Annual magazine; 150-200 pages. Circ. 1,000. No payment. Acquires simultaneous rights. Phone queries OK. Submit seasonal/holiday material 6-12 months in advance. Photocopied submissions OK. SASE. Reports in 2 weeks. Sample copy $17.50.
Nonfiction: Historical (Mexican-American history from 1848 to present); interview; personal experience (documented carefully); personal opinion; photo feature (if historical and pertinent). Send complete ms. Length: 1,500-4,500 words. Prize of $100 for best article. Captions required for b&w photos used.

JOURNAL OF MODERN LITERATURE, Temple University, 921 Humanities Bldg., Philadelphia PA 19122. (215)787-8505. Editor-in-Chief: Maurice Beebe. Managing Editor: Kathleen Zsamar. Emphasizes scholarly studies for academics interested in literature of the past 100 years. Quarterly magazine. Circ. 2,000. Buys all rights. Phone queries OK. Photocopied submissions OK. Computer printout and disk submissions OK. SASE. Reports in 8 weeks. Free sample copy.
Nonfiction: Historical (20th-century literature); informational (20th-century literature); and photo feature on art and literature. Buys 30 mss/year. Query or send complete ms. Pays $35-75.
Photos: Purchased only with accompanying nonfiction manuscript. Total purchase price for ms includes payment for photos.
Tips: Prefers not to see material on "How I started being a writer."

‡**KALEIDOSCOPE, National Literary/Art Magazine for Disabled**, Kaleidoscope Press, 318 Water St., Akron OH 44308. (216)376-6041, ext. 26. Editor: Carson W. Heiner, Jr. Semiannual magazine with international collection of literature and art by disabled people for writers, artists, and anyone interested in fine art and literature. Present disability in factual way, but not maudlin." Circ. 3,000. Pays on publication. Byline given. Buys first North American serial rights. Simultaneous queries, and photocopied and previously published submissions OK. Computer printout submissions OK. SASE. Reports in 3 months. Sample copy $2.75; writer's

guidelines for SAE and 1 first class stamp.

Nonfiction: Book excerpts, general interest, historical/nostalgic, how-to (anything relating to being disabled—adaptive aids, job market for disabled, etc.); humor, inspirational, interview/profile (on prominent disabled people in the arts), opinion, personal experience, photo feature, travel. Publishes 10 mss/year; purchases 4 mss/year. Query with clips if available or send complete ms. Length: 10,000 words maximum. Pays in contributor's copies or annual cash awards for top submissions.

Photos: No pay for photos except annual cash award for top submission. Photos of art done by disabled artists. Reviews 3x5, 5x7 8x10 and color prints. Captions and identification of subjects required.

Fiction: Experimental, fantasy, historical, horror, humorous, mainstream, mystery, religious, romance, science fiction, suspense. No erotica. Publishes 30 mss/year; purchases 8/year. Query with clips if available or send complete ms. Length: 10,000 words maximum.

Poetry: Avant-garde, free verse, haiku, light verse, traditional. No erotica. Publishes 50 poems/year; purchases 4 poems/year. Submit maximum 6 poems. Length: open. Pays in contributor's copies or annual cash award for top submissions.

Fillers: Anecdotes, short humor. Length: open.

Tips: "Study the magazine and know the editorial requirements. Avoid triteness and stereotypes in all writing. Articles about arts programs for disabled people sought. Fiction and poetry are most open to freelancers. For fiction, have strong, believable characterizations. Poetry should be vivid and free of cliches." Magazine has added a children's literature section and a column about the theater scene.

LETTERS, Mainspring Press, Box 905, Stonington ME 04681. (207)367-2484. Editor-in-Chief: Helen Nash. Publication of the Maine Writers' Workshop. For general literary audience. Quarterly magazine. Circ. 6,500. Pays on acceptance. Buys all rights. Submit seasonal/holiday material 5 months in advance. SASE. Reports in 1 month. SASE for free sample copy and submissions. Back copies are not free.

Nonfiction: "Any subject within moral standards and with quality writing style." Query. Buys 2-10 unsolicited mss/year. Length: 100-1,000 words. Pays 5¢/word.

Fiction: No pornography, confession, religious or western. Buys 5 mss/year. Pays 5¢/word.

Poetry: G.F. Bush, poetry editor. Light verse, traditional, blank verse, humorous, narrative, avant-garde, free verse and haiku. Buys 15/year. Length: 30-42 lines. Pays maximum 50¢/line.

Tips: Recent story example: "The Metamorphosis of Mrs. Blake" (April 1981). Poetry by Buckminster Fuller, Kay Boyle, George Garret, Richard Eberhart, etc.

‡LETTRES FROM LIMERICK, The International Review of Limericks & Bawdy Verse, Limerick League, Inc., 1212 Ellsworth St., Philadelphia PA 19147. (215)271-1403. Editor: J. Beauregard Pepys. Managing Editor: Roy W. West. Quarterly magazine covering limericks and bawdy verse. "Uncensored review of limericks and occasional other bawdy verse." Estab. 1982. Circ. 1,500. Pays on publication. Byline given. Buys first North American serial, one-time, simultaneous, or first or second serial (reprint) rights. Submit seasonal/holiday material 6 months in advance. Simultaneous queries and simultaneous, photocopied and previously published submissions OK "if so identified." Reports in 1 week. Sample copy $5.50.

Nonfiction: Book excerpts (limericks); historical/nostagic (on limericks); how-to (on limericks); humor; interview/profile (of famous limerick writers); personal experience (if you know a famous limerick writer); technical (on limericks). Nothing outside the limerick field. Query. Length: 300-2,500 words. Pays $25 honorarium.

LITERARY SKETCHES, Box 711, Williamsburg VA 23187. (804)229-2901. Editor: Mary Lewis Chapman. For readers with literary interests; all ages. Monthly newsletter. Circ. 500. Not copyrighted. Byline given. Buys about 12 mss/year. Pays on publication. Sample copy for SASE. Photocopied and simultaneous submissions OK. Reports in 1 month. Submit complete ms. SASE.

Nonfiction: "We use only interviews of well-known writers and biographical material on past writers. Very informal style; concise. Centennial or bicentennial pieces relating to a writer's birth, death or famous works are usually interesting. Look up births of literary figures and start from there." Length: 1,000 words maximum. Pays 1/2¢/word.

LOS ANGELES TIMES BOOK REVIEW, Times Mirror, Times Mirror Sq., Los Angeles CA 90053. (213)972-7777. Editor: Art Seidenbaum. Weekly tabloid reviewing current books. Circ. 1.3 million. Pays on publication. Byline given. Offers variable kill fee. Buys first North American serial rights. Simultaneous queries OK. Computer printout submissions OK; prefers letter quality to dot matrix. SASE. Reports in 2 weeks.

Nonfiction: No unsolicited book reviews. No requests for specific titles to review. "Query with published samples—book reviews or literary features." Buys 50 mss/year. Length: 150-1,500 words. Pays $50-250.

‡THE MALAHAT REVIEW, The University of Victoria, Box 1700, Victoria, British Columbia, Canada V8W 2Y2. Contact: Editor. Magazine published 3 times/year covering poetry, fiction, drama, criticism. Circ.

800. Pays on acceptance. Byline given. Offers full kill fee. Buys one-time rights. Photocopied submissions OK. SASE (Canadian postage or IRC). Reports in 2 weeks on queries; 1 month on mss. Sample copy $5.
Nonfiction: Interview/profile (literary/artistic). Buys 6 mss/year. Send complete ms. Length: 1,000-5,000 words. Pays $30-150.
Photos: Pays $10-50 for b&w prints. Captions required.
Fiction: Buys 20 mss/year. Send complete ms. Length: 1,000-8,000 words. Pays $30-250.
Poetry: Avant-garde, free verse, traditional. Buys 100/year. Pays $12.50.

THE MASSACHUSETTS REVIEW, Memorial Hall, University of Massachusetts, Amherst MA 01003. (413)545-0111. Editors: John Hicks and Mary Heath. Quarterly. Buys first North American serial rights. Pays on publication. Reports in 3 months maximum. Mss will not be returned unless accompanied by a self-addressed stamped envelope. Sample copy for $4.
Nonfiction: Articles on literary criticism, women, public affairs, art, philosophy, music and dance. Average length: 6,500 words. Pays $50.
Fiction: Short stories or chapters from novels when suitable for independent publication. Length: 15-22 typed pages. Pays $50.
Poetry: 35¢/line or $10 minimum.

‡**THE MICROPSYCHOLOGY NEWSLETTER**, Microsphere Enterprises, 234 Fifth Ave., New York NY 10001. (212)462-8573. Editor: Joan Virzera. Monthly literary and psychological newsletter for laypeople and professionals. Estab. 1981. Circ. 1,000. Pays on publication. Byline given. Offers 100% kill fee. Buys first North American serial rights and second serial rights. Submit seasonal/holiday material 3 months in advance. Simultaneous queries, and simultaneous, photocopied, and previously published submissions OK. Computer printout and disk submissions OK. SASE. Reports in 1 month. Sample copy $1; writer's guidelines for SASE.
Nonfiction: General interest, humor, inspirational, opinion, personal experience. "Nothing that does not conform to the theme—the importance of the seemingly trivial." Buys 100-200 mss/year. Send complete ms. Length: 2,000 words maximum. Pays variable rates and in contributor copies.
Fiction: Experimental, humorous, mainstream, novel excerpts, psychological fiction. "High quality, literary with an emphasis on the theme of the newsletter—the importance of the seemingly trivial." Buys 100-200 mss/year. Send complete ms. Length: 2,000 words maximum. Pays variable rates and in contributor copies.
Poetry: Avant-garde, free verse, haiku, light verse, traditional. Light verse and didactic poetry preferred. Buys 50-100 poems/year. No limit on number of poems submitted. Length: "short poems preferred."
Fillers: Short humor. Buys 50-100/year. Length: 500 words maximum. Pays variable rates and in contributor copies.
Tips: "Micropsychology is an area dealing with the importance of the seemingly trivial, such as minor irritations and daily frustrations that affect people on a level beyond awareness. A significant aspect of micropsychology is humor therapy—seeing problems with humor alleviates associated stress. I am looking for any well-written material conforming to this theme. Will not hesitate to publish never-published writers whose material is of high quality and applicable." No political or vulgar material.

MID-AMERICAN REVIEW, Dept. of English, Bowling Green State University, Bowling Green OH 43403. (419)372-2725. Editor: Robert Early. Semiannual literary magazine of "the highest quality fiction and poetry." Estab. 1981. Pays on publication. Byline given. Buys one-time rights. Do not query. Photocopied submissions OK. SASE. Reports in 2 months or less. Sample copy $4.50.
Fiction: William Osborn, fiction editor. Character-oriented, literary. Buys 10+ mss/year. Send complete ms. Pays $5/page.
Poetry: Mariann Hofer, poetry editor. Strong imagery, sense of concrete. Buys 60/year. Pays $5/page. Annual prize for best fiction, best poem.

‡**MSS MAGAZINE, founded by John Gardner**, SUNY Binghamton Foundation, SUNY Binghamton, Binghamton NY 13901. Editors: L.M. Rosenberg, Joanna Higgins. Managing Editor: Carol Fischler. Triquarterly magazine covering fiction, poetry, essays, illustrations. "We are looking for fiction, poetry and essays that are beautiful, thoughtful, and in some way moving. We especially want to support young and/or unpublished writers." Circ. 1,000. Pays on publication. Byline given. Buys one-time rights. Photocopied submissions OK. SASE. Sample copy $4; writer's guidelines for SASE.
Nonfiction: General interest, opinion, personal experience. "Nothing cheap or even faintly commercial." Buys 3 mss/year. Send complete ms. Pays $50-200.
Fiction: "We want wonderful fiction, not merely acceptable or publishable fiction." Buys 25 mss/year. Send

complete ms. Length: open. Pays $75-400.
Poetry: "Open to all magnificent possibilities. Nothing cheap, shoddy, sentimental, ill-made or commercial." Buys 60-100 poems/year. Submit maximum 6 poems. Length: open. Pays $25-100.

‡**THE NEW RENAISSANCE, An International Magazine of Ideas and Opinions, Emphasizing Literature and the Arts**, 9 Heath Road, Arlington MA 02174. Editor: Louise T. Reynolds. Biannual literary magazine covering literature, visual arts, ideas, opinions for general literate, sophisticated public. Circ. 1,300. Pays after publication. Buys all rights. Simultaneous queries and photocopied submissions OK. No computer printout or disk submissions. SASE. Reports in 7 weeks on queries; 7 months on mss. Sample copy $2.10.
Nonfiction: Interview/profile (literary/performing artists); opinion, literary/artistic essays. "We prefer expert opinion and/or documented non-fiction written in a style suitable for a literary magazine (i.e., *not* journalistic). Because we are a biannual, we prefer to have writers query us, with outlines, etc, and give a sample of their (published) writing." Buys 2-4 mss/year. Query with clips. Length: 14-35 pages. Pays $24-95.
Photos: State availability of photos with query letter or ms or send photos with accompanying query or ms. Pays $5-7 for 5x7 b&w prints. Captions, model release and identification of subjects required, if applicable. Buys one-time rights.
Fiction: Occasional fiction—experimental, well-crafted, serious. No "formula or plotted stories; no pulp and no woman's magazine fiction." Buys 4-10 mss/year. Send complete ms. Length: 2-35 pages. Pays $20-60.
Poetry: Stanwood Bolton, poetry editor. Avant-garde, free verse, light verse, traditional. No academic poetry; "we publish only occasional light verse; we do not want to see Hallmark Card 'verse' ". Submit maximum 6 average; 8 short, 3-4 long. Reports in 2-4 months. Buys 20-50 poems/year. Pays $10-27.
Tips: "Know your markets. We are bogged down with manuscripts that, had the writer any understanding of our publication, should have been directed elsewhere. *tnr* is a unique litmag and should be *carefully* perused. Careful reading of 1-2 issues will reveal that we have a classicist philosophy. Fiction and poetry open to freelancers. Writers most likely of breaking into *tnr* are serious writers, poets, those who feel 'compelled' to write. We don't want to see 'pop' writing, trendy writing or formula writing."

‡**THE NEW SOUTHERN LITERARY MESSENGER**, The Airplane Press, 302 S. Laurel St., Richmond VA 23220. (804)780-1244. Editor: Charles Lohmann. Managing Editor: Henry Challona. Quarterly literary tabloid featuring short stories, political satire and poetry for a generally young readership. Estab. 1981. Circ. 400. Pays on publication. Byline given. Offers $5 kill fee. Buys simultaneous rights (one reprint). Submit seasonal/holiday material 3 months in advance. Simultaneous queries and previously published submissions OK. SASE. Reports in 1 week on queries; 3 months on mss. Sample copy for $1, 6x9 SAE and 37¢ postage; writer's guidelines for 4x9 SAE and 1 first class stamp.
Fiction: Short prose, political satire. Avoid fantasy and science fiction. No formula short stories. Buys 16-20 mss/year. Query. Length: 500-3,000 words. Pays $5-10.
Poetry: Della Anderson, poetry editor. Buys 120 poems/year. Five or more poems are used per poet, per issue.

NIMROD, 2210 S. Main, Tulsa OK 74114. (918)583-1587. Editor: Francine Ringold. For readers and writers interested in good literature and art. Semiannual magazine; 120 (6x9) pages. Circ. 1,000. Acquires all rights. Byline given. Payment in contributor's copies and $5/page when funds are available. Photocopied submissions OK, but they must be very clear. No simultaneous submissions. Reports in 3 months. Query or submit complete ms. SASE.
Nonfiction: Interviews and essays. Buys 150 unsolicited mss/year. Length: open.
Fiction and Poetry: Experimental and mainstream fiction. Traditional forms of poetry; blank verse, free verse and avant-garde forms. "We are interested in quality and vigor. We often do special issues. Writers should watch for announced themes and/or query."
Tips: Recent article/story examples: "The Mind of Katherine Anne Porter"; and "The Salisburg Court Reporter" (Vol. 25, No. 1).

THE NORTH AMERICAN REVIEW, University of Northern Iowa, Cedar Falls IA 50614. (319)273-2681. Editor: Robley Wilson Jr. Quarterly. Circ. 4,000. Buys all rights for nonfiction and North American serial rights for fiction and poetry. Pays on publication. Sample copy $2. Familiarity with magazine helpful. Reports in 8-10 weeks. Query for nonfiction. SASE.
Nonfiction: No restrictions, but most nonfiction is commissioned by magazine. Rate of payment arranged.
Fiction: No restrictions; highest quality only. Length: open. Pays minimum $10/page. Fiction department closed (no manuscripts read) from April 1 to October 1. "We will not read any fiction mss between April 1, 1983 and October 1, 1984, thanks to a sizable backlog."
Poetry: Department Editor: Peter Cooley. No restrictions; highest quality only. Length: open. Pays 50¢/line minimum.

THE OHIO REVIEW, Ellis Hall, Ohio University, Athens OH 45701. (614)594-5889. Editor: Wayne Dodd. "A balanced, informed engagement of contemporary American letters, special emphasis on poetics." Published 3 times/year. Circ. 1,800. Rights acquired vary with author and material. Acquires all rights or first North American serial rights. Submit complete ms. Unsolicited material will be read only September-May. Reports in 6 to 8 weeks. Computer printout submissions OK. SASE.

Nonfiction, Fiction and Poetry: Buys essays of general intellectual and special literary appeal. Not interested in narrowly focused scholarly articles. Seeks writing that is marked by clarity, liveliness, and perspective. Interested in the best fiction and poetry. Buys 75 unsolicited mss/year. Pays minimum $5/page, plus copies.

Tips: "Make your query very brief, not gabby, one that describes some publishing history, but no extensive bibliographies."

ORBIS, The International Literary Magazine, 199 The Long Shoot, Nuneaton, Warwickshire, England CV11 6JQ. Tel. (0203)327440. Editor: Mike Shields. Quarterly magazine covering literature in English and other languages. Circ. 500 (in 30 countries). Pays on publication. Extra prizes totalling 50 pounds in each issue. Byline given. Buys first rights. Photocopied submissions OK. Computer printout and disk submissions OK. SAE and IRCs. Reports in 6 weeks. Sample copy $2.

Nonfiction: Literary criticism; how to write poetry; how to develop a literary work. "No excessively literary or academically pretentious work; keep it practical. Wild avant-garde or ultra-traditional work unlikely to be used." Buys few mss/year. "We reject more than 98% of work received for simple lack of space, so don't be disappointed." Send complete ms. Length: 1,200 words maximum. Pays 2 pounds.

Columns/Departments: Letters (not paid for); Past Master (not paid for) "poem from the past accompanied by about 100 words on 'why'. "; Poem in Progress (description of how a favorite poem was developed). Pays 2 pounds.

Fiction: "We are looking for short (1,200) pieces of original and interesting work; prose poems, mood pieces, short stories, etc. No 'magazine' or 'formula' fiction." Buys few mss/year. Send complete ms. Length: 1,200 words maximum. Pays 2 pounds.

Poetry: Free verse, light verse, traditional. "We do not specifically exclude any type of poetry, but we feel that there are far too many undistinguished haiku around, and will not publish the meaningless gobbledegook which has featured in many magazines recently. No unoriginal rhymed poetry. We are looking for original poems which communicate modern thought and expression and show an excellence of language. Length is not a major factor, but we cannot handle *very* long poems. We need American poetry; long poems; English dialect poems; translated poetry." Buys 250/year. Submit maximum 12 poems. Length: "over 100 lines may be difficult." Pays 2 pounds. US stamps cannot be used to return material from the UK; International Reply Coupons should be enclosed.

PARABOLA, 150 5th Ave., New York NY 10011. (212)924-0004. Executive Editor: Lorraine Kisly. Managing Editor: Gus Kiley. "Audience shares an interest in exploring the wisdom transmitted through myth and the great religious traditions." Quarterly magazine; 128 pages. Circ. 15,000. Buys all rights. Byline given. Pays on publication. Photocopied submissions OK. Manuscripts should be sent to the attention of the editors. SASE. Writer's guidelines for SASE.

Nonfiction: "We handle work from a wide range of perspectives, mostly related to myth or comparative religion. Don't be scholarly, don't footnote, don't be dry. We want fresh approaches to timeless subjects." Length: 5,000 words maximum. Buys 20 mss/year. Query. Pays $25-150.

Photos: Purchased with or without accompanying ms. No color. Pays $25.

Fiction: Prefers retellings of traditional stories, legends, myths. Length: 3,000 words maximum. Pays "negotiable rates."

Poetry: "Very little and only when theme-related."

THE PARIS REVIEW, 45-39 171st Place, Flushing NY 11358. Editor: George A. Plimpton. Quarterly. Buys all rights. Pays on publication. Address submissions to proper department and address. SASE.

Fiction: Study publication. No length limit. Pays up to $150. Makes award of $500 in annual fiction contest. Submit to 541 E. 72nd St., New York NY 10021.

Poetry: Study publication. Pays $10 to 25 lines; $15 to 50 lines; $25 to 100 lines; $50 thereafter. Poetry mss must be submitted to Jonathan Galassi at 541 E. 72nd St., New York NY 10021. SASE. Sample copy $6.

‡**PARTISAN REVIEW**, 121 Bay State Rd., Boston MA 02215. (617)353-4260. Editor: William Phillips. Executive Editor: Edith Kurzweil. Quarterly literary journal covering world literature, politics and contemporary culture for an intelligent public with emphasis on the arts and political/social commentary. Circ. 8,200. Pays on publication. Byline given. Photocopied submissions OK. No previously published submissions. SASE. Reports in 3 months. Sample copy $4; free writer's guidelines.

Nonfiction: Essays, book reviews. Buys 30-40 mss/year. Send complete ms. Pays $50-150.

Fiction: High quality, serious, contemporary fiction. No science fiction, mystery, confession, romantic, reli-

gious material. Buys 8-10 mss/year. Send complete ms. Pays $50-150.
Poetry: Buys 20/year. Submit maximum 6 poems. Pays $25.

‡**PERSONS MAGAZINE**, Box 3510, Hattiesburg MS 39403-3510. (601)545-2949. Managing Editor: Alec Clayton. Monthly arts and entertainment publication covering southern Mississippi (Jackson and Meridian to the Gulf Coast). Estab. 1982. Circ. 7,000. Pays on publication. Byline given. Buys first rights or second serial (reprint) rights. Simultaneous, photocopied, and previously published submissions OK. SASE. Reports in 2 months on mss. Sample copy for 9x12 SAE and 4 first class stamps; writer's guidelines for business size SAE and 1 first class stamp.
Fiction: Historical, humorous, mainstream, mystery, science fiction. "We publish one short story a month, usually with a Southern setting but not necessarily. We will publish only writers who reside in the southern states." No romance, western or erotic fiction. Send complete ms with SASE. Length: 2,000 words. Pays $25.
Tips: "We hope to soon be able to begin paying for book reviews, entertainment-related articles, and profiles of artists and musicians in southern Mississippi."

‡**PHANTASM, Literary Magazine**, Heidelberg Graphics, Box 3606W, Chico CA 95927. (916)342-6582. Editor: Larry S. Jackson. Magazine published infrequently (usually 2 times/year) covering literature/creative writing. "*Phantasm* is a multi-cultural literary magazine breaking the staid formats of traditional journals with a dash of western flavor and the dynamics of eclectism. Its audience is primarily educators, poets, writers and others interested in contemporary literature." Circ. 1,100. Pays on publication. Byline given. Buys one-time rights. Submit seasonal/holiday material 6 months in advance. No computer printout or disk submissions. SASE. Reports in 1 month on queries; 4 months on mss. Sample copy $3; writer's guidelines published in magazine.
Nonfiction: Interview/profile (poets and writers); current literary events, literary feature articles. Buys 8 mss/year. Send complete ms. Length: 500-1,800 words. Pays $2.
Photos: Send photos with accompanying query or ms. Reviews 5x7 b&w prints. Captions required.
Columns/Departments: Guest columnist—regarding contemporary literature movement or appealing to writers; book reviews; interviews. Buys 6/year. Send complete ms. Length: 800-1,500 words. Pays $2.
Fiction: Adventure, erotica, ethnic, fantasy, historical, humorous, mainstream, mystery, suspense, western. Buys 4 mss/year. Send complete ms. Length: 600-1,500 words. Pays $2.
Poetry: Phillip Hemenway, poetry editor. Avant-garde, free verse, traditional, translations. Buys 24/year. Submit maximum 5 poems. Pays $2.
Tips: Break in "by sending us your best work in congruence with the magazine's format." Feature articles, poetry, reviews open to freelancers.

PIG IRON MAGAZINE, Pig Iron Press, Box 237, Youngstown OH 44501. (216)744-2258. Editor-in-Chief: Jim Villani. Emphasizes literature/art for writers, artists and intelligent lay audience with bias towards social responsibility in the arts. Semiannual magazine. Circ. 1,500. Pays on publication. Buys one-time rights. Byline given. Submit seasonal/holiday material 4 months in advance of issue date. Photocopied and previously published submissions OK. SASE. Reports in 3 months. Sample copy $2.50; free writer's guidelines with SASE.
Nonfiction: General interest, interview, personal opinion, profile, political or alternative lifestyle/systems. Buys 3 mss/year. Query. Length: 8,000 words maximum. Pays $2/page minimum.
Photos: Submit photo material with accompanying query. Pays $2 minimum for 5x7 or 8x10 b&w glossy prints. Buys one-time rights.
Columns/Departments: Fascia: explores alternative lifestyles and systems. Buys 3 mss/year. Query. Pays $2. minimum.
Fiction: Rose Sayre, fiction editor. Fantasy, avant-garde, experimental, psychological fiction and science fiction. Buys 4-8 mss/issue. Submit complete ms. Length: 8,000 words maximum. Pays $2 minimum.
Poetry: Terry Murcko and George Peffer, poetry editors. Avant-garde and free verse. Buys 25-50/issue. Submit in batches of 10 or less. Length: open. Pays $2 minimum.
Tips: "Make query simple and direct. Send modest batches of material at frequent intervals (3-4 times per year). Let us see the range of your talent and interests by mixing up styles, subject matter. We are interested in modernistic, surreal, satirical, futuristic, political subjects."

PLOUGHSHARES, Box 529, Dept. M, Cambridge MA 02139. Editor: DeWitt Henry. For "readers of serious contemporary literature; students, educators, adult public." Quarterly magazine. Circ. 3,400. Rights purchased vary with author and material. Usually buys all rights or may buy first North American serial rights. Buys 25-50 unsolicited mss/year. Pays on publication. Sample copy $4. Photocopied submissions OK. No simultaneous submissions. Reports in 6 months. SASE.
Nonfiction, Poetry and Fiction: "Highest quality poetry, fiction, criticism." Interview and literary essays. Length: 5,000 words maximum. Pays $50. Reviews (assigned). Length: 500 words maximum. Pays $15. Fiction. Experimental and mainstream. Recent examples: Fiction from Dan Wakefield's issue (Vol. 7, No. 3&4).

Length: 300-6,000 words. Pays $5-50. Poetry. Buys traditional forms, blank verse, free verse, avant-garde forms. Length: open. Pays $10/poem.

PRAIRIE SCHOONER, Andrews Hall, University of Nebraska, Lincoln NE 68588. Editor: Hugh Luke. Quarterly. Usually acquires all rights, unless author specifies first serial rights only. Computer printout and disk submissions OK. Pays in copies of the magazine, offprints and prizes. Reports usually in 1-2 months. SASE.
Nonfiction: Uses 1 or 2 articles per issue. Subjects of literary or general interest. Does not print academic articles. Length: 5,000 words maximum.
Fiction: Uses several stories per issue.
Poetry: Uses 20-30 poems in each issue of the magazine. These may be on any subject, in any style. Occasional long poems are used, but the preference is for the shorter length. High quality necessary.

PRISM INTERNATIONAL, Department of Creative Writing, University of British Columbia, Vancouver, British Columbia, Canada V6T 1W5. Editor-in-Chief: Richard Stevenson. Managing Editor: Winowna Kent. Emphasizes contemporary literature, including translations. For university and public libraries, and private subscribers. Quarterly magazine. Circ. 1,000. Pays on publication. Buys first North American serial rights. Photocopied submissions OK. SASE and International Reply Coupons. Reports in 10 weeks. Sample copy $4.
Fiction: Experimental and traditional. Buys 5 mss/issue. Send complete ms. Length: 5,000 words maximum. Pays $15/printed page and 1 yr. subscription.
Poetry: Avant-garde and traditional. Buys 30 poems/issue. Limit submissions to batches of 6. Pays $15/printed page and 1 yr. subscription.
Drama: 1-Acts preferred. Pays $15/printed page and 1 yr. subscription.

PULPSMITH, 5 Beekman St., New York, NY 10038. Editor: Harry Smith. Managing Editor: Tom Tolnay. Roving Editor: Sidney Bernard. Digest-sized pulp-paper, four-color cover magazine that "turns a good read into a genre." Quarterly magazine. Estab. 1981. Circ. 10,000. Pays on acceptance. Byline given. Buys 150 mss/year. Buys first North American serial rights and second serial (reprint) rights. Reports in 2 months. Sample copy $1.50. SASE.
Nonfiction: Timely, topical, speculative articles on phenomena today and tomorrow—religion, sciences, sports, social, political, crime, medicine. Science Editor: Schmael Prager. Shorter pieces have better chance, but fine longer pieces may be bought. Pays $25-100.
Fiction: Special interest in stories within traditional genres—detective, science fiction, ghost, western, fantasy—but of a literary quality with strong story value: a good read. "True Story" page seeks fiction-like actual experiences, with strong flavor and lively style. Pays $25-100.
Poetry: Special interest in "story poems," with long ballads and short lyric poems of popular interest and style. Pays $5-25 (higher for longer ballads).

QUARRY, Quarry Press, Box 1061, Kingston, Ontario, Canada K7L 4Y5. (613)544-5400, ext. 165. Editor: David John Schleich. Quarterly magazine covering poetry, prose, reviews. "We seek high quality, new writers, who are aware of their genre and who are committed to their art." Circ. 1,500. Pays on publication. Byline given. Buys first North American serial rights. Simultaneous queries and photocopied submissions OK. Computer printout submission OK; prefers letter quality to dot matrix. SASE. Reports in 3 weeks on queries; 3 months on mss. Sample copy $3; writer's guidelines for business size SAE and 34¢ postage.
Nonfiction: Short stories, poetry and book reviews. "We need book reviews of Canadian work. Not interested in reviews of American or UK books. No literary criticism." Buys 100 mss/year. Send complete ms. Length: open. Pays $10/page plus one year subscription.
Fiction: Ethnic, experimental, fantasy, science fiction. "No non-literary fiction." Buys 3 mss/year. Send complete ms. Length: 10-15 pages maximum. Pays $5-10/page.
Poetry: Avant-garde, free verse, haiku, light verse, traditional. "No amateur, derivative poetry." Buys 200/year. Submit maximum 10 poems. Length: open. Pays $5-10/page.

QUEEN'S QUARTERLY, A Canadian Review, Queen's University, Kingston, Ontario, Canada K7L 3N6. (613)547-6968. Editor: Dr. Michael Fox. Quarterly magazine covering a wide variety of subjects, including: science, humanities, arts and letters, politics, and history for the educated reader. Circ. 1,900. Pays on publication. Byline given. Buys first North American serial rights. Photocopied submissions OK. Computer printout submissions OK. SASE. Reports in 2 weeks on queries; 2-3 months on mss. Sample copy $3.50; free writer's guidelines.
Fiction: Fantasy, historical, humorous, mainstream, science fiction. Buys 4-6 mss/year. Send complete ms. Length: 5,000 words maximum. Pays $25-100.
Poetry: Avant-garde, free verse, haiku, light verse, traditional. No "sentimental, religious, or first efforts by unpublished writers." Buys 25/year. Submit maximum 6 poems. Length: open. Pays $10-25.
Tips: "Poetry and fiction most open to freelancers. Include curriculum vita and brief description of what's

unique about the submission. Don't send less than the best.'' No multiple submissions. No more than 6 poems or 1 story per submission.

‡**READER'S CHOICE, Canada's Short Story Magazine**, Box 205, Station S, Toronto, Ontario, Canada M5M 4L7. (416)783-7028. Editor: Amalia Lindal. Quarterly magazine of quality short stories for mass "middle-brow" adult readers. Estab. 1982. Pays on publication. Byline given. Buys first North American serial rights. Photocopied submissions OK. SAE and IRC or Canadian postage. Reports in 2 months. Sample copy for $3 and SAE with 65¢ Canadian postage or IRC; writer's guidelines for SAE and 35¢ Canadian postage or IRC.

Fiction: Mainstream. "We are interested in contemporary stories with people who are interesting enough for our sympathy (i.e. we like them) and identification ("It could be me!"), who face a universal crisis or turning point in their lives (i.e. the kind of crisis everyone meets sooner or later). The hero/heroine must experience the crisis and emerge with a changed attitude/resolution/insight about himself or the circumstances. On finishing this absorbing story, our reader must feel he has learned something of value about coping with life or people that he didn't know or realize before. The reader, as well as the chief character, must grow." No novel excerpts or short novels. Buys 40 mss/year. Send complete ms. Length: 700-5,000 words. Pays $20-100 (about $10/printed page).

Poetry: Free verse, traditional, "those poems understood by people who seldom read poetry." Buys 16/year. Submit maximum 5 poems. Length: 8-16 lines. Pays in 2 copies.

‡**RIVER STYX MAGAZINE**, Big River Association, 7420 Cornell, St. Louis MO 63130. (314)725-0602. Editor: Jan Garden Castro. Biannual, multicultural literary magazine of contemporary prose, poetry, photography and art. Circ. 1,500. Pays on publication. Byline given. Buys first rights to publication. Submit only in October 1984 and annually in October thereafter. Reports in November. SASE. Sample copy $3.50; writer's guidelines for SASE.

Photos: "We use photos without manuscripts." Send photos and SASE in October. Pays $10 for 8x10 b&w prints. Buys one-time rights.

Fiction: Ethnic, experimental. Buys 3-4 mss/year. Query. Pays $8/page, $100 maximum.

Poetry: Avant-garde, free verse, traditional. Submit only in October 1984 and annually in October thereafter, poems international in scope. Buys 20-50 poems/year. Submit maximum 5 poems. Length: open. Pays $8/page, $100 maximum.

Tips: "Read issue #11 and #13; submit only if your work is compatible with contents and exceptional on its own terms."

‡**ROADWERK, A Journal of Travel Art**, On The Move Press, 1100 Masonic, #5, San Francisco CA 94117. (415)558-8316. Editor: James F. Prchlik. Quarterly magazine specializing in travel art "from the vagabond's, or low-budget traveler's perspective." Estab. 1982. Circ. 300. Pays on publication. Byline given. Buys one-time rights. Submit seasonal/holiday material 2 months in advance. Photocopied and previously published submissions OK. SASE. Reports in 3 weeks on queries; 2 months on mss. Sample copy for $2.50, 9x12 SAE and 50¢ postage; writer's guidelines for business-size SAE and 1 first class stamp.

Nonfiction: Personal experience, photo feature, travel and international politics from a travel perspective. Query. Length: 100-1,000 words. Pays $10 maximum.

Photos: State availability of photos. "Must be travel-related." Pays $5 for 3x5 b&w prints.

Columns/Departments: Travel Art, State of International Politics. Send complete ms. Length: 100-1,000 words. Pays $10 maximum.

Fiction: Adventure, ethnic, historical, novel excerpts—"anything dealing with travel." No pornography. Send complete ms. Length: 100-1,000 words. Pays $10 maximum.

Poetry: Avant-garde, free verse, haiku, light verse, traditional. Submit maximum 5 poems. Length: 5-100 lines. Pays $10 maximum.

Fillers: Clippings, anecdotes, newsbreaks. Length: 50-500 words. Pays $10 maximum.

SECOND COMING, Box 31249, San Francisco CA 94131. Editor-in-Chief: A.D. Winans. Semiannual magazine. Circ. 1,000. Pays in copies. Acquires one-time rights. Query first with an "honest statement of credits." No computer printout or disk submissions. SASE. Reports in 1-4 weeks. Sample copy $2.50.

Fiction: Experimental (avant-garde) and humorous. Uses 6-12 mss/year. Submit complete ms. Recent example: Article on fiction in the US (Vol. 10, No. 122). Length: 1,000-3,000 words. Pays in copies.

Poetry: Avant-garde, free verse, and surrealism. Uses 100-150/year. Limit submissions to batches of 6. No length requirement. Pays in copies.

Photos: Pays $5 token plus copies for b&w photos.

Tips: "We publish mostly veterans of the small press scene. Read at least 2 back issues."

SEWANEE REVIEW, University of the South, Sewanee TN 37375. (615)598-5931. Editor: George Core. For audience of "variable ages and locations, mostly college-educated and with interest in literature." Quarterly. Circ. 3,400. Buys all serial rights. Pays on publication. Sample copy $4.75. Returns in 4-6 weeks. No computer printout or disk submissions. SASE.

Nonfiction and Fiction: Short fiction (but not drama); essays of critical nature on literary subjects (especially modern British and American literature); essay-reviews and reviews (books and reviewers selected by the editors). Payment varies: averages $10 per printed page.

Poetry: Selections of 4 to 6 poems preferred. In general, light verse and translations are not acceptable. Maximum payment is 60¢ per line.

THE SOUTHERN REVIEW, Allen 43, Louisiana State University, Baton Rouge LA 70803. (504)388-5108. Editors: Donald E. Stanford and Lewis P. Simpson. For academic, professional, literary, intellectual audience. Quarterly. Circ. 3,000. Buys first rights. Byline given. Pays on publication. Sample copy $2. No queries. Reports in 2 to 3 months. SASE.

Nonfiction: Essays; careful attention to craftsmanship and technique and to seriousness of subject matter. "Willing to publish experimental writing if it has a valid artistic purpose. Avoid extremism and sensationalism. Essays exhibit thoughtful and sometimes severe awareness of the necessity of literary standards in our time." Emphasis on contemporary literature, especially Southern culture and history. Minimum number of footnotes. Buys 80-100 mss/year. Length: 4,000-10,000 words. Pays 3¢/word minimum. Pays $12/page for prose.

Fiction and Poetry: Short stories of lasting literary merit, with emphasis on style and technique. Length: 4,000-8,000 words. Pays minimum of 3¢/word. Pays $20/page for poetry.

SOUTHWEST REVIEW, Southern Methodist University, Dallas TX 75275. (214)692-2263. Advisory Editor: Margaret L. Hartley. Editor: Charlotte T. Whaley. For adults and college graduates with literary interests and some interest in the Southwest, but subscribers are from all over America and some foreign countries. Quarterly magazine. Circ. 1,200. Buys all rights. Byline given. Buys 65 mss/year. Pays on publication. Sample copy $1. Query for nonfiction. Submit only complete ms for fiction and poetry. Reports in 3 months. SASE.

Nonfiction and Photos: "Articles, literary criticism, social and political problems, history (especially Southwestern), folklore (especially Southwestern), the arts, etc. Articles should be appropriate for a literary quarterly; no feature stories. Critical articles should consider a writer's whole body of work, not just one book. History should use new primary sources or a new perspective, not syntheses of old material. We're regional but not provincial." Interviews with writers, historical articles, and book reviews of scholarly nonfiction. Length: 1,500-5,000 words. Pays ½¢/word. Regular columns are Regional Sketchbook (Southwestern) and Points of View (personal essays). Uses b&w photos for cover and occasional photo essays.

Fiction: No limitations on subject matter for fiction. Prefer stories of character development, of psychological penetration, rather than those depending chiefly on plot. Some experimental fiction, and mainstream fiction. Length: 1,500-5,000 words. Pays ½¢/word. The John H. McGinnis Memorial Award of $1,000 is made in alternate years for fiction and nonfiction pieces published in *SWR*.

Poetry: No limitations on subject matter. Not particularly interested in broadly humorous, religious, or sentimental poetry. Free verse, some avant-garde forms, and open to all serious forms of poetry. Length: 18 lines or shorter preferred. Pays $5 per poem. The Elizabeth Matchett Stover Memorial Award of $100 is made annually for a poem published in *SWR*.

‡**THE SPIRIT THAT MOVES US**, The Spirit That Moves Us Press, Inc., Box 1585-W, Iowa City IA 52244. (319)338-5569. Editor: Morty Sklar. Semiannual literary magazine of poetry, fiction, artwork. "We prefer work which is concerned with life and living. We don't like sensational or academic writing." Circ. 800-1,500. Pays on publication. Byline given. Buys first North American serial rights. Simultaneous queries and photocopied and previously published submissions OK for some anthologies. SASE. Reports in 1 week on queries; 1 month on mss. Sample copy for $3 and SAE; writer's guidelines for SAE and 1 first class stamp.

Photos: Morty Sklar, photo editor. "Photographs which capture a sense of life, either in mood or energy." Send photos with ms. Pays $5-10 for 4x5 and larger b&w prints. Also pays in copies. Buys one-time rights.

Poetry: Free verse, avant-garde, haiku, traditional. No skilled work without heart. Buys 25-50 poems/year. Submit maximum 5 poems. Length: open. Pays $5-10; also pays in copies.

Fiction: Ethnic, experimental, humorous, mainstream, novel excerpts, science fiction; "anything goes as long as it shows concern for life and living and is well-written. No sensational or academic material (work which is skillfully written but has little human involvement)." Buys 4-20 mss/year. Send complete ms. Length: open. Pays $10-25 and copies.

Tips: "In 1984, write first for our needs. Include SASE for reply."

‡**STAND**, Stand USA, 45 Old Peterborough Rd., Jaffrey NH 03452. Editors: Jon Silkin, Lorna Tracy, Michael Blackburn, Brendan Cleary, J. Kates. Managing Editor: Philip Bomford. International quarterly literary magazine of poetry, fiction, essays and reviews. "We are interested in literature 'in the world' rather than self-referential exercises." Circ. 6,000. Pays on publication. Byline given. Buys first North American serial

rights, one-time rights and United Kingdom serial rights. Photocopied submissions OK. SASE. Reports in 1 week to 6 months. Sample copy $3.

Nonfiction: Interview/profile (literary); opinion (political, literary). Buys 3-4 mss/year. Send complete ms. Length: 8,000 words maximum. Pays $25/1,000 words.

Fiction: Experimental, mainstream. No poorly-written material. Buys 10 mss/year. "However, as we are just winding up an extensive short-story contest, it is likely that our need for fiction will be satisfied for six months or more." Send complete ms. Length: 8,000 words maximum. Pays $25/1,000 words.

Poetry: "We do not restrict by 'type'; no workshop exercises, cocktail party chatter, journal entries." Buys 50 poems/year. Submit maximum 5 poems. Length: open. Pays $25/poem or page of verse.

Tips: "We read all submissions. We solicit material only for special issues. A writer can break in by writing well. Familiarity with the magazine is the potential writer's best guideline. Write for sample copies if you can't find them."

‡**TELESCOPE**, The Galileo Press, Box 16129, Baltimore MD 21218. (301)366-7326. Editors: Jack Stephens and Julia Wendell. Triannual literary journal of poetry, fiction, essays, book reviews, interviews and graphics. Estab. 1981. Circ. 500. Pays on acceptance. No byline given. Makes work-for-hire assignments. Photocopied submissions OK. SASE. Reports in 1 week on queries; 2 months on mss. Sample copy $2; writer's guidelines for SAE and 20¢ postage.

Nonfiction: Interview/profile, personal experience, literary criticism. Special issues include Art in the Atomic Age and Cinema's Influence on Literature. Buys 10 mss/year. Send complete ms. Length: open. Pays $3/page.

Photos: Jill Francis, photo editor. Send photos with ms. Reviews transparencies.

Fiction: Experimental, novel excerpts, science fiction, "sensitive and intelligent fiction." Buys 10 mss/year. Send complete ms. Length: open. Pays $3/page.

Poetry: Buys 75/year. Submit maximum 10 poems. Length: open. Pays 50¢/line.

TRI-QUARTERLY, 1735 Benson Ave., Northwestern University, Evanston IL 60201. (312)492-3490. Editor: Reginald Gibbons. Published 3 times/year. Publishes fiction, poetry, and essays, as well as artwork. Computer printout submissions OK; prefers letter quality to dot matrix. Buys first serial rights and non-exclusive reprint rights. Reports in 6 weeks. Pays on publication. Study magazine before submitting; enclose SASE.

Nonfiction: Query before sending essays (no scholarly or critical essays, except in special issues).

Fiction and Poetry: No prejudice against style or length of work; only seriousness and excellence are required. Buys 20-50 unsolicited mss/year.

UNDINAL SONGS, The Only International Magazine Focusing on Necrophilia and Vampirism in Modern Literature, Box 70, Oakdale NY 11769. (516)589-8715. Editors: Leilah Wendell and Kiel Stuart. Quarterly magazine. "We deal in literature whose basic concept is merging the spectres of love and death in a macabre vein." Circ. 2,000. Pays on publication. Byline given. Offers negotiable kill fee. Buys first North American serial rights. Submit seasonal/holiday material 2 months in advance. Simultaneous queries, and simultaneous, photocopied, and previously published (if so notified) submissions OK. Computer printout and disk submissions OK; prefers letter quality to dot matrix printouts. SASE. Reports in 2 weeks on queries; 3 weeks on mss. Sample copy $2.50; writer's guidelines for SAE and 1 first class stamp.

Nonfiction: Personal experience (encounters with a personified Death or a necrophilic experience that you would care to share with readers); any bits and pieces of weird or offbeat experiences, organizations or news clippings. Special issues include Annual Poetry and Graphics Contests, deadline March 1, 1984. SASE for rules. Cash awards plus publication. No science fiction, media parody or ideas that have been overdone before. Buys 12 mss/year. Send complete ms. Length: 10 pages maximum. Pays in copies or $2 maximum.

Columns/Departments: Reviews of small press books and magazines in the fantasy/horror/weird genre—fair reviews, no outright panning without at least giving credit for attempted effort. Buys 12 mss/year. Send complete ms. Length: 130 words maximum. Pays in copies.

Fiction: Macabre fantasy with a 19th Century gothic slant; Victorian weird tales; experimental (parables in the style of Edgar A. Poe); fantasy (macabre, weird); horror (all types); romance (from the viewpoint of a necrophile). "Open to many ideas, please query." No science fiction, no fiction with children as the centeral characters; no work with an overabundance of erotica. Buys 8 mss/year. Send complete ms. Length: 10 pages maximum. Pays in copies or cash. Query.

Poetry: Emotive free verse, traditional, rhyming or narrative. "Really prefer rhyming and metrically accurate work." No work with four letter words or work that is merely a run-on type of poem, limericks, blank verse or work that views death in a sorrowful light. Buys 120/year. Length: 70 lines maximum. Pays in copies or $2 maximum.

Tips: "We tend to portray a personified Death or more concretely, works that show Death as a lover. We stress the truly eerie side of human emotion and would love to see work that incorporates love in any macabre form. Be explicit without being pornographic."

UNIVERSITY OF WINDSOR REVIEW, Windsor, Ontario, Canada N9B 3P4 (519)253-4232. Editor: Eugene McNamara. For "the literate layman, the old common reader." Biannual. Circ. 300 plus. Acquires first North American serial rights. Accepts 50 mss/year. Sample copy $5 plus postage. Follow *MLA Style Sheet*. Reports in 4 to 6 weeks. Enclose SAE and International Reply Coupons.
Nonfiction and Photos: "We publish articles on literature, history, social science, etc. I think we reflect competently the Canadian intellectual scene, and are equally receptive to contributions from outside the country; I think we are good and are trying to get better." Length: about 6,000 words. Pays $25. For photos, please inquire to Evelyn McLean.
Fiction: Department Editor: Alistair MacLeod. Publishes mainstream prose with open attitude toward themes. Length: 2,000-6,000 words. Pays $25.
Poetry: Department Editor: John Ditsky. Accepts traditional forms, blank verse, free verse, and avant-garde forms. No epics. Pays $10.

THE VIRGINIA QUARTERLY REVIEW, 1 W. Range, Charlottesville VA 22903. (804)924-3124. Editor: Staige Blackford. Quarterly. Pays on publication. Reports in 4 weeks. No computer printout or disk submissions. SASE.
Nonfiction: Articles on current problems, economic, historical; literary essays. Length: 3,000-6,000 words. Byline given. Pays $10/345-word page.
Fiction: Good short stories, conventional or experimental. Length: 2,000-7,000 words. Pays $10/350-word page. Prizes offered for best short stories and poems published in a calendar year.
Poetry: Generally publishes 15 pages of poetry in each issue. No length or subject restrictions. Pays $1/line.
Tips: Prefers not to see pornography, science fiction, or fantasy.

WASCANA REVIEW, University of Regina, Saskatchewan, Canada. Editor-in-Chief: J. Chamberlain. Emphasizes literature and the arts for readers interested in serious poetry, fiction and scholarship. Semiannual magazine. Circ. 300. Pays on publication. Buys all rights. Photocopied submissions OK. SAE and International Reply Coupons. Reports in 6-8 weeks.
Nonfiction: Literary criticism and scholarship in the field of English, American, Canadian, French or German literature and drama; reviews of current books (2,000-6,000 words). Buys 65-70 unsolicited mss/year. Send complete ms. Pays $3-4/page.
Fiction: Quality fiction with an honest, meaningful grasp of human experience. Any form. Buys 2-5 mss/issue. Send complete ms. Length: 2,000-6,000 words. Pays $3/page.
Poetry: Avant-garde, free verse, haiku, light verse and traditional. Buys 10-15 poems/issue. Length: 2-100 lines. Pays $10/page.

WESTERN HUMANITIES REVIEW, University of Utah, Salt Lake City UT 84112. (801)581-7438. Editor-in-Chief: Jack Garlington. For educated readers. Quarterly magazine. Circ. 1,000. Pays on acceptance. Buys all rights. Phone queries OK. Simultaneous and photocopied submissions OK. Computer printout submissions OK. SASE. Reports in 4 weeks.
Nonfiction: Authoritative, readable articles on literature, art, philosophy, current events, history, religion, anything in the humanities. Interdisciplinary articles encouraged. Departments on film and books. "We commission book reviews." Buys 40 unsolicited mss/year. Recent article example: "Mixed Drama: Tragedy, Comedy or Whatever" (Spring 1982). Pays $50-150.
Fiction: Any type or theme. Recent short story example: "Home Economics," (Winter 1982). Buys 2 mss/issue. Send complete ms. Pays $25-150.
Poetry: Avant-garde; free verse and traditional. "We seek freshness and significance." Buys 5-10 poems/issue. Pays $50.
Tips: Do not send poetry without having a look at the magazine first.

WOMEN ARTISTS NEWS, Midmarch Associates, Box 3304 Grand Central Station, New York NY 10163. Editor: Rena Hansen. For "artists and art historians, museum and gallery personnel, students, teachers, crafts personnel, art critics, writers." Bimonthly magazine. Circ. 5,000. "Token payment as funding permits." Byline given. Submit seasonal material 1-2 months in advance. SASE. Reports in 1 month. $2.50 for sample copy.
Nonfiction: Features; informational; historical; interview; opinion; personal experience; photo feature; and technical. Query or submit complete ms. Length: 500-2,500 words.
Photos: Used with or without accompanying ms. Captions required. Query or submit contact sheet or prints. Pays $5 for 5x7 b&w prints when money is available.

THE YALE REVIEW, 1902A Yale Station, New Haven CT 06520. Editor: Kai T. Erikson. Managing Editor: Penelope Laurans. Buys first North American rights. Pays on publication. SASE.
Nonfiction and Fiction: Authoritative discussions of politics, literature and the arts. Pays $75-100. Buys quality fiction. Length: 3,000-5,000 words. Pays $75-100.

Men's

ADAM, Publishers Service, Inc., 8060 Melrose Ave., Los Angeles CA 90046. For the adult male. General subject: "Human sexuality in contemporary society." Monthly. Circ. 500,000. Buys first North American serial rights. Occasionally overstocked. Pays on publication. Writer's guidelines for SASE. Reports in 6 weeks, but occasionally may take longer. SASE.
Nonfiction: "On articles, please query first. We like hard sex articles, but research must be thorough." Length: 2,500 words. Pays $100-200.
Photos: All submissions must contain model release including parent's signature if under 21; fact sheet giving information about the model, place or activity being photographed, including all information of help in writing a photo story, and SASE. Photo payment varies, depending upon amount of space used by photo set.

‡BRITCHES, A Man's Catalog, Kearns Productions, Inc., Suite 304, 610 22nd St., San Francisco CA 94107. (415)864-5858. Editor: Michael J. Kearns. Quarterly men's fashion and lifestyle magazine—going bimonthly in 1984. Estab. 1982. Circ. 25,000. Pays on acceptance. Byline given. Buys one-time rights and "media kit reprint" rights. Simultaneous queries and simultaneous submissions OK. SASE. Reports in 1 month. Free sample copy.
Nonfiction: Expose, historical/nostalgic, how-to, humor, interview/profile, new product, technical, travel. Buys 24-30 mss/year. Query with published clips. Length: 1,000-6,000 words. Pays $50-400.
Photos: State availability of photos. Reviews contact sheets. Model release required. Buys one-time rights.
Fiction: Condensed novels, ethnic, fantasy, humorous, science fiction, suspense. Buys 10 mss/year. Query with clips of published work. Length: 1,000-5,000 words. Pays $100-400 (or more).
Poetry: Avant-garde and traditional. Buys "very few" poems/year. Submit maximum 3 poems. Length: open. Pays negotiable rates.
Fillers: Clippings, jokes, gags, short humor, newsbreaks. Buys "few" fillers/year. Length: open. Pays negotiable rates.
Tips: "Be sophisticated, light, witty, and personal. We're most open to profiles, interviews, sports and music subjects."

CAVALIER, Suite 204, 2355 Salzedo St., Coral Gables FL 33134. (305)443-2370. Editor: Douglas Allen. For "young males, 18-29, 80% college graduates, affluent, intelligent, interested in current events, ecology, sports, adventure, travel, clothing, good fiction." Monthly. Circ. 250,000. Buys first rights. Byline given. Buys 44 or more mss/year. Pays on publication or before. See past issues for general approach to take. Submit seasonal material at least 3 months in advance. Reports in 3 weeks. Computer printout and disk submissions OK "but no multiple submissions"; prefers letter quality to dot matrix printouts. SASE.
Nonfiction: Personal experience, interviews, humor, think pieces, expose and new product. "Frank—open to dealing with controversial issues." No material on Women's Lib, water sports, hunting, homosexuality or travel, "unless it's something spectacular or special." Query. Length: 2,800-3,500 words. Pays maximum $500 with photos.
Photos: Photos purchased with mss or with captions. No cheesecake.
Fiction: Department Editor: Nye Willden. Mystery, science fiction, humorous, adventure, contemporary problems "with at least one explicit sex scene per story. Very interested in female fighting." Send complete ms. Length: 2,500-3,500 words. Pays $250 maximum, "higher for special."
Tips: "Our greatest interest is in originality—new ideas, new approaches; no tired, overdone stories—both feature and fiction. We do not deal in 'hack' sensationalism but in high-quality pieces. Keep in mind the intelligent 18- to 29-year-old male reader. We will be putting more emphasis in articles and fiction on sexual themes. Serious articles, not hack sexual pornography—fiction can be very far out."

‡CHERI MAGAZINE, The All-True Sex News Magazine, 215 Lexington Ave., New York NY 10016. (212)686-9866. Editor: C.B. Lucci. Monthly erotic men's magazine for predominantly blue-collar audience aged 18-40. Circ. 750,000. Pays on publication. Byline given. Offers variable kill fee. Buys first North American serial rights and second serial (reprint) rights; makes work-for-hire assignments. Submit seasonal/holiday material 6 months in advance. Simultaneous queries, and simultaneous, photocopied and previously published submissions OK. SASE. Reports in 5 weeks on queries; 7 weeks on mss. Sample copy $2.95; writer's guidelines for business-size SAE.
Nonfiction: Jim Russell, articles editor. Book excerpts (adult-oriented); expose; general interest; historical/nostalgic (adult-oriented); how-to (adult-oriented); humor; interview/profile; new product (adult-oriented); personal experience; and photo feature. "We can't use any political expose-type stories, nor are we interested in 'my first blow job' features. Also, no S&M, fringe-sex subjects, straight sex material or personal experience." Buys 10 mss/year. Query or send complete ms. Length: 1,800-2,400 words. Pays $300-500.
Photos: Peter Hurd, photo editor. Send photos with ms. Pays variable rates for 35mm color transparencies.

Model release and identification of subjects required. Buys one-time rights.

Tips: "We're open to nearly all types of non-fiction material—writers needn't be intimidated by our highly-erotic nature and assume that we're only looking for sex stories. We're open to photo-oriented stories on new happenings in adult entertainment for the front half of our book. Articles as described above needn't be of an adult nature."

CHIC MAGAZINE, Larry Flynt Publications, 2029 Century Park E., Suite 3800, Los Angeles CA 90067. Articles Editor: Richard Warren Lewis. For men, 20-35 years old, college-educated and interested in current affairs, entertainment and sports. Monthly magazine. Circ. 250,000. Pays 1 month after acceptance. Buys exclusive English and English translation world-wide magazine rights. Pays 20% kill fee. Byline given unless writer requests otherwise. No computer printout or disk submissions. SASE. Reports in 2 months.

Nonfiction: Expose (national interest only); interview (personalities in news and entertainment); celebrity profiles. Buys 24 mss/year. Query. Length: 5,000 words. Pays $500.

Columns/Departments: Dope, Sex Life. Pays $300. Odds and Ends (front of the book shorts; study the publication first). Pays $50. Length: 100-300 words. Close Up (short Q&As) columns. Length: 1,000 words. Pays $200.

Fiction: Ted Newsom, fiction editor. Erotic, strongly plotted. Buys 12 mss/year. Send complete ms. Length: 3,500 words. Pays $300.

Tips: Prefers not to get humorous material.

ESQUIRE, 2 Park Ave., New York NY 10016. Executive Editor: Priscilla Flood. Editor: Phillip Moffitt. Monthly. Usually buys first serial rights. Pays on acceptance. Reports in 3 weeks. "We depend chiefly on solicited contributions and material from literary agencies. Unable to accept responsibility for unsolicited material." Query. SASE.

Nonfiction: Articles vary in length, but features usually average 3,000-7,000 words. Articles should be slanted for sophisticated, intelligent readers; however, not highbrow in the restrictive sense. Wide range of subject matter. Rates run roughly between $300 and $3,000, depending on length, quality, etc. Expenses are allowed, depending on the assignment.

Photos: Art Director, Robert Priest. Buys first periodical publication rights. Payment depends on how photo is used, but rates are roughly $300 for b&w; $500-750 for color. Guarantee on acceptance. Gives assignments and pays expenses.

Fiction: Rust Hills, Fiction Editor. "Literary excellence is our only criterion." Length: about 1,000-6,000 words. Payment: $350-1,500.

GALLERY, Montcalm Publishing Corp., 800 2nd Ave., New York NY 10017. (212)986-9600. Publisher: Leon Garry. Editor-in-Chief: John Bensink. Managing Editor: Marc Lichter. Design Director: Michael Monte. Monthly magazine "focusing on features of interest to the young American man." Circ. 700,000. Pays 50% on acceptance, 50% on publication. Buys first North American serial rights or will make assignments on a work-for-hire basis. Pays 25% kill fee. Byline given. Submit seasonal/holiday material 6 months in advance. Photocopied submissions OK. SASE. Reports in 1 month on queries; in 6 weeks on mss. Sample copy $3.25 plus $1.75 postage and handling.

Nonfiction: Investigative pieces, general interest, how-to, humor, interview, new products and profile. "We *do not* want to see articles on pornography." Buys 6-8 mss/issue. Query or send complete mss. Length: 1,000-6,000 words. Pays $200-1,000. "Special prices negotiated."

Photos: Send photos with accompanying mss. Pay varies for b&w contact sheets or color contact sheets and negatives. Buys one-time rights. Captions preferred; model release required.

Fiction: Adventure, erotica, experimental, humorous, mainstream, mystery and suspense. Buys 1 ms/issue. Send complete ms. Length: 500-3,000 words. Pays $250-750.

GENESIS MAGAZINE, 770 Lexington Ave., New York NY 10021. Editor: Joseph J. Kelleher. Monthly magazine. Circ. 600,000. Query. Reports in 8 weeks. SASE.

Nonfiction: Articles about serious, contemporary isssues; how-to-live-better service features; humor; celebrity interviews; features about young successful men on the rise; comment on contemporary relationships.

Photos: Photo essays of beautiful women.

GENT, Suite 204, 2355 Salzedo St., Coral Gables FL 33134. (305)443-2378. Editor: John C. Fox. Monthly magazine "for men from every strata of society." Circ. 200,000. Buys first North American serial rights. Byline given. Pays on publication. Submit complete fiction ms. Query first on non-fiction. Reports in 3-6 weeks. SASE.

Nonfiction: Looking for traditional men's subjects (cars, racing, outdoor adventure, science, gambling, etc.) as well as sex-related topics. Length: 1,500-2,500 words. Buys 70 mss/year. Pays $100-200.

Photos: B&w and color photos purchased with mss. Captions (preferred). Length: 100 words.

Fiction: Erotic. "Stories should contain a huge-breasted female character as this type of model is *Gent*'s main focus. And this character's endowments should be described in detail in the course of the story. Some of our stories also emphasize sexy, chubby women, pregnant women and their male admirers.'' Length: 1,500-3,000 words. Pays $100-200.

GENTLEMAN'S COMPANION, Larry Flynt Publications, Suite 3800, 2029 Century Park E., Los Angeles CA 90067. (213)556-9200. Managing Editor: John D. Brancato. Monthly men's magazine. Estab. 1980. Pays on acceptance. Byline given. Buys all rights. Submit seasonal/holiday material 3 months in advance. Simultaneous, photocopied, and previously published submissions OK. SASE. Reports in 1 month on queries. Writer's guidelines furnished upon request.
Nonfiction: James Gregory, articles editor. "We are looking for hard-hitting, investigative reports on a wide variety of topics. Articles should be non-sexual in orientation. A two- to five-page proposal, detailing the sources, style and direction of the article, should be submitted for approval before the finished manuscript. Writers are responsible for providing all research and back-up for articles." Buys 8-12 mss/year, usually assigned on the basis of earlier proposal. Recent article example: "Death in the Ring" (April 1983). Length: 3,000-4,000 words. Pays $300-500.
Columns/Departments: Private Affairs (sexual experience from a woman's point of view.) Buys 12 mss/year. Length: 1,500 words. Pays $50.
Fiction: Ted Newsom, fiction editor. "We will consider all fiction with a fully developed plot and characterization that includes two major erotic scenes. Plot and characterization should not be subordinated to sexual activities. The latter must grow logically from the story, rather than be forced or contrived. *GC* favors surprise endings. Science fiction is not popular here. Sexual stories about rape, incest, childhood sex and bestiality are not appropriate." Buys 12-18 unsolicited mss/year. Recent fiction example: "Into the Valley" (April 1982). Send complete ms. Length: 3,000-4,000 words. Pays $300.
Tips: "The editorial staff is open to queries from writers who can fulfill article assignments on a regular basis. Read samples of writing already appearing in magazine."

GENTLEMEN'S QUARTERLY, Condé Nast, 350 Madison Ave., New York NY 10017. Editor-in-Chief: Jack Haber. Executive Editor: Peter Carlsen. Circ. 525,000. Emphasizes fashion and service features for men in their late 20s, early 30s, with a large discretionary income. Monthly magazine. Pays $200 kill fee. Byline given. Pays on publication. Submit seasonal/holiday material 4-6 months in advance. Photocopied submissions OK. Computer printout submissions OK; prefers letter quality to dot matrix. SASE. Reports in 3 weeks.
Nonfiction: "Content is mostly geared toward self-help and service areas. Subject should cover physical fitness, grooming, nutrition, psychological matters (different types of therapy, etc.), health, travel, personality profiles, money and investment, business matters—all geared to our audience and fitting our format." Buys 2-4 mss/issue. Query with outline of story content. Length: 1,500-2,500 words. Pays $450-700.
Columns/Departments: Philip Smith, managing editor. Looking Good (physical fitness, diet, nutrition and grooming); Money (investments); Lifelines (self-help); World Wise, Destinations and Adventure (travel); Health; Westwords (West Coast matters); Home Tech (consumer electronics); Distinctively Black (black men's grooming); At Your Service and More Dash than Cash (fashion); Well Read (books); Viewpoints (the arts); Living (catchall for various stories that fit magazine format); and Pulse (details of the world at large). Buys 5-8/issue. Query with outline of story content. Length: 1,000-2,500 words. Pays $350-400 and $100 for item used in Pulse.
Tips: "The best procedure to break in is really the outline and formulating a proposal structurally in terms of content and information."

HUSTLER MAGAZINE, 2029 Century Park E., Floor 38, Los Angeles CA 90067. (213)556-9200. Articles Editor: Richard Warren Lewis. Monthly magazine. Circ. 3 million. Rights purchased vary with author and material. Usually buys exclusive English and English translation world-wide magazine rights. Buys 24 full-length mss/year. Pays on acceptance. Write for editorial guidelines. Photocopied submissions (although original is preferred) OK. Reports in 2 months. Query for nonfiction. Query or submit complete ms for other material. No computer printout or disk submissions. SASE.
Nonfiction: Will consider expose, profiles, interviews. Should be hard-hitting, probing, behind-the-scenes material. "We do not want fluff pieces or PR releases. Avoid overly complex sentence structure. Writing should nonetheless be sophisticated and contemporary, devoid of any pretensions, aggressive and down-to-earth, exhibiting no-nonsense attitude. We try to mirror the reality of our times." The publication is "sexually explicit but no pornography." Wants expose material, particularly exposes in political/celebrity/business world. Buys 1 unsolicited ms/year. Length: 5,000 words. Pays $1,200 minimum. Material also needed for reg-

---

The double dagger (‡) before a listing indicates that the listing is new in this edition. New markets are often the most receptive to freelance contributions.

ular columns, "Kinky Korner" and "Sex Play." Length: 1,500 words for "Korner"; 1,500-1,800 words for "Play." Pays $100 for "Korner"; $350 for "Play."

Photos: Photos used with mss; additional payment at usual space rates. Size: 35mm Kodachrome. Buys "total exclusive rights." Pays $300/page for color. "Check a recent copy to see our style. Slides should be sent in plastic pages. Soft-focus and diffusion are not acceptable."

Fiction: Ted Newsom, fiction editor. Considers all fiction with fully developed plot and characterization that includes at least one major erotic scene. Adventure stories preferred. Buys 6 unsolicited mss/year. Plot and characterization should not be subordinated to sexual activities. No humor or satire. Length: 5,000 words. Pays $1,000 minimum.

Tips: Recent article example: "El Salvador: The Search for John Sullivan" (July 1981). Prefers not to get humorous material.

"NEW FROM USA", Arrow Press, Inc., Suite 1251, 10 Milk St., Boston MA 02108. Editor: Alan Maxfield. Managing Editor: L.M. Martin. Monthly newsletter of the modeling profession. Promotes newcomers to the modeling field and covers consumer and sports products and trade updates for mostly male readership, 18-35 years old. Circ. 14,187. Pays on publication. Byline given. Buys one-time rights. Submit seasonal/holiday material 6 months in advance. Simultaneous and photocopied submissions OK. Send $2 in loose stamps. Reports in 1 month on queries; 6 weeks on mss. Sample copy $5 with business size SAE and $1 in loose stamps, cash or money order.

Nonfiction: L.M. Martin, articles editor. Erotica; expose (all types); gambling; how-to; new product; photo feature. "We sponsor an erotic contest. Best story wins 3-month serial with byline." Buys 6-10 mss/year. Send complete ms; include $2 in loose stamps. Length: 400 words minimum. Pays $75 minimum.

Photos: "Natural, erotic shots." Send photos with ms; include $2 in loose stamps. Pays $50-200 for b&w prints; $75 minimum for color. Model release and identification of subjects required. Buys one-time rights.

Columns/Departments: New Models, Up Coming Actresses, Best New Product. Buys 40 mss/year. Send complete ms. Length: 250-750 words. Pays $75-235.

Fiction: L.M. Martin, fiction editor. Erotica, fantasy. Buys 10 mss/year. Send complete ms; include $2 in loose stamps. Length: 350 words minimum. Pays $100 minimum.

NUGGET, Suite 204, 2355 Salzedo St., Coral Gables FL 33134. (305)443-2378. Editor: John Fox. Magazine "primarily devoted to fetishism." Buys first North American serial rights. Byline given. Pays on publication. Submit complete ms. Reports in 6 weeks. SASE.

Nonfiction: Articles on fetishism—every aspect. Length: 2,000-3,000 words maximum. Buys 20-30 mss/year. Pays $100-200.

Photos: Erotic pictorials of women—essay types in fetish clothing (leather, rubber, underwear, etc.,) or women wrestling or boxing other women or men, preferably semi- or nude. Captions or short accompanying manuscript desirable. Color or b&w photos acceptable.

Fiction: Erotic and fetishistic. Should be oriented to *Nugget's* subject matter. Length: 2,000-3,000 words. Pays $100-200.

Tips: "We require queries on articles only and the letter should be a brief synopsis of what the article is about. Originality in handling of subject is very helpful. It is almost a necessity for a freelancer to study our magazine first, be knowledgeable about the subject matter we deal with and able to write explicit and erotic fetish material."

PENTHOUSE, 909 3rd Ave., New York NY 10022. Editor-in-Chief: Bob Guccione. For male (18-34) audience; upper-income bracket, college-educated. Monthly. Circ. 5,350,000. Buys all rights. Pays 25% kill fee. Byline given. Buys 70-80 mss/year. Pays on acceptance. Photocopied submissions OK. Reports in 1 month. Query. SASE.

Nonfiction: Peter Bloch, department executive editor. Peter McCabe, senior editor, political features. Articles on general themes: money, sex, humor, politics, health, crime, etc. Male viewpoint only. Length: 5,000 words. General rates: $2,000 minimum.

Photos: Purchased without mss and on assignment. Pays $200 minimum for b&w; $350 for color. Spec sheet available from Art Director Joe Brooks.

Fiction: Kathryn Green, editor. Quality fiction. Experimental, mainstream, mystery, suspense and adventure; erotica; and science fiction. Action-oriented, central male character. Length: 3,500-6,000 words. Pays $1,500 minimum.

PENTHOUSE VARIATIONS, Penthouse International, Ltd., 909 3rd Ave., New York NY 10022. 593-3301. Editor: Victoria McCarty. Monthly magazine. *Variations* is a pleasure guide for everyone who wants to expand his horizons of enjoyment. All forms of sensuality and eroticism appear in its pages, from monogamy to menaging, from bondage to relaxation, from foreplay to romance." Circ. 400,000. Pays on acceptance. No byline given. Buys all rights. Submit seasonal/holiday material 7 months in advance. Simultaneous queries OK. Reports in 1 month on queries; 2 months on mss. Free writer's guidelines.

Nonfiction: Personal experience. "We are looking for 2,500-3,000 word, first-person, true accounts of erotic experiences, squarely focused within *one* of the pleasure variations. No fiction, articles, or short stories. No porno, favorite erotica; we are not a dirty-story clearing house." Buys 120 mss/year. Query. Length: 2,500-3,000 words. Pays $400.

Tips: "I am easily swayed by professionally neat mss style: clean ribbon, non-erasable paper, double-spacing, margins. I look for complete sentences and an electrically erotic mind sold in a business-like manner."

‡**PLATINUM, The Gentleman's Magazine,** Platinum Publishing, Inc., Suite 136, 8601 Dunwoody Place, Atlanta GA 30338. (404)998-1158. Editor: James Goode. Managing Editor: Mary C. Ward. Monthly photo essay magazine primarily for 18-34-year-old males. Circ. 350,000. Pays within 30 days after publication. By-line given. Offers 25% kill fee. Buys first North American serial rights, one-time rights, all rights, first rights, second serial (reprint) rights, and makes work-for-hire assignments. Submit seasonal/holiday material 4 months in advance. SASE. Reports in 4 or more weeks. Sample copy $3.95; writer's guidelines for SAE.

Nonfiction: Book excerpts, expose, humor, interview/profile, photo feature. No fiction, fillers or poetry. Buys 12 mss/year. Query with published clips. Length: 1,500-3,500 words. Pays 20¢/word.

Photos: Nancy Suttles, photo editor. "We are looking for photo essays, primarily of young, attractive women, who have accomplished something extraordinary, exciting and interesting in terms of sports, adventure, or unusual occupation. Subjects of these essays should be no older than mid-20s." Send photos with query. Pays $150/photo "at option of publisher." Reviews 35mm color transparencies. Captions and identification of subjects required. Buys one-time rights.

Tips: "We are looking for excellent original color transparencies, and would always like to have accompanying text. We are also looking for personality pieces on Hollywood hopefuls, new 'hot' recording artists, and established stars who have recently done something of interest which has not already received national recognition. These should be written as articles—not in interview form. We prefer that candid photography shot at the time of the interview accompanies text. On occasion we also print features on contemporary, timely social issues of national or international significance. Again, we prefer that photography accompanies text."

PLAYBOY, 919 N. Michigan, Chicago IL 60611. Managing Editor: Don Gold. Monthly. Computer printout submissions OK; prefers letter quality to dot matrix. Reports in 1 month. Buys first rights and others. SASE.

Nonfiction: James Morgan, articles editor. "We're looking for timely, topical pieces. Articles should be carefully researched and written with wit and insight. Little true adventure or how-to material. Check magazine for subject matter. Pieces on outstanding contemporary men, sports, politics, sociology, business and finance, music, science and technology, games, all areas of interest to the urban male." Query. Length: 3,000-5,000 words. On acceptance, pays $3,000 minimum. If a commissioned article does not meet standards, will pay a turn-down price of 20%. The *Playboy* interviews run between 10,000 and 15,000 words. After getting an assignment, the freelancer outlines the questions, conducts and edits the interview, and writes the introduction. Pays $4,000 minimum on acceptance. For interviews contact G. Barry Golson, Executive Editor, 747 3rd Ave., New York NY 10017.

Photos: Gary Cole, photography director, suggests that all photographers interested in contributing make a thorough study of the photography currently appearing in the magazine. Generally all photography is done on assignment. While much of this is assigned to *Playboy*'s staff photographers, approximately 50% of the photography is done by freelancers and *Playboy* is in constant search of creative new talent. Qualified freelancers are encouraged to submit samples of their work and ideas. All assignments made on an all rights basis with payments scaled from $600/color page for miscellaneous features such as fashion, food and drink, etc.; $300/b&w page; $800/color page for girl features; cover, $1,500. Playmate photography for entire project: $12,000. Assignments and submissions handled by associate editors: Jeff Cohen, Janice Moses, and James Larson, Chicago; Marilyn Grabowski, Los Angeles. Assignments made on a minimum guarantee basis. Film, processing, and other expenses necessitated by assignment honored.

Fiction: Alice Turner, Fiction Editor. Both light and serious fiction. Entertainment pieces are clever, smoothly written stories. Serious fiction must come up to the best contemporary standards in substance, idea and style. Both, however, should be designed to appeal to the educated, well-informed male reader. General types include comedy, mystery, fantasy, horror, science fiction, adventure, social-realism, "problem" and psychological stories. Fiction lengths are 3,000-6,000 words; short-shorts of 1,000 to 1,500 words are used. Pays $2,000; $1,000 short-short. Rates rise for additional acceptances. Rate for Ribald Classics is $200.

Fillers: Party Jokes are always welcome. Pays $50 each on acceptance. Also interesting items for Playboy After Hours, front section (best check it carefully before submission). The After Hours front section pays anywhere from $50 for humorous or unusual news items (submissions not returned) to $500 for original reportage. Subject matter should be new trends, fads, personalities, cultural developments. Has movie, book, record reviewers but solicits queries for short (1,000 words or less) pieces on art, places, people, trips, adventures, experiences, erotica, television—in short, open-ended. Book and record reviews are on assignment basis only. Ideas for Playboy Potpourri pay $75 on publication. Query. Games, puzzles and travel articles should be addressed to New York office.

Close-up

Mary Ward, Senior Editor
Platinum & *The Robb Report*

"Unless you know how to write yourself, how can you know what works in someone else's writing? Because I'm a writer, I take the writing aspect of the magazine very seriously." Such is the editorial philosophy that Mary Ward brings to her work as senior editor at both *Platinum*, the monthly "Gentleman's Magazine," and *The Robb Report*.

The former high school English teacher brings a combination of career experiences to her editorships. Ten years of communications know-how includes editing a community newspaper, working in PR at an ad agency, and freelancing for *The Robb Report*.

In talking about her work at *Platinum*, Ward explains that the magazine's philosophy is different from the traditional men's mag fare. "We have no total nudity, no obscene language, nothing that is sexually explicit in text or photography. We're a photo essay magazine and reach a more sophisticated readership."

With that readership (primarily 19- to 34-year-old males) in mind, Ward tackles the solicited and unsolicited manuscripts and queries that cross her desk. "I generally read all unsolicited manuscripts first. If I'm not interested, I give them to my secretary to return—assuming there's an SASE attached. If I think it might be suitable for us, I give it to the editor-in-chief with a note mentioning why I like it. If he agrees, I'll contact the writer."

As for queries, Ward prefers the no-frills approach. Letters should be "straightforward and specifically describe the slant and content of the article and how it could be illustrated with photography. Gimmicky queries go straight in the trash."

Though Ward is apt to assign a story to a writer she's worked with before, "new and unpublished writers do have a chance at *Platinum*" as long as they've taken the initiative to learn the magazine's format and content. "The ideal writer follows an editor's guidelines regarding the type of story needed; he turns in an assignment on or before deadline. And I'd like to see more of them proof their own manuscripts before submitting them," she adds.

Adherence to these tips would eliminate some of Ward's vexations on the job. "I suppose the most frustrating thing for me is to talk to a writer for 15 or 20 minutes about the type of story I want, and then have him turn in an assignment that doesn't cover it. Writers who miss the boat like that have one chance; I think twice before giving them additional assignments."

Ward's recommendations come from experience. She's written a three-act play and is currently working on the outline for a novel. She likes to keep in touch with nonfiction as well, and sometimes assigns herself a story for *Platinum*. She gets out of the office, does the research, and conducts the interviews. With knowing the reality of putting seat to chair comes respect for the process. "I have great empathy with writers because I understand how difficult it is to write. As an editor, I try to be fair with them. Our relationship is a partnership. I see my job as the main link between the concept and the finished product. I want writers to write the best possible article. After all, it's going to have their name on it—and it's going in our magazine."

PLAYERS MAGAZINE, Players International Publications, 8060 Melrose Ave., Los Angeles CA 90046. (213)653-8060. Editor: Emory Holmes. Associate Editor: Leslie Gersicoff. For the black male but "we have a high female readership—perhaps as high as 40%." Monthly magazine. Circ. 200,000. Pays on publication. Buys all rights. Submit seasonal/holiday material 6 months in advance. Photocopied submissions OK. SASE. Reports in 6 weeks minimum.
Nonfiction: "*Players* is *Playboy* in basic black." Expose; historical; humor; inspirational; sports; travel; reviews of movies, books and records; profile and interview on assignment. Recent article example: "The Glove and the Sword" (June 1982). Length: 1,000-5,000 words. Pays 6¢/word. Photos purchased on assignment (pays $25 minimum for b&w; $250 maximum per layout). Model release required.
Fiction: Adventure, erotica, fantasy, historical (black), humorous, science fiction and experimental. Recent short story example: "Rubber Sun" (April 1982). Length: 1,000-4,000 words. Pays 6¢/word.
Tips: "Follow current style with novel theme in query or article. Looking for: city, night life of cities other than New York, Chicago, Los Angeles; interviews with black political leaders; black history."

SCREW, Box 432, Old Chelsea Station, New York NY 10011. Managing Editor: Manny Neuhaus. For a predominantly male, college-educated audience; 21 through mid-40s. Tabloid newspaper. Weekly. Circ. 125,000. Buys all rights. Byline given. Buys 150-200 mss/year. Pays on publication. Free sample copy and writer's guidelines. Reports in 3 months. Submit complete ms for first-person, true confessions. Computer printout submissions OK. Query on all other material.
Nonfiction: "Sexually related news, humor, how-to articles, first-person and true confessions. Frank and explicit treatment of all areas of sex; outrageous and irreverent attitudes combined with hard information, news and consumer reports. Our style is unique. Writers should check several recent issues." Length: 1,000-3,000 words. Pays $100-200. Will also consider material for "Letter From . . . ", a consumer-oriented wrapup of commercial sex scene in cities around the country; and "My Scene," a sexual true confession. Recent article example: "Sex in Manila—A Tour of the City's Bars and Brothels." Length: 1,000-1,200 words. Pays about $40.
Photos: B&w glossy prints (8x10 or 11x14) purchased with or without mss or on assignment. Pays $10-50.
Tips: "All mss get careful attention. Those written in *Screw* style on sexual topics have the best chance."

STAG, Swank Corp., 888 7th Ave., New York NY 10106. Editor: Colette Connor. Monthly magazine covering men's entertainment with an emphasis on sex for men 18-35. Circ. 170,000. Pays on publication. Byline given. Offers 25% kill fee. Buys all rights. Submit seasonal/holiday material 6 months in advance. SASE. Reports in 1 month. Sample copy $5.
Nonfiction: Photo Features: "Subject matter of any article should lend itself to 4-6 pages of photos." Buys 8-10 non-commissioned mss/year. Query with clips of published work. Length: 2,500-3,000 words. Pays $350 minimum/article.
Photos: State availability of photos. Reviews 35mm Kodachrome transparencies. Payment varies according to usage rights.
Fiction: Buys 12 mss/year. Send complete ms. Length: 2,000 words average. Pays $300 minimum.
Tips: "We like a query that tips us off to a new sex club, strip joint, love commune etc., that would cooperate with the writer and our photographers for a feature story. For all our articles, photographs or illustrations are essential. Prefers not to see anything not dealing with sex." Read the magazine.

Military

Technical and semitechnical publications for military commanders, personnel and planners, as well as those for military families and civilians interested in Armed Forces activities are listed here. All of these publications require submissions emphasizing military or paramilitary subjects or aspects of military life.

AIR UNIVERSITY REVIEW, United States Air Force, Air University, Bldg. 1211, Maxwell Air Force Base AL 36112. (205)293-2773. Editor: Lt. Col. Donald R. Baucom, USAF. Professional military journal for military supervisory staff, command leadership personnel and top level civilians. Circ. 20,000. Not copyrighted. Byline given. Buys no mss, but gives cash awards on publication. Reports in 6 weeks. Query.
Nonfiction: "Serves as an open forum for exploratory discussion. Purpose is to present innovative thinking and stimulate dialogue concerning Air Force doctrine, strategy, tactics, and related national defense matters. Footnotes as needed. Prefer the author to be the expert. Reviews of defense-related books. Expository style. Only military and defense related matter, please; no announcements of meetings." Length: 1,500-3,500 words. Cash awards up to $150.

Photos: B&w glossy prints or charts to supplement articles are desired.
Tips: "We look for clear, concise writing."

ARMED FORCES JOURNAL, 1414 22nd St. NW, Washington DC 20037. Editor: Benjamin F. Schemmer. For "senior career officers of the US military, defense industry, Congressmen and government officials interested in defense matters, international military and defense industry." Monthly. Circ. 25,000. Buys all rights. Buys 10 unsolicited mss/year. Pays on publication. Sample copy $2.75. Photocopied submissions OK. No computer printout or disk submissions. Reports in 1 month. Submit complete ms. SASE.
Nonfiction: Publishes "national and international defense issues: weapons programs, research, personnel programs, international relations (with emphasis on defense aspect). We do not want broad overviews of a general subject; more interested in detailed analysis of a specific program or international defense issue. Our readers are decision-makers in defense matters—hence, subject should not be treated too simplistically. Be provocative. We are not afraid to take issue with our own constituency when an independent voice needs to be heard." Buys informational, profile and think pieces. No poetry, biographies, or non-defense topics. Length: 1,000-3,000 words. Pays $100/page.

ARMY MAGAZINE, 2425 Wilson Blvd., Arlington VA 22201. (703)841-4300. Editor-in-Chief: L. James Binder. Managing Editor: Poppy Walker. Emphasizes military interests. Monthly magazine. Circ. 155,000. Pays on publication. Buys all magazine rights. Byline given except for back-up research. Submit seasonal/holiday material 3 months in advance of issue date. Photocopied submissions OK. SASE. Free sample copy and writer's guidelines.
Nonfiction: Historical (military and original); humor (military feature-length articles and anecdotes); interview; new product; nostalgia; personal experience; photo feature; profile; and technical. No rehashed history. "We would like to see more pieces about interesting military personalities. We especially want material lending itself to heavy, contributor-supplied photographic treatment. The first thing a contributor should recognize is that our readership is very savvy militarily. 'Gee-whiz' personal reminiscences get short shrift, unless they hold their own in a company in which long military service, heroism and unusual experiences are commonplace. At the same time, Army readers like a well-written story with a fresh slant, whether it is about an experience in a foxhole or the fortunes of a corps in battle." Buys 12 mss/issue. Submit complete ms. Length: 4,500 words. Pays 8-12¢/word.
Photos: Submit photo material with accompanying ms. Pays $15-50 for 8x10 b&w glossy prints; $25-150 for 8x10 color glossy prints or 2¼x2¼ color transparencies, but will accept 35mm. Captions preferred. Buys all rights.
Columns/Departments: Military news; books, comment (*New Yorker*-type "Talk of the Town" items). Buys 8/issue. Submit complete ms. Length: 1,000 words. Pays $30-100.
Tips: Recent article examples: "Face Off in the Jungle—and Three Came Home" (March 1982) and an article about negotiations between US Army officers and Viet Cong for release of three POWs.

ASIA-PACIFIC DEFENSE FORUM, Commander-in-Chief, US Pacific Command, CINCPAC Staff, Box 13, Camp H. M. Smith HI 96861. (808)477-6128. Executive Editor: Lt. Col. Paul R. Stankiewicz. Editor: Phillip P. Katz. Managing Editor: Lt. Col. Soot M. Jew. For foreign military officers in Asian-Pacific and Indian Ocean countries; all services—Army, Navy, Air Force and Marines. Secondary audience—government officials, media and academicians concerned with defense issues. "We seek to enhance international professional dialogue on military training, force employment, leadership, strategy and tactics, policy matters and international cooperation." Quarterly magazine. Circ. 30,000. Pays on acceptance. Buys simultaneous, second serial (reprint) or one-time rights. Byline given. Phone queries OK. Simultaneous, photocopied and previously published submissions OK. Computer printout submissions OK; prefers letter quality to dot matrix. SASE. Reports in 3 weeks on queries; 10 weeks on mss. Free sample copy and writer's guidelines.
Nonfiction: General interest (strategy and tactics, current type forces and weapons systems, strategic balance and security issues and Asian-Pacific armed forces); historical (occasionally used, if relation to present-day defense issues is apparent); how-to (training, leadership, force employment procedures, organization); interview and personal experience (rarely used, and only in terms of developing professional military skills). "We do not want overly technical weapons/equipment descriptions, overly scholarly articles, controversial policy, and budget matters; nor do we seek discussion of in-house problem areas. We do not deal with military social life, base activities or PR-type personalities/job descriptions." Buys 2-4 mss/year. Query or send complete ms. Length: 1,000-4,000 words. Pays $25-100.
Photos: State availability of photos with ms. "We provide nearly all photos; however, will consider good quality photos with mss." Uses 5x7 or 8x10 b&w glossy prints or 35mm color transparencies. Offers no additional payment for photos accompanying mss. Buys one-time rights. Captions required.
Tips: "Develop a 'feel' for our foreign audience orientation. Provide material that is truly audience-oriented in our view and easily illustrated with photos."

AT EASE, Division of Home Missions, Assemblies of God, 1445 Boonville Ave., Springfield MO 65802. Editor: Lemuel D. McElyea. Managing Editor: Ruby M. Enyart. For military personnel. Bimonthly magazine. Circ. 15,000. Buys all rights. "We are quite limited in what we would accept from freelance writers. Everything has to be slanted to Assemblies of God readers." Pays on publication. Free sample copy and writer's guidelines. "If we can't use a submission and we think another department can, we usually let them see it before replying. Otherwise, as soon as we reject it, we return it." Query first. SASE.
Nonfiction and Photos: Materials that will interest military men and women. Must have religious value. Buys 15 unsolicited mss/year. Length: 500 to 800 words. Pays minimum of 1½¢/word.
Tips: "Give a clear statement of background faith in your query. Military experience helpful."

INFANTRY, Box 2005, Fort Benning GA 31905. (404)545-2350. Managing Editor: Albert N. Garland. Published primarily for combat arms officers and noncommissioned officers. Bimonthly magazine. Circ. 20,000. Not copyrighted. Computer printout submissions OK. Pays on publication. Payment cannot be made to US government employees. Free sample copy and writer's guidelines. Reports in 1 month.
Nonfiction: Interested in current information on US military organization, weapons, equipment, tactics and techniques; foreign armies and their equipment; lessons learned from combat experience, both past and present; solutions to problems encountered in the active Army and the Reserve components. Departments include Letters, Features and Forum, Training Notes, Book Reviews. Uses 70 unsolicited mss/year. Recent article example: "Platoon Test" (March-April 1983). Length of articles: 1,500-3,500 words. Length for Book Reviews: 500-1,000 words. Query. Accepts 75 mss/year.
Photos: Used with mss.
Tips: Start with letters to editor, book reviews to break in.

LEATHERNECK, Box 1775, Quantico VA 22134. (703)640-3171. Editor: Ronald D. Lyons. Managing Editor: Tom Bartlett. Emphasizes all phases of Marine Corps activities. Monthly magazine. Circ. 70,000. Pays on acceptance. Buys all rights. Phone queries OK. Submit seasonal/holiday material 3 months in advance of issue date. SASE. Reports in 2 weeks. Free sample copy and writer's guidelines.
Nonfiction: "All material submitted to *Leatherneck* must pertain to the U.S. Marine Corps and its members." General interest; how-to; humor; historical; interview; nostalgia; personal experience; profile; and travel. No articles on politics, subjects not pertaining to the Marine Corps, and subjects that are not in good taste. Buys 24 mss/year. Query. Length: 1,500-3,000 words. Pays $50 and up per magazine page.
Photos: "We like to receive a complete package when we consider a manuscript for publication." State availability of photos with query. No additional payment for 4x5 or 8x10 b&w glossy prints. Captions required. Buys all rights. Model release required.
Fiction: Adventure; historical; and humorous. All material must pertain to the U.S. Marine Corps and its members. Buys 3 mss/year. Query. Length: 1,000-3,000 words. Pays $50 and up per magazine page.
Poetry: Light verse and traditional. No poetry that does not pertain to the U.S. Marine Corps. Buys 40 mss/year. Length: 16-20 lines. Pays $10-20.

THE MILITARY ENGINEER, 607 Prince St., Alexandria VA 22314. (703)549-3800. Editor: John J. Kern. Bimonthly magazine. Circ. 43,000. Pays on publication. Buys all rights. Byline given. Phone queries OK. Computer printout submissions OK. SASE. Reports in 1 month. Sample copy and writer's guidelines $4.
Nonfiction: Well-written and illustrated semi-technical articles by experts and practitioners of civil and military engineering, constructors, equipment manufacturers, defense contract suppliers and architect/engineers on these subjects and on subjects of military biography and history. "Subject matter should represent a contribution to the fund of knowledge, concern a new project or method, be on R&D in these fields; investigate planning and management techniques or problems in these fields, or be of militarily strategic nature." Buys 17-20 unsolicited mss/year. Length: 1,000-2,500 words. Query.
Photos: Mss must be accompanied by 6-8 well-captioned photos, maps or illustrations; b&w, generally. Pays approximately $25/page.

MILITARY LIVING, Box 4010, Arlington VA 22204. (703)237-0203. Editor: Ann Crawford. For military personnel and their families. Monthly. Circ. 30,000. Buys first serial rights. "Very few freelance features used last year; mostly staff-written." Pays on publication. Sample copy for 50¢ in coin or stamps. "Slow to report due to small staff and workload." Submit complete ms. SASE.
Nonfiction: "Articles on military life in greater Washington DC area. We would especially like recreational features in the Washington DC area. We specialize in passing along morale-boosting information about the military installations in the area, with emphasis on the military family—travel pieces about surrounding area, recreation information, etc. We do not want to see depressing pieces, pieces without the military family in mind, personal petty complaints or general information pieces. Prefer 700 words or less, but will consider more for an exceptional feature. We also prefer a finished article rather than a query." Payment is on an honorarium basis, 1-1½¢/word.

Photos: Photos purchased with mss. 5x7 or larger b&w glossy prints only. Payment is $5 for original photos by author.

MILITARY LIVING R&R REPORT, Box 4010, Arlington VA 22204. Publisher: Ann Crawford. For "military consumers worldwide." Bimonthly newsletter. "Please state when sending submission that it is for the *R&R Report Newsletter* so as not to confuse it with our monthly magazine which has different requirements." Buys first rights, but will consider other rights. Pays on publication. Sample copy $1. SASE.
Nonfiction: "We use information on little-known military facilities and privileges, discounts around the world and travel information. Items must be short and concise. Stringers wanted around the world. Payment is on an honorarium basis. 1-1½¢/word."

MILITARY REVIEW, US Army Command and General Staff College, Fort Leavenworth KS 66027. (913)684-5642. Editor-in-Chief: Col. John D. Bloom. Managing Editor: Lt. Col. Dallas Van Hoose, Jr. Features Editor: Major S.I. Ketzis. Business Manager: Lt. Charles R. Rayhorn. Emphasizes the military for senior military officers, students and scholars. Monthly magazine. Circ. 27,000. Pays on publication. Buys one-time rights. Byline given. Phone queries OK. Photocopied submissions OK. SASE. Reports in 1 month. Free writer's guidelines.
Nonfiction: Military history, international affairs, tactics, new military equipment, strategy and book reviews. Prefers not to get material unrelated to defense subjects, poetry, or cartoons. Recently published "BAI: The Key to the Deep Battle" and "The Battle on the German Frontier" (March 1982). Buys 100-120 mss/year. Query. Length: 2,000-4,000 words. Pays $25-100.
Tips: "We need more articles from military personnel experienced in particular specialties. Examples: Tactics from a tactician, military engineering from an engineer, etc. We would appreciate receiving good quality, double-spaced letter quality computer printout submissions."

NATIONAL DEFENSE, Suite 900, 1700 N. Moore St., Arlington VA 22209. (703)522-1826. Editor: D. Ballou. For members of industry and U.S. Armed Forces. Publication of the American Defense Preparedness Association. Monthly magazine. Circ. 38,000. Buys all rights. Pays 100% kill fee. Byline given. Buys 35 unsolicited mss a year. Pays on publication. Sample copy $4; free writer's guidelines. Photocopied submissions OK. No simultaneous submissions. Reports in 1 month. Query or submit complete ms. Outline preferred. SASE.
Nonfiction: Military-related articles: weapons, systems, management and production. "We emphasize industrial preparedness for defense and prefer a news style, with emphasis on the 'why.' " Length: 1,500-2,500 words. Pays 25¢/word or more. Book reviews are sometimes used, but query is required first and no payment is made.

NATIONAL GUARD, 1 Massachusetts Ave. NW, Washington DC 20001. (202)789-0031. Editor: Major Reid K. Beveridge. For officers of the Army and Air National Guard. Monthly. Circ. 69,000. Rights negotiable. Byline given. Buys 10-12 mss/year. Pays on publication. Query. SASE.
Nonfiction: Military policy, strategy, training, equipment, logistics, personnel policies: tactics, combat lessons learned as they pertain to the Army and Air Force (and impact on Army National Guard and Air National Guard). Material must be strictly accurate from a technical standpoint. Does not publish exposes, cartoons or jokes. Recent article example: "The Thin Green Line" (March 1982). Length: 2,000-3,000 words. Payment ($75-500/article) depends on originality, amount of research involved, etc.
Photos: Photography pertinent to subject matter should accompany ms.

OFF DUTY, US: Suite C-2, 3303 Harbor Blvd., Costa Mesa CA 92626. Editor: Bruce Thorstad. Europe: Eschersheimer Landstrasse 69, Frankfurt/M, West Germany. Editor: J.C. Hixenbaugh. Pacific: Box 9869, Hong Kong. Editor: Jim Shaw. Monthly magazine for US military personnel and their families stationed around the world. Most readers 18-35 years old. Combined circ. 653,000. Computer printout and floppy disks done on Wang word procesors OK. Buys first serial or second serial rights. Pays on acceptance. Free sample copy and writer's guidelines.
Nonfiction: Three editions—American, Pacific and European. "Emphasis is on off duty travel, leisure, military shopping, wining and dining, sports, hobbies, music, and getting the most out of military life. Overseas editions lean toward foreign travel and living in foreign cultures. Also emphasize what's going on back home. In travel articles we like anecdotes, lots of description, color and dialogue. American edition uses more American trends and how-to/service material. Material with special US, Pacific or European slant should be sent to appropriate address above; material useful in all editions may be sent to US address and will be forwarded as necessary." Buys 30-50 mss/year for each of three editions. Query. Length: 1,500 words average. Also needs 500-word shorties. Pays 12¢/word for use in one edition; 15¢/word for use in 2 or more.
Photos: Bought with or without accompanying ms. Pays $25 for b&w glossy prints; $50 for color transparencies; $100 for full page color; $200 for covers. "Covers must be vertical format 35mm; larger format transparencies preferred. We don't get enough good ms/photo packages."

Tips: "All material should take into account to some extent our special audience—the US military and their dependents. Our publication is subtitled 'The Military Leisuretime Magazine,' and the stories we like best are about how to get more out of the military experience. That 'more' could range from more fun to more satisfaction to more material benefits such as military privileges. Magazine will be adding pages and buying more articles in the year ahead."

OVERSEAS!, Military Consumer Today, Inc., BismarckstraBe 17, D-6900 Heidelburg, West Germany. Editor: H.W.A. Demers. General entertainment magazine serving American and Canadian military personnel stationed throughout Europe. Specifically directed to males 18-35. Monthly magazine. Circ. 83,000. Pays on publication. Buys rights to military communities in Europe. Submit seasonal/holiday material 4 months in advance of issue date. Simultaneous and previously published submissions OK. Computer printout submissions OK. SAE and International Reply Coupons (not US postage). Sample copy for 1 International Reply Coupon.
Nonfiction: "We are a slick commercial giveaway magazine looking for flashy, sexy, young-male-interest writing and photography. In the past we've bought how-to (travel by bike, van, foot, motorcycle; how to photograph women, rock stars, traveling subjects); interview and profile articles on music and sport celebrities; and do-it-yourself-sports (skiing, kayaking, sailing, soccer, tennis). Also need some music features—rock, soul, C&W, especially on musicians soon coming to Europe. We're looking for a new kind of travel article: the 'in scenes' of Europe written up especially for our young GIs. Should include nightlife, discos, bars, informal eating out, good music scenes, rather than fancy restaurants, cathedrals, or museums. Above all, tell our servicemen where the girls are. Query with a good idea that has not been worked to death, and give a lead paragraph that indicates the style and angle to be adopted, backed by a brief outline of where the article will go. All articles must be pertinent to someone living and working in Europe, or with a slant that is neutral—i.e., profile on celebrity." Buys 5-6 unsolicited mss/year. "Writer should be able to deliver a complete package (which means he or she has a means to find photos and any other additional info pertinent to the article) on time." Length: 800-1,500 words. Pays 10¢/word.
Photos: Purchased with accompanying ms. Captions required. Pays $20 for b&w; $35 minimum for color and $150 for covers.
Tips: "Interesting travel stories with anecdotes are a good vehicle to break in, as are profiles of Americans making their mark in Europe. We are willing to consider any material that puts a premium on good, brisk and whenever possible, humorous, writing, that is written with our audience in mind."

PARAMETERS: JOURNAL OF THE U.S. ARMY WAR COLLEGE, U.S. Army War College, Carlisle Barracks PA 17013. (717)245-4943. Editor: Col. Roland R. Sullivan, U.S. Army. Readership consists of senior leadership of U.S. defense establishment, both uniformed and civilian, plus members of the media, government, industry and academe interested in scholarly articles devoted to national and international security affairs, military strategy, military leadership and management, art and science of warfare, and military history (provided it has contemporary relevance). Most readers possess graduate degree. Quarterly. Circ. 8,500. Not copyrighted; unless copyrighted by author, articles may be reprinted with appropriate credits. Byline given. Pays on publication. Reports in 6 weeks.
Nonfiction: Articles preferred that deal with current security issues, employ critical analysis, and provide solutions or recommendations. Liveliness and verve, consistent with scholarly integrity, appreciated. Theses, studies, and academic course papers should be adapted to article form prior to submission. Documentation in endnotes. Submit complete ms. Length: 5,000 words or less, preferably less. Pays $50 minimum; $100 average (including visuals).
Tips: "Research should be thorough; documentation should be complete."

PERIODICAL, Council on America's Military Past, 4970 N. Camino Antonio, Tucson AZ 85718. Editor-in-Chief: Dan L. Thrapp. Emphasizes old and abandoned forts, posts and military installations; military subjects for a professional, knowledgeable readership interested in one-time defense sites or other military installations. Quarterly magazine. Circ. 1,500. Pays on publication. Buys one-time rights. Simultaneous, photocopied and previously published (if published a long time ago) submissions OK. SASE. Reports in 3 weeks.
Nonfiction: Historical; personal experience; photo feature; technical (relating to posts, their construction/operation and military matters). Buys 4-6 mss/issue. Query or send complete ms. Length: 300-4,000 words. Pays minimum $2/page.
Photos: Purchased with or without accompanying ms. Captions required. Query. Glossy, single-weight, b&w up to 8x10. Offers no additional payment for photos accepted with accompanying ms.

THE RETIRED OFFICER MAGAZINE, 201 N. Washington St., Alexandria VA 22314. (703)549-2311. Editor: Colonel Minter L. Wilson Jr., USA-Ret. For "officers of the 7 uniformed services and their families." Monthly. Circ. 315,000. May buy all rights or first serial rights. Byline given. Pays on publication. Free sample copy and editorial requirements sheet. Photocopied submissions OK "if clean and fresh." Submit seasonal material (holiday stories in which the Armed Services are depicted) at least 4 months in advance. Reports on material accepted for publication within 6 weeks. Submit complete ms. SASE.

Nonfiction: History, humor, cultural, travel, second-career opportunities and current affairs. "Current topical subjects with particular contextual slant to the military; historical events of military significance; features pertinent to a retired military officer's milieu (second career, caveats in the business world/wives' adjusting, leisure, fascinating hobbies). True military experiences are also useful, and we tend to use articles less technical than a single-service publication might publish." Buys 45 unsolicited mss/year. Length: 1,000-2,500 words. Pays $50-300.

Photos: 8x10 b&w photos (normal halftone). Pays $10. Color photos must be suitable for color separation. Pays $50 if reproduced in color; otherwise, same as b&w. Associate editor: Marjorie J. Seng.

RUSI JOURNAL, Royal United Services Institute for Defence Studies, Whitehall SW1A 2ET, England. Editor: Jenny Shaw. Emphasizes defense and military history. Quarterly magazine. For the defense community: service officers, civil servants, politicians, journalists, academics, industrialists, etc. Circ. 6,500. Pays on publication. Buys all rights. Photocopied submissions OK. SAE and International Reply Coupons. Sample copy $10.50 or 4.50 pounds.

Nonfiction: Learned articles on all aspects of defense; historical military articles with particular reference to current defense problems; weapon technology; international relations and civil/military relations. Buys 40 unsolicited mss/year. Query. Length: 2,500-6,000 words. Pays 12.50 pounds/printed page.

Photos: No additional payment is made for photos, but they should accompany articles whenever possible.

SEA POWER, 2300 Wilson Blvd., Arlington VA 22201. Editor: James D. Hessman. Issued monthly by the Navy League of the US for naval personnel and civilians interested in naval maritime and defense matters. Buys all rights. Pays on publication. Will send free sample copy to a writer on request. Reports in 6 weeks. Query first. No computer printout or disk submissions. SASE.

Nonfiction: Factual articles on sea power in general, US industrial base, mineral resources, and the US Navy, the US Marine Corps, US Coast Guard, US merchant marine and naval services and other navies of the world in particular. Should illustrate and expound the importance of the seas and sea power to the US and its allies. Wants timely, clear, nontechnical, lively writing. Length: 500-2,500 words. No historical articles, commentaries, critiques, abstract theories, poetry or editorials. Pays $100-500 depending upon length and research involved.

Photos: Purchased with ms.

SERGEANTS, Air Force Sergeants Association, Box 31050, Temple Hills MD 20748. (301)899-3500. Editor: Belinda Reilly. Monthly magazine for the "air force enlisted (retired, active duty, reserve and guard). Features on all aspects of the Air Force and legislation affecting it." Circ. 140,000. Pays on publication. Byline given. Makes work-for-hire assignments. Submit seasonal/holiday material 2 months in advance. Simultaneous queries, and simultaneous, photocopied, and previously published submissions OK. "Computer printouts OK, but disk submissions need to be compatible to our word processors, Lanier or IBM." Reports in 1 week on queries; 1 month on mss. Free sample copy and writer's guidelines.

Nonfiction: Historical/nostalgic (war stories in Air Force involvement enlisted Air Force personnel); interview/profile (of Air Force enlisted people in high positions); personal experience (accounts of interesting Air Force experiences); technical (advances in Air Force technology); and travel (what to see and do in and around Air Force bases). No "opinion pieces on legislation or government." Buys 12 mss/year. Query with clips of published work. Length: 500-2,000 words. Pays $50/printed page.

Photos: Send photos with ms. Pays $25-250 for color transparencies; $25-50 for b&w prints. Captions, model releases and identification of subjects required. Buys one-time rights.

SOLDIER OF FORTUNE, The Journal of Professional Adventurers, Omega Group, Ltd., Box 693, Boulder CO 80306. (303)449-3750. Editor/Publisher: Robert K. Brown. Managing Editor: Jim Graves. Monthly magazine covering the military, police and the outdoors. "We take a strong stand on political issues such as maintenance of a strong national defense, the dangers of communism, and the right to keep and bear arms." Circ. 225,000. Pays on acceptance. Byline given. Offers 25% kill fee "for proven freelancers or on publication." Makes work-for-hire assignments. Submit seasonal/holiday material 6 months in advance. Simultaneous queries and photocopied submissions OK. Computer printout submissions OK; disk OK if compatible with North Star Horizon CPM. SASE. Reports in 3 months. Sample copy $4; writer's guidelines for SAE.

Nonfiction: Margaret MacDonald, articles editor. Expose (in-depth reporting from the world's hot spots—Afghanistan, Angola, etc.); general interest (critical focus on national issues—gun control, national defense); historical (soldiers of fortune, adventurers of past, history of elite units, Vietnam); how-to (outdoor equipment, weaponry, self-defense); humor (military, police); interview/profile (leaders or representatives of issues); new product (usually staff-assigned; outdoor equipment, weapons); personal experience ("I-was-there focus"); photo feature; technical (weapons, weapons systems, military tactics). Buys 75-100 mss/year. Query. Length: 2,000-4,500 words. Pays $130-550.

Photos: Send photos with ms. Pays $2.50/column inch for b&w 5x7 prints; $5/column inch for 35mm color

transparencies. Captions and identification of weapons and military equipment required. Buys first North American rights.
Columns/Departments: M.L. Jones, column/department editor. I Was There/It Happened to Me (adventure and combat stories). Buys 12 mss/year. Send complete ms. Length: 500 words maximum. Pays $50 minimum.
Tips: "All authors should have professional background in the military or police work."

THE TIMES MAGAZINE, Army Times Publishing Company, 475 School St., SW, Washington, DC 20024. (202)554-7170. Editor: Marianne Lester. Managing Editor: Barry Robinson. Monthly magazine covering current lifestyles and problems of career military families around the world. Circ. 330,000. Pays on publication. Byline given. Offers negotiable kill fee. Buys all rights. Submit seasonal/holiday material 6 months in advance. Double- or triple-spaced computer printout submissions OK. SASE. Reports in 1 month. Sample copy and writer's guidelines free for 9x12 SAE.
Nonfiction: Expose (current military); how-to (military wives); interview/profile (military); opinion (military topic); personal experience (military only); travel (of military interest). No poetry, cartoons or historical articles. Buys 100 mss/year. Query with clips of published work. Length: 1,000-3,000 words. Pays $50-300.
Photos: State availability of photos or send photos with ms. Reviews 35mm color contact sheets and prints. Caption, model releases, and identification of subjects required. Buys all rights.
Tips: "In query write a detailed description of story and how it will be told. A tentative lead is nice. Just one good story 'breaks in' a freelancer."

US NAVAL INSTITUTE PROCEEDINGS, Annapolis MD 21402. (301)268-6110. Editor-in-Chief: Clayton R. Barrow Jr. Managing Editor: Fred Rainbow. Emphasizes sea services (Navy, Marine Corps, Coast Guard) for sea services officers and enlisted personnel, other military services in the US and abroad, and civilians interested in naval/maritime affairs. Monthly magazine. Circ. 80,000. Pays on acceptance. Buys all rights. Byline given. Phone queries OK, but all material must be submitted on speculation. Submit seasonal/anniversary material at least 6 months in advance. Photocopied submissions OK. Computer printout submissions OK; "prefers typed, double-spaced mss." SASE. Reports in 2 weeks (queries); 2 months (manuscripts). Free sample copy.
Nonfiction: Informational, analytical, historical (based on primary sources, unpublished and/or first-hand experience); humor; personal opinion; photo feature; technical; professional notes; and book reviews. No poetry. Query. Length: 4,000 words maximum. Pays $200-400.
Photos: Purchased with or without accompanying ms or on assignment. Captions required. Query. Pays $15 maximum for b&w 8x10 glossy prints. "We pay $2 for each photo submitted with articles by people other than the photographer."
Columns/Departments: Fred Rainbow, managing editor. Comment and Discussion (comments 500-700 words on new subjects or ones previously covered in magazine); Professional Notes; Nobody Asked Me, But . . . (700-1,000 words, strong opinion on naval/maritime topic); and Book Reviews. Buys 35 Book Reviews; 35 Professional Notes; 100 Comment and Discussion and 10 Nobody Asked Me, But columns a year. Pays $25-150.
Fillers: Miss Laraine Missory, fillers editor. Anecdotes should be humorous actual occurrences, not previously published. Buys 25 fillers/year. Length: maximum 200 words. Pays $25 flat rate.
Tips: "The Comment and Discussion section is our bread and butter. It is a glorified letters to the editor section and exemplifies the concept of the *Proceedings* as a forum. We particularly welcome comments on material published in previous issues of the magazine. This offers the writer of the comment an opportunity to expand the discussion of a particular topic and to bring his own viewpoint into it. This feature does not pay particularly well, but it is an excellent opportunity to get one's work into print."

Music

Listed here are publications emphasizing various kinds of music (jazz, opera, bluegrass, etc.) and musicians. Additional music- (and dance-) related markets are included in the Theater, Movie, TV, and Entertainment section.

AUDIO, CBS Publications, 1515 Broadway, New York NY 10036. (212)719-6000. Editor: Eugene Pitts III. Monthly magazine covering audio equipment and technology for advanced hi-fi buffs and professionals in the industry. Circ. 140,000. Pays on publication. Byline given. Pays negotiable kill fee. Buys all rights. Photocopied submissions OK. No computer printout or disk submissions. SASE. Reports in 1 month on queries. No writer's guidelines available.

Nonfiction: How-to (construct sets or components); interview/profile (of professionals in hi-fi technology); and technical (concerning hi-fi technology and design). "This is a very technical magazine. Writers must be thoroughly knowledgeable in the field of hi-fi technology." No general or beginner articles. Buys 6 mss/year, "mostly from regular contributors." Query with clips of published work and resume. Length: 1,500-3,000 words. Pays $100-1,000 ($50-250/published page).

Photos: Reviews 35mm color transparencies and prints. "Photos are usually paid for with payment for ms." Identification of subjects required.

BEATLEFAN, The Goody Press, Box 33515, Decatur GA 30033. Editor: E.L. King. Managing Editor: Justin Stonehouse. Bimonthly magazine about the Beatles, John Lennon, Paul McCartney, George Harrison and Ringo Starr for a readership averaging 24 years of age, 53% males and 47% females. Circ. 2,400. Average issue includes 6 articles and 13 departments. Pays on publication. Byline given. Buys all rights. Submit seasonal material 4 months in advance. Simultaneous, photocopied and previously published submissions OK. Computer printout submissions OK; prefers letter quality to dot matrix. SASE. Reports in 8 weeks. Sample copy $2.

Nonfiction: Historical (factual articles concerning the early Beatles tours in the US and anything to do with the band's early career); interview (with Beatles and any associates); nostalgia (articles on collecting Beatles memorabilia and trivia); personal experience (stories of meetings with the Beatles and associates); and photo feature (current photos of McCartney, Harrison and Starr and latterday photos of Lennon). Buys 8-10 unsolicited mss/year. Send complete ms. Length: 350-2,000 words. Pays $10-35. "We are looking for regular correspondents and columnists. We also need articles with tips on memorabilia collecting, record collecting, book and record reviews. We have an anniversary issue each December (accounts of the days of the Beatlemania 1964-1966 especially needed) and in event of tours or appearances by any of the Beatles, reports from each city visited will be needed." No essays on the death of John Lennon; no poems of any type, fiction, non-Beatle material, or reviews of *old* records or books.

Photos: Send photos with ms. Pays $5-20/3x7 b&w glossy print. Offers no additional payment for photos accepted with ms. Captions required identifying subjects, places, date and photographer's name.

Columns/Departments: Book Review (any books published concerning the Beatles, foreign or domestic); Record Reviews (the Beatles together or individually; domestic or foreign; official or bootleg); Those Were the Days (articles about the Beatles that deal with generally unknown aspects or details of career together or personal lives); Collecting (articles with tips for collectors of rare records and memorabilia); Thingumybob (columns of opinion); Glass Onion (articles dealing with The Beatles' music and lyrics); Beatles Video (news and reviews of video releases); Meeting The Beatles (stories of personal encounters). Buys 2 ms/issue. Send complete ms. Length: 500 words maximum. Pays $5-25.

Fillers: Clippings (not wire service stories) and puzzles having to do with the Beatles. Buys 3 mss/issue. Pays 50¢-$5.

Tips: "We get too many submissions that are general in nature and aimed at a general audience, repeating well-worn facts and events our readers already know by heart. We need articles that are specific, detailed and authoritative and that will tell confirmed Beatlemaniacs something they don't know. Articles should not be simple rewrites of reference book chapters. Opinion pieces should lean toward analysis backed by facts and examples. Among our contributing editors are noted Beatles authors Nicholas Schaffner and Wally Podrazik and former *Mersey Beat* editor Bill Harry. This shows the level of familiarity with the subject we expect. The year 1984 will mark the 20th anniversary of Beatlemania in the USA—a natural peg for stories."

BLUEGRASS UNLIMITED, Box 111, Broad Run VA 22014. (703)361-8992. Editor-in-Chief: Peter V. Kuykendall. Managing Editor: Marion C. Kuykendall. Emphasizes old-time traditional country music for musicians and devotees of bluegrass, ages from teens through the elderly. Monthly magazine. Circ. 17,000. Pays on publication. Buys all rights. Pays variable kill fee. Byline given. Phone queries OK. Submit seasonal/holiday material 3 months in advance. Photocopied and previously published submissions OK. Computer printout and disk submissions OK. SASE. Reports in 1 month. Free sample copy and writer's guidelines.

Nonfiction: Historical, how-to, humor, informational, interview, nostalgia, personal experience, opinion, photo feature, profile and technical. Buys 20-40 mss/year. Query. Length: 500-5,000 words. Pays 4-5¢/word.

Photos: Purchased with or without accompanying ms. Query for photos. Pays $15-20/page for 5x7 or 8x10 b&w glossy prints, 35mm or 2¼x2¼ color transparencies; $100 for covers.

Columns/Departments: Record and book reviews. Buys 5-10/year. Query. Length: 100-500 words. Pays 4-5¢/word.

Fiction: Adventure and humorous. Buys 5-7 mss/year. Length: 500-2,500 words. Pays 4-5¢/word.

Tips: Prefers not to see "generalized material vaguely relating to music, e.g., a fictional piece (love story) in which hero plays guitar."

CREEM, Suite 209, 210 S. Woodward Ave., Birmingham MI 48011. (313)642-8833. Editor: Dave DiMartino. Buys all rights. Pays on publication. Query. Reports in 6 weeks. SASE.

Nonfiction: Short articles, mostly music-oriented. "Feature-length stories are mostly staff-written, but we're

open for newcomers to break in with short pieces. Freelancers are used a lot in the Beat Goes On section. Please send queries and sample articles to Mark J. Norton, submissions editor. We bill ourselves as America's Only Rock 'n' Roll Magazine." Pays $50 minimum for reviews, $300 minimum for full-length features.
Photos: Freelance photos.
Tips: "You can't study the magazine too much—our stable of writers have all come from the ranks of our readers. The writer can save his time and ours by studying what we do print—and producing similar copy that we can use immediately. Short stuff—no epics on the first try. We really aren't a good market for the professional writer looking for another outlet—a writer has to be pretty obsessed with music and/or pop culture in order to be published in our book. We get people writing in for assignments who obviously have never even read the magazine and that's totally useless to us."

FRETS MAGAZINE, GPI Publications, 20605 Lazaneo, Cupertino CA 95014. (408)446-1105. Editor: Jim Hatlo. "For amateur and professional acoustic string music enthusiasts; for players, makers, listeners and fans. Country, jazz, classical, blues, pop and bluegrass. For instrumentalists interested in banjo, mandolin, guitar, violin, upright bass, dobro, dulcimer and others." Monthly magazine. Circ. open. Pays on acceptance. Buys first rights. Prefers written queries. Submit material 4 months in advance. Computer printout submissions on 8½x11 sheets with legible type OK if not a photocopy or multiple submission. "All-caps printout unacceptable." SASE. Reports in 6 weeks. Free sample copy and writer's guidelines.
Nonfiction: General interest (artist-oriented); historical (instrument making or manufacture); how-to (instrument craft and repair); interview (with artists or historically important individuals); profile (music performer); and technical (instrument making, acoustics, instrument repair). "Prefers not to see humor; poetry; general-interest articles that really belong in a less-specialized publication; articles (about performers) that only touch on biographical or human interest angles, without getting into the 'how-to' nuts and bolts of musicianship." Buys 14 mss/year. Query with clips of published work or sample lead paragraph. Length: 1,000-2,500 words. Pays $75-150. Experimental (instrument design, acoustics). Pays $50-100.
Photos: State availability of photos. Pays $25 minimum for b&w prints (reviews contact sheets); $100 for cover shot color transparencies. Captions and credits required. Buys one-time rights.
Columns/Departments: Repair Shop (instrument craft and repair); and *FRETS* Visits (on-location visit to manufacturer). Buys 10 mss/year. Query. Length: 1,200-1,700 words. Pays $75-125, including photos.
Fillers: Newsbreaks, upcoming events, music-related news.
Tips: "We should present a wider market as we expand our focus to include ancillary areas—such as sound reinforcement for acoustic musicians, using personal computers in booking and management, recording techniques for acoustic music, and so on."

GUITAR PLAYER MAGAZINE, 20605 Lazaneo, Cupertino CA 95014. (408)446-1105. Editor: Tom Wheeler. For persons "interested in guitars; guitarists, manufacturers, guitar builders, bass players, equipment, careers, etc." Monthly magazine. Circ. 151,300. Buys first time and reprint rights. Byline given. Buys 30-40 mss/year. Pays on acceptance. Free sample copy to a writer on request. Reports in 3 weeks. Query. SASE.
Nonfiction: Publishes "wide variety of articles pertaining to guitars and guitarists: interviews, guitar craftsmen profiles, how-to features—anything amateur and professional guitarists would find fascinating and/or helpful. On interviews with 'name' performers, be as technical as possible regarding strings, guitars, techniques, etc. We're not a pop culture magazine, but a magazine for musicians." Also buys features on such subjects as a guitar museum, the role of the guitar in elementary education, personal reminiscences of past greats, technical gadgets and how to work them, analysis of flamenco, etc." Recent article example: Keith Richards cover story (January 1983). Length: open. Pays $50-200.
Photos: Photos purchased with mss. B&w glossy prints. Pays $25-50. Buys 35mm color transparencies. Pays $150 (for cover only). Buys one time rights.

HIGH FIDELITY/MUSICAL AMERICA, 825 7th Ave., New York NY 10019. Editor: William Tynan. Monthly. Circ. 40,000. Buys all rights. Pays on publication. SASE.
Nonfiction: Articles, musical and audio, are generally prepared by acknowledged writers and authorities in the field, but does use freelance material. Query with clips of published work. Length: 1,200 words maximum. Pays $150 minimum.
Photos: New b&w photos of musical personalities, events, etc.

ILLINOIS ENTERTAINER, Box 356, Mount Prospect IL 60056. (312)298-9333. Editor: Guy C. Arnston. Monthly tabloid covering music and entertainment for consumers within 100-mile radius of Chicago interested in music. Circ. 75,000. Pays on publication. Byline given. Offers 100% kill fee. Buys one-time rights. Submit seasonal/holiday material 2 months in advance. Simultaneous queries OK. Computer printout submissions OK "if letters are clear"; prefers letter quality to dot matrix; "disk submissions may be okay, check first." SASE. Reports in 1 week on queries; 1 month on mss. Sample copy $2; free writer's guidelines.
Nonfiction: Interview/profile (of entertainment figures). Recently published "Ebert & Siskel Sneak into the

Movies," "All Eyes Are on Survivor," "Cheap Trick Face to Face; One on One," "First Comics with an Eye on the Future." No Q&A interviews. Buys 200 mss/year. Query with clips of published work. Length: 500-2,000 words. Pays $15-100.

Photos: State availability of photos. Pays $10-20 for 5x7 or 8x10 b&w prints; $100 for color cover photo. Captions and identification of subjects required.

Columns/Departments: Rack Jobbing (record reviews stress record over band or genre); film reviews; book reviews. Buys 500 mss/year. Query with clips of published work. Length: 150-250 words. Pays $6-20.

Tips: "Send samples in mail (published or unpublished) with phone numbers, and be patient."

INTERNATIONAL MUSICIAN, American Federation of Musicians, 1500 Broadway, New York NY 10036. (212)869-1330. Editor: J. Martin Emerson. For professional musicians. Monthly. Byline given. Pays on acceptance. Reports in 2 months. SASE.

Nonfiction: Articles on prominent instrumental musicians (classical, jazz, rock or country). Send complete ms. Length: 1,500-2,000 words.

IT WILL STAND, Dedicated to the Preservation of Beach Music, It Will Stand Prod., 1505 Elizabeth Ave., Charlotte NC 28204. (704)377-0700. Editor: Chris Beachley. Irregular monthly magazine covering beach music (especially soul 1940-present). Circ. 1,700. Pays on acceptance. Byline given. Offers negotiable kill fee. Buys all rights. Submit seasonal/holiday material 2 months in advance. Sample copy $2.

Nonfiction: Historical/nostalgic, interview/profile, opinion, personal experience, photo feature. Buys 5 and more mss/year. Query with clips of published work or send complete ms. Length: open. Pays variable fee.

Photos: State availability of photos. Reviews color and b&w contact sheets and prints.

Tips: "Contact us for direction. We even have artist's phone numbers ready for interviews." Magazine will buy more mss as it becomes a regular monthly publication in the year ahead.

KEYBOARD MAGAZINE, 20605 Lazaneo, Cupertino CA 95014. (408)446-1105. Editor: Tom Darter. For those who play piano, organ, synthesizer, accordion, harpsichord, or any other keyboard instrument. All styles of music; all levels of ability. Monthly magazine. Circ. 75,000. Pays on acceptance. Buys all rights. Byline given. Phone queries OK. SASE. Reports in 2 weeks. Free sample copy and writer's guidelines.

Nonfiction: "We publish articles on a wide variety of topics pertaining to keyboard players and their instruments. In addition to interviews with keyboard artists in all styles of music, we are interested in historical and analytical pieces, how-to articles dealing either with music or with equipment, profiles on well-known instrument makers and their products. In general, anything that amateur and professional keyboardists would find interesting and/or useful." Buys 20 unsolicited mss/year. Recent article example: "The New Synthesizer Rock" (June 1982). Query; letter should mention topic and length of article, and describe basic approach. "It's nice (not necessary) to have a sample first paragraph." Length: approximately 2,000-5,000 words. Pays $100-200.

Tips: "Query first (just a few ideas at at time, rather than twenty). A musical background helps, and a knowledge of keyboard instruments is valuable."

MODERN DRUMMER, 1000 Clifton Ave., Clifton NJ 07013. (201)778-1700. Editor-in-Chief: Ronald Spagnardi. Features Editor: Rick Mattingly. Managing Editor: Scott K. Fish. For "student, semi-pro and professional drummers at all ages and levels of playing ability, with varied specialized interests within the field." Published 12x yearly. Circ. 45,000. Pays on publication. Buys all rights. Phone queries OK. Photocopied and previously published submissions OK. SASE. Reports in 4 weeks. Sample copy $2.25; free writer's guidelines.

Nonfiction: How-to, informational, interview, personal opinion, new product, personal experience and technical. "All submissions must appeal to the specialized interests of drummers." Buys 5-10 mss/issue. Query or submit complete ms. Length: 3,000-6,000 words. Pays $100-500.

Photos: Purchased with accompanying ms. Considers 8x10 b&w and color transparencies. Submit prints or negatives.

Columns/Departments: Jazz Drummers Workshop, Rock Perspectives, Rudimental Symposium, Complete Percussionist, Teachers Forum, Drum Soloist, Show & Studio, Strictly Technique, Book Reviews and Shop Talk. "Technical knowledge of area required for most columns." Buys 10-15 mss/issue. Query or submit complete ms. Length: 500-1,500 words. Pays $25-150. Open to suggestions for new columns and departments.

MODERN RECORDING & MUSIC, MR&M Publishing Corp., 1120 Old Country Rd., Plainview NY 11803. (516)433-6530. Editor: John Woram. Managing Editor: Ricki Zide. Monthly magazine covering semi-pro and professional recording of music for musicians, soundmen and recording engineers. Circ. 50,000. Pays second week of publication month. Buys all rights. Submit all material at least 3 months in advance. Photocopied submissions OK. SASE. Reports in 1 week. Provides sample copy "after assignment."

Nonfiction: Historical/nostalgic (recording industry); how-to (basic construction of a device using readily available parts to duplicate an expensive device in a small budget studio or at home); humor; interview/profile (musician, engineer, producer or someone in an affiliated field). Also publishes an annual buyers' guide listing

products, specs, and prices of equipment. Buys 40 mss/year. Query with clips of published work and an outline. Length: 2,000 words minimum. Pays $150-200/article.
Photos: Reviews 2¼x2¼ or 35mm color transparencies; 8x10 glossy prints or contact sheets. Pays $25 inside color; $15 inside b&w; $75 for color cover; or package payment of $150.

‡**MUSIC & SOUND OUTPUT,** Testa Communications, 220 Westbury Ave., Carle Place NY 11514. (516)334-7880. Editor: Bill Stephen. Monthly magazine covering the business of making music for musicians and soundmen. Circ. 93,000. Pays on publication. Byline given. Offers 25% kill fee. Buys first North American serial rights. Photocopied submissions OK. Computer printout and disk submissions OK. SASE. Reports in 3 weeks. Sample copy $2.50; free writer's guidelines.
Nonfiction: Book excerpts; how-to (items that aid people in surviving in the music business); humor (cartoons and satire); interview/profile (music-related); new product (instruments); opinion (reviews). Buys 75 mss/year. Query with clips. Length: 500-2,500 words. Pays $50-250.
Photos: State availability of photos. Pays $25-100 for 35mm b&w transparencies; $50-125 for 35mm color transparencies. Captions and identification of subjects required. Buys one-time rights.
Fiction: Adventure; historical (music); humorous; novel excerpts; serialized novels; suspense. Buys 8 mss/year. Query with clips. Length: 2,500-3,500 words. Pays $250-350.
Tips: "We're open to profiles/interviews. Look for the obscure or overlooked story."

MUSIC CITY NEWS, Suite 601, 50 Music Square W., Nashville TN 37203. (615)329-2200. Editor: Lee Rector. Emphasizes country music. Monthly tabloid. Circ. 100,000. Buys all rights. Phone queries OK. Submit seasonal or holiday material 2 months in advance. Photocopied submissions OK. SASE. Reports in 10 weeks. Free sample copy on request.
Nonfiction: "Interview type articles with country music personalities: question/answer, narrative/quote, etc. Focusing on new and fresh angles about the entertainer rather than biographical histories." Buys 18-24 unsolicited mss/year. Query. Length: 500-1,250 words. Pays $100-125/feature, $75/junior feature, and $50/vignettes.
Photos: Purchased on acceptance by assignment. Query. Pays $10 maximum for 8x10 b&w glossy prints.

MUSIC MAGAZINE, Barrett & Colgrass Inc., Suite 202, 56 The Esplanade, Toronto, Ontario, Canada M5E 1A7. (416)364-5938. Editor: Ulla Colgrass. Emphasizes classical music. Bimonthly magazine. Circ. 11,000. Pays on publication. Buys all rights. Byline given. Phone queries OK. Submit seasonal/holiday material 4 months in advance. Photocopied and previously published submissions (book excerpts) OK. Computer printout submissions OK; prefers letter quality to dot matrix. SAE and International Reply Coupons. Reports in 3 weeks. Sample copy and writer's guidelines $2.
Nonfiction: Interview, historical articles, photo feature and profile. "All articles should pertain to classical music and people in that world. We do not want any academic analysis or short pieces of family experiences in classical music." Query with clips of published work. Unsolicited articles will not be returned. Length: 1,500-3,500 words. Pays $100-250.
Photos: State availability of photos. Pays $15-25 for 8x10 b&w glossy prints or contact sheets; $100 for color transparencies. No posed promotion photos. "Candid lively material only." Buys one-time rights. Captions required.
Tips: Send sample of your writing, suggested subjects. Off-beat subjects are welcome, but must be thoroughly interesting to be considered. A famous person or major subject in music are your best bet.

‡**NOT JUST JAZZ, The Arts—Seen through the Eyes of the Artist,** Not Just Jazz, Inc., 314 W. 52nd St., New York NY 10019. (212)664-1915. Editor: Randy Fordyce. Bimonthly magazine covering music (particularly jazz)—all aspects with some emphasis on education; and other arts (visual, dance, etc.). "Enlightening information and entertainment by and about the people who make music and art happen." Estab. 1983 (as magazine). Circ. 50,000. Pays on publication. Byline given. Buys one-time rights. Submit seasonal/holiday material 5 months in advance. Simultaneous queries, and photocopied and simultaneous submissions OK. SASE. Reports in 2 weeks on queries; 1 month on mss. Sample copy for $1; free writer's guidelines.
Nonfiction: General interest (general for our area); humor; interview/profile. No reviews, exposes, "downers of any kind." Buys 8-10 mss/year. Send complete ms. Length: 500-2,500 words. Pays $5-75.
Fiction: Fantasy, humorous, mainstream, science fiction, all related to the arts. Buys 1-6 mss/year. Send complete ms. Length: 1,000-3,000 words. Pays $25-100.
Tips: "We are not 'artsy' and communicate in plain language. A thorough reading of a sample issue should give a reality here. If it doesn't . . . that writer could probably not write for us." Personality interviews and profiles open to freelancers. The writer should *never* come between the subject and the reader. As the business becomes more and more vertical, it becomes more important for writers to write about what they know. Research is a poor substitute for experience."

‡**OPERA CANADA**, Suite 433, 366 Adelaide St. E., Toronto, Ontario, Canada M5A 3X9. (416)363-0395. Contact: Editor. For readers who are interested in serious music; specifically, opera. Quarterly magazine. Circ. 6,000. Not copyrighted. Byline given. Buys 10 mss/year. Pays on publication. Sample copy $3. Photocopied and simultaneous submissions OK. Reports on material accepted for publication within 1 year. Returns rejected material in 1 month. Query or submit complete ms. SAE and International Reply Coupons.
Nonfiction: "Because we are Canada's only opera magazine, we like to keep 75% of our content Canadian, i.e., by Canadians or about Canadian personalities/events. We prefer informative and/or humorous articles about any aspect of music theater, with an emphasis on opera. The relationship of the actual subject matter to opera can be direct or at least related. We accept record reviews (*only* operatic recordings); book reviews (books covering any aspect of music theater); and interviews with major operatic personalities. Please, no reviews of performances. We have staff reviewers." Length (for all articles except reviews of books and records): 1,000-3,000 words. Pays $25-50. Length for reviews: 100-500 words. Pays $10.
Photos: No additional payment for photos used with mss. Captions required.

OVATION, 320 W. 57th St., New York NY 10019. Editor: Sam Chase. Monthly magazine for classical music listeners covering classical music and the equipment on which to hear it. Estab. 1980. Average issue includes 4 features plus departments. Pays on publication. Byline given. Buys all rights. Submit seasonal material 4 months in advance, SASE. Reports in 1 month. Sample copy $2.79.
Nonfiction: "We are primarily interested in interviews with and articles about the foremost classical music artists. Historical pieces will also be considered." Buys 5 unsolicited mss/year. Recent article example: "Sir Georg Solti" (February 1982). Query with clips of previously published work. Length: 800-4,500 words. Pays $5/inch.
Photos: State availability of photos. May offer additional payment for photos accepted with ms. Captions required. Buys one-time rights.

POLYPHONY MAGAZINE, 1020 W. Wilshire, Box 20305, Oklahoma City OK 73156. (405)842-5480. Bimonthly magazine about electronic music and home recording for readers who are interested in building and using electronic music instruments to perform in bands or to make recordings in their studios. Circ. 4,000. Pays on publication. Buys all rights or by arrangement. Phone queries OK. Submit seasonal material 3 months in advance. Simultaneous, photocopied and previously published submissions OK. Computer printout and disk submissions OK. SASE. Reports in 2 weeks on queries; in 3 weeks on mss. Free sample copy.
Nonfiction: General interest (music theory, electronics theory, acoustics); how-to (design and build electronic music devices, record music); interview (with progressive musicians using electronic techniques or designers of electronic music equipment); new product; and technical. No mainstream type music and artist review articles. Buys 8 mss/issue. Query with clips of previously published work. "The feature stories we use are the best area for freelancers. We need construction projects, modifications for commercial equipment, computer software for music use, and tutorials dealing with electronic music and recording studio techniques, performance, design and theory. Freelancers should write in a conversational manner; provide enough details in project articles to allow novices to complete the project; provide informative charts, graphs, drawings or photos; present material which is practical to someone working in this medium." Length: 1,000-5,000 words. Pays $35/printed page.
Photos: State availability of photos or send photos with ms. Pays $25 minimum/5x7 b&w glossy print. Captions preferred; model release required. Buys all rights or by arrangement.

PRAIRIE SUN, The Midwest Magazine of Music and Current Events, Box 885, Peoria IL 61652. (309)673-6624. Editor-in-Chief: Bill Knight. Weekly tabloid for music listeners who are also interested in films, books and general entertainment. "We have a consciously Midwest orientation, and combine music and current events." Circ. 20,000. Pays on publication. Buys first rights. Byline given. Simultaneous, photocopied and previously published submissions OK. SASE. Reports in 3 weeks. Sample copy $1.
Nonfiction: Expose (government and corporate interests); how-to (back to nature; gardening; living with less; alternative energy systems); interview (especially cultural and entertainment personalities); and profile (music personalities). Buys 30 mss/year. Query with outline. Length: 400-1,000 words. Pays $15-40.
Tips: "Creatively select themes."

RELIX MAGAZINE, Music for the Mind, Relix Magazine, Inc., Box 94, Brooklyn NY 11229. (212)645-0818. Editor: Toni A. Brown. Bimonthly magazine covering rock 'n' roll music and "specializing in Grateful Dead, Springsteen, Stones, and other top groups for readers aged 13-35." Circ. 20,000. Pays on publication. Byline given. Buys all rights. Photocopied submissions OK. No computer printout or disk submissions. SASE. Sample copy $2.
Nonfiction: Historical/nostalgic, interview/profile, new product, personal experience, photo feature, technical. Special issues include November photo special. Query with clips of published work if available or send complete ms. Length: open. Pays variable rates.
Columns/Departments: Query with clips of published work, if available, or send complete ms. Length: open.

Pays variable rates.

Fiction: Query with clips of published work, if available, or send complete ms. Length: open. Pays variable rates.

Fillers: Clippings, jokes, gags, anecdotes, short humor, newsbreaks. Length: open. Pays variable rates.

‡**ROCKBILL**, Rave Communications, 850 7th Ave., New York NY 10019. (212)977-7745. Editor: Stuart Matranga. Monthly magazine focusing on rock music and related topics for distribution at rock music clubs. Estab. 1982. Circ. 530,000. Pays on publication. Byline given. Buys one-time rights. Simultaneous queries OK. SASE. Reports in 1 month on queries; 1 week on mss. Free sample copy and writer's guidelines.
Nonfiction: Interview/profile; lifestyle and new music articles. "As long as we feel it 'fits' the magazine, we'll use any genre of writing—there are no restrictions." Buys 150 mss/year. Query with published clips. Length: 150-2,000 words. Pays $25-150.
Photos: State availability of photos. Reviews color transparencies. Captions and identification of subjects required.
Columns/Departments: Radio; Cable TV; Video. "These vary all the time. We encourage writers to create column ideas." Query with published clips. Length: open. Pays variable rates.
Fiction: "We often print fiction, if fiction is the best means of conveying certain ideas important to the magazine. Most of our fiction thus far has been inspired by and relates closely to a particular musician." Buys variable number of mss/year. Query with published clips. Length: open. Pays variable rates.
Tips: "We try to publish at least one new writer per issue. Our best advice is to keep trying to be as brilliant as possible; to think in terms of a specific subject's relation to the universe; in other words, get the big picture—but most importantly, keep writing. The best way to capture our attention is to write with integrity about something relating to rock music. Mostly, we use personality profiles, but to us, the writing and the writer's perspectives are at least as important as the stars."

ROLLING STONE, 745 5th Ave., New York NY 10151. Editor: Jann S. Wenner. "Seldom accept freelance material. All our work is assigned or done by our staff." Offers 25% kill fee. Byline given.

THE $ENSIBLE SOUND, 403 Darwin Dr., Snyder NY 14226. Editor/Publisher: John A. Horan. "All readers are high fidelity enthusiasts, and many have a high fidelity industry-related job." Quarterly magazine. Circ. 5,200. Pays on acceptance. Buys all rights. Byline given. Simultaneous, photocopied and previously published submissions OK. SASE. Reports in 2 weeks. Sample copy $2.
Nonfiction: Expose, how-to, general interest, humor, historical, interview (people in hi-fi business, manufacturers or retail); new product (all types of new audio equipment); nostalgia (articles and opinion on older equipment); personal experience (with various types of audio equipment); photo feature (on installation, or how-to tips); profile (of hi-fi equipment); and technical (pertaining to audio). "Subjective evaluations of hi-fi equipment make up 70% of our publication. Will accept 10/issue." Buys 2 mss/issue. Submit outline. Pays $25 maximum.
Columns/Departments: Bits & Pieces (short items of interest to hi-fi hobbyists); Ramblings (do-it-yourself tips on bettering existing systems); Record Reviews (of records which would be of interest to audiophiles). Query. Length: 25-400 words. Pays $5 maximum.

STEREO GUIDE, Infracom, Ltd., 6 Byng Ave., Brampton, Ontario, Canada L6Y 1L1. (416)451-8395. Editor: Maurice Holtham. Magazine published 6 times/year for home hi-fi and video enthusiasts who are not necessarily audio/video engineers. Circ. 20,000. Pays on acceptance. Byline given. Offers 100% kill fee. Buys first North American serial rights. Submit seasonal/holiday material 3 months in advance. Simultaneous queries and simultaneous and photocopied submissions OK. Reports in 3 weeks on queries; 1 month on mss. Free sample copy.
Nonfiction: General interest; how-to (understand and enjoy home hi-fi and video systems); interview/profile; technical. "Articles must show an understanding of technical subject and explain it to readers who may have limited technical ability, but are keen audiophiles. No blatantly commercial or product 'A' is superior to product 'B' articles. Showing the merits of one over the other is OK; let the reader decide which is better for him/ her." Buys 15-20 mss/year. Query with clips of published work. Length: 1,000-2,500 words. Pays $150-200.
Photos: State availability of photos. Pays $10 minimum for 8x10 b&w prints. Captions, model release and identification of subjects required. Buys one-time rights.
Columns/Departments: Would like to start special interest columns—open to ideas.

‡**TOWER RECORDS' PULSE!**, MTS, Inc., 900 Enterprise Dr., Sacramento CA 95825. (916)920-2500. Editor: Mike Farrace. Monthly tabloid covering recorded music. Estab. 1983. Circ. 50,000. Pays on publication. Byline given. Buys first rights. Simultaneous and photocopied submissions OK. Computer printout or disk submissions OK. SASE. Reports in 3 weeks. Free sample copy: writer's guidelines for SAE.
Nonfiction: Humor (trends in recorded comedy, parodies of lyrics or musical styles); interview/profile (angled toward artist's record-buying habits, write for specifics); new product (record and tape care, new hardware,

e.g., stereo and video equipment); personal experience (anecdotes about buying records, unusual experiences at concerts, encounters with musical artists). Buys 40-50 mss/year. Query or send complete ms. Length: 200-2,500 words. Pays $15-200.
Photos: State availability of photos. Reviews b&w prints. Caption and identification of subjects required. Buys one-time rights.
Fillers: Newsbreaks.
Tips: "Break in with 500-1,000 word news-oriented featurettes on recording artists or on record-product-related news. List price reductions, bonus discs, special packaging, great liner notes, etc."

TRADITION, 106 Navajo, Council Bluffs IA 51501. Editor: Robert Everhart. Emphasizes traditional country music and other aspects of pioneer living. Monthly magazine. Circ. 2,500. Pays on acceptance. Buys one-time rights. Byline given. Submit seasonal/holiday material 3 months in advance of issue date. Simultaneous, photocopied and previously published submissions OK. SASE. Reports in 1 month. Free sample copy.
Nonfiction: Historical (relating to country music); how-to (play, write, or perform country music); inspirational (on country gospel); interview (with country performers, both traditional and contemporary); nostalgia (pioneer living); personal experience (country music); and travel (in connection with country music contests or festivals). Buys 6 mss/year. Query. Length: 200-2,000 words. Pays $20-50.
Photos: State availability of photos with query. Payment is included in ms price. Uses 5x7 b&w prints. Captions and model release required. Buys one-time rights.
Poetry: Free verse and traditional. Buys 1/issue. Length: 3-15 lines. Limit submissions to batches of 3. Pays in copies.
Tips: "Material must be concerned with what we term 'real' country music as opposed to today's 'pop' country music. Freelancer must be knowledgeable of the subject; many writers don't even know who the father of country music is, let alone write about him."

TROUSER PRESS, Trans-Oceanic Trouser Press, Inc., 212 5th Ave., New York NY 10010. (212)889-7145. Editor: Scott Isler. Monthly magazine covering rock music for young, college-oriented readers. Circ. 60,000. Pays after publication. Byline given. Buys all rights. Submit seasonal/holiday material 3 months in advance. Simultaneous queries, photocopied and previously published submissions OK. SASE. Reports in 4 weeks on queries. Sample copy $1.50.
Nonfiction: Interview/profile (of band or artists), surveys of movements and new developments. Buys 90-100 mss/year. Recent article example: Cover story On Talking Heads (April 1982). Query with clips of published work. Length: 3,000 words maximum. Pays $50-75/article.
Photos: State availability of photos. Pays $15 minimum for 8x10 glossy prints, more for color slides.
Columns/Departments: Local music scene reports, concert reviews, LP reviews. Buys 100-150/year. Length: 300-350 words. Pays $10.
Tips: "I'm very concerned with quality of writing. If someone has a good portfolio of clippings and a good knowledge of music, I'm impressed. Although *Trouser Press* doesn't offer much in the way of monetary reward, our writers appreciate having an outlet for intelligent articles on a very popular subject."

Mystery

Consult the Literary and "Little" category for additional mystery markets. For information on writing mysteries see the *Mystery Writer's Handbook*, by the Mystery Writers of America (revised by Lawrence Treat, Writer's Digest Books).

ALFRED HITCHCOCK'S MYSTERY MAGAZINE, Davis Publications, Inc., 380 Lexington Ave., New York NY 10017. Editor: Cathleen Jordan. Emphasizes mystery fiction. Magazine published 13 times a year. Circ. 200,000. Buys 100 mss/year. Pays on acceptance. Buys first and second serial (reprint) rights. Byline given. Submit seasonal/holiday material 7 months in advance. Photocopied submissions OK. SASE. Reports in 2 months or less. Writer's guidelines for SASE.
Nonfiction: Buys some articles on the mystery genre and on intriguing historical mysteries, preferably unsolved ones. Length: 2,000-3000 words.
Fiction: Original and well-written mystery and crime fiction. Length: 1,000-14,000 words.

ELLERY QUEEN'S MYSTERY MAGAZINE, Davis Publications, Inc., 380 Lexington Ave., New York NY 10017. Editor: Eleanor Sullivan. Magazine published 13 times/year. Circ. 375,000. Pays on acceptance. Byline given. Submit seasonal/holiday material 7 months in advance. Simultaneous, photocopied and previously published submissions OK. SASE. Reports in 1 month. Free writer's guidelines.

Fiction: Special consideration will be given to "anything timely and original. We publish every type of mystery: the suspense story, the psychological study, the deductive puzzle—the gamut of crime and detection from the realistic (including the policeman's lot and stories of police procedure) to the more imaginative (including 'locked rooms' and impossible crimes). We need private-eye stories, but do not want sex, sadism or sensationalism-for-the-sake-of-sensationalism." No gore or horror; seldom publish parodies or pastiches. Buys 13 mss/issue. Length: 6,000 words maximum; occasionally higher but not often. Pays 3-8¢/word.

Tips: "We have a department of First Stories to encourage writers whose fiction has never before been in print. We publish an average of 20 first stories a year."

MIKE SHAYNE MYSTERY MAGAZINE, Renown Publications, Inc., Box 178, Reseda CA 91335. Editor: Charles E. Fritch. Monthly magazine. Buys non-exclusive World Magazine serial rights. Photocopied submissions OK. Reports within 3 months.

Fiction: All kinds of mystery/suspense stories; prefers the offbeat and unusual rather than the conventional and cliched; horror is OK. Pays 1½¢/word after publication.

Tips: "Avoid the cliches—the hard boiled private eye, the spouse-killer, the little old lady being threatened, the standard hitperson, the investigator miraculously solving the case by making unverified conclusions, the criminal confessing at the last minute when there's no reason for him to do so, the culprit caught by some last minute revelation no one but the author knew about, the poor sap who gets clobbered for no reason. Make it short and unusual, something we can't get any place else. *MSMM* frequently publishes first stories."

Nature, Conservation, and Ecology

The publications in this section exist for the furtherance of the natural environment—wildlife, nature preserves and the ecobalance. They do not publish recreation or travel articles except as they relate to conservation or nature. Other markets for this kind of material will be found in the Regional, Sports, and Travel, Camping, and Trailer categories, although the magazines listed there require that nature or conservation articles be slanted to their specialized subject matter and audience. Energy conservation topics for professionals are covered in the Trade Energy category.

AMERICAN FORESTS, American Forestry Association, 1319 18th St. NW, Washington DC 20036. (202)467-5810. Editor: Bill Rooney. "We are an organization for the advancement of intelligent management and use of our forests, soil, water, wildlife, and all other natural resources necessary for an environment of high quality and the well-being of all citizens." Monthly magazine. Circ. 50,000. Pays on acceptance. Buys one-time rights. Byline given. Phone queries OK, but written queries preferred. Submit seasonal/holiday material 5 months in advance. SASE. Reports in 6 weeks. Free writer's guidelines.

Nonfiction: General interest, historical, how-to, humor and inspirational. "All articles should emphasize trees, forests, wildlife or land use." Buys 5 mss/issue. Query. Length: 2,000 words. Pays $100-350.

Photos: State availability of photos. Offers no additional payment for photos accompanying mss. Uses 8x10 b&w glossy prints; 35mm or larger color transparencies. Buys one-time rights. Captions required.

Tips: "Query should have honesty, information on photo support."

AUDUBON MAGAZINE, 950 3rd Ave., New York NY 10022. "Not soliciting freelance material; practically all articles done on assignment only. We have a backlog of articles from known writers and contributors. Our issues are planned well in advance of publication and follow a theme." Pays negotiable kill fee. Byline given.

BIRD WATCHER'S DIGEST, Pardson Corp., Box 110, Marietta OH 45750. Editor: Mary B. Bowers. Focuses on birds and bird watching. Bimonthly magazine. Circ. 40,000. Pays on publication. Buys first North American serial rights and second serial rights. Photocopied and previously published submissions OK. SASE. Reports in 1 month on queries. Sample copy $2; writer's guidelines for SASE.

Nonfiction: General interest (features on species, environmental issues involving birds, endangered and threatened species); historical; how-to; humor (essays); interview (and reports on research); nostalgia; opinion; profile (outstanding or unusual bird watchers); travel (where to go to see birds); personal experience (rare sightings; observations of displays and behavior); photo feature; technical (individual species); and accompanying artwork. Buys 60-65 unsolicited mss/year. Send complete ms or send clips of previously published work with query. Length: 600-3,000 words. Pays $25/reprint and up to $50/original.

Photos: State availability of photos. Reviews 5x7 and up b&w glossy prints and 35mm and up color transparencies. Pays $10 for each b&w photo used (returnable) and $25 for full color.
Poetry: Avant-garde, free verse; light verse; and traditional. Buys 12-20 mss/year. Maximum of 5. Pays $15.
Fillers: Anecdotes. Buys 3-6 mss/issue. Length: 50-225 words. Pays $5.
Tips: "We want good ornithology, good writing. Articles on birds suited for a general interest magazine may be too basic for us. Our audience is quite knowledgeable about birds. Writers must be at least as knowledgeable."

ENVIRONMENT, 4000 Albemarle St. NW., Washington DC 20016. Managing Editor: Jane Scully. For citizens, scientists, business and government executives, teachers, high school and college students interested in environment or effects of technology and science in public affairs. Magazine published 10 times/year. Circ. 17,000. Buys all rights. Byline given. Pays on publication to professional writers. Sample copy $3.50. Photocopied submissions OK. Reports in 6-8 weeks. Query or submit 3 double-spaced copies of complete ms. SASE.
Nonfiction: Scientific and environmental material; effects of technology on society. Preferred length: 2,500-4,500 words for full-length article. Pays $100-300, depending on material. Also accepts shorter articles (1,100-1,700 words) for "Overview" section. Pays $75. "All full-length articles must be annotated (referenced) and all conclusions must follow logically from the facts and arguments presented." Prefers articles centering around policy-oriented, public decision-making, scientific and technological issues.

ENVIRONMENTAL ACTION, 1346 Connecticut Ave., Washington DC 20036. Editors: Jim Jubak, Francesca Lyman and Richard Asinof. 20% freelance written. Emphasizes grass roots citizen action and congressional/governmental activity affecting the environment for a well-educated, sophisticated, politically oriented readership. Monthly magazine. Circ. 25,000. Pays on publication. Buys all rights. Byline given. No computer printout or disk submissions. SASE. Reports in 6 weeks. Sample copy $2.50.
Nonfiction: Exposé; human interest feature; news feature; political analysis (on such issues as the urban environment, chemical pollution, public health, alternative energy, and the public interest movement). Less interested in wilderness and wildlife issues. Prefers not to see material on nature appreciation and animal rights/cruelty, or photo essays. Buys 15-20 mss/year. Query with clips of published work. Length: 1,000-2,500 words. Pays according to length.
Photos: State availability of photos. Pays $15-50 for 8x10 b&w glossy prints. Buys all rights.
Tips: "We are frequently in the market for local stories that have national significance. Because we have virtually no travel budget, we are most receptive to articles that the editors cannot do from Washington."

FORESTS & PEOPLE, Official Publication of the Louisiana Forestry Association, Louisiana Forestry Association, Drawer 5067, Alexandria LA 71301. (318)443-2558. Editor: Chuck Springstan. Quarterly magazine covering forests, forest industry, wood-related stories, wildlife for general readers, both in and out of the forest industry. Circ. 8,500. Pays on publication. Byline given. Not copyrighted. Submit seasonal/holiday material 2 months in advance. Simultaneous queries, and simultaneous, photocopied, and previously published submissions OK. Reports in 2 weeks on queries; 3 weeks on mss. Sample copy $1.50; free writer's guidelines.
Nonfiction: General interest (recreation, wildlife, crafts with wood, festivals); historical/nostalgic (logging towns, historical wooden buildings, forestry legends); interview/profile (of forest industry execs, foresters, loggers, wildlife managers, tree farmers); photo feature (of scenic forest, wetlands, logging operations); technical (innovative equipment, chemicals, operations, forestland studies, or industry profiles). No research papers. Articles may cover a technical subject but must be understandable to the general public." Buys 12 mss/year. Query with clips of published work. Length: open. Pays $50.
Photos: State availability of photos. Reviews b&w and color contact sheets. Identification of subjects required.

‡**HIGH COUNTRY NEWS,** High Country Foundation, Box K, Lander WY 82520. (307)332-6970. Editor: Dan Whipple. Biweekly tabloid covering environment and natural resource issues in the Rocky Mountain states for environmentalists, politicians, companies, etc. Circ. 4,000. Pays on publication. Byline given. Buys one-time rights. Computer printout submissions OK if "double spaced (at least) and legible"; prefers letter quality to dot matrix. Submit seasonal/holiday material 6 weeks in advance. SASE. Reports in 1 month. Free sample copy and writer's guidelines.
Nonfiction: Expose (government, corporate); historical/nostalgic; how-to (appropriate technology); humor; interview/profile; opinion; personal experience; photo feature. Special issues include those on states in the region. Buys 50 mss/year. Query. Length: 3,000 word maximum. Pays 5¢/word.
Photos: Kathy Bogan, photo editor. Send photos with ms. Reviews b&w contact sheets and prints. Captions and identification of subjects required.
Poetry: Chip Rawlins, poetry editor, Box 51, Boulder WY 82923. Avant-garde, free verse, haiku, light verse, traditional. Pays in contributor copies.

Tips: "We use a lot of freelance material, though very little from outside the Rockies. Start by writing short, 500-word news items of timely, regional interest."

‡**HYST'RY MYST'RY®MAGAZINE,** Hyst'ry Myst'ry House, Garnerville NY 10923. Editor: David Allen. Bimonthly tabloid covering historical, archaeological mysteries of research and study. Byline given. Buys one-time rights. Simultaneous queries, and photocopied and previously published submissions OK. No computer printout or disk submissions. SASE. Reports in 3 weeks. Sample copy $4.

Nonfiction: "Articles concerning mysterious aspects of history, archeology, stamps, coins, rare documents, etc. Also cover treasure hunting and exploration. No poetry. No UFO or parapsychology. All our expository articles must be scientifically oriented about supporting fact and evidence. No second-hand, warmed-over pieces taken from other people or mags. We will consider things published elsewhere before, but they must be solid." Query. Length: open. Pays negotiable rates.

Photos: State availability of photos. Reviews prints. Captions, model release, and identification of subjects required.

Columns/Departments: "We will consider columnists in the areas of treasure hunting, genealogy, exploration, or rare document dealings." Query. Length: open.

Fiction: "We are currently serializing a prototype hist'ry myst'ry novel. We will start publishing short stories based upon this format as set up in the novel. But we *will not publish* general fiction. The writer must use our format in writing his short stories. The writer must *study* our fictional style, as nothing like it is being published elsewhere and the individual writer cannot have anything in his trunk that will do."

Fillers: Jokes, gags, anecdotes, short humor relevant to history. Length: open.

INTERNATIONAL WILDLIFE, 8925 Leesburg Pike, Vienna VA 22180. Managing Editor: Jonathan Fisher. Circ. 500,000. 80% freelance written. For persons interested in natural history, outdoor adventure and the environment. Bimonthly. Buys all rights to text; usually one-time rights to photos and art. Pays on acceptance. Query. "Now assigning most articles but will consider detailed proposals for quality feature material of interest to broad audience." Reports in 2 weeks. SASE.

Nonfiction and Photos: Focus on world wildlife, environmental problems and man's relationship to the natural world as reflected in such issues as population control, pollution, resource utilization, food production, etc. Especially interested in articles on animal behavior and other natural history, little-known places, first-person experiences, timely issues. Length: 2,000-3,000 words. Pays $750 minimum. Purchase top-quality color and b&w photos; prefer 'packages' of related photos and text, but single shots of exceptional interest and sequences also considered. Prefer Kodachrome transparencies for color, 8x10 prints for b&w."

JOURNAL OF FRESHWATER, Freshwater Foundation, 2500 Shadywood Rd., Box 90, Navarre MN 55392. (612)471-7467. Editor: Linda Schroeder. Always emphasizes freshwater issues. Annual (November) magazine; 64 pages. Pays on publication. Buys all rights and one-time rights. Byline given. Phone queries OK. Reports in 6 weeks. Sample copy $6; free writer's, artist's and photographer's guidelines. SASE.

Nonfiction: Scientific, yet easy to read; how-to; general interest; humor; interview; nostalgia; photo feature; and technical. "We will consider virtually any material dealing with freshwater environment as long as it is well-written and interesting. Entries must clearly and quickly answer the reader's question 'So what's that got to do with me, my pocketbook, or my relatives?'." No "bumper-sticker" philosophies, encyclopedia articles or unresearched material, please. No articles about dam controversies, personal travelogs, fish-catching stories, or long pieces of poetry. Buys 3-5 mss/year. Submit complete ms. Length: "2,500 words or less works best." Pays $100 (more with photos or art), per 800 words used.

Photos: Submit photos with accompanying ms. Payment for photos can be included in purchase price of article. Uses 5x7 minimum b&w glossy photos or 35mm, 2¼x2¼ or larger color transparencies. Captions preferred. Buys all rights for cover photos and all or one-time rights for others. Model release required.

Fiction: Experimental and humorous. "We purchase little fiction. But we're always open to it as long as it's very water related." Pays $100 (more with photos or art)/800 words used.

Poetry: Very short; free verse; haiku; or light verse. "Prefer poetry illustrated with *excellent* photos." Buys 2-3/issue. Limit submissions to batches of 5-10. Pays $20-50.

Tips: "Study at least 2 past issues of the journal. Query us before you write the article, to save your time and ours. Introduce yourself, state story idea and why we should be interested. Give a few key facts, state main sources you expect to use, propose a deadline you can meet, and offer to round up excellent photos to illustrate."

MICHIGAN NATURAL RESOURCES MAGAZINE, State of Michigan Department of Natural Resources, Box 30034, Lansing MI 48909. (517)373-9267. Editor: Russell McKee. Managing Editor: Richard Morscheck. Bimonthly magazine covering natural resources in the Great Lakes area. Circ. 140,000. Pays on acceptance. Byline given. Offers 100% kill fee. Buys first rights. Submit seasonal/holiday material 1 year in advance. Simultaneous queries and simultaneous and photocopied submissions OK. SASE. Reports in 1 month. Sample copy for $2 and 9x12 SAE; writer's guidelines for business size SAE and one first class stamp.

Nonfiction: Historical/nostalgic, how-to, humor, technical, travel. "All material must pertain to this region's natural resources; lakes, rivers, wildlife, flora, special features, energy and industry as it relates to natural resources. No personal experience, domestic animal stories, animal rehabilitation." Buys 24 mss/year. Query with clips of published work or send complete ms. Length: 1,000-4,000 words. Pays $150-400.

Photos: Gijsbert (Nick) vanFrankenhuyzen, photo editor. "Photos submitted with an article can help sell it, but they must be razor sharp in focus." Send photos with ms. Pays $50-200 for 35mm color transparencies. Model release and identification of subjects required. Buys one-time rights.

NATIONAL PARKS, 1701 18th St. NW, Washington DC 20009. (202)265-2717. Editor: Eugenia Horstman Connally. For a highly educated audience interested in preservation of National Park System Units, natural areas and protection of wildlife habitat. Bimonthly magazine. Circ. 35,000. Pays on acceptance. Buys first North American serial rights. Submit seasonal/holiday material 5 months in advance. Computer printout submissions OK if legible; prefers letter quality to dot matrix. SASE. Reports in 4-6 weeks. Sample copy $3; free writer's guidelines with SASE.

Nonfiction: Exposé (on threats, wildlife problems to national parks); descriptive articles about new or proposed national parks and wilderness parks; brief natural history pieces describing park geology, wildlife, or plants; "adventures" in national parks (crosscountry skiing, bouldering, mountain climbing, kayaking, canoeing, backpacking); travel tips to national parks. All material must relate to national parks. No poetry or philosophical essays. Buys 6-10 unsolicited mss/year. Query or send complete ms. Length: 1,000-1,500 words. Pays $75-200.

Photos: State availability of photos or send photos with ms. Pays $25-50 for 8x10 b&w glossy prints; $35-100 for color transparencies; offers no additional payment for photos accompanying ms. Buys one-time rights. Captions required.

NATIONAL WILDLIFE, 8925 Leesburg Pike, Vienna VA 22180. Managing Editor: Mark Wexler. Emphasizes wildlife. Bimonthly magazine; 52 pages. Circ. 770,000. Pays on acceptance. Buys all rights. Submit seasonal/holiday material 6 months in advance. Previously published submissions OK. No computer printout or disk submissions. SASE. Reports in 2 weeks. Free writer's guidelines.

Nonfiction: How-to; humor; informational; interview; personal experience; photo feature and profile. Buys 8 mss/issue. Query. Length: 2,000-3,000 words. Pays $750 minimum.

Photos: John Nuhn, Photo Editor. Photos purchased with or without accompanying ms or on assignment. Pays $75 and up for 8x10 b&w glossy prints; $125 minimum for 35mm color Kodachromes.

NATURAL HISTORY, Natural History Magazine, 79th and Central Park W., New York NY 10024. Editor: Alan Ternes. For "well-educated, ecologically aware audience. Includes many professional people, scientists, scholars." Monthly. Circ. 460,000. Buys 50 mss/year. Byline given. Pays on publication. Sample copy $2.50. Submit seasonal material 6 months in advance. Query or submit complete ms. SASE.

Nonfiction: Uses all types of scientific articles except chemistry and physics—emphasis is on the biological sciences and anthropology. Prefers professional scientists as authors. "We always want to see new research findings in almost all the branches of the natural sciences—anthropology, archeology, zoology, ornithology. We find that it is particularly difficult to get something new in herpetology (amphibians and reptiles) or entomology (insects) and we would like to see material in those fields. We lean heavily toward writers who are scientists or professional science writers. High standards of writing and research. Favor an ecological slant in most of our pieces, but do not generally lobby for causes, environmental or other. Writer should have a deep knowledge of his subject. Then submit original ideas either in query or by ms. Should be able to supply high-quality illustrations." Length: 2,000-4,000 words. Pays $400-750, plus additional payment for photos used.

Photos: Uses some 8x10 b&w glossy photographs; pays $125/page maximum. Much color is used; pays $250 for inside and up to $350 for cover. Photos are purchased for one-time use.

Tips: "Learn about something in depth before you bother writing about it."

OCEANS, 315 Fort Mason, San Francisco CA 94123. Editor-in-Chief: Keith K. Howell. 100% freelance written. Publication of The Oceanic Society. For people interested in the sea. Bimonthly magazine; 72 pages. Circ. 65,000. Pays on publication. Buys one-time rights. Byline given. Submit seasonal/holiday material 4 months in advance. Simultaneous and photocopied submissions OK. SASE. Reports in 8 weeks. Sample copy $2; free writer's guidelines.

Nonfiction: "Want articles on the worldwide realm of salt water; marine life (biology and ecology), oceanography, maritime history, marine painting and other arts, geography, undersea exploration and study, voyages, ships, coastal areas including environmental problems, seaports and shipping, islands, food-fishing and aquaculture (mariculture), peoples of the sea, including anthropological materials. Writing should be simple, direct, factual, very readable (avoid dullness and pedantry, make it lively and interesting but not cute, flippant or tongue-in-cheek; avoid purple prose). Careful research, good structuring, no padding. Factual information in good, narrative style. *Oceans* is authoritative, but less technical than *Scientific American*. We do not want articles on scuba; adventuring, travel tends to be overworked. Prefer no sport fishing, boating, surfing, or other

Close-up

Bob Strohm
Executive Editor, *National Wildlife*

"I think people are as interested in nature as ever," says *National Wildlife* executive editor, Bob Strohm. "But many of them don't know as much about it as their parents or grandparents who, odds are, grew up in a small town or rural area."

It is on that general audience that *National Wildlife* focuses its attention. "We avoid writing for people who are already wildly enthusiastic about nature or know all about the wise use of resources."

And it's good writers, rather than plant or animal specialists, who can best tell the stories. Strohm, whose agricultural journalist father started the magazine 21 years ago, says that two-thirds of *NW*'s pieces are written by generalist writers, one-third by specialists in a certain field. "We're always talking with scientists about article ideas, though. And some of the most interesting stories come out of something the specialist says in passing. It may be something second nature to him, but it piques our interest."

Strohm puts great emphasis on finding and developing story ideas. In addition, his job includes budget and personnel responsibilities and editorial tasks—reviewing advanced story boards, checking copyediting, choosing photos, etc. "But it's from the ideas that everything else derives," he says.

Strohm says the magazine always needs good seasonal pieces for the winter, how-to stories, and new ways of enjoying nature. "One of the hardest things is developing a really good story idea on mammals and birds. There are few creatures with life histories that aren't ho-hum by now. Sometimes it's a matter of finding a researcher who has something new to tell us. It may be nothing more than that wolverines will range far more widely than wolves. That's something to hang a story on. And then we'll use the researcher's firsthand experience in finding this out as a means for telling the wolverine story."

Strohm says he would like to see more writers going after a story like that. "I'd like to see better reporting, less stuff gotten out of book research. More hustle in getting a story."

National Wildlife has a fairly specific article assignment process. Queries that get editorial attention detail a dynamite subject or a new angle on a tired, old subject. "The writers are specific about what they plan to do with it, and they write a query with flair. A good query letter is hard to resist," says Strohm.

The query or idea is discussed and sharpened by a group of editors. "We write a very detailed assignment letter which is our contract with the writer. We tell him how the piece should be structured; what people should be contacted; what we don't want to see in the piece. And we tell him what we'll do when the story arrives in-house. We read it and evaluate it collectively. We may ask for a rewrite. And we edit heavily."

Strohm says the average story needs a couple days of rewriting. "I wish more writers would give us finished copy. I think we get a lot of first drafts. It would be nice not to have to get the scissors and cut and paste and chop out whole paragraphs. It's always wonderful when a piece comes in and all you have to do is delete a few adjectives, add a few commas, and have it typeset. But that's rare."

purely sport-type matter. Diving okay if serious in purpose, unusual in results or story angle. We want articles on rarely visited islands, ports or shores that have great intrinsic interest, but not treated in purely travelogue style. Can use more on environmental concerns.'' Length: 1,000-6,000 words. Pays $100/page.

PACIFIC DISCOVERY, California Academy of Sciences, Golden Gate Park, San Francisco CA 94118. (415)221-5100. Editor: Sheridan Warrick. 100% freelance written. ''A journal of nature and culture around the world, read by scientists, naturalists, teachers, students, and others having a keen interest in knowing the natural world more thoroughly.'' Published quarterly by the California Academy of Sciences. Circ. 17,000. Buys first North American serial rights of articles; one-time use of photos. Usually reports within 3 months; publishes accepted articles in 3-6 months. Pays on publication. Query with 100-word summary of projected article for review before preparing finished ms. SASE.
Nonfiction and Photos: ''Subjects of articles include behavior and natural history of animals and plants, ecology, evolution, anthropology, geology, paleontology, biogeography, taxonomy, and related topics in the natural sciences. Occasional articles are published on the history of natural science, exploration, astronomy and archeology. Types of articles include discussions of individual species or groups of plants and animals that are related to or involved with one another, narratives of scientific expeditions together with detailed discussions of field work and results, reports of biological and geological discoveries and of short-lived phenomena, and explanations of specialized topics in natural science. Emphasis is on current research findings. Authors need not be scientists; however, all articles must be based, at least in part, on firsthand fieldwork.'' Length: 1,000-3,000 words. Pays 12¢/word. Color transparencies and/or b&w 8x10 prints must accompany all mss or they will not be reviewed. Send 15-30 with each ms. Photos should have both scientific and aesthetic interest, be captioned in a few sentences on a separate caption list keyed to the photos and numbered in story sequence. Half of all photos in an issue are printed in color. Some photo stories are used. Pays $30/photo. All transparencies and prints are returned soon after publication.

PACIFIC NORTHWEST, 222 Dexter Ave. N., Seattle WA 98109. Editor: Peter Potterfield. Emphasizes the arts, culture, recreation, service, and urban and rural lifestyle in the Pacific Northwest. Monthly magazine (except January and August). Buys first rights. Simultaneous and previously published submissions OK. SASE. Reports in 6 weeks. Will send writer's guidelines.
Nonfiction: Editorial material should entertain, inform or contribute to an understanding of the Pacific Northwest, including BC and Alaska. Subject matter includes travel and exploration, outdoor activities, issues in the region's development, science and the environment, arts, history, profiles of places and people, and current issues, ideas and events that concern the Northwest. Buys 4 mss/issue. Query with clips of published work. Length: 600-3,000 words. Pay starts at 10¢/word.
Photos: Send photos with or without ms. Pays $15-50 for b&w prints; $50-200 for color transparencies, 35mm or larger. Buys one-time rights. Captions preferred.
Columns/Departments: Scannings (news items); Books; Closer Look (regional issues and profiles); Travel; Food and Lodging; Back Page (photo); Calendar of Events; Letters. Query.
Tips: ''Query should have clear description of topic and relevance to Northwest with clips if writer is new to us. We look for entertaining as well as informative style and format plus original or unusual information and research. Many native, outdoors, or history submissions assume a more narrowly interested audience than we are aiming for.''

SEA FRONTIERS, 3979 Rickenbacker Causeway, Virginia Key, Miami FL 33149. (305)361-5786. Editor: Jean Bradfisch. 90-95% freelance written. ''For anyone with an interest in any aspect of the sea; its conservation, and the life it contains; professional people for the most part; people in executive positions and students.'' Bimonthly. Circ. 50,000. Buys all rights. Byline given. Buys 45-50 mss/year. Pays on publication. Sample copy $2; free writer's guidelines with SASE. Query. Will consider photocopied submissions ''if very clear.'' Reports on material within 2 months. SASE.
Nonfiction and Photos: ''Articles (with illustrations) covering interesting and little known facts about the sea, marine life, chemistry, geology, physics, fisheries, mining, engineering, navigation, influences on weather and climate, ecology, conservation, explorations, discoveries or advances in our knowledge of the marine sciences, or describing the activities of oceanographic laboratories or expeditions to any part of the world. Emphasis should be on research and discoveries rather than personalities involved.'' Length: 500-3,000 words. Pays $20-30/page. 8x10 b&w glossy prints and 35mm (or larger) color transparencies purchased with ms. Pays $50 for color used on front and $35 for the back cover. Pays $25 for color used on inside covers.
Tips: ''Query to include a paragraph or two that tells the subject, the angle or approach to be taken, and the writer's qualifications for covering this subject or the authorities with whom the facts will be checked.''

SIERRA, The Sierra Club Bulletin, 530 Bush Street, San Francisco CA 94108. (415)981-8634. Editor-in-Chief: Frances Gendlin. Senior Editor: David Gancher. 70% freelance written. Emphasizes conservation and environmental politics for people who are well-educated, activist, outdoor-oriented, and politically well-informed with a dedication to conservation. Magazine published 6 times/year; 96 pages. Circ. 340,000. Pays on publication. Byline given. Simultaneous and photocopied submissions OK. SASE. Reports in 6 weeks. Writer's guidelines.

Nonfiction: Exposé (well-documented on environmental issues of national importance such as energy, wilderness, forests, etc.); general interest (well-researched pieces on areas of particular environmental concern); historical (relevant to environmental concerns); how-to (on camping, climbing, outdoor photography, etc.); interview (with very prominent figures in the field); personal experience (by or about children and wilderness); photo feature (photo essays on threatened areas); and technical (on energy sources, wildlife management land-use, solid waste management, etc.). No "My trip to . . . " or why we must save wildlife/nature articles; no poetry or general superficial essays on environmentalism and local environmental issues. Buys 2-3 mss/issue. Query with clips of published work. Length: 800-3,000 words. Pays $200-350.

Photos: Linda Smith, art and production manager. State availability of photos. Pays $100 maximum for color transparencies; $200 for cover photos. Buys one-time rights.

Columns/Departments: Book Reviews. Buys 5 mss/year. Length: 800-2,000 words. Query. Submit queries to Jonathan King, editorial assistant.

Tips: "Queries should include an outline of how the topic would be covered, and a mention of the political appropriateness and timeliness of the article. Statements of the writer's qualifications should be included."

SNOWY EGRET, 205 S. 9th St., Williamsburg KY 40769. (606)549-0850. Editor: Humphrey A. Olsen. For "persons of at least high school age interested in literary, artistic, philosophical and historical natural history." Semiannual. Circ. less than 500. Buys first North American serial rights. Byline given. Buys 40-50 mss/year. Pays on publication. Sample copy $2. Usually reports in 2 months. SASE.

Nonfiction: Subject matter limited to material related to natural history (preferably living organisms), especially literary, artistic, philosophical, and historical aspects. Criticism, book reviews, essays, biographies. No columns. Pays $2/printed page. Send nonfiction prose mss and books for review to Humphrey A. Olsen.

Photos: No photos but drawings acceptable.

Fiction: "We are interested in considering stories or self-contained portions of novels. All fiction must be natural history or man and nature. The scope is broad enough to include such stories as Hemingway's 'Big Two-Hearted River' and Warren's 'Blackberry Winter.' " Length: maximum 10,000 words. Pays $2/printed page. Send mss for consideration and poetry and fiction books for review to Alan Seaburg, Poetry and Fiction editor, 17 Century St., West Medford MA 02155. "It is preferable to query first."

Poetry: No length limits. Pays $4/printed page, minimum $2.

Photography

CAMERA ARTS, Ziff Davis, One Park Ave., New York NY 10016. (212)725-7713. Editor: Jim Hughes. Monthly magazine "dedicated to the aesthetics of photography and excellence in image making" for "advanced amateurs and professional photographers." Estab. 1980. Circ. 100,000. Pays "between acceptance and publication." Byline given. Kill fee varies. Buys first North American serial rights or one-time rights. Queries requested, submissions of finished mss accepted, photocopied submissions OK ("neat and clean"); previously published submissions OK ("if publication and date are indicated"), but publication not likely. Computer printout submissions OK. Reports in 1 month on queries and mss. Sample copy "available on newsstands."

Nonfiction: Historical; interview/profile (outstanding individuals in the world of photography); photo features (exhibit reviews, events, issues, photographers); technical (tools of the art on an aesthetic level); and book excerpts and book reviews. Assigns or buys 40-60 mss/year. Send detailed query with clips of published work. Length: 4,000 words maximum. Pays $350-750 and up.

Photos: State availability of photos.

Columns/Departments: Perspectives; opinion (strong feelings well expressed); currents; process (technical); and books (book reviews).

Tips: "The writer must be very knowledgeable about photography as an aesthetic experience, in addition to being thoughtfully articulate in his work." No "formula stories."

‡DARKROOM TECHNIQUES, Preston Publications, Inc., Box 48312, 6366 Gross Point Rd., Niles IL 60648. (312)647-0566. Publisher: Seaton Preston. Editor: Alfred DeBat. Managing Editor: Ms. Kim Brady. Bimonthly magazine focusing mainly on darkroom techniques, photochemistry, and photographic experimentation and innovation—particularly in the areas of photographic processing, printing and reproduction—plus general user-oriented photography articles aimed at advanced workers and hobbyists. Circ. 30,000. Pays on publication. By-line given. Buys first North American serial rights. Submit seasonal/holiday material 6 months in advance. Photocopied submissions okay. Computer printout submissions OK; prefers letter quality to dot matrix. SASE. Sample copy $3; free writer's guidelines with SASE.

Nonfiction: General interest articles within above topics; how-to; technical product reviews; photo features. Query or send complete ms. Length open, but most features run approximately 2,500 words or 4-5 magazine pages. Pays $100/published page for well-researched technical articles.

Photos: Send photos with ms. Ms payment includes photo payment. Prefers color transparencies and 8x10 b&w prints. Captions, model release (where appropriate), and identification of subjects required. Buys one-time rights.

Tips: "Successful writers for our magazine are doing what they write about. They have tried the photo technique and write detailed how-to articles—new twists for use with existing materials, etc. We have a list of nearly one hundred subjects our audience has told us they'd like to read about. Ask for this idea-jogger with the writer's guidelines."

PETERSEN'S PHOTOGRAPHIC MAGAZINE, Petersen Publishing Co., 8490 Sunset Blvd., Los Angeles CA 90069. (213)657-5100. Publisher: Paul R. Farber. Editor: Karen Geller-Shinn. Emphasizes how-to photography. Monthly magazine; 100 pages. Circ. 295,000. Pays on publication. Buys all rights and one-time rights. Submit seasonal/holiday material 5 months in advance. Photocopied submissions OK. SASE. Reports in 2 months. Sample copy $2.

Nonfiction: Karen Geller-Shinn, editor. How-to (darkroom, lighting, special effects, and studio photography). "We don't cover personalities. Buys 24-50 unsolicited mss/year. Recent article example: "Isophote Mapping" (April, 1983). Send story, photos and captions. Pays $60/printed page.

Photos: Gallery Editor. Photos purchased with or without accompanying ms. Pays $25-35 for b&w and color photos. Model release and technical details required.

Tips: "We will be moving more into electronics/video uses and computers for photographers."

PHOTO INSIGHT, Suite 2, 169-15 Jamaica Ave., Jamaica NY 11432. Managing Editor: Conrad Lovelo, Jr. 82% freelance written. Emphasizes up-to-date photography contests. For amateur and professional photographers. Bimonthly newsletter; 12 pages. Circ. 2,005. Pays on publication. Buys one-time rights. Submit seasonal or holiday material 3 months in advance. Simultaneous and previously published submissions OK. SASE. Reports in 2 months. Sample copy $2.

Nonfiction: How-to on winning contests, humor, inspirational and new products (related to photography). No material on the copyright law for photographers. Buys 6-12 mss/issue. Length: features-2,000 words. Pays $35 for photo-text package. Captions required.

Photos: Portfolios accepted for publication based on themes. One photographer's portfolio/issue: 6-10 photos.

Columns/Departments: Gallery Insight (photo show reviews) and In The News (new products or seminars). Buys 2 mss/issue. Query. Length: 100-300 words. Pays $15. Open to suggestions for new columns/departments.

Poetry: Contact: Poetry Editor. Traditional. Length: 4-12 lines. Pays $5.

Fillers: Jokes, gags and anecdotes. Length: 600-800 words. Pays $5.

PHOTOGRAPHER'S FORUM, 25 W. Anapamu, Santa Barbara CA 93101. (805)966-9392. Editor-in-Chief: Glen Serbin. 50% freelance written. Emphasizes college photographic work. Quarterly magazine; 64 pages. Pays on publication. Buys all rights. Byline given. Simultaneous and previously published submissions OK. SASE. Reports in 3 weeks.

Nonfiction: Expose; interview; general interest; and historical. "Articles must deal with some aspect of photography or student photography." Interviews (how one got started, views on the different schools); profile (of schools); and photo feature. "No technical articles." Submit complete ms. Length: 1,000-3,000 words. Pays $50-100.

Photos: State availability of photos with ms. 5x7 or 8x10 b&w matte prints. Buys one-time rights. Model release is recommended.

Columns/Departments: Book Review; Historical Analysis; Interview; and School Profile. Buys 6 mss/issue. Submit complete ms. Length: 1,000-3,000 words. Pays $50-100. Open to suggestions for new columns/departments.

PHOTOMETHODS, Ziff-Davis Publishing Co., 1 Park Ave., New York NY 10016. (212)725-3942. Editorial Director: Fred Schmidt. Managing Editor: Robert Kneller. 80% freelance written. Emphasizes photography (still, cine, video) as a tool; most readers are college or technical school graduates, many readers are in science, engineering or education. Monthly magazine; 80-96 pages. Circ. 53,000. Pays on publication. Buys one-time rights. Pays 100% kill fee. Byline given. Phone queries OK. SASE. Reports in 6 weeks. Free sample copy and writer's guidelines; mention *Writer's Market* in request.

Nonfiction: How-to (application stories to help readers in his/her work); interview (emphasis on technical management); personal experience (that will benefit the reader in his/her work); photo feature (rare, but will consider); profile (emphasis on technical management); and technical (always interested in 'popularizing' highly technical applications). No material dealing with amateur photography or snapshooters. Buys 60-70

mss/year. Query. Length: 1,500-3,000 words. Pays $75-300.
Photos: Steven Karl Weininger, art director. State availability of photos with query. Offers no additional payment for photos accepted with ms. Uses 5x7 and up matte-dried or glossy b&w prints and 35mm and up color transparencies. Captions required. Buys one-time rights. Model release required.
Tips: "Our subject matter is highly specialized. An extensive background in industrial/commercial photography is preferred."

POPULAR PHOTOGRAPHY, 1 Park Ave., New York NY 10016. Editorial Director: Arthur Goldsmith. "Mostly for advanced amateur and professional photographers; most are men." Monthly. Circ. 870,000. Also publishes a picture annual and a photography hobby buyer's guide edited by Jim Hughes. "Rights purchased vary occasionally but usually buy one-time." Byline given. Buys 35-50 mss/year, "mostly from technical types already known to us." Pays on acceptance. Submit material 4 months in advance. Reports in 1 month. Query. SASE.
Nonfiction: This magazine is mainly interested in instructional articles on photography that will help photographers improve their work. This includes all aspects of photography, from theory to camera use and darkroom procedures. Utter familiarity with the subject is a prerequisite to acceptance here. It is best to submit article ideas in outline form since features are set up to fit the magazine's visual policies. "Style should be easily readable but with plenty of factual data when a technique story is involved. We're not quite as 'hardware'-oriented as some magazines. We use many equipment stories, but we often give more space to cultural and aesthetic aspects of the hobby than our competition does." Buys how-to, interviews, profiles, historical articles, photo essays. Length: 500-2,000 words. Pays $125/b&w display page; $200/color page.
Photos: Picture Editor: Monica Cipnic. Interested in seeing b&w prints of any type finish that are 8x10 or larger. Also uses any size color transparency. Usually buys one-time rights except when other agreement is made. No additional payment is made except for occasional reuse of color in "annuals." Gives few assignments.

Poetry

Publications in this category publish poetry and articles about poetry for an audience that includes poets, students and fans of the form. Many publications in the Literary and "Little" category are also interested in poetry submissions. Various other poetry markets are listed in other categories throughout the Consumer section. The Greeting Card Publishers section is another source for poets' material.

Some of these markets are also open to submissions of short stories and nonfiction related to the poetic arts.

Many of the markets that follow pay in contributor's copies, prizes or some form of remuneration other than money. Some publications may even require that you pay for the copy which features your poetry. We have included such markets because there are limited commercial outlets for poetry and these at least offer the poet some visibility.

Poetry manuscripts should have the poet's name and address typed in the upper left-hand corner. Total number of lines in the poem should appear in the upper right-hand corner. Center the title of the poem 8 to 10 lines from the top of the page. The poem should be typed, single spaced; double spaced between stanzas. The poet's name should again appear at the end of the poem. In the case where the poet submits more than one poem to the editor, each poem should always be typed on a separate sheet of paper. Always enclose SASE with poetry submissions. For more information on poetry writing, consult Judson Jerome's *The Poet's Handbook* (Writer's Digest Books).

‡**ALPHA, Arts Magazine**, Either/Or Arts Society and The Acadia Students' Union, Box 1269, Wolfville, Nova Scotia, Canada B0P 1X0. (902)542-3339. Editor: Susan Huntley. Literary and creative arts magazine publishing 4 or fewer issues/year. Circ. 1,000. Pays on publication. Byline given. Photocopied submissions OK. SASE. Reports in 1 month on queries; 3 months on mss. Sample copy for $1.50, 9x12 SAE, and $1 postage; free writer's guidelines.
Poetry: Avant-garde, free verse, haiku, light verse, traditional. Buys 45-50/year. Submit maximum 5 poems. Length: open. Pays in 2 contributor's copies.

ALURA: POETRY QUARTERLY, 29371 Jacquelyn, Livonia MI 48154. (313)427-2911. Co-editors: Ruth Lamb, Dorothy Aust. Sample copy $2.50 plus 70¢ postage. Pays 2 copies. Photocopied, simultaneous and previously published submissions OK. Byline given. "Send poems folded in a regular business envelope with 4 loose stamps instead of a SASE." 1 page is 52 lines including title, spaces, byline and town. Will use longer if exceptional; no sexual experiences. "We use 70-80 poems and average 45 poets per issue."
Poetry: Light verse, free verse, blank verse, traditional and haiku. No racial, didactic, religious or uninterpretable symbolism; no sexual experiences. "We want poems that communicate with the reader using imaginative, fresh approaches to universal themes. Some one-page articles on poetry-related subjects."
Tips: "We welcome work from unpublished poets if of good quality."

‡AMERICAN POETRY ANTHOLOGY, American Poetry Association, 1620 Seabright Ave., Box 2279, Santa Cruz CA 95063. (408)475-2010. Chief Editor: D.A. Holmes. Semiannual (hardcover) literary publication containing "all types of poetry." Estab. 1981. Circ. 6,000. Byline given. Buys one-time rights. Rights revert to author on publication. Simultaneous and photocopied submissions OK. Reports in 2 weeks. Sample copy $35; free writer's guidelines.
Poetry: Avant-garde, free verse, haiku, light verse, traditional. "We are able to consider all types. No poems requiring eccentric typesetting; scatological poems; poems over the line limit; illegible poems." Accepts 2,448 poems/year. Submit maximum 1 poem. Length: 3-20 lines. "No payment for poems, but all poems submitted are entered in the APA's Annual Poetry Contest, with a grand prize of $1,000 and over 100 other prizes."
Tips: "We particularly wish to see poems from starting or not-yet-published poets, even if their work has more feeling or energy than polish. We look less for technique, more for originality, poetic feeling and honest thought or emotion expressed in verse. We want each edition of the anthology to reveal new voices in poetry and help them gain greater public recognition."

‡ANOTHER SEASON, A Quarterly Journal, Willowwood Publishing, Box 148, Cologne MN 55322. Editor: John M. Becknell. "A journal of the Midwest that strives for an integration of ideas and interests, mainly through the use of the personal essay. The aim of *Another Season* is to better understand life through the creative, personal honesty of the essay." Estab. 1982. Circ. 500. Pays on publication. Byline given. Buys first North American serial rights. Submit seasonal/holiday material 3 months in advance. Photocopied and previously published submissions OK. Computer printout submissions OK; prefers letter quality to dot matrix. SASE. Reports in 1 month. Free sample copy and writer's guidelines.
Poetry: Free verse, traditional. "We are very selective; poetry is not our emphasis." Acquires 8 poems/year. Submit maximum 4 poems. Pays in published copies.

THE ANTIGONISH REVIEW, St. Francis Xavier University, Antigonish, Nova Scotia, Canada B2G 1C0. Editor: George Sanderson. For "those with literary interests." Quarterly magazine. Circ. 700. Pays in copies only. Not copyrighted. Photocopied submissions OK. Computer printout submissions OK. SASE. Reports in 6 weeks.
Poetry: Avant-garde and traditional. No erotic or political. Uses 30/issue.
Fiction: 1,000-10,000 words. Light critical articles 3,000-4,000 words.

APALACHEE QUARTERLY, Box 20106, Tallahassee FL 32316. Collective Editorship. For an artistic/critical audience; over 16 years of age. Quarterly magazine; 44-60 pages. Circ. 450. Acquires first rights. Uses 80 mss/year. Pays in contributor's copies. Sample copy for $2. No simultaneous submissions. Reports in 3-8 weeks. Submit complete ms. Computer printout submissions OK; prefers letter quality to dot matrix. SASE.
Poetry: Traditional forms of poetry, blank verse, free verse, avant garde forms. "No poetry told by rustic pre-bubescents in the vernacular, dead grandmother stories or poems, or stories about angst-ridden faculty members." Length: 8-100 lines. Send 3-5 poems.
Tips: "Our publication can be enjoyed by anyone with even a basic background in literature, but is not for the barely literate. We publish things that our editors would take pride in having written. Therefore, take pride in what you submit. We like avant garde writing and traditional writing, yet the traditional is difficult to master and the avant garde is impossible to attempt until the traditional has been mastered. No queries please. If it's good, send it; if it is not, don't."

ARCHER, Camas Press, Box 41, Camas Valley OR 97416. (503)445-2327. Editor: Wilfred Brown. Quarterly magazine for people who enjoy reading and/or writing poetry. There is no special slant or philosophy. Circ. 500. Pays in copies. Frequent prize contests (no entry fees). Buys one-time rights. Submit seasonal material 6 months in advance. Simultaneous and photocopied submissions OK. Computer printout submissions OK. SASE. Reports in 2 weeks. Sample copy $1.
Poetry: Avant-garde, free verse, haiku, light verse and traditional. "We're looking for imaginative and colorful verse that is relatively brief, with intended meaning not so obscure as to be unintelligible to the average reader. Brevity is usually an asset, but we do not like lines of only one or two words or only a punctuation mark, which we think detracts from what the poet is trying to say." No long poems. "We normally leave poems relat-

ing to sex, gay or lesbian attractions to other publications less conservative than *The Archer*. We do not use poems containing words long considered vulgar, even though they now are seen frequently in print.'' Buys about 300 poems/year. Submit maximum 4 poems. Length: 2 lines minimum.

Tips: ''Read thoroughly at least one copy of *The Archer*, and re-study each poem to be submitted to see if improvements might be made. Re-check carefully the typing, grammar, structure of sentences and historic, literary or other allusions to be certain that they are accurate. Do not be adverse to using punctuation marks if they add to the clarity of what is being said.''

ART AND LITERARY DIGEST, Summer address: Madoc-Tweed Art Centre, Tweed, Ontario, Canada. Winter address: 1109 N. Betty Lane, Clearwater FL 33515. Editor: Roy Cadwell. ''Our readers are the public and former students of the Art and Writing Centre. As an educational publication we welcome new writers who have something to say and want to see their name in print and get paid for it.'' No salacious material unsuitable for family audience. Quarterly. Circ. 1,000. Not copyrighted. Byline given. Pays on publication. Sample copy $1. ''Photocopied mss are accepted, but not returned. You may submit elsewhere after 1 month. Original mss must be accompanied by return envelope and unattached postage.'' No computer printout or disk submissions. SASE. ''We are no longer accepting unsolicited material other than poetry.''

‡**THE ATAVIST**, Box 5643, Berkeley CA 94705. Editors: Robert Dorsett and Loretta Ko. Semiannual magazine covering poetry and translation of poetry for poets, students of poetry, ''and a general audience that might take a delight in poetry.'' Estab. 1982. Circ. 400. Pays on publication. Byline given. Buys all rights. SASE. Reports in 4 months. Sample copy $2.25.

Poetry: ''We prefer not to advocate 'types' of poetry because it often leads to confusion. We do not wish to see off-handed poems but expect to see serious poets who take us as seriously as we take them. Translations should include the original and the source of the original.'' Buys 40-60/year. No limit as to number of poems submitted. Length: open. Pays in copies and subscription.

BEATNIKS FROM SPACE, A New Beat Journal of the Arts, The Neither/Nor Press, Box 8043, Ann Arbor MI 48107. Editor: Denis McBee. Annual magazine interfacing between science/art/modern life, with an eye on the future. ''We look for the innovative and unusual modes of presentation. We believe that the entire defense budget should be turned over to NASA!'' Circ. 1,000. Pays on publication. Byline given. Acquires one-time rights. Photocopied submissions OK. Computer printout and disk submissions OK; prefers letter quality to dot matrix. SASE. Send complete ms. Reports in 4 months. Sample copy $4.

Poetry: Avant-garde, free verse. Buys 8/year. Submit maximum 10 poems. Length: 1-1,000 lines. Pays in 1-3 copies.

Tips: ''We urge writers to purchase sample copy before submitting. We have lost money on everything we have published and can thus only pay in copies. Will trade ad space or subscriptions with other magazines. Inquire.''

BELOIT POETRY JOURNAL, Box 2, Beloit WI 53511. Editors: David Stocking, Marion Stocking, Robert Glauber. ''Our readers are people of all ages and occupations who are interested in the growing tip of poetry.'' Quarterly magazine; 40 pages. Circ. 1,100. Pays in copies of publication. Acquires all rights. Byline given. Photocopied submissions OK. Computer printout submissions OK; prefers letter quality to dot matrix. SASE. Reports in 4 months; ''actually most rejections are within a week; four months would be the maximum for a poem under serious consideration.'' Sample copy $1; SASE for writer's guidelines.

Poetry: Avant-garde; free verse; and traditional. Uses 60/year. Limit submissions to batches of 6. ''We publish the best contemporary poetry submitted, without bias as to length, form, school or subject. We are particularly interested in discovering new poets, with strong imagination and intense, accurate language.''

Tips: ''Most of the unsatisfactory submissions show no acquaintance with the high quality of the poems we publish.''

BITTERROOT, International Poetry Magazine, Blythebourne Station, Box 51, Brooklyn NY 11219. Editor: Menke Katz. Magazine published 3 times/year. Uses about 200 unsolicited mss/year. Payment in 1 contributor's copy. No computer printout or disk submissions. SASE. Regular letter-sized envelopes. Please notify of change of address immediately.

Poetry: ''We need good poetry of all kinds. If we think a poem is very good, we will publish a two-page poem; mostly however, we prefer shorter poems, not longer than one page. We always discourage cliches and stereotyped forms which imitate fixed patterns and leave no individual mark. We inspire all poets who seek their own identity; it may be realistic or fantastic, close to earth and cabalistic. We have two annual contests with awards amounting to $325. December 31 of each year is the deadline for the William Kushner award and Heershe-Dovid Badanna awards. We do not return contest entries. The winners are published.''

Tips: ''We want to see all subjects—it is *how* the poem is written which is more important than *what* the poem says.''

THE BLACK WARRIOR REVIEW, The University of Alabama, Box 2936, University AL 35486. (205)348-7839. Editor: Will Blythe. Fiction and poetry—serious, literary work only. Semiannual magazine; 128 pages. Circ. 1,500. Pays in copies, prizes. Acquires all rights. Phone queries OK. Submit material for fall by Oct. 1; for spring by Feb. 1. SASE. Reports in 2 months. Sample copy $3. Suggests looking at copy of magazine before submitting.
Poetry: Elizabeth Thomas, poetry editor. Buys 20/issue.

BLUE UNICORN, 22 Avon Rd., Kensington CA 94707. Editors: Ruth G. Iodice, B. Jo Kinnick, Harold Witt. "We appeal especially to the discriminating lover of poetry, whatever his/her taste runs to." Published 3 times/year. Magazine; 48-60 pages. Circ. 500. Pays in copies on publication. Buys one-time rights. Clear photocopied submissions OK. SASE. Reports in 3-4 months. Sample copy $3.
Poetry: "The main criterion is excellence. We like poems which communicate in a memorable way whatever is deeply felt by the poet—ones which delight with a lasting image, a unique twist of thought, and a haunting music. We don't want the hackneyed, the trite, or the banal." Uses 150 poems/year. Limit submissions to batches of 3-4. Prefers shorter verse; "rarely use poetry over 1 page in length." Pays 1 copy.

‡**CACHE REVIEW**, Cache Press, 4805 E. 29th St., Tucson AZ 85711. (602)748-0600. Editor: Steve Brady. Semiannual literary magazine of poetry, fiction, reviews, plays, interviews for "those interested in the best contemporary writing." Estab. 1982. Circ. 250-500. Pays on publication. Byline given. Buys one-time rights. Submit seasonal/holiday material 6 months in advance. Simultaneous queries and photocopied submissions OK. SASE. Reports in 1 month. Sample copy $2; writer's guidelines for letter size SAE and 1 first class stamp.
Nonfiction: Interviews with writers, editors, publishers; reviews of books—poetry, fiction—mostly small presses. Buys 10 mss/year. Send complete ms. Length: 50-3,000 words. Book reviews: 50-500 words. Pays in 2 copies.
Fiction: Char Mitchell, fiction editor. Adventure, experimental, fantasy, horror, mainstream, mystery, novel excerpts, science fiction, western. "We will consider almost anything of quality." Buys 6-8 mss/year. Length: 6,000 words maximum. Pays in 2 copies.
Poetry: Avant-garde, free verse, haiku, traditional. Buys 75 poems/year. Submit 5-10 poems. Length: 30 pages maximum. Pays in 2 copies.

‡**CALIFORNIA STATE POETRY SOCIETY QUARTERLY**, California State Poetry Society, 20350 Stanford Ave., Riverside CA 92507. (714)686-4417. Editor: James E. MacWhinney. Journal published 3 times/year "slanted to give a forum to good poetry of all types." Circ. 400. Byline given. Buys one-time rights. Computer printout submissions OK if name and address are on each sheet and if "the format does not make its handling too difficult." SASE. Reports in 3 months. Sample copy $2; free writer's guidelines with SASE.
Poetry: Avant-garde, free verse, haiku, light verse, traditional. "No overly-sentimental, self-serving poems, obscene poems for obscenity's sake or poems carelessly proof-read." Publishes 180/year. Submit maximum 5 poems. Length: 40 lines maximum "may go over if poem exceptionally fine." Pays in contributor copy.

‡**CALYX, INC., A Journal of Art & Literature by Women**, Calyx, Inc., Box B, Corvallis OR 97339. (503)753-9384. Editor: Margarita Donnelly. Triannual magazine publishing women artists and writers, fine art and literature by women. Circ. 8,000. Pays in copies. Computer printout submissions OK; prefers letter quality to dot matrix. SASE. Reports in 1 month on queries; up to 6 months on mss. Sample copy $4 and 75¢ postage; writer's guidelines for SAE and 1 first class stamp.
Poetry: "We publish serious and well-written poetry." Publishes 150 pages of poetry/year. Submit maximum 5 poems. Length: open. Pays in contributor's copies.
Fiction: Up to 5,000 words.
Reviews: Up to 800 words.

THE CAPE ROCK, Southeast Missouri State University Press, English Department, Cape Girardeau MO 63708. (314)651-2158. Editor: Harvey Hecht. For libraries and persons interested in poetry. Semiannual. Circ. 1,000. Uses 100 mss/year. Pays in contributor's copies. Sample copy $1; writer's guidelines for SASE. Photocopied submissions OK. No simultaneous submissions. Reports in 1-4 months. SASE.
Poetry: "We publish poetry—any style, subject. Avoid cuteness, sentimentality, didacticism. We have summer and winter issues and try to place poetry in the appropriate issue, but do not offer strictly seasonal issues." Photos acquired with accompanying ms with no additional payment; also used without accompanying ms. B&w only. Length: 70 lines maximum.

CEDAR ROCK, 1121 Madeline, New Braunfels TX 78130. (512)625-6002. Editor-in-Chief: David C. Yates. For "persons with an active interest in stories, poems, and ideas." Quarterly tabloid; 24-32 pages. Circ. 2,000. Pays on acceptance. Buys all rights. Byline given. Phone queries OK. Photocopied submissions OK. No computer printout or disk submissions. SASE. Reports in 3 weeks. Sample copy $2.50; writer's guidelines for SASE.

Poetry: Avant-garde, free verse, haiku, light verse and traditional. "No deliberately obscure or nature poems." Buys 200 poems/year. Limit submissions to 6 at one time. Length: 3-75 lines. Pays $2-100.
Fiction: John O'Keefe, fiction editor, 732 W. Coll, New Braunfels TX 78130. Buys 2-4/issue. Pays $2-100.
Tips: "We like stories and poems that are 'deep' (i.e., mean something important) but at the same time are readable. No 'cute' nature poems or religious stories."

CHELSEA, Box 5880, Grand Central Station, New York NY 10163. Editor: Sonia Raiziss. Acquires first North American serial rights. Pays in copies. SASE.
Poetry: Poetry of high quality. No light verse, comics, pornography, or near pornography.
Tips: "Best thing to do: Read several issues of the magazine to get the tone/content, themes, penchants, and range of contributions." Avoid sending "too many poems or stories in one submission." No guidelines.

CHICAGO REVIEW, University of Chicago, Faculty Exchange Box C, Chicago IL 60637. (312)753-3571. Editor: Keith Tuma. Readership interested in contemporary literature and criticisms. Quarterly magazine; 140 pages. Circ. 2,000. Pays in copies. Acquires all rights. Photocopied submissions OK. Computer printout submissions OK; prefers letter quality to dot matrix. SASE. Reports in 3 months. Sample copy $3.50, plus postage (75¢).
Poetry: Michael Donaghy and Steve Heminger, poetry editors. Avant-garde, free verse, translations and traditional. Uses 12/year. Limit submissions to batches of 3-5.

COMPASS Poetry & Prose, Compass, Box 51, Burwood, New South Wales 2134, Australia. Tel. (02)560-8729. Editor: Chris Mansell. Quarterly magazine covering avant-garde poetry and prose, reviews and articles. Circ. 600. Pays on publication. Byline given. Buys first Australian serial rights. Photocopied submissions OK. SASE. Reports in 3 weeks on queries; in 2 months on mss. Sample copy $5.
Nonfiction: "Accept only intelligent and well-informed reviews and articles on literature." Send complete ms. Pays $10/page maximum.
Fiction: Experimental, novel excerpts. No "formula stories of any kind." Send complete ms. Pays $10/page maximum.
Poetry: Avant-garde, free verse, haiku. Buys variable number/year. Submit maximum 6 poems. Length: open. Pays $10/page maximum.

CONNECTIONS MAGAZINE, Bell Hollow Rd., Putnam Valley NY 10579. Editor-in-Chief: Toni Ortner-Zimmerman. Annual magazine; 70 pages. Covers fine quality modern poetry, especially by women. Circ. 600. Pays in copies. SASE. Reports in 2 weeks. Sample copy for $3.50 and 75¢ postage.
Poetry: Avant-garde, free verse and traditional. Limit submissions to batches of 5. Length: 50 lines maximum.
Tips: "We do not accept cliche verse, sexist poetry, or 'cute' poems (overly sentimental)."

‡**CROTON REVIEW**, Croton Council on the Arts, Inc., Box 277, Croton-on-Hudson NY 10520. (914)271-3144. Editors: Ruth Lisa Schechter and Dan B. Thomas. Annual literary and art tabloid-size magazine. Circ. 2,000. Byline given. Pays on acceptance "if grants permit." Photocopied submissions OK. Computer printout submissions OK. SASE. Reports in 3 months or sooner. Sample copy for $3 and 80¢ postage; previous issues $2; free writer's guidelines.
Poetry: Contemporary, free verse or traditional. "No cliches; we prefer poems showing craft, substance, originality, evidence of language. Our emphasis is quality literature." Submit maximum 5-6 poems (length: 75 lines each, maximum) and short/short stories (8-16 pages). Pays in contributor copies.
Tips: "We read new material only from September-February each year. We are not a glossy-slick, commercial magazine, rather a quality, literary journal."

DEROS, 6009 Edgewood Lane, Alexandria VA 22310. (703)971-2219. Editors: Lee-lee Schlegel and Kenneth Rose. Quarterly poetry magazine devoted to those who served in Viet Nam. Estab. 1981. Circ. 200. Byline given. Acquires one-time rights. Previously published submissions OK. No computer printout or disk submissions. SASE. Reports in 1 week. Sample copy $3.
Poetry: Avant-garde, free verse, haiku, traditional. Prefers not to see anything that does not deal with Viet Nam in the form of poetry. Submit maximum 1-10 poems. Length: 35 lines. Pay: "none yet."

‡**THE DEVIL'S MILLHOPPER**, College of General Studies, University of South Carolina, Columbia SC 29208. Editor: Stephen Corey. Semiannual poetry magazine. Circ. 500. Pays on publication. Byline given. Buys first North American serial rights. Simultaneous queries and photocopied submissions OK. SASE. Reports in 2 weeks on queries; 1 month on mss. Sample copy $2.50; writer's guidelines for business size SAE and 1 first class stamp.
Poetry: All types considered. Buys 50 poems/year. Submit maximum 8 poems. Length: open. Pays in 3 copies.

‡**DREAM INTERNATIONAL QUARTERLY**, Box 271203, Escondido CA 92027. Editor: Les Jones. Australian Editor: Olive Leonard. Quarterly magazine covering dreams, sleep, "daydreams" for laypersons "to explore their mysteries." Estab. 1982. Circ. 100. Pays on publication, plus annual prizes. Byline given. Buys one-time rights and second serial (reprint) rights for previously published mss. Submit seasonal/holiday material 6 months in advance. Photocopied and previously published submissions OK. SASE. Reports in 1 month on queries; 3 months on mss. Sample copy $2; writer's guidelines $1.

Nonfiction: Book excerpts; expose; historical/nostalgic; how-to (use dreams to help self, enjoy dreaming); interviews/profiles (of researchers); opinion (on all aspects of sleep and dreams); research and experiments. Must be dream, sleep-related. Buys 20 mss/year. Send complete ms. Length: 50-2,000 words. Pays in copies.

Columns/Departments: Dreamlets (column describing dream fragments); Dreamlines (column summarizing "news" of research, experiments, etc). Buys variable number of mss. Send complete ms. Length: 10-100 words. Pays in copies.

Fiction: Dreams must be central to the story. Adventure, condensed novel, erotica, ethnic, experimental, fantasy, historical, horror, humorous, mainstream, mystery, novel excerpts, religious, romance, science fiction, serialized novels, western, parables and legends. Buys 5 mss/year. Send complete ms. Length: 100-1,500 words. Pays in copies.

Poetry: Avant-garde, free verse, haiku, light verse, traditional. Buys 20 poems/year. Length: 2-40 lines. Pays in copies.

Fillers: Clippings, jokes, gags, anecdotes, short humor, newsbreaks. Length: 20-100 words. Pays in copies.

EARTHWISE: A JOURNAL OF POETRY, Earthwise Publishing Co., Box 680-536, Miami FL 33168. (305)688-8558. Editor: Barbara Holley. Co-editor: Herman Gold. Quarterly magazine covering eclectic poetry for writers and poets. Circ. 550. Pays on publication. Buys first North American serial rights. Phone queries OK. Submit seasonal material 3 months in advance. Photocopied and previously published submissions OK. SASE. Reports in 1 month on queries; in 3 months on mss. Sample copy $2.50; free writer's guidelines.

Nonfiction: Contact: Tere Hesin, (305)532-4100. Interviews (of poets, artists and writers); profile; travel (places pertaining to the media); and how-to (pertinent to poetry). Buys 4-6 mss/year. Query with SASE. "We like to have a letter that gets to the point immediately, tells what the writer has to offer, and what he expects in return. We can deal with a person like that. Also, always enclose SASE or don't expect a reply!" Buys about 200 unsolicited mss/year. Length: 1,000 words maximum. Pays $20 maximum. "We especially need brevity, uniqueness. Avoid didacticism, use good taste. Good English and punctuation a must. Our *Earthwise Newsletter* is a good place to break in." (No submissions read from June 15 to September 15.)

Fiction: Kaye Carter, editor. "We like short stories and will be doing an issue on fables this coming fall." Buys 6 mss/year. Query with clips of previously published work. Length: 500-1,000 words. Pays $10 minimum.

Poetry: Sally Newhouse, editor. Avant-garde, free verse, haiku, light verse, traditional and eclectic. "No porno, religious, depressive or downbeat poetry; no poems about love." Buys 200-250 mss/year. Submit maximum 6 poems. Pays $2 minimum/poem on publication.

Fillers: Anecdotes, newsbreaks, short articles, translations of a specific locale (for newsletter). Buys 50 mss/year. Length: 250 words maximum. Pays $1 minimum.

Tips: "Again, send SASE and *be sure* your name and address appear on *each* sheet of work. We are holding right now, some lovely poetry which we cannot publish as we don't know its author! We accept only quality work, well-structured."

ENCORE, A Quarterly of Verse and Poetic Arts, 1121 Major Ave. NW, Albuquerque NM 87107. (505)344-5615. Editor: Alice Briley. For "anyone interested in poetry from young people in school to established poets. Good poetry on any theme." Quarterly. Circ. 500. Acquires First American rights. Byline given. Uses 300 mss/year. Pays in contributor's copies. Sample copy $1. Photocopied submissions OK, "provided the author is free to assign rights to *Encore*. Will require assurance if poem is accepted." Submit seasonal material 9-12 months in advance. Reports on material within a month. Submit complete poetry ms. Query, for short reviews. SASE.

Nonfiction, Poetry and Photos: "Particularly like poetry which illustrates the magazine's theme that poetry is a performing art. Fresh approach greatly desired." Traditional forms, blank verse, free verse, avant-garde and light verse. Limit submissions to batches of 3. Some articles on poetry related subjects. Profiles of poets, poetry reviews, technical verse writing. Length: open, but "very long articles rarely used." Prefers no larger than 5x8 b&w glossy prints with good contrast. Pays in contributor's copies. Also has poetry contests. "My poetry contests have grown considerably. Continuous contests have November 1 and May 1 deadlines. In addition, there are often very good special contests, including student contest."

Tips: "No manuscripts will be considered unless accompanied by SASE with sufficient postage for return."

‡**FEATHERED VIOLIN**, Quorum Editions, 10 N. Mill, Cranbury NJ 08512. Editor: Lee Islewright. Annual anthology of women's poetry for national distribution. Estab. 1982. Byline given. Buys second serial (reprint) rights. Simultaneous, photocopied, and previously published submissions OK. SASE. Reports in 3 weeks on queries; 6 weeks on mss.

Poetry: Avant-garde, free verse. "We want poetry by women about women's special concerns. We want nothing celebrating resignation or the changing cycles of the seasons." Buys 100/year. Submit 10-20 poems. Length: 60 lines maximum. Pays in copies.

Tips: "Include either a short biography (300 words) or a statement of poetic principle (300 words)."

FORMS, The Review of Anthropos Theophoros, Box 3379, San Francisco CA 94119. Editor: Emily McCormick. 90% freelance written. For adults interested in ideas, especially as related to all forms of art. Quarterly magazine; 100 pages. Circ. 500. Buys one-time rights. Submit seasonal/holiday material 6 months in advance of issue date. Simultaneous and photocopied submissions OK. SASE. Reports in 3 months. Sample copy $2.50.

Poetry: Avant-garde, free verse, haiku and traditional. Buys 50-60 mss/year. Limit submissions to batches of 10. Length 4-1,000 words. Pays in contributor's copies and AT membership.

Tips: Recent article/story examples: "Encounter With Early Art" (fall 1981); and "Ring in the Box" (spring 1981). The magazine will be accepting less poetry in the year ahead. No "memoirs" masked as short stories or science fiction.

GAMUT, Multidisciplinary Journal, Kyogen Publications, Suite 171, 238 Davenport Rd., Toronto, Ontario, Canada M5R 1J6. (416)929-3928. Editors: Haygo Demir, Alfredo Romano. Managing Editor: James McBain. Quarterly magazine covering the arts and humanities and "dedicated to bringing various disciplines into a single forum. Our intellectual pursuit is to break through the over-specialization in the arts, academics, and humanities." Estab. 1982. Circ. 3,000. Pays on publication. Byline given. Buys one-time rights. Submit seasonal/holiday material 2 months in advance. Simultaneous queries, and simultaneous and photocopied submissions OK. SASE. Reports in 2 weeks on queries; 1 month on mss. Sample copy $3; free writer's guidelines.

Nonfiction: Book excerpts, general interest, humor, interview/profile, opinion, photo feature and political and philosophical reviews. No articles with jargon; "the language must be able to communicate to all readers." Buys 12 mss/year. Send complete ms. Length: 800-3,000 words. Pays in copies.

Photos: Roger P. Handling, photo editor. Send photos with ms. Pays in copies for b&w contact sheet and 6x9 b&w prints.

Columns/Departments: Book Reviews; Film Reviews; Theatre; Dance, etc. "Articles, however, should review with depth. The artist's career should be taken into account. These are essays more so than reviews. Interviews with key figures." Buys 10-12 mss/year. Send complete ms. Length: 1,000-3,000 words; "interviews can be longer." Pays in copies.

Fiction: Ethnic, experimental, humorous, mainstream, novel excerpts. Buys 8 mss/year. Send complete ms. Length: 3,000 words maximum; "longer will be considered." Pays in copies.

Poetry: Avant-garde, free verse, haiku, light verse, traditional. Buys 15-20 poems/year. Submit maximum 7 poems. Length: open. Pays in copies.

Tips: "All departments are open; we strictly use freelancers. Music, dance, political essays and short fiction are particularly needed."

‡**GARGOYLE**, Paycock Press, Box 3567, Washington DC 20007. (202)333-1544. Editor: Richard Peabody Jr. Triannual literary arts journal for a literate audience generally between 17 and 45. Circ. 1,000+. Pays on publication. Byline given. Buys first North American serial rights. Photocopied and previously published submissions OK. SASE. Reports in 1 week. Sample copy $4.

Columns/Departments: Book reviews, essays, interviews. Send complete ms. Length: 1½-7 pages. Pays in contributor's copy.

Fiction: Erotica, experimental, mainstream, novel excerpts. "We're not geared toward a genre market. We don't want to see romances or derivative work." Buys 25 mss/year. Submit complete ms. Length: 700 words minimum. Pays in contributor's copy.

Poetry: Gretchen Johnsen, poetry editor. Avant-garde, free verse. "We don't print traditional rhymed verse. In fact, we're not real big on the narrative poem that is currently in vogue either." Buys 30 poems/year. Submit maximum 5 poems. Length: 1-5 lines-2 pages. Pays in contributor's copy.

Tips: "Freelancers often turn out reviews for the magazine. We provide the books on spec. We publish many young voices and are always interested in the poems or stories produced by writers under 30. We have a very broad range of interests and a very idiosyncratic and personalized way of approaching them."

GREEN'S MAGAZINE, Green's Educational Publishing, Box 3236, Regina, Saskatchewan, Canada S4P 3H1. Editor: David Green. For a general audience; "the more sentient, literate levels." Quarterly magazine. Circ. 500. Buys first North American serial rights. Byline given. Buys 48 mss/year. Pays on publication. Sample copy $3. Reports in 2 months. Submit complete ms. No computer printouts or disk submissions. SAE and International Reply Coupons.

Fiction: Mainstream, suspense, humorous, must have a realistic range in conflict areas. Slice of life situations enriched with deep characterization and more than superficial conflict. Avoid housewife, student, businessmen problems that remain "so what" in solution. Open on themes as long as writers recognize the family na-

ture of the magazine. Length: 1,000-3,000 words.
Poetry: Haiku, blank verse, free verse. Length: about 36 to 40 lines. Pays $2 to $3.

HANGING LOOSE, 231 Wyckoff St., Brooklyn NY 11217. Editors: Robert Hershon, Dick Lourie, Mark Pawlak, Ron Schreiber. Quarterly. Acquires first serial rights. Pays in copies. Sample copy $3. Reports in 2-3 months. SASE.
Poetry: Fresh, energetic poems of any length. Excellent quality. Recent work by Jack Anderson, Michael Lally, Cathy Cockrell, Carol Cox, Frances Phillips, Donna Brook, Denise Levertov.
Tips: "We strongly suggest that writers read the magazine before sending work, to save our time and theirs. Also note that artwork and book mss are by invitation only."

HAPPINESS HOLDING TANK, 1790 Grand River Ave., Okemos MI 48864. Editor: Albert Drake. For "poets of various ages, interests; other editors; students." Triannual magazine; 45 pages, (8½x11). Circ. 300-500. All rights revert to author automatically. Byline given. Payment in contributor's copies. Reports in 1-3 weeks. Not reading during summer months. Submit complete ms. Computer printout submissions OK; prefers letter quality to dot matrix. SASE. Sample copy $1.50.
Nonfiction and Poetry: Publishes "poems of various kinds, somewhat eclectic—looking for 'excellence.' Essays and articles on modern poetry. Emphasis on younger but unestablished poets: their work to date. Emphasis on information of various kinds—to make magazine useful. Interested in printing methods of all kinds." Buys informational, how-to, and poetry book reviews. Uses all forms of poetry except light verse. Now doing chapbooks and poetry posters.
Tips: "What we see repeatedly, and do not want, is a kind of poem which can best be described as a 'beginner's poem.' It's usually entitled 'Reflections' or 'Dust' or 'Spring' and has to do with death, love, etc. These are abstractions and the poet treats them in an abstract way. This kind of poem has to be written, but shouldn't be published."

HIRAM POETRY REVIEW, Box 162, Hiram OH 44234. (216)569-3211. Editors: David Fratus and Carol Donley. Published 2 times a year; magazine, 40 to 60 pages, (6x9). "Since our chief subscribers are libraries in major cities or libraries of colleges and universities, our audience is highly literate and comprises persons who are actively interested in poetry of high quality." Circ. 500. Copyrighted. Acquires all rights. Byline given. Uses approximately 75 poems a year. Payment in 2 contributor's copies plus one year's subscription. Free sample copy. Reports in 8 weeks. Submit only complete ms. SASE.
Poetry: "All forms of poetry used. No special emphasis required. Length: open, but we have printed few very long poems." Limit submissions to 4-6 to a batch.

‡INDIANA REVIEW, 316 N. Jordan Ave., Bloomington IN 47405. (812)335-3439. Editor: Clint McCown. Managing Editor: Jane Hilberry. Triannual literary magazine of contemporary poetry and fiction for a national audience. Circ. 500. Pays on publication. Byline given. Buys all rights. Photocopied submissions OK. SASE. Reports in 3 months. Sample copy $3.
Fiction: Any type of fiction with literary interest, including experimental fiction. Buys 30 mss/year. Submit complete ms. Pay is in copies: 2 copies of issue in which work appears and the rest of a year's subscription.
Poetry: Jane Hilberry, poetry editor. Avant-garde, free verse, haiku, traditional. Buys 60 poems/year. Submit maximum 8 poems. Length: open. Pay is in copies: 2 copies of issue in which work appears and the rest of a year's subscription.
Tips: "We are interested in work that demonstrates skill in the craft of writing, as well as scope or import in content. We consider variety desirable in the magazine, given that work meets our qualitative standards. Editors invariably have tastes, but we prefer to let these operate on individual works, rather than as prejudices against particular types of material. For this reason, we place few restrictions on manuscripts submitted."

JUMP RIVER REVIEW, Jump River Press, Inc., 801 Oak, Medina OH 44256. Editor: Mark Bruner. Quarterly magazine covering a literary review of the basics, behavior and human culture. Estab. 1979. Circ. 400. Pays on publication in copies. Acquires one-time rights. Phone queries OK. Submit seasonal material 3½ months in advance. Photocopied submissions OK, if not submitted elsewhere. SASE. Reports in 1-2 weeks. Query first. Sample copy $2.50; free writer's guidelines.
Nonfiction: Historical ("articles relating either historical or contemporary events to the nature of our cultural fabric"); how-to (article should be related to writing and publishing); interview (of literary figures); nostalgia (but no overly sentimental approaches); photo feature (query); and essays on the spiritual aspects of culture, ("not religious, spiritual"). Especially in need of opinion (in essay form and related to culture, literature and human behavior). Buys 2-3 mss/issue. Send complete ms. Length: approx. 900 words preferred. Pays in copies. "Poetry is most open to freelancers because we publish so much of it. We don't want driveling sentiment, confessions or pretense. Feel free to experiment. We would like to see some more forms of concrete poetry and poetry related to myth, folklife, enchantment, primalism."
Poetry: Avant-garde; free verse; traditional; and concrete. Buys 90 mss/year. Pays in copies.

Tips: "Read *Jump River Review*. We devote a portion of each issue to young writers. If you're a high school or elementary aged writer, tell us. Right now the best chance of getting accepted is with essays, drama, criticism and short prose. If there is anyone out there who can produce a 5-6 page short drama, you have a good chance of getting our interest. Letting me know if you're young or unpublished sometimes makes me more apt to spend time with your work. And read the magazine—not only does that help us keep solvent, but it also saves everyone much time in correspondence."

KANSAS QUARTERLY, Dept. of English, Kansas State University, Manhattan KS 66506. (913)532-6716. Editors: Harold W. Schneider, Ben Nyberg, John Rees, W.R. Moses. For "adults interested in creative writing, literary criticism, Midwestern history, and art." Quarterly. Circ. 1,200. Acquires all rights. Pays in contributor's copies and the chance for annual awards. Sample copy $3. Query for nonfiction. "Follow *MLA Style Sheet* and write for a sophisticated audience." Reports in about 2-4 months. SASE.
Poetry: Traditional and avant-garde forms of poetry, blank verse and free verse. Poetry themes open.
Tips: Yearly prizes (KQ/KAC) for poetry and fiction: $25 to $300; Seaton Awards annually to Kansas writers published: $25 to $250 each.

KARAMU, English Department, Eastern Illinois University, Charleston IL 61920. (217)345-5013. Editor: John Z. Guzlowski. For literate, university-educated audience. Annually. Circ. 500. Acquires first North American serial rights. Uses 24 mss/year. Pays in 2 contributor's copies. Submit complete ms. Reports on poetry, 6 weeks; fiction, 2 months. SASE. Sample copy $1.50.
Poetry: Traditional forms, free verse and avant-garde.
Fiction: "We are interested in fresh material presented in either a traditional or experimental way. If the voice heard in the fiction is original, we are interested in it."

‡**THE KINDRED SPIRIT,** Gray Cat Publications, 808 Maple, Great Bend KS 67530. (316)792-6795. Editor: Michael Hathaway. Semiannual creative writing journal of poetry, short stories, photos, b&w drawings. Estab. 1982. Circ. 1,000. Pays on publication. Byline given. Buys one-time rights. Simultaneous queries, and simultaneous, photocopied, and previously published submissions OK. SASE. Reports in 1 month. Sample copy for 9x12 SAE and 37¢ postage; writer's guidelines for business-size SAE and 1 first class stamp.
Fiction: Experimental, fantasy, horror, humorous, mainstream, mystery, science fiction, suspense. Buys 4 mss/year. Submit complete ms. Length: 5,000-7,000 words. Pays in copies.
Poetry: Free verse, haiku, light verse, traditional. Buys 100-150 poems/year. Length: open. Pays in copies.

‡**THE LAKE STREET REVIEW,** The Lake Street Review Press, Box 7188, Powderhorn Station, Minneapolis MN 55407. Editor: Kevin FitzPatrick. Semiannual literary magazine that focuses on the creative writing of Minneapolis/St. Paul poets and writers. No special slant or philosophy. Circ. 550. Pays on acceptance. Byline given. Buys first rights. Photocopied and previously published submissions OK. SASE. Reports in 2 weeks on queries; 2 months on mss. Sample copy $1.50; writer's guidelines for legal size SAE and 1 first class stamp.
Fiction: Experimental, fantasy, humorous, mainstream, novel excerpts, science fiction. Buys 10 mss/year. Submit complete ms. Length: 400-4,500 words. Length: open. Pays in 2 copies.
Poetry: Avant-garde, free verse, traditional. Buys 50 poems/year. Submit maximum 4 poems. Length: open. Pays in 2 copies.
Tips: "We're looking for writing that uses language vividly and imaginatively to explore both ordinary and extraordinary subjects or situations in new ways."

LIGHT: A POETRY REVIEW, Box 1295M, Stuyvesant PO, New York NY 10009. Editor-in-Chief: Roberta C. Gould. Irregular magazine; 64 pages. Circ. 800. Pays in copies. Acquires first North American serial rights. SASE. Reports in up to 2 years. Sample copy $1.50. Suggest writers read sample issue before contributing. Uses graphics and some 7½x5 b&w photos. "All correspondence should include SASE."
Poetry: Avant-garde, free verse and formal. Uses 40 poems/issue. Limit submissions to batches of 4. "Please mail work in normal sized business envelopes only." Length: 5-40 lines.
Tips: "We're looking for work by writers with experience. Send best works. Please—no first poems or greeting card material. Writers should have read a lot of poetry."

‡**LIGHT YEAR,** Bits Press, Department of English, Case Western Reserve University, Cleveland OH 44106. (216)795-2810. Editor: Robert Wallace. Annual publication of light verse. Estab. 1982. Circ. 1,800. Pays on publication. Byline given. Buys one-time rights. Photocopied and previously published submissions OK. Computer printout submissions OK. SASE. Reports in 2 weeks on queries; 2 months on mss. Sample copy $9 (hardbound).
Poetry: Light verse. "Poems funny, witty or just delicious. The range is from free verse to villanelles, from epigrams to ballads. We want high-quality, tight, well-crafted poems. Good models would be the light verse of Ogden Nash, Richard Armour and John Updike. Zippy and up-to-date." Buys 100-150/year. Submit any number of poems. Length: "No restrictions, but we prefer poems 2-40 lines." Pays in copies but hopes to change to

cash payment in the year ahead.

Tips: "Submit typed poems; one poem/page. *Quality* is the only criterion for acceptance."

LITERARY REVIEW, Fairleigh Dickinson University, 285 Madison Ave., Madison NJ 07940. (201)377-4050. Editors: Martin Green, Harry Keyishian and Walter Cummins. For international literary audience, largely libraries, academic readers and other poets and writers. Quarterly magazine; 128 pages. Circ. 1,000. Pays in copies. Acquires first North American serial rights. Photocopied submissions OK. Computer printout submissions OK. Reports in 2-3 months. Sample copy $3.50.
Poetry: Avant-garde, free verse and traditional. Uses 40-50/issue. Translations from contemporary non-English literature.
Tips: "We are generally open to newcomers. Quality will tell."

‡**LITTLE BALKANS REVIEW, A Southeast Kansas Literary and Graphics Quarterly**, Little Balkans Press, Inc., 601 Grandview Heights Terrace, Pittsburg KS 66762. (316)231-1589 (after 5). Regional magazine of national interest for a general and academic audience. Circ. 1,200. Pays on publication. Buys one-time rights. Submit seasonal/holiday material 8 months in advance. SASE. Simultaneous queries OK. Reports in 2 weeks on queries; 6 weeks on mss. Sample copy $2.50; writer's guidelines for business-size SAE and 1 first-class stamp.
Poetry: Gene DeGruson, poetry editor. Avant-garde, free verse, haiku, light verse, traditional. Buys 30/year. Submit maximum 5 poems. Length: 1-500 lines. Pays in copies.

‡**THE LIVING COLOR, The Magazine of Film and Fiction**, Living Color Productions, 417 Euclid Ave., Elmira NY 14905. (607)732-7509. Editor: Jack Stevenson. Bimonthly entertainment magazine that "panders to the lowest sort of audience with the lowest, most sensationalistic sort of writing and material—though we stop short of backroom pornography." Estab. 1982. Circ. 2,000. Pays on publication. Byline given. Buys one-time rights. Simultaneous queries, and simultaneous, photocopied, and previously published submissions OK. SASE. Reports in 2 weeks. Sample copy for 9x12 SAE and $1 postage; writer's guidelines for 9x12 SAE and $1 postage.
Poetry: Avant-garde, free verse. "No homosexual, lesbian poetry, no John Greenleaf Whittier, no abstract, impressionistic, off-the-wall free verse." Buys 50/year. Submit maximum 5 poems. Length: open. Pays in copies.

LOONFEATHER: MINNESOTA NORTH COUNTRY ART, Bemidji Arts Center, 5th & Bemidji, Bemidji MN 56601. Editor: Betty Rossi. Poetry Editor: William Elliott. Literary magazine published spring/summer/fall. Includes poetry, short prose, and graphics. Emphasis on northern Minnesota, though some work from outside the region accepted. Circ. 450. Pays in copies. Acquires one-time rights. Phone queries OK. Submit seasonal material 4 months in advance. Simultaneous, photocopied and previously published submissions OK. SASE. Reports in 2 months on mss.
Poetry: Free verse. No inspirational poems. Length: 40 lines or less. Uses 12 poems/issue. Prose: 3,000 words or less. No science fiction. Uss 2 mss/issue.
Tips: Theme for fall issue (November 1983) is walls/fences.

THE LYRIC, 307 Dunton Dr. SW, Blacksburg VA 24060. Editor: Leslie Mellichamp. Quarterly magazine; 26 pages. Circ. 1,000. $6/year. $2/issue. Pays in prizes only: $25-100. Acquires first North American serial rights. Submit seasonal/holiday material 3-6 months in advance. Photocopied submissions OK. SASE.
Poetry: Traditional, preferably rhymed, several light pieces/issue. "No social criticism/quarrels with the cosmos." Uses 45 poems/issue. Limit submissions to batches of 5. Length: 35 lines maximum.

MAGICAL BLEND MAGAZINE, Box 11303, San Francisco CA 94101. Editor: Lisa Shulman. Quarterly magazine covering spiritual growth. "Our readers are creative, growing people interested in alternative lifestyles and philosophies. We stress positive, uplifting, inspiring, spiritual and occult material." Circ. 6,000. Pays on publication. Byline given. Buys one-time rights. Submit seasonal/holiday material 6 months in advance. Simultaneous, photocopied and previously published submissions OK. SASE. Reports in 1 month on queries; 4 months on mss. Sample copy $3 and $1 postage; free writer's guidelines for SASE.
Poetry: Hillary Male and Mary Webster, poetry editors. Free verse, haiku, light verse and traditional. No dark, depressing or sexist poems. Buys 75/year. Length: 3-150 lines. Pays in copies.
Tips: "It's best to write material that makes one feel better about him/herself, and/or the world. We cover a broad spectrum of spiritual manifestation; however, we are basically positive and human potential-oriented. To best understand what we're looking for, read an issue of *Magical Blend*."

‡**MALINI, Pan-Asian Journal for the Literati**, 2831 Rhodelia Ave., Claremont CA 91711. (714)625-2914. Editor: Chitra Chakraborty. Bimonthly ethnic literary magazine covering Pan-Asian (India to Japan including some Pacific islands) literature and culture. Estab. 1981. Pays in 2 contributor's copies. "In the near future we

hope to pay through grant money.'' Byline given. Buys all rights. Submit seasonal/holiday material 4 months in advance. SASE. Reports in 1 month. Sample copy $1.37; writer's guidelines for legal size SAE and 1 first class stamp.

Nonfiction: Book excerpts, expose, general interest, historical/nostalgic, humor, personal experience. Does not want to see anything that does not concern Pan-Asian group. Buys 6-10 mss/year. Query. Length: 1,000-1,300 words.

Fiction: Ethnic. Buys 2-3 mss/year. Query. Length: 750-1,200 words.

Poetry: Avant-garde, free verse, haiku, light verse, traditional, translations. No monologues. Buys 18-20 poems/year. Submit maximum 6 poems. Length: 3-33 lines.

Tips: "Anybody with ethnic awareness or sensitivity and literary talent can write for us. Ordering a sample copy will be of tremendous help to prospective contributors since there is no other magazine like *Malini* in the United States.''

MANNA, Prose-Poetry, Route 8, Box 368, Sanford NC 27330. Managing Editor: Nina A. Wicker. Semiannual poetry magazine. Circ. varies. Pays in 3 prizes awarded each issue. Byline given. Rights revert to author on publication. Computer printout or disk submissions OK. SASE. Reports in 2 weeks. Sample copy $2.50.

Poetry: Avant-garde, free verse, light verse, traditional. "No sex, pornography, or gutter language." Submit maximum 5 poems. Length: 1-40 lines.

‡**MIDWEST POETRY REVIEW, A Family of Poets**, River City Publishers, Box 776, Rock Island IL 61202. (319)391-1874. Editor: Hugh Ferguson. Quarterly poetry magazine. Pays on publication. Byline given. Offers 100% kill fee. Buys first North American serial rights, one-time rights; makes work-for-hire assignments. Submit seasonal/holiday material 3 months in advance. Photocopied submissions OK. SASE. Reports in 2 weeks. Sample copy for $1 postage; writer's guidelines for business-size SAE and 1 first class stamp.

Nonfiction: Tom Tilford, articles editor. How-to (especially interested in aiding the working poet to sell his work); humor (about poetry only); interview/profile (of well-known poets); technical (skills used in writing poetry). Special issue: Fourth Annual Contest in March. Buys 4 mss/year. Query. Length: 250-750 words. Pays $25-100.

Poetry: Avant-garde, free verse, haiku, light verse, traditional. Any style; nothing blatantly erotic. Buys 300/year. Submit maximum 5 poems. Length: 3 lines minimum. Pays $5-500.

Tips: "We accept submissions only from subscribers ($12 yearly, Canada $14). Enter annual contest (March) or enter any one of three quarterly contests ($200 awards each quarterly contest; $1,300 annual awards). We are particularly interested in assisting the young or unpublished poet in breaking into print. We would like first chance to purchase your work; no simultaneous submissions.''

MILKWEED CHRONICLE, Box 24303, Minneapolis MN 55424. (612)332-3192. Editor: Emilie Buchwald. Art Director: R.W. Scholes. Tabloid published 3 times/year featuring poetry and graphics. Circ. 5,000. Pays on publication. Buys first North American serial rights. Simultaneous and photocopied submissions OK. No computer printout or disk submissions. SASE. Reports in 1 month on queries; in 2 months on mss. Sample copy $3.

Nonfiction: Photo feature (in collaboration with poetry), also first person essays by writers and artists.

Photos: Reviews contact sheets. Pays $25 for double-page graphic designs. Pays $5-$10 photo.

Poetry: Avant-garde, free verse, haiku, traditional and concrete. No religious, inspirational or poems for children. Buys 60 mss/issue. Submit 5 poems maximum. Pays $5.

Tips: "Poetry will be presented in a visually advantageous format. We are interested in seeing collaborative projects. We are looking for an individual voice, for poems of high quality." No religious, overtly political, or humorous material.

MISSISSIPPI REVIEW, Center for Writers, University of Southern Mississippi, Southern Station, Box 5144, Hattiesburg MS 39406. (601)266-4321. Editor: Frederick Barthelme. For general literary audiences, including students, libraries and writers. Published 2 times/year; 120 pages. Buys all rights. Byline given. Pays in copies. SASE. Reports in 3 months. No submissions in June-August. Sample copy $4.50.

Poetry: All types considered.

MISSISSIPPI VALLEY REVIEW, Department of English, Western Illinois University, Macomb IL 61455. Editor: Forrest Robinson. For persons active in creating, teaching or reading poetry and fiction. Magazine; 64 pages. Published twice a year. Circ. 400. "Permission to reprint must be gained from individual authors." Accepts 80-100 mss/year. Payment in 2 contributor's copies, plus a copy of the next 2 issues. Sample copy $2 plus postage. "Only excellent" photocopied submissions OK. Will consider simultaneous submissions only if the author "notifies us immediately upon receipt of an acceptance elsewhere. We try to return mss within 3 months. We do not mind writers asking for progress reports if we are a bit late. Allow for no ms reading during summer." Submit complete ms. SASE.

Poetry: John Mann, poetry editor. Loren Logsdon, fiction editor. Tries to provide a range and variety of style and subject matter. "*Writer's Market* guidelines for ms submission suggested. We publish no articles. We usually solicit our reviews."

Tips: "Our contributors are experienced writers, usually—though not always—previously published. After acceptance, we ask the contributor for credits—not before."

MODERN HAIKU, Modern Haiku, Box 1752, Madison WI 53701. Editor: Robert Spiess. Triannual magazine featuring haiku poetry and related articles and book reviews for poets and appreciators of haiku. Circ. 525. Acquires first North American serial rights. Photocopied submissions OK. SASE. Reports in 1 week on queries; in 6 weeks on mss. Sample copy $2.70; free writer's guidelines.

Nonfiction: General interest (articles of a reasonably scholarly nature related to haiku). Uses 1-3 mss/issue. Send complete ms. Pays in copies.

Poetry: Haiku and senryu. No tanka or non-haiku poetry. Uses 130-150 mss/issue. Cash prizes. "Keep in mind: A haiku is not just a mere image, it must express the thing-in-itself and have insight into the nature of the event/experience being expressed."

Tips: "Study what the haiku is from authoritative books on the subject, read *Modern Haiku,* and don't write sentimental, pretty, ego-centered, or superficial little poems under the impression that these are haiku. Submit poems on ½ sheet of paper, with one haiku on each, with name and address on each sheet. Contributors should have a basic knowledge of the inner aspects of haiku beyond the mere knowledge of its form. Simply learn what a haiku really is before submitting material. The magazine has received three consecutive award-grants for excellence from the National Endowment for the Arts."

‡**MOVING OUT, Feminist Literary and Arts Journal,** Box 21879, Detroit MI 48221. Editors: M. Kaminski, J. Gartland and A. Cherry. Annual literary magazine covering "poetry, fiction and art by women about women." Circ. 1,000. Pays on publication. Byline given. Buys first North American serial rights. Photocopied submissions OK. SASE. Reports in 2 months on queries; 6 months on mss. Sample copy for $3, or $6 for current double issue, with 9x12 SAE and 60¢ postage; writer's guidelines for SAE and 1 first class stamp.

Poetry: Avant-garde, free verse. Buys 40/year. Submit maximum 5 poems. Length: open. Pays in contributor copy.

Tips: No sexist work or work which exploits women; pornography. We publish few male writers, especially their creative work (poetry, fiction, etc.)."

‡**NEGATIVE CAPABILITY,** Negative Capability, Inc., 6116 Timberly Rd. N., Mobile AL 36609. (205)661-9114. Editor: Sue Brannan Walker. Literary quarterly covering literature, art, music, essays, reviews, photography. "We seek excellence in the arts and wish to promote new artists as well as those who are already established." Estab. 1981. Circ. 800. Pays in contributor's copy. Byline given. Buys first North American serial rights. Submit seasonal/holiday material 6 months in advance. Photocopied submissions OK. SASE. Reports in 2 weeks on queries; 6 weeks on mss. Sample copy $3.50.

Nonfiction: General interest, humor, interview/profile, personal experience. "Seeking critical essays on the poetry and/or fiction of Marge Piercy for a special book of critical essays on Marge Piercy." Buys 8 mss/year. Query or send complete ms. Length: 500-6,000 words. Pays in contributor's copy.

Fiction: Humorous, mainstream, science fiction. Buys 4 mss/year. Submit complete ms. Length: 1,000-6,000 words. Pays in contributor's copy.

Poetry: Avant-garde, free verse, haiku, light verse, traditional. Buys 1,500 poems/year. Submit maximum 5 poems. Length: open. Pays in contributor's copy.

Fillers: Short humor. Buys 5-10 mss/year. Length: open. Pays in contributor's copy.

NEW COLLAGE MAGAZINE, 5700 N. Trail, Sarasota FL 33580. (813)355-7671, ext. 203. Editor: A. McA. Miller. Co-Editor: Carol Mahler. For poetry readers. Magazine; 24 pages minimum. Triquarterly. Circ. 2,000. Acquires first rights. Uses 80 poems per year. No long fiction. Token payment or 3 contributor's copies. Sample copy $2, together with editorial guidelines sheet. Photocopied submissions OK. No simultaneous submissions. Reports in 3 weeks. SASE.

Poetry: "We want poetry as a fresh act of language. No tick-tock effusions about everyday sentiments, please. First, read a sample copy. Then, and only then, send us poems. We especially want strong poems, more in Yeats' vein than in W.C. Williams, but we are open to any poem that sustains clear imagery and expressive voice." Length: 150 lines maximum.

‡**NEW KAURI,** 2551 W. Mossman Rd., Tucson AZ 85746. (602)883-3419. Editor: Will Inman. Bilingual (Spanish/English) poetry magazine published twice/year. "*New Kauri* prints significant modern poems with social/spiritual awareness toward building crosscultural bridges." Circ. 300. Pays in 2 copies on publication. Byline given. Buys one-time rights. Simultaneous queries OK. Reports in 3 weeks. Sample copy $3; writer's guidelines $3.

Poetry: Free verse. "Accessible but not glib; well-wrought serious work. No sentimental slop, church-oriented spirituality, bigoted or polarizing notions; no cute stuff." Buys 60-70 poems/year. Submit maximum 5 po-

ems. Length: open. Pays in 2 copies.
Tips: "I want mostly intense, not tame, writing."

NEW ORLEANS REVIEW, Box 195, Loyola University, New Orleans LA 70118. (504)865-2152. Editor: John Mosier. Emphasizes art, film, and literature. Magazine published 3 times/year. Circ. 1,500. Pays on publication. Buys first North American serial rights. Byline given. SASE. Reports in 2 months. Sample copy $6.
Poetry: Buys 20/year. Payment varies.

‡**NEW VOICES, A Selection of Poetry**, Astra Publications, 24 Edgewood Terrace, Methuen MA 01844. (617)686-5381. Editor: Lorraine Moreau-Laverriere. Annual small press poetry magazine. Circ. 300. Simultaneous, photocopied, and previously published submissions OK. SASE. Reports in 3 weeks or ASAP. Sample copy $3.50; free writer's guidelines.
Poetry: Avant-garde, free verse, haiku, light verse, traditional. No "rhymed poetry, moralizing, unclear messages." Submit maximum 6 poems. Length: 3-90 lines. Pays in contributor's copy.

NEW WORLDS UNLIMITED, Box 556-WM, Saddle Brook NJ 07662. Editor-in-Chief: Sal St. John Buttaci. Managing Editor: Susan Linda Gerstle. For "professional and aspiring poets of all ages from here and abroad. We've published high school students, college students, graduates, and people from all walks of life who write good poetry." Annual hardcover anthology; 140 pages. Circ. 500-900. No payment. Obtains all rights, but may reassign following publication. Photocopied submissions OK. SASE. Reports immediately— up to 6 months. Writer's guidelines and contest rules for annual poetry contest for SASE.
Poetry: "We want previously unpublished poems rich in imagery, poems that show intelligent treatment of universal themes and reveal the poet's understanding, even limited, of the poetry craft." Avant-garde; free verse; haiku; light verse; and traditional. No "overly sentimental poems or contrived rhymes." Uses 400/issue. Limit submissions to batches of 5. Length: 2-14 lines.
Tips: "Make sure sufficient postage is placed on enclosed SASE. Poets from other countries must enclose either U.S. postage or international postal coupons."

NORTH AMERICAN MENTOR MAGAZINE, 1745 Madison St., Fennimore WI 53809. (608)822-6237. Editors: John Westburg, Mildred Westburg. 95% freelance written. For "largely mature readers, above average in education, most being fairly well-to-do; many being retired persons over 60; college personnel and professional writers or aspirants to being professional." Quarterly. A small press non-commercial publication, primarily supported by the editors, other contributors and donors. Acquires all rights. Byline given. Pays in contributor's copies. Sample copy $2. Photocopied and simultaneous submissions OK. No computer printout or disk submissions. Reports in 1 week to 6 months. SASE.
Poetry: Accepts traditional, blank and free verse, avant-garde forms and light verse. "Poetry from many cultures. We would like to see more poetry by new writers." Length: 50 lines maximum.

NORTHWEST REVIEW, 369 P.L.C., University of Oregon, Dept. of English, Eugene OR 97403. (503)686-3957. Editor-in-Chief: John Witte. 85% freelance written. For literate readership. "We have one issue per year with Northwest emphasis; the other two are of general interest to those who follow American/ world poetry and fiction." Published 3 times/year. Circ. 2,000. Pays on publication in copies. Buys first periodical rights. Phone queries OK. Photocopied submissions OK. Computer printout submissions OK "if perfectly legible"; prefers letter quality to dot matrix. SASE. Reports in 6-8 weeks. Sample copy $2.50; free writer's guidelines.
Poetry: Maxine Scates, poetry editor. Uses 20-30 poems/issue. Limit submissions to batches of 6-10.
Fiction: Deb Casey, fiction editor. Uses 5-8 stories/issue. Stories in excess of 40 pages at a disadvantage.
Tips: "Persist: the more we can see of an author's work, the better we're able to assess it."

THE OHIO JOURNAL, A Magazine of Literature and the Visual Arts, Department of English, Ohio State University, 164 W. 17th Ave., Columbus OH 43210. Editor: William Allen. Magazine; 2 times a year. Circ. 1,000. Pays in contributor's copies. Acquires all rights. Byline given. Photocopied and simultaneous submissions OK. SASE. Reports in 6 weeks. Does not accept mss during the summer months.
Poetry: David Citino. No restrictions as to category or type. Maximum length for fiction: 6,000 words. No critical studies.

OPINION, Box 3563, Bloomington IL 61701. Editor: B. Anderson. 80% freelance written. For readers 18 and older; people who have an appetite for invigorating, inspiring, thought-provoking articles. Quarterly magazine, 16 (8½x11) pages. Circ. 3,700. Not copyrighted. Byline given. Uses about 15 mss/year. Pays in contributor's copies. Sample copy 30¢. Photocopied submissions and simultaneous submissions OK. No computer printout or disk submissions. Submit complete ms. Reports in 3 to 5 weeks. SASE.
Poetry: Traditional forms, free verse and light verse.

ORPHEUS, The Magazine of Poems, Suite 204, 8812 W. Pico Blvd., Los Angeles CA 90035. (213)271-1460. Editor: P. Schneidre. Magazine published 3 times/year. Poems in English; no translations or articles. Circ. 1,800. Pays on acceptance. Byline given. Buys first rights. Photocopied submissions OK. SASE. Reports in 2 weeks. Sample copy for $4 and SAE.
Poetry: Free verse, traditional. "Nothing with the words 'crystal,' 'energy' or 'consciousness.' We don't use political or surrealistic poems." Buys 50/year. Submit maximum 10 poems. Pays $5-100.

ORPHIC LUTE, Box 2815, Newport News VA 23602. Editor: Patricia Doherty Hinnebusch. Quarterly. Circ. 200. Rights revert to author. SASE.
Nonfiction: Short articles on subjects germane to poetry. Length: 400-800 words. Pays in copies.
Poetry: Free, blank, light, and traditional verse. Personal/lyrical rather than historical/political. New metaphors, sustained metaphors; involvement of all senses; concreteness; conciseness. Editor will comment if desired. No porn; no preaching. Buys 50-70/issue. Submit 4-6 poems. Preferred length: 3-40 lines; 80 lines maximum.

PASSAGES NORTH, William Bonifas Fine Arts Center, 7th St. and 1st Ave. S., Escanaba MI 49829. (906)786-3833. Editor: Elinor Benedict. Managing Editor: Carol R. Hackenbruch. Semiannual literary tabloid (spring and fall) featuring high quality poetry, short fiction, and graphics. Circ. 1,000. Pays on publication. Byline given. Rights revert to author. Photocopied submissions OK. SASE. Reports in 2 weeks on queries; 3 weeks to 3 months on ms. Sample copy for $1 and 50¢ postage; writer's guidelines for SAE and 1 first class stamp.
Poetry: "High quality contemporary poetry." No "greeting card, heavily-rhymed, sentimental, highly traditional" poetry. Buys 60/year. Submit maximum 4 poems. Length: 40 lines maximum. Pays in 3 copies.

PHOEBE, The George Mason Review, George Mason University, 4400 University Dr., Fairfax VA 22030. (703)691-7987. Editor-in-Chief: J.W. Harchick. For the literary community. Quarterly magazine; 44-120 pages. Circ. 5,000. Pays in 2 contributor's copies on publication. Byline given. SASE. Reports in 6 weeks. Sample copy $3.
Poetry: Avant-garde, free verse, haiku and traditional. Accepts 20-30 poems/issue. Length: no more than 2 pages. Pays in contributor's copies.
Tips: "*Phoebe Magazine* is devoted to publishing works of literary excellence. Works of poetry and fiction must meet our requirements of creativity, skill and insight. We only consider the serious and creative writer; all others not meeting these criteria will be rejected outright. Those beginning writers seeking publication should be aware of our high standards; we will not settle for less. All submitted work must reflect clear and perceptive writing; cliches must be avoided; old ideas must be presented in a new and refreshing manner; all works must generate strong emotions for the reader. Read the works of contemporary poets and fiction writers to see how they meet the requirements of lucid and imagistic writing."

PIEDMONT LITERARY REVIEW, Piedmont Literary Society, Box 3656, Danville VA 24541. Editor: David Craig. Quarterly magazine featuring poetry, short fiction and reviews. Circ. 350. Pays in copies. Acquires one-time rights. Photocopied submissions OK. SASE. Reports in 2 weeks on queries; in 3 months on mss. Sample copy $2; writer's guidelines for SASE.
Nonfiction: "All submissions are given equal consideration, quality being the key factor in judging submissions. General interest; how-to (articles related to poetry and poetry analysis); and interview (with poets or writers). Buys 1-3 prose pieces/issue. Send complete ms. Length: 2,000 words maximum. Pays in copies.
Poetry: Barbara McCoy, haiku editor. Paula Christian, associate editor. Avant-garde, free verse, haiku, light verse and traditional. "We will consider any type of poetry. Lengthy poems do not stand a good chance of being published." Buys 160-200 poems/year. Submit maximum 5 poems. Length: 40 lines maximum. Pays in 1 contributor's copy.
Tips: "We publish the best from the material submitted. We try to give special attention to works of students and previously unpublished poets. Writers should indicate if they are students or previously unpublished. Our tastes are eclectic but exacting, like avant-garde surrealistic poems. We still like nature poems—It's all right to mention a tree. We will always give special attention to short humorous pieces, especially satire. If it rhymes it had better be good. Lyric and sonnets can find a home here."

PLAINS POETRY JOURNAL (PPJ), Box 2337, Bismarck ND 58502. Editor: Jane Green. Quarterly magazine. "A forum for poems and criticism demonstrating the importance of poetic form. We explore the relationship between form and content in poetry." Estab. 1981. Circ. 200. Pays on publication. Byline given.

Acquires one-time rights. Photocopied and previously published submissions OK. No computer printout or disk submissions. SASE. Reports in 1 week. Sample copy $2.50; writer's guidelines for business SAE and 1 first class stamp.

Poetry: Traditional. "No conversational, broken-prose free verse or 'Hallmark' verse. No subjects are taboo; the *poet's skill* at expression is what counts." Wants nothing but poetry and essays on poetry and poetic theory, methods and techniques. Buys 160/year. Submit maximum 10 poems. "We prefer shorter poems; exceptional long poems will be considered." Pays in 2 copies.

Tips: "We are open to poetry, and criticism or theory, but will probably publish only one piece of criticism/issue and many poems. Queries aren't necessary, but will be answered immediately. Criticism should agree with the magazine's commitment to form in poetry; if it doesn't, it had better be brilliant. We believe *how* a thing is said (using poetic tools such as meter, rhyme, alliteration, assonance, etc.) is just as important as *what* is said. Otherwise, it's mere philosophy, not poetry."

POEM, c/o U.A.H., Huntsville AL 35899. Editor: Robert L. Welker. For adults; well-educated, interested in good poetry. Published 3 times/year; magazine, 65 pages. Circ. 500. Acquires all rights. Byline given. Payment in contributor's copies. Reports in 2 months. Submit complete ms only. Computer printout and disk submissions OK. SASE.

Poetry: "We use nothing but superior quality poetry. Good taste (no pornography for its own sake) and technical proficiency. We give special attention to young and less well-known poets. Do not like poems about poems, poets, and other works of art." Traditional forms, blank verse, free verse, and avant-garde forms. Uses 200 unsolicited poems/year. Length and theme: open.

Tips: "All our contributors are unsolicited. We welcome all submissions and always hope to find an unknown who deserves publication."

POETRY, The Modern Poetry Association, Box 4348, 601 S. Morgan St., Chicago IL 60680. Editor-in-Chief: John F. Nims. Monthly magazine; 64 pages. Circ. 6,700. Pays on publication. Buys all rights. Byline given. Submit seasonal/holiday material 9 months in advance. No computer printout or disk submissions. SASE. Reports in 4-6 weeks. Sample copy $2.60; writer's guidelines for SASE.

Poetry: "We consistently publish the best poetry being written in English. All forms may be acceptable." Buys 500/year. Limit submissions to batches of 6-8. Pays $1/line.

POETRY AUSTRALIA, South Head Press, The Market Place, Berrima, NCW Australia 2577. (048)911407. Editor: Grace Perry. Managing Editor: John Millett. Quarterly magazine emphasizing poetry. Circ. approximately 2,000. Pays on publication. No byline given. Buys Australian rights. Submit seasonal/holiday material 3 months in advance. Simultaneous queries, and simultaneous and photocopied submissions OK. SASE. Reports in 1 month.

Poetry: Avant-garde, free verse, haiku, light verse and traditional. Buys "200 and more" mss/year. Submit maximum 4 poems. Length: 3-200 lines. Pays $5-10 or overseas, in copies of magazine.

POETRY CANADA REVIEW, Poetry Canada Poesie Review, Inc., Box 1280, Station A, Toronto, Ontario, Canada M5W 1G7. Editor: Clifton Whiten. Quarterly literary tabloid featuring Canadian poetry; some international. SAE and International Reply Coupons. No computer printout or disk submissions.

Poetry: Avant-garde, free verse, haiku, light verse, traditional. Buys 120/year. Submit maximum 12 poems. Pays $5 maximum.

Tips: Using 1 Internationa page/issue.

POETRY MAGAZINE, The Magazine for Poets, Spectrum Publishing, Box 20822, Portland OR 97220. (503)231-7628. Managing Editor: Greg Butkus. Consulting Editor: Mark Worden. Quarterly poetry magazine. Circ. 5,000. Pays on publication. Byline given. Acquires one-time rights. Submit seasonal/holiday material 4 months in advance. Simultaneous and photocopied submissions OK. Can process submissions on floppy disk by TRS-80 users. SASE. Reports in 2 months. Sample copy $1; free writer's guidelines with sample copy.

Nonfiction: How-to (tips for our readers on getting poems published). Buys 30-40 mss/year. Send complete ms. Length: 400-2,000 words. Pays 1/2¢/word, "unless otherwise arranged."

Poetry: Keith Van Vliet, editor. All types, but "we are tired of seeing love poems." Buys 300-400/year. Submit maximum 8 poems. Length: 40 lines maximum; "4-16 line poems get published more often." Pays in copies.

Tips: "Always send sample poems with any other articles you may submit. We like to see photos of our authors as we sometimes use them in *PM*. In *Poetry Profile* we use articles by published poets who are passing along tricks of the trade. We need more 'how-to' submissions."

POETRY TORONTO, 217 Northwood Dr., Willowdale, Ontario, Canada M2M 2K5. Editors: Maria Jacobs and Robert Billings. Monthly magazine. Circ. 600. Pays in copies. Byline given. Not copyrighted. Acquires first North American serial rights. SAE and IRCs. Reports in 6 weeks.
Poetry: B. P. Nichol, poetry editor. Avant-garde, free verse, haiku, traditional. Submit maximum 8 poems.

POETRY/LA, Peggor Press, Box 84271, Los Angeles CA 90073. (213)472-7241. Editor: Helen Friedland. Semiannual anthology in paperback format "devoted exclusively to the best poetry offered by well-known and new poets living in the Los Angeles area." Estab. 1980. Circ. 700. Byline given. Acquires first rights. Photocopied submissions OK. No computer printout or disk submissions. SASE. Reports in 2 weeks on queries; 2 months on mss. Sample copy $3.50; writer's guidelines for SAE and 1 first class stamp.
Poetry: Avant-garde, free verse, traditional. "No constraint as to subject matter or form." Buys 150/year. "Prefer about four to six poems or pages, but will consider larger submissions." Length: open. Pays in minimum of 1 copy.

‡**POET'S PRIDE**, Box 4041, Clifton NJ 07012. Editor: Karen E. Obssuth. Poetry magazine published 3 times/year for established as well as lesser-known poets. Estab. 1983. Pays on publication. Byline given. Buys one-time rights. Submit seasonal/holiday material 2 months in advance. Simultaneous queries, and simultaneous, photocopied, and previously published submissions OK. SASE. Reports in 3 weeks on queries; 6 weeks on mss. Sample copy $5; writer's guidelines for SAE and 1 first class stamp.
Nonfiction: Humor, inspirational, interview/profile, opinion, personal experience. Buys 3-6 mss/year. Send complete ms. Length: 1,000-2,500 words. Pays in contributor copy.
Poetry: Avant-garde, free verse, haiku, light verse, traditional. Nothing obscene or overly suggestive. Buys 400 poems/year. Submit maximum 10 poems "unless queried for permission." Length: 50 lines maximum. Pays in contributor copy.

PORTLAND REVIEW, Portland State University, Box 751, Portland OR 97207. (503)229-4468. Editor: Jhan Hochman. Tri- or bi-yearly magazine covering literature. Circ. 1,800. Pays on publication. Byline given. Acquires first North American serial rights. Simultaneous queries, and photocopied submissions OK. No computer printout or disk submissions. SASE. Reports in 3 weeks on queries; 4 months on mss. Sample copy $2; free writer's guidelines.
Nonfiction: Book excerpts (fiction, poetry, literary criticism); general interest; humor; interview/profile; photo feature. Buys 30 mss/year. Send complete ms. Length: 5,000 words maximum. Pays in copies.
Fiction: Erotica, ethnic, experimental, fantasy, historical, horror, humorous, mainstream, mystery, novel excerpts, science fiction, suspense, prose poems. No formula fiction. Buys 8-15 mss/year. Send complete ms. Length: 4,000 words maximum. Pays in copies.
Poetry: Avant-garde, free verse, haiku, light verse, traditional prose. Buys 50-70/year. Submit maximum 5 poems. Length: 90 lines maximum. Pays in copies.
Fillers: Aphorisms. Length: 20 words maximum. Pays in copies.

PRIMAVERA, University of Chicago, 1212 E. 59th St., Chicago IL 60637. (312)684-2742. Editor: Janet Ruth Heller. Managing Editor: Karen Peterson. Annual magazine covering literature and art by women for readers high school age and up interested in contemporary literature and art. Circ. 800. Average issue includes 6 short stories and 45 poems. Pays on publication. Byline given. Acquires first North American serial rights. Phone queries OK. SASE. Reports in 2 months on queries; in 6 months on mss. Sample copy $4; free writer's guidelines.
Poetry: Editor: Ann Gearen. Avant-garde, free verse, haiku, light verse and traditional. Buys 45 mss/year. Submit maximum 6 poems. Length: 10 page maximum. Pays 2 free copies.
Tips: "Read a recent issue. We publish a wide range of material, all by women. We're looking for new ideas and interesting styles. We do not publish scholarly articles or formula-type fiction. Read one of our issues."

PTERANODON, Lieb and Schott, Box 229, Bourbonnais IL 60914. Editors: Patricia Lieb and Carol Schott. Magazine featuring short stories, poetry and writer's workshops for poets and writers. Circ. 500. Pays on publication. Acquires first rights. Photocopied submissions OK. Computer printout submissions OK. SASE. Reports in 2 weeks on queries; in 2 months on mss. Sample copy $2.50; free writer's guidelines.
Poetry: Avant-garde, free verse, haiku, light verse, traditional and modern. Submit maximum 4 poems. Length: 3-175 lines. Pays in copies.

PUB, Ansuda Publications, Box 158, Harris IA 51345. Editor: Daniel Betz. Magazine of poetry and fiction allowing writers to express their gut-feelings and concerns. Circ. 200. Buys 20-30 unsolicited mss/year. Pays in

copies. Acquires first North American serial rights. Simultaneous, photocopied and previously published submissions OK if so indicated. SASE. Reports in 1 day on queries; in 2 months on mss. Sample copy $1.50; free writer's guidelines with SASE.
Poetry: Free verse, traditional and blank verse. "No haiku and senseless rhyming." Submit maximum 6 poems. Pays in copies.
Tips: "We are especially interested in new writers and other writers who cannot get published anywhere else. Let us know about you; you may have what we want. The poets are the ones we have trouble with. We would like to have more poetry in each issue, but many poetry submissions are just 'beautiful words' that leave no image in our minds; we'd like more concrete poetry."

PUDDING, In cooperation with Ohio Poetry Therapy Center and Library, 2384 Hardesty Drive South, Columbus OH 43204. (614)279-4188. Editor: Jennifer Groce Welch. Magazine covering poetry, and poetry and the creative arts in therapy, self-help, and the human services. Published 3 times/year. Subscribers are poets, psychologists, psychiatrists, nurses, doctors, mental health professionals, teachers, members of the clergy, and those interested in self-help. Poetry of high quality (or, for a special section of the magazine, interesting/revealing writing by students patients/clients/inmates). Articles on poetry and creative writing as discovery and therapy and poems that could evoke strong response for the reader are solicited. Authors are paid by 2 copies/piece accepted and the Featured Poet is paid $10 plus 2 author copies. Circ. 1,400. Pays on publication. Byline given. Buys one-time rights or first rights. Submit seasonal/holiday material 12 months in advance. Photocopied and previously published submissions OK if properly credited. SASE. Reports in 2 weeks on queries; 3 weeks on mss. Sample copy $3.50; writer's guidelines for business size SAE and 1 first class stamp.
Nonfiction: Book excerpts; general interest; how-to (conduct/facilitate creative writing groups); inspirational; interview/profile; opinion; personal experience; technical; and creative writing/the writing process, etc. Looking for poetry about intense human situations, e.g. disasters, employment, hunger, parenting, counseling or being counseled, teaching, topical issues, mental and physical illness, specific problems or/and solutions; and poems by professionals and their clients from the human services. Appreciates query with letter indicating "your thought on poetry as therapy, your own poems, and/or your experience with poetry as a discovery tool. Large batches appreciated." Buys 285 unsolicited mss/year. Send complete ms. Length: 100-2,000 words. Pays $10, only if article is featured.
Photos: Need photos that "evoke a poetic response."
Poetry: Avant-garde, free verse, light verse, and freewriting. No sentimental, religious, or trite themes. Buys 200 mss/year. Submit maximum 25 poems. Pays in copies.
Fillers: Anecdotes, short humor and newsbreaks. Buys a varying number/year. Length: 100 words maximum.

PULP, c/o Sage, 720 Greenwich St., New York NY 10014. Editor: Howard Sage. For writers and any persons interested in quality fiction, poetry, art. Quarterly tabloid; 16 pages. Circ. 2,000. Acquires all rights. Payment in contributor's copies. Sample copy $1, check payable to Howard Sage. Will consider photocopied submissions. No simultaneous submissions. No computer printout or disk submissions. Reports in 1 month. Submit complete ms. SASE.
Poetry: Translations of poetry welcome. Submit clear, 8x10 camera ready copy of original with translation. Brief 25-word biography should accompany all submissions. Poems on all topics as long as subject is well handled and control is deft. Traditional and avant-garde forms; free verse. Length: open.
Tips: "See sample copy before submitting. Special issues have included Hebrew, Korean, Japanese, Italian, Mozambique poetry and fiction. Interviews with Marge Piercy, Diane Wakoski, and Ralph Ellison have appeared. Special 10th anniversary issue scheduled for January 1984."

‡QUARTER MOON, C.Z. Calder, Publisher, Box 336, Warwick NY 10990. Editor: Kit Calder. Quarterly poetry and art magazine. Estab. 1982. Circ. 500. Pays on acceptance. Byline given. Not copyrighted. Buys first North American serial rights. Submit seasonal/holiday material 1 month in advance. Photocopied submissions OK. SASE. Reports in 2 weeks. Sample copy $2; writer's guidelines for business-size SAE and 1 first class stamp.
Poetry: All types. "No singsong rhymes and gushing." Buys 200/year. Submit maximum 3 poems. Length: open. Pays variable rates.

‡REBIRTH OF ARTEMIS, Astra Publications, 24 Edgewood Terrace, Methuen MA 01844. (617)686-5381. Editor: Lorraine Moreau-Laverriere. Annual poetry magazine for women by women. Estab. 1982. Circ. 500. Pays in contributor's copy. Byline given. Rights revert to author on publication. Simultaneous, photocopied and previously published submissions OK. SASE. Reports in 3 weeks. Sample copy $4.50; writer's guidelines for SASE.
Poetry: Avant-garde, free verse, haiku. No rhymed poetry. Submit maximum 6 poems/year. Length: 3 lines-2 pages. Pays in contributor's copy.

REVISTA/REVIEW INTERAMERICANA, Inter American University Press, GPO Box 3255, San Juan, Puerto Rico 00936. (809)754-8415/754-8370. Publication of the Inter American University of Puerto Rico. Editor: Gerard P. Marin. A bilingual scholarly journal oriented to Puerto Rican, Caribbean and Hispanic subjects. Poetry, short stories, reviews. Literary, contemporary, ethnic (Puerto Rican, Hispanic, Caribbean) translations, scholarly, experimental mss in either English or Spanish. Quarterly. Circ. 2,000. Acquires all rights, "but will pay 50% of money received if reprinted or quoted." Byline given. Uses about 75 mss/year. Payment in reprints (15) mailed to author. Query or submit complete ms (typed, double-spaced, clear copies) and brief bio with SASE. No simultaneous submissions. Submit seasonal material at least 6 months in advance. Reports in 6 months.
Nonfiction: "Articles on the level of educated laymen, bilingual. Book reviews. Preference to Puerto Rican and Caribbean and Latin American themes from multi-disciplinary approach." Length: maximum 10,000 words.
Photos: B&w glossy prints, 4x5 minimum. Captions required. No color.
Fiction and Poetry: Bilingual; Spanish or English. Blank verse, free verse, experimental, traditional and avant-garde forms of poetry.

THE ROMANTIST, F. Marion Crawford Memorial Society, Saracinesca House. 3610 Meadowbrook Ave., Nashville TN 37205. (615)292-9695 or 226-1890. Editor: John C. Moran. Associate Editors: Don Herron and Steve Eng. Emphasizes modern Romanticism; especially fantastic literature and art. Annual magazine. Circ. 300. Buys first rights. Byline given. Photocopied poems and previously published submissions OK. No computer printout or disk submissions. SASE. Reports in 4 weeks. Free writer's guidelines.
Nonfiction: No articles without querying first.
Poetry: Traditional and free verse. "We prefer rhymed and metered poems, but no homespun doggerel. Prefer the tradition of Swinburne, Poe, Noyes, de la Mare, Masefield, Clark Ashton Smith; especially weird or fantastic verse." Uses 15 unsolicited poems/year.
Tips: Currently over-stocked on poetry.

THE ROSE'S HOPE, 394 Lakeside Rd., Ardmore PA 19003. (215)642-9353. Editor: Peter Langman. Semiannual magazine featuring poetry for writers, high school and college students, teachers and anyone who likes poetry. Circ. 175. Pays in copies. Phone queries OK. Submit seasonal material 1 month in advance. Authors retain all rights. Simultaneous, photocopied, and previously published submissions OK. SASE. Reports in 2-3 months on mss.
Nonfiction: Historical (articles about various trends or periods in poetry or about a specific poet); how-to (read or write poetry); opinion (ideas or views about poetry or poets); and personal experience (with poetry: teaching it, being taught, trying to get published). Buys 1-2 mss/issue. Send complete ms. Length: 1,000 words maximum. Pays in copies.
Poetry: Free verse, haiku, light verse and traditional. "No originality for originality's sake. Strangeness does not mean quality. We are not interested in poets who try to write like their contemporaries. No versified sermons or poems that preach." Buys 20 mss/issue. Length: 60 lines maximum. Pays in copies. "Free verse should not be broken prose. Rather than diffuse and wandering, poems should be intense."
Tips: "Looking for the communication of something real and sincere born out of human experience. Avoid common sentimentality and moralistic tendencies. Not into difficult, obscure, or overly intellectual material—from published or unpublished poets."

RUNESTONE, Asatru Free Assembly, 3400 Village Ave., Denair CA 95316. Editor: Stephen A. McNallen. Quarterly newsletter about the religion and culture of pre-Christian Scandinavia and the Germanic lands generally, for people who follow the religion of the Vikings and related peoples, or are interested in Neo-Paganism. Circ. 400. Pays on publication. Acquires all rights. Submit seasonal material 3 months in advance. Photocopied and previously published submissions OK. Computer printout submissions OK. SASE. Reports in 2 weeks. Free sample copy.
Poetry: Free verse and traditional. "We are especially interested in skaldic poetry in the Old Norse style. Nothing too esoteric; nothing on general psychic/occult/metaphysical subjects." Buys 3 mss/year. Submit maximum 5 poems. Length: 10-20 lines. Pays in copies.
Tips: "More emphasis on 'how-to-live' matters. Study a sample copy carefully to gain an understanding of our rather unorthodox views."

SALT LICK PRESS, 5107 Martin Ave., Austin TX 78751. Editor-in-Chief: James Haining. Emphasizes literature. Published irregularly; magazine; 68 pages. Circ. 1,500. Pays in copies. Photocopied and previously published submissions OK. Computer printout submissions OK; prefers letter quality to dot matrix. SASE. Reports in 2 weeks. Sample copy $3.
Poetry: Open to all types.

SAN FERNANDO POETRY JOURNAL, Kent Publications, 18301 Halsted St., Northridge CA 91325. Editor: Richard Cloke. Managing Editors: Lori C. Smith, Shirley J. Rodecker. Quarterly poetry magazine devoted to encouraging and promoting the literary arts. Interested in social-content and current technical and scientific advances, or regressions, in poetic form. "Interested in space-age Zeitgeist: contemporary problems of peace, poverty, environment, alienation and minority rights. We focus on the outer world, seen from within, but not inwardly directed. This is a general preference; we will not reject quality poetry of any form, or genre. But our crystal ball warns of trouble ahead." Prefers not to see subjectivist, surrealist, existentialist, internalist or ultra-traditionalist material. Circ. 500. Pays on publication. Acquires one-time rights. Photocopied and previously published submissions OK. Computer printout submissions OK "if legible." SASE. Reports in 2 weeks on queries; in 5 weeks on mss. Sample copy, our choice, $2.50 (20% off to libraries and poets who offer for publication); writer's guidelines for SASE.
Poetry: Social protest-free verse. Buys 300 unsolicited poems/year. Submit maximum 5 poems. Length: 10-50 lines preferred. Will print up to 300 lines if exceptional. Pays in copies of magazine for each entry published.
Tips: "Our poetry is keyed to our space in time. No bias against meter and rhyme, if not forced or intrusive. To us, the 'me' generation is passe. The 'we' generation is emerging. We are now a tax-exempt public corporation—welcome more diversity than before."

SAN JOSE STUDIES, San Jose State University, San Jose CA 95192. (408)277-2841. Editor: Selma Burkom. For the educated, literate reader. Interdisciplinary, scholarly journal; 112 pages. Three times a year: February, May and November. Circ. 500. Acquires first serial rights. Uses about 40 mss/year (all unsolicited). $100 annual prize for the best contribution published during the year. Pays in contributor's copies. Sample copy $3.50. Reports in 2-3 months. Submit complete ms. Computer printout and disk submissions OK; prefers letter quality to dot matrix printouts. SASE.
Poetry: Traditional and avant-garde forms of poetry; blank verse and free verse. Themes and length are open.

‡**SCRIVENER, A Biannual Literary Magazine**, McGill University, Arts B-20, 853 Sherbrooke St. W., Montreal, Quebec, Canada H3A 2T6. (514)392-4483. Editor: Dan Pope. Managing Editor: Joanne Bayly. Biannual literary journal of poetry, fiction and book reviews. Circ. 1,000. Pays on publication. Byline given. Writers retain copyrights of their work. Photocopied submissions OK. SASE. Reports in 2 months. Sample copy $2.
Columns/Departments: Book reviews of Canadian books only. Buys 20 mss/year. Send complete ms. Length: 500-1,000 words. Pays in 2 copies.
Fiction: Experimental. Any serious literary fiction whether the style be traditional or experimental. No forms of mainstream entertainment, such as romance, westerns, etc. Buys 15-20 mss/year. Send complete ms. Length: 500-8,000 words. Pays in 2 copies.
Poetry: Avant-garde, free verse, haiku, traditional. Open to all styles of well-written poetry. Buys 50 mss/year. Submit maximum 10 poems. Length: 1-100 lines. Pays in 2 copies.
Tips: "Our only criterion for judgment is the literary and artistic quality of the piece. We tend towards writing that is fresh and imaginative—innovative, too."

‡**SERENADE, The Sylvan Quarterly Magazine**, Sylvan Press Publishers, Box 15125, Richmond VA 23227. (804)264-0118. Editor: Sylvia Manolatos. Managing Editor: Annette Hohman. Quarterly literary magazine featuring a collection of well-written poems for adults with an appreciation for craftsmanship in the poetic arts. "We prefer a tolerant, non-biased outlook in our subject matter." Estab. 1983. Circ. 120. Pays on publication. Byline given. Buys first North American serial rights. Submit seasonal/holiday material 3 months in advance. Photocopied submissions OK. SASE. Reports in 1 week on queries; 1 month on mss. Sample copy for $1, 5x7 SAE and 2 first class stamps; writer's guidelines for business size SAE and 2 first class stamps.
Nonfiction: Lelia Koplin and Daphne Manolatos, articles editors. Opinion (short poetic criticism); poet's biographies (short articles). No long, rhetorical articles, religious articles, pedantic viewpoints. Buys 4-6 mss/year. Send complete ms. Pays in 3 copies.
Poetry: Avant-garde, free verse, haiku, traditional. No religious or overly sentimental verse or "categorical" verse (such as verse for every species of bird, flower, musical instrument, etc.). Buys 100 poems/year. Submit maximum 4 poems. Length: 50 lines maximum. Pays in 3 copies.
Tips: "We prefer shorter poems of a serious nature with no style restrictions. Avoid hackneyed phrases and overworked subject matter such as children, religion and self-pitying confessions."

SEVEN, 3630 NW 22, Oklahoma City OK 73107. Editor: James Neill Northe. Published 4 numbers to a volume on an irregular basis. No computer printout or disk submissions. Pays on acceptance $5/poem. Sample copy $2. *Please* no amateur verse. Study your market. Universal approach, no cataloging, but definite expression in finely written lines. Not impressed by the 'chopped prose' school or 'stream of consciousness' effusions.

THE SMALL POND MAGAZINE OF LITERATURE, Box 664, Stratford CT 06497. (203)378-4066. Editor: Napoleon St. Cyr. For "some high school students, the rest college and college grad students who read us in college libraries, or, in general, the literati." Published 3 times a year. 40 pages. Circ. 300. Acquires all rights. Payment in contributor's copies. Sample copy $2.25. Will consider photocopied submissions. No simultaneous submissions. Reports in 10-30 days. SASE.
Nonfiction and Fiction: All subjects except the Vietnam War, women's lib, or science fiction. Fiction, articles, essays. 2,500-word maximum.
Poetry: Traditional and avant-garde forms of poetry, blank, free and light verse. Length: 100 lines maximum.

SOUTH DAKOTA REVIEW, Box 111, University Exchange, Vermillion SD 57069. (605)677-5229. Editor: John R. Milton. For a university audience and the college educated, although reaches others as well. Quarterly. Acquires North American serial rights and reprint rights. Byline given. Pays in contributor's copies. Reports in 4 weeks or less, except in summer. No computer printout or disk submissions. SASE.
Nonfiction: Literary criticism, with first choice going to studies of Western American literature. Occasionally uses articles on aspects of American culture or history.
Fiction: Literary, serious, very well written. Not interested in stories about sports, hunting, fishing, juvenile characters "unless very well done and original in treatment." Prefers third-person stories about adults.
Poetry: Prefers poetry which is disciplined and controlled, though open to any form (tends to prefer traditional free verse). Any length considered, but prefers 10-30 lines.
Tips: "Although most of our material is unsolicited, it generally comes from writers who like to write, or from college and university professors, not from people who try to make a living from writing. Therefore, in the technical sense, we do not cater to freelancers as such. We often find thematic numbers of the journal taking shape and will then select material supporting the general theme. We thrive on flexibility, which may cause some consternation among writers who expct a journal to publish the same kinds of material all the time."

SOU'WESTER, Department of English, Southern Illinois University, Edwardsville IL 62026. Editor: Dickie Spurgeon. For "poets, fiction writers, teachers, and anyone else connected with or interested in the small press. We publish fiction, poetry and letters. We do not have any particular editorial bias, but we do insist on meaningful, imaginative development and technical proficiency." Magazine published 3 times/year. Circ. 300. Acquires all rights. Uses about 70 mss/year. Payment in contributor's copies. Sample copy $1.50. Will consider simultaneous and photocopied submissions. Reports in 4 to 6 weeks. Submit complete ms. Computer printout submissions OK; prefers letter quality to dot matrix. SASE.
Poetry: Traditional and avant-garde forms of poetry. Length: no maximum.
Tips: "We will not operate in summers, generally."

SPARROW POVERTY PAMPHLETS, Sparrow Press, 103 Waldron St., West Lafayette, IN 47906. Editor-in-Chief: Felix Stefanile. Triannual magazine; 32 pages, one poet an issue. Circ. 800. Pays on publication. Buys first North American serial rights. "We share anthology rights. Some previously published submissions OK, but major portion of ms should be first-time original." SASE. "We read only in April and May of each year. Do not send at other times." Reports in 6 weeks. Sample copy $2.
Poetry: "No form bias. Mature, serious work in the modern manner. Poetry must be human and relevant. Only interested in mss typescript of from 20-32 pages." Buys 20-30 poems/issue, each issue devoted to one poet. Pays $25 plus royalties; 20% after cost.
Tips: "We are read by poets of standing. We emphasize the modernist tradition of clarity, intellectual vigor, and experiment with language. We are not faddist, not ideological, not NEA-funded. We are simply not a market for novices. Our authors are now in all anthologies—Untermeyer, Norton, Meridian, etc. The would-be contributor should get to know our taste, and study past issues. Only 5% of people who send bother to buy and inspect issues. This, we understand, is a better record than for most poetry journals. Poets don't seem to study markets, as prose writers learn to do."

STAR*LINE, Newsletter of the Science Fiction Poetry Association, Box 491, Nantucket MA 02554. Editor: Robert Frazier. Managing Editor: Karen Jollie. Bimonthly newsletter covering science fiction, fantasy, horror poetry for association members. Circ. 200. Pays on acceptance. Byline given. Buys one-time rights. Submit seasonal/holiday material 3 months in advance. Simultaneous and photocopied submissions OK. SASE. Reports in 2 weeks. Sample copy $1; writer's guidelines for business size SAE and 1 first class stamp.
Nonfiction: How-to (write a poem); interview/profile (of science fiction, fantasy and horror poets); opinion (science fiction and poetics). "Articles must display familiarity with the genre." Buys 4-6 mss/year. Send

complete ms. Length: 500-2,000 words. Pays $1-5/printed page and 2 complimentary copies.

Columns/Departments: Reviews (of books, chapbooks, collections of science fiction, fantasy or horror poetry); Markets (current markets for science fiction, fantasy or horror poetry). Buys 40-60 mss/year. Send complete ms. Length: 200-500 words/reviews; 20-100 words/markets. Pays $.50-2.

Poetry: Avant-garde, free verse, haiku, light verse, traditional. "Must be related to speculative fiction subjects." Buys 60-80/year. Submit maximum 3 poems. Length: 1-100 lines. Pays $1-10 and 2 complimentary copies.

Fillers: Speculative-oriented quotations, prose or poetic. Length: 10-50 words. Pays $1 minimum.

Tips: "Send us good speculative poetry. Our latitude is very broad here. Serious free verse most often accepted, but all other forms have appeared and still do. New writers always needed. We also accept b&w illustrations, spot and cover, which are sharp, reproducible and speculative (science fiction/fantasy/horror) in nature. Query with SASE for specifics to Karen Jollie, 1722 N. Mariposa Ave., Los Angeles CA 90027.

STONE COUNTRY, Box 132, Menemsha MA 02552. (617)693-5832. Editor: Judith Neeld. "If you are just beginning to write poetry, do not submit to us, please. Read the magazine carefully before submitting; it is our only accurate guideline." Magazine published 2 times/year. Acquires first North American serial rights. Byline given. Accepts 100-150 poems/year. Payment in contributor's copy plus Phillips Poetry Award ($25) for best poem published in each issue. $15 for reviews and essays. Sample copy $3.50. Reports in 2 months. Submit complete ms. No computer printout or disk submissions. "SASE, required, or we will destroy ms."

Poetry and Reviews: Reviews Editor: Robert Blake Truscott. "We publish poetry, poetry criticism and commentaries. No thematic or stylistic limitations, but we are unable to publish long narrative poems in full. We look for the immediacy of language; concrete, uncommon imagery; the undisclosed; poetry as exploration, not statement." Free verse, traditional forms, blank verse, avant-garde forms. Uses 100+ unsolicited poems/year. Length: 40 lines maximum. Limit submissions to 5 poems at a time.

TAR RIVER POETRY, East Carolina University, Department of English, Greenville NC 27834. Editor: Peter Makuck. Biannual magazine "with mix of established poets and newcomers. Quality poetry, paper, layout, drawings, in-depth reviews." 52 pages. Circ. 1,000. Pays in contributor's copies. No fee. SASE. Reports in 6-8 weeks. Sample copy $2.50.

Poetry: Free verse and fixed forms. "We do not want sentimental or flat-statement poetry. We look for skillful use of figurative lanquage." Uses 40 poems/issue. Submit in batches of 6. Length: 50 lines maximum. "We do not read mss during May-August."

TAURUS, Box 28, Gladstone OR 97027. Editor: Bruce Combs. Quarterly magazine. Estab. 1981. Circ. 400. Pays on publication. Byline given. Acquires one-time and first North American serial rights. "Clear" photocopied submissions OK. Computer printout submissions OK if legible; prefers letter quality to dot matrix. SASE. Reports in 1 week. Sample copy $2.

Poetry: Avant-garde, free verse. "Fresh, earnest, virile use of language is more important than the topic." No conservative, rhymed, religious, or sewing-circle poetry." Buys 200/year. Length: open; "but the shorter, the better." Pays 1 copy/poem page.

TENDRIL, Tendril, Inc., Box 512, Green Harbor MA 02041. (617)834-4137. Editor: George Murphy. Contributing Editors: Raymond Carver, Carolyn Forche, Richard Ford, Tess Gallagher, Brendan Galvin, William Matthews, Mekeel McBride, Heather McHugh, Lisel Mueller, Mary Robison, Diane Wakoski, Joy Williams, Tobias Wolff. Poetry and fiction magazine published 3 times/year. Circ. 1,500. Pays on publication. Acquires first North American serial rights and second reprint rights. Publishes special anthology issues annually, e.g. *The Poet's Choice*, *Poetics*. Photocopied submissions OK. Computer printout submissions OK. SASE. Sample copy $3.

Poetry and Fiction: "Reviews of *Tendril* invariably mention our eclectic nature. We are open to poetry of any length or genre. In fiction, we lean toward the clear narrative, the contemporary minimalism, but are open to work of any nature." Buys 300 mss/year. Submit maximum 4 poems, 2 stories. Pays in copies.

13TH MOON, Drawer F, Inwood Station, New York, NY 10034. Editor-in-Chief: Marilyn Hacker. A feminist literary magazine. Emphasizes quality work by women for a well-read audience. Semiannual magazine. Pays in copies. Acquires first North American serial rights. SASE. Reports in 2 months. Sample copy $5.95 plus 75¢ postage and handling.

Nonfiction: Book reviews of women authors.

Fiction: No predictable "slick" fiction, mawkish or sentimental writing, or themes based on "automatic" feminist responses. Does not accept handwritten mss or work submitted by men.

Poetry: Open to all styles. Prefers poetry written by people who *read* contemporary poetry.

TIGHTROPE, Swamp Press, 323 Pelham Rd., Amherst MA 01002.(413)253-2270. Editors: Ed Rayher and Sarah Provost. Magazine published 2 times/year for readers interested in poetry, reviews of poetry and short fiction. Circ. 200. Pays on publication. Buys one-time rights. Phone queries OK. Photocopied submissions OK. Computer printout and disk submissions OK. SASE. Reports in 6 weeks on queries; in 8 weeks on mss. Sample copy $3.
Nonfiction: Historical (poetry and writing in fiction); interview (with creative writers and artists); and opinion (reviews of poetry). Send complete ms. Pays $5/page.
Photos: Send photos with ms. Pays $5 minimum for b&w prints.
Columns/Departments: Reviews (of poetry books and prose-poetry). Send complete ms. Pays $5/page.
Fiction: Experimental, historical and mainstream. Query. Pays negotiable rate.
Poetry: Avant-garde, free verse, haiku, traditional and imagist. "No prolix abstractivism." Buys 20 mss/issue. Pays $5/page.
Tips: "We take the liberty of writing comments upon any material submitted (except art work), unless otherwise instructed. No religious material."

‡**TOUCHSTONE, New Age Journal**, Houston Writer's Guild, Box 42331, Houston TX 77042. Editor: Eugenia Riley. Publisher: William Laufer. Quarterly literary magazine "for a liberal, well-educated, upper middle class audience." Circ. 1,000. Pays on publication. Byline given. Buys first rights. Submit seasonal/holiday material 3 months in advance. Photocopied submissions OK. Computer printout submissions OK "if of readable quality (not dot matrix)." SASE. Reports in 2 weeks on queries; 6 weeks on mss. Sample copy for $1.95, 6x9 SAE and 2 first class stamps.
Poetry: Free verse, haiku, traditional. "No doggerel or obscure poetry. We seek clarity and skill; we wish to be pointed toward a universal truth." Prefers to get "nothing 'preachy,' obscure or obscene." Buys 80/year. Submit maximum 12 poems. Length: 2-32 lines. Pays in copies.
Tips: "We are actively seeking short nonfiction pieces no longer than 2,500 words pointing us toward a universal truth. We welcome quotations on cause and effect. We also use short stories, interviews and book reviews."

‡**12 SECONDS OF LAUGHTER**, 821 N. Pennsylvania St., Indianapolis IN 46208. (317)297-1222. Editor: Deborah Jaffe McGee. Managing Editor: Hal McGee. Quarterly magazine covering "the obscure, in all forms. *12 Seconds* appeals to intelligent readers who can recognize the absurd and ridiculous in all the 'serious institutions' in our society—i.e., love, sex, politics, psychology, religion, etc." Estab. 1982. Circ. 300. Pays on publication. Byline given. Buys one-time rights. Photocopied submissions OK. SASE. Reports in 3 weeks. Sample copy for 6x9 SAE and 4 first class stamps; writer's guidelines for business size SAE and 1 first class stamp.
Nonfiction: Book excerpts, offbeat; expose, subject open; opinion; personal experience; music, art in unusual forms. Acquires 5-6 mss/year. Length: 750 words maximum. Pays in contributor's copies.
Fiction: Erotica; experimental, including avant-garde, dada, and surrealism; humorous, if offbeat; novel excerpts; collage, cut-ups, fold-ins. Acquires 12-15 mss/year. Length: 1,000 words maximum. Pays in contributor's copies.
Poetry: Avant-garde, free verse. "Nothing trite, unless intended satirically. No limitations on subject matter." Acquires 4-5/year. Submit maximum 6 poems. Length: 40 lines maximum. Pays in contributor's copies and 1 year subscription.
Tips: "We are open to submissions in all subjects. All material will be read. Previous publication is not important to us. Each issue is devoted to a general theme. However, if a ms strikes us, we *can* be persuaded to publish something not particularly related to the theme."

UNMUZZLED OX, 105 Hudson St., New York NY 10013. (212)226-7170. Editor-in-Chief: Michael Andre. Emphasizes art and poetry. Quarterly magazine. Circ. 15,000. Photocopied submissions OK. SASE. Reports in 1 month. Sample copy $5.75.
Nonfiction: Interviews (artists, writers and politicians). Buys 1 ms/issue. Query.
Photos: Photos purchased on assignment only. Model release required.
Fiction: Experimental and classical. Mostly solicited.
Poetry: "Pre anti-post modernism."

UP AGAINST THE WALL, MOTHER . . . , 6009 Edgewood Ln., Alexandria VA 22310. (703)971-2219. Editor: Lee-lee Schlegel. Art Director: Sibyl Lowen. Bimonthly magazine covering "women's thoughts and feelings, especially during crisis" for "women across the country—all kinds of women." Circ. 250. Buys 300 unsolicited mss/year. Byline given. Acquires one-time rights. Previously published submissions OK. No computer printout or disk submissions. SASE. Reports in 2 weeks. Sample copy $3.

Poetry: Avant-garde, free verse, haiku, and traditional. Submit maximum 1-10 poems. Length: 30 lines. Pay: "none yet." All submissions must be poetry that deals with women in crisis.

THE VILLAGER, 135 Midland Ave., Bronxville NY 10708. (914)337-3252. Editor: Amy Murphy. Publication of the Bronxville Women's Club. For club members and families; professional people and advertisers. Monthly, October through June. Circ. 750. Acquires all rights. Pays in copies only. Sample copy $1. Submit seasonal material (Thanksgiving, Christmas, Easter) 3 months in advance. Submit only complete ms. Reports in 2 weeks. SASE. "We will accept mss from US *only*; no foreign mail."
Poetry: Traditional forms of poetry, blank verse, free verse, avant-garde forms, light verse. Length: 20 lines.

VISIONS, The International Magazine of Illustrated Poetry, Black Buzzard Press, 4705 S. 8th Rd., Arlington VA 22204. (703)892-8034. Editor: Bradley R. Strahan. Associate Editor: Shirley G. Sullivan. Art Editor: Harry Bartley. Review Editor: Harold Black. Magazine published 3 times/year covering poetry, and reviews of poetry. "Send us only your best. We showcase strong, open, imagistic poetry; vibrant work that draws the reader in, work that can be enjoyed by all people. We don't care if you're a 'big name' but poetry must be well crafted." Circ. 550. Pays on publication. Byline given. Buys one-time rights. Submit seasonal/holiday material 3 months in advance. Photocopied submissions OK. SASE. Reports in 3 weeks. Sample copy $2; writer's guidelines available with the purchase of a sample copy only.
Poetry: Avant-garde, free verse, traditional. "There will be an issue featuring poems and translations from Latin America and the troubles there (including Central America) sometime in 1984." No "God's in His Heaven and all's right with the world" poems. Nothing dry or obscure. No children's type poetry. Buys 90/year. Submit 3-9 poems. Length: 2-200 lines. Pays in copies or $5 maximum. "Cash payment only when we have a grant."
Tips: "We are striving to publish even a higher quality of poetry than previously."

VOICES INTERNATIONAL, 1115 Gillette Dr., Little Rock AR 72207. Editor-in-Chief: Clovita Rice. Quarterly magazine; 32-40 pages. Pays in copies on publication. Acquires all rights. Submit seasonal/holiday material 1 year in advance. SASE. Reports in 3 weeks. Sample copy $2.
Poetry: Free verse. Uses 200-300 unsolicited poems/year. Limit submissions to batches of 5. Length: 3-40 lines. Will consider longer ones if good.
Tips: "We accept poetry with a new approach, haunting word pictures and significant ideas. Language should be used like watercolors to achieve depth, to highlight one focal point, to be pleasing to the viewer, and to be transparent, leaving space for the reader to project his own view."

‡VOL. NO. MAGAZINE, Los Angeles Poets Press, 24721 Newhall Ave., Newhall CA 91321. (805)254-0851. Editors: Luis Campos, Richard Weekley, Jerry Davidson, Tina Landrum. Quarterly literary/visual magazine of contemporary poetry for "open minded, literary, alert audience." Estab. 1983. Circ. 300. Pays on publication. Byline given. Not copyrighted. Buys one-time rights. Simultaneous queries and simultaneous and photocopied submissions OK. SASE. Reports in 3 months. Sample copy $2; writer's guidelines $2.
Poetry: Each issue of the magazine is subtitled. December 1983 "Immigrants" (Editor: Luis Campos); March 1984 "Reboundaries" (Editor: Richard Weekley; June 1984 "Effigy" (Editor: Jerry Danielson); September 1984 "Cause and Effect" (Editor: Tina Landrum). Avant-garde, free verse, haiku, light verse, traditional. "No sentimental, loose, unimaginative work." Buys 80 poems/year. Submit maximum 6 poems. Length: 1-70 lines. Pays in 2 copies.
Tips: "Query for theme specifics. Submit fresh and concise works on the theme. We're seeking progressive and adventuresome poets who connect with reality. Black and white visuals are desired in addition to poetry."

WAVES, 79 Denham Dr., Thornhill, Ontario, Canada L4J 1P2. (416)889-6703. Editor: Bernice Lever. For university and high school English teachers and readers of literary magazines. "Our main focus is publishing poetry and fiction from writers worldwide." Magazine published 3 times/year. Circ. 1,000 plus. Acquires first North American serial rights. Byline given. Pays $5/page. Sample copy $1 cash or $2 cheque. Photocopied submissions OK. "We will read clear computer printouts—gladly;" prefers letter quality to dot matrix. No simultaneous submissions. Reports in 3-6 weeks. Submit complete ms. SAE and International Reply Coupons.
Poetry: Formal and free verse. Length: 5-150 lines.
Tips: "Read a few back issues to see the level of language—intelligent without academic dryness—in reviews. Reviews Canadian authors only. In poetry, we look for subtle control of technique, with emotion and thought input. *Waves* aims to print mss of the quality one reads in *The Atlantic* or *Paris Review*."

WEBSTER REVIEW, Webster College, Webster Groves MO 63119. (314)432-2657. Editor: Nancy Schapiro. For "academics, students, all persons interested in contemporary international literature." Magazine.

Semiannual. Circ. 1,000. Not copyrighted. Byline given. Uses 200 mss/year. Pays in copies. Free sample copy. Photocopied and simultaneous submissions OK. Reports in 1 month. SASE.
Fiction and Poetry: "Stories, poems, excerpts from novels, essays and English translations of foreign contemporary literature. Subject matter is not important, but quality is. Our emphasis is on international as well as American contemporary quality writing." No restrictions on length.

WELLSPRING, 228 A, O'Connor St., Menlo Park CA 94025. (415)326-7310. Editor: Tim Chown. Quarterly magazine featuring poetry written from a Christian perspective; a forum for Christian poets and artists. Circ. 300. Pays on publication. Acquires one-time rights. Submit seasonal material 6 months in advance. Simultaneous, photocopied and previously published submissions OK. SASE. Reports in 8 weeks. Sample copy $2.50; free writer's guidelines with SASE.
Poetry: All forms and lengths. "No poetry with jokes, silly play on words, meaningless cliches, stale imagery or language, or greeting card homilies." Buys 125-150 mss/year. Submit maximum 6 poems. Pays in copies.
Tips: "Seek to write and to submit poetry that is powerful both in its communication to the spirit and artistic beauty. Use fresh imagery, language and sound that works on more than one level; the emotional as well as the spiritual. Send 4 to 6 poems. Learn to carefully critique your own work before submitting."

‡**WHISKEY ISLAND MAGAZINE**, Cleveland State University, 1983 E. 24th St., Cleveland OH 44511. (216)687-2000. Editor: Donald Laurila. Managing Editor: Karen Hammonds. Annual literary magazine of poetry and short stories. Circ. 2,000. Byline given. Buys all rights and second serial (reprint) rights. Submit seasonal/holiday material 1 month in advance. Simultaneous queries, and simultaneous and previously published submissions OK. SASE. Reports in 2 weeks. Free sample copy and writer's guidelines.
Poetry: Free verse, light verse, traditional. "We are open to almost anything." Submit maximum 5 poems. Length: 5-40 lines.

THE WINDLESS ORCHARD, English Department, Indiana-Purdue University, Ft. Wayne IN 46805. Editor: Dr. Robert Novak. For poets and photographers. Quarterly. Circ. 300. Copyrighted in magazine's name but permission for author to reprint gladly granted. Payment in contributor's copies. Reports in 1-40 weeks. Submit complete ms. SASE.
Poetry and Photos: Avant-garde forms of poetry, free verse and haiku. Use of photos restricted to b&w.

WIND/LITERARY JOURNAL, R.F.D. 1, Box 809K, Pikeville KY 41501. (606)631-1129. Editor: Quentin R. Howard. For literary people. Triannual magazine. Circ. 500. Uses 400 mss/year. Payment in contributor's copies. Sample copy $1.50. No photocopied or simultaneous submissions. Reports in 10-20 days. Submit complete ms. SASE.
Poetry: Blank verse, traditional and avant-garde forms of poetry, free verse, haiku.

WISCONSIN REVIEW, Box 276, Dempsey Hall, University of Wisconsin-Oshkosh, Oshkosh WI 54901. (414)424-2267. Editor: Luke Gabrilska. Tri-quarterly magazine; 32 pages. Circ. 2,000. Acquires first rights. Pays in contributor's copies. Sample copy $1.50. Reports in 5 months. Submit complete ms. SASE.
Poetry: All forms and styles. "Primarily interested in material that, in one way or another, attempts to elucidate, explain, discover or otherwise untangle the manifestly complex circumstances in which we find ourselves as Americans in the 1980s."

THE WORMWOOD REVIEW, Box 8840, Stockton CA 95208. Editor: Marvin Malone. Quarterly. Circ. 700. No computer printout or disk submissions. Acquires all rights. Pays in copies or cash equivalent. Pays on publication. Sample copy $2.00. Reports in 2-8 weeks. SASE.
Poetry: Modern poetry and prose poems that communicate the temper and depth of the human scene. All styles and schools from ultra avant-garde to classical; no taboos. Especially interested in prose poems or fables. 3-500 lines.
Tips: "Be original. Be yourself. Have something to say. Say it as economically and effectively as possible. Don't be afraid of wit and intelligence."

WRIT MAGAZINE, 2 Sussex Ave., Toronto, Ontario, Canada M5S 1J5. Editor: Roger Greenwald. Circ. 700. Annual literary magazine covering high quality fiction, poetry, and translations. Computer printout submissions OK; letter quality only. Pays in copies only. SAE and IRCs or Canadian postage.
Poetry: Send complete typed ms or clear photocopy. Translators: Enclose copy of original for our reference. See magazine for detailed instructions.

WRITERS FORUM, University of Colorado, Colorado Springs CO 80907. (303)593-3155 or (303)599-4023. Editor: Alex Blackburn. Emphasizes quality fiction and poetry. For people of all ages interested in excellence in creative writing and in contemporary American literature, especially from regions west of the Mississippi. Annual book; 250 pages. Circ. 1,000. Authors retain rights. Byline given. Simultaneous, photocopied and previously published submissions OK. "Send 2 copies of all submissions, brief bio in cover letter, and SASE." Reports in 3-6 weeks. Sample copy discounted 33% to $5.95 for *Writer's Market* readers; free writer's guidelines, SASE with request.

Fiction: Mainstream, experimental. Length: 1,000-15,000 words.

Poetry: Avant-garde, free verse, and traditional, including poetic drama. Publishes 40/year. Submit in batches of 5. Length: 10-2,000 words. Payment with free copy.

Tips: "We look for originality, verbal excitement, knowledge of forms, avoidance of 'commercial' themes and approaches, also acquaintance with *Writer's Forum* itself. We give special attention to work submitted on a writer's behalf by a professional writer, teacher of writers, agent, or publisher. Please write a letter of inquiry to editor before submitting material. No submissions before October 1983 please."

XANADU, Box 773, Huntington NY 11743. Editors: Virginia Barmen, Mildred Jeffrey, Lois Walker, Anne-Ruth Baehr and Anibal Yaryura-Tobias. "For an audience interested in reading the best new poetry being written." Annual magazine; 64 pages. Circ. 750. Acquires all rights. Uses about 90 poems/year. Pays in contributor's copies. Sample copy $2. No photocopied or simultaneous submissions. "Reads only from January to June." Reports in 3 months. Submit no more than 5 poems. SASE.

Poetry: "Our main criteria for poetry are excellence of craft and clarity and force of vision. Only the highest quality contemporary poetry. We like to see up to 5 poems by a contributor at one time. Strongly realized poems rooted in human experience have an edge."

‡**YELLOW SILK, Journal of Erotic Arts,** verygraphics, Box 6374, Albany CA 94706. Editor: Lily Pond. Alternative, non-pornographic quarterly of written and visual erotica. "All persuasions; no brutality." Estab. 1981. Circ. 5,000. Pays in copies on publication. Byline given. Buys one-year rights plus possible inclusion in any anthology. Submit seasonal/holiday material 6 months in advance. Simultaneous queries and photocopied submissions OK. Computer printout submissions OK; prefers letter quality to dot matrix. SASE. Reports in 6 weeks on queries/mss. Sample copy for $3.

Poetry: Avant-garde, free verse, haiku, traditional. Fiction and essays also considered. Buys 100/year (including foreign language poems with translation). Length and number of submissions open.

Tips: Entirely freelance-written. Needs more fiction. Featured in past: W.S. Merwin, Ntozake Shange, Susan Griffin, Robert Silverberg. "Writing strength is final consideration, along with appropriateness of material. Passion, subtlety, humor and beauty are the voices of the erotic. No 'blow-by-blow' descriptions; no salacious fantasies; nothing involving brutality in any form."

Politics and World Affairs

These publications emphasize politics for the general reader interested in current events. Other categories in *Writer's Market* include publications that will also consider articles about politics and world affairs. Some of these categories are Business and Finance, Regional and General Interest.

For listings of publications geared toward the professional involved in some branch of government, see Trade Journals/Government and Public Service.

ADA REPORT, Box 5, Ada MI 49301. Editor: Don Gregory. "Political satire emphasizing the humorous side of government—federal, state, and local—particularly its foibles and its follies." Newsletter published 8 times/year. Circ. 5,000. Pays on publication. Buys all rights. Photocopied submissions OK. SASE. Free sample copy.

Nonfiction: "*Ada Report's* basic message is that people are weary of seeing the bureaucrats make a mess of things. It calls attention to government blunders, red-tape, regulations, questionable spending, and other bureaucratic excesses and abuses. In addition, it blows the whistle on governmental actions—all in a light-

---

Market conditions are constantly changing! If this is 1985 or later, buy the newest edition of *Writer's Market* at your favorite bookstore or order directly from Writer's Digest Books.

hearted vein. It confers the 'Baked Pretzel Award' for the worst examples of bureaucratic nonsense and the 'Hero Award' for actions which will save tax dollars or reduce government encroachment upon the lives of the people." Buys 60-70 unsolicited mss/year. Length 200-600 words. Pays $75-150.
Tips: "Good writing on our type of topic is the only criterion. All submissions are read. Our interest is in quality political satire."

AFRICA REPORT, 833 United Nations Plaza, New York NY 10017. (212)949-5731. Editor: Margaret A. Novicki. 60% freelance written. For US citizens, residents with a special interest in African affairs for professional, business, academic or personal reasons. Not tourist-related. Bimonthly. Circ. 10,500. Rights purchased vary with author and material. Usually buys all rights. Negotiable kill fee. Byline given unless otherwise requested. Buys 15 unsolicited mss/year. Pays on publication. Sample copy for $3.; free editorial guidelines sheet. SASE.
Nonfiction and Photos: Interested in mss on "African political, economic and cultural affairs, especially in relation to US foreign policy and business objectives. Style should be journalistic but not academic or light. Articles should not be polemical or long on rhetoric but may be committed to a strong viewpoint. I do not want tourism articles." Would like to see in-depth topical analyses of lesser known African countries, based on residence or several months' stay in the country. Recent article example: "U.S. Congo: Pragmatic Relations" (November/December 1981). Pays $150 for nonfiction. Photos purchased with or without accompanying mss with extra payment. B&w only. Pays $25. Submit 12x8 "half-plate."
Tips: "Read *Africa Report* and other international journals regularly. Become an expert on an African or Africa-related topic. Make sure your submissions fit the style, length, and level of *Africa Report*."

AMERICAN OPINION MAGAZINE, Belmont MA 02178. Managing Editor: Scott Stanley Jr. "A conservative, anti-communist journal of political affairs." Monthly except August. Circ. 35,000. Buys all rights. Kill fee varies. Byline given. Pays on publication. Sample copy $2. SASE.
Nonfiction: Articles on matters of political affairs of a conservative, anti-communist nature. "We favor highly researched, definitive studies of social, economic, political and international problems that are written with verve and originality of style." Length: 3,000-4,000 words. Pays $25/published page.

AMERICAS, Organization of American States, Editorial Offices, General Secretariat Bldg., 7th Floor, 1889 F St. NW, Washington DC 20006. Managing Editor: A.R. Williams. Official cultural organ of Organization of American States. Audience is persons interested in inter-American topics. Editions published in English and Spanish. Bimonthly. Circ. 150,000. Buys first publication and reprint rights. Byline given. Pays on publication. Free sample copy. Articles received on speculation only. Include cover letter with writer's background. Reports in 3 months. Not necessary to enclose SASE.
Nonfiction: Articles of general New World interest on travel, history, art, literature, theater, development, archeology, travel, etc. Emphasis on modern, up-to-date Latin America. Taboos are religious and political themes or articles with noninternational slant. Photos required. Recent article example: "The Shrimp's Sweet Success" (May/June 1983). Buys 36 unsolicited mss/year. Length: about 2,000 words. Pays about $200 minimum.
Tips: "Send excellent photographs in both color and b&w, keep the article short and address an international readership, not a local or national one."

‡C.L.A.S.S. MAGAZINE, C.L.A.S.S. Promotions, Inc., 15 E. 40th St., New York NY 10016. (212)685-1404. Editor: W. Franklyn Joseph. Bimonthly magazine (monthly beginning December 1983) covering Caribbean/American Third World News and Views. Circ. 150,000. Pays on publication "unless otherwise arranged." Byline given. Buys one-time rights. Submit seasonal/holiday material 4 months in advance. Simultaneous queries and previously published submissions OK. SASE. Reports in 1 month on queries; 6 weeks on mss. Free sample copy and writer's guidelines.
Nonfiction: Features, book excerpts, general interest, historical/nostalgic, inspirational, interview/profile, travel, international news, views and lifestyles in Third World countries. 90% of each issue is freelance written. Query or send complete ms. Length: 150-2,500 words. Articles over 700 words must be of international flavor in content. Pays up to $4/column inch, unless otherwise arranged.
Poetry: Avant-garde, free verse, haiku, light verse, traditional. Buys 10-20 poems/year. Submit maximum 10 poems. Length: 22-30 lines. Pays $10 minimum.
Tips: "Submit written queries; stick to Afro American/Third World interests and relate to an international audience."

CALIFORNIA JOURNAL, The California Center, 1714 Capitol Ave., Sacramento CA 95814. (916)444-2840. Editor-in-Chief: Robert Fairbanks. Managing Editor: Alice Nauman. Emphasizes analysis of California politics and government. Monthly magazine; 40 pages. Circ. 20,000. Pays on publication. Buys all rights. Byline given. Phone queries OK. Computer printout submissions OK. SASE. Reports immediately. Free sample copy.

Nonfiction: Profiles of state and local government and political analysis. No outright advocacy pieces. Buys 25 unsolicited mss/year. Query. Length: 900-3,000 words. Pays $75/printed page.
Tips: "You can break in with a phone call. But you must show deep knowledge of subject." Recent article example: "Anatomy of an Electorate" (March 1982).

CAMPAIGNS & ELECTIONS, The Journal of Political Action, Suite 602, National Press Bldg., Washington DC 20045. (202)347-2380. Editor/Publisher: Stanley Foster Reed. Managing Editor and Vice President: Robert Abeshouse. Associate Editor: Elizabeth Bartz. "Ours is the only publication on political campaigning—the art of getting elected." Quarterly journal covering political campaign management—how to get elected. "C&E is a nonpartisan 'how-to' journal on the effective management of political campaigns—be they national, state or local." Estab. 1980. Circ. 2,000. Pays within 3 weeks of publication. Byline given. Buys all rights. SASE. Reports in 2 weeks on queries; 3 weeks on mss. Sample copy $15; free writer's guidelines.
Nonfiction: Book excerpts (from books on political campaigning techniques); expose (on political campaign techniques used at any level that worked); how-to (organize specific parts of a political campaign; for example, GOTV, walking precincts, etc.); interview/profile (with top political consultants, media experts). "Writing should be highly factual, on specific campaign techniques and preferably submitted by professionals in the field of political consulting." No "partisan pieces on politics, for example, 'why the Democrats have to rally' or 'why Republicans know what America wants,' etc. Only *technique*." Buys 20 mss/year. Query with clips of published work. Length: 2,500-5,000 words. Pays $100-300/article.
Photos: Pays $10-20 for 5x7 b&w prints.
Tips: Writers should be "experienced in political campaigning and see an area in the consulting world that needs explication. Articles on how current political consulting techniques have been applied at the state or local level in a campaign are much preferred."

CONSERVATIVE DIGEST, Viguerie Communications, 7777 Leesburg Pike, Falls Church VA 22043. (703)893-1411. Editor-in-Chief: Mark Huber. 10% freelance written. Monthly magazine; 48 pages. Circ. 60,000. Pays on publication. Buys second serial and one-time rights. Pays 10% kill fee. Byline given. SASE. Simultaneous and previously published submissions OK. Reports in 3 weeks. Sample copy $2.
Nonfiction: Expose (government); how-to (political ideas); and interview. Buys 1 ms/issue. Submit complete ms. Length: 750-1,200 words. Pays 10¢/word.
Fillers: Susan Longyear, managing editor. Clippings and bureaucratic blunders. Buys 20 fillers/issue. Pays $15-25.

CONSERVATIVE REGISTER, Proud Eagle Press, Box 8453, Riverside CA 92515. (714)785-5180. Publisher/Editor-in-Chief: Paul Birchard. Editor: Alana Cross. Bimonthly Christian newspaper covering politics from a conservative viewpoint. Audience includes activist readers. Circ. 3,500. Pays on acceptance. Byline given. Buys all rights. Submit seasonal/holiday material 2 months in advance. Photocopied and previously published submissions OK. No computer printout or disk submissions. SASE. Reports in 4 weeks. Sample copy $1; writer's guidelines for business size SAE and 1 first class stamp. No material returned without SASE.
Nonfiction: Jay Sulsenbir, assignments. Expose (of government from a conservative viewpoint); general interest; inspirational (from a Christian viewpoint); interview/profile (of religious, government or business leaders); new product (on energy or consumer-related); opinion. "We prefer material which cites a governmental action or law and then projects its impact for Christians and/or conservatives in future years." No racist, bigoted or immoral material. Buys 12 unsolicited mss/year. Submit ms. Length: 100-1,000 words. Pays $5-25.
Photos: State availability of photos. Pays $5-15 for b&w 8x10 prints. Captions, model release, and identification of subjects required.
Columns/Departments: Alana Cross, column/department editor. Buys 8 mss/year. Query. Length: 1,000 maximum. Pays $25. "We will feature a Christian book review in every issue. Also, any political 'thought' piece which fits our format is carefully considered."
Fiction: J. Sulsenbir, assignments. Political satire. Limited market but will consider. No racist or immoral fiction. Buys 2 mss/year. Query. Length: 300 words maximum. Pays $5-25.
Fillers: Alana Cross, fillers editor. Anecdotes, short humor and newsbreaks. Buys 3 mss/issue. Length: 25-100 words. Pays $5-10. "Interesting factual pieces are most desired. Local religious material with national interest especially welcome."
Tips: "We are slanting our material more heavily toward a Christian publication. The emphasis is still political but it is crucial to consider impact on Christians, home life, etc. We are an excellent publication for unpublished writers. We want circulation-boosting pieces. Please document material and avoid sensationalism. We look first at material that has photos—but photos are not mandatory. Please, no phone queries. We are somewhat general in format, but specific in viewpoint. Steady income can be had for writing to meet our needs—even for new writers whom we encourage. We will not use any material over 1,000 words. Writers will have more success submitting material between 300-500 words."

‡**CRITIQUE: A JOURNAL OF CONSPIRACY & METAPHYSICS**, Critique Foundation, 2364 Valley W. Dr., Santa Rosa CA 95401. (707)526-5990. Editor: Bob Banner. Managing Editor: M. Banovitch. Quarterly journal "that explores conspiracy scenarios, behind-the-scenes-news, exposes, and unusual news that frequently create debacles within the ordinary mind set. *Critique* also explores assumptions, beliefs, and hypotheses that we use to understand ourselves, our 'world' and the metaphysical crisis of our time." Circ. 1,000. Pays on publication. Byline given. Submit seasonal/holiday material 4 months in advance. Simultaneous queries, and simultaneous, photocopied and previously published submissions OK. SASE. Reports in 2 months. Sample copy $2; free writer's guidelines.
Nonfiction: Book excerpts; expose (political, metaphysical, cultural); interview/profile (those in the specified area); personal experience (as it relates to cultural ideology). Not interested in "anything that gets published in ordinary, established media." Buys 8-25 mss/year. Send complete ms with bio/resume. Length: 200-3,000 words. Pays $15 maximum.
Tips: "We have published articles, reviews and essays that are difficult to categorize in the simplistic, dualistic Left or Right ideological camps. The material's purpose has been, and will be, to provoke critical thinking; to discriminate between valuable and manipulative information; to incite an awareness of events, trends, phases and our roles/lives within the global psyche that no ordinary consumer of ordinary media could even begin to conceive let alone use such an awareness to affect his/her life."

EUROPE, 2100 M St. NW, 707, Washington DC 20037. Editor: Webster Martin. For anyone with a professional or personal interest in Western Europe and European-US relations. Bimonthly magazine; 60 pages. Circ. 60,000. Copyrighted. Buys about 100 mss/year. Pays on acceptance. Free sample copy. Submit seasonal material 3 months in advance. Reports in 4 weeks. Query or submit complete ms. Include resume of author's background and qualifications with query or ms. SASE.
Nonfiction and Photos: Interested in current affairs (with emphasis on economics and politics), the Common Market and Europe's relations with the rest of the world. Publishes occasional cultural pieces, with European angle. High quality writing a must. "We publish anything that might be useful to people with a professional interest in Europe." Length: 500-2,000 words. Average payment is $100-325. Photos purchased with or without accompanying mss. Also purchased on assignment. Buys b&w and color. Average payment is $25-35 per b&w print, any size; $50 for inside use of color transparencies; $200-300 for color used on cover.

FOREIGN AFFAIRS, 58 E. 68th St., New York NY 10021. (212)734-0400. Editor: William P. Bundy. For academics, businessmen (national and international), government, educational and cultural readers especially interested in international affairs of a political nature. Published 5 times/year. Circ. 90,000. Buys all rights. Pays kill fee. Byline given. Buys 45 mss/year. Pays on publication. Sample copy $5 postpaid. Photocopied submissions OK. Reports in 4-6 weeks. Submit complete ms. SASE.
Nonfiction: "Articles dealing with international affairs; political, educational, cultural, economic, scientific, philosophical and social sciences. Develop an original idea in depth, with a strong thesis usually leading to policy recommendations. Serious analyses by qualified authors on subjects with international appeal." Recent article example: "Reagan and Russia" (Winter 1982/83). Buys 25 unsolicited mss/year. Length: 5,000-8,000 words. Pays $400.
Tips: "We like the writer to include his/her qualifications for writing on the topic in question (educational, past publications, relevant positions or honors), and a clear summation of the article: the argument (or area examined), and the writer's policy conclusions."

THE FREEMAN, 30 S. Broadway, Irvington-on-Hudson NY 10533. (914)591-7230. Editor: Paul L. Poirot. 60% freelance written. For "fairly advanced students of liberty and the layman." Monthly. Buys all rights, including reprint rights. Byline given. Buys 44 mss/year. Pays on publication. SASE.
Nonfiction: "We want nonfiction clearly analyzing and explaining various aspects of the free market, private enterprise, limited government philosophy, especially as pertains to conditions in the United States. Though a necessary part of the literature of freedom is the exposure of collectivistic cliches and fallacies, our aim is to emphasize and explain the positive case for individual responsibility and choice in a free economy. Especially important, we believe, is the methodology of freedom; self-improvement, offered to others who are interested. We try to avoid name-calling and personality clashes, and find satire of little use as an educational device. Ours is a scholarly analysis of the principles underlying a free market economy. No political strategy or tactics." Length: 3,500 words maximum. Pays 5¢/word.
Tips: "Facts, figures, and quotations cited should be fully documented, to their original source, if possible."

‡**GUARDIAN, Independent Radical Newsweekly**, Institute for Independent Social Journalism, 33 W. 17th St., New York NY 10011. (212)691-0404. Editor: Bill Ryan. Weekly newspaper covering news and politics for a broad left and progressive audience. Circ. 20,000. Pays on publication. Byline given. Simultaneous queries, and simultaneous and photocopied submissions OK. SASE. Reports in 3 weeks on queries; 1 month on mss. Samply copy for $1, 9x12 SAE and 5 first class stamps; writer's guidelines for business size SAE and 1 first class stamp.

Nonfiction: Ellen Davidson, articles editor. Expose (of government, corporations, etc.). "About 90% of our publication is hard news and features on current events." Buys 200 mss/year. Query with published clips. Length: 200-1,800 words. Pays $10-90.

Photos: Jill Benderly, photo editor. State availability of photos. Pays $10 for b&w prints. Captions required.

Columns/Departments: Women; Labor; The Left; Blacks. Buys 30 mss/year. Query with published clips. Length: 200-700 words. Pays $10-30.

IN THESE TIMES, Capp Street Foundation, 1300 W. Belmont Ave., Chicago IL 60657. Editor: James Weinstein. Managing Editor: Sheryl Larson. Weekly tabloid covering national and international news. Circ. 30,000. Pays on publication. Byline given. Buys variable rights. Submit seasonal/holiday material 2 months in advance. Simultaneous queries and simultaneous, photocopied, and previously published submissions OK. SASE. Reports in 6 weeks. Sample copy for SAE and 4 first class stamps.

Nonfiction: Jay Walljasper, articles editor. Book excerpts, expose, historical, interview/profile, personal experience. "The labor movement community groups, feminist and minority issues, and anti-corporate movements in general receive special emphasis." Buys 100 mss/year. Query. Length: 400-1,600 words. Pays $100 maximum.

Photos: State availability of photos. Pays $25 maximum for 8x10 b&w prints. Identification of subjects required. Buys one-time rights.

Columns/Departments: Reviews (books, film, etc.). Buys 45 mss/year. Query. Length: 400-1,600. Pays $25 maximum.

INQUIRY, 1320 G. St. SE, Washington DC 20003. (202)547-2770. Editor: Doug Bandow. Monthly magazine for "thinking people, people dissatisfied with conventional left/right analysis. Our philosophy is a deep belief in the rights and abilities of the individual, coupled with overriding skepticism about the government's ability to solve problems." Circ. 25,000. Pays on publication. Byline given. Offers "usual" 25% kill fee. Buys negotiable rights. SASE. Reports in 3 weeks on queries; 1 month on mss. Simultaneous and photocopied submissions OK. Free sample copy and writer's guidelines.

Nonfiction: Expose (of government corruption or ineptitude); political humor; profile (of political figures); "we want a blend of reporting and analysis." Special issues include winter book issue with 8-12 book reviews. No history, essays on personal opinion, Erma Bombeck humor. Also no how-to material or general nonfiction without a current events/issue angle. Buys 5-10 unsolicited mss/year. Recent article example: "The Infrastructure Scam" (February 1983). Query with clips of published work. Length: 1,000-4,500 words. Pays 10¢/word.

Columns/Departments: Law, Education, Politics, Media, Corporate State, Therapeutic State. Buys 2-3 mss/issue. Query with clips of published work. Length: 1,000-2,500 words. Pays 10¢/word.

‡**INTRIGUE, The International Journal of Reportage**, Air Crafts Limited, Inc., Box 68, Woodbridge NJ 07095. Editor: Ted Pastuszak Jr. Fortnightly newsletter and special occasional papers covering political, social and economic developments in world affairs compiled from foreign broadcasts and other diverse sources. For "a sophisticated readership of executives, journalists, and international investors." Circ. 2,000. Pays on publication. Byline given. Offers 20% kill fee. Buys first rights. Simultaneous queries OK. Computer printout submissions OK; prefers letter quality to dot matrix. SASE. Reports in 1 month on queries. Sample copy $1; free writer's guidelines.

Nonfiction: Contact: "In Cold Type" Department. Book excerpts and reviews, expose, interview/profile, personal experience, (all subjects should pertain to or concern political, social or economic events or developments); travel (arrangements to unusual places currently in the news). "Special issues include 'Islands of Intrigue,' and 'Espionage Special,' and a 'Diplomatic Edition.' With regard to our field of foreign affairs, we would prefer *not* to receive material that takes a specific political stand without including proper documentation and research. In short, we prefer reporting to editorializing." Buys less than 50 mss/year. Query with clips. Length: 700-750 words. Pays $70-140.

Columns/Departments: Airwaves (notes on international radio); ProvocaTours (travel tips to unusual places in the news); Capital Ideas (business and financial items of interest). Buys less than 50 mss/year. Query with clips of published work. Length: 700-750 words. Pays 10-20¢/word.

Fillers: Contact: "Inside Information" Department. Clippings and newsbreaks. "We're looking for interesting asides to news stories not covered by the major press." Length: 40-80 words. Pays 10-20¢/word.

Tips: "*Intrigue* is now an international fortnightly, with a particular interest in events and developments that concern foreign trade (including imports, exports, commodities, the travel industry, currency markets, etc.). All departments are open to freelancers. Since our publication is brief and confidential, writing must be concise and to the point."

‡**JOURNAL OF CONTEMPORARY STUDIES**, Institute for Contemporary Studies, 260 California St., San Francisco CA 94111. (415)398-3010. Editors: Patrick Glynn and Walter J. Lammi. Quarterly magazine covering public policy and politics, domestic and foreign, "for academics, policymakers, and informed citi-

zens with an interest in public policy and political issues and trends." Circ. 3,500. Pays on publication. Byline given. Buys all rights. Photocopied submissions OK. Reports in 6 weeks. SASE. Free sample copy.
Nonfiction: "Thoughtful, closely-argued, data-based articles on public policy and politics, written in a style suitable for both general readers and specialists." Buys 36 mss/year. Submit complete ms. Length: 4,500-7,000 words. Payment varies, depending on length and content.

THE NATION, 72 5th Ave., New York NY 10011. Editor: Victor Navasky. Weekly. Query. SASE.
Nonfiction and Poetry: "We welcome all articles dealing with the social scene, particularly if they examine it with a new point of view or expose conditions the rest of the media overlooks. Poetry is also accepted." Query. Buys 250 unsolicited mss/year. Length and payment to be negotiated. Modest rates.
Tips: "We are absolutely committed to the idea of getting more material from the boondocks. If you live somewhere where you think nothing is going on, look again! We tackle issues such as labor, national politics, consumer affairs, environmental politics, civil liberties and foreign affairs."

NATIONAL DEVELOPMENT (DESAROLLO NACIONAL), Intercontinental Publications, Inc., Box 5017, Westport CT 06880. (203)226-7463. Editor-in-Chief: Virginia Fairweather. Emphasizes 3rd world infrastructure. For government officials in 3rd world—technocrats, planners, engineers, ministers. Published 9 times/year; 120 pages. Circ. 60,000. Pays on acceptance. Buys all rights. Byline given. Phone queries OK. Previously published submissions OK. SASE. Reports in 4 weeks. Free sample copy and writer's guidelines.
Nonfiction: Technical (tourism, construction, government management, planning, power, telecommunications); informational (agriculture, economics, public works, construction management); interview; photo feature and technical. Buys 6-10 mss/issue. Query with "inclusion of suggestions for specific article topics; point out your area of expertise." Length: 1,800-5,000 words. Pays $250.
Photos: B&w and color. Captions required. Query. Total price for ms includes payment for photos.
Columns/Departments: Power technology, telecommunications, technology, water treatment, Financial Technology (finances as they might affect 3rd world governments). Buys 4 mss/issue. Query. Length: 750-1,500 words. Pays $250. Open to suggestions for new columns/departments.

NATIONAL JOURNAL, 1730 M St. NW, Washington DC 20036. (202)857-1400. Executive Director: Julie Romero. Editor: Richard Frank. "No freelance material accepted because fulltime staff produces virtually all of our material." Byline given.

NATIONAL REVIEW, 150 E. 35th St., New York NY 10016. (212)679-7330. Editor: William F. Buckley Jr. Issued fortnightly. Buys all rights. Pays 50% kill fee. Byline given. Pays on publication. Will send sample copy. Reports in a month. SASE.
Nonfiction: Kevin Lynch, articles editor. Uses articles, 1,000-3,500 words, on current events and the arts, which would appeal to a politically conservative audience. Pays $100/magazine page (900 words per page). Inquiries about book reviews, movie, play, TV reviews, or other cultural happenings, or travel should be addressed to Chilton Williamson Jr.

NEW GUARD, Young Americans for Freedom, Woodland Rd., Sterling VA 22170. (703)450-5162. Editor-in-Chief: Susan Juroe. Emphasizes conservative political ideas for readership of mostly young people with a large number of college students. Age range 14-39. Virtually all are politically conservative with interests in politics, economics, philosophy, current affairs. Mostly students or college graduates. Quarterly magazine; 48 pages. Circ. 7,000. Pays on publication. Buys all rights. Byline given. Phone queries OK. Submit seasonal/holiday material 2-3 months in advance. SASE. Reports in 1 month. Free sample copy.
Nonfiction: Expose (government waste, failure, mismanagement, problems with education or media); historical (illustrating political or economic points); interview (politicians, academics, people with conservative viewpoint or something to say to conservatives); personal opinion; and profile. Buys 40 mss/year. Submit complete ms. Length: 1,500 words maximum. Pays $40-100.
Photos: Purchased with accompanying manuscript.

THE NEW REPUBLIC, A Weekly Journal of Opinion, 1220 19th St. NW, Washington DC 20036. Contact: Editor. 50% freelance written. Circ. 100,000. Buys all rights. Byline given. Pays on publication. SASE.
Nonfiction: This liberal, intellectual publication uses 1,000- to 1,500-word comments on public affairs and arts. Pays 10¢/published word.

‡**THE NEW SOCIALIST**, New Social Publications/New Socialist Committee, Box 18026, Denver CO 80218. (303)333-1095. Editor: Phil Goodstein. Quarterly newsletter "aimed at persons interested in the history, theory, and problems of socialism and the creation of a free, classless society. A general agreement with this last goal must be reflected in articles." Circ. 500. Byline given. Makes work-for-hire assignments. Submit seasonal material 3 months in advance. Simultaneous queries and photocopied submissions OK. Reports in 2 weeks. Sample copy for SAE and 2 first class stamps; writer's guidelines for SAE and 1 first class stamp.

Nonfiction: Expose, general interest, historical, opinion, political and economic analysis, international events. Buys 4 mss/year. Send complete mss. Length: 500-5,000 words. Pays $1-50.
Tips: "We're especially interested in reports on public happenings, demonstrations, and personal experiences in any social movement."

NEWSWEEK, 444 Madison Ave., New York NY 10022. Staff-written. Unsolicited mss accepted for "My Turn," a column of opinion. Length: 1,100 words maximum. Include SASE for answer. Reports in 1 month.

‡**NUCLEAR TIMES, A Newsmagazine on the Antinuclear Weapons Movement**, Nuclear Times, Inc., 298 5th Ave., New York NY 10001. (212)563-5940. Editor: Greg Mitchell. Managing Editor: Corinna Gardner. Monthly magazine on nuclear weapons and the opposition to them. Estab. 1982. Circ. 30,000. Pays on publication. Byline given. Offers $50 kill fee. Buys one-time rights. Submit seasonal/holiday material 2 months in advance. Simultaneous queries and photocopied submissions OK. SASE. Reports in 1 month. Free sample copy.
Nonfiction: Book excerpts; general interest (on the issue); interview/profile; technical (related to the issue); news stories. No fiction. Buys 20 mss/year. Query with published clips if available or send complete ms. Length: 100-3,000 words. Pays $50-300.
Photos: Cindy Milstein, photo editor. State availability or send photos with ms. Reviews b&w contact sheet and prints. Identification of subjects required.
Columns/Departments: Send complete ms. Length: 800-1,600 words. Pays $100-200.
Tips: "We report the news on the activities and strategies of the various groups and campaigns within the antinuclear movement. We look for probing and objective journalistic style, presented in a straightforward manner, with an emphasis on timeliness."

POLITICAL PROFILES, 862 National Press Building, Washington DC 20045. Publisher: Robert J. Guttman. Managing Editor: Susan Whitmore. Publishing company featuring a newsletter and magazine style monographs on current political issues, election and campaign information. Newsletter published biweekly. Magazine varies. Pays on acceptance. Byline given. Buys all rights.
Nonfiction: Expose (investigative pieces); historical (current history); and profile (political). Query. "We are interested in assigning stories to well-established political reporters. Write a letter outlining your credentials and your availability for assignments."

THE PROGRESSIVE, 409 E. Main St., Madison WI 53703. (608)257-4626. Editor: Erwin Knoll. Monthly. Buys all rights. Byline given. Pays on publication. Reports in 2 weeks. Query. Computer printout submissions OK "if legible and double spaced"; prefers letter quality to dot matrix. SASE.
Nonfiction: Primarily interested in articles which interpret, from a progressive point of view, domestic and world affairs. Occasional lighter features. "*The Progressive* is a *political* publication. General-interest material is inappropriate." Length: 3,000 words maximum. Pays $50-200.
Tips: "Display some familiarity with our magazine, its interests and concerns, its format and style. We want query letters that fully describe the proposed article without attempting to sell it—and that give an indication of the writer's competence to deal with the subject."

PUBLIC OPINION, American Enterprise Institute, 1150 17th St. NW, Washington DC 20036. (202)862-5800. Managing Editor: Karlyn Keene. Bimonthly magazine covering public opinion for the public policy community, journalists, and academics interested in public opinion data and its meanings. Circ. 16,000. Pays on publication. Byline given. Buys all rights. Simultaneous queries OK. Reports in 1 month on queries. Sample copy $3.50.
Nonfiction: Historical (dealing with polling industry); "public policy issues, opinion polls and their meaning in relation to public policy." Buys 10-15 mss/year. Query with outline. Length: 2,500-3,000 words. Payment varies widely.

REASON MAGAZINE, Box 40105, Santa Barbara CA 93103. (805)963-5993. Editor: Robert Poole Jr. 50% freelance written. For a readership interested in individual liberty, economic freedom, private enterprise alternatives to government services and protection against inflation and depressions. Monthly. Circ. 35,000. Rights purchased vary with author and material. May buy all rights, first North American serial rights, or first serial rights. Pays 35% kill fee. Byline given. Buys 30 mss/year. Pays on publication. Sample copy $2; free guidelines for writers. "Manuscripts must be typed, double- or triple-spaced on one side of the page only. The first page (or a cover sheet) should contain an aggregate word count, the author's name and mailing address, and a brief (100- to 200-word) abstract. A short biographical sketch of the author should also be included." Photocopied submissions OK. Reports in 2 months. Query. SASE.
Nonfiction: "*Reason* deals with social, economic and political problems, supporting both individual liberty and economic freedom. Articles dealing with the following subject areas are desired: analyses of current issues and problems from a libertarian viewpoint (e.g., education, energy, victimless crimes, regulatory agencies,

foreign policy, etc.). Discussions of social change, i.e., strategy and tactics for moving toward a free society. Discussions of the institutions of a free society and how they would deal with important problems. Articles on self-preservation in today's economic, political and cultural environment. Case studies of unique examples of the current application of free-market principles." Length: 1,500-5,000 words. Book reviews are needed.

REVIEW OF THE NEWS, 395 Concord Ave., Belmont MA 02178. (617)489-0600. Editor: Scott Stanley Jr. Weekly magazine covering the news with a conservative and free market orientation. Circ. 60,000. Average issue includes capsulated news items, bylined sports, films, economic advice and overseas and congressional activities. Pays on acceptance or on publication. Byline given. Kill fee negotiated. Buys all rights. Photocopied submissions OK. SASE. Reports in 1 month on queries; in 3 weeks on mss. Sample copy $1.
Nonfiction: Expose (of government bungling); general interest (current events and politics); interview (with leading conservatives and newsmakers, heads of state, congressmen, economists and politicians); humor (satire on the news); and commentary on the news. Buys 3-4 mss/year. Query with clips of previously published work. Length: 1,500-3,000 words. Pays $150-250.

‡ROLL CALL, The Newspaper of the US Congress, 201 Massachusetts Ave. NE, Washington DC 20002. (202)546-3080. Editor: Sidney Yudain. Weekly tabloid covering national politics for Congress, congressional aides, the White House, political writers, newspeople, etc. Circ. 7,500. Pays on publication. Byline given. Buys one-time rights. Submit seasonal/holiday material 1 month in advance. Simultaneous queries OK. SASE. Reports in 2 weeks on queries; 1 month on mss. Sample copy for 9x12 SAE and 3 first class stamps.
Nonfiction: Historical/nostalgic, humor, interview/profile, personal experience and photo feature. Special issues include Anniversary Issue (June); Welcome Congress Issue (January). "No material *not* pertaining to Congress except topical satire on a national political event such as Watergate, the election, major cabinet reshuffle, etc." Buys 6 mss/year. "We will be more liberal in use of submitted material if guidelines are followed." Send complete ms. Length: 1,800 words maximum. Pays $5-25.
Photos: Send photos with ms. Pays $5 maximum for 8x10 b&w prints. Identification of subjects required.
Poetry: Light verse. No heavy, serious verse about non-political or non-Congressional subjects. Buys 12/year. Length: open. Pays $2-10.
Fillers: Jokes, gags, anecdotes, short humor. Pays $2 maximum.
Tips: "Submit well-researched original Congressional articles (oddities, statistical compilations, historical retrospectives), topical verse or topical satirical pieces and one-liners. No material far removed from Congressional political world—material or issues—we have all the 'experts' at our doorstep."

TEXAS OBSERVER, A Journal of Free Voices, 600 W. 7th, Austin TX 78701. (512)477-0746. Publisher: Ronnie Dugger. Editor: Joe Holley. Bimonthly magazine covering Texas politics and culture for a small influential audience. Circ. 12,000. Byline given. Buys first rights. Submit seasonal/holiday material 1 month in advance. Simultaneous queries, and simultaneous and photocopied submissions OK. SASE. Reports in 3 weeks. Free sample copy and writer's guidelines.
Nonfiction: Joe Holley, articles editor. Expose, interview/profile, opinion, personal experience, political analysis. Buys 100 mss/year. Query with clips of published work. Length: 200-2,000 words. Pays $10-75.
Photos: Joe Holley, photo editor. State availability of photos. Pays $10 for b&w prints. Captions, model release and identification of subjects required. Buys one-time rights.
Poetry: Joe Holley, poetry editor. Avant-garde, free verse, haiku, traditional. Buys 10/year. Length: open. Pays $25.
Tips: "We're interested in Texas literature, politics, and social issues; not interested in other topics."

TIME MAGAZINE, Rockefeller Center, New York NY 10020. Staff-written.

US NEWS & WORLD REPORT, 2300 N St. NW, Washington DC 20037. "We are presently not considering unsolicited freelance submissions."

WASHINGTON MONTHLY, 2712 Ontario Rd., NW, Washington DC 20009. (202)462-0128. Editor: Charles Peters. For "well-educated, well-read people interested in politics, the press, and government." Monthly. Circ. 35,000. Rights purchased depend on author and material. Buys all rights or first rights. Buys 20-30 mss/year. Pays on publication. Sample copy $2.25. Sometimes does special topical issues. Query or submit complete ms. Tries to report in 2-4 weeks. Computer printout and disk submissions OK; prefers letter quality to dot matrix. SASE.
Nonfiction: Responsible investigative or evaluative reporting about the US government, business, society, the press and politics. "No editorial comment/essays, please." Also no poetry, fiction or humor. Length: "average 2,000-6,000 words." Pays 5-10¢/word.
Photos: Buys b&w glossy prints.
Tips: "Best route to break in is to send 1-2 page proposal describing article and angle."

Regional

General-interest publications slanted toward residents of and visitors to a particular region are grouped below. Magazines covering a particular region of America appear first, followed by an alphabetical state/territory listing, a Canadian section, and a foreign category. In addition to city and state magazines, Sunday magazines of various newspapers are also included here. Because regional publications use little material that doesn't relate to the area they cover, they represent a limited market for writers who live outside their area. Many buy manuscripts on conservation and the natural wonders of their area; additional markets for such material will be found under the Nature, Conservation, and Ecology, and Sports headings.

Publications that report on the business climate of a region are grouped in the regional division of the Business and Finance category. Recreation and travel publications specific to a geographical area are listed in the Consumer Travel section.

For information on how to break in to regional publications, see Brian Vachon's *Writing for Regional Publications* (Writer's Digest Books).

General

COASTAL JOURNAL, (formerly *New Bedford Magazine*), Box 84 Lanesville Sta., Gloucester MA 01930. Publisher: Joe Kaknes. Editor: Dee Giles Forsythe. Bimonthly magazine primarily focusing on coastal New England from Maine to Connecticut. Pays within 1 month of publication. Submit seasonal material 6 months in advance. Computer printout submissions OK. SASE. Reports in 1 month. Sample copy $1.50; free writer's guidelines.
Nonfiction: Social, political and natural history; biography and people profiles; environmental and other pertinent public policy issues; boating, commercial fishing, and other maritime-related businesses; travel; art; education; lifestyles. Query. Length: 1,500-2,000 words. Pays approximately $100/article.
Photos: Prefers b&w glossy prints and 35mm color transparencies. Pays on publication; negotiable fee. Captions and credit lines required.
Fiction: "This magazine occasionally runs short fiction up to 3,000 words. Such manuscripts should have some connection to the sea, to the coast, or to New England's history or character. No restrictions on style; the main criterion is quality. Query or send complete ms.
Tips: "We look for the unusual story or angle, the fresh approach, the review/assessment of coastal New England related issues. Avoid overwriting and turgid style; stories should be crisp, well-researched, lively and concise. We'd like to see more contemporary pieces about events, issues or people with whom readers can identify."

‡**COUNTRY MAGAZINE, A Guide—From the Appalachians to the Atlantic**, Country Sun, Inc., Box 246, Alexandria VA 22313. (703)548-6177. Publisher: Walter Nicklin. Managing Editor: Philip Hayward. Monthly magazine of country living in the Mid-Atlantic region. "Our coverage aims at promoting an appreciation of the region, especially through writing about travel, history, outdoor sports, food, nature, the environment, gardening, the arts, and people in these states: Virginia, Maryland, Delaware, West Virginia, North Carolina, Pennsylvania and New Jersey." Circ. 60,000. Pays on publication. Byline given. Buys one-time rights. Submit seasonal/holiday material 6 months in advance. Photocopied submissions OK. SASE. Reports in 4 weeks. Sample copy for $1, 9x12 SAE and $1.22 postage; writer's guidelines for business size SAE and 1 first class stamp.
Nonfiction: Book excerpts (of regional interest); historical (mid-Atlantic history with current news peg); how-to (deal with country living: how to buy country property, how to tap a sugar maple, etc.); interview/profile (of mid-Atlantic residents); photo feature (regional); travel (mid-Atlantic—off the beaten path). Buys 120 mss/year. Query with published clips if available. Length: 1,000-2,000 words. Pays $3.50/column inch.
Photos: State availability of photos. Pays $15-25 for 35mm color transparencies and 5x7 b&w prints. Captions, model release and identification of subjects required.
Columns/Departments: The Land; The Rivers; The Bay (Chesapeake)—all deal with the natural features of the region. Buys 36 mss/year. Query with published clips if available. Length: 700-900 words. Pays $3.50/column inch.

Fiction: Historical, mainstream, and novel excerpts. No non-regional, non-country oriented fiction; "we seldom run fiction." Buys 1 ms/year. Query with published clips if available. Length: 1,200-2,000 words. Pays $3.50/column inch.

Poetry: "We seldom publish poetry." Buys 2 poems/year. Submit maximum 3 poems. Length: 50 lines maximum. Pays $25 maximum.

Tips: "Especially open to how-to, gardening and issue-oriented stories pegged to the Mid-Atlantic region."

FOCUS/MIDWEST, 8608 Olive Blvd., St. Louis MO 63132. (314)991-1698. Editor/Publisher: Charles L. Klotzer. For an educated audience in Illinois, Missouri and the Midwest. Bimonthly magazine; 28-42 pages. Circ. 5,000. Buys all rights. Pays on publication. Reports in 4-6 weeks. SASE.

Nonfiction: Controversial articles; main emphasis on Illinois and Missouri. Facts, interpretation, analyses presenting political, social, cultural and literary issues on the local, regional and national scene of direct interest to the reader in or observer of the Midwest. Investigative, informational, interview, profile, think pieces. Length: open. Pays minimum of $25.

Poetry: Blank verse and free verse. Length: open. Pays minimum of $10.

‡**THE NEW SOUTH MAGAZINE**, New South Profile, Inc., 332 Farrel Rd., Box 31592, Lafayette LA 70502. (318)981-5761. Editor: Jean E. Gonsoulin. Bimonthly magazine covering 11 Sunbelt states. Estab. 1982. Circ. 28,000. Pays on publication. Byline given. Buys all rights. Submit seasonal/holiday material 4 months in advance. Simultaneous submissions OK. SASE. Free sample copy and writer's guidelines.

Nonfiction: Interview/profile; opinion (hotels and restaurants); photo feature; technical (art and design); travel; fashion; finance. Send complete ms. Length: 200-550 words. Pays $3-4.50/column inch.

Photos: State availability or send photos with ms. Reviews color transparencies and prints. Model release and identification of subjects required.

Columns/Departments: Send complete ms. Length: 200-550 words. Pays $3-4.50/column inch.

Poetry: Light verse. Buys 4-6 poems/year. Submit maximum 2 poems. Length: 4-10 lines. Pays $15-30.

Fillers: Short humor. Buys 3-5 mss/year. Length: 5-20 words. Pays $15-30.

Tips: "All departments are open, except finance. Upon request, a quarterly outline of themes by departments is available."

NORTHWEST MAGAZINE, *The Sunday Oregonian*, 1320 SW Broadway, Portland OR 97201. Editor: Jack R. Hart. For an upscale, 25- to 49-year-old audience distributed throughout the Pacific Northwest. Weekly newspaper Sunday supplement magazine; 24-40 pages. Circ. 420,000. Buys first rights for Oregon and Washington state. Buys 400 mss/year and pays mid-month in the month following acceptance. All mss on speculation. Simultaneous submissions considered. Reports in 2 weeks. Query much preferred, but complete ms considered. Computer printout submissions OK; prefers letter quality to dot matrix. SASE. Free writer's guidelines.

Nonfiction and Photos: "Contemporary, regional articles with a strong hook to concerns of the Pacific Northwest. Cover stories usually deal with regional issues and feature professional-level reporting and writing. Personality profiles focus on young, Pacific Northwest movers and shakers. Short humor, personal essays, regional destination travel, entertainment, the arts and lifestyle stories also are appropriate. Photographs should be professional-quality black & white prints, contact sheets with negatives or Kodachrome slides. No history without a contemporary angle, boilerplate features of the type that are mailed out en masse with no specific hook to our local audience, poorly documented and highly opinionated issue stories that lack solid journalistic underpinnings, routine holiday features, or gushy essays that rhapsodize about daisies and rainbows. We expect top-quality writing and thorough, careful reporting. Contemporary writing style that features involving literary techniques like scenic construction stands the best chance." Length: 800-3,000 words. Pays $75-500/mss, $25-50 photo.

Poetry: Short poetry of distinctive quality. "Due to space limitations we are now only accepting work from Northwest poets although themes may be universal. All material must be original and not published elsewhere." Send at least 3 poems for consideration; pays $5 each on acceptance.

Tips: "Pay rates and editing standards are up, and this market will become far more competitive. However, new writers with talent and good basic language skills still are encouraged to try us. Printing quality and flexibility should improve, increasing the magazine's potential for good color photographers and illustrators."

THE ORIGINAL NEW ENGLAND GUIDE, New England Publications, Inc. Highland Mill, Box 597, Camden ME 04843. (207)236-9621. Editor: Mimi E.B. Steadman. Travel/vacation guide to New England. Annual magazine. Circ. 200,000. Pays on publication. Buys one-time rights. Deadline for queries is September 30. Computer printout or disk submissions OK; prefers letter quality to dot matrix printouts. Reports in 2-3 weeks. Sample copy $3.85. Free writer's guidelines.

Nonfiction: "We look for pieces on New England's many leisure-time choices: sports, including some of the newer interests, such as rafting, hang gliding, wind surfing, orienteering; antique shows; craft, music and art fairs; auctions; festivals and special celebrations; historical attractions; personal-experience accounts only when they offer advice on how readers may enjoy similar experiences. Our major features include information on how a certain activity may be enjoyed in all 6 New England states. We also buy shorter pieces that pertain to only 1 state. Occasionally, we run articles dealing with little-known, intriguing aspects of New England history or well-done essays on such topics as the mystique of New England or the definition of a Yankee.'' No personal—How I Spent My Vacation—material. Buys up to 28 mss/issue. Pays approximately 10¢/word. Query first with writing sample (letter, not phone). Length: 500-1,500 words.

Photos: ''Writers should feel free to include photographs (b&w prints or contact sheets or color tansparencies) with their submissions. Even if they are not of publishable quality, they are helpful in giving a visual introduction to the subject of the article and may be used in making assignments to photographers.''

Fillers: ''Fillers and short anecdotes may be as short as 50-100 words. Rarely used, however.''

Tips: Prefers ''service-oriented pieces that help New England travelers and vacationers get more from their trip. We'll be buying more manuscripts in the year ahead.''

YANKEE, Dublin NH 03444. (603)563-8111. Editor-in-Chief: Judson D. Hale. Managing Editor: John Pierce. Emphasizes the New England region. Monthly magazine. Circ. 900,000. Pays on acceptance. Buys all, first North American serial or one-time rights. Byline given. Submit seasonal/holiday material at least 4 months in advance. SASE. Reports in 4-6 weeks. Free sample copy and writer's guidelines.

Nonfiction: Historical (New England history, especially with present-day tie-in); how-to (especially for ''Forgotten Arts'' series of New England arts, crafts, etc.); humor; interview (especially with New Englanders who have not received a great deal of coverage); nostalgia (personal reminiscence of New England life); photo feature (prefer color, captions essential); profile; travel (to the Northeast only, with specifics on places, prices, etc.); current issues; antiques to look for; food. Buys 50 mss/year. Query with brief description of how article will be structured (its focus, etc.); articles must include a New England ''hook.'' Length: 1,500-3,000 words. Pays $50-700.

Photos: Purchased with accompanying ms or on assignment. (Without accompanying ms for ''This New England'' feature only; color only). Captions required. Send prints or transparencies. Pays $15 minimum for 8x10 b&w glossy prints. $125/page for 2¼x2¼ or 35mm transparencies; 4x5 for cover or centerspread. Total purchase price for ms usually includes payment for photos.

Columns/Departments: Traveler's Journal (with specifics on places, prices, etc.); Antiques to Look For (how to find, prices, other specifics); At Home in New England (recipes, gardening, crafts). Buys 10-12 mss/year. Query. Length: 1,000-2,500 words. Pays $150-400.

Fiction: Deborah Karr, fiction editor. ''Emphasis is on character development.'' Buys 12 mss/year. Send complete ms. Length: 2,000-4,000 words. Pays $750.

Poetry: Jean Burden, poetry editor. Free verse and modern. Buys 3-4 poems/issue. Send poems. Length: 32 lines maximum. Pays $35 for all rights, $25 for first magazine rights. Annual poetry contest with awards of $150, $100 and $50 for 1st, 2nd and 3rd prizes.

YANKEE MAGAZINE'S TRAVEL GUIDE TO NEW ENGLAND, Main St., Dublin NH 03444. (603)563-8111. Editor: Sharon Smith. Emphasizes travel and leisure for a readership from New England area and from all states in the union. Annual magazine. Circ. 175,000. Pays on acceptance. Buys first North American serial rights. Pays 25% kill fee. Byline given. Submit seasonal/holiday material 6-12 months in advance. Simultaneous and photocopied submissions OK. SASE. Reports in 3 weeks. Sample copy $2.50; free writer's guidelines.

Nonfiction: ''Unusual activities, places to stay, restaurants, shops, the arts, annual events, towns or areas to visit. Strict emphasis on travel discoveries within New England. Since the *Guide* is set up on a state-by-state basis, each story must be confined to activities or attractions within a single state.'' Buys 15-25 mss/issue. Query. Length: 500-2,500 words. Pays $50-300.

Photos: Picture editor. Purchased with or without accompanying ms or on assignment. Send contact sheet or transparencies plus list of stock photos on file. Pays $25-75 for b&w 8x10 glossy prints; $50-150 for 35mm or 2¼x2¼ color transparencies.

Tips: ''Send us a letter letting us know where you have been in New England and what ideas you think best fit our publication. Please don't send in suggestions if you have not bothered to obtain a copy of the magazine to see what we are all about! Send a query letter for your ideas, and explain why you are qualified to write about a given subject. Include samples. Ask for a copy of our writer's guidelines.''

Alaska

ALASKA MAGAZINE, Box 4-EEE, Anchorage AK 99509. Editor/Publisher: Tom Gresham. 90% freelance written. Monthly magazine. Computer printout submissions OK ''but some standards apply as to typewriters: new ribbon, easily readable type''; prefers letter quality to dot matrix. Pays on acceptance. Buys one-time rights. Byline given. SASE.

Nonfiction: *"Alaska Magazine's* subtitle is 'The Magazine of Life on the Last Frontier,' and, as implied, our interests are broad. Feature subjects include backpacking, resource management, sport fishing, wildlife encounters, kayaking and canoeing, trapping, cross-country skiing, snowshoeing, hunting, travel in Alaska, commercial fisheries, native affairs, mining, arts and crafts, mountaineering, bush-country life, profiles of Alaskans, history, town profiles, and wilderness photo essays. Manuscripts may run up to about 4,000 words, but we prefer shorter photo-illustrated pieces in the 1,000- to 2,000-word range. Rates for illustrated material range from $50-400, depending on length."

Photos: "We're heavy on sharp color photographs of Alaska and northwestern Canada, buying about 1,000 transparencies each year. Photos should ideally be Kodachrome slides—no duplicates, please. One-time rates are $200 for covers, $150 for 2-page spreads, $100 for full-page; and $50 for half-page.

Columns/Departments: "Regular monthly features include full-page color photos, letters, book reviews, personality profiles, bush-living tips, and short factual stories on Alaskan creatures."

NEW ALASKAN, Rt. 1, Box 677, Ketchikan AK 99901. Publisher: R.W. Pickrell. 75% freelance written. For residents of southeast Alaska. Tabloid magazine; 28 pages. Monthly. Circ. 5,500. Rights purchased vary with author and material. May buy all rights or second serial (reprint) rights. Byline given. Buys 30 mss/year. Pays on publication. Sample copy $1. Photocopied submissions OK. Submit complete ms. SASE.

Nonfiction and Photos: Bob Pickrell, articles editor. Feature material about southeast Alaska. Emphasis is on full photo or art coverage of subject. Informational, how-to, personal experience, interview, profile, inspirational, humor, historical, nostalgia, personal opinion, travel, successful business operations, new product. Length: 1,000 words minimum. Pays 1½¢/word. B&w photos purchased with or without mss. Minimum size: 5x7. Pays $5 per glossy used. Pays $2.50 per negative. Negatives are returned. Captions required.

Fiction: Bob Pickrell, articles editor. Historical fiction related to southeast Alaska. Length: open. Pays 1½¢/word.

Arizona

ARIZONA HIGHWAYS, 2039 W. Lewis Ave., Phoenix AZ 85009. (602)258-6641. Editor: Don Dedera. State-owned publication designed to help attract tourists into and through the state. Magazine. Computer printout and disk submissions OK. Pays on acceptance.

Nonfiction: Copy editor. "Article categories include first and third-person narratives dealing with contemporary events, history, anthropology, nature, special things to see and do, outstanding arts and crafts, travel, profiles, etc.; all must be Arizona oriented." Buys 6 mss/issue. Buys first rights only. Query with "a lead paragraph and brief outline of story. We deal with professionals only, so include list of current credits." Length: 1,500-2,000 words. Pays 10-30¢/word.

Photos: Picture editor. Pays $50/8x10 b&w print; $80-300 for 4x5 or larger transparencies. Buys one-time rights. "We will use 120mm (2-¼)and 35 mm when it displays exceptional quality or content. We prefer Kodachrome in 35mm. Each transparency *must* be accompanied by information attached to each photograph: where, when, what. No photography will be reviewed by the editors unless the photographer's name appears on each and every transparency."

Tips: "Writing must be professional quality, warm, sincere, in-depth, and well-peopled. Romance of the Old West feeling is important. Avoid themes that describe first trips to Arizona, Grand Canyon, the desert, etc. Emphasis to be on romance and themes that can be photographed."

ARIZONA MAGAZINE, Box 1950, Phoenix AZ 85001. (602)271-8291. Editor: Paul Schatt. For "everyone who reads a Sunday newspaper." Weekly; 60 pages. Circ. 440,000. Kill fee varies. Byline given. Buys 250 mss/year. Pays when article is scheduled for publication. For sample copy and guidelines for writers send 50¢. Photocopied submissions OK. Simultaneous submissions OK if exclusive regionally. Reports in 2 weeks. Query or submit complete ms. SASE.

Nonfiction and Photos: "General subjects that have an Arizona connection, are of interest to the West, or are of universal interest. We're looking for good writing above all and mastery of the subject by the writer. Should have an abundance of quotes and anecdotes. Some regional travel and entertainment. Outstanding profiles. We are interested in Arizona, the West, and universal subjects, not always in that order. We want to be topical and lively. We want stories that show some creativity in their approach. If story reads like a cliche Sunday Magazine story, redo it. Historical subjects are being overworked. No routine historical pieces; willing to see *the* dynamite story of how it really happened, but not any more routine stuff." Length: 1,000-3,000 words. "There is a trend to slightly shorter lead pieces, which likely will make room for more inside articles. Articles of 800-1,500 words will get fair hearings." State availability of photos. Pays $50-350. B&w and color photos purchased with or without mss or on assignment. Pays $15-25 for 8x10 b&w glossy prints; $25-80 for color (35mm or larger).

Tips: "Find a good personal subject and write about him so the reader will feel he is with the subject. Know the subject well enough to react to the material. Describe the subject in anecdotes and let him reveal himself by his quotes. Please include social security and telephone numbers.''

PHOENIX LIVING, 4621 N. 16th St., Phoenix AZ 85016. (602)279-2394. Editor: Pat Adams. Bimonthly magazine covering housing for newcomers and prospective home buyers. Circ. 70,000. Pays on acceptance. Byline given. Buys all rights. Submit seasonal/holiday material 4 months in advance. Simultaneous queries and photocopied and previously published submissions OK. Reports in 1 month. Free sample copy. Writer's guidelines for business size SAE and 1 first class stamp.
Nonfiction: General housing information, real estate, Arizona business, employment overviews, custom buildings and apartment living—all locally oriented. Buys 20 mss/year. Query with clips of published work. Length: 700-1,000 words; "longer features are assigned locally." Pays 10¢/word.
Photos: State availability of photos. Pays negotiable fee for 8x10 b&w glossy prints. Captions and model release required. Buys all rights.

PHOENIX MAGAZINE, 4707 N. 12th St., Phoenix AZ 85014. (602)248-8900. Editor: Jeff Burger. For professional, general audience. Monthly magazine. Circ. 40,000. Usually buys all rights. Occasionally pays kill fee. Byline given in most cases. Buys 120 mss/year. Pays within 2 weeks of publication. Sample copy $1.95 plus postage. January issue: Superguide to what to see and do in area; February issue: Gardening Guide, Spring/Summer Fashions; March issue: Real Estate, Arizona Lifestyle; June issue: Summer Super Guide; July issue: The Phoenix Lists; August issue: Valley Progress Report; September issue: Fall/Winter Fashions; November issue: Home Decorating. Submit special issue material 3 months in advance. Reports in 1 month. Query or submit complete ms. SASE.
Nonfiction and Photos: Predominantly features subjects unique to Phoenix life; urban affairs, arts, lifestyle, etc. Subject should be locally oriented. Informational, how-to, interview, profile, historical, photo, successful local business operations. Each issue also embraces 1 or 2 in-depth reports on crucial, frequently controversial issues that confront the community. Length: 1,000-3,000 words. Payment is negotiable. Payment for features averages $100-150. Photos are purchased with ms with no additional payment, or on assignment.
Tips: "Write for a copy of our 'Guidelines for Writers' (enclose SASE), then study magazine and send us some ideas along with samples of your work."

Arkansas

ARKANSAS TIMES, Arkansas Writers' Project, Inc., Box 34010, Little Rock AR 72203. (501)375-2985. Editor: Bob Lancaster. Monthly magazine. "We are an Arkansas magazine. We seek to appreciate, enliven and, where necessary, improve the quality of life in the state." Circ. 28,000. Pays on publication, "but with exceptions." Byline given. Pays negotiable kill fee. Not copyrighted. Buys first North American serial rights. Submit seasonal/holiday material 2 months in advance. Simultaneous, photocopied, and previously published submissions OK. SASE. Reports in 2 weeks on queries; 1 month on mss. Sample copy $3; writer's guidelines for business size SAE and 1 first class stamp.
Nonfiction: Mel White, articles editor. Book excerpts; expose (in investigative reporting vein); general interest; historical/nostalgic; humor; interview/profile; opinion; recreation; and entertainment, all relating to Arkansas. "The Arkansas angle is all-important." Buys 24 mss/year. Query. Length: 250-6,000 words. Pays $15-300.
Photos: Gloria Hodgson, photo editor. State availability of photos. Pays $5-10 for 8x10 b&w or color prints. Identification of subjects required. Buys one-time rights.
Columns/Departments: Paul Williams, column editor. Arkansas Reporter ("articles on people, places and things in Arkansas or with special interest to Arkansans). This is the department that is most open to freelancers." Buys 25 mss/year. Query. Length: 250-750 words. Pays $10-60.
Fiction: Adventure, historical, humorous, mainstream and romance. "All fiction must have an Arkansas angle." Buys 4 mss/year. Send complete ms. Length: 1,250-5,000 words. Pays $200-300.
Poetry: Paul Williams, poetry editor. Avant-garde, free verse, haiku, light verse, traditional and ballad. Buys 30-40 mss/year. Submit maximum 5 poems. Pays $50 maximum; "poems are generally without payment."

California

BAKERSFIELD LIFESTYLE, 123 Truxtun Ave., Bakersfield CA 93301. (805)325-7124. Editor & Publisher: Steve Walsh. Monthly magazine covering local lifestyles for college educated males/females 25-49 in a balanced community of industrial, agricultural and residential areas. Estab 1981. Circ. 10,000. Byline and brief bio given. Buys first North American serial rights. Simultaneous queries and simultaneous and photocopied submissions OK. Computer printout and disk submissions OK. SASE. Reports in 1 month. Sample copy $2.50.

Nonfiction: General interest (topical issues); travel (up to 1,500 words); and articles on former residents who are now successful elsewhere. No investigative reporting, politics or negative editorial. Buys 12-15 mss/year. Length: 2,500 words maximum. Pays $10.

Photos: Send photos with ms. Pays $1/photo used.

Fiction: "Anything in good taste." Buys 20 mss/year. Length: 3,000 words maximum. Pays $10 maximum.

BIG VALLEY, The San Fernando Valley Magazine, World of Communications, Inc., 16161 Roscoe Blvd., Suite 201, Sepulveda CA 91343. (213)787-2132. Editor: Denise Abbott. Monthly general interest magazine for "family-oriented upper-middle class readership." Circ. 25,000. Pays on publication. Byline given. Offers 20% kill fee. Buys first rights and second serial (reprint) rights. Submit seasonal/holiday material 3 months in advance. Photocopied and previously published submissions OK. "Letter quality computer printout submissions are acceptable." SASE. Reports in 1 month. Sample copy for 9x12 SASE; writer's guidelines for SASE.

Nonfiction: Expose, food, general interest, historical/nostalgic, home and garden, how-to, humor, interview/profile, lifestyle, personal experience, political. "Everything needs a local angle." No music, wine; no film or record reviews. Buys 80 mss/year. Query with clips of published work. Length: 1,000-2,500 words. Pays $150-500.

Photos: State availability of photos. Pays $25-100 for 35mm color transparencies and $10-25 for 8x10 b&w prints; reviews b&w contact sheet and negatives. Captions, model releases, and identification of subjects required. Buys one-time rights.

Columns/Departments: 300-400-word profiles on interesting people, places and events in the Valley are always needed. Arts column is also open to freelancers. Columns pay $25-75.

Tips: "Emphasis will be on shorter, lighter features—more articles in each issue. Query with well-conceived ideas. Remember they must have a Valley angle."

CALIFORNIA MAGAZINE, Box 69990, Los Angeles CA 90069. (213)273-7516. Executive Editors: Tom Bates and Calvin Fentress. Editor: Scott Kaufer. Publishes 12 issues/year. Buys first rights. Offers 20% kill fee. Byline given. SASE. Reports in 6 weeks. Sample copy $3.50.

Nonfiction: Fresh, original, well-written pieces with a California focus—good, solid sports articles; service pieces with a statewide appeal; political, environmental, and business issues, ambitious profiles; in addition to well-researched investigative pieces. No fiction. Recent article example: "Getting Away with Murder" (April 1982). Query with clips of published work. No phone queries. Length: 4,000-10,000 words. Pay varies.

Photos: State availability of photos. "We assign almost all photos." Buys first rights. Captions preferred; model releases required.

Columns/Departments: "Departments are written regularly by contributing editors, with the exception of Westword, an opinion page (ideas not often generated in-house, writers assigned), and California Reporter. Reporter items are timely, newsworthy close-ups which run up to 1,000 words and pay up to $250." Buys up to 30 unsolicited mss/year.

CalToday, 750 Ridder Park Dr., San Jose CA 95190. (408)920-5602. Editor: John Parkyn. For a general audience. Weekly rotogravure newspaper-magazine, published with the *San Jose Mercury News*. Circ. 290,000. Byline given. Buys 100 mss/year. Pays on acceptance. Free sample copy. Will consider photocopied and simultaneous submissions, if the simultaneous submission is out of their area. Submit seasonal material (skiing, wine, outdoor living) 3 months in advance. Reports in 4 weeks. Query. SASE.

Nonfiction and Photos: A general newspaper-magazine requiring that most subjects be related to California (especially the Bay Area) and the interests of California. Will consider subjects outside California if subject is of broad or national appeal. Length: 1,000-4,000 words. Pays $150-500. Payment varies for b&w and color photos purchased with or without mss. Captions required.

DAILY NEWS MAGAZINE, (formerly *Sunday Magazine*), *Daily News* of Los Angeles, 14539 Sylvan St., Van Nuys CA 91401. (213)873-2051. Editor: Debbie Goffa. Weekly magazine with strong Southern California slant. Circ. 150,000. Pays on publication. Byline given. Buys one-time rights regional exclusivity. Submit seasonal/holiday material 8 weeks in advance. Computer printout and disk submissions OK. SASE. Reports in 4-6 weeks. Writer's guidelines for business size SAE and 1 first class stamp.

Nonfiction: General interest; historical/nostalgic; humor; interview/profile; essay; political features; sports features; and investigative pieces. No poetry or opinion pieces, please. Buys 150-160 mss/year. Query with clips of published work. Length: 2,000-3,000 words. Pays $75-400.

HUMBOLDT COUNTY MAGAZINE, Box 3150, Eureka CA 95501. (707)445-9038. Editor and Publisher: Craig J. Beardsley. Annual magazine covering travel and tourism in Humboldt County, Northern California. This county, roughly the size of Delaware and Rhode Island combined, encompasses more than half of all the world's redwoods. Circ. 150,000. Pays on acceptance. Buys first rights only. Submit material 3 months in advance. SASE. Reports in 10 days. Sample copy $2.

Nonfiction: Reason for the publication's existence: "To educate, entertain and inform the 2.5 million visitors who travel through Humboldt County each year. Freelancers welcomed with open arms . . . if they know their subject matter." Recent articles include "Where to Go for Gifts," "The Filming of 'Salem's Lot'—When Warner Bros. Visited Humboldt," "Touring Scotia Mill," "When the Stars Stayed at Benbow Inn," etc. Query. Buys 3 unsolicited mss/year. Length: 1,500-3,000 words. Pays $200-500.

Photos: Pays $50 minimum for b&w and color.

Tips: "It's the subject matter that catches an editor's eye rather than the approach."

LOS ANGELES MAGAZINE, 1888 Century Park E., Los Angeles CA 90067. Editor: Geoff Miller. Monthly. Circ. 162,000. Buys first North American serial rights. Byline given except for short "Peoplescape" personality profiles. Query. SASE.

Nonfiction: Uses articles on how best to live (i.e., the quality of life) in the "changing, growing, diverse Los Angeles urban-suburban area; ideas, people, and occasionally places. Writer must have an understanding of contemporary living and doing in Southern California; material must appeal to an upper-income, better-educated group of people. Fields of interest include urban problems, pleasures, personalities and cultural opportunities, leisure and trends, candid interviews of topical interest; the arts. Solid research and reportage required. No essays." Length: 1,000-3,500 words. Also uses some topical satire and humor. Pays 10¢/word minimum.

Photos: Most photos assigned to local photographers. Occasionally buys photographs with mss. B&w should be 8x10. Pays $25-50 for single article photos.

‡**LOS ANGELES READER**, Suite 324, 5225 Wilshire Blvd., Los Angeles CA 90036. (213)930-1214. Editor: James Vowell. Associate Editor: Randy Michael Signor. Weekly tabloid of features, reviews and fiction for "affluent Los Angelenos interested in the arts and popular culture." Circ. 70,000. Pays on publication. Byline given. Buys one-time rights. Submit seasonal/holiday material 2 months in advance. Simultaneous queries and photocopied submissions OK. Computer printout submissions OK; prefers letter quality to dot matrix. SASE. Reports in 2 months. Sample copy $1; free writer's guidelines.

Nonfiction: Expose, general interest, historical/nostalgic, interview/profile, personal experience and photo feature. "No aimless satire." Buys "hundreds" of mss/year. Send complete ms. Length: 1,000-4,000 words. Pays $40-300.

Fiction: Randy Michael Signor, fiction editor. Adventure, confession, experimental, historical, mainstream, novel excerpts. Interested in serious fiction. Buys 4-5 mss/year. Send complete ms. Length: 1,000-4,000 words. Pays $75-200.

Tips: "Break in with submission for our Cityside page: short news items on local happenings/semi-hard news; also with book reviews for our Cityside section. We are nearly entirely a local publication and want only writing about local themes, topics, people by local writers."

‡**MONTEREY LIFE, The Magazine of California's Spectacular Central Coast**, Box 2107, Monterey CA 93942. (408)372-9200. Editor: Jeffrey Whitmore. Monthly magazine covering art, photography, regional affairs, music, sports, environment, lifestyles for "a sophisticated readership in the Central California Coast area." Circ. 20,000. Pays on acceptance. Byline given. Offers variable kill fee. Buys first North American serial rights. Submit seasonal/holiday material 3 months in advance. Simultaneous queries and simultaneous and photocopied submissions OK. SASE. Reports in 3 weeks on queries; 6 weeks on mss. Sample copy for $1.75, SAE and $1.92 postage; free writer's guidelines.

Nonfiction: Historical/nostalgic, humor, interview/profile, photo feature, travel. "All articles apply to this region, except 'getaway' which covers travel within one day's drive." Buys 75 mss/year. Query with clips if available. Length: 175-2,500 words. Pays $25-200.

Photos: State availability of photos. Pays $20-100 for color transparencies; $15-25 for 5x7 and 8x10 b&w prints. Captions, model release, and identification of subjects required. Buys one-time rights.

Columns/Departments: Community Focus. Query with clips of published work. Length: 250-1,000 words. Pays $25-40.

SACRAMENTO MAGAZINE, Box 2424, Sacramento CA 95811. Managing Editor: Betty Johannsen. Monthly magazine emphasizing a strong local angle on politics, local issues, human interest and consumer items for readers in the middle to high income brackets. Pays on acceptance within a 30-day billing period. Buys all rights. Original manuscripts only (no previously published work). Computer printout and disk submissions OK; prefers letter quality to dot matrix printouts. Absolutely no phone calls; query by letter. Reports in 6 weeks. SASE. Writer's guidelines for SASE.

Nonfiction: Local issues vital to Sacramento quality of life. Past articles have included "Gasping at Straws" (rice straw burning and its resultant air pollution) and "Missing" (the disappearance of a young sailor). Buys 15 unsolicited mss/year. Query first. Length: 200-3,000 words, depending on author, subject matter and treatment.

Photos: State availability of photos. Payment varies depending on photographer, subject matter and treatment.

Captions (including ID's, location and date) required.

Columns/Departments: Media, gourmet, profile, sports, city arts, and home & garden (850-1,250 words); City Lights (250 words).

SAN DIEGO MAGAZINE, Box 85409, San Diego CA 92138. (619)225-8953. Editor-in-Chief: Edwin F. Self. Emphasizes San Diego. Monthly magazine; 250 pages. Circ. 53,063. Pays on publication. Buys all rights. Pays negotiable kill fee. Byline given. Submit seasonal/holiday material 6 months in advance of issue date. Simultaneous and photocopied submissions OK. SASE. Reports in 2 months. Sample copy $3.
Nonfiction: Exposé (serious, documented); general interest (to San Diego region); historical (San Diego region); interview (with notable San Diegans); nostalgia; photo essay; profile; service guides; and travel. Recent article example: "San Diego TV Newscasters: The Good, the Bad and the Ludicrous." Buys 7 mss/issue. Query with clips of published work, or submit complete ms. Buys 12 unsolicited mss/year. Length: 2,000-3,000 words. Pays $500 maximum.
Photos: State availability of photos with query. Pays $25-75 b&w; $45-150 color; $250 for cover. Captions required. Buys all rights. Model release required.
Tips: "Write better lead paragraphs; write shorter, with greater clarity; wit and style appreciated; stick to basic magazine journalism principles."

‡SAN DIEGO NEWSLINE MONTHLY MAGAZINE, 3651 4th Ave., San Diego CA 92103. (619)295-0085. Editor: Larry Remer. Managing Editor: Susan Slavik. Free general interest tabloid covering politics, health, recreation and entertainment subjects in the San Diego area; also publishes weekly paid-circulation publication concentrating on "area politics for a politically active group of government and business people." Circ. 50,000. Pays on publication. Byline given. Offers 1/3 kill fee. Makes work-for-hire assignments. Simultaneous queries and photocopied and previously published submissions OK. Computer printout submissions OK. SASE. Reports in 2 weeks. Sample copy for 9x12 SAE and 80¢ postage; writer's guidelines for business size SAE and 1 first class stamp.
Nonfiction: Gregory Dennis, articles editor. Expose, interview/profile, opinion, personal experience, photo feature, "where-to" in San Diego area. "We can't use anything that doesn't have some angle on the San Diego area." Buys 50 mss/year. Query with clips if available or send complete ms. Length: 100-2,500 words. Pays $25-150.
Photos: Gregory Dennis, photo editor. "We look for professional print quality, human interest and social commentary." State availability of photos. Pays $10-15 for 8x10 b&w prints. Captions and identification of subjects required. Buys one-time rights.
Columns/Departments: Gregory Dennis, columns/departments editor. "We have a regular column of psychology and self-help articles written by professionals and laity, on topics of current interest, 600-800 words. We also accept reviews of recent books, fiction and nonfiction." Buys 25 mss/year. Query with clips if available. Length: 400-800 words. Pays $10-25.
Tips: "There will be more emphasis on pop culture and health, more subjects handled in house. The best way to break in is writing 'shorts' for our Healthy Living, Recreation, or Entertainment sections on trends, personalities and events in those fields with a San Diego area angle. We're open to lots of ideas and encourage both phone calls and letters. Also open to feature articles in these sections."

SAN FRANCISCO MAGAZINE, 973 Market St., San Francisco CA 94103. (415)777-5555. Editor: Ira Kamin. Monthly magazine covering general-interest topics for San Francisco and Northern California residents. Circ. 45,000. Pays on publication. Byline and brief bio given. Pays 25% kill fee. Buys first North American serial rights. Photocopied submissions OK. Reports in 3 weeks.
Nonfiction: General interest (lifestyles, fashion); humor; interview/profile (of person with a Northern California connection); personal experience (first-person pieces); photo feature; consumer; and science. "Topics may be of national scope. We want well-researched, well-written articles with a Northern California fix." Buys fewer than 10 unsolicited mss/year. Query with clips of published work or send complete ms. Length: 2,000-5,000 words. Pays $500 average.
Photos: State availability of photos. Reviews 35mm color transparencies and 8x10 b&w glossy prints. Negotiates pay separately for package of photos or ms/photo package.

THE SAN GABRIEL VALLEY MAGAZINE, Miller Books, 2908 W. Valley Blvd., Alhambra CA 91803. (213)284-7607. Editor-in-Chief: Joseph Miller. For upper to middle-income people who dine out often at better restaurants in Los Angeles County. Bimonthly magazine; 52 pages. Circ. 3,400. Pays on publication. Buys simultaneous, second serial (reprint) and one-time rights. Phone queries OK. Submit seasonal/holiday material 1 month in advance. Simultaneous, photocopied and previously published submissions OK. SASE. Reports in 2 weeks. Sample copy $1.
Nonfiction: Exposé (political); informational (restaurants in the valley); inspirational (success stories and positive thinking); interview (successful people and how they made it); profile (political leaders in the San Gabriel Valley); and travel (places in the valley). Interested in 500-word humor articles. Buys 18 unsolicited mss/year.

Length: 500-10,000 words. Pays 5¢/word.

Columns/Departments: Restaurants, Education, Valley News and Valley Personality. Buys 2 mss/issue. Send complete ms. Length: 500-1,500 words. Pays 5¢/word.

Fiction: Historical (successful people) and western (articles about Los Angeles County). Buys 2 mss/issue. Send complete ms. Length: 500-10,000 words. Pays 5¢/word.

Tips: "Send us a good personal success story about a valley or a California personality. We are also interested in articles on positive thinking and people who have made it."

‡**SCENE MAGAZINE, A California Picture Magazine**, Scene Publications, Inc., Suite 206, Agricultural Bldg., Embarcadero at Mission, San Francisco CA 94105. (415)986-0439. Editor: James Borton. Managing Editor: Betty Hey. Bimonthly general interest tabloid magazine covering the "people contributing to California's cultural and social landscape." Estab. 1981. Circ. 20,000. Pays on publication. Byline given. Offers $50 kill fee. Buys all rights (reserved). Submits seasonal/holiday material 3 months in advance. Simultaneous queries, and simultaneous, photocopied and "occasionally" previously published submissions OK. SASE. Reports in 3 months. Sample copy $4; free writer's guidelines.

Nonfiction: Book excerpts (especially on people involved in the arts); interview/profile; photo feature (of California "events" primarily, especially if they involve "personalities"); travel (occasional unusual and "upscale" travel pieces). No pieces not emphasizing "people," except for travel or fashion. Buys 24 mss/year. Query with clips of published work if available. Length: 1,000-2,500 words; "optimum is 2,000." Pays $75-150.

Photos: Send b&w contact sheet (preferred) or prints with ms. Identification of subjects required. Buys onetime rights.

Columns/Departments: Deborah Karff, associate editor. Portraits (full page b&w photo with small amount of text); Profile (interview with person and full page b&w photography); Feature (1 per issue, sometimes on the arts, travel, interior design, etc.); On the Scene (photo essay of California events). Buys 24 mss/year. Query with clips of published work if available. Length: 1,000-2,000 words; "Portraits are 100 words—the photograph is critical." Pays $75-150.

Fillers: Stephen K. Smith, entertainment editor. California focus, Bay area especially. Length: 300 words. "If a *good* piece covering the arts comes in, we consider running it and arrange a fee at that time."

VENTURA COUNTY & COAST REPORTER, The Reporter, VCR Inc., 2739 Buckaroo, Box 6269, Oxnard CA 93030. (805)485-0628. Editor: Nancy Cloutier. Weekly tabloid covering local news. Circ. 25,000. Pays on publication. Byline given. Buys first North American serial rights. SASE. Reports in 3 weeks.

Nonfiction: General interest; humor; interview/profile; travel (local—within 500 miles). "Local (Ventura County) slant predominates." Length: 2-5 double-spaced typewritten pages. Pays $10-25.

Photos: State availability of photos with ms. Reviews b&w contact sheet.

Columns/Departments: Boating experience (southern California). Send complete ms. Pays $10-25.

WESTWAYS, Box 2890, Terminal Annex, Los Angeles CA 90051. (213)741-4760. Managing Editor: Mary Ann Cravens. For "fairly affluent, college-educated, mobile and active southern California families. Average age of head of household is 42. Monthly. Computer printout and disk submissions OK. Buys first rights. Byline given. Pays prior to publication for mss; on publication for most photos. Reports in 2 weeks. Query. SASE.

Nonfiction: "Informative articles, well-researched and written in fresh, literate, honest style." This publication "covers all states west of the Rockies, including Alaska and Hawaii, western Canada and Mexico. We're willing to consider anything that interprets and illuminates the American West—past or present—for the Western American family. Employ imagination in treating subject. Avoid PR hand-out type style and format, and please know at least something about the magazine." Subjects include "travel, history and modern civic, cultural and sociological aspects of the West; camping, fishing, natural science, humor, first-person adventure and experience, nostalgia, profiles, and occasional unusual and offbeat pieces. Some foreign travel." Buys 665-715 unsolicited mss/year. Length: 1,000 to 1,500 words. Pays 20¢/word minimum.

Photos: Buys color and b&w photos with mss. Prefers 35mm color. Pays $25 minimum "for each b&w used as illustration"; $50/transparency.

Colorado

BOULDER DAILY CAMERA FOCUS MAGAZINE, Box 591, Boulder CO 80306. (303)442-1202. Editor-in-Chief: Barbara Baumgarten. 50% freelance written. Emphasizes subjects of particular interest to Boulder County residents. Weekly tabloid; 40 pages. Circ. 30,000. Pays on first of month following publication. Buys one-time rights. Byline given. Phone queries OK. Submit seasonal/holiday material 6-8 weeks in advance. Photocopied submissions OK. SASE. Reports in 6 weeks.

Nonfiction: Exposé (anything relevant to Boulder County that needs exposing); informational (emphasis on good writing, warmth and impact); historical (pertaining to Boulder County or Colorado in general); interview and profile (stress local angle); photo feature (featuring Boulder County or areas in Colorado and Rocky Mountain West where Boulder County residents are apt to go). Buys 100 mss/year. Query. Length: 700-2,000 words. Pays $1 a column inch and up.

Photos: Purchased with or without mss, or on assignment. Captions required. Query. Pays $8 for 8x10 b&w glossy prints; $10 for 35mm or 2¼x2¼ (or larger) color transparencies.

Tips: "We're demanding a more sophisticated, pure magazine style than we have in the past."

DENVER LIVING, Baker Publications, 2280 S. Xanadu Way, Aurora CO 80014. (303)695-8440. Publication Director: Tina Stacy. Bimonthly magazine covering housing for newcomers and others looking for new housing or upgrading their existing residence. Circ. 80,000. Pays on publication. Byline given. Buys all rights. Submit seasonal/holiday material 3 months in advance. Simultaneous queries and previously published submissions OK. SASE. Reports in 2 weeks. Sample copy free; writer's guidelines for business size SAE and 1 first class stamp.

Nonfiction: Products, services, events, landscaping, decorating, and food indigenous to the area. Recent article example: "Jobs in Denver" (January/February 1982), which won a freelance Writers' Award from *Living Magazine*. Buys 2-4 unsolicited mss/year. Query with clips of published work. Length: 200-1,000 words. Pays 20¢/word.

Photos: State availability of photos. Pays negotiable fee for 8x10 glossy prints. Captions and model release required. Buys all rights.

Columns/Departments: Discoveries (special products and services, events, book reviews, restaurant openings, the arts, shopping). Buys 42 mss/year. Query with clips of published work. Length: 150-200 words. Pays 10¢/word.

Tips: "National assignments on decorating, financing, etc., for all of Baker's city magazines are made by Tina Stacy, publication director. Payment is 20¢/word. Query her at *Living*, Suite 400, 5757 Alpha Rd., Dallas TX 75240."

Connecticut

CONNECTICUT MAGAZINE, 636 Kings Hwy., Fairfield CT 06430. (203)576-1205. Managing Editor: Cynthia M. McDonald. Monthly magazine for an affluent, sophisticated suburban audience. Pays on publication. Buys all rights. Reports in 2 months. Sample copy $2.

Nonfiction: "We want only those features which pertain specifically to Connecticut, with emphasis on service, investigative and consumer articles." No fiction or poetry. Buys 50 mss/year. Query with clips of published work and "a full, intelligent, *neat* outline of the proposed piece. The more information offered, the better the chance of an assignment." Pays $100-600.

Photos: State availability of photos. Pays $35-75 for b&w prints; $75-200 for color transparencies. Captions and model releases required.

Columns/Departments: General features, business, politics pertaining to Connecticut. Buys 50 columns/year. Query. Length: 1,000 words minimum. Pays $100-450.

Tips: "Read past issues of the magazine and submit queries relevant to our state and style. Have good solid ideas and present them in a clear and interesting manner."

NEW HAVEN ADVOCATE, The Alternative in Southern Connecticut, New Mass Media Inc., 1184 Chapel St., New Haven CT 06511. (203)789-0010. Acting Managing Editor: Louise Kennedy. Weekly tabloid "interested in reaching a very broad audience with politically progressive articles, features, investigative reports. We don't publish conservative material." Circ. 75,000. Pays mid-month following publication. Byline given. Offers negotiable kill fee. Buys one-time rights. Submit seasonal/holiday material 1 month in advance. Simultaneous queries, and simultaneous, photocopied, and previously published submissions OK. Computer printout submissions OK. SASE. Reports in 1 week on queries; 1 month on mss. Sample copy for 9x11 SAE and $1 postage.

Nonfiction: Expose, general interest, interview/profile, opinion, travel. "We use short articles on innovative technology, especially, solar energy, renewable energy; analysis of military/industrial complex; holistic health, etc." Not interested in national stories that don't have *some* local angle. Buys 40-50 mss/year. Query with clips of published work. Length: negotiable. Pays $50-300.

Photos: State availability of photos. Pays $20-75 for 5x7 b&w prints. Captions, model release and identification of subjects required.

Columns/Departments: Heleri Ziou, arts/entertainment editor. "Writers unfamiliar with paper must read it, then query with clips of published work." Length: negotiable. Pays $20-100.

Fiction: "We use very little fiction." Buys 2 mss/year. Send complete ms. Pays $50-100.

Tips: "A new section, 'The Living End,' will feature lifestyle, travel, food, fashion, humor, contests, etc. We will put more emphasis on local news."

NEW HAVEN INFO MAGAZINE, 38 Lynmoor Pl., Hamden CT 06517. (203)288-0566. Editor: Sol D. Chain. For those interested in art, music, theater, recreational activities, etc. Monthly magazine; 64 pages. Circ. 5,000. Not copyrighted. Byline given. Buys 20 mss/year. Pays on publication. Sample copy 50¢. Will consider photocopied and simultaneous submissions. Computer printout and disk submissions OK. Reports in 1 month. Query. SASE.
Nonfiction: "Most of our material is on assignment. We publish articles dealing with New Haven area events and people." Personal experience, interview, profile, historical, nostalgia. No religious, scientific or political material. Buys 10 unsolicited mss/year. Length: 350-700 words. Pays $15/page (about 350 words).

NORTHEAST MAGAZINE, *The Hartford Courant*, 179 Allyn St., Hartford CT 06103. (203)241-3701. Editor: Lary Bloom. Weekly magazine for a Connecticut audience. Circ. 300,000. Pays on acceptance. Buys 100-150 mss/year. Byline given. Buys one-time rights. Previously published submissions OK. Unsolicited ms or queries accepted; reports in 3 weeks. SASE.
Nonfiction: General interest; in-depth investigation of stories behind news; historical/nostalgic; interview/ profile (of famous or important people with Connecticut ties); and personal essays (humorous or anecdotal). No poetry. Length: 750-4,500 words. Pays $200-1,000.
Fiction: Well-written, original short stories. Length: 750-4,500 words.
Photos: Most assigned; state availability of photos. "Do not send originals."

Delaware

DELAWARE TODAY MAGAZINE, 206 E. Ayre St. Wilmington DE 19804. (302)995-7146. Editor: Peter Mucha. 80 percent freelance written. Monthly magazine covering subjects of broad interest in Delaware. 88 pages. Circ. 15,000. Pays on publication. SASE necessary. Reports in 6 weeks.
Nonfiction: Features: Human interest articles. "We want lively, vivid writing about people, organizations, communities, lifestyles, trends or events that are of special interest to people in Delaware." Service articles: "Each month we try to run an informative guide to goods or services or leisure activities. Except for travel articles, must have a Delaware tie-in." Short subjects: "When our budget permits, we will accept items that are brief, but informative, perceptive or amusing. Must relate to Delaware." In all cases, query first with writing samples. Features pay $100-200; short subjects $15-35.
Photos: Uses monthly photo essays of people and places of interest in the state. Must express local color or let readers see themselves in the subject. Pays $100-150. All photography in magazine is freelance. Pays $15-25 for b&w photo; $100-150 for photos illustrating an entire article.
Columns/Departments: Regular columns on Arts & Leisure and Business. Query first with writing samples. Pays $50-75.
Tips: "Study the magazine first, and then think big. The more people who might be interested in subject, the more likely we are to be interested."

District of Columbia

‡**THE WASHINGTON DOSSIER**, Adler International Ltd., 3301 New Mexico Ave. NW, Washington DC 20016. (202)362-5894. Editor: Sonia Adler. Senior Editor: Don Oldenburg. Monthly general interest magazine covering the Washington social and cultural scene for politicians, business people, financiers, diplomats, jet-setters, socialites, "and people who would like to be any or all of these." Circ. 40,000. Pays on acceptance. Byline given. Offers negotiable kill fee. Buys one-time rights. Submit seasonal/holiday material 4 months in advance. Simultaneous queries and photocopied and previously published submissions OK "if mentioned as such in cover letter." Computer printout submissions OK; prefers letter quality to dot matrix. SASE. Reports in 6 weeks. Sample copy $2; writers guidelines for SAE and 1 first class stamp.
Nonfiction: Book excerpts, general interest, how-to, humor, interview/profile, personal experience, photo feature, travel. Buys 45 mss/year. Query with clips or send complete ms. Length: 1,200-2,500 words. Pays 15¢ and up per assigned word.
Columns/Departments: Design for Living (focus on fashionable living, home interiors); Books by Neighbors (reviews of books by and about Washingtonians); Fashion (worked around a theme). Query with clips of published work. Length: 1,200-2,500 words, except for reviews. Pays "standard fee, except for reviews and short takes."
Fiction: "We accept very little fiction and run about 3 or 4 pieces a year. Must be about sophisticated life in

Washington. Please, no presidential assassinations, no protest marches or murder stories." Buys 3 mss/year. Query with clips of published work. Length: 1,000-2,500 words. Pays 15¢ and up per assigned word.

Poetry: Avant-garde, free verse, light verse, traditional. "No vulgar or obscene poetry, please. Anything that sounds too 60s-ish probably won't get by my desk. And due to space limitations, no epic poems." Favors poetry by Washingtonians. Buys 20-40/year. Submit maximum 5 poems. Length: open. Pays $25 maximum.

Tips: "The best bet is a solid query that gives me an idea of what the story is about, and how you would handle it. Write the query's first graph as if it were the lead paragraph of the story. Also tell me who you are, show me some clips. Propose some ideas that suit the magazine. One difficulty writers outside of the Washington area have is trying to do a piece that requires their 'presence' here. If you can't be 'here' to do a piece like that, then consider a different kind of story that doesn't need that immediacy. If you are a thorough and stylish writer who can handle 2,000 words of a feature while both informing and entertaining the reader, you can break into the magazine in any of its sections. But remember: the flavor and slant here is the nation's capital and sophistication. We are trying to broaden our base, somewhat, without losing the edge our image currently gives us as an elitist magazine of Washington's cultural and social world. We're open to substantive, even controversial, articles."

THE WASHINGTON POST, 1150 15th St. NW, Washington DC 20071. (202)334-6000. Travel Editor: Morris D. Rosenberg. Weekly travel section (Sunday). Pays on publication. Byline given. "We are now emphasizing staff-written articles, as well as quality writing from other sources. Stories are rarely assigned to freelance writers, all material comes in on spec; there is no fixed kill fee." Buys first publication rights anywhere. Query with clips of published work. Legible computer printout submissions OK. Usually reports in 3 weeks.

Nonfiction: Emphasis in on travel writing with a strong sense of place, color, anecdote, history. Length: 1,500-2,000 words.

Photos: State availability of photos with ms. "Good travel photos that illustrate and complement the article, not fuzzy vacation snapshots." Captions and identification of subjects required ("when germane").

THE WASHINGTON POST MAGAZINE, *Washington Post,* 1150 15th St., NW, Washington D.C. 20071. Managing Editor: Stephen Petranek. Weekly rotogravure featuring regional and national interest articles (Washington DC, Southern Pennsylvania, Delaware, Maryland, West Virginia and Northern Virginia) for people of all ages and all interests. Circ. 1 million (Sunday). Average issue includes 6-10 feature articles and 4-5 columns. Pays on acceptance. Byline given. Buys all rights or first North American serial rights depending on fee. Submit seasonal material 4 months in advance. Photocopied submissions OK. SASE. Reports in 6 weeks on queries; in 2 weeks on mss. Free sample copy.

Nonfiction: "Controversial and regional interest articles. We want everything from politics to the outdoors, trends and issues." Photo feature. Buys 1 ms/issue. Query with clips of previously published work. Length: 1,500-4,500 words. Pays $200-up.

Photos: Reviews 4x5 or larger b&w glossy prints and 35 mm or larger color transparencies. Offers no additional payment for photos accepted with ms. Model release required.

Fiction: Fantasy, humorous, mystery, historical, mainstream and science fiction. Buys 6 mss/year. Send complete ms. Length: 3,000 words maximum. Pays $200-$750.

THE WASHINGTONIAN MAGAZINE, 1828 L St. NW, Washington DC 20036. Editor: John A. Limpert. For active, affluent, well-educated audience. Monthly magazine; 250 pages. Circ. 120,000. Buys first rights. Buys 75 mss/year. Pays on publication. Simultaneous and photocopied submissions OK. Reports in 4-6 weeks. Query or submit complete ms. SASE.

Nonfiction and Photos: "*The Washingtonian* is written for Washingtonians. The subject matter is anything we feel might interest people interested in the mind and manners of the city. The style, as Wolcott Gibbs said, should be the author's—if he is an author, and if he has a style. The only thing we ask is thoughtfulness and that no subject be treated too reverently. Audience is literate. We assume considerable sophistication about the city, and a sense of humor." Buys how-to, personal experience, interview/profile, humor, coverage of successful business operations, think pieces and exposes. Length: 1,000-7,000 words; average feature 3,000 words. Pays 20¢/word. Photos rarely purchased with mss.

Fiction and Poetry: Department Editor: Margaret Cheney. Must be Washington-oriented. No limitations on length. Pays 10¢/word for fiction. Payment is negotiable for poetry.

Florida

‡BOCA RATON MAGAZINE, JES Publishing Corp., 140 N. Federal Highway, Box 820, Boca Raton FL 33432. (305)426-1000. Editor: Gregg Fales. Published 6 times/year—October-May. "*Boca Raton* is directed toward residents of South Palm Beach County, Florida. It examines the area's elements of the land, the sea, the

people, the culture and history; in short, the Florida experience—its industry, successes, lifestyle and beauty."
Estab. 1981. Circ. 10,000. Pays on acceptance. Byline given. Offers 100% kill fee. Buys one-time rights and
makes work-for-hire assignments. Submit seasonal/holiday material 4 months in advance. Simultaneous
queries and previously published submissions OK. SASE. Reports in 2 months on queries; 5 weeks on mss.
Sample copy for $2, #11 SAE and $1.75 postage; writer's guidelines for business size SAE.

Nonfiction: General interest (upscale, sophisticated, classy); historical/nostalgic (preferably regional); inter-
view/profile (by subject grouping, locally); photo feature (mostly on assignment); travel (usually within a
day's drive); art; lifestyle. No world travel, humor, opinion, how-to. Buys 35-45 mss/year. Query. Length:
2,000-14,000 words. Pays $100-350.

Photos: High density (or contrast), artfully composed. State availability of photos. Pays $45-150 for color
transparencies; $25-50 for b&w contact sheet and 5x7 or larger b&w prints. Captions, model release and iden-
tification of subjects required.

Columns/Departments: Regional travel (not camping) to places of unusual beauty and/or imagination; food
of elegance appropriate for Florida lifestyle. Buys 12 mss/year. Query. Length: 1,000-5,000 words. Pays
$100-450.

Fiction: Fantasy, historical, mainstream. No horror, religious, western, erotica, ethnic, romance genre. Buys
2 mss/year. Query. Length: 2,000-10,000 words. Pays $200-500.

Poetry: Etta May VanTassel, poetry editor. Free verse, light verse, traditional. Buys 12 poems/year. Submit
maximum 3 poems. Length: 8 lines minimum. Pays in 2 copies.

‡**CENTRAL FLORIDA SCENE**, Central Scene Publications, Inc., 720 W. Vassar St., Orlando FL 32804.
(305)843-6274. Editor: Nancy N. Glick. Monthly magazine covering the lifestyles of central Florida. "Our
readers are affluent, recreation and business-oriented area residents who enjoy the good life. Content is positive, upbeat." Circ. 20,000. Pays on publication. Byline given. Offers $25 kill fee. Buys one-time rights and
makes work-for-hire assignments. Submit seasonal/holiday material 4 months in advance. Simultaneous
queries, and simultaneous, photocopied and previously published submissions OK. SASE. Reports in 1
month. Sample copy for $1.50, 9x12 SAE and $1.57 postage; writer's guidelines for business size SAE and 1
first class stamp.

Nonfiction: General interest (with local slant); historical/nostalgic (local); interview/profile (local); photo feature (local); travel. Special issues include interior design; boating; shopping (expensive retail). Buys 15-20
mss/year. Query with published clips if available. Length: 750-2,500 words. Pays $35-250.

Photos: Send photos with query or ms. Pays $25-100 for 35mm color transparencies; $10 for 5x7 and larger
b&w prints. Model release and identification of subjects required. Buys negotiable rights.

Fiction: Humorous, mainstream—"only if it has a local tie-in." Buys 1-2 mss/year. Send complete ms.
Length: 1,000-3,500 words. Pays $50-300.

Fillers: Clippings, anecdotes, short humor, newsbreaks—"with a local slant."

Tips: "Focus pieces on the activities of people in Central Florida. Query with list of 5-10 article ideas."

FLORIDA GULF COAST LIVING MAGAZINE, Baker Publications Inc., Suite 809, 1211 N. Westshore
Blvd., Tampa FL 33607. Publications Director: Tina Stacy. Managing Editor: Milana McLead Petty. Magazine published 7 times/year covering real estate and related subjects for "newcomers and local residents looking for new housing in the area we cover." Circ. 70,000. Pays on acceptance. Buys all rights. Submit
seasonal/holiday material 3 months in advance. Photocopied submissions OK. SASE. Reports in 2 months.
Sample copy $2; free writer's guidelines.

Nonfiction: General interest (on housing-related subjects, interior decorating, retirement living, apartment
living, plants, landscaping, moving tips); historical (area history); how-to (build a greenhouse, decks, etc.);
and travel (interesting trips around Florida, particularly near the area we cover). No personal views. Buys 5-10
mss/year. Query with clips of published work or send complete ms. Length: 500-1,200 words. Pays $15-125.

Photos: State availability of photos or send photos with ms. "Your package will be more valuable to us if you
provide the illustrations. For color work, 35mm is acceptable." Pays $3-10 for color transparencies; $3-5 for
8x10 glossy prints. "I prefer to include photos in the total package fee." Captions and model release required.
Buys one-time rights or all rights, "depending on the subject."

Columns/Departments: Query with suggestions for new columns or departments.

Tips: "Housing features, Retirement Living, Interiors, 'Choices,' Products and Services, and other ideas, are
the departments most open to freelancers. Be sure the subject is pertinent to our magazine. Know our magazine's style and write for it."

FLORIDA KEYS MAGAZINE, FKM Publishing Co., Inc., Box 818, 6187 O/S Hwy., Marathon FL 33040.
(305)743-3721. Editor: David Ethridge. Bimonthly general interest magazine covering the Florida Keys for
residents and tourists. Circ. 7,500. Pays on publication. Byline given. Buys one-time rights. Submit seasonal/
holiday material 3 months in advance. Simultaneous queries and simultaneous and photocopied submissions
OK. SASE. Reports in 1 month. Sample copy $2.

Nonfiction: General interest, historical/nostalgic, how-to (must be Florida Keys related: how to clean a conch;

how to catch a lobster); interview/profile, new product, personal experience, photo feature, travel. Query with clips of published work. Length: 400-2,000 words. Pays $3/inch.

Photos: State availability of photos. Reviews 35mm transparencies, pays $5-20 for 5x7 b&w prints; $15-100 for 5x7 color prints. Identification of subjects required.

GULFSHORE LIFE, Gulfshore Publishing Co., Inc., 3620 Tamiami Trail N., Naples FL 33940. (813)262-6425. Editor: Molly J. Burns. For an upper-income audience of varied business and academic backgrounds; actively employed and retired; interested in travel, leisure, business, and sports, as well as local environmental issues. Monthly magazine. Circ. 18,000. Buys first rights, and requests permission for subsequent reprint rights in other publications published by the firm. Byline given. Buys 50 mss/year. Pays on publication 5¢/word. Photocopied or simultaneous submissions OK. Submit seasonal material 2 months in advance. Query. SASE.

Nonfiction: Local personalities, sports, travel, nature, environment, business, boating and fishing, historical pieces. Everything must be localized to the Southwest Coast of Florida. No political or controversial articles. Length: 1,500-2,500 words. Buys 5-10 unsolicited mss/year.

Photos: Bought separately, b&w prints or color transparencies only. Annual Contest deadline: April 1st. Each entry must convey the theme of "Life Along the Gulfshore". SASE. Cash awards and publication for winner. B&w only.

Fiction: Annual Fiction Contest deadline: March 1st. Entries must have a Florida locale; 3,500 words maximum. Cash awards and publication of winner. SASE.

Tips: "Familiarize yourself with the magazine and the location: Naples, Marco Island, Ft. Myers, Ft. Myers Beach, Sanibel-Captiva, Whiskey Creek, Punta Gorda Isles and Port Charlotte. Submissions accepted at any time."

‡**ISLAND LIFE, The Enchanting Barrier Islands of Florida's Gulf Coast**, Island Life Publications, Box X, Sanibel FL 33957. (813)472-4344. Editor: Joan Hooper. Managing Editor: Barbara Brooks. Quarterly magazine of the Barrier Islands from Longboat Key to Marco Island for upper income residents and vacationers of Florida's Gulf Coast area. Estab. 1981. Circ. 16,000. Pays on publication. Byline given. Buys second serial (reprint) rights. Submit seasonal/holiday material 6 months in advance. Simultaneous queries and simultaneous and photocopied submissions OK. SASE. Reports in 8 weeks on queries; 12 weeks on mss. Sample copy for $3, 10x13 envelope and 65¢ postage; writer's guidelines for business-size SAE and 1 first class stamp.

Nonfiction: General interest, historical/nostalgic, inspirational, interview/profile, travel. No fiction or first person experiences. "Our editorial emphasis is on the history, culture, scenic, sports, social, and leisure activities of the area." Buys 20 mss/year. Query with published clips. Length: 500-1,500 words. Pays 5¢/word.

Photos: Send photos with query or ms. Pays $5-10 for 2x3 b&w prints; $5-25 for 2x2 or 4x5 color transparencies. Captions, model release and identification of subjects required.

JACKSONVILLE MAGAZINE, Drawer 329, Jacksonville FL 32201. (904)353-0300. Bimonthly. Circ. 12,000. Buys all rights. Buys 40-45 mss/year. Pays on publication. Query. Submit seasonal material 3-6 months in advance. Reports in 3 weeks. SASE.

Nonfiction and Photos: Buys historical, photo and business articles pertaining specifically to Jacksonville. Length: usually 1,500-3,000 words. Pays $100-300. "We accept b&w glossy prints, good contrast; color transparencies." Pays $30 minimum for b&w; color terms to be arranged.

Tips: "We are reducing the length of our articles."

MIAMI MAGAZINE, Box 340008, Coral Gables FL 33134. (305)856-5011. Editor: Erica Rauzin. For involved citizens of south Florida; generally well educated. Monthly magazine. Circ. 30,000. Rights purchased vary with author and material. Usually buys first publication rights. Buys about 20 unsolicited mss/year. Pays on publication. Sample copy $1.95. Reports in 60 days. Query preferred or submit complete ms. Computer printout and disk (compatible with Apple 3) submissions OK; prefers letter quality to dot matrix printouts. SASE.

Nonfiction: Investigative pieces on the area; thorough, general features; exciting, in-depth writing. Informational, how-to, interview, profile, and expose. Strong local angle and fresh, opinionated and humorous approach. "Read the Ross/Knight piece in the January '82 issue for an example of profile/investigative piece. No travel stories from freelancers, that's mostly staff generated. We do not like to get freelance mss that are thinly disguised press releases. We don't need film because we have a regular columnist. My main thing is that writers READ the magazine first—then they'll know what to send and what not to send." Length: 3,000 words maximum. Pays $100-800.

Columns/Departments: Humor, business, books, art (all kinds) and home design. Length: 1,500 words maximum. Payment ranges from $100-150.

Tips: "We are becoming far more regional in our outlook, not just Miami, but also Key West and Ft. Lauderdale."

‡**MIAMI MENSUAL (MIAMI MONTHLY),** The International Magazine of South Florida, Quintus Communications Group, 2000 Coral Way, Miami FL 33145. (305)856-2008. Editor: Frank Soler. "The only Spanish-language monthly city magazine in the US for a sophisticated, decidedly upscale multicultural, multilingual internationally-oriented audience." City/regional magazine format. Circ. 25,000. Pays on publication. Byline given. Offers 50% kill fee. Buys all rights. Submits seasonal/holiday material 3 months in advance. Simultaneous queries, and simultaneous, photocopied and previously published submissions OK. SASE. Reports in 2 weeks. Free sample copy and writer's guidelines.

Nonfiction: Book excerpts, expose, general interest, humor, interview/profile, opinion, personal experience, photo feature, travel. Buys 50-70 mss/year. Query with published clips if available or send complete ms. Length: 1,500-3,000 words. Pays variable rates.

Photos: A. Amador, photo editor: Send photos with query or ms. Reviews b&w contact sheet, color transparencies and b&w prints. Captions, model release and identification of subjects required. Buys one-time or all rights.

Columns/Departments: Humor; Opinion; TV; Movies; Audio/Video; Books, Jet Set; Gastronomy/Wine. "All must be applicable to a highly sophisticated international audience." Buys 50-70 mss/year. Query with published clips if available or send complete ms. Length: 1,000-1,500 words. Pays variable rates.

Fiction: Adventure, condensed novels. Send complete ms. Length: open. Pays variable rates.

Tips: "We're open to feature stories about or of interest to prominent international figures in business and the arts. Our publication is equivalent to a combination of a glossy city magazine and the new *Vanity Fair*, *Connoisseur*, and *Town & Country* for Hispanics."

ORLANDO-LAND MAGAZINE, Box 2207, Orlando FL 32802. (305)644-3355. Editor-in-Chief: E.L. Prizer. Managing Editor: Carole De Pinto. Emphasizes central Florida information for "a readership made up primarily of people new to Florida—those here as visitors, traveling businessmen, new residents." Monthly magazine; 144 pages. Circ. 26,000. Pays on acceptance. Buys all rights or first North American serial rights. Byline given. Phone queries OK. Submit seasonal/holiday material 2 months in advance. Photocopied and previously published submissions OK. Computer printout and disk submissions OK. SASE. Reports in 6 weeks. Sample copy $2.

Nonfiction: Historical, how-to and informational. "Things involved in living in Florida." Pay $25-75.

Photos: B&w glossy prints. Pays $5.

Tips: "Always in need of *useful* advice-type material presented as first-person experience that relates to Central Florida area. Also, travel (excursion) pieces to places open to general public within 1 day's (there and back) journey of Orlando or experience pieces (hobbies, sports, etc.) that would not be practical for staff writers— sky diving, delta kites, etc. Must be available in Central Florida. Specialized topical columns are being added in health, environment, architecture, travel."

PALM BEACH LIFE, Box 1176, Palm Beach FL 33480. (305)837-4750. Managing Editor: Ava Van de Water. "*Palm Beach Life* caters to a sophisticated, high-income readership and reflects its interests. Readers are affluent . . . usually over 40, well-educated." Monthly. Circ. 23,000. Buys first North American rights. Pays on acceptance. Reports in 3 weeks. Query with outline. SASE. Sample copy $2.88.

Nonfiction and Photos: Subject matter involves "articles on fashion, music, art and related fields; subjects that would be of interest to the sophisticated, well-informed reader. Buys informational, feature, photo and travel articles. Length: 1,000-2,500 words. Payment varies depending on length and research. Purchases photos with mss, or on assignment. "We feature color photos, but are looking for good b&w." Captions are required. Buys 8x10 b&w glossy prints. Also buys 35mm or 2¼x2¼ transparencies and photo stories. Pay is negotiable.

Tips: "Please consider our magazine format—send for a sample copy and peruse magazine. We like stories (including good, well-written features) that appeal to upper-income, sophisticated readers."

SOUTH FLORIDA LIVING, Baker Publications, Inc., Suite 109, 700 W. Hillsboro Blvd., Deerfield Beach FL 33441. (305)428-5602. Editor: Diana Stanley. Bimonthly magazine covering real estate market in Dade, Broward, Martin and Palm Beach counties, for newcomers and home buyers. Estab. 1981. Circ. 70,000. Pays on acceptance. Byline given. Makes work-for-hire assignments. Submit seasonal/holiday material 4 months in advance. Photocopied and previously published submissions OK. SASE. Reports in 2 weeks. Sample copy and writer's guidelines free.

Nonfiction: General interest (entertainment, fine arts); historical; how-to (finance, move, build, design); moving tips; landscaping and gardening; banking; interior decorating; retirement living; and apartment living. No personal stories or articles not related to South Florida. Buys 18-20 mss/year. Query. Length: 1,500-2,000 words. Pays 20¢/word.

Photos: State availability of photos. Pays negotiable fee for 35mm color transparencies and 5x7 b&w prints. Captions and model releases required. Buys all rights.

Tips: "National assignments on decorating, financing, etc., for all of Baker's city magazines are made by Tina

Stacy, publication director. Payment is 20¢/word. Query her at: *Living*, Suite 400, 5757 Alpha Rd., Dallas TX 75240.''

‡**TALLAHASSEE MAGAZINE**, Homes & Land Publishing Corp., Box 12848, Tallahassee FL 32308. (904)222-5467. Editor: William L. Needham. Managing Editor: W.R. Lundquist. Quarterly magazine covering people, events and history in and around Florida's capital city. Circ. 15,000. Pays on publication. Offers $50 kill fee. Buys first North American serial rights. Submit seasonal/holiday material 6 months in advance. Simultaneous queries and photocopied and previously published submissions OK. Computer printout or disk submissions OK. SASE. Reports in 2 weeks on queries; 1 month on mss. Sample copy for 9x12 SAE.
Nonfiction: General interest (relating to Florida or Southeast); historical/nostalgic (for Tallahassee, North Florida, South Georgia); interview/profile (related to North Florida, South Georgia); travel (likely to appeal to Floridians). No fiction, poetry or topics unrelated to area. Buys 12 mss/year. Query. Length: 500-1,400 words. Pays 10¢/word.
Photos: State availability of photos with query letter or ms. Pays $35 minimum for 35mm color transparencies; $20 minimum for b&w prints. Model release and identification of subjects required. Buys one-time rights.
Tips: "We seek to show positive aspects of life in and around Tallahassee. Know the area. Brief author biographic note should accompany mss."

‡**TAMPA BAY MONTHLY**, Florida City Magazines, Inc. 2502 Rocky Point Dr., Tampa FL 33607. Managing Editor: Heidi A. Swanson. Associate Editor: Paula Stahel Willson. Monthly magazine for upscale Tampa Bay area readers. Circ. 25,000. Pays on publication. Byline given. Buys all rights. Submit seasonal/holiday material 3 months in advance. Simultaneous queries OK. Computer printout submissions OK; prefers letter quality to dot matrix. SASE. Reports in 6 weeks. Free sample copy and writer's guidelines.
Nonfiction: In-depth investigative, general interest, humor, historical/nostalgic, and interview/profile—pertaining to the Tampa Bay Area reader. Occasionally needs get-away pieces for Bay Area residents, fashion pieces, and food/drink articles. Buys 24-36 mss/year. Query with clips of published work. Length: 300-500 words for short articles; 3,000-5,000 words for feature articles. Pays $50-500. No fiction or poetry; no book or movie reviews.
Photos: Brian Noyes, art director. State availability of photos. Reviews contact sheets. Captions, model releases, and identification of subjects required. Buys all rights.

TROPIC MAGAZINE, Sunday Magazine of the Miami Herald, Knight Ridder, 1 Herald Plaza, Miami FL 33101. (305)350-2036. Editor: Kevin Hall. Associate Editor: Gene Weingarten. Weekly magazine covering general interest, locally-oriented topics for local readers. Circ. 500,000. Pays on publication. Byline given. Buys first rights. Submit seasonal/holiday material 2 months in advance. SASE. Reports in 6 weeks.
Nonfiction: Maggie Felser, articles editor. General interest; interview/profile (first-person); and personal experience. No fiction. Buys 20 mss/year. Query with clips of published work or send complete ms. Length: 1,500-3,000 words. Pays $400-800/article.
Photos: Debra Yates, art director. State availability of photos.

Georgia

ATLANTA JOURNAL-CONSTITUTION, Box 4689, Atlanta GA 30302. (404)526-5479. Travel Editor: Colin Bessonette. Weekly section of daily newspaper, covering travel. Circ. 509,000. Byline given. Submit seasonal/holiday material 1 month in advance. Simultaneous queries OK. SASE required.
Nonfiction: Travel (to the Southeastern US, the Caribbean, Canada, Mexico or Western Europe—any mode of transportation). Buys 18 unsolicited mss/year. Query. Length: 1,200-1,600 words. Pays $50-100.
Photos: Reviews any size b&w glossy prints. Identification of subjects required. Buys one-time rights.
Tips: "We have an extensive network of writers now. Prefer practical, useful information woven into stories on popular (not off-the-wall) destinations."

ATLANTA MAGAZINE, 6285 Barfield Rd., Atlanta GA 30328. (404)256-9800. Editor: John W. Lange. Monthly regional magazine covering the South "for educated Southerners." Computer printout submissions OK; prefers letter quality to dot matrix. Pays on acceptance. Buys first publication rights and right to reprint 1 time. Pays 10% kill fee. Byline given. SASE. Reports in 6-8 weeks. Sample copy $3.
Nonfiction: Statewide, regional and national articles are acceptable. No first person, academic or how-to. Query. Length: 2,000-4,000 words. Pays $200 minimum, $750 full length features.
Photos: State availability of photos. Buys 8x10 b&w prints or 35mm color transparencies; pay varies. Captions preferred.
Tips: Will be using "shorter stories, more topical and lively material, fewer essays, etc."

‡**ATLANTA WEEKLY**, Atlanta Newspapers, Box 4689, Atlanta GA 30302. (404)526-5415. Editor: Lee Walburn. Sunday general interest magazine. Circ. 500,000. Pays on acceptance. Byline given. Offers 40% kill fee. Buys one-time rights. Submit seasonal/holiday material 6 months in advance. Simultaneous queries and previously published submissions OK. SASE. Reports in 6 weeks. Free sample copy and writer's guidelines.
Nonfiction: Andrew Sparks, articles editor. Book excerpts, general interest, humor, interview/profile. "Articles should deal with topics of interest around Atlanta, the South and Southeast." Special issues include Home Decorating issue; Fashion issue; Christmas Gift Guide. No first-person or travel articles. Buys 100 mss/year. Query with clips if available. Length: 250-3,000 words. Pays $50-800.
Photos: Ike Hussey, photo editor. State availability of photos.
Fillers: Contact: "ETC" editor. Short humor, newsbreaks. Buys 20/year. Length: 100-200 words. Pays $15-50.

AUGUSTA SPECTATOR, Box 3168, Augusta GA 30902. (404)733-1476. Publisher: Faith Bertsche. Magazine published 3 times/year about the Augusta, Georgia and Aiken, South Carolina area for readers who are upper middle class residents, Ft. Gordon army post and medical complex personnel and visitors to the Masters Golf Tournament. Circ. 5,000. Pays on publication. Byline given. Buys one-time rights. Submit seasonal material 6 months in advance. Simultaneous, photocopied and previously published submissions OK. SASE.
Nonfiction: General interest (for people interested in golf, horses and local topical issues); historical (issues concerning the southeast coast); interview (of outstanding people of local interest); nostalgia (with a Southern flavor); profile; humor (related to the Masters, polo, birddog trials). Buys 4-6 unsolicited mss/year. Query. Length: 1,200 words minimum. Pays $25-50.
Photos: State availability of photos. Reviews 5x7 b&w glossy prints. Offers no additional payment for photos accepted with ms. Captions and model release required. Buys one-time rights.
Fiction: Adventure, humorous, mystery, romance, suspense, historical. No unnecessary violence. Buys 2 mss/issue. Send complete ms. Length: 3,000 words maximum.
Poetry: Editor: Barri Armitage. Free verse and traditional. Submit maximum 6 poems. Pays in copies.

Hawaii

ALOHA, THE MAGAZINE OF HAWAII, Davick Publishing Co., 828 Fort Street Mall, Honolulu HI 96813. Editor: Rita Gormley. For those who have been to Hawaii or those who would like to know more about Hawaii; new places to stay, eat or visit. Bimonthly magazine; 96 pages. Circ. 85,000. Pays on publication. Buys all rights. Byline given. Submit seasonal/holiday material 8 months in advance. Photocopied submissions OK. SASE. Reports in 6 weeks. Sample copy $2.75.
Nonfiction: Art, business, historical, interview, personal experience, photo feature, profile, sports and travel. "All articles must be Hawaii-related. Please, no articles on impressions of romantic sunsets or articles aimed at the tourist." Recent article example: "Knock 'Em Dead With Your Hawaii Shots" (February 1982). Buys 10 unsolicited mss/year. Query or send clips of published work. Length: 1,500-4,000 words. Pays 10¢/word.
Photos: State availability of photos. Pays $25 for 8x10 b&w glossy prints; $50 for color transparencies or $150 for covers. Buys one-time rights. Captions and model releases required for covers.
Fiction: "Any type of story as long as it has a Hawaii-related theme." Buys 1 ms/issue. Send complete ms. Length: 4,000 words maximum. Pays 10¢/word.
Poetry: Free verse, haiku and traditional. Buys 6 poems/year. Submit no more than 6. Pays $25.

‡**HONOLULU**, Honolulu Publishing Co., Ltd., 36 Merchant St., Honolulu HI 96813. (808)524-7400. Editor: Brian Nicol. Monthly magazine covering general interest topics relating to Hawaii. Circ. 35,000. Pays on acceptance. Byline given. Offers $50 kill fee. Buys one-time rights. Submit seasonal/holiday material 5 months in advance. Simultaneous queries and simultaneous and photocopied submissions OK. SASE. Sample copy for $2, 9x11 SAE and $1.50 postage.
Nonfiction: Marilyn Kim, articles editor. Expose, general interest, historical/nostalgic, photo feature (all Hawaii-related). "We run regular features on food, fashion, interior design, travel, etc., plus other timely, provocative articles. No personal experience articles." Buys 10 mss/year. Query with clips if available. Length: 2,500-5,000 words. Pays $250-400.
Photos: Jill Chen Loui, photo editor: State availability of photos. Pays $15 maximum for b&w contact sheet; $25 maximum for 35mm color transparencies. Captions and identification of subjects required. Buys one-time rights.
Columns/Departments: Marilyn Kim, column/department editor. Calabash (a light, "newsy," timely, humorous column on any Hawaii-related subject). Buys 15 mss/year. Query with clips of published work or send complete ms. Length: 250-1,000 words. Pays $25-35.

Illinois

‡**CHAMPAIGN-URBANA MAGAZINE**, Faucett Communications, Inc., 17 E. University, Champaign IL 61820. (217)352-0987. Editor: Philip M. Faucett. Monthly magazine for readers in 5 central Illinois counties surrounding the Champaign-Urbana area. Circ. 20,000. Pays on acceptance. Byline given. Offers 20% kill fee. Submit seasonal/holiday material 2 months in advance. Computer printout and disk submissions OK; prefers letter quality to dot matrix printouts. SASE. Report in 2 weeks on queries; 1 month on mss. Free sample copy and writer's guidelines.
Nonfiction: Expose, general interest, historical/nostalgic, how-to, humor, interview/profile, new product, opinion, personal experience, photo feature, travel. Special issues include Anniversay Issue, Back-to-School Issue, City/Regional Guide, Christmas Issue, Spring Issue. No religious, technical writing, fiction or poetry. Buys 50 mss/year. Query. Length: 1,000-3,000 words. Pays $50 minimum for 1,500 words.
Photos: State availability of photos. Pays $5-50 for b&w contact sheet and negatives; $5-100 for b&w prints. Identification of subjects required. Buys one-time rights.
Columns/Departments: Film Reviews, Dining Out, Astronomy, Food/Cooking, Financial, Around Town, Weather, Shopping, Health, etc. Buys 100 mss/year. Query. Length: 500 words minimum. Pays $25 minimum.
Fillers: Clippings, anecdotes, short humor. Buys 72/year. Length: 250-350 words. Pays $5 minimum.
Tips: "We encourage all writers to submit ideas of their choosing. The slant should be pointed, informative, nonfiction and sharp."

CHICAGO JOURNAL, 731 S. Dearborn St., Chicago IL 60605. (312)663-0480. Editor: Eugene Forrester. Weekly tabloid for a strong integrated and university readership (70%). Circ. 30,000. Pays on publication. Byline given. Offers kill fee "per arrangement with writer." Buys all rights. Submit seasnal/holiday material 2 months in advance. Simultaneous, photocopied, and previously published submissions OK. Computer printouts or submissions for Apple 48K Plus OK; prefers letter quality to dot matrix printouts. SASE. Reports in 1 week on queries; 2 weeks on mss. Sample copy for $1 and 10x13 SAE with 53¢ postage.
Nonfiction: Book excerpts (political of Chicago interest); expose (Chicago city-wide politics, state and federal government); how-to (rehabbing/gentrification of urban area); interview/profile (of city-wide personalities); opinion. "We seek editorial slanted to a racially integrated, sophisticed readership." No vague, general interest material that freelancers try to syndicate nationwide. Query with clips of published work. Length: 1,000-3,000 words. Pays $25-200.
Photos: Cynthia Hoffman, photo editor. State availability of photos. Pays $15-50 for 8x10 b&w prints. Buys negotiable—usually all—rights.

CHICAGO MAGAZINE, 3 Illinois Center, Chicago IL 60601. Editor-in-Chief: Allen H. Kelson. Editor: John Fink. 40% freelance written. For an audience which is "95% from Chicago area; 90% college-trained; upper income; overriding interests in the arts, dining, good life in the city and suburbs. Most are in 25 to 50 age bracket and well-read and articulate. Generally liberal inclination." Monthly. Circ. 215,000. Buys first rights. Buys about 50 mss/year. Pays on acceptance. For sample copy, send $3 to Circulation Dept. Submit seasonal material 3 months in advance. Computer printout submissions OK "if legible"; prefers letter quality to dot matrix. Reports in 2 weeks. Query; indicate "specifics, knowledge of city and market, and demonstrable access to sources." SASE.
Nonfiction and Photos: "On themes relating to the quality of life in Chicago; past, present, future." Writers should have "a general awareness that the readers will be concerned, influential longtime Chicagoans reading what the writer has to say about their city. We generally publish material too comprehensive for daily newspapers or of too specialized interest for them." Buys personal experience and think pieces, interviews, profiles, humor, spot news, historical articles, travel, and exposes. Length: 1,000-6,000 words. Pays $100-$2,500. Photos purchased with mss. Uses b&w glossy prints, 35mm color transparencies or color prints.
Fiction: Christine Newman, articles editor. Mainstream, fantasy and humorous fiction. Preferably with Chicago orientation. No word-length limits, but "no novels, please." Pays $250-500.
Tips: "Submit plainly, be businesslike and avoid cliche ideas."

CHICAGO READER, Box 11101, Chicago IL 60611. (312)828-0350. Editor: Robert A. Roth. "The *Reader* is distributed free in Chicago's lakefront neighborhoods. Generally speaking, these are Chicago's best educated, most affluent neighborhoods—and they have an unusually high concentration of young adults." Weekly tabloid; 128 pages. Circ. 117,000. Pays "by 15th of month following publication." Buys all rights. Byline given. Phone queries OK. Photocopied submissions OK. SASE. Reports "very slow," up to 1 year.
Nonfiction: "We want magazine features on Chicago topics. Will also consider reviews." Buys 500 mss/year. Submit complete ms. Length: "whatever's appropriate to the story." Pays $35-625.
Photos: By assignment only.
Columns/Departments: By assignment only.

ILLINOIS ISSUES, Sangamon State University, Springfield IL 62708. Publisher: J. Michael Lennon. Editor: Caroline Gherardini. Emphasizes Illinois government and issues for state and local government officials and staff plus citizens and businessmen concerned with Illinois and its government (local government also). Monthly magazine; 40 pages. Circ. 6,000. Pays on publication. Buys all rights. SASE. Reports in 8 weeks. Sample copy $2.50.

Nonfiction: How-to (use state services and processes as a citizen); informational (explaining state/local government agency in Illinois, detailing new process initiated by state legislation, city or county ordinance); interview (Illinois government or political leaders); and technical (related to government policy, services with issues stressed, e.g., energy). No articles on Illinois history. There is a constant need for articles about local government problems and issues that have statewide applicability. Recent article example: "The New Federalism in Illinois" (March, 1982). Buys 20 unsolicited mss/year. Query. Length: 800-5,000 words (best chance: 2,400 words). Pays 4-10¢/word.

Tips: "Local issues tied to state government in Illinois have a good chance, but writer must research to know state laws, pending legislation and past attempts that relate to the issue."

‡**ILLINOIS TIMES, Downstate Illinois' Weekly Newspaper**, Illinois Times, Inc., Box 3524, Springfield IL 62708. (217)753-2226. Editor: Fletcher Farrar Jr. Weekly tabloid covering that part of the state outside of Chicago and its suburbs for a discerning, well-educated readership. Circ. 25,000. Pays on publication. Byline given. Buys first rights. Submit seasonal/holiday material 1 month in advance. Simultaneous queries, and simultaneous, photocopied and previously published submissions OK. SASE. Reports in 2 weeks on queries; 6 weeks on mss. Sample copy 50¢.

Nonfiction: Book excerpts, expose, general interest, historical, how-to, interview/profile, opinion, personal experience, photo feature, travel "in our area," book reviews, politics, environment, energy, etc. "We are not likely to use a story that has no Illinois tie-in." Annual special issues: Lincoln (February); Health & Fitness (March); Gardening (April); Summer (June); Fall Home (September); Christmas (Books). No articles filled with "bureaucratese or generalities; no articles naively glorifying public figures or celebrity stories for celebrity's sake." Buys 100 mss/year. Query or send complete ms. Length: From 1,500 to 2,500 words maximum. Pays 4¢/word; $100 maximum.

Photos: State availability of photos. Pays $15-25 for 8x10 prints. Identification of subjects required. Buys one-time rights.

Columns/Departments: Guestwork (opinion column, any subject of personal experience with an Illinois angle). Buys 100 mss/year. Send complete ms. Length: 1,500 words maximum. Pays 4¢/word; $60 maximum.

Tips: "The ideal *IT* story is one the reader hates to put down. Good writing, in our view, is not necessarily fancy writing. It is (in the words of a colleague) whatever 'will engage the disinterested reader.' In other words, nothing dull, please. But remember that any subject—even the investment policies of public pension funds—can be made 'engaging.' It's just that some subjects require more work than others. Good illustrations are a plus. As an alternative newspaper, we prefer to treat subjects in depth or not at all. Please, no general articles that lack an Illinois angle."

Indiana

INDIANAPOLIS, 363 N. Illinois, Indianapolis IN 46204. (317)267-2986. Editor: Pegg Kennedy. Emphasizes Indianapolis-related problems/features or regional related topics. Monthly magazine. Circ. 22,000. Pays on publication. Buys one-time rights. Byline given. Queries or manuscripts. Submit seasonal/holiday material 4 months in advance. Simultaneous, photocopied and previously published submissions OK. Computer printout and disk submissions OK; prefers letter quality to dot matrix. SASE. Reports in 1 month. Sample copy $1.75.

Nonfiction: Expose (interested, but have no specifics; "we're interested in any Indianapolis-related topic including government and education"); historical (Indianapolis-related only); how-to (buying tips); humor ("broad-category for us"); inspirational (not generally but will read submitted ms); interview (Indianapolis-related person, native sons and daughters); nostalgia (Indianapolis-related); photo feature (human interest, Indianapolis-related); profile (Indianapolis-related); and travel (within a day's drive of Indianapolis). "We only want articles with Indianapolis or Central Indiana ties, no subjects outside of our region. No essays, opinions—unless they are qualified by professional credits for an opinion/essay. We aren't very interested in broad-based, national topics without a local angle. National issues can be broken into 'how does it affect Indianapolis?' or 'what does it mean for Indianapolis?' (We're big on sidebars.) Our magazine is supplemented by special guides which require general basic information: City Guide—a comprehensive directory about city services, facilities, organizations; Habitats—a guide to houses, apartments, condos; Indiana Guide—comprehensive directory that makes you want to visit a special thing/place; Office Guide—background about the commercial side of the city, growth rates, etc."; Visitors' Guide—features on things to see and do; Dining Guide—features related to dining. Buys 150 unsolicited mss/year. Query. Length: 500-3,500 words. Pays $40-200.

Photos: State availability of photos. Pays $15 for b&w; $5-35 for color transparencies. Buys one-time rights. Captions required.
Columns/Departments: Business, travel, sports.
Tips: "We are planning to expand our circulation area to include Central Indiana so that we are more of a regional magazine rather than city."

INDIANAPOLIS MONTHLY, Mayhill Publications, Inc., Box 30071, Indianapolis IN 46230. (317)259-8222. Editor: Deborah Paul. Associate Editor: Tom Collins. Monthly magazine covering subject matter of interest to those in central Indiana. All material must be upbeat, written in a lively style, of interest to Indiana residents. Circ. 24,000. Pays on publication. Byline given. Usually buys first rights. Submit seasonal/holiday material 4 months in advance. Photocopied submissions OK. Computer printout and disk submissions OK "if good, clear quality"; prefers letter quality to dot matrix printouts. SASE. Reports in 1 month. Sample copy $1.50.
Nonfiction: Expose (in-depth reporting on government, education, health, if it is fairly presented); general interest (sport, business, media, health); historical/nostalgic (pertaining to Indiana landmarks only; no first-person); design (at-home features, maximum 1,000 words about a unique home with transparencies or slides with cutlines); interview/profile (of regional personalities, success stories about Indiana natives); color photo feature (seasonal material from Indiana); travel (weekends in Indiana; no first person). Always looking for fresh angles on Indianapolis 500. No first-person narratives, movie reviews, domestic humor, poetry, cooking. Query with clips of published work or send complete ms. Length: 500-3,000 words. Pays $50-250.
Photos: Black and white glossies with good contrast. Photos to accompany ms are especially welcomed. Pays $20 for published b&w prints; variable rate for 2¼x2¼, 35mm color transparencies. Captions or identification of subjects required.
Columns/Departments: Business—success stories, unique regional business; sport—personalities or seasonal sport; media—personalities or trends in print or broadcast; health, new innovations or specialists. Query with clips of published work or send complete ms. Length: 600-1,000 words. Pays $50-150.
Fillers: Newsbreaks from or about regional personalites or institutions. Length: 300-1,000 words. Pays $50-100.
Tips: "Especially open to freelance specialized writer in areas of interior design, health, sport."

MICHIANA, Sunday Magazine of *The South Bend Tribune*, Colfax at Lafayette, South Bend IN 46626. (219)233-6161. Editor: Bill Sonneborn. 70% freelance written. For "average daily newspaper readers; perhaps a little above average since we have more than a dozen colleges and universities in our area." Weekly. Circ. 125,000. May buy first North American serial rights or simultaneous rights providing material offered will be used outside of Indiana and Michigan. Byline given. Buys 175 unsolicited mss/year. Pays on publication. Will consider photocopied submissions if clearly legible. Computer printout and disk submissions OK. Submit special material for spring and fall travel sections at least 1 month in advance. Reports in 2 weeks. Submit complete ms. SASE.
Nonfiction and Photos: "Items of general and unusual interest, written in good, clear, simple sentences with logical approach to subject. We like material oriented to the Midwest, especially Indiana, Michigan, Ohio and Illinois. We avoid all freelance material that supports movements of a political nature. We seldom use first-person humor. We can use some offbeat stuff if it isn't too far out." Length: 800-3,000 words. Payment is $50-60 minimum, with increases as deemed suitable. All mss must be accompanied by illustrations or b&w photos or 35mm or larger color transparencies.

Iowa

‡**THE IOWAN MAGAZINE**, Mid-America Publishing Corp., 214 9th St., Des Moines IA 50309. (515)282-8220. Editor: Charles W. Roberts. Quarterly magazine covering the "history, people, places, points of interest in Iowa." Circ. 22,000. Pays on publication. Byline given. Buys one-time rights. Submit seasonal/holiday material 5 months in advance. Photocopied and previously published submissions OK. Reports in 1 month. Sample copy for $3.50, 9x12 SAE and $1.75 postage; free writer's guidelines.
Nonfiction: General interest (history as in American heritage, not personal reminiscence); interview/profile, travel. No "articles from non-Iowans who come for a visit and wish to give their impression of the state." Buys 32 mss/year. Query with clips. Length: 750-3,000 words. Pays $75-350.
Photos: Send photos with ms. Pays $10-25 for b&w contact sheet; $35-50 for color transparency. Captions and identification of subjects required.
Tips: "If you are writing about Iowa, write on a specific topic. Dont be *too* general. Write a query letter with maybe two or three ideas."

Kansas

KANSAS!, Kansas Department of Economic Development, 503 Kansas Ave., 6th Floor, Topeka KS 66603. (913)296-3806. Editor: Andrea Glenn. Emphasizes Kansas "faces and places for all ages, occupations and interests." Quarterly magazine; 32 pages. Circ. 38,000. Pays on acceptance. Buys one-time rights. Byline given. Submit seasonal/holiday material 8 months in advance. Simultaneous or photocopied and previously published submissions OK. SASE. Reports in 2 months. Free sample copy and writer's guidelines.
Nonfiction: "Material must be Kansas-oriented and well-written. We run stories about Kansas people, places, and events that can be enjoyed by the general public. In other words, events must be open to the public, places also. People featured must have interesting crafts etc." General interest; interview; photo feature; profile; and travel. No exposes. Query. "Query letter should clearly outline story in mind. I'm especially interested in Kansas freelancers who can supply their own photos." Length: 5-7 pages double-spaced, typewritten copy. Pays $75-125.
Photos: "We are a full-color photo/manuscript publication." State availability of photos with query. Pays $10-25 ("generally included in ms rate") for 35mm color transparencies. Captions required.
Tips: "History and nostalgia stories do not fit into our format because they can't be illustrated well with color photography."

KANSAS CITY MAGAZINE, 5350 W. 94th Terrace, Suite 204, Prairie Village, KS 66207. (913)648-0444. Editor: William R. Wehrman. Monthly; 64-96 pages. Circ. 15,000. Freelance material is accepted if it is about Kansas City or Kansas City people. Written queries only; queries and manuscripts should be accompanied by SASE. Sample copy $1.50. Reports in 1 month. No simultaneous, photocopied, or previously published submissions accepted. Computer printout and disk (AM Comp Edit) submissions OK; prefers letter quality to dot matrix printouts.
Nonfiction: Editorial content is hard news, investigative reporting, profiles, or lengthy news features. No fiction. Short items of 250-1,250 words are considered for "City Window" column; pays $25-50. Longer stories of 2,000-8,000 words pay from $100-600, plus expenses. Columns, which include politics, theater, travel, money, and a "Postscript" essay, are from 1,600-3,000 words and pay $75-200. All material must have a demonstrable connection to Kansas City. Bylines are always given, except for "City Window" material; all rights are purchased.
Tips: Freelancers should show some previous reporting or writing experience of a professional nature.

‡**THE WICHITAN MAGAZINE**, Wichita Publishing Co., 936 N. Waco, Wichita KS 67203. (316)262-2616. Editor: Pam Porvaznik. Managing Editor: Jo Doty. Monthly magazine for upper-income Wichitans. Circ. 10,000. Pays on publication. Byline given. Offers 10% kill fee. Buys first North American serial rights. Submit seasonal/holiday material 4 months in advance. Simultaneous queries OK. No computer printout or disk submissions. SASE. Reports in 2 weeks on queries; 1 month on mss.
Nonfiction: Interview/profile; "nothing depressing or tasteless." Buys 36 mss/year. Query with clips. Length: open. Pays $100-1,000.
Photos: State availability of photos. Captions, model release and indentification of subjects required. Buys one-time rights.
Columns/Departments: Travel. Buys 36 mss/year. Query with clips of published work. Pays $150-200.
Tips: Will be using more business, more national profiles.

Kentucky

THE COURIER-JOURNAL MAGAZINE, 525 W. Broadway, Louisville KY 40202. Publisher: Barry Bingham Jr. Editor: James Pope. For general readership in Kentucky and Indiana. Weekly magazine; 52 pages. Circ. 340,000. Pays on publication. Buys one-time rights. Byline given. Submit seasonal/holiday material 2 months in advance of issue date. Simultaneous, photocopied and previously published submissions OK. SASE. Reports in 4 weeks.
Nonfiction: General interest but some link to Kentucky-Indiana region almost mandatory; photo feature; and profile. Buys 52 mss/year. Query. Length: 1,500-3,000 words. Pays $100-300.
Photos: State availability of photos. Pays $15-25 for 10x12 b&w glossy prints and $20-40 for color transparencies. Captions required. Buys one-time rights.

Louisiana

NEW ORLEANS MAGAZINE, Box 26815, New Orleans LA 70186. (504)246-2700. Editor: Linda Matys. 50% freelance written. Monthly magazine; 125 pages. Circ. 37,000. Pays on publication. Buys first-time rights. Byline given. Submit seasonal/holiday material 4 months in advance. SASE. Reports in 3 weeks.
Nonfiction: General interest; interview and profile. Buys 3 mss/issue. Submit complete ms. Length: 1,200-3,000 words. Pays $100-500.
Photos: John Maher, art director. State availability of photos with ms. Captions required. Buys one-time rights. Model release required.

‡**SHREVEPORT**, Shreveport Chamber of Commerce, Box 20074, Shreveport LA 71120-9982. (318)226-8521. Editor: Mary L. Baldwin. *Shreveport* is a monthly city magazine reflecting life and interests of the people in the Ark-La-Tex area. "The magazine strives to offer its readership solid reporting on issues affecting the quality of life in the Ark-La-Tex and feature stories on interesting events, activities or people in the area. It is written for our well-educated, upper and middle income readership in the Ark-La-Tex. Circ. 5,000. Pays on publication. Byline given. Offers negotiable kill fee. Buys first North American serial rights. Submit seasonal/holiday material 3 months in advance. "Computer printout submissions, as long as they are legible, are fine." Prefer letter quality to dot matrix printouts. SASE. Reports in 6 weeks on queries; 2 months on mss. Sample copy $1.25 and $1.50 postage; free writer's guidelines.
Nonfiction: General interest, historical/nostalgic, humor, interview/profile, new product, photo feature, travel. Special issues include Housing Guide, Oil and Gas Industry Guide, Office Guide. Buys 60-72 mss/year. Query with clips or send mss for review. Length: 1,000-4000 words. Pays $50-125.
Photos: Send photos with ms. Pays $50-100 for color transparencies; $25-75 for 8x10 color prints. Captions, model release and identification of subjects required. Buys one-time rights.
Columns/Departments: Monthly departments include Potpourri, a listing of upcoming events in the area; Arts, stories of local theater, artists, opera, etc.; Commerce, a monthly economic report from the Center for Business Research at Louisiana State University in Shreveport and stories on business trends and timely developments; Cuisine, a review by food experts of an area restaurant; and Diversions, places to go after work hours. Buys 72-96 mss/year. Query with clips of published work or seed mss for review. Length: 500-2,000 words. Pays $50-125.
Fiction: Adventure, historical, horror, humorous, science fiction, suspense. No romance or erotica. Buys 8 mss/year. Send complete ms. Length: 700-2,000 words. Pays $75-125.
Tips: "We plan to add columns on travel, health, and history."

Maine

DOWN EAST MAGAZINE, Camden ME 04843. (207)594-9544. Editor: Davis Thomas. Emphasizes Maine people, places, events and heritage. Monthly magazine. Circ. 70,000. Pays on acceptance for text; on publication for photos. Buys first North American serial rights. Pays 15% kill fee. Byline given. Phone queries OK. Submit seasonal/holiday material 6 months in advance. SASE. Reports in 1 month. Sample copy $2; free writer's guidelines if SASE provided.
Nonfiction: Submit to Manuscript Editor. "All material must be directly related to Maine: profiles, biographies, nature, gardening, nautical, travel, recreation, historical, humorous, nostalgic pieces, and photo essays and stories." Recent article example: "Close Call on the Saco River" (March 1983). Buys 40 unsolicited mss/year. Length: 600-2,500 words. Pays up to $250, depending on subject and quality.
Photos: Purchases on assignment or with accompanying ms. Each photo or transparency must bear photographer's name. Captions required. Pays page rate of $50. Accepts 35mm color transparencies and 8x10 b&w. Also purchases single b&w and color scenics for calendars. Model release required.
Columns/Departments: Short travel (600- to 1,500-word, tightly written travelogs focusing on small geographic areas of scenic, historical or local interest); I Remember (short personal accounts of some incident in Maine, less than 1,000 words); and It Happened Down East (1- or 2-paragraph, humorous Maine anecdotes). Pay depends on subject and quality.
Tips: "We depend on freelance writers for the bulk of our material—mostly on assignment and mostly from those known to us; but unsolicited submissions are valued."

MAINE LIFE, Box 111, Freedom ME 04901. Editor: George Frangoulis. For readers of all ages in urban and rural settings. 50% of readers live in Maine; balance are readers in other states who have an interest in Maine. Published 6 times/year. Circ. 30,000. Pays on publication. Buys first rights. Sample copy $1.50. Submit seasonal/holiday material 4 months in advance. Reports in 1 month. SASE.
Nonfiction: Maine travel, home and garden, wildlife and recreation, arts and culture; Maine people, business,

energy and environment, some poetry and fiction. Query. Length: 500-2,000 words. Pays 5¢/word.
Photos: B&w and color slides purchased with or without accompanying ms. Captions required.

Maryland

BALTIMORE MAGAZINE, 131 E. Redwood St., Baltimore MD 21202. (301)752-7375. Editor: Stan Heuisler. Monthly magazine; 150 pages. Circ. 50,000. Pays on publication. Buys all rights. Offers 33⅓% kill fee for assigned articles. Byline given. Written queries OK. Submit seasonal/holiday material 4 months in advance. SASE. Reports in 6 weeks. Sample copy $2; free writer's guidelines.
Nonfiction: Expose, how-to, interview, profile and consumer guides. Must have local angle. "We do not want to see any soft, non-local features." Buys 7 mss/issue. Send complete ms or clips of published work. Length: 1,000-5,000 words. Pays $100-450.
Photos: State availability of photos with ms. Uses color and b&w glossy prints. Captions preferred.
Columns/Departments: Hot Stuff (local news tips); and Tips & Touts (local unusual retail opportunities). Query.

CHESAPEAKE BAY MAGAZINE, Suite 200, 1819 Bay Ridge Ave., Annapolis MD 21403. (301)263-2662. Editor: Betty D. Rigoli. 45% freelance written. *"Chesapeake Bay Magazine* is a regional publication for those who enjoy reading about the Bay and its tributaries. Our readers are yachtsmen, boating families, fishermen, ecologists—anyone who is part of Chesapeake Bay life." Monthly magazine; 64-72 pages. Circ. 15,000. Pays either on acceptance or publication, depending on "type of article, timeliness and need." Buys all or first North American serial rights. Submit seasonal/holiday material 3 months in advance of issue date. Simultaneous (if not to magazines with overlapping circulations) and photocopied submissions OK. Computer printout submissions OK; prefers letter quality to dot matrix printouts. SASE. Reports in 1 month. Sample copy $1.50; writer's guidelines for SASE.
Nonfiction: "All material must be about the Chesapeake Bay area—land or water." How-to (fishing, hunting, and sports pertinent to Chesapeake Bay); general interest; humor (welcomed, but don't send any "dumb boater" stories where common safety is ignored); historical; interviews (with interesting people who have contributed in some way to Chesapeake Bay life: authors, historians, sailors, oystermen, etc.); nostalgia (accurate, informative and well-paced. No maudlin ramblings about "the good old days"); personal experience (drawn from experiences in boating situations, adventures, events in our geographical area); photo feature (with accompanying ms); profile (on natives of Chesapeake Bay); technical (relating to boating, hunting, fishing); and Chesapeake Bay Folklore. "We do not want material written by those unfamiliar with the Bay area, or general sea stories. No personal opinions on environmental issues or new column (monthly) material and no rehashing of familiar ports-of-call (e.g. Oxford, St. Michaels)." Recent article example: "Tangier's Flying Doctor" (March 1983). Buys 25-40 unsolicited mss/year. Query or submit complete ms. Length: 1,000-2,500 words. Pays $50-85.
Photos: Virginia Leonard, art director. Submit photo material with ms. Uses 8x10 b&w glossy prints; pays $100 for 35mm, 2¼x2¼ or 4x5 color transparencies used for cover photos; $15/color photo used inside. Captions required. Buys one-time rights with reprint permission. Model release required.
Fiction: "All fiction must deal with the Chesapeake Bay, and be written by persons familiar with some facet of bay life." Adventure; fantasy; historical; humorous; mystery; and suspense. "No general stories with Chesapeake Bay superimposed in an attempt to make a sale." Buys 8 mss/year. Query or submit complete ms. Length: 1,000-2,500 words. Pays $50-85.
Poetry: Attention: Poetry Editor. Free verse or traditional. Must be about Chesapeake Bay. "We want well-crafted, serious poetry. Do not send in short, 'inspired' sea-sick poetry or 'sea-widow' poems." Buys 2/year. Limit submissions to batches of 4. Length: 5-30 lines. Pays $10-25. Poetry used on space available basis only.
Tips: "We are a regional publication entirely about the Chesapeake Bay and its tributaries. Our readers are true 'Bay' lovers, and look for stories written by others who obviously share this love. We are particularly interested in material from the Lower Bay (Virginia) area and the Upper Bay (Maryland-Delaware) area."

‡**MARYLAND MAGAZINE**, Department of Economic and Community Development, 2525 Riva Rd., Annapolis MD 21401. (301)269-3507. Editor: Bonnie Joe Ayers. Managing Editor: D. Patrick Hornberger. Quarterly magazine promoting the state of Maryland. Circ. 30,000. Pays on acceptance. Byline given. Offers 25% kill fee. Buys all rights. Submit seasonal/holiday material 1 year in advance. Photocopied submissions OK. SASE. Reports in 6 weeks. Sample copy $2.25; writer's guidelines for business size SAE and 1 first class stamp.
Nonfiction: General interest, historical/nostalgic, humor, interview/profile, photo feature, travel. Articles on any facet of Maryland life except conservation/ecology. No poetry, fiction or controversial material or any topic *not* dealing with the State of Maryland; no trendy topics, or one that has received much publicity elsewhere. Buys 32 mss/year. Query with clips or send complete ms. Length: 800-1,800 words. Pays $100-250.

Tips: "All sections are open to freelancers; however, tendency is to purchase more historically-oriented articles from freelancers. Thoroughly research your topic, give sources (when applicable)."

Massachusetts

BOSTON GLOBE MAGAZINE, *Boston Globe,* Boston MA 02107. Editor-in-Chief: Michael J. Larkin. 25% freelance written. Weekly magazine; 44 pages. Circ. 760,000. Pays on publication. Buys one-time rights. Submit seasonal/holiday material 3 months in advance. Reports in 2-4 weeks. Computer printout submissions OK. SASE must be included with ms or queries for return.
Nonfiction: Exposé (variety of issues including political, economic, scientific, medicine and the arts); interview (not Q&A); profile; and book excerpts (first serial rights only). No travelogues or personal experience pieces. Buys 65 mss/year. Query. Length: 3,000-5,000 words. Pays $500-750.
Photos: Purchased with accompanying ms or on assignment. Captions required. Send contact sheet. "Pays standard rates according to size used."

BOSTON MAGAZINE, Municipal Publications, 1050 Park Square Bldg., Boston MA 02116. Editor-in-Chief: John Brady. Monthly magazine. For upscale readers, eager to understand and participate in the best that New England has to offer; majority are professional, college-educated, and affluent. Pays on publication. Buys one-time rights. Pays 20% kill fee. Written queries mandatory. Submit seasonal/holiday material 5 months in advance. SASE. Reports in 3 weeks.
Nonfiction: Investigative reporting (subject matter varies); profiles (of Bostonians or New Englanders); business stories; first person accounts of personal experiences. Buys fewer than 10 unsolicited mss/year. Query Charles Matthews, articles editor. Length: 1,000-6,000 words. Pays $200-1,200; more for exceptional material. For short takes, brief items of interest in Boston or throughout New England to run in the "Reporter" section, query Ric Kahn. Pays 10-20¢/word.
Photos: Stan McCray, art director. B&w and color purchased on assignment only. Query. Specifications vary. Pays $25-150 for b&w; average $275 color.
Tips: "There are many freelance writers in the Boston area and we have a large group of regular contributing writers, so our need for freelance material from writers based outside the New England area is very slight indeed. Most of all, we look for stories that no one else in our region is doing, either because the subject or the treatment of it hasn't occurred to them, or because the writer has expertise that gives her or him a special insight into the story. A *Boston* story must have a strong and specific focus on Boston or New England, be solidly reported, and be of interest to a wide variety of readers."

‡**COUNTRY SIDE,** P.A. Benjamin & Co., Box 76, Northampton, MA 01061-0076. Editor: Paul A. Benjamin. Executive Editor: Susan M. Benjamin. Bimonthly magazine covering western Massachusetts and surrounding areas. Cir. 35,000. Pays on acceptance. Byline given. Offers 20% average kill fee. Buys first North American serial, one-time or all rights. Submit seasonal/holiday material 3 months in advance. Photocopied submissions OK; previously published submissions considered "on occasion." SASE. Reports in 1 month. Free writer's guidelines; sample copy $1.
Nonfiction: Michael R. Evans, managing editor. How-to, historical, humor, interview/profile, personal experience, agriculture, industry/business, recreation, art. Buys 2-5 mss/issue. Query or send complete ms. Length: 300-2,000 words. Pays 4-10¢/published word.
Photos: Neil F. Hammer, photo editor. Pays negotiable fees for 35mm color transparencies or 8x10 b&w glossy prints. Photos purchased with or without ms. Captions and credit lines required.
Columns/Departments: Michael R. Evans, managing editor. Oddities & Endings—short articles about the unusual and interesting in western Massachusetts. Length: 50-300 words. Pays $10.
Fiction: "Only well-written material focusing specifically on the western Massachusetts area will be considered. Humor welcome." Send complete ms. Length: 300-1,500 words. Pays 4-10¢/published word.
Tips: "All material must be of interest to readers in western Massachusetts. Find the hidden, intriguing piece we haven't heard about yet. Be concise, be sharp."

NEW BEDFORD/FALL RIVER, (formerly *Gloucester*), 5 S. 6th St., New Bedford MA 02740. Editor: Dee Giles Forsythe. Bimonthly magazine primarily focusing on southeastern Massachusetts. Pays within period of publication. Submit seasonal material 6 months in advance. Computer printout submissions OK. SASE. Reports in 1 month. Sample copy $1.50; free writer's guidelines.
Nonfiction: Social, political and natural history; biography and people profiles; environmental and other pertinent public policy issues; boating, commercial fishing, and other maritime-related businesses; the arts; education; lifestyles. Query editor. Length: 1,500-2,000 words. Pays approximately $100.
Photos: Prefers b&w glossy prints; will consider 35mm color transparencies. Pays on publication; negotiable fee. Captions and credit lines required.

Fiction: "This magazine occasionally runs short fiction up to 3,000 words. Such manuscripts should have some connection to the sea, to the coast, or to southern New England's history or character. No restrictions on style; the main criterion is quality. Query or send complete ms.

Tips: "We look for the unusual story or angle, the fresh approach, the review/assessment of complex issues. Avoid overwriting and turgid style; stories should be crisp, well-researched, lively and concise. We'd like to see more contemporary type pieces about events, issues or people in the southeastern Massachusetts and Rhode Island area with whom readers can identify."

WORCESTER MAGAZINE, Box 1000, Worcester MA 01614. (617)799-0511. Editor: Dan Kaplan. Emphasizes the central Massachusetts region. Weekly tabloid; 48 pages. Estab. October 1976. Circ. 48,000. Pays on acceptance. Buys all rights. Byline given. Submit seasonal/holiday material 2 months in advance. Simultaneous and photocopied submissions OK. SASE. Reports in 2 weeks. Sample copy $1; free writer's guidelines.
Nonfiction: Expose (area government, corporate); how-to (concerning the area, homes, vacations); interview (local); personal experience; opinion (local); and photo feature. No nonlocal stories. "We leave national and general topics to national and general publications." Buys 30 mss/year. Query with clips of published work. Length: 1,000-3,500 words. Pays $50-125.
Photos: State availability of photos with query. Pays $25-75 for b&w photos. Captions preferred. Buys all rights. Model release required.

Michigan

ANN ARBOR OBSERVER, Ann Arbor Observer Company, 206 S. Main, Ann Arbor MI 48104. Editors: Don and Mary Hunt. Monthly magazine featuring stories about people and events in Ann Arbor. Circ. 38,000. Pays on publication. Byline given. Buys one-time rights. Reports in 3 weeks on queries; 4 weeks on mss. Sample copy $1.
Nonfiction: Expose, historical/nostalgic, interview/profile, personal experience and photo feature. Buys 75 mss/year. Query. Length: 100-7,000 words. Pays up to $1,200/article.
Tips: "If you have an idea for a story, write us a 100-200 word description telling us why the story is interesting and what its major point is. We are most open to investigative features of up to 5,000 words. We are especially interested in well-researched stories that uncover information about some interesting aspect of Ann Arbor."

DETROIT MAGAZINE, *The Detroit Free Press*, 321 W. Lafayette Blvd., Detroit MI 48231. (313)222-6477. Editor: Ripley Hotch. For a general newspaper readership; urban and suburban. Weekly magazine. Circ. 771,000. Computer printout and disk submissions OK. Pays within 6 weeks of publication. Buys first rights. Kill fee varies. Byline given. Reports in 3-4 weeks. SASE.
Nonfiction: "Seeking quality magazine journalism on subjects of interest to Detroit and Michigan readers: lifestyles and better living, trends, behavior, health and body, business and political intrigue, crime and cops, money, success and failure, sports, fascinating people, arts and entertainment. *Detroit Magazine* is bright and cosmopolitan in tone. Most desired writing style is literate but casual—the kind you'd like to read—and reporting must be unimpeachable." Buys 65-75 mss/year. Query or submit complete ms. "If possible, the letter should be held to one page. It should present topic, organizational technique and writing angle. It should demonstrate writing style and give some indication as to why the story would be of interest to us. It should not, however, be an extended sales pitch." Length: 2,500 words maximum. Pays $125-300.
Photos: Purchased with or without accompanying ms. Pays $25 for b&w glossy prints or color transparencies used inside; $100 for color used as cover.
Tips: "Try to generate fresh ideas, or fresh approaches to older ideas. Always begin with a query letter and not a telephone call. If sending a complete ms, be very brief in your cover letter; we really are not interested in previous publication credits. If the story is good for us, we'll know, and if the most widely published writer sends us something lousy, we aren't going to take it."

GRAND RAPIDS MAGAZINE, Suite 1040, Trust Bldg., 40 Pearl St., NW, Grand Rapids MI 49503. (616)459-4545. Editor and Publisher: John H. Zwarensteyn. Managing Editor: John J. Brosky Jr. Monthly general feature magazine serving western Michigan. Circ. 12,000. Pays 15th of month of publication. Buys first-run exclusive rights. Phone queries OK. Submit seasonal material 3 months in advance. Photocopied and previously published submissions OK. Computer printout submissions OK. SASE. Reports in 2 months.
Nonfiction: Western Michigan writers preferred. Western Michigan subjects only: government, labor, education, general interest, historical, interview/profile, nostalgia. Inspirational and personal experience pieces discouraged. No breezy, self-centered "human" pieces or "pieces not only light on style but light on hard info." Humor appreciated, but specific to region. Buys 5-8 unsolicited mss/year. Query with clips or phone query. Length: 500-4,000 words. Pays $15-150.
Photos: State availability of photos. Pays $10+/5x7 glossy print and $22+/35 or 120mm color transparen-

cies. Captions and model release required.

Fiction: Stories set in Michigan only; "only works of western Michigan writers, please." Phone queries preferred. Buys 2 mss/year. Send complete ms. Length: 1,500-3,500 words. Pays $100.

Tips: "If you live here, see John Brosky before you write. If you don't, send a letter. Free cup of coffee to first 100 writers who say they saw this listing."

MICHIGAN: The Magazine of the Detroit News, 615 Lafayette, Detroit MI 48231. (313)222-2620. Articles Editor: David Good. Weekly rotogravure featuring the state of Michigan for general interest newspaper readers. Circ. 820,000. Average issue includes 4 feature articles, departments and staff written columns. Pays on publication. Byline given. Kill fee varies. Buys first Michigan serial rights. Phone queries OK. Computer printout submissions OK; prefers letter quality to dot matrix. Submit seasonal material 2 months in advance. Simultaneous and previously published submissions OK, if other publication involved is outside of Michigan. Reports in 3 weeks on queries; in 1 month on mss.

Nonfiction: Profiles, places, topics with Michigan connections. Buys 18 unsolicited mss/year. Recent article example: "Isle Royale's Watery Graves" (March 13, 1983). Query with clips of previously published work. Length: 750-3,000 words. Pays $100 minimum.

Photos: Pays $50 minimum/5x7 b&w glossy print. Pays $100-$250/35mm or larger color transparency. Captions required.

Tips: "In query be brief as possible and include writer's qualifications on subjects. Writing style is of primary importance, even more than the subject matter."

MONTHLY DETROIT MAGAZINE, Detroit Magazine Inc., 1404 Commonwealth Bldg., Detroit MI 48226. (313)962-2350. Editor: Mike Roberts. Emphasizes Detroit area for an audience of city and suburban residents. Monthly magazine; 136 pages. Circ. 50,000. Pays on publication. Buys first North American serial rights. Kill fee by negotiation only. Byline given. Written queries preferred. Submit seasonal/holiday material 3 months in advance. SASE. Reports in 2 weeks. Sample copy $2.25; free writer's guidelines.

Nonfiction: Features, guides, service pieces, investigations and nostalgia on Detroit history, institutions, politics, neighborhoods and profiles of important metro Detroiters or ex-Detroiters. Art, music and business columns. Recent article example: "Prehistoric Detroit—Life Was Simpler in 7000 BC." Query with clips of published work. Buys 50 unsolicited mss/year. Length: 200-5,000 words. Pays $50-1,000 or 10-20¢/published word for feature articles.

Tips: "We are more receptive to shorter pieces on music, arts and history from first-time freelancers. Query letters should be as specific as possible; the writer's point of view should be stated clearly; the style of the letter should mirror the style of the proposed article; the writer's credentials to do the piece should be spelled out."

‡**WEST MICHIGAN MAGAZINE**, West Michigan Telecommunications Foundation, 7 Ionia SW, Grand Rapids MI 49503. (616) 774-0204. Editor: Jeffrey Greene. Monthly magazine covering geographical region of west Michigan; "bulk of subscribers consists of members of local public television." Circ. 18,000. Pays on publication. Byline given. Not copyrighted. Buys one-time rights. Submit seasonal/holiday material 3 months in advance. Simultaneous queries, and photocopied and previously published submissions OK. SASE. Reports in 2 weeks on queries; 1 month on mss. Free sample copy and writer's guidelines.

Nonfiction: Expose (local government and politics); general interest (to west Michigan audience); historical/nostalgic; humor; interview/profile; personal experience; photo feature. "Articles should be written in a lively style reflecting the personality of the writer." Buys 36 mss/year. Query with published clips if available. Length: 500-2,000 words. Pays $50-200.

Photos: State availability of photos. Pays $10-20 for b&w contact sheet. Identification of subjects required.

Minnesota

MPLS. ST. PAUL MAGAZINE, Suite 400, 512 Nicollet Mall, Minneapolis MN 55402. (612)339-7571. Editor-in-Chief: Brian Anderson. Managing Editor: Marla J. Kinney. 90% freelance written. For "professional people of middle-to-upper-income levels, college educated, interested in the arts, dining and the good life of Minnesota." Monthly magazine. Circ. 44,000. Pays during month of publication. Buys negotiable rights. Pays 25% maximum kill fee. Byline given except for extremely short pieces and stories that require considerable rewriting. Submit seasonal/holiday material 4 months in advance. Computer printout submissions OK; prefers double-spaced and letter quality to dot matrix. SASE. Reports in 1 month.

Nonfiction: In-depth; informational; historical; local humor; interview; profile and photo feature. "We can use any of these as long as they are related to Minneapolis-St. Paul." Buys 10 unsolicited mss/year. Query. Length: 300-3,000 words. Pays $20-500.

Photos: Maureen Ryan, art director. Purchased on assignment. Query. Pays $25-200 for b&w; $40-400 for color.

Tips: Best way for freelancer to break in is by sending a "short people feature on a local and interesting person. I like short, to-the-point, even informal queries; I hate cute, beat-around-the-bush, detailed queries. I often suggest that the writer develop a lead, followed by a couple graphs saying where the story would go. If I want to read more after the lead, then so might our readers. Submission of a 300-500 word profile on spec. should be followed in a couple weeks by a phone call. If I send a ms back I usually make suggestions for improving or scrapping the piece. If improvements are made and I see potential in the writer, then I'll make an appointment to discuss the writer's ideas for future stories. He/she may get a larger assignment on spec. at this point."

ST. PAUL PIONEER PRESS, 55 E. 4th St., St. Paul MN 55101. (612)222-5011. Feature Editor: Russ Johnson. Sunday edition of daily newspaper. Circ. 250,000. Pays on publication. Byline given. Buys one-time rights. Submit seasonal/holiday material 3 months in advance. Simultaneous ("if outside our area") and previously published submissions ("if outside our area") OK. SASE. Reports in 2 weeks.
Nonfiction: "Especially looking for articles on travel in the Midwest." Buys 20 mss/year. Send complete ms. Length: 1,000-2,000 words. Pays $50-80.
Photos: Pays $50 maximum for 35mm color transparencies; $15 maximum for 8x10 b&w glossy prints. Captions required.

Mississippi

DELTA SCENE, Box B-3, Delta State University, Cleveland MS 38733. (601)846-1976. Editor-in-Chief: Dr. Curt Lamar. Business Manager: Ms. Sherry Van Liew. For an art-oriented or history-minded audience wanting more information (other than current events) on the Mississippi Delta region. Quarterly magazine; 32 pages. Circ. 1,000. Pays on publication. Buys one-time rights. Byline given. Submit seasonal/holiday material at least 4 months in advance. Simultaneous, photocopied and previously published submissions OK. SASE. Reports in 4 weeks. Sample copy $1.50.
Nonfiction: Historical and informational articles; interviews, profiles and travel articles; technical articles (particularly in reference to agriculture). "We have a list of articles available free to anyone requesting a copy." Buys 2-3 mss/issue. Query. Length: 1,000-2,000 words. Pays $5-20.
Photos: Purchased with or without ms, or on assignment. Pays $5-15 for 5x7 b&w glossy prints or any size color or transparency.
Fiction: Humorous and mainstream. Buys 1/issue. Submit complete ms. Length: 1,000-2,000 words. Pays $10-20.
Poetry: Traditional forms, free verse and haiku. Buys 1/issue. Submit unlimited number. Pays $5-10.
Tips: "The freelancer should follow our magazine's purpose. We generally only accept articles about the Delta area of Mississippi, the state of Mississippi, and South in general. We are sponsored by a state university so no articles, poetry, etc. containing profanity or other questionable material. Nonfiction has a better chance of making it into our magazine than short stories or poetry."

Missouri

MISSOURI LIFE, The Magazine of Missouri, Missouri Life Publishing Co., Suite 500, 1205 University Ave., Columbia MO 65201. (314)449-2528. Editor: Bill Nunn. Bimonthly magazine covering Missouri people, places and history. Circ. 30,000. Pays on publication. Byline given. Buys all rights; makes work-for-hire assignments. Submit seasonal/holiday 3 months in advance. Simultaneous queries, and simultaneous, photocopied, and previously published submissions OK. SASE. Reports in 4 weeks. Sample copy $3.50; writer's guidelines for business-size SAE and 1 first class stamp.
Nonfiction: General interest, historical/nostalgic, interview/profile, personal experience, photo feature, travel. Special issues planned for St. Louis, Kansas City and Lake of the Ozarks. Buys 35-40 mss/year. Query. Length: 1,200-3,000 words. Pays $50-100.
Photos: Gina Setser, photo editor. State availability of photos. Pays $10-25 for 2x2 color transparencies and 5x7 and 8x10 b&w prints. Identification of subjects required.
Columns/Departments: "Missouri Homes" tours of interesting houses and neighborhoods around the state; "Southland" stories from the southern part of the state; "Voices" profiles of interesting Missourians; "Eastside" St. Louis area stories; "Westside" Kansas City area stories. Buys 25-30 mss/year. Query. Length: 1,000-2,500 words. Pays $50-100.
Tips: "All sections of the magazine are open to writers. If the material has anything to do with Missouri, we're interested. Keep the writing unaffected and personal."

ST. LOUIS, 7110 Oakland Ave., St. Louis MO 63117. (314)781-8787. Editor: Greg Holzhauer. Monthly magazine "by, for, and about St. Louis exclusively." Circ. 50,000. Buys all and second serial (reprint) rights.

Buys 1-2 unsolicited/mss year. Pays on publication. Photocopied submissions OK. Submit seasonal material 4 months in advance. Reports on material in 1 month. Query or submit complete ms. SASE.
Nonfiction and Photos: "Articles on the city of St. Louis, personalities, arts, recreation, media, education, politics, timely issues, urban problems/solutions, environment, etc., always related to St. Louis area. Looking for informative writing of high quality, consistent in style and timely in topic." Informational, how-to, personal experience, humor, historical, think pieces, expose, nostalgia, personal opinion. Not interested in profiles of former St. Louisans and visiting celebrities, memoirs of growing up in St. Louis, or any material that is not exclusively and wholly about St. Louis. Length: 1,000 to 5,000 words. Pays $250-700 for 8x10 b&w glossy prints purchased on assignment. "Shooting fee plus $25 minimum print used. All color on individual basis."

Montana

MONTANA MAGAZINE, Box 5630, Helena MT 59604. (406)443-2842. Publisher: Rick Graetz. For residents of Montana and out-of-state residents with an interest in Montana. Bimonthly. Pays on publication. Byline given. Sample copy $1.25; free writer's guidelines. Reports in 8 weeks. Query. SASE.
Nonfiction and Photos: Articles on life in Montana; history, recreation. "How-to, where-to." Limited usage of material on Glacier and Yellowstone National Park. Prefers articles on less-publicized areas. Personalities, profile, think pieces, nostalgia, travel, history. Length varies. Pays $40-75 for short articles with b&w photos; $75-150 for larger articles and accompanying b&w photos. Photo size: 5x7 or 8x10.
Tips: "Know Montana—especially resource issues and geographic areas within the state."

Nebraska

OMAHA MAGAZINE, Omaha, The City Magazine, Inc., Suite 207, 8424 West Center Rd., Omaha NE 68124. (402)393-3332. Editor: Teri McCarthy. Emphasizes people, events and urban survival issues for Omahans active in their city's life. Monthly magazine. Circ. 12,000. Pays on publication. Buys first North American serial rights. Byline given. Phone queries OK. Submit seasonal/holiday material 3 months in advance. Simultaneous, photocopied and previously published submissions OK. SASE. Reports in 6 months. Sample copy $3; writer's guidelines for SASE.
Nonfiction: Expose (about local issues); general interest (local or native sons in these categories: entertainment, sports, lifestyle, people, arts, consumer, food, drink, politics, business, personal finance); historical (on assignment only—usually about Omaha); how-to (throw a party, cure boredom, improve quality of life—any topic, but should have specific local application); profile (of famous or controversial Omahans); travel (emphasis on destinations); and photo feature (local). Buys 5-7 mss/issue. Query with clips of published work. Length: 1,000-2,500 words. Pays $30-100.
Photos: State availability of photos or send samples with ms. Pays $25-75 for b&w contact sheets and negatives, and for color transparencies. Captions required. Buys one-time rights.

Nevada

NEVADA MAGAZINE, Carson City NV 89710. (702)885-5416. Editor-in-Chief: Caroline J. Hadley. Managing Editor: David Moore. 50% freelance written. Bimonthly magazine published by the state of Nevada to promote tourism in the state. Circ. 63,000. Pays on publication. Buys first North American serial rights. Byline given. Phone queries OK. Submit seasonal/holiday material 4 months in advance. SASE. Reports in 2 months. Sample copy $1; free writer's guidelines.
Nonfiction: Nevada topics only. Historical, nostalgia, photo feature, people profile, recreational and travel. "We welcome stories and photos on speculation." Buys 40 unsolicited mss/year. Submit complete ms. Length: 500-2,000 words. Pays $75-300.
Photos: Send photo material with accompanying ms. Pays $10-50 for 8x10 glossy prints; $15-75 for color transparencies. Captions required and name and address labeled. Buys one-time rights.
Tips: "Keep in mind that the magazine's purpose is to promote tourism in Nevada. Keys to higher payments are quality and editing effort (more than length). Send cover letter, no photocopy."

THE NEVADAN, *The Las Vegas Review Journal*, Box 70, Las Vegas NV 89101. (702)385-4241. Editor-in-Chief: A.D. Hopkins. 15% freelance written. For Las Vegas and surrounding small town residents of all ages "who take our Sunday paper—affluent, outdoor-oriented." Weekly tabloid; 16 pages. Circ. 100,000. Pays on publication. Buys one-time rights. Byline given. Phone queries OK. Submit seasonal/holiday material 2 months in advance of issue date. Photocopied and previously published submissions OK. SASE. Reports in 3 weeks. Free sample copy and writer's guidelines; mention *Writer's Market* in request.

Nonfiction: Historical (more of these than anything else, always linked to Nevada, southern Utah, northern Arizona and Death Valley); personal experience (any with strong pioneer Nevada angle, pioneer can be 1948 in some parts of Nevada). "We buy a very few contemporary pieces of about 2,400 words with good photos. An advance query is absolutely essential for these. No articles on history that are based on doubtful sources; no current show business material; no commercial plugs." Buys 52 mss/year. Query. Length: average 2,000 words (contemporary pieces are longer). Pays $50.

Photos: State availability of photos. Pays $10 for 5x7 or 8x10 b&w glossy prints; $15 for 35 or 120mm color transparencies. Captions required. Buys one-time rights.

Tips: "Offer us articles on little-known interesting incidents in Nevada history, and good historic photos. In queries come to the point. Tell me what sort of photos are available, whether historic or contemporary, black-and-white or color transparency. Be specific in talking about what you want to write."

New Hampshire

NEW HAMPSHIRE PROFILES, Profiles Publishing Co., 109 N. Main St., Concord NH 03301. Editor: David Minnis. (603)224-5193. All articles are for and about 25- to 49-year-old, up-scale consumer oriented reader, who wants to know more about the quality of life in New Hampshire. Magazine published monthly. Approximately 96 pages. Circulation, 25,000. Pays on publication. Buys one-time rights. Computer printout and disk submissions OK. SASE. Reports in 2 months. Sample copy $2; free writer's guidelines with SASE.

Nonfiction: Interview, opinion, profile, photo feature and interesting activities. Publishes social, political, economic and cultural articles for and about the State of New Hampshire and people who live in it. "We are interested in informative, entertaining articles addressing the cost of living and the quality of life in New Hampshire." Buys 7-8 mss/issue. Query with clips of published work. Length varies from 1,000-3,000 words, depending on subject matter. Pays $125-300.

Photos: State availability of photos. Pays $15-25 for b&w 5x7 or 8x10 glossy prints; $50-150 for 2¼x2¼ or 35mm color transparencies.

Tips: "Query before submitting ms and don't send us your only copy of the ms—photocopy it."

New Jersey

ATLANTIC CITY MAGAZINE, Menus International, Inc., 1637 Atlantic Ave., Atlantic City NJ 08401. Editor: Mary Johnson. For residents and tourists interested in Atlantic City. Monthly magazine; 120 pages. Circ. 50,000. Most work done on assignment; rarely purchases unsolited mss. Pays on publication. Buys one-time rights. Byline given. Submit seasonal/holiday ideas 4 months in advance. SASE. Reports in 4 weeks. Sample copy $2 plus postage.

Nonfiction: General interest, how-to, entertainment, business, photo feature, politics, and profile. "Articles should be related to southern New Jersey in general and Atlantic City in particular. We will especially need city-related profiles, trend pieces and investigative articles. No confession articles." Buys 28 mss/year. Query and/or send clips of published work. Length: 500-5,000 words. Pays $25-500.

Photos: State availability of photos. Buys b&w prints and color transparencies. Pay varies. Captions preferred.

Columns/Departments: Art, Business, Entertainment, Nature, Sports and Real Estate, plus more. Buys 75 articles/year. Query and/or send clips of published work. Length: 1,000-3,000 words. Pays $25-300.

Tips: "Story idea must have a local angle. Letter itself should be energetic. Very little nostalgia. Include samples of published work."

NEW JERSEY MONTHLY, 7 Dumont Place, Morristown NJ 07960. Editor-in-Chief: Colleen Katz. Managing Editor: David Sarasohn. 95% freelance written. Emphasizes New Jersey interests. Monthly magazine; 100-150 pages. Circ. 95,000. Pays on publication. Buys first North American serial rights. Submit seasonal/holiday material 4 months in advance. Prefers typed submissions but will accept computer printout if letter quality. SASE. Reports in 6 weeks.

Nonfiction: Politics (government or any institution in New Jersey); general interest (unusual or significant events, national trends with NJ implications, in-depth look at situations which define a community); how-to (service pieces must cover entire state; should concentrate on living the 'better' life at reasonable cost); profiles (people who are living and doing something in New Jersey—something that affects our readers, as opposed to someone who was born in New Jersey but hasn't lived here in years); and personal experience (only if it sheds light on something going on in the state). "We like articles that are well-written and that tell a *story*." Buys 4-6 mss/issue. Query. Length: 1,000-3,500 words. Pays $250-1,250.

Columns/Departments: Departments run shorter than articles and include sports, media, health, travel, profile, books, politics, arts, history, travel (within NJ), people, and others. Buys 8-10 mss/issue. Query. Length: 1,000 words. Pays $250.

Tips: To break into *New Jersey Monthly*, "either write an impressive query letter or begin supplying good items to our gossip section *The New Jersey Informer*, or better still, promise a good, statewide service piece."

‡**THE SANDPAPER, The Newsmagazine of Southern Ocean County**, The SandPaper, Inc., 1816 Long Beach Blvd., Surf City NJ 08008. (609)494-2034. Editor: Curt Travers. Managing Editor: Cathie Cush. Weekly tabloid (monthly in January and February) covering southern New Jersey shore life. "We aim our stories at the wide variety of residents and vacationers at the Jersey shore; we shoot for objectivity." Circ. 30,000. Pays on publication. Byline given. Buys all rights; makes work-for-hire assignments. Submit seasonal/holiday material 2 months in advance. SASE. Reports in 2 weeks on queries; 6 weeks on mss. Sample copy 50¢.

Nonfiction: Expose (local, county and state government, other area institutions, chemical companies, etc.); general interest (shore, south Jersey, sports, entertainment, news); historical/nostalgic (relating to coverage area); humor; interview/profile (colorful people, also business and government leaders who have impact on our area); opinion. "All must somehow relate to life in and around southern Ocean County/the Jersey shore." No first person. "Material must be focused. We don't need a story on fishing. We would use a story on how striped bass quotas have affected the Island's annual fishing tournament." Buys 50-75 mss/year. Query with published clips. Length: 1,200-2,000 words. Pays 2-5¢/word.

Photos: State availability of photos. Pays $4-50 for b&w negatives. Identification of subjects required. Buys one-time or all rights.

Columns/Departments: Currents (250-600 word news items, local looks at national events, discoveries, ironies and oddities). Can include fiction, poetry. "SpeakEasy—our guest column—is open to anyone and any subject (except erotica); views are the author's, not ours." Buys 40 mss/year. Send complete ms. Length: 500-2,000 words. Pays $15 maximum.

Fillers: Newsbreaks. Buys 10-20 mss/year. "Mostly staff-written." Length: 250-600 words. Pays 2-4¢/word.

Tips: "SpeakEasy is open to anyone. It's our version of an editorial page, so we like opinions (even if we don't agree). We also lean heavily toward humor in this section, especially if it relates to local or national news, trends, etc. Include biographical information. While we prefer to work with published writers, and we won't give an assignment to someone who doesn't have a proven track record, we have given quite a few aspiring writers a start."

New Mexico

NEW MEXICO MAGAZINE, Bataan Memorial Bldg., Santa Fe NM 87503. (505)827-2642. Editor: Richard Sandoval. Managing Editor: Scottie King. 75% freelance written. Emphasizes New Mexico for a college-educated readership, above average income, interested in the Southwest. Monthly magazine; 64-80 pages. Circ. 72,000. Pays on acceptance for mss; on publication for photos. Buys first North American serial or one-time rights for photos/compilation. Submit seasonal/holiday material 8 months in advance. SASE. Reports in 10 days to 4 weeks. Sample copy $1.75.

Nonfiction: "New Mexico subjects of interest to travelers. Historical, cultural, humorous, nostalgic and informational articles." No columns or cartoons, no non-New Mexico subjects. Buys 5-7 mss/issue. Query. Length: 500-2,000 words. Pays $50-300.

Photos: Purchased with accompanying ms or on assignment. Captions required. Query, or send contact sheet or transparencies. Pays $30-50 for 8x10 b&w glossy prints; $30-75 for 35mm; prefers Kodachrome; (photos in plastic-pocketed viewing sheets). Model release required. SASE.

Tips: "Send a superb short (500 words) manuscript on a little-known event, aspect of history or place to see in New Mexico. Faulty research will immediately ruin a writer's chances for the future. Good style, good grammar, please! No generalized odes to the state or the Southwest. No sentimentalized, paternalistic views of Indians or Hispanics. No glib, gimmicky 'travel brochure' writing."

New York

ADIRONDACK LIFE, 420 E. Genesse St., Syracuse NY 13202. Editor: Laurie Storey. Emphasizes the Adirondack region of New York State for a readership aged 30-60, whose interests include outdoor activities, history, and natural history directly related to the Adirondacks. Bimonthly magazine; 60 pages. Circ. 50,000. Pays on publication. Buys one-time rights. Pays 20% kill fee. Byline given. Submit seasonal/holiday material 4 months in advance. Previously published book excerpts OK. SASE. Reports in 4 weeks. Sample copy $1; free writer's guidelines.

Nonfiction: Outdoor recreation (Adirondack relevance only); how-to (should relate to activities and lifestyles of the region, e.g., managing the home woodlot); informational (natural history of the region); photo feature (Adirondack relevance required); profile (Adirondack personalities); and historical (Adirondacks only). Buys 24-28 unsolicited mss/year. Query. Length: 2,500-3,500 words. Pays $100-300.

Photos: Purchased with or without mss or on assignment. Captions required (Adirondacks locale must be identified). Submit contact sheet or transparencies. Pays $15 for 8x10 glossy, semi-glossy or matte photos; $30 for 35mm or larger color transparencies, $100 for covers (color only). Credit line given.

Tips: "Start with a good query that tells us what the article offers—its narrative line and, most importantly, its relevance to the Adirondacks, which is the essential ingredient in every article. We are especially interested in material reflecting qualities of life and recreation in 'the East's last wilderness.' "

‡**AVENUE**, 30 E. 60th St., New York NY 10022. (212)758-9516. Editor: Michael Shnayerson. Managing Editor: Lisa Grunwald. Monthly magazine (except January, July and August) covering Manhattan's Upper East Side. Circ. 72,000. Pays on publication. Byline given. Offers 50% kill fee. Buys first North American serial rights. Submit seasonal/holiday material 10 weeks in advance. SASE. Reports in 1 month. Sample copy $3; free writer's guidelines.

Nonfiction: Interview/profile. "Main need is for profiles of quietly influential Upper East Siders in business or the arts. Business profiles must be of major movers and shakers, corporate or entrepreneurial." Buys 90-100 mss/year. Query with clips. Length: 2,000-3,000 words. Pays $300 minimum.

Fiction: Gary Fisketjon, fiction editor. "Only the highest quality short stories with contemporary, likely urban settings." Buys 9 mss/year. Query with clips of published work. Length: 2,000-2,500 words. Pays $400 maximum.

BUFFALO SPREE MAGAZINE, Box 38, Buffalo NY 14226. (716)839-3405. Editor: Johanna V. Shotell. For "a highly literate readership." Quarterly. Circ. 20,000. Buys first serial rights. Buys 5-8 mss/year. SASE.

Nonfiction and Fiction: Department Editor: Gary Goss. "Intellectually stimulating prose exploring contemporary social, philosophical and artistic concerns. We are not a political magazine. Matters of interest to western New York make up a significant part of what we print." Length: 1,800 words maximum. Pays $75 for a lead article. "We print fiction, but it must be brilliant." Pays approximately $75.

Poetry: Department Editor: Janet Goldenberg. "Serious, modern poetry of nature and of man's relationship with nature interests us, provided it is of the highest quality." Pays approximately $20.

COUNTY LIFE, Radius Magazines Inc., 437 Ward Ave., Mamaroneck NY 10543. (914)698-0660. Editor: Evelyn Mertens. Senior Editor: Marcia Wofsey. Monthly leisure magazine about Westchester and Fairfield lifestyles. "We reach an upscale, over 30, mostly married, highly educated readership. Our articles are geared to the needs and interests of an affluent, successful audience." Estab. 1982. Circ. 50,000. Pays on publication. Byline given. Offers approximately 25% kill fee. Buys first North American serial rights. Submit seasonal/holiday material 4 months in advance. Simultaneous queries and photocopied submissions OK; previously published submissions OK "for travel, at times." SASE. Reports in 2 months on queries; 3 months on mss. Sample copy $1.50.

Nonfiction: General interest, historical/nostalgic, humor, interview/profile, photo feature, travel (within 300-mile radius of metropolitan area). No international travel, fiction or poetry. Query with clips of published work. Length: 100-300 words. Pays $25-300.

Photos: Tricia Nostrand, photo editor. State availability of photos. Pays $75-125 for 35mm color transparencies; $50-125 for 8x10 b&w prints. Identification of subjects required. Buys one-time rights.

Columns/Departments: Nancy Delli Paoli, column/department editor. Buys 48 items/year. Query. Length: 1,500-2,000 words. Pays $100-200.

Fillers: Anecdotes, short humor, newsbreaks (*must* be about Westchester or Fairfield). Buys 80/year. Length: 100-300 words. Pays $25.

Tips: "Looking for good ideas, talent. All areas open except restaurant and movie reviews. We are interested *only* in articles on Westchester, Fairfield and Long Island."

FOCUS, 375 Park Ave., New York NY 10022. (212)628-2000. Editor: Steven De Arakie. Managing Editor: Kristine B. Schein. Annual publication featuring a guide to New York City and to New York shops for hotel guests and New York residents. Circ. 250,000. Pays on acceptance. Buys one-time rights. Phone queries OK. Sample copy $1.50.

Nonfiction: "We want reviews of antique shops, art galleries, home furnishing stores, women's shops, men's shops and restaurants. The writer must interview an owner and write a description to be approved by the owner. This is all done on assignment." Buys 120 mss/issue. Query with clips of previously published work. Length: 110 words minimum. Pays $35 minimum.

HUDSON VALLEY MAGAZINE, Box 425, Woodstock NY 12498. (914)679-5100. Editor: Joanne Michaels. Monthly. Circ. 26,000. Pays on publication. Byline given. Buys first North American serial rights,

one-time rights and second serial (reprint) rights. Submit seasonal/holiday material 3 months in advance. Simultaneous submissions OK. Computer printout or disk submissions OK. SASE. Reports in 1 month on queries.
Nonfiction: Joanne Michaels, articles editor. Book excerpts; general interest; historical/nostalgic (Hudson Valley); how-to (home improvement); interview/profile (of area personalities); photo feature; travel. No fiction or personal stories. Length: 1,500-2,000 words. Query. Pays $20-50.
Photos: State availability of photos. Reviews 5x7 b&w prints. Captions required.
Fillers: Short humor. Buys 3-6/year. Length: 500-1,000 words. Pays $10-25.

NEW BROOKLYN, Motivational Communications, 207 W. 21st St., New York NY 10011. (212)260-0800. Editor and Publisher: Barry V. Conforte. Managing Editor: Tom Bedell. Quarterly magazine covering locally oriented general-interest topics for residents of Brooklyn. Circ. 35,000. Pays on publication. Byline given. Pays average 50% kill fee. Buys first North American serial rights. Written queries only. SASE. Reports in 1 month. Sample copy $2.50; writer's guidelines for SASE.
Nonfiction: Historical; humor; interview/profile (of prominent Brooklyn personalities, business); the arts; survey pieces; health; home; community services; shopping sprees. "We're looking for light, upbeat, feature pieces of local interest. We want to present a positive image of Brooklyn. No fiction or poetry, and no topics without a link to the borough. We don't want to see any more 'I remember growing up in Brooklyn . . . ' stories." Buys 50 mss/year. Query. Length: 1,200 words minimum. Pays $50.
Photos: State availability. Pays $35 when used with ms. B&w only; color covers are assigned.
Fillers: What's New (products, events, services, whatever—items of interest to Brooklynites). Length: 250 words maximum. Pays $5.

NEW YORK AFFAIRS, Urban Research Center, New York University, 4 Washington Square N, New York NY 10003, (212)598-2984. Editor: Dick Netzer. Emphasizes urban problems. "Readers tend to be academics, public officials, corporation presidents and intellectual types." Quarterly magazine; 128 pages. Circ. 5,000. Pays on publication. Buys all rights. Phone queries OK. Photocopied submissions OK. SASE. Reports in 1 month. Sample copy $3; free writer's guidelines.
Nonfiction: Michael Winkleman, executive editor. Expose; interview (figures who are key to urban policymaking); and personal opinion. Buys 8 mss/year. Query. Length: 3,000-7,500 words. Pays $50-200. "We also have a section for short articles (250-3,000 words) called 'Side Streets' in which we run what is good about cities—humor especially. Most of our authors are academics whom we don't pay. For those whom we can't afford to pay, which includes authors of most articles and Side Streets, we pay in copies of the magazine."
Columns/Departments: Book reviews. "We don't pay reviewers. They just get to keep the book." Uses 30 pages/year. Query.
Tips: "We are looking for hard-hitting, well-written articles on general urban problems. We especially like articles that take the unconventional approach—that transit fares should be raised, or that the cost of welfare should *not* be picked up by the federal government."

NEW YORK MAGAZINE, News Group Publications, Inc. 755 2nd Ave., New York 10017. (212)880-0700. Editor: Edward Kosner. Managing Editor: Laurie Jones. Emphasizes the New York metropolitan area. Weekly magazine. Queries preferred. Pays on acceptance. Submit seasonal/holiday material 2 months in advance. Photocopied submissions OK. SASE. Reports in 1 month.
Nonfiction: Expose, general interest, interview, profile, behavior/lifestyle, health/medicine, local politics, entertainment. Pays $500-1,500.

THE NEWSDAY MAGAZINE, *Newsday*, Long Island NY 11747. (516)454-2308. Editor: Robert Keeler. Managing Editor: Stanley Green. For well-educated, affluent suburban readers. Weekly. Circ. 600,000. Buys all rights. Byline given. Pays on publication. Query. Computer printout or disk submissions OK. SASE.
Nonfiction and Photos: Graphics Director: Miriam Smith. "We buy only a limited number of freelance pieces, usually when the freelancer has a specific expertise or point of view that isn't available on *Newsday*'s own staff." No poetry or fiction. Length: 2,000-2,500 words. Pays $400-600. B&w contacts and 35mm transparencies purchased on assignment. Pays $100/page maximum for b&w; $200/page maximum for color, including cover.

OUR TOWN, East Side/West Side Communications Corp., Suite 202, 1751 2nd Ave., New York NY 10028. (212)289-8700. Editor: Kalev Pehme. Weekly tabloid covering neighborhood news of Manhattan (96th St.-14th St.). Circ. 110,000. Pays on publication. Byline given. Buys all rights. Submit seasonal/holiday material 1 month in advance. SASE.
Nonfiction: Expose (especially consumer ripoffs); historical/nostalgic (Manhattan, 14th St.-96th St.); interview/profile (of local personalities); photo feature (of local event); and animal rights. "We're looking for local news (Manhattan only, mainly 14th St.-96th St.). We need timely, lively coverage of local issues and events, focusing on people or exposing injustice and good deeds of local residents and business people. (Get *full*

names, spelled right!)" Special issues include Education (January, March and August); and Summer Camps (March). Query with clips of published work. Length: 1,000 words maximum. Pays "70¢/20-pica column-inch as published."
Photos: Pays $2-5 for 8x10 b&w prints. Buys all rights.
Tips: "Come by the office and talk to the editor. (Call first.) Bring samples of writing."

STATEN ISLAND, Motivational Communications, 207 W. 21st St., New York NY 10011. Editor/Publisher: Barry V. Conforte. Managing Editor: Tom Bedell. Quarterly magazine covering locally-oriented, general interest topics for residents of Staten Island. Circ. 25,000. Pays on publication. Byline given. Pays average 50% kill fee. Buys first North American serial rights. Written queries only. SASE. Reports in 1 month. Sample copy $2.50; writer's guidelines for SASE.
Nonfiction: Historical; humor; interview/profile (of prominent Staten Islanders or businesses); the arts (survey pieces); health; home; in-service pieces (schools, hospitals, public institutions); and shopping sprees. Also needs light feature pieces of local interest. "No fiction, poetry or nostalgia, and no topics without a link to the borough." Buys 50 mss/year. Query. Length: 1,200 words minimum. Pays $50.
Photos: State availability of photos. Pays $35 for b&w when used with ms; color covers by assignment only.
Fillers: What's New (products, services, events or whatever, of interest to Staten Islanders). Length: 250 words maximum. Pays $5.
Tips: "We also publish *New Brooklyn Magazine* and *QC: The Magazine of Queens County*. Editorial needs for these quarterlies are the same as for *Staten Island*, except for changes in reference to the particular borough."

SUBURBIA TODAY, Gannett Newspapers, One Gannett Dr., White Plains NY 10604. (914)694-5024. Editor: Neil S. Martin. Weekly Sunday supplement of the Gannett Westchester Rockland Newspapers. Estab. 1981. Circ. 200,000. Pays on publication. Buys one-time rights. Submit seasonal/holiday material 3 months in advance. Simultaneous queries, and simultaneous ("out of circulation area") and previously published submissions OK. SASE. Reports in 2 weeks.
Nonfiction: General interest (lifestyle); historical (well-written local area history); interview/profile (of well-known and less well-known personalities); and trends. Special issues include: June—summer activities; October—house design; November—jewelry and diamonds; and December—sight and sound. Buys 25 mss/year. Query with clips of published work. Length: 1,000-4,000 words. Pays $100-300.
Photos: "Most photos are taken by newspaper staff photographers." State availability of photos. Pay is open.
Tips: "We'd like to hear from specialty writers in fashion, home furnishings, leisure activities and home entertainment."

THE SUN, Eastern Suffolk Sun Corp., Bridge St., Sag Harbor NY 11963. (516)537-3474. Editor: Phyllis Stewart. Managing Editor/Features: Mary Cummings. Managing Editor/News: Patrick Boyle. Weekly newspaper. Estab. 1982. Circ. 10,000. Pays on publication. Byline given. Buys one-time rights. Simultaneous queries and previously published submissions OK. SASE. Reports in 1 month.
Nonfiction: General interest, interview/profile, opinion. No humor. Query with or without clips. Length: 250-2,000 words. Pays $25-125.

‡SYRACUSE MAGAZINE, The Syracuse Magazine, Inc., 205 S. Townsend St., Syracuse NY 13202. (315)475-7249. Editor: Marilyn Holstein. Associate Editor: J.P. Powers. Monthly magazine of Syracuse and Central New York for "above average income readers in managerial and professional positions." Circ. 12,000. Pays "within 30 days after publication." Byline given. Buys first North American rights. Submit seasonal/holiday material 3 months in advance. Simultaneous queries, and simultaneous and photocopied submissions OK. Computer printout and disk (compatible with TRS 80 Model 3) submissions OK. Reports in 3 weeks. Free sample copy and writer's guidelines.
Nonfiction: Expose (local issues); general interest; humor; interview/profile (local personalities); new product (if local); opinion; personal experience; photo feature. Not interested in ideas that do *not* concern Syracuse. Buys 120 mss/year. Query with clips. Length: 300-3,000 words. Pays $200 maximum.
Photos: Robert Pike, photo editor. State availability of photos. Reviews contact sheets. Captions, model release and identification of subjects required. Buys one-time rights.
Columns/Departments: Cityscape (trends and talk in town); Sports Shorts (local sports scene); Lively Arts (arts scene); Dining Out (local restaurant and food trends). Buys 50 mss/year. Query with clips of published work or send complete ms. Length: 800-1,500 words. Pays negotiable rates.
Tips: "We need experienced writers who are familiar with Central New York to write feature articles. Query with article ideas; do not call. Increases in our editorial budget should prove beneficial to the writer."

UPSTATE MAGAZINE, *Democrat and Chronicle*, 55 Exchange St., Rochester NY 14614. (716)232-7100. Editor: Mary Rita Kurycki. Assistant Editor: Susan Martin. Art Director: Kate Weisskopf. A Sunday magazine appearing weekly in the Sunday *Democrat and Chronicle*. A regional magazine covering topics of local interest, written for the most part by area writers. Circ. 230,000. Pays on publication. Byline given. Buys first

North American serial rights. Submit seasonal/holiday material 3 months in advance. SASE. Reports in 6-8 weeks.

Nonfiction: Investigative; general interest (places and events of local interest); historical/nostalgic; humor; interview/profile (of outstanding people in local area); personal experience; photo feature (with local angle); and travel (regional). Buys 150-200 mss/year. Query. Length: 1,000-3,000 words. Pays $60-325. Do not send fiction or fillers.

North Carolina

CAROLINA LIFESTYLE, including *Tarheel* and *Sandlapper*, Cygnet Communications, 121 College Pl., Norfolk VA 23510. (804)625-4800. Editor: Susan Spence. Monthly magazine covering North and South Carolina for well-educated, upper income area residents. Estab. 1982. Circ. 35,000. Pays on publication. Byline given. Buys all rights. Submit seasonal/holiday material 3 months in advance. Photocopied submissions OK. Queries preferred. SASE. Reports in 1 month.
Nonfiction: Interview/profile (of outstanding local residents); travel (in North and South Carolina); food; business. Buys 50 mss/year. Query with clips of published work or send complete ms "on speculation." Length: 750-2,000 words minimum. Pays 10¢/word.
Photos: State availability of photos. Pays negotiable rates for b&w and color transparencies and b&w prints.

CHARLOTTE MAGAZINE, Box 221269, Charlotte NC 28222. (704)375-8034. Editor: Catherine Osborne. Emphasizes probing, researched and upbeat articles on local people and local places. Monthly magazine. Circ. 10,000. Pays 30 days after publication. Buys first rights. SASE. Reports in 3 weeks. Sample copy $2.25.
Nonfiction: Departments: lifestyles (alternative and typical); business (spotlight successful, interesting business and people); town talk (short, local articles of interest); theater, arts. No PR promos. "We are seeking articles indicating depth and research in original treatments of subjects. Our eagerness increases with articles that give our well-educated audience significant information through stylish, entertaining prose and uniqueness of perspective. Remember our local/regional emphasis." Query or send complete ms. Length: 1,500-2,500 words. Pays $150-250 for feature articles.
Photos: State availability of photos. Buys b&w and color prints; pay negotiable. Captions preferred; model releases required.
Columns/Departments: "Will consider all types of articles." Buys 6 columns/issue. Query. Length: 1,000-2,000 words. Pays $75-150.
Fillers: Anecdotes, newsbreaks, and Carolina consumer bargains. Buys 6-8/issue. Length: 250-500 words. Pays 5¢/word.

THE NEWS AND OBSERVER, 215 S. McDowell St., Raleigh NC 27514. (919)829-4572. Editor: Claude Sitton. Managing Editor: Bob Brooks. Daily newspaper in research triangle area and eastern North Carolina. Circ. 135,000 daily; 170,000 Sunday. Pays on publication. Byline given. Buys simultaneous rights. Submit seasonal/holiday material 1 month in advance. Simultaneous queries, and simultaneous and photocopied submissions OK. SASE. Reports in 2 weeks on queries; 1 month on mss. Sample copy for 9x12 SAE and 4 first class stamps.
Nonfiction: Owen Davis, features editor. Interview/profile, travel. Send complete ms. Length: 1,200-1,500 words. Pays $35-60.
Photos: Send photos with ms. Pays $5 minimum for 8x10 b&w prints. Identification of subjects required. Buys "right to use as we see fit in news pages."

SOUTHERN EXPOSURE, Box 531, Durham NC 27702. (919)688-8167. Contact: Editor. For Southerners interested in "left-liberal" political perspective and the South; all ages; well-educated. Magazine; 72-230 pages. Bimonthly. Circ. 7,500. Buys all rights. Pays kill fee. Byline given. Buys 20 mss/year. Pays on publication. Will consider photocopied and simultaneous submissions. Submit seasonal material 2-3 months in advance. Reports in 1-2 months. "Query is appreciated, but not required." SASE.
Nonfiction and Photos: "Ours is probably the only publication about the South *not* aimed at business or the upper-class people; it appeals to all segments of the population. *And*, it is used as a resource—sold as a magazine and then as a book—so it rarely becomes dated." Needed are investigative articles about the following subjects as related to the South: politics, energy, institutional power from prisons to universities, women, labor, black people and the economy. Informational interview, profile, historical, think articles, expose, opinion and book reviews. Length: 6,000 words maximum. Pays $50-200. "Very rarely purchase photos, as we have a large number of photographers working for us." 8x10 b&w preferred; no color. Payment negotiable.
Fiction and Poetry: "Fiction should concern the South, e.g., black fiction, growing up Southern, etc." Buys

6 short stories or plays/year. Length: 6,000 words maximum. Pays $50-200. All forms of poetry accepted, if they relate to the South, its problems, potential, etc. Length: open. Pays $15-100. Buys 24 poems/year.

THE STATE, *Down Home in North Carolina*, Box 2169, Raleigh NC 27602. Editor: W.B. Wright. Monthly. Buys first rights. Sample copy $1 (for postage and handling). Pays on acceptance. Deadlines 1 month in advance. SASE.

Nonfiction and Photos: "General articles about places, people, events, history, nostalgia, general interest in North Carolina. Emphasis on travel in North Carolina; (devote features regularly to resorts, travel goals, dining and stopping places)." Will use humor if related to region. Length: average of 1,000-1,200 words. Pays $15-50, including illustration. B&w photos. Pays $3-20, "depending on use."

Ohio

BEND OF THE RIVER® MAGAZINE, 143 W. Third St., Box 239, Perrysburg OH 43551. (419)874-7534. Publishers: Christine Raizk Alexander and R. Lee Raizk. For readers interested in Ohio history, antiques, etc. Monthly magazine. Circ. 1,500. Buys one-time rights. Byline given. Buys 50-60 mss/year. Pays on publication. No photocopied or simultaneous submissions. Submit seasonal material 2 months in advance; deadline for holiday issue is October 15. Reports in 1 month. Submit complete ms. SASE. Sample copy 50¢.

Nonfiction and Photos: "We deal heavily in Ohio history. We are looking for well-researched articles about local history and modern day pioneers, doing the unusual. We'd like to see interviews with historical (Ohio) authorities; travel sketches of little-known but interesting places in Ohio; grass roots farmers; preservation. Nostalgic pieces will be considered. Our main interest is to give our readers happy thoughts and good reading. We strive for material that says 'yes' to life, past and present." No personal reflection or nostalgia. Buys 60 unsolicited mss/year. Length: 1,500 words. Pays $5-15. Purchases b&w photos with accompanying mss. Pays $1 minimum. Captions required.

Tips: "Any Toledo-area, well-researched history will be put on top of the heap! Send us any unusual piece that is either cleverly humorous, divinely inspired or thought provoking. We like articles about historical topics treated in down-to-earth conversational tones. We pay a small amount (however we're now paying more) but usually use our writers often and through the years. We're loyal." Recent article subject: the Apple Festival in Bryan, Ohio.

THE BLADE TOLEDO MAGAZINE, 541 Superior St., Toledo OH 43660. (419)245-6121. Editor: Sue Stankey. General readership. Weekly magazine; 32 pages. Circ. 210,000. Pays on publication. Buys one-time rights. Byline given. Phone queries OK. Submit seasonal/holiday material 6 months in advance. Simultaneous, photocopied and previously published submissions OK. SASE.

Nonfiction: Historical (about northwestern Ohio); informational; interview; personal·experience; and photo feature. Buys 1 ms/issue. Query. Length: 600-2,000 words. Pays $35-150.

Photos: Photos purchased with accompanying ms. Captions required. Pays $15-30 for 8x10 b&w glossy prints; $10-45 for 35mm, 2¼x2¼ or 8x10 color glossy prints. Total purchase price for ms includes payment for photos. Model release required.

Tips: "Stories should pertain to our circulation area: Toledo, northwestern Ohio and southern Michigan."

CINCINNATI MAGAZINE, Suite 900, 617 Vine St., Cincinnati OH 45202. (513)721-3300. Editor: Laura Pulfer. Emphasizes Cincinnati living. Monthly magazine; 88-120 pages. Circ. 28,000. Pays on acceptance. Buys all rights. Pays 33% kill fee. Byline given. Submit seasonal/holiday material 3 months in advance. Simultaneous, photocopied and previously published submissions OK. SASE. Reports in 3-5 weeks.

Nonfiction: How-to; informational; interview; photo feature; profile; and travel. No humor. Buys 4-5 mss/issue. Query. Length: 2,000-4,000 words. Pays $150-400.

Photos: Kay Walker, art director. Photos purchased on assignment only. Model release required.

Columns/Departments: Travel; How-To; Sports and Consumer Tips. Buys 5 mss/issue. Query. Length: 750-1,500 words. Pays $75-150.

Tips: "It helps to mention something you found particularly well done. It shows you've done your homework and sets you apart from the person who clearly is not tailoring his idea to our publication. Send article ideas that probe the whys and wherefores of major issues confronting the community, making candid and in-depth appraisals of the problems and honest attempts to seek solutions. Have a clear and well-defined subject about the city (the arts, politics, business, sports, government, entertainment); include a rough outline with proposed length; a brief background of writing experience and sample writing if available. We are looking for critical pieces, smoothly written, that ask and answer questions that concern our readers. We do not run features that are 'about' places or businesses simply because they exist. There should be a thesis that guides the writer and the reader. We want balanced articles about the city—the arts, politics, business, etc."

COLUMBUS DISPATCH SUNDAY MAGAZINE, 34 South 3rd St., Columbus OH 43216. (614)461-5250. Editor: Carol Ann Lease. 50% freelance written. Buys one-time rights. Byline given. Payment after publication. Computer printout or disk submissions OK; prefers letter quality to dot matrix printouts. SASE.
Nonfiction: "We accept offerings from beginning writers, but they must be professionally written. A good picture helps." Strong Ohio angle preferred. No history without a modern tie-in. Buys illustrated and non-illustrated articles. Length: 1,000-3,000 words. Pays $50-250. B&w photos only. Pays $10 maximum/photo.

COLUMBUS MONTHLY, 171 E. Livingston Ave., Columbus OH 43215. (614)464-4567. Editorial Director: Lenore E. Brown. Emphasizes subjects of general interest primarily to Columbus and central Ohio. Monthly magazine. Pays on publication. Buys all rights. Byline given. SASE. Reports in 1 month. Sample copy $2.65.
Nonfiction: "We want general articles which relate specifically to Columbus or central Ohio area." No humor, essays or first-person material. Buys 6 mss/issue. Query. "I like query letters which: 1. are well-written; 2. indicate the author has some familiarity with *Columbus Monthly*; 3. give me enough detail to make a decision; 4. include at least a basic bio of the writer." Buys 4-5 unsolicited mss/year. Length: 100-4,500 words. Pays $15-400.
Photos: State availability of photos. Pay varies for b&w or color prints. Model releases required.
Columns/Departments: Art, Business, Food and Drink, Movies, Politics, Sports and Theatre. Buys 2-3 columns/issue. Query. Length: 1,000-2,000 words. Pays $100-175.
Tips: "It makes sense to start small: something for our "Around Columbus" section, perhaps. Stories for that section run between 400-1,000 words." Recent article subjects: "Halle's, an off-again, on-again Columbus department store chain; and the issue of firing tenured faculty at OSU in times of financial problems."

DAYTON MAGAZINE, Dayton Area Chamber of Commerce, 1980 Kettering Tower, Dayton OH 45423. (513)226-1444. Editor: Fred Bartenstein. Bimonthly magazine covering the Dayton area and its people; "promotes the community through an honest editorial approach." Circ. 10,000. Pays on publication. Byline given. Buys first rights. Submit seasonal/holiday material 4 months in advance. SASE. Reports in 2 months. Sample copy for SAE and $1.50 postage.
Nonfiction: General interest; historical/nostalgic; how-to; humor; interview/profile; opinion; photo feature. "Must relate to Dayton area." No articles lacking local appeal or slant. Buys 36 mss/year. Query with clips of published work. Length: 1,400-3,000 words.
Photos: Send photos with ms. Payment "depends on feature." Reviews b&w and color contact sheets and color transparencies. Captions, model release and identification of subjects required. Buys one-time rights.
Columns/Departments: Buys 60 mss/year. Query with clips of published work. Length: 750-1,000 words.

THE MAGAZINE, 4th and Ludlow Sts., Dayton OH 45401. (513)225-2360. Editor: Ralph A. Morrow. Sunday supplement. Circ. 225,000. Byline given. Pays on publication. Usually reports in 2 weeks. SASE.
Nonfiction and Photos: Magazine focuses on people, places, trends. No first-person or essays. Emphasis is on color transparencies supplemented by stories. No travel. Length: open. Photos should be glossy. *"The Daily News* will evaluate articles on their own merits. Likewise with photos. Average payment per article: $125." Payments vary depending on quality of writing and photos.

OHIO MAGAZINE, Ohio Magazine, Inc., Subsidiary of Dispatch Printing Co., 40 S. 3rd St., Columbus OH 43215. Editor-in-Chief: Robert B. Smith. Managing Editor: Ellen Stein. Emphasizes news and feature material of Ohio for an educated, urban and urbane readership. Monthly magazine; 96-156 pages. Circ. 71,215. Pays on publication. Buys all rights, second serial (reprint) rights, or one-time rights. Pays 20% kill fee. Byline given "except on short articles appearing in sections." Submit seasonal/holiday material 2 months in advance. Simultaneous, photocopied and previously published submissions OK. SASE. Reports in 8 weeks. Free writer's guidelines.
Nonfiction: Features: 2,000-8,000 words. Pays $250-700. Cover pieces $600-850; Ohioana and Ohioans (should be offbeat with solid news interest; 50-250 words, pays $15-50); Short Cuts (on Ohio or Ohio-related products including mail ordering and goods or people that perform a service that are particularly amusing or offbeat; 100-300 words, pays $15-20); Ohioguide (pieces on upcoming Ohio events, must be offbeat and worth traveling for; 100-300 words, pays $10-15); Diner's Digest ("we are still looking for writers with extensive restaurant reviewing experience to do 5-10 short reviews each month in specific sections of the state on a specific topic. Fee is on a retainer basis and negotiable"); Money (covering business-related news items, profiles of prominent people in business community, personal finance—all Ohio angle; 300-1,000 words, pays $50-250); and Living (embodies dining in, home furnishings, gardening and architecture; 300-1,000 words, pays $50-250). "Send submissions for features to Robert B. Smith, editor-in-chief, or Ellen Stein, managing editor; Short Cuts, Living Ohioguide and Diner's Digest to Maryann Reilly, services editor; and Money to Ellen Stein, managing editor. No political columns and articles of limited geographical interest (must be of interest to all of Ohio). Buys 40 unsolicited mss/year.
Columns & Departments: Sports, Last Word, Travel, Fashion, and Wine, to Ellen Stein. Open to suggestions

for new columns/departments.

Photos: Lisa Griffis, art director. Rate negotiable.

Tips: "Freelancers should send a brief prospectus prior to submission of the complete article. All articles should have a definite Ohio application." Recent article examples: "Mound Builders" (February 1983); "Floods" (March 1983).

Oklahoma

‡**OKLAHOMA TODAY,** Oklahoma Department of Tourism and Recreation, Box 53384, Oklahoma City OK 73152. (405)521-2496. Editor: Sue Carter. Assistant Editor: Kate Jones. Quarterly magazine covering travel and recreation in the state of Oklahoma. "We are interested in showing off the best Oklahoma has to offer; we're serious about our travel slant, and will only very occasionally carry an article that is not travel oriented." Circ. 30,000. Pays on acceptance. Byline given. Offers 50% kill fee. Submit seasonal/holiday material 1 year in advance "depending on photographic requirements." Simultaneous queries and photocopied submissions OK. "We don't mind letter quality computer printout submissions at all—provided they are presented in ms format; that is, double spaced and on 8½x11 sheets, or a size pretty close to that. No scrolls, please." Reports in 6 weeks. Sample copy $1.75; free writer's guidelines.

Nonfiction: Book excerpts (pre-publication only, on Oklahoma topics); photo feature, travel (in Oklahoma). "We are a specialized market; no straight history or first-person reminiscences or fashion, memoirs—though just about any topic can be used if given a travel slant. Occasionally will use a well-done personality profile." Buys 25-30 mss/year. Query with clips. Length: 1,000-1,500 words. Pays $150-250.

Photos: High-quality color transparencies, b&w prints. "We are especially interested in developing contacts with photographers who either live in Oklahoma or have shot here. Send samples and price range." Free photo guidelines. Send photos with ms. Pays $50-100 for b&w and $50-250 for color; reviews 2¼ and 35mm color transparencies. Model release, identification of subjects and other information for captions required. Buys one-time rights plus right to use photos for promotional purposes.

Tips: "The best way to become a regular contributor to *Oklahoma Today* is to query us with one or more story ideas, each developed to give us an idea of your proposed slant. Clips from other publications should be included. If they've been heavily edited for good or ill, we'd appreciate seeing both the original and the published versions."

TULSA MAGAZINE, Box 1620, Tulsa OK 74101. (918)582-6000. Editor: Larry Silvey. Audience is primarily medium- to upper-income-level Tulsans. Monthly. Circulation: 6,000. Byline given. Pays on publication. Sample copy $1. Deadlines are at least 8 weeks prior to publication date, the second Monday of each month. Reports immediately. Query; "indicate name, address and phone number; specific story suggestions or types of stories you prefer; and sample of writing for style and clarity." Computer printout submissions OK; prefers letter quality to dot matrix. SASE.

Nonfiction and Photos: Articles must revolve around people or how subject affects people and must have a Tulsa area slant. Style desired is informal and lively. Length: 1,000-4,000 words. Payment is negotiable, $50-175, depending on length and research. Photos usually taken by staff or on assignment. May be purchased with mss.

Tips: "Give me an in-depth, well-researched article on a social problem facing the city of Tulsa—something we haven't already seen in the newspapers a half-dozen times. We do not print fashion or society news unless it is really out-of-the-ordinary. We prefer articles that are issue-oriented, but we are a Chamber of Commerce publication and are somewhat limited in the stands we can take."

TULSA WORLD, Box 1770, Tulsa OK 74102. (918)581-8300. Executive Editor: Bob Haring. Sunday Magazine Editor: David Averill. Sunday magazine of daily newspaper, covering travel. Pays on publication. Buys one-time rights. Simultaneous and previously published submissions OK. SASE. Reports in 3 weeks "if rejected."

Nonfiction: General interest (features); interview/profile (of Oklahoma people making good elsewhere); and travel ("lean toward locally produced material on exotic or nearby destinations"). No fiction or first-person pieces. Buys 15 mss/year. Send complete ms. Length: 300-500 words; 600-1,200 words for general-interest features and interview/profiles. Pays $75-225.

Photos: Pays $30 for any size b&w glossy prints; $50 for color transparencies or prints. Captions required.

Oregon

CASCADES EAST, 716 NE 4th St., Box 5784, Bend OR 97708. (503)382-0127. Editor: Geoff Hill. 90% freelance written. For "all ages as long as they are interested in outdoor recreation in Central Oregon: fishing, hunting, sight-seeing, hiking, bicycling, mountain climbing, backpacking, rockhounding, skiing, snowmobiling, etc." Quarterly magazine; 48 pages. Circ. 6,000 (distributed throughout area resorts and motels and to subscribers). Pays on publication. Buys all rights. Byline given. Submit seasonal/holiday material 6 months in advance of issue date. SASE. Reports in 6 weeks. Sample copy $1.50.

Nonfiction: General interest (first-person experiences in outdoor Central Oregon—with photos, can be dramatic, humorous or factual); historical (for feature, "Little Known Tales from Oregon History," with b&w photos); and personal experience (needed on outdoor subjects: dramatic, humorous or factual). "No articles that are too general, sight-seeing articles that come from a travel folder, or outdoor articles without the first-person approach." Buys 20-30 unsolicited mss/year. Query. Length: 1,000-3,000 words. Pays 3-7¢/word.

Photos: "Old photos will greatly enhance chances of selling a historical feature. First-person articles need black and white photos, also." Pays $6-12 for b&w; $15-50 for color transparencies. Captions preferred. Buys one-time rights.

Tips: "Submit stories a year or so in advance of publication. We are seasonal and must plan editorial for summer '84 in the spring of '83, etc., in case seasonal photos are needed."

Pennsylvania

ERIE & CHAUTAUQUA MAGAZINE, (formerly *Erie Magazine*), Charles H. Strong Building, 1250 Tower Lane, Erie PA 16505. (814)452-6070. Editor: Gerry B. Wallerstein. Bimonthly magazine covering Erie County, Pennsylvania and Chautauqua County, New York for upscale readers with above-average education and incomes. Circ. 20,000. Pays $35/published page for all rights upon publication. Will reassign rights to author upon written request after publication. Reports in 2-4 weeks. SASE. Sample copy $1.50; free writer's guidelines for SASE.

Nonfiction: Feature articles (usually four per issue) on "key issues affecting our coverage area, lifestyle topics, major projects or events which are of importance to our readership, area history with relevance to life today, preservation and restoration, arts and cultural subjects." Also profiles, humor and satire. Length: 2,500 words maximum for articles; 750 words maximum for personality profiles, humor and satire.

Photos: Color photos for covers by assignment only to local photographers. Will consider 8x10 b&w glossies with stories. Pays $10 per b&w photo for all rights upon publication. Model release and captions required.

Columns/Departments: Business, education, social life, arts and culture, sports and medicine items written by contributing editors. Length: 750 words maximum.

THE INQUIRER MAGAZINE, (formerly *Today Magazine*), *Philadelphia Inquirer*, Box 8263, Philadelphia PA 19101. Editor: David Boldt. Managing Editor: Carolyn White. Sunday magazine section for city and suburban readers. Weekly. Circ. 1,050,000. Pays on publication. Buys first North American serial rights. Submit seasonal/holiday material 3 months in advance of issue date. Photocopied submissions OK. Computer printout and disk submissions OK. SASE. Reports in 2 months. Free sample copy.

Nonfiction: "Most of our material is written by freelance writers. Major feature articles generally run 3,000-7,000 words. Also buy some shorter articles (500-1,000 words) for the *Our Town* section, and, occasionally short humorous articles with local angle. We use mainly articles that consist of reporting on, and analysis of, local issues and personalities. Blatant bias in favor of local writers." Buys 20-30 mss/year. Query. Pays $400-500 for major articles from first-time contributors.

Tips: "Query should have high-impact idea, evidence of an effective writing style, clear concept of story structure and reporting plan, with good clips. We will be increasingly selective and will increase what we pay for what we want." Recently published examples: "The Day the H-Bomb Hit Philadelphia," by Michael Schwartz and "The Rearming of Philadelphia," by Jack Smith.

PHILADELPHIA MAGAZINE, 1500 Walnut St., Philadelphia PA 19102. Editor: Ron Javers. For sophisticated middle- and upper-income people in the Greater Philadelphia/South Jersey area. Monthly magazine. Circ. 140,000. Buys first rights. Pays 20% kill fee. Byline given. Buys 50 mss/year. Pays on publication, or within 2 months. Free writer's guidelines for SASE. Reports in 4 weeks. Queries and mss should be sent to Ben Vagoda, articles editor. SASE.

Nonfiction: "Articles should have a strong Philadelphia focus, but should avoid Philadelphia stereotypes—we've seen them all. Lifestyles, city survival, profiles of interesting people, business stories, music, the arts, sports, local politics, stressing the topical or unusual. No puff pieces. We offer lots of latitude for style, but before you make like Norman Mailer, make sure you have something to say." Length: 1,000-7,000 words. Pays $100-1,000.

PITTSBURGH MAGAZINE, Metropolitan Pittsburgh Public Broadcasting, Inc., 4802 5th Ave., Pittsburgh PA 15213. (412)622-1360. Editor-in-Chief: Randy Rieland. "The magazine is purchased on newsstands and by subscription and is given to those who contribute $25 or more a year to public TV in western Pennsylvania."

Monthly magazine; 100 pages. Circ. 56,700. Pays on publication. Buys all rights. Pays kill fee. Byline given. Submit seasonal/holiday material 6 months in advance. SASE. Reports in 6 weeks. Sample copy $2; free writer's guidelines.

Nonfiction: Expose, lifestyle, sports, humor, informational, service, interview, nostalgia, personal experience, personal opinion and profile. No historical features, humorous or first-person material. Query or send complete ms. Length: 2,500 words. Pays $50-500.

Photos: Purchased with accompanying ms or on assignment. Captions required. Uses b&w and color. Query for photos. Model release required.

Columns/Departments: Art; books; films; dining; health; and sports. "All must relate to Pittsburgh or western Pennsylvania."

Tips: "Possible new columns coming."

THE PITTSBURGH PRESS, 34 Blvd. of Allies, Pittsburgh PA 15230. (412)263-1100. Features Editor: Louis J. Laurenzi. For general newspaper readers. Publishes 3 weekly magazines. Circ. 700,000. Not copyrighted. Byline given. Buys 10-20 mss/year. Pays on publication. Reports usually in 2 weeks. Submit complete ms. Computer printout submissions OK. SASE.

Nonfiction and Photos: Picture-oriented material for the *Roto Magazine*; family type stories for *Family Magazine*. Must be local subjects or those of good general interest. Informational, how-to, personal experience, profile, inspirational, humor, historical and nostalgia. No first-person fluff. Pays $40 minimum for features. Some additional payment for b&w and color photos used with mss.

Tips: "Submit good copy. We prefer receiving the actual manuscripts rather than suggestions for stories. We base our judgment on the whole content. We might decide in the future to accept only mss of local interest."

SUSQUEHANNA MONTHLY MAGAZINE, Susquehanna Times and Magazine, Inc., Box 75A, R.D.1, Marietta PA 17547. (717)426-2212. Editor: Richard S. Bromer. Monthly magazine about regional Lancaster County, Pennsylvania, for people in the upper middle socio-economic level who are college educated, aged 25-60, home and family and community oriented, and interested in local history and customs. Circ. 6,000. Pays on publication. Buys all rights. Phone queries OK. Submit seasonal material 2 months in advance. Simultaneous and photocopied submissions OK. Computer printout submissions OK; prefers letter quality to dot matrix. SASE. Reports in 2 months. Sample copy $2 in advance.

Nonfiction: General interest (history, business, agriculture, arts); historical (local events and personalities); nostalgia; and technical. "This material must have a special relationship to the area we cover: Lancaster County and nearby areas in Southeast Pennsylvania." No shallow, "cute," humorous, or "personal" material. Buys 60 mss/year. Send complete ms. Length: 750-2,500 words. Pays $35-75.

Photos: Offers no additional payment for photos accepted with ms. Captions preferred; model release required.

Fiction: "We use very little fiction. We would accept only if there is an obvious regional relationship."

Poetry: "We would only use if there were an obvious regional relationship."

Tips: "Read several copies of *Susquehanna Magazine* to get a feel for our style and preferred material. Write up fresh material or fresh approach to old material, e.g., historical incidents. We accept 'class' material only (informative, intellectually stimulating, accurate)—nothing trite or 'term paper.' "

South Carolina

‡**GREENVILLE MAGAZINE**, Greenville Magazine, Inc., Box 8695, Greenville SC 29604. (803)232-2380. Editor: Susan Ferguson. Monthly magazine edited for decision makers and consumers in Greenville, Spartanburg and surrounding areas. Estab. 1981. Circ. 10,000. Pays on publication. Byline given. Buys all rights. Submit seasonal/holiday material 2 months in advance. Photocopied submissions OK. SASE. Reports in 1 month. Sample copy $1.50; free writer's guidelines.

Nonfiction: Expose (investigative material); general interest; historical/nostalgic; interview/profile; photo feature; travel (seasonal). "Emphasis is on local interest events, culture, history, business and people." Buys 100 mss/year. Query with clips. Length: open. Pays $35-75.

Photos: Send photos with ms. Pays $5 maximum for 5x7 b&w prints. Captions and identification of subjects required.

Columns/Departments: Film review, book review, recipes, craft, financial, real estate (local slant). Buys 50 mss/year. Query with clips of published work. Length: open. Pays $25-50.

Fiction: "We don't, as a general rule, accept fiction." Buys 1 mss/year. Query with clips of published work. Length: open. Pays $25-50.

Fillers: Length: open. Pays $15-25.

Tennessee

MEMPHIS, Towery Press, Box 370, Memphis TN 38101. (901)345-8000. Executive Editor: Kenneth Neill. Circ. 20,000. Pays on publication. Buys all rights. Pays $35 kill fee. Byline given. Phone queries OK. Simultaneous, photocopied and previously published submissions OK. SASE. Reports in 6 weeks. Sample copy $1.50.
Nonfiction: Expose, general interest, historical, how-to, humor, interview and profiles. "Virtually all our material has strong Memphis connections." Buys 25 unsolicited mss/year. Query or submit complete ms or clips of published work. Length: 1,500-5,000 words. Pays $75-500.
Tips: "The kinds of manuscripts we most need have a sense of story (i.e., plot, suspense, character), an abundance of evocative images to bring that story alive and a sensitivity to issues at work in Memphis. Tough investigative pieces would be especially welcomed."

MID SOUTH MAGAZINE, *Commercial Appeal*, 495 Union Ave., Memphis TN 38101. (901)529-2111. Editor: Karen Brehm. Sunday newspaper supplement. Circ. 260,000. Pays after publication. Byline given. Buys one-time rights. Simultaneous queries, and photocopied and previously published submissions (if so indicated) OK. SASE. Reports in 3 weeks.
Nonfiction: General interest (with regional tie-in). Buys 12 mss/year. Query with clips of published work. Length: 1,500-2,000 words. Pays $100.
Photos: State availability of photos. Reviews color transparencies and 5x7 b&w glossy prints. "Photos are paid for with payment for ms." Buys one-time rights.
Columns/Departments: Viewpoints (political background, economic commentary, psychological issues, social issues). Buys 50 mss/year. Send complete ms. Length: 1,500-2,000 words. Pays $100.

Texas

AUSTIN LIVING, Baker Publications, Suite 207, 1805 Rutherford Lane, Austin TX 78754. (512)837-3534. Publication Director: Tina Stacy. Bimonthly magazine for newcomers and prospective homebuyers in the Austin area. Circ. 40,000. Pays on acceptance. Byline given. Buys all rights. Submit seasonal/holiday material 4 months in advance. Simultaneous queries and photocopied and previously published submissions OK. SASE. Reports in 1 week. Free sample copy; writer's guidelines for 1 business size SAE and 1 first class stamp.
Nonfiction: "Interior decorating, housing trends, financing, home building—anything of interest to home buyers or people relocating to Austin." Buys 12 mss/year. Query. Length: 2,000 words maximum. Pays 20¢/word.
Photos: State availability of photos. Pays $6 for 5x7 or 8x10 b&w glossy prints. Captions and model release required.
Tips: "National assignments on decorating, financing, etc., for all of Baker's city magazines are made by Tina Stacy, publication director." Pays 20¢/word.

D MAGAZINE, Southwest Media Corp., Suite 1200, 3988 N. Central Expressway, Dallas TX 75204. Editor: Lee Cullum. 40% freelance written. For readers in the Dallas-Fort Worth area; primarily the middle to upper income group. Monthly magazine. Circ. 70,000. Buys all rights. Pays on publication. Offers 25% kill fee on assigned stories. Byline given. Submit seasonal/holiday material 3 months in advance. Photocopied submissions OK. Computer printout and disk submissions OK; prefers letter quality to dot matrix printouts. SASE. Reports in 1 month. Sample copy $2.
Nonfiction: Informational; political; profile; travel; and business. No fiction or personal confessions. Buys 2-3 mss/issue. Query. Length: 750-4,000 words. Pays $100-1,000.
Photos: Photos purchased with accompanying ms or on assignment. Pays $25-150 for 8x10 b&w glossy prints; $50-150 for color transparencies. Model release required.
Columns/Departments: Previews (arts, entertainment, books, movies, and concert reviews); Inside Dallas (business and gossip); Dining (reviews); and Windfalls (special products and services). "All pieces must relate to Dallas and the Fort Worth area." Open to suggestions for new columns/departments.
Tips: "We want better quality writing."

DALLAS/FORT WORTH LIVING, Baker Publications, Suite 400, 5757 Alpha Rd., Dallas TX 75240. (214)239-2399. Publication Director: Tina Stacy. Bimonthly magazine covering housing and relocation for persons in the market for houses, apartments, townhouses and condominiums. Circ. 80,000. Pays on publication. Byline given. Buys all rights. Submit seasonal/holiday material 4 months in advance. Simultaneous queries OK. SASE. Reports in 6 weeks. Free sample copy; writer's guidelines for business size SAE and 1 first class stamp.
Nonfiction: How-to (decorate); new product (local "discoveries"); and technical (energy-saving devices/

methods). Buys 30 mss/year. Query with clips of published work "that show flexibility of writing style." Length: 1,000-3,000 words. Pays 20¢/word.
Photos: State availability of photos. Pays negotiable fee for color transparencies and 8x10 b&w glossy prints. Identification of subjects required. Buys all rights.
Columns/Departments: Luxury Living (customizing a new or old home). Query with clips of published work. Length: 1,000 words minimum. Pays 10¢/word.
Tips: "National assignments on decorating, financing, etc. for all of Baker's city magazines are made by Tina Stacy, publication director. Query her at *Living*, Suite 400, 5757 Alpha Rd., Dallas TX 75240."

DALLAS LIFE MAGAZINE, Sunday Magazine of *The Dallas Morning News*, Belo Corporation, Communications Center, Dallas TX 75265. (214)745-8432. Editor: Betty Cook. Weekly magazine. "We are a lively, topical, sometimes controversial city magazine devoted to informing, enlightening and entertaining our urban sunbelt readers with material which is specifically relevant to Dallas lifestyles and interests." Circ. 351,000. Pays on "scheduling." Byline given. Buys first North American serial rights or simultaneous rights. Submit seasonal/holiday material 3 months in advance. Simultaneous queries and simultaneous submissions OK ("if not competitive in our area"). Computer printout submissions OK; prefers letter quality to dot matrix. SASE. Reports in 1 month on queries; 6 weeks on mss. Sample copy $1.
Nonfiction: Exposé ("anything Dallas-related that is fully substantiated"); general interest; how-to (home, shelter and garden); humor (short); interview/profile; new product (for the home and garden). "We look for an exciting style in short, lively, fresh material that is written to indulge the reader rather than the writer. All material must, repeat *must*, have a Dallas metropolitan area frame of reference." Special issues include: Spring and fall home furnishings theme issues. Buys 15-25 unsolicited mss/year. Query with clips of published work or send complete ms. Length: 750-2,000 words. Pays $75-500.
Photos: State availability of photos. Pays $15-25 for b&w contact sheets; and $25-150 for 35mm or larger color transparencies. Captions, model release, and identification of subjects required. Buys one-time rights.
Tips: "We are focusing sharply on upwardly mobile, achievement-oriented readership in 25-45 age range."

DALLAS MAGAZINE, Dallas Chamber of Commerce, 1507 Pacific Ave., Dallas TX 75201. (214)954-1390. Editor: D. Ann Shiffler. Emphasizes business and other topics of interest to Dallas upper income business people. Monthly magazine; 84 pages. Circ. 20,000. Pays on acceptance. Buys all rights. Pays 100% kill fee "but kill fee is not offered on stories where quality is poor or editor's directions are not followed." Byline given. Submit seasonal/holiday material 3 months in advance. Photocopied submissions OK. SASE. Reports in 1 month. Sample copy $1.50.
Nonfiction: General interest (of interest to successful work-oriented men and women); historical (only on Dallas); humor (rarely accepted, but will use exceptional articles); interview (of Dallas executive or Dallas resident in an important government job or the like); profile (same as interview); and business features. "We do not want stories that underestimate our readers. Controversies involving technique or practices, not people, can be acceptable." Business issues are explored with solutions offered where appropriate. "We prefer not to see general information on such items as cooking, etc. unless the subject and/or article can be related to the Dallas business scene." Buys 3-5/mss issue. Query with "an outline that reflects preliminary research." Length: 1,000-2,500 words. Pays $100-250.
Photos: State availability of photos. Pays $75-200 for 8x10 b&w glossy prints; $75-200 for color transparencies. Captions required.
Columns/Departments: Portraits (see "interview" above); enterprise (profile of a local company and its new product, new program, new approach, etc.); ideas (how-to/self-help for business executives at work or at leisure); reviews (includes traditional cultural topics, but also critical reviews of business practices or activities).

EL PASO TODAY MAGAZINE, El Paso Chamber of Commerce, 10 Civic Center Plaza, El Paso TX 79901. (915)544-7880. Editor: Russell S. Autry. Monthly magazine "takes a positive look at El Paso people and area activities. Readers are owners and managers of El Paso businesses." Circ. 5,000. Pays on publication. Byline given. Buys first North American serial rights. Submit seasonal/holiday material 3 months in advance. Simultaneous queries and simultaneous and photocopied submissions OK. Computer printout and disk submissions OK. SASE. Reports in 3 weeks on queries; 4 weeks on mss. Free sample copy and writer's guidelines.
Nonfiction: General interest, historical/nostalgic, interview/profile, photo feature. Buys 100 mss/year. Query with clips of published work. Length: 1,000-2,500 words. Pays $100-200.
Photos: Send photos with ms. Pays $10/photo; $100 for cover photo. Captions, model releases and identification of subjects required. Buys one-time rights.
Tips: "We are actively seeking feature writers and have increased our freelance budget 7 times in the last few years."

HOUSTON CITY MAGAZINE, Southwest Media Corp., 315 W. Alabama, Houston TX 77006. (713)526-3399. Publisher: Lute Harmon. Editor: David R. Legge. Managing Editor: Ann Powell. Monthly magazine for highly upscale audience. Circ. 60,000. Pays on acceptance. Byline given. Offers 25% kill fee. Buys first

North American serial rights. Reports in 1 week. Sample copy $1.75; free writer's guidelines.
Nonfiction: Book excerpts, interview/profile (Houston angle), photo feature—have Houston or Texas angle. No poetry, religion or fiction. Buys 35-40 mss/year. Query. Length: 1,200-5,000 words. Pays $500-2,000.
Photos: Elizabeth Robben, photo editor. State availability of photos. Captions, model release and identification of subjects required. Buys one-time rights.
Columns/Departments: Attention: David R. Legge. Health, food, travel, books. Buys 36 mss/year. Query. Length: open. Pays $300-400.

HOUSTON LIVING, Baker Publications, Suite 450, 5444 Westheimer, Houston TX 77056. (713)626-2812. Publication Director: Tina Stacy. Bimonthly magazine covering housing for newcomers and other prospective home buyers in the Houston area. Circ. 80,000. Pays on acceptance. Byline and brief bio given. Buys all rights. Submit seasonal/holiday material 4 months in advance. Simultaneous queries, and photocopied and previously published submissions OK. SASE. Reports in 1 month. Free sample copy; writer's guidelines for business size SAE and 1 first class stamp.
Nonfiction: "Articles should be slanted toward buying a home. We want to run solid articles on trends, specifically slanted for the Houston area market." Buys 6 mss/year. Query with clips of published work. Length: 500-1,500 words. Pays 20¢/word (of 3 or more letters).
Photos: State availability of photos. Reviews any size b&w glossy prints.
Tips: "The writer should demonstrate lively, informative style and personal qualifications for writing on the subject. National assignments on decorating, financing, etc., for all of Baker's city magazines are made by Tina Stacy, publication director. Payment is 20¢/word. Query her at: Living, 5757 Alpha Rd., Suite 400, Dallas TX 75240."

SAN ANTONIO MAGAZINE, Greater San Antonio Chamber of Commerce, Box 1628, San Antonio TX 78296. (512)229-2108. Editor: Alice Costello. Emphasizes business and quality of life articles about San Antonio. Monthly magazine; 88 pages. Pays on publication. Buys all rights. Photocopied submissions OK. SASE. Reports in 1 month. Free sample copy and writer's guidelines.
Nonfiction: "The magazine's purpose is to tell the story of San Antonio, its businesses and its people, primarily to the membership of the Greater San Antonio Chamber of Commerce to the San Antonio community and to prospective businesses and industries. No material about the Alamo, cowboys and Indians, or any non-San Antonio topic." Buys 65 mss/year. Query or send complete ms, "query should be readable, typed and give me an element of the story, as well as some idea of the person's writing ability." Length: 800-3,000 words. Pays $75-300.
Photos: Purchased with mss or on assignment. Captions required. Query. Pays $10-25 for 8x10 b&w glossy prints. Prefers to pay according to the number of photos used in an article, a bulk rate.
Tips: "The best way to break in is to be a resident of San Antonio and, therefore, able to write on assignment or to query the editor personally. Again, we are looking for material which is related to the city of San Antonio, its people, and the business community. We consider all possible angles and tie-ins. We like to see writers who can tie national economic or business events to San Antonio and support information with figures."

‡SAN ANTONIO MONTHLY, San Antonio Publishing Corp., Box 17554, San Antonio TX 78217. (512)732-6142. Editor: Tom Bell. Associate Editor: Elizabeth Boyd. Monthly city lifestyle magazine for San Antonio metropolitan area and surrounding vicinities. Estab. 1981. Circ. 10,000. Pays on publication. Byline given. Offers negotiable kill fee. Buys first rights. Submit seasonal/holiday material 3 months in advance. Simultaneous queries, and simultaneous and previously published submissions OK. SASE. Reports in 1 month. Free sample copy.
Nonfiction: Book excerpts (Texan); expose; general interest; historical/nostalgic; interview/profile (local politicians or personalities); photo feature; travel; business, sports (with local angle); film reviews. Special issues include December, gift guide; February, spring fashion; March, annual restaurant guide; April, Fiesta guide; May, travel; August, fall fashion; September, theater guide. No "personality profiles and business articles that are all fluff and no depth. Give us an opinion, *please.*" Buys 24 mss/year. Query with published clips. Length: 500-3,500 words. Pays $25-250.
Photos: Larry Broom, art director. State availability of photos. Reviews b&w contact sheet, color transparencies and 8x10 b&w prints. Identification of subjects required. Buys one-time rights.
Columns/Departments: Sports (local only); Business (entrepreneurs, national companies based in San Antonio); What's News (short news articles on political and city issues, comments on events and personalities). Buys 24 mss/year. Query with published clips or send complete ms. Length: 250-2,500 words. Pays $25 (What's News)-75.
Tips: "Editorial features in *San Antonio Monthly* reflect a city of changing attitudes and lifestyles. As the city grows—both physically and population-wise—so does the market; our readers are middle- to upper-income, educated people, both 'new' and 'old' San Antonians. They turn to *San Antonio Monthly* to keep tap on what's changing in the city; where the city is headed, who's taking it there, and why. The best way for a freelancer to start writing for us is to bring us an *idea.* Or, several ideas. Telling us that you'd 'love to write just anything' for

us does not impress us. Instead, write us about a story idea for What's News or a department (Business or Sports are wide open) with some preliminary research. Then, follow up with a phone call, and if we like the idea, we'll have you in to talk about it. We welcome queries from freelancers, but they must be specific.''

TEXAS WEEKLY MAGAZINE, *Pasadena Citizen*, Box 6192, Pasadena TX 77506. (713)477-0221. Editor: Dick Nichols. Sunday supplement to *Pasadena Citizen*, *Clear Lake Citizen* and *Weekend Journal* (Friendswood-Pearland) emphasizing regional features. Circ. 22,500. Pays on publication. Byline given. Not copyrighted. Buys one-time rights. Submit seasonal/holiday material 2 months in advance. Simultaneous queries, and simultaneous and photocopied submissions OK. Computer printout and disk submissions OK. SASE. Reports in 2 weeks. Sample copy for 8½x11 SAE.
Nonfiction: General interest, historical/nostalgic, interview/profile. "Stories on interesting people, mainly Texas-based, greater Houston area." No poetry or fiction. Query with clips of published work, if available.
Photos: State availability of photos. "We like stories with photos. One, we like longer stories, with at least two 35mm color slides, one for the cover a vertical, one for inside either vertical or horizontal, and two to five b&w prints to accompany the article. We pay $100 flat fee for a turnkey story like this. Or, for our inside features, a shorter story with two or three b&w photos, we pay $50 flat." Captions and identification of subjects required.

ULTRA MAGAZINE, Farb Publications, Inc., Suite 200, 2000 Bering Dr., Houston TX 77057. (713)961-4132. Editor: Wendy Haskell Meyer. Monthly magazine about Texas and Texans targeted to affluent Texans. Subjects covered include: people, fashion, travel, the arts, food and wine, design interiors, entertainment and social events, all of which must have a strong Texas slant. Circ. 95,000. Pays on acceptance. Byline given. 25% kill fee on assignments not used. Submit material 4 months in advance. Do not submit simultaneous queries. SASE. Reports in 2-3 weeks. Sample copy $4; writer's guidelines for business size SAE and 1 first class stamp.
Nonfiction: General interest, interview/profile, photo features, fashion features. No fiction, poetry, investigative or political stories. Buys 60 mss/year. Query with resume and clips of published works. Length 250-2500 words. Pays minimum 20¢/word. Travel stories must have photos or state availability of photos.
Columns: Texas people and events, profiles, food and wine, the arts, homes, health, beauty, fashion, jewelry and real estate.

WESTWARD, *Dallas Times-Herald*, 1101 Pacific, Dallas TX 75202. Editor: David Eden. Weekly magazine. Circ. 400,000. Pays on publication. Byline given. Buys first North American serial rights or one-time rights. Submit seasonal/holiday material 3 months in advance. Simultaneous queries, and simultaneous (if outside circulation area) and previously published submissions OK. Computer printout or disk submissions OK. SASE. Reports in 2 months.
Nonfiction: Investigative (of Southwest interest); historical/nostalgic; interview/profile (outstanding people of regional interest); opinion (essays); photo feature (album style); and discovery pieces on out-of-the-way places. No service articles. Buys 25 unsolicited mss/year. Query. Length: 1,500-3,000 words. Pays $250-750.
Fiction: Occasional short stories or novel excerpts. Length: 1,500-3,000 words. Pays $250-750.
Photos: State availability of photos. Reviews 35mm color transparencies and 8x10 b&w glossy prints. Pays negotiable fee. Captions required. Buys one-time rights.
Tips: "Our only criterion is that we find the material interesting and well-written, although most accepted submissions have a Southwest slant." Recent article/story examples: "Route 66" and "A Secret of Military Significance."

Utah

‡**UTAH HOLIDAY**, Utah Holiday Publishing Company, 419 E. First St., Salt Lake City UT 84111. Editor: Paul Swenson. Provides provocative, under-the-surface examination of the state of Utah, its peoples, and local affairs. "Readers predominantly live along the Wasatch Front, are college educated, and are in the middle to upper income brackets. They often attend cultural events and restaurants. The readership is diverse, running the gamut from liberal to conservative." Monthly magazine; 88-36 pages. Circ. 20,000. Pays on publication. Buys first serial rights only. Pays 20% kill fee on assigned articles only. Byline given. Submit seasonal material 6 months in advance. SASE. Reports in 2 months. Free writer's guidelines. Sample copy $3. Query by letter to Managing Editor.

The double dagger (‡) before a listing indicates that the listing is new in this edition. New markets are often the most receptive to freelance contributions.

Nonfiction: Regular coverage includes investigative reporting and analysis of local issues, local general interest in entertainment, leisure, lifestyle, people, food, politics, business, travel; photo features; local history; special summer and winter visitors guides. Length: 1,000-5,000 words. Pays $50-450.
Photos: State availability of photos with query. Captions preferred.
Fiction and Poetry: Length: 1,500-5,000 words.
Tips: "If you've never written for us before, include with your query clips or copies of the first few pages of the story itself. It is essential that you study the magazine before trying to write for us."

Vermont

VERMONT LIFE MAGAZINE, 61 Elm St., Montpelier VT 05602. (802)828-3241. Editor: Charles T. Morrissey. Quarterly magazine. Circ. 120,000. Buys first rights. Byline given. Buys 60 mss/year. "Query by letter is essential." SASE.
Nonfiction: Wants articles on today's Vermont, those which portray a typical or, if possible, unique, aspect of the state or its people. Style should be literate, clear and concise. Subtle humor favored. No Vermont dialect attempts as in "Ayup," outsider's view on visiting Vermont or "Vermont cliches"—maple syrup, town meetings, or stereotyped natives. Length: average 1,500 words. Pays 20¢/word.
Photos: Buys photographs with mss and with captions and seasonal photographs alone. Prefers b&w contact sheets to look at first on assigned material. Color submissions must be 4x5 or 35mm transparencies. Buys one-time rights, but often negotiates for re-use rights also. Rates on acceptance; color, $75 inside, $200 for cover. Gives assignments but only with experienced photographers. Query in writing.
Tips: "Writers who read our magazine are given more consideration because they understand we want Vermontish articles about Vermont."

Virginia

COMMONWEALTH, Box 1710, Norfolk VA 23501. (804)625-4800. Editor: Deborah Marquardt. For urban adults interested in lifestyles and important issues in Southeastern Virginia. Monthly magazine; 96 pages. Circ. 48,000. Pays on publication. Buys all rights. Pays negotiable kill fee. Byline given. Phone queries OK. Submit seasonal/holiday material 6 months in advance. Photocopied and previously published submissions OK. SASE. Reports in 4-6 weeks. Sample copy $1.95; free writer's guidelines.
Photos: State availability of photos. Pays $20-40 minimum/5x7 color and b&w glossy prints; offers no additional payment for photos accompanying ms. Captions preferred; model releases required.
Columns/Departments: Arts/Entertainment; Business; Outdoors; People; Health; Gourmet; Lifestyle; and Travel (prefers inside story on popular or unusual local or regional spots). Buys 4 columns/issue. Query. Length: 800-1,200 words. Pays $20-100.
Fiction: "Must be about Virginia or the South." Buys 4-6 mss/year. Submit complete ms. Length: open. Pays 10¢/word.
Fillers: "No limericks or humorous ditties, please. We use them but we generate them locally."
Tips: "Visit with the editor, establish a rapport, show genuine interest in and prior knowledge of the magazine, be prepared with good ideas, show an eagerness to dig for a good story, keep in touch."

NORTHERN VIRGINIAN, 135 Park St., Box 1177, Vienna VA 22180. (703)938-0666. Reports in 30 days. Sample copy $1 (to cover postage and handling); free writer's guidelines.
Nonfiction: "Freelance manuscripts welcomed on speculation. Particularly interested in articles about or related to Northern Virginia."
Photos: "B&w photos as appropriate, with mss enhance publication probability."
Tips: "Longer articles preferred, minimum 2,500 words."

THE ROANOKER, The Magazine of Western Virginia, Leisure Publishing Co., 3424 Brambleton Ave., Box 12567, Roanoke VA 24026. (703)989-6138. Editor: Brenda McDaniel. Monthly magazine covering people and events of Western Virginia. "*The Roanoker* is a general-interest city magazine edited for the people of Roanoke, Virginia, and the surrounding area. Our readers are primarily upper-income, well-educated professionals between the ages of 35 and 60. Coverage ranges from hard news and consumer information to restaurant reviews and local history." Circ. 10,000. Pays on publication. Byline given. Buys all rights and makes work-for-hire assignments. Submit seasonal/holiday material 3 months in advance. Simultaneous queries OK. Will consider computer printout or disk submissions. SASE. Reports in 8 weeks. Sample copy $2.
Nonfiction: Expose (of government tax-supported agencies); historical/nostalgic; how-to (live better in Western Virginia); interview/profile (of well-known area personalities); photo feature; and travel (Virginia and sur-

rounding states). "We are attempting to broaden our base and provide more and more coverage of Western Virginia, i.e., that part of the state west of Roanoke. We place special emphasis on consumer-related issues and how-to articles." Periodic special sections on fashion, real estate, media, banking, investing. No think pieces or personal remembrances. Buys 100 mss/year. Query with clips of published work or send complete ms. Length: 3,000 words maximum. Pays $35-200.

Photos: Send photos with ms. Pays $5-10 for 5x7 or 8x10 b&w prints; $10 maximum for 5x7 or 8x10 color prints. Reviews color transparencies. Captions and model release required. Rights purchased vary.

Tips: "It helps if freelancer lives in the area. We will start requesting list of information sources used."

Washington

COMPASS, (formerly *Sunday Northwest*), *Tacoma News Tribune*, Box 11000, Tacoma WA 98411. (206)597-8649. Editor: Bill Smull. 60% freelance written. Sunday supplement. Circ. 100,000. Pays on publication. Byline given. Query. Reports "immediately." Computer printout submissions OK if legible and double-spaced; prefers letter quality to dot matrix. SASE.

Nonfiction and Photos: Articles and photos about Pacific Northwest, particularly the Puget Sound area. Historical, biographical, recreational stories. No fiction. Length: 1,000 words maximum. Pays $60/printed tabloid page, whether pictures, text or both. Also occasionally buys a color cover transparency for $120. Northwest subjects only.

‡**THE SEATTLE WEEKLY**, Sasquatch Publishing, 1932 1st Ave., #605, Seattle WA 98101. (206)623-3700. Editor: David Brewster. Managing Editor: Ann Senechal. Weekly tabloid covering arts, politics, food, business, sports, books with local and regional emphasis. Circ. 25,000. Pays on publication. Byline given. Offers variable kill fee. Buys first North American serial rights. Submit seasonal/holiday material 1 month in advance. Simultaneous queries OK. SASE. Reports in 1 month. Sample copy 75¢; free writer's guidelines.

Nonfiction: Book excerpts; expose; general interest; historical/nostalgic (Northwest); how-to (related to food and health); humor; interview/profile; opinion; travel; arts-related essays. Buys 25 cover stories/year. Query with published clips. Length: 700-4,000 words. Pays $75-800.

Wisconsin

FOX RIVER PATRIOT, Fox River Publishing Co., Box 54, Princeton WI 54968. (414)295-6252. Editor: Michael Jacobi. For country folks of all ages. Monthly tabloid. Circ. 6,000. Pays on publication. Buys first North American serial rights and one-time rights. Byline given. Submit seasonal/holiday material 2 months in advance. Simultaneous, photocopied and previously published submissions OK. SASE. Reports in 4 weeks. Sample copy $1.

Nonfiction: Expose, general interest, historical, how-to, humor, interview, nostalgia, personal experience, photo feature, profile, and travel. "In general, we are a country-oriented publication—we stress environment, alternative energy technology, alternative building trends, farming and gardening, etc.—submissions should be in this general area." Buys 4 mss/issue. Send complete ms. Pays $5-25.

Photos: Send photos with ms. Pays $5 for 5x7 b&w prints; $5 for 5x7 color prints. Captions preferred.

INSIGHT MAGAZINE, *Milwaukee Journal*, Box 661, Milwaukee WI 53201. (414)224-2341. Editor: Beth Slocum. Emphasizes general interest reading for a cross-section of Wisconsin and upper Michigan. Weekly magazine; 24-88 pages. Circ. 530,000. Pays on acceptance. Buys one-time rights. Byline given. Submit seasonal/holiday material at least 2 months in advance. Computer printout submissions OK; prefers letter quality to dot matrix. SASE. Reports in 3-4 weeks. Free sample copy.

Nonfiction: Humor; profiles; personal experience; provocative essays; and nostalgia. Buys 50-150 mss/year. Length: 1,000-3,000 words. Pays $200-500.

Tips: "Read the magazine and get a feel for its content. Then you might try a personal experience article, a thought-provoking essay or a lively profile. We also need 750-1,000 word fillers—examples of which you'll find in the magazine. Much of our material comes from Wisconsin writers. Generally, we're not a good market for out-of-state writers, although we may buy originals or reprints from time to time from established writers. Query with specific outline of proposed story."

MADISON MAGAZINE, Box 1604, Madison WI 53701. Editor: James Selk. General city magazine aimed at upscale audience. Magazine; 76-104 pages. Monthly. Circ. 18,500. Buys all rights. 100 mss/year. Pays on publication. Sample copy $3. Reports on material accepted for publication 10 days after publication. Returns rejected material immediately. Query. SASE.

Nonfiction and Photos: General human interest articles with strong local angles. Length: 1,000-5,000 words. Pays $25-500. Offers no additional payment for b&w photos used with mss. Captions required.

WISCONSIN TRAILS, Box 5650, Madison WI 53705. (608)831-3363. Associate Editor: Susan Pigorsch. For readers interested in Wisconsin; its natural beauty, history, recreation, contemporary issues and personalities; and the arts. Bimonthly magazine. Circ. 28,000. Rights purchased vary with author and material. Byline given. Buys 20 unsolicited mss/year. Pays on publication. Photocopied submissions OK. Guidelines available. Submit seasonal material at least 1 year in advance. Reports in 1 month. Query or send outline. SASE.
Nonfiction: "Our articles focus on some aspect of Wisconsin life; an interesting site or event, a person or industry, history or the arts. We do not use first-person essays or biographies about people who were born in Wisconsin, but made their fortunes elsewhere. Poetry exclusively on assignment. No run-of-the-mill articles that are too local for our audience, or articles about obvious places to visit in Wisconsin. We need more articles about the new and little-known." Length: 1,000-3,000 words. Pays $50-300, depending on assignment length and quality.
Photos: Purchased with or without mss or on assignment. Captions preferred. Color photos usually illustrate an activity, event, region or striking scenery. B&w photos usually illustrate a given article. Pays $10-20 each for b&w on publication. Pays $50 for inside color; pays $100 for covers and center spreads. "Transparencies; 2¼x2¼ or larger are preferred, but 35mm is OK."
Tips: "We're looking for active articles about people, places, events, and outdoor adventures in Wisconsin. We now publish one in-depth article of state-wide interest or concern per issue, and several short (1,000-word) articles about short trips, recreational opportunities, and cultural activities. We will be looking for more articles about out-of-the-way places in Wisconsin that are exceptional in some way."

Puerto Rico

WALKING TOURS OF SAN JUAN, Magazine/Guide, Caribbean World Communications, Inc., First Federal Building, Office 301, Santurce PR 00909. (809)722-1767. Editor: Al Dinhofer. Managing Editor: Julie Jewel. Magazine published 2 times/year (winter and summer). Estab. 1980. Circ. 22,000. Pays on publication. Byline given. Buys first rights. SASE. Reports in 1 month. Sample copy $4 for 9x12 SAE and $2 postage.
Nonfiction: Historical/nostalgic. "We are seeking historically based articles on San Juan. Any aspect of Spanish colonial culture, art, architecture, etc., would probably satisfy our needs. We must have sources—in fact, we will publish source material at the end of each article for reader reference." Buys 3 mss/year. Query. Length: 2,000-3,000 words. Pays $150.

Canada

ALBERTA MAGAZINE, Naylor Communications Ltd., 304-10010 105th St., Edmonton, Alberta, Canada T5J 1C4. (403)428-6164. Editor: Wayne Rothe. Bimonthly magazine for "an Alberta audience with leisure, general interest, lifestyle, consumer-type articles." Circ. 215,000. Pays on acceptance or publication. Byline given. Offers ⅓ kill fee. Buys first North American serial rights. Submit seasonal/holiday material 3 months in advance. Simultaneous queries, and simultaneous, photocopied, and previously published submissions OK. SASE. Reports in 6 weeks. Sample copy and writer's guidelines for SASE.
Nonfiction: Book excerpts; expose (of government, social or environmental issues); general interest; historical/nostalgic; humor; photo feature. Little travel. Buys 30-35 mss/year. Query with clips of published work. Length: 500-2,500 words. Pays 10-15¢/word.
Photos: State availability of photos. People, action pictures. Captions, model release and identification of subjects required. Buys one-time rights. Reviews 4x5 b&w or color prints; 35 mss color transparencies.
Columns/Departments: Upfront: "short, breezy, upbeat, concise pieces, with photos if possible—6-10 items/issue." Query with clips of published work. Length: 300-600 words. Pays 10-15¢/word.

CANADIAN GEOGRAPHIC, 488 Wilbrod St., Ottawa, Ontario Canada K1N 6M8. Publisher: J. Keith Fraser. Editor: Ross Smith. Managing Editor: Enid Byford. Circ. 120,000. Bimonthly magazine. Pays on publication. Buys first Canadian rights; interested only in first time publication. Leaflet for guidance of contributor available on request.
Nonfiction: Buys authoritative geographical articles, in the broad geographical sense, written for the average person, not for a scientific audience. Predominantly Canadian subjects by Canadian authors; non-Canadian subjects have positive Canadian involvement or appeal. Buys 30-45 unsolicited mss/year. Length: 1,200-2,500 words. Pays 12¢ minimum/word. Usual payment for articles with illustrations, $150-800 and up. Higher fees reserved for commissioned articles on which copyright remains with publisher unless otherwise agreed.

Photos: 35mm slides, 2¼x2¼ transparencies or 8x10 glossies. Pays $25-100+ for color shots, depending on published size; $12.50-40 for b&w.
Tips: "Refer to our leaflet for guidance of contributors, and pay attention to our requirements."

HAMILTON MAGAZINE, Hamilton Publishing Inc., 36 Hess St. S., Hamilton, Ontario, Canada L8P 3N1. (416)528-0436. Editor: Wayne Narciso. Managing Editor: Wayne MacPhail. Monthly magazine with lifestyle slant and some investigative reporting. Circ. 50,000. Byline given. Offers 50% kill fee. Not copyrighted. Buys first Canadian rights. Submit seasonal/holiday material 2 months in advance. Simultaneous queries, and simultaneous, photocopied, and previously published submissions OK. SASE. Reports in 2 months. Free sample copy and writer's guidelines.
Nonfiction: Book excerpts (nonfiction); expose (political); general interest; historical/nostalgic (specifically Hamilton-oriented); interview/profile; personal experience; photo feature; travel. Special needs include dining and gourmet guide, fashion supplements and audio supplements. No poetry or inspirational. Buys 30 mss/year. Query with clips of published work. Length: 2,000-5,000 words. Pays $100-400.
Photos: Send photos with ms. Pays 25-100 for color transparencies. Captions required. Buys one-time rights.
Columns/Departments: Book reviews and record reviews. Buys 20 mss/year. Query with clips of published work. Length: 2,000-5,000 words. Pays $100-400.

KEY TO TORONTO, Key Publishers Company, Ltd., 59 Front St. E., Toronto, Ontario, Canada M5E 1B3. (416)364-3333. Editor: Brian Kendall. Managing Editor: Caren Pummell. Monthly magazine covering Toronto entertainment, dining and sightseeing. Circ. 80,000. Byline given. Offers 25-50% kill fee. Buys first North American serial rights. Submit seasonal/holiday material 2 months in advance. Previously published work OK. SASE. Reports in 2 weeks on queries; 1 month on mss. Sample copy $2.50.
Nonfiction: Historical/nostalgic (pertaining to Toronto only); interview/profile. "*Key* appears free in all hotel rooms in the city and provides an informed guide for visitors. Writers must know Toronto to supply an insider's tour of activities and entertainments." Buys 48 mss/year. Length: 800-2,500 words. Pays $100-450.
Photos: State availability of photos. Pays $20-50 for 8x10 b&w prints. Page rate: $50. Identification of subjects required. Buys one-time rights.
Columns/Department: Metrobilia: satire on Toronto containing material to which visitors can relate. Buys variable number mss/year. Query with clips of published work. Length: 800 words.
Tips: Be willing to "change direction or rewrite according to the editor's needs, and do additional research. All articles require color, mood, background, as well as lots of service detail. The articles are meant to give visitors an inside look at our city and urge them to explore it."

THORNHILL MONTH MAGAZINE, Your Community Magazine, Thornhill Publications, Ltd., Box 250, Thornhill, Ontario, Canada L3T 3N3. Monthly magazine "of the people, for the people, by the people of the community of Thornhill." Circ. 16,000. Pays on publication. Byline given. Buys first rights. Photocopied and previously published submissions OK. Computer printout submissions OK. SASE. Reports in 2 weeks.
Nonfiction: Expose; humor; interview/profile; new product; personal experience; photo feature. Special issues include industrial and historical. No travel or personal experiences. Buys 80 mss/year. Query with or without clips of published work. Length: 500-1,500 words. Pays $25-60.
Photos: Send photos with ms. Captions required. Buys one-time rights.
Fiction: 500-1,000 words by local writers only.
Tips: Also publishes *Markham Month Magazine*, a community magazine parallel to *Thornhill Month*.

TORONTO LIFE, 59 Front St. E., Toronto, Ontario, Canada M5E 1B3. (416)364-3333. Editor: Marq de Villiers. Emphasizes local issues and social trends, short humor/satire, and service features for upper-income, well-educated and, for the most part, young Torontonians. Uses some fiction. Monthly magazine. Pays on acceptance. Buys first North American rights. Pays 50% kill fee "for commissioned articles only." Byline given. Phone queries OK. Reports in 3 weeks. SAE and International Reply Coupons. Sample copy $2.
Nonfiction: Uses most all types articles. Buys 17 mss/issue. Query with clips of published work. Buys about 40 unsolicited mss/year. Length: 1,000-5,000 words. Pays $400-1,500.
Photos: State availability of photos. Uses good color transparencies and clear, crisp black b&w prints. They seldom use submitted photos. Captions and model release required.
Columns/Departments: "We run about five columns an issue. They are all freelanced, though most are from regular contributors. They are mostly local in concern and cover politics, money, fine art, performing arts, movies and sports." Length: 1,200 words. Pays $400-700.

‡**WESTERN LIVING**, Comac Communications, Ltd., #303-2930 Arbutus St., Vancouver, British Columbia, Canada V6J 3Y9. (604)736-8121. Editor: Andrew Scott. Monthly general interest and home magazine for western Canadian readers interested in home design, cuisine, travel, people, etc. Circ. 215,000. Pays on acceptance. Byline given. Offers 50-100% kill fee. Buys first North American serial rights. Submit seasonal/holiday material 6 months in advance. SASE. Reports in 1 month. Free sample copy and writer's guidelines.

Nonfiction: Book excerpts (occasionally); general interest (western Canadian); historical (western Canadian); how-to (home oriented); new product (home oriented); travel; food; profiles. Ideas must be geared to the British Columbia-Alberta region. Buys 50-100 mss/year. Query with published clips. Length: 1,500-3,000 words. Pays $200-1,000.

Photos: Peter Manning, art director. Send photos with query. Pays $25-400 for color transparencies; b&w contact sheet and 8x10 b&w prints. Model release and identification of subjects required. Buys one-time rights.

WESTERN PEOPLE, Western Producer Publications, Box 2500, Saskatoon, Saskatchewan, Canada S7K 2C4. (306)665-3500. Editor: R.H.D. Phillips. Managing Editor: Mary Gilchrist. Weekly supplement to *The Western Producer*. "*Western People* is about people in western Canada, past and present. Its emphasis is rural but not necessarily agricultural." Circ. 140,000. Pays on acceptance. Byline given. Offers negotiable kill fee. Not copyrighted. Buys first North American serial rights. Sometimes buys second serial (reprint) rights. Submit seasonal/holiday material 2 months in advance. SASE; IRCs outside Canada. Reports in 2 weeks on queries; 1 month on mss. Sample copy and writer's guidelines for SAE with 37¢ Canadian postage or IRCs (48¢).

Nonfiction: Mary Gilchrist, managing editor. General interest, historical/nostalgic, humor, interview/profile, personal experience, photo feature, travel in western Canada. No opinion, book reviews. Buys 300 mss/year. Send complete ms. Length: 600-2,500 words. Pays $40-175.

Photos: Mary Gilchrist, managing editor. Photos accompanying ms increase chance of acceptance. Send photos with ms. Pays $10-50/color transparency; $5-25/b&w print and $10-50/color print. Captions and identification of subjects required. Buys one-time rights.

Columns/Departments: Mary Gilchrist, managing editor. Travel, Wildlife. Buys 50 mss/year. Query with clips of published work. Length: 600-1,500 words. Pays $100 maximum.

Fiction: Mary Gilchrist, managing editor. Adventure, historical, humorous, mainstream, science fiction, serialized novels, suspense, western. No city stories. "Our readership is rural." Buys 100 mss/year. Send complete ms. Length: 1,000-2,500 words. Pays $50-175.

Poetry: Mary Gilchrist, managing editor. Free verse, light verse, traditional. Buys 50/year. Submit maximum of 6 poems. Pays $10-50.

Fillers: Mary Gilchrist, managing editor. Short humor. Buys 50/year. Length: 100-500 words. Pays $10-50.

Tips: "Subject matter must be western Canadian. Writing must be crisp because of format (16 pages, 8x11). Best to send manuscripts rather than queries until editor is familiar with your work." Most open to profiles and contemporary issues in western Canada. "Focus on people, avoid rambling, bring the reader close to the subject."

THE WESTERN PRODUCER, Box 2500, Saskatoon, Saskatchewan, Canada. (306)665-3500. Publisher: R.H.D. Phillips. Editor: R.H.D. Phillips. 6% freelance written. Emphasizes agriculture for Western Canadian farm families. Weekly newspaper; 56-80 pages. Circ. 140,000. Pays on acceptance. Buys first North American serial rights. Byline given. Submit seasonal/holiday material 2 months in advance of issue date. Computer printouts OK; prefers letter quality to dot matrix. SASE. Reports in 2 weeks. Free writer's guidelines.

Nonfiction: General interest; historical (Western Canada); personal experience; photo feature and profile. "Urban living material not appreciated; nor is material patronizing farm people." Buys 1,200 mss/year. Submit complete ms. Pays $5-300.

Photos: Submit photos with ms. Pays $10-25 for 5x7 b&w prints. Captions and model release required. Buys one-time rights.

Fiction: Adventure, historical, humorous, mainstream, mystery, suspense, and Western Canadian subjects. Buys 40 mss/year. Length: 1,500 words maximum. Pays $25-100.

Poetry: Traditional. Buys 51/year. Pays $5-15.

Tips: "Write a story of interest to non-urban readers—and realize that 'non-urban' doesn't mean 'dodo.' "

WINDSOR THIS MONTH MAGAZINE, Box 1029, Station A, Windsor, Ontario, Canada N9A 6P4. (519)966-7411. Editor: Laura Rosenthal. 75% freelance written. "*Windsor This Month* is mailed out in a system of controlled distribution to 19,000 households in the area. The average reader is a university graduate, middle income, and active in leisure areas." Circ. 22,000. Pays on publication. Buys first North American serial rights. Phone queries OK. Submit seasonal/holiday material 3-4 months in advance. "We will accept computer printout submissions or industry-compatible magnetic media." SAE and International Reply Coupons. Reports in 4 weeks.

Nonfiction: "Windsor-oriented editorial: issues, answers, interviews, lifestyles, profiles, photo essays, opinion. How-to accepted if applicable to readership. Special inserts: design and decor, gourmet and travel featured periodically through the year." Buys 5 mss/issue. Query. Buys 15 unsolicited mss/year. Length: 500-5,000 words. Pays $20-200.

Photos: State availability of photos with query. Pays $10 for first-published and $5 thereafter for b&w prints. Captions preferred. Buys all rights.

Tips: "If experienced—arm yourself with published work and a list of 10 topics that demonstrate knowledge of the Windsor market, and query the editor. Recent article example: "The Hospice" (3-part series).

Foreign

FIESTA! TIMES, (formerly *Mexico Life*), Box 3101, Chula Vista CA 92011. (619)277-6690. Editor: O. Stanley Wulff. Monthly magazine covering Mexico and Latin America for upper-income readers with a US point of view. Circ. 20,000. Pays on publication. Byline given. Buys one-time rights. Submit seasonal/holiday material 2 months in advance. Simultaneous queries and photocopied submissions OK. Computer printout submissions OK. SASE. Reports in 1 month. Sample copy for $1.50 and 9x12 SAE.
Nonfiction: General interest, historical/nostalgic, humor, interview/profile, photo feature. "Articles on outdoor activities such as hunting and fishing. There is great reader interest in the Yucatan area. No amateurish trave experiences; no political articles." Buys 50 mss/year. Send complete ms. Length: 2,000 words maximum. Pays $25 minimum.
Tips: "Submit lively, well-researched and accurate articles on specific rather than general subjects on Mexico. Expansion will require more material."

GLIMPSES OF MICRONESIA, Box 3191, Agana, Guam 96910. Editor: Mike Malone. 90% freelance written. "A regional publication for Micronesia lovers, travel buffs and readers interested in the United States' last frontier. Our audience covers all age levels and is best described as well-educated and fascinated by our part of the world." Quarterly magazine; 100 pages. Circ. 25,000. Pays on publication. Buys first rights. Pays 10% kill fee on assignments. Byline given. Submit seasonal/holiday material 8 months in advance. Computer printout or disk submissions OK. SASE. Reports in 2 weeks. Sample copy $2; free writer's guidelines.
Nonfiction: "Range of subjects is broad, from political analysis of Micronesia's newly emerging governments to examination of traditional culture; historical (anything related to Micronesia that is lively and factual); personal experience (first-person adventure, as in our recently published piece about a sailing expedition to the uninhabited islands of the Northern Marianas); interviews/personality profiles of outstanding Micronesian or Western Pacific individuals; scientific/natural history (in lay terms); photo features (we're very photo-oriented—query us on island or Pacific themes); travel (we use one/issue about destinations in Asia and the Pacific). No articles from fly-by-night (overnight) visitors to Micronesia." Buys 30 mss/year. Query. Length: 1,500-5,000 words. Pays 5-10¢/word.
Photos: Purchased with or without accompanying ms. Pays minimum $10 for 8x10 b&w prints or $15 for 4x5 color transparencies or 35mm slides. Pay $200-300 for photo essays; $100 for covers. Captions required.
Columns/Departments: Short think-pieces on contemporary Micronesia are accepted for the "Island Views" section. Opinions are welcomed, but must be well-founded and must reflect the writer's familiarity with the subject. Length: 500-1,200 words. Pays $30.
Poetry: "Use very little, but willing to look at Pacific-related themes to be used with photos." Only traditional forms. Pays minimum $10.
Tips: "Writers living in or having first-hand experience with Micronesia and the Western Pacific are scarce. If you have that experience, have made yourself familiar with *Glimpses*, and have a good story idea, then we're willing to work with you in developing a good article."

Religious

Educational and inspirational material of interest to church members, workers and leaders within a denomination or religion is the primary interest of publications in this category. Publications intended to assist lay and professional religious workers in teaching and managing church affairs are classified in Church Administration and Ministry in the Trade Journals section. Religious magazines for children and teenagers will be found in the Juvenile, and Teen and Young Adult classifications.

Tips on writing for the religious market are available in *Writing to Inspire: A Guide to Writing and Publishing for the Expanding Religious Market*, by William Gentz, Lee Roddy, et al. (Writer's Digest Books).

‡**AGLOW, Christian Magazine for Women,** Women's Aglow Fellowship, Box I, Lynnwood WA 98036. (206)775-7282. Editor: Phyllis Mitchell. Managing Editor: Nancy Clark. Bimonthly, nondenominational

Christian, charismatic magazine for women. Pays on acceptance. Byline given. Buys all rights; will return second rights upon request. Submit seasonal/holiday material 6 months in advance. Simultaneous queries and simultaneous and photocopied submissions OK. Computer printout submissions OK. SASE. Reports in 2 months. Writer's guidelines for business-size SAE and 1 first class stamp.

Nonfiction: Humor, inspirational, personal experience, only Christian-oriented articles. "Each article should be either a testimony of or teaching about Jesus as Savior, as Baptizer in the Holy Spirit, or as guide and strength in everyday circumstances." Send complete ms. No poetry. Length: 1,000-2,000 words. Pays $35-150.

Tips: "Our rates are increasing. We are also getting better quality manuscripts."

ALIVE NOW!, The Upper Room, 1980 Grand Ave., Box 189, Nashville TN 37202. (615)327-2700. Editor: Mary Ruth Coffman. Bimonthly magazine including short prose pieces, poetry, and essays relating to a theme concerned with Christian life and action, for a general Christian audience interested in reflection and meditation. Circ. 75,000. Pays on publication. Byline given. Pays "negotiated kill fee, when applicable." Rights purchased are negotiated ("may be one-time rights, or newspaper and periodical"). Submit seasonal/holiday material 8 months in advance. Previously published work OK. Computer printout or disk submissions OK. SASE. Reports in 2 months on queries; 6 months on mss. Sample copy and writer's guidelines free, but must send SASE with request.

Nonfiction: Book excerpts, humor, inspirational and personal experience. "Send a typed, interesting story or poem that deals with personal faith journey, relations with other people and the world, questions of meaning, responsibility for the natural world, and/or thoughts on the meaning of existence. Writing should be for the young adult or mature adult, or the adult with a growing faith awareness." No polemic articles. Buys 120 unsolicited mss/year. Send complete ms. Length: 500 words maximum. Pays $5-40.

Photos: Pamela Watkins, photo editor. Send photos with ms. Pays $50-100 for 4x5 color transparencies; $15-25 for 8x10 b&w prints. Buys one-time rights.

Columns/Departments: Excerpts from devotional classics. Buys 4 mss/year. Query with clips of published work. Length: 350-800 words. Pays $25-40.

Fiction: Fantasy, humorous and religious. No confession, erotica, horror, romance or western. Buys 10 mss/year. Query with clips of published work. Length: 100-450 words. Pays $25-40.

Poetry: Avant-garde and free verse. Buys 30 poems/year. Submit maximum 5 poems. Length: 10-45 lines. Pays $5-25.

Fillers: Anecdotes and short humor. Buys 6/year. Length: 25-150 words. Pays $5-15.

Tips: "We are seeing *too* many old chestnuts, clippings, and plagiarized material now. There used to be very few."

AMERICA, 106 W. 56th St., New York NY 10019. (212)581-4640. Editor: Joseph A. O'Hare. Published weekly for adult, educated, largely Roman Catholic audience. Usually buys all rights. Byline given. Pays on acceptance. Reports in 2-3 weeks. Free writer's guidelines. SASE.

Nonfiction: "We publish a wide variety of material on politics, economics, ecology, and so forth. We are not a parochial publication, but almost all of our pieces make some moral or religious point. We are not interested in purely informational pieces or personal narratives which are self-contained and have no larger moral interest." Articles on literature, current political and social events. Length: 1,500-2,000 words. Pays $50-100.

Poetry: Length: 15-30 lines. Address to Poetry Editor.

‡THE ANNALS OF SAINT ANNE DE BEAUPRE, Basilica of St. Anne, Quebec, Canada G0A 3C0. (418)827-4538. Contact: Editor-in-Chief. 60% freelance written. Emphasizes the Catholic faith for the general public, of average education; part of the audience is made up of people who come to The Shrine of St. Anne de Beaupre. Monthly magazine; 32 pages. Circ. 60,000. Pays on acceptance. Buys first North American serial rights. Phone queries OK. Submit seasonal/holiday material 2 months in advance. SAE and International Reply Coupons. Reports in 3-4 weeks. Free sample copy and writer's guidelines.

Nonfiction: Humor (short pieces on education, family, etc.); inspirational; interview; and personal experience. No subjects that are not even indirectly related to religious education. Buys 10 mss/issue. Query. Length: 700-1,200 words. Pays $25-35.

Columns/Departments: Query. Length: 700-1,200 words. Pays $25-35. Open to suggestions for new columns/departments.

Fiction: Religious (Catholic faith). Buys 1 ms/issue. Query. Length: 700-1,200 words. Pays $25-35.

Tips: The freelancer can best break in by offering a special column or "submitting articles that fit our needs: popular Catholic life."

ASPIRE, 1819 E. 14th Ave., Denver CO 80218. Editor: Jeanne Pomranka. 50% freelance written. For teens and adults: "those who are looking for a way of life that is practical, logical, spiritual or inspirational." Monthly; 64 pages. Circ. 2,900. Buys all rights. Byline given. Buys 55-60 unsolicited mss/year. Pays following publication. Sample copy 40¢ in stamps. Submit seasonal material 6-7 months in advance. Reports in 2 weeks.

Nonfiction: Uses inspirational articles that help to interpret the spiritual meaning of life. Needs are specialized, since this is the organ of the Divine Science teaching. Personal experience, inspirational, think pieces. Also seeks material for God at Work, a department "written in the form of letters to the editor in which the writer describes how God has worked in his life or around him. Teen Talk includes short articles from teenagers to help other teenagers find meaning in life." Length: 100-1,000 words. Pays maximum 1¢/published word.
Fiction: "Anything illustrating spiritual law at work in life." Length: 250-1,000 words. Pays maximum 1¢/published word.
Poetry: Traditional, contemporary, light verse. "We use very little poetry." Length: average 8-16 lines. Pays $1-2/page.
Tips: "Avoid 'churchiness' as opposed to man's true relationship with God and his fellowmen. The latter is what we need—articles on prayer, consciousness building, faith at work, spiritual law, etc. We want good, simple, clear writing—no trite, overused phrases, no over emphasis of tragedy, but emphasis on positive, constructive attitudes that overcome such situations. Must be inspirationally written."

AXIOS, 1365 Edgecliffe Dr., Los Angeles CA 90026. (213)663-1888. Editor: Daniel J. Gorham. Monthly journal seeking spiritual articles mostly on Orthodox Christian background, either Russian, Greek, Serbian, Syrian or American. Estab. 1981. Circ. 1,989. Pays on publication. Byline given. Offers 50% kill fee. Buys all rights. Submit seasonal/holiday material 4 months in advance. Simultaneous queries, and simultaneous, photocopied, and previously published submissions OK. SASE. Reports in 1 month. Sample copy $2.
Nonfiction: Book excerpts; expose (of religious figures); general interest; historical/nostalgic; interview/profile; opinion; personal experience; photo feature; travel (Shrines, pilgrimages). Special issues include The Persecution of Christians in Iran, Russia, behind iron curtain or in Arab lands; Roman Catholic interest in the Orthodox and Episcopal Church. Nothing about the Pope or general "all-is-well-with-Christ" items. Buys 14 mss/year. Send complete ms. Length: 1,000-3,000 words. Pays 4¢/word minimum.
Columns/Departments: Reviews religious books and films. Buys 80 mss/year. Query.
Tips: "We need some hard-hitting articles on the 'political' church—the why, how and where of it and why it lacks the timelessness of the spiritual!"

BAPTIST HERALD, 1 S. 210 Summit Ave., Oakbrook Terrace IL 60181. (312)495-2000. Editor: Barbara J. Binder. For "any age from 15 and up, any educational background with mainly religious interests." Monthly. Circ. 9,000. Buys all rights. Byline given. Pays on publication. Occasionally overstocked. Free sample copy. Submit seasonal material 3-4 months in advance. SASE.
Nonfiction and Fiction: "We want articles of general religious interest. Seeking articles that are precise, concise, and honest. We hold a rather conservative religious line." Buys personal experience, interviews, inspirational and opinion articles. Length: 600 or 1,200 words. Pays $10. Buys religious and historical fiction. Length: 600 or 1,250 words. Pays $10.

BAPTIST LEADER, Valley Forge PA 19481. (215)768-2158. Editor: Vincie Alessi. For ministers, teachers, and leaders in church schools. Monthly; 64 pages. Buys first rights. Pays on acceptance. Deadlines are 8 months prior to date of issue. Reports immediately. SASE.
Nonfiction: Educational topics. How-to articles for local church school teachers. Length: 1,500-2,000 words. Pays $25-60.
Photos: Church school settings; church, worship, children's and youth activities and adult activities. Purchased with mss. B&w, 8x10; human interest and seasonal themes. Pays $15-20.

BIBLICAL ILLUSTRATOR, The Sunday School Board, 127 9th Ave. N., Nashville TN 37234. Editor: William H. Stephens. For members of Sunday School classes that use the International Sunday School Lessons and other Bible study lessons, and for adults seeking in-depth Biblical information. Quarterly. Circ. 90,000. Buys all rights. Byline given. Rarely purchases freelance material. Pays on acceptance. Reports in 2 weeks. Query. SASE.
Nonfiction and Photos: Journalistic articles and photo stories researched on Biblical subjects, such as archeology and sketches of Biblical personalities. Material must be written for laymen but research quality must be up-to-date and thorough. Should be written in a contemporary, journalistic style. Pays 4¢/word. B&w and color photos occasionally purchased with ms or on assignment. Captions required. Pays $25 for b&w, more for color.

BRIGADE LEADER, Box 150, Wheaton IL 60187. Editor: Michael Chiapperino. 50% freelance written. For men associated with Christian Service Brigade programs throughout US and Canada. Quarterly magazine; 32 pages. Buys all rights or second serial (reprint) rights. Buys 6-8 mss/year. Pays on acceptance. Submit seasonal material 5 months in advance. Photocopied submissions OK. Reports in 2 months. Query. SASE. Sample copy $1.
Nonfiction: "We are interested in articles about: problems in father-son/man-boy relationships; the holistic development of the Christian man; men as role-models for boys; helping boys to cope with their problems." In-

formational, personal experience, inspirational. Length: 900-1,500 words. Photos purchased with or without ms. Pays $25 for b&w, inside; $50-75 for b&w, cover.

‡**THE CATHEDRAL VOICE**, St. Willibrord's Press, Box 98, Highlandville MO 65669. Editor: Karl Pruter. Bimonthly magazine of the World Peace Academy. Covers peace and peace making; "we take the commandment, 'Thou Shalt Not Kill' literally. Estab. 1983. Circ. 1,200. Pays on acceptance. Byline given. Not copyrighted. Buys first North American serial rights. Submit seasonal/holiday material 2 months in advance. Simultaneous queries and photocopied submissions OK. SASE. Reports in 2 weeks. Sample copy for SAE and 2 first class stamps.
Nonfiction: Expose, general interest, historical/nostalgic, inspirational, personal experience. Length: 1,000-4,000 words. Pays $20-40.
Fiction: Religious. Length: 1,000-4,000 words. Pays $20-40.
Poetry: Free verse, light verse, traditional. Length: 24 lines maximum. Pays $10.

CATHOLIC DIGEST, Box 43090, St. Paul MN 55164. Editor: Henry Lexau. Managing Editor: Richard Reece. Monthly magazine covering the daily living of Roman Catholics for an audience that is 60% female, 40% male; 37% is college educated. Circ. 610,000. Byline given. Buys first North American serial rights or one-time reprint rights. Submit seasonal material 6 months in advance. Previously published submissions OK, if so indicated. SASE. Reports in 3 weeks.
Nonfiction: General interest (daily living and family relationships); interview (of outstanding Catholics, celebrities and locals); nostalgia (the good old days of family living); profile; religion; travel (shrines); humor; inspirational (overcoming illness, role model people); and personal experience (adventures and daily living). Buys 20 articles/issue. No queries. Send complete ms. Length: 500-3,000 words, 2,000 average. Pays on acceptance $200-400 for originals, $100 for reprints.
Columns/Departments: "Check a copy of the magazine in the library for a description of column needs. Payment varies and is made upon publication. We buy about 5/issue."
Fillers: Jokes, anecdotes and short humor. Buys 10-15 mss/issue. Length: 10-300 words. Pays $3-50 on publication.

CATHOLIC LIFE, 35750 Moravian Dr., Fraser MI 48026. Editor-in-Chief: Robert C. Bayer. Emphasizes foreign missionary activities of the Catholic Church in Burma, India, Bangladesh, the Philippines, Hong Kong, Africa, etc., for middle-aged and older audience with either middle incomes or pensions. High school educated (on the average), conservative in both religion and politics. Monthly (except July or August) magazine; 32 pages. Circ. 16,500. Pays on publication. Buys all rights. Byline given. Submit seasonal/holiday material 3-4 months in advance. Simultaneous submissions OK. SASE. Reports in 2 weeks.
Nonfiction: Informational; inspirational (foreign missionary activities of the Catholic Church; experiences, personalities, etc.). Buys 20-25 unsolicited mss/year. Query or send complete ms. Length: 1,000-1,500 words. Pays 4¢/word.
Tips: "Query with short, graphic details of what the material will cover or the personality involved in the biographical sketch. Also, we appreciate being advised on the availability of good b&w photos to illustrate the material."

CATHOLIC NEAR EAST MAGAZINE, Catholic Near East Welfare Association, 1011 1st Ave., New York NY 10022. (212)826-1480. Editor: Regina J. Clarkin. For a general audience with interest in the Near East, particularly its religious and cultural aspects. Quarterly magazine; 24 pages. Circ. 170,000. Buys first North American serial rights. Byline given. Buys 16 mss/year. Pays on publication. Free sample copy and writer's guidelines. Photocopied submissions OK if legible. Submit seasonal material (Christmas and Easter in different Near Eastern lands or rites) 6 months in advance. Reports in 3-4 weeks. Query or submit complete ms. SASE.
Nonfiction and Photos: "Cultural, territorial, devotional material on the Near East, its history, peoples and religions (especially the Eastern Rites of the Catholic Church). Style should be simple, factual, concise. Articles must stem from personal acquaintance with subject matter, or thorough up-to-date research. No preaching or speculations." Length: 1,200-1,800 words. Pays 10¢/word. "Photographs to accompany ms are always welcome; they should illustrate the people, places, ceremonies, etc., which are described in the article. We prefer color but occasionally use b&w. Pay varies depending on the quality of the photos."
Tips: "Writers please heed: stick to the Near East. Send factual articles; concise, descriptive style preferred. Not too flowery. Pictures are a big plus; if you have photos to accompany your article, please send them at the same time."

CHARISMA, The Magazine About Spirit-led Living, Plus Communications Inc., Box 2003, Winter Park FL 32790. (305)645-2022. Editor and Publisher: Stephen Strang. Senior Editor: Howard Earl. Editor-at-large: Jamie Buckingham. Associate Editor: Rob Kerby. Monthly magazine covering Christianity—especially the pentecostal/charismatic movement. Circ. 100,000. Pays on publication. Byline given. Buys first rights. Submit seasonal/holiday material 6 months in advance. SASE. Reports in 1 month. Sample copy $1.95; writer's guidelines for 9x12 SASE and 2 first class stamps.

Nonfiction: Howard Earl, articles editor. How-to (overcome fear; how to be a better parent; how to be more loving); interview/profile (well-known Christian leaders, Christian musicians); personal experience (well-known Christian personality profiles); photo feature (religious themes). Special issues include Christian music in July/August; missions in December; Bible in January. Buys 40 mss/year. Query. Length: 2,000-3,000 words. Pays $100-500. "We agree on a fee before an article is assigned. If we accept an article over the transom, we agree to the fee before acceptance. This eliminates misunderstanding."

Photos: Jody Tubbs, production coordinator. State availability of photos. Pays $35-50 for b&w contact sheet; $50-100 for 35mm color transparencies. Captions, model release, and identification of subjects (where applicable) required. Buys one-time rights.

Fiction: Howard Earl, fiction editor. Condensed novels (published by Christian publishing house; query first); religious (mainline Christian theme); serialized novels (Christian theme; "we are looking for such a novel now"). Buys 3 mss/year. Query. Length: 2,000-3,000 words (except for serialized novel). Pays $100-300 (except for serialized novel).

Tips: "Send a friendly letter that lets us get to know you. We want relationships with freelancers who will write on assignment. Our highest fees are paid for work on assignment rather than for material over the transom."

CHICAGO STUDIES, Box 665, Mundelein IL 60060. (312)566-1462. Editor: George J. Dyer. 50% freelance written. For Roman Catholic priests and religious educators. Magazine; published 3 times/year; 112 pages. Circ. 10,000. Buys all rights. Buys 30 mss/year. Pays on acceptance. Sample copy $2. Photocopied submissions OK. Submit complete ms. Reports in 6 weeks. SASE.

Nonfiction: Nontechnical discussion of theological, Biblical and ethical topics. Articles aimed at a nontechnical presentation of the contemporary scholarship in those fields. Length: 3,000-5,000 words. Pays $35-100.

THE CHRISTIAN CENTURY, 407 S. Dearborn St., Chicago IL 60605. (312)427-5380. Editor: James M. Wall. Executive Editor: Dean Peerman. Managing Editor: Linda Marie Delloff. For ecumenically-minded, progressive church people, both clergy and lay. Weekly magazine; 24-32 pages. Circ. 35,500. Pays on publication. Usually buys all rights. Query appreciated, but not essential. SASE. Reports in 1 month. Free sample copy.

Nonfiction: "We use articles dealing with social problems, ethical dilemmas, political issues, international affairs, and the arts, as well as with theological and ecclesiastical matters. We focus on concerns that arise at the juncture between church and society, or church and culture." Length: 2,500 words maximum. Payment varies, but averages $30/page.

CHRISTIAN HERALD, 40 Overlook Dr., Chappaqua NY 10514. (914)769-9000. Editor: David E. Kucharsky. 80% freelance written or commissioned. Emphasizes religious living in family and church. Monthly magazine; 64 pages. Circ. 200,000. Pays on acceptance. Buys all rights. Submit seasonal/holiday material 5-6 months in advance. Photocopied submissions OK. SASE. Sample copy $2; free writer's guidelines with SASE.

Nonfiction: How-to; informational; inspirational; interview; profile; and evangelical experience. Buys 10-20 mss/year. Query first. Length: 1,500 words. Pays $50 minimum.

Photos: Purchased with or without accompanying ms. Send transparencies. Pays $10 minimum for b&w; $25 minimum for 2¼x2¼ color transparencies.

Poetry: Meaningfully Biblical. Buys 30 poems/year. Length: 4-20 lines. Pays $10 minimum.

‡**THE CHRISTIAN HOME**, The Upper Room, 1908 Grand Ave., Box 189, Nashville TN 37202. (615)327-2700. Editor: David I. Bradley. Quarterly magazine covering family and marriage. "Our primary audience is families, teenagers and couples with many of our users being professional people responsible for Christian nurture in the area of family counseling." Circ. 52,000. Pays on acceptance. Byline given. Buys one-time rights, all rights, first rights, and second serial (reprint) rights. Submit seasonal/holiday material 1 year in advance. SASE. Reports in 1 week on queries; 1 month on ms. Free sample copy and writer's guidelines.

Nonfiction: General interest, how-to, humor, inspirational, opinion, personal experience, photo feature. Buys 110 mss/year. Send complete ms. Length: 1,200-1,400 words. Pays $20-75.

Photos: State availability of photos. Reviews b&w contact sheet and 2¼x3¼ color transparencies and prints. Model release required. Buys one-time rights.

Columns/Departments: Focus on specific issues or themes—marriage, parent as priest, single parent, exceptional child, pastor's page. Buys 30-40 mss/year. Length: 100-800 words. Pays $20-55.

Fiction: Adventure, ethnic, historical, humorous, religious. Buys 8 mss/year. Query with published clips. Length: 1,400-1,800 words. Pays $50-75.

Fillers: Jokes, anecdotes, short humor, newsbreaks. Length: 25-100 words. Pays $2-20.

Tips: "We're looking for terse writing; personal experience; and a focus on spiritual growth or how-to."

CHRISTIAN LIFE MAGAZINE, 396 E. St. Charles Rd., Wheaton IL 60188. Editor-in-Chief: Robert Walker. Executive Editor: Janice Franzen. 75% freelance written. Monthly religious magazine with strong emphasis on spiritual renewal. Circ. 100,000. Pays on publication. Buys all rights. Submit seasonal/holiday material 8-12 months in advance. SASE. Free sample copy and writer's guidelines.
Nonfiction: Adventure articles (usually in the first-person, told in narrative style); devotional (include many anecdotes, preferably from the author's own experience); general features (wide variety of subjects, with special programs of unique benefit to the community); inspirational (showing the success of persons, ideas, events and organizations); personality profiles (bright, tightly-written articles on what Christians are thinking); news (with human interest quality dealing with trends); news feature (providing interpretative analysis of person, trend, event and ideas); and trend (should be based on solid research). Pays $200 maximum.
Fiction: Short stories (with good characterization and mood); pays $200 maximum.

CHRISTIAN SINGLE, Family Ministry Dept., Baptist Sunday School Board, 127 9th Ave. North, Nashville TN 37234. (615)251-2228. Editor: Cliff Allbritton. Monthly magazine covering items of special interest to Christian single adults. "*Christian Single* is a contemporary Christian magazine that seeks to give substantive information to singles for living the abundant life. It seeks to be constructive and creative in approach." Circ. 102,000. Pays on acceptance "for immediate needs"; on publication "for unsolicited manuscripts." Byline given. Buys all rights or makes work-for-hire assignments. Submit seasonal/holiday material 12 months in advance. SASE. Reports in 6 weeks. Sample copy and writer's guidelines free.
Nonfiction: Humor (good, clean humor that applies to Christian singles); how-to (specific subjects which apply to singles; query needed); inspirational (of the personal experience type); personal experience (of single adults); photo feature (on outstanding Christian singles; query needed); and travel to places (appropriate for Christian singles; query needed). No "shallow, uninformative mouthing off. This magazine says something and people read it cover to cover." Buys 120-150 unsolicited mss/year. Query with clips of published work. Length: 300-1,200 words. Pays 4¢/word.
Tips: "We look for freshness and creativity, not duplication of what we have already done. We seek variety targeted to singles' needs. We give preference to Christian single adult writers but publish articles by *sensitive* and *informed* married writers also. Remember that you are talking to educated people who attend church."

CHRISTIANITY & CRISIS, 537 W. 121st St., New York NY 10027. (212)662-5907. Editor: Robert G. Hoyt. For professional clergy and laity; politically liberal; interested in military and foreign policy, urban and racial issues, feminism, ecology, third world problems, etc. Journal published every 2 weeks. Circ. 19,000. Rights purchased vary with author and material. Usually buys all rights. Buys 5-10 unsolicited mss a year. Pays on publication. Free sample copy. Will consider photocopied and simultaneous submissions. Computer printout submissions OK; prefers letter quality to dot matrix. Reports on material in 3 weeks. SASE.
Nonfiction: "Our articles are written in depth, by well-qualified individuals, most of whom are established figures in their respective fields and wish to reach our audience. Articles are factual and of high quality. We are less interested in 'human interest' features." Interested in articles on bio-medical ethics, new community projects, informational articles and book reviews. Length: 500-5,000 words. Pays $50-150.
Tips: "*Level*: Our audience can handle difficult materials, but avoid technical jargon. No footnotes; incorporate necessary references in text. *Tone*: Sober to breezy, as appropriate; merely polemical or politically dogmatic material not considered. *Stance*: Non-pacifist but strongly in favor of nuclear disarmament. Left of center on issues of economics, human rights, civil liberties. *Types of material*: Some reportorial, mostly analytic. *Reviews*: Must query first, giving credentials, samples."

CHRISTIANITY TODAY, 465 Gundersen Dr., Carol Stream IL 60187. Editor: V. Gilbert Beers. Emphasizes orthodox, evangelical religion. Semimonthly magazine; 55 pages. Circ. 180,000. Pays on acceptance. Usually buys all rights. Submit seasonal/holiday material 8 months in advance. Computer printout and disk submissions OK. SASE. Reports in 4-8 weeks. Free sample copy and writer's guidelines.
Nonfiction: Theological, ethical and historical and informational (not merely inspirational). Buys 4 mss/issue. Query only. Unsolicited mss not accepted and not returned. Length: 1,000-4,000 words. Pays $100 minimum.
Columns/Departments: Ministries (practical and specific, not elementary), Refiner's Fire (Christian review of the arts). Buys 12 mss/year. Send complete ms. Length: 800-900 words. Pays $100.
Tips: "We are developing more of our own mss and requiring a much more professional quality of others."

CHURCH & STATE, Americans United for Separation of Church and State, 8120 Fenton St., Silver Spring MD 20910. (301)589-3707. Managing Editor: Joseph Conn. 15% freelance written. Emphasizes religious liberty and church-state relations matters. Readership "includes the whole religious spectrum, but is predominantly Protestant and well-educated." Monthly magazine; 24 pages. Circ. 50,000. Pays on acceptance. Buys all rights. Simultaneous, photocopied and previously published submissions OK. SASE. Reports in 4 weeks. Free sample copy and writer's guidelines.
Nonfiction: Expose; general interest; historical; and interview. Buys 11 mss/year. Recent article example:

"Has the Christian Right Peaked?" (October 1981). Query. Length: 3,000 words maximum. Pays negotiable fee.

Photos: State availability of photos with query. Pays negotiable fee for b&w prints. Captions preferred. Buys one-time rights.

THE CHURCH HERALD, 1324 Lake Dr. SE, Grand Rapids MI 49506. Editor: Dr. John Stapert. Publication of the Reformed Church in America. 22 times/year; 32 pages. Circ. 62,000. Buys all rights, first serial rights, or second serial (reprint) rights. Buys about 60 mss/year. Pays on acceptance. Sample copy 50¢; free writer's guidelines. Photocopied and simultaneous submissions OK. Submit material for major Christian holidays 6 months in advance. Reports in 4 weeks. Query or submit complete ms. Computer printout submissions OK; prefers letter quality to dot matrix. SASE.

Nonfiction and Photos: "We expect all of our articles to be helpful and constructive, even when a point of view is vigorously presented. Articles on subjects such as Christianity and culture, government and politics, forms of worship, the media, ethics and business relations, responsible parenthood, marriage and divorce, death and dying, challenges on the campus, evangelism, church leadership, Christian education, Christian perspectives on current issues, spiritual growth, etc." Length: 400-1,500 words. Articles for children, 750 words. Pays 4½¢/word. Photos purchased with or without accompanying ms. Pays $20 minimum/8x10 b&w glossy print.

Fiction and Fillers: Religious fiction. Length: 400-1,500 words. Children's fiction, 750 words. Pays 4¢/word.

Poetry: Length: 30 lines maximum. Pays $15 minimum.

COLUMBIA, Drawer 1670, New Haven CT 06507. Editor: Elmer Von Feldt. For Catholic families; caters particularly to members of the Knights of Columbus. Monthly magazine. Circ. 1,342,575. Buys all rights. Buys 50 mss/year. Pays on acceptance. Free sample copy and writer's guidelines. Submit seasonal material 6 months in advance. Reports in 4 weeks. Query or submit complete ms. SASE.

Nonfiction and Photos: Fact articles directed to the Catholic layman and his family and dealing with current events, social problems, Catholic apostolic activities, education, ecumenism, rearing a family, literature, science, arts, sports and leisure. Length: 2,500-3,500 words. B&w glossy prints are required for illustration. Articles without ample illustrative material are not given consideration. Payment ranges from $400-600, including photos. Photo stories are also wanted. Pays $15/photo used and 10¢/word.

Fiction and Humor: Written from a thoroughly Christian viewpoint. Length: 3,000 words maximum. Pays $500 minimum. Humor or satire should be directed to current religious, social or cultural conditions. Length: 1,000 words. Pays $200.

COMBONI MISSIONS, 8108 Beechmont Ave., Cincinnati OH 45230. (513)474-4997. Editor: Todd Riebe, MCCJ. Quarterly magazine for those interested in Third World topics and mission efforts of the Comboni Missionaries and Comboni Missionary Sisters (formerly Verona Fathers and Sisters). Distribution 20,000. Buys all rights; first rights; or second serial (reprint) rights. Byline given. Pays on acceptance. Free sample copy. Reports in 6 weeks. SASE.

Nonfiction: Background information, human interest articles, interviews, profiles, personal experience articles, and photo features on the work of Comboni Missionaries, especially in the developing countries of Africa and Latin America and among US minority groups. Should be written knowledgeably, in a popular, conversational style, and reflect a positive outlook on efforts in social and religious fields. Length: 250-1,000 words, shorter features; 3,000 words maximum, major articles. Pays $25-200.

Photos: B&w (5x7 minimum) photos and color transparencies purchased with ms or on assignment. "We want grabbing 'people photos' with a good sense of place. We'd consider purchasing photos without ms if of a people or area (foreign) served by Comboni Missionaries. All the better if a Comboni missionary appears in the photo and is identified by his/her complete name, native country, and mission country." Captions required. Pays $8 minimum/b&w glossy print; $30/color transparency.

Tips: "We treat Third World subjects sympathetically and multi-dimensionally, and always in a Christian context. We want good, solid handling of facts and balanced, realistic stuff. We're a good market for second rights if the article fits our needs and photos are available."

COMMONWEAL, 232 Madison Ave., New York NY 10016. (212)683-2042. Editor: James O'Gara. Biweekly. Edited by Roman Catholic laymen. For college-educated audience. Special book and education issues. Circ. 20,000. Pays on acceptance. Submit seasonal material 2 months in advance. Reports in 3 weeks. "A number of our articles come in over-the-transom. I suggest a newcomer provide sufficient material to establish his or her expertise and let us know something about him/herself (credentials, tearsheets, education or past experience about yourself)." SASE. Free sample copy.

Nonfiction: "Articles on timely subjects: politics, literature and religion." Original, brightly written mss on value-oriented themes; think pieces. Buys 50 mss/year. Length: 1,000-3,000 words. Pays 2¢/word.

Poetry: Department editors: Rosemary Deen and Marie Ponsot. Contemporary and avant-garde. Length: maximum 150 lines ("long poems very rarely"). Pays $7.50-25.

COMMUNICATE, Box 600, Beaverlodge, Alberta, Canada T0H 0C0. Editor: K. Neill Foster. Monthly tabloid covering family and church activities for "a Christian (Protestant) and generally quite conservative readership; average age is about 45." Circ. 18,000. Pays on publication. Buys first-time rights. Previously published submissions OK. Send Canadian postage or International Reply Coupons with return envelope. US postage is not acceptable.
Nonfiction: News ("we're always open to short news items of international or Canadian interest"); inspirational/devotional articles, 1,500-2,000 words (on how to apply Biblical principles to daily living); and news features/human interest (on unusual religious events, activities, personalities). No material with no Christian/moral/ethical significance or features on American politicians, entertainers, etc., who are Christians." Query or send complete ms. Length: 200-2,000 words. Pays $40 maximum.
Photos: Reviews 5x7 b&w prints.
Fiction: "Any fiction we would use would illustrate the application of Christian values, or perhaps the lack thereof, in the life of an individual."
Poetry: "We're looking for poetry that is inspirational, short, and understandable."
Tips: "We are very receptive to American writers. Your best bet is to write along lines of general interest to North Americans and to avoid making your 'Americanness' obvious."

THE COMPANION OF ST. FRANCIS AND ST. ANTHONY, Conventual Franciscan Friars, Box 535, Postal Station F, Toronto, Ontario, Canada M4Y 2L8. (416)924-6349. Editor-in-Chief: Friar Philip Kelly OFM Conv. 75% freelance written. Emphasizes religious and human values and stresses Franciscan virtues—peace, simplicity, joy. Monthly magazine; 32 pages. Circ. 10,000. Pays on acceptance. Buys all rights. Phone queries OK. Submit seasonal/holiday material 6 months in advance. Computer printout submissions OK; prefers letter quality to dot matrix. SASE, Canadian postage. Reports in 3 weeks. Writer's guidelines for SAE and IRCs.
Nonfiction: Historical; how-to (medical and psychological coping); informational; inspirational; interview; nostalgia; profile; and family. No old time religion, anti-Catholic, or pro-abortion material. Buys 6 mss/issue. Send complete ms. Length: 800-1,000 words. Pays 6¢/word.
Photos: Photos purchased with accompanying ms. Captions required. Pays $8/5x7 (but all sizes accepted) b&w glossy print or color photo. Send prints. Total purchase price for ms includes payment for photos.
Fiction: Adventure; humorous; mainstream; and religious. Canadian settings preferred. Buys 6 mss/year. Send complete ms. Length: 800-1,000 words. Pays 6¢/word.
Tips: "Mss on human interest with photos are given immediate preference. In the year ahead we will be featuring shorter articles, more Canadian and Franciscan themes, and better photos." No poetry.

CONTEMPORARY CHRISTIAN MAGAZINE, (formerly *Contemporary Christian Music*), CCM Publications, Inc., Box 6300, Laguna Hills CA 92653. (714)951-9106. Editor-in-Chief/Publisher: John W. Styll. Editor: Ted Ojarovsky. Assistant Editor: Carolyn A. Burns. Monthly magazine covering contemporary Christian lifestyle. "We are a Christian publication that presents indepth profiles on vital contemporary Christians; reviews music and the arts from a Christian perspective; profiles people who support or, occasionally, challenge the Christian world view; and explores current issues to help readers better understand their faith, and how it relates to the world around them. The magazine is read primarily by 18-34 year old Christians with strong interest in music." Circ. 40,000. Pays on publication. Byline given. Pays $25 kill fee. Buys simultaneous rights. Submit seasonal/holiday material 4 months in advance. Simultaneous queries OK. SASE. Reports in 3 months. Sample copy $1.95; writer's guidelines for SASE. Address queries to editor.
Nonfiction: Book excerpts, how-to, humor, inspirational, interview/profile, current issues, arts/media, reviews, new product and personal experience. No articles unrelated to music and/or Christianity. Query with resume and clips of published work. Length: 50-2,500 words. Pays 8¢/word.
Photos: John Sutton, art director. State availability of photos. Pays negotiable rate for b&w prints or color transparencies. Identification of subjects required. Buys one-time rights.
Columns/Departments: Needs information on events, persons and news of the contemporary Christian scene in the US and worldwide. Query. Length: 10-500 words. Pays $50 maximum.

THE COVENANT COMPANION, 5101 N. Francisco Ave., Chicago IL 60625. (312)784-3000. Editor-in-Chief: James R. Hawkinson. 25% freelance written. Emphasizes Christian life and faith. Semimonthly (monthly issues July and August) magazine; 32 pages. Circ. 27,500. Pays following publication. Submit seasonal/holiday material 3 months in advance. Simultaneous, photocopied and previously published submissions OK. Computer printout submissions OK. SASE. Reports in 2-3 months. Sample copy $1.
Nonfiction: Humor; informational; inspirational (especially evangelical Christian); interviews (Christian leaders and personalities); and personal experience. "No articles promoting organizations or people not in the

church we serve (Evangelical Covenant Church)." Buys 20-30 mss/year. Length: 100-110 lines of typewritten material at 70 characters/line (double-spaced). Pays $15-35.

DAILY MEDITATION, Box 2710, San Antonio TX 78299. Editor: Ruth S. Paterson. Quarterly. Rights purchased vary. Byline given. Submit seasonal material six months in advance. Sample copy sent to writer on receipt of 50¢.
Nonfiction: Inspirational, self-improvement, nonsectarian religious articles, 500-1,600 words, showing path to greater spiritual growth.
Fillers: Length: 400 words maximum. Pays 1-1½¢/word for articles.
Poetry: Inspirational. Length: 16 lines maximum. Pays 14¢/line.
Tips: "All our material is freelance submission for consideration and we buy approximately 250 mss/year."

DAUGHTERS OF SARAH, 2716 W. Cortland, Chicago IL 60647. (312)252-3344. Editorial Coordinator: Reta Finger. Managing Editor: Pat Broughton. Bimonthly magazine covering Christian feminism. Circ. 2,500. Pays on publication. Byline given. Offers 33-50% kill fee. Buys first North American serial rights. Submit seasonal/holiday material 2 months in advance. Reports in 2 weeks on queries; 2 months on mss. Sample copy $1.25; writer's guidelines for SASE.
Nonfiction: Book excerpts (book reviews on Christian feminist books); Historical (on Christian women); humor (feminist); inspirational (biblical articles about women or feminist issues); interview/profile (of contemporary Christian women from feminist point of view); personal experience (women's—or men's—experiences from Christian feminist point of view); issues of social justice relating to women. Special issues include the male experience, women in prison, raising feminist children, sexuality, should feminists stay in the church? "No general, elementary aspects of Christian feminism. We've gone beyond that. We particularly do not want pieces about women or women's issues that are not written from a feminist and Christian point of view." Buys 5-10 mss/year. Query with or without clips of published work. Length: 500-2,000 words. (Book reviews on Christian feminist books, 100-500 words). Pays $10-50.
Fiction: Christian feminist. Buys 2-4 mss/year. Query with clips of published work. Length: 500-2,000 words. Pays $10-40.

DECISION MAGAZINE, 1300 Harmon Place, Minneapolis MN 55403. (612)338-0500. Editor: Roger C. Palms. Conservative evangelical monthly publication of the Billy Graham Evangelistic Association. Magazine; 16 pages. Circ. 3,000,000. Buys first rights on unsolicited manuscripts. Byline given. Pays on publication. Reports in 2 months. SASE.
Nonfiction: Uses some freelance material. Buys 27 full-length unsolicited mss/year. Best opportunity is in testimony area (1,800-2,200 words); buys 11 unsolicited short testimonies for "Where Are They Now?" column. Also uses short narratives, 400-800 words; buys 6 unsolicited mss/year. "Our function is to present Christ as Savior and Lord to unbelievers and present articles on deeper Christian life and human interest articles on Christian growth for Christian readers. No tangents. Center on Christ in all material."
Poetry: Uses devotional thoughts and short poems in Quiet Heart column. Positive, Christ-centered. Uses limited number of poems; send only if considered appropriate for magazine.
Tips: "The purpose of *Decision* is: 1) To set forth the Good News of salvation with such vividness and clarity that the reader will feel drawn to make a commitment to Christ; 2)To strengthen the faith of believers and to offer them hope and encouragement; and 3)To report on the ministries of the Billy Graham Evangelical Association."

THE DISCIPLE, Box 179, St. Louis MO 63166. Editor: James L. Merrell. Published by Christian Board of Publication of the Christian Church (Disciples of Christ). For ministers and church members, both young and older adults. Semimonthly, except monthly in July and December. Circ. 64,000. Buys all rights. Pays month after publication. Pays for photos at end of month of acceptance. Sample copy 35¢; free writer's guidelines. Photocopied and simultaneous submissions OK. "We've never received any computer printout submissions but we're willing to consider them." Prefers letter quality to dot matrix. Submit seasonal material at least 6 months in advance. Reports in 2 weeks to 3 months. SASE.
Nonfiction: Articles and meditations on religious themes; short pieces, some humorous. No fiction. Buys 220 unsolicited mss/year. Length: 500-800 words. Pays $10-50.
Photos: B&w glossy prints, 8x10. Occasional b&w glossy prints, any size, used to illustrate articles. Pays $10-25. Pays $35-100/cover. Occasional color. "We are looking for b&w photos of church activities—worship, prayer, dinners, etc."
Poetry: Uses 3-5 poems/issue. Traditional forms, blank verse, free verse and light verse. Length: 16 lines limit. Themes may be seasonal, historical, religious, occasionally humorous. Pays $3-20.
Tips: "We're looking for personality features about lay disciples, churches. Give good summary of story idea in query. We use articles primarily from disciples, ministers and lay persons since our magazine is written to attract the denomination. We work with more secular poets than writers and the poets write in religious themes for us."

ENGAGE/SOCIAL ACTION, 100 Maryland Ave. NE, Washington DC 20002. (202)488-5632. Editor: Lee Ranck. For "United Methodist clergy and lay people interested in in-depth analysis of social issues, with emphasis on the church's role or involvement in these issues." Monthly. Circ. 5,500. Rights purchased vary with author and material. May buy all rights. Buys 50-60 mss/year (freelance and assigned). Pays on publication. Free sample copy and writer's guidelines. Photocopied submissions OK, but prefers original. Returns rejected material in 4-5 weeks. Reports on material accepted for publication in several weeks. Query or submit complete ms. "Query to show that writer has expertise on a particular social issue, give credentials, and reflect a readable writing style." SASE.
Nonfiction: "This is the social action publication of the United Methodist Church published by the denomination's General Board of Church and Society. We publish articles relating to current social issues as well as church-related discussions. We do not publish highly technical articles or poetry. Our publication tries to relate social issues to the church—what the church can do, is doing; why the church should be involved. We only accept articles relating to social issues, e.g., war, draft, peace, race relations, welfare, police/community relations, labor, population problems, drug and alcohol problems." No devotional, 'religious,' superficial material or personal experiences. Length: 2,000 words maximum. Pays $50-75.
Tips: "Write on social issues, but not superficially; we're more interested in finding an expert (e.g., on human rights, alcohol problems, peace issues) who can write than a writer who attempts to research a complex issue."

EPIPHANY JOURNAL, Epiphany Press, Box 14727, San Francisco CA 94114. (415)431-1917. Editor: Gary Anderson. Quarterly magazine covering religious topics for the contemplative Christian. Circ. 3,000. Pays on publication. Byline given. Buys one-time rights and makes work-for-hire assignments. Submit seasonal/holiday material 6 months in advance. Simultaneous queries, and simultaneous and previously published submissions OK. Computer printout submissions OK; prefers letter quality to dot matrix. SASE. Reports in 2 weeks on queries; 2 months on mss. "Sample copy and writer's guidelines available for $4, which will be refunded with payment for your first article."
Nonfiction: Inspirational (examinations of aspects of the contemplative life, and of the Christian's role and responsibility in the modern world); interview/profile (interviews with current Christian figures; profiles of past and present figures in Christian life); and photo feature (series of artistic photos expressing a theme, e.g., "Transformation," "A Sense of the Divine," "The House of the Lord," and linked with poetry and prose). Recent article example: "The Eleventh Commandment" (summer 1981). Buys 10-20 mss/year. Query or send complete ms. Length: 2,000-8,000 words. Pays 2¢/word ($100 maximum). Also book excerpts (from forthcoming or recently published spiritual or religious works).
Columns/Departments: Book reviews (any current literature of interest to the Christian thinker). Buys 10-15 mss/year. Query or send complete ms. Length: 1,000-2,500 words. Pays 2¢/word ($30 maximum).
Tips: "Get to know our magazine, then send us a query letter or ask for an assignment suggestion. Prefers not to see first-person/anecdotal accounts."

THE EPISCOPALIAN, 1930 Chestnut St., Philadelphia PA 19103. (215)564-2010. Editor: Henry L. McCorkle. Managing Editor: Judy Mathe Foley. Monthly tabloid covering the Episcopal Church for Episcopalians. Circ. 285,000. Pays on publication. Byline given. Submit seasonal/holiday material 2 months in advance. Previously published submissions OK. SASE. Reports in 1 month. Sample copy for 2 first class stamps.
Nonfiction: Inspirational; and interview/profile (of Episcopalians participating in church or community activities). "I like action stories about people doing things and solving problems." No personal experience articles. Buys 24 mss/year. Send complete ms. Length: 1,000-1,500 words. Pays $25-200.
Photos: Pays $10 for b&w glossy prints. Identification of subjects required. Buys one-time rights.
Fillers: Newsbreaks. Buys 30/year. Length: 1,000 words minimum. Pays $25.

EVANGEL, Dept. of Christian Education, Free Methodist Headquarters, 901 College Ave., Winona Lake IN 46590. (219)267-7161. Editor: Vera Bethel. 100% freelance written. Audience is 65% female, 35% male; married, 25-31 years old, mostly city dwellers, high school graduates, mostly nonprofessional. Weekly magazine; 8 pages. Circ. 35,000. Pays on publication. Buys simultaneous, second serial (reprint) or one-time rights. Submit seasonal/holiday material 3 months in advance. Simultaneous and previously published submissions OK. Computer printout submissions OK; prefers letter quality to dot matrix. SASE. Reports in 4 weeks. Free sample copy and writer's guidelines.
Nonfiction: Interview (with ordinary person who is doing something extraordinary in his community, in service to others); profile (of missionary or one from similar service profession who is contributing significantly to society); personal experience (finding a solution to a problem common to man; coping with handicapped child, for instance, or with a neighborhood problem. Story of how God-given strength or insight saved a situation). Buys 100 mss/year. Submit complete ms. Length: 300-1,000 words. Pays $10-25.
Photos: Purchased with accompanying ms. Captions required. Send prints. Pays $5-10 for 8x10 b&w glossy prints; $2 for snapshots.
Fiction: Religious themes dealing with contemporary issues dealt with from a Christian frame of reference.

Story must "go somewhere." Buys 50 mss/year. Submit complete ms. Length: 1,200-1,500 words. Pays $35-40. SASE required.

Poetry: Free verse, haiku, light verse, traditional, religious. Buys 50/year. Limit submissions to batches of 5-6. Length: 4-24 lines. Pays $5. SASE required.

Tips: "Seasonal material will get a second look (won't be rejected so easily) because we get so little. Write an attention-grabbing lead, followed by a body of article that says something worthwhile. Relate the lead to some of the universal needs of the reader—promise in that lead to help the reader in some way. Remember that everybody is interested most in himself. Lack of SASE brands author as a nonprofessional; I seldom even bother to read the script. If the writer doesn't want the script back, it probably has no value for me, either."

THE EVANGELICAL BEACON, 1515 E. 66th St., Minneapolis MN 55423. (612)866-3343. Editor: George Keck. Denominational magazine of the Evangelical Free Church of America—evangelical Protestant readership. Published twice monthly except monthly July, August and December. Rights purchased vary with author and material. Buys all or first rights, some reprints. Pays on publication. Sample copy and writer's guidelines for 60¢. Reports on submissions in 6-8 weeks. Computer printout or disk submissions OK. SASE must be included.

Nonfiction: Articles on the church, Christ-centered human interest and personal testimony articles, well-researched on current issues of religious interest. Desire crisp, imaginative, original writing—not sermons on paper. Length: 250-2,000 words. Pays 3¢/word.

Photos: Prefers 8x10 b&w photos. Pays $7.50 minimum.

Fiction: Not much fiction used, but will consider. Length: 100-1,500 words.

Poetry: Very little poetry used. Pays variable rate, $3.50 minimum.

Tips: "Articles need to be helpful to the average Christian—encouraging, challenging, instructive. Also need material presenting reality of the Christian faith to non-Christians. Some tie-in with the Evangelical Free Church of America is helpful, but is not required."

EVANGELIZING TODAY'S CHILD, Child Evangelism Fellowship Inc., Warrenton MO 63383. (314)456-4321. Editor: Mrs. Elsie Lippy. Unsolicited articles welcomed from writers with Christian education training or experience. Our purpose—to equip Christians to win the world's children to Christ and disciple them. Our readership—Sunday school teachers, Christian education leaders and children's workers in every phase of Christian ministry to children up to 12 years old.

Photos: Submissions of photos on speculation accepted. Need photos of children or related subjects. Please include SASE. Pays $20-25 for 8x10 b&w glossy prints; $50-150 for color transparencies.

FAITH AND INSPIRATION, Seraphim Publishing Group, Inc., 720 White Plains Rd., Scarsdale NY 10583. (914)472-5500. Editor: D.M. Sheehan. 50% freelance written. Emphasizes religious and secular inspirational material for a family readership. Quarterly. Circ. 50,000. Pays on publication. Buys all rights with exceptions. Byline given. Submit seasonal/holiday material 4 months in advance of issue date. Photocopied submissions OK. SASE. Reports in 2 months. Sample copy and writer's guidelines $1.50.

Nonfiction: Inspirational; interview; personal experience (moving articles of inspiration, does not have to be religious); and profile. Buys 20 mss/issue. Submit complete ms. Length: 50-1,200 words. Pays 5¢/word.

Poems: Light verse and traditional. Buys 6 poems/issue. Limit submissions to batches of 3. Length: 5-20 lines. Pays $5-15.

Fillers: Short humor, religious, anecdotes and inspirational material. Buys 10/issue. Length: 25-100 words. Pays $5-15.

FAMILY LIFE TODAY MAGAZINE, 2300 Knoll Dr., Ventura CA 93003. (805)644-9721. Editor: Phyllis Alsdurf. 70% freelance written. Emphasizes "building strong marriages and helping Christian families deal with the realities of contemporary life." Monthly magazine; 48 pages. Circ. 50,000. Pays on publication. Byline given. Submit seasonal/holiday material 6 months in advance of issue date. Previously published submissions OK, "but we're accepting few reprints these days. Letter-type printouts OK if separated and in regular page order; prefers traditional form." SASE. Reports in 2 months. Sample copy and writer's guidelines for $1 and 9x12 SASE.

Nonfiction: All articles need to reflect a Christian value system. How-to (any family-related situation with narrow focus: how to help the hyperactive child, etc.); humor (if wholesome and family-related); interview (with person who is recognized authority in area of marriage and family life); personal experience ("when my husband lost his job," etc.); and photo feature (family-related). Buys 100 unsolicited mss/year. Query. Length: 300-1,500 words. Pays 4-5¢/word for original; 3¢/word for reprints.

Photos: State availability of photos with query. Pays $15-30 for 8x10 b&w glossy print; $35-85 for 35mm color transparencies. Buys one-time rights. Model release preferred.

Tips: "Don't send mss that offer 'pat' answers ('and they lived happily ever after') to complex family problems. Articles that show in a realistic manner the struggle a family or couple has experienced are what we look for. All mss are carefully read so no gimmicks are needed to get our attention, except a clear writing style and a timely topic. We need more articles by fathers and husbands on parenting and marriage.''

FRIDAY (OF THE JEWISH EXPONENT), 226 S. 16th St., Philadelphia PA 19102. (215)893-5745. Editor: Jane Biberman. For the Jewish community of Greater Philadelphia. Monthly literary supplement. Circ. 100,000. Buys first rights. Pays 25% kill fee. Byline given. Buys 25 unsolicited mss/year. Pays after publication. Free sample copy and writer's guidelines. Photocopied submissions OK. No simultaneous submissions. Submit special material 3 months in advance. Reports in 3 weeks. SASE.
Nonfiction and Photos: "We are interested only in articles on Jewish themes, whether they be historical, thought pieces, Jewish travel or photographic essays. Topical themes are appreciated." Length: 6-20 double-spaced pages. Pays $50 minimum.
Fiction: Short stories on Jewish themes. Length: 6-20 double-spaced pages. Pays $50 minimum.
Poetry: Traditional forms, blank verse, free verse, avant-garde forms, light verse; must relate to a Jewish theme. Length varies. Pays $15 minimum.
Tips: "Pieces on Jewish personalities—artists, musicians, authors—are most welcome." Include illustrative material.

GOOD NEWS, The Forum for Scriptural Christianity, Inc., 308 E. Main St., Wilmore KY 40390. (606)858-4661. Editor: James V. Heidinger II. Managing Editor: Ann L. Coker. For United Methodist lay people and pastors, primarily middle income; conservative and Biblical religious beliefs; broad range of political, social and cultural values. "We are the only evangelical magazine with the purpose of working within the United Methodist Church for Biblical reform and evangelical renewal." Bimonthly magazine. Circ. 15,500. Pays on acceptance. Byline given. Phone queries OK. Submit seasonal/holiday material 6 months in advance. Simultaneous submissions OK. Prefers original mss and not photostats of reprinted material. SASE. Reports in 2 months. Sample copy $1; free writer's guidelines.
Nonfiction: Historical (prominent people or churches from the Methodist/Evangelical United Brethren tradition); how-to (build faith, work in local church); humor (good taste); inspirational (related to Christian faith); personal experience (case histories of God at work in individual lives); and any contemporary issues as they relate to the Christian faith and the United Methodist Church. No sermons or secular material. Recent article: "When the Dog Bites" (March/April 1983). Buys 25 mss/year. Query with a "brief description of the article, perhaps a skeleton outline. Show some enthusiasm about the article and writing (and research). Tell us something about yourself (though not a list of credentials); whether you or the article has United Methodist tie-in." Pays $20-75.
Photos: Photos purchased with accompanying ms or on assignment. Captions required. Uses fine screen b&w glossy prints. Total purchase price for ms includes payment for photos. Payment negotiable.
Columns/Departments: Good News Book Forum. Query.
Fillers: Anecdotes, United Methodist newsbreaks and short humor. Buys 15 fillers/year. Pays $5-10.
Tips: "We are using more short articles (4-5 magazine pages), tighter writing, more visual writing, and fewer reprints."

GOOD NEWS BROADCASTER, Box 82808, Lincoln NE 68501. (402)474-4567. Editor: Theodore H. Epp. Interdenominational magazine for adults from 17 years of age and up. Monthly. Circ. 160,000. Buys first rights. Buys approximately 100 mss/year. Pays on acceptance. Sample copy and writer's guidelines for postage. Send all mss to Norman A. Olson, managing editor. Submit seasonal material at least 12 months in advance. Reports in 5 weeks. SASE required.
Nonfiction and Photos: Articles which will help the reader learn and apply Christian Biblical principles to his life. From the writer's or the subject's own experience. "Especially looking for true, personal experience 'salvation,' church, children's ages 4-10, missions, 'youth' (17 years and over), 'parents,' 'how to live the Christian life' articles, reports and interviews regarding major and interesting happenings and people in fundamental, evangelical Christian circles." Nothing rambling or sugary sweet, or without Biblical basis. Details or statistics should be authentic and verifiable. Style should be conservative but concise. Prefers that Scripture references be from the *New American Standard Version* or the *Authorized Version* or the *New Scofield Reference Bible*. Length: 1,500 words maximum. Pays 4-10¢/word. "When you can get us to assign an article to you, we pay nearer the maximum." Photos often purchased with mss. Pays $25 maximum for b&w glossies; $75 maximum for color transparencies. Photos paid on publication.
Tips: "The basic purpose of the magazine is to explain the Bible and how it is relevant to life because we believe this will accomplish one of two things—to present Christ as Saviour to the lost or to promote the spiritual growth of believers, so don't ignore our primary purposes when writing for us. Nonfiction should be Biblical and timely; at the least Biblical in principle. Use illustrations of your own experiences or of someone else's when God solved a problem similar to the reader's. Be so specific that the meanings and significance will be crystal clear to all readers."

GOSPEL CARRIER, Messenger Publishing House, Box 850, Joplin MO 64802. (417)624-7050. Editor-in-Chief: Roy M. Chappell, D.D. Denominational Sunday School take-home paper for adults, ages 20 through retirement. Quarterly publication in weekly parts; 104 pages. Circ. 3,500. Pays quarterly. Buys simultaneous, second serial and one-time rights. Byline given. Submit seasonal/holiday material 1 year in advance. Simultaneous, photocopied and previously published submissions OK. SASE. Reports in 3 months. Sample copy and writer's guidelines for 50¢.

Nonfiction: Historical (related to great events in the history of the church); informational (may explain the meaning of a Bible passage or a Christian concept); inspirational (must make a Christian point); nostalgia (religious significance); and personal experience (Christian concept). No puzzles, poems, filler material.

Fiction: Adventure; historical; romance; and religious. Must have Christian significance. Buys 13-20 mss/issue. Submit complete ms. Length: 1,500-1,800 words. Pays 1¢/word.

GUIDEPOSTS MAGAZINE, 747 3rd Ave., New York NY 10017. Editor: Van Varner. "*Guideposts* is an inspirational monthly magazine for all faiths in which men and women from all walks of life tell how they overcame obstacles, rose above failures, met sorrow, learned to master themselves, and became more effective people through the direct application of the religious principles by which they live." Buys all rights. Pays 25% kill fee for assigned articles. Buys 40-60 unsolicited mss/year. Byline given. "Most of our stories are first-person ghosted articles, so the author would not get a byline unless it was his/her story." SASE.

Nonfiction and Fillers: Articles and features should be written in simple, anecdotal style with an emphasis on human interest. Short mss of approximately 250-750 words ($25-100) would be considered for such features as "Quiet People" and general one-page stories. Full-length mss, 750-1,500 words ($200-300). All mss should be typed, double-spaced and accompanied by a stamped, self-addressed envelope. Annually awards scholarships to high school juniors and seniors in writing contest.

Tips: "The freelancer would have the best chance of breaking in by aiming for a 1-page or maybe 2-page article. That would be very short, say 2½ pages of typescript, but in a small magazine such things are very welcome. A sensitively written anecdote that could provide us with an additional title is extremely useful. And they are much easier to just sit down and write than to have to go through the process of preparing a query. They should be warm, well-written, intelligent and upbeat. We like personal narratives that are true and have some universal relevance, but the religious element does not have to be hammered home with a sledge hammer." Address short items to Nancy Schraffenberger.

HIGH ADVENTURE, 1445 Boonville Ave., Springfield MO 65802. (417)862-2781, ext. 1497. Editor: Johnnie Barnes. For boys and men. Quarterly; 16 pages. Circ. 53,000. Rights purchased vary with author and material. Buys 10-12 mss/year. Pays on acceptance. Free sample copy and writer's guidelines. Query or submit complete ms. SASE.

Nonfiction, Fiction, Photos and Fillers: Camping articles, nature stories, fiction adventure stories and jokes. Nature study and campcraft articles about 500-600 words. Buys how-to, personal experience, inspirational, humor and historical articles. Length: 1,200 words. Pays 2¢/word. Photos purchased on assignment. Adventure and western fiction wanted. Puzzles, jokes and short humor used as fillers.

‡INDIAN LIFE, Intertribal Christian Communications, Box 3765, Station B, Winnipeg, Manitoba, Canada R2W 3R6. (204)338-0311. Editor: George McPeek. Bimonthly magazine of Christian experience from a native American (Indian) point of view for readers in 30 different denominations and missions. Circ. 10,000. Pays on publication. Byline given. Buys first rights and second serial (reprint) rights. Submit seasonal/holiday material 4 months in advance. Photocopied and previously published submissions OK. Canada: SAE and IRCs outside Canada. Reports in 3 weeks on queries; 6 weeks on mss. Sample copy for 9x12 SAE and 50¢ Canadian postage; writer's guidelines for $1, business-size SAE and 37¢ Canadian postage.

Nonfiction: Historical/nostalgic (with a positive approach); inspirational; interview/profile (of Indian Christian personalities); personal experience; photo feature; general news (showing Indian achievements); human interest (wholesome, but not necessarily religious). Special edition on the Indian and alcohol (statistics, self-help programs, personal experience, etc.). No political, sexually suggestive, or negative articles on personalities, groups or points of view. Buys 12 mss/year. Query with clips. Length: 500-1,500 words. Pays $20-45; less for news items.

Photos: State availability of photos. Pays $3-5 for b&w contact sheet; $10-20 for 35mm slides or other color transparencies; $5-10 for 5x7 b&w prints. Captions, model release and identification of subjects required. Buys one-time rights.

Fiction: Adventure, confession, historical, religious, and legends with Christian applications. No explicit sex or negative themes. Buys 4-6 mss/year. Query with clips of published work. Length: 500-1,200 words. Pays $20-40.

Fillers: Clippings, jokes, anecdotes, short humor, newsbreaks. Buys 25-30/year. Length: 50-200 words. Pays $3-10.

Tips: "First person stories must be verifiable with references (including one from pastor or minister) attached. Most material is written by Indian people, but some articles by non-Indians are accepted. Maintain an Indian point of view. We seek to build a positive self-image, provide culturally-relevant material and serve as a voice for the Indian church.''

INSIGHT, The Young Calvinist Federation, Box 7244, Grand Rapids MI 49510. (616)241-5616. Editor: John Knight. Assistant Editor: Martha Kalk. For young people, 16-21, Christian backgrounds and well-exposed to the Christian faith. Monthly (except June and August) magazine; 32 pages. Circ. 23,000. Pays on publication. Buys simultaneous, second serial (reprint) and first North American serial rights. Byline given. Phone queries OK. Submit seasonal/holiday material 6 months in advance. Simultaneous, photocopied and previously published submissions OK. SASE. Reports in 4 weeks. Sample copy and writer's guidelines for 9x12 SASE.
Photos: Photos purchased without accompanying ms or on assignment. Pays $15-25/8x10 b&w glossy print; $50-200 for 35mm or larger color transparencies. Total purchase price for ms includes payment for photos.
Fiction: Humorous, mainstream and religious. ''Looks for short stories and nonfiction that lead our readers to a better understanding of how Christianity is relevant to daily life, social issues, the arts. They must do more than entertain—they must make the reader see things in a new light.'' No syrupy, sentimental, moralistic religious guidance articles. Buys 1-2 mss/issue. Send complete ms. Length: 1,000-3,000 words. Pays $45-100.
Poetry: Free verse; light verse, and traditional. Buys 10 poems/year. Length: 4-25 lines. Pays $20-25.
Fillers: Youth-oriented cartoons, jokes, gags, anecdotes, puzzles and short humor. Length: 50-300 words. Pays $10-35.
Tips: ''We are looking for shorter contributions and short, short stories.''

INTERLIT, David C. Cook Foundation, Cook Square, Elgin IL 60120. (312)741-2400, ext. 322. Editor-in-Chief: Gladys J. Peterson. 90% freelance on assignment. ''Please study publication and query before submitting mss.'' Emphasizes Christian communications and journalism especially for editors, publishers, and writers in the Third World (developing countries). Also goes to missionaries, broadcasters, and educational personnel in the U.S. Quarterly journal; 24 pages. Circ. 9,000. Pays on acceptance. Buys all rights. Photocopied submissions OK. SASE. Reports in 2 weeks. Free sample copy.
Nonfiction: Technical and how-to articles about communications, media, and literacy. Also photo features. Buys 7 mss/issue. Length: 500-1,500 words. Pays 6¢/word.
Photos: Purchased with accompanying ms only. Captions required. Query or send prints. Uses b&w.

LIBERTY, A Magazine of Religious Freedom, 6840 Eastern Ave. NW, Washington DC 20012. (202)722-6691. Editor: Roland R. Hegstad. For ''responsible citizens interested in community affairs and religious freedom.'' Bimonthly. Circ. 450,000. Buys first rights. Buys approximately 40 mss/year. Pays on acceptance. Sample copy $1. Writer's guidelines for SASE. Photocopied submissions OK. Submit seasonal material in our field 6-8 months in advance. Reports in 2-4 weeks. Query not essential, but helpful. SASE.
Nonfiction: ''Articles of national and international interest in field of religious liberty and church-state relations. Current events affecting above areas (Sunday law problems, parochial aid problems, religious discrimination by state, etc.). Current events are most important; base articles on current events rather than essay form.'' Buys how-to's, personal experience and think pieces, interviews, profiles in field of religious liberty. Length: maximum 2,500 words. Pays up to $250.
Photos: ''To accompany or illustrate articles.'' Purchased with mss; with captions only. B&w glossy prints, color transparencies. Pays $15-35. Cover photos to $250.

LIGHT AND LIFE, Free Methodist Publishing House, 901 College Ave., Winona Lake IN 46590. Managing Editor: Lyn Cryderman. 35% freelance written. Emphasizes evangelical Christianity with Wesleyan slant for a cross-section of adults. Published monthly. Magazine; 36 pages. Circ. 55,000. Pays on publication. Prefers first rights. Byline given. Submit seasonal/holiday material 6 months in advance. Previously published submissions OK. Computer printout submissions OK; prefers letter quality to dot matrix. SASE. Reports in 6 weeks. Sample copy $1.50; writer's guidelines for SASE.
Nonfiction: ''Each issue uses a lead article (warm, positive first-person account of God's help in a time of crisis; 1,500 words); a Christian living article (a fresh, lively, upbeat piece about practical Christian living; 750 words); a Christian growth article (an in-depth, lay-level article on a theme relevant to the maturing Christian; 1,500 words); a discipleship article (a practical how-to piece on some facet of Christian discipleship; 750 words).'' Buys 70-80 unsolicited mss/year. Submit complete ms. Pays 3¢/word.
Photos: Purchased without accompanying ms. Send prints. Pays $5-35 for b&w photos. Offers additional payment for photos accepted with accompanying ms.

LIGUORIAN, Liguori MO 63057. Editor: the Rev. Norman Muckerman. 50% freelance written. For families with Catholic religious convictions. Monthly. Circ. 570,000. Byline given ''except on short fillers and jokes.'' Pays on acceptance. Submit seasonal material 5-6 months in advance. Computer printout submissions OK; prefers letter quality to dot matrix. ''We ask contributors to submit printout first and send disk upon acceptance. Disk must be adaptable to TRS80, model III.'' Reports in 6-8 weeks. SASE.
Nonfiction: ''Pastoral, practical and personal approach to the problems and challenges of people today. No

travelogue approach or unresearched ventures into controversial areas. Also, no material found in secular publications—fad subjects that already get enough press, pop psychology, negative or put-down articles." Recent article examples: "REC: A New Prison Ministry" (January 1982) and "An Open Letter to Katharine Hepburn" (April 1982). Buys 60 unsolicited mss/year. Length: 400-2,000 words. Pays 7-10¢/word. Photos purchased with mss; b&w glossy prints.

LILLENAS PROGRAM BUILDERS, Lillenas Publishing Company, Box 527, Kansas City MO 64141. Editor: Paul Miller. Booklets covering program scripts, outlines, and ideas for the Sunday School and church. "We look for unique program ideas for use in Sunday Schools and churches, large and small, with an evangelical slant." Bookstore circulation. Pays on acceptance. Byline given. Buys first rights. Submit seasonal/holiday material 12 months in advance. "Only original material, no previously published submissions." SASE. Reports in 1 month. Free writer's guidelines for SAE and 20¢ postage.
Nonfiction: "Some inspirational and devotional articles suitable for readings. Skits, devotional messages, emcee ideas, banquet plans, church-related humor. Christmas is overworked; Thanksgiving is wide open. Any program you might present in your own church would have a chance in this market." No "secular subjects, such as Santa Claus, Easter Bunnies, etc." Send complete ms. Payment depends upon length and quality.
Poetry: "Recitations; poems suitable for reading aloud before an audience. Sacred poetry, only." Pays 25¢/line.
Tips: "This is a good market for beginning Christian writers. We try to answer rejections personally, and offer suggestions for better luck next time. Dozens of manuscripts are waiting for a spot, so beginners specifying rights, or copyrighting their material have less of a chance. I'm appalled at how many writers neglect SASE! We still return their manuscripts and reply to their letters, but don't look kindly on such writers, if done regularly. I personally prefer to see the manuscript. Writing a fantastic query is okay, but few can cough up a good finished product. A covering letter can be disastrous, too. The worst thing to give me is a list of meaningless credentials."

LIVE, 1445 Boonville Ave., Springfield MO 65802. (417)862-2781. Editor: Kenneth D. Barney. 100% freelance written. For adults in Assemblies of God Sunday Schools. Weekly. Circ. 225,000. Not copyrighted. Buys about 100 mss/year. Pays on acceptance. Free sample copy and writer's guidelines. Submit seasonal material 10 months in advance. Reports on material within 6 weeks. No computer printout or disk submissions. SASE.
Nonfiction and Photos: "Articles with reader appeal, emphasizing some phase of Christian living, presented in a down-to-earth manner. Biography or missionary material using fiction techniques. Historical, scientific or nature material with a spiritual lesson. Be accurate in detail and factual material. Writing for Christian publications is a ministry. The spiritual emphasis must be an integral part of your material." Prefers not to see material on highly controversial subjects. Length: 1,000 words maximum. Pays 3¢/word for first rights; 2¢/word for second rights, according to the value of the material and the amount of editorial work necessary. Color photos or transparencies purchased with mss, or on assignment. Pay open.
Fiction: "Present believable characters working out their problems according to Bible principles; in other words, present Christianity in action, without being preachy. We use very few serials, but we will consider 3-4 part stories if each part conforms to average word length for short stories. Each part must contain a spiritual emphasis and have enough suspense to carry the reader's interest from one week to the next. Stories should be true to life, but not what we would feel is bad to set before the reader as a pattern for living. Stories should not put parents, teachers, ministers or other Christian workers in a bad light. Setting, plot and action should be realistic, with strong motivation. Characterize so that the people will live in your story. Construct your plot carefully so that each incident moves naturally and sensibly toward crisis and conclusion. An element of conflict is necessary in fiction. Short stories should be written from one viewpoint only. We do not accept fiction based on incidents in the Bible." Length: 1,200-2,000 words. Pays 3¢/word for first rights; 2¢/word for second rights.
Poetry: Buys traditional, free and blank verse. Length: 12-20 lines. "Please do not send large numbers of poems at one time." Pays 20¢/line, for first rights.
Fillers: Brief, purposeful, usually containing an anecdote, and always with a strong evangelical emphasis.

LIVING WITH TEENAGERS, Baptist Sunday School Board, 127 9th Ave., Nashville TN 37234. (615)251-2273. Editor: E. Lee Sizemore. Quarterly magazine about teenagers for the Baptist parents of teenagers. Circ. 35,000. Pays within 60 days of acceptance. Buys all rights. Submit seasonal material 1 year in advance. Computer printout and disk submissions OK. Reports in 3 months. Free sample copy and writer's guidelines.
Nonfiction: "We are looking for a unique Christian element. We want a genuine insight into the teen-parent relationships." General interest (on communication; emotional problems; growing up; drugs and alcohol; leisure; sex education; spiritual growth; working teens and parents; money; family relationships; and church relationships); inspirational; personal experience. Buys 80 unsolicited mss/year. Query with clips of previously published work. Length: 600-2,100 words. Pays 4¢/published word.
Photos: Pays $15 minimum/5x7 b&w glossy print. Reviews b&w contact sheets and 2¼x2¼ and 35mm color

transparencies. "We need cover transparencies of parents with youth." Captions preferred; model release required.

Fiction: Humorous and religious, but must relate to parent-teen relationship. "No stories from the teen's point of view." Buys 2 mss/issue. Query with clips of previously published work. Length: 600-2,100 words. Pays 4¢/published word.

Poetry: Free verse, light verse, traditional and devotional and inspirational; all must relate to parent-teen relationship. Buys 3 mss/issue. Submit 5 poems maximum. Length: 33 characters maximum. Pays $1.50 plus 85¢/line for 1-7 lines; $4.30 plus 50¢/line for 8 lines minimum.

Tips: "Write in the first person. Make liberal use of illustrations and case studies. Write from the parent's point-of-view."

THE LOOKOUT, 8121 Hamilton Ave., Cincinnati OH 45231. (513)931-4050. Editor: Mark A. Taylor. 50% freelance written. For the adult and young adult of the Sunday morning Bible school. Weekly. Pays on acceptance. Byline given. Buys first or reprint rights. Simultaneous submissions OK. Computer printout submissions OK; prefers letter quality to dot matrix. SASE. Reports in 2 months. Sample copy and writer's guidelines 50¢.

Nonfiction: "Seeks stories about real people or Sunday-School classes; items that shed Biblical light on matters of contemporary controversy; and items that motivate, that lead the reader to ask, 'Why shouldn't I try that?' or 'Why couldn't our Sunday-School class accomplish this?' Should tell how real people are involved for Christ. In choosing topics, *The Lookout* considers timeliness, the church and national calendar, and the ability of the material to fit the above guidelines. Tell us about ideas that are working in your Sunday School and in the lives of its members. Remember to aim at laymen." Submit complete ms. Length: 1,200-1,800 words. Pays 3-5¢/word.

Fiction: "A short story is printed in most issues; it is usually between 1,200-1,800 words long, and should be as true to life as possible while remaining inspirational and helpful. Use familiar settings and situations."

Fillers: Inspirational or humorous shorts. "About 600-800 words is a good length for these. Relate an incident that illustrates a point without preaching. Pays 3-4¢/word.

Photos: B&w prints, 4x6 or larger. Pays $5-25. Pays $50-140 for color transparencies for covers and inside use. Needs photos of people, especially adults in a variety of settings.

THE LUTHERAN, 2900 Queen Lane, Philadelphia PA 19129. (215)438-6580. Editor: Edgar R. Trexler. General interest magazine of the Lutheran Church in America. Twice monthly, except single issues in July, August and December. Buys one-time rights. Pays on acceptance. Free sample copy and writer's guidelines. SASE.

Nonfiction: Popularly written material about human concerns with reference to the Christian faith. "We are especially interested in articles in 4 main fields: Christian ideology; personal religious life, social responsibilities; Church at work; human interest stories about people in whom considerable numbers of other people are likely to be interested." Write "primarily to convey information rather than opinions. Every article should be based on a reasonable amount of research or should explore some source of information not readily available. Most readers are grateful for simplicity of style. Sentences should be straightforward, with a minimum of dependent clauses and prepositional phrases." Length: 500-2,000 words. Pays $75-225.

Photos: Buys pix submitted with mss. Good 8x10 glossy prints. Pays $15-25. Also color for cover use. Pays up to $150.

Tips: "We need informative, detailed query letters. We also accept manuscripts on speculation only and we prefer not to encourage an abundance of query letters."

LUTHERAN FORUM, 308 W. 46th St., New York NY 10036-3894. (212)757-1292. Editor: Glenn C. Stone. For church leadership, clerical and lay. Magazine; 40 pages. Quarterly. Circ. 5,400. Rights purchased vary with author and material. Buys all rights, first North American serial rights, first serial rights, second serial (reprint) rights, simultaneous rights. Byline given. Buys 12-15 mss/year. Pays on publication. Sample copy $1.25. Will consider photocopied and simultaneous submissions. Computer printout submissions OK; prefers letter quality to dot matrix. Reports in 4-6 weeks. Query or submit complete ms. SASE.

Nonfiction: Articles about important issues and developments in the church's institutional life and in its cultural/social setting. Special interest in articles on the Christian's life in secular vocations. No purely devotional/inspirational material. Payment varies; $20 minimum. Length: 1,000-3,000 words. Informational, how-to, interview, profile, think articles and expose. Length: 500-3,000 words. Pays $20-50.

Photos: Purchased with mss or with captions only. Prefers 4x5 prints. Pays $10 minimum.

THE LUTHERAN JOURNAL, 7317 Cahill Rd., Edina MN 55435. Editor: The Rev. Armin U. Deye. Family magazine for Lutheran church members, middle age and older. Quarterly magazine; 32 pages. Circ. 115,000. Copyrighted. Byline given. Buys 12-15 mss/year. Pays on publication. Free sample copy. Will consider photocopied and simultaneous submissions. Reports in 8 weeks. Submit complete ms. SASE.

Nonfiction and Photos: Inspirational, religious, human interest, and historical articles. Interesting or unusual church projects. Informational, how-to, personal experience, interview, humor, think articles. Length: 1,500 words maximum; occasionally 2,000 words. Pays 1-3¢/word. B&w and color photos purchased with accompanying ms. Captions required. Payment varies.

Fiction and Poetry: Mainstream, religious and historical fiction. Must be suitable for church distribution. Length: 2,000 words maximum. Pays 1-1½¢/word. Traditional poetry, blank verse, free verse, related to subject matter.

THE LUTHERAN STANDARD, 426 S. 5th St., Box 1209, Minneapolis MN 55440. (612)330-3300. Editor: The Rev. Lowell G. Almen. 50% freelance written. "We are assigning more projects to specific writers in our editorial planning." For families in congregations of the American Lutheran Church. Semimonthly. Circ. 574,000. Buys first rights or multiple rights. Byline given. Buys 30-50 mss/year. Pays on acceptance. Free sample copy. Reports in 3 weeks. SASE.

Nonfiction: Inspirational articles, especially about members of the American Lutheran Church who are practicing their faith in noteworthy ways, or congregations with unusual programs. "Should be written in language clearly understandable to persons with a mid-high school reading ability." Also publishes articles that discuss current social issues and problems (crime, family life, divorce, etc.) in terms of Christian involvement and solutions. No poetry. Length: limit 1,200 words. Pays 8¢/word.

Tips: "We are interested in personal experience pieces with strong first-person approach. The ms may be on a religious and social issue, but with evident human interest using personal anecdotes and illustrations. How has an individual faced a serious problem and overcome it? How has faith made a difference in a person's life? We prefer letters that clearly describe the proposed project. Excerpts from the project or other samples of the author's work are helpful in determining whether we are interested in dealing with an author. We would appreciate it if more freelance writers seemed to have a sense of who our readers are and an awareness of the kinds of manuscripts we in fact publish."

LUTHERAN WOMEN, 2900 Queen Lane, Philadelphia PA 19129. Editor: Terry Schutz. 40% freelance written. 10 times yearly. Circ. 40,000. Decides about acceptance within 2 months. Prefers to see mss 6 months ahead of issue, at beginning of planning stage. Can consider up to 3 months before publication. SASE. Sample copy 75¢.

Nonfiction: Anything of interest to mothers—young or old—professional or other working women related to the contemporary expression of Christian faith in daily life, community action, international concerns. Family publication standards. No recipes or housekeeping hints. Length: 1,500-2,000 words. Some shorter pieces accepted. Pays up to $50 for full-length ms and photos.

Photos: Purchased with or without mss. Women; family situations; religious art objects; overseas situations related to church. Should be clear, sharp b&w. No additional payment for those used with mss. Pays $25-40 for those purchased without mss.

Fiction: Should show deepening of insight; story expressing new understanding in faith; story of human courage, self-giving, building up of community. Length: 2,000 words. Pays $30-40.

Poetry: Very little is used. "Biggest taboo for us is sentimentality. We are limited to family magazine type contributions regarding range of vocabulary, but we don't want almanac-type poetry." No limit on number of lines. Pays $20-35 minimum/poem.

MARIAN HELPERS BULLETIN, Eden Hill, Stockbridge MA 01262. (413)298-3691. Editor: the Rev. Joseph J. Sielski, M.I.C. 90% freelance written. For average Catholics of varying ages with moderate religious views and general education. Quarterly. Circ. 1,000,000. Not copyrighted. Byline given. Buys 18-24 mss/year. Pays on acceptance. Free sample copy. Reports in 4-8 weeks. Submit seasonal material 6 months in advance. SASE.

Nonfiction and Photos: "Subject matter is of general interest on devotional, spiritual, moral and social topics. Use a positive, practical and optimistic approach, without being sophisticated. We would like to see articles on the Blessed Virgin Mary." Buys informational and inspirational articles. Length: 300-900 words. Pays $25-35. Photos are purchased with or without mss; captions optional. Pays $5-10 for b&w glossy prints.

MARRIAGE & FAMILY LIVING, St. Meinrad IN 47577. (812)357-8011. Managing Editor: Ila M. Stabile. 50% freelance written. Monthly magazine. Circ. 60,000. Pays on acceptance. Buys first North American serial rights, first book reprint option and control of other reprint rights. Byline given. Query. Computer printout or disk submissions OK; prefers letter quality to dot matrix. SASE. Reports in 4-6 weeks. Sample copy 50¢.

Nonfiction: Uses 1) Articles aimed at enriching the husband-wife and parent-child relationship by expanding religious and psychological insights or sensitivity. (Note: Ecumenically Judeo-Christian but in conformity with Roman Catholicism.) Length: 1,000-2,000 words. 2) Informative articles aimed at helping the couple cope, in practical ways, with the problems of modern living. Length: 2,000 words maximum. 3) Personal essays relating amusing and/or heart-warming incidents that point up the human side of marriage and family life. No material not directly related to Christian marriage and family life. Buys 20-30 unsolicited mss/year. Length: 1,500 words maximum. Pays 7¢/word.

Photos: Mark Laurenson, art director. B&w glossy prints (5x7 or larger) and color transparencies or 35mm slides (vertical preferred). Pays $150/4-color cover photo; $50/b&w cover photo; $35/2-page spread in contents, $30 for 1 page in contents; $10 minimum. Photos of couples, families and individuals especially desirable. Model releases required.

Tips: "Query with a brief outline of article's contents and the opening couple of paragraphs. Make sure the subject matter is pertinent to our guidelines. Stay within the word limit. We prefer material to be backed up by the *facts*. We are leaning more and more toward assigned articles."

‡**MARYKNOLL MAGAZINE**, Maryknoll Fathers, Maryknoll NY 10545. (914)941-7590. Editor: Moises Sandoval. Managing Editor: Frank Maurovich. Monthly magazine of foreign mission concerns. Circ. 1.2 million. Pays on acceptance. Byline given. Buys first North American serial rights, one-time rights and makes work-for-hire assignments. Submit seasonal/holiday material 8 months in advance. SASE. Reports in 3 weeks. Free sample copy and writer's guidelines.

Nonfiction: Inspirational, interview/profile, personal experience, photo feature. Query. Length: 800-1,000 words. Pays $75-200.

Photos: Pays $35-100 for 35mm color transparencies; $15-30 for 5x7 and 8x10 b&w prints.

Tips: Freelancers can best break in "with an article about missionary work or the social, economic or political conditions in the 25 countries where we work."

MENNONITE BRETHREN HERALD, 159 Henderson Hwy., Winnipeg, Manitoba, Canada R2L 1L4. Contact: Editor. Family publication "read mainly by people of the Mennonite faith, reaching a wide cross-section of professional and occupational groups, but also including many homemakers. Readership includes people from both urban and rural communities." Biweekly. Circ. 12,000. Pays on publication. Not copyrighted. Byline given. Sample copy 75¢. Reports in 1 month. SAE and International Reply Coupons.

Nonfiction and Photos: Articles with a Christian family orientation; youth directed, Christian faith and life, current issues. Wants articles critiquing the values of a secular society, attempting to relate Christian living to the practical situations of daily living; showing how people have related their faith to their vocations. 1,500 words. Pays $25-40. Photos purchased with mss; pays $5.

THE MESSENGER OF THE SACRED HEART, 661 Greenwood Ave., Toronto, Ontario, Canada M4J 4B3. Editor: the Rev. F.J. Power, S.J. 10% freelance written. For "adult Catholics in Canada and the US who are members of the Apostleship of Prayer." Monthly. Circ. 21,000. Buys first rights. Byline given. Pays on acceptance. Sample copy $1. Submit seasonal material 3 months in advance. Reports in 1 month. SAE and International Reply Coupons. Unsolicited manuscripts, unaccompanied by return postage, will not be returned.

Nonfiction: Department Editor: Mary Pujolas. "Articles on the Apostleship of Prayer and on all aspects of Christian living." Current events and social problems that have a bearing on Catholic life, family life, Catholic relations with non-Catholics, personal problems, the liturgy, prayer, devotion to the Sacred Heart. Material should be written in a popular, nonpious style. "We are not interested in column material." Buys 12 mss/year. Length: 1,800-2,000 words. Pays 2¢ word.

Fiction: Department editor: Mary Pujolas. Wants fiction which reflects the lives, problems, preoccupations of reading audience. "Short stories that make their point through plot and characters." Length: 1,800-2,000 words. Pays 2¢/word.

THE MIRACULOUS MEDAL, 475 E. Chelten Ave., Philadelphia PA 19144. Editorial Director: the Rev. Robert P. Cawley, C.M. Quarterly. Buys first North American serial rights. Buys articles only on special assignment. Pays on acceptance. SASE. Free sample copy.

Fiction: Should not be pious or sermon-like. Wants good general fiction—not necessarily religious, but if religion is basic to the story, the writer should be sure of his facts. Only restriction is that subject matter and treatment must not conflict with Catholic teaching and practice. Can use seasonal material. Christmas stories. Length: 2,000 words maximum. Occasionally uses short-shorts from 750-1,250 words. Pays 2¢/word minimum.

Poetry: Maximum of 20 lines, preferably about the Virgin Mary or at least with religious slant. Pays 50¢/line minimum.

MODERN LITURGY, Box 444, Saratoga CA 95070. Editor: William Burns. For artists, musicians, and creative individuals who plan group worship; services; teachers of religion. Magazine; 40-48 pages. Nine times/year. Circ. 15,000. Buys all rights. Byline given. Buys 10 mss/year. Pays on publication. Sample copy $3; free writer's guidelines. "We are very receptive to computer printout or disk submissions; we prefer disk *plus* letter quality printouts." Reports in 6 weeks. Query. SASE.

Nonfiction and Fiction: Articles (historical, theological and practical) which address special interest topics in the field of liturgy; example services; liturgical art forms (music, poetry, stories, dances, dramatizations, etc.). Practical, creative ideas; and art forms for use in worship and/or religious education classrooms. "No material out of our field." Length: 750-2,000 words. Pays $5-30.

Tips: "We are opening an editorial department for books dealing with small computers. It represents a real opportunity for the author active in small computers."

THE NEW ERA, 50 E. North Temple, Salt Lake City UT 84150. (801)531-2951. Editor: Brian K. Kelly. 40-60% freelance written. For young people of the Church of Jesus Christ of Latter-Day Saints (Mormon); their church leaders and teachers. Monthly magazine; 51 pages. Circ. 180,000. Buys all rights. Byline given. Buys 100 mss/year. Pays on acceptance. Sample copy 50¢. Submit seasonal material 1 year in advance. Reports in 30 days. Query preferred. SASE.

Nonfiction and Photos: "Material that shows how the Church of Jesus Christ of Latter-Day Saints is relevant in the lives of young people today. Must capture the excitement of being a young Latter-Day Saint. Special interest in the experiences of young Mormons in other countries. No general library research or formula pieces without the *New Era* slant and feel." Uses informational, how-to, personal experience, interview, profile, inspirational, humor, historical, think pieces, travel, spot news. Length: 150-3,000 words. Pays 3-6¢/word. *For Your Information* (news of young Mormons around the world). Uses b&w photos and color transparencies with mss. Payment depends on use in magazine, but begins at $10.

Fiction: Experimental, adventure, science fiction and humorous. Must relate to young Mormon audience. Pays minimum 3¢/word.

Poetry: Traditional forms, blank verse, free verse, avant-garde forms, light verse and all other forms. Must relate to their editorial viewpoint. Pays minimum 25¢/line.

NEW WORLD OUTLOOK, Room 1351, 475 Riverside Dr., New York NY 10115. (212)870-3758. Editor: Arthur J. Moore. For United Methodist lay people; not clergy generally. Monthly magazine; 46 pages. Circ. 35,000. Buys all rights; first North American serial rights. Buys 15-20 mss/year. Pays on publication. Free sample copy and writer's guidelines. Query or submit complete ms. SASE.

Nonfiction: "Articles about the involvement of the church around the world, including the US in outreach and social concerns and Christian witness. Write with good magazine style. Facts, actualities important. Quotes. Relate what Christians are doing to meet problems. Specifics. We have too much on New York and other large urban areas. We need more good journalistic efforts from smaller places in US. Articles by freelancers in out-of-the-way places in the US are especially welcome." Length: 1,000-2,000 words. Usually pays $50-150.

Tips: "A freelancer should have some understanding of the United Methodist Church, or else know very well a local situation of human need or social problem which the churches and Christians have tried to face. Too much freelance material we get tries to paint with broad strokes about world or national issues. The local story of meaning to people elsewhere is still the best material. Avoid pontificating on the big issues. Write cleanly and interestingly on the 'small' ones."

NORTH AMERICAN VOICE OF FATIMA, Fatima Shrine, Youngstown NY 14174. Editor: Steven M. Grancini, C.R.S.P. 75% freelance written. For Roman Catholic readership. Circ. 15,000. Not copyrighted. Pays on acceptance. Free sample copy. Reports in 6 weeks. SASE.

Nonfiction, Photos and Fiction: Inspirational, personal experience, historical and think articles. Religious and historical fiction. Length: 700 words. B&w photos purchased with mss. All material must have a religious slant. Pays 1¢/word.

‡OBLATES MAGAZINE, Missionary Association of Mary Immaculate, 15 S. 59th St., Belleville IL 62222. (618)233-2238. Managing Editor: Paul Dusseault. Bimonthly religious magazine for Christian families. Circ. 500,000. Pays on acceptance. Byline given. Not copyrighted. Buys one-time rights. Submit seasonal/holiday material 6 months in advance. Simultaneous and previously published submissions OK if so noted. SASE. Reports in 1 month. Free sample copy.

Nonfiction: Inspirational, personal experience, articles on Oblates around the world. Stories should be inspirational and present Gospel values. "Don't be preachy or pious. No how-I-found-Jesus stories." Buys 12 mss/year. Send complete ms. Length: 500 words. Pays $60.

Poetry: Light verse, traditional. "Nothing that takes too much effort to decipher. Emphasis should be on inspiration and relationship with God." Buys 6 poems/year. Submit 3 poems. Length: 8-16 lines. Pays $10-20.

Tips: "Our readership is made up mostly of mature Americans who are looking for comfort, encouragement, and applicable Christian direction. They don't want to spend a lot of time wading through theology-laden or personal spiritual journey pieces. But if you can take an incident from Christ's life, for example, and parallel that with everyday living or personal experience, all in about 500 words, we're holding a couple of pages for you. This formula will also work for any Gospel theme, e.g., forgiveness, selflessness, hope. Take a look at the magazine and you'll catch on."

ONE, 6401 The Paseo, Kansas City MO 64131. (816)333-7000, ext. 210. Editor: David Best. Published by the Beacon Hill Press of Kansas City for the 18- to 23-year-old college student and career single. Monthly magazine. Circ. 18,000. Pays on acceptance. Buys first rights or second rights. Byline given. Submit seasonal material 6 months in advance. SASE. Free sample copy with 8x11½ or larger SASE. .

Nonfiction: Articles which speak to students' needs in light of their spiritual pilgrimage. How they cope on a secular campus from a Christian lifestyle. First-person articles have high priority since writers tend to communicate best that which they are in the process of learning themselves. Style should be evangelical. Material should have "sparkle." Wesleyan in doctrine. Buys interviews, profiles, inspirational and think pieces, humor, photo essays. Length: 1,500 words maximum. Pays 3½¢/word.

Photos: B&w glossy prints. Pays $20-30. Interested in photo spreads and photo essays.

Tips: "Be willing to write the article lengthwise according to our editorial needs. (Usually a one or two page article.) Be willing to send a manuscript on speculation. Be concise with description of the theme or content."

THE OTHER SIDE, Box 3948, Fredericksburg VA 22402. Co-Editors: John Alexander, Mark Olson. Assistant Editor: Kathleen Hayes. Publisher: Philip Harnden. "A magazine focusing on peace, justice, and economic liberation from a radical Christian perspective." Monthly. Circ. 14,000. Pays on acceptance. Buys all rights. Byline given. SASE. Reports in 1 month. Sample copy $1.50. Writer's guidelines available.

Nonfiction: Eunice Amarantides Smith, articles editor. "Articles on current social, political, and economic issues in the US and around the world: personality profiles, interpretative essays, interviews, how-to's, personal experiences, investigative reporting. Articles must be lively, vivid, and down-to-earth, with a radical Christian perspective." Length: 300-4,000 words. Pays $25-250.

Photos: Dan Hamlett-Leisen, art director. "Photos or photo essays illustrating current social, political, or economic reality in the US and third world." Pays $15-50 for b&w photos.

Fiction: Eunice Amarantides Smith, fiction editor. "Short stories, humor, and satire conveying insights and situations that will be helpful to Christians with a radical commitment to peace and justice. Length: 300-4,000 words. Pays $25-250.

Poetry: Rosemary Camilleri, poetry editor. "Short, creative poetry that will be thought provoking and appealing to radical Christians who have a strong commitment to peace and justice." Length: 3-100 lines. Pays $15-30.

OUR FAMILY, Oblate Fathers of St. Mary's Province, Box 249, Battleford, Saskatchewan, Canada S0M 0E0. (306)937-2131, 937-7344. Editor-in-Chief: Albert Lalonde, O.M.I. For average family men and women of high school and early college education. Monthly magazine. Circ. 13,376. Pays on acceptance. Generally purchases first North American serial rights; also buys all rights; or simultaneous, second serial (reprint); or one-time rights. Pays 100% kill fee. Byline given. Phone queries OK. Submit seasonal/holiday material 4 months in advance. Simultaneous, photocopied and previously published submissions OK. "Writer should inquire with our office before sending letter quality computer printout or disk submissions." SASE. Reports in 1 month. Sample copy $1.50; free writer's guidelines with SASE.

Nonfiction: Humor (related to family life or husband/wife relations); inspirational (anything that depicts people responding to adverse conditions with courage, hope and love); personal experience (with religious dimensions); and photo feature (particularly in search of photo essays on human/religious themes and on persons whose lives are an inspiration to others). Buys 72-88 unsolicited mss/year.

Photos: Photos purchased with or without accompanying ms. Pays $25 for 5x7 or larger b&w glossy prints and color photos (which are converted into b&w). Offers additional payment for photos accepted with ms (payment for these photos varies according to their quality). Free photo spec sheet with SASE.

Fiction: Humorous and religious. "Anything true to human nature. No romance, he-man adventure material, science fiction, moralizing or sentimentality." Buys 1-2 ms/issue. Send complete ms. Length: 750-3,000 words. Pays 7-10¢/word minimum for original material. Free fiction requirement guide with SASE.

Poetry: Avant-garde; free verse; haiku; light verse; and traditional. Buys 4-10 poems/issue. Length: 3-30 lines. Pays 75¢-$1/line.

Fillers: Jokes, gags, anecdotes and short humor. Buys 2-10 fillers/issue.

Tips: "Our pay rates have increased."

OUR SUNDAY VISITOR MAGAZINE, Noll Plaza, Huntington IN 46750. (219)356-8400. Executive Editor: Robert Lockwood. For general Catholic audience. Weekly. Circ. 340,000. Byline given. Buys 25 mss/year. Pays on acceptance. Submit seasonal material 2 months in advance. Reports in 3 weeks. Query. SASE. Free sample copy.

Nonfiction: Uses articles on Catholic-related subjects. Should explain Catholic religious beliefs in articles of human interest; articles applying Catholic principles to current problems, Catholic profiles, etc. Payment varies depending on reputation of author, quality of work and amount of research required. Length: 1,000-1,200 words. Minimum payment for major features is $100 and a minimum payment for shorter features is $50-75.

Photos: Purchased with mss; with captions only. B&w glossy prints, color transparencies, 35mm color. Pays $125/cover photo story, $75/b&w story; $25/color photo. $10/b&w photo.

PARISH FAMILY DIGEST, Our Sunday Visitor, Inc., 200 Noll Plaza, Huntington IN 46750. (219)356-8400. Editor: Patrick R. Moran. "*Parish Family Digest* is geared to the Catholic family, and to that family as a unit of the parish.'' Bimonthly magazine; 48 pages. Circ. 140,399. Pays on acceptance. Buys all rights on a work-for-hire basis. Byline given. Submit seasonal/holiday material 5 months in advance. Photocopied and previously published submissions OK. All manuscripts are retyped as edited—so it makes no difference. Computer printout submissions OK. SASE. Reports in 2 weeks for queries; 3 weeks for mss. Sample copy and writer's guidelines for postage.

Nonfiction: General interest, historical, inspirational, interview, nostalgia (if related to overall Parish involvement); and profile. No personal essays or preachy first-person ''Thou shalt's or shalt not's.'' Send complete ms. Recent article example: ''Lent: New Ways to Celebrate an Old Season'' (March/April 1982). Buys 100 unsolicited mss/year. Length: 1,000 words maximum. Pays $5-50.

Photos: State availability of photos with ms. Pays $10 for 3x5 b&w prints. Buys all rights. Captions preferred. Model release required.

Fillers: Anecdotes and short humor. Buys 6/issue. Length: 100 words maximum.

Tips: ''Know thy publication. Query with outline, title, approximate word length and possible photos. Read the magazine, get the feel of our parish family unit, or involvement, and keep manuscripts to no more than 1,000 words maximum. Original ideas usually come through as winners for the beginning writer. Avoid reference book biographicals, and write of real persons.''

PENTECOSTAL EVANGEL, The General Council of the Assemblies of God, 1445 Boonville, Springfield MO 65802. (417)862-2781. Editor: Robert C. Cunningham. Managing Editor: Richard G. Champion. 33% freelance written. Emphasizes news of the Assemblies of God for members of the Assemblies and other Pentecostal and charismatic Christians. Weekly magazine; 32 pages. Circ. 285,000. Pays on publication. Buys first rights, simultaneous, second serial (reprint) or one-time rights. Byline given. Submit seasonal/holiday material 6 months in advance. Simultaneous, photocopied and previously published submissions OK. SASE. Reports in 3 months. Free sample copy and writer's guidelines.

Nonfiction: Informational (articles on home life that convey Christian teachings); inspirational; and personal experience. Buys 5 mss/issue. Send complete ms. Length: 500-2,000 words. Pays 3¢/word maximum.

Photos: Photos purchased without accompanying ms. Pays $7.50-15/8x10 b&w glossy prints; $10-35/35mm or larger color transparencies. Total purchase price for ms includes payment for photos.

Poetry: Religious and inspirational. Buys 1 poem/issue. Limit submissions to batches of 6. Pays 20-40¢/line.

Tips: ''Break in by writing up a personal experience. We publish first-person articles concerning spiritual experiences; that is, answers to prayer for help in a particular situation. We publish personal testimonials of unusual conversions or healings through faith in Christ. All articles submitted to us should be related to religious life. We are Protestant, evangelical, Pentecostal, and any doctrines or practices portrayed should be in harmony with the official position of our denomination (Assemblies of God).''

THE PENTECOSTAL TESTIMONY, 10 Overlea Blvd., Toronto, Ontario, Canada M4H 1A5. Editor: Robert Skinner. Monthly. For church members and general readership. Circ. 22,000. Not copyrighted. Free sample copy. Submit seasonal material at least 3 months in advance. Query. SAE and International Reply Coupons.

Nonfiction: Must be written from Canadian viewpoint. Subjects preferred are contemporary public issues, events on the church calendar (Reformation month, Christmas, Pentecost, etc.) written from conservative theological viewpoint. Preferred lengths are 800-1,200 words.

Photos: Occasionally buys photographs with mss if they are vital to the article. Also buys b&w photos if they are related to some phase of the main topic of the particular issue. Should be 8x10 b&w prints.

PRAIRIE MESSENGER, Catholic Weekly, Benedictine Monks of St. Peter's Abbey, Box 190, Muenster, Saskatchewan, Canada S0K 2Y0. (306)682-5215. Editor: Andrew Britz. Saskatchewan and Manitoba Catholic weekly (48 issues/year). Covering religion, culture and social change, as well as local, national, and international events. Circ. 14,000. Pays on publication. Byline given. Not copyrighted. Makes work-for-hire assignments. Submit seasonal/holiday material 2 months in advance. Simultaneous queries and simultaneous, photocopied, and previously published submissions OK. SASE. Reports in 3 weeks on queries; 1 month on mss. Free sample copy and writer's guidelines.

Nonfiction: General interest, humor, inspirational, interview/profile, opinion, personal experience. Buys less than 10 mss/year. Send complete ms. Length: 700-1,000 words. Pays $1.45/column inch.

Photos: Send photos with ms. Pays $1.50 maximum for b&w negatives; $5.50 maximum for b&w prints. Captions and identification of subjects required. Buys one-time rights.

Columns/Departments: Books; Films; Pastoral Perspectives; Politics Today; Theological Review; Social Action (on the religious scene); Ecumenical Forum; Contemporary Family Life. Buys 20 mss/year. Send complete ms. Length: 750 words; 1,000 for center spreads. Pays $1.45/column inch or ''$22.50 for comment and analysis columns which have been requested.''

Fiction: Humorous, religious. Buys variable number mss/year. Query with clips of published work. Length: 700-1,000 words. Pays $1.45/column inch.

PRESBYTERIAN JOURNAL, Southern Presbyterian Journal Co, Inc., Box 3108, Asheville NC 28802. Editor: the Rev. G. Aiken Taylor. Business Manager: Joel Belz. "Emphasis is Presbyterian, although material appeals to religious conservatives. Highly educated readership." Weekly magazine; 24 pages. Circ. 25,000. Pays on publication. Not copyrighted. Submit seasonal/holiday material at least 2 months in advance. Simultaneous and photocopied submissions OK; might consider previously published work. SASE. Reports in 2-6 weeks. Free sample copy.

Nonfiction: General interest (must have a religious slant); humor; interview; opinion (does not necessarily have to agree with editorial policy); and personal experience (testimonials welcome). No trivia or general interest *without* theological content. Buys 1-2 mss/issue. Send complete ms. Length: 3,000 word maximum. Pays $20.

Tips: Reads, evaluates and comments on every ms. "Pieces should be *thoughtful*, embodying fresh theological insights, or fresh way of looking at old theological insights. Emphasis must be evangelical, preferably Reformed."

PRESBYTERIAN RECORD, 50 Wynford Dr., Don Mills, Ontario, Canada M3C 1J7. (416)444-1111. Editor: the Rev. James Dickey. 40-50% freelance written. For a church-oriented, family audience. Monthly magazine. Circ. 82,000. Buys 15 mss/year. Pays on publication. Free sample copy. Submit seasonal material 3 months in advance. Reports on manuscripts accepted for publication in 1 month. Returns rejected material in 8 weeks. Query. SAE and Canadian stamps.

Nonfiction and Photos: Material on religious themes. Check a copy of the magazine for style. Also, personal experience, interview, and inspirational material. No material solely American in context. Buys 10-15 unsolicited mss/year. Recent article example: "Hymn Writers and Handicaps" (December 1981). Length: 1,000-2,000 words. Pays $45-55. Pays $10-15 for b&w glossy photos. Captions required. Uses positive color transparencies for the cover. Pays $50.

PRESBYTERIAN SURVEY, Presbyterian Publishing House, 341 Ponce de Leon Ave. NE., Atlanta GA 30365. (404)873-1549. Monthly magazine covering religion, ethics, public issues for members of the Presbyterian Church. Pays on acceptance. Byline given. Offers negotiable kill fee. Buys first North American serial rights. Send queries or mss to Catherine Cottingham, associate editor. Submit seasonal/holiday material 3 months in advance. Simultaneous, photocopied and previously published submissions OK. "We are open to letter-quality printouts. We do not have capacity to use disk submissions at this time, but are now planning in that direction." SASE. Reports in 3 weeks on queries; 1 month on mss. Writer's guidelines for SASE.

Nonfiction: Book excerpts, general interest, inspirational, personal experience. "Columns are arranged at our initiative and invitation; queries about columnist opening will be pointless." Buys 50 mss/year. Query or send complete ms. Length: 1,000-2,500 words. Pays $50-150.

Tips: "A denominational merger will widen our audience from regional (17 states in the South and Southwest) to national."

PURPOSE, 616 Walnut Ave., Scottdale PA 15683. Editor: David E. Hostetler. "For adults, young and old, general audience with interests as varied as there are persons. My particular readership is interested in seeing Christianity work in tough situations." Monthly magazine. Circ. 21,500. Buys one-time rights. Byline given. Buys 175-200 unsolicited mss/year. Pays on acceptance. Free sample copy and writer's guidelines. Submit seasonal material 6 months in advance. Photocopied and simultaneous submissions OK. Reports in 6 weeks. Submit complete ms. Computer printout submissions OK if legible. SASE required.

Nonfiction and Photos: Inspirational articles from a Christian perspective. "I want material that goes to the core of human problems—morality on all levels, or lack of it in business, politics, religion, sex and any other area—and shows how the Christian faith resolves some of these problems. I don't want superficial, sentimental, or civil religion pieces. I want critical stuff that's upbeat. *Purpose* is a story paper and as such wants truth to be conveyed either through quality fiction or through articles that use the best fiction techniques to make them come alive. Our magazine has an accent on Christian discipleship. Christianity is to be applied to all of life and we expect our material to show this. We're getting too much self-centered material. I would like to see story-type articles on how people are intelligently and effectively working at some of the great human problems such as overpopulation, food shortages, international understanding, etc., motivated by their faith." Length: 200-1,200 words. Pays 1-4¢/word. Photos purchased with ms. Captions desired. Pays $5-35/b&w, depending on quality. Normal range is $7.50-15. Must be sharp enough for reproduction; prefers prints in all cases. Can use color prints at the same rate of payment.

Fiction, Poetry and Fillers: Humorous, religious and historical fiction related to the theme of magazine. "Make the effort to produce with specificity so that the story appears to take place somewhere and with real people. Should not be moralistic." Traditional poetry, blank verse, free verse and light verse. Length: 3-12 lines. Pays 50¢-$1/line. Jokes, short humor, and items up to 400 words. Pays 2¢ minimum/word.

Tips: "We are looking for articles which show Christianity slugging it out where people hurt but we want the stories told and presented professionally. Good photographs help place material with us."

QUEEN, Montfort Missionaries, 26 S. Saxon Ave., Bay Shore NY 11706. (516)665-0726. Editor: James Mc-Millan, S.M.M. Managing Editor: Roger Charest, S.M.M. Emphasizes doctrine and devotion to Mary. Bimonthly magazine; 40 pages. Circ. 8,500. Pays on acceptance. Buys all rights. Phone queries OK. Submit seasonal/holiday material 4 months in advance. SASE. Reports in 1 month.
Nonfiction: Expose (doctrinal); historical; informational; inspirational and interview. Buys 5 mss/issue. Send complete ms. Length: 1,500-2,000 words. Pays $35-45.
Poetry: Free verse and traditional forms. Marian poetry only. Buys 2/issue. Limit submissions to batches of 2. Pays in free subscription for 2 years.

REVIEW FOR RELIGIOUS, 3601 Lindell Blvd., Room 428, St. Louis MO 63108. (314)535-3048. Editor: Daniel F.X. Meenan, S.J. 100% freelance written. Bimonthly. For Roman Catholic priests, brothers and sisters. Pays on publication. Byline given. Reports in about 8 weeks. SASE.
Nonfiction: Articles on ascetical, liturgical and canonical matters only; not for general audience. Length: 2,000-8,000 words. Pays $6/page.
Tips: Writer must know about religious life in the Catholic Church, be familiar with prayer, vows and problems related to them.

ST. ANTHONY MESSENGER, 1615 Republic St., Cincinnati OH 45210. Editor-in-Chief: Norman Perry. For a national readership of Catholic families, most of them have children in grade school, high school or college. Monthly magazine; 59 pages. Circ. 350,000. Pays on acceptance. Buys first North American serial rights. Byline given. Submit seasonal/holiday material 4 months in advance. SASE. Free sample copy and writer's guidelines.
Nonfiction: How-to (on psychological and spiritual growth; family problems); humor; informational; inspirational; interview; personal experience (if pertinent to our purpose); personal opinion (limited use; writer must have special qualifications for topic); profile. Buys 12 mss/year. Length: 1,500-3,500 words. Pays 10¢/word.
Fiction: Mainstream and religious. Buys 12 mss/year. Submit complete ms. Length: 2,000-3,500 words. Pays 10¢/word.
Tips: "The freelancer should ask why his/her proposed article would be appropriate for us, rather than for *Redbook* or *Saturday Review*. We treat human problems of all kinds, but from a religious perspective. Get authoritative information (not merely library research; we want interviews with experts). Write in popular style."

ST. JOSEPH'S MESSENGER & ADVOCATE OF THE BLIND, Sisters of St. Joseph of Peace, St. Joseph's Home, Box 288, Jersey City NJ 07303. Editor-in-Chief: Sister Ursula Maphet. 50% freelance written. Quarterly magazine; 30 pages. Circ. 51,000. Pays on acceptance. Buys all rights but will reassign rights back to author after publication asking that credit line be included in next publication. Submit seasonal/holiday material 3 months in advance (no Christmas issue). Simultaneous and previously published submissions OK. Reports in 3 weeks. Free sample copy and writer's guidelines.
Nonfiction: Humor; inspirational; nostalgia; personal opinion; and personal experience. Buys 24 mss/year. Submit complete ms. Length: 300-1,500 words. Pays $3-15.
Fiction: "Fiction is our most needed area." Romance; suspense; mainstream; and religious. Buys 30 mss/year. Submit complete ms. Length: 600-1,600 words. Pays $6-25.
Poetry: Light verse, traditional. Buys 25/year. Limit submissions to batches of 10. Length: 50-300 words. Pays $5-20.

SANDAL PRINTS, 1820 Mt. Elliott, Detroit MI 48207. Editor: William La Forte. For people who are interested in the work of the Capuchins. Circ. 5,000. Not copyrighted. Pays on acceptance. Free sample copy. Reports in 1 week. Query. SASE.
Nonfiction and Photos: Material must be specifically on the contemporary apostolates and lifestyle of Capuchins (especially in the Midwest). "We do not use any general religious material; no topical subjects or themes accepted." Length: 2,500 words. Pays $25-50. Pays $5/b&w photo.
Tips: "Write about actually living Capuchins and their work. Query before writing the first word."

SCOPE, 426 S. 5th St., Box 1209, Minneapolis MN 55440. (612)330-3413. Editor: Constance Lovaas. 30% freelance written. For women of the American Lutheran Church. Monthly. Circ. 275,000. Buys first rights. Byline given. Buys 200-300 mss/year. Occasionally overstocked. Pays on acceptance. Submit seasonal material 4-5 months in advance. Reports in 4 weeks. Computer printout submissions OK but no dot matrix. SASE. Free sample copy.
Nonfiction and Photos: "The magazine's primary purpose is to be an educational tool in that it transmits the monthly Bible study material which individual women use in preparation for their group meetings. It contains articles for inspiration and growth, as well as information about the mission and concerns of the church, and material that is geared to seasonal emphasis. We are interested in articles that relate to monthly Bible study subject. We also want articles that tell how faith has affected, or can influence, the lives of women or their families. But we do not want preachy articles. We are interested in any subject that concerns women." Submit

complete ms. Length: 400-800 words. Pays $15-50. Buys 3x5 or 8x10 b&w photos with mss or with captions only. Pays $10-30.

Poetry and Fillers: "We can use interesting, brief, pithy, significant or clever filler items, but we use very little poetry and are very selective. We do not buy cute sayings of children." Pays $5-15.

Tips: "Examine a copy of *Scope* and submit a well-written manuscript that fits the obvious slant and audience. No articles built around non-Lutheran teaching and practices but may be written by non-Lutherans. I am interested in articles by and about singles and working mothers. Will read any freelance manuscript submitted, if within word limits. Prefer a manuscript to a query letter."

SEEK, Standard Publishing, 8121 Hamilton Ave., Cincinnati OH 45231. (513)931-4050, ext. 165. Editor: Leah Ann Crussell. 90% freelance written. For young and middle-aged adults who attend church and Bible classes. Sunday School paper; 8 pages. Quarterly, in weekly issues. Circ. 60,000. Byline given. Prefers first serial rights. Buys 100-150 mss/year. Pays on acceptance. Free sample copy and writer's guidelines. Submit seasonal (Christmas, Easter, New Year's) material 9-12 months in advance. Reports in 30-60 days. Query not necessary; submit complete ms. Readable computer printout submissions OK; prefers letter quality to dot matrix. SASE.

Nonfiction and Photos: "We look for articles that are warm, inspirational, devotional, of personal or human interest; that deal with controversial matters, timely issues of religious, ethical or moral nature, or first-person testimonies, true-to-life happenings, vignettes, emotional situations or problems; communication problems, and examples of answered prayers. Article must deliver its point in a convincing manner, but not be patronizing or preachy. Must appeal to either men or women. Must be alive, vibrant, sparkling and have a title that demands the article be read. Always need stories of families, marriages, problems on campus, and life testimonies." No poetry. Length: 400-1,200 words. Pays 2½¢/word. B&w photos purchased with or without mss. Pays $7.50 minimum for good 8x10 glossy prints.

Fiction: Religious fiction and religiously slanted historical and humorous fiction. Length: 400-1,200 words. Pays 2½¢/word.

Tips: Submit mss which tell of faith in action or victorious Christian living as central theme. "We select mss as far as one year in advance of publication. Complimentary copies are sent to our published writers immediately following printing."

SOCIAL JUSTICE REVIEW, 3835 Westminister Place, St. Louis MO 63108. (314)371-1653. Editor: Harvey J. Johnson. Issued bimonthly. Not copyrighted; "however special articles within the magazine may be copyrighted, or an occasional special issue has been copyrighted due to author's request." Query. SASE.

Nonfiction: Wants scholarly articles on society's economic, religious, social, intellectual and political problems with the aim of bringing Catholic social thinking to bear upon these problems. 2,500-3,500 words. Pays about $4/column.

SOLO MAGAZINE, Solo Ministries, Inc., Box 1231, Sisters OR 97759. Editor: Jerry Jones. Bimonthly magazine about today's single adults who desire to live within the framework of Christ's teachings. Circ. 20,000. Pays on publication. Submit seasonal material 8 months in advance. Accepts queries only. No unsolicited mss. Reports in 3 months on queries. Sample copy and writer's guidelines $2.50 with large magazine size SASE.

Nonfiction: Expose (showing how any group, organization or person is taking advantage of or abusing single adults); general interest (articles on travel, adventure appealing to single adults); historical (outstanding single adults in history; views of or on single adults of the past); how-to (repair, cook, garden, etc.); humor (anything that helps us laugh with others and at ourselves); inspirational (outstanding single adults who have done something inspirational); nostalgia; opinion (from a wide range of people on any topics of interest to singles; divorce, sexual attitudes and habits, viewpoints, etc.); profile (a look at outstanding Christian single adults in the *People Magazine* style); travel; new product; and personal experience. "No articles that are not in harmony with Christian principles and Christ's teachings." Buys 12-16 mss/year. Length: 200-2,000 words. Pays 5¢/word.

Columns/Departments: Relationships (how to build healthy ones, how to argue; how to break up; how to start new ones); Devotional/Bible Study (anything that would assist in the single adult's spiritual growth and development); Single Parenting (anything helpful to the single parent); and Personal Motivation/Self-Help (anything that would help motivate and challenge people to reach for their maximum). Buys 6-12 mss/year. Query. Length: 200-600 words. Pays 5¢/word.

Fiction: "To date, we have published no fiction, however, we would be open to looking at any that is not out of harmony with Christian principles or Christ's teaching." Adventure, fantasy, confession, experimental, humorous, mystery, romance, suspense, condensed novels, mainstream and religious. Query. Length: 500-2,000 words. Pays 5¢/word.

Poetry: Avant-garde, free verse, haiku, light verse and traditional. Buys 6 mss/year. Submit maximum 2 poems. Length: 5-40 lines. Pays $5-$25.

Fillers: Clippings on single adult news and newsbreaks. Buys 36 mss/year. Length: 10-100 words. Pays 5¢/ word.

Tips: "Get a copy of our magazine to know our market *before* submitting query. Ask single friends what kinds of things they would most want to see in a magazine specifically for them, and write about it. Wherever their greatest needs and interests are, there are our stories."

SONLIGHT CHRISTIAN NEWSPAPERS, (includes *Sonlight*, *Good News*, *Revival*, *Solo News*, etc.), 1415 Lake Ave. #2, Lake Worth FL 33460. Editor: Dennis Lombard. Monthly tabloids (*Sonlight*: to churches; *Good News*: to the general public; *Revival*: to prayer groups; *Solo*: to Christian singles). "*Sonlight Christian Newspapers* are generally free-distribution tabloids ministering to churches and the public, reaching all denominations, with articles by writers of all backgrounds sharing their Christian experiences and viewpoints." Circ. 20,000. Pays on publication. Byline given. Copyrighted. Buys one-time rights, simultaneous rights and second serial (reprint) rights. Submit seasonal/holiday material 3 months in advance. Simultaneous queries, and simultaneous, photocopied and previously published submissions OK. SASE. Reports in 1-3 weeks. Sample copy 50¢ plus 9x12 SASE.

Nonfiction: Book reports, historical/nostalgic, how-to, humor, inspirational, interview/profile, personal experience, photo feature, testimonies and interviews. "Our publications do *not* debate doctrine, but represent the best and the brightest of all groups. Good, bright, readable writing style is paramount, while source is not important. Read the publication and/or writer's guidelines first because these publications have a strong editorial slant. Self-help articles; testimonies of Christian experience; stories of how God has changed lives; articles on unusual ministries, churches and/or individuals; personality stories of well-known Christians; articles on prayer, unity, revival, harvest of souls, and end-times prophesy are all being sought. The reading level is nontheological, general public. Stories about prayer programs and about Christian unity (churches, ministries, individuals praying and working across denominational lines) are particularly desired at present." No preaching, doctrinal or denominational slants, criticizing of other groups or negative slants on anything. Buys 15-20 unsolicited mss/year. Send complete ms. Length: 100-1,500 words. Pays 2-10¢/word.

Photos: "Photos are welcome." Send photos with accompanying ms. Pays $1-25 for 5x7 or 8x10 b&w prints. Captions, model release, and identification of subjects required. Buys one-time rights and reprint rights.

Fillers: Clippings, anecdotes and newsbreaks. Length: 15-150 words. "We generally do not pay for fillers."

Tips: "We do not pay well yet but want to develop regulars for better pay. We are planning what we tentatively call "Neighbor News," a local community newspaper, to begin here but be 'franchised' nationwide with national capsule news and commentary, columns, features, added to local stringer-written community news. There will be literally scores of opportunities for writers to get involved."

SPIRITUAL LIFE, 2131 Lincoln Rd. NE, Washington DC 20002. (202)832-6622. Editor: the Rev. Christopher Latimer, O.C.D. 80% freelance written. "Largely Catholic, well-educated, serious readers. High percentage are priests and religious, but also some laymen. A few are non-Catholic or non-Christian." Quarterly. Circ. 17,000. Buys first rights. Buys 20 mss/year. Pays on acceptance. "Brief autobiographical information (present occupation, past occupations, books and articles published, etc.) should accompany article. Follow *A Manual of Style* (University of Chicago)." Reports in 2 weeks. SASE. Free sample copy and writer's guidelines.

Nonfiction: Serious articles of contemporary spirituality. Quality articles about man's encounter with God in the present-day world. Language of articles should be college-level. Technical terminology, if used, should be clearly explained. Material should be presented in a positive manner. Sentimental articles or those dealing with specific devotional practices not accepted. "*Spiritual Life* tries to avoid the 'popular,' sentimental approach to religion and to concentrate on a more intellectual approach. We do not want first-person accounts of spiritual experiences (visions, revelations, etc.) nor sentimental treatments of religious devotions." Buys inspirational and think pieces. No fiction or poetry. Length: 3,000-5,000 words. Pays $50 minimum. "Five contributor's copies are sent to author on publication of article." Book reviews should be sent to Rev. Steven Payne, O.C.D., Carmelite Monastery, 514 Warren St., Brookline, MA 02146.

SPIRITUALITY TODAY, Aquinas Institute, 3642 Lindell Blvd., St. Louis MO 63108. Editor: the Rev. Christopher Kiesling O.P. 25% freelance written. "For those interested in a more knowing and intense Christian life in the 20th century." Buys first North American serial rights. Byline given. Pays on publication. Query or submit complete ms. SASE. Sample copy $1; free writer's guidelines.

Nonfiction: "Articles that seriously examine important truths pertinent to the spiritual life, or Christian life, in the context of today's world. Scriptural, biographical, doctrinal, liturgical and ecumenical articles are acceptable." Buys 15 unsolicited mss/year. Recent article examples: "Can We Speak of a Distinct Charismatic Spirituality?" (Fall 1982) and "Spirituality and Social Justice: A Christological Perspective" (Winter 1982). Length: 4,000 words. Pays 1¢/word.

Tips: "Examine the journal. It is not a typical magazine. Given its characteristics, the style of writing required is not the sort that regular freelance writers usually employ."

SUNDAY DIGEST, 850 N. Grove Ave., Elgin IL 60120. Editor: Judy C. Couchman. 50% freelance written. Issued weekly for Christian adults, mainly Protestants in small churches. *Sunday Digest* provides a weekly combination of original articles and reprints, selected to help adult readers better understand the Christian faith, to keep them informed of issues and happenings within the Christian community, and to challenge them to a deeper personal commitment to Christ. Buys first rights. Pays 7¢/word minimum on acceptance. Reports in 1 month. Computer printout submissions OK; prefers letter quality to dot matrix. SASE. Free sample copy and writer's guidelines for 6½x9½ SAE and 2 first class stamps.
Nonfiction and Photos: Needs articles applying the Christian faith to personal and social problems, articles of family interest and on church subjects, personality profiles, inspirational self-help articles, personal experience articles and anecdotes. Length: 500-1,800 words. Query. "A query letter should demonstrate to me that the writer has read my publication and is offering an article that fits our editorial style or a particular standing feature." Photos help sell articles. Include color slides or b&w prints of subject and personalities featured. Action shots. Paid for separately from manuscript.
Fiction: Uses some fiction that is hard-hitting, fast-moving, with a real woven-in, not "tacked on," Christian message. Length: 1,000-1,500 words.
Poetry: If appropriate to format. Would like uplifting free-verse poetry.
Tips: "It is crucial that the writer is committed to high-quality Christian communication. Discover the publication's needs by reading *Sunday Digest*."

THESE TIMES, Review and Herald Publishing Association, 6856 Eastern Ave. NW, Washington DC 20012. (202)723-3700. Editor: Kenneth J. Holland. For the general public; adult. Monthly magazine; 32 pages. Circ. 215,000. Rights purchased vary with author and material. May buy first North American serial rights, second serial (reprint) rights or simultaneous rights. Pays 33⅓% kill fee. Byline given. Buys 75 mss/year. Pays on acceptance. Photocopied and simultaneous submissions OK. Submit seasonal material 6 months in advance. Reports in 2 weeks. Query. Computer printout and disk submissions OK. SASE. Free sample copy and writer's guidelines.
Nonfiction and Photos: Material on the relevance of Christianity and everyday life; inspirational articles. How-to; home and family problems; health; drugs, alcohol, gambling, abortion, Bible doctrine. Marriage; divorce; country living or city living. "We like the narrative style. Find a person who has solved a problem. Then, tell how he did it." No sports or theater material. Length: 250-2,500 words. Pays 8-12¢/word. B&w and color photos are purchased with or without ms, or on assignment. Pays $20-25 for b&w; $75-150 for color.
Tips: "Have two or three persons read your article, do your research thoroughly, and make your lead super-appealing."

TODAY'S CHRISTIAN PARENT, 8121 Hamilton Ave., Cincinnati OH 45231. (513)931-4050. Editor: Mrs. Mildred Mast. Quarterly. Rights purchased vary with author and material. Buys first North American serial rights and first serial rights. Pays on acceptance. No simultaneous submissions. SASE. Free sample copy and writer's guidelines for 7x9 or larger SASE.
Nonfiction: Devotional, inspirational and informational articles for the family. Also articles concerning the problems and pleasures of parents, grandparents and the entire family, and Christian childrearing. Timely articles on moral issues, ethical and social situations, in depth as much as possible in limited space. Length: 600-1,200 words. Can use short items on Christian living; and fillers serious or humorous. Very little poetry. Study magazine before submitting. Pays up to 2½¢/word.
Tips: "Write about familiar family situations in a refreshingly different way, so that help and inspiration shine through the problems and pleasures of parenthood. Ms should be crisp, tightly-written. Avoid wordiness, trite situations or formats. Slant: from a Christian perspective."

"TRUTH ON FIRE!", The Bible Holiness Movement, Box 223, Station A, Vancouver, British Columbia, Canada V6C 2M3. (604)683-1833. Editor-in-Chief: Wesley H. Wakefield. 20% freelance written. Emphasizes Evangelism and Bible teachings. Bimonthly magazine; 60 pages. Circ. 5,000. Pays on acceptance. Buys all rights. Byline given unless author requests otherwise. Simultaneous, photocopied and previously published submissions OK. SASE. Reports in 4 weeks. Free sample copy and writer's guidelines.
Nonfiction: "Evangelical articles; well-researched articles dealing with social reforms (pacifism, civil rights, religious liberty); expose (present-day slavery, cancer, tobacco, etc.); first-person testimonies of Christian experience; doctrinal articles from Wesleyan interpretation. Must observe our evangelical taboos. Nothing favoring use of tobacco, alcohol, attendance at dances or theaters; nothing in favor of abortion, divorce or remarriage; no hip language or slang; no devotional materials. Also, we do not accept Calvinistic religious or right-wing political material. Would like to see material on Christian pacifism, anti-semitism, present-day slavery, marijuana research, religious issues in Ireland, and religious articles." Recent article example: *War*, an article expounding a Scriptural view of Pacifism. "It is tightly written in easily understood language for our international readership, and is based on an evangelical viewpoint of the Scriptures." Buys 12-14 unsolicited mss/year. Length: 300-2,500 words. Pays $5-35.
Photos: Photos purchased with or without accompanying ms. Pays $5-15/5x7 b&w photos. "Subjects should

conform to our mores of dress (no jewelry, no makeup, no long-haired men, no mini-skirts, etc.).
Fillers: Newsbreaks, quotes. Length: 30-100 words. Pays $1-2.50.
Tips: "Recognize older evangelical emphasis and mores. Be direct and concise."

TWIN CIRCLE, Twin Circle Publishing, Suite 1511, 1901 Avenue of the Stars, Los Angeles CA 90067. (213)553-4911. Executive Editor: Mary Louise Frawley. Weekly tabloid covering Catholic personalities and Catholic interest topics for a mostly female Catholic readership. Circ. 76,000. Average issue includes 6-7 feature articles. Pays on publication. Byline given. Buys all rights. Submit seasonal material 2 months in advance. Simultaneous and photocopied submissions OK, if so indicated. SASE. Reports in 2 months on queries; in 1 month on mss. Free writer's guidelines with SASE. Not responsible for unsolicited manuscripts.
Nonfiction: "We are looking for articles about prominent Catholic personalities in sports, entertainment, politics and business; ethnic stories about Catholics from other countries and topical issues of concern to Catholics. We are interested in writers who are experienced and write on an ongoing basis." No theological issues. Buys 3-4 mss/issue. Length: 250-1,000 words. Pays 8¢/word.
Photos: State availability of photos. Reviews 5x7 b&w glossy prints. Price negotiated. Captions required. Rights vary.

THE UNITED BRETHREN, 302 Lake St., R.R. 1, Huntington IN 46750. (219)356-2312. Editor: Steve Dennie. Denominational monthly for conservative evangelical Christians, ages 16 and up. Circ. 5,000. Pays on acceptance. Byline given. Buys one-time rights, mostly reprint material. Submit seasonal/holiday material 6 months in advance. Photocopied and previously published submissions OK. SASE. Reports in 2 months. Sample copy $2.
Nonfiction: Historical, how-to, humor, informational, inspirational, personal experience. Must have religious slant. Length: 2,500 words maximum. Pays 1½¢/word.
Photos: Bought normally accompanying manuscript. Pays $5 for 8x10 b&w glossy prints; $3, all others. No color.
Fiction: All types, but religious slant necessary. Length: 2,000 words maximum. Pays 1½¢/word.
Poetry: Buys "a few poems, preferably rhyming." Pays 10¢/line.

THE UNITED CHURCH OBSERVER, 85 St. Clair Ave. E., Toronto, Ontario, Canada M4T 1M8. (416)925-5931. Editor: Hugh McCullum. Managing Editor: Muriel Duncan. A 60-page newsmagazine for persons associated with the United Church of Canada. Monthly. Byline usually given. Deals primarily with events, trends, and policies having religious significance. Most coverage is Canadian, but reports on international or world concerns will be considered.
Nonfiction: Occasional opinion features only. Extended coverage of major issues usually assigned to known writers. Submissions should be written as news, no more than 900 words length, accurate and well researched. Queries preferred. Pays by publication. Rates depend on subject, author, and work involved.
Photos: Buys photographs with mss. B&w should be 5x7 minimum; color 35mm or larger format. Payment varies.
Tips: "Include samples of previous *news* writing with query. Indicate ability and willingness to do research, and to evaluate that research. No opinion pieces, or poetry."

UNITED EVANGELICAL ACTION, Box 28, Wheaton IL 60189. (312)665-0500. Editor: Harold Smith. 25% freelance written. Offers "an objective evangelical viewpoint and interpretive analysis" of specific issues of consequence and concern to the American Church and updates readers on ways evangelicals are confronting those issues on the grass-roots level. Bimonthly magazine; alternating 16-20 pages. Circ. 7,100. Pays on publication. Buys all rights. Phone queries OK. SASE. Reports in 4 weeks. Free sample copy and writer's guidelines.
Nonfiction: Christopher Lutes, managing editor. Issues and trends in the Church and society that affect the ongoing witness and outreach of evangelical Christians. Content should be well thought through, and should provide practical suggestions for dealing with these issues and trends. Buys 8-10 mss/year. Query. Length: 900-2,000 words. Pays 5-8¢/word.
Tips: Editors would really like to see news (action) items that relate to the National Association of Evangelicals.

UNITED METHODIST REPORTER/NATIONAL CHRISTIAN REPORTER, Box 221076, Dallas TX 75222. (214)630-6495. Editor/General Manager: Spurgeon M. Dunnam III. The *United Methodist Reporter* is for a United Methodist national readership and *National Christian Reporter* is for a nondenominational national readership. Weekly newspaper. Circ. 487,000. Pays on acceptance. Not copyrighted. Byline given. SASE. Free sample copy and writer's guidelines.
Nonfiction: "We welcome short features, approximately 500 words. Articles need not be limited to a United Methodist angle. Write about a distinctly Christian response to human need or how a person's faith relates to a given situation." Send complete ms. Pays 4¢/word.

Photos: Purchased with accompanying ms. "We encourage the submission of good action photos (5x7 or 8x10 b&w glossy prints) of the persons or situations in the article." Pays $10.
Poetry: "Poetry welcome on a religious theme; blank verse or rhyme." Length: 2-20 lines. Pays $2.
Fillers: Crossword, other puzzles on religious or Biblical themes. Pays $5.

UNITY MAGAZINE, Unity Village MO 64065. Editor: Thomas E. Witherspoon. Publication of Unity School of Christianity. Magazine; 64 pages. Monthly. Circ. 430,000. Buys first serial rights. Buys 200 mss/year. Pays on acceptance. No photocopied or simultaneous submissions. Computer printout and disk submissions OK; prefers letter quality to dot matrix. Submit seasonal material 6-8 months in advance. Reports in 4 weeks. Submit complete ms. SASE. Free sample copy and writer's guidelines.
Nonfiction and Photos: "Inspirational articles, metaphysical in nature, about individuals who are using Christian principles in their living." Personal experience and interview. "We specialize in religious, inspirational material—anything else is rejected out of hand." Length: 3,000 words maximum. Pays minimum of 2¢/word. 4x5 or 8x10 color transparencies purchased without mss. "We are using more color photography inside." Pays $75-100.
Poetry: Traditional forms, blank verse and free verse. Pays 50¢-$1/line.
Tips: "Be innovative and use new twists on old truths."

THE UPPER ROOM, DAILY DEVOTIONAL GUIDE, The Upper Room, 1908 Grand Ave., Nashville TN 37202. (615)327-2700. Managing Editor: Mary Lou Redding. Bimonthly magazine "offering a daily inspirational message which includes a Bible reading, text, prayer, and 'Thought for the Day.' Each day's meditation is written by a different person and is usually a personal witness about discovering meaning and power for Christian living through some experience from daily life." Circ. 2,225,000 (US) +; 385,000 outside US. Pays on publication. Byline given. Offers negotiable kill fee. Buys first North American serial rights and translation rights. Submit seasonal/holiday material 1 year in advance. SASE. Reports in 3 weeks on queries; 6 months on mss. Free sample copy and writer's guidelines.
Nonfiction: Inspirational and personal experience. No poetry, lengthy "spiritual journey" stories. Buys 360 unsolicited mss/year. Send complete ms. Length: 250 words maximum. Pays $10 minimum.
Columns/Departments: Prayer Workshop—"a 2-page feature which suggests some meditation or prayer exercise. For 1984, we will feature reflection/meditation exercises about the special days of the Christian year (Epiphany, Pentecost, Ascension, All Saints' Day, etc.)." Buys 6 mss/year. Query with clips of published work. Length: 400-600 words. Pays $50-100. "All quoted material used must be documented through standard footnote material for verification. Writer should obtain permission for use of previously copyrighted material which is quoted."
Tips: "The best way to break into our magazine is to send a well-written manuscript that looks at the Christian faith in a fresh way. Standard stories and sermon illustrations are immediately rejected. We very much want to find new writers and welcome good material. Daily meditations are most open. 'Prayer Workshops' are usually assigned. Good repeat meditations can lead to work on longer assignments for our other publications, which pay more. We encourage theological diversity and especially welcome faith-perspective approaches to current social problems and controversial issues within the Christian faith."

VIRTUE, Box 850, Sisters OR 97759. (503)549-8261. Editor: Clare Forward. Bimonthly magazine about Christian life for Christian women. Circ. 85,000. Average issue includes 15 feature articles. Pays on publication. Byline given. Buys first rights. Submit seasonal material 6 months in advance. Simultaneous and previously published submissions OK, if so indicated. Computer printout and disk submissions OK; prefers letter quality to dot matrix. SASE. Reports in 2 weeks on queries; in 6 weeks on ms. Sample copy $2. Free writer's guidelines.
Nonfiction: Interviews with Christian women; current issues; how-to (upkeep and organizational tips for home); inspirational (spiritual enrichment); personal experience; and family information for husbands, wives and children. "No mystical, preachy articles and no more housewife vs. career woman articles." Recent article examples: "Menopause & Male Mid-Life Crisis" (feature); "Edith Schaeffer" (interview); and "A Plea Against Divorce" (editorial opinion). Buys 20 mss/issue. Query or send complete ms. Length: 1,000-1,500 words. Pays 5¢/word.
Photos: Reviews 3x5 b&w glossy prints. Offers additional payment for photos accepted with ms. Captions required. Buys all rights or first rights.
Columns/Departments: Opinion piece (reader editorial); foods (recipes and entertaining); and crafts, decorating, creative projects. Buys 4 mss/issue. Send complete ms. Length: 500-1,000 words. Pays 5¢/word.
Fiction: Christian adventure, humor, and romance. Buys 1 ms/issue. Send complete ms. Length: 1,000-1,500 words. Pays 5¢/word.
Fillers: Anecdotes, short humor, newsbreaks and thought-provoking family stories. Buys 2 mss/issue. Pays 5¢/word.
Tips: "We may be cutting our standard magazine size from 80 to 72 pages so we'll use fewer freelance pieces, and all pieces will have to be shorter."

VISTA, Wesleyan Publishing House, Box 2000, Marion IN 46952. Address submissions to Editor of *Vista*. Publication of The Wesleyan Church. For adults. Weekly. Circ. 60,000. Not copyrighted. "Along with mss for first use, we also accept simultaneous submissions, second rights, and reprint rights. It is the writer's obligation to secure clearance from the original publisher for any reprint rights." Pays on acceptance. Byline given. Submit material 9 months in advance. Reports in 2 months. Computer printout and disk submissions OK. "SASE for sample copy and with all manuscripts."

Nonfiction: Devotional, biographical, and informational articles with inspirational, religious, moral or educational values. Favorable toward emphasis on: "New Testament standard of living as applied to our day; soul-winning (evangelism); proper Sunday observance; Christian youth in action; Christian education in the home, the church and the college; good will to others; worldwide missions; clean living, high ideals, and temperance; wholesome social relationships. Disapprove of liquor, tobacco, theaters, dancing. Mss are judged on the basis of human interest, ability to hold reader's attention, vivid characterizations, thoughtful analysis of problems, vital character message, expressive English, correct punctuation, proper diction. Know where you are going and get there." Length: 500-1,500 words. Pays 2½¢/word for quality material.

Photos: Pays $15-40/5x7 or 8x10 b&w glossy print portraying people in action, seasonal emphasis, or scenic value. Various reader age-groups should be considered.

Fiction: Stories should have definite Christian emphasis and character-building values, without being preachy. Setting, plot and action should be realistic. Length: 1,500-1,800 words; also short-shorts and vignettes. Pays 2½¢/word for quality material.

VITAL CHRISTIANITY, Warner Press, Inc., 1200 E. 5th St., Anderson IN 46011. (317)644-7721. Editor-in-Chief: Arlo F. Newell. Managing Editor: Richard L. Willowby. Magazine covering Christian living for people attending local Church of God congregations; published 20 times/year. Circ. 40,000. Pays on acceptance. Byline given. Offers 100% kill fee. Buys first rights. Submit seasonal/holiday material 6 months in advance. Simultaneous queries OK. Computer printout and disk submissions OK but not preferable. SASE. Reports in 6 weeks. Sample copy and writer's guidelines with SAE and $1.

Nonfiction: Humor (with religious point); inspirational (religious—not preachy); interview/profile (of church-related personalities); opinion (religious/theological); personal experience (related to putting one's faith into practice). Buys 125 mss/year. Query. Length: 1,200 words maximum. Pays $10-150.

Photos: State availability of photos. Pays $50-300 for 5x7 color transparencies; $20-40 for 8x10 b&w prints. Identification of subjects (when related directly to articles) required. Buys one-time rights. Reserves the right to reprint material it has used for advertising and editorial purposes (pays second rights for editorial re-use).

Fillers: Anecdotes, short humor. Buys 100/year. Length: open. Pays $5-60.

Tips: "Fillers, personal experience, personality interviews and profiles are areas of our magazine open to free-lancers. All submissions are reviewed. The best method is to read our publication and submit similar material."

WAR CRY, The Official Organ of the Salvation Army, 799 Bloomfield Ave., Verona NJ 07044. Editor: Henry Gariepy. Weekly magazine for "persons with evangelical Christian background; members and friends of the Salvation Army; the 'man in the street.' " Circ. 280,000. Buys first rights. Pays on acceptance. SASE. Reports in 2 months. Free sample copy.

Nonfiction: Inspirational and informational articles with a strong evangelical Christian slant, but not preachy. In addition to general articles, needs articles slanted toward most of the holidays including Easter, Christmas, Mother's Day, Father's Day, etc. Buys 100 mss/year. Length: approximately 1,000-1,400 words. Pays $25-50.

Photos: Occasionally buys photos submitted with mss, but seldom with captions only. Pays $10-25 for b&w glossy prints.

Fiction: Prefers complete-in-one-issue stories, with a strong Christian slant. Can have modern or Biblical setting, but must not run contrary to Scriptural account. Length: 1,100-1,400 words. Pays 3¢/word.

Poetry: Religious or nature poems. Length: 4-24 lines. Pays $5-25.

THE WESLEYAN ADVOCATE, The Wesleyan Church Corp., Box 2000, Marion IN 46952. (317)674-3301. Editor: Dr. George E. Failing. Semimonthly magazine of the Wesleyan Church. "Reflects the devotional and doctrinal commitment of the denomination and is provided primarily for the membership and friends of The Wesleyan Church." Circ. 20,000. Pays on acceptance. Byline given. Not copyrighted. Buys first rights. Submit seasonal/holiday material 4 months in advance. SASE. Reports in 2 weeks on queries; 3 months on mss. Sample copy $1; free writer's guidelines for SASE.

Nonfiction: Inspirational; interview/profile (of people significant in or to The Wesleyan Church); personal experience (religious); Bible studies; doctrinal pieces. Special issues include youth, Easter, family, revival, missions. No "political endorsements, attacks on churches, etc." Buys 60-75 unsolicited mss/year. Recent article example: "Instant Evangelism" (Feb. 15, 1982). Query with clips of published work. Length: 200-1,500 words. Pays $5-30.

Poetry: No "doggerel and trite rhyme or verse with poor meter." Buys 10/year. Submit maximum 2 poems. Pays $2-10.

Tips: "Freelancers can best break in with a short devotional or inspirational article or through a personal experience article, accompanied by a personal letter with information about the author. We value personal integrity and a warmth that flows through any kind of article."

THE WITTENBERG DOOR, 1224 Greenfield Dr., El Cajon CA 92021. (714)440-2333. Contact: Mike Yaconelli. Bimonthly magazine for men and women, usually connected with the church. Circ. 19,000. Pays on publication. Buys all rights. Computer printout or disk submissions OK; prefers letter quality to dot matrix. SASE. Reports in 3 months. Free sample copy.
Nonfiction: Satirical or humorous articles on church renewal, Christianity, organized religion. Few book reviews. Buys about 30 mss/year. Query or submit complete ms. Length: 1,000 words maximum, 500-750 preferred. Pays $25-100.
Tips: "We look for someone who is clever, on our wave length and has some savvy about the evangelical church. We are very picky and highly selective."

WORLD ENCOUNTER, 2900 Queen Lane, Philadelphia PA 19129. (215)438-6360. Editor: The Rev. William A. Dudde. For persons who have more than average interest in, and understanding of, overseas missions and current human social concerns in other parts of the world. Quarterly magazine; 32 pages. Circ. 7,000. Buys all rights. Pays 35% kill fee. Byline given. Buys 10 mss/year. Pays on publication. Sample copy $1. Photocopied, and simultaneous submissions OK, if information is supplied on other markets being approached. Reports in 1 month. Query or submit complete ms. SASE.
Nonfiction and Photos: "This is a religious and educational publication using human interest features and think pieces related to the Christian world mission and world community. Race relations in southern Africa; human rights struggles with tyrannical regimes; social and political ferment in Latin America; resurgence of Oriental religions. Simple travelogues are not useful to us. Prospective writers should inquire as to the countries and topics of particular interest to our constituents. Material must be written in a popular style but the content must be more than superficial. It must be theologically, sociologically and anthropologically sound. We try to maintain a balance between gospel proclamation and concern for human and social development. We focus on what is happening in Lutheran groups. Our standards of content quality and writing are very high." No religious editorializing or moralizing. Recent article example: "Mission in Industrial Hong Kong" (spring 1982). Length: 500-1,800 words. Pays $35-175. B&w photos are purchased with or without accompanying mss or on assignment. Pays $10-20. Captions required.
Tips: "Write the editor, outlining your background and areas of international knowledge and interest, asking at what points they converge with our magazine's interests. Study the publication before submitting a manuscript. Too many of the pieces we receive are quite inappropriate."

Retirement

DYNAMIC YEARS, 215 Long Beach Blvd., Long Beach CA 90802. Editor: Carol Powers. Coordinating Editor: Lorena F. Farrell. 90% freelance written. "*Dynamic Years* is an official publication of the American Association of Retired Persons emphasizing stories relating to the interests of 40-60 age bracket, pre-retirees." Bimonthly. Circ. 200,000. Buys first-use or first North American rights. Pays negotiable kill fee. Byline given. Pays on acceptance. Submit seasonal material 6 months in advance. Reports in 4-6 weeks. Query or submit complete ms. "Submit only 1 ms at a time." SASE. Free sample copy.
Nonfiction: General subject matter is "financial planning, lifestyle, pre-retirement planning, health, fitness, humor, the world of work and job-related pieces, second careers, personal adjustment, sports, fashion, beauty, entertaining, generational relationships, 'people in action' with unusual activities, exciting use of leisure, investment, pensions, and travel. We do not want pieces about individuals long retired. No quizzes, poetry, or inspirational preachments. Primary concern is superb writing style, depth and accuracy of information." Buys 100 mss/year. Length: 1,000-3,000 words. Pays $150 for items, $350 minimum for short pieces, and $800-2,000 for full-length features.
Photos: State availability of photos with ms. Captions required. Pays $75 minimum for professional quality b&w. Pays $125 minimum for professional quality color slides or transparencies.

50 PLUS, 850 3rd Ave., New York NY 10022. (212)593-2100. Editor: Bard Lindeman. Managing Editor: Mark Reiter. "A service-oriented publication for men and women (age 50 and up). Readers are active, forward-looking, interested in all aspects of meaningful living in the middle and later years." Monthly. Accepts only queries from published writers. Buys all rights. Pays kill fee. Byline given. Buys 15-20 mss/year. Pays on acceptance. Sample copy $1.50 and 20¢ postage. Study magazine and needs before submitting query (indexed

in *Readers' Guide*). Submit seasonal and holiday material 6 months in advance. Reports in 6-8 weeks. SASE.
Nonfiction: "We want articles with a strong, timely service value or features about personalities or activities for people over 50 not covered in other general-interest magazines. Personal experiences, humor, second career ideas, unusual hobbies, self-fulfillment, celebrity interviews, food, fashion and controversial issues." Unusual travel stories, directly relevant to people over 50, only. Recent article example: Burt Lancaster cover story (April 1982). Length: 1,000-2,500 words. Pays $100-750 an article. "We reserve all rights to edit and rewrite to our style and space requirements.
Photos: "Photos and color transparencies must be of professional quality." Pays $50 minimum.
Fillers: Spot news, anecdotes and personality items. Pays $25-50.
Tips: "Profile a dynamic person over 50 who has news and/or service value to readers over 50, and whose current activities are meaningful or unusual to a wide range of readers."

MATURE LIVING, The Sunday School Board of the Southern Baptist Convention, 127 9th Ave. N., Nashville TN 37234. (615)251-2274. Editor: Jack Gulledge. Assistant Editor: Zada Malugen. A Christian magazine for retired senior adults 60 + . Monthly magazine; 52 pages. Pays on acceptance. Buys all rights. Byline given. Submit seasonal/holiday material at least 12-15 months in advance. SASE. Reports in 6 weeks. Free sample copy and writer's guidelines.
Nonfiction: How-to (easy, inexpensive craft articles made from easily obtained materials); informational (safety, consumer fraud, labor-saving and money-saving for senior adults); inspirational (short paragraphs with subject matter appealing to older persons); nostalgia; unique personal experiences; and travel. Buys 7-8 mss/issue. Send complete ms. Length: 400-1,400 words; prefers articles of 875 words. Pays $14-49.
Photos: Some original photos purchased with accompanying ms. Pays about $5-15 depending on size, b&w glossy prints. Model release required.
Fiction: Everyday living, humor and religious. "Must have suspense and character interaction." Buys 1 ms/ issue. Send complete ms. Length: 875-1,400 words. Pays 4¢/word.
Fillers: Short humor, religious or grandparent/grandchild episodes. Length: 125 words maximum. Pays $5.
Tips: "We want warm, creative, unique manuscripts. Presentations don't have to be moralistic or religious, but must reflect Christian standards. Don't write *down* to target audience. Speak *to* senior adults on issues that interest them. They like contemporary, good-Samaritan, and nostalgia articles. We buy some light humor. We use 140-word profiles of interesting unusual, senior adults worthy of recognition, when accompanied by a quality action b/w photo. Pays $25. Query should emphasize the uniqueness of proposed copy. Study back issues and guidelines, research and come up with creative material, that hits a need. Rewrite and refine to proper word count."

MATURE YEARS, 201 8th Ave., S., Nashville TN 37202. Editor: Daisy D. Warren. 20% freelance written. For retired persons and those facing retirement; persons seeking help on how to handle problems and privileges of retirement. Quarterly. Rights purchased vary with author and material; usually buys all rights. Buys 24 unsolicited mss/year. Pays on acceptance. Submit seasonal material 14 months in advance. Reports in 6 weeks. Submit complete ms. SASE. Free writer's guidelines.
Nonfiction: "*Mature Years* is different from the secular press in that we like material with Christian and church orientation. Usually we prefer materials that have a happy, healthy outlook regarding aging. Advocacy (for older adults) articles are at times used; some are freelance submissions. Articles deal with many aspects of pre-retirement and retirement living. Short stories and leisure-time hobbies relate to specific seasons. Give examples of how older persons, organizations, and institutions are helping others. Writing should be of interest to older adults, with Christian emphasis, though not preachy and moralizing. No poking fun or mushy, sentimental articles. We treat retirement from the religious viewpoint. How-to, humor and travel also considered." Length: 1,200-2,000 words.
Photos: 8x10 b&w glossy prints purchased with ms or on assignment.
Fiction: "We buy fiction for adults. Humor is preferred. Please, no children's stories and no stories about depressed situations of older adults." Length: 1,000-2,000 words. Payment varies, usually 4¢/word.

MODERN MATURITY, American Association of Retired Persons, 215 Long Beach Blvd., Long Beach CA 90801. Editor-in-Chief: Ian Ledgerwood. 75% freelance written. For readership over 50 years of age. Bimonthly magazine. Circ. 8 million. Pays on acceptance. Buys all rights. Byline given. Submit seasonal/holiday material 6 months in advance. SASE. Reports in 4 weeks. Free sample copy and writer's guidelines.
Nonfiction: Historical, how-to, humor, informational, inspirational, interview, new product, nostalgia, personal experience, opinion, photo feature, profile and travel. Query or send complete ms. Length: 1,000-2,000 words. Pays $1,000-2,000.
Photos: Photos purchased with or without accompanying ms. Pays $150 and up for color and $75 and up for b&w.
Fiction: Buys some fiction, but must be suitable for older readers. Send complete ms. Length: 1,000-2,000 words. Pays $1,000 minimum.

Poetry: All types. Length: 40 lines maximum. Pays $35.

Fillers: Clippings, jokes, gags, anecdotes, newsbreaks, puzzles (find-the-word, not crossword) and short humor. Pays $20 minimum.

NEW ENGLAND SENIOR CITIZEN/SENIOR AMERICAN NEWS, Prime National Publishing Corp., 470 Boston Post Rd., Weston MA 02193. Editor-in-Chief: Ira Alterman. 75% freelance written. For men and women aged 60 and over who are interested in travel, finances, retirement life styles, special legislation, nostalgia, etc. Monthly newspaper; 24-32 pages. Circ. 60,000. Pays on publication. Buys all rights. Byline given. Submit seasonal/holiday material 3 months in advance. Previously published material OK. Computer printout and disk submissions OK. SASE. Reports in 4 months. Sample copy 50¢.

Nonfiction: General interest; how-to (anything dealing with retirement years); inspirational; historical; humor; interview; nostalgia; profile; travel; personal experience; photo features; and articles about medicine relating to gerontology. Buys 10-15 mss/issue. Submit complete ms. Length: 500-1,500 words. Pays $25-50.

Photos: Purchased with ms. Captions required. Pays $5-15/5x7 or 8x10 b&w glossy print. Captions and model releases required.

Fiction: Adventure, historical, humorous, mystery, romance, suspense and religious. Buys 1 ms/issue. Submit complete ms. Length: 500-1,500 words. Pays $25-50.

Tips: "Clean, typed, top-quality copy aimed at older tastes, interests, lifestyles and memories."

PRIME TIMES, Narcup, Inc., Editorial offices: Suite 120, 2802 International Lane, Madison WI 53704. Executive Director: Steve Goldberg. Managing Editor: Glenn Deutsch. Editorial Coordinator: Ana María M. Guzmán. Quarterly magazine for people who want to redefine retirement. The audience is primarily people over 50 who were or are credit union members and want to plan and manage their retirement. Circ. 75,000. Buys first rights (pays upon acceptance) and second serial (reprint) rights (pays upon publication). Submit seasonal material 6 months in advance. Previously published submissions OK as long as they were not in another national maturity-market magazine. "We're receptive to computer printout submissions so long as the writer uses a letter-quality printer." SASE. Reports in 1 month on queries; in 6 weeks on mss. Free sample copy only with 9x12 SAE and 5 first-class stamps postage; free writer's guidelines for SASE. No exceptions.

Nonfiction: Expose and how-to (related to financial planning methods; consumer activism; health; travel; and working after retirement); interview (of people over 50 who are leading active or important retirements); opinion; profile; travel; popular arts; self-image; personal experience; and photo feature. "No rocking chair reminiscing." Buys 30-40 mss/year "of which 4-10 are from new talent. This, from well over 3,500 submissions a year." Query with clips of previously published work. Length: 500-2,500 words. Pays $50-500. SASE. "Be sure to keep a photocopy—just in case gremlins pinch the original."

Photos: Pays $25-50/8x10 b&w glossy high-contrast prints; $25-50/35mm color transparency or according to ASMP guidelines or negotiation. $7.50/cutline. Captions and model release required. Buys one-time rights. Will not reproduce color prints. SASE. "Do not send irreplaceable *anything.*"

Tips: "Query should state qualifications (such as expertise or society memberships). Freelancers should submit copy—double-spaced and typed 60 characters/line with SASE. They should also send photos, copies of photos, or other art accompanying the articles with SASE. Special issues requiring freelance work include publications on mature friendship; comparative aging (cross-cultural); second careers; money management; minorities over 50; continuing education; and the young-old *vis-à-vis* the old-old. Whether urban or rural, male or female, if attempts at humor, lightness or tongue-in-cheek seem off-target to you, they will to me, too. And we don't gloss over important matters. If you identify a problem, try to identify a solution. Every word counts. And remember that there are at least two generations reading *Prime Times*—folks over 50, and folks over 70. Most are not retired (average age: 61) and about 55% of our readers are women."

SENIOR WORLD, Senior World Publications, Inc., Suite 204, 500 Fesler St., El Cajon CA 92020-1986. (619)588-6541. Editor: Leonard J. Hansen. Managing Editor: Laura Impastato. Monthly tabloid about senior citizens for active older adults and senior citizens living in San Diego County. Circ. 103,000. Pays on publication. Rights vary. Submit seasonal material 3 months in advance. Simultaneous and photocopied submissions OK. Computer printout and disk submissions OK. SASE. Reports in 6 weeks. Sample copy $1; free writer's guidelines.

Nonfiction: Expose (government bungling of senior citizen programs or concerns); general interests; how-to (save money; fix things around the house; make money; cook for one or two); humor and cartoons (positive representation of senior citizens); interview; profile (of remarkable seniors and celebrities who are now senior citizens and still active); new product; travel; and photo feature (query). "No 'pity the poor senior' stories or 'walking 12 miles to school' stories or talking down to senior citizens." Buys 48-60 unsolicited mss/year. "We are expanding in our travel, health and feature reportage—which means we will be looking for more in these areas." Query or send complete ms. Length: 200-900 words. Pays $25-100.

Photos: State availability of photos or send photos with ms. Pays $10-50 for 8x10 b&w prints. Captions preferred; model release required. Rights vary.

Columns/Departments: "All columns currently are staff written, but we will look at proposals." Query with sample.
Tips: "Read the publication, see the very active news styles; realize that older adults and senior citizens are very active, alive and alert people. We do not use poetry, mood pieces, reveries or inspiration-type stories. You're writing to senior citizens, not down to them. They read well and understand. Make query brief—no more than one page. A good clear explanation of the article proposed and information on photos or other illustrations to go with it plus a brief paragraph or two on the writer's background and other writing credits. We are always on the lookout for good celebrity profiles of seniors and remarkable seniors who are still working and making a contribution to society. Also innovative stories about new programs, projects etc. for seniors. No inspiration pieces, reveries about grandma or growing up in Ohio, or 'cute grandkid' stories."

SEPTEMBER DAYS, Days Inns of America, Inc., 2751 Buford Hwy., NE Atlanta GA 30324. (404)325-4000. Editor: Alexandra Pieper Jones. Quarterly travel magazine for members of the September Days Club, who are 55 and older. Circ. 260,000. Pays on publication. Submit seasonal material 6 months in advance. Simultaneous and photocopied submissions OK. SASE. Reports in 3 weeks. Sample copy $2; free writer's guidelines with SASE.
Nonfiction: Travel (in the continental United States, destination stories); and photo feature (of the United States). No poems or historical pieces. Buys 4-5 mss/issue. Send complete ms. Length: 500-2,000 words. Pays negotiable fee; "depends on ms and topic."
Photos: Pays $45 and up for standard color transparencies. Captions preferred; model release required. Buys one-time rights.
Tips: "Send complete ms on spec only; do not include photos."

Romance and Confession

Romance is sweeping the nation. For more information on writing for this market, consult *Writing Romance Fiction—For Love and Money*, by Helene Schellenberg Barnhart (Writer's Digest Books).

If you haven't read a confession story in a few years, you haven't been introduced to the modern confessions. If you plan to write for this market, consult *The Confession Writer's Handbook*, by Florence K. Palmer (revised by Marguerite McClain, Writer's Digest Books).

‡**AFFAIRE DE COEUR, Leading Publication for Romance Readers and Writers**, Affaire de Coeur, Inc., 5660 Roosevelt Place, Fremont CA 94538. (415)656-4804. Editor/Publisher: Barbara N. Keenan. Monthly magazine for romance readers and writers. Estab. 1981. Circ. 3,000. Pays on publication. Byline given. Buys all rights. Submit seasonal/holiday material 3-4 months in advance. Simultaneous queries; and photocopied and previously published submissions OK. SASE. Reports in 3 weeks. Sample copy $2; writer's guidelines for SAE and 20¢ postage.
Nonfiction: Book excerpts (on romantic fiction); how-to (write romantic fiction); interview/profile (on romance authors). Nothing that doesn't pertain to romantic fiction. Buys 12 mss/year. Query. Length: varies. Pays $10-25.
Columns/Departments: Beth Rowe, Lovelore editor. Buys 12 mss/year. Query. Length: varies. Pays $10-25.
Fiction: Ann H. Wassall, senior editor. Novel excerpts, romance, serialized novels. Buys variable number mss/year. Query. Length: 1,000-1,500 words. Pays $25-50.
Fillers: Beth Rowe, fillers editor. Newsbreaks. Buys 50/year. Length: varies. Pays with credit line.

MODERN ROMANCES, Macfadden Women's Group, Inc., 215 Lexington Ave., New York NY 10016. Editor: Jean Sharbel. 100% freelance written. For blue-collar, family-oriented women, 18-35 years old. Monthly magazine; 88 pages. Circ. 200,000. Pays the last week of the month of the issue. Buys all rights. Submit seasonal/holiday material 6 months in advance. SASE. Reports in 12-16 weeks.
Nonfiction: General interest; baby and child care; how-to (homemaking subjects); humor; inspirational; and personal experience. Submit complete ms. Length: 200-1,500 words. Pay depends on merit. "Confession stories with reader identification and a strong emotional tone. No third person material." Buys 14 mss/issue. Submit complete ms. Length: 1,500-8,500 words. Pays 5¢/word.
Poetry: "Light, romantic poetry, to 24 lines." Buys 36/year. Pay "depends on merit."

ROMANTIC TIMES, The Complete Newspaper for Readers of Romantic Fiction, Romantic Times, Inc., Suite 1234, 163 Joralemon St., Brooklyn Heights NY 11201. (212)875-5019. Managing Editor: Kathryn Falk. Bimonthly newspaper covering romantic fiction for readers and writers of romantic novels. Estab. 1981. Circ. 60,000. Pays on publication. Byline given. Pays $20 kill fee. Rights purchased vary. Submit seasonal/ holiday material 6 months in advance. Simultaneous queries, and simultaneous, photocopied, and previously published submissions OK. SASE. Reports in 3 weeks. Sample copy $2.

Nonfiction: Book excerpts; historical/nostalgic (pertaining to historical novels); how-to (write romantic novels); interview/profile (with romance writers); and personal experience (How I Write Romantic Novels). "Submit an interesting, revealing interview with a long-time reader of those novels, explaining his enjoyment and recommendations. An interview with a famous author, present or past, would be most welcomed." Special issues include: Regency Issue and Romantic Suspense Issue. "At this time, no romantic fiction manuscripts. Just *articles about* this subject." Buys "at least 12" mss/year. Query. Length: 1,000-2,500 words. Pays $50.

Photos: "We need photos of writers at work or at home." State availability of photos. Pays $10 for b&w prints. Captions, model release, and identification of subjects required. Buys one-time rights.

Columns/Departments: Book reviews, gossip and historical tidbits. Query. Length: 500-1,000 words. Pays $20-30.

Tips: "The best freelancer would be one who reads or writes romantic fiction, and has a feel for what the average romantic novel fan would like to read in a newspaper devoted to this subject. We like to see in-depth, but not academic-sounding, articles on the genre of romantic fiction."

SECRETS, Macfadden Women's Group, 215 Lexington Ave., New York NY 10016. (212)340-7500. Vice President and Editorial Director: Florence J. Moriarty. Editor: Jean Press Silberg. For blue-collar family women, ages 18-35. Monthly magazine. Buys all rights. Buys about 150 mss/year. Pays on publication. No photocopied or simultaneous submissions. Submit seasonal material 4-5 months in advance. Submit only complete ms. Reports in 6 weeks. SASE.

Nonfiction and Fiction: Wants true stories of special interest to women: family, marriage and romance themes, "woman-angle articles," or self-help or inspirational fillers. "No pornographic material; no sadistic or abnormal angles." Length: 300-1,000 words for features; 1,500-7,500 words for full-length story. Occasional 10,000-worders. Pays 3¢/word for story mss. Greatest need: 4,500-6,000 words.

TRUE CONFESSIONS, Macfadden Women's Group, 215 Lexington Ave., New York NY 10016. Editor: Barbara J. Brett. For high-school-educated, blue-collar women, teens through maturity. Monthly magazine. Circ. 350,000. Buys all rights. Byline given on poetry and articles. Pays during the last week of month of issue. No photocopied or simultaneous submissions. Submit seasonal material 6 months in advance. Reports in 4 months. Submit complete ms. SASE.

Stories, Articles, and Fillers: Timely, exciting, emotional first-person stories on the problems that face today's young women. The narrators should be sympathetic, and the situations they find themselves in should be intriguing, yet realistic. Every story should have a strong romantic interest and a high moral tone, and every plot should reach an exciting climax. Careful study of a current issue is suggested. Length: 2,000-6,000 words; 5,000 word stories preferred; also book lengths of 9,000-10,000 words. Pays 5¢/word. Also, articles, regular features, and short fillers.

Poetry: Romantic poetry, free verse and traditional, of interest to women. Length: 16 lines maximum. Limit submissions to batches of 4. Pays $10 minimum.

TRUE EXPERIENCE, Macfadden Women's Group, 215 Lexington Ave., New York NY 10016. Contact: Helene Eccleston. For young marrieds, blue-collar, high school education. Interests: children, home, arts, crafts, family and self-fulfillment. Monthly magazine; 80 pages. Circ. 225,000. Buys all rights. Byline given on articles and poetry. Buys about 100 mss/year. Pays within 30 days after publication. "Study the magazine for style and editorial content." No photocopied or simultaneous submissions. Submit seasonal material 5 months in advance. Reports in 3 months. Submit complete ms. SASE.

Nonfiction: Stories on life situations, e.g., love, divorce, any real-life problems. Romance and confession, first-person narratives with strong identification for readers. Articles on health, self-help or child care. "Remember that we are contemporary. We deal with women's self-awareness, and consciousness of their roles in society." Length: 250-1,500 words for nonfiction; 1,000-7,500 words for personal narrative. Pays 3¢/word.

Poetry: Only traditional forms. Length: 4-20 lines. Payment varies.

TRUE LOVE, Macfadden Women's Group, 215 Lexington Ave., New York NY 10016. (212)340-7500. Editor: Susan O'Doherty. For young, blue-collar women. Monthly magazine; 80 pages. Circ. 225,000. Buys all rights. Byline given for nonfiction. Buys about 150 mss/year. Pays after publication. Submit seasonal material at least 6 months in advance. Reports in 12-16 weeks. Submit complete ms. SASE.

Nonfiction: Confessions, true love stories (especially young romance); problems and solutions; health problems; marital and child-rearing difficulties. Avoid graphic sex. Stories dealing with reality, current problems, everyday events, with emphasis on emotional impact. Length: 1,500-8,000 words. Pays 3¢/word. Informa-

tional and how-to articles. Length: 250-800 words. Pays 5¢/word minimum.
Tips: "The story must appeal to the average blue collar woman. It must deal with her problems and interests. Characters—especially the narrator—must be sympathetic."

TRUE ROMANCE, Macfadden Women's Group, 215 Lexington Ave., New York NY 10016. (212)340-7500. Editor: Susan Weiner. "Our readership ranges from teenagers to senior citizens. The majority are high school educated, married, have young children and also work outside the home. They are concerned with contemporary social issues, yet they are deeply committed to their husbands and children. They have high moral values and place great emphasis on love and romance." Monthly magazine. Circ. 225,000. Pays on publication. Buys all rights. Submit seasonal/holiday material at least 5 months in advance. SASE. Reports in 3 months.
Nonfiction: How-to and informational. Submit complete ms. Length: 300-1,000 words. Pays 3¢/word, special rates for short features and articles. Confession. "We want *only* true contemporary stories about relationships." Buys 13 stories/issue. Submit complete ms. Length: 2,000-7,500 words. Pays 3¢/word; slightly higher flat rate for short-shorts.
Poetry: Light verse and traditional. Buys 15/year. Length: 4-20 lines. Pays $10 minimum.
Tips: "The freelance writer is needed and welcomed. A timely, well-written story that is told by a sympathetic narrator who sees the central problem through to a satisfying resolution is all that is needed to 'break into' *True Romance*. We are always looking for good love stories."

TRUE STORY, Macfadden Women's Group, 215 Lexington Ave., New York NY 10016. Editor: Helen Vincent. 80% freelance written. For young married, blue-collar women, 20-35; high school education; increasingly broad interests; home-oriented, but looking beyond the home for personal fulfillment. Monthly magazine. Circ. 1,700,000. Buys all rights. Byline given "on articles only." Buys about 125 full-length mss/year. Pays on publication. No photocopied or simultaneous submissions. Submit seasonal material 4 months in advance. Make notation on envelope that it is seasonal material. Query for fact articles. Submit only complete mss for stories. Reports in 3-4 months. SASE.
Nonfiction, Stories and Fillers: "First-person stories covering all aspects of women's interests: love, marriage, family life, careers, social problems, etc. Nonfiction would further explore same areas. The best direction a new writer can be given is to carefully study several issues of the magazine; then submit a fresh, exciting, well-written true story. We have no taboos. It's the handling and believability that make the difference between a rejection and an acceptance." How-to, personal experience, inspirational. Nonfiction length: 1,000-2,500 words. Pays 5-10¢ or more/word. Fiction length: 1,500-10,000 words. Pays 5¢/word; $150 minimum. Also seeks material for Women are Wonderful column. Length: 1,500 words maximum. Pays 5-10¢/word. Pays a flat rate for column or departments, announced in the magazine. Query Art Director, Gus Gazzola, about all possible photo submissions.

Science

Publications classified here aim at laymen interested in technical and scientific developments and discoveries, applied science, and technical or scientific hobbies. Publications of interest to the personal computer owner/user are listed in the Home Computing category. Journals for scientists, engineers, repairmen, etc., will be found in Trade Journals.

ALTERNATIVE SOURCES OF ENERGY MAGAZINE, 107 S. Central Ave., Milaca MN 56353. Executive Editor: Donald Marier. Emphasizes alternative energy sources and the exploration and innovative use of renewable energy sources. Audience is predominantly male, age 36, college educated and concerned about energy and environmental limitations. Bimonthly magazine. Circ. 23,000. Pays on acceptance. Phone queries OK. Simultaneous, photocopied, and previously published submissions OK, "if specified at time of submission." SASE. Reports in 6 weeks. Sample copy $3.50.
Nonfiction: Larry Stoiaken, editor. How-to (plans, kits); informational (new sources of data, products); interview (any active person in field); and technical (plans, kits, designs). "We're especially interested in wind and hydro-power stories. A story (with photo support) detailing installation of low-head hydro or wind-generator with follow-up on the energy produced is higher on our readership survey than most topics." Submit an outline before complete ms. Buys 10-15 unsolicited mss/year. Recent article example: "Build Your Own Solar Electric Panel" (issue No. 53). Length: 500-3,000 words. Pays 5¢/word.
Photos: Pays $7.50, prefers b&w.

Tips: "We need well-researched articles emphasizing the practical application of alternative sources of energy: solar, water, wind, biofuels, etc. Always include addresses of all products and/or publications listed. Stay away from philosophical underpinnings; stick to how-to-do-it or rules of thumb."

COMPUTERS AND ELECTRONICS, (formerly *Popular Electronics*), 1 Park Ave., New York NY 10016. (212)725-3566. Editor-in-Chief: Art Salsberg. For computer enthusiasts, hi-fi and video, and electronics experimenters. Monthly. Circ. 500,000. Buys all rights. Pays 50% kill fee. Byline given. Buys about 75 mss/ year. Pays on acceptance. No photocopied or simultaneous submissions. Reports in 2-4 weeks. Query. Computer printout submissions OK; "disk not at this time unless arrangements agreed upon." SASE. Free writer's guidelines.
Nonfiction: "State-of-the-art" reports, how-to and tutorial articles, construction projects, etc. The writer must know what he's talking about and not depend on 'hand-out' literature from a few manufacturers or research laboratories. The writer must always bear in mind that the reader has some knowledge of computers and electronics." Informational, how-to, and technical articles. "No humor stories or superficial general-public material." Query; if a project, include a block diagram or schematic and approximate cost to builder. Length: 500-3,000 words. Pays $90-150/published page with photo, illustration, rough diagrams. B&w glossy prints preferred, though color transparencies are sometimes used.
Fillers: Electronics circuits quizzes, circuit and bench tips. Length: 100-1,000 words. Pays $10-100.
Tips: "Stronger focus on personal computers for home and small-business applications will affect writers in the year ahead."

CQ: THE RADIO AMATEUR'S JOURNAL, 76 N. Broadway, Hicksville NY 11801. (516)681-2922. Editor: Alan Dorhoffer. For the amateur radio community. Monthly journal. Circ. 100,000. Pays on publication. Buys first rights. Phone queries OK. Submit seasonal/holiday material 3 months in advance. SASE. Reports in 2-3 weeks. Free sample copy.
Nonfiction: "We are interested in articles that address all technical levels of amateur radio. Included would be basic material for newcomers and intermediate and advanced material for oldtimers. Articles may be of a theoretical, practical or anecdotal nature. They can be general interest pieces for all amateurs or they can focus in on specific topics. We would like historical articles, material on new developments, articles on projects you can do in a weekend, and pieces on long-range projects taking a month or so to complete." Length: 6-10 typewritten pages. Pays $35/published page.

ELECTRONICS TODAY INTERNATIONAL, Unit 6, 25 Overlea Blvd., Toronto, Ontario, Canada M4H 1B1. (416)423-3262. Editor: Halvor Moorshead. 40% freelance written. Emphasizes audio, electronics and personal computing for a wide-ranging readership, both professionals and hobbyists. Monthly magazine; 88 pages. Circ. 27,000. Pays on publication. Buys all rights. Byline given. Phone queries OK. Submit seasonal/ holiday material 4 months in advance. Photocopied submissions OK. SAE and International Reply Coupons. Reports in 4 weeks. Sample copy $3; free writer's guidelines.
Nonfiction: How-to (technical articles in electronics field); humor (if relevant to electronics); new product (if using new electronic techniques); and technical (on new developments, research, etc.). Buys 10 unsolicited mss/year. Recent article example: "Canada in Space" (November 1981). Query. Length: 600-3,500 words. Pays $75-100/1,000 words.
Photos: "Ideally we like to publish 2 photos or diagrams per 1,000 words of copy." State availability of photo material with query. Additional payment for photos accepted with accompanying ms. Captions required. Buys all rights.
Fillers: Puzzles (mathematical). Buys 10/year. Length: 50-250 words. Pays $15-20.

FUSION MAGAZINE, Fusion Energy Foundation, Box 1438, Radio City Station, New York NY 10101. (212)247-8439. Editor: Dr. Steven Bardwell. Managing Editor: Marjorie Mazel Hecht. Bimonthly magazine about fusion energy and nuclear energy for both lay and technical readers. Circ. 200,000. Pays on publication. Buys all rights and makes work-for-hire assignments. Phone queries OK. Photocopied and previously published submissions OK. SASE.
Nonfiction: Expose (energy, science, research, environment and anti-science); general interest (epistemology and science education); historical (science, research, technology, economics, discoveries and industrial development); humor (political satire); interview (science figures); new product (high technology and medical technology); personal experience; photo feature (advanced energy technologies); and technical (advanced technology in biology, physics, medicine, fusion, fission research, breakthroughs and international scientific work); and conference reports. Query. Length: 500-3,500 words. Pays $75 minimum.
Photos: State availability of photos. Captions and model release required. Buys all rights.
Tips: "Look through back issues to see the range of topics and styles."

MECHANIX ILLUSTRATED, 1515 Broadway, New York NY 10036. (212)719-6630. Editor: David E. Petzal. Home and Shop Editor: Burt Murphy. Managing Editor: Michael Morris. Special issues include Home

Close-up

Art Salsberg, Editorial Director
Computers & Electronics

Art Salsberg is a busy man. As editorial director of *Computers & Electronics*, "my days and nights encompass talking to writers about possible articles; distributing articles to editors for evaluation and agonizing over which ones to accept or reject; reviewing work of editors; discussing graphics approaches with artists; examining 'blues' as a final check; and reading an enormous amount of letters, industry newspapers and magazines." On top of this and sundry administrative responsibilities, he keeps in touch with his readership and their needs.

Salsberg says his readers want up-to-date information on purchasing their own computers, enhancing their current system's utility, and upgrading to more advanced systems. Reflecting these reader needs, the magazine changed its name from *Popular Electronics* to *Computers & Electronics* in 1983. "It came to the point," he says, "where computers became the single, dominant area in the magazine and the original name was no longer a true image." Currently half of the publication is devoted to personal computers, both hardware and software. "And this coverage is expected to expand," says Salsberg.

The magazine's new name has prompted additional changes writers should know about. "Our writing style is livelier; our graphics are sprightlier. And we're giving less coverage to project building and other consumer electronic areas. We focus on how something works, how to apply equipment, and what's new in the field. We assume our readers have some affinity for technical matters and want to know more than merely surface information."

And Salsberg knows the kinds of writers who are best equipped to transmit that information successfully. "The ideal writer brings his expertise to the subject; he brings fresh ideas related to our readers' interests; and he writes well and succinctly."

That kind of writer should query Salsberg with an article theme "so he can know if we want such an article. Otherwise he faces the possibility of our having such an article in-house or already commissioned to another author."

The hottest queries these days suggest a "meaty" computer-oriented topic "that relates to the latest equipment, software, applications or enhancements that have never been covered anywhere." Salsberg likes a brief summary of the topic, approximate length, and related photos/rough drawings.

It is clear that *C&E* is a specialist writer's market and author credentials are important. Salsberg wants to know a writer's formal computer/electronics training, job-related activities and published clips. An appropriate background, he says, "instills in us a sense of confidence in a writer's abilities."

To reinforce that confidence, *C&E* writers should adhere to the basics that apply to any top-notch submission. "The mechanics of an article package rank high," says Salsberg. "Copy must be typed with a fresh ribbon, double spaced with wide margins. If a computer dot-matrix printer is used, as is often the case with our authors, the matrix dot spacing should be tight. Writers should use double striking if the normal matrix is difficult to read," he says. As for deadlines, Salsberg says writers who meet them are "highly regarded, of course."

Improvement (April); Car Care (May and November); Old Houses (September); and New Cars (October). Monthly magazine; 106-180 pages. Buys first North American rights except for picture sets. Byline given. Pays on acceptance. Send SASE for copy of guidelines for writers. Reports "promptly." Query. SASE.

Nonfiction: Feature articles about inventions, electronics, alternative energy. We are seeking "more and more energy-related material." Length: 1,500-2,500 words. Pays $300 minimum. Also uses home workshop projects, kinks, etc., for Home and Shop section. Pays $75-1,000, and higher in exceptional circumstances. "We offer a varied market for all types of do-it-yourself material, ranging from simple tips on easier ways to do things to major construction projects. Furniture construction, painting, photography, gardening, concrete and masonry work or any type of building construction or repair are just a few of the subjects that interest." Pays $20-25 for an illustrated and captioned tip.

Photos: Photos should accompany mss. Pays $400 and up for transparencies of interesting mechanical subjects accepted for cover; prefers 4x5, but 2¼x2¼ square is acceptable. Inside color: $300/1 page, $500/2, $700/3, etc. Pays $35/single (b&w) feature photo involving new developments, etc., in the field. Home and Shop tips illustrated with 1 photo, $25. Captions are required. B&w picture sets, $350 maximum. Requires model releases.

Fillers: Pays $75 for half-page fillers.

Tips: "If you're planning some kind of home improvement and can write, you might consider doing a piece on it for us. Good how-to articles on home improvement are always difficult to come by. Aside from that, no particular part of the book is easier to break into than another because we simply don't care whether you've been around or been published here before. We don't care who you are or whether you have any credentials—we're in the market for good journalism and if it's convincing, we buy it."

OMNI, 909 3rd Ave., New York NY 10022. (212)593-3301. Executive Editor: Dick Teresi. Monthly magazine of the future covering science fact, fiction, and fantasy for readers of all ages, backgrounds and interests. Circ. 1,000,000. Average issue includes 3 nonfiction feature articles and 2-3 fiction articles; also monthly columns. Pays on acceptance. Offers 25% kill fee. Buys exclusive worldwide and first English rights and rights for *Omni* Anthology. Submit seasonal material 4-6 months in advance. Photocopied submissions OK. Computer printout submissions OK; prefers letter quality to dot matrix. SASE. Reports in 1 month. Free writer's guidelines with SASE (request fiction or nonfiction).

Nonfiction: "Articles with a futuristic angle, offering readers alternatives in housing, energy, transportation, medicine and communications. Executive Editor Dick Teresi explains that scientists can affect the public's perception of science and scientists by opening their minds to the new possibilities of science journalism. People want to know, want to understand what scientists are doing and how scientific research is affecting their lives and their future. *Omni* publishes articles about science in language that people can understand. We seek very knowledgeable science writers who are ready to work with scientists to produce articles that can inform and interest the general reader. Send query/proposal. Length: 2,500-3,500 words. Pays $1,250-1,500.

Photos: Art Director: Elizabeth Woodson. State availability of photos. Reviews 35mm slides and 4x5 transparencies.

Columns/Departments: Explorations (unusual travel or locations on Earth); Breakthroughs (new products); Mind (by and about psychiatrists and psychologists); Earth (environment); Life (biomedicine); Space (technology); Arts (theater, music, film, technology); Interview (of prominent person); Continuum (newsbreaks); Antimatter and UFO Update (unusual newsbreaks, paranormal); Stars (astronomy); First/Last Word (editorial/humor); Artificial Intelligence (computers); The Body (medical). Query with clips of previously published work. Length: 1,500 words maximum. Pays $700-850; $150 for Continuum and Antimatter items.

Fiction: Contact: Ellen Datlow. Fantasy and science fiction. Buys 2-3 mss/issue. Send complete ms. Length: 10,000 words maximum. Pays $850-2,000.

Tips: "Consider science fact and science fiction pictorials with a futuristic leaning. We're interested in thematic composites of excellent photos or art with exciting copy."

POPULAR MECHANICS, 224 W. 57th St., New York NY 10019. (212)262-4815. Editor: John A. Linkletter. Executive Editor: Joe Oldham. Managing Editor: William Hartford. Home and Shop Editor: Harry Wicks. Monthly magazine; 200 pages. Circ. 1,625,000. Buys all rights. Byline given. Pays "promptly." Query. SASE.

Nonfiction: Needs material on "ingenious ways readers are coping with growing energy shortages—both in their homes and in their automobiles. Principal subjects are automotive (new cars, car maintenance) and how-to (woodworking, metalworking, home improvement and home maintenance). In addition, we use features on new technology, sports, electronics, photography and hi-fi." Exciting male interest articles with strong science, exploration and adventure emphasis. Looking for reporting on new and unusual developments. The writer should be specific about what makes it new, different, better, cheaper, etc. "We are always looking for fresh ideas in home maintenance, shop technique and crafts for project pieces used in the back part of the book. The front of the book uses articles in technology and general science, but writers in that area should have background in science." Length: 300-2,000 words. Pays $300-1,500.

Photos: Dramatic photos are most important, and they should show people and things in action. Occasionally buys picture stories with short text block and picture captions. The photos must tell the story without much explanation. Topnotch photos are a must with Home and Shop Section articles. Can also use remodeling of homes, rooms and outdoor structures. Pays $25 minimum.

POPULAR SCIENCE MONTHLY, 380 Madison Ave., New York NY 10017: Editor-in-Chief: C.P. Gilmore. For the well-educated adult, interested in science, technology, new products. Monthly magazine; 180 pages. Circ. 1,850,000. Buys all rights. Pays negotiable kill fee. Byline given. Buys several hundred mss a year. Pays on acceptance. Free guidelines for writers. No photocopied or simultaneous submissions. Submit seasonal material 4 months in advance. Reports in 3 weeks. Query. SASE.
Nonfiction: "*Popular Science Monthly* is devoted to exploring (and explaining) to a nontechnical but knowledgeable readership the technical world around us. We are a 'thing'-oriented publication: things that fly or travel down a turnpike, or go on or under the sea, or cut wood, or reproduce music, or build buildings, or make pictures, or mow lawns. We are especially focused on the new, the ingenious and the useful. We are consumer-oriented and are interested in any product that adds to a man's enjoyment of his home, yard, car, boat, workshop, outdoor recreation. Some of our 'articles' are only a picture and caption long. Some are a page long. Some occupy 4 or more pages. Contributors should be as alert to the possibility of selling us pictures and short features as they are to major articles. Freelancers should study the magazine to see what we want and avoid irrelevant submissions. No biological, natural history." Recent article example: "New Powerful Portables—Best Buy in a Personal Computer." Length: 2,000 words maximum. Pays $200 a published page minimum. Prefers 8x10 b&w glossy prints. Pays $35.
Fillers: Uses shortcuts and tips for homeowners, home craftsmen, car owners, mechanics and machinists.
Tips: "Probably the easiest way to break in here is by covering a news story in science and technology that we haven't heard about yet. We need people to be acting as bird-dogs for us out there and we are willing to give the most leeway on these performances. What impresses us the most in a freelance piece—when we're thinking about uncovering a good contributor for the future—is the kind of illustrations the writer supplies. Too many of them kiss off the problem of illustrations. Nothing impresses us more than knowing that the writer can take or acquire good photos to accompany his piece. We probably buy the most freelance material in the do-it-yourself and home improvement areas."

RADIO-ELECTRONICS, 200 Park Ave. S., New York NY 10003. (212)777-6400. Managing Editor: Art Kleiman. For electronics professionals and hobbyists. Monthly magazine, 128 pages. Circ. 211,000. Buys all rights. Byline given. Pays on acceptance. Submit seasonal/holiday material 6-8 months in advance. SASE. Reports in 3 weeks. Send for "Guide to Writing."
Nonfiction: Interesting technical stories on all aspects of electronics, including video, radio, computers, communications, and stereo written from viewpoint of the electronics professional, serious experimenter, or layman with technical interests. Construction (how-to-build-it) articles used heavily. Unique projects bring top dollars. Cost of project limited only by what item will do. Emphasis on "how it works, and why." Much of material illustrated with schematic diagrams and pictures provided by author. Also high interest in how-to articles. Length: 1,000-5,000 words. Pays about $50-500.
Photos: State availability of photos. Offers no additional payment for b&w prints or 35mm color transparencies. Model releases required.
Columns/Departments: Pays $50-200/column.
Fillers: Pays $15-35.
Tips: "The simplest way to come in would be with a short article on some specific construction project. Queries aren't necessary; just send the article, 5 or 6 typewritten pages."

SCIENCE & MECHANICS, Davis Publications, 380 Lexington Ave., New York NY 10017. Editor-in-Chief: Joseph Daffron. Managing Editor: Stephen Wagner. Bimonthly. Pays on acceptance. Buys all rights. Submit seasonal material 5 months in advance of issue date. Computer printout submissions OK as long as standard paper size. SASE. Reports in 2 weeks.
Nonfiction: How-to (wood, mechanical, electronic and outdoor projects; home fix-up and repair); general interest (science, mechanics, technology, energy saving); and technical (what's new, inventions, electronics, science, technology, automotive and mechanical). Buys 14-16 mss/issue. Length: 2,500-4,000 words. Query first; rates negotiable.
Photos: "Technical and how-to material must be illustrated; would like to see drawings and diagrams, if applicable." State availability of photos with query. Captions preferred.

SCIENCE DIGEST, Hearst Magazines Division, Hearst Corp., 888 7th Ave., New York NY 10106. (212)262-7990. Editor-in-Chief: Scott DeGarmo. Executive Editor: Hazel Arnett. Emphasizes sciences and technologies for all ages with a scientific bent. Monthly magazine; 140 pages. Circ. 600,000. Pays on acceptance. Buys all magazine and periodical rights worldwide but for use only in *Science Digest* in all of its editions worldwide. Pays 25% kill fee. Byline given. Reports on queries and mss in 1 month. Sample copy $2; free writer's guidelines with SASE.

Nonfiction: Informational (authentic, timely information in all areas of science). Book excerpts, expose, interview/profile, new product, opinion, photo feature and technical. Also seeking material on computers, innovation and inventors. Length: 500-2,000 words. Buys 200 mss/year. Query with or without clips or send complete ms.

Columns/Departments: Astronomy, Speculations, Human Nature and Viewpoint. Buys about 40/year. Query with or without clips of published work or send complete ms. Length: 500-1,000 words.

Photos: Purchased with or without accompanying ms or on assignment. Send photos with accompanying query or ms. Reviews contact sheets, negatives, color transparencies and prints. Captions, model releases, and identification of subjects required. Buys all magazine and periodical rights worldwide but for use only in *Science Digest* in all of its editions worldwide.

Fillers: Amazing Scientific Facts. Length: 50-250 words. Pays $25-50.

Tips: "Our goal is to help our readers appreciate the beauty of science and the adventure of technology. Articles are geared toward the alert, inquisitive layman, fascinated by all facets of science."

SCIENCE 84, American Association for the Advancement of Science, 1101 Vermont Ave., NW, 10th Fl., Washington DC 20005. (202)842-9500. Editor: Allen L. Hammond. Managing Editor: Eric Schrier. Monthly magazine covering popular science. Circ. 725,000. Pays on acceptance. Byline given. Offers 20% kill fee. Buys all rights, shares reprint royalties. Submit seasonal/holiday material 4 months in advance. SASE. Reports in 1 month. Sample copy $2; free writer's guidelines.

Nonfiction: Susan Williams, articles editor. Book excerpts, expose, humor, profile, photo feature—"only if about science or related." Buys 80 mss/year. Query with clips. Length: 1,500-3,000 words. Pays $800-2,000.

Columns/Departments: Buys 200 mss/year. Query with clips. Length: 200-1,000 words. Pays $150-800.

Poetry: Bonnie Gordon, poetry editor. Free verse, traditional. "Science-related poetry only." Buys 10/year. Submit maximum 5 poems. Length: 50 lines maximum. Pays $400.

Tips: Wants well thought-out, well-researched, well-written, succinct query. Section most open to freelancers is Crosscurrent. Looks for grace, intelligence and wit.

SCIENTIFIC AMERICAN, 415 Madison Ave., New York NY 10017. Articles by professional scientists only. Publishes work by those already known in the field.

73 MAGAZINE, Peterborough NH 03458. (603)924-9471. Publisher: Wayne Green. For amateur radio operators and experimenters. Monthly. Buys all rights. Pays on publication. Reports on submissions within a few weeks. Query. SASE.

Nonfiction: Articles on anything of interest to radio amateurs, experimenters and computer hobbyists—construction projects. Pays $40-50/page.

Photos: Photos purchased with ms.

Tips: Query letter "should be as specific as possible. Don't hold back details that would help us make a decision. We are not interested in theoretical discussions, but in practical ideas and projects which our readers can use."

TECHNOLOGY ILLUSTRATED, 38 Commercial Wharf, Boston MA 02110. (617)227-4700. Editor: Christopher Leach. Monthly magazine of applied science "for people who are curious about the technologies and technologists around them, but who are untrained in science and engineering." Pays on acceptance. Buys all rights. Reports in 2-4 weeks.

Nonfiction: Medical technology, space and aviation, transportation, computers and electronics, communications—"anything that puts scientific knowledge to work for humankind. Articles should describe not only the *what* but also, in layman's terms, the *how*." Send SASE for writer's guidelines. Pays $1,500-2,500 for features (1,500-4,000 words); $100-750 for shorter items. Query.

TECHNOLOGY REVIEW, Alumni Association of the Massachusetts Institute of Technology, Room 10-140, Massachusetts Institute of Technology, Cambridge MA 02139. Editor-in-Chief: John I. Mattill. 20% freelance written. Emphasizes technology and its implications for scientists, engineers, managers and social scientists. Magazine published 8 times/year. Circ. 75,000. Pays on publication. Buys all rights. Phone queries OK. Submit seasonal/holiday material 6 months in advance of issue date. Simultaneous and photocopied submissions OK. SASE. Reports in 6 weeks. Sample copy $2.50.

Nonfiction: General interest, interview, photo feature and technical. Buys 5-10 mss/year. Query. Length: 1,000-10,000 words. Pays $50-750.

Columns/Departments: Book Reviews; Trend of Affairs; Society; Technology and Science and "Prospects" (guest column). Also special reports on other appropriate subjects. Buys 1 ms/issue. Query. Length: 750-1,500 words. Pays $50-300.

UFO REVIEW, Global Communications, 316 5th Ave., New York NY 10001. (212)685-4080. Editor: Timothy Beckley. Emphasizes UFOs and space science. Published 4 times/year. Tabloid. Circ. 50,000. Pays on publication. "We syndicate material to European markets and split 50-50 with writer." Phone queries OK. Photocopied submissions OK. SASE. Reports in 3 weeks. Sample copy $1.
Nonfiction: Expose (on government secrecy about UFOs). "We also want articles detailing on-the-spot field investigations of UFO landings, contact with UFOs, and UFO abductions. No lights-in-the-sky stories." Buys 1-2 mss/issue. Query. Length: 1,200-2,000 words. Pays $25-75.
Photos: Send photos with ms. Pays $5-10 for 8x10 b&w prints. Captions required.
Fillers: Clippings. Pays $2-5.
Tips: "Read the tabloid first. We get a lot of material unrelated to our subject."

UMOJA SASA NEWS JOURNAL, Pre-Professional Publications, 512 E. State St., Ithaca NY 14850. (607)272-0995. Editor: Tyrone Taborn. Managing Editor: Kim Nance. Bimonthly magazine covering technical, science and engineering for black and minority students. Circ. 15,500. Pays on publication. Byline given. Offers $25 kill fee. Buys first rights. Submit seasonal material 2 months in advance. Simultaneous queries OK. No computer printouts or disk submissions. SASE. Reports in 1 month on queries; 2 months on mss. Sample copy and writer's guidelines $3.
Nonfiction: Send complete ms only if on science or engineering. Queries demanded on all other subjects. "We are moving to a complete technical science and engineering book. Always need for computer articles, civil engineering, etc." Prefers articles with a technical slant. No travel, crime, sports, how-to, ethnic material or nontechnical personal interviews. Buys 30 mss/year. Length: 750-2,000 words. Pays $25-200/article.
Photos: Norris Smith. Send photos with ms. Pays $25-35 for b&w 8x10 prints. Buys one-time rights.
Tips: "We need articles on new developments in science and engineering. We buy for most of the entire year during late summer."

Science Fiction

Additional science fiction markets are found in the Literary and "Little" category. To learn the secrets of writing science fiction consult *Writing and Selling Science Fiction*, by the Science Fiction Writers of America (Writer's Digest Books).

‡**AMAZING® Science Fiction Stories**, (Combined with *Fantastic Magazine*), Dragon Publishing, Box 110, Lake Geneva WI 53147-0110. (414)248-3625. Editor: George H. Scithers. Production Manager: Marilyn Favaro. Bimonthly magazine of science fiction and fantasy short stories. "Audience does not need to be scientifically literate, but the authors must be, where required." Circ. 17,000. Pays on acceptance. Byline given. Buys first North American serial rights; "single, non-exclusive re-use option (with additional pay)." Photocopied submissions OK. SASE. Reports in 2 weeks. Sample copy for $1.50 and 50¢ postage; writer's guidelines $1.
Nonfiction: Interview/profile and science articles of interest to SF audiences. No "pop pseudo-science trends: The Unified Field Theory Discovered; How I Spoke to the Flying Saucer People; Interpretations of Past Visits by Sentient Beings, as Read in Glacial Scratches on Granite, etc." Buys 4-6 mss/year. Query with or without published clips. Length: 300-10,000 words. Pays 6¢/word up to 7,500 words; 4¢/word for 12,000 or more words.
Fiction: Fantasy; novel excerpts (only from established writers—query); science fiction; serialized novels (query first). Buys 60 mss/year. Send complete ms. Length: 300-20,000 words. "Anything longer, ask." Pays 6¢/word to 7,500 words; 4¢/word for 12,000 or more words.
Poetry: All are OK. No prose arranged in columns. Buys 18 poems/year. Submit maximum 3 poems. Length: 45 lines maximum; ideal length, 30 or less lines. Pays $1/line; "shades off to $30/45-line poem."

ANALOG SCIENCE FICTION/SCIENCE FACT, 380 Lexington Ave., New York NY 10017. Editor: Dr. Stanley Schmidt. 100% freelance written. For general future-minded audience. Monthly. Buys first North American and nonexclusive foreign serial rights. Byline given. Pays on acceptance. Reports in 3-4 weeks. Computer printout submissions with dark ink OK if legible; prefers letter quality to dot matrix. SASE.
Nonfiction: Illustrated technical articles dealing with subjects of not only current but future interest, i.e., with topics at the present frontiers of research whose likely future developments have implications of wide interest. Buys about 12 mss/year. Recent article example: "Mars in 1995" (June 1981). Query. Length: 5,000 words. Pays 5.75¢/word.
Fiction: "Basically, we publish science fiction stories. That is, stories in which some aspect of future science

or technology is so integral to the plot that, if that aspect were removed, the story would collapse. The science can be physical, sociological or psychological. The technology can be anything from electronic engineering to biogenetic engineering. But the stories must be strong and realistic, with believable people doing believable things—no matter how fantastic the background might be.'' Recent story example: ''Emergence'' (January 1981). Buys 60-100 unsolicited mss/year. Send complete ms on short fiction; query about serials. Length: 2,000-60,000 words. Pays 3.5-4.6¢/word for novelettes and novels; 5.75-6.9¢/word for shorts under 7,500 words.

Tips: ''In query give clear indication of central ideas and themes and general nature of story line—and what is distinctive or unusual about it. We have no hard-and-fast editorial guidelines, because science fiction is such a broad field that I don't want to inhibit a new writer's thinking by imposing 'Thou Shalt Not's.' Besides, a really good story can make an editor swallow his preconceived taboos. *Analog* will consider material submitted from any writer and consider it solely on the basis of merit. We are definitely anxious to find and develop new, capable writers. No occult or fantasy.''

EERIE COUNTRY, Box 149, Amherst Branch, Buffalo NY 14226. Editor-in-Chief: W. Paul Ganley. Modern ''pulp magazine'' published randomly emphasizing weird fantasy (swords and sorcery, supernatural horror, pure fantasy) for educated, mature readers of all ages. Circ. 200. Pays on publication. Buys first North American serial rights and right to reprint as part of entire issue. Photocopied submissions OK. SASE. ''Best time to submit is in December or summer if quicker response is desired.'' Sample copy $2.50 (make checks payable to Weirdbook Press); writer's guidelines for SASE.
Fiction: Adventure (with weird elements); experimental (maybe, if in fantasy or horror area); tightly-plotted traditional fantasy and supernatural. Buys 12 unsolicited mss/year. Submit complete ms. Length: 20,000 words maximum. Pays ¼¢/word.
Poetry: Length: 20 lines maximum. No payment.

FANTASY BOOK, Fantasy Book Enterprises, Box 4193, Pasadena CA 91106. Executive Editor: Dennis Mallonee. Editor: Nick Smith. Quarterly magazine of illustrated fantasy fiction for all ages; ''bulk of the readership is in the 17-35 range.'' Estab. 1981. Circ. 4,000. Pays on ''approval of galleys.'' Byline given. Buys first North American serial rights. Submit seasonal/holiday material 6 months in advance. Photocopied submissions OK. SASE. Reports in 2 weeks on queries; 6 weeks on mss. Sample copy $3; writer's guidelines for legal size SAE and 1 first class stamp.
Fiction: ''We will consider any story even remotely related to a genre of fantasy fiction. We look for stories with strong characterization and carefully developed plot.'' Buys 50 mss/year. Send complete ms. Length: 2,000-10,000 words. Pays 2½-4¢/word.
Poetry: Light verse, traditional. Buys 8/year. Submit maximum 4 poems. Length: open. Pays $5-20.

‡**THE HORROR SHOW**, Phantasm Press, Star Rte. 1, Box 151-T, Oak Run CA 96069. (916)472-3540. Editor: David B. Silva. Quarterly horror magazine. Estab. 1982. Circ. 500. Buys one-time rights. Computer printout or disk submissions OK; prefers letter quality to dot matrix. SASE. Reports in 3 weeks. Sample copy for $3 and $1 postage; writer's guidelines for SASE.
Columns/Departments: Wonders (fact is stranger than fiction); Tattler (reviews); Curses (letters to the editor).
Fiction: ''Stories may have a science fiction, speculative fiction or fantasy slant, as long as the overriding theme is horror. We are specifically looking for material which contains a twist or shock at the end. Do not over-indulge in sex or violence.'' Send complete ms. Length: 4,000 words maximum. Pays ¼¢/word plus contributor's copy.
Tips: ''We will work with anyone who has a good idea and is willing to adopt suggestions. This is a good opportunity for new writers to break into print.''

ISAAC ASIMOV'S SCIENCE FICTION MAGAZINE, Davis Publications, Inc., 380 Lexington Ave. New York NY 10017. (212)557-9100. Editor-in-Chief: Shawna McCarthy. 100% freelance written. Emphasizes science fiction. 13 times a year magazine; 176 pages. Circ. 150,000. Pays on acceptance. Buys first North American serial rights and foreign serial rights. Photocopied submissions OK but no simultaneous submissions. Computer printout submissions not in dot matrix OK. SASE. Reports in 2-6 weeks. Writer's guidelines for SASE.
Nonfiction: Science. Query first.
Fiction: Science fiction primarily. Some fantasy and poetry. No UFO stories or computers gone berserk. Buys 12 mss/issue. Submit complete ms. Length: 100-20,000 words. Pays 3½-5¾¢/word.
Tips: Query letters not wanted, except for nonfiction. ''Response time will be somewhat slower than in years past, and I'll be using a higher proportion of 'form' rejection slips.''

‡**THE MINNESOTAN SCIENCE FICTION READER**, 3339 Noble Ave. N., Golden Valley MN 55422. (612)529-3243. Editors: Robert Tickle, Mark D. Tabery, Matthew E. Tabery. Managing Editor: Matthew E.

Tabery. Bimonthly on science fiction and writing science fiction. Estab. 1982. Pays on acceptance. Byline given. Offers 25% kill fee. Buys first North American serial rights. Submit seasonal/holiday material 3 months in advance. Photocopied submissions OK. SASE. Reports in 1½ weeks on queries; 3 weeks on mss. Sample copy $1; writer's guidelines for business-size SAE and 1 first class stamp.

Nonfiction: How-to (write science fiction); humor (on sf/sf writing); interview/profile; convention reports; current science news. Not interested in "anything negative toward science or technology. However, the articles can be very questioning." Buys 5-7 mss/year. Query with published clips or send complete ms. Length: 600-1,200 words. Pays $3-6.

Photos: State availability or send photos with ms. Convention reports and interview/profiles should have photos. Reviews 3x3 b&w and color prints. Pays for photos with payment for ms. Captions and identification of subjects required. Buys one-time rights.

Fiction: Experimental, science fantasy, horror, humorous, mystery, science fiction, avant-garde—all science fiction related. No mainstream sf, occult or metaphysics. Buys 12-14 mss/year. Send complete ms. Length: 300-3,000 words. Pays ½¢/word. Buys first North American serial rights.

Fillers: Anecdotes, short humor, newsbreaks. Buys 12-20/year. Length: 50-200 words. Pays $.25-1. "Fillers should be about science fiction, those who write it, or what happened at a convention."

Tips: "The best way to break in to *MSFR* is through fiction. Write what you know (don't try to write a Robert L. Forward story if you failed all your science classes in high school). If you know what you're writing, this should come through in your story."

‡**NOVALIS, The Fantasy Magazine**, Headplay Press, Box 13945, Pantego Station TX 76013. (817)277-5678. Managing Editor: Walter Gammons. Bimonthly magazine of highly literate and entertaining short fiction for adults (18-45). Estab. 1982. Circ. 5,000. Pays on publication. Byline given. Offers 25% kill fee. Buys first North American serial rights and first anthology option. Submit seasonal/holiday material 4 months in advance. Photocopied submissions OK. SASE. Reports in 1 month on queries; 4 months on mss. Sample copy for $3, 9x12 SAE and 4 first class stamps; writer's guidelines for $1, 9x12 SAE and 2 first class stamps.

Nonfiction: General interest, humor, interview/profile, new product, opinion, photo feature. No political, religious or pornographic material. Buys 6 mss/year. Send complete ms. Length: 1,000-8,000 words. Pays 1-5¢/word.

Photos: Marshall Bonfire, photo editor. Pays variable rates for 4x5 color transparencies and 8x10 color prints. Captions, model release and identification of subjects required.

Columns/Departments: Buys 6 mss/year. Send complete ms. Length: 1,000-4,000 words. Pays 1-5¢/word.

Fiction: Marshall Bonfire, fiction editor. Adventure, erotica, experimental, horror, humorous, science fiction, suspense. Mainly interested in fantasy, myths, fables in the short story form. No pornography, cliches, religious, political, vignettes, scenarios. Buys 60 mss/year. Send complete ms. Length: 1,000-8,000 words. Pays 1-5¢/word.

Poetry: Marshall Bonfire, poetry editor. Avant-garde, free verse, light verse, traditional; must be fantasy. No depressing, overdramatic, political or religious poetry. Submit maximum 6 poems. Length: 8-50 lines. Pays $5-20.

Fillers: Harbinger Harris, fillers editor. Clippings, anecdotes, short humor. Buys 20/year. Length: 50-500 words. Pays $5-20.

Tips: "We look for a fantasy story with a good, fast-moving plot, good characterization, and a magnetic beginning, middle and end."

ORACLE, Science-Fiction & Fantasy Anthology Magazine, Box 19146-WM, Detroit MI 48219-0222. Editor: Dave Lillard. Quarterly magazine. "We are looking for S.F. and fantasy—particularly by newcomers." Estab. 1981. Circ. 5,000. Pays ½ on acceptance; ½ on publication. Byline given. Buys one-time rights. Previously published submissions not accepted. SASE. Reports in 1 week on queries; 2 months on mss. Sample copy $3; writer's guidelines for business size SAE and 1 first class stamp.

Fiction: Dave Lillard, fiction editor. "We welcome newcomers." No pornographic stories or those which depend on heavy sex or violence. No horror stories. Buys 70 mss/year. Send for guidelines before submitting ms. Pays 1-3¢/word.

Tips: "We will become more selective this year. Due to volume of submissions, we will be slower to respond."

‡**PANDORA, Role-Expanding Science Fiction and Fantasy**, Empire Books, Box 625, Murray KY 42071. Editors: Jean Lorrah and Lois Wickstrom. Magazine published 2 times/year covering science fiction and fantasy. Circ. 600. Pays on acceptance. Byline given. Offers $10 kill fee. Buys first North American serial rights; one-time rights on some poems. Photocopied submissions OK. Readable computer printout submissions on white 8½x11 paper OK. SASE. Reports in 2 weeks. Sample copy $2.50.

Columns/Departments: Books briefly. "We buy 200 word reviews of science fiction and fantasy books that a reader truly loves and feels are being ignored by the regular reviewers. Small press titles as well as major press titles are welcome." Buys 3-4 mss/year. Query or send complete ms. Length: 200-250 words. Pays 1¢/word.

Fiction: Experimental, fantasy, science fiction. "No pun stories. Nothing x-rated. No inaccurate science." Buys 15 mss/year. Send complete ms. Length: 1,000-5,000 words "except for controversial stories which may go to 10,000 words." Pays 1¢/word.

Poetry: Steve Tem, poetry editor. "We're over bought for at least the next year." Buys 9/year. Length: open.

Tips: "Send us a complete short story. If we like it, we'll send you a critique with suggestions, if we don't want it just the way it is, but would want it with some more work. You don't have to do exactly what we've suggested, but you should fix weak spots in your story."

‡**RISING STAR, the Science Fiction/Fantasy/Horror Writer's Newsletter**, 410 Chester Ave., Moorestown NJ 08057. Editor: John Betancourt. Monthly magazine for the science fiction, fantasy, horror writers in search of new markets. Estab. 1982. Circ. 1,000. Pays on acceptance. Byline given. Buys first North American serial rights. Submit seasonal/holiday material 2 months in advance. Photocopied submissions OK. SASE. Reports in 2 weeks. Sample copy $1.50.

Nonfiction: How-to (world building, culture constructing, etc.); interview/profile (with/of major sf/f/h writers or editors); opinion (on the future of the sf/f/h writing field); personal experience (writing for certain markets, w/editors, etc.); technical (on science or fields of interest to sf/f/h writers). "Our readers know the basic mechanics of writing; no 'how-to-prepare manuscripts, resumes, queries, etc.' " Buys 50+ mss/year. Send complete ms. Length: 2,000 words maximum. Pays in subscriptions for short material, to $50 for longer.

Poetry: Nothing mass-media related; no *Star Trek/Wars*, Hobbits, etc. Buys 48+/year. Submit maximum 3 poems. Length: 3-50 lines. SASE. Pays $1-10.

Fillers: Inspiring quotes from major sf/f/h writers. Buys 20/year. Length: 10-100 words. Pays up to $1.

Tips: "Be concise. Purple prose is as bad as not knowing what you're talking about. Say it with few words. If you don't know the field, don't submit. We like originality and informality."

SPACE AND TIME, 138 W. 70th St., New York NY 10023. Editor: Gordon Linzner. Biannual magazine covering fantasy fiction, with a broad definition of fantasy that encompasses science fiction, horror, swords and sorcery, etc. Circ. 500. Pays on acceptance. Byline given. Buys first North American serial rights. Photocopied submissions OK. SASE. Reports in 2 months. Sample copy $4.

Fiction: Fantasy, horror and science fiction. "Submit skillful writing and original ideas. We lean toward strong plot and character. No fiction based on TV shows or movies (*Star Trek*, *Star Wars*, etc.) or popular established literary characters (i.e., Conan) except as satire or other special case. No UFO, gods from space, or material of that ilk, unless you've got a drastically new slant." Buys 24 unsolicited mss/year. Length: 15,000 words maximum. Pays ¼¢/word plus contributor's copies.

Poetry: Free verse, haiku, light verse, traditional and narrative. "No poetry without a definite fantastic theme or content." Buys 12 mss/year. Submit maximum 5 poems. Length: open. Pays in contributor's copies.

Tips: "All areas are open to freelancers, but we would particularly like to see more hard science fiction, and fantasies set in 'real' historical times. No nonfiction or no fiction that cannot be considered science fiction or fantasy."

‡**SPECTRUM, The Illustrated Space Age Reader**, Headplay Press, Box 13945, Arlington TX 76013. Editor: Marshall Bonfire. Managing Editor: W. Gammons. Bimonthly magazine of science fiction and fantasy. Estab. 1982. Circ. 10,000. Pays on publication. Byline given. Buys first North American serial rights. Submit seasonal/holiday material 3 months in advance. Photocopied submissions OK. SASE. Reports in 1 month on queries; 3 months on mss. Sample copy for $3, 9x12 SAE, and 8 first class stamps; writer's guidelines for $1, legal-size SAE, and 2 first class stamps.

Nonfiction: General interest, humor, interview/profile, new product, photo feature, bizarre, experimental material with photos. Buys 12 mss/year. Send complete ms. Length: 1,000-5,000 words. Pays 5¢/word.

Photos: Bizarre, abstract and experimental photos. Send photos with ms. Pays variable rates for b&w and color contact sheet, negatives, transparencies, and 8x10 prints. Captions, model release and identification of subjects required. Buys one-time rights.

Columns/Departments: Buys 12 mss/year. Send complete ms. Length: 1,000-2,500 words. Pays 1-5¢/word.

Fiction: Erotica, experimental, fantasy, horror, humorous, mystery, suspense, authorized foreign translations. Buys mostly science fiction. No religious or political material. Buys 60-100 mss/year. Send complete ms. Length: 3,000-8,000 words. Pays 1-5¢/word.

Poetry: Avant-garde, free verse, light verse. Buys 12/year. Submit maximum 6 poems. Length: 10-50 lines. Pays $5-20.

Fillers: Harbinger Harris, fillers editor. Clippings, short humor, newsbreaks. Buys 60-100/year. Length: 50-500 words. Pays $5-25. "Trends or new developments that hold bearing on our future."

WEIRDBOOK, Box 149, Amherst Branch, Buffalo NY 14226. Editor-in-Chief: W. Paul Ganley. Emphasizes weird fantasy (swords and sorcery, supernatural horror, pure fantasy) for educated, mature readers of all ages. A modern "pulp magazine" published once or twice a year; 64 pages. Circ. 900. Pays on publication. Buys first North American serial rights and right to reprint as part of entire issue. Photocopied submissions

OK. Computer printout or disk (Apple II or III) submissions OK; prefers letter quality to dot matrix. SASE. "Best time to submit is in December or summer if quick response is desired." Sample copy $4.50; writer's guidelines for SASE.

Fiction: Adventure (with weird elements); experimental (maybe, if in fantasy or horror area); tightly-plotted traditional fantasy and supernatural. Example of recently published fiction: "Lord of the Worms," by Brian Lumley. Buys 12 unsolicited mss/year. Submit complete ms. Length: 20,000 words maximum. Pays $1/2¢$/word.

Poetry: Length: 20 lines maximum. No payment except contributor's copy.

Social Science

THE HUMANIST, American Humanist Association, 7 Harwood Dr., Amherst NY 14226. (716)839-5080. Editor: Lloyd L. Morain. Managing Editor: William J. Harnack. Bimonthly magazine covering philosophy, psychology, religion, ethics. "Discusses social issues and personal concerns in the light of humanistic ideas and developments in philosophy and science." Circ. 14,000. Pays on publication. Byline given. Buys all rights "unless arranged with author." Previously published submissions OK. No computer printout or disk submissions. SASE. Reports in 3 months on mss. Sample copy $2.50.

Nonfiction: General interest, opinion, personal experience, humanistic concerns, philosophy, controversial topics. "We like creative, upbeat articles." Buys 35 mss/year. Query or send complete ms. Length: 3,000-8,000 words. Pays variable rates from copies to $200 maximum.

Photos: "Does not buy photos; however, authors are encouraged to submit them with ms."

Columns/Departments: Humanism in Literature (humanistic slants on literature, especially contemporary). Buys 3 mss/year. Send complete ms. Length: 600-2,500 words. Pays variable rates from copies to $50 maximum.

JOURNAL OF GRAPHOANALYSIS, 111 N. Canal St., Chicago IL 60606. Editor: V. Peter Ferrara. For audience interested in self-improvement. Monthly. Buys all rights. Pays negotiable kill fee. Byline given. Pays on acceptance. Reports on submissions in 1 month. SASE.

Nonfiction: Self-improvement material helpful for ambitious, alert, mature people. Applied psychology and personality studies, techniques of effective living, etc.; all written from intellectual approach by qualified writers in psychology, counseling and teaching, preferably with degrees. Length: 2,000 words. Pays about 5¢/word.

PRACTICAL KNOWLEDGE, 111 N. Canal St., Chicago IL 60606. Editor: Lee Arnold. Bimonthly. A self-advancement magazine for active and involved men and women. Buys all rights, "but we are happy to cooperate with our authors." Pays on acceptance. Reports in 2-3 weeks. SASE.

Nonfiction and Photos: Uses success stories of famous people, past or present, applied psychology, articles on mental hygiene and personality by qualified writers with proper degrees to make subject matter authoritative. Also human interest stories with an optimistic tone. Up to 5,000 words. Photographs and drawings are used when helpful. Pays 5¢/word minimum; $10 each for illustrations.

PSYCHOLOGY TODAY, 1 Park Ave., New York NY 10016. Articles Editor: Brenda Hirsch. For intelligent laymen concerned with society and individual behavior. Monthly. Buys all rights. Pays 10% kill fee. Byline given. Each ms will be edited by staff and returned to author prior to publication for comments and approval. Author should retain a copy. Reports in 1 month. Address all queries to Articles Editor. SASE.

Nonfiction: Most mss are based on scientific research and written by scholars; freelancers are used very rarely. Primary purpose is to provide the nonspecialist with accurate, surprising and/or fresh readable information about society and behavior. Technical and specialized vocabularies should be avoided except in cases where familiar expressions cannot serve as adequate equivalents and technical expressions, when necessary, should be defined carefully for the nonexpert. References to technical literature should not be cited within article. One-page queries should usually be accompanied by one or more of the scholarly presentations or papers on which suggested story is based. Usual length of finished articles: 3,000 words. Usual payment is $550.

Tips: "Be a researcher with talent, imagination and a solid grasp of social science methodology—or a trained science journalist thoroughly knowledgeable in the field being reported."

ROSICRUCIAN DIGEST, Rosicrucian Order, AMORC, Rosicrucian Park, San Jose CA 95191. (408)287-9171, ext. 213. Editor-in-Chief: Robin M. Thompson. Emphasizes mysticism, science and the arts. For "men and women of all ages, seeking answers to life's questions." Monthly magazine. Circ. 70,000. Pays on acceptance. Buys first rights and rights to reprint. Byline given. Submit seasonal or holiday material 5 months in advance. Photocopied and previously published submissions OK. Computer printout submissions OK; "no dot matrix, please!" SASE. Reports in 1 month. Free sample copy and writer's guidelines.

Nonfiction: How to deal with life's problems and opportunities in a positive and constructive way. Informational articles—new ideas and developments in science, the arts, philosophy and thought. Historical sketches, biographies, human interest, psychology, philosophical and inspirational articles. No religious, astrological or political material or articles promoting a particular group or system of thought. Buys 20-30 mss/year. Query. Length: 1,000-1,500 words. Pays 6¢/word.

Photos: Purchased with accompanying ms. Send prints. Pays $10/8x10 b&w glossy print.

Fillers: Short inspirational or uplifting (not religious) anecdotes or experiences. Buys 6/year. Query. Length: 25-250 words. Pays 2¢/word.

Tips: "Be specific about what you want to write about—the subject you want to explore—and be willing to work with editor. Articles should appeal to worldwide circulation."

SEXOLOGY TODAY, 313 W. 53rd St., New York NY 10019. For a lay readership. Bimonthly magazine; 96 pages. Circ. 100,000. Pays on publication. Buys first serial rights. No computer printout or disk submissions. SASE. Reports in 4 weeks.

Nonfiction: "We are seeking articles to bring frank information that will help readers in their sexual experiences and relationships. Themes should be solidly educational or informative and, at the same time, entertaining. Our editorial aim is to provide helpful, accurate guidance and advice. We eschew sensationalism, but any solid attempt to bring information to our public is reviewed. Eroticism does have a place in the new *Sexology Today*. We regularly publish how-to themes with specific advice, including sexual acts. We seek articles about sexuality, psychology, sexual lifestyles, singles, new scientific breakthroughs, sociological/philosophical perspectives, first person pieces and modern appraisals of the relationship/sex theme. No straight pornography or turn-off subjects." Buys 10 unsolicited mss/year. Recent article example: "America's Incest Epidemic" (June 1982). Query with outline. Length: 1,500-2,000 words. Pays $200-250.

Tips: "We prefer queries, though we are open to completed manuscripts, no copies please, that run our word length and are compatible with our magazine's content and style. Too many writers obviously are looking for an 'easy' sell or a guaranteed column that really expresses nothing new or original. Good writing is a must. Don't press for a long-term commitment before we know you are a writer who is understanding of our editorial goals and values."

THE SINGLE PARENT, Parents Without Partners, Inc., 7910 Woodmont Ave., Bethesda MD 20814. (301)654-8850. Editor-in-Chief: Kathryn C. Gerwig. Emphasizes marriage, family, divorce, widowhood and children. Distributed to members of Parents Without Partners, plus libraries, universities, psychologists, psychiatrists, etc. Magazine, published 10 times/year; 48 pages. Circ. 220,000. Pays on publication. Rights purchased vary. Written queries only. Submit seasonal/holiday material 3 months in advance of issue date. Simultaneous, photocopied and previously published submissions OK. SASE. Reports in 6-8 weeks. Free sample copy and writer's guidelines for SASE.

Nonfiction: Informational (parenting, career development, money management, day care); interview (with professionals in the field, with people who have successfully survived the trauma of divorce); how-to (raise children alone, travel, take up a new career, home/auto fix-up). No first-hand accounts of bitter legal battles with former spouses. Buys 20 unsolicited mss/year. Query. Length: 1,000-2,000 words. Pay is negotiable.

Photos: Purchased with accompanying ms. Query. Pays negotiable rates. Model release required.

SUCCESS MAGAZINE, Suite 530, 401 N. Wabash Ave., Chicago IL 60611. Editor: Robert C. Anderson. "Average reader is 25-40, married with 2 children; working in professional, sales or management capacity; college-educated (85%) and has a strong motivation to go into business for himself. Financially, he's doing fine—but he wants to do even better." Monthly magazine. Circ. 350,000. Pays on acceptance. Rights purchased vary with author and material. Writer's guidelines with SASE.

Nonfiction: *Success* emphasizes the importance of a positive mental attitude. We publish three general categories of articles. The first is success profiles. These can be of nationally known individuals in business or industry or less recognizable people who have overcome obstacles in order to achieve success. These profiles can be either full-length—1,500-2,500 words—or short—800-1,000 words. The short profiles, which should have a topical "hook," fit our "Success Stories" department. The second type of article is the behavior piece. It deals with the philosophy and psychology of success as applied to social trends and family problems. Written in lay-

---

Market conditions are constantly changing! If this is 1985 or later, buy the newest edition of *Writer's Market* at your favorite bookstore or order directly from Writer's Digest Books.

men's language, behavior articles should focus on the latest research and developments. The third type of article is motivational and how-to. These topics include: how to overcome fear, how to start a business, how to stay healthy, goal-setting and time management. Authors of these articles must have expertise. No first-person accounts. Length: 1,500-2,500 words. Pays $250 minimum, negotiable to $1,000. Query.

TAT JOURNAL, Box 236, Bellaire OH 43906. Editor: Mark Jaqua. Biannual magazine for readers from 20-65 years old, professional and lay, who are interested in self-awareness and self-development, esoteric philosophy, psychology, and ancient cultures and sciences. Circ. 5,000. Pays on publication. Buys all rights and first North American serial rights. Simultaneous, photocopied and previously published submissions OK. SASE. Reports in 6 weeks. Sample copy $2; free writer's guidelines.
Nonfiction: Editor: Mark Jaqua. Expose (occult rip-offs, cults and spiritual gimmicks); historical (ancient cultures, sciences and religions); how-to (psychological self-change techniques); interview (of psychologists, philosophers and scientists, both professional and lay); opinion; and personal experience (new insights into the unsolved mysteries of the universe). "No articles that proselytize any one belief." Buys 5 mss/issue. Send complete ms. Length: 1,500-5,000 words. Pays $10-100.
Tips: "We want material that stimulates the reader's curiosity, allowing him to come to his own conclusions; a more psychological bent as opposed to 'New Age' or occult."

TRANSACTION/SOCIETY, Rutgers University, New Brunswick NJ 08903. (201)932-2280, ext. 83. Editor: Irving Louis Horowitz. For social scientists (policymakers with training in sociology, political issues and economics). Every 2 months. Circ. 45,000. Buys all rights. Byline given. Pays on publication. Free sample copy and writer's guidelines. Will consider photocopied submissions. No simultaneous submissions. Reports in 4 weeks. Query. SASE.
Nonfiction and Photos: Articles Editor: Karen Osborne. Photo Editor: Joan DuFault. "Articles of wide interest in areas of specific interest to the social science community. Must have an awareness of problems and issues in education, population and urbanization that are not widely reported. Articles on overpopulation, terrorism, international organizations. No general think pieces." Payment for articles is made only if done on assignment. *No payment for unsolicited articles.* Pays $200 for photographic essays done on assignment or accepted for publication.
Tips: "Submit an article on a thoroughly unique subject, written with good literary quality. Present new ideas and research findings in a readable and useful manner."

VICTIMOLOGY: An International Journal, Box 39045, Washington DC 20016. (703)528-8872. Editor-in-Chief: Emilio C. Viano. "We are the only magazine specifically focusing on the victim, on the dynamics of victimization; for social scientists, criminal justice professionals and practitioners, social workers and volunteer and professional groups engaged in prevention of victimization and in offering assistance to victims of rape, spouse abuse, child abuse, incest, abuse of the elderly, natural disasters, etc." Quarterly magazine. Circ. 2,500. Pays on publication. Buys all rights. Byline given. SASE. Reports in 6-8 weeks. Sample copy $5; free writer's guidelines.
Nonfiction: Expose, historical, how-to, informational, interview, personal experience, profile, research and technical. Buys 10 mss/issue. Query. Length: 500-5,000 words. Pays $50-150.
Photos: Purchased with accompanying ms. Captions required. Send contact sheet. Pays $15-50 for 5x7 or 8x10 b&w glossy prints.
Poetry: Avant-garde, free verse, light verse and traditional. Length: 30 lines maximum. Pays $10-25.
Tips: "Focus on what is being researched and discovered on the victim, the victim-offender relationship, treatment of the offender, the bystander-witness, preventive measures, and what is being done in the areas of service to the victims of rape, spouse abuse, neglect and occupational and environmental hazards and the elderly."

Sports

The publications listed in this category are intended for sports activists, sports fans, or both. They buy material on how to practice and enjoy both team and individual sports, material on conservation of streams and forests, and articles reporting on and analyzing professional sports.

Writers will note that several editors mention that they do not wish to see "Me 'n Joe" stories. These are detailed accounts of one hunting/fishing trip taken by the author and a buddy—starting with the friends' awakening at dawn and ending with their return home, "tired but happy."

For the convenience of writers who specialize in one or two areas of sport and outdoor writing, the publications are subcategorized by the sport or subject matter they emphasize. Publications in related categories (for example, Hunting and Fishing; Archery and Bowhunting) often buy similar material (in this case articles on bow and arrow hunting). Consequently, writers should read through this entire Sports category to become familiar with the subcategories and note the ones that contain markets for their own type of writing.

Publications concerned with horse breeding, hunting dogs or the use of other animals in sport are classified in the Animal category, while horse racing is listed here. Publications dealing with automobile or motorcycle racing will be found in the Automotive and Motorcycle category. Markets interested in articles on exercise and fitness are offered in the Health and Fitness section. Outdoor publications that exist to further the preservation of nature, placing only secondary emphasis on preserving nature as a setting for sport, are listed in the Nature, Conservation, and Ecology category. Regional magazines are frequently interested in conservation or sports material with a local angle. Camping publications are classified in the Travel, Camping, and Trailer category.

Archery and Bowhunting

ARCHERY WORLD, Suite 306, 715 Florida Ave. S., Minneapolis MN 55426. Editor: Tom Cwynar. 30-50% freelance written. For "archers of average education, hunters and target archers, experts to beginners." Subject matter is the "entire scope of archery—hunting, bowfishing, indoor target, outdoor target, field." Bimonthly. Circ. 125,000. Buys first serial rights. Buys 30-35 mss/year. Pays on publication. Will send a free sample copy to a writer on request. Tries to report in 3 weeks. Query. SASE.
Nonfiction: "Get a free sample and study it. Try, in ms, to entertain archer and show him how to enjoy his sport more and be better at it." Wants how-to, semitechnical, and hunting where-to and how-to articles. "Looking for more good technical stories and short how-to pieces." Buys 10 unsolicited mss/year. Also uses profiles and some humor. Length: 1,000-2,200 words. Payment is $50-200.
Photos: B&w glossies purchased with mss and with captions. "Like to see proofsheets and negatives with submitted stories. We make own cropping and enlargements." Color transparencies purchased. Pays $100-150 for color transparencies used on cover; $15 minimum for b&w.
Tips: "Not enough serious, talented writers pay attention to the archery/bowhunting magazines. The field is growing and in need of more qualified writers."

BOW AND ARROW, Box HH/34249 Camino Capistrano, Capistrano Beach CA 92624. Managing Editor: Dan Bisher. 75% freelance written. For archery competitors and bowhunters. Bimonthly. Buys all rights, "but will relinquish all but first American serial rights on written request of author." Byline given. Pays on acceptance. Reports on submissions in 6-8 weeks. Author must have some knowledge of archery terms. SASE.
Nonfiction: Articles: bowhunting, major archery tournaments, techniques used by champs, how to make your own tackle, and off-trail hunting tales. Likes a touch of humor in articles. "No dead animals or 'my first hunt'." Also uses one technical article per issue. Submit complete ms. Length: 1,500-2,500 words. Pays $50-200.
Photos: Purchased as package with mss; 5x7 minimum or submit contacts with negatives (returned to photographer). Pays $75-100 for cover chromes, 35mm or larger.
Tips: "Good b&w photos are of primary importance. Don't submit color prints."

BOWHUNTER MAGAZINE, 3150 Mallard Cove Lane, Fort Wayne IN 46804. (219)432-5772. Editor: M. R. James. For "readers of all ages, background and experience. All share two common passions—hunting with the bow and arrow and a love of the great outdoors." Bimonthly magazine; 96 pages. Circ. 160,000. Buys all rights. Pays on acceptance. Will send sample copy to writer on request. Write for copy of guidelines for writers. No photocopied or simultaneous submissions. "We publish a Bowhunting Annual each July and a special deer hunting issue each August. Submit seasonal material 6-8 months in advance." Reports in 4-6 weeks. Query or submit complete ms. SASE.
Nonfiction, Photos and Fillers: "Our articles are written for, by and about bowhunters and we ask that they inform as well as entertain. Most material deals with big or small game bowhunting (how-to, where to go, etc.), but we do use some technical material and personality pieces. We do not attempt to cover all aspects of archery—only bowhunting. Anyone hoping to sell to us must have a thorough knowledge of bowhunting. Next, they must have either an interesting story to relate or a fresh approach to a common subject. We would like to see more material on what is being done to combat the anti-hunting sentiment in this country." Informa-

tional, how-to, personal experience, interview, profile, humor, historical, think articles, expose, nostalgia, personal opinion, spot news, new product and technical articles. No "See what animal I bagged" or hero articles. Buys 60-70 unsolicited mss/year. Length: 200-5,000 words. Pays $25-250. Photos purchased with accompanying ms or without ms. Captions optional. Pays $10-25 for 5x7 or 8x10 b&w prints; $50 minimum for 35mm or 2¼x2¼ color. Also purchases newsbreaks of 50-500 words for $5-25. No newspaper clippings.
Tips: "The answer is simple if you know bowhunting and have some interesting, informative experiences or tips to share. Keep the reader in mind. Anticipate questions and answer them in the article. Weave information into the storyline (e.g., costs involved, services of guide or outfitter, hunting season dates, equipment preferred and why, tips on items to bring, etc.) and, if at all possible, study back issues of the magazine. We have no set formula, really, but most articles are first-person narratives and most published material will contain the elements mentioned above. We are adding more pages to two of our six regular issues so we'll probably buy a few more articles."

Basketball

BASKETBALL WEEKLY, 17820 E. Warren, Detroit MI 48224. (313)881-9554. Publisher: Roger Stanton. Editor: Mark Engel. 20 issues during season, September-May. Circ. 45,000. Buys all rights. Pays on publication. Sample copy for SASE and $1. Reports in 2 weeks. SASE.
Nonfiction, Photos and Fillers: Current stories on teams and personalities in college and pro basketball. Length: 800-1,000 words. Pays $35-75. 8x10 b&w glossy photos purchased with mss. Also uses newsbreaks. Do not send general basketball information.
Tips: "Include information about your background that qualifies you to do a particular story. More emphasis on television will affect writers in the year ahead."

EASTERN BASKETBALL, Eastern Basketball Publications, 7 May Court, West Hempstead NY 11552. (516)483-9495. Managing Editor: Rita Napolotano. Emphasizes basketball in the East for high school and college basketball enthusiasts from Maine to North Carolina. Published 12 times/year (November-May); magazine. Circ. 28,000. Pays on publication. Buys one-time rights. Phone queries OK. Reports in 6 weeks on mss. Free sample copy.
Nonfiction: "We are interested in feature stories on Eastern teams, players, coaches and issues related to the sport. Also in sports medicine, the role of the college recruit, choosing a college carefully and player profiles. Buys 1-2 mss/issue. Query or send complete ms. Length: open. Pays $50-70.
Photos: State availability of photos or send photos with ms.
Tips: "We are open to suggestions for articles on equipment, training, psychology of the star player vs. an ordinary player. Also articles such as 'What happens on the court is the end result of a lot of other things.'"

HOOP, Professional Sports Publications, 600 3rd Ave., New York NY 10016. (212)697-1460. Vice President: Pamela L. Blawie. 32-page color insert that is bound into the local magazines of each of the NBA teams. Buys all rights. "For the most part, assignments are being made to newspapermen and columnists on the pro basketball beat around the country. Features are subject to NBA approval." Sample copy $2. Reports in 1 week. SASE.
Nonfiction: Features on NBA players, officials, personalities connected with league. Length: 800-1,000 words. Pays $75-100.
Tips: "The best way for a freelancer to break in is to aim something for the local team section. That can be anything from articles about the players or about their wives to unusual off-court activities. The best way to handle this is to send material directly to the PR person for the local team. They have to approve anything that we do on that particular team and if they like it, they forward it to me. They're always looking for new material—otherwise they have to crank it all out themselves."

Bicycling

BICYCLING, Rodale Press, Inc., 33 E. Minor St., Emmaus PA 18049. Editor and Publisher: James C. McCullagh. 9 issues/year (6 monthly, 3 bimonthly); 160 pages. Circ. 240,000. Pays on publication. Buys all rights. Pays negotiable kill fee. Byline given. Submit seasonal/holiday material 5 months in advance. Computer printout submissions OK. SASE. Free writer's guidelines.
Nonfiction: How-to (on all phases of bicycle touring, bike repair, maintenance, commuting, riding technique, nutrition for cyclists, conditioning); travel (bicycling must be central here); photo feature (on cycling events of national significance); and technical (component review—query). "We are strictly a bicycling magazine. We seek readable, clear, well-informed pieces. We rarely run articles that are pure humor or inspiration but a little of either might flavor even our most technical pieces. No poetry or fiction." Buys 5-10 unsolicited mss/issue.

Query. Length: 2,500 words maximum. Pays $25-300.

Photos: State availability of photos with query letter or send photo material with ms. Pays $10-15 for b&w negatives and $15-30 for color transparencies. Pays $200 for color cover photo. Captions preferred; model release required.

Fillers: Anecdotes. Buys 1-2/issue. Length: 150-200 words. Pays $15-25.

Tips: "Fitness is becoming an increasingly important subject."

VELO-NEWS, A Journal of Bicycle Racing, Box 1257, Brattleboro VT 05301. (802)254-2305. Editor: Ed Pavelka. Monthly tabloid, (October-March, biweekly April-September) covering bicycle racing. Circ. 10,000. Pays on publication. Byline given. Buys all rights. Simultaneous queries, and simultaneous, photocopied and previously published submissions OK. Computer printout submissions OK; also phone transmissions of ASCII at 1200 band (call for specs). SASE. Reports in 2 weeks. Sample copy for 9x12 SAE.

Nonfiction: How-to (on bicycle racing); interview/profile (of people important in bicycle racing); opinion; photo feature; and technical. Buys 50 mss/year. Query. Length: 300-3,000 words. Pays $1.50/column inch.

Photos: State availability of photos. Pays $15-30 for 8x10 b&w prints. Captions and identification of subjects required. Buys one-time rights.

Boating

BAY & DELTA YACHTSMAN, Recreation Publications, 2019 Clement Ave., Alameda CA 94501. (415)865-7500. Managing Editor: Jo Ann D. Morse. 80% freelance written. Emphasizes recreational boating for small boat owners and recreational yachtsmen in northern California. Monthly tabloid newspaper; 90-166 pages. Circ. 17,000. Pays on publication. Buys first rights. Byline given. Phone queries OK. Submit seasonal/holiday material 2 months in advance. Photocopied submissions OK. Computer printout and disk submissions OK; prefers letter quality to dot matrix. SASE. Reports in 1 month. Free writer's guidelines.

Nonfiction: Historical (nautical history of northern California); how-to (modifications, equipment, supplies, rigging etc., aboard both power and sailboats); humor (no disaster or boating ineptitude pieces); informational (government legislation as it relates to recreational boating); interview; nostalgia; personal experience ("How I learned about boating from this" type of approach); photo feature (to accompany copy); profile; and travel. Buys 5-10 unsolicited mss/issue. Query. Length: 750-2,000 words. Pays $1/column inch.

Photos: Photos purchased with accompanying ms. Captions required. Pays $5 for b&w glossy or matte finish photos. Total purchase price for ms includes payment for photos.

Fiction: Adventure (sea stories, cruises, races pertaining to West Coast and points South/South West.); fantasy; historical; humorous; and mystery. Buys 2 mss/year. Query. Length: 500-1,750 words. Pays $1/column inch.

Tips: "Think of our market area: the waterways of northern California and how, why, when and where the boatman would use those waters. Think about unusual onboard application of ideas (power and sail), special cruising tips, etc. We're very interested in local boating interviews—both the famous and unknown. Write for a knowledgeable boating public."

BOATING, 1 Park Ave., New York NY 10016. (212)725-3972. Publisher: Jeff Hammond. Editor: Roy Attaway. For powerboat enthusiasts—informed boatmen, not beginners. Publishes special Boat Show issue in January; Fall show issue in September; New York National Boat Show issue in December. Monthly. Circ. 171,296. Buys first periodical rights. Buys 100 mss/year. Pays on acceptance. Submit seasonal material 6-8 months in advance. Reports in 2 months. Query. No computer printout or disk submissions. SASE.

Nonfiction: Uses articles about cruises in powerboats with b&w or color photos, that offer more than usual interest; how-to pieces illustrated with good b&w photos or drawings; piloting articles, seamanship, etc.; new developments in boating; profiles of well-known boating people; and lifestyle. "Don't talk down to the reader. Use little fantasy, emphasize the practical aspects of the subject." Length: 300-3,000 words. Pays $25-500, and varies according to subject and writer's skill.

Photos: Prefers Kodachrome 25 transparencies of happenings of interest to a national boating audience, for both cover and interior use. Pays $100-300 for one-time use "but not for anything that has previously appeared in a boating publication."

Fillers: Uses short items pertaining to boating that have an unusual quality of historical interest, timeliness, or instruction. No "funky old boats" material. Pays $50-100.

CANOE MAGAZINE, New England Publications, Highland Mill, Camden ME 04843. Editor: John Viehman. "*Canoe* represents the self-propelled water traveler." For an audience ranging from weekend canoe-camper to Olympic caliber flatwater/whitewater racing, marathon, poling, sailing, wilderness tripping or sea-cruising types. Six times/year; 72 pages. Circ. 55,000. Buys first time or all rights. Pays 25% kill fee. By-line given. Buys 30+ mss/year. Pays on publication or on acceptance by prior arrangement. Free sample copy and writer's guidelines for $1 and 9x12 SASE. "Computer printouts OK; disk submissions could well cause problems unless they're compatible with our TRS-80 or Altos hardware. All disk submissions should be checked out with us first." Reports in 60 days. Query or submit complete ms. SASE.

Nonfiction and Photos: "We publish a variety of state of the art canoeing and kayaking articles, striving for a balanced mix of stories to reflect all interests in this outdoor activity, recreational or competitive. Also interested in any articles dealing with conservation issues which may adversely affect the sport. Writing should be readable rather than academic; clever rather than endlessly descriptive. Diary type first-person style not desirable. A good, provocative lead is considered a prime ingredient. We want stories about canoeing/kayaking activities in the 50 states and Canada with which canoeists/kayakers of average or better ability can identify. Also interested in articles discussing safety aspects or instructional items. Occasional call for outdoor photography feature as relates to water accessible subjects. Please pick up and study a recent issue before querying. Also study back issues and published index (each issue) to avoid duplication. No hunting/fishing articles with minimal emphasis on the canoes involved." Length: 1,500-3,000 words. Pays $100-500. Will consider relevant book reviews (pays $25 on publication); length, 200-350 words. Short news and other items of interest, pays $25; "payment increases with accompanying photos."

Tips: "We've started a number of regular departmental stories that offer freelancers a good chance to break into our publication. Look for 1983 issues for examples."

CRUISING WORLD, Box 452, Newport RI 02840. (401)847-1588. Editor: C. Dale Nouse. 75% freelance written. For all those who cruise under sail. Monthly magazine; 200 pages. Circ. 172,000. Rights purchased vary with author and material. May buy first North American serial rights or first serial rights. Pays on publication. Reports in about 8 weeks. Submit complete ms. SASE.

Nonfiction and Photos: "We are interested in seeing informative articles on the technical and enjoyable aspects of cruising under sail. Also subjects of general interest to seafarers." Buys 135-140 unsolicited mss/year. Length: 500-3,500 words. Pays $50-500. B&w prints (5x7) and color transparencies purchased with accompanying ms.

CURRENTS, Voice of the National Organization for River Sports, National Organization for River Sports (NORS), 314 N. 20th St., Colorado Springs CO 80904. (303)473-2466. Editor: Eric Leaper. Managing Editor: Mary McCurdy. Bimonthly magazine covering river running (kayaking, rafting, canoeing). Circ. 10,000. Pays on acceptance. Byline given. Offers 25% kill fee. Buys first North American serial rights and first rights. Submit seasonal/holiday material 2 months in advance. Simultaneous queries, and simultaneous, photocopied, and previously published submissions OK. Computer printout and disk submissions OK. Disks should be 5¼" size. SASE. Reports in 2 weeks on queries; in 1 month on mss. Writer's guidelines for #10 SAE and 1 first class stamp.

Nonfiction: How-to (run rivers and fix equipment); in-depth reporting on river conservation and access issues and problems; humor (related to rivers); interview/profile (any interesting river runner); new product; opinion; personal experience; technical; travel (rivers in other countries). "We tell river runners about river conservation, river access, river equipment, how to do it, when, where, etc." No trip accounts without originality. Buys 20 mss/year. Query with or without clips of published work. Length: 500-2,500 words. Pays $12-75.

Photos: State availability of photos. Pays $10-35. Reviews b&w contact sheets or b&w negatives. Captions and identification of subjects (if racing) required. Buys one-time rights.

Columns/Departments: Book and film reviews (river-related). Buys 5 mss/year. Query with or without clips of published work or send complete ms. Length: 100-500 words. Pays $5-50.

Fiction: Adventure (river). Buys 2 mss/year. Query. Length: 1,000-2,500. Pays $25-75.

Fillers: Clippings, jokes, gags, anecdotes, short humor, newsbreaks. Buys 5/year. Length: 25-100 words. Pays $5-10.

Tips: "Go to a famous river and investigate it; find out something we don't know—especially about rivers that are *not* in Colorado or adjacent states—we already know about the ones near us."

LAKELAND BOATING, Petersen Publishing Co., 412 Longshore Dr., Ann Arbor MI 48105. (313)769-1788. Editor: David G. Brown. Managing Editor: Michael Hilts. Emphasizes pleasure boating on freshwater lakes; both sail and power boats. Monthly magazine. Circ. 46,000. Pays on publication. Buys first publication, with one reprint rights. Computer printout submissions OK if legible. SASE. Reports in 3-4 weeks. Sample copy $1.75.

Nonfiction: 2-3 "Cruise" stories/issue. Personal experience stories of power and/or sailboat cruises on freshwater lakes or rivers. Query first on stories on special events. Include sketches, maps, lists of marinas, access ramps, harbors of refuge. Length: 1,000-2,000 words. Technical articles on both sail and power boats, maintenance. "Reports on the quality of brand-name equipment should not come from freelancers." Length: 200-1,500 words.

Photos: Send photos with mss. 5x7 or 8x10 b&w can also be submitted separately. Original transparency for color stories. Captions required or identification of all pictures, prints, or transparencies. "Please stamp every transparency with name and address."
Tips: "We are a regional publication, so all stories must have a Great Lakes or Midwestern freshwater slant. This applies as much to technical articles as it does to cruise stories. Cruise stories must give reader enough information to follow in the author's wake. We don't want a 'Me 'n Joe' narrative of every breakfast and fuel stop. The waters being cruised and ports being visited are always more important than the people doing the cruising. Please query first with ideas. Biggest reason for stories being rejected is failure to meet our regional needs. We would rather spend time developing a story right from the beginning than reject an otherwise well-written manuscript."

MOTORBOATING AND SAILING, 224 W. 57th St., New York NY 10019. (212)262-8768. Editor: Peter A. Janssen. Monthly magazine covering powerboats and cruising sailboats for people who own their own boats and are active in a yachting lifestyle. Circ. 140,000. Average issue includes 8-10 feature articles. Pays on acceptance. Byline given. Buys one-time rights. SASE. Reports in 3 months.
Nonfiction: General interest (navigation, adventure, cruising); and how-to (maintenance). Buys 5-6 mss/issue. Query. Length: 2,000 words.
Photos: Reviews 5x7 b&w glossy prints and 35mm or larger color transparencies. Offers no additional payment for photos accepted with ms. Captions and model release required.

‡**NAUTICAL QUARTERLY**, Nautical Quarterly Co., 373 Park Ave. S., New York NY 10016. (212)685-9114. Editor: Joseph Gribbins. Managing Editor: Michael Levitt. Quarterly hardcover magazine covering yachting, power and sail. "We are specifically a yachting publication—not a maritime or shipping publication—with special emphasis on the best in yachts and small boats, and nautical experience, power and sail, past and present." Circ. 20,000. Pays on acceptance. Byline given. Buys first North American serial rights and all rights. Simultaneous queries, and simultaneous, photocopied, and previously published submissions OK. SASE. Reports in 2 months. Sample copy $16.
Nonfiction: Historical/nostalgic, interview/profile, opinion, personal experience, photo feature, technical. "No articles on maritime (i.e., non-yachting) subjects such as tugboats, commercial ships, lighthouses, clipper ships, etc." Buys 20-25 mss/year. Query with published clips. Length: 2,500-8,000 words. Pays $500-1,000.
Photos: Marilyn Rose, photo editor. State availability of photos or send photos with ms. Reviews 35mm color transparencies. Payment varies by arrangement with the photographer. Identification of subjects required. Buys one-time rights.
Tips: "A query, accompanied by writing samples, will succeed if both the idea and the samples suit our standards."

PACIFIC YACHTING, Power and Sail in British Columbia, S.I.P. Division, Maclean Hunter, Ltd., 1132 Hamilton St., Vancouver, British Columbia, Canada V6B 2S2. (604)687-1581. Editor: Paul Burkhart. Monthly magazine of yachting and recreational boating. Circ. 20,000. Pays mostly on publication. Byline given. Buys first and second serial (reprint) rights and makes work-for-hire assignments. Submit seasonal/holiday material 4 months in advance. Simultaneous queries, and simultaneous, photocopied, and previously published submissions OK. Computer printout and disk submissions OK. SAE and IRCs. Reports in 2 months on queries; 6 months on mss. Sample copy $2.
Nonfiction: Book excerpts, how-to, humor, interview/profile, new product, opinion, personal experience, photo feature, technical, travel. "Freelancers can break in with first-person articles about yacht and power boat adventures on the west coast of Canada accompanied by good 35mm photos. We're open to 'how-to' pieces by writers with strong technical backgrounds in the marine recreation field." No "poetry, religious, or first sailing experiences." Buys 150 mss/year. Will buy fewer stories in the year ahead. Query. Length: 100-2,000 words. Pays 10¢/word.
Photos: Send photos with ms. Reviews b&w contact sheets, b&w and color negatives, 35mm color transparencies (preferred) and prints. Captions and identification of subjects required. Buys various rights.
Columns/Departments: Scuttlebutt (news and light items, new gear, book reviews). Buys 80 mss/year. Send complete ms. Length: 100-400 words. Pays $10-40.
Fillers: Clippings, newsbreaks. Length: 100-200 words. Pays $10-25.

PLEASURE BOATING MAGAZINE, Graphcom Publishing, Inc., 1995 NE 150th St., North Miami FL 33181. (305)945-7403. Managing Editor: Bonnie J. Guerdat. Monthly magazine of recreational boating and fishing throughout the South including cruising, racing and diving subjects. Circ. 30,000. Pays on publication. Buys all rights. Phone queries OK. SASE. Reports in 1 month. Free sample copy.
Nonfiction: Technical, how-to departments on fishing, electronics, engines, etc. Features designed to entertain and inform readers in the areas of recreational boating and fishing. Pays $100 for department pieces (1,500 words) to $300 for feature-length articles (3,000 words) with color. Buys 15 unsolicited mss/year. Send com-

plete ms. Length: 500-3,000 words. Pays 5-10¢/word.
Photos: Send photos with ms. Reviews photos suitable for cover. Pays $50-150. Color transparencies requested for use with features; b&w glossies for use with department material. Buys all rights. Captions and model releases required.

POWERBOAT MAGAZINE, 15917 Strathern St., Van Nuys CA 91406. Editor: Mark Spencer. For performance-conscious boating enthusiasts. January, Buyers' Guide; February, Runabout Performance Reports; March, Offshore Performance Reports; April, Water Ski Issue; and May, Awards for Products' Excellence. Monthly. Circ. 75,000. Buys all rights or one-time North American serial rights. Pays on publication. Free sample copy. Reports in 2 weeks. Query required. SASE.
Nonfiction and Photos: Uses articles about power boats and water skiing that offer special interest to performance-minded boaters, how-to-do-it pieces with good b&w pictures, developments in boating, profiles on well-known boating and skiing individuals, competition coverage of national and major events. Length: 1,500-2,000 words. Pays $150-250/article. Photos purchased with mss. Prefers 8x10 b&w; considers vertical 35mm photos. Pays $100 for one-time cover use only.

RUDDER, Petersen Publishing Co., 318 6th St., Annapolis MD 21403. Editor: John Wooldridge. Monthly magazine covering recreational boating. Circ. 45,000. Pays on publication. Byline given. Offers standard or negotiated kill fee. Buys first North American serial rights in *Rudder* region. Submit seasonal/holiday material 6 months in advance. Simultaneous queries OK. Computer printout and disk submissions OK. SASE. Reports in 12 weeks on queries and mss. Free sample copy and writer's guidelines with SASE.
Nonfiction: Historical/nostalgic, how-to, interview/profile, opinion, personal experience and technical. Buys 60 mss/year. No poetry. Send complete ms. Length: 750-2,500 words. Pays $50-350.
Photos: Chris Larson, photo editor. State availability of photos or send photos with ms. Pays $25-300 for 35mm color transparencies; $10-50 for 8x10 b&w prints. Model release and identification of subjects required. Buys one-time rights.

SAIL, 34 Commercial Wharf, Boston MA 02110. (617)227-0888. Editor: Keith Taylor. For audience that is "strictly sailors, average age 35, above average education." Special issues: "Cruising issues, chartering issues, fitting-out issues, special race issues (e.g., America's Cup), boat show issues." Monthly magazine. Pays on publication. Buys first North American serial rights. Submit seasonal or special material at least 3 months in advance. Reports in 6 weeks. Computer printout submissions OK. SASE. Free sample copy.
Nonfiction: Patience Wales, managing editor. Wants "articles on sailing: technical, techniques and feature stories." Interested in how-to, personal experience, profiles, historical and new products. "Generally emphasize the excitement of sail and the human, personal aspect. No logs." Buys 200 mss/year (freelance and commissioned). Length: 1,500-3,000 words. Pays $100-800.
Photos: Offers additional payment for photos. Uses b&w glossy prints or color transparencies. Pays $400 if photo is used on the cover.

SAILING MAGAZINE, 125 E. Main St., Port Washington WI 53074. (414)284-3494. Editor and Publisher: William F. Schanen III. For readers 25-44, majority professionals. About 75% of them own their own sailboat. Monthly magazine; 82 pages. Circ. 35,000. Buys 24 mss/year. Pays on publication. Write for copy of guidelines for writers. Photocopied and simultaneous submissions OK. Reports in 6 weeks. Query or submit complete ms. SASE.
Nonfiction: Micca Leffingwell Hutchins, editor. "Experiences of sailing, whether cruising, racing or learning. We require no special style. We're devoted exclusively to sailing and sailboat enthusiasts, and particularly interested in articles about the trend toward cruising in the sailing world." Informational, personal experience, profile, historical, travel and book reviews. Length: open. Payment negotiable. Must be accompanied by photos.
Photos: B&w and color photos purchased with or without accompanying ms. Captions required. Flat fee for article.

‡SEA AND PACIFIC SKIPPER, Petersen Publishing Co., Suite F, 419 Old Newport Blvd., Newport Beach CA 92663. (714)645-1611. Editor: Joseph E. Brown. Managing Editor: Liz Cheston. Monthly magazine covering recreational boating primarily for the cruise boat owner. Circ. 70,000. Pays on publication. Byline given. Offers 50% kill fee. Buys first North American serial rights. Submit seasonal/holiday material 6 months in advance. Simultaneous queries OK. SASE. Reports in 6 weeks on queries; 3 months on mss. Free sample copy and writer's guidelines.
Nonfiction: Book excerpts; how-to (boating-oriented); humor; interview/profile; personal experience; photo feature; and technical. Buys 60 mss/year. Query or send complete ms. Length: 750-2,500 words. Pays $50-300.
Photos: Mike Austin, art director. State availability of photos or send photos with ms. Pays $10-50 for 8x10 b&w prints; $50-200 for 35mm color transparencies. Model release and identification of subjects required.

Buys one-time rights.

Tips: "We attempt to tell our readers how, when and where to use their boats for the most enjoyment and the greatest efficiency."

SOUNDINGS, The Nation's Boating Newspaper, Pratt St., Essex CT 06426. (203)767-0906. Editor: Christine Born. National monthly boating newspaper with nine regional editions. Features "news—hard and soft—for the recreational boating public." Circ. 80,000. Pays on "the 10th of the month of publication." Byline given. Buys one-time rights. Deadline 5th of month before issue. Simultaneous queries and simultaneous and photocopied submissions OK. SASE. Reports in 2 months on queries; 5 weeks on mss. Sample copy for 8½x11 SAE and 7 first class stamps; free writer's guidelines.

Nonfiction: General interest, historical/nostalgic, how-to, humor, interview/profile, opinion, photo feature, technical, travel. Needs charter, travel and feature stories for summer supplement. Race coverage is also used; supply full names, home towns and the full scores for the top 10 winners in each division. No personal experiences. Send complete ms. Length: 250-1,000 words. Pays $10-150.

Photos: Send photos with ms. Pays $15 minimum for 8x10 b&w prints. Identification of subjects required. Buys one-time rights.

Fillers: Short humor, newsbreaks. Length: 50-100 words. Pays $10-20.

SOUTHERN BOATING MAGAZINE, Southern Boating & Yachting, Inc., 1975 NW South River Dr., Miami FL 33125. (305)642-5350. Publisher and Editor: Skip Allen. Managing Editor: Andree Conrad. Monthly magazine; 75 pages. Circ. 25,000. Pays on publication. Buys all rights. Byline given. Phone queries OK. Submit seasonal/holiday material 2 months in advance. Photocopied submissions OK. Computer printout submissions OK; prefers letter quality to dot matrix. SASE. Reports in 3 weeks.

Nonfiction: Historical, how-to, personal experience and travel, navigation. "All articles should be related to yachting. We do want technical articles." Buys 4 mss/issue. Send complete ms. Length: 2,000-5,000 words. Pays $35-75.

Photos: State availability of photos or send photos with ms. Captions and model releases required.

Tips: "The best query device is to ask a question or series of questions that a boat owner/operator might ask, then explain how the proposed article answers those questions. Send cover letter with manuscript. Send accompanying artwork with ms. Include address and phone number where to be reached during the day. If possible, include name and address on back of photos or on slide covers. We are a boating magazine and do not publish poetry, unaccompanied cartoons, run-of-the-mill personal experiences, or cruising articles outside the magazine's region (Southern US, not California)."

TRAILER BOATS MAGAZINE, Poole Publications, Inc., Box 2307, Gardena CA 90248. (213)323-9040. Editor: Jim Youngs. Associate Editor: Jean Muckerheide. Emphasizes legally trailerable boats and related activities. Monthly magazine (Nov./Dec. issue combined); 80 pages. Circ. 80,000. Pays on publication. Buys all rights. Byline given. Submit seasonal/holiday material 3 months in advance. Computer printout submissions OK; prefers letter quality to dot matrix. SASE. Reports in 4 weeks. Sample copy $1.25; free writer's guidelines with SASE.

Nonfiction: General interest (trailer boating activities); historical (places, events, boats); how-to (repair boats, installation, etc.); humor (almost any subject); nostalgia (same as historical); personal experience; photo feature; profile; technical; and travel (boating travel on water or highways). No "How I Spent My Summer Vacation" stories not even remotely connected to trailerable boats and related activities. Buys 18-30 unsolicited mss/year. Query or send complete ms. Length: 500-3,000 words. Pays $50 minimum.

Photos: Send photos with ms. Pays $7.50-50/5x7 or 8x10 b&w glossy print; $10-100/35mm color transparency. Captions required.

Columns & Departments: Boaters Bookshelf (boating book reviews); Over the Transom (funny or strange boating photos); and Patent Pending (an invention with drawings). Buys 2/issue. Query. Length: 100-500 words. Pays $15. Mini-Cruise (short enthusiastic approach to a favorite boating spot). Need map and photographs. Length: 500-750 words. Pays $50. Open to suggestions for new columns/departments.

Fiction: Adventure, experimental, historical, humorous and suspense. "We do not use too many fiction stories but we will consider them if they fit the general editorial guidelines." Query or send complete ms. Length: 500-1,500 words. Pays $50 minimum.

Tips: "Query should contain short general outline of the intended material; what kind of photos; how the photos illustrate the piece. Write with authority covering the subject like an expert. Use basic information rather than prose, particularly in travel stories. We've added a new magazine that is a bit more freelance written: *The Western Boatman*—a bimonthly Western regional boating lifestyle magazine—13 Western states."

WATERWAY GUIDE, 93 Main St., Annapolis MD 21401. (301)268-9546. Managing Editor: Jerri Anne Hopkins. A pleasure-boater's cruising guide to the Intracoastal Waterway, East Coast waters and the Great Lakes. Annual magazine. Four regional editions.

Nonfiction: "We occasionally have a need for a special, short article on some particular aspect of pleasure cruising—such as living aboard, sailing vs. powerboating, having children or pets on board—or a particular stretch of coast—a port off the beaten track, conditions peculiar to a certain area, a pleasant weekend cruise, anchorages and so on.'' Query with ms.

Photos: State availability of photos. "We have a need for good photographs, taken from the water, of ports, inlets and points of interest. Guidelines on request with SASE.''

Tips: "Keep the query simple and friendly. Include a short bio and boating experience. Prefer to see manuscript sample attached. No personal experiences, i.e., we need information, not reminiscences.''

WOODENBOAT, Box 78, Brooklin ME 04616. Editor-in-Chief: Jonathan Wilson. Readership is composed mainly of owners, builders and designers of wooden boats. Bimonthly magazine; 160 pages. Circ. 75,000. Pays on publication. Buys first North American serial rights. Byline given "except if the material published were substantially revised and enlarged." Photocopied and previously published submissions OK. SASE. Reports in 2 months. Sample copy $3; writer's guidelines for SASE.

Nonfiction: Historical (detailed evolution of boat types of famous designers or builders of wooden boats); how-to (repair, restore, build or maintain wooden boats); informational (technical detail on repairs/restoration/construction); new product (documented by facts or statistics on performance of product); opinion (backed up by experience and experimentation in boat building, restoring, maintaining, etc.); photo feature (with in-depth captioning and identification of boats); and technical (on adhesives and other boat-building products and materials, or on particular phases of repair or boat construction). Buys 30-40 unsolicited mss/year. Recent article examples: "Custom Sawmilling," "SK1000," "Bronze, The Non-Timber" (March/April 1983). Submit complete ms. Length: 1,200-3,500 words. Pays $6/column inch.

Photos: Purchased with or without (only occasionally) accompanying ms. Captions required. Send prints, negatives or transparencies. Pays $15-75 for 8x10 high contrast b&w glossy prints; $25 minimum for color transparencies. Put name and address on all photos, slides or illustrations.

Tips: "Because we are bimonthly, and issues are scheduled well in advance, freelancers should bear in mind that if their material is accepted, it will inevitably be some time before publication can be arranged. We seek innovative and informative ideas in freelancers' manuscripts, and the degree to which research and careful attention has been paid in compiling an article must be apparent. We're not looking for scholarly treatises, rather detailed and thought-out material reflecting imagination and interest in the subject. It is important to: a) become familiar with the magazine first; read back issues to see what kinds of articles we use, and b) submit a detailed query letter; be knowledgeable, not superficial, in dealing with your subject. We relate to experience, not conjecture.''

YACHT RACING/CRUISING MAGAZINE, North American Publishing Co., 23 Leroy Ave., Box 1700, Darien CT 06820. Managing Editor: Pamela Polhemus Smith. Magazine published 10 times/year; 120 pages. Circ. 50,000. Pays on publication. Buys first North American serial rights. Byline given. Computer printout and disk submissions OK. SASE. Reports in 2 months. Sample copy $2.25.

Nonfiction: How-to for racing/cruising sailors, personal experience, photo feature, profile and travel. No travelogs. Buys 5-10 unsolicited mss/year. Query. Length: 1,000-2,500 words. Pays $125 per equivalent of one magazine page.

Tips: "Send thorough letter on what you can offer, with your experience.''

YACHTING, Ziff-Davis Publishing Co., 5 River Rd., Box 1200, Cos Cob CT 06807. Executive Editor: Marcia Wiley. For yachtsmen interested in powerboats and sailboats. Monthly. Circ. 150,000. Buys first North American serial rights. SASE.

Nonfiction: Nuts-and-bolts articles on all phases of yachting; good technical pieces on engines, electronics, and sailing gear. Buys 50-100 unsolicited mss/year. Recent article examples: "The EPIRB Explained" (March 1982) and "Baltic Ramble" (March 1982). Length: 2,500 words maximum. Article should be accompanied by 6-8 or more color transparencies.

Photos: Pays $50 for b&w photos, "more for color when used." Will accept a story without photos, if story is outstanding. See magazine for style, content.

Bowling and Billiards

BILLIARDS DIGEST, National Bowlers Journal, Inc., Suite 1801, 875 N. Michigan Ave., Chicago IL 60611. (312)266-7179. Editor: Michael Panozzo. 25% freelance written. Emphasizes billiards/pool for "readers who are accomplished players and hard core fans—also a trade readership." Bimonthly magazine; 48-70 pages. Circ. 7,000. Pays on publication. Buys all rights. Byline given. Phone queries OK. Submit seasonal/holiday material 2 months in advance of issue date. Simultaneous, photocopied and previously published submissions OK. SASE. Reports in 2 weeks. Sample copy $2; free writer's guidelines.

Nonfiction: General interest (tournament results, features on top players); historical (features on greats of the game); how-to (how to improve your game, your billiard room, billiards table maintenance); humor (anecdotes, any humorous feature dealing with billiards); interview (former and current stars, industry leaders); new product (any new product dealing with billiards, short 'blip' or feature); and profile (former and current stars—prefer current stars). No basic news stories. "We want features that provide in-depth material, including anecdotes, atmosphere and facts." Buys 3 mss/issue. Query. Length: 1,000-1,500 words. Pays $75-150.

Photos: State availability of photos with query. Pays $10-25 for 8x10 b&w glossy prints; $15-25 for 35mm or 2¼x2¼ color transparencies. Cover negotiable. Captions preferred. Buys all rights.

Tips: "The best way to break in at *Billiards Digest* is a simple query with day and night phone numbers, so we can get in touch for suggestions. Worst way is to submit ms that starts with a cliche, 'The stranger walked into the pool room . . . ' We are *very* interested in tips from stars (past and present). But query, first."

BOWLERS JOURNAL, 875 N. Michigan, Chicago IL 60611. (312)266-7171. Editor-in-Chief: Mort Luby. Managing Editor: Jim Dressel. 30% freelance written. Emphasizes bowling. Monthly magazine; 100 pages. Circ. 20,000. Pays on acceptance. Buys all rights. Phone queries OK. Submit seasonal/holiday material 2 months in advance of issue date. Photocopied submissions OK. SASE. Reports in 6 weeks. Sample copy $2.

Nonfiction: General interest (stories on top pros); historical (stories of old-time bowlers or bowling alleys); interview (top pros, men and women); and profile (top pros). "We publish some controversial matter, seek out outspoken personalities. We reject material that is too general; that is, not written for high average bowlers and bowling proprietors who already know basics of playing the game and basics of operating a bowling alley." Recent article example: "A Chip Off the Old Legend" (July 1981). Buys 2-3 unsolicited mss/year. Query. Length: 1,200-3,500 words. Pays $50-150.

Photos: State availability of photos with query. Pays $5-15 for 8x10 b&w prints; and $15-25 for 35mm or 2¼x2¼ color transparencies. Buys one-time rights.

BOWLING, 5301 S. 76th St., Greendale WI 53129. (414)421-6400, ext. 230. Editor: Rory Gillespie. Official publication of the American Bowling Congress. Monthly. Rights purchased vary with author and material. Usually buys all rights. Byline given. Pays on acceptance. Reports in 30 days. SASE. Computer printout submissions OK; prefers letter quality to dot matrix.

Nonfiction and Photos: "This is a specialized field and the average writer attempting the subject of bowling should be well-informed. However, anyone is free to submit material for approval." Wants articles about unusual ABC sanctioned leagues and tournaments, personalities, etc., featuring male bowlers. Nostalgia articles also considered. No first-person articles or material on history of bowling. Length: 500-1,200 words. Pays $25-150 per article; $10-15 per photo. No poems.

Tips: "Submit feature material on bowlers, generally amateurs competing in local leagues, or special events involving the game of bowling. Should have connection with ABC membership. Queries should be as detailed as possible so that we may get a clear idea of what the proposed story would be all about. It saves us time and the writer time. Samples of previously published material in the bowling or general sports field would help. Once we find a talented writer in a given area, we're likely to go back to him in the future. We're looking for good writers who can handle assignments professionally and promptly." No articles on professionals.

‡8 BALL NEWS, Bayside Publishing, Box 1949, Everett WA 98206. (206)353-7388. Contact: Publisher. Bimonthly tabloid covering pool and billiards news. Pays on publication. Byline given. Not copyrighted. Buys one-time rights. Submit seasonal/holiday material 2 months in advance. Photocopied submissions OK. SASE. Reports in 2 weeks on queries; less than 1 week on mss. Free sample copy.

Nonfiction: How-to and hard news on pool, bowling, barter or racquetball. Uses features on pool shooters and news of pool tournaments. Buys 24 mss/year. Send complete ms. Length: 300 words minimum. Pays minimum 50¢/column inch.

Photos: Send photos with or without ms. Pays $10-20 for 3x5 or 5x7 prints. Captions, model release and identification of subjects required.

Columns/Departments: Uses syndicated columns on pool, bowling, barter, or racquetball. Buys 70-80 mss/year. Send complete ms. Length: 300 words minimum. Pays $14-20.

Fiction: May consider fiction involving pool, bowling, barter or racquetball. Send complete ms. Length: 300 words minimum. Payment: negotiable.

Poetry: Light verse and traditional on pool, bowling, barter or racquetball. Buys 2-4 poems/year. Submit unlimited number of poems. Payment: negotiable.

Fillers: Clippings, jokes, gags, anecdotes, short humor, newsbreaks, cross word puzzles. Payment: negotiable.

Tips: "Bayside Publishing publishes four separate publications: *Northwest Bowler*, *Roundball Illustrated*, *Trader's Way*, and *8 Ball News*. Prefers material on pool, bowling, barter or racquetball."

THE WOMAN BOWLER, 5301 S. 76th St., Greendale WI 53129. (414)421-9000. Editor: Paula McMartin. Emphasizes bowling for women bowlers, ages 8-90. Monthly (except for combined July/August and December/January magazine); 48 pages. Circ. 155,000. Pays on acceptance. Buys all rights. Byline given "except on occasion, when freelance article is used as part of a regular magazine department. When this occurs, it is discussed first with the author." Phone queries OK. Submit seasonal/holiday material 2 months in advance. Photocopied and previously published submissions OK. SASE. Reports in 1 month. Free sample copy and writer's guidelines.
Nonfiction: Historical (about bowling and of national significance); interview; profile; and spot news. Buys 25 mss/year. Query. Length: 1,500 words maximum (unless by special assignment). Pays $15-50.
Photos: Purchased with accompanying ms. Identification required. Query. Pays $5-10 for b&w glossy prints. Model release required.

YABA WORLD, 5301 S. 76th St., Greendale WI 53129. (414)421-4700. Official publication of Young American Bowling Alliance. Editor: Jean Yeager. 30% freelance written. For boys and girls ages 21 and under. Monthly, November through April. Circ. 80,000. Buys all rights. Byline given "except if necessary to do extensive rewriting." Pays on publication. Reports in 3 weeks. Query. No computer printout or disk submissions. SASE.
Nonfiction and Photos: Subject matter of articles must be based on tenpin bowling and activities connected with Young American Bowling Alliance only. Audience includes youngsters down to 6 years of age, but material should feature the teenage group. Buys 3-5 unsolicited mss/year. Length: 500-800 words. Accompanying photos or art preferred. Pays $30-100/article. Photos should be 8x10 b&w glossy prints related to subject matter. Pays $5 minimum.
Tips: "We are primarily looking for feature stories on a specific person or activity. Stories about a specific person generally should center around the outstanding bowling achievements of that person in an YABA sanctioned league or tournament. Articles on special leagues for high average bowlers, physically or mentally handicapped bowlers, etc. should focus on the unique quality of the league. *YABA World* also carries articles on YABA sanctioned tournaments, but these should be more than just a list of the winners and their scores. Again, the unique feature of the tournament should be emphasized."

Football

FOOTBALL NEWS, 17820 E. Warren, Detroit MI 48224. Publisher: Roger Stanton. 10% freelance written. For avid grid fans. Weekly tabloid published during football season. 20 issues. Circ. 100,000. Not copyrighted. Pays 50% kill fee. Byline given. Buys 12-15 mss a year. Pays on publication. Will send sample copy to writer for $1. Reports in 1 month. Query first. No computer printout or disk submissions. SASE.
Nonfiction: Articles on players, officials, coaches, past and present, with fresh approach. Highly informative, concise, positive approach. Interested in profiles of former punt, pass and kick players who have made the pros. Interview, profile, historical, think articles, and exposes. "USFL league material possible. More background stories in general. Shorter pieces seem more important." No material for general audiences. Length: 800-1,000 words. Pays $50-100/ms.
Tips: "Include information about yourself that qualifies you to do a particular story."

Gambling

‡**CASINO & SPORTS**, Gamblers Book Club Press, 630 S. 11th St., Las Vegas NV 89101. (702)382-7555. Editor: Howard Schwartz. Bimonthly gambling magazine geared to casino and sports betting. Offers "inside information on how to bet; how to find an informational edge; how to spot an angle; managing your bankroll, percentage of bankroll betting, etc." Circ. 3,000. Pays on publication. Byline given. Buys one-time rights. Submit seasonal/holiday material 2 months in advance. Simultaneous queries, and simultaneous, photocopied and previously published submissions OK, "but we wish to be notified about such." SASE. Reports in 1 month. Free sample copy; writer's guidelines for SASE.
Nonfiction: Expose (gambling, cheating, hustling, bar bets, scams); historical/nostalgic (history of black games, Chinese games); how-to (gamble on individual casino games, horses, greyhounds, poker, cock fighting, golf, tennis, sports wagering); interview/profile (with famous bettors, gamblers, law enforcement personnel, ex-cheats); new product (related to gambling); personal experience (how-to hints on winning, finding illegal games); travel (gambling in other countries, rules of games, "house edges," caveats). No beginner's how-to articles. Buys 4 mss/year. Query with or without published clips. Length: 25,000 words minimum. Pays $50-100.
Tips: "Writers should do their homework and do a survey of literature and see what's already been done; what the future holds; what the new 'hot' subjects are. Remember the goal, aim and thrust of the publication."

‡**GAMBLING SCENE WEST**, Box 4483, Stanford CA 94305. (408)293-6696. Editor: Michael Wiesenberg. Managing Editor: Bill Shewman. Monthly gambling tabloid for "frequenters of card rooms and, in somewhat smaller part, casino patrons." Circ. 20,000. Pays on publication. Byline given. Buys first rights. Submit seasonal/holiday material 1 month in advance. Simultaneous queries and simultaneous, photocopied, and previously published submissions OK "if identified as such." Computer printout submissions OK. SASE. Reports in 2 weeks on queries; 2 months on mss. Sample copy $1; writer's guidelines for SAE and 1 first class stamp.

Nonfiction: Book excerpts (if pertinent); expose (of legalized, gambling-related material); historical/nostalgic (gambling in the past well-documented); humor; interview/profile (of gambling celebrities and celebrities who gamble); new product (related to gambling); opinion; personal experience (but not "my first gambling trip" or "how I lost my shirt" or "what a great gambler I am"); photo feature; technical; travel (gambling in areas other than CA, NV, NJ); card room reports; computers and gambling. Nothing derogatory to gambling or only peripherally-related to gambling. "Attitude should be that gambling is an approved activity for adults." Buys 250 mss/year. Query with clips if available or send complete ms. Length: 50-1,500 words; "if exceptional material or a subject that can't be covered in less, we sometimes use up to 3,000 words." Pays 2-5¢/word up to $50; average is $25.

Photos: "We don't pay specifically for photos, but good ones with a ms make it more likely to sell and liable to higher payment." State availability of photos or send photos with ms. Reviews 5x7 b&w prints. Captions, model release and identification of subjects required.

Columns/Departments: Celebrities, Reno entertainment, Eastern gambling scene, Southern California gambling scene. Query with clips of published work or send complete ms. Length: 500-1,500 words, sometimes more. Pays 2-5¢/word up to $50; average is $25.

Fiction: Adventure, fantasy, historical, humorous, mainstream, mystery, novel excerpts, romance, science fiction, serialized novels, suspense, and western. All must be gambling-related. Buys 2 mss/year. "Would buy more, but nothing of quality ever shows up." Send complete ms. Length: 100-3,000 words. Pays 2-5¢/word; up to $50; average is $25.

Poetry: Light verse, traditional. "No greeting-card stuff or anything not related to gambling." Buys 4/year. Length: open. Pays negotiable rates; "probably $2-10."

Fillers: Jokes, gags, anecdotes, short humor, newsbreaks. Length: 1-500 words. Pays 2-5¢/word.

Tips: "Type carefully; don't make grammatical or spelling mistakes; no handwritten mss. Don't send something that has obviously been rejected elsewhere. You *must* read the publication to sell to us."

GAMBLING TIMES MAGAZINE, 1018 N. Cole Ave:, Hollywood CA 90038. (213)463-4833. Editor: Len Miller. Address mss to Vanessa Jackson, Assistant Editor. 50% freelance written. Monthly magazine; 100 pages. Circ. 70,000. Pays on publication. Buys first North American serial rights. Byline given. Submit seasonal/holiday material 5-6 months in advance of issue date. SASE. Double-space all submissions, maximum 10 pp. Reports in 4-6 weeks. Free writer's guidelines; mention *Writer's Market* in request.

Nonfiction: How-to (related to gambling systems, betting methods, etc.); humor; photo feature (racetracks, jai alai, casinos); and travel (gambling spas and resort areas). "Also interested in investigative reports focusing on the political, economical and legal issues surrounding gambling in the US and the world and new gambling developments. No cutesy stuff. Keep your style clean, hard-edged and sardonic (if appropriate). Writers may query on any subject which is germane to our format." Buys 100 mss/year; prefers pictures with mss. Query. Pays $50-150.

Fiction: "We only use heavily gambling-related material." Buys 12 mss/year. Submit complete ms double spaced, maximum 9 pp. Pays $50-100.

Tips: "Be sure to keep photocopy of the mss sent. Know gambling thoroughly. We like short sentences and paragraphs; clear, precise, instructional material; and well-written, to-the-point material. *Pictures with mss will add $50 to the payment.* Action shots—always people shots. Photographs must show something unique to the subject in article."

‡**SYSTEMS & METHODS**, Gamblers Book Club Press, 630 S. 11th St., Las Vegas NV 89101. (702)382-7555. Editor: Howard Schwartz. Bimonthly gambling magazine geared to pari-mutuel betting. Offers "inside information on how to bet; how to find an informational edge, etc." Circ. 3,000. Pays on publication. Byline given. Buys one-time rights. Submit seasonal/holiday material 2 months in advance. Simultaneous queries, and simultaneous, photocopied and previously published submissions OK, "but we wish to be notified about such." SASE. Reports in 1 month. Free sample copy; writer's guidelines for SASE.

Nonfiction: Expose (gambling, cheating, hustling, bar bets, scams); historical/nostalgia (history of black games, Chinese games); how-to (gamble on individual casino games, horses, greyhounds, poker, cock fighting, golf, tennis, sports wagering); interview/profile (with famous bettors, gamblers, law enforcement personnel, ex-cheats); new product (related to gambling); personal experience (how-to hints on winning, finding illegal games); travel (gambling in other countries, rules of games, "house edges," caveats). No beginner's how-to articles. Buys 4 mss/year. Query with or without published clips. Length: 25,000 words minumum. Pays $50-100.

Tips: "Writers should do their homework and do a survey of literature and see what's already been done; what the future holds; what the new 'hot' subjects are. Remember the goal, aim and thrust of the publication."

General Interest

CITY SPORTS MONTHLY, "The Magazine for Active Californians," Box 3693, San Francisco CA 94119. Editor: Maggie Cloherty in northern California and 1120 Princeton Dr., Marina del Rey CA 90291. Editor: Ken Mate. Monthly controlled circulation tabloid covering participant sports for avid sports participants. Circ. in California 187,000. Two editions published monthly—one covering sports in northern California and the other for southern California's participant sportsmarket. "For the most part, we use separate writers for each magazine." Pays on publication. Byline and brief bio given. Pays negotiable kill fee. Buys one-time rights. Submit seasonal/holiday material 3 months in advance. Simultaneous queries OK; previously published submissions ("from outside readership area") OK. SASE. Reports in 1 month on queries. Sample copy $2.
Nonfiction: Interview/profile (of athletes); travel; and instructional and service pieces on sports. Special issues include: April, Tennis; May, Running; June, Outdoors and Biking; July, Water Sports; November, Skiing; December, Cross Country Skiing and Indoor Sports. Buys 60 mss/year. Query with clips of published work. Length: 1,500-2,400 words. Pays $75-300.
Photos: Pays $35-100 for 35mm color; $20 for b&w 8x10 glossy prints. Model release and identification of subjects required.

COLORADO SPORTS MONTHLY, Colorado's Oldest and Largest Sports Publication, Colorado Springs Publishing, Box 6253, Colorado Springs CO 80934. (303)630-3330. Editor: Robert Erdmann. Monthly tabloid covering Colorado's individual participation sports. "We are a regionally focused sports magazine. *All* of our stories must have a Colorado 'hook'." Circ. 30,000. Pays 30 days after publication. Buys first North American serial rights. Submit seasonal/holiday material 3 months in advance. Photocopied submissions OK. Computer printout and disk submissions OK. Reports in 1 month. Free sample copy and writer's guidelines.
Nonfiction: Expose (sports-related); general interest (but with a fresh slant); historical; how-to (must be written with clear expertise); humor ("we can always use a good laugh"); interview/profile (usually use at least 1/issue); new product (occasionally); opinion (only if it's strong, well thought out and cleverly presented); personal experience (if it is impressive); photo feature (1/issue); technical (sports-related); travel ("we publish an annual travel, i.e., sports vacations issue"); skiing; running; kayaking. No team, pro-sports, or hunting. Buys 60 mss/year. Query with clips of published work. Length: 900-2,000 words. Pays $50 minimum to "around $100, but is negotiable depending on length and difficulty of subject."
Photos: Ingrid Hart, photo editor. State availability of photos. Pays $5-75 for b&w contact sheet. Captions required. Buys one-time rights.
Columns/Departments: Bicycling; running; sports medicine; skiing. Buys 48 mss/year. Query with clips of published work. Length: 900 words. Pays $50.
Fillers: Newsbreaks (Colorado sports—or with hook). Buys 30/year. Length: 150 words minimum. Pay $15 minimum.
Tips: "The best way to break in is not to set off any alarms. Send a query with clips of work or an extended query showing writing style. We like service pieces. We like adventure stories and we love writers who have a sense of drama, irony and humor."

MICHIGAN SPORTSWOMAN, Subsidiary of the American Sportswoman, Box 32935, San Jose CA 95152. Editor: Chay Paule. Quarterly tabloid on women in Michigan sports. Seeks to promote "the dignity of the woman athlete and inform the public of her athletic prowess." Estab. 1981. Pays on publication. Byline given. Buys first North American serial rights. Simultaneous and previously published submissions OK. Computer printout and disk submissions OK. SASE. Reports in 1 month on queries; 2 weeks on mss. Sample copy for $1, 9x12 SASE; free writer's guidelines.
Nonfiction: General interest, how-to, interview/profile, sports medicine. "Articles should relate to the Michigan sportswoman." Nothing that does not show the woman athlete as a viable contributor to sports excellence. Buys 16 unsolicited mss/year. Send complete ms. Length: 500-800 words. Pays 3¢/word.
Photos: Send photos with ms. Pays $5 maximum for b&w prints. Identification of subjects required. Buys one-time rights.
Tips: "Break in with feature on an unknown amateur athlete at the top of her sport. Credentials must be verifiable."

OUTDOOR CANADA MAGAZINE, 953A Eglinton Ave. E., Toronto, Ontario, Canada M4G 4B5. (416)429-5550. Editor-in-Chief: Sheila Kaighin. 50% freelance written. Emphasizes noncompetitive outdoor recreation in Canada *only*. Published 8 times/year; magazine; 64-104 pages. Circ. 100,000. Pays on publication. Buys first rights. Submit seasonal/holiday material 5-6 months in advance of issue date. Byline given. Originals only. *SASE or material not returned*. Reports in 4 weeks. Sample copy $1.50; writer's guidelines 50¢; mention *Writer's Market* in request.

Nonfiction: Expose (only as it pertains to the outdoors, e.g. wildlife management); and how-to (in-depth, thorough pieces on how to select equipment for various subjects, or improve techniques only as they relate to outdoor subjects covered). Buys 35-40 mss/year. Submit complete ms. Length: 1,000-5,000 words. Pays $100-400.

Photos: Submit photo material with accompanying ms. Pays $5-30 for 8x10 b&w glossy prints and $35-75 for 35mm color transparencies; $150/cover. Captions preferred. Buys all rights. Model release required.

Fillers: Outdoor tips. Buys 10/year. Length: 350-500 words. Pays $25.

Tips: All submissions *must* include SASE or International Reply Coupon.

OUTSIDE, Mariah Publication Corp., 1165 N. Clark St., Chicago IL 60610. (312)951-0990. Senior Editor: David Schonauer. Emphasizes outdoor subjects. Ten issues/year; 112 pages. Circ. 200,000. Pays on publication or before. Buys first North American serial rights. Submit seasonal/holiday material 4 months in advance. SASE. Reports in 4 weeks (queries); 6 weeks (mss). Sample copy $2; free writer's guidelines.

Nonfiction: Expose (environmental/political and consumer outdoor equipment); general interest (as pertains to the outdoors); expedition and adventure stories; historical (profiles of early pioneers and expeditions); how-to (photography, equipment, techniques used in outdoor sports); humor (as pertains to outdoor activities); profiles (leaders and major figures associated with sports, politics, ecology of the outdoors); new product (hardware/software, reviews of performance of products used in camping, backpacking, outdoor sports, etc.); personal experience (major and minor expeditions and adventures); photo feature (outdoor photography); technical (of outdoor equipment); and travel (to exotic regions and cultures rarely visited). Buys 40 mss/year. Query with clips of published work. Length: 1,000-4,000 words. Pays $350-1,200.

Photos: Send photos with ms. Pays $50-200 for 35mm color transparencies. Buys one-time rights. Captions required.

Columns/Departments: Dispatches (news items); Equipage (articles on broad categories of outdoor equipment); Hardware/Software (short equipment reviews, slant to new innovative products, must include evaluation); Natural Acts (natural sciences); Destinations (travel); Law of the Land (legal and political issues that affect the outdoors). Buys 3-4/issue. Query with clips of published work. Length: 200-1,500 words. Pays $150-400.

Fiction: Adventure, fantasy and humorous. Query with clips of published work or send finished manuscript. Length: 1,000-4,000 words. Pays $250-1,000.

REFEREE, Referee Enterprises, Inc., Box 161, Franksville WI 53126. (414)632-8855. Managing Editor: Tom Hammill. For well-educated, mostly 26- to 50-year-old male sports officials. Monthly magazine. Circ. 42,000. Pays on acceptance of completed manuscript. Buys all rights. Submit seasonal/holiday material 6 months in advance. Photocopied and previously published submissions OK. Computer printout or disk submissions OK. SASE. Reports in 4 weeks. Free sample copy.

Nonfiction: How-to, informational, humor, interview, profile, personal experience, photo feature and technical. Buys 54 mss/year. Query. Length: 700-2,000 words. Pays 4-10¢/word. "No general sports articles." Recent article example: "High school basketball tournaments and the officials who *do not* receive assignments to work them" (March 1982).

Photos: Tom Hammill, managing editor. Purchased with or without accompanying ms or on assignment. Captions required. Send contact sheet, prints, negatives or transparencies. Pays $15-25 for each b&w used; $25-40 for each color used; $75-100 for color cover.

Columns/Departments: Arena (bios); Library (book reviews); and Law (legal aspects). Buys 24 mss/year. Query. Length: 200-800 words. Pays 4¢/word up to $50 maximum for Library and Law. Arena pays no fee, but full author credit is given.

Fillers: Tom Hammill, managing editor. Jokes, gags, anecdotes, puzzles and referee shorts. Query. Length: 50-200 words. Pays 4¢/word in some cases; others offer only author credit lines.

Tips: "Queries with a specific idea appeal most. It is helpful to obtain suitable photos to augment story. Don't send fluff—we need hard hitting, incisive material tailored just for our audience. Anything smacking of PR is a no sale."

SPORT, Sports Media Corp., 119 W. 40th St., New York NY 10018. (212)869-4700. Contact: Peter Griffin. Managing Editor: N.L. Cohen. Monthly magazine covering primarily college and pro sports—baseball, football, basketball, hockey, soccer, tennis, others—for sports fans. Circ. 1.25 million. Pays on acceptance. Byline given. Offers 25% kill fee. Buys first North American serial rights. Submit seasonal/holiday material 3 months in advance. No computer printout or disk submissions. SASE. Reports in 2 weeks.

Nonfiction: General interest; interview (sport interview in Q&A format); and investigative reports on the world of sports. Buys 75 mss/year. Query with clips of published work. No telephone queries. Length: 2,000-

2,500 words. Pays $1,000 minimum.

Columns/Departments: Sport Talk (briefs on news or offbeat aspects of sport). Buys 48 mss/year. Length: 250-500 words. Pays $100-150, depending on length and type of piece. Contact: Barry Shapiro.

Tips: "We are broadening subjects we're dealing with, but writers should read the magazine to find out."

SPORTING NEWS, 1212 N. Lindbergh Blvd., St. Louis MO 63132. "We do not actively solicit freelance material."

SPORTS ILLUSTRATED, Time & Life Bldg., Rockefeller Center, New York NY 10020. Articles Editor: Myra Gelband. Primarily staff-written, with small but steady amount of outside material. Weekly. Computer printout or disk submissions OK. Reports in 4 weeks. Pays on acceptance. Buys all North American rights or first North American publication rights. Byline given "except for Scorecard department." SASE.

Nonfiction: "Material falls into two general categories: regional (text that runs in editorial space accompanying regional advertising pages) and national text. Runs a great deal of regional advertising and, as a result, considerable text in that section of the magazine. Regional text does not have a geographical connotation; it can be any sort of short feature: Shopwalk, Footloose, Viewpoint, Sideline, On Deck, Spotlight, Sports Rx, Replay, Update, and Stats (400 to 1,100 words); Yesterday, Nostalgia, Reminiscence, Perspective, First Person, On the Scene (1,200-2,000 words), but it must deal with some aspect of sports. National text (1,500-6,000 words) also must have a clear sporting connection; should be personality, personal reminiscence, knowing look into a significant aspect of a sporting subject, but national text should be written for broad appeal, so that readers without special knowledge will appreciate the piece." No how-to or instructional material. Pays $400-750 for regional pieces, $1,000 and up for national text. Smaller payments are made for material used in special sections or departments.

Photos: "Do not submit photos or artwork until story is purchased." No fiction, no poetry.

Tips: "Regional text is the best section for a newcomer. National text is difficult as most of the national sections are staff-written."

THE SPORTS JOURNAL, B4-416 Meridian Rd. SE, Calgary, Alberta, Canada T2A 1X2. (403)273-5141. Editor-in-Chief: Barry A. Whetstone. 80% freelance written. Monthly tabloid; 20 pages. Circ. 30,000. Pays on publication. Buys all rights. Byline given. Phone queries OK. Submit seasonal/holiday material 1 month in advance of issue date. Simultaneous, photocopied and previously published submissions OK. SASE. Reports in 1 month. Free sample copy and writer's guidelines; mention *Writer's Market* in request.

Nonfiction: General interest; interview (sports figures); nostalgia (sports history); personal opinion (on sports-related topics); and profile. No amateur sports. Buys 15-25 mss/issue. Submit complete ms. Length: 300-350 words. Pays $25.

Photos: "We do not pay extra for photos accompanying mss, but the ms stands a much better chance for publication if photos are included." Submit photos with ms. Uses b&w prints. Buys one-time rights.

Columns/Departments: "We cover all major sports; coverage can be by league, team, or individual players." Submit complete ms. Length: 200-600 words. Pays $25.

Tips: "We will review any and all matter received, excluding quizzes, puzzles and cartoons. We have expanded this year, so we can use more articles."

SPORTS PARADE, Meridian Publishing Co., Inc., Box 2315, Ogden UT 84404. (801)394-9446. Editor: Dick Harris. Associate Editor: Peggie Bingham. Monthly magazine covering sports and general interest items. "*Sports Parade* covers all sports, but gives emphasis to participant activities including racquetball, tennis, swimming, jogging, surfing, skiing, softball, volleyball, motorcycling, boating, horseback riding, snowmobiling, and even horseshoes and wrist wrestling." Pays on acceptance. Byline given. Buys first North American serial rights. Computer printout or disk submissions OK; prefers letter quality to dot matrix. SASE. Reports in 2 weeks. Sample copy 50¢.

Nonfiction: How-to, humor, inspirational, interview/profile and success stories. "We're looking for the different twist, the unusual, the down-to-earth, and the kinds of activities that families can get involved in. Articles should have wide appeal." Query. Length: 900-1,200 words for features; 600-800 words for others. Pays 15¢/word.

Photos: "We want good, sharp, in-action photos. No snapshots. Keep in mind opportunities for cover (vertical color)." Submit photos in plastic sleeves for easy viewing. Pays $20/b&w photo; $35/color photo; "more (to be negotiated) for cover photos."

Fillers: Shorts. Buys 24/year. Length: 200-400 words.

SPORTSCAPE, The Boston Sports Journal, 1318 Beacon St., Brookline MA 02146. (617)277-3823. Editor: Todd Logan. Managing Editor: Marc Onigman. Monthly sports magazine for participants in running, racquet sports, bicycling, skiing, outdoors activities. Must have New England angle. Circ. 70,000. Pays on acceptance. Byline given. Offers 33% kill fee. Buys all rights. Submit seasonal/holiday material 6 months in advance. Simultaneous queries and simultaneous and photocopied submissions OK. Computer printout or disk submissions OK. SASE. Reports in 3 weeks on queries; 1 month on mss. Sample copy $1, 9x12 SAE and 6 first class stamps.

Nonfiction: General interest; historical/nostalgic (especially about participant sports); humor; interview/profile (not the standard "gee-whiz" approach); new product; opinion (from those qualified to offer it); and travel (participant-sports related). Fiction OK. "Participant pieces must offer something new and genuine." Recent article examples: "Solitary Cross Country Skiing" and "Running in New England." Buys 30 unsolicited mss/year. Query with clips of published work. Length: 1,800-3,500 words. Pays $200 minimum.

Photos: Jane Betts, photo editor. State availability of photos. Pays $5-20 for b&w contact sheets. Captions, model release, and identification of subjects required.

Tips: "We are looking for more participant sports stories about New England."

WOMEN'S SPORTS MAGAZINE, Women's Sports Publications, Inc., 310 Town & Country Village, Palo Alto CA 94301. Editor: Amy Rennert. Managing Editor: Lisa Schmidt. Emphasizes women's sports, fitness and health. Monthly magazine; 72 pages. Circ. 125,000. Pays on publication. Buys all rights. Submit seasonal/holiday material 3 months in advance. SASE. Reports in 1 month (queries); 6 weeks (ms). Sample copy $2; SASE for writer's guidelines.

Nonfiction: Profile, service piece, interview, how-to, historic, personal experience, personal opinion, travel, new product, reviews. "All articles should pertain to women's sports and fitness or health. All must be of national interest." Buys 5 mss/issue. Length: 2,500-3,000 words. Pays $300-500 for features.

Photos: State availability of photos. Pays about $25 for b&w prints; about $50 for 35mm color transparencies. Buys one-time rights.

Columns/Departments: Buys 6-8/issue. Query with clips of published work. Length: 500-1,500 words. Pays $50 minimum.

Fillers: Clippings, newsbreaks and health and fitness information. Length: 100-250 words.

Tips: "We prefer queries to manuscripts. The best query letters often start with a first paragraph that could be the first paragraph of the article the writer wants to do. Queries should indicate that the writer has done the preliminary research for the article and has an "angle" or something to give the article personality. Published clips help too. Freelancers can best break into *Women's Sports* by submitting short items for the Sports Pages and Active Woman's Almanac sections or opinion pieces for end zone. We are not looking for profiles of athletes that lack depth or a real understanding of the athlete; we are looking for items of concern to active women—and we interpret that broadly—from the water she drinks to women to watch or remember, from adventure/travel to event coverage."

Golf

GOLF DIGEST, 495 Westport Ave., Norwalk CT 06856. (203)847-5811. Editor: Nick Seitz. Emphasizes golfing. Monthly magazine; 130 pages. Circ. 1 million. Pays on publication. Buys all rights. Byline given. Submit seasonal/holiday material 4 months in advance. Photocopied submissions OK. SASE. Reports in 4-6 weeks.

Nonfiction: Expose, how-to, informational, historical, humor, inspirational, interview, nostalgia, opinion, profile, travel, new product, personal experience, photo feature and technical; "all on playing and otherwise enjoying the game of golf." Recent article example: "Sarazen/Anderson" (February 1982). Query. Length: 1,000-2,500 words. Pays 20¢/edited word minimum.

Photos: Pete Libby, art editor. Purchased without accompanying ms. Pays $10-150 for 5x7 or 8x10 b&w prints; $25-300/35mm color transparency. Model release required.

Poetry: Lois Hains, assistant editor. Light verse. Buys 1-2/issue. Length: 4-8 lines. Pays $15-25.

Fillers: Lois Hains, assistant editor. Jokes, gags, anecdotes. Buys 1-2/issue. Length: 2-6 lines. Pays $10-25.

GOLF MAGAZINE, Times Mirror Magazines, Inc., 380 Madison Ave., New York NY 10017. (212)687-3000. Editor: George Peper. 20% freelance written. Emphasizes golf for males, ages 15-80, college-educated, professionals. Monthly magazine; 150 pages. Circ. 750,000. Pays on acceptance. Buys all rights. Byline given. Submit seasonal/holiday material 4 months in advance. Photocopied submissions OK. No computer printout or disk submissions. SASE. Reports in 4 weeks. Sample copy $1.50.

Nonfiction: How-to (improve game, instructional tips); informational (news in golf); humor; profile (people in golf); travel (golf courses, resorts); new product (golf equipment, apparel, teaching aids); and photo feature (great moments in golf; must be special. Most photography on assignment only). Buys 4-6 unsolicited mss/year. Query. Length: 1,200-2,500 words. Pays $350-500.

Photos: Purchased with accompanying ms or on assignment. Captions required. Query. Pays $50 for 8½x11 glossy prints (with contact sheet and negatives); $75 minimum for 3x5 color prints. Total purchase price for ms includes payment for photos. Model release required.

Columns/Departments: Golf Reports (interesting golf events, feats, etc.). Buys 5-10 mss/year. Query. Length: 250 words maximum. Pays $50. Open to suggestions for new columns/departments.
Fiction: Humorous, mystery. Must be golf-related. Buys 1-2 mss/year. Query. Length: 1,200-2,000 words. Pays $350-500.
Fillers: Short humor. Length: 20-35 words. Pays $25.
Tips: "Best chance is to aim for a light piece which is not too long and is focused on a personality. Anything very technical that would require a consummate knowledge of golf, we would rather assign ourselves. But if you are successful with something light and not too long, we might use you for something heavier later. Probably the best way to break in would be by our Golf Reports section in which we run short items on interesting golf feats, events and so forth. If you send us something like that, about an important event in your area, it is an easy way for us to get acquainted."

Guns

THE AMERICAN SHOTGUNNER, Box 3351, Reno NV 89505. Publisher: Bob Thruston. Monthly. Circ. 85,000. Buys all rights. Buys 12-15 unsolicited mss/year. Pays on publication. Free sample copy and writer's guidelines. Submit special material (hunting) 3-4 months in advance. Reports on material accepted for publication in 30 days. Returns rejected material. Submit query. SASE.
Nonfiction and Photos: Sue Thruston, managing editor. All aspects of shotgunning—trap and skeet shooting and hunting, reloading, shooting clothing and shooting equipment. Emphasis is on the how-to and instructional approach. "We give the sportsman actual material that will help him to improve his game, fill his limit, or build that duck blind, etc. Hunting articles are used in all issues, year round." Length: open. Pays $75-250. No additional payment for photos used with mss. "We also purchase professional cover material. Send transparencies (originals)."

BLACK POWDER TIMES, Box 842, Mount Vernon WA 98273. (206)336-2969. Editor: Fred Holder. 25-30% freelance written. For people interested in shooting and collecting black powder guns, primarily of the muzzle-loading variety. Bimonthly magazine. 40 pages. Not copyrighted. Byline given. Pays on publication. Sample copy $2.50. Photocopied and simultaneous submissions OK. Reports in 2-4 weeks. Query. SASE.
Nonfiction: Articles on gunsmiths who make black powder guns, on shoots, on muzzle-loading gun clubs, on guns of the black powder vintage, and anything related to the sport of black powder shooting and hunting. Emphasis is on good writing and reporting. Informational, how-to, personal experience, interview, profile, historical articles and book reviews. Length: 500-2,000 words. Pays 2¢/word.

COMBAT HANDGUNS, Harris Publications Outdoor Group, 1115 Broadway, New York NY 10010. (212)686-4121. Managing Editor: Harry Kane. Bimonthly magazine covering use of handguns in combat situations and in military, police and personal defense. Readers are persons in law enforcement and the military and those interested in the uses and the history of combat firearms. Circ. 80,000. Pays on acceptance. Byline given. Buys all rights. Submit seasonal/holiday material 4 months in advance. Simultaneous queries, and photocopied and previously published submissions OK. SASE. Reports in 2 months.
Nonfiction: Book excerpts; general interest (modifications and uses in combat situations; also gun use in every area of personal defense); how-to; profile (of gunsmith schools); opinion; personal experience ("moment of truth"); photo feature and technical. Recent article examples: any gun test, any tactical scenario. Buys 20 unsolicited mss/year. Query. Length: 1,500-3,500 words. Pays $150-400.
Photos: "What I really like is photos and plenty of good ones." State availability of photos or send photos with ms. Buys first rights. B&w prints only.
Columns/Departments: Police Armory and Combat Ammo. Buys 6 mss/year. Query. Length: 500-1,000 words. Pays $100 maximum.

GUN WORLD, 34249 Camino Capistrano, Box HH, Capistrano Beach CA 92624. Editorial Director: Jack Lewis. 50% freelance written. For ages that "range from mid-20s to mid-60s; many professional types who are interested in relaxation of hunting and shooting." Monthly. Circ. 136,000. Buys all rights. Byline given. Buys 80-100 unsolicited mss/year. Pays on acceptance. Copy of editorial requirements for SASE. Submit seasonal material 4 months in advance. Reports in 6 weeks, perhaps longer. SASE.
Nonfiction and Photos: General subject matter consists of "well-rounded articles—not by amateurs—on shooting techniques, with anecdotes; hunting stories with tips and knowledge integrated. No poems or fiction. We like broad humor in our articles, so long as it does not reflect upon firearms safety. Most arms magazines are pretty deadly and we feel shooting can be fun. Too much material aimed at pro-gun people. Most of this is staff-written and most shooters don't have to be told of their rights under the Constitution. We want articles on new development; off-track inventions, novel military uses of arms; police armament and training techniques; do-it-yourself projects in this field." Buys informational, how-to, personal experience and nostalgia articles.

Pays $300 maximum. Purchases photos with mss and captions required. Wants 5x7 b&w.
Tips: "To break in, offer an anecdote having to do with proposed copy."

GUNS & AMMO MAGAZINE, Petersen Publishing Co., 8490 Sunset Blvd., Los Angeles CA 90069. Editor-in-Chief: Howard E. French. Managing Editor: E.G. Bell. Emphasizes the firearms field. Monthly magazine; 108 pages. Circ. 475,000. Pays on publication. Buys all rights. Submit seasonal/holiday material 4 months in advance. Computer printout submissions OK; dot matrix printouts must have descenders. SASE. Reports in 1 month. Free writer's guidelines.
Nonfiction: Informational and technical. Especially needs semi-technical articles on guns, shooting and reloading. Buys 7-10 mss/issue. Send complete ms. Length: 1,200-3,000 words. Pays $150-400.
Photos: Purchased with accompanying ms. Captions required. Uses 8x10 b&w glossy prints. Total purchase price for ms includes payment for photos. Model release required.

NEW BREED, The Magazine for the Bold Adventurer, New Breed Publications, Inc., 30 Amarillo Dr., Nanuet NY 10954. (914)623-8426. Editor: Harry Belil. Managing Editor: Gary Parsons. Bimonthly magazine covering military adventures, new weapons, survival. For persons interested in "where the action is—hot spots on the globe where the voice of adventure calls." Estab. 1981. Circ. 250,000. Pays on publication. Byline given. Offers 50% kill fee. Buys all rights. Photocopied and previously published submissions OK, if so indicated. SASE. Reports in 2 weeks on queries; 3 weeks on mss. Sample copy for $2, 9x12 SAE, and first class postage; free writer's guidelines.
Nonfiction: "Give us the best possible information on state-of-the-art field weaponry, combat practice and survival techniques for the professional soldier. Material should be slightly right-wing, pro-weapons (including handguns), somewhat hawkish in diplomacy, pro-freedom, pro-constitution, thus, libertarian and capitalist (in the real sense of the term) and consequently anti-totalitarian. Submit mss on all units of the armed forces, as well as soldiers of fortune, police officers and individuals who can be classified as 'New Breed.' " Special annual "combat guns" issue. Buys 80 mss/year. Send complete ms. Length: 3,000-4,000 words. Pays $125-250 for articles with b&w and color photos.

SHOTGUN SPORTS, Shotgun Sport, Inc., Box 5400, Reno NV 89513. (702)329-4519. Editor: Frank Kodl. Managing Editor: Fredi Kodl. Monthly magazine covering the sport of shotgunning. Circ. 55,000. Pays on publication. Byline given. Buys one-time rights. Submit seasonal/holiday material 3 months in advance. SASE. Reports in 1 month. Free sample copy and writer's guidelines.
Nonfiction: Book excerpts, expose, general interest, historical/nostalgic, how-to, humor, inspirational, interview/profile, new product, opinion, personal experience, photo feature, technical and travel; "all articles must be related directly to shotgunning to include trap, skeet or hunting." Buys 50-70 mss/year. Query or send complete mss. Length: open. Pays $50-200.
Photos: State availability of photos or send photos with ms. Reviews 5x7 b&w prints. "Photos included in payment for ms." Captions required.

Horse Racing

THE BACKSTRETCH, 19363 James Couzens Hwy., Detroit MI 48235. (313)342-6144. Editor: Ann Moss. Managing Editor: Ruth LeGrove. For thoroughbred horse trainers, owners, breeders, farm managers, track personnel, jockeys, grooms and racing fans who span the age range from very young to very old. Publication of United Thoroughbred Trainers of America, Inc. Quarterly magazine; 100 pages. Circ. 25,000.
Nonfiction: "*Backstretch* contains mostly general information. Articles deal with biographical material on trainers, owners, jockeys, horses and their careers on and off the track, historical track articles, etc. Unless writer's material is related to thoroughbreds and thoroughbred racing, it should not be submitted. Articles accepted on speculation basis—payment made after material is used. If not suitable, articles are returned immediately. Articles that do not require printing by a specified date are preferred. No special length requirement and amount paid depends on material. Advisable to include photos if possible. Articles should be original copies and should state whether presented to any other magazine, or whether previously printed in any other magazine. Submit complete ms. SASE. Sample copy $1. We do not buy crossword puzzles, cartoons, newspaper clippings, fiction or poetry."

‡HOOF BEATS, United States Trotting Association, 750 Michigan Ave., Columbus OH 43215. (614)224-2291. Editor: Dean A. Hoffman. Managing Editor: Edward Keys. Monthly magazine covering harness racing for the participants of the sport of harness racing. "We cover all aspects of the sport—racing, breeding, selling, etc." Circ. 26,000. Pays on publication. Byline given. Buys negotiable rights. Submit seasonal/holiday material 2 months in advance. Reports in 3 weeks.

Nonfiction: General interest, historical/nostalgic, humor, inspirational, interview/profile, new product, personal experience, photo feature. Buys 15-20 mss/year. Query. Length: open. Pays $75-200.
Photos: State availability of photos. Pays variable rates for 35mm transparencies and prints. Identification of subjects required. Buys one-time rights.
Fiction: Historical, humorous, interesting fiction with a harness racing theme. Buys 2-3 mss/year. Query. Length: open. Pays $75-200.

HUB RAIL, Hub Rail, Inc., 6320 Busch Blvd., Columbus OH 43229. (614)846-0770. Publisher and Editor: David M. Dolezal. Emphasizes harness horse racing or breeding. Bimonthly magazine; 120 pages. Circ. 10,000. Pays on publication. Buys all rights. Phone queries OK. Submit seasonal/holiday material 3 months in advance. Simultaneous and photocopied submissions OK. SASE. Reports in 4 weeks. Free sample copy and writer's guidelines.
Nonfiction: General interest, historical, humor and nostalgia. "Articles should pertain to harness racing." Buys 10 mss/year. Send clips of published work. Length: 1,000-5,000 words. Pays $50-200.
Fiction: "We use short stories pertaining to harness racing." Buys 2 mss/year. Send clips of published work. Length: 2,500-7,000 words. Pays $50-200.

RACING DIGEST, Racing Digest Publishing Co., Inc., Box 101, Dover PA 17315. (717)292-5608. Publisher: Cole Atwood. Editor: Robin Fidler. Weekly newspaper covering thoroughbred horse racing and breeding. Circ. 58,000. Pays on publication. Byline given. Makes work-for-hire assignments. Submit seasonal/holiday material 2 months in advance. Simultaneous queries, and simultaneous and photocopied submissions OK. SASE. Reports in 2 weeks. Sample copy for $2 and 9x12 SAE.
Nonfiction: Query. Length: 500-2,000 words. Pay "depends on article, assignment, etc."
Photos: State availability of photos. Reviews b&w contact sheets and prints. Captions and identification of subjects required. Buys one-time rights.

SPUR, Box 85, Middleburg VA 22117. (703)687-6314. Editor: Connie Coopersmith. Bimonthly magazine covering thoroughbred horses and the people who are involved in the business and sport of the thoroughbred industry. Circ. 10,000. Pays on publication. Byline given. Copyrighted. Buys all rights. Submit seasonal/holiday material 2½ months in advance. Simultaneous queries, and simultaneous, photocopied, and previously published submissions OK. SASE. Reports in 2 weeks on queries; 1 month on mss. Sample copy $3; writer's guidelines for business size SAE and 1 first class stamp.
Nonfiction: Historical/nostalgic, humor, interview/profile, new product, opinion, personal experience, photo feature, travel with particular emphasis on horseracing, steeplechasing and polo. "We are looking for fresh, interesting approaches to entertaining and instructing our readers. The world of the thoroughbred has many facets, including stories about personalities. No tasteless or sex types of articles." Buys 30 mss/year. Query with clips of published work, "or we will consider complete mss." Length: 300-4,000 words. Payment negotiable.
Photos: State availability of photos. Reviews color and b&w contact sheets. Captions, model releases and identification of subjects required. Buys all rights "unless otherwise negotiated."
Columns/Departments: Query or send complete ms to Editorial Assistant. Length: 100-500 words. Pays $25-50 and up.
Fillers: Anecdotes, short humor. Length: 50-100 words. Pays $25 and up.
Tips: "Writers must have a knowledge of horses, horse owners, breeding, training, racing, and riding—or the ability to obtain this knowledge from a subject and to turn out a good article."

‡THE THOROUGHBRED RECORD, Thoroughbred Publishers, Inc., Box 4240, Lexington KY 40544. (606)276-5311. Editor: Susan E. Rhodemyre. Managing Editor: Mark Simon. Weekly magazine covering thoroughbred racing/breeding. Circ. 13,000. Pays on publication. Byline given. Buys one-time rights. Simultaneous queries and photocopied submissions OK. SASE. Reports in 1 week on queries; 1 month on mss. Sample copy $2.
Nonfiction: Book excerpts, historical/nostalgic, humor, interview/profile, photo feature, and technical. Special issues include several regional and international editions scattered throughout the year. "Best approached by query from author. No first-person-type articles on anything." Query with clips or send complete ms. Length: 500-3,000 words. Pays $25 minimum; 10¢/word maximum.
Photos: Send photos with ms. Pays $25 for b&w contact sheet if published; negatives OK for submission; $50 for color contact sheet, negatives and 35mm transparencies (preferred); $150 for color cover. Identification of subjects required.

TROT, 233 Evans Ave., Toronto, Ontario, Canada M8Z 1J6. Executive Editor: Michel Corbeil. Editor: Renée St. Louis. Official publication of the Canadian Trotting Association. "Quite a number of our readers derive all their income from harness racing." Circ. 20,000. Pays on acceptance. Buys first North American serial rights. SAE and International Reply Coupons.

Nonfiction: "General material dealing with any aspect of harness racing or prominent figures in the sport. We would appreciate submissions of any general material on harness racing from anywhere in the US. Nothing dealing with strictly US subjects." Query. Length: 1,000-1,500 words. Pays $100-200.

Hunting and Fishing

ALABAMA GAME & FISH, TENNESSEE SPORTSMAN, Game & Fish Publications, Inc., Box 741, Marietta GA 30061. (404)953-9222. Editor: David Morris. Assistant Editor: Priscilla Crumpler. Monthly magazine covering game and fish indigenous to each state. Pays on publication. Byline given. Buys one-time rights. Submit seasonal material "at least 4 months in advance." Simultaneous queries OK. SASE. Reports in 2 months on queries. Sample copy $2; free writer's guidelines.
Nonfiction: How-to, interview/profile, personal experience, technical, travel—"if pertinent to 'where-to-go.' " No poems, general interest or historical. Query. Length: 1,900-2,500 words. "Payment depends on if run in one magazine only, or 2 magazines, or 3 combination."
Photos: State availability of photos or send photos with mss. Pays negotiable fee for 35mm or 2¼x2¼ color transparencies or 8x10 b&w prints. Captions required.
Tips: "Be a how-to, where-to-go, when-to-go-technical writer. Have an expertise in game and fish areas—and experience."

ALASKA OUTDOORS, Swensen's Publishing, Box 8-2222, Fairbanks AK 99708. (907)276-2670. Editor: Christopher Batin. Bimonthly magazine covering hunting and fishing in Alaska. Circ. 83,000. Pays on acceptance. Byline given. Submit seasonal/holiday material 4 months in advance. Computer printout and disk submissions OK; prefers letter quality to dot matrix. SASE. Reports in 2 weeks. Sample copy $2; writer's guidelines for 4x9½ SAE and 1 first class stamp.
Nonfiction: How-to, investigative reports on outdoor issues in Alaska, and articles on where to go to fish and hunt in Alaska. "Articles should include a sidebar that will aid the reader in duplicating your adventure. No survival-type articles or personal brushes with death." Buys 75 unsolicited mss/year. Query. Length: 800-1,800 words. Pays $50-300; "$250 minimum for article with photographic support."
Photos: Adela Johnson Ward, photo editor. Send photos with ms. Pays $10-25 for b&w contact sheets; $50-200 for 2¼x2¼ or 35mm color transparencies. Captions required. Buys one-time rights.
Tips: "Include more information and more descriptive writing, and less storytelling and Me 'n Joe type articles. No first-person accounts. Most of our writers have visited or live in Alaska. We are more than just a regional publication; we're distributed nationally."

AMERICAN FIELD, 222 W. Adams St., Chicago IL 60606. Editor: William F. Brown. Weekly. Buys first publication rights. Pays on acceptance. Free sample copy. Reports in 20 days. SASE.
Nonfiction and Photos: Interested in factual articles on breeding, rearing, development and training of hunting dogs, how-to material written to appeal to upland bird hunters, sporting dog owners, field trialers, etc. Also wants stories and articles about hunting trips in quest of upland game birds. Length: 1,000-2,500 words. Pays $50-200. Uses photos submitted with manuscripts if they are suitable; also photos submitted with captions only. Pays $5 minimum for b&w.
Fillers: Very infrequently uses some 100- to 250-word fillers. Pays $5 minimum.

THE AMERICAN HUNTER, 1600 Rhode Island Ave. NW, Washington DC 20036. Editor: Tom Fulgham. 90% freelance written. For sport hunters who are members of the National Rifle Association; all ages, all political persuasions, all economic levels. Circ. over 1,000,000. Buys first North American serial rights. Byline given. Pays on acceptance. Free sample copy and writer's guidelines. Reports in 1-3 weeks. Computer printout submissions OK; prefers letter quality to dot matrix. SASE.
Nonfiction: "Factual material on all phases of sport hunting and game animals and their habitats. Good angles and depth writing are essential. You have to *know* to write successfully here." Not interested in material on fishermen, campers or ecology buffs. Buys 200 mss/year. Prefers queries. Length: 2,000-3,000 words. Pays $25-400.
Photos: No additional payment made for photos used with mss. Pays $10-25 for b&w photos purchased without accompanying mss. Pays $40-275 for color. "Good photos with manuscripts are a must to sell here."

ANGLER, Box 12155, Oakland CA 94604. Managing Editor: Dan Blanton. 50% freelance written. Fishing magazine for western US. Bimonthly magazine. Circ. 17,600. Pays on acceptance. Buys one-time rights. Byline given. Submit seasonal/holiday material 4 months in advance of issue date. Photocopied submissions OK. SASE. Reports in 2 weeks. Sample copy $2.50; free writer's guidelines for SASE.

Nonfiction: How-to; humor; inspirational; and travel. Buys 24 mss/year. Query. Length: 1,000-3,000 words. Pays $125-250.
Fiction: Buys 3 mss/year. Query. Length: 500-2,000 words. Pays $35-100.

ARKANSAS SPORTSMAN, Game & Fish Publication, Inc., Box 741, Marietta GA 30061. (404)953-9222. Editor: David Morris. Senior Editor: Aaron Pass. Features Editor: Priscilla Crumpler. Monthly how-to, where-to, when-to hunting and fishing magazine. Estab. 1981. Pays on publication. Byline given. Buys one-time rights. Submit seasonal material 6 months in advance. Simultaneous queries and photocopied submissions OK. SASE. Reports in 3 weeks. Sample copy $2; free writer's guidelines.
Nonfiction: General interest, how-to, interview/profile, personal experience, technical, up-date on state and federal legislation. "Specific lakes or hunting lands using how-to, where-to, when-to slants or personality profiles." Buys 300-500 mss/year. Query. Length: 1,900-2,500 words. Pays $200 maximum.
Photos: "Big specimens in good color—no scenery." State availability of photos. Pays $35 minimum for 35mm color transparencies and prints; $100 minimum for covers; $20 minimum for 35mm b&w transparencies and prints. Captions required.
Fiction: Adventure. Buys 5 mss/year. Query. Length: 1,900-2,500 words. Pays $200 maximum.

BASSMASTER MAGAZINE, B.A.S.S. Publications, Box 17900, Montgomery AL 36141. (205)272-9530. Editor: Bob Cobb. Bimonthly magazine (monthly January-April) about largemouth, smallmouth, spotted bass and striped bass for dedicated beginning and advanced bass fishermen. Circ. 400,000. Pays on acceptance. Byline given. Buys all rights. Submit seasonal material 6 months in advance. Simultaneous and photocopied submissions OK, if so indicated. Letter quality printout submissions OK, "but still prefer typewritten material." SASE. Reports in 1 week. Sample copy $2; free writer's guidelines with SASE.
Nonfiction: Historical; interview (of knowledgeable people in the sport); profile (outstanding fishermen); travel (where to go to fish for bass); how-to (catch bass and enjoy the outdoors); new product (reels, rods and bass boats); and conservation related to bass fishing; "Short Cast/News & Views" (upfront regular feature covering news-related events such as new state bass records, unusual bass fishing happenings, etc.; conservation, new products and editorial viewpoints; 250-400 words). "No 'Me and Joe Go Fishing' type articles." Recent article examples: "The Weedless Wonders," how-to related material, and "Lifesaving Investment for Bassers," product report (March 1982). Query. Length: 400-2,100 words. Pays $100-300.
Photos: "We want a mixture of black and white and color photos." Pays $15 minimum for b&w prints. Pays $100-150 for color cover transparencies. Captions required; model release preferred. Buys all rights.
Fillers: Anecdotes, short humor and newsbreaks. Buys 4-5 mss/issue. Length: 250-500 words. Pays $100 minimum.
Tips: "Editorial direction continues in the short, more direct how-to article. Compact, easy-to-read information is our objective. Shorter articles with good graphics, such as how-to diagrams, step-by-step instruction, etc., will enhance a writer's articles submitted to *Bassmaster Magazine*."

CAROLINA GAME & FISH, Game & Fish Publications, Inc., Box 741, Marietta GA 30061. (404)434-0807. Editor: David Morris. Senior Editor: Aaron Pass. Monthly how-to, where-to, when-to hunting and fishing magazine covering all species. Estab. 1981. Pays on publication. Byline given. Buys one-time rights. Submit seasonal material 6 months in advance. Simultaneous queries, and photocopied submissions OK. SASE. Reports in 3 weeks. Sample copy $2; free writer's guidelines.
Nonfiction: General interest; how-to (hunting and fishing articles); humor (occasionally); interview/profile; personal experience; technical. No hiking, canoeing, backpacking, trapping or any nonhunter-related material. Buys 300-500 mss/year. Query. Pays $200 maximum.
Photos: "Big specimen species in good color—no scenery shots." State availability of photos. Pays $35 minimum for 35mm color transparencies and prints; $100 minimum for covers; $20 minimum for 35mm b&w transparencies and prints. Captions required.
Fiction: Adventure. Buys 5 mss/year. Query. Length: 1,900-2,300 words. Pays $200 maximum.
Fillers: Buys 8-10 mss/year. Query. Length: 1,000 words minimum. Pays $150 maximum.

DEER AND DEER HUNTING, The Stump Sitters, Inc., Box 1117, Appleton WI 54912. (414)734-0009. Editors: Al Hofacker and Dr. Rob Wegner. Bimonthly magazine covering deer hunting for individuals who hunt with bow, gun, or camera. Circ. 34,000. Pays on publication. Byline given. Offers $50 kill fee. Buys first North American serial rights. Submit seasonal/holiday material 2 months in advance. Simultaneous queries and photocopied submissions OK. SASE. Reports in 1 week on queries; 2 weeks on mss. Free sample copy and writer's guidelines.
Nonfiction: Historical/nostalgic; how-to (hunting techniques); interview/profile; opinion; personal experience; photo feature; technical; book review. "Our readers desire factual articles of a technical nature, that relate deer behavior and habits to hunting methodology. We focus on deer biology, management principles and practices, habitat requirements, natural history of deer, hunting techniques, and hunting ethics." No hunting "Hot Spot" or "local" articles. Buys 30 mss/year. Query with clips of published work. Length: 1,000-4,000

words. Pays $40-200.

Photos: State availability of photos. Pays $50 for 35mm color transparencies; $20 for 8x10 b&w prints. Captions and identification of subjects required. Buys one-time rights.

Columns/Departments: Review Stand (reviews of books of interest to deer hunters); Deer Browse (unusual observations of deer behavior). Buys 20 mss/year. Query. Length: 200-800 words. Pays $10-40.

Poetry: Free verse, light verse, traditional. Buys 5/year. Submit maximum 6 poems. Pays $15-40.

Fillers: Clippings, anecdotes, newsbreaks. Buys 20/year. Length: 200-800 words. Pays $10-40.

Tips: "Break in by providing material of a technical nature, backed by scientific research, and written in a style understandable to the average deer hunter. We focus primarily on white-tailed deer but periodically use material on mule deer and exotic species such as fallow deer."

FIELD AND STREAM, 1515 Broadway, New York NY 10036. Editor: Jack Samson. 50% freelance written. Monthly. Buys all rights. Byline given. Reports in 4 weeks. Query. SASE.

Nonfiction and Photos: "This is a broad-based outdoor service magazine. Editorial content ranges from very basic how-to stories that tell either in pictures or words how an outdoor technique is done or a device is made. Articles of penetrating depth about national conservation, game management, resource management, and recreation development problems. Hunting, fishing, camping, backpacking, nature, outdoor, photography, equipment, wild game and fish recipes, and other activities allied to the outdoors. The 'me and Joe' story is about dead, with minor exceptions. Both where-to and how-to articles should be well-illustrated." Especially needs conservation and environmental stories. Prefers color to b&w. Submit outline first with photos. Length: 2,000-2,500 words. Payment varies depending on the name of the author, quality of work, importance of the article. Pays $500 and up for features. *Field & Stream* also publishes regional sections with feature articles on hunting and fishing in specific areas of the country. The sections are geographically divided into Northeast, Midwest, Far West, West and South, and appear 12 months a year. Usually buys photos with mss. When purchased separately, pays $350-400 minimum for color. Buys one-time rights to photos.

Fillers: Buys "how it's done" fillers of 500-900 words. Must be unusual or helpful subjects. Pays $250 on acceptance.

FISHING AND HUNTING NEWS, Outdoor Empire Publishing Co., Inc., 511 Eastlake Ave. E., Box C-19000, Seattle WA 98109. (206)624-3845. Managing Editor: Vence Malernee. Emphasizes fishing and hunting. Weekly tabloid. Circ. 140,000. Pays on acceptance. Buys all rights. Submit seasonal/holiday material 3 months in advance. Photocopied submissions OK. Computer printout submissions OK. Free sample copy and writer's guidelines.

Nonfiction: How-to (fish and hunt successfully, things that make outdoor jaunts more enjoyable/productive); photo feature (successful fishing/hunting in the western US); informational. No first-person personal accounts of the 'me and Joe' variety or dated materials, as we are a weekly news publication." Buys 65 or more mss/year. Query. Length: 100-1,000 words. Pays $25 minimum.

Photos: Purchased with or without accompanying ms. Captions required. Submit prints or transparencies. Pays $5 minimum for b&w glossy prints; $50 minimum for 35mm or 2¼x2¼color transparencies.

Tips: "Competition in the outdoor publishing industry is very keen, and we are meeting it with increasingly timely and prognosticative articles. Writers should look for the new, the different, and the off-the-beaten track in hunting, fishing and outdoor activities."

FISHING WORLD, 51 Atlantic Ave., Floral Park NY 11001. Editor: Keith Gardner. Bimonthly. Circ. 285,000. Buys first North American serial rights. Byline given. Pays on acceptance. Free sample copy. Photocopied submissions OK. Reports in 2 weeks. Query. SASE.

Nonfiction and Photos: "Feature articles range from 1,000-2,000 words with the shorter preferred. A good selection of color transparencies and b&w glossy prints should accompany each submission. Subject matter can range from a hot fishing site to tackle and techniques, from tips on taking individual species to a story on one lake or an entire region, either freshwater or salt. However, how-to is definitely preferred over where-to, and a strong biological/scientific slant is best of all. Where-to articles, especially if they describe foreign fishing, should be accompanied by sidebars covering how to make reservations and arrange transportation, how to get there, where to stay. Angling methods should be developed in clear detail, with accurate and useful information about tackle and boats. Depending on article length, suitability of photographs and other factors, payment is up to $250 for feature articles accompanied by suitable photography. Color transparencies selected for cover use pay an additional $250. B&w or unillustrated featurettes are also considered. These can be on anything remotely connected with fishing. Length: 1,000 words. Pays $25-100 depending on length and photos. Detailed queries accompanied by photos are preferred. Cover shots are purchased separately, rather than selected from those accompanying mss. The editor favors drama rather than serenity in selecting cover shots."

FLY FISHERMAN MAGAZINE, Historical Times, Inc., 2245 Cohn, Box 8200, Harrisburg PA 17105. (717)657-9555. Founding Publisher: Donald D. Zahner. Editor: John Randolph. Associate Editor: Tom Meade. Published 6 times/year. Circ. 130,000. Pays on publication. Buys first North American magazine rights and one-time periodical rights. Written queries preferred. Submit seasonal/holiday material 6 months in advance. SASE. Reports in 6 weeks. Sample copy $2.95; writer's guidelines for SASE.

Nonfiction: How-to or where-to-go, new product, personal experience, photo feature, profile, technical and travel. Buys 30 unsolicited mss/year. Recent article example: "Brown Drakes" (April 1982). Query or submit complete ms. Length: 100-3,000 words. Pays $35-400.

Photos: Send photos with ms. Pays $30-75 for 8x10 b&w glossy prints; $40-100 for 35mm, 2¼x2¼ 4x5 color transparencies; $400 maximum for cover. Buys one-time rights. Captions required.

Columns/Departments: Casting About (where-to-go shorts); Fly Fisherman's Bookshelf (book reviews); and Fly-Tier's Bench (technical how-to). Buys 5/issue. Query or submit complete ms. Length: 100-1,500 words. Pays $35-200.

Fillers: Mini-articles (technical or nontechnical). Buys 5/issue. Length: 100-300 words. Pays $35-100.

THE FLYFISHER, 560 Legion, Idaho Falls ID 83402. (208)523-7300. Editor: Dennis G. Bitton. *"The Fly-fisher* is the official publication of the Federation of Fly Fishers, a nonprofit organization of member clubs and individuals in the US, Canada, United Kingdom, France, New Zealand, Chile and other nations. It serves an audience of sophisticated anglers." Quarterly magazine; 64 pages. Circ. 10,000. Pays on acceptance for solicited material. Buys first North American serial rights. Byline given. Submit seasonal/holiday material 75 days in advance of issue date. SASE. Reports in 4 weeks. Sample copy $3, available from FFF, Box 1088, West Yellowstone MT 59758. Writer's guidelines for SASE; write to 560 Legion, Idaho Falls ID 83402.

Nonfiction: How-to (fly fishing techniques, fly tying, tackle, etc.); general interest (any type including where to go, conservation); historical (places, people, events that have significance to fly fishing); inspirational (looking for articles dealing with Federation clubs on conservation projects); interview (articles of famous fly fishermen, fly tiers, teachers, etc.); nostalgia (articles of reminiscences on flies, fishing personalities, equipment and places); technical (about techniques of fly fishing in salt and fresh waters). "Our readers are fly fishermen and articles too basic or not innovative do not appeal to us." Buys 6-8 mss/issue. Query. Length: 500-2,500 words. Pays $50-200.

Photos: Pays $15-50 for 8x10 b&w glossy prints; $20-80 for 35mm or larger color transparencies for inside use. $100-150 for covers. Captions required. Buys one-time rights. Prefers a selection of transparencies and glossies when illustrating with a manuscript, which are purchased as a package.

Fiction: (Must be related to fly fishing). Adventure; confession; fantasy; historical; humorous; and suspense. Buys 2 mss/issue. Query. Length: 500-2,000 words. Pays $75-200.

Tips: "We make every effort to assist a writer with visuals if the idea is strong enough to develop. We will deal with freelancers breaking into the field. Our only concern is that the material be in keeping with the quality established. We prefer articles submitted by members of FFF, but do not limit our selection of good articles."

FUR-FISH-GAME, 2878 E. Main, Columbus OH 43209. Editor: Ken Dunwoody. For outdoorsmen of all ages who are interested in hunting, fishing, trapping, camping, conservation and related topics. Monthly magazine; 64-88 pages. Circ. 200,000. Buys 150 unsolicited mss/year. Pays on acceptance. Byline given. Usually buys all rights but considers reassignment to author. Prefers non-simultaneous submissions. Computer printout submissions OK. Reports in 2-4 weeks. Submit complete ms with photos and SASE. Free writer's guidelines; sample copy 60¢.

Nonfiction: "We are looking for informative, down-to-earth stories about hunting, fishing, trapping, camping, boating, conservation and related subjects. Nostalgic and historical articles are also used. Most of our stories are 'how to' and should appeal to small-town and rural readers who are true outdoorsmen. Some recent articles have told how to select an ax, catch spring crappies, trap farmland fox and build your own decoys. We also use personal experience stories and profiles, such as an article about an old-time trapper. 'Where to' stories are used occasionally if they have broad appeal and include a map and sidebar giving information on travel, lodging, etc. Length: 1,500-3,000 words. Pays $60-200 depending upon quality, photo support, and importance to magazine. Short filler stories pay $20-60. We are increasing our payment scale to writers and photographers and improving the graphics and layout of the magazine."

Photos: Send photos with ms. Photos are part of ms package and receive no additional payment. Prefer b&w but color prints or transparencies OK. Prints can be 5x7 or 8x10. Caption information required. Photos are also purchased without accompanying ms and usually pay $10-35.

Tips: "We are always looking for quality articles that tell how to hunt or fish for game animals or birds that are popular with everyday outdoorsmen but often overlooked in other publications, such as catfish, bluegill, crappie, squirrel, rabbit, crows, etc. We also use articles on standard seasonal subjects such as deer and pheasant, but need to see a fresh approach or new technique. Trapping articles, especially instructional ones, are useful all year. Articles on gun dogs, ginseng and do-it-yourself projects are also popular with our readers. An assortment of photos and/or sketches greatly enhances any ms and sidebars, where applicable, can also help. It is advisable to study the magazine carefully to get a feel for the type of stories we prefer."

GEORGIA SPORTSMAN MAGAZINE, Box 741, Marietta GA 30061. Editor: David Morris. Features Editor: Priscilla Crumpler. Emphasizes hunting and fishing and outdoor recreational opportunities in Georgia.

Monthly magazine; 64 pages. Circ. 45,000. Pays on publication. Byline given. Query. Submit seasonal material 4 months in advance. Simultaneous and "very legible" photocopied submissions OK. Source must be identified for previously published work. SASE. Reports in 4 weeks. Sample copy $2; free writer's guidelines.
Nonfiction: Expose; how-to; informational; historical (acceptable on a very small scale); humor; interviews with fishermen or hunters known statewide; nostalgia (antique weapons such as percussion guns); and articles concerning major legislation and environmental issues affecting Georgia. Length: 2,000-2,800 words. Pays $150-200.
Photos: B&w and color purchased with or without mss or on assignment.

GRAY'S SPORTING JOURNAL, 42 Bay Road, So. Hamilton MA 01982. Editor/Publisher: Ed Gray. 95% freelance written. Emphasizes hunting, fishing and conservation for sportsmen. Published 4 times/year. Magazine; 128 pages. Circ. 60,000. Buys first North American serial rights. Byline given. Computer printout submissions OK. SASE. Reports in 3 months. Sample copy $5; writer's guidelines for SASE.
Nonfiction: Articles on hunting and fishing experiences. Humor; historical; personal experience; opinion; and photo feature. Buys 7/issue. Submit complete ms. Length: 500-5,000 words. Pays $500-1,000 on publication.
Photos: Submit photo material with accompanying ms. Pays $50-300 for any size color transparencies. Captions preferred. Buys one-time rights.
Fiction: Mostly thoughtful and low-key; and humor. Submit complete ms. Length: 500-5,000 words. Pays $500-1000.
Poetry: Free verse; light verse; and traditional. Buys 1/issue. Pays $50-75.
Tips: Show that you are "someone who knows his material but is not a self-acclaimed expert; someone who can write well and with a sense of humor; someone who can share his experiences without talking down to the readers; someone who can prepare an article with focus and a creative approach to his prose." No how-to or where-to-go articles.

GREAT LAKES FISHERMAN, Great Lakes Fisherman Publishing Co., 1570 Fishinger Rd., Columbus OH 43221. (614)451-9307. Editor: Woody Earnheart. Managing Editor: Ottie M. Snyder, Jr. Monthly magazine covering how, when and where to fish in the Great Lakes region. Circ. 68,000. Pays on acceptance. Byline given. Offers $40 kill fee. Buys first North American serial rights. Submit seasonal/holiday material 3 months in advance. SASE. Reports in 5 weeks. Free sample copy and writer's guidelines.
Nonfiction: How-to (where to and when to freshwater fish). "No humor, me and Joe or subject matter outside the Great Lakes region." Buys 84 mss/year. Query with clips of published work. "Letters should be tightly written, but descriptive enough to present no surprises when the ms is received. Prefer b&w photos to be used to illustrate ms with query." Length: 1,500-2,500 words. Pays $125-200.
Photos: Send photos with ms. "Black and white photos are considered part of manuscript package and as such receive no additional payment. We consider b&w photos to be a vital part of a ms package and return more packages because of poor quality photos than any other reason. We look for four types of illustration with each article: scene (a backed off shot of fisherman); result (not the typical meat shot of angler grinning at camera with big stringer but in most cases just a single nice fish with the angler admiring the fish); method (a lure shot or illustration of special rigs mentioned in the text); and action (angler landing a fish, fighting a fish, etc.). Illustrations (line drawings) need not be finished art but should be good enough for our artist to get the idea of what the author is trying to depict." Prefers cover shots to be verticals with fish and fisherman action shots. Pays $100 minimum for 35mm color transparencies; reviews 8x10 b&w prints. Captions, model release and identification of subjects required. Buys one-time rights.
Tips: "Our feature articles are 99.9 percent freelance material. The magazine is circulated in the eight states bordering the Great Lakes, an area where one-third of the nation's licensed anglers reside. All of our feature content is how, when or where, or a combination of all three covering the species common to the region. Fishing is an age-old sport with countless words printed on the subject each year. A fresh new slant that indicates a desire to share with the reader the author's knowledge is a sale. We expect the freelancer to answer any anticipated questions the reader might have (on accommodations, launch sites, equipment needed, etc.) within the ms. We publish an equal mix each month of both warm- and cold-water articles."

GUN DOG, The Magazine of Upland Bird and Waterfowl Dogs, Gun Dog Publications, Inc., Box 68, Adel IA 50003. Editor: Dave Meisner. Bimonthly magazine covering hunting with upland and waterfowl dogs for sophisticated, "gentleman-sportsman" readers. Estab. 1981. Circ. 50,000. Pays on acceptance. Byline given. Does not give assignments. Buys first North American serial rights and one-time rights. Submit seasonal/holiday material 6 months in advance. SASE. Reports in 2 weeks on queries; 1 month on mss. Sample copy $2.95; writer's guidelines for business size SAE and 1 first class stamp.
Nonfiction: Needs "how-to," "where-to," "when-to" articles on upland bird and waterfowl hunting—pieces that entertain, inform, and instruct. Good selection of photos important. Pays $150-300. Length: 1500-3000. Always in need of short (1000-1500 word) tips on training and shotgunning, as well as humor. Pays $50-150. Little need for fiction.
Photos: State availability of photos. Reviews b&w contact sheet; no extra pay for photos submitted with mss.

Pays $150 for covers. Captions and identification of subjects required.

Tips: "Sixty percent of our publication is written by assigned columnists—the best in the business. Freelance material must meet the standards set by our columnists. Because we are so specialized, it is an absolute 'must' to have seen the magazine before trying to write for it."

LOUISIANA GAME & FISH, Game & Fish Publications, Inc., Box 741, Marietta GA 30061. (404)953-9222. Editor: David Morris. Senior Editor: Aaron Pass. Features Editor: Priscilla Crumpler. Monthly how-to, where-to, when-to fishing and hunting magazine for Louisiana. Estab. 1981. Pays on publication. Byline given. Buys one-time rights. Submit seasonal/holiday material 6 months in advance. Simultaneous queries and photocopied submissions OK. SASE. Reports in 3 weeks. Sample copy $2; free writer's guidelines.

Nonfiction: General interest, how-to, humor, interview/profile, personal experience, technical, updates on state and federal legislation. Buys 3-500 mss/year. Query. Length: 1,900-2,500 words. Pays $200 maximum.

Photos: "Big specimens in good color—no scenery." State availability of photos. Pays $35 minimum for 35mm color transparencies and prints; $20 for 35mm b&w transparencies and prints; $100 minimum for covers. Captions required.

Fiction: Adventure. Buys 5 mss/year. Query. Length: 1900-2,500 words. Pays $200 maximum.

Tips: Submit queries on specific lakes, hunting lands using how-to, where-to, when-to slant or personality profile.

MICHIGAN OUT-OF-DOORS, Box 30235, Lansing MI 48909. (517)371-1041. Editor: Kenneth S. Lowe. 50% freelance written. Emphasizes outdoor recreation, especially hunting and fishing; conservation; environmental affairs. Monthly magazine; 116 pages. Circ. 110,000. Pays on acceptance. Buys first North American serial rights. Byline given. Phone queries OK. Submit seasonal/holiday material 6 months in advance. SASE. Reports in 1 month. Sample copy $1; free writer's guidelines.

Nonfiction: Expose, historical, how-to, informational, interview, nostalgia, personal experience, personal opinion, photo feature and profile. No humor. "Stories *must* have a Michigan slant unless they treat a subject of universal interest to our readers." Buys 8 mss/issue. Send complete ms. Length: 1,000-3,000 words. Pays $60 minimum for feature stories.

Photos: Purchased with or without accompanying ms. Pays $15 minimum for any size b&w glossy prints; $60 maximum for color (for cover). Offers no additional payment for photos accepted with accompanying ms. Buys one-time rights. Captions preferred.

Tips: "Top priority is placed on true accounts of personal adventures in the out-of-doors—not simple narratives of hunting or fishing trips but well-written tales of very unusual incidents encountered while hunting, fishing, camping, hiking, etc."

MID WEST OUTDOORS, Mid West Outdoors, Ltd., 111 Shore Drive, Hinsdale (Burr Ridge) IL 60521. (312)887-7722. Editor: Gene Laulunen. Emphasizes fishing, hunting, camping and boating. Monthly tabloid. Circ. 96,000. Pays on publication. Buys simultaneous rights. Byline given. Submit seasonal material 2 months in advance. Simultaneous, photocopied and previously published submissions OK. SASE. Reports in 3 weeks. Sample copy $1; free writer's guidelines.

Nonfiction: How-to (fishing, hunting, camping in the Midwest) and where-to-go (fishing, hunting, camping within 500 miles of Chicago). "We do not want to see any articles on 'my first fishing, hunting or camping experiences,' 'Cleaning My Tackle Box,' 'Tackle Tune-up,' or 'Catch and Release.' " Buys 250 unsolicited mss/year. Send complete ms. Length: 1,000-1,500 words. Pays $15-25.

Photos: Offers no additional payment for photos accompanying ms; uses b&w prints. Buys all rights. Captions required.

Columns/Departments: Archery, Camping, Dogs, Fishing and Hunting. Open to suggestions for columns/departments. Send complete ms. Pays $20.

Tips: "Break in with a great unknown fishing hole within 500 miles of Chicago. Where, how, when and why."

MISSISSIPPI GAME & FISH, Game & Fish Publications, Box 741, Marietta GA 30061. (404)953-9222. Editor: David Morris. Monthly how-to, where-to, when-to hunting and fishing magazine. Estab. 1981. Pays on publication. Byline given. Buys one-time rights. Submit seasonal/holiday material 6 months in advance. Simultaneous queries and photocopied submissions OK. SASE. Reports in 3 weeks. Sample copy $2; free writer's guidelines.

Nonfiction: General interest; how-to; humor (occasionally); interview/profile; personal experience; technical; updates on state and federal legislation. No historical articles. Buys 300-500 mss/year. Query. Length: 1,900-2,500 words.

Photos: "Big specimen species and good color; no scenery shots." State availability of photos or send photos with ms.

Fiction: Adventure. Buys 5 mss/year. Query. Length: 1,900-2,500. Pays $200 maximum.

OHIO FISHERMAN, Ohio Fisherman Publishing Co., 1570 Fishinger Rd., Columbus OH 43221. (614)451-5769. Editor: Woody Earnheart. Managing Editor: Ottie M. Snyder, Jr. Monthly magazine covering the how, when and where of Ohio fishing. Circ. 45,000. Pays on publication. Byline given. Offers $40 kill fee. Buys first rights. Submit seasonal/holiday material 3 months in advance. SASE. Reports in 5 weeks. Free sample copy and writer's guidelines.
Nonfiction: How-to (also where to and when to fresh water fish). "Our feature articles are 99% freelance material, and all have the same basic theme—sharing fishing knowledge. No humorous or 'me and Joe' articles." Buys 84 mss/year. Query with clips of published work. Letters should be "tightly written, but descriptive enough to present no surprises when the ms is received. Prefer b&w photos to be used to illustrate ms with query." Length: 1,500-2,500 words. Pays $100-150.
Photos: 99% of covers purchased are verticals involving fishermen and fish—action preferred." Send photos with query. "We consider b&w photos to be a vital part of a ms package and return more mss because of poor quality photos than any other reason. We look for four types of illustration with each article: scene (a backed off shot of fisherman); result (not the typical meat shot of angler grinning at camera with big stringer, but in most cases just a single nice fish with the angler admiring the fish); method (a lure or illustration of special rigs mentioned in the text); and action (angler landing a fish, fighting a fish, etc.). Illustrations (line drawings) need not be finished art but should be good enough for our artist to get the idea of what the author is trying to depict." Pays $100 minimum for 35mm color transparencies (cover use); also buys 8x10 b&w prints as part of ms package—"no additional payments." Captions and identification of subjects required. Buys one-time rights.
Tips: "The specialist and regional markets are here to stay. They both offer the freelancer the opportunity for steady income. Fishing is an age-old sport with countless words printed on the subject each year. A fresh new slant that indicates a desire to share with the reader the author's knowledge is a sale. We expect the freelancer to answer any anticipated questions the reader might have (on accommodations, launch sites, equipment needed, etc.) within the ms."

ONTARIO OUT OF DOORS, 3 Church St., Toronto, Ontario, Canada M5E 1M2. (416)368-3011. Editor-in-Chief: Burton J. Myers. 75% freelance written. Emphasizes hunting, fishing, camping, and conservation. Monthly magazine; 72 pages. Circ. 55,000. Pays on acceptance. Buys all rights. Phone queries OK. Computer printout submissions OK. Submit seasonal/holiday material 3 months in advance of issue date. Reports in 6 weeks. Free sample copy and writer's guidelines; mention *Writer's Market* in request.
Nonfiction: Expose of conservation practices; how-to (improve your fishing and hunting skills); humor; photo feature (on wildlife); travel (where to find good fishing and hunting); and any news on Ontario. "Avoid 'Me and Joe' articles or funny family camping anecdotes." Buys 20-30 unsolicited mss/year. Recent article example: "Worms and Bows" (April 1982). Query. Length: 150-3,500 words. Pays $15-250.
Photos: Submit photo material with accompanying query. No additional payment for b&w contact sheets and 35mm color transparencies. "Should a photo be used on the cover, an additional payment of $150-250 is made."
Fillers: Outdoor tips. Buys 24 mss/year. Length: 20-50 words. Pays $10.
Tips: "We expect our rates to climb and our expectations on quality of submissions to become more demanding."

OUTDOOR AMERICA, Suite 1100, 1701 N. Ft. Myer Dr., Arlington VA 22209. (703)528-1818. Editor: Carol Dana. Bimonthly magazine about natural resource conservation and outdoor recreation for 50,000 members of the Izaak Walton League. Circ. 50,000. Pays on publication. Byline given. Buys first North American serial rights. Submit seasonal material 6 months in advance. Simultaneous and photocopied submissions OK, if so indicated. SASE. Reports in 2 months. Sample copy $1.50; free writer's guidelines with SASE.
Nonfiction: "We are interested in current, issue-oriented articles on resource topics, conservation, government activities that hurt or improve the land, air, water and forests, and articles about outdoor recreation such as hunting, fishing, canoeing, wilderness activities." Query with clips of previously published work. Length 2,000-2,500 words. Pays 5¢-10¢/word.
Photos: Reviews 5x7 b&w glossy prints and 35mm and larger color transparencies. Offers no additional payment for photos accepted with ms. Pays $50-75 for covers. Caption and model release required. Buys one-time rights.

‡**PENNSYLVANIA ANGLER**, Pennsylvania Fish Commission, Box 1673, Harrisburg PA 17105-1673. (717)787-2411. Editor: Art Michaels. Monthly magazine of fishing, boating and conservation topics. Circ. 65,000. Pays on acceptance. Byline given. Buys all rights. Submit seasonal/holiday material 8 months in advance. SASE. Reports in 2 weeks on queries; 2 months on mss. Free writer's guidelines for SASE. Sample copy for 9x12 SAE and 71¢ postage.
Nonfiction: How-to and where-to in fishing and boating in Pennsylvania. Technical and the latest trends in fishing. No "Me 'n' Joe" fishing articles and no hunting material. Query for articles over 1,000 words. Length: 200-1,200 words. Pays $50-150.
Photos: Pays $25 minimum for inside color; $5-10 for b&w prints. Pays $100-150 for color cover photos; $25-

50 for back cover photos.

Columns/Departments: Short subjects (with photos) related to fishing. Length: 200-250 words. Pays $50.

Tips: "Timeliness and fresh, sharply focused subjects are important for short fishing pieces, and these are the best way new writers can break in to print. Any technical fishing subject appropriate to Pennsylvania waterways is useful, and material should not exceed 200 words. Another way to break in to print here is to know Pennsylvania angling and write a detailed account of fishing a specific waterway."

PENNSYLVANIA GAME NEWS, Box 1567, Harrisburg PA 17105-1567. (717)787-3745. Editor-in-Chief: Bob Bell. 85% freelance written. Emphasizes hunting in Pennsylvania. Monthly magazine; 64 pages. Circ. 210,000. Pays on acceptance. Buys all rights. Byline given. Phone queries OK. Submit seasonal/holiday material 6 months in advance. Photocopied submissions OK. Computer printout submissions OK; prefers letter quality to dot matrix. SASE. Reports in 1 month. Free sample copy and writer's guidelines.

Nonfiction: Historical, how-to, informational, personal experience, photo feature and technical. "Must be related to outdoors in Pennsylvania." No fishing or boating material. Buys 4-8 unsolicited mss/issue. Query. Length: 2,500 words maximum. Pays $250 maximum.

Photos: Purchased with accompanying ms. Pays $5-20 for 8x10 b&w glossy prints. Model release required.

PENNSYLVANIA SPORTSMAN, Box 5196, Harrisburg PA 17110. Editor: Lou Hoffman. Covering hunting, fishing, camping, boating and conservation in Pennsylvania. Pays on publication. Buys one-time rights. Byline given. Simultaneous and previously published submissions OK. Computer printout or disk submissions OK. SASE. Reports in 3 weeks. Sample copy 75¢.

Nonfiction: How-to and where-to articles on hunting, fishing, camping and boating. No material *not* related to field sports. Buys 30-40 unsolicited mss/year. Submit complete ms or query with photos. Length 800-1,200 words. Pays $40-100.

Photos: Pays $10 for 5x7 b&w prints; $75/color cover; $20/color inside. Prefers 35mm slides. Captions and model releases are required.

Fillers: "Fillers welcome. Subjects should be different, e.g., 'How to Make A Fishy Pegbored,' 'A Camp Toaster.' We are also looking for helpful hints." Length: 300-400 words. Pays $25 each; $10 additional for b&w used with article.

PETERSEN'S HUNTING, Petersen Publishing Co., 8490 Sunset Blvd., Los Angeles CA 90069. (213)657-5100. Editor-in-Chief: Craig Boddington. Emphasizes sport hunting. Monthly magazine; 84 pages. Circ. 265,000. Pays on acceptance. Buys all rights. Submit seasonal/holiday material 6 months in advance. SASE. Reports in 2 months. Sample copy $1.50. Free writer's guidelines.

Nonfiction: How-to (how to be a better hunter, how to make hunting-related items); personal experience (use a hunting trip as an anecdote to illustrate how-to contents). Buys 15 unsolicited mss/year. Recent article example: "Outwitting Plenty-Smart Predators," (April 1982). Query. Length: 1,500-2,500 words. Pays $250-350.

Photos: Photos purchased with or without accompanying ms. Captions required. Pays $25 minimum for 8x10 b&w glossy prints; $50-150 for 2¼x2¼ or 35mm color transparencies. Total purchase price for ms includes payment for photos. Model release required.

Tips: "Write an unusual hunting story that is not often covered in other publications."

‡PRO BASS, The Bass Anglers Guide to Better Fishing, National Reporter Publishing Co., 15115 S. 76th E. Ave., Bixby OK 74008. (918)366-4441. Editor: Michael Rieke. Magazine published 8 times/year covering large mouth, small mouth and stripper bass fishing. Circ. 30,000+. Pays on acceptance. Byline given. Buys all rights. Submit seasonal/holiday material 6 months in advance. Simultaneous queries and photocopied submissions OK. SASE. Reports in 1 month. Sample copy for $1, 11x14 SAE and 3 first class stamps; writer's guidelines for business-size SAE and 1 first class stamp.

Nonfiction: Book excerpts (how-to books on bass fishing); how-to (techniques for catching all species of bass); interview/profile (offering techniques of successful bass anglers); technical (how-to for bass fishing). Buys 80 mss/year. Query or send complete ms. Length: 750-2,500 words. Pays $150-200.

Photos: Send photos with ms. Pays $25-100 for 2¼ color transparencies; reviews 8x10 b&w prints. Captions required. Buys one-time rights.

Columns/Departments: Send complete ms. Length: 500-1,000 words. Pays $100 minimum.

SALT WATER SPORTSMAN, 186 Lincoln St., Boston MA 02111. (617)426-4074. Editor-in-Chief: Barry Gibson. 85% freelance written. Emphasizes saltwater fishing. Monthly magazine; 120 pages. Circ. 100,000. Pays on acceptance. Buys first North American serial rights. Pays 100% kill fee. Byline given. Submit seasonal material 8 months in advance. No photocopied submissions. No computer printout or disk submissions. SASE. Reports in 4 weeks. Free sample copy and writer's guidelines.

Nonfiction: How-to, personal experience, technical and travel (to fishing areas). "Readers want solid how-to, where-to information written in an enjoyable, easy-to-read style. Personal anecdotes help the reader identify with the writer." Prefers new slants and "specific" information. Query. "It is helpful if the writer states experience in salt water fishing and any previous related articles. We want 1, possibly 2 well-explained ideas per query letter—not merely a listing." Buys 100 unsolicited mss/year. No fiction. Length: 1,500-2,000 words. Pays 5¢/word minimum.

Photos: Purchased with or without accompanying ms. Captions required. Uses 5x7 or 8x10 b&w prints and color slides. Pays $300 minimum for 35mm, 2¼x2¼ or 8x10 color transparencies for cover. Offers additional payment for photos accepted with accompanying ms.

Tips: "There are a lot of knowledgeable fishermen/budding writers out there who could be valuable to us with a little coaching. Many don't think they can write a story for us, but they'd be surprised. We work with writers. We want more technical and semi-technical/biology articles."

SOUTH CAROLINA WILDLIFE, Box 167, Rembert Dennis Bldg., Columbia SC 29202. (803)758-6291. Editor: John Davis. Associate Editor: Nancy Coleman. For South Carolinians interested in wildlife and outdoor activities. Bimonthly magazine; 64 pages. Circ. 60,000. Copyrighted. Byline given. Pays on publication. Free sample copy. Reports in 1 month. Submit 1 page outline and 1 page explanation. Computer printout submissions OK.

Nonfiction and Photos: Articles on outdoor South Carolina with an emphasis on preserving and protecting our natural resources. "Realize that the topic must be of interest to South Carolinians and that we must be able to justify using it in a publication, published by the state wildlife department—so if it isn't directly about hunting, fishing, a certain plant or animal, it must be somehow related to the environment and conservation. Readers prefer a broad mix of outdoor related topics (articles that illustrate the beauty of South Carolina's outdoors and those that help the reader get more for his/her time, effort, and money spent in outdoor recreation). These two general areas are the ones we most need. Subjects vary a great deal in topic, area and style, but must all have a common ground in the outdoor resources and heritage of South Carolina. Review back issues for articles by writers such as George Reiger, Joel Vance, Scott Derks, and Nancy Coleman." Query with a one-page outline citing sources, giving ideas for graphic design, explaining justification and giving an example of the first two paragraphs." Does not need any column material. Buys 9-14 unsolicited mss/year. Length: 1,000-3,000 words. Pays 10¢/word. Pays $25 for b&w glossy prints purchased with or without ms, or on assignment. Pays $50 for color.

Tips: "While our pay rates are not 'inspirational,' we need more writers in the outdoor field who take pride in the craft of writing and put a real effort toward originality and preciseness in their work. Very restricted budgeting may cause us to turn away even good material."

SOUTHERN OUTDOORS MAGAZINE, B.A.S.S. Publications, Number 1 Bell Rd., Montgomery AL 36141. Editor: Dave Precht. Emphasizes Southern outdoor activities, including hunting, fishing, boating, shooting, camping. Published 8 times/year. Circ. 200,000. Pays on acceptance. Buys all rights. SASE. Reports in 1 month. Sample copy $1.

Nonfiction: Articles should be service-oriented, helping the reader be more successful in outdoor sports. Emphasis is on techniques and trends. Some "where-to" stories purchased on Southern destinations with strong fishing or hunting theme. Buys 120 mss/year. Length: 3,000 words maximum. Pays 15¢/word.

Photos: Usually purchased with manuscripts. Pays $50 for 35mm color transparencies without ms, and $250-350 for covers.

Fillers: Needs short articles (50-500 words) with newsy slant for "Southern Shorts." Emphasis on irony and humor. Also needs humorous or thought-provoking pieces (750-1,500 words) for "S.O. Essay" feature.

Tips: "It's easiest to break in with short features of 1,200-2,000 words on 'how-to' or 'where-to' fishing and hunting topics. We buy very little first person. How-to stories should quote at least three sources, preferably from different parts of the Southeast. Query first, and send sample of your writing if we haven't done business before. Stories most likely to sell: bass fishing, deer hunting, other freshwater fishing, inshore salt-water fishing, bird and small game hunting, shooting, camping and boating."

SPORTS AFIELD, 250 W. 55th St., New York NY 10019. Editor: Tom Paugh. Managing Editor: Fred Kesting. For people of all ages whose interests are centered around the out-of-doors (hunting and fishing) and related subjects. Monthly magazine. Circ. 525,000. Buys first North American serial rights. Byline given. Pays on acceptance. "Our magazine is seasonal and material submitted should be in accordance. Fishing in spring and summer; hunting in the fall; camping in summer and fall." Submit seasonal material 6 months in advance. Reports in 1 month. Query or submit complete ms. SASE.

Nonfiction and Photos: "Informative articles and personal experiences with good photos on hunting, fishing, camping, boating and subjects such as conservation and travel related to hunting and fishing. We want first-class writing and reporting." Buys 15-17 unsolicited mss/year. Recent article example: "Buff!" (June 1981). Length: 500-2,500 words. Pays $700 minimum, depending on length and quality. Photos purchased with or without ms. Pays $50 minimum for 8x10 b&w glossy prints. Pays $50 minimum for 35mm or larger transparencies.

Fiction: Adventure, humor (if related to hunting and fishing).

Fillers: Send to Almanac editor. Payment depends on length. Almanac pays $25 and up depending on length, for newsworthy, unusual, how-to and nature items.

SPORTSMAN'S HUNTING, Harris Publications Outdoor Group, 79 Madison Ave., New York NY 10026. (212)686-4121. Editor: Lamar Underwood. Magazine published 2 times/year (early fall and mid-winter) covering hunting for hunters. Harris Publications Outdoor Group also publishes 6 annual magazines: *Hunters Hunting* (late fall), *Action Hunting* (late fall), *Backcountry Hunting* (late summer), *The Complete Deer Hunting Annual* (early fall), *Hunters Deer Hunting Annual* (late summer), and *Sportsman's Bowhunting Annual* (late summer). All submissions will be considered for the above magazines. Pays on acceptance. Byline given. Buys first North American serial rights. Submit seasonal/holiday material 4 months in advance. SASE. Reports in 3 weeks. Free sample copy; writer's guidelines for business size SAE and 1 first class stamp.
Nonfiction: Nostalgic; how-to (or where-to); personal experience ("Me and Joe" stories); and photo feature (with accompanying text). Query or send complete ms. Length: 2,000-4,000 words. Pays $250-500.
Photos: State availability of photos or send photos with ms. Pays $25-100 for color transparencies (35mm and larger); $25-100 for 8x10 glossy prints or contact sheets. Captions and model releases required. Buys one-time rights.
Tips: Study the magazines carefully. We buy almost all our material over-the-transom."

THE TEXAS FISHERMAN, Voice of the Lone Star Angler, Cordovan Corp., 5314 Bingle Road, Houston TX 77092. Editor: Larry Bozka. For freshwater and saltwater fishermen in Texas. Monthly tabloid. Circ. 55,899. Rights purchased vary with author and material. Byline given. Usually buys second serial (reprint) rights. Buys 5-8 mss/month. Pays on publication. Free sample copy and writer's guidelines. Will consider simultaneous submissions. Reports in 4 weeks. Query. SASE.
Nonfiction and Photos: General how-to, where-to, features on all phases of fishing in Texas. Strong slant on informative pieces. Strong writing. Good saltwater stories (Texas only). Length: 1,500-2,000 words. Pays $75-200, depending on length and quality of writing and photos. Mss must include 4-7 good action b&w photos or illustrations.
Tips: "Query should be a short, but complete description of the story that emphasizes a specific angle. When possible, send black and white photos with manuscripts. Good art will sell us a story that is mediocre, but even a great story can't replace bad photographs. How-to stories are preferred."

TEXAS SPORTSMAN MAGAZINE, Box 741, Marietta GA 30061. (404)953-9222. Editor: David Morris. Senior Editor: Aaron Pass. Feature Editor: Priscilla Crumpler. Monthly magazine covering Texas fishing and hunting. Pays on publication. Byline given. Buys one-time rights. Submit seasonal/holiday material 4-6 months in advance. Simultaneous queries and photocopied submissions OK. SASE. Reports in 1 month. Sample copy $2; writer's guidelines for SASE.
Nonfiction: General interest, how-to, humor, interview/profile, personal experience, photo feature, technical and travel. No articles not relating to Texas. Query with clips of published work. Length: 1,900-2,500 words.
Photos: Send photos with ms. Reviews b&w contact sheets and 35mm color transparencies. Captions required.

TURKEY CALL, Wild Turkey Bldg., Box 530, Edgefield SC 29824. (803)637-3106. Editor: Gene Smith. 30% freelance written. An educational publication for members of the National Wild Turkey Federation. Bimonthly magazine. Circ. 30,000. Buys one-time rights. Byline given. Normally pays upon publication. Sample copy $2 when supplies permit. Reports in 4 weeks. No queries necessary. Submit complete package. Wants original ms only (no carbons or other copies). Would consider letter-quality printout submissions. SASE.
Nonfiction and Photos: Feature articles dealing with the history, management, restoration, distribution and hunting of the American wild turkey. Must be accurate information and must appeal to national readership of sportsmen and wildlife management experts. No poetry or first person accounts of unremarkable hunting trips. May use some fiction that educates or entertains in a special way. Recent article example: "The Incident at Chestnut Flats" (May-June 1981). Length: 1,200-1,500 words. Pays $25 for items, $50 for short fillers of 400-500 words, $200-275 for illustrated features. "We want quality photos submitted with features." Art illustrations also acceptable. "We possibly may be using more inside color illustrations." Prefers b&w 8x10 glossies. Color transparencies also considered. Wants no typical hunter-holding-dead-turkey photos or poorly staged setups using mounted birds or domestic turkeys. Photos with how-to stories must make the techniques clear (example: how to make a turkey call; how to sculpt or carve a bird in wood). Pays $10 minimum for one-time rights on b&w photos and simple art illustrations; up to $50 for inside color, reproduced any size. Covers: Most are donated. Any purchased are negotiated.

VIRGINIA WILDLIFE, Box 11104, Richmond VA 23230. (804)257-1000. Editor: Harry L. Gillam. Send manuscripts to managing editor, Sarah Bartenstein. 50% freelance written. For sportsmen and outdoor enthusiasts. Pays on acceptance. Buys first North American serial rights. Byline given. Free sample copy and writer's guidelines. SASE (8½x11).

Nonfiction: Uses factual outdoor stories, set in Virginia. "Currently need boating subjects, women and youth in the outdoors, wildlife and nature in urban areas. Always need good fishing and hunting stories—not of the 'Me and Joe' genre, however. Slant should be to enjoy the outdoors and what you can do to improve it. Material must be applicable to Virginia, sound from a scientific basis, accurate and easily readable. No subjects which are too controversial for a state agency magazine to address; poetry and cartoons; sentimental or humorous pieces (not because they're inherently bad, but because so few writers are good at either); 'how I nursed an abandoned _____ back to health' or stories about wildlife the author has become 'pals' with." Submit photos with ms. Length: prefers approximately 1,200 words. Pays 5¢/word.

Photos: Buys photos with mss;. "and occasionally buys unaccompanied good photos." Prefers color transparencies, but also has limited need for 8x10 b&w glossy prints. Captions required. Pays $10/b&w photo; $10-15 for color.

Tips: "We are currently receiving too many anecdotes and too few articles with an educational bent—we want instructional, 'how-to' articles on hunting, fishing and outdoor sports, and also want semi-technical articles on wildlife. We are not receiving enough articles with high-quality photographs accompanying them. Catering to these needs will greatly enhance chances for acceptance of manuscripts. We have more 'backyard bird' articles than we could ever hope to use, and not enough good submissions on trapping or bird hunting. We are cutting back substantially on number of freelance, over-the-transom submissions we purchase, in favor of making assignments to writers with whom we have established relationships and articles written by our own staff. This trend is the result of our receiving too much of the same old stuff; not getting stories on areas we're trying to cover; of needing to spend less (thereby not only buying smaller percentage of total make-up of magazine, but also stockpiling less—we buy only what we think we'll need *now*); and of wanting to use the magazine as a forum for publicizing our agency's (State Game & Fish Commission) programs."

WASHINGTON FISHING HOLES, Osprey Press, Inc., Box 309, Black Diamond WA 98010. (206)630-2635. Editors: Milt Keizer, Terry Sheely. 65-75% freelance written. For anglers from 8-80, whether beginner or expert, interested in the where-to and how-to of Washington fishing. Magazine published every two months; 80 pages. Circ. 10,000. Pays on publication. Buys first North American serial rights. Submit material 45-60 days in advance. SASE. Reports in 3 weeks. Free sample copy and writer's guidelines.

Nonfiction: How-to (angling only); informational (how-to). "Articles and illustrations *must* be local, Washington angling or readily available within short distance for Washington anglers." Buys 38-52 mss/year. Query. Length: 1,000-1,500 words. Pays $50.

Photos and line art: Purchased with accompanying ms at $10 each extra. Captions required. Buys 5x7 color and b&w glossy prints or 35mm color transparencies with article. Model release required.

Fillers For '83-84: "Would like to see some pieces on striped bass fishing, angling north of Skagit River, and shad fishing in the southwestern part of Washington state."

WATERFOWLER'S WORLD, Waterfowl Publications, Ltd., Box 38306, Germantown TN 38138. (901)458-1333. Editor: Cindy Dixon. Bimonthly magazine covering duck and goose hunting for the serious hunter and experienced waterfowler, with an emphasis on improvement of skills. Circ. 25,000. Pays on publication. Buys first North American serial rights. SASE. Reports in 8 weeks. Sample copy $2.50; writer's guidelines for $1.

Nonfiction: General interest (where to hunt); how-to (market hunter's art; make regional decoys; do layout gunning); new product; and technical. Query. Length: 1,500 words. Pays $75-200.

Photos: Reviews 8x10 b&w prints and 35mm color transparencies. Pays $25/cover.

Columns/Departments: Fowlweather Gear (outdoor clothes and supplies).

WESTERN OUTDOORS, 3197-E Airport Loop, Costa Mesa CA 92626. (714)546-4370. Editor-in-Chief: Burt Twilegar. Emphasizes hunting, fishing, camping, boating for 11 Western states only, Baja California, Canada, Hawaii and Alaska. Monthly magazine; 88 pages. Circ. 150,000. Pays on publication. Buys one-time rights. Query (in writing). Submit seasonal material 4-6 months in advance. Photocopied submissions OK. Computer printout submissions are acceptable if double-spaced; prefers letter quality to dot matrix. SASE. Reports in 4-6 weeks. Sample copy $1.50; free writer's guidelines for SASE.

Nonfiction: Where-to (catch more fish, bag more game, improve equipment, etc.); informational; photo feature; and technical. "We do not accept fiction, poetry, cartoons." Buys 70 unsolicited mss/year. Query or send complete ms. Length: 1,000-2,000 words maximum. Pays $200-300.

Photos: Purchased with accompanying ms. Captions required. Uses 8x10 b&w glossy prints; prefers Kodachrome II 35mm slides. Offers no additional payment for photos accepted with accompanying ms. Pays $150 for covers.

Tips: "Provide a complete package of photos, map, trip facts and manuscript written according to our news feature format. Stick with where-to type articles. Both b&w and color photo selections make a sale more likely. We are beginning new section, 'Best In The West.' Write for details."

‡**WESTERN SALTWATER FISHERMAN**, Dyna Graphics, Inc., 6200 Yarrow Dr., Carlsbad CA 92008. (619)438-2511. Editor: Carl Calvert. Assistant Editor: Anita Spare. Monthly magazine covering saltwater fishing on the West Coast. Estab. 1981. Circ. 35,000. Pays on acceptance. Byline given. Buys all rights. Submit seasonal/holiday material 4 months in advance. SASE. Reports in 2 weeks. Sample copy $2; writer's guidelines for legal-size SAE and 1 first class stamp.

Nonfiction: General interest (fishing); how-to (fishing techniques); personal experience (angler's adventures); technical (tackle); travel (fishing in the West). Write for theme issue schedule. "We use material on techniques, species, hot spot locations, etc., for saltwater fishing on the West Coast, including South Pacific and Mexico. No informative and entertaining pieces on West Coast fishing, geared more toward the *experienced* angler than the beginner." Buys 120 mss/year. Query with or without published clips. Length: 1,500-4,000 words. Pays $75-300.

Photos: Photos are a *must* with all submitted articles. State availability of photos. Pays $15-150 (cover photos) for 2¼ color transparencies and 5x7 color prints. Captions, model release and identification of subjects required.

Columns/Departments: Shorelines (shore fishing); Angler's Adventure (experiences); Tackle Topics (equipment); Charter Trips & Tips. Buys 48 mss/year. Query with or without published clips. Length: 1,000-2,000 words. Pays $100-225.

Tips: "It helps to be 'fishing wise'. We're looking for something different in West Coast fishing—not standard fishing stories. Angler's Adventure is very open to freelancers—any battle with a large fish, rare occurrence while fishing, spectacular catches, etc. Quality says it all."

WESTERN SPORTSMAN, Box 737, Regina, Saskatchewan, Canada S4P 3A8. (306)352-8384. Editor: J.B. (Red) Wilkinson. 90% freelance written. For fishermen, hunters, campers and others interested in outdoor recreation. "Please note that our coverage area is Alberta and Saskatchewan." Quarterly magazine; 64-112 pages. Circ. 23,000. Rights purchased vary with author and material. May buy first North American serial rights or second serial (reprint) rights. Byline given. Pays on publication. Sample copy $3; free writer's guidelines. "We try to include as much information as possible on all subjects in each edition. Therefore, we usually publish fishing articles in our winter magazine along with a variety of winter stories. If material is dated, we would like to receive articles 2 months in advance of our publication date." Will consider photocopied submissions. Reports in 4 weeks. SAE and International Reply Coupons.

Nonfiction: "It is necessary that all articles can identify with our coverage area of Alberta and Saskatchewan. We are interested in mss from writers who have experienced an interesting fishing, hunting, camping or other outdoor experience. We also publish how-to and other informational pieces as long as they can relate to our coverage area. Our editors are experienced people who have spent many hours afield fishing, hunting, camping etc., and we simply cannot accept information which borders on the ridiculous. The record fish does not jump two feet out of the water with a brilliant sunset backdrop, two-pound test line, one-hour battle, a hole in the boat, tumbling waterfalls, all in the first paragraph. We are more interested in articles which tell about the average guy living on beans, guiding his own boat, stalking his game and generally doing his own thing in our part of Western Canada than a story describing a well-to-do outdoorsman traveling by motorhome, staying at an expensive lodge with guides doing everything for him except catching the fish, or shooting the big game animal. The articles that are submitted to us need to be prepared in a knowledgeable way and include more information than the actual fish catch or animal or bird kill. Discuss the terrain, the people involved on the trip, the water or weather conditions, the costs, the planning that went into the trip, the equipment and other data closely associated with the particular event in a factual manner. We like to see exciting writing, but leave out the gloss and nonsense. We're always looking for new writers. I would be very interested in hearing from writers who are experienced campers and snowmobilers." Buys 80 mss/year. Submit complete ms. Length: 1,500-3,000 words. Pays $40-225.

Photos: Photos purchased with ms with no additional payment. Also purchased without ms. Pays $10-15/5x7 or 8x10 b&w print; $100-150/35mm or larger transparency for front cover.

‡**WISCONSIN SPORTSMAN MAGAZINE**, Wisconsin Sportsman Inc., Box 2266, Oshkosh WI 54903. (414)233-1327. Editor: Tom Petrie. Bimonthly hunting and fishing magazine serving the active sportsman in Wisconsin. "Our readers require solid information on fishing and hunting in their home state." Circ. 75,000. Pays on acceptance. Byline given. Buys first North American serial rights. Submit seasonal/holiday material 6 months in advance. Simultaneous queries, and simultaneous, photocopied, and previously published submissions OK (very rarely). SASE. Reports in 3-6 weeks. Sample copy $1.

Nonfiction: Expose (Dept. of Natural Resources, poachers, etc.); historical/nostalgic (pertaining to Wisconsin); how-to (fishing and hunting); interview/profile; photo feature (wildlife of Wisconsin, etc.); technical (hunting and fishing). Buys 18-26 mss/year. Query. Length: 300-2,000 words. Pays $25-300.

Photos: Janet Wissink, photo editor. State availability of photos. Reviews transparencies and prints (8x10 glossy).

Columns/Departments: Afield in WI (little notes about what is happening in the Wisconsin outdoors). Buys 20-30 mss/year. Send complete ms. Length: 100-300 words. Pays $25-75.

Martial Arts

BLACK BELT, Rainbow Publications, Inc., 1813 Victory Place, Burbank CA 91504. (213)843-4444. Publisher: Michael James. Emphasizes martial arts for both practitioner and layman. Monthly magazine; 116 pages. Circ. 90,000. Pays on publication. Buys all rights. Submit seasonal/holiday material 6 months in advance. Photocopied submissions OK. Computer printout or disk submissions OK. SASE. Reports in 4 weeks. Free sample copy.

Nonfiction: Expose, how-to, informational, interview, new product, personal experience, profile, technical and travel. No biography, material on teachers or on new or Americanized styles. Buys 6 mss/issue. Query or send complete ms. Length: 1,200 words minimum. Pays $10-15/page of manuscript.

Photos: Very seldom purchase photos without accompanying mss. Captions required. Pays $4-7 for 5x7 or 8x10 b&w or color transparencies. Total purchase price for ms includes payment for photos. Model release required.

Fiction: Historical. Buys 1 ms/issue. Query. Pays $35-100.

Fillers: Pays $5 minimum.

Tips: "Our payment will rise, in step with the continuation of growth during the past year."

FIGHTING STARS, Rainbow Publications, 1813 Victory Place, Box 7728, Burbank CA 91510-7728. (213)843-4444. Executive Editor: Jim Coleman. Bimonthly magazine about the training and fighting techniques of the top martial artists in the world. Circ. 80,000. Pays on publication. Buys first North American serial rights. Submit seasonal martial 4 months in advance. Simultaneous and photocopied submissions OK. Computer printout submissions OK. SASE. Reports in 3-6 weeks. Free sample copy; free writer's guidelines with SASE.

Nonfiction and Photos: General interest or training articles (with standout martial artists); profiles (on championship or superior martial artists); how-to (featuring, again, top-quality martial artists). Buys 25 unsolicited mss/year. Send query or complete ms. Length: 1,200-2,000 words. Pays $75-200. State availability of photos. Most ms should be accompanied by photos. Reviews 5x7 and 8x10 b&w and color glossy prints. Can reproduce prints from negatives. Offers no additional payment for photos accepted with ms. Model releases required. Buys all rights.

Fiction: General interest (keeping with theme of fighting stars).

Tips: "We are specifically concerned with training, technical, and personality pieces involving the top martial artists in all realms, be it tournament karate, full-contact karate, judo, kendo, or any other martial arts style. We welcome articles on self-defense training, fitness, nutrition, or conditioning, as long as it deals with at least one standout martial artist. We have undergone a complete change in focus and are no longer interested in martial arts films."

INSIDE KUNG-FU, The Ultimate In Martial Arts Coverage!, Unique Publication, 7011 Sunset Blvd., Hollywood CA 90028. (213)467-1300. Editor: John Stewart. Monthly magazine covering martial arts for those with "traditional, modern, athletic and intellectual tastes. The magazine slants toward little-known martial arts, and little-known aspects of established martial arts." Circ. 100,000. Pays on publication. Byline given. Offers $35 kill fee. Buys first North American serial rights. Submit seasonal/holiday material 4 months in advance. Simultaneous queries, and simultaneous and photocopied submissions OK. SASE. Reports in 3 weeks on queries; 6 weeks on mss. Sample copy $1.75 with 9x12 SAE and 5 first class stamps; free writer's guidelines.

Nonfiction: Expose (topics relating to the martial arts); historical/nostalgic; how-to (primarily technical materials); humor; interview/profile; personal experience; photo feature; and technical. "Articles must be technically or historically accurate." No "sports coverage, first-person articles, or articles which constitute personal aggrandizement." Buys 100 mss/year. Query or send complete ms. Length: 10-15 pages, typewritten. Pays $75-100.

Photos: Send photos with accompanying ms. Reviews b&w contact sheets, b&w negatives and 8x10 b&w prints. "Photos are paid for with payment for ms." Captions and model release required. Buys one-time rights.

Fiction: Adventure, historical, humorous, mystery and suspense. "Fiction must be short (500-2,000 words) and relate to the martial arts." Buys 10 mss/year. Length: 500-2,000 words. Pays $75.

KARATE ILLUSTRATED, Rainbow Publications, Inc., 1813 Victory Place, Burbank CA 91504. (213)843-4444. Publisher: Michael James. Emphasizes karate and kung fu from the tournament standpoint and training techniques. Monthly magazine. Circ. 80,000. Pays on publication. Buys all rights. Submit seasonal/holiday material 6 months in advance. Simultaneous and photocopied submissions OK. SASE. Reports in 4-6 weeks. Free sample copy.

Nonfiction: Expose, historical, how-to, informational, interview, new product, personal experience, opinion, photo feature, profile, technical and travel. Buys 6 mss/issue. Query or submit complete ms. Pays $35-150.

Photos: Purchased with or without accompanying ms. Submit 5x7 or 8x10 b&w or color photos. Total purchase price for ms includes payment for photos.
Fiction: Historical. Query. Pays $35-150.
Fillers: Newsbreaks. Query. Pays $5.

KICK ILLUSTRATED, The Magazine for Today's Total Martial Artist, Unique Publications, 7011 Sunset Blvd., Hollywood CA 90028. (213)467-1300. Editor: Mark Shuper. Assistant Editor: Rhonda Wilson. Monthly magazine covering the martial arts. Circ. 120,000. Pays on acceptance for preferred writers. Byline given. Offers $25 kill fee. Buys first North American serial rights. Submit seasonal/holiday material 4 months in advance. Simultaneous queries, and simultaneous and photocopied submissions OK. SASE. Reports in 3 weeks on queries; in 6 weeks on mss. Sample copy for $1.50 and 9x12 SAE and 5 first class stamps; free writer's guidelines.
Nonfiction: Book excerpts; expose (of martial arts); historical/nostalgic; humor; interview/profile (with approval only); opinion; personal experience; photo feature; and technical (with approval only). *Kick Illustrated* deals specifically with all aspects of the gi disciplines of the martial arts, not with the Chinese arts or the lesser known esoteric practices which are slanted more toward *Kick's* sister publication, *Inside Kung Fu*. *Kick Illustrated* seeks a balance of the following in each issue: tradition, history, glamour, profiles and/or interviews (both by assignment only), technical, philosophical and think pieces. To date, most "how to" pieces have been done in-house. No "sports coverage, first person pieces, or articles constituting personal aggrandizement." Buys 70 mss/year. Query. Length: 1,000-2,500 words; "preferred—10-12 page ms." Pays $25-125.
Photos: Send photos with ms. Reviews b&w contact sheets, negatives and 8x10 prints. Captions and identification of subjects required. Buys one-time rights.
Tips: "Request a copy of the style guide, then follow its directions precisely. Or query with one or more ideas, and a style guide will be sent with the editor's reply."

Miscellaneous

‡**THE AMATEUR BOXER**, Taylor Publishing Corp., Box 249, Cobalt CT 06414. (203)342-4730. Editor: Bob Taylor. Bimonthly magazine for boxers, coaches and officials. Circ. 2,000. Pays on publication. Byline given. Buys first rights. Submit seasonal/holiday material 2 months in advance. Simultaneous queries, and simultaneous, photocopied and previously published submissions OK. SASE. Reports in 2 weeks on queries; 1 month on mss. Sample copy for 9x12 SAE and 54¢ postage.
Nonfiction: Interview/profile (of boxers, coaches, officials); results; tournament coverage; any stories connected with amateur boxing; photo feature; and technical. Buys 35 mss/year. Query. Length: 500-2,500 words. Pays $10-35.
Photos: State availability of photos. Pays $5-10 for b&w prints. Captions and identification of subjects required. Buys one-time rights.
Tips: "We're very receptive to new writers."

‡**AMERICAN COWBOY, The Magazine of Ranch & Rodeo**, (formerly *Hoofs and Horn*), Longhorn Publishing Co., Box 311, Walsenburg CO 81089. (303)738-1803. Publisher: Mark Day. Managing Editor: Shelley Searle. Bimonthly magazine covering all aspects of the cowboy's life for "cowboys and cowgirls who average 25 years of age and are general conservative, independent thinkers." Circ. 25,000. Pays on publication. Byline given. Buys first North American serial rights. Submit seasonal/holiday material 4 months in advance. Photocopied and previously published submissions OK. SASE. Reports in 3 weeks. Free sample copy and writer's guidelines.
Nonfiction: Expose (politics behind rodeo, ranching, western horse competition); general interest (with a western tie-in); historical/nostalgic (old-time cowboy heroes); how-to (tips from pros on road life, competition, fitness); interview/profile (of rodeo contestants as people, not just athletes); photo feature (on rodeo, rodeo contestants) and travel (to towns or areas with strong rodeo tie-in). Special issues include youth rodeo, women in rodeo, ranch cowboys, horse care and training, history of rodeo, commercial ranching. "Features/ photos of current or past rodeo contestants, particularly PRCA, WPRA, CPRA, INFR, NOTRA, NIRA, NHSRA, LBRA. Primary focus is on the personality of rodeo; statistics and records are secondary. Especially interested in rodeo-related topics like cowboys/cowgirls involved in motion pictures, entertainment, charities, off-beat rodeo news, foreign rodeo contestants. Also interested in stories on ranch cowboys and the side-ventures of rodeo contestants." Buys 15 mss/year. Query with clips or send complete ms. Length: 700-2,000 words. Pays $35-150.
Photos: State availability of photos. Pays $6-10 for 5x7 b&w prints; $50-75 for color photos or transparencies used on magazine cover. Identification of subjects required. Buys one-time rights.
Columns/Departments: Book or record reviews with western themes; pro, women's, Canadian and youth ro-

deo; guest editorials on the positives/negatives and current politics; tips on ranching. Buys 1-2 mss/year. Send complete ms. Length: 100-500 words. Pays $10-50.
Poetry: Light verse and traditional. "Nothing too corny. Our readers are down-to-earth but they are not without sophistication." Buys 1-2/year. Submit maximum 3 poems. Length: open.
Fillers: Newsbreaks. Buys 5/year. Length: 45-150 words. Pays $5-10.
Tips: "Make sure all pieces are written from an insider's point of view—our readers don't need an explanation of a cowboy's equipment; rather, they want a peek into his *specific, personal* lifestyle and thoughts. Writing profiles of students in rodeo is the easiest way to get accepted. We are usually desperate for youth news, especially from the NIRA, AJRA, NTHSRA, NLBRA, WSJRA, LSHSRA."

BALLS AND STRIKES, Amateur Softball Association, 2801 NE 50th St., Oklahoma City OK 73111. (405)424-5266. Editor: Bill Plummer III. Monthly tabloid covering amateur softball. Circ. 245,000. Pays on publication. Byline given. SASE. Reports in 3 weeks. Free sample copy.
Nonfiction: General interest, historical/nostalgic, interview/profile, technical. Query. Length: 2-3 pages. Pays $50-150.

THE BOSTON MARATHON, The Official Magazine of the B.A.A. Marathon, Boston Phoenix, Inc., 100 Massachusetts Ave., Boston MA 02115. (617)536-5390. Editor: Tory Carlson. Managing Editor: Cliff Garboden. Magazine published semiannually covering running/marathon sports. Circ. 135,000. Pays on publication. Byline given "sometimes." Buys first North American serial rights and one-time rights. Submit seasonal/holiday material 5 months in advance. Photocopied and previously published submissions OK. SASE. Reports in 1 month. Sample copy $2.50.
Nonfiction: General interest, how-to, humor, personal experience, photo feature, and technical. "No unsolicited manuscripts." Query with clips of published work. Length: 800-1,200 words. Pays negotiable fee.
Photos: State availability of photos. Pays negotiable fee for 35mm color transparencies. Caption, model release and identification of subjects required. Buys one-time rights and all rights.
Tips: This is the official race guide to the Boston Marathon. Articles, etc. must deal with the Boston Marathon.

FLORIDA RACQUET JOURNAL, Racquetball-Sports, Florida Racquet Journal, Inc., Suite 453, 843 Alderman Rd., Jacksonville FL 32211. (904)721-3660. Editor: Norm Blum. Managing Editor: Kathy Blum. Monthly tabloid covering racquetball in the state of Florida. Estab. 1981. Circ. 20,000. Pays on acceptance. Byline given. Offers $25 kill fee. Makes work-for-hire assignments. Submit seasonal/holiday material 3 months in advance. Simultaneous queries, and simultaneous and photocopied and previously published submissions OK. Computer printout and disk submissions OK. SASE. Reports in 2 weeks. Sample copy for $1 and SAE and 2 first class stamps.
Nonfiction: Book excerpts (from racquetball books); expose (of racquetball clubs); historical/nostalgic (Florida related); humor; new product; personal experience. "No how-to or instructional articles. No stories on pros unless there's a Florida angle." Query. Length: 400-900 words. Pays $10-40.
Columns/Departments: Kathy Blum, column/department editor. Horoscope, crossword puzzle, and health items—all for racquetball players. Buys 36 mss/year. Query. Length: 400-800 words. Pays $10-30.
Fiction: Humorous. Buys variable number mss/year. Query. Length: 500-1,500 words. Pays $10-30.
Poetry: Free verse. Buys variable number/year. Length: 30-60 lines. Pays $5-10.
Fillers: Clippings, jokes, gags, anecdotes, short humor, newsbreaks. Length: 30-50 words. Pays $1-5.
Tips: "We don't want your opinion—let the subject tell the story. If we like your first article we'll keep using you."

HANG GLIDING, United States Hang Gliding Association, Box 66306, Los Angeles CA 90066. (213)390-3065. Editor: Gilbert Dodgen. Monthly magazine; 72 pages. Circ. 12,000. Buys all rights. Phone queries OK. Submit seasonal/holiday material 6 weeks in advance. SASE. Reports in 2 months. Free sample copy.
Nonfiction: Technical articles on non-powered hang gliders, instruments, aerodynamics, expose, general interest, historical, how-to, humor, inspirational, interview, nostalgia, new product, experience, opinion, photo feature, profile and travel. Buys 1-2 mss/issue. Query with detailed description of subject, type of treatment, and clips of published work or send complete ms. Length: 500-2,000 words. Payment negotiable.
Photos: State availability of photos or send photos with ms. Pays variable rates for b&w negatives. Buys one-time rights. Captions and model releases required.
Fiction: Adventure, fantasy, experimental, historical, humorous, mystery and suspense. "We prefer short, to-the-point articles. We do not want anything other than articles about hang gliding." Query with clips of published work or send complete ms. Payment negotiable.
Poetry: "Anything that pertains to hang gliding." Submit in batches of 4 or 5. Length: 25 lines maximum. No pay.
Fillers: Clippings, jokes, gags, anecdotes, newsbreaks, short humor, comic strips, photos and letters to the editor.

‡**INDIANA RACQUET SPORTS**, Suite 303, 630 N. College Ave., Indianapolis IN 46204. (317)637-5683. Editor: Don Nixon. Monthly tabloid newspaper. Circ. 8,000. Pays on publication. Byline given. Submit seasonal/holiday material 2 months in advance. Simultaneous, photocopied and previously published submissions OK. SASE. Reports in 2 weeks. Sample copy for 9x12 SAE and 2 first class stamps; writer's guidelines for business-size SAE and 1 first class stamp.
Nonfiction: Health/nutrition; any racquet sport with Indiana connection—tennis, platform tennis, squash, table tennis, badminton, racquetball. Length: open. Pays $20.
Photos: Send photos with ms. Pays $5-10 for 5x7 b&w prints. Buys one-time rights.
Columns/Departments: Buys 12 mss/year. Query. Length: open. Pays $20.
Fillers: Buys 50/year. Length: 75 words maximum.

INSIDE RUNNING, 8100 Bellaire Blvd., No. 1318, Houston TX 77036. Editor/Publisher: Joanne Schmidt. Monthly tabloid covering "news and features of interest to joggers, racewalkers, and track and field athletes. We are a *Texas* magazine and our focus is on runners and running in the state." Circ. 10,000. Buys all rights. Pays on acceptance. No computer printout or disk submissions. SASE. Reports "within six weeks." Sample copy $1; writer's guidelines for SASE.
Nonfiction: "Strongly researched service pieces, profiles, race reports, and coverage of developments in the sport. We would like to discover correspondents and writers in Texas who run or have a familiarity with the sport and are looking for assignments in their area. Coverage outside Houston area badly needed. Running opportunities and scenery throughout state would be very helpful. We want very much to include capsule accounts of races from around the state for our Texas Round-up section. No personal 'How I Ran the Marathon' pieces, please." Recent article example: "A Man Behind the Scenes" (March 1982). Buys 24 unsolicited mss/year. Query, and explain your background and photographic experience. Include writing samples, if possible. Pays $20-75. "We may pay more if the writer has worked with us before and demonstrated a knowledge of our needs. We will negotiate with established writers as well."
Photos: "Strong photos earn extra payment." Pays $5 for b&w 5x7 prints "when inclusion of race results (top 10 and age group winners at least) and caption material are included."
Fiction: Pays $15-75, "depending on length, quality and originality."
Tips: "Report on races in your area or profile a local runner doing something different. Emphasize a Texas locale. We will work with writers and offer concrete, specific suggestions if the writer will follow through. Quotes and good b&w photos will give you the edge."

‡**INTERNATIONAL OLYMPIC LIFTER**, IOL Publications, 3916 Eagle Rock, Box 65855, Los Angeles CA 90065. (213)257-8762. Editor: Bob Hise. Managing Editor: Herb Glossbrenner. Bimonthly magazine covering the Olympic sport of weight lifting. Circ. 10,000. Pays on publication. Byline given. Offers $25 kill fee. Buys one-time rights or negotiable rights. Submit seasonal/holiday material 5 months in advance. Photocopied submissions OK. SASE. Reports in 6 weeks. Sample copy $1.50; writer's guidelines for SAE and 4 first class stamps.
Nonfiction: Training articles, contest reports, diet—all related to Olympic weight lifting. Buys 20-30 mss/year. Query. Length: 250-2,000 words. Pays $25-100.
Photos: Action (competition and training). State availability of photos. Pays $1-5 for 5x7 b&w prints. Identification of subjects required.
Columns/Departments: Buys 10 mss/year. Query. Length: 150-250 words. Pays $10-20.
Poetry: Keith Cain, poetry editor. Light verse, traditional—related to Olympic lifting. Buys 6-10 poems/year. Submit maximum 3 poems. Length: 12-24 lines. Pays $10-20.
Fillers: Gags, anecdotes related to weight lifting. Buys 6 mss/year. Length: 100-150 words. Pays $10-15.

THE MAINE SPORTSMAN, Box 365, Augusta ME 04330. Editor: Harry Vanderweide. 80-90% freelance written. Monthly tabloid. Circ. 18,000. Pays "shortly after publication." Byline given. Computer printout submissions OK; prefers letter quality to dot matrix. SASE. Reports in 2-4 weeks.
Nonfiction: "We publish only articles about Maine outdoor activities. Any well-written, researched, knowledgeable article about that subject area is likely to be accepted by us." Expose; how-to; general interest; interview; nostalgia; personal experience; opinion; profile; and technical. Buys 25-30 mss/issue. Submit complete ms. Length: 200-2,000 words. Pays $20-80.
Photos: "We can have illustrations drawn, but prefer 1-3 b&w photos." Submit photos with accompanying ms. Pays $5-50 for b&w print.

NATIONAL RACQUETBALL, Publication Management, Inc., 1800 Pickwick Ave., Glenview IL 60025. Publisher: Hugh Morgan. Associate Publisher/Editor: Chuck Leve. For racquetball players of all ages. Monthly magazine. Circ. 32,500. Pays on publication. Buys all rights. Byline given. Submit seasonal/holiday material 2-3 months in advance. SASE. Sample copy $2.
Nonfiction: How-to (play better racquetball or train for racquetball); interview (with players or others connected with racquetball business); opinion (usually used in letters but sometimes fullblown opinion features on is-

sues confronting the game); photo feature (on any subject mentioned); profile (short pieces with photos on women or men players interesting in other ways or on older players); health (as it relates to racquetball players—food, rest, eye protection, etc.); and fashion. No material on tournament results. Recently published articles include: "The Racquetball Cure," by Susan Nightingale (December 1981) and "How My Conditioning Went to the Dogs," by Steve Mondry (February 1982). Buys 4 mss/issue. Query with clips of published work. Length: 500-2,500 words. Pays $25-150.

Photos: State availability of photos or send photos with ms. Offers no additional payment for photos accompanying ms. Uses b&w prints or color transparencies. Buys one-time rights. Captions and model releases required.

Fiction: Adventure, humorous, mystery, romance, science fiction and suspense. "Whatever an inventive mind can do with racquetball." Buys 3 mss/year. Send complete ms. Pays $25-150.

Tips: "Break into *National Racquetball* by writing for monthly features—short pieces about racquetball players you know. We need more contributions from all over the country. Our object is national and international coverage of the sport of racquetball."

‡**PHYSIQUE, The Magazine of Bodybuilding & Fitness**, Physique, Inc., 400 E. Indian River Rd., Box 4655, Norfolk VA 23523. (804)545-7358/7365. Editor: Deborah Taylor. Managing Editor/Executive Publisher: Patricia Crabbe. Bimonthly magazine covering health and bodybuilding "for sophisticated and educated bodybuilders and fitness enthusiasts throughout the US and Canada. Its goal is to promote, report and comment on the people, events and ideas that affect the weight training environment using the finest writers and photographers in the nation." Estab. 1982. Circ. 40,000. Pays on publication. Byline given. Makes work-for-hire assignments. Submit seasonal/holiday material 2 months in advance. Simultaneous and photocopied submissions OK. SASE. Reports in 6 weeks. Sample copy for 9x12 SAE and 6 first class stamps; writer's guidelines for SAE and 1 first class stamp.

Nonfiction: Book excerpts, how-to, inspirational, interview/profile, new product, opinion, personal experience, photo feature, technical, travel. "We use detailed features on the latest information on training techniques and diet, as well as the people who are part of the bodybuilding world. We will read any and all submissions." Buys 30 mss/year. Query with published clips. Length: 800-1,500 words. Pays $75-150.

Photos: State availability of photos. Pays $10-15 for b&w; also buys color contact sheets. Captions and identification of subjects required.

Columns/Departments: Sports Injuries; Dermatology; Physique Spotlight; General Fitness "Potpourri"; Travel; Book Reviews. "Departments focus on results from national physique competitions, up-and-coming contests, nutrition, medical advice, health spas for the traveling athlete, past and rising stars, and lifestyles and important events in the fitness scene." Query with published clips. Length: 800-1,500 words. Pays $75-150.

PRORODEO SPORTS NEWS, 101 Prorodeo Dr., Colorado Springs CO 80919. (303)593-8840. Professional Rodeo Cowboys Association. Editor: Bill Crawford. Tabloid for rodeo contestants, contract members, committeemen and rodeo fans. Published every other Wednesday (1 issue in January; 1 in December). Circ. 30,000. Publishes the Annual Championship Edition, a 120-page slick paper magazine, following the National Finals Rodeo each December. Buys all rights. Clear and sharply printed computer printout submissions OK; will not read dot matrix. SASE. Reports in 2 weeks. Sample copy $1; free contributor's guidelines.

Nonfiction: News of professional rodeo, columns, interviews, features about PRCA contestants, rodeo animals, contract members and committeemen; appropriate photographs. Material must focus on a single issue; emphasis on professionalism. All material must be accurate and attributable. Avoid countrified dialect. All material must relate directly to PRCA rodeos. Recent article example: "Discarding the Myths," (February 10, 1982). "No poetry; unsolicited cartoons or other art; fiction based upon the old myths: rodeo cowboys are drunken, womanizing barroom brawlers; anything of any kind by someone who clearly does not know about professional rodeo as it exists today: a multi-million dollar, international professional sport which outdraws NFL pro football." Length: 18 column inches maximum, 800 words. Query or send complete ms.

Photos: Pays $10 for b&w 8x10 glossy prints. Rodeo action, wrecks, PRCA members involved in other activities, such as competing in other sports, receiving awards, working with disabled persons, etc. Should have complete information written on the front in the white borders. Action photos should give name and hometown of rider, score made on the ride, name or number and owner of the animal, date and place photo taken. Wreck photos should contain information as to outcome. Continuous need for mugshots, candid, unposed. Particular needs are rodeo action in all events. Pays $50 for color transparencies; $130 for color transparency used on front cover of annual.

Fiction: "Professionally written and plotted authentic rodeo fiction." Length: 40 column inches maximum, approximately 1800 words.

Tips: "We're one of the best potential markets in the business. We buy over 100 manuscripts a year, but we only buy from writers who have studied and learned to write the kind of material we publish. One year one knowledgeable and dependable freelancer got over 30 assignments, did them well and won the outstanding contributor buckle award: a gold and silver trophy buckle worth over $500 and was paid $1500+ as well."

RACING PIGEON PICTORIAL, The Racing Pigeon Publishing Co. Ltd., 19 Doughty St., London, England WCIN 2PT. Editor-in-Chief: Colin Osman. Emphasizes racing pigeons for "all ages and occupations; generally 'working class' backgrounds, both sexes." Monthly magazine. Circ. 13,000. Pays on publication. Buys first rights. Submit seasonal/holiday material 3 months in advance. Photocopied and previously published submissions OK. SAE and International Reply Coupons. Reports in 5 weeks. Sample copy $2; free writer's guidelines.

Nonfiction: Michael Shepherd, Articles Editor. How-to (methods of famous fanciers, treatment of diseases, building lofts, etc.); historical (histories of pigeon breeds); informational (practical information for pigeon fanciers); interview (with winning fanciers); and technical (where applicable to pigeons). "Don't bother, if you're not a specialist!" Buys 4 mss/issue. Submit complete ms. Length: 6,000 words minimum. Pays $30/page minimum.

Photos: Rick Osman, photo editor. Purchased with or without accompanying ms or on assignment. Captions required. Send 8x10 b&w glossy prints or 2¼x2¼ or 35mm color transparencies.

RACQUETBALL ILLUSTRATED, 7011 Sunset Blvd., Hollywood CA 90028. (213)467-1300. Editor: Rhonda Wilson. Monthly magazine about racquetball for an audience that is 18-65 years old. 55% male, upper middle class, members of private clubs. Circ. 100,000. Pays on publication. Buys first rights. Submit seasonal material 3 months in advance. Photocopied submissions OK. Reports in 1 month. Sample copy $1.50.

Nonfiction: Expose (politics of the racquetball industry); general interest; historical; how-to (turn a loser into a winner, psych out an opponent); humor; interview (of pros, unusual characters, celebrities); profile; travel; photo feature (kids in racquetball; racquetball in interesting cities). No first person or puff pieces. Instruction done only by touring pros or qualified instructors. "Find a player interesting on a national level and query. Also, we have annual special issues on shoes, racquets, balls, accessories, travel, health and instruction." No " 'first time on the court' stories." Buys 5 mss/issue. Query explaining subject matter in detail and giving background information on persons. Length: 1,500-3,000 words. Pays $100-300.

Photos: Editor: Ed Ikuta. State availability of photos. Pays $15-30 for 8x10 b&w prints. Reviews color transparencies. Offers $25-50 additional payment for photos accepted with ms. Captions preferred; model release required. Buys one-time rights.

Fiction: "We are interested in general fiction with racquetball as the theme." Buys 6 mss/year. Send complete ms. Length: 2,500 words minimum. Pays $100-300.

Fillers: Short humor. Pays $15 minimum.

Tips: "I want a variety of articles to appeal to beginners as well as advanced players, the general player as well as the hard-core player. I'm not afraid to run a controversial article. Almost sure sellers are medical or psychological stories for 'Rx for winning' column."

RACQUETS CANADA, 22A Cumberland Ave., Toronto, Ontario, Canada M4W 1J5. Editor: Tom Tebbutt. Magazine published 6 times/year covering tennis mainly but also other racquet sports. Circ. 75,000. Pays within 1 month of publication. Buys first rights. SAE and IRCs.

Nonfiction: Coverage of important international tennis, squash, or racquetball events. Articles on equipment, fitness and nutrition, tennis travel, and instruction. "Our primary focus is on tennis-related topics in Canada or of general interest to racquet sport players everywhere (i.e., not overtly American)." Query. Length: 1,000-4,000 words. Pays $150-1,000.

Photos: Coverage of important international tennis, squash, or racquetball events. Pays $50-200 for color transparency; $30-75 for b&w.

Tips: "We are concerned foremost with well-researched, entertaining writing. It's our feeling that you don't necessarily have to know the games of tennis or squash, inside and out to sell us an article. We are just as interested in off-beat sport-related pieces that other typical tennis magazines might reject, as we are in the usual athletic rhetoric. We appreciate controversial topics, for instance, or insightful profiles of people in any way related to the racquet sports. We feel our readership is generally intelligent and we wish to appeal to it on that level. No off-beat whimsy material."

THE RUNNER, 1 Park Ave., New York NY 10016. Editor-in-Chief: Marc Bloom. Emphasizes the world of running in the broadest scope with its main thrust in jogging, roadrunning and marathoning/fitness and health. Monthly magazine. Circ. 230,000. Pays on acceptance. Buys most first North American serial rights. Pays 20% kill fee. Byline given. Submit seasonal/holiday material 3 months in advance. SASE. Reports in 2-3 weeks. Free sample copy.

Nonfiction: Profiles, body science, historical, event coverage, training, lifestyle, sports medicine, phenomena and humor. Buys 5-6 mss/issue. Query with clips of published work. Length: 1,500 words and up. Pays $250 and up, usually $500 or so for 3,000 words.

Photos: State availability of photos. Pay is negotiable for b&w contact sheets and 35mm color transparencies. Buys one-time rights. Captions required.

Columns/Departments: Reviews (books, film, etc.); people; statistical listings; humor; food; medicine; and training. Regular columnists used. Buys 3-4/issue. Length: 900-1,200 words. Pays $150 and up.

Warmups: Short news items and whimsical items. Length: 100-400 words. Pays $50.
Fiction: Senior Editor: Frederika Randall. Theme should be running. Buys 2 mss/year. Send complete ms. Length: 1,500 words minimum. Price negotiable.

RUNNING TIMES, Running Times, Inc., Suite 20, 14416 Jefferson Davis Highway, Woodbridge VA 22191. (703)643-1646. Editor: Edward Ayres. Emphasizes running, jogging, holistic health and fitness. Monthly magazine; 72 pages. Circ. 100,000. Pays on publication. Buys all rights. Byline given. Submit seasonal/holiday material 3 months in advance. Simultaneous and photocopied submissions OK. SASE. Reports in 1 month. Sample copy $2.
Nonfiction: How-to (training techniques, racing techniques, self-treatment of injuries, etc.); humor; interview; photo feature; profile; and technical (written for an educated readership). "We do not want opinions or ideas which are not backed up by solid research." Buys 1-2 mss/issue. Query or send complete ms. Length: 500-2,500 words. Pays $25-400.
Photos: State availability of photos. Pays $15-40 for 5x7 or 8x10 b&w glossy prints; $30-250 for color transparencies. Captions preferred.
Fiction: Adventure, erotica, fantasy and humorous. "Subjects must involve runners or running." Buys 10 mss/year. Send complete ms or clips of published work. Length: 700-2,500 words. Pays $50-200.

SIGNPOST MAGAZINE, 16812 36th Ave. W., Lynnwood WA 98036. Publisher: Louise B. Marshall. Editor: Ann L. Marshall. About hiking, backpacking and similar trail-related activities, mostly from a Pacific Northwest viewpoint. Monthly. Will consider any rights offered by author. Buys 6 mss/year. Pays on publication. Sample copy $1. Will consider photocopied submissions. Reports in 3 weeks. Query or submit complete ms. No computer printout or disk submissions. SASE.
Nonfiction and Photos: "Most material is donated by subscribers or is staff-written. Payment for purchased material is low, but a good way to break into print or spread a particular point of view."
Tips: "We cover only *self-propelled* outdoor sports; won't consider mss about trail bikes, snowmobiles, power-er boats."

SKYDIVING, Box 189, Deltona FL 32728. (904)736-9779. Editor: Michael Truffer. Monthly tabloid featuring skydiving for sport parachutists, worldwide dealers and equipment manufacturers. Circ. 6,000. Average issue includes 3 feature articles and 3 columns of technical information. Pays on publication. Byline given. Buys one-time rights. Simultaneous, photocopied and previously published submissions OK, if so indicated. SASE. Reports in 1 month. Sample copy $2; free writer's guidelines with SASE.
Nonfiction: "Send us news and information on equipment, techniques, events and outstanding personalities who skydive. We want articles written by people who have a solid knowledge of parachuting." No personal experience or human-interest articles. Query. Length: 500-1,000 words. Pays $25-100.
Photos: State availability of photos. Reviews 5x7 and larger b&w glossy prints. Offers no additional payment for photos accepted with ms. Captions required.
Fillers: Newsbreaks. Length: 100-200 words. Pays $25 minimum.

STRENGTH & HEALTH MAGAZINE, S&H Publishing Co., Inc., Box 1707, York PA 17405. (717)767-6481. Editor-in-Chief: Bob Hoffman. Managing Editor: John Grimek. 35% freelance written. Emphasizes Olympic weightlifting and weight training. Bimonthly magazine; 74 pages. Circ. 100,000. Submit seasonal/holiday material 4-5 months in advance. SASE.
Nonfiction: Robert Dennis, Articles Editor. How-to (physical fitness routines); interview (sports figures); and profile. Buys 15 mss/year. Submit complete ms. Length: 1,500-3,000 words. Pays $50-100.
Photos: Ms. Sallie Sload, Photo Editor. Purchased with accompanying ms. Captions required. Query. Pays $5-10 for b&w glossy or matte finish; $50-100 for 2¼x2¼ color transparencies (for cover). Model release preferred.
Columns/Departments: Jan Dellinger, Department Editor. Barbells on Campus (weight training program of college or university; captioned photos required, at least one photo of prominent building or feature of campus); In the Spotlight (profile of a championship-caliber weightlifter, training photos as well as casual, family and "other sports" shots). Buys 1-2/issue. Submit complete ms. Length: 1,500-2,500 words. Pays $50-100.

THE WORLD OF RODEO AND WESTERN HERITAGE, Rodeo Construction Agency, Box 1111, Billings MT 59103. Editor-in-Chief: Jo Smith. "We reach all these facets of rodeo: Professional, all-girls rodeo, little britches, college, regional, high school rodeo, Canadian rodeo, and oldtimers rodeo. Audience age: 9-90." 12 times/year. Tabloid; 40-80 pages. Readership 50,000. Buys one-time rights. Byline given. Phone queries OK. No computer printout or disk submissions. SASE. Free sample copy and writer's guidelines.
Nonfiction: Expose (personality); historical (oldtimers and famous rodeo animals); humor (pertaining to cowboys or Western history); informational (reports on current rodeo events); interview (with controversy or strong message); photo feature (emphasis on quality rodeo action and/or drama); profile (short in-depth sketch

of person or persons); Western heritage (stories of the West and Western way of life). Query or submit complete ms. Length: 500-2,000 words. Pays $15-150.

Photos: B&w purchased with or without mss. Captions required. Send prints. Pays $5/8x10 b&w glossy with good contrast; $35-50/2¼x2¼, 35mm or 8x10 matte or glossy with good color balance.

Skiing and Snow Sports

POWDER MAGAZINE, Box 1028, Dana Point CA 92629. (714)496-5922. Executive Publisher: Steve Pezman. Creative Editor: Neil Stebbins. Managing Editor: Pat Cochran. 7/year, including two special issues: preseason equipment review and photo annual. Circ. 100,000. Rights purchased vary with author and material. May buy all rights, but will reassign rights to author after publication; or first North American serial rights; or simultaneous rights. Buys 10-15 unsolicited mss/year. Pays on publication. Sample copy for $1. Submit material late spring, early summer for publication the following season. Reports on material accepted for publication in 2 months. Phone query preferred.

Nonfiction and Photos: "We want material by or about people who reach out for the limits of the ski experience. Avoid classical ski-teaching technique problems, specific equipment tests, travel guides, or beginner-oriented articles. We try to emphasize the quality of the ski experience rather than its mechanics, logistics, or purely commercial aspects." Length: 500-2,500 words. Pays approximately 10¢/word. *Top Quality* b&w and color transparencies purchased with or without mss or on assignment. Pays approximately $25-75 b&w, full or partial page, $40-150 for color, full or partial page; $300 cover.

Fiction: Humorous, mainstream adventure and experimental fiction. Must relate to subject matter. Length: open. Pays 7-10¢/word.

Tips: "Be more creative in approaches to articles that will always interest our readers but have been done before. Review our magazine thoroughly . . . back at least 6 issues . . . before querying."

SKATING, United States Figure Skating Association, 20 First St., Colorado Springs CO 80906. (303)635-5200. Editor-in-Chief: Ian A. Anderson. Monthly magazine; 64 pages. Circ. 31,000. Pays on publication. Buys all rights. Byline given. Phone queries OK. Submit seasonal/holiday material 3 months in advance. Photocopied and previously published submissions OK. SASE. Reports in 1 month. Writer's guidelines for SASE.

Nonfiction: Historical; how-to (photograph skaters, training, exercise); humor; informational; interview; new product; personal experience; personal opinion; photo feature; profile (background and interests of national-caliber amateur skaters); technical; and competition reports. Buys 4 mss/issue. Query or send complete ms. Length: 500-1,000 words. Pays $50.

Photos: Ian Anderson, editor. Photos purchased with or without accompanying ms. Pays $15 for 8x10 or 5x7 b&w glossy prints and $35 for color transparencies. Query.

Columns/Departments: European Letter (skating news from Europe); Ice Abroad (competition results and report from outside the US); Book Reviews; People; Club News (what individual clubs are doing); and Music column (what's new and used for music for skating). Buys 4 mss/issue. Query or send complete ms. Length: 100-500 words. Pays $35. Open to suggestions for new columns/departments.

Fillers: Newsbreaks, puzzles (skating-related) and short humor. Buys 2 fillers/issue. Query. Length: 50-250 words. Pays $20.

SKI, 380 Madison Ave., New York NY 10017. (212)687-3000. Editor: Dick Needham. 15% freelance written. 8 times/year, September through April. Buys first-time rights in most cases. Pays 50% kill fee. Byline given "except when report is incorporated in 'Ski Life' department." Pays on publication. Reports in 1 month. SASE.

Nonfiction: Prefers articles of general interest to skiers, travel, adventure, how-to, budget savers, unusual people, places or events that reader can identify with. Must be authoritative, knowledgeably written, in easy, informative language and have a professional flair. Cater to middle to upper income bracket readers who are college graduates, wide travelers. No fiction or poetry. Length: 1,500-2,000 words. Pays $150-300.

Photos: Buys photos submitted with manuscripts and with captions only. Good action shots (slides only) in color for covers; pays minimum $300. B&w photos, pays $40 each; minimum $150 for photo stories. (Query on these.) Color slides. Pays $50 each; $200/page.

Tips: "Another possibility is our monthly column, Ski People, which runs 300-400-word items on unusual people who ski and have made some unique contribution to the sport. We want to see outline of how author proposes to develop story for *Ski*, sample opening page or paragraph; include previous clippings or published writing samples. Humor is welcome."

SKI RACING MAGAZINE, International Journal of Skiing, Ski Racing Inc., Box 70, Fair Haven VT 05743. (802)468-5666. Editor: Don A. Metivier. Tabloid covering major ski competition events worldwide for the serious skier and ski industry person. Published 22 times during the ski (September-April) season. Circ.

30,000. No computer printout or disk submissions. Pays on publication. Byline given. Buys one-time rights. Reports "at once, because of the time frame of events we cover." Free sample copy.

Nonfiction: "We cover only news and interviews with those making it. Prefers not to get opinion from writers." Buys 200 mss/year. Query with clips of published work. Length: "depends on the story; from minimum of a paragraph and list of top 5 finishers to maximum of 500-750 words." Pays $1/inch for news stories; $50-100 for longer assignments; negotiates fees prior to assignment on interviews.

Photos: Pays $10-25 for photos; $50 for covers, action photos, and candids for picture pages and interviews.

SKIING MAGAZINE, Ziff-Davis Publishing Co., 1 Park Ave., New York NY 10016. Editor-in-Chief: Alfred H. Greenberg. Executive Editor: Dinah B. Witchel. Published 7 times/year (September-March). Magazine; 175 pages. Circ. 430,000. Pays on acceptance. Buys first rights. Byline given. Submit seasonal/holiday material 4 months in advance. SASE. Sample copy $2.

Nonfiction: "This magazine is in the market for any material of interest to skiers. Material must appeal to and please the confirmed skier. Much of the copy is staff-prepared, but many freelance features are purchased provided the writing is fast-paced, concise and knowledgeable." Buys 10 unsolicited mss/year. Submit complete ms. Length: 1,500-3,000 words.

Photos: Rick Fiala, Art Director. Purchased with or without accompanying ms or on assignment. Send contact sheet or transparencies. Pays $125/full page for 8x10 b&w glossy or matte photos; $300 minimum/full page for 35mm transparencies, pro-rated. Model release required.

SNOW GOER, The Webb Co., 1999 Shephard Rd., St. Paul MN 55116. (612)690-7200. Editor: Jerry Bassett. Managing Editor: Bill Monn. Magazine published 4 times seasonally for snowmobilers. Circ. 2,200,000. Buys all rights. Byline given. Pays on acceptance. Submit special issue material 1 year in advance. Reports in 2 months. Query. "High-quality" computer printout submissions OK; prefers letter quality to dot matrix. SASE.

Nonfiction: General interest; historical/nostalgic; how-to (mechanical); interview/profile; personal experience; photo feature; technical; and travel. Features on snowmobiling with strong secondary story angle, such as ice fishing, mountain climbing, snow camping, conservation, rescue. Also uses features relating to man out-of-doors in winter. " 'Me and Joe' articles have to be unique for this audience." Buys 1 unsolicited mss/issue. Length: 1,000-1,500 words. Pays $100-300.

Photos: State availability of photos; send photos with ms. Pays $5-25 for 5x7 or 8x10 b&w glossy contact sheets; $15-50 for 35mm color transparencies. Offers no additional payment for photos with accompanying ms. Captions, model releases, and identification of subjects required. Buys all rights.

SNOWMOBILE CANADA, CRV Publications Canada, Ltd., Suite 221, 3414 Park Ave., Montreal, Quebec, Canada H2X 2H5. (514)282-0191. Editor: Reg Fife. Snowmobiling magazine published in September, October and November "to satisfy the needs of Canada's snowmobilers from coast to coast." Circ. 60,000. Pays on publication. Byline given. Buys first rights. Submit seasonal/holiday material "by July for fall public action." Simultaneous queries OK. Computer printout submissions OK. Reports in 1 month on queries; 2 months on mss. Free sample copy.

Nonfiction: Personal experience (on snowmobiling in Canada); photo feature (nature in winter); technical (new snowmobile developments); travel (snowmobile type). "We look for articles on nature as it relates to snowmobile use; trail systems in Canada; wilderness tips; the racing scene; ice fishing using snowmobiles, maintenance tips and new model designs." Recent article example: "Snowmobiles and Deer Yards." Buys 12 mss/year. Query or send complete ms. Length: 800-2,000 words. Pays $75-150.

Photos: Captions required. Buys one-time rights.

SNOWMOBILE MAGAZINE, Winter Sports Publications, Inc., 715 S. Florida Ave., Minneapolis MN 55426, (612)545-2662. Editor: C.J. Ramstad. Managing Editor: Dick Hendricks. Magazine published 4 times/year covering snowmobiling for snowmobilers throughout North America. Circ. 500,000. Pays on publication. Byline given. Buys all rights, but "author may request return." Simultaneous and previously published submissions OK ("if publication and date are indicated"). SASE. Reports in 1 month on mss. Free sample copy and writer's guidelines.

Nonfiction: "We want articles on travel, adventure, technology, personality and history involving snowmobiling or winter recreation." Humor; interview/profile; first person. No material on accidents. Buys 2-3 mss/year. Send complete ms. Length: 1,800-3,000 words. Pays $175-350.

Photos: Send photos with or without accompanying ms. Reviews 35mm color transparencies.

Columns/Departments: ETC. (short items pertaining to snowmobiling). Send complete ms. Length: 200-500 words. Pays $25-50 with b&w photo.

SNOWMOBILE WEST, 520 Park Ave., Box 981, Idaho Falls ID 83401. Editor: Steve James. For recreational snowmobile riders and owners of all ages. Magazine; 48 pages. Publishes six issues each winter. Circ. 125,000. Buys first North American serial rights. Pays kill fee if previously negotiated at time of assignment.

Byline given on substantive articles of two pages or more. Buys 10 mss/year. Pays on publication. Free sample copy and writer's guidelines. Reports in 2 months. Articles for one season are generally photographed and written the previous season. Query. SASE.

Nonfiction and Photos: Articles about snowtrail riding in the Western US; issues affecting snowmobilers; and maps of trail areas with good color photos and b&w. Pays 3¢/word; $5/b&w; $10/color. B&w should be 5x7 or 8x10 glossy print; color should be 35mm transparencies or larger, furnished with mss. With a story of 1,000 words, typically a selection of 5 b&w and 5 color photos should accompany. Longer stories in proportion. Length: 500-2,000 words.

Soccer

SOCCER AMERICA, Box 23704, Oakland CA 94623. (415)549-1414. Editor-in-Chief: Ms. Lynn Berling. For a wide range of soccer enthusiasts. Weekly tabloid. Circ. 10,000. Pays on publication. Buys all rights. Byline given. Submit seasonal/holiday material 14 days in advance. SASE. Reports in 1 month. Sample copy and writer's guidelines, $1.

Nonfiction: Expose (why a pro franchise isn't working right, etc.); historical; how-to; informational (news features); inspirational; interview; photo feature; profile; and technical. "No 'Why I Like Soccer' articles in 1000 words or less. It's been done!" Buys 1-2 mss/issue. Query. Length: 200-1,500 words. Pays 50¢/inch minimum.

Photos: Photos purchased with or without accompanying ms or on assignment. Captions required. Pays $12 for 5x7 or larger b&w glossy prints. Query.

SOCCER MAGAZINE, (formerly *B.C. Soccer Magazine*), Holden-Lea Soccer Publications, Ltd., 17231 57A Ave., Surrey, British Columbia, Canada V3S 5A8. (604)576-1611. Editor: David Leach. Magazine published 6 times/year covering "all aspects of amateur and professional soccer." Circ. 12,000. Pays on publication. Byline given. Buys one-time rights. Submit seasonal/holiday material 1 month in advance. Simultaneous, photocopied and previously published submissions OK. SASE. Sample copy $1.75.

Nonfiction: Short book excerpts (soccer); general interest (soccer); historical/nostalgic (British Columbian soccer); humor (shorter pieces relating to soccer); interview/profile (of soccer pro with British Columbian background); and photo feature (of traveling British Columbia teams). "Traveling teams from British Columbia, general soccer articles, e.g., the soccer mother, life of a junior coach. We need B.C. player profiles and humorous articles. We are expanding fast!" No articles on American soccer (USA). Buys 25 mss/year. Send complete ms. Length: 250-5,000 words. Pays 4-10¢/published word.

Photos: Send photos with ms. Pays $5 Canadian for b&w prints. Caption, model release, and identification of subjects required. Buys one-time rights.

Fillers: Anecdotes and short humor. "We need soccer-biased material." Buys 50/year. Length: 25-100 words. Pays 5¢/word.

Tips: "Magazine is now national with a Western Canadian bias."

Tennis

TENNIS, 495 Westport Ave., Box 5350, Norwalk CT 06856. Publisher: Francis X. Dealy Jr. Editor: Shepherd Campbell. For persons who play tennis and want to play it better. Monthly magazine. Circ. 460,000. Buys all rights. Byline given. Pays on publication. SASE.

Nonfiction and Photos: Emphasis on instructional and reader service articles, but also seeks lively, well-researched features on personalities and other aspects of the game, as well as humor. Query. Length varies. Pays $200 minimum/article, considerably more for major features. Pays $50-150/8x10 b&w glossies; $75-350/color transparencies.

TENNIS EVERYONE, 5724 W. Diversey, Chicago IL 60639. (312)745-9400. Editor: Raymond Mitchell. Monthly tabloid for Chicago and Illinois tennis players. Circ. 25,000. Pays on publication. Buys one-time rights. Phone queries OK. Simultaneous, photocopied and previously published submissions OK. SASE. Reports in 1 week. Free sample copy.

Nonfiction: How-to; interview; profile (of celebrities and professionals); new product; photo feature; technical; and events. Send complete ms. Length: 400-600 words. Pays $20 minimum.

Photos: Reviews 8x10 b&w glossy prints. Offers no additional payment for photos accepted with ms. Captions required.

Columns/Departments: Instructional, travel, fashion and exercise. Length: 400-600 words. Pays $25-$75.

TENNIS USA, Contact CBS Consumer Publishing, a Division of CBS Inc., 1515 Broadway, New York NY 10036. Publisher: Charles M. Stentiford.

TENNIS WEEK, Tennis News, Inc., 1107 Broadway, New York NY 10010. (212)741-2323. Publisher and Founder: Eugene L. Scott. Editor: Linda Pentz. Weekly newspaper; 20-32 pages. Circ. 40,000. Byline given. Pays on acceptance. Photocopied submissions OK. SASE. Reports in 2 weeks. Sample copy 50¢.
Nonfiction: "Articles should concentrate on players' lives off the court." Buys 100 mss/year. Send complete ms. Pays $25-100.
Photos: Send photos with ms. Pays $10/8x10 b&w glossy print.

THE TOURNAMENT TIMES, Western Tennis Publications, a div. of ITA, Box 4577, Santa Fe NM 87502. (505)988-7252. Editor/Publisher: Bob Raedisch. Newspaper issuing 12 main volumes with 2-4 supplements annually, covering "tennis tournaments, etc. for tennis pros and players of all levels. We mainly focus on local, national and international tournaments." Circ. varies with issues. Pays on publication. Copyright pending. Makes work-for-hire assignments "but not always." Submit seasonal/holiday material 3 months in advance. Simultaneous, photocopied, and previously published work OK. SASE. Reports in 1 month. Sample copy 50¢.
Nonfiction: Book excerpts, general interest (on players, etc.); historical/nostalgic (on tennis in the past); how-to (improve tennis strokes and play in general); humor (tennis jokes); interview/profile (of players, officials, etc.); new product (tennis items); and travel (tennis resorts). Special issues include travel, camps, equipment (all tennis) plus an explanation of tennis world structure. Buys 16 mss/year. Query. Length: 200-1,000 maximum, 50 words minimum for tennis tips. Pays $10 minimum.
Photos: State availability of photos. Pays $2 or more for b&w contact sheets. Captions preferred; model release required. Buys all rights.
Columns/Departments: "We're open to suggestions for new columns or departments." Query. Pays $10 minimum.
Tips: "We welcome coverage of tournaments and stories on national tennis happenings and players."

WORLD TENNIS MAGAZINE, CBS Consumer Publishing, a Division of CBS Inc., 1515 Broadway, New York NY 10036. Publisher: Bruce W. Gray.

Water Sports

DIVER, Seagraphic Publications, Ltd., Suite 210, 1807 Maritime Mews, Granville Island, Vancouver, British Columbia, Canada V6H 3W7. (604)681-3166. Publisher: Peter Vassilopoulos. Editor: Neil McDaniel. 60% freelance written. Emphasizes scuba diving, ocean science and technology (commercial and military diving) for a well-educated, outdoor-oriented readership. Published 8 times/year. Magazine; 56-72 pages. Circ. 25,000. Payment "follows publication." Buys first North American serial rights. Byline given. Query (by mail only). Submit seasonal/holiday material 3 months in advance of issue date. SAE and International Reply Coupons. Reports in 6 weeks.
Nonfiction: How-to (underwater activities such as photography, etc.); general interest (underwater oriented); humor; historical (shipwrecks, treasure artifacts, archeological); interview (underwater personalities in all spheres—military, sports, scientific or commercial); personal experience (related to diving); photo feature (marine life); technical (related to oceanography, commercial/military diving, etc.); and travel (dive resorts). No subjective product reports. Buys 40 mss/year. Submit complete ms. Length: 800-2,000 words. Pays $2.50/column inch.
Photos: "Features are mostly those describing dive sites, experiences, etc. Photo features are reserved more as specials, while almost all articles must be well illustrated with b&w prints supplemented by color transparencies." Submit photo material with accompanying ms. Pays $7 minimum for 5x7 or 8x10 glossy b&w prints; $15 minimum for 35mm color transparencies. Captions and model releases required. Buys one-time rights.
Columns/Departments: Book reviews. Submit complete ms. Length: 200 words maximum. Pays to $25.
Fillers: Anecdotes, newsbreaks and short humor. Buys 8-10/year. Length: 50-150 words. Pays $10.

‡**THE DIVER**, Taylor Publishing Corp., Box 249, Cobalt CT 06414. (203)342-4730. Editor: Bob Taylor. Bimonthly magazine on springboard and platform diving. Circ. 1,500. Pays on publication. Byline given. Buys first rights. Submit seasonal/holiday material 2 months in advance. SASE. Reports in 2 weeks on queries; 1 month on mss. Sample copy for 9x12 SAE and 54¢ postage.
Nonfiction: Humor; interview/profile (of divers, coaches, officials); personal experience; photo feature; technical. Buys 50 mss/year. Query. Length: 500-2,500 words. Pays $10-35.
Photos: State availability of photos. Pays $5-10 for b&w prints. Captions and identification of subjects required. Buys one-time rights.

‡**MICHIGAN DIVER**, Box 88011, Grand Rapids MI 49508. (616)455-7568. Editor: Richard Posthuma. Bimonthly magazine promoting scuba diving as a good recreational activity. Estab. 1982. Circ. 1,000. Pays on

acceptance. Byline given. Buys one-time rights, "plus subsequent reprint rights." Submit seasonal/holiday material 2 months in advance. Simultaneous queries, and simultaneous, photocopied and previously published submissions OK. SASE. Reports in 2 weeks on queries; 1 month on mss. Sample copy $1.75; free writer's guidelines.

Nonfiction: Historical/nostalgic; how-to; humor; interview/profile; personal experience; photo feature; technical; travel. "All of these should concentrate on scuba diving instruction, equipment, services, dive sites, resorts, marine live, shipwreck history, etc.—either international or preferably in the Great Lakes." Buys 35 mss/year. Send complete ms. Length: 250-1,500 words. Pays $10-75.

Photos: Send photos with ms. Pays $2-25 for b&w and color contact sheet, negatives, transparencies and prints. Captions and identification of subjects required. Buys one-time rights and subsequent one-time reprint rights with second payment.

Columns/Departments: Dive Travel; Shipwreck History; Diving Safety/Medicine; Marine Life. Buys 10 mss/year. Send complete ms. Length: 250-1,500 words. Pays $15-75.

Fillers: Clippings, jokes, gags, anecdotes, short humor, newsbreaks, cartoons, puzzles, quizzes. Buys 20/year. Length: varies. Pays $10-50.

Tips: "Although we are anxious to receive any articles related to scuba diving, the more related to the Great Lakes the better. Additional topics could include commercial diving, nautical subjects, underwater photography, environmental subjects, underwater research, dive charters and related areas."

‡**OCEAN REALM MAGAZINE, The International Journal of Sport Diving**, Ocean Realm Publishing, 2333 Brickell Ave., Miami FL 33129. (305)945-7403. Editor: Richard H. Stewart. Senior Editor: Patricia Reilly. Quarterly magazine covering all aspects of sport diving, and the ocean environment. Circ. 50,000. Pays on publication. Byline given. Buys one-time rights. Submit seasonal/holiday material 6 months in advance. Simultaneous queries OK. Computer printout or disk submissions OK; prefers letter quality to dot matrix. SASE. Reports in 1 month on queries; 6 weeks on mss. Sample copy for 9x12 SAE; free writer's guidelines.

Nonfiction: Book excerpts, expose, general interest, historical/nostalgic, how-to, humor, interview/profile, new product, opinion, personal experience, photo feature, technical, travel. Prefers not to see sailing, boating, and marine maintenance material. Buys 48 mss/year. Send complete ms. Length: 1,500-2,500 words. Pays $200-300.

Photos: State availability of "clear, sharp, colorful photos." Pays $20-50 for 35mm color transparencies; $20-50 for 8x10 b&w prints. Captions, model release and identification of subjects required.

‡**SAILBOARD NEWS, The International Journal of Boardsailing**, Sports Ink Magazines, Inc., Box 159, Fair Haven VT 05743. (802)265-8153. Editor: Mark Gabriel. Monthly boardsailing tabloid. Circ. 19,000. Pays 30 days after publication. Byline given. Buys one-time rights. Submit seasonal/holiday material 3 weeks in advance. Simultaneous queries OK. SASE. Reports in 3 weeks. Free sample copy and writer's guidelines.

Nonfiction: Book excerpts, expose, general interest, historical/nostalgic, how-to, humor, inspirational, interview/profile, new product, opinion, photo feature, technical, travel. Buys 50 mss/year. Send complete ms. Length: 750 words minimum. Pays $50-200.

Photos: Send photos with ms. Reviews b&w negatives and 8x10 prints. Identification of subjects required.

Columns/Departments: Buys 12 mss/year. Query with published clips or send complete ms.

‡**SAILORS' GAZETTE**, Coastal Communicators of St. Petersburg, Inc., Suite 107, 6727 1st Ave. S., St. Petersburg FL 33707. (813)344-1241. Editor: John Weber. Monthly tabloid covering sailing in the southeastern states for sailboat owners. Circ. 10,000. Pays on publication. Byline given. Offers 50% kill fee. Buys one-time rights. Submit seasonal/holiday material 3 months in advance. SASE. Reports in 2 weeks on queries; 3 weeks on mss. Sample copy $2; free writer's guidelines.

Nonfiction: Historical/nostalgic (sailboats with direct ties to SE states); interview/profile (with sailboat owners); personal experience (sailboat cruising in SE); photo feature (b&w on sailing or waterfront scenes in SE states); technical (sailboat maintenance, not general boat maintenance). No poetry; articles about sailboats with no connection to Southeastern states; articles about first-time sailors. Buys 125 mss/year. Query with published clips. Length: 500-2,000 words. Pays $50-250.

Photos: State availability of photos. Pays $10-25 for high contrast 8x10 b&w prints. Captions and identification of subjects required. Buys one-time rights.

Tips: "The manuscripts that we turn down are usually too general and far removed from the Southeastern themes. We're open to where-to and how-to, as it pertains to the Southeast; also interviews with cruising and racing sailors."

SCUBA TIMES, The Active Diver's Magazine, MWP Publishing Co., Box 6268, Pensacola FL 32503. (904)478-5288. Managing Editor: Meta Leckband. Publisher: M. Wallace Poole. Bimonthly magazine covering skin diving. "Our reader is the young, reasonably affluent skin diver looking for a more exciting approach to diving than he could find in the other diving magazines." Circ. 30,000 copies. Pays after publication. Byline given. Buys all rights. Simultaneous queries OK. SASE. Reports in 1 month. Sample copy $3. Writer's guidelines for business size SAE and 1 first class stamp.

Nonfiction: General interest; how-to; interview/profile ("Of 'name' people in the sport, especially if they're currently doing something radical"); new product (how to more effectively use them); personal experience (good underwater photography pieces); and travel (pertaining to diving). Especially want illustrated articles on avant-garde diving and diving travel, such as nude diving, singles only dive clubs, deep diving, etc. No articles without a specific theme or no poetry. Buys 25 mss/year. Query with clips of published work. Length: 500-1,200 words. Pays $50-250.

Photos: Amie Cox. "Underwater photography must be of the *highest* quality in order to catch our interest. We can't be responsible for unsolicited photo submissions." Pays $25-250 for 35mm color transparencies; reviews 8x10 b&w prints. Captions, model release, and identification of subjects required. Buys one-time rights, or all rights depending on the material.

Tips: "Our current contributors are among the top writers in the diving field. A newcomer must have a style that draws the reader into the article, leaves him satisfied at the end of it, and makes him want to see something else by this same author soonest! Writing for diving magazines has become a fairly sophisticated venture. The 'me and Joe went diving' type of article just won't do anymore. Writers must be able to compete with the best in order to get published. We only use contributors grounded in underwater photojournalism."

SKIN DIVER, 8490 Sunset Blvd., Los Angeles CA 90069. (213)657-5100. Editor/Publisher: Paul J. Tzimoulis. Circ. 199,555. "The majority of our contributors are divers turned writers." Buys only one-time rights. Byline given. Pays on publication. Acknowledges material immediately. All model releases and author's grants must be submitted with mss. Manuscripts reviewed are either returned to the author or tentatively scheduled for future issue. Time for review varies. Mss considered "accepted" when published; all material held on "tentatively scheduled" basis subject to change or rejection up to time of printing. Submit complete ms with photos. Computer printout submissions OK. SASE.

Nonfiction and Photos: Contact: Bonnie J. Cardone. Stories and articles directly related to skin diving activities, equipment or personalities. Features and articles equally divided into following categories: adventure, equipment, underwater photography, wrecks, treasure, spearfishing, undersea science, travel, marine life, do-it-yourself, technique and archeology. No "articles on marine life or fish-of-the-month candidates, at this time we're overstocked." Length: 1,000-2,000 words, well-illustrated by photos; b&w at ratio of 3:1 to color. Pays $50/printed page. Photos purchased with mss; b&w 8x10 glossy prints; color 35mm, 2¼x2¼ or 4x5 transparencies; do not submit color prints or negatives. All photos must be captioned and marked with name and address. Pays $50/published page for inside photos; $300/cover photo.

Tips: "The best way to get published in *Skin Diver* is to write an article on a dive spot or subject familiar to the writer, and submit good clear photos with it. We are photo-oriented; thus, sharp colorful photos often mean the difference between acceptance or rejection."

SPRAY'S WATER SKI MAGAZINE, Box 4779, Winter Park FL 32793. (305)671-0655. Editor: Harvey W. McLeod Jr. Magazine published 10 times/year for recreational through competition water skiers. Also recreational boating and safety. Circ. 80,000. Pays on publication. Byline given. Buys all rights. Submit seasonal material 3 months in advance. Photocopied and previously published submissions OK. SASE. Reports in 2 weeks. Free sample copy; writer's guidelines for SASE.

Nonfiction: Expose; general interest on speed skiing, barefoot, kite flying, tubing, knee board skiing, slalom, tricks, (jump and recreational); historical; nostalgia; profile (recreational skiers who do something unique in unusual locations or situations); travel (unique places worldwide, preferably in US); how-to (by experts); humor (short and long); personal experience (first-person motivational); and technical (from experienced person). Buys 1-2 mss/issue. Query with clips of previously published work. Pays $35-100 for short features on safety, how-to (500-1,500 words); $50-300 for longer features (3,000-4,500 words).

Photos: Reviews 35mm and larger transparencies. Offers no additional payment for photos accompanying ms. Captions and model release required. Buys all rights.

SURFER, Box 1028, Dana Point CA 92629. (714)496-5922. Editor: Paul Holmes. For teens and young adults. Slant is toward the contemporary, fast-moving and hard core enthusiasts in the sport of surfing. Monthly. Circ. 91,000. Rights purchased vary with author and material. Pays on publication. Sample copy $3. Reports on submissions in 4 weeks. Computer printout submissions OK; prefers letter quality to dot matrix. SASE.

Nonfiction: "We use anything about surfing if interesting and authoritative. Must be written from an expert's viewpoint. We're looking for good comprehensive articles on any surfing spot—especially surfing in faraway foreign lands." Length: preferably not more than 5 pages typewritten. No poetry. Pays 6-10¢/word.

Photos: Buys photos with mss or with captions only. Likes 8x10 glossy b&w proofsheets with negatives. Also uses expert color 35mm and 2¼x2¼ transparencies carefully wrapped. Pays $10-75 b&w; $25-125/35mm color or transparency.

SURFING MAGAZINE, Western Empire, 2720 Camino Capistrano, San Clemente CA 92672. (714)492-7873. Editor: David Gilovich. Monthly magazine covering all aspects of the sport of surfing. *"Surfing Magazine* is a contemporary, beach lifestyle/surfing publication. We reach the entire spectrum of surfing enthusiasts." Circ. 80,000. Pays on publication. Byline given. Buys all rights. Submit seasonal/holiday material 4 months in advance. Photocopied submissions OK. No computer printout or disk submissions. SASE. Reports in 2 weeks. Free sample copy and writer's guidelines for SAE.

Nonfiction: Book excerpts (on surfing, beach lifestyle, ocean-related); how-to (surfing-related); interview/profile (of top surfing personality); new product; photo feature (of ocean, beach lifestyle, surfing); travel (to surfing locations only). Buys 50 mss/year. Query with clips of published work or send complete ms. Length: 3,000 words maximum. Pays 10-15¢/word.

Photos: Larry Moore, photo editor. State availability of photos or send photos with ms. Pays $35-500 for 35mm color transparencies; $20-75 for b&w contact sheet and negatives. Identification of subjects required. Buys one-time rights.

Columns/Departments: Chris Carter, column/department editor. "Currents"—mini-features of current topical interest about surfing. This department includes reviews of books, films, etc. Buys 36 mss/year. Query with clips of published work, if available, or send complete ms. Length: 100-500 words. Pays $75-100.

Fiction: Adventure, humorous. No fantasy fiction. Buys 3 mss/year. Send complete ms. Length: 1,000-4,000 words. Pays 10-15¢/word.

Tips: "Begin by contributing small, mini-news features for our 'Currents' department. New editorial policy suggests that we will be more receptive than ever to bringing in new writers."

SWIMMING WORLD, 1130 W. Florence Ave., Inglewood CA 90301. (213)641-2727. Editor: Robert Ingram. 2% freelance written. For "competitors (10-24), plus their coaches, parents, and those who are involved in the enjoyment of the sport." Monthly. Circ. 40,000. Buys all rights. Byline given. Buys 10-12 mss/year. Pays on publication. Reports in 1-2 months. Query. SASE.

Nonfiction: Articles of interest to competitive swimmers, divers and water poloists, their parents and coaches. Can deal with diet, body conditioning or medicine, as applicable to competitive swimming. Nutrition and stroke and diving techniques. Psychology and profiles of athletes. Must be authoritative. Length: 1,500 words maximum. Pays $50 maximum.

Photos: Photos purchased with mss. Does not pay extra for photos with mss. 8x10 b&w only. Also photos with captions. Pays $20 maximum for b&w.

UNDERCURRENT, Box 1658, Sausalito CA 94965. (415)332-3684. Managing Editor: Ben Davison. 20-50% freelance written. Monthly consumer-oriented scuba diving newsletter; 12 pages. Circ. 13,000. Pays on publication. Buys first rights. Pays $50 kill fee. Byline given. Simultaneous (if to other than diving publisher), photocopied and previously published submissions OK. Computer printout or disk submissions OK. SASE. Reports in 4-6 weeks. Free sample copy and writer's guidelines; mention *Writer's Market* in request.

Nonfiction: Equipment evaluation; how-to; general interest; new product; and travel review. Buys 2 mss/issue. Query. Length: 2,000 words maximum. Pays $50-250.

Fillers: Buys clippings and newsbreaks. Buys 20/year. Length: 25-500 words. Pays $5-20.

THE WATER SKIER, Box 191, Winter Haven FL 33880. (813)324-4341. Editor: Duke Cullimore. Official publication of the American Water Ski Association. 15% freelance written. Published 7 times/year. Circ. 17,500. Buys North American serial rights only. Byline given. Buys limited amount of freelance material. Query. Pays on acceptance. Free sample copy. Reports on submissions within 10 days. Computer printout submissions OK "if double-spaced and standard ms requirements are followed"; prefers letter quality to dot matrix. SASE.

Nonfiction and Photos: Occasionally buys exceptionally offbeat, unusual text/photo features on the sport of water skiing. Will put more emphasis on technique, methods, etc., in the year ahead.

WORLD WATERSKIING MAGAZINE, World Publications, Box 2456, Winter Park FL 32790. (305)628-4802. Editor: Terry L. Snow. Managing Editor: Wanda K. Smith. Magazine published 7 times/year. Covers various levels of water skiing. Circ. 52,000. Pays on publication. Byline given. Buys variable rights. Submit seasonal/holiday material 6 months in advance. Simultaneous queries, and simultaneous, photocopied, and previously published submissions OK. SASE. Reports in 3 weeks. Free sample copy.

Nonfiction: Historical/nostalgic (anything dealing with water skiing); how-to (tips on equipment and repair of skis, bindings, etc.); humor ("always looking for a good laugh about water skiing); inspirational (someone who beat the odds—handicapped skier, for example); interview/profile (only on assignment); photo feature (action or special effects); technical (on assignment only); travel (picturesque water skiing sites); sports medicine. No first-person accounts or fiction. Buys 10-30 mss/year. Query with or without clips of published work. Pays $150-200/feature story; $75/medical, sports medicine; $40/tips.

Photos: Tom King, senior photographer. "We need lots of sharp photos for our annual issue in October. Send photos with ms. Prefers b&w prints or contact sheet, 35mm or 2 ¼ color slides/transparencies. Model release

and identification of subjects required. Buys negotiable rights. Buys 5-15 mss/year. Query with clips of published work. Length: 250-300 words. Pays $40-75.
Fillers: Buys 5/year. Length: 100-150 words. Pays $5-15.
Tips: "We would love to hear from good sportswriters with a lively interest in water skiing. We're especially open to features and sports medicine articles. Medical writing would require background in specialized area and proof with resume, etc."

Teen and Young Adult

The publications in this category are for young people aged 12 to 18. Publications aimed at 2- to 12-year-olds are classified in the Juvenile category. Publications for college students are listed in College, Career, and Alumni.

A good how-to resource for writing for young adults is *Writing for Children and Teenagers*, by Lee Wyndham (revised by Arnold Madison, Writer's Digest Books).

ALIVE FOR YOUNG TEENS, Christian Board of Publication, Box 179, St. Louis MO 63166. Editor: Mike Dixon. Ecumenical, mainline publication with a Protestant slant; aimed at young teens. "We especially appreciate submissions of useable quality from 12- to 15-year-olds. Those in this age range should include their age with the submission. We appreciate use of humor that early adolescents would appreciate. Please keep the age group in mind." Computer printout submissions OK; prefers letter quality to dot matrix. SASE required with all submissions. Sample copy 50¢.
Nonfiction: "Articles should concern interesting youth, church youth groups, projects and activities. There is little chance of our taking an article not accompanied by at least 3-4 captioned b&w photos." Length: 800-1,000 words. Pays 2¢/word; photos $3-5.
Fiction: "Give us fiction concerning characters in the *Alive for Young Teens* readers' age group (12-15), dealing with problems and situations peculiar to that group." Length: 100-1,200 words. Pays 2¢/word. Uses 6-10 photo features/issue. Pays $5/photo maximum.
Photos: Send photos with ms. Submit in batches. Pays $10-20 for b&w prints.
Poetry: Length: 20 lines maximum. Pays 25¢/line.
Fillers: Puzzles, riddles and daffy definitions. Pays $10 maximum.

AMERICAN NEWSPAPER CARRIER, American Newspaper Boy Press, Box 15300, Winston-Salem NC 27103. Editor: Marilyn H. Rollins. 10% freelance written. Buys all rights. Pays on acceptance. Queries not required. Computer printout submissions OK. Reports in 10 days. SASE.
Fiction: Uses a limited amount of short fiction written for teen-age newspaper carriers, male and female. It is preferable that stories be written around newspaper carrier characters. Humor, mystery and adventure plots are commonly used. No material not related to teen-age interests or stories featuring newspaper carrier contests, prizes, etc. Length: 1,000-2,000 words. "Stories are purchased with the understanding that they are original and that the *American Newspaper Carrier* purchases all rights thereto." Pays $15 minimum.

BOYS' LIFE, Boy Scouts of America, Magazine Division, National Office, 1325 Walnut Hill Lane, Irving TX 75062. (214)659-2000. Editor: Robert Hood. Monthly magazine covering Boy Scout activities for "ages 8-18—Boy Scouts, Cub Scouts, and others of that age group." Circ. 1.5 million. Pays on publication. Byline given.
Nonfiction: "Almost all articles are assigned. We do not encourage unsolicited material."
Columns/Departments: Hobby How's (1-2 paragraphs on hobby tips). Buys 60 mss/year. Send complete ms. Pays $5 minimum.
Fillers: Jokes (Think and Grin—1-3 sentences). Pays $1 minimum.

BREAD, 6401 The Paseo, Kansas City MO 64131. Editor: Gary Sivewright. Christian leisure reading magazine for junior and senior high students, published by the Division of Christian Life, Church of the Nazarene. Monthly. Pays on acceptance. Accepts simultaneous submissions. Buys first rights; sometimes second rights. Byline given. Free sample copy and editorial specifications sheet for SASE.
Nonfiction: Helpful articles in the area of developing the Christian life; first-person, "this is how I did it" stories about Christian witness. Length: up to 1,500 words. Articles must be theologically acceptable. Looking for fresh approach to basic themes. Also needs articles dealing with doctrinal subjects such as the Holy Spirit, written for the teen reader. Pays 4¢/word for first rights and 3¢/word for second rights. Works 6 months ahead of publication.
Photos: 8x10 b&w glossy prints of teens in action. Payment is $15 and up. Also considers photo spreads and essays. Uses 1 color transparency/month for cover.

Fiction: "Adventure, school, and church-oriented. No sermonizing." Length: 1,500 words maximum. Pays 4¢/word for first rights and 3¢/word for second rights.
Tips: Send complete ms by mail for consideration. Reports in 6-8 weeks. SASE.

CAMPUS LIFE MAGAZINE, Campus Life Publications, Inc., 400 E. St. Charles, Carol Stream IL 60187. Editor: Gregg Lewis. Managing Editor: Jim Long. Associate Editor: Verne Becker. For a readership of young adults, high school and college age. "Though our readership is largely Christian, *Campus Life* reflects the interests of all kids—music, bicycling, photography, cars and sports." Largely staff-written. "*Campus Life* is a Christian magazine that is *not* overtly religious. The indirect style is intended to create a safety zone with our readers and to reflect our philosophy that God is interested in all of life. Therefore, we publish message stories side by side with general interest, humor, etc." Monthly magazine. Circ. 250,000. Pays on acceptance. Buys one-time rights. Byline given. Submit seasonal/holiday material 6 months in advance. Simultaneous, photocopied and previously published submissions OK. SASE. Reports in 2 months. Sample copy $2; writer's guidelines for SASE.
Nonfiction: Contact: Lee Lueck. Personal experiences; photo features; unusual sports; humor; short items—how-to, college or career, travel, etc. Query or submit complete manuscript. Length: 500-3,000 words. Pays $100-250.
Photos: Verne Beckey, photo editor. Pays $50 minimum/8x10 b&w glossy print; $90 minimum/color transparency; $250/cover photo. Buys one-time rights.
Fiction: Contact: Lee Lueck. Stories about problems and experiences kids face. Sappy, simplistic religious stories are not acceptable.
Tips: "The best ms for a freelancer to try to sell us would be a well-written first person story (fiction or nonfiction) focusing on a common struggle young people face in any area of life—intellectual, emotional, social, physical or spiritual. Most manuscripts that miss us fail in quality or style. Since our style is distinctive, it is one of the biggest criteria in buying an article, so interested writers must study *Campus Life* to get an understanding of our audience and style. Don't submit unless you have *at least* read the magazine."

CAREER WORLD, Curriculum Innovations, Inc., 3500 Western Ave., Highland Park IL 60035. (312)432-2700. Editor: Bonnie Bekken. 30% freelance written. Emphasizes career education for junior and senior high school students at approximately 7th grade reading level. Monthly (September-May) magazine. Pays on publication. Buys all rights. Byline given. Submit seasonal/holiday material 5 months in advance. Computer printout and disk submissions OK; prefers letter quality to dot matrix printouts. SASE. Reports in 6 weeks.
Nonfiction: How-to, informational, interview, profile. Buys 20 mss/year. Query with brief outline and opening paragraphs. Length: 750-1,500 words. Pays 5¢/word minimum.
Columns/Departments: Lifestyle (worker profile), Offbeat Job (unusual occupation), New Careers. Buys 9/year. Query. Length: 300-1,500 words. Pays 4¢/word and up.
Tips: Articles must emphasize self-awareness and career exploration for students. "We like to see articles on specific occupations—preferably new or unusual—or on job getting and job holding. Follow-up activities are useful. Copy must be written simply, clearly and in a manner that appeals to young readers. We look for writing that excites the reader's imagination."

CHRISTIAN ADVENTURER, Messenger Publishing House, Box 850, Joplin MO 64802. (417)624-7050. Editor-in-Chief: Roy M. Chappell, D.D. Managing Editor: Mrs. Rosmarie Foreman. A denominational Sunday School take-home paper for teens, 13-19. Quarterly; 104 pages. Circ. 3,500. Pays quarterly. Buys simultaneous, second serial (reprint) or one-time rights. Byline given. Submit seasonal/holiday material 1 year in advance. Photocopied and previously published submissions OK. SASE. Reports in 4-6 weeks. Sample copy 50¢. Free writer's guidelines with sample copy.
Nonfiction: Historical (related to great events in the history of the church); informational (explaining the meaning of a Bible passage or a Christian concept); inspirational; nostalgia; and personal experience. Send complete ms. Length: 1,500-1,800 words. Pays 1¢/word.
Fiction: Adventure; historical; religious and romance. Length: 1,500-1,800 words. Pays 1¢/word.

CHRISTIAN LIVING FOR SENIOR HIGHS, David C. Cook Publishing Co., 850 N. Grove, Elgin IL 60120. (312)741-2400. Editor: John Conaway. "A take-home paper used in senior high Sunday School classes. We encourage Christian teens to write to us." Quarterly magazine; 4 pages. Pays on acceptance. Buys all rights. Byline given. Phone queries OK. Computer printout submissions OK. Reports in 3-5 weeks. SASE. Free sample copy and writer's guidelines.
Nonfiction: How-to (Sunday School youth projects); historical (with religious base); humor (from Christian perspective); inspirational and personality (nonpreachy); personal teen experience (Christian); poetry written by teens and photo feature (Christian subject). "Nothing not compatible with a Christian lifestyle. Since this is difficult to define, author should query doubtful topics." Buys 6 mss/issue. Submit complete ms. Length: 900-1,200 words. Pays $80; $40 for short pieces.

Fiction: Adventure (with religious theme); historical (with Christian perspective); humorous; mystery and religious. Buys 2 mss/issue. Submit complete ms. Length: 900-1,200 words. Pays $60-75. "No preachy experiences."

Photos: Sue Greer, photo editor. Photos purchased with or without accompanying ms or on assignment. Send contact sheet, prints or transparencies. Pays $20-35 for 8½x11 b&w photos; $50 minimum for color transparencies.

Tips: "Our demand for manuscripts should increase beginning in 1984, but most of these will probably be assigned rather than bought over-the-transom. Authors should query us, sending samples of their work. That way we can keep them on file for specific writing assignments."

CIRCLE K MAGAZINE, 3636 Woodview Trace, Indianapolis IN 46268. Executive Editor: Chuck Jonak. "Our readership consists almost entirely of college students interested in the concept of voluntary service. They are politically and socially aware and have a wide range of interests." Published 5 times/year. Magazine; 16 pages. Circ. 14,500. Pays on acceptance. Normally buys first North American serial rights. Byline given. Submit seasonal/holiday material 6 months in advance. SASE. Reports in 4 weeks. Free sample copy and writer's guidelines.

Nonfiction: Informational (general interest articles on any area pertinent to concerned college students); travel (Upper Midwest, 1984; Pacific Northwest, 1985); community concerns (voluntarism, youth, medical, handicapped, elderly, underprivileged). No "first-person confessions, family history or travel." Recent article example: "Drugs: An Escapable Trap" (March 1983). Query or submit complete ms. Length: 1,500-2,500 words. Pays $175-250.

Photos: Purchased with accompanying ms. Captions required. Query. Total purchase price for ms includes payment for photos.

Tips: "The new organizational theme, 'Achieve Unity Through Service,' will open the magazine to family-related features, and higher payments. Feature ideas about family concerns—in touch, in turmoil, in transition—will be needed in 1983-85. Query must be typed, and should indicate familiarity with the field and sources."

18 ALMANAC, 13-30, 505 Market St., Knoxville TN 37902. Group Editor: Keith Bellows. Annual magazine for graduating high school seniors. Circ. 750,000. Pays on acceptance. Byline given. Offers 33⅓% kill fee. Buys first North American serial rights. No computer printout or disk submissions. Reports in 1 month on written queries; in 3 weeks on mss. Free sample copy with 9x12 SASE ($1.18 postage); free writer's guidelines with SASE. March best time to query. Avoid queries that propose "articles that are too broadly conceived."

Nonfiction: "Typical topics are 'how to apply to colleges'; 'how to apply for financial aid'; 'coping with the campus'; 'how to apply for a job'; 'what the work world is like'; 'staying healthy'; and 'dealing with legal hassles.' " Query with clips of previously published work. Length: 1,000-2,500 words. Pays 10-20¢/word. "We want fact-filled articles to help students make decisions about their futures after high school. We primarily cover college, careers and practical living. We use a conversational tone that is helpful, but not condescending. New angles on old topics are encouraged. We'll become more like a true handbook with a strong emphasis on practical advice for the graduating senior."

Photos: State availability of photos.

Tips: "We rarely accept unsolicited mss."

‡EXPLORING MAGAZINE, The Journal for Explorers, Boy Scouts of America, 1325 Walnut Hill Ln., Irving TX 75062. (214)659-2365. Editor: Robert E. Hood. Executive Editor: Scott Daniels. Magazine published 4 times/year—January, March, May, September. Covers the Exploring program of the BSA. Circ. 480,000. Pays on acceptance. Byline given. Buys one-time and first rights. Submit seasonal/holiday material 6 months in advance. Simultaneous queries OK. Computer printout and disk submissions OK; prefers letter quality to dot matrix. SASE. Reports in 2 weeks. Sample copy for 8½x10 SAE and 85¢ postage; writer's guidelines for business-size SAE and 1 first class stamp.

Nonfiction: General interest, how-to (achieve outdoor skills, organize trips, meetings, etc.); interview/profile (of outstanding Explorer); travel (backpacking or canoeing with Explorers). "Nothing dealing with sex, drugs, or violence." Buys 3 mss/year. Query with clips. Length: 800-2,000 words. Pays $300-450.

Photos: Gene Daniels, photo editor. State availability of photos with query letter or ms. Reviews b&w contact sheets. Captions required. Buys one-time rights.

Tips: "Contact the local Exploring Director in your area (listed in phone book white pages under Boy Scouts of America). Find out if there are some outstanding post activities going on and then query magazine editor in Irving TX. Strive for shorter texts, faster starts and stories that lend themselves to dramatic photographs." Write for guidelines and "What is Exploring?" fact sheet.

FACE-TO-FACE, Box 801, Nashville TN 37202. (615)749-6224. Editor: Barbara Summey. For United Methodist young people, ages 15-18 inclusive. Published by the Curriculum Resources Committee of the General Board of Discipleship of The United Methodist Church. Quarterly magazine; 48 pages. Circ. 18,000. Rights purchased vary with author and material. Buys first North American serial rights, simultaneous rights, or all rights for periodical publication. Byline given. Buys about 24 mss/year. Pays on acceptance. Submit Christmas, Easter and summertime material 8-9 months in advance. Reports in 1-2 months. Computer printout submissions OK; prefers letter quality to dot matrix. SASE.

Nonfiction: "Our purpose is to speak to young persons' concerns about their faith, their purpose in life, their personal relationships, goals, and feelings. Articles and features (with photos) should be subjects of major interest and concern to high school young people. These include home and family life, school, extracurricular activities, vocation, etc. Satires, lampoons, related to the themes of an issue are also used." No material on drug abuse, abortion. Nothing that is overly pious or trite." Submit complete ms. Length: 2,500 words maximum. Pays 4¢/word.

Photos: Uses 8x10 b&w glossy prints with high impact and good contrast. Pays $15 for one-time use of b&w. "We buy stock photos and those especially taken to illustrate articles."

Fiction: Must deal with major problems and concerns of older teens, such as finding one's own identity, dealing with family and peer-group pressures, and so forth. No straight moral fiction or stories with pat answers or easy solutions used. No serials. Submit complete ms. Length: 1,800-2,500 words. Pays 4¢/word.

Poetry: Related to the theme of an issue. Free verse, blank verse, traditional and avant-garde forms. Length: 10-150 lines. Pays 50¢/line.

FREEWAY, Box 513, Glen Ellyn IL 60137. Publication Editor: Cindy Atoji. For "young adults of high school and college age." Weekly. Circ. 70,000.

Nonfiction: Needs four basic types of manuscripts: *self-help or how-to* articles with practical Christian advice on daily living; *trend* articles looking at fads and fascinations from a Christian viewpoint; *Bible exposition* written with fresh personal insights; and *true stories* on how God is working in teens' lives. Also uses humor, reporting and fillers. We use little fiction, unless it is allegory, parables or humor. About 750 words for shorter pieces; 1,000 for major articles. *Freeway* issues are planned around themes. Write for a list of current topics. Prefers first rights but buys some reprints. Purchases 100 mss/year. Byline given. Reports on material accepted for publication in 4-5 weeks. Returns rejected material in 2-3 weeks. Pays 4-7¢/word.

Photos: Whenever possible, provide clear 8x10 or 5x7 b&w photos to accompany mss (or any other available photos). Payment is $5-30.

Tips: Write to us for our "Tips to Writers" pamphlet and free sample copy. Study them, then query or send complete mss. Include information about who you are, writing qualifications and experience working with teens in your cover letter. Include SASE.

GROUP, Thom Schultz Publications, Box 481, Loveland CO 80539. (303)669-3836. Editor-in-Chief: Thom Schultz. 60% freelance written. For members and leaders of high-school-age Christian youth groups; average age 16. Magazine published 8 times/year. Circ. 60,000. Pays on publication. Buys all rights. Byline given. Phone queries OK. Submit seasonal/holiday material 5 months in advance. Special Easter, Thanksgiving and Christmas issues and college issues. Simultaneous, photocopied and previously published submissions OK. SASE. Reports in 3-4 weeks. Sample copy $1; writer's guidelines for SASE.

Nonfiction: How-to (fund-raising, membership-building, worship, games, discussions, activities, crowd breakers, simulation games); informational; (drama, worship, service projects); inspirational (issues facing young people today); interview and photo feature (group activities). Buys 3 mss/issue. Query. Length: 500-1,500 words. Pays $50-150.

Photos: Photos purchased with or without accompanying ms or on assignment. Captions required. Pays $20 minimum for 8x10 b&w glossy prints, $50 minimum for 35mm color transparencies.

Columns/Departments: Try This One (short ideas for games; crowd breakers, discussions, worships, fund raisers, service projects, etc.). Buys 6 mss/issue. Send complete ms. Length: 500 words maximum. Pays $10.

GUIDE, 6856 Eastern Ave., NW, Washington DC 20012. (202)723-3700. Editor: Penny Estes Wheeler. 90% freelance written. A Seventh-Day Adventist journal for junior youth and early teens. "Its content reflects Seventh-Day Adventist beliefs and standards. Another characteristic which probably distinguishes it from many other magazines is the fact that all its stories are nonfiction." Weekly magazine; 32 pages. Circ. 60,000. Buys first serial rights. Byline given. Buys about 350 mss/year. Pays on acceptance. Reports in 6 weeks. SASE.

Nonfiction and Poetry: Wants articles and nonfiction stories of character-building and spiritual value. All stories must be true and include dialogue. Should emphasize the positive aspects of living—faithfulness, obedience to parents, perseverance, kindness, gratitude, courtesy, etc. "We do not use stories of hunting, fishing, trapping or spiritualism." Send complete ms (include word count). Length: 1,500-2,500 words. Pays 2-4¢/word. Also buys serialized true stories. Length: 10 chapters. Buys traditional forms of poetry; also some free verse. Length: 4-16 lines. Pays 50¢-$1/line.

The double dagger (‡) before a listing indicates that the listing is new in this edition. New markets are often the most receptive to freelance contributions.

HIGHWIRE MAGAZINE, The National Student Magazine, Highwire Associates, Box 948, Lowell MA 01853. (617)458-6416. Editor-in-Chief: Bill Weber. 9 times yearly magazine covering news, lifestyles, humor, opinion, and the arts of interest to students. Estab. 1981. Circ. 100,000. Pays on publication. Byline given. Offers 25% kill fee. Buys first rights. Submit seasonal/holiday material 6 months in advance. Simultaneous queries, and simultaneous, photocopied and previously published submissions OK. Legible, double-spaced computer printout and disk submissions compatible with Apple III word processors OK. SASE. Reports in 1 month. Free sample copy and writer's guidelines.

Nonfiction: Book excerpts, expose, general interest, sports, music, video, historical/nostalgic, how-to, humor, interview/profile (of outstanding high school students), opinion, personal experience, photo feature, travel. "All categories must relate in some way to teenagers' concerns. No moralistic or cautionary tales intended to warn impressionable youngsters about the evils of the world. Direct, realistic accounts of the evils of the world are okay." Buys 100 mss/year. Query. Length: 200-2,000 words. Pays $20-500.

Photos: Emilie McCormick, art director. State availability of photos. Pays $25-150 for color transparencies and b&w or color prints. Model release and identification of subjects required. Buys one-time rights.

Columns/Departments: Nancy Rutter, senior editor. Travel: cheap ways to travel, jobs or programs with international slant; areas of interest to young people; Arts/Entertainment: reviews of books, movies, video, concerts; Profiles: of outstanding teenagers; College: first person freshman accounts, tips on unusual or good colleges; Jobs: for young people, entrepreneurs, etc. News: short news items. Buys 40 mss/year. Query. Length: 100-750 words. Pays $10-100.

Fiction: Kathleen Cushman, fiction editor. Experimental, fantasy, humorous, mainstream, romance. "We buy only to student-written work of high quality. Adult freelancers should not submit fiction." Buys 4-8 mss/year. Send complete ms. Length: 4,000 words maximum. Pays $50-250. No poetry.

Fillers: Betsy Basch, fillers editor. Clippings, anecdotes, short humor, newsbreaks. Specific categories: "A" for Effort (funny answers to real exam questions); classroom humor; funny excuses (for being late for school, absent, etc.). Buys 60-100/year. Length: 150 words maximum. Pays $10-20.

Tips: "Always identify yourself as a student, if you are one, because preference is given to student writers. We are not looking for articles written by adults that 'talk down' to students, give advice, preach, etc. *Highwire* will be paying more attention to music, video, the arts in general, television, sports, student lifestyles, fashion, dating, sex and relationships."

IN TOUCH, Wesleyan Publishing House, Box 2000, Marion IN 46952. Published to reinforce Sunday school curriculum. Most writing on assignment basis, but constantly looking for new writers. Best way to "break in" is to send unsolicited ms that shows you're "in touch" with our 13-19 year old readers. Weekly, not copyrighted. Byline given. Pays on acceptance. Queries discouraged. Submit holiday/seasonal material 9 months in advance. Computer printout submissions OK; prefers letter quality to dot matrix. SASE. Reports in 6 weeks. Free sample copy for SASE.

Nonfiction: Testimonies, observations on contemporary issues, "how to" articles, humor, and interviews with famous Christians. Length: 1,200-1,700 words. 2-3¢/word.

Fiction: Looking for "good honest fiction." Must be third person. "No Sunday school soap opera with easy out, pat answers or pollyanna fiction." Length: 1,200-1,700 words. 2-3¢/word.

Photos: Need b&w glossies of teens in variety of situations. "Seventeen," "Campus Life" cover shots, candid closeups of faces. Pays $15-25.

THE MODERN WOODMEN, 1701 1st Ave., Rock Island IL 61201. (309)786-6481. Editor: Gloria J. Bergh. For members of Modern Woodmen of America, a fraternal insurance society. Quarterly magazine; 24 pages. Circ. 325,000. Not copyrighted. Pays on acceptance. Sample copy and writer's guidelines for SASE. Photocopied and simultaneous submissions OK. No computer printout or disk submissions. Reports in 3-4 weeks. SASE.

Nonfiction: "Nonfiction may be either for children or adults with an emphasis on community involvement and family life. Our audience is broad and diverse. We want clear, educational, inspirational articles for children and young people. We don't want religious material, teen romances, teen adventure stories." Buys informational, how-to, historical, and technical articles. Buys 8-10 unsolicited mss/year. Submit complete ms. Length: 1,500-2,000 words. Also buys shorter articles of 200-500 words. Pays $40 minimum depending on quality.

Photos: B&w photos purchased with ms. Captions optional. Prefers vertical, b&w glossy photos for cover use. Payment varies with quality and need.

Fiction: Mainstream and historical fiction. Length: 1,500-2,500 words. Pays $40.

NUTSHELL, 13-30 Corp., 505 Market St., Knoxville TN 37902. Group Editor: Keith Bellows. Semiannual magazine covering all facets of the college experience, from academics, fitness, financial aid, career training, to entertainment, sports and fashion. The audience is college students, ages 18-22. Circ. 1.2 million. Pays on acceptance. Byline given. Offers 33% kill fee. Buys first North American serial rights. Simultaneous and photocopied submissions OK if so indicated. SASE. "We welcome written queries from college journalists and recent graduates. Be sure to submit ideas that have national application and enclose clips of previously published work. New angles on old topics are welcomed. *Please* analyze copies of the magazine before querying.'' Reports in 3 weeks. Free sample copy with 9x12 SASE and $1.18 postage; free writer's guidelines with SASE. January best time to query.

Nonfiction: "Recent articles have explored the future prospects for careers in space industries; highlighted the most unique campus festivals from coast to coast; examined the new boom in student businesses and explored voluntary racial segregation on campuses. We also use how-to articles that relate to the problems and experiences of college students, from learning how to study more efficiently to handling health or emotional problems.'' Query with clips of previously published work. Length: 1,500-3,500 words. Pays $150-800 and negotiable.

Photos: State availability of photos.

Columns/Departments: Campus Chronicle (100-500 words on activities of college students of special interest to a national college audience); Innovations (100-500 words on breakthroughs, experiments, or trends in various academic disciplines). Major features (1,000-3,000 words dealing with wide-ranging campus trends, or providing information of special use to students such as upcoming films; current efforts to raise the drinking age; a first person account of a computer dating experience and series of profiles of student cartoonists). Pays 10-20¢/word.

PROBE, Baptist Brotherhood Commission, 1548 Poplar Ave., Memphis TN 38104. (901)272-2461. Editor-in-Chief: Timothy C. Seanor. 5% freelance written. For "boys age 12-17 who are members of a missions organization in Southern Baptist churches.'' Monthly magazine; 32 pages. Circ. 48,000. Byline given. Pays on acceptance. Buys one-time rights. Submit seasonal/holiday material 6 months in advance. Simultaneous submissions OK. Computer printout submissions OK. SASE. Reports in 1 month. Free sample copy and writer's guidelines with 9x12 SASE ($1.18 postage).

Nonfiction: How-to (crafts, hobbies); informational (youth, religious especially); inspirational (personalities); personal experience (any first-person by teenagers—especially religious); photo feature (sports, teen subjects). No "preachy'' articles, fiction or excessive dialogue. Submit complete ms. Length: 500-1,500 words. Pays $15-45.

Photos: Purchased with accompanying ms or on assignment. Captions required. Query. Pays $10 for 8x10 b&w glossy prints.

Tips: Editorial changes include aiming for the mid-teen instead of younger teen. Will affect writers in the year ahead.

PURPLE COW, Atlanta's Newsmagazine for Teens, Purple Cow, Inc., 110 E. Andrews Dr. NW, Atlanta GA 30305. (404)233-7618/7654. Editor: Marilyn Staats. Managing Editor: Anne Goodsell. Monthly tabloid (10 issues) covering any subject of interest to the 12-18-year-old. Distributed free to high school and middle school students in metro Atlanta. Circ. 41,000. Pays on acceptance. Byline given. Buys one-time rights. Submit seasonal/holiday material 2 months in advance. Simultaneous queries, and simultaneous, photocopied, and previously published submissions OK. Computer printout and disk submissions OK. SASE. Reports in 1 month. Sample copy $1.

Nonfiction: Book excerpts; general interest; how-to (do anything—from dress fashionably to survive exams); humor; interview/profile (of people of interest to teens); personal experience (teen-related); sports (general, anecdotal—no "How to Play Soccer''); coping (different slants on drugs, sex, school, parents, peer pressure, dating, entertainment, money, etc.). Special issues include junion-senior proms and Christmas. No puzzles, games, fiction or first-person nonfiction. Buys 50 mss/year. Query with clips of published work or send complete ms. Length: 500-3,000 words. Pays $5-40.

Photos: Send photos with ms. Pays $5 for b&w transparencies and contact sheet.

Columns/Departments: Buys 5 mss/year. Length: 150-500 words. Pays $10 maximum.

Fillers: Buys 10-20/year. "Would like more.'' Length: 150 words maximum. Pays $5.

Tips: "We are written about 80% by high school students—but we want to have more adult writers. Know what you're talking about. Don't talk down. Write in a style that is neither cynical nor preachy. Have something new to say.''

SCHOLASTIC SCOPE, Scholastic Magazines, Inc., 730 Broadway, New York NY 10003. Editor: Katherine Robinson. Circ. 1,100,000. Buys all rights. Byline given. Issued weekly. 4-6th grade reading level; 15-18 age level. Reports in 4-6 weeks. SASE.

Nonfiction and Photos: Articles with photos about teenagers who have accomplished something against great odds, overcome obstacles, performed heroically, or simply done something out of the ordinary. Prefers articles about people outside New York area. Length: 400-1,200 words. Pays $125 and up.

Fiction and Drama: Problems of contemporary teenagers (drugs, prejudice, runaways, failure in school, family problems, etc.); relationships between people (interracial, adult-teenage, employer-employee, etc.) in family, job, and school situations. Strive for directness, realism, and action, perhaps carried through dialogue rather than exposition. Try for depth of characterization in at least one character. Avoid too many coincidences and random happenings. Although action stories are wanted, it's not a market for crime fiction. Occasionally uses mysteries and science fiction. Length: 400-1,200 words. Uses plays up to 15,000 words. Pays $150 minimum.

SEVENTEEN, 850 3rd Ave., New York NY 10022. Executive Editor: Ray Robinson. Monthly. Circ. 1,500,000. Buys first rights for nonfiction, features and poetry. Buys first rights on fiction. Pays 25% kill fee. Byline given. Pays on acceptance. Computer printout submissions OK; prefers letter quality to dot matrix printouts. SASE.
Nonfiction and Photos: Articles and features of general interest to young women who are concerned with the development of their own lives and the problems of the world around them; strong emphasis on topicality and helpfulness. Send brief outline and query, including a typical lead paragraph, summing up basic idea of article. Also like to receive articles and features on speculation. Length: 2,000-3,000 words. Pays $50-500 for articles written by teenagers but more to established adult freelancers. Articles are commissioned after outlines are submitted and approved. Fees for commissioned articles generally range from $350-1,500. Photos usually by assignment only. Vicky Peslak, art director.
Fiction: Dawn Raffel, fiction editor. Top-quality stories featuring teenagers—the problems, concerns and preoccupations of adolescence, which will have recognition and identification value for readers. Does not want "typical teenage" stories, but high literary quality. Avoid oversophisticated material; unhappy endings acceptable if emotional impact is sufficient. Humorous stories that do not condescend to or caricature young people are welcome. Best lengths are 2,500-3,000 words. "We publish a novelette every July (not to exceed 30 doubled-spaced manuscript pages)—sometimes with a suspenseful plot." Conducts an annual short story contest.
Poetry: By teenagers only. Pays $5-25. Submissions are nonreturnable unless accompanied by SASE.
Tips: "The best way for beginning teenage writers to crack the *Seventeen* lineup is for them to contribute suggestions and short pieces to the Free-For-All column, a literary format which lends itself to just about every kind of writing: profiles, puzzles, essays, exposes, reportage, and book reviews."

SPRINT, 850 N. Grove, Elgin IL 60120. (312)741-2400. Editor: Kristine Miller Tomasik. For junior high school age students who attend Sunday School. Weekly. Buys all rights. Buys 20-30 mss/year. Pays on acceptance. Free sample copy and writer's guidelines. SASE. Rarely considers photocopied or simultaneous submissions. Submit seasonal material for Christmas, Easter and Thanksgiving issues 1 year in advance. Reports in 3 months.
Nonfiction: Wants "very short, catchy articles (600-800 words) reporting on teen involvement in church/community projects; interviewing outstanding teens, or personalities and emotional needs of teens; etc. We are using the photo feature format increasingly to treat these topics." All mss should present a Christian approach to life. Query first for nonfiction. Pays $65-75.
Fiction: "Fiction must be believable, with realistic characters and dialogue. If your sole purpose in writing is to preach, please don't send your story to us." Stories should be 1,000-2,000 words. Pays $65-75. Submit only complete manuscripts for fiction and poetry. SASE.
Photos: Photo editor: Barbra Sheperd. Photos purchased with or without mss on assignment. Captions optional. Pays $20 for b&w glossy prints. Pays $50 for color transparencies. Color photos rarely used.

STARTING LINE, Starting Line Publications, Box 878, Reseda CA 91335. (213)345-3769. Editor/Publisher: Max Zucker. Quarterly magazine covering sports for youngsters under age 18 who participate in track and field and fitness sports. Circ. 10,000. Pays on publication. Byline given. Buys first North American serial rights. Submit seasonal/holiday material 6 months in advance. Previously published submissions OK "if from non-competing publication." Reports in 3 weeks (August-May); in 2 months (summer); "if query is of interest to us." Sample copy $1 with SASE.
Nonfiction: "Well-researched articles written for young people, coaches and teachers, and pertaining to running and other physically active sports. We like to have illustrations, charts or photos to use as a basis for our art department to create graphics." Buys 8-12 mss/year. Query with clips of published work and brief bio. Length: 200-2,000 words. Pays a variable rate.
Photos: Send photos with ms "to be used as basis for graphics."
Tips: "We're looking for a few writers whom we can depend on from issue to issue. We welcome photos with mss."

STRAIGHT, Standard Publishing Co., 8121 Hamilton Ave., Cincinnati OH 45231. (513)931-4050. Editor: Dawn Brettschneider. "Teens, age 12-19, from Christian backgrounds generally receive this publication in their Sunday School classes or through subscriptions." Weekly (published quarterly) magazine; 12 pages. Pays on acceptance. Buys all rights, or second serial (reprint) rights. Byline given. Submit seasonal/holiday material 1 year in advance. Reports in 3-6 weeks. Free sample copy; writer's guidelines with SASE. No computer printout or disk submissions. Include Social Security number on ms. SASE.
Nonfiction: Religious-oriented topics, general interest, humor, inspirational, personal experience. "We want articles that promote Christian ethics and ideals." No puzzles. Query or submit complete ms. Length: 800-

1,500 words. Pays 2¢/word.

Fiction: Adventure, historical, humorous, religious and suspense. "All fiction should have some message for the modern Christian teen." Fiction should deal with all subjects in a forthright manner, without being preachy and without talking down to teens. No tasteless manuscripts that promote anything adverse to Bible's teachings. Submit complete ms. Length: 1,000-2,000 words. Pays 2¢/word; less for reprints.

Photos: May submit photos with ms. Pays $10-20 for 8x10 b&w glossy prints. Captions required; model release should be available. Buys one-time rights.

Tips: "Don't be trite. Use unusual settings or problems. Use a lot of illustrations, a good balance of conversation, narration, and action. Style must be clear, fresh—no sermonettes or sicky-sweet fiction. Take a realistic approach to problems. Be willing to submit to editorial policies on doctrine; knowledge of the *Bible* a must. Also, be aware of teens today, and what they do. Language, clothing, and activities included in mss should be contemporary. We will be reprinting more, and picking up from other sources. We are becoming more and more selective about freelance material."

THE SUNSHINE NEWS, The Participation Magazine for Canadian High School Students, Canada Sunshine Publishing Ltd., #14A, 465 King St. E., Toronto, Ontario, Canada M5A 1L6. (416)366-7964. Editor: Wendy Reid. Monthly magazine covering "anything of interest to teenagers and especially high school students." Circ. 125,000. Pays 30 days after publication. Byline given. Buys first North American rights. Submit seasonal/holiday material 2 months in advance. Simultaneous queries, simultaneous, photocopied and previously published submissions OK. SASE; IRCs outside Canada. Reports in 2 weeks. Sample copy and writer's guidelines for 9x13 SAE.

Nonfiction: General interest; how-to (get a job, travel to Europe); humor; interview/profile; science; careers; sports; entertainment. Buys 100 mss/year. Query with clips of published work. Length: 400-1,000 words. Pays 6-10¢/word.

Photos: Send photos with ms. Reviews b&w contact sheets. Identification of subjects required. Buys one-time rights.

Fiction: Fiction accepted comes from students.

Tips: Most open to interviews with interesting high school students all across Canada. "It would be especially interesting for our readers to hear about teenagers in other countries. But I must stress that our primary interest is in publishing work by Canadian high school students. Manuscripts accepted from other people would be nonfiction 99% of the time and of course, always be of prime interest to teenagers."

'TEEN MAGAZINE, 8490 Sunset Blvd., Hollywood CA 90069. Editor: Roxanne Camron. For teenage girls. Monthly magazine; 100 pages. Circ. 1,000,000. Buys all rights. Predominantly staff-written. Freelance purchases are limited. Reports in 8-10 weeks. Computer printout submissions OK; prefers letter quality to dot matrix printouts. SASE.

Fiction: Dealing specifically with teenagers and contemporary teen issues. More fiction on emerging alternatives for young women. Suspense, humorous and romance. No prom or cheerleader stories. "Young love is all right, but teens want to read about it in more relevant settings." Length: 2,500-3,500 words. Pays $100.

Tips: "No nonfiction; no fiction with explicit language, casual references to drugs, alcohol, sex, or smoking; no fiction with too depressing outcome."

‡TEEN POWER, SP Ministries, Box 513, Glen Ellyn IL 60137. (312)668-6000. Editor: Christopher Grant. Eight-page weekly magazine for junior and senior high Christian teens. Circ. 115,000. Pays on acceptance. Byline given. Buys first rights. Submit seasonal/holiday material 9 months in advance. Photocopied and previously published submissions OK. Computer printout and disk submissions OK; prefers letter quality to dot matrix printouts. SASE. Reports in 1 month on queries; 3 weeks on mss. Sample copy and writer's guidelines for business-size SAE and one first class stamp.

Nonfiction: How-to (issues of Christian maturity); humor (general/cartoons); inspirational (young teen); interview/profile (Christian personality); personal experience (God's interaction). No reviews or non-Christian-oriented material. "Need evidence of mature, Christian integration with life; no tacked-on morals; creative presentation." Buys 40 mss/year. Send complete ms. Length: 800-1,100 words. Pays $40-90.

Photos: "Simple, bold photos illustrating the ms." Send photos with ms. Pays $5-20 for 3x5 b&w prints. Buys one-time rights.

Columns/Departments: Any mss dealing with application of Bible to everyday teen life—personal experience, expository. Buys 60 mss/year. Send complete ms. Length: 250-400 words. Pays $20-60.

Fiction: Adventure; confession (Christian insight); ethnic; fantasy; historical; humorous; religious; and suspense. Only fiction with teen Christian slant. Buys 40 mss/year. Send complete ms. Length: 800-1,100 words. Pays $60-90.

Poetry: Free verse, haiku, light verse, traditional. "No abstract, adult poetry." Buys 12/year. Length: 48 lines maximum. Pays $5-25.

Fillers: Jokes, gags, anecdotes, short humor. Buys 30/year. Length: 48-96 words. Pays $5-20.

Tips: Shorter word length and search for more varied, contemporary subjects/issues will affect writers in the year ahead.

TEENS TODAY, Church of the Nazarene, 6401 The Paseo, Kansas City MO 64131. (816)333-7000. Managing Editor: Gary Sivewright. 50% freelance written. For junior and senior high teens, to age 18, attending Church of the Nazarene Sunday School. Weekly magazine; 8 pages. Circ. 70,000. Pays on acceptance. Buys all rights. Byline given. Submit seasonal/holiday material 10 months in advance. Simultaneous, photocopied and previously published submissions OK. SASE. Reports in 6-8 weeks. Free sample copy and writer's guidelines for SASE.
Nonfiction: Humor (cartoons). Pays $5-15.
Photos: Photos purchased with or without accompanying ms or on assignment. Pays $10-25 for 8x10 b&w glossy prints. Additional payment for photos accepted with accompanying ms. Model release required.
Fiction: Adventure (if Christian principles are apparent); humorous; religious; and romance (keep it clean). Buys 1 ms/issue. Send complete ms. Length: 1,500-2,000 words. Pays 3¢/word.
Poetry: Free verse; haiku; light verse; and traditional. Buys 15 poems/year. Pays 25¢/line.
Fillers: Puzzles (religious). Buys 15 fillers/year. Pays $5-10.
Tips: "We're looking for quality nonfiction dealing with teen issues: peers, self, parents, vocation, Christian truths related to life, etc. Would also like to see more biographical sketches of outstanding Christians."

TIGER BEAT MAGAZINE, W.P. Magazines, Inc., 105 Union Ave., Cresskill NJ 07626. (201)569-5055. Editorial Director: Sharon Lee. Editor: Nancie Schwartz. For teenage girls ages 14 to 18. Monthly magazine; 80 pages. Circ. 400,000. Computer printout and disk submissions OK; prefers letter quality to dot matrix printouts. Buys all rights. Buys 10 mss/year. Pays on acceptance.
Nonfiction: Stories about young entertainers; their lives, what they do, their interests. Also service-type, self-help articles. Quality writing expected, but must be written with the 14-18 age group in mind. Length: 100-250 words depending on the topic. Pays $50-100. Send query. SASE.
Photos: Pays $25 for b&w photos used with mss; captions optional. Pays $50-75 for color used inside; $75 for cover. 35mm transparencies preferred.
Tips: "We're mostly staff-written; a freelancer's best bet is to come up with something original and exclusive that the staff couldn't do or get. *Tiger Beat*'s new format includes fashion and self-help features for teenage girls. Writing should be aimed at a 17- or 18-year-old intelligence level."

TIGER BEAT STAR, W.P. Magazine, Inc., 105 Union Ave., Cresskill NJ 07626. (201)569-5055. Editor: Ann Rasv. Associate Editor: Debi Fee. Monthly teenage fan magazine for young adults interested in movie, TV and recording stars. "It differs from other teenage fan magazines in that we feature many soap opera stars as well as the regular teenage TV, movie and music stars." Circ. 400,000. Average issue includes 20 feature interviews, gossip columns and fashion and beauty columns. Pays on acceptance. No byline given. Buys first North American serial rights. Submit seasonal material 10 weeks in advance. Previously published submissions OK, if so indicated. SASE. Reports in 2 weeks.
Nonfiction: Interview (of movie, TV and recording stars). Buys 1-2 mss/issue. Query with clips of previously published work. "Write a good query indicating your contact with the star. Investigative pieces are preferred." Length: 200-400 words. Pays $75-200.
Photos: State availability of photos. Pays $15 minimum for 5x7 and 8x10 b&w glossy prints. Pays $35 minimum for 35mm and 2¼ color transparencies. Captions and model release required. Buys all rights.
Fillers: Anecdotes and celebrity-oriented newsbreaks. Buys 5 mss/issue. Length: 100 words minimum. Pays $25 minimum.
Tips: "Be aware of our readership (teenage girls, generally ages 9-17); be 'up' on the current TV, movie and music stars; and be aware of our magazine's unique writing style (it's not geared down *too* far for the young readers or we lose attention of older girls)."

VENTURE MAGAZINE, Box 150, Wheaton IL 60187. Editor: Michael J. Chiapperino. Publication of Christian Service Brigade. For young men 12-18 years of age. Most participate in a Christian Service Brigade program. Monthly magazine except for combined issues in April/May, July/August, October/November, January/February. Circ. 22,000. Published 8 times/year. Buys first rights on unsolicited material. Buys 1-3 mss/issue. Pays on publication. Submit seasonal material 7 months in advance. Usually reports in 2-3 weeks. Query. SASE. Sample copy $1; writer's guidelines for SASE.
Nonfiction: "Family-based articles from boys' perspective; family problems, possible solutions. Interested in photo features on innovative teenage boys who do unusual things, also true-story adventures. Assigned articles deal with specific monthly themes decided by the editorial staff. Most material has an emphasis on boys in a Christian setting. No trite 'Sunday school' mss." Length: 400-1,200 words. Pays $50-100.
Photos: No additional payment is made for 8x10 b&w photos used with mss. Pays $25 for those purchased on assignment; $50-75 for b&w cover photos of boys.

Fiction: "Action-packed, suspense thrillers with Christian theme or lesson. No far-fetched plots or trite themes/settings." Length 1,000-1,800 words. Pays $50-100.

Tips: "Queries must be succinct, well written, and exciting to draw my interest. Send for sample copy; get a feel for our publication; then write something tailored specifically for us."

WORKING FOR BOYS, Box A, Danvers MA 01923. Editor: Brother Alphonsus Dwyer, C.F.X. 37% freelance written. For junior high, parents, grandparents (the latter because the magazine goes back to 1884). Quarterly magazine; 28 pages. Circ. 16,000. Not copyrighted. Buys 30 mss/year. Pays on acceptance. Submit special material (Christmas, Easter, sports, vacation time) 6 months in advance. Reports in 1 week. Submit only complete ms. Address all mss to the Associate Editor, Brother Alois, CFX, St. John's High School, Main St., Shrewsbury MA 01545. SASE. Free sample copy.

Nonfiction: "Conservative, not necessarily religious, articles. Seasonal mostly (Christmas, Easter, etc.). Cheerful, successful outlook suitable for early teenagers. Maybe we are on the 'square' side, favoring the traditional regarding youth manners: generosity to others, respect for older people, patriotism, etc. Animal articles and tales are numerous, but an occasional good dog or horse story is okay. We like to cover seasonal sports." Buys informational, how-to, personal experience, historical and travel. Length: 800-1,200 words. Pays 4¢/word.

Photos: 6x6 b&w glossy prints purchased with ms for $10 each.

Fiction: "Fiction should be wholesome and conservative." Mainstream, adventure, religious, and historical fiction. Theme: open. Length: 500-1,000 words. Pays 4¢/word.

Poetry: Length: 24 lines maximum. Pays 40¢/line.

YOUNG AMBASSADOR, The Good News Broadcasting Association, Inc., Box 82808, Lincoln NE 68501. (402)474-4567. Editor-in-Chief: Melvin A. Jones. Managing Editor: David Lambert. Emphasizes Christian living for church-oriented teens, 12-17. Monthly magazine. Circ. 80,000. Buys reprint or first North American serial rights. Byline given. Phone queries OK. Submit seasonal/holiday material at least 6 months in advance. Previously published submissions OK. No computer printout or disk submissions. SASE. Reports in 6 weeks. Free sample copy and writer's guidelines.

Nonfiction: David Lambert, managing editor. How-to (church youth group activities); interview; personal experience; photo features; inspirational and informational features on spiritual topics. Buys 3-5 mss/issue. Query or send complete ms. Length: 800-1,800 words. Pays 4-7¢/word for unsolicited mss; 7-10¢ for assigned articles. "Material that covers social, spiritual and emotional needs of teenagers. Interviews with teens who are demonstrating their faith in Christ in some unusual way. Biographical articles about teens who have overcome obstacles in their lives. No stories and articles that promote rebellious or selfish behavior in teens, or that glorify immorality."

Fiction: David Lambert, managing editor. "Needs stories involving problems common to teens in which the resolution (or lack of it) is true to our readers' experiences. Needs more stories set in unusual or exotic times and places. Spiritual interest a must, but no preaching. Most of our stories feature a protagonist 14-17 years old." Buys 35 mss/year. Query or send complete ms. Length: 2,000 words maximum. Pays 4-7¢/word.

Fillers: Puzzles on biblical themes. Send complete mss. Pays $3-10.

Tips: "Each issue follows a theme. Write for our list of themes for upcoming issues."

YOUNG AND ALIVE, Christian Record Braille Foundation, Inc., Editorial Dept., 4444 S. 52nd St., Lincoln NE 68506. Editor: Richard Kaiser. Monthly magazine for blind and visually impaired young adults (16-20) published in braille and large print for an interdenominational Christian audience. Pays on acceptance. Computer printout submissions OK; prefers letter quality to dot matrix printouts. SASE. Free writer's guidelines.

Nonfiction: Adventure, biography, camping, health, history, hobbies, nature, practical Christianity, sports and travel. "From a Christian point of view, *Young and Alive* seeks to encourage the thinking, feelings, and activities of people afflicted with sight impairment. While it's true that many blind and visually impaired young adults have the same interests as their sighted counterparts, the material should meet the needs for the sight-impaired, specifically." Recent article example: "Curacau: A Dutch Treat." Length: 800-1,400 words. Query. Pays 3¢-5¢/word.

Fiction: "All forms of stories (such as serials, parables, satire) are used. Their content, however, must be absolutely credible." Length: 800-1,400 words. Query. Pays 3¢-5¢/word.

Photos: Pays $3-$4 for b&w glossy prints.

Tips: "From my experience, I would like to see more colorful descriptions, more forceful verbs, and more intense feelings presented in the manuscripts."

YOUNG MISS, 685 3rd Ave., New York NY 10017. Editor-in-Chief: Phyllis Schneider. 75-80% freelance written. Published 10 times/year for teen girls, aged 12-17. Buys first rights. Byline given. Pays on acceptance. Editorial requirement sheet for SASE. Query on nonfiction. Reports on submissions in 6 weeks. All mss must be typed, double-spaced. Computer printout submissions OK. SASE.

Nonfiction: Deborah Purcell, features/fiction editor. Personal growth and self-improvement; all aspects of boy-girl relationships; first-person humor; quizzes; and profiles of sports, TV, film and music figures appealing to teens. Buys 10-20 unsolicited mss/year. Length: 1,500-2,000 words. Pays $25 and up for short fillers; $125 and up for features. No illustrations.

Fiction: Deborah Purcell, features/fiction editor. "All fiction should be aimed at young adults, not children; when in doubt, develop older rather than younger characters. Stories may be set in any locale or time, and stories about romance and personal dilemmas are particularly welcomed. The protagonist may be either male or female. Length: 2,500-3,000 words. Pays $350 and up.

Tips: "Queries for nonfiction should express original thought; desire and ability to do thorough research where applicable; clear understanding of the interests and needs of 12-17 year olds; fresh angles. We are not interested in lightweight nonfiction material or style except where applicable (e.g., humor). Fitness and health, fashion and beauty, pet care, and food articles are all done in-house."

Theater, Movie, TV, and Entertainment

This category features publications covering live, filmed, or videotaped entertainment, including video games, dance, and adult entertainment. For those publications whose emphasis is on music and musicians, see the Music section.

ADAM FILM WORLD, 8060 Melrose Ave., Los Angeles CA 90046. (213)653-8060. Editor: Edward S. Sullivan. For fans of X- and R-rated movies and videotapes. Magazine published 8 times/year plus 4 special issues. Circ. 250,000. Buys first North American serial rights. Buys about 12 mss/year. Pays on publication. No photocopied or simultaneous submissions. Reports on mss accepted for publication in 1-2 months. Returns rejected material in 2 weeks. Query. No computer printout or disk submissions. SASE. Sample copy $1.50.

Nonfiction: "All copy is slanted for fans of X and R movies and can be critical of this or that picture, but not critical of the genre itself. All in 4-color. Publication's main emphasis is on pictorial layouts, rather than text; layouts of stills from erotic pictures. Any article must have possibilities for illustration. We go very strong in the erotic direction, but *no* hard-core stills. We see too many fictional interviews with a fictitious porno star, and too many fantasy suggestions for erotic film plots. No think-pieces. We would consider articles on the continuing erotization of legitimate films from major studios, and the increasing legitimization of X and R films from the minors." Length: 1,000-3,000 words. Pays $80-150.

Photos: Most photos are bought on assignment from regular photographers with studio contacts, but a few 35mm slides are purchased from freelancers for use as illustrations. Pays minimum of $35/color spot photo.

Tips: "We have gone all 4-color. If necessary, we can duotone a few black/white photos."

AFTER DARK, Suite 409, 175 5th Ave., New York NY 10010. (212)246-7979. Editor: Lee Swanson. For a sophisticated audience 20-55 years old, "visually oriented, who wants to know what's news and who's making the news in the world of entertainment." Monthly. Circ. 74,000. Buys first rights. Buys about 10 mss/year. Pays on publication. Sample copy $3. Submit seasonal material 4 months in advance. Reports in 3-4 weeks. Query, including copies of previously published work; some mention of access to illustrative materials is always useful.

Nonfiction: Articles on "every area of entertainment—films, TV, theater, nightclubs, books, records. No 'think' or survey pieces about the social or psychological implications to be gleaned from some entertainment trend. The fastest approach would be to offer access to some hard-to-reach entertainment celebrity who customarily has not given interviews. However, we do not want lurid, tasteless accounts laced with sexual anecdote." Length: 500-1,500 words. Pays $150-300.

Photos: Photos with captions only. B&w glossy prints, color transparencies. Pays $20-75.

Tips: "The best way to crack *After Dark* is by doing a piece on some new trend in the entertainment world. We have people in most of the important cities, but we rely on freelancers to send us material from out-of-the-way places where new things are developing. Some of our contributing editors started out that way. Query."

‡**AFTERNOON TV**, Television Publications, 300 W. 43rd St., New York NY 10036. (212)397-5200. Editor: Diane Masters. Managing Editor: Bonnie Scheffer. Monthly magazine of soap opera and daytime TV. Circ. 240,000. Pays on publication. Byline given. Buys all rights. Submit seasonal/holiday material 5 months in advance. Photocopied submissions OK. SASE. Reports in 1 month.

Nonfiction: Interview/profile (of daytime celebrities); behind-the-scenes with producers/directors. Buys 145 mss/year. Query. Length: 2,500-3,500 words. Pays $150-175.

Photos: State availability of photos. Reviews b&w and color contact sheets. Captions, model release and identification of subjects required.

THE ALTERNATIVE MAGAZINE, (formerly *Hot Potato Magazine*), Alternative Publications, Inc., Suite 4A, 6325 N. Guilford Ave., Indianapolis IN 46220. (317)251-1754. Editor: David Lehr. Biweekly entertainment/lifestyle tabloid for the 18-40 age group. Includes human interest features preferably tied to the local market. Also includes reviews of live shows, records, films, theater, and some sports depending on personality. Circ. 30,000. Pays on publication. Byline given. Buys one-time rights and all rights. Submit seasonal/holiday material 3 months in advance. Photocopied and previously published submissions OK. No SASE. Publishers cannot return unsolicited materials. Reports in 2-4 weeks on queries; 1 month on mss. Sample copy for SAE and $1.20 postage.
Nonfiction: General interest; historical/nostalgic (on theme); interview/profile; new product (audio/video/computer, etc.); opinion; personal experience (satire, etc.). No heavy political or heavy bias/opinion mss. Buys variable number mss/year. Query with clips of published work or send complete ms. Length: open; prefer concise, yet complete ms (depending on theme). Pays $5-50.
Photos: Send photos with accompanying ms. Pays $5 for b&w or color prints (any size). Captions, model release, and identification of subjects required.
Columns/Departments: Medical/Ask Dr. Ben (questions/answers); Reviews: Movies, Albums, Midwest Music, Concerts (only local and regional); Jazz Concert Calendar. Buys variable number mss/year. Query with clips of published work or send complete ms. Length: concise. Pays $5 minimum.
Fiction: Buys 3-5 mss/year. "Query, as we use very little." Length: open. Pays variable fee.
Fillers: Short humor, newsbreaks. Buys variable number/year. Length: open. Pays variable fee.
Tips: "We are a new publication with high growth potential and an open mind. Due to the nature of our magazine, much of our material is generated locally, but we are always interested, especially in lifestyle/feature material. Queries are preferred as we cannot return mss. No SASEs."

AMERICAN FILM, American Film Institute, Kennedy Center, Washington DC 20566. (202)828-4060. Editor: Peter Biskind. 80% freelance written. For film professionals, students, teachers, film enthusiasts, culturally oriented readers. Monthly magazine. Circ. 140,000. Buys first North American serial rights. Pays kill fee. Byline given. Pays 90 days after acceptance. Sample copy $2. Will consider photocopied submissions. Submit material 3 months in advance. Reports in 1 month. Query. No computer printout or disk submissions. SASE.
Nonfiction: In-depth articles on film and television-related subjects. "Our articles require expertise and first-rate writing ability." Buys informational, profile, historical and "think" pieces. No film reviews. Buys 10 unsolicited mss/year. Length: 2,000-4,000 words. Pays $100-750.
Tips: "No 'my favorite moments in films' or other 'fanzine' type pieces."

‡**AMERICAN SQUAREDANCE**, Burdick Enterprises, Box 488, Huron OH 44839. (419)433-2188. Editors: Stan and Cathie Burdick. Monthly magazine of interviews, reviews, topics of interest to the modern square dancer. Circ. 13,000. Pays on publication. Byline given. Buys all rights. Submit seasonal/holiday material 3 months in advance. Not receptive to computer printout or disk submissions. Reports in 2 weeks on queries. Sample copy for 6x9 SAE; free writer's guidelines.
Nonfiction: General interest, historical/nostalgic, humor, inspirational, interview/profile, new product, opinion, personal experience, photo feature, travel. Must deal with square dance. Buys 6 mss/year. Send complete ms. Length: 1,000-1,500 words. Pays $10-35.
Photos: Send photos with ms. Reviews b&w prints. Captions and identification of subjects required.
Fiction: Subject related to square dancing only. Buys 1-2 mss/year. Send complete ms. Length: 2,000-2,500 words. Pays $25-35.
Poetry: Avant-garde, free verse, haiku, light verse, traditional. Square dancing subjects only. Buys 6/year. Submit maximum 3 poems. Pays $1 for 1st 4 lines; $1/verse thereafter.

ARCADE, The Electronic Entertainment Magazine, Mead Publishing Corp., 21176 S. Alameda St., Long Beach CA 90810. (213)549-2376. Editor: Sue Boyce. Monthly magazine covering video and other electronic games for all ages, all interests. "Our editorial philosophy is simple. *Arcade* is written for the video game enthusiast, the person who enjoys entertainment through electronic games. *Arcade* is sophisticated, as are our readers. We prefer to combine the varied interests of our readers into a gap-bridging whole; encompassing home video game play, coin-op commercial video games, personal home computer systems, and related topics of interest." Estab. 1982. Circ. 20,000. Pays on publication. Byline given. Buys first rights. Submit seasonal/holiday material 4 months in advance. Simultaneous queries, and simultaneous, photocopied and previously published submissions OK. Computer printout or disk submissions OK; prefers letter quality to dot matrix printouts. SASE. Reports in 1 month. Sample copy $2.25.
Nonfiction: Book excerpts (on video games and computer technology); expose (relating to video games industry or players); general interest; how-to (game playing tips); humor (preferably relating to video games or related lifestyle); interview/profile; new products (electronic games or lifestyle-oriented); opinion; travel (must

have video game hook). No poor quality writing, spelling, research, grammar, or style. "Nothing *not* related to electronic entertainment; nothing unsuitable for contemporary family reading." Buys 60 mss/year. Length: 500-3,000 words. Pays $25-100.

Photos: State availability of photos. B&w only and only with article.

Columns/Departments: Departments: video game reviews, software, hardware, movies (as they relate to player lifestyle or games), new products, Arcades, book reviews, newsfront. Buys 50 mss/year. Query with clips of published work. Length: 250-750 words. Pays up to $25.

Fillers: Jokes, gags, short humor, newsbreaks " . . . as they relate to our audience." Buys variable number/month. Length: 25-250 words. Pays up to $10.

Tips: Always query first.

‡**AUSTRALIAN VIDEO AND COMMUNICATIONS**, Incorporating *Australian Video Review*, General Magazine Company Pty., Ltd., 9 Paran Place, Glen Iris, Victoria 3146 Australia. (03)25-6456. Editor: Geoffrey M. Gold. Monthly magazine covering home video and telecommunications. Estab. 1981. Circ. 29,000. Pays on publication. Byline given. Offers 25% kill fee. Buys all Australian rights. Submit seasonal/holiday material 4 months in advance. Simultaneous queries, and photocopied and previously published submissions OK. SASE. Reports in 2 weeks. Sample copy $2.

Nonfiction: Book excerpts, historical/nostalgic, humor, interview/profile, new products and services. Special issues include Australian Video and Computer Games Annual; Australian Video Trade Reference Book 1984; Australian Video Review Annual (movies). No specifically North American material. "We require 'internationalized' material suitable for Australian readers." Buys 100 mss/year. Query with published clips. Length: 500-3,000 words. Pays $25-350.

Photos: State availability of photos. Pays $25-50 for color transparencies; $15-35 for b&w prints. Captions, model release and identification of subjects required.

Columns/Departments: New Products; Network (humorous round-up); video games. Buys 20 mss/year. Query. Length: 50-600 words. Pays $25-75.

Fiction: Buys 3 mss/year. Query.

Tips: "Contact us with suggestions and copy of previously published work. All sections are open. North American writers should become more aware of the wider international market for their material. Our Australian, New Zealand and Pacific region readers insist on locally relevant articles. At the same time, they are highly literate and wise to the international scene and appreciate foreign articles that bridge the 'national' gap."

BALLET NEWS, The Metropolitan Opera Guild, Inc., 1865 Broadway, New York NY 10023. (212)582-3285. Editor: Robert Jacobson. Managing Editor: Karl F. Reuling. Monthly magazine. Covering dance and the related fields of films, video and records. Circ. 40,000. Average issue includes 4-5 feature articles. "All are accompanied by many photos and graphics. We are writing for a dance audience who wants to better appreciate the art form. We include reviews, calendar and book reviews." Pays on publication. Byline given. Kill fee negotiable. Buys first rights. Photocopied submissions OK. SASE. Reports in 1 month. Sample copy $2.50.

Nonfiction: General interest (critical analysis, theaters); historical; interview (dancers, choreographers, entrepreneurs, costumers, stage designers); profile; travel (dance in any location); and technical (staging, practice). Query, send complete ms or send clips of previously published work. Length: 2,500 words. Pays 10¢/word.

Photos: State availability of photos or send photos with ms. Payment negotiable for b&w contact sheets.

CANADIAN THEATRE REVIEW, 4700 Keele St., Downsview, Ontario, Canada M3J 1P3. (416)667-3768. Editor-in-Chief: Robert Wallace. Managing Editor: Susan Duligal. 80% freelance written. Emphasizes theater for Canadian academics and professionals. Quarterly magazine; 144 pages. Circ. 5,000. Pays on publication. Buys one-time rights. Pays 50% kill fee. Byline given. SAE and International Reply Coupons. Reports in 10-12 weeks. Sample copy $4.

Nonfiction: Historical (theater in Canada); interview (internationally known theater figures); and photo feature (theater worldwide). Buys 40 mss/year. Length: 1,500-5,000 words. Query or submit complete ms. Pays $15/published page.

Photos: State availability of photos with query or mss.

CINEASTE MAGAZINE, A Magazine on the Art and Politics of the Cinema, 419 Park Ave. S., New York NY 10016. Editors: Gary Crowdus, Dan Georgakas, Lenny Rubenstein. Quarterly magazine covering films for filmmaking students, film lovers, and people involved in making or distributing films. Circ. 6,500. Pays on publication. Byline and brief bio given. Buys first North American serial rights. No computer printout or disk submissions. SASE. Reports in 1 month on queries. Sample copy $1; writer's guidelines for business size SAE and 1 first class stamp.

Nonfiction: Interview (of filmmakers, actors, screenwriters and directors); and social issues raised by films. Buys 6-10 mss/year. Query with clips of published work "if relevant. Query with letter should state the exact project the author wishes to undertake and his qualifications." Length: 3,000-5,000 words. Pays $20 minimum.

Columns/Departments: A Second Look (occasional feature reviewing a movie); and book reviews. Buys 6 mss/year. Send complete ms. Buys 1,000-3,000 words. Pays $10 minimum.
Tips: "Familiarity with the magazine is a must. Otherwise authors are wasting their time. We seek only high level intellectual material from people who have read the magazine and agree with its general orientation."

DANCE IN CANADA, 38 Charles St. E, Toronto, Ontario, Canada M4Y 1T1. (416)921-5169. Editor: Michael Crabb. Quarterly magazine covering dance (ballet and modern) in Canada plus limited foreign dance coverage. "A serious dance magazine providing news, analysis, opinion and criticism of dance events, films and books. Circ. 3,000. Pays within 30 days of publication. Byline given. Offers 75% kill fee. Buys first Canadian serial rights. Submit seasonal/holiday material 3 months in advance. Photocopied and previously published submissions (under special circumstances) OK. Computer printout or disk submissions OK "if there's space to copyedit"; prefers letter quality to dot matrix printouts. SASE. Reports in 2 weeks on queries; 1 month on mss. Sample copy $3; free writer's guidelines.
Nonfiction: General interest (current professional dance company news, etc.); historical/nostalgic (Canadian dance history); how-to (related to helping professional dancers in all areas); interview/profile (of leading Canadian dance people); opinion (interesting dance issues where writer has authority); personal experience (dance-related experience of interest to broad readership); photo feature ("Photo-Gallery" for Canadian dance photographers); technical (specialized aspects of dance technique with educational slant). "Nothing puffy. Prefer work from writers with broad, sound knowledge." Buys 15 mss/year. Query with clips of published work. Length: 1,000-2,500 words. Pays $50-100.
Photos: Holly Small, photo editor. State availability of photos. Pays $15-25 for 8x10 b&w prints; $25-50 for color transparencies. Captions, model release and identification of subjects required. Buys one-time rights.
Fillers: Holly Small, fillers editor. Newsbreaks. Buys 5-20/year. Length: 50-200 words. Pays $5-20.
Tips: "Provide lucid, accurate information in an engaging style likely to appeal to a broad readership, some of whom may only have a basic knowledge of dance but who love the art and want their passion fed. Dance reviewers need to have ability to give clear idea of what happened plus their own comments on the artistic worth of the performance."

DANCE MAGAZINE, 1180 Avenue of the Americas, New York NY 10036. (212)921-9300. Editor: William Como. Managing Editor: Richard Philp. Monthly. For the dance profession and members of the public interested in the art of dance, all areas of the performing art—stage performances, concerts, history, teaching, personalities—while retaining the format of an art publication. "Freelancer must have knowledge of dance; experience, technical or dance critic background. We do not encourage non-dance writers to submit articles and please . . . no poetry." Buys all rights. Pays on publication. Sample copy $3. Query with outline of knowledge of dance. No computer printout or disk submissions. SASE.
Nonfiction: Personalities, knowledgeable comment, news. No personality profiles or personal interviews. Length: 2,000-2,500 words. Pays $300 maximum.
Photos: Purchased with articles or with captions only. Pays $5-15.
Tips: "Query first, preferably by mail. Do a piece about a local company that's not too well known but growing; or a particular school that is doing well which we may not have heard about; or a local dancer who you feel will be gaining national recognition."

DANCE TEACHER NOW, SMW Communications, Inc., 1333 Notre Dame Dr., Davis CA 95616. (916)756-6222. Editor: Susan Wershing. For professional teachers of stage and ballroom dance in private studios and colleges. Bimonthly magazine. Circ. 4,500. Average issue includes 5-6 feature articles, departments, and calendar sections. Pays on acceptance. Computer printout or disk submissions OK; "the covering letter assures us the author is not shotgunning the article to a dozen publications at once." Byline given. Buys all rights. Submit seasonal material 6 months in advance. Reports in 2 months. Sample copy $2; free writer's guidelines.
Nonfiction: "Legal issues, health and dance injuries, dance techniques, business, advertising, taxes and insurance, curricula, student/teacher relations, government grants, studio equipment, concerts and recitals, departmental budgets, etc. We're leaning more toward nationally prominent people as subjects of articles." Buys 4-6 mss/issue. Query with clips of previously published work. Length: 1,000-3,000 words. Pays $100-300.
Photos: State availability of photos. Pays $20 minimum for 5x7 b&w glossy prints. Model release required. Buys all rights.
Columns/Departments: Practical Tips (3-4 paragraphs, short items of immediate practical use to the teacher). Building Your Library, and Spotlight on Successful Teachers (one per issue).
Tips: "We like complete reportage of the material with all the specifics, but personalized with direct quotes and anecdotes. The writer should speak one-to-one to the reader, but keep the national character of the magazine in mind. To achieve the practical quality in each article, the most important question in any interview is 'How?' We do not want personality profiles. Articles must include material of practical value to reader. We do not want philosophical or 'artsy' articles; straightforward reporting only."

DOWNTOWNER, R.F.D. Publications, Inc., Box 4227, Portland OR 97208. (503)620-4121. Editor: Maggi White. Weekly contemporary and upbeat tabloid. Circ. 22,000. Pays on publication. Byline given. Offers variable kill fee. Not copyrighted. Buys one-time rights. Submit seasonal/holiday material 4 months in advance. Simultaneous queries OK. No computer printout or disk submissions. SASE. Reports in 1 month.
Nonfiction: How-to, humor, interview/profile, photo feature. "The focus is interesting persons, places, things, usually requiring a local tie-in. We're not issue-oriented, but people-oriented, and we treat 'issues' through people who are dealing successfully with them." Query with clips of published work or send complete ms. Length: 750 words. Pays $25-50.
Photos: Send photos with ms. Reviews transparencies and prints. Identification of subjects required.

THE DRAMA REVIEW, New York University, 300 South Bldg., 51 W. 4th St., New York NY 10003. (212)598-2597. Editor: Michael Kirby. Emphasizes avant-garde performance art for professors, students and the general theater and dance-going public as well as professional practitioners in the performing arts. Quarterly magazine; 144 pages. Circ. 10,000. Pays on publication. Phone queries OK. Submit seasonal/holiday material 4 months in advance. Photocopied and previously published (if published in another language) submissions OK. No computer printout or disk submissions. SASE. Reports in 3 months. Sample copy $5; free writer's guidelines.
Nonfiction: Jill Dolan, managing editor. Historical (the historical avant-garde in any performance art, translations of previously unpublished plays, etc.) and informational (documentation of a particular performance). Buys 10-20 mss/issue. Query. Pays 2¢/word for translations and other material.
Photos: Jill Dolan, managing editor. Photos purchased with or without accompanying ms or on assignment. Captions required. Pays $10 for b&w photos. No additional payment for photos accepted with accompanying ms.
Tips: "No criticism in the sense of value judgments—we are not interested in the author's opinions. We are only interested in documentation theory and analysis. No criticism and scholarly, footnoted work."

DRAMATICS MAGAZINE, International Thespian Society, 3368 Central Pkwy., Cincinnati OH 45202. (513)559-1996. Editor-in-Chief: S. Ezra Goldstein. Associate Editor: Donald Corathers. 25-30% freelance written. For theater arts students, teachers and others interested in theater arts education. Magazine published monthly, September through May; 44-52 pages. Circ. 40,000. Pays on acceptance. Buys first North American serial rights. Byline given. Submit seasonal/holiday material 3 months in advance. Simultaneous, photocopied and previously published submissions OK. Computer printout or disk submissions OK; prefers letter quality to dot matrix printouts. SASE. Reports in 3 weeks. Sample copy $2; free writer's guidelines.
Nonfiction: Historical; how-to (technical theater); informational; interview; photo feature; humorous; profile; and technical. Buys 30 mss/year. Submit complete ms. Length: 1,000-3,000 words. Pays $30-150.
Photos: Purchased with accompanying ms. Uses b&w photos and color transparencies. Query. Total purchase price for ms includes payment for photos.
Fiction: Drama (one-act plays). No "children's theatre, community theatre, plays for children, Christmas plays, or plays written with no attention paid to the playwriting form." Buys 5-9 mss/year. Send complete ms. Pays $50-200.
Tips: "The best way to break in is to know our audience—drama students and teachers and others interested in theater—and to write for them. Writers who have some practical experience in theater, especially in technical areas, have a leg-up here, but we'll work with anybody who has a good idea. We like for writers to read us before they try to write for us."

DRAMATIKA, 429 Hope St., Tarpon Springs FL 33589. Editors: John and Andrea Pyros. Magazine; 40 pages. For persons interested in the theater arts. Published 2 times/year. Circ. 500-1,000. Buys all rights. Pays on publication. Sample copy $2. Query. SASE. Reports in 1 month.
Fiction: Wants "performable pieces—plays, songs, scripts, etc." Will consider plays on various and open themes. Query first. Length: 20 pages maximum. Pays about $25/piece; $5-10 for smaller pieces.
Photos: B&w photos purchased with ms with extra payment. Captions required. Pays $5. Size: 8x11.

‡**EAST CENTRAL FLORIDA, Public Broadcasting Monthly**, Community Communications, Inc., 11510 E. Colonial Dr., Orlando FL 32817. (305)273-2300. Editor: Larry Bucking. Managing Editor: Pat Schultz. Monthly magazine covering the lifestyle of Central Florida for the subscribers, financial supporters of public broadcasting in East Central Florida; "their magazine reflects their cultural bent." Estab. 1982. Circ. 24,000. Pays on publication. Byline given. Kill fee same amount as payment. Not copyrighted. Buys one-time rights. Submit seasonal/holiday material 2 months in advance. Simultaneous queries OK. SASE. Reports in 2 months. Sample copy $2; writer's guidelines for SAE.
Nonfiction: Book reviews (if book deals with region); general interest (if intent is to make life easier); interview/profile (dealing with public TV personalities); travel (query travel editor, Harriot Roberts). No unsolicited articles. Buys 30 mss/year. Query with clips if available. Pays $50-250 (negotiable).

Photos: State availability of photos with query letter or ms. Reviews 8½x11 b&w prints. Pays negotiable fee. Captions required.

Columns/Departments: Florida gardening, investments, travel, seniors, fine arts (local), foods, book reviews: All departments have an educational slant. Buys 36 items/year. Query. Length: 300-1,000 words. Pays $50-250 (negotiable).

Tips: "Writers usually are recalled once a manuscript is published. All of our material is provided by freelancers. Any section is as likely to use freelance material as another. If a writer closely follows style rules (*Associated Press Stylebook*, for example), his work will get more consideration. Editing time is becoming more valuable, rare."

ELECTRICity, THE DRUMMER and UNIVERCity, National News Bureau, 262 S. 12th St., Philadelphia PA 19107. (215)985-1990. Editors: Andrea Diehl and Harry Jay Katz. Managing Editors: Andy Edelman and Lorena Alexander. Weekly entertainment/leisure tabloids for readers aged 17-45 years. The National News Bureau syndicates to over 1,000 publications weekly. Pays on publication. Byline given. Buys all rights. Photocopied original submissions OK. Computer printout or disk submissions OK; prefers letter quality to dot matrix printouts. SASE. Reports in 3 weeks. Writer's guidelines for 8½x11 SAE and 37¢ postage.

Nonfiction: Book excerpts, general interest, how-to, interview/profile, new product, photo feature, travel. Special issues include stereo, travel, video, books, fashion, career, back-to-school. "We're looking for upbeat, feature-oriented writing that's imaginative, trendy and to the point. No hard news, political pieces or poetry." Buys 500 mss/year. Send complete ms. Length: 500-1,000 words. Pays $5-100.

Photos: Send photos with accompanying ms. Pays $5-50 for 8x10 b&w prints. Captions, model release, and identification of subjects required.

Columns/Departments: Send complete ms. Length: 500-1,000 words.

Fiction: Buys 200 mss/year. Send complete ms.

‡**EMMY MAGAZINE**, Suite 800, Academy of Television Arts & Sciences, 4605 Lankershim Blvd., N. Hollywood CA 91602. (213)506-7885. Editor: Richard Krafsur. Managing Editor: Michael Llach. Bimonthly magazine on television—a "critical—though not necessarily fault-finding—treatment of television and its effects on society, and how it might be improved." Circ. 10,000. Pays on acceptance. Byline given. Offers 20% kill fee. Buys first North American serial rights. SASE. Reports in 2 weeks on queries; 1 month on mss. Free sample copy.

Nonfiction: Expose, historical/nostalgic, humor, interview/profile, opinion—all dealing with television. No fan-type profiles of TV performers. Buys 40 mss/year. Query with published clips. Length: 2,000-3,000 words. Pays $450-1,000.

Columns/Departments: Opinion or point-of-view columns dealing with TV. Buys 18-20 mss/year. Query with published clips. Length: 800-1,500 words. Pays $300-500.

Tips: "Query with thoughtful description of what you wish to write about. Or call. In either case, we can soon establish whether or not we can do business together."

FANTASTIC FILMS, The Magazine of Imaginative Media, Box 1900, Evanston IL 60201. (312)866-7155. Editor: Michael Stein. Magazine published 6 times/year, covering science fiction films and fantasy animation, for adherents of science fiction and nostalgia, ages 7-40. Circ. 110,000. Pays "shortly after publication." Byline given. Buys first North American serial rights. Submit seasonal material 3 months in advance. Simultaneous queries OK; photocopied submission preferred. Computer printout submissions OK. SASE. Reports in 1 month.

Nonfiction: General interest (human side of filmmaking); interview/profile (of persons involved in making films); and technical (dealing with filmmaking). No movie reviews. Buys 3 mss/year. Query with clips of published work. Length: 2,000-5,000 words. Pays 3¢/word.

Photos: State availability of photos or send photos with accompanying ms. "Writer must supply all graphics to accompany article. All material will be returned."

Tips: "I prefer to deal with writers who are knowledgeable in area written about or have connections with directors, producers and special effects people."

FILM COMMENT, Film Society of Lincoln Center, 140 W. 65th St., New York NY 10023. (212)877-1800. Editor: Richard Corliss. Senior Editor: Harlan Jacobson. Bimonthly magazine covering cinema. Circ. 30,000. Pays on publication. Byline given. Buys one-time rights. Submit seasonal material 2 months in advance. No computer printout or disk submissions. SASE.

Nonfiction: Harlan Jacobson, senior editor. Book excerpts; expose; general interest (film); historical; interview/profile; new product; opinion; photo feature. "We only accept articles by writers extremely knowledgeable in film." No personal accounts of working on a film, fictional movie-inspired work. Buys 125 mss/year. Query with clips of published work. Length: 800-6,000 words. Pays $100-500.

Photos: Harlan Jacobson, senior editor. State availability of photos.

Columns/Departments: Video, Television, Books, Independents, Industry, Journals. Length: 800-2,000 words. Pays $100-250.

Tips: "The best way to break in is to have excellent writing samples, some film credentials, be already published on film somewhere, and come up with an idea well in advance of its timeliness: an interview with someone who has a new movie coming out, for example. Most open to either serious in-depth essays on older filmmakers who haven't been profiled, or right-on-the-mark trend stories or think pieces related to current films, or interviews with topical filmmakers."

FILM QUARTERLY, University of California Press, Berkeley CA 94720. (415)642-6333. Editor: Ernest Callenbach. 100% freelance written. Quarterly. Buys all rights. Byline given. Pays on publication. Query; "sample pages are very helpful from unknown writers. We must have hard-copy printout and don't care how it is produced, but we cannot use dot-matrix printouts unless done on one of the new printers that gives type-quality letters." SASE.

Nonfiction: Articles on style and structure in films, articles analyzing the work of important directors, historical articles on development of the film as art, reviews of current films and detailed analyses of classics, book reviews of film books. Must be familiar with the past and present of the art; must be competently, although not necessarily breezily, written; must deal with important problems of the art. "We write for people who like to think and talk seriously about films, as well as simply view them and enjoy them. We use no personality pieces or reportage pieces. Interviews usually work for us only when conducted by someone familiar with most of a filmmaker's work. (We don't use performer interviews.)" Recently published Daniel Greenberg's "The Reference Shelf Shuffle," analyzing deficiencies in available film reference sources (Winter 1982-83). Length: 6,000 words maximum. Pay is about 2¢/word.

Tips: "*Film Quarterly* is a specialized academic journal of film criticism, though it is also a magazine (with pictures) sold in bookstores. It is read by film teachers, students, and die-hard movie buffs, so unless you fall into one of those categories, it is very hard to write for us. Currently, we are especially looking for material on independent, documentary, etc. films not written about in the national film reviewing columns."

HIFI BUYER'S REVIEW, Box 684, Southampton NY 11968. (516)283-2360. Editor: Tom Farre. For the hi-fi enthusiast. Emphasizes "fact-filled buying and using information about hi-fi equipment." Bimonthly publication of Hampton International Communications, Inc. Magazine; 68 pages. Circ. 60,000. Buys all rights. Byline given. Buys about 36 mss/year. Pays after publication. Query with sample of work. No photocopied or simultaneous submissions. Reports in 1 month. SASE.

Nonfiction: Publishes hi-fidelity information, equipment stories and laboratory reports. Length: informational, 3,000 words. Pays $140.

Photos: Photos purchased with ms for no additional payment.

Tips: "Prospective writers must be expert in technical aspects of field, with hands-on experience with products."

HORIZON, The Magazine of the Arts, Boone, Inc., Drawer 30, Tuscaloosa AL 35402. Editor/Publisher: Gray Boone. Editorial Director: Kellee Reinhart. Monthly magazine covering the arts (fine arts, architecture, literature, theater, dance, film, music, photography, television, arts-related travel). "*Horizon* is a graphically rich arts magazine giving readers the tools and information necesary to bring the arts into their everyday lives. Our readership is upscale, highly educated, and geographically diverse. They are interested in the arts in a deeply personal way, whether it's going to the theater or collecting art for their home." Pays on publication. Byline given. Offers kill fee. Buys first North American serial rights. Submit seasonal/holiday material 4 months in advance. "This is important, as many of our articles are timed with openings, etc." SASE. Reports in 1 month. Sample copy $2; writer's guidelines for SASE.

Nonfiction: Linda Gallehugh, senior editor. Book excerpts ("relatively few"); expose ("if sound and well-documented"); historical/nostalgic ("rarely"); profiles ("no puff pieces—must be timely and interpretative"); critical essays or surveys ("must relate to something important in the contemporary cultural scene"); and photo features. "We publish no original fiction or poetry." Buys 6 unsolicited mss/year. Recent article example: "Grassroots Opera" (January/February 1982). Query with clips of published work. Length: 1,500-3,500 words. Pays $350-600.

Photos: Robin McDonald, art director. State availability of photos or send photos with ms. Reviews any size color transparencies or 8x10 prints. Identification of subjects required. Buys one-time rights.

Tips: Most open to "feature articles. When submitting ideas, consider how they could be fleshed out with sidebars, tips, and biographies so that readers could take this article and go beyond what you've written. Query letters should be well researched and to the point (not two pages long) and are best supported with clips of the writer's other publications. Timeliness and a unique angle are vital also. We take queries in writing only. Phone queries are counter-productive, because they annoy our editors, who are working on other things. Flexibility and promptness at deadlines endear writers to us."

MEDIA HISTORY DIGEST, Media Digest History Corp., c/o Editor & Publisher, 575 Lexington, New York NY 10022. Editor: Hiley H. Ward. Magazine published quarterly covering media history—newspapers,

books, film, radio-TV and magazines—for "both a specialized (history, journalism) and a general market. Articles must have high popular interest." Circ. 2,000. Buys first rights. Submit seasonal/holiday material 6 months in advance. Prefers typed mss. SASE. Reports in 2 months on queries and on mss. Sample copy $3.
Nonfiction: Historical/nostalgic—media; emphasis on people and human interest; humor (related to the media, present or historical); and interview/profile (older people's oral history). No "unreadable academic articles of narrow interest." Uses 50 mss/year. Query. Length: 500-1,500 words. Pays $50-100.
Photos: "Most of our photos would come from historical files." State availability of photos.
Fillers: Puzzles (media history quizzes, crosswords on specific topics). Pays $25-35. "We will publish regularly and expand; return to color, etc., as result of magazine being acquired by *Editor and Publisher* magazine."

PERFORMING ARTS IN CANADA, 2nd Fl., 52 Avenue Rd., Toronto, Ontario, Canada M5R 2G3. (416)921-2601. Editor: Don Rooke. For professional performers and general readers with an interest in Canadian theater, dance and music. Covers "all three major fields of the performing arts (music, theater and dance), modern and classical, plus articles on related subjects (technical topics, government arts policy, etc.)." Quarterly magazine. Circ. 66,000. Pays 1 month following publication. Buys first rights. Pays 30-50% kill fee. Byline given. Reports in 3-6 weeks. Computer printout or disk submissions OK; prefers letter quality to dot matrix printouts. SAE and International Reply Coupons. Sample copy 50¢.
Nonfiction: "Lively, stimulating, well-researched articles on Canadian performing artists or groups. We tend to be overstocked with theater pieces; most often in need of good classical music articles." No non-Canadian, non-performing arts material. Buys 30-35 mss/year. Query. Length: 1,500-2,000 words. Pays $150.
Tips: "Query with a good idea for an article—at the very least, state field of interest and two or three broad subjects that could be worked into a specific proposal for an article. Writers new to this publication should include clippings."

‡**PERFORMING ARTS NETWORK, INC.**, Suite 210, 9025 Wilshire Blvd., Beverly Hills CA 90211. Editor-in-Chief: Herbert Glass. Distributed to the theater audiences of Los Angeles, San Francisco and San Diego. Monthly magazine; 64-100 pages. Total circ. 545,000. Pays on publication. Buys all rights. Submit seasonal/holiday material 3 months in advance. SASE. Reports in 2 weeks. Sample copy $1; writer's guidelines for SASE.
Nonfiction: "Primary editorial emphasis is on the performing arts. We look for articles that will get an 'I-didn't-know-that' reaction from our readers. We also cover other aspects of both performing and visual arts. Our pages are open to your suggestions." Length: 1,000-2,000 words.

‡**PHILADELPHIA/NEW YORK ACTION NEWSPAPER**, PNS Research, Inc., Box 733, Fort Washington PA 19034. (800)523-6600, or (215)628-3030. Editor: Bob Rose. Managing Editor: George Finster. Entertainment tabloid covering sex and the commercial sex business. "We are an entertainment newspaper for sophisticated adults. Our editorial philosophy is that sex, in all of its wonderful variations, between consenting adults, is more fun than anything." Circ. 10,000. Pays on publication. Byline given; pen names are also acceptable. Buys first North American serial rights and "rights to reprint only in our own publications." Submit seasonal/holiday material 6 months in advance (specify seasonal material on outside of envelope). Photocopied submissions OK. SASE. Reports in 6 weeks on queries; 3 months on mss. Sample copy $1; writer's guidelines for business size SAE and 1 first class stamp.
Nonfiction: Personal experience (unusual sexual experience). Buys 20-25 mss/year. Query. Length: 2,500-3,000 words. Pays $100-200.
Fiction: Erotica (unusual with the emphasis on enjoyment); humorous (emphasis on sex); science fiction (emphasis on sex). "No rape stories or stories in which one or more of the sexual participants are not enjoying themselves." Buys 50 mss/year. Query or send complete ms. Length: 2,500-3,000 words. Pays $100-200.
Tips: "Send only professionally done manuscripts, wich are erotic, unusual and fun. We expect to buy mostly fiction manuscripts in the coming year. We currently have a considerable backlog of manuscripts. Writers, especially those submitting for the first time, should be patient with our response. Please inquire about the status of your manuscript in writing, not by phone."

PHOTO SCREEN, Sterling's Magazines, Inc., 355 Lexington Ave., New York NY 10017. (212)391-1400. Editor: Marsha Daly. Emphasizes TV and movie news of star personalities. Bimonthly magazine; 75 pages. Circ. 300,000. Pays on publication. Buys all rights. SASE. Reports in 6 weeks.
Nonfiction: Exposes (on stars' lives); informational (on Hollywood life); interviews (with stars); photo features (on stars' personal lives). Buys 3 mss/month. Length: 1,000 words. Query. No unsolicited mss, fiction or local personality stories. Pays $75-200.
Photos: Roger Glazer, department editor. Purchased without ms; mostly on speculation. Pays $25-35 for 8x10 b&w (glossy or matte); $50 minimum for color. Chromes only; 35mm or 2¼x2¼.

PLAYBILL MAGAZINE, 100 Avenue of the Americas, New York NY 10013. Editor-in-Chief: Ms. Joan Alleman. Monthly; free to theatergoers. "It is the only magazine in Manhattan that focuses entirely on the New York Theater." Buys first and second US magazine rights. Pays 25% kill fee. Byline given. Computer printout and disk submissions OK. SASE.

Nonfiction: "The major emphasis is on current theater and theater people. Wants sophisticated, informative prose that makes judgments and shows style. Uses unusual interviews, although most of these are staff written. Article proposal must be about a current Broadway show or star, or playwright, director, composer, etc. We do not use parody or satire. We occasionally publish 'round-up' articles—stars who play tennis, or who cook, etc. Style should be worldly and literate without being pretentious or arch; runs closer to *New Yorker* than to *Partisan Review.* Wants interesting information, written in a genuine, personal style. Humor is also welcome. Between 1,000 and 2,500 words for articles." Pays $100-400.

Tips: "We're difficult to break into and most of our pieces are assigned. We don't take any theater pieces relating to theater outside New York. The best way for a newcomer to break in is with a 750-word article for *A View From The Audience* describing how a Broadway play or musical deeply affected the writer." Pays $100.

PRE-VUE, Box 31255, Billings MT 59107. Publisher: Virginia Hansen. Editor: Valerie Hansen. "We are the cable-TV guide for southern and western Montana; our audience is as diverse as people who subscribe to cable TV." Weekly magazine; 32-48 pages. Circ. 20,000. Not copyrighted. Byline given. Pays on acceptance. Reports in 8 weeks. Query. "We have an Editwriter 7500. If the disk submission will work in this machine, it's OK. However, I would prefer standard ms form." Prefers letter quality to dot matrix printout. SASE.

Nonfiction and Photos: Valerie Hansen, department editor. "Subject matter is general, but must relate in some way to television or our reading area (Montana). We would like articles to have a beginning, middle and end; in other words, popular magazine style, heavy on the hooker lead." Informational, how-to, interview, profile, humor, historical. Feature length: 500-750 words. Pays minimum of 2¢/word. 8x10 (sometimes smaller) b&w photos purchased with mss or on assignment. Pays $3-6. Captions required.

Tips: "We're looking for work from experienced writers; we prefer writing that is short and peppy, or very informative, or humorous."

PROLOG, 104 N. St. Mary, Dallas TX 75204. (214)827-7734. Editor: Mike Firth. 10% freelance written. For "playwrights and teachers of playwriting." Quarterly newsletter; 8 pages. Circ. 300. Buys 4 mss/year. Pays on acceptance; "may hold pending final approval." Sample copy $2. Photocopied and simultaneous submissions OK. Reports in "over 3 months." Computer printout and Apple disk submissions OK; prefers letter quality "for direct pasteup, otherwise dot matrix OK." SASE.

Nonfiction: Wants "articles and anecdotes about writing, sales and production of play scripts. Style should be direct to reader (as opposed to third-person observational)." No general attacks on theater, personal problems, problems without solutions, or general interest. Pays 1¢/word.

‡R&R ENTERTAINMENT DIGEST, R&R Werbe GmbH, Bismarckstrasse 17, 6900 Heidelberg, West Germany. Editor: Tory Billard. Monthly entertainment magazine (*TV Guide* size) for Americans based in Europe (military/DoD market). "We publish 3 separate magazines—all include a common 32-page section of interest to US citizens based throughout Europe; then we have regionalized editorial for Germany, Britain and Med plus the areas encompassed by them (i.e. Med includes Spain, Greece, Italy, etc.). Covers travel, music, audio/video/photo, homemaker scene for military and DoD based throughout Europe, including Germany, the Mediterranean and Britain. "Our audience ranges from 19-year-olds, to the over-30 married couple to retirees." Circ. 190,000. Pays on publication. Byline given. Offers 50% kill fee. Buys first rights for military market in Europe only. Submit seasonal/holiday material 2 months in advance. Simultaneous queries, and simultaneous, photocopied and previously published submissions OK as long as outside the military European market. SASE. Reports in 1 month on queries; 3 weeks on mss. Writer's guidelines for legal-size SAE and postage.

Nonfiction: Humor (travel through Europe); personal experience (travel through Europe); technical (audio/video/photo, geared to market for military in Europe); travel (throughout Europe); homemaker stories; album reviews of popular and most recent albums. "Only deal with entertainment that readers can readily do. We normally don't deal in stories that have already happened, i.e., interviews of rock stars, historical pieces, etc." Buys 10 mss/year. Query with published clips. Length: 600-1,800 words. Pays $25-40/page of text "depending on the edition it is in."

Photos: State availability of photos. Pays $30 for 35mm color transparency; $20 for 5x7 or 8x10 b&w print. Buys variable rights.

Columns/Departments: Regular columns consist of European and German events occurring that month; general sports stories (how-to-oriented—not on personalities—or a big European event like Wimbledon); homemaker stories (no recipes). Buys 5-8 mss/year. Query with published clips. Length: 600-1,200 words. Pays $25-40/page text in magazine.

Fiction: Humorous (dealing with travel experiences). "We use very little fiction—mainly dealing with travel, clever homemaker pieces." Buys 1-2 mss/year. Query with published clips. Length: 600-800 words. Pays

$25-40/page of text in magazine.

Tips: "I favor freelancers who are clever, snappy writers who send in clean, easy-to-read copy, and who accompany their manuscript with a good selection of color slides."

‡**SATELLITE ORBIT, The Magazine of Satellite Entertainment & Electronics**, CommTek Publishing Company, 418 N. River, Box 1048, Hailey ID 83333. (208)788-4936. Editor: David G. Wolford. (Direct queries to Bruce Kinnaird, senior editor.) Monthly magazine covering satellite television for "an audience that is affluent, educated, and interested in reaching beyond the ordinary. Our readers are interested—and knowledgeable—in electronics of all types related to entertainment." Estab. 1982. Circ. 50,000. Pays on publication. Byline given. Offers 33% of payment for kill fee. Buys first North American serial rights, one-time rights, all rights, first rights, or makes work-for-hire assignments. Submit seasonal/holiday material 2 months in advance. Computer printout and disk submissions OK. SASE. Reports in 2 weeks. Sample copy $5 (includes 1st class mailing); writer's guidelines free for business-sized SAE and 1 first class stamp.

Nonfiction: Bruce Kinnaird, senior editor. Humor (if there is an angle); interview/profile (satellite entertainment figure); new product (in field of electronics); opinion (satellite and entertainment related); technical (innovations). "Unsolicited material will receive *no* consideration. No material about how satellite television is booming—we know that. No nostalgia." Buys 50-60 mss/year. Length: 750-2,000 words. Pays $75-500.

Photos: State availability of photos with query letter or ms. Reviews 35mm color transparencies and 8x10 b&w prints. Pays negotiable fee. Captions required. Rights negotiable.

Columns/Departments: *Profiles* of name figures who own a satellite antenna for TV reception: 750-1,000 words; short, lively piece on owner, why he bought antenna and what benefits he derives from it. *Celebrities*: 1,000-1,500 word pieces about entertainment newsmakers. Buys 24-30 items/year. Query. Pays $75-400.

Tips: "Do not make phone queries. Learn the terms of the satellite entertainment field and use those terms in a query letter. Keep track of the industry: What's new in programming? What new satellite networks are going up? Who's making news in the field? The field of satellite entertainment is relatively new, but the market for articles of this nature is going to rocket in a year or two. Initial research into the field might be a bit laborious at first, but freelancers looking for a lucrative new market would be well advised to learn the ropes of this one."

SLICK, Box 11142, San Francisco CA 94101. Editor: Mr. Jaen Anderson. Quarterly magazine covering the avant-garde scene. Circ. 20,000. Pays on publication. Byline given. Buys all rights. Submit seasonal/holiday material 4 months in advance. SASE. Reports in 6 weeks. Sample copy $1.

Nonfiction: Book excerpts, expose, general interest, inspirational, interview/profile, new product, opinion, personal experience, photo feature, travel. Emphasis on art, fashion, music, film, performance art. Buys 4-6 mss/year. Send complete ms. Length: 500-2,500 words. Pays 2¢/word; $25 maximum.

Photos: Prefers fashion and personality. Send photos and SASE with ms. Pays $10 maximum for 8x10 b&w prints. Captions, model release, and identification of subjects required. Buys all or negotiable rights.

Columns/Departments: Buys 10-20 mss/year. Send complete ms. Length: 250-500 words. Pays $10-25.

Fiction: Experimental, fantasy. Buys 2-4 mss/year. Send complete ms. Length: 5,000 words maximum. Pays $25 maximum.

SOAP OPERA DIGEST, 254 W. 31st St., New York NY 10001. Executive Editor: Meredith Brown. 25% freelance written. Biweekly magazine; 144 pages. Circ. 650,000. Pays on acceptance. Buys all rights. Submit seasonal/holiday material 4 months in advance of issue date. No photocopied submissions. Computer printout and disk submissions OK. SASE. Reports in 1 month.

Nonfiction: "Articles only directly about daytime and nighttime personalities or soap operas." Interview (no telephone interviews); nostalgia; photo features (must be recent); profiles; special interest features: health, beauty, with soap opera personalities and industry news, with a strong interest in nighttime soaps. "We are a 'newsy' magazine—not gossipy. No poorly written writing that talks down to the audience." Buys 2-3 mss/issue. Query with clips of previously published work. Length: 1,000-2,000 words. Pays $200 and up.

Photos: State availability of photos with query. Captions preferred. Buys all rights. "Writers must be good at in-depth, personality profiles. Pack as much info into a compact length. Also want humor pieces."

STARWEEK MAGAZINE, Toronto Star Newspapers, Ltd., 1 Yonge St., Toronto, Ontario, Canada M5E 1E6. (416)367-2425. Editor: Robert Crew. Weekly television newspaper supplement covering personalities, issues, technology, etc., relating to all aspects of video programming. Circ. 800,000. Pays by arrangement. Byline given. Offers 50% kill fee. Not copyrighted. Buys first rights. Submit seasonal/holiday material 6 weeks in advance. Computer printout and disk submissions OK; prefers letter quality to dot matrix printouts. SASE. Reports "as soon as possible." Sample copy for 8x11 SAE.

Nonfiction: Interview/profile (of TV personalities); technical. Buys 3,500 mss/year. Query with clips of published work. Length: 500-1,000 words. Pays $200-400.

Photos: Send photos with ms. Pays $50-100 for 8x10 b&w prints; $75-250 for 2x5 or 35mm color transparencies. Identification of subjects required. Buys one-time rights.

Tips: "I prefer to commission 'comment' or analysis pieces from writers whose credentials I know."

THIS WEEK, R.F.D. Publications, Inc., Box 4227, Portland OR 97208. (503)620-4121. Editor: Maggi White. Weekly tabloid—contemporary and upbeat. Circ. 421,000. Pays on publication. Byline given. Offers variable kill fee. Not copyrighted. Buys one-time rights. Submit seasonal/holiday material 4 months in advance. Simultaneous queries OK. No computer printout or disk submissions. SASE. Reports in 1 month.
Nonfiction: How-to, humor, interview/profile, photo feature. "We focus on interesting persons, places, things, and usually require a local tie-in. However, humor is universal. We are not issue-oriented, but people-oriented, and we treat (issues) through people who are dealing successfully with them." Query with clips of published work or send complete ms. Length: 750-1,800 words. Pays $25-100.
Photos: Send photos with ms. Reviews transparencies and prints. Identification of subjects required.

TUNED IN MAGAZINE, Jetpro Inc., Suite 8, 6867 Nancy Ridge Dr., San Diego CA 92121. (714)268-3314. Editor: Bernadette Guiniling. Weekly magazine covering TV, including cable, radio and entertainment for "entertainment-oriented San Diegans, usually between the ages of 18 and 50, of a middle-income background." Circ. 55,000. Pays on publication. Byline given. Offers kill fee. Buys one-time rights. Submit seasonal/holiday material 6 weeks in advance. Simultaneous and photocopied submissions OK. SASE. Reports in 2 weeks on queries; 1 month on mss. San Diego writers only.
Nonfiction: General interest (personality stories, TV/radio articles, entertainment); how-to (get involved in the media; to interact and be a part of it); humor (lighthearted looks at the media and entertainment technology, etc.); interview/profile (of San Diegans who made good; visiting celebrities); and new product (technological updates; services such as radio for the blind). "We're looking for sharp, snappy articles that deal with some aspect of the San Diego entertainment field, or entertainment (TV, radio, film) as it *impacts* San Diego. We run 2 freelance articles per issue, and 5 columns (4 staff-written). Query. Length: 1,200-1,500 words. Pays $75.
Photos: Send photos with accompanying ms. Captions required.
Columns/Departments: Dining Out; San Diego Nights (club/concert guides, staff-written); What's Happening (guide, staff-written); plus two other staff columns.
Tips: "Think in terms of national trends as they affect the local community, entertainment options that don't get much coverage, public-service articles, and guides."

TV GUIDE, Radnor PA 19088. Editor (National Section): David Sendler. Editor (Local Sections): Roger Youman. Managing Editor: R.C. Smith. Weekly. Circ. 20 million. Study publication. Query to Andrew Mills, Assistant Managing Editor. SASE.
Nonfiction: Wants offbeat articles about TV people and shows. This magazine is not interested in fan material. Also wants stories on the newest trends of television, but they must be written in clear, lively English. Length: 1,000-2,000 words.
Photos: Uses professional high-quality photos, normally shot on assignment, by photographers chosen by *TV Guide*. Prefers color. Pays $250 day rate against page rates—$350 for 2 pages or less.

TV GUIDE, (Canada, Inc.), 112 Merton St., Toronto, Ontario, Canada M4S 2Z7. Editor: Kenneth J. Larone. Weekly magazine covering TV listings and related articles. Circ. 1,000,000. Pays on acceptance. "Professional writers only—no amateurs, please." Buys first North American rights and promotional use. SAE and International Reply Coupons. Computer printout submissions OK; prefers letter quality to dot matrix printouts.
Nonfiction: TV personality profiles. Query. Length: 1,000-1,750 words. Pays $500-1,000.
Photos: Pays $150-500 for 35mm color transparencies.

TV PICTURE LIFE, 355 Lexington Ave., New York NY 10017. (212)391-1400. Creative Director: Robert Schartoff. Editor: Marie Morreale. Bimonthly magazine; 80 pages. 100% freelance written. Rights purchased vary with author and material. Usually buys all rights. Pays negotiable kill fee. Byline given. Pays on acceptance. Reports "immediately." Query. SASE.
Nonfiction and Photos: Celebrity interviews, profiles and angles that are provocative, enticing and truthful. Length: 1,000 words. Pays $100 minimum. Photos of celebrities purchased without ms or on assignment. Pays $25-35 minimum for photos.

TV TIME AND CHANNEL, Cable Communications Media, Inc., Box 2108, Lehigh Valley PA 18001. (215)865-6600. Production Manager: Jeff Bittner. For television and other entertainment forms. Weekly magazine; 44 pages. Pays on publication. Buys all rights. Byline given "when requested." Phone queries OK. Submit seasonal/holiday material one month in advance. Simultaneous, photocopied and previously published submissions OK. SASE. Reports in 2 weeks. Sample copy for 50¢.
Nonfiction: Expose (entertainment world and behind-the-scenes); general interest (TV related); how-to (things a TV watcher would like to know); humor; interviews (stars, producers and directors); and photo feature; fiction; opinion or whimsical humor. Wants material which looks at television with a positive viewpoint. Pays 2-7¢/word.
Photos: Uses 8x10 b&w prints. Offers no additional payment for photos accepted with ms. Captions preferred.

VIDEO, Reese Publishing Co., Inc., 160 W. 34th St., New York NY 10001 (212)947-6500. Editor: Bruce Apar. Managing Editor: Donald Pohl. Monthly magazine about home video for the person who wants to get the most from his home video equipment and keep abreast of the new products and developments in the video field. Circ. 250,008. Pays on acceptance. Buys all rights. Submit seasonal material 4 months in advance. Photocopied submissions OK. SASE. Reports in 1 month. Free sample copy.
Nonfiction: Program sections include reviews of video cassette and video disc programs and computer and video games software as well as cable programs. Also how computers and video equipment work together. How-to (use the equipment to integrate video into your lifestyle); humor; interview (with people using video in an innovative way); nostalgia (TV related); opinion; profile (celebrities who use video); travel (documenting a trip on videotape); personal experience (use of the equipment or video solving community problems); photo feature (of interior design); technical (daily use solutions); and satellite stations in the backyard. "Report on video clubs in your community. Tell us how video is used at the grassroots level or unusual specific applications of video." No trade or business articles. Buys 8 mss/issue. Query with clips of previously published work. Length: 1,000-1,500 words.
Photos: State availability of photos. Buys 8x10 b&w prints and 35mm and 2¼x2¼ color transparencies. Views contact sheets. Pays negotiable fee. Captions and model release required. Buys one-time rights.
Columns/Departments: TV Den (understanding the equipment); and Video Environment (people's home installations and interior decorating). Query with clips of previously published work. Length: 1,000-3,000 words. Pays $200 minimum.

‡**VIDEO GAMES MAGAZINE**, Pumpkin Press, 350 5th Ave., New York NY 10118. (212)947-4322. Editor: Roger C. Sharpe. Managing Editor: Susan Adamo. Monthly magazine covering home and arcade video games and computers. Estab. 1982. Circ. 100,000. Pays on publication. Byline given. Offers 20% kill fee. Buys first North American serial rights. Submit seasonal/holiday material 3 months in advance. Simultaneous queries and photocopied submissions OK. SASE. Reports in 2 weeks. Free sample copy and writer's guidelines.
Nonfiction: Book excerpts; general interest; historical/nostalgic; how-to (game tips and playing strategies); interview/profile; new product; personal experience. "We look for editorial coverage of the game, toy and computer industries—interviews, game reviews, product reviews and general business trend overviews." Special issues include Special End-of-the-Year Celebration of Games. No poetry. Buys 120 mss/year. Query with published clips. Length: 1,500-2,500 words. Pays $200-400.
Photos: Robert Sefcik, photo editor. State availability of photos. Pays $10-25 for b&w contact sheet and b&w transparencies; $50-100 for color transparencies. Captions, model release and identification of subjects required. Buys one-time rights.
Columns/Departments: Blips (short news items and mini-features on latest breaking developments); Game Efforts (product reviews); Hard Sell (system reviews); Soft Touch (computer game software reviews); Book Beat (book reviews). Buys 80 mss/year. Query with published clips. Length: 1,000-3,000 words. Pays $200-450.
Fiction: "Looking for pieces with an obvious video or computer game slant." Buys 12 mss/year. Query with published clips. Length: 1,500-3,000 words. Pays $300-500.
Tips: "Look at back issues to familiarize yourself with our editorial content and style; then submit ideas which we will respond to. Part of the problem is finding individuals who understand the uniqueness of our publication in terms of subject matter; however, everything is open for those writers who can cover the material."

‡**VIDEO GAMES PLAYER**, Carnegie Publications, 888 7th Ave., New York NY 10106. Editor: Dan Gutman. Bimonthly magazine covering video and computer games for a "14-year-old audience." Estab. 1982. Circ. 175,000. Pays on publication. Byline given. Offers 25% kill fee. Buys all rights. Submit seasonal/holiday material 4 months in advance. Simultaneous queries and photocopied submissions OK. SASE. Reports in 2 weeks.
Nonfiction: General interest; how-to (fix your Atari, make your parents like video games); humor; interview/profile; personal experience; photo feature; technical. No game reviews. Buys 48 mss/year. Query with published clips. Length: 1,000-2,500 words. Pays $200-400.
Photos: State availability of photos. Pays $15-50 for color transparencies. Captions and model release required. Buys all rights.
Columns/Departments: Feedback—column of reader opinion. Buys 6 mss/year. Send complete ms. Length: 1,000 words. Pays $50.
Fiction: Stories about video games. Buys 3-4 mss/year. Send complete ms. Length: 2,000-2,500 words. Pays $300-400.
Tips: "Send me a query with an incredible idea nobody has done before, along with published samples of work."

‡**VIDEO SWAPPER, The Video Magazine For Video Collectors**, Arena Magazine Co., 151 E. Birch St., Annandale MN 55302. (612)274-5230. Editor: Mr. Jon E. Johnson. Monthly video enthusiast's tabloid cover-

ing home video: reviews, profiles, feature reviews on gaming and technical subjects. "We strive to serve the interests of home video/video game enthusiasts and television/movie buffs." Circ. 10,000. Pays on publication. Byline given. Buys first rights. Submit seasonal/holiday material 3 months in advance. Photocopied submissions OK. Computer printout submissions OK if "close to double-spaced." SASE. Reports in 3 weeks. Free sample copy and writer's guidelines.

Nonfiction: Book excerpts; expose (investigative-type submissions); general interest; historical/nostalgic; how-to; interview/profile; new product (uses and technical subjects); opinion (in the form of reviews or commentary); technical (technical aspects of video gear). No personal experience/first person articles other than interview, profile or general interest. Query. Pays $100 maximum.

Photos: State availability of photos with query letter or ms. Pays $5-10 for 8x10 b&w prints. Model release required. Buys one-time rights.

Columns/Departments: Reviews. Query. Pays $10 minimum for short type review.

Fillers: Gags. Length: 1 page minimum, double-spaced. Pays $10.

Tips: "VS uses freelance material for nearly its entire content, and as a result it is very easy for a freelancer to break into the magazine, provided his/her material suits our editorial needs. It is advisable to query first and request a sample copy and writer's guidelines. Unsolicited submissions are acceptable. Once writers get a feel for what VS is, and we get an idea of their work, they become one of our 'family' of regular contributors. The most open areas of *Video Swapper* are Features, Reviews, Commentary and Video Gaming pieces. All areas/sections are open to new, different and fresh writers wishing to express their feelings, expertise and knowledge as it relates to the video/television/movie/personality world. Writers who know their subject should have no problem when it comes to writing for VS (providing it suits our needs). We might be stepping up our publication schedule. In that case we'll be using even more material."

VIDEO TODAY AND TOMORROW, ABC Leisure Magazines, Inc., 825 7th Ave., New York NY 10019. (212)265-8360. Editor: William Tynan. Monthly supplement bound in *High Fidelity* and *Modern Photography* covering home video. Circ. 1,000,000. Pays on acceptance. Byline given. Buys all rights. Submit seasonal/holiday material 6 months in advance. Simultaneous queries and photocopied submissions OK. SASE. Reports in 1 month. Free sample copy.

Nonfiction: General interest (on creative things being done with video); how-to (use video equipment, set-up); personal experience ("video vignettes"—must have accompanying photos); and nuts and bolts pieces on video. Buys 5-10 mss/year. Query with clips of published work. Length: 2,000 words maximum. Pays $450-600.

Photos: State availability of photos. Reviews 8x10 b&w glossy prints. Captions and model release required.

Travel, Camping, and Trailer

Publications in this category tell campers and tourists the where-tos and how-tos of travel. Publications that buy how-to camping and travel material with a conservation angle are listed in the Nature, Conservation, and Ecology classification. Regional publications are frequently interested in travel and camping material with a local angle. Hunting and fishing and outdoor publications that buy camping how-to material will be found in the Sports category. Those dealing with automobiles or other vehicles maintained for sport or as a hobby will be found in the Automotive and Motorcycle category. Many magazines in the In-Flight category are also in the market for travel articles and photos.

For how-tos on writing for the travel market, see Louise Zobel's *The Travel Writer's Handbook* (Writer's Digest Books).

‡**AAA-WORLD**, The Webb Co., 1999 Shepard Rd., St. Paul MN 55116. (612)690-7304. Editor: Don Picard. Managing Editor: Jim Carney. Bimonthly magazine of the National Automobile Association of America covering driving safety and general travel (as opposed to destination travel) topics for readers in their 50s. Eleven AAA clubs in 13 states may add regional copy to their editions of the national magazine. Queries relating to regional interests will be forwarded to the appropriate region. Circ. 1.6 million. Pays on acceptance. Byline given. Offers 25% kill fee. Buys one-time rights and non-exclusive rights. Submit seasonal/holiday material 6 months in advance. Simultaneous queries and photocopied submissions OK. SASE. Reports in 2 weeks on queries; 4 weeks on mss. Sample copy for 9x12 SAE and 71¢ postage; free writer's guidelines.

Nonfiction: General interest; how-to (driving safety, driving techniques); travel (1 travel piece/issue). No long destination pieces; first person stories; highly technical automotive maintenance features; stories aimed at younger audience. Buys 18 mss/year. Query. Length: 500-1,500 words. Pays $250-500, "except for occasional special longer pieces."

ACCENT, 1720 Washington Blvd., Box 2315, Ogden UT 84404. Editor: Dick Harris. Associate Editor: Peggie Bingham. 90% freelance written. Travel-oriented. Monthly. Circ. 600,000. "*Accent* is sold to business and industrial firms coast-to-coast who distribute it with appropriate inserts as their house magazines." Buys first rights. Buys 90-100 mss/year, 200-300 photos/year. Pays on acceptance. Computer printout and disk submissions OK. Sample copy, 50¢; free guidelines with SASE. Query with SASE.
Nonfiction and Photos: "We want travel articles—places to go, advice to travelers, new ways to travel, money-saving tips, new resorts, famous travelers and humor. Stories and photos are usually purchased as a package. Pictures are important to us in our decision on buying or rejecting material." Uses b&w glossies and color transparencies. Captions required. Feature article length: 500-1,000 words. Payment: 15¢/word, $20/b&w photo, $35/color transparency, more for color covers.
Tips: "Pictures are a very important part of our magazine. Sharp, good contrast, (colorful for color shots) often sell the piece, so make sure super-quality photos are available. Please remember we work 6 months in advance, and submit seasonal material accordingly. No poorly written copy, snapshots, several stories with ancient clippings and samples in one package—no submissions without SASE."

ASU TRAVEL GUIDE, ASU Travel Guide, Inc., 1325 Columbus Ave., San Francisco CA 94133. (415)441-5200. Managing Editor: Howard Baldwin. Quarterly guidebook covering international travel features and travel discounts for well-traveled airline employees. Circ. 37,000. Pays on publication. Byline given. Offers kill fee. Buys first North American serial rights, one-time rights, first rights, and second serial (reprint) rights and makes work-for hire assignments. Submit seasonal/holiday material 6 months in advance. Simultaneous queries and simultaneous, photocopied and previously published submissions OK. Computer printout submissions OK; prefers letter quality to dot matrix printouts. SASE. Reports in 2 months. Send SASE for writer's guidelines.
Nonfiction: International travel articles "similar to those run in consumer magazines." Not interested in amateur efforts from inexperienced traveler or personal experience articles that don't give useful information to other travelers. Buys 16-20 mss/year. Destination pieces only; no "Tips On Luggage" articles. We will be accepting fewer manuscripts and relying more on our established group of freelance contributors." Length: 1,200-1,500 words. Pays $200.
Photos: "Interested in clear, high-contrast photos; we prefer not to receive material without photos." Reviews 5x7 and 8x10 b&w prints. "Payment for photos is included in article price; photos from tourist offices are acceptable."
Tips: "Query with samples of travel writing and a list of places you've recently visited. We appreciate clean and simple style. Keep verbs in the active tense and involve the reader in what you write. Avoid 'cute' writing, excess punctuation (especially dashes and ellipses), coined words and stale cliches."

AWAY, 888 Worcester St., Wellesley MA 02181. (617)237-5200. Editor: Gerard J. Gagnon. For "members of the ALA Auto & Travel Club, interested in their autos and in travel. Ages range from approximately 20-65. They live primarily in New England." Slanted to seasons. Quarterly. Circ. 170,000. Buys first serial rights. Pays on acceptance. Submit seasonal material 6 months in advance. Reports "as soon as possible." Although a query is not mandatory, it may be advisable for many articles. No computer printout or disk submissions. SASE. Free sample copy.
Nonfiction: Articles on "travel, tourist attractions, safety, history, etc., preferably with a New England angle. Also, car care tips and related subjects." Would like a "positive feel to all pieces, but not the chamber of commerce approach." Buys both general seasonal travel and specific travel articles, for example, travel-related articles (photo hints, etc.); outdoor activities, for example, gravestone rubbing, snow sculpturing; historical articles linked to places to visit; humor with a point; photo essays. "Would like to see more nonseasonally oriented material. Most material now submitted seems suitable only for our summer issue. Avoid pieces on hunting and about New England's most publicized attractions, such as Old Sturbridge Village and Mystic Seaport." Length: 800-1,500 words, "preferably 1,000-1,200." Pays approximately 10¢/word.
Photos: Photos purchased with mss. Captions required. B&w glossy prints. Pays $5-10/b&w photo, payment on publication based upon which photos are used. Not buying color at this time.

‡**BACKPACKER**, Ziff-Davis, 1 Park Ave., New York NY 10016. (212)725-7080. Editor: J. Delves. Bimonthly magazine for backpackers who want "hard information" on equipment, skills and places to go. Circ. 180,000. Pays on acceptance. Byline given. Buys first North American serial rights and all rights. Submit seasonal/holiday material 4 months in advance. Simultaneous queries, and simultaneous and photocopied submissions OK. SASE. Reports in 1 month. Free sample copy and writer's guidelines.
Nonfiction: How-to (outdoor skills); humor; interview/profile; opinion (chiefly regarding government policies and regulations); personal experience; photo feature; technical; travel. Special issue includes October/November on ski packing. No fiction or exotic destinations. Buys 50 mss/year. Query with published clips.

Length: 1,000-4,000 words. Pays variable rates.

Photos: Erin Kenney, art director. Send photos with query or ms. Reviews 35mm color transparencies. Captions and identification of subjects required. Buys one-time rights.

Columns/Departments: Body Language; Geosphere; Forum; First Exposure; Material; Weekend Wilderness. Buys 75 mss/year. Query with published clips. Length: 1,500-2,500 words. Pays variable rates.

Fillers: Tips and Techniques. Buys 12/year. Length: 250-500 words. Pays $100 maximum.

‡**BIKEREPORT**, Bikecentennial, Inc., 113 W. Main, Missoula MT 59807. (406)721-1776. Editor: Daniel D'Ambrosio. Bimonthly bicycle touring tabloid for Bikecentennial members—all bicycle tourists. Circ. 18,000. Pays on publication. Byline given. Buys first rights. Submit seasonal/holiday material 3 months in advance. Simultaneous queries and photocopied submissions OK. SASE. Reports in 2 weeks on queries; 4 weeks on mss. Free sample copy.

Nonfiction: Historical/nostalgic (interesting spots along bike trails); how-to (bicycle); humor (touring); interview/profile (bicycle industry people); personal experience ("my favorite tour"); photo feature (bicycle); technical (bicycle); travel ("my favorite tour"). No articles on activism—biker's rights. Buys 12-15 mss/year. Query with published clips or send complete ms. Length: 800-1,500 words. Pays $35-65.

Photos: Gary MacFadden, photo editor. Bicycle, scenery, portraits. State availability of photos. Pays $5-25 for b&w and color. Model release and identification of subjects required. Buys one-time rights.

Columns/Departments: "We want to start a survival-on-the-road-while-taking-a-camping-bicycle-trip column; recipes, camping tips, etc." Buys 24-30 mss/year. Query with published clips or send complete ms. Length: 800-1,200 words. Pays $35-65.

Fiction: Adventure, experimental, historical, humorous. Not interested in anything that doesn't involve bicycles. Query with published clips or send complete ms. Length: 800-1,200 words. Pays $35-65.

Tips: "We are looking for fresh angles. We have beaten the favorite bicycle tour to death. We need copy which is bicycle-related but *not* about bicycles—people, places or things encountered on a tour. Please try us, we are small but growing. Use your imagination."

CAMPERWAYS, 550 Penllyn Pike, Blue Bell PA 19422. (215)643-2058. Editor-in-Chief: Charles E. Myers. 60% freelance written. Emphasis on recreation vehicle camping and travel. Monthly (except Dec. and Jan.) tabloid. Circ. 30,000. Pays on publication. Buys simultaneous, second serial (reprint) or regional rights. Byline given. Submit seasonal/holiday material 3-4 months in advance. Simultaneous, photocopied and previously published submissions OK. No computer printout or disk submissions. Self-addressed envelope and loose postage. Reports in 1 month. Free sample copy and writer's guidelines.

Nonfiction: Historical (when tied in with camping trip to historical attraction or area); how-to (selection, care, maintenance of RVs, accessories and camping equipment); humor; personal experience; and travel (camping destinations within 200 miles of New York-DC metro corridor). No "material on camping trips to destinations outside stated coverage area." Buys 40-50 unsolicited mss/year. Query. Length: 800-1,500 words. Pays $40-75.

Photos: "Good photos greatly increase likelihood of acceptance. Don't send snapshots, polaroids. We can't use them." Photos purchased with accompanying ms. Captions required. Uses 5x7 or 8x10 b&w glossy prints. Total purchase price for ms includes payment for photos.

Columns/Departments: Camp Cookery (ideas for cooking in RV galleys and over campfires. Should include recipes). Buys 10 mss/year. Query. Length: 500-1,000 words. Pays $25-50.

Tips: "Articles should focus on single attraction or activity or on closely clustered attractions within reach on the same weekend camping trip rather than on types of attractions or activities in general. We're looking for little-known or offbeat items. Emphasize positive aspects of camping: fun, economy, etc. We want feature items, not shorts and fillers."

CHEVRON USA, Box 6227, San Jose CA 95150. (408)296-1060. Editor: Therese Beaver. For members of the Chevron Travel Club. Quarterly. Buys first North American serial rights. Pays for articles on acceptance. Pays for photos on publication. Reports in 6 to 8 weeks. Computer printout submissions OK "if legible." SASE. Free sample copy, writer's and photographer's guidelines. Tables of contents planned approximately 1 year in advance.

Nonfiction: "We need lively, well-organized articles with sense of place and history, yet packed with see-and-do information geared toward families. Enthusiasm for, and knowledge of, subject should show. In addition to destination articles, and round-up stories, we carry general interest (circuses, ballet), photo essays and pieces on sports and the outdoors. No public relations, brochure approach; no historical treatises, personality profiles or travelogues." Buys 10 mss/issue. Recent article examples: "Memphis: Queen of the Mississippi" and "Farm And Ranch Vacations." Length: 500-1,600 words. Pays 25¢/word average.

Photos: Subject matter to illustrate copy. "Sharp, bright, original transparencies in 35mm or larger. Color only. Majority of photos must show people, but no models or setups." Pays $100-175 for inside photos; $350 for article-related front cover; $250 for non-article-related back cover.

Columns/Departments: Family Activities (600 words on craft or activity families can enjoy together); Humor (75-100 word original anecdotes on personal travel experiences). Pays $25.

DEPARTURES, The Travel Magazine of Simpsons, The Travel Magazine of Sears, The Travel Magazine of The Bay, HBC Travel Limited, Suite 909, 75 The Donway, W., Don Mills, Ontario, Canada M3C 2E9. (416)441-2080. Editor/Publisher: Dianne Dukowski. Magazine published 4 times/year (January, April, September, November) covering travel for all travel customers of Simpson, Sears, and The Bay. "Separate covers, body content the same." Estab. 1981. Circ. 125,000. Pays on acceptance. Byline given. Offers negotiable kill fee. Buys one-time rights. Simultaneous queries and previously published submissions "very occasionally" OK. Sample copy for 9x12 SAE and 2 first class stamps.
Nonfiction: How-to (take travel shots); humor (travel experience); personal experience (travel); photo feature (travel); travel. "*Departures* provides an entertaining and informative look at popular as well as little-known travel destinations around the world as seen through the eyes of top freelance writers. Articles are written in fairly lighthearted manner and are streamlined to facilitate the interest of active travelers." No articles derogatory to travel destinations. Buys 30 mss/yr. Query with clips of published work. Length: 1,000-2,000 words. Pays $200-600, plus additional for photos.
Photos: State availability of photos. Pays $10-100 for any size color transparencies. Captions required.
Fillers: Anecdotes "travel-related only." Length: 500-2,000 words. Pays $250-600.
Tips: "Please be aware that we do not solicit actual manuscripts since the editorial plan is very tight. Destinations are chosen in advance and we only require features on specific locations. Therefore, we require only listings of destinations, photographs—preferably with samples of published work relating to travel."

DISCOVERY MAGAZINE, Allstate Plaza, Northbrook IL 60062. Editor: Sarah Hoban. 75% freelance written. For motor club members; mobile families with above-average income. Quarterly. Circ. 1,000,000. Buys first North American serial rights. Pays on acceptance. Free sample copy and writer's guidelines. Submit seasonal material 8-12 months in advance. Reports in 3 weeks. Query; don't send manuscripts. Computer printout and disk submissions OK. SASE. If sample copy is desired, please send suitable envelope.
Nonfiction and Photos: "The emphasis is on visual travel features. Also automotive safety and consumer-related articles. Short pieces on restaurants must include recipes from the establishment. We're looking for polished magazine articles with useful information—not narratives of people's vacations." Recent article example "Georgia's Happy Crabbers" (spring 1983, "describing an interesting vacation activity with a specific focus; easily illustrated"). Query must be literate—clean and free of misspelling, grammatical errors; concise; enthusiastic—the writer must care about the subject and want to sell it to our publication." Buys 10-15 unsolicited mss/year. Day rate is paid; rates for existing photos depend on how the photos are used. Color transparencies (35mm or larger) are preferred. Photos should work as a story; captions required. Send transparencies by registered mail, with plenty of cardboard protection. Buys one-time rights for photography. Color photos are returned after use. Length: 1,000-2,500 words. "Rates vary, depending on type of article, ranging from $300-850 for full-length features."
Fillers: True, humorous travel anecdotes. Length: 50-150 words. Pays $10.
Tips: "No historical general articles about a big area, subjects that aren't particularly visual (we have a strong emphasis on photojournalism and our stories reflect this)."

‡ENDLESS VACATION, Endless Vacation International, Box 80260, Indianapolis IN 46280-0260. (317)846-4724. Editor: Nora Westlake. Executive Editor: Betsy Sheldon. Bimonthly travel magazine for an "audience whose interest and involvement with travel and vacationing is inherent. The readership is almost entirely made up of vacation timeshare owners and those who seek variety and quality from their vacation experiences—affluent executives and professionals." Circ. 240,000. Pays on acceptance. Byline given. Offers 25% kill fee. Buys variable rights; "mostly first North American and one-time rights." Submit seasonal/holiday material 4 months in advance. Simultaneous queries and simultaneous and previously published submissions OK. SASE. Reports in 1 month. Free sample copy and writer's guidelines.
Nonfiction: Book excerpts (on subject of travel only); how-to (travel tips, photography, sports); humor (if travel-related); interview/profile (with celebrities—travel-related); photo feature; travel. "Feature stories may focus on a specific travel location or an interesting vacation activity, but must be based on a unique or unexpected angle. Rather than a story on vacationing in the Poconos, treatment might be the Poconos as a relaxing travel base for day trips to New York City or Philadelphia. We also encourage sidebars along with the article, covering specifics such as a close-up profile of a "real" cowboy for a story on Montana, or a list of the five best-known white water tour companies as a sidebar for a story on rafting in the Rockies. Short features and featurettes run from 800-1,200 words and payment terms are the same as for major features. These stories address travel-related topics including food, health, photography, sports and more. Stories should have a specific focus—'souvenir' shopping in San Francisco's incredible warehouse of international bargains, Cost Plus on Fisherman's Wharf; the foreign flavor of Texas—a German Wurstfest in the heart of cowboy country. Articles should avoid environmentalist stance; also, no straight recitations of dry facts." Buys 6-10 mss/year. Query with published clips. Length: 1,000-1,500 words. Pays $300-900 "according to importance of story, its

length, and the author's credentials.''

Photos: Joyce Hadley, photo editor. "Most of the photography in *Endless Vacation* is supplied by professional photographers. We do not require photographs from the writers, but we will consider them if submitted. Images should be included with the original query and must be accompanied by photographer's name, model releases and full identification and/or captions. They must be 35mm, 2¼ or 4x5 transparencies. No more than 12 images should be sent." Pays negotiable rates. "We reserve the right to keep photos up to 3 or 4 months, and we will return them via registered mail." Buys one-time, exclusive rights in the industry.

Columns/Departments: Columns run frequently but not consistently and include topics such as: Food (as related to travel—how to find a good restaurant in a strange town; facts and fallacies about Mexican food); Photography (tips on photography, especially vacation photography, and camera tips—how to select the camera for your needs; how to shoot winter vacation photos); Health (leisure- and travel-related health tips—overcoming fear of flying; maintaining your fitness routine on an urban vacation); Islands (features a close-up look at one of the world's many islands—a look at Long Island; the beaches of Bora Bora; horse-and-buggy days on Michigan's Mackinac Island). Buys 6-10 mss/year. Query with published clips; indicate places of publication.

Tips: "We are looking for *specific* information that we can't get out of a guidebook or a library—*firsthand* facts presented in a colorful, readable fashion. A good, thorough query and published clips are a must to show your writing skills.''

FAMILY MOTOR COACHING, 8291 Clough Pike, Cincinnati OH 45244. (513)474-3622. Managing Editor: Terry Duschinski. 75% freelance written. Emphasizes travel by motorhome, and motorhome mechanics, maintenance and other technical information. Monthly magazine; 130 pages. Circ. 26,500. Pays on acceptance. Buys first-time, 12 months exclusive rights. Byline given. Phone queries OK. Submit seasonal/holiday material 5 months in advance. Computer printout and disk submissions OK; prefers letter quality to dot matrix printout. SASE. Reports in 2 months. Sample copy $2; free writer's guidelines.

Nonfiction: Motorhome travel and living on the road; travel (various areas of country accessible by motor coach); how-to (modify motor coach features); bus conversions, and nostalgia. Buys 12 mss/issue. Query. Length: 1,000-2,000 words. Pays $50-200.

Photos: State availability of photos with query. Offers no additional payment for b&w contact sheet(s) 35mm or 2¼x2¼ color transparencies. Captions required. B&w glossy photos should accompany non-travel articles. Buys first rights.

Tips: "Keep in mind, stories must have motorhome angle or connection. Stories about an event somewhere should allude to nearby campgrounds, etc. The stories should be written assuming that someone going there would be doing it by motorhome. We need more articles from which to select for publication. We need geographic balance and a blend of travel, technical and incidental stories. No first-person accounts of vacations.''

GREAT EXPEDITIONS, Canada's Adventure and Travel Magazine, Box 46499, Station G, Vancouver, British Columbia, Canada V6R 4G7. (604)734-4948. Editor: Lawrence Buser. Managing Editor: Marilyn Marshall. Bimonthly magazine covering adventure and travel "for people who want to discover the world around them (archaeology to climbing volcanoes); basically a how-to *National Geographic*. We focus on travel (not tourism) and adventure—a mix of Canadian and world content. We are much like a society or club—we provide services besides the basic magazine—and encourage articles and information from our readers." Circ. 4,000. Pays on publication. Byline given. Buys one-time or first rights. Submit seasonal/holiday material 6 months in advance. Simultaneous queries, and simultaneous, photocopied and previously published submissions OK. SASE; IRCs outside of Canada. Reports in 1 month. Sample copy $2; free writer's guidelines.

Nonfiction: Book reviews (travel and adventure); how-to (travel economically, do adventure trips); humor (on travel or adventure); interview/profile (travel or adventure-related); personal experience (travel or adventure); travel (economy and budget, exotic-*not* touristic!). No tourism articles. Buys 24 mss/year. Query or send complete ms. Length: 1,000-3,000 words. Pays $50 maximum. "We have limited funds and generally prefer barter instead of cash (we'll make exceptions, though, providing a free subscription for material.)''

Photos: "It is important to send photos with the manuscript. Otherwise we are reluctant to accept pieces (humor, how-to's and book reviews excepted)." Pays $10 maximum for 35mm color transparencies and 5x7 color and b&w prints. "Color reproduced in b&w for magazine." Captions required. Buys one-time rights.

Columns/Departments: Viewpoint—opinion on travel, adventure, outdoor recreation, environment. Photography—for the traveler, adventurer; equipment techniques. Health—for travelers and adventurers; how to keep healthy, be healthy. Money—best buys, best countries to visit. Length: 400-800 words. Pays $25 maximum.

Tips: "Best to send for a copy—we are rather different from most magazines because we are a network of travelers and adventurers and rely on this network for our information.''

‡**HIDEAWAYS GUIDE**, Hideaways International, Box 1459, Concord MA 01742. (617)369-0252. Editor: Michael F. Thiel. Managing Editor: Betsy Browning. Magazine published 3 times/year—March, May, September. Also publishes 4 quarterly newsletters. Features travel/leisure real estate information for upscale, affluent, educated, outdoorsy audience. Deals with unique vacation opportunities: vacation home renting, buying, exchanging, yacht/houseboat charters, country inns and small resorts. Circ. 8,000. Pays on publica-

tion. Byline given. Offers negotiable kill fee. Buys first North American serial rights, one-time rights and second serial (reprint) rights. Submit seasonal/holiday material 3 months in advance. Previously published submissions OK. Computer printout and disk submissions compatible with Wordstar program OK; prefers letter quality to dot matrix printouts. Reports in 2 weeks on queries; 3·weeks on mss. Sample copy $10; free writer's guidelines.

Nonfiction: How-to (with focus on personal experience: vacation home renting, exchanging, buying, selling, yacht and house boat chartering); travel (intimate out-of-the-way spots to visit). Articles on "learning" vacations: scuba, sailing, flying, cooking, shooting, golf, tennis, photography, etc. Buys 10 mss/year. Query. Length: 800-1,500 words. Pays $50-100.

Photos: State availability of photos with query letter or ms or send photos with accompanying query or ms. Reviews b&w prints. Pays negotiable fee. Captions and identification of subjects required. Buys one-time rights.

JOURNAL OF CHRISTIAN CAMPING, Christian Camping International, Box 646, Wheaton IL 60187. Editor: Gary L. Wall. Managing Editor: Charlyene Wall. Emphasizes the broad scope of organized camping with emphasis on Christian camping. "Leaders of youth camps and adult conferences read our magazine to get practical help in ways to run their camps." Bimonthly magazine; 32-48 pages. Circ. 6,000. Pays on acceptance. Buys all rights. Pays 25% kill fee. Byline given. SASE. Reports in 4 weeks. Sample copy $2; writer's guidelines for SASE.

Nonfiction: General interest (trends in organized camping in general and Christian camping in particular); how-to (anything involved with organized camping from repairing refrigerators, to motivating staff, to programming, to record keeping, to camper follow-up); inspirational (limited use, but might be interested in practical applications of Scriptural principles to everyday situations in camping, no preaching); interview (with movers and shakers in camping and Christian camping in particular; submit a list of basic questions first); and opinion (write a letter to the editor). Buys 30-50 mss/year. Query desired, but accepts unsolicited mss. Length: 600-2,500 words. Pays 5¢/word.

Photos: Send photos with ms. Pays $10/5x7 b&w contact sheet or print; price negotiable for 35mm color transparencies. Buys all rights. Captions required.

LEISUREGUIDE, 29901 Agoura Rd., Agoura CA 91301. Editor: Bev Dalton. An in-room hotel guidebook emphasizing information for travelers in Atlanta, Chicago, Boston, Houston, Puerto Rico, Florida Gold Coast (Ft. Lauderdale to Palm Beach), Miami, Central Florida (Orlando area), Kansas City, Milwaukee, New Orleans, and Minneapolis-St. Paul. "We try to establish a feeling of intimacy with each of our markets, so the traveler has confidence in the information we present. And we present it in a lively, readable manner. We also strive for excellence in graphics and photography." Each edition is an annual hardcover magazine; 84-200 pages. Pays on publication. Buys all rights. Byline given. Reports in 6 weeks. Sample copy $2.

Nonfiction: "We seek articles that capture the true essence of each of our cities for the sophisticated traveler who stays in luxury hotels. We occasionally publish articles of general interest to all travelers, but most articles focus on the cities themselves. We also publish a photo essay in each edition that captures an aspect or aspects of the city in a highly unique fashion." Buys about 25 mss/yr. Query. "We want to know that the writer is intimately familiar with the city involved, and that he has seen our publication and knows our sophisticated approach." SASE. Length 1,000-2,500 words. Pays $125-$350.

Photos: Purchased without ms or on assignment. Pays $50/page for b&w, $125/page for color.

Tips: "Prove to us that you can write about the city involved in a highly knowledgeable, lively fashion. Writing ability means everything. Submitting top quality color transparencies is a plus, but not necessary."

‡**LEISUREGUIDE INTERNATIONAL**, 500 Chesham House, 150 Regent St., London, W1R 5FA, England. Editor: Robert Howells. An in-room hotel guidebook emphasizing information for travelers in London, Paris, Munich, Frankfurt, Berlin and Rome. All books except London are presented in both English and the native language. Sample copy $2, from *Leisureguide*, 29901 Agoura Rd., Agoura CA 91301.

Nonfiction: "We seek articles that capture the true essence of each of our cities for the sophisticated traveler who stays in luxury hotels. We occasionally publish articles of general interest to all travelers, but most articles focus on the cities themselves. We also publish a photo essay in each edition that captures an aspect or aspects of the city in a highly unique fashion." Buys about 25 mss/yr. Query. "We want to know that the writer is intimately familiar with the city involved, and that he has seen our publication and knows our sophisticated approach." SASE. Length 1,000-2,500 words. Pays $125-$350.

Photos: Purchased without ms or on assignment. Pays $50/page for b&w, $125/page for color.

Tips: "Prove to us that you can write about the city involved in a highly knowledgeable, lively fashion. Writing ability means everything. Submitting top quality color transparencies is a plus, but not necessary."

MICHIGAN LIVING, Automobile Club of Michigan, Auto Club Dr., Dearborn MI 48126. (313)336-1211. Editor: Len Barnes. 50% freelance written. Emphasizes travel and auto use. Monthly magazine; 48 pages. Circ. 820,000. Pays on acceptance. Buys first North American serial rights. Pays 100% kill fee. Byline given. Submit seasonal/holiday material 3 months in advance. No computer printout or disk submissions. SASE. Reports in 4-6 weeks. Buys 50-60 unsolicited mss/year. Free sample copy and writer's guidelines.

Nonfiction: Travel articles on US and Canadian topics, but not on California, Florida or Arizona. Send complete ms. Length: 200-1,000 words. Pays $75-300.

Photos: Photos purchased with accompanying ms. Captions required. Pays $25-150 for color transparencies; total purchase price for ms includes payment for b&w photos.

Tips: "In addition to descriptions of things to see and do, articles should contain accurate, current information on costs the traveler would encounter on his trip. Items such as lodging, meal and entertainment expenses should be included, not in the form of a balance sheet but as an integral part of the piece. We want the sounds, sights, tastes, smells of a place or experience so one will feel he has been there and knows if he wants to go back."

THE MIDWEST MOTORIST, The Auto Club of Missouri, 12901 North Forty Dr., St. Louis MO 63141. Editor: Michael J. Right. Associate Editors: Carolyn Callison, Tim Sitek. For the motoring public. Bimonthly magazine; 32 pages. Circ. 320,000. Pays on acceptance or publication depending on the situation. Not copyrighted. Pays kill fee as agreed. Byline given. Submit seasonal/holiday material 3-4 months in advance. Simultaneous, photocopied and previously published submissions OK. SASE. Reports in 1 month. Free sample copy and writer's guidelines.

Nonfiction: General interest; historical (of Midwest regional interest); humor (motoring slant); interview, profile, travel and photo feature. No technical auto or safety stories. Buys 3 mss/issue. Query with list of credits or clips of published work. No phone queries. Buys 15 unsolicited mss/year. Length: 1,000-1,800 words. Pays $50-200.

Photos: Send photos with ms. Uses b&w contact sheets or prints and color transparencies for cover. Offers no additional payment for photos accepted with ms. Captions preferred.

Tips: "We are tired of cliche-ridden travel stories and articles on the well-known vacation spots." Recently published "Pro 'Cat' Tells How Motel Thieves Work."

MOTORHOME, 29901 Agoura Rd., Agoura CA 91301. (213)991-4980. Editor: Bill Estes. Managing Editor: Barbara Leonard. For owners and prospective buyers of motorhomes. Published 12 times/year. Circ. 100,000. Buys first time rights. Byline given. Buys 100 mss/year. Pays on publication. Submit seasonal material 3 months in advance. Reports in 1 month. SASE. Sample copy $2; free writer's guidelines.

Nonfiction and Photos: "Articles which tell the owner of a self-propelled RV about interesting places to travel, interesting things to do. Human interest and variety articles sought as well. All material must be tailored specifically for our audience." Information, personal experience, humor, historical, opinion, travel, new product and technical articles. Length: 2,500 words maximum. Pays $100-300. Photos purchased with accompanying ms or occasionally separately.

NATIONAL MOTORIST, National Automobile Club, Suite 300, 1 Market Plaza, San Francisco CA 94105. (415)777-4000. Editor: Jane M. Offers. 75% freelance written. Emphasizes motor travel in the West. Bimonthly magazine; 32 pages. Circ. 246,000. Pays on acceptance for article, layout stage for pix. Buys first publication rights. Byline given. Submit seasonal/holiday material 3 months in advance SASE. Reports in 2 weeks.

Nonfiction: Well-researched articles on care of car, travel by car. Profile/interview (of someone in transportation/energy field); and travel (interesting places and areas to visit in the 11 Western states). Buys 2-3 mss/issue. Query. Length: "around 1,100 words." Pays 10¢/word and up.

Photos: "Suggestions welcome. May accompany ms, but considered separately. Payment either with ms or separately, depending on source. Often procured from source other than author." Captions optional, "but must have caption info for pix." Send prints or transparencies. Pays $20 maximum/8x10 b&w glossy print; $30 minimum/35mm, $2\frac{1}{4}$x$2\frac{1}{4}$ or 4x5 color transparency. Model release required.

NORTHEAST OUTDOORS, Box 2180, Waterbury CT 06722. (203)755-0158. Editor: Howard Fielding. 80% freelance written. Monthly. Circ. 14,000. Buys all rights. Byline given. Pays on publication. "Queries are not required, but are useful for our planning and to avoid possible duplication of subject matter. If you have any questions, contact the editor." No "unannounced simultaneous submissions." Deadlines are on the 1st of the month preceding publication. Reports in 15-30 days. SASE. Free sample copy.

Nonfiction and Photos: Interested in articles and photos that pertain to outdoor activities in the Northeast. Recreational vehicle tips and campgrounds are prime topics, along with first-person travel experiences in the Northeast while camping. No articles on pets, product reviews or endorsements; or features on destinations outside the northeast US. Buys 50 unsolicited mss/year. "While the primary focus is on camping, we carry some related articles on outdoor topics like skiing, nature, hiking, fishing, canoeing, etc. One reader-written feature is 'My Favorite Campground'. Payment for this is $10 and writing quality need not be professional. Our pay rate for features is flexible, but generally runs from $30-50 for features without photos, and up to $80 for features accompanied by 2 or more photos. Features should be from 300-1,000 words. Premium rates are paid on the basis of quality, not length. Pays $10/8x10 b&w print."

Tips: "We're growing in advertising, as a result of more ambitious marketing and of an upturn in the economy (and hence the RV industry). This will mean increased space and an increased market for writers. Second, we're expanding our coverage—and readership—beyond merely New England. We'll be looking for more material from New York, New Jersey and Pennsylvania. A new computer typesetting system may improve our editorial and graphics capabilities."

ODYSSEY, H.M. Gousha Publications, Box 6227, San Jose CA 95150. (408)296-1060. Editor: Celia Herron. Quarterly magazine devoted to travel and leisure with national and international coverage. Pays on acceptance. Buys first North American serial rights. Submit seasonal material 1 year in advance. Computer printout submissions OK. SASE. Reports in 1 month. "If no response to query within 6 weeks, writer should feel free to offer idea elsewhere." Free sample copy and writer's guidelines.

Nonfiction: Travel and travel-related features; how-to (get started in a new sport, hobby or recreation). "We want lively, well-researched articles packed with helpful information, such as what to see and do in a given city or destination, as well as how to see it so visitors can enjoy it more fully. Descriptive detail should give a strong sense of place. We want readers to see and feel a place. The style should be friendly and informal. Personalization or anecdotes, if skillfully done, are helpful. Please study magazine before sending submission." Buys 5 unsolicited mss/issue. Query with clips of previously published work. Length, major feature: 1,200-1,700 words. Pays $240-320 (first-time contributors) for major features.

Photos: Bruce Todd, photo editor. State availability of color slides. Pays $100-175 for 2¼, 4x5 or 35mm color transparencies. Pays $350 for a front cover that is article related and $250 for a back cover not article related. Buys one-time rights. "Send photos featuring people enjoying leisure and travel." Does not assign photos.

Columns/Departments: Cities and Sights (500-600 words about US towns, museums, zoos, marketplaces, historic sights or scenic attractions); People in Travel (500-600 words about someone who travels a great deal in pursuit of career or hobby; must have color vertical photo); and Driver's Seat (about driving safety, auto maintenance). Buys 3 mss/issue. Send complete ms on spec or query with clips of previously published work. Length: 500-600 words. Pays $120 (first-time contributors) for Cities and Sights and People In Travel; $150 for solid, informative Driver's Seat articles and/or auto/safety quizzes.

Tips: "New editor is initiating a few new departments, dropping others. Also, change from bimonthly to quarterly gives us less space per year in which to run articles."

OHIO MOTORIST, Box 6150, Cleveland OH 44101. Editor: A. K. Murway Jr. 10-15% freelance written. For AAA members in 8 northeast Ohio counties. Monthly. Circ. 270,000. Buys one-time publication rights. Byline given. Buys 30 mss/year. Pays on acceptance. Submit seasonal material 2 months prior to season. Reports in 2 weeks. Submit complete ms. SASE. Free sample copy.

Nonfiction and Photos: "Travel, including foreign; automotive, highways, etc.; motoring laws and safety. No particular approach beyond brevity and newspaper journalistic treatment. Articles for travel seasons." Length: 2,000 words maximum. Pays $50-200/article including b&w photos. $125-250 for articles with color photos, transparencies any size. 8x10 b&w photos preferred. Purchased with accompanying mss. Captions required. Ohioana is major need.

Poetry: Humorous verse. Length: 4-6 lines. Pays $8-15.

PACIFIC BOATING ALMANAC, Box Q, Ventura CA 93002. (805)644-6043. Editor: William Berssen. For "Western boat owners." Published in 3 editions to cover the Pacific Coastal area. Circ. 25,000. Buys all rights. Buys 12 mss/year. Pays on publication. Sample copy $8.95. Submit seasonal material 3 to 6 months in advance. Reports in 4 weeks. Query. SASE.

Nonfiction and Photos: "This is a cruising guide, published annually in 3 editions, covering all of the navigable waters in the Pacific coast. Though we are almost entirely staff-produced, we would be interested in well-written articles on cruising and trailer-boating along the Pacific coast and in the navigable lakes and rivers of the Western states from Baja, California to Alaska inclusive." Pays $50 minimum. Pays $10/8x10 b&w glossy print.

Tips: "We are also publishers of boating books that fall within the classification of 'where-to' and 'how-to.' Authors are advised not to send mss until requested after we've reviewed a 2-4 page outline of the projected books."

‡**ROMANTIC DINING & TRAVEL LETTER**, James Dines & Co., Inc., Box 837, Belvedere CA 94920. (415)435-2774. Editor: James Dines. Monthly newsletter covering food, wine and travel. "In-depth reviews of 'special places' around the world; hotels, restaurants with detailed wine list commentary. Appeals to a very affluent audience." Pays on acceptance. Buys all rights. Submit seasonal/holiday material 4 months in advance. Simultaneous queries and simultaneous and photocopied submissions OK. Computer printout or disk submissions OK; prefers letter quality to dot matrix printouts. Reports in 3 weeks. Sample copy $3; free writer's guidelines.

Nonfiction: Travel and dining (special places only, not tourist traps or student hangouts). No budget tips or human interest articles. Buys 10-20 mss/year. Query with clips. Pays $100-1,000 ("according to quality, not length.")

Photos: State availability of photos with query letter or ms. Photos with query preferred. Reviews any size b&w or color prints. Pays negotiable fee. Identification of subjects required. Buys one-time rights.

Tips: "We are very specialized; if a writer makes a special 'discovery' of a place—a secluded hideaway, romantic restaurant, or a particularly romantic and elegant hotel—we'll want it. We want our articles to be very detailed and useful in their description. If the quality is there we will see it." Major travel features are most open to freelancers.

RV'N ON, 10417 Chandler Blvd., North Hollywood CA 91601. (213)763-4515. Editor/Publisher: Kim Ouimet. Monthly mini-newspaper, 16-22 pages, about recreational vehicles (motorhomes, campers and trailers, etc.) Official publication of the International Travel and Trailer Club, Inc. Circ. 4,750. "Payments are made quarterly." Buys one-time rights. Submit seasonal material 3 months in advance. SASE. Reports in 6 weeks. Sample copy 95¢.

Nonfiction: General interest; historical; how-to; humor; interview; nostalgia; opinion; travel; new product; personal experience; and technical. Must be geared to RVs or boats. Buys 30 mss/year. Send complete ms. Length: 100-300 words. Pays in copies.

Columns/Departments: Campfire Tales (fiction or humorous, anecdotes or short bedtime stories for children); Roadwise Driving Tips; Rolling Kitchen; An Unusual Place (places off the road worth visiting); A Most Unusual Person (release required if name used). Buys 12 mss/year. Query first. Length: 100-500 words. Pays 3¢/word-$15.

Fiction: Adventure, fantasy, historical, humorous, and suspense. Must be geared to RVs or boats. No lengthy items. No poetry or children's tales. Buys 6 mss/year. Query. Length: 200-400 words. Pays 3¢/word minimum.

Fillers: Jokes, anecdotes, short humor and newsbreaks, geared to RVs or boats. Buys 12 mss/year. Length: 25-50 words. Pays $2 maximum.

Tips: "Know motorhomes, campers, etc. and what will be of interest to owners, such as storage tips, repairs, tips of traveling with animals and children. We are anxious to have actual RVers submit material. We keep receiving general material which is scanned and returned immediately. We cannot send particular or individual replies on returns. We always know when someone is not familiar with RVs."

‡TOURING TIMES, RFD, Inc., Box 33021, Kansas City MO 64114. (816)333-1414. Editor: Norman F. Rowland. Quarterly magazine covering group travel for farmers or agribusiness people who have been on farm tours and people who have been on flower/horticultural tours. Publishes 2 editions quarterly—one for people who have traveled with Rural Route Tours International (foreign) or American Group Travel (domestic) of Kansas City; one for Southland Travel Service (flower) or Southern Farm Tours (farm) of Birmingham, Alabama. Estab. 1982. Circ. 22,000. Pays on acceptance. Byline given. Offers 1/3 kill fee. Buys one-time, simultaneous, second serial reprint and variable rights. Submit seasonal/holiday material 6 months in advance. Simultaneous queries, and simultaneous, photocopied and previously published submissions OK "if other markets are specified." Reports in 3 weeks on queries; 6 weeks on mss. Free sample copy and writer's guidelines.

Nonfiction: Historical/nostalgic; how-to (travel tips); humor; interview/profile; photo feature; travel; international recipes. "All material must be travel related to some degree and present group touring in a positive light." Special destinations: Western Europe, Southern Europe, Hawaii, South America, Australia, New Zealand. No "restaurant reviews or overly sophisticated off-the-beaten-track pieces." Buys 8 or more mss/year. Query with or without published clips or send complete ms. Length: 1,000-2,500 words. Pays $350-500.

Photos: State availability of photos. Pays $60-125 for 2¼ color transparencies. Captions, model release and identification of subjects required. Buys one-time rights.

Columns/Departments: Travel Tips; Travel Book Reviews. Query. Length: 750-1,200 words. Pays negotible rates; "we're interested in developing our book column."

Tips: "Send for sample copies in order to study our tour listings. We are making plans at present to publish four to six special destination supplements in magazine format annually. If this jells, we'll need much more freelance help. Areas we're presently serving include Alaska, Hawaii, Australia, New Zealand, Pacific Northwest, West Coast, Rockies, Canada-New England, Old South, Carolinas-Florida, American Heritage (Washington to Williamsburg), British Isles, Western Europe, Southern Europe, Scandinavia and South America. China, Spain and Caribbean (cruise) go from time to time. We're particularly interested in developing working relationships with writers who have excellent photo skills."

TRAILER LIFE, TL Enterprises, Inc., 29901 Agoura Rd., Agoura CA 90301. (213)991-4980. Associate Publisher: Don E. Brown. Editor: Bill Estes. Monthly magazine for owners and potential buyers of trailers, campers and motorhomes. Circ. 324,906. Pays on publication. Buys first rights. Phone queries OK. Submit seasonal material 4 months in advance. Computer printout submissions OK. SASE. Reports in 2 weeks on queries; in 3 weeks on mss. Free sample copy and writer's guidelines.

Nonfiction: Art of using a trailer, camper or motorhome and the problems involved. Length: 2,000 words maximum. How-to articles with step-by-step photos a necessity. Length: 800 words maximum. Combine as many operations in each photo or drawing as possible. Personal experience stories must be truly interesting. Merely living in or traveling by trailer is not enough. Uses travel articles with 3-6 good 8x10 glossy prints and several color transparencies on trips that are inexpensive or unusual, into areas which are accessible by a travel trailer or pickup camper. Photos must be top quality. Length: 1,000-2,000 words. Also uses short travel pieces, with a couple of photos of interesting places off the established routes. Length: 100-250 words. Allied interest articles are one of main interests, things that trailerists do, like boating, hiking, fishing and spelunking hobbies. A definite tie-in with travel trailers, motorhomes or pickup campers is essential. Tell the reader how their trailers fit into the sport and where they can park while there. All travel articles should include basic information on trailer parking facilities in the areas, costs, location, and time of year, etc. Payment varies "based on the quality of the material submitted and how it's used. Our rates will probably get better in the coming year."

Photos: "We are often asked by photographers about submissions of single photos. We seldom, if ever, buy photos alone; we suggest that if a photographer has a series of related good pictures either black and white or color—involving RV activity, that he wrap a story around the photos and submit the pictures and manuscript as a package. Photos should be 8x10 glossy. Prints should be numbered and the photographer identified on the back, with numbers corresponding to a caption sheet. Photos should show action and should be as close up as the subject matter will allow."

TRAILS-A-WAY, TAW Publishing Co., 1212 W. Oak St., Greenville MI 48838. (616)754-9179. Editor: Martha Higbie. Newspaper published 8 times/year on camping in the Midwest (Michigan, Ohio, Indiana). "Fun and information for campers who own recreational vehicles." Circ. 40,000. Pays on publication. Byline given. Submit seasonal/holiday material 3 months in advance. Simultaneous queries and submissions OK. Computer printout and disk submissions OK. SASE. Reports in 1 month. Sample copy 75¢; writer's guidelines for business size SAE and 1 first class stamp.

Nonfiction: How-to (use, maintain recreational vehicles—5th wheels, travel and camping trailers, pop-up trailers, motorhomes); humor; inspirational; interview/profile; new product (camp products); personal experience; photo feature; technical (on RVs); travel. March/April issue: spring camping; September/October: fall camping. "All articles should relate to RV camping in Michigan, Ohio and Indiana. No tenting or backpacking articles." Buys 16-24 mss/year. Send complete ms. Length: 750-1,500 words. Pays $50-75.

Photos: Send photos with ms. Pays $5-10 for b&w and color prints. No slides. Captions required. Buys one-time rights.

Tips: "Recently made the 40,000 circulation into three editions—Ohio edition, Michigan edition, and Indiana edition. Editorial thrust will be closer to state requirements as far as travel stories are concerned. Otherwise same general camping material will be used in all three. Payment is based on total circulation so that articles may appear in all three."

TRANSITIONS, 18 Hulst Rd., Amherst MA 01002. (413)256-0373. Editor and Publisher: Prof. Clayton A. Hubbs. A resource guide to work, study, and special interest travel abroad, for low budget travelers. Bound magazine. Circ. 15,000. Pays on publication. Rights revert to writer. Byline given. Phone queries OK. SASE. Reports in 4 weeks. Sample copy $2; writer's guidelines for SASE.

Nonfiction: How-to (find courses, inexpensive lodging and travel); interview (information on specific areas and people); personal experience (evaluation of courses, special interest and study tours, economy travel); and travel (what to see and do in specific areas of the world, new learning and travel ideas). Foreign travel only. No travel pieces for businessmen. Few destination pieces. Buys 40 unsolicited mss/issue. Query with credentials. Length: 500-1,500 words. Pays $25-75.

Photos: Send photos with ms. Pays $10-15 for 8x10 b&w glossy prints, higher for covers. No color. Offers no additional payment for photos accompanying ms, but photos increase likelihood of acceptance. Buys one-time rights. Captions required.

Columns/Departments: Studynotes (evaluation of courses or programs); Travelnotes (new ideas for offbeat independent travel); and Jobnotes (how to find it and what to expect). Buys 8/issue. Send complete ms. Length: 1,000 words maximum. Pays $10-50.

Fillers: Newsbreaks (having to do with travel, particularly offbeat educational travel and work or study abroad). Buys 5/issue. Length: 100 words maximum. Pays $5-20.

Tips: "We like nuts and bolts stuff. Real practical information, especially on how to work and cut costs abroad. Be specific: names, addresses, current costs."

THE TRAVEL ADVISOR, Box 716, Bronxville NY 10708. Editor-in-Chief: Hal E. Gieseking. 50-60% freelance written. Monthly newsletter; 6-7 pages. Owned by *Travel/Holiday* magazine. Circ. 800,000 (published as part of *Travel/Holiday*). Pays on acceptance. Buys all rights. SASE. Reports in 4 weeks. Free sample copy and writer's guidelines. No photos used.

Nonfiction: "Send us short, *very candid* items based on the writer's own travel experience—*not* written first-person. Example: a baggage rip-off in Rome; a great new restaurant in Tokyo (with prices)." Expose (candid

look at the travel industry); and how-to (good, inside information on how travelers can avoid problems, save money, etc.). Buys 50 unsolicited short 1-2 paragraph mss/year. Length: 20-150 words. Pays $20-30/item. All full-length articles are currently staff written. "We are looking for several regional correspondents in *important* worldwide travel areas who will submit short round-up reports monthly."
Tips: "*Check* facts carefully."

TRAVEL AND LEISURE, 1120 Avenue of the Americas, New York NY 10036. (212)386-5600. Editor-in-Chief: Pamela Fiori. Monthly. Circ. 925,000. Buys first worldwide serial rights. Pays 25% kill fee. Byline given unless material is assigned as research. Pays on acceptance. Reports in 2 weeks. Query. No computer printout or disk submissions. SASE.
Nonfiction: Uses articles on travel and vacation places, food, wine, shopping, sports. Nearly all articles are assigned. Length: 2,000-3,000 words. Pays $750-2,000.
Photos: Makes assignments mainly to established photographers. Pays expenses.
Tips: "New writers might try to get something in one of our regional editions (East, West, South and Midwest). They don't pay as much as our national articles ($600), but it is a good way to start. We have a need for pieces that run no more than 800-1,200 words. Regionals cover any number of possibilities from a profile of an interesting town in a certain state to unusual new attractions."

TRAVEL SMART, Communications House, Inc., Dobbs Ferry NY 10522. (914)693-4208. Editor/Publisher: H.J. Teison. Managing Editor/Publisher: Mary L. Hunt. Covers information on "budget, good-value travel." Monthly newsletter. Pays on publication. Buys all rights. Photocopied submissions OK. Computer printout submissions OK. SASE. Reports in 6 weeks. Free sample copy and writer's guidelines for #10 SASE with 37¢ postage.
Nonfiction: Mary L. Hunt, managing editor. "Interested primarily in great bargains or little-known deals on transportation, lodging, food, unusual destinations that won't break the bank. Please, no destination stories on major Caribbean islands, London, New York, no travelogues, my vacation, poetry, fillers. No photos or illustrations. Just hard facts. We are not part of 'Rosy fingers of dawn . . .' School. More like letter from knowledgeable friend who has been there." Query first. Length: 100-1,000 words. Pays "under $100."
Tips: "Send clippings of ads for bargain airfares, package tours, hotel deals in your area (outside New York only). When you travel, check out small hotels offering good prices, little known restaurants, and send us brief rundown (with prices, phone numbers, addresses) of at least 4 at one location. Information must be current and backed up with literature, etc. Include your phone number with submission, because we sometimes make immediate assignments."

TRAVEL/HOLIDAY MAGAZINE, Travel Magazine, Inc., 51 Atlantic Ave., Floral Park NY 11001. (516)352-9700. Executive Editor: Scott Shane. Managing Editor: Jim Ferri. For the active traveler with time and money to travel several times a year. Monthly magazine; 100 pages. Circ. 815,000. Pays on acceptance. Buys first North American serial rights. Byline given. Submit seasonal/holiday material 6 months in advance. Computer printout submissions OK; prefers letter quality to dot matrix printouts. SASE. Reports in 6 weeks. Sample copy $1; free writer's guidelines.
Nonfiction: Interested in travel destination articles. Send query letter/outline; clips of previously published work *must* accompany queries. Only the highest quality writing and photography are considered by the new staff. "Don't ask if we'd like to see any articles on San Francisco, France or China. Develop a specific story idea and explain why the destination is so special that we should devote space to it. Are there interesting museums, superb restaurants, spectacular vistas, etc.? Tell us how you plan to handle the piece—convey to us the mood of the city, the charm of the area, the uniqueness of the museums, etc. No food and wine, medical, photo tips, poetry or boring travelogues. Length: featurettes (1,000-1,200 words), $250 and up; features (1,500-2,000), $400 and up; "Here and There" column (750 words), $150.
Photos: B&w prints $25; color transparencies (35mm and larger) pays $75-400 depending upon use.
Tips: "Feature stories should be about major destinations: large cities, regions, etc. Featurettes can be about individual attractions, smaller cities, side trips, etc. We welcome sidebar service information. Stimulate reader interest in the subject as a travel destination through lively, entertaining and accurate writing. A good way to break in—if we're not familiar with your writing—is to send us a good idea for a featurette (a walking tour of Milan, a trip to Saba, a famous castle, etc., are featurettes we've run recently). Convey the mood of a place without being verbose; although we like good anecdotal material, our primary interest is in the destination itself, not the author's adventures. The format of the magazine has changed—do not query without having first read several recent issues. Style of the magazine has changed—we no longer use any broadbased travel pieces. Each article must have a specific angle. We are assigning articles to the best writers we can find and those writers who develop and produce good material and will continue to work with us on a regular basis. We have also become much more service-oriented in our articles."

TRAVELORE REPORT, 225 S. 15th St., Philadelphia PA 19102. (215)545-0616. Editor: Ted Barkus. For affluent travelers; businessmen, retirees, well-educated; interested in specific tips, tours, and bargain opportu-

nities in travel. Monthly newsletter; 6 pages. Buys all rights. Buys 10-20 mss/year. Pays on publication. Sample copy $1. Submit seasonal material 2 months in advance. Computer printout and disk submissions OK.
Nonfiction: "Brief insights (25-200 words) with facts, prices, names of hotels and restaurants, etc., on offbeat subjects of interest to people going places. What to do, what not to do. Supply information. We will rewrite if acceptable. We're candid—we tell it like it is with no sugar coating. Avoid telling us about places in United States or abroad without specific recommendations (hotel name, costs, rip-offs, why, how long, etc.). No destination pieces which are general with no specific 'story angle' in mind, or generally available through PR departments." Pays $5.

VISTA/USA, Box 161, Convent Station NJ 07961. (201)538-7600. Editor: Patrick Sarver. Managing Editor: Barbara OByrne. Quarterly magazine of the Exxon Travel Club. "Our publication uses articles on North American areas without overtly encouraging travel. We strive to use as literate a writing as we can in our articles, helping our readers to gain an in-depth understanding of cities, towns and areas as well as other aspects of American culture that affect the character of the nation." Circ. 900,000. Pays on acceptance. Buys first North American serial rights. Query about seasonal subjects 18 months in advance. Computer printout and disk submissions OK. SASE. Reports in 1 month. Free sample copy and writer's guidelines.
Nonfiction: General interest (geographically-oriented articles on North America focusing on the character of an area; also general articles related to travel and places); humor (related to travel or places); and photo features (photo essays on subjects such as autumn, winter, highly photogenic travel subjects; and special interest areas). "We buy feature articles on North America, Hawaii, Mexico and the Caribbean that appeal to a national audience." No articles that mention driving or follow routes on a map or articles about hotels, restaurants or annual events. Uses 7-10 mss/issue. Query with outline and clips of previously published work. Length: 1,500-2,500 words. Pays $600 minimum.
Photos: Keith Slack, art director. Send photos with ms. Pays $100 minimum for color transparencies. Captions preferred. Buys one-time rights.
Columns/Departments: Places of Interest ("on places in the US that do not have enough national significance to rate as features, along with non-North American areas; tight, straightforward prose to give the reader a vignette impression of places with as much information as is practical within a short length"). Uses 5 mss/issue. Query with clips of previously published work. Length: 100-300 words. Pays $100 maximum, depending on length.
Tips: "We are looking for readable pieces with good writing that will interest armchair travelers as much as readers who may want to visit the areas you write about. Articles should have definite themes and should give our readers an insight into the character and flavor of an area. Stories about personal experiences must impart a sense of drama and excitement or have a strong human-interest angle. Stories about areas should communicate a strong sense of what it feels like to be there. Good use of anecdotes and quotes should be included. Study the articles in the magazine to understand how they are organized, how they present their subjects, the range of writing styles, and the specific types of subjects used. Then query and enclose samples of your best writing."

WORLD TRAVELING, Midwest News Service, Inc., 30943 Club House Lane, Farmington Hills MI 48018. Editor: Theresa Mitan. Bimonthly magazine. Circ. 40,600. Pays on publication. Buys all rights. Byline given. Submit seasonal/holiday material 6 months in advance. Simultaneous submissions OK. SASE. Reports in 1 month or longer. Sample copy $2 plus postage.
Nonfiction: General interest, adventure travel (such as hang-gliding); humor; photo feature and travel. Buys 6 mss/issue. Send complete ms. Length: 1,000 words. Pays $100 for 1,000 words.
Photos: Send photos with ms. Pays $10 for b&w prints; $10 for color transparencies or prints. Buys one-time rights.
Columns & Departments: Good Restaurant Guide and Question and Answers about travel. Query or send complete ms. Length: 500 words.

Union

‡**BROTHERHOOD OF MAINTENANCE OF WAY EMPLOYES JOURNAL,** 12050 Woodward Ave., Detroit MI 48203. (313)868-0490. Editor: O.M. Berge. Associate Editor: R.J. Williamson. Monthly trade union magazine for railroad track workers. "Our readers are members of our union, and their work is on the railroad where they build and maintain the tracks, bridges and buildings." Circ. 110,000. Pays on publication. Byline given. Buys one-time, non-exclusive rights. Submit seasonal/holiday material 4 months in advance. Simultaneous queries, and simultaneous, photocopied and previously published submissions OK. SASE. Reports in 1 month. Free sample copy.
Nonfiction: Historical/nostalgic and anecdotal pieces. "All material must relate to railroad work." Buys 2-3

mss/year. Length: averages 2 typewritten pages. Pays average $40. No additional fee for photos with ms.
Photos: "Photos must be dynamic and sharp." Send photos with query or ms. Pays $10 for 4x5 b&w print used inside. Pays $100-200 for 4x5 or larger color transparencies used as cover. Must be vertical format. Identification of subjects required; caption preferred.

OCAW UNION NEWS, Box 2812, Denver CO 80201. (303)987-2229. Editor: Jerry Archuleta. Official publication of Oil, Chemical and Atomic Workers International Union. For union members. Bimonthly tabloid newspaper; 16-24 pages. Circ. 140,000. Not copyrighted. Byline given. Pays on acceptance. Reports in 30 days. Query. SASE. Free sample copy.
Nonfiction: Labor union materials, political subjects and consumer interest articles, slanted toward workers and consumers, with liberal political view. Interview, profile, think pieces and exposes. Most material is done on assignment. "We have severe space limitations." Length: 1,500-1,800 words. Pays $50-75.
Photos: No additional payment is made for 8x10 b&w glossy photos used with mss. Captions required.

UTU NEWS, United Transportation Union, 14600 Detroit Ave., Cleveland OH 44107. (216)228-9400. Editor: Art Hanford. For members of the union (250,000) working in the crafts of engineer, conductor, firemen and brakemen on North American railroads. Newspaper published 3 times/month; 4 pages. (Also one monthly tabloid; 8 pages). Pays on publication. Buys photos only. Buys all rights. Phone queries OK. Reports "at once."
Photos: Current news shots of railroad or bus accidents, especially when employees are killed or injured. Captions required. Pays $20 minimum for any size b&w glossy prints.

Women's

Women's magazines are as diverse as the people who read them. In addition to these markets, other publications that use material slanted to women's interests can be found in the following categories: Business and Finance; Child Care and Parental Guidance; Food and Drink; Hobby and Craft; Home and Garden; Lifestyles; Religious; Romance and Confession; and Sports.

THE AMERICAN MIZRACHI WOMAN, American Mizrachi Women, 817 Broadway, New York NY 10003. (212)477-4720. Executive Editor: Ruth Raisner. Editor: Micheline Ratzersdorfer. Magazine published 6 times/year "concerned with Jewish and Israeli themes, i.e., Jewish art, Jewish sociology, Jewish communities around the world to an audience with an above average educational level, a commitment to Jewish tradition and Zionism and a concern for the future of the Jewish community the world over." Circ. 50,000. Pays on publication. Buys all rights. Submit seasonal material 6 months in advance. Computer printout submissions OK "as long as it can be read by the human eye and has adequate leading and margins for editing." Prefers letter quality to dot matrix printouts. SASE. Reports in 1 month. Free sample copy and writer's guidelines.
Nonfiction: General interest; historical; interview (with notable figures in Jewish and Israeli life); nostalgia; travel; and photo feature (particularly Jewish holiday photos). "We do special holiday features for all Jewish holidays." No fiction, no memoirs about "Momma's Chicken Soup" and things of that ilk; no political analyses of the Middle East unless they can stand a six-month delay until publication; no travelogues lauding non-kosher restaurants, please." Buys 10 unsolicited mss/year. Query. Length: 1,000-2,000 words. Pays $50 maximum.
Photos: State availability of photos. Reviews 5x7 b&w glossy prints. Offers no additional payment for photos accepted with ms. Captions preferred. Buys one-time rights.
Columns/Departments: Jews Around the World (1,000-2,000 words); Life in Israel (1,000-2,000 words). Buys 5 mss/year. Query. Length: 1,000-2,000 words. Pays $50 maximum.
Poetry: Publishes rarely. Submit 3 maximum. Length: 10-50 lines. Pays $10 minimum.
Tips: "We are interested in adding to our stable of freelance writers. The best way to break in is to send a detailed query about a subject you would like to handle for the magazine. All queries will be carefully considered and answered. We've been cut from 8 to 6 issues per year for budgetary reasons, so we're buying less material. But we're still reading whatever comes in."

BRIDE'S, Conde Nast Bldg., 350 Madison Ave., New York NY 10017. (212)880-8535. Editor-in-Chief: Barbara D. Tober. For the first- or second-time bride, her family and friends, the groom and his family. Magazine published 6 times/year. Circ. 350,000. Buys all rights. Offers 20% kill fee, depending on circumstances. Byline given. Buys 10 unsolicited mss/year. Pays on acceptance. Reports in 8 weeks. Query or submit complete ms. Article outline preferred. Address mss to Features Department. Free writer's guidelines.

Nonfiction: "We want warm, personal articles, optimistic in tone, with help offered in a clear, specific way. All issues should be handled within the context of marriage. How-to features on all aspects of marriage: communications, in-laws, careers, money, sex, housework, family planning, religion, step-parenting, second marriage, reaffirmation of vows; informational articles on the realities of marriage, the changing roles of men and women, the kinds of troubles in engagement that are likely to become big issues in marriage; stories from couples or marriage authorities that illustrate marital problems and solutions to men and women both; and how-to features on wedding planning that offer expert advice. Also success stories of marriages of long duration. We're using less of the first-person piece and requiring more that articles be well researched, relying on quotes from authorities in the field." Length: 1,500-3,000 words. Pays $300-600.

Tips: "Send us a query or a well-written article that is both easy to read and offers real help for the bride as she adjusts to her new role. No first-person narratives on wedding and reception planning, home furnishings, cooking, fashion, beauty, travel. For examples of the kinds of features we want, study any issue; read articles listed in table of contents under 'Planning for Marriage.' "

CHATELAINE, 777 Bay St., Toronto, Ontario, Canada M5W 1A7. Editor-in-Chief: Mildred Istona. Monthly general-interest magazine for Canadian women, from age 20 and up. *Chatelaine* is read by one women in three across Canada, a readership that spans almost every age group but is concentrated among those 25 to 45 incuding homemakers and working women in all walks of life. Circ. over 1 million. Pays on acceptance. By-line given. Free writer's guidelines. "Writers new to us should query us with ideas for upfront columns on nutrition, fitness, relationships, feelings, and parents and kids." Pays $350 for about 1,000 words. Prefers queries for nonfiction subjects on initial contact plus a resume and writing samples. Reports within 2 weeks. All mss must be accompanied by a SASE (international reply coupons in lieu of Canadian stamps if sent from outside Canada). Sample copy $1.25 and postage.

Nonfiction: Elizabeth Parr, senior editor, articles. Submit a page or two outline/query first. Full-length major pieces run from 2,000 to 4,000 words. Pays minimum $1,000 for acceptable major article. Buys first North American serial rights in English and French (the latter to cover possible use in *Chatelaine*'s sister French-language edition, edited in Montreal for French Canada). "We look for important national Canadian subjects, examining any and all facets of Canadian life, especially as they concern or interest Canadian women; for example current issues (Women & Wages, National Disgrace, January 1982); lifestyles (Two-Income Couples: Double the Pleasure or Double the Stress? June 1981); health, both physical (Breast Cancer: More Options, New Hope, February 1982) and mental (When You're Depressed, November 1981); and relationships (The Return of Love and Marriage, October 1981). For all serious articles, deep, accurate, thorough research and rich detail are required." Also seeks full-length personal experience stories with deep emotional impact (Our Child Has Cerebral Palsy, December 1981). Pays $750. Features on beauty, food, fashion and home decorating are supplied by staff writers and editors, and unsolicited material is not considered.

Fiction: Barbara West, fiction editor. Mainstream fiction of 3,000-4,500 words. Pays $1,500 minimum. "Upbeat stories about man/woman relationships are the ones most likely to appeal. The central character should be a woman in the 25-45 age range, and the story should deal with and resolve contemporary problems and conflicts our readers relate to. We look for strong human interest, pace, emotional impact, believable characters, romance, humor. Avoid violence, too-explicit sex, science fiction, avant-garde experiments, short-shorts. Canadian settings and characters are a plus. No query necessary for fiction."

COSMOPOLITAN, Hearst Corp., 224 W. 57th St., New York NY 10019. Editor: Helen Gurley Brown. Managing Editor: Guy Flatley. For career women, ages 18-34. Monthly. Circ. 2,500,000. Buys all rights. Pays on acceptance. Not interested in receiving unsolioited manuscripts. Most material is assigned to established, known professional writers who sell regularly to top national markets, or is commissioned through literary agents.

Nonfiction: Not interested in unsolicited manuscripts; for agents and top professional writers, requirements are as follows: "We want pieces that tell an attractive, 18-34-year-old, intelligent, good-citizen girl how to have a more rewarding life—'how-to' pieces, self-improvement pieces as well as articles which deal with more serious matters. We'd be interested in articles on careers, part-time jobs, diets, food, fashion, men, the entertainment world, emotions, money, medicine and psychology and fabulous characters." Uses some first-person stories. Logical, interesting, authoritative writing is a must, as is a feminist consciousness. Length: 1,000-3,000 words. Pays $200-500 for short pieces, $500-750 for longer articles.

Photos: Photos purchased on assignment only.

Fiction: Betty Kelly, department editor. Not interested in unsolicited manuscripts; for agents and top professional writers, requirements are as follows: "Good plotting and excellent writing are important. We want short stories dealing with adult subject matter which would interest a sophisticated audience, primarily female, 18-34. We prefer serious quality fiction or light tongue-in-cheek stories on any subject, done in good taste. We love stories dealing with contemporary man-woman relationships. Short-shorts are okay but we prefer them to have snap or 'trick' endings. The formula story, the soap opera, skimpy mood pieces or character sketches are not for us." Length: short-shorts, 1,500-3,000 words; short stories, 4,000-6,000 words; condensed novels and novel excerpts. "We also use murder or suspense stories of about 25,000-30,000 words dealing with the upper class stratum of American living. A foreign background is acceptable, but the chief characters should be American." Has published the work of Agatha Christie, Joyce Carol Oates, Evan Hunter, and other established writers. Pays $1,000 minimum and up for short stories and novel excerpts; $4,500 minimum for condensed novels

FAMILY CIRCLE GREAT IDEAS, Family Circle Magazine, 488 Madison Ave., New York NY 10022. (212)593-8181. Editor: Marie T. Walsh. Managing Editor: Shari E. Hartford. Emphasizes how to: decorating, fashion and crafts. Published 9 times/year; 128 pages. Circ. 1,000,000. Pays on publication. Buys all rights. Submit seasonal/holiday material 9 months in advance. Writer's guidelines upon request with SASE. Reports in 4 weeks. Sample copy $1.95.
Nonfiction: How-to (fashion, decorating, crafts, food and beauty) and new product (for home and family). Article queries should be directed to managing editor. Buys 2 mss/issue. Query. Pays $150-350.

FAMILY CIRCLE MAGAZINE, 488 Madison Ave., New York NY 10022. (212)593-8000. Editor-in-Chief: Arthur Hettich. 60% freelance written. For women. Published 17 times/year. Usually buys all rights. Pays 25% kill fee. Byline given. Pays on acceptance. Reports in 6-8 weeks. Query. "We like to see a strong query on unique or problem-solving aspects of family life, and are especially interested in writers who have a solid background in the areas they suggest." SASE.
Nonfiction: Contact: Margaret Jaworski. Women's interest subjects such as family and social relationships, children, humor, physical and mental health, leisure-time activities, self-improvement, popular culture, travel. Service articles. For travel, interested mainly in local material. "We look for service stories told in terms of people. We want well-researched service journalism on all subjects. Length: 1,000-2,500 words. Pays $250-2,500.
Fiction: Contact: Diane Hynd, book editor. Occasionally uses fiction related to women. Buys short stories, short-shorts, vignettes. Length: 2,000-2,500 words. Payment negotiable. Minimum payment for full-length story is $2,000. Reports in 6 weeks.
Tips: Query letters should be "concise and to the point. We get some with 10 different suggestions—by the time they're passed on to all possible editors involved, weeks may go by." Also, writers should "keep close tabs on *Family Circle* and other women's magazines to avoid submitting recently run subject matter."

FARM WIFE NEWS, Box 643, Milwaukee WI 53201. (414)423-0100. Managing Editor: Ruth Benedict. For farm and ranch women of all ages; nationwide. "We are the one and only completely-dedicated-to-farm/ranch-women's magazine. Unlike some farm magazines, which only dedicate a few pages to rural women's interests, we try to make each and every issue appropriate to a farm woman's busy, unique and important life. The farm and ranch woman feels a great deal of pride in her role as the farmer, not just a farmer's partner or an assistant in the operation. Many have advanced agronomy and animal husbandry degrees and are more involved than ever." Circ. 330,000. Byline given. Buys 300 unsolicited mss/year. Pays on acceptance. Sample copy $2.25; free writer's, photographers's guidelines. Submit seasonal material 6 months in advance. No photocopied or simultaneous submissions. "Mildly receptive" to computer printout and disk submissions; prefers letter quality to dot matrix printouts. Reports in 4-6 weeks. Query stating availability of photos, etc., or submit complete ms. SASE.
Nonfiction: "We are always looking for good freelance material. Our prime consideration is that it is farm-oriented, focusing on a farm woman or a subject that would appeal especially to her. Farm and ranch women are very interested in lifestyle issues, child care and family issues. So much about rural living has been said before—'it's the best place to raise children, work together with the family, etc.'—I'm quite interested in hearing from people with a new point of view." Uses a wide variety of material: daily life, sewing, gardening, decorating, outstanding farm women, etc. Topic should always be approached from a rural woman's point of view. Informational, how-to, personal experience, interview, profile, inspirational, humor, think pieces, nostalgia, opinion, successful sideline business operations from farm and/or ranches. No "nostalgia pieces on Mom's old cookstove, the first time someone drove the Model T, etc. Looking for more unique reflections and nostalgia—new angles." Length: 1,000 words maximum. Departments and columns which also use material are: A Day in Our Lives, Besides Farming, Country Crafts, Sewing and Needlecraft, Gardening, Country Decorating, and I Remember When. Pays $45-250.
Photos: B&w photos are purchased with or without accompanying mss. Color slides and transparencies are also used. "We look for scenic, seasonal color photos and shots of farm wives at work and at play which show the life on the farm." Captions required. Payment depends on use, but begins at $40 for b&w photos; at $50 and up for color slides or transparencies.
Fiction: Mainstream, humorous. Themes should relate to subject matter. Length: 1,000 words maximum. Pays $40-150.
Poetry: Farm life related. Pays $35-60. "Please limit your submissions to 6 or less. Rural themes only."
Fillers: Word puzzles and short humor. Pays $20-45.
Tips: "Supply enough facts and your article stands a good chance of making it. Articles that require correspondence and calls for better photos, pertinent names, quotes, places or even added shaping don't survive very

well. We are under greater pressure than ever to select the very best material available and consequently, cannot take the time to wade through stacks of material sent in by one writer. If he or she cannot be selective and send in the top pieces she/he has to market, the results will be a quick skim or reading of only the top few in that writer's pile. Sorry, but we can't be a writer's complete home office in Milwaukee.''

‡**FIFTY UPWARD NETWORK, Dedicated to the 50 + Single Woman**, Network Publications, Box 4714, Cleveland OH 44126. Editor/Publisher: Nancy C. Meyer. Monthly newsletter covering the 50 + single woman. "Our newsletter is an enthusiastic 'up' publication which details the many advantages of being free, female, mature and gutsy. We are a practical, down-to-earth, supportive publication and this is the slant we would require in submissions." Estab. 1982. Pays on publication. Byline given. No kill fee: "anything accepted will be published." Simultaneous queries and previously published submissions OK "if pertinent." SASE. Reports in 2-3 weeks on queries. Sample copy for business-sized SAE and 2 first class stamps; free writer's guidelines.
Nonfiction: Interview/profile ("we cameo 50 + nationally-known women with power, talent, charm & brains"); travel (solo jaunting column). "We are open to submissions for our columns on career alternatives, Single Epicure, You & Your Money, book reviews, dating and marriage after 50, and Y.O.U. Inc. (sideline business). Send SASE for sample and writer's guidelines." No strictly feminist, or "swinging single" type articles. "Please read sample issue carefully first." Query with clips if available. "We do not require that writer has been published." Length: 800-1,000 words. Pays $20-30. "This will increase. Even though we do not pay top fees, the writer can feel certain that he/she *will* be paid."
Tips: "We suspect (although this is *not* a must) that a 50 + woman writer could lend a very pertinent and personal slant to anything submitted. Submissions should be down-to-earth, practical, believable without a definite negative slant. We are willing to give a *non-published writer* a chance so long as article is appropriate. Our newsletter has a standard column format (which could change as time passes). We are open to submissions in any of the columns previously mentioned. And also might consider a column idea not at present covered. My newsletter is in development stage. I would think it should get longer with more columns, subjects."

FLARE, 777 Bay St., Toronto, Ontario, Canada M5W 1A7. (416)596-5453. Editor: Bonnie Hurowitz. Associate Editor: Julie Beddoes. Special interest magazine published 10 times/year for 18-34-year-old Canadian working women. Covers fashion, beauty, health, careers, lifestyle features. Circ. 196,780. Pays on acceptance. Byline given. Buys first North American serial rights; buys all rights for career page material. Submit seasonal material 3 months in advance. Simultaneous, photocopied and previously published submissions OK. Reports in 1 month. Sample copy $1.
Nonfiction: General interest and profile articles no more than 3,500 words on (up-and-coming Canadians in arts, sports, politics and sciences, etc.). "All material must be for a Canadian market using Canadian research." Buys 2 mss/issue. Do not send complete mss. Query with resume and clips of previously published work. Unsolicited mss returned only if accompanied by SASE. US stamps not valid in Canada. Length: 3,500 words maximum.
Columns/Departments: Wavelength (personal essays, preferably lively and opinionated); Options (emerging trends such as shared home ownership). Buys 2 mss/issue. Length: 1,000 words. Career News: 100-word Canadian clippings, ideas, and news items for working women. Courses, conferences, solutions to problems, research findings, breakthroughs.
Fiction: Annual contest announced in September issue.
Tips: "Usually start with small items, e.g., Career News, etc."

GLAMOUR, Conde Nast, 350 Madison Ave., New York NY 10017. (212)692-5500. Editor-in-Chief: Ruth Whitney. For college-educated women, 18-35-years old. Monthly. Circ. 1.9 million; 6.5 million readers. Computer printout submissions OK "if the material is easy to read." Prefers letter quality to dot matrix printouts. SASE. Pays on acceptance. Pays 20% kill fee. Byline given. Reports within 5 weeks. Writer's guidelines available for SASE.
Nonfiction: Janet Chan, articles editor. "Editorial approach is 'how-to' with articles that are relevant in the areas of careers, health, psychology, interpersonal relationships, etc. We look for queries that are fresh and include a contemporary, timely angle. Fashion, beauty, decorating, travel, food and entertainment are all staff-written. We use 1,000-1,200 word opinion essays for our Viewpoint section. Pays $400. Our His/Hers column features generally stylish essays on relationships or comments on current mores by male and female writers in alternate months. Pays $800 for His/Hers mss. Buys first North American serial rights." Buys 10-12 mss/issue. Query "with letter that is detailed, well-focused, well-organized, and documented with surveys, statistics and research." Reports in 5 weeks. Short articles and essays (1,500-2,000 words) pay $800 and up; longer mss (2,500-3,000 words) pay $1,000 minimum on acceptance.
Tips: "We're looking for sharply focused ideas by strong writers and constantly raising our standards. We are very interested in getting new writers; and we are approachable, mainly because our range of topics is so broad."

GOOD HOUSEKEEPING, Hearst Corp., 959 8th Ave., New York NY 10019. Editor-in-Chief: John Mack Carter. Executive Editor: Mina Mulvey. Managing Editor: Mary Fiore. Mass women's magazine. Monthly; 250 pages. Circ. 5,000,000. Pays on acceptance. Buys all rights. Pays 25% kill fee. Byline given. Submit seasonal/holiday material 8 months in advance. SASE. Reports in 1 month. Sample copy $1.50. Free writer's guidelines with SASE.

Nonfiction: Joan Thursh, articles editor. Expose; how-to-informational; inspirational; interview; nostalgia; personal experience; profile. Buys 8-10 mss/issue. Query. Length: 1,500-2,500 words. Pays $500-1,500 on acceptance for articles from new writers. Regional Editor: Shirley Howard. Pays $250-350 for local interest and travel pieces of 2,000 words.

Photos: Herbert Bleiweiss, art director. Photos purchased on assignment mostly. Some short photo features with captions. Pays $50-350 for b&w; $50-400 for color photos. Query. Model release required.

Columns/Departments: Light Housekeeping & Fillers, edited by Mary Ann Littell. Humorous short-short prose and verse. Jokes, gags, anecdotes. Pays $25-100. The Better Way, edited by Bob Liles. Ideas and in-depth research. Query. Pays $25-50. "Only outstanding material has a chance here."

Fiction: Naome Lewis, fiction editor. Uses romance fiction and condensations of novels that can appear in one issue. Looks for reader identification. "Presently overstocked." Buys 3 mss/issue. "We get 1,500 short stories a month; a freelancer's odds are overwhelming—but we do look at all submissions. Send complete mss. Length: 1,000 words (short-shorts); 20,000 words (novels); average 4,000 words. Pays $1,000 minimum for fiction short-shorts; $1,250 for short stories.

Poetry: Arleen Quarfoot, poetry editor. Light verse and traditional. "Presently overstocked." Buys 3 poems/issue. Pays $5/line for poetry on acceptance.

HADASSAH MAGAZINE, 50 W. 58th St., New York NY 10019. Executive Editor: Alan M. Tigay. Monthly, except combined issues (June-July and August-September). Circ. 370,000. Buys 10 unsolicited mss/year. Buys US publication rights. Pays on publication. Reports in 6 weeks. SASE.

Nonfiction: Primarily concerned with Israel, Jewish communities around the world, and American civic affairs. Length: 1,500-2,000 words. Pays $200-400.

Photos: "We buy photos only to illustrate articles, with the exception of outstanding color from Israel which we use on our covers. We pay $175 and up for a suitable cover photo. Offers $50 for inside b&w/photo and $30 for each additional photo used in one article."

Fiction: Contact: Roselyn Bell. Short stories with strong plots and positive Jewish values. No personal memoirs, "schmaltzy" fiction, or women's magazine fiction. Length: 3,000 words maximum. Pays $300 minimum.

Tips: Of special interest are "strong fiction with a Jewish orientation; unusual experience with a Jewish community around the world—or specifically Israel."

HARPER'S BAZAAR, 1700 Broadway, New York NY 10019. Editor-in-Chief: Anthony Mazzola. For "women, late 20s and above, middle income and above, sophisticated and aware, with at least 2 years of college. Most combine families, professions, travel, often more than one home. They are active and concerned with what's happening in the arts, their communities, the world." Monthly. Circ. 684,000. All rights purchased. Query first. SASE.

Nonfiction: "We publish whatever is important to an intelligent, modern woman. Fashion questions plus beauty and health—how the changing world affects her family and herself; how she can affect it; how others are trying to do so; changing life patterns and so forth. Query us first."

‡IT'S ME, Your Large Lifestyle Magazine, Happy Hands Publishing Co., 4949 Byers, Ft. Worth TX 76107. (817)732-7494. Editor: Marilyn Thelen. Bimonthly magazine covering fashion and lifestyles for women size 16 and over. "Designed to speak to women who are larger sized, giving them information on lifestyle subjects and fashion to build their sense of self-esteem and encourage them to life a life that is both satisfying and creative. Editorially, we support the thesis that people are the size that they are by choice and that everyone should consider all the choices that life presents . . . we do not take a position that size is at issue . . . but we do stress ways to feel good about oneself by eating well, having a healthy body and dressing in a fashionable way." Circ. 200,000. Pays on acceptance. Byline given. Buys all rights. Submit seasonal/holiday material 3 months in advance. Simultaneous queries and photocopied submissions OK. SASE. Reports in 3 weeks on queries; 1 month on mss. Writer's guidelines for SASE with 1 first class stamp.

Nonfiction: Humor, inspirational, interview/profile, opinion, personal experience, travel. Uses food features (how to eat better, not thinner) self discovery features emphasizing self-worth and commitment to a better life; beauty articles (focusing on hands, feet and face). "All must be slanted to our readers." Buys 75 mss/year. Query with or without published clips. Length: 1,000 words. Pays $50-300.

Photos: State availability of photos. Reviews b&w and color contact sheets; 35mm transparencies and 3x5 b&w and color prints. Captions, model release and identification of subjects required.

Columns/Departments: Home and Garden; Crafts; Entertaining at Home; New Products; Book Reviews; Sewing; Careers/Jobs. "All must be slanted to our readers." Buys 6-8 mss/year. Query with published clips.

Length: 750-1,000 words. Pays $100-200.
Poetry: Avant-garde, free verse, haiku, light verse, traditional. Must apply to appropriate audience. Buys 20 poems/year. Submit maximum 3 poems. Length: open. Pays $10-20.
Fillers: Jokes, gags, anecdotes, short humor. Buys 100/year. Length: open. Pays $10-20.
Tips: "To write for *It's Me*, it is necessary to be comfortable with people and issues dealing with larger sizes and positive attitudes."

LADIES' HOME JOURNAL, Charter Corp., 3 Park Ave., New York NY 10016. Editor: Myrna Blyth. Senior Editor: Jan Goodwin. Monthly magazine; 200 pages. Pays on publication. Simultaneous and photocopied submissions OK. "We only accept manuscripts that are submitted to us through literary agents." Submit seasonal/holiday material 6 months in advance. Reports in 6 weeks. Free writer's guidelines.
Nonfiction: Sondra Forsyth Enos, articles editor. Expose, general interest and profile. No personal essays and memories or travel pieces. Buys 3 mss/issue. SASE. Query. Length: 2,000 words minimum. Pays $500 minimum.
Fiction: Constance Leisure, book and fiction editor. Does not consider short stories sent through the mail. "We do not have facilities that permit proper handling. Please do not send in manuscripts as we will be unable to return them."
Poetry: Janny Lehman, poetry editor. Light verse and traditional. Buys 30-50/year. Submit in batches of 6. Length: 8-15 lines. Pays $5/line.
Tips: "Send submissions directly to the department editors named above."

LADYCOM, Downey Communications, Inc., 1732 Wisconsin Ave., NW, Washington DC 20007. Editor: Sheila Gibbons. For wives of military men who live in the US or overseas. Published 10 times a year. Magazine. Circ. 475,000. Pays on publication. Buys first North American serial rights. Submit seasonal/holiday material 6 months in advance. Computer printout submissions OK; prefers leter quality to dot matrix printouts. SASE. Reports in 3 weeks. Sample copy $1. Free writer's guidelines.
Nonfiction: "All articles must have special interest for military wives. General interest articles are OK if they reflect situations our readers can relate to." How-to (crafts, food), humor, interview, personal experience, personal opinion, profile and travel. Buys 50 unsolicited mss/year. "Query letter should name sources, describe focus of article, use a few sample quotes from sources, indicate length, and should describe writer's own qualifications for doing the piece." Length: 800-2,000 words. Pays $475-600/article.
Photos: Purchased with accompanying ms and on assignment. Uses 5x7 or 8x10 b&w glossy prints; 35mm or larger color transparencies; stock photo fee payment for photo with accompanying ms. Captions and model releases are required. Query Claudia Burwell, art director.
Columns/Departments: "It Seems to Me"—personal experience pieces by military wives. "Your Travels"—highlights of life at various bases and posts. Also, "Your Pet," and "Babycom." Query. Length: 1,100-1,800 words. Rates vary.
Fiction: Mystery, romance and suspense. "Military family life or relationship themes only, please!" Buys 6-8 mss/year. Query. Length: 1,500-2,500 words. Pays $150-250.
Tips: "Our ideal contributor is a military wife who can write. However, I'm always impressed by a writer who has analyzed the market and can suggest some possible new angles for us. Sensitivity to military issues is a must for our contributors, as is the ability to write good personality profiles and/or do thorough research about military family life. We really can't stand to read gothic fiction; hints from Heloise-type material (no one does it better than she does, anyway); Erma Bombeck imitations; Vietnam War-era fiction; and parenting advice that is too personal and limited to the writer's own experience."

LADY'S CIRCLE MAGAZINE, Lopez Publications, Inc., 23 W. 26th St., New York NY 10010. Editor: Mary Terzella. For homemakers. Monthly. Buys all rights. Byline given. Pays on publication. Submit seasonal/holiday material 6 months in advance. Reports in 3 months. Query with brief outline. SASE. Free writer's guidelines for SASE.
Nonfiction: "Particularly likes first-person or as-told-to inspirational stories about people coping with or overcoming illnesses/handicaps; pieces about individuals or non-profit organizations doing good works or helping others. Also how homemakers and mothers make money at home; ways to save time and/or money. Articles on child rearing, home management, dieting, gardening, and problems of the homemaker. Each issue features how-to crafts, needlework and hobbies. Articles must be written on specific subjects and must be thoroughly researched and based on sound authority. "We don't feature travel, investments, pet care, car care or decorating pieces." Length: 2,500 words maximum. Pays $125 minimum on publication for all rights to nonfiction and fiction.
Photos: Pays $10 each for quality b&w and color photos accompanying articles.
Fiction: Emotional stories of 2,000-2,500 words. "We're looking for stories that touch the heartstrings of the readers whether the emotion be happiness, sadness, grief or triumph. These are stories that homemakers can relate to."

McCALL'S, 230 Park Ave., New York NY 10017. Editor: Robert Stein. "Study recent issues." Our publication "carefully and conscientiously services the needs of the woman reader—concentrating on matters that directly affect her life and offering information and understanding on subjects of personal importance to her." Monthly. Circ. 6,200,000. Pays on acceptance. Pays 20% kill fee. Byline given. Reports in 6 weeks. "No computer printout or disk submissions. SASE.

Nonfiction: Maureen Williams, senior editor. No subject of wide public or personal interest is out of bounds for *McCall's* so long as it is appropriately treated. The editors are seeking meaningful stories of personal experience. They are on the lookout for new research that will provide the basis for penetrating articles on the ethical, physical, material and social problems concerning readers. They are most receptive to humor. *McCall's* buys 200-300 articles/year, many in the 1,000- to 1,500-word length. Pays variable rates for nonfiction. Mrs. Helen Del Monte and Andrea Thompson are editors of nonfiction books, from which *McCall's* frequently publishes excerpts. These are on subjects of interest to women: biography, memoirs, reportage, etc. Almost all features on food, household equipment and management, fashion, beauty, building and decorating are staff-written. Query. "All manuscripts must be submitted on speculation and *McCall's* accepts no responsibility for unsolicited manuscripts."

Columns/Departments: The magazine is not in the market for new columns.

Fiction: Department Editor: Helen DelMonte. "Again the editors would remind writers of the contemporary woman's taste and intelligence. Most of all, fiction can awaken a reader's sense of identity, deepen her understanding of herself and others, refresh her with a laugh at herself, etc. *McCall's* looks for stories which will have meaning for an adult reader of some literary sensitivity. *McCall's* principal interest is in short stories; but fiction of all lengths is considered." Length: about 4,000 words. Length for short-shorts: about 2,000 words. Payment begins at $1,250.

MADEMOISELLE, 350 Madison Ave., New York NY 10017. Contact: Articles Editor. 90% freelance written. Directed to college-educated, working women 18-34. Circ. 1,000,000. Reports in 3-4 weeks. Buys first North American serial rights and all Australian rights. Pays on acceptance. Prefers written query plus samples of published work. SASE.

Nonfiction: Katherine Ames Brown, articles editor. Particular concentration on articles of interest to the intelligent young woman, including personal relationships, health, careers, travel, and current social problems. Articles should be well-researched and of good quality. Length: 1,500-3,000 words. Pays $700 minimum on acceptance.

Art: Paula Greif, art director. Commissioned work assigned according to needs. Photos of fashion, beauty, travel. Payment ranges from no-charge to an agreed rate of payment per shot, job series, or page rate. Buys all rights. Pays on publication for photos.

Fiction: Eileen Schnurr, fiction editor. High-quality fiction by both name writers and unknowns. Length: 1,500-3,000 words. Pays $700 minimum on acceptance. Uses short-shorts on occasion. "We are particularly interested in encouraging new talent, and with this aim in mind, we conduct a college fiction contest each year, open to unpublished young writers, male as well as female. A $750 award plus publication in *Mademoiselle* are awarded for the first prize-winning story; $300, for the second prize story. We are not interested in formula stories, and subject matter need not be confined to a specific age or theme."

MODERN BRIDE, 1 Park Ave., New York NY 10016. Editor: Cele G. Lalli. Managing Editor: Mary Ann Cavlin. Bimonthly. Buys first periodical publishing rights. Byline given. Pays on acceptance. Reports in 2 weeks. SASE.

Nonfiction: Uses articles of interest to brides-to-be. "We prefer articles on etiquette, marriage, and planning a home. Travel is staff-written or specially assigned. We edit everything, but don't rewrite without permission." Length: about 2,000 words. Payment is about $200 minimum.

Poetry: Occasionally buys poetry pertaining to love and marriage. Pays $15-25 for average short poem.

MS. MAGAZINE, 119 W. 40th St., New York NY 10018. (212)719-9800. Editor-in-Chief and Publisher: Patricia Carbine. Editor: Gloria Steinem. For "women and men; varying ages, backgrounds, but committed to exploring new lifestyles and changes in their roles and society." Monthly. Circ. 450,000. Rights purchased vary with author and material. Pays on acceptance. Will consider photocopied submissions. Submit seasonal material at least 3 months in advance. Reports in 5-6 weeks. SASE.

Photos: Purchased with mss, without mss, or on assignment. Payment "depends on usage." Address to Art Department.

Tips: "The Gazette section which features short news items is the easiest way to get published here, and is especially receptive to regional material from New York; but much has to be rejected because of space limitations and lack of professional standards. We use a lot of material from all over the country on politics, the women's movement, human interest features. It is possible to move from the Gazette to do other work for *Ms*."

‡**MY WEEKLY, The Magazine for Women Everywhere**, D.C. Thomson & Co., Ltd., 80 Kingsway E., Dundee, DD4 8SL, Scotland. Editor: Stewart D. Brown. Weekly entertainment magazine for women. "Enter-

tainment means we do not lecture or try to educate our readers." Circ. 756,512. Pays on acceptance. Byline given. Buys first British serial rights. Submit seasonal/holiday material 3 months in advance. Previously published submissions OK. SASE. Reports in 1 month. Free sample copy.

Nonfiction: General interest; humor (feminine, domestic); interview/profile; personal experience; photo feature. No political articles, explicit sex or anything that "attempts to lecture" the reader. Buys over 300 mss/year. Send complete ms. Length: 800-3,000 words. Pays variable rates.

Photos: Send photos with ms. Reviews 2¼x2¼ transparencies. Captions, model release and identification of subjects required. Buys one-time rights.

Fiction: Humorous; romance; serialized novels; suspense (with feminine interest); stories deling with *real* emotional, domestic problems. No material dealing explicitly with sex, violence, politics. Buys 150 mss/year. Send complete ms. Length: 1,500-6,000 words. Pays variable rates.

Fillers: Short humor (feminine). Length: 800-1,200 words. Pays variable rates.

Tips: "We invite our readers to meet and share the lives and experiences of interesting people—through both first-person articles and the interviews our writers supply. Much of this applies to our fiction, too. If our readers read *My Weekly* to 'escape,' it's to escape not into a glossy, unreal world of actresses, millionaires, politicians, but into the 'real' world of other people dealing with the problems of 'ordinary' life with dignity, warmth and humour."

‡**NEW CLEVELAND WOMAN JOURNAL**, 103 E. Bridge St., Cleveland OH 44017. (216)243-3740. Editor: Lynne Lapin. Monthly tabloid for women who work outside of the home—either for pay or as volunteers. Geared toward the managerial-level, upwardly-mobile woman. Estab. 1982. Circ. 30,000. Pays on publication. Byline given. Offers ⅓ kill fee. Buys negotiable rights. Submit seasonal/holiday material 3 months in advance. Prveiously published submissions OK "if it didn't appear in the Cleveland area or another women's magazine." SASE. Reports in 5 weeks. Writer's guidelines for business size SAE and 1 first class stamp.

Nonfiction: General interest (only as relates to working women specifically); how-to (succeed in business, manage career and family); humor (relating to working women); interview/profile (of successful women); personal experience (OK in some cases); travel (as relates to working women). No "general interest that you'd find in any newspaper. Articles must be geared toward our specific market and must offer the reader information she will benefit from." Buys 60 mss/year. Query with published clips or send complete ms. Length: 1,500 words maximum. Pays 40¢/column inch.

Photos: State availability of photos or send photos with ms. Pays $5 minimum for 8x10 b&w and color prints. Buys negotiable rights.

Columns/Departments: Buys 36 mss/year. Query with published clips or send complete ms. Length: 750-1,000 words. Pays 40¢/column inch.

Fillers: Anecdotes, short humor, newsbreaks. Buys 60/year. Length: open. Pays 40¢/column inch.

‡**NEW WOMAN**, New Woman, Inc., Drawer 189, Palm Beach FL 33480. (305)833-4583. Editor/Publisher: Margaret Harold Whitehead. Associate Editor/Publisher: Wendy Danforth. Query first *in writing*. "It is essential to familiarize yourslf with *New Woman*'s editorial format." SASE. Pays variable rates.

PIONEER WOMAN, Magazine of Pioneer Women/Na'amat, the Women's Labor Zionist Organization of America, Pioneer Women/Na'amat, 200 Madison Ave., New York NY 10016. (212)725-8010. Editor: Judith A. Sokoloff. Magazine published 5 times/year covering Jewish themes and issues; Israel; women's issues; Labor Zionism, occasional pieces dealing with social, political, economic issues usually related to Judaism. Circ. 30,000. Pays on publication. Byline given. Not copyrighted. Buys first North American serial, one-time, first and second serial (reprint) rights and makes work-for-hire assignments. SASE. Reports in 4 weeks on queries, 2 months on mss. Free sample copy and writer's guidelines.

Nonfiction: Book excerpts; expose; general interest (Jewish); historical/nostalgic; humor, inspirational, interview/profile; opinion; personal experience; photo feature; travel (Israel); art; music. "Articles must be of interest to Jewish community." Buys 35 mss/year. Query with clips of published work or send complete ms. Length: 1,000-3,000 words. Pays 5¢/word.

Photos: State availability of photos. Pays $10-30 for b&w contact sheet and 4x5 or 5x7 prints. Captions and identification of subjects required. Buys one-time rights.

Columns/Departments: Film and book reviews with Jewish themes. Buys 20-25 mss/year. Query with clips of published work or send complete ms. Length: 800-1,500 words. Pays 5¢/word.

Fiction: Adventure, ethnic, historical, humorous, mainstream, novel excerpts. "Good intelligent fiction with Jewish slant." Buys 3 mss/year. Send complete ms. Length 1,200-3,000 words. Pays 5¢/word.

Poetry: Avant-garde, free verse, traditional. Buys 5/year. Submit maximum 5 poems. Pays $10-25.

PLAYGIRL, 3420 Ocean Park Blvd., Santa Monica CA 90405. (213)450-0900. Editor: Dianne Grosskopf. Senior Editor: Pat McGilligan. Monthly entertainment magazine for 20-29 year old females. Circ. 850,000. Average issue includes 4 articles and 1 interview. Pays 1 month after acceptance. Byline given. Offers 15% kill fee. Buys all rights. Submit seasonal material 4 months in advance. Simultaneous and photocopied submissions OK, if so indicated. SASE. Reports in 1 month on queries; in 2 months on mss. Free writer's guidelines with SASE.

Nonfiction: Judy Brown, articles editor. Travel pieces; "humor for the modern woman"; exposes (related to women's issues); interview (Q&A format with major show business celebrities); articles on sexuality, hard information on credit and finances, medical breakthroughs, relationships, coping, and careers. Buys 4 mss/issue. Query with clips of previously published work. Length: 2,500 words. Pays $500-850.

Fiction: Mary Ellen Strote, fiction editor. Contemporary romance stories of 2,500 words. Send complete fiction ms. "The important thing to remember is we don't want graphic sex, and no adventure, suspense, science fiction, murder or mystery stories. We want something emotional." Pays $300 and up for fiction.

Tips: "We are not a beginner's nonfiction market. We're looking for major clips and don't really consider nonpublished writers."

REDBOOK MAGAZINE, 230 Park Ave., New York NY 10169. (212)850-9300. Editor-in-Chief: Annette Capone. Managing Editor: Jennifer Johnson. Monthly magazine; 200 pages. Circ. 4,300,000. Rights purchased vary with author and material. Reports in 4 weeks. Pays on acceptance. SASE. Free writer's guidelines on writing fiction for *Redbook* for SASE.

Nonfiction: Susan Edmiston, articles editor. Articles relevant to the magazine's readers, who are young women in the 18-34-year-old group. Also interested in submissions for Young Mother's Story. "We are interested in stories for the Young Mother series offering practical and useful information you would like to share with others on how you, as a mother and a wife, are dealing with the changing problems of marriage and family life—such as the management of outside employment, housework, time, money, the home and children. Stories also may deal with how you, as a concerned citizen or consumer, handled a problem in your community. For each 1,000-2,000 words accepted for publication, we pay $750. Mss accompanied by a large, stamped, self-addressed envelope, must be signed, and mailed to: Young Mother's Story, c/o *Redbook Magazine*. Length: articles, 3,000-3,500 words; short articles, 2,000-2,500 words. Young Mother's reports in 10-12 weeks."

Fiction: Mimi Jones, fiction editor. "Out of the 35,000 unsolicited manuscripts that we receive annually, we buy about a third of the stories (about 50/year) that appear in *Redbook* over the course of a year. We find many more stories that, for one reason or another, are not suited to our needs, but are good enough to warrant our encouraging the author to send others. Often such an author's subsequent submission turns out to be something we can use. *Redbook* looks for stories by and about men and women, realistic stories and fantasies, funny and sad stories, stories of people together and people alone; stories with familiar and exotic settings, love stories and work stories. But there are a few things common to all of them, that make them stand out from the crowd. The high quality of their writing, for one thing. The distinctiveness of their characters and plots. Stock characters and sitcom stories are not for us. We look for stories with a definite resolution or emotional resonance. Cool stylistic or intellectual experiments are of greater interest, we feel, to readers of literary magazines than of a magazine like *Redbook* that tries to offer insights into the hows and whys of day-to-day living. And all the stories reflect some aspect of the experience, the interests, or the dreams of *Redbook*'s particular readership." Short-short stories (7-9 pages, 1,400-1,600 words) are always in demand; but short stories of 10-15 pages, (3,000-5,000 words) are also acceptable. Stories 20 pages and over have a "hard fight, given our tight space limits, but we have bought longer stories that we loved." Manuscripts must be typewritten, double-spaced, and accompanied by SASE the size of the manuscript. Payment begins at $850 for short shorts; $1,000 for short stories.

Tips: "It is very difficult to break into the nonfiction section, although the Young Mother's story, which publishes short personal experience pieces (1,000-2,000 words), does depend on freelancers."

SAVVY, The Magazine for Executive Women, 111 8th Ave., New York NY 10011. (212)255-0990. Editor: Wendy Reid Crisp. Monthly magazine covering the business and personal aspects of life for highly educated, professional career women. Estab. 1980. Circ. 300,000. Average issue includes 9 features. Pays on publication. Byline given. Buys first North American serial rights. SASE. Reports in 1 month.

Nonfiction: General interest (articles should be slanted toward high level executive women who have a wide range of interests with an emphasis on their professional concerns. No "food, home, decorating or 'helpful hint' articles. Send in one or two well-developed ideas and some previously published work to show how you carry out your ideas." Recent article examples: "Technology's Heir Apparent" by Lee FroeLich and Ken Klee (March 1983): "The Lost Pepsi Generation" by Mitchell Shields (February 1983); and "Run for the Money" by Jayne Greenstein (February 1983). "We require articles on speculation before we make an assignment to a writer not known to us." Query with clips of previously published work; letters should be "concise and to the point, with the angle of the proposed article made very specific and should include SASE." Length: 1,500-3,500 words. Pays $400-850.

Photos: Art Director: Helen Winkler-Elek.

Columns/Departments: Tools of the Trade (ideas and strategies for doing business better, 500-1,500 words); and 1,000 Words (essays on anything of general interest to executive women based on personal experience, 750 words). Departments: Professional Connections (women's business networks), Health and Executive Etiquette.

SELF, Conde-Nast, 350 Madison Ave., New York NY 10017. (212)880-8834. Editor: Phyllis Starr Wilson. Managing Editor: Valorie Weaver. Monthly magazine emphasizing self improvement of emotional and physical well-being for women of all ages. Circ. 1,029,315. Average issue includes 12-20 feature articles and 3-4 columns. Pays on acceptance. Byline given. Offers 20% kill fee. Buys first North American serial rights. Submit seasonal material 4 months in advance. Simultaneous and photocopied submissions OK. No computer printout or disk submissions. SASE. Reports in 1 month. Free writer's guidelines.

Nonfiction: Well-researched service articles on self improvement, beauty, mind, the psychological angle of daily activities, health, careers, nutrition, male/female relationships and money. "We try to translate major developments and complex information in these areas into practical, personalized articles." Buys 6-10 mss/issue. Query with clips of previously published work. Length: 1,000-2,500 words. Pays $700-1,500. "We are always looking for any piece that has a psychological or behavioral side. We rely heavily on freelancers who can take an article on interior decorating, for example, and add a psychological aspect to it. Everything should relate to the whole person."

Photos: Editor: Rochelle Udell. State availability of photos. Reviews 5x7 b&w glossy prints.

Columns/Departments: Self issues (800-1,000 words on current topics of interest to women such as nutrition and diet scams, finding time for yourself, personal decision making and political issues); Health Watch (800-1,000 words on health topics); and Your Money (800-1,000 words on finance topics). Buys 1-2 mss/issue. Query. Pays $700-1,200.

Tips: "Original ideas backed up by research, not personal experiences and anecdotes, open our doors."

SPRING MAGAZINE, Rodale Press, Inc., 33 E. Minor St., Emmaus PA 18049. (215)967-5171. A nine-month per year publication emphasizing lifestyle, natural health, self-care and fitness aimed at "busy, high-energy, health-conscious, educated working women between 20 and 40. All of our articles have an underlying theme of high-level wellness—making the most of your potential, and getting the most out of life. For example, our travel pieces are about experiences with an educational or fitness benefit. Fashion stories don't talk about the hottest style—they show durable, attractive, functional and beautiful items. Career stories emphasize personal satisfaction and growth. Profiles have an 'inspirational' element—not religious, but self improvement. We don't offer miracles—we offer sensible, practical advice that our busy readers can really use." Not interested in fad fashions, crash diets, drug therapy or plastic surgery, alcohol, cigarettes, junk food, or recipes with sugar, additives, preservatives or salt. Query with clips of published work or send complete ms with SASE to articles editor. Computer printout submissions OK. Reports in three weeks on queries and six weeks on mss. Sample issue and writer's guidelines for SASE.

Nonfiction: Features of 1,500-2,500 words, including "health makeovers" (people who changed their lives to a healthier lifestyle); career, psychology, relationships, fitness and self-improvement. Pays approximately $150-$1,200) on acceptance for first North American serial rights, one-time and all rights.

Columns/Departments: New ideas for shorter columns on food, (Our "Fast and Natural" column offers recipes around a theme that take 20 minutes or less to prepare); travel (only travel stories about relatively short weekend-type experiences); fitness, etc. Length: 900-1,500 words. Pays $25-1,100. A new "High Level Wellness' section covers health, natural healing, self-care, weight control, and fitness in 1,000-word or less articles. Recent topics include "An Energizing Leg Massage," "Ten Things You Can Do Now to Prevent Health Problems Later," "Exercise for Weight Control," etc. Sources are authoritative medical experts. "We have very strict footnoting, research guidelines and, accuracy checks for all articles."

Fillers: 150-200 word fillers for our "Good Tips, Good Times" column (hints on work, childcare, travel, etc. to make life easier) and "Natural Healing Network" (natural healing experiences). Pays $15 each.

Tips: It's absolutely critical to study several issues of *Spring* before submitting a proposal or manuscript. It might also help to look at some of the other Rodale Press publications—like *Prevention* and *Bicycling*—to get a sense of where we're coming from—and translate that perspective into topics that interest today's young women. Currently, most of our columns are staff written, but we are eager to find reliable freelance writers with fresh ideas, who understand the *Spring* perspective. There are opportunities for a freelancer at *Spring* if you're a polished, professional writer, with a lively style; you've studied and understand the magazine; you have new ideas."

SUNDAY WOMAN, The King Features Syndicate, 235 E. 45th, New York NY 10017. A weekly newspaper supplement which runs in more than 50 markets in the United States with circulation of more than 3 million. Editor: Merry Clark. Sample issue and writer's guidelines for SASE.

Nonfiction: Solid, reportorial articles on topics affecting women, their families, lifestyles, relationships, careers, health, money, business. "We often run a fascinating success story about women in business or about women entrepreneurs." Also uses celebrity cover stories. No food, fashion or pet stories. 1,500-2,000 words. National focus. No poetry, fiction, essays or first-person stories. Pays $50-500 upon acceptance. Buys first North American rights. Reports in 4 weeks. "Submit previously published pieces for second serial publication by us." Include cover letter with address, phone number, and Social Security number; not responsible for mss submitted without SASE. Manuscripts should be typed and double-spaced. Computer printout submissions OK if legible; prefers letter quality to dot matrix printouts. "Query, short and to the point, with clips of published material." No phone calls.

Tips: "Women and women's roles are changing dramatically. *Sunday Woman* is reflecting this. I don't want the same old service piece or 'First Woman' stories. We're moving on from that. Writers must come up with story ideas that also reflect these changes."

VOGUE, 350 Madison Ave., New York NY 10017. (212)880-8800. Editor: Grace Mirabella. Monthly magazine for highly intelligent women. Pays variable rates on acceptance "depending on the material, our needs, and the specialization of the writer." Buys variable rights. Reports in at least 2 weeks. Byline given. SASE.
Nonfiction: Contact: Feature Editor. Uses articles and ideas for features. Fashion articles are staff-written. Material must be of high literary quality, contain good information. Query a must. Length: 500-2,500 words. "Our readers are interested not only in their appearance, but in what goes on inside them both intellectually and physically. They are contemporary American women who have deep and varied interests." Short reviews of theater, art, books, movies, TV, music, restaurants. Elaborate articles and essays. Ideal article length is 1,000-1,500 words. "Read *Vogue*, and you'll see the enormous range of subjects we cover."

‡**WOMAN MAGAZINE**, Harris Publishing, 1115 Broadway, New York NY 10010. (212)686-4121. Editor: Sherry Amatenstein. Magazine published 6 times/year covering "every aspect of a woman's life. Offers self-help orientation, guidelines on lifestyles, careers, relationships, finances, health, etc." Circ. 320,000. Pays on acceptance. Byline given. Buys all rights or first rights "if requested." Photocopied and previously published submissions OK. SASE. Reports in 2 weeks on queries; 3 weeks on mss. Sample copy $1.75; writer's guidelines for letter-size SAE and 1 first class stamp.
Nonfiction: Book excerpts (most of magazine is book reprints); how-to; humor; inspirational (how I solved a specific problem); interview/profile (short, 200-1,000 words with successful or gutsy women); personal experience (primary freelance need: how a woman took action and helped herself—emotional punch, but not "trapped housewife" material). No articles on "10 ways to pep up your marriage"—looking for unique angle. Buys 100 mss/year. Query with published clips or send complete ms. Length: 200-1,500 words. Pays $25-125.
Columns/Departments: Bravo Woman (1,000 word interviews with women who overcame numerous obstacles to start their own business); Woman in News (200 word pieces on successful women); Woman Forum (controversial issues regarding women). Query with published clips or send complete ms. Length: 200-1,000 words. Pays $20-100.
Tips: "We're for all women—ones in and out of the home. We don't condescend, neither should you. Personal experience pieces are your best bet."

WOMAN'S DAY, 1515 Broadway, New York NY 10036. Contact: Editor. 15 issues/year. Circ. over 7,000,000. Buys first and second North American serial rights. Pays negotiable kill fee. Byline given. Pays on acceptance. Reports in 2-4 weeks on queries; longer on mss. Submit detailed queries first to Rebecca Greer, articles editor. SASE.
Nonfiction: Uses articles on all subjects of interest to women—marriage, family life, child rearing, education, homemaking, money management, careers, family health, work and leisure activities. Also interested in fresh, dramatic narratives of women's lives and concerns. "These must be lively and fascinating to read." Length: 500-3,500 words, depending on material. Payment varies depending on length, and whether it's for regional or national use, etc. *Woman's Day* is planning a new feature, a full-page essay running 1,000 words. "It will be something like *Newsweek*'s 'My Turn' page, but more varied than that. We're looking for both tough, strong pieces and softer essays on matters of great and real concern to women. "We're looking for strong points of view. The topics can be controversial, but they have to be convincing. We'll look for significant issues, such as medical ethics and honesty in marriage, rather than the slight and the trivial—these will be issues that women find relevant in their lives."
Fiction: Contact department editor, Eileen Jordan. Uses high-quality, genuine human interest, romance and humor, in lengths between 1,500 and 3,000 words. Payment varies. "We pay any writer's established rate, however."
Fillers: Neighbors and Tips to Share columns also pay $50/each letter of brief practical suggestions on homemaking or child rearing. Address to the editor of the appropriate section.
Tips: "We are publishing more articles and devoting more pages to textual material. We're departing from the service format once in awhile to print 'some good reads.' We're more interested in investigative journalism."

WOMAN'S WORLD, The Woman's Weekly, Heinrich Bauer North American, Inc., 177 N. Dean St., Box 671, Englewood NJ 07631. (201)569-0006. Editor-in-Chief: Dennis Neeld. Weekly magazine covering "controversial, dramatic, and human interest women's issues" for women across the nation aged 18-60, low- to middle-income. Estab. 1981. Circ. 600,000. Pays on acceptance. Byline given. Offers negotiable kill fee. Buys first North American serial rights. Submit seasonal/holiday material 4 months in advance. Simultaneous queries, and simultaneous, photocopied and previously published submissions OK. No computer printout or disk submissions. SASE. Reports in 6 weeks on queries; 1-2 months on mss. Sample copy $1 and self-addressed mailing label; writer's guidelines for business size SAE and 1 first class stamp.

Nonfiction: Well-researched material with "a hard-news edge and topics of national scope." Reports of 1,000-2,000 words on vital trends and major issues such as women and alcohol or teen suicide; dramatic, personal women's stories; articles on self-improvement, medicine and health topics, and the economics of home, career and daily life. Features include In Real Life (true stories); Turning Point (in a woman's life); Families (how unusual families deal with problems); and the American Woman column, which profiles an uncelebrated woman who leads an exciting, unusual life. Other regular features are Opening Up (800-1,000 word discussion of an issue, pro and con, with the reader left to do her own thinking on this subject); Report (1,500-word investigative news features with national scope, statistics, etc.); Women and Crime (true stories of 1,000-1,200 on female criminals "if possible, presented with sympathetic" attitude); and Feeling Good (600-word essays on self-improvement). Queries should be addressed to Jane Bladow, articles editor.

Fiction: Elinor Nauen, fiction editor. Short story, romance and mainstream of 6,000 words and mini-mysteries of 1,200-2,000 words. "Each of our stories has a light romantic theme with a protagonist no older than forty. Each can be written from either a masculine or feminine point of view. Women characters may be single, married or divorced. Plots must be fast moving with vivid dialogue and action. The problems and dilemmas, inherent in them should be contemporary and realistic, handled with warmth and feeling. The stories must have a positive resolution." Not interested in science fiction, fantasy or historical romance. No explicit sex, graphic language or seamy settings. Humor meets with enthusiasm. Pays $1,200 on acceptance for North American serial rights for 6 months. "The mini-mysteries, at a length of 2,000 words, may feature either a 'whodunnit' or 'howdunnit' theme. The mystery may revolve around anything from a theft to a murder. However, we are not interested in sordid or grotesque crimes. Emphasis should be on intricacies of plot rather than gratuitous violence. The story must include a resolution that clearly states the villain is getting his or her comeuppance." Pays $500 on acceptance. Pays approximately 50¢ a published word on acceptance. Buys first North American serial rights. Queries with clips of published work are preferred; accepts complete mss.

Photos: State availability of photos. "State photo leads. Photos are assigned to freelance photographers." Buys one-time rights.

Tips: "Come up with good queries. Short queries are best. We have a strong emphasis on well-researched material. Writers must send research with ms including book references and phone numbers for double checking."

WOMEN IN BUSINESS, Box 8728, Kansas City MO 64114. (816)361-6621. Editor: Sharon K. Tiley. Bimonthly magazine for working women in all fields and at all levels; age 26-55; primarily members of the American Women's Association; national coverage. Circ. 110,000. Pays on acceptance. Buys all rights. Phone queries OK. Computer printout submissions "often terribly hard to read." Prefers letter quality to dot matrix printouts. SASE. Reports in 2 months. Free sample copy and writer's guidelines for 9x12 SASE with 88¢ postage.

Nonfiction: General interest, self-improvement, business trends, personal finance. Articles should be slanted toward the average working woman. No articles on women who have made it to the top or "slice of life opinions/editorials. We also avoid articles based on first-hand experiences (the 'I' stories)." Buys 25 mss/year. Query or submit complete ms. Length: 1,000-1,500 words. Pays $100-200.

Photos: State availability of photos with query or submit with accompanying ms. Pays $50-100 for 8x10 b&w glossy contact sheet; $150-250 for cover color transparency. Captions preferred. Buys all rights. Model release required.

WOMEN'S CIRCLE, Box 428, Seabrook NH 03874. Editor: Marjorie Pearl. Monthly magazine for women of all ages. Buys all rights. Byline given. Pays on acceptance. Submit seasonal material 7 months in advance. Reports in 3 months. SASE. Sample copy $1. Writer's guidelines for SASE.

Nonfiction: How-to articles of 1,000-2,000 words on handicrafts, all kinds of needlework and dolls. Also articles with b&w photos about female entrepreneurs and hobbyists. Informational approach. Needs Christmas crafts for Christmas annual. Buys 200 mss/year. Query or submit complete ms. Length: open. Pays minimum of 3¢/word, extra for photos.

Tips: "We welcome crafts and how-to directions for any media—crochet, felt, etc."

WOMEN'S WEAR DAILY, 7 E. 12th St., New York NY 10003. Completely staff-written newspaper.

WOMEN'S WORLD, B'nai B'rith Women, Inc., 1640 Rhode Island Ave., NW, Washington DC 20036. (202)857-6640. Editor: Susan Tomchin. Tabloid published 6 times/year for Jewish women concerned about Israel, Judaism, community affairs, women's issues, public affairs, the elderly, youth. Circ. 125,000. Pays on acceptance. Byline given. Offers 15% kill fee. Buys first rights. Submit seasonal/holiday material 4 months in advance. SASE. Reports in 1 month on queries; 2 months on mss. Sample copy for 9x12 SAE and 3 first class stamps.

Nonfiction: Book excerpts (on women and Judaism); general interest (on women and Judaism, social issues); Jewish historical/nostalgic; interview/profile (of interesting women or Jews); photo feature (on Judaism). Buys 4 mss/year. Query with clips of published work or send complete ms. Length: 500-1,500 words. Pays $25-100.

Close-up

Barbara Lazear Ascher, Writer

Barbara Ascher always knew she wanted to be a writer. "I wrote all through my childhood. Family and teachers encouraged and supported me when my abilities in literature and writing became apparent. I had three wonderful tutors and mentors at Bennington College. It was really a very special education, and like many things in life—it was luck."

The education may have been luck, but Ascher's skill and success as a writer are due in large part to her love of the craft. Since she began writing fulltime again two years ago, Ascher describes herself as "the most supremely happy human being on earth. I love everything about writing—the research, the reading, the interviewing." (Her return to freelancing comes after a seven-year stretch of "writing in some esoteric places, but mostly being one hundred percent involved with the grand experience of having a child"; then going to law school and spending two years with a Wall-Street-type law firm.)

"I quit to go back to writing," she says. "And writing is a way to resolve in my mind certain things I care about; at the same time, it's a way of being intimate with people. It's a strange sort of intimacy because I don't know the people out there who are reading what I write, yet I'm sharing my absolutely deepest concerns with them."

To ensure that her writing rings true, Ascher uses a test. "After every sentence or paragraph (I'm not sure of the interval), I stop and ask myself, 'Is this the absolute truth? Am I being completely honest? Is this as much of the truth as I know?' It's a good exercise because I think writing is a little bit like a child's face. If you aren't telling the truth, it shows."

Ascher admits honest writing does not come without tired seat, sore shoulders and a great deal of diligence. "And you have to write *every* day—the way a singer has to sing scales everyday. You have to keep in touch with your art, your voice, your muse. Writing regularly also keeps you from becoming frightened. I think if you stop, there's always the fear of 'have I lost it?' There are days when you agonize. It can be lonely and depressing when you aren't getting anywhere, because the reality is that writing for yourself is *not* the idea of being a writer. If you are a diarist, maybe. But the honest truth is that writing for yourself is like talking to yourself. It's just not the same."

Ascher works in an office with no telephone, "and no one knows I'm there except my husband who is my biggest fan and support." She doesn't use a computer and says she feels comfortable with her yellow legal pads and a few rounds at the typewriter. "The retyping is very important," she says, "because it's up until the very last retype that I'm catching something that could be better—it's like a jeweler polishing a stone.

Having written articles and poetry, Ascher is writing essays today. She calls this form "a wonderful combination of poetry and prose." And with it she made her debut in the *New York Times* writing the Hers column for eight weeks. "I had terrific editors there. They were ideal in that they weren't so caught up in their own voices that they couldn't hear mine. And I got letters from all sorts of people—crossing gender, economic and educational boundaries. To know you have touched people with your writing . . . that's about as fulfilling an experience as a writer can have."

Photos: State availability of photos. Pays $10-25 for 5x7 b&w prints. Identification of subjects required. Buys one-time rights.

WORKING MOTHER MAGAZINE, McCall's Publishing Co., 230 Park Ave., New York NY 10169. (212)551-9412. Editor: Vivian Cadden. Managing Editor: Mary McLaughlin. For the working mothers in this country whose problems and concerns are determined by the fact that they have children under 18 living at home. Monthly magazine; 140 pages. Circ. 500,000. Pays on acceptance. Buys all rights. Pays 20% kill fee. Byline given. Submit seasonal/holiday material 6 months in advance. SASE. Sample copy $2.

Nonfiction: Service humor (material pertinent to the working mother's predicament). "Don't just go out and find some mother who holds a job, and describe how she runs her home, manages her children and feels fulfilled. Find a working mother whose story is inherently dramatic." Buys 9-10 mss/issue. Query. Length: 750-2,000 words. Pays $300-500.

Fiction: "Stories that are relevant to working mothers' lives." We are interested in fiction if the right piece comes along, but we're still more interested in nonfiction pieces."

WORKING WOMAN, Hal Publications, Inc., 342 Madison Ave., New York NY 10017. Editor-in-Chief: Kate Rand Lloyd. Editor: Gay Bryant. Articles Editor: Julia Kagan. Monthly magazine. "We offer sophisticated, practical advice to the career-oriented working woman. Readers are not career beginners." Circ. 550,000. Pays on acceptance. Buys all rights. Pays 20% kill fee. Byline given. Submit seasonal/holiday material 6 months in advance. Computer printout submissions OK; prefers letter quality submissions only. "Tear printouts into pages and do not submit one enormous folded sheet." SASE. Reports in 6 weeks. Sample copy $2; free writer's guidelines.

Nonfiction: How-to (career strategies, managing personal life/work life, etc.); finance; business and business management; social trends—(two-career couple, generation gap in the office, etc.); health (physical and psychological); humor and essays (related to work and work situations); interview (with women in various career areas, experts in various fields); and profile. "We want subjects that have special application to career-oriented working women or are of particular interest to them." No articles on getting started, working at home, or managing a career and children/husband. "No more women truck drivers. No stale advice on getting ahead." Also no fiction, poetry, entry-level job advice, confessional articles, articles on topics not applicable to executive and professional women, or critical writing on the arts. Buys 6 mss/issue. Query with clips of published work or send complete ms. "Explain why the subject is important to our readers and why now; also, indicate how you would handle the idea and why you would be especially good to write it (i.e., what is your background?)." Length: 1,500-2,500 words. Pays $300-500.

Photos: State availability of photos with ms.

Columns/Departments: Consumer, Health, Money, On the Job, In Business, Careers, My Side, Education, Issues, Comment, MBA, Memoranda. "All columns/departments are geared to specific problems/pluses of working women." Buys 10/issue. Query with clips of published work. Length: 500-1,500 words. Pays $50-300.

Tips: "Increased coverage of 'after five' leisure topics and increased coverage of business management and especially of small business will affect writers in the year ahead. Send query letter as described above with clips of previously published work. Describe background—even if the submission is a manuscript rather than a query. What we need to know is why this article and why you? If profile, should include specific business information about the woman's work. We include much more financial how-to in our profiles of working women, not just 'nice' interview quotes. Pictures (if interview/profile) of subject helpful. We are interested only in polished, professional-level writing. Financial advice must be sophisticated—our readers know what a CD is. We have a 4-month lead time."

Trade, Technical, and Professional Journals

Notice the heading *journal* on this page. The word signals a difference between the publications listed here and those in the consumer periodicals section. *Journal* has a serious, business or technical connotation that is not necessarily associated with general-public, newsstand offerings. Trade journals sometimes have controlled circulations and their reader profiles are far easier to paint than those of *Reader's Digest* or *Redbook*.

Trade journals listed here are tied into people's occupations and educations. They may "talk shop" to retailers; provide industry and equipment reports to manufacturers; offer forums for discussion of trends and philosophies among industry experts.

Specialty writers have a haven of markets among the trade publications because it's here that technical writers come into their own. They have mastered a subject; their authority comes from an understanding of the profession or trade. Many of them are technicians, engineers, supervisors or executives who have something to say to others in their industry. Some trade journal editors are even more interested in what their writers say than how they say it.

Generalists are certainly not left out of this market, however. If a generalist writer can research a subject or a trade to the point where he can write clearly and accurately for readers who are already practitioners in the industry, he will likely find a niche in the trade journal market. Generalists can sometimes bring the freshness of a newcomer's outlook to a piece that an industry expert would handle in matter-of-fact fashion.

Most trade journal editors prefer queries to complete manuscripts. Credentials and evidence of your expertise in the field are usually a must. Your education and participation in industry activities may be your initial foot in the door. Then it's your duty to keep alert to news and trends information within the industry you write for. If you are not directly part of the trade, cultivate contacts within the industry who can be primary sources for your writing. People in the field are excellent article idea generators.

Read carefully the market listings in the 72 subject categories which follow. Note special issues or year-end reviews that the publications may have. Write for their editorial guidelines and sample copies. Tailor your queries accordingly. Consult the consumer publications introduction for some basic magazine writing tips. As a trade journal writer you speak to professionals; your writing can be nothing less.

Accounting

CA MAGAZINE, 150 Bloor St., W., Toronto, Ontario, Canada M5S 2Y2. Editor: Nelson Luscombe. Monthly magazine for accountants and financial managers. Circ. 55,000. Pays on publication for the article's copyright. No computer printout or disk submissions.
Nonfiction: Accounting, business, management and taxation. "We accept whatever is relevant to our readership, no matter the origin as long as it meets our standards. No inflation accounting articles or non-business, non-accounting articles." Length: 3,000-5,000 words. Pays $100 for feature articles, $75 for departments and 10¢/word for acceptable news items.

CASHFLOW, Coordinated Capital Resources, Inc., 1807 Glenview Rd., Glenview IL 60025. (312)998-6688. Editor: Vince DiPaolo. Magazine published 10 times/year, covering treasury professionals in organizations or "professionals who are called upon to fulfill corporate treasury functions." Almost half hold the

'Treasurer' title and the remainder are either directly or peripherally involved in treasury activities. A good number hold CPAs or other professional designations. Circ. 12,000. Pays on publication. Byline sometimes given. Buys all rights. Computer printout or disk submissions compatible with Apple Wordstar OK. SASE. Reports in 1 month. Sample copy $6; free writer's guidelines.

Nonfiction: Material must specifically relate to the interests of treasury managers. Accepts no material "without a query first." Buys 10 mss/year. Send query and outline with clips of published work. Length: 1,000-2,500 words ("set by editor when assigning article"). Pays $7/published inch.

Photos: Reviews b&w and color contact sheets, negatives, transparencies and prints. Model release and identification of subjects required.

Tips: "Opportunities are also available to cover news beats on a monthly basis. Contact editor for details."

‡CGA MAGAZINE, Suite 740, 1176 W. Georgia St., Vancouver, British Columbia, Canada V6E 4A2. (604)669-3555. 25% freelance written. For accountants and financial managers. Magazine published 12 times/year; 44 pages. Circ. 32,000. Pays on acceptance. Buys one-time rights. Byline given. Phone queries OK. Simultaneous and photocopied submissions OK. SASE. Reports in 2-4 weeks. Free sample copy and writer's guidelines.

Nonfiction: "Accounting and financial subjects of interest to highly qualified professional accountants. All submissions must be relevant to Canadian accounting. All material must be of top professional quality, but at the same time written simply and interestingly." How-to; informational; academic; research; and technical. Buys 36 mss/year. Query with outline and estimate of word count. Length: 1,500-2,000 words. Pays $100-500.

Illustrations: State availability of photos, tables, charts or graphs with query. Offers no additional payment for illustrations.

Advertising, Marketing, and PR

Trade journals for professional advertising executives, copywriters and marketing and public relations professionals are listed in this category. Those whose main interests are the advertising and marketing of specific products (such as Beverages and Bottling and Hardware) are classified under individual product categories. Journals for sales personnel and general merchandisers are found in the Selling and Merchandising category.

AD FORUM, for Consumer Marketing Management, MIN Publishing, 18 E. 53rd St., New York NY 10022. (212)888-1793. Editor: Elizabeth J. Berry. Monthly magazine covering consumer marketing for "top management down through the marketing divisions of the leading 1,000 national advertisers." Circ. 6,000. Pays on publication. No byline given; "writer is listed in masthead as contributor." Pays 50% kill fee. Buys first North American rights; "reprints must be credited to *Ad Forum*." Computer printout submissions OK. SASE. Reports in 1 month. Sample copy free.

Nonfiction: Profile (of a specific brand or company); and trend stories on consumer lifestyles or marketing management. No regional stories. Buys 12 mss/year. Query with clips of published work. Length: 800-1,600 words. Pays $200-600.

ADVERTISING AGE, 740 N. Rush, Chicago IL 60611. (312)649-5200. Managing Editor: Lauren Doherty. Currently staff-produced. Includes weekly sections devoted to one topic (i.e., marketing in Southern California; agribusiness/advertising; TV syndication trends). Much of this material is done freelance—on assignment only. Pays kill fee "based on hours spent plus expenses." Byline given "except short articles or contributions to a roundup."

ADVERTISING TECHNIQUES, ADA Publishing Co., 10 E. 39th St., New York NY 10616. (212)889-6500. Managing Editor: Lauren Bernstein. 10% freelance written. For advertising executives. Monthly magazine; 50 pages. Circ. 4,500. Pays on acceptance. Not copyrighted. Reports in 1 month. Sample copy $1.75.

Nonfiction: Articles on advertising techniques. Buys 10 mss/year. Query. Pays $25-50.

‡ADVERTISING WORLD, The Magazine For Multi-National Advertising, Directories International, Inc., Suite 610, 150 5th Ave., New York NY 10011. (212)807-1660. Editor: Bruce Kane Garson. Managing Editor: Bonnie Grande. Bimonthly magazine for advertising executives (both in advertising companies and agencies) and media executives (publishers, representatives). "*AW* talks about multi-national advertising from

a US base: how to select media, how to plan a campaign." Circ. 5,050. Pays on publication. Byline given. Makes work-for-hire assignments. Submit seasonal/holiday material 2 months in advance. Simultaneous queries OK. SASE. Reports in 2 weeks. Free sample copy.

Nonfiction: Technical (international advertising and marketing). No articles not specifically pertaining to international advertising and/or marketing. Buys 20 mss/year. Query. Length: 3-5 pages. Pays 50¢/column line.

Columns/Departments: Media Notes & Quotes: new developments on the international media front; Other Notes & Quotes: developments on international advertising front not specifically about the media. Buys few items; material usually compiled from press releases. Query. Length: short. Pays 50¢/column line.

Tips: "This is not really a freelancer's publication; our writers tend to be practitioners of international advertising, who don't rely on us for income (we pay very little and not until publication), just for prestige in the industry."

ADWEEK/WEST, 514 Shatto Place, Los Angeles CA 90020. Editor: Lee Kerry. For "people involved in advertising; media, agencies, and client organizations as well as affiliated businesses." Weekly. Buys all rights. Pays on acceptance. Reports in 1 month. Query. SASE.

Nonfiction and Photos: "Advertising in the West. Not particularly interested in success stories. We want articles by experts in advertising, marketing, communications." Length: 1,000-1,750 words. Pays up to $250 (including art). Photos purchased with mss.

AMERICAN DEMOGRAPHICS, American Demographics, Inc., Box 68, Ithaca NY 14851. (607)273-6343. Editor: Bryant Robey. Managing Editor: Caroline Eckstrom. For business executives, market researchers, media and communications people, public policymakers and those in academic world. Monthly magazine; 52 pages. Circ. 7,000. Pays on publication. Copyrighted. Buys all rights. Submit seasonal/holiday material 5-6 months in advance. Simultaneous, photocopied, and previously published submissions OK. Computer printout and disk submissions OK; prefers letter quality to dot matrix printout. SASE. Reports in 1 month on queries; in 2 months on mss. Include self-addressed stamped postcard for return word that ms arrived safely. Sample copy $5.

Nonfiction: General interest (on demographic trends, implications of changing demographics, profile of business using demographic data); how-to (on the use of demographic techniques, psychographics, understand projections, data, apply demography to business and planning). No anecdotal material or humor.

Tips: "Writer should have clear understanding of specific population trends and their implications for business and planning."

ART DIRECTION, Advertising Trade Publications, Inc., 10 E. 39th St., New York NY 10016. (212)889-6500. Managing Editor: Lauren Bernstein. 15% freelance written. Emphasis on advertising design for art directors of ad agencies (corporate, in-plant, editorial, freelance, etc.). Monthly magazine; 100 pages. Circ. 12,000. Pays on publication. Buys one-time rights. SASE. Reports in 3 months. Sample copy $3.

Nonfiction: How-to articles on advertising campaigns. Pays $25 minimum.

BUSINESS MARKETING, (formerly *Industrial Marketing*), Crain Communications, Inc., 740 N. Rush St., Chicago IL 60611. (312)649-5260. Editor: Bob Donath. Managing Editor: John A. Roberts. Monthly magazine covering the advertising, sales and promotion of business and industrial products and services for an audience in marketing/sales middle management and corporate top management. Circ. 34,000. Rights reserved. Send queries first. Submit seasonal material 3 months in advance; 1½ months in advance for spot news. SASE. Computer printout submissions without format coding OK. Reports in 1 month on queries. Sample copy $3.

Nonfiction: Expose (of marketing industry); how-to (advertise, do sales management promotion, do strategy development); interview (of industrial marketing executives); opinion (on industry practices); profile; and technical (advertising/marketing practice). "No self promotion or puff pieces." No material aimed at the general interest reader. Buys 10 mss/year. Query. Length: 1,000-2,000 words.

Photos: State availability of photos. Reviews 8x10 b&w glossy prints and color transparencies. Offers no additional payment for photos accepted with ms. Captions preferred; model release required.

Columns/Departments: Query. Length: 500-1,000 words. "Column ideas should be queried, but generally we have no need for paid freelance columnists."

Fillers: Newsbreaks. Buys 2 mss/issue. Length: 100-500 words.

CANADIAN PREMIUMS & INCENTIVES, Selling Ideas in Motivational Marketing, Maclean Hunter Publishing Company, 777 Bay St., Toronto, Ontario, Canada M5W 1A7. (416)596-5838. Editor: Ed Patrick. Publisher: Ted Wilson. Quarterly magazine covering premium/incentive programs and promotions; incentive travel. Circ. 15,850. Pays on publication. Byline given. Buys first North American serial, one-time, and first rights. Submit seasonal/holiday material 3 months in advance. Simultaneous queries OK. Computer printout and disk submissions OK. SASE or SAE and IRCs. Reports in 1 week. Sample copy $3.

Nonfiction: New product and travel (incentive). Special issues include use of business gifts. Buys 10-12 mss/year. Query with clips of published work. Length: 600-1,500 words. Pays $60-200.

Photos: Pays $15-25 for 8x10 b&w prints. Captions and identification of subjects required. Buys one-time rights.

CLIP BITS, The How-To Magazine of the Graphic Arts, Dynamic Graphics, Inc., 6000 Forest Park Dr., Peoria IL 61614. (309)688-8800. Editor: Maxine Higginbotham. Monthly magazine covering graphic arts. Circ. 11,000. Pays on acceptance. Byline given. Buys negotiable rights. Submit seasonal/holiday material 6 months in advance. Simultaneous queries, and photocopied, simultaneous and previously published submissions OK. SASE. Reports in 6 weeks on queries; 5 weeks on mss. Free sample copy and writer's guidelines.
Nonfiction: Book excerpts, how-to, interview/profile, new product, personal experience, photo feature, technical;—"anything that would be of interest to our readers, the graphic arts professionals." Buys variable number mss/year. Query with or without clips of published work. Length: 1,000-3,500 words. Pays negotiable fee.
Photos: Steve Justice, photo editor. Send photos with ms. Reviews b&w or color contact sheet or color prints (minimum size 5x7). Captions, model release and identification of subject required.
Columns/Departments: Guest Columnist: authority in field on relevant subject. Book Review: books of interest to readers; art, photography, graphics, typography, paper, color, etc. Studio Shortcuts: techniques and tips for board persons. Buys variable number items/year. Query with or without clips of published work.
Fillers: "We are interested in seeing fillers that are tips and tricks similar to Studio Shortcuts information— how-to techniques for graphic artists, designers, paste-up and keyline persons." Negotiable specifications.
Tips: "Studio Shortcuts is a collection of how-to information. Send 1, 2, a dozen or a hundred at one time. These can be any length. Outlines are not required for this department. Some of these shortcuts provide 'spin-offs' for full-length articles. Talk to professionals in the field and ask them for tips."

THE COUNSELOR MAGAZINE, Advertising Specialty Institute, NBS Bldg., 1120 Wheeler Way, Langhorne PA 19047. (215)752-4200. Editor: Theresa Crown. For executives, both distributors and suppliers, in the ad specialty industry. Monthly magazine; 250 pages. Circ. 5,000. Pays on acceptance. Copyrighted. Buys first rights. No phone queries. Submit seasonal/holiday material 3 months in advance. Simultaneous submissions, photocopied submissions and previously published work OK. Reports in two months.
Nonfiction: Contact: Managing Editor. How-to (promotional case histories); interview (with executives and government figures); profile (of executives); travel (business and technical industry material only). No "cutesy poems that attempt to spoof radio and TV advertising. We won't use them, so don't bother sending them." Buys 30 mss/year. Length: 1,000 words minimum. Query with samples. Pays $150-190.
Photos: State availability of photos. B&w photos only. Prefers contact sheet(s) and 5x7 prints. Offers no additional payment for photos accepted with ms. Captions and model releases required. Buys one-time rights.
Tips: "If a writer shows promise, we can modify his suggestions to suit our publication and provide leads. Writers must be willing to adapt or rewrite their material for a specific audience. If an article is suitable for 5 or 6 other publications, it's probably not suitable for us. The best way to break in is to write for *Imprint*, a quarterly publication we produce for the clients of ad specialty counselors. *Imprint* covers promotional campaigns— safety programs, trade show exhibits, traffic builders and sales incentives—all with a specialty advertising tie-in."

DM NEWS, THE NEWSPAPER OF DIRECT MARKETING, DM News Corp., 19 W. 21st St., New York NY 10010. (212)741-2095. Editor: Joe Fitz-Morris. Monthly tabloid about direct response marketing for users and producers of direct response marketing throughout the nation. Circ. 21,000. Pays on acceptance. Byline given. Makes work-for-hire assignments. Phone queries OK. SASE.
Nonfiction: "Come up with a newsbeat scoop and check it out with the editor." Query. Pays $50-100.
Photos: Send photos with ms. Reviews 8x10 b&w glossy prints. Offers no additional payment for photos accepted with ms. Captions and model release required. Buys one-time rights.

THE GRAPHIC MONTHLY, North Island Sound, 30 Titan Rd., Unit 6, Toronto, Ontario, Canada M82 5Y2. (416)231-4393. Editor: Tom Thompson. Bimonthly magazine covering graphic communications. "A general look at graphic communications dealing with artists through to printers. Special interest areas are high-tech and business procedures." Estab. 1980. Circ. 5,976. Pays on publication. Byline given. Makes work-for-hire assignments. Photocopied and previously published submissions OK. SASE or SAE and IRCs. Computer printout submissions OK. Reports in 2 weeks. Free sample copy and writer's guidelines.
Nonfiction: General interest; interview/profile (of a particular industry, business or personality); new product; technical (covering presswork, graphics, camera, and small business procedures). Buys 9 mss/year. Query with clips of published work. Length: 750-2,000 words. Pays $4.25/column inch.
Columns/Departments: Small Business; Paper; Electronics—publishing and graphics. Query with clips of published work. Buys 2-3 mss/year. Length: 500-750 words. Pays $4.25/column inch.

IMPRINT, The Magazine of Specialty Advertising Ideas, Advertising Specialty Institute, 1120 Wheeler Way, Langhorne PA 19047. (215)752-4200. Editor: Theresa Crown. Quarterly magazine covering specialty advertising. Circ. 50,000+. Pays on acceptance. Byline given. Pays $25 kill fee. Buys one-time rights. Submit seasonal/holiday material 6 months in advance. Simultaneous queries OK. Reports in 1 month. Free sample copy.

Nonfiction: How-to (case histories of specialty advertising campaigns); and photo feature (how ad specialties are distributed in promotions). "Emphasize effective use of specialty advertising. Avoid direct-buy situations. Stress the distributor's role in promotions. No generalized pieces on print, broadcast or outdoor advertising." Buys 10-12 mss/year. Query with clips of published work. Length: 750-1,500 words. Pays $50-150.

Photos: State availability of photos. Pays $10-25 for 5x7 b&w prints. Captions, model release and identification of subjects required.

Tips: "Query with a case history suggestion and writing samples. We can provide additional leads. All articles must be specifically geared to specialty advertising (and sometimes, premium) promotions."

INCENTIVE MARKETING, Bill Communications, Inc., 633 3rd Ave., New York NY 10017. (212)986-4800. Editor: James Hogg. For buyers of merchandise and travel used in motivational promotions. Monthly magazine; 200 pages. Circ. 37,000. Pays on acceptance. Buys all rights. No byline. SASE. Reports in 2 weeks. Sample copy and writer's guidelines $3.

Nonfiction: Informational, case histories. "No bank premium stories, please!" Buys 200 mss/year. Query. Length: 1,000-3,000 words. Pays $125-145.

Tips: "We need coverage in the West, the South and Chicago."

MAGAZINE AGE, 225 Park Ave., New York NY 10169. (212)986-7366. Editor: Wallis Wood. Monthly magazine for advertisers and advertising agencies designed to examine how they use a wide range of publications, including consumer, business, trade, farm, etc. Circ. 35,000. Pays on acceptance. Buys all rights. Reports in 2 weeks. Sample copy $3; free writer's guidelines for SASE.

Nonfiction: "We are interested in magazine advertising success and failure stories. We want marketing pieces, case histories, effective use of magazine advertising and current trends." Buys 4 mss/issue. Query first. Will not respond to handwritten inquiries. Length: 3,000 words maximum. Pays $500 maximum.

Tips: "Find an unusual aspect of print advertising."

MARKETING COMMUNICATIONS, United Business Publications, Inc., 475 Park Ave., S., New York NY 10016. Publisher: Valerie Free. 70% freelance written. Emphasizes marketing and promotion. Monthly magazine; 90 pages. Circ. 25,000. Pays on publication. Buys all rights. Byline given. Submit seasonal or holiday material 2-3 months in advance. Photocopied submissions OK (if exclusive). No computer printout or disk submissions. Reports in 2 months. Sample copy $2.50; free writer's guidelines. No materials returned.

Nonfiction: "The preferred format for feature articles is the case history approach to solving consumer marketing problems. Critical evaluations of market planning, premium and incentive programs, point-of-purchase displays, direct mail campaigns, dealer/distributor meetings, media advertising, and sales promotion tools and techniques are particularly relevant." How-to articles (develop successful product campaigns); informational (marketing case histories); profiles (on a given industry, i.e., tobacco, razors, food); technical articles (technology updates on a field of interest to marketing people). No industrial material. Buys 30 mss/year. Length: 750-1,250 words. Pays $75-400.

Photos: Prefers 8x10 b&w glossies with mss, or 2¼x2¼ color transparencies; other formats acceptable. Submit prints and transparencies. Captions required. No additional payment.

Tips: "Read our magazine and understand that we only cover major campaigns and corporations. Make specific suggestions and enclose clip samples that are appropriate and well-written."

SALES & MARKETING MANAGEMENT IN CANADA, Ingmar Communications, Ltd., Suite 303, 416 Moore Ave., Toronto, Ontario, Canada M4G 1C9. (416)424-4441. Editor: Ernie Spear. Monthly magazine. Circ. 13,000. Pays on publication. Byline given. Buys first North American serial rights. Simultaneous queries and photocopied submissions OK. Reports in 2 weeks.

Nonfiction: How-to (case histories of successful marketing campaigns). "Canadian articles only." Buys 3 mss/year. Query. Length: 800-1,500 words. Pays $200 maximum.

‡**SIGNS OF THE TIMES, The Industry Journal since 1906**, ST Publications, 407 Gilbert Ave., Cincinnati OH 45202. (513)421-2050. Editor: Tod Swormstedt. Managing Editor: Bill Dorsey. Magazine published 13 times/year; special buyer's guide between November and December issue. Circ. 15,000. Pays on publication. Byline given. Buys variable rights. Simultaneous queries, and simultaneous, photocopied, and previously published submissions OK. SASE. Reports in 2 weeks. Free sample copy and writer's guidelines.

Nonfiction: Historical/nostalgic (regarding the sign industry); how-to (carved signs, goldleaf, etc.); interview/profile (usually on assignment but interested to hear proposed topics); photo feature (query first); technical (sign engineering, etc.). Nothing "non-specific on signs, an example being a photo essay on 'signs I've seen.' We are a trade journal with specific audience interests." Buys 2-3 mss/year. Query with clips. Pays $150-250.

Photos: Send photos with ms. "Sign industry-related photos only. We sometimes accept photos with funny twists or misspellings."

VISUAL MERCHANDISING & STORE DESIGN, S.T. Publications, 407 Gilbert Ave., Cincinnati OH 45202. Associate Publisher: Pamela Gramke. Editor: Ms. P.K. Anderson. Emphasizes store design and merchandise presentation. Monthly magazine; 72 pages. Circ. 10,000. Pays on publication. Simultaneous and previously published submissions OK. No computer printout or disk submissions. SASE. Reports in 1 month.
Nonfiction: Expose; how-to (display); informational (store design, construction, merchandise presentation); interview (display directors and shop owners); profile (new and remodeled stores); new product; photo feature (window display); technical (store lighting, carpet, wallcoverings, fixtures). No "advertorials" that tout a single company's product or product line. Buys 24 mss a year. Query or submit complete ms. Length: 500-3,000 words. Pays $50-200.
Photos: Purchased with accompanying ms or on assignment.
Tips: "Be fashion and design conscious and reflect that in the article. Submit finished mss with photos or slides always. Look for stories on department and specialty store visual merchandisers and store designers (profiles, methods, views on the industry, sales promotions and new store design or remodels). The size of the publication could very well begin to increase in the year ahead. And with a greater page count, we will need to rely on an increasing number of freelancers."

ZIP MAGAZINE, North American Publishing, 545 Madison Ave., New York NY 10011. (212)371-4100. Editorial Director: Ray Lewis. Emphasizes marketing, list selection and testing, circulation, communications, and direct mail/mailing systems for mail-oriented professionals in business, industry and direct marketing. Typical articles published recently were on marketing to rural buyers, improved business-to-business communications, and justifying mailroom equipment purchases in a tight economy. Some ideas they would be interested in are "Future of Communications in General," mail-order, telephone marketing, fund raising, publication mail programs, and articles dealing with mail handling/processing. Interested in freelance stories on equipment and methods used to mail, process mail, transfer names onto and out of computers, labeling and packaging. "No clever or cute opinion or overview pieces." Published 12 times/year. Circ. 37,500. Pays on publication in some cases, acceptance in others. Copyrighted. Rights purchased vary. No phone queries. Simultaneous, photocopied and previously published submissions OK. Reports in 2 weeks. Free sample copy.
Nonfiction: General interest (about magazine circulation or direct-mail stories); how-to: (improve mailroom operation, direct-marketing case histories); interview, profile and photo features should be about mail-oriented executives and professionals. "We are not interested in personal opinion or experience articles." Buys 10-15 unsolicited mss/year. Query or send complete ms. Length: 500-1,000 words. Pays $100-200.
Photos: State availability of photos or send with ms. Accepts only b&w photos and prefers contact sheet and 4x5 glossy prints. Pays $20-l00. Captions preferred. Buys one-time rights.

Agricultural Equipment and Supplies

CUSTOM APPLICATOR, Little Publications, Suite 540, 6263 Poplar Ave., Memphis TN 38119. Editor: Tom Griffin. Managing Editor: Rob Wiley. For "firms that sell and custom apply agricultural chemicals." Circ. 17,000. Buys all rights. Pays on publication. "Query is best. The editor can help you develop the story line regarding our specific needs." SASE. No computer printout or disk submissions.
Nonfiction and Photos: "We are looking for articles on custom application firms telling others how to better perform jobs of chemical application, develop new customers, handle credit, etc. Lack of a good idea or usable information will bring a rejection." Length: 1,000-1,200 words "with 3 or 4 b&w glossy prints." Pays 20¢/word.

FARM SUPPLIER, Watt Publishing Co., Sandstone Bldg., Mount Morris IL 61054. (815)734-4171. Editor-in-Chief: Jim Klatt. For retail farm supply dealers and managers over the US. Monthly magazine; 64 pages. Circ. 20,000. Pays on acceptance. Buys all rights in competitive farm supply fields. Byline given. Phone queries OK. Submit seasonal material or query 2 months in advance. SASE. Computer printout and disk submissions OK. Reports in 2 weeks.
Nonfiction: How-to; informational; interview; new product; and photo feature. "Articles emphasizing product news, and how new product developments have been profitably resold or successfully used. We use material on successful farm dealers, particularly involving custom application, fertilizer, herbicides, etc." No

"general how-to articles that some writers blanket the industry with, inserting a word change here or there to 'customize.' " Buys 12 unsolicited mss/year. Recent article example: Feature on South Carolina fertilizer dealer (February 1982). Query. Length: 600-2,000 words. Pays $75-400. "Longer articles must include photos, charts, etc."

Photos: Purchased with accompanying ms. Submit 5x7 or 8x10 b&w prints; 35mm or larger color transparencies. Total purchase price for a ms includes payment for photos.

Tips: "Because of a constantly changing industry, *FS* attempts to work only two months in advance. Freelancers should slant stories to each season in the farm industry—examples: herbicides in January-March, feed and grain in May, application equipment in September—and should provide vertical color photos whenever possible with longer features."

Art, Design, and Collectibles

The business of art administration, architecture, environmental/package design and antique collectibles is covered in these listings. Art-related topics for the general public are located in the Consumer Art category. Antiques magazines are listed in Consumer Hobby and Craft.

THE ANTIQUES DEALER, 1115 Clifton Ave., Clifton NJ 07013. (201)779-1600. Editor: Kathy Shipp O'Brien. 90% freelance written. For antiques dealers. Monthly magazine. Circ. 7,000. Average issue includes 4 features, 5 columns. Rights purchased vary with author and material. Buys all rights. Byline given. Buys 40 mss a year. Pays on publication. Submit seasonal/holiday material 4 months in advance. Will send free sample copy to writer on request. Will consider previously published and photocopied submissions "if clear." Reports in 3 weeks. SASE.

Nonfiction: "Remember that we are a trade publication and all material must be slanted to the needs and interests of antique dealers. We publish nothing of a too general ('be a good salesman') or too limited (eastern Pennsylvania chairs) nature." Only articles of national interest to dealers; may be tutorial if by authority in one specific field (how to restore antiques; open a dealership; locate a specific antique); otherwise of broad general interest to all dealers and news of the international antique trade. Emphasis is currently on heirlooms (50-100 years old), as well as antiques (over 100 years old). Buys 2 mss/issue. Length: minimum 500 words; maximum 2-part article, about 7,000 words; 3,500 words if one-part. Pays $50/page for features; $1.50/inch for small items.

Photos: Purchased with or without accompanying mss, or on assignment. Pays $5 per b&w used inside, $10 for covers; no smaller than 5x7 (glossy). Professional quality only; no Polaroids.

Fillers: Suitable for professional dealers; any type of fillers. Length: 300-400 words. Pays approximately $15 for half-page.

Tips: "It is more important that the writer know his subject well, as a specialist or one interviewing a specialist, than that he demonstrate his writing prowess. But I am looking for good business journalists who can cover news and interviews well."

ART BUSINESS NEWS, Myers Publishing Co., 2135 Summer St., Stamford CT 06905. (203)356-1745. Editor: Vicki Wray. Managing Editor: Caroline D. Myers. Monthly tabloid covering news relating to the art and picture framing industry. Circ. 19,000. Pays on publication. Byline given. Buys all rights. Submit seasonal/holiday material 2 months in advance. Photocopied and simultaneous submissions OK. Computer printout and disk submissions OK; prefers letter quality to dot matrix printouts. Reports in 2 months. Sample copy $1.50.

Nonfiction: General interest; how-to (occasional articles, on "how-to frame" accepted); interview/profile (of persons in the art industry); new product; articles focusing on small business people—framers, art gallery management, etc. Buys 8-20 mss/year. Length: 1,000 words maximum. Pays $75-100.

ARTS MANAGEMENT, 408 W. 57th St., New York NY 10019. (212)245-3850. Editor: A.H. Reiss. For cultural institutions. Published five times/year. Circ. 6,000. Buys all rights. Byline given. Pays on publication. Mostly staff-written. Query. Reports in "several weeks." SASE.

Market conditions are constantly changing! If this is 1985 or later, buy the newest edition of *Writer's Market* at your favorite bookstore or order directly from Writer's Digest Books.

Nonfiction: Short articles, 400-900 words, tightly written, expository, explaining how art administrators solved problems in publicity, fund raising, and general administration; actual case histories emphasizing the how-to. Also short articles on the economics and sociology of the arts and important trends in the nonprofit cultural field. Must be fact-filled, well-organized and without rhetoric. Payment is 2-4¢/word. No photographs or pictures.

CANADIAN MUSEUMS ASSOCIATION, Suite 202, 280 Metcalfe St., Ottawa, Ontario, Canada K2P 1R7. (613)233-5653. Head of Communications: Elizabeth Gignac. Publishes monthly newsletter museogramme and quarterly journal *Muse*. Simultaneous submissions OK. Reports in 3 months. SAE and IRC.
Nonfiction: Must be related to the museum and art gallery field, primarily Canadian. Museology, museography, care of collections, security, environmental control, museum architecture, exhibition care and design, cataloguing and registration, conservation methods, glossaries of terminology, staff training, extension and educational services, and technical skills. Primarily concerned with the Canadian scene, with a view to the international market. Submit outline/synopsis. Consult Chicago *Manual of Style*.

INDUSTRIAL DESIGN, Design Publications, Inc., 330 W. 42nd St., 11th Fl., New York NY 10036. (212)695-4955. Managing Editor: Michael McTwigan. Subject of this publication is industrial design (of products, packaging, graphics and environments) and design management. Bimonthly magazine. Circ. 11,000. Pays on publication. Buys all rights. Byline given. Phone queries OK. Previously published work OK. Computer printout and disk submissions OK; prefers letter quality to dot matrix printouts. SASE. Sample copy $5.
Nonfiction: Expose (design related); how-to (all aspects of design and design management), interview (of important people in business and design); profile (corporate, showing value of design and/or how design is managed); design history; and new product. Recent article example: cover story on robots (January/Febuary 1982). "The writer got top pay and a bonus for hard work, extensive research, a "how-to" sidebar, and a humorous example or two." Buys 6 unsolicited mss/year. Length: 1,800 words. Query with point-by-point outline and clips of published work. Pays $100-500.
Photos: State availability of photos. Wants very good quality b&w glossy prints and contact sheets. Offers no additional payment for photos accepted with ms. Captions required.
Columns/Departments: Materials, Components, Processes; "Sourcebook" is a department of short items written from press releases. Other departments include Portfolio (new products); Visual Communications (graphics, packaging); Environments; and News and Views. Query with clips of published work. Pays $7 maximum.
Tips: "Show that you are thoroughly backgrounded on the general aspects of your topic, as well as specifics. Read the magazine."

PROGRESSIVE ARCHITECTURE, 600 Summer St., Box 1361, Stamford CT 06904. Editor: John M. Dixon. Monthly. Buys first-time rights for use in architectural press. Pays on publication. SASE.
Nonfiction and Photos: "Articles of technical professional interest devoted to architecture, interior design, and urban design and planning and illustrated by photographs and architectural drawings. Also use technical articles, which are prepared by technical authorities and would be beyond the scope of the lay writer. Practically all the material is professional, and most of it is prepared by writers in the field who are approached by the magazine for material." Pays $50-250. Buys one-time reproduction rights to b&w and color photos.

Auto and Truck

The journals below aim at automobile and truck dealers, service department personnel, or fleet operators. Publications for highway planners and traffic control experts are classified in the Government and Public Service category.

‡**AMERICAN CLEAN CAR, Serving the Car & Truck Cleaning Industries**, American Trade Magazines, 500 N. Dearborn, Chicago IL 60610. (312)337-7700. Editor: Edwin G. Schwenn. Associate Editor: Keith Kramer. Bimonthly magazine of the professional car washing industry for owners and operators of car washes. Circ. 20,000. Pays on publication. Offers negotiable kill fee. Buys first rights and second serial (reprint) rights. Submit seasonal/holiday material 3 months in advance. SASE. Reports in 2 weeks. Free sample copy and writer's guidelines.
Nonfiction: How-to (develop, maintain, improve, etc., car washes); humor (cartoons); interview/profile (industry leaders); new product (concerned with industry—no payment here); technical (maintenance of car wash equipment). "We emphasize car wash operation and use features on industry topics: Utility use and conservation, maintenance, management, customer service and advertising. A case study should emphasize how the

operator accomplished whatever he or she did—in a way that the reader can apply to his or her own operation. Mss should have no-nonsense, businesslike approach." Buys 18 mss/year. Query. Length: 500-3,000 words. Pays 6-8¢/word.

Photos: State availability of photos. Pays $6-8 for each photo used. Supply b&w contact sheet. Captions required. Buys all rights.

Columns/Departments: "Most of our columnists are from the industry or somehow related." Buys 18 mss/year. Query. Length: 500-1,000 words. Pays $50-55.

Fillers: Clippings, newsbreaks. Buys 6-12/year. Length: 200-300 words. Pays 6-8¢/word.

Tips: "Query about subjects of current interest. Be observant of car wash operations—how they are designed and equipped; how they serve customers; how (if) they advertise and promote their services. Most general articles are turned down because they are not aimed specifically to audience. Most case histories are turned down because of lack of practical purpose (nothing new or worth reporting)."

AMERICAN TRUCKER MAGAZINE, American Trucker Marketing, Box 6366, San Bernardino CA 92412. (714)889-1167. Publisher: Steve Krieger. Editor: Ryan Rees. Pays within 30 days of publication. "First time rights requested." Monthly magazine for professional truck drivers, owners, management and other trucking personnel. Articles, fillers and other materials should be generally conservative and of particular interest to the readership, of an informative or entertaining nature relating to the trucking industry. Circ. 46,700. Phone queries OK. Submit seasonal/holiday material 3 months in advance. SASE. Reports in 3 weeks. Free sample copy and writer's guidelines.

Nonfiction: Articles directed to trucking professionals that are realistic and promote a positive image of the industry. Photo features of outstanding rigs, truck maintenance and repair, business aspects of trucking. 450-2,500 words. Buys 60 articles/year. Pays standard column inch rate.

Photos: State availability of photos or send captioned photos with ms. Model release required.

Fiction: Realistic, "slice of life" for truckers, adventure and humor. Query. Length: 1,200-2,500 words. Pays standard column inch rate.

Fillers: Jokes and short humor. Length: 50-500 words. Pays standard column inch rate.

AUTO LAUNDRY NEWS, Columbia Communications, 370 Lexington Ave., New York NY 10017. (212)532-9290. Publisher/Editor: Ralph Monti. For sophisticated carwash operators. Monthly magazine; 45-100 pages. Circ. 15,000+. Pays on publication. Buys all rights. Phone queries OK. Submit seasonal/holiday material 60 days in advance. SASE. Reports in 4 weeks. Free sample copy.

Nonfiction: How-to; historical; humor; informational; new product; nostalgia; personal experience; technical; interviews; photo features; and profiles. Buys 15 mss/year. Query. Length: 1,000-2,000 words. Pays $75-175.

Tips: "Read the magazine; notice its style and come up with something interesting to the industry. Foremost, the writer has to know the industry."

AUTO TRIM NEWS, National Association of Auto Trim Shops (NAATS), 1623 N. Grand Ave., Box 86, Baldwin NY 11510. (516)223-4334. Editor: Nat Danas. Associate Editor: Dani Ben-Ari. Monthly magazine for auto trim shops, installation specialists, customizers and restylers, marine and furniture upholsterers as well as manufacturers, wholesalers, jobbers, distributors serving them. Circ. 8,000. Pays on publication. Byline given. Buys first rights. Simultaneous and previously published submissions OK. No computer printout or disk submissions. SASE. Reports in 1 month. Sample copy $1; free writer's guidelines for SAE and 2 first class stamps.

Nonfiction: How-to, interview/profile, photo feature on customizing, restoration, convertible conversions, and restyling of motor vehicles; cars, vans, trucks, motorcycles, boats and aircraft. Query or send complete ms. Length: 500-1,000 words. Pays $50-100.

Photos: State availability of photos. Pays $5 maximum for b&w print. Reviews b&w contact sheet. Captions and identification of subjects required. Buys one-time rights.

Tips: "No material dealing with engines and engine repairs. We are an aftermarket publication."

AUTOMOTIVE BOOSTER OF CALIFORNIA, Box 765, LaCanada CA 91011. (213)790-6554. Editor: Don McAnally. 3% freelance written. For members of Automotive Booster clubs, automotive warehouse distributors and automotive parts jobbers in California. Monthly. Circ. 3,500. Not copyrighted. Byline given. Pays on publication. Submit complete ms. SASE.

Nonfiction and Photos: Will look at short articles and pictures about successes of automotive parts outlets in California. Also can use personnel assignments for automotive parts people in California. Query first. Pays $1.25/column inch (about 2½¢/word); $5 for b&w photos used with mss.

AUTOMOTIVE REBUILDER MAGAZINE, Babcox Publications, Inc., 11 S. Forge St., Akron OH 44304. (216)535-6117. Editor-in-Chief: Andrew J. Doherty. Associate Editor: John Davisson. Emphasizes the automotive and heavy duty mechanical/parts rebuilding industry and jobber machine shops. Monthly magazine: 108 pages. Circ. 21,000. Pays on publication. Buys all rights. Phone queries OK. Submit seasonal/holiday material 6 weeks in advance of issue date. Simultaneous, photocopied and previously published submissions OK. SASE. Reports in 2 weeks. Free sample copy.

Nonfiction: "How-to (technical writing); humor (we particularly like humor, must be relevant to rebuilders); historical (historical automotive); inspirational (concentrate on how a rebuilder overcomes disaster or personal handicap); interview (concentrate on growth or success stories); nostalgia (only if it applies to rebuilding); personal experience (experiences with rebuilding); personal opinion (comment ·on legislation affecting rebuilders); photo feature (on machine shops; try to get people in photos, we want photojournalism, not photo illustration); profile (about individual rebuilder; perhaps the small rebuilder); technical (you must know what you're talking about, rebuilders don't just fall off Christmas trees) and articles on regulation at the state and local level (conservation of resources, air and water pollution)." Buys 8 mss/year. Query. Length: 500-1,500 words. Pays 4-6¢/word.

Columns & Departments: People (profile or close-up of industry figures welcome); Tech Notes (this entails technical how-to writing); new product ("we generally do this ourselves"); and The Forum Guest (opinions on current events relevant to rebuilders). Buys 1 ms/year. Query. Length: 200-1,500 words. Pays 4-6¢/word. Open to suggestions for columns/departments.

AUTOMOTIVE VOLUME DISTRIBUTION, (formerly *Warehouse Distribution*), 7300 N. Cicero Ave., Lincolnwood IL 60646. (312)588-7300. Editor: Larry Moore. For "specialists in the auto parts and hardware distribution field who are doing above one million dollars business per year." Published 10 times/year. Circ. 30,000. Buys all rights. Pays on publication. Most material is staff-written. Reports "within a reasonable amount of time." Computer printout and disk submissions OK; prefers letter quality to dot matrix printouts. SASE.

Nonfiction and Photos: "Business management subjects, limited to the automotive parts distribution field." No specific product stories or seasonal subjects. Query. Length: 1,500-2,000 words. Pays $200-300 "based on value to industry and the quality of the article." Photos purchased with and without mss; captions required. Wants "sharp 5x7 prints." Pays maximum $6.

Tips: Addition of hardware distributors adds new dimensions to coverage and editorial features.

THE BATTERY MAN, Independent Battery Manufacturers Association, Inc., 100 Larchwood Dr., Largo FL 33540. (813)586-1409. Editor: Celwyn E. Hopkins. Emphasizes SLI battery manufacture, applications, new developments. For battery manufacturers and retailers (garage owners, servicemen, fleet owners, etc.). Monthly magazine. Circ. 6,200. Pays on acceptance. Buys all rights. Byline given. Submit seasonal/holiday material 3 months in advance. Simultaneous, photocopied and previously published submissions OK. SASE. Reports in 6 weeks. Sample copy $2.50.

Nonfiction: Technical articles. Submit complete ms. Buys 19-24 unsolicited mss/year. Recent article examples: "The Decline of the Battery Market" (February 1981); "The Electric Boat: A Growing Market for the Battery Industry" (March 1982). Length: 1,200-1,500 words. Pays 6¢/word.

BRAKE & FRONT END, 11 S. Forge St., Akron OH 44304. (216)535-6117. Editor: Jeffrey S. Davis. 5-10% freelance written. For owners of automotive repair shops engaged in brake, wheel, suspension, chassis and frame repair, including: specialty shops; general repair shops; new car and truck dealers; gas stations; mass merchandisers and tire stores. Monthly magazine; 68 pages. Circ. 28,000. Pays on publication. Buys exclusive rights in field. Byline given. Computer printout and disk submissions OK; prefers letter quality to dot matrix printouts. SASE. Reports immediately. Sample copy and editorial schedule $3.

Nonfiction and Photos: Specialty shops taking on new ideas using new merchandising techniques; growth of business, volume; reasons for growth and success. Expansions, and unusual brake shops. Prefers no product-oriented material. Query. Length: about 800-1,500 words. Pays 7-9¢/word. Pays $8.50 for b&w glossy prints purchased with mss.

CANADIAN AUTOMOTIVE TRADE MAGAZINE, Maclean-Hunter, Ltd., 481 University Ave., Toronto, Ontario, Canada M5W 1A7. (416)596-5784. Editor-in-Chief: Doug Jordan. Emphasizes the automotive aftermarket for mechanics, service station and garage operators, new car dealers and parts jobbers. Bimonthly magazine; 60 pages. Circ. 31,000. Pays on acceptance. Buys all rights. Byline given. Phone queries OK. Submit seasonal/holiday material 2 months in advance. Photocopied submissions OK. SAE and International Reply Coupons. Reports in 2 months.

Nonfiction: Informational; new product; technical; interviews; and profiles. "We can use business articles every month from the 4 corners of Canada. Service articles can come from anywhere. We need Canadian business profiles most. No general business articles." Buys 4-6 unsolicited mss/year. Length: 600-1,400 words. Pays $100-300 (approximately $150/printed page).

Photos: Purchased with accompanying ms. Captions required. Send contact sheet and/or transparencies. Pays $5-20 for 4x5 b&w prints or 35mm color transparencies. Model release required.

CANADIAN TRANSPORTATION & DISTRIBUTION MANAGEMENT, Southam Communications, Ltd., 1450 Don Mills Rd., Don Mills, Ontario, Canada M3B 2X7. (416)445-6641. Editor: Lou Volpintesta. Monthly magazine covering physical distribution and freight transportation. Circ. 12,177. Pays on publication. Byline given. Buys second serial (reprint) rights. Simultaneous queries OK. SASE or SAE and IRCs. Reports in 3 weeks on queries; 2 weeks on mss. Free sample copy and reader profile.

Nonfiction: How-to (save distribution costs, fuel or evaluate distribution services); interview/profile; photo feature; news feature based on legislation trends, disruptions, etc. in physical distribution. Special needs include president's issue (Nov.): educational material on physical distribution for chief executives. No product descriptions or work without Canadian slant unless has international implication. No product news, literature/brochure announcements, transport company profiles—unless strong shipper slant. Buys 25 mss/year. Query with clips of published work. Length: 750-2,000 words. Pays $100-300.

Photos: State availability of photos. Reviews contact sheets; pays $10-30 for 5x7 b&w prints. Identification of subjects required. Buys all rights.

Columns/Departments: News columns: new distribution services; legislation; industry/association reaction; plant/office expansions; rates and tariffs. Buys 50 mss/year. Query. Length: 250-750 words. Pays $4/column inch (columns 13 picas wide).

Tips: "News columns and feature bank—items must be topical and timely. Writing should be terse and to the point—more interested in logical progression and tight writing than flowery prose. News stories for our columns are due the 25th of each month. The economy has affected the number of editorial pages available. That, plus cost-cutting programs we are pursuing, will mean fewer articles needed and fewer articles purchased from freelancers."

THE CHEK-CHART SERVICE BULLETIN, Box 6227, San Jose CA 95150. Associate Editor: Jo L. Phelps. 20% freelance written. Emphasizes trade news and how-to articles on automobile service for professional mechanics. Monthly newsletter; 8 pages. Circ. 20,000. Pays on acceptance. Buys all rights. No byline. Submit seasonal/holiday material 3-4 months in advance of issue date. SASE. Reports in 2 weeks. Free sample copy and writer's guidelines; mention *Writer's Market* in request.

Nonfiction: "The *Service Bulletin* is a trade newsletter, *not* a consumer magazine. How-to articles and service trade news for professional auto mechanics, also articles on merchandising automobile service. No 'do-it-yourself' articles." Also no material unrelated to car service. Buys 6 unsolicited mss/year. Recent article example: "Governor Ring Replacement—GM Diesel Roosa Master DB2 Injection Pump" (November 1982). Query with samples. Length: 700-1,100 words. Pays $75-125.

Photos: State availability of photos with query. Offers no additional payment for photos accepted with ms. Uses 8x10 b&w glossy photos. Captions and model release required. Buys all rights.

Tips: "Be willing to work in our style. Ask about subjects we would like to have covered in the future."

COLLISION, Kruzakaleidoscopix, Inc., Box 389, Franklin MA 02038. Editor: Jay Kruza. For auto dealers, auto body repairmen and managers, and tow truck operators. Magazine published every 6 weeks; 66 pages. Pays on acceptance. Buys all rights. Submit seasonal/holiday material 4 months in advance. Simultaneous, photocopied and previously published submissions OK. SASE. No computer printout or disk submissions. Reports in 2-3 weeks. Sample copy $1; free writer's guidelines.

Nonfiction: Expose (on government intervention in private enterprise via rule making; also how big business skims the cream of profitable business but fails to satisfy needs of motorist); how-to (fix a dent, a frame, repair plastics, run your business better); personal experience (regarding automotive success or failure). No general business articles, such as how to sell more, do better bookkeeping, etc. Query before submitting interview, personal opinion or technical articles. "Journalism of newsworthy material in local areas pertaining to auto body is of interest." Buys 20 or more articles/year. Length: 100-1,500 words. Pays $15-100.

Photos: "Our readers work with their hands and are more likely to be stopped by photo with story." Send photos with ms. Pays $15/first, $5/each additional for 5x7 b&w prints. Captions preferred. Model release required if not news material.

Columns & Departments: Stars and Their Cars, Personalities in Auto Dealership, Auto Body Repair Shops, Association News and Lifestyle, dealing with general human interest hobbies or past times. Almost anything that would attract readership interest. "Photos are very important. Stories that we have purchased are: 'Clearing the Farm . . . of Rattlesnakes'; 'Annual Mule Convention in Bishop, California'; and 'Cochise's Hidden Treasure.' " Buys 20/year. Query. Length: 200-500 words. Pays $25-75.

‡**FARM-TO-MARKET TRUCKERS' NEWS**, h.e.r. Publications, Ink., 2123 4th St., Sioux City IA 51101. (712)258-0782. Co-Editors: Dianne Rose and Jane Hunwardsen. Monthly trucking newspaper for company drivers, owner-operators, owners of large and small trucking firms and persons in allied industries in the Midwest. Circ. 7,000. Pays on publication. Byline given. Not copyrighted. Buys one-time rights. Submit seasonal/holiday material 2 months in advance. Simultaneous queries, and simultaneous, photocopied, and previously published submissions OK. SASE. Reports in 1 month. Sample copy $1; free writer's guidelines.

Nonfiction: Expose, general interest, historical/nostalgic, how-to, humor, interview/profile, new product,

personal experience, photo feature, technical. "Our special May Truckers' Day issue is the largest. Material should be submitted by March 15." Send complete ms. Length: 375-1,250 words. Pays $25-50.
Photos: Send photos with ms. Pays $10-25 for 5x7 prints. Captions, model release and identification of subjects required.
Tips: "Good, bright features about people in transportation are always welcome, especially when accompanied by a photo."

GO WEST MAGAZINE, 1240 Bayshore Hwy., Burlingame CA 94010. Editor: Bill Fitzgerald. 20% freelance written. Emphasizes truck transport for the truck operator who is concerned with operation, maintenance and purchase of trucks and related equipment, and running a profitable business. Monthly magazine; 80 pages. Circ. 51,000. Pays on acceptance. Buys all rights. Pays full kill fee. Byline given except "series using same format, but different locations and subjects." Phone queries OK. Submit seasonal/holiday material 6 months in advance of issue date. SASE. Reports in 2 weeks. Free sample copy; mention *Writer's Market* in request.
Nonfiction: Expose; general interest; how-to; interview; and new product. No fiction. Buys 2 mss/issue. Query. Length: 500-3,500 words. Pays $200-600.
Photos: State availability of photos with query. Pays $5-15 for b&w photos; $100 for 2¼x2¼ color transparencies. Captions required. Buys all rights.

HEAVY DUTY MARKETING, Babcox Publications, 11 S. Forge St., Akron OH 44304. (216)535-6117. Editor: Jeffrey S. Davis. Publishes 9 issues/year. Magazine about heavy duty truck parts and service. Circ. 18,000. Pays on publication. Byline given. Buys first North American serial rights. Submit seasonal material 2 months in advance. Simultaneous and photocopied submissions OK. SASE. Reports in 1 week. Sample copy $2.50.
Nonfiction: Interview (related to heavy duty truck parts and service); profile; and technical. No stories about truck fleets. Buys 12 mss/year. Query. Length: 750-3,000 words. Pays 7¢-9¢/word. "We need feature stories on established businesses in heavy duty aftermarket, including truck dealers and factory branches, trailer dealers, parts distributors and repair facilities. We also need interviews with high level executives in heavy duty parts and service."
Photos: State availability of photos. Pays $8.50 maximum for b&w negatives and contact sheets. Reviews color negatives and contact sheets. Payment negotiated. Captions required. Buys all rights.

IMPORT AUTOMOTIVE PARTS & ACCESSORIES, Import Automotive Publishers, 7637 Fulton St., North Hollywood CA 91605. (213)764-0611. Editor: John Rettie. Managing Editor: Jacquie Kreiman. Monthly magazine covering import automotive aftermarket. "We take a business editorial approach to automotive trade." Circ. 28,000. Pays on publication. Byline given. Offers negotiable kill fee. Buys all rights. Submit seasonal/holiday material 3 months in advance. Simultaneous queries OK. SASE. Sample copy and writer's guidelines for $2.
Nonfiction: Jacquie Kreiman, articles editor. How-to (service on autos); interview/profile (of automotive corporation); technical (hard parts). No non-automotive mss. Searches for "the most in-depth and up-to-date information for our industry." Buys 24 mss/year. Query with clips of published work. Length: 1,000-5,000 words. Pays $100-500.
Tips: "We do not generally consider manuscripts written specifically for our publication. We solicit from field specialists for the vast majority of our pieces. If a writer were interested and qualified, we might use for nontechnical pieces."

JOBBER/RETAILER, Bill Communications, Box 5417, Akron OH 44313. Managing Editor: Mike Mavrigian. 10% freelance written. "Readership is the automotive parts jobber who has entered the world of retailing to the automotive do-it-yourselfer and also wholesales to dealer trade. Editorial slant is business, merchandising/marketing-oriented with news secondary." Monthly tabloid; 56 pages. Circ. 31,000. Pays on publication. Buys all rights. Submit seasonal/holiday material 2-3 months in advance of issue date. Simultaneous, photocopied and previously published submissions in noncompetitive publications OK. SASE. Free sample copy and writer's guidelines; mention *Writer's Market* in request.
Nonfiction: How-to (merchandising do-it-yourself auto parts, store layout and design, transforming traditional jobber facilities to retail operations as well); interview (of jobber/retailers who have done an excellent job in retail merchandising or a particular item or product line); and technical (on do-it-yourself repairs). Buys 24 mss/year. Recent article examples: Seven Ways Employees Can Steal From You"; "Increasing Employee Productivity"; "Tooling up for Profits" (March 1982). Submit complete ms. Length: 500-1,500 words maximum. Pays $100-200.

JOBBER TOPICS, 7300 N. Cicero Ave., Lincolnwood IL 60646. (312)588-7300. Articles Editor: Jack Creighton. "A digest-sized magazine dedicated to helping its readers—auto parts jobbers and warehouse distributors—succeed in their business via better management and merchandising techniques; and a better knowledge of industry trends, activities and local or federal legislation that may influence their business activities." Monthly. Buys all rights. No byline given. Pays on acceptance. Query with outline. SASE.

Nonfiction and Photos: Most editorial material is staff-written. "Articles with unusual or outstanding automotive jobber procedures, with special emphasis on sales and merchandising; any phase of automotive parts and equipment distribution. Especially interested in merchandising practices and machine shop operations. Most independent businesses usually have a strong point or two. We like to see a writer zero in on that strong point(s) and submit an outline (or query), advising us of those points and what he intends to include in a feature. We will give him, or her, a prompt reply." Length: 2,000 words maximum. Pay based on quality and timeliness of feature. 5x7 b&w glossies or 4-color transparencies purchased with mss.

MILK AND LIQUID FOOD TRANSPORTER, Dairy Marketing Communications, N80 W12878 Fond du Lac Ave., Box 878, Menomonee Falls WI 53051. (414)255-0108. Editor: Karl F. Ohm III. Monthly magazine for owner/operators, trucking firms and management people involved in transporting bulk milk and other liquid food products in the US and Canada. Circ. 16,603. "We need more feature stories (with b&w photos and color cover shots) about owner/operators, especially in California, the Midwest, and the Northeast, who haul bulk milk from farms to dairy plants. We also need stories on liquid food hauling firms." Pays on acceptance. Byline given. Buys all rights. Submit seasonal material 3 months in advance. SASE. Computer printout submissions OK; prefers letter quality to dot matrix. No duplicate submissions. Reports in 2 weeks on queries; in 2-3 weeks on mss. Free sample copies and writer's guidelines.

Nonfiction: Expose (government regulation, state and federal); historical; interview; profile; how-to (maintenance); new product (staff written); and technical (truck maintenance). No personal opinion, humor, first-person nostalgia, travel or inspirational. "We do interpretative reporting and features on timely issues affecting the business of transporting milk and other liquid food products i.e., vegetable oils, corn sweeteners, liquid sugars and apple juice. We prefer articles that cover problems unique to haulers in a particular state. Articles about innovative milk and liquid food transporters stand a better chance of being accepted." Buys 8-10 mss/year. Query. "I like to know why the writer thinks his/her story is pertinent to my publication. I also would like to know why the writer chose a particular slant." Length: 1,500-2,500 words. Pays $200-400.

Photos: State availability of photos. Pays for b&w contact sheets and usable photos. Pays extra for color cover shot. Captions and model release required. Photo release forms are available upon request. Buys all rights.

Tips: "If freelancers take the time to study our magazine and develop a good story, they will find out that the *Milk and Liquid Food Transporter* is not a tough market to crack. If any freelancer produces a good feature (with photos) for the magazine, I will usually give him/her good contacts for generating additional, local stories or a story assignment."

MODERN TIRE DEALER, 77 N. Miller Rd., Box 5417, Akron OH 44313. (216)867-4401. Editor: Greg Smith. For independent tire dealers. Monthly tabloid, plus 2 special emphasis issue magazines; 50-page tabloid, 80-page special issues. Published 14 times annually. Buys all rights. Photocopied submissions OK. Query. Reports in 1 month. SASE. Free writer's guidelines.

Nonfiction, Photos, and Fillers: "How independent tire dealers sell tires, accessories and allied services, such as brakes, wheel alignment, shocks, mufflers. The emphasis is on merchandising and management. We prefer the writer to zero in on some specific area of interest; avoid shotgun approach." Length: 1,500 words. Pays $100-250. 8x10, 4x5, 5x7 b&w glossy prints purchased with mss.

MOTOR MAGAZINE, Hearst Corp., 555 W. 57th St., New York NY 10019. (212)262-8616. Editor: Kenneth Zino. Emphasizes auto repair. "Readers are professional auto repairmen or people who own auto repair facilities." Monthly magazine; 80-90 pages. Circ. 135,000. Pays on acceptance. Buys all rights. Pays a kill fee. Byline given. SASE. Reports in 1 month.

Nonfiction: How-to. "Writers should be able to relate their own hands-on experience to handling specific repair and technical articles." Buys 6 mss/issue. Recent article examples: "How to Fix Cadillac's V8-6-4 Engine"; "Servicing the Split-Diagonal Brake System of the Escort"; "How to Perform an Accurate Wheel Alignment"; "Diagnosing GM's THM 125 Transaxle"; "Chevy Valve Guide Restoration". Query. Length: 700-2,000 words. Pays $150-1,000.

Photos: "Photos and/or rough artwork must accompany how-to articles." State availability of photos. Uses 5x7 glossy prints. Offers no additional payment for photos accepted with ms. Captions and model releases required.

MOTOR SERVICE, Hunter Publishing Co., 950 Lee, Des Plaines IL 60016. Editor: Larry W. Carley. Monthly magazine for professional auto mechanics and the owners and service managers of repair shops, garages and fleets. Circ. 137,000. Computer printout submissions OK; prefers letter quality to dot matrix. Pays on acceptance. Buys all rights. Pays 100% kill fee. Byline given. Free sample copy.

Nonfiction: Technical how-to features in language a mechanic can enjoy and understand; management articles to help shop owners and service managers operate a better business; technical theory pieces on how something works; new technology roundups, etc. No "generic business pieces on management tips, increasing sales, employee motivation, etc." Recent articles include "Workman's Compensation Insurance; Is It a Ripoff?," "Understanding Synthetic Oils," "Diesel Diagnosis," "Servicing MacPherson Struts," "Meet GM's Self-diagnosing Computer Command Control System." Length: 1,500-2,500 words. Pays $150-300. Buys 60-70 mss/year. Query first. "Writers must know our market."

Photos: Photos and/or diagrams must accompany technical articles. Uses 5x7 b&w prints or 35mm transparencies. Offers no additional payment for photos accepted with ms. Captions and model releases required. Also buys color transparencies for cover use. Pays $50-200.

Tips: "We're always looking for new faces but finding someone who is technically knowledgeable in our field and who can also write is extremely difficult. Good tech writers are hard to find."

MUFFLER DIGEST, Box 1067SSS, Springfield MO 65805. (417)866-3917. Editor: James R. Wilder. For professional installers and manufacturers of exhaust systems and exhaust system components. Monthly magazine. Circ. 13,000. Pays on acceptance. Buys all rights. Byline given. Simultaneous and photocopied submissions OK. SASE. Reports in 1 week.

Nonfiction: How-to; humor (in the muffler field); informational; interview (good interviews with shop owners); profile (industry people); photo feature; and technical. "We're not interested in 'How I Got Ripped Off at . . .' types of features." Buys 1-5 mss/year. Query. Length: 100-1,000 words. Pays 5-10¢/word.

Photos: Gary Kennon, photo editor. Purchased with accompanying ms. Captions required. Query. Pays $5 for b&w photos.

Columns & Departments: How-To column (could be a shop-talk type of article). Query. Length: 500 words. Pays 5-10¢/word.

Tips: "We are covering the professional exhaust system installer in the US, Mexico and Canada. When we talk about professional we are talking about muffler specialty shops—Midas, Tuffy and other franchise chain operators as well as independents. We are not interested in service stations, Sears, Wards, etc. We would prefer to see more stories on successful independent installers; how did they get started, what special tricks have they picked up, what is their most successful merchandising tool, etc."

O AND A MARKETING NEWS, Box 765, LaCanada CA 91011. (213)790-6554. Editor: Don McAnally. For "service station dealers, garagemen, TBA (tires, batteries, accessories) people, oil company marketing management." Bimonthly. Circ. 15,000. Not copyrighted. Pays on publication. Reports in 1 week. SASE.

Nonfiction and Photos: "Straight news material; management, service, and merchandising applications; emphasis on news about or affecting markets and marketers *within the publication's geographic area of the 11 Western states*. No restrictions on style or slant. We could use straight news of our industry from some Western cities, notably Las Vegas, Phoenix, and Salt Lake City. Query with a letter that gives me a capsule treatment of what the story is about." Buys 25 mss/year. Length: maximum 1,000 words. Pays $1.25/column inch (about 2½¢ a word). Photos purchased with or without mss; captions required. No cartoons. Pays $5.

REFRIGERATED TRANSPORTER, Tunnell Publications, 1602 Harold St., Houston TX 77006. (713)523-8124. Editor: Gary Macklin. 5% freelance written. Monthly. Not copyrighted. Byline given "except articles which must be extensively rewritten by our staff." Pays on publication. Reports in 1 month. SASE.

Nonfiction and Photos: "Articles on fleet management and maintenance of vehicles, especially the refrigerated van and the refrigerating unit; shop tips; loading or handling systems, especially for frozen or refrigerated cargo; new equipment specifications; conversions of equipment for better handling or more efficient operations. Prefer articles with illustrations obtained from fleets operating refrigerated trucks or trailers." Pays variable rate.

Fillers: Buys newspaper clippings. "Do not rewrite."

‡**SERVICE STATION AND GARAGE MANAGEMENT**, Suite 101, 109 Vanderhoof Ave., Toronto, Ontario Canada M4G 2J2. Contact: Editor. For "service station operators and garagemen in Canada only." Monthly. Circ. 26,000. Buys first Canadian serial rights. Buys 1 or 2 articles a year. Pays on acceptance. Sample copy for 50¢. Query. Reports in 2 days. Enclose SAE and International Reply Coupons.

Nonfiction and Photos: "Articles on service station operators in Canada only; those who are doing top merchandising job. Also on specific phases of service station doings: brakes, tune-up, lubrication, etc. Solid business facts and figures; information must have human interest angles. Interested in controversial legislation, trade problems, sales and service promotions, technical data, personnel activities and changes. No general, long-winded material. The approach must be Canadian. The writer must know the trade and must provide facts and figures useful and helpful to readers. The style should be easy, simple, and friendly—not stilted." Length: 1,000 words. Payment negotiable. Photos purchased with mss and without mss "if different or novel"; captions required. Pays $5 for 5x7 or 8x10 b&w glossies.

SOUTHERN MOTOR CARGO, Box 4169, Memphis TN 38104. Editor: Mike Pennington. For "trucking management and maintenance personnel of private, contract, and for-hire carriers in 16 Southern states (Ala., Ark., Del., Fla., Ga., Ky., La., Md., Miss., N.C., Okla., S.C., Tenn., Tex., Va., and W. Va.) and the District of Columbia." Special issues include "ATA Convention," October; "Transportation Graduate Directory," January; "Mid-America Truck Show," February. Monthly. Circ. 53,000. Buys first rights within circulation area. Pays on publication (or on acceptance in certain cases). Free sample copy to sincere, interested contributors. SASE.

Nonfiction: "How a Southern trucker builds a better mousetrap. Factual newspaper style with punch in lead. Don't get flowery. No success stories. Pick one item, i.e. tire maintenance, billing procedure, etc., and show how such-and-such carrier has developed or modified it to better fit his organization. Bring in problems solved by the way he adapted this or that and what way he plans to better his present layout. Find a segment of the business that has been altered or modified due to economics or new information, such as 'due to information gathered by a new IBM process, it has been discovered that an XYZ transmission needs overhauling every 60,000 miles instead of every 35,000 miles, thereby resulting in savings of $$$ over the normal life of this transmission.' Or, 'by incorporating a new method of record keeping, claims on damaged freight have been expedited with a resultant savings in time and money.' Compare the old method with the new, itemize savings, and get quotes from personnel involved. Articles must be built around an outstanding phase of the operation and must be documented and approved by the firm's management prior to publication." Length: 1,000-3,000 words. Pays minimum 8¢ a word for "feature material."

Photos: Purchased with cutlines; glossy prints. Pays $10.

SPECIALTY & CUSTOM DEALER, Babcox Publications, 11 S. Forge St., Akron OH 44304. (216)535-6117. Publisher: Gary Gardner. Editor: Ed Kalail. "Audience is primarily jobbers and retailers of specialty automotive parts and accessories, warehouse distributors and manufacturers. Average reader has been in business for 10 years, and is store owner or manager. Educational background varies, with most readers in the high school graduate with some college category." Monthly magazine. Circ. 23,500. Pays on publication. Buys all rights. Submit seasonal or holiday material 4 months in advance. SASE. Reports in 6 weeks. Sample copy $3.

Nonfiction: Publishes informational (business techniques), interview, new product, profile, and technical articles. "No broad generalizations concerning a 'great product' without technical data behind the information. Lack of detail concerning business operations." Buys 3-5 unsolicited mss/year. Query. Length: 1,000-2,000 words. Pays $100-250.

Tips: "For the most part, an understanding of automotive products particularly in the high performance and specialty automotive market and business practices is essential. Features on a specific retailer, his merchandising techniques and unique business methods are most often used. Such a feature might include inventory control, display methods, lines carried, handling obsolete products, etc."

THE SUCCESSFUL DEALER, Kona-Cal, Inc., 707 Lake Cook Rd., Deerfield IL 60015. (312)498-3180. Editor: Denise L. Rondini. Managing Editor: R. Patricia Herron. Magazine published 6 times/year covering dealership management of medium and heavy duty trucks; construction equipment; forklift trucks; diesel engines; and truck trailers. Circ. 19,000. Pays on publication. Byline sometimes given. Buys first rights. Simultaneous queries, and simultaneous and photocopied submissions OK. SASE. Reports in 2 weeks.

Nonfiction: How-to (solve problems within the dealership); interview/profile (concentrating on business, not personality); new product (exceptional only); opinion (by readers—those in industry); personal experience (of readers); photo feature (of major events); and technical (vehicle componentry). Special issues include: March-April: American Truck Dealer Convention; September-October: Parts and Service. Query. Length: open. Pays $100-150/page.

Tips: "Phone first, then follow up with a detailed explanation of the proposed article. Allow two weeks for our response. Know dealers and dealerships, their problems and opportunities; heavy-equipment industry."

TOW-AGE, Kruzakaleidoscopix, Inc., Box 389, Franklin MA 02038. Editor: J. Kruza. For readers who run their own towing service business. Published every 6 weeks. Circ. 12,000. Buys all rights. Buys about 12 mss/year. Pays on acceptance. Sample copy $1; free writer's guidelines. Photocopied and simultaneous submissions OK. Reports in 1-4 weeks. SASE.

Nonfiction and Photos: Articles on business, legal and technical information for the towing industry. "Light reading material; short, with punch." Informational, how-to, personal experience, interview, profile. Query or submit complete ms. Length: 200-800 words. Pays $20-50. Spot news and successful business operations. Length: 100-500 words. Technical articles. Length: 100-1,000 words. Up to 8x10 b&w photos purchased with or without mss, or on assignment. Pays $15 for first photo; $5 for each additional photo in series. Captions required.

WARD'S AUTO WORLD, 28 W. Adams, Detroit MI 48226. (313)962-4433. Editor-in-Chief: David C. Smith. Managing Editor: Arthur M. Spinella. Senior Editor: Richard L. Waddell. Associate Editor: Daniel F. McCosh. Assistant Managing Editor: James W. Bush. 10% freelance written. For top and middle management in all phases of auto industry. Also adding heavy-duty vehicle coverage. Monthly magazine; 72 pages. Circ. 65,000. Pays on publication. Buys all rights. Pay varies for kill fee. Byline given. Phone queries OK. Submit

seasonal/holiday material 1 month in advance of issue date. Computer printout and disk submissions OK; prefers letter quality to dot matrix printouts. SASE. Reports in 2 weeks. Free sample copy and writer's guidelines.
Nonfiction: Expose; general interest; historical; humor; interview; new product; nostalgia; personal experience; photo feature; and technical. Few consumer-type articles. No "nostalgia or personal history type stories (like 'My Favorite Car')." Buys 4-8 mss/year. Query. Length: 700-5,000 words. Pay $100-600.
Photos: "We're heavy on graphics." Submit photo material with query. Pay varies for 8x10 b&w prints or color transparencies. Captions required. Buys one-time rights.
Tips: "Don't send poetry, how-to and 'My Favorite Car' stuff. It doesn't stand a chance. This is a business newsmagazine and operates on a news basis just like any other newsmagazine."

WAREHOUSE DISTRIBUTOR NEWS, 11 S. Forge St., Akron OH 44304. Editor: John B. Stoner. 10% freelance written. For warehouse distributors and redistributing jobbers of automotive parts and accessories, tools and equipment and supplies (all upper management personnel). Magazine; 60 pages. Monthly. Circ. 12,000. Rights purchased vary with author and material. May buy exclusive rights in field. Byline given. Buys about 12 mss/year. Pays on publication. Sample copy $2.50. Photocopied and simultaneous submissions OK. Reports at once. SASE.
Nonfiction and Photos: Automotive aftermarket distribution management articles and those on general management, success stories, etc., of interest to the industry. Articles on manufacturers and their distributors. Must be aftermarket-oriented. Each issue centers around a theme, such as rebuilt parts issue, import issue, materials handling issue, etc. Schedule changes yearly based on developments in the industry. Does not want to see freelance material on materials handling, or product information. Would be interested in merchandising articles; those on EDP startup, and interviews with prominent industry figures. Query. Length: open. Pays 5-9¢/word. B&w (5x7) photos purchased with or without ms. Captions required.

WISCONSIN MOTOR CARRIER, Wisconsin Motor Carriers Association, 125 West Doty St., Madison WI 53703. (608)255-6789. Director, Public Relations: Janice H. Thieme. Assistant Editor: Linda Scheel. Quarterly magazine covering trucking and related information. "Our readers are from the regulated for-hire and private trucking community, governmental agencies, and safety personnel." Circ. 5,000. Pays on publication. Byline given. Buys one-time rights. Submit seasonal/holiday material 3 months in advance. Simultaneous queries, and photocopied and previously published submissions ("with copyright clearance only") OK. Computer printout submissions OK. SASE. Reports in 6 weeks. Free sample copy.
Nonfiction: Book excerpts; historical/nostalgic; how-to (on engine care, driving tips, cargo control); humor; new product (alternative fuels, safety equipment); technical (tires, road building/surface testing; transportation planning; engines; future truck prototypes; fuel economy; hazardous shipments management); and fuel, safety, small communities, hazardous materials/wastes. "All must be truck or trucking/safety regulations related. We are especially interested in technical articles relating to transportation and in exploring the potential for quarterly columns on workers' compensation/insurance, safety, and equipment specifications." Special issues include safety/fuel economy. No opinions or general interest. No poems or shorts. Query. Length: 750-2,000 words. Pays $25-200.
Photos: Pays $10-25 for 5x7 b&w prints. Captions required.
Columns/Departments: Cab-over Commentary—driver's viewpoint. Buys 4 mss/year. "We're interested in establishing several columns: Maintenance, Labor Issues, Wisconsin commentary." Query. Length: 200-750 words. Pays $20-75.
Fiction: Humorous—about trucking. Query. Length: 750-1,500 words. Pays $75-150.
Tips: "Perhaps because trucking/truckers are seen as 'outlaws,' we receive a great deal of off-color humor and asphalt cowboy stories. We are a trade journal and publish only material reflecting the professional nature of our industry."

Aviation and Space

In this category are journals for aviation business executives, airport operators and aviation technicians. Publications for professional and private pilots are classified with the Aviation magazines in the Consumer Publications section.

AG-PILOT INTERNATIONAL MAGAZINE, Bio-Aeronautic Publishers, Inc. 10 N.E. Sixth, Milton-Freewater OR 97862. (503)938-5502. Editor: Tom J. Wood. Executive Editor: Rocky Kemp. Emphasizes agricultural aerial application (crop dusting). "This is intended to be a fun-to-read, technical, as well as humorous and serious publication for the Ag pilot and operator. They are our primary target." Monthly magazine; 48 pages. Circ. 10,200. Pays on publication. Buys all rights. Byline given unless writer requested holding name. Phone queries OK. Simultaneous, photocopied, and previously published (if not very recent) submissions OK. SASE. Reports in 2 weeks. Sample copy $2.

Nonfiction: Expose (of EPA, OSHA, FAA or any government function concerned with this industry); general interest; historical; interview (of well-known ag/aviation person); nostalgia; personal opinion; new product; personal experience; and photo feature. "If we receive an article, in any area we have solicited, it is quite possible this person could contribute intermittently. The international input is what we desire. Industry-related material is a must. No newspaper clippings." Send complete ms. Length: 300-1,500 words. Pays $20-100.

Photos: "We would like one b&w 5x7 (or smaller) with the manuscript, if applicable—it will help the chance of utilization." Four color. Offers no additional payment for photos accepted with ms. Captions preferred, model release required.

Columns/Departments: International (of prime interest, as they need to cultivate this area—aviation/crop dusting-related); Embryo Birdman (should be written, or appear to be written, by a first-year spray pilot); The Chopper Hopper (by anyone in the helicopter industry); Trouble Shooter (ag aircraft maintenance tips); Bio-Graphical Interview Type (of well-known person in aviation related position); and Catchin' The Corner (written by a person obviously skilled in the crop dusting field of experience or other interest-capturing material related to the industry). Send complete ms. Length: 700-1,500 words. Pays $20-100.

Poetry: Interested in all Agri-Aviation related poetry. Buys 1/issue. Submit no more than 5 at one time. Length: one 10 inch x 24 picas maximum. Pays $5-25.

Fillers: Short jokes, short humor and industry-related newsbreaks. Length: 10-100 words. Pays $5-20.

Tips: "Writers should be witty, and knowledgeable about the crop dusting aviation world. Material *must* be agricultural/aviation-oriented. Crop dusting, or nothing! We plan a Spanish language edition to all Spanish-speaking countries."

AIRPORT PRESS, J.A.J. Publishing Co., 161-15 Rockaway Blvd., Jamaica NY 11434. (212)528-8600. News Editor: Gary Stoller. Monthly business tabloid presenting US airports' viewpoint of the airline industry for airline management, employees, unions, the air freight industry, airline-related businesses, travel agents and government officials. Circ. 22,000. Pays on publication. Byline given. Offers 100% kill fee. Not copyrighted. Buys first rights. Submit seasonal/holiday material 3 months in advance. SASE. Reports in 3 weeks on queries; 1 week on mss. Sample copy $1.

Nonfiction: Expose, general interest, interview/profile, financial opinion, technical, travel, hard news. "Articles most desired: business and government issues affecting the airlines and the industry on a national basis; new airline industry developments; industry trends." Query with clips of published work or send complete ms. Length: 500-1,000 words. Pays $100-150.

Columns/Departments: General news, business, air cargo, airline sports, restaurant review, commuter airlines, labor, government, marketing, finance, US and NY airports. Query with clips of published work or send complete ms. Length: 500-1,000 words. Pays $100-150.

AIRPORT SERVICES MANAGEMENT, Lakewood Publications, 731 Hennepin Ave., Minneapolis MN 55403. (612)333-0471. Editor: Sher Jasperse. Emphasizes management of airports, airlines and airport business. Monthly magazine. Circ. 20,000. Pays on acceptance. Buys all rights. Byline given. Phone queries OK. Submit seasonal/holiday material 3 months in advance. Photocopied submissions OK, but must be industry-exclusive. Computer printout submissions OK; prefers letter quality to dot matrix. SASE. Reports in 4 weeks. Free sample copy and writer's guidelines.

Nonfiction: How-to (how to manage an airport aviation business, service organization or airline, work with local governments, etc.); interview (with a successful operator); and technical (how to manage a maintenance shop, snow removal operations, bird control, security operations). "No flying, no airport nostalgia, or product puff pieces. We don't want pieces on how one company's product solved everyone's problem. (How one airport or aviation business solved its problem with a certain type of product is okay.) No descriptions of airport construction projects (down to the square footage in the new restrooms) that don't discuss applications for other airports. All articles that begin with anything like, 'She's cute, petite and dresses like a lady, but by golly she runs the Shangrila Airport with a firm hand' are burned on the spot. Just plain 'how-to' story lines, please." Buys 40-50 mss/year, "but at least half are short (250-550 words) items for inclusion in one of our monthly departments." Query. Length: 250-2,500 words. Pays $100/published page.

Photos: State availability of photos with query. Payment for photos is included in total purchase price. Uses b&w photos.

Tips: "We're using more shorter feature articles (average 2,000 words) because I find that the longer, in-depth, issue-oriented articles are better when they are staff researched and written. No 'gee-whiz' approaches. Writing style should be lively, informal and straightforward."

‡**AVIATION EQUIPMENT MAINTENANCE**, The Irving-Cloud Publishing Co., 7300 N. Cicero Ave., Lincolnwood IL 60646. (312)588-7300. Editor: Paul Berner. Bimonthly magazine covering aircraft maintenance for mechanics and their managers. Estab. 1982. Circ. 22,000. Pays on acceptance. Byline given. Buys

all rights. Submit seasonal/holiday material 1½ months in advance. Simultaneous queries and simultaneous submissions OK. SASE. Reports in 2 weeks. Sample copy for 9x12 SAE.

Nonfiction: How-to, photo feature, technical. Uses technical, hands-on maintenance and management articles. Buys 15-20 mss/year. Send complete ms. Length: 2,000-4,000 words. Pays $200-400.

Photos: State availability of photos or send photos with ms. Payment for photos is included in payment for ms. Reviews 2¼ color transparencies and 8x10 color prints. Captions required. Buys one-time rights.

Columns/Departments: Products, Literature. Buys few mss/year. Query.

INTERLINE REPORTER, 2 W. 46th St., New York NY 10036. (212)575-9000. Editor/Publisher: Eric Friedheim. Managing Editor: Ed Sullivan. An inspirational and interesting magazine for airline employees. Buys first serial rights. Query. SASE.

Nonfiction and Photos: Wants nontechnical articles on airline activities; stories should be slanted to the sales, reservations and counter personnel. Articles on offbeat airlines and, most of all, on airline employees—those who lead an adventurous life, have a unique hobby, or have acted above and beyond the call of duty. Personality stories showing how a job has been well done are particularly welcome. Length: up to 1,200 words. Pays $50-75 for articles with photographic illustrations.

INTERNATIONAL AVIATION MECHANICS JOURNAL, 211 S. 4th St., Basin WY 82410. (307)568-2413. Editor: James Kost. For governmentally licensed airframe and powerplant mechanics involved in maintaining general aviation airplanes, and students. Monthly magazine; 72 pages. Circ. 12,319. Buys all rights. Pays within 30 days of publication. Free sample copy. Photocopied submissions OK. Reports in 30 days. SASE.

Nonfiction and Photos: Technical articles on aircraft maintenance procedures and articles helping the mechanics to be more efficient and productive. All material should be written from the point of view of an aircraft mechanic, helping him solve common field problems. Buys 30-40 mss/year. Query or submit complete ms. Informational (length: 500-2,000 words; pays $25-100); how-to (length: 100-500 words; pays $25); photo articles (length: 50-100 words; pays $20); and Technical (length: 500-4,000 words; pays $25-250).

JET CARGO NEWS, The Management Journal for Air Marketing, 5314 Bingle Rd., Houston TX 77092. (713)688-8811. Editor: Art Eddy. Designed to serve international industry concerned with moving goods by air. "It brings to shippers and manufacturers spot news of airline and aircraft development, air routes, CAB ruling, shipping techniques, innovations and rates." Monthly. Circ. 23,500. Buys all rights. Buys up to 50 mss/year. Pays on publication. Will send a sample copy and writer's guidelines on request. Will not consider photocopied or simultaneous submissions. Submit seasonal material 1 month in advance of issue date. Reports in 1 month, if postage is included. Submit complete ms. SASE.

Nonfiction: "Direct efforts to the shipper. Tell him about airline service, freight forwarder operations, innovations within the industry, new products, aircraft, and pertinent news to the industry. General news and features accepted. Use a tight magazine style. The writer must know marketing." Buys informational articles, how-to's, interviews, and coverage of successful business operations. Length: 1,500 words maximum. Pays $4/inch. 8x10 b&w glossy prints purchased with and without mss; captions required. Pays $10.

‡ROTOR & WING INTERNATIONAL, PJS Publications Inc., Box 1790, Peoria IL 61656. (309)682-6626. Editor: Don Toler. Managing Editor: David Jensen. Monthly magazine covering the international helicopter industry. "Prime audience: helicopter owners and operators; secondary audience: manufacturers. Covers all phases of the helicopter industry with special interest in Gulf of Mexico offshore operations and corporate/business use of rotorcraft." Circ. 34,000 (approximately). Pays on acceptance. Byline given. Buys all rights. Computer printout submissions OK; prefers letter quality to dot matrix. Reports in 2 weeks. Free sample copy and writer's guidelines.

Nonfiction: Interview/profile (key figures of importance to rotorcraft); technical (rotorcraft piloting and operations). No articles "pertaining to homebuilt rotorcraft, run-of-the mill rescues . . ." Buys 60 mss/year ("however, 98% come from regular freelance staff"). Query with clips. L ength: 1,500-2,000 words. Pays $250-550.

Photos: State availability of photos. "Photos are considered part of ms and not purchased separately." Reviews b&w prints. Identification of subjects required.

Tips: "Convince the editors you have a understanding of the civil helicopter industry and have experience with technical/business writing." General features and some news stringing are most open to freelancers.

Beverages and Bottling

The following journals are for manufacturers, distributors and retailers of soft drinks and alcoholic beverages. Publications for bar and tavern operators and managers of restaurants are classified in the Hotels, Motels, Clubs, Resorts and Restaurants category.

BEER WHOLESALER, Dogan Enterprises, Inc., 75 SE 4th Ave., Delray Beach FL 33444. (305)272-1223. Editor: Kenneth Breslauer. Bimonthly magazine about the beer industry for beer wholesalers, importers and brewers. Circ. 5,000. Pays on publication. Byline given. Buys all rights. Reports in 3 weeks on queries; in 2 months on mss. Sample copy $5.
Nonfiction: General interest, interview, profile, how-to and technical. "Submit articles that are business-oriented and presented in an organized manner. Dig for the unusual; what makes this beer wholesaler different? What new ideas can be used? No consumer-oriented articles such as stories on beer can collecting." Buys 3 mss/issue. Query. Length: 1,200-5,000 words. Pays $70-150.
Photos: Send photos with ms. Offers no additional payment for photos accepted with ms. Captions required. Buys all rights.

LIQUOR STORE MAGAZINE, Jobson Publishing Corp., 352 Park Ave. S., New York NY 10010. (212)685-4848. Editor: Tina Veiders. Magazine published 9 times/year about liquor retailing for retailers in the business. Circ. 50,000. Average issue includes 6 departments and 4 articles. Pays on acceptance. Buys first North American serial rights. Phone queries OK. Submit seasonal material 4 months in advance. Computer printout submissions OK. SASE. Reports in 1 week on queries; in 1 month on mss.
Nonfiction: "Articles focus on case history studies of stores, and features on merchandising, promotion, advertising, security, selling, equipment, etc. No general articles or material that do not relate to retailer's needs or contribute to his knowledge of alcoholic beverage industry." Buys 6-10 mss/year. Send complete ms. Length: 1,000-2,000 words. Pays $150-200.
Photos: Send photos with ms. Reviews 5x7 b&w glossy prints. Offers no additional payment for photos accepted with ms. Captions preferred, model release required. Buys all rights.
Tips: "We are evaluating our regular contributors, and may be more open to freelancers in future. Also, looking at budget in this area."

MID-CONTINENT BOTTLER, 10741 El Monte, Overland Park KS 66207. (913)341-0020. Publisher: Floyd E. Sageser. 3% freelance written. For "soft drink bottlers in the 20-state Midwestern area." Bimonthly. Not copyrighted. Pays on acceptance. Free sample copy. Reports "immediately." No computer printout or disk submissions. SASE.
Nonfiction and Photos: "Items of specific soft drink bottler interest with special emphasis on sales and merchandising techniques. Feature style desired." Buys 2-3 mss/year. Length: 2,000 words. Pays $15-$100. Photos purchased with mss.

MODERN BREWERY AGE, Box 5550, East Norwalk CT 06856. Editorial Director: Howard Kelly. For "brewery and beer distribution executives on the technical, administrative, and marketing levels." Buys North American serial rights. Pays on publication. Reports "at once." SASE.
Nonfiction and Photos: "Technical and business articles of interest to brewers and beer distributors." Query. Length: 5-8 double-spaced typewritten pages. Pays $50/printed page (about 3 to 3½ pages double-spaced typewritten ms)." Pays $15/published photo. Captions required.

PATTERSON'S CALIFORNIA BEVERAGE JOURNAL, Wolfer Printing Co., 422 Wall St., Los Angeles CA 90013. (213)627-4996. Editor/Associate Publisher: Harry Bradley. Monthly magazine. "We are the 'bible' to all liquor licensees in the southern California market: liquor stores, restaurants, cocktail lounges, hotels and chains. We provide in-depth coverage of industry ad campaigns, merchandising programs, new products, legislative changes, and feature articles designed to increase the subscriber profits." Circ. 17,500. Pays on acceptance. Byline given. Buys first rights. Submit seasonal/holiday material 6 months in advance. SASE. Reports in 2 weeks on queries; 1 month on mss. Sample copy $4.
Nonfiction: Book excerpts (on dealing with wine, beer or distilled spirits); historical/nostalgic (of different generic liquors); how-to (profit-making ideas); interview/profile (of important industry members); new product (alcoholic beverages); photo feature (on producing regions such as the wine country). "We're looking for regional material and pieces on profile-making and getting to know the products on the market." Query with clips of published work or send complete ms. Length: 1,200-4,000 words. Pays $50-300.
Photos: State availability of photos. Pays $25 maximum for 5x7 b&w prints. Captions, model release, and identification of subjects required. Buys one-time rights.

WINES & VINES, 1800 Lincoln Ave., San Rafael CA 94901. Editor: Philip Hiaring. For everyone concerned with the grape and wine industry including winemakers, wine merchants, growers, suppliers, consumers, etc. Monthly magazine. Circ. 6,000. Buy first North American serial rights or simultaneous rights. Pays on acceptance. Free sample copy. Submit special material (brandy, January; vineyard, February; Man-of-the-Year, March; water, April; export-import, May; enological, June; statistical, July; marketing, September; equipment and supplies, November; champagne, December) 3 months in advance. Reports in 2 weeks. SASE.
Nonfiction and Photos: Articles of interest to the trade. "These could be on grape growing in unusual areas; new winemaking techniques; wine marketing, retailing, etc." Interview, historical, spot news, merchandising techniques and technical. No stories with a strong consumer orientation as against trade orientation. Author should know the subject matter, i.e., know proper grape growing/winemaking terminology. Buys 3-4 ms/year. Recent article example: "How the French Promote Wine" (February 1982). Query. Length: 1,000-2,500 words. Pays $25-50. Pays $15 for 4x5 or 8x10 b&w photos purchased with mss. Captions required.

Book and Bookstore Trade

AB BOOKMAN'S WEEKLY, Box AB, Clifton NJ 07015. (201)772-0020. Editor-in-Chief: Jacob L. Chernofsky. For professional and specialist booksellers, acquisitions and academic librarians, book publishers, book collectors, bibliographers, historians, etc. Weekly magazine; 200 pages. Circ. 8,500. Pays on publication. Buys all rights. Byline given. Phone queries OK. Submit seasonal or holiday material 2-3 months in advance. Simultaneous and photocopied submissions OK. SASE. Reports in 1 month. Sample copy $5.
Nonfiction: How-to (for professional booksellers); historical (related to books or book trade or printing or publishing). Personal experiences, nostalgia, interviews, profiles. Query. Length: 2,500 words minimum. Pays $60 minimum.
Photos: Photos used with mss.

AMERICAN BOOKSELLER, Booksellers Publishing, Inc., 122 E. 42nd St., New York NY 10168. (212)867-9060. Editor: Ginger Curwen. This publication emphasizes the business of retail bookselling and goes to the 5,700 members of the American Booksellers Association and to more than 2,400 other readers nationwide, most of whom are involved in publishing. Monthly magazine; 48 pages. Circ. 8,700. Pays on publication. Buys all rights. Pays 25% kill fee. Byline given "except on small news stories." Submit seasonal/holiday material 3 months in advance. Computer printout submissions OK. SASE. Reports in 2 months. Sample copy $3.
Nonfiction: General interest (on bookselling); how-to (run a bookstore, work with publishers); interview (on authors and booksellers); photo feature (on book-related events); and solutions to the problems of small businesses. Recent article example: "The Book Merchant: Expert in Technical Books (April 1982). Buys 2 mss/issue. Query with clips of published work and background knowledge of bookselling. Length: 750-2,000 words. Pays $50-200.
Photos: State availability of photos. Uses b&w 5x7 matte prints and contact sheets. Pays $10-20. Uses 35mm color transparencies. Pays $10-50. Captions and model releases required.
Tips: "While we buy a number of articles for each issue, very few come from freelance writers. Since the focus of the magazine is on the business of bookselling, most of our contributors are booksellers who share their *firsthand* experience with our readers. 85% of these articles are assigned; the rest are unsolicited—but those come mainly from booksellers as well."

CHRISTIAN BOOKSELLER & LIBRARIAN, 396 E. St. Charles Rd., Wheaton IL 60188. (312)653-4200. Editor: Karen M. Ball. Emphasizes "all aspects of Christian bookselling and religious library management." Monthly magazine; 68 pages. Circ. 10,000. Pays on publication. Buys first rights. Phone queries OK. Submit seasonal/holiday material 6 months in advance of issue date. Computer printout and disk submissions OK; prefers letter quality to dot matrix printouts. SASE. Reports in 4-6 weeks. Writer's guidelines available.
Nonfiction: "*Christian Bookseller & Librarian* is a trade magazine serving religious bookstores and religious libraries. Needs articles on bookstore and library management, marketing, merchandising, personnel, finance, ministry, advertising, profiles of successful and unique bookstores and libraries, in-depth interviews with authors and publishers, interviews with musicians." Buys 36-48 mss/year. No fiction. Query. Length: 1,000-2,500 words. Pays $25-100.
Photos: "Photos are to accompany all articles." State availability of photos with query. Reviews 5x7 b&w glossy prints and contact sheets. Offers no additional payment for photos accompanying ms. Uses 2-3 b&w photos/story. Captions preferred. Buys all rights.

Fillers: Short, filler-type articles dealing with the publishing, bookseller or librarian fields.
Tips: "In queries get to the point; cut the hype; state credentials factually—tell me what you're going to write. All mss must be substantial in content, authoritatively written, and well documented where called for. Writers must exhibit knowledge and understanding of the religious retailing business and industry."

COLLEGE STORE EXECUTIVE, Box 1500, Westbury NY 11590. (516)334-3030. Editor: Marcy Kornreich. Emphasizes merchandising and marketing in the college store market. Publishes 10 issues/year tabloid; 40 pages. Circ. 8,500. Pays on publication. Buys all rights. Byline given. Submit seasonal/holiday material 2-3 months in advance of issue date. Photocopied submissions OK. No computer printout or disk submissions. SASE. Reports in 3 weeks. Must include SASE for writer's guidelines. For sample copy, use large manilla envelope only.
Nonfiction: Expose (problems in college market); general interest (to managers); how-to (advertise, manage a college store); store profile of new or remodeled location; personal experience (someone who worked for a publisher selling to bookstores); personal opinion (from those who know about the market); photo feature (on specific college bookstores in the country or outside); and technical (how to display products). No articles on the typical college student or general "how-to" articles. Recent article example: Orinda Books and JFK: A Smooth Transition (April 1983) "Spotlights an unusual bookstore operation, has good quotes and contains several useable merchandising ideas and concepts." Buys 8-10 mss/year. Query. Length: 1,000 words. Pays $2/column inch.
Photos: State availability of photos with query. Pays $5 for b&w prints. Captions preferred. Buys all rights.
Tips: "No general business advice that could apply to all retail establishments—articles must deal directly with college stores. This is a good place for someone to start—but they have to understand the market." No interviews with managers on their theories of life or public relations pieces on specific products.

‡**FINE PRINT, A Review for the Arts of the Book**, Fine Print Publishing Co., Box 3394, San Francisco CA 94119. (415)776-1530. Editor: Sandra D. Kirshenbaum. Quarterly magazine covering the arts of the book plus history of books and publishing, including printing, typography, type design, graphic design, calligraphy, bookbinding and papermaking. "We seek to cover contemporary fine book making and all related arts for printers, librarians, graphic artists, book collectors, publishers, booksellers, bookbinders, typographers, etc." Circ. 2,000. Pays on publication. Byline given. Buys first North American serial rights and "rights to publish in collections." Submit seasonal/holiday material 9 months in advance. Simultaneous queries, and simultaneous and photocopied submissions OK. SASE. Reports in 3 months on queries; 6 months on mss. Sample copy $7.50; free writer's guidelines.
Nonfiction: Interview/profile (of contemporary book artists and printers); new product (relating to printing, bookbinding, etc.); personal experience ("Book Arts Reporter" covering book events, conferences, workshops, lectures, etc.); technical (related to books, printing, typography, etc.); exhibit reviews of book-related exhibits in libraries, museums, galleries. Buys 4-5 mss/year. Query. Length: 2,000-4,000 for lead articles. Pays $150 for lead articles only; pays in copies for other articles.
Photos: State availability of photos with ms. Identification of subjects required. Buys one-time rights.
Columns/Departments: On Type (essays on typography and type design, contemporary and historical); Book Arts Profile; The Featured Book Binding; Exhibit Reviews; Recent Press Books (reviews of fine limited edition books). Query. Length: 500-1,300 words. No payment "except review copies of fine books."
Fillers: Newsbreaks. "Shoulder Notes"—"In Brief" (short notices and descriptions of events, personalities, and publications dictating to book arts).
Tips: "I need someone to conduct a regular column reviewing the best books of trade and university publishing, reviewed from the point of view of graphic arts quality and quality of production."

‡**NEW PAGES: News & Reviews of the Progressive Book Trade**, New Pages Press, 4426 S. Belsay Rd., Grand Blanc MI 48439. (313)742-9583. Editors: Grant Burns and Casey Hill. Quarterly tabloid covering independent publishing, libraries and bookstores. Pays on publication. Byline given. Buys first North American serial rights. SASE. Reports in 1 month. Sample copy $3.
Nonfiction: Interview, opinion, book reviews. "We cover the alternative press with articles, news, reviews, listings, and useful information for publishers, librarians and booksellers." Query with published clips. Length: (for book reviews) 25-250 words. Pays $5.

PUBLISHERS WEEKLY, 1180 Avenue of the Americas, New York NY 10036. (212)764-5153. Editor-in-Chief: John F. Baker. Weekly. Buys first North American rights only. Pays on publication. Reports "in several weeks." Computer printout submissions OK; prefers letter quality to dot matrix. SASE.
Nonfiction and Photos: "We rarely use unsolicited mss because of our highly specialized audience and their professional interests, but we can sometimes use news items about publishers, publishing projects, bookstores and other subjects relating to books. We will be paying increasing attention to electronic publishing." No pieces about writers or word processors. Payment negotiable; generally $150/printed page. Photos purchased with and without mss "occasionally."

Brick, Glass, and Ceramics

AMERICAN GLASS REVIEW, Box 2147, Clifton NJ 07015. (201)779-1600. Editor-in-Chief: Donald Doctorow. 10% freelance written. Monthly magazine; 24 pages. Pays on publication. Byline given. Phone queries OK. Buys all rights. Submit seasonal/holiday material 2 months in advance of issue date. SASE. Reports in 2-3 weeks. Free sample copy and writer's guidelines; mention *Writer's Market* in request.

Nonfiction: Glass plant and glass manufacturing articles. Buys 3-4 mss/year. Query. Length: 1,500-3,000 words. Pays $40-50.

Photos: State availability of photos with query. No additional payment for b&w contact sheets. Captions preferred. Buys all rights.

BRICK AND CLAY RECORD, Cahners Plaza, 1350 E. Touhy Ave., Box 5080, Des Plaines IL 60018. (312)635-8800. Editor-in-Chief: Wayne A. Endicott. For "the heavy clay products industry." Monthly. Buys all rights. Pays on publication. Query first. Reports in 15 days. SASE.

Nonfiction and Photos: "News concerning personnel changes within companies; news concerning new plants for manufacture of brick, clay pipe, refractories, drain tile, face brick, glazed tile, lightweight clay aggregate products and abrasives; news of new products, expansion, new building." Length: 1,500-2,000 words. Pays minimum $75/published page. No additional payment for photos used with mss.

Fillers: "Items should concern only news of brick, clay pipe, refractory, or abrasives plant operations. If news of personnel, should be only of top-level plant personnel. Not interested in items such as patio, motel, or home construction using brick; consumer oriented items; weddings or engagements of clay products people, unless major executives; obituaries, unless of major personnel; items concerning floor or wall tile (only structural tile); of plastics, metal, concrete, bakelite, or similar products; items concerning people not directly involved in clay plant operation." Pays minimum $6 for "full-length published news item, depending on value of item and editor's discretion. Payment is only for items published in the magazine. No items sent in can be returned."

CERAMIC INDUSTRY, Cahners Plaza, 1350 E. Touhy Ave., Box 5080, Des Plaines IL 60018. (312)635-8800. Editor-in-Chief: Wayne A. Endicott. For the ceramic industry; manufacturers of glass, porcelain enamel, whiteware and electronic/industrial and newer ceramics. Magazine; 50-60 pages. Monthly. Circ. 7,500. Buys all rights. Byline given. Buys 10-12 mss/year (on assignment only). Pays on publication. Will send free sample copy to writer on request. Reports immediately. Query first. SASE.

Nonfiction and Photos: Semitechnical, informational and how-to material purchased on assignment only. Length: 500-1,500 words. Pays $75/published page. No additional payment for photos used with mss. Captions required.

CERAMIC SCOPE, Box 48497, Los Angeles CA 90048. (213)935-1122. Editor: Mel Fiske. Associate Editor: Nancy J. Lee. Monthly magazine covering hobby ceramics business. For "ceramic studio owners and teachers, operating out of homes as well as storefronts, who have a love for ceramics, but meager business education." Also read by distributors, dealers, and supervisors of ceramic programs in institutions. Circ. 8,000. Pays on acceptance. Buys all rights. Pays $100-200. Byline given unless it is a round-up story with any number of sources. Phone queries OK. Submit seasonal/holiday material 5 months in advance. Computer printout and disk submissions OK. SASE. Reports in 2 weeks. Sample copy $1.

Nonfiction: "Articles on operating a small business specifically tailored to the ceramic hobby field; photo feature stories with in-depth information about business practices and methods that contribute to successful studio operation. We don't need articles dealing primarily with biographical material or how owner started in business."

Photos: State availability of photos or send photos with ms. Pays $5/4x5 or 5x7 glossy b&w print; $25-50/color contact sheets. Captions required.

GLASS DIGEST, 310 Madison Ave., New York NY 10017. (212)682-7681. Editor: Oscar S. Glasberg. Monthly. Buys first rights. Byline given "only industry people—not freelancers." Pays on publication "or before, if ms held too long." Will send a sample copy to a writer on request. Reports "as soon as possible." Enclose SASE for return of submissions.

Nonfiction and Photos: "Items about firms in glass distribution, personnel, plants, etc. Stories about outstanding jobs accomplished—volume of flat glass, storefronts, curtainwalls, auto glass, mirrors, windows (metal), glass doors; special uses and values; who installed it. Stories about successful glass/metal distributors, dealers, and glazing contractors—their methods, promotion work done, advertising, results." Length: 1,000-1,500 words. Pays 7¢/word, "usually more. No interest in bottles, glassware, containers, etc., but leaded and stained glass good." B&w photos purchased with mss; "8x10 preferred." Pays $7.50, "usually more."

Tips: "Find a typical dealer case history about a firm operating in such a successful way that its methods can be duplicated by readers everywhere."

NATIONAL GLASS BUDGET, LJV Corp., Box 7138, Pittsburgh PA 15213. (412)682-5136. Managing Editor: Liz Scott. Semimonthly magazine covering glass manufacturing, and glass industry news for glass manufacturers, dealers and people involved in the making, buying and selling of glass items and products. Circ. 1,650. Pays on publication. Makes work-for-hire assignments. Phone queries OK. Submit seasonal material 3 months in advance. Simultaneous and photocopied submissions OK. SASE. Reports in 1 month on queries; in 2 months on mss. Free sample copy for 9x12 SAE and 20¢ postage.

Nonfiction: Historical (about glass manufacturers, trademarks and processes); how-to (concerning techniques of glass manufacturers); interview (with glass-related people); profile; new product (glass use or glass); and technical (glass manufacture or use). Special needs include a 100th Anniversary Edition coming in 1984. No glass dealer stories, and rarely glass crafting stories. Buys 5-10 mss/year. Query. Length: 500-10,000 words. Pays $50 minimum.

Photos: State availability of photos. Pays $25 minimum for 8x10 b&w glossy prints. Offers no additional payment for photos accepted with ms. Captions preferred; model release required. Buys one-time rights.

Fillers: Anecdotes, short humor, newsbreaks and puzzles. Buys 5 mss/year. Pays $15 minimum.

Tips: "Get to know a lot about glass, how it is made and new developments."

Building Interiors

LIGHTING DIMENSIONS MAGAZINE, Suite 8, 1590 S. Coast Hwy., Laguna Beach CA 92651. (714)499-2233. Managing Editor: Barbara Hall. Magazine published seven times/year featuring entertainment lighting (for theaters, films, TV, disco, touring and laser shows) for lighting designers in all areas of entertainment, production managers, technical directors, technicians, instructors, laser specialists, holographers and manufacturers and suppliers. Circ. 10,000. Byline given. Buys first North American serial rights. Phone queries OK. Submit seasonal material 2 months in advance. Simultaneous, photocopied and previously published submissions OK. SASE. Reports in 2 weeks. Free sample copy and writer's guidelines.

Nonfiction: Interview (with well-known lighting designers); profile; how-to; photo feature; and technical. "Articles may be technical, describing new equipment or techniques. They can also be on lighting in a specific play, opera, dance production, film, TV show or nightclub installation. We also like interviews with designers and cinematographers." Buys 3 mss/issue. Send complete ms. Pays $25-150.

Photos: State availability of photos or send photos with ms. Reviews b&w glossy prints and 8x10 color glossy prints. Offers no additional payment for photos accepted with ms. Model release required. Buys one-time rights.

Tips: "It would be tremendously helpful if the writer had some theater background, knowledge of film production, etc."

MODERN FLOOR COVERINGS, Charleson Publishing Co., 124 E. 40th St., New York NY 10016. (212)682-0500. Editor: Michael Karol. Monthly tabloid featuring floor coverings, for the retail community. Circ. 30,000. Pays on acceptance. Byline given. Makes work-for-hire assignments. Submit seasonal material 6 months in advance. SASE. Reports in 2 weeks.

Nonfiction: Interview. Send complete ms. Length: 1,000-10,000 words. Pays $50-250.

PAINTING AND WALLCOVERING CONTRACTOR, (formerly *Professional Decorating & Coating Action*), Painting and Decorating Contractors of America, 7223 Lee Hwy., Falls Church VA 22046. (703)534-1201. Editor: Thomas Baker. Emphasizes the application, maintenance, restoration and removal of paint, wallcoverings, special coatings and sealants for professional painting and decorating contractors. Monthly magazine. Circ. 16,000. Pays on publication. Buys first North American serial rights. Submit seasonal or holiday material 2 months in advance. SASE. Reports in 3 weeks. Free sample copy.

Nonfiction: Publishes how-to and informational articles. Buys 17-20 mss/year. Query. Length: 2,000-2,500 words. Pays 10¢/word maximum.

Photos: Purchased with accompanying ms. Captions required. Pays $7.50 for professional quality 8x10 or 5x7 glossy b&w prints; $10 for 35mm color transparencies. Model release required.

Tips: "Gear your writing to our specializations. Query us first with precis."

WALLS & CEILINGS, 14006 Ventura Blvd., Sherman Oaks CA 91423. (213)789-8733. Editor-in-Chief: Robert Welch. Managing Editor: Don Haley. 10% freelance written. For contractors involved in lathing and plastering, drywall, acoustics, fireproofing, curtain walls, movable partitions together with manufacturers, dealers, and architects. Monthly magazine; 32 pages. Circ. 11,000. Pays on publication. Buys first North American serial rights. Byline given. Phone queries OK. Submit seasonal/holiday material 3 months in advance of issue date. SASE. Reports in 3 weeks. Sample copy $2.

Nonfiction: How-to (drywall and plaster construction and business management); and interview. Buys 5 mss/year. Query. Length: 200-1,000 words. Pays $75 maximum.

Photos: State availability of photos with query. Pays $5 for 8x10 b&w prints. Captions required. Buys one-time rights.

Business Management

The publications listed here are directed at owners of businesses and top level business executives. They cover business trends and general theory and practice of management. Publications that use similar material but have a less technical slant are listed in Business and Finance in the Consumer Publications section. Journals dealing with banking, investment, and financial management are classified in the Trade Finance category.

Journals for middle management (including supervisors and office managers) are found in Management and Supervision. Those for industrial plant managers are listed under Industrial Operation and Management, and under the names of specific industries such as Machinery and Metal Trade. Publications for office supply store operators are included with the Office Environment and Equipment journals.

EXECUTIVE REVIEW, 224 S. Michigan Ave., Chicago IL 60604. (312)922-4083. Editor-in-Chief: Harold Sabes. 5% freelance written. For management of small and middle-class companies, middle management in larger companies and enterprises. Monthly magazine; 32 pages. Circ. 25,000. Pays on publication. Buys one-time and second rights. Byline given. Submit seasonal/holiday material 6 months in advance of issue date. Simultaneous, photocopied, and previously published submissions OK. Computer printout submissions OK; prefers letter quality to dot matrix. SASE. Reports in 6 weeks. Free sample copy and writer's guidelines; mention *Writer's Market* in request.

Nonfiction: How-to (how to do it articles that will be of interest to businessmen in the operation of their companies, and ideas that can be adapted and successfully used by others); interview; personal experience (business); profile; and travel. Buys 7 mss/issue. Submit complete ms. Length: 1,000-1,500 words. Pays $15-50.

HARVARD BUSINESS REVIEW, Soldiers Field, Boston MA 02163. (617)495-6800. Editor: Kenneth R. Andrews. For top management in business and industry; younger managers who aspire to top management responsibilities; policymaking executives in government, policymakers in nonprofit organizations, and professional people interested in the viewpoint of business management. Published 6 times/year. Buys all rights. Byline given. Pays on publication. Reports in 4 to 6 weeks. SASE.

Nonfiction: Articles on business trends, techniques and problems. "*Harvard Business Review* seeks to inform executives about what is taking place in management, but it also wants to challenge them and stretch their thinking about the policies they make, how they make them, and how they administer them. It does this by presenting articles that provide in-depth analyses of issues and problems in management and, wherever possible, guidelines for thinking out and working toward resolutions of these issues and problems." Length: 3,000-6,000 words. Pays $500.

IN BUSINESS, JG Press, Inc., Box 323, Emmaus PA 18049. (215)967-4135. Editor: Jerome Goldstein. Managing Editor: Ina Pincus. Bimonthly magazine covering small businesses, their management, and new developments for small business owners or people thinking about starting out. Circ. 40,000. Pays on publication. Buys first North American serial rights. Submit seasonal material 3 months in advance. SASE. Reports in 6 weeks. Sample copy $2; free writer's guidelines.

Nonfiction: Expose (related to small business, trends and economic climate); how-to (advertise, market, handle publicity, finance, take inventory); profile (of an innovative small-scale business); new product (inventions and R&D by small businesses). "Keep how-to's in mind for feature articles; capture the personality of the business owner and the effect of that on the business operations." Buys 5 unsolicited mss/year. Recent article example: "High-Mileage, American Made" (March/April 1982). Query with clips of published work. Length: 1,000-2,000 words. Pays $75-200.

Photos: State availability of photos. Pays $25-75. Reviews contact sheets. Captions preferred; model release required.

Tips: "Get a copy of the magazine and read it carefully so you can better understand the editorial focus. Send several specific article ideas on one topic, so we can sharpen the focus. Keep in mind that the reader will be looking for specifics and transferable information."

MANAGING, Graduate School of Business, University of Pittsburgh, 1917 Cathedral of Learning, Pittsburgh PA 15260. (412)624-6667. Editor-in-Chief: Karen Hoy. Art Director: Barbara U. Dinsmore. Emphasizes business and management issues. Many of the readers are Graduate School of Business alumni; others are upper- and middle-level managers and executives in the city, tri-state region and country. Magazine published three times/year (February, June and October); 48 pages. Circ. 5,000. Pays on acceptance. Buys all rights and one-time rights. Submit seasonal/holiday material 3 months in advance. Photocopied submissions OK; previously published submissions OK, but not for full-length features. SASE. Reports in 6 weeks. Free sample copy and writer's guidelines.

Nonfiction: Profile (on corporate executive to give full picture of man and his work) and business or management-oriented features which stem from a regional base, but the story should have national impact. No "articles on personnel, sales or creativity." Buys 3-4 mss/issue. Length: 1,500-4,000 words. Query with samples. "Queries should include information about the author's previously published works and why he/she is qualified to handle the assignment. Prefer information on angle (direction) article will take, persons to be interviewed, subjects explored." Pays $100-400.

Photos: State availability of photos. Pays $10-40 for b&w contact sheets.

Columns/Departments: Your Turn (a column on personal views toward a business or management issue written with a background in the area); Management (medium-length article dealing with a particular management problem and how to solve it). Buys 1/issue. Send complete ms. Length: 500-1,500 words. Brief Cases (short synopses of interesting management research topics with humorous twist). Length: 50-100 words. Pays $25 if used.

Tips: "Our magazine is not written for the average business person. It is published three times/year so articles are in-depth and are meant to be referred to by our readers. Articles *must* have an unusual slant and contain a lot of information—information our readers can't get from the popular business publications."

MAY TRENDS, 111 S. Washington St., Park Ridge IL 60068. (312)825-8806. Editor: John E. McArdle. For owners and managers of medium- and small-sized businesses, hospitals and nursing homes, trade associations, Better Business Bureaus, educational institutions, newspapers. Publication of George S. May International Company. Magazine published without charge 3 times a year; 28-30 pages. Circulation: 30,000. Buys all rights. Byline given. Buys 10-15 mss/year. Pays on acceptance. Will send free sample copy to writer on request. Reports in 2 weeks. Returns rejected material immediately. Query or submit complete ms. Computer printout submissions OK. SASE.

Nonfiction: "We prefer articles dealing with problems of specific industries (manufacturers, wholesalers, retailers, service businesses, small hospitals and nursing homes) where contact has been made with key executives whose comments regarding their problems may be quoted. We like problem-solving articles, *not* success stories that laud an individual company." Focus is on marketing, economic and technological trends that have an impact on medium- and small-sized businesses not on the "giants"; automobile dealers coping with existing dull markets; contractors solving cost—inventory problems. Will consider material on successful business operations and merchandising techniques. Length: 2,000-3,000 words. Pays $150-250.

Tips: Query letter should tell "type of business and problems the article will deal with. We specialize in the problems of small (20-500 employees, $500,000-2,500,000 volume) businesses (manufacturing, wholesale, retail and service), plus medium and small health care facilities. We are now including nationally known writers in each issue—writers like the Vice Chairman of the Federal Reserve Bank, the US Secretary of the Treasury; names like Walter Mondale and Murray Wiedenbaum; titles like the Chairman of the Joint Chiefs of Staff. This places extra pressure on freelance writers to submit very good articles."

NATION'S BUSINESS, Chamber of Commerce of the United States, 1615 H St., NW, Washington DC 20062. (202)463-5650. Editor: Robert P. Gray. Monthly magazine covering business as related to government for business owners and executives. Circ. 800,000. Pays on acceptance. Byline given. Buys all rights. Reports in 2 months.

Nonfiction: "Trends in business and business relations with the federal government." Articles on improving different business procedures. Recent article examples: "What Small Business Wants from Congress"; "How to Choose and Use a Trademark"; "Want to be a Government Insider?" (White House Fellows Program)—April 1983. Buys 10 unsolicited mss/year. Query by mail; include phone number. Length: 1,500 words average. "Payment is subject to agreement."

Photos: State availability of photos.

‡**NPO RESOURCE REVIEW, The Nonprofit Manager's Guide to Information Resources,** NPO Management Services, Inc., Caller Box A-6, Cathedral Station, New York NY 10025. (212)678-7077. Editor: Godwyn Morris. Bimonthly newsletter covering management resources for nonprofit organizations. Estab. 1982. Pays on acceptance. Byline given. Offers $10 kill fee. Buys all rights. SASE. Reports in 3 weeks. Sample copy for $2.75, business-size SAE and 37¢ postage; writer's guidelines for business-size SAE and 1 first class stamp.

Nonfiction: Book excerpts (management and business); how-to (find and use information resources); interview/profile. Query with clips. Length: 250-1,200 words. Pays $10-100.

Tips: "We will consider anyone familiar with the workings of nonprofit organizations. Writers are free to call us for more information or to discuss ideas."

‡**PERSONNEL REPORT**, Robertson/Merrell-Information Services Group, Whitney Towers, Box 5307A, Hamden CT 06518. (203)248-2066. Director Information Services: D. Trevor Michaels. Bimonthly, biweekly, quarterly, monthly (optional frequencies). Database newsletter with information in human resource development. Pays on acceptance. Offers kill fee per individual contract. Offers first rights. Simultaneous queries and simultaneous, photocopied, and previously published submissions OK. Computer printout and disk submissions only in DEC Rainbow format OK. SASE. Reports in 1 week on queries; 4 weeks on mss.

Nonfiction: All inquiries to Director Information Services. "All material must be human resource/personnel oriented." Query. Pays variable fee, depending on nature of material.

Columns/Departments: Open column format—added as needed or with interest—includes book reviewers/seminar reviewers, all human resource oriented. Columns/departments is a new area and open. Query. Pays variable fee, depending on material.

Fillers: Clippings, newsbreaks. Fillers is new area and open. Pays variable fee, depending on nature of material.

Tips: "Submit concise, succinct, authoritative material; use qualified source material." Book reviews/summaries, article synopses are the most open for freelancers.

PURCHASOR-NEW YORK STATE, Quorum Publications, 1070 Sibley Tower, Rochester NY 14604. (716)546-7241. Managing Editor: Peter O. Allen. Monthly magazine covering industrial and commercial purchasing. Emphasizes articles on purchasing techniques and general business/management interest, with some slant toward personal improvement of business-related skills. Circ. 6,200. Pays on publication. Byline given. Offers negotiable kill fee. Buys simultaneous (limited) and first rights. Submit seasonal/holiday material 3 months in advance. Simultaneous queries, and photocopied and previously published submissions (limited) OK. Computer printout and C/PM 5¼" Osborne disk submissions OK. SASE. Reports in 1 week on queries; 1 month on mss. Sample copy for 9x12 SAE and 3 first class stamps; writer's guidelines for business sized SAE and 1 first class stamp.

Nonfiction: How-to, photo feature, technical. "Should relate to the industrial/commercial purchasing agent. As a regional magazine, we can't and don't attempt to compete with the national purchasing magazines. Regional articles (northeast US), personal development, or how-to-purchase articles are most useful. Buys 24 mss/year. Query with clips of published work. Length: 500-1,200 words. Pays $25-100.

Photos: Send photos with accompanying ms. Reviews 35mm color transparencies and 8x10 b&w prints. Captions, model release and identification of subjects required. Buys one-time rights.

Columns/Departments: Buys 24 mss/year. Query with clips of published work. Length: 1,200-1,500 words. Pays $25-50.

Fiction: Business-related humor. Buys 1-2 mss/year. Query with clips of published work. Length: 500-1,500 words. Pays $25-100.

Church Administration and Ministry

THE CHRISTIAN MINISTRY, 407 S. Dearborn St., Chicago IL 60605. (312)427-5380. Editorial Director: James M. Wall. 10% freelance written. For the professional clergy (primarily liberal Protestant). Bimonthly magazine; 40 pages. Circ. 12,000. Buys all rights. Buys 50 mss/year. Pays on publication. Free sample copy. Reports in 2 weeks. SASE.

Nonfiction: "We want articles by clergy—theologians who know the clergy audience. We are interested in articles on local church problems and in helpful how-to as well as 'think' pieces." Query. Length: 1,200-1,800 words. Pay varies, $10/page minimum.

CHURCH ADMINISTRATION, 127 9th Ave. N., Nashville TN 37234. (615)251-2060. Editor: George Clark. For Southern Baptist pastors, staff and volunteer church leaders. Monthly. Buys all rights. Byline given. Uses limited amount of freelance material. Pays on acceptance. Free sample copy and writer's guidelines upon request. SASE.

Nonfiction and Photos: "Ours is a journal for effectiveness in ministry, including church programming, organizing, and staffing; administrative skills; church financing; church food services; church facilities; communication; pastoral ministries and community needs." Length: 1,200-1,500 words. Pays 4¢/word.

Tips: "A beginning writer should first be acquainted with organization and policy of Baptist churches and with the administrative needs of Southern Baptist churches. He should perhaps interview one or several SBC pastors or staff members, find out how they are handling a certain administrative problem such as 'enlisting volunteer workers' or 'sharing the administrative load with church staff or volunteer workers.' I suggest writers compile an article showing how *several* different administrators (or churches) handled the problem, perhaps giving meaningful quotes. Submit the completed manuscript, typed 54 characters to the line, for consideration."

CHURCH MANAGEMENT—THE CLERGY JOURNAL, Box 1625, Austin TX 78767. (512)327-8501. Editor: Manfred Holck Jr. 100% freelance written. For professional clergy and church business administrators. Monthly (except June and December) magazine; 44 pages. Circ. 15,000. Pays on publication. Buys all rights. Pays 50% kill fee. Byline given. Submit seasonal/holiday material 6 months in advance of issue date. Photocopied submissions OK. SASE. Reports in 2 months. Sample copy $2.50.
Nonfiction: How-to (be a more effective minister or administrator); and inspirational (seasonal sermons). No poetry or personal experiences. Buys 4 mss/issue. Submit complete ms. Length: 1,000-1,500 words. Pays $25-35.
Columns/Departments: Stewardship; Church Administration; Sermons; Tax Planning for Clergy; and Problem Solving. Buys 2/issue. Send complete ms. Length: 1,000-1,500 words. Pays $20-35. Open to suggestions for new columns/departments.
Tips: "Send completed mss. Avoid devotional, personal stories, interviews. Readers want to know how to be more effective ministers."

CHURCH PROGRAMS FOR PRIMARIES, (formerly *Children's Church: The Leader's Guide*), 1445 Boonville Ave., Springfield MO 65807. Editor: Sinda S. Zinn. Assistant Editor: Diana Ansley. "For teachers of primary-age children in a children's church, extended session, story hour, or Bible club setting." Quarterly magazine. Circ. 4,500. Pays on acceptance. Buys one-time rights or first North American serial rights. Phone queries OK. Submit seasonal/holiday material 12-15 months in advance. Previously published submissions OK "if you tell us." Reports in 6 weeks. SASE. Free sample copy and writer's guidelines.
Nonfiction: How-to ("Get Seven Helpers Out of an Old Sock," worship through music, etc.); inspirational; and practical help for the teacher. The spiritual must be an integral part of your material and articles should reflect actual experience or observations related to working with 6- to 7-year-olds. "Articles and stories should be oriented both to children and to a church programs setting. Some how-to articles are helpful." Buys 10-12 mss/year. Submit complete ms. Length: 500-1,200 words. Pays $15-36.
Photos: Purchased with mss about handcrafted items. Offers no additional payment for photos accepted with ms.
Fiction: Most religious stories done on assignment. Buys 13 mss/issue. Query. Length: 2,000-2,200 words.
Tips: "Write, requesting a sample of our publication and a copy of our writer's guidelines."

CHURCH TRAINING, 127 9th Ave. N., Nashville TN 37234. (615)251-2843. Publisher: The Sunday School Board of the Southern Baptist Convention. Editor: Richard B. Sims. For all workers and leaders in the Church Training program of the Southern Baptist Convention. Monthly. Circ. 30,000. Buys all rights. Byline given. Buys 25 mss/year. Pays on acceptance. Will send sample copy to writer on request. Write for copy of guidelines for writers. No photocopied or simultaneous submissions. Computer printout and disk submissions OK. Reports in 6 weeks. Query with rough outline. SASE.
Nonfiction: "Articles that pertain to leadership training in the church. Success stories that pertain to Church Training. Associational articles. Informational, how-to's that pertain to Church Training." Buys 15 unsolicited mss/year. Recent article example: "Church Training" (April 1982). Length: 500-1,500 words. Pays 4¢/word.
Tips: "Write an article that reflects the writer's experience of personal growth through church training. Keep in mind the target audience: workers and leaders of Church Training organizations in churches of the Southern Baptist Convention."

EMMANUEL, 194 E. 76th St., New York NY 10021. (212)861-1076. Editor: Eugene A. La Verdiere, S.S.S. Managing Editor: Mary McCartney. Monthly. Emphasizes recent theological and spiritual development for those in Catholic Church ministry. For priests and others who share in their ministry. "*Emmanuel* addresses primarily the average priest who works in the mainstream as a general practitioner. It speaks to the majority, whose ministry is increasingly varied, but whose principal context is the parish. In doing this, it addresses secondarily the exceptional priest, who must necessarily relate to the majority." Circ. 8,500. Rights to be arranged with author. Buys 5-6 mss/year. Pays on publication. Byline given. Will consider photocopied submissions. Submit seasonal material 3 months in advance. Reports in 2 months. SASE. Free writer's guidelines.
Nonfiction: Articles of Catholic (especially priestly) spirituality; can be biographical, historical or critical. Articles on Eucharistic theology, and those which provide a solid scriptural and/or theological foundation for priestly spirituality (prayer, applied spirituality, etc.). Aims at providing today's priest and involved Catholics

with an adequate theology and philosophy of ministry in today's church. Query with clips of published work. Length: 2,500 words maximum. Usually pays $40-50.

Tips: Prefers "general articles on *positive* themes helpful to a more fulfilled and rewarding ministry. Realize audience is an educated one."

KEY TO CHRISTIAN EDUCATION, Standard Publishing, 8121 Hamilton Ave., Cincinnati OH 45231. (513)931-4050. Editor-in-Chief: Virginia Beddow. 50% freelance written. For "church leaders of all ages; Sunday-school teachers and superintendents; ministers; Christian education professors; youth workers." Quarterly magazine; 48 pages. Circ. 70,000. Pays on acceptance. Buys first North American serial rights. Byline given. Submit seasonal/holiday material 15 months in advance. Photocopied and previously published submissions OK. SASE. Reports in 4 weeks. Free sample copy and writer's guidelines.

Nonfiction: How-to (programs and projects for Christian education); informational; interview; opinion; and personal experience. Buys 10 mss/issue. Query or submit complete ms. Length: 700-2,000 words. Pays $20-60.

Photos: Purchased with accompanying ms. Submit prints. Pays $5-25 for any size glossy finish b&w prints. Total price for ms includes payment for photos. Model release required.

Fillers: Purchases short ideas on "this is how we did it" articles. Buys 10 mss/issue. Submit complete ms. Length: 50-250 words. Pays $5-10.

Tips: "Write for guidelines, sample issue and themes. Then write an article that fits one of the themes following the guidelines. Be practical. If the article pertains to a specific age group, address the article to that department editor."

‡**LEADERSHIP 100, Fresh Ideas for the Church**, Christianity Today, Inc., 465 Gundersen Dr., Carol Stream IL 60187. (312)260-6200. Editor: Dean Merrill. Bimonthly magazine covering local-church life. Estab. 1982. Circ. 50,000. Pays on acceptance. Byline given. Offers 50% kill fee. Buys first rights. Submit seasonal/holiday material 4 months in advance. Simultaneous and photocopied submissions OK. Reports in 2 weeks on queries; 6 weeks on mss.

Nonfiction: New idea, method, approach *now succeeding* in an actual church. Sample copy for 9x12 SAE; writer's guidelines for business-size SAE and 1 first class stamp. No advice, unproven suggestions in regard to church. Buys 200 mss/year. Send complete ms. Length: 150-400 words for short vignettes; 1,000-1,200 words for features (see magazine). Pays $30 maximum for vignettes; $100-125 for features.

Photos: Send photos with accompanying query or ms. Reviews b&w prints. Identification of subjects required. Buys one-time rights.

Tips: "Find a good idea in a church near you, and report it, following our format." The entire magazine is open to freelancers.

PASTORAL LIFE, Society of St. Paul, Route 224, Canfield OH 44406. Editor: Ignatius W. Staniszewski, SSP. Emphasizes priests and those interested in pastoral ministry. Magazine; 64 pages. Monthly. Circ. 8,800. Buys first rights. Byline given. Pays on acceptance. Will send sample copy to writer on request. Query with a outline before submitting ms. "New contributors are expected to include, in addition, a few lines of personal data that indicate academic and professional background." Reports in 7-10 days. SASE.

Nonfiction: "*Pastoral Life* is a professional review, principally designed to focus attention on current problems, needs, issues and all important activities related to all phases of pastoral work and life." Buys 30 unsolicited mss/year. Length: 2,000-3,400 words. Pays 3½¢/word minimum.

THE PRIEST, Our Sunday Visitor, Inc., 200 Noll Plaza, Huntington IN 46750. (219)356-8400. Editor: Father Vincent J. Giese. Managing Editor: Robert A. Willems. Monthly magazine (July-August combined issue) covering the priesthood. "Our magazine is basically for priests, by priests, although much is now being accepted from laypeople." Circ. 10,050. Pays on acceptance. Byline given. Not copyrighted. Buys one-time rights. Submit seasonal/holiday material 5 months in advance. SASE. Reports in 1 week on queries; 2 weeks on mss. Free sample copy.

Nonfiction: How-to, inspirational, interview/profile, opinion, personal experience and technical. "Material must deal with the day-to-day problems of the priest in his work in the parish. Don't pad articles." Recent articles include: "Joys and Sorrows of Ministry," and "Participation in the Eucharist by Those in an Irregular Marriage" (February 1982). Buys 60 mss/year. Send complete ms. Length: 500-3,000 words. Pays $25-150.

Fillers: Anecdotes and short humor.

‡**RELIGION TEACHER'S JOURNAL**, Twenty-Third Publications, Box 180, Mystic CT 06360. (203)536-2611. Editor: Gwen Costello. Magazine of religion (Catholic primarily) and how to teach it. "Our articles offer background information as well as practical suggestions for religion teachers. Our readers are persons of faith who are interested in how to pass on faith." Circ. 40,000. Pays on acceptance. Byline given. Publication not copyrighted. Buys first North American serial rights. Submit seasonal/holiday material 3 months in advance. Simultaneous queries, photocopied and previously published submissions OK. No computer printout or

disk submissions. SASE. Reports in 2 weeks. Sample copy for 9x12 SAE and 70¢ postage; writer's guidelines for business-size SAE and 1 first class stamp.

Nonfiction: Book excerpts, how-to (teach a class on sacraments, or Bible, etc.); humor (funny things that happened in religion class); inspirational; personal experience (successes and failures while trying to share faith); photo features. Needs for future issues: special sacrament articles; seasonal: Halloween, Thanksgiving, Christmas and Easter themes as related to teaching religion. Buys 100 mss/year. Query. Length: 1,800 words maximum. Pays $25-100.

Fiction: Humorous, religious. Buys about 10 mss/year. Query. Length: 1,800 words maximum. Pays $25-100.

Fillers: Clippings, jokes, gags, anecdotes, short humor. Buys 20 fillers/year. Length: 50-300 words. Pays $10-25.

Tips: "Write to the editor for writer's guidelines, suggest to the editor topics you would like to cover, send a sample of your written work." Break in with nonfiction. "Writers should be able to describe their own experiences of teaching religion."

SUCCESS, A Christian Education Magazine, Box 15337, Denver CO 80215. Editor: Edith Quinlan. 90% freelance written. Quarterly magazine. Byline given. Reports in 2-3 weeks. SASE. Free sample copy and writer's guidelines.

Nonfiction: "Articles should be from 500-2,000 words in length, and should provide ideas helpful to workers in Christian education. We are more interested in receiving articles from people who know Christian education, or workers who have accomplished something worthwhile in Sunday school and youth work, than from experienced writers who do not have such background. A combination of both, however, is ideal. Articles may be of a general nature, or be slanted to specific age groups, such as preschool, elementary, youth and adult." Pay: usually 3¢/word but depends on value of article to total magazine.

YOUR CHURCH, Religious Publishing Co., 198 Allendale Rd., King of Prussia PA 19406. Editor: Phyllis Mather Rice. Bimonthly magazine; 56 pages. Circ. 188,000. Pays on publication. Buys first rights. Pays 50% kill fee. Photocopied submissions OK. SASE. Reports in 2-3 months.

Nonfiction: "Articles for pastors, informative and cogently related to some aspect of being a pastor (counseling, personal finance, administration, building, etc.). No poems, sermons or devotional material." Buys 66 mss/year. Length: 5-15 typewritten pages. Pays $5/page, not to exceed $75.

Tips: "Always send a covering letter with some information about the article and the author."

THE YOUTH LEADER, 1445 Boonville Ave., Springfield MO 65802. Editor: Tom Young. For church leaders of teenagers (other than in Sunday school): staff, volunteer, appointed lay workers, adult sponsors, counselors, youth ministers. Evangelical Christianity. Secular and sacred holiday emphasis. Monthly. Circ. 4,500. Buys any rights; pays accordingly. Byline given. Buys 35-40 mss/year. Pays on acceptance. Free sample copy. Photocopied submissions OK. Submit seasonal material 4 months in advance. Reports in 6 weeks. SASE.

Nonfiction: How-to articles (e.g., "Basics of Backpacking," "Handling the Bus Trip," "Ten Ways to Better Understand Youth"); skits and role-plays; scripture choruses, ideas for youth services, projects, fund raising and socials; Bible studies and Bible study know-how; discussion starters; simulation games and activities. Avoid cliches (especially religious ones); practical rather than inspirational emphasis. Submit complete ms. Length: 100-2,000 words. Pays 3-5¢/word.

Tips: "Lead time is three and a half to four months; writing in summer, think fall, etc. Because the title of our publication is *The Youth Leader*, we get submissions for workers with children as well as teens. Because writers are more familiar with Sunday school than any other phase of church work, they write for S.S. workers. We use *neither type of submission*."

Clothing and Knit Goods

APPAREL INDUSTRY MAGAZINE, Shore Publishing, Suite 110, 6255 Barfield Rd., Atlanta GA 30328. Editor: Karen Schaffner. Managing Editor: Ray Henderson. For executive management in apparel companies with interests in equipment, government intervention in the garment industry; finance, management and training in industry. Monthly magazine; 64-125 pages. Circ. 18,600. Not copyrighted. Byline given. Buys 30 mss/year. Pays on publication. Sample copy $1. Will consider legible photocopied submissions. Reports in 1 month. Query. SASE.

Nonfiction and Photos: Articles dealing with equipment, training, finance; state and federal government, consumer interests, etc., related to the industry. "Use concise, precise language that is easy to read and understand. In other words, because the subjects are technical, keep the language comprehensible. Material must be precisely related to the apparel industry.'' Informational, interview, profile, successful business operations, technical articles. Length: 3,000 words maximum. Pays 10¢/word; $5/photo with ms.

APPAREL NEWS SOUTH, Apparel News Group, 945 S. Wall St., Los Angeles CA 90015. (800)421-8867. Editor: Anne Framroze. Tabloid published 5 times/year about the women's and children's apparel industry for retailers in 11 states of the Southeast. Average issue includes 6-10 features. Pays on publication. Byline given. Buys all rights. Submit seasonal material 2 months in advance. Simultaneous and previously published submissions OK if so indicated. Reports in 1 month.
Nonfiction: General interest (trends in fashion retailing and textile, fiber and fabrics industries); profile (of individuals and stores); and how-to (run an apparel retail store; display; manage personnel, energy, accounting and buying). Buys 2-3 mss/issue. Query with clips of previously published work and synopsis. Length: 750-1,000 words. Pays negotiable rates.
Photos: State availability of photos. Pays negotiable rate for 5x7 b&w glossy prints. Captions and model release required. Buys one-time rights.
Tips: "Query should be a brief description of the article proposed and why the writer feels it should interest me. State availability of photos with a brief explanation of why the writer is capable of doing the article. Must know the fashion retail field.''

BODY FASHIONS/INTIMATE APPAREL, Harcourt Brace Jovanovich Publications, 757 3rd Ave., New York NY 10017. (212)888-4364. Editor-in-Chief: Jill Gerson. Emphasizes information about men's and women's hosiery; women's undergarments, lingerie, sleepwear, robes, hosiery, leisurewear. For merchandise managers and buyers of store products, manufacturers and suppliers to the trade. Monthly tabloid insert, plus 10 regional market issues called *Market Maker*; 24 pages minimum. Circ. 13,500. Pays on publication. Buys all rights. Phone queries OK. Submit seasonal/holiday material 2 months in advance. Previously published submissions not accepted. SASE. Reports in 4 weeks.
Columns/Departments: New Image (discussions of renovations of *Body Fashions/Intimate Apparel* department); Creative Retailing (deals with successful retail promotions); Ad Ideas (descriptions of successful advertising campaigns). Buys 6 features/year. Query. Length: 500-2,500 words. Pays 15¢/word as edited. Open to suggestions for new columns and departments.
Photos: B&w (5x7) photos purchased without mss. Captions required. Send contact sheet, prints or negatives. Pays $5-25. Model release required.

FOOTWEAR FOCUS, National Shoe Retailers Association, 200 Madison Ave., Room 1409, New York NY 10016. (212)686-7520. Managing Editor: Anisa Mycak. Magazine published 4 times/year about shoes for shoe store owners, buyers and managers from all over the United States. The publication features articles pertaining to new methods, creative ideas, and reliable information to help them better operate their businesses. Circ. 20,000. Average issue includes 5 articles and 4 departments. Pays on acceptance. Byline given. Makes work-for-hire assignments. SASE. Reports in 1 month. Free sample copy and writer's guidelines.
Nonfiction: Contact: Editor, *Footwear Focus*. Interview (with buyers and store owners); how-to (advertise, display, create interiors, do inventory accounting, and manage data processing systems); new product (shoes and accessories); and technical (new methods of shoe manufacturing). "No generic-type articles that can be applied to any industry. No articles on salesmanship, management training, generic items, or computers.'' Buys 5 mss/year. Query with resume and clips of previously published work. "We do not accept mss.'' Length: 900-1,500 words. Pays $100-200. "We want feature articles that are personality interviews or how-to articles. They must be closely related to the shoe industry. All how-to's must pertain to some aspect of shoe retailing such as developing advertising plans, interior displays, setting up an open-to-buy or fashion merchandising.''
Tips: "Freelancers must have knowledge, experience or background in fashion merchandising and retailing, preferably in shoes. Other areas open are advertising and promotion, customer services, and buying and inventory control. We prefer article suggestions to actual manuscripts, as most freelance writing is assigned according to the editor's choice of subject and topic areas. Those writers interested in doing personal interviews and covering regional events in the shoe industry have the best opportunity, since NYC staff writers can cover only local events.''

IMPRESSIONS, Gralla Communications, Inc., Suite 112, 15400 Knoll Trail Dr., Dallas TX 75248. (214)239-3060. Editor: Carl Piazza. Monthly magazine about the imprinted sportswear industry for retailers, printers, wholesalers, manufacturers and suppliers. Circ. 25,000. Seasonal submissions should be 3 months prior to publication month. Pays on publication. Increased rates when photos or illustrations available. Phone queries OK. Buys 12 or more mss/year. Pays $100-300.
Nonfiction: Technical or general interest related to imprinted sportswear industry. Examples: screen printing of textiles (techniques, materials, etc.), direct or heat transfers printing (methods, mediums, etc.); manufacturing of equipment, imprintables (T-shirts, caps, uniforms, etc.), supplies; business management (employee management, accounting and credit, inventory control, computers, etc.); legal materials (copyright and trade-

mark rulings, sales contracts, etc.); art (preparation for transfers, screen printing, advertising, etc.); sales techniques; retailing; merchandising.

INFANT & TODDLER WEAR, Columbia Communications, 370 Lexington Ave., New York NY 10017. (212)532-9290. Editor-in-Chief: Gail Siragusa. Bimonthly magazine covering retailing and manufacturing of products for infants, for retailers and manufacturers. Circ. 14,000. Pays on publication. Byline given. Buys first North American serial rights. Submit seasonal/holiday material at least 6 months in advance. Simultaneous queries and photocopied submissions OK. Reports in 2 weeks. Free sample copy.
Nonfiction: Profile (of stores or manufacturers); and new product. No how-to material. Buys 3 unsolicited mss/year. Query with clips of published work (trade) or a writing sample. Length: 1,200-2,000 words. Pays $200 minimum.
Photos: State availability of photos. "Photos are paid for with payment for ms."
Tips: "We are keeping a file of freelancers and articles for future use. Writers may not hear from us immediately."

KIDS FASHIONS, Larkin-Pluznick-Larkin, 210 Boylston St., Chestnut Hill MA 02167. (617)964-5100. Editor: Elizabeth Cridland. Managing Editor: Katie McCarthy. Monthly magazine covering children's wear. Circ. 15,000. Pays on acceptance. Byline given. Buys all rights. Submit seasonal/holiday material 9 months in advance. SASE. Reports in 2 weeks. Free sample copy.
Nonfiction: Katie McCarthy, articles editor. How-to (on business); retailer/store profiles (of successful merchants); technical. "Knowledge of retail and/or business practices and procedures necessary." No articles previously published in apparel trade books. Buys 24 mss/year. Query with or without clips of published work. Length: 750-6,000 words. Pays $150-250.
Photos: State availability of photos. Reviews b&w contact sheet. Captions and identification of subjects required. Buys one-time rights.
Fillers: Katie McCarthy, fillers editor. Jokes, gags, short humor, newsbreaks. Buys 20/year. Length: 50-200 words. Pays variable rate.

KNITTING TIMES, National Knitted Outerwear Association, 386 Park Ave., S., New York NY 10010. (212)683-7520. Editor: Eric Hertz. For the knitting industry, from the knitter to the cutter and sewer to the machinery manufacturer, to the fiber and yarn producer, chemical manufacturer, and various other suppliers to the industry. Weekly magazine; 58 pages. Circ: 6,100. Pays on publication. Buys all rights. Submit seasonal or holiday material 1 month in advance. SASE. Reports in 1 month. Free sample copy and writer's guidelines.
Nonfiction: Historical (various parts of the knitting industry; development of machines, here and abroad); how-to (cut and sew various outer garments; knit, dye and finish; needle set-outs for various knit constructions); informational (market or show reports, trends, new fabrics, machine, fiber, yarn, chemical developments); interviews (with leading figures in the industry; may be knitter, head of fiber company, etc. Must say something significant such as new market development, import situation, projections and the like). New product (on anything in the industry such as machines, fibers, yarns, dyeing and finishing equipment, etc.). Photo features (on plants or plant layouts, how to cut and sew sweaters, skirts, etc.). Profiles (can be on industry leaders, or on operation of a company; specifically plant stories and photos). Technical (on machines, chemical processes, finishing, dyeing, spinning, texturing, etc.). Length: 750 words minimum. Query first. Pays $.70-1 an inch.
Photos: B&w glossies (8x10) purchased with mss. Query first. Pays $3 for glossies; $5/diagram.

TACK 'N TOGS MERCHANDISING, Box 67, Minneapolis MN 55440. (612)374-5200. Editor: Doug Dahl. For "retailers of products for horse and rider and Western and English fashion apparel." Monthly. Circ. 16,000. Rights purchased vary with author and material; may buy all rights. Byline given "except on simultaneous submissions, or non-exclusive articles that may appear in slightly edited form in other publications." Buys 10-12 mss/year. Pays on acceptance. Will send a sample copy to a writer on request. Write for copy of guidelines for writers. Query; "style isn't important, but substance has to be something I need—suggest angle from which writer will cover the story." Computer printout submissions OK; prefers letter quality to dot matrix. SASE.
Nonfiction and Photos: "Case histories, trends of industry." Buys informational articles, how-to's, interviews, profiles, coverage of successful business operations, and articles on merchandising techniques. No boiler-plate articles. Length: open. Pays "up to $150." B&w glossies and color transparencies purchased with mss.
Tips: "Write a letter describing a geographic area you can cover. Show some expertise in a particular phase of retail management."

TEENS & BOYS, 71 W. 35th St., New York NY 10001. 20% freelance written. For retailers, manufacturers, resident buying offices in male apparel trade. Monthly magazine; 48-100 pages. Pays on publication. Buys one-time rights. Byline given. Submit seasonal/holiday material 6 months in advance. SASE.

Nonfiction: *"Teens & Boys* is edited for large and small retailers of apparel for boys and male teenage students, aged 4-18. It forecasts style trends, reports on all aspects of retailing. All factual, carefully researched, pertinent articles presented in a lively style will be considered. No tax articles." Buys 2 mss/issue. Query with "well-detailed outline and writing samples to corporate headquarters: Attn: Katie McCarthy, Teens & Boys, 210 Boylston St., Chestnut Hill MA 02167. Retail related stories most appreciated." Length: 1,000-2,000 words. Pays $100-250.

Photos: Photos necessary with article. Payment included in article. Will accept contact sheets and negatives or 5x7, 8x10 b&w glossy prints. Captions required. Buys one-time rights.

Tips: "Phone inquiries followed up in writing are most successful. We strive for regional representation of retailers, so geographic distribution is good."

TEXTILE WORLD, Suite 420, 4170 Ashford, Dunwoody Rd. NE, Atlanta GA 30319. Editor-in-Chief: Laurence A. Christiansen. Monthly. Buys all rights. Pays on acceptance. SASE.

Nonfiction and Photos: Uses articles covering textile management methods, manufacturing and marketing techniques, new equipment, details about new and modernized mills, etc., but avoids elementary, historical, or generally well-known material. Pays $25 minimum/page. Photos purchased with accompanying ms with no additional payment, or purchased on assignment.

WEAR, The Voice of the Western Equipment & Apparel Retailer, Crow Publications Inc., 400 Livestock Exchange Bldg., Denver CO 80216. (303)296-2800. Editor/Publisher: Alex Mostrous. Biweekly magazine covering news and features of interest to small and medium sized Western wear and equipment retailers, most are proprietorships with emphasis on business, sales, economy. Circ. 15,000. Pays on publication. Byline given. Buys all rights. Submit seasonal/holiday material 2 months in advance. Simultaneous queries OK. No computer printout or disk submissions. SASE. Reports in 2 weeks. Free sample copy; editorial profile for business-sized SAE and 1 first class stamp.

Nonfiction: How-to, interview/profile, new product, photo feature. No tax columns. Buys 10 mss/year. Query. Length: 750-1,500. Pays $50/1,000 word article.

Photos: State availability of photos. Reviews color and b&w prints. Model release and identification of subjects (when applicable) required.

Columns/Departments: Tax column, personal management. Query with or without clips of published work. Length: 500-1,500 words. Pays $25 minimum.

WESTERN OUTFITTER, 5314 Bingle Rd., Houston TX 77092. (713)688-8811. Editor: Anne DeRuyter. For "owners and managers of retail stores in all 50 states and Canada. These stores sell clothing for riders and equipment for horses, both Western and English style." Monthly. Buys all rights. Pays on publication. Query. SASE.

Nonfiction: Method stories: "in-depth treatment of subjects each merchant wrestles with daily. We want stories that first describe the problem, then give details on methods used in eliminating the problem. Be factual and specific." Subjects include all aspects of retailing. "To merit feature coverage, this merchant has to be a winner. It is the uniqueness of the winner's operation that will benefit other store owners who read this magazine." Length: 1,000-1,500 words for full-length feature; 500-600 words for featurette. Pays 8-10¢/word. "Send us copies of stories you have done for other trade magazines. Send us queries based on visits to Western dealers in your territory."

Photos: "Excellent photos make excellent copy much better. Plan photos that bring to life the key points in your text. Avoid shots of store fixtures without people. Submit contact prints or 5x7 glossies. Sharp focus is a must." Captions required. "Cover photos: We will pay $50 for a color transparency if used for a cover (2¼x2¼ or 35mm). Your 35mm shots are fine for interior b&w art." Pays $10/b&w photo used with ms. Also uses "single photos, or pairs of photos that show display ideas, tricks, promotional devices that are different and that bring more business." Pays $10.

Tips: "The queries that have thought out the subject, advance some angles on which the story is built, and show that the writer has digested our detailed guidelines statement are a real pleasure to respond to."

WESTERN WEAR AND EQUIPMENT MAGAZINE, Bell Publishing, 2403 Champa, Denver CO 80205. (303)572-1777. Editor: Allen Bell. Managing Editor: Sherry Smith. For "Western and English apparel and equipment retailers, manufacturers and distributors. The magazine features retailing practices such as marketing, merchandising, display techniques, buying and selling to help business grow or improve, etc. Every issue carries feature stories on Western/English wear and equipment stores throughout the US." Monthly magazine; 50 pages. Circ. 13,000. Pays on publication. Not copyrighted. Byline given unless extensive rewriting is required. Phone queries OK. Submit seasonal/holiday material 3 months in advance. Simultaneous (to noncompeting publications), photocopied and previously published submissions OK. Computer printout and disk submissions OK. No fiction or foreign material. SASE. Free sample copy and writer's guidelines.

Nonfiction: Expose (of government as related to industry or people in industry); general interest (pertaining to Western lifestyle); interview (with Western store owners or Western personalities); new product (of interest to

Western clothing or tack retailers—send photo); and photo feature (on Western lifestyle or Western retailing operation). "We will be doing much more fashion-oriented articles and layouts." Buys 20-25/year. Query with outline. Length: 800-3,600 words. Pays $50-150.

Photos: "We buy photos with manuscripts. Occasionally we purchase photos that illustrate a unique display or store with only a cutline." State availability of photos. Captions required with "names of people or products and locations." Buys one-time rights.

Coin-Operated Machines

See the Laundry and Dry Cleaning category for related markets.

AMERICAN COIN-OP, 500 N. Dearborn St., Chicago IL 60610. (312)337-7700. Editor: Ben Russell. For owners of coin-operated laundry and drycleaning stores. Monthly magazine; 42 pages. Circ. 19,000. Rights purchased vary with author and material but are exclusive to the field. No byline. Buys 25 mss/year. Pays two weeks prior to publication. Free sample copy. Reports as soon as possible; usually in 2 weeks. Computer printout submissions OK; prefers letter quality to dot matrix. SASE.

Nonfiction and Photos: "We emphasize store operation and use features on industry topics: utility use and conservation, maintenance, store management, customer service and advertising. A case study should emphasize how the store operator accomplished whatever he did—in a way that the reader can apply to his own operation. Mss should have no-nonsense, businesslike approach." Uses informational, how-to, interview, profile, think pieces, successful business operations articles. Length: 500-3,000 words. Pays 6¢/word minimum. Pays $6 minimum for 8x10 b&w glossy photos purchased with mss. (Contact sheets with negatives preferred.)

Fillers: Newsbreaks, clippings. Length: open. Pays 3¢/word; $3 minimum.

Tips: "Query about subjects of current interest. Be observant of coin-operated laundries—how they are designed and equipped; how they serve customers; how (if) they advertise and promote their services. Most general articles turned down because they are not aimed well enough at audience. Most case histories turned down because of lack of practical purpose (nothing new or worth reporting)."

ELECTRONIC SERVICING & TECHNOLOGY, Intertec Publishing Corp., Box 12901, Overland Park KS 66212. (913)888-4664. Editor: Conrad Persson. Managing Editor: Rhonda Wickham. Monthly magazine for electronic enthusiasts who are interested in buying, building, installing, and repairing home-entertainment electronic equipment (audio, video, microcomputers, electronic games, etc.) Circ. 60,000. Pays on publication. Byline given. Buys all rights. Submit seasonal/holiday material 4 months in advance. Simultaneous queries OK. Computer printout submissions OK. Reports in 2 weeks on queries; 1 month on mss. Free sample copy and writer's guidelines.

Nonfiction: How-to (service, build, install and repair home-entertainment electronic equipment); personal experience (troubleshooting); technical (home-entertainment electronic equipment; electronic testing and servicing equipment). "Explain the techniques used carefully so that even hobbyists can understand a how-to article." Buys 36 mss/year. Send complete ms. Length: 10,000 words minimum. Pays $100-200.

Photos: "Included in payment for ms." Send photos with ms. Reviews color and b&w transparencies and b&w prints. Captions and identification of subjects required. Buys all rights.

Columns/Departments: Tina Thorpe, column/department editor. Troubleshooting Tips. Buys 12 mss/year. Send complete ms. Length: open. Pays $30-40.

GAME MERCHANDISING, Boynton & Associates, Inc., Clifton House, Clifton VA 22024. (703)830-1000. Editor: Geoffrey A. Wheeler. Monthly magazine covering the retail sale of games and related supplies. "*Game Merchandising* helps retailers and buyers stay informed on new products, industry trends, and effective sales techniques. Estab. 1981. Circ. 10,200. Pays on publication. Byline given. Buys first-time rights "in our field." Submit seasonal/holiday material 3 months in advance. Photocopied submissions and previously published work ("negotiable") OK. SASE. Reports in 3 weeks. Sample copy for 9x12 SAE; writer's guidelines for legal size SAE and 1 first class stamp.

Nonfiction: How-to (sell games most effectively); and interview/profile (of store owners/managers and industry figures). "We are slanted toward the retailer, so we prefer articles embodying hard information on the industry or the experience of successful retailers. No detailed reviews of games." Buys over 20 mss/year. Query. Length: 1,200-2,500 words. "We buy a complete editorial package of: main copy, sidebars (if needed), and illustrative material (if needed)." Pays $125-300, depending on length and degree of specialization.

Photos: "We buy photos only as part of a story package."

Columns/Departments: Tabletop Games (puzzles, board games, etc.); Electronic Games; Gaming Miniatures; and Role-playing Games. "All departments use survey articles or articles on how a particular store effectively sells that type of product." Query. Length: 1,500 words. Pays 10¢/word.

Tips: "Freelancers can best break in by querying for necessary details and writing a 'Retailer Profile' on a successful game store or game department. Once a writer has identified a suitable store, he should be able to write a good interview by adding a few questions to our standard interview form."

LEISURE TIME ELECTRONICS, Charleson Publishing Co., 124 E. 40th St., New York NY 10016. (212)953-0230. Editor: Bill Silverman. Tabloid published monthly covering electronic games and toys, personal computers and software, audio and video hardware and software, auto electronics, and personal electronics for retailers of leisure electronics. Estab. 1980. Circ. 51,000. Pays on acceptance. Byline and brief bio given. Buys "all rights in the trade." Queries requested. Reports "promptly." Free sample copy.

Nonfiction: Technical (state-of-the-art explaining technology); and merchandising (all aspects). Recent article example: "Computer Peripherals Are Becoming More Profitable" (February 1982). Buys 20 mss/year. Query with clips of published work and resume. Length: 1,500 words average. Pays rates "competitive with any national magazine."

Photos: "We ask writers to request photos from storeowners. Product photos come from manufacturers." Reviews color transparencies and 8x10 b&w glossy prints. Identification of subjects required.

Fillers: Newsbreaks. Length: 100 words maximum. Pays varying fee.

PLAY METER MAGAZINE, Skybird Publishing Co., Inc., Box 24170. New Orleans LA 70184. Publisher: Ralph Lally. Managing Editor: Laura Braddock. 25% freelance written. Trade publication for owners/operators of coin-operated amusement machine companies, e.g., pinball machines, video games, arcade pieces, jukeboxes, etc. Semimonthly magazine; 100 pages. Circ. 13,000. Pays on publication. Buys all rights. Byline given. Submit seasonal/holiday material 2 months in advance of issue date. Photocopied and previously published submissions OK. Computer printouts OK "as long as they are clear and readable." SASE. Query answered in 2 months. Sample copy $2; free writer's guidelines.

Nonfiction: How-to (get better locations for machines, promote tournaments, evaluate profitability of route, etc.); interview (with industry leaders); new product (if practical for industry, not interested in vending machines); unusual arcades (game rooms); and photo features (with some copy). "No 'puff' or 'plug' pieces about new manufacturers. Our readers want to read about how they can make more money from their machines, how they can get better tax breaks, commissions, etc. Also no stories about *playing* pinball. Our readers don't play the games per se; they buy the machines and make money from them." Recent article example: "Research and Development in US Coin-Op Manufacturing;" and "Reconditioned Pinballs Spurring Subteens' Arcade Play" (April 1, 1982). Buys 48 mss/year. Submit complete ms. Length: 250-3,000 words. Pays $30-215.

Photos: "The photography should have news value. We don't want 'stand 'em up-shoot 'em down' group shots." Pays $15 minimum for 5x7 or 8x10 b&w prints; $50 for color cover pictures. Captions preferred. Buys all rights. Art returned on request.

Tips: "*Do not* submit ms on erasable bond-type paper."

VENDING TIMES, 211 E. 43rd St., New York NY 10017. Editor: Arthur E. Yohalem. For operators of vending machines. Monthly. Circ. 14,700. Buys all rights. Pays on publication. Query. "We will discuss the story requirements with the writer in detail." SASE.

Nonfiction and Photos: Feature articles and news stories about vending operations; practical and important aspects of the business. "We are always willing to pay for good material."

Confectionery and Snack Foods

‡**BAKING TODAY,** Maclaren Publishers, Ltd., Box 109, Maclaren House, Scarbrook Rd., Croydon, CR9 1QH, United Kingdom. Editor and Publisher: Terry O'Gorman. Up to 40% freelance written. Buys variable number of mss/year. For managers and proprietors throughout the baking industry. Monthly magazine (not published August and December). Circ. 3,500. Copyrighted. SAE and IRCs. Sample copy free to serious contributors.

Nonfiction: Features on baking and allied subjects. Length: 1,000-3,000 words. Submit complete ms. Payment varies.

Photos: B&w glossies used with mss. Captions required. Query.

CANDY INDUSTRY, (formerly *Candy and Snack Industry*), HBJ Publications, 7500 Old Oak Blvd., Cleveland OH 44130. (216)243-8100. Editor: Pat Magee. For confectionery manufacturers. Monthly. Buys all rights. Reports in 2 weeks. SASE.
Nonfiction: "Feature articles of interest to large-scale candy manufacturers that deal with activities in the fields of production, packaging (including package design), merchandising; financial news (sales figures, profits, earnings), advertising campaigns in all media, and promotional methods used to increase the sale or distribution of candy." Length: 1,000-1,250 words. Pays 5¢/word; "special rates on assignments."
Photos: "Good quality glossies with complete and accurate captions, in sizes not smaller than 5x7." Pays $5; $20 for color.
Fillers: "Short news stories about the trade and anything related to candy and snacks." Pays 5¢/word; $1 for clippings.

PACIFIC BAKERS NEWS, N.E. 4791 N. Shore Rd., Belfair WA 98528. (206)275-6421. Publisher: Leo Livingston. 50% freelance written. Business newsletter for commercial bakeries in the Western states. Monthly. No computer printout or disk submissions. Pays on publication. No byline given; uses only one-paragraph news items.
Needs: Uses bakery business reports and news about bakers. Buys only brief "boiled-down news items about bakers and bakeries operating only in Alaska, Hawaii, Pacific Coast and Rocky Mountain states. Welcome clippings. Need monthly news reports and clippings about the baking industry and the donut business. No pictures, jokes, poetry or cartoons." Length: 10-200 words. Pays 6¢/word for clips and news used.

Construction and Contracting

Journals aimed at architects are included in the Art, Design, and Collectibles section. Those for specialists in the interior aspects of construction are listed under Building Interiors. Also of interest would be the markets in the Brick, Glass, and Ceramics section.

ARCHITECTURAL METALS, National Association of Architectural Metal Manufacturers, 221 N. LaSalle St., Chicago IL 60601. (312)346-1600. Editor: Jim Mruk. Managing Editor: August L. Sisco. Published winter, spring and fall. Magazine covers architectural metal applications for architects, specifiers, and other engineers involved in using architectural metal products. Circ. 15,000. Pays on acceptance. Byline given. Buys first North American serial rights and simultaneous rights on work-for-hire assignments. Simultaneous queries, and simultaneous, photocopied and previously published submissions OK. Reports in 2 weeks on queries; 1 month on mss. Free sample copy and writer's guidelines.
Nonfiction: "No articles that are too general." Number of mss bought/year "depends on need." Query with clips of published work or send complete ms. Phone queries OK. Length: 1,000 words minimum. Pays $150-400/article.
Photos: Send photos with ms. Pays $10 maximum for 5x7 b&w prints. Captions required.
Tips: "Have a knowledge of architectural metals and write clearly. Applications of hollow metal flagpoles/metal bar grating/architectural metals are all open. Keep the subject matter clear and interesting. Technical details are a must."

AUTOMATION IN HOUSING & SYSTEMS BUILDING NEWS, CMN Associates, Inc., Box 120, Carpinteria CA 93013. (805)684-7659. Editor-in-Chief: Don Carlson. Specializes in management for industrialized (manufactured) housing and volume home builders. Monthly magazine; 88 pages. Circ. 23,000. Pays on acceptance. Buys first North American or one-time rights. Phone queries OK. Computer printout submissions OK; letter quality only. SASE. Reports in 2 weeks. Free sample copy and writer's guidelines.
Nonfiction: Case history articles on successful home building companies which may be 1) production (big volume) home builders; 2) mobile home manufacturers; 3) modular home manufacturers; 4) prefabricated home manufacturers or; 5) house component manufacturers. Also uses interviews, photo features and technical articles. "No architect or plan 'dreams'. Housing projects must be built or under construction." Buys 6 mss/year. Query. Length: 1,500 words maximum. Pays $250 minimum.
Photos: Purchased with accompanying ms. Captions required. Query. No additional payment for 4x5, 5x7 or 8x10 b&w glossies or 35mm or larger color transparencies (35mm preferred).

‡**BUILDER, The Magazine of the National Association of Home Builders**, Hanley-Wood, Inc., National Housing Center, 15th and M Sts. NW, Washington DC 20005. (202)822-0390. Editor: Frank Anton. Executive

Editor: Wendy Jordan. Monthly magazine of the home building and light commercial industry for those involved with the industry. Circ. 175,000. Pays "60 days after invoice." Byline given. Offers negotiable kill fee. Buys first North American serial rights. Submit seasonal/holiday material 3 months in advance. Simultaneous queries and photocopied submissions OK. Reports in 2 weeks on queries; 1 month on mss. Free sample copy and writer's guidelines.

Nonfiction: New product, technical, business needs. No consumer-oriented material. Buys 10 mss/year. Query with published clips. Length: 500-1,200 words. Pays $100-400.

Photos: Send photos with query or ms. Reviews 4x5 color transparencies and 8x10 color prints. Identification of subjects required. Buys one-time rights.

BUILDER INSIDER, Box 191125, Dallas TX 75219-1125. (214)651-9994. Editor: Mike Anderson. Monthly; covering the entire north Texas building industry for builders, architects, contractors, remodelers and homeowners. Circ. 10,000. Free sample copy. Photocopied submissions OK. SASE.

Nonfiction: "What is current in the building industry" is the approach. Wants "advertising, business builders, new building products, building projects being developed, helpful building hints localized to the Southwest and particularly to north Texas." Submit complete ms. Length: 100-900 words. Pays $30-50.

‡**BUILDING PROFIT, The Building Magazine for Decision Makers**, WBK Publishing, Inc., 1730 Madison Rd., Cincinnati OH 45206. (513)751-0258. Editor: Sharon Pearcy. Quarterly publication of the Butler Manufacturing Company; covers pre-engineered buildings for business and community leaders considering new building construction or existing facility expansion. "Promotes the time-saving, cost-saving and energy-saving logic of pre-engineered buildings." Estab. 1981. Circ. 50,000+. Pays "within 30 days." Byline given. Buys all rights. Simultaneous queries OK. Free sample copy and writer's guidelines.

Nonfiction: How-to, interview/profile, photo feature; all pertaining to builders and building owners of pre-engineered structures. "We prefer to assign stories to freelancers with building industry writing experience." Buys 10 mss/year. Query with published clips. Length: varies with assignment. Pays $200-700.

Photos: Frank Satogata, photo editor. State availability of photos. "We assign photos and pay a day rate." Reviews color transparencies. Model release required.

Columns/Departments: Financial column (material of interest to prospective building owners). Buys 4 mss/year. Query. Length: 500-1,000 words. Pays $200-300.

Tips: "We prefer to see a freelancer's writing samples before making an assignment. Experience in the building industry is helpful. Good interviewing skills are a must."

CALIFORNIA BUILDER & ENGINEER, 4110 Transport St., Palo Alto CA 94303. Editor: John S. Whitaker. "For contractors, engineers, and machinery distributors in the heavy construction industry, and civic officials concerned with public works. Our coverage is limited to California, Hawaii, Nevada and western Arizona." Published twice a month. Circ. 12,000. Pays on publication. Not copyrighted. Reports in 3 weeks. Computer printout submissions OK; prefers letter quality to dot matrix. SASE. Free sample copy.

Nonfiction: "We are particularly interested in knowledgeable articles on nonconstruction issues that affect the large and small contractor in our region. For example: accounting for the contractor, labor issues, pending legislation or office automation. These articles must be written with rigid accuracy, often requiring specialized knowledge. We are also interested in job stories from Hawaii on heavy public construction. We are not interested in residential construction. Field experience and in-depth knowledge of the industry are essential in writing for us." Buys 4-5 unsolicited mss/year. Query. Length: 1,500-2,200 words. Pays $50/page.

Photos: Send photos with ms. Reviews 5x7 b&w glossy prints. Offers no additional payment for photos accompanying ms. Captions and model release required. Buys one-time rights.

CANADIAN BUILDING, The Business Magazine of the Building Development Industry, Maclean Hunter Ltd., 481 University Ave., Toronto, Ontario, Canada M5W 1A7. (416)596-5760. Editor: William H. Lurz. Monthly magazine covering "all building development: housing, office, shopping centers, industrial, etc." Circ. 18,500. Pays on acceptance. Byline given. Buys first publication rights. Simultaneous queries OK. Reports in 1 month. Sample copy $4.

Nonfiction: Interview/profile (of major building developer); new product; opinion; photo feature. Buys 36 mss/year. Query. Length: 800-4,000 words. Pays $200-600.

Photos: State availability of photos. Reviews 8x10 b&w prints and contact sheets and 3x5 color transparencies. Captions, model release, and identification of subjects required.

‡**CONSTRUCTION DIGEST**, Construction Digest, Inc., Box 603, Indianapolis IN 46206. (317)634-7374. Editor: Art Graham. Managing Editors: Marcia Gruver/Bill Hale. Magazine. "*CD* serves the engineered construction and public works industries in Illinois, Indiana, Ohio, Kentucky and eastern Missouri. It features bids asked, awards, planned work, job photo feature articles, industry trends, legislation, etc." Circ. 14,087. Pays on publication. Byline "depends on nature of article." Publication not copyrighted. Makes work-for-hire assignments. Reports in 2 weeks. Free sample copy and writer's guidelines.

Nonfiction: How-to, new product, photo feature, technical, "nuts & bolts" construction jobsite features. No personality/company profiles. Buys 4 mss/year. Send complete ms. Length: 175 typewritten lines, 35 character count, no maximum. Pays $75/published page.

CONSTRUCTION EQUIPMENT OPERATION AND MAINTENANCE, Box 1689, Cedar Rapids IA 52406. (319)366-1597. Editor: C.K. Parks. 15% freelance written. For users of heavy construction equipment. Bimonthly. Buys all rights. Pays on acceptance. Query. Reports in 1 month. SASE.
Nonfiction and Photos: "Articles on selection, use, operation, or maintenance of construction equipment; articles and features on the construction industry in general; job safety articles." Length: 1,000-2,000 words. Also buys a limited number of job stories with photos, and feature articles on individual contractors in certain areas of US and Canada. Length varies. Pays $50-200.

CONSTRUCTION SPECIFIER, 601 Madison St., Alexandria VA 22314. (703)684-0200. Editor: Jack Reeder. Professional society magazine for architects, engineers, specification writers and project managers. Monthly. Circ. 16,000. Buys one-time North American serial rights. Pays on publication. Free sample copy. Deadline: 60 days preceding publication on the 1st of each month. Reports in 2-3 weeks. Computer printout and disk submissions OK but "we are not compatible with minor supplier equipment." Prefers letter quality printouts; "some dot matrix OK, especially if it has real descenders." SASE. Model releases, author copyright transferral requested.
Nonfiction and Photos: "Articles on selection and specification of products, materials, practices and methods used in commercial (non-residential) construction projects, specifications as related to construction design, plus legal and management subjects." Recent article example: "Facets of Glass" (March 1983). Query. Length: 5,000 words maximum. Pays 10¢/published word, plus art. Photos desirable in consideration for publication; line art, sketches, diagrams, charts and graphs also desired. Full color transparencies may be used. Prices negotiable. 8x10 glossies, 3¼ slides preferred.
Tips: "We will get bigger and thus need good technical articles."

CONSTRUCTOR MAGAZINE (The Management Magazine for the Construction Industry), 1957 E St. NW, Washington DC 20006. Editor: Diane B. Snow. Publication of the Associated General Contractors of America for "men and women in the age range of approximately 25-70 (predominantly 40s and 50s), most with a college education. Most own or are officers in their own corporations." Monthly. Circ. 40,000. Buys all rights. Buys 5 mss/year. Pays on publication. Query or submit complete ms. "Often telephone query first is best." Reports in 2 months. SASE. Sample copy $2; free writer's guidelines.
Nonfiction: "Feature material dealing with labor, legal, technical and professional material pertinent to the construction industry. We deal only with the management aspect of the construction industry." Buys informational articles, interviews, think pieces, exposes, photo features, coverage of successful business operations, and technical articles. "Please no new product plugs, technical articles, or AGC construction project stories where the contractor wasn't an AGC member." Length: "no minimum or maximum; subject much more important than length." Pays $150 minimum.
Photos: State availability of photos. Reviews 8x10 b&w semi-glossy prints and 35mm color transparencies. Offers no additional payment for photos accompanying ms. Captions required with "action description, date, location, names of persons, general contractor's firm's name, location and AGC chapter affiliation, if applicable. Model release required. Buys all rights.

DIXIE CONTRACTOR, Box 280, Decatur GA 30031. (404)377-2683. 8-10% freelance written. For contractors, public officials, architects, engineers, and construction equipment manufacturers and dealers. Biweekly magazine; 125 pages. Circ. 10,000. Pays on publication. Buys all rights. Phone queries OK. Submit seasonal/holiday material 2 months in advance of issue date. Photocopied submissions OK. SASE. Reports in 2 weeks. Free sample copy.
Nonfiction: How-to (articles on new construction techniques and innovations); and interview (with government officials influencing construction, or prominent contractors). Buys 7 mss/year. Query or submit complete ms. Length: 1,500-2,000 words. Pays $50 minimum/published page. "Articles usually run two pages."
Photos: State availability of photos with query or ms. Captions and model release required. Buys all rights.
Columns/Departments: Labor-Management Relations in Construction. Submit complete ms. Length: 1,000-1,500 words. Pays $50 minimum.
Tips: "We are interested only in freelancers who have a business writing background. We won't reply to people who write about the West Coast, Midwest or Upper Northeast. It's a waste of our time."

ENGINEERING AND CONTRACT RECORD, Southam Communications, 1450 Don Mills Road, Toronto, Ontario, Canada M3B 2X7. (416)445-6641. Editor: Gene Lethbridge. Managing Editor: Alastair Scott. For contractors in engineered construction and aggregate producers. Monthly. Circ. 23,100. Buys Canadian rights. Pays on publication. Free sample copy. Reports in 2 weeks. No computer printout or disk submissions. SAE and International Reply Coupons.

Nonfiction: "Job stories. How to build a project quicker, cheaper, better through innovations and unusual methods. Articles on construction methods, technology, equipment, maintenance and management innovations. Management articles. Stories are limited to Canadian projects or Canadian construction firms working on projects overseas. No company profiles." Buys 6-8 mss/year. Query. Length: 800-1,000 words. Pays $200-300.
Photos: B&w 8x10 glossy prints purchased with mss or color slides or prints. Pays $15/photo b&w, $40 color.

EQUIPMENT ADVERTISER DIGEST, 100 S. College, Tyler TX 75702. (800)328-7170. Editor: Mike Craft. Monthly tabloid about the construction and heavy equipment industries for contractors and users of heavy equipment. Circ. 45,000. Average issue includes 2 feature articles, 2 columns, and profiles of companies. Pays on publication. Byline given. Offers $25 kill fee. Buys all rights. Phone queries OK. Photocopied and previously published submissions OK if so indicated. SASE. Reports in 2 weeks. Free sample copy.
Nonfiction: "We're looking for articles that cover people in the construction industry, legislation affecting the industry, regulations, finance, and operating a small business. Submit a story idea from your region that the editorial office in Tyler would not know about." Buys 1-2 mss/issue. Query with clips of previously published work and resume. Pays $150 minimum.
Photos: Reviews b&w glossy prints and negatives. Captions required. Buys one-time rights.

EXCAVATING CONTRACTOR, Cummins Publishing Co., 2520 Industrial Row, Troy MI 48084. (313)435-0770. Editor: Andrew J. Cummins. Monthly magazine about earthmoving/small business management for small earthmoving contractors and entrepreneurs. Circ. 30,000. Pays on publication. Byline given. Makes work-for-hire assignments. Phone queries OK. Submit seasonal material 2 months in advance. Previously published submissions OK; "state where." SASE. Reports in 1 month. Free sample copy and writer's guidelines.
Nonfiction: Expose (of government rip-offs of the small businessman); historical (anything on old earthmoving machines); how-to (maintain machines; move dirt more effectively); new product (innovations in the industry); and photo feature (job stories). Buys 8 mss/year. Query with clips of previously published work. Length: 500-1,500 words. Pays $25 minimum/published page. "We are a national construction publication that goes exclusively to the small earthmoving contractor. We have five departments: one is devoted to the woman's side of the business, written in an Erma Bombeck style. We also feature a good deal of articles on small business management, tax advice, etc. Read a few copies of the publication and talk to a few small contractors. Contact us and discuss the story idea. Your best bet would be a job article on how a certain small contractor tackled a particularly tough situation or used a unique approach to a problem. Special issues needing work are on winter work, and how to keep busy in the off season."
Photos: State availability of photos or send photos with ms. Reviews b&w contact sheets. Pays $25-50 for cover color contact sheets. Offers no additional payment for photos accepted with ms. Captions preferred. Buys one-time rights.
Columns/Departments: Excavator's Wife (humorous but hard-hitting articles on running a small business); Book Review (of small business or contracting-related book). Buys 12 mss/year. Query with clips of previously published work. Length: 1,000-1,800 words. Pays $25-$50.

FENCE INDUSTRY, 6255 Barfield Rd., Atlanta GA 30328. (404)256-9800. Editor/Associate Publisher: Bill Coker. For retailers and installers of fencing materials. Monthly magazine; 54-80 pages. Circ. 14,000. Buys all rights. Buys 25-35 mss/year. Pays on publication. Computer disk submissions OK if compatible with a digital system; prefers typewritten mss. Free sample copy. Reports in 3 months. Query.
Nonfiction and Photos: Case histories, as well as articles on fencing for highways, pools, farms, playgrounds, homes, industries. Surveys, and management and sales reports. Interview, profile, historical, successful business operations, and articles on merchandising techniques. No how-to articles. "They generally don't apply to installers in our industry." Buys 15-20 unsolicited mss/year. Length: open. Pays 10¢/word. Pays $10 for 5x7 b&w photos purchased with mss. Captions required.

‡**FINE HOMEBUILDING**, The Taunton Press, Inc., 52 Church Hill Rd., Box 355, Newtown CT 06470. (203)426-8171. Editor: John Lively. Bimonthly magazine covering house building, construction, design for builders, architects and serious amateurs. Circ. 134,000. Pays on publication. Byline given. Offers negotiable kill fee. Buys first rights and "use in books to be published." Computer printout submissions OK. Reports "ASAP." Sample copy $3; free writer's guidelines.
Nonfiction: Technical (unusual techniques in design or construction process). Query. Length: 2,000-3,000 words. Pays $150-900.
Columns/Departments: Reports—conferences, workshops, products or techniques that are new or unusual; Great Moments in Building History—humorous, embarrassing, or otherwise noteworthy anecdotes; Reviews—short reviews on books of building or design. Query. Length: 300-1,000 words. Pays $75-150.

JOURNAL OF COMMERCE, Box 34080, Station D, Vancouver, B.C., Canada, V6J 4M8. Editorial Director: Brian Martin. Twice-weekly tabloid aimed at a general construction and development audience in western Canada. Circ. 14,000. Buys first Canadian rights. Payment on acceptance. Query first. Enclose SAE and International Reply Coupons.
Nonfiction and Photos: Specialized stories for specific audiences. Average length: 1,500 words. Pays 15¢/word (Canadian). Pays $5 for 5x7 photos.

LOG HOME AND ALTERNATIVE HOUSING BUILDER, Log Home Builder, 16 1st Ave., Corry PA 16407. (814)664-4976. Editor: Deborah Katulich. Bimonthly magazine covering alternative housing including log home, dome home, solar and underground homes. Circ. 10,000. Pays on publication. Byline given. Buys one-time rights. Reports in 2 weeks on queries; 3 weeks on mss. Free sample copy.
Nonfiction: Technical, energy, real estate dynamics, sales, unique applications of alternative units as residential and commercial property (excluding restaurants). "We do not buy articles on how a husband and wife erected their home, or the trials and tribulations of the first-time log or dome home buyer." Buys 6 mss/year. Query. Length: 2,000-4,000 words. Pays $50-200. Buys 6 mss/year. Query. Length: 2,000-4,000 words. Pays $50-200.
Photos: Send photos with ms. Pays $15-30 for 8x10 color prints; $10-25 for 8x10 b&w prints. Captions and identification of subjects required.

LOUISIANA CONTRACTOR, Rhodes Publishing Co., Inc., 18271 Old Jefferson Hwy., Baton Rouge LA 70816. (504)292-8980. Editor: Phil Womack. Monthly magazine comprehensive covering heavy commercial, industrial, and highway construction in Louisiana, the 6th largest construction market in the US. Circ. 6,000. Pays on publication. Offers negotiable kill fee. Not copyrighted. Buys all rights. Reports in 2 weeks on queries; 2½ months on mss. Sample copy $1.50.
Nonfiction: "We are particularly interested in writers who can get clearance into a chemical plant or refinery and detail unusual maintenance job. Our feature articles are semi-technical to technical, balanced by a lot of name-dropping of subcontractors, suppliers and key job personnel. We want quotes, and we never run a story without lots of photos either taken or procured by the writer. Stories on new methods of construction and unusual projects in the state are always wanted. Nothing from anyone unfamiliar with the construction industry in Louisiana." Recent article example: "Louisiana Witnesses Concrete Resurfacing Project Near Port Hudson" (July 1981). Buys 8-12 mss/year. Query. Length: 1,000-3,500 words. Pays negotiable rate.
Photos: State availability of photos. Reviews 5x7 or 8x10 b&w glossy prints. Captions and identification of subjects required.

METAL BUILDING REVIEW, Nickerson & Collins, 1800 Oakton, Des Plaines IL 60018. (312)298-6210. Editor: Gene Adams. Monthly magazine for contractors, dealers, erectors, architects, designers and manufacturers in the metal building industry. Circ. 20,000. Pays on acceptance. No byline given. Buys first North American serial rights or all rights. Submit seasonal/holiday material 6 months in advance. Simultaneous queries, and simultaneous, photocopied and previously published submissions OK. Reports in 3 weeks. Free sample copy and writer's guidelines.
Nonfiction: How-to, interview/profile, photo feature, technical. "Freelancers can break in with on-the-job-site interviews." Query with or without clips of published work or send complete ms. Length: 1,000-3,000 words. Pays 3-6¢/word.
Photos: State availability of photos. Pays $5-10 for 5x7 b&w prints; $20-75 for 5x7 color prints. Captions, model release and identification of subjects required. Buys one-time or all rights.

‡**MHBUSINESS**, TL Enterprises, Inc., 29901 Agoura Rd., Agoura CA 91301. (219)991-4980. Editor: Michael Schneider. Managing Editor: Sheryl Davis. Monthly magazine covering manufactured housing and allied industries for people of the manufactured housing industry—dealers, manufacturers, suppliers, park management, legislators and finance experts." Circ. 20,000. Pays on publication. Byline given. Offers 50% kill fee. Buys first North American serial rights. Submit seasonal/holiday material 6 months in advance. Photocopied submissions OK. SASE. Reports in 3 weeks on queries; 6 weeks on mss. Sample copy for 9x12 SAE and 3 first class stamps; writer's guidelines for business-size SAE and 1 first class stamp.
Nonfiction: Expose (carefully done and thoroughly researched); historical/nostalgic (of companies, products or people in the MH industry itself); how-to (deal with any specific aspect of the MH business); interview/profile (of persons or companies involved in the MH industry—legislative, finance, dealerships, park management, manufacturing, supplier); new product (no payment for company promo material); opinion (controversy OK); personal experience (relative to the MH business—must be something of importance to readership; must have a point: it worked for me, it can for you. Or this is why it didn't work for me); photo feature (four-color transparencies with good captions; photo coverage of MH shows, conventions and meetings not appropriate topics for photo features); technical (photos required—four-color preferred). No general business, general anything. Buys 60 mss/year. Query with published clips; complete ms OK "but only read on speculation." Length: 1,000-2,000 words. Payment varies up to $400.

Photos: State availability of photos or send photos with ms. Reviews 35mm transparencies and 8x10 b&w prints. Captions, model release and identification of subjects required. Buys one-time or all rights; unused photos returned.

Columns/Departments: Guest Editorial; News (50-500 words maximum, b&w photos appreciated); Parade (color photos, four-color transparencies). Buys 100-120 mss/year. Query or send complete ms. Pays $10-200 "depending on where used and importance."

Tips: "Query. Phone OK; letter preferable. Send 1 or several ideas and a few lines letting us know how you plan to treat it/them. We are always looking for good authors knowledgeable in the MH industry or related industries."

‡**MID-WEST CONTRACTOR**, Construction Digest, Inc., 934 Wyandotte, Box 766, Kansas City MO 64141. (816)842-2902. Editor: John LaRoe. Biweekly magazine covering the public works and engineering construction industries in Iowa, Nebraska, Kansas and western and northeastern Missouri. Circ. 8,426. Pays on publication. Byline depends on the nature of the article. Not copyrighted. Makes work-for-hire assignments. Reports in 2 weeks. Free sample copy and writer's guidelines.

Nonfiction: How-to, new product, photo feature, technical, "nuts and bolts" construction jobsite features. Buys 4 mss/year. Send complete ms. Length: 175 typewritten lines, 35 character count, no maximum. Pays $75/published page.

P.O.B., Point of Beginning, P.O.B. Publishing Co., Box 810, Wayne MI 48184. (313)729-8400. Editor: Edwin W. Miller. Bimonthly magazine featuring articles of a technical, business, professional and general nature for the professionals and technicians of the surveying and mapping community. Circ. 58,000. Pays on publication. Byline given "with short biography, if appropriate." Offers 50% kill fee. Buys all rights or makes work-for-hire assignments. Submit seasonal/holiday material 3 months in advance. Simultaneous queries, and simultaneous and photocopied submissions OK. SASE. Reports in 1 month. Sample copy for 10x13 SAE and 7 first class stamps; writer's guidelines for business size SAE and 1 first class stamp.

Nonfiction: Contact: Sandy Goldberg. Historical/nostalgic, how-to, interview/profile, photo feature, and technical (only related to surveying, mapping, construction—profession and business of); travel (only sites of professional society meetings). Buys 12 mss/year. Query or send complete ms. Length: 1,000-4,000 words. Pays $150-400.

Photos: Contact: Sandy Goldberg. Send photos with ms. Pays $10-50 for color transparencies and prints; $5-25 for 5x7 b&w prints. Model release and identification of subjects required.

Columns/Departments: Contact: Sandy Goldberg. A Conversation With—interview of people in the field about their professional involvement, point of view. Picture·Profile—profile of people in the field slanted towards their special interest, talent, involvement that is unusual to the profession. Buys 6 mss/year. Query. Length: 1,000-2,500 words. Pays $50-200.

RESTAURANT AND HOTEL DESIGN MAGAZINE, (formerly *Restaurant Design Magazine*), Bill Communications, 633 3rd Ave., New York NY 10017. (212)986-4800, ext. 338, 355. Editor: Regina Baraban. Managing Editor: Barbara Knox. Bimonthly magazine about contract design and the restaurant business for architects, designers and restaurant and hotel executives. Circ. 33,000. Pays on acceptance. Byline given. Buys first North American serial rights. Phone queries OK. Photocopied and previously published submissions OK. SASE. Reports in 1 month on queries; in 2 months on mss. Free sample copy.

Nonfiction: Profile. Buys 4-10 mss/year. Query with clips of previously published work. Length: 1,500-2,500 words.

Tips: "We generally work very closely with a writer, directing research and focusing articles. We ask for rewriting frequently. As a result, unsolicited works seldom suit our format. Query should have clarity, brevity, knowledge of the magazine and design language. Submit quality photography with any project query so that we can determine whether or not we can use the story."

ST. LOUIS CONSTRUCTION NEWS & REVIEW, The Voice for the St. Louis Area Construction Industry, Finan Publishing Co., Inc., 130 W. Lockwood, St. Louis MO 63119. (314)961-6644. Editor: Marie A. Casey. Monthly tabloid covering all aspects of St. Louis area building design and construction and tailored to the management end of the industry. Circ. 11,000. Pays on publication. Byline given. Buys first rights and makes work-for-hire assignments. SASE. Reports in 1 month. Sample copy $2.

Nonfiction: Expose (of local, construction-related practices); interview/profile (by assignment only); photo feature (with local construction emphasis); technical. "No material unrelated to design and construction industries." Buys 2-5 mss/year. Query with clips of published work. Length: open. Pays $40-300.

Photos: Send photos with ms. Pays variable rates for 8x10 b&w glossy prints and contact sheets. Captions and identification of subjects required. Buys one-time rights.

Tips: "Break in with some story ideas and samples of expertise and experience in a specific area. Follow professional writers' general practices."

SUPERMARKET ENGINEERING MAGAZINE, The Magazine of Supermarket Design, Layout, Construction, Operations, Equipment and Fixtures. Market Publications, 39 S. LaSalle St., Chicago IL 60603. (312)263-1057. Bimonthly publication reaching managers and executives responsible for the development and operation of supermarkets. Circulation also includes independent single store supermarket operators. Circ. 15,000. Pays on publication. No byline given. Offers 100% kill fee. Buys all rights. Writer's guidelines available when article is assigned.
Nonfiction: All articles on assignment. "Query us as to availability of assignment in area covered. Send samples of case history type articles, particularly industrial type stories." Buys 6-10 mss/year.
Photos: Reviews b&w contact sheets and 4x5 transparencies. Captions required. Buys all rights. Photo requirements specified at time of assignment of articles.

WORLD CONSTRUCTION, 875 3rd Ave., New York NY 10022. (212)605-9755. Editorial Director: Ruth W. Stidger. 10-20% freelance written. For "English-speaking engineers, contractors, and government officials everywhere except the US and Canada." Monthly. Buys all rights. Byline given unless "the article is less than one page long." Pays on publication. Free sample copy. Query. Reports in 1 month. SASE.
Nonfiction: "How-to articles that stress how contractors can do their jobs faster, better or more economically. Articles are rejected when they tell only what was constructed, but not how it was constructed and why it was constructed in that way. No clippings from newspapers telling of construction projects." Length: 1,000-6,000 words. Pays $100-200/magazine page, or 5 typed ms pages, depending on content and quality.
Photos: State availability of photos. Photos purchased with mss; uses 4x5 or larger b&w glossy prints.
Tips: "At present time, we would prefer buying articles dealing with construction projects in overseas locations."

Dairy Products

DAIRY SCOPE, 3230 Vichy Ave., Napa CA 94558. Editor: Chase W. Hastings. 50% freelance written. Bimonthly magazine; 20 pages. Circ. 2,000. Pays on publication. Buys one-time rights. Photocopied submissions OK. SASE. Reports in 8 weeks. Free sample copy and writer's guidelines.
Nonfiction: How-to (new or interesting techniques in dairying and dairy processing); general interest (to the Western dairy processing industry); historical (Western dairy industry); technical (Western dairy processing); and dairy of the month. Buys 24 mss/year. Query. Length: 100-2,000 words. Pays $2.50/column inch.
Photos: State availability of photos in query. Pays $5-25 for 8x10 b&w glossy prints, contact sheets and negatives. Captions preferred. Buys one-time rights. Model release required.
Fillers: Clippings. Pays $2.

THE NATIONAL DAIRY NEWS, National Dairy News, Inc., Box 951, Madison WI 53701. (608)257-9577. Editor: Gerald Dryer. Weekly tabloid covering dairy processing and marketing. Estab. 1981. Circ. 3,000. Pays on publication. Byline given. Offers negotiable kill fee. Buys one-time rights. Submit seasonal holiday material 1 month in advance. Simultaneous queries and simultaneous, photocopied, and previously published submissions OK. SASE. Reports in 1 week on queries; 1 month on mss. Free sample copy and writer's guidelines.
Nonfiction: Margaret Patterson, articles editor. How-to (improve dairy processing and marketing ventures); humor; interview/profile; new product; photo feature; technical. "No material that has no connection at all with dairy processing, food broking, etc. That is, general info." Buys 10-40 mss/year. Send complete ms. Length: 50-2,500 words. Pays $25-300.
Photos: Margaret Patterson, photo editor. Send photos with ms. Pays $10-50 for 8x10 b&w prints. Model release and identification of subjects required.
Fillers: Margaret Patterson, fillers editor. Clippings, jokes, gags, anecdotes, short humor, newsbreaks. Length: 25-150 words. Pays $5-25.
Tips: "We are a newspaper. Submit material on innovative dairies (in your region of the country) that are of interest nationally. We'll be needing more freelance material as we're growing but can't afford more staff for a while."

Data Processing

Writers interested in programming markets should consult the Software Publishers section. For a comprehensive directory of programming opportunities, consult *Programmer's Market* (Writer's Digest Books).

‡**BUSINESS SOFTWARE MAGAZINE,** (formerly *The Power of: ES*), Management Information Source (MIS), 3543 NE Broadway, Portland OR 97232. (503)287-1462. Editors: Richard H. Mezejewski and Ron

Forbes. Bimonthly business magazine covering computer software applications in business for corporate decision makers, high level professionals, managers and business owners seeking a better understanding of the business software available to them. Estab. 1982. Circ. 50,000 + . Pays on publication. Byline given. Buys first rights. Photocopied and previously published submissions OK "in some cases." SASE. Reports in 1 month. Sample copy for 9x12 SAE; writer's guidelines for legal size SAE.

Nonfiction: General interest, how-to, interview/profile, new product, opinion, personal experience, technical. "In these categories the writer should be familiar with the product he/she is writing on. This business creates new revolutions almost daily with applications changing with the weather. A phone query is not out of line and may save time at both ends. The magazine is written to expand technical awareness and usage of business software including: database, telecommunications, electronic spreadsheet applications, word processing, graphics and more. All should be in a language even the novice will be comfortable with. No articles on computer or arcade games. Realizing execs like to pop a game disk in the personal computer now and then is not reason enough to do an article on it." Buys 8-10 mss/year. Query. Length: 1,000-2,000 words. "There are exceptions and treatments exceeding 2,000 words may be submitted. A definite query is a must. Writers of longer articles should be made aware that surgery may be needed." Pays $150-250 "with additional consideration given to longer articles."

Photos: State availability of photos. Photos purchased with ms package. Model release and identification of subjects required. Buys one-time rights.

Tips: "This market is growing rapidly. We are in need of business-oriented software application stories. Usual and unusual. Writers should be familiar with the various business-related software programs when approaching story possibilities. The feature story is the best way for a potential freelancer to break in, but being familiar with subject matter is very important. We deal with business software applications, mentioning only briefly the hardware."

CANADIAN DATASYSTEMS, 481 University Ave., Toronto, Ontario, Canada M5W 1A7. (416)596-5907. Editor: Tom Weissmann. For data processing managers, computer systems managers, systems analysts, computer programmers, corporate management and similar people concerned with the use of computers in business, industry, government and education. Monthly magazine. Circ. 30,000. Buys first Canadian rights. Pays on acceptance. Free sample copy. No photocopied or simultaneous submissions. No computer printout or disk submissions. Reports in 1 month. Enclose SAE and International Reply Coupons.

Nonfiction: Articles of technical, semi-technical and general interest within the general area of data processing. How-to features, application reports, descriptions of new techniques, surveys of equipment and services. Emphasis should be placed on the use of data processing equipment and services in Canada. Articles must be technical enough to satisfy an informed readership. Buys 20 mss/year. Query or submit complete ms. Length: 2,000 words maximum. Pays $300/feature article.

COMPUTER DEALER, Gordon Publications, Inc., Box 1952, Dover NJ 07801-0952. (201)361-9060. Editor: David Shadovitz. Sales and marketing of computer products and services for dealers, software producers, systems houses, consultants, consumer electronics outlets and business equipment dealers. Monthly magazine. Circ. 18,060. Pays on publication. Buys all rights. Phone queries OK. Submit seasonal/holiday material 6 months in advance. Previously published submissions OK. Computer printout and disk submissions OK; prefers letter quality to dot matrix printouts. SASE. Reports in 1 month. Free sample copy.

Nonfiction: How-to (sell, market, etc.); interview (with computer notables and/or where market information is revealed); and articles on capital formation, etc. Writers "must have a knowledge of marketing and the computer industry, and the ability to ferret information or restate information known in other fields in a usable, interesting and particularly applicable way to those persons engaged in selling computers and peripheral products. Prefers not to see very general marketing articles." Buys 3-6 mss/issue. Query. Length: 1,000-4,000 words. Pays $50 minimum/page; 8¢/word maximum.

Photos: "Photos (artwork) provide and spark greater reader interest, and are most times necessary to explicate text." Send photos with ms. Uses b&w 8½x11 glossy prints or 3x5 color transparencies. Offers no additional payment for photos accepted with ms. Captions and model releases required.

Columns/Departments: "Columns are solicited by editor. If writers have suggestions, please query."

COMPUTER DECISIONS, 50 Essex St., Rochelle Park NJ 07662. Editor: Mel Mandell. 10% freelance written. For computer-involved managers in industry, government, finance, academia, etc. with "emphasis on the pragmatic—here and now. Audience is well-educated, sophisticated and highly paid." Monthly. Circ. 120,000. Buys first serial rights. Pays 30% kill fee. Byline given. Pays on acceptance. Free sample copy to writer "who has a good background." Photocopied submissions OK. Reports in 4 weeks. SASE.

Nonfiction: "Mainly serious articles about raising effectiveness of information handling. Interviews. Informational, technical, think pieces, spot news. News pieces about computers and their business use. Articles should be clear and not stylized. Assertions should be well-supported by facts. We are business-oriented, witty, more interested in the widely applicable story, and less technical than most. We'll run a good article with a computer peg even if it's not entirely about computers. Business analysis done by people with good backgrounds." Buys 15 mss/year. Length: 300-1,000 words for news; 1,000-5,000 words for features. Pays 3-10¢/word. "Supply professional pictures with story."

COMPUTER DESIGN, 119 Russel St., Littleton MA 01460. Editor-in-Chief: Saul B. Dinman. Executive Editor: Michael Elphick. Managing Editor: Sydney F. Shapiro. 35% freelance written. For digital electronic design engineers and engineering managers. Monthly. Buys all rights. Pays on publication. Byline given. Free sample copy. Reports in 12 weeks. Computer printout submissions OK if letter quality. SASE.
Nonfiction: Engineering articles on the design and application of digital equipment and systems used in computing, data processing, control, automation, instrumentation and communications. "We do not accept column material from non-staff writers. All accepted material need be of value and interest to practicing design engineers." Query. Pays $30-50/page.
Tips: "Send query letter before outline or manuscript. Know the subject intimately before attempting to write an article. List suggested title, scope, and length of article and why *CD* readers would be interested."

COMPUTER GRAPHICS WORLD, 1714 Stockton St., San Francisco CA 94133. (415)398-7151. Publisher/Editor: Randall Stickrod. Monthly magazine covering computer graphics for managers in business, industry, government and institutions; readers are interested in computer graphic application and technology. Circ. 15,000. Pays on publication. Byline and brief bio given. Buys first North American serial rights; "reprints should give us credit." Simultaneous queries and photocopied submissions OK. Reports immediately. Free sample copy; "Editorial Highlights" available.
Nonfiction: Case studies, success stories in using computer graphics to solve problems. "Articles must be relevant to the needs of persons interested in applying computer graphics." Buys 25 mss/year. Query by phone or brief letter. Length: 1,500 words typical. Pays $50/printed page.
Photos: Prefers negative transparencies and 8x10 b&w glossy prints. State availability of photos or graphics. Captions required. Buys all rights.

COMPUTER MERCHANDISING, The Magazine for High Technology Retailers, Eastman Publishing, 15720 Ventura Blvd., #610, Encino CA 91436. (213)995-0436. Editor: Phillip Missimore. Managing Editor: Larry Tuck. Monthly magazine covering retailing of computers for home and small business use. "The emphasis of the magazine is to aid the growing number of computer retailers." Estab. 1981. Circ. 18,621. Pays on publication. Byline given. Submit seasonal/holiday material 3 months in advance. SASE. Reports in 2 weeks. Sample copy for 9x12 SAE.
Nonfiction: Interview/profile (of industry figures); technical (simple explanation of computers, related products); merchandising suggestions; sales training promotion tips; case histories. No articles on general topics with no relation to the retailing of computers. Buys 12 mss/year. Query. Length: 1,000-2,000 words. Pays $150-350.
Tips: Submit "query which shows research of the specifics of retailing computer products—good grasp of key issues, major names, etc."

COMPUTER RETAILING, W.R.C. Smith Publishing, 1760 Peachtree Rd., Atlanta GA 30357. (404)874-4462. Editor: Anne Bourne. Emphasizes retailing microcomputers. Monthly tabloid. Circ. 20,000. Pays on acceptance. Buys first rights. Pays 50% kill fee. Byline given. Phone queries OK. Submit seasonal/holiday material 2 months in advance. Computer printout and disk submissions OK. SASE. Reports in 2 weeks.
Nonfiction: Interested in freelancers who own microcomputer system and background in accounting, legal, medical, etc. to review software packages (provided). Also interested in interviews with local computer/software stores with unique marketing/promotion ideas. Query. Length: 750-2,000 words. Pays $100-200.
Photos: $50 for color slides of interior/exterior computer store (interesting, colorful, arty). Buys one-time rights. Captions required.
Tips: "Software review section will affect writers in the year ahead."

COMPUTERWORLD, 375 Cochituate Rd., Box 880, Framingham MA 01701. (617)879-0700. Editor: John C. Whitmarsh. 10% freelance written. For management-level computer users, chiefly in the business community, but also in government and education. Weekly. Circ. 120,000. Buys all rights. Pays negotiable kill fee; "we have to initiate the assignment in order to pay a kill fee." Pays on publication. Free sample copy, if request is accompanied by story idea or specific query; free writer's guidelines. Photocopied submissions OK, if exclusive for stated period. Submit special issue material 2 months in advance. Reports in 2-4 weeks. SASE.
Nonfiction: Articles on problems in using computers; educating computer people; trends in the industry; new,

innovative, interesting uses of computers. "We stress impact on users and need a practical approach. What does a development mean for other computer users? Most important facts first, then in decreasing order of significance. We would be interested in material on factory automation and other areas of computer usage that will impact society in general, and not just businesses. We prefer *not* to see executive appointments or financial results. We occasionally accept innovative material that is oriented to unique seasonal or geographical issues." Buys 100 mss/year. Query, "or call specific editor to ask what's needed at a particular time, establish phone rapport with individual editor." Length: 250-1,200 words. Pays 10¢/word, "except In Depth articles and feature articles for special CW publications, which pay a nominal honorarium. Consult individual editor."
Photos: B&w (5x7) glossy prints purchased with ms or on assignment. Captions required. Pays $10 minimum.
Fillers: Newsbreaks and clippings. Query. Length: 50-250 words. Pays 10¢/word.

‡**COMPUTING CANADA, Canada's Bi-Weekly Data Processing Newspaper**, Plesman Publications, Ltd., Suite 302, 211 Consumers Rd., Willowdale, Ontario, Canada M2J 4G8. (416)497-9562. Managing Editor: Grant Buckler. Biweekly tabloid covering data processing, the computer industry, and telecommunications for data processing management and professionals. Circ. 30,000. Pays on publication. Byline given. Buys one-time rights. Submit seasonal/holiday material 1 month in advance. Simultaneous queries and submissions OK. Computer printout submissions OK; prefers letter quality to dot matrix. SASE. Reports in 1 month. Free sample copy and writer's guidelines.
Nonfiction: How-to, interview/profile, current industry news. Special features (software report, office automation, computers in education, etc.) in each issue. Length: 250-1,500 words. Pays $25-100.
Tips: "Suggest a story on an industry event or trend we haven't picked up on. More use of freelance material and more coverage of the microcomputer and office automation markets will affect writers in the year ahead."

‡**DATA MANAGEMENT MAGAZINE, The Magazine for Information Processing Professionals**, Data Processing Management Association (DPMA), 505 Busse Hwy., Park Ridge IL 60068. (312)825-8124. Editor: Bill Zalud. Monthly magazine covering information processing management for professionals with corporate level responsibility for information resource and consulting services, DP service organizations and businesses with emphasis on information processing. Circ. 51,010. Pays on publication or on a negotiable basis. Byline given. Buys one-time rights. Submit seasonal/holiday material 3 months in advance. Simultaneous queries OK. Reports in 2 weeks on queries; 3 weeks on mss. Free sample copy and writer's guidelines.
Nonfiction: Interview/profile, technical. "Editorial calendar available upon request. Nothing out-dated—material must be timely." Buys 10-25 mss/year. Send complete ms. Length: 1,500-3,000 words. Pays negotiable fee.
Photos: State availability of photos with query letter or ms. Reviews 35mm color transparencies and b&w 5x7 prints. Pays negotiable fee. Captions and identification of subjects required.
Fiction: Humorous. Buys 5-10 mss/year. Send complete ms. Length: 500-1,500 words. Pays negotiable fee.
Tips: "All articles submitted to *Data Management* must contain the point of view of the information processing manager. Authors should keep in mind that our readers are professionals."

DATAMATION, Technical Publishing D & B, 875 3rd Ave., New York NY 10022. Editor: John Kirkley. Monthly magazine for scientific, engineering and commercial data processing professionals. Circ. 150,000. Pays on publication. Byline given. Pays negotiable kill fee. Buys all rights. Submit seasonal/holiday material 3 months in advance. Photocopied submissions and previously published submissions ("if indicated where") OK. SASE. Reports as soon as possible on queries. Free sample copy and writer's guidelines. "Request our list of themes for the coming year."
Nonfiction: "Horizontal publication covering all aspects of computer industry technical, managerial and sociological concerns, as well as computer industry news analysis." No general articles on computers. Buys 30 mss/year. Query with clips of published work. Length: 2,000-4,000 words. Pays $300-1,000/article.
Photos: Reviews 35mm color transparencies and 8x10 b&w prints. "No extra payment for photos—included in payment for manuscript."

‡**THE DEC PROFESSIONAL**, Professional Press, Inc., Box 362, Ambler PA 19002. (215)542-7008. Publishers: Carl B. Marbach and R.D. Mallery. Bimonthly magazine covering Digital Equipment Corp. computers. "We publish highly technical, user-written articles concerning DEC equipment. We are a forum for DEC users worldwide." Circ. 65,000. Byline given. Buys all rights. Simultaneous queries, and simultaneous, photocopied, and previously published submissions OK. "We prefer 800 or 1600 BPI mag tape as a computer printout." Free sample copy and writer's guidelines.
Nonfiction: Technical (computer related). No articles "not highly technical concerning DEC computers and related topics." Send complete ms. Length: 1,500-5,000 words. Pays $100-300.
Fiction: Fantasy, humorous. No stories unrelated to DEC equipment (games for computers).
Tips: "Send manuscript or idea, preferably on 800/1600 BPI mag tape in PIP format, or WORD-II, a RST/

RSTS/RTII floppy, or letter quality printout. No material unrelated to Digital Equipment Corporation equipment, peripherals, etc. We have no full time staff writers and rely on people in the field to submit articles.''

‡**HARDCOPY, The Magazine of Digital Equipment**, Seldin Publishing Co., Suite D, 1061 S. Melrose, Placentia CA 92670. (714)632-6924. Managing Editor: Clare P. Fleig. Monthly magazine covering Digital Equipment Corporation (DEC)-related computer equipment, software, peripherals and compatibles primarily for management-level readers with the basics in computers and computer equipment manufacturers looking for more information on how to sell, distribute or improve their computer products. Circ. 60,000. Pays on publication. Byline given. Buys all rights. Submit seasonal/holiday material 4 months in advance. Computer printout submissions OK if double-spaced. SASE. Reports in 2 weeks on queries; 2 months on mss. Sample copy for 9x12 SAE and $1.90 postage; writer's guidelines for business-size SAE and 1 first class stamp.
Nonfiction: How-to (sell product; computer-oriented management and business); interview/profile (DEC or DEC-compatible manufacturers); technical (DEC computer-oriented). No non-computer related features or computer-oriented features that do not relate in any way to Digital Equipment Corporation. Buys 24 mss/year. Query with clips. Length: 2,000-3,500 words. Pays $200-500.
Photos: Pays $10-25 for 5x7 b&w prints; $25 for 35mm color transparencies. Indentification of subjects required.
Columns/Departments: Newsbreak, Bottomline, PC Watch, Communications & Networking, New Literature—news, financial information, personal computers, communication articles, and book reviews on new automation topics. Buys 12 mss/year. Query with clips. Length: 1,500-2,500 words. Newsbreak and New Literature length: 500-750 words. Pays $50-300.
Fiction: Science fiction. "Fiction must be computer-oriented and geared to a management audience." Buys 6 mss/year. Send complete ms. Length: 2,000-3,500 words. Pays $200-500.
Tips: "We need solid technical and how-to features from contributors. Research must be thorough and the article's main point must somehow relate to DEC. For example, a market trend article should explain how DEC's market will be affected. We anticipate the size of the magazine growing about 50% in 1983 which will increase our need for freelance copy."

ICP INTERFACE SERIES, International Computer Programs, Inc., 9000 Keystone Crossing, Indianapolis IN 46240. (317)844-7461. Editor-in-Chief: Dennis Hamilton. Editors: Paul Pinella, Scott Palmer, Louis Harm and Sheila Cunningham. Seven quarterly magazines covering computer software applications and program use in the business and scientific community. Circ. 198,000. Pays on acceptance. Byline given. Buys all rights. Phone queries OK. Submit seasonal material 3 months in advance. Simultaneous and photocopied submissions OK. Computer printout submissions OK; prefers letter quality to dot matrix. Reports in 3 weeks. Free sample copy and writer's guidelines.
Nonfiction: Expose (waste, corruption, misuse of computers); interview (of major computer industry figures); opinion (of computer applications); how-to (computer solutions); humor (computer-related); new product; personal experience (case studies); and technical (application). Recent article examples: "How to Double Your Personal Productivity with a Microcomputer." No articles discussing the merits of a single product. Buys 5-10 unsolicited mss/year. Length: 1,000-3,000 words. Pays $50-$250.

INFORMATION SYSTEMS NEWS for Information Systems Management, CMP Publications, 111 E. Shore Rd., Manhasset NY 11030. (516)365-4600. Editor: James Moran. Biweekly tabloid covering hardware, software, computer communication and office automation for managers and staff of major computer installations at US corporations. Circ. over 100,000. Pays "within 30 days of acceptance." Byline given. Buys all rights. SASE. Reports in 1 month.
Nonfiction: "We're looking for articles of business-oriented news for managers of information systems." Buys 50 mss/year. Query by phone or mail. Length: 500 words minimum. Pays $150 minimum/article.
Photos: State availability of photos.
Tips: "Unsolicited manuscripts are discouraged, but clippings, queries and resumes are considered carefully. Be sure to include a phone number."

INTERFACE AGE, Computing for Business, McPheters, Wolfe & Jones, 16704 Marquardt Ave., Cerritos CA 90701. (213)926-9544. Managing Editor: Les Spindle. Monthly magazine covering microcomputers in business. "Although *Interface Age* has a wide range of readers from engineers to hobbyists, there is a distinct focus toward the businessman. Readers receive up-to-the-minute reports on new products, applications for business and programs they can apply to their own personal computer." Circ. 90,000. Buys first North American serial rights. Submit material 4 months in advance. Computer printout and disk submissions OK "after phone-consulting with editors." Reports in 6 weeks on mss. Sample copy $3.75; free writer's guidelines.
Nonfiction: "Articles should pertain to microcomputing applications in business, law, education, medicine, software, unique breakthroughs, future projections. We seek interviews/profiles of people well-known in the industry or making unusual use of microcomputers. Computer programs and sample listings must be printed with a new ribbon to get the best quality reproduction in the magazine." Buys 50-60 unsolicited mss/year. Send

complete ms. Length: 1,500-3,000 words. Pays $50-80/printed page including photos, charts, programs and listings.

Photos: Send photos, charts, listings and programs with ms.

Fillers: Book reviews (on anything concerning microcomputers). Length: 250 words minimum. Pays $20 each.

Tips: "Case study articles specifying how a particular type of business (law firm, retail store, office, etc.) implemented a computer to improve efficiency stand the best chance for acceptance. Hardware and software appraisals by qualified reviewers are also desirable. Practical and business applications, rather than home/hobbyist pursuits, are encouraged."

JOURNAL OF SYSTEMS MANAGEMENT, 24587 Bagley Road, Cleveland OH 44138. (216)243-6900. Publisher: James Andrews. 100% freelance written. For systems and procedures and management people. Monthly. Buys all serial rights. Byline given. Pays on publication. Free sample copy. Reports "as soon as possible." SASE.

Nonfiction: Articles on case histories, projects on systems, forms control, administrative practices and computer operations. No computer applications articles, humor or articles promoting a specific product. Query or submit ms in triplicate. Length: 3,000-5,000 words. Pays $25 maximum.

Tips: "We expect to receive articles over hard lines direct to our electronic terminals soon."

MINI-MICRO SYSTEMS, Cahners Publishing Co., 221 Columbus Ave., Boston MA 02116. (617)536-7780. Executive Editor: Alan R. Kaplan. Monthly magazine covering minicomputer and microcomputer industries for manufacturers and users of small computers, related equipment and software. Circ. 110,148. Pays on publication. Byline given. Buys all rights. Simultaneous queries and photocopied submissions OK. SASE. Reports in 1 month on queries. Free sample copy; free writer's guidelines for 4x9 SAE and 1 first class stamp.

Nonfiction: "Articles about highly innovative applications of computer hardware and software 'firsts'." Buys 60-100 mss/year. Query with clips of published work. Length: 500-2,500 words. Pays $70/printed page, including illustrations.

Photos: Send line art, diagrams, photos or color transparencies.

Tips: "The best way to break in is to be affiliated with a manufacturer or user of computers or a peripheral."

SMALL SYSTEMS WORLD, Hunter Publishing, 950 Lee St., Des Plaines IL 60016. (312)296-0770. Editor: Hellena Smejda. Monthly magazine covering applications of small computer systems in business. Circ. 40,000. Pays on acceptance. Byline given. Buys all rights. Submit seasonal/holiday material 4 months in advance. Reports in 2 weeks on queries. Sample copy $2.

Nonfiction: How-to (use the computer in business); and technical (organization of a data base or file system). "A writer who submits material to us should be an expert in computer applications. No material on large-scale computer equipment." No poetry. Buys 4 mss/year. Query. Length: 3,000-4,000 words. Pays $100 minimum/article.

Photos: State availability of photos.

Poetry: Payment varies/poem.

Fillers: Needs "management-oriented articles for small computer installations." Buys 5-6/year. Length: 800-1,500 words. Pays $75 average.

‡TELESYSTEMS JOURNAL, OSI Publications, Ltd., Fort Lee Executive Park, 2 Executive Dr., Fort Lee NJ 07024. (201)592-0009, (800)526-0272. Editor: Joyce Schelling. Executive Editor: Paul P. Morin. Bimonthly trade journal covering large-scale IBM main frame computers and the associated on-line software. "A forum for the exchange of technological information among computer professionals." Circ. 600. Pays on publication. Byline given. Buys all rights. Submit seasonal/holiday material 6 months in advance. Photocopied submissions OK. Reports in 6 weeks. Free sample copy and writer's guidelines.

Nonfiction: Expose (non-governmental, non-political, non-vendor); general interest (computer security, auditing and privacy controls—all areas of project planning, such as project life cycle, feasibility, design, and implementation); personal computers (articles dealing with direct hook-up to a large mainframe, and personal computers in the business world); new products (articles about IBM releases); personal experience (case studies, such as the technical story behind a major programming effort; use of a new product, including features of the product and what it accomplished for the installation; problems and/or methodology of installing or generating a system such as NCP); telecommunications (networking; philosophy and actual case implementation; latest in hardware, such as a description of, or innovative use of, 3270 and 8775 terminals and 3705 controllers); interview/profile (people involved in major software implementations; profile of the hardware and software used by an IBM shop). Special issues include Computer security for on-line systems; IBM/DB/DC; Personal computers in business; Data processing training and education, and others. Write for details. "We don't want to see articles about non-IBM or non-IBM compatible equipment; theory articles such as '37 Formulae to Use When Designing Data Structures'. We'd rather have 'How to use Bi-directional Pointers in your IMS Data Base'; articles such as 'How to Program your TRS-80'. We'd rather have 'Personal Computers and

Business Graphics'. Query or send complete ms. Length: 2,000-15,000 words. Pays $100-600.
Photos: "Send photos, diagrams, charts with manuscripts. No extra payment for photos."
Columns/Departments: Linkage Editor (column)—"We seek questions about IBM on-line software that we answer in the first available issue." Book Reviews—reviews of high tech books. Query or send complete ms. Length: 25-100 words for Linkage Editor; 300-1,000 words for Book Reviews. Pays $25 for Linkage Editor; $25-100 for Book Reviews.
Tips: "We stress the technological side of the major IBM software packages. We are interested in all aspects of computer training for these software packages; for their innovative use; for how-to's, how does it work, and for reviews of software announcements. Some examples of articles that would interest us are: 'How to Design Efficient BMS Screens for the 3270 Terminal' and 'How to Tune Your CICS/MVS System'. We also seek articles on computer security, pricing, law, and auditing. Finally, we balance our journal with articles on management topics, such as project management, capacity planning, and management strategies. All sections are open to freelancers. Our freelancers are generally computer technicians with some writing ability, or writers who are comfortable in the esoteric world of high technology. Query by telephone and establish rapport with the editor."

Dental

CONTACTS, Box 407, North Chatham NY 12132. Editor: Joseph Strack. For laboratory owners, managers, and dental technician staffs. Bimonthly. Circ. 1,200. Pays on acceptance. Byline given. Free sample copy. Reports in 1-2 weeks. SASE.
Nonfiction and Photos: Writer should know the dental laboratory field or have good contacts there to provide technical articles, how-to, and successful business operation articles. Query. Length: 1,500 words maximum. Pays 3-5¢/word. Willing to receive suggestions for columns and departments for material of 400-1,200 words. Payment for these negotiable.

DENTAL ECONOMICS, Box 3408, Tulsa OK 74101. Editor: Dick Hale. 60% freelance written. Emphasizes "practice management for dentists." Monthly magazine; 90 pages. Circ. 103,000. Pays on acceptance. Buys all rights. Byline given. "Occasionally no byline is given when it's an article combining talents of several authors, but credit is always acknowledged." Submit seasonal/holiday material 4 months in advance of issue date. Computer printout and disk submissions OK, "but we question 'exclusivity'—we must have exclusives in our field." SASE. Reports in 4 weeks. Free sample copy and writer's guidelines.
Nonfiction: Expose (closed panels, NHI); how-to (hire personnel, bookkeeping, improve production); humor (in-office type); investments (all kinds); interview (doctors in the news, health officials); personal experience (of dentists, but only if related to business side of practice); profile (a few on doctors who made dramatic lifestyle changes); and travel (only if dentist is involved). Buys 100-120 unsolicited mss/year. Query or submit complete ms. Length: 600-3,500 words. Pays $50-500.
Photos: State availability of photos with query or submit photo with ms. Pays $10 minimum for 8x10 glossy photos; $25 minimum for 35mm color transparencies. Captions and model release required. Buys all North American rights.
Columns/Departments: Viewpoint (issues of dentistry are aired here). Buys 1 ms/issue. Submit complete ms. Length: 600-1,500 words.
Tips: *DE*'s advice to freelancers is: "Talk to dentists about their problems and find an answer to one or more of them. Know the field. Read several copies of *DE* to determine slant, style and length. Write for 1 dentist, not 100,000. We're growing—need more submissions—need *objective* look at computers—both hardware and software."

DENTAL MANAGEMENT, The National Business Magazine for Dentists, HBJ Publications, 7500 Old Oak Blvd., Cleveland OH 44130. (216)243-8100. Editor: Belinda Wilson. Managing Editor: John Sabol. Monthly magazine covering business and financial aspects of dental practice, practice management, malpractice, insurance, investments, and psychologic aspects of denistry for dentists in clinical practice. Circ. 104,000. Pays on publication. Buys all rights. Byline given. SASE. Reports in 3 weeks. Writer's guidelines for SASE.
Nonfiction: Expose (bad investments, tax shelters, poor insurance deals); general interest; how-to (investments, advertising, getting new patients); interview; opinion; personal experience. No clinical mss, fiction, cartoons, poetry. Buys 100 mss/year. Query. Length: 3,000 words maximum. Pays $125/published page.
Columns/Departments: "Office Innovations' column most open to freelancers. Interview dentist or staff on tips for dentists on the business/financial aspects of dentistry. Should be innovations actually used by dental office." Buys 60/year. Send complete ms. Length: 250-500 words. Pays $25/published item.

PROOFS, The Magazine of Dental Sales and Marketing, Box 3408, Tulsa OK 74101. (918)835-3161. Publisher: Joe Bessette. Editor: Mary Elizabeth Good. Magazine published 10 times/year; combined issues July/August, November/December. Pays on publication. Byline given. Will send free sample copy on request. Query. Reports in 2 weeks. SASE.

Nonfiction: Uses short articles, chiefly on selling to dentists. Must have understanding of dental trade industry, and problems of marketing and selling to dentists and dental laboratories. Pays about $75.

TIC MAGAZINE, Box 407, North Chatham NY 12132. (518)766-3047. Editor: Joseph Strack. For dentists, dental assistants, and oral hygienists. Monthly. Buys first publication rights in the dental field. Byline given. Pays on acceptance. Reports in 2 weeks. SASE.

Nonfiction: Uses articles (with illustrations, if possible) as follows: 1. Lead feature: Dealing with major developments in dentistry of direct, vital interest to all dentists. 2. How-to-do-it pieces: Ways and means of building dental practices, improving professional techniques, managing patients, increasing office efficiency, etc. 3. Special articles: Ways and means of improving dentist-laboratory relations for mutual advantage, of developing auxiliary dental personnel into an efficient office team, of helping the individual dentist to play a more effective role in alleviating the burden of dental needs in the nation and in his community, etc. 4. General articles: Concerning any phase of dentistry or dentistry-related subjects of high interest to the average dentist. "Especially interested in profile pieces (with b&w photographs) on dentists who have achieved recognition/success in nondental fields—business, art, sport or whatever. Interesting, well-written pieces a sure bet." No material written for patients instead of dentists or "humorous" pieces about pain. Query. Length: 800-3,200 words. Pays 5¢ minimum/word.

Photos: Photo stories: 4-10 pictures of interesting developments and novel ideas in dentistry. B&w only. Pays $10 minimum/photo.

Tips: "We can use fillers of about 300 words or so. They should be pieces of substance on just about anything of interest to dentists. A psychoanalyst broke in with us recently with pieces relating to interpretations of patients' problems and attitudes in dentistry. Another writer broke in with a profile of a dentist working with an Indian tribe."

Drugs and Health Care Products

THE APOTHECARY, HealthCare Marketing Services, 334 State St., Box AP, Los Altos CA 94022. (415)941-3955. Editor: Jerold Karabensh. Managing Editor: Janet Goodman. Magazine published 6 times/year covering pharmacy. "*The Apothecary* aims to provide practical information to community retail pharmacists." Circ. 65,000. Pays on acceptance. Byline given. Buys all rights. Submit seasonal/holiday material 6-8 months in advance. Simultaneous queries and photocopied submissions OK. Computer printout submissions OK; prefers letter quality to dot matrix. SASE. Reports in 6 weeks on queries; 5 months on mss. Free sample copy and writer's guidelines.

Nonfiction: Cathryn D. Evans, articles editor. How-to (e.g., manage a pharmacy); opinion (of registered pharmacists); technical (related to drug therapy); and health-related feature stories. "We publish general health articles, but only those with some practical application for the pharmacist. No general articles not geared to our pharmacy readership; no fiction." Buys 10 mss/year. Query with clips of published work. Length: 750-3,000 words. Pays $100-350.

Columns/Departments: Cathryn D. Evans, column/department editor. Commentary (views or issues relevant to the subject of pharmacy or to pharmacists). Send complete ms. Length: 750-1,000 words. "This section unpaid; will take submissions with byline."

Fillers: Cathryn D. Evans, fillers editor. Clippings. Unpaid; usually supplied from within.

Tips: "Write according to our policy, i.e., health-related articles with emphasis on practical information for a community pharmacist, or business articles of specific relevance to a pharmacist. Suggest reading several back issues and following general feature-story tone, depth, etc. Stay away from condescending use of language. Though our articles are written in simple style, they must reflect knowledge of subject and reasonable respect for the readers' professionalism and intelligence."

CANADIAN PHARMACEUTICAL JOURNAL, 101-1815 Alta Vista Dr., Ottawa, Ontario, Canada K1G 3Y6. (613)523-7877. Associate Editor: S. Jessup Donaldson. Assistant Editor (freelance contact): Elaine Rolfe. For pharmacists. Monthly journal; 40 pages. Circ. 13,000. Pays on publication. Computer printout submissions OK; prefers letter quality to dot matrix. Reports in 2 months. Free sample copy and writer's guidelines.

Nonfiction: (relevant to Canadian pharmacy); publishes exposes (pharmacy practice, education and legislation); how-to (pharmacy business operations); historical (pharmacy practice, Canadian legislation, education);

interviews with and profiles on Canadian and international pharmacy figures. Buys 6 unsolicited mss/year. "Only buys from Canadian freelancers." Recent article example: "Ortho Pharmaceutical Takes Part in Unique Space Venture" (November 1982). Length: 200-400 words (for news notices); 800-1,200 words (for articles). Query. Payment is contingent on value; usually 12¢/word.

Photos: B&w (5x7) glossies purchased with mss. Captions required. Pays $5/photo. Model release required.

Tips: "Query with complete description of proposed article, including topic, sources (in general), length, payment requested, suggested submission date, whether photographs will be included. It is helpful if the writer has read a *recent* (1982-83) copy of the journal; we are glad to send one if required. Only Canadian writers are welcome to contribute. The letter should describe the proposed article thoroughly. References should be included where appropriate (this is vital where medical and scientific information is included). Send 4 copies of each ms. Author's degree and affiliations (if any) should be listed; author's writing background should be included (in brief form)."

DRUG TOPICS, 680 Kinderkamack Rd., Oradell NJ 07649. (201)262-3030. Editor: Valentine Cardinale. Executive Editor: Ralph M. Thurlow. For retail drug stores and wholesalers, manufacturers. Semimonthly. Circ. over 70,000. Buys all rights. Pay varies. Byline given "only for features." Pays on acceptance. Computer printout submissions OK. SASE.

Nonfiction: News of local, regional, state pharmaceutical associations, legislation affecting operation of drug stores, news of pharmacists and store managers in civic and professional activities, etc. No stories about manufacturers. Query on drug store success stories which deal with displays, advertising, promotions, selling techniques. Query. Length: 1,500 words maximum. Pays $5 and up for leads, $25 and up for short articles, $100-300 for feature articles, "depending on length and depth."

Photos: May buy photos submitted with mss. May buy news photos with captions only. Pays $10-20.

HOME HEALTH CARE BUSINESS, Cassak Publications, 2009 Morris Ave., Union NJ 07083. (201)687-8282. Editor: Laurie Cassak. For pharmacists, home health care managers and manufacturers of patient aid products. Bimonthly. Circ. 8,000. Buys all rights. Pays on publication. Free sample copy and writer's guidelines. Photocopied and simultaneous submissions OK. SASE.

Nonfiction and Photos: "Articles about existing home health care centers or opportunities for proprietors; articles about new technologies in the home care field; helpful hints for the pharmacist engaged in serving the booming consumer/home health care field. It is essential to understand your reading audience. Articles must be informative, but not extremely technical." No human interest stories. Buys informational, how-to, interview, photo articles. Query. Length: 1,000-1,500 words. Photos purchased with accompanying ms with no additional payment. Captions optional.

NARD JOURNAL, The National Association of Retail Druggists, 205 Daingerfield Rd., Alexandria VA 22314. Not currently seeking freelance material.

‡RX HOME CARE, The Journal of Home Health Care and Rehabilitation, Brentwood Publishing Corp., 825 S. Barrington Ave., Los Angeles CA 90049. (213)826-8388. Editors: Martin H. Waldman, Hal Spector. Managing Editor: Nancy Greengold. Monthly magazine of the home health care marketplace for medical equipment supply dealers. Circ. 22,000. Pays on acceptance. Byline given. Buys all rights. Submit seasonal/holiday material 4 months in advance. SASE. Reports in 4 weeks. Sample copy $5; free writer's guidelines.

Nonfiction: Equipment-oriented articles on assignment only. "Therapists, nurses and freelancers may contribute to this journal. Articles are of an educational or marketing/business nature." No write-ups of specific products or general interest stories. Buys 60 mss/year. Query with resume and published clips. Length: 1,000-2,500 words. Pays $100-300.

Columns/Departments: Management Matters (tips on running a medical equipment supply business); Sidelights (1,000-word descriptions of specific dealerships). "All mss must be assigned." Buys 20 mss/year. Query with published clips. Length: 750-1,000 words. Pays $75-100.

Tips: "Submit resume with clips of published work. We will contact you if we are interested. We are continually on the lookout for new freelancers and often keep resumes on file for months before we get back to you. The magazine is 85% freelance written. Writers skilled in marketing or business writing are most successful."

WHOLESALE DRUGS, 1111 E. 54th St., Indianapolis IN 46220. Editor: William F. Funkhouser. Bimonthly. Buys first rights. Query. SASE.

Nonfiction and Photos: Wants features on presidents and salesmen of full line wholesale drug houses throughout the country. No set style, but article should tell about both the subject and his/her company—history, type of operation, etc. Pays $50 for text and pictures. Primarily staff-written.

Education

Professional educators, teachers, coaches and school personnel—as well as other people involved with training and education—read the journals classified here. Education-related publications for students are included in the College, Career, and Alumni and Teen and Young Adult sections of Consumer Publications.

THE AMERICAN SCHOOL BOARD JOURNAL, National School Boards Association, 1055 Thomas Jefferson St. NW, Washington DC 20007. (202)337-7666. Features Editor: Jerome Cramer. Emphasizes public school administration and policymaking. For elected members of public boards of education throughout the US and Canada, and high-level administrators of same. Monthly magazine; 64 pages. Circ. 50,000. Pays on acceptance. Buys all rights. Phone queries OK. Photocopied submissions OK. Computer printout submissions OK. SASE. Reports in 6 weeks. Free sample copy and guidelines.
Nonfiction: Publishes how-to articles (solutions to problems of public school operation including political problems); interviews with notable figures in public education. "No material on how public schools are in trouble. We all know that; what we need are *answers*." Buys 20 mss/year. Query. Length: 400-2,000 words. Payment for feature articles varies, "but never less than $100."
Photos: B&w glossies (any size) and color purchased on assignment. Captions required. Pays $10-50. Model release required.

CATECHIST, Peter Li, Inc., 2451 E. River Rd., Dayton OH 45439. Editor: Patricia Fischer. Emphasizes religious education for professional and volunteer religious educators working in Catholic schools and parish programs. Monthly (July/August—April) magazine; 70 pages. Circ. 50,000. Pays on publication. Buys all rights. Submit seasonal/holiday material 3 months in advance. Computer printout and disk submissions OK. SASE. Reports in 2 months. Sample copy $2; free writer's guidelines.
Nonfiction: Publishes how-to articles (methods for teaching a particular topic or concept); informational (theology and church-related subjects, insights into current trends and developments); personal experience (in the religious classroom). Buys 45 mss/year. Query. Length: 1,500 words maximum. Pays $30-75.
Photos: Pays $15-25 for b&w 8x10 glossy prints purchased without mss. Send contact sheet.
Tips: "We like to see articles that would be of practical use for the teacher of religion or an article that results from personal experience and expertise in the field."

COACHING REVIEW, Coaching Association of Canada, 333 River Rd., Ottawa, Ontario, Canada K1L 8B9. (613)741-0036. Editor: Vic MacKenzie. For volunteer, community and paid coaches, high school and university sports personnel. Bimonthly magazine in separate English and French issues; 64 pages. Circ. 15,000. Pays on acceptance. Buys first North American rights. Pays 50-75% kill fee. Byline given unless author requests otherwise. Phone queries OK. Submit seasonal/holiday material 3 months in advance. Computer printout or disk submissions OK. Reports in 3 weeks. Free sample copy and writer's guidelines.
Nonfiction: How-to (coach-related of a general interest to all sports); humor (in coaching situations); inspirational (coaching success stories); interview (with top successful coaches); and new product (new ideas and ways of coaching). Wants "authoritative original material on coaching topics." Does not want sports stories with little or no relevance to coaching. Buys 15-20 unsolicited mss/year. Query with complete ms. Length: 1,500-2,500 words. Pays up to $200.
Photos: State availability of photos. Pays $5-25 for b&w contact sheets; $15-30 for slide size color transparencies. Captions required. Buys one-time rights.

COLLEGE UNION MAGAZINE, 825 Old Country Rd., Box 1500, Westbury NY 11590. Managing Editor: Marcy Kornreich. Emphasizes campus activity and service professionals. Published 6 times/year. Circ. 10,000. Pays on publication. Buys all rights. Queries suggested. Photocopied submissions OK. No computer printout or disk submissions. Reports in 3 weeks on queries. Must include SASE for writer's guidelines. Include large manilla envelope for sample copy.
Nonfiction: General interest (food service, computers, vending, refurbishing building); historical (history of a particular school's union); how-to (run or operate any aspect of student activities); profiles (of particular union operation); personal experience (within college union work); and photo feature (operations, game room, cultural program, whole building, lobby, theater, ballroom). No fillers. Recent article example: "Talk Isn't Cheap Anymore! The Dilemmas of Lecture Programming" (April 1983). Wants "good quotes, well-rounded treatment of the topic." No articles about students in college or anything *not* pertaining to the union, student activities, food service, housing, programming, etc. Buys 3-5 mss/year. Query. Length: 1,500 words maximum. Pays $2/column inch.
Photos: Pays $5 for 5x7 b&w prints and contact sheets.
Columns/Departments: Pinpoint (trends in campus life). Query. Length: 50-200 words.

Tips: "Submit articles aimed at professional employees who operate college unions, not students. Tightened budgets will force me to become more selective. Writers should include samples of other articles written for publication—just so I can get a feel for their abilities. Saves me time—saves them time."

CURRICULUM REVIEW AND CURRICULUM REVIEW SUBJECT REPORTS, Curriculum Advisory Service, 517 S. Jefferson St., Chicago IL 60607. (312)939-3010. Editor-in-Chief: Irene M. Goldman. Managing Editor: Charlotte H. Cox. A multidisciplinary magazine for K-12 principals, department heads, teachers, curriculum planners, superintendents; published 5 times/year (bimonthly through school year). Circ. 40,000. The *Subject Reports* (12-16 pages each) in the areas of language arts/reading, mathematics, science, and social studies are extracted from the full magazine and include computer material. Pays on publication. Byline given. Buys all rights. Photocopies and multiple queries OK, but no multiple submissions. SASE. Reports in 3-6 weeks on queries; 4 months on mss. Free sample copy and writer's guidelines.
Nonfiction: Barbara Berndt, articles editor. "How-to" articles should consider an audience of secondary educators only and describe successful teaching units or courses which might be implemented elsewhere. Other articles should focus on innovative or practical programs, teaching units, new curriculum trends, and controversial or stimulating ideas in education. Buys 45 mss/year. Length: 1,000-2,000 words. Query. Pays $25-100.
Photos: State availability of photos with query or ms. Prefers 35mm color transparencies or 8x10 b&w or color prints. Model release required. Buys all rights with ms; no additional payment.
Columns/Departments: 600 book reviews/year on an assigned basis with educational vita; textbook, supplements, media, and computer software selection in language arts/reading, mathematics, science, social studies. Emphazises secondary level. "We are looking for new treatments of educational topics. Description of specific teaching units or courses are welcome if they have broad implications for other schools. Use fresh, descriptive, plain language—no educationalese. While we need articles in all 4 areas (language arts/reading, math, science, social studies), math and science are especially welcome." Length: 300-600 words. Pays $20-50.
Tips: "In 1984 we will feature careers for the 80s and beyond, adolescent alienation, gifted education, science and societal issues, communication skills, technology, and computers. Schedule available upon request."

FORECAST FOR HOME ECONOMICS, 730 Broadway, New York NY 10003. Editorial Director: Kathy Gogick. Senior Editor: Elizabeth Forst. 10% freelance written. Monthly (September-May/June) magazine; 80 pages. Circ. 78,000. Pays on publication. Buys first rights. Pays negotiable kill fee. Byline given. Submit seasonal/holiday material 6-8 months in advance of issue date. SASE. Free writer's guidelines.
Nonfiction: Current consumer/home economics-related issues, especially energy, careers, family relations/child development, teaching techniques, health, nutrition, metrics, mainstreaming the handicapped, appealing to both boys and girls in the classroom, money management, housing, crafts, bulletin board and game ideas. Buys 3 mss/issue. Query first; do not send full-length mss. Length: 1,000-3,000 words. Pays $100 minimum.
Photos: State availability of photos with query. No additional payment for b&w glossy prints. Captions required. Model release required.
Tips: "Contributors to *Forecast* should be professional home economists, and *should* query editorial director before submitting an article. Be sure to include in your query letter "some information about your background and a list of potential articles with a 2-3 line descriptive blurb about what will be included in each article."

INSTRUCTOR MAGAZINE, 757 3rd Ave., New York NY 10017. Editor-in-Chief: Leanna Landsmann. 30% freelance written. Emphasizes elementary education. Monthly magazine; 180 pages. Circ. 269,281. Pays on acceptance. Buys all rights. Phone queries OK. Submit seasonal/holiday material 6 months in advance of issue date. Photocopied submissions OK. No computer printout or disk submissions. SASE. Reports in 6 weeks. Free writer's guidelines; mention *Writer's Market* in request.
Nonfiction: How-to articles on elementary classroom practice—practical suggestions as well as project reports. Query. Length: 750-2,500 words. No poetry.

LEARNING, The Magazine for Creative Teaching, 19 Davis Dr., Belmont CA 94002. Editor: Morton Malkofsky. 45% freelance written. Emphasizes elementary and junior high school education topics. Monthly during school year. Magazine; 150 pages. Circ. 210,000. Pays on acceptance. Buys all rights. Submit seasonal/holiday material 6 months in advance of issue date. Photocopied submissions OK. SASE. Reports in 2 months. Writer's guidelines sent upon request.
Nonfiction: "We publish manuscripts that describe innovative teaching strategies or probe controversial and significant social/political issues related to the professional and classroom interest of preschool to 8th grade teachers." How-to (classroom management, specific lessons or units or activities for children—all at the elementary and junior high level, and hints for teaching math and science); interview; new product; personal experience (from teachers in elementary and junior high schools); and profile (with teachers who are in unusual or innovative teaching situations). Strong interest in articles that deal with discipline, teaching strategy, motivation and working with parents. Recent article examples: "How Come Nobody Never Told Me I Can't Say *Ain't*" and "What Does It Take To Be A Real Teacher" (March 1982); and "For End-of-the-Year Doldrums,

Close-up

Morton Malkofsky
Editor & Publisher, *Learning*

"We look at ourselves as educators who happen to be in publishing, not publishers who happen to be, for the moment, dealing with a product—education," says *Learning* magazine editor, Morton Malkofsky.

"We started *Learning* about 11 years ago because we saw a void out there. Teachers' magazines were catering to readers' most superficial needs and interests. We wanted to deal with significant issues, and we continue to speak out on the way teachers and children should be interacting with each other—whether it's exactly what teachers want to hear or not."

Malkofsky spent eight years in the classroom and then wrote and edited material for children and teachers at the Xerox Education Group before he and a group of colleagues started the magazine. As editor and publisher he has a variety of administrative and editorial responsibilities. One of the most important is reading manuscripts.

Submissions are routed to two editors who read and make comments on whether they should be pursued for publication. "If the two of them agree it's an out-and-out 'no' then it will never get to me. If it does get to me, I'll either agree that it is in shape or needs some work. We'll talk about how the writer can make it better and then send it back for rewriting. If it's a query and there's any possibility that it may work, we tell the writer to go ahead and develop it on spec."

The mark of a can't-miss query letter, says Malkofsky, is when "the writer has some sense of who *Learning* magazine is—some sense of how we distinguish from other publications in the field."

Many of those who know the magazine best are teachers themselves. "The backbone of each issue is really made up of teachers talking to other teachers about their experiences, successful and not so successful, in the classroom. You know, teaching is a pretty lonely task. Oftentimes a teacher could have very little sense of what's going on in the classroom next door. *Learning*, in a way, provides that colleagual support."

The magazine also provides usable information for the classroom teacher. "The thing that determines whether or not I think the piece should go into publication is if I'd want my kid's teacher to read it," says Malkofsky. "The bottom line is really the kids."

Malkofsky is leery of educational reporting that is written for the general public. This is writing too often steeped in achievement test scores and how many are reading at a certain level. "Those writers miss what school should be all about. And they miss the better examples of good teaching. They tend to measure the most superficial aspects of schooling. And that just flies in the face of what we think is important," he adds.

Malkofsky is very sure of the kinds of writers *Learning* likes to hear from. "They are the ones who understand the subtleties of teaching; they know that there is something underneath the frosting of high achievement levels; they understand that teachers should help kids become independent thinkers and problem solvers. We have a very clear image of what we would like to see happening in the classroom. We try to demonstrate a respect for teachers and kids. And we'll do anything we can to support writers who will help us do that."

The Play's the Thing'' (April/May 1982). Buys 250 mss/year. Query. Length: 1,000-3,500 words. Pays $100-350.

Photos: State availability of photos with query. Offers no additional payment for 8x10 b&w glossy prints or 35mm color transparencies. Captions preferred. Buys all rights. Model release required. "Also interested in series of photos for teaching posters that present a topic or tell a story that will be of interest to children."

MEDIA & METHODS, 1511 Walnut St., Philadelphia PA 19102. Editor: Ann Caputo. For teachers who have an abiding interest in humanistic and media-oriented education, plus a core of librarians, media specialists, filmmakers, and educational computer specialists. Magazine. Monthly (September through May). Circ. 32,000. Normally buys all rights. About half of each issue is freelance material. Pays on publication. Free writer's guidelines with SASE. Will consider photocopied submissions. Computer printout or disk submissions OK. Reports in 1-2 months. Submit complete ms or query. SASE.

Nonfiction: "We are looking for the middle school, high school or college educator who has something vital and interesting to say. Subjects include practical how-to articles with broad applicability to our readers, new electronic educational technologies, and innovative, challenging, conceptual stories that deal with educational change. Our style is breezy and conversational, occasionally offbeat. We make a concentrated effort to be nonsexist. Photos welcome." Recent article example: "A Career in the Media" (April 1982). No material not appropriate for educational focus and/or lacking specific, useful information readers can use. Buys 15-25 unsolicited mss/year. Length: 1,800 words maximum. Pays $15-75.

Tips: "We look for articles that talk to educators about methods that they can put to work in the classroom. Theorizing and heavy academic philosophizing are not welcome. In the year ahead there will be more emphasis on newer technologies and expansion of editorial focus to encompass more education-related material."

MEDIA PROFILES: The Career Development Edition, (formerly *Training Film Profiles*), Olympic Media Information, 70 Hudson St., Hoboken NJ 07030. (201)963-1600. Editor: Walt Carroll. For colleges, community colleges, libraries, corporate training directors, manpower specialists, education and training services, career development centers, audiovisual specialists, administrators. Serial in magazine format, published every 2 months. Circ. 1,000. Buys all rights. Pays on publication. "Send resume of your experience in human resource development to introduce yourself." Enclose $5 for writer's guidelines and sample issue (refunded with first payment upon publication). "Wordstar" disk submissions most welcome. Reports in 2 months.

Nonfiction: "Reviews of instructional films, filmstrips, videotapes, sound-slide programs and the like. We have a highly specialized, rigid format that must be followed without exception. Besides job training areas, we are also interested in the areas of values and personal self-development, upward mobility in the world of work, social change, futuristics, management training, problem solving, and adult education. Tell us, above all, about your experience with audiovisuals, and what audiovisual hardware you have access to." Buys 200-240 mss/year. Query. Pays $10-15/review.

MEDIA PROFILES: The Health Sciences Edition, (formerly *Hospital/Health Care Training Media Profiles*), Olympic Media Information, 70 Hudson St., Hoboken NJ 07030. (201)963-1600. Publisher: Walt Carroll. 100% freelance written. For hospital education departments, nursing schools, schools of allied health, paramedical training units, colleges, community colleges, local health organizations. Serial, in magazine format, published every 2 months. Circulation: 1,000 plus. Buys all rights. Buys 240 mss/year. Computer printout submissions OK; disk submissions—"Wordstar" only. Pays on publication. Sample copies and writer's guidelines sent on receipt of your resume, background, and mention of audiovisual hardware you have access to. Enclose $5 for writer's guidelines and sample issue. (Refunded with first payment upon publication). Reports in 1 month. Query.

Nonfiction: "Reviews of all kinds of audiovisual media. We are the only review publication devoted exclusively to evaluation of audiovisual aids for hospital and health training. We have a highly specialized, definite format that must be followed in all cases. Samples should be seen by all means. Our writers should first have a background in health sciences; second, have some experience with audiovisuals; and third, follow our format precisely. Writers with advanced degrees and teaching affiliations with colleges and hospital education departments given preference. We are interested in reviews of media materials for nursing education, in-service education, continuing education, personnel training, patient education, patient care, medical problems. We will assign audiovisual aids to qualified writers and send them these to review for us. Unsolicited mss not welcome." Pays $15/review.

MOMENTUM, National Catholic Educational Association, 1077 30th St., NW, Washington DC 20007. Editor: Patricia Feistritzer. For Catholic administrators and teachers, some parents and students, in all levels of education (preschool, elementary, secondary, higher). Quarterly magazine; 48-64 pages. Circ. 14,500. Buys first magazine publishing rights only. Buys 28-36 mss/year. Pays on publication. Free sample copy. Submit material 3 months in advance. Query with outline of article. Reports in 4 weeks. SASE.

Nonfiction and Photos: "Articles concerned with educational philosophy, psychology, methodology, innovative programs, teacher training, research, financial and public relations programs, management systems—

all applicable to nonpublic schools. Book reviews on educational-religious topics. Avoid general topics or topics applicable *only* to public education. We look for a straightforward, journalistic style with emphasis on practical examples, as well as scholarly writing and statistics. All references must be footnoted, fully documented. Emphasis on professionalism." Length: 1,500-2,000 words. Pays 2¢/word. Pays $7 for b&w glossy photos purchased with mss. Captions required.

NATIONAL ON-CAMPUS REPORT, Suite 4, 607A N. Sherman Ave., Madison WI 53704. (608)249-2455. Editor: Carol Wilson. For education administrators, college student leaders, journalists, and directors of youth organizations. Monthly. Pays 25% kill fee. Pays on publication. Sample copy and writer's guidelines for SASE. Photocopied submissions OK. Reports in 1 month. SASE.
Nonfiction and Fillers: Short, timely articles relating to events and activities of college students. "No clippings of routine college news, only unusual items of possible national interest." Also buys newsbreaks and clippings related to college students and their activities. Buys 10 unsolicited mss/year. Submit complete ms. Length: 25-400 words. Pays 10-12¢/word.
Tips: "We frequently buy story ideas, if not the story itself."

PHI DELTA KAPPAN, Box 789, Bloomington IN 47402. Editor: Robert W. Cole Jr. For educators—teachers, K-12 administrators, college professors. All hold BA degrees; one-third hold doctorates. Monthly magazine; 72 pages. Circ. 140,000. Buys all rights. Pays on publication. Free sample copy. Reports in 1-2 months. SASE.
Nonfiction and Photos: Feature articles on education, emphasizing policy, trends, both sides of issues, controversial developments. Also, informational, how-to, personal experience, interview, profile, inspirational, humor, think articles, expose. "Our audience is scholarly but hard-headed." Buys 10-15 mss/year. Submit complete ms. Length: 500-4,000 words. Pays $25-$250. "We pay a fee only occasionally, and then it is usually to an author whom *we* seek out. We do welcome inquiries from freelancers, but it is misleading to suggest that we buy very much from them." Pays average photographer's rates for b&w photos purchased with mss, but captions are required. Will purchase photos on assignment. Sizes: 8x10 or 5x7 preferred.

SCHOOL ARTS MAGAZINE, 50 Portland St., Worcester MA 01608. Editor: David W. Baker. Serves arts and craft education profession, K-12, higher education and museum education programs. Written by and for art teachers. Monthly, except June, July and August. Will send a sample copy to potential writers on request. Pays on publication. Reports in 90 days. SASE.
Nonfiction and Photos: Articles, with photos, on art and craft activities in schools. Should include description and photos of activity in progress as well as examples of finished art work. Query or send complete ms. Length: 600-1,400 words. Pays $15-85.
Tips: "No articles about philosophical, psychological, or theroretical aspects of art. We need articles on actual projects done in actual classrooms by actual children. Art teachers want practical tips, not a lot of verbiage."

SCHOOL SHOP, Box 8623, Ann Arbor MI 48107. Editor: Lawrence W. Prakken. For "industrial and technical education personnel." Special issue in April deals with varying topics for which mss are solicited. Published 10 times/year. Circ. 45,000. Buys all rights. Pays on publication. Prefers authors who have "direct connection with the field of industrial and/or technical education." Submit mss to Howard Kahn, managing editor. Submit seasonal material 3 months in advance. Reports in 6 weeks. SASE.
Nonfiction and Photos: Uses articles pertinent to the various teaching areas in industrial education (woodwork, electronics, drafting, machine shop, graphic arts, computer training, etc.). "Outlook should be on innovation in educational programs, processes, or projects which directly apply to the industrial-technical education area." Buys how-tos, personal experience and think pieces, interviews, humor, coverage of new products and cartoons. Buys 135 unsolicited mss/year. Length: 500-2,000 words. Pays $15-50. B&w photos purchased with ms.

SIGHTLINES, Educational Film Library Association, Inc., 43 W. 61st St., New York NY 10023. (212)246-4533. Editor-in-Chief: Nadine Covert. 80% freelance written. Emphasizes the nontheatrical film and video world for librarians in university and public libraries, independent filmmakers and video makers, film teachers on the high school and college level, film programmers in the community, university, religious organizations, film curators in museums. Quarterly magazine; 44 pages. Circ. 3,000. Pays on publication. Buys all rights. Byline given. Phone queries OK. SASE. Reports in 2 months. Free sample copy.
Nonfiction: Informational (on the production, distribution and programming of nontheatrical films), interview (with filmmakers who work in 16mm, video; who make documentary, avant-garde, children's, and personal films), new product, and personal opinion (for regular Freedom To View column). No fanzine or feature film material. Buys 4 mss/issue. Query. Length: 4,000-6,000 words. Pay 2½¢/word.
Photos: Purchased with accompanying ms. Captions required. Offers no additional payment for photos accepted with accompanying ms. Model release required.
Columns/Departments: Who's Who in Filmmaking (interview or profile of filmmaker or video artist who

works in the nontheatrical field); Book Reviews (reviews of serious film, media, and/or library-related books); Members Reports (open to those library or museum personnel, film teachers, who are members of the Educational Film Library Association and who have creative ideas for programming films or media in institutions, have solved censorship problems, or other nuts-and-bolts thoughts on using film/media in libraries/schools). Buys 1-3 mss/issue. Query. Pays 2½¢/word. Open to suggestions for new columns or departments.

SPECIAL EDUCATION: FORWARD TRENDS, 12 Hollycroft Ave., London, NW3 7QL, England. Editor: Margaret Peter. Quarterly. Circ. 6,000. Pays token fee for commissioned articles. SAE and International Reply Coupons.
Nonfiction: Articles on the education of all types of handicapped children. "The aim of this journal of the National Council for Special Education is to provide articles on special education and handicapped children that will keep readers informed of practical and theoretical developments not only in education but in the many other aspects of the education and welfare of the handicapped. While we hope that articles will lead students and others to further related reading, their main function is to give readers an adequate introduction to a topic which they may not have an opportunity to pursue further. References should therefore be selective and mainly easily accessible ones. It is important, therefore, that articles of a more technical nature (e.g., psychology, medical, research reviews) should, whenever possible, avoid unnecessary technicalities or ensure that necessary technical terms or expressions are made clear to nonspecialists by the context or by the provision of brief additional explanations or examples. Send query that summarizes the proposed content of the article in some detail, i.e., up to 500 words." No material not related to education. Length: 2,200-3,300 words. Payment by arrangement for commissioned articles only.
Tips: "It's not easy for freelancers to break in unless they are practitioners and specialists in special education. If they have the appropriate specialized knowledge and experience, then articles in easily understood, jargon-free language are welcome, provided the depth of analysis and description are also there."

‡**TEACHING ELECTRONICS & COMPUTING**, Unit 6, 25 Overlea Blvd., Toronto, Ontario, Canada M4H 1B1. (416)423-3262. Editor: Halvor Moorshead. 50% freelance written. Articles of interest to those in the educational field. Some features are presented as (limited) copyright free teachers' notes. Tabloid published 9 times/year; 12-32 pages. Circ. 5,200. Pays on publication. Buys all rights. Byline given. Phone queries OK. Photocopied submissions OK. Free sample copy and writer's guidelines.
Nonfiction and Photos: Use of computers in education, techniques of teaching. Buys 3 unsolicited mss/year (but want many more). Recent article example "Provincial Policies in Teaching Computing." Length: 700-2,000 words. Pays 10¢/word. Author should supply photos if necessary and applicable. Pays extra for photos. Captions required. Buys all rights.

TODAY'S CATHOLIC TEACHER, 26 Reynolds Ave., Ormond Beach FL 32074. (904)672-9974. Editor-in-Chief: Ruth A. Matheny. 25% freelance written. For administrators, teachers, parents concerned with Catholic schools, both parochial and CCD. Circ. 45,000. Pays on publication. Buys all rights. Byline given. Phone queries OK. Submit seasonal/holiday material 3 months in advance of issue date. SASE. Sample copy $2; free writer's guidelines for SASE; mention *Writer's Market* in request.
Nonfiction: How-to (based on experience, particularly in Catholic situations, philosophy with practical applications); interview (of practicing educators, educational leaders); personal experience (classroom happenings); and profile (of educational leader). Buys 40-50 mss/year. Submit complete ms. Length: 800-2,000 words. Pays $15-75.
Photos: State availability of photos with ms. Offers no additional payment for 8x10 b&w glossy prints. Captions preferred. Buys one-time rights. Model release required.

TODAY'S EDUCATION, National Education Association, 1201 16th St. NW., Washington DC 20036. (202)822-7280. Editor: Bill Fisher. For elementary, secondary and higher education teachers. Annual; 192 pages. Circ. 1,700,000. Pays on acceptance. Buys all rights. SASE. Reports in 4 weeks. Free writer's guidelines.
Nonfiction: How-to (teach); descriptions of exemplary public school programs; and in-depth articles on problems of children and youth, e.g., child abuse, student suicide. Query first. Pays negotiable rates. Purchases some photos.

Electricity

Publications classified here are intended for electrical engineers; electrical contractors; and others who build, design, and maintain systems connecting and supplying homes, businesses, and industries with power. Publications for appliance servicemen and dealers will be found in the Home Furnishings and Household Goods classification.

ELECTRIC LIGHT & POWER, Technical Publishing Co., 1301 S. Grove Ave., Barrington IL 60010. (312)381-1840. Editor: Robert A. Lincicome. Managing Editor: Robert W. Smock. Monthly tabloid covering engineering and operations for electric utility executives, managers and engineers. Circ. 42,500. Pays on publication. Byline given. Buys first rights. Submit seasonal/holiday material 4 months in advance. Simultaneous queries OK. SASE. Reports in 3 weeks.
Nonfiction: Technical. "No general electricity articles or pieces discussing benefits of electrification, lighting, industrial, commercial or residential uses of electricity." Buys 24 mss/year. Query. Length: 4,000 words maximum. Pays $25-200/published page.
Photos: Send photos or copies of photos with ms.
Tips: "Writers must be familiar with electric utility technology and engineering, finance, regulation and operations."

ELECTRICAL BUSINESS, Kerrwil Publications, Ltd., 443 Mt. Pleasant Rd., Toronto, Ontario, Canada M4S 2L8. (416)482-6603. Editor-in-Chief: Randolph W. Hurst. 25% freelance written. For "marketing and operating personnel in electrical manufacturing, maintenance and construction as well as distributors." Monthly magazine. Circ. 22,000. Pays on acceptance. Buys first North American serial rights. Pays 10% kill fee. Byline given. Phone queries OK. Submit seasonal/holiday material 4 months in advance of issue date. Previously published submissions "sometimes considered." SAE and International Reply Coupons. Reports in 2 weeks. Free sample copy.
Nonfiction: Canadian electrical industry content only. How-to (problem solving, wiring, electrical construction and maintenance); general interest (to the electrical industry); interview (with electrical distributors and maintenance men); new product ("from manufacturers—we don't pay for news releases"); and technical. Query. Length: 500-1,500 words. Pays 10¢/word.
Photos: State availability of photos with query. Pays $5 for b&w photos; "negotiable" payment for color transparencies. Captions required. Buys one-time rights.

ELECTRICAL CONTRACTOR, 7315 Wisconsin Ave., Bethesda MD 20814. (301)657-3110. Editor: Larry C. Osius. 10% freelance written. For electrical contractors. Monthly. Circ. 51,000. Buys first rights, reprint rights, or simultaneous rights. Byline given. Will send free sample copy on request. Usually reports in 1 month. No computer printout or disk submissions. SASE.
Nonfiction and Photos: Installation articles showing informative application of new techniques and products. Slant is product and method contributing to better, faster, more economical construction process. Query. Length: 800-2,500 words. Pays $75/printed page, including photos and illustrative material. Photos should be sharp, reproducible glossies, 5x7 and up.

ELECTRICITY CANADA, (formerly *Electrical Contractor & Maintenance Supervisor*), 481 University Ave., Toronto, Ontario, Canada M5W 1A7. Contact: Editor. For "men who either run their own businesses or are in fairly responsible management positions. They range from university graduates to those with public school education only." Monthly. Circ. 18,000. Rights purchased vary with author and material. "Depending on author's wish, payment is either on acceptance or on publication." Free sample copy. SAE and International Reply Coupons.
Nonfiction and Photos: Editor: Ron Glen. "Articles that have some relation to electrical contracting or electrical maintenance and related business management. The writer should include as much information as possible pertaining to the electrical field. We're not interested in articles that are too general and philosophical. Don't belabor the obvious, particularly on better business management. We're interested in coverage of labor difficulties, related association business, informational articles, how-to's, profiles, coverage of successful business operations, new product pieces, or technical articles." Buys 2-3 unsolicited mss/year. Length: "no minimum or maximum." Payment depends on pre-established rate according to type of article and technical expertise of the writer. Photos purchased with mss or on assignment; captions optional.

IEEE SPECTRUM, Institute of Electrical and Electronics Engineers, Inc., 345 E. 47th St., New York NY 10017. (212)644-7555. Editor: Donald Christiansen. Senior Editor, Administration: Ronald K. Jurgen.

The double dagger (‡) before a listing indicates that the listing is new in this edition. New markets are often the most receptive to freelance contributions.

Monthly magazine covering electrical/electronics engineering for executive and staff electrical and electronics engineers in design, development, research, production, operations, maintenance, in the field of electronic and allied product manufacturing, commercial users of electronic equipment, independent research development firms, government and military departments and service/installation establishments. Circ. 240,000. Pays on acceptance. Buys all rights. Phone queries OK. Submit material 4 months in advance. Photocopied submissions OK. Computer printout or disk submissions OK; prefers letter quality to dot matrix printouts. Reports in 2 weeks. Free sample copy and writer's guidelines.

Nonfiction: Interview (about socio-technical subjects and energy); technical overviews; historical; opinion (about careers and management). No elementary business, accounting or management topics. Buys 1 ms/issue. Query. Length: 4,000-5,000 words. Pays $400-$1,500.

Columns/Departments: Relate to meetings; industrial developments and publications in the electrical or electronics engineering field. Most departmental material is staff written.

Tips: "Contact the senior editor with story ideas. Be able to exhibit a working knowledge of the magazine's charter."

PUBLIC POWER, 2301 M St. NW, Washington DC 20037. (202)775-8300. Editor: Vic Reinemer. Bimonthly. Not copyrighted. Byline given. Pays on publication. Query. "Tips for Authors" sent on request.
Nonfiction: Features on municipal and other local publicly-owned electric systems. Payment negotiable.
Photos: Uses b&w and glossy color prints.

Electronics and Communication

Listed here are publications for electronics engineers, radio and TV broadcasting managers, electronic equipment operators, and builders of electronic communication systems and equipment, including stereos, television sets, radio-TV, and cable broadcasting systems. Journals for professional announcers or communicators are found under Journalism and Entertainment and the Arts; those for electric appliance retailers are in Home Furnishings and Household Goods; publications on computer design and data processing systems are listed in Data Processing. Publications for electronics enthusiasts or stereo hobbyists will be found in Science or Music in the Consumer Publications section.

ANSWER LINE, On Page Enterprises, Box 439, Sudbury MA 01776. Editor: Stanley J. Kaplan. Managing Editor: Bette Sidlo. Quarterly newsletter focusing on telephone answering services for professional and medical offices, sales and service centers as well as small business people who need telephones monitored when they are not in. Estab. 1982. Circ. 50,000 initially. Pays on acceptance. Buys all rights. Phone queries OK. Submit seasonal material 3 months in advance. No simultaneous, photocopied or previously published submissions. SASE. Reports in 2 weeks. Free sample copy and writers' guidelines.

Fillers: Clippings, jokes, gags, anecdotes, short humor and newsbreaks. "We are particularly interested in anecdotes in the first person narrative, stories of people and their *positive* answering service experiences and newsbreaks on various developments in business communications as they relate to telephone answering service applications. "We particularly seek seasonal material for our Sept., Dec., Mar., and June editions." Buys 10-20 mss/year. Length: 75-150 words. Pays $25-40 minimum.

Tips: Submissions should be geared to telephone answering service clients with emphasis on the advantages of retaining such service. "Nothing on answering machines—they compete with our customers' services."

AUDIO VISUAL DIRECTIONS, Montage Publishing, Inc., Suite 314, 25550 Hawthorne Blvd., Torrance CA 90505. (213)373-9993. Publisher: Joy McGrath. Associate Publisher: Lloyd McGrath. Magazine published 12 times/year about the uses of audiovisuals for readers who use audiovisuals in their professional capacities in business, industry, government, health care, financial and educational institutions and civil and community service organizations, such as police, fire, museums, libraries and churches. Circ. 35,000. Pays on publication. Byline given. Buys all rights. Phone queries OK. Submit seasonal material 2 months in advance. Simultaneous and photocopied submissions OK. "We are fairly receptive to computer printout submissions as long as the lines are at least double spaced with one-inch margins." Prefers letter quality to dot matrix. Free sample copy and writer's guidelines.

Nonfiction: Nancy Scott-Price, editor. How-to. "In every issue we attempt to publish a wide variety of articles relating to all aspects of audiovisual productions as well as developments in video. We welcome all informed, well-written articles pertaining to slides, sound, video, audio, overheads, multi-image and all attendant appli-

cations." Nothing related to company profile, personnel, or promotion material. Buys 3 mss/issue.
Columns/Departments: Showbill (write-ups on schools, seminars, shows, courses and conferences dedicated to educating the A/V user); Software Solutions (showcase for professionally made software programs for training, education and internal communications); Products on Parade (news articles on "what's new" in equipment, materials and services); Anatomy of a Show (descriptive information on a current audiovisual show, what went into producing it, equipment used, and a biography on the producer); Reviews to Use (review of a current AV book); The Miracle Micro (a continuing column on the uses and applications of the personal computer); and Hi-Tek (articles focus on various audio/video techniques, and equipment in clear, understandable terms). Send complete ms. Pays $100 minimum.
Tips: "We would like to receive more audio-related articles by professionals in the field and more articles on interactive video/videodisc applications. Freelancers should have some direct involvement or experience with audiovisuals—creating or producing AV productions, scripting, using audiovisual equipment, teaching AV courses, running programs, etc. They should have some relevant information which they want to share with readers, to teach to readers, relating to audiovisuals."

BROADCAST ENGINEERING, Box 12901, Overland Park KS 66212. Editorial Director: Bill Rhodes. For "owners, managers, and top technical people at AM, FM, TV stations, cable TV operators, as well as recording studios." Monthly. Circ. 35,000. Buys all rights. Buys 50 mss/year. Pays on acceptance; "for a series, we pay for each part on publication." Free sample copy and writer's guidelines. Computer printout or disk submissions OK. Reports in 6 weeks. SASE.
Nonfiction: Wants technical features dealing with design, installation, modification, and maintenance of radio and TV broadcast equipment; interested in features of interest to communications engineers and technicians as well as broadcast management, and features on self-designed and constructed equipment for use in broadcast and communications field. "We use a technical, but not textbook, style. Our publication is mostly how-to, and it operates as a forum. We reject material that is far too general, not on target, not backed by evidence of proof, or is a sales pitch. Our Station-to-Station column provides a forum for equipment improvement and build-it-yourself tips. We pay up to $30. We're especially interested in articles on recording studios and improving facilities and techniques." Buys 10-20 unsolicited mss/year. Query. Length: 1,500-2,000 words for features. Pays $75-200.
Photos: Photos purchased with or without mss; captions required. Pays $5-10 for b&w prints; $10-100 for 2¼x2¼ or larger color transparencies.

BROADCAST MANAGEMENT/ENGINEERING, 295 Madison Ave., New York NY 10017. (212)685-5320. Editor: Robert Rivlin. 10% freelance written. For broadcast executives, general managers, chief engineers and program directors of radio and TV stations. Monthly. Circ. 30,000. Buys all rights. Byline given unless "article is used as backup for staff-written piece, which happens rarely." Buys 12-15 mss/year. Pays on publication. Reports in 4 weeks. Query. Computer printout and disk submissions compatible with Televideo Systems CPM OK; prefers letter quality to dot matrix printouts. SASE.
Nonfiction: Articles on technical trends, business trends affecting broadcasting. Particularly interested in equipment applications by broadcasters in the production of radio and television programs. Emphasis on "competitive advantage. No product puff pieces. No general management pieces or general information stories. Our readers are interested in details." Length: 1,200-3,000 words. Pays $25-100.
Tips: "To break in demonstrate a knowledge of the industry we serve. Send for an editorial schedule and sample copy of the magazine; then suggest an idea which demonstrates an understanding of our needs. Pictures, graphs, charts, schematics and other graphic material a must."

BROADCAST TECHNOLOGY, Box 420, Bolton, Ontario, Canada L0P 1A0. (416)857-6076. Editor-in-Chief: Doug Loney. 50% freelance written. Emphasizes broadcast engineering. Bimonthly magazine; 64 pages. Circ. 6,300. Pays on publication. Buys all rights. Byline given. Phone queries OK. Computer printout submissions OK; prefers letter quality to dot matrix. SAE and International Reply Coupons. Free writer's guidelines.
Nonfiction: Technical articles on developments in broadcast engineering, especially pertaining to Canada. Query. Length: 500-1,500 words. Pays $100-300.
Photos: Purchased with accompanying ms. Captions required. Query for b&w or color. Total purchase price for a ms includes payment for photos.
Tips: "Most of our outside writing is by regular contributors, usually employed fulltime in broadcast engineering. Specialized nature of magazine requires specialized knowledge on part of writer, as a rule."

BROADCASTER, 7 Labatt Ave., Toronto, Ontario, Canada M5A 3P2. (416)363-6111. Editor: Barbara Moes. For the Canadian "communications industry—radio, television, cable, ETV, advertisers and their agencies." Monthly. Circ. 7,200. Buys all rights. Byline given. Buys 50-60 mss/year. Pays on publication. Writers should submit outlines and samples of published work; sample issue will be sent for style. Photocopied and simultaneous submissions OK. Returns rejected material "as soon as possible." SAE and International

Reply Coupons.

Nonfiction: Technical and general articles about the broadcasting industry, almost exclusively Canadian. Length: 1,000-2,000 words. Pays $125-350.

Photos: Rarely purchased.

‡**CABLE COMMUNICATIONS MAGAZINE, Canada's Authoritative International Cable Television Publication**, Ter-Sat Media Publications Ltd., 4 Smetana Dr., Kitchener, Ontario, Canada N2B 3B8. (519)744-4111. Editor: Udo Salewsky. Monthly magazine covering the cable television industry. Circ. 5,700. Pays on acceptance. Byline given. Buys all rights. Submit seasonal/holiday material 1 month in advance. Photocopied submissions OK. Computer printout and disk submissions OK. Reports in 2 weeks on queries; 1 month on mss. Free sample copy and writer's guidelines.

Nonfiction: Expose, how-to, interview/profile, opinion, technical articles and informed views and comments on topical, industry related issues. No fiction. Buys 50 mss/year. Query with clips or send complete ms. Length: 1,000-4,000 words. Pays $200-800.

Columns/Departments: Buys 24 items/year. Query with clips of published work or send complete ms. Length: 1,000-1,500 words. Pays $200-300.

Tips: "Forward manuscript and personal resume. Break in with articles related to industry issues, events and new developments; analysis of current issues and events. Be able to interpret the meaning of new developments relative to the cable television industry, and their potential impact on the industry from a growth opportunity as well as a competitive point of view. Material should be well supported by facts and data."

CABLE MARKETING, The Marketing/Management Magazine for Cable Television Executives, Jobson Publishing, 352 Park Ave. South, New York NY 10010. (212)685-4848. Editor: Nicolas Furlotte. Monthly magazine for cable industry executives dealing with marketing and management topics, new trends and developments and their impact. Estab. 1981. Circ. 13,400. Pays on publication. Byline given. Buys all rights. Simultaneous queries and photocopied submissions OK. Only letter-quality computer printout submissions OK. Reports in 1 month on queries and mss. Free sample copy.

Nonfiction: How-to, interview/profile, new product, technical. "Subject areas include: advertising, promotion, public relations, direct marketing, direct sales, programming, engineering/technology, cable system case histories and profiles." No consumer-oriented, general press stories. Buys 60 mss/year. Query with clips of published work. Length: 1,000-2,500. Pays $150-500.

Columns/Departments: Cable Tech (technology, engineering, and new products); Fine Tuning (programming items with emphasis on standalone products and alternative forms of programming, also Hollywood/movie studio items); Cable Scan (news items and marketing featurettes mostly about cable system activities and developments). Buys 20 mss/year. Query with clips of published work. Length: 200-1,000 words. Pays $25-125.

Tips: "Learn something about the cable TV business before you try to write about it. Have specific story ideas. Have some field of expertise that you can draw upon (e.g., marketing or advertising)." Not interested in "reviews" of programming. Editorial focus is on the *business* of cable television.

CABLE TELEVISION BUSINESS MAGAZINE, (formerly *TVC Magazine*), Cardiff Publishing Co., 6430 S. Yosemite St., Englewood CO 80111. (303)694-1522. Managing Editor: Chuck Moozakis. Semimonthly magazine about cable television for CATV system operators and equipment suppliers. Circ. 12,000. Pays on publication. Byline given. Makes work-for-hire assignments. Phone queries OK. Reports in 2 weeks on queries; in 1 month on mss. Free sample copy.

Nonfiction: Expose (of industry corruption and government mismanagement); historical (early days of CATV); interview (of important people in the industry); how-to (manage or engineer cable systems); new product (description and application); and case history. "We use articles on all aspects of cable television from programming through government regulation to technical pieces. We use both color and black and white photos, charts and graphs. A writer should have some knowledge of cable television, then send a letter with a proposed topic." Recent article example: "Texas Turn On: Big Plans for Big D," (covered the installation of the cable system in Dallas—February 15, 1982). No first-person articles. Buys 5 mss/year. Query. Length: 1,800-3,500 words. Pays $75/page of magazine space.

Photos: State availability of photos. Pays $50/page of magazine space for contact sheets. Reviews 35mm color transparencies. Offers no additional payment for photos accepted with ms. Captions required.

‡**COMMUNICATOR'S JOURNAL, The Magazine of Applied Communications**, Communicator's Journal, Inc., Downtown Station, Box 602, Omaha NB 68101. (402)551-0444. Editor: James D. Fogarty. Publisher: James H. Beck. Bonjour. Bimonthly magazine of organizational communication for executives in public relations and advertising, marketing, training, audiovisual, design and graphics; senior business executives; editors and writers. "We stress practical articles and columns (advice)." Circ. 20,000. Pays on acceptance. Byline given. Submit seasonal/holiday material 3 months in advance. Simultaneous queries OK. SASE. Reports in 6 weeks on queries; 8 weeks on mss. Sample copy $6.

Nonfiction: How-to, new product, technical. Special issues include Video Teleconferencing; Computer Graphics; State-of-the-Art Disaster Communications. No fiction. Buys 40 mss/year. Query with published clips or send complete ms. Length: 2,000-4,000 words. Pays $100-350.
Photos: Steve Kline, photo editor. Will buy to match specific features.
Columns/Departments: People in the Business; Vantage (editorial); Digest (news briefs); Hi-Tech (shorts on technological developments); Reviews (viewing and reading). Buys 20 mss/year. Query with published clips or send complete ms. Length: 1,000 words maximum. Pays negotiable rates.
Fillers: For column material. Clippings, jokes, anecdotes, newsbreaks. Pays $15 maximum on publication only.

EE'S ELECTRONICS DISTRIBUTOR, (formerly *EIW's Electronics Distributor*), Sutton Publishing Company, Inc., 707 Westchester Ave., White Plains NY 10604. (914)949-8500. Editor-in-Chief: Edward J. Walter. Monthly tabloid for distributors of electronic parts and equipment (not hi-fi, television or computer). Circ. 15,000. Pays on publication. Byline given. Buys first North American serial rights. Photocopied submissions OK. SASE. Reports in 2 weeks. Free sample copy.
Nonfiction: Stories about specific areas of a distributor's operation such as sales, purchasing, inventory control, etc. No general columns on tax tips, government issues or inventory control. Buys 10 mss/year. Query. Length: 1,250 words typical. Pays $2/column inch, negotiable.
Photos: Send photos with ms. Pays $10-15 for b&w contact sheets. Also reviews 5x7 prints. Captions required.
Tips: "We'll be more feature- and less news-oriented in the year ahead."

ELECTRONIC BUYERS' NEWS, The High Technology Purchasing Newsweekly, 111 E. Shore Rd., Manhasset NY 11030. Editor: Paul Hyman. For purchasers in the electronics industry. Newspaper; 77 pages. Circ. 46,000. Pays on publication. Usually buys first rights. Byline given. SASE. Reports in 2 months. Rejected material not returned unless requested. Free sample copy. Accepts very little freelance material; query first. Prefer telephone queries.
Nonfiction: "Each issue features a specific theme or electronic component. Occasionally, stories are accepted from authors knowledgeable in the field." All material is aimed directly at the purchasing profession. Length: open. Pays negotiable rates.
Tips: "Writers should have a working knowledge of the electronics marketplace and/or electronics purchasing. We are always interested in ideas for news features or columns that are new, timely and informative in our field."

ELECTRONIC PACKAGING AND PRODUCTION, Cahners Publishing Co., 1350 E. Touhy Ave., Box 5080, Des Plaines IL 60018. (312)635-8800. Editor: Nikita Andreiev. 40% freelance written. Emphasizes electronic equipment fabrication for engineering and production personnel, including product testing. Monthly magazine; 150 pages. Circ. 30,000. Pays on publication. Buys all rights. Byline given. Phone queries OK. Photocopied submissions OK. SASE. Reports in 3 weeks. Free sample copy and writer's guidelines.
Nonfiction: How-to (innovative packaging, production or testing technique); interview (new features about technological trends in electronics); and technical (articles pertaining to the electronic packaging, production and testing of electronic systems and hybrids). "No single-product-oriented articles of a commercial sales-pitch nature." Buys 40 mss/year. Query or submit complete ms. Length: 1,000-2,500 words.
Photos: State availability of photos with query or submit photos with ms. Offers no additional payment for 4x5 or larger b&w or color prints. Captions preferred. Buys all rights.

ELECTRONICS & COMMUNICATIONS, Southam Communications, Ltd., 1450 Don Mills Rd., Don Mills, Ontario, Canada M3B 2X7. (416)445-6641. Associate Editor: Denis Olorenshaw. Published 6 times/year covering commercial and industrial electronics. Circ. 16,000. Pays on publication. Byline given. Buys first North American serial rights. Submit seasonal/holiday material 3 months in advance. SASE. Reports in ½ week.
Nonfiction: Interview/profile, new product, technical. Canadian only. Buys 5-6 mss/year. Query. Length: open. Pays negotiable fee.
Photos: Send photos with ms. Reviews color transparencies and prints. Payment included with ms. Identification of subjects required. Buys one-time rights.

ELECTRONICS WEST, (formerly *Arizona Electronics*), Concept Publishing, Inc., 2250 N. 16th St., Phoenix AZ 85006. (602)253-9086. Editor/Publisher: Walter J. Schuch. Monthly magazine covering a "broad spectrum of electronics for middle managers and above associated with the Southwest electronics industry (manufacturing, wholesaling and retailing)." Estab. 1981. Circ. 8,000. Pays on publication. Byline given. Submit seasonal/holiday material 3 months in advance. Simultaneous queries and photocopied submissions OK. Computer printout submissions OK. SASE. Reports in 3 weeks on queries.
Nonfiction: Historical/nostalgic (electronics-related); how-to (manage business); humor (unique applications

of electronic technology); interview/profile (of businesses and business leaders); personal experience (of managers); photo feature; and technical (written in a non-technical manner and in a marketing style). Buys 4-5 unsolicited mss/year. Query with clips of published work. Length: 1,000-2,000 words. Pays 10¢/word maximum.

Photos: State availability of photos; $10 for 8x10 b&w glossy prints. Captions and model releases required. Rights purchased are negotiable.

Tips: No articles dealing with consumer products—i.e., radio, TV, CB radios, etc., or articles dealing with electricity rather than electronics.

FIBER OPTICS AND COMMUNICATIONS NEWSLETTER, Information Gatekeepers, Inc., Suite 111, 167 Corey Rd., Brookline MA 02146. (617)739-2022. Editor: Jane Lichtenstein. Monthly newsletter covering fiber optics, communications and related fields. Circ. 500. Pays on acceptance. Buys all rights. Submit seasonal/holiday material 2 months in advance. Simultaneous queries OK. SASE. Reports in 1 month. Sample copy $10; free writer's guidelines.

Nonfiction: General interest, interview/profile, new product and technical. "We are most open to US and international news, applications, and other information directed to marketing personnel and planners in the fiber optics industry." No fiction or anything not related to fiber optics. Buys 2-3 unsolicited mss/year. Length: 600 words maximum. Pays 10¢/word minimum.

HIGH FIDELITY TRADE NEWS, 6255 Barfield Rd., Atlanta GA 30328. Editor: Timothy Martin. For "retailers, salesmen, manufacturers, and representatives involved in the high fidelity/home entertainment/video market." Monthly. Circ. 32,000. Buys all rights. Byline given. Buys 36-50 mss a year. Pays on acceptance. Free sample copy. Query; "all work by assignment only." SASE.

Nonfiction: "Dealer profiles, specific articles on merchandising of high fidelity/video/home entertainment products, market surveys, sales trends, etc." Length: "open." Pay varies "as to type of article."

Tips: "We prefer to rely on our own resources for developing story ideas. Let us know about your willingness to work and submit, if possible, some samples of previous work. Even if you're a new writer, we're still likely to try you out, especially if you know the business or live in a market area where we need coverage. Articles on merchandising, product reports, and dealer profiles."

HOME ENTERTAINING MARKETING, (formerly *Dealerscope II*), 115 2nd Ave., Waltham MA 02154. (617)890-5124. Editor: Michael Alexander. Monthly magazine covering consumer electronics for retailers and manufacturers. Circ. 25,000. Pays on publication. Byline given. Offers 50% kill fee. Submit seasonal material 3 months in advance. "We are willing to accept either computer printouts or disk submissions. However, the writer should probably call us before sending a disk to insure compatibility with our hardware." Prefers letter quality to dot matrix printouts. SASE. Reports in 1 month. Sample copy for SAE.

Nonfiction: How-to and marketing information for retailers; profiles and interviews of retailers and industry leaders; new product; personal experience in home electronics retailing; technical information relating to new products and sales; marketing analysis. No hobbyist pieces. Query with clips. Length: 750-3,000 words. Pays $100-450.

Columns/Departments: Legal, Finance, Satellite TV, Computers and Videogames, Audio, Video (Hardware and Software), Telephones, Retailing, Electronics Accessories.

LASER FOCUS, with Fiberoptic Technology, Advanced Technology Publications, Inc., 119 Russell St., Littleton MA 01460. Editor-in-Chief: Dr. Morris Levitt. Managing Editor: Leonard Phillips. Technical monthly news magazine covering all aspects of laser technology, including fiber optics for scientists, engineers, and designers involved with lasers and related products. Circ. 29,000. Pays on publication. Byline given. Buys all rights. Exclusive queries only. SASE. Reports in 2 weeks on queries; 1 month on mss. Free sample copy.

Nonfiction: How-to (design and apply lasers and fiber optics); interview/profile (of laser researchers and research facilities); technical (tutorial, design and application). Buys 40 mss/year. Query. Feature length: 2,000-4,000 words. Pays $50-150.

Columns/Departments: Applications of Lasers (special techniques involving lasers) and editorial columns (Op-Ed). Length: 750-4,000 words. Pay varies.

‡LASERS & APPLICATIONS, High Tech Publications, Inc., Suite E, 3220 W. Sepulveda Blvd., Torrance CA 90505. (213)534-3700. Editor: James Cavuoto. Monthly magazine of the laser and optical industry for engineers and designers. Estab. 1982. Circ. 20,000. Pays on acceptance. No byline given. Offers 25% kill fee. Buys all rights. SASE. Reports in 4 weeks. Sample copy $4.

Nonfiction: "We stress new applications of lasers and laser processes in medical, electronics, metalworking, communication, printing, military and other fields. Articles describe how a laser was used to perform a task better or cheaper; what kind of laser and operating conditions used; what the prognosis is for selling lasers based on this process. Particularly interested in applications of lasers in foreign countries." Query with published clips. Length: 250-1,500 words. Pays $40-200.

MARKETNEWS, The Marketing Magazine of the Canadian Consumer Electronics Industry, Hunter-Nichols Publishing Ltd., 2282 Queen St. E., Toronto, Ontario, Canada M4E 1G6. (416)690-9666. Editor: Robert Franner. Monthly controlled circulation magazine for audio, video, home computer, and car stereo retailers in Canada. "We provide both technical and business information for our readers to help them make their businesses more successful." Circ. 7,500. Pays on publication. Byline given. Offers 50% kill fee. Rights purchased "depend on nature of article." Submit seasonal/holiday material 2½ months in advance. SASE. Reports in 1 week on queries; 2 weeks on mss. Free sample copy.
Nonfiction: Interview/profile (of people in the industry); new product and technical (on audio/video equipment); merchandising sales and business articles. Buys 40 mss/year. Query. Length: 1,000-2,500 words. Pays $100-500 (Canadian funds).
Photos: State availability of photos. Pays $5-10 for 5x7 or 8x10 b&w prints. Identification of subjects required.
Tips: "Competence in the areas we cover is more important to us than flair. Mss can be tidied up here, but nothing can be done with articles which betray an ignorance of the subject."

‡**MASS HIGH TECH**, Mass Tech Times, Inc., 113 Terrace Hall Ave., Burlington MA 01830. (617)229-2768. Editor: Joeth S. Barlas. Associate Editor: Alan R. Earls. Bimonthly tabloid covering feature news of electronics, computers, biotech, systems analysis, for high-tech professionals. Estab. 1982. Circ. 30,000. Pays on publication. Byline given. Not copyrighted. Buys first North American serial rights. Submit seasonal/holiday material 1 month in advance. Simultaneous queries, and simultaneous, photocopied and previously published submissions OK "if not in our immediate market." SASE. Reports in 1 month. Sample copy for 9x12 SAE and 2 first class stamps; writer's guidelines for business size SAE and 1 first class stamp.
Nonfiction: Book excerpts; historical (technology); humor; interview/profile; new product; opinion (qualified scientist); personal experience; photo feature (needs technical orientation and strong Boston area orientation). "Material should inform without over-simplifying. Light, amusing approach is OK." Buys 50 mss/year. Send complete ms. Length: 400-1,200 words. Pays $25-100.
Photos: Send photos with ms. Pays $10-25 for 5x7 b&w prints. Captions and identification of subjects required (if appropriate). Buys one-time rights.
Columns/Departments: Buys 50 mss/year. Query "with idea" or send one sample ms. Length: 300-900 words. Pays $25-50.
Fillers: Anecdotes, short humor, newsbreaks. Buys 100 mss/year. Length: 25-100 words. Pays $5-10.
Tips: Know the Boston high tech scene or have knowledgeable contacts. Material should be plausible to trained professionals."

‡**MEDIA PROFILES: The AV Marketing Newsletter**, Olympic Media Information, 70 Hudson St., Hoboken NJ 07030. (201)963-1600. Editor: Hariet Lundgaard. Managing Editor: Walt Carroll. Quarterly newsletter covering the marketing, production and distribution of non-theatrical and educational films and video. Estab. 1983. Circ. 500. Pays on publication. Byline given. Buys all rights. Submit seasonal/holiday material 4 months in advance. Simultaneous queries, and simultaneous, photocopied, and previously published submissions OK. "Wordstar" disk submissions most welcome. SASE. Reports in 1 month. Writer's guidelines for $5 (refunded with first payment upon publication), 9x12 SAE and 4 first class stamps (includes sample issue).
Nonfiction: How-to distribute/market films, video, and other audiovisual software. "We're not interested in 'how I made' but in 'how I sell.' " Buys 50 mss/year. Query. Length: 400-2,000 words. Pays $5-50.
Tips: "Perhaps you are working for an audiovisual distribution company or are marketing your films and video on your own. Your experiences, good and bad, will interest our readers who are just like you. How did you make money (or lose it) marketing your products? We want factual reports from people who are making and selling non-theatrical films and video or slides or cassettes (pre-packaged, off-the-shelf products, not 'sponsored' or 'client-paid' ones). We're interested in those just starting out as well as those experienced in audiovisual marketing."

‡**MEDIA PROFILES: The Whole Earth Edition**, Olympic Media Information, 70 Hudson St., Hoboken NJ 07030. (201)963-1600. Editor: Walt Carroll. Managing Editor: John Githens. Quarterly magazine covering "non-theatrical films, video, slides and tapes—(news of and reviews of) in new-age, alternative, futurism, social ecology subjects for people to use for personal and group self-education." Estab. 1983. Circ. 1,000. Pays on publication. Byline given. Buys all rights. Submit seasonal/holiday material 4 months in advance. Simultaneous queries, and simultaneous, photocopied, and previously published submissions OK. "Wordstar" disk submissions most welcome. SASE. Reports in 1 month. Writer's guidelines for $5 (refunded with first payment upon publication), 9x12 SAE and 4 first class stamps (includes sample issue).
Nonfiction: How-to (get access to and get the most out of "alternative" media programs); interview/profile (film and video makers); new products (films, video, etc.); reviews and reports on films and video. Buys 50 mss/year. Query. Length: 400-2,000 words. Pays $5-50.
Tips: "By all means see a sample issue (available from us or perhaps at your local university library or public library). Though our editorial style differs markedly from most magazines, it is not difficult to follow. If

you're an interesting 'head' with access to audiovisual equipment and software, we have plenty for you to do. People who can tip us (and our readers) off to unusual, out-of-the ordinary films, video, etc., in whole earth or new age areas shouldn't fail to get in touch with us.''

MICROELECTRONICS JOURNAL, Benn Electronics Publications Ltd., Box 28, Luton, England LU1 2NT. 0582-417438. Publications Director: Philip Rathkey. For electronics engineers engaged in research design, production, applications, sales in commercial or government organizations, academics (teaching, research) and higher degree students. "Writer must be active in the microelectronics industry (including academics or higher degree students) and have either an original observation to make or be able to inform/update readers on the state-of-the-art in a specialty area, or on the activities of an organization." Bimonthly magazine; 84 pages. Circ. 1,500. Pays on publication. Buys all rights. Phone queries OK. Submit seasonal/holiday material 3 months in advance. Photocopied submissions OK. Accepts previously published work only if first English translation of foreign language paper. SAE and International Reply Coupons. Reports in 3 weeks to US. Free sample copy and writer's guidelines.
Nonfiction: Expose (technical critique of manufacturers' products, of government, commercial, trade); general interest (state-of-the-art technical/marketing articles); how-to (on new designs, applications, production, materials, technology/techniques); interview (of eminent captain of industry or government politician); nostalgia (concerning how microelectronics companies got started or techniques were invented); personal opinion (on any relevant technical/commercial subject); profile and short notes (of company research activities, university research activities); new product (assessment and evidence of product's importance); photo feature (must include write-up explaining its technical/commercial significance); technical (on integrated circuit technology and systems, memories, microprocessors, optoelectronics, infra-red, hybrid integrated circuits, microwave solid-state devices, CCD and SAW techniques, semiconductor materials and chemicals, semiconductor production equipment and processing techniques, and automatic test techniques and equipment). Buys 10-30 mss/year. Query or submit complete ms. Length: 4,000-6,000 words. Pays $60/published page including diagrams, photos, etc.
Photos: Prefers b&w 6½x4½ prints unless color is technically essential. Offers no additional payment for photos accepted with ms. Captions required.

MICROWAVES & RF, 50 Essex St., Rochelle Park NJ 07662. (201)843-0550. Editor: Walter J. Bojsza. 50% freelance written. Emphasizes radio-frequency design. "Qualified recipients are those individuals actively engaged in microwave and RF research, design, development, production, and application engineering, engineering management, administration or purchasing departments in organizations and facilities where application and use of devices, systems and techniques involve frequencies from HF through visible light." Monthly magazine; 100 pages. Circ. 50,000. Pays on publication. Buys all rights. Phone queries OK. Photocopied submissions OK. Computer printouts OK "if legible. Disks must be DEC mate or Apple II (Pie Writer or compatible word processing software)." SASE. Reports in 6 weeks. Free sample copy and writer's guidelines; mention *Writer's Market* in request.
Nonfiction: "Interested in material on research and development in microwave and RF technology and economic news that affects the industry." How-to (circuit design); new product; opinion; and technical. Buys 40 mss/year. Query. Pays $30-50/published page.
Fillers: Newsbreaks. Pays $10 (minimum).

MILITARY ELECTRONICS, ICDM of North America, Suite 104, 2065 Martin Ave., Santa Clara CA 95050. (408)727-3330. Contact: Editor. Monthly magazine for engineers, technical managers, and members of the US government and DOD, covering high technology used in military applications. Circ. 30,000. Pays on publication. Byline given. Buys all rights. Previously published work OK. Report in 6 weeks on queries; 2 months on mss. Free sample copy and writer's guidelines.
Nonfiction: Historical on military electronic applications, how-to use new technology, and explanations of new technology. Special issues on microcircuits, software, simulation, computers, electronic warfare, millimeter wave, space electronics. Query. Pays negotiable fee.

ON PAGE, On Page Enterprises, Box 439, Sudbury MA 01776. Editor: Stanley J. Kaplan. Managing Editor: Bette Sidlo. Monthly newsletter about the beeper industry (radio pocket paging) for professionals, medical people, sales people, small businessmen, municipal employees and any person whose job takes him away from the telephone and who must maintain communications. Circ. 100,000. Pays on acceptance. Buys all rights. Phone queries OK. Submit seasonal material 3 months in advance. No simultaneous, photocopied, or previously published submissions. SASE. Reports in 2 weeks. Free sample copy and writer's guidelines.
Fillers: Clippings, jokes, gags, anecdotes, short humor and newsbreaks. "We are particularly interested in anecdotes for our On Page Forum column in the first person narrative, stories of people and their beeper experiences, and newsbreaks on a variety of communication subjects of interest to people who use beepers. We especially need freelance help for our Christmas issue." Buys 10-20 mss/year. Length: 75-150 words. Pays $25-40.

Tips: "Submissions should be geared to beeper users (e.g. subject matter must be related to communications or mobility). No sarcasm or comments insulting those who carry/use beeper."

PHOTONICS SPECTRA, Optical Publishing Co., The Berkshire Common, Box 1146, Pittsfield MA 01202. (413)499-0514. Publisher: Teddi C. Laurin. Editor-in-Chief: Diane Kelley. Executive Editor: Robert S. Clark. Monthly magazine. "*Photonics Spectra* circulates monthly among scientists, engineers and managers who work in the fields of optics, electro-optics, fiber optics, vacuum technology and lasers. The magazine's purpose is to keep its readers abreast of new developments in our specific fields and related ones." Circ. 38,000. Average issue includes 20 departments, 2 or 3 contributed pieces in addition to staff reports. Photocopied submissions OK. SASE. Reports in 2 weeks on queries; in 1 month on mss. SASE. Sample copy and writer's guidelines free for SASE.

Nonfiction: "*Photonics Spectra* is a technically and scientifically-oriented publication of optics, electro-optics, fiber-optics and lasers. We offer a combination of timely news reports and feature articles examining aspects of the industries and related industries." Interview (prominent figures in the industry); profile (prominent figures in the industry); other (trends in the field, specific developments). Buys 4 unsolicited mss/year. Length: 750-3,000 words.

Photos: State availability of photos.

Columns/Departments: Query with clips of previously published work.

Tips: "Query about topic; ask for sample copy of the magazine."

PRO SOUND NEWS, International News Magazine for the Professional Sound Production Industry, Testa Communications, 220 Westbury Ave., Carle Place NY 11514. (516)334-7880. Editor: Martin Porter. Monthly tabloid covering the recording, sound reinforcement, TV and film sound industry. Circ. 12,000. Pays on publication. Byline given. Buys one-time rights. Simultaneous queries and photocopied and previously published submissions OK. SASE. Reports in 2 weeks.

Nonfiction: Query with clips of published work. Pays 10¢/word.

PROMOTION NEWSLETTER, Radio and TV, Drawer 50108, Lighthouse Point FL 33064. (305)426-4881. Editor: William N. Udell. Monthly newsletter covering promotional activities of radio and television stations. Circ. 580. Pays on acceptance. Byline may or may not be given. Not copyrighted. Buys one-time rights, non-exclusive reprints, and makes work-for-hire assignments. Submit seasonal/holiday material 3 months in advance. Simultaneous queries and simultaneous and photocopied submissions OK. Computer printout submissions OK. Reports in 2 weeks on queries; 1 month on mss. Free sample copy (while available).

Nonfiction: How-to; interview/profile (of promotional director of a busy station); photo feature. "Interested in all promotional activities of radio and TV stations; unusual examples of successful promotional events. Looking for special material for all holidays." No "fan" material. Query or send complete ms. Length: 100-500 words, sometimes more. Pays $15-150.

Photos: "Reprints of ads and other material acceptable." Send photos with ms. Pays $5 minimum for b&w contact sheets and prints. Identification of subjects required. Buys one-time rights.

Fillers: Clippings, newsbreaks. Length: 100-500 words. Pays $15-150.

RECORDING ENGINEER/PRODUCER, Box 2449, Hollywood CA 90028. (213)467-1111. Publisher: Martin Gallay. Editor: Mel Lambert. 100% freelance written. Emphasizes recording technology and concert sound for "all levels of professionals within the recording and sound industry." Bimonthly magazine; 120 pages. Circ. over 18,000. Pays on publication. Buys first publication rights. Photocopied submissions OK. SASE. Reports in 4 weeks. Sample copy $3.

Nonfiction: Interview (known engineering and producing personalities from the recording industry); new product (as related to technological advances within the recording and concert sound industry); and technical (recording and concert sound information). Buys 6 mss/issue. Query with initial outline. Pays $200-300.

SATELLITE COMMUNICATIONS, Cardiff Publishing Corp., 6430 S. Yosemite St., Englewood CO 80111. (303)694-1522. Editor: Kim E. Degnan. Emphasizes satellite communications industry. Readership includes broadcast management and engineering management, satellite industry personnel, cable television operators, government, educators, medical personnel, common carriers, military and corporate telecommunications management, spacecraft manufacturing companies. Monthly magazine. Circ. 12,500. Pays on publication. Buys all rights. Byline given. Phone queries OK. Computer printout submissions OK; prefers letter quality to dot matrix. SASE. Reports in 3 weeks. Free sample copy.

Nonfiction: Interviews (of industry figures); case studies; technical features; new satellite services, systems descriptions, and application articles; marketing articles; satellite future studies; descriptions of satellite experiments; corporate profiles, technological developments, business news; FCC policy analysis; video-teleconferencing; current issues in space communication; launches and industry conventions; demonstrations and articles on new products. No items that do not pertain to the satellite communications industry. Buys 3-6 unsolicited mss/year. Recent article example: Case study on teleconferencing (March 1982). Query. Length: 750-

2,000 words. Pays $50/published page.

Photos: Prefers b&w 5x7 glossy prints and color slides. Offers no additional payment for photos accepted with ms.

Tips: "We prefer a letter personally addressed, clear, concise, with an idea for a story in it, one page, informal but from a writer who is flexible on terms and prompt with copy. We regularly print articles by business leaders and engineers who can write, usually gratis with byline only."

‡**SAT-GUIDE, The Satellite Magazine**, CommTek Publishing Co., 419 N. River, Box 1048, Hailey ID 83333. (208)788-4936. Editor: Kathryn Carmichael. Direct queries to Bruce Kinnaird, senior editor. Monthly magazine covering satellite-related communications technologies for cable operators, programmers and distributors and those in the field of MDS, SMATV, STV, LPTV and related areas. Circ. 10,000. Pays on publication. Byline given. Offers ⅓ kill fee. Buys one-time rights, all rights, first rights; makes work-for-hire assignments. Submit seasonal/holiday material 6 weeks in advance. Computer printout and disk submissions OK. SASE. Reports in 2 weeks. Sample copy $5; writer's guidelines for business-size SAE and 1 first class stamp.

Nonfiction: How-to (upgrade business operations, break into new field, etc.); interview/profile (industry leaders); new product (hardware); opinion (of industry leaders); technical (hardware information and reviews); and new programming available to cable operators. No "fiction, nostalgia, poetry, clippings, news releases, old information, uninformed articles on 'the future of communications,' etc." Buys 20 mss/year. Query with clips. Length: 700-1,500 words. Pays $100-500.

Photos: Terry Stanton, photo editor. State availability of photos. Pays $25-150 for 8x10 b&w prints and 35mm color transparencies. Captions and identification of subjects required. Buys negotiable rights.

Columns/Departments: Industry profiles (interviews with programmers and cable operators). Buys 10 mss/year. Query with clips. Length: 700-1,200 words. Pays $100-250.

Tips: "This field is now a very lucrative one for writers, and is likely to be more so in the future. The key to success: basic research into the technological terms and pertinent areas of concern in the field of satellite communications. The areas most open to freelancers are those dealing with new hardware applications, economic concerns of cable operators and new programming planned. These topics are not as 'dry' as they seem—interesting slants and styles are duly appreciated. The field is now monopolized by a small group of freelancers who can pick and choose their assignments. Though the terminology may seem intimidating to the uninitiated, the field itself is fascinating and should be investigated."

‡**TELECOMMUNICATIONS**, Horizon House, Microwave, Inc., 610 Washington St., Dedham MA 02026. (617)326-8220. Executive Editor: Charles E. White. Managing Editor: Anthony F. Pastelis III. Monthly magazine for "concerned communications specialists interested in systems, subsystems, equipment, and services. Recognized and respected as the authoritative periodical in the field; presents a balanced mix of feature articles, case studies, industry news and products, and service information." Circ. 56,000. Pays on publication. Byline given. Buys all rights. Simultaneous queries OK. SASE. Reports in 1 month. Sample copy for 9x12 SAE. Free writer's guidelines.

Nonfiction: New product; technical; feature articles ("treating various communications' disciplines from a supervisory and end user standpoint rather than exhaustive design analysis"). Special issues include Annual Buyers' Guide. Material should not "be overly theoretical and should employ simple equations only when needed for clarity." Drawings, graphs, etc., should be included. Buys 6-9 unsolicited mss/year. Query. Pays variable rates.

Photos: "Photos should be glossy prints not exceeding 8½x11 inches."

Columns/Departments: Telecom News, Datacom Focus (items of newsworthy interest), International, West Coast, Washington DC, US Regulation and Policy, Markets and Finances, Association Reports. Query.

‡**TELEPHONE ANGLES, How to Manage an Efficient, Cost Effective, Business Telephone System**, Box 633, W. Hartford CT 06107. (203)247-6355. Editor: Bob Frank. Monthly newsletter covering the voice telecommunications industry for telecommunications users interested in managing an efficient, cost-effective business telephone system. Pays on publication. Byline given. Offers negotiable kill fee. Buys all rights. Simultaneous queries, and simultaneous, photocopied and previously published submissions OK. SASE. Reports in 1 week. Sample copy $1; writer's guidelines for SAE and 1 first class stamp.

Nonfiction: Book excerpts (telecommunications); general interest; how-to (use phone system equipment, services, etc.); interview/profile (industry leaders); new products and services; case history/applications. Buys 60 mss/year. Query. Length: 250-2,000 words. Pays 10¢/word.

TELEVISION INTERNATIONAL MAGAZINE, Box 2430, Hollywood CA 90028. (213)876-2219. Publisher/Editor: Al Preiss. For management/creative members of the TV industry. Every 2 months. Circ. 8,000 (USA); 4,000 (foreign). Rights purchased vary with author and material. Pays on publication. Will send sample copy to writer for $2. Will consider photocopied submissions. Reports in 30 days. Query. SASE.

Nonfiction and Photos: Articles on all aspects of TV programming. "This is not a house organ for the industry. We invite articles critical of TV." Length: 800-3,000 words. Pays $150-350. Column material of 600-800 words. Pays $75. Will consider suggestions for new columns and departments. Pays $25 for b&w photos purchased with mss; $35 for color transparencies.

TWO-WAY RADIO DEALER, Titsch Publishing, Box 5400TA, Denver CO 80217. Editor: Michael Mc-Cready. Monthly magazine covering the sales and service of two-way radios for dealers, service people and technicians. Circ. 11,500. Average issue includes 2-3 feature articles. Pays on publication. Byline given. Buys first North American serial rights or one-time rights. Phone queries OK. Simultaneous, photocopied and previously published submissions OK. SASE. Reports in 2 weeks on queries; in 1 month on mss. Free sample copy with 9x12 SASE and 75¢ postage.
Nonfiction: "We need very technical articles which include schematics and problem solving, and business articles concerning marketing, finance and self employment. The writer must have special knowledge of land-mobile radio use or the business of running a dealership. We want to increase the amount of freelance material used." Buys 1-2 mss/issue. Send complete ms. Length: 1,500-3,000 words. Pays $50-$250.
Photos: Reviews 5x7 b&w glossy prints and 35mm and larger color transparencies. Offers no additional payment for photos accepted with ms. Captions and model release required. Buys one-time rights.

VIDEO SYSTEMS, Box 12901, Overland Park KS 66212. (913)888-4664. Publisher: Cameron Bishop. 80% freelance written. For qualified persons engaged in professional applications of non-broadcast audio and video who have operating responsibilities and purchasing authority for equipment and software in the video systems field. Monthly magazine. Circ. 20,500. Pays on acceptance. Buys all rights. Submit seasonal/holiday material 2 months in advance of issue date. Photocopied submissions OK. SASE. Reports in 2 months. Free sample copy and writer's guidelines.
Nonfiction: General interest (about professional video); how-to (use professional video equipment); historical (on professional video); new product; and technical. Recent article example: "How-to-Shoot Video in Unusual Situations" (underwater, skydiving). No consumer video articles. Buys 2-6 unsolicited mss/year. Submit complete ms. Length: 1,000-3,000 words. Pays $125.
Photos: State availability of photos with ms. Pay varies for 8x10 b&w glossy prints; $100 maximum for 35mm color transparencies. Model release required.

VIDEOGRAPHY, United Business Publications, 475 Park Ave. S., New York NY 10016. (212)725-2300. Editor: Marjorie Costello. Monthly magazine for professional users of video and executives in the videotape and videodisc industries. Circ. 25,000. Pays 1 month after publication. Buys all rights. Phone queries OK. SASE. Reports in 1 month. Sample copy $2.
Nonfiction: Any article about the use of video in business, education, medicine, etc. Especially interested in stories about the use of new video technology to solve production problems. Also stories about cable TV and pay TV services. Buys 2 mss/issue. Query with clips of previously published work. Length: 1,000-2,500 words. Pays $100-150.
Photos: Submit photo material with accompanying query. Offers no additional payment for 5x7 b&w glossy prints or color transparencies. Captions required. Buys all rights.

VIEW MAGAZINE, The Magazine of Cable TV Programming, View Communications, 150 E. 58th St., New York NY 10022. (212)486-7111. Editor: Jane Gordon. Managing Editor: Laurence Zuckerman. Monthly magazine covering cable TV programming, marketing, advertising and production. Circ. 9,000. Pays 45 days after acceptance. Byline given. Buys all rights. Reports in 1 month. Free sample copy and writer's guidelines.
Nonfiction: General interest (issues facing the industry—pay-per-view-programming, ratings and audience measurement, consumer attitudes toward cable); trends (in children's, sports, news and entertainment programming). "We will not consider any unsolicited mss or articles not directly related to the TV industry." Buys 50 mss/year. Query with clips of published work. Length: 2,500-5,000 words. Pays $300-350 for first-time contributors.
Fillers: Buys 25/year. Length: 250-500 words. Pays $75.
Tips: "Most of *View's* feature articles are written by freelancers who understand the cable-TV business. Only writers with experience covering the entertainment industry need query."

Energy

Oil, gas, and solar energy topics are covered here as well as energy conservation for industry professionals. Electric energy publications are listed in the Electricity category.

DIESEL PROGRESS/DIESEL & GAS TURBINE WORLDWIDE, 13555 Bishop's Court, Brookfield WI 53005. Editorial Director: Robert A. Wilson. Senior Editor: J. Kane. Managing Editor: Mike Osenga. 5% freelance written. Monthly magazine; 88 pages. Circ. 25,000. Pays on publication. Buys first rights. Submit editorial material 6 weeks in advance of issue date. Previously published submissions OK. No computer printout or disk submissions. SASE. Reports in 4 weeks. Sample copy $2.
Nonfiction: "The articles we would consider from freelancers would be technical descriptions of diesel engine applications—including extensive technical descriptions of the installation, the method of operations and maintenance." Buys 10 mss/year. Query and submit clips of published work. Length: 1,600-2,400 words. Pay based on use.
Photos: "All stories are illustrated and photos of the engine installation must accompany the text, or it is really of little value." State availability of photos with query. No additional payment for 8x10 b&w glossy prints and 8x10 color glossy prints (cover only). Captions preferred. Buys all rights.

ENERGY MANAGEMENT REPORT, Box 1589, Dallas TX 75221. (214)748-4403. Editor-in-Chief: Cindy Mays. Comment by Rich McNally. 20% freelance written. Emphasizes energy for operating management of oil/gas operating companies and supply/service companies. Monthly section in *Petroleum Engineer International* and *Pipeline & Gas Journal*; 16 pages. Circ. 66,433. Pays on publication. Buys all rights. Query. No computer printout or disk submissions. SASE. Free sample copy; mention *Writer's Market* in request.
Nonfiction: Uses energy briefs and concise analysis of energy situations. "Across-the-board interpretive reporting on current energy events." Publishes briefs about energy world news, offshore energy business, energy financing, new products (price information on crude oil and gasoline). No nuclear or electric material. Pays 15¢/word.

ENERGY NEWS, Energy Publications—division of Harcourt Brace Jovanovich, Box 1589, Dallas TX 75221. (214)748-4403. Editor: Jim Watts. 5% freelance written. Emphasizes natural gas production, transmission, distribution, regulation and projects for executives or managers of energy, supply and financial companies or the government; particularly utilities. Biweekly newsletter; 4 pages. Circ. 500. Pays on publication. Buys all rights. Phone queries OK. Simultaneous and photocopied submissions OK. No computer printout or disk submissions. SASE. Reports in 4 weeks. Free sample copy and writer's guidelines.
Nonfiction: Interviews with energy industry or government leaders keyed to recent news and technical articles on natural gas projects, trends, prices or new technologies. "Can't use anything not related to natural gas or utilities." Buys 1-2 mss/issue. Length: 250 words maximum. Pays 15¢/word.

ENERGY WEEK, Energy Publications—division of Harcourt Brace Jovanovich, Box 1589, Dallas TX 75221. (214)748-4403. Editor: Cindy Mays. 5% freelance written. Emphasizes bottom-line news concerning US drilling and production with major emphasis on prices, cost, methods and operations. Biweekly newsletter; 4 pages. Circ. 500. Pays on publication. Buys all rights. Phone queries OK. Simultaneous and photocopied submissions OK. SASE. Reports in 4 weeks. Free sample copy and writer's guidelines.
Nonfiction: Interview (with energy industry trendsetters, should be keyed to recent news); and technical (new energy technologies, feasibility, costs, or technical features). "No stories dealing with the surface rather than the inner core of energy developments. Our readers are aware of news related to energy; they want to know *why* and how *they* are affected." Buys 1-2 mss/issue. Submit complete ms. Length: 250 words maximum. Pays 15¢/word.

FUEL OIL NEWS, Publex Corp,. Box 385C, Morristown NJ 07960. (201)326-9620. Editor: George Schultz. Monthly magazine about the home heating oil market. Circ. 17,000. Pays on publication. Byline given. Offers $75 kill fee. Makes work-for-hire assignments. Phone queries OK. Submit seasonal material 3 months in advance. Simultaneous, photocopied and previously published submissions OK; no disk submissions. Computer printout submissions OK; no disk submissions. Reports in 2 months. Free sample copy and writer's guidelines.
Nonfiction: Interview (industry); profile (of industry leaders); how-to (on industry methods of delivering fuel or servicing equipment); and technical. No general business articles or new product information. Buys 2 mss/issue. Query. Length: 1,000-3,000 words. Pays $70-200. "Articles should be geared to helping fuel oil dealers maintain viability in the marketplace or to some aspect of home heating or oil delivery."

Photos: State availability of photos. Pays $25 maximum for b&w contact sheets. Captions preferred; model release required. Buys all rights.

FUELOIL AND OIL HEAT, 200 Commerce Rd., Cedar Grove NJ 07009. (201)239-5800. Feature Editor: M. F. Hundley. For distributors of fuel oil, heating and air conditioning equipment dealers. Monthly. Buys first rights. Pays on publication. Reports in 2 weeks. Computer printout submissions OK; no disk submissions. SASE.
Nonfiction: Management articles dealing with fuel oil distribution and oilheating equipment selling. Cannot use articles about oil production or refining. Length: up to 2,500 words. Pays $35/printed page. "Mostly staff written."

GAS DIGEST, Box 35819, Houston TX 77035. (713)723-7456. Editor: Ken Kridner. 30% freelance written. For operating personnel of the gas industry. Monthly magazine; 24 pages. Circ. 5,000. Rights may be retained by the author. Pays on publication. Photocopied submissions OK. Reports in 1 month. Query.
Nonfiction: Applications stories; new developments. All material must be gas operations-oriented and meaningful to one working in the gas industry. How-to, technical articles. Length: 500-1,000 words. Pays 2¢/word minimum.
Photos: B&w photos purchased with ms. Pays $5 minimum.

HYDROCARBON PROCESSING, Box 2608, Houston TX 77001. Editor: Harold L. Hoffman. 95% freelance written by industry authors. For personnel in oil refining, gas and petrochemical processing; or engineering-contractors, including engineering, operation, maintenance and management phases. Special issues: January, Maintenance; April, Natural Gas Processing; September, Refining Processes; November, Petrochemical Processes. Monthly. Buys first publication rights. Write for copy of guidelines for writers. SASE.
Nonfiction: Wants technical manuscripts on engineering and operations in the industry that will help personnel. Also nontechnical articles on management, safety and industrial relations that will help technical men become managers. Length: open, "but do not waste words." Pays about $25/printed page.
Tips: "Articles must all pass a rigid evaluation of their reader appeal, accuracy and overall merit. Reader interest determines an article's value. We covet articles that will be of real job value to subscribers. Before writing, ask to see our *Author's Handbook*. You may save time and effort by writing a letter, and outline briefly what you have in mind. If your article will or won't meet our needs, we will tell you promptly."

NATIONAL PETROLEUM NEWS, 950 Lee St., Des Plaines IL 60016. (312)296-0770. Editor: Marvin Reid. For businessmen who make their living in the oil marketing industry, either as company employees or through their own business operations. Monthly magazine; 80 pages. Circ. 19,000. Rights purchased vary with author and material. Usually buys all rights. Buys 3-4 mss/year. Pays on acceptance if done on assignment. Pays on publication for unsolicited material. "The occasional freelance copy we use is done on assignment." Query. No computer printout or disk submissions. SASE.
Nonfiction and Photos: Features Editor: Thomas Olson. Material related directly to developments and issues in the oil marketing industry and "how-to" and "what-with" case studies. Informational; successful business operations. No unsolicited copy, especially with limited attribution re: information in story." Length: 2,000 words maximum. Pays $150/printed page. Payment for b&w photos "depends upon advance understanding."

OCEAN INDUSTRY, Gulf Publishing Co., Box 2608, Houston TX 77001. (713)529-4301. Editor-in-Chief: Donald M. Taylor. Associate Editors: Maretta Tubb, Ken Edmiston. Department Editor: Margaret Cashman. 25% freelance written. "Our readers are generally engineers and company executives in companies with business dealings with off-shore petroleum and deepsea mining interests." Monthly magazine. Circ. 33,000. Pays on publication. Buys all rights. Pays kill fee: "If we assign an article and it is not used, we pay full rate on estimated length." Byline given. Phone queries OK. Photocopied and previously published submissions OK. SASE. Reports in 2 months. Free sample copy and writer's guidelines.
Nonfiction: Technical articles relating to hydrocarbon exploration and development, diving, deepsea mining, oil terminals, and oil and LNG shipping. No oceanographic, fisheries, aquaculture or mariculture material. Buys 120-140 mss/year. Query. Length: 300-1,500 words. Pays $35-100/published page.
Photos: "Technical concepts are easier to understand when illustrated." State availability of photos with query. No additional payment for 5x7 or 8x10 glossy b&w or color prints. Captions required. Buys all rights.

OIL & GAS DIGEST, OGD Publishing Co., 915 Antoine, Houston TX 77024. (713)688-4429. Monthly magazine for "all phases of the petroleum industry." Circ. 36,595. Pays on publication. Byline given. Buys all rights. Simultaneous queries and simultaneous, photocopied and previously published submissions OK. SASE. Reports in 1 month. Free sample copy; writer's guidelines issued "upon assignment."
Nonfiction: "Write for editorial forecast." Buys 3-5 unsolicited mss/year. Query with clips of published work and resume. Length: assigned. Pays $6/column inch.

PETROLEO INTERNACIONAL, PennWell Publishing Co., Box 1260, Tulsa OK 74101. (918)835-3161. Editor: Gustavo Pena. Monthly magazine about the Latin American petroleum industry for the management, engineering and technical operating personnel in the oil and gas industry of the Spanish speaking world. Circ. 9,000. Average issue includes 6-7 main articles and several shorter ones. Pays on publication. Byline given. Makes work-for-hire assignments. Phone queries OK. Submit seasonal material 1 month in advance. Simultaneous, photocopied and previously published submissions OK. SASE. Reports in 2 weeks. Free sample copy and writer's guidelines.

Nonfiction: Technical (oil and gas, petrochemical industry and equipment for the petroleum industry). Query. Pays $25 minimum.

Photos: Send photos with ms. Reviews b&w prints and color prints. Offers no additional payment for photos accepted with ms. Captions required. Buys one-time rights.

Columns/Departments: "We have a section on people involved in the industry; new literature out for the industry, business in the industry, and current happenings in the petroleum industry." Pays $25 minimum.

Fillers: Newsbreaks. Pays $25 minimum.

PETROLEUM INDEPENDENT, 1101 16th St. NW, Washington DC 20036. (202)857-4775. Editor: Joe W. Taylor. For "college-educated men and women involved in high-risk petroleum ventures. Our readers drill 90% of all the exploratory oil wells in this country. They pit themselves against the major oil companies, politicians, and a dry hole rate of 9 out of 10 to try to find enough petroleum to offset imports. They are in a highly competitive, extremely expensive business and look to this magazine to help them change the political landscape, read about their friends and the activities of the Independent Petroleum Association of America, and be entertained. Contrary to popular opinion, they are not all Texans. They live in almost every state and are politically motivated. They follow energy legislation closely and involve themselves in lobbying and electoral politics." Bimonthly magazine. Circ. 15,000. Pays on acceptance. Buys all rights. Byline given "except if part of a large report compiled in-house." SASE. Reports in 2 weeks. Sample copy $1.

Nonfiction: "Articles need not be limited to oil and natural gas—but must tie in nicely." Expose (bureaucratic blunder), informational, historical (energy-related, accurate, with a witty twist), humor (we look for good humor pieces and have found a few), interview (with energy decision makers. Center with questions concerning independent petroleum industry. Send edited transcript plus tape), opinion, profile (of Independent Petroleum Association of America members), photo feature. Buys 30 mss/year. Query with brief outline. SASE. Length: 750-3,000 words. Pays $100-500. Longer articles on assignment; pay negotiable.

Photos: Reviews color and b&w transparencies. Purchased with or without accompanying ms or on assignment.

Tips: "Call first, then send outline and query. Don't write with a particular slant. Write as if for a mainstream publication."

PIPELINE & GAS JOURNAL, Box 1589, Dallas TX 75221. (214)748-4403. Editor-in-Chief: Dean Hale. 5% freelance written. Emphasizes energy transportation (oil, gas and coal slurry) by pipeline. Monthly magazine; 100 pages. Circ. 26,000. Pays on publication. Buys all rights. Phone queries OK. Photocopied submissions OK. SASE. Reports in 6-10 weeks. Free sample copy.

Nonfiction: Technical. No articles on management. Buys 5-6 mss/year. Query. Length: 800-1,500 words. Pays minimum $35/printed page.

Photos: State availability of photos with query. No additional payment for 8x10 b&w glossy prints and 5x7 or 8x10 color glossy prints. Captions required. Buys all rights. Model release required.

PIPELINE & UNDERGROUND UTILITIES CONSTRUCTION, Oildom Publishing Co. of Texas, Inc., Box 22267, Houston TX 77027. Editor: Oliver Klinger. Managing Editor: Chris Horner. Monthly magazine covering oil, gas, water, and sewer pipeline construction for contractors and construction workers who build pipelines. Circ. 13,000. No byline given. Not copyrighted. Buys first North American serial rights. Simultaneous queries and photocopied submissions OK. SASE. Reports in 2 weeks on queries; 3 weeks on mss. Sample copy for $1 and 9x12 SAE.

Nonfiction: How-to. Query with clips of published work. Length: 1,500-2,500 words. Pays $100/printed page "unless unusual expenses are incurred in getting the story."

Photos: Send photos with ms. Reviews 5x7 and 8x10 prints. Captions required. Buys one-time rights.

PIPELINE DIGEST, Universal News, Inc., Box 55225, Houston TX 77055. (713)468-2626. Publisher: H.M. Stemmer. Managing Editor: Thelma Marlowe. Semimonthly magazine of the worldwide pipeline construction industry for individuals and companies involved in construction and operation of pipelines (gas, oil, slurry, water) worldwide. Includes design and engineering projects and updated listings of projects proposed, awarded and under construction. Circ. 9,500. Pays on publication. Byline given. Previously published submissions OK. No computer printout or disk submissions. SASE. Reports in 2 weeks on queries; 2 months on mss.

Nonfiction: Interview/profile (of people in industry); new product. All material must relate to the oil and gas industry. Query with clips of published work. Length: 250-1,000 words. Pays negotiable fee.

‡**RENEWABLE ENERGY NEWS—NORTHEAST, Northeast Edition of Renewable Energy News**, Box 408, Ashfield MA 01330. (413)628-4553. Editor: Michael E.C. Gery. Monthly general interest tabloid covering renewable energy in the northeast USA primarily for northeast US subscribers interested in developments in renewable energy in the region. Pays on publication. Byline given. Not copyrighted. Buys negotiable rights. Submit seasonal/holiday material 3 months in advance. Simultaneous queries and photocopied submissions OK. SASE "if not assigned." Reports in 1 month. Sample copy for 9x12 SAE and 5 first class stamps. Writer's guidelines for business-size SAE and 1 first class stamp.

Nonfiction: General interest (on renewable energy subjects in Northeast); interview/profile (limited number); personal experience (limited number); technical (on systems in Northeast). "Will reject long personal experience stories, blatant advertising, poorly-researched articles. If in doubt, query first." Buys 30-60 mss/year. Query or send complete ms "only if it meets our guidelines." Length: 200-1,200 words. Pays $20-180.

Photos: Send photos with ms. Pays up to $25 for 5x7 and 8x10 b&w prints. Identification of subjects required. Buys one-time or negotiable rights.

Fillers: Newsbreaks. Buys "considerable number" mss/year. Length: 100-350 words. Pays $10-55.

Tips: "We're looking for renewable energy news in the Northeast. Subjects should be recent developments on matters such as solar, wood, hydro, other biomass, alcohol fuels, wind or regional appropriate technology on any scale. Specific applications preferred. Looking for specific applications in Northeast of successful or not so successful renewable energy or appropriate technology. Stories with photos stand a better chance. Short articles as welcome as those in 600-1,000 word range. Style should be news style."

SAVING ENERGY, 5411 - 117 Ave. SE, Bellevue WA 98006. (206)643-4248. Editor/Publisher: Larry Liebman. Emphasizes energy conservation, ideas and case histories aimed at business, industry and commerce. Monthly newsletter. Pays on acceptance. Buys all rights. No byline given. Phone queries OK. Computer printout and disk submissiosn OK; prefers letter quality to dot matrix printouts. SASE. Reports in 2 weeks. Free writer's guidelines.

Nonfiction: "I need good, tightly written case histories on how industry and commerce are saving energy, listing problems and solutions. The item should present an original energy saving idea. No long stories with art. Include full name and address of business so readers can contact for follow-up." How-to (conserving energy, what the problem was, how it was resolved, cost, how fast the payback was, etc.); and technical (case histories). Buys 25 unsolicited mss/year. Submit complete ms. Length: 200-800 words. Pays $10-25.

Tips: "Take potluck with a well-written item that meets specs, since the item could be shorter than the query letter after editing."

SOLAR AGE MAGAZINE, Solarvision, Inc., Church Hill, Harrisville NH 03450. (603)827-3347. Editor: William D'Alessandro. Editorial Assistant: Mary A. Cummiskey. Monthly magazine covering renewable energy resources for solar professionals, designers, installers, architects, inventors, educators, solar business executives, and state, local and federal employees in research and development. Circ. 70,000. Average issue includes 6 features articles. Pays on acceptance. Byline given. Buys first magazine and non-exclusive book rights. Phone queries OK. No computer printout or disk submissions. Reports in 1 week on queries; in 1 month on mss.

Nonfiction: Expose (of government, consumer and business); interview (of nationally known solar energy or renewable energy personalities); how-to (install solar, conserve energy, retrofit and design systems); new product; personal experience; photo feature; and technical. No "puff and politics. Articles for us should be thoroughly researched for technical accuracy but be written without jargon. Writers are encouraged to discuss the submissions and style with the editors before proceeding." Buys 20-30 mss/year. Query. Length: 2,000 words maximum. Pays $125 minimum.

Photos: B&w and color transparencies accepted. Subject matter should parallel editorial subjects listed above. All photo payments are negotiable. Photographers should present portfolios or send samples. Captions and model release required. Buys one-time and non-exclusive book rights.

Engineering and Technology

Publications for electrical engineers are classified under Electricity; journals for electronics engineers are classified under the Electronics and Communication heading.

CIVIL ENGINEERING-ASCE, American Society of Civil Engineers, 345 E. 47th St., New York NY 10017. (212)705-7507. Editor: Ned Godfrey. Monthly magazine about civil engineering for members of the American Society of Civil Engineers. Circ. 90,000. Average issue includes 7-13 features. Pays on acceptance. Byline given. Makes work-for-hire assignments. Phone queries OK. Previously published submissions OK. Reports in 2 months. Free sample copy and writer's guidelines.
Nonfiction: Technical. "Come up with articles that are timely, well-written and slanted to a Civil Engineering audience. We have an annual special issue in September on the rebuilding of America." Buys 1-2 mss/year. Query. Pays $300-1,500.
Columns/Departments: Editor: Philip DiVietro. "We want reports or news stories on conferences of interest to an engineering audience." Also, new products information. Buys 1-2 mss/year. Query. Pays $100-500.

CONTROL ENGINEERING, Technical Publishing, 1301 S. Grove Ave., Barrington IL 60010. (312)381-1840. Editor: Edward Kompass. Monthly magazine for control engineers—horizontal to industry, product and system-oriented, highly technical. Circ. 80,000. Byline usually given.
Nonfiction: New product, photo feature, technical. "We need submissions from writers who are engineers." No commercial mss. Query or send complete ms. Length: open. Pays $25/page.

DETROIT ENGINEER, 100 Farnsworth, Detroit MI 48202. Communications Coordinator: Lauri Farrell. "Our readers are mostly management-level engineers in automotive, construction, medical, technical and educational jobs." Monthly magazine. Circ. 8,000. Pays on acceptance. Buys first North American serial rights. Simultaneous, photocopied and previously published submissions OK. SASE. Reports in 3 weeks. Sample copy $1.25.
Nonfiction: General interest (technical background or basis) and technical (on the *Scientific American* level). Recent series: "Michigan Entrepreneurs" (March 1982). Buys 6 mss/year. Query or submit complete ms. Length: 1,500 words maximum. Pays negotiable fee.

‡**DIGITAL DESIGN**, Morgan-Grampian Publishing Co., 1050 Commonwealth Ave., Boston MA 02215. (617)232-5470. Editor: Jerry Borrell. Managing Editor: Bob Hirshon. Monthly magazine of computer electronics for designers and engineers of computer systems, peripherals and components. "Our readers are among the leaders in technical planning and management for computing technology." Circ. 70,000. Pays on publication. Byline given. Buys all rights "except by arrangement with editor." Reports in 2 weeks. Free sample copy and writer's guidelines.
Nonfiction: David Wilson, articles editor. How-to (design various types of systems); new product (exclusive articles on unannounced new computer products); technical. Buys 20 mss/year. Query. Length: 1,500-3,000 words. Pays $35-75/page.
Photos: "Relevant photos and other art should be submitted with manuscript. There is no additional payment." State availability of photos. Reviews 4x5 color transparencies and 8x10 b&w and color prints. Captions and identification of subjects required.
Columns/Departments: David Wilson, column/department editor. Applications Notebook (unique, useful circuit designs or microcomputer subroutines of interest to computer electronics engineers). Buys 10 mss/year. Query. Length: 500-1,500 words. Pays $70.
Tips: "Most of our material is written by engineers about their field of expertise. Non-engineers should at least be conversant in the field about which they are writing and should query an editor about their idea before proceeding. Freelancers should remember that *Digital Design* is a technical publication written specifically to help computer engineers do their job better."

ELECTRO-OPTICS MAGAZINE, (formerly, *Electro-Optical System Digest*), 1350 E. Touhy, Des Plaines IL 60018. Editor: Richard Cunningham. Monthly magazine for graduate scientists and engineers. Circ. 33,000. Buys all rights. Byline given unless anonymity requested. Pays on publication. Will send a sample copy to a writer on request. Write for copy of guidelines for writers. Will consider cassette submissions. Query with "a clear statement of why the article would be important to readers." Editorial deadlines are on the 1st of the 3rd month preceding publication. Computer printout submissions OK; prefers letter quality to dot matrix. SASE.
Nonfiction and Photos: Articles and photos on lasers, laser systems and optical systems aimed at electro-optical scientists and engineers. "Each article should serve a reader's need by either stimulating ideas, increasing

technical competence or improving design capabilities in the following areas: natural light and radiation sources, artificial light and radiation sources, light modulators, optical components, image detectors, energy detectors, information displays, image processing, information storage and processing, system and subsystem testing, materials, support equipment, and other related areas." Rejects flighty prose, material not written for readership, and irrelevant material. Pays $30/page. Submit 8x10 b&w glossies or 4x5 color transparencies with ms.

GRADUATING ENGINEER, McGraw-Hill, 1221 Avenue of the Americas, New York NY 10020. (212)997-4123. Editor: Howard Cohn. Published September-March "to help graduating engineers make the transition from campus to the working world." Circ. 85,000. Pays on acceptance. Byline given. Buys first North American serial rights. Reports in 2 weeks. Free sample copy for 9x12 SAE and $1 postage.
Nonfiction: General interest (on management, human resources); high technology; and careers, ethics, resumes, future. Special issues include Minority, Women and Computer Careers. Buys 100 mss/year. Query. Length: 2,000-3,000 words. Pays $300-500.
Photos: State availability of photos, illustrations or chàrts. Reviews 35mm color transparencies, 8x10 b&w glossy prints. Captions and model release required.

LIGHTING DESIGN & APPLICATION, 345 E. 47th St., New York NY 10017. (212)705-7922. Editor: Wanda Jankowski. 5% freelance written. For "lighting designers, architects, consulting engineers, and lighting engineers." Monthly. Circ. 13,500. Rights purchased vary with author and material. Pays kill fee. Byline given. Buys 5 mss/year. Pays on acceptance. Query. SASE.
Nonfiction: "Stories on lighting design and application, as the name implies. Specific installations reviewed in depth if they are recent, important and demonstrate good lighting. Techniques for saving energy, improving lighting quality and predicting the effect of a lighting arrangement are needed. Reports on research and tests of new ideas in lighting. Psychological factors in visibility." Length: 500-4,000 words. Pays $250-500.

THE ONTARIO TECHNOLOGIST, Ontario Association of Certified Engineering Technicians and Technologists, Suite 253, 40 Orchard View Blvd., Toronto, Ontario, Canada M4R 2G1. (416)488-1175. Editor: Ruth M. Klein. Bimonthly professional association journal covering technical processes and developments in engineering for association members, educational institutions, government and industry. Circ. 13,246. Pays on membership dues or subscription fee. Byline given. Buys first rights. Submit seasonal/holiday material 2 months in advance. Photocopied and previously published submissions OK. SASE. Reports in 1 month. Free sample copy and writer's guidelines.
Nonfiction: New product; technical (manpower news). Buys 4 mss/year. Query with clips of published work. Length: 500-1,500 words. Pays 20¢/word.
Photos: State availability of photos. Pays $25 maximum for 8x10 b&w prints. Captions and identification of subjects required. Buys one-time rights.

PARKING MAGAZINE, National Parking Association, Inc., 2000 K St. NW., Washington DC 20006. (202)296-4336. Executive Editor: Thomas G. Kobus. Editor: George V. Dragotta. 10% freelance written. "The bulk of our readers are owners/operators of off-street parking facilities in major metropolitan areas. The remainder is made up of architects, engineers, city officials, planners, retailers, contractors and service equipment suppliers." Quarterly magazine. Circ. 6,500. Pays on publication. Buys one-time rights. Submit seasonal/holiday material 3 months in advance of issue date. Simultaneous, photocopied and previously published submissions OK. Reports in 1 month. Sample copy $5.
Nonfiction: General interest (pieces on revitalization of central business districts have a high current priority); how-to (new construction, design, equipment or operational techniques); historical (could deal with some aspect of history of parking, including piece on historic garage, etc.); new product (parking-related equipment); photo feature (range of facilities in a particular city); and travel (parking in other countries). "No general, nebulous pieces or ones not dealing with most current trends in the industry." Buys 6 unsolicited mss/year. Query. Length: 1,000-5,000 words. Pays $50-500, or negotiable.
Photos: State availability of photos with query. Pays $5-25 for 8x10 b&w glossy prints and $10-50 for 2¼x2¼ or larger color transparencies. Captions preferred. Buys one-time rights. Model release required.

RESOURCE DEVELOPMENT, IBIS Holdings, Inc., Box 91760, West Vancouver, B.C., Canada V7V 4S1. (604)986-9501. Editor: Duncan Cumming. Monthly magazine covering Canadian energy and mineral exploration/development. Circ. 17,000. Pays on publication. Byline given. Pays 50% kill fee. Buys first rights or makes work-for-hire assignments. Simultaneous queries, and simultaneous, photocopied and some previously published submissions OK. SASE. Reports in 2 weeks on queries; 1 month on mss. Sample copy $2; free writer's guidelines.
Nonfiction: How-to (pertaining to energy and mineral exploration/development); interview/profile; new product; and technical (new technology). Buys 12 mss/year. Query. Length: 100-2,000 words. Pays $15-500.
Photos: State availability of photos. Pays $10-100 for 35mm and larger color transparencies; $5-20 for 5x7 and

larger b&w prints. Captions required. Buys one-time rights.

Tips: "A high level of technical or engineering writing experience is required."

THE WOMAN ENGINEER and THE MINORITY ENGINEER, Equal Opportunity Publications, Inc., 44 Broadway, Greenlawn NY 11740. (516)261-8899. Editor: James Schneider. Magazines published 4 times/ year (fall, winter, spring, summer professional edition). *Woman Engineer*: for senior year engineering students and the woman engineer. *Minority Engineer*: written for the college graduate and professional minority engineer. Circ. 10,500 each. Pays on publication. Byline given. Buys all rights. Simultaneous, photocopied, and previously published submissions OK. Computer printout and disk submissions OK; prefers typed mss and letter quality to dot matrix printouts. SASE. Sample copy and writer's guidelines available on request.

Nonfiction: General interest; how-to (land a job, keep a job, etc.); interview; opinion; personal experience; photo feature; technical (state-of-the art engineering). "We're interested in 7 to 10 articles per issue—articles dealing with career guidance and job getting for women and minority engineers." Buys 20 mss/year. Query with clips of published work or send complete ms. Length: 2,000-5,000 words.

Photos: State availability of photos or send photos with ms. Reviews b&w and color contact sheets and prints. Caption data required. Buys all rights.

Tips: "We're looking for any indication of special affinities or interests related to our magazines. We are particularly interested in hearing from Black, Hispanic, and American Indian writers. Prefers articles related to careers, not politically or socially sensitive." More profiles and role-model articles and bold graphics and art in the year ahead.

Entertainment and the Arts

The business of the entertainment/amusement industry (film, dance, theater, etc.) is covered by these publications. Journals that focus on the people and equipment of various music specialties are listed in the Trade Music section.

‡**AMERICAN ARTS**, American Council for the Arts, 570 7th Ave., New York NY 10017. (212)354-6655. Editor: William Keens. Bimonthly magazine covering arts management for nonprofit institutions nationwide. "Our readers are managers of nonprofit museums, galleries, dance companies, theaters, etc., as well as their board members and patrons. Articles focus on management concerns, such as fundraising, board policy and survival." Circ. 10,000. Pays on publication. Byline given. Buys first North American serial rights. Simultaneous queries and simultaneous and photocopied submissions OK. SASE. Reports in 6 weeks. Free sample copy, if interested in query or submission—otherwise available for $2.50 and 9x12 SAE and 88¢ postage; writer's guidelines for business-size SAE and 20¢ postage.

Nonfiction: Historical/nostalgic—historic renovations, etc.; how to (management, fundraising); humor; interview/profile (of noted figures in the art world, including artists, managers, government policy-makers); technical (financial planning, etc.); travel ("arts in various cities is a regular one-page feature"). No "articles narrow in scope, for example, those chronicling the experiences of a single organization or individual, unless author articulates broader ramifications." Buys 24 mss/year. Length: 500-2,000 words. Pays $50-150.

Photos: Bruce Peyton, photo editor. "Most photos acquired free from subjects of articles, but we hire some photographers to cover interviews." Pays $50-150 for 8x10 b&w prints from contact sheets. Captions, model release and identification of subjects required. Buys one-time rights.

Columns/Departments: "State of the Arts is a running feature with articles from freelancers covering two or three arts disciplines per issue. The focus here, unlike the rest of the magazine, is on the art itself—trends, aesthetic concerns and so forth—not on management per se." Buys 14 mss/year. Query with clips. Length: 500-750 words. Pays $50-100.

Tips: "Study the magazine. Submit queries that demonstrate an awareness of our concerns. We are particularly interested in more articles focusing on arts issues in the West, Midwest, and South with national implications." Sections most open to freelancers are "State of the Arts and special features, as well as some interviews (generally the cover story), but most of these are done by the editor."

AMUSEMENT BUSINESS, Billboard Publications, Inc., Box 24970, Nashville TN 37202. (615)748-8120. Editor: Tom Powell. Executive Editor: Steve Rogers. Emphasizes hard news of the amusement and mass entertainment industry. Read by top management. Weekly tabloid; 24-48 pages. Circ. 15,000. Pays on publication. Buys all rights. Byline sometimes given; "it depends on the quality of the individual piece." Phone queries OK. SASE. Submit seasonal/holiday material 2-3 weeks in advance.

Nonfiction: How-to (case history of successful promotions); interview; new product; and technical (how "new" devices, shows or services work at parks, fairs, auditoriums and conventions). Likes lots of financial

support data: grosses, profits, operating budgets, per-cap spending. No personality pieces or interviews with stage stars. Buys 500-1,000 mss/year. Query. Length: 400-700 words. Pays $1-2.50/published inch.
Photos: State availability of photos with query. Pays $3-5 for b&w 8x10 glossy prints. Captions required. Buys all rights. Model release required.
Columns/Departments: Auditorium Arenas; Fairs, Fun Parks; Food Concessions; Merchandise; Promotion; Shows (carnival and circus); Talent; Tourist Attractions; and Management Changes.

‡**ARABESQUE, A Magazine of International Dance**, Ibrahim Farrah, Inc., Suite 22F, 1 Sherman Square, New York NY 10023. (212)595-1677. Editor: Adam Lahm. Bimonthly magazine of ethnic dance. "The magazine takes its name from the flowing lines and patterns of Islamic art, a fitting image for the interconnectedness of all dancing forms." Circ. 6,000. Pays on publication. Byline given. Makes work-for-hire assignments. Submit seasonal/holiday material 6 months in advance. Simultaneous queries OK. SASE. Reports in 4 weeks. Sample copy $2.50.
Nonfiction: How-to, interview/profile, personal experience, technical. Buys 18 mss/year. Query with published clips. Length: 1,000-1,500 words. Pays $35-50.

BILLBOARD, The International News Weekly of Music and Home Entertainment, 1515 Broadway, New York NY 10036. (212)764-7300. 9107 Wilshire Blvd., Beverly Hills CA 90210. (213)273-7040. Editor-in-Chief/Publisher: Lee Zhito. Special Issues Editor: Ed Ochs. L.A. Bureau Chief: Sam Sutherland. Video Editor: Laura Foti. Record Review/Campus Editor: Sam Sutherland. (All Los Angeles.) Managing Editor: Adam White. Pro Equipment & Service: Radcliffe Joe. Talent and Venues: Roman Cozak. News Editor: Irv Lichtman. Radio/TV Editor: Rollye Bornstein. Executive Editor & Classical Editor: Is Horowitz. (All New York.) Country Music Editor: Kip Kirby (Nashville). International Editor: Peter Jones (London). Weekly. Buys all rights. Pays on publication. SASE.
Nonfiction: "Correspondents are appointed to send in spot amusement news covering phonograph record programming by broadcasters and record merchandising by retail dealers." Concert reviews; interviews with artists; stories on video software (both rental and merchandising).

BOXOFFICE MAGAZINE, RLD Publishing Corp., Suite 316, 1800 N. Highland Ave., Hollywood CA 90028. (213)465-1186. Editor: Alexander Auerbach. Monthly magazine about the motion picture industry for members of the film industry: theater owners, film producers, directors, financiers and allied industries. Circ. 16,000. Pays on publication. Byline given. Buys one-time rights. Phone queries OK. Submit seasonal material 2 months in advance. Simultaneous, photocopied and previously published submissions OK. Computer printout OK; "if dot matrix, use descenders. Disk unlikely—Altos 5¼" format only." SASE. Reports in 2 weeks.
Nonfiction: Expose, interview, nostalgia, profile, new product, photo feature and technical. "We are a general news magazine about the motion picture industry and are looking for stories about trends, developments, problems or opportunities facing the industry. Almost any story will be considered, including corporate profiles, but we don't want gossip or celebrity stuff." Buys 1-2 mss/issue. Query with clips of previously published work. Length: 1,500-2,500 words. Pays $75-150.
Photos: State availability of photos. Pays $10 minimum for 8x10 b&w prints. Captions required.
Tips: "Write a clear, comprehensive outline of the proposed story, and enclose a resume and clip samples. We welcome new writers but don't want to be a classroom. Know how to write."

‡**THE ELECTRIC WEENIE**, Box 25866, Honolulu HI 96825. (808)395-9600. Editor: Tom Adams. Monthly magazine covering "primarily radio, for 'personalities' world wide (however, mostly English speaking). "We mail flyers mainly to radio people, but obviously no one is excepted if he/she wants a monthly supply of first rate gags, one liners, zappers, etc." Circ. 1,000. Pays on publication. No byline given. Buys all rights. Submit seasonal/holiday material 6 months in advance. SASE. Sample copy for $1, business-size SAE and 1 first class stamp.
Fillers: Jokes, gags, short humor, one liners, etc. "SHORT is the bottom line." Uses 300/month. Pays $1/gag used.
Tips: "We like to receive in multiples of 100 if possible; not mandatory, just preferred."

‡**ENTERTAINMENT INDUSTRY WEEKLY/ENTERTAINMENT DIGEST**, Entertainment Industry Publications, Box 10804, Beverly Hills CA 90213. (213)275-6240. Editor: Lisa Galgon. Managing Editor: Steve Travis. Weekly newsletter magazine of the entertainment industry; provides total coverage of entertainment industry from performing to business. Estab. 1981. Circ. 30,000. Pays on publication. Byline given. Offers $25 kill fee. Buys all rights. Simultaneous queries, and simultaneous, photocopied, and previously published submissions OK. SASE. Reports in 1 month. Sample copy and writer's guidelines each $3.
Nonfiction: Steve Davis, articles editor. Uses any entertainment industry subject including unions, pay TV, cable, broadcast, film, music, home video, public TV, video tape/disc, advertising, commercials, casting. No fiction. Buys 60-100 mss/year. Send complete ms. Length: open. Pays variable rates.

G-STRING BEAT, Atlanta Enterprises, Box 007, Gays Mills WI 54631. Editor: Rita Atlanta. Emphasizes burlesque and allied fields of entertainment. Quarterly magazine; 48 pages. Circ. 12,000. Pays on publication. Buys all rights. SASE. Reports in 2-3 weeks.
Nonfiction: Publishes in-depth, hard-edged profiles of performers who are real people with hopes and fears. Buys 6-10 mss/year. Submit complete ms. Length: 1,000-2,500 words. Pays $75-150.
Photos: Query. "We have about 5,000 pix on hand and pix must be exceptional for us to buy."
Fiction: John Bane, Department Editor. Publishes mystery, humorous and suspense fiction. "Very little fiction is accepted because freelance writers have a limited 'feel' (no pun intended) of burlesque. The tensions of the business are rarely understood by outsiders. Would say that this is one of the hardest markets to please." Buys 2-3 mss/year. Submit complete ms. Length: 2,500-5,000 words. Pays $100-250.

THE HOLLYWOOD REPORTER, Verdugo Press, 6715 Sunset Blvd., Hollywood CA 90028. (213)464-7411. Publisher: Tichi Wilkerson. Editor: Cynthia Wilkerson. Emphasizes entertainment industry, film, TV and theater and is interested in everything to do with financial news in these areas. Daily entertainment trade publication: 25-100 pages. Circ: 20,000. SASE. Reports in 1 month. Sample copy $1.

‡**THE LONE STAR COMEDY MONTHLY**, Lone Star Publications of Humor, Suite #103, Box 29000, San Antonio TX 78229. Editor: Lauren Barnett Scharf. Monthly comedy service newsletter for professional humorists—DJs, public speakers, comedians. Includes one-liners and jokes for oral expression. Estab. 1983. Pays on publication "or before." Byline given if 2 or more jokes are used. Buys exclusive rights for 6 months from publication date. Submit seasonal/holiday material 1 month in advance. Photocopied submissions OK. SASE. Reports in 1 month. Sample copy $3.50; writer's guidelines for business-size SAE and 1 first class stamp.
Fillers: Jokes, gags, short humor. Buys 20-60/year. Length: 100 words maximum. Pays $1-5. "Submit several (no more than 20) original gags on one or two subjects only."

‡**THE NORTHWEST STAGE**, Box 8398, Moscow ID 83843. (208)882-4241. Editor: Michael Hofferber. Monthly newsletter of the performing arts for actors, directors, dancers, singers, and technical theater personnel in the Northwest. Estab. 1982. Circ. 150. Pays on publication. Byline given. Offers 50% kill fee. Not copyrighted. Buys first rights. Submit seasonal/holiday material 2 months in advance. Simultaneous queries, and simultaneous, photocopied, and previously published submissions OK. SASE. Reports in 2 months. Sample copy $1.
Nonfiction: Historical/nostalgic (NW theater, dance); how-to (theater, dance); humor (related to theater or dance); interview/profile (NW theater, dance personalities); technical (how-tos on set construction, etc.); travel (NW destinations); news about special events, auditions, openings, etc. No reviews at this time. Buys 12-24 mss/year. Query or send complete ms. Length: 50-1,000 words. Pays $2-50.
Photos: Send photos with query or ms. Pays $5-10 for 4x5 b&w prints. Captions required. Buys one-time rights.
Columns/Departments: State departments include Idaho, Montana, Oregon, northern California, Utah, Washington and British Columbia. "We publish news, notices and events coverage under each of these state headings." Buys 10-20 mss/year. Query. Length: 10-100 words. Pays $1-10.
Fillers: Clippings, jokes, newsbreaks. Buys 5/issue. Length: 10-100 words. Pays 50¢-$2.
Tips: "We would like to establish a regular cadre of stringers in principal Northwest cities who can provide news reports, profiles, features and event coverage. Freelancers should submit a query, along with either clips or a list of previous credits. Lead articles and state reports are the best break-in bets. Find interesting subjects related to theater or dance in Idaho, Montana, Utah, Oregon, Washington, northern California or British Columbia and query us about them."

PERFORMANCE, 2929 Cullen St., Fort Worth TX 76107. (817)338-9444. Publisher and Editor-in-Chief: Tom Pitts. Editor: Don Waitt. The international trade weekly for the touring entertainment industry. "*Performance* publishes tour routing information, updated on a weekly basis. These itineraries, along with box office reports, street news, industry directories, live performance reviews and industry features are of interest to our readers." Weekly magazine; also publishes industry directories once a month. Circ. 20,000. Buys all rights. Phone queries OK. Submit seasonal/holiday material 2 months in advance. Simultaneous, photocopied and previously published submissions OK. Computer printout submissions OK. SASE. Reports in 1 month. Sample copy and writer's guidelines $3.
Nonfiction: "This is a trade publication, dealing basically with the ins and outs of booking live entertainment. We are interested in adding freelancers from major cities around the US to provide us with hard news and spot information on sound, lighting, clubs, ticketing, facilities, and college news relevant to the live entertainment industry. Also publish interviews and overviews from time to time." Interviews, opinion and profile. No concert and/or show reviews. Length: ½-3 printed pages. Pays 17½-25¢/printed line.
Photos: State availability of photos with ms. B&w photos only. Captions preferred. Buys all rights.

THEATRE CRAFTS MAGAZINE, Theatre Crafts Associates, 135 5th Ave., New York NY 10010. Editor: Patricia MacKay. Magazine of the performing arts, theater, video and film. Published 9 times/year. "The primary information source for performing arts enthusiasts—working professionals and dedicated amateurs on Broadway, in regional and university theaters, summer stock, dance and opera." Circ. 27,500. Pays on acceptance. Byline given. Buys variable rights. Simultaneous queries and photocopied submissions OK. SASE. Reports in 1 month on queries; 2 months on mss. Sample copy $5; free writer's guidelines.
Nonfiction: How to; new products (and new applications of old products); technical (advances and developments in administration, design and technology). Buys 18 mss/year. Query. Length: 1,000-2,000 words. Pays $25-200.

VARIETY, 154 W. 46th St., New York NY 10036. Does not buy freelance material.

Farm

Today's farmer wears bib-overalls and claims a six-figure investment in producing foodstuffs for the country and the world. Today's farm magazines reflect this, and the successful freelance farm writer is the person who grasps this fact and turns his attention to the business end of farming.

Do you need to be a farmer to write about farming? The general consensus is yes, and no, depending on just what you're writing about. For more technical articles, most editors feel that you should have a farm background (and not just summer visits to Aunt Rhodie's farm, either) or some technical farm education. But there are plenty of writing opportunities for the general freelancer, too. Easier stories to undertake for farm publications include straight reporting of agricultural events; meetings of national agricultural organizations; or coverage of agricultural legislation. Other ideas might be articles on rural living, rural health care or transportation in small towns.

Always a commandment in any kind of writing, but possibly even more so in the farm field, is the tenet "*Study Thy Market*." The following listings for farm publications are broken down into five categories, each specializing in a different aspect of farm publishing: crops and soil management; dairy farming; general interest farming and rural life (both national and local); livestock; and miscellaneous.

The best bet for a freelancer without much farming background is probably the general interest, family-oriented magazines. These are the *Saturday Evening Posts* of the farm set. The other four categories are more specialized, dealing in only one aspect of farm production.

Where should a writer go for information about farming specialties? Go to a land-grant university; there's one in every state. Also try farming seminars or the county extension offices.

As you can see, there's no room for hayseeds in the farm writing field. But for the freelance writer who is willing to plow in and study, there's a good chance he'll find himself in the middle of a cash crop.

Crops and Soil Management

AVOCADO GROWER MAGAZINE, Rancher Publications, Box 2047, Vista CA 92083. Editor: Mark Affleck. Emphasizes avocado and subtropical fruit for growers and professionals (doctors, pilots, investors). Monthly magazine; 64 pages. Circ. 8,000. Pays on publication. Buys all rights. Pays 50% kill fee. Byline given. Phone queries OK. Submit seasonal material at least 1 month in advance. Simultaneous, photocopied and previously published submissions OK. SASE. Reports in 2-3 weeks. Sample copy $2.
Nonfiction: General interest (relative to avocado industry); historical (on avocado industry); how-to (grow av-

ocados, any interesting cultural aspects); interview (with avocado industry leader); new product (briefs only). Open to suggestions for photo features. Buys 2-3 mss/issue. Query with clips of published work or submit complete ms. Pays $1-2/column inch.

Photos: "If it can be said more explicitly with photos, use them to supplement the manuscript." State availability of photos. Pays $3-4.50 for any size b&w prints. No color. Captions preferred, model releases required for minors.

Tips: "Be thorough in the outline. I must be convinced the article has facts, readability and punch. I'm most interested in quality, completeness and readability."

‡**CRANBERRIES**, Taylor Publishing Corp., Box 249, Cobalt CT 06414. (203)342-4730. Editor: Bob Taylor. Monthly magazine covering cranberry growing and processing—anything of interest to growers. Circ. 700. Pays on publication. Byline given. "No kill fee. If we accept story, we'll work writer through. Also we'll pay for story if events make it impossible to run." Buys first rights. Submit seasonal/holiday material 1 month in advance. Simultaneous queries, and simultaneous, photocopied, and previously published submissions OK. Computer printout submissions OK; prefers letter quality to dot matrix. SASE. Reports in 2 weeks on queries; 1 month on mss. Sample copy for 8½x11 SAE and 54¢ postage.

Nonfiction: Humor, interview/profile, personal experience, photo feature, technical. Buys 50 mss/year. Query. Length: 500-2,500 words. Pays $10-35.

Photos: State availability of photos. Pays $5-10 for any size b&w print. Captions and identification of subjects required. Buys one-time rights.

Tips: "Either know your subject matter or produce material published before. However, we're very receptive to new writers." Profiles on growers open to freelancers. "While we do not pay big bucks, payment is prompt and will increase as the fortunes of the magazine go up. I also like to feel that young or beginning writers get the benefit of patience and good editing."

THE MUSHROOM NEWS, The American Mushroom Institute, Box 373, Kennett Square PA 19348. (215)388-7806. Editor: Jack Kooker. Monthly magazine covering material of interest to mushroom growers, suppliers and buyers. Circ. 1,000. Pays on publication. Byline given. Offers 25% kill fee. Buys one-time or second serial (reprint) rights or makes work-for-hire assignments. Submit seasonal/holiday material 1 month in advance. Phone queries, and simultaneous photocopied and previously published submissions OK. Reports in 2 weeks. Sample copy $1; writer's guidelines for SASE.

Nonfiction: Historical/nostalgic (of mushrooms, the mushroom industry); how-to (grow better mushrooms, make better compost, etc.); humor (farmer-oriented); interview/profile (figures of pertinence to the mushroom industry—exceptional grower, etc.); new product (of interest to mushroom growers); opinion (on the state of the mushroom industry); photo feature; technical. "Anything of interest to a mushroom grower." Buys 12 mss/year. Query. Length: 750 words minimum. Pays $2/printed column inch.

Photos: Send photos with ms. Pays $3-12 for 8x10 b&w prints. Captions and identification of subjects required. Buys one-time rights.

Columns/Departments: Buys variable number mss/year. Query. Length: 100-400 words. Pays $2/printed column inch.

Fillers: Clippings, jokes, gags, anecdotes, short humor, newsbreaks. Buys 20/year. Length: 100-400 words. Pays $2/printed column inch.

Tips: "Many of our stories are scientific, written by the scientist. An approved (by the scientist) recap of a technical article is especially desirable."

PECAN SOUTH, Publications South, Inc., 741 Piedmont Ave., Atlanta GA 30308. (404)892-6812. Editor: Ernest F. Jessee. Publisher: Rebecca H. Johnson. Bimonthly agribusiness magazine of the Southern pecan industry covering research and technology with some economic, marketing, and human-interest stories of industrial interest. Circ. 11,000. Pays on publication. Byline given. Buys one-time and first rights. Submit seasonal/holiday material 4 months in advance. Simultaneous phone queries and simultaneous submissions OK. SASE. Reports in 1 month. Sample copy $3; free writer's guidelines.

Nonfiction: General interest (in the Southeast); how-to (grow, market, promote, handle problems in culture, etc.), interview/profile (of notables or recognized contributors to industries); opinion (of experts only); personal experience (of reputable growers or researchers); technical (new tools, techniques, plant varieties, chemicals, equipment, etc.). Special issues: irrigation (May); marketing (September); equipment (November). No "home gardening material, commercially slanted stories, or information not of widespread industry interest in the Southeast." Buys variable number mss/year. Query. Length: 900-6,000 words. Pays $25-150.

Photos: Send photos with ms. Pays $10 maximum for b&w contact sheet and 8x10 prints; reviews 8x10 color prints. Captions required. Buys one-time rights.

Tips: "Discuss material with us by phone before writing; submit completed works well in advance of copy deadlines; include charts, photos and illustrations. We need more grower and related stories in both wholesale and retail categories. Marketing, shipping and economic features are also needed. Very long features (8-10 typed pages) are rarely welcome from freelancers."

POTATO GROWER OF IDAHO, Harris Publishing, Inc., Box 981, Idaho Falls ID 83401. (208)522-5187. Editor: Steve James. 25% freelance written. Emphasizes material slanted to the potato grower and the business of farming related to this subject—packing, shipping, processing, research, etc. Monthly magazine; 40-72 pages. Circ. 17,000. Pays on publication. Buys all rights. Byline given. Phone queries OK. Submit seasonal/ holiday material 6 weeks in advance. Photocopied submissions and previously published work OK. SASE. Reports in 1 month. Free sample copy and editorial guidelines.
Nonfiction: Expose (facts, not fiction or opinion, pertaining to the subject); how-to (do the job better, cheaper, faster, etc.); informational articles; interviews ("can use one of these a month, but must come from state of Idaho since this is a regional publication, telling the nation 'how Idaho grows potatoes' "); all types of new product articles pertaining to the subject; photo features (story can be mostly photos, but must have sufficient outlines to carry technical information); technical articles (all aspects of the industry of growing, storage, processing, packing and research of potatoes in general, but must relate to the Idaho potato industry). Buys 12 mss/ year. Query. Length: 750 words minimum. Pays 3¢/word.
Photos: B&w glossies (any size) purchased with mss or on assignment; use of color limited. Captions required. Query if photos are not to be accompanied by ms. Pays $5 minimum; $25 for color used on cover. Model release required.
Tips: "Choose one vital, but small, aspect of the industry; research that subject, slant it to fit the readership and/or goals of the magazine. All articles on research must have valid source for foundation. Material must be general in nature about the subject or specific in nature about Idaho potato growers. Write a query letter, noting what you have in mind for an article; be specific."

‡**SINSEMILLA TIPS, Domestic Grower's Journal**, New Moon Publishing, 1106 NW Van Buren, Box 2046, Corvallis OR 97339. (503)757-2532. Editor: Thomas Alexander. Quarterly magazine tabloid covering the domestic cultivation of marijuana. Circ. 5,000. Pays on publication. Byline given. "Some writers desire to be anonymous for obvious reasons." Not copyrighted. Buys one-time rights. Submit seasonal/holiday material 2 months in advance. SASE. Reports in 2 months. Sample copy $3.
Nonfiction: Book excerpts and reviews; expose (on political corruption); general interest; how-to; interview/ profile; opinion; personal experience; technical. Send complete ms. Length: 500-2,000 words. Pays $25-100.
Photos: Send photos with ms. Pays $10-20 for b&w prints. Captions optional. Model release required. Buys all rights.

SOYBEAN DIGEST, Box 27300, 777 Craig Rd., St. Louis MO 63141. (314)432-1600. Editor: Gregg Hillyer. 75% freelance written. Emphasizes soybean production and marketing. Monthly magazine. Circ. 160,000. Pays on acceptance. Buys all rights. Byline given. Phone queries OK. Submit seasonal material 2 months in advance of issue date. Reports in 3 weeks. Sample copy 50¢; mention *Writer's Market* in request.
Nonfiction: How-to (soybean production and marketing); and new product (soybean production and marketing). Buys over 100 mss/year. Query or submit complete ms. Length: 1,000 words. Pays $50-350.
Photos: State availability of photos with query. Pays $25-100 for 5x7 or 8x10 b&w prints and $50-200 for 35mm color transparencies and up to $350 for covers. Captions and/or manuscript required. Buys all rights.

TOBACCO REPORTER, 3000 Highwoods Blvd. #300, Box 95075, Raleigh NC 27625. Editor: Anne Shelton. For tobacco growers, processors, warehousemen, exporters, importers, manufacturers and distributors of cigars, cigarettes, and tobacco products. Monthly. Buys all rights. Pays on publication. SASE.
Nonfiction and Photos: Uses exclusive original material on request only. Pays 10-15¢/word. Pays $3 for photos purchased with mss.
Fillers: Wants clippings on new tobacco product brands, local tobacco distributors, smoking and health, and the following relating to tobacco and tobacco products: job promotions, obituaries, honors, equipment, etc. Pays $5-10/clipping on use only.

WINE WEST, (formerly *Redwood Rancher*), Box 498, Geyserville CA 95441. (703)433-7306. Editor/Publisher: Mildred Howie. Almost 100% freelance written. For entire West coast and for those who make, grow and enjoy wine. Circ. 2,500. Covers western Mexico through western Canada and as far as east Texas. Buys 35-45 mss/year. Byline given. Pays on publication. Photocopied and simultaneous submissions are not accepted. Prefers query before submitting ms. SASE. Reports in 2-4 weeks.
Nonfiction and Photos: Must be wine oriented. Technical articles on viticulturists and wine ecology. "Features and articles in *Wine West* are involved with western wine districts, the people, the practices and the lifestyle." Length: 300-3,000 words. Pays $2.50/inch; $10 for b&w photos only purchased with mss.

Dairy Farming

Publications for dairy farmers are classified here. Publications for farmers who raise animals for meat, wool, or hides are included in the Livestock category. Other magazines that buy material on dairy herds are listed in the General Interest Farming and Rural Life classification. Journals for dairy products retailers are found under Dairy Products.

BUTTER-FAT, Fraser Valley Milk Producers' Cooperative Association, Box 9100, Vancouver, British Columbia, Canada V6B 4G4. (604)420-6611. Editor: C.A. Paulson. Managing Editor: T.W. Low. Bimonthly magazine emphasizing this dairy cooperative's processing and marketing operations for dairy farmers and dairy workers in British Columbia. Circ. 3,300. Pays on acceptance. Byline given. Makes work-for-hire assignments. Phone queries preferred. Submit seasonal material 4 months in advance. Simultaneous, photocopied and previously published submissions OK. Reports in 1 week on queries; in 1 month on mss. Free sample copy and writer's guidelines.
Nonfiction: Interview (character profile with industry leaders); local nostalgia; opinion (of industry leaders); profile (of association members and employees).
Photos: Reviews 5x7 b&w negatives and contact sheets. Offers $10/published photo. Captions required. Buys all rights.
Columns/Departments: "We want articles on the people, products, business of producing, processing, marketing dairy foods in this province." Query first. Buys 3 mss/issue. Length: 500-1,500 words. Pays 7¢/word.
Poetry: Free verse, light verse and traditional. Buys 1 ms/year. Submit maximum 10 poems. Pays $10-25.
Fillers: Jokes, short humor and quotes. Buys 5 mss/issue. Pays $10.
Tips: "Make an appointment to come by and see us!"

DAIRY GOAT JOURNAL, Box 1808, Scottsdale AZ 85252. Editor: Kent Leach. 40% freelance written. Monthly for breeders and raisers of dairy goats. Pays on publication. Free sample copy. Reports in 1 month. Query. Computer printout and disk submissions OK. SASE.
Nonfiction and Photos: Uses articles, items, and photos that deal with dairy goats, and the people who raise them; goat dairies and shows. How-to articles up to 1,000 words. Buys 12-25 unsolicited mss/year. Pays by arrangement. Also buys 5x7 or 8x10 b&w photos for $1-15.
Tips: "In query give the thrust or point of the article, what illustrations may be available, how soon it might be finished—and if payments are expected, state how much or if negotiable."

THE DAIRYMAN, Box 819, Corona CA 91720. Editor: Dennis J. Halladay. For large herd dairy farmers. Monthly. Buys reprint rights. Pays on publication. Free sample copy. Reports in 3 weeks. Computer printout submissions OK. SASE.
Nonfiction and Photos: Uses articles on anything related to dairy farming, preferably anything new and different or substantially unique in operation, for US subjects. Acceptance of foreign dairy farming stories based on potential interest of readers. No politics, religion, food or cinema/arts. Recent article example: "Seven Reasons Why You Should Use A.I." Buys 5-10 unsolicited mss/year; would possibly buy 20-25. Pays $2/printed inch. Buys b&w photos with mss only, pays $10 each. Buys color with or without mss, pays $20-50 each. Also buys drawings, sketches, and other art used to illustrate story. Greater use of freelance material and some use of 4-color art inside with stories in the year ahead.
Tips: "Break in by sending us something . . . we're very informal about freelancers. Just send us the story and a proof, and we'll say yes or no. We only publish material concerning dairying—no pigs, horses, beef cattle or otherwise. We don't care about the upper Midwest, or upper Atlantic Coast. Our readers are the best dairymen in the world; stories should reflect the modern times of the industry."

DAIRYMEN'S DIGEST (Southern Region Edition), Box 5040, Arlington TX 76011. Editor: Phil Porter. For commercial dairy farmers and their families, throughout the central US, with interests in dairy production and marketing. Magazine; 32 pages. Monthly. Circ. 9,000. Not copyrighted. Byline given. Buys 34 mss/year. Pays on publication. Will send free sample copy to writer on request. Reports in 3 weeks. Computer printout or disk submissions OK. SASE.
Nonfiction and Photos: Emphasis on dairy production and marketing. Buys articles of general interest to farm families, especially dairy-oriented. Seeks unusual accomplishments and satisfactions resulting from determination and persistence. Must be positive and credible. Needs fresh ideas, profile, personal experience articles. Buys some historical, inspirational or nostalgia. Also articles of interest to farm wives. "I don't want to see material that is not related to dairying or milk marketing." Length: 50-1,500 words. Pay varies from $10-125, plus additional amount for photos, depending on quality.

‡**DAIRYNEWS**, Dairylea Cooperative, Inc., 831 James St., Syracuse NY 13203. (315)476-9101. Editor: David C. Jicha. Monthly magazine for dairy farmers in the northeastern US. Circ. 20,364. Pays on publication. Byline given. Submit seasonal/holiday material 2 months in advance. Simultaneous queries, and simultaneous, photocopied and previously published submissions OK. Computer printout submissions OK; prefers letter quality to dot matrix. SASE. Reports in 1 month on queries; 2 months on mss. Free sample copy. **Nonfiction:** How-to, interview/profile, photo feature, technical. No profiles on non-members—check with *Dairynews* first. Buys 5-7 mss/year. Query. Length: open. Pays $50-150.

ONTARIO MILK PRODUCER, Ontario Milk Marketing Board, 50 Maitland St., Toronto, Ontario, Canada M5W 1K2. (416)920-2700. Editor: Karen Sample. Monthly magazine covering dairy farm management. Circ. 17,000. Pays on acceptance. Byline given. Buys first rights. Submit seasonal/holiday material 2 months in advance. Simultaneous queries OK. Computer printout submissions OK. SASE; IRCs outside Canada. Reports in 1 week on queries; 2 weeks on mss. Free sample copy. **Nonfiction:** How-to, interview/profile, technical. No material on farm computers or generalized farming information. "We are specifically dairy-oriented." Priority given to Canadian material. Buys 55 mss/year. Query. Length: 200-3,000 words. Pays $50-700. **Photos:** Send photos with ms. Pays $10-25 for 2¼x2¼ color transparencies or 5x7 b&w prints. Captions, model release, and identification of subject required. **Columns/Departments:** Buys 1-2 mss/year. Query. Length: 500-1,000 words. Pays $25-100. **Fillers:** Clippings, gags. Buys 12/year. Length: 20-200 words. Pays $5-25.

General Interest Farming and Rural Life

The publications listed here are read by farm families or farmers in general and contain material on sophisticated agricultural and business techniques. Magazines that specialize in the raising of crops are in the Crops and Soil Management classification; publications that deal exclusively with livestock raising are classified in the Livestock category. Magazines for farm suppliers are grouped under Agricultural Equipment and Supplies.

National

AGRI NEWS, Rochester Post-Bulletin, 18 1st Ave. SE, Rochester MN 55901. (507)285-7707. Editor: Myron Williams. Managing Editor: William Boyne. Weekly newspaper for southeastern Minnesota and northeastern Iowa farmers interested in changes in agriculture, people in agriculture, and agriculture worldwide. Circ. 18,000. Pays on publication. Byline given. Not copyrighted. Buys first rights. Submit seasonal/holiday material 1 month in advance. Simultaneous queries OK. "We prefer typed copy, although letter quality computer printouts are acceptable. No disk submissions." SASE. Reports in 3 weeks. Sample copy for 9x12 SAE and 5 first class stamps; writer's guidelines for 5x9 envelope and 2 first class stamps. **Nonfiction:** Interview/profile (of anyone involved in agriculture); opinion (news analysis—ag related); technical; and features on agriculture. "Stories should be written in an objective, but in-depth newspaper style which is hard-hitting, clear and interesting to read. We take the view that the farmer is sophisticated enough to read professionally written pieces and not rambling stories about life in the country." No homespun writing, articles written for urban readers, or first-person stories. Buys 150 mss/year. Query with clips of published work. Length: 800-1,000 words. Pays $1.50/printed inch. **Columns/Departments:** "Our editorial page is in need of additional copy to keep it fresh, interesting and opinionated. We're always interested in viewing new column material about a variety of subjects as they pertain to agriculture. Queries will always be viewed closely and not just filed away." Buys 150 mss/year. Query with clips of published work. Length: 800-1,000 words. Pays $1.50/printed inch. **Tips:** "We may buy less freelance material later in the year because of additions to our staff—more staff writers means less dependence on freelancers."

AGWAY COOPERATOR, Box 4933, Syracuse NY 13221. (315)477-6488. Editor: James E. Hurley. For farmers. Published 9 times/year. Pays on acceptance. Usually reports in 1 week. SASE. **Nonfiction:** Should deal with topics of farm or rural interest in the Northeastern US. Length: 1,200 words maximum. Pays $100, usually including photos.

BLAIR AND KETCHUM'S COUNTRY JOURNAL, William Blair, Box 870, Manchester VT 05255. Editor: Richard Ketchum. Managing Editor: Thomas Rawls. Monthly magazine featuring country living for people who live in the country or who are thinking about moving there, small and part-time farmers. Circ. 275,000. Average issue includes 8-10 feature articles and 10 departments. Pays on acceptance. Byline given. Buys first North American serial and reprint rights. Submit seasonal material 6 months in advance. Photocopied submissions OK. SASE. Reports in 1 month.

Nonfiction: Opinion (essays); profile (people who are outstanding in terms of country living); how-to (2,000-2,500 words on practical gardening, energy, and animal care); and technical (new developments in a certain category). Buys 8-10 mss/issue. Query with clips of previously published work. Length: 2,000-2,500 words. Pays $400-500.

Photos: State availability of photos. Reviews 5x7 and 8x10 b&w glossy prints and 35mm or larger color transparencies. Captions and model release required. Buys one-time rights.

Poetry: Free verse, light verse and traditional. Buys 1 ms/issue. Pays $2/line.

‡**FARM INDUSTRY NEWS**, Webb Publishing, 1999 Shepard Rd., St. Paul MN 55116. (612)690-7284. Editor: Robert Moraczewski. Managing Editor: William Gergen. Magazine published 10 times/year. Covers product news, buying information. "We treat high volume farmers as purchasing agents rather than producers. Our stories provide farmers with in-depth information on new products they may consider buying." Circ. 450,000. Pays on acceptance. Byline given. Buys one-time rights. SASE. Reports in 3 weeks. Free sample copy and writer's guidelines. Sunbelt and Midwest editions.

Nonfiction: Interview/profile, new product, technical. No production stories, fiction or poetry. "Please study the publication before submitting stories." Query or send complete ms. Length: 500-1,500 words. Pays $50-400.

Photos: Reviews b&w contact sheets, 35mm color transparencies or 8x10 b&w prints. Payment depends on use and is included with ms. Captions and indentification of subjects required.

Tips: "Read the magazine, then query with specific idea and contacts. Good photographs showing a product and human involvement help in selling an article." Phone queries OK.

FARM JOURNAL, 230 W. Washington Square, Philadelphia PA 19105. Contact: Editor. "The business magazine of American agriculture" is published 14 times/year with many regional editions. Material bought for one or more editions depending upon where it fits. Buys all rights. Byline given "except when article is too short or too heavily rewritten to justify one." Payment made on acceptance and is the same regardless of editions in which the piece is used. SASE.

Nonfiction: Timeliness and seasonableness are very important. Material must be highly practical and should be helpful to as many farmers as possible. Farmers' experiences should apply to one or more of these 8 basic commodities: corn, wheat, milo, soybeans, cotton, dairy, beef and hogs. Technical material must be accurate. No farm nostalgia. Query to describe a new idea that farmers can use. Length: 500-1,500 words. Pays 10-20¢/word published.

Photos: Much in demand either separately or with short how-to material in picture stories and as illustrations for articles. Warm human interest pix for covers—activities on modern farms. For inside use, shots of homemade and handy ideas to get work done easier and faster, farm news photos, and pictures of farm people with interesting sidelines. In b&w, 8x10 glossies are preferred; color submissions should be 2¼x2¼ for the cover, and 35mm for inside use. Pays $50 and up for b&w shot; $75 and up for color.

Tips: "*Farm Journal* now publishes in hundreds of editions reflecting geographic, demographic, and economic sectors of the farm market."

FARM MONEY MANAGEMENT, Box 67, Minneapolis MN 55440. (612)374-5200. Editor: Craig Sabatka. Bimonthly magazine covering farm finance and economics for high-income farmers, agricultural lenders, farm managers and agricultural consultants. Estab. 1980. Circ. 60,000. Pays on acceptance. Byline given. Buys all rights. Submit seasonal/holiday queries 3 months in advance. Simultaneous queries, and simultaneous ("if so indicated"), photocopied, and previously published submissions OK. Computer printout submissions OK; prefers letter quality to dot matrix. SASE. Reports in 1 month. Sample copy free; writer's guidelines for business size SAE and 1 first class stamp.

Nonfiction: Needs articles on estate planning, tax planning, marketing, hedging, record keeping, computer applications, leasing, off-farm-investment and financing improvements, as well as features and profiles of farmers or lenders. Buys 15 mss/year. Query or send complete ms. Length: 1,000-2,500 words. Pays average $200.

Photos: Reviews 35mm color transparencies and 5x7 or 8x10 b&w glossy prints.

‡**FERTILIZER PROGRESS**, The Fertilizer Institute, 1015 18th St. NW, Washington DC 20036. (202)861-4900. Editor: Thomas E. Waldinger. Managing Editor: Kathleen S. Haffey. Bimonthly magazine covering fertilizer, farm chemical and allied industries for business and management, with emphasis on the retail market. Circ. 22,000. Pays on publication. Byline given. Offers 2½¢/word kill fee. Buys all rights. Submit seasonal/holiday material 2 months in advance. Photocopied submissions OK. SASE. Reports in 2 weeks on queries; 3 weeks on mss. Free sample copy.

Nonfiction: Articles on sales, services, credit, products, equipment, merchandising, production, regulation, research, environment. Also news about people, companies, trends, and developments. No "highly technical or philosophic pieces; we want relevance—something the farm retail dealer can sink his teeth into." No material not related to fertilizer, farm chemical and allied industries, or to the retail market. Send complete ms. Length: 400-2,500 words. Pays $40-250.

Photos: Send photos with ms. Pays $5-20 for 5x7 b&w and color prints. Captions and identification of subjects required.

Columns/Departments: Elements of Success (productive agronomic advice for dealers to use in selling to farmers); Fit to be Tried (ideas that really work); Worth Repeating (agricultural-related editorial commentary). Send complete ms. Length: 500-750 words. Pays $40-60.

THE FURROW, Deere & Co., John Deere Rd., Moline IL 61265. Executive Editor: Ralph E. Reynolds. Magazine published 8 times/year. For commercial farmers and ranchers. Circ. 1.1 million. Pays on acceptance. Buys all rights. Submit seasonal/holiday material at least 6 months in advance. SASE. Reports in 2 weeks. Free sample copy and writer's guidelines.

Nonfiction: George R. Sollenberger, North American editor. "We want articles describing new developments in the production and marketing of crops and livestock. These could be classified as how-to, informational and technical, but all must have a news angle. All articles should include some interviews, but we rarely use straight interviews. We publish articles describing farmers' personal experiences with new practices. We occasionally use photo features related to agriculture." Buys 10-15 mss/year. Submit complete ms. Length: 600-1,500 words. Pays $200-500.

Photos: Wayne Burkart, art editor. Original color transparencies (no copies) or color negatives of any size used only with mss. Captions required. Send negatives or transparencies with ms. No additional payment.

THE NATIONAL FUTURE FARMER, Box 15130, Alexandria VA 22309. (703)360-3600. Editor-in-Chief: Wilson W. Carnes. Managing Editor: Michael Wilson. Bimonthly magazine for members of the Future Farmers of America who are students of vocational agriculture in high school, ranging in age from 14-21; major interest in careers in agriculture/agribusiness and other youth interest subjects. Circ. 475,073. Pays on acceptance. Buys all rights. Byline given. Submit seasonal/holiday material 3-4 months in advance. Computer printout submissions OK; prefers letter quality to dot matrix. SASE. Usually reports in 3 weeks. Free sample copy and writer's guidelines.

Nonfiction: Contact: Michael Wilson. How-to for youth (outdoor-type such as camping, hunting, fishing); informational (getting money for college, farming; other help for youth). Informational, personal experience and interviews are used only if FFA members or former members are involved. Recent article example: "A Tale of Two Star Farmers" (February/March 1983). Buys 15 unsolicited mss/year. Query or send complete ms. Length: 1,000 words maximum. Pays 4-6¢/word.

Photos: Purchased with mss (5x7 or 8x10 b&w glossies; 35mm or larger color transparencies). Pays $7.50 for b&w; $30-40 for inside color; $100 for cover.

Tips: "Find an FFA member who has done something truly outstanding that will motivate and inspire others, or provide helpful information for a career in farming, ranching or agribusiness. We are also very interested in stories on the latest trends in agriculture and how those trends may affect our readers. As a result of cutbacks in money for pages, we're accepting mss now that are tighter and more concise."

SUCCESSFUL FARMING, 1716 Locust St., Des Moines IA 50336. (515)284-2693. Editor: Richard Krumme. Magazine of farm management published for top farmers. 13 times/year. Circ. 680,000. Buys all rights. Pays on acceptance. Reports in 2 weeks. SASE.

Nonfiction: Semi-technical articles on the aspects of farming with emphasis on how to apply this information to one's own farm. "Most of our material is too limited and unfamiliar for freelance writers, except for the few who specialize in agriculture, have a farm background and a modern agricultural education." Recent article example: "Why Chickens Will Be King at the Meat Counter" (February 1983). Buys 100 unsolicited mss/year. Query with outline. Length: about 1,500 words maximum. Pays $250-600.

Photos: Jim Galbraith, art director, prefers 8x10 b&w glossies to contacts; color should be transparencies, not prints. Buys exclusive rights. Assignments are given, and sometimes a guarantee, provided the editors can be sure the photography will be acceptable. Pays expenses.

Local

AcreAGE, Malheur Publishing Co., Box 130, Ontario OR 97914. (503)889-5387. Editor: Dick Yost. Monthly tabloid covering anything and everything relating to farming and ranching for all rural boxholders in southern Idaho and eastern Oregon. Circ. 40,000. Pays on acceptance. Byline given. Buys one-time rights. Computer printout submissions OK "if have *quality* dot matrix printer. We use Myro-Comp word processors and as such have no way of utilizing disk submissions." SASE. Reports in 3 weeks. Sample copy $1.

Nonfiction: General interest (on farming and ranching); how-to (install fence, irrigate, plant, harvest, etc.); interview/profile (of leaders in agriculture); personal experience (better ways to farm and ranch). No nostalgic pieces. "About 50% of our articles are technical pieces about such things as ag chemicals, irrigation, etc. These pieces are difficult for writers lacking a good ag background and proximity to a university or research center specializing in such work. No mss on 'how nice (or bad) it is to be a farmer or rancher.' " Buys 24 mss/year. Query or send complete ms. Length: 9 typewritten pages maximum. Pays $1-1.25/inch.

Photos: Pays $7 minimum for 5x7 (minimum) b&w glossy prints. Identification of subjects required.

Tips: "Avoid telling the obvious, e.g., 'Holsteins are a breed of cow that gives lots of milk.' Writers will have better luck breaking in with human interest features (farm-ranch oriented). Past articles have included a power hang-glider (ultralight) pilot who used his machine to check irrigation lines; Landsat satellites for water and crop management; an old-time threshing bee; and a farmer who collects antique farm machinery. The majority of our articles deal with farming and ranching in the southern Idaho, eastern Oregon region."

BUCKEYE FARM NEWS, Ohio Farm Bureau Federation, Box 479, Columbus OH 43216. (614)225-8906. Editor: Jack K. Hill. Managing Editor: Ellen Russell. Emphasizes agricultural policy pertaining to Ohio farmers. Monthly magazine; 48 pages. Circ. 92,000. Pays on acceptance. Buys all rights. Byline given. Prefers Ohio writers. Phone queries OK. Submit holiday/seasonal material 3 months in advance. Simultaneous, photocopied and previously published submissions OK. SASE. Reports in 3 weeks. Free sample copy.

Nonfiction: Exposes (of government, agriculture); humor (light pieces about farm life); informational (but no nuts-and-bolts farming); inspirational ("as long as they're not too heavy"); opinion; and interview. Buys 5 unsolicited mss/year. Query. Length: 500-2,000 words. Pays $25-100.

Photos: B&w and color purchased with mss or on assignment. Captions required. Send prints and transparencies. Pays $5-10 for b&w.

‡**COUNTRY ESTATE**, Northern Miner Press Ltd., RR1, Terra Cotta, Ontario, Canada L0P 1N0. (Editorial Only). (416)838-2800. Editor: Michael Pembry. Bimonthly magazine covering country living for upper income country homeowners. "Subjects must inform or entertain this specific audience." Circ. 40,000 (within 50 miles of Toronto). Pays on publication. Byline given. Buys first North American serial rights. Simultaneous queries and photocopied and simultaneous submissions OK. SASE. Reports in 1 month. Sample copy for $2 and 9x11 SAE and 60¢ postage or IRC; writer's guidelines for 30¢ postage or IRC.

Nonfiction: Historical/nostalgic; how-to; humor (on country living); interview/profile (country personalities in S. Ontario); personal experience; photo feature. "All subjects must relate to country living and people in Ontario, especially areas within 50 miles of Toronto." No "articles written for a very general audience." Buys 30 mss/year. Query. Length: 500-1,500 words. Pays $75-150.

Photos: Stae availability of photos with query letter or ms, or send photos with accompanying ms. Reviews transparencies and 5x7 prints. Payment included with article. Captions required. Buys one-time rights.

Tips: "Have a good grasp of our audience. Pick a subject which really relates specifically to country living in Ontario. Submit clean, edited material. Articles with good photos always preferred."

‡**EASTERN/WESTERN ONTARIO FARMER, First with the Farm News in Ontario**, Bowes Publishers, Box 7400, Station E, London, Ontario, Canada N5Y 4X3. (519)473-0010. Editor: Robert Way. Publisher: James O. Johnston. Two separate weekly tabloids covering Ontario agriculture—crops, all livestock, horticulture. "Weekly farm news, profiles on farm leaders, farm management advice, achievements, commodity markets. Aimed at helping farmers in day-to-day operation of farm. Common sense approach to subject matter." Circ. 9,022 *Eastern*; 26,913 *Western*. Pays on publication. Byline given. Buys first North American serial rights. Reports in 1 week. Sample copy for mailing cost.

Nonfiction: Interview/profile, personal experience on farm women and life on the farm. Buys 80 mss/year. Send complete ms. "Computer disk submissions acceptable as long as compatible with Compugraphic MDT 350 terminal for editing." Length: 750-1,000 words. Pays $65 maximum.

Photos: Send photos with ms. Reviews b&w prints (head and shoulders) of farm women. Photo purchase included in $65 fee. Identification of subjects required. Buys one-time rights.

Tips: "Our own reporters handle news reporting. We want features on farm women only. Send in query or call about an interesting farm woman to see if we haven't already done story on her. Check with editor." Break in with women's features (farming). "Explore wife's contributions to family farm, community, charities—any unusual talents, abilities."

FARM & FOREST, Henley Publishing, Ltd., Box 130, Woodstock, New Brunswick, Canada E0J 2B0. (506)328-8863. Editor: Gordon F. Catt. Monthly tabloid for residents of Atlantic Canada engaged or interested in agriculture and forestry in the province. Circ. 5,000. Pays on publication. Byline given. Pays 50% kill fee. Not copyrighted. Buys one-time rights. Submit seasonal/holiday material 4 months in advance. Photocopied and previously published submissions OK. SASE. Reports in 2 weeks on queries; 1 month on mss. Sample copy $1; writer's guidelines for business size SAE and 32¢ Canadian postage.

Nonfiction: General interest; historical/nostalgic; how-to (better ways to harvest, house cattle, adapt machinery); interview/profile (people in regional farming, forestry); technical. No opinion pieces or inspirational material. "We are looking for freelancers living in our area who can write profiles of regional people in the agriculture and forestry industries. We will also contract with freelancers to cover specific events in our province. Submit articles on farm forestry outside our primary distribution areas as long as they tie in with what's happening here." Buys 12 mss/year. Query. Length: 500-1,200 words. Pays 5¢/word, except for special advance contracts.

Photos: State availability of photos. Pays $5-10 for 5x7 b&w prints. Captions and identification of subjects required.

Fiction: Children's stories—emphasis on animals, rural life. "No 'cute' calves and baby animal stories." No erotica, fantasy, romance, horror. Buys 12 mss/year. Query. Length: 500-1,000 words. Pays 5¢/word.

Poetry: Free verse, haiku, light verse, traditional. "No erotica." Buy 12/year. Submit maximum 2 poems. Length: 6-20 lines. Pays $3.

Tips: "Change to monthly publication means we'll purchase fewer mss, and those we use will have to be tighter in length and of definite interest to our readers who are mostly in Canada's Atlantic Provinces region and its agricultural and forest industries."

FARM FOCUS, Box 128 Yarmouth, Nova Scotia, Canada B5A 4B1. Bimonthly magazine read by farmers, people in agribusiness, and in government agricultural agencies. "It is the only farm and agricultural paper that is distributed throughout Atlantic Canada." Circ. 11,500. Pays on publication. Buys first or second rights. SAE and International Reply Coupons.

Nonfiction: "Any American developments that could have an impact on the Canadian agricultural scene." No "re-writes on agricultural bulletins, scientific papers." Buys 100 unsolicited mss/year. Send complete ms. Length: 800-1,400 words. Pays 3¢-7¢/word.

Photos: Pays $5 for 5x7 b&w prints.

Tips: "At the present time it is not easy for a freelance writer to break into the limited field we service, but copy on any government policies that would affect agriculture, new innovations in agriculture, or about individuals or groups that have been successful by flying in the face of tradition, would be of interest. Articles should be as concise as possible and written so the layman can understand them."

FLORIDA GROWER & RANCHER, 723 E. Colonial Dr., Orlando FL 32803. Editor: Frank Abrahamson. For citrus grove managers and production managers, vegetable growers and managers, livestock raisers; all agricultural activities in state. Monthly magazine. Circ. 32,500. Buys all rights. Pays on publication. Reports in 30 days. Query. SASE.

Nonfiction and Photos: Articles on production and industry-related topics. In-depth and up-to-date. Writer must know the market and write specifically for it. Informational, how-to, personal experience, interview, profile, opinion, successful business operations. Buys a minimum of outside material due to fulltime staff additions. Length: 500-1,500 words for features; 100 words or less for short items. Pays "competitive rates." B&w illustrations desirable with features. Color illustrations purchased only occasionally.

INDIANA PRAIRIE FARMER, a Farm Progress Publication, Box 41281, Indianapolis IN 46241. (317)248-0681. Editor: Paul Queck. Semimonthly magazine covering farm management, production technology and policy for owners of farms, farm workers, and agribusiness people. Controlled circ. 89,500. Pays on acceptance. No byline given. Buys first North American serial rights. Submit seasonal/holiday material 6 months in advance. Reports in 2 weeks. Free sample copy.

Nonfiction: "We are a farm business magazine using articles on farm management and production with emphasis on farmer interviews." Buys 20-25 mss/year. Length: 600-1,200 words. Pays $75-150.

Photos: Send photos with ms. Pays $100-150 for 35mm color transparencies; $15-25 for 8x10 b&w prints. B&w photo payment included in payment for ms. Captions and model release required. Buys first rights.

IOWA REC NEWS, Suite 48, 8525 Douglas, Urbandale IA 50322. (515)276-5350. Editor: Mary Harding. Emphasizes energy issues for residents of rural Iowa. Monthly magazine. Circ. 125,000. Pays on publication. Not copyrighted. Simultaneous, photocopied and previously published submissions OK. Computer printout and disk submissions OK. SASE.

Nonfiction: General interest, historical, humor, nostalgia (farm) and photo features. Recent article example: "Kinnick: An Unforgettable Iowan." Buys 18 unsolicited mss/year. Send complete ms. Pays $50-75.

Tips: "The easiest way to break into our magazine is: include a couple paragraphs about the author, research a particular subject well, or, be very funny. Reading and knowing about farm people is important. Stories that touch the senses or can improve the lives of the readers are highly considered."

‡**LANCASTER FARMING**, Box 366, Lititz PA 17543. (717)626-1164. Editor: Sheila M. Miller. Weekly newspaper covering farming and agribusiness news. Circ. 40,000. Pays on publication. Byline given. Buys one-time rights. Photocopied submissions OK. SASE. Sample copy for 10x13 SAE and $2.50 postage.

Nonfiction: How-to, interview/profile, new product, personal experience, home and youth. "We provide the latest market news, analysis of agricultural market trends, state and federal news as it affects farmers, how-to features dealing with farm and cropland management, and personality features. Articles need to be technically sound and written for the experienced farmer." No unsolicited mss. "Our market is regionalized to Pennsylvania, Maryland, Delaware and New Jersey and specifically agriculture." Buys less than 30 mss/year. Query with published clips. Length: 1,000-2,500 words. Pays variable rates; average $50.
Photos: State availability of photos. Pays $5-10 for 4x5 b&w prints. Captions required. Buys one-time rights.
Fillers: Jokes. Buys 50/year. Length: 10-50 words. Pays $5.
Tips: "The best way for a freelancer to break into our publication is through a farm feature. Articles can be on a farm family that is doing an outstanding job, special livestock accomplishments, etc. We also welcome stories on new developments in farm machinery, plant and livestock genetics, innovative farming practices—but query first."

MICHIGAN FARMER, 3303 W. Saginaw St., Lansing MI 48901. (517)321-9393. Associate Editor: Dave Weinstock. 10-20% freelance written. Semimonthly. Buys first North American rights. Byline given. Pays on acceptance. Reports in 1 month. Query. SASE.
Nonfiction: Uses problem solving articles of interest and value to Michigan farmers, which discuss Michigan agriculture and the people involved in it. Also articles for home section about Michigan farm housewives and what they are doing. Lucid, easy-to-understand writing is desired. Length depends on topic. Rates are $1/column inch minimum; special stories bring higher rates.
Photos: Buys some b&w singles; also a few color transparencies, for cover use. Pays $5-10 each for b&w, depending on quality. Pays $60 for selected cover transparencies of identifiable Michigan farm or rural scenes; accepts only verticals.

MISSOURI RURALIST, Harvest Publishing, Suite 600, 2103 Burlington, Columbia MO 65202. Editor: Larry Harper. Managing Editor: Joe Link. Semimonthly magazine featuring Missouri farming for people who make their living at farming. Pays on acceptance. Byline given. Buys first North American serial rights and all rights in Missouri. Photocopied submissions OK. Computer printout or disk submissions OK; prefers letter quality to dot matrix printouts. SASE. Reports in 1 month. Sample copy $1.50.
Nonfiction: "We use articles valuable to the Missouri farmer, discussing Missouri agriculture and people involved in it, including housewives. Technical articles must be written in an easy-to-read style. The length depends on the topic." No corny cartoons or poems on farmers. Query. Pays $60/published page.
Photos: State availability of photos. Pays $5-10 for 5x7 b&w glossy prints. Pays $60 maximum for 35mm transparencies for covers. Captions required.
Fillers: Newsbreaks. Length: 100-500 words. Pays $60/printed page.

N.D. REC MAGAZINE, N.D. Association of RECs, Box 727, Mandan ND 58554. (701)663-6501. Editor-in-Chief: Leland Ulmer. Managing Editor: Dennis Hill. Monthly magazine covering rural electric program and rural North Dakota lifestyle. "Our magazine goes to the 70,000 North Dakotans who get their electricity from rural electric cooperatives. We cover rural lifestyle, energy conservation, agriculture, farm family news, and other features of importance to this predominantly agrarian state. Of course, we represent the views of our statewide association." Circ. 74,000. Pays on publication; "acceptance for assigned features." Byline given. Buys first North American serial rights. Submit seasonal/holiday material 6 months in advance. Simultaneous queries OK. Computer printout submissions OK; prefers letter quality to dot matrix. SASE. Reports in 2 weeks. Sample copy for 9x12 SAE with $1.37 postage.
Nonfiction: Dennis Hill, managing editor. Expose (subjects of ND interest dealing with rural electric, agriculture, rural lifestyle); historical/nostalgic (ND events or people only); how-to (save energy, weatherize homes, etc.); interview/profile (on great leaders of the rural electric program, agriculture); opinion (why family farms should be saved, the rural electric program, agriculture); opinion (why family farms should be saved, etc.). No fiction that does not relate to our editorial goals. Buys 10-12 mss/year. Length: open. Pays $35-300.
Photos: Dennis Hill, managing editor. "We need 5x7 b&w glossy prints for editorial material. Transparencies needed for cover, ag/rural scenes only—ND interest." Pays $25 maximum for 35mm color transparencies; $5 minimum for 5x7 b&w prints. Captions and identification of subjects required. Buys one-time rights.
Columns/Departments: Dennis Hill, managing editor. Guest Spot: Guest opinion page, preferably about 700-850 words, about issues dealing with agriculture, rural social issues, and the rural electric program. Buys 12 mss/year. Length: 700-1,000 words. Pays $35-75.

‡**NEW ENGLAND FARMER**, NEF Publishing Co., Box 391, St. Johnsbury VT 05819. (802)748-8908. Editor: Dan Hurley. Managing Editor: Thomas Gilson. Monthly tabloid covering New England agriculture for farmers. Circ. 13,052. Pays on publication. Byline given. Buys all rights and makes-work-for-hire assignments. Submit seasonal/holiday material 2 months in advance. Previously published submissions OK. SASE. Reports in 3 months. Free sample copy.
Nonfiction: How-to, interview/profile, opinion, technical. No romantic views of farming. "We use on-the-

farm interviews with good b&w photos that combine technical information with human interest. No poetics!"
Buys 150 mss/year. Send complete ms. Pays $40-100.
Photos: Send photos with ms. Payment for photos is included in payment for articles. Reviews b&w contact
sheet and 8x10 b&w prints.
Tips: "Good, accurate stories needing minimal editing, with art, of interest to commercial farmers in New
England are welcome."

THE OHIO FARMER, 1350 W. 5th Ave., Columbus OH 43212. (614)486-9637. Editor: Andrew Stevens.
For Ohio farmers and their families. Biweekly magazine; 50 pages. Circ. 103,000. Usually buys all rights.
Buys 5-10 mss/year. Pays on publication. Sample copy $1; free writer's guidelines. Will consider photocopied
submissions. Reports in 2 weeks. Submit complete ms. SASE.
Nonfiction and Photos: Technical and on-the-farm stories. Buys informational, how-to, personal experience.
Length: 600-700 words. Pays $15. Photos purchased with ms with no additional payment, or without ms. Pays
$5-25 for b&w; $35-100 for color. Size: 4x5 for b&w glossies; transparencies or 8x10 prints for color.
Tips: "We are now doing more staff-written stories. We buy very little freelance material."

RURAL KENTUCKIAN, Official Magazine of Kentucky Association of Electric Cooperatives, Box
32170, Louisville KY 40232. (502)451-2430. Editor: Gary W. Luhr. Monthly magazine covering rural electrification for a general audience. Circ. 260,000. Pays on acceptance. Byline given. Not copyrighted. Buys first
rights. Submit seasonal/holiday material 3 months in advance. Simultaneous queries, and simultaneous, photocopied, and previously published submissions OK. Computer printout and disk submissions OK. SASE. Reports in 2 weeks. Sample copy for SAE and 3 first class stamps; writer's guidelines for SAE and 1 first class
stamp.
Nonfiction: General interest; historical/nostalgic (with Kentucky angle); how-to (general consumer interest);
humor (suitable for general audience); interview/profile (with Kentucky angle); photo feature (with Kentucky
angle). Buys 12-20 mss/year. Query or send complete ms. Length: 800-2,000 words. Pays $50-150.
Photos: State availability of photos. Reviews color slide transparencies and 8x10 b&w prints. "Payment included in payment for ms." Identification of subjects required. Buys one-time rights.
Tips: "We are glad to receive inquires or material from freelancers. Preference is given to Kentucky writers
and former residents. No fiction or poetry."

RURAL MONTANA, Montana Associated Utilities, Inc., Box 1641, Great Falls MT 59403. (406)454-1412.
Editor: Martin L. Erickson. Emphasizes rural life. For farmers, ranchers and rural dwellers. Monthly magazine; 32 pages. Circ. 58,000. Pays on publication. Buys one-time rights. Phone queries OK. Simultaneous,
photocopied, and previously published submissions OK. SASE. Reports in 3 weeks.
Nonfiction: How-to, informational, historical, humor, inspirational, nostalgic and travel articles; interviews
and photo features. Query. Length: 500-2,000 words. Pays $15 minimum.
Photos: Purchased with mss or on assignment. Captions required. Query. Pays $10 minimum for 8x10 (or 5x7
minimum) b&w glossies. Model release required.

WYOMING RURAL ELECTRIC NEWS, 340 West B St., Casper WY 82601. (307)234-6152. Editor: Gale
Eisenhauer. For audience of primarily farmers and ranchers. Monthly magazine; 16 pages. Circ. 28,500. Not
copyrighted. Byline given. Buys 12-15 mss/year. Pays on publication. Free sample copy. Will consider photo-
copied and simultaneous submissions. Submit seasonal material 2 months in advance. Reports in 3-4 weeks.
SASE.
Nonfiction, Photos and Fiction: Wants energy-related material, "people" features, historical pieces about
Wyoming and the West, things of interest to Wyoming's rural people. Buys informational, humor, historical,
nostalgia and photo mss. Submit complete ms. Length for nonfiction and fiction: 1,200-1,500 words. Pays
$10-25. Photos purchased with accompanying ms with no additional payment, or purchased without ms. Cap-
tions required. Pays $10 for cover photos. B&w preferred. Buys some experimental, western, humorous and
historical fiction. Pays $25.
Tips: "Study an issue or two of the magazine to become familiar with our focus and the type of freelance material we're using. Submit entire manuscript. Don't submit a regionally-set story from some other part of the
country and merely change the place names to Wyoming. Photos, illustrations (if appropriate) are always
welcomed."

Livestock

Farmers who raise cattle, sheep or hogs for meat, wool or hides are the audience for these journals. Publications for farmers who raise other animals are listed
in the Miscellaneous category; many magazines in the General Interest Farming and

Rural Life classification buy material on raising livestock. Magazines for dairy farmers are included under Dairy Farming. Publications dealing with raising horses, pets or other pleasure animals are found under Animal in the Consumer Publications section.

BEEF, The Webb Co., 1999 Shepard Rd., St. Paul MN 55116. (612)647-7374. Editor-in-Chief: Paul D. Andre. Managing Editor: Warren Kester. Monthly magazine. For readers who have the same basic interest—making a living feeding cattle or running a cow herd. Circ. 120,000. Pays on acceptance. Buys one-time rights. Byline given. Phone queries OK. Submit seasonal material 3 months in advance. Computer printout or disk submissions OK. SASE. Reports in 2 months. Free sample copy and writer's guidelines.
Nonfiction: How-to and informational articles on doing a better job of producing feeding cattle, market building, managing, and animal health practices. Material must deal with cattle-beef only. Buys 8-10 mss/year. Query. Length: 500-2,000 words. Pays $25-250.
Photos: B&w glossies (8x10) and color transparencies (35mm or 2¼x2¼) purchased with or without mss. Captions required. Query or send contact sheet or transparencies. Pays $10-50 for b&w; $25-100 for color. Model release required.
Tips: "Be completely knowledgeable about cattle feeding and cowherd operations. Know what makes a story. We want specifics, not a general roundup of an operation. Pick one angle and develop it fully."

BLACKS UNLIMITED INC., Box 578, Webster City IA 50595. Editor: Greg Garwood. Monthly magazine published for North American cattlemen interested in Angus cattle or Angus cross cattle such as Brangus and Chiangus. The publication reaches purebred breeders as well as commercial cattlemen. Circ. 12,000. Pays on publication. Rights negotiable. Phone queries OK. Submit seasonal material 2 months in advance. Simultaneous, photocopied and previously published submissions OK. Reports in 2 weeks. Free sample copy and writer's guidelines.
Nonfiction: Expose, general interest, how-to, interview, opinion, profile, travel, new product, photo feature, and research in breeding cattle. Buys 4 mss/issue. Query. Length: 2,000-2,500 words. Pays $25-500.
Photos: State availability of photos. Reviews b&w contact sheets. Payment negotiable.

POLLED HEREFORD WORLD, 4700 E. 63rd St., Kansas City MO 64130. (816)333-7731. Editor: Ed Bible. For "breeders of Polled Hereford cattle—about 80% registered breeders, 5% commercial cattle breeders; remainder are agribusinessmen in related fields." Monthly. Circ. 20,000. Not copyrighted. Buys "no unsolicited mss at present." Pays on publication. Free sample copy. Photocopied submissions OK. Computer printout and disk submissions OK; prefers letter quality to dot matrix printouts. Submit seasonal material "as early as possible: 2 months preferred." Reports in 1 month. Query first for reports of events and activities. Query first or submit complete ms for features. SASE.
Nonfiction: "Features on registered or commercial Polled Hereford breeders. Some on related agricultural subjects (pastures, fences, feeds, buildings, etc.). Mostly technical in nature; some human interest. Our readers make their living with cattle, so write for an informed, mature audience." Buys informational articles, how-to's, personal experience articles, interviews, profiles, historical and think pieces, nostalgia, photo features, coverage of successful business operations, articles on merchandising techniques, and technical articles. Length: "varies with subject and content of feature." Pays about 5¢/word ("usually about 50¢/column inch, but can vary with the value of material").
Photos: Purchased with mss, sometimes purchased without mss, or on assignment; captions required. "Only good quality b&w glossies accepted; any size. Good color prints or transparencies." Pays $2 for b&w, $2-25 for color. Pays $25 for color covers.

SHEEP! MAGAZINE, Rt. 1, Box 78, Helenville WI 53137. (414)593-8385. Editor: Dave Thompson. Monthly magazine. "We're looking for clear, concise, useful information for sheep raisers who have a few sheep to a 1,000 ewe flock." Circ. 7,500. Pays on publication. Byline given. Offers $30 kill fee. Buys first rights or makes work-for-hire assignments. Submit seasonal/holiday material 3 months in advance. Computer printout and disk submissions OK. SASE. Reports in 1 month. Sample copy for 9x12 SAE with postage.
Nonfiction: Book excerpts; information on personalities and/or political, legal or environmental issues affecting the sheep industry); how-to (on innovative lamb and wool marketing and promotion techniques, efficient record-keeping systems or specific aspects of health and husbandry. "Health and husbandry articles should be written by someone with extensive experience or appropriate credentials—i.e., a veterinarian or animal scientist."); profiles (on experienced sheep producers who detail the economics and management of their operation); features (on small businesses that promote wool products and stories about local and regional sheep producer's groups and their activities); new products (of value to sheep producers; should be written by someone who has used them); technical (on genetics, health and nutrition). First-person narratives. Buys 50 mss/year. Query with clips of published work or send complete ms. Length: 750-2,500 words. Pays $35-115.
Photos: "Color—vertical compositions of sheep and/or people—for our cover. Use only b&w inside magazine. B&w, 35mm photos or other visuals improve your chances of a sale." Pays $50 maximum for 35mm col-

or transparencies; $5-30 for 5x7 b&w prints. Identification of subjects required. Buys all rights.
Tips: "We will buy more articles from freelancers as our editorial pages expand."

SIMMENTAL SHIELD, Box 511, Lindsborg KS 67456. Publisher: Chester Peterson Jr. Editor: Jim Cotton. Official publication of American Simmental Association. Readers are purebred cattle breeders and/or commercial cattlemen. Monthly; 150 pages. Circ. 7,000. Buys all rights. Pays on publication. Will send free sample copy to writer on request. January is AI issue; July is herd sire issue; December is brood cow issue. Submit material 3-4 months in advance. Reports in 1 week. Query first or submit complete ms. SASE.
Nonfiction, Photos, and Fillers: Farmer experience; management articles with emphasis on ideas used and successful management ideas based on cattleman who owns Simmental. Research: new twist to old ideas or application of new techniques to the Simmental or cattle business. Wants articles that detail to reader how to make or save money or pare labor needs. Buys informational, how-to, personal experience, interview, profile, humor, think articles. Rates vary, but equal or exceed those of comparable magazines. Photos purchased with accompanying ms with no additional payment. Interest in cover photos; accepts 35mm if sharp, well-exposed.
Tips: "Articles must involve Simmental and/or beef breeding cattle."

Miscellaneous

AMERICAN BEE JOURNAL, Dadant and Sons, Inc., 51 S. 2nd St., Hamilton IL 62341. (217)847-3324. Editor: Joe Graham. Monthly magazine about beekeeping for hobbyist beekeepers, commercial beekeepers and researchers. Circ. 20,000. Average issue includes 8-10 nonscientific articles and 1-2 scientific articles by researchers. Pays on publication. Byline given. Buys all rights. Submit seasonal material 2 months in advance. Previously published submissions OK, if so indicated. SASE. Reports in 2 weeks. Free sample copy.
Nonfiction: General interest (articles that deal with beekeeping management; honey packing and handling; bee diseases; other products of the hive such as royal jelly, pollen and beeswax; pesticide hazards to honeybees; and occasional articles on beekeeping as a business). No general information about beekeeping. Recent article example: "Assembly Line Nuc Making" (March 1982). Buys 20-40 unsolicited mss/year. Send complete ms. Length: 1,200-1,500 words. Pays 2½¢/word minimum.
Photos: Send photos with ms. Pays $5 minimum for 5x7 b&w glossy prints. Captions and model release required.
Fillers: Newsbreaks. Buys 1-2 mss/issue. Pays 2½¢/word minimum.

GLEANINGS IN BEE CULTURE, Box 706, Medina OH 44258. Editor: Lawrence R. Goltz. For beekeepers. Monthly. Buys first North American serial rights. Pays on publication. Writer's guidelines available upon request/SASE. Reports in 15-90 days. SASE.
Nonfiction and Photos: Interested in articles giving new ideas on managing bees. Also uses success stories about commercial beekeepers. No "how I began beekeeping" articles. No highly advanced, technical and scientific abstracts or impractical advice. Length: 3,000 words maximum. "We'll be changing format to allow for approximately 35% more copy space for articles." Pays $23/published page. Sharp b&w photos pertaining to honeybees purchased with mss. Can be any size, prints or enlargements, but 4x5 or larger preferred. Pays $3-5/picture.
Tips: "Do an interview story on commercial beekeepers who are cooperative enough to furnish accurate, factual information on their operations."

THE SUGAR PRODUCER, Harris Publishing, Inc., 520 Park, Box 981, Idaho Falls ID 83401. (208)522-5187. Editor: Steve James. 25% freelance written. Bimonthly magazine covering the growing, storage, use and by-products of the sugar beet. Circ. 19,000. Pays on publication. Buys all rights. Byline given. Phone queries OK. Photocopied submissions and previously published work OK. SASE. Reports in 30 days. Free sample copy and writer's guidelines.
Nonfiction: "This is a trade magazine, not a farm magazine. It deals with the business of growing sugar beets, and the related industry. All articles must tell the grower how he can do his job better, or at least be of interest to him, such as historical, because he is vitally interested in the process of growing sugar beets, and the industries related to this." Expose (pertaining to the sugar industry or the beet grower); how-to (all aspects of growing, storing and marketing the sugar beet); interview; profile; personal experience; technical (material source must accompany story—research and data must be from an accepted research institution). Query or send complete ms. Length: 750-2,000 words. Pays 3¢/word.
Photos: Purchased with mss. Captions required. Pays $5 for any convenient size b&w; $10 for color print or transparency; $25 for color shot used on cover. Model release required.

Finance

The magazines listed below deal with banking, investment, and financial management. Publications that use similar material but have a less technical slant are listed in Consumer Publications under Business and Finance.

ABA BANKING JOURNAL, 345 Hudson St., New York NY 10014. (212)620-7200. Editor: Lyman B. Coddington. Managing Editor: William Streeter. Executive Editor: Joe W. Kizzia. 15-20% freelance written. Monthly magazine; 150 pages. Circ. 41,000. Pays on publication. Query. Photocopied submissions OK. SASE. Reports in 4-6 weeks. Sample copy sent to writer "only if a manuscript is commissioned."
Nonfiction: How-to; new product; and articles dealing with banking. Buys 24-36 mss/year. Query. Average length: 2,000 words. Pays $100/magazine page, including headlines, photos and artwork.
Photos: State availability of photos with query. Uses 8x10 b&w glossy prints and 35mm color transparencies. Buys one-time rights.

AMERICAN BANKER, 1 State St. Plaza, New York NY 10004. (212)943-0400. Editor: William Zimmerman. Managing Editor: Robert Casey. Daily tabloid covering banking and finance for top management of banks, savings banks, savings and loans, and other financial service institutions. Circ. 21,800. Pays on publication. Byline given. Buys all rights. Simultaneous and previously published ("depending on where published") submissions OK. Reports in 1 month.
Nonfiction: Patricia Stundza, features editor. Book excerpts; technical (relating to banking/finance). No "non-banking or non-business-oriented articles—must be specific." Query. Length: 1,500-3,000 words. Pays $75-200.
Photos: State availability of photos. Pays $100 minimum for 8x10 b&w prints. Captions and identification of subjects required. Buys one-time rights.

‡BANK DIRECTOR & STOCKHOLDER, Box 6847, Orlando FL 32853. Executive Editor: William P. Seaparke. 20% freelance written. Semi-annual journal; 20 pages. Circ. 8,000. Pays on publication. Buys all rights. Pays 50% kill fee. Byline given. SASE. Reports in 3 months.
Nonfiction: Case studies of financial problems which would be of interest to corporate directors and shareholders, particularly banking institutions or financial corporations. Recent article example: "How Will Banks Fare in the Prestige Card Market?" (February 1983). Buys a few unsolicited mss/year. Query. Length: 500-3,000 words. Payment varies.
Photos: State availability of photos with query. Pays $10-100 for 5x7 b&w glossy prints; $20-200 for 35mm color transparencies. Captions and model release required. Buys all rights.
Columns/Departments: Economy; interview; and energy. Query. Length: 600-3,000 words. Pays $20 minimum. Open to suggestions for new columns/departments.

BANK SYSTEMS & EQUIPMENT, 1515 Broadway, New York NY 10036. Editor: Joan Prevete Hyman. For bank, savings and loan association, mutual savings banks and credit union operations executives. Monthly. Circ. 22,000. Buys all rights. Byline given. Pays on publication. Query for style sheet and specific article assignment. Mss should be triple-spaced on one side of paper only with wide margin at left-hand side of the page. SASE.
Nonfiction: Third-person case history articles and interviews as well as material related to systems, operations and automation. Charts, systems diagrams, artist's renderings of new buildings, etc., may accompany ms and must be suitable for reproduction. Prefers one color only. Length: open. Pays $100 for each published page.
Photos: 5x7 or 8x10 single-weight glossies. Candids of persons interviewed, views of bank, bank's data center, etc. Captions required. "We do not pay extra for photos."
Tips: "Writers can break in by covering telecommunications in banks and thrifts."

BENEFITS CANADA, Pension Fund Investment and Employee Benefit Management, Maclean Hunter Ltd., 777 Bay St., Toronto, Ontario, Canada M5W 1A7. (416)596-5958. Editor: Robin Schiele. Bimonthly magazine covering money management, investment management, pension fund administration, employee benefits industry for experts in the field. "However, there is a degree of overlap between the investment and benefits sides. Knowledge of each side should be assumed in the readership." Circ. 13,000. Pays on acceptance. Byline given. Buys first North American serial rights. Reports in 2 weeks on queries; 1 month on mss. Free sample copy.
Nonfiction: Interview/profile and opinion (of figures in pension fund, investments or employee benefits); technical (investment or employee benefit administration). Query with clips of published work or send complete ms. Length: 1,000-2,200 words. Pays $125-400.

BIOTECHNOLOGY INVESTMENT OPPORTUNITIES, High Tech Publishing Co., Box 266, Brattleboro VT 05301. (802)869-2833. Editor: Philip T. DiPeri. Monthly newsletter covering investment opportunities in high technology aimed at "sophisticated, well-informed investors seeking calculated-risk investments. Identifies and analyzes emerging investment opportunities in genetic engineering,; follows trends and conditions having significant impact on the development and commercial application of leading-edge biotechnology research. Emphasis is on new enterprise formation, capital formation, emerging markets and applications." Circ. 1,000. Pays on publication. Byline given. Buys all rights. Simultaneous queries and simultaneous, photocopied and previously published submissions OK. SASE. Reports in 2 weeks. Sample copy and writer's guidelines for business size SAE and 1 first class stamp.
Nonfiction: Interview/profile (high technology, capital providers, firms, idea/research/patent generators); new product (potential commercialization of research concepts and ideas); technical (new patents with commercial possibilities, related instrumentation); current research efforts in various high technology areas. Special issues include bimonthly supplements providing in-depth reporting of important aspect of investing in genetic engineering and high technology. Buys 150 mss/year. Send complete ms. Length: 25-500 words. Pays 10-25¢/word.
Columns/Departments: New patents (in genetic engineering with commercial possibilities); new applications (of biotech processes and products); people (briefs on the principal players in biotechnology). Buys 100 mss/year. Send complete ms. Length: 25-500 words. Pays 10-25¢/word.
Fillers: Newsbreaks. Buys 10/year. Length: 25-500 words. Pays 10-25¢/word.
Tips: "Submit completed manuscript or, if extensive investigation or research is needed, query first. We're looking for newsletter-style writing with a high proportion of nouns and verbs over adjectives and adverbs."

CANADIAN BANKER, The Canadian Bankers' Association, Box 282, T-D Centre, Toronto, Ontario, Canada M5K 1K2. Editor: Brian O'Brien. 90% freelance written. Emphasizes banking in Canada. Bimonthly magazine. Circ. 45,000. Buys first North American serial rights. Byline given. SAE and International Reply Coupons. Reports in 1 month.
Nonfiction: Informational articles on international banking and economics; interviews, nostalgic and opinion articles; book reviews. Query. Length: 750-2,000 words. Pays $100-300. "Freelancer should be an authority on the subject. Most contributors are bankers, economists and university professors."

COMMODITIES MAGAZINE, 219 Parkade, Cedar Falls IA 50613. (319)677-6341. Publisher: Merrill Oster. Editor-in-Chief: Darrell Jobman. For private, individual futures traders, brokers, exchange members, agribusinessmen, bankers, anyone with an interest in futures or commodity options. Monthly magazine; 104-128 pages. Circ. 50,000. Buys all rights. Byline given. Pays on publication. Free sample copy. Photocopied submissions OK. Computer printout submissions OK. Reports in 1 month. Query or submit complete ms. SASE.
Nonfiction and Photos: Articles analyzing specific commodity futures and options trading strategies; fundamental and technical analysis of individual commodities and markets; interviews, book reviews, "success" stories; news items. Material on new legislation affecting commodities, trading, any new trading strategy ("results must be able to be substantiated"); personalities. No "homespun" rules for trading and simplistic approaches to the commodities market. Treatment is always in-depth and broad. Informational, how-to, interview, profile, technical. "Articles should be written for a reader who has traded commodities for one year or more; should not talk down or hypothesize. Relatively complex material is acceptable." No get-rich-quick gimmicks, astrology articles or general, broad topics. Buys 30-40 mss/year. Length: No maximum or minimum; 1,500 words optimum. Pays $50-1,000, depending upon author's research and writing quality.
Tips: "Writers must have a solid understanding and appreciation for futures or options trading. We will have more financial and stock index features as well as new options contracts that will require special knowledge and experience."

FLORIDA BANKER, Box 6847, Orlando FL 32853. Executive Editor: William P. Seaparke. 60% freelance written. Monthly magazine; 52 pages. Circ. 7,300. Pays on publication. Buys all rights. Pays 50% kill fee. Byline given. Computer printout or disk submissions OK. SASE. Reports in 3 months. Sample copy and writer's guidelines $2 prepaid.
Nonfiction: General interest (banking-oriented); historical (on banking); how-to (anything in banking industry or trade); inspirational (occasionally, must deal with banking); interview; nostalgia; photo feature; profile; technical; and travel. Recent article example: "Industrial Development Bonds: What's the Outlook?" (February 1983). Buys 12-25 unsolicited mss/year. Query. Length: 500-3,000 words. Payment varies.
Photos: State availability of photos with query. Pays $10-100 for 5x7 b&w glossy prints; $20-200 for 35mm color transparencies. Captions and model release required. Buys all rights. Loans usage back to photographers on agreement.
Columns/Departments: Economy; interviews; and technology in banking. Query. Length: 600-3,000 words. Pays $25 minimum. Open to suggestions for new columns/departments.

ILLINOIS BANKER, Illinois Bankers Association, Suite 1100, 205 W. Randolph, Chicago IL 60606. (312)984-1500. Editor: Cindy L. Altman. Editorial Assistant: Anetta Gauthier. Monthly magazine about banking for top decision makers and executives, bank officers, title and insurance company executives, elected officials, and individual subscribers interested in banking products and services. Circ. 3,000. Pays on acceptance. Byline given. Buys first rights. Phone queries OK. Submit material by the 10th of the month prior to publication. Simultaneous submissions OK. Reports in 2 weeks. Free sample copy and writer's guidelines.
Nonfiction: Interview (ranking government and banking leaders); personal experience (along the lines of customer relations); and technical (specific areas of banking). "The purpose of the publication is to educate, inform, and guide its readers in the activities and projects of their banks and those of their fellow bankers, while keeping them aware of any developments within the banking industry and other related fields. Any clear, fresh approach geared to a specific area of banking, such as agricultural bank management, credit, lending, marketing and trust is what we want." Buys 4-5 unsolicited mss/year. Send complete ms. Length: 825-3,000 words. Pays $50-100.
Fillers: Jokes, anecdotes and financial puzzles. Buys 8 mss/year. Pays $15-50.
Tips: "Cutbacks in purchasing have made us more selective."

MERGERS & ACQUISITIONS, 229 S. 18th St., Philadelphia PA 19103. Editor: Alexandra Lajoux. For presidents and other high corporate personnel, financiers, buyers, stockbrokers, accountants and related professionals. Quarterly. Buys all rights. Byline given. Pays 21 days after publication. Query must be with outline. Include 50-word autobiography with mss. SASE. Will send a free sample copy to qualified writers on request.
Nonfiction: "Articles on merger and acquisition techniques (taxes, SEC regulations, anti-trust, etc.), case studies or surveys and roundups emphasizing analysis and description of trends and implications thereof. Case histories should contain 20-60 facts/1,000 words (real names, dates, places, companies, etc.). Technical articles should be well researched and documented." Buys 2-4 unsolicited mss/year. Recent article example: "Cable TV Acquisitions" (Winter 1982). Length: maximum 3,000-6,000 words. Pays $100; "more for articles by professional freelance writers."
Tips: "We prefer actual practitioners in the M&A field—investment bankers, auditors, tax lawyers, etc. to write for us. Freelancers with a business writing background are welcome to submit projects for Case Studies of deals."

MONEYFAX, National Association of Financial Consultants, Ivy Publications, Box 1, Ischua NY 14746. (716)557-8900. Editor: Jeffrey Brisky. Monthly newsletter covering financing, loans, real estate, leasing and mortgages. Byline given. Buys all rights. Submit seasonal/holiday material 2 months in advance. Simultaneous queries, and simultaneous and previously published submissions OK. Computer printout submissions OK. SASE. Reports in 1 week on queries; 3 weeks on mss. Sample copy and writer's guidelines free for business size SAE and 28¢ postage.
Nonfiction: Expose (of loan frauds); how-to (get loans); and humor (money jokes). "No non-financial material." Query. Length: 300-1,000 words. Pay is negotiable.
Columns/Departments: "We're interested in anything regarding financing, real estate, leasing or loan brokerage." Query. Length: 300-1,000 words. Pay is negotiable.
Fillers: Clippings, news for immediate release, jokes, and newsbreaks (anything about financing and money brokerage). Length: open. Pay is negotiable.

MOUNTAIN STATES BANKER, Mountain States Publishing Co., Suite 900, 912 Baltimore, Kansas City MO 64105. (816)421-7941. Editor: Sharon Smith. Monthly magazine for bankers and others interested in financial services. Features new techniques and developments for improving banking performance. Circ. 2,000. Pays on publication. Byline given. Buys all rights. Submit seasonal/holiday material 4 months in advance. Simultaneous queries and simultaneous, photocopied, and previously published submissions OK. SASE. Reports in 2 weeks on queries; 1 month on mss. Sample copy $3; writer's guidelines for business size SAE and 1 first class stamp.
Nonfiction: How-to, interview/profile, opinion, technical. Buys 10-20 mss/year. Send complete ms. Length: 500-2,500 words. Pays $50-200.
Photos: State availability of photos. Pays negotiable rate for b&w contact sheets and prints. Captions and identification of subjects required. Buys one-time rights.
Columns/Departments: "All columns and departments are written inhouse."

THE NABW JOURNAL, Suite 1400, 500 N. Michigan Ave., Chicago IL 60611. (312)661-1700. Contact: Editor. Bimonthly magazine for members of the National Association of Bank Women. Circ. 30,000. Pays on acceptance. Byline given. Buys all rights. Submit seasonal/holiday material 3 months in advance. Simultaneous queries and photocopied submissions OK. SASE. Reports in 1 month. Free sample copy.
Nonfiction: Women's issues, banking, management. Buys 8-10 mss/year. Query with clips of published work. Length: 1,000-5,000 words. Pays $200-500.

Photos: State availability of photos. Pays variable rates for 5x7 b&w prints. Captions and model release required.

Fishing

COMMERCIAL FISHERIES NEWS, Box 37, Stonington ME 04681. (207)367-2396. Managing Editor: Robin Alden Peters. 33% freelance written. Emphasizes commercial fisheries. Monthly newspaper with New England wide coverage; 52 pages. Circ. 8,500. Pays on publication. Byline given. SASE. Reports in 2 weeks. Sample copy $1.25.
Nonfiction: "Material strictly limited to coverage of commercial fishing, technical and general; occasional environment, business, etc. articles as they relate to commercial fishing in New England." Buys 10 unsolicited mss/year. Query. Pays $50-150.

FISHING GAZETTE, Fishing Gazette Publishing Corp., 461 8th Ave., New York NY 10001. (212)324-0959. Editorial Offices: Fishing Gazette, Box 907, Rockland ME 04841. (207)594-9592. Editor: David R. Getchell, Sr. Publisher: David P. Jackson. Monthly magazine for those with commercial fishing interests: fishermen, importers, exporters, processors, manufacturers, fleet owners, freezers, shippers, purveyors. Circ. 19,000. Pays upon acceptance, in most cases. Byline given. First North American rights only. Reports in 2 weeks. Free sample copy and editorial guidelines.
Nonfiction: Articles cover all aspects of commercial fishing: human interest, gear, methods, new vessels, shore facilities, processing, marketing, research. No stories on sport fishing. Buys 50 mss/year. Query preferred, or send complete ms. Length: 500-1,500 words. Pays 12¢/word.
Photos: State availability of photos. Uses 5x7 and 8x10 b&w glossy prints, and color slides, 35mm and larger. Detailed captions required. Pays $10 minimum for b&w; $25 minimum for color; $150 minimum for color cover.
Tips: "We will be using a great deal of illustrative material in the year ahead: b&w photos, color, diagrams, sketches, graphs, etc. Our direction will be toward pictorial display rather than lengthy text, so we will be looking for high-quality illustrations of all sorts."

NATIONAL FISHERMAN, Diversified Communications, 21 Elm St., Camden ME 04843. (207)236-4342. Editor-in-Chief: James W. Fullilove. Managing Editor: Linda S. Stanley. 75% freelance written. For amateur and professional boatbuilders, commercial fishermen, armchair sailors, bureaucrats and politicians. Monthly tabloid; 120 pages. Circ. 63,000. Pays in month of acceptance. Buys one-time rights. Byline given. Phone queries OK. Submit seasonal/holiday material 3 months in advance of issue date. Photocopied submissions OK. Computer printout submissions OK if double spaced; prefers letter quality to dot matrix. SASE. Reports in 4 weeks. Free sample copy and writer's guidelines; mention *Writer's Market* in request.
Nonfiction: Expose; how-to; general interest; humor; historical; inspirational; interview; new product; nostalgia, personal experience; opinion; photo feature; profile; and technical. Especially needs articles on commercial fishing techniques (problems, solutions, large catches, busts); gear development; and marine historical and offbeat articles. No articles about sailboat racing, cruising and sportfishing. Buys 50 unsolicited mss/year. Submit complete ms. Length: 100-3,500 words.
Photos: State availability of photos with ms. Pays $5-15 for 5x7 or 8x10 b&w prints; color cover photo pays $250. Buys one-time rights.
Columns/Departments: Boatyard news (photos with captions of new boats, commercial fishboats favored); fishing highlights (short articles on catches); marine book review. Buys 5/issue. Submit complete ms. Length: 50-1,000 words. Pays $10 or 5¢/word minimum, whichever is more.
Tips: "We are soliciting more business-related articles."

PACIFIC FISHING, Pacific Fishing Partnership, 1515 NW 51st St., Seattle WA 98107. (206)789-5333. Editors: Ken Talley, Doug McNair. Monthly business magazine for commercial fishermen and others in the West Coast commercial fishing industry. *Pacific Fishing* views the fisherman as a small businessman and covers all aspects of the industry, including harvesting, processing and marketing. Circ. 10,000. Pays on publication. Byline given. Offers negotiable kill fee. Buys one-time rights or makes arrangements with publisher. Queries highly recommended. Reports in 1 month. Free sample copy and writer's guidelines.
Nonfiction: Interview/profile, technical (usually with a business hook or slant). "Articles must be concerned specifically with *commercial* fishing." Buys 20 mss/year. Query. Length: 1,500-3,000 words. Pays 7-10¢/word.

Florists, Nurseries, and Landscaping

AMERICAN CHRISTMAS TREE JOURNAL, 611 E. Wells St., Milwaukee WI 53202. (414)276-6410. Editors: Phil Jones and Jane A Svinicki. Quarterly magazine. Circ. 1,800-2,000. Byline given. Pays on publication. Simultaneous, photocopied and previously published submissions OK. Reports in 1 month. Free sample copy and writer's guidelines.
Nonfiction: How-to, interview, job safety (any farm equipment); vocational techniques, new product (chemicals, equipment, tags, shearing knives and chain saws, etc.); personal experience, profile and technical (foresters, researchers). Query. Length: 2,000 words minimum. Pays $50.

‡**DESIGN FOR PROFIT**, Florafax International, Inc., 4175 S. Memorial Dr., Box 45745, Tulsa OK 74145. (918)622-8415. Editor: Ginger Holsted. Quarterly magazine covering trends in the floral industry. "The publication is designed to be a creative sales tool for retail florists." Circ. 15,000. No byline given. Buys all rights. Submit seasonal/holiday material 4 months in advance. Simultaneous queries, and simultaneous and photocopied submissions OK. SASE. Reports in 2 weeks on queries; 3 months on mss. Free sample copy and writer's guidelines.
Nonfiction: Historical/nostalgic (themes tying into floral arranging); how-to (floral designs—how to carry through themes, innovative ideas); interview/profile (prominent individuals in the profession); new product; personal experience (unique, unusual, outstanding in industry); photo feature. Note: features or news/features only. Buys variable number of mss/year. Query with published clips. Length: 300 words maximum. Pays negotiable rates.
Photos: Send photos with query or ms. Pays negotiable rates for 4x5 transparencies and prints. Captions, model release and identification of subjects required. Buys all rights.
Poetry: Avant-garde, free verse, haiku, light verse, traditional. Buys variable number of poems/year. Submit unlimited number of poems. Length: 30 lines maximum. Pays negotiable rates.

FLORIST, Florists' Transworld Delivery Association, 29200 Northwestern Hwy., Box 2227, Southfield MI 48037. (313)355-9300. Editor-in-Chief: William P. Golden. Managing Editor: Bill Gubbins. 5% freelance written. For retail florists, floriculture growers, wholesalers, researchers and teachers. Monthly magazine; 96 pages. Circ. 25,000. Pays on acceptance. Buys one-time rights. Pays 10-25% kill fee. Byline given "unless the story needs a substantial rewrite." Phone queries OK. Submit seasonal/holiday material 3-4 months in advance of issue date. Simultaneous, photocopied and previously published submissions OK. Computer printout or disk submissions OK. SASE. Reports in 1 month.
Nonfiction: How-to (more profitably run a retail flower shop, grow and maintain better-quality flowers, etc.); general interest (to floriculture and retail floristry); and technical (on flower and plant growing, breeding, etc.). Buys 5 unsolicited mss/year. Query with clips of published work. Length: 1,200-3,000 words. Pays 10¢/word.
Photos: "We do not like to run stories without photos." State availability of photos with query. Pays $10-25 for 5x7 b&w photos or color transparencies. Buys one-time rights.
Tips: "Send samples of published work with query. Suggest several ideas in query letter. We're now paying more for freelance material."

FLOWER NEWS, 549 W. Randolph St., Chicago IL 60606. (312)236-8648. Managing Editor: Lauren Cerniglia. For retail, wholesale florists, floral suppliers, supply jobbers, growers. Weekly newspaper; 40 pages. Circ. 14,500. Pays on acceptance. Copyrighted. Byline given. Submit seasonal/holiday material at least 2 months in advance. Photocopied and previously published submissions OK. SASE. Reports "immediately." Free sample copy and writer's guidelines.
Nonfiction: How-to articles (increase business, set up a new shop, etc.; anything floral-related without being an individual shop story); informational (general articles of interest to industry); and technical (grower stories related to industry, but not individual grower stories). No articles on "protecting your business from crime; how to get past-due accounts to pay; attitudes for salespeople." Submit complete ms. Length: 3-5 typed pages. Pays $10.
Photos: "We do not buy individual pictures. They may be enclosed with ms at regular ms rate (b&w only)."

FLOWERS &, Suite 314, 12233 W. Olympic Blvd., Los Angeles CA 90064. Publisher and Editor-in-Chief: Barbara Cady. Published by Teleflora Inc., for members of the floriculture industry. Positioned as "the magazine with a new approach to the floriculture industry." Monthly. Circ. 20,900. Buys one-time rights in floral trade magazine field. Byline given unless "article is not thorough enough but portions are included in another article." Most articles are staff-written. Pays on acceptance. Reports in 3 weeks. Must send query letter with proposed, brief outline first. SASE.

Nonfiction: Articles dealing with floral retailing, merchandising of product, sales promotion, management, designing, shop remodeling, display techniques, etc. Also, allied interests such as floral wholesalers, growers, tradespeople, gift markets, etc. Covers general interest stories and news about retail business, finances and taxes. All articles must be thoroughly researched and professionally relevant. Buys 5 unsolicited mss/year. Length: 1,000-3,000 words. Pays approximately 14¢/published word.

Tips: "Queries should be brief and to the point, include author's qualifications and past published experience plus a brief outline detailing the proposed article. We prefer to see no unsolicited manuscripts without prior query."

GARDEN SUPPLY RETAILER, Miller Publishing, Box 67, Minneapolis MN 55440. (612)374-5200. Managing Editor: Claude Chmiel. Staff Editor: Kay Melchisedech Olson. Monthly magazine for lawn and garden retailers. Circ. 40,000. Pays on acceptance. Submit seasonal/holiday material 6 months in advance. Previously published submissions "in different fields" OK. Prefers double spaced, typewritten manuscripts. "We will not guarantee reading material submitted in other forms." SASE. Reports in 2 weeks. Sample copy $2.

Nonfiction: "We aim to provide retailers with management, merchandising, tax planning and computer information. No technical advice on how to care for lawns, plants, lawn mowers." Buys 10-15 mss/year. Query with clips of published work or send complete ms. Length: 750 words. Pays $150-300.

Photos: Send photos with ms. Reviews color negatives and transparencies, and 5x7 b&w prints. Captions and identification of subjects required.

Tips: "Articles that tell a retailer specific information on how to make more money will always get our attention, but we cannot guarantee using or returning all manuscripts. I'll look at anything that tells small retailers how to run a more profitable business, but I can't guarantee I'll return all manuscripts. Query letters get tiresome and numerous. Photos with articles are always welcome."

‡**THE LANDSCAPE CONTRACTOR, Official Publication of the Illinois Landscape Contractors Association**, Better Business Communicators, 4A East Wilson St., Batavia IL 60510. (312)879-0765. Editor: Bonnie Zaruba. Monthly magazine covering landscaping, landscape architecture and horticulture—business articles as they pertain to the landscape contracting profession, or allied fields. Circ. 2,000. Pays on publication. Byline given. Buys first North American serial rights. Submit seasonal/holiday material 4 months in advance. Simultaneous queries, and simultaneous, photocopied, and previously published submissions OK. SASE. Reports in 2 weeks on queries; 6 weeks on mss. Sample copy for 9x12 SAE and 5 first class stamps.

Nonfiction: Expose (government/landscaping); how-to (photos, trade shows); interview/profile (of business/owner in field); new product (or method of doing job); technical (as related to horticulture/landscaping). "No light, general interest pieces; no 'how the businessman can save time' articles." Buys 10 mss/year. Send complete ms. Length: 1,250-3,750 words. Pays $60-180.

Photos: Send photos with ms. Pays $8-15 for 5x7 and 8x10 b&w prints. Captions and identification of subjects required. Buys one-time rights.

LAWN CARE INDUSTRY, Harcourt Brace Jovanovich, Inc., 7500 Old Oak Blvd., Cleveland OH 44130. (216)243-8100. Editor: Jerry Roche. 10% freelance written. For lawn care businessmen. Monthly tabloid; 40 pages. Circ. 12,000. Pays on acceptance. Buys all rights. Phone queries OK. Submit seasonal/holiday material 3 months in advance of issue date. Simultaneous and photocopied submissions OK. Computer printout and disk submissions OK. SASE. Reports in 2 weeks. Free sample copy.

Nonfiction: General interest (articles related to small business operation); how-to (run a lawn care business); interview (with lawn care operator or industry notable); new product (helping to better business practices); and profile (of lawn care businessmen). Buys 3 mss/issue. Query. Length: 500-1,000 words. Pays $50-250.

Photos: State availability of photos with query. Pays $10-100 for 5x7 glossy b&w prints; $50-250 for 35mm color transparencies. Captions required. Buys one-time rights.

Tips: "Because of change of address, we *may* be accepting more freelance material from the East Coast."

ORNAMENTALS SOUTH, Publications South, Inc., 741 Piedmont Ave., Atlanta GA 30308. (404)892-6812. Editor: Ernest F. Jessee. Publisher: Rebecca H. Johnson. Bimonthly agribusiness magazine of the nursery industry covering research and technology with some economic, marketing, and human-interest stories of industrial interest. Circ. 9,000. Pays on publication. Byline given. Buys one-time and first rights. Submit seasonal/holiday material 4 months in advance. Simultaneous phone queries and simultaneous submissions OK. SASE. Reports in 1 month. Sample copy $3; free writer's guidelines.

Nonfiction: General interest (in the Southeast); how-to (grow, market, promote, handle problems in culture, etc.), interview/profile (of notables or recognized contributors to industries); opinion (of experts only); personal experience (of reputable growers or researchers); technical (new tools, techniques, plant varieties, chemicals, equipment, etc.). No "home gardening material, commercially slanted stories, or information not of widespread industry interest in the Southeast." Buys variable number mss/year. Query. Length: 900-6,000 words. Pays $25-150.

Photos: Send photos with ms. Pays $10 maximum for b&w contact sheet and 8x10 prints; reviews 8x10 color prints. Captions required. Buys one-time rights.
Tips: "Discuss material with us by phone before writing; submit completed works well in advance of copy deadlines; include charts, photos and illustrations. We need more grower and related stories in both wholesale and retail categories. Marketing, shipping and economic features are also needed. Very long features (8-10 typed pages) are rarely welcome from freelancers."

WESTERN LANDSCAPING NEWS, Hester Communications, Inc., Box 19531, Irvine CA 92713. (714)549-4834. Associate Publisher/Editor: Steve McGonigal. Published for the Western landscaping and irrigation industry. Monthly magazine; 64 pages. Circ. 17,000 + . Pays on publication. Buys all rights. Submit seasonal/holiday material 4 months in advance. Photocopied and previously published submissions OK. SASE. Reports in 4 weeks. Free sample copy.
Nonfiction: How-to (ideas for the average contractor on design, product selection, planning, irrigation, selecting nursery stock, management and marketing, etc.); interview (with respected person in industry in the West or someone promoting or improving the industry); personal opinion (government regulations, etc.); profile (Western landscapers who have unusual qualities); personal opinion (only when author is known and respected in industry); and technical (write in lay terms). "If you're intent on writing for us, interview an expert and let him form the basis of your article." Buys 1 ms/issue. Query. Length: 1,200-3,000 words. Pays only writers who are not industry professionals.
Photos: "Ours is basically a visual industry. When we're talking about an interesting landscape design, we'd like to picture it." State availability of photos and/or landscape plans. Reviews b&w 5x7 or 8x10 prints and 35mm color transparencies. Captions and model releases required.

Food Products, Processing, and Service

In this list are journals for food wholesalers, processors, warehousers, caterers, institutional managers, and suppliers of grocery store equipment. Publications for grocery store operators are classified under Groceries. Journals for food vending machine operators are found under Coin-Operated Machines.

MEAT PLANT MAGAZINE, 9701 Gravois Ave., St. Louis MO 63123. (314)638-4050. Editor: Tony Nolan. For meat processors, locker plant operators, freezer provisioners, portion control packers, meat dealers, and food service (food plan) operators. Monthly. Pays on publication. Reports in 2 weeks. SASE for return of submissions.
Nonfiction, Photos, and Fillers: Buys feature-length articles and shorter subjects pertinent to the field. Length: 1,000-1,500 words for features. Pays 5¢/word. Pays $5 for photos.

PRODUCE NEWS, 2185 Lemoine Ave., Fort Lee NJ 07024. Editor: Melvina Bauer. For commercial growers and shippers, receivers, and distributors of fresh fruits and vegetables, including chain store produce buyers and merchandisers. Weekly. Circ. 5,300. Pays on publication. Free sample copy. Deadline is Wednesday afternoon before Friday press day. SASE.
Nonfiction: News stories (about the produce industry.) Buys profiles, spot news, coverage of successful business operations, articles on merchandising techniques. Query. Pays $1/column inch for original material, 40¢/column inch for clippings.
Photos: B&w glossies purchased with ms or caption.

QUICK FROZEN FOODS, Harcourt Brace Jovanovich, 7500 Oak Blvd., Cleveland OH 44130. (216)243-8100. Editor: Ron Stevens. Senior Associate Editor: C. Ross Chamberlain. 5-10% freelance written. For executives of processing plants, distributors, warehouses, transport companies, retailers and food service operators involved in frozen foods. Monthly magazine; 100 pages. Circ. 25,000. Pays on acceptance. Buys all rights. Pays kill fee up to full amount if reasons for kill are not fault of author. Byline given unless it is work-for-hire or ghostwriting. Submit seasonal/holiday material 3 months in advance of issue date. SASE. Reports in 1 week. Free sample copy; mention *Writer's Market* in request.
Nonfiction: Interview; new product; photo feature; profile; and technical. Buys 12 mss/year. Query or submit complete ms. Length: 1,500-3,000 words. Pays 5¢/word. "For special circumstances will offer flat rate for package which may be higher than word rate."
Photos: State availability of photos with query or ms. Pays $5 for 4x5 b&w smooth prints. Captions required. Buys all rights.

QUICK FROZEN FOODS INTERNATIONAL, E.W. Williams Publishing Co., 80 8th Ave., New York NY 10011. (212)989-1101. Editor: Sam Martin. Quarterly magazine covering frozen foods outside US— "every phase of frozen food manufacture, retailing, food service, brokerage, transport, warehousing, merchandising, providing it is outside the US, though we will print stories about US firms that sell abroad, but that must be emphasis." Circ. 10,000. Pays on acceptance. Byline given. Offers kill fee "if satisfactory, we will pay promised amount. If bungled, half." Buys first rights or second serial (reprint) rights. Submit seasonal/ holiday material 6 months in advance. Photocopied submissions OK ("if not under submission elsewhere"). Computer printout submissions OK; prefers letter quality to dot matrix. SASE. Sample copy for $1 and SAE.
Nonfiction: Book excerpts; general interest; historical/nostalgic; interview/profile; new product (from overseas); personal experience; photo feature; technical; travel. No articles peripheral to frozen food industry such as taxes, insurance, government regulation, safety, etc. Buys 20-30 mss/year. Query or send complete ms. Length: 500-4,000 words. Pays 3¢/word or by arrangement.
Photos: "Prefer photos with all articles." State availability of photos or send photos with accompanying ms. Pays $7 for 5x7 b&w prints (contact sheet if many shots). Captions and identification of subject required. Buys all rights. "Release on request."
Columns/Departments: News or analysis or frozen foods abroad. Buys 20 columns/year. Query. Length: 500-1,500 words. Pays by arrangement.
Fillers: Newsbreaks. Length: 100-500 words. Pays $5-20.
Tips: "Always query (though we will buy unsolicited manuscripts if they are suitable). A recent freelancer visited Poland before the crackdown and reported on state of frozen foods in stores—turned out to be a scoop. Same reporter did the same on recent trip to Israel. Another did the same for China; all queried in advance."

SNACK FOOD, HBJ Publications, Inc., 1 E. 1st St., Duluth MN 55802. (218)727-8511. Editor-in-Chief: Jerry L. Hess. 10-15% freelance written. For manufacturers and distributors of snack foods. Monthly magazine; 60 pages. Circ. 10,000. Pays on acceptance. Buys first North American serial rights. Occasional byline. Phone queries OK. Photocopied submissions OK. SASE. Reports in 2-3 weeks. Free sample copy and writer's guidelines.
Nonfiction: Informational, interview, new product, nostalgia, photo feature, profile and technical articles. "We use an occasional mini news-feature or personality sketch." Length: 300-600 words for mini-features; 1,000-1,500 words for longer features. Pays 10-12¢/word.
Photos: Purchased with accompanying ms. Captions required. Pays $15 for 5x7 b&w photos; $15-20 for 4x5 color transparencies. Total purchase price for a ms includes payment for photos. Buys all rights.
Tips: "Query should contain specific lead and display more than a casual knowledge of our audience."

THE WISCONSIN RESTAURATEUR, Wisconsin Restaurant Association, 122 W. Washington, Madison WI 53703. (603)251-3663. Editor: Jan La Rue. Emphasizes restaurant industry for restaurateurs, hospitals, institutions, food service students, etc. Monthly magazine "except November/December combined." Circ. 3,600. Pays on acceptance. Buys all rights or one-time rights. Pays 10% kill fee. Byline given. Phone queries OK. Submit seasonal/holiday material 2-3 months in advance. Previously published work OK; "indicate where." SASE. Reports in 3 weeks. Free sample copy and writer's guidelines with large post paid envelope.
Nonfiction: Interested in expose, general interest, historical, how-to, humor, inspirational, interview, nostalgia, opinion, profile, travel, new product, personal experience, photo feature and technical articles pertaining to restaurant industry. "No features on nonmember restaurants." Buys 1 ms/issue. Query with "copyright clearance information and a note about the writer in general." Length: 700-1,500 words. Pays $10-20.
Photos: Fiction and how-to article mss stand a better chance for publication if photo is submitted. State availability of photos. Pays $15 for b&w 8x10 glossy prints. Model releases required, captions are not.
Columns/Departments: Spotlight column provides restaurant member profiles. Buys 6/year. Query. Length: 500-1,500 words. Pays $5-10.
Fiction: Likes experimental, historical and humorous stories related to food service only. Buys 12 mss/year. Query. Length: 1,000-3,000 words. Pays $10-20.
Poetry: Uses all types of poetry, but must have food service as subject. Buys 6-12/year. No more than 5 submissions at one time. Length: 10-50 lines. Pays $5-10.
Fillers: Uses clippings, jokes, gags, anecdotes, newsbreaks, and short humor. No puzzles or games. Buys 12/ year. Length: 50-500 words. Pays $2.50-7.50.

Funeral Services

C & S (Casket and Sunnyside), Funeral Services Publication, 274 Madison Ave., New York NY 10016. (212)685-8310. Contact: Editor. 10% freelance written. "This magazine is circulated to funeral directors of all ages, more and more who are becoming college educated." Published 10 times/year; 48 pages. Circ. 8,500.

Pays on publication. Buys all rights. Byline given. Submit seasonal/holiday material 2 months in advance of issue date. SASE. Reports in 2 weeks.

Nonfiction: General interest (stories on mortuaries); historical (articles dealing with embalming, early funeral vehicles and ambulances, etc.); how-to (handle difficult or unusual restorative art or embalming cases); inspirational (public relations achievements); and "short items or new products in the funeral field." Buys 20 mss/year. Query. Length: 2,500-3,500 words. Pays $75.

Photos: State availability of photos with query. Pays $5 for 5x7 or 8x10 b&w prints. Captions required. Buys all rights.

Fillers: Clippings, obituaries and items concerning various activities of funeral directors. Buys 10-15/issue. Pays $3.

Tips: "We appreciate a straightforward inquiry, indicating concisely what the author proposes to write about. We are interested in receiving stories on new or remodeled mortuaries."

CANADIAN FUNERAL DIRECTOR, Peter Perry Publishing, Ltd., Suite 5, 1658 Victoria Park Ave., Scarboro, Ontario, Canada M1R 1P7. (416)755-7050. Managing Editor: Peter Perry. 15% freelance written. Emphasizes funeral home operation. Monthly magazine; 60 pages. Circ. 1,700. Pays on publication. Buys one-time rights. Byline given. Phone queries OK. Reports in 30-60 days. Simultaneous and photocopied submissions and previously published work OK. SASE. Reports in 3 weeks.

Nonfiction: Informational, historical, interview, personal opinion, profile, photo feature, technical. Buys 12 mss a year. Query. Length: 200-1,500 words. Pays $75/1,000 words.

Photos: Purchased with or without ms. Captions required. Query or send contact sheet. Pays $5-10/5x7 or 8x10 b&w glossies.

Tips: "Canadian writers only need query, with Canadian subject material."

Government and Public Service

Below are journals for individuals who provide governmental services, either in the employ of local, state, or national governments or of franchised utilities. Included are journals for city managers, politicians, civil servants, firefighters, police officers, public administrators, urban transit managers, utilities managers, etc.

Journals for professionals in the arena of world affairs are found in the International Affairs section. Publications for lawyers are found in the Law category. Journals for teachers and school administrators are found in Education. Those for private citizens interested in politics, government, and public affairs are classified with the Politics and World Affairs magazines in the Consumer Publications section.

BOUNTY HUNTER INTERNATIONAL, Manhunter, American Police Academy, Bureau of Research, Box 9935, Washington DC 20015. (202)293-9088. Editor: Col. Fred Pearson. Managing Editor: James Gordon. Bimonthly magazine featuring stories of missing persons still missing or who have rewards posted. Circ. 10,000. Pays on acceptance. Byline given. Buys all rights. Submit seasonal/holiday material 2 months in advance. Simultaneous queries and simultaneous and previously published submissions OK. SASE. Reports in 2 weeks. Sample copy for $1 and 8x11 SAE; writer's guidelines for $1 and 8x11 SAE.

Nonfiction: Expose (of runaway children being abused); interview/profile (captures by police or citizens); personal experience (how a person found a missing or wanted fugitive); photo feature (of missing or wanted persons). Buys 50-100 mss/year. Send complete ms. Length 600-2,000 words. Pays $15-100.

COMMUNITY ANIMAL CONTROL, K.B.R. Publications, Box 43488, Tucson AZ 85733. (602)622-5259. Editor: Katherine B. Morgan. Bimonthly magazine covering animal welfare/animal control for an "audience of professionals and governmental officials who deal with the public's pets, *not* the pet-owning public." Estab. 1982. Circ. 7,350. Pays on acceptance. Byline given. Buys first North American serial rights, simultaneous, and second serial (reprint) rights. Submit seasonal/holiday material 4 months in advance. Simultaneous queries, and simultaneous, photocopied, and previously published submissions OK. SASE. Reports in 2 weeks. Free sample copy.

Nonfiction: Book excerpts, expose, historical, how-to, interview/profile, technical. "No profiles of dear ladies running animal rescue societies." Buys 6-8 mss/year. Query with or without clips of published work. Length: 600-2,000 words. Pays $50.

Photos: State availability of photos. Pays $5-10 for b&w prints; reviews b&w contact sheets. Model release required. Buys one-time rights.

Columns/Departments: Book Reviews. Buys 2 mss/year. Query. Length: 200-1,000 words. Pays $10-25.

‡**CRIMINAL JUSTICE CAREER DIGEST**, Checkpoint, Inc. Box 565, Phoenix AZ 85001. (602)582-2002. Editor: I. Gayle Shuman. Managing Editor: Joseph C. Kelly. Monthly career assistance publication covering criminal justice topics and lists of current criminal justice career openings across the US. Estab. 1981. Circ. 1,200. Pays on acceptance. Byline given. Buys one-time rights. Submit seasonal/holiday material 3 months in advance. Simultaneous queries, and simultaneous, photocopied and previously published submissions OK. SASE. Reports in 2 weeks on queries; 8 weeks on mss. Sample copy for $2.50, 9x12 SAE and 54¢ postage; free writer's guidelines.

Nonfiction: I. Gayle Shuman, Catherine D. Schultz, articles editors. General interest; historical/nostalgic; how-to (improve one's job satisfaction—career advancement/promotion/training); inspirational; interview/profile; new trends in criminal justice. No highly opinionated articles. Buys 36 mss/year. Query with or without published clips. Length: 1,000-2,500 words. Pays $20-100; negotiable.

Photos: Joseph C. Kelly, photo editor. State availability of phots. Pays $10 minimum for b&w contact sheet and 5x7 and 8x10 b&w prints. Captions and model release required.

Fillers: Jokes, anecdotes. Buys 20-30/year. Length: 10-20 words. Pays $5. "Must contain a criminal justice slant."

Editor's Note: As we go to press, we have learned from the staff of the *Criminal Justice Career Digest* that the magazine has ceased publication.

FIRE ENGINEERING, 375 3rd Ave., New York NY 10022. Editor: Jerry Laughlin. For commissioners, chiefs and other officers of paid, volunteer, industrial and military fire departments and brigades. Buys first serial rights. Byline given. Pays on acceptance. Computer printout and disk (Apple only) submissions OK. Reports in 3 weeks.

Nonfiction and Photos: Wants articles on fire suppression, fire prevention, fire administration, and any other subject that relates to fire service. Buys 115 unsolicited mss/year. Length: 750-1,500 words. Pays $75-200. Inside photos used only with articles. Particular need for color photos for cover; small print or slide satisfactory for submission, but must always be a vertical or capable of being cropped to vertical. Transparency required if accepted. Pays $125 for color shots used on cover.

Tips: "Some freelancers hesitate to write because they have never written an article. We encourage them to set down the facts as though they were talking to someone. We take care of putting the article into our style. We wll use more fire reports in the year ahead."

FOREIGN SERVICE JOURNAL, 2101 E St., NW, Washington DC 20037. (202)338-4045. Editor: Stephen R. Dujack. For Foreign Service personnel and others interested in foreign affairs and related subjects. Monthly (July/August combined). Buys first North American rights. Computer printout submissions OK; prefers letter quality to dot matrix printouts. Byline given. Pays on publication. SASE.

Nonfiction: Uses articles on "international relations, internal problems of the State Department and Foreign Service, diplomatic history, articles on Foreign Service experiences. Much of our material is contributed by those working in the fields we reach. Informed outside contributions are welcomed, however." Query. Buys 5-10 unsolicited mss/year. Length: 1,000-4,000 words. Pays 2-6¢/word.

‡**FOUNDATION NEWS, The Magazine of Philanthropy**, Council on Foundations, 1828 L St. NW, Washington DC 20036. (202)466-6512. Editor: Arlie Schardt. Managing Editor: Kathleen Hallahan. Bimonthly magazine covering the world of philanthropy, nonprofit organization and their relation to current events. Read by staff and executives of hospitals, colleges and universities, and various nonprofit organizations. Circ. 16,500. Pays on acceptance. Byline given. Offers negotiable kill fee. Not copyrighted. Buys all rights. Submit seasonal/holiday material 3 months in advance. Simultaneous queries and previously published submissions OK. SASE. Reports in 4 weeks on queries; 3 weeks on mss.

Nonfiction: Book excerpts, expose, general interest, historical/nostalgic, how-to, humor, interview/profile, photo feature. Special issue on the role of religion in American life and how religious giving affects social welfare, culture, health conditions, etc. Buys 25 mss/year. Query. Length: 500-3,000 words. Pays $200-2,000.

Photos: State availability of photos. Pays negotiable rates for b&w contact sheet and prints. Captions and identification of subjects required. Buys one-time rights; "some rare requests for second use."

Columns/Departments: Buys 12 mss/year. Query. Length: 900-1,400 words. Pays $100-500.

Tips: "Writers should be able to put current events into the perspective of how nonprofits affect them and are affected by them."

THE GRANTSMANSHIP CENTER NEWS, The Grantsmanship Center, 1031 S. Grand Ave., Los Angeles CA 90015. (213)749-4721. Editor: Sam Orr. Emphasizes fundraising, philanthropy, grants process and nonprofit management for professionals in government, foundations and nonprofit organizations. Bimonthly magazine; 104 pages. Circ. 15,000. Pays on acceptance. Makes assignments on a work-for-hire basis. Pays variable kill fee. Byline given. Simultaneous, photocopied and previously published submissions OK. No computer printout or disk submissions. SASE. Reports in 2 months. Sample copy $4.65.

Nonfiction: Expose, general interest, how-to and interview. "Familiarity with the field is an asset." Recent article example: "A Primer on Mailing Lists" (November/December 1982). Buys 4-5 mss/issue. Query with clips of published work. Length: 1,500-10,000 words. Pays $200-$2,000.

Photos: State availability of photos. Uses b&w contact sheets and color transparencies. Offers no additional payment for photos accepted with ms. Captions preferred; model release required. Buys all rights.

LAW AND ORDER, Hendon Co., 5526 N. Elston, Chicago IL 60630. (312)792-1838. Editor: Bruce W. Cameron. Monthly magazine covering the administration and operation of law enforcement agencies, directed to police chiefs and supervisors. Circ. 26,000. Pays on publication. Byline given. Buys first North American serial rights. Submit seasonal/holiday material 3 months in advance. Photocopied submissions OK. No simultaneous queries. Computer printout submissions OK. Reports in 1 month. Sample copy for 9x12 SAE.

Nonfiction: General police interest; how-to (do specific police assignments); new product (how applied in police operation); technical (specific police operation). Special issues include Buyers Guide (January); Communications (February); Training (March); International (April); Administration (May); Small Departments (June); Police Science (July); Equipment (August); Weapons (September); Mobile Patrol (November); Working with Youth (December). No articles dealing with courts (legal field) or convicted prisoners. No nostalgic, financial, travel or recreational material. Buys 20-30 mss/year. Length: 1,000-3,000 words. Pays $50-300.

Photos: Send photos with ms. Reviews transparencies and prints. Identification of subjects required. Buys all rights.

Tips: "*L&O* is a respected magazine that provides up-to-date information that chiefs can use. Writers must know their subject as it applies to this field. Case histories are well received. We are upgrading quality for editorial—stories *must* show some understanding of law enforcement field."

PLANNING, American Planning Association, 1313 E. 60th St., Chicago IL 60637. (312)955-9100. Editor: Sylvia Lewis. Emphasizes urban planning for adult, college-educated readers who are university faculty or students; or regional and urban planners in city, state or federal agencies or in private business. Published 11 times/year. Circ. 25,000. Pays on publication. Buys all rights or first serial rights. Byline given. Phone queries OK. Photocopied and previously published submissions OK. SASE. Reports in 5 weeks. Free sample copy and writer's guidelines.

Nonfiction: Expose (on government or business, but on topics related to planning, housing, land use, zoning); general interest (trend stories on cities, land use, government); historical (historic preservation); how-to (successful government or citizen efforts in planning; innovations; concepts that have been applied); technical (detailed articles on the nitty-gritty of planning, zoning, transportation but no footnotes or mathematical models). Also needs news stories up to 500 words. "It's best to query with a fairly detailed, one-page letter. We'll consider any article that's well written and relevant to our audience. Articles have a better chance if they are timely and related to planning and land use and if they appeal to a national audience. All articles should be written in magazine feature style." Buys 2 features, 1 news story and 2 book reviews/issue. Length: 500-2,000 words. Pays $50-200. "We pay freelance writers and photographers only."

Photos: "We prefer that authors supply their own photos, but we sometimes take our own or arrange for them in other ways." State availability of photos. Pays $25 minimum for 8x10 matte or glossy prints and $100 for cover photos. Captions preferred. Buys one-time rights.

Columns/Departments: Planners Library (book reviews). Books assigned by book review editor. Buys 1 review/issue. Query. Length: 500-1,000 words. Pays $25.

POLICE PRODUCT NEWS, Dyna Graphics, Inc., Box 847, 6200 Yarrow Dr., Carlsbad CA 92008. (714)438-2511. Editor: Carl Calvert. For all law enforcement personnel. Monthly magazine. Circ. 50,000. Pays on publication. Buys all rights. Byline given. SASE. Reports in 1 week. Sample copy $2; free writer's guidelines.

Nonfiction: Expose, historical, how-to, humor, interview, profile (of police departments around the country); new product (testing/evaluation/opinion); and technical. "All material must be clearly related to law enforcement." Buys 54 unsolicited mss/year. Send query and clips of published work. Length: 1,000-2,500 words. Pays $100-400.

Photos: State availability of photos. Pays $10-25 for b&w 8x10 glossy prints and $25-100 for color transparencies. Model release required.

Columns/Departments: 750-1,500 words. Pays $50-150.

POLICE TIMES/COMMAND MAGAZINE, 1100 NE 125th St., North Miami FL 33161. (305)891-1700. Editor: Gerald Arenberg. 90% freelance written. For "law enforcement officers: federal, state, county, local and private security." Magazine published eight times/year. Circ. 87,000. Buys all rights. Buys 50-100 mss/year. Pays on publication. Sample copy for $1 postage. Reports "at once." Computer printout and disk submissions OK. SASE.

Nonfiction and Photos: Interested in articles about local police departments all over the nation. In particular, short articles about what the police department is doing, any unusual arrests made, acts of valor of officers in the performance of duties, etc. Also articles on any police subject from prisons to reserve police. "We prefer newspaper style. Short and to the point. No fiction. Photos and drawings are a big help." Length: 300-1,200 words. Pays $5-15—up to $25 in some cases based on 1¢/word. Uses b&w Polaroid and 8x10 b&w glossy prints, "if of particular value." Pays $5-15 for each photo used.

STATE LEGISLATURES, National Conference of State Legislatures, Suite 1500, 1125 17th St., Denver CO 80202. (303)623-6600. Associate Editor: Dan Pilcher. Emphasizes current issues facing state legislatures for legislators, legislative staff members and close observers of state politics and government. Magazine published 10 times/year; 32 pages. Pays on acceptance. Buys all rights. Byline given. SASE. Reports in 1 month. Free sample copy.
Nonfiction: "We're interested in original reporting on the responses of states (particularly state legislatures) to current problems, e.g., tax reform, health care, energy, consumer protection. We seldom publish articles that deal exclusively with one state; our usual approach is to survey and compare the actions of states across the country." Query preferred, but will consider complete ms. Pays $300-450, depending on length.

SUPERINTENDENT'S PROFILE & POCKET EQUIPMENT DIRECTORY, Profile Publications, 220 Central Ave., Box 43, Dunkirk NY 14048. (716)366-4774. Editor: Robert Dyment. Monthly magazine covering "outstanding" town, village, county and city highway superintendents and Department of Public Works Directors throughout New York state only. Circ. 2,500. Pays on publication. No byline given "except sometimes for excellent material." Buys one-time rights. Submit seasonal/holiday material 3 months in advance. Simultaneous queries OK. Computer printout submissions OK; prefers letter quality to dot matrix. SASE. Reports in 2 weeks on queries; 1 month on mss. Sample copy for 9x12 SAE and 2 first class stamps.
Nonfiction: John Powers, articles editor. Interview/profile (of a highway superintendent or DPW director in NY state who has improved department operations through unique methods or equipment); technical. Special issues include winter maintenance profiles. No fiction. Buys 20 mss/year. Query. Length: 1,500-2,000 words. Pays $75 for a full-length ms. "Pays more for excellent material. All manuscripts will be edited to fit our format and space limitations."
Photos: John Powers, photo editor. State availability of photos. Pays $5-10 for b&w contact sheets; reviews 5x7 prints. Captions and identification of subjects required. Buys one-time rights.
Tips: "We are a widely read and highly respected state-wide magazine, and although we can't pay high rates, we expect quality work. Too many freelance writers are going for the expose rather than the meat and potato type articles that will help readers. We will have a need for more manuscripts and photos because of two new publications being launched."

THE TROOPER, Publication of the Maryland Troopers Association, Brent-Wyatt Associates, 97 Davis Straits Rd., Falmouth MA 02540. (617)540-5051. Editor: Donna Costa. Managing Editor: Gail McPhee. Quarterly magazine covering law enforcement for members of Maryland's law enforcement community. Circ. 5,000. Pays on publication. Byline given. Not copyrighted. Buys all rights. Simultaneous queries, and simultaneous, photocopied, and previously published submissions OK. Reports in 1 month. Free sample copy and writer's guidelines.
Nonfiction: Expose, general interest, historical/nostalgic, how-to, humor, inspirational, interview/profile, new product, personal experience, photo feature, technical. Query with clips of published work. Length: 2,500 words maximum. Pays 10¢/word maximum.
Photos: Send photos with ms. Pays $50 maximum for b&w and color contact sheets, negatives, transparencies, and prints. Captions, model release, and identification of subjects required. Buys one time or all rights.
Fiction: Adventure, humorous, mystery, suspense. Query with clips of published work. Length: 2,000-2,500 words. Pays 10¢/word.
Fillers: Anecdotes, short humor, newsbreaks.

THE VOLUNTEER FIREMAN, A Fire Service Publication, Publico, Box 220783, Charlotte NC 28222. (704)535-8200. Editor: Pattie Toney. Managing Editor: Martha Tatum. Quarterly magazine for volunteer fire fighters nation wide covering fire safety/protection, news of saves and special fire ground situations. Estab. 1981. Circ. 20,000. Pays on publication. Byline given. Photocopied submissions OK. SASE. Reports in 1 month. Sample copy for 9x12 SAE and 2 first class stamps; writer's guidelines for $1, 9x12 SAE, and 2 first class stamps.
Nonfiction: Expose; general interest; historical/nostalgic; how-to (raise funds for volunteer fire departments); humor; interview/profile; new product; opinion; personal experience; photo feature; technical. "We want 'glamor' articles. We want good, exciting and honest news. No mom 'n' pop, picnic news, etc." Length: 200-1,500 words. Pays $10-105.
Photos: L.P. Coleman, photo editor. Send photos with ms. Pays $5-25 for 5x7 b&w prints. Captions, model release, and identification of subjects required.
Columns/Departments: News, features, product reviews. Buys 8-10 ms/year. Length: 100-750 words. Pays $5-52.50.
Fillers: Clippings, anecdotes, short humor, newsbreaks. Buys 20/year. Length: 25-100 words. Pays $1.75-10.

Tips: "Writers should keep our readership in mind. Volunteer fire fighters are highly interested in ways to save other people's lives while not harming their own."

WESTERN FIRE JOURNAL, Suite 7, 9072 E. Artesia Blvd., Bellflower CA 90706. (213)866-1664. Editor: Heidi M. Ziolkowski. For fire chiefs of paid and volunteer departments in metropolitan and small communities located in the West, Southwest, North Central and some Midwest states. Also read by other fire department officers and personnel. Monthly magazine; 66 pages. Circ. 5,500. Pays on publication. Buys first North American serial rights. Cannot purchase material already published in the fire-service press. Byline given. Phone queries OK. Absolutely *no* multiple submissions. "They're much more trouble than they're worth—both to the editor and the writer." Computer printout and disk submissions OK. SASE. Reports in 6 weeks. Sample copy $2; free writer's guidelines.
Nonfiction: How-to (develop or build a new piece of fire protection equipment or facility); interview (leaders recognized in fire protection with something constructive to say); and technical (new ideas in fire protection techniques, management training and prevention). "We are doing quite a few series, so that leaves less room for freelanced articles." Buys 15 unsolicited mss/year. Query. Pays $1.50-2/inch.
Photos: State availability of photos with query. Pays $6 for 8x10 b&w matte or glossy prints or $30 for 35mm color transparencies (for covers only). Captions preferred. Buys one-time rights.
Tips: "If you send me something that could have been published in the Sunday supplement of your local paper, it's just not going to make it in our magazine. You've got to realize professional fire service people are not interested in reading 'cute' human interest pieces. They've heard the same stories many times already. Call me and ask for our specific needs (they change monthly). If I am not in the office, try again. We can't afford to return calls regarding queries. But if you call, I'll be happy to talk with you. Please include an SASE. If we buy your piece, it will more than pay for the stamps; if we don't it will guarantee its return."

WISCONSIN SHERIFF & DEPUTY, Wisconsin Sheriffs & Deputy Sheriffs Association, Box 145, Chippewa Falls WI 54729. (715)723-7173. Editor: Don Saunders. Quarterly magazine covering law enforcement in Wisconsin. Circ. 3,000. Pays on publication. Byline given. Offers 25% kill fee. Buys one-time, first and second serial (reprint) rights. Submit seasonal/holiday material 2 months in advance. Photocopied and previously published submissions OK. Reports in 1 month. Writer's guidelines for business size SAE with 20¢ postage.
Nonfiction: Articles about Wisconsin Sheriffs' Departments, professional matters that would be of interest to sheriffs and deputy sheriffs. "Tell our readers what sheriffs and deputy sheriffs are doing to improve law enforcement and crime prevention in Wisconsin's 72 counties." No general matter of interest to sheriffs and deputy sheriffs. Query with clips of published work. Length: 1,000-1,500. Pays $25-100.
Photos: State availability of photos. "Photos of Wisconsin sheriffs and/or deputy sheriffs in action, unless accompanied by article." Pays $5-15 for 8x10 b&w prints. Captions and identification of subjects required. Buys one-time rights.

YOUR VIRGINIA STATE TROOPER MAGAZINE, Box 2189, Springfield VA 22152. (703)451-2524. Editor: Geraldine A. Lash. Biannual magazine covering police topics for troopers, police, libraries, legislators and businesses. Circ. 10,000. Pays on acceptance. Byline given. Buys first North American serial rights and all rights on assignments. Submit seasonal/holiday material 2 months in advance. Simultaneous and photocopied submissions OK. Computer printout submissions OK. Reports in 4 weeks on mss.
Nonfiction: Book excerpts; expose (consumer or police-related); general interest; nutrition/health; historical/nostalgic; how-to (energy saving); humor; interview/profile (notable police figures); opinion; personal experience; technical (radar); and other (recreation). All articles must be police related. Buys 40-45 mss/year. Query with clips of published work or send complete ms. Length: 2,500 maximum words. Pays $250 maximum/article (10¢/word).
Photos: Send photos with ms. Pays $25 maximum/5x7 b&w glossy print. Captions and model release required. Buys one-time rights.
Fiction: Adventure, humorous, mystery, novel excerpts, and suspense. All articles must be police related. Buys 4 mss/year. Send complete ms. Length: 2,500 words minimum. Pays $250 maximum (10¢/word) on acceptance.

Market conditions are constantly changing! If this is 1985 or later, buy the newest edition of *Writer's Market* at your favorite bookstore or order directly from Writer's Digest Books.

Groceries

The journals that follow are for owners and operators of retail food stores. Journals for food wholesalers, packers, warehousers and caterers are classified with the Food Products, Processing, and Service journals. Publications for food vending machine operators are found in the Coin-Operated Machines category.

CANADIAN GROCER, Maclean-Hunter Ltd., Maclean Hunter Building, 777 Bay St., Toronto, Ontario, Canada M5W 1A7. (416)596-5772. Editor: George H. Condon. Monthly magazine about supermarketing and food retailing for Canadian chain and independent food store managers, owners, buyers, executives, food brokers, food processors and manufacturers. Circ 16,000. Pays on publication. Byline given. Buys first Canadian rights. Phone queries OK. Submit seasonal material 2 months in advance. Previously published submissions OK. SAE and International Reply Coupons. Reports in 2 weeks. Sample copy $4.
Nonfiction: Interview (national trendsetters in marketing, finance or food distribution); technical (store operations, equipment and finance); and news features on supermarkets. "Freelancers should be well versed on the supermarket industry. We don't want unsolicited material. Writers with business and/or finance expertise are preferred. Know the retail food industry and be able to write concisely and accurately on subjects relevant to our readers: food store managers, senior corporate executives, etc. A good example of an article would be 'How a Six Store Chain of Supermarkets Improved Profits 2% and Kept Customers Coming.' " Buys 14 mss/year. Query with clips of previously published work. Pays $25-175.
Photos: State availability of photos. Pays $5-15 for 8x10 b&w glossy prints. Captions preferred. Buys one-time rights.

ENTRÉE, Fairchild, 7 E. 12th St., New York NY 10003. (212)741-4009. Editor: Geri Brin. Managing Editor: Debra Kent. Monthly magazine covering "trends in cooking, housewares and food industry news, new products in the gourmet and lifestyle areas for specialty retailers and buyers of gourmet housewares and food, and executives and managers in the gourmet product industry." Estab. 1980. Circ. 15,000. Average issue includes 5-11 features, 5 columns, a calendar, news and 50% advertising. Pays on publication. Byline given. Kill fee varies. Buys all rights. Phone queries OK. SASE. Reports in 6 weeks on queries; in 1 week on mss. Sample copy $2.
Nonfiction: Profile (of major retailers); how-to (handle a business situation as explained by retailers of "gourmet products"); new product ("hot product categories"); photo feature; and technical (cookware and specialty food in terms retailers can apply to their businesses). No first person; humor; unsolicited stories on obscure retailers; or general pieces of any kind. Buys 2-3 mss/issue. Query. Length: 1,500-3,000 words. Pays $250-400.
Photos: Editor: Mare Earley. Pays $20 for 8x10 b&w glossy prints. Color photos negotiable. Captions required.
Columns/Departments: Sizzlers (about people); Simmer (on news); Menu Makers (cookbook reviews); and Bright Ideas (on new products).
Tips: "We've expanded heavily into specialty foods, as opposed to gourmet housewares, which was our main thrust three years ago. Now, we're presenting a balance of food and housewares. In addition, we're much more interested in experienced *trade* writers rather than experienced consumer magazine writers. We've rejected stories from successful consumer writers becaus they simply don't meet the requirements of a *business* magazine. *Entrée* is actively searching for qualified, experienced trade writers. We use two to three freelancers every issue, and now wish to establish a core of regular writers we can rely on. Our problem is that, while writers are in abundance, experienced *trade* writers are not. We need a writer who can thoroughly analyze a market, whether it be cutlery, cheese, pâté or ice cream machines. We need someone who can do in-depth retail profiles with major retailers. Most important, we're not particularly interested in hearing queries. We'd rather interview qualified writers who can accept *our* assignments month after month. A typical feature pays $400."

FLORIDA FOOD DEALER, Retail Grocers Association of Florida, Box 3310, Ocala FL 32678-3310. (904)732-8439. Editor: Andy Williams. Managing Editor: Bill Weaver. Monthly magazine covering the Florida retail supermarket and convenience store industry. Circ. 4,000. Byline given. Offers negotiable kill fee. Buys first North American serial rights. Submit seasonal/holiday material 2 months in advance. Simultaneous queries and photocopied and previously published submissions OK. Computer printout or disk submissions OK; prefers letter quality to dot matrix. SASE. Reports in 1 week on queries, 2 weeks on mss. Sample copy $1.
Nonfiction: Historical/nostalgic; how-to; inspirational; interview/profile; new product; personal experience; technical—Florida angle. "Conservative business-oriented." Special issues include new equipment (July); dairy (May) security. No coupon handling, consumer tips, recipes. Buys 12 mss/year. Query. Length: 500-1,500 words. Pays $50-150.
Tips: "Know supermarket and convenience store industry from owner's standpoint."

GROCER'S SPOTLIGHT, Shamie Publishing Co., 22725 Mack Ave., St. Clair Shores MI 48080. (313)779-4940. Editor: Joe Scheringer. Monthly tabloid about the supermarket industry for operators, chain and independent wholesalers, food brokers and manufacturers. Circ. 75,000. Pays on publication. Byline given. Buys all rights. Phone queries OK. Submit seasonal material 2 months in advance. Simultaneous and photocopied submissions OK. SASE. Reports in 3 weeks. Free sample copy and writer's guidelines.
Nonfiction: Interview. Query. Pays $5/column inch.
Photos: State availability of photos with query. Uses b&w and color.
Columns/Departments: Query. Pays $1/column inch.

GROCERY DISTRIBUTION MAGAZINE, The Magazine of Physical Distribution and Plant Development for the Food Industry, Market Publications, 39 S. La Salle St., Chicago IL 60603. (312)263-1057. Bimonthly magazine reaching managers and executives responsible for food warehousing operations and distribution. Circ. 15,000. Pays on publication. No computer printout or disk submissions. No byline given. Offers 100% kill fee. Buys all rights. "Will furnish guidelines to writer when article assigned."
Nonfiction: "All articles on assignment. Query us as to availability of assignment in area covered. Send samples of case history type articles, particularly industrial type stories. No general business-type subjects, inasmuch as our audience is engaged in high-level transactions and not suitable targets for general fare." Buys 6-10 mss/year.
Photos: Reviews b&w contact sheets and 4x5 transparencies. Captions required. Buys all rights. "Photo requirements specified at time of assignment of articles."
Tips: "We want to develop more case histories on reader operations, need more inquiries from writers."

HEALTH FOODS BUSINESS, Howmark Publishing Corp., 567 Morris Ave., Elizabeth NJ 07208 (201)353-7373. Editor-in-Chief: Alan Richman. 20% freelance written. For owners and managers of health food stores. Monthly magazine; 100 pages. Circ. over 8,000. Pays on publication. Byline given "if story quality warrants it." Phone queries OK. "Query us about a good health foods store in your area. We use many store profile stories." Simultaneous and photocopied submissions OK if exclusive to their field. Previously published work OK, but please indicate when and where material appeared previously. Computer printout submissions OK if double-spaced and in upper and lower case; prefers letter quality to dot matrix. SASE. Reports in 1 month. Sample copy $2.50; plus $2 for postage and handling.
Nonfiction: Exposés (government hassling with health food industry); how-to (unique or successful retail operators); informational (how or why a product works; technical aspects must be clear to laymen); historical (natural food use); interviews (must be prominent person in industry or closely related to the health food industry); and photo features (any unusual subject related to the retailer's interests). Buys 1-2 mss/issue. Query for interviews and photo features. Will consider complete ms in other categories. Length: long enough to tell the whole story without padding. Pays $50 and up for feature stories, $75 and up for store profiles.
Photos: "Most articles must have photos included"; negs and contact sheet OK. Captions required. No additional payment.

IGA GROCERGRAM, Fisher-Harrison Corp., 338 N. Elm St., Greensboro NC 27401. (919)378-9651. Editor: Bonnie McElveen-Hunter. Managing Editor: Leslie P. Daisy. Monthly magazine for independent grocery retailers and wholesalers. Circ. 11,000. Pays on publication. Byline given. Buys first rights. Submit seasonal/holiday material 3 months in advance. No computer printout or disk submissions. SASE. Reports in 2 weeks on queries; 1 month on mss. Free sample copy.
Nonfiction: Book excerpts, interview/profile, new product, technical. "All articles must concentrate on the independent grocery business." Buys 25-35 mss/year. Query with clips of published work. Pays $25-500.
Photos: Send photos with ms. Reviews b&w contact sheets and color transparencies. Buys one-time rights.

PENNSYLVANIA GROCER, 1355 Old York Rd., Abington PA 19001. (215)228-0808. Editor: John McNelis. For grocers, their families and employees, store managers; food people in general. Monthly magazine; 16 pages. Circ. 3,000. Byline given. Pays on publication. Sample copy 75¢. Reports in 30 days. SASE.
Nonfiction and Photos: Articles on food subjects in retail food outlets; mainly local, in Pennsylvania and surrounding areas. Informational, interviews, profiles, historical, successful business operations, new product, merchandising techniques and technical articles. Buys 12-15 unsolicited mss/year. Query or submit complete ms. Length: 500-900 words. Pays $25. Pays $25 maximum for minimum of 2 b&w photos purchased with ms.
Tips "We need graphics and will use more color."

WHOLE FOODS, The Voice of the Natural Foods Industry, Hester Communications, Inc., Suite 250, 1700 E. Dyer Rd., Santa Ana CA 92705. (714)549-4834. Editors: Jan Kingaard, Anita Fieldman. Monthly magazine edited for health food retailers, food cooperative managers, natural food restaurant owners, organic growers and nutritionists. Byline given on articles and columns; photocredits also. Buys first North American rights. Submit seasonal material 3 months in advance. Photocopied submissions OK. Computer printout submissions OK "if highly readable." Prefers double-spaced letter quality to dot matrix. SASE. Reports in 1 month. Pays on acceptance. Length: 500-2,000 words. Writer's guidelines and sample copy available with 9x12 SASE. "Good freelancers wanted."

Nonfiction: Editorial content targets product knowledge and aids retailers in making responsible and profitable inventory selection through nutritional education, market awareness and merchandising expertise. Feature articles explain products, including manufacturing procedures, proper storage and preparation, as well as nutritional benefits. Consumer tearouts expand product understanding beyond the retailer; health connection reviews research on the critical link between nutrition and health that is impacting the scientific and medical communities and ultimately the natural/health foods industry. Industry members speak out about the industry issues in the Debate department. Calendar, book reviews, industry news and product showcase are written in-house. No consumer-oriented pieces other than one-subject consumer tearouts (i.e. "Everything You Need To Know About Tofu . . . or Sprouts . . ."). Not interested in undocumented, unreferenced, experiential pieces unless company or store profile of success (or specifics about failure). Wants "higher quality, compact, documentable work." Testimonials/healing stories NOT wanted."

Photos: Photos desirable with ms. Provide captions and model release if appropriate.

Tips: "We are in the market for qualified freelancers who submit on-target pieces which do not require considerable editing, retyping, etc. Writer should read three issues of the magazine and have observed the operation of a health food store prior to beginning any work. Industry exclusive a must for all submissions. We will provide list of competitors' magazines."

Grooming Products and Services

AMERICAN HAIRDRESSER/SALON OWNER, Suite 1000, 100 Park Ave., New York NY 10017. (212)532-5588. Editor: Louise Cotter. For beauty salon owners and operators. Monthly. Buys all rights. Pays on publication. Computer printout or disk submissions OK; prefers letter quality to dot matrix printouts. SASE.

Nonfiction: Profiles, how-to and management. Technical material is mainly staff written. "We are not interested unless material is directly related to the needs of beauty salon professionals."

WOMAN BEAUTIFUL, Allied Publications, Inc., Drawer 189, Palm Beach FL 33480. (305)833-4593. Editor: Wendy Wagman. For "students at beauty schools and people who go to beauty salons." Used as a recruiting tool at cosmetology schools. Bimonthly magazine; 16 pages. Pays on acceptance. Buys one-time rights. Simultaneous submissions OK. Sample copy $1. Free writer's guidelines. Reports in 4 weeks. SASE.

Nonfiction: "Articles on hairstyling, beauty, and women's fashion." Interested in some new product articles; interviews (with famous hairstylists) and anything related to celebrities and hairstyles. Occasionally uses a history piece such as an article on the history of wigs. Buys 2 mss/issue. Length: 400-800 words. Pays 5¢/published word. Send complete ms.

Columns/Departments: What's New. Pays 5¢/published word.

Hardware

In this classification are journals for general hardware wholesalers and retailers, locksmiths, and retailers of miscellaneous special hardware items. Journals specializing in the retailing of hardware for a certain trade, such as plumbing or automotive supplies, are classified with the other publications for that trade.

HARDWARE AGE, Chilton Co., Chilton Way, Radnor PA 19089. (215)964-4275. Editor: Jay Holtzman. Managing Editor: Wendy Ampolsk. 5% freelance written. Emphasizes retailing, distribution and merchandising of hardware and building materials. Monthly magazine; 180 pages. Circ. 71,000. Buys first North American serial rights. No guarantee of byline. Simultaneous, photocopied and previously published submissions OK, if exclusive in the field. SASE. Reports in 1-2 months. Sample copy and writer's guidelines $1; mention *Writer's Market* in request.

Nonfiction: Wendy Ampolsk, managing editor. How-to more profitably run a hardware store or a department within a store. "We particularly want stories on local hardware stores and home improvement centers, with photos. Stories should concentrate on one particular aspect of how the retailer in question has been successful." Also want technical pieces (will consider stories on retail accounting, inventory management and business management by qualified writers). Buys 5-10 unsolicited mss/year. Submit complete ms. Length: 500-3,000 words. Pays $75-200.

Photos: "We like store features with b&w photos. Usually use b&w for small freelance features." Send photos with ms. Pays $25 for 4x5 glossy b&w prints. Captions preferred. Buys one-time rights.
Columns/Departments: Retailers' Business Tips; Wholesalers' Business Tips; Moneysaving Tips. Query or submit complete ms. Length: 1,000-1,250 words. Pays $100-150. Open to suggestions for new columns/departments.

HARDWARE MERCHANDISER, The Irving-Cloud Publishing Co., 7300 N. Cicero, Lincolnwood IL 60646. (312)674-7300. Editor: James W. Stapleton. Managing Editor: Pamela Taylor. Monthly tabloid covering hardware, home center and hardlines market for owners and managers of hardware stores, home centers, and executives of businesses serving them. Circ. 65,000. Pays on acceptance. Buys first North American serial rights. SASE. Reports in 1 month on queries. Free sample copy.
Nonfiction: Profile (of hardware business). Buys 10 mss/year. Query or send complete ms "on speculation; enough to tell the story."
Photos: Send photos with ms. Reviews 35mm or larger color transparencies. "Photos are paid for as part of article payment."

HARDWARE MERCHANDISING, Maclean-Hunter Co., Ltd., 481 University Ave., Toronto, Ontario, Canada M5W 1A7. (416)596-5797. For hardware and building supply retailers throughout Canada. Circ. 17,000. Contact: Editor-in-Chief. Canadian freelancers should contact the editor at above address for more information. No computer printout or disk submissions.

HARDWARE RETAILING, The Hardware Home Center Magazine, National Retail Hardware Association, 770 N. High School Rd., Indianapolis IN 46224. (317)248-1261. Editor: John Hammond. Managing Editor: Ellen Hackney. Monthly magazine covering hardware stores, home centers, consumer building material dealers. Circ. 65,000. Pays on acceptance. Byline given. Buys one-time rights. Photocopied submissions OK. Computer printout submissions OK. Reports in 2 weeks on queries; 3 weeks on mss. Free sample copy.
Nonfiction: How-to (manage your retail hardware/home center business). "Expert articles on specific management problems and opportunities." No column material. "We have too many columns now and it seems we constantly receive suggested columns." Buys 10 mss/year. Send complete ms. Length: open. Pays $50-150.
Tips: "We have an increasing interest in management articles directed to the consumer-oriented lumber yard."

SOUTHERN HARDWARE, 1760 Peachtree Rd., NW, Atlanta GA 30357. (404)874-4462. Editor-in-Chief: Ralph E. Kirby. 50% freelance written. For retailers of hardware and allied lines, located in the Southern states. Monthly magazine; 80 pages. Circ. 16,500. Pays on acceptance. Buys all rights. Phone queries OK. Submit seasonal/holiday material 3 months in advance of issue date. SASE. Free sample copy and writer's guidelines; mention *Writer's Market* in request.
Nonfiction: How-to (how a store can achieve greater results in selling lines or a line of merchandise). "No articles on history of business." Query. Length: 500-1,000 words. Pays $95-200.
Photos: State availability of photos with query. Offers no additional payment for 5x7 or 8x10 b&w prints. Buys all rights.

Home Furnishings and Household Goods

APPLIANCE SERVICE NEWS, 110 W. Saint Charles Rd., Box 789, Lombard IL 60148. Editor: William Wingstedt. For professional service people whose main interest is repairing major and portable household appliances. Their jobs consist of either service shop owner, service manager or service technician. Monthly "newspaper style" publication. Circ. 41,000. Buys all rights. Byline given. Pays on publication. Sample copy $1.50. Will consider simultaneous submissions. Reports in about 1 month. SASE.
Nonfiction and Photos: James Hodl, associate editor. "Our main interest is in technical articles about appliances and their repair. Material should be written in a straightforward, easy-to-understand style. It should be crisp and interesting, with a high informational content. Our main interest is in the major and portable appliance repair field. We are not interested in retail sales." Query. Length: open. Pays $200-300/feature. Pays $10 for b&w photos used with ms. Captions required.

CHINA GLASS & TABLEWARE, Ebel-Doctorow Publications, Inc., Box 2147, Clifton NJ 07015. (201)779-1600. Editor-in-Chief: Susan Grisham. 30% freelance written. Monthly magazine for buyers, merchandise managers, and specialty store owners who deal in tableware, dinnerware, glassware, flatware, and

other tabletop accessories. Pays on publication. Buys one-time rights. Byline given. Phone queries OK. Submit seasonal/holiday material 3 months in advance of issue date. No computer printout or disk submissions. SASE. Reports in 2-3 weeks. Free sample copy and writer's guidelines; mention *Writer's Market* in request.
Nonfiction: General interest (on store successes, reasons for a store's business track record); interview (personalities of store owners; how they cope with industry problems; why they are in table ware); technical (on the business aspects of retailing china, glassware and flatware). "Bridal registry material always welcomed." No articles on how-to or gift shops. Buys 2-3 mss/issue. Query. Length: 1,500-3,000 words. Pays $40-50/page.
Photos: State availability of photos with query. No additional payment for b&w contact sheets or color contact sheets. Captions required. Buys one-time rights.
Fillers: Clippings. Buys 2/issue. Pays $3-5.
Tips: "Show imagination in the query; have a good angle on a story—that makes it unique from the competition's coverage and requires less work on the editor's part for rewriting a snappy beginning."

FURNITURE WORLD/SOUTH, Towse Publishing Co., 127 E. 31st St., New York NY 10016. (212)686-3910. Editor: Phillip Mazzurco. Monthly magazine covering the furniture industry for retailers and manufacturers. Pays on publication. Byline given. Not copyrighted. Buys one-time rights. Submit seasonal/holiday material 1 month in advance. SASE. Reports in 1 month. Free sample copy and writer's guidelines.
Nonfiction: General interest (economics affecting furniture and housing industries); interview/profile (of successful retailers, manufacturers); technical. Query. Pays $50/published page.
Photos: State availability of photos. Reviews b&w negatives and prints. Captions required. Buys one-time rights.
Columns/Departments: Interviews with top industry leaders about economic future of furniture industry.

GIFTS & DECORATIVE ACCESSORIES, 51 Madison Ave., New York NY 10010. (212)689-4411. Editor-in-Chief: Phyllis Sweed. Managing Editor: Douglas Gilbert-Neiss. 10% freelance written. Published primarily for quality gift retailers. Monthly magazine; 250 pages. Circ. 33,000. Pays on publication. No byline. Buys all rights. Submit seasonal/holiday material 6 months in advance of issue date. Photocopied submissions OK. No computer printout or disk submissions. SASE. Reports "as soon as possible." Free writer's guidelines.
Nonfiction: "Merchandising how-to stories of quality stores—how they have solved a particular merchandising problem, or successfully displayed or promoted a particularly difficult area." Nothing about discount stores or mass merchants. No cartoons, poems or think pieces. Buys 6 unsolicited mss/year. Query or submit complete ms. Length: 500-1,500 words. Pays $75-200.
Photos: "Photos should illustrate merchandising points made in a story." Pays $7.50-10 for good 5x7 glossy b&w prints; $15-25 for 4x5 color transparencies or 35mm transparencies. Captions required. Buys all rights.
Tips: "We're always in the market for a good story from the West or Southwest."

GIFTWARE BUSINESS, 1515 Broadway, New York NY 10036. (212)764-7317. Editor: Rita Guarna. For "merchants (department store buyers, specialty shop owners) engaged in the resale of giftware, china and glass, decorative accessories." Monthly. Circ. 36,800. Buys all rights. Byline given "by request only." Pays on acceptance. Query or submit complete ms. Will consider photocopied submissions. SASE.
Nonfiction: "Retail store success stories. Describe a single merchandising gimmick. We are a tabloid format—glossy stock. Descriptions of store interiors are less important than sales performance unless display is outstanding. We're interested in articles on aggressive selling tactics. We cannot use material written for the consumer." Buys coverage of successful business operations and merchandising techniques. Length: 750 words maximum.
Photos: Purchased with mss and on assignment; captions required. "Individuals are to be identified." Reviews b&w glossy prints (preferred) and color transparencies.

HOME FURNISHINGS, (formerly *Southwest Homefurnishings News*), 4313 N. Central Expressway, Box 64545, Dallas TX 75206. (214)526-7757. Editor: Tina Berres Filipski. Biannual magazine for home furnishings retail dealers, manufacturers, their representatives, and others in related fields. Circ. 15,000. Pays on acceptance. No simultaneous submissions. No computer printout or disk submissions. SASE.
Nonfiction: Informational articles about retail selling; success and problem solving stories in the retail business; economic and legislative-related issues, etc. "No profiles of people out of our area or nonmembers of the association. No trite, over-used features on trends, lighthearted features." Query. Length: open; appropriate to subject and slant. Pays 15¢/word. "Extensive research projects done on assignment negotiated in addition to the per-word rate; particularly interested in articles related to the Southwest." Photos desirable.

HOME LIGHTING & ACCESSORIES, Box 2147, Clifton NJ 07015. (201)779-1600. Editor-in-Chief: Herb Ballinger. 35% freelance written. For lighting stores/departments. Monthly magazine. Circ. 7,000. Pays on publication. Buys all rights. Phone queries OK. Submit seasonal/holiday material 6 months in advance of issue date. SASE. Free sample copy.

Nonfiction: How-to (run your lighting store/department, including all retail topics); interview (with lighting retailers); personal experience (as a businessperson involved with lighting); opinion (about business approaches and marketing); profile (of a successful lighting retailer/lamp buyer); and technical (concerning lighting or lighting design). Buys 30 mss/year. Query. Pays $60/published page.

Photos: State availability of photos with query. Offers no additional payment for 5x7 or 8x10 b&w glossy prints. Pays additional $90 for color transparencies used on cover. Captions required.

HOUSEHOLD AND PERSONAL PRODUCTS INDUSTRY, 26 Lake St., Ramsey NJ 07446. Editor: Hamilton C. Carson. 5-10% freelance written. For "manufacturers of soaps, detergents, cosmetics and toiletries, waxes and polishes, insecticides, and aerosols." Monthly. Circ. 14,000. Not copyrighted. Buys 3 to 4 mss a year, "but would buy more if slanted to our needs." Pays on publication. Will send a sample copy to a writer on request. Will consider photocopied submissions. Submit seasonal material 2 months in advance. Query. No computer printout or disk submissions. SASE.

Nonfiction and Photos: "Technical and semitechnical articles on manufacturing, distribution, marketing, new products, plant stories, etc., of the industries served. Some knowledge of the field is essential in writing for us." Buys informational articles, interviews, photo features, spot news, coverage of successful business operations, new product articles, coverage of merchandising techniques, and technical articles. No articles slanted toward consumers. Query with clips of published work. Length: 500-2,000 words. Pays $10-200. 5x7 or 8x10 b&w glossies purchased with mss. Pays $10.

LINENS, DOMESTICS AND BATH PRODUCTS, 370 Lexington Ave., New York NY 10017. (212)532-9290. Editor: Marc R. Dick. For department stores, mass merchandisers, specialty stores and bath boutiques. Published 6 times/year. Buys all rights. Pays on publication. Reports in 4-6 weeks. SASE.

Nonfiction and Photos: Merchandising articles that educate the buyer on sales and fashion trends, promotions, industry news, styles; in-depth articles with photos on retail stores/departments for bath accessories, linens and sheets, tablecloths, napkins and place mats, towels, and comforters. Especially focusing on interesting promotions and creative displays within these departments. Buys 6-10 mss/year. Length: 700-1,500 words. Pays $150-250. Photos purchased with mss.

NATIONAL HOME CENTER NEWS, Lebhar-Friedman, Inc., 425 Park Ave., New York NY 10022. (212)371-9400. Editor: Wyatt Kash. Biweekly tabloid covering "business news in the $60 billion retail building supply and do-it-yourself home improvement industry." Circ. 28,000. Pays on publication. Byline given in some cases. Rights purchased are negotiable. Submit seasonal/holiday material 1 month in advance. Simultaneous queries, and simultaneous and photocopied submissions OK. Computer printout submissions OK, "as long as the copy is easily read and edited. We have no ability, however, to receive stories via computer, or wire. (We *do* use facsimile machines.)" Reports in 2 weeks.

Nonfiction: "We use very little freelance material. Please write first. Query editor on possible story ideas concerning specific retail building supply/home center companies, housing, home improvements and home improvement products." No how-to stories on running a business, or on do-it-yourself projects. "We're looking for business stories on actual companies, or on trends regarding home improvement products sales and merchandising of interest to retailers and wholesalers of those products."

Tips: "In the past, we tended to survey only retailers about what was happening in the retail building supply/home improvement market. We are now surveying wholesalers and manufacturers as well as retailers."

‡PROFESSIONAL FURNITURE MERCHANT MAGAZINE, The Business Magazine for Progressive Furniture Retailers, Vista Publications, 9600 W. Sample Rd., Coral Springs FL 33065. (305)753-7400. Editor: Ms. Sandy Evans. Managing Editor: Julia McNair Docke. Monthly magazine covering the furniture industry from a retailer's perspective. In-depth features on direction, trends, certain retailers doing outstanding jobs, analyses of areas affecting industry (housing, economy, etc.). Circ. 20,000. Pays on publication. Byline given. Buys one-time rights. Submit seasonal/holiday material 3 months in advance. Simultaneous queries and submissions OK. SASE. Reports in 1 month. Sample copy and guidelines $6.

Nonfiction: Expose (relating to or affectng furniture industry); how-to (business-oriented how-to control cash flow, inventory, market research, etc.); interview/profile (furniture retailers); photo feature (special furniture category). No general articles, fiction or personal experience. Buys 24 mss/year. Send complete ms. Length: 1,000-2,400 words. Pays $150 maximum.

Photos: State availablity of photos. Pays $5 maximum for 3x5 color transparencies; $5 maximum for 3x5 b&w prints. Captions, model release and identification of subjects required.

Tips: "Read the magazine. Send manuscript specifically geared to furniture retailers, with art (photos or drawings) specified." Break in with features. "First, visit a furniture store, talk to the owner, discover what he's interested in."

RETAILER AND MARKETING NEWS, Box 191105, Dallas TX 75219-1105. (214)651-9959. Editor: Michael J. Anderson. For "retail dealers and wholesalers in appliances, TV's, furniture, consumer electronics, records, air conditioning, housewares, hardware and all related businesses." Monthly. Circ. 10,000. Free sample copy. Photocopied submissions OK. SASE.

Nonfiction: "How a retail dealer can make more profit" is the approach. Wants "sales promotion ideas, advertising, sales tips, business builders and the like, localized to the Southwest and particularly to north Texas." Submit complete ms. Length: 100-900 words. Pays $30-50.

SEW BUSINESS, Box 1331, Ft. Lee NJ 07024. Editor: Christina Holmes. For retailers of home-sewing, quilting and needlework merchandise. "We are the only glossy magazine format in the industry—including homesewing, art needlework and a new *Quilt Quarterly* supplement." Monthly. Circ. 17,000. Not copyrighted. Pays on publication. Free sample copy and writer's guidelines. Reports in 5 weeks on queries; in 6 weeks on ms. SASE.

Nonfiction and Photos: Articles on department store or fabric, needlework, or quilt, shop operations, including coverage of art needlework, piece goods, patterns, quilting, sewing accessories and all other notions. Interviews with buyers—retailers on their department or shop. "Stories must be oriented to provide interesting information from a *trade* point of view. Looking for retailers doing something different or offbeat, something that another retailer could put to good use in his own operation. Best to query editor first to find out if a particular article might be of interest to us." Buys 25 unsolicited mss/year. Query. Length: 750-1,500 words. Pays $100 minimum. Photos purchased with mss. "Should illustrate important details of the story." Sharp 5x7 b&w glossies. Offers no additional payment for photos accompanying ms.

UNFINISHED FURNITURE MAGAZINE, United States Exposition Corp., 1850 Oak St., Northfield IL 60093. (312)446-8434. Editor: Lynda Utterback. Bimonthly magazine for unfinished furniture retailers, distributors and manufacturers throughout the US, Canada, England, Australia and Europe. Circ. 6,000. Pays on publication. Byline give. Buys all rights. Submit seasonal/holiday material 6 months in advance. Simultaneous queries and simultaneous and photocopied submissions OK. Computer printout and disk submissions OK. Reports in 3 weeks on queries; 1 month on mss. Free sample copy and writer's guidelines.

Nonfiction: How-to, interview/profile, new product, personal experience, technical (as these relate to the furniture industry). Production distribution, marketing, advertising and promotion of unfinished furniture and current happenings in the industry. "No poetic pieces about trees." Buys 10 unsolicited mss/year. Send complete ms. Length: 2,000. Pays $50-100. Pays $5 for b&w photos.

Hospitals, Nursing, and Nursing Homes

In this section are journals for nurses; medical and nonmedical nursing homes; clinical and hospital staffs; and laboratory technicians and managers. Journals publishing technical material on new discoveries in medicine and information for physicians in private practice are listed in the Medical category. Publications that report on medical trends for the consumer are in the Health and Science categories.

AMERICAN JOURNAL OF NURSING, 555 West 57th St., New York NY 10019. (212)582-8820. Editor: Mary B. Mallison, RN. Managing Editor: Ellen Goldensohn. Monthly magazine covering nursing and health care. Circ. 360,000. Pays on publication. Byline given. Simultaneous queries OK. Computer printout and disk submissions OK; prefers letter quality to dot matrix printouts. Reports in 3 weeks on queries, 4 months on mss. Sample copy $3; free writer's guidelines.

Nonfiction: How-to, satire, new product, opinion, personal experience, photo feature, technical. No material other than nursing care and nursing issues. "Nurse authors mostly accepted for publication." Query. Length: 1,000-1,500 words. Pays $20 minimum/published page.

Photos: Forbes Linkhorn, art editor. Reviews b&w and color transparencies and prints. Model release and identification of subjects required. Buys variable rights.

Columns/Departments: Buys 12 mss/year. Query with or without clips of published work.

DIMENSIONS IN HEALTH SERVICE, Canadian Hospital Association, Suite 100, 17 York St., Ottawa, Ontario, Canada K1N 9J6. (613)238-8005. Executive Editor: Jean-Claude Martin. Managing Editor: Ruta Siulys. Monthly magazine for health care administration. Circ. 11,500. Pays on publication. Byline given. Buys first rights. Submit seasonal/holiday material 3 months in advance. Simultaneous queries and previously published submissions OK. SASE. Reports in 3 weeks on queries; 1 month on mss. Sample copy $2 (Canada); $3 (US); free writer's guidelines.

Nonfiction: How-to (improve patient care, manage health facilities); interview/profile (of figures in Canadian health field); technical (health services). No US-oriented articles or analysis of "sensitive" areas in the Canadian health care field, i.e. labor negotiations in Quebec. Recent editoral themes: Manpower; Emergency Services, Interconnect; Finance/Cost Control; Computers; I.C.U./C.C.U.; Laundry/Houskeeping; Safety and Security; Design & Construction; Food Services; Community Services, Fundraising; Technology; Communications; Infection Control; Conventions; Purchasing; Geriatrics; and Rehabilitation. Buys 10 mss/year. Query. Length: 800-3,000 words. Pays $100-300.

Photos: State availability of photos. Pays $15 minimum for 2x2 color transparencies; $15-30 for prints; $15-30 for 2x2 b&w transparencies and prints. Captions required. Buys one-time rights.

Tips: "Emphasize Canadian or international aspects. Write with easy reading style, a bit of humor, and include *photos*."

‡**HEALTHCARE HORIZONS, The National Newspaper for Health Care Professionals**, Horizon Four, Box 1069, San Pedro CA 90733. (213)547-4456. Editor: Dawn A. Bruner. Biweekly newspaper covering nursing, healthcare, hospitals. "A national forum for health care professionals dealing with these interesting and dedicated people as human beings, their working and personal lifestyles, what they do and what they think." Circ. 250,000. Pays on publication. Byline given. Buys first North American serial rights, one-time rights, all rights, first rights and second serial (reprint) rights. Submit seasonal/holiday material 3 months in advance. Photocopied, simultaneous, and previously published submissions OK. SASE. Reports in 2 weeks on queries; 1 month on mss. Sample copy for 9x12 SAE and 54¢ postage; writer's guidelines for business size SAE and 1 first class stamp.

Nonfiction: Book excerpts (books about healthcare/wellness/healthcare professionals); general interest (all types including finance/lifestyle); historical/nostalgic (healthcare yesterday vs. healthcare today); humor (about healthcare professionals/hospitals); interview/profile (of healthcare professionals—*not* doctors); new product (of use to hospitals and healthcare professionals); opinion (of healthcare professionals about their profession—constructive criticism); personal experience (positive experiences of general interest about healthcare professionals); technical (clinical/technical medical advances/procedures equipment); travel (combining travel/work, offseason buys, unusual places to go, health and travel). Future special issues: Christmas/healthcare and graduation. No "stories about doctors, especially when not inclusive of the rest of the healthcare team; or dry, too-technical material. Buys 150-200 mss/year. Query or send complete ms. Length: 100-1,500 words. Pays $1-80.

Photos: Send photos with ms. Pays $10 for 5x7 or 8x10 b&w print. Captions, model releases and identification of subjects required. Buys one-time rights.

Columns/Departments: Puzzles—crossword/word games with medical theme; Dialogue—opinions about healthcare with constructive format. Buys 50 items/year. Send complete ms. Length: 50-1,000 words. Pays $1-80.

Poetry: Avant-garde, free verse, haiku, light verse, traditional. "Will accept poetry that deals with healthcare/hospitals/healthcare professionals *only*. Buys 15 poems/year. Submit maximum 2 poems. Length: 2-40 lines. Pays $1-80.

Fillers: Clippings and newsbreaks. Buys 20 fillers/year. Length: 50-500 words. Pays $1-80.

Tips: "We like the human touch whenever possible and prefer in-depth stories about the people in the health care field—especially nurses. The area most available to freelancers is the feature area. An unusual, well-written article, accompanied by photos, is the prime target. The article should be of interest to the healthcare professional, not just about professionals and their world. Beginning contributors would fare better if submitting a finished manuscript on a specific topic. If the article concept is more general in nature, it would be wise to submit a query, as we may have information on file, or have used such a topic in the recent past. Technical articles should always be accompanied by a bibliography source listing. We especially look for diversity of opinion, backed by strong substantiation."

HOSPITAL SUPERVISOR'S BULLETIN, Bureau of Business Practice, 24 Rope Ferry Rd., Waterford CT 06386. Editor: Patricia Ryan. For non-medical hospital supervisors. Semimonthly newsletter; 8 pages. Circ. 8,000. Pays on acceptance. Buys all rights. No byline. Submit seasonal/holiday material 6 months in advance. Photocopied submissions OK. SASE. Reports in 4 weeks. Free sample copy and writer's guidelines.

Nonfiction: Publishes interviews with non-medical hospital department heads. "You should ask supervisors to pinpoint current problems in supervision, tell how they are trying to solve these problems and what results they're getting—backed up by real examples from daily life." Also publishes interviews on people problems and good methods of management. People problems include the areas of training, planning, evaluating, counseling, discipline, motivation, supervising the undereducated, getting along with the medical staff, etc., with emphasis on good methods of management. No material on hospital volunteers. "We prefer 6- to 8-page typewritten articles, based on interviews." Pays 12¢/word after editing.

HOSPITALS, American Hospital Publishing, Inc., 211 E. Chicago Ave., Chicago IL 60611. (312)951-1100. Editor: Daniel Schechter. Managing Editor: Wesley Curry. Bimonthly magazine featuring hospitals and health care systems. Circ. 95,000. Average issue includes 4-5 articles. Pays on acceptance. Byline given. Buys first North American serial rights. Phone queries OK. Submit seasonal material 4 months in advance. Photocopied submissions OK. Computer printout and Wang disk submissions OK. Reports in 2 weeks on queries; in 2 months on mss. Free sample copy and writer's guidelines.

Nonfiction: How-to and new product. "Articles must address issues of the management of health care institutions." Buys 10-12 unsolicited mss/year. "Moving to staff-written magazine in the year ahead." Query with "reasonably detailed summary or outline of proposed article." Length: 3,000 words maximum. Pays $250-500.

Columns/Departments: "Columns are published on cost containment, architecture and design, and long-term care. Another column includes short features on innovative hospital programs."

JOURNAL OF NURSING CARE, Technomic Publishing Co., 265 Post Rd., W., Box 913, Westport CT 06881. (203)226-7203. Editor: Gerald C. Melson. Monthly magazine covering nursing and related subject matter for Licensed Practical Nurses. Circ. 15,000. Average issue includes 5-7 departments and 5 articles. Byline given. Submit seasonal material 3 months in advance. Simultaneous and photocopied submissions OK. Computer printout and disk submissions OK; prefers letter quality to dot matrix printouts but either acceptable. SASE. Free sample copy and writer's guidelines.

Nonfiction: Historical (patient care); interview; opinion; profile; how-to (health-related matters); humor; inspirational; new product; personal experience; photo feature; and technical. "We prefer at least 4 double-spaced, typed pages or longer. The biggest problem is that articles, while good, are usually too short for publication. Drawings and/or photographs are quite helpful." Buys 20 mss/year. Send complete ms. Length: 800-4,400 words.

Photos: State availability of photos.

NURSINGWORLD JOURNAL, (formerly *Nursing Job News*), Prime National Publishing Corp., 470 Boston Post Rd., Weston MA 02193. Editor: Karen Rafeld. Contains reviews of all the pertinent nursing and healthcare articles plus news and feature stories about nursing. Each issue also contains the latest career and employment opportunities in selected hospitals in specific states. "We accept feature articles dealing with the issues and concerns of the profession and mss describing the problems and opportunities in specific types of nursing, for example, oncology nursing. Monthly journal, 24-72 pages. Circ. 40,000. Pays on publication. Buys one-time rights. Byline given. Phone queries OK. Submit seasonal/holiday material 1-3 months in advance. Previously published work OK. SASE. Reports in 4 months. Sample copy $2.

Nonfiction: General interest; how-to; interview (with nurses, students); opinion; profile; travel; personal experience; photo feature; employment; and issues or concerns. All articles must be related to nursing or hospitals. Buys 1 mss/issue. Send complete ms. Length: 1,500 words maximum. Pays $50 minimum.

Photos: Pays $5-15 each b&w 5x7 or 8x10 glossy print. Captions and model releases required.

Columns/Departments: Open to suggestions for new columns or departments.

RN, 680 Kinderkamack Rd., Oradell NJ 07649. (201)262-3030. Editor: James A. Reynolds. For registered nurses, mostly hospital-based but also in physicians' offices, public health, schools, industry. Monthly magazine; 120 pages. Circ. 375,000. Buys all rights. Pays 25% kill fee for specifically commissioned material. Byline given. Pays on publication. Submit seasonal/holiday material 8 months in advance. Free writer's guidelines. Reports in 6-8 weeks. SASE. Sample copy $2.

Nonfiction: "If you are a nurse who writes, we would like to see your work. Editorial content: diseases, clinical techniques, surgery, therapy, equipment, drugs, etc. These should be thoroughly researched and sources cited. Personal anecdotes, experiences, observations based on your relations with doctors, hospitals, patients and nursing colleagues. Our style is simple and direct, not preachy. Do include examples and case histories that relate the reader to her own nursing experience. Talk mostly about people, rather than things. Dashes of humor or insight are always welcome. Include photos where feasible." Buys 100 mss/year. Query or submit complete ms. Length: 1,000-2,000 words. Pays $100-300.

Photos: "We want good clinical illustration." Send photos with ms. Pays $25 minimum/b&w contact sheet; $35 minimum/35mm color transparency. Captions required; model release required. Buys all rights.

TODAY'S OR NURSE, Slack, Inc., 6900 Grove Rd., Thorofare NJ 08086. (609)848-1000. Editor: Judith B. Paquet, RN. Monthly magazine covering general interest, features and scientific information for operating room nurses. Circ. 35,000. Pays on publication. Byline given. Buys all rights. Submit seasonal material 4 months in advance. Computer printout submissions OK. Reports in 3 weeks on queries; 2 months on mss. Free sample copy and writer's guidelines.

Nonfiction: General interest, how-to, humor, personal experience, technical. Must be pertinent to operating room nurses. No travel material. Query with clips of published work or send complete ms. Length: 500-1,000 words. Pays 10¢/word.

Photos: Send photos with ms. Pays $5-25 for 35mm or 2¼x2¼ b&w transparencies and 8x10 b&w prints; $10-250 for color. Model release and identification of subjects required.

Columns/Departments: Humor, how-to, profiles, human interest, reviews—all about or pertaining to OR nurses. Buys 18 mss/year. Query with clips of published work or send complete ms. Length: 500-2,500 words. Pays $50-200.

Tips: "We're looking for timely, useful, original articles pertaining to operating room nurses. Illustrated material is best. Page budget will be slightly less and columns contracted in the year ahead."

Hotels, Motels, Clubs, Resorts, Restaurants

Hotel and restaurant management is the subject covered in these publications for owners, managers and operators of these establishments. Journals for manufacturers and distributors of bar and beverage supplies are classified in the Beverages and Bottling category. For publications slanted to food wholesalers, processors, and caterers, see Food Products, Processing, and Service.

BARTENDER, Bartender Publishing Corp., Box 593, Livingston NJ 07039. (201)227-4330. Publisher: Raymond P. Foley. Editor: Jaclyn M. Wilson. Emphasizes liquor and bartending for bartenders, tavern owners and owners of restaurants with liquor licenses. Bimonthly magazine; 50 pages. Estab. June 1979. Circ. 15,000. Pays on publication. Buys all rights. Byline given. Phone queries OK. Submit seasonal/holiday material 3 months in advance. Simultaneous, photocopied, and previously published submissions OK. SASE. Reports in 2 months. Sample copies $2.50.

Nonfiction: General interest, historical, how-to, humor, interview (with famous ex-bartenders); new products, nostalgia, personal experience, unique bars, opinion, new techniques, new drinking trends, photo feature, profile, travel and bar sports. Send complete ms. Length: 100-1,000 words.

Photos: Send photos with ms. Pays $7.50-50 for 8x10 b&w glossy prints; $10-75 for 8x10 color glossy prints. Caption preferred and model release required.

Columns/Departments: Bar of the Month; Bartender of the Month; Drink of the Month; New Drink Ideas; Bar Sports; Quiz; Bar Art; Wine Cellar Tips of the Month (from prominent figures in the liquor industry); One For The Road (travel); Collectors (bar or liquor related items); Photo Essays. Query. Length: 200-1,000 words. Pays $50-200.

Fillers: Clippings, jokes, gags, anecdotes, short humor, newsbreaks and anything relating to bartending and the liquor industry. Length: 25-100 words. Pays $5-25.

Tips: "To break in, absolutely make sure that your work will be of interest to all bartenders across the country. Your style of writing should reflect the audience you are addressing."

FLORIDA HOTEL & MOTEL NEWS, The Official Publication of the Florida Hotel & Motel Association, Accommodations, Inc., Box 1529, Tallahassee FL 32302. (904)224-2888. Editor: Mrs. Jayleen Woods. Monthly magazine for managers in the lodging industry (every licensed hotel, motel and resort in Florida). Circ. 6,500. Pays on publication. Byline given. Offers $50 kill fee. Buys all rights and makes work-for-hire assignments. Submit seasonal/holiday material 3 months in advance. Photocopied submissions OK. SASE. Reports in 1 month. Sample copy for 9x12 SAE and 3 first class stamps; writer's guidelines for business size SAE and 1 first class stamp.

Nonfiction: General interest (business, finance, taxes); historical/nostalgic (old Florida hotel reminiscences); how-to (improve management, housekeeping procedures, guest services, security and coping with common hotel problems); humor (hotel-related anecdotes); inspirational (succeeding where others have failed); interview/profile (of unusual hotel personalities); new product (industry-related and non-brand preferential); photo feature (queries only); technical (emerging patterns of hotel accounting, telephone systems, etc.); travel (transportation and tourism trends only—no scenics or site visits); property renovations and maintenance techniques. Buys 10-12 mss/year. Query with clips of published work. Length: 750-2,500 words. Pays $50-200 "depending on type of article and amount of research."

Photos: Send photos with ms. Pays $25-100 for 4x5 color transparencies; $10-15 for 5x7 b&w prints. Captions, model release and identification of subjects required.

Tips: "We prefer feature stories on properties or personalities holding current membership in the Florida Hotel & Motel Association. Memberships and/or leadership brochures are available (SASE) on request. We're open to articles showing how Mom & Dad management copes with inflation and rising costs of energy systems, repairs, renovations, new guest needs and expectations."

FOODSERVICE MARKETING, The Magazine for Independent Operators, EIP, Inc., 2132 Fordem Ave., Madison WI 53704. (608)244-3528. Editor: Jeanette Riechers. Monthly magazine covering management and marketing of independently owned and operated restaurants. Circ. 106,000. Pays on acceptance. No byline given. Offers negotiable kill fee. Buys first North American serial rights. Submit seasonal/holiday material 6 months in advance. Photocopied submissions OK. Computer printout submissions OK; prefers letter quality to dot matrix. SASE. Reports in 2 months. Sample copy $2.50.

Nonfiction: How-to (improve management of independent restaurant; marketing techniques, promotions, etc.); interview/profile (with independent restaurateur; needs a strong angle). "Send us a query on a successful independent restaurateur with an effective marketing program, unusual promotions, interesting design and decor, etc." No restaurant reviews, consumer-oriented material, non-restaurant-oriented management articles. Buys variable number mss/year. Length: open. Pays variable fee.

Photos: State availability of photos. Captions, model release and identification of subjects required. Buys all rights.

‡**THE INN BUSINESS**, Kerch Publications, Ltd., 621 B Mt. Pleasant Rd., Toronto, Ontario, Canada M4S 2M5. Contact: Editor. For resort, hotel and motel owners and managers. Bimonthly. Circ. 10,000. Buys one-time rights. Pays on publication. Reports in 6 weeks. SASE or International Reply Coupons.

Nonfiction: Informational, technical and how-to articles. Canadian content required. Interviews, successful business operations, new products, and merchandising techniques. Length: open. Pays 5¢/word.

INNKEEPING WORLD, Box 15480, Seattle WA 98115. Editor/Publisher: Charles Nolte. 50% freelance written. Emphasizes the lodging industry worldwide. Newsletter published 10 times a year; 8 pages. Circ. 2,000. Pays on acceptance. Buys one-time rights. No byline. Submit seasonal/holiday material 1 month in advance of issue date. SASE. Reports in 4 weeks. Free sample copy and writer's guidelines (provide SASE).

Nonfiction: Articles on "managing," "marketing" and "sales promotion." Buys 20-25 unsolicited mss/ year. Query with "thorough description of article and SASE." Length: 100-1,000 words. Pays 12¢/word. Special reports: "The Guest Speaks"; interviews with well-traveled people, their positive comments on hotels/motels; and "Management"; interviews with successful hotel managers for innkeeping wisdom. Buys 2/issue. Length: 100-1,000 words. Pays 12¢/word.

Columns/Departments: Advertising/Promotion; Marketing; Cutting Expenses; Guest Relations; Staff Relations; successful operation case histories; and news, trends and ideas (for fillers). Buys 2/issue. Length: 50-500 words. Pays 12¢/word.

MEETINGS & CONVENTIONS, Ziff-Davis Publishing Co., 1 Park Ave., New York NY 10016. Editor-in-Chief: Mel Hosansky. 15% freelance written. For association and corporate executives who plan sales meetings, training meetings, annual conventions, incentive travel trips, and any other kind of off-premises meeting. Monthly magazine; 150 pages. Circ. 74,500. Pays on acceptance. Buys first rights. Photocopied submissions and previously published work (if not published in a competing publication) OK. No computer printout or disk submissions. SASE. Reports in 1-2 months.

Nonfiction: "Publication is basically how-to. We tell how to run better meetings; where to hold them, etc. Must be case history, talking about specific meeting." No destination write-ups. Buys 7-10 unsolicited mss/ year. Query. Length: 250-2,000 words. Pays $100-500.

Photos: Uses b&w slides. Query.

RESTAURANT HOSPITALITY, Penton IPC, Penton Plaza, 1111 Chester Ave., Cleveland OH 44114. (216)696-7000. Editor: Stephen Michaelides. Managing Editor: Michael DeLuca. Monthly magazine covering the commercial foodservice industry for owners and operators of independent restaurants, hotel foodservices, and executives of national and regional restaurant chains. Circ. 85,000. Average issue includes 10-12 features. Pays on acceptance. Byline given. Buys exclusive rights. Query first. SASE. Reports in 1 week. Free sample copy for 9x12 SASE.

Nonfiction: Michael DeLuca, managing editor. General interest (articles that advise operators how to run their operations profitably and efficiently); interview (with operators); profile. No restaurant reviews. Buys 20 mss/ year. Query with clips of previously published work and a short bio. Length: 500-1,500 words. Pays $100/ published page.

Photos: Send color photos with manuscript. Captions required.

Tips: "We're accepting fewer queried stories, but assigning more to our regular freelancers. We need new angles on old stories and we like to see pieces on emerging trends, technologies in the restaurant industry. Stories on psychology, consumer behavior, managerial problems and solutions, how-to's on buying insurance, investing (our readers have a high degree of disposable income), design elements. They don't want to read how to open a restaurant or why John Smith is so successful. We are accepting 100-150 word pieces with photos (slides preferred; will accept b&w) for our Restaurant People department. Should be light, humorous, anecdotal." Byline given. Pays $75.

TEXAS FOOD & SERVICE NEWS, (formerly *Chuck Wagon*), Texas Restaurant Association, Box 1429, Austin TX 78767. (512)444-6543. Editor: Kate Fox. Magazine published 10 times/year about the Texas food service industry for restaurant owners and operators in Texas. Circ. 6,700. Pays on acceptance. Byline given. Buys one-time rights. Written queries preferred. Submit seasonal material 2 months in advance. Photocopied submissions OK. Computer printout or disk submissions OK. SASE. Reports in 1 month. Free sample copy.
Nonfiction: Interview, profile, how-to, humor and personal experience. "The magazine spotlights many general categories (economy, energy, labor relations, new products and staff editorials) in short columns. Therefore, we appreciate getting good, terse articles with a how-to-improve-your-business slant. These we prefer with sharp, black and white photos. All articles should be substantiated with plenty of facts or specific examples. Avoid too much vocabulary. Opt for shorter sentences and shorter words." No restaurant critiques. Query. Length: 1,000-1,500 words. Pays $15-50.
Columns/Departments: Send complete ms. Open to suggestions for new columns or departments.
Tips: "All of our readers are business people, seeking to improve their operations. We like to feature specific areas of food service, such as hiring mentally disabled workers; serving health food; computers; and catering to the senior citizen market. The magazine is adopting a more and more professional approach to the food service industry. In other words, articles must contain ideas and information that will make money."

Industrial Operation and Management

Industrial plant managers, executives, distributors and buyers read the journals that follow. Subjects include equipment, supplies, quality control, and production engineering. Some industrial management journals are also listed under the names of specific industries, such as Machinery and Metal Trade. Publications for industrial supervisors are listed in Management and Supervision.

COMPRESSED AIR, 253 E. Washington Ave., Washington NJ 07882. Senior Editor: Robert Seeley. 75% freelance written. Emphasizes general industrial/technology subjects for engineers and managers. Monthly magazine; 48 pages. Circ. 150,000. Buys all rights. SASE. Reports in 4-6 weeks. Free sample copy, editorial schedule, and writer's guidelines; mention *Writer's Market* in request.
Nonfiction: "Articles must be reviewed by experts in the field." How-to (save costs with air power); and historical (engineering). Recent article example: "The Resurgence of Cogeneration" (March 1982). Buys 20 mss/year. Query with clips of previously published work. Pays negotiable fee.
Photos: State availability of photos in query. Payment for 8x10 glossy b&w photos is included in total purchase price. Captions required. Buys all rights.
Tips: "We are presently looking for freelancers with a track record in industrial/technology writing. Editorial schedule is developed well in advance and relies heavily on article ideas from contributors. Resume and samples help. Writers with access to authorities preferred; prefer interviews over library research. The magazine's name doesn't reflect its contents; suggest writers request sample copies."

INDUSTRIAL CHEMICAL NEWS, Bill Communications, 633 3rd Ave., New York NY 10025. (212)986-4800. Editor: Irvin Schwartz. Managing Editor: Pamela Hunt. Monthly magazine covering the scientific, business industrial aspects of chemistry for chemists working in industry. Circ. 40,000. Pays on publication. Byline given. Pays $100 kill fee. Buys all rights. No computer printout or disk submissions. SASE. Reports within weeks. Free sample copy and writer's guidelines.
Nonfiction: Expose (of government or industry matters); interview/profile (related to the chemical industry); personal experience (of a chemist's work life); photo feature (of a chemical development); and technical overviews (chemical or biological). "The features in *ICN* are written in an informative and fresh style. We do not intend to burden our readers with complex technical jargon when the facts can be told more simply and other publications cover research articles. But neither do we want a basic story; we must tell them something new, something they must know. The features emphasize examples and details of how the research was actually accomplished (equipment used, dollars spent, etc.). Always, the emphasis is our readers: How will the industrial chemist learn from the information?" Buys 3-6 unsolicited mss/year. Query with clips of published work. Length: 1,000-3,000 words. Pays $200-500.
Photos: State availability of photos. "It would be helpful if the author could supply the artwork or recommend material that could be used to clearly portray points made in the written material." Buys one-time rights.
Columns/Departments: Book reviews (new books); employment briefs ("news items on chemical careers"); and news ("broad topic of interest to chemists"). Length: 300-3,000 words.

INDUSTRIAL FABRIC PRODUCTS REVIEW, Industrial Fabrics Assoc., Suite 450, 345 Cedar Bldg., St. Paul MN 55101. (612)222-2508. Editor: Brian Becker. Director of Publications: Mike Coughlin. Monthly magazine covering industrial textiles for company owners, salespersons, and researchers in a variety of industrial textile areas. Circ. 6,000. Pays on publication. Byline given. Buys all rights. Submit seasonal/holiday material 4 months in advance. Simultaneous queries, and photocopied and previously published submissions OK. SASE. Reports in 2 weeks. Sample copy free "after query and phone conversation."
Nonfiction: Technical, marketing, and other topics "related to any aspect of industrial fabric industry from fiber to finished fabric product." Special issues include new products, industrial products and equipment. No historical or apparel oriented articles. Buys 12 mss/year. Query with phone number. Length: 1,200-3,000 words. Pays $75/published page.
Photos: State availability of photos. Reviews 8x10 b&w glossy prints. Pay is negotiable. Model release and identification of subjects required. Buys one-time rights.

INDUSTRIAL MANAGEMENT, Clifford/Elliot Ltd., 277 Lakeshore Rd., E., Oakville, Ontario, Canada L6J 6J3. (416)842-2884. Editor: Carol Radford. Managing Editor: Jackie Roth. Monthly magazine for Canada's manufacturing industries providing "management information and innovations in the areas of industrial and labor relations, product development, new production technology, motivaton, communications, etc." Circ. 21,000. Pays on acceptance. Byline given. Offers 50% kill fee. Buys first North American serial rights. Simultaneous queries and photocopied submissions OK. Reports in 2 weeks on queries, 1 month on mss. Free sample copy and writer's guidelines.
Nonfiction: How-to (management, productivity improvement, problem solving); interview/profile (industry leaders); new product. "All articles must have a manufacturing management angle and must be written by CAnadian freelancers." Buys 15-20 mss/year. Query. Length: 1,000-3,000. Pays $400-800.

INDUSTRY WEEK, Penton/IPC, Inc., 1111 Chester Ave., Cleveland OH 44114, (216)696-7000. Editor-in-Chief: Stanley Modic. 5-10% freelance written. Emphasizes manufacturing and related industries for top or middle management (administrating, production, engineering, finance, purchasing or marketing) throughout industry. Biweekly magazine; 120 pages. Circ. 300,000. Pays on publication. Buys all rights. Byline given depending on length of article. Phone queries OK. Submit seasonal or holiday material 3 months in advance. Simultaneous and photocopied submissions OK. SASE. Reports in 4 weeks. Sample copy $2.
Nonfiction: Robert W. Gardner, managing editor. How-to and informational articles (should deal with areas of interest to manager audience, e.g., developing managerial skills or managing effectively). "No product news or case histories, please." Length: 1,000-4,000 words. Pays $300/first 1,000 words; $100/additional 1,000 words. Buys 5-10/year. Query. No product news or clippings.
Photos: Nick Dankovich, art director. B&w and color purchased with ms or on assignment. Query. Pays $35 minimum. Model release required.

INSULATION OUTLOOK, National Insulation Contractors Association, Suite 410, 1025 Vermont NW, Washington DC 20005. (202)783-6278. Managing Editor: M. Brown. Monthly magazine about general business, commercial and industrial insulation for the insulation industry in the United States and abroad. Publication is read by engineers, specifiers, buyers, contractors, and union members in the industrial and commercial insulation field. There is also representative distribution to public utilities, and energy-related industries. Pays on publication. Byline given. Buys first rights. Phone queries OK. Written queries should be short and simple, with samples of writing attached. Submit seasonal material 6 months in advance. Simultaneous, photocopied and previously published submissions OK. SASE. Sample copy $2; free writer's guidelines. "Give us a call. If there seems to be compatibility, we will send a free issue sample so the writer can see directly the type of publication he or she is dealing with."
Columns/Departments: Query. Pays $50-300.

PLANT MANAGEMENT & ENGINEERING, MacLean Hunter Bldg; 777 Bay St., Toronto, Ontario, Canada M5W 1A7. Editor: William Roebuck. For Canadian plant managers and engineers. Monthly magazine. Circ. 26,000. Pays on acceptance. Buys first Canadian rights. SAE and International Reply Coupons. Computer printout submissions OK; prefers letter quality to dot matrix. Reports in 2-3 weeks. Free sample copy with SAE only.
Nonfiction: How-to, technical and management technique articles. Must have Canadian slant. No generic articles that appear to be rewritten from textbooks. Buys less than 20 unsolicited mss/year. Query. Pays 12¢/word minimum.
Photos: State availability of photos with query. Pays $25-50 for b&w prints; $50-100 for 2¼x2¼ or 35mm color transparencies. Captions preferred. Buys one-time rights.
Tips: Query first by letter. "Read the magazine. Know the Canadian readers' special needs. Case histories and interviews only—no theoretical pieces. We have incorporated *Modern Power and Engineering Magazine* (effective April 1983) and as a result will expand our plant engineering and technical content."

PRODUCTION ENGINEERING, Penton Plaza, Cleveland OH 44114. (216)696-7000. Managing Editor: Donald E. Hegland. Executive Editor: John McRainey. 50% freelance written. For "men and women in production engineering—the engineers who plan, design and improve manufacturing operations." Monthly magazine; 100 pages. Circ. 95,000. Pays on publication. Buys exclusive North American first rights. Byline given "unless, by prior arrangement, an author contributed a segment of a broader article, he might not be bylined." Phone queries OK. Photocopied submissions OK, if exclusive. Computer printout submissions OK. SASE. Reports in 2 weeks. Free sample copy and writer's guidelines.
Nonfiction: How-to (engineering, data for engineers); personal experience (from *very* senior production or manufacturing engineers only); and technical (technical news or how-to). "We're interested in solid, hard-hitting technical articles on the gut issues of manufacturing. Not case histories, but no-fat treatments of manufacturing concepts, innovative manufacturing methods, and state-of-the-art procedures. Our readers also enjoy articles that detail a variety of practical solutions to some specific, everyday manufacturing headache." Buys 2 mss/issue. Query. Length: 800-3,000 words. Pays $25-150.

PURCHASING EXECUTIVE'S BULLETIN, Bureau of Business Practice, 24 Rope Ferry Rd., Waterford CT 06386. (203)442-4365. Editor: Claire Sherman. Managing Editor: Wayne Muller. For purchasing managers and purchasing agents. Semimonthly newsletter; 4 pages. Circ. 5,500. Pays on acceptance. Buys all rights. Submit seasonal/holiday material 3 months in advance. Reports in 2 weeks. Free sample copy and writer's guidelines.
Nonfiction: How-to (better cope with problems confronting purchasing executives); and direct interviews detailing how purchasing has overcome problems and found better ways of handling departments. No derogatory material about a company; no writer's opinions; no training or minority purchasing articles. "We don't want material that's too elementary (things any purchasing executive already knows)." Buys 2-3 mss/issue. Query. Length: 750-1,000 words.
Tips: "Make sure that a release is obtained and attached to a submitted article."

‡QUALITY CONTROL SUPERVISOR'S BULLETIN, Natonal Foremen's Institute, 24 Rope Ferry Rd., Waterford CT 06386. (800)243-0876. Editor: Steven J. Finn. Biweekly newsletter for quality control supervisors. Circ. 10,000. Pay on acceptance. No byline given. Buys all rights. SASE. Reports in 2 weeks on queries; 1 month on mss. Free sample copy and writer's guidelines.
Nonfiction: How-to and interview. "Articles with a strong how-to slant that make use of direct quotes whenever possible." Buys 70 mss/year. Query. Length: 800-1,100 words. Pays 8-14¢/word.
Tips: "Write for our freelancer guidelines and follow them closely. We're looking for steady freelancers (especially those from Canada and the western US) to whom we can provide leads on a regular basis."

SEMICONDUCTOR INTERNATIONAL, Cahners Publishing Co., 1350 E. Touhy Ave., Box 5080, Des Plaines IL 60018. (312)635-8800. Editor: Donald J. Levinthal. Monthly magazine covering semiconductor industry processing, assembly and testing technology subjects for semiconductor industry processing engineers and management. "Technology stories that cover all phases of semiconductor product manufacturing and testing are our prime interest." Circ. 26,000. Pays on publication. "News items are paid for upon acceptance." Byline given. Buys all rights and makes work-for-hire assignments. Computer printout submissions OK. Reports in 2 weeks. Free sample copy and writer's guidelines.
Nonfiction: Technical and news pertaining to the semiconductor industry in the US and overseas. No "articles that are commercial in nature or product oriented." Buys 50 mss/year (including feature articles and news). Query with "your interest and capabilities" or send complete ms. Length: 2,500 words maximum.
Photos: State availability of photos or send photos with ms. Reviews 8x10 b&w prints. Captions and identification of subjects required.
Columns/Departments: "News of the semiconductor industry as it pertains to technology trends is of interest. Of special interest is news of the semiconductor industry in foreign countries such as Japan, England, Germany, France, Netherlands." Buys 30-40 mss/year. Query. Length: 200-1,500 words. Pays 15¢/word for accepted, edited copy.

WEIGHING & MEASUREMENT, Key Markets Publishing Co., Box 5867, Rockford IL 61125. (815)399-6970. Editor: David M. Mathieu. For users of industrial scales and meters. Bimonthly magazine; 32 pages. Circ. 15,000. Pays on acceptance. Buys all rights. Pays 20% kill fee. Byline given. Reports in 2 weeks. Free sample copy.
Nonfiction: Interview (with presidents of companies); personal opinion (guest editorials on government involvement in business, etc.); profile (about users of weighing and measurement equipment); and technical. Buys 25 mss/year. Query on technical articles; submit complete ms for general interest material. Length: 750-2,500 words. Pays $45-125.

WIRE BUSINESS, (formerly *Rod, Wire & Fastener*), Business Information Services, Inc., 20 Pine Mountain Rd., Ridgefield CT 06877. (203)748-6529. Editorial Director: Dick Callahan. Bimonthly magazine covering wire and fiber optics for middle and upper management. Emphasis is on business and personalities. Circ. 12,000. Pays on acceptance. Byline given. Buys one-time rights. Reports in 2 months on queries; 3 weeks on mss. Free sample copy.

Nonfiction: Interview/profile, photo feature, and technical. "No how-to or general business topics." Buys 24 mss/year. Query with clips of published work ("preferably bylined"). Length: 1,000-5,000 words. Pays $300-500/article.

Photos: State availability of photos. Pays $50-100 for b&w contact sheets or 5x7 prints.

Tips: "We are most open to profiles of individuals or companies in the wire business. Writers do not have to have a technical background. We want *Forbes-* or *Barron's*-type articles stressing business aspects of companies."

Insurance

BUSINESS INSURANCE, 740 N. Rush Street, Chicago IL 60611. Editor: Kathryn J. McIntyre. For "corporate risk, employee benefit and financial executives, insurance brokers and agents, and insurance company executives interested in commercial insurance, risk and benefit financing, safety, security, employee benefits." Special issues on self-insurance, safety, pensions, health and life benefits, brokers, reinsurance, international insurance. Weekly. Circ. 41,000. Buys all rights. Pays negotiable kill fee. Byline given. Buys 50 mss/year. Pays on publication. Submit seasonal or special material 2 months in advance. Reports in 2 weeks. Query. SASE.

Nonfiction: "We publish material on corporate insurance and employee benefit programs and related subjects. We take everything from the buyers' point of view, rather than that of the insurance company, broker or consultant who is selling something. Items on insurance companies, insurance brokers, property/liability insurance, union contract (benefit) settlements, group life/health/medical plans, of interest—provided the *commercial* insurance or benefits angle is clear. Special emphasis on corporate risk management and employee benefits administration requires that freelancers discuss with us their proposed articles. Length is subject to discussion with contributor." Pays $7/column inch or negotiated fee.

Tips: "Send a detailed proposal including story angle and description of sources."

LINES MAGAZINE, Reliance Insurance Co., 4 Penn Center, Philadelphia PA 19103. Editor: Patricia McLaughlin. 30% freelance written. Emphasizes insurance and business for "Reliance employees and independent insurance agents interested in business trends and opinion." Quarterly magazine; 28 pages. Circ. 11,000. Pays on acceptance. Copyrighted. Submit seasonal/holiday material 2 months in advance of issue date. SASE. Reports in 2 weeks. Free sample copy; mention *Writer's Market* in request.

Nonfiction: Features that relate to insurance, more general pieces about business, and usually 1-2 general interest pieces per issue. Buys 10 mss/year. Query with clips of previously published work. Length: 800-2,000 words.

Fillers: Newsbriefs for wraparound, original or clipped from a newspaper or magazine. Length: 50-200 words.

‡PROFESSIONAL AGENT MAGAZINE, Professional Insurance Agents, 400 N. Washington St., Alexandria VA 22314. (703)836-9340. Editor/Publisher: Janice J. Artandi. Monthly magazine covering insurance/ small business for independent insurance agents. Circ. 40,000. Pays on acceptance. Byline given. Buys exclusive rights in the industry. Submit seasonal/holiday material 3 months in advance. Simultaneous queries, and simultaneous, photocopied, and previously published submissions OK. SASE. Reports in 1 month. Sample copy for SAE.

Nonfiction: Expose, general interest, historical/nostalgic, how-to, inspirational, interview/profile, photo feature, technical. Special issues on life insurance and computer interface. Buys 12 mss/year. Query with published clips or send complete ms. Length: 1,000-3,000 words. Pays $100-300.

Photos: State availability of photos. Pays $35-200 for 5x7 b&w prints; $50-300 for 35mm color transparencies. Captions, model release and identification of subjects required. Buys one-time rights.

Columns/Departments: Book reviews. Query with published clips or send complete ms. Length: 1,000 words minimum.

International Affairs

These publications cover global relations, international trade, economic analysis and philosophy for business executives and government officials involved in foreign affairs. Consumer publications on related subjects are listed in Politics and World Affairs.

‡**AFRICUS, Africa's International Business Magazine**, TransNational Publications, Box 43587, Washington DC 20010. (202)234-7800. Executive Editor: Justice Zormelo. Senior Editor: Dominic Kwang Ntube. Publisher: Jeffrey Jackson. Bimonthly trade journal. TransNational Publications also publishes *Trade Leads Bulletin* (monthly), *Africa Business & Economic Review* (weekly), and *Buyer's Guide* (annual). Provides economic analysis and business and trade leads, and covers US and international business activities. Buys one-time rights. Pays on publication. Byline given. Previously published submissions OK. Free sample copy and writer's guidelines with postage. Query with clips of published work or send complete ms to executive editor.
Nonfiction: Interview/profile, new product, and how-to articles on cultural differences. Opinion and personal experience on development economics and international economics on US and African markets. Also articles on tourism, technology, banking, and the transfer system from the United States to an African country. No fiction, poetry or politics. Length: varies. Pays negotiable rates.
Photos: Writers should send photos with accompanying query or ms. Captions and identification of subjects required.
Fillers: Uses clippings from other magazines and newspapers.
Tips: "Writers should be aware of the focus of the magazine. Our focus is to open up the African markets for the United States and to open up the US markets for Africa." Writers should request the schedule of monthly focuses. "A good knowledge of Africa," an international economics and finance background, and a general education on Africa and economics will be an advantage for writers submitting articles to *Africus*.

PROBLEMS OF COMMUNISM, US Information Agency, P/PMP, Room 402, 400 C St., SW, Washington DC 20547. (202)485-2230. Editor: Paul A. Smith Jr. For scholars and decision-makers in all countries of the world with higher education and a serious interest in foreign area studies and international relations. Circ. 27,000. Not copyrighted. Pays 20% kill fee. Byline given. Buys 60-70 mss/year. Pays on acceptance. Free sample copy. Photocopied submissions OK. Reports in 3 months.
Nonfiction: "*Problems of Communism* is one of a very few journals devoted to objective, dispassionate discourse on a highly unobjective, passionately debated phenomenon: communism. It is maintained as a forum in which qualified observers can contribute to a clearer understanding of the sources, nature and direction of change in the areas of its interest. It has no special emphasis or outlook and represents no partisan point of view. Standards of style are those appropriate to the field of international scholarship and journalism. We use intellectually rigorous studies of East-West relations, and/or related political, economic, social and strategic trends in the USSR, China and their associated states and movements. Length is usually 5,000 words. Essay reviews of 1,500 words cover new books offering significant information and analysis. Emphasis throughout *Problems of Communism* is on original research, reliability of sources and perceptive insights. We do not publish political statements or other forms of advocacy or apologetics for particular forms of belief." Query or submit complete ms. Pays $600/article; $250/essay reviews.
Photos: Pays minimum $45 for b&w glossy prints.

Jewelry

AMERICAN JEWELRY MANUFACTURER, 825 7th Ave., 8th Floor, New York NY 10019. (212)245-7555. Editor: Steffan Aletti. For jewelry manufacturers, as well as manufacturers of supplies and tools for the jewelry industry; their representatives, wholesalers and agencies. Monthly. Circ. 5,000. Buys all rights (with exceptions). Byline given. Free sample copy and writer's guidelines. Will consider photocopied submissions. Computer printout or disk submissions OK. Submit seasonal material 3 months in advance. Reports in 1 month. Query. SASE.
Nonfiction and Photos: "Topical articles on manufacturing; company stories; economics (e.g., rising gold prices). Story must inform or educate the manufacturer. Occasional special issues on timely topics, e.g., gold; occasional issues on specific processes in casting and plating. We reject material that is not specifically pointed at our industry; e.g., articles geared to jewelry retailing or merchandising, not to manufacturers." Informational, how-to, interview, profile, historical, exposé, successful business operations, new product, merchandising techniques, technical. Buys 5-10 unsolicited mss/year. Length: open. Payment "usually around

$50/printed page.'' B&w photos purchased with ms. 5x7 minimum.
Tips: ''Query first; we have accepted some general business articles, but not many.''

CANADIAN JEWELLER, 777 Bay St., Toronto, Ontario, Canada M5W 1A7. Editor: Simon Hally. Monthly magazine for members of the jewelry trade, primarily retailers. Circ. 6,000. Pays on acceptance. Buys first Canadian serial rights. SAE and International Reply Coupons.
Nonfiction: Wants ''stories on the jewelry industry internationally. No stories on the US jewelry business.'' Query. Length: 200-2,000 words. Pays $40-500.
Photos: Reviews 5x7 and 8x10 b&w prints and 35mm and 2¼x2¼ color transparencies. ''We pay more if usable photos accompany ms. Payment is based on space used in the book including both text and photos.''

THE DIAMOND REGISTRY BULLETIN, 30 W. 47th St., New York NY 10036. Editor-in-Chief: Joseph Schlussel. 15% freelance written. Monthly newsletter. Pays on publication. Buys all rights. Submit seasonal/holiday material 1 month in advance of issue date. Simultaneous and previously published submissions OK. SASE. Reports in 3 weeks. Sample copy $5.
Nonfiction: Prevention advice (on crimes against jewelers); how-to (ways to increase sales in diamonds, improve security, etc.); and interview (of interest to diamond dealers or jewelers). Submit complete ms. Length: 50-500 words. Pays $10-150.
Tips: ''We seek ideas to increase sales of diamonds.''

WATCH AND CLOCK REVIEW, 2403 Champa St., Denver CO 80205. (303)296-1600. Managing Editor: Jayne L. Barrick. 20% freelance written. The magazine of watch/clock sales and service. Monthly magazine; 68 pages. Circ. 16,000. Pays on publication. Buys first rights. Byline given. Submit seasonal/holiday material 3 months in advance of issue date. SASE. Reports in 2-3 weeks. Free sample copy.
Nonfiction: Articles on successful watch/clock manufacturers and retailers; merchandising and display; profiles of industry leaders. Buys 15 mss/year. Query. Length: 1,000-2,000 words. Pays $50-150.
Photos: Submit photo material with accompanying ms. No additional payment for b&w glossy prints. Captions preferred. Buys first rights. Model release required.
Columns/Departments: Buys 7/issue. Pays $50-150. Open to suggestions for new columns/departments.
Tips: ''Brevity is helpful in a query. Find the right subject—an interesting clock shop, a jewelry store with unique watch displays, a street clock of antiquarian interest, etc.''

Journalism

Both paying and nonpaying markets of the writing trade are included here. Writers wishing to contribute material to these publications should query about requirements before submitting their work.

BOOK ARTS REVIEW, The Center for Book Arts, 15 Bleecker St., New York NY 10012. (212)460-9768. Managing Editor: Bryan Johnson. Emphasizes bookbinding and exploring the arts of the book. Quarterly newsletter; 6 pages. Circ. 1,000. Pays in copies. ''Rights revert to artist.'' Byline given. Submit seasonal/holiday material 3 months in advance. Simultaneous, photocopied and previously published submissions OK. Computer printout submissions OK. Reports in 2 months. SASE.
Nonfiction: Reviews (exhibitions, lectures, conferences, shows, etc. dealing with printing, bookbinding, papermaking, calligraphy or preservation); interview (with book artists) and technical (e.g., ''William Blake's Method of Printing''). No censorship, fiction or material dealing with writing. Query. Pays in copies.

‡**BOOK DEALERS WORLD**, American Bookdealers Exchange, Box 2525, La Mesa CA 92041. (619)698-8970. Editor: Al Galasso. Quarterly magazine covering writing, self-publishing and marketing books by mail. Circ. 15,000. Pays on publication. Byline given. Buys one-time rights. Simultaneous and previously published submissions OK. SASE. Reports in 1 month. Sample copy $1.
Nonfiction: Book excerpts (how-to, mail order, direct mail, publishing); how-to (home business by mail, advertising); interview/profile (of successful self-publishers). Positive articles on self-publishing, new writing angles, marketing, etc. Buys 10 mss/year. Send complete ms. Length: 1,000-1,500 words. Pays $20-40.
Columns/Departments: Print Perspective (about new magazines and newsletters); From The Source (items of interest to mail order entrepreneurs). Buys 20 mss/year. Send complete ms. Length: 500-1,000 words. Pays $10-20.
Fillers: Clippings. ''Fillers to do with writing, publishing or books.'' Buys 6/year. Length: 100-250 words. Pays $5-10.

Close-up

Thomas Middleton, Writer

"Writers have a responsibility to language," says *Saturday Review* columnist, Thomas Middleton. "This is not to say that there's anything wrong with using dialect or dreadful grammar—if you're writing about someone who uses it. But to use language sloppily is a shame."

It is precisely this philosophy—nurtured by a "father who imbued me with a love of language"—that Middleton brings to his columns on language in The *Los Angeles Times* and *Verbatim, The Language Quarterly*, as well as *SR*. Middleton has publicly cultivated his language habit since he started doing double-crostics for *SR* in 1966.

It is in his columns, however, that he looks at language critically. "It does change; you can't hold it still. But I do believe in knowing the rules of how grammar works and how language works. When you know the rules, then you can break them with common sense. I'm clearly at odds with the National Council of Teachers of English on this," says Middleton. "They think the rules are crippling to creativity. I don't think so at all—any more than I think learning to dance is crippling to creativity."

Middleton finds one way to learn what "works" in language is to study the good writers. "I have savored such writers as Thurber, E.B. White and Ring Lardner. I'm a slow reader and often play the parts I'm reading. One of my objections to a lot of modern writing is that so much of it is overwritten. And I have a sneaky feeling that the people who overwrite are speed readers. They don't have a chance to savor phrases. They're whipping along getting the sense of the thing. We slow readers come along a wonderful phrase and think, 'Isn't that terrific?' This kind of natural outgrowth of being a stupid reader has helped me a lot with my own writing."

In addition to reading the language, Middleton listens to it. Column ideas come from everyday conversations, letters from readers, and even the newspaper. He tells of the time he got a column idea from the Sunday *Peanuts* comic strip. "Peppermint Patty was telling Marcy that she'd seen the word 'fiddlesticks' written on her father's paper and she didn't know what it meant. That got me started on a column about words and phrases that die out."

Middleton currently puts his ideas to paper via a TRS-80, Model 3 computer—"a wonderful, new experience in writing for someone who has never been able to compose at the typewriter." But for all the positive, technological innovation in the writing/publishing field these days, Middleton is aware of a disturbing trend. "I'm depressed by the appalling lack of editorial expertise. Books coming out of the best publishing houses in the United States have the most terrible solecisms in them. Obviously, nobody's catching these things. I have a feeling that even proofreaders these days are speed readers. And you just can't be a speed proofreader.

"I think we (writers, editors, publishers) all have a duty to language. And I'm disturbed by a kind of sloppiness that's permitted. Language survives mostly through written records. We affect that language, and what we do with it is terribly important."

Tips: "In the year ahead we'll be using more success-oriental pieces on self-publishing and marketing books along with more in-depth interviews."

THE CALIFORNIA PUBLISHER, Suite 1040, 1127 11th St., Sacramento CA 95814. (916)443-5991. Editor: Jackie Nava. Monthly tabloid read by publishers, journalism teachers, editors and managers in newspaper publishing in California. Byline given. Computer printout (letter quality only) submissions OK.
Nonfiction: In-depth stories or articles designed to inform and amuse California newspaper publishers. Sample topics include: newsprint shortage, changing role of papers, historical profiles on California journalism greats, success stories, role of minorities in the newspaper field, profiles on California newspapers, and technological advances. No general "humorous" material. "If it isn't specific to *California* journalism, we don't want it." Query. Length: 2,000 words maximum. Pays $25-30.
Photos: Reviews b&w glossy prints.
Tips: "Go on; query us! Stories used will be read by all the newspaper publishers who count in the state of California. We'd like to showcase first-effort, good writing talent."

CANADIAN AUTHOR & BOOKMAN, Canadian Authors Association, Suite 412, 131 Bloor St. W., Toronto, Ontario, Canada M5S 1R1. Editor: Anne Osborne. 75% freelance written. "For writers—all ages, all levels of experience." Quarterly magazine; 32 pages. Circ. 5,000. Pays on publication. Buys first Canadian rights. Byline given. Written queries only. Computer printout submissions OK. SASE (Canadian stamps); sample copy $3.50.
Nonfiction: How-to (on writing, selling; the specifics of the different genres—what they are and how to write them); informational (the writing scene—who's who and what's what); interview (on writers, mainly leading ones, but also those with a story that can help others write and sell more often); and opinion. No personal, lightweight writing experiences; no fillers. Query with immediate pinpointing of topic, length (if ms is ready), and writer's background. Length: 800-1,500 words. Pays 1¢/word.
Photos: We're after an interesting-looking magazine and graphics are a decided help. State availability of photos with query. Offers no additional payment for b&w photos accepted with ms. Buys one-time rights.
Poetry: High quality. "Major poets publish with us—others need to be as good." Buys 60 poems/year. Pays $2.
Tips: "We dislike 1) material that condescends to its reader; 2) articles that advocate on adversarial approach to writer-editor relationships. We agree that there is a time and place for such an approach, but good sense should prevail."

CHILDREN'S LITERATURE, The Children's Literature Foundation, Box 370, Windham Center CT 06280. (203)456-1900. Editor: Francelia Butler. Managing Editor: John C. Wandell. Annual journal; 250-300 pages. Circ. 3,500. Pays in reprints. Byline given. Phone queries OK. Submit seasonal/holiday material 1 year in advance. SASE. Reports in 1 month.
Nonfiction: Scholarly or critical essays. Manuscripts must conform to MLA Handbook. Uses 20 mss/issue. Query or send complete ms. Length: 7,500 words.
Photos: State availability of photos. Uses 4x5 or 8x10 b&w glossy prints. Captions and permission to publish required.
Columns/Departments: Book Review Articles (send to David L. Greene, Chairman, English Department, Piedmont College, Demorest GA). Uses 20/year. Query. Length: 3,000 words. Open to suggestions for new columns/departments.

‡**THE CHRISTIAN WRITER, The Professional Writing Magazine for Christians**, Box 5650, Lakeland FL 33803. (813)644-3548. Editor: Thomas A Noton. Managing Editor: Karen Hull. Monthly writing magazine aimed at a Christian audience. "We reach Christians who desire to write or are writers. Our aim is to help create the professional approach to this craft." Estab. 1982. Circ. 10,000. Offers no payment. Byline given. Acquires one-time rights. Submit seasonal/holiday material 4 months in advance. Simultaneous queries, and photocopied submissions OK. SASE. Reports in 2 weeks on queries; 4 weeks on mss. Free sample copy and writer's guidelines.
Nonfiction: How-to (specifics on authoring, selling, related subjects); humor (rare); inspirational (limited); interview/profile (top Christian authors); new product (electronic writing); personal experience (some). Material on conferences, workshops, clubs, etc. for annual "Service Guide. We receive too many 'This Is My Life' articles. We want more specific articles helping others overcome specialized problems in authoring." Buys 36 mss/year. Query with published clips. Length: 1,200-3,500 words. No payment.
Tips: "We're looking for freelancers who have answers for specific problems in writing, marketing, querying, rewriting, editing or self-publishing. We are only interested in professionalism as it applies to the craft of writing. Although we use the Christian influence, we do not deal with it directly. We deal with the craft, its problems and answers."

COLLEGE PRESS REVIEW, E.W. Scripps School of Journalism, Ohio University, Athens OH 45701. (614)594-5013. Editor: J. William Click. For members of College Media Advisers, staffs, editors and faculty advisers; staff members of student publications, journalism professors and others interested in the student communication media. Quarterly. Circ. 1,500. Acquires all rights. No payment. Sample copy $2.50; free writer's guidelines. Send two copies of manuscript. Photocopied submissions OK. No simultaneous submissions. Reports in 1-3 months. Query or submit complete ms. SASE.
Nonfiction and Photos: Articles by, about, and of interest to college publication staffs, editors, and faculty advisers. Articles should focus on the editing, advising and production of college newspapers, magazines and yearbooks. "We like to use articles on research and thoughtful opinion in the student communications media and related areas. We also like to use features on journalism techniques. The writer should write in a readable style. We will accept no manuscripts that read like term papers." Topical subjects of interest include use of new technology on campus publications; case studies of censorship problems at private schools; tips on purchasing new equipment; improving graphic appearance; improving fact gathering and writing. No first-person or ego trip pieces. Length: 3,000 words maximum. B&w glossy photos used with ms. Captions required.

COLUMBIA JOURNALISM REVIEW, 700 Journalism Bldg., Columbia University, New York NY 10027. (212)280-5595. Managing Editor: Gloria Cooper. "We welcome queries concerning media issues and performance. *CJR* also publishes book reviews. We emphasize in-depth reporting, critical analysis, and good writing. All queries are read by editors."

CREATIVE YEARS With Writer's Opportunities, (formerly *Writer's Opportunities*), Coronado Publishers, #40, 2490 SW 14th Dr., Gainesville FL 32608. (904)373-7445. Editor: Eloise Cozens Henderson. Assistant Editor: Natalie Cornell. Bimonthly magazine for new and unpublished writers. Circ. 2,000. Pays on publication. Buys one-time rights. Submit seasonal/holiday material 3 months in advance. Simultaneous submissions OK. SASE. Reports in 3 weeks on queries; 3 months on mss. Sample copy $2; writer's guidelines for SASE.
Nonfiction: General interest, historical/nostalgic, interview, humor, inspirational, opinion, personal experience. "We feature regular tips on writing nostalgia, short stories, articles, recipes, poetry, and are open to other subjects." No sports, space, obscenity, profanity, or liquor/drug related articles. Buys 30 mss/year. Length: 450-500 words. Send complete ms. Pays presently in copies only.
Fiction: Humorous, historical, religious. No sports, space, obscenity, profanity, liquor/drug related mss. Buys 30 mss/year. Length: 450-500 words. Send complete ms. Pays in copies only.
Poetry: Light verse, traditional. No far out, agnostic, atheist, etc. poetry. Buys 12/year. Pays in copies only.
Tips: Especially needs Biblical quiz and other puzzle material.

EDITOR & PUBLISHER, 575 Lexington Ave., New York NY 10022. (212)752-7050. Editor: Robert U. Brown. For newspaper publishers, editors, executives, employees and others in communications, marketing, advertising, etc. Weekly magazine; 60 pages. Circ. 29,000. Pays on publication. Sample copy $1. SASE.
Nonfiction: Department Editor: Jerome H. Walker Jr. Uses newspaper business articles and news items; also newspaper personality features and printing technology. Query.
Fillers: "Amusing typographical errors found in newspapers." Pays $2.

EMPIRE, for the SF Writer, c/o Unique Graphics, 1025 55th St., Oakland CA 94608. (415)655-3024. Editor: Millea Kenin. Quarterly magazine covering writing, editing, and publishing science fiction and fantasy. "*Empire's* aim is to assist, entertain, and inform science fiction and fantasy writers." Circ. 1,500. Pays on publication. Byline given. Acquires first English language serial rights. Simultaneous queries and photocopied submissions OK. "We are completely receptive to computer printout submissions as long as they are NOT dot matrix. Dot matrix printouts will be returned unread." SASE. Reports in 1 month. Sample copy $2, payable to Unique Graphics.
Nonfiction: Expose (of publishing industry); how-to (on specific writing techniques and skills); humor (about the writing life; "If you find any, send it to us."); inspirational (what to do after the electricity has been cut off; how to believe in yourself; how to learn from rejections); interview/profile (of writers, editors, agents, publishers, filmmakers); personal experience ("how I wrote and sold"); technical (science fact with application to science fiction). "We use articles about writing, editing, and publishing science fiction; our material is written by professional SF writers for would-be professional SF writers. We are not interested in general articles for the beginning writer. We take a practical 'nuts-and-bolts approach." Buys 32 mss/year. Send complete ms. Length: 1,000-3,500 words. Pays in copies and a one-year subscription. Pay negotiable to regular contributors.
Fiction: Crazy Diamonds. "Each issue contains 1 story written by a subscriber and 3 critiques of the story by professional SF writers. We use no other fiction." Buys 4 mss/year. Length: 3,500 words maximum, shorter preferred. Pays in copies and subscription.
Poetry: "Short humorous verse used as fillers. Must be SF-related."
Tips: "There has been a change of ownership. No official changes of policy are contemplated, but the new edi-

torial staff has its own viewpoint. (We always reply with a personal note, so you'll soon learn what we're looking for.)''

FEED/BACK, THE CALIFORNIA JOURNALISM REVIEW, 1600 Holloway, San Francisco CA 94132. (415)469-2086. Editor: David M. Cole. 40-50% freelance written. For the working journalist, the journalism student, the journalism professor and the journalistic layman. Magazine; 60 pages. Quarterly. Circ. 1,750. By-line given. Pays in subscriptions and copies. Sample copy $1. Will consider photocopied and simultaneous submissions. Reports in 1 month. Query. SASE.
Nonfiction and Photos: In-depth views of California journalism. Criticism of journalistic trends throughout the country, but with a local angle. Reviews of books concerning journalism. Informational, interview, profile, humor, historical, think pieces, expose, nostalgia, spot news, successful (or unsuccessful) business operations, new product, technical; all must be related to journalism. "Articles must focus on the news media and be of interest to professional journalists—they are our audience. We like articles that examine press performance—strengths and weaknesses; we also like personality articles on offbeat or little-known editors and journalists who escape national attention." Rejects articles that are not documented, or those in which the subject matter is not pertinent, or those which show personal prejudice not supported by evidence. Length: 1,000-5,000 words. B&w glossies (8x10 or 11x14) used with or without mss. Pays in subscriptions and/or copies, tearsheets for all material.

FOLIO: The Magazine for Magazine Management, 125 Elm St., Box 697, New Canaan CT 06840. Editor-in-Chief: J. Hanson. Mostly staff written. Computer printout or disk submissions OK; prefers letter quality to dot matrix printouts.
Tips: "In the year ahead we will have more editorial pages and more *assigned* freelance work."

FREELANCE WRITER'S REPORT, The Newsletter for Florida Freelance Writers, Cassell Communications Inc., Florida Freelance Writers Association, 214 Solaz Ave., Port St. Lucie FL 33452. (305)878-2328. Editor: Dana K. Cassell. Monthly newsletter covering writing and marketing advice for freelance writers. Estab. 1982. Pays on publication. Byline given. Buys first North American serial, simultaneous, first or second serial (reprint) rights. "We retain reprint rights for FFWA, writer may resell elsewhere." Submit seasonal/holiday material 2 months in advance. Simultaneous queries and simultaneous, photocopied, and previously published work OK. Computer printout submissions OK. SASE. Reports in 1 month. Sample copy $2.50.
Nonfiction: Book excerpts (on writing profession); how-to (market, write, research); interview (of writers or editors); new product (only those pertaining to writers); photojournalism; promotion and administration of a writing business. No humor, fiction or poetry. Buys 36 mss/year. Query or send complete ms. Length: 750 words maximum. Pays 10¢/word.
Tips: "Write in terse newsletter style, eliminate flowery adjectives and edit mercilessly. Send something that will help Florida writers increase profits from writing output—must be a proven method."

‡THE INKLING, Inkling Publications, Inc., Box 128, Alexandria MN 56308. (612)762-2020. Editors: Marilyn Bailey and Betty Ulrich. Managing Editor: John Hall. Monthly newsletter covering advice, guidance and inspiration for writers and poets. "The *INKLING* is both informative and motivational, providing a forum for writers. 'Well-written' articles and timely market news are the main criteria." Circ. 2,400. Pays on publication. Byline given. Buys one-time rights. Submit seasonal/holiday material 3 months in advance. Simultaneous queries OK. SASE. Reports in 2 weeks on queries; 1 month on mss. Sample copy $2; writer's guidelines for business-sized SAE and 1 first class stamp.
Nonfiction: How-to (on the business and approach to writing); inspirational; interview/profile; opinion; personal experience. "The Best Of *INKLING*" annaul will print material previously published in monthly *INKLING*'s. Buys 6-10 mss/year. Send complete ms. Length: 500-1,200 words. Pays $15-50.
Poetry: Avant-garde, free verse, haiku, light verse, traditional. "The *INKLING* runs two poetry contests each year—spring and fall. Winner and 2nd place cash prizes and two Honorable Mentions." Buys 4 poems/year. Submit maximum 3 poems. Length: 25 lines maximum. Pays $15-25.
Tips: "Query first with an outline. Articles must be *well* written and slanted toward the business (or commitment) of writing and/or being a writer." Break in with informative "interviews with established writers. In-depth, particularly reporting interviewee's philosophy on writing, how (s)he got started, how (s)he 'does it.' Tape interviews, transcribe, then edit!"

THE JOURNALISM EDUCATOR, School of Journalism, University of North Carolina, Chapel Hill NC 27514. (919)962-4084. Editor: Thomas A. Bowers. For journalism professors, administrators, and a growing number of professional journalists in the US and Canada. Published by the Association for Education in Journalism and Mass Communication. Founded by the American Society of Journalism School Administrators. Quarterly. Byline given. SASE.
Nonfiction: "We do accept some unsolicited manuscripts dealing with our publication's specialized area—problems of administration and teaching in journalism education. Because we receive more articles than we

can use from persons working in this field, we do not need to encourage freelance materials, however. A writer, generally, would have to be in journalism/communications teaching or in some media work to have the background to write convincingly about the subjects this publication is interested in. The writer also should become familiar with the content of recent issues of this publication." Nothing not directly connected with journalism education at the four-year college and university level. Maximum length: 2,500 words. Does not pay.

JOURNALISM QUARTERLY, School of Journalism, Ohio University, Athens OH 45701. (614)594-6710. Editor: Guido H. Stempel III. 100% freelance written. For members of the Association for Education in Journalism and other academicians and journalists. Quarterly. Usually acquires all rights. Circ. 4,800. Photocopied submissions OK. Computer printout submissions OK. Free writer's guidelines. Reports in 4-6 months. SASE.
Nonfiction: Research in mass communication. Recent articles include "How Newspaper Editors Reacted To *Post's* Pulitzer Prize Hoax." No essays or opinion pieces. Length: 4,000 words maximum. Submit complete ms "in triplicate." No payment.
Tips: "Query letters don't really help either the author or me very much. We can't make commitments on the basis of query letters, and we are not likely to reject or discourage the manuscript either unless it is clearly outside our scope. Do a good piece of research. Write a clear, well-organized manuscript."

‡MECHANICS, (A Writer's Quarterly), Box 207, Hyde Park NY 12538. Editor: Virginia (Ginger) Bisanz. Quarterly magazine covering all aspects of writing (including writing exercises). "The emphasis is tri-focal: 1) Workshop/Workbook; 2) Little Magazine; 3) Networking: opinions, problems, advice." Estab. 1983. Circ. "growing." Pays on publication. Byline given. Offers ½ kill fee, if assigned. Buys one-time rights; but first rights for New Lines. Submit seasonal/holiday material 4 months in advance. Simultaneous queries, and simultaneous, photocopied and previously published submissions OK except for New Lines section. SASE. Reports in 3 weeks on queries; 1 month on mss. Sample copy $4; writer's guidelines for business sized SAE and 1 first class stamp.
Nonfiction: Book excerpts; historical/nostalgic (if applicable); how-to (writing, writing exercises); humor; inspirational (if applicable); interview/profile; new product; opinion; personal experience; photo feature. All nonfiction, except completed exercises, must pertain to writing. 95% freelance written. Query with clips if available or send complete ms. Length: open. Preference given to short, terse pieces. Pays $5-25.
Photos: Richard Bisanz, photo editor. Send photos with ms.
Columns/Departments: Workbench, Mechanics, Back to the Drawing Board, Showroom, New Lines (fiction/poetry). Query with clips of published work or send complete ms. Length: varies. Pays $5-25.
Fiction: "Any well-written, entertaining, and/or thought provoking material for our New Lines section. Submissions will be individually, and personally edited. We emphasize revision vs. rejection." No porno, cynical or downbeat material. Buys 16-32 mss/year or "more depending on their length." Query with clips of published work or send complete ms. Length: open. Prefers short pieces. Pays $25.
Poetry: "All/any" type of poetry. No "unintelligible, esoterically coded missives." Buys 16-32 poems/year. Submit maximum 10 poems. Pays $5.
Fillers: Jokes, anecdotes, short humor, newsbreaks (that deal with writing). Buys 8-16 fillers/year. Length: open. Pays $5.
Tips: "The personal touch is essential. Communicate with us and you'll get a response—about revisions, queries, submissions. Be yourself. Share your failures and successes. Get us excited about writing through your writing (fiction and nonfiction). We're more than a little/literary magazine, we're a reader participation workbook/magazine for communicators. And we are becoming as much a service to writers as a Workbook Magazine."

MEDICAL COMMUNICATIONS, A.H. Robins Co., Box 26609, Richmond VA 23261. (804)257-2966. Editor: Howard M. Smith. For members of the American Medical Writers Association, physicians, medical libraries, journal and medical news editors, pharmaceutical writers, editors, and advertising people, and other communicators in medical and allied fields. Quarterly. 32- to 48-page digest-size magazine. Circ. 3,000. Acquires first North American serial rights. Byline. Uses 6-8 mss/issue. Pays 3 contributor's copies. Sample copy for $1.25. Reports in 6 weeks. Query. SASE.
Nonfiction: Articles related to any aspect of medical communications. No clinical articles. May be either philosophic or how-to. "We are more of a journal than a magazine, but like to take a less formal approach." Uses fairly serious, simple, straightforward style. Humor and special features accepted. Footnotes if required. "No clinical manuscripts." Length: 1,500-3,000 words. Tables and figures are used with mss, if needed.
Tips: "We're especially interested in articles on subjects not usually covered in other journals aimed at medical writers/editors: translation, indexing, speaking. We accept few articles resting on a humorous base. Most of our members are experienced, literate and literary-minded writers and editors. Only the best writing holds their interest; the topic must be important to them, too."

PHILATELIC JOURNALIST, 154 Laguna Court, St. Augustine Shores FL 32084. (904)797-3513. Editor: Gustav Detjen Jr. For "journalists, writers, columnists in the field of stamp collecting. *The Philatelic Journalist* is mainly read by philatelic writers, professionals and amateurs, including all of the members of the Society of Philaticians, an international group of philatelic journalists." Bimonthly. Circ. 1,000. Not copyrighted. Pays on publication. Free sample copy. Will consider photocopied submissions. Submit seasonal material 2 months in advance. Reports in 2 weeks. Query. SASE.
Nonfiction and Photos: "Articles concerned with the problems of the philatelic journalist, how to publicize and promote stamp collecting, how to improve relations between philatelic writers and publishers and postal administrations. Philatelic journalists, many of them amateurs, are very much interested in receiving greater recognition as journalists, and in gaining greater recognition for the use of philatelic literature by stamp collectors. Any criticism should be coupled with suggestions for improvement." Buys profiles and opinion articles. Length: 250-500 words. Pays $15-30. Photos purchased with ms; captions required.

PRO/COMM, The Professional Communicator, published by Women in Communications, Inc., Box 9561, Austin TX 78766. (512)345-8922. Editor: Ruth Massingill. Associate Editor: Gene T. Krane. 95% freelance written; mostly by WICI members and without pay. Monthly January-August; combination September/October and November/December issues; 8-12 pages. Circ. more than 12,000. Byline given. Photocopied and previously published submissions OK. SASE. Reports in 4 weeks. Sample copy $1.50.
Nonfiction: General interest (media, freedom of information, legislation related to communications); how-to (improve graphics, take better photos, write a better story, do investigative reporting, sell ideas, start a magazine or newspaper, improve journalism education, reach decision-making jobs, etc.); personal experience (self-improvement, steps to take to reach management-level jobs); profile (people of interest because of their work in communications); and technical (advancements in print or electronic media). Query. Length: 1,000-1,500 words.
Photos: Offers no additional payment for photos accepted with mss. State availability of photos with query. Uses b&w photos. Captions required.

‡**PUBLISHING TRADE, Serving Non-Consumer Publications**, Northfield Publishing, 1495 Oakwood, Des Plaines IL 60016. (312)298-7291. Editor: Gordon F. Bieberle. Bimonthly magazine covering non-consumer magazine and tabloid publishing. Circulated to more than 5,000 publishers, editors, ad managers, circulation managers, production managers and art directors of non-consumer magazines and tabloids." Estab. 1982. Circ. 5,000. Pays on publication. Byline given. Buys first North American serial rights and makes work-for-hire assignments. Submit seasonal/holiday material 6 months in advance. SASE. Reports in 2 months on queries. "Do not send ms without prior query." Sample copy $4.
Nonfiction: How-to (write, sell advertising, manage production, manage creative and sales people, etc.); interview/profile (*only* after assignment—must be full of "secrets" of success and how-to detail); personal experiences (only after assignment); new product (no payment); technical (aspects of magazine publishing). "Features deal with every aspect of publishing, including: creating an effective ad sales team; increasing ad revenue; writing effective direct-mail circulation promotion; improving 4-color reproduction quality; planning and implementing ad sales strategies; buying printing; gathering unique information; writing crisp, clear articles with impact; designing publications with visual impact." No general interest. "Everything must be keyed directly to our typical reader—a 39-year-old publisher/editor producing a trade magazine for 30,000 special interest readers." Buys 12 mss/year. Query. Length: 600-2,000 words. Pays $50-100.
Photos: Send photos with ms. Reviews b&w contact sheets. Payment included in payment for ms. Captions, model release and identification of subjects required. Buys first rights.
Tips: "Articles must present practical, useful, new information in how-to detail, so readers can do what the articles discuss. Articles that present problems and discuss how they were successfully solved also are welcome. These must carry many specific examples to flesh out general statements."

‡**QUOTE/UNQUOTE, The Editors' Magazine**, Newspaper, Inc., Box 1550, Princeton NJ 08540. (609)924-6650, 428-7910. Editors: Jerry Bellune/Edward D. Miller. Bimonthly magazine covering journalistic topics for editors, publishers, writers, designers and educators. "Subjects should be topical and of concern to editors, particularly newspaper editors." Estab. 1983. Circ. 3,000. Pays on acceptance. Byline given. "We think kill fees are unfair. If we accept a writer's outline, he or she is guaranteed payment." Buys first North American serial rights. Submit seasonal/holiday material 3 months in advance. Reports in 2 weeks. Sample copy $5; free writer's guidelines.
Nonfiction: Book excerpts (journalistic or news subjects only); expose (of questionable journalistic practices); how-to (practical advice on news management, other areas of concern to editors); humor (about journalism); interview/profile (of important or controversial journalistic figures); opinion (if well-founded on the evidence); personal experience (if other editors would profit or gain insight from it); technical (trends and effects of technology on journalism). Special issues include journalism education, newspaper design, investigative reporting, newsroom management. Buys 50-100 mss/year. Query. Length: 500-3,000 words. Pays $100-2,000.
Photos: State availability of photos. Pays $75-300 for b&w contact sheet; $150-500 for color transparencies.

Columns/Departments: Ideas and trends involving libel and First Amendment law, newspaper technology and design, newspaper management, marketing and advertising. Buys 25-30 mss/year. Query. Length: 500-1,000 words. Pays $100-250.

Tips: "Most of our contributors, like most of our readers, are working journalists, many of them current or former newspaper editors. We also publish contributions from journalism educators and reporters. Please query us by mail, stating topic and treatment in a few sentences. If it looks like our kind of material, we will request an outline from you. Once the outline is agreed on, you will be assured of being paid."

Editor's Note: As we go to press, we have learned from editors of *Quote/Unquote* that the magazine is no longer being published.

THE REVIEW OF BOOKS AND RELIGION, Editorial Office, Box 1460, Lexington KY 40591. (606)255-9591. Editor: Kendig Brubaker Cully. Tabloid published monthly, except August and December, reviewing religion—ecumenically conceived—and related fields. Circ. 10,000. "We do not pay for reviews. Reviewer keeps book." Byline given. Submit seasonal holiday material 3 months in advance. SASE. Reports in 1 month. Sample copy available from: *The Review of Books and Religion*, Business Office, Forward Movement Publications, 412 Sycamore St., Cincinnati OH 45202.

Nonfiction: Book reviews. "Write concerning qualifications for reviewing serious works."

Fiction: Query. "Only religious thematic material, broadly understood and not longer than 1,000 words." No payment for fiction and articles.

Poetry: Avant-garde, free-verse, haiku, light verse, traditional (religious imagery only). "We do not pay for poetry." Submit maximum 2 poems.

ST. LOUIS JOURNALISM REVIEW, 8606 Olive Blvd., St. Louis MO 63132. (314)991-1699. Publisher: Charles L. Klotzer. Bimonthly tabloid newspaper critiquing St. Louis media, print, broadcasting and cable primarily by working journalists and others. Occasionally buys articles on national media criticism. No taboos. Circ. 14,000. Buys all rights. Byline given. SASE.

Nonfiction: "We buy material which analyzes, critically, St. Louis area and, less frequently, national media institutions, personalities, or trends." Payment depends.

SAN FRANCISCO REVIEW OF BOOKS, 1111 Kearny St., San Francisco CA 94133. Editor: Ron Nowicki. For a college-educated audience interested in books and publishing. Bimonthly magazine; 40 pages. Circ. 20,000. Acquires all rights. Byline given. Uses about 180 mss/year. Payment in contributor's copies and subscription. Sample copy $1. No photocopied or simultaneous submissions. Reports on material accepted for publication in 4-6 weeks. Query for nonfiction; submit complete ms for book reviews. SASE.

Nonfiction: Book reviews; articles about authors, books and their themes. Contains "Western Publisher" supplement. "No glib, slick writing. Primarily serious; humor occasionally acceptable. No restrictions on language provided it is germane to the book or article." Interviews, profiles, historical and think articles. Length: 1,000 words maximum for reviews; 2,000 words maximum for articles.

SCIENCE FICTION CHRONICLE, Algol Press, Box 4175, New York NY 10163. (212)643-9011. Editor: Andrew Porter. Monthly magazine about science fiction publishing for science fiction readers, editors, writers, et al., who are interested in keeping up with the latest developments and news in science fiction. Publication also includes market reports and media news. Circ. 3,000. Pays on publication. Makes work-for-hire assignments. Phone queries OK. Submit seasonal material 4 months in advance. Computer printout submissions OK; prefers letter quality to dot matrix. SASE. Reports in 1 week. Sample copy $1.75.

Nonfiction: Expose (science fiction which is more investigative than sensational); new product; and photo feature. No articles about UFO's, interviews or "news we reported six months ago." Buys 15 unsolicited mss/year. Send complete ms. Length: 100-500 words. Pays 3¢/word.

Photos: Send photos with ms. Pays $5-15 for 4x5 and 8x10 b&w prints. Captions preferred. Buys one-time rights.

Tips: "News of publishers and booksellers is most needed from freelancers."

SMALL PRESS REVIEW, Box 100, Paradise CA 95969. Editor: Len Fulton. Associate Editor: Ellen Ferber. For "people interested in small presses and magazines, current trends and data; many libraries." Monthly. Circ. 3,000. Accepts 50-200 mss/year. Byline given. Free sample copy. "Query if you're unsure." Reports in 1 to 2 months. SASE.

Nonfiction and Photos: "News, short reviews, photos, short articles on small magazines and presses. Get the facts and know your mind well enough to build your opinion into the article." Uses how-to's, personal experience articles, interviews, profiles, spot news, historical articles, think pieces, photo pieces, and coverage of merchandising techniques. Length: 100-200 words. Uses b&w glossy photos.

WEST COAST REVIEW OF BOOKS, Rapport Publishing Co., Inc., 6565 Sunset Blvd., Hollywood CA 90028. (213)464-2662. Editor: D. David Dreis. Bimonthly magazine for book consumers. "Provocative arti-

cles based on specific subject matter, books and author retrospectives.'' Circ. 80,000. Pays on publication. By-line given. Offers $50 kill fee. Buys all rights. SASE. Sample copy $2.
Nonfiction: General interest, historical/nostalgic, profile (author retrospectives). ''No individual book reviews.'' Buys 12 mss/year. Query. Length: open.
Tips: ''There must be a reason (current interest, news events, etc.) for any article here. Example: 'The Jew-Haters' was about anti-semitism which was written up in six books; all reviewed and analyzed under that umbrella title. Under no circumstances should articles be submitted unless query has been responded to.'' No phone calls.

‡**WORD PROCESSING NEWS,** (formerly *W.P. News*), Word of Mouth Enterprises, #210, 211 E. Olive Ave., Burbank CA 91501. (213)845-7809. Publisher: Barbara Elman. Managing Editor: Glenn Schiffman. Associate Editor: Judith Lovejoy. Bimonthly nesletter covering writing on computers and general computer information. ''Audience owns or is interested in writing on computers instead of typewriter.'' Estab. 1982. Circ. 1,500 + . Pays on publication. Byline given. Buys first North American, one-time rights or second serial (reprint) rights. Simultaneous queries, and simultaneous, photocopied, and previously published submissions OK. ''Computer printout submissions not okay. Telecommunications may be okay—query first with details on contributor's system.'' Reports ''ASAP.'' Sample copy $2; writer's guidelines available.
Nonfiction: Book excerpts and reviews; general interest; how-to (tips on using word processing for specific computer or type of writing); humor; interview/profile; new product; opinion; personal experience (''all articles have personal slant''). ''Each issue focuses on different type of writing (script, freelance, self-publish). SASE for list of future and back issues.'' No ''how to choose a computer/word processor—most readers already have one.'' Query with clips if available or send complete ms. Buys 20 mss/year. Length: 250-2,000 words. Pays 5¢/word.
Columns/Departments: A Writer's Point of View—personal experiences; Choices—program and system comparisons; Another Writer's POV—interviews. Query with clips if available or send complete ms. Length: varies. Pays 5¢/word.
Fillers: Clippings, anecdotes, newsbreaks. Buys 20 fillers/year. Length: 25-100 words. Pays $15-20.
Tips: ''Send for sample or subscribe and check out style. Send query and/or ms direct. Already published writers should include information on where it was printed. We're buying *more* articles from contributors and seeking reviewers with many brands of computer. We're growing dramatically and hope to become monthly before 1984.''

THE WRITER, 8 Arlington St., Boston MA 02116. Editor: Sylvia K. Burack. Monthly. Pays on acceptance. Uses little freelance material. SASE.
Nonfiction: Articles of instruction for writers. Length: about 2,000 words. Pays good rates, on acceptance.

WRITER'S DIGEST, 9933 Alliance Rd., Cincinnati OH 45242. (513)984-0717. Editor: William Brohaugh. Associate Editor: Rose Adkins. Monthly magazine about writing and publishing. ''Our readers write fiction, poetry, nonfiction, plays and all kinds of creative writing. They're interested in improving their writing skills, improving their salesmanship, and finding new outlets for their talents.'' Circ. 150,000. Pays on acceptance. Buys first North American serial rights for one-time editorial use, microfilm/microfiche use, and magazine promotional use. Pays 20% kill fee. Byline given. Submit seasonal/holiday material 8 months in advance. Previously published and photocopied submissions OK. ''Computer disk submissions are possible a few years down the line. We'll accept computer printout submissions, of course—but they *must* be readable. That's the rule behind any submission to any magazine. We strongly recommend letter-quality. Only *one* dot-matrix submission has made its way into print in *WD*—and that from a regular.'' SASE. Reports in 1 month. Sampie copy $2; writer's guidelines for SASE.
Nonfiction: ''Our mainstay is the how-to article—that is, an article telling how to write and sell more of what you write. For instance, how to write compelling leads and conclusions, how to improve your character descriptions, how to become more efficient and productive. Be alert in spotting the new opportunities for writers and be concise in letting the reader know how to write for that market, and how to market the article once it's written. We like plenty of examples, anecdotes and $$$ in our articles—so other writers can actually see what's been done successfully by the author of a particular piece. We like our articles to speak directly to the reader through the use of the first-person voice. Don't submit an article on what five book editors say about writing mysteries. Instead, submit an article on how you cracked the mystery market, and how our readers can do the same. But don't limit the article to your experiences; include the opinions of those five editors to give your article increased depth and authority.'' General interest (about writing); how-to (writing and marketing techniques that work); humor (short pieces); inspirational; interview and profile (query first); new product; personal experience (marketing and freelancing experiences). ''We can always use articles on fiction technique, and solid articles on poetry or poets are always welcome. We also use a 'Money-Maker' feature regularly. These articles point out ways to make extra cash doing things such as writing resumes and freelance editing.'' No articles titled ''So You Want to Be a Writer''—first-person pieces that ramble without giving a lesson or something read-

ers can learn from in the sharing of the story. Buys 90-100 mss/year. Queries are preferred, but complete mss are OK. Length: 500-3,000 words. Pays 10¢/word minimum

Photos: "All things being equal, photos do make a difference, especially for interviews and profiles. State availability of photos or send contact sheet with ms." Pays $25 for 5x7 or larger b&w prints. Captions required.

Columns/Departments: And You Can Quote Me, uses authors' quotes; depending on length, pays $2-5/quote (include source). Chronicle, first-person narratives of writing adventures; length: 1,200-1,500 words; pays 10¢/word. The Writing Life; length: 50-800 words; pays 10¢/word. Trends/Topics, short, unbylined news items about topics and issues that affect writers; pays 10¢/word. My First Sale, an "occasional" department; a first-person account of how a writer broke into print; length: 1,000 words. For First Sale items, use a narrative, anecdotal style to tell a tale that is both inspirational and instructional. Before you submit a My First Sale item, make certain that your story contains a solid lesson that will benefit other writers; pays 10¢/word. Buys approximately 200 Writing Life section, Trends/Topics and shorter pieces/year. Send complete ms.

Poetry: Light verse about "the writing life"—joys and frustrations of writing. "We are also considering poetry other than short light verse—but related to writing, publishing, other poets and authors, etc." Buys 2/issue. Submit poems in batches of 4-6. Length: 2-20 lines. Pays $5-50/poem.

Fillers: Anecdotes and short humor, primarily for use in The Writing Life column. Uses 2/issue. Length: 50-200 words. Pays 10¢/word.

‡**WRITER'S LIFELINE**, Box 1641, Cornwall, Ontario, Canada K6H 5V6. Contact: Editor. Monthly magazine "aimed at freelance writers of all ages and interests." Acquires first rights. Previously published submissions OK. SAE and International Reply Coupons.

Nonfiction: "Articles on all aspects of writing and publishing." Send complete ms. Length: 500 words maximum. Payment: 3 free issues in which article appears.

Fiction: Must be tied in to writing and publishing. Poetry published. Payment: 3 free issues in which story or poem appears.

Tips: "Writer should show evidence of his qualification to write on subject. All articles should be pegged to current concerns of writers: self-publishing, hitting local markets, anecdotes of new writer breaking in, and preparing book reviews are among articles we have published recently."

WRITER'S YEARBOOK, 9933 Alliance Rd., Cincinnati OH 45242. Editor: William Brohaugh. Associate Editor: Rose Adkins. Newsstand annual for freelance writers, journalists, and teachers of creative writing. "We provide information to help our readers become more skilled at writing and successful at selling their writing." Buys first North American serial rights and (occasionally) reprint rights. Pays 20% kill fee. Byline given. Buys 10-15 unsolicited mss/year. Pays on acceptance. "Writers should query in spring with ideas for the following year." Send detailed query or outline of what you have in mind. Previously published (book reprints) and high-quality photocopied submissions OK. SASE.

Nonfiction: "We want articles that reflect the current state of writing in America. Trends, inside information, money-saving and money-making ideas for the freelance writer. Material on writer's hardware—typewriters, cameras, recorders, etc.—and how it can be used to make writing easier or more lucrative. We try to touch on the various facets of writing in each issue of the *Yearbook*—from fiction to poetry to playwriting, and any other endeavor a writer can pursue. How-to articles—that is, articles that explain in detail how to do something—are very important to us. For example, you could explain how to establish mood in fiction, how to improve interviewing techniques, how to write for and sell to specialty magazines, or how to construct and market a good poem. We are also interested in the writer's spare time—what she/he does to retreat occasionally from the writing wars; where and how to refuel and replenish the writing spirit. 'How Beats the Heart of a Writer' features are of interest to us, if written warmly, in first person, by a writer who has had considerable success. We also want big interviews or profiles, always with good pictures. Articles on writing techniques that are effective today are always welcome." Recent article examples: "Tune in Your Creativity and Let the Ideas Come to You (how to tap your creativity) and "Rapid Transit" (how to write clear, smooth transitions between scenes in fiction and nonfiction), both appeared in the 1983 edition. Length: 750-4,500 words. "The manuscripts we use in the *Yearbook* are usually similar to the material we buy for *Writer's Digest*. The extra space available in the *Yearbook*, however, allows us to cover topics in greater length and depth." Pays 10¢/word minimum.

Photos: Interviews and profiles must be accompanied by high-quality photos. B&w only; depending on use, pays $20-50/published photo. Captions required.

WRITING!, Curriculum Innovations, Inc., 3500 Western Ave., Highland Park IL 60035. Editor: Bonnie Bekken. Monthly magazine (September through May) covering writing skills for junior and senior high school students. Pays on publication. Buys all rights. Byline given. Submit seasonal/holiday material 5 months in advance. Computer printout submissions OK; prefers letter quality to dot matrix. SASE. Reports in 6 weeks.

Nonfiction: Interviews wth professional writers. Should stress the writer's introduction into the craft and his/her own reading preferences as a student. Query with brief outline. Length 1,000-1,500 words. Pays 5¢/word minimum.

Laundry and Dry Cleaning

Some journals in the Coin-Operated Machines category are also in the market for material on laundries and dry cleaning establishments.

AMERICAN DRYCLEANER, 500 N. Dearborn St., Chicago IL 60610. (312)337-7700. Editor: Earl V. Fischer. For professional drycleaners. Monthly. Circ. 28,000. Buys all rights or industry-exclusive rights. Pays on publication. Will send free sample copy to writers with specific queries. Reports "promptly." SASE.
Nonfiction and Photos: Articles on all aspects of running a drycleaning business. "These can be narratives about individual drycleaners and how they are handling, say, advertising, counter service, customer relations, cleaning, spot removal, pressing, inspection, packaging, paperwork, or general business management; interpretive reports about outside developments, such as textile innovations or government reglations affecting drycleaners; or how-to articles offering practical help to cleaners on any facet of their business. The important thing is that the reader find practical benefit in the article, whichever type submitted." No basic advertising and public relations material. "We have regulars for this who know our industry." Pays a minimum of 6¢/published word. Recent article example: "Adding a Coin-op Laundry: One Cleaner's Experience" (March 1982). Photos purchased with mss; quality 8x10 or 5x7 b&w glossies. Photos should help tell story. No model releases required. Pays $6 minimum.
Tips: "I would like each query letter to state as specifically as possible the proposed subject matter. It would help to get a theme sentence or brief outline of the proposed article. Also helpful would be a statement of whether (and what sort of) photos or other illustrations are available. Anyone with the type of article that our readers would find helpful can break into the publication. Find a successful drycleaner—one with unusually satisfied customers, for example, or one that seems to be making a lot of money. Find out what makes that cleaner so successful. Tell us about it in specific, practical terms, so other cleaners will be able to follow suit. Articles should help our readers operate their drycleaning businesses more successfully; the appropriateness and practical value of information given are more important than writing style. We anticipate more space to fill and plan to increase emphasis in the year ahead on field reports. We prefer *short* reports about *small* cleaning companies doing *one thing* well enough for others to want to know about it and how they might do the same. Reports can range from less than 250 words up to any length the writer can justify."

AMERICAN LAUNDRY DIGEST, American Trade Magazines, Inc., 500 N. Dearborn St., Chicago IL 60610. (312)337-7700. Editor: Larry Kai Ebert. 13-26% freelance written. For a professional laundering, linen supply, uniform rental audience. Monthly magazine; 52 pages. Circ. 17,100. Pays 2 weeks prior to publication. Buys all rights. Phone queries OK. Photocopied submissions OK. SASE. Reports in 2 weeks. Free sample copy and writer's guidelines.
Nonfiction: How-to articles about how laundrymen have cut costs, increased production, improved safety, gained sales, etc. "Interviews with laundrymen about how they run a successful plant would be welcome." Query. Length: 300-3,000 words. Pays minimum of 5¢/word.
Photos: B&w glossies (8x10 preferred; 5x7 acceptable) purchased with mss. Send contact sheet. Pays minimum of $5.

INDUSTRIAL LAUNDERER, Suite 613, 1730 M St. NW, Washington DC 20036. (202)296-6744. Editor: David A. Ritchey. 15-20% freelance written. For decisionmakers in the industrial laundry industry. Publication of the Institute of Industrial Launderers, Inc. Magazine; 124 pages. Monthly. Circ. 2,500. Buys all rights. Pays on acceptance. Sample copies $1; limited sample copies available. Write for copy of guidelines for writers. Reports in 1 week. Query. SASE.
Nonfiction and Photos: General interest pieces for the industrial laundry industry; labor news, news from Washington; book reviews on publications of interest to people in this industry. Technical advancements and "people" stories. Informational, personal experience, interview, profile, historical, successful business operations, merchandising techniques. No "general business articles or articles not specifically related to the industrial laundry industry." Buys 5-10 unsolicited mss/year. Length: 750 words minimum. Payment negotiable. No additional payment for 8x10 b&w glossies used with ms. Pays $5 minimum for those purchased on assignment. Captions required.

Law

‡**THE ALTMAN & WEIL REPORT TO LEGAL MANAGEMENT**, Altman & Weil Publications, Inc., Box 472, Ardmore PA 19003. (215)649-4646. Editor: Robert I. Weil. Monthly newsletter covering law office purchases (equipment, insurance services, space, etc.). Circ. 2,200. Pays on publication. Byline given. Buys

all rights; "sometimes" second serial (reprint) rights. Photocopied and previously published submissions OK. Reports in 4 weeks on queries; 6 weeks on mss. Sample copy for business size SAE and 1 first class stamp. **Nonfiction:** How-to (buy, use, repair); interview/profile; new product. Buys 6 mss/year. Query. Length: 500-2,500 words. Pays $125/published page.

Photos: State availability of photos. Reviews b&w prints; payment is included in payment for ms. Captions and model release required. Buys one-time rights.

BARRISTER, American Bar Association Press, 1155 E. 60th St., Chicago IL 60637. (312)947-4072. Editor: Anthony Monahan. For young lawyers who are members of the American Bar Association, concerned about practice of law, improvement of the profession and service to the public. Quarterly magazine; 64 pages. Circ. 155,000. Pays on acceptance. Buys all rights, first serial rights, second serial (reprint) rights, or simultaneous rights. Photocopied submissions OK. SASE. Reports in 4-6 weeks. Free sample copy.

Nonfiction: "As a magazine of ideas and opinion, we seek material that will help readers in their interrelated roles of attorney and citizen; major themes in legal and social affairs." Especially needs expository or advocacy articles; position should be defended clearly in good, crisp, journalistic prose. "We would like to see articles on issues such as the feasibility of energy alternatives to nuclear power, roles of women and minorities in law, the power and future of multinational corporations; national issues such as gun control; aspects of the legal profession such as salary comparisons, use of computers in law practice." Recent article example: "Are You Meant to Be a Partner?" No humorous court reporter anecdote material or political opinion articles. Buys 20-25 unsolicited mss/year. Length: 3,000-4,000 words. Query with a working title and outline of topic. "Be specific." Pays $300-450.

Photos: Donna Tashjian, photo editor. B&w photos and color transparencies purchased without accompanying ms. Pays $35-150.

Tips: "We urge writers to think ahead about new areas of law and social issues: sexual habits, work habits, corporations, etc."

‡**CALIFORNIA LAWYER**, The State Bar of California, 555 Frankiin St., San Francisco CA 94102. (415)561-8286. Editor-in-Chief: Diana L. Diamond. Associate Editor: Jonathan Maslow. Monthly magazine. Law-related articles and general-interest subjects of appeal to attorneys. Estab. 1981. Circ. 90,000. Pays on acceptance. Byline given. Offers ⅓ kill fee. Buys one-time and first rights. Simultaneous queries, and simultaneous and photocopied submissions OK. Computer printout submissions OK. Reports in 2 weeks on queries; 3 weeks on mss. Sample copy for 8½x11 SAE and $1.50 postage; writer's guidelines for SAE and 1 first class stamp.

Nonfiction: Book excerpts, general interest, historical, humor, interview/profile, opinion, technical, travel, personal finance advice, personal effectiveness. Buys 36 mss/year. Query with clips if available. Length: 2,000-3,000 words (features). Pays $300-550.

Photos: Jan Leonard, photo editor. State availability of photos with query letter or manuscript. Reviews prints. Identification of subjects required.

Columns/Departments: Business of Practice; After Hours; Profile; Money; Effectiveness. Buys 100/year. Query with clips if available. Length: 1,000-1,500 words. Pays $150-300.

Tips: "We are interested in concise, well-written and well-researched articles on recent trends in the legal profession, legal aspects of issues of current concern, as well as general-interest articles of potential appeal and benefit to the state's lawyers. We would like to see a description or outline of your proposed idea, including a list of possible information sources."

‡**THE CHAMPION**, National Association of Criminal Defense Lawyers, Suite 320, 2600 S. Loop West, Houston TX 77054. (713)666-2777. Editor: Louis F. Linden. Published 10 times/year. Magazine of defense of criminal cases for an audience almost exclusively criminal defense lawyers. Circ. 2,400. Pays on acceptance. Byline given. Publication not copyrighted. Buys one-time rights. Photocopied and previously published submissions OK. Computer printout submissions OK. SASE. Reports in 1½ weeks. Free sample copy.

Nonfiction: Historical, how-to, profile, technical. "We stress material of practical use to the criminal defense lawyer. The freelancer should produce articles of substantive legal or technical merit which address issues of a controversial nature in the criminal justice system." No articles purporting to explain law to lay-persons. Buys 5 mss/year. Query. Length: 1,000-2,500 words. Pays $50.

Photos: State availability of photos. "Legal articles most often do not lend themselves to use of photos. Therefore, finding photos as graphic enhancement of the publication is difficult. Photos are used for explanatory purposes primarily and graphic purposes secondarily." Pays $10 for 5x7 b&w glossy prints. Captions required with description of the subject matter.

LEGAL ECONOMICS, Box 11418, Columbia SC 29211. Managing Editor/Art Director: Delmar L. Roberts. For the practicing lawyer. Bimonthly magazine; 64-92 pages. Circ. 23,000. Rights purchased vary with author and material. Usually buys all rights. Byline given. Pays on publication. Free writer's guidelines. Sample copy $2.50 (make check payable to American Bar Association). Returns rejected material in 90 days, if requested. Query. SASE.

Nonfiction and Photos: "We assist the practicing lawyer in operating and managing his office in an efficient and economical manner by providing relevant articles and editorial matter written in a readable and informative style. Editorial content is intended to aid the lawyer by conveying management methods that will allow him or her to provide legal services to clients in a prompt and efficient manner at reasonable cost. Typical topics of articles include timekeeping systems; word processing systems; microcomputers; client/lawyer relations; office equipment; computerized research; compensation of partners and associates; information retrieval; and use of paralegals." No articles on basic technology, such as, "Why You Need Word Processing in the Law Office." Pays $50-200. Pays $25-40 for b&w photos purchased with mss; $45-50 for color; $75 up for cover transparencies.

Tips: "We normally do not publish thematic issues. However, we have published a special computer issue. Based on its reception, we may have another in the coming year—or a thematic issue on another topic."

THE NATIONAL LAW JOURNAL, New York Law Publishing Company, 111 8th Ave., New York NY 10011. (212)741-8300. Editor: Timothy Robinson. Managing Editor: Barry Adler. Weekly newspaper for the legal profession. Circ. 37,000. Pays on publication. Byline given. Offers $75 kill fee. Buys all rights. Reports in 1 month. Simultaneous queries OK. SASE. Reports in 3 weeks on queries; 5 weeks on mss. Sample copy $1.50.

Nonfiction: Expose (on subjects of interest to lawyers); humor (relating to legal topics); and interview/profile (of lawyers or judges of note). "The bulk of our freelance articles are 2,000-2,500 word profiles of prominent lawyers, or trend stories relating to the legal profession. We also buy a steady stream of short, spot-news stories on local court decisions or lawsuits; often, these come from legal affairs writers on local newspapers. No articles without a legal angle." Buys 60 mss/year. Query with clips of published work or send complete ms. Length: 1,500-3,000 words. Pays $300-500.

Tips: "For those who are not covering legal affairs on a regular basis, the best way into *The National Law Journal* is probably through our 'On Trial' feature. Every week, we print a sort of reporter's notebook on some proceeding currently underway in a courtroom. These stories come from all around the country, and range from gory murder trials to a night in small claims court. They usually run about 1,000 words, and are stylistically quite flexible. We also use op-ed pieces on subjects of legal interest, many of which come from freelancers. Writers interested in doing an op-ed piece should query first."

‡**THE PENNSYLVANIA LAWYER**, Pennsylvania Bar Association, 100 South St., Box 186, Harrisburg PA 17108. (717)238-6715. Editor: Francis J. Fanucci. Assistant Editor: Donald C. Sarvey. Magazine published 7 times/year as a service to the legal profession. Circ. 24,000. Pays on acceptance. Byline given. Buys negotiable rights; generally first rights. Submit seasonal/holiday material 5 months in advance. Simultaneous queries and previously published submissions OK. Reports in 2 weeks. Free sample copy.

Nonfiction: General interest, how-to, humor, interview/profile, new product, personal experience. All features must relate in some way to lawyers or the practice of law. Buys 12-18 mss/year. Query. Length: 800-2,500 words. Pays $75-250.

STUDENT LAWYER, American Bar Association, 1155 E. 60th St., Chicago IL 60637. (312)947-4087. Editor: Lizanne Poppens. Monthly (September-May) magazine; 60 pages. Circ. 45,000. Pays on publication. Buys first rights. Pays negotiable kill fee. Byline given. Submit seasonal/holiday material 2 months in advance of issue date. Photocopied submissions OK. Reports in 2 weeks. Sample copy $1; free writer's guidelines.

Nonfiction: Expose (government, law, education and business); profiles (prominent persons in law-related fields); opinion (on matters of current legal interest); essays (on legal affairs); interviews and photo features. Recent article examples: "Today's Law Students, Tomorrow's Robots," and "This Land Is Our Land" (September 1981). Buys 5 mss/issue. Query. Length: 3,000-5,000 words. Pays $250-600.

Photos: State availability of photos with query. Pays $50-75 for 8x10 b&w prints; $50-200 for color. Model release required.

Columns/Departments: Briefly (short stories on unusual and interesting developments in the law); Legal Aids (unusual approaches and programs connected to teaching law students and lawyers); Esq. (brief profiles of people in the law); Status (news stories on legal education, programs and personalities); Pro Se (opinion slot for authors to wax eloquent on such topics as a legal issue, a civil rights conflict, the state of the union); and Et Al. (column for short features that fit none of the above categories). Buys 4-8 mss/issue. Length: 50-1,500 words. Pays $25-250.

Fiction: "We buy fiction only when it is very good and deals with issues of law in the contemporary world, or offers insights into the inner workings of lawyers. No mystery or science fiction accepted."

Tips: "*Student Lawyer* actively seeks good, new writers. Legal training definitely not essential; writing talent is. The writer should not think we are a law review; we are a features magazine with the law (in the broadest sense) as the common denominator. Past articles concerned gay rights, prison reform, the media, pornography, capital punishment, and space law. Find issues of national scope and interest to write about; be aware of subjects the magazine has already covered and propose something new. Write clearly and well."

Leather Goods

LUGGAGE & TRAVELWARE, Business Journals, 22 S. Smith St., Norwalk CT 06855. (203)853-6015. Editor: Roger Zimmer. Monthly magazine covering luggage, leather goods and travel accessories for specialty and department store retailers and mass merchandisers. Circ. 9,000. Pays on publication. Byline given. Not copyrighted. Simultaneous queries and simultaneous and photocopied submissions OK. SASE. Reports in 2 weeks. Free sample copy.
Nonfiction: "We're looking for timely features and business-oriented articles on merchandising display and retailing." No material that is not tied in fairly close to the industry. Length: 6-8 typewritten pages. Pays $200-300.

SHOE SERVICE, SSIA Service Corp., 154 W. Hubbard St., Chicago IL 60610. (312)670-3732. Editor: T.J. Donnelly. Monthly magazine for business people who own and operate small shoe repair shops. Circ. 6,500. Pays on publication. Byline given. Buys exclusive industry rights. Submit seasonal/holiday material 3 months in advance. Simultaneous queries, and photocopied and previously published submissions OK. Computer printout submissions OK. SASE. Reports in 6 weeks. Sample copy $1.
Nonfiction: How-to (run a profitable shop); interview/profile (of an outstanding or unusual person on shoe repair); business articles (particulary about small business practices in a service/retail shop). Buys 12-24 mss/year. Query with clips of published work or send complete ms. Length: 500-2,000 words. Pays $25-100.
Photos: "Photos will help sell an article." State availability of photos. Pays $10-30 for 8x10 b&w prints. Captions, model release and identification of subjects required.
Tips: "Visit some shoe repair shops to get an idea of the kind of person who reads *Shoe Service*. Profiles are the easiest to sell to us if you can find a repairer we think is unusual. We are hoping to go to computerized typeset in the next year, which would, among other things, make compatible disks acceptable."

Library Science

AMERICAN LIBRARIES, 50 E. Huron St., Chicago IL 60611. (312)944-6780. Editor: Arthur Plotnik. For librarians. "A highly literate audience. They are for the most part practicing professionals with down-to-earth interest in people and current trends." Published 11 times a year. Circ. 39,000. Buys first North American serial rights. Pays negotiable kill fee. Byline given. Will consider photocopied submissions if not being considered elsewhere at time of submission. Letter quality computer printout submissions OK. Submit seasonal material 6 months in advance. Reports in 10 weeks. SASE.
Nonfiction and Photos: "Material reflecting the special and current interests of the library profession. Nonlibrarians should browse recent journals in the field, available on request in medium-sized and large libraries everywhere. Topic and/or approach must be fresh, vital, or highly entertaining. Library memoirs and stereotyped stories about old maids, overdue books, fines, etc., are unacceptable. Our first concern is with the American Library Association's activities, and how they relate to the 39,000 reader/members. Tough for an outsider to write on this topic, but not to supplement it with short, offbeat or profoundly significant library stories and features. No fillers. Recent article example: "Online Encyclopedias: Are They Ready for Libraries?" (March 1983). Will look at all good b&w, well-lit photos of library situations, and at color transparencies for possible cover use." Buys 10-15 mss/year. Pays $25-150 for briefs and articles. Pays $25-75 for b&w photos.
Tips: "You can break in with a sparkling, 300-word report on a true, offbeat library event, use of new technology, or with an exciting photo and caption. Though stories on public libraries are always of interest, we especially need arresting material on academic and school libraries."

EMERGENCY LIBRARIAN, Dyad Services, Box 46258, Stn. G, Vancouver, British Columbia, Canada V6R 4G6. Co-Editors: Carol Ann Haycock; Ken Haycock. Bimonthly magazine. Circ. 3,000. Pays on publication. Photocopied submissions OK. SAE and International Reply Coupons. Reports in 4-6 weeks. Free writer's guidelines.
Nonfiction: Emphasis is on improvement of library service for children and young adults in school and public libraries. Also annotated bibliographies. Buys 3 mss/issue. Query. No multiple submissions. Length: 1,000-3,500 words. Pays $50.
Columns/Departments: Book Reviews (of professional materials in education, librarianship). Query. Length: 100-300 words. Payment consists of book reviewed.

LIBRARY JOURNAL, 1180 Avenue of the Americas, New York NY 10036. Editor-in-Chief: John N. Berry III. For librarians (academic, public, special). 115-page magazine published every 2 weeks. Circ. 30,000.

Buys all rights. Buys 50-100 mss/year (mostly from professionals in the field). Pays on publication. Submit complete ms. SASE.

Nonfiction and Photos: *"Library Journal* is a professional magazine for librarians. Freelancers are most often rejected because they submit one of the following types of article: 'A wonderful, warm, concerned, loving librarian who started me on the road to good reading and success'; 'How I became rich, famous, and successful by using my public library'; 'Libraries are the most wonderful and important institutions in our society, because they have all of the knowledge of mankind—praise them.' We need material of greater sophistication, dealing with issues related to the transfer of information, access to it, or related phenomena. (Current hot ones are copyright, censorship, the decline in funding for public institutions, the local politics of libraries, trusteeship, etc.)" Professional articles on criticism, censorship, professional concerns, library activities, historical articles and spot news. Outlook should be from librarian's point of view. Recent artcle example: "The Generalist Concept" (April 15, 1982). Buys 50-65 unsolicited mss/year. Length: 1,500-2,000 words. Pays $50-250. Payment for b&w glossy photos purchased without accompanying mss is $30. Must be at least 5x7. Captions required.

MEDIA: LIBRARY SERVICES JOURNAL, 127 9th Ave. N., Nashville TN 37234. (615)251-2752. Editor: Floyd B. Simpson. For adult leaders in church organizations and people interested in library work (especially church library work). Quarterly magazine; 50 pages. Circ. 17,500. Pays on publication. Buys all rights. Byline given. Phone queries OK. Submit seasonal/holiday material 14 months in advance. Previously published submissions OK. SASE. Reports in 1 month. Free sample copy and writer's guidelines.

Nonfiction: "Primarily interested in articles that relate to the development of church libraries in providing media and services to support the total program of a church and in meeting individual needs. We publish personal experience accounts of services provided, promotional ideas, exciting things that have happened as a result of implementing an idea or service; human interest stories that are library-related; media education (teaching and learning with a media mix). Articles should be practical for church library staffs and for teachers and other leaders of the church." Buys 15-20 mss/issue. Query. Pays 4¢/word.

WILSON LIBRARY BULLETIN, 950 University Ave., Bronx NY 10452. (212)588-8400. Editor: Milo Nelson. For professional librarians and those interested in the book and library worlds. Monthly (September-June). Circ. 30,000. Buys North American serial rights only. Pays on publication. Sample copies may be seen on request in most libraries. "Ms must be original copy, double-spaced; additional photocopy or carbon is appreciated. Computer printout submissions OK; prefers letter quality to dot matrix. Deadlines are a minimum 2 months before publication." Reports in 8-12 weeks. SASE.

Nonfiction: Uses articles "of interest to librarians throughout the nation and around the world. Style must be lively, readable and sophisticated, with appeal to modern professionals; facts must be thoroughly researched. Subjects range from the political to the comic in the world of media and libraries, with an emphasis on the human as well as the technical aspects of any story. No condescension: no library stereotypes." Recent article example: "The Free Library of Philadelphia: Making th Hard Choices" (September 1980). Buys 30 mss/year. Send complete ms. Length: 2,500-6,000 words. Pays about $100-250, "depending on the substance of article and its importance to readers."

Tips: "The best way you can break in is with a first-rate b&w photo and caption information on a library, library service, or librarian that departs completely from all stereotypes and the commonplace. Note: Libraries have changed! You'd better first discover what is now commonplace."

Lumber and Woodworking

B.C. LUMBERMAN MAGAZINE, Box 34080, Station D, Vancouver, British Columbia, Canada, V6J 4M8. (403)731-1171. Editorial Director: Brian Martin. 60% freelance written. For the logging and sawmilling industries of Western Canada and the Pacific Northwest of the United States. Monthly magazine; 75 pages. Circ. 8,500. Pays on acceptance. Buys first Canadian rights. Query first. Submit seasonal/holiday material 2 months in advance of issue date. Reports in 2 weeks.

Nonfiction: How-to (technical articles on any aspect of the forest industry); general interest (anything of interest to persons in forest industries in western Canada or US Pacific Northwest); interview (occasionally related to leading forestry personnel); and technical (forestry). No fiction or history. Buys 8 mss/issue. Query with clips of published work. Average length: 1,500 words. Pays 15¢/word (Canadian).

Photos: State availability of photos with query. Pays $5-25 for b&w negatives and $50-80 for 8x10 glossy color prints. Captions required. Buys first Canadian rights.

NORTHERN LOGGER AND TIMBER PROCESSOR, Northeastern Loggers' Association, Box 69, Old Forge NY 13420. (315)369-3078. Associate Editor: Eric A. Johnson. Monthly magazine of the forest industry in the Northern US (Maine to Minnesota and South to Virginia and Missouri). We are not a technical journal, but are more information and entertainment-oriented.'' Circ. 10,300. Pays on publication. Byline given. Copyrighted. Buys all rights. Submit seasonal/holiday material 3 months in advance. Photocopied and previously published submissions OK. ''Any computer printout submission that can be easily read is acceptable.'' SASE. Reports in 2 weeks. Free sample copy.

Nonfiction: Expose, general interest, historical/nostalgic, how-to, interview/profile, new product, opinion. ''We only buy feature articles and those should contain some technical or historical material relating to the forest products industry.'' Buys 12-15 mss/year. Query. Length: 500-2,500 words. Pays $25-125.

Photos: Send photos with ms. Pays $20-35 for 35mm color transparencies; $5-15 for 5x7 b&w prints. Captions and identification of subjects required.

Tips: ''We accept most any subject dealing with this part of the country's forest industry from historical to logging, firewood, and timber processing.''

WOOD & WOOD PRODUCTS, 300 W. Adams St., Chicago IL 60606. (312)977-7269. Editor: Harry Urban. 10-15% freelance written. For owners and managers of furniture, cabinet, and other wood product manufacturing companies. Monthly magazine; 100 pages. Circ. 35,000. Pays on publication. Buys all rights unless otherwise specified. Byline given. Phone queries OK. Submit material 3 months in advance of issue date. SASE. Free sample copy, writer's guidelines, and annual story schedule.

Nonfiction: Expose (of upcoming government regulations); how-to (increase production, efficiency, and profits); new product (one offering truly new technology, not just a new cap screw); photo feature (how-to, plant story); and technical. No articles on hobbyist woodworking or small woodcraft shops. Buys 15 mss/year. Query with clips of published work; ''give full information on story and indicate whether any competition is interested in story or has turned it down.'' Length: 500-1,500 words. Pays $150-200.

Photos: State availability of photos with query. Offers no additional payment for b&w contact sheets or prints 35mm color transparencies. Captions required.

Columns/Departments: Production Ideas (efficiency tips, how a company solved a problem); and Trends & News (news items). Query. Length: 100-150 words. Pays $50-150.

Tips: ''Find a good story and offer us an exclusive, with good color transparencies and snappy writing. Query first. To us, a good story is one about a new product or technique which will help woodworkers save money.''

Machinery and Metal Trade

ASSEMBLY ENGINEERING, Hitchcock Publishing Co., Wheaton IL 60187. Editor: Terrance Thompson. 30% freelance written. For design and manufacturing engineers and production personnel concerned with assembly problems in manufacturing plants. Monthly. Buys first publication rights. Pays on publication. Sample copy will be sent on request. ''Query on leads or ideas. We report on ms decision as soon as review is completed and provide edited proofs for checking by author, prior to publication.'' SASE.

Nonfiction and Photos: Wants features on design engineering and production practices for the assembly of manufactured products. Material should be submitted on ''exclusive rights'' basis. Subject areas include selection, specification, and application of fasteners, mounting hardware, electrical connectors, wiring, hydraulic and pneumatic fittings, seals and gaskets, adhesives, joining methods (soldering, welding, brazing, etc.) and assembly equipment; specification of fits and tolerances; joint design; design and shop assembly standards; time and motion study (assembly line); quality control in assembly; layout and balancing of assembly lines; assembly tool and jig design; programming assembly line operations; working conditions, incentives, labor costs, and union relations as they relate to assembly line operators; hiring and training of assembly line personnel; supervisory practices for the assembly line. Also looking for news items on assembly-related subjects, and for unique or unusual ''ideas'' on assembly components, equipment, processes, practices and methods. ''We want only technical articles, not PR releases.'' Requires good quality photos or sketches, usually close-ups of specific details. Pays $30 minimum/published page.

AUTOMATIC MACHINING, 228 N. Winton Rd., Rochester NY 14610. (716)654-8964. Editor: Donald E. Wood. For metalworking technical management. Buys all rights. Byline given. Query. Computer printout or disk submissions OK. SASE.

Nonfiction: ''This is not a market for the average freelancer. A personal knowledge of the trade is essential. Articles deal in depth with specific job operations on automatic screw machines, chucking machines, high production metal turning lathes and cold heading machines. Part prints, tooling layouts always required, plus written agreement of source to publish the material. Without personal background in operation of this type of equipment, freelancers are wasting time. No material researched from library sources.'' Length: ''no limit.'' Pays $20/printed page.

Tips: "In the year ahead there will be more emphasis on plant and people news so less space will be available for conventional articles."

CANADIAN MACHINERY AND METALWORKING, 777 Bay St., Toronto, Ontario, Canada M5W 1A7. (416)596-5714. Editor: Nick Hancock. Monthly. Buys first Canadian rights. Pays on acceptance. Query. SAE and International Reply Coupons.
Nonfiction: Technical and semitechnical articles dealing with metalworking operations in Canada and in the US, if of particular interest to Canadian readers. Accuracy and service appeal to readers is a must. Pays minimum 18¢/word.
Photos: Purchased with mss and with captions only. Pays $10 minimum for b&w features.

FOUNDRY MANAGEMENT AND TECHNOLOGY, Penton Plaza, Cleveland OH 44114. (216)696-7000. Editor: J.C. Miske. Monthly. Byline given. Reports in 2 weeks. SASE.
Nonfiction and Photos: Uses articles describing operating practice in foundries written to interest companies producing metal castings. Buys 7-10 unsolicited mss/year. Length: 3,000 words maximum. Pays $35-50/printed page. Uses illustrative photographs with article; uses "a great deal of 4-color photos."

INDUSTRIAL MACHINERY NEWS, Hearst Business Media Corp., IMN Division, 29516 Southfield Rd., Box 5002, Southfield MI 48086. (313)557-0100. Editorial Manager: Evelyn Dzmelyk. Emphasizes metalworking for buyers, specifiers, manufacturing executives, engineers, management, plant managers, production managers, master mechanics, designers and machinery dealers. Monthly tabloid; 200 pages. Circ. 175,000. Pays on publication. Buys first North American serial rights. Submit seasonal/holiday material 3 months in advance. Simultaneous, photocopied and previously published submissions OK. SASE. Reports in 3-6 weeks. Sample copy $3.
Nonfiction and Photos: Articles on "metal removal, metal forming, assembly, finishing, inspection, application of machine tools, technology, measuring, gauging equipment, small cutting tools, tooling accessories, materials handling in metalworking plants, safety programs. We give our publication a newspaper feel—fast reading with lots of action or human interest photos." Buys how-to's. Pays $25 minimum. Length: open. Photos purchased with mss; captions required. Pays $5 minimum.
Fillers: Puzzles, jokes, short humor. Pays $5 minimum.
Tips: "We're looking for stories on old machine tools—how they're holding up and how they're being used. We're also interested in metalworking machinery and equipment application articles that illustrate techniques geared to improving efficiency and productivity in the plant."

MODERN MACHINE SHOP, 6600 Clough Pike, Cincinnati OH 45244. Editor: Ken Gettelman. Monthly. Byline given. Pays 30 days following acceptance. Query. Reports in 5 days. SASE.
Nonfiction: Uses articles dealing with all phases of metal manufacturing and machine shop work, with photos. No general articles. "Ours is an industrial publication, and contributing authors should have a working knowledge of the metalworking industry." Buys 10 unsolicited mss/year. Length: 800-3,000 words. Pays current market rate.
Tips: "The use of articles relating to computers in manufacturing is growing."

POWER TRANSMISSION DESIGN, 1111 Chester Ave., Cleveland OH 44114. (216)696-0300. Editor: LaVerne Leonard. 20% freelance written. Emphasizes industrial motion and control systems. Monthly magazine: 96 pages. Circ. 50,600. Pays on publication. Buys first-time publication rights and nonexclusive republication rights. Byline given all features. Phone queries OK. Submit seasonal/holiday material 5 months in advance. Photocopied submissions OK. Reports in 1 month. Free sample copy.
Nonfiction: Articles on design, selection and maintenance of industrial/mechanical power-transmission systems and components. Buys 10-12 unsolicited mss/year. Query with description of technical questions to be answered by article. Include "why new" information. Length: 1,500-7,500 words. Pays $50-200.

PRODUCTS FINISHING, 6600 Clough Pike, Cincinnati OH 45244. Editor: G. Thos. Robison. Monthly. Buys all rights. Byline given "except on press releases from agencies." Pays within 30 days after acceptance. Reports in 1 week. SASE.
Nonfiction: Uses "material devoted to the finishing of metal and plastic products. This includes the cleaning, plating, polishing and painting of metal and plastic products of all kinds. Articles can be technical and must be practical. Technical articles should be on processes and methods. Particular attention given to articles describing novel approaches used by product finishers to control air and water pollution, and finishing techniques that reduce costs." Pays 8¢ minimum/word.
Photos: Wants photographs dealing with finishing methods or processes. Pays $10 minimum for each photo used.

33 METAL PRODUCING, McGraw-Hill Bldg., 36th Floor, 1221 Avenue of the Americas, New York NY 10020. (212)997-3330. Editor: Joseph L. Mazel. For "operating managers (from turn foreman on up), engineers, metallurgical and chemical specialists, and corporate officials in the steelmaking industry. Work areas for these readers range from blast furnace and coke ovens into and through the steel works and rolling mills. *33*'s readers also work in nonferrous industries and foundries." Monthly. Buys all rights. Pays on publication. Free sample copy. Query. Reports in 3 weeks. SASE.

Nonfiction: Case histories of primary metals producing equipment in use, such as smelting, blast furnace, steelmaking, rolling. "Broadly speaking, *33 Metal Producing* concentrates its editorial efforts in the areas of technique (what's being done and how it's being done), technology (new developments), and equipment (what's being used). Your article should include a detailed explanation (who, what, why, where and how) and the significance (what it means to operating manager, engineer, or industry) of the techniques, technology or equipment being written about. In addition, your readers will want to know of the problems you experienced during the planning, developing, implementing and operating phases. And, it would be especially beneficial to tell of the steps you took to solve the problems or roadblocks encountered. You should also include all cost data relating to implementation, operation, maintenance, etc., wherever possible. Benefits (cost savings, improved manpower utilization, reduced cycle time, increased quality, etc.) should be cited to gauge the effectiveness of the subject being discussed. The highlight of any article is its illustrative material. This can take the form of photographs, drawings, tables, charts, graphs, etc. Your type of illustration should support and reinforce the text material. It should not just be an added, unrelated item. Each element of illustrative material should be identified and contain a short description of exactly what is being presented. We reject material that lacks in-depth knowledge of the technology on operations involved in metal producing." Pays $50/published page. Minimum 5x7 b&w glossies purchased with mss.

Maintenance and Safety

EQUIPMENT MANAGEMENT, 7300 N. Cicero Ave., Lincolnwood IL 60646. (312)588-7300. Editor: Greg Sitek. 10% freelance written. Magazine; 76-110 pages. Monthly. Circ. 55,000. Rights purchased vary with author and material. Usually buys all rights. Buys 12 mss/year. Pays on publication. Free sample copy. No photocopied or simultaneous submissions. Computer printout submissions OK; prefers letter quality to dot matrix. Reports in 4 weeks. Query with outline. SASE.

Nonfiction and Photos: "Our focus is on the effective management of equipment through proper selection, careful specification, correct application and efficient maintenance. We use job stories, technical articles, safety features, basics and shop notes. No product stories or 'puff' pieces." Length: 2,000-5,000 words. Pays $25/printed page minimum, without photos. Uses 35mm and 2¼x2¼ or larger color transparencies with mss. Pays $50/printed page when photos are furnished by author.

Tips: "Know the equipment, how to manage it, and how to maintain/service/repair it."

PEST CONTROL MAGAZINE, 7500 Old Oak Blvd., Cleveland OH 44130. (216)243-8100. Editor: Jerry Mix. For professional pest control operators and sanitation workers. Monthly magazine; 68 pages. Circ. 15,000. Buys all rights. Buys 12+ mss/year. Pays on publication. Submit seasonal material 2 months in advance. Reports in 30 days. Query or submit complete ms. SASE.

Nonfiction and Photos: Business tips, unique control situations, personal experience (stories about 1-man operations and their problems) articles. Must have trade or business orientation. No general information type of articles desired. Buys 3 unsolicited mss/year. Length: 4 double-spaced pages. Pays $150 minimum. Regular columns use material oriented to this profession. Length: 8 double-spaced pages. No additional payment for photos used with mss. Pays $50-150 for 8x10 color or transparencies.

Management and Supervision

This category includes trade journals for middle management business and industrial managers, including supervisors and office managers. Journals for business executives and owners are classified under Business Management. Those for industrial plant managers are listed in Industrial Operation and Management.

CONSTRUCTION SUPERVISION & SAFETY LETTER, (formerly *Construction Foreman's & Supervisor's Letter*), CL Bureau of Business Practice, 24 Rope Ferry Rd., Waterford CT 06386. (203)442-4365. Contact: Editor. Emphasizes all aspects of construction supervision. Semimonthly newsletter; 4 pages. Buys all rights. Phone queries OK. Submit seasonal material at least 4 months in advance. SASE. Reports in 4-6 weeks. Free sample copy and writer's guidelines.

Nonfiction: Publishes solid interviews with construction managers or supervisors on how to improve a single aspect of the supervisor's job. Recent article example: "Prevent Idleness on the Job." Buys 100 unsolicited mss/year. Length: 360-720 words. Pays 7-10¢/word.

Photos: B&w head and shoulders "mug shots" of person interviewed purchased with mss. Send prints. Pays $10.

EMPLOYEE RELATIONS AND HUMAN RESOURCES BULLETIN, (formerly *Employee Relations Bulletin*), Bureau of Business Practice, 24 Rope Ferry Rd., Waterford CT 06386. Supervisory Editor: Barbara Kelsey. For personnel, human resources and employee relations managers on the executive level. Semimonthly newsletter; 8 pages. Circ. 3,000. Pays on acceptance. Buys all rights. No byline. Phone queries OK. Submit seasonal/holiday material 6 months in advance. Photocopied submissions OK. Computer printout submissions OK; prefers letter quality to dot matrix. SASE. Reports in 1 month. Free sample copy and writer's guidelines.

Nonfiction: Interviews about all types of business and industry such as banks, insurance companies, public utilities, airlines, consulting firms, etc. Interviewee should be a high level company officer—general manager, president, industrial relations manager, etc. Writer must get signed release from person interviewed showing that article has been read and approved by him/her, before submission. Some subjects for interviews might be productivity improvement, communications, compensation, government regulations, safety and health, grievance handling, human relations techniques and problems, etc. No general opinions and/or philosophy of good employee relations or general good motivation/morale material. Buys 3 mss/issue. Query. Length: 700-2,000 words. Pays 10¢/word after editing.

THE FOREMAN'S LETTER, Bureau of Business Practice, 24 Rope Ferry Rd., Waterford CT 06386. (203)442-4365. Editor: Carl Thunberg. For industrial supervisors. Semimonthly. Buys all rights. Pays on acceptance. Interested in regular stringers (freelance). Computer printout submissions OK "provided guidelines are met." SASE. Comprehensive guidelines available.

Nonfiction: Interested primarily in direct in-depth interviews with industrial supervisors in the US and Canada. Subject matter would be the interviewee's techniques for becoming a more effective manager, bolstered by illustrations out of the interviewee's own job experiences. Slant would be toward informing readers how to solve a particular supervisory problem. "Our aim is to offer information which, hopefully, readers may apply to their own professional self-improvement. No copy that focuses on the theme that 'happy workers are productive workers.' " Buys 15-20 unsolicited mss/year. Length: 600-1,200 words. Pays 8¢-14½¢/word "after editing for all rights."

Photos: Buys photos submitted with mss. "Captions needed for identification only." Head and shoulders, any size b&w glossy from 2x3 up. Pays $10.

Tips: "Study our editorial guidelines carefully. Emulate the style of sample issues. Write a how-to article focusing on one specific topic. A new freelancer should be willing to rewrite submissions if neccessary. Editor will offer suggestions. An effort will be made to cultivate freelancers who comply the *closest* to editorial guidelines."

HI-TECH MANAGER'S BULLETIN, TEM, (formerly *Supervision for Technology and Electronics Management*), Bureau of Business Practice, Inc. 24 Rope Ferry Rd., Waterford CT 06386. (203)442-4365. Editor: Sally Wagner. Managing Editor: Wayne Muller. Bimonthly newsletter for technical supervisors wishing to improve their managerial skills in high technology fields. Pays on acceptance. No byline given. Buys all rights. Reports in 2 weeks on queries, 6 weeks on mss. Free sample copy and writer's guidelines.

Nonfiction: How-to (solve a supervisory problem on the job); interview (of top-notch supervisors and managers). "Sample topics could include: how-to increase productivity, cut costs, achieve better teamwork, help employees adapt to change." No articles about company programs. Buys 72 mss/year. Query. "A resume and sample of work are helpful." Length: 750-1,000 words. Pays 8-14¢/word.

Tips: "We need interview-based articles that emphasize direct quotes. Each article should include a reference to the interviewee's company (location, size, products, function of the interviewee's department and number of employees under his control). Define a problem and show how the supervisor solved it. Write in a light, conversational style, talking directly to technical supervisors who can benefit from putting the interviewee's tips into practice."

LE BUREAU, Suite 1000, 1001 de Maisonneuve W., Montreal, Quebec, Canada H3A 3E1. (514)845-5141. Editor: Paul Saint-Pierre, C.Adm. For "office executives." Published 6 times/year. Circ. 7,500. Buys all rights. Byline given. Buys about 10 mss/year. Pays on acceptance. Query or submit complete ms. Submit seasonal material "between 1 and 2 months" in advance of issue date. SAE and International Reply Coupons.

Nonfiction and Photos: "Our publication is published in the French language. We use case histories on new office systems, applications of new equipment, articles on personnel problems. Material should be exclusive and above-average quality." Buys personal experience articles, interviews, think pieces, coverage of successful business operations, and new product articles. Length: 500-1,000 words. Pays $75-150. B&w glossies purchased with mss. Pays $25 each.

MANAGE, 2210 Arbor Blvd., Dayton OH 45439. (513)294-0421. Editor-in-Chief: Douglas E. Shaw. 60% freelance written. For first-line and middle management and scientific/technical managers. Quarterly magazine; 36 pages. Circ. 72,000. Pays on acceptance. Buys North American magazine rights with reprint privileges; book rights remain with the author. Phone queries OK. SASE. Reports in 1 month. Free sample copy and writer's guidelines.
Nonfiction: "All material published by *Manage* is in some way management-oriented. Most articles concern one or more of the following categories: communications; cost reduction; economics; executive abilities; health and safety; human relations; job status; labor relations; leadership; motivation and productivity; and professionalism. Articles should be specific and tell the manager how to apply the information to his job immediately. Be sure to include pertinent examples, and back up statements with facts and, where possible, charts and illustrations. *Manage* does not want essays or academic reports, but interesting, well-written and practical articles for and about management." Buys 6 mss/issue. Submit complete ms. Length: 600-2,000 words. Pays 5¢/word.
Tips: "Keep current on management subjects; submit timely work."

‡**OFFICE ADMINISTRATION AND AUTOMATION**, (Incorporating *Administrative Management* and *Word Processing & Information Systems*), Geyer-McAllister Publications, Inc., 51 Madison Ave., New York NY 10010. (212)689-4411. Editor: Walter A. Kleinschrod. Executive Editor: Walter J. Presnick. Monthly business publication covering office systems, equipment, personnel, and management for administrators and systems specialists in charge of office operations. Estab. 1983. Circ. 65,000. Pays on publication. Byline given. Offers negotiable kill fee. Buys all rights. Photocopied submissions OK. SASE. Reports in 1 month. Sample copy $3.50; free writer's guidelines.
Nonfiction: Book excerpts, how-to, new product, opinion, and photo feature. No "college thesis" articles. Buys 50 mss/year. Query. Length: 500-2,000 words. Pays $350 maximum.
Photos: Send photos with ms. Pays $50 maximum for 8x10 b&w prints; $75 maximum for 4x5 color transparencies. Captions, model release, and identificaton of subjects required. Buys one-time rights.
Tips: "Analyze and interpret clearly, especially if subject is technical. Assume readers have years of experience in the field."

PERSONNEL ADVISORY BULLETIN, Bureau of Business Practice, 24 Rope Ferry Rd., Waterford CT 06386. (203)442-4365. Editor: John Fuller. Emphasizes all aspects of personnel management for personnel managers in all types and sizes of companies, both white collar and industrial. Semimonthly newsletter; 4 pages. Pays on acceptance. Buys all rights. Phone queries OK. Submit seasonal/holiday material 4 months in advance of issue date. SASE. Reports in 2 weeks. Free sample copy and writer's guidelines.
Nonfiction: Interviews with personnel managers or human resource executives on topics of current interest in the personnel field. No articles on training programs, hiring and interviewing, discipline, or absenteeism/tardiness control. Buys 30 mss/year. Query with brief, specific outline. Length: 800-1,000 words. Pays 10¢/word after editing.
Tips: "It's very easy to break in. Just query by phone or letter (preferably phone) and we'll discuss the topic. Especially need writers in the Midwest and West. Send for guidelines and sample first, though, so we can have a coherent conversation."

PRODUCTIVITY IMPROVEMENT BULLETIN, PIB, Bureau of Business Practice, 24 Rope Ferry Rd., Waterford CT 06386. (203)442-4365. Editor: Paula Brisco. Semimonthly newsletter covering productivity improvement techniques of interest to middle and top management. Pays on acceptance. No byline given. Buys all rights. Reports in 2 weeks on queries; 1 month on mss. Free sample copy and writer's guidelines.
Nonfiction: Interviews with managers from business or industry discussing productivity innovations. No articles on general management theory. Buys 50 mss/year. Query. Length: 1,000-2,000 words. Pays 8-14¢/word "after editing."
Columns/Departments: "Personal Productivity column uses interview-based copy explaining specific measures our readers can take to increase their effectiveness." Buys 12 mss/year. Query. Length: 800-1,200 words. Pays 8-14¢/word.
Tips: "Lead story articles *must* cover a 'problem-process-solution-results' format as described in the writer's guidelines. Be willing to rewrite, if necessary. Topics should be well focused. (Check with us before doing the write-up. We like to talk to freelancers.) Writing should be conversational; use the 'you' approach. Use subheads and questions to guide the reader through your piece. Articles on activities of a specific company are subject to its approval."

SALES MANAGER'S BULLETIN, The Bureau of Business Practice, 24 Rope Ferry Rd., Waterford CT 06386. Editor: Paulette Withers. For sales managers and salespeople interested in getting into sales management. Newsletter published twice a month; 8 pages. Pays on acceptance. Phone queries from regulars OK. Submit seasonal/holiday material 6 months in advance. Original submissions only. SASE. Reports in 2 weeks. Free sample copy and writer's guidelines only when accompanied by SASE.

Nonfiction: How-to (motivate salespeople, cut costs, create territories, etc.); interview (with working sales managers who use innovative techniques); and technical (marketing stories based on interviews with experts). No articles on territory management, saving fuel in the field, or public speaking skills. Break into this publication by reading the guidelines and sample issue. Follow the directions closely and chances for acceptance go up dramatically. One easy way to start is with an interview article ("Here's what sales executives have to say about . . ."). Recent article example: "Increasing Sales Productivity Through Call Card Analysis" (March 1983). Buys 5 unsolicited mss/year. Query is vital to acceptance; "send a simple postcard explaining briefly the subject matter, the interviewees (if any), slant, length, and date of expected completion, accompanied by a SASE." Length: 800-1,500. Pays 10-15¢/word.

Tips: "Freelancers should always request samples and writer's guidelines, accompanied by SASE. Requests without SASE are discarded immediately. Examine the sample, and don't try to improve on our style. Write as we write. The more time a writer can save the editors, the greater his or her chance of a sale and repeated sales, when queries may not be necessary any longer."

SECURITY MANAGEMENT, American Society for Industrial Security, Suite 1200, 1655 N. Fort Myers Dr., Arlington VA 22209. (703)522-5800. Editor: Shari Mendelson Gallery. Senior Editor: Mary Alice Crawford. Managing Editor: Pamela Blumgart. Monthly professional magazine of the security business (i.e., protecting assets from loss). Circ. 19,000. Pays on publication. Byline given. Buys all rights. Submit seasonal/holiday material 6 months in advance. Simultaneous queries and simultaneous, photocopied, and previously published submissions to noncompetitive magazines OK. Computer printout or disk submissions OK. SASE. Reports in 3 weeks on queries; 10 weeks on mss. Sample copy $3; writer's guidelines for business size SAE and 1 first class stamp.

Nonfiction: Mary Alice Crawford, articles editor. Book excerpts, how-to, interview/profile, opinion, personal experience, photo feature, technical. Case studies, analytical pieces, and new approaches to persistent security problems such as access control, computer security. No humor. "Send a coherent outline query." Buys 5-10 mss/year. Query with or without clips of published work. Length: 1,500-5,000 words. Pays 10¢/word; $250 maximum.

Photos: State availability of photos. Reviews b&w and color contact sheets and prints, color transparencies.

Fillers: David Raths, fillers editor. Clippings, anecdotes, newsbreaks. Buys variable number/year. Length: 50-200 words. Pays $5-25.

Tips: "We need more substantive, technical articles, not cursory overviews."

SECURITY MANAGEMENT: PROTECTING PROPERTY, PEOPLE & ASSETS, (formerly *Security Management—Plant and Property Protection*), Bureau of Business Practice, 24 Rope Ferry Rd., Waterford CT 06386. Editor: Alex Vaughn. Emphasizes security for industry. "All material should be slanted toward security directors, preferably industrial, but some retail and institutional as well." Semimonthly newsletter; 4 pages. Circ. 3,000. Pays on acceptance. Buys all rights. Phone queries OK. Photocopied submissions OK. SASE. Reports in 2 weeks. Free sample copy and writer's guidelines.

Nonfiction: Interview (with security professionals only). "Articles should be tight and specific. They should deal with new security techniques or new twists on old ones." Buys 2 mss/issue. Query. Length: 750-1,000 words. Pays 10¢/word.

SUPERVISION, 424 N. 3rd St., Burlington IA 52601. Publisher: Bertrand G. Houle. Editorial Supervisor: Doris J. Ruschill. Editor: Barbara Boeding. 65% freelance written. For first-line foremen, supervisors and office managers. Monthly magazine; 24 pages. Circ. 13,100. Pays on publication. Buys all rights. Previously published submissions OK. SASE. Reports in 3 weeks. Free sample copy and writer's guidelines; mention *Writer's Market* in request.

Nonfiction: How-to (cope with supervisory problems, discipline, absenteeism, safety, productivity, goal setting, etc.); personal experience (unusual success story of foreman or supervisor). No sexist material written from only a male viewpoint. Buys 12 mss/issue. Query. Length: 1,500-1,800 words. Pays 4¢/word.

Tips: "Query to be brief, but long enough to give a clear picture of material and approach being used. We are particularly interested in writers with first-hand experience—current or former supervisors who are also good writers. Following AP stylebook would be helpful." Uses no photos or advertising.

TRAINING, The Magazine of Human Resources Development, 731 Hennepin Ave., Minneapolis MN 55403. (612)333-0471. Managing Editor: Jack Gordon. Monthly magazine for persons who train people in business, industry, government and health care. Circ. 42,000. Rights purchased vary with author and material. Usually buys all rights. Buys 10-20 mss/year; pays on acceptance. Will consider photocopied submissions. No simultaneous submissions. Computer printout submissions OK; prefers letter quality to dot matrix. Works three months in advance. Reports in 6 weeks. Query only. SASE. Write for sample copy and editorial guidelines.

Nonfiction and Photos: Articles on management and techniques of employee training. "Material should discuss a specific training problem or need; why the need existed, how it was met, alternatives considered, criteria for success, etc. Should furnish enough data for readers to make an independent judgment about the appropriateness of the solution and identify implications for their own situations. We want names and specific details on all techniques and programs used." Would like to see "articles relating general business concerns to specific training and development functions; interesting examples of successful training and management development programs; articles about why certain types of the above seem to fail; profiles of trainers who have moved into upper-level executive positions; emerging trends in the training and development field." Informational, how-to. Recent article example: "Computer Literacy for Managers: Will Trainers Accept the Challenge?" (February 1983). No puff or "gee whiz" material. Buys 5 unsolicited mss/year. Length: 1,200-2,500 words. Training Today: Reports on research, opinions or events of significance to human resources development professionals; length; 300-700 words. No extra payment for photos. Prefers b&w or color transparencies, with captions. Pays negotiable rates.

UTILITY SUPERVISION AND SAFETY LETTER, (formerly *Utility Supervision*), US Bureau of Business Practice, 24 Rope Ferry Rd., Waterford CT 06386. (203)442-4365. Editor: DeLoris Lidestri. Emphasizes all aspects of utility supervision. Semimonthly newsletter; 4 pages. Pays on acceptance. Buys all rights. Phone queries OK. Submit seasonal material 4 months in advance. SASE. Reports in 4-6 weeks. Free sample copy and writer's guidelines.

Nonfiction: Publishes how-to (interview on a single aspect of supervision with utility manager/supervisor concentrating on how reader/supervisor can improve in that area). Buys 100 mss/year. Query. Length: 500-1,000 words. Pays 8-12¢/word.

Photos: Purchased with accompanying ms. Pays $10 for b&w prints of "head and shoulders 'mug shot' of person interviewed." Total purchase price for ms includes payment for photos.

WAREHOUSING SUPERVISOR'S BULLETIN, WSB, Bureau of Business Practice, Inc. 24 Rope Ferry Rd., Waterford CT 06386. (203)442-4365. Editor: Sally Wagner. Managing Editor: Wayne Muller. Biweekly newsletter covering traffic, materials handling and distribution for warehouse supervisors "interested in becoming more effective on the job." Pays on acceptance. No byline given. Buys all rights. Reports in 2 weeks on queries; 6 weeks on mss. Free sample copy and writer's guidelines.

Nonfiction: How-to (increase efficiency, control or cut costs, cut absenteeism or tardiness, increase productivity, raise morale); interview (of warehouse supervisors who have solved problems on the job). No descriptions of company programs, noninterview articles, textbook-like descriptions, union references. Buys 50 mss/year. Query. "A resume and sample of work are helpful." Length: 800-1,200 words. Pays 8-14¢/word.

Tips: "Interview-based articles must emphasize direct quotes. They should also include a reference to the interviewee's company (location, size, products, function of the interviewee's department and number of employees under his control). Focus articles on one problem and get the interviewee to pinpoint the best way to solve it. Write in a light, conversational style, talking directly to warehouse supervisors who can benefit from putting the interviewee's tips into practice."

Marine Industries and Water Navigation

THE BOATING INDUSTRY, 850 3rd Ave., New York NY 10022. Editor and Publisher: Charles A. Jones. Managing Editor: Olga Badillo. For "boating retailers and distributors." Monthly. Circ. 26,300. Buys all rights. Byline given. Buys 10-15 feature mss/year. "Interested in good column material, too." Pays on publication. "Best practice is to check with managing editor first on story ideas for go-ahead." Submit seasonal material 3-4 months in advance. Reports in 2 months. SASE.

Nonfiction and Photos: No clippings. Pays 9-15¢/word. B&w glossy photos purchased with mss.

CANADIAN SHIPPING AND MARINE ENGINEERING, Suite 204, 5200 Dixie Rd., Mississauga, Ontario, Canada L4W 1E4. Editor: Patrick Brophy. Monthly magazine covering ship building, repair and operation. Circ. 3,800. Pays on publication. Buys first Canadian rights. SAE and International Reply Coupons.

Nonfiction: "*Competent, authoritative*, technical or historical material dealing with maritime subjects of interest to Canadian readers." Query or send complete ms. Length: 1,000-2,000 words. Pays 10-12¢/word.

Photos: Uses 5x7 b&w prints and 35mm or larger color transparencies or prints with articles.

SEAWAY REVIEW, The Business Magazine of the Great Lakes/St. Lawrence Seaway, Transportation System, Harbor Island, Maple City Postal Station MI 49664. Production office: 8715 Parmater Rd., Elmira MI 49730. Publisher: Jacques LesStrang. Managing Editor: Michelle Cortright. 10% freelance written. For "the entire Great Lakes maritime community, executives of companies that ship via the Great Lakes, traffic managers, transportation executives, federal and state government officials and manufacturers of maritime equipment." Quarterly magazine. Circ. 15,500. Pays on publication. Buys first North American serial rights. Submit seasonal material 2 months in advance of issue date. Photocopied submissions OK. Computer printout or disk submissions OK. SASE. Reports in 3 weeks. Sample copy $3.
Nonfiction: "Articles dealing with Great Lakes shipping, shipbuilding, marine technology, economics of 8 states in Seaway region (Michigan, Minnesota, Illinois, Indiana, Ohio, New York, Pennsylvania and Wisconsin), and Canada (Ontario, Quebec), port operation, historical articles dealing with Great Lakes shipping, current events dealing with commercial shipping on lakes, etc." No subjects contrary to our editorial statement. Submit complete ms. Length: 1,000-4,000 words. Pay "varies with value of subject matter and knowledgeability of author, $50 to $250."
Photos: State availability of photos with query. Pays $10-150 for 8x10 glossy b&w prints; $10-50 for 8x10 glossy color prints or transparencies. Captions required. Buys one-time rights. Buys "hundreds" of freelance photos each year.
Fillers: Clippings and spot news relating to ports and the Great Lakes. Buys 3/issue. Length: 50-500 words. Pays $5-50.

THE WORK BOAT, H.L. Peace Publications, Box 2400, Covington LA 70434. (504)893-2930. Publisher/Editor: Harry L. Peace. Managing Editor: Rick Martin. Monthly. Buys all rights. Pays on acceptance. Query. Reports in 1 month. SASE. Sample copy $3; writer's guidelines for SASE.
Nonfiction: "Articles on waterways, river terminals, barge line operations, work boat construction and design, barges, offshore oil vessels and tugs. Best bet for freelancers: One-angle article showing in detail how a barge line, tug operator or dredging firm solves a problem of either mechanical or operational nature. This market is semitechnical and rather exacting. Such articles must be specific, containing firm name, location, officials of company, major equipment involved, by brand name, model, power, capacity and manufacturer; with color or b&w photos." Length: 1,000-2,000 words. Pays $150 minimum.
Photos: 5x5 or 5x7 b&w; 4x5 color prints only. No additional payment for photos accompanying ms. Captions and model release required. Buys one-time rights.

Medical

Herein are publications for the private physician and journals reporting on new discoveries in medicine. Journals for nurses, laboratory technicians, and other medical workers are included with the Hospitals, Nursing, and Nursing Homes journals. Publications for druggists and drug wholesalers and retailers are grouped with the Drugs and Health Care Products journals. Publications that report on medical trends for the consumer can be found in the Health and Science categories.

APA MONITOR, 1200 17th St. NW, Washington DC 20036. Editor: Jeffrey Mervis. Associate Editor: Kathleen Fisher. For psychologists and other social scientists and professionals interested in behaviorial sciences and mental health area. Monthly newspaper. Circ. 70,000. Buys first serial rights. Computer printout submissions OK; prefers letter quality to dot matrix printouts. Pays on publication. Free sample copy.
Nonfiction: News and feature articles about issues facing psychology both as a science and a mental health profession; political, social and economic developments in the behavioral sciences area. Interview, profile and historical pieces. No personal views, reminiscences or satire. Buys 10-15 mss/year. Query. Length: 300-3,000 words.

CANADIAN DOCTOR, 1450 Don Mills Rd., Don Mills, Ontario, Canada M3B 2X7. (416)445-6641. Editor-in-Chief: Kimberly Coffman. Assistant Editor: Ellen Gardner. Monthly magazine; 100 pages. Circ. 36,000. Pays on publication. Buys all rights. Byline given. SAE and International Reply Coupons are essential for return of material. Computer printout submissions OK; prefers letter quality to dot matrix printouts. No disk submissions. Reports in 3 weeks. Free sample copy and writer's guidelines.
Nonfiction: How-to (run a physician's practice efficiently); interview (with Canadian doctors, perhaps those who have moved to US); personal experience (from Canadian doctors); personal opinion (from Canadian doctor about the profession); profile (of Canadian doctor); and medical lifestyles (only on assignment). No human interest or lifestyle pieces. Buys 50 unsolicited mss/year. Query with outline of article, "preferably in point

form so that editors can add/change to meet needs." Length: 1,000-2,500 words. Pays 20¢/word.
Photos: State availability of photos with query. Pays $15 for b&w glossy prints; $25 for color. Captions required. Buys one-time rights. Model release required.
Tips: "We are a Canadian magazine aimed at a Canadian audience, 36,000 + . We have different problems (a health insurance scheme for one, based on fee-for-service, and which varies from one province to another), but we can learn about medical business management from anywhere. In the year ahead there will be great emphasis on practice management and brass tacks of business procedures needed for an efficient and profitable medical practice."

DIAGNOSTIC IMAGING, Miller Freeman, 500 Howard St., San Francisco CA 94105. Publisher: Thomas Kemp. Editor: Peter Ogle. Monthly news magazine covering radiology, nuclear medicine and ultrasound for physicians and chief technicians in diagnostic professions. Circ. 24,000. Average issue includes 2-3 features. Pays on acceptance. Byline given. Buys all rights. Phone queries OK. "Written query should be well written, concise and contain a brief outline of proposed article and a description of the approach or perspective the author is taking." Submit seasonal material 1 month in advance. Simultaneous and photocopied submissions OK. SASE. Reports in 2 weeks. Free sample copy.
Nonfiction: "We are interested in topical news features in the areas of radiology, nuclear medicine, and ultrasound, especially news of state and federal legislation, new products, insurance, regulations, medical literature, professional meetings and symposia and continuing education." Buys 10-12 mss/year. Query with clips of previously published work. Length: 1,000-2,000 words. Pays 10¢/word minimum.
Photos: Reviews 5x7 b&w glossy prints and 35mm and larger color transparencies. Offers no additional payment for photos accepted with ms. Captions required. Buys one-time rights.

EMERGENCY, Box 159, Carlsbad CA 92008. Managing Editor: Carl Calbert. 40% freelance written. Emphasizes emergency medical services for anyone involved in emergency services, including ambulance personnel, paramedics, search and rescue personnel, emergency room personnel, law enforcement personnel and firefighters. Monthly magazine; 84 pages. Circ. 40,000. Pays on publication. Buys all rights. Byline and biographical information given. Submit seasonal/holiday material 4 months in advance of issue date. SASE. Reports in 2 months. Free sample copy and writer's guidelines.
Nonfiction: How-to (better execute a certain emergency procedure, guidelines for emergency medical techniques). Recent article example: "Airway Management in Prehospital Care." Buys 24 unsolicited mss/year. Query. Length: 800-3,000 words. Pays $50-175.
Photos: State availability of photos with query. Pays $15 minimum for 5x7 b&w glossy prints; $25-35 for 35mm color transparencies. Captions required. Buys all rights. Buys 1-2 cover color transparencies/year. Pays $100-150.
Columns/Departments: News Briefs (short items of interest to emergency personnel); and Funds and Grants (allocated for improvement of emergency care). Buys 10/year. Query. Length: 50-100 words. Pays $1/inch. Open to suggestions for new columns/departments.
Tips: "All articles are carefully reviewed; therefore, any well-written article, especially one including 35mm transparencies, has a good chance of being published."

FACETS, American Medical Association Auxiliary, Inc., 535 N. Dearborn St., Chicago IL 60610. (312)751-6166. Editor: Kathleen T. Jordan. For physicians' spouses. Magazine published 5 times/year; 32 pages. Circ. 90,000. Pays on acceptance. Buys first rights. Submit seasonal/holiday material 4 months in advance of issue date. Simultaneous, photocopied and previously published submissions OK. SASE. Reports in 6 weeks. Free sample copy and writer's guidelines.
Nonfiction: All articles must be related to the experiences of physicians' spouses. Current health issues; financial topics; physicians' family circumstances; business management; leadership how-to's. Buys 8 mss/year. Query with clear outline of article—what points will be made, what conclusions drawn, what sources will be used. No personal experience or personality stories. Length: 1,000-2,500 words. Pays $300-800.
Photos: State availability of photos with query. Uses 8x10 glossy b&w prints and 2¼x2¼ color transparencies.
Tips: Uses "articles only on specified topical matter; with good sources, not hearsay or opinion, but credibility. Since we use only nonfiction articles and have a limited readership, we must relate factual material."

GENETIC ENGINEERING NEWS, The Information Source of the Biotechnology Industry, Mary Ann Liebert, Inc., 157 E. 86th St., New York NY 10028. (212)289-2393. Editor: Peter Wesley Dorfman. Bimonthly tabloid featuring articles on industry and research in all areas of biotechnology such as recombinant DNA and hybridoma technology. Circ. 10,000. Pays on acceptance. Byline given. Buys all rights. Computer printout submissions OK if double spaced; prefers letter quality to dot matrix printout. SASE. Reports in 6 weeks on queries; 1 month on mss.
Nonfiction: Interview/profile (of corporate executives, academicians or researchers); new product; technical (any articles relating to biotechnology with emphasis on application); and financial (Wall Street analysis,

etc.—of new companies). No company personnel changes or rewritten press releases. Buys 75 mss/year. Query with clips of published work. Length: 1,000-1,200 words. "All negotiable."
Photos: Send photos with ms. Pays negotiable fee for b&w contact sheets. Identification of subjects required.
Tips: "Writers submitting queries must be extremely knowledgeable in the field and have direct access to hard news. In late 1983 we will increase the frequency of our publication."

HEALTH INDUSTRY TODAY, (formerly *Surgical Business*), Box 1487, Union NJ 07083. Editor: David Cassak. For medical/surgical dealers and dealer/salesmen. Monthly magazine; 92 pages. Circ. 7,000. Buys exclusive industry rights. Byline given. Buys 5-10 mss/year. Pays on publication. Free sample copy and writer's guidelines. Will consider photocopied and simultaneous submissions. Query or submit complete ms. SASE.
Nonfiction and Photos: "We publish articles touching on all aspects of healthcare supply, from company and individual profiles to market studies, and from government regulatory action and its impact to coming trends. We are also interested in new technologies and products, but from a marketing perspective, not a technical one. Keep in mind that we deal with the marketing (or selling) of healthcare supplies to hospitals, doctors, and the home healthcare trade, and that our readers are, for the most part, sophisticated businessmen. We insist that submitted articles demonstrate an understanding of the issues that affect the industry." No general articles on finances (especially around tax time) or selling that could apply to a variety of fields. No additional payment for b&w photos used with mss. Length: approximately 2,500 words. Pays 10¢/word or negotiable fee.
Tips: "We are always eager to receive quality freelance submissions and would gladly enter into a long-term arrangement with a freelancer whose work we like. Submitted articles can relieve a burden on our own staff and give our publication a wider perspective. The problem we encounter with most freelancers, however, quality of writing aside, is that they want to write general articles that they can submit to a number of publications, and thus do not want to write articles of sufficient sophistication for our readers. Simply put, the articles are so general in approach, they rarely provide any real information at all for anyone even slightly exposed to the field. Know either the publication or the field. We encourage freelancers to write for a sample copy of our publication."

THE MAYO ALUMNUS, Mayo Clinic, 200 SW 1st St., Rochester MN 55901. (507)284-2511. Editor: Rosemary A. Klein. For physicians, scientists, and medical educators who trained at the Mayo Clinic. Quarterly magazine; 48 pages. Circ. 10,000. Pays on acceptance. Buys all rights. Submit seasonal/holiday material 6 months in advance of issue date. Previously published submissions OK. SASE. Reports in 2 months. Free sample copy; mention *Writer's Market* in request.
Nonfiction: "We're interested in seeing interviews with members of the Mayo Alumni Association—stories about Mayo-trained doctors/educators/scientists/researchers who are interesting people doing interesting things in medicine, surgery or hobbies of interest, etc." Query with clips of published work. Length: 1,000-3,000 words. Pays 15¢/word, first 1,500 words. Maximum payment is $275.
Photos: "We need art and must make arrangements if not provided with the story." Pays $10 for b&w photos. State availability of photos with query. Captions preferred. Buys all rights.

MD MAGAZINE, MD Publications, Inc., 30 E. 60th St., New York NY 10022. (212)355-5432. Editor: A.J. Vogl. Managing Editor: Barbara Guidos. Monthly magazine of information and culture for practicing physicians. Circ. 170,000. Pays on acceptance. Byline given. Offers 25% kill fee. Buys one-time rights. Simultaneous queries OK. Not receptive to computer printout and disk submissions. SASE. Reports in 1 week on queries; 2 weeks on mss. Free sample copy and writer's guidelines.
Nonfiction: General interest; historical/nostalgic; interview/profile (of physicians); photo feature; technical (medicine); travel. Buys 120 mss/year. Query with clips of published work. Length: 750-3,000 words. Pays $250-700.
Photos: Barbara Floria, photo editor. State availability of photos. Pays ASMP rates for b&w contact sheet and 35mm color transparencies. Captions, model release and identification of subjects required.
Tips: "I'm especially looking for lively writing on contemporary subjects."

THE MEDICAL POST, 481 University Ave., Toronto, Ontario, Canada M5W 1A7. Editor: Derek Cassels. For the medical profession. Biweekly. Will send sample copy to medical writers only. Buys first Canadian serial rights. Pays on publication. SAE and International Reply Coupons.
Nonfiction: Uses newsy, factual reports of medical developments. Must be aimed at professional audience, and written in newspaper style. Length: 300-800 words. Pays 17¢/word.
Photos: Uses photos with mss or captions only, of medical interest; pays $10 up.

MEDICAL TIMES, Romaine Pierson Publishers, Inc. 80 Shore Rd., Port Washington NY 11050. (516)883-6350. Editors: A.J. Bollet, M.D., and A.H.Bruckheim, M.D. Managing Editor: Susan Carr Jenkins. Monthly magazine covering clinical medical subjects for primary care physicians in private practice. Circ. 100,000. Pays on acceptance. Byline given. Offers 100% kill fee. Buys all rights and makes work-for-hire assignments.

Submit seasonal/holiday material 6 months in advance. Simultaneous queries OK. Not receptive to computer printout or disk submissions. Reports in 1 month on queries; 2 months on mss. Sample copy $5; writer's guidelines for business size SAE and 1 first class stamp.

Nonfiction: "We accept only clinical medical and medicolegal material. It is useless to send us any material that is not related directly to medicine." Buys 100 mss/year. Query. Length: 500-2,500 words. Pays $25-300.

Photos: State availability of photos. Pays variable rates for 2x2 b&w and color transparencies, and 4x5 or 8x10 b&w and color prints. Model release and identification of subjects required.

Fillers: Anecdotes. "Must be true, unpublished, and medically oriented." Buys 25/year. Length: 25-200 words.

Tips: "A query letter is a must. 99% of our material is 'invited.' "

THE NEW PHYSICIAN, 1910 Association Dr., Reston VA 22091. Editor: Keith Haglund. 20% freelance written. For medical students, interns and residents. Published 9 times/year; 56 pages. Circ. 80,000. Buys all rights. Buys 6-12 mss/year. Pays on publication. Free sample copy. Will consider simultaneous submissions. Computer printout submissions OK; no disk submissions. Reports in 4-8 weeks. Query. SASE.

Nonfiction and Photos: "Articles on social, political, economic issues in medicine/medical education. Our readers need more than a superficial, simplistic look into issues that affect them. We want skeptical, accurate, professional contributors to do well-researched, comprehensive reports, and offer new perspectives on health care problems." Not interested in material on "my operation," or encounters with physicians, or personal experiences as physician's patient, investment/business advice for physicians, or highly technical material. Occasionally publishes special topic issues, such as those on death and dying and alternatives in medical training. Informational articles, interviews and exposes are sought. Length: 500-3,500 words. Pays $25-400. Pays $10-35 for b&w photos used with mss. Captions required.

Tips: "Our magazine demands real sophistication on the issues we cover because we are a professional journal. Those freelancers we publish reveal in their queries and ultimately in their mss a willingness and an ability to look deeply into the issues in question and not be satisfied with a cursory review of those issues."

‡NUCLEUS SCIENCE JOURNAL, Queens College/City University of New York, Kissena & Melbourne Ave., Box 67, Flushing NY 11367. Editor: Mark A. Young. Managing Editor: Lisa C. Bogdonoff. Annual scientific journal covering biology, chemistry, medicine and natural science. Circ. 7,000. Pays on publication. Byline given. Buys all rights. Submit seasonal material 3 months in advance. Simultaneous queries, and simultaneous, photocopied, and previously published submissions OK. SASE. Reports in 2 weeks on queries; 4 weeks on mss. Sample copy $1; free writer's guidelines.

Nonfiction: Mark A. Young, articles editor. Book excerpts; interview/profile (with scientists who have made significant contributions to furthering an understanding of science); photo feature. Buys 20 mss/year. Query with or without published clips. Length: open. Pays $50 minimum; sometimes pays in copies; sometimes commissions articles.

Photos: Louis Wenger, photo editor. Reviews b&w contact sheet. Payment depends on photo.

Fillers: Nat Soloman, fillers editor. Anecdotes, newsbreaks. Buys 10/year. Length: open.

Tips: "Well written scientific 'journal style' articles are what we seek. Articles should be slanted toward laymen and scientists alike. Articles on medical topics written by M.D.'s are especially welcome."

ONCOLOGY TIMES, Herlitz Publications, Inc. 404 Park Ave. S., New York NY 10016. (212)532-9400. Editor: Jonathan S. Wood. Monthly tabloid covering cancer research with a clinical emphasis for oncologists and allied professionals. Circ. 23,000. Pays on acceptance. Byline given. Buys all rights. Reports in 2 weeks on queries; 1 week on mss. Free sample copy and writer's guidelines.

Nonfiction: Articles on cancer research—some basic, primarily clinical. News interviews and features based on meetings and current literature reviews. No anecdotal stories. No unsolicited mss. Buys 240 mss/year. Query with clips of published work. Length: 750-1,500 words. Pays $150 minimum.

Tips: "Get some medical writing experience; I am generally pretty flexible with new writers, but I can't over emphasize the need for a working knowledge of medicine. If there is an upcoming meeting in your area (directly related to cancer), let me know; if it's your first contact, send *resume* and clips (copies OK)."

PHYSICIAN'S MANAGEMENT, Harcourt Brace Jovanovich Health Care Publications, 7500 Old Oak Blvd., Cleveland OH 44130. (216)243-8100. Editor: Bob Feigenbaum. Emphasizes finances, investments, estate and retirement planning, small office administration, practice management, leisure time, computers, automobiles, and taxes for primary care physicians in private practice. Monthly magazine. Circ. 110,000. Pays on acceptance. Buys first rights. Submit seasonal or holiday material 5 months in advance. "Computer printout submission is fine, as long as it is readable and spacing between lines is sufficient to permit editing. Strongly prefer submissions to be on standard 8½x11 paper and letter quality. Dislike computer paper, particularly long sheets." SASE. Reports in 2-4 weeks.

Nonfiction: *Physician's Management* is a practice management-economic publication, not a clinical one." Publishes how-to articles (limited to medical practice management); informational (when relevant to audi-

ence); personal experience articles (if written by a physician). No fiction; clinical material; satire that portrays MD in an unfavorable light; or soap opera, "real-life" articles. Length: 1,500-5,000 words. Buys 20-25/issue. Query. Pays $125/printed page. Use of charts, tables, graphs, sidebars, and photos strongly encouraged.
Tips: "Talk to doctors first about their practices, financial interests, and day-to-day nonclinical problems and then query us. Use of an MD byline helps tremendously! Also, the ability to write a concise, well-structured and well-researched magazine article is essential. Freelancers who think like patients fail with us. Those who can think like MDs are successful. Our magazine is growing significantly. The opportunities for good writers will, therefore, increase greatly."

PODIATRY MANAGEMENT, 401 N. Broad St., Philadephia PA 19108. (215)925-9744. Publisher: Scott C. Borowsky. Editor: Barry Block, D.P.M. Managing Editor: M.J. Goldberg. Bimonthly business magazine for practicing podiatrists. "Aims to help the doctor of podiatric medicine to build a bigger, more successful practice, to conserve and invest his money, to keep him posted on the economic, legal and sociological changes that affect him." Estab. 1981. Circ. 9,000. Pays on publication. Byline given. Offers 50% kill fee. Buys first North American and second serial (reprint) rights. Submit seasonal/holiday material 4 months in advance. Simultaneous queries, and simultaneous, photocopied, and previously published submissions OK. SASE. Reports in 2 weeks. Sample copy $2; free writer's guidelines.
Nonfiction: General interest (taxes, investments, estate planning, recreation hobbies); how-to (establish and collect fees, practice management, organize office routines, supervise office assistants, handle patient relations); interview/profile; personal experience. "These subjects are the mainstay of the magazine, but offbeat articles and humor are always welcome." Buys 25 mss/year. Query. Length: 1,000-2,500 words. Pays $150-350.
Photos: State availability of photos. Pays $10 for b&w contact sheet. Buys one-time rights.

PRIVATE PRACTICE, Box 12489, Oklahoma City OK 73157. Executive Editor: Karen C. Murphy. . For "medical doctors in private practice." Monthly. Buys first North American serial rights. "If an article is assigned, it is paid for in full, used or killed." Byline given "except if it was completely rewritten or a considerable amount of additional material is added to the article." Pays on acceptance. Query. "We accept computer printout submissions as long as they meet our other requirements of being first American serial rights, etc." SASE.
Nonfiction and Photos: "Articles that indicate importance of maintaining freedom of medical practice or which detail outside interferences in the practice of medicine, including research, hospital operation, drug manufacture, etc. Straight reporting style. No cliches, no scare words, no flowery phrases to cover up poor reporting. Stories must be actual, factual, precise, correct. Copy should be lively and easy-to-read. Also publish travel and leisure." No general short humor, poetry or short stories. "Please, no first-person humor or other type of personal experiences with your doctor—i.e., my account of when my doctor told me I needed my first operation, etc." Buys 50-60 unsolicited mss/year. Length: up to 2,500 words. Pays "usual minimum $150." Photos purchased with mss only. B&w glossies, 8x10. Payment "depends on quality, relevancy of material, etc."
Tips: "The article we are most likely to buy will be a straight report on some situation where the freedom to practice medicine has been enhanced, or where it has been intruded on to the detriment of good health."

SURGICAL ROUNDS, Romaine Pierson Publishers, Inc., 80 Shore Rd., Port Washington NY 11050. (516)883-6350. Editor: Mark M. Ravitch, MD. Managing Editor: Randolph P. Savicky. Monthly magazine for surgeons and surgical specialists throughout the country, including all surgical interns, all surgical residents, all surgical faculty in medical schools, plus fulltime hospital and private practice surgeons, and operating room supervisors. Circ. 70,000. Pays on acceptance. Byline given. Buys all rights. Reports in 1 month. Sample copy $5; free writer's guidelines.
Nonfiction: How-to (practical, everyday clinical applications). "Articles for 'The Surgeon's Laboratory' should demonstrate a particular procedure step-by-step and be amply and clearly illustrated with intraoperative color photographs and anatomical drawings." Buys 80 mss/year. Query with clips of published work. Length: 1,000-4,000 words. Pays $150-400.
Poetry: Only poetry related to hospital, physician or operative experience. Buys 6/year. Pays $25.

‡**THE SURGICAL TECHNOLOGIST**, Association of Surgical Technologists, Caller No. E, Littleton CO 80120. (303)978-9010. Editor: William Teatsch. Bimonthly magazine covering surgery, operating room issues, and legal, social and ethical implications. "Makes available the total picture of advanced operating room techniques, health care issues, educational programs, new instruments, supplies and equipment." Circ. 11,000. Pays on acceptance. Byline given. Buys all rights. Submit seasonal/holiday material 6 months in advance. Simultaneous queries and simultaneous, photocopied and previously published submissions OK. Reports in 2 weeks. Free sample copy and writer's guidelines.
Nonfiction: Book excerpts, expose, general interest, historical/nostalgic, how-to, humor, inspirational, interview/profile, new product, opinion, personal experience, photo feature, technical, travel. Buys "unlimited"

number mss/year. Query with clips if available or send complete ms. Length: 1,000-6,000 words. Pays $100-300.

Photos: State availability of photos or send photos with ms. Reviews all types of photos. Pays $25-100.

Fiction: Surgical humorous.

Mining and Minerals

AMERICAN GOLD NEWS, Box 457, Ione CA 95640. (209)274-2196. Editor: Luckii Ludwig. 25% freelance written. For anyone interested in gold, gold mining, gold companies, gold stocks, gold history, gold coins, the future of gold in our economy. Monthly tabloid newspaper; 20 pages. Circ. 3,500. Not copyrighted. Byline given. Pays on publication. Sample copy and writer's guidelines for $1. No photocopied or simultaneous submissions. Computer printout and disk submissions OK. Submit seasonal material (relating to seasonal times in mining country) 2 months in advance. Reports in 2-4 weeks. Query or submit complete ms. SASE.

Nonfiction and Photos: "This is not a literary publication. We want information on any subject pertaining to gold told in the most simple, direct and interesting way." How to build gold mining equipment; history of mines (with pix); history of gold throughout the US; financial articles on gold philosophy in money matters; picture stories of mines, mining towns, mining country. Would like to see more histories of mines, from any state. No fiction. Recent article example: "The Gold of Hornitos" (January 1983). Buys 12-24 unsolicited mss/year. Length: 500-2,000 words. Pays $10-50. B&w photos purchased with or without ms. Must be sharp (if not old historical photos). Pays $2.50-25. Captions required.

Tips: New editor, new guidelines, and "big PR push to increase subscribers and advertising" will affect writers in the year ahead.

COAL AGE, 1221 Avenue of the Americas, New York NY 10020. Editor: Joseph F. Wilkinson. For supervisors, engineers and executives in coal mining. Monthly. Circ. 20,000. Buys all rights. Pays on publication. Query. Reports in 2-3 weeks. SASE.

Nonfiction: Uses some technical (operating type) articles; some how-to pieces on equipment maintenance; management articles. Pays $200/page.

‡**COAL INDUSTRY NEWS, Coal's National Newspaper**, Whitney Communications Corp., 850 3rd Ave., New York NY 10022. (212)715-2600. Editor: Gene Smith. Managing Editor: Nick Snow. Biweekly tabloid covering all coal-related news and companies "aimed at decision-makers and upper echelon of coal/energy industry and government officials who deal with the industry." Circ. 12,000. Pays on publication. Byline given. Offers negotiable kill fee. Buys one-time rights. Simultaneous queries, and simultaneous and previously published submissions OK. Reports in 2 weeks. Free sample copy.

Nonfiction: General interest; how-to (case histories or reports on new technology); interview/profile; new product; technical (not too technical). Write for schedule of special supplements. No material on heavy technology. Buys 20-30 mss/year. Query. Length: 500-1,500 words. Pays $71.25/column.

Photos: State availability of photos. Pays $5 for 8x10 b&w print. Captions and identification of subjects required.

Tips: "A simple query in writing or by phone will get immediate response. All areas are open. Stress is on newspaper format—we are not technically-oriented."

KENTUCKY COAL JOURNAL, Box 573, Frankfort KY 40602. (502)223-1619. Editor: Mike Bennett. Monthly tabloid about coal mining: specifically the constrictions placed on the industry by federal and state bureaus regulating it, and market conditions. Circ. 10,000. Pays on publication. Byline given. Buys one-time rights. Phone queries OK. No computer printout or disk submissions. Submit seasonal material 1 month in advance. Photocopied and previously published submissions OK. Reports in 1 week. Free sample copy.

Nonfiction: Expose (of government); historical (of old coal mines); opinion; profile (of Kentucky coal mines and miners); humor; new product (revolutionary); and photo feature. "We have been called an example of 'personal journalism' meaning we inject comments, viewpoints, etc., into just about anything that's printed. We first took up for the small, independent operator; now we have become the unofficial spokesman for the entire Kentucky coal industry, although our circulation is national." No fictional or highly technical articles. Buys 2-3 mss/issue. Send complete ms. Length: 300 words minimum. Pays $25-300.

Photos: State availability of photos. Pay $15 minimum for any size b&w glossy prints. Captions required. Buys one-time rights.

Tips: "Tell us about a unique coal venture, mine or person. Tell us how to bust a particular bureaucracy. Or write a timely, factual story that fits into our editorial philosophy. We do not object to an adversary point of view, but no diatribes, please. If you have a valid and logical reason for opposing something, fine. Reading a copy of the *Coal Journal* will help. We don't want anything that does not relate directly to coal—preferably Kentucky coal."

Music

ASCAP IN ACTION, A Publication of the American Society of Composers, Authors and Publishers, 1 Lincoln Plaza, New York NY 10023. (212)595-3050. Editor: Merry Aronson. Magazine published 3 times/year covering music and its creators and publishers, ASCAP members, the music industry, college libraries, and foreign performing rights organizations. Circ. 50,000. Pays on acceptance. Byline "generally given." Buys first North American serial rights. Photocopied submissions OK. Reports in 1 month. Free sample copy.
Nonfiction: Profile (of an individual or event); publishing trends; and performing rights issues. No articles on BMI members or music people who are not writers." Buys 10-15 mss/year. Query with clips of published work. Length: 3,000-3,500 words. Pays $350.
Photos: "Whenever possible we get free use of photos through publicity agents; otherwise we buy." State availability of photos. Reviews color transparencies and 8x10 glossy prints. Captions required. Buys one-time rights.
Fillers: Anecdotes and short humor (music-oriented). Pays negotiable fee.

‡CADENCE, Cadence Jazz & Blues Magazine, Ltd., Cadence Building, Redwood NY 13679. (315)287-2852. Editor: Robert D. Rusch. Monthly jazz and blues trade magazine published for serious jazz and blues fans who are writers, performers, producers and record collectors. Pays on acceptance. Byline given. Buys all rights. Simultaneous queries, and simultaneous and photocopied submissions OK. SASE. Reports in weeks. Sample copy $2.
Nonfiction: Interview/profile. "We only use interviews (Q&A) and oral histories" related to jazz and blues. Query or send complete ms. Length: variable. Pays variable rates.
Photos: Reviews prints. Identification of subjects required.

THE CHURCH MUSICIAN, 127 9th Ave. N., Nashville TN 37234. (615)251-2953. Editor: William Anderson. 30% freelance written. Southern Baptist publication. For Southern Baptist church music leaders. Monthly. Circ. 20,000. Buys all rights. Pays on acceptance. Free sample copy. No query required. Reports in 2 months. SASE.
Nonfiction: Leadership and how-to features, success stories, articles on Protestant church music. "We reject material when the subject of an article doesn't meet our needs. And they are often poorly written, or contain too many 'glittering generalities' or lack creativity." Length: maximum 1,300 words. Pays up to 4¢/word.
Photos: Purchased with mss; related to mss content only. "We use only b&w glossy prints."
Fiction: Inspiration, guidance, motivation, morality with Protestant church music slant. Length: to 1,300 words. Pays up to 3½¢/word.
Poetry: Church music slant, inspirational. Length: 8-24 lines. Pays $5-15.
Fillers: Puzzles, short humor. Church music slant. No clippings. Pays $5-15.
Tips: "I'd advise a beginning writer to write about his or her experience with some aspect of church music; the social, musical, and spiritual benefits from singing in a choir; a success story about their instrumental group; a testimonial about how they were enlisted in a choir—especially if they were not inclined to be enlisted at first. A writer might speak to hymn singers—what turns them on and what doesn't. Some might include how music has helped them to talk about Jesus as well as sing about Him. We would prefer most of these experiences be related to the church, of course, although we include many articles by freelance writers whose affiliation is other than Baptist. A writer might relate his experience with a choir of blind or deaf members. Some people receive benefits from working with unusual children—retarded, or culturally deprived, emotionally unstable, and so forth. Photographs are valuable here."

CLAVIER, 1418 Lake Street, Evanston IL 60204. (312)328-6000. Editor: Lee Prater Yost. Magazine; 48 pages. 10 times a year. Buys all rights. Pays on publication. Free sample copy. No simultaneous submissions. "Suggest query to avoid duplication." No computer printout or disk submissions. SASE.
Nonfiction and Photos: Wants "articles aimed at teachers of piano and organ. Must be written from thoroughly professional point of view. Avoid, however, the thesis-style subject matter and pedantic style generally found in scholarly journals. We like fresh writing, practical approach. We can use interviews with concert pianists and organists. An interview should not be solely a personality story, but should focus on a subject of interest to musicians. Any word length. Photos may accompany ms." Buys 65+ unsolicited mss/year. Pays $35/printed page. Need color photos for cover, such as angle shots of details of instruments, other imaginative photos, with keyboard music themes."

THE INSTRUMENTALIST, 1418 Lake St., Evanston IL 60204. Editor: Kenneth L. Neidig. For instrumental music educators. Monthly. Circ. 22,527. Buys all rights. Byline given. Buys 200 mss/year. Pays on publication. Sample copy $2. Submit seasonal material 4 months in advance. New Products (February); Summer Camps, Clinics, Workshops (March); Marching Bands (June); Back to School (September); Fundraising (October). Reports on material accepted for publication within 4 months. Returns rejected material within 3 months. Query. SASE.

Nonfiction and Photos: "Practical information of immediate use to instrumentalists. Not articles 'about music and musicians,' but articles by musicians who are sharing knowledge, techniques, experience. 'In-service education.' Professional help for instrumentalists in the form of instrumental clinics, how-to articles, new trends, practical philosophy. Most contributions are from professionals in the field." Interpretive photojournalism. "Query for mss over 1,000 words." Length: 100-1,500 words. Pays according to length (approximately $25-45/printed page), plus 2 contributor's copies. Quality b&w prints. Pays $5-10. Color: 35mm and up. Pays $50-75 if used for cover.

MUSIC EDUCATORS JOURNAL, 1902 Association Dr., Reston VA 22091. (703)860-4000. Editor: Rebecca Taylor. For music educators in elementary and secondary schools and universities. Monthly (September-May) magazine. Circ. 55,000. Pays only for solicited articles by authors outside the music education field. Byline given. "Prefer typed manuscripts, but will consider computer printouts not submitted simultaneously to another journal." SASE. Reports in 6-8 weeks. Free author's guidesheet.

Nonfiction: "*MEJ* is the communications organ for the members of Music Educators National Conference. We publish articles on music education at all levels—not about individual schools, but about broad issues, trends, instructional techniques. Particularly interested in issue-oriented articles, pieces on individual aspects of American and non-Western music, and up-beat interviews with musicians, composers and innovative teachers." No articles on personal awards or group tours. Length: 1,000-3,000 words. Query the editor.

Tips: "Our readers are experts in music education, so accuracy and complete familiarity with the subject is essential. A selection of appropriate professional-quality 8x10 b&w glossy prints submitted with a manuscript greatly increases the chances of acceptance."

OPERA NEWS, 1865 Broadway, New York NY 10023. Editor: Robert Jacobson. For all people interested in opera; opera singers, opera management people, administrative people in opera, opera publicity people, artists' agents; people in the trade and interested laymen. Monthly magazine (May-November); biweekly (December-April). Circ. 105,000. Copyrighted. Pays negotiable kill fee. Byline given. Pays on publication. Sample copy $2.50. Query. No telephone inquiries. SASE.

Nonfiction and Photos: Most articles are commissioned in advance. In summer, uses articles of various interests on opera; in the fall and winter, articles that relate to the weekly broadcasts. Emphasis is on high quality in writing and an intellectual interest in the opera-oriented public. Informational, how-to, personal experience, interview, profile, humor, historical, think pieces, personal opinion; opera reviews. Length: 2,500 words maximum. Pays 11¢/word for features; 9¢/word for reviews. Pays minimum of $25 for photos purchased on assignment. Captions required.

‡**SONGS OF A SERVANT, Musicians Serving God**, Prime Composition, 5253 Clinton Blvd., Jackson MS 39209. (601)922-5941. Editor: Patricia Jane Prime. Managing Editor: W. Davis Prime. Triquarterly magazine of Christian music "for musicians of small to mid-range memberships of churches. The musicians are volunteers and have a wide range of training." Estab. 1982. Circ. 5,000. Pays on acceptance. Byline given. Offers $5 kill fee. Buys one-time rights. Submit seasonal/holiday material 5 months in advance. Simultaneous queries, and simultaneous and previously published submissions OK. SASE. Reports in 6 weeks. Sample copy $3; writer's guidelines 30¢.

Nonfiction: General interest, historical/nostalgic, humor, inspirational, interview/profile, personal experience, photo feature, technical. "All articles should be written with the small to mid-range membership of churches in mind (volunteer leadership with no training to college degrees). We want articles about small church choirs with successful or unique music ministries. We want articles of an entertaining nature about large church programs. We want articles on choir organization and leadership (tied in with small churches). We want articles on choirs (large and small, Presbyterian and other denominations). We want articles on performers. We will even consider articles of an inspirational nature." No articles on "how to start a Bell Choir on $2,000 or more. In other words, articles directed toward large church choir directors with unlimited budgets or pastors planning a service." Buys 6 mss/year. Send complete ms. Length: 500-2,000 words. Pays $20-100.

Photos: Send photos with ms. Pays $5-25 for 8x10 b&w prints. Captions, model release and identification of subjects required. Buys all rights.

Columns/Departments: "Music Reviews, printed and records, for Christian performers and choirs. The slant should be on listening or performance by a performer or small choir. Emphasis should be on how to obtain the reviewed materials." Buys 3 mss/year. Query. Length: 500-1,000 words. Pays $20-50.

Fillers: Short humor. Buys 9-12 mss/year. Length: 50-500 words. Pays $5.

Tips: "We are also looking for articles on a series basis: articles on leadership (motivation), conducting, music theory (keep in mind the small church, articles may be along line of self taught lessons that could be photocopied and passed out to be worked on at home). Please, submit ideas befor sending series articles."

SYMPHONY MAGAZINE, American Symphony Orchestra League, 633 E St., NW, Washington DC 20004. (202)628-0099. Editor: Robin Perry Allen. Associate Editor: Chester Lane. Bimonthly magazine covering symphony orchestras in North America and the classical music industry for members of the association, including managers, conductors, board members, musicians, volunteer association members, music businesses, schools, libraries, etc. Circ. 14,500. Pays on publication. Byline given. Pays negotiable kill fee. Buys all rights. Simultaneous queries, and photocopied and previously published submissions OK. Reports in 1 month. Free sample copy.

Nonfiction: How-to (put together a symphony); interview/profile (conductors and personalities in the field); technical (budgeting, tour planning); and "thoughtful, reflective looks at the state of the classical music industry." Buys 20 mss/year. Query with clips of published work. Length: 2,500-3,000 words. Pays $50-300.

Photos: "We prefer action shots and informal shots." State availability of photos. Pays $25-50 for 8x10 glossy prints. Captions required.

UP BEAT MAGAZINE, Maher Publications, Inc., 222 W. Adams St., Chicago IL 60606. Editor: Herb Nolan. Managing Editor: Al DeGenova. Magazine published 10 times/year about the musical instrument and sound equipment industry for retailers of musical instruments and sound equipment. Circ. 11,200. Average issue includes 8 features and 3-4 columns. Pays on publication. Byline given. Offers 50%-100% kill fee. Buys all rights. Phone queries OK. Submit seasonal material 2½ months in advance. Simultaneous and photocopied submissions OK. SASE. Reports in 2 weeks. Sample copy $2.50.

Nonfiction: Interview; profile; how-to; new product; and technical. "We want breezy how-to articles dealing with the musical instrument industry, slanted toward retailers. Articles are largely based on phone interviews with successful music industry people (retailers and manufacturers); some interpret trends in musical taste and how they affect the equipment industry. Articles should be clear and incisive, with depth and hard business advice." Buys 40 mss/year. Query with clips of previously published work. Length: 1,000-3,000 words. Pays $75-125.

Photos: Send photos with ms. Pays $15-25 for 8x10 b&w glossy prints. Buys one-time rights.

Columns/Departments: Money, Management, Clinics, Promotions, Education, Selling. "Department articles should be based on interviews with knowledgeable music industry figures." Buys 4 mss/issue. Query with clips of previously published work. Length: 1,000-2,800 words. Pays $50-125.

Tips: "All articles should be well-researched, with quotes from successful retailers and manufacturers of musical instruments and sound equipment."

Office Environment and Equipment

GEYER'S DEALER TOPICS, 51 Madison Ave., New York NY 10010. (212)689-4411. Editor: C. Edwin Shade. For independent office equipment and stationery dealers, and special purchasers for store departments handling stationery and office equipment. Monthly. Buys all rights. Pays kill fee. Byline given. Pays on publication. Reports "immediately." No computer printout or disk submissions. SASE.

Nonfiction and Photos: Articles on dealer efforts in merchandising and sales promotion; programs of stationery and office equipment dealers. Problem-solving articles related to retailers of office supplies, social stationery items, office furniture and equipment and office machines. Must feature specified stores. Pays $100 minimum but quality of article is real determinant. Query. Length: 300-1,000 words. B&w glossies are purchased with accompanying ms with no additional payment.

MARKING INDUSTRY MAGAZINE, Marking Deviles Publishing Co., 2640 N. Halsted, Chicago IL 60614. (312)528-6600. Editor: David Hachmeister. Monthly magazine for manufacturers and dealers of marking products. Pays on acceptance. Byline given. Rights purchased vary. Simultaneous queries, and simultaneous, photocopied and previously published submissions OK. Reports in 2 weeks. Free sample copy and writer's guidelines.

Nonfiction: How-to, inspirational, interview/profile, new products, technical. "We publish a promotional quarterly for which we need cartoons, jokes and fillers. Nothing controversial." Buys 12-18 mss/year. Query with clips of published work. Length: 4,000 words maximum. Pays $25 minimum.

Photos: State availability of photos. Buys one-time rights.

Fillers: Jokes, short humor. Buys 20/year. Pays $30 minimum.

‡**SECRETARY'S WORLD**, Farrington House, 30 S. Main St., Concord NH 03301. (603)228-1240. Editor: Alice Downey. Monthly magazine "devoted to enriching the position of the secretary. Our magazine is for secretaries and about secretaries" and their work-related interests and concerns. Estab. 1983. Circ. 100,000+. Pays within 30 days after acceptance. Byline given. Buys one-time or variable rights. Submit seasonal/holiday material 3 months in advance. Simultaneous queries, and simultaneous, photocopied, and previously

published submissions OK. SASE. Reports in 4-6 weeks on queries. Sample copy for $1 and 9x12 SAE.
Nonfiction: "We are looking for practical work-related articles written in a lively fashion. Relevance to the work world of the secretary is the key criteria for a publishable piece. Articles should be chock full of examples and anecdotes that reflect secretarial work and the profession. In particular we are looking for articles that concern office dynamics; new products; better, quicker and healthier methods of work; occupational health; office automation; job enrichment ideas and analyses of present needs and future trends in the secretarial field. We will include first person stories, how tos, interviews and features on secretaries in various work settings. The slant we request is a constructive one where readers are offered positive examples and practical solutions to the problems and challenges they face in their work." Buys 90 mss/year. "Experienced writers" should query with published clips. Length: 1,000-2,500 words. Pays $250-500.
Columns/Departments: A Day in the Life . . . (first person narrative); After Hours (the one section in the magazine that is not specifically work-related—short pieces on meals and menus, recreational activities, fashion, travel, even hobbies are fine here); Reviews and Resources (book reviews and previews of resources and reference works about secretaries); News and Notes; Office of the Secretary (100-150-word tips and time-savers). Length: 500-950 words. Pays $50-250; Office of the Secretary pays $15 and gift subscription.
Tips: "We're really depending on freelancers for quality articles. In particular, we're looking for writers who can write on the technical aspects and various skill areas of the secretarial world—accounting tips, filing and mail sort procedures, word processing, etc. Secretaries, especially, are encouraged to submit queries."

‡**THE SPOKESMAN**, National Office Machine Dealers Association (NOMDA), 810 Lively Blvd., Box 707, Wood Dale IL 60191. (312)860-9400. Editor: Mary Jane Grube. Editorial Assistant: Vivian Fotos. Monthly magazine covering office machines, equipment and products for independent office machine dealers. Circ. 6,200. Pays on publication. Byline given. Offers $25 kill fee. Buys all rights. Submit seasonal/holiday material 3 months in advance. Simultaneous queries and photocopied and previously published submissions OK "if never published in another trade-related magazine." Computer printout submissions OK; prefers standard typewritten pages. SASE. Reports in 2 weeks. Free sample copy and writer's guidelines.
Nonfiction: How-to (better manage your dealership, improve sales and service, motivate personnel, effectively advertise, train end users, market products, etc.); interview/profile, new product, personal experience (if our readers learn something from it or can apply it to business); technical, "State of the Industry" articles including all fields in the office machine business. No "extremely technical articles or stories that are not dealer-oriented." Wants nothing not related to the office machine industry or beneficial to office machine dealers. Buys variable number of mss/year. Query with clips or send completed ms. Length: open. Pays $50 minimum.
Photos: Send photos with ms. Pays $5 maximum for 3x5 b&w print; $7 maximum for 3x5 color print. Captions required. Buys one-time rights.
Columns/Departments: "We are looking to expand our monthly columns/departments in which we will accept freelance material." Financial Notes (covers all areas of finance/budgeting/taxes, general impact of the economy on dealers); High Technology (articles on computer technology, hardware and software). "We are developing new monthly departments on promotion and store image for which we will accept freelance material." Buys variable number mss/year. Query with clips or send complete ms. Length: 1,250-3,000 words. Pays $50 minimum.
Tips: "We will encourage and help any writer who has interest and knowledge in the office machine and equipment field. Writers may query by phone and seek story ideas and writing guidelines."

WESTERN OFFICE DEALER, 41 Sutter St., San Francisco CA 94104. Editor: Robert B. Frier. Monthly magazine; 60-70 pages. Circ. 9,000. Copyrighted. Byline given. Buys 12 mss/year. Pays on acceptance. Sample copy $2. No photocopied or simultaneous submissions. Submit seasonal (merchandising) material 4 months in advance. Reports in 1 week. Query or submit complete ms. No computer printout or disk submissions. SASE.
Nonfiction and Photos: "Our main interest is in how Western retailers of stationery and office products can do a better selling job. We use how-to-do-it merchandising articles showing dealers how to sell more stationery and office products to more people at a greater profit. Seasonal merchandising articles always welcome, if acceptable." Informational, how-to, personal experience, interview, successful business operations. "We only want material pertaining to successful merchandising activities." Length: 1,000-1,500 words. Pays 2¢/word. Pays $5 for b&w photos used with mss; 3x5 minimum. Captions required.

Packing, Canning, and Packaging

Journals in this category are for packaging engineers and others concerned with new methods of packing, canning, and packaging foods in general. Other publications that buy similar material are found under the Food Products, Processing, and Service heading.

PACKAGE PRINTING, North American Publishing Co., 401 N. Broad St., Philadelphia PA 19108. Editor: Hennie Shore. 50% freelance written. Emphasizes "any sort of package printing (gravure, flexo, offset) for the plant superintendent or general manager of the company's package printing department." Monthly magazine; 88 pages. Circ. 10,000. Pays on publication. Buys all rights. Pays 33% kill fee. Byline given. Phone queries OK. Simultaneous and photocopied submissions OK. Computer printout and disk submissions OK. SASE. Reports in 2 weeks. Sample copy $1.
Nonfiction: "Generally a 'plant' story on the operation of the printing department of a packaging concern. The writer may not know a flexographic machine from a gravure machine or any other, but we expect him to interview the plant manager and get all the technical as well as 'people' details. How is the package printed? What is the paper/film/foil used? How many? What kinds? Names and speed of all machines used; number of employees in production; everything relating to the manufacture and printing of any sort of package (look in any supermarket for 1,000 examples of packages)." No general, broad subjects that could affect any industry or market. "Much of our editorial is now written inhouse or by agencies." Query. Pays $75/printed page.
Photos: State availability of photos with query. Captions required. Buys all rights.

THE PACKER, Box 2939, Shawnee Mission KS 66201. (913)381-6310. Editor: Paul Campbell. 10% freelance written. For shippers, fruit and vegetable growers, wholesalers, brokers, retailers. Newspaper; 36 pages. Weekly. Circ. 16,000. Buys all rights. Buys about 10 mss/year. Pays on publication. Will send free sample copy to writer on request. Write for copy of guidelines for writers. Will consider simultaneous submissions. Reports in 2 weeks. Returns rejected material in 1 month. Query or submit complete ms. SASE.
Nonfiction: Articles on growing techniques, merchandising, marketing, transportation, refrigeration. Emphasis is on the "what's new" approach in these areas. Length: 1,000 words. Pays $40 minimum.
Tips: "It's important to be a good photographer, too. Have features on new growing, merchandising or shipping techniques."

Paint

Additional journals that buy material on paint, wallpaper, floor covering, and decorating products stores are listed under Building Interiors.

AMERICAN PAINTING CONTRACTOR, American Paint Journal Co., 2911 Washington Ave., St. Louis MO 63103. (314)534-0301. Editor-in-Chief: John L. Cleveland. For painting and decorating contractors, inplant maintenance painting department heads, architects and paint specifiers. Monthly magazine; 80 pages. Circ. 25,000. Buys all rights. Phone queries OK. Submit seasonal/holiday material 2 months in advance. Simultaneous and photocopied submissions OK. SASE. Reports in 3 weeks. Free sample copy and writer's guidelines.
Nonfiction: Historical, how-to, humor, informational, new product, personal experience, opinion and technical articles; interviews, photo features and profiles. Buys 10-15 unsolicited mss/year. "Freelancers should be able to write well and have some understanding of the painting and decorating industry. We do not want general theme articles such as 'How to Get More Work Out of Your Employee' unless they relate to a problem within the painting and decorating industry. Query before submitting copy." Length: 1,000-2,500 words. Pays $150-200.
Photos: B&w and color purchased with mss or on assignment. Captions required. Send contact sheets, prints or transparencies. Pays $15-35.

DECORATIVE PRODUCTS WORLD, American Paint Journal Co., 2911 Washington, St. Louis MO 63103. (314)534-0301. Editor: Rick Hirsch. Editorial Director: John Cleveland. Monthly magazine about decorating outlets for retailers of paint, wallpaper and related items. Circ. 33,000. Pays on publication. Byline given. Submit seasonal material 3 months in advance. Reports in 1 month. Free sample copy and writer's guidelines.
Nonfiction: Profile (of stores). "Find stories that will give useful information for our readers. We are basically a service to our readers and our articles reflect that." Buys 1-2 mss/issue. Length: varies. Query. Pays $150.
Photos: "Photos must accompany a story in order to be published." State availability of photos. Pays $10 maximum for b&w prints. Pays $25 maximum for color transparencies. Captions required. Buys one-time rights.
Fillers: Short humor. Buys 3 mss/issue. Pays $4 maximum.

Paper

FORET ET PAPIER, 1001 de Maisonneuve W., Montreal, Quebec, Canada H3A 3E1. (514)845-5141. Editor: Paul Saint-Pierre, C. Adm. For engineers and technicians engaged in the making of paper. Bimonthly magazine; 50 pages. Circ. 7,000. Rights purchased vary with author and material. Buys first North American serial rights, second serial (reprint) rights, and simultaneous rights. Buys about 12 mss/year. Pays on acceptance. Will consider photocopied submissions. Free sample copy. Reports on mss accepted for publication in 1 week. Returns rejected material in 2 days. SASE.
Nonfiction and Photos: Uses technical articles on papermaking. Buys informational, how-to, personal experience, interview, photo and technical articles. Length: 1,000 words maximum. Pays $25-150. Photos purchased with accompanying ms with extra payment or purchased on assignment. Captions required. Pays $25 for b&w. Color shots must be vertical. Pays $150 maximum for color cover shots.

PAPER TRADE JOURNAL, Vance Publishing Co., 133 E. 58th St., New York NY 10022. Editor: Jeremiah E. Flynn. Managing Editor: Carol Brusslan. Semimonthly magazine about the pulp and paper industry for the top management of paper mills. Circ. 11,500. Pays on publication. Byline given. Buys first North American serial rights. Submit seasonal material 3 months in advance. SASE. Reports in 2 weeks. Free sample copy.
Nonfiction: Profile, how-to, new product and technical. Buys 8 unsolicited mss/year. Query. Length: 1,500 words. Pays $125.
Columns/Departments: Query.
Fillers: Clippings. Buys 250 mss/year. Pays $1.

PAPERBOARD PACKAGING, 7500 Old Oak Blvd., Cleveland OH 44130. (216)243-8100. Editor: Mark Arzoumanian. For "managers, supervisors, and technical personnel who operate corrugated box manufacturing, folding cartons converting and rigid box companies and plants." Monthly. Circ. 15,000. Buys all rights. Pays on publication. Will send a sample copy to a writer on request. Will consider photocopied submissions. Submit seasonal material 3 months in advance. Query. SASE.
Nonfiction and Photos: "Application articles, installation stories, etc. Contact the editor first to establish the approach desired for the article. Especially interested in packaging systems using composite materials, including paper and other materials." Buys technical articles. Length: open. Pays "$75/printed page (about 1,000 words to a page), including photos. We do not pay for commercially oriented material. We do pay for material if it is not designed to generate business for someone in our field. Will not pay photography costs, but will pay cost of photo reproductions for article."

PULP & PAPER CANADA, Southam Communications, Ltd., 310 Victoria Ave., Montreal, Quebec, Canada H3Z 2M9. (514)487-2302. Editor: Peter N. Williamson. Managing Editor: Graeme Rodden. Monthly magazine. Circ. 12,000. Pays on publication. Byline given. Offers kill fee according to prior agreement. Buys first North American serial rights. Submit seasonal/holiday material 2 months in advance. Simultaneous queries OK. SASE. Reports in 2 weeks on queries; 3 weeks on mss. Sample copy $3 (Canada), $5 (other countries); free writer's guidelines.
Nonfiction: How-to (related to processes and procedures in the industry); interview/profile (of Canadian leaders in pulp and paper industry); technical (relevant to modern pulp and/or paper industry). "Negative editorial approaches should be substantiated by a recognized authority on the subject." No fillers; short industry news items; product news items. Buys 10 mss/year. Query with or without clips of published work or send complete ms. Length: 1,500-5,000 words (with photos). Pays $120 (Canadian funds)/published page, including photos, graphics, charts, etc.

Pets

Listed here are publications for professionals in the pet industry: wholesalers, manufacturers, suppliers, retailers, owners of pet specialty stores, pet groomers, aquarium retailers, distributors, and those interested in the fish industry. Publications for pet owners are listed in the Animal section of Consumer Publications.

PET AGE, H.H. Backer Associates, Inc., 207 S. Wabash Ave., Chicago IL 60604. (312)663-4040. Editor: Sue Bush. Monthly magazine about the pet industry for pet retailers. Circ. 16,000. Pays on acceptance. Byline given. Buys all rights. Submit seasonal material 6 months in advance. SASE. Reports in 6 weeks. Sample copy $2.50; free writer's guidelines.
Nonfiction: Profile (of a successful, well-run pet retail operation). Buys 25-30 mss/year. "Query as to the

name and location of a pet operation you wish to profile and why the operation is successful, why it would make a good feature." Length: 1,600-2,000 words. Pays $80 minimum.

Photos: State availability of photos. Reviews 5x7 b&w glossy prints and color transparencies. Offers no additional payment for photos accepted with ms. Captions required. Buys all rights.

Columns/Departments: Fish Care, Retailing, Government Action, Bird Care, New Products and Industry News.

PET BUSINESS, Pet Business, Inc., 7330 NW 66th, Miami FL 33166. Publisher: Robert L. Behme. For the complete pet industry—retailers, groomers, breeders, manufacturers, wholesalers and importers. Monthly magazine; 30 pages. Circ. 18,500. Pays on acceptance. Not copyrighted. Previously published submissions OK. Computer printout submission OK "as long as it is readable, easy to edit and well written. But there are exceptions—we hate dot matrix." SASE. Reports in 3 weeks. Sample copy $1; free writer's guidelines.

Nonfiction: General interest (to retailers—what a store is doing, etc.); historical (when there is a reason—death, sale, etc.); how-to (sell more, retailer ideas); interview (with successful stores and manufacturers); opinion (with background); photo feature (on occasion). No news of stores. Buys 15-30 mss/year. "We will consider anything if queried first." Length: 600-1,500 words. Pays $35-250.

Photos: State availability of photos. Pays $5 for 5x7 or larger b&w prints; and $30 for any size color prints. Captions required.

Columns/Departments: "We're interested in ideas that relate to retailing,.e.g., dogs, cats, small animals—but it must be on a retail, not hobby, level." Open to suggestions for new columns/departments. Query. Pays $100.

Tips: "We are looking at international editions."

THE PET DEALER, Howmark Publishing Corp., 567 Morris Ave., Elizabeth NJ 07208. (201)353-7373. Editor-in-Chief: William G. Reddan. 15% freelance written. Emphasizes merchandising, marketing and management for owners and managers of pet specialty stores, departments, and pet groomers and their suppliers. Monthly magazine; 80 pages. Circ. 11,000. Byline given. Pays on publication. Phone queries OK. Submit seasonal/holiday material 3 months in advance of issue date. Computer printout submissions OK; prefers letter quality to dot matrix printouts. No disk submissions. SASE. Reports in 1 week. Free sample copy and writer's guidelines.

Nonfiction: How-to (store operations, administration, merchandising, marketing, management, promotion, and purchasing). Consumer pet articles—lost pets, best pets, humane themes—*not* welcome. Emphasis is on *trade* merchandising and marketing of pets and supplies. Buys 8 unsolicited mss/year. Recent article example: "The Tickets are High Here—That's Wetzel's Two Worlds" (March 1983). Length: 800-1,200 words. Pays $50-100.

Photos: Submit photo material with ms. No additional payment for 5x7 b&w glossy prints. "Six photos with captions required." Buys one-time rights.

Tips: "We're interested in store profiles outside the New York, New Jersey, Connecticut, Pennsylvania metro areas. Photos are of key importance. Articles focus on new techniques in merchandising or promotion. Submit query letter first, with writing background summarized; include samples. We seek one-to-one, interview-type features on retail pet store merchandising. Indicate the availability of the proposed article, your willingness to submit on exclusive or first-in-field basis, and whether you are patient enough to await payment on publication."

PETS/SUPPLIES/MARKETING, Harcourt Brace Jovanovich Publications, 1 E. 1st St., Duluth MN 55802. (218)727-8511. Editor: David Kowalski. For independent pet retailers, chain franchisers, livestock and pet supply wholesalers, manufacturers of pet products. Monthly magazine. Circ. 14,200. Pays on publication. Buys first rights. Phone queries OK. Submit seasonal/holiday material 4 months in advance. Photocopied submissions OK. SASE. Reports in 2 months. Free writer's guidelines. Sample copy $2.

Nonfiction: How-to (merchandise pet products, display, set up window displays, market pet product line); interviews (with pet store retailers); opinion (of pet industry members or problems facing the industry); photo features (of successful pet stores or effective merchandising techniques and in-store displays); profiles (of successful retail outlets engaged in the pet trade); technical articles (on more effective pet retailing; e.g., building a central filtration unit, constructing custom aquariums or display areas). Business management articles must deal specifically with pet shops and their own unique merchandise and problems. Length: 1,000-2,000 words. Buys 1-2 mss/issue. Query. Pays 10¢/word.

Photos: Purchased with or without mss or on assignment. "We prefer 5x7 or 8x10 b&w glossies. But we will accept contact sheets and standard print sizes. For color, we prefer 35mm kodachrome transparencies or 2¼x2¼." Pays $10 for b&w; $25 for color. Captions and model release required.

Columns/Departments: Suggestions for new columns or departments should be addressed to the editor. No clippings, please.

Tips: "We want articles which stress professional retailing, provide insight into successful shops, and generally capture the excitement of an exciting and sometimes controversial industry. All submissions are read. However an initial query could save time and energy and ensure a publishable article."

Photography

AMERICAN CINEMATOGRAPHER, A.S.C. Holding Corp., Box 2230, Hollywood CA 90028. (213)876-5080. Editor: Richard Patterson. Associate Editor: George Turner. An international journal of film and video production techniques "addressed to creative, managerial, and technical people in all aspects of production. Its function is to disseminate practical information about the creative use of film and video equipment, and it strives to maintain a balance between technical sophistication and accessibility." 120 pages. Circ. 25,000. Pays on publication. Buys all rights. Phone queries OK. Simultaneous and photocopied submissions OK. Computer printout submissions OK "provided they are adequately spaced." SASE.
Nonfiction: Descriptions of new equipment and techniques or accounts of specific productions involving unique problems or techniques; historical articles detailing the production of a classic film, the work of a pioneer or legendary cinematographer or the development of a significant technique or type of equipment. Also discussions of the aesthetic principles involved in production techniques. Recent article examples: "The Electronic Optical Printer," "Inside the Khmer Rouge," "The Making of Gunga Din," and "Photographic Composition for Best Friends." Length: 1,500 to 6,000 words. Pays approximately 5¢/word.
Photos: B&w and color purchased with mss. No additional payment.
Tips: "Queries must describe writer's qualifications and include writing samples. We hope to make more use of freelance writers."

AMERICAN PREMIERE, Suite 205, 8421 Wilshire Blvd., Beverly Hills CA 90211. Editor: Susan Royal. Monthly trade magazine (except January and August) "for and about persons in the film industry—executives, producers, directors, actors, and all others associated." Circ. 25,000. Pays on publication. Byline given. Pays negotiable kill fee. Buys first North American rights. Submit seasonal/holiday material 2 months in advance. Sample copy $3 (address request to "Circulation"); writer's guidelines for business size SAE and 1 first class stamp.
Nonfiction: Investigative; historical; how-to (incorporate yourself, read a contract, etc.); humor (satire); interview/profile (directors, producers, businesses, top persons in the industry); personal experience; photo feature ("Photo Albums"); and other themes associated with the film industry. "Only business-oriented articles." No fan material or gossip. Recent article example: "The New Media and Its Impact on the Film Industry" (Vol. III, No. 1). Buys 7-20 unsolicited mss/year. Query with "limited samples" of published work and resumé. Length: 1,200-3,000 words. Pays $50-150.
Photos: State availability of photos. Reviews color transparencies and b&w prints. "Photos are paid for with payment for ms." Captions and model release required.
Fillers: Anecdotes, short humor and newsbreaks. "Must relate directly to the film industry." Buys 100+/year. Length: 50-150 words. Pays $10 maximum.
Tips: "Writers should be well-versed on the workings of the film industry. We're interested in people who can pen statistical, but not boring, articles."

NEW YORK PHOTO DISTRICT NEWS, A Monthly Newspaper for the Professional Photographer, Rm. 816, 156 5th Ave., New York NY 10010. (212)243-8664. Editor: Anne M. Russell. Monthly tabloid covering professional commercial photography. "We are *not* a technical publication. We provide professional photographers with business and legal news and industry features. Circ. 12,800. Pays on publication. Byline given. Buys first North American serial rights. Submit seasonal/holiday material 3 months in advance. Simultaneous queries and photocopied submissions OK. Computer printout submissions OK "as long as the quality is good enough to read easily." SASE. Reports in 1 month. Sample copy $2.
Nonfiction: Humor, interview/profile, new product, opinion, personal experience, photo feature, technical, travel—"all photographic industry-oriented. We particularly appreciate hearing from writers who have the initiative to come up with their own feature ideas." No amateur, technical, how-to mss. Buys 120 mss/year. Length: 1,000-2,500 words. Pays $75-125.
Photos: Send photos with ms. Pays $10 maximum for 8x10 b&w prints or contact sheet. Captions required. Buys one-time rights.
Tips: "We are increasing in size and need more material. I'd also like to expand our national coverage, especially from the West Coast."

ON LOCATION MAGAZINE, On Location Publishing, Inc., Suite 501, 6777 Hollywood Blvd., Hollywood CA 90028. (213)467-1268. Editor-in-Chief: Steven Bernard. Managing Editor: Arthur G. Insana. Monthly trade magazine covering film and videotape production for producers, directors, production managers, cinematographers and sound, lighting, motion picture and video equipment suppliers. Circ. 23,300. Pays on publication. Byline given. Buys all rights. Submit seasonal/holiday and special issue material 4 months in advance. Simultaneous queries and photocopied submissions OK. SASE. Reports in 3 weeks. Free sample copy; editorial forecasts and writer's guidelines for business size SAE and 1 first class stamp.
Nonfiction: General interest (unique locations); how-to (use innovations and unusual techniques); technical

(semi-technical articles, naming equipment brand names). No interviews with performers. Buys 10-12 mss/year. Query with clips of published work to managing editor. Length 1,500-2,000 words. Pays $100-300.
Photos: State availability of photos. "Usually the unit publicist will help get photos."
Fillers: Short humor. "Must be right on target. Writer must know cinematography well." Buys 5/year. Length: 500 words minimum. Pays $50-75.
Tips: "Query should include a strong hook and convince us that the filming location is unique. We like to have a feeling that the writer was on the set if possible, or the best re-creation thereof when the film was shot. The same applies to video production and commercial shoots. Talk with a director, cinematographer and set designer to find out how they solved problems down to the finest details. We use many regional correspondents. Our most successful editorial develops with the direction or thrust towards the 'hands-on' person."

PHOTO LAB MANAGEMENT, PLM Publishing, Inc., 1312 Lincoln Blvd., Santa Monica CA 90406. (213)451-1344. Editor: Ron Leach. Associate Editor: Patrice Apodaca. Bimonthly magazine covering process chemistries, process control, process equipment and marketing/administration for photo lab owners, managers and management personnel. Circ. 8,600. Pays on publication. Byline and brief bio given. Buys first North American serial rights. Submit seasonal/holiday material 6 months in advance. SASE. Reports on queries in 6 weeks. Free sample copy and writer's guidelines for business size SAE and 1 first class stamp.
Nonfiction: Interview/profile (lab or lab managers); personal experience (lab manager); technical; and management or administration. Buys 12-15 mss/year. Query with brief biography. Length: 1,200-1,800 words. Pays $48/published page.
Photos: Reviews 35mm color transparencies and 4-color prints suitable for cover. "We're looking for outstanding cover shots of things to do with photo finishing."
Tips: "Send a query if you have some background in the industry or a willingness to dig out information and research for a top-quality article that really speaks to our audience."

PHOTO WEEKLY, Billboard Publications, Inc., 1515 Broadway, New York NY 10036. (212)764-7415. Editor: Willard Clark. Weekly photography tabloid featuring industry news for photographic retailers and photofinishers. Circ. 15,000. Pays on acceptance. Byline given. Buys one-time rights.

‡PHOTOFLASH, Models & Photographers Newsletter, Box 7946, Colorado Springs CO 80933. Managing Editor: Ron Marshall. Quarterly newsletter of photographic modeling and glamour photography "for models, photographers, publishers, picture editors, modeling agents, advertising agencies, and others involved in the interrelated fields of modeling and photography." Pays on publication. Byline given. Buys one-time rights. Submit seasonal/holiday material 6 months in advance. Simultaneous queries, and simultaneous, photocopied, and previously published submissions OK. SASE. Reports in 3 months on queries; 4 months on mss. Sample copy $4.
Nonfiction: Interview/profile (of established and rising professionals in the field, especially models); photo feature; technical (illustrating/explaining photographic and modeling "tricks"). Send complete ms. "We prefer photo-illustrated text packages."
Photos: Send photos with ms. "Payment is for the complete photo-text package; it includes a credit line, contributor copies and up to $15-25 depending on quality, completeness, etc. of the submissions." Reviews 8x10 b&w prints. Captions and model release required.

PHOTOGRAPHER'S MARKET NEWSLETTER, F&W Publishing Corp., 9933 Alliance Rd., Cincinnati OH 45242. (513)984-0717. Editor: Robert D. Lutz. Monthly newsletter on freelance photography covering "markets and marketing techniques and strategies for amateur and professional photographers who want to begin selling or sell more of their work." Estab. 1981. Pays on publication. Byline given. Buys one-time rights. Simultaneous and previously published submissions OK. Computer printout submissions OK. SASE. Reports in 2 weeks on queries; 1 month on mss. Sample copy $3.50.
Nonfiction: How-to (sell photos); interview/profile (photography professionals); personal experience (in photo marketing); photo feature (previously published work); technical (must relate to selling). No purely technical material on cameras, film, equipment. Buys 12 mss/year. Query. Length: 1,500-2,000 words plus photos. Pays $75-125.
Photos: State availability of photos. Reviews 8x10 b&w prints; payment included with purchase price. Captions required.
Columns/Departments: SOLD. "We reprint previously published photos with first-person 'story-behind-the-sale.' Tell how you made a first, big or remarkable sale." Buys 12 mss/year. Query with clips of published work. Length: 100-300 words. Pays $25 minimum.
Tips: "Experimentation with format may lead to a need for more *shorter* pieces."

PHOTOMETHODS, Ziff-Davis Publishing Co., 1 Park Ave., New York NY 10016. (212)725-3942. Editorial Director: Fred Schmidt. For professional and in-plant image-makers (still, film, video, AV) and visual communications managers. Monthly magazine; 80-96 pages. Circ. 50,000. Pays on publication. Buys one-time rights. Pays 100% kill fee. Byline given. Phone queries OK. Computer printout submissions OK "as long as pages are ripped and collated." SASE. Free sample copy and writer's guidelines.

Nonfiction: How-to and photo features (solve problems with image-making techniques: photography, etc.); technical management; informational (to help the reader use photography, cine and video); interviews (with working pros); personal experience (in solving problems with photography, cine and video); profiles (well-known personalities in imaging); and technical (on photography, cine and video). No material written for the amateur photographer. Buys 5 mss/issue. Length: 1,500-3,000 words. Pays $75 minimum.

Photos: Steven Karl Weininger, art director. B&w photos (5x7 up matte or dried glossy) and color (35mm transparencies minimum or 8x10 print) purchased with or without mss, or on assignment. Captions required. Query or submit contact sheet. Pays $35 for b&w; $50 for color; more for covers. Model release required.

Tips: "You can get my attention by knowing who we are and what we publish. Anything sent must be professionally packaged: neatly typed, well organized; and have patience. Don't come across as a writer we cannot live without. Don't contact us unless you know the magazine and the type of articles we publish. No unsolicited mss. Please query first."

THE RANGEFINDER, 1312 Lincoln Blvd., Santa Monica CA 90406. (213)451-8506. Editor: Ronald Leach. Associate Editor: Patrice Apodaca. Emphasizes professional photography. Monthly magazine; 100 pages. Circ. 48,500. Pays on publication. Buys first North American serial rights. Phone queries OK. Submit seasonal material 4 months in advance. Byline given. SASE. Reports in 6 weeks. Sample copy $2.50; free writer's guidelines.

Nonfiction: How-to (solve a photographic problem; such as new techniques in lighting, new poses or setups); interview; and technical. "Articles should contain practical, solid information. Issues should be covered in depth. Look thoroughly into the topic." No opinion, experience or biographical articles. Buys 5 mss/issue. Query with outline. Length: 800-1,200 words. Pays $60/published page.

Photos: State availability of photos with query. Captions preferred. Buys one-time rights. Model release required.

Tips: "Exhibit some knowledge of photography. Introduce yourself with a well-written letter and a great story idea."

TECHNICAL PHOTOGRAPHY, PTN Publishing Corp., 101 Crossways Park West, Woodbury NY 11797. Editor-in-Chief: Don Garbera. 50% freelance written. Publication of the "on-staff (in-house) industrial, military and government still, cinema, video and AV professional who must produce (or know where to get) visuals of all kinds." Monthly magazine; 64 pages. Circ. 60,000. Pays on publication. Buys first North American serial rights. Byline given "except when it needs complete rewrite or when supplied through public relations agency." SASE. Reports in 4 weeks. Free sample copy.

Nonfiction: How-to; interview; photo feature; profile (detailed stories about in-house operations); and technical. "All manuscripts must relate to industrial, military or government production of visuals." Buys 75-110 mss/year. Query. Length: "as long as needed to get the information across." Pays $50-350 minimum/display page.

Photos: Offers no additional payment for photos purchased with ms. Captions required. Query.

Plumbing, Heating, Air Conditioning, and Refrigeration

Publications for fuel oil dealers who also install heating equipment are classified with the Energy journals.

AIR CONDITIONING, HEATING AND REFRIGERATION NEWS, Box 2600, Troy MI 48099. (313)362-3700. Editor-in-Chief: Gordon D. Duffy. Managing Editor: John O. Sweet. 20% freelance written. "An industry newspaper that covers both the technology and marketing of air conditioning, heating and refrigeration." Weekly tabloid. Circ. 28,000. Pays on publication. Buys all rights. Phone queries OK. "Query to be a short precis of the story containing a slant writer plans to take—not something vague like 'I'll give you what you want.' We can add or delete from a 'known' better than a 'maybe.' " Submit seasonal/holiday material 1 month in advance of issue date. Simultaneous and photocopied submissions OK. Reports in 2-3 weeks. Free sample copy.

Nonfiction: How-to (basic business management applied to contracting operations; sophisticated technical problems in heating, air conditioning, and refrigeration); interview (check first); nostalgia; profile; and technical. Buys 2-4 mss/issue. Query. Length: 1,500 words maximum. Pays $1.50-2.25/column inch.

Photos: State availability of photos with query or ms. Pays $10-35 for 5x7 or 8x10 b&w glossy prints. Captions required. Buys all rights.

CONTRACTOR MAGAZINE, Berkshire Common, Pittsfield MA 01201. Editor: Seth Shepard. For mechanical contractors and wholesalers. Newspaper; 50 (11x15) pages. Twice monthly. Circ. 46,100. Copyrighted. Buys 8 mss/year. Pays on publication. Sample copy for $3. Photocopied submissions OK. No simultaneous submissions. Reports in 1 month. Query first or submit complete ms. SASE.
Nonfiction and Photos: Articles on materials, use, policies, and business methods of the air conditioning, heating, plumbing contracting industry. Topics covered include: interpretive reports, how-to, informational, interview, profile, think articles, expose, spot news, successful business operations, merchandising techniques, labor. Pays $300 maximum. 5x7 b&w glossies purchased with or without ms. Pays $10. Captions required.

DOMESTIC ENGINEERING MAGAZINE, Construction Press, 135 Addison St., Elmhurst IL 60126. Editor: Stephen J. Shafer. Managing Editor: Donald Michard. Emphasizes plumbing, heating, air conditioning and piping for contractors, and for mechanical contractors in these specialties. Gives information on management, marketing and merchandising. Monthly magazine; 100 pages. Circ. 40,000. Pays on acceptance. Buys all rights, simultaneous rights, or first rights. Simultaneous, photocopied and previously published submissions OK. SASE. Reports in 1 month. Sample copy $4.
Nonfiction: How-to (some technical in industry areas). Expose, interview, profile, personal experience, photo feature and technical articles are written on assignment only and should be about management, marketing and merchandising for plumbing and mechanical contracting businesssmen. Buys 12 mss/year. Query. Pays $25 minimum.
Photos: State availability of photos. Pays $10 minimum for b&w prints (reviews contact sheets) and color transparencies.

FLORIDA FORUM, FRSA Services Corp., Drawer 4850, Winter Park FL 32793. (305)671-3772. Editor: Gerald Dykhuisen. Monthly magazine covering the roofing, sheet metal and air conditioning industries. Circ. 8,100. Pays on publication. Byline given. Buys one-time rights. Submit seasonal/holiday material 2 months in advance. Simultaneous queries, and simultaneous, photocopied and previously published submissions OK. Computer printout submissions OK; disk submissions OK "if compatible with IBM System 6." Reports in 2 weeks. Free sample copy.
Nonfiction: General interest, historical/nostalgic, humor, interview/profile, new product, opinion, personal experience, technical. Buys 12 mss/year. Send complete ms. Length: open. Pays variable rates.
Photos: Send photos with ms. Pays variable rates for b&w prints.
Columns/Departments: Buys 12 mss/year. Send complete ms. Length: open. Pays variable rates.

HEATING, PLUMBING, AIR CONDITIONING, 1450 Don Mills Rd., Don Mills, Ontario, Canada M3B 2X7. (416)445-6641. Editor: Ronald H. Shuker. For mechanical contractors; plumbers; warm air heating, refrigeration, ventilation, air conditioning and insulation contractors; wholesalers; architects; consulting and mechanical engineers who are in key management or specifying positions in the plumbing, heating, air conditioning and refrigeration industries in Canada. Monthly. Circ. 12,500. Pays on publication. Free sample copy. Reports in 2 months. For a prompt reply, "enclose a sheet on which is typed a statement either approving or rejecting the suggested article which can either be checked off, or a quick answer written in and signed and returned."
Nonfiction and Photos: News, technical, business management and "how-to" articles that will inform, educate and motivate readers who design, manufacture, install, sell, service, maintain or supply all mechanical components and systems in residential, commercial, institutional and industrial installations across Canada. Length: 1,000-1,500 words. Pays 10-20¢/word. Photos purchased with mss. Prefers 5x7 or 8x10 glossies.
Tips: "Topics must relate directly to the day-to-day activities of *HPAC* readers in Canada. Must be detailed, with specific examples, quotes from specific people or authorities—show depth. Specifically want material from other parts of Canada besides Southern Ontario. Not really interested in material from US unless specifically related to Canadian readers' concerns. Primarily want articles that show *HPAC* readers how they can increase their sales and business step-by-step based on specific examples of what others have done."

SNIPS MAGAZINE, 407 Mannheim Rd., Bellwood IL 60104. (312)544-3870. Editor: Nick Carter. For sheet metal, warm air heating, ventilating, air conditioning, and roofing contractors. Monthly. Buys all rights.

The double dagger (‡) before a listing indicates that the listing is new in this edition. New markets are often the most receptive to freelance contributions.

"Write for detailed list of requirements before submitting any work." SASE.

Nonfiction: Material should deal with information about contractors who do sheet metal, warm air heating, air conditioning, ventilation and roofing work; also about successful advertising campaigns conducted by these contractors and the results. Length: "prefers stories to run less than 1,000 words unless on special assignment." Pays 2¢ each for first 500 words, 1¢ each for additional words.

Photos: Pays $2 each for small snapshot pictures, $4 each for usable 8x10 pictures.

Printing

AMERICAN PRINTER, 300 W. Adams St., Chicago IL 60606. Editor: Elizabeth G. Berglund. 45-60% freelance written. For qualified personnel active in any phase of the graphic arts industry. Monthly. Circ. 80,000. Buys all rights, unless otherwise specified in writing at time of purchase. Byline given. Pays on publication. Free sample copy. Submit seasonal material 2 months in advance. "Study publication before writing." SASE.

Nonfiction: Management, and technical subjects with illustrations pertinent to the graphic arts industry. Query. Length: 1,500-3,000 words. Pays $200-450.

Photos: Purchased with mss; also news shots of graphic arts occurrences. Uses 5x7 or 8x10 glossy prints. Pays $25-40.

Fillers: Clippings about product installations, plant openings, acquisitions and purchases, business reorganization. Particularly interested in items on newspapers; not interested in personnel announcements. Pays $5-15.

HIGH VOLUME PRINTING, Innes Publishing Co., Box 368, Northbrook IL 60062. (312)564-5940. Editor: Virgil J. Busto. Bimonthly magazine for book and magazine publishers, large commercial printing plants with 20 or more employees. Aimed at telling the reader what he needs to know to manage his company or department more efficiently and more profitably. Circ. 20,000. Pays on publication. Byline given. Buys one-time rights and makes work-for-hire assignments. Simultaneous queries OK. Reports in 2 weeks. Free sample copy and writer's guidelines.

Nonfiction: How-to (printing production techniques); interview/profile (of trade personalities); new product (printing, auxiliary equipment, plant equipment); photo feature (case histories featuring unique equipment); technical (printing product research and development); shipping, publishing distribution methods. No product puff. Buys 12 mss/year. Query. Length: 700-3,000 words. Pays $50-200.

Photos: Send photos with ms. Pays $25-100 for 3x5 and larger b&w prints; $25-150 for any size color transparencies and prints. Captions, model release, and identification of subjects required.

Tips: "Feature articles covering actual installations and industry trends are most open to freelancers. Be familiar with the industry, spend time in the field, attend industry meetings and trade shows where equipment is displayed."

IN-PLANT PRINTER, Innes Publishing, Box 368, Northbrook IL 60062. (312)564-5940. Editor: Bill Esler. Bimonthly magazine covering in-house print shops. Circ. 35,000. Pays on publication. Byline "usually" given. Buys first and second serial (reprint) rights. Reports in 2 months. Submit seasonal/holiday material 2 months in advance. Photocopied and previously published submissions OK. Computer printout submissions OK. Reports in 2 weeks. Free sample copy and writer's guidelines.

Nonfiction: Book excerpts, how-to, case history. "No nebulous management advice; undetailed stories lacking in concrete information. No human interest material." Buys 18 mss/year. Query or send complete ms. Length: 1,500-3,000 words. Pays $100-250.

Photos: Send photos with ms. "No additional payment is made for photos with ms, unless negotiated." Captions required. Buys all rights.

IN-PLANT REPRODUCTIONS, North American Publishing Co., 401 N. Broad St., Philadelphia PA 19108. (215)574-9600. Editor: Ida Crist. Assistant Editor: Anita McKelvey. Monthly magazine about in-plant printing management for printing departments in business, government, education and industry. These graphic arts facilities include art, composition, camera, platemaking, press, and finishing equipment, xerographic and other business communications systems. Circ. 40,000. Pays on publication. Byline given. Buys first North American serial rights or all rights. Phone queries OK. SASE. Reports in 1 month. Sample copy $5.

Nonfiction: Interview, profile, how-to, and technical. Buys 4 mss/issue. Query. Length: 500-2,500 words. Pays $75-200.

INSTANT PRINTER, Innes Publishing, 425 Huehl Rd., Bldg. 11B, Northbrook IL 60062. (312)564-5940. Editor: Daniel Witte. Bimonthly magazine covering the instant/retail printing industry for owners/operators of instant print shops. "We are primarily concerned with ways to be successful, ways to avoid failure, ways to make lots of money, and what to do with the money. Basically we try to focus on the needs and concerns of the entrepreneurial type." Estab. 1982. Circ. 17,000. Pays on publication. Byline given. Buys first North American serial rights with option for future use. Submit seasonal/holiday material 6 months in advance. Photocopied and previously published submissions OK. SASE. Reports in 2 weeks on queries; 1 month on mss. Sample copy $3; free writer's guidelines.

Nonfiction: Book excerpts (primarily on small business-related or graphic arts-related topics); general interest (anything about taxing the small business, regulating small businesses); how-to (focus on more efficient ways to do everyday things instant printers do: technical, business, financial); interview/profile (case histories of successful instant printers with angle on unique or special services); personal experience (any small printer who has tried marketing some new or unique service, successful or not); technical (any printing-related topic). Buys 18-25 mss/year. Query with or without clips of published work or send complete ms. Pays $200 maximum.

Photos: State availability of photos. Pays $50 maximum for b&w contact sheets, slides or 3x5 prints; $100 maximum for color contact sheets, slides, or 3x5 prints. Captions, model release, and identification of subjects required. Buys all rights.

Columns/Departments: Promotion—about advertising/promotion techniques used by instant printers (with samples); Computers—information about computers and software for instant printers. Buys 6 mss/year. Query with or without clips or send complete ms. Length: 1,000 words maxmimum. Pays $75 maximum.

Fillers: Clippings, anecdotes, newsbreaks, printing or marketing hints. Pays $10 maximum.

Tips: "I would suggest reading copies of our magazine, as well as related publications, e.g., *Inc.*, *Entrepreneur*, *Business Week*, any graphic arts mag, for style."

NEWSPAPER PRODUCTION, North American Publishing Co., 401 N. Broad St., Philadelphia PA 19108. (215)574-9600. Demographic edition of *Printing Impressions*. Editor-in-Chief: Alan Tepper. For the newspaper industry; production personnel through management to editor and publisher. Bimonthly demographic section magazine; 8-24 pages. Circ. 17,500. Pays on publication. Buys all rights. Phone queries OK. Photocopied submissions OK, "but please identify if simultaneous elsewhere." SASE. Reports in 3 weeks.

Nonfiction: Publishes production case histories and how-to articles (production techniques); nothing about the editorial side of newspapers. Length: 1,500 words minimum. Query or submit complete ms. Pays $50-175.

Photos: B&w and color purchased with or without mss, or on assignment. Captions required. Query or submit contact sheet or prints. Additional payment for those used with mss computed into article's length. Model release required.

PLAN AND PRINT, 10116 Franklin Ave., Franklin Park IL 60131. (312)671-5356. Editor-in-Chief: James C. Vebeck. 50% freelance written. For commercial reproduction companies, in-plant reproduction, printing, drafting and design departments of business and industry and architects. Monthly magazine. Circ. 23,000. Pays on publication. Buys all rights. Byline given. Submit seasonal/holiday material 4-6 months in advance of issue date. No computer printout or disk submissions. SASE. Reports in 2 weeks. Free sample and writer's guidelines.

Nonfiction: How-to (how certain problems may have been solved; new methods of doing certain kinds of reproduction and/or design/drafting/computer-aided design work); and technical (must relate to industry). "Strong interest in computer-aided design." Buys 50 mss/year. Query with clips of previously published work. Length: 250-5,000 words. Pays $25-300.

Photos: State availability of photos with query. Pays $5-10 for 8x10 b&w glossy prints. Captions required. Buys all rights. Model release required.

Columns/Departments: Open to suggestions for new columns/departments.

Poetry: Light verse related to the industry. Buys 6/year. Length: 4-12 lines. Pays $8 maximum.

PRINTING VIEWS, For the Midwest Printer, Midwest Publishing, 8328 N. Lincoln, Skokie IL 60077. (312)539-8540. Editor: Len Berman. Managing Editor: Mary Lou Parker. Monthly magazine about printing and graphic arts for commercial printers, typographers, platemakers, engravers and other trade people. Circ. 15,000. Average issue includes 3-4 articles. Pays on publication. Byline given. Buys one-time rights. Phone queries OK. Computer printout submissions OK; prefers letter quality to dot matrix printouts. SASE. Reports in 2 weeks. Sample copy $1.

Nonfiction: Mary Lou Parker, nonfiction editor. Interview (possibly with graphic arts personnel); new product (in graphic arts in a Midwest plant); management/sales success in Midwest printing plant; and technical (printing equipment). Buys 8 mss/year. Query with clips of previously published work. "We will entertain query letters; no unsolicited manuscripts." Length: 2-9 typed pages. Pays $100-150.

Photos: State availability of photos. Reviews b&w contact sheets. Offers additional payment for photos accepted with ms. Captions preferred. Buys one-time rights.

SCREEN PRINTING, 407 Gilbert Ave., Cincinnati OH 45202. (513)421-2050. Editor: Tamas S. Frecska. For the screen printing industry, including screen printers (commercial, industrial and captive shops), suppliers and manufacturers, ad agencies and allied professions. Monthly magazine; 120 pages. Circ. 11,000. Buys all rights. Byline given. Pays on publication. Free writer's guidelines. Reporting time varies. SASE.

Nonfiction and Photos: "Since the screen printing industry covers a broad range of applications and overlaps other fields in the graphic arts, it's necessary that articles be of a significant contribution, preferably to a specific area of screen printing. Subject matter is fairly open, with preference given to articles on administration or technology; trends and developments. We try to give a good sampling of technical business and management articles; articles about unique operations. We also publish special features and issues on important subjects, such as material shortages, new markets and new technology breakthroughs. While most of our material is nitty-gritty, we appreciate a writer who can take an essentially dull subject and encourage the reader to read on through concise, factual, 'flairful' and creative, expressive writing. Interviews are published after consultation with and guidance from the editor." Interested in stories on unique approaches by some shops. No general, promotional treatment of individual companies. Buys 6-10 unsolicited mss/year. Length: 1,500-2,000 words. Pays minimum of $150 for major features; minimum of $75 for minor features; minimum of $50 for back of book articles. Cover photos negotiable; b&w or color. Published material becomes the property of the magazine.

THE TYPOGRAPHER, Typographers International Association, Suite 101, 2262 Hall Pl. NW., Washington DC 20007. (202)965-3400. Editor: Geoff Lindsay. Bimonthly tabloid of the commercial typesetting industry for owners and executives of typesetting firms. Circ. 8,500. Pays on publication. Byline given. Buys one-time rights. Simultaneous queries, and simultaneous, photocopied and previously published submissions OK. Computer printout submissions OK. Reports in 1 week. Free sample copy.

Nonfiction: Book excerpts, historical/nostalgic, how-to, interview/profile, new product, opinion, personal experience, photo feature, technical. "All articles should relate to typesetting management." No opinion pieces. Buys 20 mss/year. Query with clips of published work. Length: 1,000-2,000 words. Pays $50-150.

Photos: State availability of photos. Pays $20-35 for 5x7 b&w prints. Captions and identification of subjects required.

Columns/Departments: Sales column (how to improve sales of typesetting). Buys 15 mss/year. Query with clips of published work. Length: 1,200 words minimum. Pays $50-100.

WORLD-WIDE PRINTER, North American Publishing Co., 401 N. Broad St., Philadelphia PA 19108. Editor: Mark Michelson. Emphasizes printing and printing technology for printers; packagers; and publishers of newspapers, books, magazines, any and all printed matter in all parts of the world. Distributed internationally. Bimonthly magazine; 110 pages. Circ. 17,000. Pays on publication. Buys all rights. Phone queries OK. Submit seasonal/holiday material 2 months in advance. Simultaneous, photocopied and previously published submissions OK, if identified as to other possible placement. Reports in 3 weeks. Sample copy $5.

Nonfiction: Technical material only. "Knowledge of printing technology is absolutely necessary in the writer, even if the subject is only an interview or plant story." Buys 2-3 mss/issue. Query. Length: 500-1,000 words. Pays $25-150.

Photos: State availability of photos. Pays $5 for b&w 5x7 prints.

Real Estate

AREA DEVELOPMENT MAGAZINE, 525 Northern Blvd., Great Neck NY 11021. (516)829-8990. Editor-in-Chief: Tom Bergeron. Emphasizes corporate facility planning and site selection for industrial chief executives worldwide. Monthly magazine; 110-190 pages. Circ. 33,000. Pays when edited. Buys first rights. Byline given. Photocopied submissions OK. Computer printout submissions OK. No disk submissions. Reports in 1-3 weeks. Free sample copy and writer's guidelines.

Nonfiction: How-to (case histories of companies; experiences in site selection and all other aspects of corporate facility planning); historical (if it deals with corporate facility planning); interview (corporate executives and industrial developers); related areas of site selection and facility planning such as taxes, labor, government, energy, architecture and finance. Buys 8-10 mss/yr. Query. Pays $25-35/ms page; rates for illustrations depend on quality and printed size.

Photos: State availability of photos with query. Prefer 8x10 or 5x7 b&w glossy prints. Captions preferred.

Tips: "Articles must be accurate, objective (no puffery) and useful to our industrial executive readers. Avoid any discussion of the merits or disadvantages of any particular areas or communities."

BUSINESS FACILITIES, (formerly *American Industrial Properties Report*), BUS FAC Publishing Co., 90 Monmouth St., Box 2060, Red Bank NJ 07701. (201)842-7433. Editor: Eric C. Peterson. Magazine published 10 times/year (March/April, July/August combined issues) covering economic development, industrial and commercial real estate. "Emphasis is on news and trends, including market conditions, economics, finance, legislation, innovations—anything that could affect the economic development practitioner on a national, regional or local level.'' Circ. 35,000. Pays on acceptance. Byline given. Buys all rights. Simultaneous queries, and simultaneous and photocopied submissions OK. Computer printout submissions OK; prefers letter quality to dot matrix printouts. SASE. Reports in 1 month on queries, 2 weeks on mss. Free sample copy and writer's guidelines.

Nonfiction: General interest (newsy case histories); how-to (innovations, construction features, operation of facilities); interview/profile (of top corporate real estate, development and government figures); technical (construction and operation techniques). No mss that are too generic. Buys under 20 mss/year. Query. Length: 1,000-3,000 words. Pays $100-400.

Photos: Send photos with ms. Pays negotiable rate. Reviews b&w contact sheets with negatives and 5x7 or 8x10 prints, and color transparencies. Identification of subjects required. Buys one-time rights.

Tips: ''We buy a limited amount of freelance material, so such material must be exceptional or should give us an 'in' with a top development or corporate or governmental official—an exclusive, in other words. Easiest way to turn us off is to telephone; please write. Know something about the field—any field. Don't submit material that your next door neighbor can understand. In this business, you're talking to established experts—and you should have solid expertise, too. Our name change has broadened our field of coverage somewhat. A writer should query to find out how.''

COMMUNITY DEVELOPMENT PUBLICATIONS, Suite 100, 8555 16th St., Silver Spring MD 20910. (301) 588-6380. Various newsletters for government officials and industry executives in housing-community development—housing production; local growth; housing market; managing housing; community development programs; neighborhoods and home improvement; real estate. Pays end of month after publication. SASE if return desired. Sample copy and writer's guidelines for SASE.

Fillers: Uses contributions of significant newspaper clippings on housing, community development, and real estate; substantive actions and litigations that would be of interest to housing, community development, and real estate professionals beyond immediate area. Particularly wants regular contributors for multistates, region, or at least a full state, especially state capitals. Buys 500-1,000 clippings. Normally pays $2.75 for each use of an accepted clipping.

FINANCIAL FREEDOM REPORT, National Institute of Financial Planning, Suite C, 1831 Fort Union Blvd., Salt Lake City UT 84121. (801)943-1280. Chairman of the Board: Mark O. Haroldsen. Managing Editor: Michael Hansen. For ''professional and nonprofessional investors, and would-be investors in real estate— real estate brokers, insurance companies, investment planners, truck drivers, housewives, doctors, architects, contractors, etc. The magazine's content is presently expanding to interest and inform the readers about other ways to put their money to work for them.'' Monthly magazine; 72 pages. Circ. 50,000. Pays on publication. Buys all rights. Phone queries OK. Simultaneous submissions OK. Computer printout submissions OK. SASE. Reports in 2 weeks. Sample copy $3; free writer's guidelines.

Nonfiction: How-to (find real estate bargains, finance property, use of leverage, managing property, developing market trends, goal setting, motivational); and interviews (success stories of those who have relied on own initiative and determination in real estate market or other business endeavors, e.g., Ray Kroc of McDonald's). Buys 10-15 unsolicited mss/year. Query with clips of published work or submit complete ms. Length: 1,500-4,500 words. ''If the topic warranted a two- or three-parter, we would consider it.'' Pays 5-10¢/word.

Photos: Send photos with ms. Uses b&w 8x10 matte prints. Offers no additional payment for photos accepted with ms. Captions required.

Tips: ''We would like to find several specialized writers in our field of real estate investments.''

PANORAMA, The Real Estate Magazine, (formerly *Real Estate Canada*), The Canadian Real Estate Association, 99 Duncan Mill Rd., Don Mills, Ontario, Canada M1N 2X5. (416)445-9910. Editor: E. Mack Parliament. Quarterly real estate magazine. Circ. 50,000. Pays on publication. Byline given. Buys all rights. Simultaneous and previously published submissions OK. Reports in 2 weeks on queries; 1 month on mss. Sample copy for 9x12 SAE.

Nonfiction: How-to (make sales and operate a successful real estate business); interview/profile; personal experience; photo feature. No articles on other than real estate subjects. Recent article example: ''Here's How Bigger Businesses Are Built.'' Buys 10 unsolicited mss/year. Send complete ms. Length: 1,000-4,000 words. Pays variable fee; ''depends on quality.''

Photos: Send photos with ms. Reviews 5x7 b&w and color prints. Captions required. Buys one-time rights.

PROPERTIES MAGAZINE, 4900 Euclid Ave., Cleveland OH 44103. (216)431-7666. Editor: Gene Bluhm. Monthly. Buys all rights. Pays on publication. Query. SASE.

Nonfiction and Photos: Wants articles of real estate and construction news value. Interested primarily in articles relating to northeastern Ohio. Length: up to 900 words. Buys photographs with mss, 5x7 preferred.

SOUTHWEST REAL ESTATE NEWS, Communication Channels, Inc., Suite 240, 18601 LBJ Freeway, Mesquite TX 75150. (214)270-6651. Editor: Jim Mitchell. Managing Editor: Sheryl Roberts. Monthly newspaper about commercial and industrial real estate for professional real estate people, including realtors, developers, mortgage bankers, corporate real estate executives, architects, contractors and brokers. Circ. 16,000. Average issue includes 4 columns, 20-50 short news items, 2-5 special articles and 10 departments. Pays on publication. Byline given. Buys all rights. Phone queries OK. Submit seasonal material 2 months in advance. Photocopied submissions OK. Computer printout submissions OK; "dot matrix OK with legible descenders." SASE. Reports in 4-6 weeks. Free sample copy and writer's guidelines.

Nonfiction: "We're interested in hearing from writers in major cities in the states that we cover, which are TX, OK, CO, NM, LA, AZ, AR, southern Nevada and southern California. We are particularly interested in writers with newspaper experience or real estate background. Assignments are made according to our editorial schedule which we will supply upon request. Most open to freelancers are city reviews and special articles. Contact the staff to discuss ideas first. No unsolicited material." Buys 3-5 mss/issue. Query. Pays $100-400.

Columns/Departments: Offices; Shopping Centers; Industrials; Multiplexes; Leases; Sales and Purchases; Mortgage and Financial; Realty Operations; Residentials; and People in the News. No newspaper clippings. Buys 3 mss/issue. Query. Length: 1,000-5,000 words. Pays $75-100.

‡TIME SHARING INDUSTRY REVIEW, Box 4301920, South Miami FL 33143. (305)667-0202. Managing Editor: William L. Coulter. Monthly newspaper for professionals involved in the time sharing industry. Pays on acceptance. Buys all rights. Reports in 1 month. Sample copy and writer's guidelines $1.

Nonfiction: Well-researched news features about new developments, marketing trends, financing, sales strategies, consumer profiles, interviews with key industry personalities, etc. Query. Length: 1,000-5,000 words. Pays according to length.

Photos: Pays extra for photo used.

Tips: "We are an international publication covering every aspect of this dynamic, rapidly-growing industry. We need freelance writers with solid business or real estate writing experience in every location where time sharing is part of the vacation scene. Send three clips demonstrating your best work, along with a brief resume. If you're convincing, we'll send you our writer's guidelines and give you an assignment. We're also interested in story ideas you generate on your own."

Selling and Merchandising

In this category are journals for sales personnel and merchandisers interested in how to sell products successfully. Journals in nearly every other category of this Trade Journal section also buy sales-related material if it is slanted to the specialized product or industry they deal with, such as clothing or paint. Publications for advertising and marketing professionals will be found under Advertising, Marketing, and PR.

AGENCY SALES MAGAZINE, Box 16878, Irvine CA 92713. (714)752-5231. Editor: Dan Bayless. 60% freelance written. For independent sales representatives and the manufacturers they represent. Publication of Manufacturers' Agents National Association. Monthly magazine. Circ. 15,000. Rights purchased vary with author and material. May buy all rights or simultaneous rights. Byline given. Buys 30 mss/year. Pays on publication. Free sample copy and writer's guidelines. Will consider photocopied or simultaneous submissions. Computer printout submissions OK. Reports in 2 months. Query. SASE.

Nonfiction and Photos: Articles on independent sales representatives, the suppliers and customers, and their operations and manufacturers who sell through sales agents. Must be about independent selling from the agent's or manufacturer's point of view. Uses how-to, profile, interview, successful business techniques. "Articles about selling should not be too general—specifics a must." Buys 5 maximum unsolicited mss/year. Length: 500-2,500 words. Ideal length is 1,500 words. Pays $50-100. Photos purchased with accompanying ms with extra payment. Captions required. B&w glossies only. Pays $10-15. Size: 3x5, 8x10.

THE AMERICAN SALESMAN, 424 N. 3rd St., Burlington IA 52601. Publisher: Bertrand G. Houle. Editorial Supervisor: Doris J. Ruschill. Editor: Barbara Boeding. 95% freelance written. For distribution through company sales representatives. Monthly magazine; 44 pages. Circ. 4,050. Pays on publication. Buys all rights. No computer printout or disk submissions. Free sample copy and writer's guidelines; mention *Writer's Market* in request.

Nonfiction: Sales seminars, customer service and followup, closing sales, sales presentations, handling objections, competition, telephone usage and correspondence, managing your territory and new innovative sales concepts. No sexist material, illustration written from only a salesman's viewpoint. No mss dealing with supervisory problems. Query. Length: 900-1,200 words. Pays 3-5¢/word. Uses no photos or advertising. Follow AP Stylebook.

ARMY/NAVY STORE AND OUTDOOR MERCHANDISER, 567 Morris Ave., Elizabeth NJ 07208. (201)353-7373. Editor: Alan Richman. 15-20% freelance written. For the owners of army/navy surplus and outdoor goods stores. Circ. 5,400. Byline given. Buys 30 mss/year. Pays on publication. SASE. Reports in 1 month. Sample copy $2 plus $1.50 postage and handling.
Nonfiction and Photos: Articles on the methods stores use to promote items; especially on how army/navy items have become fashion items, and the problems attendant to catering to this new customer. Sources of supply, how they promote, including windows, newspapers, etc. Writer's guidelines are available. Length: 1,000-2,000 words. Pays $50-125. "Most articles—especially on stores—must have photos included; minimum 5x7 b&w glossies with captions."
Tips: "The best material always has a unique—but not forced—slant. Play up the special things a store does to succeed—whether it's display, pricing policy, emphasis on certain merchandise, advertising or whatever. Be specific."

‡**THE AUCTION BOTTOM LINE®** , "All About Auctions and Auctioneering", Auction Marketing Network, Box 100, New Paris OH 45347. (513)437-7071. Editor: Dave Kessler. Bimonthly tabloid. "We're the world's largest circulation publication for auctions and auctioneers." Estab. 1981. Circ. 30,000 + . Pays on publication. Byline given. Buys one-time rights, all rights, first rights, second serial (reprint) rights, and makes work-for-hire assignments. Submit seasonal/holiday material 1 month in advance. Simultaneous queries and photocopied submissions OK. SASE. Reports in 2 weeks; "by phone if we want the article." Sample copy for 9x12 SAE and 88¢ first class postage. Writer's guidelines for 4x9 SAE and 1 first class stamp. Guidelines will be sent with free copies.
Nonfiction: How-to (do it successfully, make it work under difficult circumstances, etc.); photo feature (auction action, auctioneers at work, crowd, interesting items being sold); features. "Women in auctioneering are not a novelty anymore. Write about their professional ability to take charge and sell. Don't write 'cutesy poo.' Academicians don't read our publications. Keep it simple. Keep it accurate. Keep it coming. No straight puff pieces on 'how great I am'. Writers should run the interview and decide what's worth printing, and what's helpful to readers." Buys several mss/year. Query with or without published clips. Length: "Enough words to tell the story clearly." Pays $1.50 per column inch.
Photos: State availability of photos—or "we'll suggest photo ideas." Pays $5 for each photo published with article. Reviews b&w contact sheet and prints. Identification of subjects required. Buys all rights.
Tips: "A brief query letter about your article idea seems to be the best way for us to size up your idea and your writing ability. Be sure to include your phone number (work and home) as I prefer to call to firm up assignment, make suggestions on particular slant, give you tips on side bars, etc. But if it's hot—call us. We are open from front page to back. Features on interesting or unique auctions are wanted. Articles showing how public benefits from auctions are needed. We look forward to going monthly when we can staff up to handle everything. At that time we'll need more good freelance articles."

AUTOMOTIVE AGE, Freed-Crown-Lee Publishing, 6931 Van Nuys Blvd., Van Nuys CA 92405. (213)873-1320. Editor: George-Ann Rosenberg. For owners and management of new car dealerships. Monthly magazine designed to inform readers of management techniques, systems and products to make car dealerships more profitable. Circ. 35,000. Buys all rights. Byline given. Phone queries OK. SASE. Reports in 2 weeks. Free sample copy.
Nonfiction: Publishes articles related to retail sales, auto repair, or management of new car dealerships; informational articles (sales techniques, dealership/retail promotions). "Clean, sophisticated copy that talks to the audience on a professional level." Buys 1-3 mss/issue. Query with brief bio of author if unfamiliar to editor. Length: 300-2,000 words. Pays $5/column inch.
Photos: Pays $15-25/b&w photo used with articles, columns or departments; $50-150 color.
Tips: "Understand the new car dealer's business needs and interests and address those in accurate, well-researched articles."

CONVENIENCE STORE NEWS, BMT Publications, Inc., 254 W. 31st St., New York NY 10001. (212)594-4120. Editor: Barbara J. Bagley. For convenience-store chain executives, middle-management and owner/operators; franchisors and franchisees; convenience store managers, wholesalers, distributors, service merchandisers, food brokers and manufacturers involved in the food retailing and convenience store business. Tabloid published 16 times/year. Circ. 48,000. Pays on publication. Buys all rights. Phone queries OK. Query for submission of seasonal/holiday material. Reports on queries in 1-2 weeks. Free sample copy and writer's guidelines.
Nonfiction: General interest, how-to, interview, profile and photo feature. Interested in news about convenience stores and chains, their personnel, operations and product mix trends, promotions and legislative activi-

ties on all levels of government that affect the operations of these businesses. Buys 90 unsolicited mss/year. Query. Pays $3/column inch.

Photos: Send photos with ms. Pays $5 for b&w glossy prints; $35 for contact sheet and negatives, "provided at least 1 photo is used." Captions required.

Columns/Departments: Store Managers Section. Buys 16-20 mss/issue. Query. Length: 4 double-spaced ms pages maximum. Pays $3/column inch.

Fillers: Newsbreaks ("in our industry only"). Length: 1-2 pages, double-spaced.

INFO FRANCHISE NEWSLETTER, 11 Bond St., St. Catharines, Ontario, Canada L2R 4Z4 or 736 Center St., Lewiston NY 14092. (716)754-4669. Editor-in-Chief: E.L. Dixon Jr. Managing Editor: Jean Baird. Monthly newsletter; 8 pages. Circ. 5,000. Pays on publication. Buys all rights. Photocopied submissions OK. SASE. Reports in 4 weeks.

Nonfiction: "We are particularly interested in receiving articles regarding franchise legislation, franchise litigation, franchise success stories, and new franchises. Both American and Canadian items are of interest. We do not want to receive any information which is not fully documented; or articles which could have appeared in any newspaper or magazine in North America. An author with a legal background, who could comment upon such things as arbitration and franchising, or class actions and franchising would be of great interest to us." Expose; how-to; informational; interview; profile; new product; personal experience and technical. Buys 10-20 mss/year. Length: 25-1,000 words. Pays $10-300.

KEY NEWSLETTER, Voice Publications, 1016 S. Fly Ave., Goreville IL 62939-9720. (618)995-2027. Editor-in-Chief: Bernard Lyons. 5% freelance written, "but would like to see more." Emphasizes direct marketing/mail order, specifically for those using classified columns of national magazines. Quarterly newsletter; 16 pages. Pays on acceptance. Buys all rights. Submit seasonal/holiday material 4 months in advance of issue date. Photocopied submissions OK. SASE. Reports in 24 hours. One sample copy, $5; mention *Writer's Market* in request.

Nonfiction: Expose (fraud in mail order/direct marketing); historical (old classified ads); how-to (write classified ads, match markets, increase response to ads); humor (funny classifieds); inspirational (examples of successful classifieds, personal stories of successful mail order through classifieds); interview (with successful mail order/direct market persons using classifieds); new product (if of help to small business); personal experience (summary of test results); profile (successful users of classifieds, written in first person); and technical (math for mail order/direct marketing). Buys 10 mss/year. Submit complete ms. Length: 50-1,500 words. Pays $10-75.

Tips: "We do not cover want-ads, but only classified ads in the national publications, those that you find on the newsstand. To break in find a consistent mail order advertiser; write up his or her experiences, including start, problems, ad response, etc.; mail it to us today, without anything more than the clearest and simplest language describing the who, why, what, where, when and how."

NON-FOODS MERCHANDISING, Charleson Publishing Co., 124 E. 40th St., New York NY 10024. Editor: Donna Italiano. 10% freelance written. For buyers, manufacturers, and distributors of health and beauty aids and general merchandise (non-foods) in the supermarket. Monthly tabloid; 75 pages. Circ. 20,000. Pays on publication. Buys all rights. Byline given on major features. Photocopied submissions OK. SASE.

Nonfiction: "Reports on aspects of our business." Analytical trends, historical, interview, profile, how-to and new product. Buys 2 mss/issue. Query with clips of published work. Length: 2,000-6,000 words. Pays $150-350.

Photos: "No extra fee paid for photos included with ms." Uses color slides and b&w prints. Buys all rights.

‡ON THE UPBEAT, A Few Thoughts to Help People Who Sell for a Living Recharge Their Batteries, The Economics Press, Inc., 12 Daniel Rd., Fairfield NJ 07006. (201)227-1224. Editor: Diane Cody. Monthly magazine "serving as a refresher for veteran salespeople and a training tool for new salespeople." Circ. 36,851. Pays on acceptance. Offers 100% kill fee. Buys all rights. Submit seasonal/holiday material 3 months in advance. Photocopied submissions OK. Computer printout and disk submissions OK. Reports in 6 weeks. Free sample copy and writer's guidelines.

Nonfiction: Historical/nostalgic (incidents involving historical figures that highlight a positive personality trait); humor (wholesome jokes, cute stories—any subject); personal experience (anecdotes/stories about selling or about a helpful salesperson); travel (anecdotes about traveling salespeople or helpful techniques to make the most of travel time, etc.). Original material only. Buys 60-100 mss/year. Send complete ms. Length: 50-300 words. Pays $20-50.

Fillers: Buys 60-100/year. Length: 50-300 words. Pays $20-50.

Tips: "True stories/anecdotes about sales experience, either from the salesperson's viewpoint or the buyer's, are always welcome. Story should be unusual and serve as an example of a technique salespeople should use or stay away from. *On the Upbeat* is a business publication. Please stay away from subjects unrelated to working/ business, etc. However, jokes, cute stories may be on any *wholesome* subject."

PHOTO MARKETING, 3000 Picture Place, Jackson MI 49201. Executive Editor: Monica Smiley. For camera store dealers, photofinishers, manufacturers and distributors of photographic equipment. Publication of the Photo Marketing Association, International. Monthly magazine; 75 pages. Circ. 15,000. Buys all rights. Pays on publication. Reports in 21 days. Query with outline and story line. SASE.
Nonfiction and Photos: Business features dealing with photographic retailing or photofinishing operations, highlighting unique aspects, promotional programs, special problems. Buys 12 unsolicited mss/year. Length: 300-500 typewritten lines. Pays 5-7¢/word minimum. Pays $10-15/published 5x7 glossy photo.
Tips: Query to have: "indications that freelancer understands who our reader is—the businessperson who needs advice; intent by freelancer to tailor article to our market by talking to/interviewing people in photo business. Writers should send us a list of articles they have prepared, with descriptions, and their qualifications/background. If they're doing an article on selling techniques, for example, I'd like to know who they talked with or if they've worked in retailing to get info."

PRIVATE LABEL, The Magazine for House Brands and Generics, E.W. Williams Publishing Co., 80 8th Ave., New York NY 10011. (212)989-1101. Editor: Sam Martin. Managing Editor: Mark Edgar. Bimonthly magazine covering food and non-food private label and generic products. Circ. 25,000. Pays on acceptance. Byline given. Offers 50-100% kill fee "depending on circumstances." Buys first rights and second serial (reprint) rights. Submit seasonal/holiday material 4 months in advance. Photocopied submissions OK "if not under submission elsewhere." Computer printout submissions OK; prefers letter quality to dot matrix printouts. SASE. Reports in "weeks." Sample copy for $1 and SAE.
Nonfiction: Book excerpts (if segments are appropriate); general interest; historical/nostalgic; how-to; interview/profile; personal experience; photo feature; travel. "We use feature articles showing how retailers promote, buy, display, sell, and feel about their store brands (private label and generic products). We're always interested in coverage of areas more than 300 miles from New York. No articles on peripheral topics such as taxes, insurance, safety, etc." Buys 30-40 mss/year. Query or send complete ms. Length: 500-4,000 words; Pays 3¢/word; "flat fee by special arrangement."
Photos: "We prefer articles with photos." Send photos with ms. Pays $7 minimum for 5x7 b&w prints; reviews contact sheets (if large selection). Captions and identification of subjects required. Buys all rights; "release on request."
Tips: "We are wide open to freelancers who can line up store permission (preferably headquarters) for feature articles on philosophy, purchase, consumer attitudes, retailer attitudes, display, and promotion of private label and generic products."

‡**PROFESSIONAL SELLING**, 24 Rope Ferry Rd., Waterford CT 06386. (203)442-4365. Editor: Paulette S. Withers. Bimonthly newsletter for sales professionals covering industrial or wholesale sales. "Provides field sales personnel with both the basics and current information that can help them better perform the sales function." Pays on acceptance. No byline given. Buys all rights. Submit seasonal/holiday material 4 months in advance. SASE. Reports in 2 weeks. Sample copy for business-size SAE and 1 first class stamp; writer's guidelines available for same.
Nonfiction: How-to (successful sales techniques); interview/profile (interview-based articles). "We buy only interview-based material." Buys 12-15 mss/year. Query. Length: 800-1,000 words.
Tips: "Only the lead article is open to freelancers. That must be based on an interview with an actual sales professional. Freelancers may occasionally interview sales managers, but the slant must be toward field sales *not* management."

SALESMAN'S OPPORTUNITY MAGAZINE, 6 N. Michigan Ave., Chicago IL 60602. Managing Editor: Jack Weissman. 30% freelance written. "For anyone who is interested in making money, full or spare time, in selling or in independent business program." Monthly magazine. Circ. 190,000. Pays on publication. Buys all rights. Byline given. Submit seasonal/holiday material 6 months in advance of issue date. SASE. Free sample copy and writer's guidelines.
Nonfiction: "We use articles dealing with sales techniques, sales psychology or general self-improvement topics." How-to; inspirational; and interview (with successful salespeople who are selling products offered by direct selling firms, especially concerning firms which recruit salespeople through *Salesman's Opportunity Magazine*). Articles on self-improvement should deal with specifics rather than generalities. Would like to have more articles that deal with overcoming fear, building self-confidence, increasing personal effectiveness, and other psychological subjects. Submit complete ms. Buys 35-50 unsolicited mss/year. Length: 250-900 words. Pays $20-35.
Photos: State availability of photos with ms. Offers no additional payment for 8x10 b&w glossy prints. Captions required. Buys all rights. Model release required.
Tips: "Many articles are too academic for our audience. We look for free-and-easy style in simple language which is packed with useful information, drama and inspiration. Check the magazine before writing. We can't use general articles. The only articles we buy deal with material that is specifically directed to readers who are

opportunity seekers—articles dealing with direct sales programs or successful ventures that others can emulate. Try to relate the article to the actual work in which the reader is engaged."

SELLING DIRECT, (formerly *Specialty Salesman Magazine*), Communications Channels, Inc., 6255 Barfield Rd., Atlanta GA 30328. (404)256-9800. Publisher: William Hood. Editor: Susan Spann. 75% advertising, 25% freelance written. For independent businessmen and women who sell door-to-door, store-to-store, office-to-office and by the party plan method as well as through direct mail and telephone solicitation; selling products and services. Monthly magazine; 50-100 pages. Circ. 500,000. Pays on publication. Buys all rights. Byline given. Submit seasonal/holiday material 3 months in advance of issue date. Computer printout and disk submissions OK "if compatible with Digital Corp.'s Decmate." SASE. Reports in 3 months. Free sample copy and writer's guidelines.
Nonfiction: How-to (sell better; increase profits); historical (related to the history of various kinds of sales pitches, anecdotes, etc.); inspirational (success stories, "rags to riches" type of stories); with no additional payment. Photos purchased with accompanying ms. Buys 30 unsolicited mss/year. Query or submit complete ms. Length: 500-1,500 words. Pays 10¢/word.
Columns/Departments: Ideas Exchange (generated from our readers). Submit complete ms. Open to suggestions for new columns/departments.
Fillers: Jokes, gags, anecdotes and short humor. Buys 2/issue. Length: 150-500 words. Pays $10 for each published item.
Tips: No general articles on "How to be a Super Salesperson." Writers should concentrate on one specific aspect of selling and expand on that.

STORES, National Retail Merchants Association, 100 W. 31st St., New York NY 10001. (212)244-8780. Editor: Joan Bergmann. Managing Editor: Carol Ellen Messenger. Monthly magazine about retail issues for top retail management. Circ. 25,000. Pays on publication. Byline given. Buys all rights. Reports in 2 weeks on queries; in 2 months on mss. Free sample copy and writer's guidelines.
Nonfiction: Buys 8-10 mss/issue. Query with clips of previously published work. Length: 1,000 words minimum. Pays 12¢/word.
Photos: Send photos with ms on assigned story. Pays $5 for each b&w used. Buys all rights.
Tips: "Send writing samples and background; assignments sometimes are given on the basis of writing style."

VIDEO BUSINESS, CES Publishing, 135 W. 50th St., New York NY 10020. (212)794-0500. Editor: John HuBach. Managing Editor: Frank Moldstad. Associate Editor: Steven Friedlander. Monthly magazine covering home video industry. Also covers video game and home computer industries. Estab. 1981. Circ. 26,000. Pays on publication. Byline given. Buys all rights in the industry. Simultaneous queries and previously published submissions OK ("indicate where and when published"). Computer printout submissions OK. SASE. Reports in 1 month. Free sample copy.
Nonfiction: Informational pieces (on marketing, merchandising and selling themes). No "technical articles or how-tos dealing with cutting costs, managing people, etc." Buys 10 mss/year. Query. Length: 1,500-2,000 words. Pays 12.5¢/word.
Photos: State availability of photos.
Tips: "Our style has become more upbeat. Writers should avoid 'dry' language."

WALLCOVERINGS MAGAZINE, Publishing Dynamics, Inc., 2 Selleck St., Stamford CT 06902. Publisher/Editor: Martin A. Johnson. Associate Publisher: Robert Johnson. Managing Editor: Dorianne Russo. Associate Editors: Laura Beal and Richard Bomber. Monthly trade journal of the flexible wallcoverings industry. Circ. 10,000. Submit query on all nonfiction article ideas. Computer printout and disk submissions OK. Buys all rights. SASE. Sample copy $2.
Nonfiction: Articles about manufacturers, distributors, retailers who sell wallcoverings. Query with clips of previously published work.
Photos: On assignment. 8x10 b&w prints or contact sheets with negatives. Rates negotiable. Model release required.

Sport Trade

AMERICAN BICYCLIST AND MOTORCYCLIST, 461 8th Ave., New York NY 10001. (212)563-3430. Editor: Stan Gottlieb. For bicycle sales and service shops. Monthly. Circ. 10,068. Buys all rights. "Only staff-written articles are bylined, except under special circumstances." Pays on publication.
Nonfiction: Typical story describes (very specifically) unique traffic-builder or merchandising ideas used with success by an actual dealer. Articles may also deal exclusively with moped sales and service operation

within conventional bicycle shop. Emphasis is on showing other dealers how they can follow a similar pattern and increase their business. Articles may also be based entirely on repair shop operation, depicting efficient and profitable service systems and methods. Buys 8 mss/year. Query. Length: 1,000-2,800 words. Pays 5¢/word, plus "bonus for outstanding manuscript."

Photos: Relevant b&w photos illustrating principal points in article purchased with ms; 5x7 minimum. No transparencies. Pays $5 per photo. Captions required. Buys all rights.

AMERICAN FIREARMS INDUSTRY, American Press Media Association, Inc., 2801 E. Oakland Park Blvd., Ft. Lauderdale FL 33306. Specializes in the sporting arms trade. Monthly magazine. Circ. 30,000. Pays on publication. Buys all rights. Submit all material with SASE. No computer printout or disk submissions. Reports in 2 weeks.

Nonfiction: R.A. Lesmeister, articles editor. Publishes informational, technical and new product articles. No general firearms subjects. Query. Length: 900-1,500 words. Pays $100-150.

Photos: B&w 8x10 glossy prints. "Ms price includes payment for photos."

AMERICAN HOCKEY AND ARENA MAGAZINE, Amateur Hockey Association of the United States, 2997 Broadmoor Valley Rd., Colorado Springs CO 80906. (303)576-4990. Publisher: Hal Trumble. Managing Editor: Jeff Mordhorst. Monthly magazine covering hockey equipment and arena components for teams, coaches and referees of the Amateur Hockey Association of the United States, ice facilities in the US and Canada, buyers, schools, colleges, pro teams, and park and recreation departments. Circ. 35,000. Pays on publication. Byline given. Makes work-for-hire assignments. Phone queries OK. Submit seasonal material 4 months in advance. Photocopied and previously published submissions OK. SASE. Reports in 1 month. Sample copy $2.

Nonfiction: General interest, profile, new product and technical. Query. Length: 500-3,000 words. Pays $50 minimum.

Photos: Reviews 5x7 b&w glossy prints and color slides. Offers no additional payment for photos accepted with ms. Captions preferred. Buys one-time rights.

Columns/Departments: Rebound Shots (editorial); Americans in the Pros (US players in the NHL); College Notes; Rinks and Arenas (arena news); Equipment/Sports Medicine; Referees Crease; Coaches Playbook; For the Record; Features (miscellaneous). Query.

ARCHERY RETAILER, Suite 306, 715 Florida Ave., S., Minneapolis MN 55426. (414)276-6600. Editor: Richard Sapp. Emphasizes archery retailing. Magazine published 6 times/year. Circ. 15,000. Pays on publication. Buys one-time rights. Byline given. Phone queries OK, "but prefer mail queries." Submit seasonal/holiday material 4 months in advance. SASE. Reports in 3 weeks. Free sample copy and writer's guidelines.

Nonfiction: How-to (better buying, selling, displaying, advertising, etc.); interview; profile. Features on sporting goods retail and specifically the marketing of archery equipment and accessories. "No stories about dinky shops selling because they love archery but have no idea of profitability." Query. Length: 500-1,250 words. Pays $50-150.

Photos: Purchased with or without accompanying ms. Captions required. Pays $10-25 for 8x10 b&w glossies.

Tips: "Our primary purchases are shop features these days—stories on successful archery dealers. We're looking for writing that entertains as well as informs."

BICYCLE BUSINESS JOURNAL, 1904 Wenneca, Box 1570, Fort Worth TX 76101. Editor: Walt Jarvis. Monthly. Circ. 10,000. Not copyrighted. Pays on publication. SASE.

Nonfiction and Photos: Stories about dealers who service what they sell, emphasizing progressive, successful sales ideas in the face of rising costs and increased competition. Length: 5 double-spaced pages maximum. Also includes moped dealerships. B&w glossy photo a must; vertical photo preferred. "One 8x10 photo is sufficient." Query.

Tips: "We are demanding greater professionalism and more content and research in freelance material."

BICYCLE DEALER SHOWCASE, Box 19531, Irvine CA 92713. Editor: John Francis. For bicycle/moped dealers and industry personnel. Monthly magazine; 90-110 pages. Circ. 13,000. Buys all rights. Buys about 6-12 mss/year. Pays on publication. Free sample copy and writer's guidelines with SASE. Submit seasonal material 2 months in advance. Reports in 3-4 weeks. Query or submit complete ms. Computer printout and disk submissions OK. SASE.

Nonfiction: Articles dealing with marketing bicycle products; financing, better management techniques, current trends, as related to bicycle equipment or selling. Material must be fairly straightforward, with a slant toward economic factors or marketing techniques. Informational, how-to, interview, profile, humor, successful business operations, merchandising techniques, technical. Length: 500-1,000 words. Pays $100 "or more, depending on the work involved."

Photos: 8x10 b&w glossy prints purchased with mss. Pays $10 minimum/photo.

Tips: "Bigger freelance budget. We judge the writer's style, ability and command of the facts by his query. If the query is good, the writer is good. Know what you're talking about, be open to suggestions and keep in constant touch, whether you have an article in mind or not. No simultaneous submissions.''

‡**CATCHLINE**, Ski Business News, Drawer 5007, Bend OR 97708. (503)382-6978. Editor: Tom Healy. Managing Editor: Ken Asher. Newsletter published 18 times/year covering the ski resort business. Estab. 1983. Pays on publication. Buys first North American serial rights. Submit seasonal/holiday material 2 months in advance. Photocopied submissions OK. Computer printout submissions OK. ''We will soon be able to interface our typesetting equipment to most micros and word processors.'' SASE. Reports in 3 weeks. Sample copy $1; free writer's guidelines.
Nonfiction: Book excerpts, expose, general interest, how-to, interview/profile, new product, photo feature, technical. No fiction. Send complete ms. Length: 50-500 words. Pays $10-100.
Photos: Send photos with accompanying ms. Pays $10-30 for 35mm color transparencies; $10-30 for 5x7 color prints; $2-7 for 5x7 b&w prints. Captions, model release on cover shots and identification of subjects required. Buys one-time rights.
Tips: ''Send us a timely, informative article that will be of interest to ski business people. We are just getting started. If we are highly successful, we will pass along our successful financial status to our writers by way of larger payments.''

FISHING TACKLE RETAILER, B.A.S.S. Publications, 1 Bell Rd., Montgomery AL 36141. (205)272-9530. Editor: Dave Ellison. Quarterly magazine ''designed to promote the economic health of retail sellers of freshwater and saltwater angling equipment.'' Circ. 22,000. Byline usually given. Buys all rights. Submit seasonal/holiday material 6 months in advance. SASE. Reports in 6 weeks. Sample copy $2; writer's guidelines for standard size SAE and 1 first class stamp.
Nonfiction: How-to (merchandising and management techniques); technical (how readers can specifically benefit from individual technological advances); success stories (how certain fishing tackle retailers have successfully overcome business difficulties and their advice to their fellow retailers). Articles must directly relate to the financial interests of the magazine's audience. Buys 100 mss/year. Query with clips of published work. Length: 50-3,000 words. Pays $10-600.
Photos: State availability of photos. Payment included with ms.
Columns/Departments: Retail Pointers (200-300 words) and Profit Strategy (750-900 words)—how-to tips, should be accompanied by illustration. Buys variable number mss/year.

FITNESS INDUSTRY, (formerly *Racquetball Industry*), Industry Publishers, Inc., 1545 NE 123rd St., North Miami FL 33161. (305)893-8771. Executive Editor: Michael J. Keighley. Bimonthly magazine about the fitness industry. Includes racquetball, dancercize, running, bicycling, swimming, and aerobocize. For retailers and business people in the industry. Circ. 18,500. Pays on publication. Byline given. Buys all rights. Submit seasonal material 2 months in advance. SASE. Reports in 6 weeks. Sample copy $2.50; free writer's guidelines.
Nonfiction: ''Content must be general, not featuring one specific manufacturing company or individual shop case-study. Articles can feature products, such as an examination of women's racquetball apparel, but must include industry-wide information, not pertaining specifically to the product of one manufacturer. Design, display, merchandising techniques, retailing procedures, shop layout and lighting are among those categories that would be of interest to our readers.'' Query. Length: 2,000-2,500 words. Pays 5¢/word.

GOLF COURSE MANAGEMENT, Golf Course Superintendents Association of America, 1617 St. Andrews, Lawrence KS 66044. (913)841-2240. Editor: Zahid Iqbal. Monthly magazine covering golf course and turf management. Circ. 15,000. Byline given. Buys all rights. Submit seasonal/holiday material 6 months in advance. Simultaneous queries, and simultaneous submissions OK. Reports in 2 weeks on queries; 1 month on mss. Free sample copy and writer's guidelines.
Nonfiction: Book excerpts, historical/nostalgic, interview/profile, personal experience, technical. ''All areas that relate to the golf course superintendent—whether features or scholarly pieces related to turfgrass management. We prefer all submissions to be written SIMPLY.'' Special issues include January ''conference issue''—features on convention cities used each year. Buys 20 mss/year. Query with clips of published work. Length: 1,500-3,000 words. Pays $100-300.
Photos: Send photos with ms. Pays $50-250 for color, 4x5 transparencies preferred. Captions, model release and identification of subjects required. Buys one-time rights.
Tips: ''Call communications department (913)841-2240, offer idea, follow with outline, writing samples. Response from us immediate.''

GOLF INDUSTRY, Industry Publishers, Inc., 1545 NE 123rd St., North Miami FL 33161. (305)893-8771. Executive Editor: Michael J. Keighley. Emphasizes the golf industry for country clubs, pro-owned golf shops, real estate developments, municipal courses, military and schools. Bimonthly magazine; 75 pages. Circ. 17,000. Pays on publication. Buys all rights. Submit seasonal/holiday material 2-3 months in advance. No computer printout or disk submissions. SASE. Reports "usually in 6-8 weeks." Sample copy $2.50. Free writer's guidelines.

Nonfiction: Publishes informational articles "dealing with a specific facet of golf club or pro shop operations, e.g., design, merchandising, finances, etc." Buys 20 mss/year. Submit complete ms. Length: 2,500 words maximum. Pays 5¢/word.

Tips: "Since we don't make freelance assignments, a query is not particularly important. We would rather have a complete ms which conforms to our policy of general, but informative, articles about one specific facet of the business of golf merchandising, financing, retailing, etc. Well-done mss, if not used immediately, are often held in our files for use in a future issue. We never publish articles concentrating on one specific manufacturer, or extolling the virtues of one product over another. We seldom feature one club or retail outlet. We don't deal with the game itself, but with the business end of the game."

GOLF SHOP OPERATIONS, 495 Westport Ave., Norwalk CT 06856. (203)847-5811. Editor: Nick Romano. For golf professionals and shop operators at public and private courses, resorts, driving ranges, and golf specialty shops. Magazine published 6 times/year. Circ. 12,500. Byline given. Pays on publication. Free sample copy. Photocopied submissions OK. Computer printout and disk submissions OK. Submit seasonal material (for Christmas and other holiday sales, or profiles of successful professionals) 3 months in advance. Reports in 1 month.

Nonfiction: "We emphasize improving the golf professional's knowledge of his profession. Articles should describe how pros are buying, promoting, merchandising and displaying wares in their shops that might be of practical value to fellow professionals. Must be aimed only at the pro audience." How-to, profile, successful business operation, merchandising techniques. Buys 6-8 mss/year. Phone queries preferred. Pays $150-175.

Photos: "Pictures are mandatory with all manuscript submissions." Captions required.

Tips: "I'm less inclined to assign anything unless the person can handle a camera. The profile pieces must have decent photos. We're really looking for the freelancers that understand the golf business. This helps us in that we won't have to rewrite a lot or have the writer go back and ask the obvious questions."

MOTORCYCLE DEALER & TRADE, Brave Beaver Pressworks, Ltd., 290 Jarvis St., Toronto, Ontario, Canada M5B 2C5. (416)977-6318. Editor: Christopher Knowles. Editorial Director: Georgs Kolesnikovs. Monthly tabloid covering the Canadian motorcycle business. Circ. 2,500. Pays on acceptance or publication; "depends on the situation." Byline given. Offers 50% kill fee. Buys one-time rights. Submit seasonal/holiday material 2 months in advance. Simultaneous queries, and simultaneous and photocopied submissions OK. SASE. Reports in 2 weeks. Free sample copy and writer's guidelines.

Nonfiction: How-to (relative to retail m/c business); interview/profile (of successful m/c businessmen); and new product (re: motorcycles). "Since most of our readers are dealers, we publish many stories of the how-to variety—how to sell, display, insure your premises, etc." No articles "that pertain solely to US situations." Buys 8 mss/year. Query with clips of published work. Length: 500-1,000 words. Pays "in the neighborhood of $100."

Photos: State availability of photos. Pays $10-35 for b&w contact sheets or negatives. Identification of subjects required.

Tips: "We're primarily interested in articles to help motorcycle dealers do their job better. Humorous articles about the business also welcome. We prefer very fast-paced stories jam-packed with useful information. No puff pieces, please."

MOTORCYCLE DEALERNEWS, Hester Communications, 1700 E. Dyer Rd., Santa Ana CA 92714. (714)549-4834. Associate Editors: John Brumm, Fred Clements. Monthly magazine "dedicated to informing motorcycle dealers of more effective ways of doing business." Circ. 15,000. Pays on publication. Byline given. Buys first rights. Submit seasonal/holiday material 3 months in advance. Simultaneous queries and photocopied submissions OK. SASE. Reports in 1 month. Sample copy for 9x12 SAE and 3 first class stamps; writer's guidelines for business size SAE and 1 first class stamp.

Nonfiction: General interest (business insurance, finance, displays, legislation, advertising); how-to (sell motorcycles, manage motorcycle dealerships); interview/profile. "We are also looking for articles that examine a problem and offer a solution that would be of help to dealers. Not interested in general nonspecific articles; concrete thoughts and examples are a must." Buys 8 mss/year. Query with clips of published work. "Follow up by phone." Length: 1,200-2,000 words. Pays $125-175.

Photos: State availability of photos. Reviews 5x7 b&w prints. "Photos paid for with payment for ms." Captions required. Buys all rights.

Tips: "For increased readability, manuscripts should include sidebars, summaries, pictures/captions, etc."

PGA MAGAZINE, Professional Golfer's Association of America, 100 Avenue of Champions, Palm Beach Gardens FL 33410. (305)626-3600. Editor: William A. Burbaum. Monthly magazine about golf for 14,000 club professionals and apprentices nationwide. Circ. 18,500. Average issue includes 8-10 articles and 6 departments. Pays on acceptance. Byline given. Phone queries OK. Submit seasonal material 3 months in ad-

vance. Photocopied and previously published submissions OK. Reports in 3 weeks. Free sample copy.
Nonfiction: Historical (great moments in golf revisited); profile (success stories); how-to (instructional, PGA member teaching techniques); inspirational (personal success stories); and photo feature (great golf courses). Buys 15 mss/year. Query with outline and clips of previously published work. Length: 900-1,500 words. Pays 15¢/word minimum. "Exhibit knowledge and interest in the professional business and in other needs of today's club professional."
Photos: Pays $10-25/b&w contact sheets. Pays $25-50/35mm inside color transparencies; $150 for cover photos. Captions and model release required. Buys all rights.

POOL & SPA NEWS, Leisure Publications, 3923 W. 6th St., Los Angeles CA 90020. (213)385-3926. Editor-in-Chief: J. Field. 40% freelance written. Emphasizes news of the swimming pool and spa industry for pool builders, pool retail stores and pool service firms. Semimonthly magazine. Circ. 10,000. Pays on publication. Buys all rights. Phone queries OK. Photocopied submissions OK. No computer printout or disk submissions. SASE. Reports in 2 weeks.
Nonfiction: Interview, new product, profile, and technical. Length: 500-2,000 words. Pays 8¢/word. Pays $8 per b&w photo used.

‡**RODEO NEWS, Voice of the International Professional Rodeo Association**, Rodeo News, Inc., Box 587, Pauls Valley OK 73075. (405)238-3310. Managing Editor: Chuck Smith. Rodeo magazine published 11 times/year and covering the entire industry. Circ. 14,500. Pays on publication. Byline given. Buys all rights. Submit seasonal/holiday material 3 months in advance. Simultaneous submissions OK. SASE. Reports in 2 weeks on queries; 3 weeks on mss. Free sample copy and writer's guidelines.
Nonfiction: New product, opinion, photo feature. Buys 10 mss/year. Send complete ms. Length: 250-1,500 words. Pays 5¢/word.
Photos: Send photos with ms. Reviews 5x7 b&w and color prints. Captions required.

RVB, RECREATIONAL VEHICLE BUSINESS, 29901 Agoura Rd., Agoura CA 91301. Editor: Michael Schneider. Managing Editor: Sheryl Davis. 50% freelance written. For men and women of the RV industry, primarily those involved in the sale of trailers, motorhomes, pickup campers, and vans to the public. Also, owners and operators of trailer supply stores, plus manufacturers and executives of the RV industry nationwide and in Canada. Monthly magazine; 100 pages. Circ. 20,000. Buys first North American rights. Pays on publication. Free sample copy and writer's guidelines. Reports in 4 weeks. SASE.
Nonfiction and Photos: "Stories that show trends in the industry; success stories of particular dealerships throughout the country; news stories on new products; accessories (news section); how to sell; how to increase profits, be a better businessman. Interested in broadbased, general interest material of use to all RV retailers, rather than mere trade reporting." Informational, how-to, personal experience, interview, profile, humor, think articles, successful business operations, and merchandising techniques. Buys 75 mss/year. Query. Length: 1,000-2,000 words. Pays $150-350. Shorter items for regular columns or departments run 800 words. Pays $50-125. Photos purchased with accompanying ms with no additional payment. Captions required.
Columns/Departments: Dealer/industry items from over the country; newsbreaks. Length: 100-200 words; with photos, if possible. Payment based on length.
Tips: A "more broad-based approach" will affect writers in the year ahead.

THE SHOOTING INDUSTRY, 291 Camino de la Reina, San Diego CA 92108. (619)297-8521. Editor: J. Rakusan. For manufacturers, dealers, sales representatives of archery and shooting equipment. Monthly. Buys all rights. Byline given. Pays on publication. Free sample copy. Reports in 2-3 weeks. SASE.
Nonfiction and Photos: Articles that tell "secrets of my success" based on experience of individual gun dealer; articles of advice to help dealers sell more guns and shooting equipment. Also, articles about and of interest to manufacturers and top manufacturers' executives. Buys about 135 mss/year. Query. Length: 3,000 words maximum. Pays $100-200. Photos essential; b&w glossies purchased with ms.

SKI BUSINESS, 975 Post Rd., Darien CT 06820. Editor: Bob Gillen. Tabloid magazine published 11 times/year. For ski retailers. Circ. 18,000. Byline given, except on "press releases and round-up articles containing passages from articles submitted by several writers." Pays on publication. Submit seasonal material 3 weeks in advance. Reports in 1 month. Free sample copy available to qualified writers. SASE.
Nonfiction: Will consider ski shop case studies; mss about unique and successful merchandising ideas; and ski area equipment rental operations. "All material should be slanted toward usefulness to the ski shop operator. Always interested in interviews with successful retailers." Uses round-ups of preseason sales and Christmas buying across the country during September to December. Would like to see reports on what retailers in major markets are doing. Buys about 150 mss/year. Query first. Pays $50-200.
Photos: Photos purchased with accompanying mss. Buys b&w glossy 8x10 photos. Pays minimum of $25/photo; more for color and 35mm transparencies.

SKIING TRADE NEWS, 1 Park Ave., New York NY 10016. Editor: Rick Kahl. For ski shop owners. Annual magazine; 270 pages. Also publishes a tabloid 9 times/year. Circ. about 11,600. Buys first North American serial rights. Pays on acceptance. Reports in 1 month. SASE.
Nonfiction: Factual how-to or success articles about buying at the ski trade shows, merchandising ski equipment, keeping control of inventory, etc. Buys 10 mss/year. Query. Length: 1,000 words. Pays 12¢/word.
Tips: "Find a ski shop that is a success, one that does something differently and makes money at it. Research the reasons for the shop's success and query. More focused attention to marketing strategies and business management will affect writers in the year ahead."

THE SPORTING GOODS DEALER, 1212 N. Lindbergh Blvd., St. Louis MO 63132. (314)997-7111. President/Chief Executive Officer: Richard Waters. Editor: Gary Goldman. For members of the sporting goods trade: retailers, manufacturers, wholesalers, representatives. Monthly magazine. Circ. 27,000. Buys second serial (reprint) rights. Buys about 15 mss/year. Pays on publication. Sample copy $1 (refunded with first ms); free writer's guidelines. Will not consider photocopied or simultaneous submissions. Reports in 2 weeks. Query. SASE.
Nonfiction and Photos: "Articles about specific sporting goods retail stores, their promotions, display techniques, sales ideas, merchandising, timely news of key personnel; expansions, new stores, deaths—all in the sporting goods trade. Specific details on how individual successful sporting goods stores operate. What specific retail sporting goods stores are doing that is new and different. We would also be interested in features dealing with stores doing an outstanding job in retailing of baseball, fishing, golf, tennis, camping, firearms/hunting and allied lines of equipment. Query on these." Successful business operations, merchandising techniques. Does not want to see announcements of doings and engagements. Length: open. Pays $2 per 100 published words. Also looking for material for the following columns: Terse Tales of the Trade (store news); Selling Slants (store promotions); Open for Business (new retail sporting goods stores or sporting goods departments). All material must relate to specific sporting goods stores by name, city, and state; general information is not accepted. Pays minimum of $3.50 for sharp clear b&w photos; size not important. These are purchased with or without mss. Captions optional, but identification requested.
Fillers: Clippings. These must relate directly to the sporting goods industry. Pays 1-2¢/published word.

SPORTS MERCHANDISER, W.R.C. Smith Publishing Co., 1760 Peachtree Rd. NW, Atlanta GA 30357. (404)874-4462. Editor: Eugene R. Marnell. For retailers and wholesalers of sporting goods in all categories; independent stores, chains, specialty stores, department store departments. Monthly tabloid; 100 pages. Circ. 30,000. Pays on acceptance, buys all rights. Submit seasonal/holiday material 4-6 months in advance. SASE. Reports in 4 months.
Nonfiction: "Articles telling how retailers are successful in selling a line of products, display ideas, successful merchandising programs, inventory operations, and advertising program successes. No articles on business history. Query to be one-page with card (reply) enclosed. Letters to state full name of contact, address, etc. and describe type of business relative to volume, inventory, positioning in local market. Tell particular slant author believes most interesting." Length: 1,000-2,000 words. Pays $75-175.
Photos: State availability of photos with query. Offers no additional payment for 5x7 or 8x10 b&w prints. Captions required. Buys all rights.
Tips: "The retail order season is almost six months opposite the retail buying season (i.e., consumer buying). Lead time for ordering is six months—sometimes more on hardgoods and softgoods. Other products have full-year ordering cycle. Hence, query will help everyone."

SPORTS RETAILER, 1699 Wall St., Mt. Prospect IL 60056. (312)439-4000. Managing Editor: Thomas L. Quigley. For owners and managers of retail sporting goods stores. Monthly. Circ. 19,000. Buys first North American serial rights. Buys 18 mss/year. Pays on publication. Free editorial calendar and writer's guidelines. Submit seasonal material 4 months in advance. SASE.
Nonfiction and Photos: Articles on "full-line and specialty sporting goods stores. Informational articles, how-to; articles on retail sporting goods advertising, promotions, in-store clinics/workshops; employee hiring and training; merchandising techniques. Articles should cover one aspect of store operation in depth." Query with clips of previously published work. Length: 1,500-2,000 words. Pays $50-175. B&w glossy prints should accompany ms. 5x7 minimum. Captions required. Color transparencies acceptable. Pays $100 for cover transparency.
Tips: "Practice photography! Most stories, no matter how good, are useless without quality photos. They can be submitted as contact sheets with negatives to hold down writer's cost."

SPORTS TRADE CANADA, Page Publications, Ltd., 380 Wellington St. W., Toronto, Ontario, Canada M5V 1E3. (416)593-0608. Editor: Jamie Howe. For sporting goods retailers, manufacturers, wholesalers, jobbers, department and chain stores, camping equipment dealers, bicycle sales and service, etc. Magazine published 7 times/year. Circ. 9,800. Pays on publication. Buys first rights. Reports in 2 months. SAE and International Reply Coupons.

Nonfiction: Technical and informational articles. Articles on successful Canadian business operations, new products, merchandising techniques; interviews. No US-oriented articles. Query. No computer printout or disk submissions. Length: 1,200-2,000 words. Pays 10¢/word or $60/published page.

Tips: Submit Canadian-oriented articles only; "new sales help techniques are best."

SWIMMING POOL AGE & SPA MERCHANDISER, Communication Channels, Inc., 6255 Barfield Rd., Atlanta GA 30328. (404)256-9800. Editor: Bill Gregory. Emphasizes pool, spa, and hot tub industry. Monthly tabloid. Circ. 15,000. Pays on publication. Buys first rights for industry. Phone queries OK. Submit seasonal/holiday material 3 months in advance.

Nonfiction: Expose (if in industry, company frauds); how-to (do more business, installation techniques, service and repairs, tips, etc.); interview (with people and groups within the industry); photo feature (pool/spa/tub construction or special use); technical (should be prepared with expert within the industry); industry news; market research reports. Buys 10-20 unsolicited mss/year. Query. Length: 250-1,500 words. Pays 10¢/word.

Photos: Purchased with accompanying ms or on assignment. Captions required. Query or send contact sheet. Will accept 35mm transparencies of good quality.

Fiction: Humor about the industry. Length: 1,000 words maximum. Pays 10¢/word.

Columns/Departments: "Short news on personality items always welcome." Association News, Continuing Education.

TENNIS INDUSTRY, Industry Publishers, Inc., 1545 NE 123 St., North Miami FL 33161. (305)893-8771. Editor: Michael J. Keighley. Emphasizes the tennis industry for department store divisionals, teaching pros, pro shop managers, specialty shop managers, country club managers, coaches, athletic directors, etc. Monthly magazine; 200 pages. Circ. 19,000. Pays on publication. Buys all rights. Submit seasonal/holiday material 2-3 months in advance. Previously published submissions OK. SASE. Reports "usually in 6-8 weeks." Sample copy $2.50; free writer's guidelines.

Nonfiction: Publishes informational articles dealing "with specific facets of the tennis club or pro shop operation, e.g., design, merchandising, finances, etc." Buys 20 mss/year. Submit complete ms. Length: 2,500 words maximum. Pays 5¢/word.

Tips: "Since we do not make freelance assignments, a query is not particularly important. We would rather have a complete ms which conforms to our policy of general, but informative articles about one specific facet of the business of tennis merchandising, financing, retailing, etc. Well-done manuscripts, if not used immediately, are often held in our files for use in a future issue. We never publish articles concentrating on one specific manufacturer, or extolling the virtues of one product over another. We seldom feature one club or retail outlet. We don't deal with the game itself, but with the business end of the game."

‡WILDLIFE HARVEST MAGAZINE, For Game Breeders and Hunting Resorts, Arrowhead Hunt Club, R#1, Box 28, Goose Lake IA 52750. Editor: John M. Mullin. Monthly magazine of private enterprise game bird hunting resorts and wildlife habitats. Aimed mostly for North American Gamebird Association members. Circ. 1,460. Pays on acceptance. Byline given. Buys one-time and first rights. Submit seasonal/holiday material 2 months in advance. Photocopied submissions OK. SASE. Reports in 3 weeks on queries; 2 months on mss. Sample copy for $1.25 and 6x9 SAE.

Nonfiction: How-to (pen-rear game birds, develop and operate a bird hunting resort); photo feature (NAGA member game farms and private enterprise hunting resorts). No general conservation articles or travel articles. Buys 3-4 mss/year. Query. Length: 2,000 words maximum. Pays $40-200.

Photos: "Photos should depict private enterprise, commercial game farms or hunting resorts." Send photos with query. Payment for photos is included in payment for ms. Reviews 3x5 or 5x7 b&w or color prints (if good contrast). Captions preferred; identification of subjects required.

Tips: "We would buy more articles if they were of the right subject and people." Contact the editor for a listing of NAGA members or game farm enterprises in your state. Open to picture stories about a *member* game bird farm or member hunting preserve. "Most freelance writers don't work well for our magazine. They don't seem to want to go to a specific operation for a story."

Stone and Quarry Products

For a list of related markets, see the Mining and Minerals category.

CONCRETE, Eyre & Spottiswoode Publications Ltd., 32 Swan Court, Leatherhead, Surrey KT22 8AH, England. (01). Editor: R.J. Barfoot. Emphasizes civil engineering and building and construction. Monthly magazine; 60 pages. Circ. 9,000. Pays on publication. Phone queries OK. Photocopied submissions OK. Free sample copy.

Nonfiction: Historical, new product, and technical articles dealing with concrete and allied industries. Query or submit complete ms. Length: 1,000-3,000 words.

CONCRETE CONSTRUCTION MAGAZINE, 426 South Westgate, Addison IL 60101. Editor: M.K. Hurd. For general and concrete contractors, architects, engineers, concrete producers, cement manufacturers, distributors and dealers in construction equipment, testing labs. Monthly magazine; 80 pages average. Circ. 72,000. Buys all rights. "Bylines are used only by prearrangement with the author." Pays on acceptance. Buys 8-10 mss/year. Free sample copy and writer's guidelines. Photocopied submissions OK. Reports in 1-2 months. Submit query with topical outline. SASE.
Nonfiction and Photos: "Our magazine has one major emphasis: cast-in-place (site cast) concrete. Our articles deal with tools, techniques and materials that result in better handling, better placing, and ultimately an improved final product. We are particularly firm about not using proprietary names in any of our articles. Manufacturer and product names are never mentioned; only the processes or techniques that might be of help to the concrete contractor, the architect or the engineer dealing with the material. We do use reader response cards to relay reader interest to manufacturers." Does not want to see job stories or promotional material. Pays $200/2-page article. Prefers 1,000-2,000 words with 2-3 illustrations. Photos are used only as part of a completed ms.
Tips: "Condensed, totally factual presentations preferred."

CONCRETE INTERNATIONAL: DESIGN AND CONSTRUCTION, American Concrete Institute, 22400 W. Seven Mile Rd., Detroit MI 48219. (313)532-2600. Monthly magazine about concrete for design engineers, management and construction people. Circ. 17,000. Pays on publication. Buys all rights, first rights, second serial rights, and makes assignments on a work-for-hire basis. Phone queries OK. Submit seasonal material 4 months in advance. SASE. Reports in 2 weeks on queries; in 1 month on mss. Free sample copy and writer's guidelines.
Nonfiction: Historical (concrete structures); how-to (concrete construction, new methods, techniques); new product (concrete-related); and technical (concrete-related). Query. Length: 300-5,000 words. Pays $100/printed page.
Photos: State availability of photos or send photos with ms. Reviews b&w contact sheets and 5x7 and 8x10 prints. Offers no additional payment for photos accepted with ms. Captions and model release required. Buys one-time rights.
Columns/Departments: Legal (related to concrete construction); Problems, Solutions and Practices; and Management Techniques. Query. Length: 600-1,000 words.

MINE AND QUARRY, Ashire Publishing Ltd., 42 Gray's Inn Rd., London, England WC1X 8LR. Editor: Cyril C. Middor. Monthly magazine; for senior management at mines and quarries. 80 pages. Circ. 4,600. Buys all rights. Phone queries OK. Submit seasonal/holiday material 2 months in advance. Simultaneous, photocopied and previously published submissions OK. Computer printout and disk submissions OK. SAE and International Reply Coupons. Reports in 2 months. Free sample copy and writer's guidelines.
Nonfiction: Technical and new product articles related to the industry. Buys 10 mss/year. Submit complete ms. Length: 200-1,000 words. Pays $10-20.
Photos: B&w glossy prints and color transparencies purchased with or without mss. Captions required. Send contact sheet, prints or transparencies. Pays $3-6.

STONE IN AMERICA, American Monument Association, 6902 N. High St., Worthington OH 43085. (614)885-2713. Managing Editor: Bob Moon. Monthly magazine for the retailers of upright memorials in the US and Canada. Circ. 2,600. Pays on publication. Buys one-time rights. Phone queries preferred. SASE. Reports in 1 month. Free sample copy and writer's guidelines.
Nonfiction: How-to (run a monument business); informational (major news within the industry, monuments as an art form); profile (successful retailers); and technical. Buys 30-40 mss/year. Length: 1,500-2,000 words. Query. Pays $150-400.
Photos: Pays $20-50 for 5x7 or 8x10 b&w glossy prints.
Columns/Departments: Businss Brief (small business practices); Retail Report (successful retailers); Panorama (industry news and features). Length: 2,000 words maximum.

Toy, Novelty, and Hobby

CREATIVE PRODUCT NEWS, Box 584, Lake Forest IL 60045. (312)234-5052. Editor: Linda F. McKee. Monthly tabloid for retailers of crafts, needlework, and art materials for fine art, hobby art, and doll house miniatures. Circ. 28,000. Pays on acceptance. Byline given. Buys first North American serial rights. Submit seasonal/holiday material 7 months in advance. Simultaneous queries and photocopied submissions OK. SASE. Reports in 1 month. Free sample copy.

Nonfiction: "We need only one thing: packages containing 4-6 photos and 200- 500-word descriptions. Topic should be demonstration of a new art or craft technique; photos must show finished article, supplies used and procedure." Buys 12 mss/year. Query with clips of published work. Pays $50.

Tips: "Our total concern is what's new. Submit only ideas that are truly new."

MINIATURES & DOLL MAGAZINE, (formerly *Miniatures Dealer Magazine*), Boynton & Associates Inc., Clifton House, Clifton VA 22024. (703)830-1000. Editor: Rebecca Beatty. For "retailers in the dollhouse/miniatures and collectible doll trade. Our readers are generally independent, small store owners who don't have time to read anything that does not pertain specifically to their own problems." Monthly magazine; 80 pages. Circ. 7,000. Pays on publication. Buys all rights. Byline given. Phone queries OK. Submit seasonal/holiday material 4 months in advance. Photocopied and previously published submissions OK; simultaneous submissions (if submitted to publications in different fields) OK. SASE. Reports in 2 months. Sample copy $1.50; free writer's guidelines (SASE).

Nonfiction: How-to (unique articles—for example, how to finish a dollhouse exterior—are acceptable if they introduce new techniques or ideas; show the retailer how learning this technique will help sell dollhouses); profiles of miniatures and/or doll shops; business information pertaining to small store retailers. Buys 4-6 mss/issue. Query or send complete ms. "In query, writer should give clear description of intended article, when he could have it to me plus indication that he has studied the field, and is not making a 'blind' query. Availability of photos should be noted." Pay negotiable.

Photos: "Photos must tie in directly with articles." State availability of photos. Pays $7 for each photo used. Prefers 5x7 b&w glossy prints (reviews contact sheets); and $25 for 2¼x2¼ color transparencies. Buys very few color photos. Captions preferred; model release preferred.

Tips: "The best way for a freelancer to break in is to study several issues of our magazine, then try to visit a miniatures and/or doll shop and submit an *M&D* Visits . . . article. This is a regular feature that can be written by a sharp freelancer who takes the time to study and follow the formula this feature uses. Also, basic business articles for retailers—inventory control, how to handle bad checks, etc., that are written with miniatures and doll dealers in mind, are always needed."

MODEL RETAILER MAGAZINE, Clifton House, Clifton VA 22024. (703)830-1000. Editor: Geoffrey Wheeler. 60-70% freelance written. "For hobby store owners—generally well-established small business persons, fairly well educated, and very busy." Monthly magazine. Circ. 6,700. Pays on publication. Buys "first-time rights in our field." Byline given. Phone queries OK (no collect calls, please), but prefers written queries. Submit seasonal/holiday material 3 months in advance of issue date. Simultaneous, photocopied and previously published submissions OK; Computer printout submissions OK; prefers letter quality to dot matrix printouts. SASE. Reports in 2 weeks. Sample copy $1.50; free writer's guidelines.

Nonfiction: Retailer profiles; articles on store management, marketing, merchandising, advertising; and photo feature (if photos tie in with marketing techniques or hobby store operation, etc.). "No company profiles, "human interest" stories, self-publicity articles, reports on trade shows. (We do those ourselves)." Buys 3-5 mss/issue. Query. Length: 1,200-2,500 words. Pays for complete article package of: main copy, side bars (if needed), working headline, and illustrative material (if needed). Range: $125-300, depending on length and degree of specialization.

Photos: "Photos that illustrate key points and are of good quality will help the article, particularly if it concerns business operation. Photos are paid for as part of total article package."

THE STAMP WHOLESALER, Box 706, Albany OR 97321. Editor/Publisher: Jim Magruder. 80% freelance written. For small-time independent businessmen; many are part-time and/or retired from other work. Published 26 times/year; 80 pages. Circ. 9,000. Buys all rights. Byline given. Buys 60 mss/year. Pays on publication. Will send free sample copy to writer on request. Reports in 10 weeks. Submit complete ms. SASE.

Nonfiction: How-to information on how to deal more profitably in postage stamps for collections. Emphasis on merchandising techniques and how to make money. Does not want to see any so-called "humor" items from nonprofessionals. Length: 1,000-1,500 words. Pays 3¢/word minimum.

Tips: "Send queries on business stories. Send manuscript on stamp dealer stories. We need stories to help dealers make and save money."

Travel

AIRFAIR INTERLINE MAGAZINE, The Authority On Interline Travel, Airline Marketing, Inc., 25 W. 39th St., New York NY 10018. (212)840-6714. Editor: Julie Barker. Assistant Editor: Nancy Mattia. Monthly magazine covering travel information for airline employees; describing travel packages by air, land or ship and including information on hotels and restaurants. Circ. 26,000. Pays on publication. Byline given. Buys first North American serial rights. Submit seasonal/holiday material 2 months in advance. Simultaneous queries, and simultaneous and photocopied submissions OK. SASE. Reports in 6 months on queries; 4 months on mss. Free sample copy and writer's guidelines.
Nonfiction: Travel (should concentrate on foreign destinations). Buys 20 mss/year. Query with clips of published work. Length: 2,000 words maximum. Pays $75 maximum.

ASTA TRAVEL NEWS, 488 Madison Ave., New York NY 10022. Editor: Patrick Arton. Managing Editor: Kathi Froio. 75% freelance written. Emphasizes travel, tourism and transportation. Monthly magazine; 120 pages. Circ. 19,500. Pays on acceptance. Buys all rights. Submit seasonal/holiday material 3 months in advance of issue date. Photocopied submissions OK. Reports in 4 weeks.
Nonfiction: How-to; interview; new product; profile; technical; and travel. No first-person personal experience. Buys 75 mss/year. Query. Length: 500-3,000 words. Pays $50-250.
Photos: Submit photo material with accompanying query. No additional payment for b&w prints or color transparencies. Captions required.

BUS RIDE, Friendship Publications, Inc., Box 1472, Spokane WA 99210. (509)328-9181. Editor: William A. Luke. Magazine published 8 times/year covering bus transportation. Circ. 12,500. Byline given. Not copyrighted. No computer printout or disk submissions. SASE. Sample copy $2.75; free writer's guidelines.
Nonfiction: How-to (on bus maintenance, operations, marketing); new product; technical. Only bus transportation material is acceptable. Query. Length: 500-1,500 words. No payment from publication; "writer may receive payment from company or organization featured."
Photos: State availability of photos. Reviews b&w 8x10 prints. Captions required.
Fillers: Newsbreaks. Length: 50-100 words.
Tips: "A freelancer can contact bus companies, transit authorities, suppliers and products for the bus industry to write articles which would be accepted by our publication."

BUS TOURS MAGAZINE, The Magazine of Bus Tours and Long Distance Charters, National Bus Trader, Inc., Rt. 3, Box 349B (Theater Rd.), Delavan WI 53115. (414)728-2691. Editor: Larry Plachno. Managing Editor: Lucinda Schreiner. Bimonthly magazine for bus companies and tour brokers who design or sell bus tours. Circ. 6,500. Pays as arranged. Byline given. Not copyrighted. Buys rights as arranged. Submit seasonal/holiday material 9 months in advance. Simultaneous queries OK. Reports in 1 month. Free sample copy and writer's guidelines.
Nonfiction: Historical/nostalgic, how-to, humor, interview/profile, new product, personal experience, travel; all on bus tours. Buys 10 mss/year. Query. Length: open. Pays negotiable fee.
Photos: State availability of photos. Reviews 35mm transparencies and 6x9 or 8x10 prints. Caption, model release and identification of subjects required.
Columns/Departments: Bus Tour Marketing; Buses and the Law. Buys 15-20 mss/year. Query. Length: 1-1½ pages.
Tips: "Most of our feature articles are written by freelancers under contract from local convention and tourism bureaus. Specifications on request. Writers should query local bureaus regarding their interest. Must have extensive background and knowledge of bus tours."

‡BUS WORLD, Motor Coach Photo-Feature Magazine, Sunrise Enterprises, Box 39, Woodland Hills CA 91365. (213)710-0208. Editor: Ed Stauss. Quarterly trade journal covering the transit and intercity bus industries. "*Bus World* is edited to inform and entertain people who have an interest in buses—bus owners, managers, drivers, enthusiasts, and historians. With extensive photographic coverage, *Bus World* describes the function and lore of the bus industry including intercity, transit, tour, and charter." Circ. 5,000. Pays on publication. Byline given. Buys first North American serial rights. Submit seasonal/holiday material 6 months in advance. Simultaneous queries, and simultaneous, photocopied, and previously published submissions OK. SASE. Reports in 3 weeks. Sample copy $1; writer's guidelines for SAE and 1 first class stamp.
Nonfiction: Historical/nostalgic, humor, interview/profile, new product, opinion, personal experience, photo feature, technical. "Author must show an understanding of the bus industry. Coverage includes descriptions of new vehicles, surveys of operating systems, first-person experiences with transit and intercity operations, and reviews of historic equipment and systems. Primary coverage is North America." No tourist or travelog viewpoints. Buys 8-12 mss/year. Query. Length: 500-2,000 words. Pays $20-60.
Photos: "Photos should be sharp and clear." State availability of photos. "No separate payment for photos.

We buy photos with manuscripts under one payment." Reviews 35mm color transparencies and 8x10 b&w prints. Captions required. Buys one-time rights.

Fillers: Cartoons. Buys 4-6/year. Pays $10-25.

Tips: "Be employed in or have a good understanding of the bus industry. Be enthusiastic about buses—their history and future—as well as current events. Acceptable material will be held until used and will not be returned unless requested by sender. Unacceptable and excess material will be returned only if accompanied by suitable SASE."

INCENTIVE TRAVEL MANAGER, Brentwood Publishing Corp., 825 S. Barrington Ave., Los Angeles CA 90049. (213)826-8388. Editor: Ben Kalb. Monthly magazine covering incentive travel for corporate executives in charge of incentive travel. Circ. 40;000. Pays "on edited word count, which falls between acceptance and publication." Byline given. Buys all rights. SASE. Reports "when an assignment is available."

Nonfiction: General interest (incentive travel, planning, setting up, selecting destinations); interview/profile (of executives); travel (destination updates); and literature. Buys 150 mss/year. Query or send resume. Length: 2,000-2,500 words average. Pays 10-12¢/word.

Tips: "Not interested in travel articles geared for average tourist or travel agent. Must report on incentive group that has gone to destination. If you don't know what incentive travel is, learn it, and then query us."

NATIONAL BUS TRADER, The Magazine of Bus Equipment for the United States and Canada, Rt. 3, Box 349B (Theater Rd.), Delavan WI 53115. (414)728-2691. Editor: Larry Plachno. Monthly magazine for manufacturers, dealers and owners of buses and motor coaches. Circ. 3,500. Pays on either acceptance or publication. Byline given. Not copyrighted. Buys rights "as required by writer." Simultaneous queries and simultaneous, photocopied and previously published submissions OK. Computer printout and disk submissions OK. Reports in 1 month. Free sample copy.

Nonfiction: Historical/nostalgic (on old buses); how-to (maintenance repair); new products; photo features; technical (aspects of mechanical operation of buses). "We are finding that more and more firms and agencies are hiring freelancers to write articles to our specifications. We are more likely to run them if someone else pays." No material that does NOT pertain to bus tours or bus equipment. Buys 3-5 unsolicited mss/year. Query. Length: varies. Pays variable rate.

Photos: State availability of photos. Reviews 5x7 or 8x10 prints and 35mm transparencies. Captions, model release and identification of subjects required.

Columns/Departments: Bus maintenance; Buses and the Law; Regulations; Bus of the Month. Buys 20-30 mss/year. Query. Length: 1-1½ pages. Pays variable rate.

Tips: "We are a very technical publication. Writers should submit qualifications showing extensive background in bus vehicles. We're always looking for new column ideas. We probably will add more pages in the next year which will require more editorial."

PACIFIC TRAVEL NEWS, 274 Brannan St., San Francisco CA 94107. (415)397-0070. Publisher: William Hewes. Editor: Phyllis Elving. 10% freelance written. For travel trade—travel agencies, transportation companies. Monthly. Circ. 25,000. Buys one-time rights for travel trade publication. Pays on publication unless material is for future use; then on acceptance. Query about assignment. Reports in 4 weeks. SASE.

Nonfiction: Area covered is from Hawaii west to Pakistan, south to Australia and New Zealand. "We are primarily interested in reporting on destinations in the Pacific Ocean area from the standpoint of their tourism attractions, facilities and plans for the future—written with little essay and more facts so that the information is useful to the travel agent in selling tickets to the Pacific area. We are not interested in how-to articles, such as how to sell, decorate your windows, keep your staff happy, cut costs." Pays $300 maximum.

Photos: Purchased with mss or captions only. Related to travel attractions, activities within Pacific area. Sometimes general travel-type photos, other times specific photos related to hotels, tours, tour equipment, etc. Buys mainly b&w glossy, 5x7 or larger. Also buys about 18 color transparencies/year, 35mm top quality. Pays up to $20 for b&w; up to $50 for inside color; $100 for color used on cover.

‡RVBUSINESS, TL Enterprises, Inc., 29901 Agoura Rd., Agoura CA 91301. (213)991-4980. Editor: Michael Schneider. Managing Editor: Sheryl Davis. Monthly magazine covering the recreational vehicle and allied industries for "people of the RV industry—dealers, manufacturers, suppliers, park management, legislators and finance experts." Circ. 20,000. Pays on publication. Byline given. Offers 50% kill fee. Buys first North American serial rights. Submit seasonal/holiday material 6 months in advance. Photocopied submissions OK. SASE. Reports in 3 weeks on queries; 6 weeks on mss. Sample copy for 9x12 SAE and 3 first class stamps; writer's guidelines for business-size SAE and 1 first class stamp.

Nonfiction: Expose (carefully done and thoroughly researched); historical/nostalgic (companies, products or people pertaining to the RV industry itself); how-to (deal with any specific aspect of the RV business); interview/profile (persons or companies involved with the industry—legislative, finance, dealerships, park management, manufacturing, supplier); new product (no payment for company promo material—Product Spotlight usually requires interview with company spokesperson, firsthand experience with product; specifics and verification of statistics required—must be factual); opinion (controversy OK); personal experience (must be something of importance to readership—must have a point: it worked for me, it can for you; or this is why it didn't work for me); photo feature (four-color transparencies required with good captions; photo coverage of RV shows, conventions and meetings not appropriate topics for photo feature); technical (photos required, four-color preferred). No general business articles. Buys 60 mss/year. Query with published clips. Send complete ms—"but only read on speculation." Length: 1,000-2,000 words. Pays variable rate up to $400.

Photos: State availability of photos with query or send photos with ms. Reviews 35mm transparencies and 8x10 b&w prints. Captions, model release, and identification of subjects required. Buys one-time or all rights; unused photos returned.

Columns/Departments: Guest editorial; News (50-500 words maximum, b&w photos appreciated); RV People (color photos/four-color transparencies; this section lends itself to fun, upbeat copy). Buys 100-120 mss/year. Query or send complete ms. Pays $10-200 "depending on where used and importance."

Tips: "Query. Phone OK; letter preferable. Send 1 or several ideas and a few lines letting us know how you plan to treat it/them. We are always looking for good authors knowledgeable in the RV industry or related industries."

THE STAR SERVICE, Sloane Travel Agency Reports, Box 15610, Fort Lauderdale FL 33318. (305)472-8794. Editor: Robert D. Sloane. Editorial manual sold to travel agencies on subscription basis. Buys all rights. Buys about 4,000 reports/year. Pays 15 days prior to publication. "Write for instruction sheet and sample report form. Initial reports sent by a new correspondent will be examined for competence and criticized as necessary upon receipt; but once established, a correspondent's submissions will not usually be acknowledged until payment is forwarded, which can often be several months, depending on immediate editorial needs." Query. Computer printout and disk submissions OK "if standard 5½" diskette." SASE.

Nonfiction: "Objective, critical evaluations of worldwide hotels and cruise ships suitable for North Americans, based on inspections. Forms can be provided to correspondents so no special writing style is required, only perception, experience and judgment in travel. No commercial gimmick—no advertising or payment for listings in publication is accepted." With query, writer should "*outline experience in travel and writing and specific forthcoming travel plans, time available for inspections.* Leading travel agents throughout the world subscribe to Star Service. No credit or byline is given correspondents due to delicate subject matter often involving negative criticism of hotels. We would like to emphasize the importance of reports being based on current experience and the importance of reporting on a substantial volume of hotels, not just isolated stops (since staying in hotel is not a requisite) in order that work be profitable for both publisher and writer. Experience in travel writing and/or travel industry is desirable." Length: "up to 350 words, if submitted in paragraph form; varies if submitted on printed inspection form." Pays $10-15/report (higher for ships) used. "Guarantees of acceptance of set numbers of reports may be made on establishment of correspondent's ability and reliability, but always on prior arrangement. Higher rates of payment sometimes arranged, after correspondent's reliability is established."

THE TRAVEL AGENT, 2 W. 46th St., New York NY 10036. Editor/Publisher: Eric Friedheim. For "travel agencies and travel industry executives." Semiweekly. Circ. 35,000. Not copyrighted. Pays on acceptance. Query. Reports "immediately." SASE.

Nonfiction and Photos: Uses trade features slanted to travel agents, sales and marketing people, and executives of transportation companies such as airlines, ship lines, etc. No travelogues such as those appearing in newspapers and consumer publications. Articles should show how agent and carriers can sell more travel to the public. Length: up to 2,500 words. Pays $50-100. Photos purchased with ms.

TRAVELAGE MIDAMERICA, Official Airlines Guide, Inc., A Dun & Bradstreet Co., Suite 2416 Prudential Plaza, Chicago IL 60601. (312)861-0432. Editor/Publisher: Martin Deutsch. Managing Editor: Linda Ball. 10% freelance written. "For travel agents in the 13 midAmerica states and in Ontario and Manitoba." Biweekly magazine. Circ. 13,000. Pays on publication. Buys one-time rights. Submit seasonal/holiday material 3 months in advance of issue date. Simultaneous, photocopied and previously published submissions OK. "Not pleased with computer printout submissions." Prefers letter quality to dot matrix printouts. Query first. SASE. Reports in 2 weeks. Free sample copy and writer's guidelines.

Nonfiction: "News on destinations, hotels, operators, rates and other developments in the travel business." Also runs human interest features on retail travel agents in the readership area. No stories that don't contain prices; no queries that don't give detailed story lines. No general destination stories, especially ones on "do-it-yourself" travel. Buys 12-15 mss/year. Query. Length: 400-1,500 words. Pays $1.50/column inch.

Photos: State availability of photos with query. Pays $1.50/column inch for glossy b&w prints.

TRAVELAGE WEST, Official Airline Guides, Inc., 582 Market St., San Francisco CA 94104. Executive Editor: Donald C. Langley. 5% freelance written. For travel agency sales counselors in the Western US and Canada. Weekly magazine. Circ. 25,000. Pays on publication. Buys all rights. Pays kill fee. Byline given. Submit seasonal/holiday material 2 months in advance. Computer printout and disk submissions OK. SASE.

Reports in 4 weeks. Free writer's guidelines.

Nonfiction: Travel. Buys 40 mss/year. Query. Length: 1,000 words maximum. Pays $1.50/column inch. "No promotional approach or any hint of do-it-yourself travel. Emphasis is on news, not description. No static descriptions of places, particularly resort hotels."

Tips: "Query to be a straightforward description of the proposed story, including (1) an indication of the news angle, no matter how tenuous and (2) a recognition by the author that we run a trade magazine for travel agents, not a consumer book. I am particularly turned off by letters that try to get me all worked up about the 'beauty' or excitement of some place. Authors planning to travel might discuss with us a proposed angle before they go; otherwise their chances of gathering the right information are slim."

Veterinary

MODERN VETERINARY PRACTICE, American Veterinary Publications, Inc., Drawer KK, 300 E. Canon Perdido, Santa Barbara CA 93102. For graduate veterinarians. Monthly magazine; 90 pages. Circ. 22,000. Pays on publication. Buys all rights. Phone queries OK. Submit seasonal/holiday material 3 months in advance. Computer printout submissions OK; prefers letter quality to dot matrix printouts. SASE. Reports in 4 weeks. Sample copy $2.50.

Nonfiction: How-to articles (clinical medicine, new surgical procedures, business management); informational (business management, education, government projects affecting practicing veterinarians, special veterinary projects); interviews (only on subjects of interest to veterinarians; query first); technical articles (clinical reports, technical advancements in veterinary medicine and surgery). Buys 12-15 unsolicited mss/year. Submit complete ms, but query first on ideas for pieces other than technical or business articles. Pays $25/page.

Photos: B&w glossies (5x7 or larger) and color transparencies (5x7) used with mss. No additional payment.

Tips: "Contact practicing veterinarians or veterinary colleges. Find out what interests the clinician, and what new procedures and ideas might be useful in a veterinary practice. Better yet, collaborate with a veterinarian. Most of our authors are veterinarians or those working with veterinarians in a professional capacity. Knowledge of the interests and problems of practicing veterinarians is essential."

VETERINARY ECONOMICS MAGAZINE, Box 13265, Edwardsville KS 66113. (913)422-5010. Editor: Mike Sollars. For all practicing veterinarians in the US. Monthly. Buys exclusive rights in the field. Pays on publication. SASE.

Nonfiction and Photos: Uses case histories telling about good business practices on the part of veterinarians. Also, articles about financial problems, investments, insurance and similar subjects of particular interest to professionals. "We reject articles with superficial information about a subject instead of carefully researched and specifically directed articles for our field." Pays negotiable rates.

VETERINARY MEDICINE/SMALL ANIMAL CLINICIAN, 144 N. Nettleton Ave., Bonner Springs KS 66012. (913)441-6167. Executive Editor: Ray Ottinger. 5% freelance written. For graduate veterinarians, student veterinarians, animal health technicians, libraries, representatives of drug companies and research personnel. Monthly magazine; 160 pages. Circ. 18,500. Pays on publication. Buys first North American serial rights. Byline given. Phone queries OK. Submit seasonal/holiday material 5-6 months in advance of issue date. Previously published submissions OK. Prefers typewritten rather than computer printout submissions. SASE. Reports in 2-3 weeks. Free writer's guidelines.

Nonfiction: Accepts only articles dealing with medical case histories, practice management, business, taxes, insurance, investments. Photo feature (new hospital, floor plan, new equipment; remodeled hospital). No "cutesy" stories about animals. Buys 3 mss/issue. Submit complete ms. Length: 1,500-5,000 words. Pays $50-200.

Photos: State availability of photos with ms. Reviews b&w and color glossy prints, and 35mm color transparencies. Captions required. Buys one-time US and reprint rights. Model release required.

Scriptwriting

Scriptwriters are made, not born. There is practically no substitute for involvement in the production, management and business end of the dramatic form if you intend to write in it. Writing for local theater or radio may be the credentials that will make a producer take a second look at your script. The star-studded scriptwriting field is highly competitive. Learning firsthand the goings-on behind the curtain or camera can only give you an edge. For tips and techniques on how to break in and write for TV, radio, film and theater, consult *The Complete Book of Scriptwriting*, by J. Michael Straczynski (Writer's Digest Books) and the bimonthly scriptwriting column in *Writer's Digest* magazine.

Business and Educational Writing

Virtually all the firms listed in this section responded to our question about predictions for their companies with a resounding, "Increased sales and growth!" Many of them are broadening their outlooks by entering the computer software market. The entries for companies interested in software include a software subhead and information on the kinds of programs (most often in the education market) they want.

Companies of all sizes are using technical scriptwriters to develop training and industrial films and videotape presentations for employees and customers. Some educational firms are concentrating on video cassettes for the school market. One producer suggested that classroom teachers often have good ideas for educational scripts.

Several producers offered tips for scriptwriters, the most oft-repeated being a request for "visual scripts"—words on a page that translate into telling drama and dialogue. A related comment was the need for good verbal skills. Other producers mentioned the importance of conducting adequate research for a script. And many stressed absolute adherence to deadlines.

Above all, become familiar with the particular firm you plan to query. What else have they produced? Arrange for a screening that will help you define their audiences, formats and style. Contact local producers directly. Write to out-of-town firms for a list of their clients in your area. If they are interested in your writing, you may be able to view their AV material at a local company or school that uses it. Be sure that your script idea fits with their established image. A resume that establishes you as a writer and writing samples that prove it are very important in this business. Read carefully the market listings detailing how to make initial contact with a production company.

A.V. MEDIA CRAFTSMAN, INC., Suite 600, 110 E. 23rd St., New York NY 10010. (212)228-6644. President: Carolyn Clark. Produces training material for corporations and educational material for publishers. Works with New York area writers only. Buys 15-20 scripts/year. Query with samples and resume. Reports immediately. Buys all rights.
Needs: "Most of our projects are 10-15 minute training scripts with related study materials for corporations and educational publishers. We create multi-screen presentations for conferences as well." Produces slide shows, sound filmstrips, multiscreen shows, multimedia kits, overhead transparencies, tapes and cassettes, films in many formats, and teaching machine programs. Pays in outright purchase of $350-500, for scripts.
Tips: "Accept changes, do accurate research, and enjoy the subject matter. Write—do *not* call."

DOM ALBI ASSOCIATES, INC., Suite 1C, 251 W. 92nd St., New York NY 10025. (212)799-2202. President: Dom Albi. Produces material for corporate and business audiences. Buys 20-30 scripts/year. Query or submit resume listing types of clients. Buys all rights.

Needs: Produces 16mm films, multimedia programs and videotape slide presentations. Payment negotiable.
Tips: "We expect our writers to spend as much time on concept and purpose, as they do on finished script."

ALLEGRO FILM PRODUCTIONS, INC., Box 25195, Tamarac FL 33320. President: Mr. J. Forman. Produces for the general and school markets. Buys 3-20 scripts/year. Submit resume. Computer printout submissions OK. Buys all rights.
Needs: Science films for education, films for industry and government, and documentaries. Produces 16mm and 35mm films. Pays negotiable fee.

‡**AMERICAN MEDIA INC.**, 5911 Meredith Dr., Des Moines IA 50324. (515)278-1078. President: Arthur R. Bauer. Produces material for trainees in the areas of—but not exclusive—productivity, retail, banking, supervision, infield selling, management and customer relations. Buys 3 scripts/year. Buys all rights. SASE. Reports in 2 months. Free catalog.
Needs: Scripts for 30-minute dramatic films, how-to in nature. Topics include: motivation, interviewing, communication, blue-collar supervision. Produces 16mm films, tapes and cassettes. Submit synopsis/outline and resume, or completed script. Pays royalty or in outright purchase; "too many variables to be specific."
Tips: Material must be how-to in content and entertaining. Looks for "ability to meet deadlines, and the talent of formulating a script with beginning and climax proceeding to a definite end."

ANCO/BOSTON, INC., 441 Stuart St., Boston MA 02116. (617)267-9700. Director, Instructional Systems: R. Hoyt. Produces for the industrial and business communities. Submit resume. SASE. Buys all rights.
Needs: "Technical or business-oriented material on specific subjects for specific customized needs." Produces charts, sound filmstrips, multimedia kits, overhead transparencies and cassettes and slides.

ANIMATION ARTS ASSOCIATES, INC., 2225 Spring Garden St., Philadelphia PA 19130. (215)563-2520. Contact: Harry E. Ziegler Jr. For "government, industry, engineers, doctors, scientists, dentists, general public, military." Send "resume of credits for motion picture and filmstrip productions. Buys average 12 scripts/year. The writer should have scriptwriting credits for training, sales, promotion, public relations." SASE.
Needs: Produces 3½-minute 8mm and 16mm film loops; 16mm and 35mm films (ranging from 5-40 minutes); 2¼x2¼ or 4x5 slides; and teaching machine programs for training, sales, industry and public relations. Pay dependent on client's budget.
Tips: "Send us a resume listing writing and directing credits for films and sound/slide programs."

ARZTCO PICTURES, INC., 15 E. 61st St., New York NY 10021. (212)753-1050. President/Producer: Tony Arzt. Produces material for industrial, education, and home viewing audiences (TV specials and documentaries). Buys 8-10 scripts/year. Buys all rights. Previously produced material OK ("as sample of work only"). SASE, "however, we will only comment in writing on work that interests us." Reports in 3 weeks.
Needs: Business films, sales, training, promotional, educational. "Also interested in low-budget feature film scripts." 16mm and 35mm films and videotapes and cassettes. Submit synopsis/outline or completed script and resume. Pays in accordance with Writers Guild standards.
Tips: "We would like writers to understand that we cannot find time to deal with each individual submission in great detail. If we feel your work is right for us, you will definitely hear from us. We're looking for writers with originality, skill in turning out words, and a sense of humor when appropriate. We prefer to work with writers available in the New York metropolitan area."

‡**ASSOCIATED AUDIO VISUAL**, 2821 Central, Evanston IL 60201. (312)866-6780. President/Creative Director: Ken Solomon. Vice President/Executive Producer: Sharon Spence. Produces material for corporate/industrial/TV commercials and programs. Buys 6-12 scripts/year. Buys all rights. Computer printout and disk submissions OK; prefers letter quality to dot matrix printouts. SASE. Reports in 1 month. Catalog for 8x10 SAE and 1 first class stamp.
Needs: Open. Produces 16mm films, slides, tapes and cassettes. "Call first; then send samples." Pays in negotiable outright purchase.
Tips: "Be persistent, have *produced* samples on film or tape rather than scripts." Looks for "intelligence, humor, contemporary, visual and verbal skills; a fast researcher."

AUDIO-VIDEO CORP., 213 Broadway, Menands NY 12204. (518)449-7213. Senior Producer: Jennifer Novosel. Produces material for TV commercial audiences, and sales and informational film screenings. "We purchase 20 scripts annually, with our need increasing." Query with samples or submit resume. SASE. Reports in 6 weeks. Buys first rights.
Needs: Scripts for 10- to 30-minute programs for audiences ranging from educational, business and consumer groups to nonprofit organizations. "At least half of the material is of a humorous nature, or is otherwise informative and thought-provoking. We seek imagination, motivation, experience, and after receiving numer-

ous responses from this listing, we would prefer to narrow down our writers' file to those in the New York State-New England area. Menands is a suburb of Albany, New York and we will be providing production services to our offices across the rest of the state. While our market primarily encompasses the Northeast, our requirements span a spectrum of subjects. With our recent expansion, we need access to a pool of freelance writers experienced in producing film scripts that are creative and practical.'' Produces videotapes, 16mm films, multimedia kits and slide sets. Pays $30-80/minute of finished program.

Tips: ''The realities of budgets in the current economy naturally restrict production extravaganzas. It is essential to come up with a clever, concise script that lends itself well to the location and studio budget priorities of the project. Having a visual sense is a bonus and sometimes essential for a 'fresh' approach, but inexperience in this realm should not be a restraint to a good writer.''

A/V CONCEPTS CORP., 30 Montauk Blvd., Oakdale NY 11769. (516)567-7229. Editor: Joyce W. Masterson. Produces material for el-hi students, both those on grade level and in remedial situations. Employs the media of filmstrip and personal computers. Computer—disk based—language arts, mathematics and reading. Query with resume and samples. SASE. Reports on outline in 1 month; on final scripts in 6 weeks. Buys all rights. Catalog for SASE.

Needs: ''Authors must receive a set of our specifications before submitting material. Manuscripts must be written using our lists of vocabulary words, and must meet readability formula requirements provided by us. Length of manuscript and subjects will vary according to grade level for which material is prepared. Basically, we want articles and stories that will motivate people to read. Authors must be highly creative and highly disciplined. We are interested in mature content material.'' Pays $100.

Software: Interested in original educational computer programs for the Apple II plus 48K.

Tips: ''If possible, contact the editor or editorial department by phone and 'meet' the company through 'personal' contact.''

‡AVEKTA PRODUCTIONS, Suite 2177, 2 Penn Plaza, New York NY 10001. (212)760-4222. Producer: William Avgerakis. Produces material for industrial and broadcast television. Buys 2-3 scripts/year. Computer printout and disk submissions OK. Buys all rights. SASE. Reports in 1 month.

Needs: Produces 16-35mm films; tapes and cassettes. Query with samples. Pays $500-2,000 outright purchase.

BACHNER PRODUCTIONS, INC., 45 W. 45th St., New York NY 10036. (212)354-8760. Produces 16mm and 35mm films; videotape programs; and 2-inch, 1-inch, and ¾-inch cassettes. Not copyrighted. Does not accept unsolicited material. Prospective writer usually must have experience in subject related to proposed film, and needs knowledge of videotape or film requirements. Sometimes will use good writer without specialized experience and then supply all necessary research. SASE.

Needs: Produces training and sales films and documentaries. Subject matter and style depend on client requirements. ''Sometimes clients supply outlines and research from which our writers work. We usually pay Writers Guild scale, depending on usage and what is supplied by us. Price varies with assignments.''

Tips: ''Writer should have knowledge of film dialogue writing, and recognize that there is ''less money available for experimentation. You must write with budgets in mind.''

‡BARTON FILM COMPANY, 4853 Waller St., Jacksonville FL 32205. (904)389-4541. President: Donald E. Barton. Produces material for various audiences. Works with average 6 writers/year. Buys all rights. Submissions returned with SASE. Reports in 4 weeks.

Needs: Documentary and sales-motivation material—16mm films and video tape. Query with samples. Pays $850-2,500.

BLACKSIDE, INC., 238 Huntington Ave., Boston MA 02115. (617)536-6900. President: Henry Hampton. Produces material for ''all types'' of audiences. ''Query only. No scripts are accepted unless they're requested.'' Buys all rights.

Needs: Produces silent and sound filmstrips, 16mm and 35mm films, multimedia kits, overhead transparencies, phonograph records, tapes and cassettes, slide sets, and teaching machine programs.

BNA COMMUNICATIONS, INC., 9417 Decoverly Hall Rd., Rockville MD 20850. (301)948-0540. Producer/Director: Pare Lorentz Jr. Produces material primarily for business, industry and government; ''client-sponsored films approach specific audiences.'' Buys 7-12 scripts, works with 3-4 writers/year. Buys ''usually all rights—but other arrangements have been made.'' Reports in 1 month. Free catalog.

Needs: ''Presently under control.'' 16mm films, slides, and tapes, cassettes and videodiscs. Query with samples. ''Find out what we do before you query.'' Pays negotiable fee.

Tips: ''We're looking for writers with the ability to grasp the subject and develop a relatively simple treatment, particularly if the client is not motion-savvy. Don't overload with tricks . . . unless the show is about tricks. Most good scripts have some concept of a beginning, middle and end. We are interested in good *dialogue* writers.''

BOARD OF JEWISH EDUCATION OF NEW YORK, 426 W. 58th St., New York NY 10019. (212)245-8200. Director, Multimedia Services and Materials Development: Yaakov Reshef. Produces material for Jewish schools, youth groups, temples and synagogues; for audience from kindergarten to old age. Buys 12-15 scripts/year. Submit outline/synopsis or resume. SASE. Reports in 3 months. Buys first rights or all rights.
Needs: General, educational and informational. "Generally, length is up to 20-25 minutes maximum; most material geared to 10-12 years old and up. Jewish background needed." Produces sound filmstrips, 16mm films, tapes and cassettes, and slide sets. Pays 10-15% royalty or $500 minimum/outright purchase.

BOUCHARD, WALTON PRODUCTIONS, Bishop's Rd., Kingston MA 02364. (617)585-8069. Script Supervisor: Betsy B. Walton. Produces material on contract base for business and industrial clients. Works with 4-6 writers/year. Buys "specific rights for intended use." SASE. Reports in 3 weeks on queries; 2 weeks on mss.
Needs: "We are currently researching the production of generic materials in marine related fields, i.e., safety, training." Sound filmstrips (LaBelle Commpaks). Query with samples. Pays negotiable fee, "per project/budget."
Tips: "Our requirements are usually technical and specific. Flexibility and good research habits, combined with the ability to logically present targeted subject matter, are more essential than off-the-wall creativity. We prefer experienced writers with excellent technical skills, a simple, direct style, and the ability to write for the ear, and with the eye. We do not interview freelance writers until we have a specific need. We welcome samples with cover letters for our files. No phone calls, please. Print writers usually have a difficult time making the transition to *scriptwriting*. (It is very different!) Exercises in *visualizing* words and ideas help. Practice."

ROBERT J. BRADY CO., Routes 197 & 450, Bowie MD 20715. Editor-in-Chief: David T. Culverwell. Produces books, audiovisual packages and computer software for professionals and paraprofessionals in allied health, nursing, emergency care, fire service and microcomputer science. Will buy rights or sign standard contracts. Free catalog. "We are always eager to develop new writers who can blend both book skills and audiovisual skills." Query. Produces books, manuals, computer software, sound filmstrips, films, videotapes, overhead transparencies, audio tapes and cassettes, and 35mm slides.
Needs: Educational materials for allied health, nursing, emergency medicine, microcomputer science and fire service training. "Our company deals with instructional rather than informational-type programs." Pays $200-1,200/script.
Tips: "Send a resume with samples of writing ability and grasp of subject."

ALDEN BUTCHER PRODUCTIONS, 6331 Hollywood Blvd., Hollywood CA 90028. (213)467-6045. Personnel Manager: Cynthia Butcher. Produces material for commercial/industrial and entertainment audiences. Buys 20 scripts/year. Deals mainly with local clients. Uses *only* local writers. Buys all rights. SASE. Reports in 1 month.
Needs: "Depends upon contracts closed." Produces multi-media slide shows and some video programs. Looks for "the ability to easily communicate with an industrial client and translate that into a script that meets their communication objectives the first time." Query with samples and resume. Pays "according to production budget on an individual basis."
Tips: "Clients are looking more and more for a production company to provide creative approaches as a part of a bidding process. Often it is important for a writer to be involved in this speculative process prior to writing the actual script. This way they can help develop the style and approach with how and what they would write in mind."

CALIFORNIA COMMUNICATIONS, 6900 Santa Monica Blvd., Los Angeles CA 90038. (213)466-8511. Editorial Director: Bill Muster. Produces material for corporations, industry and service industry. Submit resume. "No unsolicited manuscripts." SASE. Reports in 2 weeks. Buys all rights.
Needs: Produces industrial sound filmstrips, 16mm films, multi-media kits, slides, and AV multi image shows and videotapes. "We work on assignment only." Pays in outright purchase of "approximately $100/minute minimum."

PAUL CARTER PRODUCTIONS, INC., 638 Congress St., Portland ME 04101. (207)772-7401. President: Paul Carter. Produces material for industry and education. Query with samples and resume. SASE. Reports in 1 week. Buys all rights.
Needs: Interested in "energy education, appropriate technology, environment—15-30 minutes, documentary." Produces sound filmstrips and 16mm films. Pays in outright purchase of $100-250/minute (negotiable).
Tips: Looking for writers with "understanding of the audience, subject and filmmaking process. Clearly understood and defined objectives for the piece."

‡**CATHEDRAL FILMS, INC.**, 2282 Townsgate Rd., Westlake Village CA 91359. (805)495-7418. Contact: Candace Hunt. Produces material for church and school audiences. Works with variable number of writers/

year. Buys all rights and AV rights. Previously produced material OK "except from other AV media." SASE. Reports in 4 weeks on queries; 8 weeks on mss. Catalog for SAE and 54¢ postage.

Needs: Various Christian, religious, educational and/or dramatic material. All ages. Produces 16mm films, sound filmstrips and video. Submit synopsis/outline or complete script. Pays variable rates.

‡**CLEARVUE, INC.**, 5711 N. Milwaukee Ave., Chicago IL 60646. (312)775-9433. Executive Vice President: W.O. McDermed. Produces educational material for grades K-12. Buys 20-30 scripts/year. Buys all or first rights. Previously produced material OK. SASE. Reports in 2 weeks on queries; 1 month on submissions. Free catalog.

Needs: Educational material for grades K-12. Produces filmstrips (silent and sound), multimedia kits, overhead transparencies, phonograph records, study prints, tapes and cassettes. Query. Pays in outright purchase.

Tips: "Know the specific objectives of the program; have an outline of teaching experience and list of programs published." Looks for "ability to meet needs of market place."

CLEARWATER PRODUCTIONS, Suite 201, 45 W. Broadway, Eugene OR 97401. (503)683-5200. Owner: Douglas C. Daggett. Produces training, sales, and PR sound-slide shows. Buys 10-20 AV scripts/year; works with 3-6 writers/year. Query with samples and resume. SASE. Buys all rights.

Needs: Slides. Pays in outright purchase.

Tips: Seeks "writers with imagination, humor and the ability to let the visuals tell the story."

COMMAND PRODUCTIONS, 99 Lafayette Ave., White Plains NY 10603. (914)948-6868. Executive Producer: G. Stromberg. Produces material for business clients. Works with 10 writers/year. Submit resume, sample script and long range goals. SASE. Buys all rights.

Needs: Technical and nontechnical business presentations and customized training programs. Produces sound filmstrips, video productions, multimedia kits, overhead transparencies, slides, booklets and brochures. Pays by outright purchase.

COMMUNICATION CORPORATION, INC., 711 4th St. NW, Washington DC 20001. (202)638-6550. President: Jeff Whatley. Produces material for corporations, federal agencies, schools, industry and broadcast industry. Query with samples. SASE. Reports in 2 weeks. Buys all rights.

Needs: Material needs include "5-30 minute expository films and slide shows. Voice-over narrations, proposals and treatments." Produces 8mm film loops, silent and sound filmstrips, 16mm films, multimedia kits, tapes and cassettes, and slides. Pays in outright purchase of $100-3,000.

COMPASS FILMS, 6 Florence Ln., Newton NJ 07860. Executive Producer: Robert Whittaker. Produces material for educational, industrial and general adult audiences. Specializes in Marine films, stop motion and special effects with a budget . . . and worldwide filming in difficult locations. Works with 4 writers/year. Query with samples or submit resume. SASE. Reports in 6 weeks. Buys all rights.

Needs: Scripts for 10- to 30-minute business films, and general documentary and theatrical feature films. "We would like to consider theatrical stories for possible use for feature films. We also would like to review writers to develop existing film treatments and ideas with strong dialogue." Also needs (ghost writers) editors and researchers. Produces 16mm and 35mm films. Payment negotiable, depending on experience.

Tips: Writer/photographers receive higher consideration "because we could also use them as still photographers on location and they could double-up as rewrite men . . . and ladies."

COMPRENETICS, INC., 5805 Uplander Way, Culver City CA 90230. (213)204-2080. President: Ira Englander. "Target audience varies, however, programs are designed for health care audiences only. This ranges from entry level health workers with minimal academic background to continuing education programs for physicians and health professionals. In the cultural area, all levels." Buys approximately 10-20 scripts/ year. Query with samples or submit resume. SASE. Reports in 1 month. Buys all rights.

Needs: "Films are generally 10 to 20 minutes in length and tend to have a dramatic framework. Subject topics include all educational areas with emphasis on health and medical films, manpower and management training and multi-cultural education. Our staff normally does subject matter research and content review which is provided for the writer who is then required to provide us with an outline or film treatment for review. Due to the extensive review procedures, writers are frequently required to modify through three or four drafts before final approval." Produces sound filmstrips, 16mm films, and tapes and cassettes. Pays $1,000-5,000.

‡**CORONADO STUDIOS**, #600, 3550 Biscayne Blvd., Miami FL 33137. (305)573-7250. President: Fred L. Singer. Produces material for the general public, various specialized audiences. Buys 50 commercials/year; 15 corporate films/year. "We commission custom scripts that have no value to anyone but our clients." Computer printout submissions OK; no disk submissions. SASE. Reports in 2 weeks on queries; 1 month on submissions.

Needs: "We will need an indeterminate number of scripts for commercials and corporate films." Produces 16mm films, video tapes. Query with samples. Pays in outright purchase; "depends on nature of job."

‡CORONET FILMS, 65 E. South Water St., Chicago IL 60601. (312)977-4018. Creative Director: Mel Waskin. Produces material for school audiences, kindergarten through college. "The films we produce are only for educational purposes." Buys 25-50 scripts/year. Buys all rights. "All scripts assigned. No original material purchased. Nothing accepted (or wanted) on spec." Reports in 1 month. Writers must be in Chicago area.
Needs: "Specific needs not for publication. In general, all scripts are voice-over, educational, about 10-20 minutes long." Produces 16mm films. Query with samples (voice-over only) or submit resume. Computer printout submissions OK; no disk submissions. Pays in $50-1,500 outright purchase. "Price depends on how much work is required, whether script is just a rewrite or a full new production."
Tips: "All script samples submitted should be voice-over approach and on an educational or training theme." Looks for "clarity, organizational ability, informality of style, varied educational background, ability to explain complex subjects in clear, simple ways, and a good sense of 'style' and drama in narrative writing."

CORY SOUND CO., 1255 Howard St., San Francisco CA 94103. (415)861-4004. Owner: Phil Markinson. Produces material for various audiences. Buys all rights. Computer printout submissions OK; prefers letter quality to dot matrix printouts. SASE. Reports in 1 week.
Needs: Tapes and cassettes. Query. Pays in outright purchase.

THE CREATIVE ESTABLISHMENT, 115 W. 31st St., New York NY 10001. (212)563-3337. Script Writer: Dale Wilson. Produces material for business meetings and industrial audiences. Works with approximately 10 writers/year. Buys all rights. SASE. "We don't return unsolicited material; material is held on file." Reports "when needed. Material is always specific to project. We cannot project future needs." 8mm and 16mm film loops, 16mm and 35mm films, sound filmstrips, slides, and multi-image and live shows. Submit synopsis/outline or completed script and resume. Pays in outright purchase.

CREATIVE PRODUCTIONS, INC., 200 Main St., Orange NJ 07050. (212)290-9075. Contact: Gus Nichols, Bill Griffing. Produces material for industrial, business and medical clients. Buys variable number of scripts/yr. Query with resume and "background that is appropriate for specific project we may have." Computer printout submissions OK; prefers letter quality to dot matrix printouts. SASE. Buys all rights.
Needs: "We can use staff writers/associate producers with AV experience. We may consider help from time to time on a project basis. The writer must have the ability to create visual sequences as well as narrative. Flexibility is a must; treatments might be technical, humorous, etc." Produces sound filmstrips, 16mm films, slides, video and multi-image shows. Pays salary to writers added to the staff; a negotiable fee to freelancers.

CREATIVE VISUALS, Division of Gamco Industries, Inc., Box 1911, Big Spring TX 79720. (915)267-6327. Vice President, Research and Development: Judith Rickey. Free catalog and author's guidelines. "Provide a list of your educational degrees and majors. Explain your teaching experience, including subjects taught, grades taught, and the number of years you have taught. Please describe any writing experience, and, if possible, include a sample of your published educational material currently on the market. We ask for this information because we have found that our best authors are usually experienced classroom teachers who are writing in their subject area. Once we have information about your background, we will ask you for the subject and titles of your proposed series."
Software: Produces microcomputer software and sound filmstrips, cassettes and reproducible books relating to microcomputer software.
Needs: Education (grades K-12, all subjects areas). Pays royalty; usually 5 or 10% of net sales.

RAUL DA SILVA & OTHER FILMMAKERS, 311 E. 85th St., New York NY 10028. Creative Director: Raul da Silva. Produces material for business, industry, institutions, education and entertainment audiences. "We strive for excellence in both script and visual interpretation. We produce quality only, and bow to the budget-conscious clients who cannot or will not afford quality." Submit resume. "Generally works on assignment only. We have a selection of writers known to us already. Cannot handle unsolicited mail/scripts." Rights purchased vary. "If possible, we share profits with writers, particularly when resale is involved."
Needs: "We produce both types of material: on assignment from clients (one-shot communications) and proprietary AV materials which resell." Produces 8mm and 16mm film loops, silent and sound filmstrips, 16mm and 35mm films, multimedia kits, phonograph records, tapes and cassettes and slides. Pays 10% royalty; also pays in outright purchase of 10% of total budget. Pays in accordance with Writers Guild standards.
Tips: "We are impressed with scripts that have received recognition in writing competition. We also welcome resumes from writers who have credentials and credits with other producers. From these we will select our future writers." Looks for "knowledge of medium, structure, style, cohesiveness (mastery of continuity), clarity, obvious love for the language and intelligence."

NICHOLAS DANCY PRODUCTIONS, INC., 333 W. 39th St., New York NY 10018. (212)564-9140. President: Nicholas Dancy. Produces material for general audiences, employees, members of professional groups, members of associations, and special customer groups. Buys 5-10 scripts/year; works with 5-10 writers/year. Buys all rights. Reports in 1 month.

Needs: "We use scripts for films or videotapes from 15 minutes to 1 hour for corporate communications, sales, orientation, corporate image, medical, documentary, training." 16mm films, slides, and tapes and cassettes (audio tapes and videotapes). Query with resume. "No unsolicited material. Our field is too specialized." Pays in outright purchase of $800-5,000.

Tips: "Writers should have knowledge of business and industry and professions, ability to work with clients and communicators, fresh narrative style, creative use of dialogue, good skills in accomplishing research, and a professional approach to production."

ALFRED DE MARTINI EDUCATIONAL FILMS, 414 4th Ave., Haddon Heights NJ 08035. (609)547-2800. President: Alfred De Martini. Produces material for schools, colleges, universities, libraries and museums. "We're informal, creative, earthy, realistic, productive and perfection-oriented." Submit synopsis/outline or completed script. SASE. Reports in 1 month. Buys all rights. Free catalog for SASE.

Needs: Subject topics include "educational material on art, travel and history from secondary to adult level." Produces silent and sound filmstrips, multimedia kits, and tapes and cassettes. Pays in outright purchase of $100-$2,500. "Fee is established in advance with writers."

Tips: Interested in "imagination, brevity, uniqueness of style and ascertaining objectives."

MARK DRUCK PRODUCTIONS, 300 E. 40th St., New York NY 10016. (212)682-5980. Produces audiovisuals for "mostly industrial audiences." Produces 16mm films, multimedia kits and videotape industrials. Subjects: retail items, drugs, travel, industrial products, etc. Material is sometimes copyrighted. "The whole production belongs to the client. No unsolicited scripts; only resumes, lists of credits, etc. The freelance writer must have some expertise in the subject, and in writing AV scripts." SASE.

General: Pays $500/reel minimum. "Writer will be expected to produce outline, treatment and shooting script."

THE DURASELL CORPORATION, 360 Lexington Ave., New York NY 10017. President: Albert A. Jacoby. Produces AV material for sales presentations, meetings, and training programs—primarily for consumer package goods companies. Buys 30-50 scripts/year; works with 6-10 writers/year. Buys all rights.

Needs: Video, meetings, sound filmstrips, slides and tapes. Must send letter and resume first. Pays in outright purchase. ("Freelancer sets fee.")

Tips: "Freelancers must be fast, creative, organized, enthusiastic, experienced, talented. Demonstrate heavy experience in AV sales meetings scripts and in creative multi-image sales meetings."

EDUCATIONAL FILM CENTER, 5101 F Backlick Rd., Box 1017, Annandale VA 22003. (703)750-0560. Chief Writer: Ruth Pollak. Produces dramatic and documentary material for commercial, government, broadcast, schools and communities. Works with 5-20 writers/year. Buys all rights. Computer printout submissions OK. SASE. Reports in 1 month.

Needs: "Strong dramatic screenplays, especially for family/children audience." Query with samples. Pays in outright purchase or by commercial arrangement.

EDUCATIONAL IMAGES LTD., Box 367, Lyons Falls NY 13368. (315)348-8211. Executive Director: Dr. Charles R. Belinky. Produces material for schools, K-college and graduate school, public libraries, parks, nature centers, etc. Buys 50 scripts/yr. Buys all AV rights. Free catalog. Query with a meaningful sample of proposed program. Computer printout submissions OK. Produces sound filmstrips, multimedia kits and slide sets.

Needs: Slide sets and filmstrips on science, natural history, anthropology and social studies. "We are looking primarily for complete AV programs; will consider slide collections to add to our files. This requires high quality, factual text and pictures." Pays $150 minimum.

Software: Science-related material.

Tips: The writer/photographer is given high consideration. "Once we express interest, follow up! Potential contributors lose many sales to us by not following up on initial query. Don't waste our time and yours if you can't deliver."

‡EDUCATIONAL INSIGHTS, 150 W. Carob St., Compton CA 90220. (213)637-2131. Director of Development: Terry Garnholz. Educational publisher. Averages 50 titles/year. Pays 5% minimum royalty; buys some mss outright. No advance. Simultaneous and photocopied submissions OK. SASE. Reports in 1 month. Free catalog.

Needs: Educational areas. Query or submit outline/synopsis and sample chapters or script.

EFFECTIVE COMMUNICATION ARTS, INC., 47 W. 57th St., New York NY 10019. (212)688-6225. Vice President: W.J. Comcowich. Produces "imaginative technical films" for the general public; medical education and science students. Buys 30-40 scripts/year. Query with resume of specific titles and descriptions of

scripts written—objectives, format, audience, etc. Computer printout and disk submissions OK; prefers letter quality to dot matrix printouts. "Explain what the films accomplished—how they were better than the typical." Buys all rights.
Needs: "Primarily 10- to 30-minute films on science, medicine and technology. We also need 3- to 5-minute films on product promotion. A writer must have the ability to 'translate' technical material and supply scripts with detailed visuals. Films on science and medicine are becoming even more technically oriented. Writers must have ability to do independent research." Produces sound filmstrips, models, 16mm films, videodiscs, multimedia kits, tapes and cassettes, slides, and allied print materials. Pays by negotiation based on the project's budget.

THE EPISCOPAL RADIO-TV FOUNDATION, INC., 3379 Peachtree Rd. NE, Atlanta GA 30326. (404)233-5419. President/Executive Director: The Rev. Louis C. Schueddig. Produces materials for educational and religious organizations. Catalog for SASE.
Needs: 16mm films and tapes and cassettes.

FILMS FOR CHRIST ASSOCIATION, INC., 5310 N. Eden Rd., Elmwood IL 61529. (309)565-7266. Production Manager: Paul Taylor. Produces material for use by churches (interdenominational), schools (both secular and parochial), and missions. Most films are 20-90 minutes in length. Previously published submissions OK. Computer printout submissions OK; disk submissions OK if Lanier format only. Free catalog.
Needs: Produces 16mm films, sound filmstrips, slides and books. Documentaries and dramas. Particularly interested in scripts or script ideas dealing with such subjects as: Creation vs. evolution, archaeology, science and the Bible, apologetics, Christian living and evangelism. Also interested in good scripts for evangelistic children's films. Query. Prefers brief one-page synopsis. Payment negotiable.

‡FILMS FOR THE HUMANITIES, INC., Box 2053, Princeton NJ 08540. (609)452-1128. Vice President, Editorial: Stephen Mantell. Produces material for a junior high, high school, college, business and industry audience. Buys 50-75 scripts/year; works with 5-10 writers/year. Previously produced material OK. SASE.
Needs: Produces sound filmstrips, multimedia kits, tapes and cassettes. Submit resume and sample material; "we assign topics."
Tips: "We assign writing in line with our curriculum and editorial program needs."

FLIPTRACK LEARNING SYSTEMS, Division of Mosaic Media, Inc., 526 N. Main St., Box 711, Glen Ellyn IL 60137. (312)790-1117. Publisher: F. Lee McFadden. Estab. 1981. Produces training tapes for microcomputer equipment and business software. Buys 25 scripts/year. Works with 5-10 writers/year. Buys all rights. Computer printout and disk submissions OK. SASE. Reports in 3 weeks. Free product literature.
Needs: Spoken voice audio cassette scripts geared to the adult or mature student in a business setting and to the first-time microcomputer user. "Programming ability may be helpful." Produces audio cassettes and reference manuals. Query with resume and samples if available. Pays negotiable royalty; buys some scripts outright.
Tips: Looks for "ability to organize lesson content logically, develop carefully sequenced lessons and write step-by-step audio scripts in narrative form. Experience in writing training material for the adult learner is more important than a deep knowledge of the microcomputer. Business orientation is a help. We are expanding, along with the microcomputer market."

FLORIDA PRODUCTION CENTER, 150 Riverside Ave., Jacksonville FL 32202. (904)354-7000. Tampa office: 4010 N. Nebraska Ave., Tampa FL 33603. Outside Florida call (800)237-4490. Inside Florida call (813)237-1200. Vice President: Lou DiGiusto. Director of Marketing: Edward S. Epstein. Produces material for business, industry, government and education. Buys 24 scripts/year. Query with samples and resume. SASE. Buys all rights. Previously produced material OK.
Needs: "General script needs. Training programs and industrial motivation. Six training of 10 minutes and 10 industrial—some with image-type slant, others with informational slant." Produces 8mm film loops, silent and sound filmstrips, 16-35mm films, multimedia kits, tapes and cassettes, slides, teaching machine programs and videotape presentations. Pays in outright purchase "depending on project."

‡FORMAT 2, 232 1st Ave., Pittsburgh PA 15222. (412)281-6620. President: Ed Jacob. Produces material for an industrial, corporate, sales and training audience. Buys 10 scripts/year. Buys all rights. Previously published material OK.
Needs: Produces multimedia slides, tapes and cassettes. Submit completed script and resume. Pays in outright purchase.
Tips: Looks for AV understanding.

PAUL FRENCH & PARTNERS, INC., Rt. 5, Gabbettville Rd., LaGrange GA 30240. (404)882-5581. Contact: Paul French. Query or submit resume. SASE. Reports in 2 weeks. Buys all rights.

Needs: Wants to see multi-screen scripts (all employee attitude related) and/or multi-screen AV sales meeting scripts or resumes. Produces silent and sound filmstrips, 16mm films, multimedia kits, phonograph records, tapes and cassettes, and slides. Pays in outright purchase of $500-$5,000. Payment is in accordance with Writers Guild standards.

FRIED PRODUCTIONS, 768 Farmington Ave., Farmington CT 06032. (203)674-8221. President: Joel Fried. Executive Producer: Roy Shaw. Vice President, Industrial Division: Pat Fox. Production Assistant: David Sherer. "We produce programs that are aimed at the high school/college/cable TV market." Query; "tell us what your idea is, and why you can write on this particular subject." Computer printout or disk submissions OK. SASE. Buys all rights. Pays by cash and/or royalty.
Needs: "Education is very important to us. You should be familiar with the market and what subjects are of interest to today's students. We are open to any good idea. Original script ideas for cable production also of interest." Buys 20-40 scripts/yr. Subjects include vocational education and academics, chemistry, career awareness, physics and biology, horticulture, sex education—just about any area. Produces videotapes, 6mm sound filmstrips, overhead transparencies, slides, study prints, teaching machine programs and multimedia kits. Pays by the project.
Software: "Computer software ideas are needed for the home or school market."
Tips: "Please let us hear your ideas. All queries are answered."

GATEWAY PRODUCTIONS INC., 304 E. 45th St., New York NY 10017. (212)286-0770. Produces material for corporate communications, over-the-air commercial television, cable and the international business community. Submit resume. SASE. Buys "non-theatrical rights under corporation client's name."
Needs: "Scripts are developed through research of each client's needs. Length is usually 10-30 minutes. Subject matter and style vary." Produces 16mm films and video. Payment is "based on overall production budget and negotiation of flat fee."
Tips: Interested in "strong visualization capability, fresh concepts, research capability, client rapport and especially professionalism. Most people who write for us come to us through referrals and are actually working in the New York metropolitan area."

‡**GESSLER PUBLISHING CO., INC.**, 900 Broadway, New York NY 10003. (212)673-3113. President: Seth C. Levin. Produces material for foreign language students—French, Spanish, German, Italian, Latin and ESL. Buys about 25 scripts/year. Buys all rights. Previously published material OK "occasionally. Do not send disk submission without documentation." SASE. Reports in 3 weeks on queries; 2 months on submissions.
Needs: "Filmstrips to create an interest in learning a foreign language and its usefulness in career objectives; also culturally insightful filmstrips on French, German, Italian and Spanish-speaking countries." Produces sound filmstrips, multimedia kits, overhead transparencies, games, realia, tapes and cassettes, computer software.
Software: Submit synopsis/outline or software with complete documentation, introduction, objectives. Pays in outright purchase and royalties.
Tips: "Be organized in your presentation; be creative but keep in mind that your audience is primarily in the junior/senior high school age bracket."

ROBERT GILMORE ASSOCIATES, INC., 990 Washington St., Dedham MA 02026. (617)329-6633. Produces materials for industrial training and sales promotion. "We are interested to learn of writers in the New England area with experience in writing for videotape and film industrial production."
Needs: 16mm and 35mm films and slides.

GRIFFIN COMMUNICATIONS, INC., 802 Wabash Ave., Chesterton IN 46304. (219)926-8602. President: Michael J. Griffin. Produces material for business and industry. Submit resume. Computer printout and disk submissions OK. SASE. Reports in 2 weeks. Buys all rights.
Needs: "Griffin Communications is a full service communications company specializing in the development of marketing, advertising and training programs for a wide variety of business and industrial clients. The vast majority of our audiovisual presentations must be motivational or inspirational as much as informational. Our programs encompass various media including films, filmstrips, multi-image presentations, brochures, media advertising, training manuals, point-of-purchase displays, etc. Each of our programs is designed to achieve specific objectives. We do not produce generic programs for mass distribution. Each communication program is custom designed and produced." Produces charts; sound filmstrips; films; multimedia kits; overhead transparencies; tapes and cassettes; and slides. "Because of complex array of programs, payment varies on assignment."
Tips: "Those writers with the best chance of breaking in with our company will have multiple talents in a wide variety of applications. Show your best work in different media. Potential contributors should show a unique ability to approach communication problems with fresh, exciting ideas. The 'poetic ego' should not get in the

way of the expressed objective. There is a tremendous amount of room for creativity, but it must be channeled toward specific business goals.''

HAYES SCHOOL PUBLISHING CO., INC., 321 Pennwood Ave., Wilkinsburg PA 15221. (412)371-2373. 2nd Vice President: Clair N. Hayes III. Produces material for school teachers, principals, elementary through high school. Buys all rights. Catalog for SASE. Query. Produces charts, workbooks, teachers' handbooks, posters, bulletin board material, computer software, and liquid duplicating books.
Needs: Education material only. (''Particularly interested in books or software relating to computers.'') Pays $25 minimum.

IDEAL SCHOOL SUPPLY CO., Affiliate of Westinghouse Learning Corp., 11000 S. Lavergne Ave., Oak Lawn IL 60453. (312)425-0800. Manager, Product Development: Barbara Stiles. Produces material for preschool, primary and elementary students. ''The majority of our product line comes from outside sources, most of them practicing classroom teachers.'' Occasionally these products are edited by freelance talent. Writers and editors are also used for some special development projects. Query with resume which will be filed for future reference. Free catalog.
Needs: ''Style, length and format vary according to grade level and subject matter of material.'' Produces manipulatives, games, models, printed material, multimedia kits, and cassette programs.

IMAGE INNOVATIONS, INC., 14 Buttonwood Dr., Somerset NJ 08873. President: Mark A. Else. Produces material for business, education and general audiences. Query with samples. Computer printout and disk submissions OK; CPT only. Prefers letter quality to dot matrix printouts. SASE. Reports in 2 weeks. Buys all rights.
Needs: Subject topics include education, sales and public relations. Produces sound filmstrips, 16mm films, multimedia kits, ½ and ¾-inch video, and tapes and cassettes. Pays in outright purchase of $500-5,000.

IMAGE MARKETING SERVICES, INC., 95-97 Compark Rd., Centerville OH 45459. (513)434-3974. President: Dale R. Mercer. Produces material for business, industry, institutions, and the general public. Arrange ''advance appointment with samples.'' Buys all rights.
Needs: Produces silent and sound filmstrips; multimedia kits; tapes and cassettes; and slides. Pays negotiable outright purchase ''based on assignment budget.''

IMAGE MEDIA, 3249 Hennepin Ave. S, Minneapolis MN 55408. (612)827-6500. Creative Director: A.M. Rifkin. Query with samples. SASE. Reports in 2 weeks. Rights purchased ''depend on project.''
Needs: Produces silent and sound filmstrips, 16mm films, tapes and cassettes, and slides. Pays in outright purchase.

IMPERIAL INTERNATIONAL LEARNING CORP., Box 548, Kankakee IL 60901. Director of Manuscript Development: Spencer Barnard. Educational AV publisher producing a variety of instructional aids for grades K through high school. Draws mainly from freelance sources on an assignment basis. Seeks authors skilled in writing sound filmstrips, cassette tape and multimedia programs and microcomputer programs. ''Writers should submit a query letter which includes background and professional writing experience. Indicate that you understand our particular market.'' Reports in 6 weeks.
Needs: Sound filmstrips; slides; tapes and cassettes; Spirit master worksheets and teacher's manuals. Reading and math are main areas of concentration. Pays fee within 1 month after acceptance of ms. Contract provided.
Software: Educational. Looking for ''innovative ideas to make the microcomputer challenge pupils to think; also ideas for the efficient management of instruction, testing, tracking results, etc.''
Tips: ''Offer concrete evidence that specific needs and requirements of the company would be met. Manuscripts need to be well researched. Stories should be intriguing with modern themes and illustrations.''

‡INSIGHT! INC., 100 E. Ohio St., Chicago IL 60611. (312)467-4350. President: Neal Cochran. Produces material for all audiences, depending on type of client. Buys over 200 scripts/year from more than 30 writers. Buys all rights. Disk submissions OK ''as long as compatible with our format.'' SASE.
Needs: ''Depends on contract awarded to Insight! Films, videotapes, filmstrips and, most important, shows of all types.'' Produces 16mm films, sound filmstrips, multimedia kits, multimedia and ''book'' shows, overhead transparencies, slides. No educational materials. Query with samples. Pays in outright purchase.

INSTRUCTIONAL DYNAMICS INC., Suite 1100, 666 N. Lake Shore Dr., Chicago IL 60611. Director, Multimedia Products: Linda Phillips. For early learning through college level. ''Writer should have valid background and experience that parallels the specific assignment. Would like to have vita as first contact. We keep on file and activate as needs arise. We use a substantial group of outside talent to supplement our in-house staff.'' SASE. Buys all rights.
Needs: Silent filmstrips, sound filmstrips, multimedia kits, overhead transparencies, phonograph records,

prerecorded tapes and cassettes, 2x2 slides, study prints, hard copy and videotapes. "Requirements for these vary depending upon assignments from our clients. Payment depends on contractual arrangements with our client and also varies depending on medium or multimedia involved."

INSTRUCTOR BOOKS, 1 E. 1st St., Duluth MN 55802. Editorial Director: John Bradley. "US and Canadian school supervisors, principals, and teachers purchase items in our line for instructional purposes." Buys all rights. Writer should have "experience in preparing materials for elementary students, including suitable teaching guides to accompany them, and demonstrate knowledge of the appropriate subject areas, or demonstrate ability for accurate and efficient research and documentation." Query. SASE. Free catalog.
Needs: "Elementary curriculum enrichment—all subject areas. Display material, copy and illustration should match interest and reading skills of children in grades for which material is intended. Production is limited to printed matter: posters, charts, duplicating masters, resource handbooks, teaching guides." Length: 6,000-12,000 words. "Standard contract, but fees vary considerably, depending on type of project."
Tips: "Writers who reflect current educational practices can expect to sell to us."

JEAN-GUY JACQUE ET COMPAGNIE, 1463 Tamarind Ave., Hollywood CA 90028. (213)462-6474. Owner: J.G. Jacque. Produces TV commercials (animation and puppet animation). Query with samples. SASE. Reports in 3 weeks. Buys all rights.
Needs: Produces 16mm and 35mm films. Pays according to Writers Guild standards.

PAUL S. KARR PRODUCTIONS, 2949 W. Indian School Rd., Box 11711, Phoenix AZ 85017. Utah Division Box 1254, 1024, No. 250 Orem UT 84057. (801)225-8485/226-8209. (602)266-4198. Produces films and materials for industry, business, education, TV and cable programming. Query. "Do not submit material unless requested." Buys all rights. Works on co-production ventures.
Needs: Produces 16mm films. Payment varies.
Tips: "One of the best ways for a writer to become a screenwriter is to create a situation with a client that requires a film. He then can assume the position of an associate producer, work with an experienced professional producer in putting the film into being, and in that way learn about filmmaking and chalk up some meaningful credits."

KEN-DEL PRODUCTIONS, INC., 111 Valley Rd., Wilmington DE 19804-1397. (302)655-7488. President: Ed Kennedy. Produces material for "elementary, junior high, high school, and college level, as well as interested organizations and companies." Query. SASE.
Needs: "Topics of the present (technology, cities, traffic, transit, pollution, ecology, health, water, race, genetics, consumerism, fashions, communications, education, population control, waste, future sources of food, undeveloped sources of living, food, health, etc.); topics of the future; how-to series (everything for the housewife, farmer, banker or mechanic, on music, art, sports, reading, science, love, repair, sleep—on any subject); and material handling." Produces sound filmstrips; 8mm, 16mm, and 35mm films; 16mm film loops; phonograph records; prerecorded tapes and cassettes; slides and videotapes in ¾" U-matic, ½" VHS, ½" BETA cassettes.

KIMBO EDUCATIONAL-UNITED SOUND ARTS, INC., 10-16 N. 3rd Ave., Box 477, Long Branch NJ 07740. (201)229-4949. Contact: James Kimble or Amy Laufer. Produces materials for the educational market (early childhood, special education, music, physical education, dance, and preschool children 6 months and up). Buys approximately 12-15 scripts/year; works with approximately 12-15 writers/year. Buys all rights or first rights. Previously produced material OK "in some instances." SASE. Reports in 1 month. Free catalog.
Needs: "For the next two years we will be concentrating on a few new special education products, general early chilhood-movement-oriented products, new albums in the dance field and more. Each will be an album/cassette with accompanying teacher's manual and, if warranted, manipulatives." Phonograph records and cassettes; "all with accompanying manual or teaching guides." Query with samples and synopsis/outline or completed script. Pays 5-7% royalty on lowest wholesale selling price, and in outright purchase. Both negotiable.
Tips: "We look for creativity first. Having material that is educationally sound is also important. Being organized is certainly helpful. Fitness is growing rapidly in popularity and will always be a necessary thing. Children will always need to be taught the basic fine and gross motor skills. Capturing interest while reaching these goals is the key."

‡**KOCH/MARSCHALL PRODUCTIONS, INC.**, 1718 N. Mohawk St., Chicago IL 60614. (312)664-6482. President: Phillip Koch. Produces material for teenage, health education and general audiences. Buys 3 scripts/year; works with 5 writers/year. Buys all rights. Previously published material OK. No computer printout or disk submissions. SASE. Reports in 6 weeks.
Needs: "We are looking for original, feature-length film scripts for both comedy and drama." Produces 16mm films. Query. Pays in accordance with Writers Guild standards.

Tips: "Submit only your very best work sample. We have a greater respect for an original idea than a commercial one. But a writer must also recognize the commercial aspect of his work." Looks for "originality, attention to craft and technique, good working attitude."

L & M PRODUCTIONS, INC., 2110 Superior, Cleveland OH 44114. (216)621-0754. Contact: Ben Ball. Produces material for large corporate meetings. Buys all rights. SASE.
Needs: Multi-image. Multimedia kits, slides, and tapes and cassettes. Query with samples and resume. Pays in outright purchase on a "per-job basis."

BRIEN LEE & COMPANY, 2025 N. Summit Ave., Milwaukee WI 53202. (414)277-7600. Also 33 W. 54th St., New York NY 10019. (212)307-7810. President/Creative Director: Brien Lee. Produces custom audiovisual material for business; industry; arts/non-profit; advertising and public relations agencies; business associations; special entertainment oriented projects. Buys average 5 scripts/yr. Submit an example of your scripting ability as well as a resume. Computer printout submissions OK; disk OK if compatible. SASE. Reports in 1 month, sometimes leading to an interview and an assignment. Buys all rights.
Needs: "People who understand what 'AV' is all about . . . words, pictures, sound. Motivational, informational, clear-cut, straightforward . . . writing that is literate, but never so good it could stand on its own without the pictures or sound. Usually writing for one narrator, plus additional voices and/or characters. No hype." Produces filmstrips, multi-image presentations, and mixed media presentations, slide-sound programs.
Recent Productions: *The New World of Kirby*, *On the Move* for Borden Company, *Aul Dealer Meeting*, Pabst *New Company* introduction.

WILLIAM V. LEVINE ASSOCIATES, INC., 31 E. 28th St., New York NY 10016. (212)683-7177. President: William V. Levine. Presentations for business and industry. Firm emphasizes "creativity and understanding of the client's goals and objectives." Will interview writers after submission of resume and/or sample AV scripts. Specifically seeks writers with offbeat or humorous flair. Buys 1-2 scripts/month. Previously published material OK. Query with resume. "We prefer New York City-area based writers only." SASE. Buys all rights.
Needs: Business-related scripts *on assignment* for specific clients for use at sales meetings or for desk-top presentations. Also uses theme-setting and inspirational scripts with inherent messages of business interest. Produces charts, sound and silent filmstrips, 16mm films, multimedia kits, tapes and cassettes, slide sets and live industrial shows. Pays $500-2,500.

J.B. LIPPINCOTT CO., Audiovisual Media Department, East Washington Sq., Philadelphia PA 19105. (215)574-4235. Contact: H.M. Eisler. Produces materials for nursing students and medical students. Buys 15-25 scripts/yr. Works with approximately 25 writers/year. Disk submissions OK if compatible with TRS-80 and IBM-PC. Buys all rights. SASE. Reports in 2 weeks on queries; 4 weeks on submissions. Free catalog.
Needs: "High-level instruction in medical/surgical topics for pre-service and in-service professional education." 16mm films, sound filmstrips, slides (rarely) and video materials. Query. Negotiates pay.

LORI PRODUCTIONS, INC., 6430 Sunset Blvd., Hollywood CA 90028. (213)466-7567. Produces material for industrial clients. Buys 5-10 scripts/year. Query with resume. SASE. Reports in 3 weeks. Buys all rights.
Needs: "We produce industrial films (sales, corporate image, training, safety), which generally run from 6-20 minutes in length." Seeks writers with a "clean, concise writing style; a familiarity with film production; and experience with industrial films." Works with Los Angeles-area writers *only*. Produces 16mm films, live corporate shows, multi-image presentations, and sales meetings. Pays by outright purchase of $500-2,000.

LYONS STUDIOS, INC., 200 W. 9th St., Wilmington DE 19801. (302)654-6146. Contact: P. Coleman DuPont. Produces material for business and industry. Submit completed script with resume. SASE. Reports in 2 weeks. Buys all rights.
Needs: Subject topics include "business/industrial presentations—both educational and motivational." Produces multimedia presentations, video programs and collateral materials. Pays in outright purchase of $200-$1,000.
Tips: "Submit complete scripts with description of objectives, audience, time and budget required. We want honest estimates of time and budget needs; clean, terse style—conversational copy."

‡MCKNIGHT PUBLISHING CO., Box 2854, Bloomington IL 61701. (309)663-1341. Contact: Vice President, Editorial. Produces material for industrial arts, vocational education, vocational guidance, home economics *in schools*, grades 7-14. Produces 10-20 products/year; 1-2 FS/CS, 8-15 textbooks, 1-3 miscellaneous. Buys all rights. Previously produced material OK. SASE. Reports in 1 month on queries; 6 weeks on submissions. Free catalog.
Needs: FS/CS programs to sell with proven textbooks, and to established customers. Produces sound filmstrips. Query with samples and submit synopsis/outline. Pays royalty.
Tips: Looks for "a track record; knowledge of subject matter *as it is taught in our markets*."

THE MCMANUS COMPANY, Box 446, Greens Farms CT 06436. (203)255-3301. President: John F. McManus. National Advertising, Marketing and Public Relations Agency. Produces material for consumers, corporate management and trade associations. Query with resume. Rights purchased "depend upon project and usage."
Needs: "Our needs are based on specific assignment, mostly business oriented." Produces 16mm and 35mm films, radio commercial tapes and cassettes.
Tips: "We maintain a complete and up-to-date file of talent availabilities." Interested in creativity, originality and realism.

MAGNETIX CORP., 770 W. Bay St., Winter Garden FL 32787. (305)656-4494. President: John Lory. Produces material for the general public. "Personal contact must be made due to wide variety of very specific scripts we require." Buys all rights.
Needs: Produces tapes and cassettes: 20- to 30-minute audio programs with sound effects written to be sold to general public as a souvenir with some educational value. "Writers must have the ability to dramatize our subjects using sound effects, etc." Pays $300 minimum. Recent production: *Shuttle to Tomorrow* (booklet with audio cassette).

MARSHFILM ENTERPRISES, INC., Box 8082, Shawnee Mission KS 66208. (816)523-1059. President: Joan K. Marsh. Produces material for elementary and junior/senior high school students. Buys 8-16 scripts/year. Buys all rights.
Needs: 50 frame; 15 minutes/script. Sound filmstrips. Query "only." Pays in outright purchase of $250-500/script.

ED MARZOLA & ASSOCIATES, 11846 Ventura Blvd., Studio City CA 91604. Creative Director: William Case. Produces material for broadcast and industrial audiences. Query with samples or submit resume. SASE. Reports in 2 weeks.
Needs: "We now produce television programs and feature-length films for theatrical release." Produces 16mm and 35mm films and videotaped presentations. "We negotiate each case individually." Pays according to Writers Guild standards.

MASTER MEDIA, INC., 5097 Chamblee-Tucker Rd., Atlanta/Tucker GA 30084. (404)491-0330. President: Dave Causey. Produces materials for "a wide variety of audiences. In addition to regular commercial production, we have a unique relationship with Christian audiences in single showings, workshops and seminars." Buys approximately 6-10 scripts/year. Buys variable rights, "depending upon use and the economics involved." Previously produced material OK. SASE. Reports in 2 weeks.
Needs: Devotional topics, comedy, human interest, travel, hunger and human rights; material on growing old, senior citizens; the Christian perspective; 12-28 minutes in length. "We are very interested at this point in scripts dealing with human conditions, social problems and human rights. Religious, especially Christian, content material is needed. We need, now, a script with impact on world hunger." 16mm films, multimedia kits, slides, tapes and cassettes and multi-image materials. Submit synopsis/outline or completed script. Pays negotiable fee. "We do an average of two a month."
Tips: "Writers need to think visually, that is, subject development should not be too abstract. The multi-image medium is becoming more content-oriented instead of the initial visual excitement from graphics syndrome. We see an increasing need for scripts with a 'message,' or emotional and entertainment values in the 12-28 minute range."

MAXFILMS, INC. 2525 Hyperion Ave., Los Angeles CA 90027. (213)662-3285. President: Kel Christiansen. Vice President: Sid Glenar. Produces educational material for audiences "from high-school to college graduate level in our educational film division, to all business and technical people in our industrial division. We also produce made-for-television movies and documentaries, and quality scripts and ideas in these areas are actively sought. The amount of material we use varies greatly from year to year, but on the average, perhaps 5-10 educational/industrial scripts are bought each year, with an additional 15-20 story ideas and scripts for TV movies or documentaries." Query or submit outline/synopsis, "a statement about the audience for which it is intended and the present extent of its development." SASE. Reports in 3 weeks. Rights purchased vary.
Needs: "The primary criterion for educational material is that the subject matter have entertainment as well as educational value. This does not preclude straight educational-informational scripts, but they must be entertainingly presented. Scripts or concepts for television movies must have appeal for an adult audience and have a story concept that is either unique or of current social interest. If the same concept has appeal for children as well, so much the better." Produces 16mm and 35mm films. Payment varies according to rights purchased.
Tips: "We are willing to work with new writers who show promise. About one-half of the story concepts and scripts we buy are from new writers."

MEDICAL MULTIMEDIA CORP., 211 E. 43rd St., New York NY 10017. (212)986-0180. Administrative Assistant: Ruth Shiffer. Produces for the medical and paramedical professions. Buys 10-12 scripts/year. Query

with resume; "scripts are purchased on assignment." Buys all rights.
Needs: "Style and format vary; however, all writing is for the medical health sciences profession." Produces charts, sound filmstrips, 16mm film, multimedia kits, tapes and cassettes, videotapes, slides and teaching machine programs. Pays $200-2,000.

‡**MEETING MAKERS, INC.**, 215 Lexington Ave., New York NY 10016. (212)679-5100. President: Sam Sugarman. Produces material for salespeople. Buys 30 scripts/year; works with 5 writers/year. Buys all rights; no residual fees unless more work is done. Previously produced material OK. SASE. Reports in a few weeks.
Needs: Sales meetings, new product introductions. Produces slides, multimedia shows. Query with samples or submit completed script and resume. Pays in outright purchase.
Tips: Contributors must "have experience in writing for multi-screen, multi-projector shows—AV only." Looks for "writers with ability to get along with clients and an understanding of marketing."

MERIWETHER PUBLISHING LTD. (CONTEMPORARY DRAMA SERVICE), Box 457, Downers Grove IL 60515. President: Arthur Zapel.
Needs: "We publish 'how-to' materials in filmstrip, game and cassette formats. We prefer materials for high school and college level students. Elementary-age-level materials are very limited." Christian activity book mss accepted. Query. Letter-quality computer printout submissions OK. Pays royalty; buys some mss outright.
Recent titles: *Radio Plays for Taping*, by Stuart Sheeley; *Ten Practice Monologs for Stand-Up Comedians*, by Bill Majeski; *Variety Show to Go!*, by Stephanie Shute (book).
Tips: "We publish a wide variety of speech contest materials for high school students."

MODE-ART PICTURES, INC., 3075 W. Liberty Ave., Pittsburgh PA 15216. (412)343-8700. Chairman: James L. Baker. Produces material for "all" audiences. Buys 5-10 scripts/year, but "each year is different." Query; "we write by contract." SASE. Reports in 3 weeks. Buys all rights.
Needs: Produces sound filmstrips, 16mm and 35mm films, slide sets, and teaching machine programs. "We seek writers who are flexible and willing to work. Good writers in our field are hard to find." Pays $1,000-5,000.

MONTAGE COMMUNICATIONS, 1556 N. Fairfax Ave., Los Angeles CA 90046. (213)851-8010. President: Stan Ono. Produces material for corporate audiences. Query with samples and resume. SASE. Reports in 1 month. Buys all rights.
Needs: Subject topics include 10-15 minute scripts for training, marketing, sales. Produces training materials, e.g. workbooks; sound filmstrips; 16mm films; multimedia kits; tapes and cassettes; slides; and video. Pays in outright purchase.

BENJAMIN MORSE INC., 16 Aberdeen St., Boston MA 02215. (617)262-1550. President: Nat Morse. Produces material for industry and education. Query with samples and resume. Does not return unsolicited material—"cannot handle volume." Reports in 2 weeks. Buys all rights. Free catalog.
Needs: Produces charts; 16mm and 35mm film loops; silent and sound filmstrips; models; multimedia kits; overhead transparencies; tapes and cassettes; slides; study prints; teaching machine programs; and special effects. Pays "depending on job."
Tips: Especially interested in "someone who writes for 'the ear' and not 'the eye.' "

MOTIVATION MEDIA, INC., 1245 Milwaukee Ave., Glenview IL 60025. (312)297-4740. Executive Producer: Frank Stedronsky. Produces customized material for salespeople, customers, corporate/industrial employees and distributors. Query with samples. SASE. Reports in 1 month. Buys all rights.
Needs: Material for all audiovisual media—particularly marketing-oriented (sales training, sales promotional, sales motivational) material. Produces sound filmstrips, 16mm films, multimedia sales meeting programs, tapes and cassettes and slide sets. Pays $150-5,000.

MRC FILMS, Div. McLaughlin Research Corp., 71 W. 23rd St., New York NY 10010. (212)989-1750. Executive Producer: Larry Mollot. "Audience varies with subject matter, which is wide and diverse." Writer "should have an ability to visualize concepts and to express ideas clearly in words. Experience in film or filmstrip scriptwriting is desirable. Write us, giving some idea of background. Submit samples of writing. We are looking for new talent. No unsolicited material accepted. Work upon assignment only." Query. SASE.
Needs: "Industrial, documentary, educational and television films. Also, public relations, teaching and motivational filmstrips. Some subjects are highly technical in the fields of aerospace and electronics. Others are on personal relationships, selling techniques, ecology, etc. A writer with an imaginative visual sense is important." Produces 16mm films, silent and sound filmstrips, video programs, and tapes and cassettes. "Fee depends on nature and length of job. Typical fees: $600-1,200 for script for 10-minute film; $1,200-2,000 for script for 20-minute film; $1,500-3,000 for script for 30-minute film. For narration writing only, the range is $300-600 for a 10-minute film; $500-900 for a 20-minute film; $600-1,200 for a 30-minute film. For

scriptwriting services by the day, fee is $80-150 per day. All fees may be higher on specific projects with higher budgets.''

MULTI-MEDIA PRODUCTIONS, INC., Box 5097, Stanford CA 94305. Program Director: Mark Vining. Produces interactive instructional material for elementary (grades 4-6) and secondary (grades 9-12) schools, business and industry. Buys 30-35 scripts/year. Query with samples, if available. Computer printout submissions OK; prefers letter quality to dot matrix printouts. No disk submissions. Reports in 6 weeks. Buys all rights. Free catalog.
Needs: ''Material suitable for general high school and elementary school social studies curricula: history, biography, sociology, psychology, anthropology, archeology and economics. Style should be straightforward, lively, objective and interactive.'' Approximate specifications: 50 frames, 10-15 minutes/program part; 2 sentences and 1 visual per frame; 1- or 2-part programs. Writer supplies script, slides for filmstrip, and teacher's manual (as per our format). Pays royalties quarterly, based on 15½% of return on each program sold. ''We like to avoid programs geared to a travelogue, generalized approach to foreign countries, and programs that deal with nebulous, values-oriented subject matter. Programs with a central academic theme sell best. Program subjects should be adaptable to videotape format and to student-interactive instructional methods.''
Recent Production: *The Man From Deer Creek: The Story of Ishi*, sound filmstrip and video presentation.

‡**BURT MUNK & COMPANY**, 666 Dundee Rd., Northbrook IL 60062. (312)564-0855. President: Burton M. Munk. Produces material for industrial, sales training, product information, and education (schools). Works with approximately 10 writers/year. Buys all rights. Does not return material ''all our work is 'made to order' for specific client needs—we are a custom house.''
Needs: Sound filmstrips, slides, tapes and cassettes, 16mm films, videotapes. ''We will contact individual writers who seem suitable for our projects.'' Makes outright purchase.

HENRY NASON PRODUCTIONS, INC., 555 W. 57th St., New York NY 10019. (212)757-5437. President: Henry Nason. Produces custom audiovisual presentations for corporate clients. Query with samples or contact for personal interview. SASE. Reports in 1 month. Buys all rights.
Needs: ''Usually 10- to 15-minute scripts on corporate subjects, such as sales, marketing, employee benefits, products, systems, public affairs, etc. Usually freestanding audiovisual modules. The style should be clear and relaxed, well-researched and organized. Writers must live in the New York City area.'' Produces slide and multimedia presentations. Pays ''an average of 8-10% of the production budget.''

NATIONAL PARK SERVICE, DIVISION OF AV ARTS, Harpers Ferry Center, Harpers Ferry WV 25425. Production Manager: Bob Morris. Produces materials for the general public. Buys 5-25 scripts/year. Buys all rights. SASE. Reports in 1 month.
Needs: 16mm and 35mm films, multimedia kits, slide shots, and tapes and cassettes. Submit resume. Pays in outright purchase; negotiable.
Tips: ''We're looking for writers with an understanding and appreciation of the wildlife environment, ability for interpretation and historical reenactments.''

NETWORK COMMUNICATIONS LTD., (formerly Advision Communications Ltd.), 14524 85th Ave., Edmonton, Alberta, Canada T5R 3Z4. (403)489-1044. President: R. Schwartz. Produces material for cable TV, advertising, government, etc. Submit resume and sample concept or script. SASE. Reports in 3 weeks.
Needs: ''Most productions are 10-15 minutes in length and subject matter is naturally dependent upon the project. Produces cable programs, industrial films and TV commercials (35mm, 16mm or videotape).'' Pays by ''hourly rate, percentage of budget dependent upon project.''

NEW ORIENT MEDIA, 103 N. 2nd St. W., Dundee, IL 60118. (312)428-6000. General Manager: Dennis Maxwell. Produces material for pharmaceutical, automotive, communications and industrial audiences. Submit resume. SASE. Reports in 2 weeks. Buys all rights.
Needs: ''Primarily sales oriented multi-image programs—training oriented films and slide programs.'' Produces sound filmstrips; 8mm and 16mm films; phonograph records; tapes and cassettes; slides and multi-image. Buys ''40-50 scripts/year. We also buy research from writers.'' Pays in outright purchase by negotiation.
Tips: ''We like unusual approaches that reflect a futuristic approach to communications. Writers have to be willing to come to us for input.''

NYSTROM, 3333 N. Elston Ave., Chicago IL 60618. (312)463-1144. Editorial Director: Darrell A. Coppock. Produces material for school audiences (kindergarten through 12th grade). Required credentials depend on topics and subject matter and approach desired. Query. Computer printout and disk submissions OK. SASE. Free catalog.
Needs: Educational material on social studies, earth and life sciences, career education, reading, language arts

and mathematics. Produces charts, sound filmstrips, models, multimedia kits, overhead transparencies and realia. Pays according to circumstances.

OCEAN REALM VIDEO PRODUCTIONS, 2333 Brickell Ave., Miami FL 33129, (305)285-0252. President: Richard H. Stewart. Produces ocean-related material for broad and narrow-cast audience. Works with 8 writers/year. Buys all rights and first rights. Previously produced material OK. SASE. Reports in 1 month. **Needs:** Tapes and cassettes. Query with samples.

ORIGIN, INC., 4466 Laclede, St. Louis MO 63108. (314)533-0010. President: Carla Lane. Creative Director: George Johnson. Produces material for corporate training, sales POP, conventions, magazine videoformat, personnel, financial, paperwork, procedures and communications testing. Rights purchased by assignment. SASE. Reports in 2 weeks.
Needs: "All material is produced according to client needs." Charts; 35mm films; silent and sound filmstrips; slides; tapes and cassettes; teaching machine programs; video and videodisc; and stage. Query or query with samples and resume. Pays by contract.
Tips: Looks for writers with "imagination, creativity and logical progression of thought. Have the ability to understand complicated business functions in minimum time."

OUR SUNDAY VISITOR, INC., Audiovisual Dept., 200 Noll Plaza, Huntington IN 46750. (219)356-8400. Contact: Director of Religious Education. Produces material for students (kindergarten through 12th grade), adult religious education groups and teacher trainees. "We are very concerned that the materials we produce meet the needs of today's church." Query. SASE. Free catalog.
Needs: "Proposals for projects should be no more than 2 pages in length, in outline form. Programs should display up-to-date audiovisual techniques and cohesiveness. Broadly speaking, material should deal with religious education, including liturgy and daily Christian living, as well as structured catechesis. It must not conflict with sound Catholic doctrine, and should reflect modern trends in education." Produces charts, sound filmstrips, phonograph records, tapes and cassettes and multimedia kits. "Work-for-hire and royalty arrangements possible."
Tips: "We're interested in two types of background: audiovisual and religious education. Very few people have both, and cannot be expected to perform equally well in each area. We want the best in either field."

‡PENTAGRAM PRODUCTIONS INC., Suite 5, 1526 Pontium Ave., Los Angeles CA 90025. (213)472-1004. President: Frank Keeney. Produces material for students, mainly teenagers, age range 11-18. Buys 4 scripts/year, each approximately 15 minute narrated duration. Buys all rights. No submissions; resumes only and they must be from general Los Angeles area.
Needs: Four 15-minute filmstrips written to teenage level. Subject matter to be student-motivation to study English, math, history and science. Produces sound filmstrips. Query with resume. Pays 50% when half-completed, balance on completion.
Tips: Contributors "must be willing to demonstrate that they can write for a teenage level. We can usually tell with one written page. We furnish outlines and often much of the research material. Writers should not state they can write for a teenage level if without previous experience, or at least they should be willing to demonstrate ability and be able to accept an assignment with minimum of instruction."

PHOTOCOM PRODUCTIONS, Box 3135, Pismo Beach CA 93449. Creative Services Director: B. L. Pattison. Produces material for schools, junior high to university level. Query with outline/synopsis. "Do *not* send resume or samples of what you've done for other companies. We want to know what you can do for *us* not what you've done for someone else!" Computer printout submissions OK. SASE. Reports in 3 weeks. Buys average 20 scripts/yr. Buys filmstrip rights. Free guidelines.
Needs: "We're most interested in how-to's in vocational areas that can be used in high school shop classes or adult education classes. Material that we've been buying is 60-70 frames long and the narration runs about 8-9 minutes. We want variety in the individual frame lengths though, mostly short, snappy narrations with some medium length frames and very few long ones." Produces sound filmstrips, multimedia kits, cassettes, and slide sets. Pays 10-15% royalty or $200 minimum/script. Royalty payments begin after sales.
Tips: Writer/photographers receive high consideration. So do beginning AV writers. "We're small and so can give special attention to first timers who show potential: we're a good place to get your start, but you *must* be a professional in your attitude! Send us ideas you can accomplish on time and in a professional manner."

PHOTOSCOPE, INC., (formerly Media Management Corp.), 12 W. 27th St., Fl. 12, New York NY 10001. (212)696-0880. President: Geoffrey Carter. Vice President: Carswell Berlin. Produces material for a corporate audience. Buys 10 scripts/year. Buys all rights. Computer printout submissions OK. SASE.
Needs: Produces slides and multi-image. Looks for "imagination, coherency, clarity." Query with samples. Buys scripts outright for negotiable rate.

PREMIER FILM & RECORDING CORP., 3033 Locust, St. Louis MO 63103. (314)531-3555. Secretary/ Treasurer: Grace Dalzell. Produces material for the corporate community; religious organizations; political arms; and hospital and educational groups. Buys 50-100 scripts/year. Buys all rights; "very occasionally the writer retains rights." Previously produced material OK; "depends upon original purposes and markets." SASE. Reports "within a month or as soon as possible."
Needs: "Our work is all custom-produced with the needs being known only as required." 35mm film loops, super 8mm and 35mm films; silent and sound filmstrips; multimedia kits; overhead transparencies; phonograph records; slides; tapes and cassettes; and "LaBelle Filmstrips (a specialty)." Submit complete script and resume. Pays in accordance with Writers Guild standards or by outright purchase of $100 to "any appropriate sum."
Tips: "Always place *occupational pursuit*, name, address, and phone number in upper right hand corner of resume without fail. We're looking for writers with creativity, good background, and a presentable image."

‡PRENTICE-HALL MEDIA, INC., 150 White Plains Rd., Tarrytown NY 10591. (914)631-8300. Managing Editor: Sandra Carr Grant. Produces material for secondary, post-secondary vocational and science students. Buys 50 scripts/year. Buys all rights. Previously produced material OK. SASE. Reports in 1 month. Catalog for SAE.
Needs: "We will be looking for audio-visual treatments for high technology training." Sound filmstrips. Query with samples or submit synopsis/outline. Pays by outright purchase of $350 minimum.
Tips: "We look for clarity of language, ability to write 'visual' scripts, and facility with technical subject matter."

BILL RASE PRODUCTIONS, INC., 955 Venture Ct., Sacramento CA 95825. (916)929-9181. President: Bill Rase. Produces material for business education and mass audience. Buys 20 scripts maximum/year. Buys all rights. SASE. Reports "when an assignment is available."
Needs: Produces silent and sound filmstrips, multimedia kits, slides, cassettes, videotapes and video productions. Submit resume, sample page or 2 of script, and description of expertise. Pays negotiable rate in 30 days.
Tips: "Call and ask for Bill Rase personally. Must be within 100 miles and thoroughly professional."

REGENTS PUBLISHING CO., 2 Park Ave., New York NY 10016. See listing in Book Publisher section.

RESCO, 99 Draper Ave., Meriden CT 06450. (203)238-4709. Producer: Mr. Ronald F. LaVoie. Produces material for "all types of audiences based on subject matter—no pornography of any type." Submit resume. SASE. Reports immediately. Buys all rights. "Contingencies between writer, producer and/or client can be negotiated as well."
Needs: "Scripting for sound slide productions 16-18 minutes long. Subject topics include education, religion, business, technical, medical and general." Produces 8mm film loops (special request); sound filmstrips, overhead transparencies; tapes and cassettes; and sound slides. Pays 5% royalties; outright purchase of $25-$2,500; by negotiation or pre-contract. Pays in accordance with Writers Guild standards.
Tips: Writers should demonstrate "flexible grammarian interface with subject material, self starter creativity, intuitiveness, in-depth detail with minimal use of grammar and immense imagination as well as conceptual visualization."

RHYTHMS PRODUCTIONS, Whitney Bldg., Box 34485, Los Angeles CA 90034. President: R.S. White. "Our audience is generally educational, with current projects in elementary early childhood." Query. "We need to know a writer's background and credits and to see samples of his work." SASE.
Needs: Teacher resource books; phonograph records. "Content is basic to the resource books; educational background is a necessity. For our phonograph records, we accept only fully produced tapes of a professional quality. If tapes are sent, include return postage."

‡DENNIS RIZZUTO ASSOCIATES, 29-30 161st St., Flushing NY 11358. (212)359-5555. President: Ms. Terry Viola. Produces material for industrial, public relations audiences. Buys all rights. SASE. Reports in 1 month.
Needs: Produces 16mm films, multimedia kits, slides, video productions. Query or submit synopsis/outline or completed script, and resume. Pays in outright purchase or on project basis.
Tips: Looks for "a working knowledge of specific AV format."

‡SANDY CORP., 1500 W. Big Beaver Rd., Troy MI 48084. (313)569-0800. Human Resources Executive: Rachel E. Vert. Produces material for sales and technical/automotive audiences. Works with 50 freelance writers. Buys all rights. SASE. Reports in 1 month on queries.
Needs: Articles up to 500 words on how Chevrolet or GMC Truck dealers are doing an outstanding job of selling cars and trucks, servicing cars and trucks, participating in community activities, recognizing employee achievement—can use b&w glossies of story events. Produces various publications (samples on request). Sub-

mit outline/synopsis. Makes outright purchase of $100 minimum.

Tips: "Submit only if you have good relationship with local Chevrolet or GMC Truck dealership and can write copy/take pictures reflecting a professional knowledge of the business."

JIM SANT' ANDREA MIDWEST INC., 875 N. Michigan Ave., Chicago IL 60611. General Manager: W.R. Kaufman. Associate Creative Director: Shirley Shannon. Produces business communications presentations of all kinds. Submit resume. "We like to keep resumes on file." Buys all rights.
Needs: Subject types include business; technical; medical; and general. Produces multimedia, films, slides, videotape and live shows. Pays by project requirements.
Tips: Writers should show "originality, marketing savvy, good grasp of subject matter and be able to work with producer and client well."

SAVE THE CHILDREN, 54 Wilton Rd., Westport CT 06880. (203)226-7272. Producer: Joseph Loya. Generally buys all rights, "but it depends on project. We use work only written for specific assignments." Produces 16mm films, tapes and cassettes, 2¼x2¼ slides and posters and displays.
Needs: General (radio and TV); and education (high school, college and adult). Pays $250-500 minimum/assignment.

SAXTON COMMUNICATIONS GROUP LTD., 605 3rd Ave., New York NY 10016. (212)953-1300. Creative Director: Charles Reich. Produces material for industrial, consumer and sales audiences, AV presentations, meetings. Submit resume. SASE.
Needs: "We work with more than 10 outside writers regularly. We buy copy and scripts for approximately 30 projects/year."

‡SCOTT RESOURCES, INC., Box 2121, Fort Collins CO 80522. (303)484-7445. Director of Sales: Kathleen Steffens. Produces material for public and private school audiences. Works with 3-5 authors/year. Buys all rights. Previously produced material OK. SASE. Reports in 2 weeks. Free catalog.
Needs: "We will be developing audio visual materials for existing rock, fossil and mineral collections." Produces 35mm film loops, silent filmstrips, slides, study prints, tapes and cassettes. Query with samples. Pays 6-12% royalty.

SCREENSCOPE, INC., #204, 3600 M St. NW, Washington DC 20007. (202)965-6900. Vice President for Production: Jim Hristakos. Produces material for schools, industry and libraries. Submit resume. SASE. Reports in 1 month. Buys all rights.
Needs: "For education we need a script which can communicate to many grade levels. Style, format, length, etc. are discussed with producer and client." Produces 16mm and 35mm films and slides. Buys 20 scripts/year. Pays in outright purchase.

‡PETER SIMMONS PRODUCTIONS, 452 Pleasant St., Watertown MA 02192. (617)923-4314. Producer: Adrienne Schure. Produces material for private corporations—their employees, sales people or potential customers. "We produce approximately 25 slide shows and/or films and/or videotapes each year . . . and we're growing." Buys all rights. SASE. Reports in 2 weeks on queries; 1 week on submissions. Free catalog.
Needs: "Our slide shows vary in length from 7 to 25 minutes. Format is generally narration, sometimes interspersed with testimonials from clients, etc. Videotape scripts are more complex, obviously including dialogue. Our clients are a wide variety of companies from the private sector: computer companies, electronics manufacturers, food handlers, colleges." Produces 16mm films, sound filmstrips, slides. Query with samples. Buys in outright purchase.
Tips: "Send us a sample of yor work, then follow up with a phone call. We would prefer writers with a background in the visual media and an ability to write a 'visual' script."

PHOEBE T. SNOW PRODUCTIONS, INC., 240 Madison Ave., New York NY 10016. (212)679-8756. Creative Director: Deborah R. Herr. Produces material for corporate uses, sales force, in-house training, etc. Buys 20-40 scripts/year. Buys all rights. Computer printout submissions OK; prefers letter quality to dot matrix printouts. No disk submissions. SASE. Reports in 2 weeks on queries; 1 month on mss.
Needs: 16mm films, sound filmstrips and slides. Query with samples and resume. Pays in outright purchase.
Tips: "Have some understanding of AV for corporations. This is not the educational field. We're looking for creative writers who work with speed and can take direction. Be aware of short deadlines and some low budgets."

JOE SNYDER & COMPANY LTD., 155 W. 68th St., New York NY 10023. (212)595-5925. Chairman: Joseph H. Snyder. Produces material for corporations, management seminars and employee training. Submit resume. SASE. Reports in 1 month. Buys all rights.
Needs: Subject topics include "education; motivation; management; productivity; speaking and writing.

Produces multimedia kits, tapes and cassettes, and slides. Payment is in accordance with Writers Guild standards.
Tips: Especially interested in "sharpness and clarity."

SOUTH CAROLINA EDUCATIONAL TELEVISION NETWORK, Drawer L, Columbia SC 29250. (803)758-7261. Associate Director for State Agencies: Ms. Sandra V. Pedlow. Produces material for the general public; training and career development for business and industry; college courses; and on-going adult education in fields of medicine and technical education. Query or submit resume. SASE. Reports in 2 weeks. Buys all rights.
Needs: "The Division of Continuing Education works in all media. Since, as a state agency, we work with other state agencies of varying needs, style, format, length, etc. are determined for each individual project." Produces 16mm films, multimedia kits, slides, videotape, live in-studio television productions, teleconferences and related printed materials for training programs. Payment "depends on funding governed by South Carolina state law guidelines."
Tips: "If possible come in for an interview and bring in samples of previous work."

SPENCER PRODUCTIONS, INC., 234 5th Ave., New York NY 10001. (212)697-5895. General Manager: Bruce Spencer. Produces material for high school students, college students and adults. Occasionally uses freelance writers with considerable talent. Query. SASE.
Needs: 16mm films, prerecorded tapes and cassettes. Satirical material only. Pay is negotiable.
Tips: "For a further insight into our philosophy, read *Don't Ged Mad . . . Get Even*, by our executive producer, Alan Abel."

SPOTLIGHT PRESENTS, INC., 20 E. 46th St., New York NY 10017. (212)986-5520. Producer/President: Carmine Santandrea. Produces material for corporate employees, trade association members and the general public. Query with samples and resume. SASE. Reports in 3 weeks. Buys all rights. Free catalog for SASE.
Needs: "We specialize in multi-image productions (3-30 projectors), 5-15 minutes in length. Subject topics: business, corporate image, new product introductions, and general. Frequently need proposals written." Produces sound filmstrips; 16mm and 35mm films; multimedia kits; overhead transparencies; slides and video. "Freelancers supply approximately 20 scripts/year and approximately 60 proposals/year." Pays in outright purchase of $50-$125/running minute.
Tips: "Submit samples indicative of range of writing experience, e.g., proposals, multimedia and film." Writers should show "reliability, thoroughness, creativity and responsiveness to suggestions."

AL STAHL ANIMATED, 1600 Broadway, New York NY 10019. (212)265-2942. President: Al Stahl. Produces industrial, sales promotion, educational and television commercial material. Query. SASE. Buys first rights. Free catalog.
Needs: "We specialize in making movies from slides, and in converting slide shows and multimedia (three or more screens) into a one-screen movie." Produces 8mm and 16mm films, and multimedia kits. Pays by outright purchase.

‡**STARR PHOTO PRODUCTIONS, INC.**, 2727 Ponce de Leon, Coral Gables FL 33134. (305)446-3300. Production Manager: Lucy Morris. Produces material for a corporate audience. Works with 6 writers/year. Buys all rights. "Prefer personal inquiries only."
Needs: Produces slides. Query. Pays $150-15,000 in outright purchase.
Tips: Looks for "professional writers with a track record."

E.J. STEWART, INC., 525 Mildred Ave., Primos PA 19018. (215)626-6500. "Our firm is a television production house providing programming for the broadcast, industrial, educational and medical fields. Government work is also handled." Buys 50 scripts/year. Buys all rights. Computer printout submissions OK. SASE. Reports "when needed."
Needs: "We produce programming for our clients' specific needs. We do not know in advance what our needs will be other than general scripts for commercials and programs depending upon requests that we receive from clients." Videotapes. Submit resume only. Pays in negotiable outright purchase.

TALCO PRODUCTIONS, 279 E. 44th St., New York NY 10017. (212)697-4015. President: Alan Lawrence. Produces for TV, also videotape and films for schools, foundations, industrial organizations and associations. Buys all rights. "We maintain a file of writers and call on those with experience in the general category. We do not accept unsolicited mss. No computer printout or disk submissions. We prefer to receive a writer's resume listing credits. If his background merits, we will be in touch when a project seems right." Produces sound filmstrips, films, videotapes, phonograph records, tapes and cassettes, and slide sets.
Needs: General (client-oriented productions to meet specific needs); education (peripheral market); business (public relations, documentaries, industrial); foreign language (we sometimes dub client's shows for a specific non-English speaking market). Payment runs $500 and up; usually Writers Guild minimums apply.

TEL-AIR INTERESTS, INC., 1755 N.E. 149th St., Miami FL 33181. (305)944-3268. President: Grant H. Gravitt. Produces material for groups and theatrical and TV audiences. Submit resume. SASE. Buys all rights. **Needs:** "Documentary films on education, travel and sports." Produces films and videotape. Pays in outright purchase.

TELSTAR, INC., 366 N. Prior Ave., St. Paul MN 55104. Editor: Dr. Victor Kerns. Produces video material for adult, college-level audience, in industry and continuing education. Buys video recording rights. Query. No computer printout or disk submissions. Produces instructional videotapes not intended for broadcast. **Needs:** Education (curricular materials for small group or independent study); business (training and development material); communication skills. Looks for "the ability to chapterize/pace the instruction." Pays $100 plus royalties.

ROGER TILTON FILMS, INC., 315 6th Ave., San Diego CA 92101. (619)233-6513. Production Manager: Robert T. Hitchcox. Audience "varies with client." Submit resume. SASE. "We do not accept unrequested scripts. We will request samples if a writer is being considered." Reports in 2 weeks. Buys all rights. **Needs:** "Scripts are all on contract basis with specific details supplied by us or our clients. Subjects run full spectrum of topics and audiences." Produces sound filmstrips, 16mm, 35mm and 65mm films and video cassettes. Pays in outright purchase; "depends on project, quoted in advance." **Tips:** Writers must demonstrate "ability to work within the constraints of the client."

TROLL ASSOCIATES, 320 Rt. 17, Mahwah NJ 07430. (201)529-4000. Contact: M. Schecter. Produces material for elementary and high school students. Buys approximately 200 scripts/year. Query or submit outline/synopsis. SASE. Reports in 3 weeks. Buys all rights. Free catalog. **Needs:** Produces silent and sound filmstrips, multimedia kits, tapes and cassettes, and books. Pays royalty or by outright purchase.

TUTOR/TAPE, 107 France St., Toms River NJ 08753. President: Richard R. Gallagher. Produces and publishes cassettes, filmstrips and visual aids including slides and transparencies for the college market. Buys average 5 scripts/yr. "We are the largest publisher of pre-recorded educational cassettes for the college market. We are capable of handling everything from writer to recording to packaging to marketing in a totally vertically integrated production-marketing publishing organization." Computer printout and disk submissions OK. SASE. Reports in 1 week. **Needs:** 10- to 25-page scripts for 15- to 30-minute educational messages on college topics, including business, management, marketing, personnel, advertising, accounting, economics, and other related material. We also seek remedial and study skills material useful to college students and suitable for audio presentation. Send brief synopsis or short outline stating credentials, education or experience. Pays 15% royalty or in outright purchase. **Tips:** "Writers should submit material relevant to students in college who need assistance in passing difficult courses, or interesting material which supplements college textbooks and enhances class work."

UNIVERSITY OF WISCONSIN STOUT TELEPRODUCTION CENTER, 800 S. Broadway, Menomonie WI 54751. (715)232-1649. Director of Instructional Television: David Conyer. Produces "TV material for primary; secondary; post secondary; and general audiences. We produce instructional and public television programs for national, regional and state distribution." Query with resume and samples of TV scripts. Computer printout and disk submissions OK. SASE. Buys all rights. Free catalog. **Needs:** "Our clients fund programs in a 'series' format which tend to be 4-6 programs each." Produces 16mm films for TV. "I need materials from writers who have experience in instructional TV. At present, we are looking for writers who have instructional television writing experience in early childhood and computer instruction. We also have a need for writers in Wisconsin and Minnesota whom we can call on to write one or multi program/series in instructional television." **Recent Productions:** *Let Me See* (award-winning first grade science series); *Out & About* (a kindergarten series). **Tips:** Especially interested in "experience, time commitment to the project, willingness to work with producer/director(s) to meet content committee requests."

VIDEOCOM, INC., 502 Sprague St., Dedham MA 02026. (617)329-4080. President: Clifford Jones. Executive Producer: Karen Clair. Produces materials for broadcast, industrial and educational audiences. Buys 25 scripts/year. Query with samples. Buys all rights. **Needs:** "Scripts and copy for broadcast and industrial clients ranging from commercials to marketing and training programs and printed materials. We look for originality in the ability to understand problems and in the design of a solution." Produces videotape (all formats), films, slide presentations and printed materials. Pays by outright purchase.

VISUAL EDUCATION CORP., Box 2321, Princeton NJ 08540. Vice President: William J. W̶ material for colleges, elementary and high schools. Query with resume, samples, and range of fee̶ sions will not be returned; "we like to keep a file of freelancers on whom we can call." Reports in 1̶ Buys all rights.
Needs: "Most of our audiovisual work is in filmstrips of about 80 frames (10 minutes). Topics range from lan̶ guage arts to social studies and home economics. Editorial developers of college and high school textbooks̶ Need editors and writers with the ability to write clearly to the grade level." Produces textbooks, sound film-strips, films, teacher's guides and student activity material, multimedia kits. Pays variable fee based on the length of chapters assigned.

VISUAL HORIZONS, 180 Metro Park, Rochester NY 14623. (716)424-5300. President: Stanley Feingold. Produces material for general audiences. Buys 50 programs/year. Query with samples. SASE. Reports in 5 months. Free catalog.
Needs: Business, medical and general subjects. Produces silent and sound filmstrips, multimedia kits, slide sets, and videotapes. Payment negotiable.

VOCATIONAL EDUCATION PRODUCTIONS, California Polytechnic State University, San Luis Obispo CA 93407. Contact: Annie Waltz Kubicka. "We specialize in agricultural media." Query. SASE.
Needs: Produces sound filmstrips, multimedia kits, tapes and cassettes, and 35mm slide sets. "We usually fur-nish script development pages for the typing of final drafts, just to make it easier to work with the script. Our productions deal almost exclusively with agricultural subjects. Since we sell around the world, we cannot focus on a limited regional topic. Total length of our filmstrips is about 10 minutes, or 50-70 frames. Avoid talking down to the viewer. Technical accuracy is an absolute must." Pays $300/script for a series of 3-6; $400-600 for a single script.
Recent Productions: The Beef Management Practices Series, Swine Management Series and *Contemporary Floristry*.

ZELMAN STUDIOS LTD., 623 Cortelyou Rd., Brooklyn NY 11218. (212)941-5500. General Manager: Jerry Krone. Produces material for business, education and fundraising audiences. Query with samples and re-sume. SASE. Reports in 1 month. Buys all rights.
Needs: Produces film loops; silent and sound filmstrips; films; tapes and cassettes; and slides. Pays in outright purchase "by agreement, based on talent and turnaround."

Playwriting

Theater in America continues to respond to a diverse audience. And playwrights today have more outlets than ever for their work. Community theaters, university theater departments, radio theater productions, and the blossoming of regional the-ater continue to reaffirm our fascination with watching and listening to life depicted on stage. Regional theater especially—in Louisville, Seattle, Milwaukee, Cambridge and elsewhere—is giving us an honest look at ourselves. Even the houses in New York are taking notice of the original productions coming out of regional theaters.

Despite the healthy state of the dramatic form, many of the individual play-houses listed in this *Writer's Market* tell us they are stretched to their budget limits and must increasingly depend on NEA grants and private funding in order to keep reading and producing original scripts. With that, they have offered playwrights this advice: "Be aware of increasing production costs, especially for small/local theaters that are usually the ones most open to producing new scripts."

Playhouse managers continue to stress involvement with theater if you plan to write for theater. Attend plays at the house you're interested in; watch audience re-action to characters and themes. Know the theater's stage and casting limitations. Enter playwriting competitions. Participate in workshops for the chance to learn from professional criticism.

Some universities offer playwright-in-residence grants. Investigate the options in your area and be willing to travel if necessary. As a beginning playwright *you* must sell your play.

...e marketing of your work. If the theater you're interested in
...nd *Julius Caesar*, it will probably not be receptive to your ex-
...ket your work with an audience in mind.
...udience is essential to the *writing* of your play as well. If you're
...theater, consider your audience very carefully. Don't write
... have real joys, fears and expectations—just like the rest of us.
...at although you're writing for a younger audience, the actors
will ....

Finally, have patience. One rejection slip does not label your writing as unpro-
ducible. Tennessee Williams failed with his play, *Battle of Angels*; in addition, he had
written at least seven full-length plays and many one-acts before his first notable
success, *The Glass Menagerie*.

The closest thing to a playwright's Bible is the *Dramatists Sourcebook* (Theatre
Communications Group, 355 Lexington Ave., New York City 10017). It lists theaters
that consider unsolicited playscripts, festivals and contests, conferences and workshops, and playwriting opportunities in film, radio and video. Two other useful directories are the *Theatre Directory* (Theatre Communications Group) listing nearly 200
professional nonprofit theaters and *New York's Other Theatre: A Guide to Off Off
Broadway* (Off Off Broadway Alliance, Room 206, 162 W. 56th St., New York City
10019) giving information on its 90 member theaters.

‡**ACADEMY THEATRE**, 1137 Peachtree St. NE, Atlanta GA 30309. (404)873-2518. Artistic Director:
Frank Wittow. Produces 10 plays/year. Plays performed in Academy Theatre—415 seats thrust stage, and in
Academy Lab Theatre, 100 seats, flexible stage. Professional productions tour the Southeast for elementary,
high school, college and community audiences. Submit complete ms. "We accept unsolicited, year-round submissions." Computer printout submissions OK. Reports in 4 months. Buys negotiable rights. Pays negotiable
royalty. SASE.
Needs; "Full length plays, one acts, children's plays, adaptations, translations, original plays of contemporary
significance, plays that go beyond the conventions of naturalism; Transformational plays: actors playing multiple roles. Prefer small cast; unit set. Follow standard playwright submission guidelines and standard preparation of script." No sitcom love affairs, triangles; plays with very large casts. Special programs: "Academy
Playwrights Lab is an ongoing program of workshop productions of previously unproduced full length and one
act plays by Southeastern playwrights. Deadline is open. The Atlanta New Play Project is sponsored each June
by the Academy and other local theaters. The project includes staged readings, workshops, full productions as
plays in progress with a forum for discussion of new works. Southeastern playwrights are specifically desired
for this project."

ACTORS THEATRE OF LOUISVILLE, 316 W. Main St., Louisville KY 40202. Producing-Director: Jon
Jory. Actors Theatre of Louisville is a resident professional theater operating under a L.O.R.T. "D" contract
for a 35-week season from September to June. Subscription audience of 18,000 from diverse backgrounds.
"We accept plays of all types and lengths. ATL rarely produces original musicals or children's shows. The theater complex houses 2 stages, a 637-seat thrust stage and a 161-seat three-quarter arena stage. Unsolicited manuscripts are welcomed throughout the year. Each season new plays comprise our fall Shorts festival and the
Humana Festival of New American Plays each spring." Pays negotiable rate. Submit mss (computer printout
submissions OK) with SASE and cover letter to Julie Beckett Crutcher, Literary Manager.

‡**ALASKA REPERTORY THEATRE**, Suite 201, 705 W. 6th Ave., Anchorage AK 99501. (907)276-2327.
Artistic Director: Robert J. Farley. Produces 4-5 plays/year. Professional plays performed for Alaskan audi-
ences. Submit complete ms. Reports in 5 months. Pays 3%+ royalty "depending on work." SASE.
Needs: Produces all types of plays.

ALLEY THEATRE, 615 Texas Ave., Houston TX 77002. A resident professional theater; large stage seating
798; arena stage seating 296.
Needs: "Good plays of no more than 2½ hours in length. Cast restriction of no more than 15 actors. No musicals." Pays variable royalty arrangements. Send complete script. SASE. Reports in 4 months. Produces 6-8
plays/year.
Recent Play Productions: *Red Blue Grass Western Flyer Show*, by Conn Fleming; *If That Mockingbird Don't
Sing*, by William Whitehead; *Paradise*, by Monty Philip Holamon.

Close-up

Julie Jensen, Playwright

According to Julie Jensen, theater people make the best playwrights. "It's a difficult form to master," she says, "and if you're not hanging around plays all the time, you miss it."

Jensen has been hanging around plays both as an actor and a writer since the early 70s. Both her one-act and full-length plays have been performed at colleges; her scripts have won awards in national playwriting competitions and received professional staged readings and productions in New York, Detroit and Los Angeles. She also teaches theater at St. Mary's College in Indiana.

"I've written stories and tried my hand at a novel," she says. "But I write two pages of the story, and then I think 'now they can start talking' and that's the real fun—and of course, it ends up being a play."

Jensen is especially intrigued with black dialect and has written several black plays. Having grown up in rural southern Utah, she also writes "gothic Utah" plays and sees a link between the strong character and struggle for survival of the Utahn and black cultures.

She's also tuned in to the culture of women. "And I write women better than men," she says. Characters are important to Jensen. "I set them up so the audience can understand and predict things about them. Then I throw the characters some sort of curve, and see if they really behave in the way I've set it up. The characters do themselves pretty much, though. You tinker with the pacing and rewrite; but once you have the way they sound and the things they do, they do their own play."

The real key to writing a play, says Jensen, is always to do it differently. "Sometimes you start with a set of images, or a scene. Sometimes a thought like 'wouldn't this be funny?' The trick is

to trick yourself out of yourself, so you don't rewrite your last play. You can't do that, though the temptation is there. You think this was successful before, so it must be the answer. But every time is different, so you have to reinvent the process."

Jensen says a big part of the playwriting process is getting produced. And to do that there's no substitute for *really* understanding and seeing theater in your area and around the country. "You can join the Dramatists Guild and become familiar with the Theatre Communications Group in New York City; but you have to be out there, too."

And when you know what's out there, you have to market yourself. "It means pounding the pavement; it means sending out an inordinate number of manuscripts; it's expensive. It's different from submitting fiction or poetry, because if you're convinced you have something good, you get fifty copies of it and send them out with a bio all at the same time. If you sit around waiting for someone to respond, you'll never get produced. You have to do it in a mass way."

Jensen says there are great rewards in getting a play produced "and seeing what was in your imagination captured on stage exactly the way you wanted. But the most exciting thing in terms of production," she adds, "is not to be associated with the production at all—and then to be surprised at how wonderfully the actors saw it. And that, in fact, they saw things you didn't see."

ALLIANCE THEATRE, 1280 Peachtree St., Atlanta GA 30309. Artistic Director: Fred Chappell. "We are a professional Equity Theater." Produces 16 plays/year for a general audience. Also have season for young audiences. Submit complete ms. No computer printout or disk submissions. Reply in 3-5 months. Buys variable rights. Pays royalty on variable fee/performance. SASE.
Needs: "Full-length; up to 10 cast members, drama, comedy or musical. No situation comedy or dinner theater."

‡**AMERICAN RADIO THEATRE**, Suite 104, 1616 W. Victory Blvd., Glendale CA 91201. (213)246-6584. Story Editor: Dudley Knight. Produces and distributes original radio theater presentations to non-commercial and public radio stations nationwide. "Radio drama for general audience. Anthology programs cover many subjects and genres, occasional mature subjects requiring discretionary listening." Buys 13-26 half-hour scripts. Pays Writers Guild minimum rates. "Writers receive a cassette copy of the produced form of their script. Some material will be selected from the A.R.T. Annual Radio Script Writing Competition." Buys first radio broadcast rights and "right to use script material for educational purposes. We do accept adaptations of public domain material if outstandingly executed. Original material designed for audio medium is preferred." SASE. "Fourth class book rate is no longer acceptable to the post office. Use third class to save money on SASE. A script is not a book." Reports in 6 weeks on queries; 10 weeks on mss. Catalog for business-size SAE and 1 first class stamp.
Needs: "Thirty-minute radio scripts on any subject matter. We encourage minority writers to submit plays on minority problems or situations of interest to a general audience." Query or submit synopsis/outline and resume. Pays in outright purchase and in accordance with Writers Guild standards at the time of purchase."
Tips: "Characters and situations should be believable within the context of the genre selected. Authors are encouraged to use sound effects and to be aware that the plays will be recorded in stereo. Avoid gratuitous violence, sex, frank language, and propaganda which cannot be justified within the context of the characters or which is unessential to the plot. We still receive a lot of stage plays that authors haven't taken the time to convert. Unless they're great we won't bother with them."

‡**AMERICAN REPERTORY THEATRE**, 64 Brattle St., Cambridge MA 02138. (617)495-2678. Artistic Director: Robert Brustein. Produces 6 plays/year. "We produce our main season at the Loeb Drama Center; occasionally we produce other plays elsewhere on the Harvard campus. All productions are professional." Query with synopsis. Reports in 5 months. Buys "exclusive performance rights for a negotiable period of time." Pays 5% maximum royalty. SASE.
Needs: "We produce classics, neglected works from the past, and new plays with a substantial poetic dimension that reflects upon the social, economic, political, philosophical or aesthetic problems of today. We have a permanent professional company of a dozen actors, from which all our productions are cast. No standard Broadway fare, strictly realistic dramas, dramatized anecdotes or biographies."
Tips: "Our theater has a highly individualized aesthetic outlook, so we will not be interested in looking at material that may be perfectly suited to a theater with more eclectic tastes."

AMERICAN STAGE FESTIVAL, Box 225, Milford NH 03055. Artistic Director: Larry Carpenter. "The ASF is a central New England professional theater (professional equity company) with a 3 month summer season (June-August)" for audience of all ages, interests, education and sophistication levels. Query with synopsis. Produces musicals (20%) and nonmusicals (80%) (5 are mainstage and 10 are children's productions); 40% are originals. Royalty option and subsequent amount of gross: optional. SASE. Reports in 3 months.
Needs: "The Festival can do comedies, musicals and dramas. However, the most frequent problems come from plays not fitting into the resident acting company system (all men, all young, for example) and/or that are bolder in language and action than a general mixed audience will accept. We emphasize plays that move; long and philosophical discussion-oriented plays are generally not done. We have a 40 foot proscenium stage with 30 foot wings, but no fly system. Festival plays are chosen to present scale and opportunities for scenic and costume projects far beyond the 'summer theater' type of play. No saga/heavy dramas." Length: Mainstage: 2-3 acts; children's productions: 50 minutes.
Recent Productions: *Artichoke*, by Joanna Glass; and *Almost an Eagle*, by Michael Kimberley.
Tips: Writers could improve submissions with "dramatic action, complexity, subplot and a unique statement. Try to get a staged reading of the script before submitting the play to us. Our audiences prefer plays that deal with human problems presented in a conventional manner."

AMERICAN THEATRE ARTS, 6240 Hollywood Blvd., Dept. W, Hollywood CA 90028. (213)466-2462. Artistic Director: Don Eitner. Produces 9 plays/year. Plays performed in a 99-seat Equity Waiver house for the general public. Submit complete ms. "Submit script sized SASE for return of manuscript. Submit copies only—not original manuscripts. Submit bound copies, not loose pages secured only with paper clips or rubber bands." Reports in 3 months minimum. "If show goes on to full Equity production, percentage arrangement is worked out with author." Pays $100 minimum royalty. SASE.
Needs: No restrictions as to genres, topics, or styles.

ARENA STAGE, 6th and Maine Ave. SW, Washington DC 20024. Wants original plays, solicited or submitted through agents. Otherwise, writers may submit a letter of inquiry with a synopsis of the play. "Plays with relevance to the human situation—which cover a multitude of dramatic approaches—are welcome here." Produces 8 works a year; 15% musicals, 85% non-musicals. 50% are originals. Pays 5% of gross. Query. Computer printout submissions OK, "as long as they are easily readable." Reports in 4 months. SASE.

‡**ART CRAFT PLAY CO.**, Box 1058, Cedar Rapids IA 52406. (319)364-6311. Averages 5-10 plays/year for junior and senior high school. Query or send complete ms. Buys amateur rights. Pays $100-1,000.

ARTS CLUB THEATRE, 1585 Johnston St., Vancouver, British Columbia, Canada V6H 3R9. (604)687-5315. Artistic Director: Bill Millerd. Produces 14 plays/year. Plays performed in 3 theaters seating 500, 200 and 175 respectively, for a diverse adult audience. Stock professional company operating year-round. Tours British Columbia and occasionally goes on national tours. Submit complete ms. Computer printout submissions OK; prefers letter quality to dot matrix printouts. Reports in 2 months. "If interested, we ask for first production plus future rights." Pays 8% royalty, or commission: from $1,000-5,000. SASE or SAE and IRCs.
Needs: Full-length plays for adult audiences. Comedies and plays about concerns of the region. Well-made plays as opposed to experimental; realistic over fantasy. "We are interested in plays that are well-suited to our 200 seat intimate space. Such plays usually are one-set, and have limited number of characters (not more than 8) and have a strong story line."
Recent Production: *Talking Dirty*, by Sherman Snukal ("a sexual satire which takes a close look at the contemporary lifestyles of hip, young sophisticates who inhabit the trendy neighborhoods of Canadian cities.")
Tips: "As a theater that operates in Canada, we are of course more interested in Canadian works. But we are definitely interested in good plays no matter where they are written. We are *not* a theater that only does Canadian work. We are also very interested in original revue material (both musical and non-musical) to suit our new 175-seat Arts Club Revue Theatre."

BAKER'S PLAY PUBLISHING CO., 100 Chauncy St., Boston MA 02111. Editor: John B. Welch. Plays performed by amateur groups, high schools, children's theater, churches and community theater groups. "We are the largest publisher of chancel drama in the world." Submit complete script. Computer printout submissions OK. Publishes 18-25 straight plays; all originals. Pay varies; outright purchase price to split in production fees. SASE. Reports in 2-3 months.
Needs: "One-acts (specifically for competition use). Quality children's theater scripts. Chancel drama for easy staging—voice plays ideal. Long plays only if they have a marketable theme. Include as much stage direction in the script as possible." Emphasis on large female cast desired. No operettas for elementary school production.
Recent Titles: *Love is Murder*, by Tim Kelly; *Jonah and the German Whale*, by Earl Reimer; *That Was No Lady, That Was a Private Eye*, by Dennis Snee; and *Voices From the High School*, by Peter Dee.

BARTER THEATRE, Main St., Abingdon VA 24210. Artistic Director/Producer: Rex Partington.
Needs: "Good plays, particularly comedies." Two or three acts, preferably, but will consider good quality plays of shorter length. Pays 5% royalties. Send complete script. SASE.

‡**BERKELEY STAGE COMPANY**, Box 2327, Berkeley CA 94702-0327. (415)548-4728. Artistic Director: Angela Paton. "Address scripts to Robert MacDougall." Produces 5-10 plays/year. Plays performed for general public at professional (LOA Equity) theater, 1111 Addison St., Berkeley CA. Submit complete ms. Reports in 8 months. Buys "negotiated percentage of future rights." Pays $35-50/performance or negotiable fees. SASE.
Needs: "We prefer small casts and a unit set. No restrictions as to theme or content. Musicals should be accompanied by a cassette tape. No one act plays."
Tips: "We are a small house (110 seats) in a very flexible space. Extravagant plays are not really appropriate."

‡**JAN BRUNGARD**, Box 1452, Haines City FL 33844. (813)422-4042. Artistic Director: N.R. March. Produces 3 plays/year. "We have a 500-seat auditorium for our community theater. We play to a large segment of retired people who are primarily from the Midwest and eastern seaboard." Query with synopsis or submit complete ms. Computer printout submissions OK. No disk submissions. Reports in 3 weeks. Pays $25-50/performance. SASE.
Needs: Comedies and dramas; 2 or 3 acts or 2 or 3 one acts for a one evening bill. "We want plays that deal with the interaction of the older generation and the younger one, or simply with the problems the younger generation has in dealing with life. We are particularly looking for a 'love in the mobile home park' play—one that might deal with a widow and widower and the problems inherent with that type of romance." Prefers one set or simple unit sets. "Not too heavy on the men; no costume or period plays. No political or religious plays. No obscenity beyond a possible 'hell or damn.' Innuendos are fine. No overt sex. Difficult to cast blacks, but we would welcome a play that shows them in roles other than domestics."

Tips: "We have decided to produce 1-2 plays by new writers in a season. A play where old age is presented with humor and dignity, as well as a few tears thrown in would be a sure winner. Frantic comedies are also well accepted (boy meets and loses girl through mix-ups, etc.). Our audience wants a happy ending. If the play has a message, it must be one with hope, not futility. Strong characters with well-defined personality traits (whiner, yeller, nervous, etc.) are popular with both our actors and the audience.''

GERT BUNCHEZ AND ASSOCIATES, INC., 7730 Carondelet, St. Louis MO 63105. President: Gert Bunchez. "We feel that the time is propitious for the return of stories to radio. It is our feeling that it is not necessary to 'bring back' old programs, and that there certainly should be contemporary talent to write mystery, detective, suspense, children's stories, soap operas, etc. We syndicate radio properties to advertisers and stations. Requirements are plays with sustaining lead characters, 5 minutes to 30 minutes in length, suitable for radio reproduction. Disclaimer letter must accompany scripts." SASE.

CASA MANANA MUSICALS, INC., 3101 W. Lancaster, Box 9054, Fort Worth TX 76107. (817)332-9319. Producer/General Manager: Bud Franks. Produces 12 plays/year. "All performances are staged at Casa Manana Theatre, and are community funded." Query. Computer printout submissions OK. No disk submissions. Reports in 2 months. Produces Summer Musicals (uses Equity people only), Theatre for Youth and new plays. Theater-in-the-round or proscenium.
Needs: Scripts of all kinds.

‡**CASSETTE BOOK COMPANY**, Box 7111, Pasadena CA 91109. (213)799-4139. Editor: Lynne Urban. Produces material for all ages. Buys 12-20 mss/year. Buys all rights. Previously produced submissions OK. SASE. Reports in 1 month on queries; 2 months on mss. Free catalog. Writer's guidelines available for SASE.
Needs: "The only mss we buy are romance stories." Query. Pays royalty or in outright purchase.

‡**CENTERSTAGE PRESS, INC.**, Suite B-150, 4638 E. Shea Blvd., Phoenix AZ 85028. (602)996-2982. Editor: Chuck Lakin. Estab. 1982. Publishes 15 musical plays/season. Plays are designed for family viewing. Query with synopsis or send complete ms. SASE. "Although we publish *only* musicals, plays submitted to us need not be fully scored." Reports in 4 weeks on query/synopsis; 2 months on mss. Buys all rights "for a specified period of time as stated in a contract agreement between the Press and the author(s)." Pays 50% royalty; division of royalties between author(s); lyrics and music on a contract by contract basis.
Needs: "Our basic rule for musicals is: There is no basic rule. Many of our plays have running times of an hour to an hour and a half. But there are always exceptions and it depends upon the story, *always*. We do not accept standard children's musicals. Plays can be based upon classics, new interpretations of classic stories, totally original subjects of interest to young people, and basically anything else under the sun. We do not have any limitations on cast, props and staging. But most schools do. An author should keep this in mind when writing. Simplified staging is always popular with us, so that schools or community theaters that *do* have budgets can add to the show what they want to see, rather than what the story demands. We prefer our shows to be in straight narrative form. No complicated flashbacks. Music should be contemporary (no hard rock, please) and the lyrics equally straightforward. Nothing flowery and Reincarnated Shakespeares need not apply." Not interested in modern musicals about Herpes, or organized crime (unless it's a spoof and very light); nothing so heavy that seven-year-olds can't grasp a portion of and nothing so frilly as to bore their parents to tears.

THE CHANGING SCENE THEATER, 1527½ Champa St., Denver CO 80202. Director: Alfred Brooks. Year-round productions in theater space. Cast may be made up of both professional and amateur actors. For public audience; age varies, but mostly youthful, and interested in taking a chance on new and/or experimental works. No limit to subject matter or story themes. Emphasis is on the innovative. "Also, we require that the playwright be present for at least one performance of his work, if not for the entire rehearsal period. We have a small stage area, but are able to convert to round, semi-round or environmental. Prefer to do plays with limited sets and props." 1-act, 2-act and 3-act. Produces 8-10 nonmusicals a year; all are originals. "We do not pay royalties, or sign contracts with playwrights. We function on a performance share basis of payment. Our theater seats 76; the first 50 seats go to the theater, the balance is divided among the participants in the production. The performance share process is based on the entire production run, and not determined by individual performances. We do not copyright our plays." Send complete script. No computer printout or disk submissions. SASE. Reporting time varies; usually several months.
Recent Productions: *The Last Prostitute*, by William Borden (subsequent NY production); *Last Night's Lightning*, by David Erickson (subsequent production at U.C./Irvine); *The Death of Galatea*, by Michael Hulett; and *The Last Slumber Party*, by Laura Shamas.
Tips: "We are experimental: open to young artists who want to test their talents and open to experienced artists who want to test new ideas/explore new techniques. Dare to write 'strange and wonderful' well-thought-out scripts. We want upbeat ones. Consider that we have a small performance area when submitting."

CHELSEA THEATER CENTER, 407 W. 43rd St., Third Floor, New York NY 10036. Artistic Director: Robert Kalfin. Looking for full-length plays "that stretch the bounds of the theater in form and content. No limita-

tion as to size of cast or physical production.'' Pays for a 6-month renewable option for an off-Broadway production. Works 10 months in advance. No unsolicited mss. Essential to submit advance synopsis. SASE.
Recent Productions: *Hijinks!* adapted from Clyde Fitch's *Captain Jinks of the Horse Marines*; *Monsieur Amilcar*, by Yves Jamiaque (emotional bankruptcy of the leisure class); *Dona Rosita*, by Federico Garcia Lorca (withering of the human spirit); and *The Upper Depths*, by David Steven Rapapport.

‡**CHILDREN'S RADIO THEATRE**, #302, 1609 Connecticut Ave. NW, Washington DC 20009. (202)234-4136. Artistic Directors: Joan Bellsey, Doris Indyke, David Thompson, Lee Cioffi. Produces 10 plays/year. ''Children's Radio Theatre produces plays to be broadcast on radio nationwide. The plays are intended for a family listening audience.''
Needs: ''We like to receive a sample script and specific treatments.'' Reports in 3 months. ''Each project is negotiated separately.'' Pays $100-400. ''We produce half-hour radio plays covering a wide range of topics including, fairy tales, folk tales, musicals, adaptations, pop, original, and commissioned plays. We are interested in material targeted for children 5-15. There are character limitations in radio plays—no more then 5 major characters. Contact Children's Radio Theatre before sending *any* material.''

‡**CIRCLE REPERTORY CO.**, 161 Avenue of the Americas, New York NY 10013. (212)691-3210. Literary Manager: Robert Meiksins. Acting Artistic Director: Rod Marriott. Produces 6 mainstage plays; 10 projects in process/year; weekly company readings. Plays performed for Circle Repertory subscribers. Submit complete ms. Computer printout submissions OK. Reports in 12 weeks. Buys ''first right of refusal agreed upon with Artistic Director.'' Pays variable fee. SASE.
Needs: Lyric naturalism, full-lengths, one acts, American plays; plays with relatively small casts.
Tips: ''Open to traditional and experimental writers exploring the human condition.''

‡**CIRCUIT PLAYHOUSE/PLAYHOUSE ON THE SQUARE**, 2121 Madison Ave., Memphis TN 38104. (901)725-0776. Artistic Director: Jackie Nichols. Produces 2 plays/year. Professional plays performed for the Memphis/Mid-South area. Member of the Theatre Communications Group. A play contest is held each fall. Submit complete ms. Reports in 3 months. Buys ''percentage of royalty rights for 2 years.'' Pays $500-1,000 in outright purchase.
Needs: All types; limited to single or unit sets. Cast of 20 or fewer.
Tips: ''Each play is read by three readers through the extended length of time a script is kept. Preference is given to scripts for the southeastern region of the US.''

THE CITADEL THEATRE, 9828-101 A Ave., Edmonton, Alberta, Canada T5J 3C6. (403)426-4811. General Managers: Mr. W.C. Fipke. Produces 17 plays/year. Plays performed on 3 stages: Shoctor (seating 700), Rice (seating 250), Zeidler (seating 240). Fourth stage to open July 1984 seating 750. Staging includes proscenium, thrust, arena. Educational touring company for all ages. Annual audience over 250,000. Submit complete ms. Computer printout submissions OK. Reports in 1 month. Pays 5% royalty. SASE.
Needs: Casts limited to 20 for both musicals and straight plays. ''We will examine each submission on its own merits.''

THE CLEVELAND PLAY HOUSE, Box 1989, Cleveland OH 44106. (216)795-7000. Dramaturg: Peter Sander. Plays performed in professional LORT theater for the general public. ''Ours is a long-standing resident company performing in 3 theaters presenting an eclectic season of commercial plays, musicals, and contemporary and traditional classics with occasional American and world premiers.'' Submit complete script. Produces 8 musicals (12%) and nonmusicals (88%) a year; 25% are originals. Buys stock rights, and sometimes first class options. Payment varies. SASE. Reports in 6 months.
Needs: ''No restrictions. Vulgarity and gratuitous fads are not held in much esteem. Cast size should be small to moderate. Plays intended for arena stages are not appropriate. Musicals should be geared for actors, not singers. One-act plays are rarely performed. Plays of an extremely experimental nature are almost never selected.'' No first drafts; works-in-progress; unfinished manuscripts. Length: 3 acts.

CONTEMPORARY DRAMA SERVICE, Box 457, Downers Grove IL 60515. Editor: Arthur L. Zapel. Plays performed with amateur performers for age level junior high to adult. ''We publish reader's theater and other modern forms of drama.'' Publishes 25-30 plays/year; (80%) 1-act plays, (20%) 3-act plays. Both originals and adaptations. Submit synopsis or complete script. Letter quality computer printout submissions OK. Pays negotiable royalty up to 10%. SASE. Reports in 1 month. Catalog for $1 postage.
Needs: ''We prefer scripts that can be produced in schools or churches where staging materials are limited. In the church field we are looking for chancel drama for presentation at various holidays: Thanksgiving, Mother's Day, Christmas, Easter, etc. School drama materials can be reader's theater adaptations, drama rehearsal scripts, simple dialogues and short action plays. Emphasis on humor. We like a free and easy style. Nothing too formal. We publish elementary material for church school.''
Recent Titles: *Lucky, Lucky Hudson and the 12th Street Gang*, by Tim Kelly (comedy); *A Yankee Hokey Pok-*

ey, by Virginia Meeks (musical); and *How to Make Sunday School Fun for Everyone*, by Evelyn Witter (book).
Tips: "There is very little written for mime performers. We are trying to find more scripts that may be used by specialist performers of all types."

THE CRICKET THEATRE, 528 Hennepin Ave., Minneapolis MN 55403. (612)333-5241. Associate Artistic Director: Sean Michael Dowse. Audiences consist of adults and students. Submit complete ms. Computer printout submissions OK. "Must include SASE." Reports in 7 months. Buys production rights for selected dates. Produces 6 plays, main stage; 5-7 plays, Works-in-Progress; musicals (14%) and nonmusicals (86%) a year; 64% are originals. Produces plays by living American playwrights only. Only full-length plays will be considered for production.
Needs: "There are no content or form restrictions for scripts of the main season. For Works-in-Progress, any kind of a script is welcomed provided there is a spark of a good play in it. Works-in-Progress productions are seminars, readings and staged readings depending on the availability of the playwright. The focus is on the text and not the fully staged, polished performance as with the main season. All Works-in-Progress playwrights are brought to Minneapolis to join in the play's rehearsal and revision process. Works-in-Progress cannot use plays currently under option or that have had full professional productions. Such plays will be considered only for the main season." No children's plays or large Broadway-type musicals. Cast limit: 9.

‡**DALLAS THEATER CENTER**, 3636 Turtle Creek Blvd., Dallas TX 75219. (214)526-8210. Artistic Director: Mary Sue Jones. Produces 4 plays/year; professional plays performed for a regional audience. Submit complete ms. Reports in 6 months. "Standard rights recommendation is 5% for 5 years; but it is negotiable." Pays $25 minimum/performance. SASE.
Needs: "We prefer full length, but there is no specific style or genre. We rarely produce a play with a cast larger than 14 due to the limitations of the space. The stage is small and low and very intimate." No TV situation comedies or dinner theater material. "We appreciate it very much when a script is neatly typed and well bound. The readability of the material is very important."

‡**DENVER CENTER THEATRE COMPANY**, 1050 13th St., Denver CO 80204. (303)893-4200. Artistic Director: Edward Payson Call. Produces 12 plays/year. Professional regional repertory plays (LORT B) performed in the only major regional theater in the Rocky Mountain West. Also, professional tours possible, both regionally and nationally. Submit complete ms. Reports in 2 months. Buys negotiable rights. Pays negotiable royalty. SASE.
Needs: "One act and full length comedies, dramas, musicals, and adaptations. The Denver Center Theatre Company is especially eager to see plays of regional interest."

THE DRAMATIC PUBLISHING CO., 4150 N. Milwaukee Ave., Chicago IL 60641. (312)545-2062. Publishes about 40 new titles/year. "We have a large amateur market (i.e. high schools, colleges, churches, children and community theatres). Will also consider submissions suitable for cable television." Submit complete ms. Computer printout submissions OK. Reports in 6-8 weeks. Buys amateur and stock theatrical rights as well as rights for cable TV. Pays royalty or by outright purchase. SASE.
Needs: "Props, staging, etc. should be simple so that any group could perform it no matter how limited the budget or space. Casts can be any size. Must run at least 30 minutes playing time."
Recent Titles: *Whose Life Is It, Anyway?*, by Brian Clark; *Clumsy Custard Horror Show*, by William Gleason and *Good*, by C.P. Taylor.
Tips: "Risque or objectionable material presented in an abrupt or unsympathetic manner tends to limit acceptability and appeal."

‡**EAST WEST PLAYERS**, 4424 Santa Monica Blvd., Los Angeles CA 90029. (213)660-0366. Artistic Director: Mako. Produces 5-6 plays/year. Professional plays performed in an Equity waiver house for all audiences. Query with synopsis or submit complete ms. Reports in 3 weeks on query and synopsis; 2 months on mss. Buys standard Dramatist's Guild contract rights. Pays $200 in outright purchase or 2-6% of house receipts (ticket prices vary). SASE.
Needs: "We prefer plays dealing with Asian-American themes. The majority of the important roles should be playable by Asian-American actors; our acting company is 98 percent Asian." No fluff, TV sitcom-type material.
Tips: "East West Players was founded by a group of Asian-American actors weary of playing stereotypes in theater and film. Submitting writers should bear this in mind and refrain from wallowing in 'exoticism.' "

ELDRIDGE PUBLISHING CO., Drawer 216, Franklin OH 45005. (513)746-6531. Editor/General Manager: Kay Myerly. Plays performed in high schools and churches; some professional—but most are amateur productions. Publishes plays for all age groups. Publishes 15-20 plays/year; (2%) musicals; 100% originals. Send synopsis or complete script. Buys all rights "unless the author wishes to retain some rights." Pays $100-125 for 1-act plays; $350 for 3-acts. Also royalty contracts for topnotch plays. SASE. Reports in 60 days.

Needs: "We are looking for good straight comedies which will appeal to high school and junior-high age groups. We do not publish anything which can be suggestive. Most of our plays are published with a hanging indentation—2 ems. All stage, scenery and costume plots must be included." No run-of-the-mill plots. Length: 1-acts from 25-30 minutes; 2-acts of around 2 hours; and skits of 10-15 minutes.
Recent Titles: *Don't Rock the Boat*, by Tim Kelly (comedy); *Dickerson for Senate*, by Ev Miller (comedy-drama); and *King Lud*, by Guy Guyon (comedy).

‡**THE EMPTY SPACE**, 919 E. Pike, Seattle WA 98122. (206)325-4379. Artistic Director: M. Burke Walker. Produces 6 plays/year. Professional plays for subscriber base and single ticket Seattle audience. Query with synopsis before sending script. Computer printout submissions OK. Reports in 3 months. LOA Theater. SASE.
Needs: "Other things besides linear, narrative realism; but we are interested in that as well; no restriction on subject matter. Generally we opt for broader, more farcical comedies and harder-edged, uncompromising dramas. We have a flexible stage; no trap-door system and a low ceiling that makes 2-story sets a bit awkward. We like to go places we've never been before." No commercial musicals.

‡**ENCORE THEATRE**, 5170 Cote St. Catherine Rd., Montreal, Quebec, Canada H3W 1M7. (514)737-1738. Artistic Director: Jack Roberts. Produces 5-6 plays/year. Plays performed on a wide studio arena stage in a Jewish cultural center seating 270. The audience is subscription based. Submit complete ms. Reports in 3 months. Buys performance rights in the municipality of Montreal for a minimum of 18 months. Pays 10% royalty. SASE.
Needs: Full-length plays of all genres. No restrictions as to style or topic. No plays requiring more than 7 actors.

SAMUEL FRENCH, INC., 25 W. 45th St., New York NY 10036. Editor: Lawrence Harbison. "We publish 10-15 manuscripts a year from freelancers. We are the world's largest publisher of plays. In addition to publishing plays, we also act as agents in the placement of plays for professional production—eventually in New York (hopefully)." Pays on royalty basis. Submit complete ms (bound). "ALWAYS type your play in the standard, accepted stageplay ms format used by all professional playwrights in the US. If in doubt: send $2 to the attention of Lawrence Harbison for a copy of *Guidelines*. Require a minimum of 2 months to report." SASE.
Needs: "We are willing at all times to read the work of freelancers. As publishers, we prefer simple-to-stage, light, happy romantic comedies or mysteries. If your work does not fall into this category, we would be reading it for consideration for agency representation. No 25-page 'full-length' plays; no children's plays to be performed *by* children; no puppet plays; no adaptations of public domain children's stories; no verse plays; no large-cast historical (costume) plays; no seasonal and/or religious plays; no 'high school' plays; no TV, film or radio scripts; no translations of foreign plays requiring large casts."
Recent Titles: *Beyond Therapy*, by Christopher Durang (Broadway comedy); *Squirrels*, by David Mamet (one-act play); *Squabbles*, by Marshall Karp (light, romantic comedy).

HIPPODROME THEATRE, 25 SE 2nd Pl., Gainesville FL 32601. (904)373-5968. Artistic Co-Director: Kerry McKenney. Produces 17 plays/year (Mainstage, 2nd Stage, Theatre-in-Education, Tour) for subscription audience and tours throughout Florida and the Southeast. Query with synopsis. Computer printout submissions OK. Reports in 4 months. Buys negotiable rights. Pays royalty. SASE.
Needs: One-act or full-length plays with contemporary concerns. No limitations in terms of genre, topic, or style. Cast seldom exceeds 12.
Tips: "Plays submitted by professional recommendation or by agents receive reading priority."

WILLIAM E. HUNT, 801 West End Ave., New York NY 10025. Interested in reading scripts for stock production, off-Broadway and even Broadway production. "Small cast, youth-oriented, meaningful, technically adventuresome; serious, funny, far-out. Must be about people first, ideas second. No political or social tracts." No individual 1-act, anti-black, anti-Semitic, or anti-gay plays. "I do not want 1920, 1930, or 1940 plays disguised as modern by 'modern' language. I do not want plays with 24 characters, plays with 150 costumes, plays about symbols instead of people. I do not want plays which are really movie or TV scripts." Pays royalties on production. Off-Broadway, 5%; on Broadway, 5%, 7½% and 10%, based on gross. No royalty paid if play is selected for a showcase production. Reports in "a few weeks." SASE.
Recent Productions: *Miss Stanwyck Is Still in Hiding*, by Larry Puchall and Reigh Hagen; and *The Wonderful Ice Cream Suit*, by Ray Bradbury.

‡**INVISIBLE THEATRE**, 1400 N. 1st Ave., Tucson AZ 85719. (602)882-9721. Artistic Director: Susan Claassen. Produces 5-7 plays/year. Semi-professional regional theater for liberal, college-educated audiences. Plays performed in 70-100 seat non-equity theater with small production budget. Query with synopsis. Reports in 6 months. Buys non-professional rights. Pays 10% of royalty.
Needs: "Two act plays, generally contemporary, some historical, comedies, drama, small musicals, wide

range of topics. Limited to plays with small casts of 10 or less, strong female roles, simple sets, minimal props." No large musicals, complex set designs, casts larger than 15.

‡**THE LOST IN THE FOG PLAYERS**, Box 673, Mendocino CA 95460. (707)964-9194. Secretary: Stan Barr. Produces material for an adult radio audience. Works with 12 writers/year. Buys negotiable rights. Previously produced submissions OK. Computer printout submissions OK. SASE. Reports in 2 weeks on queries; 1 month on mss.
Needs: Radio drama scripts—24-26 minutes in length. Any subject in good taste for an adult radio listening audience. Submit completed script. Pays negotiable rates plus copy tape of radio drama.
Tips: "Read some old radio drama scripts from the '40s and '50s. Follow a standard format for typing both dialogue and sound effects. Keep a copy of your work."

LUNCHBOX THEATRE, Box 9027, Bow Valley Sq. II, Calgary, Alberta, Canada T2P 2W4. (403)265-4292. Artistic Director: Bartley Bard. Produces 8 plays/year. Professional company performs at lunchtime for downtown workers, shoppers, school groups—everyone. Submit complete ms. Reports in 2 months. Pays $25 and up/performance. Returns scripts once or twice a year. "In the meantime, we mail out letters."
Needs: One-acts only. "Must be 45-50 minutes in length. Emphasis on fast-paced comedies. Small cast plays given more consideration. Generally, *one* set." No 'dead baby' plays, plays containing overt physical violence, 'prairie dramas,' or 'kitchen sink dramas.'

‡**MCCARTER THEATRE COMPANY**, 91 University Place, Princeton NJ 08540. (609)452-6619. Artistic Director: Nagle Jackson. Submit plays to Robert Lanchester. Produces 2 full productions, 6 readings/year. "One play performed on our main stage, a LORT B professional, regional theater; one on our Stage Two, a smaller auditorium; six readings for a small, but extremely loyal and supportive audience." Submit complete ms. Reports in 2 months. Buys negotiable rights. Pays negotiable fees. SASE.
Needs: All genres considered.

MAGIC THEATRE, INC., Bldg. 314, Fort Mason, San Francisco CA 94123. (415)441-8001. General Director: John Lion. Administrative Director: Marcia O'Dea. Dramaturg: Martin Esslin. "Oldest experimental theater in California." For public audience, generally college-educated. General cross-section of the area with an interest in alternative theater. Plays produced in the off Broadway manner. Cast is part Equity, part non-Equity. Produces 8 plays/year. Submit complete ms. SASE.
Needs: "The playwright should have an approach to his writing with a specific intellectual concept in mind or specific theme of social relevance. We don't want to see scripts that would be television or 'B' movies-oriented. 1- or 2-act plays considered. We pay $500 against 5% of gross."
Recent Productions: *Buried Child* and *True West*, by Sam Shepard; *Winterplay* and *Stuck* by Adele Edling Shank; and *The Man Who Killed the Buddha*, by Martin Epstein.

MANHATTAN THEATRE CLUB, 321 E. 73 St., New York NY 10021. Literary Manager: Jonathan Alper. A three-theater performing arts complex classified as Off-Broadway, using professional actors. "We present a wide range of new work, from this country and abroad, to a subscription audience. We want plays about contemporary problems and people. No special requirements. No verse plays or historical dramas or large musicals. Very heavy set shows or multiple detailed sets are out. We prefer shows with casts not more than 15. No skits, but any other length is fine." Payment is negotiable. Query with synopsis. SASE. Reports in 6 months. Produces 10 plays/year.
Recent Productions: *No End of Blame*, by Howard Barker; *Mass Appeal*, by Bill Davis; and *Crimes of the Heart*, by Beth Henley.

TOM MARKUS, Artistic Director, Virginia Museum Theatre, Boulevard and Grove Ave., Richmond VA 23221. For public, well-educated, conservative, adventurous audiences. Professional resident theater. Standard format of presentation. Light comedies, musicals, and dramas with small casts. 2-act and 3-act plays considered. No 1-acts. Payment is negotiable. For a premiere, theater requires share in future income. Produces one new script/year. Send complete script. Reports in 3-5 months. SASE.

MIDWEST PLAYWRIGHTS' PROGRAM, 2301 Franklin Ave., Minneapolis MN 55406. (612)332-7481. Artistic Director: Dale Wasserman. "Each summer, the MPP moves to a different state in the designated 12-state area: North Dakota, South Dakota, Illinois, Indiana, Iowa, Kansas, Michigan, Minnesota, Missouri, Nebraska, Ohio, Wisconsin. It is an extensive two-week workshop focusing on the development of a script and the playwright. The plays are given staged readings at the site of the workshop and an additional reading (some staged, some informal) at a prestigious regional theatre." Submit complete ms—work in progress. Announcements of playwrights in 5 months. Pays $500 stipend; room and board; partial travel. SASE.
Needs: "We are interested in playwrights with talent, ambitions for a professional career in theater, and scripts which could benefit from an intensive developmental process involving professional dramaturgs, directors and

actors. A playwright needs to be affiliated with the Midwest (must be documented if they no longer reside in the Midwest); MPP accepts scripts between Aug. 15 and Nov. 1 of each year. Full lengths and one-acts. No produced materials—"a script which has gone through a similar process which would make our work redundant (O'Neill Conference scripts, for instance)."

BRUCE E. MILLAN/DETROIT REPERTORY THEATRE, 13103 Woodrow Wilson, Detroit MI 48238. (313)868-1347. Artistic Director: Bruce E. Millan. Produces 4-5 plays/year. Plays performed professionally. "Our audience is mixed: 40% black, 60% white; mostly middle class professionals with college backgrounds." Submit complete ms. Reports in 6 months. Pays for production plus $15-25/performance. SASE. **Needs:** "We interracially cast without bloodline or sex distinctions when and where possible." No one-acts or musicals.

MILWAUKEE REPERTORY THEATRE, 929 N. Water St., Milwaukee WI 53202. (414)273-7121. Artistic Director: John Dillon. Produces 10-12 plays/year. Plays performed principally in a 504-seat, three-quarter thrust theater. Submit complete ms. "The best time to submit is in the fall." Reports in 1 month. SASE. **Needs:** "The Milwaukee Repertory Theater has a long tradition of supporting new writers and producing new plays. Our main interest is in straight plays dealing with serious themes. While we're happy to receive plays that have been produced elsewhere, we are particularly interested in working with playwrights, which means that if a playwright would like to do further work on an already-produced script, we would be especially interested. As part of our ongoing commitment to playwrights, we have severalplaywrights-in-residence whose work we produce on a regular basis. Because of budgetary and space limitations, we seldom do musicals."

‡DICK MUELLER/THE FIREHOUSE THEATER, 514 S. 11th St., Omaha NB 68102. (402)346-6009. Artistic Director: Dick Mueller. Produces 7 plays/year.
Needs: "We produce at the Firehouse Dinner Theatre in Omaha. Our interest in new scripts is the hope of finding material that can be proven here at our theater and then go on from here to find its audience." Submit complete ms. Reporting times vary; depends on work load. Buys negotiable rights. Pays $100/week or negotiable rates. SASE.
Tips: "We are a small theater so certainly size and cost is a consideration. Quality is also a consideration. We can't use heavy drama in this theater. We might, however, consider a production if it were a good script and use another theater."

NASHVILLE ACADEMY THEATRE, 724 2nd Ave. S., Nashville TN 37210. (615)254-9103. Artistic Director: Dr. Guy Keeton. Produces both amateur and professional productions in a studio situation and in a 696-seat theater. Age groups performed for are: Kindergarten through 4th grade, 5th grade through 8th, and 9th grade to adult. "We are considered a family theater. Although we select plays for different age groups, we feel that any age should enjoy any play we do on some level. In the past we have produced murder mysteries, Shakespeare, plays of the supernatural, fairy tales, *The Mikado* dance-drama, musical comedy, serious drama, chamber theater, contemporary children's drama—almost anything you can think of." Reports in 2 months. Produces 6 musicals (15%) and nonmusicals (85%) a year; 15% are originals. Buys exclusive performance rights for middle Tennessee, one year prior to and during their production. Pays $10-35/performance. SASE. **Needs:** "We prefer a variety of styles and genres. Length is usually limited to one hour. We are interested in quality new scripts of the old fairy tales for our younger audiences. There is no limit on topics. Interested in musicals also." Wants a richness of language and mood in their productions. No intermissions. Fluid and fast moving. Must have at least some literary merit. No or little obscenity. Cast size: 5-20 players. No limits in staging.

NATIONAL RADIO THEATRE, Suite 502A, 600 N. McClurg Ct., Chicago IL 60611. (312)751-1625. Assistant to Producer: Janice Cooper. Produces material for an adult, well-educated audience. Buys 20-30 scripts/year. Buys first rights. Previously produced material OK. Reports in 1 month on queries; 6 months on mss. SASE.
Needs: "One-hour plays written specifically for radio; topics may vary—however, plots cannot be static (i.e., we do not accept 'dramatic dialogues'); plays must conform to our audience: adult, highly literate." Submit complete script. Pays negotiable rate.

‡THE NEW AMERICAN THEATER, 117 S. Wyman St., Rockford IL 61101. (815)963-9454. Artistic Director: J.R. Sullivan. Produces 6 plays/year. "The New American Theater is a professional resident theater company with a subscription audience. It is located in a predominantly middle class midwestern town with significant minority populations." Submit complete ms. Computer printout submissions OK. No disk submissions. Reports in 3 months. Buys negotiable rights. Pays royalty based on number of performances. SASE. **Needs:** Productions at N.A.T. over the last three years: *Morning's At Seven, Bedroom Farce, The Miser, A Life, Whose Life Is It Anyway, A Man for All Seasons, Wild Oats, Talley's Folly, On Golden Pond, Da, Room*

Service, *Deathtrap*, and more. No limitations "that would affect script submissions." Open to format, etc. No opera.

Tips: "We look for 'well made' plays exploring past and present American and international social themes."

THE NEW PLAYWRIGHTS' THEATRE OF WASHINGTON, 1742 Church St. NW, Washington DC 20036. (202)232-1122. Artistic Director: Harry M. Bagdasian. Literary Manager: Ms. Lloyd Rose. Produces 5 musicals (20%) and straight plays (80%) and 26 readings/year. "Plays are produced in professional productions for general Washington audiences." Submit complete ms, "typed to form, suitably bound." Reports in 6-8 months. "Rights purchased and financial arrangements are individually negotiated." SASE, acknowledgement postcard.

Needs: "All styles, traditional to experimental, straight plays to musicals and music-dramas, revues and cabaret shows, and full-lengths only. No verse plays. Cast: maximum of 12. Staging: performance space adaptable.

THE NEXT MOVE THEATRE, 1 Boylston Pl., Boston MA 02116. (617)423-7588. Producing Director: Steven Warnick. Produces 4-5 plays/year—5-6 adults'. Plays performed for the greater Boston and New England general public. Submit complete ms. No computer printout submissions. "Must be in a tightly bound folder, double spaced with an inserted synopsis listing characters, acts, scenes, etc." Reports in 6 months. Pays .5-5% royalty. SASE.

Needs: Shows for adults ranging from totally improvised musical revues to plays dealing with infertility (*Ashes*), apartheid (*The Blood Knot*), or the situation in Ireland (*Saints and Martyrs*). The company has also written and performed 2 musical revues (*This End Up* and *This End Up: 1980*)—both dealing with modern day issues in Boston and other parts of the country. The Next Move has performed full-lengths and an evening of one-acts (*The Real Inspector Hound* and *A Separate Peace*). And, of the 14 plays produced thus far, over half have been new plays or adaptations." Cast: 10-14 maximum, with possible double-casting.

NORTH LIGHT REPERTORY, 2300 Green Bay Rd., Evanston IL 60201. (312)869-7732. Associate Art Director: Mary F. Monroe. "We are a LORT theater using professional artistic personnel with a season that runs from September through June, located just outside Chicago with a subscription audience. We are committed to producing new plays of high quality rather than pure entertainment or more commercial fare. Audience is college age and over, broad range of socio-economic and religious backgrounds." Query with synopsis. Computer printout submissions OK; prefers letter quality to dot matrix printouts. Reports in 3 months. Produces 5 nonmusicals a year; 50-75% are originals. Rights purchased vary. SASE.

Needs: "New plays of high quality. Plays may vary in genre and topic. Full-length and prefer a cast size of 10 or less with doubling. Though accessibility is an issue, we rate substance as a higher concern for our audience. We have a 298-seat house with a small proscenium/thrust stage allowing for some use of multiple sets but only the suggestion of levels, e.g. a second story home, etc. Our budget and other resources restrict very elaborate staging but we are fortunate to have talented and creative designers. Solely commercial work or dinner theatre material is not appropriate for our audiences. We emphasize work which speaks to the human condition and is often contemporary. Musicals often require larger budgets than we are able to provide and are not favored by us unless their requirements are minimal."

Recent Productions: *The Rear Column*, by Simon Gray; *Les Belles Soeurs*, and *The Impromptu of Outrement*, by Michael Tramblay; *The Promise*, by Aleksei Arbuzov; and *Children*, by A.R. Gurney, Jr.

Tips: "We are most concerned with language and characterization."

ODYSSEY THEATRE ENSEMBLE, 12111 Ohio Ave., Los Angeles CA 90025. (213)826-1626. Artistic Director: Ron Sossi. Produces 12 plays/year. Plays performed in a 3-theater facility. "All three theaters are Equity waiver; Odyssey 1 and 2 each have 99 seats, while Odyssey 3 has 72 seats. We have a subscription audience of 1,800 who subscribe to a six-play season, and are offered a discount on our remaining non-subscription plays. Remaining seats are sold to the general public." Query with synopsis. Reports in 8 months. Buys negotiable rights. Pays 5-7% royalty or $25-35/performance. SASE. "We will *not* return scripts without SASE."

Needs: Full-length plays only with "either an innovative form, or extremely provocative subject matter. We desire more theatrical pieces that explore possibilities of the live theater experience."

‡**OLD GLOBE THEATRE**, Box 2171, San Diego CA 92112. (619)231-1941. Artistic Director: Jack O'Brien. Produces 12 plays/year. "We are a LORT B professional house. Our plays are produced for a single ticket and subscription audience of 250,000, a large cross section of southern California, including visitors from the LA area." Submit complete ms through agent only. Reports in 2 months. Buys negotiable rights. Pays 6-10% royalty. SASE.

Needs: "We are looking for contemporary, realistic, theatrical dramas and comedies and request that all submissions be full-length plays at this time." Prefers smaller cast and single sets, and "to have the playwright submit the play he has written rather than to enforce any limitations. No musicals or large cast historical dramas."

Tips: "Get back to theatricality. I am tired of reading screenplays."

OLD LOG THEATER, Box 250, Excelsior MN 55331. Producer: Don Stolz. Produces 2-act and 3-act plays for "a professional cast. Public audiences, usually adult. Interested in contemporary comedies. No more than 2 sets. Cast not too large." Produces about 14 plays/year. Payment by Dramatists Guild agreement. Send complete script. SASE.

ONE ACT THEATRE COMPANY, 430 Mason St., San Francisco CA 94102. (415)421-6162. Artistic Director: Ric Prindle. Produces 30 plays/year. Professional productions performed for a subscription and community audience—30-40 age group, especially. Reports in 6 weeks. Buys negotiable rights. Pays negotiable rate. SASE.
Needs: "One-act plays only: 60 minutes maximum. Comedy and drama, wide stylistic range. We will consider plays with provocative themes."
Tips: "Don't overwrite. Make sure there is conflict and resolution. Make your characters believable. Create a plot, a genuine problem."

O'NEILL THEATER CENTER'S NATIONAL PLAYWRIGHTS CONFERENCE, Suite 901, 234 W. 44th St., New York NY 10036. (212)382-2790. Artistic Director: Lloyd Richards. Develops staged readings of 12 stage plays, 4 teleplays/year for a general audience. "Our theater is located in Waterford, Connecticut and we operate under an Equity LORT(C) Contract. We have 3 theaters: Barn-250 seats, Amphitheatre-300 seats, Instant Theater-150." Submit complete ms. Decision in approximately 2 months. "We have an option on the script from time of acceptance until one month *after* the four-week summer conference is completed. After that, all rights revert back to the author." Pays $200 stipend plus room, board and transportation. SASE. "Interested writers should send us a self-addressed-stamped envelope and request our updated guidelines. We accept script submissions from September 15-December 1st of each year. Conference takes place during four weeks in July and August each summer."
Needs: "We do staged readings of new American plays. We use modular sets for all plays, minimal lighting, minimal props and no costumes. We do script-in-hand readings with professional actors and directors."

JOSEPH PAPP PRODUCER, New York Shakespeare Festival, 425 Lafayette St., New York NY 10003. (212)598-7100. Literary Manager, Play Department: Morgan Jenness. Interested in full-length plays and musical works. No restrictions as to style, historical period, traditional or experimental forms, etc. New works produced on 5 stages at the Public Theater. Produces about 20 plays/year; 90% are originals. Unsolicited material accepted *only* if recommended by legitimate source in theater, music or other professionally related fields. Standard option and production agreements. Reports in 6 weeks. SASE.

‡PEOPLE'S LIGHT & THEATRE COMPANY, 39 Conestoga Rd., Malvern PA 19355. (215)647-1900. Producing Director: Danny S. Fruchter. Produces 6 full-length, 10-12 one-act plays/year. "LOA Actors' Equity plays are produced in Malvern 30 miles outside Philadelphia in 350-seat main stage and 80-seat second stage. Our audience is mainly suburban, some from Philadelphia. We do a 5 or 6 show subscription season, plus a New Play Festival each summer." Query with synopsis. SASE is a must. Reports in 10 months. Buys "rights to production in our theater, sometimes for local touring." Pays 2-5% royalty.
Needs: "We will produce anything that interests us." Prefers single set, maximum cast of 12 (for full length), fewer for one act. No musicals, mysteries, domestic comedies.

PERFORMANCE PUBLISHING CO., 978 N. McLean Blvd., Elgin IL 60120. Editor: Virginia Butler. "We publish one-, two- and three-act plays and musicals suitable for stock, community, college, high school and children's theater. We're looking for comedies, mysteries, dramas, farces, etc. with modern dialogue and theme. Plays for and about high school students are usually the most remunerative and we publish 50% high school, 15% children's theater and 35% for the balance of the market. The new writer is advised to obtain experience by limiting himself to one-acts until he has been published. We offer a standard royalty contract for amateur, stock, and community theater licensing rights." Publishes 40 plays/year; (15%) musicals and (85%) straight plays. Authors should retain a copy of any script mailed. Computer printout submissions OK. Include SASE. Reports in 3 months.
Needs: "Budgets are limited and production costs are escalating. Sets should be kept simple but innovative."
Recent Titles: *How the West Was Fun*, by James Seay (western comedy/melodrama); *Lindy*, book and lyrics by R. Eugene Jackson, music by David Ellis (country-rock theme); and *Long Live Rock and Roll*, by Cynthia Mercati (nostalgic 50's comedy).
Tips: "Our interest in the new writer and editorial guidance is unique in the field. The new writer needs to read more successful plays and see more to learn technique. Plot structure should be a primary concern."

PIONEER DRAMA SERVICE, 2171 S. Colorado Blvd., Box 22555, Denver CO 80222. (303)759-4297. Publisher: Shubert Fendrich. Plays are performed by high school, junior high and adult groups, colleges, and recreation programs for audiences of all ages. "We are one of the largest full-service play publishers in the country in that we handle straight plays, musicals, children's theater and melodrama." Publishes 15 plays/

year; (40%) musicals and (60%) straight plays. Submit synopsis or complete script. Buys all rights. Pays "usually 10% royalty on copy sales; 50% of production royalty and 50% of subsidiary rights with some limitations on first-time writers." SASE. Reports in 30-60 days.

Needs: "We are looking for adaptations of great works in the public domain or plays on subjects of current interest. We use the standard 1-act and 3-act format, 2-act musicals, melodrama in all lengths and plays for children's theater (plays to be done by adult actors for children)." Length: 1-acts of 30-45 minutes; 2-act musicals and 3-act comedies from 90 minutes to 2 hours; and children's theater of 1 hour. No "heavily domestic comedy or drama, simplistic children's plays, shows with multiple sets or that hang heavily on special effects, plays with a primarily male cast, highly experimental works, or plays which lean strongly on profanity or sexual overtones."

Recent Titles: *Hospital*, by Tim Kelly (comedy); *One Day at a Time* (based on episodes from the Embassy Television series), adapted by Shubert Fendrich; *Lovesong*, by Robert Lehan (one act).

PLAYERS PRESS, INC., Box 1132, Studio City CA 91604. Senior Editor: Robert W. Gordon. "We deal in all areas and handle works for film, television as well as theater. But all works must be in stage play format for publication." Submit complete ms. No computer printout or disk submissions. "Must have SASE or play will not be returned. All submissions must have been produced and should include a flyer and/or program with dates of performance." Reports in 3 months. Buys negotiable rights. "We prefer all area rights." Pays variable royalty "according to area; approximately 10-75% of gross receipts." Also pays in outright purchase of $100-25,000 or $5-5,000/performance.

Needs: "We prefer comedies, musicals, and children's theater, but are open to all genres. We will rework the ms after acceptance. We are interested in the quality, not the format."

Recent Titles: *A Matter of Degree*, by Anson Campbell; and *The Berringsford Experiment*, by Marvin R. Wilson, Jr.

PLAYS, The Drama Magazine for Young People, 8 Arlington St., Boston MA 02116. Editor: Sylvia K. Burack. Publishes approximately 80 1-act plays each season to be performed by junior and senior high, middle grades, lower grades. Can use comedies, farces, melodramas, skits, mysteries and dramas, plays for holidays and other special occasions, such as Book Week; adaptations of classic stories and fables; historical plays; plays about other lands; puppet plays; folk and fairy tales; creative dramatics; and plays for conservation, ecology or human rights programs. Mss should follow the general style of *Plays*. Stage directions should not be typed in capital letters or underlined. No incorrect grammar or dialect. Characters with physical defects or speech impediments should not be included. Desired lengths for mss are: Junior and Senior high—20 double spaced ms pages (25 to 30 minutes playing time). Middle Grades—12 to 15 pages (25 to 20 minutes playing time). Lower Grades—6 to 10 pages (8 to 15 minutes playing time). Pays "good rates on acceptance." Reports in 2-3 weeks. SASE. "Manuscript specification sheet sent on request."

‡PLAYWRIGHTS' PLATFORM, INC., 355 Boylston St., Boston MA 02116. (617)267-6180. Artistic Director: David Moore, Jr. Produces 30 plays/season. "Selected scripts are developed through cold, rehearsed, and staged reading, as well as no-frills productions. All activities professional. Audiences general and professional." Indicate with synopsis if Massachusetts or New England writer; submit complete ms if Massachusetts writer. Reports in 3 months. Program credit given only (in case of eventual fall production or publication). Playwright honoraria *average* $20 for script program.

Needs: May work with all new playwriting talent. Seeking new voices, unusual visions. "Emphasis is on high textual/performance value." Readings and workshops employ minimal props, costumes, lights, sets.

Tips: "Playwrights of real promise afforded access to first-class directors and actors with considerable dramaturgical support available. Theatrical characters and events are *not* ultimately 'real', but rather of extraordinary human circumstance and values."

‡PRINCETON LOVE ROMANCES, 685 Rt. 202, Morristown NJ 07960. (201)539-6990. Editor: Marjorie Meacham. Estab. 1982. Produces material for women who are currently enjoying romantic fiction novels and true romance stories. "We are looking for at least 200 fiction stories per year, and at least as many true stories." Buys all rights. "We will consider reprints, condensations." Previously produced material OK. SASE. Reports in 2 weeks on queries; 6 weeks on submissions. Free catalog.

Needs: "We produce 60 minute cassettes to be played on an ordinary tape recorder/player. These stories will either be true love or fiction stories." Produces audio tapes and cassettes. Submit completed script. "Request writer's guidelines first (free); then submit completed work." Pays $250 in outright purchase. "We generally purchase a writer's first submission for a flat $250. Thereafter, our price becomes negotiable."

Tips: "Study our guidelines thoroughly before submitting." Writer must have "ability to make the story come alive when *spoken*. We believe that women's entertainment fiction will become increasingly sensual, and expect to be near the front of this trend."

‡RAFT THEATRE, 432 W. 42nd St., New York NY 10036. (212)947-8389. Artistic Director: Martin Zurla. Produces 10 plays/year. Plays performed are professional: showcase (AEA), with mini-contract, Off-Broadway; intended for general audiences. Submit complete ms. Computer printout submissions OK. Reports in 2 months. Pays on year option and royalty (on individual basis).

Needs: "We have *no* restrictions on content, theme, style or length. Prefer scripts that have six or *fewer* characters and limited set and scene changes (due to performing space); and scripts that are typed in professional play-script format (theme, structure, format, etc.)."

Tips: "We are looking for writers tht respect their craft and present their work in like manner. We prefer works that set their own trends and not those that follow other trends. We normally look for scripts that deal with human issues and cover a wide scope and audience, and not the so-called commercial property."

READ MAGAZINE, 245 Long Hill Rd., Middletown CT 06457. (203)347-7251. Editor: Edwin A. Hoey. 10% freelance written. For junior high school students. Biweekly magazine; 32 pages. Circ. 500,000. Rights purchased vary with author and material. May buy second serial (reprint) rights or all rights. Byline given. Buys 10 mss/year. Pays on publication. Free sample copy and writer's guidelines. Will consider photocopied submissions. No simultaneous submissions. Reports in 6 weeks. Submit complete ms. SASE.

Drama and Fiction: First emphasis is on plays; second on fiction with suspense, adventure, or teenage identification themes. "No preachy material. Plays should have 12 to 15 parts and not require complicated stage directions, for they'll be used mainly for reading aloud in class. Remember that we try to be educational as well as entertaining." No kid detective stories or plays. No obscenity. Pays $50 minimum.

‡RECORDED BOOKS, Box 79, Charlotte Hall MD 20622. (301)868-7856. Manager: Sandy Spencer. Produces material for a general reading public. Produces 3-4 cassette books/month. Buys recording rights only on a royalty basis, usually through agents or publishers. Previously produced material OK if previously unproduced in audio form. SASE. Reports in 2 weeks on queries; 6 weeks on submissions. Free catalog for "booklet-size" SAE and 71¢ postage.

Needs: "All recordings are made from unabridged material, usually fiction or general interest (history, biography, firsthand narratives). Produces audio tapes and cassettes. Query. Pays 10% maximum royalty.

SEATTLE REPERTORY THEATRE, Seattle Center, Box B, Seattle WA 98109. (206)447-4730. "The Seattle Repertory Theatre is currently looking for new, unproduced plays for its main stage and for its New Plays in Process Project. Playwrights should send a professional resume, plot synopsis and several pages of dialogue to Alison Harris, Literary Manager."

SHAW FESTIVAL CANADA, Box 774, Niagara-on-the-Lake, Ontario, Canada L0S 1J0. Artistic Director: Christopher Newton. Produces 8 plays/year. "Professional summer festival operating three theaters (Festival: 845 seats, Court House: 370 seats and Royal George: 250 seats). We also host some music and some winter rentals. Mandate is based on the works of G.B. Shaw and his contemporaries." Submit complete ms. Reports in 3 months. "We prefer to hold rights for Canada and northeastern US, also potential to tour." Pays 5-6% royalty. SASE or SAE and IRCs.

Needs: "In addition to mandate above, we are expanding into operettas in the period. Modern work that has connection of theme and/or setting to the period (late 19th to mid-20th century). We operate a repertory company of up to 65 actors, and have sophisticated production facilities."

‡SOHO REPERTORY THEATRE, 19 Mercer St., New York NY 10013. (212)925-2588. Co-Artistic Directors: Jerry Engelbach and Marlene Swartz. Produces 4-10 full productions and 8-10 staged readings/year. Plays performed off-off-Broadway. "The audience is well-educated, mature, and composed of regular theatergoers." Query with synopsis. "We prefer that queries/synopses be submitted by a director interested in staging the play, but will accept author queries, too." Computer printout submissions OK. Reports in 6 weeks. Rights for full-length plays: percentage of author's royalties on future earnings, credit in published script and on future programs; for staged readings: none. Pays up to $200 for limited run performance rights. Pays $500 for future right to option. SASE.

Needs: "Unusual plays not likely to be seen elsewhere; including rarely produced classics; revivals of superior modern works; new plays that utilize contemporary theater techniques; and musicals and mixed media pieces that are noncommercial. Writers should keep in mind that our stage is a thrust, not a proscenium." Desires "full-length works that are physical, three-dimensional, and that use heightened language, are witty and sophisticated, and that demonstrate a high quality of dramatic craft. No sitcoms, featherweight pieces for featherbrained audiences, drawing room plays, pedantic political pieces, works that do not require the audience to think, or pieces more suited to television or the printed page than to the live stage."

Tips: "Most of the plays submitted to us are too conventional. Look us up in the Theatre Communications Group's *Theatre Profiles* to see what kind of work we have done, and use the most unusual productions as a guideline. The most interesting contemporary theater pieces are stylistically eclectic and very active. Dialogue is terse and direct. Sets are rarely realistic. The audience's imagination is constantly challenged, and they leave the theater feeling that they've had a physical, as well as intellectual/aesthetic, experience. Such works are rare, which is why we reject a thousand scripts for each one we produce."

SOUTHEASTERN ACADEMY OF THEATRE AND MUSIC, DBA ACADEMY THEATRE, 581 Peachtree St. NE., Atlanta GA 30308. (404)873-2518. Artistic Director: Frank Wittow. Produces 10-16 plays/year. Plays performed on a professional mainstage for the Academy's Theatre for Youth and Children's Theatre, and for the Academy's School of Performing Arts lab theater. Query with synopsis or agented submissions. Reports in 6 months. Buys "usually sole and exclusive right to produce play within a 100-mile radius of the metro Atlanta area for up to 3 years." Pays 5% royalty or $5-100/performance. SASE.
Needs: "Full-length, small cast shows which provide interesting challenges for actors. Plays which deal with new approaches to naturalism, transformational plays. One-acts considered for lab theater (minimal royalty)." Cast: 12 maximum. Minimal or simple sets. "Deal with basic, honest emotions. Delve into social issues in a subtle manner. Provide thought-provoking material which deals with the human condition and allows for greater self-awareness." No musicals/revues or frivolous, light comedies.
Tips: "The Academy Theatre is devoted to exploring human behavior, through physical and emotional involvement, for the purpose of greater self-awareness, for the purpose of making people more social, more able to live with each other."

STAGE ONE: The Louisville Children's Theatre, 2117 Payne St., Louisville KY 40206. (502)895-9486. Producing Director: Moses Goldberg. Produces 6-7 plays/year. Plays performed by an Equity company for young audiences aged 4-18; usually does different plays for different age groups within that range. Submit complete ms. Computer printout submission OK; disks OK if on 8" dual density. Reports in 4 months. Pays negotiable royalty or $15-50/performance. SASE.
Needs: "Good plays for young audiences of all types: adventure, fantasy, realism, serious problem plays about growing up or family entertainment. Maximum running time is 90 minutes." Cast: 10 maximum. "Honest, visual potentiality, worthwhile story and characters are necessary. An awareness of children and their schooling is a plus." No "campy material or anything condescending to children. No musicals unless they are fairly limited in orchestration."

STAGE WEST EDMONTON, 16615 109th Ave., Edmonton, Alberta, Canada T5P 4K8. (403)484-0841. Director of Production: William Fisher. Produces 6 plays/year. Plays performed in dinner theater. Submit complete ms. No computer printout or disk submissions. Reports in 2 months. Pays 6% royalty. SASE or SAE and IRCs.
Needs: Comedies, musical comedies, mystery-thrillers. Cast: 9 maximum. Stage lights: 52. About 100 minutes playing time: preferably 3 acts. "No commentary or political plays, unless in a humorous vein."

CHARLES STILWILL, Managing Director, Community Playhouse, Box 433, Waterloo IA 50704. (319)235-0367. Plays performed at Waterloo Community Playhouse with a volunteer cast. "We are one of few community theaters with a commitment to new scripts. We do at least one a year. We are the largest community theater per capita in the country." We have 5,000 season members. Average attendance at main stage shows is 5,600; at studio shows 2,240. We try to fit the play to the theater. We do a wide variety of plays. Looking for good plays with more roles for women than men. Our public isn't going to accept nudity, too much sex, too much strong language. We don't have enough black actors to do all-black shows. We have done plays with as few as 2 characters, and as many as 61." Produces 14 plays; 1-3 musicals and 7-11 nonmusicals a year; 1-4 originals. "On the main stage we usually pay between $300 and $500. In our studio we usually pay between $50 and $300. We are now also producing children's theater. We are looking for good adaptations of name children's shows and very good shows for about 15 kids (10-14 year-olds) that don't necessarily have a name. We produce children's theater with both adult and child actors." Send synopsis or complete script. SASE. "Reports negatively within 10 months, but acceptance takes longer because we try to fit a wanted script into the balanced season."
Recent Productions: *Johnny Blue, How do You do?*, by Jean Klein (communication between generations); *A Servant's Christmas*, by John Fenn (young Jewish girl servant in a Christian household); a new version of *Hansel and Gretl*, by Pat Stilwill.

‡**THEATER OF THE OPEN EYE**, 316 E. 88th St., New York NY 10028. (212)534-6363. Artistic Director: Jean Erdman. Produces 3 plays/year. "The Open Eye is a professional, Equity, 99-seat, off-off Broadway theater. Our audiences include a broad spectrum of ages and backgrounds." Query with synopsis or submit complete ms with SASE. Reports in 2 months. "Plays originally produced at the Theater of the Open Eye mentioned in program of subsequent productions. We retain all rights for 6 months after production at the Open Eye." Pays $300-500 in outright purchase. SASE.
Needs: "The Open Eye looks for plays that stretch the boundaries of theatrical convention, especially those incorporating music, dance, mime or masks. 'Total theater' pieces. Plays written to outside specifications rather than out of the playwright's own experiences are rarely exciting theater. We tend to avoid casts larger than ten and have a limited scenic budget." No "family" dramas, sitcoms, children's theater, "straight" musicals. "Plans for the next three years call for an increased emphasis on developmental works, new plays, and unique forms—while continuing a commitment to dance and total theater."

25TH STREET THEATRE, Box 542, Saskatoon, Saskatchewan, Canada S7K 3L6. Artistic Directors: Andras Tahn, Layne Coleman, Linda Griffiths. Produces 7 plays/year. At least 7 new Canadian plays produced/premiered per season running from September to May. "These are full mainstage professional productions serving a subscription (season ticket) audience of 2,000 per show. Theater also mounts one major tour of Saskatchewan per season." Submit complete ms. Reports in 6 weeks. Buys first professional production rights with an option to tour the play and first refusal rights on remounts in the Saskatchewan region to be held for 2 years. Pays 10% of gross; buys some scripts outright for $500-1,500 "depending on whether writer is established or new." SASE or SAE and IRCs.

Needs: "Our objective is to produce new plays by new writers with special emphasis on Canadian work. Anything worthy will be produced but only the best new work finds its way onto the mainstage." Prefers to do small cast plays due to budget restrictions. No badly written plays or plays with no writer behind them.

Tips: "In Canada the trend is toward openness! Anything goes. The theater is hungry for new solid professional work. The audiences are becoming more demanding; plays have to be able to compete on the international market."

Screenwriting

It's a heady thought to dream of writing for the television or motion picture screen. It's the talented and the persevering who make it happen. Playwriting and educational/industrial scriptwriting opportunities are available for beginners at local levels. But TV and film markets aren't as accessible. For writers without a Los Angeles connection, the chances for breaking in to the field are slim.

There may be additional opportunities for scriptwriters with the continuing growth of the cable TV market—local cable systems hover just under the 5,000 mark; nearly 50 cable services currently originate cable programming. The concept of cable is that viewers should be able to watch what they want to watch when they want to watch it. This is reflected in the specialty networks entering the market—business, health, religion, entertainment and other special interests are being attended to. In addition, some cable systems produce local programs along with the national networks (CNN, ESPN, etc.) they carry. The ability of viewers and the cable industry itself to accommodate and sustain the sheer volume of material will determine how many networks will survive.

It is unclear, yet, just how big the cable market will be for freelance scriptwriters. It may be that much already-produced material will be used. Keep in touch with industry trends in the business pages of the *New York Times* and the weekly arts tabloid, *Variety*.

Production companies interested in receiving scripts for cable TV are identified with an asterisk to the left of the listing. Sometimes these local independent producers feed a particular cable network by doing scripts for which the network itself has neither facility nor equipment. Many of these markets are interested in how-to and educational programming.

But the largest number of independent producers per square mile is located in Los Angeles. If you have some other writing credits, you might want to approach these people. It's a good idea to register your script with the Writers Guild of America (8955 Beverly Blvd., Los Angeles 90048, or 555 W. 57th St., New York City 10019) prior to submitting it. Often ideas, rather than entire scripts, are sold to networks or producers—so don't be surprised if *your* dialogue doesn't make it to the screen.

Some producers seek only scripts submitted through agents. (See the Authors' Agents section in the Appendix for more information.) For a compendium of screenwriting information that includes a guide to literary agents, producers and directors, consult the *1983 Scriptwriter's Market* (Joshua Publishing Co., Suite 306, 8033 Sunset Blvd., Hollywood CA 90046).

Format for the screenplay calls for a typed, single-spaced (triple-spaced between the dialogue of different characters) manuscript. Set margins at 15 and 75 (pica)—18 and 90 (elite) and allow 125-150 pages for a two-hour feature film (90 pages for 90 minutes).

A good screenplay avoids stereotypes and cliches. It features originality and a solid story idea. It proves the writer can handle characterization, dialogue, plot construction, conflict and resolution.

For more information on writing for television, consult *The TV Scriptwriter's Handbook*, by Alfred Brenner (Writer's Digest Books).

‡**BEST FILM & VIDEO CORP.**, Suite 462, 98 Cutter Mill Rd., Great Neck NY 11021. (516)487-4515. President: Roy Winnick. Produces material for a general audience. Number of scripts and writers varies/year. Buys negotiable rights. Previously produced material OK. SASE. Reports in 1 month. "Produce, develop, program and distribute full spectrum series and one-time shows on any subject." TV programs. Submit resume and 1-2 page treatment or development. Pays royalty.

‡*CENTERPOINT PRODUCTIONS**, Suite 455, 3575 Cahuenga Blvd. W., Los Angeles CA 90068. (213)850-1250. Director of Movies and Mini-Series: Carla Kettner. Produces material for network television and cable networks. "We option approximately 50 pieces of material annually." Buys all rights. Previously produced material OK. SASE. Reports in 3 weeks on queries; 2 months on submissions.
Needs: Network-acceptable material. Produces films for movies of the week and TV series; tapes for cable shows—concerts, cable network shows. Submit synopsis/outline or completed scripts and resume. Pays in accordance with Writers Guild standards.
Tips: "If in the Los Angeles area, call first. If you don't have an agent, you will have to sign a release form which we can send to you or you can sign if you drop off your script." Looks for talent.

*CHRISTIAN BROADCASTING NETWORK**, Virginia Beach VA 23463. (804)424-7777. Director of Program Development: David Freyss. Produces material for a general mass audience as well as Christian audiences. Second largest cable network in the nation. Producer of *Another Life* and *700 Club*. "We are planning over 12 different programs: some one-shot, some series, women's programs, dramas based on Bible characters, and holiday shows. Mostly staff-written but will consider freelance treatments." Buys negotiable rights. Previously produced material OK. Send to Tom Rogeberg, Director of Operations, CBN Cable Network. SASE. Reports in 2 weeks.
Needs: Secular and Christian. Dramatic, service, educational, children's, feature films, informational shows, film adaptations of books. Query and request release form to submit an idea or script. Buys some ideas outright; flat fee for treatment, outline or script.
Tips: "We're looking for writers with strong television/film background who have screenwriting experience. A basic belief in the Bible is necessary."

CINE/DESIGN FILMS, INC., 255 Washington St., Denver CO 80203. (303)777-4222. Producer/Director: Jon Husband. Produces educational material for general, sales training and theatrical audiences. Buys 8-10 scripts/year. Phone query OK: "original solid ideas are encouraged." Computer printout submissions OK. Rights purchased vary.
Needs: "Motion picture outlines in the theatrical, documentary, sales or educational areas. We are seeking theatrical scripts in the low-budget area that are possible to produce for under $1,500,000. We seek flexibility and personalities who can work well with our clients." Produces 16mm and 35mm films. Pays $100-200/screen minute on 16mm productions. Theatrical scripts negotiable.
Tips: "Understand the marketing needs of film production today."

CINETUDES, 295 W. 4th St., New York NY 10014. (212)966-4600. President: Christine Jurzykowski. Produces material for TV. Works with 20 writers/year. Query with samples or submit resume. SASE. Reports in 2 weeks. Buys all rights.
Needs: Feature length screenplays (theatrical/TV); theatrical shorts; children's programming. "We look for the willingness to listen, and past experience in visual writing." Produces 16mm and 35mm films and videotape. Pays by outright purchase, or pays daily rates.

CONCORDIA PUBLISHING HOUSE, Product Development Division, 3558 S. Jefferson Ave., St. Louis MO 63118. (314)664-7000. Produces religious material for preschool through adult audiences, for institutional and home use. "Writer must have demonstrated skills in writing producible material for print and the audio and visual fields. Competence in the content area is necessary. Initial query is preferred in view of existing production commitments and necessity to maintain a satisfactory product mix. Do not send completed manuscripts or multiple submissions." SASE.
Needs: Manuscripts and scripts for educational and religious subjects. "The content areas relate to the requirements of religious and moral guidance instruction. The emphasis may be curricular, quasi-curricular or enriching." Produces books, silent and sound filmstrips, 16mm films, multimedia kits, overhead transparencies,

phonograph records, tapes and cassettes, 35mm slides and study prints. "Most writers are paid on a royalty basis."
Tips: "Send a prospectus of project to be evaluated as to producibility, market, etc."

PIERRE COSSETTE CO., 8899 Beverly Blvd., Los Angeles CA 90048. (213)278-3366. Writers worked with "varies from year to year." Rights purchased "depends on situation." Previously produced material OK. SASE. Reports on queries.
Needs: TV. "Mostly, scripts are handled through agents. Query first; then if we're interested, we will ask for a submission." Pay "depends on situation."

DILLY INTERNATIONAL PRODUCTIONS, (formerly Murdock Productions), Vernon Manor Hotel, Cincinnati OH 45219. (513)281-5900. Contact: Dilly Segal. Estab. 1981. Produces material for a general TV audience. Buys all rights. Reports "immediately or takes option."
Needs: Magazine-format shows—visually interesting. "You must know the structure of TV scripting. Take college courses to learn before submitting." Submit treatment. Pays negotiable royalty; buys some scripts outright for a negotiable rate; "guaranteed deal for a series."
Tips: "There is not much money in writing for cable TV now, but in a couple of years there will be."

WALT DISNEY PRODUCTIONS, 500 S. Buena Vista St., Burbank CA 91521. (213)840-1000. Director of Creative Affairs: David Ehrman. Produces material for an audience of children through adults. Buys 20 scripts/year. Buys all rights. SASE. Reports in 2 weeks on queries; 1 month on submissions.
Needs: Screenplays, teleplays, treatments, outlines, fantasies, high adventure, optimistic dramas and comedies. 35mm films and TV. Query. Pays in accordance with Writers Guild standards.
Tips: "Outside submissions must ordinarily come through an accredited literary agent of the Writers Guild of America. Disney will only entertain G- or PG-rated material. We look for strong characters, an unusual storyline and strong dialogue. A good many scripts suffer from episodic story construction. In other words the writer tells the story in a 'and then they did this' fashion. Characters sometimes tend to be cardboard or stereotypes. Writers should strive for original tales or perhaps a new variation on an old theme."

ECHO FILM PRODUCTIONS, INC., Suite 200, 413 W. Idaho St., Boise ID 83702. (208)336-0349. Producer: Tyler Nelson. Produces material for "local TV audiences, national TV audiences concerned with the environment, national and worldwide audiences concerned with sports and action film documentaries." Buys 2-6 scripts/year. Query. SASE. Reports in 1 week. Buys all rights.
Needs: "We're seeking theatrical and entertainment scripts oriented toward the West, sports and environment/wildlife." Avoid "overwriting and flowery wording." Produces 16mm films. Pays negotiable rate.

*ETERNAL WORD TELEVISION NETWORK, 5817 Old Leeds Rd., Birmingham AL 35210. (205)956-9537. Director of Programming: Virginia Dominick. Estab. 1981. Produces material with a Catholic focus on everyday living. "Spiritual growth network which airs 2 hours Catholic and 2 hours family entertainment nightly. This network does not solicit funds on the air. Support comes from donations. Founded by Mother Angelica who has an active book ministry." SASE. Reports in 4 months.
Needs: "We would like to see scripts in all forms and formats: drama, talk shows, panel discussions and original ideas." Half-hour programs or specials for cable television with uplifting, inspirational themes. Submit synopsis/outline of script. "May hold the script for up to 1 year."
Tips: "We want scripts that promote strong social values, or with religious themes."

*FACET COMMUNICATIONS, 1223 Central Pkwy., Cincinnati OH 45214. (513)381-4033. Contact: Georgia Mathis. Estab. 1981. Produces material for a general TV audience. Works with variable number of writers/year. SASE. Computer printout submissions OK. Reports in 3 weeks.
Needs: "We're considering 30- and 60-minute program ideas for single showing and series on how-to and educational topics. If pilot is to be produced, writers will be put under contract, then paid after program is sold—possibly 1 year later." Submit proposal including concept, time frame, frequency, probable audience and background research. Pays set amount plus percentage of profits.

*FILMCREATIONS, INC., 6627 Kentucky Dr., West Jordan UT 84084. (801)969-5798. Producer/Director: Robert N. Hatch. Produces material for TV—commercial, cable and public and educational. Works with 2-4 writers/year. Submit synopsis/outline or complete script. SASE. Reports in 2 months. Buys all or first rights.
Needs: "Material should be suitable for television special or pilot programming, or suitable for public television or educational film release. Drama is preferable." Produces 16mm films. Buys scripts outright for $500-10,000. "All material is purchased on a submission basis."
Tips: "Strong emphasis is given to material of a dramatic nature, in which central conflict and rich characterizations are prominent. For educational release, the subject matter must be didactic."

Close-up

Virginia Dominick
Producer & Programming Director
Eternal Word Television Network

According to Virginia Dominick, producer and programming director of the Eternal Word Television Network, Catholic programming on a national level came to a halt when Bishop Sheen died. "There was a need for the Church to respond to 51 million Catholics in the United States."

Enter EWTN. Begun by Mother Angelica as a production house for religious programming, the faith ministry has grown to be *the* Catholic cable network. It airs two hours of Catholic and two hours of family entertainment nightly. "We serve both as an informative tool for those interested in learning why Catholics believe what they believe, and as an alternative for people concerned about crummy television programming," says Dominick, who comes to her multi-faceted job with experience in television news programming and public relations.

Serving as programming director and producer, Dominick is busy with a variety of network-related responsibilities—planning productions, contracting for syndicated programming, reviewing demo tapes.

Dominick says she is fortunate because when a script comes in, she can look at it from the eye of both producer and director. She can decide whether a script is right for the network "and if it's something our facilities can handle. We're at a handicap because we don't have field equipment and our studio is small. Our budgets are very low," she adds. (And the network does not solicit funds on the air.)

Unproduced scriptwriters, therefore, have a good chance to break in to scriptwriting for EWTN "as long as they understand the limitations of the network's studio. We're set up beautifully to do teleconferencing and any kind of in-house work that could be done in a 15-by-30 foot studio. But if you want the parting of the Red Sea, that's just not possible—except figuratively."

What *is* right for EWTN are scripts with uplifting, wholesome themes that keep in mind the studio's limitations. "It doesn't have to have a religious tone. We look for beauty—whether it's in drama, dance, music, or art. There are so many places to go to hear how bad things are. We're just not interested in that. And it doesn't mean we live in an ethereal, surrealistic world, either. It's true sometimes you have to say life stinks, and there's nothing you can do about it. But that's not to say you can't have a story of a terminally-ill patient or a script about the kind of conflict resolution he goes through. I guess our overall philosophy is that God is in the midst of all that."

In the scripts she receives, Dominick is distressed about the careless use of profanity, when it has no value to the writing. "That's not to say you can't have a 'damn' or 'hell' in the script, but make it mean something."

Dominick also admits to being automatically biased against scripts replete with incorrect grammar and misspelled words. "A script is much like a résumé," she says. "You are submitting your services in the same way. And you are exhibiting the actual creativity of your work."

GOLDEN IMAGE MOTION PICTURE CORP., Suite 1000, 9000 Sunset Blvd., Los Angeles CA 90069. (213)550-8710. Contact: Sandy Cobe. Buys all rights. Previously produced material OK "if from another medium."
Needs: Submit synopsis/outline "with SASE for return." Pays in outright purchase.

GOLDSHOLL ASSOCIATES, 420 Frontage Rd., Northfield IL 60093. (312)446-8300. President: M. Goldsholl. Query. Buys all rights.
Needs: Scripts for industrial PR films. Also interested in original screenplays, and short stories to be made into screenplays. "Describe your material before sending it. Do not send 'fantasy' scripts!" Produces sound film-strips, 16mm and 35mm films, multimedia kits, tapes and cassettes, and 35mm slide sets. Pays 5-10% of budget.
Tips: "Write your ideas clearly. Know the visual world."

LIROL TV PRODUCTIONS, 6335 Homewood Ave., Los Angeles CA 90028. (213)467-8111. Contact: Morlene Keller. Writers worked with "varies from year to year." Buys all rights.
Needs: TV syndication only. Submit synopsis/outline. Pays in accordance with Writers Guild standards.

METROMEDIA PRODUCERS CORP., 5746 Sunset Blvd., Hollywood CA. (213)462-7111. Story Editor: Michael Brown. "We use a lot of material. All material must be represented by a literary agent or an established production company." Buys negotiable rights; "depends on the project." Previously produced material OK, "as we are also a distributing company." Reporting time "depends on volume. If it's something we really like, we may call the writer the day material is received."
Needs: Wide variety. TV. Query with samples and resume, or submit synopsis/outline or completed script. Pays in accordance with Writers Guild standards.
Recent Production: *Little Gloria, Happy At Last* (NBC mini-series).

MULTI-MEDIA INTERNATIONAL, 8915 Yolanda Ave., Northridge CA 91324. (213)993-7816. Contact: Bob Cawley. Vice President: Rena Winters. Works with 10 writers/year and buys 3-5 scripts and synopses/year. Buys all rights or arranges package deal with writers for creator fees throughout series in TV, or for film. "We contact writers whose ideas we like as soon as possible. Please enclose SASE with submissions for return of material, in case we can't use it."
Needs: 35mm films and TV. "We're looking for top drawer action-adventure. We're interested in material that can be produced for between $3 million and $6 million." Submit synopsis/outline or complete script. Pays ("depending on the situation") royalty, in outright purchase, or in accordance with Writers Guild standards.
Tips: "If we can't use a script or synopsis that we feel has potential, *sometimes* we will make notations with suggestions as to how the script could be made stronger, or if we aren't using that particular kind of material at the time, we may refer the writer to someone who is."

*NICKELODEON, Warner Amex Satellite Entertainment, 1133 Avenue of the Americas, New York NY 10036. (212)944-4250. Manager of Acquisitions: Eileen Opatut. Produces material for age-specific audience aged 2 to 16. Now in 11½ million homes. Buys negotiable rights. SASE. Reports in 1 month.
Needs: "Entertaining and educational programs for cable TV. Value filled, non-violent material desired." Submit resume and programming ideas (2-3 page explanations). Pays variable rate.

‡*PACE FILMS, INC., 411 E. 53rd Ave., New York NY 10022. (212)755-5486. President: R. Vanderbes. Produces material for a general theatrical audience. Buys all rights. Previously produced material OK. SASE. Reports in 2 month.
Needs: Theatrical motion pictures. Produces 35mm films, cable tapes and cassettes. Query with samples; submit synopsis/outline or completed script. Pays in accordance with Writers Guild standards.

‡PAULIST PRODUCTIONS, Box 1057, Pacific Palisades CA 90272. (213)454-0688. Contact: Story Department. "*Insight* is geared toward older teens and adults of all faiths. Our 'Capital Cities Family Specials' are geared towards senior high school students." Buys 15-20 ½-hour scripts/year. SASE. Reports in 1 month. Catalog for 10x14 SAE and 88¢ postage.
Needs: 16mm films and television shows. Submit completed script through agent only. "We are not interested in unsolicited manuscripts. *Insight* scripts are donated. Our teenage specials allow for small stipend to writer."
Tips: "Watch *Insight* and our 'Capital Cities Family Specials' enough so that you have a strong sense of the sort of material we are interested in producing." Looks for "wit, originality of theme and approach, an unsentimental, yet strong and hopefully positive manner of approaching subject matter. Intelligent, literate, un-cliche-ridden writing."

‡*RESTON REPERTORY TELEVISION THEATRE, Box 2400, Reston VA 22090. (703)437-0764. Executive Producer: Sharon Cohen. Produces material for a cable audience. Buys 2-3 scripts/year. "We negotiate with playwright on the basis of a percentage of resulting sales; no outright purchase or rights." SASE. Reports in 3 weeks on queries; 4 months on submissions.

Needs: "Original scripts—no adaptations. Casts should be kept small, and playing time may be 30 minutes to 2 hours. All scripts considered within the limits of good taste." Produces ¾" tapes and cassettes. Submit complete script. Pay "negotiable with playwright."

Tips: "We are especially looking for writers who understand how to use the medium of television to its best advantage."

‡**TANNEBRING ROSE**, #100, 10400 N. Central, Dallas TX 75231. (214)363-3464. Development: Steve Pullin. Produces material for TV/film audience. Buys 10 scripts/year. Buys all rights and first rights. SASE. Reports in 3 weeks on queries; 6 weeks on submissions.

Needs: Produces 16mm and 35mm films, videotape productions. Query or submit synopsis/outline and completed script. Pays in accordance with Writers Guild standards.

‡*****TELEVISION PRODUCTION SERVICES CORP.**, 381 Horizon Dr., Edison NJ 08817. (201)287-3626. Executive Director/Producer: R.S. Burks. Produces material for major market distributor networks, etc. Buys 50-100 scripts/year. Buys all rights. Previously produced material OK. Computer printout submissions OK; prefers letter quality to dot matrix printouts. SASE. Reports in 2 weeks. Catalog for 8x10 SAE and 4 first class stamps.

Needs: "We do video music for record companies, MTV, HBO, etc. We use treatments of story ideas from the groups management. We also do commercials for over the air broadcast and cable." Submit synopsis/outline or completed script, and resume.

Tips: Looks for rewrite flexibility and availability. "We have the capability of transmission electronically over the phone modem to our printer or directly onto disk for storage."

BOB THOMAS PRODUCTIONS, Box 1787, Wayne NJ 07470. (201)696-7500. New York Office: 60 E. 42nd St., New York NY 10165. (212)221-3602. President: Robert G. Thomas. Buys all rights. "Send introductory letter explaining ideas. Submit outline or rough draft for film. If possible, we will contact the writer for further discussion." SASE.

Needs: 35mm films for entertainment for a general audience (theater type). General subject matter and made-for-TV films. Pays "dependent on agreements between both parties."

*****UNITED JEWISH APPEAL/FEDERATION OF JEWISH PHILANTHROPIES**, 130 E. 59th St., New York NY 10022. (212)980-1000. Public Relations: Art Portnow. Produces material for people interested in Jewish topics and a Jewish audience. Buys 4 TV ideas and 2-3 scripts/year. Buys negotiable rights. Previously produced material OK. Computer printout and disk submissions OK; prefers letter quality to dot matrix printouts. Reports in 1 month.

Needs: Audiovisual materials for group showing, scripts for commercial and cable TV and radio programs. "Writer must be well-versed in Judaic tradition and customs." Produces slides/sound shows, video, radio, films. Query with sample or resume and sample of script from a completed program. Does not return samples. Buys scripts outright for $100-500; "varies with length and requirement of the script."

Tips: "Unique ideas are welcome here. New angles on holidays are always of interest. Additional per diem freelance writing assignments for news release work and the like is also available."

UNITED PRODUCTIONS LIMITED, Box 5942, Sherman Oaks CA 91403. Contact: Patrick Roberts. Buys "several" scripts/year.

Needs: Produces 35mm films and TV. Not interested in plays, period pieces, musicals. "Interested in mostly location shootings. Keep budget in mind!" Submit synopsis or complete script. Pays negotiable royalty.

Tips: "My advice to novice scriptwriters is to concentrate on content. Don't worry about camera angles, scene numbers, etc. The director will take care of that. Just give me a good story and a strong believable character—one that the reader will immediately 'care' for."

‡**WORLD WIDE PICTURES**, 2520 W. Olive, Burbank CA 91505. (213)843-1300. Executive Producer: Bill Brown. Produces material for a Christian audience. Buys 2-3 documentaries/year and 1 feature film every other year. Buys first rights. SASE. Reports in 1 month.

Needs: Religious material, church history, Biblical subjects, prophecy, evangelistic topics, Christian living material. Produces documentaries for TV, feature films for theater and church. Submit treatment. Pays in negotiable outright purchase.

Tips: Worldwide Pictures is a branch of the Billy Graham Evangelistic Association. Stories must be consistent with Dr. Graham's theology. "We do not use material sent on submission, but assign projects to freelance writers."

Software Publishers

If the more than 200 computer systems on the market are the body of the current technological revolution, then the software for these systems is the soul.

Computer programs which allow computers to play a game, solve a problem, or edit a manuscript are the latest outlet for a writer's creativity.

Software is the nutrient of the computer industry. Just as magazine and book publishers need quality manuscripts to quench their readers' thirsts, so do software publishers need top-notch programs to satisfy the appetites of business and home computer users. And as video games continue to be replaced by home computers in America's family rooms, the market for quality programs will grow.

Some industry estimates suggest that software is already a billion-dollar-a-year business. The time for getting in on the ground floor is now. For freelancers, that usually means contacting hardware manufacturers who produce programs for their machines, or independent software publishers in the business of marketing programs for one or several computer systems.

Writers (also known as programmers, authors and inventors—depending on the newspaper/magazine you are reading) of computer programs are logical thinkers who own or use a computer and know how to program it. Some of them program out of necessity (perhaps none of the programs on the market is designed to keep track of the inventory for your new poultry farm); others are following a creative drive (the same one that motivates novelists, biographers, poets, etc.). These are writers who not only understand how a computer works, but know what to tell it when it doesn't.

The independent software publishers listed below are looking for freelance writers. Says one software evaluation director, "Software companies cannot afford full time programmers when so many outstanding programs are being written by freelancers." Another firm's marketing director observes that "the freelance author is certainly in a seller's market as the number of firms to market programs seems only exceeded by the sea of consumers."

The software writer's job, then, is to translate his ideas into programs with entertainment, utility, educational and business/professional applications. From there, it's a matter of submitting them to appropriate companies.

The listings below have been prepared from questionnaires that software publishers completed indicating their freelance needs. Read the market listings carefully, noting the systems the publishers serve, the formats they work in, and how they want to be contacted. Some firms require an outline and complete documentation with an initial program submission; others prefer a query with resume and credits; still others accept only demo disks. Wherever they are available, write for programmer's guidelines.

Be aware of what rights you sell to a software publisher interested in your program. If a firm buys nonexclusive rights, you will be able to continue selling your program through other channels; if it buys machine-specific rights, you can sell another version of your program to a different publisher serving other computer systems. If a publisher wants irrevocable rights to your program, it means it's his forever.

Payment for software is usually on a royalty basis and parallels that in the book publishing industry. Royalties average 10-30% of net sales, with game programs generally in the 10-20% range. With sales breaking anticipated projections, the profit potential is high.

Knowing your market is as important in the software industry as in the traditional world of the printed word. Write for company catalogs; better yet, use some of their programs. Note whether they stress technical complexity, graphics, animation or color. To make a sale, your program will have to "fit" with their already-established image and product line. Submit only those kinds of programs they specify need in their *Writer's Market* listing.

In addition to the independent software publishers listed here, there are hundreds of other outlets for your programs including hardware manufacturers, book publishers, and computer magazines. For a comprehensive guide to selling your software, consult the *1984 Programmer's Market*, edited by Brad McGehee (Writer's Digest Books).

Then get busy. The program the world's been waiting for may right now be jelling in your own creative drive.

‡**ABERSOFT**, 7, MaesAfallen, Bow St., Nr. Aberystwyth Dyfed, SY24 5BA, England. Contact: C.J. Jones-Steele, Partner. Estab. 1981. Software publisher producing games and serious software for ZX81, ZXSpectrum, Atari and Lynx (cassette) systems. Currently publishes 9 programs. Send program outline and documentation or cassette. Reports in 1 week. Buys variable British rights. Pays 10-25% royalty.
Needs: High quality original arcade games. No "software written in BASIC!" Looks for animation features.
Recent Programs: Adventure (textual adventure-type program filling the full storage capacity of each machine); Forth (implementation of the computer language FORTH).
Tips: "Fully debug and document programs before submission."

‡**A-BIT-BETTER SOFTWARE**, Box 28, Laurel MD 20707. (301)953-7256. President: Troy L. Hummon. Estab. 1982. Software publisher producing educational, entertainment, professional/business and utilities programming aids for Atari 400/800. Currently publishes 2 programs. Send demo disk. Reports in 2 weeks. Negotiable rights. No simultaneous or previously published submissions. Pays up to 25% royalty.
Needs: Data application programs; games; educational programs. Looks for audio, animation, color, user friendly and logical use features.
Recent Programs: *Magic Mail* (mailing list data base program capable of searching and sorting on any field in a matter of seconds); *Fast Pak* (disk utilities package containing seven popular utility needs).
Tips: "Write user friendly code. Make the program operate in a logical manner. Provide explicit and easy-to-understand documentation. Add a bit of imagination and diversity."

‡**ACTIVISION, INC.**, Drawer No. 7286, Mountain View CA 94039. Contact: Hugh Bowen. Software publisher producing recreational material for Atari 2600, Atari 400 and Intellivision. Currently has issued over 25 programs; "some freelance." Query with resume and credits and send demo disk. Reports in 3 weeks on queries; 5 weeks on programs. Buys all rights. No simultaneous or previously published submissions. Pays by individual arrangement.
Needs: Recreational programs for all ages. No business programs. Use assembly language only. Looks for audio, animation, color, strong graphics and action features.
Recent Programs: *River Raid* (scrolling river scene; "you pilot a jet through a dangerous river facing enemy ships, planes and helicopters"); *Keystone Kapers* ("you chase criminals through old-time department store leaping over obstacles and collecting bags of gold and cash left in your path").
Tips: "We seek the best graphics and game play for original concepts."

‡**ADVENTURE INTERNATIONAL**, Division of Scott Adams, Inc., Box 3435, Longwood FL 32750. (305)862-6917. Editor: Mark Sprague. Software publisher producing entertainment, professional/business and utility material for TRS-80, TRS-color, IBM, Atari, Apple, CP/M and Commodore systems. Currently publishes 150 programs. 95% freelance. Query with resume and credits; send demo disk and documentation. Reports in 2 weeks. Buys all rights and first rights. Pays 7-25% royalty or makes outright purchase. Free programmer's guidelines.
Needs: Business and education programs. Looks for audio, animation, color and speed features.
Recent Programs: *Preppie* (action game of recovering golf balls in an alligator-filled river); *Sea Dragon* (game puts you in command of a nuclear submarine armed with missiles).
Tips: "Call editor first."

‡**ALPHA SOFTWARE CORP.**, 12 New England Executive Park, Burlington MA 01803. (617)229-2924. Vice President: George Lechter. Estab. 1981. Software publisher producing educational, entertainment and professional/business material for IBM PC and Apple II (5¼" floppy). Currently publishes 8 programs; 100% freelance. Send query, resume and credits; demo disk; or program outline and documentation. Reports in 2 weeks. Buys flexible rights "depending on situation." Simultaneous and previously published submissions OK. Pays 10-45% royalty or pays by combination of royalty and outright purchase. Free programmer's guidelines.
Needs: Business, games and special programs. Looks for appropriate features.

Recent Programs: *The Apple-IBM Connection* (communications); *Data Base Manager II* (file management).
Tips: "Concentrate on quality work."

‡**APROPOS TECHNOLOGY**, Suite 821, 350 N. Lantana, Camarillo CA 93010. (805)482-3604. Contact:
Paul Johnson, owner. Estab. 1982. Software publisher/hardware manufacturer producing educational and entertainment material for Sinclair ZX-81, Timex/Sinclair 1000, Commodore VIC-20 (cassette). Currently
publishes 6 programs; 100% freelance. Send program outline and documentation. Reports in 2 weeks on
queries and outlines; 4 weeks on programs. Buys all rights or makes royalty agreement. Simultaneous and previously published submissions OK. Pay "depends on the program." Programmer's guidelines for business-
size SAE and 1 first class stamp.
Needs: "Everything—but especially thought-provoking word games." Looks for audio, animation and color
features.
Recent Programs: Small Artificial Intelligence program using key word responses; Typing Teacher program
using animation and an almost unlimited string of text.
Tips: "Supply superior documentation and it will sell. Make a demo to distribute to dealers, etc."

‡**AV CONCEPTS CORP.**, 30 Montauk Blvd., Oakdale NY 11769. (516)567-7227. President: P.J. Solimene.
Software publisher producing educational material for Apple II amd 48K, Apple IIe, and Franklin Ace 1000
systems. Currently publishes 19 programs; 100% freelance. Send demo disk. Reports in 2 weeks on queries; 4
weeks on outlines; 6 weeks on programs. Buys all rights. Simultaneous and previously published submissions
OK. Makes outright purchase; amounts "depending on depth of program." Free programmer's guidelines.
Needs: Math and reading programs—must be educationally sound.
Recent Programs: *TAC-AFFIX* (language arts); *TAC-Vocabulary*; *TAC-PAT*; *Contained Reading*.
Tips: "Call in advance for a review of our needs."

‡**AVANT GARDE CREATIONS, INC.**, Box 30160, Eugene OR 97403. President: Mary Carol Smith. Software publisher producing educational, entertainment, professional/business material and utilities for programmers of Apple II (11e), Atari, VIC 20, Commodore 64, IBM-PC, TI994A. Currently publishes 120 programs;
63% freelance. Send query, resume and credits, demo disk, program outline and documentation or description
or reference to published products. Reports in 1 week. Buys all rights. Simultaneous and previously published
submissions OK. Pays 10-25% royalty or combination of advance/guarantees and royalties. Free programmer's guidelines.
Needs: Education (primary and elementary) programs; translations from Apple to other machines. Looks for
audio, animation, color, user friendliness, clear concise screens, documentation features.
Recent Programs: *Jump Jet* (high action challenging arcade game); *Golf 2* (unique computer sport—swing,
direct and play golf on the computer).
Tips: "Compare your program to what's already on the market. Just because it works, doesn't mean it's marketable. Test it on friends and associates before sending it. Talk to us before you finalize it."

‡**BRAM, INC.**, 18779 Kenlake Place, NE, Seattle WA 98155. (206)644-3425. Contact: Product Manager.
Estab. 1981. Software publisher producing entertainment material for Atari 400/800/1200 systems. Currently
publishes 2 programs. Send demo disk or program outline and documentation. Reports in 2 weeks. Buys all
rights and first rights. Simultaneous submissions OK. Pays 10-40% royalty.
Needs: Games. No business programs. Looks for audio, animation, color features.
Recent Programs: *Attack at EP-CYG-4* (space adventure); *Zombie*.

‡**BRØDERBUND SOFTWARE, INC.**,1938 4th St., San Rafael CA 94901. (415)456-6424. Vice President,
Product Development: Gary Carlston. Software publisher producing entertainment and personal productivity
material for Apple, Atari, IBM, Commodore 64, VIC-20, TI 99/4 systems. Currently publishes 35 programs;
70% freelance. Query with detailed outline of works in progress or send demo disk with necessary documentation. Reports in 3 weeks on queries; 1 week on programs. Buys all rights. Simultaneous and previously
published submissions OK. Pays 10-25% royalty. Free programmer's guidelines.
Needs: Games. No business, occult, board games, utilities or programs in poor taste. Looks for animation, col-
or, game play and originality.
Recent Programs: *Choplifter!*; *Lode Runner*.

‡**THE BUSINESS DIVISION**, Box 3435, Longwood FL 32750. (305)862-6917. Software publisher producing professional/business material for IBM PC, TRS-80 and CP/M systems. Currently publishes 10 programs;
100% freelance. Send demo disk or program outline and documentation. Reports in 10 weeks on queries; 3
weeks on outlines and programs. Buys negotiable rights. No simultaneous submissions. Previously published
submissions OK. Pays negotiable royalty. Free programmer's guidelines.
Needs: Accounting, communication, data base management—aimed at sophisticated home users and small
business. "Don't send us anything unless it does something better than existing products."

Recent Programs: *Maxi Stat* (sophisticated statistical analysis package); *Maxi C.R.A.S.* (check register accounting system).

‡**CENTAUR**, 501 Jackson, Charleston IL 61920. (217)348-8055. Marketing Director: John Best. Estab. 1981. Software publisher producing entertainment material for CP/M based computers and hobby (TRS-80 Apple) computers. Currently publishes 4 programs; all freelance. Send program outline and documentation. Reports in 2 weeks. Buys all rights. Simultaneous submissions OK. Pays 10-30% royalty. Programmer's guidelines for business-size SAE and 1 first class stamp.
Needs: Games for all ages. "No educational games unless something very new and different. No business software or anything written in BASIC." Looks for enjoyability.
Recent Programs: Swords and sorcery-type game; video-type game; space-type game.
Tips: "Give us good documentation. We can provide excellent marketing as long as the program is worth it."

‡**CLOAD PUBLICATIONS, INC.**, Box 1448, Santa Barbara CA 93102. (805)962-6271. Publisher: Robin Sager. Software publisher producing educational and entertainment material for TRS-80, Mod. I and III and 4 on *Cload Magazine*; TRS-80 Color Computer on *Chromasette Magazine*. Currently publishes 500 programs; 98% freelance. Query for information or send demo disk. Reports in 2 weeks on queries and outlines; 2 months on programs. Buys all rights. Makes outright purchase of $50-300. Free programmer's guidelines.
Needs: Games, utilities, practical programs, tutorials. No "serious business programs requiring lots of back-up." Looks for audio, animation, color (Chromasette); no bugs.

‡**COMM DATA COMPUTER HOUSE, INC.**, 320 Summit Ave., Milford MI 48042. (313)685-0113. Software Coordinator: Larry Jones. Software publisher producing educational and entertainment material for Commodore VIC 20, Commodore Pet and Commodore 64. Currently publishes 130 programs; 60% freelance. Send demo disk or program outline and documentation. Reports in 4 weeks on outlines; 2 weeks on programs. Buys all rights and first rights. Pays 10-30% royalty; or makes outright purchase of $50-300. "Comm Data must be granted exclusive rights, with non-performance (by Comm Data) being the only allowable out of the contract." Free programmer's guidelines.
Needs: Games (must be machine code and fast); educational (consumer market—prime buyers are parents of children ages 3-14). No software which requires add-ons (such as memory expansion) to the computer. Looks for audio, animation, color, graphics and user friendliness.
Recent Programs: *Munch Word* (educational type Pacman); *Geography Smash* (educational game); *Pagasus Odyssey* (arcade-style game).
Tips: "Request programmer's guidelines. Software must really be slick to be acceptable. We reject approximately 90-95% of all software submitted because it is too amateurish."

‡**COMMUNITREE GROUP**, 1150 Bryant, San Francisco CA 94103. Contact: Chief Executive Officer. Software publisher producing telecommunications/networking material in Forth or machine languages for various systems. Currently publishes 2 programs; 50% freelance. Query with resume and credits. Reports in 1 month on queries; 2 months on outlines; 4 months on programs. Buys all rights. No simultaneous or previously published submissions. Pays royalty or makes outright purchase—negotiated on a case-by-case basis.
Needs: "Contact us for specific details." Not interested in games software.

‡**COMPUTER ENGINEERING SERVICES**, The Jarrett Company, Box 1222, Show Low AZ 85901. (602)537-7522. Contact: John Jarrett, owner. Software publisher/hardware manufacturer producing educational, entertainment and professional/business material for Timex-Sinclair, VIC 20, Commodore 64, Apple II + , TRS-80 (cassette and documentation). Currently publishes 16 programs; 60% freelance. Send program outlines, documentation and cassette. Reports in 1 week on queries; 2 weeks on outlines and programs. Buys either exclusive or nonexclusive rights. Previously published submissions OK. Pays 10-30% royalty.
Needs: Specialized business programs; would "love educational, or games, relating to Christian beliefs." No pornographic (sex related) or extremely violent programs. Looks for audio, animation, color features and thought in program design.
Recent Programs: *Mutual Fund Advisor* (business program in BASIC for those interested or dealing with no load mutual funds); *ZX-Data Finder* (program in Sinclair BASIC dealing with file handling).

‡**COMPUTER PALACE/ROYAL SOFTWARE**, 2160 W. 11th Ave., Eugene OR 97402. (503)683-5361. Contact: Donald Marr. Estab. 1982. Retail and mail order sales firm offering educational, entertainment and professional/business material for Atari (tape and disk) systems. Currently publishes 2 programs; 50% freelance. Send demo disk or program outline and documentation. Reports in 2 weeks—1 month on programs. Buys all rights. Simultaneous and previously published submissions OK.
Needs: Children and adult programs—educational, games or business. No pornography. Looks for audio, animation, color and graphics features.
Recent Programs: *Super Mailer-Business Program* (allows user to add to the data line, sort by name, zip and

edit, modify or print any combination of entries. Its features also include the merging of files, wild card search and the ability to use any printer); *Meteor Storm* (arcade action game—fast action game; makes extensive use of the player missile graphics and sound routines. You must guide your fighter ship from the rescue ship through the meteors, debris, and the random space storms to the city. You score points as you pick up survivors from each city. If you save all the people in one city you advance on to the next level).

‡**COMPUTER SKILL BUILDERS**, Box 42050, Tucson AZ 85733. (602)323-7500. Managing Editor: Bill Crider. Software publisher producing educational material for Apple, IBM, TRS-80, Commodore, Atari systems (disk only). Currently publishes about 100 programs. Send demo disk or program outline and documentation. Reports in 2 weeks on queries; 1 month on outlines; 2 months on programs. Buys all rights. Previously published submissions OK. Pays negotiable royalty. Programmer's guidelines for business-size SAE and 1 first class stamp.
Needs: Educational programs, all subjects and ages. Looks for audio, animation, color and "state of the art" features.
Recent Programs: *Greeting Cards* and *Math Skill Builders*.
Tips: "Query first."

‡**CRAWFORD DATA SYSTEMS**, Box 705, Somis CA 93066. Contact: J.C. Moule, owner. Estab. 1981. Software publisher producing professional/business material for Apple and IBM PC. Currently produces no freelance-written programs. Query with resume and credits or send program outline and documentation. Reports in 1 week on queries and outlines; 2 weeks on programs. Buys all rights. Simultaneous and previously published submissions OK. Pays 10-30% royalty or makes outright purchase of $1,000 minimum; no maximum. Free programmer's guidelines.
Needs: "All our programs are targeted for the knowledgeable, active investor or speculator in stocks and or options. Eighty percent of our customers speculate, trade, or advise as their primary occupation." Prefers programs written in Pascal; BASIC OK; compiled BASIC OK if source code submitted. Looks for ease of use for the computer novice.
Recent Programs: *OPTIONX*™ (computes fair value, hedge ratio, actual volatility, etc.—all parameters of interest to an option writer or speculator.
Tips: "We are only interested in working with programmers who already understand the stock market. No proprietary trading schemes, please. Your program should be based on published investment principles."

‡**DIGITAL MARKETING CORP.**, 2363 Boulevard Circle, Walnut Creek CA 94595. (415)947-1000. Marketing Communications Specialist: Franette Armstrong. Software publisher producing educational, entertainment, professional/business and utility material for most CA/M, CP/M-86, MS-DOS systems. Currently publishes over 30 programs; 100% freelance. Author information brochure for business-size SAE and 75¢. Reports in 2 weeks on queries; 8 weeks on outlines and programs. Buys all rights. Simultaneous and previously published submissions OK. Pays variable royalty.
Needs: Business, medical-dental and legal programs. Looks for integration.
Recent Programs: *Databook II and Personal Datebook* (schedules appointments); *Bibliography* (compares citations in a ms with entries in a reference file).
Tips: "Request our author information brochure."

‡**DYNCOMP, INC.**, 1427 Monroe Ave., Rochester NY 14618. President: F. Ruckelschul. Software publisher producing educational, entertainment and professional/business material for most computer systems (diskette/disk, cassette). Currently publishes about 200 programs; 50% freelance. Send demo disk or program outline and documentation. Reports in 1 week. Buys all rights. Simultaneous and previously published submissions OK. Pays 10-20% royalty.
Needs: "A wide range of programs." No pornography.
Recent Programs: *Basic Scientific Subroutines* and *Hodge Podge Alphabet*.

‡**EDUCATIONAL SOFTWARE, INC.**, 4565 Cherry Vale Ave., Soquel CA 95073. (408)476-4901. Contact: Sylvia Smith, Marketing. Software publisher producing educational, entertainment and business material for Atari, Commodore 64, VIC 20, TI 99/4A, IBM PC. Currently publishes 38 programs; 50% freelance. Send demo disk or program outline and documentation. Reports in 1 month on queries and outlines; 2 months on programs. Buys all rights. Previously published submissions OK. Pays 10% maximum royalty. Free programmer's guidelines.
Needs: Games (interested in foreign language programs, home business programs). "All programs must complement our already existing product line. No violent or unfriendly programs of any kind." Looks for audio, animation, color, and excellent graphics features.
Recent Programs: *Sam Tutorial* (program on how to use the S.A.M. from Don't Ask—teaches how to make Sam speak, sing and combine graphics with voice); *Music Major* (teaches fundamentals of music via comprehensive lessons).

Tips: "Be familiar with our products and our image. Programmers will need lots of creativity if their software is going to stand out among the deluge of programs available for publishers to choose from."

‡**FEROX MICROSYSTEMS, INC.**, Suite 611, 1701 N. Fort Meyers Dr., Arlington VA 22209. (703)841-0800. President: Rusty Luhring. Software publisher producing professional/business material for Pascal systems. Currently publishes 5 programs. Query with resume and credits. Reports in 4 weeks on queries; 3 weeks on outlines; 10 weeks on programs. Buys variable rights. Simultaneous and previously published submissions OK. Pays variable rates.
Needs: Business, financial modeling applications—games geared toward financial analysts. No foreign language or educational programs for high school students.
Recent Programs: *DSS/F* (financial modeling program); *GraphPower* (plotter graphics program).
Tips: "Write a communications package, data base management all in Pascal."

‡**HARTHUN ENGINEERING & RESEARCH, INC.**, Box 111, Albany KY 42602. President: Ken Harthun. Estab. 1982. Software publisher and hardware design firm producing educational and professional/business material for VIC-20, Sinclair 2X81, TS 1000 systems (cassette, listings). Currently publishes 25 programs. Send demo cassette or program outline and documentation. Reports in 2-3 weeks on queries; 4-6 weeks on outlines; 1-2 weeks on programs. Buys first rights. Previously published submissions OK ("only if writer holds copyright and has right to re-sell"). Pays 10-25% royalty.
Needs: Statistical analysis for businesspeople; accounting for small businesses; basic skills for school children from grade 1 to high school. No games. Looks for audio, color and ease-of-use features.
Recent Programs: *Histogram* (plots bar charts of input statistical data); *Artificial Intelligence Demo* (basic look at how a machine can be taught to "think" on a basic level).
Tips: "Write the programs so that someone who has never used a computer before could easily perform the required actions. Be sure that the program does not allow erroneous data to 'crash' it."

‡**HUMAN SYSTEMS DYNAMICS**, Suite 222, 9010 Reseda Blvd., Northridge CA 91324. (213)993-8536. Director: Virginia Lawrence. Software publisher producing educational, professional/business material, and statistical analysis for research for Apple II and III, IBM PC, and CP/M systems. Currently publishes 6 programs. Send program outlines and documentation. Reports in 3 weeks on queries; 2 months on outlines and programs. Buys all rights. Simultaneous and previously published submissions OK. Pays royalty.
Needs: Statistical analysis for scientific researchers, forecasters or teachers of statistics; any programs helpful to research and development personnel; forecasting for business. No games, accounting—anything not technical. Looks for easy-to-use features that lead to sophisticated results.
Recent Programs: General Statistics, including 5-way cross tabulation; program to plot any equation graphically.
Tips: "We need high quality software. We are providing mainframe flexibility on micros, but we are not sacrificing ease of use."

‡**INFOCOM, INC.**, 55 Wheeler St., Cambridge MA 02138. (617)492-1031. Contact: Michael Berlyn, Software Acquisition. Software publisher producing entertainment material for Apple II; Atari 400, 800; Commodore 64; DEC Rainbow; IBM PC; NEC PC-8000, APC; TRS-80 Model I and III; Osborne; CP/M 8''; PDP-11; TI Professional (disk). Currently publishes 7 programs. Send query, resume and credits. Reports in 1 week on queries; 2 weeks on outlines; 3 weeks on programs. Buys all rights. No simultaneous or previously published submissions. Pays negotiable rates "depending on situation and product."
Needs: Games—good stories for text adventures and different approaches to graphics games in general. "No 'Me too' products. We're not interested in doing another version of Pac-man or Frogger." Looks for originality.
Recent Programs: *Suspended*™ (a text adventure written by a published science fiction author); *Witness*™ (a text adventure in the mystery genre, a '30s period piece). "Both programs were staff written and accept full sentence input including adjectives, nouns, verbs, articles, etc."
Tips: "Make sure that the program could run on most popular machines. For us to produce/publish a product which was designed to run on only one machine, the program would have to be far above the average."

‡**INTERNATIONAL PUBLISHING AND SOFTWARE**, 3948 Chesswood Dr., Downsview, Ontario, Canada M3J 2W6. (416)636-9409. Product Manager: Bob Fraser. Estab. 1982. Software publisher producing educational, entertainment and professional/business material for TS1000/ZX81; TS2000/Spectrum; VIC 20; Commodore 64 systems. Currently publishes 70 programs; 90% freelance. Send program outline and documentation. Reports in 1 week on queries and outlines; 3 weeks on programs. Buys all rights. Simultaneous and previously published submissions OK. Pays royalty. Free programmer's guidelines.
Needs: "We're willing to look at anything submitted." Looks for quality features.
Recent Program: *Fastload* (load and save programs).

‡LINK SYSTEMS, 1640 19th St., Santa Monica CA 90404. Production Editor: Pat Merryman. Software publisher producing educational, professional/business and utility material for Apple and IBM-PC. Currently produces 6 programs; 66% freelance. Send query, demo disk or program outline and documentation. Reports in 2 weeks on query; 4 weeks on outline; 8 weeks on programs. Buys all rights. Simultaneous submissions OK. Pays royalty or makes outright purchase.
Needs: Business programs. No games. Looks for simplicity in programs.
Recent Programs: *Datafax*; *Datalink*.
Tips: "Keep it simple to explain to new computer users. Documentation must be easy to read."

‡MASTERWORKS SOFTWARE, 25834 Narbonne, Lomita CA 90274. (213)539-7486. Contact: Thomas R. Heffernan, Sales/Marketing. Software publisher producing professional/business material for IBM and Apple computers. Currently publishes 11 programs. Send query, resume and credits, demo disk or program outline and documentation. Reports in 1 week. Buys first, all and negotiable rights. Simultaneous and previously published submissions OK. Pays royalty or makes outright purchase.
Needs: Games, business programs. No products competing with current line. Looks for menu-driven, user friendly programs.
Tips: "Get defined interests before beginning production."

‡NEW CLASSICS SOFTWARE, 239 Fox Hill Rd., Denville NJ 07834. (201)625-8838. President: George Blank. Software publisher producing educational programs for TRS-80, Apple II, IBM PC (diskette only) systems. Currently publishes 6 programs; 100% freelance. Send demo disk. Reports in 2 months on queries; 3 weeks on outlines; 1 week on programs. Buys negotiable rights. Simultaneous and previously published submissions OK. Pays royalty or makes outright purchase.
Needs: Programs in all areas of secondary education. No games; items that would sell for less than $50.
Recent Programs: *Pascal 80* (Pascal language for school use); *Accounting* (school accounting package).
Tips: "Our writers must have expert knowledge of curriculum areas plus serious programming skills."

‡NORELL DATA SYSTEMS CORP., 3400 Wilshire Blvd., Los Angeles CA 90010. (213)257-2026. President: Melvin Norell. Estab. 1982. Software publisher producing educational, entertainment, professional/business and utilities material for IBM Personal Computer, Apple II, Sony SMC-70 (disk). Currently publishes 25 programs; 60% freelance. Send program outline and documentation. Reports in 1 week on queries; 2 weeks on outlines and programs. Buys all rights. Simultaneous and previously published submissions OK. Pays 10-25% royalty. Free programmer's guidelines.
Needs: Entertainment, utilities, home applications and language programs. "We will look at everything." Looks for animation and color features.
Recent Programs: *The Phantom's Revenge* (text adventure game); *Easy Calc Electronic Spreadsheet*.
Tips: "Check with us for marketing/research advice. We can provide you with specifications on what to develop."

‡OPTIMIZED SYSTEMS SOFTWARE, INC., 10379 Lansdale Ave., Cupertino CA 95014. (408)446-3099. Technical Director: Bill Wilkinson. Estab. 1981. Software publisher producing professional/business and systems (languages, OS) material for Atari, Apple, Commodore 64 (diskette). Currently publishes 8 programs; 63% freelance. Send demo disk or program outline and preliminary documentation. Reports in 1 week on queries; 2-4 weeks on outlines and programs. Buys all rights. Simultaneous submissions OK. Pays 5-12% royalty on retail price, makes outright purchase of $3,000-20,000, or combination of both.
Needs: Business and home applications; graphics utilities; vertical market packages; word processor programs. "We would like to acquire an entire line of adventure games (graphics preferred)." No arcade games. Looks for portability, compatibility and ease of use.
Recent Programs: *Action!* (Pascal-like language—fastest 8-bit language ever); *OSS Integer BASIC* (integer-only BASIC, 95% compatible with Atari BASIC—written to gain speed).
Tips: "Please, no more me-too programs. No more data base programs in poorly-written BASIC. Programs *must* be well commented for later maintenance."

‡PHOENIX SOFTWARE, INC., 64 Lake Zurich Dr., Lake Zurich IL 60047. (312)438-4850. General Manager: Judy Wessel. Estab. 1981. Software publisher producing entertainment, professional/business and utility material for Apple II, Atari 400/800 and IBM-PC (5¼" floppy). Currently publishes 10 programs; 80% freelance. Send demo disk or program outline and documentation. Reports in 1-2 weeks on queries and outlines; 2-3 weeks on programs. Author retains copyrights, etc. Phoenix Software buys exclusive marketing rights. Simultaneous and previously published submissions OK. Pays 15-25% royalty.
Needs: Original, arcade-type games. "We discourage authors from doing 'better' versions of popular arcade games, i.e., a better Asteroids, Pac-man, Defender, etc. Arcade games should be written in assembly for speed. Other software may be written in BASIC or other higher level languages." Looks for audio, animation, color, speed, and also attract mode.

Recent Programs: *Sherwood Forest* (graphic adventure game for the Apple Computer where the player must solve a series of puzzles in order to win the hand of Maid Marian); *Forms Foundry* (business software designed to print forms used in everyday business, i.e., P.O.'s, invoices, statements, etc.).
Tips: "On games look for an original idea; they should be colorful and fun to play—easy enough for the most unskilled but increasingly difficult so that none can survive. Business software must be designed so that non-programmers can use it, menu driven, prompted, etc."

‡**PRACTICAL PROGRAMS**, 1104 Aspen Dr., Toms River NJ 08753. (201)349-6070. Software Specialist: Gerry Wagner. Software publisher producing professional/business material for the TRS-80, Model 1/3/4, cassette/diskette. Currently publishes 20 programs; 50% freelance. Send demo disk or program outline and documentation; "if program looks good, format for documentation will be sent." Reports in 1 week on queries and outline; 2 weeks on programs. Buys non-exclusive rights; pays 10-20% royalty. Simultaneous and previously published submissions OK, "as long as program has no encumberances on it." Royalty "depends on programmer support—full support and documentation is 20%." Programmer's guidelines available for $5 on a single density TRS-80 NewDos 80 V2.0 diskette.
Needs: Practical programs for home, small business, specific vertical markets. No games, no education. Looks for practicality, utility and usefulness features.
Recent Programs: *Mail Order Generator*; *Family Budget*; *Computer of Calories*.
Tips: "Be willing to document in our prescribed format. Make program user friendly (menus, error checks). Thoroughly test program in as many environments as possible."

‡**RAINBOW COMPUTING, INC.**, 19517 Business Center Dr., Northridge CA 91324. (213)849-0300. Assistant Marketing Manager: Tina Day. Software publisher producing entertainment, professional/business and utility material for Apple II Plus, Apple IIe (DOS 3.3). Currently publishes 5 programs; 100% freelance. Send program outline and documentation. Reports in 2 weeks on queries; 3-4 weeks on outlines; 4-6 weeks on programs. "We pay 15-20% royalty to publish program." Simultaneous and previously published submissions OK.
Needs: Business, utility, educational programs. Looks for audio, animation, color and good error-trapping.
Recent Programs: *Poor Man's Graphics Tablet* (graphics utility); *Rainbow Graphics* (graphics utility).
Tips: "We need good, easy-to-understand documentation and good error-trapping."

‡**SAVANT SOFTWARE, INC.**, Box 440278, Houston TX 77244. (713)556-8363. Vice President: John E. Dutra. Estab. 1982. Software publisher producing professional/business material for IBM PC and Apple II. Currently publishes 8 programs. Send demo disk. Reports in 2 weeks. Buys negotiable rights. Pays negotiable rates "depending on program."
Needs: Technical and financial programs. No games. Looks for ease-of-use in programs.
Recent Programs: *Option Calc* (options analysis and valuation); *Graphics Utility* (utility program to easily use graphics capability of IBM PC).
Tips: "We look for quality, user friendly, IBM PC or PC compatible material."

‡**SIMULUSION**, Box 894, Lemon Grove CA 92045. Contact: Conan LaMotte, owner. Estab. 1983. Software publisher producing professional/business material for TS1000, TS1500, TS2016, TS2048, ZX81, ZX80 (cassette). Currently publishes 16 packages. Send program outline and documentation. Reports in 4 weeks. Pays 10% royalty for non-exclusive rights. Simultaneous and previously published submissions OK. Programmer's guidelines for legal size SAE and 1 first class stamp.
Needs: Arcade-style games with extensive graphics and high speed. Strategy games and fantasy/science fiction games that will appeal to board gamers. Programs for general home use. No slow, cumbersome BASIC programs. Prefers programs in machine-code or assembly language; otherwise, BASIC. Looks for animation and fast response time features.
Recent Programs: *Escape from Stalag Luft III* (16K strategy game for the TS1000 and ZX81. As a P.O.W. you must plan escapes, and hide tunnels, wirecutters, disguises, etc. from the guards directed by the computer); *The ZX81 Home Computer Package* (four 1K programs: *Billboard* scrolls messages, *Composer* plays music, *Etch-a-Screen* writes pictures, and *Checkbook Balancer*).
Tips: "We are interested in programs you have designed, not in copies of existing software, or programs that are rewritten from magazine listings."

‡**SIRIUS SOFTWARE, INC.**, 10364 Rockingham Dr., Sacramento CA 95826. (916)366-1195. Product Manager: Ernest Brock. Estab. 1981. Software publisher producing educational and entertainment material for Apple, Atari 400/800/1200, VIC-20, Commodore 64, IBM-PC, TI-99/4A. Currently publishes 40 programs; 50% freelance. Send program outline and documentation. Reports in 1 week on queries and outlines; 1 month on programs. Buys all rights. No simultaneous or previously published submissions. Pays 3-21% royalty. Free programmer's guidelines.
Needs: Games—fast action, adventure and educational in assembly language. No business software or game

ideas without a program. Looks for audio, animation and color features.

Tips: "Programs must be at least as good as current best sellers. Do some research before you submit your game."

‡**SOUTHWESTERN DATA SYSTEMS,** Suite E, 10761 Woodside, Santee CA 92071. (619)562-3670. Contact: Tom Burns, Software Evaluation. Software publisher producing educational, entertainment, professional/business, communications and utilities material for Apple II and IBM P/C (5¼" diskettes). Currently publishes 24 programs; 80% freelance. Send demo disk or program outline and documentation. Reports in 2 weeks on queries; 8 weeks on programs. Buys all rights. Simultaneous and previously published submissions OK. Pays 10-25% royalty.

Needs: Utilities (programming aids); communications (electronic mail). No business programs. Looks for audio, animation, color and other features as they apply.

Recent Programs: *Routine Machine* (installs machine language subroutines automatically in Applesoft programs); *Ascii Express The Professional* (versatile communications program available for the Apple—supports all modems, all communication devices, all 80 column cards, etc.).

Tips: "The commercial appeal of the product must reach the largest audience possible—in short, can anybody use it?"

‡**SPECTRAL ASSOCIATES,** 3418 S. 90th St., Tacoma WA 98409. (206)581-6938. Manager: Cindy Shackleford. Estab. 1981. Software publisher producing educational, entertainment, and professional/business material for TRS-80, TDPSystem 100, Dragon 32 systems (cassette, disk, ROMPAC). Currently publishes over 50 programs; 50% freelance. Query with resume and credits, or send demo disk, or program outline and documentation. Reports in 1 month. Simultaneous and previously published submissions OK. Pays royalty. Programmer's guidelines for business-size SAE and 1 first class stamp.

Needs: Games, foreign languages for high schoolers, accounting, utilities, and a flex disk operating system. "We will accept all software submissions in 6809 and 6502 machine language." Looks for color and graphics features.

Recent Programs: *Lancer*; *Lunar Rover Patrol*; *Math Drill Math Flasher* (math education); *Keys of the Wizard Maze Escape* (adventure game).

Tips: "Appeal to the demands of the public in color graphics. Freelance software market is increasing for arcade-type games and good, educational programs."

‡**SUPERSOFT, INC.,** Box 1628, Champaign IL 61820. (217)359-2112. Marketing Director: Stephen Hagler. Software publisher producing educational, professional/business and languages/language compilers for most CP/M-80, CP/M-86 and MS DOS compatible systems. Currently publishes 30 programs; 50% freelance. Query with resume and credits. Reports in 1 week on queries; 4 months on outlines and programs. Buys variable rights. Simultaneous submissions OK. Pays royalty; average is 15% of net sales.

Needs: Business programs and programming languages for CP/M-80, CP/M-86; MS DOS (IBM PC DOS) and Apple DOS. Looks for completeness.

Recent Programs: *Personal Data Base* (data base/filing program for IBM PC); *BASIC Compiler* (superset of standard BASIC, native code compiler).

Tips: "Write something with a potential to Sell!"

‡**JOHN WILEY & SONS, INC.,** 605 3rd Ave., New York NY 10158. (212)856-6540. Software publisher producing educational, professional/business and engineering software for IBM, Apple II, TRS 80-I, II, III, H-P, Commodore 64, VIC 20, Atari. Currently publishes 7 programs; 100% freelance. Send program outline and documentation or demo disk. Reports in 4 weeks on queries; 2 months on outlines; 3 months on programs. Buys all rights. Previously published submissions OK. Pays 10-20% royalty or makes outright purchase "depending on the program." Free programmer's guidelines.

Needs: Consumer programs and programs in unique business areas (not spread sheet). No games. Looks for animation and use of the computer's capabilities.

Recent Programs: *Buy or Lease* (program for companies considering purchase or lease of capital equipment); *Personal Investment Analysis* (mortgage; retirement fund, tax-free securities, etc.).

Tips: "Send complete information on programs that have wide audience appeal, or unique specialized market (high priced). Information should include competition and machine requirements."

Greeting Card Publishers

To write for this market, your research must be ongoing. Study the card racks at your book or department store. Look at cards with a critical eye—who is the audience for this card? Why does it "work"? Write for a company's guidelines or current needs list. Send SASE for a copy of the *Artists & Writers Market List* available from the National Association of Greeting Card Publishers, Suite 300, 600 Pennsylvania Ave., Washington DC 20003. Read *A Guide to Greeting Card Writing*, edited by Larry Sandman (Writer's Digest Books), and *How to Make Money Writing Little Articles, Anecdotes, Hints, Recipes, Light Verse and Other Fillers*, by Connie Emerson (Writer's Digest Books).

To submit conventional greeting card material, type or neatly print your verses on either 4x6 or 3x5 slips of paper or file cards. For humorous or studio card ideas, either fold sheets of paper into card dummies about the size and shape of an actual card, or use file cards. For ideas that use attachments, try to get the actual attachment and put it on your dummy; if you can't, suggest the attachment. For mechanical card ideas, you must make a workable mechanical dummy. Most companies will pay more for attachment and mechanical card ideas.

Neatly print or type your idea on the dummy as it would appear on the finished card. Type your name and address on the back of each dummy or card, along with an identification number (which helps both you and the editor in keeping records). Always maintain records of where and when ideas were submitted; use a file card for each idea.

Submit 5-15 ideas at a time (this constitutes a "batch"). Quality, not quantity, should be your guideline. Keep the file cards for each batch together until rejected ideas are returned. You may want to code each submission so you can identify how many you have sent and where.

Listings below cover publishers' requirements for verse, gags and other product ideas. Artwork requirements are also covered when a company is interested in a complete package of art and idea.

AMBERLEY GREETING CARD CO., Box 36159, Cincinnati OH 45236. Editor: Ned Stern. Submit ideas in batches of 10-20 on regular 3x5 cards. No conventional cards. Reports in 3-4 weeks. Buys all rights. SASE. Free market list revised about every 6 months (include SASE with request).
Humorous, Studio and Promotions: Buys all kinds of studio and humorous everyday cards. Birthday studio is still the best selling caption. We never get enough. We look for belly laugh humor. All types of risque are accepted. No ideas with attachments. We prefer short and snappy ideas. The shorter gags seem to sell best. No seasonal cards. Buys 200 items/year. Pays $40."

AMERICAN GREETINGS CORP., 10500 American Rd., Cleveland OH 44144. Editorial Director: Karen Middaugh. Submit ideas in batches of 10-15.
Needs: "Interested in *fresh*, well-written material for cards, promotions, new concepts, new products. Will review copy ideas for our stable of characters: Ziggy, Holly Hobbie, Strawberry Shortcake, Sherman on the Mount, Himself the Elf, etc. Please study these characters before submitting."
Other Product Lines: Will consider ideas and copy for posters, plaques, calendars, invitations and announcements, serious as well as humorous and cute.

ARTFORMS CARD CORPORATION, #7, 3150 Skokie Valley Rd., Highland Park IL 60035. (312)433-0532. Editor: Ms. Bluma K. Marder. Buys "about 60-70 messages"/year. Submit ideas in batches of 10. Submit seasonal/holiday material 6 months in advance. SASE. Reports in 3 weeks. Buys common law and statutory copyright rights. Market list available for legal size SASE.
Needs: Conventional; humorous; informal; inspirational; sensitivity; studio; messages for Jewish Greeting Cards such as Bar/Bat Mitzvah, Jewish New Year and Chanukah; Wedding, Sympathy, Anniversary, Get Well and Birthday. No insults or risque greetings. Pays $15-25/card idea.
Other Product Lines: Gift wrap for Chanukah and year 'round use.
Recent Verse: "Praying that you/And the ones you hold dear/Will all be inscribed/For a Happy New Year."
Tips: "Do research on Judaism so greeting is not questionable to a religious market; also, if Biblical quotes are

used, make sure references are correct. We look for simple messages that pertain directly to subject matter. Humorous cards are selling well."

CAROLYN BEAN PUBLISHING, LTD., 120 2nd St., San Francisco CA 94105. (415)957-9574. President: John C.W. Carroll. "We are just opening to message-bearing cards, so we don't have a history yet." Submit seasonal/holiday material 18 months in advance. SASE. Reports in 6 weeks. Buys exclusive card rights; negotiates others. Pays on acceptance or publication. Free writer's guidelines.
Needs: Conventional holiday and occasions; humorous; informal; studio ("our cards are artistically sophisticated); general, occasion-oriented messages. Looks for sophisticated, witty, and/or sensitive material. No Hallmark-type, "hearts and flowers" messages or heavy Christian messages. Pays $15-30. "These terms are negotiable."

BLUE MOUNTAIN ARTS, INC., Dept. WM, Box 1007, Boulder CO 80306. Contact: Editorial Staff. Buys 50-75 items/year. SASE. Reports in 3-5 months. Buys all rights. Pays on publication.
Needs: Inspirational (without being religious); and sensitivity ("primarily need sensitive and sensible writings about love, friendships, families, philosophies, etc.—written with originality and universal appeal"). Pays $150.
Other Product Lines: Calendars, gift books and greeting books. Payment varies.
Tips: "Get a feel for the Blue Mountain Arts line prior to submitting material. Our needs differ from other card publishers; we do not use rhymed verse, preferring instead a more honest person-to-person style. We use unrhymed, sensitive poetry and prose on the deep significance and meaning of life and relationships. A very limited amount of freelance material is selected each year, either for publication on a notecard or in a gift anthology, and the selection prospects are highly competitive. But new material is always welcome and each manuscript is given serious consideration."

BRILLIANT ENTERPRISES, 117 W. Valerio St., Santa Barbara CA 93101. Contact: Editorial Dept. Buys all rights. Submit words and art in black on 5½x3½ horizontal, thin white paper in batches of no more than 15. Reports "usually in 2 weeks." SASE. Catalog and sample set for $1.
Needs: Post cards. Messages should be "of a highly original nature, emphasizing subtlety, simplicity, insight, wit, profundity, beauty, and felicity of expression. Accompanying art should be in the nature of oblique commentary or decoration rather than direct illustration. Messages should be of universal appeal, capable of being appreciated by all types of people and of being easily translated into other languages. Since our line of cards is highly unconventional, it is essential that freelancers study it before submitting." No "topical references, subjects limited to American culture, or puns." Limit of 17 words/card. Pays $40 for "complete ready-to-print word and picture design."
Recent Verse: "Maybe I'm lucky to be going so slowly,/Because I may be going in the wrong direction."
Tips: For further tips, study Ashleigh Brilliant's 3 books: *I May Not Be Totally Perfect, But Parts of Me Are Excellent, I Have Abandoned My Search for Truth, and Am Now Looking for a Good Fantasy,* and *Appreciate Me Now, and Avoid the Rush* ($5.95 each postpaid).

CONTENOVA, 1239 Adanac St., Vancouver, British Columbia, Canada V6A 2C8. (604)253-4444. Editor: F. Hird-Rutter. Submit ideas on 3x5 cards or small mock-ups in batches of 10. Reports in 3-6 weeks. Buys world rights. Pays on acceptance. Current needs list for SAE and International Reply Coupon. Do *not* send US postage stamps.
Needs: Humorous, studio, both risque and nonrisque. "The shorter, the better." Birthday, belated birthday, get well, anniversary, thank you, congratulations, miss you, new job, etc. Seasonal ideas needed for Christmas by March; Valentine's Day (September). Pays $50.

DRAWING BOARD GREETING CARDS, INC., 8200 Carpenter Freeway, Dallas TX 75247. (214)637-0390. Editorial Director: Jimmie Fitzgerald. Submit ideas on 3x5 cards, typed, with name and address on each card. SASE. Reports in 2 weeks. Pays on acceptance.
Needs: Conventional, humorous, informal, inspirational, everyday, seasonal, and studio cards. No 'blue' or sex humor. Pays $30-80.
Other Product Lines: Calendars. Pays $200-600.

D. FORER & CO., INC., 105 E. 73rd St., New York NY 10021. (212)879-6600. Editor: Barbara Schaffer. SASE. Reports in 2 weeks. Not copyrighted. Pays on acceptance. One-time market list for SAE and 1 first class stamp..
Needs: Humorous, studio. Pays $20.

FRAN MAR GREETING CARDS, LTD., Box 1057, Mt. Vernon NY 10550. (914)664-5060. President: Stan Cohen. Buys 100-300 items/year. Submit ideas in small batches (no more than 15 in a batch) on 3x5 sheets or cards. SASE. "Copy will not be returned without SASE enclosed with submissions." Reports in 1-2 weeks.

Buys all rights. Pays on the 15th of the month following acceptance. Market list for SASE.
Needs: Invitations (all categories), thank you notes (all categories), humorous pads and stationery.
Other Product Lines: Stationery, novelty card concepts, captions, novelty pad captions. Pays $25/card idea.
Recent Verses: Pad concept: (pad all green except for 2 eyes at the bottom). Caption: "This is not a pad, somebody squashed my froggie." Invitation: "A surprise party/Come help us surprise the pants off—."
Tips: Send "short copy—with a punch. Pads should be functional and/or funny."

HALLMARK CARDS, INC., Contemporary Design Department, #303, Box 580, Kansas City MO 64141. Contact: Editor, Contemporary. Submit ideas either on card mock-ups or 3x5 cards; 10-20/batch. SASE. Reports in 2-3 weeks. Buys all rights. Pays on acceptance. Market list for SASE.
Needs: Studio cards. Pays $78 maximum. "Avoid heavily masculine humor as our buyers are mostly female."
Recent Verse: "You're at that perfect age!/Somewhere between 'I Can't Wait a Minute!'/ and 'Wait a Minute, I Can't!'/Happy Birthday!"
Tips: "Don't send non-humorous material. The funnier the better: material with a good me-to-you message sells best for us."

LEANIN' TREE PUBLISHING CO., Box 9500, Boulder CO 80301. (303)530-1442. Contact: Greeting Card Editor. Submit ideas (not more than 15) on 3x5 cards. SASE. Reports in 2 months or sooner. May hold good ideas indefinitely. Pays $25 on publication. Market list for SASE.
Needs: Birthday, friendship, get well, anniversary, thank you, romantic love, Christmas, Valentines, Easter, Mother's Day, Father's Day.
Tips: "We publish western, inspirational and contemporary (not studio) cards. Do not send art suggestions. Become familiar with our card lines before submitting."

MAINE LINE CO., Box 418, Rockport ME 04856. (207)236-8536. Vice President: P. Ardman. Buys 100-200 card designs (copy and artwork)/year. Submit seasonal/holiday material 1 year in advance. SASE. Reports in 1 month. Buys negotiable but primarily greeting card rights. Pays ½ on acceptance and ½ on publication. Current market list for 9x12 SAE and 60¢ postage.
Needs: Humorous, informal, inspirational (not religious, but spiritual and motivational OK), sensitivity, Christmas. Pays $10-100 or 2.5% royalty. "Our fees/advances/royalties are individually negotiated. Basically, flat fee paid for executing our idea; advance/royalty for freelancer's concept/execution."
Other Product Lines: Calendars, greeting books, postcards, posters. Pays $10-400.
Tips: "We most often do a series, so submitting a concept and some examples is better than random lines. Cards do not need rhyming verses, but *sendable* funny or thought-provoking words, with universal appeal. The newer and more original the better—nothing you've seen before. We are looking for unusual, highly imaginative writers."

MARK I GREETING CARDS, 1733 W. Irving Park Rd., Chicago IL 60613. Editor: Alex H. Cohen. Buys all rights. Reports in 2 weeks. SASE.
Needs: Sensitivity, humorous and studio. "The verse should fit the cards; humorous for the studio cards; sensitive for the 'Tenderness' line. Also interested in Christmas (both sensitivity and studio), and Valentine's Day (sensitivity and studio), Mother's Day and Father's Day (studio and sensitivity), graduation (studio)." Pays $35 for studio ideas; $35-50 for sensitivity ideas; and $125-150 for color photographs.

MISTER B GREETING CARD CO., 3305 NW 37th St., Miami FL 33142. (305)638-8808. Editor: Harry Gee. Buys variable amount items/year. Submit seasonal/holiday material 9 months in advance. SASE. Reports in 2 weeks. Buys variable rights. Pays on publication. Current market list for business-sized SAE and 20¢ postage.
Needs: Conventional, humorous, sensitivity, soft line, special programs. "We're always looking for new ideas and subject matter." Pays 5% royalty after production expense or variable rate.
Other Product Lines: Bumper stickers, plaques, postcards, posters, promotions. Pays variable rates.

OATMEAL STUDIOS, Box 138, Rochester VT 05767. (802)767-3325. Editor: Helene Lehrer. Buys everyday (birthday, friendship, anniversary, get well) and seasonal (Christmas, Valentine's, Mother's Day, Father's Day, Easter) material. Submit seasonal/holiday material 10 months in advance. SASE. Reports in 2 weeks. Pays on acceptance. One-time market list for business sized SAE and 20¢ postage.
Needs: Humorous (clever and *very* funny); also warm and sensitive (not too sentimental). Pays $25 minimum.
Tips: "We are looking for writers to send us copy that will be funny enough to knock us off our feet, something with some zing to it. We also need material that is warm and sensitive, more serious but still cheerful; however not *too* sentimental."

THE PARAMOUNT LINE, INC., Box 678, Pawtucket RI 02862. Editor: Dolores Riccio. Submit ideas in batches of no more than 10-12. Submit seasonal/holiday material 10 months in advance. SASE. Reports in 3 weeks. Buys all rights. Pays on acceptance. Instruction sheet for SASE.

Needs: Announcements (everyday—all titles); conventional (everyday, seasonal 4-, 6-, and 8-line verses, general and family); humorous (everyday, seasonal, general and family titles); informal (everyday, seasonal, general and family titles); inspirational (religious and non-religious); invitations (everyday, all titles, Christmas, confirmation, communion); juvenile (everyday, seasonal, general and family titles); sensitivity (contemporary prose: love, general, wish, inspirational, compliment, etc.); studio (everyday, seasonal, general titles); and contemporary promotions. Rates upon request.

Other Product Lines: Greeting books and promotions.

Tips: "Study the market; use conversational, contemporary language; include SASE; send 10-12 items at a time, on 3x5 cards."

‡**PORTAL PUBLICATIONS, LTD.**, 21 Tamal Vista Blvd., Corte Madera CA 94925. (415)924-5652. Editor: André Sala. Buys 150 greeting card lines/year. SASE. Reports in 8 weeks. Pays on acceptance. Free guidelines.

Needs: Conventional, humorous, informal, invitations, sensitivity, soft line, studio, Pays $50/card idea.

RED FARM STUDIO, 334 Pleasant St., Box 347, Pawtucket RI 02860. Editor: Claudia Scott. Send 6-12 submissions at 1 time. Submit ideas in batches of 6 or more on 3x5 index cards. SASE. Reports in 1-2 weeks. Pays on acceptance. Pay varies.

Needs: Material for birthday, wedding, new baby, get well, retirement, graduation, anniversary, Mother's Day, Father's Day, and Easter. Pay varies.

Other Product Lines: Coloring books, paintables, placemats, gift wrap and note paper. No studio-type or related subjects.

Recent Verse: "Happy Birthday, Grandmother/With many happy memories/of every hour spent with you . . . /and many loving wishes/for life's best things . . . just for you!"

REED STARLINE CARD CO., 3331 Sunset Blvd., Los Angeles CA 90026. (213)663-3161. Submit seasonal/holiday material 1 year in advance. SASE. Reports in 2 weeks. Pays on acceptance. Free market list.

Needs: Announcements, humorous, informal, invitations and studio. No verse or jingles-type material. Pays $40/card idea.

Tips: "Study the current trends on card racks to determine the type of card that is selling."

SANGAMON GREETING CARD CO., Rt. 48 W., Taylorville IL 62568. (217)824-2261. Verse Editor: Mary Munyon. "We purchase large amounts of material." Submit seasonal/holiday material right after holiday. SASE. Reports in 4-6 weeks. Buys all rights. Pays on acceptance. "If the writer sends a sample of his work and I am interested, I will personally keep in contact with him as to our needs. (We work in season order.)"

Needs: Birth announcements (very little), conventional (all types), humorous (all types), informal (all categories), inspirational (all categories), invitations (showers, parties), juvenile (all types), sensitivity (birthday, Valentine's Day—most lines), soft line (all types), studio (some—use for promo series), humorous gags that are easily illustrated. Pays $1.50/line (verse); $15/gag.

VAGABOND CREATIONS, INC., 2560 Lance Dr., Dayton OH 45409. Editor: George F. Stanley Jr. Buys all rights. Submit seasonal material any time; "we try to plan ahead a great deal in advance." Submit on 3x5 cards. "We don't want artwork—only ideas." Reports in same week usually. May hold ideas 3 or 4 days. SASE for return of submissions.

Needs: Christmas, Valentine's, graduation, everyday, Mother's Day and Father's Day verse. "The current style of the new 'Sophisticates' greeting card line is graphics only on the front with a short tie-in punch line on the inside of the card. General rather than specific subject matter." Buys 50 items/year. Pays $10 "for beginners; up to $15 for regular contributors."

Other Product Lines: Interested in receiving copy for mottoes, humorous buttons, and postcards. "On buttons we like double-entendre expressions—preferably short. We don't want the protest button or a specific person named. We pay $10 for each button idea." Mottoes should be written in the first-person about situations at the job, about the job, confusion, modest bragging, drinking habits, etc. Pays $10 for mottoes.

Tips: "Our audience includes college students and their contemporaries . . . and young moderns. Writers can tailor their efforts by checking racks in college bookstores and discussing what college students are requesting with card buyers in these stores."

Appendix

The Business of Freelancing

There are some things about the writing business that ring true whether you are writing advertising copy for Bozell & Jacobs, the final draft of your novel for Harper & Row, or an exposé for *Esquire*. These appendix pages put you in touch with a modicum of generalization—standards flexible enough to be modified to fit a particular editor's wants. These are the guidelines with which most of the publishing community can live; these are the tips and treatments they expect professional writers to know.

Manuscript Mechanics

It's a grand thing to dream of seeing a story with your byline in one of the major national magazines. The actual *writing* of it may be a bit difficult, but once you have it down in good shape on a rough draft, the rest is a snap . . . you *think*. There is still one very important—though often irksome—chore to do.

Sometimes it's a little difficult to climb off that lofty, creative plane of writing and find the old bugaboo of simple manuscript mechanics staring you in the eye. It's a comedown. It's irritating. It's bothersome. But it's a necessary evil and the quicker you start using the right way, the easier it is to live with.

Type of Paper. One of the things to consider is the paper. It must measure 8½x11 inches. That's a standard size and editors are adamant; they don't want off-beat colors and sizes.

There's a wide range of white, 8½x11 papers. The cheaper ones are all wood content. They will suffice but they are not recommended. Your best bet is a good 25 percent cotton fiber content paper. It has quality feel, smoothness, shows type neatly and holds up under erasing. Editors almost unanimously discourage the use of erasable bond for manuscripts, as it tends to smear when handled. Where weight of the paper is concerned, don't use less than a 16-pound bond, and 20-pound is preferred.

File Copies. Always make a carbon or photocopy of your manuscript before you send it off to a publisher. You might even want to make several photocopies while the original manuscript is still fresh and crisp looking—as insurance against losing a submission in the mails, and as a means of circulating the same manuscript to other editors for reprint sales after the original has been accepted for publication. (Inform editors that the manuscript offered for reprint should *not* be used before it has first appeared in the original publication buying it, of course.) Some writers keep their original manuscript as a file copy, and submit a good-quality photocopy of the manuscript to an editor, with a personal note explaining that it is *not* a simultaneous or multiple submission. They tell the editor that he may toss the manuscript if it is of no interest to him, and reply with a self-addressed postcard (also enclosed). This costs a writer some photocopy expense, but saves on the postage bill—and may speed the manuscript review process in some editorial offices.

Type Characters. Another firm rule: for manuscripts, always type double space, using either elite or pica type. The slightly larger pica type is easier to read and many editors prefer it, but they don't object to elite. They *do* dislike (and often will refuse) hard-to-read or unusual typewritten characters, such as script, italics, Old English, all capitals, unusual letter styles, etc.

Page Format. Do not use a cover sheet; nor should you use a binder—unless you are submitting a play or television or movie script. Instead, in the upper left corner of page one list your name, address and phone number on four single-spaced lines. In the upper right corner, on three single-spaced lines, indicate the approximate word count for the manuscript, the rights you are offering for sale, and your copyright notice (© 1984 Joe Jones). It is *not* necessary to indicate that this is page one. Its format is self-evident.

On every page after the first, type your last name, a dash, and the page number in the upper left corner (page two, for example, would be: Jones—2). Then drop down two double-spaces and begin copy. If you are using a pseudonym, type your real name, followed by your pen name in parentheses, then a dash and the page number in the upper left corner of every page after page one. (page two, for example, would be: Jones (Smith) —2)

If you are submitting novel chapters, leave one third of the first page of each chapter blank before typing the title. Subsequent pages should include in the upper left margin the author's last name, a shortened form of the book's title and a chapter number. Use arabic numerals for chapter titles.

How to Estimate Wordage. To estimate wordage, count the exact number of words on the first three pages of your manuscript (in manuscripts up to 25 pages), divide the total by 3 and multiply the result by the number of pages. Carry the total to the nearest 100 words. For example, say you have a 12-page manuscript with totals of 303, 316 and 289 words on the first three pages. Divide your total of 908 by 3 to get 302. Now multiply 302 x 12 pages and you get 3,624. Your approximate wordage, therefore, will be 3,600 words. On manuscripts over 25 pages, count five pages instead of three, then follow the same process, dividing by 5 instead of 3.

Now, flip the lever to double-space and center the title in capital letters halfway down the page. To center, set the tabulator to stop in the exact left-right center of the page. Count the letters in the title (including spaces and punctuation) and backspace half that number. Centered one double-space under that, type "by" and centered one double-space under that, your name or pseudonym.

Margins should be about 1¼ inches on all sides of each full page of typewritten manuscript. Paragraph indentation is five or six letter spaces, consistently.

Now, after the title and byline block, drop down three double-spaces, paragraph indent and start your story.

Concluding Page. Carry on just as you have on other pages after page one. After your last word and period on this page, however, skip three double-spaces and then center the words "The End" or, more commonly, the old telegrapher's symbol of — 30—meaning the same thing.

Special Points to Keep in Mind. Always use a good dark black (*not* colored) typewriter ribbon and clean your keys frequently. If the enclosures in the letters a, b, d, e, g, etc. get inked-in, your keys need cleaning. Keep your manuscript neat *always*. Occasional retyping over erasures is acceptable, but strikeovers are bad and give a manuscript a sloppy, careless appearance. Sloppy typing is viewed by many editors as an index to sloppy work habits—and the likelihood of careless research and writing. Strive for a clean, professional-looking manuscript that reflects pride in your work.

Jones--2

Title of Manuscript (optional)

    Begin the second page, and all following pages, in this manner--
with a page-number line (as above) that includes your name, in case
loose manuscript pages get shuffled by mistake. You may include the
title of your manuscript or a shortened version of the title to identify
the Jones manuscript this page 2 belongs to.

Joe Jones
1234 My Street
Anytown, U.S.A.
Tel. 123/456-7890

About 3,000 words
First Serial Rights
© 1984 Joe Jones

YOUR STORY OR ARTICLE TITLE HERE

by
Joe Jones

    The manuscript begins here--about halfway down the first page.
It should be cleanly typed, double spaced, using either elite or
pica type. Use one side of the paper only, and leave a margin of
about 1-1/4 inches on all four sides.

NEATNESS COUNTS. Here are sample pages of a manuscript ready for submission to an editor. If the author uses a pseudonym, it should be placed on the title page only in the byline position; the author's real name must always appear in the top left corner of the title page—for manuscript mailing and payment purposes. On subsequent pages, list the real name, then the pen name in parentheses, followed by a dash and the page number.

Computer-related Submissions. Because of the increased efficiency they afford the writing, revising and editing process, computers (word processors) are becoming a tool of the writing trade. Hard copy computer printouts and disk submissions are the newest result of the computer revolution's impact on writers.

Most editors are receptive to computer printout submissions if the type is letter quality (as opposed to dot matrix); double spaced with wide margins; and generally easy to read. Fewer editors at this point are ready to accept disk submissions because of the complications involved with system compatibility. Manuscripts submitted in disk form will likely become more popular with writers and editors as the interfacing of equipment becomes more sophisticated. Those editors who do welcome disk submissions often request that a hard copy of the manuscript accompany the disk.

Many listings in this edition of *Writer's Market* include information about editors' preferences regarding computer-related submissions. If no information is given, be sure to check with an editor before sending a computer printout or disk submission.

Mailing Your Manuscript. Except when working on assignment from a magazine, or when under contract to do a book for a publisher, always enclose a self-addressed return envelope and the correct amount of postage with your manuscript. Manuscript pages should be held together with a paper clip only—never stapled together. When submitting poetry, the poems should be typed single space (double space between stanzas), one poem per page. Long poems requiring more than a page should be on sheets paper-clipped together.

Most editors won't object too much if manuscripts under six pages are folded in thirds and letter-mailed. However, there is a marked *preference* for flat mailing (in large envelopes) of manuscripts of six or more pages. You will need two 9x12 gummed or clasped mailing envelopes: one for the return of the manuscript and any accompanying material, and another to send out the manuscript, photos and return envelope. It is acceptable to fold the 9x12 return envelope in half to fit inside the outer envelope. To prevent accidental loss of stamps, affix—don't paperclip—them to the return envelope.

Mark your envelope, as desired with FIRST CLASS MAIL, or SPECIAL FOURTH CLASS RATE: MANUSCRIPT. First Class mail costs more but assures better handling and faster delivery. Special Fourth Class mail is handled the same as Parcel Post, so wrap it well. Also, the Special Fourth Class Rate only applies in the US, and to manuscripts that weigh one pound or more (otherwise, there is no price break).

For lighter weight manuscripts, First Class mail is recommended because of the better speed and handling. First Class mail is handled the same as Air Mail.

For foreign publications and publishers, including the expanding Canadian markets, always enclose an International Reply Coupon (IRC), determined by the weight of the manuscript at the post office.

Insurance is available, but payable only on typing fees or the tangible value of what is in the package, i.e., writing paper, so your best insurance is to keep a copy of what you send.

First Class mail is forwarded or returned automatically; however, Special Fourth Class Rate mail is not. To make sure you get your submission back if undeliverable, print "Return Postage Guaranteed" under your return address.

Cover Letters. At the Special Fourth Class rate, you may enclose a personal letter with your manuscript; but you must also add enough First Class postage to cover the letter and mark FIRST CLASS LETTER ENCLOSED on the outside.

In most cases, a brief cover letter is helpful in personalizing the submission. Nothing you say will make the editor decide in your favor (the manuscript must stand by itself in that regard), so don't use the letter to make a sales pitch. But you may want to tell an editor something about yourself, your publishing history, or any particular qualifications you have for writing the enclosed manuscript. If you are doing an exposé on, say, nursing home irregularities—it would be useful to point out that you have worked as a volunteer in nursing homes for six years. If you have queried the editor on the article earlier, he probably already has the background information—so the note should be a brief reminder: "Here is the piece on nursing homes we discussed earlier. I look forward to hearing from you at your earliest convenience."

If the manuscript is a photocopy, be sure to indicate whether or not it is a multiple submission. An editor is likely to assume it is, unless you tell him otherwise—and many are offended by writers using this marketing tactic (though when agents use it, that seems to be OK).

When submitting a manuscript to a newspaper—even the Sunday magazine section—be sure to include a cover note inquiring about the paper's rates for freelance submissions. Newspaper editors are deluged regularly by PR offices and "free" writers who submit material for ego and publicity purposes. Make sure your submission is not part of that crowd, or you may find it in print without even an acknowledgment—much less a check.

Query Letters. If you have an article idea that seems "right" for a particular publication, you should contact the editor with a query. A query letter is a powerful tool. It can open doors or deny entry to the published land. Though no query alone will sell a manuscript, a bad one may squelch your chances of even a cursory look from an editor. A good query letter can be your right of passage.

Granted, the specifics of a query depend on your manuscript content, the audience you hope to reach, and the particular slant you are taking. But some general guidelines may help you structure your book or article proposal in a way that reflects your professionalism.

• A query letter should both inform and excite an editor—not only about an article/book idea, but about the prospect of your writing the manuscript.

• The lead paragraph may either succinctly capsule the idea, your slant and intent; or show the editor your style and topic by writing a representative excerpt. (The latter lead paragraph would be double spaced; with the rest of the query single-spaced.)

• Subsequent paragraphs should provide examples, facts and anecdotes that support the writing of the manuscript and verify your ability/qualification to do it.

• The closing paragraph might include a direct request to do the article/book; it may specify the date the manuscript can be completed and possibly a proposed length.

In general, query letters are single-spaced; and whenever possible, they should be limited to one typed page. They should be addressed to the current editor by name and be accompanied by SASE. Published writing samples and a list of credits may also be attached if appropriate. Accuracy in spelling, grammar and writing mechanics is essential.

See the sample query letter that resulted in a story sold to *Woman's Day*.

Submitting Photos by Mail. When submitting black & white prints with your manuscript, send 8x10 glossies unless the editor indicates otherwise. Stamp or print your name, address and phone number on the back of each print or contact sheet. Don't use a heavy felt tip pen because the ink will seep through the print.

Buy some sturdy 9x12 envelopes. Your photo dealer should have standard print mailers in stock; some may be pre-stamped with "Photos—Do Not Bend" and contain two cardboard inserts. You can also pick up corrugated cardboard inserts from your local grocery store. Place your print(s) between two cardboard inserts, wrap two rubber bands around the bundle, and insert it with your manuscript into the envelope.

When sending many prints (say, 25-50 for a photo book), mail them in a sturdy cardboard box; 8x10 print paper boxes are perfect. Add enough cardboard inserts to fill the carton after the prints and manuscript are in place, and cover the box with wrapping paper. Send rare or extremely valuable photos only when an editor specifically requests them; then send them in a fiberboard mailing case with canvas straps,

Query Letter Sample

Jane Chestnutt
Health and Medical Editor
Woman's Day
1515 Broadway
New York, New York 10036

Dear Jane:

A young mother wheeling her baby in the sunshine looks perfectly ordinary; so does a teenager shooting baskets in his high school gym. The fact that there's nothing unusual in either one's appearance is a miracle, for they both have scoliosis, a lateral curvature of the spine. Without recently developed surgical techniques to correct this disorder, neither the baby nor the baskets would have been possible. Pregnancy-related back strain would have crippled this mother, and the teen would have spent his high school years encased in a body cast.

Scoliosis affects 10 percent of all school age children; of those affected 85 percent are girls. Cases can range from mild to severe, and many scoliosis victims share a common destiny. If the curvature is left untreated, deformity and disability occur. The disorder often creates psychological problems as well as physical ones, including feelings of isolation and rejection. However, debility can be prevented by early treatment.

An article about scoliosis makes good sense for two reasons. First, the topic insures audience interest, since many readers of Woman's Day have children who are approaching the vulnerable years for this disorder. Second, scoliosis is newsworthy because several exciting, new treatments are supplanting older, incapacitating therapies.

The article would include a description of the early signs of scoliosis, instructions to parents about screening their children for symptoms, a summary of standard treatments and the latest information about medical advances against scoliosis, such as electrical stimulation, an improved version of the Harrington rod and electrospinal instrumentation. Several case histories, including those of the young mother and the teenager mentioned above, would add interest. The teenager's situation is especially remarkable, as he plays sports in school during the day and plugs himself into a small transmitter at night for treatment of his curvature with internal electric stimulation.

Among the physicians I expect to interview are: Dr. Martin Gruber, who recently performed the first experimental electrical implant surgery for scoliosis on Long Island; Dr. Morley Herbert, a Canadian research scientist who invented the surgical implant technique, and Dr. Walter Bobechko, a surgeon who has performed over 200 operations for scoliosis using the improved Harrington rod.

I hope you'll agree that this topic will make an informative, interesting article. I'm looking forward to hearing from you about it.

Sincerely,

Adrienne

Adrienne Popper

Ms. Popper's actual letter, of course, carried her address and the date. The query letter is used with her permission.

available at most photo stores. Tell the editor to return the photos in the same case or return the empty case itself if the photos are kept.

For color transparencies, 35mm is the universally accepted size. Few buyers will look at color prints. (Check each market listing individually for exact preferences from editors). To mail transparencies, use slotted acetate sheets, which hold twenty slides and offer protection from scratches, moisture, dirt and dust—available in standard sizes from most photo supply houses. Do not use glass mounts. Put your name, address and phone number on each transparency. Mail the transparencies just as you would prints, using corrugated cardboard. If a number of sheets are being sent, use a cardboard box. Because transparencies are irreplaceable (unless you have internegatives or duplicates made), be sure to insure the package.

One additional note about photo submissions. When you mail photos or transparencies to an editor, you are giving him permission to use any or all of the visuals according to the conditions and payment rates he has included in his *Writer's Market* listing. If he says, "We would like to consider these indefinitely", he may use them at any time—unless you respond in writing, voicing an objection or asking for their return.

Photo Captions. Prints and transparencies should always be captioned when submitted for consideration with a manuscript. For prints, type the caption on a sheet of paper and tape it to the bottom of the back of the print. The caption should fold over the front of the photo so that the buyer can fold it back for easy reading. Masking tape allows the editor to easily remove the copy for typesetting.

You can also type the captions on a separate sheet of paper, and assign each an index number corresponding with its photos. A third method, but not generally preferred, is to tape the caption to the back of the print.

Captions for transparencies 2¼x2¼ or larger can be typed on thin strips of paper and inserted in the acetate sleeve protecting the transparency. For 35mm transparencies, type the captions on a separate sheet and assign corresponding numbers.

Enclosing return postage with photos sent through the mail is more than a professional courtesy; it also helps assure that you'll get the photos back. Most writer/photographers enclose a self-addressed stamped envelope (SASE—same size as the envelope used for the submission) with their material. Never drop loose stamps into the original envelope, nor fasten them to one of the prints with a staple or paper clip. You can, however, enclose a small coin envelope (available at hobby stores) with return postage in it rather than attaching stamps to the return envelope.

Once your photos are properly packaged, speed and safe handling in the mail will be your main concerns. Most writers prefer First Class mail because it ensures both speed and safety of prints, but a cheaper rate can be allowed for the return of the material. A cover letter and manuscript can be mailed with any package sent first class. More information is available from the Postal Service.

Mailing Book Manuscripts. Do not bind your book manuscript pages in any way. They should be mailed loose in a box (a ream-size stationery box is perfect) without binding. To ensure a safe return, enclose a self-addressed label and suitable postage in stamps clipped to the label. If your manuscript is returned, it will either come back in your original box, or—increasingly likely today—in an insulated bag-like mailer, with your label and postage used thereon. Many publishing houses open the box a manuscript is mailed in, and toss the box (if it has not been damaged in the mails, or in the opening already); they then read and circulate the manuscript as necessary for editorial consideration, and finally route it through the mail room back to you with a letter or rejection slip. This kind of handling makes it likely that a freshly typed manuscript will be in rough shape even after one or two submissions. So it is wise to have several photocopies made of a book-length manuscript while it is still fresh—and to circulate those to publishers, rather than risk an expensive retyping job in the midst of your marketing effort. As mentioned above, indicate in a cover note that the submission is not a multiple submission if such is the case.

Postage by the Page

By Carolyn Hardesty

To assist you in using the right amount of postage for your manuscript's journey to and from an editorial office, consult the rates listed below. This chart is designed to tell you the correct amount of postage for manuscripts up to 70 pages. The weight of paper used to determine these figures was 20 pound, a paper with a respectable heft for impressing editors plus enough strength to tolerate repeated paper clip snaps if, alas, the piece is sent to several publications.

The chart shows first-class mailing costs. The middle columns give number of pages plus mailing envelope and SASE, and number of pages plus SASE (for return trips).

On the odd chance you mail very short manuscripts in large envelopes or perhaps submit a few large photos, you will be assessed an additional seven cents under the regulations for odd-sized mail (large envelope, two ounces or less).

Beyond the first 20¢ ounce, the increments are by 17¢ leaps. The exception is the fee for oversized envelopes; if this applies to you, add that denomination to your cache.

FIRST-CLASS POSTAGE RATES

ounces	9x12 envelope, 9x12 SASE number of pages	9x12 SASE (for return trips) number of pages	first-class postage
2	1 to 4	3 to 8	$ .37
3	5 to 10	9 to 12	.54
4	11 to 16	13 to 19	.71
5	17 to 21	20 to 25	.88
6	22 to 27	26 to 30	1.05
7	28 to 32	31 to 35	1.22
8	33 to 38	36 to 41	1.39
9	39 to 44	42 to 46	1.56
10	45 to 49	47 to 52	1.73
11	50 to 55	53 to 57	1.90
12	56 to 61	58 to 63	2.07

For short manuscripts or long queries, use a business-size envelope and up to five pages with a 20¢ stamp. If you are including a business-size SASE, four pages is the limit.

● First class packages weighing more than 12 ounces are charged according to geographical zones. This is true also for all weights of fourth class (or book rate) mail.

● Four captionless 5x7 photographs or two 8x10 photographs will increase the weight of your package by one ounce.

● Stamps of 20¢ and 17¢ denominations are available singly, by the sheet and in rolls of 500 and 3,000 (for the extremely prolific writer). Twenty cent stamps are also available in books of 6 and 20 and in rolls of 100.

● Insurance (to recover typing fees) is 45¢ for a $20 liability, 85¢ for up to $50, and $1.25 for coverage to $100.

● Certified mail costs 75¢.

● International Reply Coupons (IRCs) for Canadian and overseas submissions are generally available only at larger post offices.

● Record any changes in postal rates in pencil as they occur.

Carolyn Hardesty *is a freelance writer whose tendency to "overstamp" led her to develop the time- and money-saving "Postage by the Page."*

Book manuscripts can be mailed Fourth Class Manuscript Rate, but that can be slow and have an additional mauling effect on the package in the mails. When doing so, if you include a letter, state this on the outer wrapping and add appropriate postage to your manuscript postal rate. Most writers use First Class, secure in the feeling that their manuscript is in an editorial office within a few days. Some send book manuscripts using the United Parcel Service, which can be less expensive than First Class mail when you drop the package off at UPS yourself. The drawback here is that UPS cannot legally carry First Class mail, so you will have to send your cover letter a few days before giving UPS the manuscript, and both will arrive at about the same time. Check with UPS in your area to see if it has benefits for you. The cost depends on the weight of your manuscript and the delivery distance.

The tips and recommendations made here are based upon what editors prefer. Give editors what they prefer and you won't be beginning with a strike or two against you before the manuscript is even read.

The Waiting Game. The writer who sends off a story, article or book manuscript to an editor should turn immediately to other ideas and try to forget about the submission. Unless you are on assignment, or under contract to do a book—in which case, a phone call to your editor saying the manuscript is in the mail is quite appropriate—it's best to use your time productively on other writing projects, and let the submission take care of itself. But one day you realize it's been too long. According to the *Writer's Market* listing, your editor responds to submissions in a maximum of four weeks—and it's been six already, and you haven't heard a word. Will inquiring about it jeopardize a possible sale? Are they really considering it, or has the editor had an accident and your manuscript is at the bottom of a huge stack of unread mail?

If you have had no report from a publisher by the maximum reporting time given in a *WM* listing, allow six weeks' grace period and then write a brief letter to the editor asking if your manuscript (give the title, a brief description, and the date you mailed it) has in fact reached his office. If so, is it still under consideration? Your concern at this point is the mails: Is the manuscript safely delivered? Don't act impatient with an editor—who may be swamped, or short-handed, or about to give your manuscript a second reading. The wrong word or attitude from you at this point could be hazardous to your manuscript's health. Be polite, be professional. Enclose another SASE to expedite a reply. This is usually enough to stir a decision if matters are lagging in an editorial office, even during rush season (which is year 'round).

If you still hear nothing from a publisher one month after your follow-up, send the editor a short note asking if he received your previous follow-up, and include a photocopy of that second letter. If, after another month, you are still without word, send a polite letter saying that you are withdrawing the manuscript from consideration (include the title, date of submission, and dates of follow-up correspondence), and ask that the manuscript be returned immediately in the SASE your original correspondence included.

Rejection Slips. It is possible you will get a quick response from an editor in the form of a rejection. Rejection slips or letters should not be taken as a *personal* rejection. Direct your energy toward writing manuscripts, not writing attacking letters.

Whether disappointment comes from delayed editorial responses or rejection—never write in anger. Be cool, professional, and set about the business of finding another publisher for your work. The advantage of having a clean photocopy of the manuscript in your files at this point cannot be overstated. Move on to another publisher with it, using a personal cover letter and the same methods outlined above. In the meantime, continue working on your other writing projects.

Authors' Agents. If you have sold a reasonable number of articles, stories and manuscripts on your own, you may want to consider the services of an agent. An agent is a literary broker who frees you up to do the writing, while he makes sales and negotiates the best possible deals for you in the publishing world. He may or may not charge reading, criticism or marketing fees for his services, over and above his commission.

INTRODUCTORY OFFER
SAVE $3.00

Since 1920 *WRITER'S DIGEST* has been showing writers how to write publishable material and find the choice markets for it. Each monthly issue features:

- Hundreds of fresh markets for your writing. We list the names and addresses of editors, what types of writing they are currently buying, how much they pay, and how to get in touch with them. Get first crack at the new markets, while they are hungry for manuscripts.

- Professional insights, advice, and "how to" information from successful writers. Learn their techniques for writing and selling publishable material.

- Monthly expert columns about the writing *and* selling of fiction, nonfiction, and poetry.

A $3.00 DISCOUNT. Subscribe through this special introductory offer, and you will receive a full year (12 issues) of *WRITER'S DIGEST* for only $15 — that's a $3.00 savings off the $18 basic subscription rate. If you enclose payment with your order, and save us the expense of billing you, we will add an *extra issue* to your subscription, absolutely *free*.

GUARANTEE: If you are not satisfied with your subscription at any time, you may cancel it and receive a full refund for all unmailed issues due to you.

(Detach and mail today)

SUBSCRIPTION ORDER FORM

Yes, I want to know the techniques that professional writers use to write and sell publishable material. I want the latest market information, "how to" advice and other information that will help me get published. Start my subscription to WRITER'S DIGEST today.

Please check appropriate boxes:

☐ Send me a year (12 issues) of WRITER'S DIGEST for only $15 (a $3 discount off the basic subscription and cover price).

☐ I want to save even more. Send me two years of WRITER'S DIGEST for *only* $29 *(a $7 discount).*

(Please remit in U.S. dollars or equivalent. Outside of U.S. add $4.50 per year.)

☐ Payment Enclosed *(you get an extra issue for saving us billing postage).*

☐ Please Bill Me.

☐ Extend My Present Subscription

☐ New Subscription

Send my subscription to:

Name

Address

City   State   Zip

Please allow 5 weeks for first issue delivery.

PWM84-1

THE WORLD'S LEADING MAGAZINE FOR WRITERS

Would you like to:

- get up-to-the-minute reports on where to sell what you write?

- receive the advice of editors and professional writers about what to write and how to write it to increase your chances for getting published?

- read interviews with leading authors that reveal their secrets of success?

- hear what experts have to say about writing and selling fiction, non-fiction, and poetry?

 get a special introductory price for all this?

(See other side for details.)

NO POSTAGE
NECESSARY
IF MAILED
IN THE
UNITED STATES

BUSINESS REPLY CARD
FIRST CLASS   PERMIT NO. 481   CINCINNATI, OHIO

POSTAGE WILL BE PAID BY ADDRESSEE

Subscription Department
205 West Center Street
Marion, Ohio 43306

Having an agent is not the answer to your writing problems. Some writers prefer to find publishers on their own; hire attorneys for advice and contract review; and keep the 10-15% agent commission on domestic sales for themselves.

Finding an agent to handle your writing is not easy. Many accept new clients only through referrals; others represent only published writers. According to a survey by Author Aid/Research Associates International, 80% of the agents who read manuscripts from unpublished writers charge a fee for the service; 15% will not read any unsolicited manuscripts. There are agents who do not charge fees, however. And you should try to work with them first. Consult the *Literary Agents of North America: 1983-84 Marketplace* (Author Aid/Research Associates International, 350 E. 52nd St., New York City 10022) for a list of over 450 currently active agents (including those who do and do not charge fees) in the U.S. and Canada.

Two organizations, the Independent Literary Agents (ILA) and the Society of Authors' Representatives (SAR), may provide you with additional information on securing an agent's services. The SAR publishes a pamphlet called, "The Literary Agent," which explains the role of the agent and how to get one, and lists the current SAR membership. The pamphlet is free with a #10 SASE.

The Business of Writing

Writing is an occupation with many hidden costs. In addition to the time a writer spends over a typewriter actually *writing*, many hours and miles are logged doing research, soliciting materials, conducting interviews, communicating with editors, and rounding out the corners of a manuscript. While readers, and to some extent editors, are oblivious to these background tasks, the Internal Revenue Service need not be. Such costs can become deductible writing expenses at income tax time.

For the Records. Though the deadline for filing your tax return is April 15, you should maintain careful records all year. To arrive at verifiable figures, you will need two things: *records and receipts*. For tax purposes, good records are not only helpful; they are *required* by law. Receipts are the foundation that careful record keeping is built upon.

At tax time each year, a freelance writer normally reports his business activities on tax Schedule C ("Profit or Loss From Business or Profession"); the resulting figure for income is entered on Form 1040. In addition, if your writing or editing work nets you $400 or more in earnings, you must file a Schedule SE and pay self-employment tax, which makes you eligible for Social Security benefits. Furthermore, if you think your taxes from freelancing will be $100 or more, you are required to pay your taxes in quarterly installments. To do this, you file a declaration of estimated tax using Form 1040-ES ("Declaration Voucher") and use the envelopes the IRS provides to mail in your estimated taxes every three months.

It's not as complicated as it may sound, but one thing is certain: to document all these tax liabilities at the end of the year, you must have accurate records.

Tax laws don't require any particular type of records, as long as they are permanent, accurate and complete, and they clearly establish income, deductions, credits, etc. It's remarkably easy to overlook deductible expenses unless you record them at the time they are paid and keep receipts for them. Since some assets are subject to depreciation (typewriter, desk, files, tape recorder, camera equipment, etc.), you also need records of the purchase prices you used to determine depreciation allowances.

Finally, you need good records in case the IRS audits you and asks you to explain items reported on your return. Memos, scribbled notes or sketchy records that merely approximate income, deductions, or other pertinent items affecting your taxes are simply *not* adequate. You must have a record supported by sales slips, invoices, receipts, bank deposit slips, canceled checks, and other documents.

Records for Credit Purposes. You and the IRS are not the only ones interested in the well-being of your business. Banks, credit organizations, suppliers of materials, and others often require information on the condition of your finances when you apply for credit—if, for example, you want to buy a house.

In fact, freelance writers, in the eyes of many lending institutions, might as well be totally unemployed. Some writers have taken on fulltime jobs just to qualify for financing for a home, even when the "steady" job might produce less income than freelancing.

A Simple Bookkeeping System. There are almost as many different ways of keeping records as there are record-keepers to keep them. For a freelance writer, normally a simple type of "single-entry" bookkeeping that requires only one account book to record the flow of income and expense is completely adequate. At the heart of this single-entry system is the journal. It is an accounting book, available at any stationery store (the *Writer's Digest Diary* can be used, too), in which all the everyday transactions of your freelance business are recorded. Each transaction is set forth clearly, including the date, a description of the transaction, and the amount entered in the proper column—either "income" or "expense":

Income entries will include whatever funds you receive, either by cash or check. Expense entries might include payments you make for writing supplies, photocopying, postage, repairs, dues paid to writers' organizations, travel expenses, books and magazine subscriptions, photo developing and printing, etc.—whatever you have to spend as a business expense.

The Receipt File. Now comes the really important part: for each income entry you make, keep a copy of a receipt, an invoice, or some other record to substantiate that entry. For each expense entry, keep a canceled check, a receipt, or some other document. By keeping your record complete with some type of document to support *every* entry, your record is foolproof.

A partitioned, envelope-type folder works well for keeping receipts in order. If a receipt does not clearly indicate which entry it refers to, make a note on it and date it before filing it. That way, you can locate it quickly.

Business Banking. To record your income as accurately as possible, it is best to deposit all the money you receive in a separate bank account. This will give you deposit slips to verify the entries in your journal. Furthermore, you should make all payments by check, if possible, so that your business expenses will be well documented. If you have to pay cash, keep receipts on file.

Any record must be retained as long as it may be material to the administration of any law. Statutes of limitations for various legal purposes vary from state to state, but if you keep your records on file for seven to ten years, you will seldom run into difficulty. Records supporting items on a tax return should be kept for at least three years, although keeping them indefinitely is a good idea.

What's Deductible. Among your deductible expenses, don't overlook the following writing-related costs:

● **All writing supplies**, including paper, carbons, pens, ribbons, envelopes, copying costs, postage, photo developing and printing costs, and recording tapes.

● **Repairs and maintenance of writing equipment**, including typewriter, tape recorder and camera.

● **Courses and conferences attended to enhance you as a professional writer.** It's important to realize, though, that you can't deduct courses you take to *become* a writer. The IRS rule is that courses must be "refresher" or professionally improving in nature to count. Besides deducting the costs of these, also deduct mileage (at 20¢ a mile)—or actual car expenses, whichever is greater—cost of tickets for public transportation; cost of hotel/motel rooms; and costs of meals.

● **Courses taken as research on subjects you are writing about.** To establish that a course is for research, it would help if you had documentation from the potential publisher of your writings—such as a favorable response to a query. Even if the magazine should not publish what you write, the response will show the research was done in good faith.

● **Writing books, magazines and other references.**

Date	Description	Expense		Income	
JAN. 4	Regional Supply – 1ream of paper	5	80		
5	Photocopying – _Analog_ story		95		
5	Postage – story sent to Analog	1	15		
8	_Economic Bulletin_ – for March article & photos			450	00
10	Billy's Bookstore – 1984 Writer's Market	18	95		
14	Reed Real Estate – for editing 4th-quarter newsletter			225	00
15	Renewal of _IWD_ subscription	15	00		
18	Billy's – 20 manila envelopes	1	80		
21	Mountain Press – for editing _Survival Handbook_.			575	00
21	Aardvark & Son – for developing photos for _Am. Horse J._ article	9	55		
25	Regional Supply – Typewriter ribbons	15	20		
28	Fee for Western Writer's Conf.	24	50		
30	_American Horse Journal_ – for February article			325	00
	JAN. TOTALS	92	50	1,575	00

A typical single-entry page in a bookkeeping journal that records a freelance writer's income and expense transactions.

- **Dues paid for membership in writers' organizations.**
- **Home office expenses.** In the past, writers using a portion of their home dining room or living room have been allowed to deduct a percentage of home costs as "office" expenses. This is no longer allowed. To take a home office deduction today, you must have a portion of your dwelling set aside _solely for writing on a regular basis._ The same rule applies to a separate structure on your property. For example, you may not use a portion of your garage for writing and a portion for parking your car. If your car goes in, your home office expense is out.

Example: If you rent a five-room apartment for $300 a month and use one room exclusively for writing, you are entitled to deduct one-fifth of the rent which comes to $60 a month, or $720 a year. Add to this one-fifth of your heating bill and one-fifth of your electric bill and watch the deductions mount up. Keep a list, too, of long-distance phone bills arising from your writing.

If you own your home and use one room for writing, you can deduct the allocated expenses of operating that room. Among these allowable expenses are interest on mortgage, real estate taxes, repairs or additions to the home, cost of utilities, home insurance premiums, and depreciation on the room.

Example: If you own a seven-room house, one room used for writing, one-seventh of the total cost of the house can be depreciated, as well as one-seventh of the above mentioned expenses.

Note: There is a limit to home office expenses. You may not exceed in deductible expenses the amount of your gross income. If you made $1,000 last year, you can't deduct any more than that in home office expenses—no matter how much they came to. Just $1,000 in this case.

● **Mileage.** Take 20¢ a mile for the first 15,000 miles you travel on writing-related missions and 11¢ a mile for miles traveled over 15,000. Or you may take the actual cost of operating your car—gas, oil, tires, maintenance and depreciation. (See below for figuring depreciation.) If you use your car 100 percent for writing, the total cost of operating it is deductible. Compare mileage deduction to cost deduction, and use the one that gives you the bigger break.

What May Be Depreciated. You can count depreciation of your typewriter, desk, chair, lamps, tape recorder, files, camera equipment, photocopier, or anything else related to your writing which costs a considerable amount of money and which has a useful life of more than one year.

You have a couple of ways to recover these capital expenses. For most property placed into service after 1980, costs can be recovered in a relatively short period of time using the Accelerated Cost Recovery System (ACRS). Under this system, eligible capital expenses can be recovered by applying pre-determined percentages over a 3-, 5-, or 10-year period, depending on the category into which your property falls. Most of a writer's tangible property would likely be considered 3- or 5-year property. The accelerated cost recovery of 3-year property is 25% of its original cost in the first year; 38% in the second year; 37% in the third year. For 5-year recovery property, deductions are 15% the first year; 22% the second year; and 21% for each of the last 3 years.

Along with using the ACRS, you are eligible to take an additional deduction called an investment tax credit (ITC) for furniture, equipment, and other depreciable assets used in your writing business. This is subtracted from your total tax liability. For assets categorized as 3-year property, the ITC is a 6% deduction from any tax you owe. For 5-year property, the credit is 10%.

The IRS gives you yet another option for recovering your capital expenses. For tax years beginning after 1981, you may deduct up to $5,000 of normally depreciable property in the year you buy the typewriter, word processor or whatever. However, if you elect to take this deduction, you forfeit the investment tax credit.

There are other options, requirements and regulations that can affect the figuring of your taxes. It's wise to consult with a tax professional who is aware of the current percentages and category definitions involved in figuring your taxes. It will be important to calculate your tax both ways—using the $5,000 deduction and the ACRS/tax investment credit combination—in deciding which method best fits your situation.

Self-Employment Earnings. If after deductions you earn $400 or more, you are required to pay a Social Security tax of .0935 of the first $35,700 of your earnings. And you must fill out and submit a Schedule SE (for "self-employment").

Finally, save your rejection slips. Though they may be unpleasant reminders, keep them in a folder. Look at them as professional communiques from publishers, not personal rejection letters. If you are subjected to a tax audit, these letters will help establish you as a working writer.

Rights and the Writer

Selling Rights to Your Writing. Initially, a writer may have little say in the rights sold to an editor. The beginning writer, in fact, can jeopardize a sale by haggling with an editor who is likely to have other writers on call who are anxious to please. As long as there are more writers than there are markets, this situation will remain the same.

As a writer acquires skill, reliability, and professionalism on the job, however, that writer becomes more valued to editors—and rights become a more important consideration. Though a beginning writer will accept modest payment just to get in print, an experienced writer soon learns that he cannot afford to give away good writing just to see a byline. At this point a writer must become concerned with selling reprints of articles already sold to one market, or using sold articles as chapters in a book on the same topic, or seeking markets for the same material overseas, offering work to TV or the movies. Dramatic rights can be meaningful for both fiction and nonfiction writers. Jame Michener's bestselling *Space* was bought by CBS for a ten-hour mini series. The movie *Doctor Detroit* is based on a story that appeared in *Esquire* magazine.

What Editors Want. And so it is that writers should strive to keep as many rights to their work as they can from the outset, because before you can resell any piece of writing you must own the rights to negotiate. If you have sold "all rights" to an article, for instance, it can be reprinted *without* your permission, and without additional payment to you. What an editor buys, therefore, will determine whether you can resell your own work. Here is a list of the rights most editors and publishers seek.

● **First Serial Rights.** The word serial here does not mean publication in installments, but refers to the fact that libraries call periodicals "serials" because they are published in serial or continuing fashion. *First serial rights* means the writer offers the newspaper or magazine (both of which are periodicals) the right to publish the article, story or poem the first time in their periodical. All other rights to the material belong to the writer. Variations on this right are, for example, First North American Serial rights. Some magazines use this purchasing technique to obtain the right to publish first in both America and Canada since many American magazines are circulated in Canada. If they had purchased only First U.S. Serial Rights, a Canadian magazine could come out with prior or simultaneous publication of the same material. When material is excerpted from a book which is to be published and it appears in a magazine or newspaper prior to book publication, this is also called First Serial Rights.

● **One-Time Rights.** This differs from First Serial Rights in that the buyer has no guarantee he will be the first to publish the work. One-time rights most often applies to photos, but occasionally writing, too.

● **Second Serial (Reprint) Rights.** This gives a newspaper or magazine the opportunity to print an article, poem or story after it has already appeared in some other newspaper or magazine. The term is also used to refer to the sale of part of a book to a newspaper or magazine after a book has been published, whether or not there has been any first serial publication (income derived from second serial rights to book material is often shared 50/50 by author and book publisher).

● **All Rights.** Some magazines, either because of the top prices they pay for material, or the fact that they have book publishing interests or foreign magazine connections, sometimes buy All Rights. A writer who sells an article, story or poem to a magazine under these terms, forfeits the right to use his material in its present form elsewhere himself. If you sign a "work-for-hire" agreement, you sign away all rights and the copyright to the company making the assignment. If the writer thinks he may want to use his material later (perhaps in book form), he must avoid submitting to these types of markets, or refuse payment and withdraw his material if he discovers it later. Or ask the editor whether he's willing to buy only first rights instead of all rights before you agree to an assignment or a sale. Some editors will reassign rights to a writer after a given period—say, one year. It's worth an inquiry in writing.

● **Simultaneous Rights.** This term covers articles and stories which are sold to publications (primarily religious magazines) which do not have overlapping circulations. A Baptist publication, for example, might be willing to buy Simultaneous Rights to a Christmas story which they like very much, even though they know a Presbyterian magazine may be publishing the same story in one of its Christmas issues. Publications which will buy simultaneous rights indicate this fact in their listings in *Writer's Market*. Always advise an editor when the material you are sending is a Simultaneous Submission.

● **Foreign Serial Rights.** Can you resell a story you have had published in America to a foreign magazine? If you sold only First U.S. Serial Rights to the American magazine, yes, you are free to market your story abroad. This presumes, of course, that the foreign magazine does buy material which has previously appeared in an American periodical.

● **Syndication Rights.** This is a division of serial rights. For example, a book publisher may sell the rights to a newspaper syndicate to print a book in twelve installments in, say, each of twenty United States newspapers. If they did this prior to book publication it would be syndicating First Serial Rights to the book. If they did this after book publication, they would be syndicating Second Serial Rights to the book.

● **Dramatic, Television and Motion Picture Rights.** This means the writer is selling his material for use on the stage, in television, or in the movies. Often a one-year "option" to buy such rights is offered (generally for 10% of the total price), and the interested party then tries to sell the idea to other people—actors, directors, studios or television networks, etc.—who become part of the project, which then becomes a script. Some properties are optioned over and over again, but fail to become dramatic productions. In such cases, the writer can sell his rights again and again—as long as there is interest in the material. Though dramatic, TV and motion picture rights are more important to the fiction writer than to the nonfiction writer, producers today are increasingly interested in "real-life" material; many biographies and articles that are slices of real life are being dramatized. For example, motion picture rights to Nicholas Gage's book, *Eleni* (an account of his mother's life and torture by Communists in a post-World War II Greek village), were bought for $850,000.

Communicate and Clarify. Before submitting material to a market, check its listing in this book to see what rights are purchased. Most editors will discuss rights they wish to purchase before an exchange of money occurs. Some buyers are adamant about what rights they will accept; others will negotiate. In any case, the rights purchased should be stated specifically *in writing* sometime during the course of the sale, usually in a letter or memo of agreement. *Note*: If no rights are transferred in writing, and the material is sold for use in a collective work (that is, a work that derives material from a number of contributors), you are authorizing unlimited use of the piece in that work or in subsequent issues or updates of the work. Thus, you can't collect reprint fees if the rights weren't spelled out in advance, in writing.

Give as much attention to the rights you haven't sold as you do the rights you have sold. Be aware of the rights you retain, with an eye out for additional sales.

Whatever rights you sell or don't sell, make sure all parties involved in any sale understand the terms of the sale. Clarify what is being sold *before* any actual sale, and do it in writing. Communication, coupled with these guidelines and some common sense, will preclude misunderstandings with editors over rights.

Copyrighting Your Writing. The new copyright law, effective since January 1, 1978, protects your writing, unequivocally recognizes the creator of the work as its owner, and grants the creator all the rights, benefits and *privileges* that ownership entails.

In other words, the moment you finish a piece of writing—whether it be short story, article, novel, poem or even paragraph—the law recognizes that only you can decide how it is to be used.

This law gives writers power in dealing with editors and publishers, but they should understand how to use that power. They should also understand that certain circumstances can complicate and confuse the concept of ownership. Writers must be wary of these circumstances, or risk losing ownership of their work.

Here are answers to commonly asked questions about copyright law:

● **To what rights am I entitled under copyright law?** The law gives you, as creator of your work, the right to print, reprint and copy the work; to sell or distribute copies of the work; to prepare "derivative works"—dramatizations, translations, musical arrangement, novelizations, etc.; to record the work; and to perform or display literary, dramatic or musical works publicly. These rights give you control over how your work is used, and assure you that you receive payment for any use of your work.

If, however, you create the work as a "work-for-hire," you *do not* own any of these rights. The person or company that commissioned the work-for-hire owns the copyright. The work-for-hire agreement will be discussed in more detail later.

● **When does copyright law take effect, and how long does it last?** A piece of writing is copyrighted the moment it is put to paper. Protection lasts for the life of the author plus 50 years, thus allowing your heirs to benefit from your work. For material written by two or more people, protection lasts for the life of the last survivor plus 50 years. The life-plus-50 provision applies if the work was created or registered with the Copyright Office after Jan. 1, 1978, when the updated copyright law took effect. The old law protected works for a 28-year term, and gave the copyright owner the option to renew the copyright for an additional 28 years at the end of that term. Works copyrighted under the old law that are in their second 28-year term automatically receive an additional 19 years of protection (for a total of 75 years). Works in their first term also receive the 19-year extension, but must still be renewed when the first term ends.

If you create a work anonymously or pseudonymously, protection lasts for 100 years after the work's creation, or 75 years after its publication, whichever is shorter. The life-plus-50 coverage takes effect, however, if you reveal your identity to the Copyright Office any time before the original term of protection runs out.

Works created on a for-hire basis are also protected for 100 years after the work's creation or 75 years after its publication, whichever is shorter.

● **Must I register my work with the Copyright Office to receive protection?** No. Your work is copyrighted whether or not you register it, although registration offers certain advantages. For example, you must register the work before you can bring an infringement suit to court. You can register the work *after* an infringement has taken place, and *then* take the suit to court, but registering after the fact removes certain rights from you. You can sue for actual damages (the income or other benefits lost as a result of the infringement), but you can't sue for statutory damages and you can't recover attorney's fees unless the work has been registered with the Copyright Office *before* the infringement took place. Registering before the infringement also allows you to make a stronger case when bringing the infringement to court.

If you suspect that someone might infringe on your work, register it. If you doubt that an infringement is likely (and infringements are relatively rare), you might save yourself the time and money involved in registering the material.

● **I have an article that I want to protect fully. How do I register it?** Request the proper form from the Copyright Office. Send the completed form, a $10 registration fee, and one copy (if the work is unpublished; two if it's published) of the work to the Register of Copyrights, Library of Congress, Washington, D.C. 20559. You needn't register each work individually. A group of articles can be registered simultaneously (for a single $10 fee) if they meet these requirements: They must be assembled in orderly form (simply placing them in a notebook binder is sufficient); they must bear a single title ("Works by Joe Jones," for example); they must represent the work of one person (or one set of collaborators); and they must be the subject of a single claim to copyright. No limit is placed on the number of works that can be copyrighted in a group.

● **If my writing is published in a "collective work"—such as a magazine— does the publication handle registration of the work?** Only if the publication owns the piece of writing. Although the copyright notice carried by the magazine covers its contents, you must register any writing to which *you* own the rights if you want the additional protection registration provides.

Collective works are publications with a variety of contributors. Magazines, newspapers, encyclopedias, anthologies, etc., are considered collective works. If you sell something to a collective work, state specifically—*in writing*—what rights you're selling. If you don't, you are automatically selling the nonexclusive right to use the writing in the collective work and in any succeeding issues or revisions of it. For example, a magazine that buys your article without specifying in writing the rights purchased can reuse the article in that magazine—but in no other, not even in another magazine put out by the same publisher—without repaying you. The same is true for other collective works, so always detail *in writing* what rights you are selling before actually making the sale.

When contributing to a collective work, ask that your copyright notice be placed on or near your published manuscript (if you still own the manuscript's rights). Prominent display of your copyright notice on published work has two advantages: It signals to readers and potential reusers of the piece that it belongs to you, and not to the collective work in which it appears; and it allows you to register all published works bearing such notice with the Copyright Office as a group for a single $10 fee. A published work *not* bearing notice indicating you as copyright owner can't be included in a group registration.

Display of copyright notice is especially important when contributing to an uncopyrighted publication—that is, a publication that doesn't display a copyright symbol and doesn't register with the Copyright Office. You risk losing copyright protection on material that appears in an uncopyrighted publication. Also, you have no legal recourse against a person who infringes on something that is published without appropriate copyright notice. That person has been misled by the absence of the copyright notice and can't be held liable for his infringement. Copyright protection remains in force on material published in an uncopyrighted publication without benefit of copyright notice if the notice was left off only a few copies, if you asked (in writing) that the notice be included and the publisher didn't comply, or if you register the work and make a reasonable attempt to place the notice on any copies that haven't been distributed after the omission was discovered.

Official notice of copyright consists of the symbol ©, the word "Copyright," or the abbreviation "Copr."; the name of the copyright owner or owners; and the year date of first publication (for example, "© 1984 by Joe Jones").

• **Under what circumstances should I place my copyright notice on unpublished works that haven't been registered?** Place official copyright notice on the first page of *any* manuscript, a procedure intended not to stop a buyer from stealing your material (editorial piracy is very rare, actually), but to demonstrate to the editor that you understand your rights under copyright law, that you own that particular manuscript, and that you want to retain your ownership after the manuscript is published. Seeing this notice, an editor might be less apt to try to buy all rights from you. Remember, you want to retain your rights to any writing.

• **How do I transfer copyright?** A transfer of copyright, like the sale of any property, is simply an exchange of the property for payment. The law stipulates, however, that the transfer of any exclusive rights (and the copyright is the most exclusive of exclusive rights) must be made in writing to be valid. Various types of exclusive rights exist, as outlined above. Usually it is best not to sell your copyright. If you do, you lose control over use of the manuscript, and forfeit future income from its use.

• **What is a "work-for-hire agreement"?** This is a work that another party commissions you to do. Two types of for-hire works exist: Work done as a regular employee of a company, and commissioned work that is specifically called a "work-for-hire" in writing at the time of assignment. The phrase "work-for-hire" or something close must be used in the written agreement, though you should watch for similar phrasings. The work-for-hire provision was included in the new copyright law so that no writer could unwittingly sign away his copyright. The phrase "work-for-hire" is a bright red flag warning the writer that the agreement he's about to enter into will result in loss of rights to any material created under the agreement.

Some editors offer work-for-hire agreements when making assignments, and expect writers to sign them routinely. By signing them, you forfeit the potential for additional income from a manuscript through reprint sales, or sale of other rights. Be careful, therefore, in signing away your rights in a "work-for-hire" agreement. Many articles written as works-for-hire or to which all rights have been sold are never resold, but if you retain the copyright, you might try to resell the article—something you wouldn't be motivated to do if you forfeited your rights to the piece.

● **Can I get my rights back if I sell all rights to a manuscript, or if I sell the copyright itself?** Yes. You or certain heirs can terminate the transfer of rights 40 years after creation or 35 years after publication of a work by serving written notice to the person to whom you transferred rights within specified time limits. Consult the Copyright Office for the procedural details. This may seem like a long time to wait, but remember that some manuscripts remain popular (and earn royalties and other fees) for much longer than 35 years.

● **Must all transfers be in writing?** Only work-for-hire agreements and transfers of exclusive rights *must* be in writing. However, getting any agreement in writing before the sale is wise. Beware of other statements about what rights the buyer purchases that may appear on checks, writer's guidelines or magazine mastheads. If the publisher makes such a statement elsewhere, you might insert a phrase like "No statement pertaining to purchase of rights other than the one detailed in this letter—including masthead statements or writer's guidelines—applies to this agreement" into the letter that outlines your rights agreement. Some publishers put their terms in writing on the back of a check that, when endorsed by the writer, becomes a "contract." This is a dubious legal maneuver, which many writers sidestep by not signing the check—yet depositing it in their bank accounts with the notation FOR DEPOSIT ONLY.

● **Are ideas and titles copyrightable?** No. Nor can information be copyrighted. Only the actual expression of ideas or information can be copyrighted. You can't copyright the idea to do a solar energy story, and you can't copyright information about building solar energy converters. But you can copyright the article that results from that idea and that information.

● **Where do I go for more information about copyright law?** Write the Copyright Office (Library of Congress, Washington, D.C. 20559) for a free Copyright Information Kit. Call (not collect) the Copyright Public Information Office at (202)287-8700 weekdays between 8:30 a.m. and 5:00 p.m. if you need forms for registration of a claim to copyright. The Copyright Office will answer specific questions, but won't provide legal advice. For more information about copyright and other law, consult *Law and the Writer*, edited by Kirk Polking and Leonard S. Meranus (Writer's Digest Books).

How Much Should I Charge?

As a freelance writer, sooner or later you are going to be faced with the happy dilemma of being asked to quote a price for handling a writing or editing assignment for a local company or institution or even a regional or national organization. Or, you may have decided to actively pursue those prospects in your community who might need—and buy your writing skills either on a temporary or seasonal basis. What follows is a checklist of writing jobs you might want to consider in your own corner of the world—and rates that have been reported to us by freelancers doing similar duties in various parts of the United States. Prices quoted here are by no means fixed; the rates in your own marketplace may be higher or lower, depending on demand and other local variables. Therefore, consider the rates quoted here as guidelines, not fixed fees.

How do you find out what the local going rate is? If possible, contact writers or friends in a related business or agency that employs freelancers to find out what has been paid for certain kinds of jobs in the past. Or try to get the prospective client to quote his budget for a specific project before you name your price.

When setting your own fees, keep two factors in mind: (1) how much you want to earn for your time; and (2) how much you think the client is willing or able to pay for the job. How much you want to earn for your time should take into consideration not only an hourly rate for the time you actually spend writing, but also the time involved in meeting with the client, doing research, and, where necessary, handling details with a printer or producer. One way to figure your hourly rate is to determine what an annual salary might be for a staff person to do the same job you are bidding on, and figure an hourly wage on that. If, for example, you think the buyer would have to pay a staff person $20,000 a year, divide that by 2,000 (approximately 40 hours per week for 50 weeks) and you will arrive at $10 an hour. Then add on another 20% to cover the amount of fringe benefits that an employer normally pays in Social Security, unemployment insurance, paid vacations, hospitalization, retirement funds, etc. Then add on another dollars per hour figure to cover your actual overhead expense for office space, equipment, supplies; plus time spent on professional meetings, readings and making unsuccessful proposals. (Add up one year's expense and divide by the number of hours per year you work on freelancing. In the beginning you may have to adjust this to avoid pricing yourself out of the market.)

Regardless of the method by which you arrive at your fee for the job, be sure to get a letter of agreement signed by both parties covering the work to be done and the fee to be paid.

You will, of course, from time to time handle certain jobs at less than desirable rates because they are for a social cause you believe in, or because the job offers you additional experience or exposure to some profitable client for the future. Some clients pay hourly rates, others pay flat fees for the job; both kinds of rates are listed when the data were available so you have as many pricing options as possible. More details on many of the freelance jobs listed below are contained in *Jobs for Writers*, edited by Kirk Polking (Writer's Digest Books)—which tells how to get writing jobs, how to handle them most effectively, and how to get a fair price for your work.

Advertising copywriting: Advertising agencies and the advertising departments of large companies need part-time help in rush seasons; but newspapers, radio and TV stations also need copywriters for their smaller business customers who do not have an agency. Depending on the client and the job, the following rates could apply: $10-$35 per hour, $100 per day, $200 and up per week, $100-$500 as a monthly retainer.

Annual reports: A brief report with some economic information and an explanation of figures, $20-$35 per hour; a report that must meet Securities and Exchange Commission (SEC) standards and reports that use legal language could bill at $40-$50 per hour. Some writers who provide copywriting up to 3,000 words charge flat fees ranging from $1,500-$7,500.

Anthology editing: 3%-15% of royalties.

Article manuscript critique: 3,000 words, $30.

Arts reviewing: for weekly newspapers, $5-$15; for dailies, $25 and up; for Sunday supplements, $100-$200; regional arts events summaries for national trade magazines $15-$50; arts calendar compiling for local newspapers, $4 per hour.

Associations: miscellaneous writing projects, small associations, $5-$15 per hour; larger groups, up to $60 per hour; or a flat fee per project, such as $250-$500 for 10-12 page magazine articles, or $500-$1,500 for a 10-page booklet.

Audio cassette scripts: $150 for 20 minutes, assuming written from existing client materials; no additional research or meetings; otherwise $75-$100 per minute, $750 minimum.

Audiovisuals: see film strips, motion pictures, slide films, video programs.

Book, as-told-to (ghostwriting): author gets full advance and 50% of author's royalties; subject gets 50%. Hourly rate for subjects who are self-publishing ($8-$30 per hour).

Book, ghostwritten, without as-told-to credit: For clients who are either self-publishing or have no royalty publisher lined up; $5,000 and up with one-fourth down payment, one-fourth when book half finished, one-fourth at three quarters mark and last fourth of payment when manuscript completed.

Book content editing: $10-$25 per hour and up; $600-$3,000 per manuscript, based on size and complexity of the project.

Book copyediting: $7.50-$9 per hour and up; occasionally $1 per page.

Book indexing: $8-$15 per hour, or a flat fee, or by the entry.

Book jacket blurb writing: $60-$75 for selling front cover copy plus inside and back cover copy summarizing content and tone of the book.

Book manuscript reading, nonspecialized subjects: $20-$50 for a half page summary and recommendation. *Specialized subject:* $100-$350 and up, depending on complexity of project.

Book proofreading: $6.50 per hour and up; sometimes 30-40¢ per page.

Book research: $5-$20 per hour and up, depending on complexity.

Book reviews: byline and the book only, on small papers; to $25-$125 on larger publications.

Book rewriting: $7.50-$12 per hour and up; sometimes $5 per page. Some writers have combination ghostwriting and rewriting short-term jobs for which the pay could be $350 per day and up.

Business booklets, announcement folders: writing and editing, $25-$1,000 depending on size, research, etc. Average 8½x11" brochure, $100-$200.

Business facilities brochure: 12-16 pages, $1,000-$2,000.

Business letters: such as those designed to be used as form letters to improve customer relations, $15 per hour.

Business meeting guide and brochure: 4 pages, $120; 8-12 pages, $200.

Business writing: On the local or national level, this may be advertising copy, collateral materials, speechwriting, films, public relations or other jobs—see individual entries on these subjects for details. General business writing rates could range from $20-$50 per hour; $100-$200 per day.

Catalogs for business: $60-$75 per printed page; more if many tables or charts must be reworked for readability and consistency.

Collateral materials for business: see business booklets, catalogs, etc.

Comedy writing for night club entertainers: *Gags only*, $2-$7 each. *Routines:* $100-$500 per minute. Some new comics may try to get a five-minute routine for $150; others will pay $1,500 for a five-minute bit from a top writer.

Commercial reports for businesses, insurance companies, credit agencies: $2-$6 per page; $3-$15 per report on short reports.

Company newsletters and inhouse publications: writing and editing 2-4 pages, $100-$500; 12-32 pages, $500-$1,000.

Consultation on communications: $250 per day plus expenses for nonprofit, social service and religious organizations.

Consultation to business: on writing, PR, $25-$50 per hour.

Contest judging: short manuscripts, $5 per entry; with one-page critique, $10-$25.

Corporate history: up to 5,000 words, $1,000-$3,000.

Corporate profile: up to 3,000 words, $1,250-$2,500.

Dance criticism: $25-$400 per article (see also Arts reviewing.)

Direct-mail catalog copy: $10-$30 per page for 3-20 blocks of copy per page of a 24-48 page catalog.

Direct-mail packages: copywriting direct mail letter, response card, etc., $300-$3,000 depending on writer's skill, reputation.

Editing: see book editing, company newsletters, magazines, etc.

Educational consulting and educational grant and proposal writing: $100-$500 per day and sometimes up to 5-10% of the total grant funds depending on whether writing only is involved or also research and design of the project itself.

Educational films: see films.

Encyclopedia articles: entries in some reference books, such as biographical encyclopedias, 500-2,000 words and pay ranges from $60-$80 per 1,000 words. Specialists' fees vary.

English teachers—lay reading for: $4-$6 per hour.

Filmstrip script: $75-$100 per minute, $750 minimum.

Financial presentation for a corporation: 20-30 minutes, $1,500-$4,500.

Flyers for tourist attractions, small museums, art shows: $25 and up for writing a brief bio, history, etc.

Fund-raising campaign brochure: at least $2,000 for 20 hours' research and 30 hours to write, get it approved, lay out and produce with printer.

Gags: see comedy writing.

Genealogical research: $5-$25 per hour.

Ghostwriting: $15-$40 per hour; $5-$10 per page, $200 per day plus expenses. Ghostwritten trade journal article under someone else's byline, $250-$400. Ghostwritten books: see book, as-told-to (ghostwriting and book, ghostwritten, without as-told-to credit).

Ghostwriting a corporate book: 6 months' work, $13,000-$25,000.

Ghostwriting speeches: see speeches.

Government public information officer: part-time, with local governments, $10-$15 per hour; or a retainer for so many hours per period.

Histories, family: fees depend on whether the writer need only edit already prepared notes or do extensive research and writing; and the length of the work, $500-$5,000.

House organ editing: see company newsletters and inhouse publications.

Industrial promotions: $15-$40 per hour. See also business writing.

Job application letters: $10-$25.

Lectures to local librarians or teachers: $50-$100.

Lectures to school classes: $25-$50.

Lectures at national conventions by well-known authors: $300-$1,000 and up, plus expenses; less for panel discussions.

Magazine column: 200 words, $25. Larger circulation publications pay more.

Magazine editing: religious publications, $200-$500 per month.

Magazine stringing: 20¢-$1 per word based on circulation. Daily rate: $200 plus expenses; weekly rate: $750 plus expenses. Also $7.50-$35 per hour plus expenses.

Manuscript consultation on book proposals: $25-$35 per hour.

Manuscript criticism: $5-$20 per 16-line poem; $12-$30 per article or short story of up to 3,000 words; book outlines and sample chapters of up to 20,000 words, $125.

Manuscript typing: 65¢-$1.25 per page with one copy.

Market research survey reports: $10 per report; $8-$30 per hour; writing results of studies or reports, $500-$1,200 per day.

Medical editing: $15-$25 per hour.

Medical proofreading: $7-$10 per hour.

Medical writing: $15 per hour.

New product release: $300-$500 plus expenses.

Newsletters: see company newsletters and retail business newsletters.

Newspaper column, local: 80¢ per column inch to $5 for a weekly; $7.50 for dailies of 4,000-6,000 circulation; $10-$12.50 for 7,000-10,000 dailies; $15-$20 for 11,000-25,000 dailies; and $25 and up for larger dailies.

Newspaper reviews of art, music, drama: see arts reviewing.

Newspaper stringing: 50¢-$2.50 per column inch up to $4-$5 per column inch for some national publications. Also publications like *National Enquirer* pay lead fees up to $250 for tips on page one story ideas.

Newspaper ads for small business: $25 for a small, one-column ad, or $10 per hour and up.

Obituary copy: where local newspapers permit lengthier than normal notices paid for by the funeral home (and charged to the family), $15. Writers are engaged by funeral homes.

Opinion research interviewing: $4-$5.50 per hour or $15-$25 per completed interview.

Permission fees to publishers to reprint article or story: $10-$100.

Photo brochures: $700-$15,000 flat fee for photos and writing.

Political writing: see public relations and speechwriting.

Press release: 1-3 pages, $50-$200.

Printers' camera ready typewritten copy: negotiated with individual printers, but see also manuscript typing services above.

Product literature: per page, $100-$150.

Programmed instruction consultant fees: $300-$700 per day; $50 per hour.

Programmed instruction materials for business: $50 per hour for inhouse writing and editing; $500-$700 a day plus expenses for outside research and writing. *Alternate method:* $2,000-$5,000 per hour of programmed training provided, depending on technicality of subject.

Public relations for business: $200-$400 per day plus expenses.

Public relations for conventions: $500-$1,500 flat fee.

Public relations for libraries: small libraries, $5-$10 per hour; larger cities, $35 an hour and up.

Public relations for nonprofit or proprietary organizations: small towns, $100-$500 monthly retainers.

Public relations for politicians: small town, state campaigns, $10-$30 per hour; incumbents, congressional, gubernatorial and other national campaigns, $25-$75 per hour.

Public relations for schools: $10 per hour and up in small districts; larger districts have fulltime staff personnel.

Radio advertising copy: small towns, up to $5 per spot, $100-$250 per week for a four- to six-hour day; larger cities, $250-$400 per week.

Radio continuity writing: $5 per page to $150 per week, part-time.

Radio documentaries: $200 for 60 minutes, local station.

Radio editorials: $10-$30 for 90-second to two-minute spots.

Radio interviews: for National Public Radio, up to 3 minutes, $25; 3-10 minutes, $40-$75; 10-60 minutes, $125 to negotiable fees. Small radio stations would pay approximately 50% of the NPR rate; large stations, double the NPR rate.

Readings by poets, fiction writers: $25-$300 depending on the author.

Record album cover copy: $100-$250 flat fee.

Recruiting brochure: 8-12 pages, $500-$1,500.

Research for writers or book publishers: $10-$30 an hour and up. Some quote a flat fee of $300-$500 for a complete and complicated job.

Restaurant guide features: short article on restaurant, owner, special attractions, $15; interior, exterior photos, $15.

Resumé writing: $45-$100 per resumé.

Retail business newsletters for customers: $175-$300 for writing four-page publications. Some writers work with a local printer and handle production details as well, billing the client for the total package. Some writers also do their own photography.

Sales brochure: 12-16 pages, $750-$3,000.

Sales letter for business or industry: $150 for one or two pages.

Scripts for nontheatrical films for education, business, industry: prices vary among producers, clients, and sponsors and there is no standardization of rates in the field. Fees include $75-$120 per minute for one reel (10 minutes) and corresponding increases with each successive reel; approximately 10% of the production cost of films that cost the producer more than $1,500 per release minute.

Services brochure: 12-18 pages, $1,250-$2,000.

Shopping mall promotion: $500 monthly retainer up to 15% of promotion budget for the mall.

Short story manuscript critique: 3,000 words, $30.

Slide film script: $75-$100 per minute, $750 minimum.

Slide/single image photos: $75 flat fee.

Slide/tape script: $75-$100 per minute, $750 minimum.

Special news article: for business' submission to trade publication, $250-$400 for 1,000 words.

Slide presentation for an educational institution: $1,000 flat fee.

Speech for owner of a small business: $100 for six minutes.

Speech for owners of larger businesses: $500-$1,500 for 10-15 minutes.

Speech for local political candidate: $150-$250 for 15 minutes.

Speech for statewide candidate: $500-$800.

Speech for national candidate: $1,000 and up.

Syndicated newspaper column, self-promoted: $2-$8 each for weeklies; $5-$25 per week for dailies, based on circulation.

Teaching adult education course: $7-$15 class hour.

Teaching college course or seminar: $15-$30 per class hour.

Teaching creative writing in school: $15-$60 per hour of instruction, or $1,200 for a 10 session class of 25 students; less in recessionary times.

Teaching journalism in high school: proportionate to salary scale for fulltime teacher in the same school district.

Teaching home-bound students: $5 per hour.

Technical writing: $15-$30 per hour.

Technical typing: 65¢-$1 per double-spaced page.

Translation, commercial: a final draft in one of the common European languages, $2\frac{1}{2}$-$4\frac{1}{2}$¢ per English word.

Translation for government agencies: some pay $1\frac{1}{2}$-2¢ per English word.

Translation, literary: $40-$60 per thousand English words.

Translation through translation agencies: less $33\frac{1}{3}$% for agency commission.

TV documentary: 30-minute five-six page proposal outline, $250 and up; 15-17 page treatment, $1,000 and up; less in smaller cities.

TV editorials: $35 and up for 1-minute, 45 seconds (250-300 words).

TV instruction taping: $150 per 30-minute tape; $25 residual each time tape is sold.

TV news film still photo: $3-$6 flat fee.

TV news story: $16-$25 flat fee.

TV filmed news and features: from $10-$20 per clip for 30-second spot; $15-$25 for 60-second clip; more for special events.

TV, national and local public stations: $35-$100 per minute down to a flat fee of $100-$500 for a 30- to 60-minute script.

TV scripts: 60 minutes, prime time, Writers Guild March 1981 rates, $6,065; 30 minutes, $4,718.

Video script: $75-$100 per minute, $750 minimum.

Writer-in-schools: Arts council program, $125 per day plus expenses; personal charges vary from $25 per day to $100 per hour depending on school's ability to pay.

Writer's workshop: lecturing and seminar conducting, $100-$200 per day; local classes, $50 per student for 10 sessions.

Glossary

All Rights. See "Rights and the Writer."

Assignment. Editor asks a writer to do a specific article for which he usually names a price for the completed manuscript.

B&W. Abbreviation for black & white photograph.

Bimonthly. Every two months. See also *semimonthly*.

Biweekly. Every two weeks.

Book packager. Draws all the elements of a book together, from the initial concept to writing and marketing strategies, then sells the book package to a book publisher and/or movie producer.

Caption. Originally a title or headline over a picture but now a description of the subject matter of a photograph, including names of people where appropriate. Also called cutline.

Chapbook. A small booklet, usually paperback, of poetry, ballads or tales.

Clean copy. Free of errors, cross-outs, wrinkles, smudges.

Clippings. News items of possible interest to trade magazine editors.

Clips. Published writing samples with documentation of where they appeared. May be actual copy or photocopy.

Column inch. All the type contained in one inch of a typeset column.

Compatible. The condition which allows one type of computer/word processor to share information or communicate with another type of machine.

Concept. A statement that summarizes a screenplay or teleplay—before the outline or treatment is written.

Contributor's copies. Copies of the issues of a magazine sent to an author in which his/her work appears.

Co-publishing. An arrangement (usually contractual) in which author and publisher share publication costs and profits.

Copy editing. Editing the manuscript for grammar, punctuation and printing style as opposed to subject content.

Copyright. A means to protect an author's work. See "Rights and the Writer."

Correspondent. Writer away from the home office of a newspaper or magazine who regularly provides it with copy.

Cutline. See *caption*.

Disk. A round, flat magnetic plate on which computer data may be stored.

Dot matrix. Printed type whose individual characters are composed of a matrix or pattern of tiny dots.

El-hi. Elementary to high school.

Epigram. A short, witty, sometimes paradoxical saying.

Erotica. Usually fiction that is sexually-oriented; although it could be art on the same theme.

Fair use. A provision of the copyright law that says short passages from copyrighted material may be used without infringing on the owner's rights.

Feature. An article giving the reader background information on the news. Also used by magazines to indicate a lead article or distinctive department.

Filler. A short item used by an editor to "fill" out a newspaper column or a page in a magazine. It could be a timeless news item, a joke, an anecdote, some light verse or short humor, a puzzle, etc.

First North American serial rights. See "Rights and the Writer."

Formula story. Familiar theme treated in a predictable plot structure—such as boy meets girl, boy loses girl, boy gets girl.

Gagline. The caption for a cartoon, or the cover teaser line and the punchline on the inside of a studio greeting card.

Ghostwriter. A writer who puts into literary form, an article, speech, story or book based on another person's ideas or knowledge.

Glossy. A black & white photograph with a shiny surface as opposed to one with a non-shiny matte finish.

Gothic novel. One in which the central character is usually a beautiful young girl, the setting is an old mansion or castle; there is a handsome hero and a real menace, either natural or supernatural.

Hard copy. The printed copy (usually on paper) of a computer's output.

Hardware. All the mechanically-integrated components of a computer that are not software. Circuit boards, transistors, and the machines that are the actual computer are the hardware.

Honorarium. A token payment. It may be a very small amount of money, or simply a byline and copies of the publication in which your material appears.

Illustrations. May be photographs, old engravings, artwork. Usually paid for separately from the manuscript. See also *package sale*.

International Postal Reply Coupons. Can be purchased at your local post office and enclosed with your letter or manuscript to a foreign publisher to cover his postage cost when replying.

Invasion of privacy. Cause for suits against some writers who have written about persons (even though truthfully) without their consent.

Kill fee. A portion of the agreed-on price for a complete article that was assigned but which was subsequently cancelled.

Letter quality. Finely printed type whose appearance is typewriter quality.

Libel. A false accusation; or any published statement or presentation that tends to expose another to public contempt, ridicule, etc. Defenses are truth; fair comment on the matter of public interest; and privileged communication—such as a report of legal proceedings or a client's communication to his lawyer.

Little magazine. Publications of limited circulation, usually on literary or political subject matter.

Machine language. Symbols that can be used directly by a computer.

Microcomputer. A small computer system capable of performing various specific tasks with data it receives. Personal computers are microcomputers.

Model release. A paper signed by the subject of a photograph (or his guardian, if a juvenile) giving the photographer permission to use the photograph, editorially or for advertising purposes or for some specific purpose as stated.

Ms. Abbreviation for manuscript.

Mss. Abbreviation for more than one manuscript.

Multiple submissions. Some editors of non-overlapping circulation magazines, such as religious publications, are willing to look at manuscripts which have also been submitted to other editors at the same time. See individual listings for which editors these are. No multiple submissions should be made to larger markets paying good prices for original material, unless it is a query on a highly topical article requiring an immediate response and that fact is so stated in your letter.

Novelette. A short novel, or a long short story; 7,000 to 15,000 words approximately.

One-time rights. See "Rights and the Writer."

Outline. Of a book is usually a summary of its contents in five to fifteen double-spaced pages; often in the form of chapter headings with a descriptive sentence or two under each one to show the scope of the book. Of a screenplay or teleplay is a scene-by-scene narrative description of the story (10-15 pages for a ½-hour teleplay; 15-25 pages for a 1-hour teleplay; 25-40 pages for a 90-minute teleplay; 40-60 pages for a 2-hour feature film or teleplay).

Over-the-transom. Refers to unsolicited material submitted to a book publisher, magazine editor, etc., by a freelance writer. These submissions are said to come in "over-the-transom."

Package sale. The editor wants to buy manuscript and photos as a "package" and pay for them in one check.

Page rate. Some magazines pay for material at a fixed rate per published page, rather than so much per word.

Payment on acceptance. The editor sends you a check for your article, story or poem as soon as he reads it and decides to publish it.

Payment on publication. The editor decides to buy your material but doesn't send you a check until he publishes it.

Pen name. The use of a name other than your legal name on articles, stories, or books where you wish to remain anonymous. Simply notify your post office and bank that you are using the name so that you'll receive mail and/or checks in that name.

Photo feature. A feature in which the emphasis is on the photographs rather than any accompanying written material.

Photocopied submissions. Are acceptable to some editors instead of the author's sending his original manuscript. See also *multiple submissions*.

Plagiarism. Passing off as one's own, the expression of ideas, words to another.

Program. A series of instructions written in symbols and codes that a computer "reads" in order to perform a specific task.

Public domain. Material which was either never copyrighted or whose copyright term has run out.

Publication not copyrighted. Publication of an author's work in such a publication places it in the public domain, and it cannot subsequently be copyrighted. See "Rights and the Writer."

Query. A letter to an editor eliciting his interest in an article you want to write.

Reporting times. The number of days, weeks, etc., it takes an editor to report back to the author on his query or manuscript.

Reprint rights. See "Rights and the Writer."

Round-up article. Comments from, or interviews with, a number of celebrities or experts on a single theme.

Royalties, standard hardcover book. 10% of the retail price on the first 5,000 copies sold; 12½% on the next 5,000 and 15% thereafter.

Royalties, standard mass paperback book. 4 to 8% of the retail price on the first 150,000 copies sold.

SAE. Self-addressed envelope.

SASE. Self-addressed, stamped envelope.

Screenplay. Script for a film intended to be shown in theaters.

Second serial rights. See "Rights and the Writer."

Semimonthly. Twice a month.

Semiweekly. Twice a week.

Serial. Published periodically, such as a newspaper or magazine.

Sidebar. A feature presented as a companion to a straight news report (or main magazine article) giving sidelights on human-interest aspects, (or) sometimes elucidating just one aspect of the story.

Simultaneous submissions. Submissions of the same article, story or poem to several publications at the same time.

Slant. The approach of a story or article so as to appeal to the readers of a specific magazine. Does, for example, this magazine always like stories with an upbeat ending? Or does that one like articles aimed only at the blue-collar worker?

Slides. Usually called transparencies by editors looking for color photographs.

Slush pile. A collective term for the stack of unsolicited, or misdirected manuscripts received by an editor or book publisher.

Software. Programs and related documentation for use with a particular computer system.

Speculation. The editor agrees to look at the author's manuscript with no assurance that it will be bought.

Stringer. A writer who submits material to a magazine or newspaper from a specific geographical location.

Style. The way in which something is written—for example, short, punchy sentences of flowing, narrative description or heavy use of quotes of dialogue.

Subsidiary rights. All those rights, other than book publishing rights included in a book contract—such as paperback, book club, movie rights, etc.

Subsidy publisher. A book publisher who charges the author for the cost to typeset and print his book, the jacket, etc., as opposed to a royalty publisher which pays the author.

Syndication rights. A book publisher may sell the rights to a newspaper syndicate to print a book in installments in one or more newspapers.

Synopsis. Of a book is a summary of its contents. Of a screenplay or teleplay is a summary of the story. See *Outline*.

Tabloids. Newspaper format publication on about half the size of the regular newspaper page, such as *National Enquirer*.

Tearsheet. Page from a magazine or newspaper containing your printed story, article, poem or ad.

Teleplay. A dramatic story written to be performed on television.

Transparencies. Positive color slides; not color prints.

Treatment. Synopsis of a proposed television or film script (40-60 pages for a 2-hour feature film or teleplay). More detailed than an outline.

Uncopyrighted publication. Publication of an author's work in such a publication potentially puts it in the public domain.

Unsolicited manuscript. A story, article, poem or book that an editor did not specifically ask to see.

User friendly. Easy to handle and use. Refers to computer hardware designed with the user in mind.

Vanity publisher. See *subsidy publisher*.

Word processor. A computer that produces typewritten copy via automated typing, text-editing, and storage and transmission capabilities.

Index

C

U

V

X, Y, Z

Other Writer's Digest Books

General Writing
  Getting the Words Right: How to Revise, Edit, and Rewrite, by Theodore Cheney $13.95
  How to Get Started in Writing, by Peggy Teeters $10.95
  International Writers' & Artists' Yearbook, (paper) $10.95
  Law and the Writer, edited by Polking and Meranus (paper) $7.95
  Make Every Word Count, by Gary Provost (paper) $6.95
  Teach Yourself to Write, by Evelyn Stenbock $12.95
  Treasury of Tips for Writers, edited by Marvin Weisbord (paper) $6.95
  Writer's Encyclopedia, edited by Kirk Polking $19.95
  Writer's Resource Guide, edited by Bernadine Clark $16.95
  Writing for the Joy of It, by Leonard Knott $11.95
Magazine/News Writing
  The Complete Guide to Writing Nonfiction, edited by Glen Evans $24.95
  Craft of Interviewing, by John Brady $9.95
  Magazine Writing: The Inside Angle, by Art Spikol $12.95
  Stalking the Feature Story, by William Ruehlmann $9.95
  Write On Target, by Connie Emerson $12.95
  Writing and Selling Non-Fiction, by Hayes B. Jacobs $12.95
Fiction Writing
  Fiction Is Folks: How to Create Unforgettable Characters, by Robert Newton Peck $11.95
  Fiction Writer's Help Book, by Maxine Rock $12.95
  Fiction Writer's Market, $17.95
  Handbook of Short Story Writing, edited by Dickson and Smythe (paper) $6.95
  How to Write Best-Selling Fiction, by Dean R. Koontz $13.95
  How to Write a Play, by Raymond Hull $13.95
  How to Write Short Stories that Sell, by Louise Boggess $9.95
  Writing the Novel: From Plot to Print, by Lawrence Block $10.95
  Writing Romance Fiction—For Love and Money, by Helene S. Barnhart $14.95
Special Interest Writing
  Children's Picture Book: How to Write It, How to Sell It, by Ellen E.M. Roberts $17.95
  Complete Book of Scriptwriting, by J. Michael Straczynski $14.95
  How to Write and Sell Your Personal Experiences, by Lois Duncan $10.95
  How to Write and Sell (Your Sense of) Humor, by Gene Perret $12.95
  How to Write "How-To" Books and Articles, by Raymond Hull (paper) $8.95
  Mystery Writer's Handbook, edited by Lawrence Treat (paper) $8.95
  The Poet and the Poem, by Judson Jerome $13.95
  The Poet's Handbook, by Judson Jerome $11.95
  Programmer's Market, edited by Brad M. McGehee (paper) $16.95
  TV Scriptwriter's Handbook, by Alfred Brenner $12.95
  Travel Writer's Handbook, by Louise Purwin Zobel $13.95
  Writing and Selling Science Fiction, compiled by The Science Fiction Writers of America (paper) $7.95
  Writing for Children & Teenagers, by Wyndham/Madison $11.95
  Writing to Inspire, by Gentz, Roddy, et al $14.95
The Writing Business
  Complete Handbook for Freelance Writers, by Kay Cassill $14.95
  How to Be a Successful Housewife/Writer, by Elaine Fantle Shimberg $10.95
  How You Can Make $20,000 a Year Writing, by Nancy Hanson (paper) $6.95
  Jobs for Writers, edited by Kirk Polking $11.95
  Writer's Survival Guide: How to Cope with Rejection, Success, and 99 Other Hang-Ups of the Writing Life, by Jean and Veryl Rosenbaum $12.95

To order directly from the publisher, include $1.50 postage and handling for 1 book and 50¢ for each additional book. Allow 30 days for delivery.

Writer's Digest Books, Department B
9933 Alliance Road, Cincinnati, OH 45242

Prices subject to change without notice.